THE RIVERSIDE
ANTHOLOGY
OF LITERATURE

THE RIVERSIDE ANTHOLOGY OF LITERATURE

OF LITERATURE

SECOND EDITION

DOUGLAS HUNT

University of Missouri

HOUGHTON MIFFLIN COMPANY

BOSTON

DALLAS   GENEVA, ILLINOIS   PALO ALTO   PRINCETON, NEW JERSEY

Printed in the U.S.A.

Library of Congress Catalog Card Number: 90–83058

ISBN: 0–395–47285–7

ABCDEFGHIJ-D-9876543210

ACKNOWLEDGMENTS

SHORT FICTION

Chinua Achebe. "Civil Peace" copyright © 1973 by Chinua Achebe. From *Girls at War and Other Stories* by Chinua Achebe. Reprinted by permission of Doubleday & Company, Inc. Extract from *Chants of Saints: A Gathering of Afro-American Literature, Art and Scholarship,* ed. by Harper and Steptoe. Reprinted by permission of Chinua Achebe.

Margaret Atwood. Extracts from *Second Words* by Margaret Atwood. Copyright © 1972 by O. W. Toad Limited. Reprinted by permission of Beacon Press. Copyright © 1982 by O. W. Toad Limited. Reprinted by permission of Stoddard Publishing Co. Limited, 34 Lesmill Rd., Don Mills, Ont. Canada. Extract from *Survival* by Margaret Atwood. Copyright © 1972 by House of Anansi Press. Reprinted by permission of Stoddart Publishing Co. Limited, 34 Lesmill Rd. Don Mills, Ontario, Canada. "Rape Fantasies": Reprinted by permission of Margaret Atwood. Originally published in the short story collection "Dancing Girls," McClelland and Stewart. From "Dancing Girls" by Margaret Atwood. Used by permission of the Canadian Publishers, McClelland and Stewart, Toronto.

W. H. Auden. Excerpt from *Forewords and Afterwords* by W. H. Auden. Copyright © 1973 by W. H. Auden. Reprinted by permission of Random House, Inc.

Toni Cade Bambara. "The Lesson": From *Gorilla, My Love* by Toni Cade Bambara. Copyright © 1972 by Toni Cade Bambara. Reprinted by permission of Random House, Inc. Extract from *The Writer on Her Work,* ed. by J. Sternburg. Reprinted by permission of Toni Cade Bambara.

Jorge Luis Borges. Extract from "Prologue to Herman Melville's *Bartleby*" by Jorge Luis Borges, translated by Ronald Christ. Reprinted by permission of the translator and the Estate of Jorge Luis Borges. All rights reserved. "The Aleph": From THE ALEPH AND OTHER STORIES 1939–1969 by Jorge Luis Borges, edited and translated by Norman Thomas di Giovanni in collaboration with the author. English translation copyright © 1968, 1969, 1970 by Emece Editores, S. A. and Norman Thomas di Giovanni. Reprinted by permission of the publisher, Dutton, an imprint of New American Library, a division of Penguin Books USA Inc.

Raymond Carver. "Why Don't You Dance?": Copyright © 1980 by Raymond Carver. Reprinted from *What We Talk About When We Talk About Love* by Raymond Carver, by permission of Alfred A. Knopf Inc. Excerpt from introduction by Raymond Carver from *The Best American Short Stories 1986* edited by Shannon Ravenel. Copyright © 1986 by Houghton Mifflin Company. Reprinted by permission of Houghton Mifflin Co.

Anton Chekhov. "Lady with a Pet Dog": From *The Portable Chekhov,* edited and translated by Avrahm Yarmolinsky. Copyright 1947, © 1968 by The Viking Press. Renewed © 1975 by Avrahm Yarmolinsky. Reprinted by permission of the publisher, Viking Penguin, a division of Penguin Books USA Inc.

(Acknowledgments continue on p. 1661)

CONTENTS

Preface   xxi

SHORT FICTION ANTHOLOGY

POETRY ANTHOLOGY

Reading Poetry: Giving the Poem Its Second Life   448

A Further Reading list follows the selections of each major author.

DRAMA ANTHOLOGY

PREFACE

The Second Edition of *The Riverside Anthology of Literature,* like the first, presents students with a diverse selection of high-quality works. To that end, it includes many of the best-known authors in the Anglo-American tradition as well as a number of contemporary writers whose reputations are not yet settled, and a healthy selection of writers from Europe, Latin America, and Africa. The Second Edition includes nine new authors in its list of 103 and fresh selections from fourteen of the retained authors.

The Riverside Anthology of Literature, Second Edition, keeps the spotlight on works and writers but includes a good deal of unobtrusive apparatus. The elements of literature are discussed in the introductions to the three genres and (often in lesson-length essays) in the Handbook of Literature (pages 1592–1620). After the selections of each major author is a new Further Reading list, a brief bibliography of secondary sources students may find useful in reading or writing about the selection. These references have been chosen with accessibility in mind—intellectual accessibility for undergraduates and physical accessibility in libraries with limited holdings. The "Counterpoints" that follow sometimes give one writer's view of another, sometimes a writer's comment on the underpinnings of his or her own work: collectively, they provide a lively and varied picture of how writers view their art, a picture that raises provocative questions for class discussion.

Because writing about literature is an important way of learning about it, the Writing About Literature section (pages 1621–1642) shows one interpreter's struggle to come to grips with a prose poem, first in an informal journal entry, then in a draft and revision of a short essay, then in a research paper. The Instructor's Resource Manual for *The Riverside Anthology of Literature,* Second Edition, offers over 350 questions appropriate for journal writing, short essays, or class discussion. Each question is "answered" with an essay of 200 to 500 words that shows where the question is likely to lead the student who pursues it. Sample student essays, with instructor's comments, on eighteen of these questions are collected in the package of Sample Student Papers, new to this edition.

Listed after each work is the earliest date of publication we could confirm; works published posthumously, however, are followed by the generally recognized date of composition. For translated works, we have given the date of the first publication in the original language, followed by the date of the English translation we are printing. In glossing the works themselves, we have aimed to give only the information needed to make them comprehensible: words easily found in a dictionary are not glossed, nor is every potentially unfamiliar reference.

I owe special thanks to Carolyn Perry (University of Missouri) for her many contributions to both the first and the second editions—including assembling the bibliographies, writing most of the biographical sketches of the authors, drafting portions of the handbook section, collecting and commenting on sample student papers, and generally holding the project together. For their excellent work on the Instructor's Resource Manual, I thank Melody Richardson Daily (University of Missouri), W. Raymond Smith (Indiana University), and Victor Bowman (University of Massachusetts). Marcia Sankey's tenacity in searching out dates of publication for the first edition continues to benefit the second, as does Glenn Hopp's (Howard Payne University) work finding material on dramatists. For useful reviews of the second edition, I want to thank

Therese Brychta, Truckee Meadows Community College, NV
Mary Ellen Byrne, Ocean County College, NJ
Angela G. Dorenkamp, Assumption College, MA
Robert J. Forman, St. John's University, NY
Marjorie Ginsberg, The University of Iowa
LaVerne González, San Jose State University
Darlene J. Gravett, Gardner-Webb College, NC
Michael S. Gregory, San Francisco State University
James A. Grimshaw, Jr., East Texas State University
Stephen Hahn, William Paterson College, NJ
John D. Hain, Tennessee Temple University
William C. Hamlin, University of Missouri-St. Louis
Stephen Jama, II, El Camino Community College, CA
Carol Jamieson, Niagara County Community College, NY
John H. Knight, Viterbo College, WI
Patricia C. Knight, Amarillo College, TX
Eugene P. Kretschmer, San Joaquin Delta College, CA
Douglas Krienke, Sam Houston State University, TX
James S. Leonard, The Citadel, SC
Jill L. Levenson, Trinity College, Ontario
Tom Lisk, University of South Carolina-Sumter
Dianne C. Luce, Midlands Technical College, SC
Dennis B. Martin, Cape Cod Community College, MA
Richard B. Maxwell, Foothill College, CA
John G. Parks, Miami University, OH
Susan Petit, College of San Mateo, CA
Joseph Powell, Central Washington University
A. R. Price, Jr., Virginia Polytechnic Institute and State University
Compton Rees, The University of Connecticut
Martin B. Shichtman, Eastern Michigan University
Sandra W. Tomlinson, Galveston College, TX

Julia Watson, University of Montana
Eileen H. Watts, La Salle University, PA
John Webster, University of Washington
Sid Young, Galveston College, TX

Houghton Mifflin, if it will not blush at being praised in its own print, should be thanked for sparing no effort to bring outstanding contemporary writers into *The Riverside Anthology of Literature,* Second Edition. I am particularly grateful to the editorial staff for making the second edition a better book, in several respects, than the first.

DOUG HUNT

THE RIVERSIDE
ANTHOLOGY
OF LITERATURE

SHORT
FICTION

Reading Fiction: The Tale Inside the Portrait

For some scholars, the analysis of a short story is an exact procedure requiring instruments nearly as specialized as a surgeon's. For them the chief implements are terms, and they might describe a story as "a *bildungsroman* with a double plot and with two round and three flat characters, narrated primarily from the third-person limited point of view (by an unreliable narrator) but twice allowing comments from omniscient point of view." Though you may hope that no such sentence will ever pass your lips, the terms can be useful, and many are defined and discussed in the Handbook (pages 1592–1620). But let's begin with a simpler critical tool that, like a jackknife, will serve in almost every situation.

This tool is the distinction between two traditions of storytelling, traditions that affect not only fiction, but poetry and drama as well. We will call the first "the tradition of the tale"; the second, "the tradition of the portrait." The short story, as we will see, is an offspring of both traditions, and this parentage provides the story with two quite different dimensions in which to grow.

THE TRADITIONAL TALE

The very word *tale* reminds us that the tradition we associate with it is far older than writing. In the prehistory of language, *tale* is a close cousin of *tell*, and we

ought to bear in mind the word's long association with the human voice. Although we now find tales printed in books, the printed page is not their native habitat. More natural to them is the environment that gave us the "fairy tales" recorded by the Grimms in the early nineteenth century. These pioneering folklorists discovered a great cauldron of stories that illiterate peasants had been cooking up for centuries in the Black Forest of Germany. The Grimm fairy tales, it is worth remembering, were largely products of the dark, told by firelight in a latitude where winter nights are very long.

In the dark, the listeners were essentially alone with their imaginations and with the speaker's voice. We realize the importance of the voice when we read "The Juniper Tree," a story filled with sounds: the voices of several characters, the "klipp klapp, klipp klapp" of a mill, the "hick hack, hick hack" of men chiseling a millstone, the repeated bird songs, and the crash of chest lid decapitating one character and of a dropped millstone crushing another. It is a cliché to talk about the storyteller casting a spell, but we should remember that the word *spell*, like the word *tale,* originally referred to a recitation or an incantation and later to the effects of the incantation. The peasant storytellers who recited their tales for the brothers Grimm had memorized them word for word, as a sorcerer would memorize a magical formula. Innovations were possible, of course, and a story would change gradually over decades of telling, but a traditional tale was not to be loosely paraphrased. The telling, the spell, required certain syllables in a certain order. In this respect, the traditional tale is more like a poem or song than it is like most modern novels, which are not made to be read aloud, let alone memorized.

And what are traditional tales about? Consider a familiar example, "Cinderella." Even in the relatively tame version presented by Walt Disney, we can see that this tale compresses into a small space some of our deepest hopes and fears. Cinderella experiences the things we have feared since childhood, some of which we continue to fear as adults: our mother's death, captivity in the power of pitiless strangers (the stepmother and the stepsisters), squalor, ugliness, neglect. She also experiences things we only wish for: communication with animals, the revelation of our hidden beauty and nobility, perfect love. In the unexpurgated version recorded by the brothers Grimm, she also experiences the pleasure of taking a gruesome revenge. One of the step sisters, in order to get the tiny slipper on, cuts off her big toe; the other cuts off her heel. Lamed for life by their own efforts, they then have their eyes pecked out by the pigeons who are Cinderella's allies. Deep wishes and fears include things that the Disney organization prefers to suppress.

In a pragmatic century like ours, many people dismiss the tale as "unrealistic," but the dismissal is a bit too hasty. Cinderella's glass slippers and fairy godmother may be bits of fantasy, like the special effects in a Steven Spielberg film, but what about the abusiveness of her stepmother, the avarice and jealousy of her stepsisters, her loneliness, her desire to escape, to be rescued by a lover, to have her revenge? Nathaniel Hawthorne, who worked very consciously in the tradition of the tale, said that its business was not to reproduce the surface appearance of life, but to reach beneath that surface to reveal "the truth of the human heart." And, in fact, psychologists and psychiatrists have found tales, like dreams, to be important clues to the workings of our subconscious minds.

Whether a hope or fear is less real than an automobile, for example, or a blue smock, is a difficult question. Suffice it for now to say that it is real in a different dimension of experience. In a very short story written about 1922, the German writer Franz Kafka shows how a single moment may be the intersection between two incompatible dimensions of reality.

On Parables

There were many who complained that the words of the wise were always mere parables, and of no use in daily life, which is the only life that we have. When the wise man says: "Go across", he does not mean that one should cross over to the other side of the street, which is at least something that one could manage if the result were worth the effort; he means some fabulous yonder, something that is unknown to us and that even he cannot designate more precisely, and therefore something that cannot help us down here in the very least. All these parables mean really no more than that the inconceivable is inconceivable, and that we knew already. But the cares that we actually have to struggle with every day are a different matter.

One man then said: "Why do you resist? If you followed the parables, then you would become parables yourselves, and thus free of your daily cares."

Another said: "I bet that is also a parable."

The first said: "You have won."

The second said: "But unfortunately only in parable."

The first said: "No, in reality. In parable you have lost."

We might use Kafka's geometry and say that the business of the tale is primarily to be true "in parable" rather than "in reality."

THE MARRIAGE OF THE TALE AND THE PORTRAIT

We expect the tale (like the dream) to be a true reflection of our wishes, hopes, and fears, but we do not expect it to correspond to the realities we see around us at high noon. On the other hand, we do not live our entire lives in the dimly lit passages of our dreams. We have eyes that see and minds that analyze, and there are, as Kafka's second man says, "the cares that we actually have to struggle with every day." The early masters of modern fiction found ways to do justice to this side of our nature, too. They brought into the story images from ordinary life: the sight, smell, and texture of the world, as well as (or even in place of) the sound of the storyteller's voice. Daniel Defoe, one of the fathers of the English novel, had such a good eye for realistic detail that he was able to convince most of his contemporary readers that *Robinson Crusoe* (1719) and *Moll Flanders* (1722) were true stories. Indeed, there is so much of the real world in *Moll Flanders* that it is very hard to classify. Some scholars see it as a "tale" into which Defoe worked many elements from daily life in order to create a salable hoax. Other scholars see it as an essentially factual portrait of a reformed thief and prostitute whom the author interviewed in prison. Every reader of Defoe's novels knows that the pleasure they give comes from the illusion, at least, that we are reading about things that really happened.

The Frenchman Guy de Maupassant (1850–1893) was one of the earliest proponents of the short story as a serious portrait of ordinary life, "the revelation of the real, contemporary man." For Maupassant, the story does not begin in traditions about princesses, goblins, and glass mountains, nor in emotions that the writer wishes to express. It begins in close observation of the daily routines and habits of real people, the sort of observation we might expect of a first-rate journalist or biographer. Maupassant learned to write under the instruction of Gustave Flaubert, who used to set him exercises in verbal portraiture:

> "When you pass," he would say, "a grocer seated at his shop door, a janitor smoking a pipe, a stand of hackney coaches, show me that grocer and that janitor, their whole physical appearance, including also a description of their whole moral nature, so that I cannot confound them with any other grocer or janitor; make me see, in one word, that a certain cab horse does not resemble the fifty others that follow or precede it."

The influence of realists like Maupassant and Flaubert has been profound. The traditional tale could take place "once upon a time" in no particular location and could include characters too dazzlingly good or evil to resemble the people we meet on the streets. On every page of most modern short stories, however, you will find precise observations about a particular setting and particular characters. Indeed, half the pleasure of reading a short story may come from the accuracy with which the writer records what he or she has seen, heard, smelled, felt, and tasted.

Skill at portraying the external world is essential for a writer like Maupassant, but the writer is not merely a camera or a tape recorder, recording a flat reality. The short story is descended from the tale as well as from the portrait, and it manages, sometimes miraculously, to speak truly both "in reality" and "in parable." The literary realist finds the raw materials of art in the external world but discards much and reassembles the rest into what Maupassant calls a "personal vision of life," a vision that leads us once again into deep hopes and fears. Consider, for example, the opening paragraph of Maupassant's "The String":

> Along all the roads around Goderville the peasants and their wives were coming towards the little town, for it was market-day. The men walked with plodding steps, their bodies bent forward at each thrust of their long bowed legs. They were deformed by hard work, by the pull of the heavy plough which raises the left shoulder and twists the torso, by the reaping of the wheat which forces the knees apart to get a firm stand, by all the slow and strenuous labors of life on the farm. Their blue smocks, starched, shining as if varnished, ornamented with a little design in white at the neck and wrists, puffed about their bony bodies, seemed like balloons ready to carry them off. From each smock a head, two arms, and two feet protruded.

This paragraph, which we might be inclined to rush through on our way to the "real story," is constructed from details any observer might have seen in a French market town in the 1870s; it embodies, however, Maupassant's "personal vision." In this vision of life (characteristic of the nineteenth-century realists), people are not just shaped by their environment, but deformed by it. Their hard lives unsuit them for great joy, leaving them small and pitiable pleasures. The shining blue smocks with little designs in white seem misplaced on their bony, plodding bodies. Life in Goderville is squeezed down into a narrow emotional range, incapable of producing ecstasy or tragedy. Maupassant's description of Goderville is so precise that a knowledgeable French person of the period could probably have placed the imaginary village very accurately on a real map of France, listed its principal products, and estimated its population. But it is not merely the geography "in reality" that is accurate. We can also place Goderville in the geography of our imaginations. It is a hell on earth. Or to put the case as a nineteenth-century realist might have, it is a statement that earth is hell, unredeemed and unredeemable. Goderville is a miniature world painted in such a way that we recognize it as being simultaneously true to external reality and true to the writer's dark vision. Into this world, four paragraphs later, Maupassant introduces his protagonist.

> Maître Hauchecorne, of Bréaute, had just arrived at Goderville. He was directing his steps towards the square, when he perceived upon the ground a little piece of string. Maître Hauchecorne, economical like a true Norman, thought that everything useful ought to be picked up, and he stooped painfully, for he suffered from rheumatism. He took up the bit of string from the ground and was beginning to roll it carefully when he noticed Maître Malandain, the harness-maker, on the threshold of his door, looking at him. They had once had a quarrel on the subject of a halter, and they had remained on bad terms, being both good haters. Maître Hauchecorne was seized with a sort of shame to be seen thus by his enemy, picking a bit of string out of the dirt. He hid his find quickly under his smock, and slipped it into his trouser pocket; then he pretended to be still looking on the ground for something which he did not find, and he went towards the market, his head thrust forward, bend double by his pain.

Here again is a paragraph that we might pass over carelessly on our way to the plot, but we should stop to relish it. It is a brilliant portrait: we learn more about a man in these 150 words than we will ever learn about most of our neighbors. We see his miserliness, his physical pain, his capacity for hatred, and above all his pride—the pride of a man who has nothing but pride to comfort him. Maupassant learned Flaubert's lessons in realism admirably, but what he saw around him was rarely admirable: deformed bodies and spirits in a world that offers little room for joy.

"Too bleak," we may say, and many readers of Maupassant's own time did say so, preferring stories that would amuse them or uplift them. Maupassant's response was to say that he was a realistic artist and that he had no choice but to consider the life around him and present his findings about it: "Let us rise to the heights of poetry when we criticize an idealist, and show him that his dream is commonplace, vulgar, not mad enough or magnificent enough. But if we criticize a naturalist, let us show him wherein the truth in life differs from the truth in his book."

By blending features of the portrait and the tale, the short story creates a special challenge for the reader. In Kafka's terms, it claims to give us the truth both "in reality" and "in parable." It claims to connect the observable details of ordinary life with what Hawthorne called "the truth of the human heart" and Maupassant called "the deep, hidden meanings of events."

A SHORT STORY EXAMINED

On the one hand, the tale tradition, as we have seen, overleaps the details of ordinary reality, concerns itself very little with particular characters or settings, depends on the spell cast by the words of the narrator, and goes directly to the heart's truth. The portrait tradition, on the other hand, embraces everyday reality, relishes the exact description of individual characters in a particularized setting, and builds credibility by reporting almost scientifically on the data given by the senses. To see how these apparently contrary traditions work in a story, let's examine a very short example, Elizabeth Tallent's "No One's a Mystery" (1985).

No One's a Mystery

For my eighteenth birthday Jack gave me a five-year diary with a latch and a little key, light as a dime. I was sitting beside him scratching at the lock, which didn't seem to want to work, when he thought he saw his wife's Cadillac in the distance, coming toward us. He pushed me down onto the dirty floor of the pickup and kept one hand on my head while I inhaled the musk of his cigarettes in the dashboard ashtray and sang along with Rosanne Cash on the tape deck. We'd been drinking tequila and the bottle was between his legs, resting up against his crotch, where the seam of his Levi's was bleached linen-white, though the Levi's were nearly new. I don't know why his Levi's always bleached like that, along the seams and at the knees. In a curve of cloth his zipper glinted, gold.

"It's her," he said. "She keeps the lights on in the daytime. I can't think of a single habit in a woman that irritates me more than that." When he saw that I was going to stay still he took his hand from my head and ran it through his own dark hair.

"Why does she?" I said.

"She thinks it's safer. Why does she need to be safer? She's driving exactly fifty-five miles an hour. She believes in those signs:

'Speed Monitored by Aircraft.' It doesn't matter that you can look up and see that the sky is empty."

"She'll see your lips move, Jack. She'll know you're talking to someone."

"She'll think I'm singing along with the radio."

He didn't lift his hand, just raised the fingers in salute while the pressure of his palm steadied the wheel, and I heard the Cadillac honk twice, musically; he was driving easily eighty miles an hour. I studied his boots. The elk heads stitched into the leather were bearded with frayed thread, the toes were scuffed, and there was a compact wedge of muddy manure between the heel and the sole—the same boots he'd been wearing for the two years I'd known him. On the tape deck Rosanne Cash sang, "Nobody's into me, no one's a mystery."

"Do you think she's getting famous because of who her daddy is or for herself?" Jack said.

"There are about a hundred pop tops on the floor, did you know that? Some little kid could cut a bare foot on one of these, Jack."

"No little kids get into this truck except for you."

"How come you let it get so dirty?"

"'How come,'" he mocked. "You even sound like a kid. You can get back into the seat now, if you want. She's not going to look over her shoulder and see you."

"How do you know?"

"I just know," he said. "Like I know I'm going to get meat loaf for supper. It's in the air. Like I know what you'll be writing in that diary."

"What will I be writing?" I knelt on my side of the seat and craned around to look at the butterfly of dust printed on my jeans. Outside the window Wyoming was dazzling in the heat. The wheat was fawn and yellow and parted smoothly by the thin dirt road. I could smell the water in the irrigation ditches hidden in the wheat.

"Tonight you'll write, 'I love Jack. This is my birthday present from him. I can't imagine anybody loving anybody more than I love Jack.'"

"I can't."

"In a year you'll write, 'I wonder what I ever really saw in Jack. I wonder why I spent so many days just riding around in his pickup. It's true he taught me something about sex. It's true there wasn't ever much else to do in Cheyenne.'"

"I won't write that."

"In two years you'll write, 'I wonder what that old guy's name was, the one with the curly hair and the filthy dirty pickup truck and time on his hands.'"

"I won't write that."

"No?"

"Tonight I'll write, 'I love Jack. This is my birthday present from him. I can't imagine anybody loving anybody more than I love Jack.'"

"No, you can't," he said. "You can't imagine it."

"In a year I'll write, 'Jack should be home any minute now. The table's set—my grandmother's linen and her old silver and the yellow candles left over from the wedding—but I don't know if I can wait until after the trout à la Navarra to make love to him.'"

"It must have been a fast divorce."

"In two years I'll write, 'Jack should be home by now. Little Jack is hungry for his supper. He said his first word today besides "Mama" and "Papa." He said "kaka."'"

Jack laughed. "He was probably trying to finger-paint with kaka on the bathroom wall when you heard him say it."

"In three years I'll write, 'My nipples are a little sore from nursing Eliza Rosamund.'"

"Rosamund. Every little girl should have a middle name she hates."

"'Her breath smells like vanilla and her eyes are just Jack's color of blue.'"

"That's nice." Jack said.

"So, which one do you like?"

"I like yours," he said. "But I believe mine."

"It doesn't matter. I believe mine."

"Not in your heart of hearts, you don't."

"You're wrong."

"I'm not wrong," he said. "And her breath would smell like your milk, and it's kind of a bittersweet smell, if you want to know the truth."

As a portrait of a particular time and place and of two particular characters, the story deserves high marks. Wyoming in midsummer in the 1980s comes to us through the gates of our senses. For our eyes, Tallent provides the bleached Levi's with the gold zipper, the pop tops littering the floor of the pickup, the frayed elk heads and the manure on Jack's boots, the "fawn and yellow wheat," and much more. For our nose, she provides the musk of old cigarettes and the smell of water in the irrigation ditches. For our ears, she provides the scratching of the key in the lock of the diary, the musical honk of the Cadillac, the Rosanne Cash song on the radio. (The song, "It Hasn't Happened Yet," dates the story precisely: it was a favorite on country stations in 1982.) For our sense of touch, she gives us the faint pressure of the key on the girl's hand ("light as a dime") and the heavier pressure of Jack's hand on her head. Like Defoe, Tallent does a convincing job of impersonation: we have the illusion of experiencing a real place through the consciousness of a well-defined person.

Actually, the portraiture in the story is so convincing that we seem to see and understand more than the story's narrator does. Eighteen and infatuated, can the girl really see Jack as clearly as we do? Can she see all the warnings that a disinterested observer would see in the cheap diary, the litter of pop tops, the casual handling of a speeding truck, the frayed and manure-encrusted boots, the confident deception of a wife, the contempt for an orderly life? Like Maupassant's portrait of Maître Hauchecorne, Tallent's portrait of Jack reveals him more completely than life reveals our neighbors to us.

But the story attempts something more than an accurate portrait of characters in a setting. It speaks "in reality," but it also whispers "in parable." In reality, we might care very little about two individuals in Cheyenne, Wyoming, in 1982. Our involvement with the story depends on Tallent's ability to make the portrait work simultaneously as a tale that speaks directly to our hopes and fears. The situation that Jack and the narrator are in has to become *our* situation, universal rather than particular. How does Tallent accomplish this transformation?

Two moments in the story are crucial. The first comes when Jack complains that his wife drives with the lights on in the daytime:

> "She thinks it's safer. Why does she need to be safer? She's driving exactly fifty-five miles an hour. She believes in those signs: 'Speed Monitored by Aircraft.' It doesn't matter that you can look up and see that the sky is empty."

In the portrait tradition, Jack's comment on his wife functions as a characterization of himself. A man who criticizes someone for being cautious and law abiding is announcing that he is neither. We could let the comment rest there and never concern ourselves with any other meaning that may lurk in the passage. But something about the language tells us that we are not entirely in Wyoming anymore: ". . . you can look up and see that the sky is empty." Jack intends this sentence only "in reality"; he is thinking of no force more sublime than the highway patrol. Tallent, however, makes it echo "in parable." When a man like Jack says that the sky is empty, a reader familiar with Scripture may think of Psalm 53:1: "The fool says in his heart 'There is no God.'" The equation of God with a flying highway patrol and of sinners with speeders is admittedly slapstick theology, but there you are: Tallent has a sense of humor.

Once we notice the implications of Jack's claim that the sky is empty, we see that this story is concerned with the life of all people who break the rules, who don't play it safe. Jack and the girl have not only placed themselves on the other side of one or two state laws, they have rejected the idea of lawfulness. They won't be constrained by society's rules; they will act on their impulses. They have put themselves outside the shelter of correct behavior, as even the most upright of us inevitably does at some point in our lives. So now we have a tale running beside our portrait, and the question the tale poses is "What does the universe do to those who abandon the safety of the rules?" If the answer is that it crushes them like insects, then the narrator, of whom Tallent makes us rather fond, is in a great deal of trouble.

This brings us to the second key point in the story, which comes precisely midway. The narrator, who has been reporting on the world from the dirty floor of Jack's truck, gets up, examines the "butterfly of dust" on her jeans, and takes a look outside. What she sees hardly suggests a crushing universe:

> Outside the window Wyoming was dazzling in the heat. The wheat was fawn and yellow and parted smoothly by the thin dirt road. I could smell the water in the irrigation ditches hidden in the wheat.

The imagery and the language suddenly brighten, as though a cloud had passed over. "In reality" there is a clear-enough explanation: our narrator has been in a cramped, dark place; when she emerges into the sunlight, her eyes should be dazzled. "In parable," in the emotional world of the tale, we have turned a corner. We are encouraged to hope. Perhaps the universe is not in the business of crushing the outlaw, the sinner, the "wild" teenage girl. Perhaps it has something else in store for them (for us).

In the dialogue that fills the second half of the story, Jack and the narrator invent their own tales about the future. Jack's version is darker, not because he imagines a celestial patrol swooping down in retribution, but because experience has made him cynical. The girl offers a brighter story, a fairy-tale ending complete with grandmother's old linen and a daughter whose middle name seems to come straight from a romance: Rosamund, whose "breath smells like vanilla and her eyes are just Jack's color of blue."

From this point on, the story becomes a dialogue between fear and hope. Jack likes the girl's vision of redemption by love, but he doesn't believe it. In fact, he knows that in her "heart of hearts," she can't entirely believe it either. She, in turn, knows that Jack can't entirely *doubt* it, and in the last paragraph of the story, we feel him move very slightly in the direction of hope. He isn't willing to imagine an Eliza Rosamund with breath that smells like vanilla, but he is willing to imagine her existence: ". . . her breath would smell like your milk, and it's a kind of a bittersweet smell, if you want to know the truth." Here is another sentence that lives one life in reality and another in parable. Jack would know the smell of milk on a baby's breath; it is part of his portrait as a man who has been in at least one marriage. But the sentence is also the ambivalent closing to the tale dimension of the story. Tallent has created a universe that is neither as harsh as the one Maupassant gives us in "The String" nor as kind as the one Disney gives us in "Cinderella." Like Eliza Rosamund's breath, it is bittersweet. The sweetness *might* prevail.

Your reading of "No One's a Mystery" will probably be different from mine. What we bring to a story affects what we take from it, and I've no intention of insisting that my interpretation is better than yours. I do want to suggest, however, that in the world of the short story *everyone's* a mystery. No matter how literally the characters are portrayed, no matter how exact the setting they are placed in, their presence in a tale gives them another dimension that opens onto our hopes and fears.

JACOB GRIMM

(1785–1863)

WILHELM GRIMM

(1786–1859)

THE JUNIPER TREE

translated from the German by Margaret Hunt and James Stern

It is now long ago, quite two thousand years, since there was a rich man who had a beautiful and pious wife, and they loved each other dearly. They had, however, no children, though they wished for them very much, and the woman prayed for them day and night, but still they had none. Now there was a court-yard in front of their house in which was a juniper tree, and one day in winter the woman was standing beneath it, paring herself an apple, and while she was paring herself the apple she cut her finger, and the blood fell on the snow. "Ah," said the woman, and sighed right heavily, and looked at the blood before her, and was most unhappy, "ah, if I had but a child as red as blood and as white as snow!" And while she thus spoke, she became quite happy in her mind, and felt just as if that were going to happen. Then she went into the house, and a month went by and the snow was gone, and two months, and then everything was green, and three months, and then all the flowers came out of the earth, and four months, and then all the trees in the wood grew thicker, and the green branches were all closely entwined, and the birds sang until the wood resounded and the blossoms fell from the trees, then the fifth month passed away and she stood under the juniper tree, which smelt so sweetly that her heart leapt, and she fell on her knees and was beside herself with joy, and when the sixth month was over the fruit was large and fine, and then she was quite still, and the seventh month she snatched at the juniper-berries and ate them greedily, then she grew sick and sorrowful, then the eighth month passed, and she called her husband to her, and wept and said: "If I die, then bury me beneath the juniper tree." Then she was quite comforted and happy until the next month was over, and then she had a child as white as snow and as red as blood, and when she beheld it she was so delighted that she died.

Then her husband buried her beneath the juniper tree, and he began to weep sore; after some time he was more at ease, and though he still wept he could bear it, and after some time longer he took another wife.

By the second wife he had a daughter, but the first wife's child was a little son, and he was as red as blood and as white as snow. When the woman looked at her daughter she loved her very much, but then she looked at the little boy and it seemed to cut her to the heart, for the thought came into her mind that he would always stand in her way, and she was for ever thinking how she could get all the fortune for her daughter, and the Evil One filled her mind with this till she was quite wroth with the little boy and she pushed him from one corner to the other and slapped him here and cuffed him there, until the poor child was in continual terror, for when he came out of school he had no peace in any place.

One day the woman had gone upstairs to her room, and her little daughter went up too, and said: "Mother, give me an apple." "Yes, my child," said the woman, and gave her a fine apple out of the chest, but the chest had a great heavy lid with a great sharp iron lock. "Mother," said the little daughter, "is brother not to have one too?" This made the woman angry, but she said: "Yes, when he comes out of school." And when she saw from the window that he was coming, it was just as if the Devil entered into her, and she snatched at the apple and took it away again from her daughter, and said: "You shall not have one before your brother." Then she threw the apple into the chest, and shut it. Then the little boy came in at the door, and the Devil made her say to him kindly: "My son, will you have an apple?" and she looked wickedly at him. "Mother," said the little boy, "how dreadful you look! Yes, give me an apple." Then it seemed to her as if she were forced to say to him: "Come with me," and she opened the lid of the chest and said: "Take out an apple for yourself," and while the little boy was stooping inside, the Devil prompted her, and crash! she shut the lid down, and his head flew off and fell among the red apples. Then she was overwhelmed with terror, and thought: "If I could but make them think that it was not done by me!" So she went upstairs to her room to her chest of drawers, and took a white handkerchief out of the top drawer, and set the head on the neck again, and folded the handkerchief so that nothing could be seen, and she set him on a chair in front of the door, and put the apple in his hand.

After this Marlinchen came into the kitchen to her mother, who was standing by the fire with a pan of hot water before her which she was constantly stirring round. "Mother," said Marlinchen, "brother is sitting at the door, and he looks quite white, and has an apple in his hand. I asked him to give me the apple, but he did not answer me, and I was quite frightened." "Go back to him," said her mother, "and if he will not answer you, give him a box on the ear." So Marlinchen went to him and said: "Brother, give me the apple." But he was silent, and she gave him a box on the ear, whereupon his head fell off. Marlinchen was terrified, and began crying and screaming, and ran to her mother, and said: "Alas, mother, I have knocked my brother's head off!" and she wept and wept and could not be comforted. "Marlinchen," said the mother, "what have you done? but be quiet and let no one know it; it cannot be helped now, we will make him into black-puddings." Then the mother took the little boy and chopped him in pieces, put him into the pan and made him into black-puddings; but Marlinchen stood by weeping and weeping, and all her tears fell into the pan and there was no need of any salt.

Then the father came home, and sat down to dinner and said: "But where is my son?" And the mother served up a great dish of black-puddings, and Marlinchen wept and could not leave off. Then the father again said: "But where is my son?" "Ah," said the mother, "he has gone across the country to his mother's great uncle; he will stay there awhile." "And what is he going to do there? He did not even say good-bye to me."

"Oh, he wanted to go, and asked me if he might stay six weeks, he is well taken care of there." "Ah," said the man, "I feel so unhappy lest all should not be right. He ought to have said good-bye to me." With that he began to eat and said: "Marlinchen, why are you crying? Your brother will certainly come back." Then he said: "Ah, wife, how delicious this food is, give me some more." And the more he ate the more he wanted to have, and he said: "Give me some more, you shall have none of it. It seems to me as if it were all mine." And he ate and ate and threw all the bones under the table, until he had finished the whole. But Marlinchen went away to her chest of drawers, and took her best silk handkerchief out of the bottom drawer, and got all the bones from beneath the table, and tied them up in her silk hand-kerchief, and carried them outside the door, weeping tears of blood. Then she lay down under the juniper tree on the green grass, and after she had lain down there, she suddenly felt light-hearted and did not cry any more. Then the juniper tree began to stir itself, and the branches parted asunder, and moved together again, just as if someone were rejoicing and clapping his hands. At the same time a mist seemed to arise from the tree, and in the center of this mist it burned like a fire, and a beautiful bird flew out of the fire singing magnificently, and he flew high up in the air, and when he was gone, the juniper tree was just as it had been before, and the handkerchief with the bones was no longer there. Marlinchen, however, was as gay and happy as if her brother were still alive. And she went merrily into the house, and sat down to dinner and ate.

But the bird flew away and lighted on a goldsmith's house, and began to sing:

> "My mother she killed me,
> My father he ate me,
> My sister, little Marlinchen,
> Gathered together all my bones,
> Tied them in a silken handkerchief,
> Laid them beneath the juniper tree,
> Kywitt, kywitt, what a beautiful bird am I!"

The goldsmith was sitting in his workshop making a golden chain, when he heard the bird which was sitting singing on his roof, and very beautiful the song seemed to him. He stood up, but as he crossed the threshold he lost one of his slippers. But he went away right up the middle of the street with one shoe on and one sock; he had his apron on, and in one hand he had the golden chain and in the other the pincers, and the sun was shining brightly on the street. Then he went right on and stood still, and said to the bird: "Bird," said he then, "how beautifully you can sing! Sing me that piece again." "No," said the bird, "I'll not sing it twice for nothing! Give me the golden chain, and then I will sing it again for you." "There," said the goldsmith, "there is the golden chain for you, now sing me that song again." Then the bird came and took the golden chain in his right claw, and went and sat in front of the goldsmith, and sang:

> *"My mother she killed me,*
> *My father he ate me,*
> *My sister, little Marlinchen,*
> *Gathered together all my bones,*
> *Tied them in a silken handkerchief,*
> *Laid them beneath the juniper tree,*
> *Kywitt, kywitt, what a beautiful bird am I!"*

Then the bird flew away to a shoemaker, and lighted on his roof and sang:

> *"My mother she killed me,*
> *My father he ate me,*
> *My sister, little Marlinchen,*
> *Gathered together all my bones,*
> *Tied them in a silken handkerchief,*
> *Laid them beneath the juniper tree,*
> *Kywitt, kywitt, what a beautiful bird am I!"*

The shoemaker heard that and ran out of doors in his shirt sleeves, and looked up at his roof, and was forced to hold his hand before his eyes lest the sun should blind him. "Bird," said he, "how beautifully you can sing!" Then he called in at his door: "Wife, just come outside, there is a bird, look at that bird, he certainly can sing." Then he called his daughter and children, and apprentices, boys and girls, and they all came up the street and looked at the bird and saw how beautiful he was, and what fine red and green feathers he had, and how like real gold his neck was, and how the eyes in his head shone like stars. "Bird," said the shoemaker, "now sing me that song again." "Nay," said the bird, "I do not sing twice for nothing; you must give me something." "Wife," said the man, "go to the garret, upon the top shelf there stands a pair of red shoes, bring them down." Then the wife went and brought the shoes. "There, bird," said the man, "now sing me that piece again." Then the bird came and took the shoes in his left claw, and flew back on the roof, and sang:

> *"My mother she killed me,*
> *My father he ate me,*
> *My sister, little Marlinchen,*
> *Gathered together all my bones,*
> *Tied them in a silken handkerchief,*
> *Laid them beneath the juniper tree,*
> *Kywitt, kywitt, what a beautiful bird am I!"*

And when he had finished his song he flew away. In his right claw he had the chain and in his left the shoes, and he flew far away to a mill, and the mill went "klipp klapp, klipp klapp, klipp klapp," and in the mill sat twenty miller's men hewing a stone, and cutting, hick hack, hick hack, hick hack, and the mill went klipp klapp, klipp klapp, klipp klapp. Then the bird went and sat on a lime-tree which stood in front of the mill, and sang:

> *"My mother she killed me,"*

Then one of them stopped working,

> *"My father he ate me,"*

Then two more stopped working and listened to that,

> *"My sister, little Marlinchen,"*

Then four more stopped,

> *"Gathered together all my bones,*
> *Tied them in a silken handkerchief,"*

Now eight only were hewing,

> *"Laid them beneath"*

Now only five,

> *"The juniper tree,"*

And now only one,

> *"Kywitt, kywitt, what a beautiful bird am I!"*

Then the last stopped also, and heard the last words. "Bird," said he, "how beautifully you sing! Let me, too, hear that. Sing that once more for me."

"Nay," said the bird, "I will not sing twice for nothing. Give me the millstone, and then I will sing it again."

"Yes," said he, "if it belonged to me only, you should have it."

"Yes," said the others, "if he sings again he shall have it." Then the bird came down, and the twenty millers all set to work with a beam and raised the stone up. And the bird stuck his neck through the hole, and put the stone on as if it were a collar, and flew on to the tree again, and sang:

> *"My mother she killed me,*
> *My father he ate me,*
> *My sister, little Marlinchen,*
> *Gathered together all my bones,*
> *Tied them in a silken handkerchief,*
> *Laid them beneath the juniper tree,*
> *Kywitt, kywitt, what a beautiful bird am I!"*

And when he had done singing, he spread his wings, and in his right claw he had the chain, and in his left the shoes, and round his neck the millstone, and he flew far away to his father's house.

In the room sat the father, the mother, and Marlinchen at dinner, and the father said: "How light-hearted I feel, how happy I am!" "Nay," said the mother, "I feel so uneasy, just as if a heavy storm were coming." Marlinchen, however, sat weeping and weeping, and then came the bird flying, and as it seated itself on the roof the father said: "Ah, I feel so truly happy, and the sun is shining so beautifully outside, I feel just as if I were about to see some old friend again." "Nay," said the woman, "I feel so anxious, my teeth chatter, and I seem to have fire in my veins." And she tore her stays open, but Marlinchen sat in a corner crying, and held her plate before her eyes and cried till it was quite wet. Then the bird sat on the juniper tree, and sang:

"My mother she killed me,"

Then the mother stopped her ears, and shut her eyes, and would not see or hear, but there was a roaring in her ears like the most violent storm, and her eyes burnt and flashed like lightning:

"My father he ate me,"

"Ah, mother," says the man, "that is a beautiful bird! He sings so splendidly, and the sun shines so warm, and there is a smell just like cinnamon."

"My sister, little Marlinchen,"

Then Marlinchen laid her head on her knees and wept without ceasing, but the man said: "I am going out, I must see the bird quite close." "Oh, don't go," said the woman, "I feel as if the whole house were shaking and on fire." But the man went out and looked at the bird:

"Gathered together all my bones,
Tied them in a silken handkerchief,
Laid them beneath the juniper tree,
Kywitt, kywitt, what a beautiful bird am I!"

On this the bird let the golden chain fall, and it fell exactly round the man's neck, and so exactly round it that it fitted beautifully. Then he went in and said: "Just look what a fine bird that is, and what a handsome golden chain he has given me, and how pretty he is!" But the woman was terrified, and fell down on the floor in the room, and her cap fell off her head. Then sang the bird once more:

"My mother she killed me,"

"Would that I were a thousand feet beneath the earth so as not to hear that!"

"My father he ate me,"

Then the woman fell down again as if dead.

"My sister, little Marlinchen,"

"Ah," said Marlinchen, "I too will go out and see if the bird will give me anything," and she went out.

*"Gathered together all my bones,
    Tied them in a silken handkerchief,"*

Then he threw down the shoes to her.

*"Laid them beneath the juniper tree,
    Kywitt, kywitt, what a beautiful bird am I!"*

Then she was light-hearted and joyous, and she put on the new red shoes, and danced and leaped into the house. "Ah," said she, "I was so sad when I went out and now I am so light-hearted; that is a splendid bird, he has given me a pair of red shoes!" "Well," said the woman, and sprang to her feet and her hair stood up like flames of fire, "I feel as if the world were coming to an end! I, too, will go out and see if my heart feels lighter." And as she went out at the door, crash! the bird threw down the millstone on her head, and she was entirely crushed by it. The father and Marlinchen heard what had happened and went out, and smoke, flames and fire were rising from the place, and when that was over, there stood the little brother, and he took his father and Marlinchen by the hand, and all three were right glad, and they went into the house to dinner, and ate.

1812

Further Reading

Auden, W. H. "Grimm and Andersen." *Forewords and Afterwords.* New York: Random, 1943. 198–207. • Bottigheimer, Ruth. *Grimms' Bad Girls and Bold Boys: The Moral and Social Vision of the Tales.* New Haven: Yale UP, 1987. • Mueller, Gerhard O. W. "The Criminologicial Significance of the Grimms' Fairy Tales." *Fairy Tales and Society: Illusion, Allusion, and Paradigm.* Ed. Ruth Bottigheimer. Philadelphia: U of Pennsylvania P, 1986. 217–27, spec. 223. • Michaelis-Jena, Ruth. "Oral Tradition and the Brothers Grimm." *Folklore* 82 (Winter 1971): 265–75. • Ellis, John M. "Introduction: The Problem of the Status of the Tales." *One Fairy Story Too Many: The Brothers Grimm and Their Tales.* Chicago: U of Chicago P, 1983. 1–12.

The German "fairy tales" collected by the Grimm brothers rarely have fairies in them, and they are not stories primarily for children. They are folk tales, dictated to the two German scholars by people who had first heard them told in cottages lacking even kerosene lamps to keep the darkness back. The tales developed under these circumstances paid less heed to what Randall Jarrell calls "the learned principle of reality" than to a more "primary" psychological truth.

Randall Jarrell: On the Truth in Fairy Tales

The wish is the first truth about us, since it represents not that learned principle of reality which half-governs our workaday hours, but the primary principle of pleasure which governs infancy, sleep, daydreams— and, certainly, many stories. Reading stories, we cannot help remembering Groddeck's "We have to reckon with what exists, and dreams, daydreams too, are also facts; if anyone really wants to investigate realities, he cannot do better than to start with such as these. If he neglects them, he will learn little or nothing of the world of life." If wishes were stories, beggars would read; if stories were true, our saviors would speak to us in parables. Much of our knowledge of, our compensation for, "the world of life" comes from stories; and the stories themselves are part of "the world of life." Shakespeare wrote:

> *This is an art*
> *Which does mend nature, change it rather, but*
> *The art itself is nature . . .*

and Goethe, agreeing, said: "A work of art is just as much a work of nature as a mountain."

In showing that dreams sometimes both satisfy our wishes and punish us for them, Freud compares the dreamer to the husband and wife in the fairy tale of The Three Wishes: the wife wishes for a pudding, the husband wishes it on the end of her nose, and the wife wishes it away again. A contradictory family! But it is this family—wife, husband, and pudding—which the story must satisfy: the writer is, and is writing for, a doubly- or triply-natured creature, whose needs, understandings, and ideals—whether they are called id, ego, and superego, or body, mind, and soul—contradict one another.

The truths that he systematized, Freud said, had already been discovered by the poets; the tears of things, the truth of things, are there in their fictions. And yet, as he knew, the root of all stories is in Grimm, not in La Rochefoucauld; in dreams, not in cameras and tape recorders. . . .

NATHANIEL HAWTHORNE

(1804–1864)

THE BIRTHMARK

In the latter part of the last century there lived a man of science, an eminent proficient in every branch of natural philosophy, who not long before our story opens had made experience of a spiritual affinity more attractive than any chemical one. He had left his laboratory to the care of an assistant, cleared his fine countenance from the furnace smoke, washed the stain of acids from his fingers, and persuaded a beautiful woman to become his wife. In those days, when the comparatively recent discovery of electricity and other kindred mysteries of Nature seemed to open paths into the region of miracle, it was not unusual for the love of science to rival the love of woman in its depth and absorbing energy. The higher intellect, the imagination, the spirit, and even the heart might all find their congenial aliment in pursuits which, as some of their ardent votaries believed, would ascend from one step of powerful intelligence to another, until the philosopher should lay his hand on the secret of creative force and perhaps make new worlds for himself. We know not whether Aylmer possessed this degree of faith in man's ultimate control over Nature. He had devoted himself, however, too unreservedly to scientific studies ever to be weaned from them by any second passion. His love for his young wife might prove the stronger of the two; but it could only be by intertwining itself with his love of science and uniting the strength of the latter to his own.

Such a union accordingly took place, and was attended with truly remarkable consequences and a deeply impressive moral. One day, very soon after their marriage, Aylmer sat gazing at his wife with a trouble in his countenance that grew stronger until he spoke.

"Georgiana," said he, "has it never occurred to you that the mark upon your cheek might be removed?"

"No, indeed," said she, smiling; but, perceiving the seriousness of his manner, she blushed deeply. "To tell you the truth, it has been so often called a charm that I was simple enough to imagine it might be so."

"Ah, upon another face perhaps it might," replied her husband; "but never on yours. No, dearest Georgiana, you came so nearly perfect from the hand of Nature that this slightest possible defect, which we hesitate whether to term a defect or a beauty, shocks me, as being the visible mark of earthly imperfection."

"Shocks you, my husband!" cried Georgiana, deeply hurt; at first reddening with momentary anger, but then bursting into tears. "Then why did you take me from my mother's side? You cannot love what shocks you!"

To explain this conversation, it must be mentioned that in the centre of Georgiana's left cheek there was a singular mark, deeply interwoven, as it were, with the texture and substance of her face. In the usual state of her complexion—a healthy though delicate bloom—the mark wore a tint of deeper crimson, which imperfectly defined its shape amid the surrounding rosiness. When she blushed it gradually became more indistinct, and finally vanished amid the triumphant rush of blood that bathed the whole cheek with its brilliant glow. But if any shifting motion caused her to turn pale there was the mark again, a crimson stain upon the snow, in what Aylmer sometimes deemed an almost fearful distinctness. Its shape bore not a little similarity to the human hand, though of the smallest pygmy size. Georgiana's lovers were wont to say that some fairy at her birth hour had laid her tiny hand upon the infant's cheek, and left this impress there in token of the magic endowments that were to give her such sway over all hearts. Many a desperate swain would have risked life for the privilege of pressing his lips to the mysterious hand. It must not be concealed, however, that the impression wrought by this fairy sign-manual varied exceedingly according to the difference of temperament in the beholders. Some fastidious persons—but they were exclusively of her own sex—affirmed that the bloody hand, as they chose to call it, quite destroyed the effect of Georgiana's beauty and rendered her countenance even hideous. But it would be as reasonable to say that one of those small blue stains which sometimes occur in the purest statuary marble would convert the Eve of Powers to a monster. Masculine observers, if the birthmark did not heighten their admiration, contented themselves with wishing it away, that the world might possess one living specimen of ideal loveliness without the semblance of a flaw. After his marriage,—for he thought little or nothing of the matter before,— Aylmer discovered that this was the case with himself.

Had she been less beautiful,—if Envy's self could have found aught else to sneer at,—he might have felt his affection heightened by the prettiness of this mimic hand, now vaguely portrayed, now lost, now stealing forth again and glimmering to and fro with every pulse of emotion that throbbed within her heart; but, seeing her otherwise so perfect, he found this one defect grow more and more intolerable with every moment of their united lives. It was the fatal flaw of humanity which Nature, in one shape or another, stamps ineffaceably on all her productions, either to imply that they are temporary and finite, or that their perfection must be wrought by toil and pain. The crimson hand expressed the ineludible grip in which mortality clutches the highest and purest of earthly mould, degrading them into kindred with the lowest, and even with the very brutes, like whom their visible frames return to dust. In this manner, selecting it as the symbol of his wife's liability to sin, sorrow, decay, and death, Aylmer's sombre imagination was not long in rendering the birthmark a frightful object, causing him more trouble and horror than ever Georgiana's beauty, whether of soul or sense, had given him delight.

At all the seasons which should have been their happiest he invariably, and without intending it, nay, in spite of a purpose to the contrary, reverted to this one disastrous topic. Trifling as it at first appeared, it so connected itself with innumerable trains of thought and modes of feeling that it became the central point of all. With the morning twilight Aylmer opened his eyes upon his wife's face and recognized the symbol of imperfection; and when they sat together at the evening hearth his eyes wandered stealthily to her cheek, and beheld, flickering with the blaze of the wood fire, the spectral hand that wrote mortality where he would fain have worshipped. Georgiana soon learned to shudder at his gaze. It needed but a glance with the peculiar expression that his face often wore to change the roses of her cheek into a deathlike paleness, amid which the crimson hand was brought strongly out, like a bass relief of ruby on the whitest marble.

Late one night, when the lights were growing dim so as hardly to betray the stain on the poor wife's cheek, she herself, for the first time, voluntarily took up the subject.

"Do you remember, my dear Aylmer," said she, with a feeble attempt at a smile, "have you any recollection, of a dream last night about this odious hand?"

"None! none whatever!" replied Aylmer, starting; but then he added, in a dry, cold tone, affected for the sake of concealing the real depth of his emotion, "I might well dream of it; for, before I fell asleep, it had taken a pretty firm hold of my fancy."

"And you did dream of it?" continued Georgiana, hastily; for she dreaded lest a gush of tears should interrupt what she had to say. "A terrible dream! I wonder that you can forget it. Is it possible to forget this one expression?—'It is in her heart now; we must have it out!' Reflect, my husband; for by all means I would have you recall that dream."

The mind is in a sad state when Sleep, the all-involving, cannot confine her spectres within the dim region of her sway, but suffers them to break forth, affrighting this actual life with secrets that perchance belong to a deeper one. Aylmer now remembered his dream. He had fancied himself with his servant Aminadab, attempting an operation for the removal of the birthmark; but the deeper went the knife, the deeper sank the hand, until at length its tiny grasp appeared to have caught hold of Georgiana's heart; whence, however, her husband was inexorably resolved to cut or wrench it away.

When the dream had shaped itself perfectly in his memory Aylmer sat in his wife's presence with a guilty feeling. Truth often finds its way to the mind close muffled in robes of sleep, and then speaks with uncompromising directness of matters in regard to which we practise an unconscious self-deception during our waking moments. Until now he had not been aware of the tyrannizing influence acquired by one idea over his mind, and of the lengths which he might find in his heart to go for the sake of giving himself peace.

"Aylmer," resumed Georgiana, solemnly, "I know not what may be the cost to both of us to rid me of this fatal birthmark. Perhaps its removal may cause cureless deformity; or it may be the stain goes as deep as life itself. Again: do we know that there is a possibility, on any terms, of unclasping the firm grip of this little hand which was laid upon me before I came into the world?"

"Dearest Georgiana, I have spent much thought upon the subject," hastily interrupted Aylmer. "I am convinced of the perfect practicability of its removal."

"If there be the remotest possibility of it," continued Georgiana, "let the attempt be made, at whatever risk. Danger is nothing to me; for life, while this hateful mark makes me the object of your horror and disgust,— life is a burden which I would fling down with joy. Either remove this dreadful hand, or take my wretched life! You have deep science. All the world bears witness of it. You have achieved great wonders. Cannot you remove this little, little mark, which I cover with the tips of two small fingers? Is this beyond your power, for the sake of your own peace, and to save your poor wife from madness?"

"Noblest, dearest, tenderest wife," cried Aylmer, rapturously, "doubt not my power. I have already given this matter the deepest thought— thought which might almost have enlightened me to create a being less perfect than yourself. Georgiana, you have led me deeper than ever into the heart of science. I feel myself fully competent to render this dear cheek as faultless as its fellow; and then, most beloved, what will be my triumph when I shall have corrected what Nature left imperfect in her fairest work! Even Pygmalion, when his sculptured woman assumed life, felt not greater ecstasy than mine will be."

"It is resolved, then," said Georgiana, faintly smiling. "And, Aylmer, spare me not, though you should find the birthmark take refuge in my heart at last."

Her husband tenderly kissed her cheek—her right cheek—not that which bore the impress of the crimson hand.

The next day Aylmer apprised his wife of a plan that he had formed whereby he might have opportunity for the intense thought and constant watchfulness which the proposed operation would require; while Georgiana, likewise, would enjoy the perfect repose essential to its success. They were to seclude themselves in the extensive apartments occupied by Aylmer as a laboratory, and where, during his toilsome youth, he had made discoveries in the elemental powers of Nature that had roused the admiration of all the learned societies in Europe. Seated calmly in this laboratory, the pale philosopher had investigated the secrets of the highest cloud region and of the profoundest mines; he had satisfied himself of the causes that kindled and kept alive the fires of the volcano; and had explained the mystery of the fountains, and how it is that they gush forth, some so bright and pure, and others with such rich medicinal virtues, from the dark bosom of the earth. Here, too, at an earlier period, he had studied the wonders of the human frame, and attempted to fathom the very process by which Nature assimilates all her precious influences from earth and air, and from the spiritual world, to create and foster man, her masterpiece. The latter pursuit, however, Aylmer had long laid aside in unwilling recognition of the truth—

against which all seekers sooner or later stumble—that our great creative Mother, while she amuses us with apparently working in the broadest sunshine, is yet severely careful to keep her own secrets, and, in spite of her pretended openness, shows us nothing but results. She permits us, indeed, to mar, but seldom to mend, and, like a jealous patentee, on no account to make. Now, however, Aylmer resumed these half-forgotten investigations; not, of course, with such hopes or wishes as first suggested them; but because they involved much physiological truth and lay in the path of his proposed scheme for the treatment of Georgiana.

As he led her over the threshold of the laboratory, Georgiana was cold and tremulous. Aylmer looked cheerfully into her face, with intent to reassure her, but was so startled with the intense glow of the birthmark upon the whiteness of her cheek that he could not restrain a strong convulsive shudder. His wife fainted.

"Aminadab! Aminadab!" shouted Aylmer, stamping violently on the floor.

Forthwith there issued from an inner apartment a man of low stature, but bulky frame, with shaggy hair hanging about his visage, which was grimed with the vapors of the furnace. This personage had been Aylmer's underworker during his whole scientific career, and was admirably fitted for that office by his great mechanical readiness, and the skill with which, while incapable of comprehending a single principle, he executed all the details of his master's experiments. With his vast strength, his shaggy hair, his smoky aspect, and the indescribable earthiness that incrusted him, he seemed to represent man's physical nature; while Aylmer's slender figure, and pale, intellectual face, were no less apt a type of the spiritual element.

"Throw open the door of the boudoir, Aminadab," said Aylmer, "and burn a pastil."

"Yes, master," answered Aminadab, looking intently at the lifeless form of Georgiana; and then he muttered to himself, "If she were my wife, I'd never part with that birthmark."

When Georgiana recovered consciousness she found herself breathing an atmosphere of penetrating fragrance, the gentle potency of which had recalled her from her deathlike faintness. The scene around her looked like enchantment. Aylmer had converted those smoky, dingy, sombre rooms, where he had spent his brightest years in recondite pursuits, into a series of beautiful apartments not unfit to be the secluded abode of a lovely woman. The walls were hung with gorgeous curtains, which imparted the combination of grandeur and grace that no other species of adornment can achieve; and, as they fell from the ceiling to the floor, their rich and ponderous folds, concealing all angles and straight lines, appeared to shut in the scene from infinite space. For aught Georgiana knew, it might be a pavilion among the clouds. And Aylmer, excluding the sunshine, which would have interfered with his chemical processes, had supplied its place with perfumed lamps, emitting flames of various hue, but all uniting in a soft, impurpled radiance. He now knelt by his wife's side, watching her earnestly, but without alarm; for he was confident in his science, and felt that he could draw a magic circle round her within which no evil might intrude.

"Where am I? Ah, I remember," said Georgiana, faintly, and she placed her hand over her cheek to hide the terrible mark from her husband's eyes.

"Fear not, dearest!" exclaimed he. "Do not shrink from me! Believe me, Georgiana, I even rejoice in this single imperfection, since it will be such a rapture to remove it."

"O, spare me!" sadly replied his wife. "Pray do not look at it again. I never can forget that convulsive shudder."

In order to soothe Georgiana, and, as it were, to release her mind from the burden of actual things, Aylmer now put in practice some of the light and playful secrets which science had taught him among its profounder lore. Airy figures, absolutely bodiless ideas, and forms of unsubstantial beauty came and danced before her, imprinting their momentary footsteps on beams of light. Though she had some indistinct idea of the method of these optical phenomena, still the illusion was almost perfect enough to warrant the belief that her husband possessed sway over the spiritual world. Then again, when she felt a wish to look forth from her seclusion, immediately, as if her thoughts were answered, the procession of external existence flitted across a screen. The scenery and the figures of actual life were perfectly represented, but with that bewitching yet indescribable difference which always makes a picture, an image, or a shadow so much more attractive than the original. When wearied of this, Aylmer bade her cast her eyes upon a vessel containing a quantity of earth. She did so, with little interest at first; but was soon startled to perceive the germ of a plant shooting upward from the soil. Then came the slender stalk; the leaves gradually unfolded themselves; and amid them was a perfect and lovely flower.

"It is magical!" cried Georgiana. "I dare not touch it."

"Nay, pluck it," answered Aylmer,—"pluck it, and inhale its brief perfume while you may. The flower will wither in a few moments and leave nothing save its brown seed vessels; but thence may be perpetuated a race as ephemeral as itself."

But Georgiana had no sooner touched the flower than the whole plant suffered a blight, its leaves turning coal-black as if by the agency of fire.

"There was too powerful a stimulus," said Aylmer, thoughtfully.

To make up for this abortive experiment, he proposed to take her portrait by a scientific process of his own invention. It was to be effected by rays of light striking upon a polished plate of metal. Georgiana assented; but, on looking at the result, was affrighted to find the features of the portrait blurred and indefinable; while the minute figure of a hand appeared where the cheek should have been. Aylmer snatched the metallic plate and threw it into a jar of corrosive acid.

Soon, however, he forgot these mortifying failures. In the intervals of study and chemical experiment he came to her flushed and exhausted, but seemed invigorated by her presence, and spoke in glowing language of the resources of his art. He gave a history of the long dynasty of the alchemists, who spent so many ages in quest of the universal solvent by which the golden principle might be elicited from all things vile and base. Aylmer appeared to believe that, by the plainest scientific logic, it was altogether within the limits of possibility to discover this long-sought medium; "but," he added, "a philosopher who should go deep enough to acquire the power would attain too lofty a wisdom to stoop to the exercise of it." Not less singular were his opinions in regard to the elixir vitae. He more than intimated that it was at his option to concoct a liquid that should prolong life for years, perhaps interminably; but that it would produce a discord in Nature which all the world, and chiefly the quaffer of the immortal nostrum, would find cause to curse.

"Aylmer, are you in earnest?" asked Georgiana, looking at him with amazement and fear. "It is terrible to possess such power, or even to dream of possessing it."

"O, do not tremble, my love," said her husband. "I would not wrong either you or myself by working such inharmonious effects upon our lives; but I would have you consider how trifling, in comparison, is the skill requisite to remove this little hand."

At the mention of the birthmark, Georgiana, as usual, shrank as if a red-hot iron had touched her cheek.

Again Aylmer applied himself to his labors. She could hear his voice in the distant furnace room giving directions to Aminadab, whose harsh, uncouth, misshapen tones were audible in response, more like the grunt or growl of a brute than human speech. After hours of absence, Aylmer reappeared and proposed that she should now examine his cabinet of chemical products and natural treasures of the earth. Among the former he showed her a small vial, in which, he remarked, was contained a gentle yet most powerful fragrance, capable of impregnating all the breezes that blow across a kingdom. They were of inestimable value, the contents of that little vial; and, as he said so, he threw some of the perfume into the air and filled the room with piercing and invigorating delight.

"And what is this?" asked Georgiana, pointing to a small crystal globe containing a gold-colored liquid. "It is so beautiful to the eye that I could imagine it the elixir of life."

"In one sense it is," replied Aylmer; "or rather, the elixir of immortality. It is the most precious poison that ever was concocted in this world. By its aid I could apportion the lifetime of any mortal at whom you might point your finger. The strength of the dose would determine whether he were to linger out years, or drop dead in the midst of a breath. No king on his guarded throne could keep his life if I, in my private station, should deem that the welfare of millions justified me in depriving him of it."

"Why do you keep such a terrific drug?" inquired Georgiana in horror.

"Do not mistrust me, dearest," said her husband, smiling; "its virtuous potency is yet greater than its harmful one. But see! here is a powerful cosmetic. With a few drops of this in a vase of water, freckles may be washed away as easily as the hands are cleansed. A stronger infusion would take the blood out of the cheek, and leave the rosiest beauty a pale ghost."

"Is it with this lotion that you intend to bathe my cheek?" asked Georgiana, anxiously.

"O, no," hastily replied her husband; "this is merely superficial. Your case demands a remedy that shall go deeper."

In his interviews with Georgiana, Aylmer generally made minute inquiries as to her sensations, and whether the confinement of the rooms and the temperature of the atmosphere agreed with her. These questions had such a particular drift that Georgiana began to conjecture that she was already subjected to certain physical influences, either breathed in with the fragrant air or taken with her food. She fancied likewise, but it might be altogether fancy, that there was a stirring up of her system—a strange, indefinite sensation creeping through her veins, and tingling, half painfully, half pleasurably, at her heart. Still, whenever she dared to look into the mirror, there she beheld herself pale as a white rose and with the crimson birthmark stamped upon her cheek. Not even Aylmer now hated it so much as she.

To dispel the tedium of the hours which her husband found it necessary to devote to the processes of combination and analysis, Georgiana turned over the volumes of his scientific library. In many dark old tomes she met with chapters full of romance and poetry. They were the works of the philosophers of the middle ages, such as Albertus Magnus, Cornelius Agrippa, Paracelsus, and the famous friar who created the prophetic Brazen Head. All these antique naturalists stood in advance of their centuries, yet were imbued with some of their credulity, and therefore were believed, and perhaps imagined themselves to have acquired from the investigation of Nature a power above Nature, and from physics a sway over the spiritual world. Hardly less curious and imaginative were the early volumes of the Transactions of the Royal Society, in which the members, knowing little of the limits of natural possibility, were continually recording wonders or proposing methods whereby wonders might be wrought.

But to Georgiana, the most engrossing volume was a large folio from her husband's own hand, in which he had recorded every experiment of his scientific career, its original aim, the methods adopted for its development, and its final success or failure, with the circumstances to which either event was attributable. The book, in truth, was both the history and emblem of his ardent, ambitious, imaginative, yet practical and laborious life. He handled physical details as if there were nothing beyond them; yet spiritualized them all and redeemed himself from materialism by his strong and eager aspiration towards the infinite. In his grasp the veriest clod of earth assumed a soul. Georgiana, as she read, reverenced Aylmer and loved him more profoundly than ever, but with a less entire dependence on his judgment than heretofore. Much as he had accomplished, she could not but observe that his most splendid successes were almost invariably failures, if compared with the ideal at which he aimed. His brightest diamonds were the merest pebbles, and felt to be so by himself, in comparison with the inestimable gems which lay hidden beyond his reach. The volume, rich with achievements that had won renown for its author, was yet as melancholy a record as ever mortal hand had penned. It was the sad confession and continual exemplification of the shortcomings of the composite man, the spirit burdened with clay and working in matter, and of the despair that assails the higher nature at finding itself so miserably thwarted by the earthly part. Perhaps every man of genius, in whatever sphere, might recognize the image of his own experience in Aylmer's journal.

So deeply did these reflections affect Georgiana that she laid her face upon the open volume and burst into tears. In this situation she was found by her husband.

"It is dangerous to read in a sorcerer's books," said he with a smile, though his countenance was uneasy and displeased. "Georgiana, there are pages in that volume which I can scarcely glance over and keep my senses. Take heed lest it prove detrimental to you."

"It has made me worship you more than ever," said she.

"Ah, wait for this one success," rejoined he, "then worship me if you will. I shall deem myself hardly unworthy of it. But come, I have sought you for the luxury of your voice. Sing to me, dearest."

So she poured out the liquid music of her voice to quench the thirst of his spirit. He then took his leave with a boyish exuberance of gayety, assuring her that her seclusion would endure but a little longer, and that the result was already certain. Scarcely had he departed when Georgiana felt irresistibly impelled to follow him. She had forgotten to inform Aylmer of a symptom which for two or three hours past had begun to excite her attention. It was a sensation in the fatal birthmark, not painful, but which induced a restlessness throughout her system. Hastening after her husband, she intruded for the first time into the laboratory.

The first thing that struck her eye was the furnace, that hot and feverish worker, with the intense glow of its fire, which by the quantities of soot clustered above it seemed to have been burning for ages. There was a distilling apparatus in full operation. Around the room were retorts, tubes, cylinders, crucibles, and other apparatus of chemical research. An electrical machine stood ready for immediate use. The atmosphere felt oppressively close, and was tainted with gaseous odors which had been tormented forth by the processes of science. The severe and homely simplicity of the apartment, with its naked walls and brick pavement, looked strange, accustomed as Georgiana had become to the fantastic elegance of her boudoir. But what chiefly, indeed almost solely, drew her attention, was the aspect of Aylmer himself.

He was pale as death, anxious and absorbed, and hung over the furnace as if it depended upon his utmost watchfulness whether the liquid which it was distilling should be the draught of immortal happiness or misery. How different from the sanguine and joyous mien that he had assumed for Georgiana's encouragement!

"Carefully now, Aminadab; carefully, thou human machine; carefully, thou man of clay," muttered Aylmer, more to himself than his assistant. "Now, if there be a thought too much or too little, it is all over."

"Ho! ho!" mumbled Aminadab. "Look, master! look!"

Aylmer raised his eyes hastily, and at first reddened, then grew paler than ever, on beholding Georgiana. He rushed towards her and seized her arm with a grip that left the print of his fingers upon it.

"Why do you come hither? Have you no trust in your husband?" cried he, impetuously. "Would you throw the blight of that fatal birthmark over my labors? It is not well done. Go, prying woman! go!"

"Nay, Aylmer," said Georgiana with the firmness of which she possessed no stinted endowment, "it is not you that have a right to complain. You mistrust your wife; you have concealed the anxiety with which you watch the development of this experiment. Think not so unworthily of me, my husband. Tell me all the risk we run, and fear not that I shall shrink; for my share in it is far less than your own."

"No, no, Georgiana!" said Aylmer, impatiently; "it must not be."

"I submit," replied she, calmly. "And, Aylmer, I shall quaff whatever draught you bring me; but it will be on the same principle that would induce me to take a dose of poison if offered by your hand."

"My noble wife," said Aylmer, deeply moved, "I knew not the height and depth of your nature until now. Nothing shall be concealed. Know, then, that this crimson hand, superficial as it seems, has clutched its grasp into your being with a strength of which I had no previous conception. I have already administered agents powerful enough to do aught except to change your entire physical system. Only one thing remains to be tried. If that fails us we are ruined."

"Why did you hesitate to tell me this?" asked she.

"Because, Georgiana," said Aylmer, in a low voice, "there is danger."

"Danger? There is but one danger—that this horrible stigma shall be left upon my cheek!" cried Georgiana. "Remove it, remove it, whatever be the cost, or we shall both go mad!"

"Heaven knows your words are too true," said Aylmer, sadly. "And now, dearest, return to your boudoir. In a little while all will be tested."

He conducted her back and took leave of her with a solemn tenderness which spoke far more than his words how much was now at stake. After his departure Georgiana became rapt in musings. She considered the character of Aylmer and did it completer justice than at any previous moment. Her heart exulted, while it trembled, at his honorable love—so pure and lofty that it would accept nothing less than perfection nor miserably make itself contented with an earthlier nature than he had dreamed of. She felt how much more precious was such a sentiment than that meaner kind which would have borne with the imperfection for her sake, and have been guilty of treason to holy love by degrading its perfect idea to the level of the actual; and with her whole spirit she prayed that, for a single moment, she might satisfy his highest and deepest conception. Longer than one moment she well knew it could not be; for his spirit was ever on the march, ever ascending, and each instant required something that was beyond the scope of the instant before.

The sound of her husband's footsteps aroused her. He bore a crystal goblet containing a liquor colorless as water, but bright enough to be the draught of immortality. Aylmer was pale; but it seemed rather the consequence of a highly-wrought state of mind and tension of spirit than of fear or doubt.

"The concoction of the draught has been perfect," said he, in answer to Georgiana's look. "Unless all my science have deceived me, it cannot fail."

"Save on your account, my dearest Aylmer," observed his wife, "I might wish to put off this birthmark of mortality by relinquishing mortality itself in preference to any other mode. Life is but a sad possession to those who have attained precisely the degree of moral advancement at which I stand. Were I weaker and blinder, it might be happiness. Were I stronger, it might be endured hopefully. But, being what I find myself, methinks I am of all mortals the most fit to die."

"You are fit for heaven without tasting death!" replied her husband. "But why do we speak of dying? The draught cannot fail. Behold its effect upon this plant."

On the window seat there stood a geranium diseased with yellow blotches which had overspread all its leaves. Aylmer poured a small quantity of the liquid upon the soil in which it grew. In a little time, when the roots of the plant had taken up the moisture, the unsightly blotches began to be extinguished in a living verdure.

"There needed no proof," said Georgiana, quietly. "Give me the goblet. I joyfully stake all upon your word."

"Drink, then, thou lofty creature!" exclaimed Aylmer, with fervid admiration. "There is no taint of imperfection on thy spirit. Thy sensible frame, too, shall soon be all perfect."

She quaffed the liquid and returned the goblet to his hand.

"It is grateful," said she, with a placid smile. "Methinks it is like water from a heavenly fountain; for it contains I know not what of unobtrusive fragrance and deliciousness. It allays a feverish thirst that had parched me for many days. Now, dearest, let me sleep. My earthly senses are closing over my spirit like the leaves around the heart of a rose at sunset."

She spoke the last words with a gentle reluctance, as if it required almost more energy than she could command to pronounce the faint and lingering syllables. Scarcely had they loitered through her lips ere she was lost in slumber. Aylmer sat by her side, watching her aspect with the emotions proper to a man the whole value of whose existence was involved in the process now to be tested. Mingled with this mood, however, was the philosophic investigation characteristic of the man of science. Not the minutest symptom escaped him. A heightened flush of the cheek, a slight irregularity of breath, a quiver of the eyelid, a hardly perceptible tremor through the frame,—such were the details which, as the moments passed, he wrote down in his folio volume. Intense thought had set its stamp upon every previous page of that volume; but the thoughts of years were all concentrated upon the last.

While thus employed, he failed not to gaze often at the fatal hand, and not without a shudder. Yet once, by a strange and unaccountable impulse, he pressed it with his lips. His spirit recoiled, however, in the very act; and Georgiana, out of the midst of her deep sleep, moved uneasily and murmured as if in remonstrance. Again Aylmer resumed his watch. Nor was it without avail. The crimson hand, which at first had been strongly visible upon the marble paleness of Georgiana's cheek, now grew more faintly outlined. She remained not less pale than ever; but the birthmark, with every breath that came and went lost somewhat of its former distinctness. Its presence had been awful; its departure was more awful still. Watch the stain of the rainbow fading out of the sky, and you will know how that mysterious symbol passed away.

"By Heaven! it is well nigh gone!" said Aylmer to himself, in almost irrepressible ecstasy. "I can scarcely trace it now. Success! success! And now it is like the faintest rose color. The slightest flush of blood across her cheek would overcome it. But she is so pale!"

He drew aside the window curtain and suffered the light of natural day to fall into the room and rest upon her cheek. At the same time he heard a gross, hoarse chuckle, which he had long known as his servant Aminadab's expression of delight.

"Ah, clod! ah, earthly mass!" cried Aylmer, laughing in a sort of frenzy, "you have served me well! Matter and spirit—earth and heaven—have both done their part in this! Laugh, thing of the senses! You have earned the right to laugh."

These exclamations broke Georgiana's sleep. She slowly unclosed her eyes and gazed into the mirror which her husband had arranged for that purpose. A faint smile flitted over her lips when she recognized how barely perceptible was now that crimson hand which had once blazed forth with such disastrous brilliancy as to scare away all their happiness. But then her eyes sought Aylmer's face with a trouble and anxiety that he could by no means account for.

"My poor Aylmer!" murmured she.

"Poor? Nay, richest, happiest, most favored!" exclaimed he. "My peerless bride, it is successful! You are perfect!"

"My poor Aylmer," she repeated, with a more than human tenderness, "you have aimed loftily; you have done nobly. Do not repent that, with so high and pure a feeling, you have rejected the best the earth could offer. Aylmer, dearest Aylmer, I am dying!"

Alas! it was too true! The fatal hand had grappled with the mystery of life, and was the bond by which an angelic spirit kept itself in union with a mortal frame. As the last crimson tint of the birthmark—that sole token of human imperfection—faded from her cheek, the parting breath of the now perfect woman passed into the atmosphere, and her soul, lingering a moment near her husband, took its heavenward flight. Then a hoarse, chuckling laugh was heard again! Thus ever does the gross fatality of earth exult in its invariable triumph over the immortal essence which, in this dim sphere of half development, demands the completeness of a higher state. Yet, had Aylmer reached a profounder wisdom, he need not thus have flung away the happiness which would have woven his mortal life of the selfsame texture with the celestial. The momentary circumstance was too strong for him; he failed to look beyond the shadowy scope of time, and, living once for all in eternity, to find the perfect future in the present.

1846

Further Reading

Melville, Herman. "Hawthorne and His Mosses. By a Virginian Spending His Summer in Vermont." *Hawthorne: The Critical Heritage.* Ed. J. Donald Crowley. New York: Barnes, 1970. 111–26. • Crowley, J. Donald, ed. Introduction. *Nathaniel Hawthorne: A Collection of Criticism.* By J. Donald Crowley. New York: McGraw, 1975. 1–10. • Way, Brian. "Art and the Spirit of Anarchy: A Reading of Hawthorne's Short Stories." *Nathaniel Hawthorne: New Critical Essays.* Ed. A. Robert Lee. Totowa, N.J.: Barnes, 1982. 11–29, spec. 14–15. • Heilman, R. B. "Hawthorne's 'The Birthmark': Science as Religion." *South Atlantic Quarterly* 48 (1949): 573–83. • Horne, Lewis B. "The Heart, The Hand and 'The Birthmark.'" *American Transcendental Quarterly* 1 (1969): 38–41.

Nathaniel Hawthorne, who was very aware of the realistic tradition in fiction, chose to concentrate his attention on "romances" that present "the truth of the human heart." At first, some readers may be inclined to dismiss these romances as simple fairy stories, but as Herman Melville points out, a Hawthorne story has psychological complexities beneath its rather simple plot and sometimes bright surface.

Herman Melville: On the Blackness of Hawthorne's Themes

For spite of all the Indian-summer sunlight on the hither side of Hawthorne's soul, the other side—like the dark half of the physical sphere—is shrouded in a blackness, ten times black. But this darkness but gives more effect to the ever-moving dawn, that for ever advances through it, and circumnavigates his world. Whether Hawthorne has simply availed himself of this mystical blackness as a means to the wondrous effects he makes it to produce in his lights and shades; or whether there really lurks in him, per-haps unknown to himself, a touch of Puritanic gloom,—this, I cannot alto-gether tell. Certain it is, however, that this great power of blackness in him derives its force from its appeals to that Calvinistic sense of Innate Deprav-ity and Original Sin, from whose visitations, in some shape or other, no deeply thinking mind is always and wholly free. For, in certain moods, no man can weigh this world without throwing in something, somehow like Original Sin, to strike the uneven balance. At all events, perhaps no writer has ever wielded this terrific thought with greater terror than this same harmless Hawthorne. Still more: this black conceit pervades him through and through. You may be witched by his sunlight,—transported by the bright gildings in the skies he builds over you; but there is the blackness of darkness beyond; and even his bright gildings but fringe and play upon the edges of thunder-clouds.

EDGAR ALLAN POE

(1809–1849)

THE TELL-TALE HEART

True!—nervous—very, very dreadfully nervous I had been and am; but why *will* you say that I am mad? The disease had sharpened my senses—not destroyed—not dulled them. Above all was the sense of hearing acute. I heard all things in the heaven and in the earth. I heard many things in hell. How, then, am I mad? Hearken! and observe how healthily—how calmly I can tell you the whole story.

It is impossible to say how first the idea entered my brain; but once conceived, it haunted me day and night. Object there was none. Passion there was none. I loved the old man. He had never wronged me. He had never given me insult. For his gold I had no desire. I think it was his eye! yes, it was this! One of his eyes resembled that of a vulture—a pale blue eye, with a film over it. Whenever it fell upon me, my blood ran cold; and so by degrees—very gradually—I made up my mind to take the life of the old man, and thus rid myself of the eye for ever.

Now this is the point. You fancy me mad. Madmen know nothing. But you should have seen *me*. You should have seen how wisely I proceeded—with what caution—with what foresight—with what dissimulation I went to work! I was never kinder to the old man than during the whole week before I killed him. And every night, about midnight, I turned the latch of his door and opened it—oh, so gently! And then, when I had made an opening suf-ficient for my head, I put in a dark lantern, all closed, closed, so that no light shone out, and then I thrust in my head. Oh, you would have laughed to see how cunningly I thrust it in! I moved it slowly—very, very slowly, so that I might not disturb the old man's sleep. It took me an hour to place my whole head within the opening so far that I could see him as he lay upon his bed. Ha!—would a madman have been so wise as this? And then, when my head was well in the room, I undid the lantern cautiously—oh, so cautiously—cautiously (for the hinges creaked)—I undid it just so much that a single thin ray fell upon the vulture eye. And this I did for seven long nights—every night just after midnight—but I found the eye always closed; and so it was impossible to do the work; for it was not the old man who vexed me, but his Evil Eye. And every morning, when the day broke, I went boldly into the chamber, and spoke courageously to him, calling him by name in a hearty tone, and inquiring how he had passed the night. So you see he would have been a very profound old man, indeed, to suspect that every night, just at twelve, I looked in upon him while he slept.

Upon the eighth night I was more than usually cautious in opening the door. A watch's minute hand moves more quickly than did mine. Never before that night had I *felt* the extent of my own powers—of my sagacity. I could scarcely contain my feelings of triumph. To think that there I was, opening the door, little by little, and he not even to dream of my secret deeds or thoughts. I fairly chuckled at the idea; and perhaps he heard me; for he moved on the bed suddenly, as if startled. Now you may think that I drew back—but no. His room was as black as pitch with the thick darkness (for the shutters were close fastened, through fear of robbers), and so I knew that he could not see the opening of the door, and I kept pushing it on steadily, steadily.

I had my head in, and was about to open the lantern, when my thumb slipped upon the tin fastening, and the old man sprang up in the bed, crying out—"Who's there?"

I kept quite still and said nothing. For a whole hour I did not move a muscle, and in the meantime I did not hear him lie down. He was still sitting up in the bed listening;—just as I have done, night after night, hearkening to the death watches in the wall.

Presently I heard a slight groan, and I knew it was the groan of mortal terror. It was not a groan of pain or of grief—oh, no!—it was the low stifled sound that arises from the bottom of the soul when overcharged with awe. I knew the sound well. Many a night, just at midnight, when all the world slept, it has welled up from my own bosom, deepening, with its dreadful echo, the terrors that distracted me. I say I knew it well. I knew what the old man felt, and pitied him, although I chuckled at heart. I knew that he had been lying awake ever since the first slight noise, when he had turned in the bed. His fears had been ever since growing upon him. He had been trying to fancy them causeless, but could not. He had been saying to himself—"It is nothing but the wind in the chimney—it is only a mouse crossing the floor," or "it is merely a cricket which has made a single chirp." Yes, he has been trying to comfort himself with these suppositions; but he had found all in vain. *All in vain;* because Death, in approaching him, had stalked with his black shadow before him, and enveloped the victim. And it was the mournful influence of the unperceived shadow that caused him to feel—although he neither saw nor heard—to *feel* the presence of my head within the room.

When I had waited a long time, very patiently, without hearing him lie down, I resolved to open a little—a very, very little crevice in the lantern. So I opened it—you cannot imagine how stealthily, stealthily—until, at length, a single dim ray, like the thread of the spider, shot from out the crevice and full upon the vulture eye.

It was open—wide, wide open—and I grew furious as I gazed upon it. I saw it with perfect distinctness—all a dull blue, with a hideous veil over it that chilled the very marrow in my bones; but I could see nothing else of the old man's face or person: for I had directed the ray as if by instinct, precisely upon the damned spot.

And now have I not told you that what you mistake for madness is but over-acuteness of the senses?—now, I say, there came to my ears a low, dull, quick sound, such as a watch makes when enveloped in cotton. I knew *that* sound well too. It was the beating of the old man's heart. It increased my fury, as the beating of a drum stimulates the soldier into courage.

But even yet I refrained and kept still. I scarcely breathed. I held the lantern motionless. I tried how steadily I could maintain the ray upon the eye. Meantime the hellish tattoo of the heart increased. It grew quicker and quicker, and louder and louder every instant. The old man's terror *must* have been extreme! It grew louder, I say, louder every moment!—do you mark me well? I have told you that I am nervous: so I am. And now at the dead hour of the night, amid the dreadful silence of that old house, so strange a noise as this excited me to uncontrollable terror. Yet, for some minutes longer I refrained and stood still. But the beating grew louder, louder! I thought the heart must burst. And now a new anxiety seized me —the sound would be heard by a neighbor! The old man's hour had come! With a loud yell, I threw open the lantern and leaped into the room. He shrieked once—once only. In an instant I dragged him to the floor, and pulled the heavy bed over him. I then smiled gaily, to find the deed so far done. But, for many minutes, the heart beat on with a muffled sound. This, however, did not vex me; it would not be heard through the wall. At length it ceased. The old man was dead. I removed the bed and examined the corpse. Yes, he was stone, stone dead. I placed my hand upon the heart and held it there many minutes. There was no pulsation. He was stone dead. His eye would trouble me no more.

If still you think me mad, you will think so no longer when I describe the wise precautions I took for the concealment of the body. The night waned, and I worked hastily, but in silence. First of all I dismembered the corpse. I cut off the head and the arms and the legs.

I then took up three planks from the flooring of the chamber, and deposited all between the scantlings. I then replaced the boards so cleverly, so cunningly, that no human eye—not even *his*—could have detected anything wrong. There was nothing to wash out—no stain of any kind—no blood-spot whatever. I had been too wary for that. A tub had caught all—ha! ha!

When I had made an end of these labors, it was four o'clock—still dark as midnight. As the bell sounded the hour, there came a knocking at the street door. I went down to open it with a light heart—for what had I *now* to fear? There entered three men, who introduced themselves, with perfect suavity, as officers of the police. A shriek had been heard by a neighbor during the night; suspicion of foul play had been aroused; information had been lodged at the police office, and they (the officers) had been deputed to search the premises.

I smiled,—for *what* had I to fear? I bade the gentlemen welcome. The shriek, I said, was my own in a dream. The old man, I mentioned, was absent in the country. I took my visitors all over the house. I bade them search—search *well*. I led them, at length, to *his* chamber. I showed them his treasures, secure, undisturbed. In the enthusiasm of my confidence, I brought chairs into the room, and desired them *here* to rest from their fatigues, while I myself, in the wild audacity of my perfect triumph, placed my own seat upon the very spot beneath which reposed the corpse of the victim.

The officers were satisfied. My *manner* had convinced them. I was singularly at ease. They sat, and while I answered cheerily, they chatted familiar things. But, ere long, I felt myself getting pale and wished them gone. My head ached, and I fancied a ringing in my ears: but still they sat and still chatted. The ringing became more distinct:—it continued and became more distinct: I talked more freely to get rid of the feeling: but it continued and gained definitiveness—until, at length, I found that the noise was *not* within my ears.

No doubt I now grew *very* pale;—but I talked more fluently, and with a heightened voice. Yet the sound increased—and what could I do? It was *a low, dull, quick sound—much such a sound as a watch makes when enveloped in cotton.* I gasped for breath—and yet the officers heard it not. I talked more quickly—more vehemently; but the noise steadily increased. I arose and argued about trifles, in a high key and with violent gesticulations, but the noise steadily increased. Why *would* they not be gone? I paced the floor to and fro with heavy strides, as if excited to fury by the observation of the men—but the noise steadily increased. Oh God! what *could* I do? I foamed —I raved—I swore! I swung the chair upon which I had been sitting, and grated it upon the boards, but the noise arose over all and continually increased. It grew louder—louder—*louder!* And still the men chatted pleasantly, and smiled. Was it possible they heard not? Almighty God!— no, no! They heard!—they suspected!—they *knew!*—they were making a mockery of my horror!—this I thought, and this I think. But any thing was better than this agony! Any thing was more tolerable than this derision! I could bear those hypocritical smiles no longer! I felt that I must scream or die!—and now—again!—hark! louder! louder! louder! *louder!*—

"Villains!" I shrieked, "dissemble no more! I admit the deed!—tear up the planks!—here, here!—it is the beating of his hideous heart!"

1843

Further Reading

E. Arthur Robinson. "Poe's 'The Tell-Tale Heart.' " *Nineteenth-Century Fiction* 19.4 (Mar. 1965): 369–78. • Halliburton, David. "Tales." *Edgar Allan Poe: A Phenomenological View.* Princeton: Princeton UP, 1973. 193–374, spec. 333–38. • Hoffman, Daniel. "Grotesques and Arabesques." *Poe Poe Poe Poe Poe Poe Poe.* Garden City, N.Y.: Doubleday, 1972. 205–32, spec. 226–32. • Gargano, James W. "The Question of Poe's Narrators." *The Recognition of Edgar Allan Poe.* Ed. Eric W. Carlson. Ann Arbor: U of Michigan P, 1966. 308–16. • Ketterer, David. "Grotesques and *Politian.*" *The Rationale of Deception in Poe.* Baton Rouge: Louisiana State UP, 1979. 74–117, spec. 103–06.

Many of Edgar Allan Poe's stories, like the Grimms' fairy tales, owe less allegiance to the external realities of life than to the internal realities of the psyche: dreams, nightmares, wishes, and fears. As Poe noted in a review of Nathaniel Hawthorne's stories, this allegiance to internal reality requires the story to cast something like a spell over the reader.

Edgar Allan Poe: On Unity in the Tale

The ordinary novel is objectionable, from its length, for reasons already stated in substance. As it cannot be read at one sitting, it deprives itself, of course, of the immense force derivable from *totality.* Worldly interests intervening during the pauses of perusal, modify, annul, or counteract, in a greater or less degree, the impressions of the book. But simple cessation in reading would, of itself, be sufficient to destroy the true unity. In the brief tale, however, the author is enabled to carry out the fulness of his intention, be it what it may. During the hour of perusal the soul of the reader is at the writer's control. There are no external or extrinsic influences—resulting from weariness or interruption.

A skillful literary artist has constructed a tale. If wise, he has not fashioned his thoughts to accommodate his incidents; but having conceived, with deliberate care, a certain unique or single *effect* to be wrought out, he then invents such incidents—he then combines such events as may best aid him in establishing this preconceived effect. If his very initial sentence tend not to the outbringing of this effect, then he has failed in his first step. In the whole composition there should be no word written, of which the tendency, direct or indirect, is not to the one pre-established design. And by such means, with such care and skill, a picture is at length painted which leaves in the mind of him who contemplates it with a kindred art, a sense of the fullest satisfaction. The idea of the tale has been presented unblemished, because undisturbed; and this is an end unattainable by the novel.

HERMAN MELVILLE

(1819–1891)

BARTLEBY THE SCRIVENER

A STORY OF WALL STREET

I am a rather elderly man. The nature of my avocations for the last thirty years has brought me into more than ordinary contact with what would seem an interesting and somewhat singular set of men, of whom as yet nothing that I know of has ever been written:—I mean the law-copyists or scriveners. I have known very many of them, professionally and privately, and if I pleased, could relate divers histories, at which good-natured gentlemen might smile, and sentimental souls might weep. But I waive the biographies of all other scriveners for a few passages in the life of Bartleby, who was a scrivener and the strangest I ever saw, or heard of. While of other law-copyists I might write the complete life, of Bartleby nothing of that sort can be done. I believe that no materials exist for a full and satisfactory biography of this man. It is an irreparable loss to literature. Bartleby was one of those beings of whom nothing is ascertainable, except from the original sources, and in his case those are very small. What my own astonished eyes saw of Bartleby, *that* is all I know of him, except, indeed, one vague report which will appear in the sequel.

Ere introducing the scrivener, as he first appeared to me, it is fit I make some mention of myself, my *employés*, my business, my chambers, and general surroundings; because some such description is indispensable to an adequate understanding of the chief character about to be presented.

Imprimis.[1] I am a man who, from his youth upward, has been filled with a profound conviction that the easiest way of life is the best. Hence, though I belong to a profession proverbially energetic and nervous, even to turbulence, at times, yet nothing of that sort have I ever suffered to invade my peace. I am one of those unambitious lawyers who never addresses a jury, or in any way draws down public applause; but in the cool tranquillity of a

---

1. In the first place.

snug retreat, do a snug business among rich men's bonds and mortgages and title-deeds. All who know me, consider me an eminently *safe* man. The late John Jacob Astor, a personage little given to poetic enthusiasm, had no hesitation in pronouncing my first grand point to be prudence; my next, method. I do not speak it in vanity, but simply record the fact, that I was not unemployed in my profession by the late John Jacob Astor; a name which, I admit, I love to repeat, for it hath a rounded and orbicular sound to it, and rings like unto bullion. I will freely add, that I was not insensible to the late John Jacob Astor's good opinion.

Some time prior to the period at which this little history begins, my avocations had been largely increased. The good old office, now extinct in the State of New York, of a Master in Chancery, had been conferred upon me. It was not a very arduous office, but very pleasantly remunerative. I seldom lose my temper; much more seldom indulge in dangerous indignation at wrongs and outrages; but I must be permitted to be rash here and declare, that I consider the sudden and violent abrogation of the office of Master in Chancery, by the new Constitution, as a——premature act; inasmuch as I had counted upon a life-lease of the profits, whereas I only received those of a few short years. But this is by the way.

My chambers were upstairs at No.——Wall street. At one end they looked upon the white wall of the interior of a spacious skylight shaft, penetrating the building from top to bottom. This view might have been considered rather tame than otherwise, deficient in what landscape painters call "life." But if so, the view from the other end of my chambers offered, at least, a contrast, if nothing more. In that direction my windows commanded an unobstructed view of a lofty brick wall, black by age and everlasting shade; which wall required no spy-glass to bring out its lurking beauties, but for the benefit of all near-sighted spectators, was pushed up to within ten feet of my window panes. Owing to the great height of the surrounding buildings, and my chambers being on the second floor, the interval between this wall and mine not a little resembled a huge square cistern.

At the period just preceding the advent of Bartleby, I had two persons as copyists in my employment, and a promising lad as an office-boy. First, Turkey; second, Nippers; third, Ginger Nut. These may seem names, the like of which are not usually found in the Directory. In truth they were nicknames, mutually conferred upon each other by my three clerks, and were deemed expressive of their respective persons or characters. Turkey was a short, pursy Englishman of about my own age, that is, somewhere not far from sixty. In the morning, one might say, his face was of a fine florid hue, but after twelve o'clock, meridian—his dinner hour—it blazed like a grate full of Christmas coals; and continued blazing—but, as it were, with a gradual wane—till 6 o'clock P.M. or thereabouts, after which I saw no more of the proprietor of the face, which, gaining its meridian with the sun, seemed to set with it, to rise, culminate, and decline the following day, with the like regularity and undiminished glory. There are many singular coincidences I have known in the course of my life, not the least among which was the fact, that exactly when Turkey displayed his fullest beams from his red and radiant countenance, just then, too, at that critical moment, began the daily period when I considered his business capacities as seriously disturbed for the remainder of the twenty-four hours. Not that he was absolutely idle, or averse to business then; far from it. The difficulty was, he was apt to be altogether too energetic. There was a strange, inflamed, flurried, flighty recklessness of activity about him. He would be incautious in dipping his pen into his inkstand. All his blots upon my documents, were dropped there after twelve o'clock, meridian. Indeed, not only would he be reckless and sadly given to making blots in the afternoon, but some days he went further, and was rather noisy. At such times, too, his face flamed with augmented blazonry, as if cannel coal had been heaped on anthracite. He made an unpleasant racket with his chair; spilled his sand-box; in mending his pens, impatiently split them all to pieces, and threw them on the floor in a sudden passion; stood up and leaned over his table, boxing his papers about in a most indecorous manner, very sad to behold in an elderly man like him. Nevertheless, as he was in many ways a most valuable person to me, and all the time before twelve o'clock, meridian, was the quickest, steadiest creature, too, accomplishing a great deal of work in a style not easy to be matched—for these reasons, I was willing to overlook his eccentricities, though indeed, occasionally, I remonstrated with him. I did this very gently, however, because, though the civilest, nay, the blandest and most reverential of men in the morning, yet in the afternoon he was disposed, upon provocation, to be slightly rash with his tongue, in fact, insolent. Now, valuing his morning services as I did, and resolving not to lose them—yet, at the same time, made uncomfortable by his inflamed ways after twelve o'clock; and being a man of peace, unwilling by my admonitions to call forth unseemly retorts from him—I took upon me, one Saturday noon (he was always worse on Saturdays), to hint to him, very kindly, that perhaps now that he was growing old, it might be well to abridge his labours; in short, he need not come to my chambers after twelve o'clock, but, dinner over, had best go home to his lodgings and rest himself till tea-time. But no; he insisted upon his afternoon devotions. His countenance became intolerably fervid, as he oratorically assured me—gesticulating, with a long ruler, at the other side of the room—that if his services in the morning were useful, how indispensable, then, in the afternoon?

"With submission, sir," said Turkey on this occasion, "I consider myself your right-hand man. In the morning I but marshal and deploy my columns; but in the afternoon I put myself at their head, and gallantly charge the foe, thus!"—and he made a violent thrust with the ruler.

"But the blots, Turkey," intimated I.

"True,—but, with submission, sir, behold these hairs! I am getting old. Surely, sir, a blot or two of a warm afternoon is not to be severely urged against grey hairs. Old age—even if it blot the page—is honourable. With submission, sir, we *both* are getting old."

This appeal to my fellow-feeling was hardly to be resisted. At all events,

I saw that go he would not. So I made up my mind to let him stay, resolving, nevertheless, to see to it, that during the afternoon he had to do with my less important papers.

Nippers, the second on my list, was a whiskered, sallow, and, upon the whole, rather piratical-looking young man of about five and twenty. I always deemed him the victim of two evil powers—ambition and indigestion. The ambition was evinced by a certain impatience of the duties of a mere copyist—an unwarrantable usurpation of strictly professional affairs, such as the original drawing up of legal documents. The indigestion seemed betokened in an occasional nervous testiness and grinning irritability, causing the teeth to audibly grind together over mistakes committed in copying; unnecessary maledictions, hissed, rather than spoken, in the heat of business; and especially by a continual discontent with the height of the table where he worked. Though of a very ingenious mechanical turn, Nippers could never get this table to suit him. He put chips under it, blocks of various sorts, bits of pasteboard, and at last went so far as to attempt an exquisite adjustment by final pieces of folded blotting-paper. But no invention would answer. If, for the sake of easing his back, he brought the table lid at a sharp angle well up toward his chin, and wrote there like a man using the steep roof of a Dutch house for his desk—then he declared that it stopped the circulation in his arms. If now he lowered the table to his waistbands, and stooped over it in writing, then there was a sore aching in his back. In short, the truth of the matter was, Nippers knew not what he wanted. Or, if he wanted anything, it was to be rid of a scrivener's table altogether. Among the manifestations of his diseased ambition was a fondness he had for receiving visits from certain ambiguous-looking fellows in seedy coats, whom he called his clients. Indeed I was aware that not only was he, at times, considerable of a ward-politician, but he occasionally did a little business at the Justices' courts, and was not unknown on the steps of the Tombs. I have good reason to believe, however, that one individual who called upon him at my chambers, and who, with a grand air, he insisted was his client, was no other than a dun, and the alleged title-deed, a bill. But with all his failings, and the annoyances he caused me, Nippers, like his compatriot Turkey, was a very useful man to me; wrote a neat, swift hand; and, when he chose, was not deficient in a gentlemanly sort of deportment. Added to this, he always dressed in a gentlemanly sort of way; and so, incidentally, reflected credit upon my chambers. Whereas with respect to Turkey, I had much ado to keep him from being a reproach to me. His clothes were apt to look oily and smell of eating-houses. He wore his pantaloons very loose and baggy in summer. His coats were execrable; his hat not to be handled. But while the hat was a thing of indifference to me, inasmuch as his natural civility and deference, as a dependent Englishman, always led him to doff it the moment he entered the room, yet his coat was another matter. Concerning his coats, I reasoned with him; but with no effect. The truth was, I suppose, that a man with so small an income, could not afford to sport such a lustrous face and a lustrous coat at one and the same time. As

Nippers once observed, Turkey's money went chiefly for red ink. One winter day I presented Turkey with a highly-respectable looking coat of my own, a padded grey coat, of a most comfortable warmth, and which buttoned straight up from the knee to the neck. I thought Turkey would appreciate the favour, and abate his rashness and obstreperousness of afternoons. But no. I verily believe that buttoning himself up in so downy and blanketlike a coat had a pernicious effect upon him; upon the same principle that too much oats are bad for horses. In fact, precisely as a rash, restive horse is said to feel his oats, so Turkey felt his coat. It made him insolent. He was a man whom prosperity harmed.

Though concerning the self-indulgent habits of Turkey I had my own private surmises, yet touching Nippers I was well persuaded that whatever might be his faults in other respects, he was, at least, a temperate young man. But, indeed, nature herself seemed to have been his vintner, and at his birth charged him so thoroughly with an irritable, brandy-like disposition, that all subsequent potations were needless. When I consider how, amid the stillness of my chambers, Nippers would sometimes impatiently rise from his seat, and stooping over his table, spread his arms wide apart, seize the whole desk, and move it, and jerk it, with a grim, grinding motion on the floor, as if the table were a perverse voluntary agent, intent on thwarting and vexing him; I plainly perceive that for Nippers, brandy and water were altogether superfluous.

It was fortunate for me that, owing to its peculiar cause— indigestion—the irritability and consequent nervousness of Nippers, were mainly observable in the morning, while in the afternoon he was comparatively mild. So that Turkey's paroxysms only coming on about twelve o'clock, I never had to do with their eccentricities at one time. Their fits relieved each other like guards. When Nippers's was on, Turkey's was off; and *vice versa*. This was a good natural arrangement under the circumstances.

Ginger Nut, the third on my list, was a lad some twelve years old. His father was a carman, ambitious of seeing his son on the bench instead of a cart, before he died. So he sent him to my office as student at law, errand boy, and cleaner and sweeper, at the rate of one dollar a week. He had a little desk to himself, but he did not use it much. Upon inspection, the drawer exhibited a great array of the shells of various sorts of nuts. Indeed, to this quick-witted youth the whole noble science of the law was contained in a nut-shell. Not the least among the employments of Ginger Nut, as well as one which he discharged with the most alacrity, was his duty as cake and apple purveyor for Turkey and Nippers. Copying law papers being proverbially a dry, husky sort of business, my two scriveners were fain to moisten their mouths very often with Spitzenbergs to be had at the numerous stalls nigh the Custom House and Post Office. Also, they sent Ginger Nut very frequently for that peculiar cake—small, flat, round, and very spicy— which he had been named by them. Of a cold morning, when business was but dull, Turkey would gobble up scores of these cakes, as if they were mere wafers—indeed they sell them at the rate of six or eight for a penny—the scrape of his pen blending with the crunching of the crisp particles in his mouth. Of all the fiery afternoon blunders and flurried rashness of Turkey, was his once moistening a ginger-cake between his lips, and clapping it on to a mortgage for a seal. I came within an ace of dismissing him then. But he mollified me by making an oriental bow and saying—"With submission, sir, it was generous of me to find you in stationery on my own account."

Now my original business—that of a conveyancer and title hunter, and drawer-up of recondite documents of all sorts—was considerably increased by receiving the master's office. There was now great work for scriveners. Not only must I push the clerks already with me, but I must have additional help. In answer to my advertisement, a motionless young man one morning stood upon my office threshold, the door being open, for it was summer. I can see that figure now—pallidly neat, pitiably respectable, incurably forlorn! It was Bartleby.

After a few words touching his qualifications, I engaged him, glad to have among my corps of copyists a man of so singularly sedate an aspect, which I thought might operate beneficially upon the flighty temper of Turkey, and the fiery one of Nippers.

I should have stated before that ground glass folding-doors divided my premises into two parts, one of which was occupied by my scriveners, the other by myself. According to my humour I threw open these doors, or closed them. I resolved to assign Bartleby a corner by the folding-doors, but on my side of them, so as to have this quiet man within easy call, in case any trifling thing was to be done. I placed his desk close up to a small side-window in that part of the room, a window which originally had afforded a lateral view of certain grimy back-yards and bricks, but which, owing to subsequent erections, commanded at present no view at all, though it gave some light. Within three feet of the panes was a wall, and the light came down from far above, between two lofty buildings, as from a very small opening in a dome. Still further to a satisfactory arrangement, I procured a high green folding screen, which might entirely isolate Bartleby from my sight, though not remove him from my voice. And thus, in a manner, privacy and society were conjoined.

At first Bartleby did an extraordinary quantity of writing. As if long famishing for something to copy, he seemed to gorge himself on my documents. There was no pause for digestion. He ran a day and night line, copying by sun-light and by candle-light. I should have been quite delighted with his application, had he been cheerfully industrious. But he wrote on silently, palely, mechanically.

It is, of course, an indispensable part of a scrivener's business to verify the accuracy of his copy, word by word. Where there are two or more scriveners in an office, they assist each other in this examination, one reading from the copy, the other holding the original. It is a very dull, wearisome, and lethargic affair. I can readily imagine that to some sanguine temperaments it would be altogether intolerable. For example, I cannot credit that the mettlesome poet Byron would have contentedly sat down with Bartleby to examine a law document of, say, five hundred pages, closely written in a crimpy hand.

Now and then, in the haste of business, it had been my habit to assist in comparing some brief document myself, calling Turkey or Nippers for this purpose. One object I had in placing Bartleby so handy to me behind the screen, was to avail myself of his services on such trivial occasions. It was on the third day, I think, of his being with me, and before any necessity had arisen for having his own writing examined, that, being much hurried to complete a small affair I had in hand, I abruptly called to Bartleby. In my haste and natural expectancy of instant compliance, I sat with my head bent over the original on my desk, and my right hand sideways, and somewhat nervously extended with the copy, so that immediately upon emerging from his retreat, Bartleby might snatch it and proceed to business without the least delay.

In this very attitude did I sit when I called to him, rapidly stating what it was I wanted him to do—namely, to examine a small paper with me. Imagine my surprise, nay, my consternation, when without moving from his privacy, Bartleby in a singularly mild, firm voice, replied, "I would prefer not to."

I sat awhile in perfect silence, rallying my stunned faculties. Immediately it occurred to me that my ears had deceived me, or Bartleby had entirely misunderstood my meaning. I repeated my request in the clearest tone I could assume. But in quite as clear a one came the previous reply, "I would prefer not to."

"Prefer not to," echoed I, rising in high excitement, and crossing the room with a stride. "What do you mean? Are you moonstruck? I want you to help me compare this sheet here—take it," and I thrust it towards him.

"I would prefer not to," said he.

"I looked at him steadfastly. His face was leanly composed; his grey eye dimly calm. Not a wrinkle of agitation rippled him. Had there been the least uneasiness, anger, impatience or impertinence in his manner; in other words, had there been anything ordinarily human about him, doubtless I should have violently dismissed him from the premises. But as it was, I should have as soon thought of turning my pale plaster-of-paris bust of Cicero out of doors. I stood gazing at him awhile, as he went on with his own writing, and then reseated myself at my desk. This is very strange, thought I. What had one best do? But my business hurried me. I concluded to forget the matter for the present, reserving it for my future leisure. So calling Nippers from the other room, the paper was speedily examined.

A few days after this, Bartleby concluded four lengthy documents, being quadruplicates of a week's testimony taken before me in my High Court of Chancery. It became necessary to examine them. It was an important suit, and great accuracy was imperative. Having all things arranged, I called Turkey, Nippers and Ginger Nut from the next room, meaning to place the four copies in the hands of my four clerks, while I should read from the original. Accordingly Turkey, Nippers and Ginger Nut had taken their seats in a row, each with his document in hand, when I called to Bartleby to join this interesting group.

"Bartleby! quick, I am waiting."

I heard a slow scrape of his chair legs on the uncarpeted floor, and soon he appeared standing at the entrance of his hermitage.

"What is wanted?" said he mildly.

"The copies, the copies," said I hurriedly. "We are going to examine them. There"—and I held toward him the fourth quadruplicate.

"I would prefer not to," he said, and gently disappeared behind the screen.

For a few moments I was turned into a pillar of salt, standing at the head of my seated column of clerks. Recovering myself, I advanced toward the screen, and demanded the reason for such extraordinary conduct.

"*Why* do you refuse?"

"I would prefer not to."

With any other man I should have flown outright into a dreadful passion, scorned all further words, and thrust him ignominiously from my presence. But there was something about Bartleby that not only strangely disarmed me, but in a wonderful manner touched and disconcerted me. I began to reason with him.

"These are your own copies we are about to examine. It is labour saving to you, because one examination will answer for your four papers. It is common usage. Every copyist is bound to help examine his copy. Is it not so? Will you not speak? Answer!"

"I prefer not to," he replied in a flute-like tone. It seemed to me that while I had been addressing him, he carefully revolved every statement that I made; fully comprehended the meaning; could not gainsay the irresistible conclusion; but, at the same time, some paramount consideration prevailed with him to reply as he did.

"You are decided, then, not to comply with my request—a request made according to common usage and common sense?"

He briefly gave me to understand that on that point my judgment was sound. Yes: his decision was irreversible.

It is not seldom the case that when a man is browbeaten in some unprecedented and violently unreasonable way, he begins to stagger in his own plainest faith. He begins, as it were, vaguely to surmise that, wonderful as it may be, all the justice and all the reason are on the other side. Accordingly, if any disinterested persons are present, he turns to them for some reinforcement for his own faltering mind.

"Turkey," said I, "what do you think of this? Am I not right?"

"With submission, sir," said Turkey, with his blandest tone, "I think that you are."

"Nippers," said I, "what do *you* think of it?"

"I think I should kick him out of the office."

(The reader of nice perceptions will here perceive that, it being morning, Turkey's answer is couched in polite and tranquil terms but Nippers's reply in ill-tempered ones. Or, to repeat a previous sentence, Nippers's ugly mood was on duty, and Turkey's off.)

"Ginger Nut," said I, willing to enlist the smallest suffrage in my behalf, "what do *you* think of it?"

"I think, sir, he's a little *luny*," replied Ginger Nut, with a grin.

"You hear what they say," said I, turning towards the screen, "come forth and do your duty."

But he vouchsafed no reply. I pondered a moment in sore perplexity. But once more business hurried me. I determined again to postpone the consideration of this dilemma to my future leisure. With a little trouble we made out to examine the papers without Bartleby, though at every page or two, Turkey deferentially dropped his opinion that this proceeding was quite out of the common; while Nippers, twitching in his chair with a dyspeptic nervousness, ground out between his set teeth occasional hissing maledictions against the stubborn oaf behind the screen. And for his (Nippers's) part, this was the first and the last time he would do another man's business without pay.

Meanwhile Bartleby sat in his hermitage, oblivious to everything but his own peculiar business there.

Some days passed, the scrivener being employed upon another lengthy work. His late remarkable conduct led me to regard his ways narrowly. I observed that he never went to dinner; indeed that he never went any where. As yet I had never of my personal knowledge known him to be outside of my office. He was a perpetual sentry in the corner. At about eleven o'clock though, in the morning, I noticed that Ginger Nut would advance towards the opening in Bartleby's screen, as if silently beckoned thither by a gesture invisible to me where I sat. The boy would then leave the office jingling a few pence, and reappear with a handful of ginger-nuts which he delivered in the hermitage, receiving two of the cakes for his trouble.

He lives, then, on ginger-nuts, thought I; never eats a dinner, properly speaking; he must be a vegetarian then; but no; he never eats even vegetables, he eats nothing but ginger-nuts. My mind then ran on in reveries concerning the probable effects upon the human constitution of living entirely on ginger-nuts. Ginger-nuts are so called because they contain ginger as one of their peculiar constituents, and the final flavouring one. Now what was ginger? A hot, spicy thing. Was Bartleby hot and spicy? Not at all. Ginger, then, had no effect upon Bartleby. Probably he preferred it should have none.

Nothing so aggravates an earnest person as a passive resistance. If the individual so resisted be of a not inhumane temper, and the resisting one perfectly harmless in his passivity; then, in the better moods of the former, he will endeavour charitably to construe to his imagination what proves impossible to be solved by his judgment. Even so, for the most part, I regarded Bartleby and his ways. Poor fellow! thought I, he means no mischief; it is plain he intends no insolence; his aspect sufficiently evinces that his eccentricities are involuntary. He is useful to me. I can get along with him. If I turn him away, the chances are he will fall in with some less indulgent employer, and then he will be rudely treated, and perhaps driven forth miserably to starve. Yes. Here I can cheaply purchase a delicious self-approval. To befriend Bartleby; to humour him in his strange wilfulness, will cost me little or nothing, while I lay up in my soul what will eventually prove a sweet morsel for my conscience. But this mood was not invariable with me. The passiveness of Bartleby sometimes irritated me. I felt strangely goaded on to encounter him in new opposition, to elicit some angry spark from him answerable to my own. But indeed I might as well have essayed to strike fire with my knuckles against a bit of Windsor soap. But one afternoon the evil impulse in me mastered me, and the following little scene ensued:

"Bartleby," said I, "when those papers are all copied, I will compare them with you."

"I would prefer not to."

"How? Surely you do not mean to persist in that mulish vagary?"

No answer.

I threw open the folding-doors near by, and turning upon Turkey and Nippers, exclaimed in an excited manner:

"He says, a second time, he won't examine his papers. What do you think of it, Turkey?"

It was afternoon, be it remembered. Turkey sat glowing like a brass boiler, his bald head steaming, his hands reeling among his blotted papers.

"Think of it?" roared Turkey; "I think I'll just step behind his screen, and black his eyes for him!"

So saying, Turkey rose to his feet and threw his arms into a pugilistic position. He was hurrying away to make good his promise, when I detained him, alarmed at the effect of incautiously rousing Turkey's combativeness after dinner.

"Sit down, Turkey," said I, "and hear what Nippers has to say. What do you think of it, Nippers? Would I not be justified in immediately dismissing Bartleby?"

"Excuse me, that is for you to decide, sir. I think his conduct quite unusual, and indeed unjust, as regards Turkey and myself. But it may only be a passing whim."

"Ah," exclaimed I, "You have strangely changed your mind then—you speak very gently of him now."

"All beer," cried Turkey; "gentleness is effects of beer—Nippers and I dined together to-day. You see how gentle *I* am, sir. Shall I go and black his eyes?"

"You refer to Bartleby, I suppose. No, not to-day, Turkey," I replied; "pray, put up your fists."

I closed the doors, and again advanced towards Bartleby. I felt additional incentives tempting me to my fate. I burned to be rebelled against again. I remembered that Bartleby never left the office.

"Bartleby," said I, "Ginger Nut is away; just step round to the Post Office, won't you? (it was but a three minutes' walk), and see if there is anything for me."

"I would prefer not to."

"You *will* not?"

"I *prefer* not."

I staggered to my desk, and sat there in a deep study. My blind inveteracy returned. Was there any other thing in which I could procure myself to be ignominiously repulsed by this lean, penniless wight?—my hired clerk? What added thing is there, perfectly reasonable, that he will be sure to refuse to do?

"Bartleby!"

No answer.

"Bartleby," in a louder tone.

No answer.

"Bartleby," I roared.

Like a very ghost, agreeably to the laws of magical invocation, at the third summons, he appeared at the entrance of his hermitage.

"Go to the next room, and tell Nippers to come to me."

"I prefer not to," he respectfully and slowly said, and mildly disappeared.

"Very good, Bartleby," said I, in a quiet sort of serenely severe self-possessed tone, intimating the unalterable purpose of some terrible retribution very close at hand. At the moment I half intended something of the kind. But upon the whole, as it was drawing towards my dinner-hour, I thought it best to put on my hat and walk home for the day, suffering much from perplexity and distress of mind.

Shall I acknowledge it? The conclusion of this whole business was, that it soon became a fixed fact of my chambers, that a pale young scrivener, by the name of Bartleby, had a desk there; that he copied for me at the usual rate of four cents a folio (one hundred words); but he was permanently exempt from examining the work done by him, that duty being transferred to Turkey and Nippers, out of compliment doubtless to their superior acuteness; moreover, said Bartleby was never on any account to be despatched on the most trivial errand of any sort; and that even if entreated to take upon him such a matter, it was generally understood that he would prefer not to—in other words, that he would refuse point-blank.

As days passed on, I became considerably reconciled to Bartleby. His steadiness, his freedom from all dissipation, his incessant industry (except when he chose to throw himself into a standing revery behind his screen), his great stillness, his unalterableness of demeanour under all circumstances, made him a valuable acquisition. One prime thing was this,—*he was always there*;—first in the morning, continually through the day, and the last at night. I had a singular confidence in his honesty. I felt my most precious papers perfectly safe in his hands. Sometimes to be sure I could not, for the very soul of me, avoid falling into sudden spasmodic passions with him. For it was exceeding difficult to bear in mind all the time those strange peculiarities, privileges, and unheard of exemptions, forming the tacit stipulations on Bartleby's part under which he remained in my office. Now and then, in the eagerness of despatching pressing business, I would inadvertently summon Bartleby, in a short, rapid tone, to put his finger, say, on the incipient tie of a bit of red tape with which I was about compressing some papers. Of course, from behind the screen the usual answer, "I prefer not to," was sure to come; and then, how could a human creature with the common infirmities of our nature, refrain from bitterly exclaiming upon such perverseness—such unreasonableness. However, every added repulse of this sort which I received only tended to lessen the probability of my repeating the inadvertence.

Here it must be said, that according to the custom of most legal gentlemen occupying chambers in densely-populated law buildings, there were several keys to my door. One was kept by a woman residing in the attic, which person weekly scrubbed and daily swept and dusted my apartments. Another was kept by Turkey for convenience sake. The third I sometimes carried in my own pocket. The fourth I knew not who had.

Now, one Sunday morning I happened to go to Trinity Church, to hear a celebrated preacher, and finding myself rather early on the ground, I thought I would walk round to my chambers for awhile. Luckily I had my key with me; but upon applying it to the lock, I found it resisted by something inserted from the inside. Quite surprised, I called out; when to my consternation a key was turned from within; and thrusting his lean visage at me, and holding the door ajar, the apparition of Bartleby appeared, in his shirt sleeves, and otherwise in a strangely tattered dishabille, saying quietly that he was sorry, but he was deeply engaged just then, and—preferred not admitting me at present. In a brief word or two, he moreover added, that perhaps I had better walk round the block two or three times, and by that time he would probably have concluded his affairs.

Now, the utterly unsurmised appearance of Bartleby, tenanting my law-chambers of a Sunday-morning, with his cadaverously gentlemanly *nonchalance*, yet withal firm and self-possessed, had such a strange effect upon me, that incontinently I slunk away from my own door, and did as desired. But not without sundry twinges of impotent rebellion against the mild effrontery of this unaccountable scrivener. Indeed, it was his wonderful mildness chiefly, which not only disarmed me, but unmanned me, as it were. For I consider that one, for the time, is in a way unmanned when he tranquilly permits his hired clerk to dictate to him, and order him away from his own premises. Furthermore, I was full of uneasiness as to what Bartleby could possibly be doing in my office in his shirt sleeves, and in an otherwise dismantled condition of a Sunday morning. Was anything amiss going on? Nay, that was out of the question. It was not to be thought of for a moment that Bartleby was an immoral person. But what could he be doing there—

copying? Nay again, whatever might be his eccentricities, Bartleby was an eminently decorous person. He would be the last man to sit down to his desk in any state approaching to nudity. Besides, it was Sunday; and there was something about Bartleby that forbade the supposition that he would by any secular occupation violate the proprieties of the day.

Nevertheless, my mind was not pacified; and full of a restless curiosity, at last I returned to the door. Without hindrance I inserted my key, opened it, and entered. Bartleby was not to be seen. I looked around anxiously, peeped behind his screen; but it was very plain that he was gone. Upon more closely examining the place, I surmised that for an indefinite period Bartleby must have ate, dressed, and slept in my office, and that too without plate, mirror, or bed. The cushioned seat of a ricketty old sofa in one corner bore the faint impress of a lean, reclining form. Rolled away under his desk, I found a blanket; under the empty grate, a blacking box and brush; on a chair, a tin basin, with soap and a ragged towel; in a newspaper a few crumbs of ginger-nuts and a morsel of cheese. Yes, thought I, it is evident enough that Bartleby has been making his home here, keeping bachelor's hall all by himself. Immediately then the thought came sweeping across me, What miserable friendlessness and loneliness are here revealed! His poverty is great; but his solitude, how horrible! Think of it. Of a Sunday, Wall street is deserted as Petra; and every night of every day it is an emptiness. This building too, which of week-days hums with industry and life, at nightfall echoes with sheer vacancy, and all through Sunday is forlorn. And here Bartleby makes his home; sole spectator of a solitude which he has seen all populous—a sort of innocent and transformed Marius[2] brooding among the ruins of Carthage![3]

For the first time in my life a feeling of overpowering stinging melancholy seized me. Before, I had never experienced aught but a not-unpleasing sadness. The bond of a common humanity now drew me irresistibly to gloom. A fraternal melancholy! For both I and Bartleby were sons of Adam. I remembered the bright silks and sparkling faces I had seen that day, in gala trim, swan-like sailing down the Mississippi of Broadway; and I contrasted them with the pallid copyist, and thought to myself, Ah, happiness courts the light, so we deem the world is gay; but misery hides aloof, so we deem that misery there is none. These sad fancyings—chimeras, doubtless, of a sick and silly brain—led on to other and more special thoughts, concerning the eccentricities of Bartleby. Presentiments of strange discoveries hovered round me. The scrivener's pale form appeared to me laid out, among uncaring strangers, in its shivering winding sheet.

Suddenly I was attracted by Bartleby's closed desk, the key in open sight left in the lock.

---

2. Gaius Marius, a powerful Roman general, alive between 155 (?) B.C. and 86 B.C.
3. Ancient city and state on the northern coast of Africa, in the Bay of Tunis; northeast of the modern Tunis.

I mean no mischief, seek the gratification of no heartless curiosity, thought I; besides, the desk is mine, and its contents, too, so I will make bold to look within. Everything was methodically arranged, the papers smoothly placed. The pigeon holes were deep, and, removing the files of documents, I groped into their recesses. Presently I felt something there, and dragged it out. It was an old bandana handkerchief, heavy and knotted. I opened it, and saw it was a savings' bank.

I now recalled all the quiet mysteries which I had noted in the man. I remembered that he never spoke but to answer; that though at intervals he had considerable time to himself, yet I had never seen him reading—no, not even a newspaper; that for long periods he would stand looking out, at his pale window behind the screen, upon the dead brick wall; I was quite sure he never visited any refectory or eating-house; while his pale face clearly indicated that he never drank beer like Turkey, or tea and coffee even, like other men; that he never went anywhere in particular that I could learn; never went out for a walk, unless indeed that was the case at present; that he had declined telling who he was, or whence he came, or whether he had any relatives in the world; that though so thin and pale, he never complained of ill health. And more than all, I remembered a certain unconscious air of pallid—how shall I call it?—of pallid haughtiness, say, or rather an austere reserve about him, which had positively awed me into my tame compliance with his eccentricities, when I had feared to ask him to do the slightest incidental thing for me, even though I might know, from his long-continued motionlessness, that behind his screen he must be standing in one of those dead-wall reveries of his.

Revolving all these things, and coupling them with the recently discovered fact that he made my office his constant abiding place and home, and not forgetful of his morbid moodiness; revolving all these things, a prudential feeling began to steal over me. My first emotions had been those of pure melancholy and sincerest pity; but just in proportion as the forlornness of Bartleby grew and grew to my imagination, did that same melancholy merge into fear, that pity into repulsion. So true it is, and so terrible, too, that up to a certain point the thought or sight of misery enlists our best affections; but, in certain special cases, beyond that point it does not. They err who would assert that invariably this is owing to the inherent selfishness of the human heart. It rather proceeds from a certain hopelessness of remedying excessive and organic ill. To a sensitive being, pity is not seldom pain. And when at last it is perceived that such pity cannot lead to effectual succour, common sense bids the soul be rid of it. What I saw that morning persuaded me that the scrivener was the victim of innate and incurable disorder. I might give alms to his body; but his body did not pain him; it was his soul that suffered, and his soul I could not reach.

I did not accomplish the purpose of going to Trinity Church that morning. Somehow, the things I had seen disqualified me for the time from church-going. I walked homeward, thinking what I would do with Bartleby. Finally, I resolved upon this:—I would put certain calm questions to him the next morning, touching his history, &c., and if he declined to answer them openly and unreservedly (and I supposed he would prefer not), then to give him a twenty dollar bill over and above whatever I might owe him, and tell him his services were no longer required; but that if in any other way I could assist him, I would be happy to do so, especially if he desired to return to his native place, wherever that might be, I would willingly help to defray the expenses. Moreover, if, after reaching home, he found himself at any time in want of aid, a letter from him would be sure of a reply.

The next morning came.

"Bartleby," said I, gently calling to him behind his screen.

No reply.

"Bartleby," said I, in a still gentler tone, "come here; I am not going to ask you to do anything you would prefer not to do—I simply wish to speak to you."

Upon this he noiselessly slid into view.

"Will you tell me, Bartleby, where you were born?"

"I would prefer not to."

"Will you tell me *anything* about yourself?"

"I would prefer not to."

"But what reasonable objection can you have to speak to me? I feel friendly towards you."

He did not look at me while I spoke, but kept his glance fixed upon my bust of Cicero, which, as I then sat, was directly behind me, some six inches above my head.

"What is your answer, Bartleby?" said I, after waiting a considerable time for a reply, during which his countenance remained immovable, only there was the faintest conceivable tremor of the white attenuated mouth.

"At present I prefer to give no answer," he said, and retired into his hermitage.

It was rather weak in me I confess, but his manner on this occasion nettled me. Not only did there seem to lurk in it a certain calm disdain, but his perverseness seemed ungrateful, considering the undeniable good usage and indulgence he had received from me.

Again I sat ruminating what I should do. Mortified as I was at his behaviour, and resolved as I had been to dismiss him when I entered my office, nevertheless I strangely felt something superstitious knocking at my heart, and forbidding me to carry out my purpose, and denouncing me for a villain if I dared to breathe one bitter word against this forlornest of mankind. At last, familiarly drawing my chair behind his screen, I sat down and said: "Bartleby, never mind then about revealing your history; but let me entreat you, as a friend, to comply as far as may be with the usages of this office. Say now you will help to examine papers to-morrow or next day: in short, say now that in a day or two you will begin to be a little reasonable:— say so, Bartleby."

"At present I would prefer not to be a little reasonable," was his mildly cadaverous reply.

Just then the folding-doors opened, and Nippers approached. He seemed suffering from an unusually bad night's rest, induced by severer indigestion than common. He overheard those final words of Bartleby.

"*Prefer not*, eh?" gritted Nippers—"I'd *prefer* him, if I were you, sir," addressing me—"I'd *prefer* him; I'd give him preferences, the stubborn mule! What is it, sir, pray, that he *prefers* not to do now?"

Bartleby moved not a limb.

"Mr. Nippers," said I, "I'd prefer that you would withdraw for the present."

Somehow, of late I had got into the way of involuntarily using this word "prefer" upon all sorts of not exactly suitable occasions. And I trembled to think that my contact with the scrivener had already and seriously affected me in a mental way. And what further and deeper aberration might it not yet produce? This apprehension had not been without efficacy in determining me to summary means.

As Nippers, looking very sour and sulky, was departing, Turkey blandly and deferentially approached.

"With submission, sir," said he, "yesterday I was thinking about Bartleby here, and I think that if he would but prefer to take a quart of good ale every day, it would do much towards mending him, and enabling him to assist in examining his papers."

"So you have got the word, too," said I, slightly excited.

"With submission, what word, sir," asked Turkey, respectfully crowding himself into the contracted space behind the screen, and by so doing, making me jostle the scrivener. "What word, sir?"

"I would prefer to be left alone here," said Bartleby, as if offended at being mobbed in his privacy.

"*That's* the word, Turkey," said I—"*that's* it."

"Oh, *prefer*? oh, yes—queer word. I never used it myself. But, sir, as I was saying, if he would but prefer—"

"Turkey," interrupted I, "you will please withdraw."

"Oh certainly, sir, if you prefer that I should."

As he opened the folding-door to retire, Nippers at his desk caught a glimpse of me, and asked whether I would prefer to have a certain paper copied on blue paper or white. He did not in the least roguishly accent the word prefer. It was plain that it involuntarily rolled from his tongue. I thought to myself, surely I must get rid of a demented man, who already has in some degree turned the tongues, if not the heads, of myself and clerks. But I thought it prudent not to break the dismission at once.

The next day I noticed that Bartleby did nothing but stand at his window in his dead-wall revery. Upon asking him why he did not write, he said that he had decided upon doing no more writing.

"Why, how now? what next?" exclaimed I, "do no more writing?"

"No more."

"And what is the reason?"

"Do you not see the reason for yourself?" he indifferently replied.

I looked steadfastly at him, and perceived that his eyes looked dull and glazed. Instantly it occurred to me, that his unexampled diligence in copying by his dim window for the first few weeks of his stay with me might have temporarily impaired his vision.

I was touched. I said something in condolence with him. I hinted that, of course, he did wisely in abstaining from writing for a while, and urged him to embrace that opportunity of taking wholesome exercise in the open air. This, however, he did not do. A few days after this, my other clerks being absent, and being in a great hurry to despatch certain letters by the mail, I thought that, having nothing else earthly to do, Bartleby would surely be less inflexible than usual, and carry these letters to the Post Office. But he blankly declined. So, much to my inconvenience, I went myself.

Still added days went by. Whether Bartleby's eyes improved or not, I could not say. To all appearance, I thought they did. But when I asked him if they did, he vouchsafed no answer. At all events, he would do no copying. At last, in reply to my urgings, he informed me that he had permanently given up copying.

"What!" exclaimed I; "suppose your eyes should get entirely well— better than ever before—would you not copy then?"

"I have given up copying," he answered and slid aside.

He remained, as ever, a fixture in my chamber. Nay—if that were possible—he became still more of a fixture than before. What was to be done? He would do nothing in the office: why should he stay there? In plain fact, he had now become a millstone to me, not only useless as a necklace, but afflictive to bear. Yet I was sorry for him. I speak less than truth when I say that, on his own account, he occasioned me uneasiness. If he would but have named a single relative or friend, I would instantly have written, and urged their taking the poor fellow away to some convenient retreat. But he seemed alone, absolutely alone in the universe. A bit of wreckage in the mid-Atlantic. At length, necessities connected with my business tyrannized over all other considerations. Decently as I could, I told Bartleby that in six days' time he must unconditionally leave the office. I warned him to take measures, in the interval, for procuring some other abode. I offered to assist him in this endeavour, if he himself would but take the first step towards a removal. "And when you finally quit me, Bartleby," added I. "I shall see that you go away not entirely unprovided. Six days from this hour, remember."

At the expiration of that period, I peeped behind the screen, and lo! Bartleby was there.

I buttoned up my coat, balanced myself; advanced slowly towards him, touched his shoulder, and said, "The time has come; you must quit this place; I am sorry for you; here is money; but you must go."

"I would prefer not," he replied, with his back still towards me.

"You *must*."

He remained silent.

Now I had an unbounded confidence in this man's common honesty. He had frequently restored to me sixpences and shillings carelessly dropped upon the floor, for I am apt to be very reckless in such shirt-button affairs. The proceeding then which followed will not be deemed extraordinary.

"Bartleby," said I, "I owe you twelve dollars on account; here are thirty-two; the odd twenty are yours.—Will you take it?" and I handed the bills towards him.

But he made no motion.

"I will leave them here then," putting them under a weight on the table. Then taking my hat and cane and going to the door, I tranquilly turned and added—"After you have removed your things from these offices, Bartleby, you will of course lock the door—since every one is now gone for the day but you—and if you please, slip your key underneath the mat, so that I may have it in the morning. I shall not see you again; so good-bye to you. If hereafter in your new place of abode I can be of any service to you, do not fail to advise me by letter. Good-bye, Bartleby, and fare you well."

But he answered not a word; like the last column of some ruined temple, he remained standing mute and solitary in the middle of the otherwise deserted room.

As I walked home in a pensive mood, my vanity got the better of my pity. I could not but highly plume myself on my masterly management in getting rid of Bartleby. Masterly I call it, and such it must appear to any dispassionate thinker. The beauty of my procedure seemed to consist in its perfect quietness. There was no vulgar bullying, no bravado of any sort, no choleric hectoring, no striding to and fro across the apartment, jerking out vehement commands for Bartleby to bundle himself off with his beggarly traps. Nothing of the kind. Without loudly bidding Bartleby depart—as an inferior genius might have done—I *assumed* the ground that depart he must; and upon that assumption built all I had to say. The more I thought over my procedure, the more I was charmed with it. Nevertheless, next morning, upon awakening, I had my doubts,—I had somehow slept off the fumes of vanity. One of the coolest and wisest hours a man has, is just after he awakes in the morning. My procedure seemed as sagacious as ever,—but only in theory. How it would prove in practice—there was the rub. It was truly a beautiful thought to have assumed Bartleby's departure; but, after all, that assumption was simply my own, and none of Bartleby's. The great point was, not whether I had assumed that he would quit me, but whether he would prefer so to do. He was more a man of preferences than assumptions.

After breakfast, I walked down town, arguing the probabilities *pro* and *con*. One moment I thought it would prove a miserable failure, and Bartleby would be found all alive at my office as usual; the next moment it seemed certain that I should see his chair empty. And so I kept veering about. At the corner of Broadway and Canal Street, I saw quite an excited group of people standing in earnest conversation.

"I'll take odds he doesn't," said a voice as I passed.

"Doesn't go?—done!" said I, "put up your money."

I was instinctively putting my hand in my pocket to produce my own, when I remembered that this was an election day. The words I had overheard bore no reference to Bartleby, but to the success or non-success of some candidate for the mayoralty. In my intent frame of mind, I had, as it were, imagined that all Broadway shared in my excitement, and were debating the same question with me. I passed on, very thankful that the uproar of the street screened my momentary absent-mindedness.

As I had intended, I was earlier than usual at my office door. I stood listening for a moment. All was still. He must be gone. I tried the knob. The door was locked. Yes, my procedure had worked to a charm; he indeed must be vanished. Yet a certain melancholy mixed with this: I was almost sorry for my brilliant success. I was fumbling under the door mat for the key, which Bartleby was to have left there for me, when accidentally my knee knocked against a panel, producing a summoning sound, and in response a voice came to me from within—"Not yet; I am occupied."

It was Bartleby.

I was thunderstruck. For an instant I stood like the man who, pipe in mouth, was killed one cloudless afternoon long ago in Virginia, by summer lightning; at his own warm open window he was killed, and remained leaning out there upon the dreamy afternoon, till some one touched him, and he fell.

"Not gone!" I murmured at last. But again obeying that wondrous ascendency which the inscrutable scrivener had over me—and from which ascendency, for all my chafing, I could not completely escape—I slowly went down stairs and out into the street, and while walking round the block, considered what I should next do in this unheard-of perplexity. Turn the man out by an actual thrusting I could not; to drive him away by calling him hard names would not do; calling in the police was an unpleasant idea; and yet, permit him to enjoy his cadaverous triumph over me,—this too I could not think of. What was to be done? or, if nothing could be done, was there anything further that I could *assume* in the matter? Yes, as before I had prospectively assumed that Bartleby would depart, so now I might retrospectively assume that departed he was. In the legitimate carrying out of this assumption, I might enter my office in a great hurry, and pretending not to see Bartleby at all, walk straight against him as if he were air. Such a proceeding would in a singular degree have the appearance of a home-thrust. It was hardly possible that Bartleby could withstand such an application of the doctrine of assumptions. But, upon second thought, the success of the plan seemed rather dubious. I resolved to argue the matter over with him again.

"Bartleby," said I, entering the office, with a quietly severe expression, "I am seriously displeased. I am pained, Bartleby. I had thought better of you. I had imagined you of such a gentlemanly organization, that in any delicate dilemma a slight hint would suffice—in short, an assumption; but it appears I am deceived. Why," I added, unaffectedly starting, "you have not even touched that money yet," pointing to it, just where I had left it the evening previous.

He answered nothing.

"Will you, or will you not, quit me?" I now demanded in a sudden passion, advancing close to him.

"I would prefer *not* to quit you," he replied, gently emphasizing the *not*.

"What earthly right have you to stay here? Do you pay any rent? Do you pay my taxes? Or is this property yours?"

He answered nothing.

"Are you ready to go on and write now? Are your eyes recovered? Could you copy a small paper for me this morning? or help examine a few lines? or step round to the Post Office? In a word, will you do any thing at all, to give a colouring to your refusal to depart the premises?"

He silently retired into his hermitage.

I was now in such a state of nervous resentment that I thought it but prudent to check myself, at present, from further demonstrations. Bartleby and I were alone. I remembered the tragedy of the unfortunate Adams and the still more unfortunate Colt in the solitary office of the latter; and how poor Colt, being dreadfully incensed by Adams, and imprudently permitting himself to get wildly excited, was at unawares hurried into his fatal act—an act which certainly no man could possibly deplore more than the actor himself. Often it had occurred to me in my ponderings upon the subject, that had that altercation taken place in the public street, or at a private residence, it would not have terminated as it did. It was the circumstance of being alone in a solitary office, upstairs, of a building entirely unhallowed by humanizing domestic associations—an uncarpeted office, doubtless, of a dusty, haggard sort of appearance;—this it must have been, which greatly helped to enhance the irritable desperation of the hapless Colt.

But when this old Adam of resentment rose in me and tempted me concerning Bartleby, I grappled him and threw him. How? Why, simply by recalling the divine injunction: "A new commandment give I unto you, that ye love one another." Yes, this it was that saved me. Aside from higher considerations, charity often operates as a vastly wise and prudent principle—a great safeguard to its possessor. Men have committed murder for jealousy's sake, and anger's sake, and hatred's sake, and selfishness' sake, and spiritual pride's sake; but no man that ever I heard of, ever committed a diabolical murder for sweet charity's sake. Mere self-interest, then, if no better motive can be enlisted, should, especially with high-tempered men, prompt all beings to charity and philanthropy. At any rate, upon the occasion in question, I strove to drown my exasperated feelings towards the scrivener by benevolently construing his conduct. Poor fellow, poor fellow! thought I, he doesn't mean any thing; and besides, he has seen hard times, and ought to be indulged.

I endeavoured also immediately to occupy myself, and at the same time to comfort my despondency. I tried to fancy that in the course of the morning, at such time as might prove agreeable to him, Bartleby, of his own free accord, would emerge from his hermitage, and take up some decided line of march in the direction of the door. But no. Half-past twelve o'clock came; Turkey began to glow in the face, overturn his inkstand, and become generally obstreperous; Nippers abated down into quietude and courtesy; Ginger Nut munched his noon apple; and Bartleby remained standing at his window in one of his profoundest dead-wall reveries. Will it be credited? Ought I to acknowledge it? That afternoon I left the office without saying one further word to him.

Some days now passed, during which at leisure intervals I looked a little into "Edwards on the Will," and "Priestley on Necessity." Under the circumstances, those books induced a salutary feeling. Gradually I slid into the persuasion that these troubles of mine, touching the scrivener, had been all predestinated from eternity, and Bartleby was billeted upon me for some mysterious purpose of an all-wise Providence, which it was not for a mere mortal like me to fathom. Yes, Bartleby, stay there behind your screen, thought I; I shall persecute you no more; you are harmless and noiseless as any of these old chairs; in short, I never feel so private as when I know you are here. At least I see it, I feel it; I penetrate to the predestinated purpose of my life. I am content. Others may have loftier parts to enact; but my mission in this world, Bartleby, is to furnish you with office room for such period as you may see fit to remain.

I believe that this wise and blessed frame of mind would have continued with me had it not been for the unsolicited and uncharitable remarks obtruded upon me by my professional friends who visited the rooms. But thus it often is, that the constant friction of illiberal minds wears out at last the best resolves of the more generous. Though to be sure, when I reflected upon it, it was not strange that people entering my office should be struck by the peculiar aspect of the unaccountable Bartleby, and so be tempted to throw out some sinister observations concerning him. Sometimes an attorney having business with me, and calling at my office, and finding no one but the scrivener there, would undertake to obtain some sort of precise information from him touching my whereabouts; but without heeding his idle talk, Bartleby would remain standing immovable in the middle of the room. So, after contemplating him in that position for a time, the attorney would depart, no wiser than he came.

Also, when a Reference was going on, and the room full of lawyers and witnesses and business was driving fast, some deeply occupied legal gentleman present, seeing Bartleby wholly unemployed, would request him to run round to his (the legal gentleman's) office and fetch some papers for him. Thereupon, Bartleby would tranquilly decline, and yet remain idle as before. Then the lawyer would give a great stare, and turn to me. And what could I say? At last I was made aware that all through the circle of my professional acquaintance, a whisper of wonder was running round, having reference to the strange creature I kept at my office. This worried me very much. And as the idea came upon me of his possibly turning out a long-lived man, and keep occupying my chambers, and denying my authority; and perplexing my visitors; and scandalizing my professional reputation; and casting a general gloom over the premises; keeping soul and body together to the last upon his savings (for doubtless he spent but half a dime a day), and in the end perhaps outlive me, and claim possession of my office by right of his perpetual occupancy: as all these dark anticipations crowded upon me more and more, and my friends continually intruded their relentless remarks upon the apparition in my room, a great change was wrought in me. I resolved to gather all my faculties together, and for ever rid me of this intolerable incubus.[4]

Ere resolving any complicated project, however, adapted to this end, I first simply suggested to Bartleby the propriety of his permanent departure. In a calm and serious tone, I commended the idea to his careful and mature consideration. But having taken three days to meditate upon it, he apprised me that his original determination remained the same; in short, that he still preferred to abide with me.

What shall I do? I now said to myself, buttoning up my coat to the last button. What shall I do? what ought I to do? what does conscience say I *should* do with this man, or rather ghost? Rid myself of him, I must; go, he shall. But how? You will not thrust him, the poor, pale, passive mortal,—you will not thrust such a helpless creature out of your door? you will not dishonour yourself by such cruelty? No, I will not, I cannot do that. Rather would I let him live and die here, and then mason up his remains in the wall. What then will you do? For all your coaxing, he will not budge. Bribes he leaves under your own paper-weight on your table; in short, it is quite plain that he prefers to cling to you.

Then something severe, something unusual must be done. What! surely you will not have him collared by a constable, and commit his innocent pallor to the common jail? And upon what ground could you procure such a thing to be done?—a vagrant, is he? What! he a vagrant, a wanderer, who refuses to budge? It is because he will *not* be a vagrant, then, that you seek to count him *as* a vagrant. That is too absurd. No visible means of support: there I have him. Wrong again: for indubitably he *does* support himself, and that is the only unanswerable proof that any man can show of his possessing the means so to do. No more then. Since he will not quit me, I must quit him. I will change my offices; I will move elsewhere;

---

4. Something that is nightmarishly oppressive; a nightmare.

and give him fair notice, that if I find him on my new premises I will then proceed against him as a common trespasser.

Acting accordingly, next day I thus addressed him: "I find these chambers too far from the City Hall; the air is unwholesome. In a word, I propose to remove my offices next week, and shall no longer require your services. I tell you this now, in order that you may seek another place."

He made no reply, and nothing more was said.

On the appointed day I engaged carts and men, proceeded to my chambers, and having but little furniture, everything was removed in a few hours. Throughout all, the scrivener remained standing behind the screen, which I directed to be removed the last thing. It was withdrawn; and being folded up like a huge folio, left him the motionless occupant of a naked room. I stood in the entry watching him a moment, while something from within me upbraided me.

I re-entered, with my hand in my pocket—and—and my heart in my mouth.

"Good-bye, Bartleby; I am going—good-bye, and God some way bless you; and take that," slipping something in his hand. But it dropped upon the floor and then—strange to say—I tore myself from him whom I had so longed to be rid of.

Established in my new quarters, for a day or two I kept the door locked, and started at every footfall in the passages. When I returned to my rooms after any little absence, I would pause at the threshold for an instant, and attentively listen, ere applying my key. But these fears were needless. Bartleby never came nigh me.

I thought all was going well, when a perturbed looking stranger visited me, inquiring whether I was the person who had recently occupied rooms at No.——Wall street.

Full of forebodings, I replied that I was.

"Then sir," said the stranger, who proved a lawyer, "you are responsible for the man you left there. He refuses to do any copying, he refuses to do anything; and he says he prefers not to; and he refuses to quit the premises."

"I am very sorry, sir," said I, with assumed tranquillity, but an inward tremor, "but, really, the man you allude to is nothing to me—he is no relation or apprentice of mine, that you should hold me responsible for him."

"In mercy's name, who is he?"

"I certainly cannot inform you. I know nothing about him. Formerly I employed him as a copyist; but he has done nothing for me now for some time past."

"I shall settle him then,—good morning, sir."

Several days passed, and I heard nothing more; and though I often felt a charitable prompting to call at the place and see poor Bartleby, yet a certain squeamishness of I know not what withheld me.

All is over with him, by this time, thought I at last, when through another week no further intelligence reached me. But coming to my room the day after, I found several persons waiting at my door in a high state of nervous excitement.

"That's the man—here he comes," cried the foremost one, whom I recognized as the lawyer who had previously called upon me alone.

"You must take him away, sir, at once," cried a portly person among them, advancing upon me, and whom I knew to be the landlord of No.——Wall street. "These gentlemen, my tenants, cannot stand it any longer; Mr. B——," pointing to the lawyer, "has turned him out of his room, and he now persists in haunting the building generally, sitting upon the banisters of the stairs by day, and sleeping in the entry by night. Everybody here is concerned; clients are leaving the offices; some fears are entertained of a mob; something you must do, and that without delay."

Aghast at this torrent, I fell back before it, and would fain have locked myself in my new quarters. In vain I persisted that Bartleby was nothing to me—no more than to any one else there. In vain:—I was the last person known to have anything to do with him, and they held me to the terrible account. Fearful then of being exposed in the papers (as one person present obscurely threatened) I considered the matter, and at length said, that if the lawyer would give me a confidential interview with the scrivener, in his (the lawyer's) own room, I would that afternoon strive my best to rid them of the nuisance they complained of.

Going up stairs to my old haunt, there was Bartleby silently sitting upon the banister at the landing.

"What are you doing here, Bartleby?" said I.

"Sitting upon the banister," he mildly replied.

I motioned him into the lawyer's room, who then left us.

"Bartleby," said I, "are you aware that you are the cause of great tribulation to me, by persisting in occupying the entry after being dismissed from the office?"

No answer.

"Now one of two things must take place. Either you must do something, or something must be done to you. Now what sort of business would you like to engage in? Would you like to re-engage in copying for some one?"

"No; I would prefer not to make any change."

"Would you like a clerkship in a dry-goods store?"

"There is too much confinement about that. No, I would not like a clerkship; but I am not particular."

"Too much confinement," I cried, "why you keep yourself confined all the time!"

"I would prefer not to take a clerkship," he rejoined, as if to settle that little item at once.

"How would a bartender's business suit you? There is no trying of the eyesight in that."

"I would not like it at all; though, as I said before, I am not particular."

His unwonted wordiness inspirited me. I returned to the charge.

"Well then, would you like to travel through the country collecting bills for the merchants? That would improve your health."

"No, I would prefer to be doing something else."

"How then would going as a companion to Europe to entertain some young gentleman with your conversation,—how would that suit you?"

"Not at all. It does not strike me that there is anything definite about that. I like to be stationary. But I am not particular."

"Stationary you shall be then," I cried, now losing all patience, and for the first time in all my exasperating connection with him fairly flying into a passion. "If you do not go away from these premises before night, I shall feel bound—indeed I *am* bound—to—to—to quit the premises myself!" I rather absurdly concluded, knowing not with what possible threat to try to frighten his immobility into compliance. Despairing of all further efforts, I was precipitately leaving him, when a final thought occurred to me—one which had not been wholly unindulged before.

"Bartleby," said I, in the kindest tone I could assume under such exciting circumstances, "will you go home with me now—not to my office, but my dwelling—and remain there till we can conclude upon some convenient arrangement for you at our leisure? Come, let us start now, right away."

"No: at present I would prefer not to make any change at all."

I answered nothing; but effectually dodging every one by the suddenness and rapidity of my flight, rushed from the building, ran up Wall street toward Broadway, and then jumping into the first omnibus was soon removed from pursuit. As soon as tranquillity returned I distinctly perceived that I had now done all that I possibly could, both in respect to the demands of the landlord and his tenants, and with regard to my own desire and sense of duty, to benefit Bartleby, and shield him from rude persecution. I now strove to be entirely care-free and quiescent; and my conscience justified me in the attempt; though indeed it was not so successful as I could have wished. So fearful was I of being again hunted out by the incensed landlord and his exasperated tenants, that, surrendering my business to Nippers, for a few days I drove about the upper part of the town and through the suburbs, in my rockaway;[5] crossed over to Jersey City and Hoboken, and paid fugitive visits to Manhattanville and Astoria. In fact I almost lived in my rockaway for the time.

When again I entered my office, lo, a note from the landlord lay upon the desk. I opened it with trembling hands. It informed me that the writer had sent to the police, and had Bartleby removed to the Tombs as a vagrant. Moreover, since I knew more about him than any one else, he wished me to appear at that place, and make a suitable statement of the facts. These tidings had a conflicting effect upon me. At first I was indignant; but at last almost approved. The landlord's energetic, summary dis-

---

5. A four-wheeled carriage with two seats and a standing top.

position had led him to adopt a procedure which I do not think I would have decided upon myself; and yet as a last resort, under such peculiar circumstances, it seemed the only plan.

As I afterwards learned, the poor scrivener, when told that he must be conducted to the Tombs, offered not the slightest obstacle, but in his own pale, unmoving way silently acquiesced.

Some of the compassionate and curious bystanders joined the party; and headed by one of the constables, arm-in-arm with Bartleby, the silent procession filed its way through all the noise, and heat, and joy of the roaring thoroughfares at noon.

The same day I received the note I went to the Tombs, or, to speak more properly, the Halls of Justice. Seeking the right officer, I stated the purpose of my call, and was informed that the individual I described was indeed within. I then assured the functionary that Bartleby was a perfectly honest man, and greatly to be a compassionated (however unaccountable) eccentric. I narrated all I knew, and closed by suggesting the idea of letting him remain in as indulgent confinement as possible till something less harsh might be done—though indeed I hardly knew what. At all events if nothing else could be decided upon, the alms-house must receive him. I then begged to have an interview.

Being under no disgraceful charge, and quite serene and harmless in all his ways, they had permitted him freely to wander about the prison, and especially in the inclosed grass-platted yards thereof. And so I found him there, standing all alone in the quietest of the yards, his face toward a high wall—while all around, from the narrow slits of the jail windows, I thought I saw peering out upon him the eyes of murderers and thieves.

"Bartleby!"

"I know you," he said, without looking around,—"and I want nothing to say to you."

"It was not I that brought you here, Bartleby," said I, keenly pained at his implied suspicion. "And to you, this should not be so vile a place. Nothing reproachful attaches to you by being here. And see, it is not so sad a place as one might think. Look, there is the sky and here is the grass."

"I know where I am," he replied, but would say nothing more, and so I left him.

As I entered the corridor again a broad, meat-like man in an apron accosted me, and jerking his thumb over his shoulder said—"Is that your friend?"

"Yes."

"Does he want to starve? If he does, let him live on the prison fare, that's all."

"Who are you?" asked I, not knowing what to make of such an unofficially speaking person in such a place.

"I am the grub-man. Such gentlemen as have friends here, hire me to provide them with something good to eat."

"Is this so?" said I, turning to the turnkey.

He said it was.

"Well then," said I, slipping some silver into the grub-man's hands (for so they called him), "I want you to give particular attention to my friend there: let him have the best dinner you can get. And you must be as polite to him as possible."

"Introduce me, will you?" said the grub-man, looking at me with an expression which seemed to say he was all impatience for an opportunity to give a specimen of his breeding.

Thinking it would prove of benefit to the scrivener, I acquiesced; and asking the grub-man his name, went up with him to Bartleby.

"Bartleby, this is Mr. Cutlets; you will find him very useful to you."

"Your sarvant, sir, your sarvant," said the grub-man, making a low salutation behind his apron. "Hope you find it pleasant here, sir;—spacious grounds—apartments, sir—hope you'll stay with us some time—try to make it agreeable. May Mrs. Cutlets and I have the pleasure of your company to dinner, sir, in Mrs. Cutlets' private room?"

"I prefer not to dine to-day," said Bartleby, turning away. "It would disagree with me; I am unused to dinners." So saying, he slowly moved to the other side of the inclosure and took up a position fronting the dead-wall.

"How's this?" said the grub-man, addressing me with a stare of astonishment. "He's odd, ain't he?"

"I think he is a little deranged," said I, sadly.

"Deranged? deranged is it? Well now, upon my word, I thought that friend of yourn was a gentleman forger; they are always pale and genteel-like, them forgers. I can't help pity 'em—can't help it, sir. Did you know Monroe Edwards?" he added touchingly, and paused. Then, laying his hand pityingly on my shoulder, sighed, "he died of the consumption at Sing-Sing.[6] So you weren't acquainted with Monroe?"

"No, I was never socially acquainted with any forgers. But I cannot stop longer. Look to my friend yonder. You will not lose by it. I will see you again."

Some few days after this, I again obtained admission to the Tombs, and went through the corridors in quest of Bartleby; but without finding him.

"I saw him coming from his cell not long ago," said a turnkey, "maybe he's gone to loiter in the yards."

So I went in that direction.

"Are you looking for the silent man?" said another turnkey passing me. "Yonder he lies—sleeping in the yard there. 'Tis not twenty minutes since I saw him lie down."

---

6. Founded in 1825, Sing-Sing is a state prison for men that became infamous for its harsh measures during the late 1800s.

The yard was entirely quiet. It was not accessible to the common prisoners. The surrounding walls, of amazing thickness, kept off all sounds behind them. The Egyptian character of the masonry weighed upon me with its gloom. But a soft imprisoned turf grew under foot. The heart of the eternal pyramids, it seemed, wherein by some strange magic, through the clefts grass-seed, dropped by birds, had sprung.

Strangely huddled at the base of the wall—his knees drawn up, and lying on his side, his head touching the cold stones—I saw the wasted Bartleby. But nothing stirred. I paused; then went close up to him; stooped over, and saw that his dim eyes were open; otherwise he seemed profoundly sleeping. Something prompted me to touch him. I felt his hand, when a tingling shiver ran up my arm and down my spine to my feet.

The round face of the grub-man peered upon me now. "His dinner is ready. Won't he dine to-day, either? Or does he live without dining?"

"Lives without dining," said I, and closed the eyes.

"Eh!—He's asleep, ain't he?"

"With kings and counsellors," murmured I.

There would seem little need for proceeding further in this history. Imagination will readily supply the meagre recital of poor Bartleby's interment. But ere parting with the reader, let me say, that if this little narrative has sufficiently interested him, to awaken curiosity as to who Bartleby was, and what manner of life he led prior to the present narrator's making his acquaintance, I can only reply, that in such curiosity I fully share—but am wholly unable to gratify it. Yet here I hardly know whether I should divulge one little item of rumour, which came to my ear a few months after the scrivener's decease. Upon what basis it rested, I could never ascertain; and hence, how true it is I cannot now tell. But inasmuch as this vague report has not been without a certain strange suggestive interest to me, however sad, it may prove the same with some others; and so I will briefly mention it. The report was this: that Bartleby had been a subordinate clerk in the Dead Letter Office at Washington, from which he had been suddenly removed by a change in the administration. When I think over this rumour I cannot adequately express the emotions which seize me. Dead letters! Does it not sound like dead men? Conceive a man by nature and misfortune prone to a pallid hopelessness: can any business seem more fitted to heighten it than that of continually handling these dead letters, and assorting them for the flames? For by the cartload they are annually burned. Sometimes from out the folded paper the pale clerk takes a ring:—the finger it was meant for, perhaps, moulders in the grave; a bank-note sent in swiftest charity:—he whom it would relieve, nor eats nor hungers any more; pardon for those who died despairing; hope for those who died unhoping; good tidings for those who died stifled by unrelieved calamities. On errands of life, these letters speed to death.

Ah Bartleby! Ah humanity!

1853

Further Reading

Borges, Jorge Luis. "Prologue to Herman Melville's 'Bartleby.'" Trans. Ronald Christ. *Review* 17 (Spring 1976): 24–25. • Lewis, R. B. W. "Melville After *Moby-Dick*: The Tales." *Modern Critical Views: Herman Melville.* Ed. Harold Bloom. New York: Chelsea, 1986. 77–90. • Forst, Graham Nicol. "Up Wall Street Towards Broadway: The Narrator's Pilgrimage in Melville's 'Bartleby the Scrivener.'" *Studies in Short Fiction* 24.3 (Summer 1987): 263–70. • Marcus, Mordecai. "Melville's Bartleby as Psychological Double." *College English* 23.5 (Feb. 1962): 365–68. • Franklin, H. Bruce. "Bartleby: The Ascetic's Advent." *The Wake of the Gods.* Stanford: Stanford UP, 1963. 126–36.

Herman Melville's fiction sometimes combines the realism of the typical nineteenth-century novel with a surrealism that reaches back toward the folk-tale or forward toward such twentieth-century writers as Franz Kafka. Argentinian writer Jorge Luis Borges, himself no stranger to such a melding of styles, notes that "Bartleby" mixes these elements in a surprising way.

Jorge Luis Borges: On Melville and the Irrational

Moby Dick is written in a romantic dialect of English, an impassioned dialect that alternates or combines rhetorical schemes of Shakespeare and Thomas De Quincey, of Browne and Carlyle; "Bartleby" is written in a calm, even droll diction whose deliberate application to an infamous subject matter seems to prefigure Kafka. Nevertheless, between both fictions, there is a secret, central affinity. In the former, Ahab's monomania disturbs and finally destroys all the men on the boat; in the latter, Bartleby's frank nihilism contaminates his companions and even the stolid man who tells Bartleby's story, the man who pays him for his imaginary labors. It is as if Melville had written: "It is enough that one man is irrational for others to be irrational and for the universe to be irrational." The history of the universe teems with confirmations of this fear.

"Bartleby" belongs to the volume entitled *The Piazza Tales* (New York and London, 1856). About another narrative in that book, John Freeman observes that it could not be fully understood until Joseph Conrad published certain analogous works, almost half a century later. I would observe that the work of Kafka projects a curious, hind light on "Bartleby." "Bartleby" already defines a genre that Kafka would re-invent and quarry around 1919: the genre of fantasies of conduct and feeling or, as it is unfortunately termed today, the psychological. Beyond that, the opening pages of "Bartleby" do not foreshadow Kafka; rather, they allude to or repeat Dickens. . . . In 1849, Melville had published *Mardi*, an entangled and even unreadable novel, but one whose basic argument anticipates the obsessions and the mechanism of *The Castle, The Trial* and *Amerika*: it presents an infinite persecution across an infinite sea.

GUSTAVE FLAUBERT

(1821–1880)

A SIMPLE HEART

translated from the French by Robert Baldick

1

For half a century the women of Pont-l'Évêque envied Mme Aubain her maidservant Félicité.

In return for a hundred francs a year she did all the cooking and the housework, the sewing, the washing, and the ironing. She could bridle a horse, fatten poultry, and churn butter, and she remained faithful to her mistress, who was by no means an easy person to get on with.

Mme Aubain had married a young fellow who was good-looking but badly-off, and who died at the beginning of 1809, leaving her with two small children and a pile of debts. She then sold all her property except for the farms of Toucques and Geffosses, which together brought in five thousand francs a year at the most, and left her house at Saint-Melaine for one behind the covered market which was cheaper to run and had belonged to her family.

This house had a slate roof and stood between the alley-way and a lane leading down to the river. Inside there were differences in level which were the cause of many a stumble. A narrow entrance-hall separated the kitchen from the parlor, where Mme Aubain sat all day long in a wicker easy-chair by the window. Eight mahogany chairs were lined up against the white-painted wainscoting, and under the barometer stood an old piano loaded with a pyramid of boxes and cartons. On either side of the chimney-piece, which was carved out of yellow marble in the Louis Quinze style, there was a tapestry-covered arm-chair, and in the middle was a clock designed to look like a temple of Vesta. The whole room smelt a little musty, as the floor was on a lower level than the garden.

On the first floor was "Madame's" bedroom—very spacious, with a patterned wallpaper of pale flowers and a portrait of "Monsieur" dressed in what had once been the height of fashion. It opened into a smaller room in which there were two cots, without mattresses. Then came the drawing-room, which was always shut up and full of furniture covered with dust-sheets. Next there was a passage leading to the study, where books and papers filled the shelves of a book-case in three sections built round a big writing-table of dark wood. The two end panels were hidden under pen-and-ink drawings, landscapes in gouache, and etchings by Audran, souvenirs of better days and bygone luxury. On the second floor a dormer window gave light to Félicité's room, which looked out over the fields.

Every day Félicité got up at dawn, so as not to miss Mass, and worked until evening without stopping. Then, once dinner was over, the plates and dishes put away, and the door bolted, she piled ashes on the log fire and went to sleep in front of the hearth, with her rosary in her hands. Nobody could be more stubborn when it came to haggling over prices, and as for cleanliness, the shine on her saucepans was the despair of all the other servants. Being of a thrifty nature, she ate slowly, picking up from the table the crumbs from her loaf of bread—a twelve pound loaf which was baked specially for her and lasted twenty days.

All the year round she wore a kerchief of printed calico fastened behind with a pin, a bonnet which covered her hair, grey stockings, a red skirt, and over her jacket a bibbed apron such as hospital nurses wear.

Her face was thin and her voice was sharp. At twenty-five she was often taken for forty; once she reached fifty, she stopped looking any age in particular. Always silent and upright and deliberate in her movements, she looked like a wooden doll driven by clock-work.

2

Like everyone else, she had had her love-story.

Her father, a mason, had been killed when he fell off some scaffolding. Then her mother died, and when her sisters went their separate ways, a farmer took her in, sending her, small as she was, to look after the cows out in the fields. She went about in rags, shivering with cold, used to lie flat on the ground to drink water out of the ponds, would be beaten for no reason at all, and was finally turned out of the house for stealing thirty sous, a theft of which she was innocent. She found work at another farm, looking after the poultry, and as she was liked by her employers the other servants were jealous of her.

One August evening—she was eighteen at the time—they took her off to the fête at Colleville. From the start she was dazed and bewildered by the noise of the fiddles, the lamps in the trees, the medley of gaily colored dresses, the gold crosses and lace, and the throng of people jigging up and down. She was standing shyly on one side when a smart young fellow, who had been leaning on the shaft of a cart, smoking his pipe, came up and asked her to dance. He treated her to cider, coffee, griddle-cake, and a silk neckerchief, and imagining that she knew what he was after, offered to see her home. At the edge of a field of oats, he pushed her roughly to the ground. Thoroughly frightened, she started screaming for help. He took to his heels.

Another night, on the road to Beaumont, she tried to get past a big, slow-moving wagon loaded with hay, and as she was squeezing by she recognized Théodore.

He greeted her quite calmly, saying that she must forgive him for the way he had behaved to her, as "it was the drink that did it."

She did not know what to say in reply and felt like running off.

Straight away he began talking about the crops and the notabilities of the commune, saying that his father had left Colleville for the farm at Les Écots, so that they were now neighbors.

"Ah!" she said.

He added that his family wanted to see him settle but that he was in no hurry and was waiting to find a wife to suit his fancy. She lowered her head. Then he asked her if she was thinking of getting married. She answered with a smile that it was mean of him to make fun of her.

"But I'm not making fun of you!" he said. "I swear I'm not!"

He put his left arm round her waist, and she walked on supported by his embrace. Soon they slowed down. There was a gentle breeze blowing, the stars were shining, the huge load of hay was swaying about in front of them, and the four horses were raising clouds of dust as they shambled along. Then, without being told, they turned off to the right. He kissed her once more and she disappeared into the darkness.

The following week Théodore got her to grant him several rendezvous.

They would meet at the bottom of a farm-yard, behind a wall, under a solitary tree. She was not ignorant of life as young ladies are, for the animals had taught her a great deal; but her reason and an instinctive sense of honor prevented her from giving way. The resistance she put up inflamed Théodore's passion to such an extent that in order to satisfy it (or perhaps out of sheer naïveté) he proposed to her. At first she refused to believe him, but he swore that he was serious.

Soon afterwards he had a disturbing piece of news to tell her: the year before, his parents had paid a man to do his military service for him, but now he might be called up again any day, and the idea of going into the army frightened him. In Félicité's eyes this cowardice of his appeared to be a proof of his affection, and she loved him all the more for it. Every night she would steal out to meet him, and every night Théodore would plague her with his worries and entreaties.

In the end he said that he was going to the Prefecture himself to make inquiries, and that he would come and tell her how matters stood the following Sunday, between eleven and midnight.

At the appointed hour she hurried to meet her sweetheart, but found one of his friends waiting for her instead.

He told her that she would not see Théodore again. To make sure of avoiding conscription, he had married a very rich old woman, Mme Lehoussais of Toucques.

Her reaction was an outburst of frenzied grief. She threw herself on the ground, screaming and calling on God, and lay moaning all alone in the open until sunrise. Then she went back to the farm and announced her intention of leaving. At the end of the month, when she had received her wages, she wrapped her small belongings up in a kerchief and made her way to Pont-l'Évêque.

In front of the inn there, she sought information from a woman in a widow's bonnet, who, as it happened, was looking for a cook. The girl did not know much about cooking, but she seemed so willing and expected so little that finally Mme Aubain ended up by saying: "Very well, I will take you on."

A quarter of an hour later Félicité was installed in her house.

At first she lived there in a kind of fearful awe caused by "the style of the house" and the memory of "Monsieur" brooding over everything. Paul and Virginie, the boy aged seven and the girl barely four, seemed to her to be made of some precious substance. She used to carry them about pick-a-back, and when Mme Aubain told her not to keep on kissing them she was cut to the quick. All the same, she was happy now, for her pleasant surroundings had dispelled her grief.

On Thursdays, a few regular visitors came in to play Boston, and Félicité got the cards and the foot-warmers ready beforehand. They always arrived punctually at eight, and left before the clock struck eleven.

Every Monday morning the second-hand dealer who lived down the alley put all his junk out on the pavement. Then the hum of voices began to fill the town, mingled with the neighing of horses, the bleating of lambs, the grunting of pigs, and the rattle of carts in the streets.

About midday, when the market was in full swing, a tall old peasant with a hooked nose and his cap on the back of his head would appear at the door. This was Robelin, the farmer from Geffosses. A little later, and Liébard, the farmer from Toucques, would arrive—a short, fat, red-faced fellow in a grey jacket and leather gaiters fitted with spurs.

Both men had hens or cheeses they wanted to sell to "Madame." But Félicité was up to all their tricks and invariably outwitted them, so that they went away full of respect for her.

From time to time Mme Aubain had a visit from an uncle of hers, the Marquis de Grémanville, who had been ruined by loose living and was now living at Falaise on his last remaining scrap of property. He always turned up at lunch-time, accompanied by a hideous poodle who dirtied all the furniture with its paws. However hard he tried to behave like a gentleman, even going so far as to raise his hat every time he mentioned "my late father," the force of habit was usually too much for him, for he would start pouring himself one glass after another and telling bawdy stories. Félicité used to push him gently out of the house, saying politely: "You've had quite enough, Monsieur de Grémanville. See you another time!" and shutting the door on him.

She used to open it with pleasure to M. Bourais, who was a retired solicitor. His white tie and his bald head, his frilled shirt-front and his ample brown frock-coat, the way he had of rounding his arm to take a pinch of snuff, and indeed everything about him made an overwhelming impression on her such as we feel when we meet some outstanding personality.

As he looked after "Madame's" property, he used to shut himself up with her for hours in "Monsieur's" study. He lived in dread of compromising his reputation, had a tremendous respect for the Bench, and laid claim to some knowledge of Latin.

To give the children a little painless instruction, he made them a present of a geography book with illustrations. These represented scenes in different parts of the world, such as cannibals wearing feather head-dresses, a monkey carrying off a young lady, Bedouins in the desert, a whale being harpooned, and so on.

Paul explained these pictures to Félicité, and that indeed was all the education she ever had. As for the children, they were taught by Guyot, a poor devil employed at the Town Hall, who was famous for his beautiful handwriting, and who had a habit of sharpening his penknife on his boots.

When the weather was fine the whole household used to set off early for a day on the Geffosses farm.

The farm-yard there was on a slope, with the house in the middle; and the sea, in the distance, looked like a streak of grey. Félicité would take some slices of cold meat out of her basket, and they would have their lunch in a room adjoining the dairy. It was all that remained of a country house which had fallen into ruin, and the wallpaper hung in shreds, fluttering in the draught. Mme Aubain used to sit with bowed head, absorbed in her memories, so that the children were afraid to talk. "Why don't you run along and play?" she would say, and away they went.

Paul climbed up into the barn, caught birds, played ducks and drakes on the pond, or banged with a stick on the great casks, which sounded just like drums.

Virginie fed the rabbits, or scampered off to pick cornflowers, showing her little embroidered knickers as she ran.

One autumn evening they came home through the fields. The moon, which was in its first quarter, lit up part of the sky, and there was some mist floating like a scarf over the winding Toucques. The cattle, lying out in the middle of the pasture, looked peacefully at the four people walking by. In the third field a few got up and made a half circle in front of them.

"Don't be frightened!" said Félicité, and crooning softly, she stroked the back of the nearest animal. It turned about and the others did the same. But while they were crossing the next field they suddenly heard a dreadful bellowing. It came from a bull which had been hidden by the mist, and which now came towards the two women.

Mme Aubain started to run.

"No! No!" said Félicité. "Not so fast!"

All the same they quickened their pace, hearing behind them a sound of heavy breathing which came nearer and nearer. The bull's hooves thudded like hammers on the turf, and they realized that it had broken into a gallop. Turning around, Félicité tore up some clods of earth and flung them at its eyes. It lowered its muzzle and thrust its horns forward, trembling with rage and bellowing horribly.

By now Mme Aubain had got to the end of the field with her two children and was frantically looking for a way over the high bank. Félicité was still backing away from the bull, hurling clods of turf which blinded it, and shouting: "Hurry! Hurry!"

Mme Aubain got down into the ditch, pushed first Virginie and then Paul up the other side, fell once or twice trying to climb the bank, and finally managed it with a valiant effort.

The bull had driven Félicité back against a gate, and its slaver was spurting into her face. In another second it would have gored her, but she just had time to slip between two of the bars, and the great beast halted in amazement.

This adventure was talked about at Pont-l'Évêque for a good many years, but Félicité never prided herself in the least on what she had done, as it never occurred to her that she had done anything heroic.

Virginie claimed all her attention, for the fright had affected the little girl's nerves, and M. Poupart, the doctor, recommended sea-bathing at Trouville.

In those days the resort had few visitors. Mme Aubain made inquiries, consulted Bourais, and got everything ready as though for a long journey.

Her luggage went off in Liébard's cart the day before she left. The next morning he brought along two horses, one of which had a woman's saddle with a velvet back, while the other carried a cloak rolled up to make a kind of seat on its crupper. Mme Aubain sat on this, with Liébard in front. Félicité looked after Virginie on the other horse, and Paul mounted M. Lechaptois's donkey, which he had lent them on condition they took great care of it.

The road was so bad that it took two hours to travel the five miles to Toucques. The horses sank into the mud up to their pasterns and had to jerk their hind-quarters to get out; often they stumbled in the ruts, or else they had to jump. In some places, Liébard's mare came to a sudden stop, and while he waited patiently for her to move off again, he talked about the people whose properties bordered the road, adding moral reflections to each story. For instance, in the middle of Toucques, as they were passing underneath some windows set in a mass of nasturtiums, he shrugged his shoulders and said:

"There's a Madame Lehoussais lives here. Now instead of taking a young man, she . . . ."

Félicité did not hear the rest, for the horses had broken into a trot and the donkey was galloping along. All three turned down a bridle-path, a gate swung open, a couple of boys appeared, and everyone dismounted in front of a manure-heap right outside the farm-house door.

Old Mother Liébard welcomed her mistress with every appearance of pleasure. She served up a sirloin of beef for lunch, with tripe and black pudding, a fricassee of chicken, sparkling cider, a fruit tart and brandy-plums, garnishing the whole meal with compliments to Madame, who seemed to be enjoying better health, to Mademoiselle, who had turned into a "proper little beauty," and to Monsieur Paul, who had "filled out a lot." Nor did she forget their deceased grandparents, whom the Liébards had known personally, having been in the family's service for several generations.

Like its occupants, the farm had an air of antiquity. The ceiling-beams were worm-eaten, the walls black with smoke, and the window-panes grey with dust. There was an oak dresser laden with all sorts of odds and ends— jugs, plates, pewter bowls, wolf-traps, sheep-shears, and an enormous syringe which amused the children. In the three yards outside there was not a single tree without either mushrooms at its base or mistletoe in its branches. Several had been blown down and had taken root again in the middle; all of them were bent under the weight of their apples. The thatched roofs, which looked like brown velvet and varied in thickness, weathered the fiercest winds, but the cart-shed was tumbling down. Mme Aubain said that she would have it seen to, and ordered the animals to be reharnessed.

It took them another half-hour to reach Trouville. The little caravan dismounted to make their way along the Écores, a cliff jutting right out over the boats moored below; and three minutes later they got to the end of the quay and entered the courtyard of the Golden Lamb, the inn kept by Mère David.

After the first few days Virginie felt stronger, as a result of the change of air and the sea-bathing. Not having a costume, she went into the water in her chemise and her maid dressed her afterwards in a customs officer's hut which was used by the bathers.

In the afternoons they took the donkey and went off beyond the Roches-Noires, in the direction of Hennequeville. To begin with, the path went uphill between gentle slopes like the lawns in a park, and then came out on a plateau where pastureland and ploughed fields alternated. On either side there were holly-bushes standing out from the tangle of brambles, and here and there a big dead tree spread its zigzag branches against the blue sky.

They almost always rested in the same field, with Deauville on their left, Le Havre on their right, and the open sea in front. The water glittered in the sunshine, smooth as a mirror, and so still that the murmur it made was scarcely audible; unseen sparrows could be heard twittering, and the sky covered the whole scene with its huge canopy. Mme Aubain sat doing her needlework, Virginie plaited rushes beside her, Félicité gathered lavender, and Paul, feeling profoundly bored, longed to get up and go.

Sometimes they crossed the Toucques in a boat and hunted for shells. When the tide went out, sea-urchins, ormers, and jelly-fish were left behind; and the children scampered around, snatching at the foam-flakes carried on the wind. The sleepy waves, breaking on the sand, spread themselves out along the shore. The beach stretched as far as the eye could see, bounded on the land side by the dunes which separated it from the Marais, a broad meadow in the shape of an arena. When they came back that way, Trouville, on the distant hillside, grew bigger at every step, and with its medley of oddly assorted houses seemed to blossom out in gay disorder.

On exceptionally hot days they stayed in their room. The sun shone in dazzling bars of light between the slats of the blind. There was not a sound to be heard in the village, and not a soul to be seen down in the street. Everything seemed more peaceful in the prevailing silence. In the distance caulkers were hammering away at the boats, and the smell of tar was wafted along by a sluggish breeze.

The principal amusement consisted in watching the fishingboats come in. As soon as they had passed the buoys, they started tacking. With their canvas partly lowered and their foresails blown out like balloons they glided through the splashing waves as far as the middle of the harbor, where they suddenly dropped anchor. Then each boat came alongside the quay, and the crew threw ashore their catch of quivering fish. A line of carts stood waiting, and women in cotton bonnets rushed forward to take the baskets and kiss their men.

One day one of these women spoke to Félicité, who came back to the inn soon after in a state of great excitement. She explained that she had found one of her sisters—and Nastasie Barette, now Leroux, made her appearance, with a baby at her breast, another child holding her right hand, and on her left a little sailor-boy, his arms akimbo and his cap over one ear.

Mme Aubain sent her off after a quarter of an hour. From then on they were forever hanging round the kitchen or loitering about when the family went for a walk, though the husband kept out of sight.

Félicité became quite attached to them. She bought them a blanket, several shirts, and a stove; and it was clear that they were bent on getting all they could out of her.

This weakness of hers annoyed Mme Aubain, who in any event disliked the familiar way in which the nephew spoke to Paul. And so, as Virginie had started coughing and the good weather was over, she decided to go back to Pont-l'Évêque.

M. Bourais advised her on the choice of a school; Caen was considered the best, so it was there that Paul was sent. He said good-bye bravely, feeling really rather pleased to be going to a place where he would have friends of his own.

Mme Aubain resigned herself to the loss of her son, knowing that it was unavoidable. Virginie soon got used to it. Félicité missed the din he used to make, but she was given something new to do which served as a distraction; from Christmas onwards she had to take the little girl to catechism every day.

3

After genuflecting at the door, she walked up the center aisle under the nave, opened the door of Mme Aubain's pew, sat down, and started looking about her.

The choir stalls were all occupied, with the boys on the right and the girls on the left, while the curé stood by the lectern. In one of the stained-glass windows in the apse the Holy Ghost looked down on the Virgin; another window showed her kneeling before the Infant Jesus; and behind the tabernacle there was a wood-carving of St. Michael slaying the dragon.

The priest began with a brief outline of sacred history. Listening to him, Félicité saw in imagination the Garden of Eden, the Flood, the Tower of Babel, cities burning, peoples dying, and idols being overthrown; and his dazzling vision left her with a great respect for the Almighty and profound fear of His wrath.

Then she wept as she listened to the story of the Passion. Why had they crucified Him, when He loved children, fed the multitudes, healed the blind, and had chosen out of humility to be born among the poor, on the litter of a stable? The sowing of the seed, the reaping of the harvest, the pressing of the grapes—all those familiar things of which the Gospels speak had their place in her life. God had sanctified them in passing, so that she loved the lambs more tenderly for love of the Lamb of God, and the doves for the sake of the Holy Ghost.

She found it difficult, however, to imagine what the Holy Ghost looked like, for it was not just a bird but a fire as well, and sometimes a breath. She wondered whether that was its light she had seen flitting about the edge of the marshes at night, whether that was its breath she had felt driving the clouds across the sky, whether that was its voice she had heard in the sweet music of the bells. And she sat in silent adoration, delighting in the coolness of the walls and the quiet of the church.

Of dogma she neither understood nor even tried to understand anything. The curé discoursed, the children repeated their lesson, and she finally dropped off to sleep, waking up suddenly at the sound of their sabots clattering across the flagstones as they left the church.

It was in this manner, simply by hearing it expounded, that she learnt her catechism, for her religious education had been neglected in her youth. From then on she copied all Virginie's observances, fasting when she did and going to confession with her. On the feast of Corpus Christi the two of them made an altar of repose together.

The preparations for Virginie's first communion caused her great anxiety. She worried over her shoes, her rosary, her missal, and her gloves. And how she trembled as she helped Mme Aubain to dress the child!

All through the Mass her heart was in her mouth. One side of the choir was hidden from her by M. Bourais, but directly opposite her she could see the flock of maidens, looking like a field of snow with their white crowns perched on top of their veils; and she recognized her little darling from a distance by her dainty neck and her rapt attitude. The bell tinkled. Every head bowed low, and there was a silence. Then, to the thunderous accompaniment of the organ, choir and congregation joined in singing the *Agnus Dei*. Next the boys' procession began, and after that the girls got up from their seats. Slowly, their hands joined in prayer, they went towards the brightly lit altar, knelt on the first step, received the Host one by one, and went back to their places in the same order. When it was Virginie's turn, Félicité leant forward to see her, and in one of those imaginative flights born of real affection, it seemed to her that she herself was in the child's place. Virginie's face became her own, Virginie's dress clothed her, Virginie's heart was beating in her breast; and as she closed her eyes and opened her mouth, she almost fainted away.

Early next morning she went to the sacristy and asked M. le Curé to give her communion. She received the sacrament with all due reverence, but did not feel the same rapture as she had the day before.

Mme Aubain wanted her daughter to possess every accomplishment, and since Guyot could not teach her English or music, she decided to send her as a boarder to the Ursuline Convent at Honfleur.

Virginie raised no objection, but Félicité went about sighing at Madame's lack of feeling. Then she thought that perhaps her mistress was right: such matters, after all, lay outside her province.

Finally the day arrived when an old wagonette stopped at their door, and a nun got down from it who had come to fetch Mademoiselle. Félicité hoisted the luggage up on top, gave the driver some parting instructions, and put six pots of jam, a dozen pears, and a bunch of violets in the boot.

At the last moment Virginie burst into a fit of sobbing. She threw her arms round her mother, who kissed her on the forehead, saying: "Come now, be brave, be brave." The step was pulled up and the carriage drove away.

Then Mme Aubain broke down, and that evening all her friends, M. and Mme Lormeau, Mme Lechaptois, the Rochefeuille sisters, M. de Houppeville, and Bourais, came in to console her.

To begin with she missed her daughter badly. But she had a letter from her three times a week, wrote back on the other days, walked round her garden, did a little reading, and thus contrived to fill the empty hours.

As for Félicité, she went into Virginie's room every morning from sheer force of habit and looked round it. It upset her not having to brush the child's hair any more, tie her bootlaces, or tuck her up in bed; and she missed seeing her sweet face all the time and holding her hand when they went out together. For want of something to do, she tried making lace, but her fingers were too clumsy and broke the threads. She could not settle to anything, lost her sleep, and, to use her own words, was "eaten up inside."

To "occupy her mind," she asked if her nephew Victor might come and see her, and permission was granted.

He used to arrive after Mass on Sunday, his cheeks flushed, his chest bare, and smelling of the countryside through which he had come. She laid a place for him straight away, opposite hers, and they had lunch together. Eating as little as possible herself, in order to save the expense, she stuffed him so full of food that he fell asleep after the meal. When the first bell for vespers rang, she woke him up, brushed his trousers, tied his tie, and set off for church, leaning on his arm with all a mother's pride.

His parents always told him to get something out of her—a packet of brown sugar perhaps, some soap, or a little brandy, sometimes even money. He brought her his clothes to be mended, and she did the work gladly, thankful for anything that would force him to come again.

In August his father took him on a coasting trip. The children's holidays were just beginning, and it cheered her up to have them home again. But Paul was turning capricious and Virginie was getting too old to be addressed familiarly—a state of affairs which put a barrier of constraint between them.

Victor went to Morlaix, Dunkirk, and Brighton in turn, and brought her a present after each trip. The first time it was a box covered with shells, the second a coffee cup, the third a big gingerbread man. He was growing quite handsome, with his trim figure, his little moustache, his frank open eyes, and the little leather cap that he wore on the back of his head like a pilot. He kept her amused by telling her stories full of nautical jargon.

One Monday—it was the fourteenth of July 1819, a date she never forgot—Victor told her that he had signed on for an ocean voyage, and that on the Wednesday night he would be taking the Honfleur packet to join his schooner, which was due to sail shortly from Le Havre. He might be away, he said, for two years.

The prospect of such a long absence made Félicité extremely unhappy, and she felt she must bid him godspeed once more. So on the Wednesday evening, when Madame's dinner was over, she put on her clogs and swiftly covered the ten miles between Pont-l'Évêque and Honfleur.

When she arrived at the Calvary she turned right instead of left, got lost in the shipyards, and had to retrace her steps. Some people she spoke to advised her to hurry. She went right round the harbor, which was full of boats, constantly tripping over moorings. Then the ground fell away, rays of light criss-crossed in front of her, and for a moment, she thought she was going mad, for she could see horses up in the sky.

On the quayside more horses were neighing, frightened by the sea. A derrick was hoisting them into the air and dropping them into one of the boats, which was already crowded with passengers elbowing their way between barrels of cider, baskets of cheese, and sacks of grain. Hens were cackling and the captain swearing, while a cabin-boy stood leaning on the cats-head, completely indifferent to it all. Félicité, who had not recognized him, shouted: "Victor!" and he raised his head. She rushed forward, but at that very moment the gangway was pulled ashore.

The packet moved out of the harbor with women singing as they hauled it along, its ribs creaking and heavy waves lashing its bows. The sail swung round, hiding everyone on board from view, and against the silvery, moonlit sea the boat appeared as a dark shape that grew ever fainter, until at last it vanished in the distance.

As Félicité was passing the Calvary, she felt a longing to commend to God's mercy all that she held most dear; and she stood there praying for a long time, her face bathed in tears, her eyes fixed upon the clouds. The town was asleep, except for the customs officers walking up and down. Water was pouring ceaselessly through the holes in the sluice-gate, making as much noise as a torrent. The clocks struck two.

The convent parlor would not be open before daybreak, and Madame would be annoyed if she were late; so, although she would have liked to give a kiss to the other child, she set off for home. The maids at the inn were just waking up as she got to Pont-l'Évêque.

So the poor lad was going to be tossed by the waves for months on end! His previous voyages had caused her no alarm. People came back from England and Brittany; but America, the Colonies, the Islands, were all so far away, somewhere at the other end of the world.

From then on Félicité thought of nothing but her nephew. On sunny days she hoped he was not too thirsty, and when there was a storm she was afraid he would be struck by lightning. Listening to the wind howling in the chimney or blowing slates off the roof, she saw him being buffeted by the very same storm, perched on the top of a broken mast, with his whole body bent backwards under a sheet of foam; or again—and these were reminiscences of the illustrated geography book—he was being eaten by savages, captured by monkeys in the forest, or dying on a desert shore. But she never spoke of her worries.

Mme Aubain had worries of her own about her daughter. The good nuns said that she was an affectionate child, but very delicate. The slightest emotion upset her, and she had to give up playing the piano.

Her mother insisted on regular letters from the convent. One morning when the postman had not called, she lost patience and walked up and down the room, between her chair and the window. It was really extraordinary! Four days without any news!

Thinking her own example would comfort her, Félicité said:

"I've been six months, Madame, without news."

"News of whom?"

The servant answered gently:

"Why—of my nephew."

"Oh, your nephew!" And Mme Aubain started pacing up and down again, with a shrug of her shoulders that seemed to say: "I wasn't thinking of him—and indeed, why should I? Who cares about a young, good-for-nothing cabin-boy? Whereas my daughter—why, just think!"

Although she had been brought up the hard way, Félicité was indignant with Madame, but she soon forgot. It struck her as perfectly natural to lose one's head where the little girl was concerned. For her, the two children were of equal importance; they were linked together in her heart by a single bond, and their destinies should be the same.

The chemist told her that Victor's ship had arrived at Havana: he had seen this piece of information in a newspaper.

Because of its association with cigars, she imagined Havana as a place where nobody did anything but smoke, and pictured Victor walking about among crowds of Negroes in a cloud of tobacco-smoke. Was it possible, she wondered, "in case of need" to come back by land? And how far was it from Pont-l'Évêque? To find out she asked M. Bourais.

He reached for his atlas, and launched forth into an explanation of latitudes and longitudes, smiling like the pedant he was at Félicité's bewilderment. Finally he pointed with his pencil at a minute black dot inside a ragged oval patch, saying:

"There it is."

She bent over the map, but the network of colored lines meant nothing to her and only tired her eyes. So when Bourais asked her to tell him what was puzzling her, she begged him to show her the house where Victor was living. He threw up his hands, sneezed, and roared with laughter, delighted to come across such simplicity. And Félicité—whose intelligence was so limited that she probably expected to see an actual portrait of her nephew —could not make out why he was laughing.

It was a fortnight later that Liébard came into the kitchen at market-time, as he usually did, and handed her a letter from her brother-in-law. As neither of them could read, she turned to her mistress for help.

Mme Aubain, who was counting the stitches in her knitting, put it down and unsealed the letter. She gave a start, and, looking hard at Félicité, said quietly:

"They have some bad news for you. . . . Your nephew. . . ."

He was dead. That was all the letter had to say.

Félicité dropped on to a chair, leaning her head against the wall and closing her eyelids, which suddenly turned pink. Then, with her head bowed, her hands dangling, and her eyes set, she kept repeating:

"Poor little lad! Poor little lad!"

Liébard looked at her and sighed. Mme Aubain was trembling slightly. She suggested that she should go and see her sister at Trouville, but Félicité shook her head to indicate that there was no need for that.

There was a silence. Old Liébard thought it advisable to go.

Then Félicité said:

"It doesn't matter a bit, not to them it doesn't."

Her head fell forward again, and from time to time she unconsciously picked up the knitting needles lying on the work table.

Some women went past carrying a tray full of dripping linen.

Catching sight of them through the window, she remembered her own washing; she had passed the lye through it the day before and today it needed rinsing. So she left the room.

Her board and tub were on the bank of the Toucques. She threw a pile of chemises down by the water's edge, rolled up her sleeves, and picked up her battledore. The lusty blows she gave with it could be heard in all the neighboring gardens.

The fields were empty, the river rippling in the wind; at the bottom long weeds were waving to and fro, like the hair of corpses floating in the water. She held back her grief, and was very brave until the evening; but in her room she gave way to it completely, lying on her mattress with her face buried in the pillow and her fists pressed against her temples.

Long afterwards she learnt the circumstances of Victor's death from the captain of his ship. He had gone down with yellow fever, and they had bled him too much at the hospital. Four doctors had held him at once. He had died straight away, and the chief doctor had said:

"Good! There goes another!"

His parents had always treated him cruelly. She preferred not to see them again, and they made no advances, either because they had forgotten about her or out of the callousness of the poor.

Meanwhile Virginie was growing weaker. Difficulty in breathing, fits of coughing, protracted bouts of fever, and mottled patches on the cheekbones all indicated some deepseated complaint. M. Poupart had advised a stay in Provence. Mme Aubain decided to follow this suggestion, and, if it had not been for the weather at Pont-l'Évêque, she would have brought her daughter home at once.

She arranged with a jobmaster to drive her out to the convent every Tuesday. There was a terrace in the garden, overlooking the Seine, and there Virginie, leaning on her mother's arm, walked up and down over the fallen vineleaves. Sometimes, while she was looking at the sails in the distance, or at the long stretch of horizon from the Château de Tancarville to the lighthouses of Le Havre, the sun would break through the clouds and make her blink. Afterwards they would rest in the arbor. Her mother had secured a little cask of excellent Malaga, and, laughing at the idea of getting tipsy, Virginie used to drink a thimbleful, but no more.

Her strength revived. Autumn slipped by, and Félicité assured Mme Aubain that there was nothing to fear. But one evening, coming back from some errand in the neighborhood, she found M. Poupart's gig standing at the door. He was in the hall, and Mme Aubain was trying on her bonnet.

"Give me my foot-warmer, purse, gloves. Quickly now!"

Virginie had pneumonia and was perhaps past recovery.

"Not yet!" said the doctor; and the two of them got into the carriage with snowflakes swirling around them. Night was falling and it was very cold.

Félicité rushed into the church to light a candle, and then ran after the gig. She caught up with it an hour later, jumped lightly behind, and hung on to the fringe. But then a thought struck her: the courtyard had not been locked up, the burglars might get in. So she jumped down again.

At dawn the next day she went to the doctor's. He had come home and gone out again on his rounds. Then she waited at the inn, thinking that somebody who was a stranger to the district might call there with a letter. Finally, when it was twilight, she got into the coach for Lisieux.

The convent was at the bottom of a steep lane. When she was halfway down the hill, she heard a strange sound which she recognized as a deathbell tolling.

"It's for somebody else," she thought, as she banged the door-knocker hard.

After a few minutes she heard the sound of shuffling feet, the door opened a little way, and a nun appeared.

The good sister said with an air of compunction that "she had just passed away." At that moment the bell of Saint-Léonard was tolled more vigorously than ever.

Félicité went up to the second floor. From the doorway of the room she could see Virginie lying on her back, her hands clasped together, her mouth open, her head tilted back under a black crucifix that leant over her, her face whiter than the curtains that hung motionless on either side. Mme Aubain was clinging to the foot of the bed and sobbing desperately. The Mother Superior stood on the right. Three candlesticks on the chest of drawers added touches of red to the scene, and fog was whitening the windows. Some nuns led Mme Aubain away.

For two nights Félicité never left the dead girl. She said the same prayers over and over again, sprinkled holy water on the sheets, then sat down again to watch. At the end of her first vigil she noticed that the child's face had gone yellow, the lips were turning blue, the nose looked sharper, and the eyes were sunken. She kissed them several times, and would not have been particularly surprised if Virginie had opened them again: to minds like hers the supernatural is a simple matter. She laid her out, wrapped her in a shroud, put her in her coffin, placed a wreath on her, and spread out her hair. It was fair and amazingly long for her age. Félicité cut off a big lock, half of which she slipped into her bosom, resolving never to part with it.

The body was brought back to Pont-l'Évêque at the request of Mme Aubain, who followed the hearse in a closed carriage.

After the Requiem Mass, it took another three-quarters of an hour to reach the cemetery. Paul walked in front, sobbing. Then came M. Bourais, and after him the principal inhabitants of the town, the women all wearing long black veils, and Félicité. She was thinking about her nephew; and since she had been unable to pay him these last honors, she felt an added grief, just as if they were burying him with Virginie.

Mme Aubain's despair passed all bounds. First of all she rebelled against God, considering it unfair of Him to have taken her daughter from her—for she had never done any harm, and her conscience was quite clear. But was it? She ought to have taken Virginie to the south; other doctors would have saved her life. She blamed herself, wished she could have joined her daughter, and cried out in anguish in her dreams. One dream in particular obsessed her. Her husband, dressed like a sailor, came back from a long voyage, and told her amid tears that he had been ordered to take Virginie away—whereupon they put their heads together to discover somewhere to hide her.

One day she came in from the garden utterly distraught. A few minutes earlier—and she pointed to the spot—father and daughter had appeared to her, doing nothing, but simply looking at her.

For several months she stayed in her room in a kind of stupor. Félicité scolded her gently, telling her that she must take care of herself for her son's sake, and also in remembrance of "her."

"Her?" repeated Mme Aubain, as if she were waking from a sleep. "Oh, yes, of course! You don't forget her, do you!" This was an allusion to the cemetery, where she herself was strictly forbidden to go.

Félicité went there every day. She would set out on the stroke of four, going past the houses, up the hill, and through the gate, until she came to Virginie's grave. There was a little column of pink marble with a tablet at its base, and a tiny garden enclosed by chains. The beds were hidden under a carpet of flowers. She watered their leaves and changed the sand, going down on her knees to fork the ground thoroughly. The result was that when Mme Aubain was able to come here, she experienced a feeling of relief, a kind of consolation.

Then the years slipped by, each one like the last, with nothing to vary the rhythm of the great festivals: Easter, the Assumption, All Saints' Day. Domestic events marked dates that later served as points of reference. Thus in 1825 a couple of glaziers whitewashed the hall; in 1827 a piece of the roof fell into the courtyard and nearly killed a man; and in the summer of 1828 it was Madame's turn to provide the bread for consecration. About this time Bourais went away in a mysterious fashion; and one by one the old acquaintances disappeared: Guyot, Liébard, Mme Lechaptois, Robelin, and Uncle Grémanville, who had been paralyzed for a long time.

One night the driver of the mail-coach brought Pont-l'Évêque news of the July Revolution. A few days later a new subprefect was appointed. This was the Baron de Larsonnière, who had been a consul in America, and who brought with him, besides his wife, his sister-in-law and three young ladies who were almost grown-up. They were to be seen on their lawn, dressed in loose-fitting smocks; and they had a Negro servant and a parrot. They paid a call on Mme Aubain, who made a point of returning it. As soon as Félicité saw them coming, she would run and tell her mistress. But only one thing could really awaken her interest, and that was her son's letters.

He seemed to be incapable of following any career and spent all his time in taverns. She paid his debts, but he contracted new ones, and the sighs Mme Aubain heaved as she knitted by the window reached Félicité at her spinning wheel in the kitchen.

The two women used to walk up and down together beside the espalier, forever talking of Virginie and debating whether such and such a thing would have appealed to her, or what she would have said on such and such an occasion.

All her little belongings were in a cupboard in the children's bedroom. Mme Aubain went through them as seldom as possible. One summer day she resigned herself to doing so, and the moths were sent fluttering out of the cupboard.

Virginie's frocks hung in a row underneath a shelf containing three dolls, a few hoops, a set of toy furniture, and the wash-basin she had used. Besides the frocks, they took out her petticoats, her stockings, and her handkerchiefs, and spread them out on the two beds before folding them up again. The sunlight streamed in on these pathetic objects, bringing out the stains and showing up the creases made by the child's movements. The air was warm, the sky was blue, a blackbird was singing, and everything seemed to be utterly at peace.

They found a little chestnut-colored hat, made of plush with a long nap; but the moths had ruined it. Félicité asked if she might have it. The two women looked at each other and their eyes filled with tears. Then the mistress opened her arms, the maid threw herself into them, and they clasped each other in a warm embrace, satisfying their grief in a kiss which made them equal.

It was the first time that such a thing had happened, for Mme Aubain was not of a demonstrative nature. Félicité was as grateful as if she had received a great favor, and henceforth loved her mistress with dog-like devotion and religious veneration.

Her heart grew softer as time went by.

When she heard the drums of a regiment coming down the street she stood at the door with a jug of cider and offered the soldiers a drink. She looked after the people who went down with cholera. She watched over the Polish refugees, and one of them actually expressed a desire to marry her. But they fell out, for when she came back from the Angelus one morning, she found that he had got into her kitchen and was calmly eating an oil-and-vinegar salad.

After the Poles it was Père Colmiche, an old man who was said to have committed fearful atrocities in '93. He lived by the river in a ruined pig-sty. The boys of the town used to peer at him through the cracks in the walls, and threw pebbles at him which landed on the litter where he lay, constantly shaken by fits of coughing. His hair was extremely long, his eyelids inflamed, and on one arm there was a swelling bigger than his head. Félicité brought him some linen, tried to clean out his filthy hovel, and even wondered if she could install him in the wash-house without annoying Madame. When the tumor had burst, she changed his dressings every day, brought him some cake now and then, and put him out in the sun on a truss of hay. The poor old fellow would thank her in a faint whisper, slavering and trembling all the while, fearful of losing her and stretching his hands out as soon as he saw her moving away.

He died, and she had a Mass said for the repose of his soul.

That same day a great piece of good fortune came her way. Just as she was serving dinner, Mme de Larsonnière's Negro appeared carrying the parrot in its cage, complete with perch, chain, and padlock. The Baroness had written a note informing Mme Aubain that her husband had been promoted to a Prefecture and they were leaving that evening; she begged her to accept the parrot as a keepsake and a token of her regard.

This bird had engrossed Félicité's thoughts for a long time, for it came from America, and that word reminded her of Victor. So she had asked the Negro all about it, and once she had even gone so far as to say:

"How pleased Madame would be if it were hers!"

The Negro had repeated this remark to his mistress, who, unable to take the parrot with her, was glad to get rid of it in this way.

4

His name was Loulou. His body was green, the tips of his wings were pink, his poll blue, and his breast golden.

Unfortunately he had a tiresome mania for biting his perch, and also used to pull his feathers out, scatter his droppings everywhere, and upset his bath water. He annoyed Mme Aubain, and so she gave him to Félicité for good.

Félicité started training him, and soon he could say: "Nice boy! Your servant, sir! Hail, Mary!" He was put near the door, and several people who spoke to him said how strange it was that he did not answer to the name of Jacquot, as all parrots were called Jacquot. They likened him to a turkey or a block of wood, and every sneer cut Félicité to the quick. How odd, she thought, that Loulou should be so stubborn, refusing to talk whenever any-one looked at him!

For all that, he liked having people around him, because on Sundays, while the Rochefeuille sisters, M. Houppeville, and some new friends—the apothecary Onfroy, M. Varin, and Captain Mathieu—were having their game of cards, he would beat on the window-panes with his wings and make such a din that it was impossible to hear oneself speak.

Bourais's face obviously struck him as terribly funny, for as soon as he saw it he was seized with uncontrollable laughter. His shrieks rang round the courtyard, the echo repeated them, and the neighbors came to their windows and started laughing too. To avoid being seen by the bird, M. Bourais used to creep along by the wall, hiding his face behind his hat, until he got to the river, and then come into the house from the garden. The looks he gave the parrot were far from tender.

Loulou had once been cuffed by the butcher's boy for poking his head into his basket; and since then he was always trying to give him a nip through his shirt. Fabu threatened to wring his neck, although he was not a cruel fellow, in spite of his tattooed arms and bushy whiskers. On the contrary, he rather liked the parrot, so much so indeed that in a spirit of jovial cama-raderie he tried to teach him a few swear-words. Félicité, alarmed at this development, put the bird in the kitchen. His little chain was removed and he was allowed to wander all over the house.

Coming downstairs, he used to rest the curved part of his beak on each step and then raise first his right foot, then his left; and Félicité was afraid that this sort of gymnastic performance would make him giddy. He fell ill and could neither talk nor eat for there was a swelling under his tongue such as hens sometimes have. She cured him by pulling this pellicule out with her finger-nails. One day M. Paul was silly enough to blow the smoke of his cigar at him; another time Mme Lormeau started teasing him with the end of her parasol, and he caught hold of the ferrule with his beak. Finally he got lost.

Félicité had put him down on the grass in the fresh air, and left him there for a minute. When she came back, the parrot had gone. First of all she looked for him in the bushes, by the river, and on the rooftops, paying no attention to her mistress's shouts of: "Be careful, now! You must be mad!" Next she went over all the gardens in Pont-l'Évêque, stopping passersby and asking them: "You don't happen to have seen my parrot by any chance?" Those who did not know him already were given a description of the bird. Suddenly she thought she could make out something green flying about behind the mills at the foot of the hill. But up on the hill there was nothing to be seen. A pedlar told her that he had come upon the parrot a short time before in Mère Simon's shop at Saint-Melaine. She ran all the way there, but no one knew what she was talking about. Finally she came back home, worn out, her shoes falling to pieces, and death in her heart. She was sitting beside Madame on the garden-seat and telling her what she had been doing, when she felt something light drop on her shoulder. It was Loulou! What he had been up to, no one could discover: perhaps he had just gone for a little walk round the town.

Félicité was slow to recover from this fright, and indeed never really got over it.

As the result of a chill she had an attack of quinsy, and soon after that her ears were affected. Three years later she was deaf, and she spoke at the top of her voice, even in church. Although her sins could have been proclaimed over the length and breadth of the diocese without dishonor to her or offense to others, M. le Curé thought it advisable to hear her confession in the sacristy.

Imaginary buzzings in the head added to her troubles. Often her mistress would say: "Heavens, how stupid you are!" and she would reply: "Yes, Madame," at the same time looking all around her for something.

The little circle of her ideas grew narrower and narrower, and the pealing of bells and the lowing of cattle went out of her life. Every living thing moved about in a ghostly silence. Only one sound reached her ears now, and that was the voice of the parrot.

As if to amuse her, he would reproduce the click-clack of the turn-spit, the shrill call of a man selling fish, and the noise of the saw at the joiner's across the way; and when the bell rang he would imitate Mme Aubain's "Félicité! The door, the door!"

They held conversations with each other, he repeating *ad nauseam* the three phrases in his repertory, she replying with words which were just as disconnected but which came from the heart. In her isolation, Loulou was almost a son or a lover to her. He used to climb up her fingers, peck at her lips, and hang on to her shawl; and as she bent over him, wagging her head from side to side as nurses do, the great wings of her bonnet and the wings of the bird quivered in unison.

When clouds banked up in the sky and there was a rumbling of thunder, he would utter piercing cries, no doubt remembering the sudden downpours in his native forests. The sound of the rain falling roused him to frenzy. He would flap excitedly around, shoot up to the ceiling, knocking everything over, and fly out of the window to splash about in the garden. But he would soon come back to perch on one of the firedogs, hopping about to dry his feathers and showing tail and beak in turn.

One morning in the terrible winter of 1837, when she had put him in front of the fire because of the cold she found him dead in the middle of his cage, hanging head down with his claws caught in the bars. He had probably died of a stroke, but she thought he had been poisoned with parsley, and despite the absence of any proof, her suspicions fell on Fabu.

She wept so much that her mistress said to her: "Why don't you have him stuffed?"

Félicité asked the chemist's advice, remembering that he had always been kind to the parrot. He wrote to Le Havre, and a man called Fellacher agreed to do the job. As parcels sometimes went astray on the mail-coach, she decided to take the parrot as far as Honfleur herself.

On either side of the road stretched an endless succession of apple trees, all stripped of their leaves, and there was ice in the ditches. Dogs were barking around the farms; and Félicité, with her hands tucked under her mantlet, her little black sabots, and her basket, walked briskly along the middle of the road.

She crossed the forest, passed Le Haut-Chêne, and got as far as Saint-Gatien.

Behind her, in a cloud of dust, and gathering speed as the horses galloped downhill, a mail-coach swept along like a whirlwind. When he saw this woman making no attempt to get out of the way, the driver poked his head out above the hood, and he and the postilion shouted at her. His four horses could not be held in and galloped faster, the two leaders touching her as they went by. With a jerk of the reins the driver threw them to one side, and then, in a fury, he raised his long whip and gave her such a lash, from head to waist, that she fell flat on her back.

The first thing she did on regaining consciousness was to open her basket. Fortunately nothing had happened to Loulou. She felt her right cheek burning, and when she touched it her hand turned red; it was bleeding.

She sat down on a heap of stones and dabbed her face with her handkerchief. Then she ate a crust of bread which she had taken the precaution of putting in her basket, and tried to forget her wound by looking at the bird.

As she reached the top of the hill at Ecquemauville, she saw the lights of Honfleur twinkling in the darkness like a host of stars, and the shadowy expanse of the sea beyond. Then a sudden feeling of faintness made her stop; and the misery of her childhood, the disappointment of her first love, the departure of her nephew, and the death of Virginie all came back to her at once like the waves of a rising tide, and, welling up in her throat, choked her.

When she got to the boat she insisted on speaking to the captain, and without telling him what was in her parcel, asked him to take good care of it.

Fellacher kept the parrot a long time. Every week he promised it for the next; after six months he announced that a box had been sent off, and nothing more was heard of it. It looked as though Loulou would never come back, and Félicité told herself: "They've stolen him for sure!"

At last he arrived—looking quite magnificent, perched on a branch screwed into a mahogany base, one foot in the air, his head cocked to one side, and biting a nut which the taxidermist, out of love of the grandiose, had gilded.

Félicité shut him up in her room.

This place, to which few people were ever admitted, contained such a quantity of religious bric-à-brac and miscellaneous oddments that it looked like a cross between a chapel and a bazaar.

A big wardrobe prevented the door from opening properly. Opposite the window that overlooked the garden was a little round one looking on to the courtyard. There was a table beside the bed, with a water-jug, a couple of combs, and a block of blue soap in a chipped plate. On the walls there were rosaries, medals, several pictures of the Virgin, and a holy-water stoup made out of a coconut. On the chest of drawers, which was draped with a cloth just like an altar, was the shell box Victor had given her, and also a watering-can and a ball, some copy-books, the illustrated geography book, and a pair of ankle-boots. And on the nail supporting the looking-glass, fastened by its ribbons, hung the little plush hat.

Félicité carried this form of veneration to such lengths that she even kept one of Monsieur's frock-coats. All the old rubbish Mme Aubain had no more use for, she carried off to her room. That was how there came to be artificial flowers along the edge of the chest of drawers, and a portrait of the Comte d'Artois in the window-recess.

With the aid of a wall-bracket, Loulou was installed on a chimney-breast that jutted out into the room. Every morning when she awoke, she saw him in the light of the dawn, and then she remembered the old days, and the smallest details of insignificant actions, not in sorrow but in absolute tranquillity.

Having no intercourse with anyone, she lived in the torpid state of a sleep-walker. The Corpus Christi processions roused her from this condition, for she would go round the neighbors collecting candlesticks and mats to decorate the altar of repose which they used to set up in the street.

In church she was forever gazing at the Holy Ghost, and one day she noticed that it had something of the parrot about it. This resemblance struck her as even more obvious in a colorprint depicting the baptism of Our Lord. With its red wings and its emerald-green body, it was the very image of Loulou.

She bought the print and hung it in the place of the Comte d'Artois, so that she could include them both in a single glance. They were linked together in her mind, the parrot being sanctified by this connection with the Holy Ghost, which itself acquired new life and meaning in her eyes. God the Father could not have chosen a dove as a means of expressing Himself, since doves cannot talk, but rather one of Loulou's ancestors. And although Félicité used to say her prayers with her eyes on the picture, from time to time she would turn slightly towards the bird.

She wanted to join the Children of Mary, but Mme Aubain dissuaded her from doing so.

An important event now loomed up—Paul's wedding.

After starting as a lawyer's clerk, he had been in business, in the Customs, and in Inland Revenue, and had even begun trying to get into the Department of Woods and Forests, when, at the age of thirty-six, by some heaven-sent inspiration, he suddenly discovered his real vocation—in the Wills and Probate Department. There he proved so capable that one of the auditors had offered him his daughter in marriage and promised to use his influence on his behalf.

Paul, grown serious-minded, brought her to see his mother. She criticized the way things were done at Pont-l'Évêque, put on airs, and hurt Félicité's feelings. Mme Aubain was relieved to see her go.

The following week came news of M. Bourais's death in an inn in Lower Brittany. Rumors that he had committed suicide were confirmed, and doubts arose as to his honesty. Mme Aubain went over her accounts and was soon conversant with the full catalogue of his misdeeds—embezzlement of interest, secret sales of timber, forged receipts, etc. Besides all this, he was the father of an illegitimate child, and had had "relations with a person at Dozule."

These infamies upset Mme Aubain greatly. In March 1853 she was afflicted with a pain in the chest; her tongue seemed to be covered with a film; leeches failed to make her breathing any easier; and on the ninth evening of her illness she died. She had just reached the age of seventy-two.

She was thought to be younger because of her brown hair, worn in bandeaux round her pale, pock-marked face. There were few friends to mourn her, for she had a haughty manner which put people off. Yet Félicité wept for her as servants rarely weep for their masters. That Madame should die before her upset her ideas, seemed to be contrary to the order of things, monstrous and unthinkable.

Ten days later—the time it took to travel hot-foot from Besançon—the heirs arrived. The daughter-in-law ransacked every drawer, picked out some pieces of furniture, and sold the rest; and then back they went to the Wills and Probate Department.

Madame's arm-chair, her pedestal table, her foot-warmer, and the eight chairs had all gone. Yellow squares in the center of the wall-panels showed where the pictures had hung. They had carried off the two cots with their mattresses, and no trace remained in the cupboard of all Virginie's things. Félicité climbed the stairs to her room, numbed with sadness.

The next day there was a notice on the door, and the apothecary shouted in her ear that the house was up for sale.

She swayed on her feet, and was obliged to sit down.

What distressed her most of all was the idea of leaving her room, which was so suitable for poor Loulou. Fixing an anguished look on him as she appealed to the Holy Ghost, she contracted the idolatrous habit of kneeling in front of the parrot to say her prayers. Sometimes the sun, as it came through the little window, caught his glass eye, so that it shot out a great luminous ray which sent her into ecstasies.

She had a pension of three hundred and eighty francs a year which her mistress had left her. The garden kept her in vegetables. As for clothes, she had enough to last her till the end of her days, and she saved on lighting by going to bed as soon as darkness fell.

She went out as little as possible, to avoid the second-hand dealer's shop where some of the old furniture was on display. Ever since her fit of giddiness, she had been dragging one leg; and as her strength was failing, Mère Simon, whose grocery business had come to grief, came in every morning to chop wood and pump water for her.

Her eyes grew weaker. The shutters were not opened any more. Years went by, and nobody rented the house and nobody bought it.

For fear of being evicted, Félicité never asked for any repairs to be done. The laths in the roof rotted, and all through one winter her bolster was wet. After Easter she began spitting blood.

When this happened Mère Simon called in a doctor. Félicité wanted to know what was the matter with her, but she was so deaf that only one word reached her: "Pneumonia." It was a word she knew, and she answered gently: "Ah! like Madame," thinking it natural that she should follow in her mistress's footsteps.

The time to set up the altars of repose was drawing near.

The first altar was always at the foot of the hill, the second in front of the post office, the third about halfway up the street. There was some argument as to the siting of this one, and finally the women of the parish picked on Mme Aubain's courtyard.

The fever and the tightness of the chest grew worse. Félicité fretted over not doing anything for the altar. If only she could have something put on it! Then she thought of the parrot. The neighbors protested that it would not be seemly, but the curé gave his permission, and this made her so happy that she begged him to accept Loulou, the only thing of value she possessed, when she died.

From Tuesday to Saturday, the eve of Corpus Christi, she coughed more and more frequently. In the evening her face looked pinched and drawn, her lips stuck to her gums, and she started vomiting. At dawn the next day, feeling very low, she sent for a priest.

Three good women stood by her while she was given extreme unction. Then she said that she had to speak to Fabu.

He arrived in his Sunday best, very ill at ease in this funereal atmosphere.

"Forgive me," she said, making an effort to stretch out her arm. "I thought it was you who had killed him."

What could she mean by such nonsense? To think that she had suspected a man like him of murder! He got very indignant and was obviously going to make a scene.

"Can't you see," they said, "that she isn't in her right mind any more?"

From time to time Félicité would start talking to shadows. The women went away. Mère Simon had her lunch.

A little later she picked Loulou up and held him out to Félicité, saying: "Come now, say good-bye to him."

Although the parrot was not a corpse, the worms were eating him up. One of his wings was broken, and the stuffing was coming out of his stomach. But she was blind by now, and she kissed him on the forehead and pressed him against her cheek. Mère Simon took him away from her to put him on the altar.

5

The scents of summer came up from the meadows; there was a buzzing of flies; the sun was glittering in the river and warming the slates of the roof. Mère Simon had come back into the room and was gently nodding off to sleep.

The noise of church bells woke her up; the congregation was coming out from vespers. Félicité's delirium abated. Thinking of the procession, she could see it as clearly as if she had been following it.

All the school-children, the choristers, and the firemen were walking along the pavements, while advancing up the middle of the street came the church officer armed with his halberd, the beadle carrying a great cross, the schoolmaster keeping an eye on the boys, and the nun fussing over her little girls—three of the prettiest, looking like curly-headed angels, were throwing rose-petals into the air. Then came the deacon, with both arms outstretched, conducting the band, and a couple of censer-bearers who turned round at every step to face the Holy Sacrament, which the curé, wearing his splendid chasuble, was carrying under a canopy of poppy-red velvet held aloft by four churchwardens. A crowd of people surged along behind, between the white cloths covering the walls of the houses, and eventually they got to the bottom of the hill.

A cold sweat moistened Félicité's temples. Mère Simon sponged it up with a cloth, telling herself that one day she would have to go the same way.

The hum of the crowd increased in volume, was very loud for a moment, then faded away.

A fusillade shook the window-panes. It was the postilions saluting the monstrance. Félicité rolled her eyes and said as loud as she could: "Is he all right?"—worrying about the parrot.

She entered into her death-agony. Her breath, coming ever faster, with a rattling sound, made her sides heave. Bubbles of froth appeared at the corners of her mouth, and her whole body trembled.

Soon the booming of the ophicleides, the clear voices of the children, and the deep voices of the men could be heard near at hand. Now and then everything was quiet, and the tramping of feet, deadened by a carpet of flowers, sounded like a flock moving across pasture-land.

The clergy appeared in the courtyard. Mère Simon climbed on to a chair to reach the little round window, from which she had a full view of the altar below.

It was hung with green garlands and adorned with a flounce in English needlepoint lace. In the middle was a little frame containing some relics, there were two orange-trees at the corners, and all the way along stood silver candlesticks and china vases holding sunflowers, lilies, peonies, fox-gloves, and bunches of hydrangea. This pyramid of bright colors stretched from the first floor right down to the carpet which was spread out over the pavement. Some rare objects caught the eye: a silver-gilt sugar-basin wreathed in violets, some pendants of Alençon gems gleaming on a bed of moss, and two Chinese screens with landscape decorations. Loulou, hidden under roses, showed nothing but his blue poll, which looked like a plaque of lapis lazuli.

The churchwardens, the choristers, and the children lined up along the three sides of the courtyard. The priest went slowly up the steps and placed his great shining gold sun on the lace altar-cloth. Everyone knelt down. There was a deep silence. And the censers, swinging at full tilt, slid up and down their chains.

A blue cloud of incense was wafted up into Félicité's room. She opened her nostrils wide and breathed it in with a mystical, sensuous fervor. Then she closed her eyes. Her lips smiled. Her heart-beats grew slower and slower, each a little fainter and gentler, like a fountain running dry, an echo fading away. And as she breathed her last, she thought she could see, in the opening heavens, a gigantic parrot hovering above her head.

1877

Further Reading

Debray-Genette, Raymode. "Narrative Figures of Speech in 'A Simple Heart.'" Trans. Mark W. Andrews. *Critical Essays on Gustave Flaubert.* Ed. Laurence M. Porter. Boston: Hall, 1986. 165–86. • Nadeau, Maurice. "Three Tales." *The Greatness of Flaubert.* Trans. Barbara Bray. New York: Library, 1972. 249–60, spec. 252–54 • Lytle, Andrew. "Three Ways of Making a Saint: A Reading of *Three Tales* by Flaubert." *Southern Review* 20.3 (July 1984): 495–527, spec. 519–27. • Roe, David. "Trois Contes." *Gustave Flaubert.* New York: St. Martin's, 1989. 87–98, spec. 95–98. • Ginsburg, Michal Peled. "The Last Works." *Flaubert Writing: A Study in Narrative Strategy.* Stanford: Stanford UP, 1986. 154–78, spec. 170–75.

Gustave Flaubert is one of the founders of literary realism, a movement that insisted on the most scrupulous observation of the details of ordinary life. Flaubert's example has inspired several generations of fiction writers, including the Southern novelist Flannery O'Conner, who mixes Flaubertian realism into stories that are sometimes macabre.

Flannery O'Connor: On Flaubert's Use of Setting

All the sentences in *Madame Bovary* could be examined with wonder, but there is one in particular that always stops me in admiration. Flaubert has just shown us Emma at the piano with Charles watching her. He says, "She struck the notes with aplomb and ran from top to bottom of the keyboard without a break. Thus shaken up, the old instrument, whose strings buzzed, could be heard at the other end of the village when the window was open, and often the bailiff's clerk, passing along the highroad, bareheaded and in list slippers, stopped to listen, his sheet of paper in his hand."

The more you look at a sentence like that, the more you can learn from it. At one end of it, we are with Emma and this very solid instrument "whose strings buzzed," and at the other end of it we are across the village with this very concrete clerk in his list slippers. With regard to what happens to Emma in the rest of the novel, we may think that it makes no difference that the instrument has buzzing strings or that the clerk wears list slippers and has a piece of paper in his hand, but Flaubert had to create a believable village to put Emma in. It's always necessary to remember that the fiction writer is much less *immediately* concerned with grand ideas and bristling emotions than he is with putting list slippers on clerks.

HENRY JAMES

(1843–1916)

THE MIDDLE YEARS

1

The April day was soft and bright, and poor Dencombe, happy in the conceit of reasserted strength, stood in the garden of the hotel, comparing, with a deliberation in which, however, there was still something of languor, the attractions of easy strolls. He liked the feeling of the south, so far as you could have it in the north, he liked the sandy cliffs and the clustered pines, he liked even the colourless sea. "Bournemouth as a health-resort" had sounded like a mere advertisement, but now he was reconciled to the prosaic. The sociable country postman, passing through the garden, had just given him a small parcel, which he took out with him, leaving the hotel to the right and creeping to a convenient bench that he knew of, a safe recess in the cliff. It looked to the south, to the tinted walls of the Island, and was protected behind by the sloping shoulder of the down. He was tired enough when he reached it, and for a moment he was disappointed; he was better, of course, but better, after all, than what? He should never again, as at one or two great moments of the past, be better than himself. The infinite of life had gone, and what was left of the dose was a small glass engraved like a thermometer by the apothecary. He sat and stared at the sea, which appeared all surface and twinkle, far shallower than the spirit of man. It was the abyss of human illusion that was the real, the tideless deep. He held his packet, which had come by book-post, unopened on his knee, liking, in the lapse of so many joys (his illness had made him feel his age), to know that it was there, but taking for granted there could be no complete renewal of the pleasure, dear to young experience, of seeing one's self "just out." Dencombe, who had a reputation, had come out too often and knew too well in advance how he should look.

His postponement associated itself vaguely, after a little, with a group of three persons, two ladies and a young man, whom, beneath him, straggling and seemingly silent, he could see move slowly together along the sands. The gentleman had his head bent over a book and was occasionally brought to a stop by the charm of this volume, which, as Dencombe could perceive even at a distance, had a cover alluringly red. Then his companions, going a little further, waited for him to come up, poking their parasols into the beach, looking around them at the sea and sky and clearly sensible of the beauty of the day. To these things the young man with the book was still more clearly indifferent; lingering, credulous, absorbed, he was an object of envy to an observer from whose connection with literature all such artlessness had faded. One of the ladies was large and mature; the other had the spareness of comparative youth and of a social situation possibly inferior. The large lady carried back Dencombe's imagination to the age of crinoline; she wore a hat of the shape of a mushroom, decorated with a blue veil, and had the air, in her aggressive amplitude, of clinging to a vanished fashion or even a lost cause. Presently her companion produced from under the folds of a mantle a limp, portable chair which she stiffened out and of which the large lady took possession. This act, and something in the movement of either party, instantly characterised the performers—they performed for Dencombe's recreation—as opulent matron and humble dependant. What, moreover, was the use of being an approved novelist if one couldn't establish a relation between such figures; the clever theory, for instance, that the young man was the son of the opulent matron, and that the humble dependant, the daughter of a clergyman or an officer, nourished a secret passion for him? Was that not visible from the way she stole behind her protectress to look back at him?—back to where he had let himself come to a full stop when his mother sat down to rest. His book was a novel; it had the catchpenny cover, and while the romance of life stood neglected at his side he lost himself in that of the circulating library. He moved mechanically to where the sand was softer, and ended by plumping down in it to finish his chapter at his ease. The humble dependant, discouraged by his remoteness, wandered, with a martyred droop of the head, in another direction, and the exorbitant lady, watching the waves, offered a confused resemblance to a flying-machine that had broken down.

When his drama began to fail Dencombe remembered that he had, after all, another pastime. Though such promptitude on the part of the publisher was rare, he was already able to draw from its wrapper his "latest," perhaps his last. The cover of "The Middle Years" was duly meretricious, the smell of the fresh pages the very odour of sanctity; but for the moment he went no further—he had become conscious of a strange alienation. He had forgotten what his book was about. Had the assault of his old ailment, which he had so fallaciously come to Bournemouth to ward off, interposed utter blankness as to what had preceded it? He had finished the revision of proof before quitting London, but his subsequent fortnight in bed had passed the sponge over colour. He couldn't have chanted to himself a single sentence, couldn't have turned with curiosity or confidence to any particular page. His subject had already gone from him, leaving scarcely a superstition behind. He uttered a low moan as he breathed the chill of this dark void, so desperately it seemed to represent the completion of a sinister process. The tears filled his mild eyes; something precious had passed away. This was the pang that had been sharpest during the last few years—the sense of ebbing time, of shrinking opportunity; and now he felt not so much that his last chance was going as that it was gone indeed. He had done all that he should ever do, and yet he had not done what he wanted. This was the laceration—that practically his career was over: it was as violent as a rough hand at his throat. He rose from his seat nervously, like a creature hunted by a dread; then he fell back in his weakness and nervously opened his book. It was a single volume; he preferred single volumes and aimed at a rare compression. He began to read, and little by little, in this occupation, he was pacified and reassured. Everything came back to him, but came back with a wonder, came back, above all, with a high and magnificent beauty. He read his own prose, he turned his own leaves, and had, as he sat there with the spring sunshine on the page, an emotion peculiar and intense. His career was over, no doubt, but it was over, after all, with *that*.

He had forgotten during his illness the work of the previous year; but what he had chiefly forgotten was that it was extraordinarily good. He dived once more into his story and was drawn down, as by a siren's hand, to where, in the dim underworld of fiction, the great glazed tank of art, strange silent subjects float. He recognised his motive and surrendered to his talent. Never, probably, had that talent, such as it was, been so fine. His difficulties were still there, but what was also there, to his perception, though probably, alas! to nobody's else, was the art that in most cases had surmounted them. In his surprised enjoyment of this ability he had a glimpse of a possible reprieve. Surely its force was not spent—there was life and service in it yet. It had not come to him easily, it had been backward and roundabout. It was the child of time, the nursling of delay; he had struggled and suffered for it, making sacrifices not to be counted, and now that it was really mature was it to cease to yield, to confess itself brutally beaten? There was an infinite charm for Dencombe in feeling as he had never felt before that diligence *vincit omnia*. The result produced in his little book was somehow a result beyond his conscious intention: it was as if he had planted his genius, had trusted his method, and they had grown up and flowered with this sweetness. If the achievement had been real, however, the process had been painful enough. What he saw so intensely to-day, what he felt as a nail driven in, was that only now, at the very last, had he come into possession. His development had been abnormally slow, almost grotesquely gradual. He had been hindered and retarded by experience, and for long periods had only groped his way. It had taken too much of his life to produce too little of his art. The art had come, but it had come after everything else. At such a rate a first existence was too short—long enough only to collect material; so that to fructify, to use the material, one must have a second age, an extension. This extension was what poor Dencombe sighed for. As he turned the last leaves of his volume he murmured: "Ah for another go!—ah for a better chance!"

The three persons he had observed on the sands had vanished and then reappeared; they had now wandered up a path, an artificial and easy ascent, which led to the top of the cliff. Dencombe's bench was half-way down, on a sheltered ledge, and the large lady, a massive, heterogeneous person, with bold black eyes and kind red cheeks, now took a few moments to rest. She wore dirty gauntlets and immense diamond ear-rings; at first she looked vulgar, but she contradicted this announcement in an agreeable off-hand tone. While her companions stood waiting for her she spread her skirts on the end of Dencombe's seat. The young man had gold spectacles, through which, with his finger still in his red-covered book, he glanced at the volume, bound in the same shade of the same colour, lying on the lap of the original occupant of the bench. After an instant, Dencombe understood that he was struck with a resemblance, had recognised the gilt stamp on the crimson cloth, was reading "The Middle Years," and now perceived that somebody else had kept pace with him. The stranger was startled, possibly even a little ruffled, to find that he was not the only person who had been favoured with an early copy. The eyes of the two proprietors met for a moment, and Dencombe borrowed amusement from the expression of those of his competitor, those, it might even be inferred, of his admirer. They confessed to some resentment—they seemed to say: "Hang it, has he got it *already*?—Of course he's a brute of a reviewer!" Dencombe shuffled his copy out of sight while the opulent matron, rising from her repose, broke out: "I feel already the good of this air!"

"I can't say I do," said the angular lady. "I find myself quite let down."

"I find myself horribly hungry. At what time did you order lunch?" her protectress pursued.

The young person put the question by. "Doctor Hugh always orders it."

"I ordered nothing to-day—I'm going to make you diet," said their comrade.

"Then I shall go home and sleep. *Qui dort dine!*"

"Can I trust you to Miss Vernham?" asked Doctor Hugh of his elder companion.

"Don't I trust *you?*" she archly inquired.

"Not too much!" Miss Vernham, with her eyes on the ground, permitted herself to declare. "You must come with us at least to the house," she went on, while the personage on whom they appeared to be in attendance began to mount higher. She had got a little out of ear-shot; nevertheless Miss Vernham became, so far as Dencombe was concerned, less distinctly audible to murmur to the young man: "I don't think you realise all you owe the Countess!"

Absently, a moment, Doctor Hugh caused his gold-rimmed spectacles to shine at her.

"Is that the way I strike you? I see—I see!"

"She's awfully good to us," continued Miss Vernham, compelled by her interlocutor's immovability to stand there in spite of his discussion of private matters. Of what use would it have been that Dencombe should be sensitive to shades had he not detected in that immovability a strange influence from the quiet old convalescent in the great tweed cape? Miss Vernham appeared suddenly to become aware of some such connection, for she added in a moment: "If you want to sun yourself here you can come back after you've seen us home."

Doctor Hugh, at this, hesitated, and Dencombe, in spite of a desire to pass for unconscious, risked a covert glance at him. What his eyes met this time, as it happened, was on the part of the young lady a queer stare, naturally vitreous, which made her aspect remind him of some figure (he couldn't name it) in a play or a novel, some sinister governess or tragic old maid. She seemed to scrutinise him, to challenge him, to say, from general spite: "What have you got to do with us?" At the same instant the rich humour of the Countess reached them from above: "Come, come, my little lambs, you should follow your old *bergère!*" Miss Vernham turned away at this, pursuing the ascent, and Doctor Hugh, after another mute appeal to Dencombe and a moment's evident demur, deposited his book on the bench, as if to keep his place or even as a sign that he would return, and bounded without difficulty up the rougher part of the cliff.

Equally innocent and infinite are the pleasures of observation and the resources engendered by the habit of analysing life. It amused poor Dencombe, as he dawdled in his tepid air-bath, to think that he was waiting for a revelation of something at the back of a fine young mind. He looked hard at the book on the end of the bench, but he wouldn't have touched it for the world. It served his purpose to have a theory which should not be exposed to refutation. He already felt better of his melancholy; he had, according to his old formula, put his head at the window. A passing Countess could draw off the fancy when, like the elder of the ladies who had just retreated, she was as obvious as the giantess of a caravan. It was indeed general views that were terrible; short ones, contrary to an opinion sometimes expressed, were the refuge, were the remedy. Doctor Hugh couldn't possibly be anything but a reviewer who had understandings for early copies with publishers or with newspapers. He reappeared in a quarter of an hour, with visible relief at finding Dencombe on the spot, and the gleam of white teeth in an embarrassed but generous smile. He was perceptibly disappointed at the eclipse of the other copy of the book; it was a pretext the less for speaking to the stranger. But he spoke notwithstanding; he held up his own copy and broke out pleadingly:

"*Do* say, if you have occasion to speak of it, that it's the best thing he has done yet!"

Dencombe responded with a laugh: "Done yet" was so amusing to him, made such a grand avenue of the future. Better still, the young man took *him* for a reviewer. He pulled out "The Middle Years" from under his cape, but instinctively concealed any tell-tale look of fatherhood. This was partly because a person was always a fool for calling attention to his work. "Is that what you're going to say yourself?" he inquired of his visitor.

"I'm not quite sure I shall write anything. I don't, as a regular thing— I enjoy in peace. But it's awfully fine."

Dencombe debated a moment. If his interlocutor had begun to abuse him he would have confessed on the spot to his identity, but there was no harm in drawing him on a little to praise. He drew him on with such success that in a few moments his new acquaintance, seated by his side, was confessing candidly that Dencombe's novels were the only ones he could read a second time. He had come the day before from London, where a friend of his, a journalist, had lent him his copy of the last—the copy sent to the office of the journal and already the subject of a "notice" which, as was pretended there (but one had to allow for "swagger") it had taken a full quarter of an hour to prepare. He intimated that he was ashamed for his friend, and in the case of a work demanding and repaying study, of such inferior manners; and, with his fresh appreciation and inexplicable wish to express it, he speedily became for poor Dencombe a remarkable, a delightful apparition. Chance had brought the weary man of letters face to face with the greatest admirer in the new generation whom it was supposable he possessed. The admirer, in truth, was mystifying, so rare a case was it to find a bristling young doctor—he looked like a German physiologist—enamoured of literary form. It was an accident, but happier than most accidents, so that Dencombe, exhilarated as well as confounded, spent half an hour in making his visitor talk while he kept himself quiet. He explained his premature possession of "The Middle Years" by an allusion to the friendship of the publisher, who, knowing he was at Bournemouth for his health, had paid him this graceful attention. He admitted that he had been ill, for Doctor Hugh would infallibly have guessed it; he even went so far as to wonder whether he mightn't look for some hygienic "tip" from a personage combining so bright an enthusiasm with a presumable knowledge of the remedies now in vogue. It would shake his faith a little perhaps to have to take a doctor seriously who could take *him* so seriously, but he enjoyed this gushing modern youth and he felt with an acute pang that there would still be work to do in a world in which such odd combinations were presented. It was not true, what he had tried for renunciation's sake to believe, that all the combinations were exhausted. They were not, they were not—they were infinite: the exhaustion was in the miserable artist.

Doctor Hugh was an ardent physiologist, saturated with the spirit of the age—in other words he had just taken his degree; but he was independent and various, he talked like a man who would have preferred to love literature best. He would fain have made fine phrases, but nature had denied him the trick. Some of the finest in "The Middle Years" had struck him inordinately, and he took the liberty of reading them to Dencombe in support of his plea. He grew vivid, in the balmy air, to his companion, for whose deep refreshment he seemed to have been sent; and was particularly ingenuous in describing how recently he had become acquainted, and how instantly infatuated, with the only man who had put flesh between the ribs of an art that was starving on superstitions. He had not yet written to him —he was deterred by a sentiment of respect. Dencombe at this moment felicitated himself more than ever on having never answered the photographers. His visitor's attitude promised him a luxury of intercourse, but he surmised that a certain security in it, for Doctor Hugh, would depend not a little on the Countess. He learned without delay with what variety of Countess they were concerned, as well as the nature of the tie that united the curious trio. The large lady, an Englishwoman by birth and the daughter of a celebrated baritone, whose taste, without his talent, she had inherited, was the widow of a French nobleman and mistress of all that remained of the handsome fortune, the fruit of her father's earnings, that had constituted her dower. Miss Vernham, an odd creature but an accomplished pianist, was attached to her person at a salary. The Countess was generous, independent, eccentric; she travelled with her minstrel and her medical man. Ignorant and passionate, she had nevertheless moments in which she was almost irresistible. Dencombe saw her sit for her portrait in Doctor Hugh's free sketch, and felt the picture of his young friend's relation to her frame itself in his mind. This young friend, for a representative of the new psychology, was himself easily hypnotised, and if he became abnormally communicative it was only a sign of his real subjection. Dencombe did accordingly what he wanted with him, even without being known as Dencombe.

Taken ill on a journey in Switzerland the Countess had picked him up at an hotel, and the accident of his happening to please her had made her offer him, with her imperious liberality, terms that couldn't fail to dazzle a practitioner without patients and whose resources had been drained dry by his studies. It was not the way he would have elected to spend his time, but it was time that would pass quickly, and meanwhile she was wonderfully kind. She exacted perpetual attention, but it was impossible not to like her. He gave details about his queer patient, a "type" if there ever was one, who had in connection with her flushed obesity and in addition to the morbid strain of a violent and aimless will a grave organic disorder; but he came back to his loved novelist, whom he was so good as to pronounce more essentially a poet than many of those who went in for verse, with a zeal excited, as all his indiscretion had been excited, by the happy chance of Dencombe's sympathy and the coincidence of their occupation. Dencombe had confessed to a slight personal acquaintance with the author of "The Middle Years," but had not felt himself as ready as he could have wished when his companion, who had never yet encountered a being so privileged, began to be eager for particulars. He even thought that Doctor Hugh's eye at that moment emitted a glimmer of suspicion. But the young man was too inflamed to be shrewd and repeatedly caught up the book to exclaim: "Did you notice this?" or "Weren't you immensely struck with that?" "There's a beautiful passage toward the end," he broke out; and again he laid his hand upon the volume. As he turned the pages he came upon something else, while Dencombe saw him suddenly change colour. He had taken up, as it lay on the bench, Dencombe's copy instead of his own, and his neighbour immediately guessed the reason of his start. Doctor Hugh looked grave an instant; then he said: "I see you've been altering the text!" Dencombe was a passionate corrector, a fingerer of style; the last thing he ever arrived at was a form final for himself. His ideal would have been to publish secretly, and then, on the published text, treat himself to the terrified revise, sacrificing always a first edition and beginning for posterity and even for the collectors, poor dears, with a second. This morning, in "The Middle Years," his pencil had pricked a dozen lights. He was amused at the effect of the young man's reproach; for an instant it made him change colour. He stammered, at any rate, ambiguously; then, through a blur of ebbing consciousness, saw Doctor Hugh's mystified eyes. He only had time to feel he was about to be ill again—that emotion, excitement, fatigue, the heat of the sun, the solicitation of the air, had combined to play him a trick, before, stretching out a hand to his visitor with a plaintive cry, he lost his senses altogether.

Later he knew that he had fainted and that Doctor Hugh had got him home in a bath-chair, the conductor of which, prowling within hail for custom, had happened to remember seeing him in the garden of the hotel. He had recovered his perception in the transit, and had, in bed, that afternoon, a vague recollection of Doctor Hugh's young face, as they went together, bent over him in a comforting laugh and expressive of something more than a suspicion of his identity. That identity was ineffaceable now, and all the more that he was disappointed, disgusted. He had been rash, been stupid, had gone out too soon, stayed out too long. He oughtn't to have exposed himself to strangers, he ought to have taken his servant. He felt as if he had fallen into a hole too deep to descry any little patch of heaven. He was confused about the time that had elapsed—he pieced the fragments together. He had seen his doctor, the real one, the one who had treated him from the first and who had again been very kind. His servant was in and out on tiptoe, looking very wise after the fact. He said more than once something about the sharp young gentleman. The rest was vagueness, in so far as it wasn't despair. The vagueness, however, justified itself by dreams, dozing anxieties from which he finally emerged to the consciousness of a dark room and a shaded candle.

"You'll be all right again—I know all about you now," said a voice near him that he knew to be young. Then his meeting with Doctor Hugh came back. He was too discouraged to joke about it yet, but he was able to perceive, after a little, that the interest of it was intense for his visitor. "Of course I can't attend you professionally—you've got your own man, with whom I've talked and who's excellent," Doctor Hugh went on. "But you must let me come to see you as a good friend. I've just looked in before going to bed. You're doing beautifully, but it's a good job I was with you on the cliff. I shall come in early to-morrow. I want to do something for you. I want to do everything. You've done a tremendous lot for me." The young man held his hand, hanging over him, and poor Dencombe, weakly aware of this living pressure, simply lay there and accepted his devotion. He couldn't do anything less—he needed help too much.

The idea of the help he needed was very present to him that night, which he spent in a lucid stillness, an intensity of thought that constituted a reaction from his hours of stupor. He was lost, he was lost—he was lost if he couldn't be saved. He was not afraid of suffering, of death; he was not even in love with life; but he had had a deep demonstration of desire. It came over him in the long, quiet hours that only with "The Middle Years" had he taken his flight; only on that day, visited by soundless processions, had he recognised his kingdom. He had had a revelation of his range. What he dreaded was the idea that his reputation should stand on the unfinished. It was not with his past but with his future that it should properly be concerned. Illness and age rose before him like spectres with pitiless eyes: how was he to bribe such fates to give him the second chance? He had had the one chance that all men have—he had had the chance of life. He went to sleep again very late, and when he awoke Doctor Hugh was sitting by his head. There was already, by this time, something beautifully familiar in him.

"Don't think I've turned out your physician," he said; "I'm acting with his consent. He has been here and seen you. Somehow he seems to trust me. I told him how we happened to come together yesterday, and he recognises that I've a peculiar right."

Dencombe looked at him with a calculating earnestness. "How have you squared the Countess?"

The young man blushed a little, but he laughed. "Oh, never mind the Countess!"

"You told me she was very exacting."

Doctor Hugh was silent a moment. "So she is."

"And Miss Vernham's an *intrigante*."

"How do you know that?"

"I know everything. One *has* to, to write decently!"

"I think she's mad," said limpid Doctor Hugh.

"Well, don't quarrel with the Countess—she's a present help to you."

"I don't quarrel," Doctor Hugh replied. "But I don't get on with silly women." Presently he added: "You seem very much alone."

"That often happens at my age. I've outlived, I've lost by the way."

Doctor Hugh hesitated; then surmounting a soft scruple: "Whom have you lost?"

"Every one."

"Ah, no," the young man murmured, laying a hand on his arm.

"I once had a wife—I once had a son. My wife died when my child was born, and my boy, at school, was carried off by typhoid."

"I wish I'd been there!" said Doctor Hugh simply.

"Well—if you're here!" Dencombe answered, with a smile that, in spite of dimness, showed how much he liked to be sure of his companion's whereabouts.

"You talk strangely of your age. You're not old."

"Hypocrite—so early!"

"I speak physiologically."

"That's the way I've been speaking for the last five years, and it's exactly what I've been saying to myself. It isn't till we *are* old that we begin to tell ourselves we're not!"

"Yet I know I myself am young," Doctor Hugh declared.

"Not so well as I!" laughed his patient, whose visitor indeed would have established the truth in question by the honesty with which he changed the point of view, remarking that it must be one of the charms of age—at any rate in the case of high distinction—to feel that one has laboured and achieved. Doctor Hugh employed the common phrase about earning one's rest, and it made poor Dencombe, for an instant, almost angry. He recovered himself, however, to explain, lucidly enough, that if he, ungraciously, knew nothing of such a balm, it was doubtless because he had wasted inestimable years. He had followed literature from the first, but he had taken a lifetime to get alongside of her. Only to-day, at last, had he begun to *see,* so that what he had hitherto done was a movement without a direction. He had ripened too late and was so clumsily constituted that he had had to teach himself by mistakes.

"I prefer your flowers, then, to other people's fruit, and your mistakes to other people's successes," said gallant Doctor Hugh. "It's for your mistakes I admire you."

"You're happy—you don't know," Dencombe answered.

Looking at his watch the young man had got up; he named the hour of the afternoon at which he would return. Dencombe warned him against committing himself too deeply, and expressed again all his dread of making him neglect the Countess—perhaps incur her displeasure.

"I want to be like you—I want to learn by mistakes!" Doctor Hugh laughed.

"Take care you don't make too grave a one! But do come back," Dencombe added, with the glimmer of a new idea.

"You should have had more vanity!" Doctor Hugh spoke as if he knew the exact amount required to make a man of letters normal.

"No, no—I only should have had more time. I want another go."

"Another go?"

"I want an extension."

"An extension?" Again Doctor Hugh repeated Dencombe's words, with which he seemed to have been struck.

"Don't you know?—I want to what they call 'live.'"

The young man, for good-bye, had taken his hand, which closed with a certain force. They looked at each other hard a moment. "You *will* live," said Doctor Hugh.

"Don't be superficial. It's too serious!"

"You *shall* live!" Dencombe's visitor declared, turning pale.

"Ah, that's better!" And as he retired the invalid, with a troubled laugh, sank gratefully back.

All that day and all the following night he wondered if it mightn't be arranged. His doctor came again, his servant was attentive, but it was to his confident young friend that he found himself mentally appealing. His collapse on the cliff was plausibly explained, and his liberation, on a better basis, promised for the morrow; meanwhile, however, the intensity of his meditations kept him tranquil and made him indifferent. The idea that occupied him was none the less absorbing because it was a morbid fancy. Here was a clever son of the age, ingenious and ardent, who happened to have set him up for connoisseurs to worship. This servant of his altar had all the new learning in science and all the old reverence in faith; wouldn't he therefore put his knowledge at the disposal of his sympathy, his craft at the disposal of his love? Couldn't he be trusted to invent a remedy for a poor artist to whose art he had paid a tribute? If he couldn't, the alternative was hard: Dencombe would have to surrender to silence, unvindicated and undivined. The rest of the day and all the next he toyed in secret with this sweet futility. Who would work the miracle for him but the young man who could combine such lucidity with such passion? He thought of the fairy-tales of science and charmed himself into forgetting that he looked for a magic that was not of this world. Doctor Hugh was an apparition, and that placed him above the law. He came and went while his patient, who sat up, followed him with supplicating eyes. The interest of knowing the great author had made the young man begin "The Middle Years" afresh, and would help him to find a deeper meaning in its pages. Dencombe had told him what he "tried for;" with all his intelligence, on a first perusal, Doctor Hugh had failed to guess it. The baffled celebrity wondered then who in the world *would* guess it: he was amused once more at the fine, full way with which an intention could be missed. Yet he wouldn't rail at the general mind to-day—consoling as that ever had been: the revelation of his own slowness had seemed to make all stupidity sacred.

Doctor Hugh, after a little, was visibly worried, confessing, on inquiry, to a source of embarrassment at home. "Stick to the Countess—don't mind me," Dencombe said, repeatedly; for his companion was frank enough about the large lady's attitude. She was so jealous that she had fallen ill—she resented such a breach of allegiance. She paid so much for his fidelity that she must have it all: she refused him the right to other sympathies, charged him with scheming to make her die alone, for it was needless to point out how little Miss Vernham was a resource in trouble. When Doctor Hugh mentioned that the Countess would already have left Bournemouth if he hadn't kept her in bed, poor Dencombe held his arm tighter and said with decision: "Take her straight away." They had gone out together, walking back to the sheltered nook in which, the other day, they had met. The young man, who had given his companion a personal support, declared with emphasis that his conscience was clear—he could ride two horses at once. Didn't he dream, for his future, of a time when he should have to ride five hundred? Longing equally for virtue, Dencombe replied that in that golden age no patient would pretend to have contracted with him for his whole attention. On the part of the Countess was not such an avidity lawful? Doctor Hugh denied it, said there was no contract but only a free understanding, and that a sordid servitude was impossible to a generous spirit; he liked moreover to talk about art, and that was the subject on which, this time, as they sat together on the sunny bench, he tried most to engage the author of "The Middle Years." Dencombe, soaring again a little on the weak wings of convalescence and still haunted by that happy notion of an organised rescue, found another strain of eloquence to plead the cause of a certain splendid "last manner," the very citadel, as it would prove, of his reputation, the stronghold into which his real treasure would be gathered. While his listener gave up the morning and the great still sea appeared to wait, he had a wonderful explanatory hour. Even for himself he was inspired as he told of what his treasure would consist—the precious metals he would dig from the mine, the jewels rare, strings of pearls, he would hang between the columns of his temple. He was wonderful for himself, so thick his convictions crowded; but he was still more wonderful for Doctor Hugh, who assured him, none the less, that the very pages he had just published were already encrusted with gems. The young man, however, panted for the combinations to come, and, before the face of the beautiful day, renewed to Dencombe his guarantee that his profession would hold itself responsible for such a life. Then he suddenly clapped his hand upon his watch-pocket and asked leave to absent himself for half an hour. Dencombe waited there for his return, but was at last recalled to the actual by the fall of a shadow across the ground. The shadow darkened into that of Miss Vernham, the young lady in attendance on the Countess; whom Dencombe, recognising her, perceived so clearly to have come to speak to him that he rose from his bench to acknowledge the civility. Miss Vernham indeed proved not particularly civil; she looked strangely agitated, and her type was now unmistakable.

"Excuse me if I inquire," she said, "whether it's too much to hope that you may be induced to leave Doctor Hugh alone." Then, before Dencombe, greatly disconcerted, could protest: "You ought to be informed that you stand in his light; that you may do him a terrible injury."

"Do you mean by causing the Countess to dispense with his services?"

"By causing her to disinherit him." Dencombe stared at this, and Miss Vernham pursued, in the gratification of seeing she could produce an impression: "It has depended on himself to come into something very handsome. He has had a magnificent prospect, but I think you've succeeded in spoiling it."

"Not intentionally, I assure you. Is there no hope the accident may be repaired?" Dencombe asked.

"She was ready to do anything for him. She takes great fancies, she lets herself go—it's her way. She has no relations, she's free to dispose of her money, and she's very ill."

"I'm very sorry to hear it," Dencombe stammered.

"Wouldn't it be possible for you to leave Bournemouth? That's what I've come to ask of you."

Poor Dencombe sank down on his bench. "I'm very ill myself, but I'll try!"

Miss Vernham still stood there with her colourless eyes and the brutality of her good conscience. "Before it's too late, please!" she said; and with this she turned her back, in order, quickly, as if it had been a business to which she could spare but a precious moment, to pass out of his sight.

Oh, yes, after this Dencombe was certainly very ill. Miss Vernham had upset him with her rough, fierce news; it was the sharpest shock to him to discover what was at stake for a penniless young man of fine parts. He sat trembling on his bench, staring at the waste of waters, feeling sick with the directness of the blow. He was indeed too weak, too unsteady, too alarmed; but he would make the effort to get away, for he couldn't accept the guilt of interference, and his honour was really involved. He would hobble home, at any rate, and then he would think what was to be done. He made his way back to the hotel and, as he went, had a characteristic vision of Miss Vernham's great motive. The Countess hated women, of course; Dencombe was lucid about that; so the hungry pianist had no personal hopes and could only console herself with the bold conception of helping Doctor Hugh in order either to marry him after he should get his money or to induce him to recognise her title to compensation and buy her off. If she had befriended him at a fruitful crisis he would really, as a man of delicacy, and she knew what to think of that point, have to reckon with her.

At the hotel Dencombe's servant insisted on his going back to bed. The invalid had talked about catching a train and had begun with orders to pack; after which his humming nerves had yielded to a sense of sickness. He consented to see his physician, who immediately was sent for, but he wished it to be understood that his door was irrevocably closed to Doctor Hugh. He had his plan, which was so fine that he rejoiced in it after getting back to bed. Doctor Hugh, suddenly finding himself snubbed without mercy, would, in natural disgust and to the joy of Miss Vernham, renew his allegiance to the Countess. When his physician arrived Dencombe learned that he was feverish and that this was very wrong: he was to cultivate calmness and try, if possible, not to think. For the rest of the day he wooed stupidity; but there was an ache that kept him sentient, the probable sacrifice of his "extension," the limit of his course. His medical adviser was anything but pleased; his successive relapses were ominous. He charged this personage to put out a strong hand and take Doctor Hugh off his mind—it would contribute so much to his being quiet. The agitating name, in his room, was not mentioned again, but his security was a smothered fear, and it was not confirmed by the receipt, at ten o'clock that evening, of a telegram which his servant opened and read for him and to which, with an address in London, the signature of Miss Vernham was attached. "Beseech you to use all influence to make our friend join us here in the morning. Countess much the worse for dreadful journey, but everything may still be saved." The two ladies had gathered themselves up and had been capable in the afternoon of a spiteful revolution. They had started for the capital, and if the elder one, as Miss Vernham had announced, was very ill, she had wished to make it clear that she was proportionately reckless. Poor Dencombe, who was not reckless and who only desired that everything should indeed be "saved," sent this missive straight off to the young man's lodging and had on the morrow the pleasure of knowing that he had quitted Bournemouth by an early train.

Two days later he pressed in with a copy of a literary journal in his hand. He had returned because he was anxious and for the pleasure of flourishing the great review of "The Middle Years." Here at least was something adequate—it rose to the occasion; it was an acclamation, a reparation, a critical attempt to place the author in the niche he had fairly won. Dencombe accepted and submitted; he made neither objection nor inquiry, for old complications had returned and he had had two atrocious days. He was convinced not only that he should never again leave his bed, so that his young friend might pardonably remain, but that the demand he should make on the patience of beholders would be very moderate indeed. Doctor Hugh had been to town, and he tried to find in his eyes some confession that the Countess was pacified and his legacy clinched; but all he could see there was the light of his juvenile joy in two or three of the phrases of the newspaper. Dencombe couldn't read them, but when his visitor had insisted on repeating them more than once he was able to shake an unintoxicated head. "Ah, no; but they would have been true of what I *could* have done!"

"What people 'could have done' is mainly what they've in fact done," Doctor Hugh contended.

"Mainly, yes; but I've been an idiot!" said Dencombe.

Doctor Hugh did remain; the end was coming fast. Two days later Dencombe observed to him, by way of the feeblest of jokes, that there would now be no question whatever of a second chance. At this the young man stared; then he exclaimed: "Why, it has come to pass—it has come to pass! The second chance has been the public's—the chance to find the point of view, to pick up the pearl!"

"Oh, the pearl!" poor Dencombe uneasily sighed. A smile as cold as a winter sunset flickered on his drawn lips as he added: "The pearl is the unwritten—the pearl is the unalloyed, the *rest,* the lost!"

From that moment he was less and less present, heedless to all appearance of what went on around him. His disease was definitely mortal, of an action as relentless, after the short arrest that had enabled him to fall in with Doctor Hugh, as a leak in a great ship. Sinking steadily, though this visitor, a man of rare resources, now cordially approved by his physician, showed endless art in guarding him from pain, poor Dencombe kept no reckoning of favour or neglect, betrayed no symptom of regret or speculation. Yet toward the last he gave a sign of having noticed that for two days Doctor Hugh had not been in his room, a sign that consisted of his suddenly opening his eyes to ask of him if he had spent the interval with the Countess.

"The Countess is dead," said Doctor Hugh. "I knew that in a particular contingency she wouldn't resist. I went to her grave."

Dencombe's eyes opened wider. "She left you 'something handsome'?"

The young man gave a laugh almost too light for a chamber of woe. "Never a penny. She roundly cursed me."

"Cursed you?" Dencombe murmured.

"For giving her up. I gave her up for *you.* I had to choose," his companion explained.

"You chose to let a fortune go?"

"I chose to accept, whatever they might be, the consequences of my infatuation," smiled Doctor Hugh. Then, as a larger pleasantry: "A fortune be hanged! It's your own fault if I can't get your things out of my head."

The immediate tribute to his humour was a long, bewildered moan; after which, for many hours, many days, Dencombe lay motionless and absent. A response so absolute, such a glimpse of a definite result and such a sense of credit worked together in his mind and, producing a strange commotion, slowly altered and transfigured his despair. The sense of cold submersion left him—he seemed to float without an effort. The incident was extraordinary as evidence, and it shed an intenser light. At the last he signed to Doctor Hugh to listen, and, when he was down on his knees by the pillow, brought him very near.

"You've made me think it all a delusion."

"Not your glory, my dear friend," stammered the young man.

"Not my glory—what there is of it! It *is* glory—to have been tested, to have had our little quality and cast our little spell. The thing is to have made somebody care. You happen to be crazy, of course, but that doesn't affect the law."

"You're a great success!" said Doctor Hugh, putting into his young voice the ring of a marriage-bell.

Dencombe lay taking this in; then he gathered strength to speak once more. "A second chance—*that's* the delusion. There never was to be but one. We work in the dark—we do what we can—we give what we have. Our doubt is our passion and our passion is our task. The rest is the madness of art."

"If you've doubted, if you've despaired, you've always 'done' it," his visitor subtly argued.

"We've done something or other," Dencombe conceded.

"Something or other is everything. It's the feasible. It's *you!*"

"Comforter!" poor Dencombe ironically sighed.

"But it's true," insisted his friend.

"It's true. It's frustration that doesn't count."

"Frustration's only life," said Doctor Hugh.

"Yes, it's what passes." Poor Dencombe was barely audible, but he had marked with the words the virtual end of his first and only chance.

1893

Further Reading

James, Henry. Preface to *The Princess Casamassima*. *The Art of the Novel: Critical Prefaces*. New York: Scribner's, 1934. 59–78. • Wagenknecht, Edward. *The Tales of Henry James*. New York: Ungar, 1984. 75–97, spec. 75–77. • Vaid, Krishna Baldev. "Anecdotes (Also Parables)." *Technique in the Tales of Henry James*. Cambridge: Harvard UP, 1964. 192–213, spec. 207–13. • Westbrook, Perry D. "The Supersubtle Fry." *Nineteenth-Century Fiction* 8.2 (Sept. 1953): 134–40, spec. 134–37. • Tintner, Adeline R. "Shakespeare." *The Book World of Henry James: Appropriating the Classics*. Ann Arbor: UMI Research, 1987. 1–50, spec. 44–50 ("*The Tempest* and 'The Middle Years'").

In writers like Flaubert and Maupassant we find a strain of realism that keeps us firmly grounded in the external world. In Henry James we find a strain devoted to delineating the consciousness of characters realistically. Such psychological realism presents the writer with the special problem of creating a consciousness interesting enough to bear examination. As James points out in the preface to his novel The Princess Casamassima, *one requirement is that the character be perceptive; but this is not enough.*

Henry James: On Limiting the Protagonist's Insight

I recognise at the same time, and in planning "The Princess Casamassima" felt it highly important to recognise, the danger of filling too full any supposed and above all any obviously limited vessel of consciousness. If persons either tragically or comically embroiled with life allow us the comic or tragic value of their embroilment in proportion as their struggle is a measured and directed one, it is strangely true, none the less, that beyond a certain point they are spoiled for us by this carrying of a due light. They may carry too much of it for our credence, for our compassion, for our derision. They may be shown as knowing too much and feeling too much—not certainly for their remaining remarkable, but for their remaining "natural" and typical, for their having the needful communities with our own precious liability to fall into traps and be bewildered. It seems probable that if we were never bewildered there would never be a story to tell about us; we should partake of the superior nature of the all-knowing immortals whose annals are dreadfully dull so long as flurried humans are not, for the positive relief of bored Olympians, mixed up with them. Therefore it is that the wary reader for the most part warns the novelist against making his characters too *interpretative* of the muddle of fate, or in other words too divinely, too priggishly clever. "Give us plenty of bewilderment," this monitor seems to say, "so long as there is plenty of slashing out in the bewilderment too. But don't, we beseech you, give us too much intelligence; for intelligence—well, *endangers;* endangers not perhaps the slasher himself, but the very slashing, the subject-matter of any self-respecting story. It opens up too many considerations, possibilities, issues; it *may* lead the slasher into dreary realms where slashing somehow fails and falls to the ground."

GUY DE MAUPASSANT

(1850–1893)

THE STRING

translated from the French by Ernest Boyd

Along all the roads around Goderville the peasants and their wives were coming towards the little town, for it was market-day. The men walked with plodding steps, their bodies bent forward at each thrust of their long bowed legs. They were deformed by hard work, by the pull of the heavy plough which raises the left shoulder and twists the torso, by the reaping of the wheat which forces the knees apart to get a firm stand, by all the slow and strenuous labors of life on the farm. Their blue smocks, starched, shining as if varnished, ornamented with a little design in white at the neck and wrists, puffed about their bony bodies, seemed like balloons ready to carry them off. From each smock a head, two arms, and two feet protruded.

Some led a cow or a calf at the end of a rope, and their wives, walking behind the animal, whipped its haunches with a leafy branch to hasten its progress. They carried on their arms large wicker-baskets, out of which here a chicken and there a duck thrust forth its head. The women walked with a quicker, livelier step than their husbands. Their spare, straight figures were wrapped in a scanty little shawl, pinned over their flat bosoms, and their heads were enveloped in a piece of white linen tightly pressed on the hair and surmounted by a cap.

Then a wagon passed, its nag's jerky trot shaking up and down two men seated side by side and a woman in the bottom of the vehicle, the latter holding on to the sides to lessen the stiff jolts.

The square of Goderville was filled with a milling throng of human beings and animals. The horns of the cattle, the rough-napped top-hats of the rich peasants, and the headgear of the peasant women stood out in the crowd. And the clamorous, shrill, shouting voices made a continuous and savage din dominated now and again by the robust lungs of some countryman's laugh, or the long lowing of a cow tied to the wall of a house.

The scene smacked of the stable, the dairy and the dung-heap, of hay and sweat, and gave forth that sharp, unpleasant odor, human and animal, peculiar to the people of the fields.

Maître Hauchecorne, of Bréauté, had just arrived at Goderville. He was directing his steps towards the square, when he perceived upon the ground a little piece of string. Maître Hauchecorne, economical like a true Norman, thought that everything useful ought to be picked up, and he stooped painfully, for he suffered from rheumatism. He took up the bit of string from the ground and was beginning to roll it carefully when he noticed Maître Malandain, the harness-maker, on the threshold of his door, looking at him. They had once had a quarrel on the subject of a halter, and they had remained on bad terms, being both good haters. Maître Hauchecorne was seized with a sort of shame to be seen thus by his enemy, picking a bit of string out of the dirt. He hid his find quickly under his smock, and slipped it into his trouser pocket; then he pretended to be still looking on the ground for something which he did not find, and he went towards the market, his head thrust forward, bent double by his pain.

He was soon lost in the noisy and slowly moving crowd, which was busy with interminable bargainings. The peasants looked at cows, went away, came back, perplexed, always in fear of being cheated, not daring to decide, watching the vendor's eye, ever trying to find the trick in the man and the flaw in the beast.

The women, having placed their great baskets at their feet, had taken out the poultry, which lay upon the ground, tied together by the feet, with terrified eyes and scarlet crests.

They listened to offers, stated their prices with a dry air and impassive face, or perhaps, suddenly deciding on some proposed reduction, shouted to the customer who was slowly going away: "All right, Maître Anthime, I'll let you have it for that."

Then little by little the square was deserted, the church bell rang out the hour of noon, and those who lived too far away went to the different inns.

At Jourdain's the great room was full of people eating, and the big yard was full of vehicles of all kinds, gigs, wagons, nondescript carts, yellow with dirt, mended and patched, some with their shafts rising to the sky like two arms, others with their shafts on the ground and their backs in the air.

Behind the diners seated at table, the immense fireplace, filled with bright flames, cast a lively heat on the backs of the row on the right. Three spits were turning on which were chickens, pigeons, and legs of mutton; and an appetizing odor of roast meat and gravy dripping over the nicely browned skin rose from the fireplace, lightening all hearts and making the mouth water.

All the aristocracy of the plough ate there, at Maître Jourdain's, tavern keeper and horse dealer, a clever fellow and well off.

The dishes were passed and emptied, as were the jugs of yellow cider. Everyone told his affairs, his purchases, and sales. They discussed the crops. The weather was favorable for the greens but rather damp for the wheat.

Suddenly the drum began to beat in the yard, before the house. Everybody rose, except a few indifferent persons, and ran to the door, or to the windows, their mouths still full, their napkins in their hands.

After the public crier had stopped beating his drum, he called out in a jerky voice, speaking his phrases irregularly:

"It is hereby made known to the inhabitants of Goderville, and in general to all persons present at the market, that there was lost this morning, on the road to Benzeville, between nine and ten o'clock, a black leather pocketbook containing five hundred francs and some business papers. The finder is requested to return same to the Mayor's office or to Maître Fortuné Houlbrèque of Manneville. There will be twenty francs' reward."

Then the man went away. The heavy roll of the drum and the crier's voice were again heard at a distance.

Then they began to talk of this event discussing the chances that Maître Houlbrèque had of finding or not finding his pocketbook.

And the meal concluded. They were finishing their coffee when the chief of the gendarmes appeared upon the threshold.

He inquired:

"Is Maître Hauchecorne, of Bréauté, here?"

Maître Hauchecorne, seated at the other end of the table, replied: "Here I am."

And the officer resumed:

"Maître Hauchecorne, will you have the goodness to accompany me to the Mayor's office? The Mayor would like to talk to you."

The peasant, surprised and disturbed, swallowed at a draught his tiny glass of brandy, rose, even more bent than in the morning, for the first steps after each rest were specially difficult, and set out, repeating: "Here I am, here I am."

The Mayor was waiting for him, seated in an armchair. He was the local lawyer, a stout, solemn man, fond of pompous phrases.

"Maître Hauchecorne," said he, "you were seen this morning picking up, on the road to Benzeville, the pocketbook lost by Maître Houl-brèque, of Manneville."

The countryman looked at the Mayor in astonishment, already terrified by this suspicion resting on him without his knowing why.

"Me? Me? I picked up the pocketbook?"

"Yes, you, yourself."

"On my word of honor, I never heard of it."

"But you were seen."

"I was seen, me? Who says he saw me?"

"Monsieur Malandain, the harness-maker."

The old man remembered, understood, and flushed with anger.

"Ah, he saw me, the clodhopper, he saw me pick up this string, here, Mayor." And rummaging in his pocket he drew out the little piece of string.

But the Mayor, incredulous, shook his head.

"You will not make me believe, Maître Hauchecorne, that Monsieur Malandain, who is a man we can believe, mistook this string for a pocketbook."

The peasant, furious, lifted his hand, spat at one side to attest his honor, repeating:

"It is nevertheless God's own truth, the sacred truth. I repeat it on my soul and my salvation."

The Mayor resumed:

"After picking up the object, you went on staring, looking a long while in the mud to see if any piece of money had fallen out."

The old fellow choked with indignation and fear.

"How anyone can tell—how anyone can tell—such lies to take away an honest man's reputation! How can anyone——"

There was no use in his protesting, nobody believed him. He was confronted with Monsieur Malandain, who repeated and maintained his affirmation. They abused each other for an hour. At his own request, Maître Hauchecorne was searched. Nothing was found on him.

Finally the Mayor, very much perplexed, discharged him with the warning that he would consult the Public Prosecutor and ask for further orders.

The news had spread. As he left the Mayor's office, the old man was surrounded and questioned with a serious or bantering curiosity, in which there was no indignation. He began to tell the story of the string. No one believed him. They laughed at him.

He went along, stopping his friends, beginning endlessly his statement and his protestations, showing his pockets turned inside out, to prove that he had nothing.

They said:

"Ah, you old rascal!"

And he grew angry, becoming exasperated, hot and distressed at not being believed, not knowing what to do and endlessly repeating himself.

Night came. He had to leave. He started on his way with three neighbors to whom he pointed out the place where he had picked up the bit of string; and all along the road he spoke of his adventure.

In the evening he took a turn in the village of Bréauté, in order to tell it to everybody. He only met with incredulity.

It made him ill all night.

The next day about one o'clock in the afternoon, Marius Paumelle, a hired man in the employ of Maître Breton, husbandman at Ymauville, returned the pocketbook and its contents to Maître Houlbrèque of Manneville.

This man claimed to have found the object in the road; but not knowing how to read, he had carried it to the house and given it to his employer.

The news spread through the neighborhood. Maître Hauchecorne was informed of it. He immediately went the circuit and began to recount his story completed by the happy climax. He triumphed.

"What grieved me so much was not the thing itself, as the lying. There is nothing so shameful as to be placed under a cloud on account of a lie."

He talked of his adventure all day long, he told it on the highway to people who were passing by, in the inn to people who were drinking there, and to persons coming out of church the following Sunday. He stopped strangers to tell them about it. He was calm now, and yet something disturbed him without his knowing exactly what it was. People seemed to wink at him while they listened. They did not seem convinced. He had the feeling that remarks were being made behind his back.

On Tuesday of the next week he went to the market at Goderville, urged solely by the necessity he felt of discussing the case.

Malandain, standing at his door, began to laugh on seeing him pass. Why?

He approached a farmer from Criquetot, who did not let him finish, and giving him a poke in the stomach said to his face:

"You clever rogue."

Then he turned his back on him.

Maître Hauchecorne was confused, why was he called a clever rogue?

When he was seated at the table, in Jourdain's tavern he commenced to explain "the affair."

A horse-dealer from Monvilliers called to him:

"Come, come, old sharper, that's an old trick; I know all about your piece of string!"

Hauchecorne stammered:

"But the pocketbook was found."

But the other man replied:

"That'll do to tell, pop. One man finds a thing, and another man brings it back. No one is any the wiser, so you get out of it."

The peasant stood choking. He understood. They accused him of having had the pocketbook returned by a confederate, by an accomplice.

KATE CHOPIN

(1851–1904)

DÉSIRÉE'S BABY

As the day was pleasant, Madame Valmondé drove over to L'Abri to see Désirée and the baby.

It made her laugh to think of Désirée with a baby. Why, it seemed but yesterday that Désirée was little more than a baby herself; when Monsieur in riding through the gateway of Valmondé had found her lying asleep in the shadow of the big stone pillar.

The little one awoke in his arms and began to cry for "Dada." That was as much as she could do or say. Some people thought she might have strayed there of her own accord, for she was of the toddling age. The prevailing belief was that she had been purposely left by a party of Texans, whose canvas-covered wagon, late in the day, had crossed the ferry that Coton Maïs kept, just below the plantation. In time Madame Valmondé abandoned every speculation but the one that Désirée had been sent to her by a beneficent Providence to be the child of her affection, seeing that she was without child of the flesh. For the girl grew to be beautiful and gentle, affectionate and sincere,—the idol of Valmondé.

It was no wonder, when she stood one day against the stone pillar in whose shadow she had lain asleep, eighteen years before, that Armand Aubigny riding by and seeing her there, had fallen in love with her. That was the way all the Aubignys fell in love, as if struck by a pistol shot. The wonder was that he had not loved her before; for he had known her since his father brought him home from Paris, a boy of eight, after his mother died there. The passion that awoke in him that day, when he saw her at the gate, swept along like an avalanche, or like a prairie fire, or like anything that drives headlong over all obstacles.

Monsieur Valmondé grew practical and wanted things well considered: that is, the girl's obscure origin. Armand looked into her eyes and did not care. He was reminded that she was nameless. What did it matter about a name when he could give her one of the oldest and proudest in Louisiana? He ordered the *corbeille* from Paris, and contained himself with what patience he could until it arrived; then they were married.

Madame Valmondé had not seen Désirée and the baby for four weeks. When she reached L'Abri she shuddered at the first sight of it, as she always did. It was a sad looking place, which for many years had not known the gentle presence of a mistress, old Monsieur Aubigny having married and buried his wife in France, and she having loved her own land too well ever to leave it. The roof came down steep and black like a cowl, reaching out beyond the wide galleries that encircled the yellow stuccoed house. Big, solemn oaks grew close to it, and their thick-leaved, far-reaching branches shadowed it like a pall. Young Aubigny's rule was a strict one, too, and under it his negroes had forgotten how to be gay, as they had been during the old master's easy-going and indulgent lifetime.

The young mother was recovering slowly, and lay full length, in her soft white muslins and laces, upon a couch. The baby was beside her, upon her arm, where he had fallen asleep, at her breast. The yellow nurse woman sat beside a window fanning herself.

Madame Valmondé bent her portly figure over Désirée and kissed her, holding her an instant tenderly in her arms. Then she turned to the child.

"This is not the baby!" she exclaimed, in startled tones. French was the language spoken at Valmondé in those days.

"I knew you would be astonished," laughed Désirée, "at the way he has grown. The little *cochon de lait!* Look at his legs, mamma, and his hands and fingernails,—real fingernails. Zandrine had to cut them this morning. Isn't it true, Zandrine?"

The woman bowed her turbaned head majestically, "Mais si, Madame."

"And the way he cries," went on Désirée, "is deafening. Armand heard him the other day as far away as La Blanche's cabin."

Madame Valmondé had never removed her eyes from the child. She lifted it and walked with it over to the window that was lightest. She scanned the baby narrowly, then looked as searchingly at Zandrine, whose face was turned to gaze across the fields.

"Yes, the child has grown, has changed," said Madame Valmondé, slowly, as she replaced it beside its mother. "What does Armand say?"

Désirée's face became suffused with a glow that was happiness itself.

"Oh, Armand is the proudest father in the parish, I believe, chiefly because it is a boy, to bear his name; though he says not,—that he would have loved a girl as well. But I know it is n't true. I know he says that to please me. And mamma," she added, drawing Madame Valmondé's head down to her, and speaking in a whisper, "he has n't punished one of them —not one of them—since baby is born. Even Négrillon, who pretended to have burnt his leg that he might rest from work—he only laughed, and said Négrillon was a great scamp. Oh, mamma, I'm so happy; it frightens me."

What Désirée said was true. Marriage, and later the birth of his son had softened Armand Aubigny's imperious and exacting nature greatly. This was what made the gentle Désirée so happy, for she loved him desperately. When he frowned she trembled, but loved him. When he smiled, she asked no greater blessing of God. But Armand's dark, handsome face had not often been disfigured by frowns since the day he fell in love with her.

When the baby was about three months old, Désirée awoke one day to the conviction that there was something in the air menacing her peace. It was at first too subtle to grasp. It had only been a disquieting suggestion; an air of mystery among the blacks; unexpected visits from far-off neighbors who could hardly account for their coming. Then a strange, an awful change in her husband's manner, which she dared not ask him to explain. When he spoke to her, it was with averted eyes, from which the old love-light seemed to have gone out. He absented himself from home; and when there, avoided her presence and that of her child, without excuse. And the very spirit of Satan seemed suddenly to take hold of him in his dealings with the slaves. Désirée was miserable enough to die.

She sat in her room, one hot afternoon, in her *peignoir*, listlessly drawing through her fingers the strands of her long, silky brown hair that hung about her shoulders. The baby, half naked, lay asleep upon her own great mahogany bed, that was like a sumptuous throne, with its satin-lined half-canopy. One of La Blanche's little quadroon boys—half naked too—stood fanning the child slowly with a fan of peacock feathers. Désirée's eyes had been fixed absently and sadly upon the baby, while she was striving to penetrate the threatening mist that she felt closing about her. She looked from her child to the boy who stood beside him, and back again; over and over. "Ah!" It was a cry that she could not help; which she was not conscious of having uttered. The blood turned like ice in her veins, and a clammy moisture gathered upon her face.

She tried to speak to the little quadroon boy; but no sound would come, at first. When he heard his name uttered, he looked up, and his mistress was pointing to the door. He laid aside the great, soft fan, and obediently stole away, over the polished floor, on his bare tiptoes.

She stayed motionless, with gaze riveted upon her child, and her face the picture of fright.

Presently her husband entered the room, and without noticing her, went to a table and began to search among some papers which covered it.

"Armand," she called to him, in a voice which must have stabbed him, if he was human. But he did not notice. "Armand," she said again. Then she rose and tottered towards him. "Armand," she panted once more, clutching his arm, "look at our child. What does it mean? tell me."

He coldly but gently loosened her fingers from about his arm and thrust the hand away from him. "Tell me what it means!" she cried despairingly.

"It means," he answered lightly, "that the child is not white; it means that you are not white."

A quick conception of all that this accusation meant for her nerved her with unwonted courage to deny it. "It is a lie; it is not true, I am white! Look at my hair, it is brown; and my eyes are gray, Armand, you know they are gray. And my skin is fair," seizing his wrist. "Look at my hand; whiter than yours, Armand," she laughed hysterically.

"As white as La Blanche's," he returned cruelly; and went away leaving her alone with their child.

When she could hold a pen in her hand, she sent a despairing letter to Madame Valmondé.

"My mother, they tell me I am not white. Armand has told me I am not white. For God's sake tell them it is not true. You must know it is not true. I shall die. I must die. I cannot be so unhappy, and live."

The answer that came was as brief:

"My own Désirée: Come home to Valmondé; back to your mother who loves you. Come with your child."

When the letter reached Désirée she went with it to her husband's study, and laid it open upon the desk before which he sat. She was like a stone image: silent, white, motionless after she placed it there.

In silence he ran his cold eyes over the written words. He said nothing.

"Shall I go, Armand?" she asked in tones sharp with agonized suspense.

"Yes, go."

"Do you want me to go?"

"Yes, I want you to go."

He thought Almighty God had dealt cruelly and unjustly with him; and felt, somehow, that he was paying Him back in kind when he stabbed thus into his wife's soul. Moreover he no longer loved her, because of the unconscious injury she had brought upon his home and his name.

She turned away like one stunned by a blow, and walked slowly towards the door, hoping he would call her back.

"Good-by, Armand," she moaned.

He did not answer her. That was his last blow at fate.

Désirée went in search of her child. Zandrine was pacing the sombre gallery with it. She took the little one from the nurse's arms with no word of explanation, and descending the steps, walked away, under the live-oak branches.

It was an October afternoon; the sun was just sinking. Out in the still fields the negroes were picking cotton.

Désirée had not changed the thin white garment nor the slippers which she wore. Her hair was uncovered and the sun's rays brought a golden gleam from its brown meshes. She did not take the broad, beaten road which led to the far-off plantation of Valmondé. She walked across a deserted field, where the stubble bruised her tender feet, so delicately shod, and tore her thin gown to shreds.

She disappeared among the reeds and willows that grew thick along the banks of the deep, sluggish bayou; and she did not come back again.

Some weeks later there was a curious scene enacted at L'Abri. In the centre of the smoothly swept back yard was a great bonfire. Armand Aubigny sat in the wide hallway that commanded a view of the spectacle; and it was he who dealt out to a half dozen negroes the material which kept this fire ablaze.

A graceful cradle of willow, with all its dainty furbishings, was laid upon the pyre, which had already been fed with the richness of a priceless *layette*. Then there were silk gowns, and velvet and satin ones added to these; laces, too, and embroideries; bonnets and gloves; for the *corbeille* had been of rare quality.

The last thing to go was a tiny bundle of letters; innocent little scribblings that Désirée had sent to him during the days of their espousal. There was the remnant of one back in the drawer from which he took them. But it was not Désirée's; it was part of an old letter from his mother to his father. He read it. She was thanking God for the blessing of her husband's love:—

"But, above all," she wrote, "night and day, I thank the good God for having so arranged our lives that our dear Armand will never know that his mother, who adores him, belongs to the race that is cursed with the brand of slavery."

1893

Further Reading

Seyersted, Per, Ed. Introduction. *The Complete Works of Kate Chopin.* Vol. 1. By Per Seyersted. Baton Rouge: Louisiana State UP, 1969. 21–33. • Skaggs, Peggy. "Bayou Folks." *Kate Chopin.* Boston: Twayne, 1985. 12–26, spec. 25–26. • Ewell, Barbara C. *"Bayou Folk:* A Louisiana Local Colorist." *Kate Chopin.* New York: Ungar, 1986. 51–84, spec. 69–72. • Wolff, Cynthia Griffin. "Kate Chopin and the Fiction of Limits: 'Désirée's Baby.'" *Southern Literary Journal* 10.2 (Spring 1978): 123–33. • Arner, Robert D. "Pride and Prejudice: Kate Chopin's 'Désirée's Baby.'" *Mississippi Quarterly* 25.2 (Spring 1972): 131–40.

Kate Chopin was an admirer and translator of the fiction of Guy de Maupassant, and so—far more than most of her contemporaries—was affected by the French realists' frank treatment of social themes and minute fidelity to details of setting and character. Her irritation with the more romantic fiction being produced in America shows in her comment on a group of writers that included the poet James Whitcomb Riley and Lew Wallace, author of The Robe.

Kate Chopin: On the Western Association of Writers

Provincialism in the best sense of the word stamps the character of this association of writers, who gather chiefly from the State of Indiana and meet annually at Spring Fountain Park. It is an ideally beautiful spot, a veritable garden of Eden in which the disturbing fruit of the tree of knowledge still hangs unplucked. The cry of the dying century has not reached this body of workers, or else it has not been comprehended. There is no doubt in their souls, no unrest: apparently an abiding faith in God as he manifests himself through the sectional church, and an overmastering love of their soil and institutions.

Most of them are singers. Their native streams, trees, bushes and birds, the lovely country life about them, form the chief burden of their often too sentimental songs. . . .

Among these people are to be found an earnestness in the acquirement and dissemination of book-learning, a clinging to past and conventional standards, an almost Creolean sensitiveness to criticism and a singular ignorance of, or disregard for, the value of the highest art forms.

There is a very, very big world lying not wholly in northern Indiana, nor does it lie at the antipodes, either. It is human existence in its subtle, complex, true meaning, stripped of the veil with which ethical and conventional standards have draped it. When the Western Association of Writers with their earnestness of purpose and poetic insights shall have developed into students of true life and true art, who knows but they may produce a genius such as America has not yet known.

ANTON CHEKHOV

(1860–1904)

THE LADY WITH THE PET DOG

translated from the Russian by Avrahm Yarmolinsky

1

A new person, it was said, had appeared on the esplanade: a lady with a pet dog. Dmitry Dmitrich Gurov, who had spent a fortnight at Yalta and had got used to the place, had also begun to take an interest in new arrivals. As he sat in Vernet's confectionery shop, he saw, walking on the esplanade, a fair-haired young woman of medium height, wearing a beret; a white Pomeranian was trotting behind her.

And afterwards he met her in the public garden and in the square several times a day. She walked alone, always wearing the same beret and always with the white dog; no one knew who she was and everyone called her simply "the lady with the pet dog."

"If she is here alone without husband or friends," Gurov reflected, "it wouldn't be a bad thing to make her acquaintance."

He was under forty, but he already had a daughter twelve years old, and two sons at school. They had found a wife for him when he was very young, a student in his second year, and by now she seemed half as old again as he. She was a tall, erect woman with dark eyebrows, stately and dignified and, as she said of herself, intellectual. She read a great deal, used simplified spelling in her letters, called her husband, not Dmitry, but Dimitry, while he privately considered her of limited intelligence, narrow-minded, dowdy, was afraid of her, and did not like to be at home. He had begun being unfaithful to her long ago—had been unfaithful to her often and, probably for that reason, almost always spoke ill of women, and when they were talked of in his presence used to call them "the inferior race."

It seemed to him that he had been sufficiently tutored by bitter experience to call them what he pleased, and yet he could not have lived without "the inferior race" for two days together. In the company of men he was bored and ill at ease, he was chilly and uncommunicative with them; but when he was among women he felt free, and knew what to speak to them about and how to comport himself; and even to be silent with them was no strain on him. In his appearance, in his character, in his whole make-up there was something attractive and elusive that disposed women in his favor and allured them. He knew that, and some force seemed to draw him to them, too.

Oft-repeated and really bitter experience had taught him long ago that with decent people—particularly Moscow people—who are irresolute and slow to move, every affair which at first seems a light and charming adventure inevitably grows into a whole problem of extreme complexity, and in the end a painful situation is created. But at every new meeting with an interesting woman this lesson of experience seemed to slip from his memory, and he was eager for life, and everything seemed so simple and diverting.

One evening while he was dining in the public garden the lady in the beret walked up without haste to take the next table. Her expression, her gait, her dress, and the way she did her hair told him that she belonged to the upper class, that she was married, that she was in Yalta for the first time and alone, and that she was bored there. The stories told of the immorality in Yalta are to a great extent untrue; he despised them, and knew that such stories were made up for the most part by persons who would have been glad to sin themselves if they had had the chance; but when the lady sat down at the next table three paces from him, he recalled these stories of easy conquests, of trips to the mountains, and the tempting thought of a swift, fleeting liaison, a romance with an unknown woman of whose very name he was ignorant suddenly took hold of him.

He beckoned invitingly to the Pomeranian, and when the dog approached him, shook his finger at it. The Pomeranian growled; Gurov threatened it again.

The lady glanced at him and at once dropped her eyes.

"He doesn't bite," she said and blushed.

"May I give him a bone?" he asked; and when she nodded he inquired affably, "Have you been in Yalta long?"

"About five days."

"And I am dragging out the second week here."

There was a short silence.

"Time passes quickly, and yet it is so dull here!" she said, not looking at him.

"It's only the fashion to say it's dull here. A provincial will live in Belyov or Zhizdra and not be bored, but when he comes here it's 'Oh, the dullness! Oh, the dust!' One would think he came from Granada."

She laughed. Then both continued eating in silence, like strangers, but after dinner they walked together and there sprang up between them the light banter of people who are free and contented, to whom it does not matter where they go or what they talk about. They walked and talked of the strange light on the sea: the water was a soft, warm, lilac color, and there was a golden band of moonlight upon it. They talked of how sultry it was after a hot day. Gurov told her that he was a native of Moscow, that he had studied languages and literature at the university, but had a post in a bank; that at one time he had trained to become an opera singer but had given it up, that he owned two houses in Moscow. And he learned from her that she had grown up in Petersburg, but had lived in S—— since her marriage two years previously, that she was going to stay in Yalta for about another month, and that her husband, who needed a rest, too, might perhaps come to fetch her. She was not certain whether her husband was a member of a Government Board or served on a Zemstvo Council, and this amused her. And Gurov learned too that her name was Anna Sergeyevna.

Afterwards in his room at the hotel he thought about her—and was certain that he would meet her the next day. It was bound to happen. Getting into bed he recalled that she had been a schoolgirl only recently, doing lessons like his own daughter; he thought how much timidity and angularity there was still in her laugh and her manner of talking with a stranger. It must have been the first time in her life that she was alone in a setting in which she was followed, looked at, and spoken to for one secret purpose alone, which she could hardly fail to guess. He thought of her slim, delicate throat, her lovely gray eyes.

"There's something pathetic about her, though," he thought, and dropped off.

2

A week had passed since they had struck up an acquaintance. It was a holiday. It was close indoors, while in the street the wind whirled the dust about and blew people's hats off. One was thirsty all day, and Gurov often went into the restaurant and offered Anna Sergeyevna a soft drink or ice cream. One did not know what to do with oneself.

In the evening when the wind had abated they went out on the pier to watch the steamer come in. There were a great many people walking about the dock; they had come to welcome someone and they were carrying bunches of flowers. And two peculiarities of a festive Yalta crowd stood out: the elderly ladies were dressed like young ones and there were many generals.

Owing to the choppy sea, the steamer arrived late, after sunset, and it was a long time tacking about before it put in at the pier. Anna Sergeyevna peered at the steamer and the passengers through her lorgnette as though looking for acquaintances, and whenever she turned to Gurov her eyes were shining. She talked a great deal and asked questions jerkily, forgetting the next moment what she had asked; then she lost her lorgnette in the crush.

The festive crowd began to disperse; it was now too dark to see people's faces; there was no wind any more, but Gurov and Anna Sergeyevna still stood as though waiting to see someone else come off the steamer. Anna Sergeyevna was silent now, and sniffed her flowers without looking at Gurov.

"The weather has improved this evening," he said. "Where shall we go now? Shall we drive somewhere?"

She did not reply.

Then he looked at her intently, and suddenly embraced her and kissed her on the lips, and the moist fragrance of her flowers enveloped him; and at once he looked round him anxiously, wondering if anyone had seen them.

"Let us go to your place," he said softly. And they walked off together rapidly.

The air in her room was close and there was the smell of the perfume she had bought at the Japanese shop. Looking at her, Gurov thought: "What encounters life offers!" From the past he preserved the memory of carefree, good-natured women whom love made gay and who were grateful to him for the happiness he gave them, however brief it might be; and of women like his wife who loved without sincerity, with too many words, affectedly, hysterically, with an expression that it was not love or passion that engaged them but something more significant; and of two or three others, very beautiful, frigid women, across whose faces would suddenly flit a rapacious expression—an obstinate desire to take from life more than it could give, and these were women no longer young, capricious, unreflecting, domineering, unintelligent, and when Gurov grew cold to them their beauty aroused his hatred, and the lace on their lingerie seemed to him to resemble scales.

But here there was the timidity, the angularity of inexperienced youth, a feeling of awkwardness; and there was a sense of embarrassment, as though someone had suddenly knocked at the door. Anna Sergeyevna, "the lady with the pet dog," treated what had happened in a peculiar way, very seriously, as though it were her fall—so it seemed, and this was odd and inappropriate. Her features drooped and faded, and her long hair hung down sadly on either side of her face; she grew pensive and her dejected pose was that of a Magdalene in a picture by an old master.

"It's not right," she said. "You don't respect me now, you first of all."

There was a watermelon on the table. Gurov cut himself a slice and began eating it without haste. They were silent for at least half an hour.

There was something touching about Anna Sergeyevna; she had the purity of a well-bred, naive woman who has seen little of life. The single candle burning on the table barely illumined her face, yet it was clear that she was unhappy.

"Why should I stop respecting you, darling?" asked Gurov. "You don't know what you're saying."

"God forgive me," she said, and her eyes filled with tears. "It's terrible."

"It's as though you were trying to exonerate yourself."

"How can I exonerate myself? No. I am a bad, low woman; I despise myself and I have no thought of exonerating myself. It's not my husband but myself I have deceived. And not only just now; I have been deceiving myself for a long time. My husband may be a good, honest man, but he is a flunkey! I don't know what he does, what his work is, but I know he is a flunkey! I was twenty when I married him. I was tormented by curiosity; I wanted something better. 'There must be a different sort of life,' I said to myself. I wanted to live! To live, to live! Curiosity kept eating at me—you don't understand it, but I swear to God I could no longer control myself; something was going on in me; I could not be held back. I told my husband I was ill, and came here. And here I have been walking about as though in a daze, as though I were mad; and now I have become a vulgar, vile woman whom anyone may despise."

Gurov was already bored with her; he was irritated by her naive tone, by her repentance, so unexpected and so out of place, but for the tears in her eyes he might have thought she was joking or play-acting.

"I don't understand, my dear," he said softly. "What do you want?"

She hid her face on his breast and pressed close to him.

"Believe me, believe me, I beg you," she said, "I love honesty and purity, and sin is loathsome to me; I don't know what I'm doing. Simple people say, 'The Evil One has led me astray.' And I may say of myself now that the Evil One has led me astray."

"Quiet, quiet," he murmured.

He looked into her fixed, frightened eyes, kissed her, spoke to her softly and affectionately, and by degrees she calmed down, and her gaiety returned; both began laughing.

Afterwards when they went out there was not a soul on the esplanade. The town with its cypresses looked quite dead, but the sea was still sounding as it broke upon the beach; a single launch was rocking on the waves and on it a lantern was blinking sleepily.

They found a cab and drove to Oreanda.

"I found out your surname in the hall just now: it was written on the board—von Dideritz," said Gurov. "Is your husband German?"

"No; I believe his grandfather was German, but he is Greek Orthodox himself."

At Oreanda they sat on a bench not far from the church, looked down at the sea, and were silent. Yalta was barely visible through the morning mist; white clouds rested motionlessly on the mountaintops. The leaves did not stir on the trees, cicadas twanged, and the monotonous muffled sound of the sea that rose from below spoke of the peace, the eternal sleep awaiting us. So it rumbled below when there was no Yalta, no Oreanda here; so it rumbles now, and it will rumble as indifferently and as hollowly when we are no more. And in this constancy, in this complete indifference to the life and death of each of us, there lies, perhaps, a pledge of our eternal salvation, of the unceasing advance of life upon earth, of unceasing movement towards perfection. Sitting beside a young woman who in the dawn seemed so lovely, Gurov, soothed and spellbound by these magical surroundings—the sea, the mountains, the clouds, the wide sky—thought how everything is really beautiful in this world when one reflects: everything except what we think or do ourselves when we forget the higher aims of life and our own human dignity.

A man strolled up to them—probably a guard—looked at them and walked away. And this detail, too, seemed so mysterious and beautiful. They saw a steamer arrive from Feodosia, its lights extinguished in the glow of dawn.

"There is dew on the grass," said Anna Sergeyevna, after a silence.

"Yes, it's time to go home."

They returned to the city.

Then they met every day at twelve o'clock on the esplanade, lunched and dined together, took walks, admired the sea. She complained that she slept badly, that she had palpitations, asked the same questions, troubled now by jealousy and now by the fear that he did not respect her sufficiently. And often in the square or the public garden, when there was no one near them, he suddenly drew her to him and kissed her passionately. Complete idleness, these kisses in broad daylight exchanged furtively in dread of someone's seeing them, the heat, the smell of the sea, and the continual flitting before his eyes of idle, well-dressed, well-fed people, worked a complete change in him; he kept telling Anna Sergeyevna how beautiful she was, how seductive, was urgently passionate; he would not move a step away from her, while she was often pensive and continually pressed him to confess that he did not respect her, did not love her in the least, and saw in her nothing but a common woman. Almost every evening rather late they drove somewhere out of town, to Oreanda or to the waterfall; and the excursion was always a success, the scenery invariably impressed them as beautiful and magnificent.

They were expecting her husband, but a letter came from him saying that he had eye-trouble, and begging his wife to return home as soon as possible. Anna Sergeyevna made haste to go.

"It's a good thing I am leaving," she said to Gurov. "It's the hand of Fate!"

She took a carriage to the railway station, and he went with her. They were driving the whole day. When she had taken her place in the express, and when the second bell had rung, she said, "Let me look at you once more—let me look at you again. Like this."

She was not crying but was so sad that she seemed ill and her face was quivering.

"I shall be thinking of you—remembering you," she said. "God bless you; be happy. Don't remember evil against me. We are parting forever—it has to be, for we ought never to have met. Well, God bless you."

The train moved off rapidly, its lights soon vanished, and a minute later there was no sound of it, as though everything had conspired to end as

quickly as possible that sweet trance, that madness. Left alone on the platform, and gazing into the dark distance, Gurov listened to the twang of the
grasshoppers and the hum of the telegraph wires, feeling as though he had
just waked up. And he reflected, musing, that there had now been another
episode or adventure in his life, and it, too, was at an end, and nothing was
left of it but a memory. He was moved, sad, and slightly remorseful: this
young woman whom he would never meet again had not been happy with
him; he had been warm and affectionate with her, but yet in his manner, his
tone, and his caresses there had been a shade of light irony, the slightly
coarse arrogance of a happy male who was, besides, almost twice her age.
She had constantly called him kind, exceptional, high-minded; obviously he
had seemed to her different from what he really was, so he had involuntarily
deceived her.

Here at the station there was already a scent of autumn in the air; it was
a chilly evening.

"It is time for me to go north, too," thought Gurov as he left the platform. "High time!"

3

At home in Moscow the winter routine was already established; the
stoves were heated, and in the morning it was still dark when the children
were having breakfast and getting ready for school, and the nurse would
light the lamp for a short time. There were frosts already. When the first
snow falls, on the first day the sleighs are out, it is pleasant to see the white
earth, the white roofs; one draws easy, delicious breaths, and the season
brings back the days of one's youth. The old limes and birches, white with
hoar-frost, have a good-natured look; they are closer to one's heart than
cypresses and palms, and near them one no longer wants to think of mountains and the sea.

Gurov, a native of Moscow, arrived there on a fine frosty day, and when
he put on his fur coat and warm gloves and took a walk along Petrovka, and
when on Saturday night he heard the bells ringing, his recent trip and the
places he had visited lost all charm for him. Little by little he became
immersed in Moscow life, greedily read three newspapers a day, and
declared that he did not read the Moscow papers on principle. He already
felt a longing for restaurants, clubs, formal dinners, anniversary celebrations, and it flattered him to entertain distinguished lawyers and actors, and
to play cards with a professor at the physicians' club. He could eat a whole
portion of meat stewed with pickled cabbage and served in a pan, Moscow
style.

A month or so would pass and the image of Anna Sergeyevna, it
seemed to him, would become misty in his memory, and only from time to
time he would dream of her with her touching smile as he dreamed of
others. But more than a month went by, winter came into its own, and eve-

rything was still clear in his memory as though he had parted from Anna Sergeyevna only yesterday. And his memories glowed more and more vividly. When in the evening stillness the voices of his children preparing their lessons reached his study, or when he listened to a song or to an organ playing in a restaurant, or when the storm howled in the chimney, suddenly everything would rise up in his memory; what had happened on the pier and the early morning with the mist on the mountains, and the steamer coming from Feodosia, and the kisses. He would pace about his room a long time, remembering and smiling; then his memories passed into reveries, and in his imagination the past would mingle with what was to come. He did not dream of Anna Sergeyevna, but she followed him about everywhere and watched him. When he shut his eyes he saw her before him as though she were there in the flesh, and she seemed to him lovelier, younger, tenderer than she had been, and he imagined himself a finer man than he had been in Yalta. Of evenings she peered out at him from the bookcase, from the fireplace, from the corner—he heard her breathing, the caressing rustle of her clothes. In the street he followed the women with his eyes, looking for someone who resembled her.

Already he was tormented by a strong desire to share his memories with someone. But in his home it was impossible to talk of his love, and he had no one to talk to outside; certainly he could not confide in his tenants or in anyone at the bank. And what was there to talk about? He hadn't loved her then, had he? Had there been anything beautiful, poetical, edifying, or simply interesting in his relations with Anna Sergeyevna? And he was forced to talk vaguely of love, of women, and no one guessed what he meant; only his wife would twitch her black eyebrows and say, "The part of a philanderer does not suit you at all, Dimitry."

One evening, coming out of the physicians' club with an official with whom he had been playing cards, he could not resist saying:

"If you only knew what a fascinating woman I became acquainted with at Yalta!"

The official got into his sledge and was driving away, but turned suddenly and shouted:

"Dmitry Dmitrich!"

"What is it?"

"You were right this evening: the sturgeon was a bit high."

These words, so commonplace, for some reason moved Gurov to indignation, and struck him as degrading and unclean. What savage manners, what mugs! What stupid nights, what dull, humdrum days! Frenzied gambling, gluttony, drunkenness, continual talk always about the same thing! Futile pursuits and conversations always about the same topics take up the better part of one's time, the better part of one's strength, and in the end there is left a life clipped and wingless, an absurd mess, and there is no escaping or getting away from it—just as though one were in a madhouse or a prison.

Gurov, boiling with indignation, did not sleep all night. And he had a headache all the next day. And the following nights too he slept badly; he sat up in bed, thinking, or paced up and down his room. He was fed up with his children, fed up with the bank; he had no desire to go anywhere or to talk of anything.

In December during the holidays he prepared to take a trip and told his wife he was going to Petersburg to do what he could for a young friend—and he set off for S——. What for? He did not know, himself. He wanted to see Anna Sergeyevna and talk with her, to arrange a rendezvous if possible.

He arrived at S—— in the morning, and at the hotel took the best room, in which the floor was covered with gray army cloth, and on the table there was an inkstand, gray with dust and topped by a figure on horseback; its hat in its raised hand and its head broken off. The porter gave him the necessary information: von Dideritz lived in a house of his own on Staro-Goncharnaya Street, not far from the hotel: he was rich and lived well and kept his own horses; everyone in the town knew him. The porter pronounced the name: "Dridiritz."

Without haste Gurov made his way to Staro-Goncharnaya Street and found the house. Directly opposite the house stretched a long gray fence studded with nails.

"A fence like that would make one run away," thought Gurov, looking now at the fence, now at the windows of the house.

He reflected: this was a holiday, and the husband was apt to be at home. And in any case, it would be tactless to go into the house and disturb her. If he were to send her a note, it might fall into her husband's hands, and that might spoil everything. The best thing was to rely on chance. And he kept walking up and down the street and along the fence, waiting for the chance. He saw a beggar go in at the gate and heard the dogs attack him; then an hour later he heard a piano, and the sound came to him faintly and indistinctly. Probably it was Anna Sergeyevna playing. The front door opened suddenly, and an old woman came out, followed by the familiar white Pomeranian. Gurov was on the point of calling to the dog, but his heart began beating violently, and in his excitement he could not remember the Pomeranian's name.

He kept walking up and down, and hated the gray fence more and more, and by now he thought irritably that Anna Sergeyevna had forgotten him, and was perhaps already diverting herself with another man, and that that was very natural in a young woman who from morning till night had to look at that damn fence. He went back to his hotel room and sat on the couch for a long while, not knowing what to do, then he had dinner and a long nap.

"How stupid and annoying all this is!" he thought when he woke and looked at the dark windows: it was already evening. "Here I've had a good sleep for some reason. What am I going to do at night?"

He sat on the bed, which was covered with a cheap gray blanket of the kind seen in hospitals, and he twitted himself in his vexation:

"So there's your lady with the pet dog. There's your adventure. A nice place to cool your heels in."

That morning at the station a playbill in large letters had caught his eye. *The Geisha* was to be given for the first time. He thought of this and drove to the theater.

"It's quite possible that she goes to first nights," he thought.

The theater was full. As in all provincial theaters, there was a haze above the chandelier, the gallery was noisy and restless; in the front row, before the beginning of the performance the local dandies were standing with their hands clasped behind their backs; in the Governor's box the Governor's daughter, wearing a boa, occupied the front seat, while the Governor himself hid modestly behind the portiere and only his hands were visible; the curtain swayed; the orchestra was a long time tuning up. While the audience was coming in and taking their seats, Gurov scanned the faces eagerly.

Anna Sergeyevna, too, came in. She sat down in the third row, and when Gurov looked at her his heart contracted, and he understood clearly that in the whole world there was no human being so near, so precious, and so important to him; she, this little, undistinguished woman, lost in a provincial crowd, with a vulgar lorgnette in her hand, filled his whole life now, was his sorrow and his joy, the only happiness that he now desired for himself, and to the sounds of the bad orchestra, of the miserable local violins, he thought how lovely she was. He thought and dreamed.

A young man with small side-whiskers, very tall and stooped, came in with Anna Sergeyevna and sat down beside her; he nodded his head at every step and seemed to be bowing continually. Probably this was the husband whom at Yalta, in an access of bitter feeling, she had called a flunkey. And there really was in his lanky figure, his side-whiskers, his small bald patch, something of a flunkey's retiring manner; his smile was mawkish, and in his buttonhole there was an academic badge like a waiter's number.

During the first intermission the husband went out to have a smoke; she remained in her seat. Gurov, who was also sitting in the orchestra, went up to her and said in a shaky voice, with a forced smile:

"Good evening!"

She glanced at him and turned pale, then looked at him again in horror, unable to believe her eyes, and gripped the fan and the lorgnette tightly together in her hands, evidently trying to keep herself from fainting. Both were silent. She was sitting, he was standing, frightened by her distress and not daring to take a seat beside her. The violins and the flute that were being tuned up sang out. He suddenly felt frightened: it seemed as if all the people in the boxes were looking at them. She got up and went hurriedly to the exit; he followed her, and both of them walked blindly along the corridors and up and down stairs, and figures in the uniforms prescribed for magistrates, teachers, and officials of the Department of Crown Lands, all wearing badges, flitted before their eyes, as did also ladies, and fur coats on hangers; they were conscious of drafts and the smell of stale tobacco. And Gurov, whose heart was beating violently, thought:

"Oh, Lord! Why are these people here and this orchestra!"

And at that instant he suddenly recalled how when he had seen Anna Sergeyevna off at the station he had said to himself that all was over between them and that they would never meet again. But how distant the end still was!

On the narrow, gloomy staircase over which it said "To the Amphitheatre," she stopped.

"How you frightened me!" she said, breathing hard, still pale and stunned. "Oh, how you frightened me! I am barely alive. Why did you come? Why?"

"But do understand, Anna, do understand—" he said hurriedly, under his breath. "I implore you, do understand—"

She looked at him with fear, with entreaty, with love; she looked at him intently, to keep his features more distinctly in her memory.

"I suffer so," she went on, not listening to him. "All this time I have been thinking of nothing but you; I live only by the thought of you. And I wanted to forget, to forget; but why, oh, why have you come?"

On the landing above them two high school boys were looking down and smoking, but it was all the same to Gurov; he drew Anna Sergeyevna to him and began kissing her face and hands.

"What are you doing, what are you doing!" she was saying in horror, pushing him away. "We have lost our senses. Go away today; go away at once—I conjure you by all that is sacred, I implore you—People are coming this way!"

Someone was walking up the stairs.

"You must leave," Anna Sergeyevna went on in a whisper. "Do you hear, Dmitry Dmitrich? I will come and see you in Moscow. I have never been happy; I am unhappy now, and I never, never shall be happy, never! So don't make me suffer still more! I swear I'll come to Moscow. But now let us part. My dear, good, precious one, let us part!"

She pressed his hand and walked rapidly downstairs, turning to look round at him, and from her eyes he could see that she really was unhappy. Gurov stood for a while, listening, then when all grew quiet, he found his coat and left the theater.

4

And Anna Sergeyevna began coming to see him in Moscow. Once every two or three months she left S—— telling her husband that she was going to consult a doctor about a woman's ailment from which she was suffering—and her husband did and did not believe her. When she arrived in

Moscow she would stop at the Slavyansky Bazar Hotel, and at once send a man in a red cap to Gurov. Gurov came to see her, and no one in Moscow knew of it.

Once he was going to see her in this way on a winter morning (the messenger had come the evening before and not found him in). With him walked his daughter, whom he wanted to take to school; it was on the way. Snow was coming down in big wet flakes.

"It's three degrees above zero, and yet it's snowing," Gurov was saying to his daughter. "But this temperature prevails only on the surface of the earth; in the upper layers of the atmosphere there is quite a different temperature."

"And why doesn't it thunder in winter, papa?"

He explained that, too. He talked, thinking all the while that he was on his way to a rendezvous, and no living soul knew of it, and probably no one would ever know. He had two lives, an open one, seen and known by all who needed to know it, full of conventional truth and conventional falsehood, exactly like the lives of his friends and acquaintances; and another life that went on in secret. And through some strange, perhaps accidental, combination of circumstances, everything that was of interest and importance to him, everything that was essential to him, everything about which he felt sincerely and did not deceive himself, everything that constituted the core of his life, was going on concealed from others; while all that was false, the shell in which he hid to cover the truth—his work at the bank, for instance, his discussions at the club, his references to the "inferior race," his appearances at anniversary celebrations with his wife—all that went on in the open. Judging others by himself, he did not believe what he saw, and always fancied that every man led his real, most interesting life under cover of secrecy as under cover of night. The personal life of every individual is based on secrecy, and perhaps it is partly for that reason that civilized man is so nervously anxious that personal privacy should be respected.

Having taken his daughter to school, Gurov went on to the Slavyansky Bazar Hotel. He took off his fur coat in the lobby, went upstairs, and knocked gently at the door. Anna Sergeyevna, wearing his favorite gray dress, exhausted by the journey and by waiting, had been expecting him since the previous evening. She was pale, and looked at him without a smile, and he had hardly entered when she flung herself on his breast. That kiss was a long, lingering one, as though they had not seen one another for two years.

"Well, darling, how are you getting on there?" he asked. "What news?"

"Wait; I'll tell you in a moment—I can't speak."

She could not speak; she was crying. She turned away from him, and pressed her handkerchief to her eyes.

"Let her have her cry; meanwhile I'll sit down," he thought, and he seated himself in an armchair.

Then he rang and ordered tea, and while he was having his tea she remained standing at the window with her back to him. She was crying out of sheer agitation, in the sorrowful consciousness that their life was so sad; that they could only see each other in secret and had to hide from people like thieves! Was it not a broken life?

"Come, stop now, dear!" he said.

It was plain to him that this love of theirs would not be over soon, that the end of it was not in sight. Anna Sergeyevna was growing more and more attached to him. She adored him, and it was unthinkable to tell her that their love was bound to come to an end some day; besides, she would not have believed it!

He went up to her and took her by the shoulders, to fondle her and say something diverting, and at that moment he caught sight of himself in the mirror.

His hair was already beginning to turn gray. And it seemed odd to him that he had grown so much older in the last few years, and lost his looks. The shoulders on which his hands rested were warm and heaving. He felt compassion for this life, still so warm and lovely, but probably already about to begin to fade and wither like his own. Why did she love him so much? He always seemed to women different from what he was, and they loved in him not himself, but the man whom their imagination created and whom they had been eagerly seeking all their lives; and afterwards, when they saw their mistake, they loved him nevertheless. And not one of them had been happy with him. In the past he had met women, come together with them, parted from them, but he had never once loved; it was anything you please, but not love. And only now when his head was gray he had fallen in love, really, truly—for the first time in his life.

Anna Sergeyevna and he loved each other as people do who are very close and intimate, like man and wife, like tender friends; it seemed to them that Fate itself had meant them for one another, and they could not understand why he had a wife and she a husband; and it was as though they were a pair of migratory birds, male and female, caught and forced to live in different cages. They forgave each other what they were ashamed of in their past, they forgave everything in the present, and felt that this love of theirs had altered them both.

Formerly in moments of sadness he had soothed himself with whatever logical arguments came into his head, but now he no longer cared for logic; he felt profound compassion, he wanted to be sincere and tender.

"Give it up now, my darling," he said. "You've had your cry; that's enough. Let us have a talk now, we'll think up something."

Then they spent a long time taking counsel together, they talked of how to avoid the necessity for secrecy, for deception, for living in different cities, and not seeing one another for long stretches of time. How could they free themselves from these intolerable fetters?

"How? How?" he asked, clutching his head. "How?"

And it seemed as though in a little while the solution would be found, and then a new and glorious life would begin; and it was clear to both of them that the end was still far off, and that what was to be most complicated and difficult for them was only just beginning.

1899

Further Reading

Nabokov, Vladimir. "Anton Chekhov." *Lectures on Russian Literature.* Ed. Fredson Bowers. New York: Harcourt, 1981. 245–95, spec. 255–63. • Smith, Virginia Llewellyn. "The Lady with the Dog." *Anton Chekhov and the Lady with the Dog.* London: Oxford UP, 1973. 212–19. • Stowell, H. Peter. "Chekhov the Impressionist: 1899–1904." *Literary Impressionism, James and Chekhov.* Athens: U of Georgia P, 1980. 120–66, spec. 120–35. • Pritchett, V. S. "Books in General: *My Life.*" *New Statesman and Nation* 25 (27 Mar. 1943): 209. • Welty, Eudora. "Reality in Chekhov's Stories." *The Eye of the Story: Selected Essays and Reviews.* New York: Random, 1977. 61–81.

Anton Chekhov's fidelity to the details of external reality seems to put his fiction at a pole opposite that of writers of tales and fantasies that express an inward reality. As Virginia Woolf observes, however, Chekhov's stories reveal his soul, a soul she admires but cannot be entirely sympathetic with.

Virginia Woolf: On Inconclusiveness Themes in Chekhov

The emphasis is laid upon such unexpected places that at first it seems as if there were no emphasis at all; and then, as the eyes accustom themselves to twilight and discern the shapes of things in a room we see how complete the story is, how profound, and how truly in obedience to his vision Tchekov has chosen this, that, and the other, and placed them together to compose something new. But it is impossible to say 'this is comic', or 'that is tragic', nor are we certain, since short stories, we have been taught, should be brief and conclusive, whether this, which is vague and inconclusive, should be called a short story at all. . . . In every great Russian writer we seem to discern the features of a saint, if sympathy for the sufferings of others, love towards them, endeavour to reach some goal worthy of the most exacting demands of the spirit constitute saintliness. It is the saint in them which confounds us with a feeling of our own irreligious triviality, and turns so many of our famous novels to tinsel and trickery. The conclusions of the Russian mind, thus comprehensive and compassionate, are inevitably, perhaps, of the utmost sadness. More accurately indeed we might speak of the inconclusiveness of the Russian mind. It is the sense that there is no answer, that if honestly examined life presents question after question which must be left to sound on and on after the story is over in hopeless interrogation that fills us with a deep, and finally it may be with a resentful, despair. They are right perhaps; unquestionably they see further than we do and without our gross impediments of vision. But perhaps we see something that escapes them, or why should this voice of protest mix itself with our gloom? The voice of protest is the voice of another and an ancient civilization which seems to have bred in us the instinct to enjoy and fight rather than to suffer and understand.

CHARLOTTE PERKINS GILMAN

(1860–1935)

THE YELLOW WALLPAPER

It is very seldom that mere ordinary people like John and myself secure ancestral halls for the summer.

A colonial mansion, a hereditary estate, I would say a haunted house and reach the height of romantic felicity—but that would be asking too much of fate!

Still I will proudly declare that there is something queer about it.

Else, why should it be let so cheaply? And why have stood so long untenanted?

John laughs at me, of course, but one expects that.

John is practical in the extreme. He has no patience with faith, an intense horror of superstition, and he scoffs openly at any talk of things not to be felt and seen and put down in figures.

John is a physician, and *perhaps*—(I would not say it to a living soul, of course, but this is dead paper and a great relief to my mind)—*perhaps* that is one reason I do not get well faster.

You see, he does not believe I am sick! And what can one do?

If a physician of high standing, and one's own husband, assures friends and relatives that there is really nothing the matter with one but temporary nervous depression—a slight hysterical tendency—what is one to do?

My brother is also a physician, and also of high standing, and he says the same thing.

So I take phosphates or phosphites—whichever it is—and tonics, and air and exercise, and journeys, and am absolutely forbidden to "work" until I am well again.

Personally, I disagree with their ideas.

Personally, I believe that congenial work, with excitement and change, would do me good.

But what is one to do?

I did write for a while in spite of them; but it *does* exhaust me a good deal—having to be so sly about it, or else meet with heavy opposition.

I sometimes fancy that in my condition, if I had less opposition and more society and stimulus—but John says the very worst thing I can do is to think about my condition, and I confess it always makes me feel bad.

So I will let it alone and talk about the house.

The most beautiful place! It is quite alone, standing well back from the road, quite three miles from the village. It makes me think of English places that you read about, for there are hedges and walls and gates that lock, and lots of separate little houses for the gardeners and people.

There is a *delicious* garden! I never saw such a garden—large and shady, full of box-bordered paths, and lined with long grape-covered arbors with seats under them.

There were greenhouses, but they are all broken now.

There was some legal trouble, I believe, something about the heirs and co-heirs; anyhow, the place has been empty for years.

That spoils my ghostliness, I am afraid, but I don't care—there is something strange about the house—I can feel it.

I even said so to John one moonlight evening, but he said what I felt was a draught, and shut the window.

I get unreasonably angry with John sometimes. I'm sure I never used to be so sensitive. I think it is due to this nervous condition.

But John says if I feel so I shall neglect proper self-control; so I take pains to control myself—before him, at least, and that makes me very tired.

I don't like our room a bit. I wanted one downstairs that opened onto the piazza and had roses all over the window, and such pretty old-fashioned chintz hangings! But John would not hear of it.

He said there was only one window and not room for two beds, and no near room for him if he took another.

He is very careful and loving, and hardly lets me stir without special direction.

I have a schedule prescription for each hour in the day; he takes all care from me, and so I feel basely ungrateful not to value it more.

He said he came here solely on my account, that I was to have perfect rest and all the air I could get. "Your exercise depends on your strength, my dear," said he, "and your food somewhat on your appetite; but air you can absorb all the time." So we took the nursery at the top of the house.

It is a big, airy room, the whole floor nearly, with windows that look all ways, and air and sunshine galore. It was nursery first, and then playroom and gymnasium, I should judge, for the windows are barred for little children, and there are rings and things in the walls.

The paint and paper look as if a boys' school had used it. It is stripped off—the paper—in great patches all around the head of my bed, about as far as I can reach, and in a great place on the other side of the room low down. I never saw a worse paper in my life. One of those sprawling, flamboyant patterns committing every artistic sin.

It is dull enough to confuse the eye in following, pronounced enough constantly to irritate and provoke study, and when you follow the lame uncertain curves for a little distance they suddenly commit suicide —plunge off at outrageous angles, destroy themselves in unheard-of contradictions.

The color is repellent, almost revolting: a smouldering unclean yellow, strangely faded by the slow-turning sunlight. It is a dull yet lurid orange in some places, a sickly sulphur tint in others.

No wonder the children hated it! I should hate it myself if I had to live in this room long.

There comes John, and I must put this away—he hates to have me write a word.

We have been here two weeks, and I haven't felt like writing before, since that first day.

I am sitting by the window now, up in this atrocious nursery, and there is nothing to hinder my writing as much as I please, save lack of strength.

John is away all day, and even some nights when his cases are serious.

I am glad my case is not serious!

But these nervous troubles are dreadfully depressing.

John does not know how much I really suffer. He knows there is no reason to suffer, and that satisfies him.

Of course it is only nervousness. It does weigh on me so not to do my duty in any way!

I meant to be such a help to John, such a real rest and comfort, and here I am a comparative burden already!

Nobody would believe what an effort it is to do what little I am able—to dress and entertain, and order things.

It is fortunate Mary is so good with the baby. Such a dear baby!

And yet I *cannot* be with him, it makes me so nervous.

I suppose John never was nervous in his life. He laughs at me so about this wallpaper!

At first he meant to repaper the room, but afterward he said that I was letting it get the better of me, and that nothing was worse for a nervous patient than to give way to such fancies.

He said that after the wallpaper was changed it would be the heavy bedstead, and then the barred windows, and then that gate at the head of the stairs, and so on.

"You know the place is doing you good," he said, "and really, dear, I don't care to renovate the house just for a three months' rental."

"Then do let us go downstairs," I said. "There are such pretty rooms there."

Then he took me in his arms and called me a blessed little goose, and said he would go down cellar, if I wished, and have it whitewashed into the bargain.

But he is right enough about the beds and windows and things.

It is as airy and comfortable a room as anyone need wish, and, of course, I would not be so silly as to make him uncomfortable just for a whim.

I'm really getting fond of the big room, all but that horrid paper.

Out of one window I can see the garden—those mysterious deep-shaded arbors, the riotous old-fashioned flowers, and bushes and gnarly trees.

Out of another I get a lovely view of the bay and a little private wharf belonging to the estate. There is a beautiful shaded lane that runs down there from the house. I always fancy I see people walking in these numer-ous paths and arbors, but John has cautioned me not to give way to fancy in the least. He says that with my imaginative power and habit of story-making, a nervous weakness like mine is sure to lead to all manner of excited fancies, and that I ought to use my will and good sense to check the tendency. So I try.

I think sometimes that if I were only well enough to write a little it would relieve the press of ideas and rest me.

But I find I get pretty tired when I try.

It is so discouraging not to have any advice and companionship about my work. When I get really well, John says we will ask Cousin Henry and Julia down for a long visit; but he says he would as soon put fireworks in my pillow-case as to let me have those stimulating people about now.

I wish I could get well faster.

But I must not think about that. This paper looks to me as if it *knew* what a vicious influence it had!

There is a recurrent spot where the pattern lolls like a broken neck and two bulbous eyes stare at you upside down.

I get positively angry with the impertinence of it and the everlasting-ness. Up and down and sideways they crawl, and those absurd unblinking eyes are everywhere. There is one place where two breadths didn't match, and the eyes go all up and down the line, one a little higher than the other.

I never saw so much expression in an inanimate thing before, and we all know how much expression they have! I used to lie awake as a child and get more entertainment and terror out of blank walls and plain furniture than most children could find in a toy-store.

I remember what a kindly wink the knobs of our big old bureau used to have, and there was one chair that always seemed like a strong friend.

I used to feel that if any of the other things looked too fierce I could always hop into that chair and be safe.

The furniture in this room is no worse than inharmonious, however, for we had to bring it all from downstairs. I suppose when this was used as a playroom they had to take the nursery things out, and no wonder! I never saw such ravages as the children have made here.

The wallpaper, as I said before, is torn off in spots, and it sticketh closer than a brother—they must have had perseverance as well as hatred.

Then the floor is scratched and gouged and splintered, the plaster itself is dug out here and there, and this great heavy bed, which is all we found in the room, looks as if it had been through the wars.

But I don't mind it a bit—only the paper.

There comes John's sister. Such a dear girl as she is, and so careful of me! I must not let her find me writing.

She is a perfect and enthusiastic housekeeper, and hopes for no better profession. I verily believe she thinks it is the writing which made me sick!

But I can write when she is out, and see her a long way off from these windows.

There is one that commands the road, a lovely shaded winding road, and one that just looks off over the country. A lovely country, too, full of great elms and velvet meadows.

This wallpaper has a kind of sub-pattern in a different shade, a particularly irritating one, for you can only see it in certain lights, and not clearly then.

But in the places where it isn't faded and where the sun is just so—I can see a strange, provoking, formless sort of figure that seems to skulk about behind that silly and conspicuous front design.

There's sister on the stairs!

Well, the Fourth of July is over! The people are all gone, and I am tired out. John thought it might do me good to see a little company, so we just had Mother and Nellie and the children down for a week.

Of course I didn't do a thing. Jennie sees to everything now.

But it tired me all the same.

John says if I don't pick up faster he shall send me to Weir Mitchell in the fall.

But I don't want to go there at all. I had a friend who was in his hands once, and she says he is just like John and my brother, only more so!

Besides, it is such an undertaking to go so far.

I don't feel as if it was worthwhile to turn my hand over for anything, and I'm getting dreadfully fretful and querulous.

I cry at nothing, and cry most of the time.

Of course I don't when John is here, or anybody else, but when I am alone.

And I am alone a good deal just now. John is kept in town very often by serious cases, and Jennie is good and lets me alone when I want her to.

So I walk a little in the garden or down that lovely lane, sit on the porch under the roses, and lie down up here a good deal.

I'm getting really fond of the room in spite of the wallpaper. Perhaps *because* of the wallpaper.

It dwells in my mind so!

I lie here on this great immovable bed—it is nailed down, I believe—and follow that pattern about by the hour. It is as good as gymnastics, I assure you. I start, we'll say, at the bottom, down in the corner over there where it has not been touched, and I determine for the thousandth time that I *will* follow that pointless pattern to some sort of a conclusion.

I know a little of the principle of design, and I know this thing was not arranged on any laws of radiation, or alternation, or repetition, or symmetry, or anything else that I ever heard of.

It is repeated, of course, by the breadths, but not otherwise.

Looked at in one way, each breadth stands alone; the bloated curves and flourishes—a kind of "debased Romanesque" with delirium tremens go waddling up and down in isolated columns of fatuity.

But, on the other hand, they connect diagonally, and the sprawling outlines run off in great slanting waves of optic horror, like a lot of wallowing sea-weeds in full chase.

The whole thing goes horizontally, too, at least it seems so, and I exhaust myself trying to distinguish the order of its going in that direction.

They have used a horizontal breadth for a frieze, and that adds wonderfully to the confusion.

There is one end of the room where it is almost intact, and there, when the crosslights fade and the low sun shines directly upon it, I can almost fancy radiation after all—the interminable grotesque seems to form around a common center and rush off in headlong plunges of equal distraction.

It makes me tired to follow it. I will take a nap, I guess.

I don't know why I should write this.

I don't want to.

I don't feel able.

And I know John would think it absurd. But I *must* say what I feel and think in some way—it is such a relief!

But the effort is getting to be greater than the relief.

Half the time now I am awfully lazy, and lie down ever so much. John says I mustn't lose my strength, and has me take cod liver oil and lots of tonics and things, to say nothing of ale and wine and rare meat.

Dear John! He loves me very dearly, and hates to have me sick. I tried to have a real earnest reasonable talk with him the other day, and tell him how I wish he would let me go and make a visit to Cousin Henry and Julia.

But he said I wasn't able to go, nor able to stand it after I got there; and I did not make out a very good case for myself, for I was crying before I had finished.

It is getting to be a great effort for me to think straight. Just this nervous weakness, I suppose.

And dear John gathered me up in his arms, and just carried me upstairs and laid me on the bed, and sat by me and read to me till it tired my head.

He said I was his darling and his comfort and all he had, and that I must take care of myself for his sake, and keep well.

He says no one but myself can help me out of it, that I must use my will and self-control and not let any silly fancies run away with me.

There's one comfort—the baby is well and happy, and does not have to occupy this nursery with the horrid wallpaper.

If we had not used it, that blessed child would have! What a fortunate escape! Why, I wouldn't have a child of mine, an impressionable little thing, live in such a room for worlds.

I never thought of it before, but it is lucky that John kept me here after all; I can stand it so much easier than a baby, you see.

Of course I never mention it to them any more—I am too wise—but I keep watch for it all the same.

There are things in that wallpaper that nobody knows about but me, or ever will.

Behind that outside pattern the dim shapes get clearer every day.

It is always the same shape, only very numerous.

And it is like a woman stooping down and creeping about behind that pattern. I don't like it a bit. I wonder—I begin to think—I wish John would take me away from here!

It is so hard to talk with John about my case, because he is so wise, and because he loves me so.

But I tried it last night.

It was moonlight. The moon shines in all around just as the sun does.

I hate to see it sometimes, it creeps so slowly, and always comes in by one window or another.

John was asleep and I hated to waken him, so I kept still and watched the moonlight on that undulating wallpaper till I felt creepy.

The faint figure behind seemed to shake the pattern, just as if she wanted to get out.

I got up softly and went to feel and see if the paper *did* move, and when I came back John was awake.

"What is it, little girl?" he said. "Don't go walking about like that— you'll get cold."

I thought it was a good time to talk, so I told him that I really was not gaining here, and that I wished he would take me away.

"Why, darling!" said he. "Our lease will be up in three weeks, and I can't see how to leave before.

"The repairs are not done at home, and I cannot possibly leave town just now. Of course, if you were in any danger, I could and would, but you really are better, dear, whether you can see it or not. I am a doctor, dear, and I know. You are gaining flesh and color, your appetite is better, I feel really much easier about you."

"I don't weigh a bit more," said I, "nor as much; and my appetite may be better in the evening when you are here but it is worse in the morning when you are away!"

"Bless her little heart!" said he with a big hug. "She shall be as sick as she pleases! But now let's improve the shining hours by going to sleep, and talk about it in the morning!"

"And you won't go away?" I asked gloomily.

"Why, how can I, dear? It is only three weeks more and then we will take a nice little trip of a few days while Jennie is getting the house ready. Really, dear, you are better!"

"Better in body perhaps—" I began, and stopped short, for he sat up straight and looked at me with such a stern, reproachful look that I could not say another word.

"My darling," said he, "I beg of you, for my sake and for our child's sake, as well as for your own, that you will never for one instant let that idea enter your mind! There is nothing so dangerous, so fascinating, to a temperament like yours. It is a false and foolish fancy. Can you not trust me as a physician when I tell you so?"

So of course I said no more on that score, and we went to sleep before long. He thought I was asleep first, but I wasn't, and lay there for hours trying to decide whether that front pattern and the back pattern really did move together or separately.

On a pattern like this, by daylight, there is a lack of sequence, a defiance of law, that is a constant irritant to a normal mind.

The color is hideous enough, and unreliable enough, and infuriating enough, but the pattern is torturing.

You think you have mastered it, but just as you get well under way in following, it turns a back-somersault and there you are. It slaps you in the face, knocks you down, and tramples upon you. It is like a bad dream.

The outside pattern is a florid arabesque, reminding one of a fungus. If you can imagine a toadstool in joints, an interminable string of toadstools, budding and sprouting in endless convolutions—why, that is something like it.

That is, sometimes!

There is one marked peculiarity about this paper, a thing nobody seems to notice but myself, and that is that it changes as the light changes.

When the sun shoots in through the east window—I always watch for that first long, straight ray—it changes so quickly that I never can quite believe it.

That is why I watch it always.

By moonlight—the moon shines in all night when there is a moon—I wouldn't know it was the same paper.

At night in any kind of light, in twilight, candlelight, lamplight, and worst of all by moonlight, it becomes bars! The outside pattern, I mean, and the woman behind it is as plain as can be.

I didn't realize for a long time what the thing was that showed behind, that dim sub-pattern, but now I am quite sure it is a woman.

By daylight she is subdued, quiet. I fancy it is the pattern that keeps her so still. It is so puzzling. It keeps me quiet by the hour.

I lie down ever so much now. John says it is good for me, and to sleep all I can.

Indeed he started the habit by making me lie down for an hour after each meal.

It is a very bad habit, I am convinced, for you see, I don't sleep.

And that cultivates deceit, for I don't tell them I'm awake—oh, no!

The fact is I am getting a little afraid of John.

He seems very queer sometimes, and even Jennie has an inexplicable look.

It strikes me occasionally, just as a scientific hypothesis, that perhaps it is the paper!

I have watched John when he did not know I was looking, and come into the room suddenly on the most innocent excuses, and I've caught him several times *looking at the paper*! And Jennie too. I caught Jennie with her hand on it once.

She didn't know I was in the room, and when I asked her in a quiet, a very quiet voice, with the most restrained manner possible, what she was doing with the paper, she turned around as if she had been caught stealing, and looked quite angry—asked me why I should frighten her so!

Then she said that the paper stained everything it touched, that she had found yellow smooches on all my clothes and John's and she wished we would be more careful!

Did not that sound innocent? But I know she was studying that pattern, and I am determined that nobody shall find it out but myself!

Life is very much more exciting now than it used to be. You see, I have something more to expect, to look forward to, to watch. I really do eat better, and am more quiet than I was.

John is so pleased to see me improve! He laughed a little the other day, and said I seemed to be flourishing in spite of my wallpaper.

I turned it off with a laugh. I had no intention of telling him it was *because* of the wallpaper—he would make fun of me. He might even want to take me away.

I don't want to leave now until I have found it out. There is a week more, and I think that will be enough.

I'm feeling so much better!

I don't sleep much at night, for it is so interesting to watch developments; but I sleep a good deal during the daytime.

In the daytime it is tiresome and perplexing.

There are always new shoots on the fungus, and new shades of yellow all over it. I cannot keep count of them, though I have tried conscientiously.

It is the strangest yellow, that wallpaper! It makes me think of all the yellow things I ever saw—not beautiful ones like buttercups, but old, foul, bad yellow things.

But there is something else about that paper—the smell! I noticed it the moment we came into the room, but with so much air and sun it was not bad. Now we have had a week of fog and rain, and whether the windows are open or not, the smell is here.

It creeps all over the house.

I find it hovering in the dining-room, skulking in the parlor, hiding in the hall, lying in wait for me on the stairs.

It gets into my hair.

Even when I go to ride, if I turn my head suddenly and surprise it—there is that smell!

Such a peculiar odor, too! I have spent hours in trying to analyze it, to find what it smelled like.

It is not bad—at first—and very gentle, but quite the subtlest, most enduring odor I ever met.

In this damp weather it is awful. I wake up in the night and find it hanging over me.

It used to disturb me at first. I thought seriously of burning the house —to reach the smell.

But now I am used to it. The only thing I can think of that it is like is the *color* of the paper! A yellow smell.

There is a very funny mark on this wall, low down, near the mopboard. A streak that runs round the room. It goes behind every piece of furniture, except the bed, a long, straight, even *smooch*, as if it had been rubbed over and over.

I wonder how it was done and who did it, and what they did it for. Round and round and round—round and round and round—it makes me dizzy!

I really have discovered something at last.

Through watching so much at night, when it changes so, I have finally found out.

The front pattern *does* move—and no wonder! The woman behind shakes it!

Sometimes I think there are a great many women behind, and sometimes only one, and she crawls around fast, and her crawling shakes it all over.

Then in the very bright spots she keeps still, and in the very shady spots she just takes hold of the bars and shakes them hard.

And she is all the time trying to climb through. But nobody could climb through that pattern—it strangles so; I think that is why it has so many heads.

They get through and then the pattern strangles them off and turns them upside down, and makes their eyes white!

If those heads were covered or taken off it would not be half so bad.

I think that woman gets out in the daytime!

And I'll tell you why—privately—I've seen her!

I can see her out of every one of my windows!

It is the same woman, I know, for she is always creeping, and most women do not creep by daylight.

I see her in that long shaded lane, creeping up and down. I see her in those dark grape arbors, creeping all around the garden.

I see her on that long road under the trees, creeping along, and when a carriage comes she hides under the blackberry vines.

I don't blame her a bit. It must be very humiliating to be caught creeping by daylight!

I always lock the door when I creep by daylight. I can't do it at night, for I know John would suspect something at once.

And John is so queer now that I don't want to irritate him. I wish he would take another room! Besides, I don't want anybody to get that woman out at night but myself.

I often wonder if I could see her out of all the windows at once.

But, turn as fast as I can, I can only see out of one at one time.

And though I always see her, she *may* be able to creep faster than I can turn! I have watched her sometimes away off in the open country, creeping as fast as a cloud shadow in a wind.

If only that top pattern could be gotten off from the under one! I mean to try it, little by little.

I have found out another funny thing, but I shan't tell it this time! It does not do to trust people too much.

There are only two more days to get this paper off, and I believe John is beginning to notice. I don't like the look in his eyes.

And I heard him ask Jennie a lot of professional questions about me. She had a very good report to give.

She said I slept a good deal in the daytime.

John knows I don't sleep very well at night, for all I'm so quiet!

He asked me all sorts of questions, too, and pretended to be very loving and kind.

As if I couldn't see through him!

Still, I don't wonder he acts so, sleeping under this paper for three months.

It only interests me, but I feel sure John and Jennie are affected by it.

Hurrah! This is the last day, but it is enough. John is to stay in town over night, and won't be out until this evening.

Jennie wanted to sleep with me—the sly thing; but I told her I should undoubtedly rest better for a night all alone.

That was clever, for really I wasn't alone a bit! As soon as it was moon-light and that poor thing began to crawl and shake the pattern, I got up and ran to help her.

I pulled and she shook. I shook and she pulled, and before morning we had peeled off yards of that paper.

A strip about as high as my head and half around the room.

And then when the sun came and that awful pattern began to laugh at me, I declared I would finish it today!

We go away tomorrow, and they are moving all my furniture down again to leave things as they were before.

Jennie looked at the wall in amazement, but I told her merrily that I did it out of pure spite at the vicious thing.

She laughed and said she wouldn't mind doing it herself, but I must not get tired.

How she betrayed herself that time!

But I am here, and no person touches this paper but Me—not *alive*!

She tried to get me out of the room—it was too patent! But I said it was so quiet and empty and clean now that I believed I would lie down again and sleep all I could, and not to wake me even for dinner—I would call when I woke.

So now she is gone, and the servants are gone, and the things are gone, and there is nothing left but that great bedstead nailed down, with the canvas mattress we found on it.

We shall sleep downstairs tonight, and take the boat home tomorrow.

I quite enjoy the room, now it is bare again.

How those children did tear about here!

This bedstead is fairly gnawed!

But I must get to work.

I have locked the door and thrown the key down into the front path.

I don't want to go out, and I don't want to have anybody come in, till John comes.

I want to astonish him.

I've got a rope up here that even Jennie did not find. If that woman does get out, and tries to get away, I can tie her!

But I forgot I could not reach far without anything to stand on!

This bed will *not* move!

I tried to lift and push it until I was lame, and then I got so angry I bit off a little piece at one corner—but it hurt my teeth.

Then I peeled off all the paper I could reach standing on the floor. It sticks horribly and the pattern just enjoys it! All those strangled heads and bulbous eyes and waddling fungus growths just shriek with derision!

I am getting angry enough to do something desperate. To jump out of the window would be admirable exercise, but the bars are too strong even to try.

Besides I wouldn't do it. Of course not. I know well enough that a step like that is improper and might be misconstrued.

I don't like to *look* out of the windows even—there are so many of those creeping women, and they creep so fast.

I wonder if they all come out of that wallpaper as I did?

But I am securely fastened now by my well-hidden rope—you don't get *me* out in the road there!

I suppose I shall have to get back behind the pattern when it comes night, and that is hard!

It is so pleasant to be out in this great room and creep around as I please!

I don't want to go outside. I won't, even if Jennie asks me to.

For outside you have to creep on the ground, and everything is green instead of yellow.

But here I can creep smoothly on the floor, and my shoulder just fits in that long smooch around the wall, so I cannot lose my way.

Why, there's John at the door!

It is no use, young man, you can't open it!

How he does call and pound!

Now he's crying to Jennie for an axe.

It would be a shame to break down that beautiful door!

"John, dear!" said I in the gentlest voice. "The key is down by the front steps, under a plantain leaf!"

That silenced him for a few moments.

Then he said, very quietly indeed, "Open the door, my darling!"

"I can't," said I. "The key is down by the front door under a plantain leaf!" And then I said it again, several times, very gently and slowly, and said it so often that he had to go and see, and he got it of course, and came in. He stopped short by the door.

"What is the matter?" he cried. "For God's sake, what are you doing!"

I kept on creeping just the same, but I looked at him over my shoulder.

"I've got out at last," said I, "in spite of you and Jane. And I've pulled off most of the paper, so you can't put me back!"

Now why should that man have fainted? But he did, and right across my path by the wall, so that I had to creep over him every time!

1892

Further Reading

Lane, Ann J. "The Fictional World of Charlotte Perkins Gilman." *The Charlotte Perkins Gilman Reader*. Ed. Ann J. Lane. New York: Pantheon, 1980. ix–xlii.
• Hedges, Elaine. Afterword. *The Yellow Wallpaper*. By Charlotte Gilman. Old Westbury, N.Y.: Feminist, 1973. 37–63. • Schumaker, Conrad. " 'Too Terribly

Good to Be Printed': Charlotte Gilman's 'The Yellow Wallpaper.'" *American Literature* 57 (Dec. 1985): 588–98. • Schopp-Schilling, Beate. "'The Yellow Wallpaper': A Rediscovered 'Realistic' Story." *American Literary Realism* 8.3 (Summer 1975): 284–86. • MacPike Loralee. "Environment as Psychopathological Symbolism in 'The Yellow Wallpaper.'" *American Literary Realism* 8 (Summer 1975): 286–88.

"The Yellow Wallpaper" can be seen as a story of obsession, related therefore to Edgar Allan Poe's "The Tell-Tale Heart." But the psychological state of Charlotte Perkins Gilman is of more than literary interest. Gilman herself was a double victim of what we now would call depression: a victim once from the disease, and once again from the failure of others to understand the disease. In her autobiography Gilman records the "nervous prostration" she experienced in 1886.

Charlotte Perkins Gilman: On Her Own "Nervous Prostration"

Presently we moved to a better house, on Humboldt Avenue near by, and a German servant girl of unparalleled virtues was installed. Here was a charming home; a loving and devoted husband; an exquisite baby, healthy, intelligent and good; a highly competent mother to run things; a wholly satisfactory servant—and I lay all day on the lounge and cried. . . .

In those days a new disease had dawned on the medical horizon. It was called "nervous prostration." No one knew much about it, and there were many who openly scoffed, saying it was only a new name for laziness. To be recognizably ill one must be confined to one's bed, and preferably in pain.

That a heretofore markedly vigorous young woman, with every comfort about her, should collapse in this lamentable manner was inexplicable. "You should use your will," said earnest friends. I had used it, hard and long, perhaps too hard and too long; at any rate it wouldn't work now.

"Force some happiness into your life," said one sympathizer. "Take an agreeable book to bed with you, occupy your mind with pleasant things." She did not realize that I was unable to read, and that my mind was exclusively occupied with unpleasant things. This disorder involved a growing melancholia, and that, as those know who have tasted it, consists of every painful mental sensation, shame, fear, remorse, a blind oppressive confusion, utter weakness, a steady brainache that fills the conscious mind with crowding images of distress. . . .

"If you would get up and do something you would feel better," said my mother. I rose drearily, and essayed to brush up the floor a little, with a dustpan and small whiskbroom, but soon dropped those implements exhausted, and wept again in helpless shame.

EDITH WHARTON

(1862–1937)

ROMAN FEVER

1

From the table at which they had been lunching two American ladies of ripe but well-cared-for middle age moved across the lofty terrace of the Roman restaurant and, leaning on its parapet, looked first at each other, and then down on the outspread glories of the Palatine and the Forum, with the same expression of vague but benevolent approval.

As they leaned there a girlish voice echoed up gaily from the stairs leading to the court below. "Well, come along, then," it cried, not to them but to an invisible companion, "and let's leave the young things to their knitting"; and a voice as fresh laughed back: "Oh, look here, Babs, not actually *knitting*—" "Well, I mean figuratively," rejoined the first. "After all, we haven't left our poor parents much else to do. . . ." and at that point the turn of the stairs engulfed the dialogue.

The two ladies looked at each other again, this time with a tingle of smiling embarrassment, and the smaller and paler one shook her head and colored slightly.

"Barbara!" she murmured, sending an unheard rebuke after the mocking voice in the stairway.

The other lady, who was fuller, and higher in color, with a small determined nose supported by vigorous black eyebrows, gave a good-humored laugh. "That's what our daughters think of us!"

Her companion replied by a deprecating gesture. "Not of us individually. We must remember that. It's just the collective modern idea of Mothers. And you see—" Half-guiltily she drew from her handsomely mounted black handbag a twist of crimson silk run through by two fine knitting needles. "One never knows," she murmured. "The new system has certainly given us a good deal of time to kill; and sometimes I get tired just looking—even at this." Her gesture was now addressed to the stupendous scene at their feet.

The dark lady laughed again, and they both relapsed upon the view, contemplating it in silence, with a sort of diffused serenity which might have been borrowed from the spring effulgence of the Roman skies. The luncheon hour was long past, and the two had their end of the vast terrace to themselves. At its opposite extremity a few groups, detained by a lingering look at the outspread city, were gathering up guidebooks and fumbling for tips. The last of them scattered, and the two ladies were alone on the air-washed height.

"Well, I don't see why we shouldn't just stay here," said Mrs. Slade, the lady of the high color and energetic brows. Two derelict basket chairs stood near, and she pushed them into the angle of the parapet, and settled herself in one, her gaze upon the Palatine. "After all, it's still the most beautiful view in the world."

"It always will be, to me," assented her friend Mrs. Ansley, with so slight a stress on the "me" that Mrs. Slade, though she noticed it, wondered if it were not merely accidental, like the random underlinings of old-fashioned letter writers.

"Grace Ansley was always old-fashioned," she thought; and added aloud, with a retrospective smile: "It's a view we've both been familiar with for a good many years. When we first met here we were younger than our girls are now. You remember?"

"Oh, yes, I remember," murmured Mrs. Ansley, with the same undefinable stress. "There's that headwaiter wondering," she interpolated. She was evidently far less sure than her companion of herself and of her rights in the world.

"I'll cure him of wondering," said Mrs. Slade, stretching her hand toward a bag as discreetly opulent-looking as Mrs. Ansley's. Signing to the headwaiter, she explained that she and her friend were old lovers of Rome, and would like to spend the end of the afternoon looking down on the view —that is, if it did not disturb the service? The headwaiter, bowing over her gratuity, assured her that the ladies were most welcome, and would be still more so if they would condescend to remain for dinner. A full-moon night, they would remember. . . .

Mrs. Slade's black brows drew together, as though references to the moon were out of place and even unwelcome. But she smiled away her frown as the headwaiter retreated. "Well, why not? We might do worse. There's no knowing, I suppose, when the girls will be back. Do you even know back from *where*? I don't!"

Mrs. Ansley again colored slightly. "I think those young Italian aviators we met at the Embassy invited them to fly to Tarquinia for tea. I suppose they'll want to wait and fly back by moonlight."

"Moonlight—moonlight! What a part it still plays. Do you suppose they're as sentimental as we were?"

"I've come to the conclusion that I don't in the least know what they are," said Mrs. Ansley. "And perhaps we didn't know much more about each other."

"No; perhaps we didn't."

Her friend gave her a shy glance. "I never should have supposed you were sentimental, Alida."

"Well, perhaps I wasn't." Mrs. Slade drew her lids together in retrospect; and for a few moments the two ladies, who had been intimate since childhood, reflected how little they knew each other. Each one, of course, had a label ready to attach to the other's name; Mrs. Delphin Slade, for instance, would have told herself, or anyone who asked her, that Mrs. Horace Ansley, twenty-five years ago, had been exquisitely lovely—no, you wouldn't believe it, would you? . . . though, of course, still charming, distinguished. . . . Well, as a girl she had been exquisite; far more beautiful than her daughter Barbara, though certainly Babs, according to the new standards at any rate, was more effective—had more *edge*, as they say. Funny where she got it, with those two nullities as parents. Yes; Horace Ansley was—well, just the duplicate of his wife. Museum specimens of old New York. Good-looking, irreproachable, exemplary. Mrs. Slade and Mrs. Ansley had lived opposite each other—actually as well as figuratively—for years. When the drawing-room curtains in No. 20 East 73rd Street were renewed, No. 23, across the way, was always aware of it. And of all the movings, buyings, travels, anniversaries, illnesses—the tame chronicle of an estimable pair. Little of it escaped Mrs. Slade. But she had grown bored with it by the time her husband made his big *coup* in Wall Street, and when they bought in upper Park Avenue had already begun to think: "I'd rather live opposite a speakeasy for a change; at least one might see it raided." The idea of seeing Grace raided was so amusing that (before the move) she launched it at a woman's lunch. It made a hit, and went the rounds—she sometimes wondered if it had crossed the street, and reached Mrs. Ansley. She hoped not, but didn't much mind. Those were the days when respectability was at a discount, and it did the irreproachable no harm to laugh at them a little.

A few years later, and not many months apart, both ladies lost their husbands. There was an appropriate exchange of wreaths and condolences, and a brief renewal of intimacy in the half-shadow of their mourning; and now, after another interval, they had run across each other in Rome, at the same hotel, each of them the modest appendage of a salient daughter. The similarity of their lot had again drawn them together, lending itself to mild jokes, and the mutual confession that, if in old days it must have been tiring to "keep up" with daughters, it was now, at times, a little dull not to.

No doubt, Mrs. Slade reflected, she felt her unemployment more than poor Grace ever would. It was a big drop from being the wife of Delphin Slade to being his widow. She had always regarded herself (with a certain conjugal pride) as his equal in social gifts, as contributing her full share to the making of the exceptional couple they were: but the difference after his death was irremediable. As the wife of the famous corporation lawyer, always with an international case or two on hand, every day brought its exciting and unexpected obligation: the impromptu entertaining of eminent colleagues from abroad, the hurried dashes on legal business to London, Paris or Rome, where the entertaining was so handsomely reciprocated; the amusement of hearing in her wake: "What, that handsome woman with the good clothes and the eyes is Mrs. Slade—*the* Slade's wife? Really? Generally the wives of celebrities are such frumps."

Yes; being *the* Slade's widow was a dullish business after that. In living up to such a husband all her faculties had been engaged; now she had only her daughter to live up to, for the son who seemed to have inherited his father's gifts had died suddenly in boyhood. She had fought through that agony because her husband was there, to be helped and to help; now, after the father's death, the thought of the boy had become unbearable. There was nothing left but to mother her daughter; and dear Jenny was such a perfect daughter that she needed no excessive mothering. "Now with Babs Ansley I don't know that I *should* be so quiet," Mrs. Slade sometimes half-enviously reflected; but Jenny, who was younger than her brilliant friend, was that rare accident, an extremely pretty girl who somehow made youth and prettiness seem as safe as their absence. It was all perplexing—and to Mrs. Slade a little boring. She wished that Jenny would fall in love—with the wrong man, even; that she might have to be watched, out-maneuvered, rescued. And instead, it was Jenny who watched her mother, kept her out of drafts, made sure that she had taken her tonic. . . .

Mrs. Ansley was much less articulate than her friend, and her mental portrait of Mrs. Slade was slighter, and drawn with fainter touches. "Alida Slade's awfully brilliant; but not as brilliant as she thinks," would have summed it up; though she would have added, for the enlightenment of strangers, that Mrs. Slade had been an extremely dashing girl; much more so than her daughter, who was pretty, of course, and clever in a way, but had none of her mother's—well, "vividness," someone had once called it. Mrs. Ansley would take up current words like this, and cite them in quotation marks, as unheard-of audacities. No; Jenny was not like her mother. Sometimes Mrs. Ansley thought Alida Slade was disappointed; on the whole she had had a sad life. Full of failures and mistakes; Mrs. Ansley had always been rather sorry for her. . . .

So these two ladies visualized each other, each through the wrong end of her little telescope.

2

For a long time they continued to sit side by side without speaking. It seemed as though, to both, there was a relief in laying down their somewhat futile activities in the presence of the vast Memento Mori[1] which faced them. Mrs. Slade sat quite still, her eyes fixed on the golden slope of the Palace of the Caesars, and after a while Mrs. Ansley ceased to fidget with her bag, and she too sank into meditation. Like many intimate friends, the two ladies had never before had occasion to be silent together, and Mrs. Ansley was slightly embarrassed by what seemed, after so many years, a new stage in their intimacy, and one with which she did not yet know how to deal.

Suddenly the air was full of that deep clangor of bells which periodically covers Rome with a roof of silver. Mrs. Slade glanced at her wrist-watch. "Five o'clock already," she said, as though surprised.

Mrs. Ansley suggested interrogatively: "There's bridge at the Embassy at five." For a long time Mrs. Slade did not answer. She appeared to be lost in contemplation, and Mrs. Ansley thought the remark had escaped her.

---

1. Reminder, memory of death.

But after a while she said, as if speaking out of a dream: "Bridge, did you say? Not unless you want to. . . . But I don't think I will, you know."

"Oh, no," Mrs. Ansley hastened to assure her. "I don't care to at all. It's so lovely here; and so full of old memories, as you say." She settled herself in her chair, and almost furtively drew forth her knitting. Mrs. Slade took sideway note of this activity, but her own beautifully cared-for hands remained motionless on her knee.

"I was just thinking," she said slowly, "what different things Rome stands for to each generation of travelers. To our grandmothers, Roman fever; to our mothers, sentimental dangers—how we used to be guarded! —to our daughters, no more dangers than the middle of Main Street. They don't know it—but how much they're missing!"

The long golden light was beginning to pale, and Mrs. Ansley lifted her knitting a little closer to her eyes. "Yes; how we were guarded!"

"I always used to think," Mrs. Slade continued, "that our mothers had a much more difficult job than our grandmothers. When Roman fever stalked the streets it must have been comparatively easy to gather in the girls at the danger hour; but when you and I were young, with such beauty calling us, and the spice of disobedience thrown in, and no worse risk than catching cold during the cool hour after sunset, the mothers used to be put to it to keep us in—didn't they?"

She turned again toward Mrs. Ansley, but the latter had reached a delicate point in her knitting. "One, two, three—slip two; yes, they must have been," she assented, without looking up.

Mrs. Slade's eyes rested on her with a deepened attention. "She can knit—in the face of *this!* How like her. . . ."

Mrs. Slade leaned back, brooding, her eyes ranging from the ruins which faced her to the long green hollow of the Forum, the fading glow of the church fronts beyond it, and the outlying immensity of the Colosseum. Suddenly she thought: "It's all very well to say that our girls have done away with sentiment and moonlight. But if Babs Ansley isn't out to catch that young aviator—the one who's a Marchese—then I don't know anything. And Jenny has no chance beside her. I know that too. I wonder if that's why Grace Ansley likes the two girls to go everywhere together? My poor Jenny as a foil—!" Mrs. Slade gave a hardly audible laugh, and at the sound Mrs. Ansley dropped her knitting.

"Yes—?"

"I—oh, nothing. I was only thinking how your Babs carries everything before her. That Campolieri boy is one of the best matches in Rome. Don't look so innocent, my dear—you know he is. And I was wondering, ever so respectfully, you understand . . . wondering how two such exemplary characters as you and Horace had managed to produce anything quite so dynamic." Mrs. Slade laughed again, with a touch of asperity.

Mrs. Ansley's hands lay inert across her needles. She looked straight out at the great accumulated wreckage of passion and splendor at her feet.

But her small profile was almost expressionless. At length she said: "I think you overrate Babs, my dear."

Mrs. Slade's tone grew easier. "No; I don't. I appreciate her. And perhaps envy you. Oh, my girl's perfect; if I were a chronic invalid I'd—well, I think I'd rather be in Jenny's hands. There must be times . . . but there! I always wanted a brilliant daughter . . . and never quite understood why I got an angel instead."

Mrs. Ansley echoed her laugh in a faint murmur. "Babs is an angel too."

"Of course—of course! But she's got rainbow wings. Well, they're wandering by the sea with their young men; and here we sit . . . and it all brings back the past a little too acutely."

Mrs. Ansley had resumed her knitting. One might almost have imagined (if one had known her less well, Mrs. Slade reflected) that, for her also, too many memories rose from the lengthening shadows of those august ruins. But no; she was simply absorbed in her work. What was there for her to worry about? She knew that Babs would almost certainly come back engaged to the extremely eligible Campolieri. "And she'll sell the New York house, and settle down near them in Rome, and never be in their way . . . she's much too tactful. But she'll have an excellent cook, and just the right people in for bridge and cocktails . . . and a perfectly peaceful old age among her grandchildren."

Mrs. Slade broke off this prophetic flight with a recoil of self-disgust. There was no one of whom she had less right to think unkindly than of Grace Ansley. Would she never cure herself of envying her? Perhaps she had begun too long ago.

She stood up and leaned against the parapet, filling her troubled eyes with the tranquilizing magic of the hour. But instead of tranquilizing her the sight seemed to increase her exasperation. Her gaze turned toward the Colosseum. Already its golden flank was drowned in purple shadow, and above it the sky curved crystal clear, without light or color. It was the moment when afternoon and evening hang balanced in mid-heaven.

Mrs. Slade turned back and laid her hand on her friend's arm. The gesture was so abrupt that Mrs. Ansley looked up, startled.

"The sun's set. You're not afraid, my dear?"

"Afraid—?"

"Of Roman fever or pneumonia? I remember how ill you were that winter. As a girl you had a very delicate throat, hadn't you?"

"Oh, we're all right up here. Down below, in the Forum, it does get deathly cold, all of a sudden . . . but not here."

"Ah, of course you know because you had to be so careful." Mrs. Slade turned back to the parapet. She thought: "I must make one more effort not to hate her." Aloud she said: "Whenever I look at the Forum from up here, I remember that story about a great-aunt of yours, wasn't she? A dreadfully wicked great-aunt?"

"Oh, yes; great-aunt Harriet. The one who was supposed to have sent her young sister out to the Forum after sunset to gather a night-blooming flower for her album. All our great-aunts and grandmothers used to have albums of dried flowers."

Mrs. Slade nodded. "But she really sent her because they were in love with the same man—"

"Well, that was the family tradition. They said Aunt Harriet confessed it years afterward. At any rate, the poor little sister caught the fever and died. Mother used to frighten us with the story when we were children."

"And you frightened *me* with it, that winter when you and I were here as girls. The winter I was engaged to Delphin."

Mrs. Ansley gave a faint laugh. "Oh, did I? Really frighten you? I don't believe you're easily frightened."

"Not often; but I was then. I was easily frightened because I was too happy. I wonder if you know what that means?"

"I—yes . . . ." Mrs. Ansley faltered.

"Well, I suppose that was why the story of your wicked aunt made such an impression on me. And I thought: 'There's no more Roman fever, but the Forum is deathly cold after sunset—especially after a hot day. And the Colosseum's even colder and damper.' "

"The Colosseum—?"

"Yes. It wasn't easy to get in, after the gates were locked for the night. Far from easy. Still, in those days it could be managed; it *was* managed, often. Lovers met there who couldn't meet elsewhere. You knew that?"

"I—I dare say. I don't remember."

"You don't remember? You don't remember going to visit some ruins or other one evening, just after dark, and catching a bad chill? You were supposed to have gone to see the moon rise. People always said that expedition was what caused your illness."

There was a moment's silence; then Mrs. Ansley rejoined: "Did they? It was all so long ago."

"Yes. And you got well again—so it didn't matter. But I suppose it struck your friends—the reason given for your illness, I mean—because everybody knew you were so prudent on account of your throat, and your mother took such care of you. . . . You *had* been out late sight-seeing, hadn't you, that night?"

"Perhaps I had. The most prudent girls aren't always prudent. What made you think of it now?"

Mrs. Slade seemed to have no answer ready. But after a moment she broke out: "Because I simply can't bear it any longer—!"

Mrs. Ansley lifted her head quickly. Her eyes were wide and very pale. "Can't bear what?"

"Why—your not knowing that I've always known why you went."

"Why I went—?"

"Yes. You think I'm bluffing, don't you? Well, you went to meet the man I was engaged to—and I can repeat every word of the letter that took you there."

While Mrs. Slade spoke Mrs. Ansley had risen unsteadily to her feet. Her bag, her knitting and gloves, slid in a panic-stricken heap to the ground. She looked at Mrs. Slade as though she were looking at a ghost.

"No, no—don't," she faltered out.

"Why not? Listen, if you don't believe me. 'My one darling, things can't go on like this. I must see you alone. Come to the Colosseum immediately after dark tomorrow. There will be somebody to let you in. No one whom you need fear will suspect'—but perhaps you've forgotten what the letter said?"

Mrs. Ansley met the challenge with an unexpected composure. Steadying herself against the chair she looked at her friend, and replied: "No; I know it by heart too."

"And the signature? 'Only *your* D.S.' Was that it? I'm right, am I? That was the letter that took you out that evening after dark?"

Mrs. Ansley was still looking at her. It seemed to Mrs. Slade that a slow struggle was going on behind the voluntarily controlled mask of her small quiet face. "I shouldn't have thought she had herself so well in hand," Mrs. Slade reflected, almost resentfully. But at this moment Mrs. Ansley spoke. "I don't know how you knew. I burnt that letter at once."

"Yes; you would, naturally—you're so prudent!" The sneer was open now. "And if you burnt the letter you're wondering how on earth I know what was in it. That's it, isn't it?"

Mrs. Slade waited, but Mrs. Ansley did not speak.

"Well, my dear, I know what was in that letter because I wrote it!"

"You wrote it?"

"Yes."

The two women stood for a minute staring at each other in the last golden light. Then Mrs. Ansley dropped back into her chair. "Oh," she murmured, and covered her face with her hands.

Mrs. Slade waited nervously for another word or movement. None came, and at length she broke out: "I horrify you."

Mrs. Ansley's hands dropped to her knee. The face they uncovered was streaked with tears. "I wasn't thinking of you. I was thinking—it was the only letter I ever had from him!"

"And I wrote it. Yes; I wrote it! But I was the girl he was engaged to. Did you happen to remember that?"

Mrs. Ansley's head drooped again. "I'm not trying to excuse myself . . . I remembered. . . ."

"And still you went?"

"Still I went."

Mrs. Slade stood looking down on the small bowed figure at her side. The flame of her wrath had already sunk, and she wondered why she had ever thought there would be any satisfaction in inflicting so purposeless a wound on her friend. But she had to justify herself.

"You do understand? I'd found out—and I hated you, hated you. I knew you were in love with Delphin—and I was afraid; afraid of you, of your quiet ways, your sweetness . . . your . . . well, I wanted you out of the way, that's all. Just for a few weeks; just till I was sure of him. So in a blind fury I wrote that letter . . . I don't know why I'm telling you now."

"I suppose," said Mrs. Ansley slowly, "it's because you've always gone on hating me."

"Perhaps. Or because I wanted to get the whole thing off my mind." She paused. "I'm glad you destroyed the letter. Of course I never thought you'd die."

Mrs. Ansley relapsed into silence, and Mrs. Slade, leaning above her, was conscious of a strange sense of isolation, of being cut off from the warm current of human communion. "You think me a monster!"

"I don't know. . . . It was the only letter I had, and you say he didn't write it?"

"Ah, how you care for him still!"

"I cared for that memory," said Mrs. Ansley.

Mrs. Slade continued to look down at her. She seemed physically reduced by the blow—as if, when she got up, the wind might scatter her like a puff of dust. Mrs. Slade's jealousy suddenly leapt up again at the sight. All these years the woman had been living on that letter. How she must have loved him, to treasure the mere memory of its ashes! The letter of the man her friend was engaged to. Wasn't it she who was the monster?

"You tried your best to get him away from me, didn't you? But you failed; and I kept him. That's all."

"Yes. That's all."

"I wish now I hadn't told you. I'd no idea you'd feel about it as you do; I thought you'd be amused. It all happened so long ago, as you say; and you must do me the justice to remember that I had no reason to think you'd ever taken it seriously. How could I, when you were married to Horace Ansley two months afterward? As soon as you could get out of bed your mother rushed you off to Florence and married you. People were rather surprised —they wondered at its being done so quickly; but I thought I knew. I had an idea you did it out of *pique*—to be able to say you'd got ahead of Delphin and me. Girls have such silly reasons for doing the most serious things. And your marrying so soon convinced me that you'd never really cared."

"Yes. I suppose it would," Mrs. Ansley assented.

The clear heaven overhead was emptied of all its gold. Dusk spread over it, abruptly darkening the Seven Hills. Here and there lights began to twinkle through the foliage at their feet. Steps were coming and going on the deserted terrace—waiters looking out of the doorway at the head of the stairs, then reappearing with trays and napkins and flasks of wine. Tables were moved, chairs straightened. A feeble string of electric lights flickered out. Some vases of faded flowers were carried away, and brought back replenished. A stout lady in a dust coat suddenly appeared, asking in broken Italian if anyone had seen the elastic band which held together her tattered Baedeker.[2] She poked with her stick under the table at which she had lunched, the waiters assisting.

The corner where Mrs. Slade and Mrs. Ansley sat was still shadowy and deserted. For a long time neither of them spoke. At length Mrs. Slade began again: "I suppose I did it as a sort of joke—"

"A joke?"

"Well, girls are ferocious sometimes, you know. Girls in love especially. And I remember laughing to myself all that evening at the idea that you were waiting around there in the dark, dodging out of sight, listening for every sound, trying to get in—Of course I was upset when I heard you were so ill afterward."

Mrs. Ansley had not moved for a long time. But now she turned slowly toward her companion. "But I didn't wait. He'd arranged everything. He was there. We were let in at once," she said.

Mrs. Slade sprang up from her leaning position. "Delphin there? They let you in?—Ah, now you're lying!" she burst out with violence.

Mrs. Ansley's voice grew clearer, and full of surprise. "But of course he was there. Naturally he came—"

"Came? How did he know he'd find you there? You must be raving!"

Mrs. Ansley hesitated, as though reflecting. "But I answered the letter. I told him I'd be there. So he came."

Mrs. Slade flung her hands up to her face. "Oh, God—you answered! I never thought of your answering. . . ."

"It's odd you never thought of it, if you wrote the letter."

"Yes. I was blind with rage."

Mrs. Ansley rose, and drew her fur scarf about her. "It is cold here. We'd better go. . . . I'm sorry for you," she said, as she clasped the fur about her throat.

The unexpected words sent a pang through Mrs. Slade. "Yes; we'd better go." She gathered up her bag and cloak. "I don't know why you should be sorry for me," she muttered.

Mrs. Ansley stood looking away from her toward the dusky secret mass of the Colosseum. "Well—because I didn't have to wait that night."

Mrs. Slade gave an unquiet laugh. "Yes; I was beaten there. But I oughtn't to begrudge it to you, I suppose. At the end of all these years. After all, I had everything; I had him for twenty-five years. And you had nothing but that one letter that he didn't write."

Mrs. Ansley was again silent. At length she turned toward the door of the terrace. She took a step, and turned back, facing her companion.

"I had Barbara," she said, and began to move ahead of Mrs. Slade toward the stairway.

1936

---

2. A guidebook named after Karl Baedeker (1801–1859), a publisher of guidebooks to Europe.

Further Reading

Wharton, Edith. "Telling a Short Story." *The Writing of Fiction*. New York: Scribner's, 1925. 31–58. • Lewis, R. B. W. "A Writer of Short Stories." *Modern Critical Views: Edith Wharton*. Ed. Harold Bloom. New York: Chelsea, 1986. 9–28. • Hutchison, Percy. "Mrs. Wharton's New Stories and Other Recent Works of Fiction." *New York Times Book Review* 26 Apr. 1936: 6. • Petry, Alice Hall. "A Twist of Crimson Silk: Edith Wharton's 'Roman Fever.'" *Studies in Short Fiction* 24.2 (Spring 1987): 163–66.

For practical reasons, few short stories involve a span of years as long as that Edith Wharton covers in "Roman Fever," and few undertake as much development of the principal characters. The story appears to press the limits of what can be done in short fiction, and it is thus worthwhile to see Wharton's own assessment of what those limits are.

Edith Wharton: On the Difficulty of Moral Drama in the Short Story

There are at least two reasons why a subject should find expression in novel-form rather than as a tale; but neither is based on the number of what may be conveniently called incidents, or external happenings, which the narrative contains. There are novels of action which might be condensed into short stories without the loss of their distinguishing qualities. The marks of the subject requiring a longer development are, first, the gradual unfolding of the inner life of its characters, and secondly the need of producing in the reader's mind the sense of the lapse of time. Outward events of the most varied and exciting nature may without loss of probability be crowded into a few hours, but moral dramas usually have their roots deep in the soul, their rise far back in time; and the suddenest-seeming clash in which they culminate should be led up to step by step if it is to explain and justify itself.

There are cases, indeed, when the short story may make use of the moral drama at its culmination. If the incident dealt with be one which a single retrospective flash sufficiently lights up, it is qualified for use as a short story; but if the subject be so complex, and its successive phases so interesting, as to justify elaboration, the lapse of time must necessarily be suggested, and the novel-form becomes appropriate.

JAMES JOYCE

(1882–1941)

ARABY

North Richmond Street, being blind, was a quiet street except at the hour when the Christian Brothers' School set the boys free. An uninhabited house of two storeys stood at the blind end, detached from its neighbours in a square ground. The other houses of the street, conscious of decent lives within them, gazed at one another with brown imperturbable faces.

The former tenant of our house, a priest, had died in the back drawing-room. Air, musty from having been long enclosed, hung in all the rooms, and the waste room behind the kitchen was littered with old useless papers. Among these I found a few paper-covered books, the pages of which were curled and damp: *The Abbot,* by Walter Scott, *The Devout Communicant* and *The Memoirs of Vidocq.* I liked the last best because its leaves were yellow. The wild garden behind the house contained a central apple-tree and a few straggling bushes under one of which I found the late tenant's rusty bicycle-pump. He had been a very charitable priest; in his will he had left all his money to institutions and the furniture of his house to his sister.

When the short days of winter came dusk fell before we had well eaten our dinners. When we met in the street the houses had grown sombre. The space of sky above us was the colour of ever-changing violet and towards it the lamps of the street lifted their feeble lanterns. The cold air stung us and we played till our bodies glowed. Our shouts echoed in the silent street. The career of our play brought us through the dark muddy lanes behind the houses where we ran the gauntlet of the rough tribes from the cottages, to the back doors of the dark dripping gardens where odours arose from the ashpits, to the dark odorous stables where a coachman smoothed and combed the horse or shook music from the buckled harness. When we returned to the street, light from the kitchen windows had filled the areas. If my uncle was seen turning the corner we hid in the shadow until we had seen him safely housed. Or if Mangan's sister came out on the doorstep to call her brother in to his tea we watched her from our shadow peer up and down the street. We waited to see whether she would remain or go in and, if she remained, we left our shadow and walked up to Mangan's steps resign-edly. She was waiting for us, her figure defined by the light from the half-opened door. Her brother always teased her before he obeyed and I stood by the railings looking at her. Her dress swung as she moved her body and the soft rope of her hair tossed from side to side.

Every morning I lay on the floor in the front parlour watching her door. The blind was pulled down to within an inch of the sash so that I could not be seen. When she came out on the doorstep my heart leaped. I ran to the hall, seized my books and followed her. I kept her brown figure always in my eye and, when we came near the point at which our ways diverged, I quickened my pace and passed her. This happened morning after morning. I had never spoken to her, except for a few casual words, and yet her name was like a summons to all my foolish blood.

Her image accompanied me even in places the most hostile to romance. On Saturday evenings when my aunt went marketing I had to go to carry some of the parcels. We walked through the flaring streets, jostled by drunken men and bargaining women, amid the curses of labourers, the shrill litanies of shop-boys who stood on guard by the barrels of pigs' cheeks, the nasal chanting of street-singers, who sang a *come-all-you* about O'Donovan Rossa, or a ballad about the troubles in our native land. The noises converged in a single sensation of life for me: I imagined that I bore my chalice[1] safely through a throng of foes. Her name sprang to my lips at moments in strange prayers and praises which I myself did not understand. My eyes were often full of tears (I could not tell why) and at times a flood from my heart seemed to pour itself out into my bosom. I thought little of the future. I did not know whether I would ever speak to her or not or, if I spoke to her, how I could tell her of my confused adoration. But my body was like a harp and her words and gestures were like fingers running upon the wires.

One evening I went into the back drawing-room in which the priest had died. It was a dark rainy evening and there was no sound in the house. Through one of the broken panes I heard the rain impinge upon the earth, the fine incessant needles of water playing in the sodden beds. Some distant lamp or lighted window gleamed below me. I was thankful that I could see so little. All my senses seemed to desire to veil themselves and, feeling that I was about to slip from them, I pressed the palms of my hands together until they trembled, murmuring: "*O love! O love!*" many times.

At last she spoke to me. When she addressed the first words to me I was so confused that I did not know what to answer. She asked me was I going to *Araby*. I forgot whether I answered yes or no. It would be a splendid bazaar, she said she would love to go.

"And why can't you?" I asked.

While she spoke she turned a silver bracelet round and round her wrist. She could not go, she said, because there would be a retreat that week in her convent. Her brother and two other boys were fighting for their caps and I was alone at the railings. She held one of the spikes, bowing her head towards me. The light from the lamp opposite our door caught the white curve of her neck, lit up her hair that rested there and, falling, lit up the hand upon the railing. It fell over one side of her dress and caught the white border of a petticoat, just visible as she stood at ease.

"It's well for you," she said.

"If I go," I said, "I will bring you something."

---

1. A cup or goblet, especially one used to contain the consecrated wine of the Eucharist.

What innumerable follies laid waste my waking and sleeping thoughts after that evening! I wished to annihilate the tedious intervening days. I chafed against the work of school. At night in my bedroom and by day in the classroom her image came between me and the page I strove to read. The syllables of the word *Araby* were called to me through the silence in which my soul luxuriated and cast an Eastern enchantment over me. I asked for leave to go to the bazaar on Saturday night. My aunt was surprised and hoped it was not some Freemason affair. I answered few questions in class. I watched my master's face pass from amiability to sternness; he hoped I was not beginning to idle. I could not call my wandering thoughts together. I had hardly any patience with the serious work of life which, now that it stood between me and my desire, seemed to me child's play, ugly monotonous child's play.

On Saturday morning I reminded my uncle that I wished to go to the bazaar in the evening. He was fussing at the hallstand, looking for the hatbrush, and answered me curtly:

"Yes, boy, I know."

As he was in the hall I could not go into the front parlour and lie at the window. I left the house in bad humour and walked slowly toward the school. The air was pitilessly raw and already my heart misgave me.

When I came home to dinner my uncle had not yet been home. Still it was early. I sat staring at the clock for some time and, when its ticking began to irritate me, I left the room. I mounted the staircase and gained the upper part of the house. The high cold empty gloomy rooms liberated me and I went from room to room singing. From the front window I saw my companions playing below in the street. Their cries reached me weakened and indistinct and, leaning my forehead against the cool glass, I looked over at the dark house where she lived. I may have stood there for an hour, seeing nothing but the brown-clad figure cast by my imagination, touched discreetly by the lamplight at the curved neck, at the hand upon the railings and at the border below the dress.

When I came downstairs again I found Mrs. Mercer sitting at the fire. She was an old garrulous woman, a pawnbroker's widow, who collected used stamps for some pious purpose. I had to endure the gossip of the teatable. The meal was prolonged beyond an hour and still my uncle did not come. Mrs. Mercer stood up to go: she was sorry she couldn't wait any longer, but it was after eight o'clock and she did not like to be out late, as the night air was bad for her. When she had gone I began to walk up and down the room, clenching my fists. My aunt said:

"I'm afraid you may put off your bazaar for this night of Our Lord."

At nine o'clock I heard my uncle's latchkey in the halldoor. I heard him talking to himself and heard the hallstand rocking when it had received the weight of his overcoat. I could interpret these signs. When he was midway through his dinner I asked him to give me the money to go to the bazaar. He had forgotten.

"The people are in bed and after their first sleep now," he said.

I did not smile. My aunt said to him energetically:

"Can't you give him the money and let him go? You've kept him late enough as it is."

My uncle said he was very sorry he had forgotten. He said he believed in the old saying: "All work and no play makes Jack a dull boy." He asked me where I was going and, when I had told him a second time he asked me did I know *The Arab's Farewell to his Steed*. When I left the kitchen he was about to recite the opening lines of the piece to my aunt.

I held a florin tightly in my hand as I strode down Buckingham Street towards the station. The sight of the streets thronged with buyers and glaring with gas recalled to me the purpose of my journey. I took my seat in a third-class carriage of a deserted train. After an intolerable delay the train moved out of the station slowly. It crept onward among ruinous houses and over the twinkling river. At Westland Row Station a crowd of people pressed to the carriage doors; but the porters moved them back, saying that it was a special train for the bazaar. I remained alone in the bare carriage. In a few minutes the train drew up beside an improvised wooden platform. I passed out on to the road and saw by the lighted dial of a clock that it was ten minutes to ten. In front of me was a large building which displayed the magical name.

I could not find any sixpenny entrance and, fearing that the bazaar would be closed, I passed in quickly through a turnstile, handing a shilling to a weary-looking man. I found myself in a big hall girdled at half its height by a gallery. Nearly all the stalls were closed and the greater part of the hall was in darkness. I recognised a silence like that which pervades a church after a service. I walked into the centre of the bazaar timidly. A few people were gathered about the stalls which were still open. Before a curtain, over which the words *Café Chantant* were written in coloured lamps, two men were counting money on a salver. I listened to the fall of the coins.

Remembering with difficulty why I had come I went over to one of the stalls and examined porcelain vases and flowered tea-sets. At the door of the stall a young lady was talking and laughing with two young gentlemen. I remarked their English accents and listened vaguely to their conversation.

"O, I never said such a thing!"

"O, but you did!"

"O, but I didn't!"

"Didn't she say that?"

"Yes. I heard her."

"O, there's a . . . fib!"

Observing me the young lady came over and asked me did I wish to buy anything. The tone of her voice was not encouraging; she seemed to have spoken to me out of a sense of duty. I looked humbly at the great jars that stood like eastern guards at either side of the dark entrance to the stall and murmured:

"No, thank you."

The young lady changed the position of one of the vases and went back to the two young men. They began to talk of the same subject. Once or twice the young lady glanced at me over her shoulder.

I lingered before her stall, though I knew my stay was useless, to make my interest in her wares seem the more real. Then I turned away slowly and walked down the middle of the bazaar. I allowed the two pennies to fall against the sixpence in my pocket. I heard a voice call from one end of the gallery that the light was out. The upper part of the hall was now completely dark.

Gazing up into the darkness I saw myself as a creature driven and derided by vanity; and my eyes burned with anguish and anger.

1914

Further Reading

Garrett, Peter K. Introduction. *Twentieth Century Interpretations of Dubliners.* Ed. Garrett. Englewood Cliffs: Prentice, 1968. 1–17. • Beck, Warren. "Araby." *Joyce's Dubliners: Substance, Vision, and Art.* Durham: Duke UP, 1969. 96–109. • Collins, Ben L. "'Araby' and the 'Extended Simile.'" *Twentieth Century Interpretations of Dubliners.* Ed. Peter K. Garrett. Englewood Cliffs: Prentice, 1968. 93–99. • Stone, H. "'Araby' and the Writings of James Joyce." *Antioch Review* 25.3 (Fall 1965): 375–410. • Roberts, R. P. "'Araby' and the Palimpsest of Criticism, or Through a Glass Eye Darkly." *Antioch Review* 26.4 (Winter 1966–67): 469–89.

James Joyce's fiction often presents moments of sudden insight, when ordinary things are suddenly seen fresh and take on new significance. In Joyce's novel A Portrait of the Artist as a Young Man, *the protagonist Stephen Dedalus attempts to define philosophical terms from St. Thomas Aquinas by referring to such moments. His definitions shed some light on the consciousness of the protagonist in "Araby."*

James Joyce: Stephen Dedalus on "Claritas" in a Work of Art

The connotation of the word—Stephen said—is rather vague. Aquinas uses a term which seems to be inexact. It baffled me for a long time. It would lead you to believe that he had in mind symbolism or idealism, the supreme quality of beauty being a light from some other world, the idea of which the matter was but the shadow, the reality of which it was but the symbol. I thought he might mean that *claritas* was the artistic discovery and representation of the divine purpose in anything or a force of generalization which would make the esthetic image a universal one, make it outshine its proper conditions. But that is literary talk. I understand it so. When you have apprehended that basket as one thing and have then analysed it according to its form and apprehended it as a thing you make the only synthesis which is logically and esthetically permissible. You see that it is that thing which it is and no other thing. The radiance of which he speaks in the scholastic *quidditas,* the *whatness* of a thing. This supreme quality is felt by the artist when the esthetic image is first conceived in his imagination. The mind in that mysterious instant Shelley likened beautifully to a fading coal. The instant wherein that supreme quality of beauty, the clear radiance of the esthetic image, is apprehended luminously by the mind which has been arrested by its wholeness and fascinated by its harmony is the luminous silent stasis of esthetic pleasure, a spiritual state very like to that cardiac condition which the Italian physiologist Luigi Galvani, using a phrase almost as beautiful as Shelley's, called the enchantment of the heart.—

VIRGINIA WOOLF

(1882–1941)

SOLID OBJECTS

The only thing that moved upon the vast semicircle of the beach was one small black spot. As it came nearer to the ribs and spine of the stranded pilchard boat, it became apparent from a certain tenuity in its blackness that this spot possessed four legs; and moment by moment it became more unmistakable that it was composed of the persons of two young men. Even thus in outline against the sand there was an unmistakable vitality in them; an indescribable vigour in the approach and withdrawal of the bodies, slight though it was, which proclaimed some violent argument issuing from the tiny mouths of the little round heads. This was corroborated on closer view by the repeated lunging of a walking-stick on the right-hand side. 'You mean to tell me. . . You actually believe . . .' thus the walking-stick on the right-hand side next the waves seemed to be asserting as it cut long straight stripes on the sand.

'Politics be damned!' issued clearly from the body on the left-hand side, and, as these words were uttered, the mouths, noses, chins, little moustaches, tweed caps, rough boots, shooting coats, and check stockings of the two speakers became clearer and clearer; the smoke of their pipes went up into the air; nothing was so solid, so living, so hard, red, hirsute and virile as these two bodies for miles and miles of sea and sandhill.

They flung themselves down by the six ribs and spine of the black pilchard boat. You know how the body seems to shake itself free from an argument, and to apologise for a mood of exaltation; flinging itself down and expressing in the looseness of its attitude a readiness to take up with something new—whatever it may be that comes next to hand. So Charles, whose stick had been slashing the beach for half a mile or so, began skimming flat pieces of slate over the water; and John, who had exclaimed 'Politics be damned!' began burrowing his fingers down, down, into the sand. As his hand went further and further beyond the wrist, so that he had to hitch his sleeve a little higher, his eyes lost their intensity, or rather the background of thought and experience which gives an inscrutable depth to the eyes of grown people disappeared, leaving only the clear transparent surface, expressing nothing but wonder, which the eyes of young children display. No doubt the act of burrowing in the sand had something to do with it. He remembered that, after digging for a little, the water oozes round your finger-tips; the hole then becomes a moat; a well; a spring; a secret channel to the sea. As he was choosing which of these things to make it, still working his fingers in the water, they curled round something hard —a full drop of solid matter—and gradually dislodged a large irregular lump, and brought it to the surface. When the sand coating was wiped off, a green tint appeared. It was a lump of glass, so thick as to be almost opaque; the smoothing of the sea had completely worn off any edge or shape, so that it was impossible to say whether it had been bottle, tumbler or window-pane; it was nothing but glass; it was almost a precious stone. You had only to enclose it in a rim of gold, or pierce it with a wire, and it became a jewel; part of a necklace, or a dull, green light upon a finger. Perhaps after all it was really a gem; something worn by a dark Princess trailing her finger in the water as she sat in the stern of the boat and listened to the slaves singing as they rowed her across the Bay. Or the oak sides of a sunk Elizabethan treasure-chest had split apart, and, rolled over and over, over and over, its emeralds had come at last to shore. John turned it in his hands; he held it to the light; he held it so that its irregular mass blotted out the body and extended right arm of his friend. The green thinned and thickened slightly as it was held against the sky or against the body. It pleased him; it puzzled him; it was so hard, so concentrated, so definite an object compared with the vague sea and the hazy shore.

Now a sigh disturbed him—profound, final, making him aware that his friend Charles had thrown all the flat stones within reach, or had come to the conclusion that it was not worth while to throw them. They ate their sandwiches side by side. When they had done, and were shaking themselves and rising to their feet, John took the lump of glass and looked at it in silence. Charles looked at it too. But he saw immediately that it was not flat, and filling his pipe he said with the energy that dismisses a foolish strain of thought,

'To return to what I was saying—'

He did not see, or if he had seen would hardly have noticed, that John after looking at the lump for a moment, as if in hesitation, slipped it inside his pocket. That impulse, too, may have been the impulse which leads a child to pick up one pebble on a path strewn with them, promising it a life of warmth and security upon the nursery mantelpiece, delighting in the sense of power and benignity which such an action confers, and believing that the heart of the stone leaps with joy when it sees itself chosen from a million like it, to enjoy this bliss instead of a life of cold and wet upon the high road. 'It might so easily have been any other of the millions of stones, but it was I, I, I!'

Whether this thought or not was in John's mind, the lump of glass had its place upon the mantelpiece, where it stood heavy upon a little pile of bills and letters, and served not only as an excellent paperweight, but also as a natural stopping place for the young man's eyes when they wandered from his book. Looked at again and again half consciously by a mind thinking of something else, any object mixes itself so profoundly with the stuff of thought that it loses its actual form and recomposes itself a little differently in an ideal shape which haunts the brain when we least expect it. So John found himself attracted to the windows of curiosity shops when he was out walking, merely because he saw something which reminded him of the lump of glass. Anything, so long as it was an object of some kind, more or less round, perhaps with a dying flame deep sunk in its mass, anything—china, glass, amber, rock, marble—even the smooth oval egg of a prehistoric bird would do. He took, also, to keeping his eyes upon the ground, especially in the neighbourhood of waste land where the household refuse is thrown away. Such objects often occurred there—thrown away, of no use to anybody, shapeless, discarded. In a few months he had collected four or five specimens that took their place upon the mantelpiece. They were useful, too, for a man who is standing for Parliament upon the brink of a brilliant career has any number of papers to keep in order—addresses to constituents, declarations of policy, appeals for subscriptions, invitations to dinner, and so on.

One day, starting from his rooms in the Temple to catch a train in order to address his constituents, his eyes rested upon a remarkable object lying half-hidden in one of those little borders of grass which edge the bases of vast legal buildings. He could only touch it with the point of his stick through the railings; but he could see that it was a piece of china of the most remarkable shape, as nearly resembling a starfish as anything—shaped, or broken accidentally, into five irregular but unmistakable points. The colouring was mainly blue, but green stripes or spots of some kind overlaid the blue, and lines of crimson gave it a richness and lustre of the most attractive kind. John was determined to possess it; but the more he pushed, the further it receded. At length he was forced to go back to his rooms and improvise a wire ring attached to the end of a stick, with which, by dint of great care and skill, he finally drew the piece of china within reach of his hands. As he seized hold of it he exclaimed in triumph. At that moment the clock struck. It was out of the question that he should keep his appointment. The meeting was held without him. But how had the piece of china been broken into this remarkable shape? A careful examination put it beyond doubt that the star shape was accidental, which made it all the more strange, and it seemed unlikely that there should be another such in existence. Set at the opposite end of the mantelpiece from the lump of glass that had been dug from the sand, it looked like a creature from another world—freakish and fantastic as a harlequin. It seemed to be pirouetting through space, winking light like a fitful star. The contrast between the china so vivid and alert, and the glass so mute and contemplative, fascinated him, and wondering and amazed he asked himself how the two came to exist in the same world, let alone to stand upon the same narrow strip of marble in the same room. The question remained unanswered.

He now began to haunt the places which are most prolific of broken china, such as pieces of waste land between railway lines, sites of demolished houses, and commons in the neighbourhood of London. But china is seldom thrown from a great height; it is one of the rarest of human actions. You have to find in conjunction a very high house, and a woman of such reckless impulse and passionate prejudice that she flings her jar or pot straight from the window without thought of who is below. Broken china was to be found in plenty, but broken in some trifling domestic accident, without purpose or character. Nevertheless, he was often astonished, as he came to go into the question more deeply, by the immense variety of shapes to be found in London alone, and there was still more cause for wonder and speculation in the differences of qualities and designs. The finest specimens he would bring home and place upon his mantelpiece, where, however, their duty was more and more of an ornamental nature, since papers needing a weight to keep them down became scarcer and scarcer.

He neglected his duties, perhaps, or discharged them absentmindedly, or his constitutents when they visited him were unfavourably impressed by the appearance of his mantelpiece. At any rate he was not elected to represent them in Parliament, and his friend Charles, taking it much to heart and hurrying to condole with him, found him so little cast down by the disaster that he could only suppose that it was too serious a matter for him to realise all at once.

In truth, John had been that day to Barnes Common, and there under a furze bush had found a very remarkable piece of iron. It was almost identical with the glass in shape, massy and globular, but so cold and heavy, so black and metallic, that it was evidently alien to the earth and had its origin in one of the dead stars or was itself the cinder of a moon. It weighed his pocket down; it weighed the mantelpiece down; it radiated cold. And yet the meteorite stood upon the same ledge with the lump of glass and the star-shaped china.

As his eyes passed from one to another, the determination to possess objects that even surpassed these tormented the young man. He devoted himself more and more resolutely to the search. It he had not been consumed by ambition and convinced that one day some newly-discovered rubbish heap would reward him, the disappointments he had suffered, let alone the fatigue and derision, would have made him give up the pursuit. Provided with a bag and a long stick fitted with an adaptable hook, he ransacked all deposits of earth; raked beneath matted tangles of scrub; searched all alleys and spaces between walls where he had learned to expect to find objects of this kind thrown away. As his standard became higher and his taste more severe the disappointments were innumerable, but always some gleam of hope, some piece of china or glass curiously marked or broken, lured him on. Day after day passed. He was no longer young. His career —that is his political career—was a thing of the past. People gave up visiting him. He was too silent to be worth asking to dinner. He never talked to anyone about his serious ambitions; their lack of understanding was apparent in their behaviour.

He leaned back in his chair now and watched Charles lift the stones on the mantelpiece a dozen times and put them down emphatically to mark what he was saying about the conduct of the Government, without once noticing their existence.

'What was the truth of it, John?' asked Charles suddenly, turning and facing him. 'What made you give it up like that all in a second?'

'I've not given it up,' John replied.

'But you've not a ghost of a chance now,' said Charles roughly.

'I don't agree with you there,' said John with conviction. Charles looked at him and was profoundly uneasy; the most extraordinary doubts possessed him; he had a queer sense that they were talking about different things. He looked round to find some relief for his horrible depression, but the disorderly appearance of the room depressed him still further. What was that stick, and the old carpet bag hanging against the wall? And then those stones? Looking at John, something fixed and distant in his expression alarmed him. He knew only too well that his mere appearance upon the platform was out of the question.

'Pretty stones,' he said as cheerfully as he could; and saying that he had an appointment to keep, he left John—for ever.

1921

Further Reading

Woolf, Virginia. "Modern Fiction." *Collected Essays.* Vol. 2. New York: Harcourt, 1967. 103–10. • Brace, Marjorie. "Worshipping Solid Objects: The Pagan World of Virginia Woolf." *Accent Anthology: Selections from "Accent, a Quarterly of New Literature 1940–1945."* Ed. Kerker Quinn and Charles Shattuck. New York: Harcourt, 1946. 489–95. • Watson, Robert A. " 'Solid Objects' as Allegory." *Virginia Woolf Miscellany* 16 (Spring 1981): 3–4. • Fleishman, Avrom. "Forms of the Woolfian Short Story." *Virginia Woolf: Re-evaluation and Continuity.* Ed. Ralph

Freedman. Berkeley: U of California P, 1980. 44–70, spec. 54–55. • Welty, Eudora. "Mirrors for Reality." *New York Times Book Review* 16 Apr. 1944: 3.

Like the impressionist painters whom she admired, Virginia Woolf was impatient with the conventions of realism, which she felt could distort reality rather than convey it accurately. Her rebellion against these conventions is manifest in both her fiction and such critical writings as her essay "Modern Fiction," from which the following passage is taken.

Virginia Woolf: On Her Rejection of Traditional Fiction

So much of the enormous labour of providing the solidity, the likeness to life, of the story is not merely labour thrown away but labour misplaced to the extent of obscuring and blotting out the light of the conception. The writer seems constrained, not by his own free will but by some powerful and unscrupulous tyrant who has him in thrall, to provide a plot, to provide comedy, tragedy, love interest, and an air of probability embalming the whole so impeccable that if all his figures were to come to life they would find themselves dressed down to the last button of their coats in the fashion of the hour. The tyrant is obeyed; the novel is done to a turn. But sometimes, more and more often as time goes by, we suspect a momentary doubt, a spasm of rebellion, as the pages fill themselves in the customary way. Is life like this? Must novels be like this?

Look within and life, it seems, is very far from being 'like this'. Examine for a moment an ordinary mind on an ordinary day. The mind receives a myriad impressions—trivial, fantastic, evanescent, or engraved with the sharpness of steel. From all sides they come, an incessant shower of innumerable atoms; and as they fall, as they shape themselves into the life of Monday or Tuesday, the accent falls differently from of old; the moment of importance came not here but there; so that, if a writer were a free man and not a slave, if he could write what he chose, not what he must, if he could base his work upon his own feeling and not upon convention, there would be no plot, no comedy, no tragedy, no love interest or catastrophe in the accepted style, and perhaps not a single button sewn on as the Bond Street tailors would have it. Life is not a series of gig-lamps symmetrically arranged; life is a luminous halo, a semi-transparent envelope surrounding us from the beginning of consciousness to the end. Is it not the task of the novelist to convey this varying, this unknown and uncircumscribed spirit, whatever aberration or complexity it may display, with as little mixture of the alien and external as possible? We are not pleading merely for courage and sincerity; we are suggesting that the proper stuff of fiction is a little other than custom would have us believe it.

FRANZ KAFKA

(1883–1924)

A HUNGER ARTIST

translated from the Russian by Willa and Edwin Muir

During these last decades the interest in professional fasting has markedly diminished. It used to pay very well to stage such great performances under one's own management, but today that is quite impossible. We live in a different world now. At one time the whole town took a lively interest in the hunger artist; from day to day of his fast the excitement mounted; everybody wanted to see him at least once a day; there were people who bought season tickets for the last few days and sat from morning till night in front of his small barred cage; even in the nighttime there were visiting hours, when the whole effect was heightened by torch flares; on fine days the cage was set out in the open air, and then it was the children's special treat to see the hunger artist; for their elders he was often just a joke that happened to be in fashion, but the children stood open-mouthed, holding each other's hands for greater security, marveling at him as he sat there pallid in black tights, with his ribs sticking out so prominently, not even on a seat but down among straw on the ground, sometimes giving a courteous nod, answering questions with a constrained smile, or perhaps stretching an arm through the bars so that one might feel how thin it was, and then again withdrawing deep into himself, paying no attention to anyone or anything, not even to the all-important striking of the clock that was the only piece of furniture in his cage, but merely staring into vacancy with half-shut eyes, now and then taking a sip from a tiny glass of water to moisten his lips.

Besides casual onlookers there were also relays of permanent watchers selected by the public, usually butchers, strangely enough, and it was their task to watch the hunger artist day and night, three of them at a time, in case he should have some secret recourse to nourishment. This was nothing but a formality, instituted to reassure the masses, for the initiates knew well enough that during his fast the artist would never in any circumstances, not even under forcible compulsion, swallow the smallest morsel of food: the honor of his profession forbade it. Not every watcher, of course, was capable of understanding this, there were often groups of night watchers who were very lax in carrying out their duties and deliberately huddled together in a retired corner to play cards with great absorption, obviously intending to give the hunger artist the chance of a little refreshment, which they supposed he could draw from some private hoard. Nothing annoyed the artist more than such watchers; they made him miserable; they made his fast seem unendurable; sometimes he mastered his feebleness sufficiently to sing during their watch for as long as he could keep going, to show them how unjust their suspicions were. But that was of little use; they only wondered at his cleverness in being able to fill his mouth even while singing. Much more to his taste were the watchers who sat close up to the bars, who were not content with the dim night lighting of the hall but focused him in the full glare of the electric pocket torch given them by the impresario. The harsh light did not trouble him at all, in any case he could never sleep properly, and he could always drowse a little, whatever the light, at any hour, even when the hall was thronged with noisy onlookers. He was quite happy at the prospect of spending a sleepless night with such watchers; he was ready to exchange jokes with them, to tell them stories out of his nomadic life, anything at all to keep them awake and demonstrate to them again that he had no eatables in his cage and that he was fasting as not one of them could fast. But his happiest moment was when the morning came and an enormous breakfast was brought them, at his expense, on which they flung themselves with the keen appetite of healthy men after a weary night of wakefulness. Of course there were people who argued that this breakfast was an unfair attempt to bribe the watchers, but that was going rather too far, and when they were invited to take on a night's vigil without a breakfast, merely for the sake of the cause, they made themselves scarce, although they stuck stubbornly to their suspicions.

Such suspicions, anyhow, were a necessary accompaniment to the profession of fasting. No one could possibly watch the hunger artist continuously, day and night, and so no one could produce first-hand evidence that the fast had really been rigorous and continuous; only the artist himself could know that, he was therefore bound to be the sole completely satisfied spectator of his own fast. Yet for other reasons he was never satisfied; it was not perhaps mere fasting that had brought him to such skeleton thinness that many people had regretfully to keep away from his exhibitions, because the sight of him was too much for them, perhaps it was dissatisfaction with himself that had worn him down. For he alone knew, what no other initiate knew, how easy it was to fast. It was the easiest thing in the world. He made no secret of this, yet people did not believe him, at the best they set him down as modest, most of them, however, thought he was out for publicity or else was some kind of cheat who found it easy to fast because he had discovered a way of making it easy, and then had the impudence to admit the fact, more or less. He had to put up with all that, and in the course of time had got used to it, but his inner dissatisfaction always rankled, and never yet, after any term of fasting—this must be granted to his credit—had he left the cage of his own free will. The longest period of fasting was fixed by his impresario at forty days, beyond that term he was not allowed to go, not even in great cities, and there was good reason for it, too. Experience had proved that for about forty days the interest of the public could be stimulated by a steadily increasing pressure of advertisement, but after that the town began to lose interest, sympathetic support began notably to fall off; there were of course local variations as between one town and another or one country and another, but as a general rule forty days marked the limit.

So on the fortieth day the flower-bedecked cage was opened, enthusiastic spectators filled the hall, a military band played, two doctors entered the cage to measure the results of the fast, which were announced through a megaphone, and finally two young ladies appeared, blissful at having been selected for the honor, to help the hunger artist down the few steps leading to a small table on which was spread a carefully chosen invalid repast. And at this very moment the artist always turned stubborn. True, he would entrust his bony arms to the outstretched helping hands of the ladies bending over him, but stand up he would not. Why stop fasting at this particular moment, after forty days of it? He had held out for a long time, an illimitably long time; why stop now, when he was in his best fasting form, or rather, not yet quite in his best fasting form? Why should he be cheated of the fame he would get for fasting longer, for being not only the record hunger artist of all time, which presumably he was already, but for beating his own record by a performance beyond human imagination, since he felt that there were no limits to his capacity for fasting? His public pretended to admire him so much, why should it have so little patience with him; if he could endure fasting longer, why shouldn't the public endure it? Besides, he was tired, he was comfortable sitting in the straw, and now he was supposed to lift himself to his full height and go down to a meal the very thought of which gave him a nausea that only the presence of the ladies kept him from betraying, and even that with an effort. And he looked up into the eyes of the ladies who were apparently so friendly and in reality so cruel, and shook his head, which felt too heavy on its strengthless neck. But then there happened yet again what always happened. The impresario came forward, without a word—for the band made speech impossible—lifted his arms in the air above the artist, as if inviting Heaven to look down upon its creature here in the straw, this suffering martyr, which indeed he was, although in quite another sense; grasped him round the emaciated waist, with exaggerated caution, so that the frail condition he was in might be appreciated; and committed him to the care of the blenching ladies, not without secretly giving him a shaking so that his legs and body tottered and swayed. The artist now submitted completely; his head lolled on his breast as if it had landed there by chance; his body was hollowed out; his legs in a spasm of self-preservation clung close to each other at the knees, yet scraped on the ground as if it were not really solid ground, as if they were only trying to find solid ground; and the whole weight of his body, a feather-weight after all, relapsed onto one of the ladies, who, looking round for help and panting a little—this post of honor was not at all what she had expected it to be—first stretched her neck as far as she could to keep her face at least free from contact with the artist, when finding this impossible, and her more fortunate companion not coming to her aid but merely holding extended on her own trembling hand the little bunch of knucklebones that was the artist's, to the great delight of the spectators burst into tears and had to be replaced by an attendant who had long been stationed in readiness. Then came the food, a little of which the impresario managed to get between the artist's lips, while he sat in a kind of half-fainting trance, to the accompaniment of cheerful patter designed to distract the public's attention from the artist's condition; after that, a toast was drunk to the public, supposedly prompted by a whisper from the artist in the impresario's ear; the band confirmed it with a mighty flourish, the spectators melted away, and no one had any cause to be dissatisfied with the proceedings, no one except the hunger artist himself, he only, as always.

So he lived for many years, with small regular intervals of recuperation, in visible glory, honored by the world, yet in spite of that troubled in spirit, and all the more troubled because no one would take his trouble seriously. What comfort could he possibly need? What more could he possibly wish for? And if some good-natured person, feeling sorry for him, tried to console him by pointing out that his melancholy was probably caused by fasting, it could happen, especially when he had been fasting for some time, that he reacted with an outburst of fury and to the general alarm began to shake the bars of his cage like a wild animal. Yet the impresario had a way of punishing these outbreaks which he rather enjoyed putting into operation. He would apologize publicly for the artist's behavior, which was only to be excused, he admitted, because of the irritability caused by fasting; a condition hardly to be understood by well-fed people; then by natural transition he went on to mention the artist's equally incomprehensible boast that he could fast for much longer than he was doing; he praised the high ambition, the good will, the great self-denial undoubtedly implicit in such a statement; and then quite simply countered it by bringing out photographs, which were also on sale to the public, showing the artist on the fortieth day of a fast lying in bed almost dead from exhaustion. This perversion of the truth, familiar to the artist though it was, always unnerved him afresh and proved too much for him. What was a consequence of the premature ending of his fast was here presented as the cause of it! To fight against this lack of understanding, against a whole world of nonunderstanding, was impossible. Time and again in good faith he stood by the bars listening to the impresario, but as soon as the photographs appeared he always let go and sank with a groan back on to his straw, and the reassured public could once more come close and gaze at him.

A few years later when the witnesses of such scenes called them to mind, they often failed to understand themselves at all. For meanwhile the aforementioned change in public interest had set in; it seemed to happen almost overnight; there may have been profound causes for it, but who was going to bother about that; at any rate the pampered hunger artist suddenly found himself deserted one fine day by the amusement seekers, who went streaming past him to other more favored attractions. For the last time the impresario hurried him over half of Europe to discover whether the old interest might still survive here and there; all in vain; everywhere, as if by secret agreement, a positive revulsion from professional fasting was in evidence. Of course it could not really have sprung up so suddenly as all that, and many premonitory symptoms which had not been sufficiently remarked or suppressed during the rush and glitter of success now came retrospectively to mind, but it was now too late to take any countermeasures. Fasting would surely come into fashion again at some future date, yet that was no comfort for those living in the present. What, then, was the hunger artist to do? He had been applauded by thousands in his time and could hardly come down to showing himself in a street booth at village fairs, and as for adopting another profession, he was not only too old for that but too fanatically devoted to fasting. So he took leave of the impresario, his partner in an unparalleled career, and hired himself to a large circus; in order to spare his own feelings he avoided reading the conditions of his contract.

A large circus with its enormous traffic in replacing and recruiting men, animals and apparatus can always find a use for people at any time, even for a hunger artist, provided of course that he does not ask too much, and in this particular case anyhow it was not only the artist who was taken on but his famous and long-known name as well, indeed considering the peculiar nature of his performance, which was not impaired by advancing age, it could not be objected that here was an artist past his prime, no longer at the height of his professional skill, seeking a refuge in some quiet corner of a circus; on the contrary, the hunger artist averred that he could fast as well as ever, which was entirely credible, he even alleged that if he were allowed to fast as he liked, and this was at once promised him without more ado, he could astound the world by establishing a record never yet achieved, a statement which certainly provoked a smile among the other professionals, since it left out of account the change in public opinion, which the hunger artist in his zeal conveniently forgot.

He had not, however, actually lost his sense of the real situation and took it as a matter of course that he and his cage should be stationed, not in the middle of the ring as a main attraction, but outside, near the animal cages, on a site that was after all easily accessible. Large and gaily painted placards made a frame for the cage and announced what was to be seen inside it. When the public came thronging out in the intervals to see the animals, they could hardly avoid passing the hunger artist's cage and stopping there for a moment, perhaps they might even have stayed longer had not those pressing behind them in the narrow gangway, who did not understand why they should be held up on their way toward the excitements of the menagerie, made it impossible for anyone to stand gazing quietly for any length of time. And that was the reason why the hunger artist, who had of course been looking forward to these visiting hours as the main achievement of his life, began instead to shrink from them. At first he could hardly wait for the intervals; it was exhilarating to watch the crowds come streaming his way, until only too soon—not even the most obstinate self-deception, clung to almost consciously, could hold out against the fact—the conviction was borne in upon him that these people, most of them, to judge from their actions, again and again, without exception, were all on their way to the menagerie. And the first sight of them from the distance remained the best. For when they reached his cage he was at once deafened by the storm of shouting and abuse that arose from the two contending factions, which renewed themselves continuously, of those who wanted to stop and stare at him—he soon began to dislike them more than the others—not out of real interest but only out of obstinate self-assertiveness, and those who wanted to go straight on to the animals. When the first great rush was past, the stragglers came along, and these, whom nothing could have prevented from stopping to look at him as long as they had breath, raced past with long strides, hardly even glancing at him, in their haste to get to the menagerie in time. And all too rarely did it happen that he had a stroke of luck, when some father of a family fetched up before him with his children, pointed a finger at the hunger artist and explained at length what the phenomenon meant, telling stories of earlier years when he himself had watched similar but much more thrilling performances, and the children, still rather uncomprehending, since neither inside nor outside school had they been sufficiently prepared for this lesson—what did they care about fasting?— yet showed by the brightness of their intent eyes that new and better times might be coming. Perhaps, said the hunger artist to himself many a time, things would be a little better if his cage were set not quite so near the menagerie. That made it too easy for people to make their choice, to say nothing of what he suffered from the stench of the menagerie, the animals' restlessness by night, the carrying past of raw lumps of flesh for the beasts of prey, the roaring at feeding times, which depressed him continually. But he did not dare to lodge a complaint with the management; after all, he had the animals to thank for the troops of people who passed his cage, among whom there might always be one here and there to take an interest in him, and who could tell where they might seclude him if he called attention to his existence and thereby to the fact that, strictly speaking, he was only an impediment on the way to the menagerie.

A small impediment, to be sure, one that grew steadily less. People grew familiar with the strange idea that they could be expected, in times like these, to take an interest in a hunger artist, and with this familiarity the ver- dict went out against him. He might fast as much as he could, and he did so; but nothing could save him now, people passed him by. Just try to explain to anyone the art of fasting! Anyone who has no feeling for it cannot be made to understand it. The fine placards grew dirty and illegible, they were torn down; the little notice board telling the number of fast days achieved, which at first was changed carefully every day, had long stayed at the same figure, for after the first few weeks even this small task seemed pointless to the staff; and so the artist simply fasted on and on, as he had once dreamed of doing, and it was no trouble to him, just as he had always foretold, but no one counted the days, no one, not even the artist himself, knew what records he was already breaking, and his heart grew heavy. And when once in a time some leisurely passer-by stopped, made merry over the old figure on the board and spoke of swindling, that was in its way the stupidest lie ever invented by indifference and inborn malice, since it was not the hunger artist who was cheating; he was working honestly, but the world was cheating him of his reward.

Many more days went by, however, and that too came to an end. An overseer's eye fell on the cage one day and he asked the attendants why this perfectly good cage should be left standing there unused with dirty straw inside it; nobody knew, until one man, helped out by the notice board, remembered about the hunger artist. They poked into the straw with sticks and found him in it. "Are you still fasting?" asked the overseer. "When on earth do you mean to stop?" "Forgive me, everybody," whispered the hunger artist; only the overseer, who had his ear to the bars, understood him. "Of course," said the overseer, and tapped his forehead with a finger to let the attendants know what state the man was in, "we forgive you." "I always wanted you to admire my fasting," said the hunger artist. "We do admire it," said the overseer, affably. "But you shouldn't admire it," said the hunger artist. "Well, then we don't admire it," said the overseer, "but why shouldn't we admire it?" "Because I have to fast, I can't help it," said the hunger artist. "What a fellow you are," said the overseer, "and why can't you help it?" "Because," said the hunger artist, lifting his head a little and speaking, with his lips pursed, as if for a kiss, right into the overseer's ear, so that no syllable might be lost, "because I couldn't find the food I liked. If I had found it, believe me, I should have made no fuss and stuffed myself like you or anyone else." These were his last words, but in his dimming eyes remained the firm though no longer proud persuasion that he was still continuing to fast.

"Well, clear this out now!" said the overseer, and they buried the hunger artist, straw and all. Into the cage they put a young panther. Even the most insensitive felt it refreshing to see this wild creature leaping around the cage that had so long been dreary. The panther was all right. The food he liked was brought him without hesitation by the attendants; he seemed not even to miss his freedom; his noble body, furnished almost to the bursting point with all that it needed, seemed to carry freedom around with it too; somewhere in his jaws it seemed to lurk; and the joy of life streamed with such ardent passion from his throat that for the onlookers it was not easy to stand the shock of it. But they braced themselves, crowded round the cage, and did not want ever to move away.

1924

Further Reading

Rubinstein, William C. "Franz Kafka: A Hunger Artist." *Monatshefte* 44.1 (Jan. 1952): 13–19. • Steinhauer, Harry. "Hungering Artist or Artist in Hungering:

Kafka's 'A Hunger Artist.'" *Criticism* 4.1 (Winter 1962): 28–43. • Spann, Meno. "Franz Kafka's Leopard." *Germanic Review* 34.2 (April 1959): 85–104. See also "The Last Metamorphoses." *Franz Kafka*. Boston: Twayne, 1976. 164–73.
   • Waidson, H. M. "The Starvation-Artist and the Leopard." *Germanic Review* 35.4 (Dec. 1960): 262–69. • Muir, Edwin. "Franz Kafka." *Kafka: A Collection of Critical Essays*. Ed. Ronald Gray. Englewood Cliffs: Prentice, 1962. 33–44.

Franz Kafka's stories are extreme instances of the dual nature of fiction, its attempt to deal simultaneously with the concrete details of the external world and the writer's impressions of an internal life. Flannery O'Connor, whose "grotesque" fiction is in some ways like Kafka's, often used Kafka as a point of reference when she attempted to teach others how fiction works.

Flannery O'Connor: On Realism in Fantasy

Fiction is an art that calls for the strictest attention to the real—whether the writer is writing a naturalistic story or a fantasy. I mean that we always begin with what is or with what has an eminent possibility of truth about it. Even when one writes a fantasy, reality is the proper basis of it. A thing is fantastic because it is so real, so real that it is fantastic. Graham Greene has said that he can't write, "I stood over a bottomless pit," because that couldn't be true, or "Running down the stairs I jumped into a taxi," because that couldn't be true either. But Elizabeth Bowen can write about one of her characters that "she snatched at her hair as if she heard something in it," because that is eminently possible.

I would even go so far as to say that the person writing a fantasy has to be even more strictly attentive to the concrete detail than someone writing in a naturalistic vein—because the greater the story's strain on the credulity, the more convincing the properties in it have to be.

A good example of this is a story called "The Metamorphosis" by Franz Kafka. This is a story about a man who wakes up one morning to find that he has turned into a cockroach overnight, while not discarding his human nature. The rest of the story concerns his life and feelings and eventual death as an insect with human nature, and this situation is accepted by the reader because the concrete detail of the story is absolutely convincing. The fact is that this story describes the dual nature of man in such a realistic fashion that it is almost unbearable. The truth is not distorted here, but rather, a certain distortion is used to get at the truth.

D. H. LAWRENCE

(1885–1930)

THE BLIND MAN

Isabel Pervin was listening for two sounds—for the sound of wheels on the drive outside and for the noise of her husband's footsteps in the hall. Her dearest and oldest friend, a man who seemed almost indispensable to her living, would drive up in the rainy dusk of the closing November day. The trap had gone to fetch him from the station. And her husband, who had been blinded in Flanders, and who had a disfiguring mark on his brow, would be coming in from the outhouses.

He had been home for a year now. He was totally blind. Yet they had been very happy. The Grange was Maurice's own place. The back was a farmstead, and the Wernhams, who occupied the rear premises, acted as farmers. Isabel lived with her husband in the handsome rooms in front. She and he had been almost entirely alone together since he was wounded. They talked and sang and read together in a wonderful and unspeakable intimacy. Then she reviewed books for a Scottish newspaper, carrying on her old interest, and he occupied himself a good deal with the farm. Sightless, he could still discuss everything with Wernham, and he could also do a good deal of work about the place—menial work, it is true, but it gave him satisfaction. He milked the cows, carried in the pails, turned the separator, attended to the pigs and horses. Life was still very full and strangely serene for the blind man, peaceful with the almost incomprehensible peace of immediate contact in darkness. With his wife he had a whole world, rich and real and invisible.

They were newly and remotely happy. He did not even regret the loss of his sight in these times of dark, palpable joy. A certain exultance swelled his soul.

But as time wore on, sometimes the rich glamour would leave them. Sometimes, after months of this intensity, a sense of burden overcame Isabel, a weariness, a terrible *ennui*, in that silent house approached between a colonnade of tall-shafted pines. Then she felt she would go mad, for she could not bear it. And sometimes he had devastating fits of depression, which seemed to lay waste his whole being. It was worse than depression— a black misery, when his own life was a torture to him, and when his presence was unbearable to his wife. The dread went down to the roots of her soul as these black days recurred. In a kind of panic she tried to wrap herself up still further in her husband. She forced the old spontaneous cheerfulness and joy to continue. But the effort it cost her was almost too much. She knew she could not keep it up. She felt she would scream with the strain, and would give anything, anything, to escape. She longed to possess her husband utterly; it gave her inordinate joy to have him entirely to herself. And yet, when again he was gone in a black and massive misery, she could not bear him, she could not bear herself; she wished she could be snatched away off the earth altogether, anything rather than live at this cost.

Dazed, she schemed for a way out. She invited friends, she tried to give him some further connection with the outer world. But it was no good. After all their joy and suffering, after their dark, great year of blindness and solitude and unspeakable nearness, other people seemed to them both shallow, rattling, rather impertinent. Shallow prattle seemed presumptuous. He became impatient and irritated, she was wearied. And so they lapsed into their solitude again. For they preferred it.

But now, in a few weeks' time, her second baby would be born. The first had died, an infant, when her husband first went out to France. She looked with joy and relief to the coming of the second. It would be her salvation. But also she felt some anxiety. She was thirty years old, her husband was a year younger. They both wanted the child very much. Yet she could not help feeling afraid. She had her husband on her hands, a terrible joy to her, and a terrifying burden. The child would occupy her love and attention. And then, what of Maurice? What would he do? If only she could feel that he, too, would be at peace and happy when the child came! She did so want to luxuriate in a rich, physical satisfaction of maternity. But the man, what would he do? How could she provide for him, how avert those shattering black moods of his, which destroyed them both?

She sighed with fear. But at this time Bertie Reid wrote to Isabel. He was her old friend, a second or third cousin, a Scotchman, as she was a Scotchwoman. They had been brought up near to one another, and all her life he had been her friend, like a brother, but better than her own brothers. She loved him—though not in the marrying sense. There was a sort of kinship between them, an affinity. They understood one another instinctively. But Isabel would never have thought of marrying Bertie. It would have seemed like marrying in her own family.

Bertie was a barrister and a man of letters, a Scotchman of the intellectual type, quick, ironical, sentimental, and on his knees before the woman he adored but did not want to marry. Maurice Pervin was different. He came of a good old country family—the Grange was not a very great distance from Oxford. He was passionate, sensitive, perhaps over-sensitive, wincing—a big fellow with heavy limbs and a forehead that flushed painfully. For his mind was slow, as if drugged by the strong provincial blood that beat in his veins. He was very sensitive to his own mental slowness, his feelings being quick and acute. So that he was just the opposite to Bertie, whose mind was much quicker than his emotions, which were not so very fine.

From the first the two men did not like each other. Isabel felt that they *ought* to get on together. But they did not. She felt that if only each could have the clue to the other there would be such a rare understanding between them. It did not come off, however. Bertie adopted a slightly ironical attitude, very offensive to Maurice, who returned the Scotch irony with English resentment, a resentment which deepened sometimes into stupid hatred.

This was a little puzzling to Isabel. However, she accepted it in the course of things. Men were made freakish and unreasonable. Therefore, when Maurice was going out to France for the second time, she felt that, for her husband's sake, she must discontinue her friendship with Bertie. She wrote to the barrister to this effect. Bertram Reid simply replied that in this, as in all other matters, he must obey her wishes, if these were indeed her wishes.

For nearly two years nothing had passed between the two friends. Isabel rather gloried in the fact; she had no compunction. She had one great article of faith, which was, that husband and wife should be so important to one another, that the rest of the world simply did not count. She and Maurice were husband and wife. They loved one another. They would have children. Then let everybody and everything else fade into insignificance outside this connubial felicity. She professed herself quite happy and ready to receive Maurice's friends. She was happy and ready: the happy wife, the ready woman in possession. Without knowing why, the friends retired abashed, and came no more. Maurice, of course, took as much satisfaction in this connubial absorption as Isabel did.

He shared in Isabel's literary activities, she cultivated a real interest in agriculture and cattle-raising. For she, being at heart perhaps an emotional enthusiast, always cultivated the practical side of life and prided herself on her mastery of practical affairs. Thus the husband and wife had spent the five years of their married life. The last had been one of blindness and unspeakable intimacy. And now Isabel felt a great indifference coming over her, a sort of lethargy. She wanted to be allowed to bear her child in peace, to nod by the fire and drift vaguely, physically, from day to day. Maurice was like an ominous thunder-cloud. She had to keep waking up to remember him.

When a little note came from Bertie, asking if he were to put up a tombstone to their dead friendship, and speaking of the real pain he felt on account of her husband's loss of sight, she felt a pang, a fluttering agitation of re-awakening. And she read the letter to Maurice.

"Ask him to come down," he said.

"Ask Bertie to come here!" she re-echoed.

"Yes—if he wants to."

Isabel paused for a few moments.

"I know he wants to—he'd only be too glad," she replied. "But what about you, Maurice? How would you like it?"

"I should like it."

"Well—in that case——But I thought you didn't care for him——"

"Oh, I don't know. I might think differently of him now," the blind man replied. It was rather abstruse to Isabel.

"Well, dear," she said, "if you're quite sure——"

"I'm sure enough. Let him come," said Maurice.

So Bertie was coming, coming this evening, in the November rain and darkness. Isabel was agitated, racked with her old restlessness and indecision. She had always suffered from this pain of doubt, just an agonizing sense of uncertainty. It had begun to pass off, in the lethargy of maternity. Now it returned, and she resented it. She struggled as usual to maintain her calm, composed, friendly bearing, a sort of mask she wore over all her body.

A woman had lighted a tall lamp beside the table and spread the cloth. The long dining-room was dim, with its elegant but rather severe pieces of old furniture. Only the round table glowed softly under the light. It had a rich, beautiful effect. The white cloth glistened and dropped its heavy, pointed lace corners almost to the carpet, the china was old and handsome, creamy-yellow, with a blotched pattern of harsh red and deep blue, the cups large and bell-shaped, the teapot gallant. Isabel looked at it with superficial appreciation.

Her nerves were hurting her. She looked automatically again at the high, uncurtained windows. In the last dusk she could just perceive outside a huge fir-tree swaying its boughs: it was as if she thought it rather than saw it. The rain came flying on the window panes. Ah, why had she no peace? These two men, why did they tear at her? Why did they not come—why was there this suspense?

She sat in a lassitude that was really suspense and irritation. Maurice, at least, might come in—there was nothing to keep him out. She rose to her feet. Catching sight of her reflection in a mirror, she glanced at herself with a slight smile of recognition, as if she were an old friend to herself. Her face was oval and calm, her nose a little arched. Her neck made a beautiful line down to her shoulder. With hair knotted loosely behind, she had something of a warm, maternal look. Thinking this of herself, she arched her eyebrows and her rather heavy eyelids, with a little flicker of a smile, and for a moment her grey eyes looked amused and wicked, a little sardonic, out of her transfigured Madonna face.

Then, resuming her air of womanly patience—she was really fatally self-determined—she went with a little jerk towards the door. Her eyes were slightly reddened.

She passed down the wide hall and through a door at the end. Then she was in the farm premises. The scent of dairy, and of farm-kitchen, and of farm-yard and of leather almost overcame her: but particularly the scent of dairy. They had been scalding out the pans. The flagged passage in front of her was dark, puddled, and wet. Light came out from the open kitchen door. She went forward and stood in the doorway. The farm-people were at tea, seated at a little distance from her, round a long, narrow table, in the centre of which stood a white lamp. Ruddy faces, ruddy hands holding food, red mouths working, heads bent over the tea-cups: men, land-girls, boys: it was tea-time, feeding-time. Some faces caught sight of her. Mrs. Wernham, going round behind the chairs with a large black teapot, halting slightly in her walk, was not aware of her for a moment. Then she turned suddenly.

"Oh, is it Madam!" she exclaimed. "Come in, then, come in! We're at tea." And she dragged forward a chair.

"No, I won't come in," said Isabel. "I'm afraid I interrupt your meal."

"No—no—not likely, Madam, not likely."

"Hasn't Mr. Pervin come in, do you know?"

"I'm sure I couldn't say! Missed him, have you, Madam?"

"No, I only wanted him to come in," laughed Isabel, as if shyly.

"Wanted him, did ye? Get up, boy—get up, now—"

Mrs. Wernham knocked one of the boys on the shoulder. He began to scrape to his feet, chewing largely.

"I believe he's in top stable," said another face from the table.

"Ah! No, don't get up. I'm going myself," said Isabel.

"Don't you go out of a dirty night like this. Let the lad go. Get along wi' ye, boy," said Mrs. Wernham.

"No, no," said Isabel, with a decision that was always obeyed. "Go on with your tea, Tom. I'd like to go across to the stable, Mrs. Wernham."

"Did ever you hear tell!" exclaimed the woman.

"Isn't the trap late?" asked Isabel.

"Why, no," said Mrs. Wernham, peering into the distance at the tall, dim clock. "No, Madam—we can give it another quarter or twenty minutes yet, good—yes, every bit of a quarter."

"Ah! It seems late when darkness falls so early," said Isabel.

"It do, that it do. Bother the days, that they draw in so," answered Mrs. Wernham. "Proper miserable!"

"They are," said Isabel, withdrawing.

She pulled on her overshoes, wrapped a large tartan shawl around her, put on a man's felt hat, and ventured out along the causeways of the first yard. It was very dark. The wind was roaring in the great elms behind the outhouses. When she came to the second yard the darkness seemed deeper. She was unsure of her footing. She wished she had brought a lantern. Rain blew against her. Half she liked it, half she felt unwilling to battle.

She reached at last the just visible door of the stable. There was no sign of a light anywhere. Opening the upper half, she looked in: into a simple well of darkness. The smell of horses, and ammonia, and of warmth was startling to her, in that full night. She listened with all her ears but could hear nothing save the night, and the stirring of a horse.

"Maurice!" she called, softly and musically, though she was afraid. "Maurice—are you there?"

Nothing came from the darkness. She knew the rain and wind blew in upon the horses, the hot animal life. Feeling it wrong, she entered the stable and drew the lower half of the door shut, holding the upper part close. She did not stir, because she was aware of the presence of the dark hind-quarters of the horses, though she could not see them, and she was afraid. Something wild stirred in her heart.

She listened intensely. Then she heard a small noise in the distance—

far away, it seemed—the chink of a pan, and a man's voice speaking a brief word. It would be Maurice, in the other part of the stable. She stood motionless, waiting for him to come through the partition door. The horses were so terrifyingly near to her, in the invisible.

The loud jarring of the inner door-latch made her start; the door was opened. She could hear and feel her husband entering and invisibly passing among the horses near to her, darkness as they were, actively intermingled. The rather low sound of his voice as he spoke to the horses came velvety to her nerves. How near he was, and how invisible! The darkness seemed to be in a strange swirl of violent life, just upon her. She turned giddy.

Her presence of mind made her call, quietly and musically:

"Maurice! Maurice—dea-ar!"

"Yes," he answered. "Isabel?"

She saw nothing, and the sound of his voice seemed to touch her.

"Hello!" she answered cheerfully, straining her eyes to see him. He was still busy, attending to the horses near her, but she saw only darkness. It made her almost desperate.

"Won't you come in, dear?" she said.

"Yes, I'm coming. Just half a minute. *Stand over—now!* Trap's not come, has it?"

"Not yet," said Isabel.

His voice was pleasant and ordinary, but it had a slight suggestion of the stable to her. She wished he would come away. Whilst he was so utterly invisible, she was afraid of him.

"How's the time?" he asked.

"Not yet six," she replied. She disliked to answer into the dark. Presently he came very near to her, and she retreated out of doors.

"The weather blows in here," he said, coming steadily forward, feeling for the doors. She shrank away. At last she could dimly see him.

"Bertie won't have much of a drive," he said, as he closed the doors.

"He won't indeed!" said Isabel calmly, watching the dark shape at the door.

"Give me your arm, dear," she said.

She pressed his arm close to her, as she went. But she longed to see him, to look at him. She was nervous. He walked erect, with face rather lifted, but with a curious tentative movement of his powerful, muscular legs. She could feel the clever, careful, strong contact of his feet with the earth, as she balanced against him. For a moment he was a tower of darkness to her, as if he rose out of the earth.

In the house-passage he wavered and went cautiously, with a curious look of silence about him as he felt for the bench. Then he sat down heavily. He was a man with rather sloping shoulders, but with heavy limbs, powerful legs that seemed to know the earth. His head was small, usually carried high and light. As he bent down to unfasten his gaiters and boots he did not look blind. His hair was brown and crisp, his hands were large, reddish, intelligent, the veins stood out in the wrists; and his thighs and knees seemed massive. When he stood up his face and neck were surcharged with blood, the veins stood out on his temples. She did not look at his blindness.

Isabel was always glad when they had passed through the dividing door into their own regions of repose and beauty. She was a little afraid of him, out there in the animal grossness of the back. His bearing also changed, as he smelt the familiar indefinable odour that pervaded his wife's surroundings, a delicate, refined scent, very faintly spicy. Perhaps it came from the potpourri bowls.

He stood at the foot of the stairs, arrested, listening. She watched him, and her heart sickened. He seemed to be listening to fate.

"He's not here yet," he said. "I'll go up and change."

"Maurice," she said, "you're not wishing he wouldn't come, are you?"

"I couldn't quite say," he answered. "I feel myself rather on the qui vive."

"I can see you are," she answered. And she reached up and kissed his cheek. She saw his mouth relax into a slow smile.

"What are you laughing at?" she said roguishly.

"You consoling me," he answered.

"Nay," she answered. "Why should I console you? You know we love each other—you know *how* married we are! What does anything else matter?"

"Nothing at all, my dear."

He felt for her face and touched it, smiling.

"*You're* all right, aren't you?" he asked anxiously.

"I'm wonderfully all right, love," she answered. "It's you I am a little troubled about, at times."

"Why me?" he said, touching her cheeks delicately with the tips of his fingers. The touch had an almost hypnotizing effect on her.

He went away upstairs. She saw him mount into the darkness, unseeing and unchanging. He did not know that the lamps on the upper corridor were unlighted. He went on into the darkness with unchanging step. She heard him in the bath-room.

Pervin moved about almost unconsciously in his familiar surroundings, dark though everything was. He seemed to know the presence of objects before he touched them. It was a pleasure to him to rock thus through a world of things, carried on the flood in a sort of blood-prescience. He did not think much or trouble much. So long as he kept this sheer immediacy of blood-contact with the substantial world he was happy, he wanted no intervention of visual consciousness. In this state there was a certain rich positivity, bordering sometimes on rapture. Life seemed to move in him like a tide lapping, lapping, and advancing, enveloping all things darkly. It was a pleasure to stretch forth the hand and meet the unseen object, clasp it, and possess it in pure contact. He did not try to remember, to visualize. He did not want to. The new way of consciousness substituted itself in him.

The rich suffusion of this state generally kept him happy, reaching its culmination in the consuming passion for his wife. But at times the flow would seem to be checked and thrown back. Then it would beat inside him like a tangled sea, and he was tortured in the shattered chaos of his own blood. He grew to dread this arrest, this throw-back, this chaos inside himself, when he seemed merely at the mercy of his own powerful and conflicting elements. How to get some measure of control or surety, this was the question. And when the question rose maddening in him, he would clench his fists as if he would *compel* the whole universe to submit to him. But it was in vain. He could not even compel himself.

Tonight, however, he was still serene, though little tremors of unreasonable exasperation ran through him. He had to handle the razor very carefully, as he shaved, for it was not at one with him, he was afraid of it. His hearing also was too much sharpened. He heard the woman lighting the lamps on the corridor, and attending to the fire in the visitors' room. And then, as he went to his room, he heard the trap arrive. Then came Isabel's voice, lifted and calling, like a bell ringing:

"Is it you, Bertie? Have you come?"

And a man's voice answered out of the wind:

"Hello, Isabel! There you are."

"Have you had a miserable drive? I'm so sorry we couldn't send a closed carriage. I can't see you at all, you know."

"I'm coming. No, I liked the drive—it was like Perthshire. Well, how are you? You're looking fit as ever, as far as I can see."

"Oh, yes," said Isabel. "I'm wonderfully well. How are you? Rather thin, I think——"

"Worked to death—everybody's old cry. But I'm all right, Ciss. How's Pervin?—isn't he here?"

"Oh, yes, he's upstairs changing. Yes, he's awfully well. Take off your wet things; I'll send them to be dried."

"And how are you both, in spirits? He doesn't fret?"

"No—no, not at all. No, on the contrary, really. We've been wonderfully happy, incredibly. It's more than I can understand—so wonderful: the nearness, and the peace——"

"Ah! Well, that's awfully good news——"

They moved away. Pervin heard no more. But a childish sense of desolation had come over him, as he heard their brisk voices. He seemed shut out—like a child that is left out. He was aimless and excluded, he did not know what to do with himself. The helpless desolation came over him. He fumbled nervously as he dressed himself, in a state almost of childishness. He disliked the Scotch accent in Bertie's speech, and the slight response it found on Isabel's tongue. He disliked the slight purr of complacency in the Scottish speech. He disliked intensely the glib way in which Isabel spoke of their happiness and nearness. It made him recoil. He was fretful and beside himself like a child, he had almost a childish nostalgia to be included in the life circle. And at the same time he was a man, dark and powerful and infuriated by his own weakness. By some fatal flaw, he could not be by himself, he had to depend on the support of another. And this very dependence enraged him. He hated Bertie Reid, and at the same time he knew the hatred was nonsense, he knew it was the outcome of his own weakness.

He went downstairs. Isabel was alone in the dining-room. She watched him enter, head erect, his feet tentative. He looked so strong-blooded and healthy and, at the same time, cancelled. Cancelled—that was the word that flew across her mind. Perhaps it was his scar suggested it.

"You heard Bertie come, Maurice?" she said.

"Yes—isn't he here?"

"He's in his room. He looks very thin and worn."

"I suppose he works himself to death."

A woman came in with a tray—and after a few minutes Bertie came down. He was a little dark man, with a very big forehead, thin, wispy hair, and sad, large eyes. His expression was inordinately sad—almost funny. He had odd, short legs.

Isabel watched him hesitate under the door, and glance nervously at her husband. Pervin heard him and turned.

"Here you are, now," said Isabel. "Come, let us eat."

Bertie went across to Maurice.

"How are you, Pervin?" he said, as he advanced.

The blind man stuck his hand out into space, and Bertie took it.

"Very fit. Glad you've come," said Maurice.

Isabel glanced at them, and glanced away, as if she could not bear to see them.

"Come," she said. "Come to table. Aren't you both awfully hungry? I am, tremendously."

"I'm afraid you waited for me," said Bertie, as they sat down.

Maurice had a curious monolithic way of sitting in a chair, erect and distant. Isabel's heart always beat when she caught sight of him thus.

"No," she replied to Bertie. "We're very little later than usual. We're having a sort of high tea, not dinner. Do you mind? It gives us such a nice long evening, uninterrupted."

"I like it," said Bertie.

Maurice was feeling, with curious little movements, almost like a cat kneading her bed, for his plate, his knife and fork, his napkin. He was getting the whole geography of his cover into his consciousness. He sat erect and inscrutable, remote-seeming. Bertie watched the static figure of the blind man, the delicate tactile discernment of the large, ruddy hands, and the curious mindless silence of the brow, above the scar. With difficulty he looked away, and without knowing what he did, picked up a little crystal bowl of violets from the table, and held them to his nose.

"They are sweet-scented," he said. "Where do they come from?"

"From the garden—under the windows," said Isabel.

"So late in the year—and so fragrant! Do you remember the violets under Aunt Bell's south wall?"

The two friends looked at each other and exchanged a smile, Isabel's eyes lighting up.

"Don't I?" she replied. "*Wasn't* she queer!"

"A curious old girl," laughed Bertie. "There's a streak of freakishness in the family, Isabel."

"Ah—but not in you and me, Bertie," said Isabel. "Give them to Maurice, will you?" she added, as Bertie was putting down the flowers. "Have you smelled the violets, dear? Do!—they are so scented."

Maurice held out his hand, and Bertie placed the tiny bowl against his large, warm-looking fingers. Maurice's hand closed over the thin white fingers of the barrister. Bertie carefully extricated himself. Then the two watched the blind man smelling the violets. He bent his head and seemed to be thinking. Isabel waited.

"Aren't they sweet, Maurice?" she said at last, anxiously.

"Very," he said. And he held out the bowl. Bertie took it. Both he and Isabel were a little afraid, and deeply disturbed.

The meal continued. Isabel and Bertie chatted spasmodically. The blind man was silent. He touched his food repeatedly, with quick, delicate touches of his knife-point, then cut irregular bits. He could not bear to be helped. Both Isabel and Bertie suffered: Isabel wondered why. She did not suffer when she was alone with Maurice. Bertie made her conscious of a strangeness.

After the meal the three drew their chairs to the fire, and sat down to talk. The decanters were put on a table near at hand. Isabel knocked the logs on the fire, and clouds of brilliant sparks went up the chimney. Bertie noticed a slight weariness in her bearing.

"You will be glad when your child comes now, Isabel?" he said.

She looked up to him with a quick wan smile.

"Yes, I shall be glad," she answered. "It begins to seem long. Yes, I shall be very glad. So will you, Maurice, won't you?" she added.

"Yes, I shall," replied her husband.

"We are both looking forward so much to having it," she said.

"Yes, of course," said Bertie.

He was a bachelor, three or four years older than Isabel. He lived in beautiful rooms overlooking the river, guarded by a faithful Scottish man-servant. And he had his friends among the fair sex—not lovers, friends. So long as he could avoid any danger of courtship or marriage, he adored a few good women with constant and unfailing homage, and he was chivalrously fond of quite a number. But if they seemed to encroach on him, he withdrew and detested them.

Isabel knew him very well, knew his beautiful constancy, and kindness, also his incurable weakness, which made him unable ever to enter into close contact of any sort. He was ashamed of himself because he could not marry, could not approach women physically. He wanted to do so. But he could not. At the centre of him he was afraid, helplessly and even brutally afraid. He had given up hope, had ceased to expect any more that he could escape his own weakness. Hence he was a brilliant and successful barrister, also a *littérateur* of high repute, a rich man, and a great social success. At the centre he felt himself neuter, nothing.

Isabel knew him well. She despised him even while she admired him.

She looked at his sad face, his little short legs, and felt contempt of him. She looked at his dark grey eyes, with their uncanny, almost childlike, intuition, and she loved him. He understood amazingly—but she had no fear of his understanding. As a man she patronized him.

And she turned to the impassive, silent figure of her husband. He sat leaning back, with folded arms, and face a little uptilted. His knees were straight and massive. She sighed, picked up the poker, and again began to prod the fire, to rouse the clouds of soft brilliant sparks.

"Isabel tells me," Bertie began suddenly, "that you have not suffered unbearably from the loss of sight."

Maurice straightened himself to attend but kept his arms folded.

"No," he said, "not unbearably. Now and again one struggles against it, you know. But there are compensations."

"They say it is much worse to be stone deaf," said Isabel.

"I believe it is," said Bertie. "Are there compensations?" he added, to Maurice.

"Yes. You cease to bother about a great many things." Again Maurice stretched his figure, stretched the strong muscles of his back, and leaned backwards, with uplifted face.

"And that is a relief," said Bertie. "But what is there in place of the bothering? What replaces the activity?"

There was a pause. At length the blind man replied, as out of a negligent, unattentive thinking:

"Oh, I don't know. There's a good deal when you're not active."

"Is there?" said Bertie. "What, exactly? It always seems to me that when there is no thought and no action, there is nothing."

Again Maurice was slow in replying.

"There is something," he replied. "I couldn't tell you what it is."

And the talk lapsed once more, Isabel and Bertie chatting gossip and reminiscence, the blind man silent.

At length Maurice rose restlessly, a big obtrusive figure. He felt tight and hampered. He wanted to go away.

"Do you mind," he said, "if I go and speak to Wernham?"

"No—go along, dear," said Isabel.

And he went out. A silence came over the two friends. At length Bertie said:

"Nevertheless, it is a great deprivation, Cissie."

"It is, Bertie. I know it is."

"Something lacking all the time," said Bertie.

"Yes, I know. And yet—and yet—Maurice is right. There is something else, something *there*, which you never knew was there, and which you can't express."

"What is there?" asked Bertie.

"I don't know—it's awfully hard to define it—but something strong and immediate. There's something strange in Maurice's presence—indefinable—but I couldn't do without it. I agree that it seems to put one's mind to sleep. But when we're alone I miss nothing; it seems awfully rich, almost splendid, you know."

"I'm afraid I don't follow," said Bertie.

They talked desultorily. The wind blew loudly outside, rain chattered on the window-panes, making a sharp drum-sound because of the closed, mellow-golden shutters inside. The logs burned slowly, with hot, almost invisible small flames. Bertie seemed uneasy, there were dark circles round his eyes. Isabel, rich with her approaching maternity, leaned looking into the fire. Her hair curled in odd, loose strands, very pleasing to the man. But she had a curious feeling of old woe in her heart, old, timeless night-woe.

"I suppose we're all deficient somewhere," said Bertie.

"I suppose so," said Isabel wearily.

"Damned, sooner or later."

"I don't know," she said, rousing herself. "I feel quite all right, you know. The child coming seems to make me indifferent to everything, just placid. I can't feel that there's anything to trouble about, you know."

"A good thing, I should say," he replied slowly.

"Well, there it is. I suppose it's just Nature. If only I felt I needn't trouble about Maurice, I should be perfectly content——"

"But you feel you must trouble about him?"

"Well——I don't know——" She even resented this much effort.

The night passed slowly. Isabel looked at the clock. "I say," she said. "It's nearly ten o'clock. Where can Maurice be? I'm sure they're all in bed at the back. Excuse me a moment."

She went out, returning almost immediately.

"It's all shut up and in darkness," she said. "I wonder where he is. He must have gone out to the farm——"

Bertie looked at her.

"I suppose he'll come in," he said.

"I suppose so," she said. "But it's unusual for him to be out now."

"Would you like me to go out and see?"

"Well——if you wouldn't mind. I'd go, but——" She did not want to make the physical effort.

Bertie put on an old overcoat and took a lantern. He went out from the side door. He shrank from the wet and roaring night. Such weather had a nervous effect on him: too much moisture everywhere made him feel almost imbecile. Unwilling, he went through it all. A dog barked violently at him. He peered in all the buildings. At last, as he opened the upper door of a sort of intermediate barn, he heard a grinding noise, and looking in, holding up his lantern, saw Maurice, in his shirt-sleeves, standing listening, holding the handle of a turnip-pulper. He had been pulping sweet roots, a pile of which lay dimly heaped in a corner behind him.

"That you, Wernham?" said Maurice, listening.

"No, it's me," said Bertie.

A large, half-wild grey cat was rubbing at Maurice's leg. The blind man stooped to rub its sides. Bertie watched the scene, then unconsciously entered and shut the door behind him. He was in a high sort of barnplace, from which, right and left, ran off the corridors in front of the stalled cattle. He watched the slow, stooping motion of the other man, as he caressed the great cat.

Maurice straightened himself.

"You came to look for me?" he said.

"Isabel was a little uneasy," said Bertie.

"I'll come in. I like messing about doing these jobs."

The cat had reared her sinister, feline length against his leg, clawing at his thigh affectionately. He lifted her claws out of his flesh.

"I hope I'm not in your way at all at the Grange here," said Bertie, rather shy and stiff.

"My way? No, not a bit. I'm glad Isabel has somebody to talk to. I'm afraid it's I who am in the way. I know I'm not very lively company. Isabel's all right, don't you think? She's not unhappy, is she?"

"I don't think so."

"What does she say?"

"She says she's very content—only a little troubled about you."

"Why me?"

"Perhaps afraid that you might brood," said Bertie, cautiously.

"She needn't be afraid of that." He continued to caress the flattened grey head of the cat with his fingers. "What I am a bit afraid of," he resumed, "is that she'll find me a dead weight, always alone with me down here."

"I don't think you need think that," said Bertie, though this was what he feared himself.

"I don't know," said Maurice. "Sometimes I feel it isn't fair that she's saddled with me." Then he dropped his voice curiously. "I say," he asked, secretly struggling, "is my face much disfigured? Do you mind telling me?"

"There is the scar," said Bertie, wondering. "Yes, it is a disfigurement. But more pitiable than shocking."

"A pretty bad scar, though," said Maurice.

"Oh, yes."

There was a pause.

"Sometimes I feel I am horrible," said Maurice, in a low voice, talking as if to himself. And Bertie actually felt a quiver of horror.

"That's nonsense," he said.

Maurice again straightened himself, leaving the cat.

"There's no telling," he said. Then again, in an odd tone, he added: "I don't really know you, do I?"

"Probably not," said Bertie.

"Do you mind if I touch you?"

The lawyer shrank away instinctively. And yet, out of very philanthropy, he said, in a small voice: "Not at all."

But he suffered as the blind man stretched out a strong, naked hand to him. Maurice accidentally knocked off Bertie's hat.

"I thought you were taller," he said, starting. Then he laid his hand on Bertie Reid's head, closing the dome of the skull in a soft, firm grasp, gathering it, as it were; then, shifting his grasp and softly closing again, with a fine, close pressure, till he had covered the skull and the face of the smaller man, tracing the brows, and touching the full, closed eyes, touching the small nose and the nostrils, the rough, short moustache, the mouth, the rather strong chin. The hand of the blind man grasped the shoulder, the arm, the hand of the other man. He seemed to take him, in the soft, travelling grasp.

"You seem young," he said quietly, at last.

The lawyer stood almost annihilated, unable to answer.

"Your head seems tender, as if you were young," Maurice repeated. "So do your hands. Touch my eyes, will you?—touch my scar."

Now Bertie quivered with revulsion. Yet he was under the power of the blind man, as if hypnotized. He lifted his hand, and laid the fingers on the scar, on the scarred eyes. Maurice suddenly covered them with his own hand, pressed the fingers of the other man upon his disfigured eye-sockets, trembling in every fibre, and rocking slightly, slowly, from side to side. He remained thus for a minute or more, whilst Bertie stood as if in a swoon, unconscious, imprisoned.

Then suddenly Maurice removed the hand of the other man from his brow, and stood holding it in his own.

"Oh, my God," he said, "we shall know each other now, shan't we? We shall know each other now."

Bertie could not answer. He gazed mute and terror-struck, overcome by his own weakness. He knew he could not answer. He had an unreasonable fear, lest the other man should suddenly destroy him. Whereas Maurice was actually filled with hot, poignant love, the passion of friendship. Perhaps it was this very passion of friendship which Bertie shrank from most.

"We're all right together now, aren't we?" said Maurice. "It's all right now, as long as we live, so far as we're concerned?"

"Yes," said Bertie, trying by any means to escape.

Maurice stood with head lifted, as if listening. The new delicate fulfilment of mortal friendship had come as a revelation and surprise to him, something exquisite and unhoped-for. He seemed to be listening to hear if it were real.

Then he turned for his coat.

"Come," he said, "we'll go to Isabel."

Bertie took the lantern and opened the door. The cat disappeared. The two men went in silence along the causeways. Isabel, as they came, thought their footsteps sounded strange. She looked up pathetically and anxiously for their entrance. There seemed a curious elation about Maurice. Bertie was haggard, with sunken eyes.

"What is it?" she asked.

"We've become friends," said Maurice, standing with his feet apart, like a strange colossus.

"Friends!" re-echoed Isabel. And she looked again at Bertie. He met her eyes with a furtive, haggard look; his eyes were as if glazed with misery.

"I'm so glad," she said, in sheer perplexity.

"Yes," said Maurice.

He was indeed so glad. Isabel took his hand with both hers, and held it fast.

"You'll be happier now, dear," she said.

But she was watching Bertie. She knew that he had one desire—to escape from this intimacy, this friendship, which had been thrust upon him. He could not bear it that he had been touched by the blind man, his insane reserve broken in. He was like a mollusc whose shell is broken.

1920

Further Reading

Lawrence, D. H. "Why the Novel Matters."*D. H. Lawrence: Selected Literary Criticism*. Ed. Anthony Beal. New York: Viking, 1966. 102–07. • Abolin, Nancy. "Lawrence's 'The Blind Man': The Reality of Touch." In *D. H. Lawrence: A Critical Survey*. Ed. Harry T. Moore. London: Forum, 1969. 215–20. • Vowles, Richard B. "D. H. Lawrence's 'The Blind Man.'" *Explicator* 11.3 (Dec. 1952): 14. • Marks, W. S., III. "The Psychology of Regression in D. H. Lawrence's 'The Blind Man.'" *Literature and Psychology* 17.4 (1967): 177–92. • Breen, Judith Puchner. "D. H. Lawrence, World War I, and the Battle Between the Sexes: A Reading of 'The Blind Man' and 'Tickets, Please.'" *Women's Studies* 13.1–2 (1986): 63–74.

Anyone who has read D. H. Lawrence's short stories or novels knows that his writing strongly appeals to the senses and that the life of the senses is one of his major themes. In a posthumously published essay entitled "Why the Novel Matters," he fully explained his view that fiction allows us to understand the truths of living inside a body.

D. H. Lawrence: On the Truths of the Body

We have curious ideas of ourselves. We think of ourselves as a body with a spirit in it, or a body with a soul in it, or a body with a mind in it. *Mens sana in corpore sano.* The years drink up the wine, and at last throw the bottle away, the body, of course, being the bottle.

It is a funny sort of superstition. Why should I look at my hand, as it so cleverly writes these words, and decide that it is a mere nothing compared to the mind that directs it? Is there really any huge difference between my hand and my brain? Or my mind? My hand is alive, it flickers with a life of its own. It meets all the strange universe in touch, and learns a vast number of things, and knows a vast number of things. My hand, as it writes these words, slips gaily along, jumps like a grasshopper to dot an *i*, feels the table rather cold, gets a little bored if I write too long, has its own rudiments of thought, and is just as much *me* as is my brain, my mind, or my soul. Why should I imagine that there is a *me* which is more *me* than my hand is? Since my hand is absolutely alive, me alive.

Whereas, of course, as far as I am concerned, my pen isn't alive at all. My pen *isn't me* alive. Me alive ends at my finger-tips. . . .

If you are a philosopher, you talk about infinity, and the pure spirit which knows all things. But if you pick up a novel, you realize immediately that infinity is just a handle to this self-same jug of a body of mine; while as for knowing, if I find my finger in the fire, I know that fire burns, with a knowledge so emphatic and vital, it leaves Nirvana merely a conjecture. Oh, yes, my body, me alive, *knows,* and knows intensely. And as for the sum of all knowledge, it can't be anything more than an accumulation of all the things I know in the body, and you, dear reader, know in the body.

KATHERINE ANNE PORTER

(1890–1980)

THE JILTING OF GRANNY WEATHERALL

She flicked her wrist neatly out of Doctor Harry's pudgy careful fingers and pulled the sheet up to her chin. The brat ought to be in knee breeches. Doctoring around the country with spectacles on his nose! "Get along now, take your schoolbooks and go. There's nothing wrong with me."

Doctor Harry spread a warm paw like a cushion on her forehead where the forked green vein danced and made her eyelids twitch. "Now, now, be a good girl, and we'll have you up in no time."

"That's no way to speak to a woman nearly eighty years old just because she's down. I'd have you respect your elders, young man."

"Well, Missy, excuse me." Doctor Harry patted her cheek. "But I've got to warn you, haven't I? You're a marvel, but you must be careful or you're going to be good and sorry."

"Don't tell me what I'm going to be. I'm on my feet now, morally speaking. It's Cornelia. I had to go to bed to get rid of her."

Her bones felt loose, and floated around in her skin, and Doctor Harry floated like a balloon around the foot of the bed. He floated and pulled down his waistcoat and swung his glasses on a cord. "Well, stay where you are, it certainly can't hurt you."

"Get along and doctor your sick," said Granny Weatherall. "Leave a well woman alone. I'll call for you when I want you. . . . Where were you forty years ago when I pulled through milk-leg[1] and double pneumonia? You weren't even born. Don't let Cornelia lead you on," she shouted, because Doctor Harry appeared to float up to the ceiling and out. "I pay my own bills, and I don't throw my money away on nonsense!"

She meant to wave good-by, but it was too much trouble. Her eyes closed of themselves, it was like a dark curtain drawn around the bed. The pillow rose and floated under her, pleasant as a hammock in a light wind. She listened to the leaves rustling outside the window. No, somebody was swishing newspapers: no, Cornelia and Doctor Harry were whispering together. She leaped broad awake, thinking they whispered in her ear.

"She was never like this, *never* like this!" "Well, what can we expect?" "Yes, eighty years old. . . ."

Well, and what if she was? She still had ears. It was like Cornelia to whisper around doors. She always kept things secret in such a public way. She was always being tactful and kind. Cornelia was dutiful; that was the trouble with her. Dutiful and good: "So good and dutiful," said Granny, "that I'd like to spank her." She saw herself spanking Cornelia and making a fine job of it.

"What'd you say, Mother?"

Granny felt her face tying up in hard knots.

"Can't a body think, I'd like to know?"

"I thought you might want something."

"I do. I want a lot of things. First off, go away and don't whisper."

She lay and drowsed, hoping in her sleep that the children would keep out and let her rest a minute. It had been a long day. Not that she was tired. It was always pleasant to snatch a minute now and then. There was always so much to be done, let me see: tomorrow.

Tomorrow was far away and there was nothing to trouble about. Things were finished somehow when the time came; thank God there was always a little margin over for peace: then a person could spread out the plan of life and tuck in the edges orderly. It was good to have everything clean and folded away, with the hair brushes and tonic bottles sitting straight on the white embroidered linen: the day started without fuss and the pantry shelves laid out with rows of jelly glasses and brown jugs and white stone-china jars with blue whirligigs and words painted on them: coffee, tea, sugar, ginger, cinnamon, allspice: and the bronze clock with the lion on top nicely dusted off. The dust that lion could collect in twenty-four hours! The box in the attic with all those letters tied up, well, she'd have to

---

1. A painful condition in women after childbirth that causes great swelling of the leg because of clotting and inflammation of the femoral veins.

go through that tomorrow. All those letters—George's letters and John's letters and her letters to them both—lying around for the children to find afterwards made her uneasy. Yes, that would be tomorrow's business. No use to let them know how silly she had been once.

While she was rummaging around she found death in her mind and it felt clammy and unfamiliar. She had spent so much time preparing for death there was no need for bringing it up again. Let it take care of itself now. When she was sixty she had felt very old, finished, and went around making farewell trips to see her children and grandchildren, with a secret in her mind: This is the very last of your mother, children! Then she made her will and came down with a long fever. That was all just a notion like a lot of other things, but it was lucky too, for she had once for all got over the idea of dying for a long time. Now she couldn't be worried. She hoped she had better sense now. Her father had lived to be one hundred and two years old and had drunk a noggin of strong hot toddy on his last birthday. He told the reporters it was his daily habit, and he owed his long life to that. He had made quite a scandal and was very pleased about it. She believed she'd just plague Cornelia a little.

"Cornelia! Cornelia!" No footsteps, but a sudden hand on her cheek. "Bless you, where have you been?"

"Here, Mother."

"Well, Cornelia, I want a noggin of hot toddy."

"Are you cold, darling?"

"I'm chilly, Cornelia. Lying in bed stops the circulation. I must have told you that a thousand times."

Well, she could just hear Cornelia telling her husband that Mother was getting a little childish and they'd have to humor her. The thing that most annoyed her was that Cornelia thought she was deaf, dumb, and blind. Little hasty glances and tiny gestures tossed around her and over her head saying, "Don't cross her, let her have her way, she's eighty years old," and she sitting there as if she lived in a thin glass cage. Sometimes Granny almost made up her mind to pack up and move back to her own house where nobody could remind her every minute that she was old. Wait, wait, Cornelia, till your own children whisper behind your back!

In her day she had kept a better house and had got more work done. She wasn't too old yet for Lydia to be driving eighty miles for advice when one of the children jumped the track, and Jimmy still dropped in and talked things over: "Now, Mammy, you've a good business head, I want to know what you think of this?. . ." Old. Cornelia couldn't change the furniture around without asking. Little things, little things! They had been so sweet when they were little. Granny wished the old days were back again with the children young and everything to be done over. It had been a hard pull, but not too much for her. When she thought of all the food she had cooked, and all the clothes she had cut and sewed, and all the gardens she had made —well, the children showed it. There they were, made out of her, and they couldn't get away from that. Sometimes she wanted to see John again and point to them and say, Well, I didn't do so badly, did I? But that would have to wait. That was for tomorrow. She used to think of him as a man, but now all the children were older than their father, and he would be a child beside her if she saw him now. It seemed strange and there was something wrong in the idea. Why, he couldn't possibly recognize her. She had fenced in a hundred acres once, digging the post holes herself and clamping the wires with just a negro boy to help. That changed a woman. John would be looking for a young woman with the peaked Spanish comb in her hair and the painted fan. Digging post holes changed a woman. Riding country roads in the winter when women had their babies was another thing: sitting up nights with sick horses and sick negroes and sick children and hardly ever losing one. John, I hardly ever lost one of them! John would see that in a minute, that would be something he could understand, she wouldn't have to explain anything!

It made her feel like rolling up her sleeves and putting the whole place to rights again. No matter if Cornelia was determined to be everywhere at once, there were a great many things left undone on this place. She would start tomorrow and do them. It was good to be strong enough for everything, even if all you made melted and changed and slipped under your hands, so that by the time you finished you almost forgot what you were working for. What was it I set out to do? she asked herself intently, but she could not remember. A fog rose over the valley, she saw it marching across the creek swallowing the trees and moving up the hill like an army of ghosts. Soon it would be at the near edge of the orchard, and then it was time to go in and light the lamps. Come in, children, don't stay out in the night air.

Lighting the lamps had been beautiful. The children huddled up to her and breathed like little calves waiting at the bars in the twilight. Their eyes followed the match and watched the flame rise and settle in a blue curve, then they moved away from her. The lamp was lit, they didn't have to be scared and hang on to Mother any more. Never, never never more. God, for all my life I thank Thee. Without Thee, my God, I could never have done it. Hail, Mary, full of grace.

I want you to pick all the fruit this year and see that nothing is wasted. There's always someone who can use it. Don't let good things rot for want of using. You waste life when you waste good food. Don't let things get lost. It's bitter to lose things. Now, don't let me get to thinking, not when I am tired and taking a little nap before supper. . . .

The pillow rose about her shoulders and pressed against her heart and the memory was being squeezed out of it: oh, push down the pillow, somebody; it would smother her if she tried to hold it. Such a fresh breeze blowing and such a green day with no threats in it. But he had not come, just the same. What does a woman do when she has put on the white veil and set out the white cake for a man and he doesn't come? She tried to remember. No, I swear he never harmed me but in that. He never harmed me but in that . . . and what if he did? There was the day, the day, but a whirl of dark smoke rose and covered it, crept up and over into the bright field where everything was planted so carefully in orderly rows. That was hell, she knew hell when she saw it. For sixty years she had prayed against remembering him and against losing her soul in the deep pit of hell, and now the two things were mingled in one and the thought of him was a smoky cloud from hell that moved and crept in her head when she had just got rid of Doctor Harry and was trying to rest a minute. Wounded vanity, Ellen, said a sharp voice in the top of her mind. Don't let your wounded vanity get the upper hand of you. Plenty of girls get jilted. You were jilted, weren't you? Then stand up to it. Her eyelids wavered and let in streamers of blue-gray light like tissue paper over her eyes. She must get up and pull the shades down or she'd never sleep. She was in bed again and the shades were not down. How could that happen? Better turn over, hide from the light, sleeping in the light gave you nightmares. "Mother, how do you feel now?" and a stinging wetness on her forehead. But I don't like having my face washed in cold water!

Hapsy? George? Lydia? Jimmy? No, Cornelia, and her features were swollen and full of little puddles. "They're coming, darling, they'll all be here soon." Go wash your face, child, you look funny.

Instead of obeying, Cornelia knelt down and put her head on the pillow. She seemed to be talking but there was no sound. "Well, are you tongue-tied? Whose birthday is it? Are you going to give a party?"

Cornelia's mouth moved urgently in strange shapes. "Don't do that, you bother me, daughter."

"Oh, no, Mother. Oh, no. . . ."

Nonsense. It was strange about children. They disputed your every word. "No what, Cornelia?"

"Here's Doctor Harry."

"I won't see that boy again. He just left five minutes ago."

"That was this morning, Mother. It's night now. Here's the nurse."

"This is Doctor Harry, Mrs. Weatherall. I never saw you look so young and happy!"

"Ah, I'll never be young again—but I'd be happy if they'd let me lie in peace and get rested."

She thought she spoke up loudly, but no one answered. A warm weight on her forehead, a warm bracelet on her wrist, and a breeze went on whispering, trying to tell her something. A shuffle of leaves in the everlasting hand of God, He blew on them and they danced and rattled. "Mother, don't mind, we're going to give you a little hypodermic." "Look here, daughter, how do ants get in this bed? I saw sugar ants yesterday." Did you send for Hapsy too?

It was Hapsy she really wanted. She had to go a long way back through a great many rooms to find Hapsy standing with a baby on her arm. She seemed to herself to be Hapsy also, and the baby on Hapsy's arm was Hapsy and himself and herself, all at once, and there was no surprise in the meeting. Then Hapsy melted from within and turned flimsy as gray gauze and the baby was a gauzy shadow, and Hapsy came up close and said, "I thought you'd never come," and looked at her very searchingly and said, "You haven't changed a bit!" They leaned forward to kiss, when Cornelia began whispering from a long way off, "Oh, is there anything you want to tell me? Is there anything I can do for you?"

Yes, she had changed her mind after sixty years and she would like to see George. I want you to find George. Find him and be sure to tell him I forgot him. I want him to know I had my husband just the same and my children and my house like any other woman. A good house too and a good husband that I loved and fine children out of him. Better than I hoped for even. Tell him I was given back everything he took away and more. Oh, no, oh, God, no, there was something else besides the house and the man and the children. Oh, surely they were not all? What was it? Something not given back. . . . Her breath crowded down under her ribs and grew into a monstrous frightening shape with cutting edges; it bored up into her head, and the agony was unbelievable: Yes, John, get the Doctor now, no more talk, my time has come.

When this one was born it should be the last. The last. It should have been born first, for it was the one she had truly wanted. Everything came in good time. Nothing left out, left over. She was strong, in three days she would be as well as ever. Better. A woman needed milk in her to have her full health.

"Mother, do you hear me?"

"I've been telling you—"

"Mother, Father Connolly's here."

"I went to Holy Communion only last week. Tell him I'm not so sinful as all that."

"Father just wants to speak to you."

He could speak as much as he pleased. It was like him to drop in and inquire about her soul as if it were a teething baby, and then stay on for a cup of tea and a round of cards and gossip. He always had a funny story of some sort, usually about an Irishman who made his little mistakes and confessed them, and the point lay in some absurd thing he would blurt out in the confessional showing his struggles between native piety and original sin. Granny felt easy about her soul. Cornelia, where are your manners? Give Father Connolly a chair. She had her secret comfortable understanding with a few favorite saints who cleared a straight road to God for her. All as surely signed and sealed as the papers for the new Forty Acres. Forever . . . heirs and assigns forever. Since the day the wedding cake was not cut, but thrown out and wasted. The whole bottom dropped out of the world, and there she was blind and sweating with nothing under her feet and the walls falling away. His hand had caught her under the breast, she had not fallen, there was the freshly polished floor with the green rug on it, just as before. He had cursed like a sailor's parrot and said, "I'll kill him for you." Don't lay a hand on him, for my sake leave something to God. "Now, Ellen, you must believe what I tell you. . . ."

So there was nothing, nothing to worry about any more, except sometimes in the night one of the children screamed in a nightmare, and they both hustled out shaking and hunting for the matches and calling, "There, wait a minute, here we are!" John, get the doctor now, Hapsy's time has come. But there was Hapsy standing by the bed in a white cap. "Cornelia, tell Hapsy to take off her cap. I can't see her plain."

Her eyes opened very wide and the room stood out like a picture she had seen somewhere. Dark colors with the shadows rising towards the ceiling in long angles. The tall black dresser gleamed with nothing on it but John's picture, enlarged from a little one, with John's eyes very black when they should have been blue. You never saw him, so how do you know how he looked? But the man insisted the copy was perfect, it was very rich and handsome. For a picture, yes, but it's not my husband. The table by the bed had a linen cover and a candle and a crucifix. The light was blue from Cornelia's silk lampshades. No sort of light at all, just frippery. You had to live forty years with kerosene lamps to appreciate honest electricity. She felt very strong and she saw Doctor Harry with a rosy nimbus around him.

"You look like a saint, Doctor Harry, and I vow that's as near as you'll ever come to it."

"She's saying something."

"I heard you, Cornelia. What's all this carrying-on?"

"Father Connolly's saying—"

Cornelia's voice staggered and bumped like a cart in a bad road. It rounded corners and turned back again and arrived nowhere. Granny stepped up in the cart very lightly and reached for the reins, but a man sat beside her and she knew him by his hands, driving the cart. She did not look in his face, for she knew without seeing, but looked instead down the road where the trees leaned over and bowed to each other and a thousand birds were singing a Mass. She felt like singing too, but she put her hand in the bosom of her dress and pulled out a rosary, and Father Connolly murmured Latin in a very solemn voice and tickled her feet. My God, will you stop that nonsense? I'm a married woman. What if he did run away and leave me to face the priest by myself? I found another a whole world better. I wouldn't have exchanged my husband for anybody except St. Michael himself, and you may tell him that for me with a thank you in the bargain.

Light flashed on her closed eyelids, and a deep roaring shook her. Cornelia, is that lightning? I hear thunder. There's going to be a storm. Close all the windows. Call the children in. . . . "Mother, here we are, all of us." "Is that you, Hapsy?" "Oh, no, I'm Lydia. We drove as fast as we could." Their faces drifted above her, drifted away. The rosary fell out of her hands and Lydia put it back. Jimmy tried to help, their hands fumbled together, and Granny closed two fingers around Jimmy's thumb. Beads wouldn't do, it must be something alive. She was so amazed her thoughts ran round and round. So, my dear Lord, this is my death and I wasn't even thinking about it. My children have come to see me die. But I can't, it's not time. Oh, I always hated surprises. I wanted to give Cornelia the amethyst set—Cornelia, you're to have the amethyst set, but Hapsy's to wear it when she wants, and, Doctor Harry, do shut up. Nobody sent for you. Oh, my dear Lord, do wait a minute. I meant to do something about the Forty Acres, Jimmy doesn't need it and Lydia will later on, with that worthless husband of hers. I meant to finish the altar cloth and send six bottles of wine to Sister Borgia for her dyspepsia. I want to send six bottles of wine to Sister Borgia, Father Connolly, now don't let me forget.

Cornelia's voice made short turns and tilted over and crashed. "Oh, Mother, oh, Mother, oh, Mother. . . ."

"I'm not going. Cornelia. I'm taken by surprise. I can't go."

You'll see Hapsy again. What about her? "I thought you'd never come." Granny made a long journey outward, looking for Hapsy. What if I don't find her? What then? Her heart sank down and down, there was no bottom to death, she couldn't come to the end of it. The blue light from Cornelia's lampshade drew into a tiny point in the center of her brain, it flickered and winked like an eye, quietly it fluttered and dwindled. Granny lay curled down within herself, amazed and watchful, staring at the point of light that was herself; her body was now only a deeper mass of shadow in an endless darkness and this darkness would curl around the light and swallow it up. God, give a sign!

For the second time there was no sign. Again no bridegroom and the priest in the house. She could not remember any other sorrow because this grief wiped them all away. Oh, no, there's nothing more cruel than this—I'll never forgive it. She stretched herself with a deep breath and blew out the light.

1929

Further Reading

Welty, Eudora. "The Eye of the Story." *Katherine Anne Porter: A Collection of Critical Essays.* Ed. Robert Penn Warren. Englewood Cliffs: Prentice, 1979. 72–80. • Cobb, Joann P. "Pascal's Wager and Two Modern Losers." *Philosophy and Literature* 2.3 (Fall 1979). *Modern Critical Views: Katherine Anne Porter.* Ed. Harold Bloom. New York: Chelsea, 1986. 97–106. • Wiesenfarth, Joseph. "Internal Opposition in Porter's 'Granny Weatherall.'" *Critique* 11.2 (1969): 47–55. • Wolfe, Peter. "The Problems of Granny Weatherall." *CLA Journal* 11.2 (Dec. 1967): 142–48. • Unrue, Darlene Harbour. "The Rural Southwest." *Understanding Katherine Anne Porter.* Columbia: U of South Carolina P, 1988. 69–89, spec. 75–78.

"The Jilting of Granny Weatherall" reveals Katherine Anne Porter's ability to give us the world from the perspective of a particular character. Part

of her ability to produce such a convincing perspective comes from her awareness (shown in the journal entry below) of her own mental processes, particularly the coexistence in her mind of the past and the present. As Eudora Welty points out, the result is narration that seems to look "through the gauze of the passing scene, not distracted by the immediate and transitory."

Katherine Anne Porter: On Memory

Perhaps in time I shall learn to live more deeply and consistently in that undistracted center of being where the will does not intrude, and the sense of time passing is lost, or has no power over the imagination. Of the three dimensions of time, only the past is "real" in the absolute sense that it has occurred, the future is only a concept, and the present is that fateful split second in which all action takes place. One of the most disturbing habits of the human mind is its willful and destructive forgetting of whatever in its past does not flatter or confirm its present point of view. I must very often refer far back in time to seek the meaning or explanation of today's smallest event, and I have long since lost the power to be astonished at what I find there. This constant exercise of memory seems to be the chief occupation of my mind, and all my experience seems to be simply memory, with continuity, marginal notes, constant revision and comparison of one thing with another. Now and again thousands of memories converge, harmonize, arrange themselves around a central idea in a coherent form, and I write a story.

Eudora Welty: On Porter's Break with Surface Realism

Most good stories are about the interior of our lives, but Katherine Anne Porter's stories take place there; they show surface only at her choosing. Her use of the physical world is enough to meet her needs and no more; she is not wasteful with anything. This artist, writing her stories with a power that stamps them to their last detail on the memory, does so to an extraordinary degree without sensory imagery.

I have the most common type of mind, the visual, and when first I began to read her stories it stood in the way of my trust in my own certainty of what was there that, for all my being bowled over by them, I couldn't see them happening. This was a very good thing for me. As her work has done in many other respects, it has shown me a thing or two about the eye of fiction, about fiction's visibility and invisibility, about its clarity, its radiance. . . .

Katherine Anne Porter shows us that we do not have to see a story happen to know what is taking place. For all we are to know, she is not looking at it happen herself when she writes it; for her eyes are always looking through the gauze of the passing scene, not distracted by the immediate and transitory; her vision is reflective.

Her imagery is as likely as not to belong to a time other than the story's present, and beyond that it always differs from it in nature; it is *memory* imagery, coming into the story from memory's remove. It is a distilled, a reformed imagery, for it is part of a language made to speak directly of premonition, warning, surmise, anger, despair.

JAMES THURBER

(1894–1961)

THE CATBIRD SEAT

Mr. Martin bought the pack of Camels on Monday night in the most crowded cigar store on Broadway. It was theater time and seven or eight men were buying cigarettes. The clerk didn't even glance at Mr. Martin, who put the pack in his overcoat pocket and went out. If any of the staff at F & S had seen him buy the cigarettes, they would have been astonished, for it was generally known that Mr. Martin did not smoke, and never had. No one saw him.

It was just a week to the day since Mr. Martin had decided to rub out Mrs. Ulgine Barrows. The term "rub out" pleased him because it suggested nothing more than the correction of an error—in this case an error of Mr. Fitweiler. Mr. Martin had spent each night of the past week working out his plan and examining it. As he walked home now he went over it again. For the hundredth time he resented the element of imprecision, the margin of guesswork that entered into the business. The project as he had worked it out was casual and bold, the risks were considerable. Something might go wrong anywhere along the line. And therein lay the cunning of his scheme. No one would ever see in it the cautious, painstaking hand of Erwin Martin, head of the filing department at F & S, of whom Mr. Fitweiler had once said, "Man is fallible but Martin isn't." No one would see his hand, that is, unless it were caught in the act.

Sitting in his apartment, drinking a glass of milk, Mr. Martin reviewed his case against Mrs. Ulgine Barrows, as he had every night for seven nights. He began at the beginning. Her quacking voice and braying laugh had first profaned the halls of F & S on March 7, 1941 (Mr. Martin had a head for dates). Old Roberts, the personnel chief, had introduced her as the newly appointed special adviser to the president of the firm, Mr. Fitweiler. The woman had appalled Mr. Martin instantly, but he hadn't shown it. He had given her his dry hand, a look of studious concentration, and a faint smile. "Well," she had said, looking at the papers on his desk, "are you lifting the oxcart out of the ditch?" As Mr. Martin recalled that moment, over his milk, he squirmed slightly. He must keep his mind on her crimes as a special adviser, not on her peccadillos as a personality. This he found difficult to do, in spite of entering an objection and sustaining it. The faults of the woman as a woman kept chattering on in his mind like an unruly witness. She had, for almost two years now, baited him. In the halls, in the elevator, even in his own office, into which she romped now and then like a circus horse, she was constantly shouting these silly questions at him. "Are you lifting the oxcart out of the ditch? Are you tearing up the pea patch? Are you hollering down the rain barrel? Are you scraping around the bottom of the pickle barrel? Are you sitting in the catbird seat?"

It was Joey Hart, one of Mr. Martin's two assistants, who had explained what the gibberish meant. "She must be a Dodger fan," he had said. "Red Barber announces the Dodger games over the radio and he uses those expressions—picked 'em up down South." Joey had gone on to explain one or two. "Tearing up the pea patch" meant going on a rampage; "sitting in the catbird seat" meant sitting pretty, like a batter with three balls and no strikes on him. Mr. Martin dismissed all this with an effort. It had been annoying, it had driven him near to distraction, but he was too solid a man to be moved to murder by anything so childish. It was fortunate, he reflected as he passed on to the important charges against Mrs. Barrows, that he had stood up under it so well. He had maintained always an outward appearance of polite tolerance. "Why, I even believe you like the woman," Miss Paird, his other assistant, had once said to him. He had simply smiled.

A gavel rapped in Mr. Martin's mind and the case proper was resumed. Mrs. Ulgine Barrows stood charged with willful, blatant, and persistent attempts to destroy the efficiency and system of F & S. It was competent, material, and relevant to review her advent and rise to power. Mr. Martin had got the story from Miss Paird, who seemed always able to find things out. According to her, Mrs. Barrows had met Mr. Fitweiler at a party, where she had rescued him from the embraces of a powerfully built drunken man who had mistaken the president of F & S for a famous retired Middle Western football coach. She had led him to a sofa and somehow worked upon him a monstrous magic. The aging gentleman had jumped to the conclusion there and then that this was a woman of singular attainments, equipped to bring out the best in him and in the firm. A week later he had introduced her into F & S as his special adviser. On that day confusion got its foot in the door. After Miss Tyson, Mr. Brundage, and Mr. Bartlett had been fired and Mr. Munson had taken his hat and stalked out, mailing in his resignation later, old Roberts had been emboldened to speak to Mr. Fitweiler. He mentioned that Mr. Munson's department had been "a little disrupted" and hadn't they perhaps better resume the old system there? Mr. Fitweiler had said certainly not. He had the greatest faith in

Mrs. Barrows' ideas. "They require a little seasoning, a little seasoning, is all," he had added. Mr. Roberts had given it up. Mr. Martin reviewed in detail all the changes wrought by Mrs. Barrows. She had begun chipping at the cornices of the firm's edifice and now she was swinging at the foundation stones with a pickaxe.

Mr. Martin came now, in his summing up, to the afternoon of Monday, November 2, 1942—just one week ago. On that day, at 3 P.M., Mrs. Barrows had bounced into his office. "Boo!" she had yelled. "Are you scraping around the bottom of the pickle barrel?" Mr. Martin had looked at her from under his green eyeshade, saying nothing. She had begun to wander about the office, taking it in with her great, popping eyes. "Do you really need *all* these filing cabinets?" she had demanded suddenly. Mr. Martin's heart had jumped. "Each of these files," he had said, keeping his voice even, "plays an indispensable part in the system of F & S." She had brayed at him, "Well, don't tear up the pea patch!" and gone to the door. From there she had bawled, "But you sure have got a lot of fine scrap in here!" Mr. Martin could no longer doubt that the finger was on his beloved department. Her pickaxe was on the upswing, poised for the first blow. It had not come yet; he had received no blue memo from the enchanted Mr. Fitweiler bearing nonsensical instructions deriving from the obscene woman. But there was no doubt in Mr. Martin's mind that one would be forthcoming. He must act quickly. Already a precious week had gone by. Mr. Martin stood up in his living room, still holding his milk glass. "Gentlemen of the jury," he said to himself, "I demand the death penalty for this horrible person."

The next day Mr. Martin followed his routine, as usual. He polished his glasses more often and once sharpened an already sharp pencil, but not even Miss Paird noticed. Only once did he catch sight of his victim; she swept past him in the hall with a patronizing "Hi!" At five-thirty he walked home, as usual, and had a glass of milk, as usual. He had never drunk anything stronger in his life—unless you could count ginger ale. The late Sam Schlosser, the S of F & S, had praised Mr. Martin at a staff meeting several years before for his temperate habits. "Our most efficient worker neither drinks nor smokes," he had said. "The results speak for themselves." Mr. Fitweiler had sat by, nodding approval.

Mr. Martin was still thinking about that red-letter day as he walked over to the Schrafft's on Fifth Avenue near Forty-sixth Street. He got there, as he always did, at eight o'clock. He finished his dinner and the financial page of the *Sun* at a quarter to nine, as he always did. It was his custom after dinner to take a walk. This time he walked down Fifth Avenue at a casual pace. His gloved hands felt moist and warm, his forehead cold. He transferred the Camels fom his overcoat to a jacket pocket. He wondered, as he did so, if they did not represent an unnecessary note of strain. Mrs. Barrows smoked only Luckies. It was his idea to puff a few puffs on a Camel (after the rubbing-out), stub it out in the ashtray holding her lipstick-stained

Luckies, and thus drag a small red herring across the trail. Perhaps it was not a good idea. It would take time. He might even choke, too loudly.

Mr. Martin had never seen the house on West Twelfth Street where Mrs. Barrows lived, but he had a clear enough picture of it. Fortunately, she had bragged to everybody about her ducky first-floor apartment in the perfectly darling three-story red-brick. There would be no doorman or other attendants; just the tenants of the second and third floors. As he walked along, Mr. Martin realized that he would get there before nine-thirty. He had considered walking north on Fifth Avenue from Schrafft's to a point from which it would take him until ten o'clock to reach the house. At that hour people were less likely to be coming in or going out. But the procedure would have made an awkward loop in the straight thread of his casualness, and he had abandoned it. It was impossible to figure when people would be entering or leaving the house, anyway. There was a great risk at any hour. If he ran into anybody, he would simply have to place the rubbing-out of Ulgine Barrows in the inactive file forever. The same thing would hold true if there were someone in her apartment. In that case he would just say that he had been passing by, recognized her charming house and thought to drop in.

It was eighteen minutes after nine when Mr. Martin turned into Twelfth Street. A man passed him, and a man and a woman talking. There was no one within fifty paces when he came to the house, halfway down the block. He was up the steps and in the small vestibule in no time, pressing the bell under the card that said "Mrs. Ulgine Barrows." When the clicking in the lock started, he jumped forward against the door. He got inside fast, closing the door behind him. A bulb in a lantern hung from the hall ceiling on a chain seemed to give a monstrously bright light. There was nobody on the stair, which went up ahead of him along the left wall. A door opened down the hall in the wall on the right. He went toward it swiftly, on tiptoe.

"Well, for God's sake, look who's here!" bawled Mrs. Barrows, and her braying laugh rang out like the report of a shotgun. He rushed past her like a football tackle, bumping her. "Hey, quit shoving!" she said, closing the door behind them. They were in her living room, which seemed to Mr. Martin to be lighted by a hundred lamps. "What's after you?" she said. "You're as jumpy as a goat." He found he was unable to speak. His heart was wheezing in his throat. "I—yes," he finally brought out. She was jabbering and laughing as she started to help him off with his coat. "No, no," he said. "I'll put it here." He took it off and put it on a chair near the door. "Your hat and gloves, too," she said. "You're in a lady's house." He put his hat on top of the coat. Mrs. Barrows seemed larger than he had thought. He kept his gloves on. "I was passing by," he said. "I recognized —is there anyone here?" She laughed louder than ever. "No," she said, "we're all alone. You're as white as a sheet, you funny man. Whatever *has* come over you? I'll mix you a toddy." She started toward a door across the room. "Scotch-and-soda be all right? But say, you don't drink, do you?" She turned and gave him her amused look. Mr. Martin pulled himself together. "Scotch-and-soda will be all right," he heard himself say. He could hear her laughing in the kitchen.

Mr. Martin looked quickly around the living room for the weapon. He had counted on finding one there. There were andirons and a poker and something in a corner that looked like an Indian club. None of them would do. It couldn't be that way. He began to pace around. He came to a desk. On it lay a metal paper knife with an ornate handle. Would it be sharp enough? He reached for it and knocked over a small brass jar. Stamps spilled out of it and it fell to the floor with a clatter. "Hey," Mrs. Barrows yelled from the kitchen, "are you tearing up the pea patch?" Mr. Martin gave a strange laugh. Picking up the knife, he tried its point against his left wrist. It was blunt. It wouldn't do.

When Mrs. Barrows reappeared, carrying two highballs, Mr. Martin, standing there with his gloves on, became acutely conscious of the fantasy he had wrought. Cigarettes in his pocket, a drink prepared for him—it was all too grossly improbable. It was more than that; it was impossible. Somewhere in the back of his mind a vague idea stirred, sprouted. "For heaven's sake, take off those gloves," said Mrs. Barrows. "I always wear them in the house," said Mr. Martin. The idea began to bloom, strange and wonderful. She put the glasses on a coffee table in front of a sofa and sat on the sofa. "Come over here, you odd little man," she said. Mr. Martin went over and sat beside her. It was difficult getting a cigarette out of the pack of Camels, but he managed it. She held a match for him, laughing. "Well," she said, handing him his drink, "this is perfectly marvelous. You with a drink and a cigarette."

Mr. Martin puffed, not too awkwardly, and took a gulp of the highball. "I drink and smoke all the time," he said. He clinked his glass against hers. "Here's nuts to that old windbag, Fitweiler," he said, and gulped again. The stuff tasted awful, but he made no grimace. "Really, Mr. Martin," she said, her voice and posture changing, "you are insulting our employer." Mrs. Barrows was now all special adviser to the president. "I am preparing a bomb," said Mr. Martin, "which will blow the old goat higher than hell." He had only had a little of the drink, which was not strong. It couldn't be that. "Do you take dope or something?" Mrs. Barrows asked coldly. "Heroin," said Mr. Martin. "I'll be coked to the gills when I bump that old buzzard off." "Mr. Martin!" she shouted, getting to her feet. "That will be all of that. You must go at once." Mr. Martin took another swallow of his drink. He tapped his cigarette out in the ashtray and put the pack of Camels on the coffee table. Then he got up. She stood glaring at him. He walked over and put on his hat and coat. "Not a word about this," he said, and laid an index finger against his lips. All Mrs. Barrows could bring out was "Really!" Mr. Martin put his hand on the doorknob. "I'm sitting in the catbird seat," he said. He stuck his tongue out at her and left. Nobody saw him go.

Mr. Martin got to his apartment, walking, well before eleven. No one saw him go in. He had two glasses of milk after brushing his teeth, and he felt elated. It wasn't tipsiness, because he hadn't been tipsy. Anyway, the walk had worn off all effects of the whisky. He got in bed and read a magazine for a while. He was asleep before midnight.

Mr. Martin got to the office at eight-thirty the next morning, as usual. At a quarter to nine, Ulgine Barrows, who had never before arrived at work before ten, swept into his office. "I'm reporting to Mr. Fitweiler now!" she shouted. "If he turns you over to the police, it's no more than you deserve!" Mr. Martin gave her a look of shocked surprise. "I beg your pardon?" he said. Mrs. Barrows snorted and bounced out of the room, leaving Miss Paird and Joey Hart staring after her. "What's the matter with that old devil now?" asked Miss Paird. "I have no idea," said Mr. Martin, resuming his work. The other two looked at him and then at each other. Miss Paird got up and went out. She walked slowly past the closed door of Mr. Fitweiler's office. Mrs. Barrows was yelling inside, but she was not braying. Miss Paird could not hear what the woman was saying. She went back to her desk.

Forty-five minutes later, Mrs. Barrows left the president's office and went into her own, shutting the door. It wasn't until half an hour later that Mr. Fitweiler sent for Mr. Martin. The head of the filing department, neat, quiet, attentive, stood in front of the old man's desk. Mr. Fitweiler was pale and nervous. He took his glasses off and twiddled them. He made a small, bruffing sound in his throat. "Martin," he said, "you have been with us more than twenty years." "Twenty-two, sir," said Mr. Martin. "In that time," pursued the president, "your work and your—uh—manner have been exemplary." "I trust so, sir," said Mr. Martin. "I have understood, Martin," said Mr. Fitweiler, "that you have never taken a drink or smoked." "That is correct, sir," said Mr. Martin. "Ah, yes." Mr. Fitweiler polished his glasses. "You may describe what you did after leaving the office yesterday, Martin," he said. Mr. Martin allowed less than a second for his bewildered pause. "Certainly, sir," he said. "I walked home. Then I went to Schrafft's for dinner. Afterward I walked home again. I went to bed early, sir, and read a magazine for a while. I was asleep before eleven." "Ah, yes," said Mr. Fitweiler again. He was silent for a moment, searching for the proper words to say to the head of the filing department. "Mrs. Barrows," he said finally, "Mrs. Barrows has worked hard, Martin, very hard. It grieves me to report that she has suffered a severe breakdown. It has taken the form of a persecution complex accompanied by distressing hallucinations." "I am very sorry, sir," said Mr. Martin. "Mrs. Barrows is under the delusion," continued Mr. Fitweiler, "that you visited her last evening and behaved yourself in an—uh—unseemly manner." He raised his hand to silence Mr. Martin's little pained outcry. "It is the nature of these psychological diseases," Mr. Fitweiler said, "to fix upon the least likely and most innocent party as the—uh—source of persecution. These matters are not for the lay mind to grasp, Martin. I've just had my psychiatrist, Dr. Fitch, on the phone. He would not, of course, commit himself, but he made enough generalizations to substantiate my suspicions. I suggested to Mrs. Barrows when she had completed her—uh—story to me this morning, that she visit Dr. Fitch, for I suspected a condition at once. She flew, I regret to say, into a rage, and demanded—uh—requested that I call you on the carpet. You may not know, Martin, but Mrs. Barrows had planned a reorganization of your department—subject to my approval, of course, subject to my approval. This brought you, rather than anyone else, to her mind—but again that is a phenomenon for Dr. Fitch and not for us. So, Martin, I am afraid Mrs. Barrows' usefulness here is at an end." "I am dreadfully sorry, sir," said Mr. Martin.

It was at this point that the door to the office blew open with the suddenness of a gas-main explosion and Mrs. Barrows catapulted through it. "Is the little rat denying it?" she screamed. "He can't get away with that!" Mr. Martin got up and moved discreetly to a point beside Mr. Fitweiler's chair. "You drank and smoked at my apartment," she bawled at Mr. Martin, "and you know it! You called Mr. Fitweiler an old windbag and said you were going to blow him up when you got coked to the gills on your heroin!" She stopped yelling to catch her breath and a new glint came into her popping eyes. "If you weren't such a drab, ordinary little man," she said, "I'd think you'd planned it all. Sticking your tongue out, saying you were sitting in the catbird seat, because you thought no one would believe me when I told it! My God, it's really too perfect!" She brayed loudly and hysterically, and the fury was on her again. She glared at Mr. Fitweiler. "Can't you see how he has tricked us, you old fool? Can't you see his little game?" But Mr. Fitweiler had been surreptitiously pressing all the buttons under the top of his desk and employees of F & S began pouring into the room. "Stockton," said Mr. Fitweiler, "you and Fishbein will take Mrs. Barrows to her home. Mrs. Powell, you will go with them." Stockton, who had played a little football in high school, blocked Mrs. Barrows as she made for Mr. Martin. It took him and Fishbein together to force her out of the door into the hall, crowded with stenographers and office boys. She was still screaming imprecations at Mr. Martin, tangled and contradictory imprecations. The hubbub finally died out down the corridor.

"I regret that this has happened," said Mr. Fitweiler. "I shall ask you to dismiss it from your mind, Martin." "Yes, sir," said Mr. Martin, anticipating his chief's "That will be all" by moving to the door. "I will dismiss it." He went out and shut the door, and his step was light and quick in the hall. When he entered his department he had slowed down to his customary gait, and he walked quietly across the room to the W20 file, wearing a look of studious concentration.

1942

James Thurber: Two Cartoons

"It's Our *Own* Story *Exactly*! He Bold as a Hawk, She Soft as the Dawn"

"All Right, Have It Your Way—You Heard a Seal Bark"

Further Reading

Yates, Norris W. "James Thurber's Little Man and Liberal Citizen." *The American Humorist: Conscience of the Twentieth Century.* Ames: Iowa State UP, 1964. 275–98. • Tobias, Richard. "The Beast in the Marges of the Mind." *The Art of James Thurber.* Athens: Ohio, 1969. 81–101, spec. 91–93. • Long, Robert Emmet. "The Further Range: Thurber's Other Stories." *James Thurber.* New York: Continuum, 1988. 75–106, spec. 75–77. • Kane, Thomas S. "A Note on the Chronology of 'The Catbird Seat.'" *CEA Critic* (Apr. 1968): 8–9. • Underwood, Marylyn. "Thurber's 'The Catbird Seat.'" *The Explicator* 40.4 (Summer 1982): 49–50.

In addition to being one of The New Yorker's *funniest writers, James Thurber was an accomplished—though untrained and unorthodox— cartoonist. His stories, sketches, and cartoons often presented the conflict between two distinct character types: the Thurber woman and the Thurber man.*

WILLIAM FAULKNER

(1897–1962)

BARN BURNING

The store in which the Justice of the Peace's court was sitting smelled of cheese. The boy, crouched on his nail keg at the back of the crowded room, knew he smelled cheese, and more: from where he sat he could see the ranked shelves close-packed with the solid, squat, dynamic shapes of tin cans whose labels his stomach read, not from the lettering which meant nothing to his mind but from the scarlet devils and the silver curve of fish— this, the cheese which he knew he smelled and the hermetic meat which his intestines believed he smelled coming in intermittent gusts momentary and brief between the other constant one, the smell and sense just a little of fear because mostly of despair and grief, the old fierce pull of blood. He could not see the table where the Justice sat and before which his father and his father's enemy (*our enemy* he thought in that despair; *ourn! mine and hisn both! He's my father!*) stood, but he could hear them, the two of them that is, because his father had said no word yet:

"But what proof have you, Mr. Harris?"

"I told you. The hog got into my corn. I caught it up and sent it back to him. He had no fence that would hold it. I told him so, warned him. The next time I put the hog in my pen. When he came to get it I gave him enough wire to patch up his pen. The next time I put the hog up and kept it. I rode down to his house and saw the wire I gave him still rolled on to the spool in his yard. I told him he could have the hog when he paid me a dollar pound fee. That evening a nigger came with the dollar and got the hog. He was a strange nigger. He said, 'He say to tell you wood and hay kin burn.' I said, 'What?' 'That whut he say to tell you,' the nigger said. 'Wood and hay kin burn.' That night my barn burned. I got the stock out but I lost the barn."

"Where is the nigger? Have you got him?"

"He was a strange nigger, I tell you. I don't know what became of him."

"But that's not proof. Don't you see that's not proof?"

"Get that boy up here. He knows." For a moment the boy thought too that the man meant his older brother until Harris said, "Not him. The little one. The boy," and, crouching, small for his age, small and wiry like his father, in patched and faded jeans even too small for him, with straight, uncombed, brown hair and eyes gray and wild as storm scud, he saw the men between himself and the table part and become a lane of grim faces, at the end of which he saw the Justice, a shabby, collarless, graying man in spectacles, beckoning him. He felt no floor under his bare feet; he seemed to walk beneath the palpable weight of the grim turning faces. His father, stiff in his black Sunday coat donned not for the trial but for the moving, did not even look at him. *He aims for me to lie,* he thought, again with that frantic grief and despair. *And I will have to do hit.*

"What's your name, boy?" the Justice said.

"Colonel Sartoris Snopes," the boy whispered.

"Hey?" the Justice said. "Talk louder. Colonel Sartoris? I reckon anybody named for Colonel Sartoris in this country can't help but tell the truth, can they?" The boy said nothing. *Enemy! Enemy!* he thought; for a moment he could not even see, could not see that the Justice's face was kindly nor discern that his voice was troubled when he spoke to the man named Harris: "Do you want me to question this boy?" But he could hear, and during those subsequent long seconds while there was absolutely no sound in the crowded little room save that of quiet and intent breathing it was as if he had swung outward at the end of a grape vine, over a ravine, and at the top of the swing had been caught in a prolonged instant of mesmerized gravity, weightless in time.

"No!" Harris said violently, explosively. "Damnation! Send him out of here!" Now time, the fluid world, rushed beneath him again, the voices coming to him again through the smell of cheese and sealed meat, the fear and despair and the old grief of blood:

"This case is closed. I can't find against you, Snopes, but I can give you advice. Leave this country and don't come back to it."

His father spoke for the first time, his voice cold and harsh, level, without emphasis: "I aim to. I don't figure to stay in a country among people who . . ." he said something unprintable and vile, addressed to no one.

"That'll do," the Justice said. "Take your wagon and get out of this country before dark. Case dismissed."

His father turned, and he followed the stiff black coat, the wiry figure walking a little stiffly from where a Confederate provost's man's[1] musket ball had taken him in the heel on a stolen horse thirty years ago, followed the two backs now, since his older brother had appeared from somewhere in the crowd, no taller than the father but thicker, chewing tobacco steadily, between the two lines of grim-faced men and out of the store and across the worn gallery and down the sagging steps and among the dogs and half-grown boys in the mild May dust where as he passed a voice hissed:

"Barn burner!"

Again he could not see, whirling; there was a face in a red haze, moon-like, bigger than the full moon, the owner of it half again his size, he leaping in the red haze toward the face, feeling no blow, feeling no shock when his head struck the earth, scrabbling up and leaping again, feeling no blow this time either and tasting no blood, scrabbling up to see the other boy in full flight and himself already leaping into pursuit as his father's hand jerked him back, the harsh, cold voice speaking above him: "Go get in the wagon."

It stood in a grove of locusts and mulberries across the road. His two hulking sisters in their Sunday dresses and his mother and her sister in calico and sunbonnets were already in it, sitting on and among the sorry residue of the dozen and more movings which even the boy could remember—the battered stove, the broken beds and chairs, the clock inlaid with mother-of-pearl, which would not run, stopped at some fourteen minutes past two o'clock of a dead and forgotten day and time, which had been his mother's dowry. She was crying, though when she saw him she drew her sleeve across her face and began to descend from the wagon. "Get back," the father said.

"He's hurt. I got to get some water and wash his . . ."

"Get back in the wagon," his father said. He got in too, over the tail-gate. His father mounted to the seat where the older brother already sat and struck the gaunt mules two savage blows with the peeled willow, but without heat. It was not even sadistic; it was exactly that same quality which in later years would cause his descendants to overrun the engine before putting a motor car into motion, striking and reining back in the same movement. The wagon went on, the store with its quiet crowd of grimly watching men dropped behind; a curve in the road hid it. *Forever* he thought. *Maybe he's done satisfied now, now that he has . . .* stopping himself, not to say it aloud even to himself. His mother's hand touched his shoulder.

"Does hit hurt?" she said.

"Naw," he said. "Hit don't hurt. Lemme be."

"Can't you wipe some of the blood off before hit dries?"

"I'll wash to-night," he said. "Lemme be, I tell you."

The wagon went on. He did not know where they were going. None of them ever did or ever asked, because it was always somewhere, always a house of sorts waiting for them a day or two days or even three days away.

---

1. Provost's man: a military policeman.

Likely his father had already arranged to make a crop on another farm before he . . . Again he had to stop himself. He (the father) always did. There was something about his wolf-like independence and even courage when the advantage was at least neutral which impressed strangers, as if they got from his latent ravening ferocity not so much a sense of dependability as a feeling that his ferocious conviction in the rightness of his own actions would be of advantage to all whose interest lay with his.

That night they camped, in a grove of oaks and beeches where a spring ran. The nights were still cool and they had a fire against it, of a rail lifted from a nearby fence and cut into lengths—a small fire, neat, niggard almost, a shrewd fire; such fires were his father's habit and custom always, even in freezing weather. Older, the boy might have remarked this and wondered why not a big one; why should not a man who had not only seen the waste and extravagance of war, but who had in his blood an inherent voracious prodigality with material not his own, have burned everything in sight? Then he might have gone a step farther and thought that that was the reason: that niggard blaze was the living fruit of nights passed during those four years in the woods hiding from all men, blue or gray, with his strings of horses (captured horses, he called them). And older still, he might have divined the true reason: that the element of fire spoke to some deep mainspring of his father's being, as the element of steel or of powder spoke to other men, as the one weapon for the preservation of integrity, else breath were not worth the breathing, and hence to be regarded with respect and used with discretion.

But he did not think this now and he had seen those same niggard blazes all his life. He merely ate his supper beside it and was already half asleep over his iron plate when his father called him, and once more he followed the stiff back, the stiff and ruthless limp, up the slope and on to the starlit road where, turning, he could see his father against the stars but without face or depth—a shape black, flat, and bloodless as though cut from tin in the iron folds of the frockcoat which had not been made for him, the voice harsh like tin and without heat like tin:

"You were fixing to tell them. You would have told him." He didn't answer. His father struck him with the flat of his hand on the side of the head, hard but without heat, exactly as he had struck the two mules at the store, exactly as he would strike either of them with any stick in order to kill a horse fly, his voice still without fear or anger: "You're getting to be a man. You got to learn. You got to learn to stick to your own blood or you ain't going to have any blood to stick to you. Do you think either of them, any man there this morning, would? Don't you know all they wanted was a chance to get at me because they knew I had them beat? Eh?" Later, twenty years later, he was to tell himself, "If I had said they wanted only truth, justice, he would have hit me again." But now he said nothing. He was not crying. He just stood there. "Answer me," his father said.

"Yes," he whispered. His father turned.

"Get on to bed. We'll be there tomorrow."

Tomorrow they were there. In the early afternoon the wagon stopped before a paintless two-room house identical almost with the dozen others it had stopped before even in the boy's ten years, and again, as on the other dozen occasions, his mother and aunt got down and began to unload the wagon, although his two sisters and his father and brother had not moved.

"Likely hit ain't fitten for hawgs," one of the sisters said.

"Nevertheless, fit it will and you'll hog it and like it," his father said. "Get out of them chairs and help your Ma unload."

The two sisters got down, big, bovine, in a flutter of cheap ribbons; one of them drew from the jumbled wagon bed a battered lantern, the other a worn broom. His father handed the reins to the older son and began to climb stiffly over the wheel. "When they get unloaded, take the team to the barn and feed them." Then he said, and at first the boy thought he was still speaking to his brother: "Come with me."

"Me?" he said.

"Yes," his father said. "You."

"Abner," his mother said. His father paused and looked back—the harsh level stare beneath the shaggy, graying, irascible brows.

"I reckon I'll have a word with the man that aims to begin tomorrow owning me body and soul for the next eight months."

They went back up the road. A week ago—or before last night, that is —he would have asked where they were going, but not now. His father had struck him before last night but never before had he paused afterward to explain why; it was as if the blow and the following calm, outrageous voice still rang, repercussed, divulging nothing to him save the terrible handicap of being young, the light weight of his few years, just heavy enough to prevent his soaring free of the world as it seemed to be ordered but not heavy enough to keep him footed solid in it, to resist it and try to change the course of its events.

Presently he could see the grove of oaks and cedars and the other flowering trees and shrubs, where the house would be, though not the house yet. They walked beside a fence massed with honeysuckle and Cherokee roses and came to a gate swinging open between two brick pillars, and now, beyond a sweep of drive, he saw the house for the first time and at that instant he forgot his father and the terror and despair both, and even when he remembered his father again (who had not stopped) the terror and despair did not return. Because, for all the twelve movings, they had sojourned until now in a poor country, a land of small farms and fields and houses, and he had never seen a house like this before. *Hit's big as a courthouse* he thought quietly, with a surge of peace and joy whose reason he could not have thought into words, being too young for that: *They are safe from him. People whose lives are a part of this peace and dignity are beyond his touch, he no more to them than a buzzing wasp: capable of stinging for a little moment but that's all; the spell of this peace and dignity rendering even the barns and stable and cribs which belong to it impervious to the puny flames he might contrive . . .* this, the peace and joy, ebbing for an instant as he looked again at the stiff black back, the stiff and implacable limp of the figure which was not dwarfed by the house, for the reason that it had never looked big anywhere and which now, against the serene columned backdrop, had more than ever that impervious quality of something cut ruthlessly from tin, depthless, as though, sidewise to the sun, it would cast no shadow. Watching him, the boy remarked the absolutely undeviating course which his father held and saw the stiff foot come squarely down in a pile of fresh droppings where a horse had stood in the drive and which his father could have avoided by a simple change of stride. But it ebbed only for a moment, though he could not have thought this into words either, walking on in the spell of the house, which he could even want but without envy, without sorrow, certainly never with that ravening and jealous rage which unknown to him walked in the ironlike black coat before him: *Maybe he will feel it too. Maybe it will even change him now from what maybe he couldn't help but be.*

They crossed the portico. Now he could hear his father's stiff foot as it came down on the boards with clocklike finality, a sound out of all proportion to the displacement of the body it bore and which was not dwarfed either by the white door before it, as though it had attained to a sort of vicious and ravening minimum not to be dwarfed by anything—the flat, wide, black hat, the formal coat of broadcloth which had once been black but which had now that friction-glazed greenish cast of the bodies of old house flies, the lifted sleeve which was too large, the lifted hand like a curled claw. The door opened so promptly that the boy knew the Negro must have been watching them all the time, an old man with neat grizzled hair, in a linen jacket, who stood barring the door with his body, saying, "Wipe yo foots, white man, fo you come in here. Major ain't home nohow."

"Get out of my way, nigger," his father said, without heat too, flinging the door back and the Negro also and entering, his hat still on his head. And now the boy saw the prints of the stiff foot on the doorjamb and saw them appear on the pale rug behind the machinelike deliberation of the foot which seemed to bear (or transmit) twice the weight which the body compassed. The Negro was shouting "Miss Lula! Miss Lula!" somewhere behind them, then the boy, deluged as though by a warm wave by a suave turn of carpeted stair and a pendant glitter of chandeliers and a mute gleam of gold frames, heard the swift feet and saw her too, a lady—perhaps he had never seen her like before either—in a gray, smooth gown with lace at the throat and an apron tied at the waist and the sleeves turned back, wiping cake or biscuit dough from her hands with a towel as she came up the hall, looking not at his father at all but at the tracks on the blond rug with an expression of incredulous amazement.

"I tried," the Negro cried. "I tole him to . . ."

"Will you please go away?" she said in a shaking voice. "Major de Spain is not at home. Will you please go away?"

His father had not spoken again. He did not speak again. He did not even look at her. He just stood stiff in the center of the rug, in his hat, the shaggy iron-gray brows twitching slightly above the pebble-colored eyes as he appeared to examine the house with brief deliberation. Then with the same deliberation he turned; the boy watched him pivot on the good leg and saw the stiff foot drag round the arc of the turning, leaving a final long and fading smear. His father never looked at it, he never once looked down at the rug. The Negro held the door. It closed behind them, upon the hysteric and indistinguishable woman-wail. His father stopped at the top of the steps and scraped his boot clean on the edge of it. At the gate he stopped again. He stood for a moment, planted stiffly on the stiff foot, looking back at the house. "Pretty and white, ain't it?" he said. "That's sweat. Nigger sweat. Maybe it ain't white enough yet to suit him. Maybe he wants to mix some white sweat with it."

Two hours later the boy was chopping wood behind the house within which his mother and aunt and the two sisters (the mother and aunt, not the two girls, he knew that; even at this distance and muffled by walls the flat loud voices of the two girls emanated an incorrigible idle inertia) were setting up the stove to prepare a meal, when he heard the hooves and saw the linen-clad man on a fine sorrel mare, whom he recognized even before he saw the rolled rug in front of the Negro youth following on a fat bay carriage horse—a suffused, angry face vanishing, still at full gallop, beyond the corner of the house where his father and brother were sitting in the two tilted chairs; and a moment later, almost before he could have put the axe down, he heard the hooves again and watched the sorrel mare go back out of the yard, already galloping again. Then his father began to shout one of the sisters' names, who presently emerged backward from the kitchen door dragging the rolled rug along the ground by one end while the other sister walked behind it.

"If you ain't going to tote, go on and set up the wash pot," the first said.

"You, Sarty!" the second shouted. "Set up the wash pot!" His father appeared at the door, framed against that shabbiness, as he had been against that other bland perfection, impervious to either, the mother's anxious face at his shoulder.

"Go on," the father said. "Pick it up." The two sisters stooped, broad, lethargic; stooping, they presented an incredible expanse of pale cloth and a flutter of tawdry ribbons.

"If I thought enough of a rug to have to git hit all the way from France I wouldn't keep hit where folks coming in would have to tromp on hit," the first said. They raised the rug.

"Abner," the mother said. "Let me do it."

"You go back and git dinner," his father said. "I'll tend to this."

From the woodpile through the rest of the afternoon the boy watched them, the rug spread flat in the dust beside the bubbling wash-pot, the two sisters stooping over it with that profound and lethargic reluctance, while the father stood over them in turn, implacable and grim, driving them though never raising his voice again. He could smell the harsh homemade lye they were using; he saw his mother come to the door once and look toward them with an expression not anxious now but very like despair; he saw his father turn, and he fell to with the axe and saw from the corner of his eye his father raise from the ground a flattish fragment of field stone and examine it and return to the pot, and this time his mother actually spoke: "Abner. Abner. Please don't. Please, Abner."

Then he was done too. It was dusk; the whippoorwills had already begun. He could smell coffee from the room where they would presently eat the cold food remaining from the mid-afternoon meal, though when he entered the house he realized they were having coffee again probably because there was a fire on the hearth, before which the rug now lay spread over the backs of the two chairs. The tracks of his father's foot were gone. Where they had been were now long, water-cloudy scoriations resembling the sporadic course of a Lilliputian mowing machine.

It still hung there while they ate the cold food and then went to bed, scattered without order or claim up and down the two rooms, his mother in one bed, where his father would later lie, the older brother in the other, himself, the aunt, and the two sisters on pallets on the floor. But his father was not in bed yet. The last thing the boy remembered was the depthless, harsh silhouette of the hat and coat bending over the rug and it seemed to him that he had not even closed his eyes when the silhouette was standing over him, the fire almost dead behind it, the stiff foot prodding him awake. "Catch up the mule," his father said.

When he returned with the mule his father was standing in the black door, the rolled rug over his shoulder. "Ain't you going to ride?" he said.

"No. Give me your foot."

He bent his knee into his father's hand, the wiry, surprising power flowed smoothly, rising, he rising with it, on to the mule's bare back (they had owned a saddle once; the boy could remember it though not when or where) and with the same effortlessness his father swung the rug up in front of him. Now in the starlight they retraced the afternoon's path, up the dusty road rife with honeysuckle, through the gate and up the black tunnel to the drive to the lightless house, where he sat on the mule and felt the rough warp of the rug drag across his thighs and vanish.

"Don't you want me to help?" he whispered. His father did not answer and now he heard again that stiff foot striking the hollow portico with that wooden and clocklike deliberation, that outrageous overstatement of the weight it carried. The rug, hunched, not flung (the boy could tell that even in the darkness) from his father's shoulder struck the angle of wall and floor with a sound unbelievably loud, thunderous, then the foot again, unhurried and enormous; a light came on in the house and the boy sat, tense, breathing steadily and quietly and just a little fast, though the foot itself did not increase its beat at all, descending the steps now; now the boy could see him.

"Don't you want to ride now?" he whispered. "We kin both ride now," the light within the house altering now, flaring up and sinking. *He's coming down the stairs now,* he thought. He had already ridden the mule up beside the horse block; presently his father was up behind him and he doubled the reins over and slashed the mule across the neck, but before the animal could begin to trot the hard, thin arm came round him, the hard, knotted hand jerking the mule back to a walk.

In the first red rays of the sun they were in the lot, putting plow gear on the mules. This time the sorrel mare was in the lot before he heard it at all, the rider collarless and even bareheaded, trembling, speaking in a shaking voice as the woman in the house had done, his father merely looking up once before stooping again to the hame he was buckling, so that the man on the mare spoke to his stooping back:

"You must realize you have ruined that rug. Wasn't there anybody here, any of your women . . ." he ceased, shaking, the boy watching him, the older brother leaning now in the stable door, chewing, blinking slowly and steadily at nothing apparently. "It cost a hundred dollars. But you never had a hundred dollars. You never will. So I'm going to charge you twenty bushels of corn against your crop. I'll add it in your contract and when you come to the commissary you can sign it. That won't keep Mrs. de Spain quiet but maybe it will teach you to wipe your feet off before you enter her house again."

Then he was gone. The boy looked at his father, who still had not spoken or even looked up again, who was now adjusting the logger-head in the hame.

"Pap," he said. His father looked at him—the inscrutable face, the shaggy brows beneath which the gray eyes glinted coldly. Suddenly the boy went toward him, fast, stopping as suddenly. "You done the best you could!" he cried. "If he wanted hit done different why didn't he wait and tell you how? He won't git no twenty bushels! He won't git none! We'll gether hit and hide hit! I kin watch . . ."

"Did you put the cutter back in that straight stock like I told you?"

"No, sir," he said.

"Then go do it."

That was Wednesday. During the rest of that week he worked steadily, at what was within his scope and some which was beyond it, with an industry that did not need to be driven nor even commanded twice; he had this from his mother, with the difference that some at least of what he did he liked to do, such as splitting wood with the half-size axe which his mother and aunt had earned, or saved money somehow, to present him with at Christmas. In company with the two older women (and on one afternoon, even one of the sisters), he built pens for the shoat and the cow which were a part of his father's contract with the landlord, and one afternoon, his father being absent, gone somewhere on one of the mules, he went to the field.

They were running a middle buster now, his brother holding the plow straight while he handled the reins, and walking beside the straining mule, the rich black soil shearing cool and damp against his bare ankles, he thought *Maybe this is the end of it. Maybe even that twenty bushels that seems hard to have to pay for just a rug will be a cheap price for him to stop forever and always from being what he used to be;* thinking, dreaming now, so that his brother had to speak sharply to him to mind the mule: *Maybe he even won't collect the twenty bushels. Maybe it will all add up and balance and vanish—corn, rug, fire; the terror and grief, the being pulled two ways like between two teams of horses— gone, done with for ever and ever.*

Then it was Saturday; he looked up from beneath the mule he was harnessing and saw his father in the black coat and hat. "Not that," his father said. "The wagon gear." And then, two hours later, sitting in the wagon bed behind his father and brother on the seat, the wagon accomplished a final curve, and he saw the weathered paintless store with its tattered tobacco- and patent-medicine posters and the tethered wagons and saddle animals below the gallery. He mounted the gnawed steps behind his father and brother, and there again was the lane of quiet, watching faces for the three of them to walk through. He saw the man in spectacles sitting at the plank table and he did not need to be told this was a Justice of the Peace; he sent one glare of fierce, exultant, partisan defiance at the man in collar and cravat now, whom he had seen but twice before in his life, and that on a galloping horse, who now wore on his face an expression not of rage but of amazed unbelief which the boy could not have known was at the incredible circumstance of being sued by one of his own tenants, and came and stood against his father and cried at the Justice: "He ain't done it! He ain't burnt . . ."

"Go back to the wagon," his father said.

"Burnt?" the Justice said. "Do I understand this rug was burned too?"

"Does anybody here claim it was?" his father said. "Go back to the wagon." But he did not, he merely retreated to the rear of the room, crowded as that other had been, but not to sit down this time, instead, to stand pressing among the motionless bodies, listening to the voices:

"And you claim twenty bushels of corn is too high for the damage you did to the rug?"

"He brought the rug to me and said he wanted the tracks washed out of it. I washed the tracks out and took the rug back to him."

"But you didn't carry the rug back to him in the same condition it was in before you made the tracks on it."

His father did not answer, and now for perhaps half a minute there was no sound at all save that of breathing, the faint, steady suspiration of complete and intent listening.

"You decline to answer that, Mr. Snopes?" Again his father did not answer. "I'm going to find against you, Mr. Snopes. I'm going to find that you were responsible for the injury to Major de Spain's rug and hold you liable for it. But twenty bushels of corn seems a little high for a man in your circumstances to have to pay. Major de Spain claims it cost a hundred dollars. October corn will be worth about fifty cents. I figure that if Major de Spain can stand a ninety-five dollar loss on something he paid cash for, you can stand a five-dollar loss you haven't earned yet. I hold you in damages to

Major de Spain to the amount of ten bushels of corn over and above your contract with him, to be paid to him out of your crop at gathering time. Court adjourned."

It had taken no time hardly, the morning was but half begun. He thought they would return home and perhaps back to the field, since they were late, far behind all other farmers. But instead his father passed on behind the wagon, merely indicating with his hand for the older brother to follow with it, and crossed the road toward the blacksmith shop opposite, pressing on after his father, overtaking him, speaking, whispering up at the harsh, calm face beneath the weathered hat: "He won't git no ten bushels neither. He won't git one. We'll . . ." until his father glanced for an instant down at him, the face absolutely calm, the grizzled eyebrows tangled above the cold eyes, the voice almost pleasant, almost gentle:

"You think so? Well, we'll wait till October anyway."

The matter of the wagon—the setting of a spoke or two and the tightening of the tires—did not take long either, the business of the tires accomplished by driving the wagon into the spring branch behind the shop and letting it stand there, the mules nuzzling into the water from time to time, and the boy on the seat with the idle reins, looking up the slope and through the sooty tunnel of the shed where the slow hammer rang and where his father sat on an upended cypress bolt, easily, either talking or listening, still sitting there when the boy brought the dripping wagon up out of the branch and halted it before the door.

"Take them on to the shade and hitch," his father said. He did so and returned. His father and the smith and a third man squatting on his heels inside the door were talking, about crops and animals; the boy, squatting too in the ammoniac dust and hoof-parings and scales of rust, heard his father tell a long and unhurried story out of the time before the birth of the older brother even when he had been a professional horsetrader. And then his father came up beside him where he stood before a tattered last year's circus poster on the other side of the store, gazing rapt and quiet at the scarlet horses, the incredible poisings and convolutions of tulle and tights and the painted leers of comedians, and said, "It's time to eat."

But not at home. Squatting beside his brother against the front wall, he watched his father emerge from the store and produce from a paper sack a segment of cheese and divide it carefully and deliberately into three with his pocket knife and produce crackers from the same sack. They all three squatted on the gallery and ate, slowly, without talking; then in the store again, they drank from a tin dipper tepid water smelling of the cedar bucket and of living beech trees. And still they did not go home. It was a horse lot this time, a tall rail fence upon and along which men stood and sat and out of which one by one horses were led, to be walked and trotted and then cantered back and forth along the road while the slow swapping and buying went on and the sun began to slant westward, they—the three of them—watching and listening, the older brother with his muddy eyes and his steady, inevitable tobacco, the father commenting now and then on certain of the animals, to no one in particular.

It was after sundown when they reached home. They ate supper by lamplight, then, sitting on the doorstep, the boy watched the night fully accomplish, listening to the whippoorwills and the frogs, when he heard his mother's voice: "Abner! No! No! Oh, God. Oh, God. Abner!" and he rose, whirled, and saw the altered light through the door where a candle stub now burned in a bottle neck on the table and his father, still in the hat and coat, at once formal and burlesque as though dressed carefully for some shabby and ceremonial violence, emptying the reservoir of the lamp back into the five-gallon kerosene can from which it had been filled, while the mother tugged at his arm until he shifted the lamp to the other hand and flung her back, not savagely or viciously, just hard, into the wall, her hands flung out against the wall for balance, her mouth open and in her face the same quality of hopeless despair as had been in her voice. Then his father saw him standing in the door.

"Go to the barn and get that can of oil we were oiling the wagon with," he said. The boy did not move. Then he could speak.

"What . . ." he cried. "What are you . . ."

"Go get that oil," his father said. "Go."

Then he was moving, running, outside the house, toward the stable: this the old habit, the old blood which he had not been permitted to choose for himself, which had been bequeathed him willy nilly and which had run for so long (and who knew where, battening on what of outrage and savagery and lust) before it came to him. *I could keep on,* he thought. *I could run on and on and never look back, never need to see his face again. Only I can't. I can't,* the rusted can in his hand now, the liquid sploshing in it as he ran back to the house and into it, into the sound of his mother's weeping in the next room, and handed the can to his father.

"Ain't you going to even send a nigger?" he cried. "At least you sent a nigger before!"

This time his father didn't strike him. The hand came even faster than the blow had, the same hand which had set the can on the table with almost excruciating care flashing from the can toward him too quick for him to follow it, gripping him by the back of his shirt and on to tiptoe before he had seen it quit the can, the face stooping at him in breathless and frozen ferocity, the cold, dead voice speaking over him to the older brother who leaned against the table, chewing with that steady, curious, sidewise motion of cows:

"Empty the can into the big one and go on. I'll catch up with you."

"Better tie him up to the bedpost," the brother said.

"Do like I told you," the father said. Then the boy was moving, his bunched shirt and the hard, bony hand between his shoulder-blades, his toes just touching the floor, across the room and into the other one, past the sisters sitting with spread heavy thighs in the two chairs over the cold hearth, and to where his mother and aunt sat side by side on the bed, the aunt's arms about his mother's shoulders.

"Hold him," the father said. The aunt made a startled movement. "Not you," the father said. "Lennie. Take hold of him. I want to see you do it." His mother took him by the wrist. "You'll hold him better than that. If he gets loose don't you know what he is going to do? He will go up yonder." He jerked his head toward the road. "Maybe I'd better tie him."

"I'll hold him," his mother whispered.

"See you do then." Then his father was gone, the stiff foot heavy and measured upon the boards, ceasing at last.

Then he began to struggle. His mother caught him in both arms, he jerking and wrenching at them. He would be stronger in the end, he knew that. But he had no time to wait for it. "Lemme go!" he cried. "I don't want to have to hit you!"

"Let him go!" the aunt said. "If he don't go, before God, I am going up there myself!"

"Don't you see I can't?" his mother cried. "Sarty! Sarty! No! No! Help me, Lizzie!"

Then he was free. His aunt grasped at him but it was too late. He whirled, running, his mother stumbled forward on to her knees behind him, crying to the nearer sister: "Catch him, Net! Catch him!" But that was too late too, the sister (the sisters were twins, born at the same time, yet either of them now gave the impression of being, encompassing as much living meat and volume and weight as any other two of the family) not yet having begun to rise from the chair, her head, face, alone merely turned, presenting to him in the flying instant an astonishing expanse of young female features untroubled by any surprise even, wearing only an expression of bovine interest. Then he was out of the room, out of the house, in the mild dust of the starlit road and the heavy rifeness of honeysuckle, the pale ribbon unspooling with terrific slowness under his running feet, reaching the gate at last and turning in, running, his heart and lungs drumming, on up the drive toward the lighted house, the lighted door. He did not knock, he burst in, sobbing for breath, incapable for the moment of speech; he saw the astonished face of the Negro in the linen jacket without knowing when the Negro had appeared.

"De Spain!" he cried, panted. "Where's . . ." then he saw the white man too emerging from a white door down the hall. "Barn!" he cried. "Barn!"

"What?" the white man said. "Barn?"

"Yes!" the boy cried. "Barn!"

"Catch him!" the white man shouted.

But it was too late this time too. The Negro grasped his shirt, but the entire sleeve, rotten with washing, carried away, and he was out that door too and in the drive again, and had actually never ceased to run even while he was screaming into the white man's face.

Behind him the white man was shouting, "My horse! Fetch my horse!" and he thought for an instant of cutting across the park and climbing the fence into the road, but he did not know the park nor how high the vine-massed fence might be and he dared not risk it. So he ran on down the drive, blood and breath roaring; presently he was in the road again though he could not see it. He could not hear either: the galloping mare was almost upon him before he heard her, and even then he held his course, as if the very urgency of his wild grief and need must in a moment more find him wings, waiting until the ultimate instant to hurl himself aside and into the weed-choked roadside ditch as the horse thundered past and on, for an instant in furious silhouette against the stars, the tranquil early summer night sky which, even before the shape of the horse and rider vanished, stained abruptly and violently upward: a long, swirling roar incredible and soundless, blotting the stars, and he springing up and into the road again, running again, knowing it was too late yet still running even after he heard the shot and, an instant later, two shots, pausing now without knowing he had ceased to run, crying "Pap! Pap!", running again before he knew he had begun to run, stumbling, tripping over something and scrabbling up again without ceasing to run, looking backward over his shoulder at the glare as he got up, running on among the invisible trees, panting, sobbing, "Father! Father!"

At midnight he was sitting on the crest of a hill. He did not know it was midnight and he did not know how far he had come. But there was no glare behind him now and he sat now, his back toward what he had called home for four days anyhow, his face toward the dark woods which he would enter when breath was strong again, small, shaking steadily in the chill darkness, hugging himself into the remainder of his thin, rotten shirt, the grief and despair now no longer terror and fear but just grief and despair. *Father. My father,* he thought. "He was brave!" he cried suddenly, aloud but not loud, no more than a whisper: "He was! He was in the war! He was in Colonel Sartoris' cav'ry!" not knowing that his father had gone to that war a private in the fine old European sense, wearing no uniform, admitting the authority of and giving fidelity to no man or army or flag, going to war as Malbrouck himself did: for booty—it meant nothing and less than nothing to him if it were enemy booty or his own.

The slow constellations wheeled on. It would be dawn and then sun-up after a while and he would be hungry. But that would be tomorrow and now he was only cold, and walking would cure that. His breathing was easier now and he decided to get up and go on, and then he found that he had been asleep because he knew it was almost dawn, the night almost over. He could tell that from the whippoorwills. They were everywhere now among the dark trees below him, constant and inflectioned and ceaseless, so that, as the instant for giving over to the day birds drew nearer and nearer, there was no interval at all between them. He got up. He was a little stiff, but walking would cure that too as it would the cold, and soon there would be the sun. He went on down the hill, toward the dark woods within which the liquid silver voices of the birds called unceasing—the rapid and urgent beating of the urgent and quiring heart of the late spring night. He did not look back.

1939

Further Reading

Warren, Robert Penn. "William Faulkner." *William Faulkner: Three Decades of Criticism*. Ed. Frederick J. Hoffman and Olga W. Vickery. East Lansing: Michigan State UP, 1960. • Howell, Elmo. "Colonel Sartoris Snopes and Faulkner's Aristocrats: A Note on 'Barn Burning.'" *Carolina Quarterly* 11.3 (Summer 1959): 13–19. • Franklin, Phyllis. "Sarty Snopes and 'Barn Burning.'" *Mississippi Quarterly* 21.3 (Summer 1968): 189–93. • Wilson, Gayle Edward. "'Being Pulled Two Ways': The Nature of Sarty's Choice in 'Barn Burning.'" *Mississippi Quarterly* 24.3 (Summer 1971): 279–88. • Stein, William Bysshe. "Faulkner's Devil." *Modern Language Notes* 76.8 (Dec. 1961): 731–32.

Ab Snopes, the protagonist in "Barn Burning," is the founder of a clan of ne'er-do-wells who appear repeatedly in William Faulkner's fiction. Colonel Sartoris is the father of a clan that produces many of Faulkner's more high-minded characters. Faulkner's comments on the Father of Evil may illuminate aspects of both characters.

William Faulkner: On the Role of Satan

During all this time, the angels (with one exception; God had probably had trouble with this one before) merely looked on and watched—the serene and blameless seraphim. . . . Because they were white, immaculate, negative, without past, without thought or grief or regrets or hopes, except that one—the splendid dark incorrigible one, who possessed the arrogance and pride to demand with, and the temerity to object with, and the ambition to substitute with—not only to decline to accept a condition just because it was a fact, but to want to substitute another condition in its place.

But this one's opinion of man was even worse than that of the negative and shining ones. This one not only believed that man was incapable of anything but baseness, this one believed that baseness had been inculcated in man to be used for base personal aggrandizement by them of a higher and more ruthless baseness. So God used the dark spirit too. He did not merely cast it shrieking out of the universe, as He could have done. Instead, He used it. He already presaw the long roster of the ambition's ruthless avatars—Genghis and Caesar and William and Hitler and Barca and Stalin and Bonaparte and Huey Long. But He used more—not only the ambition and the ruthlessness and the arrogance to show man what to revolt against, but also the temerity to revolt and the will to change what one does not like. Because He presaw the long roster of the other avatars of that rebellious and uncompromising pride also, the long roster of names longer and more enduring than those of the tyrants and oppressors.

ERNEST HEMINGWAY

(1899–1961)

HILLS LIKE WHITE ELEPHANTS

The hills across the valley of the Ebro[1] were long and white. On this side there was no shade and no trees and the station was between two lines of rails in the sun. Close against the side of the station there was the warm shadow of the building and a curtain, made of strings of bamboo beads, hung across the open door into the bar, to keep out flies. The American and the girl with him sat at a table in the shade, outside the building. It was very hot and the express from Barcelona would come in forty minutes. It stopped at this junction for two minutes and went on to Madrid.

"What should we drink?" the girl asked. She had taken off her hat and put it on the table.

"It's pretty hot," the man said.

"Let's drink beer."

"Dos cervezas," the man said into the curtain.

"Big ones?" a woman asked from the doorway.

"Yes. Two big ones."

The woman brought two glasses of beer and two felt pads. She put the felt pads and the beer glasses on the table and looked at the man and the girl. The girl was looking off at the line of hills. They were white in the sun and the country was brown and dry.

"They look like white elephants," she said.

"I've never seen one," the man drank his beer.

"No, you wouldn't have."

"I might have," the man said. "Just because you say I wouldn't have doesn't prove anything."

The girl looked at the bead curtain. "They've painted something on it," she said. "What does it say?"

"Anis del Toro. It's a drink."

"Could we try it?"

The man called "Listen" through the curtain. The woman came out from the bar.

"Four reales."

"We want two Anis del Toro."

"With water?"

"Do you want it with water?"

"I don't know," the girl said. "Is it good with water?"

"It's all right."

"You want them with water?" asked the woman.

---

1. River in the north of Spain.

"Yes, with water."

"It tastes like licorice," the girl said and put the glass down.

"That's the way with everything."

"Yes," said the girl. "Everything tastes of licorice. Especially all the things you've waited so long for, like absinthe."

"Oh, cut it out."

"You started it," the girl said. "I was being amused. I was having a fine time."

"Well, let's try and have a fine time."

"All right. I was trying. I said the mountains looked like white elephants. Wasn't that bright?"

"That was bright."

"I wanted to try this new drink. That's all we do, isn't it—look at things and try new drinks?"

"I guess so."

The girl looked across at the hills.

"They're lovely hills," she said. "They don't really look like white elephants. I just meant the coloring of their skin through the trees."

"Should we have another drink?"

"All right."

The warm wind blew the bead curtain against the table.

"The beer's nice and cool," the man said.

"It's lovely," the girl said.

"It's really an awfully simple operation, Jig," the man said. "It's not really an operation at all."

The girl looked at the ground the table legs rested on.

"I know you wouldn't mind it, Jig. It's really not anything. It's just to let the air in."

The girl did not say anything.

"I'll go with you and I'll stay with you all the time. They just let the air in and then it's all perfectly natural."

"Then what will we do afterward?"

"We'll be fine afterward. Just like we were before."

"What makes you think so?"

"That's the only thing that bothers us. It's the only thing that's made us unhappy."

The girl looked at the bead curtain, put her hand out and took hold of two of the strings of beads.

"And you think then we'll be all right and be happy."

"I know we will. You don't have to be afraid. I've known lots of people that have done it."

"So have I," said the girl. "And afterward they were all so happy."

"Well," the man said, "if you don't want to you don't have to. I wouldn't have you do it if you didn't want to. But I know it's perfectly simple."

"And you really want to?"

"I think it's the best thing to do. But I don't want you to do it if you don't really want to."

"And if I do it you'll be happy and things will be like they were and you'll love me?"

"I love you now. You know I love you."

"I know. But if I do it, then it will be nice again if I say things are like white elephants, and you'll like it?"

"I'll love it. I love it now but I just can't think about it. You know how I get when I worry."

"If I do it you won't ever worry?"

"I won't worry about that because it's perfectly simple."

"Then I'll do it. Because I don't care about me."

"What do you mean?"

"I don't care about me."

"Well, I care about you."

"Oh, yes. But I don't care about me. And I'll do it and then everything will be fine."

"I don't want you to do it if you feel that way."

The girl stood up and walked to the end of the station. Across, on the other side, were fields of grain and trees along the banks of the Ebro. Far away, beyond the river, were mountains. The shadow of a cloud moved across the field of grain and she saw the river through the trees.

"And we could have all this," she said. "And we could have everything and every day we make it more impossible."

"What did you say?"

"I said we could have everything."

"We can have everything."

"No, we can't."

"We can have the whole world."

"No, we can't."

"We can go everywhere."

"No, we can't. It isn't ours any more."

"It's ours."

"No, it isn't. And once they take it away, you never get it back."

"But they haven't taken it away."

"We'll wait and see."

"Come on back in the shade," he said. "You mustn't feel that way."

"I don't feel any way," the girl said. "I just know things."

"I don't want you to do anything that you don't want to do—"

"Nor that isn't good for me," she said. "I know. Could we have another beer?"

"All right. But you've got to realize—"

"I realize," the girl said. "Can't we maybe stop talking?"

They sat down at the table and the girl looked across at the hills on the dry side of the valley and the man looked at her and at the table.

"You've got to realize," he said, "that I don't want you to do it if you don't want to. I'm perfectly willing to go through with it if it means anything to you."

"Doesn't it mean anything to you? We could get along."

"Of course it does. But I don't want anybody but you. I don't want any one else. And I know it's perfectly simple."

"Yes, you know it's perfectly simple."

"It's all right for you to say that, but I do know it."

"Would you do something for me now?"

"I'd do anything for you."

"Would you please please please please please please please stop talking?"

He did not say anything but looked at the bags against the wall of the station. There were labels on them from all the hotels where they had spent nights.

"But I don't want you to," he said, "I don't care anything about it."

"I'll scream," the girl said.

The woman came out through the curtains with two glasses of beer and put them down on the damp felt pads. "The train comes in five minutes," she said.

"What did she say?" asked the girl.

"That the train is coming in five minutes."

The girl smiled brightly at the woman, to thank her.

"I'd better take the bags over to the other side of the station," the man said. She smiled at him.

"All right. Then come back and we'll finish the beer."

He picked up the two heavy bags and carried them around the station to the other tracks. He looked up the tracks but could not see the train. Coming back, he walked through the barroom, where people waiting for the train were drinking. He drank an Anis at the bar and looked at the people. They were all waiting reasonably for the train. He went out through the bead curtain. She was sitting at the table and smiled at him.

"Do you feel better?" he asked.

"I feel fine," she said. "There's nothing wrong with me. I feel fine."

1927

Further Reading

Wilson, Edmund. "Hemingway: Gauge of Morale." *Modern Critical Views: Ernest Hemingway.* Ed. Harold Bloom. New York: Chelsea, 1985. 17–33. • Trilling, Lionel. Commentary on "Hills Like White Elephants." *The Exploration of Literature: A Reader with Commentaries.* Garden City, N.Y.: Doubleday, 1967. 729–32. • Maynard, Reid. "Leitmotif and Irony in Hemingway's "Hills Like White Elephants." *University Review* 37.4 (Summer 1971): 273–75. • Lid, Richard W. "Hemingway and the Need for Speech." *Modern Fiction Studies* 8.4 (Winter 1962–63): 401–07. • Kobler, J. F. "Hemingway's 'Hills Like White Elephants.'" *Explicator* 38.4 (Summer 1980): 6–7.

In many of Ernest Hemingway's stories the point of view is largely objective and the dialogue is only occasionally supported by glimpses into the unspoken thoughts of the characters. Hemingway enthusiasts like Eudora Welty applaud Hemingway's reluctance to comment directly on the story or use the omniscient point of view. Others, like Virginia Woolf, are less enthusiastic.

Eudora Welty: On Hemingway's Brilliant Use of Dialogue

Part of Hemingway's power comes straight out of this conditioning he imposes on his stories. In San Francisco there's a painting by Goya, who himself used light, action, and morality dramatically, of course. The bull ring and the great tossing wall of spectators are cut in diagonal half by a great shadow of afternoon. There lies the wonder of the painting—the opaque paired with the clear, golden sun; half of the action, with dense, clotting shade. It's like this in Hemingway's plots.

In the same way, one power of Hemingway's famous use of conversation derives from the fact that it's often in translated or broken sentences—a shadow inserted between the direct speakers. It is an obscuring and at the same time a magical touch; it illuminates from the side. It makes us aware of the fact that communication is going on.

As we now picture Hemingway's story, isn't it something like this—not transparent, not radiant from the front; but from the side, from without his story, from a moral source, comes its beam of light; and his story is not radiant, but spotlighted.

Virginia Woolf: On Hemingway's Overuse of Dialogue

For some reason the book of short stories does not seem to us to go as deep or to promise as much as the novel. Perhaps it is the excessive use of dialogue, for Mr. Hemingway's use of it is surely excessive. A writer will always be chary of dialogue because dialogue puts the most violent pressure upon the reader's attention. He has to hear, to see, to supply the right tone, and to fill in the background from what the characters say without any help from the author. Therefore, when fictitious people are allowed to speak it must be because they have something so important to say that it stimulates the reader to do rather more than his share of the work of creation. But, although Mr. Hemingway keeps us under the fire of dialogue constantly, his people, half the time, are saying what the author could say much more economically for them. At last we are inclined to cry out with the little girl in 'Hills Like White Elephants': 'Would you please please please please please please please stop talking?'

JORGE LUIS BORGES

(1899–1986)

THE ALEPH

translated from the Spanish by Anthony Kerrigan

O God, I could be bounded in a nutshell and count myself a King of infinite space.

Hamlet, II, 2.

But they will teach us that Eternity is the Standing still of the Present Time, a *Nunc-stans* (as the Schools call it); which neither they, nor any else understand, no more than they would a *Hic-stans* for an Infinite greatness of Place.

Leviathan, IV, 46.

On the incandescent February morning Beatriz Viterbo died, after a death agony so imperious it did not for a moment descend into sentimentalism or fear, I noticed that the iron billboards in the Plaza Constitución[1] bore new advertisements for some brand or other of Virginia tobacco; I was saddened by this fact, for it made me realize that the incessant and vast universe was already moving away from her and that this change was the first in an infinite series. The universe would change but I would not, I thought with melancholy vanity; I knew that sometimes my vain devotion had exasperated her; now that she was dead, I could consecrate myself to her memory, without hope but also without humiliation. I thought of how the thirtieth of April was her birthday; to visit her house in Calle Garay on that day and pay my respects to her father and Carlos Argentino Daneri, her first cousin, would be an act of courtesy, irreproachable and perhaps even unavoidable. I would wait, once again, in the twilight of the overladen entrance hall, I would study, one more time, the particulars of her numerous portraits: Beatriz Viterbo in profile, in color; Beatriz wearing a mask, during the Car-

---

1. Constitution Square, the main plaza in Mexico City.

nival of 1921; Beatriz at her First Communion; Beatriz on the day of her wedding to Roberto Alessandri; Beatriz a little while after the divorce, at a dinner in the Club Hípico; Beatriz with Delia San Marco Porcel and Carlos Argentino; Beatriz with the Pekingese which had been a present from Villegas Haedo; Beatriz from the front and in a three-quarter view, smiling, her hand under her chin. . . . I would not be obliged, as on other occasions, to justify my presence with moderate-priced offerings of books, with books whose pages, finally, I learned to cut beforehand, so as to avoid finding, months later, that they were still uncut.

Beatriz Viterbo died in 1929. From that time on, I never let a thirtieth of April go by without a visit to her house. I used to arrive there around seven-fifteen and stay about twenty-five minutes. Every year I came a little later and stayed a little longer. In 1933 a torrential rain worked to my advantage: they were forced to invite me to dine. I did not fail to avail myself of this advantageous precedent. In 1934, I appeared, just after eight, with a honey nutcake from Santa Fe. With the greatest naturalness, I remained for supper. And thus, on these melancholy and vainly erotic anniversaries, Carlos Argentino Daneri began gradually to confide in me.

Beatriz was tall, fragile, lightly leaning forward: there was in her walk (if the oxymoron is acceptable) a kind of gracious torpor, the beginnings of an ecstasy. Carlos Argentino is rosy, important, gray-haired, fine-featured. He holds some subordinate position or other in an illegible library in the south side suburbs. He is authoritarian, but also ineffective. Until very recently, he took advantage of nights and holidays to avoid going out of his house. At a remove of two generations, the Italian *s* and the copious gesticulation of the Italians survive in him. His mental activity is continuous, impassioned, versatile, and altogether insignificant. He abounds in useless analogies and fruitless scruples. He possesses (as did Beatriz) long, lovely, tapering hands. For several months he was obsessed with Paul Fort, less with his ballads than with the idea of irreproachable glory. "He is the Prince of the poets of France," he would repeat fatuously. "You will set yourself against him in vain; no, not even your most poisoned barb will reach him."

The thirtieth of April, 1941, I allowed myself to add to the gift of honey nutcake a bottle of Argentine cognac. Carlos Argentino tasted it, judged it "interesting," and, after a few glasses, launched on a vindication of modern man.

"I evoke him," he said with rather inexplicable animation, "in his studio-laboratory, in the city's watchtowers, so to say, supplied with telephones, telegraphs, phonographs, radiotelephone apparatus, cinematographic equipment, magic lanterns, glossaries, timetables, compendiums, bulletins. . . ."

He remarked that for a man of such faculties the act of travel was useless. Our twentieth century had transformed the fable of Mohammed and the mountain: the mountains, now, converged upon the modern Mohammed.

His ideas seemed so inept to me, their exposition so pompous and so vast, that I immediately related them to literature: I asked him why he did not write them down. Foreseeably he replied that he had already done so: these concepts, and others no less novel, figured in the Augural Canto, or more simply, the Prologue Canto, of a poem on which he had been working for many years, without publicity, without any deafening to-do, putting his entire reliance on those two props known as work and solitude. First, he opened the floodgates of the imagination; then he made use of a sharp file. The poem was titled *The Earth;* it consisted of a description of the planet, wherein, naturally, there was no lack of picturesque digression and elegant apostrophe.

I begged him to read me a passage, even though brief. He opened a drawer in his desk, took out a tall bundle of pages from a pad, each sheet stamped with the letterhead of the Juan Crisóstomo Lafinur Library, and, with sonorous satisfaction, read out:

> *I have seen, like the Greek, the cities of men and their fame,*
> *Their labor, days of various light, hunger's shame;*
> *I correct no event, falsify no name,*
> *But the voyage I narrate is . . .* autour de ma chambre.

"By all lights an interesting strophe," he opined. "The first line wins the applause of the professor, the academician, the Hellenist, if not of superficial pedants, who form, these last, a considerable sector of public opinion. The second passes from Homer to Hesiod (the entire verse an implicit homage, writ on the façade of the resplendent building, to the father of didactic poetry), not without rejuvenating a procedure whose lineage goes back to Scripture, that of enumeration, congeries or conglomeration. The third line—Baroquism? Decadentism? Purified and fanatical cult of form?—is composed of two twin hemistichs. The fourth, frankly bilingual, assures me the unconditional support of every spirit sensitive to the gay lure of graceful play. I say nothing of the rare rhyme, nor of the learning which permits me—without any pedantry!—to accumulate, in four lines, three erudite allusions encompassing thirty centuries of compressed literature: first to the *Odyssey,* second to *Works and Days,* third to the immortal bagatelle proffered us through the idling of the Savoyard's pen. . . . Once more I have understood that modern art requires the balsam of laughter, the *scherzo.* Decidedly, Goldoni has the floor!"

He read me many another stanza, each of which obtained his approbation and profuse commentary, too. There was nothing memorable in any of them. I did not even judge them very much worse than the first one. There had been a collaboration, in his writing, between application, resignation, and chance; the virtues which Daneri attributed to them were posterior. I realized that the poet's labor lay not with the poetry, but with the invention of reasons to make the poetry admirable; naturally, this ulterior and subsequent labor modified the work for him, but not for others. Daneri's oral style was extravagant; his metric heaviness hindered his transmitting that extravagance, except in a very few instances, to the poem.*

Only once in my life have I had occasion to examine the fifteen thousand dodecasyllabic verses of the *Poly-Olbion*, that topographic epic poem in which Michael Drayton recorded the flora, fauna, hydrography, orography, military and monastic history of England; I am sure that this considerable, but limited, production is less tedious than the vast congeneric enterprise of Carlos Argentino. The latter proposed to put into verse the entire face of the planet; in 1941, he had already dispatched several hectares of the State of Queensland, in addition to one kilometer of the course of the River Ob, a gasometer north of Veracruz, the main business houses in the parish of La Concepción, the villa owned by Mariana Cambaceres de Alvear on Eleventh of September street, in Belgrano, and an establishment devoted to Turkish baths not far from the famous Brighton Aquarium. He read me from his poem certain laborious passages concerning the Australian zone; these large and formless alexandrines lacked the relative agitation of the Preface. I copy one stanza:

> *Know ye. To the right hand of the routinary post*
> *(Coming, of course, from the North-northwest)*
> *One wearies out a skeleton—Color? White-celeste—*
> *Which gives the sheep run an ossuary cast.*

"Two audacious strokes," he cried out in exultation, "redeemed, I can hear you muttering, by success! One, the epithet *routinary*, which accurately proclaims, *en passant*,[2] the inevitable tedium inherent in pastoral and farming chores, a tedium which neither georgic poetry nor our already laureled *Don Segundo* ever ventured to denounce in this way, in red-hot heat. The other, the energetic prosaicism of *one wearies out a skeleton*, a phrase which the prudish will want to excommunicate in horror, but which the critic with virile taste will appreciate more than his life. For the rest, the entire line is of high carat, the highest. The second hemistich engages the reader in the most animated converse; it anticipates his lively curiosity, places a question in his mouth and answers it . . . instantly. And what do you tell me of that find of mine: *white-celeste*? This picturesque neologism insinuates the sky, which is a very important factor in the Australian landscape. Without this evocation, the colors of the sketch would be much too somber, and the reader would find himself com-

---

* Among my memories are also some lines of a satire in which he lashed out unsparingly at bad poets. After accusing them of dressing their poems in the warlike armor of erudition, and of flapping in vain their unavailing wings, he concluded with this verse: "But they forget, alas, one foremost fact—BEAUTY!"

Only the fear of creating an army of implacable and powerful enemies dissuaded him (he told me) from fearlessly publishing this poem. [author's note]

2. In passing.

pelled to close the book, wounded in the innermost part of his soul by a black and incurable melancholy."

Toward midnight, I took my leave.

Two Sundays later, Daneri called me on the telephone, for the first time in his life, I believe. He proposed that we meet at four o'clock, "to drink a glass of milk together, in the salon-bar next door, which the progressivism of Zunino and of Zungri—the proprietors of my house, you will recall—is causing to be inaugurated on the corner. Truly, a confectionery shop you will be interested in knowing about." I accepted, with more resignation than enthusiasm. There was no difficulty in finding a table; the "salon-bar," inexorably modern, was just slightly less atrocious than what I had foreseen; at the neighboring tables an excited public mentioned the sums which Zunino and Zungri had invested without batting an eye. Carlos Argentino feigned astonishment over some wonder or other in the lighting installations (which he doubtless already knew about), and he said to me, with a certain severity:

"You'll have to admit, no matter how grudgingly, that these premises vie successfully with the most renowned of Flores."

Then, he reread me four or five pages of his poem. He had made corrections in accordance with a depraved principle of verbal ostentation: where he had formerly written *azurish*,[3] he now put *azuritic, azuritish,* and even *azury.* The word *lacteous* proved not ugly enough for him; in the course of an impetuous description of a wool washer, he preferred *lactary, lactinous, lactescent, lactiferous.*[4] . . . He bitterly reviled the critics; later, in a more benign spirit, he compared them to persons "who dispose of no precious metals, nor steam presses, nor rolling presses, nor sulphuric acids for minting treasures, but who can *indicate* to *others* the *site* of a treasure." Next he censured *prologomania*[5] "which the Prince of Talents,[6] in the graceful prefacing of his *Don Quixote,* already ridiculed." He nevertheless admitted to me now that by way of frontispiece to the new work a showy prologue, an accolade signed by the feather pen of a bird of prey, of a man of weight, would be most convenient. He added that he planned to bring out the initial cantos of his poems. I understood, then, the singular telephonic invitation; the man was going to ask me to preface his pedantic farrago.[7] My fears proved unfounded: Carlos Argentino observed, with rancorous admiration, that he did not misuse the epithet in denominating as *solid* the prestige achieved in all circles by Álvaro Melián Lafinur, man of letters, who would, if I insisted on it, delightfully prologue the poem. So as to avoid the most unpardonable of failures, I was to make myself spokesman for two undeniable merits: formal perfection and scientific rigor, "inasmuch as this

---

3. A light purplish blue.
4. Producing and/or secreting milk.
5. Daneri's opinion of overkill on the part of the author in explaining his text.
6. Miguel de Cervantes (1547–1616), Spanish author of *Don Quixote.*
7. A medley or an arrangement.

vast garden of tropes, figures of speech, and elegance, allows no single detail which does not confirm the severe truth." He added that Beatriz had always enjoyed herself with Álvaro.

I assented, assented profusely. For greater conviction, I promised to speak to Álvaro on Thursday, rather than wait until the following Monday: we could meet at the small supper that usually climaxes every reunion of the Writers' Club. (There are no such suppers, but it is an irrefutable fact that the reunions do take place on Thursdays, a point which Carlos Argentino Daneri would find confirmed in the daily newspapers, and which lent a certain reality to the phrase.) Adopting an air halfway between divinatory and sagacious, I told him that before taking up the question of a prologue, I would delineate the curious plan of the book. We took our leave of each other. As I turned the corner into Calle Bernardo de Irigoyen, I impartially considered the alternatives before me: a) I could talk to Álvaro and tell him how that cousin of Beatriz' (this explicatory euphemism would allow me to say her name) had elaborated a poem which seemed to dilate to infinity the possibilities of cacophony and chaos; b) I could fail to speak to Álvaro altogether. I foresaw, lucidly, that my indolence would choose b.

From early Friday morning the telephone began to disquiet me. It made me indignant to think that this instrument, which in other days had produced the irrecoverable voice of Beatriz, could lower itself to being a receptacle for the useless and perhaps even choleric complaints of that deceived man Carlos Argentino Daneri. Luckily, nothing awful occurred —except the inevitable animosity inspired by that man, who had imposed on me a delicate mission and would later forget me altogether.

The telephone lost its terrors; but then toward the end of October, Carlos Argentino called me again. He was terribly agitated; at first I could not identify the voice. Sadly and yet wrathfully he stammered that the now uncurbed Zunino and Zungri, under the pretext of enlarging their outrageous confectionery, were going to demolish his house.

"The house of my fathers! My house, the inveterate house of the Calle Garay!" he went on repeating, perhaps forgetting his grief in the melody.

It was not difficult for me to share his grief. Once past forty, every change is a detestable symbol of the passage of time. Besides, at stake was a house that, for me, infinitely alluded to Beatriz. I wanted to bring out this most delicate point; my interlocutor did not hear me. He said that if Zunino and Zungri persisted in their absurd proposal, Doctor Zunni, his lawyer, would enter an action *ipso facto*[8] for damages and would oblige them to pay one hundred thousand *pesos nacionales*[9] in compensation.

I was impressed to hear the name of Zunni: his practice, out of his office at the corner of Caseros and Tacuarí, was of a proverbial and solemn reliability. I asked if Zunni had already taken charge of the matter. Daneri

---

8. By that very fact.
9. National coins; in other words, in domestic currency.

said he would speak to him that very afternoon. He hesitated, and then, in that level, impersonal voice to which we all have recourse for confiding something very intimate, he told me that in order to finish the poem the house was indispensable to him, for in one of the cellar corners there was an Aleph. He indicated that an Aleph is one of the points in space containing all points.

"It's in the dining-room cellar," he explained, his diction grown hasty from anxiety. "It's mine, it's mine; I discovered it in childhood, before I was of school age. The cellar stair is steep, and my aunt and uncle had forbidden me to go down it. But someone said that there was a world in the cellar. They were referring, I found out later, to a trunk, but I understood there was a world there. I descended secretly, went rolling down the forbidden stairs, fell off. When I opened my eyes I saw the Aleph."

"The Aleph?" I echoed.

"Yes, the place where, without any possible confusion, all the places in the world are found, seen from every angle. I revealed my discovery to no one, and I returned there. The child could not understand that this privilege was proffered him so that the man might chisel out the poem! Zunino and Zungri will not dislodge me, no, a thousand times no. With the code of laws in hand, Doctor Zunni will prove that my Aleph is *inalienable*."

I attempted to reason with him.

"But, isn't the cellar very dark?"

"Really, truth does not penetrate a rebellious understanding. If all the places on earth are in the Aleph, the Aleph must also contain all the illuminations, all the lights, all the sources of light."

"I will go and see it at once."

I hung up, before he could issue a prohibition. The knowledge of one fact is enough to allow one to perceive at once a whole series of confirming traits, previously unsuspected. I was astonished not to have understood until that moment that Carlos Argentino was a madman. All the Viterbos, for that matter . . . Beatriz (I often say so myself) was a woman, a girl, of an almost implacable clairvoyance, but there was about her a negligence, a distraction, a disdain, a real cruelty, which perhaps called for a pathological explanation. The madness of Carlos Argentino filled me with malicious felicity; in our innermost beings, we had always detested each other.

In Calle Garay, the serving woman asked me if I would be kind enough to wait. The child was, as always, in the cellar, developing photographs. Next to the flower vase without a single flower in it, atop the useless piano, there smiled (more timeless than anachronic) the great portrait of Beatriz, in dull colors. No one could see us; in an access of tender despair I went up close and told her:

"Beatriz, Beatriz Elena, Beatriz Elena Viterbo, beloved Beatriz, Beatriz lost forever, it's me, Borges."

A little later Carlos came in. He spoke with a certain dryness. I understood that he was incapable of thinking of anything but the loss of the Aleph.

"A glass of the pseudo-cognac," he ordered, "and then you can duck into the cellar. As you already know, the dorsal decubitus is imperative. And so are darkness, immobility, and a certain ocular accommodation. You lie down on the tile floor and fix your eyes on the nineteenth step of the pertinent stairs. I leave, lower the trap door, and you're alone. Quite likely— it should be easy!—some rodent will scare you! In a few minutes you will see the Aleph. The microcosm of alchemists and cabalists, our proverbial concrete friend, the *multum in parvo!*"[10]

Once we were in the dining room he added:

"Of course if you don't see it, your incapacity in no way invalidates my testimony. . . . Now, down with you. Very shortly you will be able to engage in a dialogue with *all* of the images of Beatriz."

I rapidly descended, tired of his insubstantial words. The cellar, barely wider than the stairs, had much of a well about it. I gazed about in search of the trunk of which Carlos Argentino had spoken. Some cases with bottles in them and some canvas bags cluttered one corner. Carlos picked up one of the bags, folded it in half and placed it exactly in a precise spot.

"A humble pillow," he explained, "but if I raise it one centimeter, you won't see a thing, and you'll be left abashed and ashamed. Stretch your bulk out on the floor and count off nineteen steps."

I complied with his ridiculous requisites; and at last he went away. Carefully he closed the trap door; the darkness, despite a crevice which I discovered later, seemed total. And suddenly I realized the danger I ran: I had allowed myself to be buried by a madman, after having drunk some poison! Behind the transparent bravado of Carlos was the intimate terror that I would not see the prodigy; to defend his delirium, to avoid knowing that he was mad, Carlos *had to kill me.* A confused malaise swept over me; I attempted to attribute it to my rigid posture rather than to the operation of a narcotic. I closed my eyes; opened them. Then I saw the Aleph.

I arrive, now, at the ineffable center of my story. And here begins my despair as a writer. All language is an alphabet of symbols whose use presupposes a past shared by all the other interlocutors. How, then, transmit to others the infinite Aleph, which my fearful mind scarcely encompasses? The mystics, in similar situations, are lavish with emblems: to signify the divinity, a Persian speaks of a bird that in some way is all birds; Alanus de Insulis speaks of a sphere whose center is everywhere and whose circumference is nowhere; Ezekiel,[11] of an angel with four faces who looks simultaneously to the Orient and the Occident, to the North and the South. (Not vainly do I recall these inconceivable analogies; they bear some relation to the Aleph.) Perhaps the gods would not be against my finding an equivalent image, but then this report would be contaminated with literature, with falsehood. For the rest, the central problem is unsolvable: the enumera-

---

10. A great deal in a small space.
11. One of the major Hebrew prophets; see Ezekiel 1:5–6.

tion, even if only partial, of an infinite complex. In that gigantic instant I saw millions of delightful and atrocious acts; none astonished me more than the fact that all of them together occupied the same point, without superposition and without transparency. What my eyes saw was simultaneous: what I shall transcribe is successive, because language is successive. Nevertheless, I shall cull something of it all.

In the lower part of the step, toward the right, I saw a small iridescent sphere, of almost intolerable brilliance. At first I thought it rotary; then I understood that this movement was an illusion produced by the vertiginous sights it enclosed. The Aleph's diameter must have been about two or three centimeters, but Cosmic Space was in it, without diminution of size. Each object (the mirror's glass, for instance) was infinite objects, for I clearly saw it from all points in the universe. I saw the heavy-laden sea; I saw the dawn and the dusk; I saw the multitudes of America; I saw a silver-plated cobweb at the center of a black pyramid; I saw a tattered labyrinth (it was London); I saw interminable eyes nearby looking at me as if in a mirror; I saw all the mirrors in the planet and none reflected me; in an inner patio in the Calle Soler I saw the same paving tile I had seen thirty years before in the entranceway to a house in the town of Fray Bentos; I saw clusters of grapes, snow, tobacco, veins of metal, steam; I saw convex equatorial deserts and every grain of sand in them; I saw a woman at Inverness whom I shall not forget: I saw her violent switch of hair, her proud body, the cancer in her breast; I saw a circle of dry land on a sidewalk where formerly there had been a tree; I saw a villa in Adrogué; I saw a copy of the first English version of Pliny, by Philemon Holland, and saw simultaneously every letter on every page (as a boy I used to marvel that the letters in a closed book did not get mixed up and lost in the course of a night); I saw night and day contemporaneously; I saw a sunset in Querétaro which seemed to reflect the color of a rose in Bengal; I saw my bedroom with nobody in it; I saw in a study in Alkmaar a terraqueous[12] globe between two mirrors which multiplied it without end; I saw horses with swirling manes on a beach by the Caspian Sea at dawn; I saw the delicate bone structure of a hand; I saw the survivors of a battle sending out post cards; I saw a deck of Spanish playing cards in a shopwindow in Mirzapur; I saw the oblique shadows of some ferns on the floor of a hothouse; I saw tigers, emboli, bison, ground swells, and armies; I saw all the ants on earth; I saw a Persian astrolabe; in a desk drawer I saw (the writing made me tremble) obscene, incredible, precise letters, which Beatriz had written Carlos Argentino; I saw an adored monument in La Chacarita cemetery; I saw the atrocious relic of what deliciously had been Beatriz Viterbo; I saw the circulation of my obscure blood; I saw the gearing of love and the modifications of death; I saw the Aleph from all points; I saw the earth in the Aleph and in the earth the Aleph once more and the earth in the Aleph; I saw my face and my viscera; I saw your face and

---

12. Consisting of land and water.

felt vertigo and cried because my eyes had seen that conjectural and secret object whose name men usurp but which no man has gazed on: the inconceivable universe.

I felt infinite veneration, infinite compassion.

"You must be good and dizzy from peering into things that don't concern you," cried a hateful, jovial voice. "Even if you rack your brains, you won't be able to pay me back in a century for this revelation. What a formidable observatory, eh, Borges!"

Carlos Argentino's feet occupied the highest step. In the half-light I managed to get up and to stammer:

"Formidable, yes, formidable."

The indifference in the sound of my voice surprised me. Anxiously Carlos Argentino insisted:

"You saw it all, in colors?"

It was at that instant that I conceived my revenge. Benevolently, with obvious pity, nervous, evasive, I thanked Carlos Argentino for the hospitality of his cellar and urged him to take advantage of the demolition of his house to get far away from the pernicious capital, which is easy on no one, believe me, on no one! I refused, with suave energy, to discuss the Aleph; I embraced him on leaving, and repeated that the country and its quiet are two grand doctors.

In the street, on the Constitución stairs, in the subway, all the faces struck me as familiar. I feared that not a single thing was left to cause me surprise; I was afraid I would never be quit of the impression that I had "returned." Happily, at the end of a few nights of insomnia, forgetfulness worked in me again.

P.S. March 1, 1943
Six months after the demolition of the building in Calle Garay, Procusto Publishers did not take fright at the length of Argentino's considerable poem and launched upon the reading public a selection of "Argentino Extracts." It is almost needless to repeat what happened: Carlos Argentino Daneri received Second Prize, of the National Prizes for Literature.* First Prize was awarded to Doctor Aita; Third, to Doctor Mario Bonfanti; incredibly, my book *The Cards of the Cardsharp* did not get a single vote. Once again incomprehension and envy won the day! For a long time now I have not been able to see Daneri; the daily press says he will soon give us another volume. His fortunate pen (no longer benumbed by the Aleph) has been consecrated to versifying the epitomes of Doctor Acevedo Díaz.

I would like to add two further observations: one, on the nature of the Aleph; the other, on its name. As is well known, the latter is the name of the first letter of the alphabet of the sacred language. Its application to the

_____
* "I received your pained congratulations," he wrote me. "You rage, my poor friend, with envy, but you must confess—even if it chokes you!—that this time I have crowned my cap with the reddest of feathers; my turban with the most *caliph* of rubies." [author's note]

cycle of my story does not appear mere chance. For the cabala, this letter signifies the En-Sof, the limitless and pure divinity; it has also been said that it has the form of a man who points out heaven and earth, to indicate that the inferior world is the mirror and map of the superior; for the *Mengenlehre,* it is the symbol of transfinite numbers, in which the whole is no greater than any of its parts. I wanted to know: Had Carlos Argentino chosen this name, or had he read it, *applied to another point where all points converge,* in some one of the innumerable texts revealed to him by the Aleph in his house? Incredible as it may seem, I believe there is (or was) another Aleph, I believe that the Aleph in the Calle Garay was a false Aleph.

Here are my reasons. Toward 1867, Captain Burton held the office of British Consul in Brazil. In July, 1942, Pedro Henríquez Ureña discovered, in a library at Santos, a manuscript by Burton dealing with the mirror which the Orient attributes to Iskandar Zu al-Karnayn, or Alexander Bicornis of Macedonia. In its glass the entire world was reflected. Burton mentions other artifices of like kind: the septuple goblet of Kai Josru; the mirror which Tarik Benzeyad found in a tower (*The Thousand and One Nights,* 272); the mirror which Lucian of Samosata was able to examine on the moon (*True History,* I, 26); the diaphanous spear which the first book of Capella's *Satyricon* attributes to Jupiter; the universal mirror of Merlin, "round and hollow . . . and seemed a world of glass" (*The Faerie Queene,* III, 2, 19). And he adds these curious words: "But the former (besides the defect of not existing) are mere instruments of optics. The Faithful who attend the Mosque of Amr, in Cairo, know very well that the universe is in the interior of one of the stone columns surrounding the central courtyard. . . . No one, of course, can see it, but those who put their ears to the surface claim to hear, within a short time, its workaday rumor. . . . The mosque dates from the seventh century; the columns come from other, pre-Islamic, temples, for as ibn-Khaldûn has written: '*In republics founded by nomads, the assistance of foreigners is indispensable in all that concerns masonry.*' "

Does that Aleph exist in the innermost recess of a stone? Did I see it when I saw all things, and have I forgotten it? Our minds are porous with forgetfulness; I myself am falsifying and losing, through the tragic erosion of the years, the features of Beatriz.

trans. 1970

Further Reading

Dembo, L. S. Interview. *The Contemporary Writer.* Ed. L. S. Dembo and Cyrena N. Pondrom. Madison: U of Wisconsin P, 1972. 113–21. • Barrenchea, Ana María. "Borges: Life and Works." *Borges the Labyrinth Maker.* Ed. and trans. Robert Lima. New York: New York UP, 1965. 1–22. • Bell-Villada, Gene H. "*El Aleph* III: The

Visionary Experience." *Borges and His Fiction: A Guide to His Mind and Art.* Chapel Hill: U of North Carolina P, 1981. 202–37, spec. 219–29. • McBride, Mary. "Jorge Luis Borges, Existentialist: 'The Aleph' and the Relativity of Human Perception." *Studies in Short Fiction* 14.4 (Fall 1977): 401–03. • Murillo, L. A. "The Labyrinths of Jorge Luis Borges: An Introduction to the Stories of *The Aleph." Modern Language Quarterly* 20.3 (Sept. 1959): 259–66.

The fiction of Jorge Luis Borges, like that of several other contemporary Latin American writers, is built on lines very different from those that characterize the realistic fiction of his North American contemporaries Hemingway and Steinbeck. We can get some sense of the tone and method of Borges' work from comments he made during an interview with L. S. Dembo.

Jorge Luis Borges: On Philosophical Quandaries

Q. One of your chief themes seems to be the ability of the mind to influence or recreate reality. Are you in fact a philosophic idealist or do you simply delight in paradoxes made possible by idealistic reasoning, or both?

A. Well, my father—I seem to be referring to him all the time; I greatly loved him, and I think of him as living—my father was a professor of psychology, and I remember—I was quite a small boy—when he began trying to teach me something of the puzzles that constitute the idealistic philosophy. And I remember once he explained to me, or he tried to explain to me, with a chessboard, the paradoxes of Xeno, Achilles and the Tortoise, and so on. I also remember that he held an orange in his hand and asked me, "Would you think of the taste of the orange as belonging to it?" And I said, "Well, I hardly know that. I suppose I'd have to taste the orange. I don't think the orange is tasting itself all the time." He replied, "That's quite a good answer," and then he went on to the color of the orange and asked, "Well, if you close your eyes, and if I put out the light, what color is the orange?" He didn't say a word about Berkeley or Hume, but he was really teaching me the philosophy of idealism, although, of course, he never used those words, because he thought they might scare me away. But he was teaching me a good many things, and he taught them as if they were of no importance at all. He was teaching me philosophy and psychology—that was his province—and he used William James as his textbook. He was teaching me all those things, and yet not allowing me to suspect that he was teaching me something.

Q. But you would say that you more or less were brought up on idealism?

A. Yes, and now when people tell me that they're down-to-earth and they tell me that I should be down-to-earth and think of reality, I wonder why a dream or an idea should be less real than this table for example, or why Macbeth should be less real than today's newspaper. I cannot quite understand this. I suppose if I had to define myself, I would define myself as an idealist, philosophically speaking. But I'm not sure I have to define myself. I'd rather go on wondering and puzzling about things, for I find that very enjoyable.

JOHN STEINBECK

(1902–1968)

THE CHRYSANTHEMUMS

The high grey-flannel fog of winter closed off the Salinas Valley from the sky and from all the rest of the world. On every side it sat like a lid on the mountains and made of the great valley a closed pot. On the broad, level land floor the gang plows bit deep and left the black earth shining like metal where the shares had cut. On the foothill ranches across the Salinas River, the yellow stubble fields seemed to be bathed in pale cold sunshine, but there was no sunshine in the valley now in December. The thick willow scrub along the river flamed with sharp and positive yellow leaves.

It was a time of quiet and of waiting. The air was cold and tender. A light wind blew up from the southwest so that the farmers were mildly hopeful of a good rain before long; but fog and rain do not go together.

Across the river, on Henry Allen's foothill ranch there was little work to be done, for the hay was cut and stored and the orchards were plowed up to receive the rain deeply when it should come. The cattle on the higher slopes were becoming shaggy and rough-coated.

Elisa Allen, working in her flower garden, looked down across the yard and saw Henry, her husband, talking to two men in business suits. The three of them stood by the tractor shed, each man with one foot on the side of the little Fordson. They smoked cigarettes and studied the machine as they talked.

Elisa watched them for a moment and then went back to her work. She was thirty-five. Her face was lean and strong and her eyes were as clear as water. Her figure looked blocked and heavy in her gardening costume, a man's black hat pulled low down over her eyes, clodhopper shoes, a figured print dress almost completely covered by a big corduroy apron with four big pockets to hold the snips, the trowel and scratcher, the seeds and the knife she worked with. She wore heavy leather gloves to protect her hands while she worked.

She was cutting down the old year's chrysanthemum stalks with a pair of short and powerful scissors. She looked down toward the men by the tractor shed now and then. Her face was eager and mature and handsome; even her work with the scissors was over-eager, over-powerful. The chrysanthemum stems seemed too small and easy for her energy.

She brushed a cloud of hair out of her eyes with the back of her glove, and left a smudge of earth on the cheek in doing it. Behind her stood the neat white farm house with red geraniums close-banked around it as high as the windows. It was a hard-swept looking little house, with hard-polished windows, and a clean mud-mat on the front steps.

Elisa cast another glance toward the tractor shed. The strangers were getting into their Ford coupe. She took off a glove and put her strong fingers down into the forest of new green chrysanthemum sprouts that were growing around the old roots. She spread the leaves and looked down among the close-growing stems. No aphids were there, no sowbugs or snails or cutworms. Her terrier fingers destroyed such pests before they could get started.

Elisa started at the sound of her husband's voice. He had come near quietly, and he leaned over the wire fence that protected her flower garden from cattle and dogs and chickens.

"At it again," he said. "You've got a strong new crop coming."

Elisa straightened her back and pulled on the gardening glove again. "Yes. They'll be strong this coming year." In her tone and on her face there was a little smugness.

"You've got a gift with things," Henry observed. "Some of those yellow chrysanthemums you had this year were ten inches across. I wish you'd work out in the orchard and raise some apples that big."

Her eyes sharpened. "Maybe I could do it, too. I've a gift with things, all right. My mother had it. She could stick anything in the ground and make it grow. She said it was having planters' hands that knew how to do it."

"Well, it sure works with flowers," he said.

"Henry, who were those men you were talking to?"

"Why, sure, that's what I came to tell you. They were from the Western Meat Company. I sold those thirty head of three-year-old steers. Got nearly my own price, too."

"Good," she said. "Good for you."

"And I thought," he continued, "I thought how it's Saturday afternoon, and we might go into Salinas for dinner at a restaurant, and then to a picture show—to celebrate, you see."

"Good," she repeated. "Oh, yes. That will be good."

Henry put on his joking tone. "There's fights tonight. How'd you like to go to the fights?"

"Oh, no," she said breathlessly. "No, I wouldn't like fights."

"Just fooling, Elisa. We'll go to a movie. Let's see. It's two now. I'm going to take Scotty and bring down those steers from the hill. It'll take us maybe two hours. We'll go in town about five and have dinner at the Cominos Hotel. Like that?"

"Of course I'll like it. It's good to eat away from home."

"All right, then. I'll go get up a couple of horses."

She said, "I'll have plenty of time to transplant some of these sets, I guess."

She heard her husband calling Scotty down by the barn. And a little later she saw the two men ride up the pale yellow hillside in search of the steers.

There was a little square sandy bed kept for rooting the chrysanthemums. With her trowel she turned the soil over and over, and smoothed it and patted it firm. Then she dug ten parallel trenches to receive the sets. Back at the chrysanthemum bed she pulled out the little crisp shoots, trimmed off the leaves of each one with her scissors and laid it on a small orderly pile.

A squeak of wheels and plod of hoofs came from the road. Elisa looked up. The country road ran along the dense bank of willows and cottonwoods that bordered the river, and up this road came a curious vehicle, curiously drawn. It was an old spring-wagon, with a round canvas top on it like the cover of a prairie schooner. It was drawn by an old bay horse and a little grey-and-white burro. A big stubble-bearded man sat between the cover flaps and drove the crawling team. Underneath the wagon, between the hind wheels, a lean and rangy mongrel dog walked sedately. Words were painted on the canvas in clumsy, crooked letters. "Pots, pans, knives, sisors, lawn mores. Fixed." Two rows of articles and the triumphantly definitive "Fixed" below. The black paint had run down in little sharp points beneath each letter.

Elisa, squatting on the ground, watched to see the crazy, loose-jointed wagon pass by. But it didn't pass. It turned into the farm road in front of her house, crooked old wheels skirling and squeaking. The rangy dog darted from between the wheels and ran ahead. Instantly the two ranch shepherds flew out at him. Then all three stopped, and with stiff and quivering tails, with taut straight legs, with ambassadorial dignity, they slowly circled, sniffing daintily. The caravan pulled up to Elisa's wire fence and stopped. Now the newcomer dog, feeling outnumbered, lowered his tail and retired under the wagon with raised hackles and bared teeth.

The man on the wagon seat called out. "That's a bad dog in a fight when he gets started."

Elisa laughed. "I see he is. How soon does he generally get started?"

The man caught up her laughter and echoed it heartily. "Sometimes not for weeks and weeks," he said. He climbed stiffly down, over the wheel. The horse and the donkey drooped like unwatered flowers.

Elisa saw that he was a very big man. Although his hair and beard were greying, he did not look old. His worn black suit was wrinkled and spotted with grease. The laughter had disappeared from his face and eyes the moment his laughing voice ceased. His eyes were dark, and they were full of the brooding that gets in the eyes of teamsters and of sailors. The calloused hands he rested on the wire fence were cracked, and every crack was a black line. He took off his battered hat.

"I'm off my general road, ma'am," he said. "Does this dirt road cut over across the river to the Los Angeles highway?"

Elisa stood up and shoved the thick scissors in her apron pocket. "Well, yes, it does, but it winds around and then fords the river. I don't think your team could pull through the sand."

He replied with some asperity. "It might surprise you what them beasts can pull through."

"When they get started?" she asked.

He smiled for a second. "Yes. When they get started."

"Well," said Elisa, "I think you'll save time if you go back to the Salinas road and pick up the highway there."

He drew a big finger down the chicken wire and made it sing. "I ain't in any hurry, ma'am. I go from Seattle to San Diego and back every year. Takes all my time. About six months each way. I aim to follow nice weather."

Elisa took off her gloves and stuffed them in the apron pocket with the scissors. She touched the under edge of her man's hat, searching for fugitive hairs. "That sounds like a nice kind of a way to live," she said.

He leaned confidentially over the fence. "Maybe you noticed the writing on my wagon. I mend pots and sharpen knives and scissors. You got any of them things to do?"

"Oh, no," she said quickly. "Nothing like that." Her eyes hardened with resistance.

"Scissors is the worst thing," he explained. "Most people just ruin scissors trying to sharpen 'em but I know how. I got a special tool. It's a little bobbit kind of thing, and patented. But it sure does the trick."

"No. My scissors are all sharp."

"All right, then. Take a pot," he continued earnestly, "a bent pot, or a pot with a hole. I can make it like new so you don't have to buy no new ones. That's a saving for you."

"No," she said shortly. "I tell you I have nothing like that for you to do."

His face fell to an exaggerated sadness. His voice took on a whining undertone. "I ain't had a thing to do today. Maybe I won't have no supper tonight. You see I'm off my regular road. I know folks on the highway clear from Seattle to San Diego. They save their things for me to sharpen up because they know I do it so good and save them money."

"I'm sorry," Elisa said irritably. "I haven't anything for you to do."

His eyes left her face and fell to searching the ground. They roamed about until they came to the chrysanthemum bed where she had been working. "What's them plants, ma'am?"

The irritation and resistance melted from Elisa's face. "Oh, those are chrysanthemums, giant whites and yellows. I raise them every year, bigger than anybody around here."

"Kind of a long-stemmed flower? Looks like a quick puff of colored smoke?" he asked.

"That's it. What a nice way to describe them."

"They smell kind of nasty till you get used to them," he said.

"It's a good bitter smell," she retorted, "not nasty at all."

He changed his tone quickly. "I like the smell myself."

"I had ten-inch blooms this year," she said.

The man leaned farther over the fence. "Look. I know a lady down the road a piece, has got the nicest garden you ever seen. Got nearly every kind of flower but no chrysanthemums. Last time I was mending a copper-bottom washtub for her (that's a hard job but I do it good), she said to me, 'If you ever run acrost some nice chrysanthemums I wish you'd try to get me a few seeds.' That's what she told me."

Elisa's eyes grew alert and eager. "She couldn't have known much about chrysanthemums. You can raise them from seed, but it's much easier to root the little sprouts you see there."

"Oh," he said. "I s'pose I can't take none to her, then."

"Why yes you can," Elisa cried. "I can put some in damp sand, and you can carry them right along with you. They'll take root in the pot if you keep them damp. And then she can transplant them."

"She'd sure like to have some, ma'am. You say they're nice ones?"

"Beautiful," she said. "Oh, beautiful." Her eyes shone. She tore off the battered hat and shook out her dark pretty hair. "I'll put them in a flower pot, and you can take them right with you. Come into the yard."

While the man came through the picket gate Elisa ran excitedly along the geranium-bordered path to the back of the house. And she returned carrying a big red flower pot. The gloves were forgotten now. She kneeled on the ground by the starting bed and dug up the sandy soil with her fingers and scooped it into the bright new flower pot. Then she picked up the little pile of shoots she had prepared. With her strong fingers she pressed them into the sand and tamped around them with her knuckles. The man stood over her. "I'll tell you what to do," she said. "You remember so you can tell the lady."

"Yes, I'll try to remember."

"Well, look. These will take root in about a month. Then she must set them out, about a foot apart in good rich earth like this, see?" She lifted a handful of dark soil for him to look at. "They'll grow fast and tall. Now remember this. In July tell her to cut them down, about eight inches from the ground."

"Before they bloom?" he asked.

"Yes, before they bloom." Her face was tight with eagerness. "They'll come right up again. About the last of September the buds will start."

She stopped and seemed perplexed. "It's the budding that takes the most care," she said hesitantly. "I don't know how to tell you." She looked deep into his eyes, searchingly. Her mouth opened a little, and she seemed to be listening. "I'll try to tell you," she said. "Did you ever hear of planting hands?"

"Can't say I have, ma'am."

"Well, I can only tell you what it feels like. It's when you're picking off the buds you don't want. Everything goes right down into your fingertips. You watch your fingers work. They do it themselves. You can feel how it is. They pick and pick the buds. They never make a mistake. They're with the plant. Do you see? Your fingers and the plant. You can feel that, right up your arm. They know. They never make a mistake. You can feel it. When you're like that you can't do anything wrong. Do you see that? Can you understand that?"

She was kneeling on the ground looking up at him. Her breast swelled passionately.

The man's eyes narrowed. He looked away, self-consciously. "Maybe I know," he said. "Sometimes in the night in the wagon there—"

Elisa's voice grew husky. She broke in on him. "I've never lived as you do, but I know what you mean. When the night is dark—why, the stars are sharp-pointed, and there's quiet. Why, you rise up and up! Every pointed star gets driven into your body. It's like that. Hot and sharp and—lovely."

Kneeling there, her hand went out toward his legs in the greasy black trousers. Her hesitant fingers almost touched the cloth. Then her hand dropped to the ground. She crouched low like a fawning dog.

He said, "It's nice, just like you say. Only when you don't have no dinner, it ain't."

She stood up then, very straight, and her face was ashamed. She held the flower pot out to him and placed it gently in his arms. "Here. Put it in your wagon, on the seat, where you can watch it. Maybe I can find something for you to do."

At the back of the house she dug in the can pile and found two old and battered aluminum saucepans. She carried them back and gave them to him. "Here, maybe you can fix these."

His manner changed. He became professional. "Good as new I can fix them." At the back of his wagon he set a little anvil, and out of an oily tool box dug a small machine hammer. Elisa came through the gate to watch him while he pounded out the dents in the kettles. His mouth grew sure and knowing. At a difficult part of the work he sucked his under-lip.

"You sleep right in the wagon?" Elisa asked.

"Right in the wagon, ma'am. Rain or shine I'm dry as a cow in there."

"It must be nice," she said. "It must be very nice. I wish women could do such things."

"It ain't the right kind of a life for a woman."

Her upper lip raised a little, showing her teeth. "How do you know? How can you tell?" she said.

"I don't know, ma'am," he protested. "Of course I don't know. Now here's your kettles, done. You don't have to buy no new ones."

"How much?"

"Oh, fifty cents'll do. I keep my prices down and my work good. That's why I have all them satisfied customers up and down the highway."

Elisa brought him a fifty-cent piece from the house and dropped it in his hand. "You might be surprised to have a rival some time. I can sharpen scissors, too. And I can beat the dents out of little pots. I could show you what a woman might do."

He put his hammer back in the oily box and shoved the little anvil out of sight. "It would be a lonely life for a woman, ma'am, and a scarey life, too, with animals creeping under the wagon all night." He climbed over the singletree, steadying himself with a hand on the burro's white rump. He settled himself in the seat, picked up the lines. "Thank you kindly, ma'am," he said. "I'll do like you told me; I'll go back and catch the Salinas road."

"Mind," she called, "if you're long in getting there, keep the sand damp."

"Sand, ma'am? . . . Sand? Oh, sure. You mean round the chrysanthemums. Sure I will." He clucked his tongue. The beasts leaned luxuriously into their collars. The mongrel dog took his place between the back wheels. The wagon turned and crawled out the entrance road and back the way it had come, along the river.

Elisa stood in front of her wire fence watching the slow progress of the caravan. Her shoulders were straight, her head thrown back, her eyes half-closed, so that the scene came vaguely into them. Her lips moved silently, forming the words "Good-bye—goodbye." Then she whispered. "That's a bright direction. There's a glowing there." The sound of her whisper startled her. She shook herself free and looked about to see whether anyone had been listening. Only the dogs had heard. They lifted their heads toward her from their sleeping in the dust, and then stretched out their chins and settled asleep again. Elisa turned and ran hurriedly into the house.

In the kitchen she reached behind the stove and felt the water tank. It was full of hot water from the noonday cooking. In the bathroom she tore off her soiled clothes and flung them into the corner. And then she scrubbed herself with a little block of pumice, legs and thighs, loins and chest and arms, until her skin was scratched and red. When she had dried herself she stood in front of a mirror in her bedroom and looked at her body. She tightened her stomach and threw out her chest. She turned and looked over her shoulder at her back.

After a while she began to dress, slowly. She put on her newest under-clothing and her nicest stockings and the dress which was the symbol of her prettiness. She worked carefully on her hair, pencilled her eyebrows and rouged her lips.

Before she was finished she heard the little thunder of hoofs and the shouts of Henry and his helper as they drove the red steers into the corral. She heard the gate bang shut and set herself for Henry's arrival.

His step sounded on the porch. He entered the house calling "Elisa, where are you?"

"In my room, dressing. I'm not ready. There's hot water for your bath. Hurry up. It's getting late."

When she heard him splashing in the tub, Elisa laid his dark suit on the bed, and shirt and socks and tie beside it. She stood his polished shoes on the floor beside the bed. Then she went to the porch and sat primly and stiffly down. She looked toward the river road where the willow-line was still yellow with frosted leaves so that under the high grey fog they seemed a thin band of sunshine. This was the only color in the grey afternoon. She sat unmoving for a long time. Her eyes blinked rarely.

Henry came banging out of the door, shoving his tie inside his vest as he came. Elisa stiffened and her face grew tight. Henry stopped short and looked at her. "Why—why, Elisa. You look so nice!"

"Nice? You think I look nice? What do you mean by 'nice'?"

Henry blundered on. "I don't know. I mean you look different, strong and happy."

"I am strong? Yes, strong. What do you mean 'strong'?"

He looked bewildered. "You're playing some kind of a game," he said helplessly. "It's a kind of a play. You look strong enough to break a calf over your knee, happy enough to eat it like a watermelon."

For a second she lost her rigidity. "Henry! Don't talk like that. You didn't know what you said." She grew complete again. "I'm strong," she boasted. "I never knew before how strong."

Henry looked down toward the tractor shed, and when he brought his eyes back to her, they were his own again. "I'll get out the car. You can put on your coat while I'm starting."

Elisa went into the house. She heard him drive to the gate and idle down his motor, and then she took a long time to put on her hat. She pulled it here and pressed it there. When Henry turned the motor off she slipped into her coat and went out.

The little roadster bounced along on the dirt road by the river, raising the birds and driving the rabbits into the brush. Two cranes flapped heavily over the willow-line and dropped into the riverbed.

Far ahead on the road Elisa saw a dark speck. She knew. She tried not to look as they passed it, but her eyes would not obey. She whispered to herself sadly, "He might have thrown them off the road. That wouldn't have been much trouble, not very much. But he kept the pot," she explained. "He had to keep the pot. That's why he couldn't get them off the road."

The roadster turned a bend and she saw the caravan ahead. She swung full around toward her husband so she could not see the little covered wagon and the mismatched team as the car passed them.

In a moment they had left behind them the man who had not known or needed to know what she said, the bargainer. She did not look back.

To Henry, she said loudly, to be heard above the motor, "It will be good, tonight, a good dinner."

"Now you're changed again," Henry complained. He took one hand from the wheel and patted her knee. "I ought to take you in to dinner oftener. It would be good for both of us. We get so heavy out on the ranch."

"Henry," she asked, "could we have wine at dinner?"

"Sure. Say! That will be fine."

She was silent for a while; then she said, "Henry, at those prize fights do the men hurt each other very much?"

"Sometimes a little, not often. Why?"

"Well, I've read how they break noses, and blood runs down their chests. I've read how the fighting gloves get heavy and soggy with blood."

He looked round at her. "What's the matter, Elisa? I didn't know you read things like that." He brought the car to a stop, then turned to the right over the Salinas River bridge.

"Do any women ever go to the fights?" she asked.

"Oh, sure, some. What's the matter, Elisa? Do you want to go? I don't think you'd like it, but I'll take you if you really want to go."

She relaxed limply in the seat. "Oh, no. I don't want to go. I'm sure I don't." Her face was turned away from him. "It will be enough if we can have wine. It will be plenty." She turned up her coat collar so he could not see that she was crying weakly—like an old woman.

1938

Further Reading

Davis, Robert Murray. Introduction. *Steinbeck: A Collection of Critical Essays.* Englewood Cliffs, N.J.: Prentice-Hall, 1972. 1–17. • Marcus, Mordecai. "The Lost Dream of Sex and Children in 'The Chrysanthemums.' " *Modern Fiction Studies* 11.1 (Spring 1965): 54–58. • Sweet, Charles A. "Ms. Eliza Allen and Steinbeck's 'The Chrysanthemums.' " *Modern Fiction Studies* 20.2 (Summer 1974): 210–14. • McMahan, Elizabeth E. " 'The Chrysanthemums': Study of a Woman's Sexuality." *Modern Fiction Studies* 14.4 (Winter 1968–69): 453–58.

Like many writers who lived through the Great Depression of the 1930s, John Steinbeck directly observed the suffering caused by economic and social injustice, and much of his best work has an element of protest about it. His readers sometimes disagree about whether the protest note or the note of optimism (sounded below in an interview with The Paris Review) *is dominant.*

John Steinbeck: On the Writer's Duty to Encourage

It is the fashion now in writing to have every man defeated and destroyed. And I do not believe all men are destroyed. I can name a dozen who were not and they are the ones the world lives by. It is true of the spirit as it is of battles—the defeated are forgotten, only the winners come themselves into the race. The writers of today, even I, have a tendency to celebrate the destruction of the spirit and god knows it is destroyed often enough. But the beacon thing is that sometimes it is not. And I think I can take time right now to say that. There will be great sneers from the neurosis belt of the south, from the hard-boiled writers, but I believe that the great ones, Plato, Lao Tze, Buddha, Christ, Paul, and the great Hebrew prophets are not remembered for negation or denial. Not that it is necessary to be remembered but there is one purpose in writing that I can see, beyond simply doing it interestingly. It is the duty of the writer to lift up, to extend, to encourage. If the written word has contributed anything at all to our developing species and our half developed culture, it is this: Great writing has been a staff to lean on, a mother to consult, a wisdom to pick up stumbling folly, a strength in weakness and a courage to support sick cowardice. And how any negative or despairing approach can pretend to be literature I do not know. It is true that we are weak and sick and ugly and quarrelsome but if that is all we ever were, we would millenniums ago have disappeared from the face of the earth, and a few remnants of fossilized jaw bones, a few teeth in strata of limestone would be the only mark our species would have left on the earth. . . .

It is too bad we have not more humor about this. After all it is only a book and no worlds are made or destroyed by it.

ZORA NEALE HURSTON

(1903–1960)

SPUNK

1

A giant of a brown-skinned man sauntered up the one street of the village and out into the palmetto thickets with a small pretty woman clinging lovingly to his arm.

"Looka theah, folkses!" cried Elijah Mosley, slapping his leg gleefully. "Theah they go, big as life an' brassy as tacks."

All the loungers in the store tried to walk to the door with an air of nonchalance but with small success.

"Now pee-eople!" Walter Thomas gasped. "Will you look at 'em!"

"But that's one thing Ah likes about Spunk Banks—he ain't skeered of nothin' on God's green footstool—*nothin'!* He rides that log down at sawmill jus' like he struts 'round wid another man's wife—jus' don't give a kitty. When Tes' Miller got cut to giblets on that circle-saw, Spunk steps right up and starts ridin'. The rest of us was skeered to go near it."

A round-shouldered figure in overalls much too large came nervously in the door and the talking ceased. The men looked at each other and winked.

"Gimme some soda-water. Sass'prilla Ah reckon," the newcomer ordered, and stood far down the counter near the open pickled pig-feet tub to drink it.

Elijah nudged Walter and turned with mock gravity to the new-comer.

"Say, Joe, how's everything up yo' way? How's yo' wife?"

Joe started and all but dropped the bottle he was holding. He swallowed several times painfully and his lips trembled.

"Aw 'Lige, you oughtn't to do nothin' like that," Walter grumbled. Elijah ignored him.

"She jus' passed heah a few minutes ago goin' thata way," with a wave of his hand in the direction of the woods.

Now Joe knew his wife had passed that way. He knew that the men lounging in the general store had seen her, moreover, he knew that the men knew *he* knew. He stood there silent for a long moment staring blankly, with his Adam's apple twitching nervously up and down his throat. One could actually *see* the pain he was suffering, his eyes, his face, his hands, and even the dejected slump of his shoulders. He set the bottle down upon the counter. He didn't bang it, just eased it out of his hand silently and fiddled with his suspender buckle.

"Well, Ah'm goin' after her to-day. Ah'm goin' an' fetch her back. Spunk's done gone too fur."

He reached deep down into his trouser pocket and drew out a hollow ground razor, large and shiny, and passed his moistened thumb back and forth over the edge.

"Talkin' like a man, Joe. 'Course that's *yo'* fambly affairs, but Ah like to see grit in anybody."

Joe Kanty laid down a nickel and stumbled out into the street.

Dusk crept in from the woods. Ike Clarke lit the swinging oil lamp that was almost immediately surrounded by candle-flies. The men laughed boisterously behind Joe's back as they watched him shamble woodward.

"You oughtn't to said whut you said to him, 'Lige—look how it worked him up," Walter chided.

"And Ah hope it did work him up. Tain't even decent for a man to take and take like he do."

"Spunk will sho' kill him."

"Aw, Ah doan know. You never kin tell. He might turn him up an' spank him fur gettin' in the way, but Spunk wouldn't shoot no unarmed man. Dat razor he carried outa heah ain't gonna run Spunk down an' cut him, an' Joe ain't got the nerve to go to Spunk with it knowing he totes that Army .45. He makes that break outa heah to bluff us. He's gonna hide that razor behind the first palmetto root an' sneak back home to bed. Don't tell me nothin' 'bout that rabbit-foot colored man. Didn't he meet Spunk an' Lena face to face one day las' week an' mumble sumthin' to Spunk 'bout lettin' his wife alone?"

"What did Spunk say?" Walter broke in. "Ah like him fine but tain't right the way he carries on wid Lena Kanty, jus' 'cause Joe's timid 'bout fightin'."

"You wrong theah, Walter. Tain't 'cause Joe's timid at all, it's 'cause Spunk wants Lena. If Joe was a passle of wile cats Spunk would tackle the job just the same. He'd go after *anything* he wanted the same way. As Ah wuz sayin' a minute ago, he tole Joe right to his face that Lena was his. 'Call her and see if she'll come. A woman knows her boss an' she answers when he calls.' 'Lena, ain't I yo' husband?' Joe sorter whines out. Lena looked at him real disgusted but she don't answer and she don't move outa her tracks. Then Spunk reaches out an' takes hold of her arm an' says: 'Lena, youse mine. From now on Ah works for you an' fights for you an' Ah never wants you to look to nobody for a crumb of bread, a stitch of close or a shingle to go over yo' head, but *me* long as Ah live. Ah'll git the lumber foh owah house to-morrow. Go home an' git yo' things together!'

" 'Thass mah house,' Lena speaks up. 'Papa gimme that.'

" 'Well,' says Spunk, 'doan give up whut's yours, but when youse inside doan forgit youse mine, an' let no other man git outa his place wid you!'

"Lena looked up at him with her eyes so full of love that they wuz runnin' over, an' Spunk seen it an' Joe seen it too, and his lip started to tremblin' and his Adam's apple was galloping up and down his neck like a race horse. Ah bet he's wore out half a dozen Adam's apples since Spunk's been on the job with Lena. That's all he'll do. He'll be back heah after while swallowin' an' workin' his lips like he wants to say somethin' an' can't."

"But didn't he do *nothin'* to stop 'em?"

"Nope, not a frazzlin' thing—jus' stood there. Spunk took Lena's arm and walked off jus' like nothin' ain't happened and he stood there gazin' after them till they was outa sight. Now you know a woman don't want no man like that. I'm jus' waitin' to see whut he's goin' to say when he gits back."

2

But Joe Kanty never came back, never. The men in the store heard the sharp report of a pistol somewhere distant in the palmetto thicket and soon Spunk came walking leisurely, with his big black Stetson set at the same rakish angle and Lena clinging to his arm, came walking right into the general store. Lena wept in a frightened manner.

"Well," Spunk announced calmly, "Joe came out there wid a meat axe an' made me kill him."

He sent Lena home and led the men back to Joe—crumpled and limp with his right hand still clutching his razor.

"See mah back? Mah close cut clear through. He sneaked up an' tried to kill me from the back, but Ah got him, an' got him good, first shot," Spunk said.

The men glared at Elijah, accusingly.

"Take him up an' plant him in Stony Lonesome," Spunk said in a careless voice. "Ah didn't wanna shoot him but he made me do it. He's a dirty coward, jumpin' on a man from behind."

Spunk turned on his heel and sauntered away to where he knew his love wept in fear for him and no man stopped him. At the general store later on, they all talked of locking him up until the sheriff should come from Orlando, but no one did anything but talk.

A clear case of self-defense, the trial was a short one, and Spunk walked out of the court house to freedom again. He could work again, ride the dangerous log-carriage that fed the singing, snarling, biting circle-saw; he could stroll the soft dark lanes with his guitar. He was free to roam the woods again; he was free to return to Lena. He did all these things.

3

"Whut you reckon, Walt?" Elijah asked one night later. "Spunk's gittin' ready to marry Lena!"

"Naw! Why, Joe ain't had time to git cold yit. Nohow Ah didn't figger Spunk was the marryin' kind."

"Well, he is," rejoined Elijah. "He done moved most of Lena's things —and her along wid 'em—over to the Bradley house. He's buying it. Jus' like Ah told yo' all right in heah the night Joe was kilt. Spunk's crazy 'bout Lena. He don't want folks to keep on talkin' 'bout her—thass reason he's rushin' so. Funny thing 'bout that bob-cat, wan't it?"

"What bob-cat, 'Lige? Ah ain't heered 'bout none."

"Ain't cher? Well, night befo' las' as they was goin' to bed, a big black bob-cat, black all over, you hear me, *black,* walked round and round that house and howled like forty, an' when Spunk got his gun an' went to the winder to shoot it, he says it stood right still an' looked him in the eye, an' howled right at him. The thing got Spunk so nervoused up he couldn't shoot. But Spunk says twan't no bob-cat nohow. He says it was Joe done sneaked back from Hell!"

"Humph!" sniffed Walter, "he oughter be nervous after what he done. Ah reckon Joe come back to dare him to marry Lena, or to come out an' fight. Ah bet he'll be back time and again, too. Know what Ah think? Joe wuz a braver man than Spunk."

There was a general shout of derision from the group.

"Thass a fact," went on Walter. "Lookit whut he done; took a razor an' went out to fight a man he knowed toted a gun an' wuz a crack shot, too; 'nother thing Joe wuz skeered of Spunk, skeered plumb stiff! But he went jes' the same. It took him a long time to get his nerve up. Tain't nothin' for Spunk to fight when he ain't skeered of nothin'. Now, Joe's done come back to have it out wid the man that's got all he ever had. Y'all know Joe ain't never had nothin' nor wanted nothin' besides Lena. It musta been a h'ant cause ain't nobody never seen no black bob-cat."

"'Nother thing," cut in one of the men, "Spunk was cussin' a blue streak to-day 'cause he 'lowed dat saw wuz wobblin'—almos' got 'im once. The machinist come, looked it over an' said it wuz alright. Spunk musta been leanin' t'wards it some. Den he claimed somebody pushed 'im but twan't nobody close to 'im. Ah wuz glad when knockin' off time came. I'm skeered of dat man when he gits hot. He'd beat you full of button holes as quick as he'd look atcher."

4

The men gathered the next evening in a different mood, no laughter. No badinage this time.

"Look, 'Lige, you goin' to set up wid Spunk?"

"Naw, Ah reckon not, Walter. Tell yuh the truth, Ah'm a li'l bit skittish. Spunk died too wicket—died cussin' he did. You know he thought he was done outa life."

"Good Lawd, who'd he think done it?"

"Joe."

"Joe Kanty? How come?"

"Walter, Ah b'leeve Ah will walk up thata way an' set. Lena would like it Ah reckon."

"But whut did he say, 'Lige?"

Elijah did not answer until they had left the lighted store and were strolling down the dark street.

"Ah wuz loadin' a wagon wid scantlin' right near the saw when Spunk fell on the carriage but 'fore Ah could git to him the saw got him in the body —awful sight. Me an' Skint Miller got him off but it was too late. Anybody could see that. The fust thing he said wuz: 'He pushed me, 'Lige—the dirty hound pushed me in the back!'—he was spittin' blood at ev'ry breath. We laid him on the sawdust pile with his face to the East so's he could die easy. He helt mah han' till the last, Walter, and said: 'It was Joe, 'Lige . . . the dirty sneak shoved me . . . he didn't dare come to mah face . . . but Ah'll git the son-of-a-wood louse soon's Ah get there an' make hell too hot for him . . . Ah felt him shove me . . .!' Thass how he died."

"If spirits kin fight, there's a powerful tussle goin' on somewhere ovah Jordan 'cause Ah b'leeve Joe's ready for Spunk an' ain't skeered any more —yas, Ah b'leeve Joe pushed 'im mahself."

They had arrived at the house. Lena's lamentations were deep and loud. She had filled the room with magnolia blossoms that gave off a heavy sweet odor. The keepers of the wake tipped about whispering in frightened tones. Everyone in the village was there, even old Jeff Kanty, Joe's father, who a few hours before would have been afraid to come within ten feet of him, stood leering triumphantly down upon the fallen giant as if his fingers had been the teeth of steel that laid him low.

The cooling board consisted of three sixteen-inch boards on saw horses, a dingy sheet was his shroud.

The women ate heartily of the funeral baked meats and wondered who would be Lena's next. The men whispered coarse conjectures between guzzles of whiskey.

1927

Further Reading

Hemenway, Robert. "Zora Neale Hurston and the Eatonville Anthropology." *The Harlem Renaissance Remembered.* Ed. A. W. Bontemps. New York: Dodd, 1972. 190–214. • Bone, R. A. "Three Versions of the Pastoral." *Down Home: A History of Afro-American Short Fiction from Its Beginnings to the End of the Harlem Renaissance.* New York: Putnam's, 1975. 139–70. • Howard, Lillie P. "Marriage: Zora Neale Hurston's System of Values." *CLA Journal* 21.2 (Dec. 1977): 256–68, spec. 256–60. • Lowe, John. "Hurston, Humor, and the Harlem Renaissance." *The Harlem Renaissance Re-examined.* Ed. Victor A. Kramer. New York: AMS, 1987. 238–83. • Ikonné, Chidi. "Zora Neale Hurston." *From DuBois to Van Vechten: The Early New Negro Literature: 1903–1926.* Westport, Conn.: Greenwood, 1981. 183–87.

Hurston's writing, like that of Langston Hughes, provoked controversy because it presents black culture in America as something separate from white culture and because it describes aspects of black life that could reinforce negative stereotypes. Richard Wright's review of Their Eyes Were Watching God *points out the danger of Hurston's methods. The final paragraph of Hurston's autobiography is her most eloquent defense.*

Richard Wright: On Hurston's Use of the "Quaint" in Negro Life

Miss Hurston can write; but her prose is cloaked in that facile sensuality that has dogged Negro expression since the days of Phillis Wheatley. Her dialogue manages to catch the psychological movements of the Negro folk-mind in their pure simplicity, but that's as far as it goes.

Miss Hurston *voluntarily* continues in her novel the tradition which was *forced* upon the Negro in the theater, that is, the minstrel technique that makes the "white folks" laugh. Her characters eat and laugh and cry and work and kill; they swing like a pendulum eternally in that safe and narrow orbit in which America likes to see the Negro live: between laughter and tears. . . .

The sensory sweep of her novel carries no theme, no message, no thought. In the main, her novel is not addressed to the Negro, but to a white audience whose chauvinistic tastes she knows how to satisfy. She exploits that phase of Negro life which is "quaint," the phase which evokes a piteous smile on the lips of the "superior" race.

Zora Neale Hurston: On Tolerance and Patience

I have no race prejudice of any kind. My kinfolks, and my "skin-folks" are dearly loved. My own circumference of everyday life is there. But I see their same virtues and vices everywhere I look. So I give you all my right hand of fellowship and love, and hope for the same from you. In my eyesight, you lose nothing by not looking just like me. I will remember you all in my good thoughts, and I ask you kindly to do the same for me. Not only just me. You, who play the zig-zag lightning of power over the world, and the grumbling thunder in your wake, think kindly of those who walk in the dust. And you who walk in humble places, think kindly too, of others. There has been no proof in the world so far that you would be less arrogant if you held the lever of power in your hands. Let us all be kissing-friends. Consider that with tolerance and patience, we godly demons may breed a noble world in a few hundred generations or so. Maybe all of us who do not have the good fortune to meet, or meet again, in this world, will meet at a barbecue.

RICHARD WRIGHT

(1908–1960)

BIG BLACK GOOD MAN

Through the open window Olaf Jenson could smell the sea and hear the occasional foghorn of a freighter; outside, rain pelted down through an August night, drumming softly upon the pavements of Copenhagen, inducing drowsiness, bringing dreamy memory, relaxing the tired muscles of his work-wracked body. He sat slumped in a swivel chair with his legs outstretched and his feet propped atop an edge of his desk. An inch of white ash tipped the end of his brown cigar and now and then he inserted the end of the stogie into his mouth and drew gently upon it, letting wisps of blue smoke eddy from the corners of his wide, thin lips. The watery gray irises behind the thick lenses of his eyeglasses gave him a look of abstraction, of absentmindedness, of an almost genial idiocy. He sighed, reached for his half-empty bottle of beer, and drained it into his glass and downed it with a long slow gulp, then licked his lips. Replacing the cigar, he slapped his right palm against his thigh and said half aloud:

"Well, I'll be sixty tomorrow. I'm not rich, but I'm not poor either . . . Really, I can't complain. Got good health. Traveled all over the world and had my share of the girls when I was young . . . And my Karen's a good wife. I own my home. Got no debts. And I love digging in my garden in the spring . . . Grew the biggest carrots of anybody last year. Ain't saved much money, but what the hell . . . Money ain't everything. Got a good job. Night portering ain't too bad." He shook his head and yawned. "Karen and I could of had some children, though. Would of been good company . . . 'Specially for Karen. And I could of taught 'em languages . . . English, French, German, Danish, Dutch, Swedish, Norwegian, and Spanish . . ." He took the cigar out of his mouth and eyed the white ash critically. "Hell of a lot of good language learning did me . . . Never got anything out of it. But those ten years in New York were fun . . . Maybe I could of got rich if I'd stayed in America . . . Maybe. But I'm satisfied. You can't have everything."

Behind him the office door opened and a young man, a medical student occupying room number nine, entered.

"Good evening," the student said.

"Good evening," Olaf said, turning.

The student went to the keyboard and took hold of the round, brown knob that anchored his key.

"Rain, rain, rain," the student said.

"That's Denmark for you," Olaf smiled at him.

"This dampness keeps me clogged up like a drainpipe," the student complained.

"That's Denmark for you," Olaf repeated with a smile.

"Good night," the student said.

"Good night, son," Olaf sighed, watching the door close.

Well, my tenants are my children, Olaf told himself. Almost all of his children were in their rooms now . . . Only seventy-two and forty-four were missing . . . Seventy-two might've gone to Sweden . . . And forty-four was maybe staying at his girl's place tonight, like he sometimes did . . . He studied the pear-shaped blobs of hard rubber, reddish brown like ripe fruit, that hung from the keyboard, then glanced at his watch. Only room thirty, eighty-one, and one hundred and one were empty . . . And it was almost midnight. In a few moments he could take a nap. Nobody hardly ever came looking for accommodations after midnight, unless a stray freighter came in, bringing thirsty, women-hungry sailors. Olaf chuckled softly. Why in hell was I ever a sailor? The whole time I was at sea I was thinking and dreaming about women. Then why didn't I stay on land where women could be had? Hunh? Sailors are crazy . . .

But he liked sailors. They reminded him of his youth, and there was something so direct, simple, and childlike about them. They always said straight out what they wanted, and what they wanted was almost always women and whisky . . . "Well, there's no harm in that . . . Nothing could be more natural," Olaf sighed, looking thirstily at his empty beer bottle. No; he'd not drink any more tonight; he'd had enough; he'd go to sleep . . .

He was bending forward and loosening his shoelaces when he heard the office door crack open. He lifted his eyes, then sucked in his breath. He did not straighten; he just stared up and around at the huge black thing that filled the doorway. His reflexes refused to function; it was not fear; it was just simple astonishment. He was staring at the biggest, strangest, and blackest man he'd ever seen in all his life.

"Good evening," the black giant said in a voice that filled the small office. "Say, you got a room?"

Olaf sat up slowly, not to answer but to look at this brooding black vision; it towered darkly some six and a half feet into the air, almost touching the ceiling, and its skin was so black that it had a bluish tint. And the sheer bulk of the man! . . . His chest bulged like a barrel; his rocklike and humped shoulders hinted of mountain ridges; the stomach ballooned like a threatening stone; and the legs were like telephone poles . . . The big black cloud of a man now lumbered into the office, bending to get its buffalolike head under the door frame, then advanced slowly upon Olaf, like a stormy sky descending.

"You got a room?" the big black man asked again in a resounding voice.

Olaf now noticed that the ebony giant was well dressed, carried a wonderful new suitcase, and wore black shoes that gleamed despite the raindrops that peppered their toes.

"You're American?" Olaf asked him.

"Yeah, man; sure," the black giant answered.

"Sailor?"

"Yeah. American Continental Lines."

Olaf had not answered the black man's question. It was not that the hotel did not admit men of color; Olaf took in all comers—blacks, yellows, whites, and browns . . . To Olaf, men were men, and, in his day, he'd worked and eaten and slept and fought with all kinds of men. But this particular black man . . . Well, he didn't seem human. Too big, too black, too loud, too direct, and probably too violent to boot . . . Olaf's five feet seven inches scarcely reached the black giant's shoulder and his frail body weighed less, perhaps, than one of the man's gigantic legs . . . There was something about the man's intense blackness and ungainly bigness that frightened and insulted Olaf; he felt as though this man had come here expressly to remind him how puny, how tiny, and how weak and how white he was. Olaf knew, while registering his reactions, that he was being irrational and foolish; yet, for the first time in his life, he was emotionally determined to refuse a man a room solely on the basis of the man's size and color . . . Olaf's lips parted as he groped for the right words in which to couch his refusal, but the black giant bent forward and boomed:

"I asked you if you got a room. I got to put up somewhere tonight, man."

"Yes, we got a room," Olaf murmured.

And at once he was ashamed and confused. Sheer fear had made him yield. And he seethed against himself for his involuntary weakness. Well, he'd look over his book and pretend that he'd made a mistake; he'd tell this hunk of blackness that there was really no free room in the hotel, and that he was so sorry . . . Then, just as he took out the hotel register to make believe that he was poring over it, a thick roll of American bank notes, crisp and green, was thrust under his nose.

"Keep this for me, will you?" the black giant commanded. "Cause I'm gonna get drunk tonight and I don't wanna lose it."

Olaf stared at the roll; it was huge, in denominations of fifties and hundreds. Olaf's eyes widened.

"How much is there?" he asked.

"Two thousand six hundred," the giant said. "Just put it into an envelope and write 'Jim' on it and lock it in your safe, hunh?"

The black mass of man had spoken in a manner that indicated that it was taking it for granted that Olaf would obey. Olaf was licked. Resentment clogged the pores of his wrinkled white skin. His hands trembled as he picked up the money. No; he couldn't refuse this man . . . The impulse to deny him was strong, but each time he was about to act upon it something thwarted him, made him shy off. He clutched about desperately for an idea. Oh yes, he could say that if he planned to stay for only one night, then he could not have the room, for it was against the policy of the hotel to rent rooms for only one night . . .

"How long are you staying? Just tonight?" Olaf asked.

"Naw. I'll be here for five or six days, I reckon," the giant answered offhandedly.

"You take room number thirty," Olaf heard himself saying. "It's forty kroner a day."

"That's all right with me," the giant said.

With slow, stiff movements, Olaf put the money in the safe and then turned and stared helplessly up into the living, breathing blackness looming above him. Suddenly he became conscious of the outstretched palm of the black giant; he was silently demanding the key to the room. His eyes downcast, Olaf surrendered the key, marveling at the black man's tremendous hands . . . He could kill me with one blow, Olaf told himself in fear.

Feeling himself beaten, Olaf reached for the suitcase, but the black hand of the giant whisked it out of his grasp.

"That's too heavy for you, big boy; I'll take it," the giant said.

Olaf let him, He thinks I'm nothing . . . He led the way down the corridor, sensing the giant's lumbering presence behind him. Olaf opened the door of number thirty and stood politely to one side, allowing the black giant to enter. At once the room seemed like a doll's house, so dwarfed and filled and tiny it was with a great living blackness . . . Flinging his suitcase upon a chair, the giant turned. The two men looked directly at each other now. Olaf saw that the giant's eyes were tiny and red, buried, it seemed, in muscle and fat. Black cheeks spread, flat and broad, topping the wide and flaring nostrils. The mouth was the biggest that Olaf had ever seen on a human face; the lips were thick, pursed, parted, showing snow-white teeth. The black neck was like a bull's . . . The giant advanced upon Olaf and stood over him.

"I want a bottle of whisky and a woman," he said. "Can you fix me up?"

"Yes," Olaf whispered, wild with anger and insult.

But what was he angry about? He'd had requests like this every night from all sorts of men and he was used to fulfilling them; he was a night porter in a cheap, water-front Copenhagen hotel that catered to sailors and students. Yes, men needed women, but this man, Olaf felt, ought to have a special sort of woman. He felt a deep and strange reluctance to phone any of the women whom he habitually sent to men. Yet he had promised. Could he lie and say that none was available? No. That sounded too fishy. The black giant sat upon the bed, staring straight before him. Olaf moved about quickly, pulling down the window shades, taking the pink coverlet off the bed, nudging the giant with his elbow to make him move as he did so . . . That's the way to treat 'im . . . Show 'im I ain't scared of 'im . . . But he was still seeking for an excuse to refuse. And he could think of nothing. He felt hypnotized, mentally immobilized. He stood hesitantly at the door.

"You send the whisky and the woman quick, pal?" the black giant asked, rousing himself from a brooding stare.

"Yes," Olaf grunted, shutting the door.

Goddamn, Olaf sighed. He sat in his office at his desk before the phone. Why did *he* have to come here? . . . I'm not prejudiced . . . No, not at all . . . But . . . He couldn't think any more. God oughtn't make men as big and black as that . . . But what the hell was he worrying about? He'd sent women of all races to men of all colors . . . So why not a woman to the black giant? Oh, only if the man were small, brown, and intelligent-looking . . . Olaf felt trapped.

With a reflex movement of his hand, he picked up the phone and dialed Lena. She was big and strong and always cut him in for fifteen per cent instead of the usual ten per cent. Lena had four small children to feed and clothe. Lena was willing; she was, she said, coming over right now. She didn't give a good goddamn about how big and black the man was . . .

"Why you ask me that?" Lena wanted to know over the phone. "You never asked that before . . ."

"But this one is *big*," Olaf found himself saying.

"He's just a man," Lena told him, her voice singing stridently, laughingly over the wire. "You just leave that to me. You don't have to do anything. *I'll* handle 'im."

Lena had a key to the hotel door downstairs, but tonight Olaf stayed awake. He wanted to see her. Why? He didn't know. He stretched out on the sofa in his office, but sleep was far from him. When Lena arrived, he told her again how big and black the man was.

"You told me that over the phone," Lena reminded him.

Olaf said nothing. Lena flounced off on her errand of mercy. Olaf shut the office door, then opened it and left it ajar. But why? He didn't know. He lay upon the sofa and stared at the ceiling. He glanced at his watch; it was almost two o'clock . . . She's staying in there a long time . . . Ah, God, but he could do with a drink . . . Why was he so damned worked up and nervous about a nigger and a white whore? . . . He'd never been so upset in all his life. Before he knew it, he had drifted off to sleep. Then he heard the office door swinging creakingly open on its rusty hinges. Lena stood in it, grim and businesslike, her face scrubbed free of powder and rouge. Olaf scrambled to his feet, adjusting his eyeglasses, blinking.

"How was it?" he asked her in a confidential whisper.

Lena's eyes blazed.

"What the hell's that to you?" she snapped. "There's your cut," she said, flinging him his money, tossing it upon the covers of the sofa. "You're sure nosy tonight. You wanna take over my work?"

Olaf's pasty cheeks burned red.

"You go to hell," he said, slamming the door.

"I'll meet you there!" Lena's shouting voice reached him dimly.

He was being a fool; there was no doubt about it. But, try as he might, he could not shake off a primitive hate for that black mountain of energy, of muscle, of bone; he envied the easy manner in which it moved with such a creeping and powerful motion; he winced at the booming and commanding voice that came to him when the tiny little eyes were not even looking at him; he shivered at the sight of those vast and clawlike hands that seemed always to hint of death . . .

Olaf kept his counsel. He never spoke to Karen about the sordid doings at the hotel. Such things were not for women like Karen. He knew instinctively that Karen would have been amazed had he told her that he was worried sick about a nigger and a blonde whore . . . No; he couldn't talk to anybody about it, not even the hard-bitten old bitch who owned the hotel. She was concerned only about money; she didn't give a damn about how big and how black a client was as long as he paid his room rent.

Next evening, when Olaf arrived for duty, there was no sight or sound of the black giant. A little later after one o'clock in the morning he appeared, left his key, and went out wordlessly. A few moments past two the giant returned, took his key from the board, and paused.

"I want that Lena again tonight. And another bottle of whisky," he said boomingly.

"I'll call her and see if she's in," Olaf said.

"Do that," the black giant said and was gone.

He thinks he's God, Olaf fumed. He picked up the phone and ordered Lena and a bottle of whisky, and there was a taste of ashes in his mouth. On the third night came the same request: Lena and whisky. When the black giant appeared on the fifth night, Olaf was about to make a sarcastic remark to the effect that maybe he ought to marry Lena, but he checked it in time . . . After all, he could kill me with one hand, he told himself.

Olaf was nervous and angry with himself for being nervous. Other black sailors came and asked for girls and Olaf sent them, but with none of the fear and loathing that he sent Lena and a bottle of whisky to the giant . . . All right, the black giant's stay was almost up. He'd said that he was staying for five or six nights; tomorrow night was the sixth night and that ought to be the end of this nameless terror.

On the sixth night Olaf sat in his swivel chair with his bottle of beer and waited, his teeth on edge, his fingers drumming the desk. But what the hell am I fretting for? . . . The hell with 'im . . . Olaf sat and dozed. Occasionally he'd awaken and listen to the foghorns of freighters sounding as ships came and went in the misty Copenhagen harbor. He was half asleep when he felt a rough hand on his shoulder. He blinked his eyes open. The giant, black and vast and powerful, all but blotted out his vision.

"What I owe you, man?" the giant demanded. "And I want my money."

"Sure," Olaf said, relieved, but filled as always with fear of this living wall of black flesh.

With fumbling hands, he made out the bill and received payment, then gave the giant his roll of money, laying it on the desk so as not to let his hands touch the flesh of the black mountain. Well, his ordeal was over. It was past two o'clock in the morning. Olaf even managed a wry smile and muttered a guttural "Thanks" for the generous tip that the giant tossed him.

Then a strange tension entered the office. The office door was shut and Olaf was alone with the black mass of power, yearning for it to leave. But the black mass of power stood still, immobile, looking down at Olaf. And Olaf could not, for the life of him, guess at what was transpiring in that mysterious black mind. The two of them simply stared at each other for a full two minutes, the giant's tiny little beady eyes blinking slowly as they seemed to measure and search Olaf's face. Olaf's vision dimmed for a second as terror seized him and he could feel a flush of heat overspread his body. Then Olaf sucked in his breath as the devil of blackness commanded:

"Stand up!"

Olaf was paralyzed. Sweat broke on his face. His worst premonitions about this black beast were coming true. This evil blackness was about to attack him, maybe kill him . . . Slowly Olaf shook his head, his terror permitting him to breathe:

"What're you talking about?"

"Stand up, I say!" the black giant bellowed.

As though hypnotized, Olaf tried to rise; then he felt the black paw of the beast helping him roughly to his feet.

They stood an inch apart. Olaf's pasty-white features were glued to the giant's swollen black face. The ebony ensemble of eyes and nose and mouth and cheeks looked down at Olaf, silently; then, with a slow and deliberate movement of his gorillalike arms, he lifted his mammoth hands to Olaf's throat. Olaf had long known and felt that this dreadful moment was coming; he felt trapped in a nightmare. He could not move. He wanted to scream, but could find no words. His lips refused to open; his tongue felt icy and inert. Then he knew that his end had come when the giant's black fingers slowly, softly encircled his throat while a horrible grin of delight broke out on the sooty face . . . Olaf lost control of the reflexes of his body and he felt a hot stickiness flooding his underwear . . . He stared without breathing, gazing into the grinning blackness of the face that was bent over him, feeling the black fingers caressing his throat and waiting to feel the sharp, stinging ache and pain of the bones in his neck being snapped, crushed . . . He knew all along that I hated 'im . . . Yes, and now he's going to kill me for it, Olaf told himself with despair.

The black fingers still circled Olaf's neck, not closing, but gently massaging it, as it were, moving to and fro, while the obscene face grinned into his. Olaf could feel the giant's warm breath blowing on his eyelashes and he felt like a chicken about to have its neck wrung and its body tossed to flip and flap dyingly in the dust of the barnyard . . . Then suddenly the black giant withdrew his fingers from Olaf's neck and stepped back a pace, still grinning. Olaf sighed, trembling, his body seeming to shrink; he waited. Shame sheeted him for the hot wetness that was in his trousers. Oh, God, he's teasing me . . . He's showing me how easily he can kill me . . . He swallowed, waiting, his eyes stones of gray.

The giant's barrel-like chest gave forth a low, rumbling chuckle of delight.

"You laugh?" Olaf asked whimperingly.

"Sure I laugh," the giant shouted.

"Please don't hurt me," Olaf managed to say.

"I wouldn't hurt you, boy," the giant said in a tone of mockery. "So long."

And he was gone. Olaf fell limply into the swivel chair and fought off losing consciousness. Then he wept. He was showing me how easily he could kill me . . . He made me shake with terror and then laughed and left . . . Slowly, Olaf recovered, stood, then gave vent to a string of curses:

"Goddamn 'im! My gun's right there in the desk drawer; I should of shot 'im. Jesus, I hope the ship he's on sinks . . . I hope he drowns and the sharks eat 'im . . ."

Later, he thought of going to the police, but sheer shame kept him back; and, anyway, the giant was probably on board his ship by now. And he had to get home and clean himself. Oh, Lord, what could he tell Karen? Yes, he would say that his stomach had been upset . . . He'd change clothes and return to work. He phoned the hotel owner that he was ill and wanted an hour off; the old bitch said that she was coming right over and that poor Olaf could have the evening off.

Olaf went home and lied to Karen. Then he lay awake the rest of the night dreaming of revenge. He saw that freighter on which the giant was sailing; he saw it springing a dangerous leak and saw a torrent of sea water flooding, gushing into all the compartments of the ship until it found the bunk in which the black giant slept. Ah, yes, the foamy, surging waters would surprise that sleeping black bastard of a giant and he would drown, gasping and choking like a trapped rat, his tiny eyes bulging until they glittered red, the bitter water of the sea pounding his lungs until they ached and finally burst . . . The ship would sink slowly to the bottom of the cold, black, silent depths of the sea and a shark, a *white* one, would glide aimlessly about the shut portholes until it found an open one and it would slither inside and nose about until it found that swollen, rotting, stinking carcass of the black beast and it would then begin to nibble at the decomposing mass of tarlike flesh, eating the bones clean . . . Olaf always pictured the giant's bones as being jet black and shining.

Once or twice, during these fantasies of cannibalistic revenge, Olaf felt a little guilty about all the many innocent people, women and children, all white and blonde, who would have to go down into watery graves in order that that white shark could devour the evil giant's black flesh . . . But, despite feelings of remorse, the fantasy lived persistently on, and when Olaf found himself alone, it would crowd and cloud his mind to the exclusion of all else, affording him the only revenge he knew. To make me suffer just for the pleasure of it, he fumed. Just to show me how strong he was . . . Olaf learned how to hate, and got pleasure out of it.

Summer fled on wings of rain. Autumn flooded Denmark with color. Winter made rain and snow fall on Copenhagen. Finally spring came, bringing violets and roses. Olaf kept to his job. For many months he feared the return of the black giant. But when a year had passed and the giant had not put in an appearance, Olaf allowed his revenge fantasy to peter out, indulging in it only when recalling the shame that the black monster had made him feel.

Then one rainy August night, a year later, Olaf sat drowsing at his desk, his bottle of beer before him, tilting back in his swivel chair, his feet resting atop a corner of his desk, his mind mulling over the more pleasant aspects of his life. The office door cracked open. Olaf glanced boredly up and around. His heart jumped and skipped a beat. The black nightmare of terror and shame that he had hoped that he had lost forever was again upon him . . . Resplendently dressed, suitcase in hand, the black looming mountain filled the doorway. Olaf's thin lips parted and a silent moan, half a curse, escaped them.

"Hi," the black giant boomed from the doorway.

Olaf could not reply. But a sudden resolve swept him: this time he would even the score. If this black beast came within so much as three feet of him, he would snatch his gun out of the drawer and shoot him dead, so help him God . . .

"No rooms tonight," Olaf heard himself announcing in a determined voice.

The black giant grinned; it was the same infernal grimace of delight and triumph that he had had when his damnable black fingers had been around his throat . . .

"Don't want no room tonight," the giant announced.

"Then what are you doing here?" Olaf asked in a loud but tremulous voice.

The giant swept toward Olaf and stood over him; and Olaf could not move, despite his oath to kill him . . .

"What do you want then?" Olaf demanded once more, ashamed that he could not lift his voice above a whisper.

The giant still grinned, then tossed what seemed the same suitcase upon Olaf's sofa and bent over it; he zippered it open with a sweep of his clawlike hand and rummaged in it, drawing forth a flat, gleaming white object done up in glowing cellophane. Olaf watched with lowered lids, wondering what trick was now being played on him. Then, before he could defend himself, the giant had whirled and again long, black, snakelike fingers were encircling Olaf's throat . . . Olaf stiffened, his right hand clawing blindly for the drawer where the gun was kept. But the giant was quick.

"Wait," he bellowed, pushing Olaf back from the desk.

The giant turned quickly to the sofa and, still holding his fingers in a wide circle that seemed a noose for Olaf's neck, he inserted the rounded fingers into the top of the flat, gleaming object. Olaf had the drawer open and his sweaty fingers were now touching his gun, but something made him freeze. The flat, gleaming object was a shirt and the black giant's circled fingers were fitting themselves into its neck . . .

"A perfect fit!" the giant shouted.

Olaf stared, trying to understand. His fingers loosened about the gun. A mixture of a laugh and a curse struggled in him. He watched the giant plunge his hands into the suitcase and pull out other flat, gleaming shirts.

"One, two, three, four, five, six," the black giant intoned, his voice crisp and businesslike. "Six nylon shirts. And they're all yours. One shirt for each time Lena came . . . See, Daddy-O?"

The black, cupped hands, filled with billowing nylon whiteness, were extended under Olaf's nose. Olaf eased his damp fingers from his gun and pushed the drawer closed, staring at the shirts and then at the black giant's grinning face.

"Don't you like 'em?" the giant asked.

Olaf began to laugh hysterically, then suddenly he was crying, his eyes so flooded with tears that the pile of dazzling nylon looked like snow in the dead of winter. Was this true? Could he believe it? Maybe this too was a trick? But, no. There were six shirts, all nylon, and the black giant had had Lena six nights.

"What's the matter with you, Daddy-O?" the giant asked. "You blowing your top? Laughing and crying . . ."

Olaf swallowed, dabbed his withered fists at his dimmed eyes; then he realized that he had his glasses on. He took them off and dried his eyes and sat up. He sighed, the tension and shame and fear and haunting dread of his fantasy went from him, and he leaned limply back in his chair . . .

"Try one on," the giant ordered.

Olaf fumbled with the buttons of his shirt, let down his suspenders, and pulled the shirt off. He donned a gleaming nylon one and the giant began buttoning it for him.

"Perfect, Daddy-O," the giant said.

His spectacled face framed in sparkling nylon, Olaf sat with trembling lips. So he'd not been trying to kill me after all.

"You want Lena, don't you?" he asked the giant in a soft whisper. "But I don't know where she is. She never came back here after you left—"

"I know where Lena is," the giant told him. "We been writing to each other. I'm going to her house. And, Daddy-O, I'm late." The giant zippered the suitcase shut and stood a moment gazing down at Olaf, his tiny little red eyes blinking slowly. Then Olaf realized that there was a compassion in that stare that he had never seen before.

"And I thought you wanted to kill me," Olaf told him. "I was scared of you . . ."

"Me? Kill you?" the giant blinked. "When?"

"That night when you put your fingers about my throat—"

"What?" the giant asked, then roared with laughter. "Daddy-O, you're a funny little man. I wouldn't hurt you. I like you. You a *good* man. You helped me."

Olaf smiled, clutching the pile of nylon shirts in his arms.

"You're a good man too," Olaf murmured. Then loudly: "You're a big black good man."

"Daddy-O, you're crazy," the giant said.

He swept his suitcase from the sofa, spun on his heel, and was at the door in one stride.

"Thanks!" Olaf cried after him.

The black giant paused, turned his vast black head, and flashed a grin.

"Daddy-O, drop dead," he said and was gone.

1957

Further Reading

Burgum, Edwin Berry. "The Art of Richard Wright's Short Stories." *Five Black Writers.* Ed. Donald B. Gibson. New York: New York UP, 1970. 36–49. • Felgar, Robert. "*Eight Men.*" *Richard Wright.* Boston: Twayne, 1980. 156–73, spec.

160–64. • Margolies, Edward. "The Short Stories: *Uncle Tom's Children; Eight Men.*" *The Art of Richard Wright.* Carbondale: Southern Illinois UP, 1969. 57–89, spec. 87–89. • Brignano, Russell Carl. "New Directions? A Postscript." *Richard Wright: An Introduction to the Man and His Works.* Pittsburgh: U of Pittsburgh P, 1970. 166–72, spec. 170–71. • Howe, Irving. "Richard Wright: A Word of Farewell." *New Republic* 144 (13 Feb. 1961): 17–18.

Most of Richard Wright's fiction has been praised or criticized because of the author's very strong political commitments, his desire to speak not only for American blacks, but for oppressed people throughout the world. At times the political theme of a Wright story may overwhelm the reader and make it hard to notice his fine workmanship, particularly his use of clear and evocative imagery. When we examine some of the haiku Wright wrote toward the end of his life, we better appreciate his strong interest in what the five senses can reveal.

Richard Wright: Six Haiku

Just enough of rain
To bring the smell of silk
From umbrellas

The spring lingers
In the scent of a damp log
Rotting in the sun.

The green cockleburs
Caught in the thick wooly hair
Of the black boy's head.

Winter rain at night
Sweetening the taste of bread
And spicing the soup.

The dog's violent sneeze
Fails to rouse a single fly
On his mangy back.

The crow flew so fast
That he left his lonely caw
Behind in the fields.

EUDORA WELTY

(b. 1909)

LIVVIE

Solomon carried Livvie twenty-one miles away from her home when he married her. He carried her away up on the Old Natchez Trace into the deep country to live in his house. She was sixteen—an only girl, then. Once people said he thought nobody would ever come along there. He told her himself that it had been a long time, and a day she did not know about, since that road was a traveled road with *people* coming and going. He was good to her, but he kept her in the house. She had not thought that she could not get back. Where she came from, people said an old man did not want anybody in the world to ever find his wife, for fear they would steal her back from him. Solomon asked her before he took her, "Would she be happy?"—very dignified, for he was a colored man that owned his land and had it written down in the courthouse; and she said, "Yes, sir," since he was an old man and she was young and just listened and answered. He asked her, if she was choosing winter, would she pine for spring, and she said, "No indeed." Whatever she said, always, was because he was an old man . . . while nine years went by. All the time, he got old, and he got so old he gave out. At last he slept the whole day in bed, and she was young still.

It was a nice house, inside and outside both. In the first place, it had three rooms. The front room was papered in holly paper, with green palmettos from the swamp spaced at careful intervals over the walls. There was fresh newspaper cut with fancy borders on the mantel-shelf, on which were propped photographs of old or very young men printed in faint yellow—Solomon's people. Solomon had a houseful of furniture. There was a double settee, a tall scrolled rocker and an organ in the front room, all around a three-legged table with a pink marble top, on which was set a lamp with three gold feet, besides a jelly glass with pretty hen feathers in it. Behind the front room, the other room had the bright iron bed with the polished knobs like a throne, in which Solomon slept all day. There were snow-white curtains of wiry lace at the window, and a lace bed-spread belonged on the bed. But what old Solomon slept so sound under was a big feather-stitched piece-quilt in the pattern "Trip Around the World," which had twenty-one different colors, four hundred and forty pieces, and a thousand yards of thread, and that was what Solomon's mother made in her life and old age. There was a table holding the Bible, and a trunk with a key. On the wall were two calendars, and a diploma from somewhere in Solomon's family, and under that Livvie's one possession was nailed, a picture of the little white baby of the family she worked for, back in Natchez before she was married. Going through that room and on to the kitchen, there was a big wood stove and a big round table always with a wet top and with the knives and forks in one jelly glass and the spoons in another, and a cut-glass vine-gar bottle between, and going out from those, many shallow dishes of pick-led peaches, fig preserves, watermelon pickles and blackberry jam always sitting there. The churn sat in the sun, the doors of the safe were always both shut, and there were four baited mouse-traps in the kitchen, one in every corner.

The outside of Solomon's house looked nice. It was not painted, but across the porch was an even balance. On each side there was one easy chair with high springs, looking out, and a fern basket hanging over it from the ceiling, and a dishpan of zinnia seedlings growing at its foot on the floor. By the door was a plow-wheel, just a pretty iron circle, nailed up on one wall and a square mirror on the other, a turquoise-blue comb stuck up in the frame, with the wash stand beneath it. On the door was a wooden knob with a pearl in the end, and Solomon's black hat hung on that, if he was in the house.

Out front was a clean dirt yard with every vestige of grass patiently uprooted and the ground scarred in deep whorls from the strike of Livvie's broom. Rose bushes with tiny blood-red roses blooming every month grew in threes on either side of the steps. On one side was a peach tree, on the other a pomegranate. Then coming around up the path from the deep cut of the Natchez Trace below was a line of bare crape-myrtle trees with every branch of them ending in a colored bottle, green or blue. There was no word that fell from Solomon's lips to say what they were for, but Livvie knew that there could be a spell put in trees, and she was familiar from the time she was born with the way bottle trees kept evil spirits from coming into the house—by luring them inside the colored bottles, where they can-not get out again. Solomon had made the bottle trees with his own hands over the nine years, in labor amounting to about a tree a year, and without a sign that he had any uneasiness in his heart, for he took as much pride in his precautions against spirits coming in the house as he took in the house, and sometimes in the sun the bottle trees looked prettier than the house did.

It was a nice house. It was in a place where the days would go by and surprise anyone that they were over. The lamplight and the firelight would shine out the door after dark, over the still and breathing country, lighting the roses and the bottle trees, and all was quiet there.

But there was nobody, nobody at all, not even a white person. And if there had been anybody, Solomon would not have let Livvie look at them, just as he would not let her look at a field hand, or a field hand look at her. There was no house near, except for the cabins of the tenants that were for-bidden to her, and there was no house as far as she had been, stealing away down the still, deep Trace. She felt as if she waded a river when she went, for the dead leaves on the ground reached as high as her knees, and when she was all scratched and bleeding she said it was not like a road that went anywhere. One day, climbing up the high bank, she had found a graveyard without a church, with ribbon-grass growing about the foot of an angel (she had climbed up because she thought she saw angel wings), and in the sun, trees shining like burning flames through the great caterpillar nets which enclosed them. Scarey thistles stood looking like the prophets in the Bible in Solomon's house. Indian paint brushes grew over her head, and the mourning dove made the only sound in the world. Oh for a stirring of the leaves, and a breaking of the nets! But not by a ghost, prayed Livvie, jumping down the bank. After Solomon took to his bed, she never went out, except one more time.

Livvie knew she made a nice girl to wait on anybody. She fixed things to eat on a tray like a surprise. She could keep from singing when she ironed, and to sit by a bed and fan away the flies, she could be so still she could not hear herself breathe. She could clean up the house and never drop a thing, and wash the dishes without a sound, and she would step outside to churn, for churning sounded too sad to her, like sobbing, and if it made her home-sick and not Solomon, she did not think of that.

But Solomon scarcely opened his eyes to see her, and scarcely tasted his food. He was not sick or paralyzed or in any pain that he mentioned, but he was surely wearing out in the body, and no matter what nice hot thing Livvie would bring him to taste, he would only look at it now, as if he were past seeing how he could add anything more to himself. Before she could beg him, he would go fast asleep. She could not surprise him any more, if he would not taste, and she was afraid that he was never in the world going to taste another thing she brought him—and so how could he last?

But one morning it was breakfast time and she cooked his eggs and grits, carried them in on a tray, and called his name. He was sound asleep. He lay in a dignified way with his watch beside him, on his back in the middle of the bed. One hand drew the quilt up high, though it was the first day of spring. Through the white lace curtains a little puffy wind was blowing as if it came from round cheeks. All night the frogs had sung out in the swamp, like a commotion in the room, and he had not stirred, though she lay wide awake and saying "Shh, frogs!" for fear he would mind them.

He looked as if he would like to sleep a little longer, and so she put back the tray and waited a little. When she tiptoed and stayed so quiet, she surrounded herself with a little reverie, and sometimes it seemed to her when she was so stealthy that the quiet she kept was for a sleeping baby, and that she had a baby and was its mother. When she stood at Solomon's bed and looked down at him, she would be thinking, "He sleeps so well," and she would hate to wake him up. And in some other way, too, she was afraid to wake him up because even in his sleep he seemed to be such a strict man.

Of course, nailed to the wall over the bed—only she would forget who it was—there was a picture of him when he was young. Then he had a fan of hair over his forehead like a king's crown. Now his hair lay down on his head, the spring had gone out of it. Solomon had a lightish face, with eyebrows scattered but rugged, the way privet grows, strong eyes, with second sight, a strict mouth, and a little gold smile. This was the way he looked in his clothes, but in bed in the daytime he looked like a different and smaller man, even when he was wide awake, and holding the Bible. He looked like somebody kin to himself. And then sometimes when he lay in sleep and she stood fanning the flies away, and the light came in, his face was like new, so smooth and clear that it was like a glass of jelly held to the window, and she could almost look through his forehead and see what he thought.

She fanned him and at length he opened his eyes and spoke her name, but he would not taste the nice eggs she had kept warm under a pan.

Back in the kitchen she ate heartily, his breakfast and hers, and looked out the open door at what went on. The whole day, and the whole night before, she had felt the stir of spring close to her. It was as present in the house as a young man would be. The moon was in the last quarter and out-side they were turning the sod and planting peas and beans. Up and down the red fields, over which smoke from the brush-burning hung showing like a little skirt of sky, a white horse and a white mule pulled the plow. At inter-vals hoarse shouts came through the air and roused her as if she dozed ne-glectfully in the shade, and they were telling her, "Jump up!" She could see how over each ribbon of field were moving men and girls, on foot and mounted on mules, with hats set on their heads and bright with tall hoes and forks as if they carried streamers on them and were going to some place on a journey—and how as if at a signal now and then they would all start at once shouting, hollering, cajoling, calling and answering back, running, being leaped on and breaking away, flinging to earth with a shout and lying motionless in the trance of twelve o'clock. The old women came out of the cabins and brought them the food they had ready for them, and then all worked together, spread evenly out. The little children came too, like a bouncing stream overflowing the fields, and set upon the men, the women, the dogs, the rushing birds, and the wave-like rows of earth, their little voices almost too high to be heard. In the middle distance like some white and gold towers were the haystacks, with black cows coming around to eat their edges. High above everything, the wheel of fields, house, and cabins, and the deep road surrounding like a moat to keep them in, was the turning sky, blue with long, far-flung white mare's-tail clouds, serene and still as high flames. And sound asleep while all this went around him that was his, Solomon was like a little still spot in the middle.

Even in the house the earth was sweet to breathe. Solomon had never let Livvie go any farther than the chicken house and the well. But what if she would walk now into the heart of the fields and take a hoe and work until she fell stretched out and drenched with her efforts, like other girls, and laid her cheek against the laid-open earth, and shamed the old man with her humbleness and delight? To shame him! A cruel wish could come in unin-vited and so fast while she looked out the back door. She washed the dishes and scrubbed the table. She could hear the cries of the little lambs. Her mother, that she had not seen since her wedding day, had said one time, "I rather a man be anything, than a woman be mean."

So all morning she kept tasting the chicken broth on the stove, and when it was right she poured off a nice cupful. She carried it in to Solomon, and there he lay having a dream. Now what did he dream about? For she saw him sigh gently as if not to disturb some whole thing he held round in his mind, like a fresh egg. So even an old man dreamed about something pretty. Did he dream of her, while his eyes were shut and sunken, and his small hand with the wedding ring curled close in sleep around the quilt? He might be dreaming of what time it was, for even through his sleep he kept track of it like a clock, and knew how much of it went by, and waked up knowing where the hands were even before he consulted the silver watch that he never let go. He would sleep with the watch in his palm, and even holding it to his cheek like a child that loves a plaything. Or he might dream of journeys and travels on a steamboat to Natchez. Yet she thought he dreamed of her; but even while she scrutinized him, the rods of the foot of the bed seemed to rise up like a rail fence between them, and she could see that people never could be sure of anything as long as one of them was asleep and the other awake. To look at him dreaming of her when he might be going to die frightened her a little, as if he might carry her with him that way, and she wanted to run out of the room. She took hold of the bed and held on, and Solomon opened his eyes and called her name, but he did not want anything. He would not taste the good broth.

Just a little after that, as she was taking up the ashes in the front room for the last time in the year, she heard a sound. It was somebody coming. She pulled the curtains together and looked through the slit.

Coming up the path under the bottle trees was a white lady. At first she looked young, but then she looked old. Marvelous to see, a little car stood steaming like a kettle out in the field-track—it had come without a road.

Livvie stood listening to the long, repeated knockings at the door, and after a while she opened it just a little. The lady came in through the crack, though she was more than middle-sized and wore a big hat.

"My name is Miss Baby Marie," she said.

Livvie gazed respectfully at the lady and at the little suitcase she was holding close to her by the handle until the proper moment. The lady's eyes were running over the room, from palmetto to palmetto, but she was saying, "I live at home . . . out from Natchez . . . and get out and show these pretty cosmetic things to the white people and the colored people both . . . all around . . . years and years. . . . Both shades of powder and rouge. . . . It's the kind of work a girl can do and not go clear 'way from home . . ." And the harder she looked, the more she talked. Suddenly she turned up her nose and said, "It is not Christian or sanitary to put feathers in a vase," and then she took a gold key out of the front of her dress and began unlocking the locks on her suitcase. Her face drew the light, the way it was covered with intense white and red, with a little patty-cake of white between the wrinkles by her upper lip. Little red tassels of hair bobbed under the rusty wires of her picture-hat, as with an air of triumph and secrecy she now drew open her little suitcase and brought out bottle after bottle and jar after jar, which she put down on the table, the mantel-piece, the settee, and the organ.

"Did you ever see so many cosmetics in your life?" cried Miss Baby Marie.

"No'm," Livvie tried to say, but the cat had her tongue.

"Have you ever applied cosmetics?" asked Miss Baby Marie next.

"No'm," Livvie tried to say.

"Then look!" she said, and pulling out the last thing of all, "Try this!" she said. And in her hand was unclenched a golden lipstick which popped open like magic. A fragrance came out of it like incense, and Livvie cried out suddenly, "Chinaberry flowers!"

Her hand took the lipstick, and in an instant she was carried away in the air through the spring, and looking down with a half-drowsy smile from a purple cloud she saw from above a chinaberry tree, dark and smooth and neatly leaved, neat as a guinea hen in the dooryard, and there was her home that she had left. On one side of the tree was her mama holding up her heavy apron, and she could see it was loaded with ripe figs, and on the other side was her papa holding a fish-pole over the pond, and she could see it transparently, the little clear fishes swimming up to the brim.

"Oh, no, not chinaberry flowers—secret ingredients," said Miss Baby Marie. "My cosmetics have secret ingredients—not chinaberry flowers."

"It's purple," Livvie breathed, and Miss Baby Marie said, "Use it freely. Rub it on."

Livvie tiptoed out to the wash stand on the front porch and before the mirror put the paint on her mouth. In the wavery surface her face danced before her like a flame. Miss Baby Marie followed her out, took a look at what she had done, and said, "That's it."

Livvie tried to say "Thank you" without moving her parted lips where the paint lay so new.

By now Miss Baby Marie stood behind Livvie and looked in the mirror over her shoulder, twisting up the tassels of her hair. "The lipstick I can let you have for only two dollars," she said, close to her neck.

"Lady, but I don't have no money, never did have," said Livvie.

"Oh, but you don't pay the first time. I make another trip, that's the way I do. I come back again—later."

"Oh," said Livvie, pretending she understood everything so as to please the lady.

"But if you don't take it now, this may be the last time I'll call at your house," said Miss Baby Marie sharply. "It's far away from anywhere, I'll tell you that. You don't live close to anywhere."

"Yes'm. My husband, he keep the *money*," said Livvie, trembling. "He is strict as he can be. He don't know *you* walk in here—Miss Baby Marie!"

"Where is he?"

"Right now, he in yonder sound asleep, an old man. I wouldn't ever ask him for anything."

Miss Baby Marie took back the lipstick and packed it up. She gathered up the jars for both black and white and got them all inside the suitcase, with the same little fuss of triumph with which she had brought them out. She started away.

"Goodbye," she said, making herself look grand from the back, but at the last minute she turned around in the door. Her old hat wobbled as she whispered, "Let me see your husband."

Livvie obediently went on tiptoe and opened the door to the other room. Miss Baby Marie came behind her and rose on her toes and looked in.

"My, what a little tiny old, old man!" she whispered, clasping her hands and shaking her head over them. "What a beautiful quilt! What a tiny old, old man!"

"He can sleep like that all day," whispered Livvie proudly.

They looked at him awhile so fast asleep, and then all at once they looked at each other. Somehow that was as if they had a secret, for he had never stirred. Livvie then politely, but all at once, closed the door.

"Well! I'd certainly like to leave you with a lipstick!" said Miss Baby Marie vivaciously. She smiled in the door.

"Lady, but I told you I don't have no money, and never did have."

"And never will?" In the air and all around, like a bright halo around the white lady's nodding head, it was a true spring day.

"Would you take eggs, lady?" asked Livvie softly.

"No, I have plenty of eggs—plenty," said Miss Baby Marie.

"I still don't have no money," said Livvie, and Miss Baby Marie took her suitcase and went on somewhere else.

Livvie stood watching her go, and all the time she felt her heart beating in her left side. She touched the place with her hand. It seemed as if her heart beat and her whole face flamed from the pulsing color of her lips. She went to sit by Solomon and when he opened his eyes he could not see a change in her. "He's fixin' to die," she said inside. That was the secret. That was when she went out of the house for a little breath of air.

She went down the path and down the Natchez Trace a way, and she did not know how far she had gone, but it was not far, when she saw a sight. It was a man, looking like a vision—she standing on one side of the Old Natchez Trace and he standing on the other.

As soon as this man caught sight of her, he began to look himself over. Starting at the bottom with his pointed shoes, he began to look up, lifting his peg-top pants the higher to see fully his bright socks. His coat long and wide and leaf-green he opened like doors to see his high-up tawny pants and his pants he smoothed downward from the points of his collar, and he wore a luminous baby-pink satin shirt. At the end, he reached gently above his wide platter-shaped round hat, the color of a plum, and one finger touched at the feather, emerald green, blowing in the spring winds.

No matter how she looked, she could never look so fine as he did, and she was not sorry for that, she was pleased.

He took three jumps, one down and two up, and was by her side.

"My name is Cash," he said.

He had a guinea pig in his pocket. They began to walk along. She stared on and on at him, as if he were doing some daring spectacular thing, instead of just walking beside her. It was not simply the city way he was dressed that made her look at him and see hope in its insolence looking back. It was not only the way he moved along kicking the flowers as if he could break through everything in the way and destroy anything in the world, that made her eyes grow bright. It might be, if he had not appeared the way he did appear that day she would never have looked so closely at him, but the time people come makes a difference.

They walked through the still leaves of the Natchez Trace, the light and the shade falling through trees about them, the white irises shining like candles on the banks and the new ferns shining like green stars up in the oak branches. They came out at Solomon's house, bottle trees and all. Livvie stopped and hung her head.

Cash began whistling a little tune. She did not know what it was, but she had heard it before from a distance, and she had a revelation. Cash was a field hand. He was a transformed field hand. Cash belonged to Solomon. But he had stepped out of his overalls into this. There in front of Solomon's house he laughed. He had a round head, a round face, all of him was young, and he flung his head up, rolled it against the mare's-tail sky in his round hat, and he could laugh just to see Solomon's house sitting there. Livvie looked at it, and there was Solomon's black hat hanging on the peg on the front door, the blackest thing in the world.

"I been to Natchez," Cash said, wagging his head around against the sky. "*I* taken a trip, *I* ready for Easter!"

How was it possible to look so fine before the harvest? Cash must have stolen the money, stolen it from Solomon. He stood in the path and lifted his spread hand high and brought it down again and again in his laughter. He kicked up his heels. A little chill went through her. It was as if Cash was bringing that strong hand down to beat a drum or to rain blows upon a man, such an abandon and menace were in his laugh. Frowning, she went closer to him and his swinging arm drew her in at once and the fright was crushed from her body, as a little match-flame might be smothered out by what it lighted. She gathered the folds of his coat behind him and fastened her red lips to his mouth, and she was dazzled by herself then, the way he had been dazzled at himself to begin with.

In that instant she felt something that could not be told—that Solomon's death was at hand, that he was the same to her as if he were dead now. She cried out, and uttering little cries turned and ran for the house.

At once Cash was coming, following after, he was running behind her. He came close, and halfway up the path he laughed and passed her. He even picked up a stone and sailed it into the bottle trees. She put her hands over her head, and sounds clattered through the bottle trees like cries of outrage. Cash stamped and plunged zigzag up the front steps and in at the door.

When she got there, he had stuck his hands in his pockets and was turning slowly about in the front room. The little guinea pig peeped out. Around Cash, the pinned-up palmettos looked as if a lazy green monkey had walked up and down and around the walls leaving green prints of his hands and feet.

She got through the room and his hands were still in his pockets, and she fell upon the closed door to the other room and pushed it open. She ran to Solomon's bed, calling "Solomon! Solomon!" The little shape of the old man never moved at all, wrapped under the quilt as if it were winter still.

"Solomon!" She pulled the quilt away, but there was another one under that, and she fell on her knees beside him. He made no sound except a sigh, and then she could hear in the silence the light springy steps of Cash walking and walking in the front room, and the ticking of Solomon's silver watch, which came from the bed. Old Solomon was far away in his sleep, his face looked small, relentless, and devout, as if he were walking somewhere where she could imagine the snow falling.

Then there was a noise like a hoof pawing the floor, and the door gave a creak, and Cash appeared beside her. When she looked up, Cash's face was so black it was bright, and so bright and bare of pity that it looked sweet to her. She stood up and held up her head. Cash was so powerful that his presence gave her strength even when she did not need any.

Under their eyes Solomon slept. People's faces tell of things and places not known to the one who looks at them while they sleep, and while Solomon slept under the eyes of Livvie and Cash his face told them like a mythical story that all his life he had built, little scrap by little scrap, respect. A beetle could not have been more laborious or more ingenious in the task of its destiny. When Solomon was young, as he was in his picture overhead, it was the infinite thing with him, and he could see no end to the respect he would contrive and keep in a house. He had built a lonely house, the way he would make a cage, but it grew to be the same with him as a great monumental pyramid and sometimes in his absorption of getting it erected he was like the builder-slaves of Egypt who forgot or never knew the origin and meaning of the thing to which they gave all the strength of their bodies and used up all their days. Livvie and Cash could see that as a man might rest from a life-labor he lay in his bed, and they could hear how, wrapped in his quilt, he sighed to himself comfortably in sleep, while in his dreams he might have been an ant, a beetle, a bird, an Egyptian, assembling and carrying on his back and building with his hands, or he might have been an old man of India or a swaddled baby, about to smile and brush all away.

Then without warning old Solomon's eyes flew wide open under the hedge-like brows. He was wide awake.

And instantly Cash raised his quick arm. A radiant sweat stood on his temples. But he did not bring his arm down—it stayed in the air, as if something might have taken hold.

It was not Livvie—she did not move. As if something said "Wait," she stood waiting. Even while her eyes burned under motionless lids, her lips parted in a stiff grimace, and with her arms stiff at her sides she stood above the prone old man and the panting young one, erect and apart.

Movement when it came came in Solomon's face. It was an old and strict face, a frail face, but behind it, like a covered light, came an animation that could play hide and seek, that would dart and escape, had always escaped. The mystery flickered in him, and invited from his eyes. It was that very mystery that Cash with his quick arm would have to strike, and that Livvie could not weep for. But Cash only stood holding his arm in the air, when the gentlest flick of his great strength, almost a puff of his breath, would have been enough, if he had known how to give it, to send the old man over the obstruction that kept him away from death.

If it could not be that the tiny illumination in the fragile and ancient face caused a crisis, a mystery in the room that would not permit a blow to fall, at least it was certain that Cash, throbbing in his Easter clothes, felt a pang of shame that the vigor of a man would come to such an end that he could not be struck without warning. He took down his hand and stepped back behind Livvie, like a round-eyed schoolboy on whose unsuspecting head the dunce cap has been set.

"Young ones can't wait," said Solomon.

Livvie shuddered violently, and then in a gush of tears she stooped for a glass of water and handed it to him, but he did not see her.

"So here come the young man Livvie wait for. Was no prevention. No prevention. Now I lay eyes on young man and it come to be somebody I know all the time, and been knowing since he were born in a cotton patch, and watched grow up year to year, Cash McCord, growed to size, growed up to come in my house in the end—ragged and barefoot."

Solomon gave a cough of distaste. Then he shut his eyes vigorously, and his lips began to move like a chanter's.

"When Livvie married, her husband were already somebody. He had paid great cost for his land. He spread sycamore leaves over the ground from wagon to door, day he brought her home, so her foot would not have to touch ground. He carried her through his door. Then he growed old and could not lift her, and she were still young."

Livvie's sobs followed his words like a soft melody repeating each thing as he stated it. His lips moved for a little without sound, or she cried too fervently, and unheard he might have been telling his whole life, and then he said, "God forgive Solomon for sins great and small. God forgive Solomon for carrying away too young girl for wife and keeping her away from her people and from all the young people would clamor for her back."

Then he lifted up his right hand toward Livvie where she stood by the bed and offered her his silver watch. He dangled it before her eyes, and she hushed crying; her tears stopped. For a moment the watch could be heard ticking as it always did, precisely in his proud hand. She lifted it away. Then he took hold of the quilt; then he was dead.

Livvie left Solomon dead and went out of the room. Stealthily, nearly without noise, Cash went beside her. He was like a shadow, but his shiny shoes moved over the floor in spangles, and the green downy feather shone like a light in his hat. As they reached the front room, he seized her deftly as a long black cat and dragged her hanging by the waist round and round him, while he turned in a circle, his face bent down to hers. The first moment, she kept one arm and its hand stiff and still, the one that held Solomon's watch. Then the fingers softly let go, all of her was limp, and the watch fell somewhere on the floor. It ticked away in the still room, and all at once there began outside the full song of a bird.

They moved around and around the room and into the brightness of the open door, then he stopped and shook her once. She rested in silence in his trembling arms, unprotesting as a bird on a nest. Outside the redbirds were flying and criss-crossing, the sun was in all the bottles on the prisoned trees, and the young peach was shining in the middle of them with the bursting light of spring.

1943

Further Reading

Welty, Eudora. "Writing and Analyzing a Story." *The Eye of the Story: Selected Essays and Reviews.* New York: Random, 1977. 107–15. • Porter, Katherine Anne. Introduction. *Selected Stories of Eudora Welty.* New York: Modern Library, 1941. xi–xxii. • Appel, Alfred, Jr. "The 'Season of Dreams' and the Natchez Trace." *A Season of Dreams: The Fiction of Eudora Welty.* Baton Rouge: Louisiana State UP, 1965. 172–204, spec. 193–99. • Smith, Julian. " 'Livvie'—Eudora Welty's Song of Solomon." *Studies in Short Fiction* 5.1 (Fall 1967): 73–74. • Neault, D. James. "Time in the Fiction of Eudora Welty." *A Still Moment: Essays on the Art of Eudora Welty.* Ed. John F. Desmond. Metuchen, N.J.: Scarecrow, 1978. 35–50, spec. 39–40.

The atmosphere of a story by Eudora Welty is often more important than its plot or characters. Her own comments on writing fiction emphasize the need to achieve an effect that goes beyond the more mechanical aspects of storytelling.

Eudora Welty: On the Addition of Meaning to Experience

How can I express outside fiction what I think this reality of fiction is?

As a child I was led, an unwilling sightseer, into Mammoth Cave in Kentucky, and after our party had been halted in the blackest hole yet and our guide had let us wait guessing in cold dark what would happen to us, suddenly a light was struck. And we stood in a prism. The chamber was bathed in color, and there was nothing else, we and our guide alike were blotted out by radiance. As I remember, nobody said boo. Gradually we could make out that there was a river in the floor, black as night, which appeared to come out of a closet in the wall; and then, on it, a common rowboat, with ordinary countrified people like ourselves sitting in it, mute, wearing hats, came floating out and on by, and exited into the closet in the opposite wall. I suppose they were simply a party taking the more expensive tour. As we tourists mutually and silently stared, our guide treated us to a recitation on bats, how they lived in uncounted numbers down here and reached light by shooting up winding mile-high chimneys through rock, never touching by so much as the crook of a wing. He had memorized the speech, and we didn't see a bat. Then the light was put out—just as it is after you've had your two cents' worth in the Baptistry of Florence, where of course more happens: the thing I'm trying here to leave out. As again we stood damp and cold and not able to see our feet, while we each now had something of our own out of it, presumably, what I for one remember is how right I had been in telling my parents it would be a bore. For I was too ignorant to know there might be more, or even less, in there than I could see unaided. . . .

Without the act of human understanding—and it is a double act through which we make sense to each other—experience is the worst kind of emptiness; it is obliteration, black or prismatic, as meaningless as was indeed that loveless cave. Before there is meaning, there has to occur some personal act of vision. And it is this that is continuously projected as the novelist writes, and again as we, each to ourselves, read.

If this makes fiction sound full of mystery, I think it's fuller than I know how to say. Plot, characters, setting, and so forth, are not what I'm referring to now; we all deal with those as best we can. The mystery lies in the use of language to express human life.

In writing, do we try to solve this mystery? No, I think we take hold of the other end of the stick. In very practical ways, we rediscover the mystery. We even, I might say, take advantage of it.

MARGUERITE YOURCENAR

(1913–1987)

HOW WANG-FO WAS SAVED

translated from the French by Alberto Manguel and Marguerite Yourcenar

The old painter Wang-Fo and his disciple Ling were wandering along the roads of the Kingdom of Han.

They made slow progress because Wang-Fo would stop at night to watch the stars and during the day to observe the dragonflies. They carried hardly any luggage, because Wang-Fo loved the image of things and not the things themselves, and no object in the world seemed to him worth buying, except brushes, pots of lacquer and China ink, and rolls of silk and rice paper. They were poor, because Wang-Fo would exchange his paintings for a ration of boiled millet, and paid no attention to pieces of silver. Ling, his disciple, bent beneath the weight of a sack full of sketches, bowed his back with respect as if he were carrying the heavens' vault, because for Ling the sack was full of snow-covered mountains, torrents in spring, and the face of the summer moon.

Ling had not been born to trot down the roads, following an old man who seized the dawn and captured the dusk. His father had been a banker who dealt in gold, his mother the only child of a jade merchant who had left her all his worldly possessions, cursing her for not being a son. Ling had grown up in a house where wealth made him shy: he was afraid of insects, of thunder and the face of the dead. When Ling was fifteen, his father chose a bride for him, a very beautiful one because the thought of the happiness he was giving his son consoled him for having reached the age in which the night is meant for sleep. Ling's wife was as frail as a reed, childish as milk, sweet as saliva, salty as tears. After the wedding, Ling's parents became discreet to the point of dying, and their son was left alone in a house painted vermilion, in the company of his young wife who never stopped smiling and a plum tree that blossomed every spring with pale-pink flowers. Ling loved this woman of a crystal-clear heart as one loves a mirror that will never tarnish, or a talisman that will protect one forever. He visited the teahouses to follow the dictates of fashion, and only moderately favored acrobats and dancers.

One night, in the tavern, Wang-Fo shared Ling's table. The old man had been drinking in order to better paint a drunkard, and he cocked his head to one side as if trying to measure the distance between his hand and his bowl. The rice wine undid the tongue of the taciturn craftsman, and that night Wang spoke as if silence were a wall and words the colors with which to cover it. Thanks to him, Ling got to know the beauty of the drunkards' faces blurred by the vapors of hot drink, the brown splendor of the roasts unevenly brushed by tongues of fire, and the exquisite blush of wine stains strewn on the tablecloths like withered petals. A gust of wind broke the window: the downpour entered the room. Wang-Fo leaned out to make Ling admire the livid zebra stripes of lightning, and Ling, spellbound, stopped being afraid of storms.

Ling paid the old painter's bill, and as Wang-Fo was both without money and without lodging, he humbly offered him a resting place. They walked away together; Ling held a lamp whose light projected unexpected fires in the puddles. That evening, Ling discovered with surprise that the walls of his house were not red, as he had always thought, but the color of an almost rotten orange. In the courtyard, Wang-Fo noticed the delicate shape of a bush to which no one had paid any attention until then, and compared it to a young woman letting down her hair to dry. In the passageway, he followed with delight the hesitant trail of an ant along the cracks in the wall, and Ling's horror of these creatures vanished into thin air. Realizing that Wang-Fo had just presented him with the gift of a new soul and a new vision of the world, Ling respectfully offered the old man the room in which his father and mother had died.

For many years now, Wang-Fo had dreamed of painting the portrait of a princess of olden days playing the lute under a willow. No woman was sufficiently unreal to be his model, but Ling would do because he was not a woman. Then Wang-Fo spoke of painting a young prince shooting an arrow at the foot of a large cedar tree. No young man of the present was sufficiently unreal to serve as his model, but Ling got his own wife to pose under the plum tree in the garden. Later on, Wang-Fo painted her in a fairy costume against the clouds of twilight, and the young woman wept because it was an omen of death. As Ling came to prefer the portraits painted by Wang-Fo to the young woman herself, her face began to fade, like a flower exposed to warm winds and summer rains. One morning, they found her hanging from the branches of the pink plum tree: the ends of the scarf that was strangling her floated in the wind, entangled with her hair. She looked even more delicate than usual, and as pure as the beauties celebrated by the poets of days gone by. Wang-Fo painted her one last time, because he loved the green hue that suffuses the face of the dead. His disciple Ling mixed the colors and the task needed such concentration that he forgot to shed tears.

One after the other, Ling sold his slaves, his jades, and the fish in his pond to buy his master pots of purple ink that came from the West. When the house was emptied, they left it, and Ling closed the door of his past behind him. Wang-Fo felt weary of a city where the faces could no longer teach him secrets of ugliness or beauty, and the master and his disciple walked away together down the roads of the Kingdom of Han.

Their reputation preceded them into the villages, to the gateway of fortresses, and into the atrium of temples where restless pilgrims halt at dusk. It was murmured that Wang-Fo had the power to bring his paintings to life by adding a last touch of color to their eyes. Farmers would come and beg him to paint a watchdog, and the lords would ask him for portraits of their best warriors. The priests honored Wang-Fo as a sage; the people feared him as a sorcerer. Wang enjoyed these differences of opinion which gave him the chance to study expressions of gratitude, fear, and veneration.

Ling begged for food, watched over his master's rest, and took advantage of the old man's raptures to massage his feet. With the first rays of the sun, when the old man was still asleep, Ling went in pursuit of timid landscapes hidden behind bunches of reeds. In the evening, when the master, disheartened, threw down his brushes, he would carefully pick them up. When Wang became sad and spoke of his old age, Ling would smile and show him the solid trunk of an old oak; when Wang felt happy and made jokes, Ling would humbly pretend to listen.

One day, at sunset, they reached the outskirts of the Imperial City and Ling sought out and found an inn in which Wang-Fo could spend the night. The old man wrapped himself up in rags, and Ling lay down next to him to keep him warm because spring had only just begun and the floor of beaten earth was still frozen. At dawn, heavy steps echoed in the corridors of the inn; they heard the frightened whispers of the innkeeper and orders shouted in a foreign, barbaric tongue. Ling trembled, remembering that the night before, he had stolen a rice cake for his master's supper. Certain that they would come to take him to prison, he asked himself who would help Wang-Fo ford the next river on the following day.

The soldiers entered carrying lanterns. The flames gleaming through the motley paper cast red and blue lights on their leather helmets. The string of a bow quivered over their shoulders, and the fiercest among them suddenly let out a roar for no reason at all. A heavy hand fell on Wang-Fo's neck, and the painter could not help noticing that the soldiers' sleeves did not match the color of their coats.

Helped by his disciple, Wang-Fo followed the soldiers, stumbling along uneven roads. The passing crowds made fun of these two criminals who were certainly going to be beheaded. The soldiers answered Wang's questions with savage scowls. His bound hands hurt him, and Ling in despair looked smiling at his master, which for him was a gentler way of crying.

They reached the threshold of the Imperial Palace, whose purple walls rose in broad daylight like a sweep of sunset. The soldiers led Wang-Fo through countless square and circular rooms whose shapes symbolized the seasons, the cardinal points, the male and the female, longevity, and the prerogatives of power. The doors swung on their hinges with a musical note, and were placed in such a manner that one followed the entire scale when crossing the palace from east to west. Everything combined to give an impression of superhuman power and subtlety, and one could feel that here the simplest orders were as final and as terrible as the wisdom of the ancients. At last, the air became thin and the silence so deep that not even a man under torture would have dared to scream. A eunuch lifted a tapestry; the soldiers began to tremble like women, and the small troop entered the chamber in which the Son of Heaven sat on a high throne.

It was a room without walls, held up by thick columns of blue stone. A garden spread out on the far side of the marble shafts, and each and every flower blooming in the greenery belonged to a rare species brought here from across the oceans. But none of them had any perfume, so that the Celestial Dragon's meditations would not be troubled by fine smells. Out of respect for the silence in which his thoughts evolved, no bird had been allowed within the enclosure, and even the bees had been driven away. An enormous wall separated the garden from the rest of the world, so that the wind that sweeps over dead dogs and corpses on the battlefield would not dare brush the Emperor's sleeve.

The Celestial Master sat on a throne of jade, and his hands were wrinkled like those of an old man, though he had scarcely reached the age of twenty. His robe was blue to symbolize winter, and green to remind one of spring. His face was beautiful but blank, like a looking glass placed too high, reflecting nothing except the stars and the immutable heavens. To his right stood his Minister of Perfect Pleasures, and to his left his Counselor of Just Torments. Because his courtiers, lined along the base of the columns, always lent a keen ear to the slightest sound from his lips, he had adopted the habit of speaking in a low voice.

"Celestial Dragon," said Wang-Fo, bowing low, "I am old, I am poor, I am weak. You are like summer; I am like winter. You have Ten Thousand Lives; I have but one, and it is near its close. What have I done to you? My hands have been tied, these hands that never harmed you."

"You ask what you have done to me, old Wang-Fo?" said the Emperor.

His voice was so melodious that it made one want to cry. He raised his right hand, to which the reflections from the jade pavement gave a pale sea-green hue like that of an underwater plant, and Wang-Fo marveled at the length of those thin fingers, and hunted among his memories to discover whether he had not at some time painted a mediocre portrait of either the Emperor or one of his ancestors that would now merit a sentence of death. But it seemed unlikely because Wang-Fo had not been an assiduous visitor at the Imperial Court. He preferred the farmers' huts or, in the cities, the courtesans' quarters and the taverns along the harbor where the dockers liked to quarrel.

"You ask me what it is you have done, old Wang-Fo?" repeated the Emperor, inclining his slender neck toward the old man waiting attentively. "I will tell you. But, as another man's poison cannot enter our veins except through our nine openings, in order to show you your offenses I must take you with me down the corridors of my memory and tell you the story of my life. My father had assembled a collection of your work and hidden it in the most secret chamber in the palace, because he judged that the people in your paintings should be concealed from the world since they cannot lower their eyes in the presence of profane viewers. It was in those same rooms that I was brought up, old Wang-Fo, surrounded by solitude. To prevent my innocence from being sullied by other human souls, the restless crowd of my future subjects had been driven away from me, and no one was allowed to pass my threshold, for fear that his or her shadow would stretch out and touch me. The few aged servants that were placed in my service showed themselves as little as possible; the hours turned in circles; the colors of your paintings bloomed in the first hours of the morning and grew pale at dusk. At night, when I was unable to sleep, I gazed at them, and for nearly ten years I gazed at them every night. During the day, sitting on a carpet whose design I knew by heart, I dreamed of the joys the future had in store for me. I imagined the world, with the Kingdom of Han at the center, to be like the flat palm of my hand crossed by the fatal lines of the Five Rivers. Around it lay the sea in which monsters are born, and farther away the mountains that hold up the heavens. And to help me visualize these things I used your paintings. You made me believe that the sea looked like the vast sheet of water spread across your scrolls, so blue that if a stone were to fall into it, it would become a sapphire; that women opened and closed like flowers, like the creatures that come forward, pushed by the wind, along the paths of your painted gardens; and that the young, slim-waisted warriors who mount guard in the fortresses along the frontier were themselves like arrows that could pierce my heart. At sixteen I saw the doors that separated me from the world open once again; I climbed onto the balcony of my palace to look at the clouds, but they were far less beautiful than those in your sunsets. I ordered my litter; bounced along roads on which I had not foreseen either mud or stones, I traveled across the provinces of the Empire without ever finding your gardens full of women like fireflies, or a woman whose body was in itself a garden. The pebbles on the beach spoiled my taste for oceans; the blood of the tortured is less red than the pomegranates in your paintings; the village vermin prevented me from seeing the beauty of the rice fields; the flesh of mortal women disgusted me like the dead meat hanging from the butcher's hook, and the coarse laughter of my soldiers made me sick. You lied, Wang-Fo, you old impostor. The world is nothing but a mass of muddled colors thrown into the void by an insane painter, and smudged by our tears. The Kingdom of Han is not the most beautiful of kingdoms, and I am not the Emperor. The only empire which is worth reigning over is that which you alone can enter, old Wang, by the road of One Thousand Curves and Ten Thousand Colors. You alone reign peacefully over mountains covered in snow that cannot melt, and over fields of daffodils that cannot die. And that is why, Wang-Fo, I have conceived a punishment for you, for you whose enchantment has filled me with disgust at everything I own, and with desire for everything I shall never possess. And in order to lock you up in the only cell from which there is no escape, I have decided to have your eyes burned out, because your eyes, Wang-Fo, are the two magic gates that open onto your kingdom. And as your hands are the two roads of ten forking paths that lead to the heart of your kingdom, I have decided to have your hands cut off. Have you understood, old Wang-Fo?"

Hearing the sentence, Ling, the disciple, tore from his belt an old knife and leaped toward the Emperor. Two guards immediately seized him. The Son of Heaven smiled and added, with a sigh: "And I also hate you, old Wang-Fo, because you have known how to make yourself beloved. Kill that dog."

Ling jumped to one side so that his blood would not stain his master's robe. One of the soldiers lifted his sword and Ling's head fell from his neck like a cut flower. The servants carried away the remains, and Wang-Fo, in despair, admired the beautiful scarlet stain that his disciple's blood made on the green stone floor.

The Emperor made a sign and two eunuchs wiped Wang's eyes.

"Listen, old Wang-Fo," said the Emperor, "and dry your tears, because this is not the time to weep. Your eyes must be clear so that the little light that is left to them is not clouded by your weeping. Because it is not only the grudge I bear you that makes me desire your death; it is not only the cruelty in my heart that makes me want to see you suffer. I have other plans, old Wang-Fo. I possess among your works a remarkable painting in which the mountains, the river estuary, and the sea reflect each other, on a very small scale certainly, but with a clarity that surpasses the real landscapes themselves, like objects reflected on the walls of a metal sphere. But that painting is unfinished, Wang-Fo; your masterpiece is but a sketch. No doubt, when you began your work, sitting in a solitary valley, you noticed a passing bird, or a child running after the bird. And the bird's beak or the child's cheeks made you forget the blue eyelids of the sea. You never finished the frills of the water's cloak, or the seaweed hair of the rocks. Wang-Fo, I want you to use the few hours of light that are left to you to finish this painting, which will thus contain the final secrets amassed during your long life. I know that your hands, about to fall, will not tremble on the silken cloth, and infinity will enter your work through those unhappy cuts. I know that your eyes, about to be put out, will discover bearings far beyond all human senses. This is my plan, old Wang-Fo, and I can force you to fulfill it. If you refuse, before blinding you, I will have all your paintings burned, and you will be like a father whose children are slaughtered and all hopes of posterity extinguished. However, believe, if you wish, that this last order stems from nothing but my kindness, because I know that the silken scroll is the only mistress you ever deigned to touch. And to offer you brushes, paints, and inks to occupy your last hours is like offering the favors of a harlot to a man condemned to death."

Upon a sign from the Emperor's little finger, two eunuchs respectfully brought forward the unfinished scroll on which Wang-Fo had outlined the image of the sea and the sky. Wang-Fo dried his tears and smiled, because that small sketch reminded him of his youth. Everything in it spoke of a fresh new spirit which Wang-Fo could no longer claim as his, and yet something was missing from it, because when Wang had painted it he had not yet looked long enough at the mountains or at the rocks bathing their naked flanks in the sea, and he had not yet penetrated deep enough into the sadness of the evening twilight. Wang-Fo selected one of the brushes which a slave held ready for him and began spreading wide strokes of blue onto the unfinished sea. A eunuch crouched by his feet, mixing the colors; he carried out his task with little skill, and more than ever Wang-Fo lamented the loss of his disciple Ling.

Wang began by adding a touch of pink to the tip of the wing of a cloud perched on a mountain. Then he painted onto the surface of the sea a few small lines that deepened the perfect feeling of calm. The jade floor became increasingly damp, but Wang-Fo, absorbed as he was in his painting, did not seem to notice that he was working with his feet in water.

The fragile rowboat grew under the strokes of the painter's brush and now occupied the entire foreground of the silken scroll. The rhythmic sound of the oars rose suddenly in the distance, quick and eager like the beating of wings. The sound came nearer, gently filling the whole room, then ceased, and a few trembling drops appeared on the boatman's oars.

The red iron intended for Wang's eyes lay extinguished on the executioner's coals. The courtiers, motionless as etiquette required, stood in water up to their shoulders, trying to lift themselves onto the tips of their toes. The water finally reached the level of the imperial heart. The silence was so deep one could have heard a tear drop.

It was Ling. He wore his everyday robe, and his right sleeve still had a hole that he had not had time to mend that morning before the soldiers' arrival. But around his neck was tied a strange red scarf.

Wang-Fo said to him softly, while he continued painting, "I thought you were dead."

"You being alive," said Ling respectfully, "how could I have died?"

And he helped his master into the boat. The jade ceiling reflected itself in the water, so that Ling seemed to be inside a cave. The pigtails of submerged courtiers rippled up toward the surface like snakes, and the pale head of the Emperor floated like a lotus.

"Look at them," said Wang-Fo sadly. "These wretches will die, if they are not dead already. I never thought there was enough water in the sea to drown an Emperor. What are we to do?"

"Master, have no fear," murmured the disciple. "They will soon be dry again and will not even remember that their sleeves were ever wet. Only the Emperor will keep in his heart a little of the bitterness of the sea. These people are not the kind to lose themselves inside a painting."

And he added: "The sea is calm, the wind high, the seabirds fly to their nests. Let us leave, Master, and sail to the land beyond the waves."

"Let us leave," said the old painter.

Wang-Fo took hold of the helm, and Ling bent over the oars. The sound of rowing filled the room again, strong and steady like the beating of a heart. The level of the water dropped unnoticed around the large vertical rocks that became columns once more. Soon only a few puddles glistened in the hollows of the jade floor. The courtiers' robes were dry, but a few wisps of foam still clung to the hem of the Emperor's cloak.

The painting finished by Wang-Fo was leaning against a tapestry. A rowboat occupied the entire foreground. It drifted away little by little, leaving behind it a thin wake that smoothed out into the quiet sea. One could no longer make out the faces of the two men sitting in the boat, but one could still see Ling's red scarf and Wang-Fo's beard waving in the breeze.

The beating of the oars grew fainter, then ceased, blotted out by the distance. The Emperor, leaning forward, a hand above his eyes, watched Wang's boat sail away till it was nothing but an imperceptible dot in the paleness of the twilight. A golden mist rose and spread over the water. Finally the boat veered around a rock that stood at the gateway to the ocean; the shadow of a cliff fell across it; its wake disappeared from the deserted surface, and the painter Wang-Fo and his disciple Ling vanished forever on the jade-blue sea that Wang-Fo had just created.

1938, trans. 1984

Further Reading

Yourcenar, Marguerite. "From the Orient to Politics." *With Open Eyes: Conversations with Matthieu Galey.* Trans. Arthur Goldhammer. Boston: Beacon, 1984. 85–91. • Horn, Pierre L. *Marguerite Yourcenar.* Boston: Twayne, 1985. 20–23. • Farrell, C. Frederick, Jr., and Edith R. Farrell. *Marguerite Yourcenar in Counterpoint.* Lanham, Md.: UP of America, 1983. • Shurr, Georgia. "Experimental Fiction Continued." *Marguerite Yourcenar: A Reader's Guide.* Lanham, Md.: UP of America, 1987. 21–31, spec. 29–31.

The theme of human perfectability runs through Yourcenar's fiction and through her conversation. It found its most famous expression in Memoirs of Hadrian, *a psychological novel in the form of a long letter from the Roman Emperor Hadrian (*A.D. *76–138) to his successor, Marcus Aurelius. In the passage below, the great humanistic ruler, who was officially deified by the state, explains his own feelings of divinity.*

Marguerite Yourcenar: On the Human Achievement of Divinity

And it was at about this time that I began to feel myself divine. Don't misunderstand me: I was still, and more than ever, the same man, fed by the fruits and flesh of earth, and giving back to the soil their unconsumed residue, surrendering to sleep with each revolution of the stars, and nearly beside myself when too long deprived of the warming presence of love. My strength and agility, both of mind and of body, had been carefully maintained by purely human disciplines. What more can I say except that all that was lived as god-like experience? The dangerous experiments of youth were over, and its haste to seize the passing hour. At forty-eight I felt free of impatience, assured of myself, and as near perfection as my nature would permit, in fact, eternal. Please realize that all this was wholly on the plane of the intellect; the delirium, if I must use the term, came later on. I was god, to put it simply, because I was man. The titles of divinity which Greece conferred upon me thereafter served only to proclaim what I had long since ascertained for myself. I even believe that I could have felt myself god had I been thrown into one of Domitian's prisons, or confined to the pits of a mine. If I make bold to such pretensions, it is because the feeling seems to me hardly extraordinary, and in no way unique. Others besides me have felt it, or will do so in time to come.

RALPH ELLISON

(b. 1914)

DID YOU EVER DREAM LUCKY?

After the hurried good-bys the door had closed and they sat at the table with the tragic wreck of the Thanksgiving turkey before them, their heads turned regretfully toward the young folks' laughter in the hall. Then they could hear the elevator open and shut and the gay voices sinking swiftly beneath the floor and they were left facing one another in a room suddenly quiet with disappointment. Each of them, Mary, Mrs. Garfield, and Portwood, missed the young roomers, but in his disappointment Portwood had said something about young folks being green and now Mary was challenging him.

"Green," she said, "shucks, you don't know nothing about green!"

"Just wait a minute now," Portwood said, pushing back from the table, "Who don't? Who you talking about?"

"I'm talking about you," Mary said. "Them chillun is gone off to the dance, so *I must* be talking 'bout you. And like I *shoulda* said, you don't even know green when you see it."

"Let me get on out of here," Portwood said, getting up. "Mrs. Garfield, she's just tuning up to lie. I can't understand why we live here with an ole lying woman like her anyway. And contentious with it too. Talking 'bout *I* don't know nothing 'bout green. Why, I been meeting green folks right at the dam' station for over twenty-five years. . . ."

"Sit down, man. Just sit on back down," said Mary, placing her hand upon the heavy cut-glass decanter. "You got nowhere in this whole wide world to go—probably cause you make so much noise with your mouth . . ."

Mrs. Garfield smiled with gentle amusement. She'd been through it all before. A retired cook whose husband was dead, she had roomed with Mary almost as long as Portwood and knew that just as this was his way of provoking Mary into telling a story, it was Mary's way of introducing the story she would tell. She watched Mary cut her eyes from Portwood's frowning face to look through the window to where, far beyond the roofs of Harlem, mist-shrouded buildings pierced the sky. It was raining.

"It's gon' be cold out there on the streets this winter," Mary said. "I guess you know all about that."

"Don't be signifying at me," Portwood said. "You must aim to *lie* me into the streets. Well, I ain't even thinking about moving."

"You'll move," Mary said. "You'll be glad to move. And you still won't know nothing 'bout green."

"Then you tell us, Miss Mary," Mrs. Garfield said. "Don't pay Portwood any mind."

Portwood sat down, shaking his head hopelessly. "Now she's bound to lie. Mrs. Garfield, you done *guaranteed* she go' lie. And just look at her," he said, his voice rising indignantly, "sitting there looking like a lady preacher or something!"

"Portwood, I done tole you 'bout your way of talking," Mary began, but suddenly the stern façade of her face collapsed and they were all laughing.

"Hush, y'all," Mary said, her eyes gleaming. "Hush!"

"Don't try to laugh out of it," Portwood said, "I maintain these youngsters nowadays is green. They black and trying to git to heaven in a Cadillac. They think their education proves that we old southern folks is fools who don't know nothing 'bout life or loving or nothing 'bout living in the world. They green, I tell you! How we done come this far and lived this long if we didn't learn nothing 'bout life? Answer me that!"

"Now, Portwood," Mrs. Garfield said gently, "They're not that bad, the world just looks different to their eyes."

"Don't tell me, I see 'em when they get off the trains. Long as I been a Red Cap I've seen thousands of 'em, and dam' nigh everyone of 'em is green. And just cause these here is rooming with you, Moms, don't make 'em no different. Here you done fixed this fine Thanksgiving dinner and they caint hardly finish it for rushing off somewhere. Too green to be polite. Don't even know there ain't no other ole fool woman like you renting rooms in Harlem who'll treat 'em like kinfolks. Don't tell me 'bout . . ."

"Shh," Mrs. Garfield said, as the sound of voices leaving the elevator came to them, "they might be coming back."

They listened. The voices grew gaily up the hall, then blending with a remote peel of chimes, faded beyond a further wall. Mrs. Garfield sighed as they looked at one another guiltily.

"Shucks," Portwood said, "by now they just about beating the door down, trying to get into that dance. Like I was telling y'all . . ."

"Hush, Portwood!" Mary said. "What *green?*" She said singing full-throatedly now, her voice suddenly folk-toned and deep with echoes of sermons and blue trombones, "Lawd *I* was green. That's what I'm trying to tell you. Y'all hear me? *I, Me, Mary Raaaam-bo*, was green."

"You telling me?" Portwood laughed. "Is you telling *me?*" Nevertheless he leaned forward with Mrs. Garfield now, surrendering once more to Mary's once-upon-a-time antiphonal spell, waiting to respond to her stated theme: green.

"Here y'all," she said, beckoning for their glasses with one hand and lifting the decanter with the other. "Git some wine in y'all's stomachs so's it can warm y'alls' old-time blood."

They drank ceremoniously with lowered eyes, waiting for Mary's old contralto to resume its flight, its tragic-comic ascendence.

"Sho, I was green," she continued. "Green as anybody what ever left the farm and come to town. Shucks, here you criticizing those youngsters for rushing to the dance 'cause they hope to win that auto—that ain't nothing, not to what I done. Cause like them chillun and everybody else, I was after money. And I was full grown, too. Times was hard. My husband had done died and I couldn't get nothing but part-time work and didn't nobody have enough to eat. My daughter Lucy and me couldn't even afford a ten cents movies so we could go forget about it. So Lawd, this evening we're sitting in the window watching the doings down in the streets. Y'all know how it gits round here in the summertime, after it has been hot all day and has cooled off a bit: Folks out strolling or hanging on the stoops and hollering out the windows, chillun yelling and ripping and romping and begging for pennies to buy that there shaved ice with the red sirup poured over it. Dogs barking—y'all know how it is round here in the summertime. All that talk and noise and Negroes laughing loud and juke boxes blaring and like-a-that. Well, it's 'bout that time on one of them kinda days, and one of them store-front churches is just beginning to jump. You can hear them clapping their hands and shouting and the tambourines is a-shaking and a-beating, and that ole levee camp trombone they has is going *Wah-wah, Wah-wah, Wah-wah-wah!* Y'all know, just like it really has something to do with the good Lawd's business—when all of a sudden two autos decides to see which is the toughest."

"A wreck?" Portwood said. "What the newspapers call a *collision?*"

"That's it," Mary said, sipping her wine, "one of the biggest smashups you ever seen. Here we is up in the window on the fourth floor and it's happening right down below us. Why, it's like two big bulls has done charged and run head-on. I tell you, Mrs. Garfield, it was something! Here they is," she said, shifting two knives upon the cloth, "one's coming thisa way, and the other's coming thata way, and when they gits right here, WHAM! They done come together and something flies out of there like a cannon ball. Then for a second it gets real quiet. It's like everybody done stopped to take a breath at the same time—all except those clapping hands and tambourines and that ole nasty-mouthed trombone (that fool was sounding like he done took over and started preaching the gospel by now). Then, Lawd," she said, rocking forward for emphasis, "*glass is falling, dust* is rising, *women* is screaming—Oh, such a commotion. Then all of a sudden all you can hear is Negroes' feet slapping the sidewalks . . ."

"Never mind them feet," Portwood said, "what was it that flew out of there?"

"I'm fixing to tell you now, fool. When the cars come together me and Lucy sees that thing bust outa there like a comet and fly off to one side somewhere. Lucy said, 'Mama, did you see what I seen?' 'Come on, chile,' I says, 'Let's us get ourselfs on down there!' And good people, that's when we started to move! Lawd, we flew down them stairs. I didn't even take time to pull off my apron or my house shoes. Just come a-jumping. Oh, it was a sight, I tell you. Everybody and his brother standing round trying to see if anybody was killed and measuring the skid marks and waiting for the ambulance to come—the man coulda died before that ambulance got there——"

"Well, how about it, Moms, was anybody hurt?"

"Yes, they was, but I ain't your mama, an ole rusty Negro like you! Sho' they was hurt. One man was all cut up and bleeding and the other knocked cold as a big deep freeze. They thought he was dead.

"But me and Lucy don't waste no time with none of that. We gets busy looking for what we seen shoot out of them cars. I whispers, 'Chile, where did it hit?' And she points over near the curb. And sho 'nough, when I starts slow-dragging my leg along the gutter my foot hits against something heavy, and when I hears it clink together my heart almost flies out of my mouth . . ."

"My Lord, Miss Mary! What was it?" Mrs. Garfield said, her eyes intense. "You don't mean to tell me it was——"

Mary gave her a flat look. "I'm goin' to tell you," she said, taking a taste of wine. "I give y'all my word I'm gon' tell you—I calls to Lucy, 'Gal, come over here a minute,' justa looking 'round to see if anybody'd seen me. And she come and I whispers to her, 'Now don't let on we found anything, just get on the other side of me and make like you trying to kick me on the foot. Go on, gal,' I says, 'Don't argue with me—And watch out for my bunion!' And Lawd, she kicks that bag and this time I'm sho, 'cause I hear that sweet metal-like sound. 'What you think it is' I says and she leans close to me, eyes done got round as silver dollars, says, 'Mother' (always called me *mother* steada 'mama,' when she was excited or trying to be proper or something) says, 'Mother, that's money!' 'Shhh, fool,' I tole her, 'you don't have to tell *eve'y*body.'

" 'But, Mother, what are we going to do?'

" 'Just stand still a secon', I says. 'Just quiet down. Don't move. Take it easy! Make out like you watching what they doing over yonder with those cars. Gimme time to figure this thing out . . .'"

She laughed. "Lawd, I was sweating by the gallon. Here I am standing in the street with my foot on a bag full of somebody's money! I don't know what to do. By now the police is all around us and I don't know when whichever one of them men who was hurt is gonna rise up and start yelling for it. I tell you, I musta lost five pounds in five minutes, trying to figure out the deal."

"Miss Mary, I wish I could have seen you," Mrs. Garfield said.

"Well, I'm glad you didn't; I was having trouble enough. Oh it was agonizing. Everytime somebody walks toward us I almost faint. And Lucy, she's turning this-away and that-away, real fast, like she's trying to invent a new dance. 'Do something, Mother,' she says. 'Please hurry up and do something!' Till finally I caint stand it and just flops down on the curbstone and kicks the bag kinda up under my skirts. Lawd, today!" she sang, then halted to inspect Portwood, who, with his head on his arms, laughed in silent glee. "What's the matter with you, fool?"

"Go on, tell the lie," Portwood said. "Don't mind poor me. You really had larceny in your heart that day."

"Well," Mary grinned, "'bout this time old Miz Brazelton, a meddlesome ole lady who lived across the hall from me, she comes up talking 'bout, 'Why, Miss Mary, don't you know a woman of your standing in the community oughtn't to be sitting on the curb like some ole common nobody?' Like all Mary Rambo's got to do is worry 'bout what somebody might think about her—I looks and I knows the only way to git rid of the fool is to bawl her out. 'Look here, Miz Brazelton,' I says, 'this here's my own ole rusty tub I'm sitting on and long as I can haul it 'round without your help I guess I can put it down wherever I please . . .' "

"You a rough woman, Moms," Portwood said with deep resonance, his face a judicial frown. "Rough!"

"I done tole you 'bout calling me Moms!" Mary warned.

"Just tell the lie," Portwood said. "Then what happen?"

"I know that type," Mrs. Garfield said. "With them you do sometimes have to be radical."

"You know it too?" Mary said. "Radical sho is the word. You shoulda seen her face. I really didn't want to hurt that ole woman's feelings, but right then I had to git shed of the fool.

"Well, she leaves and I'm still sitting there fighting with myself over what I oughta do. Should I report what we'd found, or just take it on upstairs? Not that I meant to be dishonest, you know, but like everybody else in New York if something-for-nothing comes along, I wanted to be the one to git it. Besides, anybody fool enough to have that much money riding around with him in a car *deserves* to lose it."

"He sho dam' do," Portwood said. "He *dam'* sho do!"

"Well, all at once Lucy shakes me and here comes the ambulance, justa screaming.

" 'Mother, we better go,' Lucy says. And me I don't know *what* to do. By now the cops is pushing folks around and I knows soon as they see me they bound to find out what kinda egg this is I'm nesting on. Then all of a sudden it comes over me that I'm still wearing my apron! Lawd, I reaches down and touches that bag and my heart starts to going ninety miles a minute. It feels like a heapa money! And when I touches that thick cloth bag you can hear it clinking together. 'Lucy, chile,' I whispers, 'stand right in front of me while the ole lady rolls this heavy stuff up in her apron . . .' "

"Oh, Miss Mary," Mrs. Garfield said, shaking her head, "You'd given in to the devil."

"I'm in his arms, girl, in his hairy arms! And Lucy in on the deal. She's hurrying me up and I picks up that bag and no sooner'n I do, here comes a cop!"

"Oh my Jesus, Miss Mary!" cried Mrs. Garfield.

"Woman," said Mary, "you don't know; you have no *idea*. He's one of these tough-looking young cops, too. One of them that thinks he has to beat you up just to prove he's in command of things. Here he comes, swinging up to Lucy like a red sledge hammer, telling folks to move along— Ain't seen *me*, cause I'm still sitting down. And when he comes up to Lucy I starts to moaning like I'm sick: 'Please, mister officer,' I says, kinda hiding my face, 'we just fixin' to leave.' Well, suh, his head shoots round Lucy like a turkey gobbler's and he sees me. Says, 'What's the matter, madam, wuz you in this wreck?'—and in a real nice voice too. Then Lucy—Lawd, that Lucy was smart; up to that time I didn't know my chile could lie. But Lucy looks the cop dead in the eye and says, 'Officer, we be going in a minute. My mother here is kinda nauchus from looking at all that blood.' "

"Oh, Miss Mary, she didn't say that!"

"She sho did, and it worked! Why the cop bends down and tries to help me to my feet and I says, 'Thank you, officer, just let me rest here a second and I be all right.' Well, suh, he leaves us and goes on off. But by now I got the bag in my apron and gets up moaning and groaning and starts out across the street, kinda bent over like, you know, with Lucy helping me along. Lawd, that bag feels like a thousand pounds. And everytime I takes a step it gets heavier. And on top of that, looks like we never going to cross the street, cause everybody in the block is stopping us to ask what's wrong: 'You sick Miss Mary?'; 'Lucy, what done happen to your mother?'; 'Do she want a doctor?'; 'Po' thing, she done got herself overexcited'—and all likea that. Shucks! I'm overexcited, all right, that bag's 'bout to give me a nervous breakdown!

"When we finally make it up to the apartment, I'm so beat that I just flops into a chair and sits there panting. Don't even take the bag outa my apron, and Lucy, she's having a fit. 'Open it up, Mother, let's see what's in it,' she says. But I figures we better wait, cause after all, they might miss the money and come searching for it. You see, after I done worked so hard gitting it up there, I had decided to keep it sho 'nough . . ."

"You had given in to the devil," Mrs. Garfield said.

"Who?" said Mary, reaching for the wine, "I'm way, *way* past the giving-in stage."

"This world is surely a trial," Mrs. Garfield mused. "It truly is."

"And you can say that again," said Mary, "cause it's the agonizing truth."

"What did you do then, Miss Mary?"

"Pass me your glass, Portwood," Mary said, reaching for the decanter.

"Never mind the wine," said Portwood, covering his glass with his hand. "Get back to what *happened!*"

"Well, we goes to the bathroom—wait, don't say it!" she warned, giving Portwood a frown. "We goes to the bathroom and I gits up on a chair and drops that bag dead into the flush box."

"Now Miss Mary, really!"

"Girl, yes! I knowed wouldn't nobody think to look for it up there. It coulda been hid up in heaven somewhere. Sho! I dropped it in there, then I sent Lucy on back downstairs to see if anybody'd missed it. She musta hung 'round there for over an hour. Police and the newspaper people come and made pictures and asked a heapa questions and everything, but nothing 'bout the bag. Even after the wreckers come and dragged that pile of brand new junk away—still nothing 'bout the bag."

"Everything going in y'all's favor," Portwood said.

"Uhhuh, everything going our way."

"Y'all had it made, Moms," Portwood said, "Why you never tole this lie before?"

"The devil is truly powerful," Mrs. Garfield said, "Almost as powerful as the Lord. Even so, it's strange nobody missed *that* much money!"

"Now that's what me and Lucy thought . . ."

Portwood struck the table, "What I want to know is how much money was in the bag?"

"I'm coming to that in a second," Mary said.

"Yeah, but why you taking so long?"

"Who's telling this lie, Portwood, me or you?" said Mary.

"You was 'til you got off the track."

"Don't forget your manners, Portwood," Mrs. Garfield said.

"I'm not, but looks like to me y'all think money ought to be as hard to get in a lie somebody's telling as it is to get carrying folks' bags."

"Or as 'tis to git you to hush your mouth," said Mary. "Anyway, we didn't count it right then. We was scaird. I knowed I was doing wrong, holding on to something wasn't really mine. But that wasn't stopping me."

"Y'all was playing a little finders-keepers," Portwood said, resting back.

"Yeah, and concentrating on the keeping part."

"But why didn't you just *look* at the money, Miss Mary?"

"Cause we mighta been tempted to spend some of it, girl."

"Yeah, and y'all mighta give yourself away," Portwood said.

"Ain't it the truth! And that bag was powerful enough as it was. It was really working on us. Me and Lucy just sitting 'round like two ole hens on a nest, trying to guess how much is in it. Then we tries to figure whether it was dollars or fifty-centies. Finally we decides that it caint be less'n five or ten dollar gold pieces to weigh so much."

"But how on earth could you resist looking at it?" Mrs. Garfield said.

"Scaird, chile; scaird; We was like a couple kids who somebody's done give a present and tole 'em it would disappear if they opened it before Christmas. And know something else, neither one of us ever had to go to the bathroom so much as when us had that bag up there in that flush box. I got to flushing it just to hear it give out that fine clinking sound."

Portwood groaned, "I know you was gon' lie," he said. "I *knowed* it."

"Hush, man, hush!" Mary laughed. "I know our neighbors musta got sick and tired of hearing us flush that thing. But I tell you, everytime I pulled the chain it was like ringing up money in the cash register! I tell you, it was disintegrating! Whew! I'd go in there and stay a while and come out. Next thing I know there'd be Lucy going in. Then we got shamed and started slipping past one another. She'd try to keep hid from me, and me from her. I tell you, that stuff was working on us like a dose of salts! Why, after a few days I got so I couldn't work, just sat 'round thinking 'bout that doggone bag. And naturally, I done most of my thinking up there on the throne."

"Didn't I tell you she was tuning up to lie," Portwood laughed. "If she don't stop I'm dead gon' call the police."

"This here's the agonizing truth I'm telling y'all," said Mary.

"I wouldn't have been able to stand it, Miss Mary. I would have had to get it over with."

"They shoulda been looking for it by now," Portwood said, "all that money."

"That's what us thought," said Mary. "And we got to figuring why they didn't. First we figgers maybe it was because the man who was hurt so bad had died. But then we seen in the papers that he got well . . ."

"Maybe they was gangsters," Portwood said.

"Yeah, we thought of that too; gangsters or bootleggers."

"Yeah, yeah, either one of them coulda been carrying all that money—or gamblers even."

"Sho they could. Me and Lucy figgered that maybe they thought the cops had took the money or that they was trying to find it theyselves on the q.t., y'know."

"Miss Mary, you were either very brave or very reckless."

"Neither one, girl," Mary said, "just broke and hongry. And don't talk about brave, shucks, we was scaird to answer the doorbell at night. Let me tell you, we was doing some tall figuring. Finally I got so I couldn't eat and Lucy couldn't sleep. We was evil as a coupla lady bears at cubbing time."

"You just couldn't stand all that prosperity, huh, Moms?"

"It was a burden, all right. And everytime we pulled the chain it got a few dollars more so."

Mrs. Garfield smiled. "Mr. Garfield often said that the possession of great wealth brought with it the slings and arrows of outrageous responsibility."

"Mrs. Garfield," Mary mused, "you know you had you a right smart man in him? You really did. And looks like when you got stuff saved up like that you got the responsibility of keeping some of it circulating. Even without looking at it we got to figuring how to spend it. Lucy, she wants to go into business. Why she *almost* persuaded me to see about buying a building and opening a restaurant! And as if *that* wasn't enough trouble to git into, she decides she's goin' take the third floor and open her a beauty shop. Oh, we had it all planned!" She shook her head.

"And y'all still ain't looked at it," Portwood said.

"Still ain't seen a thing."

"Dam!"

"You had marvelous self-control," Mrs. Garfield said.

"Yeah, I did," Mary said, "until that day Lucy went to the dentist. Seems I just couldn't hold out no longer. Seems like I got to thinking 'bout that bag and couldn't stop. I looked at the newspaper and all those ads. Reminded me of things I wanted to buy; looked out the window and saw autos; I tried to read the Bible and as luck would have it I opened it to where it says something 'bout 'Store ye up riches in heaven,' or 'Cast your bread upon the waters.' It really had me on a merry-go-round. I just had to take a peep! So I went and pulled down all the shades and started the water running in the tub like I was taking me a bath—turned on every faucet in the house—then I climbed up there with a pair of scissors and reached in and raised that bag up and just looked at it awhile.

"It had done got *cooold!* It come up *cooold,* with the water dripping off it like some old bucket been deep down in a well. Done turned green with canker, y'all!! I just couldn't resist it no longer. I really couldn't, I took them scissors and snipped me a piece outa that bag and took me a good, *looong* look. And let me tell you, dear people, after I looked I was so excited I had to get down from there and put myself to bed. My nerves just couldn't take it . . . ."

"It surely must have been an experience, Miss Mary."

"Woman, you don't know. You really don't know. You hear me? *I had to go to bed!*"

"Heck, with that much money you could afford to go to bed," said Portwood.

"Wait, le'me tell you. I'm laying up there moaning and groaning when here come Lucy and she's in one of her talking moods. Soon as I seen her I knowed pretty soon she was going to want to talk 'bout that bag and I truly dreaded telling her that I'd done looked into it without her. I says, 'Baby, I don't feel so good. You talk to me later' . . . But y'all think that stopped her? Shucks, all she does is to go get me a bottle of cold beer she done brought me and start to running her mouth again. And, just like I knowed she was gon' do, she finally got round to talking 'bout that bag. What ought we to buy *first,* she wants to know. Lawd, that pore chile, whenever she got her mind set on a thing! Well suh, I took me a big swoller of beer and just lay there like I was thinking awhile."

"You were really good companions," Mrs. Garfield said. "There is nothing like young people to make life rich and promising. Especially if they're your own children. If only Mr. Garfield and I . . . ."

"Mrs. Garfield, let her finish this lie," Portwood said, "*then* we can talk about you and Mr. Garfield."

"Oh, of course," Mrs. Garfield said, "I'm sorry, Miss Mary, you know I didn't really mean to interrupt."

"Pay that pore fool no min'," Mary said. "I wish I had Lucy with me right this minit!"

"Is this lie about money or chillun," Portwood said. "Y'all here'bout to go serious. I want to know what you tole Lucy *then.* What did y'all start out to buy?"

"If you hadn't started monkeying with Mrs. Garfield you'da learned by now," Mary said. "Well, after I lay there and thought awhile I tole her, 'Well, baby, if you want to know the truth 'bout what I think, *I* think we oughta buy us an auto.'

"Well suh, you coulda knocked her over with a feather. 'A car!' she says, 'why Mother, I didn't know you was interested in a car. We don't want to be like these ole ignorant Negroes who buy cars and don't have anything to go with it and no place to keep it,' she says. Says, 'I'm certainly surprised at you, Mother. I never would've dreamed you wanted a *car,* not the very first thing.'

"Oh, she was running off a mile a minute. And looking at me like she done caught me kissing the preacher or the iceman or somebody! 'We want to be practical,' she says, 'We don't want to throw our money away . . .'

"Well, it almost killed me. 'Lucy, honey,' I says, 'that's just what your mama's trying to do, be practical. That's why I say let's git us an auto.'

" 'But, Mama,' she says, 'a car isn't practical at all.'

" 'Oh yes it is,' I says, 'Cause how else is we gon' use two sets of auto chains?'——

"And do y'all know," said Mary, sitting up suddenly and balancing the tips of her fingers on her knees, her face a mask of incredulity, "I had to hop outa bed and catch that chile before she swayed dead away in a faint!"

"Yeah," Portwood laughed, falling back in his chair, "and you better hop up from there and catch me."

Mrs. Garfield's voice rose up girlishly, "Oh Miss Mary," she laughed, "you're just fooling."

Mary's bosom heaved, "I wish I was, girl," she said, "I sho wish I was."

"How 'bout that? Tire chains," Portwood said. "All that larceny for some dam' tire chain!"

"Fool," said Mary, "didn't I tell you you didn't know nothing 'bout green? There *I* was thinking I done found me a bird nest on the ground. C'mon now," she said chuckling at the gullibility of all mankind, "let's us finish the wine."

Portwood winked at Mrs. Garfield. "Hey, Moms, tell us something . . ."

"I ain't go' tell you again that I ain't yo' mama," said Mary.

"I just want you to tell us one last thing . . ."

Mary looked at him warily, "What is it? I got no more time for your foolishness now, I got to git up from here and fix for them chillun."

"Never mind them youngsters," said Portwood, "just tell us if you ever dreamed lucky?"

Mary grinned, "Ain't I just done tole you?" she said. "Sho I did, but I woke up cold in hand. Just the same though," she added thoughtfully, "I still hope them youngsters win that there auto."

"Yes," Mrs. Garfield said, "And wouldn't it be a comfort, Miss Mary? Just to know that they *can* win one, I mean . . . ?"

Mary said that it certainly would be.

1954

Further Reading

Stern, Richard G. *Shadow and Act.* Ed. Ralph Ellison. New York: Random, 1964. 3–23. • O'Meally, Robert G. "Visions and Revisions: New Fiction." *The Craft of*

Ralph Ellison. Cambridge: Harvard UP, 1980. 105–18, spec. 109–13. • Rovit, Earl H. "Ralph Ellison and the American Comic Tradition." *Five Black Writers: Essays on Wright, Ellison, Baldwin, Hughes, and LeRoi Jones.* Ed. Donald B. Gibson. New York: New York UP, 1970. 108–15. • Ostendorf, Berndt, "Anthropology, Modernism, and Jazz." *Modern Critical Views: Ralph Ellison.* Ed. Harold Bloom. New York: Chelsea, 1986, 145–72.

"Did You Ever Dream Lucky?" belongs to a tradition of humorous storytelling that is characteristically American. Margaret Atwood, a Canadian, has defined that tradition more clearly than many American humorists could.

Margaret Atwood: On American Humor

American humour is a different kettle of fish. Classically, it has been Tall Tale or Wooden Nutmeg humour. The three roles available are the con-man or sharpie, sucker or dupe, and audience, and the idea is for the sharpie to put one over on the dupe, with the audience admiring the con-man's superior cunning and laughing at the dupe's gullibility. In Tall Tale, the audience itself plays dupe until the tallness of the tale is finally revealed. A simple con-man story is Mark Twain's famous Jumping Frog tale; a more complicated rendition is the episode in Owen Wister's *Virginian*, where the cowboy hero wins his duel, not with pistols but by telling an absurd story and sucking the villain into believing it. The "audience" is both the reading audience and an audience of "cultivated" easterners who have gathered to listen. Both audiences are flattered by being able to perceive themselves as more astute than the dupe. Then there's the King and the Duke and their Royal Nonesuch in *Huckleberry Finn*, with the audience in the book playing dupe and the reading audience laughing; and the Connecticut Yankee, putting things over on the "gentlemen" of King Arthur's Court. "Gentlemen" get short shrift in American humour; in fact they are distrusted as generally as they are in the rest of American literature, and are likely to be exposed as fakes, pretenders, snobs or ninnies. Real admiration is reserved for the con-men, who are just as likely to have a "regional" accent and play their tricks on city slickers as they are to be travelling salesmen pulling a fast one on the farmer's daughter (a wonderful variation occurs in Flannery O'Connor's story of the Bible salesman who steals the crippled woman's wooden leg). Faulkner's Compsons are Southern Gentlemen and have a kind of crumbling nobility, but it's the lowbrow Snopeses who make the sharp horse trades and end up with the money.

One of the charms of James Thurber is that he reverses the roles: in "Sitting in the Catbird Seat,"[1] the potential dupe turns the tables on the

---

1. The published title of this Thurber story is "The Catbird Seat." See pages 206–212.

con-lady, and time and again the ineffectual Walter Mittys end up, if not top dog, at least unduped.

In American humour the desired pattern is not one of right, correct, "gentlemanly" behaviour; instead it is a pattern suited to a highly competitive, individualistic society: you have to be smart enough to take care of yourself and not let the other guy outsmart you. Better still, you should have the wit to do it to him.

NADINE GORDIMER

(b. 1923)

THE CATCH

His thin strong bony legs passed by at eye level every morning as they lay, stranded on the hard smooth sand. Washed up thankfully out of the swirl and buffet of the city, they were happy to lie there, but because they were accustomed to telling the time by their nerves' response to the different tensions of the city—children crying in flats, lorries going heavily, and bicycles jangling for early morning, skid of tyres, sound of frying, and the human insect noise of thousands talking and walking and eating at midday —the tensionless shore keyed only to the tide gave them a sense of timelessness that, however much they rejoiced mentally, troubled their habit-impressed bodies with a lack of pressure. So the sound of his feet, thudding nearer over the sand, passing their heads with the deep sound of a man breathing in the heat above the rolled-up, faded trousers, passing away up the beach and shrinking into the figure of an Indian fisherman, began to be something to be waited for. His coming and going divided the morning into three; the short early time before he passed, the time when he was actually passing, and the largish chunk of warm midday that followed when he had gone.

After a few days, he began to say good morning, and looking up they found his face, a long head with a shining dark dome surrounded with curly hair given a stronger liveliness by the sharp coarse strokes of grey hairs, the beautiful curved nose handed out so impartially to Indians, dark eyes slightly bloodshot from the sun, a wide muscular mouth smiling on strong uneven teeth that projected slightly like the good useful teeth of an animal. But it was by his legs they would have known him; the dark, dull-skinned feet with the few black hairs on the big toe, the long hard shaft of the shin tightly covered with smooth shining skin, the pull of the tendons at his ankle like the taut ropes that control the sails of a ship.

They idly watched him go, envious of his fisherman's life not because they could ever really have lived it themselves, but because it had about it the frame of their holiday freedom. They looked at him with the curious respect people feel for one who has put a little space between himself and the rest of the world. 'It's a good life,' said the young man, the words not quite hitting the nail of this respect. 'I can just see *you* . . .,' said the girl, smiling. She saw him in his blue creased suit, carrying a bottle of gin wrapped in brown paper, a packet of bananas, and the evening paper.

'He's got a nice open face,' said the young man. 'He wouldn't have a face like that if he worked as a waiter at the hotel.'

But when they spoke to him one morning when he was fishing along the surf for chad right in front of them, they found that he like themselves was only on holiday from a more complicated pattern of life. He worked five or six miles away at the sugar refinery, and this was his annual two weeks. He spent it fishing, he told them, because that was what he liked to do with his Sundays. He grinned his strong smile, lifting his chin out to sea as he swung his spoon glittering into the coming wave. They stood by like children, tugging one another back when he cast his line, closing in to peer with their hands behind their backs when he pulled in the flat silver fish and pushed the heads into the sand. They asked him questions, and he answered with a kind of open pleasure, as if discounting his position as a man of skill, a performer before an audience, out of friendliness. And they questioned animatedly, feeling the knowledge that he too was on holiday was a sudden intimacy between them, like the discovery between strangers that they share a friend. The fact that he was an Indian troubled them hardly at all. They almost forgot he *was* an Indian. And this too, though they did not know it, produced a lightening of the heart, a desire to do conversational frolics with a free tongue the way one stretches and kicks up one's legs in the sun after confinement in a close dark room.

'Why not get the camera?' said the girl, beginning to help with the fish as they were brought in. And the young man went away over the sand and came back adjusting the complications of his gadget with the seriousness of the amateur. He knelt in the wet sand that gave beneath his weight with a wet grinding, trying to catch the moment of skill in the fisherman's face. The girl watched quietly, biting her lip for the still second when the camera blinked. Aware but not in the least self-conscious of the fact that he was the subject, the Indian went on with his fishing, now and then parenthetically smiling his long-toothed smile.

The tendrils of their friendship were drawn in sharply for a moment when, putting his catch into a sack, he inquired naturally, 'Would you like to buy one for lunch, sir?' Down on his haunches with a springy strand of hair blowing back and forth over his ear, he could not know what a swift recoil closed back through the air over his head. He wanted to sell something. Disappointment as much as a satisfied dig in the ribs from opportunist prejudice stiffened them momentarily. Of course, he was not in quite the same position as themselves, after all. They shifted their attitude slightly.

'Well, we live at the hotel, you see,' said the girl.

He tied the mouth of the sack and looked up with a laugh. 'Of course!'

he smiled, shaking his head. 'You couldn't cook it.' His lack of embarrassment immediately made things easy.

'Do you ever sell fish to the hotel?' asked the young man. 'We must keep a look out for it.'

'No—no, not really,' said the Indian. 'I don't sell much of my fish—mostly we eat it up there,' he lifted his eyebrows to the hills, brilliant with cane. 'It's only sometimes I sell it.'

The girl felt the dismay of having mistaken a privilege for an imposition. 'Oh well,' she smiled at him charmingly, 'that's a pity. Anyway, I suppose the hotel has to be sure of a regular supply.'

'That's right,' he said. 'I only fish in my spare time.'

He was gone, firmly up the beach, his strong feet making clefts in the sand like the muscular claws of a big strong-legged bird.

'You'll see the pictures in a few days,' shouted the girl. He stopped and turned with a grin. 'That's nothing,' he said. 'Wait till I catch something big. Perhaps soon I'll get something worth taking.'

He was 'their Indian'. When they went home they might remember the holiday by him as you might remember a particular holiday as the one when you used to play with a spaniel on the beach every day. It would be, of course, a nameless spaniel, an ownerless spaniel, an entertaining creature existing nowhere in your life outside that holiday, yet bound with absolute intimacy within that holiday itself. And, as an animal becomes more human every day, so every day the quality of their talk with the Indian had to change; the simple question-and-answer relation that goes with the celluloid pop of a ping-pong ball and does so well for all inferiors, foreigners, and children became suddenly a toy (the Indian was grown-up and might smile at it). They did not know his name, and now, although they might have asked the first day and got away with it, it was suddenly impossible, because he didn't ask them theirs. So their you's and he's and I's took on the positiveness of names, and yet seemed to deepen their sense of communication by the fact that they introduced none of the objectivity that names must always bring. He spoke to them quite a lot about Johannesburg, to which he assumed they must belong, as that was his generalization of city life, and he knew, sympathetically, that they were city people. And although they didn't live there, but somewhere near on a smaller pattern, they answered as if they did. They also talked a little of his life; or rather of the processes of the sugar refinery from which his life depended. They found it fascinating.

'If I were working, I'd try and arrange for you to come and see it,' he said, pausing, with his familiar taking his own time, and then looking directly smiling at them, his head tilted a little, the proud, almost rueful way one looks at two attractive children. They responded to his mature pleasure in them with a diffusion of warm youth that exuded from their skin as sweat is released at the touch of fear. 'What a fascinating person he is!' they would say to one another, curious.

But mostly they talked about fishing, the sea, and the particular stretch of coast on which they were living. The Indian knew the sea—at home the couple would have said he 'loved' it—and from the look of it he could say whether the water would be hot or cold, safe or nursing an evil grievance of currents, evenly rolling or sucking at the land in a fierce backwash. He knew, as magically to them as a diviner feeling the pull of water beneath the ground, where the fish would be when the wind blew from the east, when it didn't blow at all, and when clouds covered in from the hills to the horizon. He stood on the slippery rocks with them and saw as they did, a great plain of heaving water, empty and unreadable as infinity; but *he* saw a hard greedy life going on down in there, shining plump bodies gaping swiftly close together through the blind green, tentacles like dark hands feeling over the deep rocks. And he would say, coming past them in his salt-stiff old trousers that seemed to put to shame clothes meekly washed in soap and tap-water, 'Over there at the far rocks this morning.'

They saw him most days; but always only in the morning. By afternoon they had had enough of the beach, and wanted to play golf on the closely green course that mapped inland through the man-high cane as though a barber had run a pair of clippers through a fine head of hair, or to sit reading old hotel magazines on the porch whose windows were so bleared with salt air that looking through them was like seeing with the opaque eyes of an old man. The beach was hot and far away; one day after lunch when a man came up from the sand and said as he passed their chairs, 'There's someone looking for you down there. An Indian's caught a huge salmon and he says you've promised to photograph it for him,'—they sat back and looked at one another with a kind of lazy exasperation. They felt weak and unwilling, defeating interest.

'Go on,' she said. 'You must go.'

'It had to be right after lunch,' he grumbled, smiling.

'Oh go on,' she insisted, head tilted. She herself did not move, but remained sitting back with her chin dropped to her chest, while he fetched the camera and went jogging off down the steep path through the bush. She pictured the salmon. She had never seen a salmon: it would be pink and powerfully agile; how big? She could not imagine.

A child came racing up from the beach, all gasps. 'Your husband says,' saying it word for word, 'he says you must come down right away and you must bring the film with you. It's in the little dressing-table drawer under his handkerchiefs.' She swung out of her chair as if she had been ready to go. The small boy ran before her all the way down to the beach, skidding on the stony path. Her husband was waving incoherently from the sand, urgent and excited as a waving flag. Not understanding, she began to hurry too.

'Like this!' he was shouting. 'Like this! Never seen anything like it! It must weigh eighty pounds—' his hands sized out a great hunk of air.

'But where?' she cried impatiently, not wanting to be told, but to see.

'It's right up the beach. He's gone to fetch it. I'd forgotten the film was finished, so when I got there, it was no use. I had to come back, and he said he'd lug it along here.' Yet he hadn't been able to leave the beach to get the film himself; he wanted to be there to show the fish to anyone who came along; he couldn't have borne to have someone see it without him, who had seen it first.

At last the Indian came round the paw of the bay, a tiny black stick-shape detected moving alive along the beached waterline of black drift-sticks, and as he drew nearer he took on a shape, and then, more distinctly, the shape divided, another shape detached itself from the first, and there he was—a man hurrying heavily with a huge fish slung from his shoulder to his heels. 'O-o-h!' cried the girl, knuckle of her first finger caught between her teeth. The Indian's path wavered, as if he staggered under the weight, and his forearms and hands, gripping the mouth of the fish, were bent stiff as knives against his chest. Long strands of grey curly hair blew over from the back of his head along his bright high forehead, that held the sun in a con-centric blur of light on its domed prominence.

'Go and help him,' the girl said to her husband, shaming him. He was standing laughing proudly, like a spectator watching the winner come in at a race. He was startled he hadn't gone himself: 'Shall I?' he said, already going.

They staggered up with the fish between them, panting heavily, and dropped the dead weight of the great creature with a scramble and thud upon the sand. It was as if they had rescued someone from the sea. They stood back that they might feel the relief of their burden, and the land might receive the body. But what a beautiful creature lay there! Through the powdering of sand, mother-of-pearl shone up. A great round glass eye looked out.

'Oh, get the sand off it!' laughed the girl. 'Let's see it properly.'

Exhausted as he was, he belonged to the fish, and so immediately the Indian dragged it by the tail down to the rill of the water's edge, and they cupped water over it with their hands. Water cleared it like a cloth wiping a film from a diamond; out shone the magnificent fish, stiff and handsome in its mail of scales, glittering a thousand opals of colour, set with two brilliant deep eyes all hard clear beauty and not marred by the capability of expres-sion which might have made a reproach of the creature's death; a king from another world, big enough to shoulder a man out of the way; dead, cap-tured, astonishing.

The child came up and put his forefinger on its eye. He wrinkled his nose, smiling and pulling a face, shoulders rising. 'It can't see!' he said joyously. The girl tried it; smooth, firm, resilient eye; like a butterfly wing bright under glass.

They all stood, looking down at the fish, that moved very slightly in the eddy of sand as the thin water spread out softly round its body and then drew gently back. People made for them across the sand. Some came down from the hotel; the piccanin caddies left the golf course. Interest spread like a net, drawing in the few, scattered queer fish of the tiny resort, who avoided one another in a gesture of jealous privacy. They came to stand and stare, prodding a tentative toe at the real fish, scooped out of his sea. The men tried to lift it, making terse suggestions about its weight. A hundred, seventy, sixty-five they said with assurance. Nobody really knew. It was a wonderful fish. The Indian, wishing to take his praise modestly, busied himself with practical details, explaining with serious charm, as if he were quoting a book or someone else's experience, how such a fish was landed, and how rarely it was to be caught on that part of the coast. He kept his face averted, down over the fish, like a man fighting tears before strangers.

'Will it bite? Will it bite?' cried the children, putting their hands inside its rigid white-lipped mouth and shrieking. 'Now that's enough,' said a mother.

'Sometimes there's a lovely stone, here,' the Indian shuffled nearer on his haunches, not touching but indicating with his brown finger a place just above the snout. He twisted his head to the girl. 'If I find it in this one, I'll bring it for you. It makes a lovely ring.' He was smiling to her.

'I want a picture taken with the fish,' she said determinedly, feeling the sun very hot on her head.

Someone had to stand behind her, holding it up. It was exactly as tall as she was; the others pointed with admiration. She smiled prettily, not looking at the fish. Then the important pictures were to be taken: the Indian and his fish.

'Just a minute,' he said, surprisingly, and taking a comb out of his pocket, carefully smoothed back his hair under his guiding hand. He lifted the fish by the gills with a squelch out of the wet sand, and some pictures were taken. 'Like this?' he kept saying anxiously, as he was directed by the young man to stand this way or that.

He stood tense, as if he felt oppressed by the invisible presence of some long-forgotten backdrop and palmstand. 'Smile!' demanded the man and the girl together, anxiously. And the sight of them, so concerned for his picture, released him to smile what was inside him, a strong, wide smile of pure achievement, that gathered up the unequal components of his face— his slim fine nose, his big ugly horse-teeth, his black crinkled-up eyes, and scribbled boldly a brave moment of whole man.

After the pictures had been taken, the peak of interest had been touched; the spectators' attention, quick to rise to a phenomenon, tended to sink back to its level of ordinary, more dependable interests. Wonderment at the fish could not be sustained in its purely specific projection; the remarks became more general and led to hearsay stories of other catches, other unusual experiences. As for the Indian, he had neglected his fish for his audience long enough. No matter how it might differ as an experience, as a fish it did not differ from other fish. He worried about it being in the full hot sun, and dragged it a little deeper into the sea so that the wavelets might flow over it. The mothers began to think that the sun was too hot for their children, and straggled away with them. Others followed, talking about the fish, shading the backs of their necks with their hands. 'Half past two,' said someone. The sea glittered with broken mirrors of hurtful light. 'What do you think you'd get for it?' asked the young man, slowly fitting his camera into its case.

'I'll get about two-pound-ten.' The Indian was standing with his hands on hips, looking down at the fish as if sizing it up.

So he *was* going to sell it! 'As much as that?' said the girl in surprise. With a slow, deliberate movement that showed that the sizing up had been a matter of weight rather than possible profit, he tried carrying the fish under his arm. But his whole body bent in an arc to its weight. He let it slither to the sand.

'Are you going to try the hotel?' she asked; she expected something from the taste of this fish, a flavour of sentiment.

He smiled, understanding her. 'No,' he said indulgently, 'I might. But I don't think they'd take it. I'll try somewhere else. *They* might want it.' His words took in vaguely the deserted beach, the one or two tiny holiday cottages. 'But where else?' she insisted. It irritated her although she smiled, this habit of other races of slipping out of one's questioning, giving vague but adamant assurances of sureties which were supposed to be hidden but that one knew perfectly well did not exist at all. 'Well, there's the boarding-house at Bailey's River—the lady there knows me. She often likes to take my fish.'

Bailey's River was the next tiny place, about a mile away over the sands. 'Well, I envy them their eating!' said the girl, giving him her praise again. She had taken a few steps back over the sand, ready to go; she held out her hand to draw her husband away. 'When will I see the picture?' the Indian stayed them eagerly. 'Soon, soon, soon!' they laughed. And they left him, kneeling beside his fish and laughing with them.

'I don't know how he's going to manage to carry that great thing all the way to Bailey's,' said the young man. He was steering his wife along with his hand on her little nape. 'It's only a mile!' she said. 'Ye-es! But—?' 'Oh, they're strong. They're used to it,' she said, shaking her feet free of the sand as they reached the path.

When they got back to the hotel, there was a surprise for them. As though the dam of their quiet withdrawal had been fuller than they thought, fuller than they could withstand, they found themselves toppling over into their old stream again, that might run on pointlessly and busy as the brook for ever and ever. Three friends from home up-country were there, come on an unexpected holiday to a farm a mile or two inland. They had come to look them up, as they would no doubt every day of the remainder of the holiday; and there would be tennis, and picnic parties, and evenings when they would laugh on the veranda round a table spiked with bottles and glasses. And so they were swept off from something too quiet and sure to beckon them back, looking behind them for the beckon, but already twitching to the old familiar tune. The visitors were shown the hotel bedroom, and walked down the broken stone steps to the first tee of the little golf course. They were voracious with the need to make use of everything they saw; bouncing on the beds, hanging out of the window, stamping on the tee, and assuring that they'd be there with their clubs in the morning.

After a few rounds of drinks at the close of the afternoon, the young man and his wife suddenly felt certain that they had had a very dead time indeed up till now, and the unquiet gnaw of the need to 'make the best'—of time, life, holidays, anything—was gleefully hatched to feed on them again. When someone suggested that they all go into Durban for dinner and a cinema, they were excited. 'All in our car!' the girl cried. 'Let's all go together.'

The women had to fly off to the bedroom to prepare themselves to meet the city, and while the men waited for them, talking quieter and closer on the veranda, the sun went down behind the cane, the pale calm sea thinned into the horizon and turned long straight shoals of light foam to glass on the sand, pocked, farther up, by shadow. When they drove off up the dusty road between the trees they were steeped in the first dark. White stones stood out; as they came to the dip in the road where the stream ran beneath, they saw someone sitting on the boulder that marked the place, and as they slowed and bumped through, the figure moved slightly with a start checked before it could arrest their attention. They were talking. 'What was that?' said one of the women, without much interest. 'What?' said the young man, braking in reflex. 'It's just an old Indian with a sack or something,' someone else broke off to say. The wife, in the front seat, turned:

'Les!' she cried. 'It's him, with the fish!'

The husband had pulled up the car, skidded a little sideways on the road, its two shafts of light staring up among the trees. He sat looking at his wife in consternation. 'But I wonder what's the matter?' he said. 'I don't know!' she shrugged, in a rising tone. 'Who is it?' cried someone from the back.

'An Indian fisherman. We've spoken to him on the beach. He caught a huge salmon today.'

'We know him well,' said the husband; and then to her: 'I'd better back and see what's wrong.' She looked down at her handbag. 'It's going to make us awfully late, if you hang about,' she said. 'I won't hang about!' He reversed in a long jerk, annoyed with her or the Indian, he did not know. He got out, banging the door behind him. They all twisted, trying to see through the rear window. A silence had fallen in the car; the woman started to hum a little tune, faded out. The wife said with a clear little laugh: 'Don't think we're crazy. This Indian is really quite a personality. We forgot to tell you about the fish—it happened only just before you came. Everyone was there looking at it—the most colossal thing I've ever seen. And Les took some pictures of him with it; I had one taken too!'

'So why the devil's the silly fool sitting there with the thing?'

She shrugged. 'God knows,' she said, staring at the clock.

The young husband appeared at the window; he leaned conspiratorially into the waiting faces, with an unsure gesture of the hand. 'He's stuck,' he explained with a nervous giggle. 'Can't carry the thing any farther.' A little way behind him the figure of the Indian stood uncertainly, supporting the long dark shape of the fish. 'But why didn't he sell it?' said the wife, exasperated. 'What can *we* do about it?'

'Taking it home as a souvenir, of course,' said a man, pleased with his joke. But the wife was staring, accusing, at the husband. 'Didn't he try to sell it?' He gestured impatiently. 'Of course. But what does it matter? Fact is, he couldn't sell the damn thing, and now he can't carry it home.' 'So what do you want to do about it?' her voice rose indignantly. 'Sit here all night?' 'Shh,' he frowned. He said nothing. The others kept the studiedly considerate silence of strangers pretending not to be present at a family argument. Her husband's silence seemed to be forcing her to speak. 'Where does he live?' she said in resigned exasperation. 'Just off the main road,' said the husband, pat.

She turned with a charmingly exaggerated sense of asking a favour. 'Would you mind awfully if we gave the poor old thing a lift down the road?' 'No. No . . . Good Lord, no,' they said in a rush. 'There'll be no time to have dinner,' someone whispered.

'Come on and get in,' the young man called over his shoulder, but the Indian still hung back, hesitant. '*Not* the fish!' whispered the wife urgently after her husband. 'Put the fish in the boot!'

They heard the wrench of the boot being opened, the thud of the lid coming down again. Then the Indian stood with the young husband at the door of the car. When he saw her, he smiled at her quickly.

'So your big catch is more trouble than it's worth,' she said brightly. The words seemed to fall hard upon him; his shoulders dropped as if he suddenly realized his stiff tiredness; he smiled and shrugged.

'Jump in,' said the husband heartily, opening the door of the driver's seat and getting in himself. The Indian hesitated, his hand on the back door. The three in the back made no move.

'No, there's no room there,' said the girl clearly, splintering the pause. 'Come round the other side and get in the front.' Obediently the fisherman walked through the headlights—a moment of his incisive face against the light—and opened the door at her side.

She shifted up. 'That's right,' she said, as he got in.

His presence in the car was as immediate as if he had been drawn upon the air. The sea-starched folds of his trousers made a slight harsh rubbing noise against the leather of the seat, his damp old tweed jacket smelled of warm wool, showed fuzzy against the edge of light. He breathed deeply and slowly beside her. In her clear voice she continued to talk to him, to ask him about his failure to sell the fish.

'The catch was more trouble than it was worth,' he said once, shaking his head, and she did not know whether he had just happened to say what she herself had said, or whether he was consciously repeating her words to himself.

She felt a stab of cold uncertainty, as if she herself did not know what she had said, did not know what she had meant, or might have meant. Nobody else talked to the Indian. Her husband drove the car. She was furious with them for leaving it all to her: the listening of the back of the car was as rude and blatant as staring.

'What will you do with the salmon now?' she asked brightly, and 'I'll probably give it away to my relations,' he answered obediently.

When they got to a turn-off a short distance along the main road, the Indian lifted his hand and said quickly, 'Here's the place, thank you.' His hand sent a little whiff of fish into the air. The car scudded into the dust at the side of the road, and as it did so, the door swung open and he was out.

He stood there as if his body still held the position he had carefully disciplined himself to in the car, head hunched a bit, hands curled as if he had had a cap he might perhaps have held it before him, pinned there by the blurs of faces looking out at him from the car. He seemed oddly helpless, standing while the young husband opened the boot and heaved the fish out.

'I must thank you very much,' he kept saying seriously. 'I must thank you.'

'That's all right,' the husband smiled, starting the car with a roar. The Indian was saying something else, but the revving of the engine drowned it. The girl smiled down to him through the window, but did not turn her head as they drove off.

'The things we get ourselves into!' she said, spreading her skirt on the seat. She shook her head and laughed a high laugh. 'Shame! The poor thing! What on earth can he do with the great smelly fish now?'

And as if her words had touched some chord of hysteria in them all, they began to laugh, and she laughed with them, laughed till she cried, gasping all the while, 'But what have I said? Why are you laughing at me? What have I said?'

1952

Further Reading

Hurwitt, Jannika. "The Art of Fiction 77: Nadine Gordimer." *The Paris Review* 88 (1983): 82–127. • Haugh, Robert F. "The Meticulous Vision: Sojourners and Fat Ladies." *Nadine Gordimer.* New York: Twayne, 1974. 19–33, spec. 26–29. • Barkham, John. "African Smiles." *Saturday Review* 35 (24 May 1952): 22. • Githii, Ethel W. "Nadine Gordimer's *Selected Stories*." *Critique* 22.3 (1981): 45–54.

*Like Henry James and Doris Lessing, Nadine Gordimer is remarkably suc-
cessful in developing the inner lives of her characters. The political context
in which she creates this development is worth noting: many of her central
characters are, like her, middle-class South African whites, confronting or
failing to confront the injustices of their society. In a 1984 interview with
Jannika Hurwitt, she discussed her method of characterization.*

Nadine Gordimer: On Moral Judgment of Characters

Hurwitt: I noticed that almost all of the white women in your *Selected
Stories* are physically and mentally both highly unattractive and
middle-class. Does this reflect the way in which you view white
colonialists in your country?

Gordimer: I don't make such judgments about people. After all, I'm a
white colonial woman myself, of colonial descent. Perhaps I
know us too well through myself. But if somebody is partly frivolous or superficial, has moments of cruelty or self-doubt, I
don't write them off, because I think that absolutely everybody
has what are known as human failings. My black characters are
not angels either. All this role-playing that is done in a society
like ours—it's done in many societies, but it's more noticeable
in ours—sometimes the role is forced upon you. You fall into
it. It's a kind of song-and-dance routine, and you find yourself,
and my characters find themselves, acting out these preconceived, ready-made roles. But, of course, there are a large
number of white women of a certain kind in the kind of society
that I come from who . . . well, the best one can say of them is
that one can excuse them because of their ignorance of what
they have allowed themselves to become. I see the same kind of
women here in the U.S. You go into one of the big stores here
and you can see these extremely well-dressed, often rather dis-
satisfied-looking, even sad-looking middle-aged women, rich,
sitting trying on a dozen pairs of shoes; and you can see they're
sitting there for the morning. And it's a terribly agonizing decision, but maybe the heel should be a little higher or maybe . . .
should I get two pairs? And a few blocks away it's appalling to
see in what poverty and misery other people are living in this
city, New York. Why is it that one doesn't criticize that American woman the same way one does her counterpart in South
Africa? For me, the difference is that the rich American represents class difference and injustice, while in South Africa the
injustice is based on both class *and* race prejudice.

JOSÉ DONOSO

(b. 1924)

PASEO

translated from the Spanish by Lorraine O'Grady Freeman

1

This happened when I was very young, when my father and Aunt Mathilda, his maiden sister, and my uncles Gustav and Armand were still living. Now they are all dead. Or I should say, I prefer to think they are all dead: it is too late now for the questions they did not ask when the moment was right, because events seemed to freeze all of them into silence. Later they were able to construct a wall of forgetfulness or indifference to shut out everything, so that they would not have to harass themselves with impotent conjecture. But then, it may not have been that way at all. My imagination and my memory may be deceiving me. After all, I was only a child then, with whom they did not have to share the anguish of their inquiries, if they made any, nor the result of their discussions.

What was I to think? At times I used to hear them closeted in the library, speaking softly, slowly, as was their custom. But the massive door screened the meaning of their words, permitting me to hear only the grave and measured counterpoint of their voices. What was it they were saying? I used to hope that, inside there, abandoning the coldness which isolated each of them, they were at last speaking of what was truly important. But I had so little faith in this that, while I hung around the walls of the vestibule near the library door, my mind became filled with the certainty that they had chosen to forget, that they were meeting only to discuss, as always, some case in jurisprudence relating to their specialty in maritime law. Now I think that perhaps they were right in wanting to blot out everything. For why should one live with the terror of having to acknowledge that the streets of a city can swallow up a human being, leaving him without life and without death, suspended as it were, in a dimension more dangerous than any dimension with a name?

One day, months after, I came upon my father watching the street from the balcony of the drawing room on the second floor. The sky was close, dense, and the humid air weighed down the large, limp leaves of the ailanthus trees. I drew near my father, eager for an answer that would contain some explanation.

"What are you doing here, Papa?" I murmured.

When he answered, something closed over the despair on his face, like the blow of a shutter closing on a shameful scene.

"Don't you see? I'm smoking . . ." he replied.

And he lit a cigarette.

It wasn't true. I knew why he was peering up and down the street, his eyes darkened, lifting his hand from time to time to stroke his smooth chestnut whiskers: it was in hope of seeing them reappear, returning under the trees of the sidewalk, the white bitch trotting at heel.

Little by little I began to realize that not only my father but all of them, hiding from one another and without confessing even to themselves what they were doing, haunted the windows of the house. If someone happened to look up from the sidewalk he would surely have seen the shadow of one or another of them posted beside a curtain, or faces aged with grief spying out from behind the window panes.

In those days the street was paved with quebracho[1] wood, and under the ailanthus trees a clangorous streetcar used to pass from time to time. The last time I was there neither the wooden pavements nor the streetcars existed any longer. But our house was still standing, narrow and vertical like a little book pressed between the bulky volumes of new buildings, with shops on the ground level and a crude sign advertising knitted undershirts covering the balconies of the second floor.

When we lived there all the houses were tall and slender like our own. The block was always happy with the games of children playing in the patches of sunshine on the sidewalks, and with the gossip of the servant girls on their way back from shopping. But our house was not happy. I say it that way, "it was not happy" instead of "it was sad," because that is exactly what I mean to say. The word "sad" would be wrong because it has too definite a connotation, a weight and a dimension of its own. What took place in our house was exactly the opposite: an absence, a lack, which because it was unacknowledged was irremediable, something that, if it weighed, weighed by not existing.

My mother died when I was only four years old, so the presence of a woman was deemed necessary for my care. As Aunt Mathilda was the only woman in the family and she lived with my uncles Armand and Gustav, the three of them came to live at our house, which was spacious and empty.

Aunt Mathilda discharged her duties towards me with that propriety which was characteristic of everything she did. I did not doubt that she loved me, but I could never feel it as a palpable experience uniting us. There was something rigid in her affections, as there was in those of the men of the family. With them, love existed confined inside each individual, never breaking its boundaries to express itself and bring them together. For them to show affection was to discharge their duties to each other perfectly, and above all not to inconvenience, never to inconvenience. Perhaps to express love in any other way was unnecessary for them now, since they had so long a history together, had shared so long a past. Perhaps the tenderness they felt in the past had been expressed to the point of satiation and found itself stylized now in the form of certain actions, useful symbols

---

1. A variety of South American tree with very hard wood.

which did not require further elucidation. Respect was the only form of contact left between those four isolated individuals who walked the corridors of the house which, like a book, showed only its narrow spine to the street.

I, naturally, had no history in common with Aunt Mathilda. How could I, if I was no more than a child then who could not understand the gloomy motivations of his elders? I wished that their confined feeling might overflow and express itself in a fit of rage, for example, or with some bit of foolery. But she could not guess this desire of mine because her attention was not focused on me: I was a person peripheral to her life, never central. And I was not central because the entire center of her being was filled up with my father and my uncles. Aunt Mathilda was born the only woman, an ugly woman moreover, in a family of handsome men, and on realizing that for her marriage was unlikely, she dedicated herself to looking out for the comfort of those three men, by keeping house for them, by taking care of their clothes and providing their favorite dishes. She did these things without the least servility, proud of her role because she did not question her brothers' excellence. Furthermore, like all women, she possessed in the highest degree the faith that physical well-being is, if not principal, certainly primary, and that to be neither hungry nor cold nor uncomfortable is the basis for whatever else is good. Not that these defects caused her grief, but rather they made her impatient, and when she saw affliction about her she took immediate steps to remedy what, without doubt, were errors in a world that should be, that had to be, perfect. On another plane, she was intolerant of shirts which were not stupendously well-ironed, of meat that was not of the finest quality, of the humidity that owing to someone's carelessness had crept into the cigar-box.

After dinner, following what must have been an ancient ritual in the family, Aunt Mathilda went upstairs to the bedrooms, and in each of her brothers' rooms she prepared the beds for sleeping, parting the sheets with her bony hands. She spread a shawl at the foot of the bed for that one, who was subject to chills, and placed a feather pillow at the head of this one, for he usually read before going to sleep. Then, leaving the lamps lighted beside those enormous beds, she came downstairs to the billiard room to join the men for coffee and for a few rounds, before, as if bewitched by her, they retired to fill the empty effigies of the pajamas she had arranged so carefully upon the white, half-opened sheets.

But Aunt Mathilda never opened my bed. Each night, when I went up to my room, my heart thumped in the hope of finding my bed opened with the recognizable dexterity of her hands. But I had to adjust myself to the less pure style of the servant girl who was charged with doing it. Aunt Mathilda never granted me that mark of importance because I was not her brother. And not to be "one of my brothers" seemed to her a misfortune of which many people were victims, almost all in fact, including me, who after all was only the son of one of them.

Sometimes Aunt Mathilda asked me to visit her in her room where she sat sewing by the tall window, and she would talk to me. I listened attentively. She spoke to me about her brothers' integrity as lawyers in the intricate field of maritime law, and she extended to me her enthusiasm for their wealth and reputation, which I would carry forward. She described the embargo on a shipment of oranges, told of certain damages caused by miserable tugboats manned by drunkards, of the disastrous effects that arose from the demurrage of a ship sailing under an exotic flag. But when she talked to me of ships her words did not evoke the hoarse sounds of ships' sirens that I heard in the distance on summer nights when, kept awake by the heat, I climbed to the attic, and from an open window watched the far-off floating lights, and those blocks of darkness surrounding the city that lay forever out of reach for me because my life was, and would ever be, ordered perfectly. I realize now that Aunt Mathilda did not hint at this magic because she did not know of it. It had no place in her life, as it had no place in the life of anyone destined to die with dignity in order afterward to be installed in a comfortable heaven, a heaven identical to our house. Mute, I listened to her words, my gaze fastened on the white thread that, as she stretched it against her black blouse, seemed to capture all of the light from the window. I exulted at the world of security that her words projected for me, that magnificent straight road which leads to a death that is not dreaded since it is exactly like this life, without anything fortuitous or unexpected. Because death was not terrible. Death was the final incision, clean and definitive, nothing more. Hell existed, of course, but not for us. It was rather for chastising the other inhabitants of the city and those anonymous seamen who caused the damages that, when the cases were concluded, filled the family coffers.

Aunt Mathilda was so removed from the idea of fear that, since I now know that love and fear go hand in hand, I am tempted to think that in those days she did not love anyone. But I may be mistaken. In her rigid way she may have been attached to her brothers by a kind of love. At night, after supper, they gathered in the billiard room for a few games. I used to go in with them. Standing outside that circle of imprisoned affections, I watched for a sign that would show me the ties between them did exist, and did, in fact, bind. It is strange that my memory does not bring back anything but shades of indeterminate grays in remembering the house, but when I evoke that hour, the strident green of the table, the red and white of the balls and the little cube of blue chalk become inflamed in my memory, illumined by the low lamp whose shade banished everything else into dusk. In one of the family's many rituals, the voice of Aunt Mathilda rescued each of the brothers by turn from the darkness, so that they might make their plays.

"Now, Gustav . . ."

And when he leaned over the green table, cue in hand, Uncle Gustav's face was lit up, brittle as paper, its nobility contradicted by his eyes, which were too small and spaced too close together. Finished playing, he returned to the shadow, where he lit a cigar whose smoke rose lazily until it was dissolved in the gloom of the ceiling. Then his sister said: "All right, Armand . . ."

And the soft, timid face of Uncle Armand, with his large sky-blue eyes concealed by gold-rimmed glasses, bent down underneath the light. His game was generally bad because he was "the baby," as Aunt Mathilda sometimes referred to him. After the comments aroused by his play he took refuge behind his newspaper and Aunt Mathilda said: "Pedro, your turn . . ."

I held my breath when I saw him lean over to play, held it even more tightly when I saw him succumb to his sister's command. I prayed, as he got up, that he would rebel against the order established by his sister's voice. I could not see that this order was in itself a kind of rebellion, constructed by them as a protection against chaos, so that they might not be touched by what can be neither explained nor resolved. My father, then, leaned over the green cloth, his practiced eye gauging the exact distance and positions of the billiards. He made his play, and making it, he exhaled in such a way that his mustache stirred about his half-opened mouth. Then he handed me his cue so I might chalk it with the blue cube. With this minimal role that he assigned to me, he let me touch the circle that united him with the others, without letting me take part in it more than tangentially.

Now it was Aunt Mathilda's turn. She was the best player. When I saw her face, composed as if from the defects of her brothers' faces, coming out of the shadow, I knew that she was going to win. And yet . . . had I not seen her small eyes light up that face so like a brutally clenched fist, when by chance one of them succeeded in beating her? That spark appeared because, although she might have wished it, she would never have permitted herself to let any of them win. That would be to introduce the mysterious element of love into a game that ought not to include it, because affection should remain in its place, without trespassing on the strict reality of a carom shot.

2

I never did like dogs. One may have frightened me when I was very young, I don't know, but they have always displeased me. As there were no dogs at home and I went out very little, few occasions presented themselves to make me uncomfortable. For my aunt and uncles and for my father, dogs, like all the rest of the animal kingdom, did not exist. Cows, of course, supplied the cream for the dessert that was served in a silver dish on Sundays. Then there were the birds that chirped quite agreeably at twilight in the branches of the elm tree, the only inhabitant of the small garden at the rear of the house. But animals for them existed only in the proportion in which they contributed to the pleasure of human beings. Which is to say that dogs, lazy as city dogs are, could not even dent their imagination with a possibility of their existence.

Sometimes, on Sunday, Aunt Mathilda and I used to go to Mass early to take communion. It was rare that I succeeded in concentrating on the sacrament, because the idea that she was watching me without looking generally occupied the first place of my conscious mind. Even when her eyes were directed to the altar, or her head bowed before the Blessed Sacrament, my every movement drew her attention to it. And on leaving the church she told me with sly reproach that it was without doubt a flea trapped in the pews that prevented me from meditating, as she had suggested, that death is the good foreseen end, and from praying that it might not be painful, since that was the purpose of masses, novenas and communions.

This was such a morning. A fine drizzle was threatening to turn into a storm, and the quebracho pavements extended their shiny fans, notched with streetcar rails, from sidewalk to sidewalk. As I was cold and in a hurry to get home I stepped up the pace beside Aunt Mathilda, who was holding her black mushroom of an umbrella above our heads. There were not many people in the street since it was so early. A dark-complexioned gentleman saluted us without lifting his hat, because of the rain. My aunt was in the process of telling me how surprised she was that someone of mixed blood had bowed to her with so little show of attention, when suddenly, near where we were walking, a streetcar applied its brakes with a screech, making her interrupt her monologue. The conductor looked out through his window:

"Stupid dog!" he shouted.

We stopped to watch.

A small white bitch escaped from between the wheels of the streetcar and, limping painfully, with her tail between her legs, took refuge in a doorway as the streetcar moved on again.

"These dogs," protested Aunt Mathilda. "It's beyond me how they are allowed to go around like that."

Continuing on our way, we passed by the bitch huddled in the corner of a doorway. It was small and white, with legs which were too short for its size and an ugly pointed snout that proclaimed an entire genealogy of misalliances: the sum of unevenly matched breeds which for generations had been scouring the city, searching for food in the garbage cans and among the refuse of the port. She was drenched, weak, trembling with cold or fever. When we passed in front of her I noticed that my aunt looked at the bitch, and the bitch's eyes returned her gaze.

We continued on our way home. Several steps further I was on the point of forgetting the dog when my aunt surprised me by abruptly turning around and crying out: "Psst! Go away!"

She had turned in such absolute certainty of finding the bitch following us that I trembled with the mute question which arose from my surprise: How did she know? She couldn't have heard her, since she was following us at an appreciable distance. But she did not doubt it. Perhaps the look that had passed between them of which I saw only the mechanics—the bitch's head raised slightly toward Aunt Mathilda, Aunt Mathilda's slightly inclined toward the bitch—contained some secret commitment? I do not know. In any case, turning to drive away the dog, her peremptory "psst" had the sound of something like a last effort to repel an encroaching destiny. It is possible that I am saying all this in the light of things that happened later, that my imagination is embellishing with significance what was only trivial. However, I can say with certainty that in that moment I felt a strangeness, almost a fear of my aunt's sudden loss of dignity in condescending to turn around and confer rank on a sick and filthy bitch.

We arrived home. We went up the stairs and the bitch stayed down below, looking up at us from the torrential rain that had just been unleashed. We went inside, and the delectable process of breakfast following communion removed the white bitch from my mind. I have never felt our house so protective as that morning, never rejoiced so much in the security derived from those old walls that marked off my world.

In one of my wanderings in and out of the empty sitting rooms, I pulled back the curtain of a window to see if the rain promised to let up. The storm continued. And, sitting at the foot of the stairs still scrutinizing the house, I saw the white bitch. I dropped the curtain so that I might not see her there, soaked through and looking like one spellbound. Then, from the dark outer rim of the room, Aunt Mathilda's low voice surprised me. Bent over to strike a match to the kindling wood already arranged in the fireplace, she asked: "Is it still there?"

"What?"

I knew what.

"The white bitch . . ."

I answered yes, that it was.

3

It must have been the last storm of the winter, because I remember quite clearly that the following days opened up and the nights began to grow warmer.

The white bitch stayed posted on our doorstep scrutinizing our windows. In the mornings, when I left for school, I tried to shoo her away, but barely had I boarded the bus when I would see her reappear around the corner or from behind the mailbox. The servant girls also tried to frighten her away, but their attempts were as fruitless as mine, because the bitch never failed to return.

Once, we were all saying goodnight at the foot of the stairs before going up to bed. Uncle Gustav had just turned off the lights, all except the one on the stairway, so that the large space of the vestibule had become peopled with the shadowy bodies of furniture. Aunt Mathilda, who was entreating Uncle Armand to open the window of his room so a little air could come in, suddenly stopped speaking, leaving her sentence unfinished, and the movements of all of us, who had started to go up, halted.

"What is the matter?" asked Father, stepping down one stair.

"Go on up," murmured Aunt Mathilda, turning around and gazing into the shadow of the vestibule.

But we did not go up.

The silence of the room was filled with the sweet voice of each object: a grain of dirt trickling down between the wallpaper and the wall, the creaking of polished woods, the quivering of some loose crystal. Someone, in addition to ourselves, was where we were. A small white form came out of the darkness near the service door. The bitch crossed the vestibule, limping slowly in the direction of Aunt Mathilda, and without even looking at her, threw herself down at her feet.

It was as though the immobility of the dog enabled us to move again. My father came down two stairs. Uncle Gustav turned on the light. Uncle Armand went upstairs and shut himself in his room.

"What is this?" asked my father.

Aunt Mathilda remained still.

"How could she have come in?" she asked aloud.

Her question seemed to acknowledge the heroism implicit in having either jumped walls in that lamentable condition, or come into the basement through a broken pane of glass, or fooled the servants' vigilance by creeping through a casually opened door.

"Mathilda, call one of the girls to take her away," said my father, and went upstairs followed by Uncle Gustav.

We were left alone looking at the bitch. She called a servant, telling the girl to give her something to eat and the next day to call a veterinarian.

"Is she going to stay in the house?" I asked.

"How can she walk in the street like that?" murmured Aunt Mathilda. "She has to get better so we can throw her out. And she'd better get well soon because I don't want animals in the house."

Then she added: "Go upstairs to bed."

She followed the girl who was carrying the dog out.

I sensed that ancient drive of Aunt Mathilda's to have everything go well about her, that energy and dexterity which made her sovereign of immediate things. Is it possible that she was so secure within her limitations that for her the only necessity was to overcome imperfections, errors not of intention or motive, but of condition? If so, the white bitch was going to get well. She would see to it because the animal had entered the radius of her power. The veterinarian would bandage the broken leg under her watchful eye, and protected by rubber gloves and an apron, she herself would take charge of cleaning the bitch's pustules with disinfectant that would make her howl. But Aunt Mathilda would remain deaf to those howls, sure that whatever she was doing was for the best.

And so it was. The bitch stayed in the house. Not that I saw her, but I could feel the presence of any stranger there, even though confined to the lower reaches of the basement. Once or twice I saw Aunt Mathilda with the rubber gloves on her hands, carrying a vial full of red liquid. I found a plate with scraps of food in a passage of the basement where I went to look for the bicycle I had just been given. Weakly, buffered by walls and floors, at times the suspicion of a bark reached my ears.

One afternoon I went down to the kitchen. The bitch came in, painted like a clown with red disinfectant. The servants threw her out without paying her any mind. But I saw that she was not hobbling any longer, that her tail, limp before, was curled up like a feather, leaving her shameless bottom in plain view.

That afternoon I asked Aunt Mathilda: "When are you going to throw her out?"

"Who?" she asked.

She knew perfectly well.

"The white bitch."

"She's not well yet," she replied.

Later I thought of insisting, of telling her that surely there was nothing now to prevent her from climbing the garbage cans in search of food. I didn't do it because I believe it was the same night that Aunt Mathilda, after losing the first round of billiards, decided that she did not feel like playing another. Her brothers went on playing, and she, ensconced in the leather sofa, made a mistake in calling their names. There was a moment of confusion. Then the thread of order was quickly picked up again by the men, who knew how to ignore an accident if it was not favorable to them. But I had already seen.

It was as if Aunt Mathilda were not there at all. She was breathing at my side as she always did. The deep, silencing carpet yielded under her feet as usual and her tranquilly crossed hands weighed on her skirt. How is it possible to feel with the certainty I felt then the absence of a person whose heart is somewhere else? The following nights were equally troubled by the invisible slur of her absence. She seemed to have lost all interest in the game and left off calling her brothers by their names. They appeared not to notice it. But they must have, because their games became shorter and I noticed an infinitesimal increase in the deference with which they treated her.

One night, as we were going out of the dining room, the bitch appeared in the doorway and joined the family group. The men paused before they went into the library so that their sister might lead the way to the billiard room, followed this time by the white bitch. They made no comment, as if they had not seen her, beginning their game as they did every night.

The bitch sat down at Aunt Mathilda's feet. She was very quiet. Her lively eyes examined the room and followed the players' strategies as if all of that amused her greatly. She was fat now and had a shiny coat. Her whole body, from her quivering snout to her tail ready to waggle, was full of an abundant capacity for fun. How long had she stayed in the house? A month? Perhaps more. But in that month Aunt Mathilda had forced her to get well, caring for her not with displays of affection but with those hands of hers which could not refrain from mending what was broken. The leg was well. She had disinfected, fed and bathed her, and now the white bitch was whole.

In one of his plays Uncle Armand let the cube of blue chalk fall to the floor. Immediately, obeying an instinct that seemed to surge up from her picaresque past, the bitch ran toward the chalk and snatched it with her mouth away from Uncle Armand, who had bent over to pick it up. Then followed something surprising: Aunt Mathilda, as if suddenly unwound, burst into a peal of laughter that agitated her whole body. We remained frozen. On hearing her laugh, the bitch dropped the chalk, ran towards her with tail waggling aloft, and jumped up onto her lap. Aunt Mathilda's laugh relented, but Uncle Armand left the room. Uncle Gustav and my father went on with the game: now it was more important than ever not to see, not to see anything at all, not to comment, not to consider oneself alluded to by these events.

I did not find Aunt Mathilda's laugh amusing, because I may have felt the dark thing that had stirred it up. The bitch grew calm sitting on her lap. The cracking noises of the balls when they hit seemed to conduct Aunt Mathilda's hand first from its place on the edge of the sofa, to her skirt, and then to the curved back of the sleeping animal. On seeing that expression-less hand reposing there, I noticed that the tension which had kept my aunt's features clenched before, relented, and that a certain peace was now softening her face. I could not resist. I drew closer to her on the sofa, as if to a newly kindled fire. I hoped that she would reach out to me with a look or include me with a smile. But she did not.

4

When I arrived from school in the afternoon, I used to go directly to the back of the house and, mounting my bicycle, take turn after turn around the narrow garden, circling the pair of cast-iron benches and the elm tree. Behind the wall, the chestnut trees were beginning to display their light spring down, but the seasons did not interest me, for I had too many serious things to think about. And since I knew that no one came down into the garden until the suffocation of midsummer made it imperative, it seemed to be the best place for meditating about what was going on inside the house.

One might have said that nothing was going on. But how could I remain calm in the face of the entwining relationship which had sprung up between my aunt and the white bitch? It was as if Aunt Mathilda, after hav-ing resigned herself to an odd life of service and duty, had found at last her equal. And as women-friends do, they carried on a life full of niceties and pleasing refinements. They ate bonbons that came in boxes wrapped frivo-lously with ribbons. My aunt arranged tangerines, pineapples and grapes in tall crystal bowls, while the bitch watched her as if on the point of criticizing her taste or offering a suggestion.

Often when I passed the door of her room, I heard a peal of laughter like the one which had overturned the order of her former life that night. Or I heard her engage in a dialogue with an interlocutor whose voice I did not hear. It was a new life. The bitch, the guilty one, slept in a hamper near her bed, an elegant, feminine hamper, ridiculous to my way of thinking, and followed her everywhere except into the dining room. Entrance there was forbidden her, but waiting for her friend to come out again, she followed her to the billiard room and sat at her side on the sofa or on her lap, exchanging with her from time to time complicitory glances.

How was it possible? I used to ask myself: why had she waited until now to go beyond herself and establish a dialogue? At times she appeared insecure about the bitch, fearful that, in the same way she had arrived one fine day, she might also go, leaving her with all this new abundance weighing on her hands. Or did she still fear for her health? These ideas, which now seem to clear, floated blurred in my imagination while I listened to the gravel of the path crunching under the wheels of my bicycle. What was not blurred, however, was my vehement desire to become gravely ill, to see if I might also succeed in harvesting some kind of relationship. Because the bitch's illness had been the cause of everything. If it had not been for that, my aunt might have never joined in league with her. But I had a constitution of iron, and furthermore it was clear that Aunt Mathilda's heart did not have room for more than one love at a time.

My father and my uncles did not seem to notice any change. The bitch was very quiet and, abandoning her street ways, seemed to acquire manners more worthy of Aunt Mathilda. But still, she had somehow preserved all the sauciness of a female of the streets. It was clear that the hardships of her life had not been able to cloud either her good humor or her taste for adventure which, I felt, lay dangerously dormant inside her. For the men of the house it proved easier to accept her than to throw her out, since this would have forced them to revise their canons of security.

One night, when the pitcher of lemonade had already made its appearance on the console table of the library, cooling that corner of the shadow, and the windows had been thrown open to the air, my father halted abruptly at the doorway of the billiard room.

"What is that?" he exclaimed, looking at the floor.

The three men stopped in consternation to look at a small, round pool on the waxed floor.

"Mathilda!" called Uncle Gustav.

She went to look and then reddened with shame. The bitch had taken refuge under the billiard table in the adjoining room. Walking over to the table my father saw her there, and changing direction sharply, he left the room, followed by his brothers.

Aunt Mathilda went upstairs. The bitch followed her. I stayed in the library with a glass of lemonade in my hand, and looked out at the summer sky, listening to some far-off siren from the sea, and to the murmur of the city stretched out under the stars. Soon I heard Aunt Mathilda coming down. She appeared with her hat on and with her keys chinking in her hand.

"Go up and go to bed," she said. "I'm going to take her for a walk on the street so that she can do her business."

Then she added something strange: "It's such a lovely night."

And she went out.

From that night on, instead of going up after dinner to open her brothers' beds, she went to her room, put her hat tightly on her head and came downstairs again, chinking her keys. She went out with the bitch without explaining anything to anyone. And my uncles and my father and I stayed behind in the billiard room, and later we sat on the benches of the garden, with all the murmuring of the elm tree and the clearness of the sky weighing down on us. These nocturnal walks of Aunt Mathilda's were never spoken of by her brothers. They never showed any awareness of the change that had occurred inside our house.

In the beginning Aunt Mathilda was gone at the most for twenty minutes or half an hour, returning to take whatever refreshment there was and to exchange some trivial commentary. Later, her sorties were inexplicably prolonged. We began to realize, or I did at least, that she was no longer a woman taking her dog out for hygienic reasons: outside there, in the streets of the city, something was drawing her. When waiting, my father furtively eyed his pocket watch, and if the delay was very great Uncle Gustav went up to the second floor pretending he had forgotten something there, to spy for her from the balcony. But still they did not speak. Once, when Aunt Mathilda stayed out too long, my father paced back and forth along the path that wound between the hydrangeas. Uncle Gustav threw away a cigar which he could not light to his satisfaction, then another, crushing it with the heel of his shoe. Uncle Armand spilled a cup of coffee. I watched them, hoping that at long last they would explode, that they would finally say something to fill the minutes that were passing by one after another, getting longer and longer and longer without the presence of Aunt Mathilda. It was twelve-thirty when she arrived.

"Why are you all waiting up for me?" she asked, smiling.

She was holding her hat in her hand, and her hair, ordinarily so well-groomed, was mussed. I saw that a streak of mud was soiling her shoes.

"What happened to you?" asked Uncle Armand.

"Nothing," came her reply, and with it she shut off any right of her brothers to meddle in those unknown hours that were now her life. I say they were her life because, during the minutes she stayed with us before going up to her room with the bitch, I perceived an animation in her eyes, an excited restlessness like that in the eyes of the animal: it was as though they had been washed in scenes to which even our imagination lacked access. Those two were accomplices. The night protected them. They belonged to the murmuring sound of the city, to the sirens of the ships which, crossing the dark or illuminated streets, the houses and factories and parks, reached my ears.

Her walks with the bitch continued for some time. Now we said good night immediately after dinner, and each one went up to shut himself in his room, my father, Uncle Gustav, Uncle Armand and I. But no one went to sleep before she came in, late, sometimes terribly late, when the light of dawn was already striking the top of our elm. Only after hearing her close the door of her bedroom did the pacing with which my father measured his room cease, or was the window in one of his brothers' rooms finally closed to exclude that fragment of the night which was no longer dangerous.

Once I heard her come up very late, and as I thought I heard her singing softly, I opened my door and peeked out. When she passed my room, with the white bitch nestled in her arms, her face seemed to me surprisingly young and unblemished, even though it was dirty, and I saw a rip in her skirt. I went to bed terrified, knowing this was the end.

I was not mistaken. Because one night, shortly after, Aunt Mathilda took the dog out for a walk after dinner, and did not return.

We stayed awake all night, each one in his room, and she did not come back. No one said anything the next day. They went—I presume—to their office, and I went to school. She wasn't home when we came back and we sat silently at our meal that night. I wonder if they found out something definite that very first day. But I think not, because we all, without seeming to, haunted the windows of the house, peering into the street.

"Your aunt went on a trip," the cook answered me when I finally dared to ask, if only her.

But I knew it was not true.

Life continued in the house just as if Aunt Mathilda were still living there. It is true that they used to gather in the library for hours and hours, and closeted there they may have planned ways of retrieving her out of that night which had swallowed her. Several times a visitor came who was clearly not of our world, a plainclothesman perhaps, or the head of a stevedore's union come to pick up indemnification for some accident. Sometimes their voices rose a little, sometimes there was a deadened quiet, sometimes their voices became hard, sharp, as they fenced with the voice I did not know. But the library door was too thick, too heavy for me to hear what they were saying.

trans. 1969

Further Reading

McMurray, George R. "The Short Stories." *José Donoso.* Boston: Twayne, 1979. 34–58. • Tatum, Charles M. "The Child Point of View in Donoso's Fiction." *Journal of Spanish Studies: Twentieth Century* (Winter 1973): 187–96. • Callan, Richard J. "Animals as Mana Figures in José Donoso's 'Paseo' and 'Santelices.' " *Essays in Literature* (Spring 1975): 115–23, spec. 115–19. • Maurer, Robert. "Unbridled Pegasus." *Saturday Review* (9 July 1977): 30–31.

"Paseo" is a story that invites the reader to find symbolic meanings for certain details. Straining after symbolic reading can often lead the reader astray, however. Flannery O'Connor, whose fiction is comparable to José Donoso's in its use of symbolism, wrote very clearly on the way that symbols accumulate meaning in a story.

Flannery O'Connor: On Letting Symbols Gather Meaning

In good fiction, certain of the details will tend to accumulate meaning from the action of the story itself, and when this happens they become symbolic in the way they work. I once wrote a story called "Good Country People," in which a lady Ph.D. has her wooden leg stolen by a Bible salesman whom she has tried to seduce. Now I'll admit that, paraphrased in this way, the situation is simply a low joke. The average reader is pleased to observe anybody's wooden leg being stolen. But without ceasing to appeal to him and without making any statements of high intention, this story does manage to operate at another level of experience, by letting the wooden leg accumulate meaning. Early in the story, we're presented with the fact that the Ph.D. is spiritually as well as physically crippled. She believes in nothing but her own belief in nothing, and we perceive that there is a wooden part of her soul that corresponds to her wooden leg. Now of course this is never stated. The fiction writer states as little as possible. The reader makes this connection from things he is shown. He may not even know that he makes the connection, but the connection is there nevertheless and it has its effect on him. As the story goes on, the wooden leg continues to accumulate meaning. The reader learns how the girl feels about her leg, how her mother feels about it, and how the country woman on the place feels about it; and finally, by the time the Bible salesman comes along, the leg has accumulated so much meaning that it is, as the saying goes, loaded. And when the Bible salesman steals it, the reader realizes that he has taken away part of the girl's personality and has revealed her deeper affliction to her for the first time.

If you want to say that the wooden leg is a symbol, you can say that. But it is a wooden leg first, and as a wooden leg it is absolutely necessary to the story. It has its place on the literal level of the story, but it operates in depth as well as on the surface. It increases the story in every direction, and this is essentially the way a story escapes being short.

FLANNERY O'CONNOR

(1925–1964)

A GOOD MAN IS HARD TO FIND

The grandmother didn't want to go to Florida. She wanted to visit some of her connections in east Tennessee and she was seizing every chance to change Bailey's mind. Bailey was the son she lived with, her only boy. He was sitting on the edge of his chair at the table, bent over the orange sports section of the *Journal*. "Now look here, Bailey," she said, "see here, read this," and she stood with one hand on her thin hip and the other rattling the newspaper at his bald head. "Here this fellow that calls himself The Misfit is aloose from the Federal Pen and headed toward Florida and you read here what it says he did to these people. Just you read it. I wouldn't take my children in any direction with a criminal like that aloose in it. I couldn't answer to my conscience if I did."

Bailey didn't look up from his reading so she wheeled around then and faced the children's mother; a young woman in slacks, whose face was as broad and innocent as a cabbage and was tied around with a green headkerchief that had two points on the top like rabbit's ears. She was sitting on the sofa, feeding the baby his apricots out of a jar. "The children have been to Florida before," the old lady said. "You all ought to take them somewhere else for a change so they would see different parts of the world and be broad. They never have been to east Tennessee."

The children's mother didn't seem to hear her, but the eight-year-old boy, John Wesley, a stocky child with glasses, said, "If you don't want to go to Florida, why dontcha stay at home?" He and the little girl, June Star, were reading the funny papers on the floor.

"She wouldn't stay at home to be queen for a day," June Star said without raising her yellow head.

"Yes, and what would you do if this fellow, The Misfit, caught you?" the grandmother asked.

"I'd smack his face," John Wesley said.

"She wouldn't stay at home for a million bucks," June Star said. "Afraid she'd miss something. She has to go everywhere we go."

"All right, Miss," the grandmother said. "Just remember that the next time you want me to curl your hair."

June Star said her hair was naturally curly.

The next morning the grandmother was the first one in the car, ready to go. She had her big black valise that looked like the head of a hippopotamus in one corner, and underneath it she was hiding a basket with Pitty Sing, the cat, in it. She didn't intend for the cat to be left alone in the house for three days because he would miss her too much and she was afraid he might brush against one of the gas burners and accidentally asphyxiate himself. Her son, Bailey, didn't like to arrive at a motel with a cat.

She sat in the middle of the back seat with John Wesley and June Star on either side of her. Bailey and the children's mother and the baby sat in the front and they left Atlanta at eight forty-five with the mileage on the car at 55890. The grandmother wrote this down because she thought it would be interesting to say how many miles they had been when they got back. It took them twenty minutes to reach the outskirts of the city.

The old lady settled herself comfortably, removing her white cotton gloves and putting them up with her purse on the shelf in front of the back window. The children's mother still had on slacks and still had her head tied up in a green kerchief, but the grandmother had on a navy blue straw sailor hat with a bunch of white violets on the brim and a navy blue dress with a small white dot in the print. Her collar and cuffs were white organdy trimmed with lace and at her neckline she had pinned a purple spray of cloth violets containing a sachet. In case of an accident, anyone seeing her dead on the highway would know at once that she was a lady.

She said she thought it was going to be a good day for driving, neither too hot nor too cold, and she cautioned Bailey that the speed limit was fifty-five miles an hour and that the patrolmen hid themselves behind bill-boards and small clumps of trees and sped out after you before you had a chance to slow down. She pointed out interesting details of the scenery: Stone Mountain; the blue granite that in some places came up to both sides of the highway; the brilliant red clay banks slightly streaked with purple; and the various crops that made rows of green lace-work on the ground. The trees were full of silver-white sunlights and the meanest of them sparkled. The children were reading comic magazines and their mother had gone back to sleep.

"Let's go through Georgia fast so we won't have to look at it much," John Wesley said.

"If I were a little boy," said the grandmother, "I wouldn't talk about my native state that way. Tennessee has the mountains and Georgia has the hills."

"Tennessee is just a hillbilly dumping ground," John Wesley said, "and Georgia is a lousy state too."

"You said it," June Star said.

"In my time," said the grandmother, folding her thin veined fingers, "children were more respectful of their native states and their parents and everything else. People did right then. Oh look at the cute little pickaninny!" she said and pointed to a Negro child standing in the door of a shack. "Wouldn't that make a picture, now?" she asked and they all turned and looked at the little Negro out of the back window. He waved.

"He didn't have any britches on," June Star said.

"He probably didn't have any," the grandmother explained. "Little niggers in the country don't have things like we do. If I could paint, I'd paint that picture," she said.

The children exchanged comic books.

The grandmother offered to hold the baby and the children's mother passed him over the front seat to her. She set him on her knee and bounced him and told him about the things they were passing. She rolled her eyes and screwed up her mouth and stuck her leathery thin face into his smooth bland one. Occasionally he gave her a faraway smile. They passed a large cotton field with five or six graves fenced in the middle of it, like a small island. "Look at the graveyard!" the grandmother said, pointing it out. "That was the old family burying ground. That belonged to the plantation."

"Where's the plantation?" John Wesley asked.

"Gone With the Wind," said the grandmother. "Ha. Ha."

When the children finished all the comic books they had brought, they opened the lunch and ate it. The grandmother ate a peanut butter sandwich and an olive and would not let the children throw the box and the paper napkins out the window. When there was nothing else to do they played a game by choosing a cloud and making the other two guess what shape it suggested. John Wesley took one the shape of a cow and June Star guessed a cow and John Wesley said, no, an automobile, and June Star said he didn't play fair, and they began to slap each other over the grandmother.

The grandmother said she would tell them a story if they would keep quiet. When she told a story, she rolled her eyes and waved her head and was very dramatic. She said once when she was a maiden lady she had been courted by a Mr. Edgar Atkins Teagarden from Jasper, Georgia. She said he was a very good-looking man and a gentleman and that he brought her a watermelon every Saturday afternoon with his initials cut in it, E.A.T. Well, one Saturday, she said, Mr. Teagarden brought the watermelon and there was nobody at home and he left it on the front porch and returned in his buggy to Jasper, but she never got the watermelon, she said, because a nigger boy ate it when he saw the initials, E.A.T.! This story tickled John Wesley's funny bone and he giggled and giggled but June Star didn't think it was any good. She said she wouldn't marry a man that just brought her a watermelon on Saturday. The grandmother said she would have done well to marry Mr. Teagarden because he was a gentleman and had bought Coca-Cola stock when it first came out and that he had died only a few years ago, a very wealthy man.

They stopped at The Tower for barbecued sandwiches. The Tower was a part-stucco and part-wood filling station and dance hall set in a clearing outside of Timothy. A fat man named Red Sammy Butts ran it and there were signs stuck here and there on the building and for miles up and down the highway saying, TRY RED SAMMY'S FAMOUS BARBECUE. NONE LIKE FAMOUS RED SAMMY'S! RED SAM! THE FAT BOY WITH THE HAPPY LAUGH. A VETERAN! RED SAMMY'S YOUR MAN!

Red Sammy was lying on the bare ground outside The Tower with his head under a truck while a gray monkey about a foot high, chained to a small chinaberry tree, chattered nearby. The monkey sprang back into the tree and got on the highest limb as soon as he saw the children jump out of the car and run toward him.

Inside, The Tower was a long dark room with a counter at one end and tables at the other and dancing space in the middle. They all sat down at a broad table next to the nickelodeon and Red Sam's wife, a tall burnt-brown woman with hair and eyes lighter than her skin, came and took their order. The children's mother put a dime in the machine and played "The Tennessee Waltz," and the grandmother said that tune always made her want to dance. She asked Bailey if he would like to dance but he only glared at her. He didn't have a naturally sunny disposition like she did and trips made him nervous. The grandmother's brown eyes were very bright. She swayed her head from side to side and pretended she was dancing in her chair. June Star said play something she could tap to so the children's mother put in another dime and played a fast number and June Star stepped out onto the dance floor and did her tap routine.

"Ain't she cute?" Red Sam's wife said, leaning over the counter. "Would you like to come be my little girl?"

"No, I certainly wouldn't," June Star said. "I wouldn't live in a broken-down place like this for a million bucks!" and she ran back to the table.

"Ain't she cute?" the woman repeated, stretching her mouth politely.

"Aren't you ashamed?" hissed the grandmother.

Red Sam came in and told his wife to quit lounging on the counter and hurry up with these people's order. His khaki trousers reached just to his hip bones and his stomach hung over them like a sack of meal swaying under his shirt. He came over and sat down at a table nearby and let out a combination sigh and yodel. "You can't win," he said. "You can't win," and he wiped his sweating red face off with a gray handkerchief. "These days you don't know who to trust," he said. "Ain't that the truth?"

"People are certainly not nice like they used to be," said the grandmother.

"Two fellers come in here last week," Red Sammy said, "driving a Chrysler. It was an old beat-up car but it was a good one and these boys looked all right to me. Said they worked at the mill and you know I let them fellers charge the gas they bought? Now why did I do that?"

"Because you're a good man!" the grandmother said at once.

"Yes'm, I suppose so," Red Sam said as if he were struck with this answer.

His wife brought the orders, carrying the five plates all at once without a tray, two in each hand and one balanced on her arm. "It isn't a soul in this green world of God's that you can trust," she said. "And I don't count nobody out of that, not nobody," she repeated, looking at Red Sammy.

"Did you read about that criminal, The Misfit, that's escaped?" asked the grandmother.

"I wouldn't be a bit surprised if he didn't attack this place right here," said the woman. "If he hears about it being here, I wouldn't be none surprised to see him. If he hears it's two cent in the cash register, I wouldn't be a tall surprised if he. . . ."

"That'll do," Red Sam said. "Go bring these people their Co'-Colas," and the woman went off to get the rest of the order.

"A good man is hard to find," Red Sammy said. "Everything is getting terrible. I remember the day you could go off and leave your screen door unlatched. Not no more."

He and the grandmother discussed better times. The old lady said that in her opinion Europe was entirely to blame for the way things were now. She said the way Europe acted you would think we were made of money and Red Sam said it was no use talking about it, she was exactly right. The children ran outside into the white sunlight and looked at the monkey in the lacy chinaberry tree. He was busy catching fleas on himself and biting each one carefully between his teeth as if it were a delicacy.

They drove off again into the hot afternoon. The grandmother took cat naps and woke up every few minutes with her own snoring. Outside of Toombsboro she woke up and recalled an old plantation that she had visited in this neighborhood once when she was a young lady. She said the house had six white columns across the front and that there was an avenue of oaks leading up to it and two little wooden trellis arbors on either side in front where you sat down with your suitor after a stroll in the garden. She recalled exactly which road to turn off to get to it. She knew that Bailey would not be willing to lose any time looking at an old house, but the more she talked about it, the more she wanted to see it once again and find out if the little twin arbors were still standing. "There was a secret panel in this house," she said craftily, not telling the truth but wishing that she were, "and the story went that all the family silver was hidden in it when Sherman[1] came through but it was never found. . . ."

"Hey!" John Wesley said. "Let's go see it! We'll find it! We'll poke all the woodwork and find it! Who lives there? Where do you turn off at? Hey Pop, can't we turn off there?"

"We never have seen a house with a secret panel!" June Star shrieked. "Let's go to the house with the secret panel! Hey, Pop, can't we go see the house with the secret panel!"

"It's not far from here, I know," the grandmother said. "It wouldn't take over twenty minutes."

Bailey was looking straight ahead. His jaw was as rigid as a horseshoe. "No," he said.

The children began to yell and scream that they wanted to see the house with the secret panel. John Wesley kicked the back of the front seat

---

1. William T. Sherman (1820–1891), American Union General who blazed a trail of destruction through the South during the Civil War.

and June Star hung over her mother's shoulder and whined desperately into her ear that they never had any fun even on their vacation, that they could never do what THEY wanted to do. The baby began to scream and John Wesley kicked the back of the seat so hard that his father could feel the blows in his kidney.

"All right!" he shouted and drew the car to a stop at the side of the road. "Will you all shut up? Will you all shut up for one second? If you don't shut up, we won't go anywhere."

"It would be very educational for them," the grandmother murmured.

"All right," Bailey said, "but get this. This is the only time we're going to stop for anything like this. This is the one and only time."

"The dirt road that you have to turn down is about a mile back," the grandmother directed. "I marked it when we passed."

"A dirt road," Bailey groaned.

After they had turned around and were headed toward the dirt road, the grandmother recalled other points about the house, the beautiful glass over the front doorway and the candle lamp in the hall. John Wesley said that the secret panel was probably in the fireplace.

"You can't go inside this house," Bailey said. "You don't know who lives there."

"While you all talk to the people in front, I'll run around behind and get in a window," John Wesley suggested.

"We'll all stay in the car," his mother said.

They turned onto the dirt road and the car raced roughly along in a swirl of pink dust. The grandmother recalled the times when there were no paved roads and thirty miles was a day's journey. The dirt road was hilly and there were sudden washes in it and sharp curves on dangerous embankments. All at once they would be on a hill, looking down over the blue tops of trees for miles around, then the next minute, they would be in a red depression with the dust-coated trees looking down on them.

"This place had better turn up in a minute," Bailey said, "or I'm going to turn around."

The road looked as if no one had traveled on it in months.

"It's not much farther," the grandmother said and just as she said it, a horrible thought came to her. The thought was so embarrassing that she turned red in the face and her eyes dilated and her feet jumped up, upsetting her valise in the corner. The instant the valise moved, the newspaper top she had over the basket under it rose with a snarl and Pitty Sing, the cat, sprang onto Bailey's shoulder.

The children were thrown to the floor and their mother, clutching the baby, was thrown out the door onto the ground; the old lady was thrown into the front seat. The car turned over once and landed right-side-up in a gulch on the side of the road. Bailey remained in the driver's seat with the cat—gray-striped with a broad white face and an orange nose—clinging to his neck like a caterpillar.

As soon as the children saw they could move their arms and legs, they scrambled out of the car, shouting, "We've had an ACCIDENT!" The grand-mother was curled up under the dashboard, hoping she was injured so that Bailey's wrath would not come down on her all at once. The horrible thought she had had before the accident was that the house she had remem-bered so vividly was not in Georgia but in Tennessee.

Bailey removed the cat from his neck with both hands and flung it out the window against the side of a pine tree. Then he got out of the car and started looking for the children's mother. She was sitting against the side of the red gutted ditch, holding the screaming baby, but she only had a cut down her face and a broken shoulder. "We've had an ACCIDENT!" the chil-dren screamed in a frenzy of delight.

"But nobody's killed," June Star said with disappointment as the grandmother limped out of the car, her hat still pinned to her head but the broken front brim standing up at a jaunty angle and the violet spray hang-ing off the side. They all sat down in the ditch, except the children, to recover from the shock. They were all shaking.

"Maybe a car will come along," said the children's mother hoarsely.

"I believe I have injured an organ," said the grandmother, pressing her side, but no one answered her. Bailey's teeth were clattering. He had on a yellow sport shirt with bright blue parrots designed in it and his face was as yellow as the shirt. The grandmother decided that she would not mention that the house was in Tennessee.

The road was about ten feet above and they could see only the tops of the trees on the other side of it. Behind the ditch they were sitting in there were more woods, tall and dark and deep. In a few minutes they saw a car some distance away on top of a hill, coming slowly as if the occupants were watching them. The grandmother stood up and waved both arms dra-matically to attract their attention. The car continued to come on slowly, disappeared around a bend and appeared again, moving even slower, on top of the hill they had gone over. It was a big black battered hearselike automobile. There were three men in it.

It came to a stop just over them and for some minutes, the driver looked down with a steady expressionless gaze to where they were sitting, and didn't speak. Then he turned his head and muttered something to the other two and they got out. One was a fat boy in black trousers and a red sweat shirt with a silver stallion embossed on the front of it. He moved around on the right side of them and stood staring, his mouth partly open in a kind of loose grin. The other had on khaki pants and a blue striped coat and a gray hat pulled down very low, hiding most of his face. He came around slowly on the left side. Neither spoke.

The driver got out of the car and stood by the side of it, looking down at them. He was an older man than the other two. His hair was just beginning to gray and he wore silver-rimmed spectacles that gave him a scholarly look. He had a long creased face and didn't have on any shirt or undershirt. He had on blue jeans that were too tight for him and was holding a black hat and a gun. The two boys also had guns.

"We've had an ACCIDENT!" the children screamed.

The grandmother had the peculiar feeling that the bespectacled man was someone she knew. His face was as familiar to her as if she had known him all her life but she could not recall who he was. He moved away from the car and began to come down the embankment, placing his feet carefully so that he wouldn't slip. He had on tan and white shoes and no socks, and his ankles were red and thin. "Good afternoon," he said. "I see you all had you a little spill."

"We turned over twice!" said the grandmother.

"Oncet," he corrected. "We seen it happen. Try their car and see will it run, Hiram," he said quietly to the boy with the gray hat.

"What you got that gun for?" John Wesley asked. "Whatcha gonna do with that gun?"

"Lady," the man said to the children's mother, "would you mind calling them children to sit down by you? Children make me nervous. I want all you all to sit down right together there where you're at."

"What are you telling us what to do for?" June Star asked.

Behind them the line of woods gaped like a dark open mouth. "Come here," said their mother.

"Look here now," Bailey began suddenly, "we're in a predicament! We're in. . . ."

The grandmother shrieked. She scrambled to her feet and stood staring.

"You're The Misfit!" she said. "I recognized you at once!"

"Yes'm," the man said, smiling slightly as if he were pleased in spite of himself to be known, "but it would have been better for all of you, lady, if you hadn't of reckernized me."

Bailey turned his head sharply and said something to his mother that shocked even the children. The old lady began to cry and The Misfit reddened.

"Lady," he said, "don't you get upset. Sometimes a man says things he don't mean. I don't reckon he meant to talk to you thataway."

"You wouldn't shoot a lady, would you?" the grandmother said and removed a clean handkerchief from her cuff and began to slap at her eyes with it.

The Misfit pointed the toe of his shoe into the ground and made a little hole and then covered it up again. "I would hate to have to," he said.

"Listen," the grandmother almost screamed, "I know you're a good man. You don't look a bit like you have common blood. I know you must come from nice people!"

"Yes mam," he said, "finest people in the world." When he smiled he showed a row of strong white teeth. "God never made a finer woman than my mother and my daddy's heart was pure gold," he said. The boy with the red sweat shirt had come around behind them and was standing with his gun at his hip. The Misfit squatted down on the ground. "Watch them children, Bobby Lee," he said. "You know they make me nervous." He looked at the six of them huddled together in front of him and he seemed to be embarrassed as if he couldn't think of anything to say. "Ain't a cloud in the sky," he remarked, looking up at it. "Don't see no sun but don't see no cloud neither."

"Yes, it's a beautiful day," said the grandmother. "Listen," she said, "you shouldn't call yourself The Misfit because I know you're a good man at heart. I can just look at you and tell."

"Hush!" Bailey yelled. "Hush! Everybody shut up and let me handle this!" He was squatting in the position of a runner about to sprint forward but he didn't move.

"I pre-chate that, lady," The Misfit said and drew a little circle in the ground with the butt of his gun.

"It'll take a half a hour to fix this here car," Hiram called, looking over the raised hood of it.

"Well, first you and Bobby Lee get him and that little boy to step over yonder with you," The Misfit said, pointing to Bailey and John Wesley. "The boys want to ask you something," he said to Bailey. "Would you mind stepping back in them woods there with them?"

"Listen," Bailey began, "we're in a terrible predicament! Nobody realizes what this is," and his voice cracked. His eyes were as blue and intense as the parrots in his shirt and he remained perfectly still.

The grandmother reached up to adjust her hat brim as if she were going to the woods with him but it came off in her hand. She stood staring at it and after a second she let it fall on the ground. Hiram pulled Bailey up by the arm as if he were assisting an old man. John Wesley caught hold of his father's hand and Bobby Lee followed. They went off toward the woods and just as they reached the dark edge, Bailey turned and supporting himself against a gray naked pine trunk, he shouted, "I'll be back in a minute, Mamma, wait on me!"

"Come back this instant!" his mother shrilled but they all disappeared into the woods.

"Bailey Boy!" the grandmother called in a tragic voice but she found she was looking at The Misfit squatting on the ground in front of her. "I just know you're a good man," she said desperately. "You're not a bit common!"

"Nome, I ain't a good man," The Misfit said after a second as if he had considered her statement carefully, "but I ain't the worst in the world neither. My daddy said I was a different breed of dog from my brothers and sisters. 'You know,' Daddy said, 'it's some that can live their whole life out without asking about it and it's others has to know why it is, and this boy is one of the latters. He's going to be into everything!' " He put on his black hat and looked up suddenly and then away deep into the woods as if he were embarrassed again. "I'm sorry, I don't have on a shirt before you ladies," he said, hunching his shoulders slightly. "We buried our clothes that we had on when we escaped and we're just making do until we can get better. We borrowed these from some folks we met," he explained.

"That's perfectly all right," the grandmother said. "Maybe Bailey has an extra shirt in his suitcase."

"I'll look and see terrectly," The Misfit said.

"Where are they taking him?" the children's mother screamed.

"Daddy was a card himself," The Misfit said. "You couldn't put anything over on him. He never got in trouble with the Authorities though. Just had the knack of handling them."

"You could be honest too if you'd only try," said the grandmother. "Think how wonderful it would be to settle down and live a comfortable life and not have to think about somebody chasing you all the time."

The Misfit kept scratching in the ground with the butt of his gun as if he were thinking about it. "Yes'm, somebody is always after you," he murmured.

The grandmother noticed how thin his shoulder blades were just behind his hat because she was standing up looking down on him. "Do you ever pray?" she asked.

He shook his head. All she saw was the black hat wiggle between his shoulder blades. "Nome," he said.

There was a pistol shot from the woods, followed closely by another. Then silence. The old lady's head jerked around. She could hear the wind move through the tree tops like a long satisfied insuck of breath. "Bailey Boy!" she called.

"I was a gospel singer for a while," The Misfit said. "I been most everything. Been in the arm service, both land and sea, at home and abroad, been twict married, been an undertaker, been with the railroads, plowed Mother Earth, been in a tornado, seen a man burnt alive oncet," and he looked up at the children's mother and the little girl who were sitting close together, their faces white and their eyes glassy; "I even seen a woman flogged," he said.

"Pray, pray," the grandmother began, "pray, pray. . . ."

"I never was a bad boy that I remember of," The Misfit said in an almost dreamy voice, "but somewheres along the line I done something wrong and got sent to the penitentiary. I was buried alive," and he looked up and held her attention to him by a steady stare.

"That's when you should have started to pray," she said. "What did you do to get sent to the penitentiary that first time?"

"Turn to the right, it was a wall," The Misfit said, looking up again at the cloudless sky. "Turn to the left, it was a wall. Look up it was a ceiling, look down it was a floor. I forget what I done, lady. I set there and set there, trying to remember what it was I done and I ain't recalled it to this day. Oncet in a while, I would think it was coming to me, but it never come."

"Maybe they put you in by mistake," the old lady said vaguely.

"Nome," he said. "It wasn't no mistake. They had the papers on me."

"You must have stolen something," she said.

The Misfit sneered slightly. "Nobody had nothing I wanted," he said. "It was a head-doctor at the penitentiary said what I had done was kill my daddy but I known that for a lie. My daddy died in nineteen ought nineteen of the epidemic flu and I never had a thing to do with it. He was buried in the Mount Hopewell Baptist churchyard and you can go there and see for yourself."

"If you would pray," the old lady said, "Jesus would help you."

"That's right," The Misfit said.

"Well then, why don't you pray?" she asked trembling with delight suddenly.

"I don't want no hep," he said. "I'm doing all right by myself."

Bobby Lee and Hiram came ambling back from the woods. Bobby Lee was dragging a yellow shirt with bright blue parrots in it.

"Thow me that shirt, Bobby Lee," The Misfit said. The shirt came flying at him and landed on his shoulder and he put it on. The grandmother couldn't name what the shirt reminded her of. "No, lady," The Misfit said while he was buttoning it up, "I found out the crime don't matter. You can do one thing or you can do another, kill a man or take a tire off his car, because sooner or later you're going to forget what it was you done and just be punished for it."

The children's mother had begun to make heaving noises as if she couldn't get her breath. "Lady," he asked, "would you and that little girl like to step off yonder with Bobby Lee and Hiram and join your husband?"

"Yes, thank you," the mother said faintly. Her left arm dangled helplessly and she was holding the baby, who had gone to sleep, in the other. "Hep that lady up, Hiram," The Misfit said as she struggled to climb out of the ditch, "and Bobby Lee, you hold onto that little girl's hand."

"I don't want to hold hands with him," June Star said. "He reminds me of a pig."

The fat boy blushed and laughed and caught her by the arm and pulled her off into the woods after Hiram and her mother.

Alone with The Misfit, the grandmother found that she had lost her voice. There was not a cloud in the sky nor any sun. There was nothing around her but woods. She wanted to tell him that he must pray. She opened and closed her mouth several times before anything came out. Finally she found herself saying, "Jesus. Jesus," meaning, Jesus will help you, but the way she was saying it, it sounded as if she might be cursing.

"Yes'm," The Misfit said as if he agreed. "Jesus thrown everything off balance. It was the same case with Him as with me except He hadn't committed any crime and they could prove I had committed one because they had the papers on me. Of course," he said, "they never shown me my papers. That's why I sign myself now. I said long ago, you get you a signature and sign everything you do and keep a copy of it. Then you'll know what you done and you can hold up the crime to the punishment and see do they match and in the end you'll have something to prove you ain't been treated right. I call myself The Misfit," he said, "because I can't make what all I done wrong fit what all I gone through in punishment."

There was a piercing scream from the woods, followed closely by a pistol report. "Does it seem right to you, lady, that one is punished a heap and another ain't punished at all?"

"Jesus!" the old lady cried. "You've got good blood! I know you wouldn't shoot a lady! I know you come from nice people! Pray! Jesus, you ought not to shoot a lady. I'll give you all the money I've got!"

"Lady," The Misfit said, looking beyond her far into the woods, "there never was a body that give the undertaker a tip."

There were two more pistol reports and the grandmother raised her head like a parched old turkey hen crying for water and called, "Bailey Boy, Bailey Boy!" as if her heart would break.

"Jesus was the only One that ever raised the dead," The Misfit continued, "and He shouldn't have done it. He thrown everything off balance. If He did what He said, then it's nothing for you to do but throw away everything and follow Him, and if He didn't then it's nothing for you to do but enjoy the few minutes you got left the best way you can—by killing somebody or burning down his house or doing some other meanness to him. No pleasure but meanness," he said and his voice had become almost a snarl.

"Maybe He didn't raise the dead," the old lady mumbled, not knowing what she was saying and feeling so dizzy that she sank down in the ditch with her legs twisted under her.

"I wasn't there so I can't say He didn't," The Misfit said. "I wisht I had of been there," he said, hitting the ground with his fist. "It ain't right I wasn't there because if I had of been there I would of known. Listen Lady," he said in a high voice, "if I had of been there I would of known and I wouldn't be like I am now." His voice seemed about to crack and the grandmother's head cleared for an instant. She saw the man's face twisted close to her own as if he were going to cry and she murmured, "Why, you're one of my babies. You're one of my own children!" She reached out and touched him on the shoulder. The Misfit sprang back as if a snake had bitten him and shot her three times through the chest. Then he put his gun down on the ground and took off his glasses and began to clean them.

Hiram and Bobby Lee returned from the woods and stood over the ditch, looking down at the grandmother who half sat and half lay in a puddle of blood with her legs crossed under her like a child's and her face smiling up at the cloudless sky.

Without his glasses, The Misfit's eyes were red-rimmed and pale and defenseless-looking. "Take her off and throw her where you thrown the others," he said, picking up the cat that was rubbing itself against his leg.

"She was a talker, wasn't she?" Bobby Lee said, sliding down the ditch with a yodel.

"She would of been a good woman," The Misfit said, "if it had been somebody there to shoot her every minute of her life."

"Some fun!" Bobby Lee said.

"Shut up, Bobby Lee," The Misfit said. "It's no real pleasure in life."

1955

Further Reading

Dowell, Bob. "The Moment of Grace in the Fiction of Flannery O'Connor." *College English* 27.3 (Dec. 1965): 235–39. • Doxey, William S. "A Dissenting Opinion of Flannery O'Connor's 'A Good Man Is Hard to Find.' " *Studies in Short Fiction* 10.2 (Spring 1973): 199–204. • Feeley, Kathleen, SSND. " 'The New Jesus': Alienated Modern Man." *Flannery O'Connor: Voice of the Peacock.* New York: Fordham UP, 1982. 52–84, spec. 69–76. • Eggenschwiler, David. "Demons and Neuroses." *The Christian Humanism of Flannery O'Connor.* Detroit: Wayne State UP, 1972. 31–70, spec. 46–52. • Browning, Preston M., Jr. " 'A Good Man Is Hard to Find.' " *Flannery O'Connor.* Carbondale: Southern Illinois UP, 1974, 40–71, spec. 54–59.

Flannery O'Connor was sometimes irritated by the interpretations imposed on her stories by teachers and literary critics. In remarks made at Hollins College before a reading of "A Good Man Is Hard to Find," she cited a teacher who had told his class that the grandmother in the story is "a witch, even down to the cat." Like this teacher's students, O'Connor rejected such an over-simple view.

Flannery O'Connor: On the Effect of a Key Gesture

This same teacher was telling his students that morally the Misfit was several cuts above the Grandmother. He had a really sentimental attachment to the Misfit. But then a prophet gone wrong is almost always more interesting than your grandmother, and you have to let people take their pleasures where they find them.

It is true that the old lady is a hypocritical old soul; her wits are no match for the Misfit's, nor is her capacity for grace equal to his; yet I think the unprejudiced reader will feel that the Grandmother has a special kind of

triumph in this story which instinctively we do not allow to someone altogether bad.

I often ask myself what makes a story work, and what makes it hold up
as a story, and I have decided that it is probably some action, some gesture
of a character that is unlike any other in the story, one which indicates
where the real heart of the story lies. This would have to be an action or a
gesture which was both totally right and totally unexpected; it would have to
be one that was both in character and beyond character; it would have to
suggest both the world and eternity. The action or gesture I'm talking
about would have to be on the anagogical level, that is, the level which has to
do with the Divine life and our participation in it. It would be a gesture that
transcended any neat allegory and might have been intended or any pat
moral categories a reader could make. It would be a gesture which somehow made contact with mystery.

YUKIO MISHIMA

(1925–1970)

SWADDLING CLOTHES

translated from the Japanese by Ivan Morris

He was always busy, Toshiko's husband. Even tonight he had to dash off to
an appointment, leaving her to go home alone by taxi. But what else could a
woman expect when she married an actor—an attractive one? No doubt
she had been foolish to hope that he would spend the evening with her.
And yet he must have known how she dreaded going back to their house,
unhomely with its Western-style furniture and with the bloodstains still
showing on the floor.

Toshiko had been oversensitive since girlhood: that was her nature. As
the result of constant worrying she never put on weight, and now, an adult
woman, she looked more like a transparent picture than a creature of flesh
and blood. Her delicacy of spirit was evident to her most casual
acquaintance.

Earlier that evening, when she had joined her husband at a night club,
she had been shocked to find him entertaining friends with an account of
'the incident.' Sitting there in his American-style suit, puffing at a cigarette,
he had seemed to her almost a stranger.

'It's a fantastic story,' he was saying, gesturing flamboyantly as if in an
attempt to outweigh the attractions of the dance band. 'Here this new
nurse for our baby arrives from the employment agency, and the very first
thing I notice about her is her stomach. It's enormous—as if she had a pillow stuck under her kimono! No wonder, I thought, for I soon saw that she

could eat more than the rest of us put together. She polished off the contents of our rice bin like that. . . .' He snapped his fingers. ' "Gastric dilation"—that's how she explained her girth and her appetite. Well, the day before yesterday we heard groans and moans coming from the nursery. We rushed in and found her squatting on the floor, holding her stomach in her two hands, and moaning like a cow. Next to her our baby lay in his cot, scared out of his wits and crying at the top of his lungs. A pretty scene, I can tell you!'

'So the cat was out of the bag?' suggested one of their friends, a film actor like Toshiko's husband.

'Indeed it was! And it gave me the shock of my life. You see, I'd completely swallowed that story about "gastric dilation." Well, I didn't waste any time. I rescued our good rug from the floor and spread a blanket for her to lie on. The whole time the girl was yelling like a stuck pig. By the time the doctor from the maternity clinic arrived, the baby had already been born. But our sitting room was a pretty shambles!'

'Oh, that I'm sure of!' said another of their friends, and the whole company burst into laughter.

Toshiko was dumbfounded to hear her husband discussing the horrifying happening as though it were no more than an amusing incident which they chanced to have witnessed. She shut her eyes for a moment and all at once she saw the newborn baby lying before her: on the parquet floor the infant lay, and his frail body was wrapped in bloodstained newspapers.

Toshiko was sure that the doctor had done the whole thing out of spite. As if to emphasize his scorn for this mother who had given birth to a bastard under such sordid conditions, he had told his assistant to wrap the baby in some loose newspapers, rather than proper swaddling. This callous treatment of the newborn child had offended Toshiko. Overcoming her disgust at the entire scene, she had fetched a brand-new piece of flannel from her cupboard and, having swaddled the baby in it, had lain him carefully in an armchair.

This all had taken place in the evening after her husband had left the house. Toshiko had told him nothing of it, fearing that he would think her oversoft, oversentimental; yet the scene had engraved itself deeply in her mind. Tonight she sat silently thinking back on it, while the jazz orchestra brayed and her husband chatted cheerfully with his friends. She knew that she would never forget the sight of the baby, wrapped in stained newspapers and lying on the floor—it was a scene fit for a butchershop. Toshiko, whose own life had been spent in solid comfort, poignantly felt the wretchedness of the illegitimate baby.

I am the only person to have witnessed its shame, the thought occurred to her. The mother never saw her child lying there in its newspaper wrappings, and the baby itself of course didn't know. I alone shall have to preserve that terrible scene in my memory. When the baby grows up and wants to find out about his birth, there will be no one to tell him, so long as I preserve silence. How strange that I should have this feeling of guilt! After all, it was I who took him up from the floor, swathed him properly in flannel, and laid him down to sleep in the armchair.

They left the night club and Toshiko stepped into the taxi that her husband had called for her. 'Take this lady to Ushigomé,' he told the driver and shut the door from the outside. Toshiko gazed through the window at her husband's smiling face and noticed his strong, white teeth. Then she leaned back in the seat, oppressed by the knowledge that their life together was in some way too easy, too painless. It would have been difficult for her to put her thoughts into words. Through the rear window of the taxi she took a last look at her husband. He was striding along the street toward his Nash car, and soon the back of his rather garish tweed coat had blended with the figures of the passers-by.

The taxi drove off, passed down a street dotted with bars and then by a theatre, in front of which the throngs of people jostled each other on the pavement. Although the performance had only just ended, the lights had already been turned out and in the half dark outside it was depressingly obvious that the cherry blossoms decorating the front of the theatre were merely scraps of white paper.

Even if that baby should grow up in ignorance of the secret of his birth, he can never become a respectable citizen, reflected Toshiko, pursuing the same train of thoughts. Those soiled newspaper swaddling clothes will be the symbol of his entire life. But why should I keep worrying about him so much? Is it because I feel uneasy about the future of my own child? Say twenty years from now, when our boy will have grown up into a fine, carefully educated young man, one day by a quirk of fate he meets that other boy, who then will also have turned twenty. And say that the other boy, who has been sinned against, savagely stabs him with a knife. . . .

It was a warm, overcast April night, but thoughts of the future made Toshiko feel cold and miserable. She shivered on the back seat of the car.

No, when the time comes I shall take my son's place, she told herself suddenly. Twenty years from now I shall be forty-three. I shall go to that young man and tell him straight out about everything—about his newspaper swaddling clothes, and about how I went and wrapped him in flannel.

The taxi ran along the dark wide road that was bordered by the park and by the Imperial Palace moat. In the distance Toshiko noticed the pinpricks of light which came from the blocks of tall office buildings.

Twenty years from now that wretched child will be in utter misery. He will be living a desolate, hopeless, poverty-stricken existence—a lonely rat. What else could happen to a baby who has had such a birth? He'll be wandering through the streets by himself, cursing his father, loathing his mother.

No doubt Toshiko derived a certain satisfaction from her somber thoughts: she tortured herself with them without cease. The taxi approached Hanzomon and drove past the compound of the British Embassy. At that point the famous rows of cherry trees were spread out before Toshiko in all their purity. On the spur of the moment she decided to go and view the blossoms by herself in the dark night. It was a strange decision for a timid and unadventurous young woman, but then she was in a strange state of mind and she dreaded the return home. That evening all sorts of unsettling fancies had burst open in her mind.

She crossed the wide street—a slim, solitary figure in the darkness. As a rule when she walked in the traffic Toshiko used to cling fearfully to her companion, but tonight she darted alone between the cars and a moment later had reached the long narrow park that borders the Palace moat. Chidorigafuchi, it is called—the Abyss of the Thousand Birds.

Tonight the whole park had become a grove of blossoming cherry trees. Under the calm cloudy sky the blossoms formed a mass of solid whiteness. The paper lanterns that hung from wires between the trees had been put out; in their place electric light bulbs, red, yellow, and green, shone dully beneath the blossoms. It was well past ten o'clock and most of the flower-viewers had gone home. As the occasional passers-by strolled through the park, they would automatically kick aside the empty bottles or crush the waste paper beneath their feet.

Newspapers, thought Toshiko, her mind going back once again to those happenings. Bloodstained newspapers. If a man were ever to hear of that piteous birth and know that it was he who had lain there, it would ruin his entire life. To think that I, a perfect stranger, should from now on have to keep such a secret—the secret of a man's whole existence. . . .

Lost in these thoughts, Toshiko walked on through the park. Most of the people still remaining there were quiet couples; no one paid her any attention. She noticed two people sitting on a stone bench beside the moat, not looking at the blossoms, but gazing silently at the water. Pitch black it was, and swathed in heavy shadows. Beyond the moat the somber forest of the Imperial Palace blocked her view. The trees reached up, to form a solid dark mass against the night sky. Toshiko walked slowly along the path beneath the blossoms hanging heavily overhead.

On a stone bench, slightly apart from the others, she noticed a pale object—not, as she had at first imagined, a pile of cherry blossoms, nor a garment forgotten by one of the visitors to the park. Only when she came closer did she see that it was a human form lying on the bench. Was it, she wondered, one of those miserable drunks often to be seen sleeping in public places? Obviously not, for the body had been systematically covered with newspapers, and it was the whiteness of those papers that had attracted Toshiko's attention. Standing by the bench, she gazed down at the sleeping figure.

It was a man in a brown jersey who lay there, curled up on layers of newspapers, other newspapers covering him. No doubt this had become his normal night residence now that spring had arrived. Toshiko gazed down at the man's dirty, unkempt hair, which in places had become hopelessly matted. As she observed the sleeping figure wrapped in its newspapers, she was inevitably reminded of the baby who had lain on the floor in its wretched swaddling clothes. The shoulder of the man's jersey rose and fell in the darkness in time with his heavy breathing.

It seemed to Toshiko that all her fears and premonitions had suddenly taken concrete form. In the darkness the man's pale forehead stood out, and it was a young forehead, though carved with the wrinkles of long poverty and hardship. His khaki trousers had been slightly pulled up; on his sockless feet he wore a pair of battered gym shoes. She could not see his face and suddenly had an overmastering desire to get one glimpse of it.

She walked to the head of the bench and looked down. The man's head was half buried in his arms, but Toshiko could see that he was surprisingly young. She noticed the thick eyebrows and the fine bridge of his nose. His slightly open mouth was alive with youth.

But Toshiko had approached too close. In the silent night the newspaper bedding rustled, and abruptly the man opened his eyes. Seeing the young woman standing directly beside him, he raised himself with a jerk, and his eyes lit up. A second later a powerful hand reached out and seized Toshiko by her slender wrist.

She did not feel in the least afraid and made no effort to free herself. In a flash the thought had struck her. Ah, so the twenty years have already gone by! The forest of the Imperial Palace was pitch dark and utterly silent.

1966

Further Reading

Shabecoff, Philip. "You've Heard of Yukio Mishima." *New York Times Magazine* 2 August 1970: 6ff. • Scott-Stokes, Henry. *The Life and Death of Yukio Mishima.* New York: Farrar, 1974. • Yourcenar, Marguerite. *Mishima: A Vision of the Void.* Trans. Alberto Manguel. New York: Farrar, 1986. • Petersen, Gwen Boardman. "Mishima Yukio." *The Moon in the Water: Understanding Tanizaki, Kawabata, and Mishima.* Honolulu: UP of Hawaii, 1979. 201–336, spec. 241.

The clash in "Swaddling Clothes" between Western and Japanese values is a theme reflected in much of Yukio Mishima's fiction; it figured importantly in his life as well. In an interview conducted a few months before his death, Mishima discussed the relation between his Japanese spirit and his Westernized way of life.

Yukio Mishima: On Trying to Reclaim Japanese Culture

"If you look at my house, it seems completely Westernized," he said after a pause. "But I am living in a double house. You can see only the visible house. But I also live in an invisible house which you cannot see. Let me give you a simple explanation for the Western civilization you see here.

"Here are two floors of a house. How to get from the first to the second floor is the basic problem. In Western culture, the solution is to make a stairway. Then anyone can climb up from the ground floor.

"The stairway is a method—not technique, not civilization, but method inherited from the ancient Greeks. They adopted this method in building their culture.

"Since the 19th century, the Japanese have learned the Western way of using a stairway. We've imported this stairway, this method, from the West and with the method we immediately imported all the trappings of Western civilization to modernize our country.

"But in our own Oriental way of thinking, there is no stairway at all. We never believed in method. It has been said of Noh acting that its highest discipline is a flower. How can you reach a flower? There is no method. You can only try hard by yourself. Independently. A teacher may suggest something but he cannot help you. So it is with climbing to the second floor. You must try hard to climb by your own enthusiasm and ambition. Maybe you will jump up. Maybe you will climb a pillar. But you must decide yourself and not rely on method . . ."

"Another way of thinking is Indian. The Indian meditates about how to reach the second floor and after a while reaches the conclusion that he already is there. That is an illusion. But the Japanese can actually climb to the second floor. . . . But I would like to ask the Japanese people: "We think we have climbed to the second floor. But can we be sure? Can we really certify that this is the second floor? I believe Europeans can certify their results and say they have reached the second floor because they built the stairway. But if we borrow the stairway, the second floor is not our second floor—at best it is borrowed." . . .

Before the war, he said, writers used to serve up the raw stuff of life to tradition-bound Japanese society. Now, the Japanese people feel liberated and free. They are materialistic and wealthy and want nothing but to enjoy life without limitation. Of course, Mishima added, all this freedom and enjoyment is artificial. This is also true of the writer. He has no raw material to offer because his life, too, is "artificial" canned food.

"So I reached the conclusion that we must search for and find something genuine and pure—something 'raw' not only in our minds but in our history. I want to touch fire, but there is no fire in our present society. Who is the one in Greek myth who took fire from the mountain? Yes, Prometheus. I want to be Prometheus."

GABRIEL GARCÍA MÁRQUEZ

(b. 1928)

A VERY OLD MAN WITH ENORMOUS WINGS

A TALE FOR CHILDREN

translated from the Spanish by Gregory Rabassa

On the third day of rain they had killed so many crabs inside the house that Pelayo had to cross his drenched courtyard and throw them into the sea, because the newborn child had a temperature all night and they thought it was due to the stench. The world had been sad since Tuesday. Sea and sky were a single ash-gray thing and the sands of the beach, which on March nights glimmered like powdered light, had become a stew of mud and rotten shellfish. The light was so weak at noon that when Pelayo was coming back to the house after throwing away the crabs, it was hard for him to see what it was that was moving and groaning in the rear of the courtyard. He had to go very close to see that it was an old man, a very old man, lying face down in the mud, who, in spite of his tremendous efforts, couldn't get up, impeded by his enormous wings.

Frightened by that nightmare, Pelayo ran to get Elisenda, his wife, who was putting compresses on the sick child, and he took her to the rear of the courtyard. They both looked at the fallen body with mute stupor. He was dressed like a ragpicker. There were only a few faded hairs left on his bald skull and very few teeth in his mouth, and his pitiful condition of a drenched great-grandfather had taken away any sense of grandeur he might have had. His huge buzzard wings, dirty and half-plucked, were forever entangled in the mud. They looked at him so long and so closely that Pelayo and Elisenda very soon overcame their surprise and in the end found him familiar. Then they dared speak to him, and he answered in an incomprehensible dialect with a strong sailor's voice. That was how they skipped over the inconvenience of the wings and quite intelligently concluded that he was a lonely castaway from some foreign ship wrecked by the storm. And yet, they called in a neighbor woman who knew everything about life and death to see him, and all she needed was one look to show them their mistake.

"He's an angel," she told them. "He must have been coming for the child, but the poor fellow is so old that the rain knocked him down."

On the following day everyone knew that a flesh-and-blood angel was held captive in Pelayo's house. Against the judgment of the wise neighbor woman, for whom angels in those times were the fugitive survivors of a celestial conspiracy, they did not have the heart to club him to death. Pelayo watched over him all afternoon from the kitchen, armed with his bailiff's club, and before going to bed he dragged him out of the mud and locked him up with the hens in the wire chicken coop. In the middle of the night, when the rain stopped, Pelayo and Elisenda were still killing crabs. A short time afterward the child woke up without a fever and with a desire to eat. Then they felt magnanimous and decided to put the angel on a raft with fresh water and provisions for three days and leave him to his fate on the high seas. But when they went out into the courtyard with the first light of dawn, they found the whole neighborhood in front of the chicken coop having fun with the angel, without the slightest reverence, tossing him things to eat through the openings in the wire as if he weren't a supernatural creature but a circus animal.

Father Gonzaga arrived before seven o'clock, alarmed at the strange news. By that time onlookers less frivolous than those at dawn had already arrived and they were making all kinds of conjectures concerning the captive's future. The simplest among them thought that he should be named mayor of the world. Others of sterner mind felt that he should be promoted to the rank of five-star general in order to win all wars. Some visionaries hoped that he could be put to stud in order to implant on earth a race of winged wise men who could take charge of the universe. But Father Gonzaga, before becoming a priest, had been a robust woodcutter. Standing by the wire, he reviewed his catechism in an instant and asked them to open the door so that he could take a close look at that pitiful man who looked more like a huge decrepit hen among the fascinated chickens. He was lying in a corner drying his open wings in the sunlight among the fruit peels and breakfast leftovers that the early risers had thrown him. Alien to the impertinences of the world, he only lifted his antiquarian eyes and murmured something in his dialect when Father Gonzaga went into the chicken coop and said good morning to him in Latin. The parish priest had his first suspicion of an imposter when he saw that he did not understand the language of God or know how to greet His ministers. Then he noticed that seen close up he was much too human: he had an unbearable smell of the outdoors, the back side of his wings was strewn with parasites and his main feathers had been mistreated by terrestrial winds, and nothing about him measured up to the proud dignity of angels. Then he came out of the chicken coop and in a brief sermon warned the curious against the risks of being ingenuous. He reminded them that the devil had the bad habit of making use of carnival tricks in order to confuse the unwary. He argued that if wings were not the essential element in determining the difference between a hawk and an airplane, they were even less so in the recognition of angels. Nevertheless, he promised to write a letter to his bishop so that the latter would write to his primate so that the latter would write to the Supreme Pontiff in order to get the final verdict from the highest courts.

His prudence fell on sterile hearts. The news of the captive angel spread with such rapidity that after a few hours the courtyard had the bustle of a marketplace and they had to call in troops with fixed bayonets to disperse the mob that was about to knock the house down. Elisenda, her spine all twisted from sweeping up so much marketplace trash, then got the idea of fencing in the yard and charging five cents admission to see the angel.

The curious came from far away. A traveling carnival arrived with a flying acrobat who buzzed over the crowd several times, but no one paid any attention to him because his wings were not those of an angel but, rather, those of a sidereal bat. The most unfortunate invalids on earth came in search of health: a poor woman who since childhood had been counting her heartbeats and had run out of numbers; a Portuguese man who couldn't sleep because the noise of the stars disturbed him; a sleepwalker who got up at night to undo the things he had done while awake; and many others with less serious ailments. In the midst of that shipwreck disorder that made the earth tremble, Pelayo and Elisenda were happy with fatigue, for in less than a week they had crammed their rooms with money and the line of pilgrims waiting their turn to enter still reached beyond the horizon.

The angel was the only one who took no part in his own act. He spent his time trying to get comfortable in his borrowed nest, befuddled by the hellish heat of the oil lamps and sacramental candles that had been placed along the wire. At first they tried to make him eat some mothballs, which, according to the wisdom of the wise neighbor woman, were the food prescribed for angels. But he turned them down, just as he turned down the papal lunches that the penitents brought him, and they never found out whether it was because he was an angel or because he was an old man that in the end he ate nothing but eggplant mush. His only supernatural virtue seemed to be patience. Especially during the first days, when the hens pecked at him, searching for the stellar parasites that proliferated in his wings, and the cripples pulled out feathers to touch their defective parts with, and even the most merciful threw stones at him, trying to get him to rise so they could see him standing. The only time they succeeded in arousing him was when they burned his side with an iron for branding steers, for he had been motionless for so many hours that they thought he was dead. He awoke with a start, ranting in his hermetic[1] language and with tears in his eyes, and he flapped his wings a couple of times, which brought on a whirlwind of chicken dung and lunar dust and a gale of panic that did not seem to be of this world. Although many thought that his reaction had been one not of rage but of pain, from then on they were careful not to annoy him, because the majority understood that his passivity was not that of a hero taking his ease but that of a cataclysm in repose.

Father Gonzaga held back the crowd's frivolity with formulas of maidservant inspiration while awaiting the arrival of a final judgment on the nature of the captive. But the mail from Rome showed no sense of urgency. They spent their time finding out if the prisoner had a navel, if his dialect had any connection with Aramaic,[2] how many times he could fit on

---

1. Occult, mysterious.
2. An ancient Semitic language dating from the seventh century B.C.

the head of a pin, or whether he wasn't just a Norwegian with wings. Those meager letters might have come and gone until the end of time if a providential event had not put an end to the priest's tribulations.

It so happened that during those days, among so many other carnival attractions, there arrived in town the traveling show of the woman who had been changed into a spider for having disobeyed her parents. The admission to see her was not only less than the admission to see the angel, but people were permitted to ask her all manner of questions about her absurd state and to examine her up and down so that no one would ever doubt the truth of her horror. She was a frightful tarantula the size of a ram and with the head of a sad maiden. What was most heart-rending, however, was not her outlandish shape but the sincere affliction with which she recounted the details of her misfortune. While still practically a child she had sneaked out of her parents' house to go to a dance, and while she was coming back through the woods after having danced all night without permission, a fearful thunderclap rent the sky in two and through the crack came the lightning bolt of brimstone that changed her into a spider. Her only nourishment came from the meatballs that charitable souls chose to toss into her mouth. A spectacle like that, full of so much human truth and with such a fearful lesson, was bound to defeat without even trying that of a haughty angel who scarcely deigned to look at mortals. Besides, the few miracles attributed to the angel showed a certain mental disorder, like the blind man who didn't recover his sight but grew three new teeth, or the paralytic who didn't get to walk but almost won the lottery, and the leper whose sores sprouted sunflowers. Those consolation miracles, which were more like mocking fun, had already ruined the angel's reputation when the woman who had been changed into a spider finally crushed him completely. That was how Father Gonzaga was cured forever of his insomnia and Pelayo's courtyard went back to being as empty as during the time it had rained for three days and crabs walked through the bedrooms.

The owners of the house had no reason to lament. With the money they saved they built a two-story mansion with balconies and gardens and high netting so that crabs wouldn't get in during the winter, and with iron bars on the windows so that angels wouldn't get in. Pelayo also set up a rabbit warren close to town and gave up his job as bailiff for good, and Elisenda bought some satin pumps with high heels and many dresses of iridescent silk, the kind worn on Sunday by the most desirable women in those times. The chicken coop was the only thing that didn't receive any attention. If they washed it down with creolin and burned tears of myrrh inside it every so often, it was not in homage to the angel but to drive away the dungheap stench that still hung everywhere like a ghost and was turning the new house into an old one. At first, when the child learned to walk, they were careful that he not get too close to the chicken coop. But then they began to lose their fears and got used to the smell, and before the child got his second teeth he'd gone inside the chicken coop to play, where the wires were falling apart. The angel was no less standoffish with him than with other mortals, but he tolerated the most ingenious infamies with the patience of a dog who had no illusions. They both came down with chicken pox at the same time. The doctor who took care of the child couldn't resist the temptation to listen to the angel's heart, and he found so much whistling in the heart and so many sounds in his kidneys that it seemed impossible for him to be alive. What surprised him most, however, was the logic of his wings. They seemed so natural on that completely human organism that he couldn't understand why other men didn't have them too.

When the child began school it had been some time since the sun and rain had caused the collapse of the chicken coop. The angel went dragging himself about here and there like a stray dying man. They would drive him out of the bedroom with a broom and a moment later find him in the kitchen. He seemed to be in so many places at the same time that they grew to think that he'd been duplicated, that he was reproducing himself all through the house, and the exasperated and unhinged Elisenda shouted that it was awful living in that hell full of angels. He could scarcely eat and his antiquarian eyes had also become so foggy that he went about bumping into posts. All he had left were the bare cannulae of his last feathers. Pelayo threw a blanket over him and extended him the charity of letting him sleep in the shed, and only then did they notice that he had a temperature at night, and was delirious with the tongue twisters of an old Norwegian. That was one of the few times they became alarmed, for they thought he was going to die and not even the wise neighbor woman had been able to tell them what to do with dead angels.

And yet he not only survived his worst winter, but seemed improved with the first sunny days. He remained motionless for several days in the farthest corner of the courtyard, where no one would see him, and at the beginning of December some large, stiff feathers began to grow on his wings, the feathers of a scarecrow, which looked more like another misfortune of decrepitude. But he must have known the reason for those changes, for he was quite careful that no one should notice them, that no one should hear the sea chanteys that he sometimes sang under the stars. One morning Elisenda was cutting some bunches of onions for lunch when a wind that seemed to come from the high seas blew into the kitchen. Then she went to the window and caught the angel in his first attempts at flight. They were so clumsy that his fingernails opened a furrow in the vegetable patch and he was on the point of knocking the shed down with the ungainly flapping that slipped on the light and couldn't get a grip on the air. But he did manage to gain altitude. Elisenda let out a sigh of relief, for herself and for him, when she saw him pass over the last houses, holding himself up in some way with the risky flapping of a senile vulture. She kept watching him even when she was through cutting the onions and she kept on watching until it was no longer possible for her to see him, because then he was no longer an annoyance in her life but an imaginary dot on the horizon of the sea.

1968

Further Reading

McMurray, George R. "Fantasy Prevails." *Gabriel García Márquez*. New York: Ungar, 1977. 108–28, spec. 116–19. • Gerlach, John. "The Logic of Wings: García Márquez, Todorov, and the Endless Resources of Fantasy." *Bridges to Fantasy*. Ed. George E. Slusser, Eric S. Rabkin, and Robert Scholes. Carbondale: Southern Illinois UP, 1982. 121–30. • Janes, Regina. "Intermezzi: Innocent Eréndira and Her Friends." *Gabriel García Márquez: Revolutions in Wonderland*. Columbia: U of Missouri P, 1981. 70–87, spec. 74–76. • Williams, Raymond L. "The Incredible and Sad Tale of Innocent Eréndira and Her Heartless Grandmother (1972)." *Gabriel García Márquez*. Boston: Twayne, 1984. 92–109, spec. 93–97. • Millington, Mark. "Aspects of Narrative Structure in *The Incredible and Sad Story of Innocent Eréndira and Her Heartless Grandmother*." *Gabriel García Márquez: New Readings*. Ed. Bernard McGuirk and Richard Cardwell. Cambridge, Eng.: Cambridge UP, 1987. 117–33, spec. 117–23.

The term "magical realism" is often associated with Gabriel García Márquez's fiction. His account of the origin of this "journalistic trick" is given in an interview with Peter Stone for The Paris Review.

Gabriel García Márquez: On Matter-of-Factness in Fantasy

Interviewer: How would you describe the search for a style that you went through after *Leaf Storm* and before you were able to write *One Hundred Years of Solitude*? . . .

García Márquez: . . . After *The Evil Hour* I did not write anything for five years. I had an idea of what I always wanted to do, but there was something missing and I was not sure what it was until one day I discovered the right tone—the tone that I eventually used in *One Hundred Years of Solitude*. It was based on the way my grandmother used to tell her stories. She told things that sounded supernatural and fantastic, but she told them with complete naturalness. When I finally discovered the tone I had to use, I sat down for eighteen months and worked every day.

Interviewer: How did she express the "fantastic" so naturally?

García Márquez: What was most important was the expression she had on her face. She did not change her expression at all when telling her stories, and everyone was surprised. In previous attempts to write *One Hundred Years of Solitude*, I tried to tell the story without believing in it. I discovered that what I had to do was believe in them myself and write them with the same expression with which my grandmother told them: with a brick face.

Interviewer: There also seems to be a journalistic quality to that technique or tone. You describe seemingly fantastic events in such minute detail that it gives them their own reality. Is this something you have picked up from journalism?

García Márquez: That's a journalistic trick which you can also apply to literature. For example, if you say that there are elephants flying in the sky, people are not going to believe you. But if you say that there are four hundred and twenty-five elephants in the sky, people will probably believe you. *One Hundred Years of Solitude* is full of that sort of thing. That's exactly the technique my grandmother used. I remember particularly the story about the character who is surrounded by yellow butterflies. When I was very small there was an electrician who came to the house. I became very curious because he carried a belt with which he used to suspend himself from the electrical posts. My grandmother used to say that every time this man came around, he would leave the house full of butterflies. But when I was writing this, I discovered that if I didn't say the butterflies were yellow, people would not believe it. When I was writing the episode of Remedios the Beauty going to heaven, it took me a long time to make it credible. One day I went out to the garden and saw a woman who used to come to the house to do the wash and she was putting out the sheets to dry and there was a lot of wind. She was arguing with the wind not to blow the sheets away. I discovered that if I used the sheets for Remedios the Beauty, she would ascend. That's how I did it, to make it credible. The problem for every writer is credibility. Anybody can write anything so long as it's believed.

ALICE MUNRO

(b. 1930)

CIRCLE OF PRAYER

Trudy threw a jug across the room. It didn't reach the opposite wall; it didn't hurt anybody, it didn't even break.

This was the jug without a handle—cement-colored with brown streaks on it, rough as sandpaper to the touch—that Dan made the winter he took pottery classes. He made six little handleless cups to go with it. The jug and the cups were supposed to be for sake, but the local liquor store doesn't carry sake. Once, they brought some home from a trip, but they didn't really like it. So the jug Dan made sits on the highest open shelf in the kitchen, and a few odd items of value are kept in it. Trudy's wedding ring and her engagement ring, the medal Robin won for all-round excellence in Grade 8, a long, two-strand necklace of jet beads that belonged to Dan's mother and was willed to Robin. Trudy won't let her wear it yet.

Trudy came home from work a little after midnight; she entered the house in the dark. Just the little stove light was on—she and Robin always left that on for each other. Trudy didn't need any other light. She climbed up on a chair without even letting go of her bag, got down the jug, and fished around inside it.

It was gone. Of course. She had known it would be gone.

She went through the dark house to Robin's room, still with her bag over her arm, the jug in her hand. She turned on the overhead light. Robin groaned and turned over, pulled the pillow over her head. Shamming.

"Your grandmother's necklace," Trudy said. "Why did you do that? Are you insane?"

Robin shammed a sleepy groan. All the clothes she owned, it seemed, old and new and clean and dirty, were scattered on the floor, on the chair, the desk, the dresser, even on the bed itself. On the wall was a huge poster showing a hippopotamus, with the words underneath "Why Was I Born So Beautiful?" And another poster showing Terry Fox running along a rainy highway, with a whole cavalcade of cars behind him. Dirty glasses, empty yogurt containers, school notes, a Tampax still in its wrapper, the stuffed snake and tiger Robin had had since before she went to school, a collage of pictures of her cat Sausage, who had been run over two years ago. Red and blue ribbons that she had won for jumping, or running, or throwing basketballs.

"You answer me!" said Trudy. "You tell me why you did it!"

She threw the jug. But it was heavier than she'd thought, or else at the very moment of throwing it she lost conviction, because it didn't hit the wall; it fell on the rug beside the dresser and rolled on the floor, undamaged.

You threw a jug at me that time. You could have killed me.

Not at you. I didn't throw it at you.

You could have killed me.

Proof that Robin was shamming: She started up in a fright, but it wasn't the blank fright of somebody who'd been asleep. She looked scared, but underneath that childish, scared look was another look—stubborn, calculating, disdainful.

"It was so beautiful. And it was valuable. It belonged to your grandmother."

"I thought it belonged to me," said Robin.

"That girl wasn't even your friend. Christ, you didn't have a good word to say for her this morning."

"You don't know who is my friend!" Robin's face flushed a bright pink and her eyes filled with tears, but her scornful, stubborn expression didn't change. "I knew her. I talked to her. So get out!"

Trudy works at the Home for Mentally Handicapped Adults. Few people call it that. Older people in town still say "the Misses Weir's house," and a number of others, including Robin—and, presumably, most of those her age—call it the Half-Wit House.

The house has a ramp now for wheelchairs, because some of the mentally handicapped may be physically handicapped as well, and it has a swimming pool in the back yard, which caused a certain amount of discussion when it was installed at taxpayers' expense. Otherwise the house looks pretty much the way it always did—the white wooden walls, the dark-green curlicues on the gables, the steep roof and dark screened side porch, and the deep lawn in front shaded by soft maple trees.

This month, Trudy works the four-to-midnight shift. Yesterday afternoon, she parked her car in front and walked up the drive thinking how nice the house looked, peaceful as in the days of the Misses Weir, who must have served iced tea and read library books, or played croquet, whatever people did then.

Always some piece of news, some wrangle or excitement, once you get inside. The men came to fix the pool but they didn't fix it. They went away again. It isn't fixed yet.

"We don't get no use of it, soon summer be over," Josephine said.

"It's not even the middle of June, you're saying summer'll be over," Kelvin said. "You think before you talk. Did you hear about the young girl that was killed out in the country?" he said to Trudy.

Trudy had started to mix two batches of frozen lemonade, one pink and one plain. When he said that, she smashed the spoon down on the frozen chunk so hard that some of the liquid spilled over.

"How, Kelvin?"

She was afraid she would hear that a girl was dragged off a country road, raped in the woods, strangled, beaten, left there. Robin goes running along the country roads in her white shorts and T-shirt, a headband on her flying hair. Robin's hair is golden; her legs and arms are golden. Her cheeks and limbs are downy, not shiny—you wouldn't be surprised to see a cloud of pollen delicately floating and settling behind her when she runs. Cars hoot at her and she isn't bothered. Foul threats are yelled at her, and she yells foul threats back.

"Driving a truck," Kelvin said.

Trudy's heart eased. Robin doesn't know how to drive yet.

"Fourteen years old, she didn't know how to drive," Kelvin said. "She got in the truck, and the first thing you know, she ran it into a tree. Where was her parents? That's what I'd like to know. They weren't watching out for her. She got in the truck when she didn't know how to drive and ran it into a tree. Fourteen. That's too young."

Kelvin goes uptown by himself; he hears all the news. He is fifty-two years old, still slim and boyish-looking, well-shaved, with soft, short, clean dark hair. He goes to the barbershop every day, because he can't quite manage to shave himself. Epilepsy, then surgery, an infected bone-flap, many more operations, a permanent mild difficulty with feet and fingers, a gentle head fog. The fog doesn't obscure facts, just motives. Perhaps he shouldn't be in the Home at all, but where else? Anyway, he likes it. He says he likes it. He tells the others they shouldn't complain; they should be more careful, they should behave themselves. He picks up the soft-drink cans and beer bottles that people have thrown into the front yard—though of course it isn't his job to do that.

When Janet came in just before midnight to relieve Trudy, she had the same story to tell.

"I guess you heard about that fifteen-year-old girl?"

When Janet starts telling you something like this, she always starts off with "I guess you heard." *I guess you heard Wilma and Ted are breaking up,* she says. *I guess you heard Alvin Stead had a heart attack.*

"Kelvin told me," Trudy said. "Only he said she was fourteen."

"Fifteen," Janet said. "She must've been in Robin's class at school. She didn't know how to drive. She didn't even get out of the lane."

"Was she drunk?" said Trudy. Robin won't go near alcohol, or dope, or cigarettes, or even coffee, she's so fanatical about what she puts into her body.

"I don't think so. Stoned, maybe. It was early in the evening. She was home with her sister. Their parents were out. Her sister's boyfriend came over—it was his truck, and he either gave her the keys to the truck or she took them. You hear different versions. You hear that they sent her out for something, they wanted to get rid of her, and you hear she just took the keys and went. Anyway, she ran it right into a tree in the lane."

"Jesus," said Trudy.

"I know. It's so idiotic. It's getting so you hate to think about your kids growing up. Did everybody take their medication okay? What's Kelvin watching?"

Kelvin was still up, sitting in the living room watching TV.

"It's somebody being interviewed. He wrote a book about schizophrenics," Trudy told Janet.

Anything he comes across about mental problems, Kelvin has to watch, or try to read.

"I think it depresses him, the more he watches that kind of thing," Janet said. "Do you know I found out today I have to make five hundred roses out of pink Kleenex for my niece Laurel's wedding? For the car. She said I promised I'd make the roses for the car. Well, I didn't. I don't remember promising a thing. Are you going to come over and help me?"

"Sure," said Trudy.

"I guess the real reason I want him to get off the schizophrenics is I want to watch the old *Dallas*," said Janet. She and Trudy disagree about this. Trudy can't stand to watch those old reruns of *Dallas,* to see the characters, with their younger, plumper faces, going through tribulations and bound up in romantic complications they and the audience have now forgotten all about. That's what's so hilarious, Janet says; it's so unbelievable it's wonderful. All that happens and they just forget about it and go on. But to Trudy it doesn't seem so unbelievable that the characters would go from one thing to the next thing—forgetful, hopeful, photogenic, forever changing their clothes. That it's not so unbelievable is the thing she really can't stand.

Robin, the next morning, said, "Oh, probably. All those people she hung around with drink. They party all the time. They're self-destructive. It's her own fault. Even if her sister told her to go, she didn't have to go. She didn't have to be so stupid."

"What was her name?" Trudy said.

"Tracy Lee," said Robin with distaste. She stepped on the pedal of the garbage tin, lifted rather than lowered the container of yogurt she had just emptied, and dropped it in. She was wearing bikini underpants and a T-shirt that said "If I Want to Listen to an Asshole, I'll Fart."

"That shirt still bothers me," Trudy said. "Some things are disgusting but funny, and some things are more disgusting than funny."

"What's the problem?" said Robin. "I sleep alone."

Trudy sat outside, in her wrapper, drinking coffee while the day got hot. There is a little brick-paved space by the side door that she and Dan always called the patio. She sat there. This is a solar-heated house, with big panels of glass in the south-sloping roof—the oddest-looking house in town. It's odd inside, too, with the open shelves in the kitchen instead of cupboards, and the living room up some stairs, looking out over the fields at the back. She and Dan, for a joke, gave parts of it the most conventional, suburban-sounding names—the patio, the powder room, the master bedroom. Dan always had to joke about the way he was living. He built the house himself—Trudy did a lot of the painting and staining—and it was a success. Rain didn't leak in around the panels, and part of the house's heat really did come from the sun. Most people who have the ideas, or ideals, that Dan has aren't very practical. They can't fix things or make things; they don't understand wiring or carpentry, or whatever it is they need to understand. Dan is good at everything—at gardening, cutting wood, building a house. He is especially good at repairing motors. He used to travel around getting jobs as an auto mechanic, a small-engines repairman. That's how he ended up here. He came here to visit Marlene, got a job as a mechanic, became a working partner in an auto-repair business, and before he knew it —married to Trudy, not Marlene—he was a small-town businessman, a member of the Kinsmen. All without shaving off his nineteen-sixties beard or trimming his hair any more than he wanted to. The town was too small and Dan was too smart for that to be necessary.

Now Dan lives in a townhouse in Richmond Hill with a girl named Genevieve. She is studying law. She was married when she was very young, and has three little children. Dan met her three years ago when her camper broke down a few miles outside of town. He told Trudy about her that night. The rented camper, the three little children hardly more than babies, the lively little divorced mother with her hair in pigtails. Her bravery, her poverty, her plans to enter law school. If the camper hadn't been easily fixed, he was going to invite her and her children to spend the night. She was on her way to her parents' summer place at Pointe au Baril.

"Then she can't be all that poor," Trudy said.

"You can be poor and have rich parents," Dan said.

"No, you can't."

Last summer, Robin went to Richmond Hill for a month's visit. She came home early. She said it was a madhouse. The oldest child has to go to a special reading clinic, the middle one wets the bed. Genevieve spends all her time in the law library, studying. No wonder. Dan shops for bargains, cooks, looks after the children, grows vegetables, drives a taxi on Saturdays and Sundays. He wants to set up a motorcycle-repair business in the garage, but he can't get a permit; the neighbors are against it.

He told Robin he was happy. Never happier, he said. Robin came home firmly grownup—severe, sarcastic, determined. She had some slight, steady grudge she hadn't had before. Trudy couldn't worm it out of her, couldn't tease it out of her; the time when she could do that was over.

Robin came home at noon and changed her clothes. She put on a light, flowered cotton blouse and ironed a pale-blue cotton skirt. She said that some of the girls from the class might be going around to the funeral home after school.

"I forgot you had that skirt," said Trudy. If she thought that was going to start a conversation, she was mistaken.

The first time Trudy met Dan, she was drunk. She was nineteen years old, tall and skinny (she still is), with a wild head of curly black hair (it is cropped short now and showing the gray as black hair does). She was very tanned, wearing jeans and a tie-dyed T-shirt. No brassière and no need. This was in Muskoka in August, at a hotel bar where they had a band. She was camping with girlfriends. He was there with his fiancée, Marlene. He had taken Marlene home to meet his mother, who lived in Muskoka on an island in an empty hotel. When Trudy was nineteen, he was twenty-eight. She danced around by herself, giddy and drunk, in front of the table where he sat with Marlene, a meek-looking blonde with a big pink shelf of bosom all embroidered in little fake pearls. Trudy just danced in front of him until he got up and joined her. At the end of the dance, he asked her name, and took her back and introduced her to Marlene.

"This is Judy," he said. Trudy collapsed, laughing, into the chair beside Marlene's. Dan took Marlene up to dance. Trudy finished off Marlene's beer and went looking for her friends.

"How do you do?" she said to them. "I'm Judy!"

He caught up with her at the door of the bar. He had ditched Marlene when he saw Trudy leaving. A man who could change course quickly, see the possibilities, flare up with new enthusiasm. He told people later that he was in love with Trudy before he even knew her real name. But he told Trudy that he cried when he and Marlene were parting.

"I have feelings," he said. "I'm not ashamed to show them."

Trudy had no feelings for Marlene at all. Marlene was over thirty—what could she expect? Marlene still lives in town, works at the Hydro office, is not married. When Trudy and Dan were having one of their conversations about Genevieve, Trudy said, "Marlene must be thinking I got what's coming to me."

Dan said he had heard that Marlene had joined the Fellowship of Bible Christians. The women weren't allowed makeup and had to wear a kind of bonnet to church on Sundays.

"She won't be able to have a thought in her head but forgiving," Dan said.

Trudy said, "I bet."

This is what happened at the funeral home, as Trudy got the story from both Kelvin and Janet.

The girls from Tracy Lee's class all showed up together after school. This was during what was called the visitation, when the family waited beside Tracy Lee's open casket to receive friends. Her parents were there, her married brother and his wife, her sister, and even her sister's boyfriend who owned the truck. They stood in a row and people lined up to say a few words to them. A lot of people came. They always do, in a case like this. Tracy Lee's grandmother was at the end of the row in a brocade-covered chair. She wasn't able to stand up for very long.

All the chairs at the funeral home are upholstered in this white-and-gold brocade. The curtains are the same, the wallpaper almost matches. There are little wall-bracket lights behind heavy pink glass. Trudy has been there several times and knows what it's like. But Robin and most of these girls had never been inside the place before. They didn't know what to expect. Some of them began to cry as soon as they got inside the door.

The curtains were closed. Soft music was playing—not exactly church music but it sounded like it. Tracy Lee's coffin was white with gold trim, matching all the brocade and the wallpaper. It had a lining of pleated pink satin. A pink satin pillow. Tracy Lee had not a mark on her face. She was not made up quite as usual, because the undertaker had done it. But she was wearing her favorite earrings, turquoise-colored triangles and yellow crescents, two to each ear. (Some people thought that was in bad taste.) On the part of the coffin that covered her from the waist down, there was a big heart-shaped pillow of pink roses.

The girls lined up to speak to the family. They shook hands, they said sorry-for-your-loss, just the way everybody else did. When they got through that, when all of them had let the grandmother squash their cool hands between her warm, swollen, freckled ones, they lined up again, in a straggling sort of way, and began to go past the coffin. Many were crying now, shivering. What could you expect? Young girls.

But they began to sing as they went past. With difficulty at first, shyly, but with growing confidence in their sad, sweet voices, they sang:

> *"Now, while the blossom still clings to the vine,*
> *I'll taste your strawberries, I'll drink your sweet wine—"*

They had planned the whole thing, of course, beforehand; they had got that song off a record. They believed that it was an old hymn.

So they filed past, singing, looking down at Tracy Lee, and it was noticed that they were dropping things into the coffin. They were slipping the rings off their fingers and the bracelets from their arms, and taking the earrings out of their ears. They were undoing necklaces, and bowing to pull chains and long strands of beads over their heads. Everybody gave something. All this jewellery went flashing and sparkling down on the dead girl, to lie beside her in her coffin. One girl pulled the bright combs out of her hair, let those go.

And nobody made a move to stop it. How could anyone interrupt? It was like a religious ceremony. The girls behaved as if they'd been told what to do, as if this was what was always done on such occasions. They sang, they wept, they dropped their jewellery. The sense of ritual made every one of them graceful.

The family wouldn't stop it. They thought it was beautiful.

"It was like church," Tracy Lee's mother said, and her grandmother said, "All those lovely young girls loved Tracy Lee. If they wanted to give their jewellery to show how they loved her, that's their business. It's not anybody else's business. I thought it was beautiful."

Tracy Lee's sister broke down and cried. It was the first time she had done so.

Dan said, "This is a test of love."

Of Trudy's love, he meant. Trudy started singing, "Please release me, let me go—"

She clapped a hand to her chest, danced in swoops around the room, singing. Dan was near laughing, near crying. He couldn't help it; he came and hugged her and they danced together, staggering. They were fairly drunk. All that June (it was two years ago), they were drinking gin, in between and during their scenes. They were drinking, weeping, arguing, explaining, and Trudy had to keep running to the liquor store. Yet she can't remember ever feeling really drunk or having a hangover. Except that she felt so tired all the time, as if she had logs chained to her ankles.

She kept joking. She called Genevieve "Jenny the Feeb."

"This is just like wanting to give up the business and become a potter," she said. "Maybe you should have done that. I wasn't really against it. You gave up on it. And when you wanted to go to Peru. We could still do that."

"All those things were just straws in the wind," Dan said.

"I should have known when you started watching the Ombudsman on TV," Trudy said. "It was the legal angle, wasn't it? You were never so interested in that kind of thing before."

"This will open life up for you, too," Dan said. "You can be more than just my wife."

"Sure. I think I'll be a brain surgeon."

"You're very smart. You're a wonderful woman. You're brave."

"Sure you're not talking about Jenny the Feeb?"

"No, you. You, Trudy. I still love you. You can't understand that I still love you."

Not for years had he had so much to say about how he loved her. He loved her skinny bones, her curly hair, her roughening skin, her way of coming into a room with a stride that shook the windows, her jokes, her clowning, her tough talk. He loved her mind and her soul. He always would. But the part of his life that had been bound up with hers was over.

"That is just talk. That is talking like an idiot!" Trudy said. "Robin, go back to bed!" For Robin in her skimpy nightgown was standing at the top of the steps.

"I can hear you yelling and screaming," Robin said.

"We weren't yelling and screaming," Trudy said. "We're trying to talk about something private."

"What?"

"I told you, it's something private."

When Robin sulked off to bed, Dan said, "I think we should tell her. It's better for kids to know. Genevieve doesn't have any secrets from her kids. Josie's only five, and she came into the bedroom one afternoon—"

Then Trudy did start yelling and screaming. She clawed through a cushion cover. "You stop telling me about your sweet fucking Genevieve and her sweet fucking bedroom and her asshole kids—you shut up, don't tell me anymore! You're just a big dribbling mouth without any brains. I don't care what you do, just shut up!"

Dan left. He packed a suitcase; he went off to Richmond Hill. He was back in five days. Just outside of town, he had stopped the car to pick Trudy a bouquet of wildflowers. He told her he was back for good, it was over.

"You don't say?" said Trudy.

But she put the flowers in water. Dusty pink milkweed flowers that smelled like face powder, black-eyed Susans, wild sweet peas, and orange lilies that must have got loose from old disappeared gardens.

"So you couldn't stand the pace?" she said.

"I knew you wouldn't fall all over me," Dan said. "You wouldn't be you if you did. And what I came back to is you."

She went to the liquor store, and this time bought champagne. For a month—it was still summer—they were back together being happy. She never really found out what had happened at Genevieve's house. Dan said he'd been having a middle-aged fit, that was all. He'd come to his senses. His life was here, with her and Robin.

"You're talking like a marriage-advice column," Trudy said.

"Okay. Forget the whole thing."

"We better," she said. She could imagine the kids, the confusion, the friends—old boyfriends, maybe—that he hadn't been prepared for. Jokes and opinions that he couldn't understand. That was possible. The music he liked, the way he talked—even his hair and his beard—might be out of style.

They went on family drives, picnics. They lay out in the grass behind the house at night, looking at the stars. The stars were a new interest of Dan's; he got a map. They hugged and kissed each other frequently and tried out some new things—or things they hadn't done for a long time— when they made love.

At this time, the road in front of the house was being paved. They'd built their house on a hillside at the edge of town, past the other houses, but trucks were using this street quite a bit now, avoiding the main streets, so the town was paving it. Trudy got so used to the noise and constant vibration she said she could feel herself jiggling all night, even when everything was quiet. Work started at seven in the morning. They woke up at the bottom of a river of noise. Dan dragged himself out of bed then, losing the hour of sleep that he loved best. There was a smell of diesel fuel in the air.

She woke up one night to find him not in bed. She listened to hear noises in the kitchen or the bathroom, but she couldn't. She got up and walked through the house. There were no lights on. She found him sitting outside, just outside the door, not having a drink or a glass of milk or a cof-fee, sitting with his back to the street.

Trudy looked out at the torn-up earth and the huge stalled machinery. "Isn't the quiet lovely?" she said.

He didn't say anything.

Oh. Oh.

She realized what she'd been thinking when she found his side of the bed empty and couldn't hear him anywhere in the house. Not that he'd left her, but that he'd done worse. Done away with himself. With all their happiness and hugging and kissing and stars and picnics, she could think that.

"You can't forget her," she said. "You love her."

"I don't know what to do."

She was glad just to hear him speak. She said, "You'll have to go and try again."

"There's no guarantee I can stay," he said. "I can't ask you to stand by."

"No," said Trudy. "If you go, that's it."

"If I go, that's it."

He seemed paralyzed. She felt that he might just sit there, repeating what she said, never be able to move or speak for himself again.

"If you feel like this, that's all there is to it," she said. "You don't have to choose. You're already gone."

That worked. He stood up stiffly, came over, and put his arms around her. He stroked her back.

"Come back to bed," he said. "We can rest for a little while yet."

"No. You've got to be gone when Robin wakes up. If we go back to bed, it'll just start all over again."

She made him a thermos of coffee. He packed the bag he had taken with him before. All Trudy's movements seemed skillful and perfect, as they never were, usually. She felt serene. She felt as if they were an old couple, moving in harmony, in wordless love, past injury, past forgiving. Their goodbye was hardly a ripple. She went outside with him. It was between four-thirty and five o'clock; the sky was beginning to lighten and the birds to wake, everything was drenched in dew. There stood the big harmless machinery, stranded in the ruts of the road.

"Good thing it isn't last night—you couldn't have got out," she said. She meant that the road hadn't been navigable. It was just yesterday that they had graded a narrow track for local traffic.

"Good thing," he said.

Goodbye.

"All I want is to know why you did it. Did you just do it for show? Like your father—for show? It's not the necklace so much. But it was a beautiful thing—I love jet beads. It was the only thing we had of your grandmother's. It was your right, but you have no right to take me by surprise like that. I deserve an explanation. I always loved jet beads. Why?"

"I blame the family," Janet says. "It was up to them to stop it. Some of the stuff was just plastic—those junk earrings and bracelets—but what Robin threw in, that was a crime. And she wasn't the only one. There were birthstone rings and gold chains. Somebody said a diamond cluster ring, but I don't know if I believe that. They said the girl inherited it, like Robin. You didn't ever have it evaluated, did you?"

"I don't know if jet is worth anything," Trudy says.

They are sitting in Janet's front room, making roses out of pink Kleenex.

"It's just stupid," Trudy says.

"Well. There is one thing you could do," says Janet. "I don't hardly know how to mention it."

"What?"

"Pray."

Trudy'd had the feeling, from Janet's tone, that she was going to tell her something serious and unpleasant, something about herself—Trudy—that was affecting her life and that everybody knew except her. Now she wants to laugh, after bracing herself. She doesn't know what to say.

"You don't pray, do you?" Janet says.

"I haven't got anything against it," Trudy says. "I wasn't brought up to be religious."

"It's not strictly speaking religious," Janet says. "I mean, it's not connected with any church. This is just some of us that pray. I can't tell you the names of anybody in it, but most of them you know. It's supposed to be secret. It's called the Circle of Prayer."

"Like at high school," Trudy says. "At high school there were secret societies, and you weren't supposed to tell who was in them. Only I wasn't."

"I was in everything going." Janet sighs. "This is actually more on the serious side. Though some people in it don't take it seriously enough, I don't think. Some people, they'll pray that they'll find a parking spot, or they'll pray they get good weather for their holidays. That isn't what it's for. But that's just individual praying. What the Circle is really about is, you phone up somebody that is in it and tell them what it is you're worried about, or upset about, and ask them to pray for you. And they do. And they phone one other person that's in the Circle, and they phone another and it goes all around, and we pray for one person, all together."

Trudy throws a rose away. "That's botched. Is it all women?"

"There isn't any rule it has to be. But it is, yes. Men would be too embarrassed. I was embarrassed at first. Only the first person you phone knows your name, who it is that's being prayed for, but in a town like this nearly everybody can guess. But if we started gossiping and ratting on each other it wouldn't work, and everybody knows that. So we don't. And it does work."

"Like how?" Trudy says.

"Well, one girl banged up her car. She did eight hundred dollars' damage, and it was kind of a tricky situation, where she wasn't sure her insurance would cover it, and neither was her husband—he was raging mad—but we all prayed, and the insurance came through without a hitch. That's only one example."

"There wouldn't be much point in praying to get the necklace back when it's in the coffin and the funeral's this morning," Trudy says.

"It's not up to you to say that. You don't say what's possible or impossible. You just ask for what you want. Because it says in the Bible, 'Ask and it shall be given.' How can you be helped if you won't ask? You can't, that's for sure. What about when Dan left—what if you'd prayed then? I wasn't in the Circle then, or I would have said something to you. Even if I knew you'd resist it, I would have said something. A lot of people resist. Now, even—it doesn't sound too great with that girl, but how do you know, maybe even now it might work? It might not be too late."

"All right," says Trudy, in a hard, cheerful voice. "All right." She pushes all the floppy flowers off her lap. "I'll just get down on my knees right now and pray that I get Dan back. I'll pray that I get the necklace back and I get Dan back, and why do I have to stop there? I can pray that Tracy Lee never died. I can pray that she comes back to life. Why didn't her mother ever think of that?"

Good news. The swimming pool is fixed. They'll be able to fill it tomorrow. But Kelvin is depressed. Early this afternoon—partly to keep them from bothering the men who were working on the pool—he took Marie and Josephine uptown. He let them get ice-cream cones. He told them to pay attention and eat the ice cream up quickly, because the sun was hot and it would melt. They licked at their cones now and then, as if they had all day. Ice cream was soon dribbling down their chins and down their arms. Kelvin had grabbed a handful of paper napkins, but he couldn't wipe it up fast enough. They were a mess. A spectacle. They didn't care. Kelvin told them they weren't so pretty that they could afford to look like that.

"Some people don't like the look of us anyway," he said. "Some people don't even think we should be allowed uptown. People just get used to seeing us and not staring at us like freaks and you make a mess and spoil it."

They laughed at him. He could have cowed Marie if he had her alone, but not when she was with Josephine. Josephine was one who needed some old-fashioned discipline, in Kelvin's opinion. Kelvin had been in places where people didn't get away with anything like they got away with here. He didn't agree with hitting. He had seen plenty of it done, but he didn't agree with it, even on the hand. But a person like Josephine could be shut up in her room. She could be made to sit in a corner, she could be put on bread and water, and it would do a lot of good. All Marie needed was a talking-to—she had a weak personality. But Josephine was a devil.

"I'll talk to both of them," Trudy says. "I'll tell them to say they're sorry."

"I want for them to *be* sorry," Kelvin says. "I don't care if they say they are. I'm not taking them ever again."

Later, when all the others are in bed, Trudy gets him to sit down to play cards with her on the screened veranda. They play Crazy Eights. Kelvin says that's all he can manage tonight; his head is sore.

Uptown, a man said to him, "Hey, which one of them two is your girlfriend?"

"Stupid," Trudy says. "He was a stupid jerk."

The man talking to the first man said, "Which one you going to marry?"

"They don't know you, Kelvin. They're just stupid."

But they did know him. One was Reg Hooper, one was Bud DeLisle. Bud DeLisle that sold real estate. They knew him. They had talked to him in the barbershop; they called him Kelvin. "Hey, Kelvin, which one you going to marry?"

"Nerds," says Trudy. "That's what Robin would say."

"You think they're your friend, but they're not," says Kelvin. "How many times I see that happen."

Trudy goes to the kitchen to put on coffee. She wants to have fresh coffee to offer Janet when she comes in. She apologized this morning, and Janet said all right, I know you're upset. It really is all right. Sometimes you think they're your friend, and they are.

She looks at all the mugs hanging on their hooks. She and Janet shopped all over to find them. A mug with each one's name. Marie, Josephine, Arthur, Kelvin, Shirley, George, Dorinda. You'd think Dorinda would be the hardest name to find, but actually the hardest was Shirley. Even the people who can't read have learned to recognize their own mugs, by color and pattern.

One day, two new mugs appeared, bought by Kelvin. One said Trudy, the other Janet.

"I'm not going to be too overjoyed seeing my name in that lineup," Janet said. "But I wouldn't hurt his feelings for a million dollars."

For a honeymoon, Dan took Trudy to the island on the lake where his mother's hotel was. The hotel was closed down, but his mother still lived there. Dan's father was dead, and she lived there alone. She took a boat with an outboard motor across the water to get her groceries. She sometimes made a mistake and called Trudy Marlene.

The hotel wasn't much. It was a white wooden box in a clearing by the shore. Some little boxes of cabins were stuck behind it. Dan and Trudy stayed in one of the cabins. Every cabin had a wood stove. Dan built a fire at night to take off the chill. But the blankets were damp and heavy when he and Trudy woke up in the morning.

Dan caught fish and cooked them. He and Trudy climbed the big rock behind the cabins and picked blueberries. He asked her if she knew how to make a piecrust, and she didn't. So he showed her, rolling out the dough with a whiskey bottle.

In the morning there was a mist over the lake, just as you see in the movies or in a painting.

One afternoon, Dan stayed out longer than usual, fishing. Trudy kept busy for a while in the kitchen, rubbing the dust off things, washing some jars. It was the oldest, darkest kitchen she had ever seen, with wooden racks for the dinner plates to dry in. She went outside and climbed the rock by herself, thinking she would pick some blueberries. But it was already dark under the trees; the evergreens made it dark, and she didn't like the idea of wild animals. She sat on the rock looking down on the roof of the hotel, the old dead leaves and broken shingles. She heard a piano being played. She scrambled down the rock and followed the music around to the front of the building. She walked along the front veranda and stopped at a window, looking into the room that used to be the lounge. The room with the blackened stone fireplace, the lumpy leather chairs, the horrible mounted fish.

Dan's mother was there, playing the piano. A tall, straight-backed old woman, with her gray-black hair twisted into such a tiny knot. She sat and played the piano, without any lights on, in the half-dark, half-bare room.

Dan had said that his mother came from a rich family. She had taken piano lessons, dancing lessons; she had gone around the world when she was a young girl. There was a picture of her on a camel. But she wasn't playing a classical piece, the sort of thing you'd expect her to have learned. She was playing "It's Three O'Clock in the Morning." When she got to the end, she started in again. Maybe it was a special favorite of hers, something she had danced to in the old days. Or maybe she wasn't satisfied yet that she had got it right.

Why does Trudy now remember this moment? She sees her young self looking in the window at the old woman playing the piano. The dim room, with its oversize beams and fireplace and the lonely leather chairs. The clattering, faltering, persistent piano music. Trudy remembers that so clearly and it seems she stood outside her own body, which ached then from the punishing pleasures of love. She stood outside her own happiness in a tide of sadness. And the opposite thing happened the morning Dan left. Then she stood outside her own unhappiness in a tide of what seemed unreasonably like love. But it was the same thing, really, when you got outside. What are those times that stand out, clear patches in your life—what do they have to do with it? They aren't exactly promises. Breathing spaces. Is that all?

She goes into the front hall and listens for any noise from upstairs.

All quiet there, all medicated.

The phone rings right beside her head.

"Are you still there?" Robin says. "You're not gone?"

"I'm still here."

"Can I run over and ride back with you? I didn't do my run earlier because it was so hot."

You threw the jug. You could have killed me.

Yes.

Kelvin, waiting at the card table, under the light, looks bleached and old. There's a pool of light whitening his brown hair. His face sags, waiting. He looks old, sunk into himself, wrapped in a thick bewilderment, nearly lost to her.

"Kelvin, do you pray?" says Trudy. She didn't know she was going to ask him that. "I mean, it's none of my business. But, like for anything specific?"

He's got an answer for her, which is rather surprising. He pulls his face up, as if he might have felt the tug he needed to bring him to the surface.

"If I was smart enough to know what to pray for," he says, "then I wouldn't have to."

He smiles at her, with some oblique notion of conspiracy, offering his halfway joke. It's not meant as comfort, particularly. Yet it radiates—what he said, the way he said it, just the fact that he's there again, radiates, expands the way some silliness can, when you're very tired. In this way, when she was young, and high, a person or a moment could become a lily floating on the cloudy river water, perfect and familiar.

1986

Further Reading

Slopen, Beverley. "PW Interviews: Alice Munro." *Publisher's Weekly* 230 (22 Aug. 1986): 70. • Blodgett, E. D. "Fiction as Destiny: *The Progress of Love.*" *Alice Munro.* Boston: Twayne, 1988. 130–52, spec. 148–50. • Levene, Mark. Review. *University of Toronto Quarterly* 57.1 (Fall 1987): 7–9. • Mallinson, Jean. "Alice Munro's *The Progress of Love.*" *West Coast Review* 21.3 (Winter 1977): 52–58. • Tyler, Anne. "Canadian Club." *New Republic* 195 (15, 22 Sept. 1986): 54–55.

Alice Munro's stories reflect life in small towns in southwest Ontario, a region that retains something of a frontier flavor and encourages independence. Life there may also make a person feel more isolated and vulnerable than a more cosmopolitan life would. Margaret Atwood, another Canadian writer, has attempted to define the effects of isolation on Canada's fiction.

Margaret Atwood: On the Theme of Survival in Canadian Literature

The central symbol for Canada—and this is based on numerous instances of its occurrence in both English and French Canadian literature—is undoubtedly Survival, *la Survivance.* Like the Frontier and The Island, it is a multi-faceted and adaptable idea. For early explorers and settlers, it meant bare survival in the face of "hostile" elements and/or natives: carving out a place and a way of keeping alive. But the word can also suggest survival of a crisis or disaster, like a hurricane or a wreck, and many Canadian poems have this kind of survival as a theme; what you might call 'grim' survival as opposed to 'bare' survival. For French Canada after the English took over it became cultural survival, hanging on as a people, retaining a religion and a language under an alien government. And in English Canada now while the Americans are taking over it is acquiring a similar meaning. There is another use of the word as well: a survival can be a vestige of a vanished order which has managed to persist after its time is past, like a primitive reptile. This version crops up in Canadian thinking too, usually among those who believe that Canada is obsolete.

But the main idea is the first one: hanging on, staying alive. Canadians are forever taking the national pulse like doctors at a sickbed: the aim is not to see whether the patient will live well but simply whether he will live at all. Our central idea is one which generates, not the excitement and sense of adventure or danger which The Frontier holds out, not the smugness and/or sense of security, of everything in its place, which The Island can offer, but an almost intolerable anxiety. Our stories are likely to be tales not of those who made it but of those who made it back, from the awful experience—the North, the snowstorm, the sinking ship—that killed everyone else. The survivor has no triumph or victory but the fact of his survival; he has little after his ordeal that he did not have before, except gratitude for having escaped with his life.

CHINUA ACHEBE

(b. 1930)

CIVIL PEACE

Jonathan Iwegbu counted himself extra-ordinarily lucky. 'Happy survival!' meant so much more to him than just a current fashion of greeting old friends in the first hazy days of peace. It went deep to his heart. He had come out of the war with five inestimable blessings—his head, his wife Maria's head and the heads of three out of their four children. As a bonus he also had his old bicycle—a miracle too but naturally not to be compared to the safety of five human heads.

The bicycle had a little history of its own. One day at the height of the war it was commandeered 'for urgent military action'. Hard as its loss would have been to him he would still have let it go without a thought had he not had some doubts about the genuineness of the officer. It wasn't his disreputable rags, nor the toes peeping out of one blue and one brown canvas shoe, nor yet the two stars of his rank done obviously in a hurry in biro, that troubled Jonathan; many good and heroic soldiers looked the same or worse. It was rather a certain lack of grip and firmness in his manner. So Jonathan, suspecting he might be amenable to influence, rummaged in his raffia bag and produced the two pounds with which he had been going to buy firewood which his wife, Maria, retailed to camp officials for extra stock-fish and corn meal, and got his bicycle back. That night he buried it in the little clearing in the bush where the dead of the camp, including his own youngest son, were buried. When he dug it up again a year later after the surrender all it needed was a little palm-oil greasing. 'Nothing puzzles God,' he said in wonder.

He put it to immediate use as a taxi and accumulated a small pile of Biafran money ferrying camp officials and their families across the four-mile stretch to the nearest tarred road. His standard charge per trip was six pounds and those who had the money were only glad to be rid of some of it in this way. At the end of a fortnight he had made a small fortune of one hundred and fifteen pounds.

Then he made the journey to Enugu and found another miracle waiting for him. It was unbelievable. He rubbed his eyes and looked again and it was still standing there before him. But, needless to say, even that monumental blessing must be accounted also totally inferior to the five heads in the family. This newest miracle was his little house in Ogui Overside. Indeed nothing puzzles God! Only two houses away a huge concrete edifice some wealthy contractor had put up just before the war was a mountain of rubble. And here was Jonathan's little zinc house of no regrets built with mud blocks quite intact! Of course the doors and windows were missing and five sheets off the roof. But what was that? And anyhow he had returned to Enugu early enough to pick up bits of old zinc and wood and soggy sheets of cardboard lying around the neighbourhood before thousands more came out of their forest holes looking for the same things. He got a destitute carpenter with one old hammer, a blunt plane and a few bent and rusty nails in his tool bag to turn this assortment of wood, paper and metal into door and window shutters for five Nigerian shillings or fifty Biafran pounds. He paid the pounds, and moved in with his overjoyed family carrying five heads on their shoulders.

His children picked mangoes near the military cemetery and sold them to soldiers' wives for a few pennies—real pennies this time—and his wife started making breakfast akara balls for neighbours in a hurry to start life again. With his family earnings he took his bicycle to the villages around and bought fresh palm-wine which he mixed generously in his rooms with the water which had recently started running again in the public tap down the road, and opened up a bar for soldiers and other lucky people with good money.

At first he went daily, then every other day and finally once a week, to the offices of the Coal Corporation where he used to be a miner, to find out what was what. The only thing he did find out in the end was that that little house of his was even a greater blessing than he had thought. Some of his fellow ex-miners who had nowhere to return at the end of the day's waiting just slept outside the doors of the offices and cooked what meal they could scrounge together in Bournvita tins. As the weeks lengthened and still nobody could say what was what Jonathan discontinued his weekly visits altogether and faced his palm-wine bar.

But nothing puzzles God. Came the day of the windfall when after five days of endless scuffles in queues and counterqueues in the sun outside the Treasury he had twenty pounds counted into his palms as ex-gratia award for the rebel money he had turned in. It was like Christmas for him and for many others like him when the payments began. They called it (since few could manage its proper official name) *egg-rasher.*

As soon as the pound notes were placed in his palm Jonathan simply closed it tight over them and buried fist and money inside his trouser pocket. He had to be extra careful because he had seen a man a couple of days earlier collapse into near-madness in an instant before that oceanic crowd because no sooner had he got his twenty pounds than some heartless ruffian picked it off him. Though it was not right that a man in such an extremity of agony should be blamed yet many in the queues that day were able to remark quietly at the victim's carelessness, especially after he pulled out the innards of his pocket and revealed a hole in it big enough to pass a thief's head. But of course he had insisted that the money had been in the other pocket, pulling it out too to show its comparative wholeness. So one had to be careful.

Jonathan soon transferred the money to his left hand and pocket so as to leave his right free for shaking hands should the need arise, though by fixing his gaze at such an elevation as to miss all approaching human faces he made sure that the need did not arise, until he got home.

He was normally a heavy sleeper but that night he heard all the neighbourhood noises die down one after another. Even the night watchman who knocked the hour on some metal somewhere in the distance had fallen silent after knocking one o'clock. That must have been the last thought in Jonathan's mind before he was finally carried away himself. He couldn't have been gone for long, though, when he was violently awakened again.

'Who is knocking?' whispered his wife lying beside him on the floor.

'I don't know,' he whispered back breathlessly.

The second time the knocking came it was so loud and imperious that the rickety old door could have fallen down.

'Who is knocking?' he asked them, his voice parched and trembling.

'Na tief-man and him people,' came the cool reply. 'Make you hopen de door.' This was followed by the heaviest knocking of all.

Maria was the first to raise the alarm, then he followed and all their children.

'*Police-o! Thieves-o! Neighbours-o! Police-o! We are lost! We are dead! Neighbours, are you asleep? Wake up! Police-o!*'

This went on for a long time and then stopped suddenly. Perhaps they had scared the thief away. There was total silence. But only for a short while.

'You done finish?' asked the voice outside. 'Make we help you small. Oya, everybody!'

'*Police-o! Tief-man-so! Neighbours-o! we done loss-o! Police-o! . . .*'

There were at least five other voices besides the leader's.

Jonathan and his family were now completely paralysed by terror. Maria and the children sobbed inaudibly like lost souls. Jonathan groaned continuously.

The silence that followed the thieves' alarm vibrated horribly. Jonathan all but begged their leader to speak again and be done with it.

'My frien,' said he at long last, 'we don try our best for call dem but I tink say dem all done sleep-o . . . So wetin we go do now? Sometaim you wan call soja? Or you wan make we call dem for you? Soja better pass police. No be so?'

'Na so!' replied his men. Jonathan thought he heard even more voices now than before and groaned heavily. His legs were sagging under him and his throat felt like sandpaper.

'My frien, why you no de talk again. I de ask you say you wan make we call soja?'

'No'.

'Awrighto. Now make we talk business. We no be bad tief. We no like for make trouble. Trouble done finish. War done finish and all the kata-kata wey de for inside. No Civil War again. This time na Civil Peace. No be so?'

'Na so!' answered the horrible chorus.

'What do you want from me? I am a poor man. Everything I had went with this war. Why do you come to me? You know people who have money. We . . .'

'Awright! We know say you no get plenty money. But we sef no get even anini. So derefore make you open dis window and give us one hundred pound and we go commot. Orderwise we de come for inside now to show you guitar-boy like dis . . .'

A volley of automatic fire rang through the sky. Maria and the children began to weep aloud again.

'Ah, missisi de cry again. No need for dat. We done talk say we na good tief. We just take our small money and go nwayorly. No molest. Abi we de molest?'

'At all!' sang the chorus.

'My friends,' began Jonathan hoarsely. 'I hear what you say and I thank you. If I had one hundred pounds . . .'

'Lookia my frien, no be play we come play for your house. If we make mistake and step for inside you no go like am-o. So derefore . . .'

'To God who made me; if you come inside and find one hundred pounds, take it and shoot me and shoot my wife and children. I swear to God. The only money I have in this life is this twenty-pounds *egg-rasher* they gave me today . . .'

'Ok. Time de go. Make you open dis window and bring the twenty pound. We go manage am like dat.'

There were now loud murmurs of dissent among the chorus: 'Na lie de man de lie; e get plenty money . . . Make we go inside and search properly well . . . Wetin be twenty pound? . . .'

'Shurrup!' rang the leader's voice like a lone shot in the sky and silenced the murmuring at once. 'Are you dere? Bring the money quick!'

'I am coming,' said Jonathan fumbling in the darkness with the key of the small wooden box he kept by his side on the mat.

At the first sign of light as neighbours and others assembled to commiserate with him he was already strapping his five-gallon demijohn to his bicycle carrier and his wife, sweating in the open fire, was turning over akara balls in a wide clay bowl of boiling oil. In the corner his eldest son was rinsing out dregs of yesterday's palm-wine from old beer bottles.

'I count it as nothing,' he told his sympathizers, his eyes on the rope he was tying. 'What is *egg-rasher*? Did I depend on it last week? Or is it greater than other things that went with the war? I say, let *egg-rasher* perish in the flames! Let it go where everything else has gone. Nothing puzzles God.'

1971

Further Reading

Carroll, David. *Chinua Achebe.* New York: Twayne, 1970. • Brown, Lloyd W. "Cultural Norms and Modes of Perception in Achebe's Fiction." *Critical Perspectives on Chinua Achebe.* Ed. C. L. Innes and Bernth Lindfurs. Washington, D.C.: Three Continents, 1978. 22–36. • Lindfurs, Bernth. "The Palm-Oil with Which Achebe's Words Are Eaten." *Folklore in Nigerian Literature.* New York: Africana, 1973. 73–93. • Morell, Karen L., ed. *In Person: Achebe, Awoohur, and Soyinka.* Seattle: African Studies Program of the U of Washington, 1975.

An African writer with international stature like Chinua Achebe's natu-rally assumes the role of educator to Europeans and Americans who, Achebe says, tend to assume that there was no African culture until Europeans brought one. His impatience with this assumption was in his mind when he delivered a lecture at the University of Massachusetts, from which this excerpt is taken.

Chinua Achebe: On Customs and Superstitions

It was a fine autumn morning at the beginning of this academic year such as encouraged friendliness to passing strangers. Brisk youngsters were hurry-ing in all directions, many of them obviously freshmen in their first flush of enthusiasm. An older man, going the same way as I, turned and remarked to me how very young they came these days. I agreed. Then he asked me if I was a student too. I said no, I was a teacher. What did I teach? African literature. Now that was funny, he said, because he never had thought of Africa as having that kind of stuff, you know. By this time I was walking much faster. "Oh well," I heard him say finally, behind me, "I guess I have to take your course to find out."

A few weeks later I received two very touching letters from high school children in Yonkers, New York, who—bless their teacher—had just read *Things Fall Apart*. One of them was particularly happy to learn about the customs and superstitions of an African tribe.

I propose to draw from these rather trivial encounters rather heavy conclusions which at first sight might seem somewhat out of proportion to them: But only at first sight.

The young fellow from Yonkers, perhaps partly on account of his age but I believe also for much deeper and more serious reasons, is obviously unaware that the life of his own tribesmen in Yonkers, New York, is full of odd customs and superstitions and, like everybody else in his culture, imagines that he needs a trip to Africa to encounter those things.

The other person being fully my own age could not be excused on the grounds of his years. Ignorance might be a more likely reason; but here again I believe that something more willful than a mere lack of information was at work. For did not that erudite British historian and Regius Professor at Oxford, Hugh Trevor Roper, pronounce a few years ago that African history did not exist?

If there is something in these utterances more than youthful experience, more than a lack of factual knowledge, what is it? Quite simply it is the desire—one might indeed say the need—in Western psychology to set up Africa as a foil to Europe, a place of negations at once remote and vaguely familiar in comparison with which Europe's own state of spiritual grace will be manifest.

ELENA PONIATOWSKA

(b. 1933)

A LITTLE FAIRY TALE

translated from the Spanish by Magda Bogin

From time to time we would hear about the wild boar and I would look down at the forest. We lived up above in a house held back by a retaining wall that kept us from falling down onto the sea of trees, but to me they looked so strong that I was sure they would support us with their branches if the wall ever collapsed. I could see them from my window. They were different at different times of day: at noon so thick that the sun's rays bounced off without penetrating them; a single black, ominous tree at night; and at dawn a pale green lake emerging through the mist. In my head I could hear old Madame Dot saying, "The woods are dark," drawing out the "a" of dark into a long, terrifying tunnel. "The woods are daaaaaaark. Very very daaaaaaark." Sofia, who was always the stronger one, or at any rate less morbidly inclined than I, would say, "Don't listen to her. She's old. She just doesn't want us going down to gather wild strawberries." Sofia had a special predilection for the tiny, aromatic strawberries that grow at the foot of trees. She never waited, but ate them on the spot, so that by the time we got back home our basket would be empty. Even on the way uphill she'd still be saying, "Pass me the basket. I'll carry it," finishing them off by the fistful, leaves and all.

I've always liked to put my hands in cracks and crevices; to dig. I can spend hours standing at the sink pulling garbage from the drain, along with leaves, tangled hair, dirt and hardened soap. The closer I get to unclogging it the more excited I become. As the feeling of satisfaction rises through my body, filling my mouth, I think of our revolutionary generals shouting to their men: "Nail them, lay into them, let them have it, kill the sons of bitches," and I feel I'm doing something useful equal to what they did, although I'm not completely sure that what they did was right. In the forest, while Sofia gathered strawberries, I would stop to stroke the rough bark, to plunge my hands into the damp earth, to cut the stems of mushrooms with their fascinating texture; crack; I'd stroke them with my index finger for a long time, watching their skin stiffen like the leaves of certain plants that tighten and close on themselves. "You and your poisons," Sofia would shout with her mouth full. Sometimes I would find a dark black truffle beneath a bed of musty leaves. "You're going to turn into a mushroom," she'd say. But I didn't move. Bent over the earth, crouched on all fours, looking and sniffing, when I found what I was looking for I'd scratch and scratch with a little stick: crack, crack, crack, pulling out the worms and all the other little forest creatures. I pulled them from their dens so I could see them and feel them walk across my palm, so I could feel their sharp little feet. I didn't want to hurt them. When I was done I closed up the holes, fortified their dwelling places, put them back in their homes. I wanted to see them and feel them but that's all. And when Sofia called, "Come here, there are piles of them here!" I never went, because I couldn't tear myself away from the damp moss, the lichen, but above all the moss that is like the earth's softest hair, its childhood down, a sweet delicate fleece that went back and forth across my face.

When the news broke the whole village was stunned. The boar had gored Berta. They brought her up from the woods thin and transparent after a two-day search. She had been wounded in the stomach and died in their arms on the way uphill. She was wearing a white dress and they had found her basket almost full. *She* didn't eat the berries. The boar had bitten her. Or charged her. Or who knows. The long and short of it is that she had bled to death and neither Sofia nor I was allowed to see her. The peasants made her a stretcher out of branches and covered her with foliage. Her whole face was hidden with green leaves so no one would be left with the image, the expression fear had stamped there. For days no one in the village talked of anything but the wild boar and how on Sunday, a holy day, a posse would go down into the forest to avenge her death. Someone had seen the bloody eyes of the beast glowing through the branches. Berta's father would lead the hunters, not her fiancé who had fled drunk and crazed, arms flailing, to Cahors.

"You're not to go into the woods ever again, is that clear, girls?"

For days I circled Madame Dot's windowless house. I wanted to speak to her. But she never came out. I never saw her open the door, and her broom still stood to one side, leaning, in the same place. The pail filled with cobwebs. The chickens cackled untended, left to fend for themselves. Finally one Thursday—Thursdays are always good days, white and round, days for talking—I saw her stooped back just ahead on the path, her shoulders covered by her black shawl.

"Madame Dot, Madame Dot!"

I walked her to her house and she invited me in. The broom was still leaning against the wall. No one had swept. She knew that I wanted to ask about the woods, which is to say, about the wild boar. She offered me a small low chair and I liked having to crouch down to sit in it the way I do when I'm looking for mushrooms in the earth. Outside a cold wind was blowing. She told me in her cracked voice that the boar's eyes were always red and that his hairs stood on end, almost like a porcupine's. She said he was black and thick and weighed a lot in the dark. "He charges like a huge pig." She pulled her shawl across her chest to protect herself from an imaginary attack. "He has hooves like the devil. Didn't you know that the devil has hooves?"

"What I want to know is why he killed Berta."

"For her flower."

"Her flower? What flower?"

"The black flower that grows between a woman's legs."

She saw the terror on my lips and said gently: "Yes, a tiny black flower. You don't have yours yet."

Madame Dot's old nose lengthened into a hook.

"That's what wild boars hunt. That's what they eat."

"Eat?"

"Yes, they tear it out by the roots, once and for all."

I ran out of there as fast as I could and didn't stop for weeks and weeks until I was twenty-three. The day of my wedding was also my birthday. The guests all remarked on the coincidence and offered double congratulations. "How nice to be getting married on the day you were born." They told me I was being born again to love. People are clever. Besides, it was a Sunday, but I prefer Thursdays. Guests like Sundays. My mother in her ramblings always spoke of the week of four Thursdays, and she made up a secret one just for me, in French: *la semaine des quatre jeudis*.[1] But I live in Mexico and have only been to France two times and the French are very exact about their days; they never lose track. On my wedding day she lifted my organdy veil and whispered in my ear, "Now you'll really have your week of four Thursdays."

I thought the veil was holding me aloft and with a smile I stretched out my arms that were swathed in white. He struck head-on from his powerful tuxedo. I saw him coming straight toward me from the dark, his head lowered. I heard the rumble of his hooves. When he was a few yards away I could see his eyes glowing red beneath his thick black eyebrows. On the broad planes of his thinker's brow I saw the erect hairs. Like a porcupine's. He breathed into my face as his moustached mouth drew close. I who had begun to caress the fascinating texture of mushrooms, to feel their damp beneath my fingertips, fell backwards: crack, crack, crack, and when he put his arms around me I fell down, down onto a steep path that descended to the deepest reaches of the woods. My screams must have pierced the thin walls of the hotel because the next morning an old woman with a hooked nose and a broom came rushing toward me. "You must be the new bride."

And just as speedily she handed me a white cup of herb tea. "Drink this. It will clean out your stomach."

I almost spilled it when he entered haughtily on his gleaming hooves and in the noon heat of Mérida immediately announced, slamming his fist on the table: "It's better to visit the ruins at dusk when the sun is going down."

Without taking her eyes off me the old lady insisted, "Drink your tea. Can't you see you've spilled your honeymoon?"

Then she brought us the menu. "It's almost dinner time. May I recommend tacos stuffed with black beans, with pheasant, venison or wild boar?"

He ordered tacos with wild boar and ate them lost in concentration. I washed down a bowl of lime soup, cleansing myself with its consoling water. The sky had turned purple from the heat.

"Can I bring you anything else?"

"And this old hag—why's she being so attentive?" he asked, wiping his moustache that was rotting in sauce. I didn't know how to tell him that women like me have always had a fairy godmother.

The same scream was heard again that night, but over the years it grew fainter and less frequent. I gave birth to some little bisons who took their first wobbly steps holding on to my arm. Now that my hair has begun to

---

1. A week of four Thursdays.

turn white my only wish is to return to the house in the mountains and go down to the forest with my basket; to walk beneath the arching trees, the thick ferns, to tread the ochres and yellows, choose the path, put my hands into the earth, find the truffle and feel the little creatures who make their home in the dense weeds. But I'm afraid it's only an illusion, a fairy tale that I will have to try again in my next incarnation—because we're all given a second chance, aren't we? It's only fair, after all; you can always start over again, meet up with some other animal, a unicorn for example, or a lion with a flat head like in the tapestries or a swan like Leda's that made love to her by covering her with its wings, or a deer. It doesn't always have to be a wild boar, does it? A fairy tale, yes, because it's late now and I don't have what it takes for all this jousting, and the little dog laughed to see such sport, right? and all I know is that they all lived everly happily after and had many children and rode in a carriage, and all the king's horses and all the king's men, do you want me to tell it all over again?

1986

Further Reading

Bearse, Grace M. "Interview with Elena Poniatowska." *Hispania* 64 (Mar. 1981): 135–36. • Marting, Diane E. "Elena Poniatowska." *Women Writers of Spanish America.* New York: Greenwood, 1987. 313–15. • Flori, Mónica. "Visions of Women: Symbolic Physical Portrayal as Social Commentary in the Short Fiction of Elena Poniatowska." *Third Woman* 2.2 (1984): 77–83.

When a contemporary author like Elena Poniatowska calls one of her stories a fairy tale, she is setting up specific expectations in her reader. She may fulfill these expectations, violate them, or do both at once. A very clear explanation of what the expectations are is found in W. H. Auden's introduction to an edition of the Grimms' fairy tales.

W. H. Auden: On the Form and Function of Fairy Tales

A fairy story, as distinct from a merry tale, or an animal story, is a serious tale with a human hero and a happy ending. The progression of its hero is the reverse of the tragic hero's: at the beginning he is either socially obscure or despised as being stupid or untalented, lacking in the heroic virtues, but at the end, he has surprised everyone by demonstrating his heroism and winning fame, riches, and love. Though ultimately he succeeds, he does not do so without a struggle in which his success is in doubt, for opposed to him are not only natural difficulties like glass mountains, or barriers of flame, but also hostile wicked powers, stepmothers, jealous brothers and witches. In many cases, indeed, he would fail were he not assisted by friendly powers who give him instructions or perform tasks for him which he cannot do himself; that is, in addition to his own powers, he needs luck, but this luck is not fortuitous but dependent upon his character and his actions. The tale ends with the establishment of justice; not only are the good rewarded but also the evil are punished. . . .

In the folk tale, as in the Greek epic and tragedy, situation and character are hardly separable; a man reveals what he is in what he does, or what happens to him is a revelation of what he is. In modern literature, what a man is includes all the possibilities of what he may become, so that what he actually does is never a complete revelation. . . .

Broadly speaking, and in most cases, the fairy tale is a dramatic projection in symbolic images of the life of the psyche, and it can travel from one country to another, one culture to another culture, whenever what it has to say holds good for human nature in both, despite their differences. Insofar as the myth is valid, the events of the story and its basic images will appeal irrespective of the artistic value of their narration; a genuine myth, like the Chaplin clown, can always be recognized by the fact that its appeal cuts across all differences between highbrow and lowbrow tastes. Further, no one conscious analysis can exhaust its meaning.

RAYMOND CARVER

(1938–1988)

WHY DON'T YOU DANCE?

In the kitchen, he poured another drink and looked at the bedroom suite in his front yard. The mattress was stripped and the candy-striped sheets lay beside two pillows on the chiffonier. Except for that, things looked much the way they had in the bedroom—nightstand and reading lamp on his side of the bed, nightstand and reading lamp on her side.

His side, her side.

He considered this as he sipped the whiskey.

The chiffonier stood a few feet from the foot of the bed. He had emptied the drawers into cartons that morning, and the cartons were in the living room. A portable heater was next to the chiffonier. A rattan chair with a decorator pillow stood at the foot of the bed. The buffed aluminum kitchen set took up a part of the driveway. A yellow muslin cloth, much too large, a gift, covered the table and hung down over the sides. A potted fern was on the table, along with a box of silverware and a record player, also gifts. A big console-model television set rested on a coffee table, and a few feet away from this stood a sofa and chair and a floor lamp. The desk was pushed against the garage door. A few utensils were on the desk, along with a wall clock and two framed prints. There was also in the driveway a carton with cups, glasses, and plates, each object wrapped in newspaper. That morning he had cleared out the closets, and except for the three cartons in the living room, all the stuff was out of the house. He had run an extension cord on out there and everything was connected. Things worked, no different from how it was when they were inside.

Now and then a car slowed and people stared. But no one stopped. It occurred to him that he wouldn't, either.

"It must be a yard sale," the girl said to the boy.

This girl and this boy were furnishing a little apartment.

"Let's see what they want for the bed," the girl said.

"And for the TV," the boy said.

The boy pulled into the driveway and stopped in front of the kitchen table.

They got out of the car and began to examine things, the girl touching the muslin cloth, the boy plugging in the blender and turning the dial to MINCE, the girl picking up a chafing dish, the boy turning on the television set and making little adjustments.

He sat down on the sofa to watch. He lit a cigarette, looked around, flipped the match into the grass.

The girl sat on the bed. She pushed off her shoes and lay back. She thought she could see a star.

"Come here, Jack. Try this bed. Bring one of those pillows," she said.

"How is it?" he said.

"Try it," she said.

He looked around. The house was dark.

"I feel funny," he said. "Better see if anybody's home."

She bounced on the bed.

"Try it first," she said.

He lay down on the bed and put the pillow under his head.

"How does it feel?" she said.

"It feels firm," he said.

She turned on her side and put her hand to his face.

"Kiss me," she said.

"Let's get up," he said.

"Kiss me," she said.

She closed her eyes. She held him.

He said, "I'll see if anybody's home."

But he just sat up and stayed where he was, making believe he was watching the television.

Lights came on in houses up and down the street.

"Wouldn't it be funny if," the girl said and grinned and didn't finish.

The boy laughed, but for no good reason. For no good reason, he switched the reading lamp on.

The girl brushed away a mosquito, whereupon the boy stood up and tucked in his shirt.

"I'll see if anybody's home," he said. "I don't think anybody's home. But if anybody is, I'll see what things are going for."

"Whatever they ask, offer ten dollars less. It's always a good idea," she said. "And, besides, they must be desperate or something."

"It's a pretty good TV," the boy said.

"Ask them how much," the girl said.

The man came down the sidewalk with a sack from the market. He had sandwiches, beer, whiskey. He saw the car in the driveway and the girl on the bed. He saw the television set going and the boy on the porch.

"Hello," the man said to the girl. "You found the bed. That's good."

"Hello," the girl said, and got up. "I was just trying it out." She patted the bed. "It's a pretty good bed."

"It's a good bed," the man said, and put down the sack and took out the beer and the whiskey.

"We thought nobody was here," the boy said. "We're interested in the bed and maybe in the TV. Also maybe the desk. How much do you want for the bed?"

"I was thinking fifty dollars for the bed," the man said.

"Would you take forty?" the girl asked.

"I'll take forty," the man said.

He took a glass out of the carton. He took the newspaper off the glass. He broke the seal on the whiskey.

"How about the TV?" the boy said.

"Twenty-five."

"Would you take fifteen?" the girl said.

"Fifteen's okay. I could take fifteen," the man said.

The girl looked at the boy.

"You kids, you'll want a drink," the man said. "Glasses in that box. I'm going to sit down. I'm going to sit down on the sofa."

The man sat on the sofa, leaned back, and stared at the boy and the girl.

The boy found two glasses and poured whiskey.

"That's enough," the girl said. "I think I want water in mine."

She pulled out a chair and sat at the kitchen table.

"There's water in that spigot over there," the man said. "Turn on that spigot."

The boy came back with the watered whiskey. He cleared his throat and sat down at the kitchen table. He grinned. But he didn't drink anything from his glass.

The man gazed at the television. He finished his drink and started another. He reached to turn on the floor lamp. It was then that his cigarette dropped from his fingers and fell between the cushions.

The girl got up to help him find it.

"So what do you want?" the boy said to the girl.

The boy took out the checkbook and held it to his lips as if thinking.

"I want the desk," the girl said. "How much money is the desk?"

The man waved his hand at this preposterous question.

"Name a figure," he said.

He looked at them as they sat at the table. In the lamplight, there was something about their faces. It was nice or it was nasty. There was no telling.

"I'm going to turn off this TV and put on a record," the man said. "This record-player is going, too. Cheap. Make me an offer."

He poured more whiskey and opened a beer.

"Everything goes," said the man.

The girl held out her glass and the man poured.

"Thank you," she said. "You're very nice," she said.

"It goes to your head," the boy said. "I'm getting it in the head." He held up his glass and jiggled it.

The man finished his drink and poured another, and then he found the box with the records.

"Pick something," the man said to the girl, and he held the records out to her.

The boy was writing the check.

"Here," the girl said, picking something, picking anything, for she did not know the names on these labels. She got up from the table and sat down again. She did not want to sit still.

"I'm making it out to cash," the boy said.

"Sure," the man said.

They drank. They listened to the record. And then the man put on another.

Why don't you kids dance? he decided to say, and then he said it. "Why don't you dance?"

"I don't think so," the boy said.

"Go ahead," the man said. "It's my yard. You can dance if you want to."

Arms about each other, their bodies pressed together, the boy and the girl moved up and down the driveway. They were dancing. And when the record was over, they did it again, and when that one ended, the boy said, "I'm drunk."

The girl said, "You're not drunk."

"Well, I'm drunk," the boy said.

The man turned the record over and the boy said, "I am."

"Dance with me," the girl said to the boy and then to the man, and when the man stood up, she came to him with her arms wide open.

"Those people over there, they're watching," she said.

"It's okay," the man said. "It's my place," he said.

"Let them watch," the girl said.

"That's right," the man said. "They thought they'd seen everything over here. But they haven't seen this, have they?" he said.

He felt her breath on his neck.

"I hope you like your bed," he said.

The girl closed and then opened her eyes. She pushed her face into the man's shoulder. She pulled the man closer.

"You must be desperate or something," she said.

Weeks later, she said: "The guy was about middle-aged. All his things right there in his yard. No lie. We got real pissed and danced. In the driveway. Oh, my God. Don't laugh. He played us these records. Look at this record-player. The old guy gave it to us. And all these crappy records. Will you look at this shit?"

She kept talking. She told everyone. There was more to it, and she was trying to get it talked out. After a time, she quit trying.

1981

Further Reading

Simpson, Mona. "The Art of Fiction 76: Raymond Carver." *The Paris Review* 88 (1983): 192–221. • Saltzman, Arthur M. "What We Talk About When We Talk About Love." *Understanding Raymond Carver.* U of South Carolina P, 1988. 100–23, spec. 101–04. • Marsh, Meredith. "The Mutability of the Heart." *New Republic* 184.17 (25 Apr. 1981): 38–40. • Atlas, James. "Less Is Less." *Atlantic* 247.6 (June 1981): 96–98. • Stull, William L. "Beyond Hopelessville: Another Side of Raymond Carver." *Philological Quarterly* 64.1 (Winter 1985): 1–15.

Raymond Carver has often been seen as an experimenter with fictional technique: a "minimalist" who attempts to strip his story to the barest elements. In fact, Carver was uncomfortable with this view of his fiction and saw himself as a fairly traditional writer, following especially in the tradition of Anton Chekhov. In his introduction to The Best American Short Stories of 1986, *Carver gives a clear explanation of his own standards as a reader and writer of short fiction.*

Raymond Carver: On His Standards for the Short Story

I lean toward realistic, "life-like" characters—that is to say, people—in realistically detailed situations. I'm drawn toward the traditional (some would call it old-fashioned) methods of storytelling: one layer of reality unfolding and giving way to another, perhaps richer layer; the gradual accretion of meaningful detail; dialogue that not only reveals something about character but advances the story. I'm not very interested, finally, in haphazard revelations, attenuated characters, stories where method or technique is all—stories, in short, where nothing much happens, or where what *does* happen merely confirms one's sour view of a world gone out of control. Too, I distrust the inflated language that some people pile on when they write fiction. I believe in the efficacy of the concrete word, be it noun or verb, as opposed to the abstract or arbitrary or slippery word—or phrase, or sentence. I tried to steer away from stories that, in my terms, didn't seem to be *written* well, stories where the words seemed to slide into one another and blur the meaning. If that happens, if the reader loses his way and his interest, for whatever reason, the story suffers and usually dies. *Abjure carelessness in writing*, just as you would in life.

The present volume is not to be seen as a holding action against slipshod writing or poorly conceived and executed stories. But it does, by virtue of its contents, stand squarely against that brand of work. I believe it is safe to say that the day of the campy, or crazy, or trivial, stupidly written account of inconsequential acts that don't count for much in the world has come and gone. And we should all be grateful that it *has* passed on. I deliberately tried to pick stories that rendered, in a more or less straightforward manner, what it's like out there. I wanted the stories I selected to throw some light on what it is that makes us and keeps us, often against great odds, recognizably human.

JOYCE CAROL OATES
(b. 1938)

WHERE ARE YOU GOING,
WHERE HAVE YOU BEEN?

to Bob Dylan

Her name was Connie. She was fifteen and she had a quick nervous giggling habit of craning her neck to glance into mirrors or checking other people's faces to make sure her own was all right. Her mother, who noticed everything and knew everything and who hadn't much reason any longer to look at her own face, always scolded Connie about it. "Stop gawking at yourself, who are you? You think you're so pretty?" she would say. Connie would raise her eyebrows at these familiar complaints and look right through her mother, into a shadowy vision of herself as she was right at that moment: she knew she was pretty and that was everything. Her mother had been pretty once too, if you could believe those old snapshots in the album, but now her looks were gone and that was why she was always after Connie.

"Why don't you keep your room clean like your sister? How've you got your hair fixed—what the hell stinks? Hair spray? You don't see your sister using that junk."

Her sister June was twenty-four and still lived at home. She was a secretary in the high school Connie attended, and if that wasn't bad enough—with her in the same building—she was so plain and chunky and steady that Connie had to hear her praised all the time by her mother and her mother's sisters. June did this, June did that, she saved money and helped clean the house and cooked and Connie couldn't do a thing, her mind was all filled with trashy daydreams. Their father was away at work most of the time and when he came home he wanted supper and he read the newspaper at supper and after supper he went to bed. He didn't bother talking much to them, but around his bent head Connie's mother kept picking at her until Connie wished her mother were dead and she herself were dead and it were all over. "She makes me want to throw up sometimes," she complained to her friends. She had a high, breathless, amused voice which made everything she said sound a little forced, whether it was sincere or not.

There was one good thing: June went places with girlfriends of hers, girls who were just as plain and steady as she, and so when Connie wanted to do that her mother had no objections. The father of Connie's best girl-friend drove the girls the three miles to town and left them off at a shopping plaza, so that they could walk through the stores or go to a movie, and when he came to pick them up again at eleven he never bothered to ask what they had done.

They must have been familiar sights, walking around that shopping plaza in their shorts and flat ballerina slippers that always scuffed the sidewalk, with charm bracelets jingling on their thin wrists; they would lean together to whisper and laugh secretly if someone passed by who amused or interested them. Connie had long dark blond hair that drew anyone's eye to it, and she wore part of it pulled up on her head and puffed out and the rest of it she let fall down her back. She wore a pullover jersey blouse that looked one way when she was at home and another way when she was away from home. Everything about her had two sides to it, one for home and one for anywhere that was not home: her walk that could be childlike and bobbing, or languid enough to make anyone think she was hearing music in her head, her mouth which was pale and smirking most of the time, but bright and pink on these evenings out, her laugh which was cynical and drawling at home—"Ha, ha, very funny"—but high-pitched and nervous anywhere else, like the jingling of the charms on her bracelet.

Sometimes they did go shopping or to a movie, but sometimes they went across the highway, ducking fast across the busy road, to a drive-in restaurant where older kids hung out. The restaurant was shaped like a big bottle, though squatter than a real bottle, and on its cap was a revolving figure of a grinning boy who held a hamburger aloft. One night in midsummer they ran across, breathless with daring, and right away someone leaned out a car window and invited them over, but it was just a boy from high school they didn't like. It made them feel good to be able to ignore him. They went up through the maze of parked and cruising cars to the bright-lit, fly-infested restaurant, their faces pleased and expectant as if they were entering a sacred building that loomed out of the night to give them what haven and what blessing they yearned for. They sat at the counter and crossed their legs at the ankles, their thin shoulders rigid with excitement, and listened to the music that made everything so good: the music was always in the background like music at a church service, it was something to depend upon.

A boy named Eddie came in to talk with them. He sat backward on his stool, turning himself jerkily around in semicircles and then stopping and turning again, and after a while he asked Connie if she would like something to eat. She said she did and so she tapped her friend's arm on her way out —her friend pulled her face up into a brave droll look—and Connie said she would meet her at eleven, across the way. "I just hate to leave her like that," Connie said earnestly, but the boy said that she wouldn't be alone for long. So they went out to his car and on the way Connie couldn't help but let her eyes wander over the windshields and faces all around her, her face gleaming with a joy that had nothing to do with Eddie or even this place; it might have been the music. She drew her shoulders up and sucked in her breath with the pure pleasure of being alive, and just at that moment she happened to glance at a face just a few feet from hers. It was a boy with shaggy black hair, in a convertible jalopy painted gold. He stared at her and then his lips widened into a grin. Connie slit her eyes at him and turned away, but she couldn't help glancing back and there he was still watching her. He wagged a finger and laughed and said, "Gonna get you, baby," and Connie turned away again without Eddie noticing anything.

She spent three hours with him, at the restaurant where they ate hamburgers and drank Cokes in wax cups that were always sweating, and then down an alley a mile or so away, and when he left her off at five to eleven only the movie house was still open at the plaza. Her girlfriend was there, talking with a boy. When Connie came up the two girls smiled at each other and Connie said, "How was the movie?" and the girl said, "*You* should know." They rode off with the girl's father, sleepy and pleased, and Connie couldn't help but look at the darkened shopping plaza with its big empty parking lot and its signs that were faded and ghostly now, and over at the drive-in restaurant where cars were still circling tirelessly. She couldn't hear the music at this distance.

Next morning June asked her how the movie was and Connie said, "So-so."

She and that girl and occasionally another girl went out several times a week that way, and the rest of the time Connie spent around the house—it was summer vacation—getting in her mother's way and thinking, dreaming, about the boys she met. But all the boys fell back and dissolved into a single face that was not even a face, but an idea, a feeling, mixed up with the urgent insistent pounding of the music and the humid night air of July. Connie's mother kept dragging her back to the daylight by finding things for her to do or saying, suddenly, "What's this about the Pettinger girl?"

And Connie would say nervously, "Oh, her. That dope." She always drew thick clear lines between herself and such girls, and her mother was simple and kindly enough to believe her. Her mother was so simple, Connie thought, that it was maybe cruel to fool her so much. Her mother went scuffling around the house in old bedroom slippers and complained over the telephone to one sister about the other, then the other called up and the two of them complained about the third one. If June's name was mentioned her mother's tone was approving, and if Connie's name was mentioned it was disapproving. This did not really mean she disliked Connie and actually Connie thought that her mother preferred her to June because she was prettier, but the two of them kept up a pretense of exasperation, a sense that they were tugging and struggling over something of little value to either of them. Sometimes, over coffee, they were almost friends, but something would come up—some vexation that was like a fly buzzing suddenly around their heads—and their faces went hard with contempt.

One Sunday Connie got up at eleven—none of them bothered with church—and washed her hair so that it could dry all day long, in the sun. Her parents and sisters were going to a barbecue at an aunt's house and Connie said no, she wasn't interested, rolling her eyes to let her mother know just what she thought of it. "Stay home alone then," her mother said sharply. Connie sat out back in a lawn chair and watched them drive away, her father quiet and bald, hunched around so that he could back the car out, her mother with a look that was still angry and not at all softened through the windshield, and in the back seat poor old June all dressed up as if she didn't know what a barbecue was, with all the running yelling kids and the flies. Connie sat with her eyes closed in the sun, dreaming and dazed with the warmth about her as if this were a kind of love, the caresses of love, and her mind slipped over onto thoughts of the boy she had been with the night before and how nice he had been, how sweet it always was, not the way someone like June would suppose but sweet, gentle, the way it was in movies and promised in songs; and when she opened her eyes she hardly knew where she was, the back yard ran off into weeds and a fence line of trees and behind it the sky was perfectly blue and still. The asbestos "ranch house" that was now three years old startled her—it looked small. She shook her head as if to get awake.

It was too hot. She went inside the house and turned on the radio to drown out the quiet. She sat on the edge of her bed, barefoot, and listened for an hour and a half to a program called XYZ Sunday Jamboree, record after record of hard, fast, shrieking songs she sang along with, interspersed by exclamations from "Bobby King": "An' look here you girls at Napoleon's—Son and Charley want you to pay real close attention to this song coming up!"

And Connie paid close attention herself, bathed in a glow of slow-pulsed joy that seemed to rise mysteriously out of the music itself and lay languidly about the airless little room, breathed in and breathed out with each gentle rise and fall of her chest.

After a while she heard a car coming up the drive. She sat up at once, startled, because it couldn't be her father so soon. The gravel kept crunching all the way in from the road—the driveway was long—and Connie ran to the window. It was a car she didn't know. It was an open jalopy, painted a bright gold that caught the sunlight opaquely. Her heart began to pound and her fingers snatched at her hair, checking it, and she whispered "Christ, Christ," wondering how bad she looked. The car came to a stop at the side door and the horn sounded four short taps as if this were a signal Connie knew.

She went into the kitchen and approached the door slowly, then hung out the screen door, her bare toes curling down off the step. There were two boys in the car and now she recognized the driver: he had shaggy, shabby black hair that looked crazy as a wig and he was grinning at her.

"I ain't late, am I?" he said.

"Who the hell do you think you are?" Connie said.

"Toldja I'd be out, didn't I?"

"I don't even know who you are."

She spoke sullenly, careful to show no interest or pleasure, and he spoke in a fast bright monotone. Connie looked past him to the other boy, taking her time. He had fair brown hair, with a lock that fell onto his forehead. His sideburns gave him a fierce, embarrassed look, but so far he hadn't even bothered to glance at her. Both boys wore sunglasses. The driver's glasses were metallic and mirrored everything in miniature.

"You wanta come for a ride?" he said.

Connie smirked and let her hair fall loose over one shoulder.

"Don'tcha like my car? New paint job," he said. "Hey."

"What?"

"You're cute."

She pretended to fidget, chasing flies away from the door.

"Don'tcha believe me, or what?" he said.

"Look, I don't even know who you are," Connie said in disgust.

"Hey, Ellie's got a radio, see. Mine's broke down." He lifted his friend's arm and showed her the little transistor the boy was holding, and now Connie began to hear the music. It was the same program that was playing inside the house.

"Bobby King?" she said.

"I listen to him all the time. I think he's great."

"He's kind of great," Connie said reluctantly.

"Listen, that guy's *great*. He knows where the action is."

Connie blushed a little, because the glasses made it impossible for her to see just what this boy was looking at. She couldn't decide if she liked him or if he was just a jerk, and so she dawdled in the doorway and wouldn't come down or go back inside. She said, "What's all that stuff painted on your car?"

"Can'tcha read it?" He opened the door very carefully, as if he was afraid it might fall off. He slid out just as carefully, planting his feet firmly on the ground, the tiny metallic world in his glasses slowing down like gelatine hardening and in the midst of it Connie's bright green blouse. "This here is my name, to begin with," he said. ARNOLD FRIEND was written in tarlike black letters on the side, with a drawing of a round grinning face that reminded Connie of a pumpkin, except it wore sunglasses. "I wanta introduce myself, I'm Arnold Friend and that's my real name and I'm gonna be your friend, honey, and inside the car's Ellie Oscar, he's kinda shy." Ellie brought his transistor radio up to his shoulder and balanced it there. "Now these numbers are a secret code, honey," Arnold Friend explained. He read off the numbers 33, 19, 17 and raised his eyebrows at her to see what she thought of that, but she didn't think much of it. The left rear fender had been smashed and around it was written, on the gleaming gold background: DONE BY CRAZY WOMAN DRIVER. Connie had to laugh at that. Arnold Friend was pleased at her laughter and looked up at her. "Around the other side's a lot more—you wanta come and see them?"

"No."

"Why not?"

"Why should I?"

"Don'tcha wanta see what's on the car? Don'tcha wanta go for a ride?"

"I don't know."

"Why not?"

"I got things to do."

"Like what?"

"Things."

He laughed as if she had said something funny. He slapped his thighs. He was standing in a strange way, leaning back against the car as if he were balancing himself. He wasn't tall, only an inch or so taller than she would be if she came down to him. Connie liked the way he was dressed, which was the way all of them dressed: tight faded jeans stuffed into black, scuffed boots, a belt that pulled his waist in and showed how lean he was, and a white pullover shirt that was a little soiled and showed the hard small muscles of his arms and shoulders. He looked as if he probably did hard work, lifting and carrying things. Even his neck looked muscular. And his face was a familiar face, somehow: the jaw and chin and cheeks slightly darkened, because he hadn't shaved for a day or two, and the nose long and hawklike, sniffing as if she were a treat he was going to gobble up and it was all a joke.

"Connie, you ain't telling the truth. This is your day set aside for a ride with me and you know it," he said, still laughing. The way he straightened and recovered from his fit of laughing showed that it had been all fake.

"How do you know what my name is?" she said suspiciously.

"It's Connie."

"Maybe and maybe not."

"I know my Connie," he said, wagging his finger. Now she remembered him even better, back at the restaurant, and her cheeks warmed at the thought of how she sucked in her breath just at the moment she passed him —how she must have looked at him. And he had remembered her. "Ellie and I come out here especially for you," he said. "Ellie can sit in back. How about it?"

"Where?"

"Where what?"

"Where're we going?"

He looked at her. He took off the sunglasses and she saw how pale the skin around his eyes was, like holes that were not in shadow but instead in light. His eyes were like chips of broken glass that catch the light in an amiable way. He smiled. It was as if the idea of going for a ride somewhere, to some place, was a new idea to him.

"Just for a ride, Connie sweetheart."

"I never said my name was Connie," she said.

"But I know what it is. I know your name and all about you, lots of things," Arnold Friend said. He had not moved yet but stood still leaning back against the side of his jalopy. "I took a special interest in you, such a pretty girl, and found out all about you like I know your parents and sister are gone somewheres and I know where and how long they're going to be gone, and I know who you were with last night, and your best girlfriend's name is Betty. Right?"

He spoke in a simple lilting voice, exactly as if he were reciting the words to a song. His smile assured her that everything was fine. In the car Ellie turned up the volume on his radio and did not bother to look around at them.

"Ellie can sit in the back seat," Arnold Friend said. He indicated his friend with a casual jerk of his chin, as if Ellie did not count and she should not bother with him.

"How'd you find out all that stuff?" Connie said.

"Listen: Betty Schultz and Tony Fitch and Jimmy Pettinger and Nancy Pettinger," he said, in a chant. "Raymond Stanley and Bob Hutter—"

"Do you know all those kids?"

"I know everybody."

"Look, you're kidding. You're not from around here."

"Sure."

"But—how come we never saw you before?"

"Sure you saw me before," he said. He looked down at his boots, as if he were a little offended. "You just don't remember."

"I guess I'd remember you," Connie said.

"Yeah?" He looked up at this, beaming. He was pleased. He began to mark time with the music from Ellie's radio, tapping his fists lightly together. Connie looked away from his smile to the car, which was painted so bright it almost hurt her eyes to look at it. She looked at that name, ARNOLD FRIEND. And up at the front fender was an expression that was familiar—MAN THE FLYING SAUCERS. It was an expression kids had used the year before, but didn't use this year. She looked at it for a while as if the words meant something to her that she did not yet know.

"What're you thinking about? Huh?" Arnold Friend demanded. "Not worried about your hair blowing around in the car, are you?"

"No."

"Think I maybe can't drive good?"

"How do I know?"

"You're a hard girl to handle. How come?" he said. "Don't you know I'm your friend? Didn't you see me put my sign in the air when you walked by?"

"What sign?"

"My sign." And he drew an X in the air, leaning out toward her. They were maybe ten feet apart. After his hand fell back to his side the X was still in the air, almost visible. Connie let the screen door close and stood perfectly still inside it, listening to the music from her radio and the boy's blend together. She stared at Arnold Friend. He stood there so stiffly relaxed, pretending to be relaxed, with one hand idly on the door handle as if he were keeping himself up that way and had no intention of ever moving again. She recognized most things about him, the tight jeans that showed his thighs and buttocks and the greasy leather boots and the tight shirt, and even that slippery friendly smile of his, that sleepy dreamy smile that all the boys used to get across ideas they didn't want to put into words. She recognized all this and also the singsong way he talked, slightly mocking, kidding, but serious and a little melancholy, and she recognized the way he tapped one fist against the other in homage of the perpetual music behind him. But all these things did not come together.

She said suddenly, "Hey, how old are you?"

His smile faded. She could see then that he wasn't a kid, he was much older—thirty, maybe more. At this knowledge her heart began to pound faster.

"That's a crazy thing to ask. Can'tcha see I'm your own age?"

"Like hell you are."

"Or maybe a coupla years older, I'm eighteen."

"Eighteen?" she said doubtfully.

He grinned to reassure her and lines appeared at the corners of his mouth. His teeth were big and white. He grinned so broadly his eyes became slits and she saw how thick the lashes were, thick and black as if painted with a black tarlike material. Then he seemed to become embarrassed, abruptly, and looked over his shoulder at Ellie. "*Him*, he's crazy," he said. "Ain't he a riot, he's a nut, a real character." Ellie was still listening to the music. His sunglasses told nothing about what he was thinking. He wore a bright orange shirt unbuttoned halfway to show his chest, which was a pale, bluish chest and not muscular like Arnold Friend's. His shirt collar was turned up all around and the very tips of the collar pointed out past his chin as if they were protecting him. He was pressing the transistor radio up against his ear and sat there in a kind of daze, right in the sun.

"He's kinda strange," Connie said.

"Hey, she says you're kinda strange! Kinda strange!" Arnold Friend cried. He pounded on the car to get Ellie's attention. Ellie turned for the first time and Connie saw with shock that he wasn't a kid either—he had a fair, hairless face, cheeks reddened slightly as if the veins grew too close to the surface of his skin, the face of a forty-year-old baby. Connie felt a wave of dizziness rise in her at this sight and she stared at him as if waiting for something to change the shock of the moment, make it all right again. Ellie's lips kept shaping words, mumbling along with the words blasting in his ear.

"Maybe you two better go away," Connie said faintly.

"What? How come?" Arnold Friend cried. "We come out here to take you for a ride. It's Sunday." He had the voice of the man on the radio now. It was the same voice, Connie thought. "Don'tcha know it's Sunday all day and honey, no matter who you were with last night today you're with Arnold Friend and don't you forget it!—Maybe you better step out here," he said, and this last was in a different voice. It was a little flatter, as if the heat was finally getting to him.

"No. I got things to do."

"Hey."

"You two better leave."

"We ain't leaving until you come with us."

"Like hell I am—"

"Connie, don't fool around with me. I mean, I mean, don't fool *around*," he said, shaking his head. He laughed incredulously. He placed his sunglasses on top of his head, carefully, as if he were indeed wearing a wig, and brought the stems down behind his ears. Connie stared at him, another wave of dizziness and fear rising in her so that for a moment he wasn't even in focus but was just a blur, standing there against his gold car, and she had the idea that he had driven up the driveway all right but had come from nowhere before that and belonged nowhere and that everything about him and even about the music that was so familiar to her was only half real.

"If my father comes and sees you—"

"He ain't coming. He's at a barbecue."

"How do you know that?"

"Aunt Tillie's. Right now they're—uh—they're drinking. Sitting around," he said vaguely, squinting as if he were staring all the way to town and over to Aunt Tillie's back yard. Then the vision seemed to get clear and he nodded energetically. "Yeah. Sitting around. There's your sister in a blue dress, huh? And high heels, the poor sad bitch—nothing like you, sweetheart! And your mother's helping some fat woman with the corn, they're cleaning the corn—husking the corn—"

"What fat woman?" Connie cried.

"How do I know what fat woman, I don't know every goddam fat woman in the world!" Arnold laughed.

"Oh, that's Mrs. Hornby . . . Who invited her?" Connie said. She felt a little light-headed. Her breath was coming quickly.

"She's too fat. I don't like them fat. I like them the way you are, honey," he said, smiling sleepily at her. They stared at each other for a while, through the screen door. He said softly, "Now what you're going to do is this: you're going to come out that door. You're going to sit up front with me and Ellie's going to sit in the back, the hell with Ellie, right? This isn't Ellie's date. You're my date. I'm your lover, honey."

"What? You're crazy—"

"Yes, I'm your lover. You don't know what that is, but you will," he said. "I know that too. I know all about you. But look: it's real nice and you couldn't ask for nobody better than me, or more polite. I always keep my word. I'll tell you how it is, I'm always nice at first, the first time. I'll hold you so tight you won't think you have to try to get away or pretend anything because you'll know you can't. And I'll come inside you where it's all secret and you'll give in to me and you'll love me—"

"Shut up! You're crazy!" Connie said. She backed away from the door. She put her hands against her ears as if she'd heard something terrible, something not meant for her. "People don't talk like that, you're crazy," she muttered. Her heart was almost too big now for her chest and its pumping made sweat break out all over her. She looked out to see Arnold Friend pause and then take a step toward the porch lurching. He almost fell. But, like a clever drunken man, he managed to catch his balance. He wobbled in his high boots and grabbed hold of one of the porch posts.

"Honey?" he said. "You still listening?"

"Get the hell out of here!"

"Be nice, honey. Listen."

"I'm going to call the police—"

He wobbled again and out of the side of his mouth came a fast spat curse, an aside not meant for her to hear. But even this "Christ!" sounded forced. Then he began to smile again. She watched this smile come, awkward as if he were smiling from inside a mask. His whole face was a mask, she thought wildly, tanned down onto his throat but then running out as if he had plastered makeup on his face but had forgotten about his throat.

"Honey—? Listen, here's how it is. I always tell the truth and I promise you this: I ain't coming in that house after you."

"You better not! I'm going to call the police if you—if you don't—"

"Honey," he said, talking right through her voice, "honey, I'm not coming in there but you are coming out here. You know why?"

She was panting. The kitchen looked like a place she had never seen before, some room she had run inside but which wasn't good enough, wasn't going to help her. The kitchen window had never had a curtain, after three years, and there were dishes in the sink for her to do—probably —and if you ran your hand across the table you'd probably feel something sticky there.

"You listening, honey? Hey?"

"—going to call the police—"

"Soon as you touch the phone I don't need to keep my promise and can come inside. You won't want that."

She rushed forward and tried to lock the door. Her fingers were shaking. "But why lock it," Arnold Friend said gently, talking right into her face. "It's just a screen door. It's just nothing." One of his boots was at a strange angle, as if his foot wasn't in it. It pointed out to the left, bent at the ankle. "I mean, anybody can break through a screen door and glass and wood and iron or anything else if he needs to, anybody at all and specially Arnold Friend. If the place got lit up with a fire honey you'd come runnin' out into my arms, right into my arms an' safe at home—like you knew I was your lover and'd stopped fooling around. I don't mind a nice shy girl but I don't like no fooling around." Part of those words were spoken with a slight rhythmic lilt, and Connie somehow recognized them—the echo of a song from last year, about a girl rushing into her boyfriend's arms and coming home again—

Connie stood barefoot on the linoleum floor, staring at him. "What do you want?" she whispered.

"I want you," he said.

"What?"

"Seen you that night and thought, that's the one, yes sir. I never needed to look any more."

"But my father's coming back. He's coming to get me. I had to wash my hair first—" She spoke in a dry, rapid voice, hardly raising it for him to hear.

"No, your Daddy is not coming and yes, you had to wash your hair and you washed it for me. It's nice and shining and all for me, I thank you, sweetheart," he said, with a mock bow, but again he almost lost his balance. He had to bend and adjust his boots. Evidently his feet did not go all the way down; the boots must have been stuffed with something so that he would seem taller. Connie stared out at him and behind him Ellie in the car, who seemed to be looking off toward Connie's right into nothing. This Ellie said, pulling the words out of the air one after another as if he were just discovering them, "You want me to pull out the phone?"

"Shut your mouth and keep it shut," Arnold Friend said, his face red from bending over or maybe from embarrassment because Connie had seen his boots. "This ain't none of your business."

"What—what are you doing? What do you want?" Connie said. "If I call the police they'll get you, they'll arrest you—"

"Promise was not to come in unless you touch that phone, and I'll keep that promise," he said. He resumed his erect position and tried to force his shoulders back. He sounded like a hero in a movie, declaring something important. He spoke too loudly and it was as if he were speaking to someone behind Connie. "I ain't made plans for coming in that house where I don't belong but just for you to come out to me, the way you should. Don't you know who I am?"

"You're crazy," she whispered. She backed away from the door but did not want to go into another part of the house, as if this would give him permission to come through the door. "What do you . . . You're crazy, you . . ."

"Huh? What're you saying, honey?"

Her eyes darted everywhere in the kitchen. She could not remember what it was, this room.

"This is how it is, honey; you come out and we'll drive away, have a nice ride. But if you don't come out we're gonna wait till your people come home and then they're all going to get it."

"You want that telephone pulled out?" Ellie said. He held the radio away from his ear and grimaced, as if without the radio the air was too much for him.

"I toldja shut up, Ellie," Arnold Friend said, "you're deaf, get a hearing aid, right? Fix yourself up. This little girl's no trouble and's gonna be nice to me, so Ellie keep to yourself, this ain't your date—right? Don't hem him in on me. Don't hog. Don't crush. Don't bird dog. Don't trail me," he said in a rapid meaningless voice, as if he were running through all the expressions he'd learned but was no longer sure which one of them was in style, then rushing on to new ones, making them up with his eyes closed, "Don't crawl under my fence, don't squeeze in my chipmunk hole, don't sniff my glue, suck my popsicle, keep your own greasy fingers on yourself!" He shaded his eyes and peered in at Connie, who was backed against the kitchen table. "Don't mind him honey he's just a creep. He's a dope. Right? I'm the boy for you and like I said you come out here nice like a lady and give me your hand, and nobody else gets hurt, I mean, your nice old bald-headed daddy and your mummy and your sister in her high heels. Because listen: why bring them in this?"

"Leave me alone," Connie whispered.

"Hey, you know that old woman down the road, the one with the chickens and stuff—you know her?"

"She's dead!"

"Dead? What? You know her?" Arnold Friend said.

"She's dead—"

"Don't you like her?"

"She's dead—she's—she isn't there any more—"

"But don't you like her, I mean, you got something against her? Some grudge or something?" Then his voice dipped as if he were conscious of a rudeness. He touched the sunglasses perched on top of his head as if to make sure they were still there. "Now you be a good girl."

"What are you going to do?"

"Just two things, or maybe three," Arnold Friend said. "But I promise it won't last long and you'll like me the way you get to like people you're close to. You will. It's all over for you here, so come on out. You don't want your people in any trouble, do you?"

She turned and bumped against a chair or something, hurting her leg, but she ran into the back room and picked up the telephone. Something roared in her ear, a tiny roaring, and she was so sick with fear that she could do nothing but listen to it—the telephone was clammy and very heavy and her fingers groped down to the dial but were too weak to touch it. She began to scream into the phone, into the roaring. She cried out, she cried for her mother, she felt her breath start jerking back and forth in her lungs as if it were something Arnold Friend were stabbing her with again and again with no tenderness. A noisy sorrowful wailing rose all about her and she was locked inside it the way she was locked inside this house.

After a while she could hear again. She was sitting on the floor with her wet back against the wall.

Arnold Friend was saying from the door, "That's a good girl. Put the phone back."

She kicked the phone away from her.

"No, honey. Pick it up. Put it back right."

She picked it up and put it back. The dial tone stopped.

"That's a good girl. Now you come outside."

She was hollow with what had been fear, but what was now just an emptiness. All that screaming had blasted it out of her. She sat, one leg cramped under her, and deep inside her brain was something like a pinpoint of light that kept going and would not let her relax. She thought, I'm not going to see my mother again. She thought, I'm not going to sleep in my bed again. Her bright green blouse was all wet.

Arnold Friend said, in a gentle-loud voice that was like a stage voice. "The place where you came from ain't there any more, and where you had in mind to go is canceled out. This place you are now—inside your daddy's house—is nothing but a cardboard box I can knock down any time. You know that and always did know it. You hear me?"

She thought, I have got to think. I have to know what to do.

"We'll go out to a nice field, out in the country here where it smells so nice and it's sunny," Arnold Friend said. "I'll have my arms tight around you so you won't need to try to get away and I'll show you what love is like, what it does. The hell with this house! It looks solid all right," he said. He ran a fingernail down the screen and the noise did not make Connie shiver, as it would have the day before. "Now put your hand on your heart, honey.

Feel that? That feels solid too, but we know better, be nice to me, be sweet like you can because what else is there for a girl like you but to be sweet and pretty and give in?—and get away before her people come back?"

She felt her pounding heart. Her hand seemed to enclose it. She thought for the first time in her life that it was nothing that was hers, that belonged to her, but just a pounding, living thing inside this body that wasn't really hers either.

"You don't want them to get hurt," Arnold Friend went on. "Now get up, honey. Get up all by yourself."

She stood.

"Now turn this way. That's right. Come over here to me—Ellie, put that away, didn't I tell you? You dope. You miserable creepy dope," Arnold Friend said. His words were not angry but only part of an incantation. The incantation was kindly. "Now come out through the kitchen to me honey, and let's see a smile, try it, you're a brave sweet little girl and now they're eating corn and hot dogs cooked to bursting over an outdoor fire, and they don't know one thing about you and never did and honey you're better than them because not a one of them would have done this for you."

Connie felt the linoleum under her feet; it was cool. She brushed her hair back out of her eyes. Arnold Friend let go of the post tentatively and opened his arms for her, his elbows pointing in toward each other and his wrists limp, to show that this was an embarrassed embrace and a little mocking, he didn't want to make her self-conscious.

She put out her hand against the screen. She watched herself push the door slowly open as if she were safe back somewhere in the other doorway, watching this body and this head of long hair moving out into the sunlight where Arnold Friend waited.

"My sweet little blue-eyed girl," he said, in a half-sung sigh that had nothing to do with her brown eyes but was taken up just the same by the vast sunlit reaches of the land behind him and on all sides of him, so much land that Connie had never seen before and did not recognize except to know that she was going to it.

1970

Further Reading

Wagner, Linda W. "Joyce Carol Oates: The Changing Shapes of Her Realities." *Great Lakes Review* 5.2 (Winter 1979): 15–23. • Urbanski, Marie. "Existential Allegory: Joyce Carol Oates's 'Where Are You Going, Where Have You Been?' " *Studies in Short Fiction* 15.2 (Spring 1978): 200–03. • Quirk, Tom. "A Source for 'Where Are You Going, Where Have You Been?' " *Studies in Short Fiction* 18.4 (Fall 1981): 413–19. • Hurley, C. Harold. "Cracking the Secret Code in Oates's 'Where

Are You Going, Where Have You Been?' " *Studies in Short Fiction* 24.1 (Winter 1987): 62–66. • Wegs, Joyce M. " 'Don't You Know Who I Am?' : The Grotesque in Oates's 'Where Are You Going, Where Have You Been?' " *Journal of Narrative Technique* 5 (1975): 66–72.

When she discusses her intentions as a writer, Joyce Carol Oates shows us that she is equally anxious to avoid simple spontaneity (the unreflective reporting of emotions and events) and strict rationality (the production of stories that are embodied ideas). A story like "Where Are You Going, Where Have You Been?" may exemplify her notion that a story, like a dream, can be suspended somewhere between logic and effusion.

Joyce Carol Oates: On the Short Story as a "Dream Verbalized"

In our time, in the Seventies, we are chided for being too intellectual, too clinical, if we do not surrender to the tyranny of the Present. Our art, if it is careful, if it makes a rational and even calculated point, is considered a betrayal of the spontaneous joy of life—living—which is always non-rational or anti-rational, as if only the more primitive levels of our brains are truly human. All this is a mistake. More than that, it is a waste: it is a waste that intelligent people should earnestly deny their intelligence, extolling the impulsive and the sensuous and the "original." In making a blunt distinction between a life of action and a life of reflection, Sartre is insisting that the materials of life cannot become translated immediately into the materials of art; the two belong to entirely different dimensions.

Any remarks about the short story made by a writer of short stories are bound to be autobiographical, if they are at all honest. For me the short story is an absolutely undecipherable fact. Years ago I believed that art was rational, at bottom, that it could be seen to "make sense," that it had a definite relationship with philosophical inquiry, though its aim was not necessarily to resolve philosophical doubt. Now I am not so sure: certain short stories, certain works of fiction, are obviously more rational than others, more reducible to an essence. But others are mysterious and fluid and unpossessible, like certain people. The short story is a dream verbalized, arranged in space and presented to the world, imagined as a sympathetic audience (and not, as the world really is, a busy and indifferent crowd): the dream is said to be some kind of manifestation of desire, so the short story must also represent a desire, perhaps only partly expressed, but the most interesting thing about it is its mystery.

TONI CADE BAMBARA

(b. 1939)

THE LESSON

Back in the days when everyone was old and stupid or young and foolish and me and Sugar were the only ones just right, this lady moved on our block with nappy hair and proper speech and no makeup. And quite naturally we laughed at her, laughed the way we did at the junk man who went about his business like he was some big-time president and his sorry-ass horse his secretary. And we kinda hated her too, hated the way we did the winos who cluttered up our parks and pissed on our handball walls and stank up our hallways and stairs so you couldn't halfway play hide-and-seek without a goddamn gas mask. Miss Moore was her name. The only woman on the block with no first name. And she was black as hell, cept for her feet, which were fish-white and spooky. And she was always planning these boring-ass things for us to do, us being my cousin, mostly, who lived on the block cause we all moved North the same time and to the same apartment then spread out gradual to breathe. And our parents would yank our heads into some kinda shape and crisp up our clothes so we'd be presentable for travel with Miss Moore, who always looked like she was going to church, though she never did. Which is just one of the things the grownups talked about when they talked behind her back like a dog. But when she came calling with some sachet she'd sewed up or some gingerbread she'd made or some book, why then they'd all be too embarrassed to turn her down and we'd get handed over all spruced up. She'd been to college and said it was only right that she should take responsibility for the young ones' education, and she not even related by marriage or blood. So they'd go for it. Specially Aunt Gretchen. She was the main gofer in the family. You got some ole dumb shit foolishness you want somebody to go for, you send for Aunt Gretchen. She been screwed into the go-along for so long, it's a blood-deep natural thing with her. Which is how she got saddled with me and Sugar and Junior in the first place while our mothers were in a la-de-da apartment up the block having a good ole time.

So this one day Miss Moore rounds us all up at the mailbox and it's puredee hot and she's knockin herself out about arithmetic. And school suppose to let up in summer I heard, but she don't never let up. And the starch in my pinafore scratching the shit outta me and I'm really hating this nappy-head bitch and her goddamn college degree. I'd much rather go to the pool or to the show where it's cool. So me and Sugar leaning on the mailbox being surly, which is a Miss Moore word. And Flyboy checking out what everybody brought for lunch. And Fat Butt already wasting his peanut-butter-and-jelly sandwich like the pig he is. And Junebug punchin on Q.T.'s arm for potato chips. And Rosie Giraffe shifting from one hip to the other waiting for somebody to step on her foot or ask her if she from Georgia so she can kick ass, preferably Mercedes'. And Miss Moore asking us do we know what money is, like we a bunch of retards. I mean real money, she say, like it's only poker chips or monopoly papers we lay on the grocer. So right away I'm tired of this and say so. And would much rather snatch Sugar and go to the Sunset and terrorize the West Indian kids and take their hair ribbons and their money too. And Miss Moore files that remark away for next week's lesson on brotherhood, I can tell. And finally I say we oughta get to the subway cause it's cooler and besides we might meet some cute boys. Sugar done swiped her mama's lipstick, so we ready.

So we heading down the street and she's boring us silly about what things cost and what our parents make and how much goes for rent and how money ain't divided up right in this country. And then she gets to the part about we all poor and live in the slums, which I don't feature. And I'm ready to speak on that, but she steps out in the street and hails two cabs just like that. Then she hustles half the crew in with her and hands me a five-dollar bill and tells me to calculate 10 percent tip for the driver. And we're off. Me and Sugar and Junebug and Flyboy hangin out the window and hollering to everybody, putting lipstick on each other cause Flyboy a faggot anyway, and making farts with our sweaty armpits. But I'm mostly trying to figure how to spend this money. But they all fascinated with the meter ticking and Junebug starts laying bets as to how much it'll read when Flyboy can't hold his breath no more. Then Sugar lays bets as to how much it'll be when we get there. So I'm stuck. Don't nobody want to go for my plan, which is to jump out at the next light and run off to the first bar-b-que we can find. Then the driver tells us to get the hell out cause we there already. And the meter reads eighty-five cents. And I'm stalling to figure out the tip and Sugar say give him a dime. And I decide he don't need it bad as I do, so later for him. But then he tries to take off with Junebug foot still in the door so we talk about his mama something ferocious. Then we check out that we on Fifth Avenue and everybody dressed up in stockings. One lady in a fur coat, hot as it is. White folks crazy.

"This is the place," Miss Moore say, presenting it to us in the voice she uses at the museum. "Let's look in the windows before we go in."

"Can we steal?" Sugar asks very serious like she's getting the ground rules squared away before she plays. "I beg your pardon," say Miss Moore, and we fall out. So she leads us around the windows of the toy store and me and Sugar screamin, "This is mine, that's mine, I gotta have that, that was made for me, I was born for that," till Big Butt drowns us out.

"Hey, I'm goin to buy that there."

"That there? You don't even know what it is, stupid."

"I do so," he say punchin on Rosie Giraffe. "It's a microscope."

"Whatcha gonna do with a microscope, fool?"

"Look at things."

"Like what, Ronald?" ask Miss Moore. And Big Butt ain't got the first notion. So here go Miss Moore gabbing about the thousands of bacteria in a drop of water and the somethinorother in a speck of blood and the million and one living things in the air around us is invisible to the naked eye. And what she say that for? Junebug go to town on that "naked" and we rolling. Then Miss Moore ask what it cost. So we all jam into the window smudgin it up and the price tag say $300. So then she ask how long'd take for Big Butt and Junebug to save up their allowances. "Too long," I say. "Yeh," adds Sugar, "outgrown it by that time." And Miss Moore say no, you never out-grow learning instruments. "Why, even medical students and interns and," blah, blah, blah. And we ready to choke Big Butt for bringing it up in the first damn place.

"This here costs four hundred eighty dollars," say Rosie Giraffe. So we pile up all over her to see what she pointin out. My eyes tell me it's a chunk of glass cracked with something heavy, and different-color inks dripped into the splits, then the whole thing put into a oven or something. But for $480 it don't make sense.

"That's a paperweight made of semi-precious stones fused together under tremendous pressure," she explains slowly, with her hands doing the mining and all the factory work.

"So what's a paperweight?" asks Rosie Giraffe.

"To weigh paper with, dumbbell," say Flyboy, the wise man from the East.

"Not exactly," say Miss Moore, which is what she say when you warm or way off too. "It's to weigh paper down so it won't scatter and make your desk untidy." So right away me and Sugar curtsy to each other and then to Mercedes who is more the tidy type.

"We don't keep paper on top of the desk in my class," say Junebug, fig-uring Miss Moore crazy or lyin one.

"At home, then," she say. "Don't you have a calendar and a pencil case and a blotter and a letter-opener on your desk at home where you do your homework?" And she know damn well what our homes look like cause she nosys around in them every chance she gets.

"I don't even have a desk," say Junebug. "Do we?"

"No. And I don't get no homework neither," says Big Butt.

"And I don't even have a home," say Flyboy like he do at school to keep the white folks off his back and sorry for him. Send this poor kid to camp posters, is his specialty.

"I do," says Mercedes. "I have a box of stationery on my desk and a picture of my cat. My godmother bought the stationery and the desk. There's a big rose on each sheet and the envelopes smell like roses."

"Who wants to know about your smelly-ass stationery," say Rosie Giraffe fore I can get my two cents in.

"It's important to have a work area all your own so that . . ."

"Will you look at this sailboat, please," say Flyboy, cuttin her off and pointin to the thing like it was his. So once again we tumble all over each other to gaze at this magnificent thing in the toy store which is just big enough to maybe sail two kittens across the pond if you strap them to the posts tight. We all start reciting the price tag like we in assembly. "Hand-crafted sailboat of fiberglass at one thousand one hundred ninety-five dollars."

"Unbelievable," I hear myself say and am really stunned. I read it again for myself just in case the group recitation put me in a trance. Same thing. For some reason this pisses me off. We look at Miss Moore and she lookin at us, waiting for I dunno what.

"Who'd pay all that when you can buy a sailboat set for a quarter at Pop's, a tube of glue for a dime, and a ball of string for eight cents? It must have a motor and a whole lot else besides," I say. "My sailboat cost me about fifty cents."

"But will it take water?" say Mercedes with her smart ass.

"Took mine to Alley Pond Park once," say Flyboy. "String broke. Lost it. Pity."

"Sailed mine in Central Park and it keeled over and sank. Had to ask my father for another dollar."

"And you got the strap," laugh Big Butt. "The jerk didn't even have a string on it. My old man wailed on his behind."

Little Q.T. was staring hard at the sailboat and you could see he wanted it bad. But he too little and somebody'd just take it from him. So what the hell. "This boat for kids, Miss Moore?"

"Parents silly to buy something like that just to get all broke up," say Rosie Giraffe.

"That much money it should last forever," I figure.

"My father'd buy it for me if I wanted it."

"Your father, my ass," say Rosie Giraffe getting a chance to finally push Mercedes.

"Must be rich people shop here," say Q.T.

"You are a very bright boy," say Flyboy. "What was your first clue?" And he rap him on the head with the back of his knuckles, since Q.T. the only one he could get away with. Though Q.T. liable to come up behind you years later and get his licks in when you half expect it.

"What I want to know is," I says to Miss Moore though I never talk to her, I wouldn't give the bitch that satisfaction, "is how much a real boat costs? I figure a thousand'd get you a yacht any day."

"Why don't you check that out," she says, "and report back to the group?" Which really pains my ass. If you gonna mess up a perfectly good swim day least you could do is have some answers. "Let's go in," she say like she got something up her sleeve. Only she don't lead the way. So me and Sugar turn the corner to where the entrance is, but when we get there I kinda hang back. Not that I'm scared, what's there to be afraid of, just a toy store. But I feel funny, shame. But what I got to be shamed about? Got as much right to go in as anybody. But somehow I can't seem to get hold of the door, so I step away from Sugar to lead. But she hangs back too. And I look at her and she looks at me and this is ridiculous. I mean, damn, I have never ever been shy about doing nothing or going nowhere. But then Mercedes steps up and then Rosie Giraffe and Big Butt crowd in behind and shove, and next thing we all stuffed into the doorway with only Mercedes squeezing past us, smoothing out her jumper and walking right down the aisle. Then the rest of us tumble in like a glued-together jigsaw done all wrong. And people lookin at us. And it's like the time me and Sugar crashed into the Catholic church on a dare. But once we got in there and everything so hushed and holy and the candles and the bowin and the hand-kerchiefs on all the drooping heads, I just couldn't go through with the plan. Which was for me to run up to the altar and do a tap dance while Sugar played the nose flute and messed around in the holy water. And Sugar kept givin me the elbow. Then later teased me so bad I tied her up in the shower and turned it on and locked her in. And she'd be there till this day if Aunt Gretchen hadn't finally figured I was lyin about the boarder takin a shower.

Same thing in the store. We all walkin on tiptoe and hardly touchin the games and puzzles and things. And I watched Miss Moore who is steady watchin us like she waitin for a sign. Like Mama Drewery watches the sky and sniffs the air and takes note of just how much slant is in the bird forma-tion. Then me and Sugar bump smack into each other, so busy gazing at the toys, 'specially the sailboat. But we don't laugh and go into our fat-lady bump-stomach routine. We just stare at that price tag. Then Sugar run a finger over the whole boat. And I'm jealous and want to hit her. Maybe not her, but I sure want to punch somebody in the mouth.

"Watcha bring us here for, Miss Moore?"

"You sound angry, Sylvia. Are you mad about something?" Givin me one of them grins like she tellin a grown-up joke that never turns out to be funny. And she's lookin very closely at me like maybe she plannin to do my portrait from memory. I'm mad, but I won't give her that satisfaction. So I slouch around the store bein very bored and say, "Let's go."

Me and Sugar at the back of the train watchin the tracks whizzin by large then small then gettin gobbled up in the dark. I'm thinkin about this tricky toy I saw in the store. A clown that somersaults on a bar then does chin-ups just cause you yank lightly at his leg. Cost $35. I could see me askin my mother for a $35 birthday clown. "You wanna who that costs what?" she'd say, cocking her head to the side to get a better view of the hole in my head. Thirty-five dollars could buy new bunk beds for Junior and Gretchen's boy. Thirty-five dollars and the whole household could go visit Granddaddy Nelson in the country. Thirty-five dollars would pay for the rent and the piano bill too. Who are these people that spend that much for performing clowns and $1000 for toy sailboats? What kinda work they do and how they live and how come we ain't in on it? Where we are is who we are, Miss Moore always pointin out. But it don't necessarily have to be that way, she always adds then waits for somebody to say that poor people have to wake up and demand their share of the pie and don't none of us know what kind of pie she talking about in the first damn place. But she ain't so smart cause I still got her four dollars from the taxi and she sure ain't gettin it. Messin up my day with this shit. Sugar nudges me in my pocket and winks.

Miss Moore lines us up in front of the mailbox where we started from, seem like years ago, and I got a headache for thinkin so hard. And we lean all over each other so we can hold up under the draggy ass lecture she always finishes us off with at the end before we thank her for borin us to tears. But she just looks at us like she readin tea leaves. Finally she say, "Well, what did you think of F.A.O. Schwarz?"

Rosie Giraffe mumbles, "White folks crazy."

"I'd like to go there again when I get my birthday money," says Mercedes, and we shove her out the pack so she has to lean on the mailbox by herself.

"I'd like a shower. Tiring day," say Flyboy.

Then Sugar surprises me by sayin, "You know, Miss Moore, I don't think all of us here put together eat in a year what that sailboat costs." And Miss Moore lights up like somebody goosed her. "And?" she say, urging Sugar on. Only I'm standin on her foot so she don't continue.

"Imagine for a minute what kind of society it is in which some people can spend on a toy what it would cost to feed a family of six or seven. What do you think?"

"I think," say Sugar pushing me off her feet like she never done before, cause I whip her ass in a minute, "that this is not much of a democracy if you ask me. Equal chance to pursue happiness means an equal crack at the dough, don't it?" Miss Moore is besides herself and I am disgusted with Sugar's treachery. So I stand on her foot one more time to see if she'll shove me. She shuts up, and Miss Moore looks at me, sorrowfully I'm thinkin. And somethin weird is goin on, I can feel it in my chest.

"Anybody else learn anything today?" lookin dead at me. I walk away and Sugar has to run to catch up and don't even seem to notice when I shrug her arm off my shoulder.

"Well, we got four dollars anyway," she says.

"Uh hunh."

"We could go to Hascombs and get half a chocolate layer and then go to the Sunset and still have plenty money for potato chips and ice cream sodas."

"Uh hunh."

"Race you to Hascombs," she say.

We start down the block and she gets ahead which is O.K. by me cause I'm going to the West End and then over to the Drive to think this day through. She can run if she want to and even run faster. But ain't nobody gonna beat me at nuthin.

1972

Further Reading

Tate, Claudia, ed. *Black Women Writers at Work*. New York: Continuum, 1983. 174–87. • Vertreace, Martha M. "Toni Cade Bambara: The Dance of Character and Community." *American Women Writing Fiction: Memory, Identity, Family, Space.* Ed. Mickey Pearlman. Lexington: UP of Kentucky, 1989. 154–71. • Hargrove, Nancy D. "Youth in Toni Cade Bambara's *Gorilla, My Love*." *Women Writers of the Contemporary South.* Ed. Peggy Whitman Prenshaw. Jackson: UP of Mississippi, 1984. 214–32, spec. 220–23. • Burks, Ruth Elizabeth. "From Baptism to Resurrection: Toni Cade Bambara and the Incongruity of Language." *Black Women Writers (1950–1980): A Critical Evaluation.* Ed. Mari Evans. Garden City, N.Y.: Doubleday, 1984. 48–57. • Bryan, C. D. B. Review. *New York Times Book Review* 15 Oct. 1972: 31.

Some of Toni Cade Bambara's subjects, in the hands of another writer, could develop into political invective. The poverty of the children in "The Lesson" is, after all, serious business. Bambara's own explanation of why she avoids turning a story into a merely political statement gives us some insight into her goals as a writer.

Toni Cade Bambara: On Wholesomeness Versus Hatred

The greatest challenge in writing, then, in the earlier stages was to strike a balance between candor, honesty, integrity, and truth—terms that are fairly synonymous for crossword puzzlers and thesaurus ramblers but hard to equate as living actions. Speaking one's mind, after all, does not necessarily mean one is in touch with the truth or even with the facts. Being honest and frank in terms of my own where—where I'm at a given point in my political/spiritual/etc. development—is not necessarily in my/our interest to utter, not necessarily in the interest of health, wholesomeness. Certain kinds of poisons, for example—rage, bitterness, revenge—don't need to be in the atmosphere, not to mention in my mouth. I don't, for example, hack up racists and stuff them in metaphorical boxes. I do not wish to lend them energy, for one thing. Though certainly there are "heavies" that people my stories. But I don't, for example, conjure up characters for the express purpose of despising them, of breaking their humps in public. I used to be astounded at Henry James et al., so nice nasty about it too, soooo refined. Gothic is of no interest to me. I try not to lend energy to building grotesqueries, depicting morbid relationships, dramatizing perversity. Folks come up to me 'lowing as how since I am a writer I would certainly want to hear blah, blah, blah, blah. They dump shit all over me, tell me about every ugly overheard and lived-through nightmare imaginable. They've got the wrong writer. The kid can't use it. I straightaway refer them to the neighborhood healer, certain that anyone so intoxicated would surely welcome a cleansing. But they persist—"Hey, this is for real, square business. The truth." I don't doubt that the horror tales are factual. I don't even doubt that ugly is a truth for somebody . . . somehow. But I'm not convinced that ugly is *the* truth that can save us, redeem us. The old folks teach that. Be triflin' and ugly and they say, "Deep down, gal, you know that ain't right," appealing to a truth about our deep-down nature. Good enough for me. Besides, I can't get happy writing ugly weird. If I'm not laughing while I work, I conclude that I am not communicating nourishment, since laughter is the most sure-fire healant I know. I don't know all my readers, but I know well for whom I write. And I want for them no less than I want for myself—wholesomeness.

MARGARET ATWOOD

(b. 1939)

RAPE FANTASIES

The way they're going on about it in the magazines you'd think it was just invented, and not only that but it's something terrific, like a vaccine for cancer. They put it in capital letters on the front cover, and inside they have these questionnaires like the ones they used to have about whether you were a good enough wife or an endomorph or an ectomorph, remember that? with the scoring upside down on page 73, and then these numbered do-it-yourself dealies, you know? RAPE, TEN THINGS TO DO ABOUT IT, like it was ten new hairdos or something. I mean, what's so new about it?

So at work they all have to talk about it because no matter what magazine you open, there it is, staring you right between the eyes, and they're beginning to have it on the television, too. Personally I'd prefer a June Allyson movie anytime but they don't make them anymore and they don't even have them that much on the Late Show. For instance, day before yesterday, that would be Wednesday, thank god it's Friday as they say, we were sitting around in the women's lunch room—the *lunch* room, I mean you'd think you could get some peace and quiet in there—and Chrissy closes up the magazine she's been reading and says, "How about it, girls, do you have rape fantasies?"

The four of us were having our game of bridge the way we always do, and I had a bare twelve points counting the singleton with not that much of a bid in anything. So I said one club, hoping Sondra would remember about the one club convention, because the time before when I used that she thought I really meant clubs and she bid us up to three, and all I had was four little ones with nothing higher than a six, and we went down two and on top of that we were vulnerable. She is not the world's best bridge player. I mean, neither am I but there's a limit.

Darlene passed but the damage was done, Sondra's head went round like it was on ball bearings and she said, "*What* fantasies?"

"Rape fantasies," Chrissy said. She's a receptionist and she looks like one; she's pretty but cool as a cucumber, like she's been painted all over with nail polish, if you know what I mean. Varnished. "It says here all women have rape fantasies."

"For Chrissake, I'm eating an egg sandwich," I said, "and I bid one club and Darlene passed."

"You mean, like some guy jumping you in an alley or something," Sondra said. She was eating her lunch, we all eat our lunches during the game, and she bit into a piece of that celery she always brings and started to chew away on it with this thoughtful expression in her eyes and I knew we might as well pack it in as far as the game was concerned.

"Yeah, sort of like that," Chrissy said. She was blushing a little, you could see it even under her makeup.

"I don't think you should go out alone at night," Darlene said, "you put yourself in a position," and I may have been mistaken but she was looking at me. She's the oldest, she's forty-one though you wouldn't know it and neither does she, but I looked it up in the employees' file. I like to guess a person's age and then look it up to see if I'm right. I let myself have an extra pack of cigarettes if I am, though I'm trying to cut down. I figure it's harmless as long as you don't tell. I mean, not everyone has access to that file, it's more or less confidential. But it's all right if I tell you, I don't expect you'll ever meet her, though you never know, it's a small world. Anyway.

"For *heaven's* sake, it's only *Toronto*," Greta said. She worked in Detroit for three years and she never lets you forget it, it's like she thinks she's a war hero or something, we should all admire her just for the fact that she's still walking this earth, though she was really living in Windsor the whole time, she just worked in Detroit. Which for me doesn't really count. It's where you sleep, right?

"Well, do you?" Chrissy said. She was obviously trying to tell us about hers but she wasn't about to go first, she's cautious, that one.

"I certainly don't," Darlene said, and she wrinkled up her nose, like this, and I had to laugh. "I think it's disgusting." She's divorced, I read that in the file too, she never talks about it. It must've been years ago anyway. She got up and went over to the coffee machine and turned her back on us as though she wasn't going to have anything more to do with it.

"Well," Greta said. I could see it was going to be between her and Chrissy. They're both blondes, I don't mean that in a bitchy way but they do try to outdress each other. Greta would like to get out of Filing, she'd like to be a receptionist too so she could meet more people. You don't meet much of anyone in Filing except other people in Filing. Me, I don't mind it so much, I have outside interests.

"Well," Greta said, "I sometimes think about, you know my apartment? It's got this little balcony, I like to sit out there in the summer and I have a few plants out there. I never bother that much about locking the door to the balcony, it's one of those sliding glass ones, I'm on the eighteenth floor for heaven's sake, I've got a good view of the lake and the CN Tower and all. But I'm sitting around one night in my housecoat, watching TV with my shoes off, you know how you do, and I see this guy's feet, coming down past the window, and the next thing you know he's standing on the balcony, he's let himself down by a rope with a hook on the end of it from the floor above, that's the nineteenth, and before I can even get up off the chesterfield he's inside the apartment. He's all dressed in black with black gloves on"—I knew right away what show she got the black gloves off because I saw the same one—"and then he, well, you know."

"You know what?" Chrissy said, but Greta said, "And afterwards he tells me that he goes all over the outside of the apartment building like that, from one floor to another, with his rope and his hook . . . and then he goes out to the balcony and tosses his rope, and he climbs up it and disappears."

"Just like Tarzan," I said, but nobody laughed.

"Is that all?" Chrissy said. "Don't you ever think about, well, I think about being in the bathtub, with no clothes on . . ."

"So who takes a bath in their clothes?" I said, you have to admit it's stupid when you come to think of it, but she just went on, ". . . with lots of bubbles, what I use is Vitabath, it's more expensive but it's so relaxing, and my hair pinned up, and the door opens and this fellow's standing there . . ."

"How'd he get in?" Greta said.

"Oh, I don't know, through a window or something. Well, I can't very well get out of the bathtub, the bathroom's too small and besides he's blocking the doorway, so I just lie there, and he starts to very slowly take his own clothes off, and then he gets into the bathtub with me."

"Don't you scream or anything?" said Darlene. She'd come back with her cup of coffee, she was getting really interested. "I'd scream like bloody murder."

"Who'd hear me?" Chrissy said. "Besides, all the articles say it's better not to resist, that way you don't get hurt."

"Anyway you might get bubbles up your nose," I said, "from the deep breathing," and I swear all four of them looked at me like I was in bad taste, like I'd insulted the Virgin Mary or something. I mean, I don't see what's wrong with a little joke now and then. Life's too short, right?

"Listen," I said, "those aren't *rape* fantasies. I mean, you aren't getting *raped*, it's just some guy you haven't met formally who happens to be more attractive than Derek Cummins"—he's the Assistant Manager, he wears elevator shoes or at any rate they have these thick soles and he has this funny way of talking, we call him Derek Duck—"and you have a good time. Rape is when they've got a knife or something and you don't want to."

"So what about you, Estelle," Chrissy said, she was miffed because I laughed at her fantasy, she thought I was putting her down. Sondra was miffed too, by this time she'd finished her celery and she wanted to tell about hers, but she hadn't got in fast enough.

"All right, let me tell you one," I said. "I'm walking down this dark street at night and this fellow comes up and grabs my arm. Now it so happens that I have a plastic lemon in my purse, you know how it always says you should carry a plastic lemon in your purse? I don't really do it, I tried it once but the darn thing leaked all over my checkbook, but in this fantasy I have one, and I say to him, 'You're intending to rape me, right?' and he nods, so I open my purse to get the plastic lemon, and I can't find it! My purse is full of all this junk, Kleenex and cigarettes and my change purse and my lipstick and my driver's license, you know the kind of stuff; so I ask him to hold out his hands, like this, and I pile all this junk into them and down at the bottom there's the plastic lemon, and I can't get the top off. So I hand it to him and he's very obliging, he twists the top off and hands it back to me, and I squirt him in the eye."

I hope you don't think that's too vicious. Come to think of it, it is a bit mean, especially when he was so polite and all.

"*That's* your rape fantasy?" Chrissy says. "I don't believe it."

"She's a card," Darlene says, she and I are the ones that've been here the longest and she never will forget the time I got drunk at the office party and insisted I was going to dance under the table instead of on top of it, I did a sort of Cossack number but then I hit my head on the bottom of the table—actually it was a desk—when I went to get up, and I knocked myself out cold. She's decided that's the mark of an original mind and she tells everyone new about it and I'm not sure that's fair. Though I did do it.

"I'm being totally honest," I say. I always am and they know it. There's no point in being anything else, is the way I look at it, and sooner or later the truth will come out so you might as well not waste the time, right? "You should hear the one about the Easy-Off Oven Cleaner."

But that was the end of the lunch hour, with one bridge game shot to hell, and the next day we spent most of the time arguing over whether to start a new game or play out the hands we had left over from the day before, so Sondra never did get a chance to tell about her rape fantasy.

It started me thinking though, about my own rape fantasies. Maybe I'm abnormal or something, I mean I have fantasies about handsome strangers coming in through the window too, like Mr. Clean, I wish one would, please god somebody without flat feet and big sweat marks on his shirt, and over five feet five, believe me being tall is a handicap though it's getting better, tall guys are starting to like someone whose nose reaches higher than their belly button. But if you're being totally honest you can't count those as rape fantasies. In a real rape fantasy, what you should feel is this anxiety, like when you think about your apartment building catching on fire and whether you should use the elevator or the stairs or maybe just stick your head under a wet towel, and you try to remember everything you've read about what to do but you can't decide.

For instance, I'm walking along this dark street at night and this short, ugly fellow comes up and grabs my arm, and not only is he ugly, you know, with a sort of puffy nothing face, like those fellows you have to talk to in the bank when your account's overdrawn—of course I don't mean they're all like that—but he's absolutely covered in pimples. So he gets me pinned against the wall, he's short but he's heavy, and he starts to undo himself and the zipper gets stuck. I mean, one of the most significant moments in a girl's life, it's almost like getting married or having a baby or something, and he sticks the zipper.

So I say, kind of disgusted, "Oh for Chrissake," and he starts to cry. He tells me he's never been able to get anything right in his entire life, and this is the last straw, he's going to go jump off a bridge.

"Look," I say, I feel so sorry for him, in my rape fantasies I always end up feeling sorry for the guy, I mean there has to be something *wrong* with them, if it was Clint Eastwood it'd be different but worse luck it never is. I was the kind of little girl who buried dead robins, know what I mean? It used to drive my mother nuts, she didn't like me touching them, because of the germs I guess. So I say, "Listen, I know how you feel. You really should do something about those pimples, if you got rid of them you'd be quite good looking, honest; then you wouldn't have to go around doing stuff like this. I had them myself once," I say, to comfort him, but in fact I did, and it ends up I give him the name of my old dermatologist, the one I had in high school, that was back in Leamington, except I used to go to St. Catharines for the dermatologist. I'm telling you, I was really lonely when I first came here; I thought it was going to be such a big adventure and all, but it's a lot harder to meet people in a city. But I guess it's different for a guy.

Or I'm lying in bed with this terrible cold, my face is all swollen up, my eyes are red and my nose is dripping like a leaky tap, and this fellow comes in through the window and *he* has a terrible cold too, it's a new kind of flu that's been going around. So he says, "I'b goig do rabe you"—I hope you don't mind me holding my nose like this but that's the way I imagine it—and he lets out this terrific sneeze, which slows him down a bit, also I'm no object of beauty myself, you'd have to be some kind of pervert to want to rape someone with a cold like mine, it'd be like raping a bottle of LePages mucilage the way my nose is running. He's looking wildly around the room, and I realize it's because he doesn't have a piece of Kleenex! "Id's ride here," I say, and I pass him the Kleenex, god knows why he even bothered to get out of bed, you'd think if you were going to go around climbing in windows you'd wait till you were healthier, right? I mean, that takes a certain amount of energy. So I ask him why doesn't he let me fix him a Neo-Citran and scotch, that's what I always take, you still have the cold but you don't feel it, so I do and we end up watching the Late Show together. I mean, they aren't all sex maniacs, the rest of the time they must lead a normal life. I figure they enjoy watching the Late Show just like anybody else.

I do have a scarier one though . . . where the fellow says he's hearing angel voices that're telling him he's got to kill me, you know, you read about things like that all the time in the papers. In this one I'm not in the apartment where I live now, I'm back in my mother's house in Leamington and the fellow's been hiding in the cellar, he grabs my arm when I go downstairs to get a jar of jam and he's got hold of the axe too, out of the garage, that one is really scary. I mean, what do you say to a nut like that?

So I start to shake but after a minute I get control of myself and I say, is he sure the angel voices have got the right person, because I hear the same angel voices and they've been telling me for some time that I'm going to give birth to the reincarnation of St. Anne who in turn has the Virgin Mary and right after that comes Jesus Christ and the end of the world, and he wouldn't want to interfere with that, would he? So he gets confused and listens some more, and then he asks for a sign and I show him my vaccination mark, you can see it's sort of an odd-shaped one, it got infected because I scratched the top off, and that does it, he apologizes and climbs out the coal chute again, which is how he got in in the first place, and I say to myself there's some advantage in having been brought up a Catholic even though I haven't been to church since they changed the service into English, it just isn't the same, you might as well be a Protestant. I must write to Mother and tell her to nail up that coal chute, it always has bothered me. Funny, I couldn't tell you at all what this man looks like but I know exactly what kind of shoes he's wearing, because that's the last I see of him, his shoes going up the coal chute, and they're the old-fashioned kind that lace up the ankles, even though he's a young fellow. That's strange, isn't it?

Let me tell you though I really sweat until I see him safely out of there and I go upstairs right away and make myself a cup of tea. I don't think about that one much. My mother always said you shouldn't dwell on unpleasant things and I generally agree with that, I mean, dwelling on them doesn't make them go away. Though not dwelling on them doesn't make them go away either, when you come to think of it.

Sometimes I have these short ones where the fellow grabs my arm but I'm really a Kung-Fu expert, can you believe it, in real life I'm sure it would just be a conk on the head and that's that, like getting your tonsils out, you'd wake up and it would be all over except for the sore places, and you'd be lucky if your neck wasn't broken or something, I could never even hit the volleyball in gym and a volleyball is fairly large, you know?—and I just go *zap* with my fingers into his eyes and that's it, he falls over, or I flip him against a wall or something. But I could never really stick my fingers in anyone's eyes, could you? It would feel like hot jello and I don't even like cold jello, just thinking about it gives me the creeps. I feel a bit guilty about that one, I mean how would you like walking around knowing someone's been blinded for life because of you?

But maybe it's different for a guy.

The most touching one I have is when the fellow grabs my arm and I say, sad and kind of dignified, "You'd be raping a corpse." That pulls him up short and I explain that I've just found out I have leukemia and the doctors have only given me a few months to live. That's why I'm out pacing the streets alone at night, I need to think, you know, come to terms with myself.

I don't really have leukemia but in the fantasy I do, I guess I chose that particular disease because a girl in my grade four class died of it, the whole class sent her flowers when she was in the hospital. I didn't understand then that she was going to die and I wanted to have leukemia too so I could get flowers. Kids are funny, aren't they? Well, it turns out that he has leukemia himself, and *he* only has a few months to live, that's why he's going around raping people, he's very bitter because he's so young and his life is being taken from him before he's really lived it. So we walk along gently under the street lights, it's spring and sort of misty, and we end up going for coffee, we're happy we've found the only other person in the world who can understand what we're going through, it's almost like fate, and after a while we just sort of look at each other and our hands touch, and he comes back with me and moves into my apartment and we spend our last months together before we die, we just sort of don't wake up in the morning, though I've never decided which one of us gets to die first. If it's him I have to go on and fantasize about the funeral, if it's me I don't have to worry about that, so it just about depends on how tired I am at the time. You may not believe this but sometimes I even start crying. I cry at the ends of movies, even the ones that aren't all that sad, so I guess it's the same thing. My mother's like that too.

The funny thing about these fantasies is that the man is always someone I don't know, and the statistics in the magazines, well, most of them anyway, they say it's often someone you do know, at least a little bit, like your boss or something—I mean, it wouldn't be *my* boss, he's over sixty and I'm sure he couldn't rape his way out of a paper bag, poor old thing, but it might be someone like Derek Duck, in his elevator shoes, perish the thought—or someone you just met, who invites you up for a drink, it's getting so you can hardly be sociable anymore, and how are you supposed to meet people if you can't trust them even that basic amount? You can't spend your whole life in the Filing Department or cooped up in your own apartment with all the doors and windows locked and the shades down. I'm not what you would call a drinker but I like to go out now and then for a drink or two in a nice place, even if I am by myself, I'm with Women's Lib on that even though I can't agree with a lot of other things they say. Like here for instance, the waiters all know me and if anyone, you know, bothers me. . . . I don't know why I'm telling you all this, except I think it helps you get to know a person, especially at first, hearing some of the things they think about. At work they call me the office worry wart, but it isn't so much like worrying, it's more like figuring out what you should do in an emergency, like I said before.

Anyway, another thing about it is that there's a lot of conversation, in fact I spend most of my time, in the fantasy that is, wondering what I'm going to say and what he's going to say, I think it would be better if you could get a conversation going. Like, how could a fellow do that to a person he's just had a long conversation with, once you let them know you're human, you have a life too, I don't see how they could go ahead with it, right? I mean, I know it happens but I just don't understand it, that's the part I really don't understand.

1977

Further Reading

Rosenberg, Jerome H. "Home Ground, Foreign Territory." *Margaret Atwood.* Boston: Twayne, 1984. 95–133, spec. 120–25. • Thompson, Lee Briscoe. "Minuets and Madness: Margaret Atwood's *Dancing Girls.*" *The Art of Margaret Atwood: Essays in Criticism.* Ed. Arnold E. Davidson and Cathy N. Davidson. Toronto: House of Anansi Press, 1981. 107–22, spec. 115–16. • Hill, Douglas. "Violations." *Canadian Forum* 57 (Dec.–Jan. 1977–78): 35. • Spettigue, D. O. Review. *Queen's Quarterly* 85.3 (Autumn 1978): 516–18. • Van Spanckeren, Kathryn, and Jan Garden Castro, eds. *Margaret Atwood: Vision and Forms.* Carbondale: Southern Illinois UP, 1988.

Margaret Atwood likes to call herself a storyteller rather than a writer of fiction. Her reason is that she sees a clear connection between her writing and the oral storytelling she grew up with.

Margaret Atwood: On Spoken and Written Stories

Think of a simple joke; now think of the same joke told, first well and then badly. It's the timing, isn't it? And the gestures, the embellishments, the tangents, the occasion, the expression on the face of the teller, and whether you like him or not. Literary critics talking about fiction may call these things style, voice and narrative technique and so forth, but you can trace them all back to that moment when the tribe or the family is sitting around the fire or the dinner table and the story-teller decides to add something, leave something out or vary the order of telling in order to make the story a little better. Writing on the page is after all just a notation, and all literature, like all music, is oral by nature.

Neither of my parents are writers, but both of them are very good story-tellers; and since they're both from Nova Scotia, I'd like to illustrate one kind of story. . . .

I used to hear around the dinner table when I was growing up. Anyone from rural Nova Scotia is well-steeped in what we now call the oral tradition but which they didn't call anything of the sort. Sometimes they called these stories "yarns"; sometimes they didn't call them anything. They were just things that had once happened.

For instance, there was the ingenious man who lived down around the South Shore and built a circular barn for his cows. The cows spent the night facing outwards, with their rear ends all facing inwards towards the centre of the circle, which made mucking out the barn more efficient. Each cow had its own door, and the doors, equidistant around the perimeter of the circle, were worked by a central pulley. Every morning people would gather from miles around to watch the cows being let out of the barn. At the sound of a horn, the doors would all fly upwards at once, and the cows, urged on by little boys with switches, would squirt out of the barn like drops from a lemon. Or so my father said.

ALICE WALKER

(b. 1944)

EVERYDAY USE

for your grandmamma

I will wait for her in the yard that Maggie and I made so clean and wavy yesterday afternoon. A yard like this is more comfortable than most people know. It is not just a yard. It is like an extended living room. When the hard clay is swept clean as a floor and the fine sand around the edges lined with tiny, irregular grooves, anyone can come and sit and look up into the elm tree and wait for the breezes that never come inside the house.

Maggie will be nervous until after her sister goes: she will stand hopelessly in corners, homely and ashamed of the burn scars down her arms and legs, eying her sister with a mixture of envy and awe. She thinks her sister has held life always in the palm of one hand, that "no" is a word the world never learned to say to her.

You've no doubt seen those TV shows where the child who has "made it" is confronted, as a surprise, by her own mother and father, tottering in weakly from backstage. (A pleasant surprise, of course: What would they do if parent and child came on the show only to curse out and insult each other?) On TV mother and child embrace and smile into each other's faces. Sometimes the mother and father weep, the child wraps them in her arms and leans across the table to tell how she would not have made it without their help. I have seen these programs.

Sometimes I dream a dream in which Dee and I are suddenly brought together on a TV program of this sort. Out of a dark and soft-seated limousine I am ushered into a bright room filled with many people. There I meet a smiling, gray, sporty man like Johnny Carson who shakes my hand and tells me what a fine girl I have. Then we are on the stage and Dee is embracing me with tears in her eyes. She pins on my dress a large orchid, even though she has told me once that she thinks orchids are tacky flowers.

In real life I am a large, big-boned woman with rough, man-working hands. In the winter I wear flannel nightgowns to bed and overalls during the day. I can kill and clean a hog as mercilessly as a man. My fat keeps me hot in zero weather. I can work outside all day, breaking ice to get water for washing; I can eat pork liver cooked over the open fire minutes after it comes steaming from the hog. One winter I knocked a bull calf straight in the brain between the eyes with a sledge hammer and had the meat hung up to chill before nightfall. But of course all this does not show on television. I am the way my daughter would want me to be: a hundred pounds lighter, my skin like an uncooked barley pancake. My hair glistens in the hot bright lights. Johnny Carson has much to do to keep up with my quick and witty tongue.

But that is a mistake. I know even before I wake up. Who ever knew a Johnson with a quick tongue? Who can even imagine me looking a strange white man in the eye? It seems to me I have talked to them always with one foot raised in flight, with my head turned in whichever way is farthest from them. Dee, though. She would always look anyone in the eye. Hesitation was no part of her nature.

"How do I look, Mama?" Maggie says, showing just enough of her thin body enveloped in pink skirt and red blouse for me to know she's there, almost hidden by the door.

"Come out into the yard," I say.

Have you ever seen a lame animal, perhaps a dog run over by some careless person rich enough to own a car, sidle up to someone who is ignorant enough to be kind to him? That is the way my Maggie walks. She has been like this, chin on chest, eyes on ground, feet in shuffle, ever since the fire that burned the other house to the ground.

Dee is lighter than Maggie, with nicer hair and a fuller figure. She's a woman now, though sometimes I forget. How long ago was it that the other house burned? Ten, twelve years? Sometimes I can still hear the flames and feel Maggie's arms sticking to me, her hair smoking and her dress falling off her in little black papery flakes. Her eyes seemed stretched open, blazed open by the flames reflected in them. And Dee. I see her standing off under the sweet gum tree she used to dig gum out of; a look of concentration on her face as she watched the last dingy gray board of the house fall in toward the red-hot brick chimney. Why don't you do a dance around the ashes? I'd wanted to ask her. She had hated the house that much.

I used to think she hated Maggie, too. But that was before we raised the money, the church and me, to send her to Augusta to school. She used to read to us without pity; forcing words, lies, other folks' habits, whole lives upon us two, sitting trapped and ignorant underneath her voice. She washed us in a river of make-believe, burned us with a lot of knowledge we didn't necessarily need to know. Pressed us to her with the serious way she read, to shove us away at just the moment, like dimwits, we seemed about to understand.

Dee wanted nice things. A yellow organdy dress to wear to her graduation from high school; black pumps to match a green suit she'd made from an old suit somebody gave me. She was determined to stare down any disaster in her efforts. Her eyelids would not flicker for minutes at a time. Often I fought off the temptation to shake her. At sixteen she had a style of her own: and knew what style was.

I never had an education myself. After second grade the school was closed down. Don't ask me why: in 1927 colored asked fewer questions than they do now. Sometimes Maggie reads to me. She stumbles along good-naturedly but can't see well. She knows she is not bright. Like good looks and money, quickness passed her by. She will marry John Thomas (who has mossy teeth in an earnest face) and then I'll be free to sit here and I guess just sing church songs to myself. Although I never was a good singer. Never could carry a tune. I was always better at a man's job. I used to love to milk till I was hooked in the side in '49. Cows are soothing and slow and don't bother you, unless you try to milk them the wrong way.

I have deliberately turned my back on the house. It is three rooms, just like the one that burned, except the roof is tin; they don't make shingle roofs any more. There are no real windows, just some holes cut in the sides, like the portholes in a ship, but not round and not square, with rawhide holding the shutters up on the outside. This house is in a pasture, too, like the other one. No doubt when Dee sees it she will want to tear it down. She wrote me once that no matter where we "choose" to live, she will manage to come see us. But she will never bring her friends. Maggie and I thought about this and Maggie asked me, "Mama, when did Dee ever *have* any friends?"

She had a few. Furtive boys in pink shirts hanging about on washday after school. Nervous girls who never laughed. Impressed with her they worshiped the well-turned phrase, the cute shape, the scalding humor that erupted like bubbles in lye. She read to them.

When she was courting Jimmy T she didn't have much time to pay to us, but turned all her faultfinding power on him. He *flew* to marry a cheap city girl from a family of ignorant flashy people. She hardly had time to recompose herself.

When she comes I will meet—but there they are!

Maggie attempts to make a dash for the house, in her shuffling way, but I stay her with my hand. "Come back here," I say. And she stops and tries to dig a well in the sand with her toe.

It is hard to see them clearly through the strong sun. But even the first glimpse of leg out of the car tells me it is Dee. Her feet were always neat-looking, as if God himself had shaped them with a certain style. From the other side of the car comes a short, stocky man. Hair is all over his head a foot long and hanging from his chin like a kinky mule tail. I hear Maggie suck in her breath. "Uhnnnh," is what it sounds like. Like when you see the wriggling end of a snake just in front of your foot on the road. "Uhnnnh."

Dee next. A dress down to the ground, in this hot weather. A dress so loud it hurts my eyes. There are yellows and oranges enough to throw back the light of the sun. I feel my whole face warming from the heat waves it throws out. Earrings gold, too, and hanging down to her shoulders. Bracelets dangling and making noises when she moves her arm up to shake the folds of the dress out of her armpits. The dress is loose and flows, and as she walks closer, I like it. I hear Maggie go "Uhnnnh" again. It is her sister's hair. It stands straight up like the wool on a sheep. It is black as night and around the edges are two long pigtails that rope about like small lizards disappearing behind her ears.

"Wa-su-zo-Tean-o!" she says, coming on in that gliding way the dress makes her move. The short stocky fellow with the hair to his navel is all grinning and he follows up with "Asalamalakim,[1] my mother and sister!" He moves to hug Maggie but she falls back, right up against the back of my chair. I feel her trembling there and when I look up I see the perspiration falling off her chin.

"Don't get up," says Dee. Since I am stout it takes something of a push. You can see me trying to move a second or two before I make it. She turns, showing white heels through her sandals, and goes back to the car. Out she peeks next with a Polaroid. She stoops down quickly and lines up picture after picture of me sitting there in front of the house with Maggie cowering behind me. She never takes a shot without making sure the house is included. When a cow comes nibbling around the edge of the yard she snaps it and me and Maggie *and* the house. Then she puts the Polaroid in the back seat of the car, and comes up and kisses me on the forehead.

Meanwhile Asalamalakim is going through motions with Maggie's hand. Maggie's hand is as limp as a fish, and probably as cold, despite the sweat, and she keeps trying to pull it back. It looks like Asalamalakim wants to shake hands but wants to do it fancy. Or maybe he don't know how people shake hands. Anyhow, he soon gives up on Maggie.

"Well," I say. "Dee."

"No, Mama," she says. "Not 'Dee,' Wangero Leewanika Kemanjo!"

"What happened to 'Dee'?" I wanted to know.

"She's dead," Wangero said. "I couldn't bear it any longer, being named after the people who oppress me."

"You know as well as me you was named after your aunt Dicie," I said. Dicie is my sister. She named Dee. We called her "Big Dee" after Dee was born.

---

1. A Muslim greeting sounded phonetically. Likewise, Wa-su-zo-Tean-o is an African greeting.

"But who was *she* named after?" asked Wangero.

"I guess after Grandma Dee," I said.

"And who was she named after?" asked Wangero.

"Her mother," I said, and saw Wangero was getting tired. "That's about as far back as I can trace it," I said. Though, in fact, I probably could have carried it back beyond the Civil War through the branches.

"Well," said Asalamalakim, "there you are."

"Uhnnnh," I heard Maggie say.

"There I was not," I said, "before 'Dicie' cropped up in our family, so why should I try to trace it that far back?"

He just stood there grinning, looking down on me like somebody inspecting a Model A car. Every once in a while he and Wangero sent eye signals over my head.

"How do you pronounce this name?" I asked.

"You don't have to call me by it if you don't want to," said Wangero.

"Why shouldn't I?" I asked. "If that's what you want us to call you, we'll call you."

"I know it might sound awkward at first," said Wangero.

"I'll get used to it," I said. "Ream it out again."

Well, soon we got the name out of the way. Asalamalakim had a name twice as long and three times as hard. After I tripped over it two or three times he told me to just call him Hakim-a-barber. I wanted to ask him was he a barber, but I didn't really think he was, so I didn't ask.

"You must belong to those beef-cattle peoples down the road," I said. They said "Asalamalakim" when they met you, too, but they didn't shake hands. Always too busy: feeding the cattle, fixing the fences, putting up salt-lick shelters, throwing down hay. When the white folks poisoned some of the herd the men stayed up all night with rifles in their hands. I walked a mile and a half just to see the sight.

Hakim-a-barber said, "I accept some of their doctrines, but farming and raising cattle is not my style." (They didn't tell me, and I didn't ask, whether Wangero (Dee) had really gone and married him.)

We sat down to eat and right away he said he didn't eat collards and pork was unclean. Wangero, though, went on through the chitlins and corn bread, the greens and everything else. She talked a blue streak over the sweet potatoes. Everything delighted her. Even the fact that we still used the benches her daddy made for the table when we couldn't afford to buy chairs.

"Oh, Mama!" she cried. Then turned to Hakim-a-barber. "I never knew how lovely these benches are. You can feel the rump prints," she said, running her hands underneath her and along the bench. Then she gave a sigh and her hand closed over Grandma Dee's butter dish. "That's it!" she said. "I knew there was something I wanted to ask you if I could have." She jumped up from the table and went over in the corner where the churn stood, the milk in it clabber by now. She looked at the churn and looked at it.

"This churn top is what I need," she said. "Didn't Uncle Buddy whittle it out of a tree you all used to have?"

"Yes," I said.

"Uh huh," she said happily. "And I want the dasher, too."

"Uncle Buddy whittle that, too?" asked the barber.

Dee (Wangero) looked up at me.

"Aunt Dee's first husband whittled the dash," said Maggie so low you almost couldn't hear her. "His name was Henry, but they called him Stash."

"Maggie's brain is like an elephant's," Wangero said, laughing. "I can use the churn top as a centerpiece for the alcove table," she said, sliding a plate over the churn, "and I'll think of something artistic to do with the dasher."

When she finished wrapping the dasher the handle stuck out. I took it for a moment in my hands. You didn't even have to look close to see where hands pushing the dasher up and down to make butter had left a kind of sink in the wood. In fact, there were a lot of small sinks; you could see where thumbs and fingers had sunk into the wood. It was beautiful light yellow wood, from a tree that grew in the yard where Big Dee and Stash had lived.

After dinner Dee (Wangero) went to the trunk at the foot of my bed and started rifling through it. Maggie hung back in the kitchen over the dishpan. Out came Wangero with two quilts. They had been pieced by Grandma Dee and then Big Dee and me had hung them on the quilt frames on the front porch and quilted them. One was in the Lone Star pattern. The other was Walk Around the Mountain. In both of them were scraps of dresses Grandma Dee had worn fifty and more years ago. Bits and pieces of Grandpa Jarrell's Paisley shirts. And one teeny faded blue piece, about the size of a penny matchbox, that was from Great Grandpa Ezra's uniform that he wore in the Civil War.

"Mama," Wangero said sweet as a bird. "Can I have these old quilts?"

I heard something fall in the kitchen, and a minute later the kitchen door slammed.

"Why don't you take one or two of the others?" I asked. "These old things was just done by me and Big Dee from some tops your grandma pieced before she died."

"No," said Wangero. "I don't want those. They are stitched around the borders by machine."

"That'll make them last better," I said.

"That's not the point," said Wangero. "These are all pieces of dresses Grandma used to wear. She did all this stitching by hand. Imagine!" She held the quilts securely in her arms, stroking them.

"Some of the pieces, like those lavender ones, come from old clothes her mother handed down to her," I said, moving up to touch the quilts. Dee (Wangero) moved back just enough so that I couldn't reach the quilts. They already belonged to her.

"Imagine!" she breathed again, clutching them closely to her bosom.

"The truth is," I said, "I promised to give them quilts to Maggie, for when she marries John Thomas."

She gasped like a bee had stung her.

"Maggie can't appreciate these quilts!" she said. "She'd probably be backward enough to put them to everyday use."

"I reckon she would," I said. "God knows I been saving 'em for long enough with nobody using 'em. I hope she will!" I didn't want to bring up how I had offered Dee (Wangero) a quilt when she went away to college. Then she had told me they were old-fashioned, out of style.

"But they're *priceless*!" she was saying now, furiously; for she has a temper. "Maggie would put them on the bed and in five years they'd be in rags. Less than that!" "She can always make some more," I said. "Maggie knows how to quilt."

Dee (Wangero) looked at me with hatred. "You just will not understand. The point is these quilts, *these* quilts!"

"Well," I said, stumped. "What would you do with them?"

"Hang them," she said. As if that was the only thing you *could* do with quilts.

Maggie by now was standing in the door. I could almost hear the sound her feet made as they scraped over each other.

"She can have them, Mama," she said, like somebody used to never winning anything, or having anything reserved for her. "I can 'member Grandma Dee without the quilts."

I looked at her hard. She had filled her bottom lip with checker-berry snuff and it gave her face a kind of dopey, hangdog look. It was Grandma Dee and Big Dee who taught her how to quilt herself. She stood there with her scarred hands hidden in the folds of her skirt. She looked at her sister with something like fear but she wasn't mad at her. This was Maggie's portion. This was the way she knew God to work.

When I looked at her like that something hit me in the top of my head and ran down to the soles of my feet. Just like when I'm in church and the spirit of God touches me and I get happy and shout. I did something I never had done before: hugged Maggie to me, then dragged her on into the room, snatched the quilts out of Miss Wangero's hands and dumped them into Maggie's lap. Maggie just sat there on my bed with her mouth open.

"Take one or two of the others," I said to Dee.

But she turned without a word and went out to Hakim-a-barber.

"You just don't understand," she said, as Maggie and I came out to the car.

"What don't I understand?" I wanted to know.

"Your heritage," she said. And then she turned to Maggie, kissed her, and said, "You ought to try to make something of yourself, too, Maggie. It's really a new day for us. But from the way you and Mama still live you'd never know it."

She put on some sunglasses that hid everything above the tip of her nose and her chin.

Maggie smiled; maybe at the sunglasses. But a real smile, not scared.

After we watched the car dust settle I asked Maggie to bring me a dip of snuff. And then the two of us sat there just enjoying, until it was time to go in the house and go to bed.

1973

Further Reading

Walker, Alice. "In Search of Our Mothers' Gardens." *In Search of Our Mothers' Gardens: Womanist Prose.* New York: Harcourt, 1983. 231–43. • Callahan, John F. "The Higher Ground of Alice Walker." *New Republic* 171 (14 Sept. 1974): 21–22. • Baker, Houston A., Jr., and Charlotte Pierce-Baker. "Patches: Quilts and Community in Alice Walker's 'Everyday Use.' " *Southern Review* 21.3 (July 1985): 706–20. • Christian, Barbara. "Alice Walker: The Black Woman Artist as Wayward." *Black Women Writers (1950–1980): A Critical Evaluation.* Ed. Mari Evans. Garden City, N.Y.: Doubleday, 1984. 457–77, spec. 462–63.

The contrast between the way that Dee and her mother view the world in "Everyday Use" comes largely from the differences between them in age, experience, and hardship. In a 1981 interview with Kay Bonetti, Walker discussed a somewhat comparable contrast of age and experience between two renowned singers.

Alice Walker: On Integrity and Experience

I was reading another book yesterday by Ellen Willis, who writes the rock column in *The New Yorker,* and for the *Voice*—the *Village Voice.* Here's a woman who has spent her whole life listening to rock and roll, and loves it, and knows every record ever cut, and so forth. And yet she talks about how it took her years and years and years and years to understand—because she played a Bessie Smith record over and over, and she played one of Bessie's songs called, I think, "Electric Chair Blues"—that Bessie was able to put more energy and more integrity and more substance in one line of that song than Janis Joplin was able to put in all the songs that she sang, and many of them of course were Bessie's songs.

Now why is that?

It certainly can't be said that Janis did not have energy, in her own struggle, you know. But Bessie did have it harder, and did have it longer, and had to really surmount, in her life, the things that really Janis succumbed to. I regret very much that Janis Joplin didn't live to be an old woman. Think of what she would have been able to sing, if she had been an old woman, singing.

LOUISE ERDRICH

(b. 1954)

SNARES

It began after church with Margaret and her small granddaughter, Lulu, and was not to end until the long days of Lent and a hard-packed snow. There were factions on the reservation, a treaty settlement in the Agent's hands. There were Chippewa who signed their names in the year 1924, and there were Chippewa who saw the cash offered as a flimsy bait. I was one and Fleur Pillager, Lulu's mother, was another who would not lift her hand to sign. It was said that all the power to witch, harm, or cure lay in Fleur, the lone survivor of the old Pillager clan. But as much as people feared Fleur, they listened to Margaret Kashpaw. She was the ringleader of the holdouts, a fierce, one-minded widow with a vinegar tongue.

Margaret Kashpaw had knots of muscles in her arms. Her braids were thin, gray as iron, and usually tied strictly behind her back so they wouldn't swing. She was plump as a basket below and tough as roots on top. Her face was gnarled around a beautiful sharp nose. Two shell earrings caught the light and flashed whenever she turned her head. She had become increasingly religious in the years after her loss, and finally succeeded in dragging me to the Benediction Mass, where I was greeted by Father Damien, from whom I occasionally won small sums at dice.

"Grandfather Nanapush," he smiled, "at last."

"These benches are a hardship for an old man," I complained. "If you spread them with soft pine-needle cushions I'd have come before."

Father Damien stared thoughtfully at the rough pews, folded his hands inside the sleeves of his robe.

"You must think of their unyielding surfaces as helpful," he offered. "God sometimes enters the soul through the humblest parts of our anatomies, if they are sensitized to suffering."

"A god who enters through the rear door," I countered, "is no better than a thief."

Father Damien was used to me, and smiled as he walked to the altar. I adjusted my old bones, longing for some relief, trying not to rustle for fear of Margaret's jabbing elbow. The time was long. Lulu probed all my pockets with her fingers until she found a piece of hard candy. I felt no great presence in this cold place and decided, as my back end ached and my shoulders stiffened, that our original gods were better, the Chippewa characters who were not exactly perfect but at least did not require sitting on hard boards.

When mass was over and the smell of incense was thick in all our clothes, Margaret, Lulu, and I went out into the starry cold, the snow and stubble fields, and began the long walk to our homes. It was dusk. On either side of us the heavy trees stood motionless and blue. Our footsteps squeaked against the dry snow, the only sound to hear. We spoke very little, and even Lulu ceased her singing when the moon rose to half, poised like a balanced cup. We knew the very moment someone else stepped upon the road.

We had turned a bend and the footfalls came unevenly, just out of sight. There were two men, one mixed-blood or white, from the drop of his hard boot soles, and the other one quiet, an Indian. Not long and I heard them talking close behind us. From the rough, quick tension of the Indian's language, I recognized Lazarre. And the mixed-blood must be Clarence Morrissey. The two had signed the treaty and spoke in its favor to anyone they could collar at the store. They even came to people's houses to beg and argue that this was our one chance, our good chance, that the government would withdraw the offer. But wherever Margaret was, she slapped down their words like mosquitoes and said the only thing that lasts life to life is land. Money burns like tinder, flows like water. And as for promises, the wind is steadier. It is no wonder that, because she spoke so well, Lazarre and Clarence Morrissey wished to silence her. I sensed their bad intent as they passed us, an unpleasant edge of excitement in their looks and greetings.

They went on, disappeared in the dark brush.

"Margaret," I said, "we are going to cut back." My house was close, but Margaret kept walking forward as if she hadn't heard.

I took her arm, caught the little girl close, and started to turn us, but Margaret would have none of this and called me a coward. She grabbed the girl to her. Lulu, who did not mind getting tossed between us, laughed, tucked her hand into her grandma's pocket, and never missed a step. Two years ago she had tired of being carried, got up, walked. She had the balance of a little mink. She was slippery and clever, too, which was good because when the men jumped from the darkest area of brush and grappled with us half a mile on, Lulu slipped free and scrambled into the trees.

They were occupied with Margaret and me, at any rate. We were old enough to snap in two, our limbs dry as dead branches, but we fought as though our enemies were the Nadouissouix kidnappers of our childhood. Margaret uttered a war cry that had not been heard for fifty years, and bit Lazarre's hand to the bone, giving a wound which would later prove the death of him. As for Clarence, he had all he could do to wrestle me to the ground and knock me half unconscious. When he'd accomplished that, he tied me and tossed me into a wheelbarrow, which was hidden near the road for the purpose of lugging us to the Morrissey barn.

I came to my sense trussed to a manger, sitting on a bale. Margaret was roped to another bale across from me, staring straight forward in a rage, a line of froth caught between her lips. On either side of her, shaggy cows chewed, and shifted their thumping hooves. I rose and staggered, the weight of the manger on my back. I planned on Margaret biting through my ropes with her strong teeth, but then the two men entered.

I'm a talker, a fast-mouth who can't keep his thoughts straight, but lets fly with words and marvels at what he hears from his own mouth. I'm a smart one. I always was a devil for convincing women. And I wasn't too bad a shot, in other ways, at convincing men. But I had never been tied up before.

"*Booshoo*," I said. "Children, let us loose, your game is too rough!"

They stood between us, puffed with their secrets.

"Empty old windbag," said Clarence.

"I have a bargain for you," I said, looking for an opening. "Let us go and we won't tell Pukwan." Edgar Pukwan was the tribal police. "Boys get drunk sometimes and don't know what they're doing."

Lazarre laughed once, hard and loud. "We're not drunk," he said. "Just wanting what's coming to us, some justice, money out of it."

"Kill us," said Margaret. "We won't sign."

"Wait," I said. "My cousin Pukwan will find you boys, and have no mercy. Let us go. I'll sign and get it over with, and I'll persuade the old widow."

I signaled Margaret to keep her mouth shut. She blew air into her cheeks. Clarence looked expectantly at Lazarre, as if the show were over, but Lazarre folded his arms and was convinced of nothing.

"You lie when it suits, skinny old dog," he said, wiping at his lips as if in hunger. "It's her we want, anyway. We'll shame her so she shuts her mouth."

"Easy enough," I said, smooth, "now that you've got her tied. She's plump and good-looking. Eyes like a doe! But you forget that we're together, almost man and wife."

This wasn't true at all, and Margaret's face went rigid with tumbling fury and confusion. I kept talking.

"So of course if you do what you're thinking of doing you'll have to kill me afterward, and that will make my cousin Pukwan twice as angry since I owe him a fat payment for a gun which he lent me and I never returned. All the same," I went on—their heads were spinning—"I'll forget you bad boys ever considered such a crime, something so terrible that Father Damien would nail you on boards just like in the example on the wall in church."

"Quit jabbering," Lazarre stopped me in a deadly voice.

It was throwing pebbles in a dry lake. My words left no ripple. I saw in his eyes that he intended us great harm. I saw his greed. It was like watching an ugly design of bruises come clear for a moment and reconstructing the evil blows that made them.

I played my last card.

"Whatever you do to Margaret you are doing to the Pillager woman!" I dropped my voice. "The witch, Fleur Pillager, is her own son's wife."

Clarence was too young to be frightened, but his mouth hung in interested puzzlement. My words had a different effect on Lazarre, as a sudden light shone, a consequence he hadn't considered.

I cried out, seeing this, "Don't you know she can think about you hard enough to stop your heart?" Lazarre was still deciding. He raised his fist and swung it casually and tapped my face. It was worse not to be hit full on.

"Come near!" crooned Margaret in the old language. "Let me teach you how to die."

But she was trapped like a fox. Her earrings glinted and spun as she hissed her death song over and over, which signaled something to Lazarre, for he shook himself angrily and drew a razor from his jacket. He stropped it with fast, vicious movements while Margaret sang shriller, so full of hate that the ropes should have burned, shriveled, fallen from her body. My struggle set the manger cracking against the barn walls and further confused the cows, who bumped each other and complained. At a sign from Lazarre, Clarence sighed, rose, and smashed me. The last I saw before I blacked out, through the tiny closing pinhole of light, was Lazarre approaching Margaret with the blade.

When I woke, minutes later, it was to worse shock. For Lazarre had sliced Margaret's long braids off and was now, carefully, shaving her scalp. He started almost tenderly at the wide part, and then pulled the edge down each side of her skull. He did a clean job. He shed not one drop of her blood.

And I could not even speak to curse them. For pressing my jaw down, thick above my tongue, her braids, never cut in this life till now, were tied to silence me. Powerless, I tasted their flat, animal perfume.

It wasn't much later, or else it was forever, that we walked out into the night again. Speechless, we made our way in fierce pain down the road. I was damaged in spirit, more so than Margaret. For now she tucked her shawl over her naked head and forgot her own bad treatment. She called out in dread each foot of the way, for Lulu. But the smart, bold girl had hidden till all was clear and then run to Margaret's house. We opened the door and found her sitting by the stove in a litter of scorched matches and kindling. She had not the skill to start a fire, but she was dry-eyed. Though very cold, she was alert and then captured with wonder when Margaret slipped off her shawl.

"Where is your hair?" she asked.

I took my hand from my pocket. "Here's what's left of it. I grabbed this when they cut me loose." I was shamed by how pitiful I had been, relieved when Margaret snatched the thin gray braids from me and coiled them round her fist.

"I knew you would save them, clever man!" There was satisfaction in her voice.

I set the fire blazing. It was strange how generous this woman was to me, never blaming me or mentioning my failure. Margaret stowed her braids inside a birchbark box and merely instructed me to lay it in her grave, when that time occurred. Then she came near the stove with a broken mirror from beside her washstand and looked at her own image.

"My," she pondered, "my." She put the mirror down. "I'll take a knife to them."

And I was thinking too. I was thinking I would have to kill them.

But how does an aching and half-starved grandfather attack a young, well-fed Morrissey and a tall, sly Lazarre? Later, I rolled up in blankets in the corner by Margaret's stove, and I put my mind to this question throughout that night until, exhausted, I slept. And I thought of it first thing next morning, too, and still nothing came. It was only after we had some hot *gaulette* and walked Lulu back to her mother that an idea began to grow.

Fleur let us in, hugged Lulu into her arms, and looked at Margaret, who took off her scarf and stood bald, face burning again with smoldered fire. She told Fleur all of what happened, sparing no detail. The two women's eyes held, but Fleur said nothing. She put Lulu down, smoothed the front of her calico shirt, flipped her heavy braids over her shoulders, tapped one finger on her perfect lips. And then, calm, she went to the washstand and scraped the edge of her hunting knife keen as glass. Margaret and Lulu and I watched as Fleur cut her braids off, shaved her own head, and folded the hair into a quilled skin pouch. Then she went out, hunting, and didn't bother to wait for night to cover her tracks.

I would have to go out hunting too.

I had no gun, but anyway that was a white man's revenge. I knew how to wound with barbs of words, but had never wielded a skinning knife against a human, much less two young men. Whomever I missed would kill me, and I did not want to die by their lowly hands.

In fact, I didn't think that after Margaret's interesting kindness I wanted to leave this life at all. Her head, smooth as an egg, was ridged delicately with bone, and gleamed as if it had been buffed with a flannel cloth. Maybe it was the strangeness that attracted me. She looked forbidding, but the absence of hair also set off her eyes, so black and full of lights. She reminded me of that queen from England, of a water snake or a shrewd young bird. The earrings, which seemed part of her, mirrored her moods like water, and when they were still rounds of green lights against her throat I seemed, again, to taste her smooth, smoky braids in my mouth.

I had better things to do than fight. So I decided to accomplish revenge as quickly as possible. I was a talker who used my brains as my weapon. When I hunted, I preferred to let my game catch itself.

Snares demand clever fingers and a scheming mind, and snares had never failed me. Snares are quiet, and best of all snares are slow. I wanted to give Lazarre and Morrissey time to consider why they had to strangle. I thought hard. One- or two-foot deadfalls are required beneath a snare so that a man can't put his hand up and loosen the knot. The snares I had in mind also required something stronger than a cord, which could be broken, and finer than a rope, which even Lazarre might see and avoid. I pondered this closely, yet even so I might never have found the solution had I not gone to mass with Margaret and grown curious about the workings of Father Damien's pride and joy, the piano in the back of the church, the instrument whose keys he breathed on, polished, then played after services, and sometimes alone. I had noticed that his hands usually stayed near the middle of the keyboard, so I took the wires from either end.

In the meantime, I was not the only one concerned with punishing Lazarre and Clarence Morrissey. Fleur was seen in town. Her thick skirts brushed the snow into clouds behind her. Though it was cold she left her head bare so everyone could see the frigid sun glare off her skull. The light reflected in the eyes of Lazarre and Clarence, who were standing at the door of the pool hall. They dropped their cue sticks in the slush and ran back to Morrissey land. Fleur walked the four streets, once in each direction, then followed.

The two men told of her visit, how she passed through the Morrissey house touching here, touching there, sprinkling powders that ignited and stank on the hot stove. How Clarence swayed on his feet, blinked hard, and chewed his fingers. How Fleur stepped up to him, drew her knife. He smiled foolishly and asked her for supper. She reached forward and trimmed off a hank of his hair. Then she stalked from the house, leaving a taste of cold wind, and then chased Lazarre to the barn.

She made a black silhouette against the light from the door. Lazarre pressed against the wood of the walls, watching, hypnotized by the sight of Fleur's head and the quiet blade. He did not defend himself when she approached, reached for him, gently and efficiently cut bits of his hair, held his hands, one at a time, and trimmed the nails. She waved the razor-edged knife before his eyes and swept a few eyelashes into a white square of flour sacking that she then carefully folded into her blouse.

For days after, Lazarre babbled and wept. Fleur was murdering him by use of bad medicine, he said. He showed his hand, the bite that Margaret had dealt him, and the dark streak from the wound, along his wrist and inching up his arm. He even used that bound hand to scratch his name from the treaty, but it did no good.

I figured that the two men were doomed at least three ways now. Margaret won the debate with her Catholic training and decided to damn her soul by taking up the ax, since no one else had destroyed her enemies. I begged her to wait for another week, all during which it snowed and thawed and snowed again. It took me that long to arrange the snare to my satisfaction, near Lazarre's shack, on a path both men took to town.

I set it out one morning before anyone stirred, and watched from an old pine twisted along the ground. I waited while the smoke rose in a silky feather from the tiny tin spout on Lazarre's roof. I had to sit half a day before Lazarre came outside, and even then it was just for wood, nowhere near the path. I had a hard time to keep my blood flowing, my stomach still. I ate a handful of dry berries Margaret had given me, and a bit of pounded meat. I doled it to myself and waited until finally Clarence showed. He walked the trail like a blind ghost and stepped straight into my noose.

It was perfect, or would have been if I had made the deadfall two inches wider, for in falling Clarence somehow managed to spread his legs and straddle the deep hole I'd cut. It had been invisible, covered with snow, and yet in one foot-peddling instant, the certain knowledge of its construction sprang into Clarence's brain and told his legs to reach for the sides. I don't know how he did it, but there he was poised. I waited, did not show myself. The noose jerked enough to cut slightly into the fool's neck, a too-snug fit. He was spread-eagled and on tiptoe, his arms straight out. If he twitched a finger, lost the least control, even tried to yell, one foot would go, the noose constrict.

But Clarence did not move. I could see from behind my branches that he didn't even dare to change the expression on his face. His mouth stayed frozen in shock. Only his eyes shifted, darted fiercely and wildly, side to side, showing all the agitation he must not release, searching desperately for a means of escape. They focused only when I finally stepped toward him, quiet, from the pine.

We were in full view of Lazarre's house, face to face. I stood before the boy. Just a touch, a sudden kick, perhaps no more than a word, was all that it would take. But I looked into his eyes and saw the knowledge of his situation. Pity entered me. Even for Margaret's shame, I couldn't do the thing I might have done.

I turned away and left Morrissey still balanced on the ledge of snow.

What money I did have, I took to the trading store next day. I bought the best bonnet on the reservation. It was black as a coal scuttle, large, and shaped the same.

"It sets off my doe eyes," Margaret said and stared me down.

She wore it every day, and always to mass. Not long before Lent and voices could be heard: "There goes Old Lady Coalbucket." Nonetheless, she was proud, and softening day by day, I could tell. By the time we got our foreheads crossed with ashes, she consented to be married.

"I hear you're thinking of exchanging the vows," said Father Damien as I shook his hand on our way out the door.

"I'm having relations with Margaret already," I told him, "that's the way we do things."

This had happened to him before, so he was not even stumped as to what remedy he should use.

"Make a confession, at any rate," he said, motioning us back into the church.

So I stepped into the little box and knelt. Father Damien slid aside the shadowy door. I told him what I had been doing with Margaret and he stopped me partway through.

"No more details. Pray to Our Lady."

"There is one more thing."

"Yes?"

"Clarence Morrissey, he wears a scarf to church around his neck each week. I snared him like a rabbit."

Father Damien let the silence fill him.

"And the last thing," I went on. "I stole the wire from your piano."

The silence spilled over into my stall, and I was held in its grip until the priest spoke.

"Discord is hateful to God. You have offended his ear." Almost as an afterthought, Damien added, "And his commandment. The violence among you must cease."

"You can have the wire back," I said. I had used only one long strand. I also agreed that I would never use my snares on humans, an easy promise. Lazarre was already caught.

Just two days later, while Margaret and I stood with Lulu and her mother inside the trading store, Lazarre entered, gesturing, his eyes rolled to the skull. He stretched forth his arm and pointed along its deepest black vein and dropped his jaw wide. Then he stepped backward into a row of traps that the trader had set to show us how they worked. Fleur's eye lit, her white scarf caught the sun as she turned. All the whispers were true. Fleur had scratched Lazarre's figure into a piece of birchbark, drawn his insides, and rubbed a bit of rouge up his arm until the red stain reached his heart. There was no sound as he fell, no cry, no word, and the traps of all types that clattered down around his body jumped and met for a long time, snapping air.

1987

Further Reading

Berkley, Miriam. "*Publisher's Weekly* Interviews: Louise Erdrich." *Publisher's Weekly* 230.7 (15 Aug. 1986): 58–59. • Strouse, Jean. "In the Heart of the Heartland." *New York Times Book Review* 2 Oct. 1988: 1ff. • Flavin, Louise. "Louise Erdrich's *Love Medicine*: Loving Over Time and Distance." *Critique* 31.1 (Fall 1989): 55–64. • Magalaner, Marvin. "Louise Erdrich: Of Cars, Time, and the River." *American Women Writing Fiction*. Ed. Mickey Pearlman. Lexington: UP of Kentucky, 1988. 94–112.

We typically think of the fiction writer as a person who works out his or her fictional world in isolation, but Louise Erdrich and her husband, Michael Dorris, are successful novelists and short story writers who work in close cooperation. Dorris says that "nothing goes out of the house without the other person saying that this is the best way to say it." Erdrich explained the process to an interviewer for Publisher's Weekly.

Louise Erdrich: On Collaborative Writing

We'll be talking about a character or a scenario and one of us will write a draft: a sentence, a paragraph, a page, a chapter. Then the other person takes it and goes over it with a red pencil. The person who wrote the draft takes it back, tries again, sometimes four or five drafts' worth, until in the case of all three books [Erdrich's two novels and Dorris's forthcoming one], we sit down and read them aloud over a period of a week or so, and do the final paring and achieve consensus, on, literally, every word.

In the course of it, we'll continuously plot and continuously talk about who the characters are, what they eat, what clothes they wear, what their favorite colors are and what's going to happen to them. In that way, I think it's a true kind of collaboration: we both really influence the course of the book. We can't look back and say which one made it go this way or that way, because you can't remember. You just remember that you had that exciting conversation.

LEIGH ALLISON WILSON

(b. 1957)

THE RAISING

1

Of the eight matrons perched like pigeons around two identical card tables, Mrs. Bertram Eastman was the lone childless woman. Her husband, in whom—she was sure—the fault lay, only confounded this burden she'd borne for thirty years, fixing a funny look on his face every time the subject came up and saying, in a voice soft as solemnity itself, "Spare the child and spare the rod, Mrs. Eastman." But he was like that, a nitwit, and half the time she never knew what he was talking about. Still, being a woman of industry, Mrs. Eastman took up the slack of impotence by becoming an expert on children and motherhood. She was renowned in the gin rummy set, in the Daughters of the Confederacy set, and perhaps in the whole area of East Tennessee, renowned and widely quoted for her running commentary on child-rearing.

"A child is like a new boot," she'd say and pause with the dramatic flair of a born talker. "You take that boot and wear it and at first it blisters your foot, pains you all over, but the time comes it fits like a glove and you got a dutiful child on your hands." What she had missed in experience, Mrs. Eastman overcame with pithy insight; what she lacked as human collateral in a world of procreation, Mrs. Eastman guaranteed with sheer volume. She was a specialist in armchair mothering.

A steady hum of a general nature had settled over the women playing at both tables, punctuated by an occasional snap of a card, but like a foghorn in the midst of a desert the voice of Mrs. Eastman rose and fell in every ear. She was explaining, for the third time since seven o'clock, the circumstances that led to Little Darryl, the Melungeon orphan boy, who would come to live at her house the very next morning. A child! In her own home! She couldn't get over it. Her brain worked at the idea with a violence akin to despair turning upside-down and her hair, from some internal cue, dropped onto her forehead a large, stiff curl that flopped from side to side as if to let off steam. Mrs. Eastman, although not fat, was a formidable personage, stout and big-boned and not unlike the bouncer in a hard-bitten country bar. Mr. Eastman was the tiniest man in Hawklen County. Just yesterday he had come home and told her, out of the blue, that he was bringing Little Darryl out from Eastern State and into their home—one two three and like a bolt of electricity she was a mother. She couldn't get over it.

Little Darryl was thirteen years old and of "origin unknown," a poor abandoned charity case dumped from orphanage to orphanage since the day his faceless mother—unfit and unwed, Mrs. Eastman knew for a certainty—dropped him off in the middle of the canned-goods section of the Surgoinsville A&P. He was discovered beside the creamed corn, eating an unhealthy peanut butter and jelly sandwich. The "origin unknown" part delighted Mrs. Eastman: Little Darryl would be *her* child, sprung as mysteriously and as certainly into her care as a baby of her own making. O, she would make a lawyer out of him, distill the taint of his blood like meltwater. She would recreate the boy in her own image and watch him tower among men in her old age.

"Smart as a *whip*, the social worker told Mr. Eastman," Mrs. Eastman said in a loud, confidential voice. At her table were old Mrs. Cowan, the Methodist preacher's wife; Mrs. Jenkins, the wife of the Jenkins Hardware Jenkinses; and Mrs. Talley, wife of Hubert Talley, the local butcher. Mrs. Eastman had given each one advice, off and on, for thirty years, from Mrs. Talley's redheaded boy who was thirty years old and no good, right down to Mrs. Jenkins's six-year-old who still sucked her thumb and was a "mistake."

"You said that ten minutes ago, Eloise," Mrs. Jenkins told Mrs. Eastman, "and you said he was a genius before that." Mrs. Jenkins was playing

North to Mrs. Eastman's South. "You said he was a genius that wasn't understood and you ain't even met him yet."

"Made him a lawyer already, too," said Mrs. Talley, looking calmly over Mrs. Jenkins's shoulder, her lips screwed up in concentration.

"Ida Mae Talley!" cried Mrs. Jenkins. "Put you in the East and straightway you cheat left and right."

"For your general information," Mrs. Eastman said and tossed her curl, like a hook, back up into her beehive hairdo, "for your edification, Little Darryl scored in the 'excessively bright' range on three different tests."

"I am most certainly not cheating," said Mrs. Talley. "I seen those kings three minutes ago."

"God loves all the little children, smart and stupid, black and white," old Mrs. Cowan said with a smile so bright that her lips appeared to retreat back into her gums. She was the simple-minded member of the women's club although, somehow, her children had grown up to be wildly successful bankers and businessmen in the county, as if to intimate that children, even life, were too muddled a factor to control entirely. For this reason old Mrs. Cowan said nothing that was really heard, did nothing that was really seen, and existed in the main as a hand in gin rummy, or as a how-de-do on the Methodist Church steps every Sunday morning. She was incapable of taking sound advice, given in good faith, by even the best of friends. Deep in her bowels Mrs. Eastman believed her to be the most wicked woman of her acquaintance, the most deceitful as well as the most dangerous, and to hold, somewhere behind her idiocy, a hidden ace in the hole.

"God may be well and good on Sundays," Mrs. Eastman said, leveling her eyes like shotgun bores toward old Mrs. Cowan's western position. "But God Hisself don't have to raise no boy geniuses at a moment's notice. Pass me one of those green mints, Vivian." She stretched her free hand toward Mrs. Jenkins. "The white ones give me the morning sickness."

"They come in the same box, Eloise. Green and white. In the same damn box." Mrs. Jenkins, whose mints and home provided this evening's entertainment for the club, shut her cards with a click, laid them carefully facedown on the table, then folded her arms like hemp cord and stared at Mrs. Eastman. She looked ready to pounce in panther fashion across the table, to defend her territory with a beast's wit. Mrs. Eastman had on her patient expression, the one she recommended for children with colic.

"I only meant to point out that I *read* somewheres that they put more dye in the white mints than they do in the green, that's all. They start out gray and add twice't the dye to turn them white. Scientific fact. Twenty schoolchildren alone have died in Detroit, Michigan, from a pound of white mints. Now think about *that*."

"All I know," said Mrs. Jenkins, rising clumsily from her chair, "is we've had these same mints for fifteen years and I never heard a word till now. I'm going to put whip cream on my Jell-O if you'll excuse me."

"I didn't read it till last week," Mrs. Eastman called over her shoulder, then she lowered her voice until only the whole room could hear: "Don't either of you tell a dead man, but she's on par*ticu*lar edge tonight strictly because her boy was found pig drunk, with a hair ribbon in his mouth, underneath the II-E overpass. No clothes on him anywhere."

"O," said old Mrs. Cowan. "He was the finest acolyte our church ever had."

"No more he ain't," Mrs. Eastman said happily. "Comes of no discipline."

"Now, now," Mrs. Talley said, watching herself thumb through Mrs. Jenkins's cards. "You ain't exactly the one, Eloise"—here she paused to exchange one of her cards with one in the other pile—"you ain't exactly the one to pass judgment on a drunk, now are you?"

"Well, Mrs. Ida *Mae* Talley." Mrs. Eastman sneered on the "Mae." "Are you sinuating that my husband is a drunk?"

"That's for you to know, Eloise," she said, "and me to hear over coffee."

The truth of the matter was that, although Mr. Eastman sat in his law office with the door shut to clients and associates alike and drank corn whiskey from a Dixie cup, reading obscure poetry and even more obscure philosophy from dusty, dead-looking bindings, he was not a drunk. He was merely partial to alcohol, had told Mrs. Eastman more than once that he and whiskey were blood-related, on better terms with one another than anyone living or dead he'd ever known. Mrs. Eastman believed him through a rare faculty of reflexive apathy, a sixth sense she applied to all situations beyond her ken and control. Once, when Mr. Eastman brought home a litter of eight mongrel dogs, payment for services rendered from one of his poverty clients (who were the only ones he seemed to have, crowded into his office anteroom with chickens and moonshine and quart jars full of pennies clutched under their arms, the room always a three-ring circus to the point that each newly hired legal secretary had but to walk in the door before she quit and walked back out), Mrs. Eastman, in a reflex as immediate as a sneeze, stepped on the dogs' tails, ate the dogs' fur in her potatoes and greens, got nipped on the calves in the middle of dogfights, and she never knew the difference. The dogs existed only as the vaguest of doubts in her mind, much as the person and behavior of Mr. Eastman, and eventually, one by one, the dogs skulked emphatically from the premises and trotted off westward, as if in search of something that either would caress them passionately or kick them viciously. Leave bad enough alone, Mrs. Eastman always said, as well as, Never look a gifted horse in the mouth.

"Leave bad enough alone *I* always say," Mrs. Eastman told Mrs. Talley. "If I had a boy thirty year old and still at home, I wouldn't make no sinuations on nobody else."

"The best, O! O!" said old Mrs. Cowan, almost luringly. "The best acolyte we ever had."

Both women stared at her.

"Attention ladies!" Mrs. Jenkins called from the kitchen door. She held a tray of eight green Jell-O molds, each topped with pear-shaped smidgens of whipped cream. "Laura June here wants to say goodnight," she said. "Say goodnight, Laura June." Laura June, who was under the tray in her mother's hands, just stood and looked stupidly at the seven crooked smiles fastened maternally on the faces of the women's club. Under her arm showed the hind legs and tail of a tabby cat, and she wore a pink nightgown, hiked up at the waist from the furious squirms of the cat. Because her thumb was plunged up to the knuckle into her mouth, Laura June had difficulty saying goodnight, so she just stood and stared, stupidly, at all the smiles.

"That there is what I call a real teddy bear," Mrs. Talley said sweetly. "What's that there teddy bear's name, honey?"

Laura June turned her head in the direction of Mrs. Talley, squinting her eyes, and the cat, as though synchronized puppetlike to her movements, turned its head around and squinted at the women with two uneven green eyes that matched the color of the Jell-O. One of its eyes had an ugly yellow pustule on the rim, making the whole eye look like an open wound in the act of rankling. Laura June unplugged her mouth long enough to say "Name's Darryl Lee Roy," then she quickly plugged the thumb back, as if any second something more important might fall out into the open.

"Why isn't that just the cutest thing!" Mrs. Eastman cried and clapped her hands in the air over the card table. "Come over here, honey, Mama Eastman has a secret for you." Laura June stayed put; the cat blinked its eyes and only one of them opened again. It appeared to be winking suggestively at Mrs. Eastman. "I have a little boy coming to my house that has the very same name," she said. "Little Darryl."

"Time for Laura June to go to bed," said Mrs. Jenkins. "Go to bed, Laura June." Laura June turned obediently toward a door across the room and stalked stiff-legged across the wooden slats with the cat's head bouncing behind her like a gibbous growth. At the door she stopped, facing the room, and caught Mrs. Eastman's eye. There was an expression of malignancy on her face. She dropped the thumb and the hand wandered with a will of its own to the side of her face where it started to scratch a cheek. It might have been a large, pink spider dropped incredibly there to spin a cobweb.

"It's a lie!" she shouted abruptly and the cat meowed and then both were gone into the dark recesses of the house.

2

The mountains spliced at the southernmost tip of the city limits, then diverged northward to form the east and west boundaries of Hawklenville where Mr. Bertram Eastman lived. An ambitious person could climb to the top of that southern splice—named Devil's Nose by the first Methodist settlers—could sit on one of the numerous granite slabs found there, and he would notice that the town appears to be a discolored blemish in the middle of a dark green arrowhead. If that person were ambitious indeed, he would climb a tree and see the land beyond the mountains, land welling out for miles, green with tobacco, brown with freshly tilled soil, and still farther, the cusp of something huge and dusky-blue. But he would see no people. Though these mountains were the town's sole measure of eminent height, a stranger well-versed in the world would point out that they were only foothills, mere knurls in the great body of the Appalachians. Still, from their summits, one could see no people. They are *that* high, Mr. Eastman often said, but quietly and mostly to himself, they are high enough.

From his small back porch, or from what might have been a porch had he chosen to call it one, preferring the word *veranda* because it "sounded like a sigh," Mr. Eastman was watching the last tendrils of light skid away over the top of the mountains. Mr. Eastman, a man not balding but bald, sat in a plastic lawn chair and sipped corn whiskey from a Dixie cup. His shoulders cocked slightly forward and his head tilted slightly backward, giving him the appearance (as the more flexible gossips of the town were quick to mimic) of neither coming nor going. At the moment, though, he was poised over a precipice, at the edge of something, and somehow the boy, Little Darryl, was the nub to which his mind clung. Tomorrow he would come and tomorrow something—he didn't know what—something would happen, for tomorrow Little Darryl would come.

Beads of sweat, tiny as dewdrops, eased from the crown of his head and slid unhindered down the back of his neck. So quickly did they fall, and so brazenly, they could have been the tears of a brokenhearted old woman too tired for pretense. Night had fallen and the mountains crouched against the sky, darker even than the night.

Experience had taught Mr. Eastman that the mountains themselves were deceptive, mute purveyors of nothing but bulk. To the tourist, as he had been when he first brought his wife to the town, they were beautiful, rumpled across the horizon like an immense and living snake. He recalled an incident from those earlier days. They had been walking down Main Street, he and his newly-wed wife, he arm in arm with a woman who was so striking and so lovely, all the more so because of her height and his lack of it, that he thought he might be crushed under the weight of his own pride. They had walked in silence for many minutes, nodding sociably at the passerby, when he noticed the mountains around them, as though for the first time.

"They are like a great undulating serpent, Eloise," he told her, and he was trying to profess his love for her and for their new home. Her eyes almost the color of ripe raspberries, she looked first at the mountains, then down at him, and she stared into his face with an expression that may have been utter tenderness. At last she fluttered her eyelashes and, looking vaguely toward the mountains, said: "Do tell." The mountains were no longer beautiful to Mr. Eastman, hadn't been perhaps from the incident on:

and neither was his wife. No longer did he see the mountains surge upward as living things, no longer was the town, nor the county of Hawklen, a place where north and south and west and east converged into only one thing: the place to be. He had been deceived.

This boy, this Little Darryl, would be his salvation.

"Yoo-hoo!" came his wife's voice through the entranceway, through the hallway, through the kitchen and onto the back veranda where he started, like a frightened sparrow, in the lawn chair. "I'm home!"

Mr. Eastman bent down and set his Dixie cup on the floor, then he placed his hands, one grottoed in the bowl of the other, into his lap. Patiently, keenly, like a man for whom time was as yet unborn, he waited to be found out by his wife. An excess of amplified noise, her greeting was meant for the house and not for him, but in a short time she would work her way through every room until she found him out. She was tenacious in that way, could find anything lost, stolen, or converted, except the truth. She had a gift of activity at its most inessential whereabouts, a kind of feverish sprinting in place that left her wrung-out and triumphant and as blind as a newt. Mr. Eastman believed he was safe from her, his wife of thirty years, because, when you got right down to it, she didn't know shit from apple butter; and without distinctions the rage to live was merely a delirious murmur. Despite the sounds of a bull ox, Mrs. Eastman, he felt, was a murmurer.

"*There* you are," Mrs. Eastman said and poked her head between the screen door and the door frame. It hung there in space like a giant full moon whose face had a coarse, sketchy expression. The least cloud would obscure any resemblance to humanity it may have had. Or so it seemed to Mr. Eastman who sat quietly with his hands in his lap.

"Here I am," Mr. Eastman said.

Here and there across the backyard a group of crickets screeched to one another in duets, in off-beat duets, in those insistent and eerie cries of utterly invisible creatures involved in communication. *Cheezit!* they said. *Cheezit!*

"Listen to those bugs," Mrs. Eastman said and stepped onto the veranda. She let the screen door slam shut behind her, its springs squealing, and the crickets paused for a measure, then started back up again. With her hands fastened securely onto her hips, elbows akimbo, she peered out into the backyard in order to pin down the source of the sound coming from everywhere and nowhere. "I declare they sound like they're in painful love. Bugs do fall in love and set up house together just like anybody. It's nature is what it is." Mr. Eastman said nothing and sat tight, as if he were just hanging in a closet without any insides; he wanted to pat his wife kindly on the cheek or else smack her very hard in the middle of her face. But he did nothing at all, could have been dead except for the heart pounding madly between the places he breathed.

"Buddy Ruth Quarles run off this morning with that retarded taxicab driver. Took almost everything they owned. In case you're interested."

She slapped and killed a periwinkle green insect, then continued on in a cheerful tone. A dollop of hair ticked coquettishly onto her forehead. "Took the TV, took the radio, took the silverware. Took the sofa and the phonograph. Took ever light bulb in the house. Didn't take that half-grown boy of hers. Last anybody saw of Mr. Quarles, he took off down II-E with a butcher knife, wearing a pair of socks and green pants. He had to borrow the butcher knife. Mr. Eastman, are you listening to me?"

"No, Mrs. Eastman," he said. "I am not."

"Ida Mae said she hadn't known the taxicab driver but three weeks, and him so simple to begin with. They did it with a U-Haul hitched to the taxicab."

"Mrs. Eastman," said Mr. Eastman.

"Can't figure out, though, what she *sees* in him. He had that wart in the corner of his eye. Puckered and bobbed ever time he opened his mouth. I can't figure it. And him so simple too."

Mr. Eastman reached for his Dixie cup, squinting out into the night settled over his yard. It appeared to him to be the inside of a huge window-less box set on its side out in the middle of nowhere. The stars, pricking out relentlessly, didn't fit into his picture.

"I foretold it long ago. Time and again I said, If he don't kill her first, he won't never know where she'll be or what she's doing there. I foretold it twice in the past two years. If she's not six feet under, I said, no telling where she is. There you have it."

"Perhaps she's happy, Mrs. Eastman."

"Well *I like that*!" Mrs. Eastman cried and stomped three paces to the edge of the veranda, then stomped the three paces back. She was furious, looking at him as she might at some bear who still hibernated in the chafe of summer, and her hair bristled like burs along the top of her head. "Happy, Mr. Eastman, is what those bugs have. Any *nor*mal human being might know that already. Any *nor*mal human being might know that happy is a word the government made up. What will our son think? I'll tell you what he'll think, he'll think his daddy's shoes are too little to grow into, that's what. You'll be a stigmatism to him all the days of his life!"

Again, Mr. Eastman sat tight. Thought and action in his wife, usually by tongue but sometimes otherwise, were almost simultaneous in her, rather like thunder and lightning, and Mr. Eastman was forever surprised by the coincidence. For him there was by necessity a gap between the two, first deep thought and much later decisive action. And it was true: it had taken him thirty years to secure a son.

"Do you hear me, Bertram Eastman?" she asked. Stomping up and back, her hair at loose ends, her shadow stomping crabbed and backward behind her through the light from the house, she made Mr. Eastman want to shout; want to scream out madly; made him want to take the box of his backyard and the night and his wife and fling the whole of them over that impenetrable black scar of the mountains. Instead he said absolutely noth-ing and, too, the silence within him grew absolute.

"Do you *hear* me?"

"I hear you very well, Mrs. Eastman."

"Our son is a responsibility. He's a responsibility for bad and for worse, for sickness and disease, forever and forever, till the dead do us part. He's responsibility is what this boy's made of."

"I know what little boys are made of," he said, raising himself to leave. So soaked with sweat was the back of his collar that it crept toward his collarbone and felt like a cold hand at his throat. Out in the yard the crickets seemed to have gone mad in the interim of their conversation. *Cheezit!* *cheezit! cheezit!* they sang. Cheee-*zit!* If his wife said anything, he couldn't hear her for the crickets.

3

Little Darryl's people, the Melungeons, came from Goins Hollow, a cul-de-sac at the base of Devil's Nose from whence there was only one exit: a deep green bottleneck steeped in poison ivy and ridden with underbrush and so utterly hidden that the inhabitants themselves were known to leave and never return, set suddenly adrift in the outside world. Brown-eyed and maize-colored, they wedlocked themselves, cheated on themselves, coalesced with abandon, and produced either geniuses or idiots. They had no in-betweens. They loved each other or they killed each other, and still they endured in Goins Hollow; their endurance preceded the first Methodist settlers by many hand-counted years. On a vivid autumn day the smoke of their fires, beckoning upward like unformed fingers, was clearly visible from the town of Hawklenville, but not one soul in Hawklenville ever looked at it.

The Melungeon blood, although not their experience, was fecund as a loam in the body of Little Darryl, the orphan, and by the age of five he knew the appetites of a very old man. He knew when to lie outright and when to tell a lie honestly, when to cheat and when to win fairly. He knew when to be given and when to steal someone blind. He even knew when to attack a problem face-forward, and when to beat a noble retreat into the next county. He was thirteen years old, of a conspicuous unknown origin, and he had lived in nine separate orphanages, one of which burned down mysteriously.

"They got the papers that's stuck to me," Little Darryl told the orphan boys who sat roosting on the next cot, "and there ain't nothing but for me to go with them. They got the papers."

"You could burn them papers," suggested the littlest boy, writhing himself in embarrassment so that the row of boys tilted sideways like a wave washing through. Each little boy had a scar of some kind on some part of his body, and each boy loved Little Darryl with a passion that drew blood. He had seen to that.

"You would, would you," said Little Darryl and leaned over and flipped the littlest boy's nose until he bellowed out. "They got the machines that can resurrect a million a me. You burn one paper and they make ten more. You burn ten papers and they fill a library with them. You burn down a library and they fill the whole shittin' world with paper. They got you up one side and down the other."

"You could run away from here," a boy with a cauliflower ear said, "could run to Kingdom Come from here."

The littlest boy sniffed and said: "That's what I meant back then."

"I already done that once't," Little Darryl said. "They come at me with three cop cars and six guns. They had the papers that's stuck to me. The highest mountain and the lowest hole, they got you if they got them papers that they think is you."

"*I* don't have no papers on *me*," said the boy with a cauliflower ear. He let out a yell and thumped his chest to prove himself. All the little boys fell to scuffling, then they cheered and the cot skittered a few inches along the floor.

"It's because you ain't never done nothing worth the proving of it," Little Darryl said and smacked the boy on his cauliflower ear. They all settled down after that.

"These here people I ain't never seen nor seen their house might think they know what my paper says, but they don't know me. I reckon I got the upper hand under them, I reckon I know who I am." Little Darryl puffed himself up with air, standing slack-kneed on the bed with his shoes on. "I seen worse predicaments." The little boys stared up at him with the expressions of crows strung on a telephone wire. They flapped their arms and stared. "I seen the worser and the worst and they's nothing I seen that could make me forget myself in it. Pain's nothing to the forgetting yourself from it. I know who I am."

"Darryl!" cried the social worker. "Get your shoes off that bed and on the floor." She had on a pink polyester pantsuit that clung to her legs and gave the appearance of a second skin shedding off from the waist down.

"Boooo," said all the little boys, punching each other.

"It's my bed," Little Darryl said. "I'll stand on my own bed with anything on."

"You go home today and you know it. Effective at seven o'clock A.M. it wasn't your bed any more."

"I'll stand on anybody's bed with anything on."

"Let's go," the social worker said grimly. With her free arm cocked in a triangle just above her waist, she held open the door and looked as if the least movement would make her pants disappear. The little boys waited expectantly, booing softly.

"I seen worse than you look on Monday morning," said Little Darryl and got down off the bed. The little boys cheered, scuffled, grew into a wad of arms and legs on top of the cot. At the door Little Darryl looked back into the dormitory room, then he spat viciously on the floor.

"I seen even worser," he said, but the little boys, scuffling, didn't look up again.

4

"Excessively bright! Excessively bright!" Mrs. Eastman sang aloud, scattering motes of dust helter-skelter with her mud-colored feather-duster. The dust settled down again just inches ahead of Mrs. Eastman's movement across the table. "O my boy, O yes *my* boy, O he is ex—*press*—ive—ly—bright!"

Up at cock's crow that morning (the cock one of Mr. Eastman's poverty payments), Mrs. Eastman rampaged through the dawn inside her house with a vengeance and a joy. She had attacked her floors and her ceilings, her walls, her knickknacks. She'd made, then unmade, then made again her beds. She did the same with Little Darryl. First he was a lawyer, then he was a president, then he was a brain surgeon. Nothing suited. She couldn't get over it, she was electrified. And when the doorbell rang she thought she'd liked to have had a heart murmur. With the hand that held the duster pressed against her chest, she prayed to God and sneezed violently. Dust floated everywhere like tiny messengers. A feeling came to her, at the base of her spine, and it said, Practice makes perfect! Pretty is as pretty does! These were the exact sentiments she had expressed, intuitively, to the women's club off and on for thirty years: real mothering would be her forte. She sneezed once more and felt powerful.

By the second ring from the doorbell Mrs. Eastman was prepared, so much so that when she opened the door she had on her wisdom expression, the one she recommended for children with homesickness. On her porch stood a pair of pink polyester pants and Little Darryl, who wore an over-sized Prince Albert coat, collar turned up, and a brown fedora hat, brim turned down. His eyes peeped out from under his hat as though from inside a tank turret. Mrs. Eastman said the first thing to come to her mind.

"I didn't know he was such a colored child," she said and smiled maternally. The eyes inside the hat seemed to look through Mrs. Eastman and onto the entranceway carpet. "I could've mistook you for a pickaninny, little boy," she said sweetly.

"They's two people said that to me before and lived," said Little Darryl.

"I'll be running right along," the social worker told Mrs. Eastman, "if you'll just sign these documents. I already stopped by your husband's office."

"The outside of it looked more like one of them goddamn saloons to me," Little Darryl snarled, spitting through his teeth at a fly on the porch. "Smell't of it, too."

"We don't curse in this home, Darryl. We are gentlemen and ladies in this home. Gentlemen and ladies don't curse or spit."

He looked at her, his eyes slightly askew.

"Sign here," said the social worker, and Mrs. Eastman did.

"You might think that's me right there," Little Darryl said through his teeth. Mrs. Eastman could have sworn it came from the paper itself. "But I know where I stand."

"Why of course you do!" Mrs. Eastman cried. "You're on the door-step of your very own home!" She gave Little Darryl a hug, agitated by the goodness welling inside her like a carbonation, and he stood stiffly as a hanged man.

"From now on you touch me by permission," he said out of a corner of his mouth.

When they looked up the social worker was long gone.

"Food," said Mrs. Eastman. "You must be hungry, little boys are always hungry. They are hungry until they reach the age of twenty and then they are modern afterward."

"I've eat but I could do it again if it was a roast beef with string beans."

Without another word Mrs. Eastman clucked and herded Little Darryl into the kitchen of her house. On his way he picked up two china cats, pil-fering them into the pocket of his Prince Albert. A look of sublime pleas-ure, which Mrs. Eastman mistook for good adjustment, showed above the coat collar. He sidled up to a kitchen window, gazed sullenly onto the back-yard with a hooded pucker around his eyes.

"Gentlemen don't wear hats on in their homes," said Mrs. Eastman. Her hands gripped and sliced on the roast as if performing an emergency operation on a still-live body.

"Lady," said Little Darryl, his eyes directed toward the backyard. "I don't like you. I don't like your house, I don't like your husband. The onliest thing to keep me from the murder of you is if'n you pretend you don't see hear smell feel nor taste me. Do you understand me in that head a hair?"

"But I'm your mother." Mrs. Eastman paused, an expression of some awful recognition shrouding her nose and eyes and mouth. "Pretty is as pretty does," she said.

"You're nuts," he said, "and my mother was a thought my daddy thought for about three seconds. Serve me that roast beef with ketchup on it." He sat down at the table, pulling out a jackknife; the silver spoon and knife already on a place mat, he put in his pocket. He left the fork where it was.

"God loves all the little children," Mrs. Eastman said and her voice sounded very far away. "Black and white, smart and stupid."

"Serve it with ketchup and some mayo on the side, lady." In a rapid, choppy movement Little Darryl flipped open the jackknife and let the blade hang, for an instant, in the air like an unkept promise. "That God of yourn loves because they got the papers on Him a million years ago. You don't a bit more know who He is than you think you know who I am. I know worser."

"You!" screeched Mrs. Eastman. "You're a mistake!" Her hair and nerves were all unstrung. "I'm not your mother, you won't be a lawyer, you won't be." She couldn't think, and immediately, in a reflexive action, she shifted gears into the vaguest of doubts. Outside the rooster crooned an offbeat love song. "I'm going to call my husband," said Mrs. Eastman, dispassionately.

"Serve me the roast beef first," Little Darryl said, and Mrs. Eastman did, filling a plate with greasy slices that hunkered on top of each other in an orgy of flesh. "I ain't afraid of nobody that'd marry you."

While Mrs. Eastman was gone Little Darryl ate the roast beef and when he finished he roamed around, pocketing certain valuables. Inside the refrigerator he found a hamhock. He put it inside the coat, down near the waistline. Inside a drawer he found the silverware, and he put it all, including a soup ladle, into the front left pocket of the Prince Albert. It bulged outward like a cancerous tumor. He put the remains of the roast beef and a bottle of ketchup into the front right pocket. By the time Mrs. Eastman got back, there was very little left in her kitchen.

"He's on his way home," Mrs Eastman told him, as if the matter were settled at last.

"Whoopee," said Little Darryl. He clinked when he spoke. "You're going to have to go upstairs." Briefly, but certainly, he flashed the jackknife in front of Mrs. Eastman. It caused her to remember a story she'd heard quite a time ago. "You're going to have to show me where your jewry is up there. I'll take my chances with them papers this time."

"You're just a little boy," Mrs. Eastman said. "Just a little children."

"They's bigger than me that's less. Upstairs, lady."

Mrs. Eastman breathed heavily up the stairs, and she felt her heart make little leaps, as though it might creep onto her tongue and expose something. Each crack in the wood of the floor struck her as the place to be, each piece of dust looked like the safest of sizes, and she studied them with the vigilance of a scientist. In the bedroom she had a horrible thought.

"You wouldn't hurt a lady would you?" she asked, but Little Darryl was already rooting through her dressing table. "You wouldn't hurt a lady *would you?*" she asked, a little louder. She got up on her bed and held tightly as a tick to the wood of the headboard. "*Would you?*"

Little Darryl turned around, his hands full of rings and bracelets and necklaces that dangled like liquids through his fingers. Along the lines of his face there slithered a configuration of sheer hatred.

"Lady," he said, almost tenderly, "I wouldn't touch a hair a your head for anything anywhere," and then he disappeared out of the bedroom.

"Rape!" Mrs. Eastman cried, but her heart wasn't in it.

When Mr. Eastman came home all he could hear were his wife's screams, and all he could see was a brown figure in the distance, the plumes of a rooster sticking out like an exhaust under its arms, and all he could think would be forever silent.

1983

Leigh Allison Wilson   443

Further Reading

Wilson, Leigh Allison, et al. "A Stubborn Sense of Place." *Harper's Magazine* 273 (Aug. 1986): 35–45, spec. 45. • Grumbach, Doris. "Single-Fisted Intensity." *Georgia Review* 37.4 (Winter 1983): 889–93, spec. 91–92. • Morris, Gregory. "A Metaphorical Resonance." *Prairie Schooner* 58.3 (Fall 1984): 113–14. • "Notes on Current Books." *Virginia Quarterly Review* 59.3 (Summer 1983): 79–100, spec. 90.

The characters in Leigh Allison Wilson's story are developed largely through what Flannery O'Connor calls their "manners—good and bad" and especially their speech. O'Connor's description of the uses and abuses of Southern speech and demeanor provide a useful perspective for discussing "The Raising."

Flannery O'Connor: On Southern Idiom and the Short Story

There are two qualities that make fiction. One is the sense of mystery and the other is the sense of manners. You get the manners from the texture of existence that surrounds you. The great advantage of being a Southern writer is that we don't have to go anywhere to look for manners; bad or good, we've got them in abundance. We in the South live in a society that is rich in contradiction, rich in irony, rich in contrast, and particularly rich in its speech. . . .

There is nothing worse than the writer who doesn't *use* the gifts of the region, but wallows in them. Everything becomes so Southern that it's sickening, so local that it is unintelligible, so literally reproduced that it conveys nothing. The general gets lost in the particular instead of being shown through it.

However, when the life that actually surrounds us is totally ignored, when our patterns of speech are absolutely overlooked, then something is out of kilter. The writer should then ask himself if he is not reaching out for a kind of life that is artificial to him.

An idiom characterizes a society, and when you ignore the idiom, you are very likely ignoring the whole social fabric that could make a meaningful character. You can't cut characters off from their society and say much about them as individuals. You can't say anything meaningful about the mystery of a personality unless you put that personality in a believable and significant social context. And the best way to do this is through the character's own language. When the old lady in one of Andrew Lytle's stories says contemptuously that she has a mule that is older than Birmingham, we get in that one sentence a sense of a society and its history. A great deal of the Southern writer's work is done for him before he begins, because our history lives in our talk. In one of Eudora Welty's stories a character says, "Where I come from, we use fox for yard dogs and owls for chickens, but we sing true." Now there is a whole book in that one sentence; and when the people of your section can talk like that, and you ignore it, you're just not taking advantage of what's yours.

POETRY

ANTH

Reading Poetry: Giving the Poem Its Second Life

Poetry, like all art, has three lives. The first begins and ends in the process of composition, during which (many poets have said) the poem is not so much *made* as *discovered*. Randall Jarrell, discussing the composition of "The Woman at the Washington Zoo" (1960), talks about things that "came into" the poem, as if of their own free will, and began gradually to arrange themselves into patterns plain "even to the writer." For some poets, only this first life of the poem is truly interesting: they do not reread their old poems.

The second life of a poem comes when a reader or listener experiences through the poem a discovery comparable to the poet's. Jarrell's poem provides a fairly clear example. The speaker in the poem is a government office worker dressed in a navy-blue dress, a dull dress acceptable to the "Deputy Assistant Chief" for whom she works. At the Washington Zoo she sees women from India dressed in brilliant saris and watching a brilliantly spotted leopard. "They look back at the leopard like the leopard," the woman says. Jarrell's poem allows us to see in that moment what the woman sees, to discover the visual connections among herself in her dull dress, the sari-clad women, and the leopard. It allows us to discover the deeper connection between humans and animals that these sights suggests. We, too, long for movement and color. A part of us is stifled by

the enclosed office and the navy-blue dress. Jarrell doesn't give us a lecture on human nature; he gives us images and allows us the pleasure of discovering ways they are connected. In reading a poem, we give it a second life. We become partners of the poet, co-creators.

The third life is perhaps the most important: the poem's life after we first discover it, after we cease to "study" it or consciously to appreciate it. The music that moves us most stays with us when it is not being played, and the poetry that counts for most is that which comes back to us unbidden, months after we see the printed page. In this third life the poem may accumulate unexpected meanings and may be fragmented and distorted by a faulty memory, but it is alive. It becomes so much a part of our minds that it shapes our perceptions of other poems, of language, of the world itself.

The first life of poetry does not depend on our active participation, but the second and third lives obviously do. How can we become partners with the poet, discovering in the poem something akin to what she or he discovered? How can we articulate these discoveries? There are certainly no pat answers to these questions: every reader must eventually find his or her own way. There are, however, at least four approaches that have frequently helped readers discover what they might otherwise have missed:

- Read the poem in light of other poems.
- Read the poem in light of the author's other works.
- Read the poem in light of its internal contrasts.
- Live with the poem.

READ THE POEM IN THE LIGHT OF OTHER POEMS

Robert Frost, whose poetry is widely admired both by other poets and by the general public, once said that "a poem is best read in the light of all other poems ever written."

> We read A the better to read B (we have to start somewhere; we may get very little out of A). We read B the better to read C, C the better to read D, D the better to get something more out of A. Progress is not the aim, but circulation. The thing is to get among the poems where they hold each other apart in their places as the stars do.

Perhaps the key phrase here is "hold each other *apart*." When we first begin to read poetry, we tend to think of it as one thing. Poems are lumped together in our minds into an amorphous mass called "poetry," which we like or dislike. As we learn more, we begin to see individual poems holding each other, so to speak, at arm's length, connected and separated at the same time. We find that some poems appeal to us more than do others, and we become increasingly capable of articulating the relationship of one poem to poems around it.

To get a clearer understanding of Frost's notion of "circulation" among poems that "hold each other apart in their places as the stars do," let's examine two poems that belong to a loosely defined constellation and one that may stand on its edge. In the process, we will discuss the sound, imagery, theme, and tone of the poems in question.

Perhaps we should begin with the poem that stands nearest the constellation's center, a 1916 poem by Ezra Pound that sounds like the product of an earlier century.

Alba

When the nightingale to his mate
Sings day-long and night late
My love and I keep state
In bower,
In flower,
'Till the watchman on the tower
Cry:

<blockquote>
<pre>
        "Up! Thou rascal, Rise,
     I see the white
          Light
     And the night
               Flies."
</pre>
</blockquote>

The word used for a title, *alba*, may not be familiar to you, and since you are not likely to find a complete definition in your dictionary, let's examine one from the *Princeton Encyclopedia of Poetry and Poetics:*

> A dawn song, ordinarily expressing the regret of two lovers that day has come so soon to separate them. It has no fixed metrical form but each stanza usually ends with the word *alba*. The earliest examples in Provençal and in French date from the end of the 12th century. The alba probably grew out of the medieval watchman's cry, announcing from his tower the passing of the night hours and the return of the day.

A fuller definition might tell us that in Provence (now a region of France) in the twelfth and thirteenth centuries, troubadours were busy composing songs about illicit love affairs: the adulterous lovers in these poems have reason to regret the dawn. A fuller definition would also point out that *alba* is the Provençal word for dawn—derived from, and essentially identical to, the Latin word for white (notice the "white/Light"). Pound's poem is clearly in the medieval tradition, a translation or recreation of a Provençal alba, and the tradition shapes its sound, imagery, tone, and theme.

Consider first the sound. The medieval troubadours sang their poems, accompanied, typically, by a lute. To them, the sound was at least as important as the sense. Rhyme is especially important to the singer and songwriter, and you'll notice that Pound uses it copiously at the ends of his lines. In the traditional way that we describe end rhyme, we would say that Pound's poem rhymes *aaa/bbb/cdddc* (assuming that "Cry" is really part of the line that follows it). The end rhyme is not the only conspicuous sound effect, however. Notice the balance of "day-long" against "night late" in the second line and the way that the long *i* sound dominates the last six lines: *cry, rise, I, white, light, night, flies.* Readers who look at a poem like "Alba" and wonder what its point is should remember that sound is sometimes "point" enough.

The imagery in a poem is its representation of things that the eye can see, the ear hear, the nose smell, and so forth. In the case of Pound's poem, the imagery is deliberately uninventive. The nightingale's nocturnal song appears in so many poems from the twelfth century through the nineteenth that the bird may be said to belong to poetry as much as it does to nature. The watchman on his tower is, as we have seen, written into the definition of an alba. Pound is not interested in introducing into his poem the sights, smells, and sounds of an actual medieval village. He is following the lead of the troubadours, who left us very little information about the everyday realities of Provençal life.

This brings us to tone and theme. *Tone* is usually defined as the writer's implied attitude toward the audience and the subject; *theme,* as the central idea of a literary work. Is there a well-defined tone in "Alba"? In one sense the answer might be no. Pound is essentially absent from this poem: we do not feel that he has expressed any personal attitude toward the lovers or toward the dawn. He has simply made a song out of traditional material. In another sense the poem borrows its tone as well as its images from the models on which it is drawn. The poem is exuberant and joyful, a celebration of life and love. "Up!" Thou rascal, Rise," the watchman shouts, and there is nothing in his voice but the good cheer of a conspirator. It is as though conscience had not yet been invented.

Is there a theme? Once again, we may not feel that Pound is advancing any idea of its own, any personal theme. Inherent in the alba, however, is a traditional theme: the idea that the lovers (and therefore all of us) must claim our private pleasures before time takes them away from us. The rising sun stands, in this sense, for Father Time with his scythe.

The alba constellation of poems is therefore connected by theme to a neighbor that we might call the *carpe diem* ("seize the day") constellation, which has existed at least since the days of the Latin poet Horace (65–8 B.C.). The poems in this constellation do not ordinarily contain reminders of the dawn or watchman's cries, but they contain constant reminders that time is passing. One of the most famous poems in the constellation is Robert Herrick's "To the Virgins, to Make Much of Time" (1648). Since Herrick's theme will make a guest appearance in a moment, you should hear its first stanza:

> Gather ye rosebuds while ye may,
>   Old time is still a-flying;
> And this same flower that smiles today
>   Tomorrow will be dying.

Horace, Herrick, Pound, and several nameless troubadours of medieval Provence have shaken hands over the theme of seizing our pleasures before they are consumed by encroaching time. Like the nightingale, this theme has become a creature of poetry as much as a creature of the world.

Now let's return to the "dawn song" proper to compare to Pound's poem a much more modern-sounding one, written by Richard Wilbur in 1969:

A Late Aubade

> You could be sitting now in a carrel
> Turning some liver-spotted page,

Or rising in an elevator-cage
Toward Ladies' Apparel.

You could be planting a raucous bed
Of salvia, in rubber gloves,
Or lunching through a screed of someone's loves
With pitying head,

Or making some unhappy setter
Heel, or listening to a bleak
Lecture on Schoenberg's serial technique.
Isn't this better?

Think of all the time you are not
Wasting, and would not care to waste,
Such things, thank God, not being to your taste.
Think what a lot

Of time, by woman's reckoning,
You've saved, and so may spend on this,
You who had rather lie in bed and kiss
Than anything.

It's almost noon, you say? If so,
Time flies, and I need not rehearse
The rosebuds-theme of centuries of verse.
If you *must* go,

Wait for a while, then slip downstairs
And bring us up some chilled white wine,
And some blue cheese, and crackers, and some fine
Ruddy-skinned pears.

The word *aubade* is a synonym for *alba,* differing (some authorities say) in that the medieval aubade tended to be a joyous dawn song, the alba a more regretful one. The theme here is very like that in the alba: "The rosebuds-theme of centuries of verse." (Wilbur is having a good deal of fun by suggesting that the best way to "seize the day" may be to spend it in bed.) The sound, too, is in some ways reminiscent of Pound's poem. Wilbur's poem is songlike in that it has rhymed stanzas *(abba)* with regular meter (three lines of iambic tetrameter, the fourth of iambic dimeter). In sound and theme, the poem declares that it is linked to the work of the troubadours.

But in imagery and tone, the poem takes a new direction. Consider the way that Wilbur imports into his poem images we could never find in a medieval aubade or alba. Some of the images don't fit because they belong so definitely to our century: a study carrel, an elevator cage, rubber gloves, a lecture on atonal music. Some don't fit because they are presented in words that haven't the conventional prettiness of words long associated with poetry: a "page" might appear in a troubadour's aubade, but it surely wouldn't be "liver-spotted." A dog might appear, but not one being trained to "heel." Perhaps half the pleasure of this poem comes from the friction caused by Wilbur's pushing into the medieval dawn song a series of words and pictures that jar badly with the world of bowers, flowers, and watchtowers. You'll notice the speaker's request in the last stanza introduces some far less jarring imagery.

What can we say about the tone? The speaker in the poem has clearly articulated attitudes toward his subject and his audience. The intrusions of the world with all its modern trappings are to him merely distractions from what matters: this woman, those pears, these pleasures. But he certainly speaks with more amusement than anger when he describes to his lover the trivialness of what she might otherwise be doing. And he compliments her by expecting her not only to catch the drift of his argument but to recognize its poetic ancestry: "Time flies, and I need not rehearse/The rosebuds-theme of centuries of verse." The speaker's tone is adult, amused, calm, playful, and we feel that this is the poet's tone as well.

This tone shows as well in the title, "A Late Aubade." The aubade is "late," of course, because it is approaching noon, making a dawn song untimely. It is also late because aubades belong properly to an earlier century. The speaker and the poet are both self-consciously ignoring the clock.

Our poem from the edge of the alba-aubade constellation is from Adrienne Rich's 1984 collection, *The Fact of a Doorframe:*

Living in Sin

She had thought the studio would keep itself;
no dust upon the furniture of love.
Half heresy, to wish the taps less vocal,
the panes relieved of grime. A plate of pears,
a piano with a Persian shawl, a cat
stalking the picturesque amusing mouse
had risen at his urging.
Not that at five each separate stair would writhe
under the milkman's tramp; that morning light
so coldly would delineate the scraps
of last night's cheese and three sepulchral bottles;
that on the kitchen shelf among the saucers
a pair of beetle-eyes would fix her own—
envoy from some village in the moldings . . .
Meanwhile, he, with a yawn
sounded a dozen notes upon the keyboard,
declared it out of tune, shrugged at the mirror,
rubbed at his beard, went out for cigarettes;
while she, jeered by the minor demons,

pulled back the sheets and made the bed and found
a towel to dust the table-top,
and let the coffee-pot boil over on the stove.
By evening she was back in love again,
though not so wholly but throughout the night
she woke sometimes to feel the daylight coming
like a relentless milkman up the stairs.

Though this poem is related to the other two by its presentation of two
lovers at dawn, Rich is clearly not writing in the Provençal tradition. The
sound of her poem is certainly not that of a troubadour's song: there are no
rhymes, and the long lines, running together in still longer sentences, contrast sharply with the spritely rhythms of Wilbur's poem and (especially)
Pound's. In fact, Rich is writing what is called, somewhat cryptically, "blank
verse": unrhymed lines of iambic pentameter. Note the regular stresses in
these lines:

no dust upon the furniture of love.   (line 2)
so coldly would delineate the scraps   (line 10)
By evening she was back in love again,   (line 24)

Note, too, that the lines have their own internal harmonies of sound. Listen
to the interplay of *n-* and *uh-* sounds in line 2, the interplay of *c-* and *l-*
sounds in line 10, and the interplay of *b*'s and *n*'s in line 24. Rich's lines
have a self-conscious "music" in them, but it is not the music of the light-
hearted lyrical poem. Blank verse of this sort has repeatedly been used for
the graver subjects of English poetry.

The imagery in this poem, like the imagery in Wilbur's, contrasts the
ideal world with the real, but Rich's real world is considerably more sinister
and depressing. For our eyes we have dust on the furniture, grime on the
window, scraps of cheese and empty wine bottles, the eyes of insects crawling among the saucers. For our ears we have a dozen notes from an out-of-
tune piano and the ominous "tramp" of the milkman's foot on the stairs.

Obviously, the tone of Rich's poem is much darker than the tone of
Pound's or Wilbur's. Here everything seems to forebode unhappiness.
Contrast the "chilled white wine" of "A Late Aubade" to the "sepulchral
bottles" of "Living in Sin," and you will see that we have moved from an
essentially joyful poem to an essentially sorrowful one. We have also moved
away from the "rosebuds-theme." We might disagree about precisely what
the theme is. Is it that love can come into conflict with conscience? Is it
that the reality of love is disenchanting? Is it that we can't escape conscience? Whichever we choose, it won't be a theme borrowed from Provençal poetry. When the watchman calls at the break of dawn in "Alba," he

does not sound like a troubled conscience or a warning of unhappiness to come. But in Rich's poem the five-o'clock sound of the "relentless milk-man" on the stairs suggests the misery of disillusionment. By comparing the milkman to the guard on his tower, we come to a clearer understanding of both poems.

"The thing," says Frost, "is to get among the poems where they hold each other apart in their places as the stars do." His image nicely expresses the way that most of us learn our way around poetry. We start with individual poems that remind us of other poems, either by shared characteristics or by contrasts. Eventually we begin to define constellations (alba, confessional poem, sonnet, meditation, dramatic monologue, and so on) that help us see a new poem in relation to many others. The constellations are admittedly ill defined and overlapping, and one needs to remember that they only crudely correspond to the true relationships among the stars, but they are tremendously helpful when we need to orient ourselves. Readers who know what an alba is, for example, will find something very familiar not only in "A Late Aubade," but in John Donne's "The Sun Rising." They may find that their knowledge helps them read not only "Living in Sin," but John Milton's "Methought I saw my late espoused saint," Edna St. Vincent Millay's "Recuerdo," and Robert Browning's "Meeting at Night" and "Parting at Morning." Readers familiar with the *carpe diem* theme will find that it helps them find connections to more poems than we can begin to list.

READ THE POEM IN THE LIGHT OF THE AUTHOR'S OTHER WORKS

The most significant constellation in which to place a poem may be a collection of the poet's own works. In fact, some poems conceal a good part of their meaning until we see them in such a context. Take, for example, the following 1975 poem by Louise Glück:

> Still Life
>
> Father has his arm around Tereze.
> She squints. My thumb
> is in my mouth: my fifth autumn.
> Near the copper beech
> the spaniel dozes in shadows.
> Not one of us does not avert his eyes.
>
> Across the lawn, in full sun, my mother
> stands behind her camera.

We may immediately like this poem for nostalgic reasons. Many of us remember being periodically lined up facing the bright sun in poses suitable for the family album. The poem simultaneously brings back the experience of posing for such pictures and the experience of looking at them. It can give us, therefore, a sweet pleasure.

It is only when you have read several of Glück's poems that you realize that there is more to this one than first appears. If you look at the half-dozen poems collected on pages 916–921, you'll see that sweet nostalgia is not at all typical of Glück's work. In poems like "For My Mother," "The Apple Trees," and "Metamorphosis," we get a view of the difficulties, pains, and separations of family life. For example, consider these lines from "The Apple Trees":

> In the dark room your son sleeps.
> The walls are green, the walls
> are spruce and silence.
> I wait to see how he will leave me.

This is not the view of the happy, inseparable family that the photo album is supposed to present, and when we think again about "Still Life" we realize what a disturbing poem it is.

Through the first six lines the picture seems a standard one: young family squinting into the sun, with dog and beech tree. Then, significantly set off by the blank line, a reminder of who is *not* in the picture: the mother, from whose perspective, we suddenly realize, we have been viewing the entire scene. This is the family as the mother sees it, as she tries to preserve it, on film at least, for reasons no one else seems quite to understand. "Not one of us does not avert his eyes" now seems a more sinister line; the mother gazes intently through the viewfinder at a family that does not look back at her.

When I realized this much, I saw a dimension of the poem that had entirely escaped me on first reading. When she looks at the photograph, Glück (now a grown woman, now—in fact—a mother) is seeing the family as her mother had seen it thirty years before. She is seeing *herself*, even, through her mother's eyes, as a thumb-sucking five-year-old who will inevitably grow up, move away, call less frequently, become a stranger, become a mother herself of a daughter who will grow up to repeat the cycle. The sad look into the past and future is captured in the moment of looking at the photograph. Until we read the poem in light of other Glück poems, however, much of it escapes us.

READ THE POEM IN THE LIGHT OF ITS INTERNAL CONTRASTS

As we see very clearly in "Still Life," poems often articulate a tension: the family versus the mother, the public world versus the private relationship, the gritty surroundings versus the internal joy. Sometimes the best way into a poem is to begin by identifying a key tension. Here, for example, is a poem by Emily Dickinson in which the tension is expressed clearly in rhythm and rhyme:

> A Bird came down the Walk—
> He did not know I saw—
> He bit an Angleworm in halves
> And ate the fellow, raw,
>
> And then he drank a Dew
> From a convenient Grass—
> And then hopped sidewise to the Wall
> To let a Beetle pass—
>
> He glanced with rapid eyes
> That hurried all around—
> They looked like frighted Beads, I thought—
> He stirred his Velvet Head
>
> Like one in danger, Cautious,
> I offered him a Crumb
> And he unrolled his feathers
> And rowed him softer home—
>
> Than Oars divide the Ocean,
> Too silver for a seam—
> Or Butterflies, off Banks of Noon
> Leap, plashless as they swim.

The contrast between the nursery-rhyme quality of the first half of the poem and the more complex second half strikes us immediately. The first two stanzas are built on the same pattern: lines in iambic meter (ta-TUM, ta-Tum, ta-Tum—mechanically—with an extra foot in the third line of the stanza). The obvious full rhymes would delight a five-year-old: *saw/raw* and *grass/pass* remind me of Mother Goose's *dock/clock* and *muffet/tuffet*. The little manlike bird, too, is straight from the nursery: reminiscent of Peter Rabbit on and off his best behavior. Even those of us whose experience with poetry is very limited know exactly where we stand through the second stanza.

Then we discover that we are not standing where the poem is. The third stanza misses the expected rhyme almost entirely (is *around/head* a rhyme at all?), and the poem staggers into the fourth stanza with what textbooks call an enjambment:

> They looked like frighted Beads, I thought—
> He stirred his Velvet Head
>
> Like one in danger, Cautious,
> I offered him a Crumb

Even the syntax has become unclear. Who is cautious, the bird or the poet, or both? The poem seems to be reeling as if it had been boxed on the ears. The mechanical iambic meter is blurred by an occasional extra syllable at the end ("Like one in danger, Cautious"), and when the rhymes return, they are unpredictable slant rhymes (*crumb/home, seam/swim*). The form that had been so confident and comfortable has shifted, and the effect is somewhat eerie—like the effect of music shifting to a minor key.

The difference in form between the first and second half of the poem corresponds to a difference in the way the bird is viewed. At first it is a comical mechanical thing, as birds seem to be when we see them on the ground. But when the bird flies it becomes something else again, and we begin to see the mystery of it.

Contrasts within the poem need not involve meter or rhyme, of course. William Stafford's "Traveling Through the Dark" is written in a free verse virtually indistinguishable from the prose,[1] so it does not provide an opportunity for such a dramatic change in form:

> Traveling through the dark I found a deer
> dead on the edge of the Wilson River road.
> It is usually best to roll them into the canyon:
> that road is narrow; to swerve might make more dead.
>
> By glow of the tail-light I stumbled back of the car
> and stood by the heap, a doe, a recent killing;
> she had stiffened already, almost cold.
> I dragged her off; she was large in the belly.
>
> My fingers touching her side brought me the reason—
> her side was warm; her fawn lay there waiting,
> alive, still, never to be born.
> Beside that mountain road I hesitated.
>
> The car aimed ahead its lowered parking lights;
> under the hood purred the steady engine.

---

1. Though I say the poem is in free verse, a careful listener will find this is an oversimplification. Notice that the second and fourth lines of each stanza contain a very faint rhyme and that the poem's last two lines suggest a rhyme with their *r* and *v* sounds.

> I stood in the glare of the warm exhaust turning red;
> around our group I could hear the wilderness listen.
>
> I thought hard for all of us—my only swerving—,
> then pushed her over the edge into the river.

The great tension is between two realities, two systems of life. On one hand are efficiency and responsibility, unglamorous virtues that we learn to admire when we face danger or loss. The protagonist's statement that "to swerve might make more dead" could be the motto of the dedicated soldier, reformer, or surgeon, all of whom occasionally need to view life with utter detachment in order to serve their cause. On the other hand, there are emotions warmer than efficiency and deeper than good judgment. Where on the scale of rational decision making is the protagonist to weigh what he feels when he touches the doe's side: ". . . her fawn lay there waiting,/alive, still, never to be born"? Stafford's poem is strong because he does full justice to both sides of the conflict.

Another tension is at work in the style of the poem. Stafford has a large theme here, one that could fly off into sentimentality in one direction ("What a torment life is for us sensitive souls who are alert to brutality!") or into tough-guy clichés in another ("You can't make omelets without breaking eggs"). To avoid these failings, he stays very close to literal reality. The incident takes place on the Wilson River road, which runs from Portland to Tillamook and which the state calls Highway 6. Many of the Oregonians who drive it would say, in precisely the same words, that they had to "swerve" to avoid a "heap" in the road, or that "it is usually best to roll them into the canyon." The flat accuracy of Stafford's language and setting provide a background against which a few passages assume a particularly sharp profile. Take, for example, these lines from the fourth quatrain:

> The car aimed ahead its lowered parking lights;
> under the hood purred the steady engine.
> I stood in the glare of the warm exhaust turning red . . .

Immediately after the description of the dead doe, warmed from the inside by a living fawn, we get this description of a truly dead object, an automobile, the embodiment of efficiency. But so restrained has Stafford's language been to this point that little touches—"aimed," "purred the steady engine," "the warm exhaust turning red"—make the automobile seem like a living thing, slightly demonic. The effect is not flashy: the car never stops being a car, but the poem steps up its emotional intensity. Now we are ready to see the larger emotions and thoughts that the restrained language of this poem opens out on. Now we will read Stafford's "I thought hard for all of us—my only swerving" with a sense that "all of us" reaches beyond one man, one doe, one car, and whatever passengers may be in it, and that "swerving" has acquired new meaning. We may go back to the title of the poem and realize that Stafford's plain title "Traveling Through the Dark" symbolizes the terrifying freedom of a life in which we have to make moral choices by the faint light of our human judgment.

LIVE WITH THE POEM

The faint light of judgment leaves some poems unilluminated, and I should leave this introduction with a reminder that poems often affect us for reasons we will never understand. Full appreciation of poetry has to go beyond fully conscious appreciation, and many poems need to be lived with over a period of weeks or months while they do their work unanalyzed. Here I can only give an example from my own experience. A few years ago I discovered the following poem:

> The Castle of My Heart
>
> Cleanse and refresh the castle of my heart
> Where I have lived for long with little joy.
> For Falsest Danger, with its counterpart
> Sorrow, has made this siege its long employ.
>
> Now lift the siege, for in your bravest part
> Full power exists, most eager for employ;
> Cleanse and refresh the castle of my heart
> Where I have lived for long with little joy.
>
> Do not let Peril play its lordly part;
> Show up the bad game's bait, and its employ.
> Nor, for a moment, strut as future's toy.
> Advance, and guard your honor and my art.
>
> Cleanse and refresh the castle of my heart.

There is little to say about the poem. It is in the form of a rondel, an elaborate French invention in which both lines and rhymes rearrange themselves from stanza to stanza like keys juggled on a key ring. It was composed by Charles D'Orléans, probably after his release in 1440 from twenty-five years of captivity as an English prisoner of war. Louise Bogan translated it from the French in 1966, when she was sixty-eight years old and nearing the end of a life remarkable for its devotion to art, its fierce independence, and its frequent solitude. She never published the translation.

There are things about the poem I do not understand. It seems to be a prayer addressed to God, but how odd it is to say that "full power" exists in God's "bravest part" (as if there were a cowardly part) or that He "strut[s] as future's toy." When I try to reason about the poem, I cannot tell if it is addressed to God or to some part of the poet's soul or to another person, a lover, real or imagined. Perhaps it is addressed to all three simultaneously. Finally this difficulty makes no difference, since the poem works on me without my having to understand it completely. What makes a difference is that almost every day the poem comes back to me in fragments. Sometimes when I recite the lines I think of the literal castles, smelly and unromantic, where Charles D'Orléans "lived for long with little joy." Sometimes I think of Louise Bogan's poetry, austere and beautiful and undervalued ("Advance, and guard your honor and my art"). Generally, however, I let the music of the poem do its work without interference. "Cleanse and refresh the castle of my heart": it is a well-crafted line, but it is also something more. It is a prayer that seems to rise spontaneously from a part of us that analysis cannot reach.

WILLIAM SHAKESPEARE

(1564–1616)

[NOT MARBLE, NOR THE GILDED MONUMENTS]

Not marble, nor the gilded monuments
Of princes shall outlive this pow'rful rhyme,
But you shall shine more bright in these conténts
Than unswept stone, besmear'd with sluttish time.
When wasteful war shall statues overturn,   5
And broils root out the work of masonry,
Nor Mars his sword nor war's quick fire shall burn
The living record of your memory.
'Gainst death and all-oblivious enmity
Shall you pace forth; your praise shall still find room   10
Even in the eyes of all posterity
That wear this world out to the ending doom.
    So, till the judgment that yourself arise,
    You live in this, and dwell in lovers' eyes.

(Sonnet 55) 1609

[SINCE BRASS, NOR STONE, NOR EARTH, NOR BOUNDLESS SEA]

Since brass, nor stone, nor earth, nor boundless sea
But sad mortality o'er-sways their power,
How with this rage shall beauty hold a plea,
Whose action is no stronger than a flower?
O how shall summer's honey breath hold out   5
Against the wreckful siege of batt'ring days,
When rocks impregnable are not so stout,
Nor gates of steel so strong, but Time decays?
O fearful meditation! where, alack,
Shall Time's best jewel from Time's chest lie hid?   10
Or what strong hand can hold his swift foot back?
Or who his spoil of beauty can forbid?

Sonnet 55: 4. *sluttish:* dirty and slovenly.   6. *broils:* quarrels, battles.   7. *Nor . . . nor:*
neither . . . nor. *Mars his:* Mars'.   9. *all-oblivious:* all-obliterating.   *Sonnet 65:* 10. *chest:*
treasure chest.

O, none, unless this miracle have might,
That in black ink my love may still shine bright.

(Sonnet 65) 1609

[THAT TIME OF YEAR THOU MAYST IN ME BEHOLD]

That time of year thou mayst in me behold
When yellow leaves, or none, or few, do hang
Upon those boughs which shake against the cold,
Bare ruin'd choirs, where late the sweet birds sang.
In me thou seest the twilight of such day   5
As after sunset fadeth in the west,
Which by and by black night doth take away,
Death's second self, that seals up all in rest.
In me thou seest the glowing of such fire,
That on the ashes of his youth doth lie,   10
As the deathbed whereon it must expire,
Consum'd with that which it was nourish'd by.
   This thou perceiv'st, which makes thy love more strong,
   To love that well which thou must leave ere long.

(Sonnet 73) 1609

[O, NEVER SAY THAT I WAS FALSE OF HEART]

O, never say that I was false of heart,
Though absence seem'd my flame to qualify;
As easy might I from myself depart
As from my soul, which in thy breast doth lie:
That is my home of love; if I have ranged   5
Like him that travels I return again,
Just to the time, not with the time exchang'd,
So that myself bring water for my stain.
Never believe, though in my nature reign'd
All frailties that besiege all kinds of blood,   10
That it could so preposterously be stain'd,
To leave for nothing all thy sum of good;
   For nothing this wide universe I call,
   Save thou, my rose; in it thou art my all.

(Sonnet 109) 1609

Sonnet 109:   2. *qualify:* to diminish or make less complete.   7. *just . . . time:* faithful to the appointed time.   *altered:* changed.   10. *blood:* temperament.   12. *for:* in exchange for.

[WHEN MY LOVE SWEARS THAT SHE IS MADE OF TRUTH]

When my love swears that she is made of truth,
I do believe her, though I know she lies,
That she might think me some untutor'd youth,
Unlearnéd in the world's false subtleties.
Thus vainly thinking that she thinks me young,   5
Although she knows my days are past the best,
Simply I credit her false-speaking tongue:
On both sides thus is simple truth suppress'd.
But wherefore says she not she is unjust?
And wherefore say not I that I am old?   10
Oh, love's best habit is in seeming trust,
And age in love loves not t' have years told.
Therefore I lie with her and she with me,
And in our faults by lies we flattered be.

(Sonnet 138) 1609

O MISTRESS MINE, WHERE ARE YOU ROAMING?

O mistress mine, where are you roaming?
Oh, stay and hear! your true Love's coming,
    That can sing both high and low:
Trip no further, pretty sweeting;
Journeys end in lovers' meeting,   5
    Every wise man's son doth know.

What is love? 'tis not hereafter;
Present mirth hath present laughter;
    What's to come is still unsure:
In delay there lies no plenty: 10
Then come kiss me, sweet-and-twenty,
    Youth's a stuff will not endure.

1599

COME AWAY, COME AWAY, DEATH

Come away, come away, death,
    And in sad cypress let me be laid.
Fly away, fly away, breath;

Sonnet 138: 1. *truth:* faithfulness.   7. *simply:* naively.   9. *unjust:* unfaithful.

I am slain by a fair cruel maid.
My shroud of white, stuck all with yew,   5
    O, prepare it!
My part of death, no one so true
    Did share it.

Not a flower, not a flower sweet,
    On my black coffin let there be strown.   10
Not a friend, not a friend greet
    My poor corpse, where my bones shall be thrown.
A thousand thousand sighs to save,
    Lay me, O, where
Sad true lover never find my grave,   15
    To weep there!

1602

FEAR NO MORE THE HEAT O' THE SUN

Fear no more the heat o' the sun,
    Nor the furious winter's rages;
Thou thy worldly task hast done,
    Home art gone, and ta'en thy wages:
Golden lads and girls all must,   5
As chimney-sweepers, come to dust.

Fear no more the frown o' the great;
    Thou art past the tyrant's stroke;
Care no more to clothe and eat;
    To thee the reed is as the oak: 10
The scepter, learning, physic, must
All follow this, and come to dust.

Fear no more the lightning flash,
    Nor the all-dreaded thunder stone;
Fear not slander, censure rash;   15
    Thou hast finished joy and moan:
All lovers young, all lovers must
Consign to thee, and come to dust.

No exorciser harm thee!
Nor no witchcraft charm thee!   20
Ghost unlaid forbear thee!
Nothing ill come near thee!
Quiet consummation have;
And renownéd be thy grave!

1611

Further Reading

Willen, Gerald, and Victor B. Reed, eds. *A Casebook on Shakespeare's Sonnets*. New York: Crowell, 1964. • Muir, Kenneth. *Shakespeare's Sonnets*. London: Allen, 1979. • Weiser, David K. *Mind in Character: Shakespeare's Speaker in the Sonnets*. Columbia: U of Missouri P, 1987. • Klause, John. "Shakespeare's *Sonnets*: Age in Love and Goring of Thoughts." *Studies in Philology* 53.3 (Summer 1983): 300–24. • Auden, W. H. "Music in Shakespeare." *The Dyer's Hand and Other Essays*. New York: Random, 1962. 500–27. • Nolan, Edward F. "Shakespeare's 'Fear No More the Heat O' Th' Sun.'" *Explicator* 11.1 (Oct. 1952): 4.

Shakespeare's lyrics do what they do so well that they periodically become a reference point in debates about what poetry ought to be doing. In the 1930s such influential poets as T. S. Eliot and Ezra Pound were writing poems more intellectual, ironic, and "objective" than the lyrics Shakespeare had written so well. A. E. Housman delivered his address on "The Name and Nature of Poetry" partly in answer to such poets. A dismayed proponent of the new poetry reported that he would have to work fifteen years to undo the damage Housman had done in one hour.

A. E. Housman: On the Separation of Poetry and Thought

Poetry is not the thing said but a way of saying it. Can it then be isolated and studied by itself? For the combination of language with its intellectual content, its meaning, is as close a union as can well be imagined. Is there such a thing as pure unmingled poetry, poetry independent of meaning?

. . . Even Shakespeare, who had so much to say, would sometimes pour out his loveliest poetry in saying nothing.

> Take O take those lips away
>   That so sweetly were forsworn,
> And those eyes, the break of day,
>   Lights that do mislead the morn;
> But my kisses bring again,
>   bring again,
> Seals of love, but seal'd in vain,
>   seal'd in vain.

That is nonsense, but it is ravishing poetry. When Shakespeare fills such poetry with thought, and thought which is worthy of it, as in 'Fear no more the heat o' the sun' or 'O mistress mine, where are you roaming?' those songs, the very summits of lyrical achievement, are indeed greater and more moving poems, but I hardly know how to call them more poetical.

. . . Poetry indeed seems to me more physical than intellectual. A year or two ago, in common with others, I received from America a request that I would define poetry. I replied that I could no more define poetry than a terrier can define a rat, but that I thought we both recognised the object by the symptoms which it provokes in us. One of these symptoms was described in connexion with another object by Elipaz the Temanite: 'A spirit passed before my face: the hair of my flesh stood up.' Experience has taught me, when I am shaving in the morning, to keep watch over my thoughts, because, if a line of poetry strays into my memory, my skin bristles so that the razor ceases to act. This particular symptom is accompanied by a shiver down the spine; there is another which consists in a constriction of the throat and a precipitation of water to the eyes; and there is a third which I can only describe by borrowing a phrase from one of Keats's last letters, where he says, speaking of Fanny Brawne, 'everything that reminds me of her goes through me like a spear'. The seat of this sensation is the pit of the stomach.

JOHN DONNE

(1572–1631)

THE RELIC

When my grave is broke up again
Some second guest to entertain
(For graves have learned that woman-head,
To be to more than one a bed)
   And he that digs it spies   5
A bracelet of bright hair about the bone,
   Will he not let us alone,
And think that there a loving couple lies,
Who thought that this device might be some way
To make their souls, at the last busy day,   10
Meet at this grave, and make a little stay?

If this fall in a time, or land,
Where mis-devotion doth command,
Then he that digs us up will bring

"The Relic": 13. *mis-devotion:* idolatry.

Us to the Bishop and the King   15
    To make us relics; then
Thou shalt be a Mary Magdalen, and I
    A something else thereby;
All women shall adore us, and some men;
And, since at such time miracles are sought,   20
I would have that age by this paper taught
What miracles we harmless lovers wrought.
    First, we loved well and faithfully,
    Yet knew not what we loved, nor why;
    Difference of sex no more we knew,   25
    Than our guardian angels do;
        Coming and going, we
Perchance might kiss, but not between those meals;
    Our hands ne'er touched the seals
Which nature, injured by late law, sets free.   30
These miracles we did; but now, alas,
All measure, and all language, I should pass,
Should I tell what a miracle she was.

                                                        1633

THE CANONIZATION

For God's sake, hold your tongue, and let me love,
    Or chide my palsy, or my gout,
My five gray hairs, or ruined fortune flout,
    With wealth your state, your mind with arts improve,
        Take you a course, get you a place,   5
        Observe his honor, or his grace,
Or the King's real, or his stamped face
    Contemplate; what you will, approve,
        So you will let me love.

Alas, alas, who's injured by my love?   10
    What merchant's ships have my sighs drowned?
Who says my tears have overflowed his ground?
    When did my colds a forward spring remove?
        When did the heats which my veins fill
        Add one more to the plaguy bill?   15
Soldiers find wars, and lawyers find out still

"The Canonization": 7. *stamped face:* the likeness on a coin.   8. *approve*: try out.   15. *plaguy
bill:* the list of those dead from the plague; Donne is possibly referring to the plague of 1592,
which struck London while he was living there.

Litigious men, which quarrels move,
   Though she and I do love.

Call us what you will, we are made such by love;
   Call her one, me another fly,   20
We're tapers too, and at our own cost die,
   And we in us find the eagle and the dove.
      The phoenix riddle hath more wit
      By us; we two being one, are it.
So, to one neutral thing both sexes fit.   25
   We die and rise the same, and prove
   Mysterious by this love.

We can die by it, if not live by love,
   And if unfit for tombs and hearse
Our legend be, it will be fit for verse;   30
   And if no piece of chronicle we prove,
      We'll build in sonnets pretty rooms;
      As well a well-wrought urn becomes
The greatest ashes, as half-acre tombs,
   And by these hymns, all shall approve   35
   Us *canonized* for Love.

And thus invoke us: "You, whom reverend love
   Made one another's hermitage;
You, to whom love was peace, that now is rage;
   Who did the whole world's soul extract, and drove   40
      Into the glass of your eyes
      (So made such mirrors, and such spies,
That they did all to you epitomize)
   Countries, towns, courts: beg from above
   A pattern of your love!"   45

1633

A VALEDICTION:
FORBIDDING MOURNING

As virtuous men pass mildly away,
   And whisper to their souls to go,
Whilst some of their sad friends do say,
   "The breath goes now," and some say, "No,"

"The Canonization": 22. *eagle . . . dove:* the powerful and the meek; the two also represent
righteousness and mercy, which, in medieval literature, produced peace.   23. *phoenix:* a
mythical bird that was both male and female, and that self-procreated by burning in fire and
then rising again from the ashes.

So let us melt, and make no noise, 5
    No tear-floods, nor sigh-tempests move;
'Twere profanation of our joys
    To tell the laity our love.

Moving of the earth brings harms and fears,
    Men reckon what it did and meant; 10
But trepidation of the spheres,
    Though greater far, is innocent.

Dull sublunary lovers' love
    (Whose soul is sense) cannot admit
Absence, because it doth remove 15
    Those things which elemented it.

But we, by a love so much refined
    That our selves know not what it is,
Inter-assured of the mind,
    Care less, eyes, lips, and hands to miss. 20

Our two souls therefore, which are one,
    Though I must go, endure not yet
A breach, but an expansion,
    Like gold to airy thinness beat.

If they be two, they are two so 25
    As stiff twin compasses are two:
Thy soul, the fixed foot, makes no show
    To move, but doth, if the other do;

And though it in the center sit,
    Yet when the other far doth roam, 30
It leans, and hearkens after it,
    And grows erect, as that comes home.

Such wilt thou be to me, who must,
    Like the other foot, obliquely run;
Thy firmness makes my circle just, 35
    And makes me end where I begun.

1633

THE GOOD-MORROW

I wonder, by my troth, what thou and I
Did, till we loved? were we not weaned till then?
But sucked on country pleasures, childishly?

"*Valediction*": 12. *innocent:* innocuous.

Or snorted we in the Seven Sleepers' den?
'Twas so; but this, all pleasures fancies be.   5
If ever any beauty I did see,
Which I desired, and got, 'twas but a dream of thee.

And now good-morrow to our waking souls,
Which watch not one another out of fear;
For love, all love of other sights controls,   10
And makes one little room an everywhere.
Let sea-discoverers to new worlds have gone,
Let maps to others, worlds on worlds have shown,
Let us possess one world, each hath one, and is one.

My face in thine eye, thine in mine appears,   15
And true plain hearts do in the faces rest;
Where can we find two better hemispheres,
Without sharp north, without declining west?
Whatever dies was not mixed equally;
If our two loves be one, or, thou and I   20
Love so alike that none do slacken, none can die.

1633

THE SUN RISING

    Busy old fool, unruly sun,
      Why dost thou thus,
Through windows, and through curtains, call on us?
Must to thy motions lovers' seasons run?
    Saucy pedantic wretch, go chide   5
    Late schoolboys, and sour prentices,
  Go tell court-huntsmen that the King will ride,
  Call country ants to harvest offices;
Love, all alike, no season knows, nor clime,
Nor hours, days, months, which are the rags of time.   10

    Thy beams, so reverend and strong
      Why shouldst thou think?
I could eclipse and cloud them with a wink,
But that I would not lose her sight so long:
    If her eyes have not blinded thine,   15
    Look, and tomorrow late, tell me
  Whether both the Indias of spice and mine
  Be where thou leftst them, or lie here with me.

"*The Good-morrow*": 4. *Seven Sleepers:* according to legend, seven Christian youths who took refuge in a cave to escape persecution during the rule of Decius; they awakened two centuries later.   "*The Sun Rising*": 6. *prentices:* apprentices.   17. *Indias:* the East Indies, known for its spices, and the West Indies, known for its gold mines.

Ask for those kings whom thou saw'st yesterday,
And thou shalt hear, All here in one bed lay.   20

    She's all states, and all princes I,
      Nothing else is.
Princes do but play us; compared to this,
All honor's mimic, all wealth alchemy.
    Thou, sun, art half as happy as we,   25
      In that the world's contracted thus;
   Thine age asks ease, and since thy duties be
   To warm the world, that's done in warming us.
Shine here to us, and thou art everywhere;
This bed thy center is, these walls thy sphere.   30

1633

THE FLEA

Mark but this flea, and mark in this
How little that which thou deny'st me is;
It sucked me first, and now sucks thee,
And in this flea our two bloods mingled be;
Thou know'st that this cannot be said   5
A sin, nor shame, nor loss of maidenhead,
    Yet this enjoys before it woo,
    And pampered swells with one blood made of two,
    And this, alas, is more than we would do.

Oh stay, three lives in one flea spare,   10
Where we almost, yea more than married are.
This flea is you and I, and this
Our marriage bed, and marriage temple is;
Though parents grudge, and you, we're met
And cloistered in these living walls of jet.   15
    Though use make you apt to kill me,
    Let not to that, self-murder added be,
    And sacrilege, three sins in killing three.

Cruel and sudden, hast thou since
Purpled thy nail in blood of innocence?   20
Wherein could this flea guilty be,
Except in that drop which it sucked from thee?
Yet thou triumph'st, and say'st that thou
Find'st not thyself, nor me, the weaker now;
    'Tis true; then learn how false, fears be;   25
    Just so much honor, when thou yield'st to me,
    Will waste, as this flea's death took life from thee.

1633

[DEATH BE NOT PROUD, THOUGH SOME HAVE CALLED THEE]

Death be not proud, though some have called thee
Mighty and dreadful, for thou art not so;
For those whom thou think'st thou dost overthrow
Die not, poor death, nor yet canst thou kill me.
From rest and sleep, which but thy pictures be,   5
Much pleasure; then from thee much more must flow,
And soonest our best men with thee do go,
Rest of their bones, and soul's delivery.
Thou art slave to fate, chance, kings, and desperate men,
And dost with poison, war, and sickness dwell;   10
And poppy or charms can make us sleep as well,
And better than thy stroke; why swell'st thou then?
One short sleep past, we wake eternally,
And death shall be no more; death, thou shalt die.

(Holy Sonnet 10) 1633

[BATTER MY HEART, THREE-PERSONED GOD]

Batter my heart, three-personed God; for You
As yet but knock, breathe, shine, and seek to mend;
That I may rise and stand, o'erthrow me, and bend
Your force, to break, blow, burn, and make me new.
I, like an usurped town, to another due,   5
Labor to admit You, but Oh, to no end!
Reason, Your viceroy in me, me should defend,
But is captived, and proves weak or untrue.
Yet dearly I love You, and would be loved fain,
But am betrothed unto Your enemy: 10
Divorce me, untie or break that knot again,
Take me to You, imprison me, for I,
Except You enthrall me, never shall be free,
Nor ever chaste, except You ravish me.

(Holy Sonnet 14) 1633

HYMN TO GOD MY GOD, IN MY SICKNESS

Since I am coming to that holy room
    Where, with Thy choir of saints for evermore,
I shall be made Thy music; as I come

I tune the instrument here at the door,
And what I must do then, think here before.   5

Whilst my physicians by their love are grown
   Cosmographers, and I their map, who lie
Flat on this bed, that by them may be shown
   That this is my southwest discovery
   Per fretum febris, by these straits to die,   10

I joy, that in these straits, I see my West;
   For, though their currents yield return to none,
What shall my West hurt me? As West and East
   In all flat maps (and I am one) are one,
   So death doth touch the resurrection.   15

Is the Pacific Sea my home? Or are
   The Eastern riches? Is Jerusalem?
Anyan, and Magellan, and Gibraltar,
   All straits, and none but straits, are ways to them,
   Whether where Japhet dwelt, or Cham, or Shem.   20

We think that Paradise and Calvary,
   Christ's cross, and Adam's tree, stood in one place;
Look, Lord, and find both Adams met in me;
   As the first Adam's sweat surrounds my face,
   May the last Adam's blood my soul embrace.   25

So, in his purple wrapped, receive me, Lord;
   By these his thorns give me his other crown;
And, as to others' souls I preached Thy word,
   Be this my text, my sermon to mine own;
   Therefore that he may raise the Lord throws down.   30

1635

Further Reading

Kermode, Frank. *Discussions of John Donne*. Boston: Heath, 1962. • Gardner,
Helen, ed. *John Donne: The Divine Poems*. 2nd ed. New York: Oxford UP, 1978.
• Warnke, Frank J. *John Donne*. Boston: Twayne, 1987. • Martz, Louis L.
"Meditative Action and 'The Metaphysick Style.'" *The Poem of the Mind: Essays on*

---

9. *southwest discovery:* the Straits of Magellan.   10. *Per fretum febris:* through the raging, or
strait, of fever.   18. *Anyan:* the Bering Strait.   20. *Japhet, Cham, Shem:* the sons of Noah
who populated Europe, Africa, and Asia respectively.

Poetry, English and American. New York: Oxford UP, 1966. 33–53, spec. 40–43.
• Kerrigan, William. "The Fearful Accommodations of John Donne." *Modern Critical Views: John Donne and the Seventeenth-Century Metaphysical Poets.* Ed. Harold Bloom. New York: Chelsea, 1986. 37–50, spec. 40–44. • Anthony, J. Philip. "Donne's 'The Relique.'" *Explicator* 44.2 (Winter 1986): 13–15.

Shakespeare's songs and sonnets approach pure lyricism, but the "metaphysical" poems of some of his contemporaries and immediate successors (including John Donne and George Herbert) replace direct, simple themes with subjects and ideas far more subtle and emotionally complex. A poet like A. E. Housman is naturally unsympathetic to this sort of poetry; a poet like T. S. Eliot admires it.

A. E. Housman: On Wit Versus Poetry

There was a whole age of English in which the place of poetry was usurped by something very different which possessed the proper and specific name of wit: wit not in its modern sense, but as defined by Johnson, 'a combination of dissimilar images, or discovery of occult resemblances in things apparently unlike'. Such discoveries are no more poetical than anagrams; such pleasure as they give is purely intellectual and is intellectually frivolous; but this was the pleasure principally sought and found in poems by the intelligentsia of fifty years and more of the seventeenth century. Some of the writers who purveyed it to their contemporaries were, by accident, considerable poets; and though their verse was generally inharmonious, and apparently cut into lengths and tied into faggots by deaf mathematicians, some little of their poetry was beautiful and even superb. But it was not by this that they captivated and sought to captivate. Simile and metaphor, things inessential to poetry, were their great engrossing preoccupation, and were prized the more in proportion as they were further fetched. They did not mean these accessories to be helpful, to make their sense clearer or their conceptions more vivid; they hardly even meant them for ornament, or cared whether an image had any independent power to please: their object was to startle by novelty and amuse by ingenuity a public whose one wish was to be so startled and amused. The pleasure, however luxurious, of hearing St Mary Magdalene's eyes described as

> Two walking baths, two weeping motions,
> Portable and compendious oceans,

was not a poetic pleasure; and poetry, as a label for this particular commodity, is not appropriate.

T. S. Eliot: On Intellectual Versus Reflective Poetry

The difference [between a passage by Herbert and one by Tennyson] is not a simple difference of degree between poets. It is something which had happened to the mind of England between the time of Donne or Lord Herbert of Cherbury and the time of Tennyson and Browning; it is the difference between the intellectual poet and the reflective poet. Tennyson and Browning are poets, and they think; but they do not feel their thought as immediately as the odour of a rose. A thought to Donne was an experience; it modified his sensibility. When a poet's mind is perfectly equipped for its work, it is constantly amalgamating disparate experience; the ordinary man's experience is chaotic, irregular, fragmentary. The latter falls in love, or reads Spinoza, and these two experiences have nothing to do with each other, or with the noise of the typewriter or the smell of cooking; in the mind of the poet these experiences are always forming new wholes.

JOHN MILTON

(1608–1674)

[WHEN I CONSIDER HOW MY LIGHT IS SPENT]

When I consider how my light is spent
  Ere half my days, in this dark world and wide,
  And that one talent which is death to hide
  Lodged with me useless, though my soul more bent
To serve therewith my Maker, and present   5
  My true account, lest he returning chide;
  "Doth God exact day-labor, light denied?"
  I fondly ask; but Patience to prevent
That murmur, soon replies, "God doth not need
  Either man's work or his own gifts; who best   10
  Bear his mild yoke, they serve him best. His state
Is kingly. Thousands at his bidding speed
  And post o'er land and ocean without rest:
  They also serve who only stand and wait."

(Sonnet 16) 1652

ON THE LATE MASSACRE IN PIEDMONT

Avenge, O Lord, thy slaughtered saints, whose bones
  Lie scattered on the Alpine mountains cold,
  Even them who kept thy truth so pure of old
  When all our fathers worshiped stocks and stones,
Forget not: in thy book record their groans   5
  Who were thy sheep and in their ancient fold
  Slain by the bloody Piedmontese that rolled
  Mother with infant down the rocks. Their moans
The vales redoubled to the hills, and they
  To Heaven. Their martyred blood and ashes sow   10
  O'er all th' Italian fields where still doth sway
The triple tyrant: that from these may grow
  A hundredfold, who having learnt thy way
  Early may fly the Babylonian woe.

(Sonnet 18) 1655

[METHOUGHT I SAW MY LATE ESPOUSÉD SAINT]

Methought I saw my late espouséd saint
  Brought to me like Alcestis from the grave,
  Whom Jove's great son to her glad husband gave,
  Rescued from Death by force, though pale and faint.
Mine, as whom washed from spot of child-bed taint   5
  Purification in the Old Law did save,
  And such, as yet once more I trust to have
  Full sight of her in heaven without restraint,
Came vested all in white, pure as her mind.
  Her face was veiled; yet to my fancied sight   10
  Love, sweetness, goodness, in her person shined
So clear as in no face with more delight.

"Massacre": The massacre of the Vaudois, a Protestant sect founded by Peter Valdres in the twelfth century, resulted from a dispute over land rights involving villages bordering France and Italy. In 1655 the Duke of Savoy sent the Marquis of Pianezza to expel the Vaudois, and when the villagers fled, Pianezza pursued and massacred nearly 2,000 of them. Cromwell took up the Vaudois cause and had Milton write letters of protest to several European countries. Meanwhile, the Vaudois regained strength and won several battles against the Piedmontese troops. A treaty that restored the ancient rights of the Vaudois was signed within months of the massacre.   8. *Mother with infant:* an account of the massacre by one of Cromwell's agents records three separate incidents in which a woman and her child were hurled down the rocks to their deaths.   12. *tyrant:* the Pope with his three-tiered crown.   14. *Babylonian:* Puritans often identified Roman Catholicism with the Babylon of *Revelation*.
"Methought": 2. *Alcestis:* in Euripides' *Alcestis*, she gives her life for her husband; Hercules ("Jove's great son") brings her back to life by wrestling with death.   6. *purification:* Old Testament purification of a woman after childbirth.

But O, as to embrace me she inclined,
I waked, she fled, and day brought back my night.

(Sonnet 23) ca. 1658

from PARADISE LOST, Book IX

Satan, having compassed the earth, with meditated guile returns as a mist by night into Paradise, enters into the serpent sleeping. Adam and Eve in the morning go forth to their labours, which Eve proposes to divide in several places, each labouring apart: Adam consents not, alleging the dangers lest that enemy, of whom they were forewarned, should attempt her found alone. Eve, loath to be thought not circumspect or firm enough, urges her going apart, the rather desirous to make trial of her strength; Adam at last yields. . . . [Milton's summary]

Oft he to her his charge of quick return
Repeated; she to him as oft engaged   400
To be returned by noon amid the bower,
And all things in best order to invite
Noontide repast, or afternoon's repose.
O much deceived, much failing, hapless Eve,
Of thy presumed return! Event perverse!   405
Thou never from that hour in Paradise
Found'st either sweet repast, or sound repose;
Such ambush hid among sweet flowers and shades
Waited with hellish rancor imminent
To intercept thy way, or send thee back   410
Despoiled of innocence, of faith, of bliss.
For now, and since first break of dawn, the fiend,
Mere serpent in appearance, forth was come,
And on his quest, where likeliest he might find
The only two of mankind, but in them   415
The whole included race, his purposed prey.
In bower and field he sought, where any tuft
Of grove or garden-plot more pleasant lay,
Their tendance or plantation for delight;
By fountain or by shady rivulet   420
He sought them both, but wished his hap might find
Eve separate; he wished, but not with hope
Of what so seldom chanced; when to his wish,
Beyond his hope, Eve separate he spies,
Veiled in a cloud of fragrance, where she stood,   425
Half spied, so thick the roses bushing round

"Paradise Lost": 419. *tendance:* object of care.

About her glowed, oft stooping to support
Each flower of slender stalk, whose head though gay
Carnation, purple, azure, or specked with gold,
Hung drooping unsustained, them she upstays   430
Gently with myrtle band, mindless the while
Herself, though fairest unsupported flower,
From her best prop so far, and storm so nigh.
Nearer he drew, and many a walk traversed
Of stateliest covert, cedar, pine, or palm;   435
Then voluble and bold, now hid, now seen
Among thick-woven arborets and flowers
Embordered on each bank, the hand of Eve:
Spot more delicious than those gardens feigned
Or of revived Adonis, or renowned   440
Alcinous, host of old Laertes' son,
Or that, not mystic, where the sapient king
Held dalliance with his fair Egyptian spouse.
Much he the place admired, the person more.
As one who long in populous city pent,   445
Where houses thick and sewers annoy the air,
Forth issuing on a summer's morn to breathe
Among the pleasant villages and farms
Adjoined, from each thing met conceives delight,
The smell of grain, or tedded grass, or kine,   450
Or dairy, each rural sight, each rural sound:
If chance with nymphlike step fair virgin pass,
What pleasing seemed, for her now pleases more,
She most, and in her look sums all delight.
Such pleasure took the serpent to behold   455
This flowery plat, the sweet recess of Eve
Thus early, thus alone; her heavenly form
Angelic, but more soft, and feminine,
Her graceful innocence, her every air
Of gesture or least action overawed   460
His malice, and with rapine sweet bereaved
His fierceness of the fierce intent it brought:
That space the evil one abstracted stood
From his own evil, and for the time remained

---

436. *voluble:* gliding easily; rolling.   438. *hand:* handiwork.   440. *Adonis:* a youth loved by
Venus and killed by a boar; his death and revival are celebrated in seasonal rites.
441. *Alcinous:* king of Phaeacia who entertained Odysseus; Odysseus was "stopped still" by
the beauty of his garden. *Laertes' son:* Odysseus; Laertes gave up kingship to take up gardening.   442. *sapient king:* Solomon, another Old Testament figure led to sin by love of
his wife.   456. *plat:* patch of ground.

Stupidly good, of enmity disarmed,   465
Of guile, of hate, of envy, of revenge.
But the hot Hell that always in him burns,
Though in mid Heaven, soon ended his delight,
And tortures him now more, the more he sees
Of pleasure not for him ordained: then soon   470
Fierce hate he recollects, and all his thoughts
Of mischief, gratulating, thus excites:
    "Thoughts, whither have ye led me? with what sweet
Compulsion thus transported to forget
What hither brought us? hate, not love, nor hope   475
Of Paradise for Hell, hope here to taste
Of pleasure, but all pleasure to destroy,
Save what is in destroying; other joy
To me is lost. Then let me not let pass
Occasion which now smiles; behold alone   480
The woman, opportune to all attempts,
Her husband, for I view far round, not nigh,
Whose higher intellectual more I shun,
And strength, of courage haughty, and of limb
Heroic built, though of terrestrial mold;   485
Foe not informidable, exempt from wound,
I not; so much hath Hell debased, and pain
Enfeebled me, to what I was in Heaven.
She fair, divinely fair, fit love for gods,
Not terrible, though terror be in love   490
And beauty, not approached by stronger hate,
Hate stronger, under show of love well feigned,
The way which to her ruin now I tend."
    So spake the enemy of mankind, enclosed
In serpent, inmate bad, and toward Eve   495
Addressed his way, not with indented wave,
Prone on the ground, as since, but on his rear,
Circular base of rising folds, that towered
Fold above fold a surging maze; his head
Crested aloft, and carbuncle his eyes;   500
With burnished neck of verdant gold, erect
Amidst his circling spires, that on the grass
Floated redundant. Pleasing was his shape,
And lovely; never since of serpent kind
Lovelier, not those that in Illyria changed   505

---

472. *gratulating:* expressing joy. 500. *carbuncle:* red garnet, a mineral associated with the underworld. 505. *Illyria:* the Adriatic region.

Hermione and Cadmus, or the god
In Epidaurus; nor to which transformed
Ammonian Jove, or Capitoline was seen,
He with Olympias, this with her who bore
Scipio, the height of Rome. With tract oblique   510
At first, as one who sought access, but feared
To interrupt, sidelong he works his way.
As when a ship by skillful steersman wrought
Nigh river's mouth or foreland, where the wind
Veers oft, as oft so steers, and shifts her sail: 515
So varied he, and of his tortuous train
Curled many a wanton wreath in sight of Eve,
To lure her eye: she busied heard the sound
Of rustling leaves, but minded not, as used   520
To such disport before her through the field,
From every beast, more duteous at her call,
Than at Circean call the herd disguised.
He bolder now, uncalled before her stood:
But as in gaze admiring; oft he bowed   525
His turret crest, and sleek enameled neck,
Fawning, and licked the ground whereon she trod.
His gentle dumb expression turned at length
The eye of Eve to mark his play: he, glad
Of her attention gained, with serpent tongue
Organic, or impulse of vocal air,   530
His fraudulent temptation thus began.
   "Wonder not, sovereign mistress, if perhaps
Thou canst, who art sole wonder; much less arm
Thy looks, the heaven of mildness, with disdain,
Displeased that I approach thee thus, and gaze   535
Insatiate, I thus single, nor have feared
Thy awful brow, more awful thus retired.
Fairest resemblance of thy Maker fair,
Thee all things living gaze on, all things thine
By gift, and thy celestial beauty adore   540
With ravishment beheld, there best beheld
Where universally admired: but here
In this enclosure wild, these beasts among,
Beholders rude, and shallow to discern

---

506. *Hermione . . . Cadmus:* both were metamorphosed into serpents.   507. *Epidaurus:* a
god of medicine who, in serpent form, went to Rome to stop the plague.   508. *Ammonian
Jove:* while in serpent form, fathered Alexander the Great. *Capitoline:* Jupiter Capitolinus, who
took a serpent form to father Scipio, the greatest general of the Roman Republic.
509. *Olympias:* mother of Alexander the Great.   522. *Circean:* allegorically, any form of
excess that reduces men to beasts.

Half what in thee is fair, one man except,   545
Who sees thee? (and what is one?) who shouldst be seen
A goddess among gods, adored and served
By angels numberless, thy daily train."

*Eve, wondering to hear the Serpent speak, asks how he attained to human
speech and such understanding, not till now; the Serpent answers that by
tasting of a certain tree in the garden he attained both to speech and reason,
till then void of both. Eve requires him to bring her to that tree, and finds it
to be the tree of knowledge forbidden. The Serpent now grown bolder, with
many wiles and arguments induces her at length to eat; she, pleased with the
taste, deliberates a while whether to impart thereof to Adam or not, at last
brings him of the fruit; relates what persuaded her to eat thereof. Adam at
first amazed, but perceiving her lost, resolves through vehemence of love to
perish with her and, extenuating the trespass, eats also of the fruit.* [Milton's summary]

In recompense (for such compliance bad
Such recompense best merits), from the bough   995
She gave him of that fair enticing fruit
With liberal hand; he scrupled not to eat,
Against his better knowledge, not deceived,
But fondly overcome with female charm.
Earth trembled from her entrails, as again   1000
In pangs, and Nature gave a second groan,
Sky lowered, and muttering thunder, some sad drops
Wept at completing of the mortal sin
Original; while Adam took no thought,
Eating his fill, nor Eve to iterate   1005
Her former trespass feared, the more to soothe
Him with her loved society; that now
As with new wine intoxicated both,
They swim in mirth, and fancy that they feel
Divinity within them breeding wings   1010
Wherewith to scorn the Earth. But that false fruit
Far other operation first displayed,
Carnal desire inflaming; he on Eve
Began to cast lascivious eyes, she him
As wantonly repaid; in lust they burn,   1015
Till Adam thus 'gan Eve to dalliance move:
    "Eve, now I see thou art exact of taste,
And elegant, of sapience no small part,
Since to each meaning savor we apply,

1018. *sapience:* the Latin word *sapere* means both "to taste" and "to be wise."

And palate call judicious. I the praise   1020
Yield thee, so well this day thou hast purveyed.
Much pleasure we have lost, while we abstained
From this delightful fruit, nor known till now
True relish, tasting; if such pleasure be
In things to us forbidden, it might be wished,   1025
For this one tree had been forbidden ten.
But come; so well refreshed, now let us play,
As meet is, after such delicious fare;
For never did thy beauty, since the day
I saw thee first and wedded thee, adorned   1030
With all perfections, so enflame my sense
With ardor to enjoy thee, fairer now
Than ever, bounty of this virtuous tree."
   So said he, and forbore not glance or toy
Of amorous intent, well understood   1035
Of Eve, whose eye darted contagious fire.
Her hand he seized, and to a shady bank,
Thick overhead with verdant roof embowered
He led her, nothing loath; flowers were the couch,
Pansies, and violets, and asphodel,   1040
And hyacinth—Earth's freshest, softest lap.
There they their fill of love and love's disport
Took largely, of their mutual guilt the seal,
The solace of their sin, till dewy sleep
Oppressed them, wearied with their amorous play.   1045
   Soon as the force of that fallacious fruit,
That with exhilarating vapor bland
About their spirits had played, and inmost powers
Made err, was now exhaled, and grosser sleep
Bred of unkindly fumes, with conscious dreams   1050
Encumbered, now had left them, up they rose
As from unrest, and each the other viewing,
Soon found their eyes how opened, and their minds
How darkened. Innocence, that as a veil
Had shadowed them from knowing ill, was gone;   1055
Just confidence, and native righteousness,
And honor from about them, naked left
To guilty Shame; he covered, but his robe
Uncovered more. So rose the Danite strong,
Herculean Samson, from the harlot-lap   1060
Of Philistean Dalilah, and waked

1036. *Of:* by. 1050. *unkindly:* unnatural.

Shorn of his strength; they destitute and bare
Of all their virtue. Silent, and in face
Confounded, long they sat, as strucken mute;
Till Adam, though not less than Eve abashed,   1065
At length gave utterance to these words constrained:
    "O Eve, in evil hour thou didst give ear
To that false worm, of whomsoever taught
To counterfeit man's voice, true in our fall,
False in our promised rising; since our eyes   1070
Opened we find indeed, and find we know
Both good and evil, good lost, and evil got:
Bad fruit of knowledge, if this be to know,
Which leaves us naked thus, of honor void,
Of innocence, of faith, of purity,   1075
Our wonted ornaments now soiled and stained,
And in our faces evident the signs
Of foul concupiscence; whence evil store,
Even shame, the last of evils; of the first
Be sure then. How shall I behold the face   1080
Henceforth of God or angel, erst with joy
And rapture so oft beheld? Those heavenly shapes
Will dazzle now this earthly with their blaze
Insufferably bright. O might I here
In solitude live savage, in some glade   1085
Obscured, where highest woods, impenetrable
To star or sunlight, spread their umbrage broad,
And brown as evening! Cover me, ye pines,
Ye cedars, with innumerable boughs
Hide me, where I may never see them more!   1090
But let us now, as in bad plight, devise
What best may for the present serve to hide
The parts of each from other, that seem most
To shame obnoxious, and unseemliest seen;
Some tree whose broad smooth leaves together sewed,   1095
And girded on our loins, may cover round
Those middle parts, that this newcomer, Shame,
There sit not, and reproach us as unclean."
    So counseled he, and both together went
Into the thickest wood; there soon they chose   1100
The figtree, not that kind for fruit renowned,
But such as at this day, to Indians known,
In Malabar or Deccan spreads her arms

1094. *obnoxious:* exposed.

Branching so broad and long, that in the ground
The bended twigs take root, and daughters grow 1105
About the mother tree, a pillared shade
High overarched, and echoing walks between;
There oft the Indian herdsman, shunning heat,
Shelters in cool, and tends his pasturing herds
At loopholes cut through thickest shade. Those leaves 1110
They gathered, broad as Amazonian targe,
And with what skill they had, together sewed,
To gird their waist; vain covering, if to hide
Their guilt and dreaded shame! O how unlike
To that first naked glory! Such of late 1115
Columbus found th' American, so girt
With feathered cincture, naked else and wild
Among the trees on isles and woody shores.
Thus fenced, and, as they thought, their shame in part
Covered, but not at rest or ease of mind, 1120
They sat them down to weep; nor only tears
Rained at their eyes, but high winds worse within
Began to rise, high passions, anger, hate,
Mistrust, suspicion, discord, and shook sore
Their inward state of mind, calm region once 1125
And full of peace, now tossed and turbulent:
For Understanding ruled not, and the Will
Heard not her lore, both in subjection now
To sensual Appetite, who, from beneath
Usurping over sovereign Reason, claimed 1130
Superior sway. From thus distempered breast,
Adam, estranged in look and altered style,
Speech intermitted thus to Eve renewed:
    "Would thou hadst hearkened to my words, and stayed
With me, as I besought thee, when that strange 1135
Desire of wandering, this unhappy morn,
I know not whence possessed thee! we had then
Remained still happy, not as now, despoiled
Of all our good, shamed, naked, miserable.
Let none henceforth seek needless cause to approve 1140
The faith they owe; when earnestly they seek
Such proof, conclude, they then begin to fail."
    To whom, soon moved with touch of blame, thus Eve:
"What words have passed thy lips, Adam severe?
Imput'st thou that to my default, or will 1145

———
1140. *approve:* prove.   1141. *owe:* own.

Of wandering, as thou call'st it, which who knows
But might as ill have happened, thou being by,
Or to thyself perhaps? Hadst thou been there,
Or here th' attempt, thou couldst not have discerned
Fraud in the serpent, speaking as he spake;   1150
No ground of enmity between us known,
Why he should mean me ill, or seek to harm?
Was I to have never parted from thy side?
As good have grown there still a lifeless rib.
Being as I am, why didst not thou, the head,   1155
Command me absolutely not to go,
Going into such danger, as thou saidst?
Too facile then, thou didst not much gainsay,
Nay, didst permit, approve, and fair dismiss.
Hadst thou been firm and fixed in thy dissent,   1160
Neither had I transgressed, nor thou with me."
    To whom, then first incensed, Adam replied:
"Is this the love, is this the recompense
Of mine to thee, ingrateful Eve, expressed
Immutable when thou were lost, not I,   1165
Who might have lived and joyed immortal bliss,
Yet willingly chose rather death with thee?
And am I now upbraided as the cause
Of thy transgressing? not enough severe,
It seems, in thy restraint! What could I more?   1170
I warned thee, I admonished thee, foretold
The danger, and the lurking enemy
That lay in wait: beyond this had been force,
And force upon free will hath here no place.
But confidence then bore thee on, secure   1175
Either to meet no danger, or to find
Matter of glorious trial; and perhaps
I also erred in overmuch admiring
What seemed in thee so perfect, that I thought
No evil durst attempt thee! but I rue   1180
That error now, which is become my crime,
And thou th' accuser. Thus it shall befall
Him who, to worth in women overtrusting,
Lets her will rule; restraint she will not brook,
And, left to herself, if evil thence ensue,   1185
She first his weak indulgence will accuse."
    Thus they in mutual accusation spent
The fruitless hours, but neither self-condemning;
And of their vain contést, appeared no end.

1667

Further Reading

Bush, Douglas, ed. *The Complete Poetry of John Milton*. Boston: Houghton, 1965.
• Ricks, Christopher. *Milton's Grand Style*. London: Oxford UP, 1963. • Lewis,
C. S. *A Preface to Paradise Lost*. London: Oxford UP, 1942. • Nardo, Anna K.
Milton's Sonnets and the Ideal Community. Lincoln: U of Nebraska P, 1979. • Stroup,
Thomas B. " 'When I Consider': Milton's Sonnet XIX." *Studies in Philology* 69.2
(Apr. 1972): 242–58. • Knott, John R., Jr. "The Biblical Matrix of Milton's
'On the Late Massacre in Piedmont.' " *Philological Quarterly* 62.2 (Spring 1983):
259–62.

*John Milton's great stature among English poets has not kept readers from
finding fault with some aspects of his poetry. Some readers, like T. S. Eliot,
have objected that Milton's language and imagery are vague. Others, like
Samuel Taylor Coleridge, have found in the supposed vagueness some
unexpected virtues.*

T. S. Eliot: On the Sound of Milton's Poetry

The most important fact about Milton, for my purpose, is his blindness. I
do not mean that to go blind in middle life is itself enough to determine the
whole nature of a man's poetry. Blindness must be considered in conjunction with Milton's personality and character, and the peculiar education
which he received. It must also be considered in connection with his devotion to, and expertness in, the art of music. Had Milton been a man of very
keen senses—I mean of *all* the five senses—his blindness would not have
mattered so much. But for a man whose sensuousness, such as it was, had
been withered early by book-learning, and whose gifts were naturally aural;
it mattered a great deal. It would seem, indeed, to have helped him to concentrate on what he could do best.

    At no period is the visual imagination conspicuous in Milton's poetry.
. . . Milton's images do not give a sense of particularity, nor are the separate
words developed in significance. His language is, if one may use the term
without disparagement, *artificial* and *conventional*.

    O'er the smooth enamel'd green . . .

      . . . paths of this drear wood
    The nodding horror of whose shady brows
    Threats the forlorn and wandering passenger.

('Shady brow' here is a diminution of the value of the two words from their use in the line from *Dr. Faustus*

> *Shadowing more beauty in their airy brows.*)

The imagery in *L'Allegro* and *Il Penseroso* is all general:

> *While the ploughman near at hand,*
> *Whistles o'er the furrowed land,*
> *And the milkmaid singeth blithe,*
> *And the mower whets his scythe,*
> *And every shepherd tells his tale,*
> *Under the hawthorn in the dale.*

It is not a particular ploughman, milkmaid, and shepherd that Milton sees (as Wordsworth might see them); the sensuous effect of these verses is entirely on the ear, and is joined to the concepts of ploughman, milkmaid, and shepherd.

Samuel Taylor Coleridge: On Milton's Imagination

The poet should paint to the imagination, not to the fancy; and I know no happier case to exemplify the distinction between these two faculties. Masterpieces of the former mode of poetic painting abound in the writings of Milton, ex. gr.

> "The fig-tree; not that kind for fruit renown'd,
> But such as at this day, to Indians known,
> In Malabar or Decan spreads her arms
> Branching so broad and long, that in the ground
> The bended twigs take root, *and daughters grow*
> *About the mother tree, a pillar'd shade*
> *High over-arch'd, and* ECHOING WALKS BETWEEN:
> *There oft the Indian Herdsman, shunning heat,*
> *Shelters in cool, and tends his pasturing herds*
> *At loop holes cut through thickest shade.*"
>
> *Paradise Lost*, ix, 1100–1110

This is *creation* rather than *painting*, or if painting, yet such, and with such co-presence of the whole picture flash'd at once upon the eye, as the sun paints in a camera obscura. But the poet must likewise understand and command what Bacon calls the *vestigia communia* of the senses, the latency of all in each, and more especially as by a magical *penna duplex*, the excitement of vision by sound and the exponents of sound. Thus "THE ECHOING WALKS BETWEEN," may be almost said to reverse the fable in tradition of the head of Memnon, in the Egyptian statue. Such may be deservedly entitled the *creative words* in the world of imagination.

ANDREW MARVELL

(1621–1678)

EYES AND TEARS

1

How wisely nature did decree,
With the same eyes to weep and see!
That, having viewed the object vain,
They might be ready to complain.

2

And, since the self-deluding sight,   5
In a false angle takes each height;
These tears which better measure all,
Like wat'ry lines and plummets fall.

3

Two tears, which sorrow long did weigh
Within the scales of either eye,   10
And then paid out in equal poise,
Are the true price of all my joys.

4

What in the world most fair appears,
Yea even laughter, turns to tears:
And all the jewels which we prize,   15
Melt in these pendants of the eyes.

5

I have through every garden been,
Amongst the red, the white, the green;
And yet, from all the flow'rs I saw,
No honey, but these tears could draw.   20

8. *plummet:* a plumb, a weight suspended to establish a vertical line. 11. *poise:* equal weight.

6

So the all-seeing sun each day
Distils the world with chemic ray;
But finds the essence only showers,
Which straight in pity back he pours.

7

Yet happy they whom grief doth bless,   25
That weep the more, and see the less:
And, to preserve their sight more true,
Bathe still their eyes in their own dew.

8

So Magdalen, in tears more wise
Dissolved those captivating eyes,   30
Whose liquid chains could flowing meet
To fetter her Redeemer's feet.

9

Not full sails hasting loaden home,
Nor the chaste lady's pregnant womb,
Nor Cynthia teeming shows so fair,   35
As two eyes swoll'n with weeping are.

10

The sparkling glance that shoots desire,
Drenched in these waves, does lose its fire.
Yea oft the Thund'rer pity takes
And here the hissing lightning slakes.   40

11

The incense was to heaven dear,
Not as a perfume, but a tear.
And stars show lovely in the night,
But as they seem the tears of light.

12

Ope then mine eyes your double sluice,   45
And practise so your noblest use.
For others too can see, or sleep;
But only human eyes can weep.

_____

22. *chemic:* chemical or alchemic.

13

Now like two clouds dissolving, drop,
And at each tear in distance stop: 50
Now like two fountains trickle down;
Now like two floods o'erturn and drown.

14

Thus let your streams o'erflow your springs,
Till eyes and tears be the same things:
And each the other's difference bears;   55
These weeping eyes, those seeing tears.

1681

THE DEFINITION OF LOVE

1

My Love is of a birth as rare
    As 'tis, for object, strange and high;
It was begotten by Despair,
    Upon Impossibility.

2

Magnanimous Despair alone   5
    Could show me so divine a thing,
Where feeble Hope could ne'er have flown,
    But vainly flapped its tinsel wing.

3

And yet I quickly might arrive
    Where my extended soul is fixed;   10
But Fate does iron wedges drive,
    And always crowds itself betwixt.

4

For Fate with jealous eye does see
    Two perfect loves, nor lets them close;
Their union would her ruin be,   15
    And her tyrannic pow'r depose.

5

And therefore her decrees of steel
    Us as the distant poles have placed,
(Though Love's whole world on us doth wheel),
    Not by themselves to be embraced,   20

Unless the giddy heaven fall,
   And earth some new convulsion tear,
And, us to join, the world should all
   Be cramped into a planisphere.

7

As lines, so loves oblique, may well   25
   Themselves in every angle greet:
But ours, so truly parallel,
   Though infinite, can never meet.

Therefore the love which us doth bind,
   But Fate so enviously debars,   30
Is the conjunction of the mind,
   And opposition of the stars.

                                                          1681

A DIALOGUE BETWEEN
THE SOUL AND BODY

Soul.   O, who shall from this dungeon raise
         A soul enslaved so many ways?
         With bolts of bones, that fettered stands
         In feet, and manacled in hands;
         Here blinded with an eye, and there   5
         Deaf with the drumming of an ear;
         A soul hung up, as 'twere, in chains
         Of nerves, and arteries, and veins;
         Tortured, besides each other part,
         In a vain head, and double heart?   10

Body. O, who shall me deliver whole
         From bonds of this tyrannic soul?
         Which, stretched upright, impales me so
         That mine own precipice I go;
         And warms and moves his needless frame,   15
         (A fever could but do the same,)
         And, wanting where its spite to try,
         Has made me live to let me die
         A body that could never rest
         Since this ill spirit it possessed.   20

───────

"Definition of Love": 24. *planisphere:* a flat representation of a sphere with the poles united.

Soul. What magic could me thus confine
　　　Within another's grief to pine?
　　　Where, whatsoever it complain,
　　　I feel, that cannot feel, the pain;
　　　And all my care itself employs,　　　　　　　　　25
　　　That to preserve which me destroys;
　　　Constrained not only to endure
　　　Diseases, but, what's worse, the cure;
　　　And, ready oft the port to gain,
　　　Am shipwrecked into health again.　　　　　　　30

Body. But Physic yet could never reach
　　　The maladies thou me dost teach;
　　　Whom first the cramp of hope does tear,
　　　And then the palsy shakes of fear;
　　　The pestilence of love does heat,　　　　　　　　35
　　　Or hatred's hidden ulcer eat;
　　　Joy's cheerful madness does perplex,
　　　Or sorrow's other madness vex;
　　　Which knowledge forces me to know,
　　　And memory will not forego;　　　　　　　　　　40
　　　What but a soul could have the wit
　　　To build me up for sin so fit?
　　　So architects do square and hew
　　　Green trees that in the forest grew.

　　　　　　　　　　　　　　　　　　　　　　　1681

TO HIS COY MISTRESS

Had we but world enough, and time,
This coyness, lady, were no crime.
We would sit down, and think which way
To walk, and pass our long love's day.
Thou by the Indian Ganges' side　　　　　　　　　　5
Shouldst rubies find: I by the tide
Of Humber would complain. I would
Love you ten years before the flood,
And you should, if you please, refuse
Till the conversion of the Jews;　　　　　　　　　　10
My vegetable love should grow
Vaster than empires and more slow;
An hundred years should go to praise

"Mistress": 7. *Humber:* a small river that runs through Marvell's hometown of Hull.

Thine eyes, and on thy forehead gaze;
Two hundred to adore each breast,   15
But thirty thousand to the rest;
An age at least to every part,
And the last age should show your heart.
For, lady, you deserve this state,
Nor would I love at lower rate.   20
    But at my back I always hear
Time's wingèd chariot hurrying near,
And yonder all before us lie
Deserts of vast eternity.

Thy beauty shall no more be found,   25
Nor, in thy marble vault, shall sound
My echoing song; then worms shall try
That long-preserved virginity,
And your quaint honour turn to dust,
And into ashes all my lust: 30
The grave's a fine and private place,
But none, I think, do there embrace.
    Now therefore, while the youthful hue
Sits on thy skin like morning dew,
And while thy willing soul transpires   35
At every pore with instant fires,
Now let us sport us while we may,
And now, like am'rous birds of prey,
Rather at once our time devour,
Than languish in his slow-chapped power.   40
Let us roll all our strength and all
Our sweetness up into one ball,
And tear our pleasures with rough strife,
Through the iron gates of life;
Thus, though we cannot make our sun   45
Stand still, yet we will make him run.

1681

BERMUDAS

Where the remote Bermudas ride,
In the ocean's bosom unespied,

"Mistress": 29. *quaint:* fastidious.   *"Bermudas"*: Inspired by the Puritan zeal and cheerfulness
of his friends, the Oxenbridges, Marvell wrote "Bermudas" while he was a guest in their
house. The Oxenbridges returned to England in 1641 after two extended stays in the islands.

From a small boat, that rowed along,
The listening winds received this song:

   "What should we do but sing His praise,   5
That led us through the wat'ry maze,
Unto an isle so long unknown,
And yet far kinder than our own?

Where He the huge sea-monsters wracks,
That lift the deep upon their backs;   10
He lands us on a grassy stage,
Safe from the storms, and prelate's rage.
He gave us this eternal spring,
Which here enamels every thing,
And sends the fowls to us in care,   15
On daily visits through the air;
He hangs in shades the orange bright,
Like golden lamps in a green night,
And does in the pom'granates close
Jewels more rich than Ormus shows;   20
He makes the figs our mouths to meet,
And throws the melons at our feet;
But apples plants of such a price.
No tree could ever bear them twice;
With cedars chosen by His hand,   25
From Lebanon, He stores the land,
And makes the hollow seas, that roar,
Proclaim the ambergris on shore;
He cast (of which we rather boast)
The Gospel's pearl upon our coast,   30
And in these rocks for us did frame
A temple where to sound His name.
Oh! let our voice His praise exalt,
Till it arrive at Heaven's vault,
Which, thence (perhaps) rebounding, may   35
Echo beyond the Mexique Bay."

   Thus sung they, in the English boat,
An holy and a cheerful note;
And all the way, to guide their chime,
With falling oars they kept the time.   40

                              1681

---

20. *Ormus:* a trading center for pearls and jewels in the Persian Gulf.   23. *apples:* pineapples.
36. *Mexique Bay:* Gulf of Mexico.

Further Reading

Eliot, T. S. "Andrew Marvell." *The Critical Heritage*. Ed. Elizabeth Story Donno. London: Routledge, 1978. 362–74. • Craze, Michael. *The Life and Lyrics of Andrew Marvell*. New York: Barnes, 1978. • Pequigney, Joseph. "Marvell's 'Soul' Poetry." *Tercentenary Essays in Honor of Andrew Marvell*. Ed. Kenneth Friedenreich. Hamden, Ct.: Archer, 1977. 76–104, spec. 86–93. • Crider, Richard. "Marvell's Valid Logic." *College Literature* 15.3 (1988): 224–32. • Summers, Joseph H. "Some Apocalyptic Strains in Marvell's Poetry." *Tercentenary Essays in Honor of Andrew Marvell*. Ed. Kenneth Friedenreich. Hamden, Ct.: Archer, 1977. 180–203, spec. 198–200. • Hyman, Lawrence W. *Andrew Marvell*. New York: Twayne, 1964.

Andrew Marvell's poetic reputation was not great at the time of his death (it was overshadowed by his political reputation). In the eighteenth and nineteenth centuries, he was thought of as a distinctly minor poet. Three hundred years after his birth, however, his reputation rose because the rising generation of poets (and especially T. S. Eliot) found in his work qualities they wished to emulate in their own.

T. S. Eliot: On Marvell's "Tough Reasonableness"

The wit of the Caroline poets . . . is more than a technical accomplishment, or the vocabulary and syntax of an epoch; it is, what we have designated tentatively as wit, a tough reasonableness beneath a slight lyric grace . . . . There is here an equipoise, a balance and proportion of tones, which, while it cannot raise Marvell to the level of Dryden or Milton, extorts an approval which these poets do not receive from us, and bestows a pleasure at least different in kind than what they can often give. It is what makes Marvell a classic; or a classic at least in a sense in which Gray and Collins are not; for the latter, with all their accredited purity, are comparatively poor in shades of feeling to contrast and unite.

. . . With our eye still on Marvell, we can say that wit is not erudition; it is sometimes stifled by erudition, as in much of Milton. It is not cynicism, though it has a kind of toughness which may be confused with cynicism by the tender-minded. It is confused with erudition because it belongs to an educated mind, rich in generations of experience. It involves, probably, a recognition, implicit in the expression of every experience, of the other kinds of experience which are possible, which we find as clearly in the greatest as in poets like Marvell. . . . [T]hat precise taste of Marvell's . . . finds for him the proper degree of seriousness for every subject which he treats . . . .

But later poets, who would have been the better for Marvell's quality, were without it; even Browning seems oddly immature, in some way, beside Marvell. And nowadays we find occasionally good irony, or satire, which lacks wit's internal equilibrium, because their voices are essential protests against some outside sentimentality or stupidity; or we find serious poets who seem afraid of acquiring wit, lest they lose intensity. The quality which Marvell had, this modest and certainly impersonal virtue—whether we call it wit or reason, or even urbanity— . . . . is something precious and needed and apparently extinct; it is what should preserve the reputation of Marvell.

Trained as a lawyer, seasoned as a soldier, and involved in U.S. politics both as librarian of Congress and assistant secretary of state, Archibald MacLeish was part of the poetic generation that appreciated and understood Marvell's attitude toward life. "You, Andrew Marvell" does justice to Marvell's "tough reasonableness" and at the same time responds to what MacLeish and others felt to be a shallow optimism in the American character.

Archibald MacLeish

(1892–1982)

YOU, ANDREW MARVELL

And here face down, beneath the sun
And here upon earth's noonward height
To feel the always coming on
The always rising of the night

To feel creep up the curving east   5
The earthy chill of dusk and slow
Upon those under lands the vast
And ever climbing shadow grow

And strange at Ecbatan the trees
Take leaf by leaf the evening strange   10
The flooding dark about their knees
The mountains over Persia change

And now at Kermanshah the gate
Dark empty and the withered grass
And through the twilight now the late   15
Few travelers in the westward pass

And Baghdad darken and the bridge
Across the silent river gone

And through Arabia the edge
Of evening widen and steal on   20

And deepen on Palmyra's street
The wheel rut in the ruined stone
And Lebanon fade out and Crete
High through the clouds and overblown

And over Sicily the air   25
Still flashing with the landward gulls
And loom and slowly disappear
The sails above the shadowy hulls

And Spain go under and the shore
Of Africa the gilded sand   30
And evening vanish and no more
The low pale light across that land

Nor now the long light on the sea

And here face downward in the sun
To feel how swift how secretly   35
The shadow of the night comes on. . . .

1930

ALEXANDER POPE

(1688–1744)

SOUND AND SENSE

But most by Numbers judge a Poet's song,
And smooth or rough, with them, is right or wrong;
In the bright Muse tho' thousand charms conspire,
Her Voice is all these tuneful fools admire;   340
Who haunt *Parnassus* but to please their ear,
Not mend their minds; as some to Church repair,
Not for the doctrine, but the music there.
These equal syllables alone require,
Tho' oft' the ear the open vowels tire;   345
While expletives their feeble aid do join;
And ten low words oft' creep in one dull line;
While they ring round the same unvary'd chimes,

"Sound and Sense": 337. *Numbers:* versification.   341. *Parnassus:* a mountain in Greece sacred to the Muses.

With sure returns of still-expected rhymes.
Where-e'er you find *the cooling western breeze,*   350
In the next line, it *whispers thro' the trees;*
If crystal streams *with pleasing murmurs creep,*
The reader's threaten'd (not in vain) with *sleep.*
Then, at the last, and only couplet fraught
With some unmeaning thing they call a Thought,   355
A needless *Alexandrine* ends the song,
That like a wounded snake, drags its slow length along.
Leave such to tune their own dull rhimes, and know
What's roundly smooth, or languishingly slow;
And praise the easy vigor of a line,   360
Where *Denham's* strength, and *Waller's* sweetness join.
True ease in writing comes from art, not chance,
As those move easiest who have learn'd to dance.
'Tis not enough no harshness gives offence,
The sound must seem an echo to the sense.   365
Soft is the strain when *Zephyr* gently blows,
And the smooth stream in smoother numbers flows;
But when loud surges lash the sounding shore,
The hoarse, rough verse should like the torrent roar.
When *Ajax* strives, some rock's vast weight to throw,   370
The line too labours, and the words move slow;
Not so, when swift *Camilla* scours the plain,
Flies o'er th' unbending corn, and skims along the main.
Hear how *Timotheus'* various lays surprise,   375
And bid alternate passions fall and rise!

(An Essay on Criticism, *part 2, ll. 337–375)   1711*

THE GAME OF OMBRE

Close by those meads, for ever crown'd with flow'rs,
Where *Thames* with pride surveys his rising tow'rs,
There stands a structure of majestic frame,

"*Sound and Sense*": 361. *Denham and Waller:* seventeenth-century poets; Pope claimed that
the Elizabethans could produce "nothing so even, sweet, and flowing, as Mr. Waller; nothing
so majestic, so correct, as Sir John Denham." 336. *Zephyr:* the west wind.   370. *Ajax:* hero
in Virgil's *Aeneid* known for his roughness and strength.   372. *Camilla:* female warrior in
Virgil's *Aeneid* whose life was saved when her father attached her to a javelin and hurled her
across a river.   374. *Timotheus:* a bard known for his music, which was so passionate it could
drive one to rage or tranquillity.   "*Ombre*": Ombre is a three-handed card game in which the
player naming trumps tries to take more tricks than the other two players combined. When
spades are trumps, the three highest ranked cards (the Matadores) are the ace of spades
(Spadille), the deuce of spades (Manille), and the ace of clubs (Basto). Thereafter, the cards
rank as in bridge, except that in nontrump suits, aces are low.   2. *Thames:* a river in
Southern England that runs through London.

Which from the neighb'ring *Hampton* takes its name.
Here *Britain*'s statesman oft' the fall foredoom   5
Of foreign tyrants, and of nymphs at home;
Here thou, great *Anna!* whom three realms obey,
Dost sometimes counsel take—and sometimes Tea.
  Hither the heroes and the nymphs resort,
To taste a while the pleasures of a Court;   10
In various talk th' instructive hours they past,
Who gave the ball, or paid the visit last:
One speaks the glory of the *British* Queen,
And one describes a charming *Indian* screen;
A third interprets motions, looks, and eyes;   15
At ev'ry word a reputation dies.
Snuff, or the fan, supply each pause of chat,
With singing, laughing, ogling, and all that.
  Mean while declining from the noon of day,
The sun obliquely shoots his burning ray;   20
The hungry Judges soon the sentence sign,
And wretches hang that Jury-men may dine;
The merchant from th' *Exchange* returns in peace,
And the long labours of the Toilet cease.—
Belinda now, whom thirst of fame invites,   25
Burns to encounter two adventrous Knights,
At *Ombre* singly to decide their doom;
And swells her breast with conquests yet to come.
Strait the three bands prepare in arms to join,
Each band the number of the sacred nine.   30
Soon as she spreads her hand, th' aerial guard
Descend, and sit on each important card:
First *Ariel* perch'd upon a Matadore,
Then each, according to the rank they bore;
For *Sylphs*, yet mindful of their ancient race,   35
Are, as when women, wondrous fond of place.
  Behold, four Kings in majesty rever'd,
With hoary whiskers and a forky beard:
And four fair Queens whose hands sustain a flow'r,
Th' expressive emblem of their softer pow'r;   40
Four Knaves in garbs succinct, a trusty band,
Caps on their heads, and halberds in their hand
And particolour'd troops, a shining train,
Draw forth to combat on the velvet plain.
  The skilful nymph reviews her force with care;   45

---

4. *Hampton:* a section of London surrounding Hampton Court, the largest of royal palaces.
7. *Anna:* Queen Anne, ruler of Great Britain and Ireland.

Let Spades be trumps, she said, and trumps they were.
    Now move to war her sable Matadores,
In show like leaders of the swarthy Moors.
Spadillio first, unconquerable Lord!
Led off two captive trumps, and swept the board.   50
As many more *Manillio* forc'd to yield,
And march'd a victor from the verdant field.
Him *Basto* follow'd, but his fate more hard
Gain'd but one trump and one *Plebeian* card.
With his broad sabre next, a chief in years,   55
The hoary Majesty of Spades appears;
Puts forth one manly leg, to sight reveal'd;
The rest, his many-colour'd robe conceal'd.
The rebel-Knave, who dares his prince engage,
Proves the just victim of his royal rage.   60
Ev'n mighty *Pam* that Kings and Queens o'erthrew,
And mow'd down armies in the fights of *Lu,*
Sad chance of war! now, destitute of aid,
Falls undistinguish'd by the victor Spade!
    Thus far both armies to *Belinda* yield;   65
Now to the Baron fate inclines the field.
His warlike *Amazon* her host invades,
Th' imperial consort of the crown of Spades.
The Club's black Tyrant first her victim dy'd,
Spite of his haughty mien, and barb'rous pride: 70
What boots the regal circle on his head,
His giant limbs, in state unwieldy spread;
That long behind he trails his pompous robe,
And, of all monarchs, only grasps the globe?
    The Baron now his Diamonds pours apace;   75
Th' embroider'd King who shows but half his face,
And his refulgent Queen, with pow'rs combin'd,
Of broken troops an easy conquest find.
Clubs, Diamonds, Hearts, in wild disorder seen,
With throngs promiscuous strow the level green.   80
Thus when dispers'd a routed army runs,
Of *Asia*'s troops, and *Africa*'s sable sons,
With like confusion different nations fly,
In various habits, and of various dye,
The pierc'd battalions dis-united fall,   85
In heaps on heaps; one fate o'erwhelms them all.
    The Knave of Diamonds tries his wily arts,

61. *Pam:* Knave of Clubs; strongest card in the card game Loo (Lu).   67. *Amazon:* Queen of
Spades.

And wins (oh shameful chance) the Queen of Hearts.
At this, the blood the virgin's cheek forsook,
A livid paleness spreads o'er all her look;
She sees, and trembles at th' approaching ill,
Just in the jaws of ruin, and *Codille*.
And now, (as oft' in some distemper'd state)
On one nice Trick depends the gen'ral fate.
An Ace of Hearts steps forth: The King unseen
Lurk'd in her hand, and mourn'd his captive Queen:
He springs to vengeance with an eager pace,
And falls like thunder on the prostrate Ace.
The nymph exulting fills with shouts the sky,
The walls, the woods, and long canals reply.
  Oh thoughtless mortals! ever blind to fate,
Too soon dejected, and too soon elate!
Sudden, these honours shall be snatch'd away,
And curs'd for ever this victorious day.

          (The Rape of the Lock, *canto 3, ll. 1–104*) *1714*

EPISTLE TO MISS BLOUNT

On her leaving the Town after the Coronation

As some fond virgin, whom her mother's care
Drags from the town to wholsom country air,
Just when she learns to roll a melting eye,
And hear a spark, yet think no danger nigh;
From the dear man unwilling she must sever,
Yet takes one kiss before she parts for ever.
Thus from the world fair *Zephalinda* flew,
Saw others happy, and with sighs withdrew;
Not that their pleasures caus'd her discontent,
She sigh'd not that They stay'd, but that She went.
  She went, to plain-work and to purling brooks,
Old-fashion'd halls, dull aunts, and croaking rooks,
She went from Op'ra, park, assembly, play,
To morning walks, and pray'rs three hours a day:
To part her time 'twixt reading and Bohea,
To muse, and spill her solitary Tea,
Or o'er cold coffee trifle with the spoon,

"*Ombre*": 92. *Codille:* defeat, failure to take five tricks of nine.   "*Epistle to Miss Blount*": This poem was written for Teresa Blount, the sister of Pope's close friend, Martha Blount. The coronation suggested was that of George I in 1714.   4. *spark:* a fop or beau.   7. *Zephalinda:* a fanciful name adopted by Teresa Blount.   15. *Bohea:* an expensive tea.

Count the slow clock, and dine exact at noon;
Divert her eyes with pictures in the fire,
Hum half a tune, tell stories to the squire;   20
Up to her godly garret after sev'n,
These starve and pray, for that's the way to heav'n.
    Some Squire, perhaps, you take delight to rack;
Whose game is Whisk, whose treat a toast in sack,
Who visits with a gun, presents you birds,   25
Then gives a smacking buss, and cries—No words!
Or with his hound comes hollowing from the stable,
Makes love with nods, and knees beneath a table;
Whose laughs are hearty, tho' his jests are coarse,
And loves you best of all things—but his horse.   30
    In some fair evening, on your elbow laid,
You dream of triumphs in the rural shade;
In pensive thought recall the fancy'd scene,
See Coronations rise on ev'ry green,
Before you pass th' imaginary sights   35
Of Lords, and Earls, and Dukes, and garter'd Knights;
While the spread Fan o'ershades your closing eyes,
Then give one flirt, and all the vision flies.
Thus vanish sceptres, coronets, and balls,
And leave you in lone woods, or empty walls.   40
    So when your slave, at some dear, idle time,
(Not plagu'd with headachs, or the want of rhime)
Stands in the streets, abstracted from the crew,
And while he seems to study, thinks of you:
Just when his fancy points your sprightly eyes,   45
Or sees the blush of *Parthenissa* rise,
Gay pats my shoulder, and you vanish quite;
Streets, chairs, and coxcombs, rush upon my sight;
Vext to be still in town, I knit my brow,
Look sow'r, and hum a song—as you may now.   50

                                                      1717

TIMON'S VILLA

At *Timon*'s Villa let us pass a day,
Where all cry out, 'What sums are thrown away!'   100
So proud, so grand; of that stupendous air,

"*Epistle*": 26. *buss:* kiss.   46. *Parthenissa:* Martha Blount.   47. *Gay:* the poet, John Gay.
Timon's Villa: Pope presents in the person of Timon a synthesis of several wealthy men whose estates grossly insulted good taste.

Soft and *Agreeable* come never there.
Greatness, with *Timon,* dwells in such a draught
As brings all *Brobdignag* before your thought.
To compass this, his building is a Town,   105
His pond an Ocean, his parterre a Down:
Who but must laugh, the Master when he sees,
A puny insect, shiv'ring at a breeze!
Lo! what huge heaps of littleness around!
The whole, a labour'd quarry above ground.   110
Two *Cupids* squirt before: a Lake behind
Improves the keenness of the Northern wind.
His Gardens next your admiration call,
On ev'ry side you look, behold the Wall!
No pleasing Intricacies intervene,   115
No artful wildness to perplex the scene;
Grove nods at grove, each Alley has a brother,
And half the platform just reflects the other.
The suff'ring eye inverted Nature sees,
Trees cut to Statues, Statues thick as trees,   120
With here a Fountain, never to be play'd,
And there a Summer-house, that knows no shade.
Here *Amphitrite* sails thro' myrtle bow'rs;
There *Gladiators* fight, or die in flow'rs;
Un-water'd see the drooping sea-horse mourn,   125
And swallows roost in *Nilus'* dusty Urn.
    My Lord advances with majestic mien,
Smit with the mighty pleasure, to be seen:
But soft—by regular approach—not yet—
First thro' the length of yon hot Terrace sweat;   130
And when up ten steep slopes you've dragg'd your thighs,
Just at his Study-door he'll bless your eyes.
    His *Study?* with what Authors is it stor'd?
In Books, not Authors, curious is my Lord;
To all their *dated Backs* he turns you round: 135
These *Aldus* printed, those *Da Suëil* has bound.
Lo some are *Vellom,* and the rest as good
For all his Lordship knows, but they are Wood.
For *Locke* or *Milton* 'tis in vain to look,
These shelves admit not any modern book.   140
    And now the Chappel's silver bell you hear,
That summons you to all the pride of Pray'r:

---

104. *Brobdignag:* the land of giants in Swift's *Gulliver's Travels* (1726).   123. *Amphitrite:*
Greek goddess of the sea, Poseidon's wife.   126. *Nilus'* . . . *urn:* the urn from which the river
god Nile should pour water.   136. *Aldus, Da Suëil:* European men prominent in the
book-making business.

Light quirks of Musick, broken and uneven,
Make the soul dance upon a Jig to Heav'n.
On painted Ceilings you devoutly stare,   145
Where sprawl the Saints of *Verrio,* or *Laguerre,*
On gilded clouds in fair expansion lie,
And bring all Paradise before your eye.
To rest, the Cushion and soft Dean invite,
Who never mentions Hell to ears polite.   150
   But hark! the chiming Clocks to dinner call;
A hundred footsteps scrape the marble Hall:
The rich Buffet well-colour'd *Serpents* grace,
And gaping *Tritons* spew to wash your face.
Is this a dinner? this a Genial room?   155
No, 'tis a Temple, and a Hecatomb;
A solemn Sacrifice, perform'd in state,
You drink by measure, and to minutes eat.
So quick retires each flying course, you'd swear
Sancho's dread Doctor and his Wand were there.   160
Between each Act the trembling salvers ring,
From soup to sweetwine, and *God bless the King.*
In plenty starving, tantaliz'd in state,
And complaisantly help'd to all I hate,
Treated, caress'd, and tir'd, I take my leave,   165
Sick of his civil Pride from Morn to Eve;
I curse such lavish cost, and little skill,
And swear no Day was ever past so ill.
   Yet hence the *Poor* are cloath'd, the *Hungry* fed;
Health to himself, and to his Infants bread   170
The Lab'rer bears: What his hard Heart denies,
His charitable Vanity supplies.

(Epistle to Richard Boyle, Earl of Burlington, *ll. 99–172*)   *1731*

Further Reading

Clark, Donald B. *Alexander Pope.* New York: Twayne, 1967. • Hooker, Edward
Niles. "Pope on Wit: The Essay on Criticism." *Essential Articles for the Study of
Alexander Pope.* Ed. Maynard Mack. Hamden, Ct: Archon, 1964. 175–97. • Brooks,

---

146. *Verrio, Laguerre:* fashionable court artists.   154. *Tritons:* like mermaids, half human and
half fish; water was ejected from their open mouths into a fountain.   160. *Sancho's . . . Wand:* In Cervantes' *Don Quixote,* the doctor steals away the food Sancho longs for.

Cleanth. "The Case of Miss Arabella Fermor." *Pope: A Collection of Critical Essays.* Ed. J. V. Guerinot. Englewood Cliffs, NJ: Prentice, 1972. 93–110. • Pollack, Ellen. " 'The Rape of the Lock': A Reification of the Myth of Passive Womanhood." *The Poetics of Sexual Myth: Gender and Ideology in the Verse of Swift and Pope.* Chicago: U of Chicago P, 1985. 77–107. • Pope, Alexander. "Epistle IV (To Burlington)." *Epistles to Several Persons.* Ed. F. W. Bateson. London: Methuen, 1961. 127–56, 170–74. • Hibbard, G. R. *Essential Articles for the Study of Alexander Pope.* Ed. Maynard Mack. Hamden, Ct: Archon, 1964. 401–37.

The "tough reasonableness" of Andrew Marvell's poetry became, in the decades that followed, something almost exactly opposed to the metaphysical wit of Donne and Herbert. By the time of Alexander Pope, reasonableness had become devotion to Reason, and wit had come to mean taste and judgment:

> *Some to conceit alone their taste confine,*
> *And glittering thoughts struck out at every line;*
> *Pleased with a work where nothing's just or fit;*
> *One glaring chaos and wild heap of wit.*
> *Poets, like painters, thus, unskilled to trace*
> *The naked Nature and the living grace,*
> *With gold and jewels cover every part,*
> *And hide with ornaments their want of art.*
> *True wit is nature to advantage dress'd:*
> *What oft was thought, but ne'er so well express'd.*

(An Essay on Criticism, ll. 289–298)

As the century wore on and the first stirring of the Romantic revolution began, some people began to question whether Pope, for all his brilliance, was a poet at all. The reputation of the neoclassical poets sank in the nineteenth and the early twentieth centuries, for reasons well stated by A. E. Housman in "The Name and Nature of Poetry" (1933).

A. E. Housman: On the Frosty Perfection of Pope

The literature of the eighteenth century in England is an admirable and most enjoyable thing. It has a greater solidity of excellence than any before or after; and although the special task and characteristic achievement of the age was the invention and establishment of a healthy, workmanlike, athletic prose, to supersede the cumbrous and decorated and self-admiring prose of a Milton or a Jeremy Taylor, and to become a trustworthy implement for accurate thinking and the serious pursuit of truth, yet in verse also it created masterpieces, and perhaps no English poem of greater than lyric length, not even 'The Nonne's Priest's Tale' or 'The Ancient Mariner', is quite so perfect as 'The Rape of the Lock'. But the human faculty which dominated the eighteenth century and informed its literature was the intelligence, and that involved, as Arnold says, 'some repressing and silencing of poetry', 'some touch of frost to the imaginative life of the soul'. Man had ceased to live from the depths of his nature; he occupied himself for choice with thoughts which do not range beyond the sphere of the understanding; he lighted the candles and drew down the blind to shut out that patroness of poets, the moon. The writing of poetry proceeded, and much of the poetry written was excellent literature; but excellent literature which is also poetry is not therefore excellent poetry, and the poetry of the eighteenth century was most satisfactory when it did not try to be poetical. . . .

To poets of the eighteenth century high and impassioned poetry did not come spontaneously, because the feelings which foster its birth were not then abundant and urgent in the inner man; but they girt up their loins and essayed a lofty strain at the bidding of ambition. The way to write real poetry, they thought, must be to write something as little like prose as possible; they devised for the purpose what was called a 'correct and splendid diction', which consisted in always using the wrong word instead of the right, and plastered it as ornament, with no thought of propriety, on whatever they desired to dignify. It commanded notice and was not easy to mistake; so the public mind soon connected it with the notion of poetry and came in course of time to regard it as alone poetical.

WILLIAM BLAKE

(1757–1827)

THE LAMB

Little Lamb, who made thee?
Dost thou know who made thee?
Gave thee life & bid thee feed,
By the stream & o'er the mead;
Gave thee clothing of delight,   5
Softest clothing wooly bright;
Gave thee such a tender voice,
Making all the vales rejoice!
Little Lamb, who made thee?
Dost thou know who made thee?   10

Little Lamb, I'll tell thee,
Little Lamb, I'll tell thee!
He is called by thy name,

For he calls himself a Lamb:
He is meek & he is mild,   15
He became a little child:
I a child & thou a lamb,
We are calléd by his name.
     Little Lamb, God bless thee.
     Little Lamb, God bless thee.   20

(Songs of Innocence)   *1789*

THE CHIMNEY SWEEPER

When my mother died I was very young,
And my father sold me while yet my tongue
Could scarcely cry " 'weep! 'weep! 'weep! 'weep!"
So your chimneys I sweep & in soot I sleep.

There's little Tom Dacre, who cried when his head   5
That curl'd like a lambs back, was shav'd, so I said,
"Hush, Tom! never mind it, for when your head's bare,
You know that the soot cannot spoil your white hair."

And so he was quiet, & that very night,
As Tom was a-sleeping he had such a sight!   10
That thousands of sweepers, Dick, Joe, Ned, & Jack,
Were all of them lock'd up in coffins of black;

And by came an Angel who had a bright key,
And he open'd the coffins & set them all free;
Then down a green plain, leaping, laughing they run,   15
And wash in a river and shine in the Sun;

Then naked & white, all their bags left behind,
They rise upon clouds, and sport in the wind.
And the Angel told Tom, if he'd be a good boy,
He'd have God for his father & never want joy.   20

And so Tom awoke; and we rose in the dark
And got with our bags & our brushes to work.
Tho' the morning was cold, Tom was happy & warm;
So if all do their duty, they need not fear harm.

(Songs of Innocence)   *1789*

THE LITTLE BLACK BOY

My mother bore me in the southern wild,
And I am black, but O! my soul is white;

White as an angel is the English child:
But I am black as if bereav'd of light.

My mother taught me underneath a tree,   5
And sitting down before the heat of day,
She took me on her lap and kisséd me,
And pointing to the east, began to say:

"Look on the rising sun: there God does live,
And gives his light, and gives his heat away;   10
And flowers and trees and beasts and men receive
Comfort in morning, joy in the noon day.

"And we are put on earth a little space,
That we may learn to bear the beams of love,
And these black bodies and this sun-burnt face   15
Is but a cloud, and like a shady grove.

"For when our souls have learn'd the heat to bear,
The cloud will vanish; we shall hear his voice,
Saying: 'Come out from the grove, my love & care,
And round my golden tent like lambs rejoice.' "   20

Thus did my mother say, and kisséd me;
And thus I say to little English boy:
When I from black and he from white cloud free,
And round the tent of God like lambs we joy,

I'll shade him from the heat till he can bear   25
To lean in joy upon our father's knee;
And then I'll stand and stroke his silver hair,
And be like him, and he will then love me.

(Songs of Innocence) 1789

THE TYGER

Tyger! Tyger! burning bright
In the forests of the night,
What immortal hand or eye
Could frame thy fearful symmetry?

In what distant deeps or skies   5
Burnt the fire of thine eyes?
On what wings dare he aspire?
What the hand, dare seize the fire?

And what shoulder, & what art,
Could twist the sinews of thy heart?   10

And when thy heart began to beat,
What dread hand? & what dread feet?

What the hammer? what the chain?
In what furnace was thy brain?
What the anvil? what dread grasp   15
Dare its deadly terrors clasp?

When the stars threw down their spears,
And water'd heaven with their tears,
Did he smile his work to see?
Did he who made the Lamb make thee?   20

Tyger! Tyger! burning bright
In the forests of the night,
What immortal hand or eye
Dare frame thy fearful symmetry?

(Songs of Experience)   1794

THE SICK ROSE

O Rose, thou art sick.
The invisible worm
That flies in the night
In the howling storm

Has found out thy bed   5
Of crimson joy,
And his dark secret love
Does thy life destroy.

(Songs of Experience)   1794

A POISON TREE

I was angry with my friend:
I told my wrath, my wrath did end.
I was angry with my foe:
I told it not, my wrath did grow.

And I waterd it in fears,   5
Night & morning with my tears;
And I sunnéd it with smiles,
And with soft deceitful wiles.

And it grew both day and night,
Till it bore an apple bright.   10

And my foe beheld it shine,
And he knew that it was mine,

And into my garden stole,
When the night had veild the pole;
In the morning glad I see   15
My foe outstretchd beneath the tree.

(Songs of Experience) 1794

LONDON

I wander thro' each charter'd street,
Near where the charter'd Thames does flow,
And mark in every face I meet
Marks of weakness, marks of woe.

In every cry of every man,   5
In every Infant's cry of fear,
In every voice, in every ban,
The mind-forg'd manacles I hear.

How the Chimney-sweeper's cry
Every blackning Church appalls;   10
And the hapless Soldier's sigh
Runs in blood down Palace walls.

But most thro' midnight streets I hear
How the youthful Harlot's curse
Blasts the new-born Infant's tear,   15
And blights with plagues the Marriage hearse.

(Songs of Experience) 1794

AUGURIES OF INNOCENCE

To see a World in a Grain of Sand
And a Heaven in a Wild Flower
Hold Infinity in the palm of your hand
And Eternity in an hour
A Robin Red breast in a Cage   5
Puts all Heaven in a Rage
A dove house filld with doves & Pigeons
Shudders Hell thro all its regions
A dog starvd at his Masters Gate
Predicts the ruin of the State   10

___

"London": 1. *charter'd:* legally authorized, or hired out. 16. *plagues:* evils of prostitution.

A Horse misusd upon the Road
Calls to Heaven for Human blood
Each outcry of the hunted Hare
A fibre from the Brain does tear
A Skylark wounded in the wing   15
A Cherubim does cease to sing
The Game Cock clipd & armd for fight
Does the Rising Sun affright
Every Wolfs & Lions howl
Raises from Hell a Human Soul   20
The wild deer wandring here & there
Keeps the Human Soul from Care
The Lamb misusd breeds Public strife
And yet forgives the Butchers Knife
    The Bat that flits at close of Eve   25
Has left the Brain that wont Believe
The Owl that calls upon the Night
Speaks the Unbelievers fright
He who shall hurt the little Wren
Shall never be belovd by Men   30
He who the Ox to wrath has movd
Shall never be by Woman lovd
The wanton Boy that kills the Fly
Shall feel the Spiders enmity
He who torments the Chafers sprite   35
Weaves a Bower in endless Night
The Catterpiller on the Leaf
Repeats to thee thy Mothers grief
Kill not the Moth nor Butterfly
For the Last Judgment draweth nigh   40
He who shall train the Horse to War
Shall never pass the Polar Bar
The Beggers Dog & Widows Cat
Feed them & thou wilt grow fat
The Gnat that sings his Summers song   45
Poison gets from Slanders tongue
The poison of the Snake & Newt
Is the sweat of Envys Foot
The Poison of the Honey Bee
Is the Artists Jealousy   50
The Princes Robes & Beggars Rags
Are Toadstools on the Misers Bags
A truth thats told with bad intent

---

35. *Chafers:* beetles.

Beats all the Lies you can invent
It is right it should be so   55
Man was made for Joy & Woe
And when this we rightly know
Thro the World we safely go
Joy & Woe are woven fine
A Clothing for the Soul divine   60
Under every grief & pine
Runs a joy with silken twine
The Babe is more than swadling Bands
Throughout all these Human Lands
Tools were made & Born were hands   65
Every Farmer Understands
Every Tear from Every Eye
Becomes a Babe in Eternity
This is caught by Females bright
And returned to its own delight   70
The Bleat the Bark Bellow & Roar
Are Waves that Beat on Heavens Shore
The Babe that weeps the Rod beneath
Writes Revenge in realms of death
The Beggars Rags fluttering in Air   75
Does to Rags the Heavens tear
The Soldier armd with Sword & Gun
Palsied strikes the Summers Sun
The poor Mans Farthing is worth more
Than all the Gold on Africs Shore   80
One Mite wrung from the Labrers hands
Shall buy & sell the Misers Lands
Or if protected from on high
Does that whole Nation sell & buy
He who mocks the Infants Faith   85
Shall be mock'd in Age & Death
He who shall teach the Child to Doubt
The rotting Grave shall neer get out
He who respects the Infants faith
Triumphs over Hell & Death   90
The Childs Toys & the Old Mans Reasons
Are the Fruits of the Two seasons
The Questioner who sits so sly
Shall never know how to Reply
He who replies to words of Doubt   95
Doth put the Light of Knowledge out
The Strongest Poison ever known
Came from Caesars Laurel Crown

Nought can deform the Human Race
Like to the Armours iron brace   100
When Gold & Gems adorn the Plow
To peaceful Arts shall Envy Bow
A Riddle or the Crickets Cry
Is to Doubt a fit Reply
The Emmets Inch & Eagles Mile   105
Make Lame Philosophy to smile
He who Doubts from what he sees
Will neer Believe do what you Please
If the Sun & Moon should doubt
Theyd immediately Go out   110
To be in a Passion you Good many do
But no Good if a Passion is in you
The Whore & Gambler by the State
Licencd build that Nations Fate
The Harlots cry from Street to Street   115
Shall weave Old Englands winding Sheet
The Winners Shout the Losers Curse
Dance before dead Englands Hearse
Every Night & every Morn
Some to Misery are Born   120
Every Morn & every Night
Some are Born to sweet delight
Some are Born to sweet delight
Some are Born to Endless Night
We are led to Believe a Lie   125
When we see not Thro the Eye
Which was Born in a Night to perish in a Night
When the Soul Slept in Beams of Light
God Appears & God is Light
To those poor Souls who dwell in Night   130
But does a Human Form Display
To those Who Dwell in Realms of day.

1800–1808

AND DID THOSE FEET

And did those feet in ancient time
Walk upon England's mountains green?
And was the holy Lamb of God
On England's pleasant pastures seen?

"Auguries of Innocence": 105. *Emmets:* ants.

And did the Countenance Divine   5
Shine forth upon our clouded hills?
And was Jerusalem builded here,
Among these dark Satanic Mills?

Bring me my Bow of burning gold:
Bring me my Arrows of desire: 10
Bring me my Spear: O clouds unfold!
Bring me my Chariot of fire!

I will not cease from Mental Fight,
Nor shall my Sword sleep in my hand,
Till we have built Jerusalem   15
In England's green & pleasant Land.

1804

Further Reading

Grant, John E., ed. *Discussions of William Blake*. Boston: Heath, 1961. • Paley,
Morton D., ed. *Songs of Innocence and Experience: A Collection of Critical Essays*.
Englewood Cliffs, NJ: Prentice, 1969. • Mankowitz, Wolf. "The Songs of Experi-
ence." *William Blake: Songs of Innocence and Experience*. Ed. Margaret Bottrall.
London: Macmillan, 1970. 123–35. • Nurmi, Martin K. "Fact and Symbol in 'The
Chimney Sweeper.'" *Blake: A Collection of Critical Essays*. Ed. Northrop Frye.
Englewood Cliffs, NJ: Prentice, 1966. 15–22. • Beer, John. *Blake's Humanism*.
Manchester, Eng.: Manchester UP, 1968. 197–201. • Raine, Kathleen. *William
Blake*. New York: Oxford UP, 1970.

When William Blake was writing his Songs of Innocence *and* Songs of
Experience, *most other poets were still writing verse in the style of Alexander Pope. Eighteenth-century critics were inclined to talk about poetry as
a sort of dignified clothing for the poet's thoughts, which were what really
mattered. Blake and a few of his contemporaries wrote poetry on entirely
different principles, ones that appeal more strongly to readers like A. E.
Housman.*

A. E. Housman: On Blake's Revolt Against Intellect

Meaning is of the intellect, poetry is not. If it were, the eighteenth century
would have been able to write it better. As matters actually stand, who are
the English poets of that age in whom pre-eminently one can hear and

recognise the true poetic accent emerging clearly from the contemporary dialect? These four: Collins, Christopher Smart, Cowper, and Blake. And what other characteristic had these four in common? They were mad. Remember Plato: 'He who without the Muses' madness in his soul comes knocking at the door of poesy and thinks that art will make him anything fit to be called a poet, finds that the poetry which he indites in his sober senses is beaten hollow by the poetry of madmen.'. . .

Collins and Cowper, though they saw the inside of madhouses, are not supposed to have written any of their poetry there; and Blake was never mad enough to be locked up. But elements of their nature were more or less insurgent against the centralised tyranny of the intellect, and their brains were not thrones on which the great usurper could sit secure. And so it strangely came to pass that in the eighteenth century, the age of prose and of unsound or unsatisfying poetry, there sprang up one well of the purest inspiration. For me the most poetical of all poets is Blake. I find his lyrical note as beautiful as Shakespeare's and more beautiful than anyone else's; and I call him more poetical than Shakespeare, even though Shakespeare has so much more poetry, because poetry in him preponderates more than in Shakespeare over everything else, and instead of being confounded in a great river can be drunk pure from a slender channel of its own. Shakespeare is rich in thought, and his meaning has power of itself to move us, even if the poetry were not there: Blake's meaning is often unimportant or virtually non-existent, so that we can listen with all our hearing to his celestial tune.

WILLIAM WORDSWORTH

(1770–1850)

TINTERN ABBEY

Composed a Few Miles Above Tintern Abbey on Revisiting the Banks of the Wye During a Tour. July 13, 1798

Five years have passed; five summers, with the length
Of five long winters! and again I hear
These waters, rolling from their mountain-springs
With a soft inland murmur. Once again
Do I behold these steep and lofty cliffs,   5
That on a wild secluded scene impress
Thoughts of more deep seclusion; and connect
The landscape with the quiet of the sky.
The day is come when I again repose
Here, under this dark sycamore, and view   10

These plots of cottage ground, these orchard tufts,
Which at this season, with their unripe fruits,
Are clad in one green hue, and lose themselves
'Mid groves and copses. Once again I see
These hedgerows, hardly hedgerows, little lines   15
Of sportive wood run wild; these pastoral farms,
Green to the very door; and wreaths of smoke
Sent up, in silence, from among the trees!
With some uncertain notice, as might seem
Of vagrant dwellers in the houseless woods,   20
Or of some Hermit's cave where by his fire
The Hermit sits alone.

                 These beauteous forms,
Through a long absence, have not been to me
As is a landscape to a blind man's eye;   25
But oft, in lonely rooms, and 'mid the din
Of towns and cities, I have owed to them,
In hours of weariness, sensations sweet,
Felt in the blood, and felt along the heart;
And passing even into my purer mind,   30
With tranquil restoration—feelings too
Of unremembered pleasure; such, perhaps,
As have no slight or trivial influence
On that best portion of a good man's life,
His little, nameless, unremembered, acts   35
Of kindness and of love. Nor less, I trust,
To them I may have owed another gift,
Of aspect more sublime; that blessed mood,
In which the burthen of the mystery,
In which the heavy and the weary weight   40
Of all this unintelligible world,
Is lightened—that serene and blessed mood,
In which the affections gently lead us on—
Until, the breath of this corporeal frame
And even the motion of our human blood   45
Almost suspended, we are laid asleep
In body, and become a living soul;
While with an eye made quiet by the power
Of harmony, and the deep power of joy,
We see into the life of things.   50

                 If this
Be but a vain belief, yet, oh! how oft—
In darkness and amid the many shapes
Of joyless daylight; when the fretful stir
Unprofitable, and the fever of the world,   55

Have hung upon the beatings of my heart—
How oft, in spirit, have I turned to thee,
O sylvan Wye! thou wanderer through the woods,
How often has my spirit turned to thee!

    And now, with gleams of half-extinguished thought,   60
With many recognitions dim and faint,
And somewhat of a sad perplexity,
The picture of the mind revives again;
While here I stand, not only with the sense
Of present pleasure, but with pleasing thoughts   65
That in this moment there is life and food
For future years. And so I dare to hope,
Though changed, no doubt, from what I was when first
I came among these hills; when like a roe
I bounded o'er the mountains, by the sides   70
Of the deep rivers, and the lonely streams,
Wherever nature led—more like a man
Flying from something that he dreads than one
Who sought the thing he loved. For nature then
(The coarser pleasures of my boyish days,   75
And their glad animal movements all gone by)
To me was all in all.—I cannot paint
What then I was. The sounding cataract
Haunted me like a passion; the tall rock,
The mountain, and the deep and gloomy wood,   80
Their colors and their forms, were then to me
An appetite; a feeling and a love,
That had no need of a remoter charm,
By thought supplied, nor any interest
Unborrowed from the eye.—That time is past,   85
And all its aching joys are now no more,
And all its dizzy raptures. Not for this
Faint I, nor mourn nor murmur; other gifts
Have followed; for such loss, I would believe,
Abundant recompense. For I have learned   90
To look on nature, not as in the hour
Of thoughtless youth; but hearing oftentimes
The still, sad music of humanity,
Nor harsh nor grating, though of ample power
To chasten and subdue. And I have felt   95
A presence that disturbs me with the joy
Of elevated thoughts; a sense sublime
Of something far more deeply interfused,
Whose dwelling is the light of setting suns,
And the round ocean and the living air,   100

And the blue sky, and in the mind of man:
A motion and a spirit, that impels
All thinking things, all objects of all thought,
And rolls through all things. Therefore am I still
A lover of the meadows and the woods,   105
And mountains; and of all that we behold
From this green earth; of all the mighty world
Of eye, and ear—both what they half create,
And what perceive; well pleased to recognize
In nature and the language of the sense   110
The anchor of my purest thoughts, the nurse,
The guide, the guardian of my heart, and soul
Of all my moral being.

     Nor perchance,
If I were not thus taught, should I the more   115
Suffer my genial spirits to decay:
For thou art with me here upon the banks
Of this fair river; thou my dearest Friend,
My dear, dear Friend; and in thy voice I catch
The language of my former heart, and read   120
My former pleasures in the shooting lights
Of thy wild eyes. Oh! yet a little while
May I behold in thee what I was once,
My dear, dear Sister! and his prayer I make,
Knowing that Nature never did betray   125
The heart that loved her; 'tis her privilege,
Through all the years of this our life, to lead
From joy to joy: for she can so inform
The mind that is within us, so impress
With quietness and beauty, and so feed   130
With lofty thoughts, that neither evil tongues,
Rash judgments, nor the sneers of selfish men,
Nor greetings where no kindness is, nor all
The dreary intercourse of daily life,
Shall e'er prevail against us, or disturb   135
Our cheerful faith, that all which we behold
Is full of blessings. Therefore let the moon
Shine on thee in thy solitary walk;
And let the misty mountain winds be free
To blow against thee: and, in after years,   140
When these wild ecstasies shall be matured
Into a sober pleasure; when thy mind
Shall be a mansion for all lovely forms,

-----

119. *Friend:* his sister, Dorothy.

Thy memory be as a dwelling place
For all sweet sounds and harmonies; oh! then,   145
If solitude, or fear, or pain, or grief
Should be thy portion, with what healing thoughts
Of tender joy wilt thou remember me,
And these my exhortations! Nor, perchance—
If I should be where I no more can hear   150
Thy voice, nor catch from thy wild eyes these gleams
Of past existence—wilt thou then forget
That on the banks of this delightful stream
We stood together; and that I, so long
A worshiper of Nature, hither came   155
Unwearied in that service; rather say
With warmer love—oh! with far deeper zeal
Of holier love. Nor wilt thou then forget,
That after many wanderings, many years
Of absence, these steep woods and lofty cliffs,   160
And this green pastoral landscape, were to me
More dear, both for themselves and for thy sake!

1798

SHE DWELT AMONG THE UNTRODDEN WAYS

She dwelt among the untrodden ways
   Beside the springs of Dove,
A maid whom there were none to praise
   And very few to love:

A violet by a mossy stone   5
   Half hidden from the eye!
—Fair as a star, when only one
   Is shining in the sky.

She lived unknown, and few could know
   When Lucy ceased to be;   10
But she is in her grave, and, oh,
   The difference to me!

1800

STRANGE FITS OF PASSION HAVE I KNOWN

Strange fits of passion have I known:
And I will dare to tell,

But in the Lover's ear alone,
What once to me befell.

When she I loved looked every day   5
Fresh as a rose in June,
I to her cottage bent my way,
Beneath an evening-moon.

Upon the moon I fixed my eye,
All over the wide lea;   10
With quickening pace my horse drew nigh
Those paths so dear to me.

And now we reached the orchard-plot;
And, as we climbed the hill,
The sinking moon to Lucy's cot   15
Came near, and nearer still.

In one of those sweet dreams I slept,
Kind Nature's gentlest boon!
And all the while my eyes I kept
On the descending moon.   20

My horse moved on; hoof after hoof
He raised, and never stopped:
When down behind the cottage roof,
At once, the bright moon dropped.

What fond and wayward thoughts will slide   25
Into a Lover's head!
"O mercy!" to myself I cried,
"If Lucy should be dead!"

                                                          1800

THERE WAS A BOY

   There was a Boy: ye knew him well, ye cliffs
And islands of Winander!—many a time
At evening, when the earliest stars began
To move along the edges of the hills,
Rising or setting, would he stand alone   5
Beneath the trees or by the glimmering lake,
And there, with fingers interwoven, both hands
Pressed closely palm to palm, and to his mouth
Uplifted, he, as through an instrument,
Blew mimic hootings to the silent owls,   10
That they might answer him; and they would shout
Across the watery vale, and shout again,
Responsive to his call, with quivering peals,

And long halloos and screams, and echoes loud,
Redoubled and redoubled, concourse wild   15
Of jocund din; and, when a lengthened pause
Of silence came and baffled his best skill,
Then sometimes, in that silence while he hung
Listening, a gentle shock of mild surprise
Has carried far into his heart the voice   20
Of mountain torrents; or the visible scene
Would enter unawares into his mind,
With all its solemn imagery, its rocks,
Its woods, and that uncertain heaven, received
Into the bosom of the steady lake.   25

   This Boy was taken from his mates, and died
In childhood, ere he was full twelve years old.
Fair is the spot, most beautiful the vale
Where he was born; the grassy churchyard hangs
Upon a slope above the village school,   30
And through that churchyard when my way has led
On summer evenings, I believe that there
A long half hour together I have stood
Mute, looking at the grave in which he lies!

                                                                  1800

THE WORLD IS TOO MUCH WITH US

The world is too much with us; late and soon,
Getting and spending, we lay waste our powers;
Little we see in Nature that is ours;
We have given our hearts away, a sordid boon!
This Sea that bares her bosom to the moon,   5
The winds that will be howling at all hours,
And are up-gathered now like sleeping flowers,
For this, for everything, we are out of tune;
It moves us not.—Great God! I'd rather be
A Pagan suckled in a creed outworn;   10
So might I, standing on this pleasant lea,
Have glimpses that would make me less forlorn;
Have sight of Proteus rising from the sea;
Or hear old Triton blow his wreathéd horn.

                                                                  1807

"*The World Is Too Much with Us*": 13. *Proteus:* a sea god in Greek mythology.   14. *Triton:* a
gigantic god in Greek mythology; he dwelt on the ocean floor and blew a shell trumpet to
raise or quiet storms.

COMPOSED UPON WESTMINSTER BRIDGE, SEPTEMBER 3, 1802

Earth has not anything to show more fair:
Dull would he be of soul who could pass by
A sight so touching in its majesty;
This City now doth, like a garment, wear
The beauty of the morning; silent, bare,   5
Ships, towers, domes, theaters, and temples lie
Open unto the fields, and to the sky;
All bright and glittering in the smokeless air.
Never did sun more beautifully steep
In his first splendor, valley, rock, or hill;   10
Ne'er saw I, never felt, a calm so deep!
The river glideth at his own sweet will:
Dear God! the very houses seem asleep;
And all that mighty heart is lying still!

1807

RESOLUTION AND INDEPENDENCE

1

There was a roaring in the wind all night;
The rain came heavily and fell in floods;
But now the sun is rising calm and bright;
The birds are singing in the distant woods;
Over his own sweet voice the Stock-dove broods;   5
The Jay makes answer as the Magpie chatters;
And all the air is filled with pleasant noise of waters.

2

All things that love the sun are out of doors;
The sky rejoices in the morning's birth;
The grass is bright with rain-drops;—on the moors 10
The hare is running races in her mirth;
And with her feet she from the plashy earth
Raises a mist; that, glittering in the sun,
Runs with her all the way, wherever she doth run.

3

I was a Traveller then upon the moor;   15
I saw the hare that raced about with joy;
I heard the woods and distant waters roar;

Or heard them not, as happy as a boy:
The pleasant season did my heart employ:
My old remembrances went from me wholly;   20
And all the ways of men, so vain and melancholy.

4

But, as it sometimes chanceth, from the might
Of joy in minds that can no further go,
As high as we have mounted in delight
In our dejection do we sink as low;   25
To me that morning did it happen so;
And fears and fancies thick upon me came;
Dim sadness—and blind thoughts, I knew not, nor could name.

5

I heard the sky-lark warbling in the sky;
And I bethought me of the playful hare: 30
Even such a happy Child of earth am I;
Even as these blissful creatures do I fare;
Far from the world I walk, and from all care;
But there may come another day to me—
Solitude, pain of heart, distress, and poverty.   35

6

My whole life I have lived in pleasant thought,
As if life's business were a summer mood;
As if all needful things would come unsought
To genial faith, still rich in genial good;
But how can He expect that others should   40
Build for him, sow for him, and at his call
Love him, who for himself will take no heed at all?

7

I thought of Chatterton, the marvellous Boy,
The sleepless Soul that perished in his pride;
Of Him who walked in glory and in joy   45
Following his plough, along the mountain-side:
By our own spirits are we deified:
We Poets in our youth begin in gladness;
But thereof come in the end despondency and madness.

---

43. *Chatterton:* Thomas Chatterton (1752–1770): after a brief period of literary success, he
declined into poverty and committed suicide at age seventeen.   45. *Him:* Robert Burns
(1759–1796), the great Scottish lyric poet who grew up doing heavy farm labor and died at the
height of his career.

8

8

Now, whether it were by peculiar grace,   50
A leading from above, a something given,
Yet it befell that, in this lonely place,
When I with these untoward thoughts had striven,
Beside a pool bare to the eye of heaven   55
I saw a Man before me unawares:
The oldest man he seemed that ever wore grey hairs.

9

As a huge stone is sometimes seen to lie
Couched on the bald top of an eminence;
Wonder to all who do the same espy,
By what means it could thither come, and whence;   60
So that it seems a thing endued with sense:
Like a sea-beast crawled forth, that on a shelf
Of rock or sand reposeth, there to sun itself;

10

Such seemed this Man, not all alive nor dead,
Nor all asleep—in his extreme old age: 65
His body was bent double, feet and head
Coming together in life's pilgrimage;
As if some dire constraint of pain, or rage
Of sickness felt by him in times long past,
A more than human weight upon his frame had cast.   70

11

Himself he propped, limbs, body, and pale face,
Upon a long grey staff of shaven wood:
And, still as I drew near with gentle pace,
Upon the margin of that moorish flood
Motionless as a cloud the old Man stood,   75
That heareth not the loud winds when they call;
And moveth all together, if it move at all.

12

At length, himself unsettling, he the pond
Stirred with his staff, and fixedly did look
Upon the muddy water, which he conned,   80
As if he had been reading in a book:
And now a stranger's privilege I took;
And, drawing to his side, to him did say,
"This morning gives us promise of a glorious day."

13

A gentle answer did the old Man make,   85
In courteous speech which forth he slowly drew:
And him with further words I thus bespake,
"What occupation do you there pursue?
This is a lonesome place for one like you."
Ere he replied, a flash of mild surprise   90
Broke from the sable orbs of his yet-vivid eyes.

14

His words came feebly, from a feeble chest,
But each in solemn order followed each,
With something of a lofty utterance drest—
Choice word and measured phrase, above the reach   95
Of ordinary men; a stately speech;
Such as grave Livers do in Scotland use,
Religious men, who give to God and man their dues.

15

He told, that to these waters he had come
To gather leeches, being old and poor: 100
Employment hazardous and wearisome!
And he had many hardships to endure:
From pond to pond he roamed, from moor to moor;
Housing, with God's good help, by choice or chance;
And in this way he gained an honest maintenance.   105

16

The old Man still stood talking by my side;
But now his voice to me was like a stream
Scarce heard; nor word from word could I divide;
And the whole body of the Man did seem
Like one whom I had met with in a dream;   110
Or like a man from some far region sent,
To give me human strength, by apt admonishment.

17

My former thoughts returned: the fear that kills;
And hope that is unwilling to be fed;
Cold, pain, and labor, and all fleshly ills;   115
And mighty Poets in their misery dead.

---

97. *grave Livers:* those who live serious lives.

—Perplexed, and longing to be comforted,
My question eagerly did I renew,
"How is it that you live, and what is it you do?"

18

He with a smile did then his words repeat;   120
And said that, gathering leeches, far and wide
He travelled; stirring thus about his feet
The waters of the pools where they abide.
"Once I could meet with them on every side;
But they have dwindled long by slow decay;   125
Yet still I persevere, and find them where I may."

19

While he was talking thus, the lonely place,
The old Man's shape, and speech—all troubled me:
In my mind's eye I seemed to see him pace
About the weary moors continually,   130
Wandering about alone and silently.
While I these thoughts within myself pursued,
He, having made a pause, the same discourse renewed.

20

And soon with this he other matter blended,
Cheerfully uttered, with demeanor kind,   135
But stately in the main; and, when he ended,
I could have laughed myself to scorn to find
In that decrepit Man so firm a mind.
"God," said I, "be my help and stay secure;
I'll think of the Leech-gatherer on the lonely moor!"   140

1807

MY HEART LEAPS UP

My heart leaps up when I behold
    A rainbow in the sky:
So was it when my life began;
So is it now I am a man;

So be it when I shall grow old,   5
    Or let me die!
The Child is father of the Man;
And I could wish my days to be
Bound each to each by natural piety.

1807

Further Reading

Wordsworth, William. "Wordsworth's Preface, Lyrical Ballads 1805." *Lyrical Ballads 1805*. 2nd ed. Ed. Derek Roper. London: Macdonald, 1976. 18–48. • Barrell, John. "The Uses of Dorothy: 'The Language of the Sense' in 'Tintern Abbey.' " *Poetry, Language and Politics*. Manchester, Eng.: Manchester UP, 1988. 137–67. • Ferguson, Frances C. "The Lucy Poems: Wordsworth's Quest for a Poetic Object." *English Literary History* 40.4 (Winter 1973): 532–48. • Kroeber, Karl. "A New Reading of 'The World Is Too Much with Us.' " *Studies in Romanticism* 2 (1962–63): 183–88. • Ferry, David. "Some Characteristics of Wordsworth's Style." *Wordsworth: A Collection of Critical Essays*. Ed. M. H. Abrams. Englewood Cliffs, NJ: Prentice, 1972. 35–44. • Taylor, Irene. "By Peculiar Grace: Wordsworth in 1802." *The Evidence of the Imagination*. Ed. Donald H. Reiman et al. New York: New York UP, 1978. 119–41.

William Wordsworth was among the most revolutionary figures in the history of English poetry. Pope and the other major writers of the Age of Reason had built a citadel of literary taste based on what we would now call sophistication: their poems were typically formal, emotionally cool, and skeptical about human nature—distinctly the products of the city and the university. Wordsworth introduced (or reintroduced) England to poetry that rejected sophistication, looked to nature for inspiration, and attempted a more direct expression of basic human emotions. The impetus for this Romantic revolution was political and psychological as well as artistic, as we can see in the following excerpts from a letter to John Wilson and from the preface to Lyrical Ballads.

William Wordsworth: On Poetry and Human Nature

You begin what you say . . . with this observation, that nothing is a fit subject for poetry which does not please. But here follows a question. Does not please whom? Some have little knowledge of natural imagery of any kind, and, of course, little relish for it; some are disgusted with the very mention of the words "pastoral poetry," "sheep," or "shepherds"; some cannot tolerate a poem with a ghost or any supernatural agency in it; others would shrink from an animated description of the pleasures of love, as from a thing carnal and libidinous; some cannot bear to see delicate and refined feelings ascribed to men in low conditions of society, because their vanity and self-love tell them that these belong only to themselves and men like themselves in dress, station, and way of life; others are disgusted with the naked language of some of the most interesting passions of men, because either it is indelicate, or gross, or vulgar. . . . I return then to the question, please whom? or what? I answer, human nature, as it has been and ever will be. But where are we to find the best measure of this? I answer, from within; by stripping our own hearts naked, and by looking out of ourselves towards men who lead the simplest lives, and those most according to nature; men who have never known false refinements, wayward and artificial desires, false criticisms, effeminate habits of thinking and feeling, or who, having known these things, have outgrown them. This latter class is the·most to be depended upon, but it is very small in number. . . . You have given me praise for having reflected faithfully in my Poems the feelings of human nature. I would fain hope that I have done so. But a great Poet ought to do more than this: he ought, to a certain degree, to rectify men's feelings, to give them new compositions of feeling, to render their feelings more sane, pure, and permanent, in short, more consonant to nature, that is, to eternal nature, and the great moving spirit of things. He ought to travel before men occasionally as well as at their sides.

William Wordsworth: On Poetry and the "Overthrow of Powerful Emotions"

I have said that Poetry is the spontaneous overflow of powerful feelings: it takes its origin from emotion recollected in tranquillity: the emotion is contemplated till by a species of reaction the tranquillity gradually disappears, and an emotion, kindred to that which was before the subject of contemplation, is gradually produced, and does itself actually exist in the mind. In this mood successful composition generally begins, and in a mood similar to this it is carried on; but the emotion, of whatever kind and in whatever degree, from various causes is qualified by various pleasures, so that in describing any passions whatsoever, which are voluntarily described, the mind will upon the whole be in a state of enjoyment. Now, if Nature be thus cautious in preserving in a state of enjoyment a being thus employed, the Poet ought to profit by the lesson thus held forth to him, and ought especially to take care, that whatever passions he communicates to his Reader, those passions, if his Reader's mind be sound and vigorous, should always be accompanied with an overbalance of pleasure. Now the music of harmonious metrical language, the sense of difficulty overcome, and the blind association of pleasure which has been previously received from works of rhyme or metre of the same or similar construction, an indistinct perception perpetually renewed of language closely resembling that of real life, and yet, in the circumstance of metre, differing from it so widely, all these imperceptibly make up a complex feeling of delight, which is of the most important use in tempering the painful feeling which will always be found intermingled with powerful descriptions of the deeper passions.

SAMUEL TAYLOR COLERIDGE

(1772–1834)

THE AEOLIAN HARP

Composed at Clevedon, Somersetshire

My pensive Sara! thy soft cheek reclined
Thus on mine arm, most soothing sweet it is
To sit beside our Cot, our Cot o'ergrown
With white-flowered Jasmin, and the broad-leaved Myrtle,
(Meet emblems they of Innocence and Love!)   5
And watch the clouds, that late were rich with light,
Slow saddening round, and mark the star of eve
Serenely brilliant (such should Wisdom be)
Shine opposite! How exquisite the scents
Snatched from yon bean-field! and the world *so* hushed!   10
The stilly murmur of the distant Sea
Tells us of silence.

             And that simplest Lute,
Placed length-ways in the clasping casement, hark!
How by the desultory breeze caressed,   15
Like some coy maid half yielding to her lover,
It pours such sweet upbraiding, as must needs
Tempt to repeat the wrong! And now, its strings
Boldlier swept, the long sequacious notes
Over delicious surges sink and rise,   20
Such a soft floating witchery of sound
As twilight Elfins make, when they at eve
Voyage on gentle gales from Fairy-Land,
Where Melodies round honey-dropping flowers,
Footless and wild, like birds of Paradise,   25
Nor pause, nor perch, hovering on untamed wing!
O! the one Life within us and abroad,
Which meets all motion and becomes its soul,
A light in sound, a sound-like power in light,
Rhythm in all thought, and joyance everywhere—   30
Methinks, it should have been impossible
Not to love all things in a world so filled;
Where the breeze warbles, and the mute still air
Is Music slumbering on her instrument.

    And thus, my Love! as on the midway slope   35
Of yonder hill I stretch my limbs at noon,

Whilst through my half-closed eyelids I behold
The sunbeams dance, like diamonds, on the main,
And tranquil muse upon tranquility:
Full many a thought uncalled and undetained,   40
And many idle flitting phantasies,
Traverse my indolent and passive brain,
As wild and various as the random gales
That swell and flutter on this subject Lute!

    And what if all of animated nature   45
Be but organic Harps diversely framed,
That tremble into thought, as o'er them sweeps
Plastic and vast, one intellectual breeze,
At once the Soul of each, and God of all?
    But thy more serious eye a mild reproof   50
Darts, O belovéd Woman! nor such thoughts
Dim and unhallowed dost thou not reject,
And biddest me walk humbly with my God.
Meek Daughter in the family of Christ!
Well hast thou said and holily dispraised   55
These shapings of the unregenerate mind;
Bubbles that glitter as they rise and break
On vain Philosophy's aye-babbling spring.
For never guiltless may I speak of him,
The Incomprehensible! save when with awe   60
I praise him, and with Faith that inly *feels;*
Who with his saving mercies healéd me,
A sinful and most miserable man,
Wildered and dark, and gave me to possess
Peace, and this Cot, and thee, heart-honored Maid!   65

1796

KUBLA KHAN

Or a vision in a dream. A Fragment

In Xanadu did Kubla Khan
A stately pleasure dome decree:
Where Alph, the sacred river, ran
Through caverns measureless to man
    Down to a sunless sea.   5

"*Kubla Khan*": 1. *Xanadu:* where Kublai Khan had his summer capital.   *Kubla Khan:* Kublai
Khan, the first Mongol emperor of China, visited and served by Marco Polo during the
thirteenth century.

So twice five miles of fertile ground
With walls and towers were girdled round:
And there were gardens bright with sinuous rills,
Where blossomed many an incense-bearing tree;
And here were forests ancient as the hills,   10
Enfolding sunny spots of greenery.

But oh! that deep romantic chasm which slanted
Down the green hill athwart a cedarn cover!
A savage place! as holy and enchanted
As e'er beneath a waning moon was haunted   15
By woman wailing for her demon lover!
And from this chasm, with ceaseless turmoil seething,
As if this earth in fast thick pants were breathing,
A mighty fountain momently was forced:
Amid whose swift half-intermitted burst   20
Huge fragments vaulted like rebounding hail,
Or chaffy grain beneath the thresher's flail:
And 'mid these dancing rocks at once and ever
It flung up momently the sacred river.
Five miles meandering with a mazy motion   25
Through wood and dale the sacred river ran,
Then reached the caverns measureless to man,
And sank in tumult to a lifeless ocean:
And 'mid this tumult Kubla heard from far
Ancestral voices prophesying war!   30

    The shadow of the dome of pleasure
    Floated midway on the waves;
    Where was heard the mingled measure
    From the fountain and the caves.
It was a miracle of rare device,   35
A sunny pleasure dome with caves of ice!

    A damsel with a dulcimer
    In a vision once I saw:
    It was an Abyssinian maid,
    And on her dulcimer she played,   40
    Singing of Mount Abora.
    Could I revive within me
    Her symphony and song,
    To such a deep delight 'twould win me,
That with music loud and long,   45
I would build that dome in air,

---

39. *Abyssinian:* Ethiopian. 41. *Mount Abora:* Mount Amara in Abyssinia, referred to by
Milton in *Paradise Lost* 4:281.

That sunny dome! those caves of ice!
And all who heard should see them there,
And all should cry, Beware! Beware!
His flashing eyes, his floating hair!   50
Weave a circle round him thrice,
And close your eyes with holy dread,
For he on honey-dew hath fed,
And drunk the milk of Paradise.

                                                    1797

THE RIME OF THE ANCIENT MARINER

Part 1

An ancient Mariner
meeteth three Gallants
bidden to a wedding-feast,
and detaineth one.

It is an ancient Mariner
And he stoppeth one of three.
—"By thy long gray beard and glittering eye
Now wherefore stopp'st thou me?

The Bridegroom's doors are opened wide,   5
And I am next of kin;
The guests are met, the feast is set:
May'st hear the merry din."

He holds him with his skinny hand,
"There was a ship," quoth he.   10
"Hold off! unhand me, graybeard loon!"
Eftsoons his hand dropped he.

The Wedding-Guest is
spellbound by the eye of the
old seafaring man, and
constrained to hear his
tale.

He holds him with his glittering eye—
The Wedding Guest stood still,
And listens like a three years' child: 15
The Mariner hath his will.

The Wedding Guest sat on a stone:
He cannot choose but hear;
And thus spake on that ancient man,
The bright-eyed Mariner.   20

"The ship was cheered, the harbor cleared,
Merrily did we drop
Below the kirk, below the hill,
Below the lighthouse top.

The Mariner tells how the
ship sailed southward

The Sun came up upon the left,   25
Out of the sea came he!

"The Rime of the Ancient Mariner": 12. *Eftsoons:* at once.   23. *kirk:* church.

with a good wind and fair weather, till it reached the Line.

And he shone bright, and on the right
Went down into the sea.

Higher and higher every day,
Till over the mast at noon—"   30
The Wedding Guest here beat his breast,
For he heard the loud bassoon.

The Wedding-Guest heareth the bridal music; but the Mariner continueth his tale.

The bride hath paced into the hall,
Red as a rose is she;
Nodding their heads before her goes   35
The merry minstrelsy.

The Wedding Guest he beat his breast,
Yet he cannot choose but hear;
And thus spake on that ancient man,
The bright-eyed Mariner.   40

The ship driven by a storm toward the south pole.

"And now the STORM-BLAST came, and he
Was tyrannous and strong;
He struck with his o'ertaking wings,
And chased us south along.

With sloping masts and dipping prow,   45
As who pursued with yell and blow
Still treads the shadow of his foe,
And forward bends his head,
The ship drove fast, loud roared the blast,
And southward aye we fled.   50

And now there came both mist and snow,
And it grew wondrous cold:
And ice, mast-high, came floating by,
As green as emerald.

The land of ice, and of fearful sounds, where no living thing was to be seen.

And through the drifts the snowy clifts   55
Did send a dismal sheen:
Nor shapes of men nor beasts we ken—
The ice was all between.

The ice was here, the ice was there,
The ice was all around: 60
It cracked and growled, and roared and howled,
Like noises in a swound!

Till a great sea-bird, called the Albatross, came

At length did cross an Albatross,
Through the fog it came;

---

55. *clifts:* fissures.   62. *swound:* swoon.

As if it had been a Christian soul,   65
We hailed it in God's name.

It ate the food it ne'er had eat,
And round and round it flew.
The ice did split with a thunder-fit;
The helmsman steered us through!   70

*through the snow-fog, and
was received with great joy
and hospitality.*

*And lo! the Albatross
proveth a bird of good
omen, and followeth the
ship as it returned
northward through fog
and floating ice.*

And a good south wind sprung up behind;
The Albatross did follow,
And every day, for food or play,
Came to the mariners' hollo!

In mist or cloud, on mast or shroud,   75
It perched for vespers nine;
Whiles all the night, through fog-smoke white,
Glimmered the white Moon-shine."

*The ancient Mariner
inhospitably killeth the
pious bird of good omen.*

"God save thee, ancient Mariner!
From the fiends, that plague thee thus!—   80
Why look'st thou so?"—With my crossbow
I shot the ALBATROSS.

Part 2

The Sun now rose upon the right:
Out of the sea came he,
Still hid in mist, and on the left   85
Went down into the sea.

And the good south wind still blew behind,
But no sweet bird did follow,
Nor any day for food or play
Came to the mariners' hollo!   90

*His shipmates cry out
against the ancient
Mariner, for killing the
bird of good luck.*

And I had done a hellish thing,
And it would work 'em woe:
For all averred, I had killed the bird
That made the breeze to blow.
Ah wretch! said they, the bird to slay,   95
That made the breeze to blow!

*But when the fog cleared
off, they justify the same,
and thus make themselves
accomplices in the crime.*

Nor dim nor red, like God's own head,
The glorious Sun uprist:
Then all averred, I had killed the bird
That brought the fog and mist.   100
'Twas right, said they, such birds to slay,
That bring the fog and mist.

*The fair breeze continues;
the ship enters the Pacific*

The fair breeze blew, the white foam flew,
The furrow followed free;

We were the first that ever burst   105
Into that silent sea.

Down dropped the breeze, the sails dropped down,
'Twas sad as sad could be;
And we did speak only to break
The silence of the sea!   110

All in a hot and copper sky,
The bloody Sun, at noon,
Right up above the mast did stand,
No bigger than the Moon.

Day after day, day after day,   115
We stuck, nor breath nor motion;
As idle as a painted ship
Upon a painted ocean.

Water, water, everywhere,
And all the boards did shrink;   120
Water, water, everywhere,
Nor any drop to drink.

The very deep did rot: O Christ!
That ever this should be!
Yea, slimy things did crawl with legs   125
Upon the slimy sea.

About, about, in reel and rout
The death-fires danced at night;
The water, like a witch's oils,
Burnt green, and blue and white.   130

And some in dreams assuréd were
Of the Spirit that plagued us so;
Nine fathom deep he had followed us
From the land of mist and snow.

And every tongue, through utter drought,   135
Was withered at the root;
We could not speak, no more than if
We had been choked with soot.

Ah! well-a-day! what evil looks
Had I from old and young!   140
Instead of the cross, the Albatross
About my neck was hung.

Part 3

The ancient Mariner
beholdeth a sign in the element afar off.

There passed a weary time. Each throat
Was parched, and glazed each eye.
A weary time! a weary time!   145
How glazed each weary eye,
When looking westward, I beheld
A something in the sky.

At first it seemed a little speck,
And then it seemed a mist;   150
It moved and moved, and took at last
A certain shape, I wist.

A speck, a mist, a shape, I wist!
And still it neared and neared:
As if it dodged a water sprite,   155
It plunged and tacked and veered.

At its nearer approach, it
seemeth him to be a ship;
and at a dear ransom he
freeth his speech from the
bonds of thirst.

With throats unslaked, with black lips bake
We could nor laugh nor wail;
Through utter drought all dumb we stood!
I bit my arm, I sucked the blood,   160
And cried, A sail! a sail!

With throats unslaked, with black lips bake
Agape they heard me call:

A flash of joy;

Gramercy! they for joy did grin,
And all at once their breath drew in,   165
As they were drinking all.

And horror follows. For
can it be a ship that comes
onward without wind or
tide?

See! see! (I cried) she tacks no more!
Hither to work us weal;
Without a breeze, without a tide,
She steadies with upright keel!   170

The western wave was all aflame.
The day was well nigh done!
Almost upon the western wave
Rested the broad bright Sun;
When that strange shape drove suddenly   175
Betwixt us and the Sun.

It seemeth him but the
skeleton of a ship:

And straight the Sun was flecked with bars,
(Heaven's Mother send us grace!)
As if through a dungeon grate he peered
With broad and burning face.   180

---

155. *sprite:* a spirit that haunted the water.   157. *Unslaked:* parched.   164. *Gramercy:*
exclamation of surprise and thanks.   168. *weal:* good.

Alas! (though I, and my heart beat loud)
How fast she nears and nears!
Are those *her* sails that glance in the Sun,
Like restless gossameres?

And its ribs are seen as bars on the face of the setting Sun. The Spectre-Woman and her Death-mate, and no other on board the skeleton-ship. Like vessel, like crew.

Are those *her* ribs through which the Sun   185
Did peer, as through a grate?
And is that Woman all her crew?
Is that a DEATH? and are there two?
Is DEATH that woman's mate?

Her lips were red, *her* looks were free,   190
Her locks were yellow as gold:
Her skin was as white as leprosy,
The Nightmare LIFE-IN-DEATH was she,
Who thicks man's blood with cold.

Death and Life-in-Death have diced for the ship's crew, and she (the latter) winneth the ancient Mariner.

The naked hulk alongside came,   195
And the twain were casting dice;
"The game is done! I've won! I've won!"
Quoth she, and whistles thrice.

No twilight within the courts of the Sun.

The Sun's rim dips; the stars rush out:
At one stride comes the dark;   200
With far-heard whisper, o'er the sea,
Off shot the specter-bark.

At the rising of the Moon,

We listened and looked sideways up!
Fear at my heart, as at a cup,
My lifeblood seemed to sip!   205
The stars were dim, and thick the night,
The steersman's face by his lamp gleamed white;
From the sails the dew did drip—
Till clomb above the eastern bar
The hornéd Moon, with one bright star   210
Within the nether tip.

One after another,

One after one, by the star-dogged Moon,
Too quick for groan or sigh,
Each turned his face with ghastly pang,
And cursed me with his eye.   215

His ship-mates drop down dead.

Four times fifty living men,
(And I heard nor sigh nor groan)
With heavy thump, a lifeless lump,
They dropped down one by one.

But Life-in-Death begins her work on the ancient Mariner.

The souls did from their bodies fly—   220
They fled to bliss or woe!
And every soul, it passed me by,
Like the whizz of my cross-bow!

Part 4

*The Wedding-Guest
feareth that a Spirit is
talking to him;*

"I fear thee, ancient Mariner!
I fear thy skinny hand!
And thou art long, and lank, and brown,
As is the ribbed sea-sand.

225

*But the ancient Mariner
assureth him of his bodily
life, and proceedeth to
relate his horrible
penance.*

I fear thee and thy glittering eye,
And thy skinny hand, so brown."—
Fear not, fear not, thou Wedding Guest!
This body dropped not down.

230

Alone, alone, all, all alone,
Alone on a wide wide sea!
And never a saint took pity on
My soul in agony.

235

*He despiseth the creatures
of the calm.*

The many men, so beautiful!
And they all dead did lie:
And a thousand thousand slimy things
Lived on; and so did I.

*And envieth that they
should live, and so many
lie dead.*

I looked upon the rotting sea,
And drew my eyes away;
I looked upon the rotting deck,
And there the dead men lay.

240

I looked to heaven, and tried to pray;
But or ever a prayer had gushed,
A wicked whisper came, and made
My heart as dry as dust.

245

I closed my lids, and kept them close,
And the balls like pulses beat,
For the sky and the sea, and the sea and the sky
Lay like a load on my weary eye,
And the dead were at my feet.

250

*But the curse liveth for
him in the eye of the dead
men.*

The cold sweat melted from their limbs,
Nor rot nor reek did they:
The look with which they looked on me
Had never passed away.

255

An orphan's curse would drag to hell
A spirit from on high;
But oh! more horrible than that
Is the curse in a dead man's eye!
Seven days, seven nights, I saw that curse,
And yet I could not die.

260

The moving Moon went up the sky,
And nowhere did abide:
Softly she was going up,   265
And a star or two beside—

Her beams bemocked the sultry main,
Like April hoar-frost spread;
But where the ship's huge shadow lay,
The charméd water burnt alway   270
A still and awful red.

Beyond the shadow of the ship,
I watched the water snakes:
They moved in tracks of shining white,
And when they reared, the elfish light   275
Fell off in hoary flakes.

Within the shadow of the ship
I watched their rich attire:
Blue, glossy green, and velvet black,
They coiled and swam; and every track   280
Was a flash of golden fire.

O happy living things! no tongue
Their beauty might declare:
A spring of love gushed from my heart,
And I blessed them unaware: 285
Sure my kind saint took pity on me,
And I blessed them unaware.

The self-same moment I could pray;
And from my neck so free
The Albatross fell off, and sank   290
Like lead into the sea.

Part 5

Oh sleep! it is a gentle thing,
Beloved from pole to pole!
To Mary Queen the praise be given!
She sent the gentle sleep from Heaven,   295
That slid into my soul.

The silly buckets on the deck,
That had so long remained,
I dreamt that they were filled with dew;
And when I awoke, it rained.   300

In his loneliness and fixedness he yearneth toward the journeying Moon, and the stars that still sojourn, yet still move onward; and everywhere the blue sky belongs to them, and is their appointed rest, and their native country and their own natural homes, which they enter unannounced, as lords that are certainly expected and yet there is a silent joy at their arrival.

By the light of the Moon he beholdeth God's creatures of the great calm.

Their beauty and their happiness.

He blesseth them in his heart.

The spell begins to break.

By grace of the holy Mother, the ancient Mariner is refreshed with rain.

---

297. *silly:* simple; here, useless.

My lips were wet, my throat was cold,
My garments all were dank;
Sure I had drunken in my dreams,
And still my body drank.

I moved, and could not feel my limbs: 305
I was so light—almost
I thought that I had died in sleep,
And was a blessèd ghost.

He heareth sounds and seeth strange sights and commotions in the sky and the element.

And soon I heard a roaring wind:
It did not come anear;   310
But with its sound it shook the sails,
That were so thin and sere.

The upper air burst into life!
And a hundred fire-flags sheen,
To and fro they were hurried about!   315
And to and fro, and in and out,
The wan stars danced between.

And the coming wind did roar more loud,
And the sails did sigh like sedge;
And the rain poured down from one black cloud;   320
The Moon was at its edge.

The thick black cloud was cleft, and still
The Moon was at its side:
Like waters shot from some high crag,
The lightning fell with never a jag,   325
A river steep and wide.

The loud wind never reached the ship,
Yet now the ship moved on!
Beneath the lightning and the Moon
The dead men gave a groan.   330

The bodies of the ship's crew are inspired and the ship moves on;

They groaned, they stirred, they all uprose,
Nor spake, nor moved their eyes;
It had been strange, even in a dream,
To have seen those dead men rise.

The helmsman steered, the ship moved on;   335
Yet never a breeze up-blew;
The mariners all 'gan work the ropes,
Where they were wont to do;

---

314. *sheen:* shone.

They raised their limbs like lifeless tools—
We were a ghastly crew.   340

The body of my brother's son
Stood by me, knee to knee:
The body and I pulled at one rope,
But he said nought to me.

*But not by the souls of the
men, nor by daemons of
earth or middle air, but by
a blessed troop of angelic
spirits, sent down by the
invocation of the
guardian saint.*
"I fear thee, ancient Mariner!"   345
Be calm, thou Wedding Guest!
'Twas not those souls that fled in pain,
Which to their corses came again,
But a troop of spirits blest:

For when it dawned—they dropped their arms,   350
And clustered round the mast;
Sweet sounds rose slowly through their mouths,
And from their bodies passed.

Around, around, flew each sweet sound,
Then darted to the Sun;   355
Slowly the sounds came back again,
Now mixed, now one by one.

Sometimes a-dropping from the sky
I heard the sky-lark sing;
Sometimes all little birds that are,   360
How they seemed to fill the sea and air
With their sweet jargoning!

And now 'twas like all instruments,
Now like a lonely flute;
And now it is an angel's song,   365
That makes the heavens be mute.

It ceased; yet still the sails made on
A pleasant noise till noon,
A noise like of a hidden brook
In the leafy month of June,   370
That to the sleeping woods all night
Singeth a quiet tune.

Till noon we quietly sailed on,
Yet never a breeze did breathe:
Slowly and smoothly went the ship,   375
Moved onward from beneath.

---

348. *corses:* corpses.

The lonesome Spirit from
the South Pole carries on
the ship as far as the Line,
in obedience to the angelic
troop, but still requireth
vengeance.

Under the keel nine fathom deep,
From the land of mist and snow,
The spirit slid: and it was he
That made the ship to go.   380
The sails at noon left off their tune,
And the ship stood still also.

The Sun, right up above the mast,
Had fixed her to the ocean:
But in a minute she 'gan stir,   385
With a short uneasy motion—
Backwards and forwards half her length
With a short uneasy motion.

Then like a pawing horse let go,
She made a sudden bound: 390
It flung the blood into my head,
And I fell down in a swound.

The Polar Spirit's
fellow-daemons, the invisible inhabitants of the
element, take part in his
wrong; and two of them
relate one to the other, that
penance long and heavy
for the ancient Mariner
hath been accorded to the
Polar Spirit, who
returneth southward.

How long in that same fit I lay,
I have not to declare;
But ere my living life returned,   395
I heard and in my soul discerned
Two voices in the air.

"Is it he?" quoth one, "Is this the man?
By him who died on cross,
With his cruel bow he laid full low   400
The harmless Albatross.

The spirit who bideth by himself
In the land of mist and snow,
He loved the bird that loved the man
Who shot him with his bow."   405

The other was a softer voice,
As soft as honey-dew:
Quoth he, "The man hath penance done,
And penance more will do."

Part 6

FIRST VOICE

"But tell me, tell me! speak again,   410
Thy soft response renewing—
What makes that ship drive on so fast?
What is the ocean doing?"

SECOND VOICE

"Still as a slave before his lord,
The ocean hath no blast;   415
His great bright eye most silently
Up to the Moon is cast—

If he may know which way to go;
For she guides him smooth or grim.
See, brother, see! how graciously   420
She looketh down on him."

FIRST VOICE

The Mariner hath been cast into a trance; for the angelic power causeth the vessel to drive northward faster than human life could endure.

"But why drives on that ship so fast,
Without or wave or wind?"

SECOND VOICE

"The air is cut away before,
And closes from behind.   425

Fly, brother, fly! more high, more high!
Or we shall be belated:
For slow and slow that ship will go,
When the Mariner's trance is abated."

The supernatural motion is retarded; the Mariner awakes, and his penance begins anew.

I woke, and we were sailing on   430
As in a gentle weather:
'Twas night, calm night, the moon was high;
The dead men stood together.

All stood together on the deck,
For a charnel-dungeon fitter: 435
All fixed on me their stony eyes,
That in the Moon did glitter.

The pang, the curse, with which they died,
Had never passed away:
I could not draw my eyes from theirs,   440
Nor turn them up to pray.

The curse is finally expiated.

And now this spell was snapped: once more
I viewed the ocean green,
And looked far forth, yet little saw
Of what had else been seen—   445

Like one, that on a lonesome road
Doth walk in fear and dread,
And having once turned round walks on,
And turns no more his head;
Because he knows, a frightful fiend   450
Doth close behind him tread.

Samuel Taylor Coleridge   **545**

But soon there breathed a wind on me,
Nor sound nor motion made:
Its path was not upon the sea,
In ripple or in shade.   455

It raised my hair, it fanned my cheek
Like a meadow-gale of spring—
It mingled strangely with my fears,
Yet it felt like a welcoming.

Swiftly, swiftly flew the ship,   460
Yet she sailed softly too:
Sweetly, sweetly blew the breeze—
On me alone it blew.

And the ancient Mariner
beholdeth his native
country.

Oh! dream of joy! is this indeed
The lighthouse top I see?   465
Is this the hill? is this the kirk?
Is this mine own countree?

We drifted o'er the harbor-bar,
And I with sobs did pray—
O let me be awake, my God!   470
Or let me sleep alway.

The harbor-bay was clear as glass,
So smoothly it was strewn!
And on the bay the moonlight lay,
And the shadow of the Moon.   475

The rock shone bright, the kirk no less,
That stands above the rock:
The moonlight steeped in silentness
The steady weathercock.

And the bay was white with silent light,   480
Till rising from the same,
Full many shapes, that shadows were,
In crimson colors came.

The angelic spirits leave
the dead bodies,

A little distance from the prow
Those crimson shadows were: 485
I turned my eyes upon the deck—
Oh, Christ! what saw I there!

And appear in their own
forms of light.

Each corse lay flat, lifeless and flat,
And, by the holy rood!
A man all light, a seraph-man,   490
On every corse there stood.

This seraph-band, each waved his hand;
It was a heavenly sight!
They stood as signals to the land,
Each one a lovely light;   495

This seraph-band, each waved his hand,
No voice did they impart—
No voice; but oh! the silence sank
Like music on my heart.

But soon I heard the dash of oars,   500
I heard the Pilot's cheer;
My head was turned perforce away
And I saw a boat appear.

The Pilot and the Pilot's boy,
I heard them coming fast: 505
Dear Lord in Heaven! it was a joy
The dead men could not blast.

I saw a third—I heard his voice:
It is the Hermit good!
He singeth loud his godly hymns   510
That he makes in the wood.
He'll shrieve my soul, he'll wash away
The Albatross's blood.

Part 7

The Hermit of the Wood,

This Hermit good lives in that wood
Which slopes down to the sea.   515
How loudly his sweet voice he rears!
He loves to talk with marineres
That come from a far countree.

He kneels at morn, and noon, and eve—
He hath a cushion plump: 520
It is the moss that wholly hides
The rotted old oak stump.

The skiff-boat neared: I heard them talk,
"Why, this is strange, I trow!
Where are those lights so many and fair,   525
That signal made but now?"

Approacheth the ship with
wonder.

"Strange, by my faith!" the Hermit said—
"And they answered not our cheer!
The planks looked warped! and see those sails,
How thin they are and sere!   530

I never saw aught like to them,
Unless perchance it were

Brown skeletons of leaves that lag
My forest-brook along;
When the ivy tod is heavy with snow,   535
And the owlet whoops to the wolf below,
That eats the she-wolf's young."

"Dear Lord! it hath a fiendish look,"
The Pilot made reply,
"I am a-feared"—"Push on, push on!"   540
Said the Hermit cheerily.

The boat came closer to the ship,
But I nor spake nor stirred;
The boat came close beneath the ship,
And straight a sound was heard.   545

The ship suddenly sinketh.   Under the water it rumbled on,
Still louder and more dread:
It reached the ship, it split the bay;
The ship went down like lead.

The ancient Mariner is   Stunned by that loud and dreadful sound,   550
saved in the Pilot's boat.   Which sky and ocean smote,
Like one that hath been seven days drowned
My body lay afloat;
But swift as dreams, myself I found
Within the Pilot's boat.   555

Upon the whirl, where sank the ship,
The boat spun round and round;
And all was still, save that the hill
Was telling of the sound.

I moved my lips—the Pilot shrieked   560
And fell down in a fit;
The holy Hermit raised his eyes,
And prayed where he did sit.

I took the oars: the Pilot's boy,
Who now doth crazy go,   565
Laughed loud and long, and all the while
His eyes went to and fro.
"Ha! ha!" quoth he, "full plain I see,
The Devil knows how to row."

---

535. *tod:* bushy clump.

And now, all in my own countree,   570
I stood on the firm land!
The Hermit stepped forth from the boat,
And scarcely he could stand.

*The ancient Mariner
earnestly entreateth the
Hermit to shrieve him; and
the penance of life falls on
him.*

"O shrieve me, shrieve me, holy man!"
The Hermit crossed his brow.   575
"Say quick," quoth he, "I bid thee say—
What manner of man art thou?"

Forthwith this frame of mine was wrenched
With a woeful agony,
Which forced me to begin my tale;   580
And then it left me free.

*And ever and anon
throughout his future life
an agony constraineth him
to travel from land to
land,*

Since then, at an uncertain hour,
That agony returns:
And till my ghastly tale is told,
This heart within me burns.   585

I pass, like night, from land to land;
I have strange power of speech;
That moment that his face I see,
I know the man that must hear me:
To him my tale I teach.   590

What loud uproar bursts from that door!
The wedding guests are there:
But in the garden-bower the bride
And bridemaids singing are:
And hark the little vesper bell,   595
Which biddeth me to prayer!

O Wedding Guest! this soul hath been
Alone on a wide wide sea:
So lonely 'twas, that God himself
Scarce seeméd there to be.   600

O sweeter than the marriage feast,
'Tis sweeter far to me,
To walk together to the kirk
With a goodly company!

To walk together to the kirk,   605
And all together pray,
While each to his great Father bends,
Old men, and babes, and loving friends
And youths and maidens gay!

And to teach, by his own
example, love and
reverence to all things that
God made and loveth.

Farewell, farewell! but this I tell 610
To thee, thou Wedding Guest!
He prayeth well, who loveth well
Both man and bird and beast.

He prayeth best, who loveth best
All things both great and small; 615
For the dear God who loveth us,
He made and loveth all.

The Mariner, whose eye is bright,
Whose beard with age is hoar,
Is gone: and now the Wedding Guest 620
Turned from the bridegroom's door.

He went like one that hath been stunned,
And is of sense forlorn:
A sadder and a wiser man,
He rose the morrow morn. 625

1797–1798

FROST AT MIDNIGHT

The Frost performs its secret ministry,
Unhelped by any wind. The owlet's cry
Came loud—and hark, again! loud as before
The inmates of my cottage, all at rest,
Have left me to that solitude, which suits 5
Abstruser musings: save that at my side
My cradled infant slumbers peacefully.
'Tis calm indeed! so calm, that it disturbs
And vexes meditation with its strange
And extreme silentness. Sea, hill, and wood, 10
This populous village! Sea, and hill, and wood,
With all the numberless goings-on of life,
Inaudible as dreams! the thin blue flame
Lies on my low-burnt fire, and quivers not;
Only that film, which fluttered on the grate, 15
Still flutters there, the sole unquiet thing.
Methinks its motion in this hush of nature

"*The Rime of the Ancient Mariner*": 624. *forlorn*: deprived, denied.   "*Frost at Midnight*":
7. *infant*: Coleridge's son Hartley.   15. *film*: an ember or ash lingering on the grate;
according to folklore, it foretells the arrival of an unexpected guest, a stranger.

Gives it dim sympathies with me who live,
Making it a companionable form,
Whose puny flaps and freaks the idling Spirit   20
By its own mood interprets, everywhere
Echo or mirror seeking of itself,
And makes a toy of Thought.

                But O! how oft,
How oft, at school, with most believing mind,   25
Presageful, have I gazed upon the bars,
To watch that fluttering *stranger!* and as oft
With unclosed lids, already had I dreamt
Of my sweet birthplace, and the old church tower,
Whose bells, the poor man's only music, rang   30
From morn to evening, all the hot Fair-day,
So sweetly, that they stirred and haunted me
With a wild pleasure, falling on mine ear
Most like articulate sounds of things to come!
So gazed I, till the soothing things, I dreamt,   35
Lulled me to sleep, and sleep prolonged my dreams!
And so I brooded all the following morn,
Awed by the stern preceptor's face, mine eye
Fixed with mock study on my swimming book:
Save if the door half opened, and I snatched   40
A hasty glance, and still my heart leaped up,
For still I hoped to see the *stranger's* face,
Townsman, or aunt, or sister more beloved,
My playmate when we both were clothed alike!

   Dear Babe, that sleepest cradled by my side,   45
Whose gentle breathings, heard in this deep calm,
Fill up the intersperséd vacancies
And momentary pauses of the thought!
My babe so beautiful! it thrills my heart
With tender gladness, thus to look at thee,   50
And think that thou shalt learn far other lore,
And in far other scenes! For I was reared
In the great city, pent 'mid cloisters dim,
And saw nought lovely but the sky and stars.
But *thou*, my babe! shalt wander like a breeze   55
By lakes and sandy shores, beneath the crags
Of ancient mountain, and beneath the clouds,
Which image in their bulk both lakes and shores

---

26. *presageful:* foretelling. 38. *preceptor's:* schoolmaster's.

And mountain crags: so shalt thou see and hear
The lovely shapes and sounds intelligible 60
Of that eternal language, which thy God
Utters, who from eternity doth teach
Himself in all, and all things in himself.
Great universal Teacher! he shall mold
Thy spirit, and by giving make it ask. 65

   Therefore all seasons shall be sweet to thee,
Whether the summer clothe the general earth
With greenness, or the redbreast sit and sing
Betwixt the tufts of snow on the bare branch
Of mossy apple tree, while the nigh thatch 70
Smokes in the sun-thaw; whether the eave-drops fall
Heard only in the trances of the blast,
Or if the secret ministry of frost
Shall hang them up in silent icicles,
Quietly shining to the quiet Moon. 75

1798

Further Reading

Radley, Virginia L. *Samuel Taylor Coleridge*. Boston: Twayne, 1966. • Milne,
Fred L. "Coleridge's 'Kubla Khan': A Metaphor for the Creative Process." *South
Atlantic Review* 51.4 (Nov. 1986): 17–29. • Frieden, Ken. "Conversational Pretense
in 'Kubla Khan.'" *Genius and Monologue*. Ithaca: Cornell UP, 1985. • Boulger,
James D., ed. *Twentieth Century Interpretations of "The Rime of the Ancient Mariner."*
Englewood Cliffs, NJ: Prentice, 1969. • Wolfson, Susan J. "The Language of
Interpretation." *Modern Critical Views: Samuel Taylor Coleridge*. Ed. Harold Bloom.
New York: Chelsea, 1986. 201–08. • Reed, Arden. "Frost at Midnight." *Romantic
Weather: The Climates of Coleridge and Baudelaire*. Hanover, N.H.: UP of New
England, 1983.

*Samuel Taylor Coleridge was in some ways a more radical rebel against
eighteenth-century taste than Wordsworth himself. While Wordsworth kept
returning to nature and strong emotion as the source of poetry, Coleridge
looked primarily to a poetic unity above the tangle of the natural world, created by the imagination. Coleridge's theories eventually became more intricate than his poems, but we can see their kernel in his comment on the origins
of Lyrical Ballads.*

---

67. *general:* generative.

Samuel Taylor Coleridge: On the "Willing Suspension of Disbelief"

During the first year that Mr. Wordsworth and I were neighbours, our conversations turned frequently on the two cardinal points of poetry, the power of exciting the sympathy of the reader by a faithful adherence to the truth of nature, and the power of giving the interest of novelty by the modifying colors of imagination. The sudden charm, which accidents of light and shade, which moon-light or sun-set diffused over a known and familiar landscape, appeared to represent the practicability of combining both. These are the poetry of nature. The thought suggested itself (to which of us I do not recollect) that a series of poems might be composed of two sorts. In the one, the incidents and agents were to be, in part at least, supernatural; and the excellence aimed at was to consist in the interesting of the affections by the dramatic truth of such emotions, as would naturally accompany such situations, supposing them real. And real in *this* sense they have been to every human being who, from whatever source of delusion, has at any time believed himself under supernatural agency. For the second class, subjects were to be chosen from ordinary life; the characters and incidents were to be such, as will be found in every village and its vicinity, where there is a meditative and feeling mind to seek after them, or to notice them, when they present themselves.

In this idea originated the plan of the "Lyrical Ballads"; in which it was agreed, that my endeavours should be directed to persons and characters supernatural, or at least romantic; yet so as to transfer from our inward nature a human interest and a semblance of truth sufficient to procure for these shadows of imagination that willing suspension of disbelief for the moment, which constitutes poetic faith. With this view I wrote "The Ancient Mariner," and was preparing among other poems, "The Dark Ladie," and the "Christabel," in which I should have more nearly realized my ideal, than I had done in my first attempt.

JOHN KEATS

(1795–1821)

WHEN I HAVE FEARS THAT I MAY CEASE TO BE

When I have fears that I may cease to be
  Before my pen has gleaned my teeming brain,

Before high-pilèd books, in charactery,
    Hold like rich garners the full ripened grain;
When I behold, upon the night's starred face;   5
    Huge cloudy symbols of a high romance,
And think that I may never live to trace
    Their shadows, with the magic hand of chance;
And when I feel, fair creature of an hour,
    That I shall never look upon thee more,   10
Never have relish in the faery power
    Of unreflecting love;—then on the shore
Of the wide world I stand alone, and think
Till Love and Fame to nothingness do sink.

1818

ODE ON MELANCHOLY

1

No, no, go not to Lethe, neither twist
    Wolf's-bane, tight-rooted, for its poisonous wine;
Nor suffer thy pale forehead to be kissed
    By nightshade, ruby grape of Proserpine;
Make not your rosary of yew-berries,   5
    Nor let the beetle, nor the death-moth be
        Your mournful Psyche, nor the downy owl
A partner in your sorrow's mysteries;
    For shade to shade will come too drowsily,
        And drown the wakeful anguish of the soul.   10

2

But when the melancholy fit shall fall
    Sudden from heaven like a weeping cloud,
That fosters the droop-headed flowers all,
    And hides the green hill in an April shroud;
Then glut thy sorrow on a morning rose,   15
    Or on the rainbow of the salt sand-wave,
        Or on the wealth of globèd peonies;
Or if thy mistress some rich anger shows,
    Emprison her soft hand, and let her rave,
        And feed deep, deep upon her peerless eyes.   20

"Ode on Melancholy": 1. *Lethe:* in Greek mythology, one of the rivers of Hades. Those who
drank from it forgot their former lives.   4. *Proserpine:* queen of Hades.   7. *Psyche:*
personification of the soul in Greek mythology, often symbolized by a butterfly.

She dwells with Beauty—Beauty that must die;
    And Joy, whose hand is ever at his lips
Bidding adieu; and aching Pleasure nigh,
    Turning to poison while the bee-mouth sips:
Ay, in the very temple of Delight   25
    Veiled Melancholy has her sovran shrine,
        Though seen of none save him whose strenuous tongue
Can burst Joy's grape against his palate fine:
His soul shall taste the sadness of her might,
    And be among her cloudy trophies hung.   30

1819

LA BELLE DAME SANS MERCI

Ah, what can ail thee, wretched wight,
    Alone and palely loitering;
The sedge is withered from the lake,
    And no birds sing.

Ah, what can ail thee, wretched wight,   5
    So haggard and so woe-begone?
The squirrel's granary is full,
    And the harvest's done.

I see a lily on thy brow
    With anguish moist and fever dew,   10
And on thy cheek a fading rose
    Fast withereth too.

I met a lady in the meads,
    Full beautiful, a faery's child:
Her hair was long, her foot was light,   15
    And her eyes were wild.

I set her on my pacing steed,
    And nothing else saw all day long;
For sideways would she lean, and sing
    A faery's song.   20

I made a garland for her head,
    And bracelets too, and fragrant zone;
She looked at me as she did love,
    And made sweet moan.

She found me roots of relish sweet,   25
    And honey wild, and manna dew,

And sure in language strange she said,
   I love thee true.

She took me to her elfin grot,
   And there she gazed and sighèd deep,   30
And there I shut her wild sad eyes—
   So kissed to sleep.

And there we slumbered on the moss,
   And there I dreamed, ah woe betide
The latest dream I ever dreamed   35
   On the cold hill side.

I saw pale kings, and princes too,
   Pale warriors, death-pale were they all;
Who cried—"La belle Dame sans merci
   Hath thee in thrall!"   40

I saw their starved lips in the gloom,
   With horrid warning gapèd wide,
And I awoke, and found me here
   On the cold hill side.

And this is why I sojourn here,   45
   Alone and palely loitering,
Though the sedge is withered from the lake,
   And no birds sing.

1819

ODE TO A NIGHTINGALE

1

My heart aches, and a drowsy numbness pains
   My sense, as though of hemlock I had drunk,
Or emptied some dull opiate to the drains
   One minute past, and Lethe-wards had sunk:
'Tis not through envy of thy happy lot,   5
   But being too happy in thine happiness,—
      That thou, light-wingèd Dryad of the trees,
        In some melodious plot
   Of beechen green, and shadows numberless,
      Singest of summer in full-throated ease.   10

"Ode to a Nightingale": 4. *Lethe-wards:* toward the river in Hades whose water brings
forgetfulness.

O, for a draught of vintage! that hath been
  Cool'd a long age in the deep-delvèd earth,
Tasting of Flora and the country green,
  Dance, and Provençal song, and sunburnt mirth!
O for a breaker full of the warm South,   15
  Full of the true, the blushful Hippocrene,
    With beaded bubbles winking at the brim,
      And purple-stainèd mouth;
  That I might drink, and leave the world unseen,
    And with thee fade away into the forest dim: 20

3

Fade far away, dissolve, and quite forget
  What thou among the leaves hast never known,
The weariness, the fever, and the fret
  Here, where men sit and hear each other groan;
Where palsy shakes a few, sad, last gray hairs,   25
  Where youth grows pale, and spectre-thin, and dies;
    Where but to think is to be full of sorrow
      And leaden-eyed despairs,
  Where Beauty cannot keep her lustrous eyes,
    Or new Love pine at them beyond tomorrow.   30

4

Away! away! for I will fly to thee,
  Not charioted by Bacchus and his pards,
But on the viewless wings of Poesy,
  Though the dull brain perplexes and retards:
Already with thee! tender is the night,   35
  And haply the Queen-Moon is on her throne,
    Clustered around by all her starry fays;
      But here there is no light,
Save what from heaven is with the breezes blown
    Through verdurous glooms and winding mossy ways.   40

5

I cannot see what flowers are at my feet,
  Nor what soft incense hangs upon the boughs,
But, in embalmèd darkness, guess each sweet
  Wherewith the seasonable month endows

---

13. *Flora:* Roman goddess of flowers.   16. *Hippocrene:* in Greek mythology, a fountain
sacred to the Muses and the source of poetic inspiration.   32. *Bacchus:* Greek god of wine.
pards: leopards.

The grass, the thicket, and the fruit-tree wild;   45
    White hawthorn, and the pastoral eglantine;
        Fast fading violets covered up in leaves;
           And mid-May's eldest child,
The coming musk-rose, full of dewy wine,
    The murmurous haunt of flies on summer eves.   50

6

Darkling I listen; and for many a time
    I have been half in love with easeful Death,
Called him soft names in many a musèd rhyme,
    To take into the air my quiet breath;
Now more than ever seems it rich to die,   55
    To cease upon the midnight with no pain,
    While thou art pouring forth thy soul abroad
        In such an ecstasy!
Still wouldst thou sing, and I have ears in vain—
    To thy high requiem become a sod.   60

7

Thou wast not born for death, immortal Bird!
    No hungry generations tread thee down;
The voice I hear this passing night was heard
    In ancient days by emperor and clown:
Perhaps the self-same song that found a path   65
    Through the sad heart of Ruth, when, sick for home,
        She stood in tears amid the alien corn;
           The same that oft-times hath
Charmed magic casements, opening on the foam
    Of perilous seas, in faery lands forlorn.   70

8

Forlorn! the very word is like a bell
    To toll me back from thee to my sole self!
Adieu! the fancy cannot cheat so well
    As she is famed to do, deceiving elf.
Adieu! adieu! thy plaintive anthem fades   75
    Past the near meadows, over the still stream,
        Up the hill-side; and now 'tis buried deep
           In the next valley-glades:
    Was it a vision, or a waking dream?
    Fled is that music:—Do I wake or sleep?   80

1820

---

66. *Ruth:* the Old Testament account can be found in Ruth 2:1–7.

ODE ON A GRECIAN URN

1

Thou still unravished bride of quietness,
    Thou foster-child of silence and slow time,
Sylvan historian, who canst thus express
    A flowery tale more sweetly than our rhyme:
What leaf-fringed legend haunts about thy shape   5
    Of deities or mortals, or of both,
        In Tempe or the dales of Arcady?
    What men or gods are these? what maidens loth?
What mad pursuit? What struggle to escape?
        What pipes and timbrels? What wild ecstasy?   10

2

Heard melodies are sweet, but those unheard
    Are sweeter; therefore, ye soft pipes, play on;
Not to the sensual ear, but, more endeared,
    Pipe to the spirit ditties of no tone:
Fair youth, beneath the trees, thou canst not leave   15
    Thy song, nor ever can those trees be bare;
        Bold Lover, never, never canst thou kiss,
Though winning near the goal—yet, do not grieve;
    She cannot fade, though thou hast not thy bliss,
        For ever wilt thou love, and she be fair!   20

3

Ah, happy, happy boughs! that cannot shed
    Your leaves, nor ever bid the Spring adieu;
And, happy melodist, unwearièd,
    For ever piping songs for ever new;
More happy love! more happy, happy love!   25
    For ever warm and still to be enjoyed,
        For ever panting, and for ever young;
All breathing human passion far above,
    That leaves a heart high-sorrowful and cloyed,
        A burning forehead, and a parching tongue.   30

4

Who are these coming to the sacrifice?
    To what green altar, O mysterious priest,
Lead'st thou that heifer lowing at the skies,

"Ode on a Grecian Urn": 7. *Tempe:* a beautiful and sublime valley in eastern Greece. *Arcady:* Arcadia, an isolated region in Greece known for its rustic simplicity.

And all her silken flanks with garlands drest?
What little town by river or sea shore,   35
    Or mountain-built with peaceful citadel,
        Is emptied of this folk, this pious morn?
And, little town, thy streets for evermore
    Will silent be; and not a soul to tell
        Why thou art desolate, can e'er return.   40

                        5

O Attic shape! Fair attitude! with brede
    Of marble men and maidens overwrought,
With forest branches and the trodden weed;
    Thou, silent form, dost tease us out of thought
As doth eternity: Cold Pastoral!   45
    When old age shall this generation waste,
        Thou shalt remain, in midst of other woe
Than ours, a friend to man, to whom thou say'st,
    "Beauty is truth, truth beauty—that is all
        Ye know on earth, and all ye need to know."   50

                                                                1820

TO AUTUMN

                        1

Season of mists and mellow fruitfulness,
    Close bosom-friend of the maturing sun:
Conspiring with him how to load and bless
    With fruit the vines that round the thatch-eves run;
To bend with apples the mossed cottage-trees,   5
    And fill all fruit with ripeness to the core;
        To swell the gourd, and plump the hazel shells
With a sweet kernel; to set budding more,
    And still more, later flowers for the bees,
        Until they think warm days will never cease,   10
            For Summer has o'er-brimmed their clammy cells.

                        2

Who hath not seen thee oft amid thy store?
    Sometimes whoever seeks abroad may find
Thee sitting careless on a granary floor,
    Thy hair soft-lifted by the winnowing wind;   15
Or on a half-reaped furrow sound asleep,
    Drowsed with the fume of poppies, while thy hook
        Spares the next swath and all its twinèd flowers:

And sometimes like a gleaner thou dost keep
   Steady thy laden head across a brook;   20
  Or by a cider-press, with patient look,
     Thou watchest the last oozings hours by hours.

3

Where are the songs of Spring? Ay, where are they?
   Think not of them, thou hast thy music too,—
While barrèd clouds bloom the soft-dying day,   25
And touch the stubble-plains with rosy hue;
Then in a wailful choir the small gnats mourn
   Among the river sallows, borne aloft
     Or sinking as the light wind lives or dies;
And full-grown lambs loud bleat from hilly bourn;   30
  Hedge-crickets sing; and now with trebel soft
  The red-breast whistles from a garden-croft;
  And gathering swallows twitter in the skies.

1820

Further Reading

Hirst, Wolf Z. *John Keats.* Boston: Twayne, 1981. • Watts, Cedric. *A Preface to Keats.*
New York: Longman, 1985. • Elliott, Nathaniel. "Keats' 'When I Have Fears.' "
Ariel 10.1 (Jan. 1979): 3–10. • Stillinger, Jack, ed. *Keats' Odes.* Englewood Cliffs,
NJ: Prentice, 1968. • Vendler, Helen. "The Strenuous Tongue: The 'Ode on
Melancholy.' " *The Odes of John Keats.* Cambridge: Harvard UP, 1983. 153–90.

*Born a generation after Wordsworth and Coleridge, John Keats responded
strongly to their emphasis on the sensuous dimension of poetry. So strong,
in fact, was this response that some readers have doubted that there was anything beneath the beautifully wrought surface. William Butler Yeats, for
instance, gives us this picture of Keats:*

   I see a schoolboy, when I think of him,
   With face and nose pressed to a sweetshop window,
   For certainly he sank into his grave,
   His senses and his heart unsatisfied;
   And made—being poor, ailing and ignorant,
   Shut out from all the luxury of the world,

"To Autumn": 28. *sallows:* low-growing willows.   30. *bourn:* realm or domain.

The coarse-bred son of a livery stable keeper—
Luxuriant song.

Ego Dominus Tuus

Keats's letters, including the following one to John Taylor, show the deeper thought other readers find at work in the poems.

John Keats: On the Development of the Spirit

. . . axioms in philosophy are not axioms until they are proved upon our pulses. We read fine things but never feel them to the full until we have gone the same steps as the Author. . . .

I compare human life to a large Mansion of Many Apartments, two of which I can only describe, the doors of the rest being as yet shut upon me. The first we step into we call the infant or thoughtless Chamber, in which we remain as long as we do not think—We remain there a long while, and notwithstanding the doors of the second Chamber remain wide open, showing a bright appearance, we care not to hasten to it; but are at length imperceptibly impelled by the awakening of this thinking principle within us—we no sooner get into the second Chamber, which I call the Chamber of Maiden-Thought, than we become intoxicated with the light and atmosphere, we see nothing but pleasant wonders, and think of delaying there for ever in delight: However among the effects this breathing is father of is that tremendous one of sharpening one's vision into the heart and nature of Man —of convincing one's nerves that the world is full of Misery and Heartbreak, Pain, Sickness and oppression—whereby this Chamber of Maiden Thought becomes gradually darken'd and at the same time on all sides of it many *doors* are set open—but all dark—all leading to dark passages—We see not the balance of good and evil. We are in a Mist. *We* are now in that state—We feel the 'burden of the Mystery'. To this Point was Wordsworth come, as far as I can conceive when he wrote *Tintern Abbey* and it seems to me that his genius is explorative of those dark Passages. Now if we live, and go on thinking, we too shall explore them—he is a Genius and superior to us, in so far as he can, more than we, make discoveries, and shed a light in them—Here I must think Wordsworth is deeper than Milton— though I think it has depended more upon the general and gregarious advance of intellect, than individual greatness of Mind.

ALFRED, LORD TENNYSON

(1809–1892)

MARIANA

'Mariana in the moated grange.'
MEASURE FOR MEASURE

With blackest moss the flower-plots
   Were thickly crusted, one and all:
The rusted nails fell from the knots
   That held the pear to the gable-wall.
The broken sheds look'd sad and strange: 5
   Unlifted was the clinking latch;
   Weeded and worn the ancient thatch
Upon the lonely moated grange.
      She only said, 'My life is dreary,
        He cometh not,' she said;   10
      She said, 'I am aweary, aweary,
        I would that I were dead!'

Her tears fell with the dews at even;
   Her tears fell ere the dews were dried;
She could not look on the sweet heaven,   15
   Either at morn or eventide.
After the flitting of the bats,
   When thickest dark did trance the sky,
   She drew her casement-curtain by,
And glanced athwart the glooming flats.   20
      She only said, 'The night is dreary,
        He cometh not,' she said;
      She said, 'I am aweary, aweary,
        I would that I were dead!'

Upon the middle of the night,   25
   Waking she heard the night-fowl crow:
The cock sung out an hour ere light:
   From the dark fen the oxen's low
Came to her: without hope of change,
   In sleep she seem'd to walk forlorn,   30
   Till cold winds woke the gray-eyed morn
About the lonely moated grange.
      She only said, 'The day is dreary,
        He cometh not,' she said;

She said, 'I am aweary, aweary,   35
    I would that I were dead!'

About a stone-cast from the wall
    A sluice with blacken'd waters slept,
And o'er it many, round and small,
    The cluster'd marish-mosses crept.   40
Hard by a poplar shook alway,
    All silver-green with gnarled bark:
    For leagues no other tree did mark
The level waste, the rounding gray.
    She only said, 'My life is dreary,   45
        He cometh not,' she said;
    She said, 'I am aweary, aweary,
        I would that I were dead!'

And ever when the moon was low,
    And the shrill winds were up and away,   50
In the white curtain, to and fro,
    She saw the gusty shadow sway.
But when the moon was very low,
    And wild winds bound within their cell,
    The shadow of the poplar fell   55
Upon her bed, across her brow.
    She only said, 'The night is dreary,
        He cometh not,' she said;
    She said, 'I am aweary, aweary,
        I would that I were dead!'   60

All day within the dreamy house,
    The doors upon their hinges creak'd;
The blue fly sung in the pane, the mouse
Behind the mouldering wainscot shriek'd,
Or from the crevice peer'd about.   65
    Old faces glimmer'd thro' the doors,
    Old footsteps trod the upper floors,
Old voices called her from without.
    She only said, 'My life is dreary,
        He cometh not,' she said;   70
    She said, 'I am aweary, aweary,
        I would that I were dead!'

The sparrow's chirrup on the roof,
    The slow clock ticking, and the sound
Which to the wooing wind aloof   75
    The poplar made, did all confound
Her sense; but most she loathed the hour
    When the thick-moted sunbeam lay

Athwart the chambers, and the day
Was sloping toward his western bower.   80
    Then, said she, 'I am very dreary,
      He will not come,' she said;
    She wept, 'I am aweary, aweary,
      Oh God, that I were dead!'

1830

THE KRAKEN

Below the thunders of the upper deep;
Far, far beneath in the abysmal sea,
His ancient, dreamless, uninvaded sleep
The Kraken sleepeth: faintest sunlights flee
About his shadowy sides: above him swell   5
Huge sponges of millennial growth and height;
And far away into the sickly light,
From many a wondrous grot and secret cell
Unnumber'd and enormous polypi
Winnow with giant arms the slumbering green.   10
There hath he lain for ages and will lie
Battening upon huge seaworms in his sleep,
Until the latter fire shall heat the deep;
Then once by man and angels to be seen,
In roaring he shall rise and on the surface die.   15

1830

ULYSSES

It little profits that an idle king,
By this still hearth, among these barren crags,
Matched with an aged wife, I mete and dole
Unequal laws unto a savage race,
That hoard, and sleep, and feed, and know not me.   5
I cannot rest from travel; I will drink
Life to the lees. All times I have enjoyed
Greatly, have suffered greatly, both with those
That loved me, and alone; on shore, and when
Through scudding drifts the rainy Hyades   10

"*The Kraken*": *Kraken:* a mythical Norwegian sea-beast; see also Revelation 13:1.
"*Ulysses*": *Ulysses:* also known as Odysseus. Tennyson wrote this poem just after the death of
his close friend, Arthur Hallam. It is based on Homer's *Odyssey*, Book 11: 100–137, and on
Dante's *Inferno*, Canto 26.   10. *Hyades:* a group of stars; their rising with the sun was
associated with the beginning of the rainy season.

Vext the dim sea. I am become a name;
For always roaming with a hungry heart
Much have I seen and known—cities of men
And manners, climates, councils, governments,
Myself not least, but honored of them all,— 15
And drunk delight of battle with my peers,
Far on the ringing plains of windy Troy.
I am a part of all that I have met;
Yet all experience is an arch wherethrough
Gleams that untraveled world whose margin fades 20
For ever and for ever when I move.
How dull it is to pause, to make an end,
To rust unburnished, not to shine in use!
As though to breathe were life! Life piled on life
Were all too little, and of one to me 25
Little remains; but every hour is saved
From that eternal silence, something more,
A bringer of new things; and vile it were
For some three suns to store and hoard myself,
And this gray spirit yearning in desire 30
To follow knowledge like a sinking star,
Beyond the utmost bound of human thought.
    This is my son, mine own Telemachus,
To whom I leave the scepter and the isle,
Well-loved of me, discerning to fulfill 35
This labor, by slow prudence to make mild
A rugged people, and through soft degrees
Subdue them to the useful and the good.
Most blameless is he, centered in the sphere
Of common duties, decent not to fail 40
In offices of tenderness, and pay
Meet adoration to my household gods,
When I am gone. He works his work, I mine.
    There lies the port; the vessel puffs her sail;
There gloom the dark, broad seas. My mariners, 45
Souls that have toiled, and wrought, and thought with me,
That ever with a frolic welcome took
The thunder and the sunshine, and opposed
Free hearts, free foreheads—you and I are old;
Old age hath yet his honor and his toil. 50
Death closes all; but something ere the end,
Some work of noble note, may yet be done,
Not unbecoming men that strove with gods.
The lights begin to twinkle from the rocks;
The long day wanes; the slow moon climbs; the deep 55
Moans round with many voices. Come, my friends,
'Tis not too late to seek a newer world.

Push off, and sitting well in order smite
The sounding furrows; for my purpose holds
To sail beyond the sunset, and the baths   60
Of all the western stars, until I die.
It may be that the gulfs will wash us down;
It may be we shall touch the Happy Isles,
And see the great Achilles, whom we knew.
Though much is taken, much abides; and though   65
We are not now that strength which in old days
Moved earth and heaven, that which we are, we are,
One equal temper of heroic hearts,
Made weak by time and fate, but strong in will
To strive, to seek, to find, and not to yield.   70

1842

'BREAK, BREAK, BREAK . . .'

Break, break, break,
  On thy cold gray stones, O Sea!
And I would that my tongue could utter
  The thoughts that arise in me.

O well for the fisherman's boy,   5
  That he shouts with his sister at play!
O well for the sailor lad,
  That he sings in his boat on the bay!

And the stately ships go on
  To their haven under the hill;   10
But O for the touch of a vanish'd hand,
  And the sound of a voice that is still!

Break, break, break,
  At the foot of thy crags, O Sea!
But the tender grace of a day that is dead   15
  Will never come back to me.

1842

TEARS, IDLE TEARS

  Tears, idle tears, I know not what they mean,
  Tears from the depth of some divine despair

"Ulysses": 63. *Happy Isles:* islands supposedly west of the known world where the souls of the virtuous meet after death.   64. *Achilles:* in Greek mythology, one of the chief heroes of the Trojan War.

Rise in the heart, and gather to the eyes,
In looking on the happy autumn-fields,
And thinking of the days that are no more.   5

    Fresh as the first beam glittering on a sail,
That brings our friends up from the underworld,
Sad as the last which reddens over one
That sinks with all we love below the verge;
So sad, so fresh, the days that are no more.   10

Ah, sad and strange as in dark summer dawns
The earliest pipe of half-awakened birds
To dying ears, when unto dying eyes
The casement slowly grows a glimmering square;
So sad, so strange, the days that are no more.   15

    Dear as remembered kisses after death,
And sweet as those by hopeless fancy feigned
On lips that are for others; deep as love,
Deep as first love, and wild with all regret;
O Death in Life, the days that are no more!   20

1847

NOW SLEEPS THE CRIMSON PETAL

    Now sleeps the crimson petal, now the white;
Nor waves the cypress in the palace walk;

Nor winks the gold fin in the porphyry font.
The firefly wakens; waken thou with me.

    Now droops the milk-white peacock like a ghost,   5
And like a ghost she glimmers on to me.

    Now lies the Earth all Danaë to the stars,
And all thy heart lies open unto me.

    Now slides the silent meteor on, and leaves
A shining furrow, as thy thoughts in me.   10

    Now folds the lily all her sweetness up,
And slips into the bosom of the lake.
So fold thyself, my dearest, thou, and slip
Into my bosom and be lost in me.

1847

"*Now Sleeps the Crimson Petal*": 7. *Danaë:* in Greek mythology, while Danae was imprisoned in a tower, she was visited by Zeus in the form of a shower of gold.

'COME DOWN, O MAID . . .'

'Come down, O maid, from yonder mountain height:
What pleasure lives in height (the shepherd sang)
In height and cold, the splendour of the hills?
But cease to move so near the Heavens, and cease
To glide a sunbeam by the blasted Pine,   5
To sit a star upon the sparkling spire;
And come, for Love is of the valley, come,
For Love is of the valley, come thou down
And find him; by the happy threshold, he,
Or hand in hand with Plenty in the maize,   10
Or red with spirted purple of the vats,
Or foxlike in the vine; nor cares to walk
With Death and Morning on the silver horns,
Nor wilt thou snare him in the white ravine,
Nor find him dropt upon the firths of ice,   15
That huddling slant in furrow-cloven falls
To roll the torrent out of dusky doors:
But follow; let the torrent dance thee down
To find him in the valley; let the wild
Lean-headed Eagles yelp alone, and leave   20
The monstrous ledges there to slope, and spill
Their thousand wreaths of dangling water-smoke,
That like a broken purpose waste in air:
So waste not thou; but come; for all the vales
Await thee; azure pillars of the hearth   25
Arise to thee; the children call, and I
Thy shepherd pipe, and sweet is every sound,
Sweeter thy voice, but every sound is sweet;
Myriads of rivulets hurrying thro' the lawn,
The moan of doves in immemorial elms,   30
And murmuring of innumerable bees.'

1847

from IN MEMORIAM

2

Old Yew, which graspest at the stones
   That name the under-lying dead,
   Thy fibres net the dreamless head,
Thy roots are wrapt about the bones.

The seasons bring the flower again.   5
   And bring the firstling to the flock;

And in the dusk of thee, the clock
Beats out the little lives of men.

O not for thee the glow, the bloom,
  Who changest not in any gale,   10
  Nor branding summer suns avail
To touch thy thousand years of gloom:

And gazing on thee, sullen tree,
  Sick for thy stubborn hardihood,
  I seem to fail from out my blood   15
And grow incorporate into thee.

7

Dark house, by which once more I stand
  Here in the long unlovely street,
  Doors, where my heart was used to beat
So quickly, waiting for a hand.

A hand that can be clasp'd no more—   5
  Behold me, for I cannot sleep,
  And like a guilty thing I creep
At earliest morning to the door.

He is not here; but far away
  The noise of life begins again,   10
  And ghastly thro' the drizzling rain
On the bald street breaks the blank day.

11

Calm is the morn with a sound,
  Calm as to suit a calmer grief,
  And only thro' the faded leaf
The chestnut pattering to the ground:

Calm and deep peace on this high wold,   5
  And on these dews that drench the furze,
  And all the silvery gossamers
That twinkle into green and gold:

Calm and still light on yon great plain
  That sweeps with all its autumn bowers,   10
  And crowded farms and lessening towers,
To mingle with the bounding main:

Calm and deep peace in this wide air,
  These leaves that redden to the fall;
  And in my heart, if calm at all,   15
If any calm, a calm despair:

Calm on the seas, and silver sleep,
    And waves that sway themselves in rest,
    And dead calm in that noble breast
Which heaves but with the heaving deep.   20

20

The lesser griefs that may be said,
    That breathe a thousand tender vows,
    Are but as servants in a house
Where lies the master newly dead;

Who speak their feeling as it is,   5
    And weep the fulness from the mind:
    'It will be hard,' they say, 'to find
Another service such as this.'

My lighter moods are like to these,
    That out of words a comfort win;   10
    But there are other griefs within,
And tears that at their fountain freeze;

For by the hearth the children sit
    Cold in that atmosphere of Death,
    And scarce endure to draw the breath,   15
Or like to noiseless phantoms flit:

But open converse is there none,
    So much the vital spirits sink
    To see the vacant chair, and think,
'How good! how kind! and he is gone.'   20

39

Old warder of these buried bones,
    And answering now my random stroke
    With fruitful cloud and living smoke,
Dark yew, that graspest at the stones

And dippest toward the dreamless head,   5
    To thee too comes the golden hour
    When flower is feeling after flower;
But Sorrow—fixt upon the dead,

And darkening the dark graves of men,—
    What whisper'd from her lying lips?   10
    Thy gloom is kindled at the tips,
And passes into gloom again.

1850

Further Reading

Critical Essays on the Poetry of Tennyson. Ed. John Killham. London: Routledge, 1960. • Hughes, Linda K. "Dramatis and Private Personae: 'Ulysses' Revisited." *Victorian Poetry* 17.3 (Autumn 1979): 192–203. • Storch, R. F. "The Fugitive from the Ancestral Hearth: Tennyson's 'Ulysses.' " *Texas Studies in Literature and Language* 12.2 (Summer 1971): 281–97. • Assad, Thomas J. "Tennyson's 'Break, Break, Break.'" *Tulane Studies in English* 12 (1962): 71–80. • Hunt, John Dixon, ed. *Tennyson: In Memoriam.* London: Macmillan, 1970. • Ricks, Christopher. *Tennyson.* 2nd. ed. Berkeley: U of California P, 1989.

After he became Poet Laureate in 1850, Lord Tennyson became increasingly identified with the "authorized" view of Victorian life. Many of his later poems were patriotic, optimistic, and very popular; few of these are now read. His twentieth-century readers, led by such influential poets as T. S. Eliot, have found the other side of Tennyson far more interesting.

T. S. Eliot: On Tennyson as an "Instinctive Rebel"

In ending we must go back to the beginning and remember that *In Memoriam* would not be a great poem, or Tennyson a great poet, without the technical accomplishment. Tennyson is the great master of metric as well as of melancholia; I do not think any poet in English has ever had a finer ear for vowel sound, as well as a subtler feeling for some moods of anguish:

> Dear as remember'd kisses after death,
> And sweet as those by hopeless fancy feign'd
> On lips that are for others; deep as love,
> Deep as first love, and wild with all regret.

And this technical gift of Tennyson's is no slight thing. Tennyson lived in a time which was already acutely time-conscious: a great many things seemed to be happening, railways were being built, discoveries were being made, the face of the world was changing. That was a time busy in keeping up to date. It had, for the most part, no hold on permanent things, on permanent truths about man and God and life and death. The surface of Tennyson stirred about with his time; and he had nothing to which to hold fast except his unique and unerring feeling for the sounds of words. But in this he had something that no one else had. Tennyson's surface, his technical accomplishment, is intimate with his depths: what we most quickly see about Tennyson is that which moves between the surface and the depths, that which is of slight importance. By looking innocently at the surface we are most likely to come to the depths, to the abyss of sorrow. Tennyson is not only a minor Virgil, he is also with Virgil as Dante saw him, a Virgil among the Shades, the saddest of all English poets, among the Great in Limbo, the most instinctive rebel against the society in which he was the most perfect conformist.

ROBERT BROWNING

(1812–1889)

MY LAST DUCHESS

Ferrara

That's my last duchess painted on the wall,
Looking as if she were alive. I call
That piece a wonder, now: Frà Pandolf's hands
Worked busily a day, and there she stands.
Will't please you sit and look at her? I said   5
"Frà Pandolf" by design, for never read
Strangers like you that pictured countenance,
The depth and passion of its earnest glance,
But to myself they turned (since none puts by
The curtain I have drawn for you, but I)   10
And seemed as they would ask me, if they durst,
How such a glance came there; so, not the first
Are you to turn and ask thus. Sir, 'twas not
Her husband's presence only, called that spot
Of joy into the Duchess' cheek: perhaps   15
Frà Pandolf chanced to say "Her mantle laps
Over my lady's wrist too much," or "Paint
Must never hope to reproduce the faint
Half-flush that dies along her throat": such stuff
Was courtesy, she thought, and cause enough   20
For calling up that spot of joy. She had
A heart—how shall I say?— too soon made glad,
Too easily impressed; she liked whate'er
She looked on, and her looks went everywhere.

"My Last Duchess": Ferrara: a center of culture during the early Italian Renaissance.   3. *Frà Pandolf:* an imaginary artist, intended to represent a number of early Renaissance painters; "Frà" (brother) was the title given to monks and friars.

Sir, 'twas all one! My favor at her breast,   25
The dropping of the daylight in the West,
The bough of cherries some officious fool
Broke in the orchard for her, the white mule
She rode with round the terrace—all and each
Would draw from her alike the approving speech,   30
Or blush, at least. She thanked men—good! but thanked
Somehow—I know not how—as if she ranked
My gift of a nine-hundred-years-old name
With anybody's gift. Who'd stoop to blame
This sort of trifling? Even had you skill   35
In speech—which I have not—to make your will
Quite clear to such an one, and say, "Just this
Or that in you disgusts me; here you miss,
Or there exceed the mark"—and if she let
Herself be lessoned so, nor plainly set   40
Her wits to yours, forsooth, and made excuse,
—E'en then would be some stooping; and I choose
Never to stoop. Oh sir, she smiled, no doubt,
Whene'er I passed her; but who passed without
Much the same smile? This grew; I gave commands;   45
Then all smiles stopped together. There she stands
As if alive. Will 't please you rise? We'll meet
The company below, then. I repeat,
The Count your master's known munificence
Is ample warrant that no just pretense   50
Of mine for dowry will be disallowed;
Though his fair daughter's self, as I avowed
At starting, is my object. Nay, we'll go
Together down, sir. Notice Neptune, though,
Taming a sea-horse, thought a rarity,   55
Which Claus of Innsbruck cast in bronze for me!

                                                                          1842

MEETING AT NIGHT

1

The grey sea and the long black land;
And the yellow half-moon large and low;
And the startled little waves that leap
In fiery ringlets from their sleep,

"*My Last Duchess*": 54. *Neptune:* in Roman mythology, the god of the sea.   56. *Claus of Innsbruck:* another imaginary artist.

As I gain the cove with pushing prow, 5
And quench its speed i' the slushy sand.

2

Then a mile of warm sea-scented beach;
Three fields to cross till a farm appears;
A tap at the pane, the quick sharp scratch
And blue spurt of a lighted match, 10
And a voice less loud, thro' its joys and fears,
Than the two hearts beating each to each!

1845

PARTING AT MORNING

Round the cape of a sudden came the sea,
And the sun looked over the mountain's rim:
And straight was a path of gold for him,
And the need of a world of men for me.

1845

FRA LIPPO LIPPI

I am poor brother Lippo, by your leave!
You need not clap your torches to my face.
Zooks, what's to blame? you think you see a monk!
What, 'tis past midnight, and you go the rounds,
And here you catch me at an alley's end 5
Where sportive ladies leave their doors ajar?
The Carmine's my cloister: hunt it up,
Do—harry out, if you must show your zeal,
Whatever rat, there, haps on his wrong hole,
And nip each softling of a wee white mouse, 10
Weke, weke, that's crept to keep him company!
Aha, you know your betters! Then, you'll take
Your hand away that's fiddling on my throat,
And please to know me likewise. Who am I?
Why, one, sir, who is lodging with a friend 15
Three streets off—he's a certain . . . how d'ye call?
Master—a . . . Cosimo of the Medici,

"Frà Lippo Lippi": Frà Lippo Lippi: (1406–1469); a Florentine artist and Carmelite monk.
Browning obtained most of his information from Giorgio Vasari's gossipy *Lives of the
Painters.* 3. *Zooks:* an exclamation of vexation or surprise. 17. *Cosimo of the Medici:* a
Florentine banker who practically ruled Florence by his wealth, also a patron of the arts.

I' the house that caps the corner. Boh! you were best!
Remember and tell me, the day you're hanged,
How you affected such a gullet's gripe!   20
But you, sir, it concerns you that your knaves
Pick up a manner nor descredit you:
Zooks, are we pilchards, that they sweep the streets
And count fair prize what comes into their net?
He's Judas to a tittle, that man is!   25
Just such a face! Why, sir, you make amends.
Lord, I'm not angry! Bid your hangdogs go
Drink out this quarter-florin to the health
Of the munificent House that harbors me
(And many more beside, lads! more beside!)   30
And all's come square again. I'd like his face—
His, elbowing on his comrade in the door
With the pike and lantern—for the slave that holds
John Baptist's head a-dangle by the hair
With one hand ("Look you, now," as who should say)   35
And his weapon in the other, yet unwiped!
It's not your chance to have a bit of chalk,
A wood-coal or the like? or you should see!
Yes, I'm the painter, since you style me so.
What, brother Lippo's doings, up and down,   40
You know them and they take you? like enough!
I saw the proper twinkle in your eye—
'Tell you, I liked your looks at very first.
Let's sit and set things straight now, hip to haunch.
Here's spring come, and the nights one makes up bands   45
To roam the town and sing out carnival,
And I've been three weeks shut within my mew,
A-painting for the great man, saints and saints
And saints again. I could not paint all night—
Ouf! I leaned out of window for fresh air.   50
There came a hurry of feet and little feet,
A sweep of lute-strings, laughs, and whiffs of song—
Flower o' the broom,
Take away love, and our earth is a tomb!
Flower o' the quince,   55
I let Lisa go, and what good in life since?
Flower o' the thyme—and so on. Round they went.
Scarce had they turned the corner when a titter
Like the skipping of rabbits by moonlight—three slim shapes,
And a face that looked up . . . zooks, sir, flesh and blood,   60

_____
23. *pilchards:* common Mediterranean fish.

That's all I'm made of! Into shreds it went,
Curtain and counterpane and coverlet,
All the bed-furniture—a dozen knots,
There was a ladder! Down I let myself,
Hands and feet, scrambling somehow, and so dropped,   65
And after them. I came up with the fun
Hard by Saint Laurence, hail fellow, well met—
Flower o' the rose,
If I've been merry, what matter who knows?
And so as I was stealing back again   70
To get to bed and have a bit of sleep
Ere I rise up to-morrow and go work
On Jerome knocking at his poor old breast
With his great round stone to subdue the flesh,
You snap me of the sudden. Ah, I see!   75
Though your eye twinkles still, you shake your head—
Mine's shaved—a monk, you say—the sting's in that!
If Master Cosimo announced himself,
Mum's the word naturally; but a monk!
Come, what am I a beast for? tell us, now!   80
I was a baby when my mother died
And father died and left me in the street.
I starved there, God knows how, a year or two
On fig-skins, melon-parings, rinds and shucks,
Refuse and rubbish. One fine frosty day,   85
My stomach being empty as your hat,
The wind doubled me up and down I went.
Old Aunt Lapaccia trussed me with one hand,
(Its fellow was a stinger as I knew)
And so along the wall, over the bridge,   90
By the straight cut to the convent. Six words there,
While I stood munching my first bread that month:
"So, boy, you're minded," quoth the good fat father
Wiping his own mouth, 't was refection-time—
"To quit this very miserable world?   95
Will you renounce" . . . "the mouthful of bread?" thought I;
By no means! Brief, they made a monk of me;
I did renounce the world, its pride and greed,
Palace, farm, villa, shop and banking-house,
Trash, such as these poor devils of Medici   100
Have given their hearts to—all at eight years old.
Well, sir, I found in time, you may be sure,

---

67. *Saint Laurence:* San Lorenzo, a church in Florence.   73. *Jerome:* Saint Jerome (340–420)
whom Lippi painted for Cosimo.   88. *Aunt Lapaccia:* Lippi's aunt who placed him in the
Carmelite monastery after he was orphaned.

'T was not for nothing—the good bellyful,
The warm serge and the rope that goes all round,
And day-long blessed idleness beside!   105
"Let's see what the urchin's fit for"—that came next.
Not overmuch their way, I must confess.
Such a to-do! They tried me with their books:
Lord, they'd have taught me Latin in pure waste!
Flower o' the clove,   110
All the Latin I construe is, "amo," I love!
But, mind you, when a boy starves in the streets
Eight years together, as my fortune was,
Watching folk's faces to know who will fling
The bit of half-stripped grape-bunch he desires,   115
And who will curse or kick him for his pains—
Which gentleman processional and fine,
Holding a candle to the Sacrament,
Will wink and let him lift a plate and catch
The droppings of the wax to sell again,   120
Or holla for the Eight and have him whipped—
How say I? nay, which dog bites, which lets drop
His bone from the heap of offal in the street—
Why, soul and sense of him grow sharp alike,
He learns the look of things, and none the less   125
For admonition from the hunger-pinch.
I had a store of such remarks, be sure,
Which, after I found leisure, turned to use.
I drew men's faces on my copy-books,
Scrawled them within the antiphonary's marge,   130
Joined legs and arms to the long music-notes,
Found eyes and nose and chin for A's and B's,
And made a string of pictures of the world
Betwixt the ins and outs of verb and noun,
On the wall, the bench, the door. The monks looked black.   135
"Nay," quoth the Prior, "turn him out, d'ye say?
In no wise. Lose a crow and catch a lark.
What if at last we get our man of parts,
We Carmelites, like those Camaldolese
And Preaching Friars, to do our church up fine   140
And put the front on it that ought to be!"
And hereupon he bade me daub away.
Thank you! my head being crammed, the walls a blank,

---

139. *Camaldolese:* Benedictine religious order.   140. *Preaching Friars:* Dominican religious
order.

Never was such prompt disemburdening.
First, every sort of monk, the black and white,   145
I drew them, fat and lean: then, folk at church,
From good old gossips waiting to confess
Their cribs of barrel-droppings, candle-ends—
To the breathless fellow at the altar-foot,
Fresh from his murder, safe and sitting there   150
With the little children round him in a row
Of admiration, half for his beard and half
For that white anger of his victim's son
Shaking a fist at him with one fierce arm,
Signing himself with the other because of Christ   155
(Whose sad face on the cross sees only this
After the passion of a thousand years)
Till some poor girl, her apron o'er her head,
(Which the intense eyes looked through) came at eve
On tiptoe, said a word, dropped in a loaf,   160
Her pair of earrings and a bunch of flowers
(The brute took growling), prayed, and so was gone.
I painted all, then cried " 'Tis ask and have;
Choose, for more's ready!"—laid the ladder flat,
And showed my covered bit of cloister-wall.   165
The monks closed in a circle and praised loud
Till checked, taught what to see and not to see,
Being simple bodies—"That's the very man!
Look at the boy who stoops to pat the dog!
That woman's like the Prior's niece who comes   170
To care about his asthma: it's the life!"
But there my triumph's straw-fire flared and funked;
Their betters took their turn to see and say:
The Prior and the learned pulled a face
And stopped all that in no time. "How? what's here?   175
Quite from the mark of painting, bless us all!
Faces, arms, legs and bodies like the true
As much as pea and pea! it's devil's-game!
Your business is not to catch men with show,
With homage to the perishable clay,   180
But lift them over it, ignore it all,
Make them forget there's such a thing as flesh.
Your business is to paint the souls of men—
Man's soul, and it's a fire, smoke . . . no, it's not
It's vapor done up like a new-born babe—   185
(In that shape when you die it leaves your mouth)
It's . . . well, what matters talking, it's the soul!
Give us no more of body than shows soul!

Here's Giotto, with his Saint a-praising God,
That sets us praising—why not stop with him?   190
Why put all thoughts of praise out of our head
With wonder at lines, colors, and what not?
Paint the soul, never mind the legs and arms!
Rub all out, try at it a second time.
Oh, that white smallish female with the breasts,   195
She's just my niece . . . Herodias, I would say—
Who went and danced and got men's heads cut off!
Have it all out!" Now, is this sense, I ask?
A fine way to paint soul, by painting body
So ill, the eye can't stop there, must go further   200
And can't fare worse! Thus, yellow does for white
When what you put for yellow's simply black,
And any sort of meaning looks intense
When all beside itself means and looks nought.
Why can't a painter lift each foot in turn,   205
Left foot and right foot, go a double step,
Make his flesh liker and his soul more like,
Both in their order? Take the prettiest face,
The Prior's niece . . . patron-saint—is it so pretty
You can't discover if it means hope, fear,   210
Sorrow or joy? won't beauty go with these?
Suppose I've made her eyes all right and blue,
Can't I take breath and try to add life's flash,
And then add soul and heighten them threefold?
Or say there's beauty with no soul at all—   215
(I never saw it—put the case the same—)
If you get simple beauty and nought else,
You get about the best thing God invents:
That's somewhat: and you'll find the soul you have missed,
Within yourself, when you return him thanks.   220
"Rub all out!" Well, well, there's my life, in short,
And so the thing has gone on ever since.
I'm grown a man no doubt, I've broken bounds:
You should not take a fellow eight years old
And make him swear to never kiss the girls.   225
I'm my own master, paint now as I please—
Having a friend, you see, in the Corner-house!
Lord, it's fast holding by the rings in front—
Those great rings serve more purposes than just
To plant a flag in, or tie up a horse!   230

---

189. *Giotto* (1276–1337); an early medieval Italian painter, sculptor, and architect who became one of the leaders of the Italian Renaissance.   196. *Herodias:* see Matthew 14:1–12.

And yet the old schooling sticks, the old grave eyes
Are peeping o'er my shoulder as I work,
The heads shake still—"It's art's decline, my son!
You're not of the true painters, great and old;
Brother Angelico's the man, you'll find;   235
Brother Lorenzo stands his single peer:
Fag on at flesh, you'll never make the third!"
Flower o' the pine,
You keep your mistr . . . manners, and I'll stick to mine!
I'm not the third, then: bless us, they must know!   240
Don't you think they're the likeliest to know,
They with their Latin? So, I swallow my rage,
Clench my teeth, suck my lips in tight, and paint
To please them—sometimes do and sometimes don't;
For, doing most, there's pretty sure to come   245
A turn, some warm eve finds me at my saints—
A laugh, a cry, the business of the world—
(Flower o' the peach,
Death for us all, and his own life for each!)
And my whole soul revolves, the cup runs over,   250
The world and life's too big to pass for a dream,
And I do these wild things in sheer despite,
And play the fooleries you catch me at,
In pure rage! The old mill-horse, out at grass
After hard years, throws up his stiff heels so,   255
Although the miller does not preach to him
The only good of grass is to make chaff.
What would men have? Do they like grass or no—
May they or mayn't they? all I want's the thing
Settled for ever one way. As it is,   260
You tell too many lies and hurt yourself:
You don't like what you only like too much,
You do like what, if given you at your word,
You find abundantly detestable.
For me, I think I speak as I was taught;   265
I always see the garden and God there
A-making man's wife: and, my lesson learned,
The value and significance of flesh,
I can't unlearn ten minutes afterwards.

     You understand me: I'm a beast, I know.   270
But see, now—why, I see as certainly
As that the morning-star's about to shine,

---

235. *Angelico . . . Lorenzo:* Fra Angelico (1387–1455) and Lorenzo Monaco (1370–1425),
both painters of the traditional, acceptable medieval style.

What will hap some day. We've a youngster here
Comes to our convent, studies what I do,
Slouches and stares and lets no atom drop: 275
His name is Guidi—he'll not mind the monks—
They call him Hulking Tom, he lets them talk—
He picks my practice up—he'll paint apace,
I hope so—though I never live so long,
I know what's sure to follow. You be judge! 280
You speak no Latin more than I, belike;
However, you're my man, you've seen the world
—The beauty and the wonder and the power,
The shapes of things, their colors, lights and shades,
Changes, surprises—and God made it all! 285
—For what? Do you feel thankful, ay or no,
For this fair town's face, yonder river's line,
The mountain round it and the sky above,
Much more the figures of man, woman, child,
These are the frame to? What's it all about? 290
To be passed over, despised? or dwelt upon,
Wondered at? oh, this last of course!—you say.
But why not do as well as say, paint these
Just as they are, careless what comes of it?
God's works—paint any one, and count it crime 295
To let a truth slip. Don't object, "His works
Are here already; nature is complete:
Suppose you reproduce her (which you can't)
There's no advantage! you must beat her, then."
For, don't you mark? we're made so that we love 300
First when we see them painted, things we have passed
Perhaps a hundred times nor cared to see;
And so they are better, painted—better to us,
Which is the same thing. Art was given for that;
God uses us to help each other so, 305
Lending our minds out. Have you noticed, now,
Your cullion's hanging face? A bit of chalk,
And trust me but you should, though! How much more,
If I drew higher things with the same truth!
That were to take the Prior's pulpit-place, 310
Interpret God to all of you! Oh, oh,
It makes me mad to see what men shall do
And we in our graves! This world's no blot for us,
Nor blank; it means intensely, and means good:

---

276. *Guidi:* Tommaso Guidi or Masaccio (1401–1429) was probably a teacher, rather than
pupil of Lippi; he revolted against the medieval theory of art and was called the father of
modern painting.

To find its meaning is my meat and drink.   315
"Ay, but you don't so instigate to prayer!"
Strikes in the Prior: "when your meaning's plain
It does not say to folk—remember matins,
Or, mind you fast next Friday!" Why, for this
What need of art at all? A skull and bones,   320
Two bits of stick nailed crosswise, or, what's best,
A bell to chime the hour with, does as well.
I painted a Saint Laurence six months since
At Prato, splashed the fresco in fine style:
"How looks my painting, now the scaffold's down?"   325
I ask a brother: "Hugely," he returns—
"Already not one phiz of your three slaves
Who turn the Deacon off his toasted side,
But's scratched and prodded to our heart's content,
The pious people have so eased their own   330
With coming to say prayers there in a rage:
We get on fast to see the bricks beneath.
Expect another job this time next year,
For pity and religion grow i' the crowd—
Your painting serves its purpose!" Hang the fools!   335

—That is—you'll not mistake an idle word
Spoke in a huff by a poor monk, God wot,
Tasting the air this spicy night which turns
The unaccustomed head like Chianti wine!
Oh, the church knows! don't misreport me, now!   340
It's natural a poor monk out of bounds
Should have his apt word to excuse himself:
And hearken how I plot to make amends.
I have bethought me: I shall paint a piece
. . . There's for you! Give me six months, then go, see   345
Something in Sant' Ambrogio's! Bless the nuns!
They want a cast o' my office. I shall paint
God in the midst, Madonna and her babe,
Ringed by a bowery flowery angel-brood,
Lilies and vestments and white faces, sweet   350
As puff on puff of grated orris-root
When ladies crowd to Church at midsummer.
And then i' the front, of course a saint or two—
Saint John, because he saves the Florentines,

---

323. *Saint Lawrence:* Executed by being roasted alive, St. Lawrence is said to have asked his
tormentors to turn him because he was well done on one side.   324. *Prato:* A town near
Florence.   346. *Sant' Ambrogio's:* The next forty-two lines describe Lippi's *Coronation of the
Virgin,* painted for the altar at the Cathedral of Sant' Ambrogio and now displayed in the
Uffizi museum.

Saint Ambrose, who puts down in black and white   355
The convent's friends and gives them a long day,
And Job, I must have him there past mistake,
The man of Uz (and Us without the z,
Painters who need his patience). Well, all these
Secured at their devotion, up shall come   360
Out of a corner when you least expect,
As one by a dark stair into a great light,
Music and talking, who but Lippo! I!—
Mazed, motionless and moonstruck—I'm the man!
Back I shrink—what is this I see and hear?   365
I, caught up with my monk's-things by mistake,
My old serge gown and rope that goes all round,
I, in this presence, this pure company!
Where's a hole, where's a corner for escape?
Then steps a sweet angelic slip of a thing   370
Forward, puts out a soft palm—"Not so fast!"
—Addresses the celestial presence, "nay—
He made you and devised you, after all,
Though he's none of you! Could Saint John there draw—
His camel-hair make up a painting-brush?   375
We come to brother Lippo for all that,
Iste perfecit opus!" So, all smile—
I shuffle sideways with my blushing face
Under the cover of a hundred wings
Thrown like a spread of kirtles when you're gay   380
And play hot cockles, all the doors being shut,
Till, wholly unexpected, in there pops
The hothead husband! Thus I scuttle off
To some safe bench behind, not letting go
The palm of her, the little lily thing   385
That spoke the good word for me in the nick,
Like the Prior's niece . . . Saint Lucy, I would say.
And so all's saved for me, and for the church
A pretty picture gained. Go, six months hence!
You hand, sir, and good-bye: no lights, no lights!   390
The street's hushed, and I know my own way back,
Don't fear me! There's the gray beginning. Zooks!

                                                                        1855

---

375. *camel-hair:* "And John was clothed with camel hair. . . ." Mark 1:6.   377. *Iste perfecit opus!*: "This one accomplished the work." The words appear on a scroll painted in front of the figure Browning identifies as Lippi.   381. *hot cockles:* "A rustic game in which one player lay face downwards, or knelt down with his eyes covered, and being struck in the back by the others in turn, guessed who struck him." (*Oxford English Dictionary*).

TWO IN THE CAMPAGNA

1

I wonder do you feel today
    As I have felt since, hand in hand,
We sat down on the grass, to stray
    In spirit better through the land,
This morn of Rome and May?   5

2

For me, I touched a thought, I know,
    Has tantalized me many times,
(Like turns of thread the spiders throw
    Mocking across our path) for rhymes
To catch and let go.   10

3

Help me to hold it! First it left
    The yellowing fennel, run to seed
There, branching from the brickwork's cleft,
    Some old tomb's ruin: yonder weed
Took up the floating weft,   15

4

Where one small orange cup amassed
    Five beetles—blind and green they grope
Among the honey-meal: and last,
    Everywhere on the grassy slope
I traced it. Hold it fast!   20

5

The champaign with its endless fleece
    Of feathery grasses everywhere!
Silence and passion, joy and peace,
    An everlasting wash of air—
Rome's ghost since her decease.   25

6

Such life here, through such lengths of hours,
    Such miracles performed in play,
Such primal naked forms of flowers,
    Such letting nature have her way
While heaven looks from its towers!   30

7

How say you? Let us, O my dove,
　　Let us be unashamed of soul,
As earth lies bare to heaven above!
　　How is it under our control
To love or not to love? 　　　　　　　　　　　　　35

8

I would that you were all to me,
　　You that are just so much, no more.
Nor yours nor mine, nor slave nor free!
　　Where does the fault lie? What the core
O' the wound, since wound must be? 　　　　　　40

9

I would I could adopt your will,
　　See with your eyes, and set my heart
Beating by yours, and drink my fill
　　At your soul's springs—your part my part
In life, for good and ill. 　　　　　　　　　　　　45

10

No. I yearn upward, touch you close,
　　Then stand away. I kiss your cheek,
Catch your soul's warmth—I pluck the rose
　　And love it more than tongue can speak—
Then the good minute goes. 　　　　　　　　　　50

11

Already how am I so far
　　Out of that minute? Must I go
Still like the thistle-ball, no bar,
　　Onward, whenever light winds blow,
Fixed by no friendly star? 　　　　　　　　　　　55

12

Just when I seemed about to learn!
　　Where is the thread now? Off again!
That old trick! Only I discern—
　　Infinite passion, and the pain
Of finite hearts that yearn. 　　　　　　　　　　60

1855

Further Reading

DeVane, William Clyde. *A Browning Handbook*. New York: Appleton, 1955. •
Honan, Park. *Browning's Characters: A Study in Poetic Technique*. New Haven: Yale
UP, 1961. • Jerman, B. R. "Browning's Witless Duke." *The Browning Critics*. Ed.
Boyd Litzinger and K. L. Knickerbocker. Lexington: U of Kentucky P, 1965.
329–35. • Perrine, Laurence. "Browning's Shrewd Duke." *The Browning Critics*.
Ed. Boyd Litzinger and K. L. Knickerbocker. Lexington: U of Kentucky P, 1965.
336–42. • Shaw, W. David. "Character and Philosophy in 'Fra Lippo Lippi.' "
Victorian Poetry 2.2 (Spring 1964): 127–32. • *Robert Browning: A Collection of Critical
Essays*. Ed. Philip Drew. Boston: Houghton, 1966.

*During the period of Browning's greatest popularity, which extended into
the early years of the twentieth century, he had a reputation as a "difficult"
poet, largely because the public's experience was largely with the lyric tradition in which Wordsworth and Keats had worked. Readers who expected a
poem to be a direct expression of the poet's own emotions were often baffled by
Browning's poems, and the process of educating the public in how to read
them became a small industry. Among the best explanations was that offered
in Professor Samuel Silas Curry's* Browning and the Dramatic Monologue *(1908).*

Samuel Silas Curry: On Browning's New Literary Form

The monologue, as Browning has exemplified it, is one end of a
conversation. A definite speaker is conceived in a definite, dramatic
situation. Usually we find also a well-defined listener, though his
character is understood entirely from the impression he produces
upon the speaker. We feel that this listener has said something and
that his presence and character influence the speaker's thought,
words, and manner. The conversation does not consist of abstract
remarks, but takes place in a definite situation as a part of human
life.

We must realize the situation, the speaker, the hearer, before the
meaning can become clear; and it is the failure to do this which has
caused many to find Browning obscure.

For example, observe Browning's "Confessions."

CONFESSIONS

What is he buzzing in my ears?
   "Now that I come to die,

Do I view the world as a vale of tears?"
   Ah, reverend sir, not I!

What I viewed there once, what I view again   5
   Where the physic bottles stand
On the table's edge,—is a suburb lane,
   With a wall to my bedside hand.

That lane sloped, much as the bottles do,
   From a house you could descry   10
O'er the garden-wall: is the curtain blue
   Or green to a healthy eye?

To mine, it serves for the old June weather
   Blue above lane and wall;
And that farthest bottle labelled "Ether"   15
   Is the house o'er-topping all.

At a terrace, somewhere near the stopper,
   There watched for me, one June,
A girl: I know, sir, it's improper,
   My poor mind's out of tune.   20

Only, there was a way . . . you crept
   Close by the side, to dodge
Eyes in the house, two eyes except:
   They styled their house "The Lodge."

What right had a lounger up their lane?   25
   But, by creeping very close,
With the good wall's help,—their eyes might strain
   And stretch themselves to Oes,

Yet never catch her and me together,
   As she left the attic, there,   30
By the rim of the bottle labelled "Ether,"
   And stole from stair to stair,

And stood by the rose-wreathed gate. Alas,
   We loved, sir—used to meet:
How sad and bad and mad it was—   35
But then, how it was sweet!

Here, evidently, the speaker, who has "come to die," has been aroused by
some "reverend sir," who has been expostulating with him and uttering
conventional phrases about the vanity of human life. Such superficial pes-
simism awakens protest, and the dying man remonstrates in the words of
the poem.

    The speaker is apparently in bed and hardly believes himself fully pos-
sessed of his senses. He even asks if the curtain is "green or blue to a

healthy eye," as if he feared to trust his judgment, lest it be perverted by disease.

An abrupt beginning is very characteristic of a monologue, and when given properly, the first words arrest attention and suggest the situation.

After the speaker's bewildered repetition of the visitor's words and his blunt answer "not I," which says such views are not his own, he talks of his "bedside hand," turns a row of bottles into a street, and tells of the sweetest experience of his life. He refuses to say that it was not sweet; he will not allow an abnormal condition such as his sickness to determine his views of life. The result is an introspection of the deeper hope found in the heart of man.

The poem is not an essay or a sermon, it is not the lyric expression of a mood; it portrays the conflict of individual with individual and reveals the deepest motives of a character. It is not a dialogue, but only one end of a conversation, and for this reason it more intensely and definitely focuses attention. We see deeper into the speaker's spirit and view of life, while we recognize the superficiality of the creed of his visitor. The monologue thus is dramatic. It interprets human experience and character.

WALT WHITMAN

(1819–1892)

---

from SONG OF MYSELF

5

I believe in you my soul, the other I am must not abase itself to you,
And you must not be abased to the other.

Loafe with me on the grass, loose the stop from your throat,
Not words, not music or rhyme I want, not custom or lecture, not
    even the best,
Only the lull I like, the hum of your valvèd voice.   5

I mind how once we lay such a transparent summer morning,
How you settled your head athwart my hips and gently turn'd over
    upon me,
And parted the shirt from my bosom-bone, and plunged your tongue
    to my bare-stript heart,
And reach'd till you felt my beard, and reach'd till you held my feet.   10

Swiftly arose and spread around me the peace and knowledge that
    pass all the argument of the earth,
And I know that the hand of God is the promise of my own,

And I know that the spirit of God is the brother of my own,
And that all the men ever born are also my brothers, and the women
    my sisters and lovers,   15
And that a kelson of the creation is love,
And limitless are leaves stiff or drooping in the fields,
And brown ants in the little wells beneath them,
And mossy scabs of the worm fence, heap'd stones, elder, mullein
    and poke-weed.   20

1855

THE WOUND-DRESSER

1

An old man bending I come among new faces,
Years looking backward resuming in answer to children,
Come tell us old man, as from young men and maidens that love me,
(Arous'd and angry, I'd thought to beat the alarum, and urge relent
    less war,
But soon my fingers fail'd me, my face droop'd and I resign'd myself,   5
To sit by the wounded and soothe them, or silently watch the dead;)
Years hence of these scenes, of these furious passions, these chances,
Of unsurpass'd heroes, (was one side so brave? the other was equally
    brave;)
Now be witness again, paint the mightiest armies of earth,
Of those armies so rapid so wondrous what saw you to tell us?   10
What stays with you latest and deepest? of curious panics,
Of hard-fought engagements or sieges tremendous what deepest
    remains?

2

O maidens and young men I love and that love me,
What you ask of my days those the strangest and sudden your talking
    recalls,
Soldier alert I arrive after a long march cover'd with sweat and dust,   15
In the nick of time I come, plunge in the fight, loudly shout in the
    rush of successful charge,
Enter the captur'd works—yet lo, like a swift-running river they fade,
Pass and are gone they fade—I dwell not on soldiers' perils or
    soldiers' joys,
(Both I remember well—many the hardships, few the joys, yet I was
    content.)

"*Song of Myself*": 16. *Kelson:* a line of timber which holds the floorboards to the keel, the principal structure of a ship which runs through its center.

But in silence, in dreams' projections,   20
While the world of gain and appearance and mirth goes on,
So soon what is over forgotten, and waves wash the imprints off the
    sand,
With hinged knees returning I enter the doors, (while for you up
    there,
Whoever you are, follow without noise and be of strong heart.)

Bearing the bandages, water and sponge,   25
Straight and swift to my wounded I go,
Where they lie on the ground after the battle brought in,
Where their priceless blood reddens the grass the ground,
Or to the rows of the hospital tent, or under the roof'd hospital,
To the long rows of cots up and down each side I return,   30
To each and all one after another I draw near, not one do I miss,
An attendant follows holding a tray, he carries a refuse pail,
Soon to be fill'd with clotted rags and blood, emptied, and fill'd
    again.

I onward go, I stop,
With hinged knees and steady hand to dress wounds,   35
I am firm with each, the pangs are sharp yet unavoidable,
One turns to me his appealing eyes—poor boy! I never knew you,
Yet I think I could not refuse this moment to die for you, if that
    would save you.

3

On, on I go, (open doors of time! open hospital doors!)
The crush'd head I dress, (poor crazed hand tear not the bandage
    away,)   40
The neck of the cavalry-man with the bullet through and through I
    examine,
Hard the breathing rattles, quite glazed already the eye, yet life
    struggles hard,
(Come sweet death! be persuaded O beautiful death!
In mercy come quickly.)

From the stump of the arm, the amputated hand,
I undo the clotted lint, remove the slough, wash off the matter and
    blood,   45
Back on his pillow the soldier bends with curv'd neck and side-falling
    head,
His eyes are closed, his face is pale, he dares not look on the bloody
    stump,
And has not yet look'd on it.

I dress a wound in the side, deep, deep,
But a day or two more, for see the frame all wasted and sinking,   50
And the yellow-blue countenance see.

Walt Whitman   *591*

I dress the perforated shoulder, the foot with the bullet-wound,
Cleanse the one with a gnawing and putrid gangrene, so sickening, so
    offensive,
While the attendant stands behind aside me holding the tray and pail.

I am faithful, I do not give out,   55
The fractur'd thigh, the knee, the wound in the abdomen,
These and more I dress with impassive hand, (yet deep in my breast a
    fire, a burning flame.)

4

Thus in silence in dreams' projections,
Returning, resuming, I thread my way through the hospitals,
The hurt and wounded I pacify with soothing hand,   60
I sit by the restless all the dark night, some are so young,
Some suffer so much, I recall the experience sweet and sad,
(Many a soldier's loving arms about this neck have cross'd and rested,
Many a soldier's kiss dwells on these bearded lips.)

1865

WHEN I HEARD THE LEARN'D ASTRONOMER

When I heard the learn'd astronomer,
When the proofs, the figures, were ranged in columns before me,
When I was shown the charts and diagrams, to add, divide, and
    measure them.
When I sitting heard the astronomer where he lectured with much
    applause in the lecture-room,
How soon unaccountable I became tired and sick,   5
Till rising and gliding out I wander'd off by myself,
In the mystical moist night-air, and from time to time,
Look'd up in perfect silence at the stars.

1865

A NOISELESS PATIENT SPIDER

A noiseless patient spider,
I mark'd where on a little promontory it stood isolated,
Mark'd how to explore the vacant vast surrounding,
It launch'd forth filament, filament, filament, out of itself,
Ever unreeling them, ever tirelessly speeding them.   5

And you O my soul where you stand,
Surrounded, detached, in measureless oceans of space,

Ceaselessly musing, venturing, throwing, seeking the spheres to
   connect them,
Till the bridge you will need be form'd, till the ductile anchor hold,
Till the gossamer thread you fling catch somewhere, O my soul.   10

1868

Further Reading

Jarrell, Randall. "Some Lines from Whitman." *Critical Essays on Walt Whitman.* Ed.
James Woodress. Boston: Hall, 1983. 231–43. • Killingsworth, M. Jimmie.
Whitman's Poetry of the Body. Chapel Hill: U of North Carolina P, 1989. • Miller,
James E., Jr. *Walt Whitman.* New York: Twayne, 1962. • Aspiz, Harold. *Walt
Whitman and the Body Beautiful.* Urbana: U of Illinois P, 1980. • Eckly, Witton.
"Whitman's 'A Noiseless Patient Spider.' " *Explicator* 22 (Nov. 1963): 20. •
Lindfors, Bernth. "Whitman's 'When I Heard the Learn'd Astronomer.' " *Walt
Whitman Review* 10 (Mar. 1964): 19–21.

*The impact of Walt Whitman's poetry has inspired a wide range of admirers
and imitators. In the 1880s, William Butler Yeats showed himself to be a
poetic rebel by walking around Dublin with a copy of* Leaves of Grass *in
his pocket. Later Pablo Neruda of Chile and Federico García Lorca of
Spain spread Whitman's influence to Spanish-language poetry. Among
twentieth-century Americans, Whitman's influence is so pervasive that
almost every poet has to make his or her peace with the Whitmanesque
"epic" style. The following comments by Randall Jarrell and W. S. Merwin show that poets may make this peace in very different ways.*

Randall Jarrell: On Whitman as an Epic Poet

Whitman is more coordinate and parallel than anybody, is *the* poet of parallel present participles, of twenty verbs joined by a single subject: all this
helps to give his work its feeling of raw hypnotic reality, of being that world
which also streams over us joined only by *ands,* until we supply the subordi-
nating conjunctions; and since as children we see the *ands* and not the
becauses, this method helps to give Whitman some of the freshness of childhood. How inexhaustibly interesting the world is in Whitman! Arnold all
his life kept wishing that he could see the world "with a plainness as near, as
flashing" as that with which Moses and Rebekah and the Argonauts saw it.
He asked with elegiac nostalgia, "Who can see the green earth any more /

As she was by the sources of Time?"—and all the time there was somebody alive who saw it so, as plain and near and flashing, and with a kind of calm, pastoral, Biblical dignity and elegance as well, sometimes. The *thereness* and *suchness* of the world are incarnate in Whitman as they are in few other writers.

They might have put on his tombstone WALT WHITMAN: HE HAD HIS NERVE. He is the rashest, the most inexplicable and unlikely—the most impossible, one wants to say—of poets. He somehow *is* in a class by himself, so that one compares him with other poets about as readily as one compares *Alice* with other books. (Even his free verse has a completely different effect from anybody else's.) Who would think of comparing him with Tennyson or Browning or Arnold or Baudelaire?—it is Homer, or the sagas, or something far away and long ago, that comes to one's mind only to be dismissed; for sometimes Whitman *is* epic, just as *Moby Dick* is, and it surprises us to be able to use truthfully this word that we have misused so many times.

W. S. Merwin: On Whitman as a Propagandist

ED FOLSOM: . . . I'm wondering if some of that positivism in Whitman is that he refused ever to set his past aside and begin again?

WSM: . . . Both Whitman's strength and his weakness is that he is basically a rhetorical poet. And he's rhetorical not only in the obvious sense that all poetry is rhetorical, but in the sense of rhetoric as public speech: you decide on a stance and then you bring in material to flesh out that stance, to give details to your position. This is one of the things that makes me uneasy about Whitman. The stance is basically *there;* and much of the poetry simply adds detail to it. So many of the moments in Whitman that I really love are exceptions to this. Yet to my mind, these exceptions occur far too infrequently. Most of the time he's making a speech. The whole *Leaves of Grass* in a sense is a speech. It's a piece of emotional propaganda about an emotional approach to a historical moment. It's almost set up in a way which makes it impossible for it to develop, to deepen, or to reflect on itself and come out with sudden new perspectives.

Certainly that urge to write propaganda is one I not only understand but sympathize with. But I think it's an urge that doesn't often make poetry. Of course poetry should never be completely devoid of the desire to make something happen—it would only be decoration then—and that desire to make something happen is the part of you that is writing propaganda: so it's always there. After all, there is a kind of desperate hope built into poetry now; one really wants, hopelessly, to save the world and one tries to say everything that can be said for the things that one loves, while there's still time. But I don't think it can be messianic, you know; poets can't go out and preach on the street corners to save the world.

EF: What about some of the poems of the "Drum Taps" period like "The Wound-Dresser"?

WSM: They're some of my favorite passages, because his theory won't support him there. He's simply paying attention to what he sees in front of him. I find those poems both sharper and more moving than many other things in Whitman.

CHARLES BAUDELAIRE

(1821–1867)

TO THE READER

translated from the French by Robert Lowell

Infatuation, sadism, lust, avarice
possess our souls and drain the body's force;
we spoonfeed our adorable remorse,
like whores or beggars nourishing their lice.

Our sins are mulish, our confessions lies;   5
we play to the grandstand with our promises,
we pray for tears to wash our filthiness,
importantly pissing hogwash through our styes.

The devil, watching by our sickbeds, hissed
old smut and folk-songs to our soul, until   10
the soft and precious metal of our will
boiled off in vapor for this scientist.

Each day his flattery makes us eat a toad,
and each step forward is a step to hell,
unmoved, though previous corpses and their smell   15
asphyxiate our progress on this road.

Like the poor lush who cannot satisfy,
we try to force our sex with counterfeits,
die drooling on the deliquescent tits,
mouthing the rotten orange we suck dry.   20

Gangs of demons are boozing in our brain—
ranked, swarming, like a million warrior-ants,

they drown and choke the cistern of our wants;
each time we breathe, we tear our lungs with pain.

If poison, arson, sex, narcotics, knives   25
have not yet ruined us and stitched their quick,
loud patterns on the canvas of our lives,
it is because our souls are still too sick.

Among the vermin, jackals, panthers, lice,
gorillas and tarantulas that suck   30
and snatch and scratch and defecate and fuck
in the disorderly circus of our vice,

there's one more ugly and abortive birth.
It makes no gestures, never beats its breast,
yet it would murder for a moment's rest,   35
and willingly annihilate the earth.

It's BOREDOM. Tears have glued its eyes together.
You know it well, my Reader. This obscene
beast chain-smokes yawning for the guillotine—
you—hypocrite Reader—my double—my brother!   40

1857, trans. 1961

CORRESPONDENCES

translated from the French by Richard Howard

The pillars of Nature's temple are alive
and sometimes yield perplexing messages;
forests of symbols between us and the shrine
remark our passage with accustomed eyes.

Like long-held echoes, blending somewhere else   5
into one deep and shadowy unison
as limitless as darkness and as day,
the sounds, the scents, the colors correspond.

There are odors succulent as young flesh,
sweet as flutes, and green as any grass,   10
while others—rich, corrupt and masterful—

possess the power of such infinite things
as incense, amber, benjamin and musk,
to praise the senses' raptures and the mind's.

1857, trans. 1982

BY ASSOCIATION

translated from the French by Richard Howard

These warm fall nights I breathe, eyes closed, the scent
of your welcoming breasts, and thereupon appears
the coast of maybe Malabar—some paradise
besotted by the sun's monotonous fire;

an idle isle where Nature grants to men   5
with bodies slim and strong, to women who
meet your eye with amazing willingness,
the rarest trees, the ripest fruit; and then,

guided by your fragrance to enchanted ground,
I glimpse a harbor filled with masts and sails   10
still troubled by the slow-receding tide,

while the aroma of green tamarinds
dilates my nostrils as it drifts to sea
and mingles in my soul with the sailors' song.

1857, trans. 1982

A PHANTOM

translated from the French by Richard Howard

1 The Shadows

Dejection has its catacombs
to which Fate has abandoned me;
no light comes, and I am left
with Night, a sullen cell-mate—

as if a scoffing God had forced   5
my hand to fresco . . . silhouettes!
Here with grisly appetite
I grill and devour my heart,

but then a shape looms, shining,
and as it moves it modifies: 10
a lovely . . . something—is there not

all the East in its easy way?
I know my visitor! *She* comes,
black—yet how that blackness glows!

2 The Perfume

Reader, you know how a church can reek   15
from one grain of incense you inhale
with careful greed—remember the smell?
Or the stubborn musk of an old sachet?

The spell is cast, the magic works,
and the present is the past—restored!   20
So a lover from beloved flesh
plucks subtle flowers of memory . . .

In bed her heavy resilient hair
—a living censer, like a sachet—
released its animal perfume,   25

and from discarded underclothes
still fervent with her sacred body's
form, there rose a scent of fur.

3 The Frame

As the fine frame completes a canvas
(even one from a master's hand),   30
adding an indefinable magic
by dividing art from mere nature,

so jewels, mirrors, metals, gold
invariably suited her loveliness—
none violated the lustre she had,   35
and each thing seemed to set her off.

You might have said, sometimes, she thought
objects longed to make love to her,
so greedily she slaked her nakedness

on the kisses of linen sheets and silk,   40
revealing with each movement all
the unstudied grace of a marmoset.

4 The Portrait

Look what Death and Disease have made
of our old flame: a heap of ashes.
My god, how horrible! What's left   45
of eyes so soft yet so intense,

of kisses stronger than any drug,
of a mouth that used to drown my heart,
of all our glowing exaltation?
Precious little—barely a sketch   50

fading in a solitude like mine,
erased a little more each day
by disrespectful Time that wipes
out Life and Art; yet even Time
cannot force me to forget Her   55
who was my glory and my Joy!

1857, trans. 1982

THE KING OF THE RAINY COUNTRY

translated from the French by Edna St. Vincent Millay

A rainy country this, that I am monarch of,—
A rich but powerless king, worn-out while yet a boy;
For whom in vain the falcon falls upon the dove;
Not even his starving people's groans can give him joy;
Scorning his tutors, loathing his spaniels, finding stale   5
His favourite jester's quips, yawning at the droll tale.
His bed, for all its *fleurs de lis,* looks like a tomb;
The ladies of the court, attending him, to whom
He, being a prince, is handsome, see him lying there
Cold as a corpse, and lift their shoulders in despair: 10
No garment they take off, no garter they leave on
Excites the gloomy eye of this young skeleton.
The royal alchemist, who makes him gold from lead,
The baser element from out the royal head
Cannot extract; nor can those Roman baths of blood,   15
For some so efficacious, cure the hebetude
Of him, along whose veins, where flows no blood at all,
For ever the slow waters of green Lethe crawl.

1857, trans. 1932

THE LITTLE OLD WOMEN

to Victor Hugo

translated from the French by Richard Howard

1

In murky corners of old cities where
everything—horror too—is magical,

"*The King of the Rainy Country*": 7. "*fleurs de lis:* lilies.   16. *hebetude:* lethargy or dullness of
the mind.   18. *Lethe:* the mythic, underworld river of forgetfulness.

I study, servile to my moods, the odd
and charming refuse of humanity.

These travesties were women once—Laïs   5
or Eponine! Love them, pathetic freaks,
hunchbacked and crippled—for they still have souls!
In ragged skirts and threadbare finery

they creep, tormented by the wicked gusts,
cowering each time an omnibus   10
thunders past, and clutching a reticule
as if it were a relic sewn with spells.

Whether they mince like marionettes or drag
themselves along like wounded animals,
they dance—against their will, the creatures dance—   15
sad bells on which a merciless Devil tugs.

They waver, but their eyes are gimlet-sharp
and gleam like holes where water sleeps at night—
the eyes of a child, a little girl who laughs
in sacred wonder at whatever shines!   20

—The coffins of old women are often the size
of a child's, have you ever noticed? Erudite
Death, by making the caskets match, suggests
a tidy symbol, if in dubious taste,

and when I glimpse one of these feeble ghosts   25
at grips with Paris and its murderous swarm,
it always seems to me the poor old thing
is slowly crawling toward a second crib;

or else those ill-assorted limbs propose
a problem in geometry: to fit   30
so many crooked corpses, how many times
must the workman alter a coffin's shape?

Those eyes are cisterns fed by a million tears,
or crucibles cracked by an ore that has gone cold:
irresistible their sovereignty   35
to one who suckled at disaster's dugs!

2

A Vestal at defunct *Frascati*'s shrine;
a priestess of Thalia whose memory survives

---

5. *Laïs . . . Eponine:* Greek courtesans known for their beauty.   37. *Frascati:* a central Italian
town known for its palaces of the Roman aristocracy.   38. *Thalia:* in Greek mythology, the
Muse of comedy and idyllic poetry.

only in one long-dead prompter's mind;
the profligate of *Tivoli* in her prime;   40

this one a martyr to her fatherland,
that one her husband's victim, and one more
doomed by her son to a Madonna's grief—
all could make a river of their tears.

And all beguile me, but especially   45
those who, honeying their pain, implore
Addiction that had once lent them its wings:
'Mighty Hippogriff, let me fly again!'

3

Little old women! I remember one
I had trailed for hours, until the sky   50
went scarlet as a wound, and she sat down
lost in thought on a public-garden bench,

listening to the tunes our soldiers play—
brazen music for daylight's waning gold
(and yet such martial measures stir the soul,   55
granting a kind of glory to the crowd) . . .

Upright and proud she sat, and greedily
drank in the military airs, her eyes
like some old eagle's brightening beneath
the absent laurel on her marble brow!   60

4

And so you wander, stoic and inured
to all the uproar of the heedless town:
broken-hearted mothers, trollops, saints,
whose names were once the order of the day,

embodiments of glory and of grace!   65
Who knows you now? From doorways, derelicts
murmur obscene endearments as you pass,
and mocking children caper at your heels . . .

Poor wizened spooks, ashamed to be alive,
you hug the walls, sickly and timorous,   70
and no one greets you, no one says goodbye
to rubbish ready for eternity!

But I who at a distance follow you
and anxiously attend your failing steps

---

40. *Tivoli:* a central Italian town known for its temples and famous villas.

as if I had become your father—mine   75
are secret pleasures you cannot suspect!

I see first love in bloom upon your flesh,
dark or luminous I see your vanished days—
my teeming heart exults in all your sins
and all your virtues magnify my soul!   80

Flotsam, my family—ruins, my race!
Each night I offer you a last farewell!
Where will you be tomorrow, ancient Eves
under God's undeviating paw?

1861, trans. 1982

THE ALBATROSS

translated from the French by Richard Wilbur

Often, for pastime, mariners will ensnare
The albatross, that vast sea-bird who sweeps
On high companionable pinion where
Their vessel glides upon the bitter deeps.

Torn from his native space, this captive king   5
Flounders upon the deck in stricken pride,
And pitiably lets his great white wing
Drag like a heavy paddle at his side.

This rider of winds, how awkward he is, and weak!
How droll he seems, who was all grace of late!   10
A sailor pokes a pipestem into his beak;
Another, hobbling, mocks his trammeled gait.

The Poet is like this monarch of the clouds,
Familiar of storms, of stars, and of all high things;
Exiled on earth amidst its hooting crowds,   15
He cannot walk, borne down by his giant wings.

1861, trans. 1955

Further Reading

Peyre, Henri, ed. *Baudelaire: A Collection of Critical Essays*. Englewood Cliffs, NJ:
Prentice, 1962. • Carter, A. E. *Charles Baudelaire*. Boston: Twayne, 1977. 56–101.

• Hyslop, Lois Boe. *Baudelaire: Man of His Time*. New Haven: Yale UP, 1980. •
De Man, Paul. "Anthropomorphism and Trope in the Lyric." *Modern Critical Views: Charles Baudelaire*. Ed. Harold Bloom. New York: Chelsea, 1987. 125–42. • Caws, Mary Ann. "Insertion in an Oval Frame: Poe Circumscribed by Baudelaire." *Modern Critical Views: Charles Baudelaire*. Ed. Harold Bloom. New York: Chelsea, 1987. 101–23, spec. 110–118.

About the time that Whitman in America was expressing an all-embracing exuberance, the Frenchman Charles Baudelaire was expressing a darker view of life. The common view of the poet as a "bohemian" outsider stems partly from the "dandyism" Baudelaire expresses in the following passage from his journal, an attitude adopted by the later French symbolists Arthur Rimbaud, Paul Verlaine, and Stéphane Mallarmé.

Charles Baudelaire: On Middle-Class Values

translated from the French by David Paul

. . . universal ruin, or universal progress—I don't care which you call it—will manifest itself not so much in political institutions, as in the debasement of the human heart. Need I say that what is left of political systems will struggle feebly in the clutches of universal animality, and that governments, in order to hold on to their power, will be forced to resort to means that would make our humanity today, hardened as it is, shudder with horror? Then the son will run away from his family not at eighteen, but at twelve years of age, emancipated by his gluttonous precocity; he will run away, not in search of heroic adventures, not to deliver some captive maiden from a prison tower, nor to immortalize some garret with the sublimity of his thought, but in order to found his own business, get rich, and set up in competition with his infamous papa. Then, anything resembling virtue, anything at all indeed which is not a rage for money, will be deemed contemptible, ridiculous. Your spouse, your chaste better half, oh Bourgeois, she who provides the legitimate poetry of your life, will introduce an irreproachable infamy into her legality, become the loving and vigilant guardian of your strong-boxes, and be none other than the perfect ideal of the kept woman. Your daughter, prematurely nubile, will dream in her cradle of selling herself for a million. And you yourself, Bourgeois—even less of a poet than you are today—you will find no cause for reproach in that. For there are things in man which prosper and strengthen in proportion as other qualities shrink and grow enfeebled; and thanks to the progress of these times, there will be nothing left of your compassion but your bowels! These times are perhaps quite near; who knows if they are not already come, and the coarsening of our natures is the only obstacle that prevents us from truly appreciating the atmosphere we are now breathing!

For my part, though I feel a ridiculous touch of the prophet in me sometimes, I know I will never have the charity of a physician. Astray in this foul world, shoved by the crowd, I feel like one prematurely worn out, who sees, in the depths of time behind him only bitterness and disappointment, ahead only a tumult with nothing new in it, whether of enlightenment or suffering. In the evening, when such a man has snatched from fate a few pleasant hours, and lulled by the digestive process, forgetting the past—as far as he can—content with the moment and resigned to the future, exhilarated by his own nonchalance and dandyism, proud to be not quite as base as those who pass by, he can say, as he gazes at the smoke of his cigar: How should I care what become of these conscious entities?

EMILY DICKINSON

(1830–1886)

[I LIKE A LOOK OF AGONY]

I like a look of Agony,
Because I know it's true—
Men do not sham Convulsion,
Nor simulate, a Throe—

The Eyes glaze once—and that is Death—   5
Impossible to feign
The Beads upon the Forehead
By homely Anguish strung.

1861

[WILD NIGHTS—WILD NIGHTS!]

Wild Nights—Wild Nights!
Were I with thee
Wild Nights should be
Our luxury!

Futile—the Winds—   5
To a Heart in port—
Done with the Compass—
Done with the Chart!

Rowing in Eden—
Ah, the Sea!   10

Might I but moor—Tonight—
In Thee!

ca. 1861

[OF BRONZE—AND BLAZE—]

Of Bronze—and Blaze—
The North—Tonight—
So adequate—it forms—
So preconcerted with itself
So distant—to alarms—   5
An Unconcern so sovereign
To Universe, or me—
Infects my simple spirit
With Taints of Majesty—
Till I take vaster attitudes—   10
And strut upon my stem—
Disdaining Men, and Oxygen,
For Arrogance of them—

My Splendors, are Managerie—
But their Competeless Show   15
Will entertain the Centuries
When I, am long ago,
An Island in dishonored Grass—
Whom none but Daisies, know.

1861?

[THE SOUL SELECTS HER OWN SOCIETY—]

The Soul selects her own Society—
Then—shuts the Door—
To her divine Majority—
Present no more—

Unmoved—she notes the Chariots—pausing—   5
At her low Gate—
Unmoved—an Emperor be kneeling
Upon her Mat—

I've known her—from an ample nation—
Choose One—   10
Then—close the Valves of her attention—
Like Stone—

1862

[WHAT SOFT—CHERUBIC CREATURES—]

What Soft—Cherubic Creatures—
These Gentlewomen are—
One would as soon assault a Plush—
Or violate a Star—

Such Dimity Convictions—   5
A Horror so refined
Of freckled Human Nature—
Of Deity—ashamed—

It's such a common—Glory—
A Fisherman's—Degree—   10
Redemption—Brittle Lady—
Be so—ashamed of Thee—

1862

[I DIED FOR BEAUTY—BUT WAS SCARCE]

I died for Beauty—but was scarce
Adjusted in the Tomb
When One who died for Truth, was lain
In an adjoining Room—

He questioned softly "Why I failed"?   5
"For Beauty", I replied—
"And I—for Truth—Themself are One—
We Brethren, are", He said—

And so, as Kinsmen, met a Night—
We talked between the Rooms—   10
Until the Moss had reached our lips—
And covered up—our names—

1862

[IT WAS NOT DEATH, FOR I STOOD UP]

It was not Death, for I stood up,
And all the Dead, lie down—
It was not Night, for all the Bells
Put out their Tongues, for Noon.

It was not Frost, for on my Flesh   5
I felt Siroccos—crawl—

Nor Fire—for just my Marble feet
Could keep a Chancel, cool—

And yet, it tasted, like them all,
The Figures I have seen   10
Set orderly, for Burial,
Reminded me, of mine—

As if my life were shaven,
And fitted to a frame,
And could not breathe without a key,   15
And 'twas like Midnight, some—

When everything that ticked—has stopped—
And Space stares all around—
Or Grisly frosts—first Autumn morns,
Repeat the Beating Ground—   20

But, most, like Chaos—Stopless—cool—
Without a Chance, or Spar—
Or even a Report of Land—
To justify Despair.

1862

[THE HEART ASKS PLEASURE—FIRST—]

The Heart asks Pleasure—first—
And then—Excuse from Pain—
And then—those little Anodynes
That deaden suffering—

And then—to go to sleep—   5
And then—if it should be
The will of its Inquisitor
The privilege to die—

1862

[BECAUSE I COULD NOT STOP FOR DEATH—]

Because I could not stop for Death—
He kindly stopped for me—
The Carriage held but just Ourselves—
And Immortality.

We slowly drove—He knew no haste   5
And I had put away

My labor and my leisure too,
For His Civility—

We passed the School, where Children strove
At Recess—in the Ring— 10
We passed the Fields of Gazing Grain—
We passed the Setting Sun—

Or rather—He passed Us—
The Dews drew quivering and chill—
For only Gossamer, my Gown— 15
My Tippet—only Tulle—

We paused before a House that seemed
A Swelling of the Ground—
The Roof was scarcely visible—
The Cornice—in the Ground— 20

Since then—'tis Centuries—and yet
Feels shorter than the Day
I first surmised the Horses' Heads
Were toward Eternity—

1863

[MY LIFE HAD STOOD—A LOADED GUN—]

My Life had stood—a Loaded Gun—
In Corners—till a Day
The Owner passed—identified—
And carried Me away—

And now We roam in Sovereign Woods— 5
And now We hunt the Doe—
And every time I speak for Him—
The Mountains straight reply—

And do I smile, such cordial light
Upon the Valley glow— 10
It is as a Vesuvian face
Had let its pleasure through—

And when at Night—Our good Day done—
I guard My Master's Head—
'Tis better than the Eider-Duck's 15
Deep Pillow—to have shared—

To foe of His—I'm deadly foe—
None stir the second time—

On whom I lay a Yellow Eye—
Or an emphatic Thumb—   20

Though I than He—may longer live
He longer must—than I—
For I have but the power to kill,
Without—the power to die—

                                                         1863

[A NARROW FELLOW IN THE GRASS]

A narrow Fellow in the Grass
Occasionally rides—
You may have met Him—did you not
His notice sudden is—

The Grass divides as with a Comb—   5
A spotted shaft is seen—
And then it closes at your feet
And opens further on—

He likes a Boggy Acre
A Floor too cool for Corn—   10
Yet when a Boy, and Barefoot—
I more than once at Noon
Have passed, I thought, a Whip lash
Unbraiding in the Sun
When stooping to secure it   15
It wrinkled, and was gone—

Several of Nature's People
I know, and they know me—
I feel for them a transport
Of cordiality—   20

But never met this Fellow
Attended, or alone
Without a tighter breathing
And Zero at the Bone—

                                                         1865

[MY LIFE CLOSED TWICE BEFORE ITS
CLOSE—]

My life closed twice before its close—
It yet remains to see

If Immortality unveil
A third event to me

So huge, so hopeless to conceive   5
As these that twice befell.
Parting is all we know of heaven,
And all we need of hell.

1865

Further Reading

Wilbur, Richard. "Sumptuous Destitution." *Responses: Prose Pieces: 1953–1976.*
New York: Harcourt, 1976. 3–15. • Johnson, Thomas H. *Emily Dickinson: An*
Interpretive Biography. Cambridge: Harvard UP, 1955. • Wolff, Cynthia Griffin.
Emily Dickinson. New York: Knopf, 1986. • Miller, Ruth. *The Poetry of Emily*
Dickinson. Middletown: Wesleyan UP, 1968. • Rich, Adrienne. "Vesuvius at Home:
The Power of Emily Dickinson." *Critical Essays on Emily Dickinson.* Ed. Paul J.
Ferlazzo. Boston: Hall, 1984. 175–95.

Though Emily Dickinson is sometimes seen as an American Romantic poet,
she can hardly be considered a disciple of Wordworth or Keats. If we had to
name the poet whose work shaped hers most strongly, it would probably be the
hymnist Isaac Watts, whose quatrain of four iambic feet gives the basic
rhythm to most of her poems. A simple hymnist, however, she was not, and
readers soon find that the apparently simple form undergoes a metamorpho-
sis to reflect strong tensions: religious feelings versus skepticism, Romantic
optimism versus disillusioned wit, strong emotions versus formal restraint.
Most of her work was unpublished in her lifetime, known only to a small
circle of correspondents; but when Amherst, Massachusetts, celebrated its
bicentenary, it became clear that Dickinson had become the town's most
famous citizen. Louise Bogan and Richard Wilbur were among those pay-
ing tribute to her.

Louise Bogan: On Dickinson's Mysticism

Poets down the centuries, visited by that power which the ancients call *the*
Muse, have described their experience in much the same way as the mystic
describes his ecstatic union with Divine Truth. This experience has been
rendered at length, and dramatically, by Dante, as well as by St. John of the
Cross; and certain poems in the literature of every language attest to
moments when, for the poet, "the deep and primal life which he shares with

all creation has been roused from its sleep." And both poets and mystics have described with great poignance that sense of deprivation and that shutting away from grace which follows the loss of the vision (or of the inspiring breath), which is called, in the language of mysticism, "the dark night of the soul."

Certainly one of the triumphs brought about by the emergence of the Romantic spirit, in English poetry, at the end of the eighteenth century, was a freeing and an enlargement of poetic vision, and in the nineteenth century we come upon a multiplication of poets whose spiritual perceptions were acute. . . . By examining the work of these poets—to whom the imagination, the creative spirit of man, was of utmost importance—we find that the progress of the mystic toward illumination, and of the poet toward the full depth and richness of his insight, is much alike. Both work from the world of reality, toward the realm of Essence; from the microcosm to the macrocosm. Both have an intense and accurate sense of their surroundings; there is nothing vague or floating in their perception of reality; it is indeed as though they saw "through, not with, the eye." And they are filled with love for the beauty they perceive in the world of time—"this remarkable world" as Emily Dickinson called it; and concerning death they are neither fearful nor morbid—how could they be, since they feel immortality behind it? They document life's fearful limitations from which they suffer, but they do not mix self-pity with the account of their suffering (which they describe, like their joy, in close detail). They see the world in a grain of sand and Heaven in a wild flower; and now and again they bring eternity into focus, as it were, in a phrase of the utmost clarity. In the work of Emily Dickinson such moments of still and halted perception are many. The slant of light on a winter day, the still brilliance of a summer noon, the sound of the wind before the rain—she speaks of these, and we share the shock of insight, the slight dislocation of serial events, the sudden shift from the Manifold into the One.

Richard Wilbur: On Dickinson's Struggle with Calvinism

At some point Emily Dickinson sent her whole Calvinist vocabulary into exile, telling it not to come back until it would subserve her own sense of things.

Of course, that is not a true story, but it is a way of saying what I find most remarkable in Emily Dickinson. She inherited a great and overbearing vocabulary, which, had she used it submissively, would have forced her to express an established theology and psychology. But she would not let that vocabulary write her poems for her. There lies the real difference between a poet like Emily Dickinson and a fine versifier like Isaac Watts. To be sure, Emily Dickinson also wrote in the meters of hymnody, and paraphrased the Bible, and made her poems turn on great words like Immortality and Salvation and Election. But in her poems those great words are not merely being themselves; they have been adopted, for expressive purposes; they have been taken personally, and therefore redefined. . . .

At the age of seventeen, after a series of revival meetings at Mount Holyoke Seminary, Emily Dickinson found that she must refuse to become a professing Christian. To some modern minds this may seem to have been a sensible and necessary step; and surely it was a step toward becoming such a poet as she became. But for her, no pleasure in her own integrity could then eradicate the feeling that she had betrayed a deficiency, a want of grace. In her letters to Abiah Root she tells of the enhancing effect of conversion on her fellow-students, and says of herself in a famous passage:

> I am one of the lingering bad ones, and so do I slink away, and pause
> and ponder, and ponder and pause, and do work without knowing
> why, not surely for this brief world, and more sure it is not for heaven,
> and I ask what this message *means* that they ask for so very eagerly: *you*
> know of this depth and fulness, will you try to tell me about it?

There is humor in that, and stubbornness, and a bit of characteristic lurking pride: but there is also an anguished sense of having separated herself, through some dry incapacity, from spiritual community, from purpose, and from magnitude of life. As a child of evangelical Amherst, she inevitably thought of purposive, heroic life as requiring a vigorous faith. Out of such a thought she later wrote:

> The abdication of Belief
> Makes the Behavior small—
> Better an ignis fatuus
> Than no illume at all—

That hers *was* a species of religious personality goes without saying; but by her refusal of such ideas as original sin, redemption, hell, and election, she made it impossible for herself—as Whicher observed—"to share the religious life of her generation." She became an unsteady congregation of one.

CHRISTINA ROSSETTI

(1830–1894)

IN AN ARTIST'S STUDIO

One face looks out from all his canvases,
  One selfsame figure sits or walks or leans:
  We found her hidden just behind those screens,

That mirror gave back all her loveliness.
A queen in opal or in ruby dress,   5
   A nameless girl in freshest summer-greens,
   A saint, an angel—every canvas means
The same one meaning, neither more nor less.
He feeds upon her face by day and night,
   And she with true kind eyes looks back on him,   10
Fair as the moon and joyful as the light:
   Not wan with waiting, not with sorrow dim;
Not as she is, but was when hope shone bright;
   Not as she is, but as she fills his dream.

1861

SONG

When I am dead, my dearest,
   Sing no sad songs for me;
Plant thou no roses at my head,
   Nor shady cypress tree:
Be the green grass above me   5
   With showers and dewdrops wet;
And if thou wilt, remember,
   And if thou wilt, forget.

I shall not see the shadows,
   I shall not feel the rain;   10
I shall not hear the nightingale
   Sing on, as if in pain:
And dreaming through the twilight
   That doth not rise nor set,
Haply I may remember,   15
   And haply may forget.

1862

L.E.L.

"Whose heart was breaking for a little love."

Downstairs I laugh, I sport and jest with all:
   But in my solitary room above
I turn my face in silence to the wall;
   My heart is breaking for a little love.

"L.E.L.": L.E.L., Letitia Elizabeth Landon (1802–38), a popular poet.

Tho' winter frosts are done,
And birds pair every one,
And leaves peep out, for springtide is begun.

I feel no spring, while spring is wellnigh blown,
I find no nest, while nests are in the grove:
Woe's me for mine own heart that dwells alone, 10
My heart that breaketh for a little love.
While golden in the sun
Rivulets rise and run,
While lilies bud, for springtide is begun.

All love, are loved, save only I; their hearts 15
Beat warm with love and joy, beat full thereof:
They cannot guess, who play the pleasant parts,
My heart is breaking for a little love.
While beehives wake and whirr,
And rabbit thins his fur, 20
In living spring that sets the world astir.

I deck myself with silks and jewelry,
I plume myself like any mated dove:
They praise my rustling show, and never see
My heart is breaking for a little love. 25
While sprouts green lavender
With rosemary and myrrh,
For in quick spring the sap is all astir.

Perhaps some saints in glory guess the truth,
Perhaps some angels read it as they move, 30
And cry one to another full of ruth,
"Her heart is breaking for a little love."
Tho' other things have birth,
And leap and sing for mirth,
When springtime wakes and clothes and feeds the earth. 35

Yet saith a saint: "Take patience for thy scathe;"
Yet saith an angel: "Wait, for thou shalt prove
True best is last, true life is born of death,
O thou, heart-broken for a little love.
Then love shall fill thy girth, 40
And love make fat thy dearth,
When new spring builds new heaven and clean new earth."

1863

GOOD FRIDAY

Am I a stone and not a sheep
   That I can stand, O Christ, beneath Thy Cross,
   To number drop by drop Thy Blood's slow loss,
And yet not weep?

Not so those women loved   5
   Who with exceeding grief lamented Thee;
   Not so fallen Peter weeping bitterly;
Not so the thief was moved;

Not so the Sun and Moon
   Which hid their faces in a starless sky,   10
A horror of great darkness at broad noon—
   I, only I.

Yet give not o'er,
   But seek Thy sheep, true Shepherd of the flock;
Greater than Moses, turn and look once more   15
   And smite a rock.

1864

LIFE AND DEATH

Life is not sweet. One day it will be sweet
   To shut our eyes and die:
Nor feel the wild flowers blow, nor birds dart by
   With flitting butterfly,
Nor grass grow long above our heads and feet,   5
Nor hear the happy lark that soars sky high,
Nor sigh that spring is fleet and summer fleet,
   Nor mark the waxing wheat,
Nor know who sits in our accustomed seat.

Life is not good. One day it will be good   10
   To die, then live again;
To sleep meanwhile: so not to feel the wane
Of shrunk leaves dropping in the wood,
Nor hear the foamy lashing of the main,
Nor mark the blackened bean-fields, nor where stood   15
   Rich ranks of golden grain
Only dead refuse stubble clothe the plain:
Asleep from risk, asleep from pain.

1866

BY THE SEA

Why does the sea moan evermore?
    Shut out from heaven it makes its moan,
It frets against the boundary shore;
    All earth's full rivers cannot fill
    The sea, that drinking thirsteth still.   5

Sheer miracles of loveliness
    Lie hid in its unlooked-on bed:
Anemones, salt, passionless,
    Blow flower-like; just enough alive
    To blow and multiply and thrive.   10

Shells quaint with curve, or spot, or spike,
    Encrusted live things argus-eyed,
All fair alike, yet all unlike,
    Are born without a pang, and die
    Without a pang, and so pass by.   15

1866

"THEY DESIRE A BETTER COUNTRY"

1

I would not if I could undo my past,
    Tho' for its sake my future is a blank;
    My past for which I have myself to thank,
For all its faults and follies first and last.
I would not cast anew the lot once cast,   5
    Or launch a second ship for one that sank,
    Or drug with sweets the bitterness I drank,
Or break by feasting my perpetual fast.
I would not if I could: for much more dear
    Is one remembrance than a hundred joys,   10
    More than a thousand hopes in jubilee;

2

What seekest thou, far in the unknown land?
    In hope I follow joy gone on before;
    In hope and fear persistent more and more,
As the dry desert lengthens out its sand.   15
Whilst day and night I carry in my hand
    The golden key to ope the golden door
    Of golden home; yet mine eye weepeth sore,
For long the journey is that makes no stand.
And who is this that veiled doth walk with thee?   20

Lo, this is Love that walketh at my right;
    One exile holds us both, and we are bound
To selfsame home-joys in the land of light.
Weeping thou walkest with him; weepeth he?—
    Some sobbing weep, some weep and make no sound.   25

3

A dimness of a glory glimmers here
    Thro' veils and distance from the space remote,
    A faintest far vibration of a note
Reaches to us and seems to bring us near;
Causing our face to glow with braver cheer,   30
    Making the serried mist to stand afloat,
    Subduing languor with an antidote,
And strengthening love almost to cast out fear:
Till for one moment golden city walls
    Rise looming on us, golden walls of home,   35
Light of our eyes until the darkness falls;
    Then thro' the outer darkness burdensome
I hear again the tender voice that calls,
    "Follow me hither, follow, rise, and come."

1869

PASSING AND GLASSING

    All things that pass
    Are woman's looking-glass;
They show her how her bloom must fade,
And she herself be laid
With withered roses in the shade;   5
    With withered roses and the fallen peach,
    Unlovely, out of reach
        Of summer joy that was.

    All things that pass
    Are woman's tiring-glass;   10
The faded lavender is sweet,
Sweet the dead violet
Culled and laid by and cared for yet;
The dried-up violets and dried lavender
Still sweet, may comfort her,   15
    Nor need she cry Alas!

    All things that pass
    Are wisdom's looking-glass;
Being full of hope and fear, and still
Brimful of good or ill,   20

According to our work and will;
    For there is nothing new beneath the sun;
    Our doings have been done,
        And that which shall be was.

1881

Further Reading

Woolf, Virginia. "I Am Christina Rossetti." *Collected Essays* IV. New York: Harcourt, 1967. 54–60. • Bellas, Ralph A. *Christina Rossetti.* Boston: Twayne, 1977. • Rosenblum, Dolores. *Christina Rossetti: The Poetry of Endurance.* Carbondale: Southern Illinois UP, 1986. • Stevenson, Lionel. "Christina Rossetti." *The Pre-Raphaelite Poets.* Chapel Hill: U of North Carolina P, 1972. 78–122. • McGann, Jerome J. "The Religious Poetry of Christina Rossetti." *Critical Inquiry* 10.1 (Sept. 1983): 127–44.

Christina Rossetti's poems reveal a tension between the sensuous appeal notable among the pre-Raphaelites (including her brother Dante Gabriel Rossetti and Algernon Charles Swinburne) and a deep religious commitment. Virginia Woolf's well-known tribute to Rossetti's work shows a clear insight into this conflict.

Virginia Woolf: On Rossetti's Virtues

O Christina Rossetti, I have humbly to confess that though I know many of your poems by heart, I have not read your works from cover to cover. I have not followed your course and traced your development. I doubt indeed that you developed very much. You were an instinctive poet. You saw the world from the same angle always. Years and the traffic of the mind with men and books did not affect you in the least. You carefully ignored any book that could shake your faith or any human being who could trouble your instincts. You were wise perhaps. Your instinct was so sure, so direct, so intense that it produced poems that sing like music in one's ears—like a melody by Mozart or an air by Gluck. Yet for all its symmetry, yours was a complex song. When you struck your harp many strings sounded together. Like all instinctives you had a keen sense of the visual beauty of the world. Your poems are full of gold dust and "sweet geraniums' varied brightness"; your eye noted incessantly how rushes are "velvet-headed", and lizards have a "strange metallic mail"—your eye, indeed, observed with a sensual pre-

Raphaelite intensity that must have surprised Christina the Anglo-Catholic. But to her you owed perhaps the fixity and sadness of your muse. The pressure of a tremendous faith circles and clamps together these little songs. Perhaps they owe to it their solidity. Certainly they owe to it their sadness—your God was a harsh God, your heavenly crown was set with thorns. No sooner have you feasted on beauty with your eyes than your mind tells you that beauty is vain and beauty passes. Death, oblivion, and rest lap round your songs with their dark wave. And then, incongruously, a sound of scurrying and laughter is heard. There is the patter of animals' feet and the odd guttural notes of rooks and the snufflings of obtuse furry animals grunting and nosing. For you were not a pure saint by any means. You pulled legs; you tweaked noses. You were at war with all humbug and pretence. Modest as you were, still you were drastic, sure of your gift, convinced of your vision. A firm hand pruned your lines; a sharp ear tested their music. Nothing soft, otiose, irrelevant cumbered your pages. In a word, you were an artist.

GERARD MANLEY HOPKINS

(1844–1889)

THE WINDHOVER

To Christ Our Lord

I caught this morning morning's minion, king-
   dom of daylight's dauphin, dapple-dawn-drawn Falcon, in his
      riding
   Of the rolling level underneath him steady air, and striding
High there, how he rung upon the rein of a wimpling wing
In his ecstasy! then off, off forth on swing,   5
   As a skate's heel sweeps smooth on a bow-bend: the hurl and
      gliding
   Rebuffed the big wind. My heart in hiding
Stirred for a bird,—the achieve of, the mastery of the thing!

Brute beauty and valour and act, oh, air, pride, plume, here
   Buckle! AND the fire that breaks from thee then, a billion   10
Times told lovelier, more dangerous, O my chevalier!

Windhover: a kestrel or small hawk.

No wonder of it: sheer plod makes plough down sillion
Shine, and blue-bleak embers, ah my dear,
    Fall, gall themselves, and gash gold-vermilion.

1877

PIED BEAUTY

Glory be to God for dappled things—
    For skies of couple-colour as a brinded cow;
        For rose-moles all in stipple upon trout that swim;
Fresh-firecoal chestnut-falls; finches' wings;
    Landscape plotted and pieced—fold, fallow, and plough,   5
        And all trades, their gear and tackle and trim.
All things counter, original, spare, strange;
    Whatever is fickle, freckled (who knows how?)
        With swift, slow; sweet, sour; adazzle, dim;
He fathers-forth whose beauty is past change: 10
                    Praise him.

1877

GOD'S GRANDEUR

The world is charged with the grandeur of God.
    It will flame out, like shining from shook foil;
    It gathers to a greatness, like the ooze of oil
Crushed. Why do men then now not reck his rod?
Generations have trod, have trod, have trod;   5
    And all is seared with trade; bleared, smeared with toil;
    And wears man's smudge and shares man's smell: the soil
Is bare now, nor can foot feel, being shod.

And for all this, nature is never spent;
    There lives the dearest freshness deep down things;   10
And though the last lights off the black West went
    Oh, morning, at the brown brink eastward, springs—
Because the Holy Ghost over the bent
    World broods with warm breast and with ah! bright wings.

1877

"The Windhover": 12. *sillion:* the ridge between furrows of a plowed field.   "Pied Beauty":
2. *brinded:* streaked.   "God's Grandeur": 2. *shook foil:* Hopkins explained that he meant gold
leaf and compared it to lightning.   4. *reck his rod:* pay attention to the commands of God.

THE SEA AND THE SKYLARK

On ear and ear two noises too old to end
   Trench—right, the tide that ramps against the shore;
   With a flood or a fall, low lull-off or all roar,
Frequenting there while moon shall wear and wend.

Left hand, off land, I hear the lark ascend,   5
   His rash-fresh re-winded new-skeinèd score
   In crisps of curl off wild winch whirl, and pour
And pelt music, till none's to spill nor spend.

How these two shame this shallow and frail town!
   How ring right out our sordid turbid time,   10
Being pure! We, life's pride and cared-for crown,

   Have lost that cheer and charm of earth's past prime:
Our make and making break, are breaking, down
   To man's last dust, drain fast towards man's first slime.

1877

THOU ART INDEED JUST, LORD

Justus quidem tu es, Domine, si disputem tecum:
verum justa loquar ad te: Quare
via impiorum prosperatur?

Thou art indeed just, Lord, if I contend
With thee; but, sir, so what I plead is just.
Why do sinners' ways prosper? and why must
Disappointment all I endeavour end?
   Wert thou my enemy, O thou my friend,   5
How wouldst thou worse, I wonder, than thou dost
Defeat, thwart me? Oh, the sots and thralls of lust
Do in spare hours more thrive than I that spend,
Sir, life upon thy cause. See, banks and brakes
Now, leavèd how thick! lacèd they are again   10
With fretty chervil, look, and fresh wind shakes
Them; birds build—but not I build; no, but strain,
Time's eunuch, and not breed one work that wakes.
Mine, O thou lord of life, send my roots rain.

1889

"Thou Art Indeed Just, Lord": Justus quidem . . . prosperatur: "Righteous art thou, O Lord, when
I plead with thee: yet let me talk with thee of thy judgments: Wherefore doth the way of the
wicked prosper?" Jeremiah 12:1.

Further Reading

Mariani, Paul. *A Commentary on the Complete Works of Gerard Manley Hopkins.* Ithaca: Cornell UP, 1970. • Bump, Jerome. *Gerard Manley Hopkins.* Boston: Twayne, 1982. • Boyle, Robert. *Metaphor in Hopkins.* Chapel Hill: U of North Carolina P, 1960. • Hartman, Geoffrey H., ed. *Hopkins: A Collection of Critical Essays.* Englewood Cliffs, NJ: Prentice, 1966. • Sulloway, Alison G. "'New Nazareths in Us': The Making of a Victorian Gentleman." *Gerard Manley Hopkins and the Victorian Temper.* New York: Columbia UP, 1972. 115–57, spec. 151–54. • *Studies in the Literary Imagination* 21.1 (Spring 1988): entire issue.

The poetry of Gerard Manley Hopkins is hymnlike in more ways than one. It is full of the bright side of a deep religious faith and is written (as Hopkins said in a letter to his brother) to be "performed" aloud. Hopkins believed that his much-discussed "sprung rhythm" was part of a long tradition of oral poetry, a tradition that includes both nursery rhymes and the Old English "The Seafarer."

Gerard Manley Hopkins: On the Oral Nature of Poetry

Every art then and every work of art has its own play or performance. The play or performance of a stageplay is the playing it on the boards, the stage: reading it, much more writing it, is not its performance. The performance of a symphony is not the scoring it however elaborately; it is in the concert room, by the orchestra, and then and there only. A picture is performed, or performs, when anyone looks at it in the proper and intended light. A house performs when it is now built and lived in. To come nearer: books play, perform, or are played and performed when they are read; and ordinarily by one reader, alone, to himself, with the eyes only. Now we are getting to it, George. Poetry was originally meant for either singing or reciting; a record was kept of it; the record could be, was, read, and that in time by one reader, alone, to himself, with the eyes only. This reacted on the art: what was to be performed under these conditions, for these conditions ought to be and was composed and calculated. Sound-effects were intended, wonderful combinations even; but they bear the marks of having been meant for the whispered, not even whispered, merely mental performance of the closet, the study, and so on. You follow, Edward Joseph? You do: then we are there. This is not the true nature of poetry, the darling child of speech, of lips and spoken utterance: it must be spoken; *till it is spoken it is not performed,* it does not perform, it is not itself.

Richard Wilbur: On Hopkins's Cataloguing

That is what the cataloguing impulse almost always expresses—a longing to possess the whole world, and to praise it, or at least to feel it. We see this most plainly and perfectly in the Latin canticle *Benedicite, omnia opera domini.* The first verses of that familiar canticle are:

> O all ye Works of the Lord, bless ye the Lord: praise him,
> and magnify him for ever.
> O ye Angels of the Lord, bless ye the Lord: praise him,
> and magnify him for ever.
> O ye Heavens, bless ye the Lord: praise him and magnify
> him for ever.
> O ye Waters that be above the firmament, bless ye the Lord:
> praise him and magnify him forever.

I need not go on to the close, because I am sure that you all know the logic of what follows. All the works of the Lord are called upon in turn—the sun, moon, and stars, the winds and several weathers of the sky, the creatures of earth and sea, and lastly mankind. There is nothing left out. The canticle may not speak of crushed laurel leaves and sycamores, but it does say more comprehensively, "O all ye Green Things upon the Earth, bless ye the Lord"; it may not speak of foxes and of young cows in a mountain stream, but it does say, "O all ye Beasts and Cattle, bless ye the Lord.". . .

It is interesting to compare the strategy of the *Benedicite* to that of another and more personal poem of catalogue and praise, Gerard Manley Hopkins's "curtal sonnet" "Pied Beauty.". . . As in the old canticle, God is praised first and last; but what lies between is very different. Hopkins does not give us an inventory of the creation; rather, he sets out to celebrate one kind of beauty—pied beauty, the beauty of things that are patchy, particolored, variegated. And in his tally of variegated things there is no hierarchy or other logic: his mind jumps, seemingly at random, from sky to trout to chestnuts to finches, and finally, by way of landscape, to the gear and tackle of the various trades. The poem *sets out,* then, to give scattered examples of a single class of things; and yet in its final effect this is a poem of universal praise. Why does it work out that way?

It works that way, for one thing, because of the randomness which I have just pointed out; when a catalogue has a random air, when it seems to have been assembled by chance, it implies a vast reservoir of other things that might just as well have been mentioned. In the second place, Hopkins's poem may begin with dappled things, but when we come to "gear and tackle and trim," the idea of variegation is far less clear, and seems to be yielding to that of *character*. When, in the next line, Hopkins thanks God for "All things counter, original, spare, strange," we feel the poem opening out toward the celebration of the rich and quirky particularity of all things whatever.

A. E. HOUSMAN
(1859–1936)

LOVELIEST OF TREES, THE CHERRY NOW

Loveliest of trees, the cherry now
Is hung with bloom along the bough,
And stands about the woodland ride
Wearing white for Eastertide.

Now, of my threescore years and ten,   5
Twenty will not come again,
And take from seventy springs a score,
It only leaves me fifty more.

And since to look at things in bloom
Fifty springs are little room,   10
About the woodlands I will go
To see the cherry hung with snow.

1896

TO AN ATHLETE DYING YOUNG

The time you won your town the race
We chaired you through the market-place;
Man and boy stood cheering by,
And home we brought you shoulder-high.

To-day, the road all runners come,   5
Shoulder-high we bring you home,
And set you at your threshold down,
Townsman of a stiller town.

Smart lad, to slip betimes away
From fields where glory does not stay   10

And early though the laurel grows
It withers quicker than the rose.

Eyes the shady night has shut
Cannot see the record cut,
And silence sounds no worse than cheers   15
After earth has stopped the ears:

Now you will not swell the rout
Of lads that wore their honours out,
Runners whom renown outran
And the name died before the man.   20

So set, before its echoes fade,
The fleet foot on the sill of shade,
And hold to the low lintel up
The still-defended challenge-cup.

And round that early-laurelled head   25
Will flock to gaze the strengthless dead,
And find unwithered on its curls
The garland briefer than a girl's.

1896

TERENCE, THIS IS STUPID STUFF

'Terence, this is stupid stuff:
You eat your victuals fast enough;
There can't be much amiss, 'tis clear,
To see the rate you drink your beer.
But oh, good Lord, the verse you make,   5
It gives a chap the belly-ache.
The cow, the old cow, she is dead;
It sleeps well, the horned head:
We poor lads, 'tis our turn now
To hear such tunes as killed the cow.   10
Pretty friendship 'tis to rhyme
Your friends to death before their time
Moping melancholy mad:
Come, pipe a tune to dance to, lad.'

Why, if 'tis dancing you would be,   15
There's brisker pipes than poetry.
Say, for what were hop-yards meant,
Or why was Burton built on Trent?
Oh many a peer of England brews
Livelier liquor than the Muse,   20
And malt does more than Milton can

To justify God's ways to man.
Ale, man, ale's the stuff to drink
For fellows whom it hurts to think:
Look into the pewter pot   25
To see the world as the world's not.
And faith, 'tis pleasant till 'tis past:
The mischief is that 'twill not last.
Oh I have been to Ludlow fair
And left my necktie God knows where,   30
And carried half-way home, or near,
Pints and quarts of Ludlow beer:
Then the world seemed none so bad,
And I myself a sterling lad;
And down in lovely muck I've lain,   35
Happy till I woke again.
Then I saw the morning sky:
Heigho, the tale was all a lie;
The world, it was the old world yet,
I was I, my things were wet,   40
And nothing now remained to do
But begin the game anew.

      Therefore, since the world has still
Much good, but much less good than ill,
And while the sun and moon endure   45
Luck's a chance, but trouble's sure,
I'd face it as a wise man would,
And train for ill and not for good.
'Tis true, the stuff I bring for sale
Is not so brisk a brew as ale: 50
Out of a stem that scored the hand
I wrung it in a weary land.
But take it: if the smack is sour,
The better for the embittered hour;
It should do good to heart and head   55
When your soul is in my soul's stead;
And I will friend you, if I may,
In the dark and cloudy day.

      There was a king reigned in the East:
There, when kings will sit to feast,   60
They get their fill before they think
With poisoned meat and poisoned drink.
He gathered all that springs to birth
From the many-venomed earth;
First a little, thence to more   65

He sampled all her killing store;
And easy, smiling, seasoned sound,
Sate the king when healths went round.
They put arsenic in his meat
And stared aghast to watch him eat; 70
They poured strychnine in his cup
And shook to see him drink it up:
They shook, they stared as white's their shirt:
Them it was their poison hurt.
—I tell the tale that I heard told. 75
Mithridates, he died old.

1896

IS MY TEAM PLOUGHING

'Is my team ploughing,
    That I was used to drive
And hear the harness jingle
    When I was man alive?'

Ay, the horses trample, 5
    The harness jingles now;
No change though you lie under
    The land you used to plough.

'Is football playing
    Along the river shore, 10
With lads to chase the leather,
    Now I stand up no more?'

Ay, the ball is flying,
    The lads play heart and soul;
The goal stands up, the keeper 15
    Stands up to keep the goal.

'Is my girl happy,
    That I thought hard to leave,
And has she tired of weeping
    As she lies down at eve?' 20

Ay, she lies down lightly,
    She lies not down to weep:
Your girl is well contented.
    Be still, my lad, and sleep.

'Is my friend hearty, 25
    Now I am thin and pine,

And has he found to sleep in
    A better bed than mine?'

Yes, lad, I lie easy,
    I lie as lads would choose;   30
I cheer a dead man's sweetheart,
    Never ask me whose.

1896

ON MOONLIT HEATH

On moonlit heath and lonesome bank
    The sheep beside me graze;
And yon the gallows used to clank
    Fast by the four cross ways.

A careless shepherd once would keep   5
    The flocks by moonlight there,
And high amongst the glimmering sheep
    The dead man stood on air.

They hang us now in Shrewsbury jail:
    The whistles blow forlorn,   10
And trains all night groan on the rail
    To men that die at morn.

There sleeps in Shrewsbury jail to-night,
    Or wakes, as may betide,
A better lad, if things went right,   15
    Than most that sleep outside.

And naked to the hangman's noose
    The morning clocks will ring
A neck God made for other use
    Than strangling in a string.   20

And sharp the link of life will snap,
    And dead on air will stand
Heels that held up as straight a chap
    As treads upon the land.

So here I'll watch the night and wait   25
    To see the morning shine,
When he will hear the stroke of eight
    And not the stroke of nine;

And wish my friend as sound a sleep
    As lads I did not know,   30

That shepherded the moonlit sheep
  A hundred years ago.

1896

COULD MAN BE DRUNK FOR EVER

Could man be drunk for ever
  With liquor, love, or fights,
Lief should I rouse at morning
  And lief lie down of nights.

But men at whiles are sober   5
  And think by fits and starts,
And if they think, they fasten
  Their hands upon their hearts.

1922

WHEN FIRST MY WAY

When first my way to fair I took
  Few pence in purse had I,
And long I used to stand and look
  At things I could not buy.

Now times are altered: if I care   5
  To buy a thing, I can;
The pence are here and here's the fair,
  But where's the lost young man?

—To think that two and two are four
  And neither five nor three   10
The heart of man has long been sore
  And long 'tis like to be.

1922

STARS, I HAVE SEEN THEM FALL

Stars, I have seen them fall,
  But when they drop and die
No star is lost at all
  From all the star-sown sky.
The toil of all that be   5
  Helps not the primal fault;
It rains into the sea,
  And still the sea is salt.

1936

A. E. Housman   629

Further Reading

Ricks, Christopher, ed. *A. E. Housman: A Collection of Critical Essays.* Englewood Cliffs, NJ: Prentice, 1968. • Haber, Tom Burns. *A. E. Housman.* New York: Twayne, 1967. • Stevenson, John W. "The Pastoral Setting in the Poetry of A. E. Housman." *South Atlantic Quarterly* 55 (Oct. 1956): 487–500. • Leggett, B. J. "The Poetry of Insight: Persona and Point of View in Housman." *Victorian Poetry* 14.4 (Winter 1976): 325–39.

A. E. Housman's anti-intellectual attitude toward poetry (see p. 467) made him cut a peculiar figure in the literary world. Professionally, he was a Latin professor who entered into hair-splitting scholarly disputes with great gusto. As a poet, on the other hand, he seemed distrustful of intellectualization, or uninterested in it. These peculiar attitudes and a very distinctive style made him a subject of controversy and sometimes parody, as the following poems show.

Ezra Pound

(1885–1972)

MR. HOUSMAN'S MESSAGE

O woe, woe,
People are born and die,
We also shall be dead pretty soon
Therefore let us act as if we were
                 dead already.   5

The bird sits on the hawthorn tree
But he dies also, presently.
Some lads get hung, and some get shot.
Woeful is this human lot.
             Woe! woe, etcetera. . . .   10

London is a woeful place,
Shropshire is much pleasanter.
Then let us smile a little space
Upon fond nature's morbid grace.
            Oh, Woe, woe, woe, etcetera. . . .   15

1911

Hugh Kingsmill

(1889–1949)

WHAT, STILL ALIVE

What, still alive at twenty-two,
A clean upstanding chap like you?
Sure, if your throat 'tis hard to slit,
Slit your girl's, and swing for it.

Like enough, you won't be glad,   5
When they come to hang you, lad:
But bacon's not the only thing
That's cured by hanging from a string.

So, when the spilt ink of the night
Spreads o'er the blotting pad of light,   10
Lads whose job is still to do
Shall whet their knives, and think of you.

ca. 1927

W. H. Auden

(1907–1973)

A. E. HOUSMAN

No one, not even Cambridge, was to blame
(Blame if you like the human situation):
Heart-injured in North London, he became
The Latin Scholar of his generation.

Deliberately he chose the dry-as-dust.   5
Kept tears like dirty postcards in a drawer;
Food was his public love, his private lust
Something to do with violence and the poor.

In savage foot-notes on unjust editions
He timidly attacked the life he led,   10
And put the money of his feelings on

The uncritical relations of the dead,
Where only geographical divisions
Parted the coarse hanged soldier from the don.

1939

WILLIAM BUTLER YEATS

(1865–1939)

THE LAKE ISLE OF INNISFREE

I will arise and go now, and go to Innisfree,
And a small cabin build there, of clay and wattles made:
Nine bean-rows will I have there, a hive for the honey-bee,
And live alone in the bee-loud glade.

And I shall have some peace there, for peace comes dropping slow,   5
Dropping from the veils of the morning to where the cricket sings;
There midnight's all a glimmer, and noon a purple glow,
And evening full of the linnet's wings.

I will arise and go now, for always night and day
I hear lake water lapping with low sounds by the shore;   10
While I stand on the roadway, or on the pavements gray,
I hear it in the deep heart's core.

1892

THE FOLLY OF BEING COMFORTED

One that is ever kind said yesterday:
'Your well-beloved's hair has threads of grey,
And little shadows come about her eyes;
Time can but make it easier to be wise
Though now it seems impossible, and so   5
All that you need is patience.'
                      Heart cries, 'No,
I have not a crumb of comfort, not a grain.
Time can but make her beauty over again:
Because of that great nobleness of hers   10
The fire that stirs about her, when she stirs,
Burns but more clearly. O she had not these ways
When all the wild summer was in her gaze.'

O heart! O heart! if she'd but turn her head,
You'd know the folly of being comforted.

1903

THE WILD SWANS AT COOLE

The trees are in their autumn beauty,
The woodland paths are dry,
Under the October twilight the water
Mirrors a still sky;
Upon the brimming water among the stones   5
Are nine-and-fifty swans.

The nineteenth autumn has come upon me
Since I first made my count;
I saw, before I had well finished,
All suddenly mount   10
And scatter wheeling in great broken rings
Upon their clamorous wings.

I have looked upon those brilliant creatures,
And now my heart is sore.
All's changed since I, hearing at twilight,   15
The first time on this shore,
The bell-beat of their wings above my head,
Trod with a lighter tread.

Unwearied still, lover by lover,
They paddle in the cold   20
Companionable streams or climb the air;
Their hearts have not grown old;
Passion or conquest, wander where they will,
Attend upon them still.

But now they drift on the still water,   25
Mysterious, beautiful;
Among what rushes will they build,
By what lake's edge or pool
Delight men's eyes when I awake some day
To find they have flown away?   30

1917

THE SCHOLARS

Bald heads forgetful of their sins,
Old, learned, respectable bald heads

Edit and annotate the lines
That young men, tossing on their beds,
Rhymed out in love's despair   5
To flatter beauty's ignorant ear.

All shuffle there; all cough in ink;
All wear the carpet with their shoes;
All think what other people think;
All know the man their neighbor knows.   10
Lord, what would they say
Did their Catullus walk that way?

                                                              1917

THE CAT AND THE MOON

The cat went here and there
And the moon spun round like a top,
And the nearest kin of the moon,
The creeping cat, looked up.
Black Minnaloushe stared at the moon,   5
For, wander and wail as he would,
The pure cold light in the sky
Troubled his animal blood.
Minnaloushe runs in the grass
Lifting his delicate feet.   10
Do you dance, Minnaloushe, do you dance?
When two close kindred meet,
What better than call a dance?
Maybe the moon may learn,
Tired of that courtly fashion,   15
A new dance turn.
Minnaloushe creeps through the grass
From moonlit place to place,
The sacred moon overhead
Has taken a new phase.   20
Does Minnaloushe know that his pupils
Will pass from change to change,
And that from round to crescent,
From crescent to round they range?
Minnaloushe creeps through the grass   25
Alone, important and wise,

"*The Cat and the Moon*": *The Cat and the Moon* appears in Yeats's play by the same name.
5. *Minnaloushe*: a black Persian cat belonging to a friend of Yeats.

And lifts to the changing moon
His changing eyes.

1918

THE SECOND COMING

Turning and turning in the widening gyre
The falcon cannot hear the falconer;
Things fall apart; the centre cannot hold;
Mere anarchy is loosed upon the world,
The blood-dimmed tide is loosed, and everywhere   5
The ceremony of innocence is drowned;
The best lack all conviction, while the worst
Are full of passionate intensity.

Surely some revelation is at hand;
Surely the Second Coming is at hand.   10
The Second Coming! Hardly are those words out
When a vast image out of *Spiritus Mundi*
Troubles my sight: somewhere in sands of the desert
A shape with lion body and the head of a man,
A gaze blank and pitiless as the sun,   15
Is moving its slow thighs, while all about it

Reel shadows of the indignant desert birds.
The darkness drops again; but now I know
That twenty centuries of stony sleep
Were vexed to nightmare by a rocking cradle,   20
And what rough beast, its hour come round at last,
Slouches towards Bethlehem to be born?

1921

LEDA AND THE SWAN

A sudden blow: the great wings beating still
Above the staggering girl, her thighs caressed
By the dark webs, her nape caught in his bill,
He holds her helpless breast upon his breast.

How can those terrified vague fingers push   5
The feathered glory from her loosening thighs?

"The Second Coming": 12. *Spiritus Mundi*: "The Spirit of the World," the psychic pool of
images that all human minds share and draw from.   *"Leda and the Swan"*: *Leda*: impregnated
by Zeus in the form of a swan, became the mother of Helen of Troy.

And how can body, laid in that white rush,
But feel the strange heart beating where it lies?

A shudder in the loins engenders there
The broken wall, the burning roof and tower   10
And Agamemnon dead.
                    Being so caught up,
So mastered by the brute blood of the air,
Did she put on his knowledge with his power
Before the indifferent beak could let her drop?   15

1924

SAILING TO BYZANTIUM

1

That is no country for old men. The young
In one another's arms, birds in the trees,
—Those dying generations—at their song,
The salmon-falls, the mackerel-crowded seas,
Fish, flesh, or fowl, commend all summer long   5
Whatever is begotten, born, and dies.
Caught in that sensual music all neglect
Monuments of unageing intellect.

2

An aged man is but a paltry thing,
A tattered coat upon a stick, unless   10
Soul clap its hands and sing, and louder sing
For every tatter in its mortal dress,
Nor is there singing school but studying
Monuments of its own magnificence;
And therefore I have sailed the seas and come   15
To the holy city of Byzantium.

3

O sages standing in God's holy fire
As in the gold mosaic of a wall,
Come from the holy fire, perne in a gyre,
And be the singing-masters of my soul.   20
Consume my heart away; sick with desire

"Sailing to Byzantium": Byzantium: for a BBC broadcast in 1931, Yeats wrote: "Byzantium was
the center of European civilization and the source of its spiritual philosophy, so I symbolize
the search for spiritual life by a journey to that city."

And fastened to a dying animal
It knows not what it is; and gather me
Into the artifice of eternity.

4

Once out of nature I shall never take   25
My bodily form from any natural thing,
But such a form as Grecian goldsmiths make
Of hammered gold and gold enamelling
To keep a drowsy Emperor awake;
Or set upon a golden bough to sing   30
To lords and ladies of Byzantium
Of what is past, or passing, or to come.

1928

AMONG SCHOOL CHILDREN

1

I walk through the long schoolroom questioning;
A kind old nun in a white hood replies;
The children learn to cipher and to sing,
To study reading-books and histories,
To cut and sew, be neat in everything   5
In the best modern way—the children's eyes
In momentary wonder stare upon
A sixty-year-old smiling public man.

2

I dream of a Ledaean body, bent
Above a sinking fire, a tale that she   10
Told of a harsh reproof, or trivial event
That changed some childish day to tragedy—
Told, and it seemed that our two natures blent
Into a sphere from youthful sympathy,
Or else, to alter Plato's parable,   15
Into the yolk and white of the one shell.

"*Among School Children*": 9. *Ledaean:* "like Helen of Troy," Leda's daughter.   15. *Plato's parable:* in his *Symposium,* Plato explains the origin of love between men and women: once the two sexes were united in one body, with four arms and legs, which moved by rolling; it was so big and powerful that the gods decided each one had to be divided "as you might divide an egg with a hair." Each half was unhappy and longed for the other, however, and this longing is love.

3

And thinking of that fit of grief or rage
I look upon one child or t'other there
And wonder if she stood so at that age—
For even daughters of the swan can share   20
Something of every paddler's heritage—
And had that color upon cheek or hair,
And thereupon my heart is driven wild:
She stands before me as a living child.

4

Her present image floats into the mind—   25
Did Quattrocento finger fashion it
Hollow of cheek as though it drank the wind
And took a mess of shadows for its meat?
And I though never of Ledaean kind
Had pretty plumage once—enough of that,   30
Better to smile on all that smile, and show
There is a comfortable kind of old scarecrow.

5

What youthful mother, a shape upon her lap
Honey of generation had betrayed,
And that must sleep, shriek, struggle to escape   35
As recollection or the drug decide,
Would think her son, did she but see that shape
With sixty or more winters on its head,
A compensation for the pang of his birth,
Or the uncertainty of his setting forth?   40

6

Plato thought nature but a spume that plays
Upon a ghostly paradigm of things;
Solider Aristotle played the taws
Upon the bottom of a king of kings;
World-famous golden-thighed Pythagoras   45
Fingered upon a fiddle-stick or strings
What a star sang and careless Muses heard:
Old clothes upon old sticks to scare a bird.

---

26. *Quattrocento:* the 1400s in Italy, which was one of the greatest times of artistic creation.
41. *Aristotle:* in contrast to Plato, who located reality in Ideal forms, Aristotle believed reality
was found in the natural world.   43. *Pythagoras:* a sixth-century philosopher and mathematician who believed that the underlying truth of things was numerical; his mathematical theory
of music led to the legend that he possessed a golden bone that allowed him to hear the music
of the spheres.

7

Both nuns and mothers worship images,
But those the candles light are not as those   50
That animate a mother's reveries,
But keep a marble or a bronze repose.
And yet they too break hearts—O Presences
That passion, piety or affection knows,
And that all heavenly glory symbolize—   55
O self-born mockers of man's enterprise;

8

Labor is blossoming or dancing where
The body is not bruised to pleasure soul,
Nor beauty born out of its own despair,
Nor blear-eyed wisdom out of midnight oil.   60
O chestnut-tree, great-rooted blossomer,
Are you the leaf, the blossom or the bole?
O body swayed to music, O brightening glance,
How can we know the dancer from the dance?

1928

CRAZY JANE TALKS WITH THE BISHOP

I met the Bishop on the road
And much said he and I.
'Those breasts are flat and fallen now,
Those veins must soon be dry;
Live in a heavenly mansion,   5
Not in some foul sty.'

'Fair and foul are near of kin,
And fair needs foul,' I cried.
'My friends are gone, but that's a truth
Nor grave nor bed denied,   10
Learned in bodily lowliness
And in the heart's pride.

'A women can be proud and stiff
When on love intent;
But Love has pitched his mansion in   15
The place of excrement;
For nothing can be sole or whole
That has not been rent.'

1933

Further Reading

Jeffares, A. Norman. *A Commentary on the Collected Poems of W. B. Yeats.* Stanford: Stanford UP, 1968. • Ellman, Richard. *Yeats: The Man and the Masks.* New York: Norton, 1979. • Stauffer, Donald A. "The Reading of a Lyric Poem." *Kenyon Review* 11.3 (Summer 1949): 426–40. • Shaw, Priscilla Washburn. " 'Leda and the Swan' as Model." *Modern Critical Views: W. B. Yeats.* Ed. Harold Bloom. New York: Chelsea, 1986. 35–40. • Bradford, Curtis. "Yeats's Byzantium Poems: A Study of Their Development." *PMLA* 75.1 (Mar. 1960): 110–25, spec. 110–18. • Lensing, George S. " 'Among School Children': Questions as Conclusions." *College Literature* 13.1 (1986): 1–8.

Certainly one of the key figures in defining the character of poetry in the first half of the twentieth century, William Butler Yeats edited The Oxford Book of Modern Verse *in 1936. In the introduction, he explained the new generation's movement away from the influence of such nineteenth-century figures as Gerard Manley Hopkins and Thomas Hardy.*

William Butler Yeats: On the Revolt Against Victorian Poetry

All these writers were, in the eye of the new generation, in so far as they were known, Victorian, and the new generation was in revolt. But one writer, almost unknown to the general public—I remember somebody saying at his death 'no newspaper has given him an obituary notice'—had its entire uncritical admiration, Walter Pater. That is why I begin this book with the famous passage from his essay on Leonardo da Vinci. Only by printing it in *vers libre* can one show its revolutionary importance. Pater was accustomed to give each sentence a separate page of manuscript, isolating and analysing its rhythm; Henley wrote certain 'hospital poems,' not included in this book, in *vers libre,* but did not permit a poem to arise out of its own rhythm as do Turner and Pound at their best and as, I contend, Pater did. [T]his passage . . . dominated a generation, a domination so great that all over Europe from that day to this men shrink from Leonardo's masterpiece as from an over-flattered woman. . . .

The revolt against Victorianism meant to the young poet a revolt against irrelevant descriptions of nature, the scientific and moral discursiveness of *In Memoriam*—'When he should have been broken-hearted', said Verlaine, 'he had many reminiscences'—the political eloquence of

Swinburne, the psychological curiosity of Browning, and the poetical diction of everybody. Poets said to one another over their black coffee—a recently imported fashion—'We must purify poetry of all that is not poetry', and by poetry they meant poetry as it had been written by Catullus, a great name at that time, by the Jacobean writers, by Verlaine, by Baudelaire. Poetry was a tradition like religion and liable to corruption, and it seemed that they could best restore it by writing lyrics technically perfect, their emotion pitched high, and as Pater offered instead of moral earnestness life lived as 'a pure gem-like flame' all accepted him for master.

Yeats's arrangement into lines of the above-mentioned Walter Pater sentence was printed as the first "poem" in The Oxford Book of Modern Verse.

Walter Pater

(1839–1894)

MONA LISA

She is older than the rocks among which she sits;
Like the Vampire,
She has been dead many times,
And learned the secrets of the grave;
And has been a diver in deep seas,   5
And keeps their fallen day about her;
And trafficked for strange webs with Eastern merchants;
And, as Leda,
Was the mother of Helen of Troy,
And, as St. Anne,   10
Was the mother of Mary;
And all this has been to her but as the sound of lyres and flutes,
And lives
Only in the delicacy
With which it has moulded the changing lineaments,   15
And tinged the eyelids and the hands.

1939

If Yeats was in some ways a typical "modern" poet, he was also very different from his contemporaries, in ways touched on in this passage from his autobiography.

William Butler Yeats: On Making a New Religion

I was unlike others of my generation in one thing only. I am very religious, and deprived by Huxley and Tyndall, whom I detested, of the simple-minded religion of my childhood, I had made a new religion, almost an infallible church of poetic tradition, of a fardel of stories, and of personages, and of emotions, inseparable from their first expression, passed on from generation to generation by poets and painters with some help from philosophers and theologians. I wished for a world, where I could discover this tradition perpetually, and not in pictures and in poems only, but in tiles round the chimney-piece and in the hangings that kept out the draft. I had even created a dogma: "Because those imaginary people are created out of the deepest instinct of man, to be his measure and his norm, whatever I can imagine those mouths speaking may be the nearest I can go to truth." When I listened they seemed always to speak of one thing only: they, their loves, every incident of their lives, were steeped in the supernatural. Could even Titian's "Ariosto" that I loved beyond other portraits have its grave look, as if waiting for some perfect final event, if the painters before Titian had not learned portraiture, while painting into the corner of compositions full of saints and Madonnas, their kneeling patrons? At seventeen years old I was already an old-fashioned brass cannon full of shot, and nothing had kept me from going off but a doubt as to my capacity to shoot straight.

EDWIN ARLINGTON ROBINSON

(1869–1935)

RICHARD CORY

Whenever Richard Cory went down town,
   We people on the pavement looked at him:
He was a gentleman from sole to crown,
   Clean favored, and imperially slim.

And he was always quietly arrayed,   5
   And he was always human when he talked;
But still he fluttered pulses when he said,
   "Good-morning," and he glittered when he walked.

And he was rich—yes, richer than a king,
   And admirably schooled in every grace: 10

In fine, we thought that he was everything
    To make us wish that we were in his place.

So on we worked, and waited for the light,
    And went without the meat, and cursed the bread;
And Richard Cory, one calm summer night,   15
    Went home and put a bullet through his head.

                                     1896–1897

MINIVER CHEEVY

Miniver Cheevy, child of scorn,
    Grew lean while he assailed the seasons;
He wept that he was ever born,
    And he had reasons.

Miniver loved the days of old   5
    When swords were bright and steeds were prancing;
The vision of a warrior bold
    Would set him dancing.

Miniver sighed for what was not,
    And dreamed, and rested from his labors;   10
He dreamed of Thebes and Camelot,
    And Priam's neighbors.

Miniver mourned the ripe renown
    That made so many a name so fragrant;
He mourned Romance, now on the town,   15
    And Art, a vagrant.

Miniver loved the Medici,
    Albeit he had never seen one;
He would have sinned incessantly
    Could he have been one.   20

Miniver cursed the commonplace
    And eyed a khaki suit with loathing;
He missed the medieval grace
    Of iron clothing.

Miniver scorned the gold he sought,   25
    But sore annoyed was he without it;

"Miniver Cheevy":   11. *Thebes:* a Greek city and the site of many mythical events, including the stories of Oedipus, Antigone, and the Sphinx. *Camelot:* the legendary location of King Arthur's court.   12. *Priam:* king of Troy during the Trojan War.   17. *Medici:* merchant princes of the Italian Renaissance who by their wealth ruled Florence for nearly 200 years. They are known for their cruelty and as patrons of the arts.

Miniver thought, and thought, and thought,
    And thought about it.

Miniver Cheevy, born too late,
    Scratched his head and kept on thinking;   30
Miniver coughed, and called it fate,
    And kept on drinking.

1910

EROS TURANNOS

She fears him, and will always ask
    What fated her to choose him;
She meets in his engaging mask
    All reasons to refuse him;
But what she meets and what she fears   5
Are less than are the downward years,
Drawn slowly to the foamless weirs
    Of age, were she to lose him.

Between a blurred sagacity
    That once had power to sound him,   10
And Love, that will not let him be
    The Judas that she found him,
Her pride assuages her almost,
As if it were alone the cost.—
He sees that he will not be lost,   15
    And waits and looks around him.

A sense of ocean and old trees
    Envelops and allures him;
Tradition, touching all he sees,
    Beguiles and reassures him;   20
And all her doubts of what he says
Are dimmed with what she knows of days—
Till even prejudice delays
    And fades, and she secures him

The falling leaf inaugurates   25
    The reign of her confusion:
The pounding wave reverberates
    The dirge of her illusion;
And home, where passion lived and died,
Becomes a place where she can hide,   30

"Eros Turannos": Eros Turannos: "Love, the Tyrant."

While all the town and harbor side
   Vibrate with her seclusion.

We tell you, tapping on our brows,
   The story as it should be,—
As if the story of a house   35
   Were told, or ever could be;
We'll have no kindly veil between
Her visions and those we have seen,—
As if we guessed what hers have been,
   Or what they are or would be.   40

Meanwhile we do no harm; for they
   That with a god have striven,
Not hearing much of what we say,
   Take what the god has given;
Though like waves breaking it may be   45
Or like a changed familiar tree,
Or like a stairway to the sea
   Where down the blind are driven.

1916

THE MILL

The miller's wife had waited long,
   The tea was cold, the fire was dead;
And there might yet be nothing wrong
   In how he went and what he said:
"There are no millers any more,"   5
   Was all that she had heard him say;
And he had lingered at the door
   So long that it seemed yesterday.

Sick with a fear that had no form
   She knew that she was there at last;   10
And in the mill there was a warm
   And mealy fragrance of the past.
What else there was would only seem
   To say again what he had meant;
And what was hanging from a beam   15
   Would not have heeded where she went.

And if she thought it followed her,
   She may have reasoned in the dark
That one way of the few there were
   Would hide her and would leave no mark: 20
Black water, smooth above the weir

Like starry velvet in the night,
Though ruffled once, would soon appear
The same as ever to the sight.

1920

MR. FLOOD'S PARTY

Old Eben Flood, climbing alone one night
Over the hill between the town below
And the forsaken upland hermitage
That held as much as he should ever know
On earth again of home, paused warily.   5
The road was his with not a native near;
And Eben, having leisure, said aloud,
For no man else in Tilbury Town to hear:

'Well, Mr. Flood, we have the harvest moon
Again, and we may not have many more;   10
The bird is on the wing, the poet says,
And you and I have said it here before.
Drink to the bird.' He raised up to the light
The jug that he had gone so far to fill,
And answered huskily: 'Well, Mr. Flood,   15
Since you propose it, I believe I will.'

Alone, as if enduring to the end
A valiant armor of scarred hopes outworn,
He stood there in the middle of the road
Like Roland's ghost winding a silent horn.   20
Below him, in the town among the trees,
Where friends of other days had honored him,
A phantom salutation of the dead
Rang thinly till old Eben's eyes were dim.

Then, as a mother lays her sleeping child   25
Down tenderly, fearing it may awake,
He set the jug down slowly at his feet
With trembling care, knowing that most things break;
And only when assured that on firm earth
It stood, as the uncertain lives of men   30
Assuredly did not, he paced away,
And with his hand extended paused again:

"Mr. Flood's Party": 20. *Roland:* from the medieval *Song of Roland;* Roland was a commander
in Charlemagne's army, defeated because he was too proud to sound his horn for help.

'Well, Mr. Flood, we have not met like this
In a long time; and many a change has come
To both of us, I fear, since last it was   35
We had a drop together. Welcome home!'
Convivially returning with himself,
Again he raised the jug up to the light;
And with an acquiescent quaver said:
'Well, Mr. Flood, if you insist, I might.   40

'Only a very little, Mr. Flood—
For auld lang syne. No more, sir; that will do.'
So, for the time, apparently it did,
And Eben evidently thought so too;
For soon amid the silver loneliness   45
Of night he lifted up his voice and sang,
Secure, with only two moons listening,
Until the whole harmonious landscape rang—

'For auld lang syne.' The weary throat gave out,
The last word wavered, and the song was done.   50
He raised again the jug regretfully
And shook his head, and was again alone.
There was not much that was ahead of him,
And there was nothing in the town below—
Where strangers would have shut the many doors   55
That many friends had opened long ago.

1921

THE SHEAVES

Where long the shadows of the wind had rolled,
Green wheat was yielding to the change assigned;
And as by some vast magic undivined
The world was turning slowly into gold.
Like nothing that was ever bought or sold   5
It waited there, the body and the mind;
And with a mighty meaning of a kind
That tells the more the more it is not told.

So in a land where all days are not fair,
Fair days went on till on another day   10
A thousand golden sheaves were lying there,
Shining and still, but not for long to stay—

"Mr. Flood's Party": 42. *auld lang syne*: "old long since," the good old days.

As if a thousand girls with golden hair
Might rise from where they slept and go away.

1925

Further Reading

Murphy, Francis, ed. *Edwin Arlington Robinson: A Collection of Critical Essays.*
Englewood Cliffs, NJ: Prentice, 1970. • Winters, Yvor. *Edwin Arlington Robinson.*
New York: New Directions, 1971. • Anderson, Wallace L. *Edwin Arlington Robinson:
A Critical Introduction.* Boston: Houghton, 1967. • Sullivan, Winifred H. "The
Double-Edged Irony of E. A. Robinson's 'Miniver Cheevy.'" *Colby Library Quarterly*
22.3 (Sept. 1986): 185–91. • Allen, James L., Jr. "Symbol and Theme in 'Mr.
Flood's Party.' " *Mississippi Quarterly* 15.4 (Fall 1962): 139–43.

*Edwin Arlington Robinson was master of a tone related to A. E. Housman's
in some ways, but distinctly his own. No one has identified this tone more
accurately than Robert Frost.*

Robert Frost: On Robinson's Humor

The first poet I ever sat down with to talk about poetry was Ezra Pound. It
was in London in 1913. The first poet we talked about, to the best of my
recollection, was Edwin Arlington Robinson. I was fresh from America and
from having read *The Town Down the River.* Beginning at that book, I have
slowly spread my reading of Robinson twenty years backward and forward,
about equally in both directions.

I remember the pleasure with which Pound and I laughed over the
fourth "thought" in

> Miniver thought, and thought, and thought,
> And thought about it.

Three "thoughts" would have been "adequate" as the critical praise-
word then was. There would have been nothing to complain of, if it had
been left at three. The fourth made the intolerable touch of poetry. With
the fourth, the fun began. . . .

There is more to it than the number of "thoughts." There is the way
the last one turns up by surprise round the corner, the way the shape of the
stanza is played with, the easy way the obstacle of verse is turned to advantage. The mischief is in it.

One pauses half afraid—
To say for certain that he played

a man as sorrowful as Robinson. His death was sad to those who knew him, but nowhere near as sad as the lifetime of poetry to which he attuned our ears. Nevertheless, I say his much-admired restraint lies wholly in his never having let grief go further than it could in play. So far shall grief go, so far shall philosophy go, so far shall confidences go, and no further. Taste may set the limit. Humor is a surer dependence.

ROBERT FROST

(1874–1963)

HOME BURIAL

He saw her from the bottom of the stairs
Before she saw him. She was starting down,
Looking back over her shoulder at some fear.
She took a doubtful step and then undid it
To raise herself and look again. He spoke   5
Advancing toward her: "What is it you see
From up there always?—for I want to know."
She turned and sank upon her skirts at that,
And her face changed from terrified to dull.
He said to gain time: "What is it you see?"   10
Mounting until she cowered under him.
"I will find out now—you must tell me, dear."
She, in her place, refused him any help,
With the least stiffening of her neck and silence.
She let him look, sure that he wouldn't see,   15
Blind creature; and awhile he didn't see.
But at last he murmured, "Oh," and again, "Oh."

"What is it—what?" she said.

                    "Just that I see."

"You don't," she challenged. "Tell me what it is."   20

"The wonder is I didn't see at once.
I never noticed it from here before.
I must be wonted to it—that's the reason.
The little graveyard where my people are!

So small the window frames the whole of it.   25
Not so much larger than a bedroom, is it?
There are three stones of slate and one of marble,
Broad shouldered little slabs there in the sunlight
On the sidehill. We haven't to mind *those*.
But I understand: it is not the stones,   30
But the child's mound——"

                    "Don't, don't, don't, don't," she cried.

She withdrew, shrinking from beneath his arm
That rested on the banister, and slid downstairs;   35
And turned on him with such a daunting look,
He said twice over before he knew himself:
"Can't a man speak of his own child he's lost?"

"Not you!—Oh, where's my hat? Oh, I don't need it!
I must get out of here. I must get air.—   40
I don't know rightly whether any man can."

"Amy! Don't go to someone else this time.
Listen to me. I won't come down the stairs."
He sat and fixed his chin between his fists.
"There's something I should like to ask you, dear."   45

"You don't know how to ask it."

                  "Help me, then."

Her fingers moved the latch for all reply.

"My words are nearly always an offense.
I don't know how to speak of anything   50
So as to please you. But I might be taught,
I should suppose. I can't say I see how.
A man must partly give up being a man
With womenfolk. We could have some arrangement
By which I'd bind myself to keep hands off   55
Anything special you're a-mind to name.
Though I don't like such things 'twixt those that love.
Two that don't love can't live together without them.
But two that do can't live together with them."
She moved the latch a little. "Don't—don't go.   60
Don't carry it to someone else this time.
Tell me about it if it's something human.
Let me into your grief. I'm not so much
Unlike other folks as your standing there
Apart would make me out. Give me my chance.   65
I do think, though, you overdo it a little.
What was it brought you up to think it the thing

To take your mother-loss of a first child
So inconsolably—in the face of love.
You'd think his memory might be satisfied——"   70

"There you go sneering now!"

                   "I'm not, I'm not!

You make me angry. I'll come down to you.
God, what a woman! And it's come to this,
A man can't speak of his own child that's dead."   75

"You can't because you don't know how to speak.
If you had any feelings, you that dug
With your own hand—how could you?—his little grave;
I saw you from that very window there,
Making the gravel leap and leap in air,   80
Leap up, like that, like that, and land so lightly
And roll back down the mound beside the hole.
I thought, Who is that man? I didn't know you.
And I crept down the stairs and up the stairs
To look again, and still your spade kept lifting.   85
Then you came in. I heard your rumbling voice
Out in the kitchen, and I don't know why,
But I went near to see with my own eyes.
You could sit there with the stains on your shoes
Of the fresh earth from your own baby's grave   90
And talk about your everyday concerns.
You had stood the spade up against the wall
Outside there in the entry, for I saw it."

"I shall laugh the worst laugh I ever laughed.
I'm cursed. God, if I don't believe I'm cursed."   95

"I can repeat the very words you were saying:
'Three foggy mornings and one rainy day
Will rot the best birch fence a man can build.'
Think of it, talk like that at such a time!
What had how long it takes a birch to rot   100
To do with what was in the darkened parlor?
You *couldn't* care! The nearest friends can go
With anyone to death, comes so far short
They might as well not try to go at all.
No, from the time when one is sick to death,   105
One is alone, and he dies more alone.
Friends make pretense of following to the grave,
But before one is in it, their minds are turned
And making the best of their way back to life
And living people, and things they understand.   110

But the world's evil. I won't have grief so
If I can change it. Oh, I won't, I won't!"

"There, you have said it all and you feel better.
You won't go now. You're crying. Close the door.
The heart's gone out of it: why keep it up?   115
Amy! There's someone coming down the road!"

"*You*—oh, you think the talk is all. I must go—
Somewhere out of this house. How can I make you—"

"If—you—do!" She was opening the door wider.
"Where do you mean to go? First tell me that.   120
I'll follow and bring you back by force. I *will!*—"

                                                               1914

THE WOOD-PILE

Out walking in the frozen swamp one gray day,
I paused and said, "I will turn back from here.
No, I will go on farther—and we shall see."
The hard snow held me, save where now and then
One foot went through. The view was all in lines   5
Straight up and down of tall slim trees
Too much alike to mark or name a place by
So as to say for certain I was here
Or somewhere else: I was just far from home.
A small bird flew before me. He was careful   10
To put a tree between us when he lighted,
And say no word to tell me who he was
Who was so foolish as to think what *he* thought.
He thought that I was after him for a feather—
The white one in his tail; like one who takes   15
Everything said as personal to himself.
One flight out sideways would have undeceived him.
And then there was a pile of wood for which
I forgot him and let his little fear
Carry him off the way I might have gone,   20
Without so much as wishing him good-night.
He went behind it to make his last stand.
It was a cord of maple, cut and split
And piled—and measured, four by four by eight.
And not another like it could I see.   25
No runner tracks in this year's snow looped near it.
And it was older sure than this year's cutting,
Or even last year's or the year's before.

The wood was gray and the bark warping off it
And the pile somewhat sunken. Clematis   30
Had wound strings round and round it like a bundle.
What held it, though, on one side was a tree
Still growing, and on one a stake and prop,
These latter about to fall. I thought that only
Someone who lived in turning to fresh tasks   35
Could so forget his handiwork on which
He spent himself, the labor of his ax,
And leave it there far from a useful fireplace
To warm the frozen swamp as best it could
With the slow smokeless burning of decay.   40

1914

NOTHING GOLD CAN STAY

Nature's first green is gold,
Her hardest hue to hold.
Her early leaf's a flower;
But only so an hour.
Then leaf subsides to leaf.   5
So Eden sank to grief,
So dawn goes down to day.
Nothing gold can stay.

1916

BIRCHES

When I see birches bend to left and right
Across the lines of straighter darker trees,
I like to think some boy's been swinging them.
But swinging doesn't bend them down to stay.
Ice-storms do that. Often you must have seen them   5
Loaded with ice a sunny winter morning
After a rain. They click upon themselves
As the breeze rises, and turn many-colored
As the stir cracks and crazes their enamel.
Soon the sun's warmth makes them shed crystal shells   10
Shattering and avalanching on the snow-crust—
Such heaps of broken glass to sweep away
You'd think the inner dome of heaven had fallen.
They are dragged to the withered bracken by the load,
And they seem not to break; though once they are bowed   15
So low for long, they never right themselves:

You may see their trunks arching in the woods
Years afterwards, trailing their leaves on the ground
Like girls on hands and knees that throw their hair
Before them over their heads to dry in the sun. 20
But I was going to say when Truth broke in
With all her matter-of-fact about the ice-storm
I should prefer to have some boy bend them
As he went out and in to fetch the cows—
Some boy too far from town to learn baseball, 25
Whose only play was what he found himself,
Summer or winter, and could play alone.
One by one he subdued his father's trees
By riding them down over and over again
Until he took the stiffness out of them, 30
And not one but hung limp, not one was left
For him to conquer. He learned all there was
To learn about not launching out too soon
And so not carrying the tree away
Clear to the ground. He always kept his poise 35
To the top branches, climbing carefully
With the same pains you use to fill a cup
Up to the brim, and even above the brim.
Then he flung outward, feet first, with a swish,
Kicking his way down through the air to the ground. 40
So was I once myself a swinger of birches.
And so I dream of going back to be.
It's when I'm weary of considerations,
And life is too much like a pathless wood
Where your face burns and tickles with the cobwebs 45
Broken across it, and one eye is weeping
From a twig's having lashed across it open.
I'd like to get away from earth awhile
And then come back to it and begin over.
May no fate willfully misunderstand me 50
And half grant what I wish and snatch me away
Not to return. Earth's the right place for love:
I don't know where it's likely to go better.
I'd like to go by climbing a birch tree,
And climb black branches up a snow-white trunk 55
Toward heaven, till the tree could bear no more,
But dipped its top and set me down again.
That would be good both going and coming back.
One could do worse than be a swinger of birches.

1916

STOPPING BY WOODS ON A
SNOWY EVENING

Whose woods these are I think I know.
His house is in the village though;
He will not see me stopping here
To watch his woods fill up with snow.

My little horse must think it queer   5
To stop without a farmhouse near
Between the woods and frozen lake
The darkest evening of the year.

He gives his harness bells a shake
To ask if there is some mistake.   10
The only other sound's the sweep
Of easy wind and downy flake.

The woods are lovely, dark and deep.
But I have promises to keep,
And miles to go before I sleep,   15
And miles to go before I sleep.

1923

ACQUAINTED WITH THE NIGHT

I have been one acquainted with the night.
I have walked out in rain—and back in rain.
I have outwalked the furthest city light.

I have looked down the saddest city lane.
I have passed by the watchman on his beat   5
And dropped my eyes, unwilling to explain.

I have stood still and stopped the sound of feet
When far away an interrupted cry
Came over houses from another street,

But not to call me back or say good-bye;   10
And further still at an unearthly height,
One luminary clock against the sky

Proclaimed the time was neither wrong nor right.
I have been one acquainted with the night.

1928

NEITHER OUT FAR NOR IN DEEP

The people along the sand
All turn and look one way.
They turn their back on the land.
They look at the sea all day.

As long as it takes to pass   5
A ship keeps raising its hull;
The wetter ground like glass
Reflects a standing gull.

The land may vary more;
But wherever the truth may be—   10
The water comes ashore,
And the people look at the sea.

They cannot look out far.
They cannot look in deep.
But when was that ever a bar   15
To any watch they keep?

                                        1932

DEPARTMENTAL

An ant on the tablecloth
Ran into a dormant moth
Of many times his size.
He showed not the least surprise.
His business wasn't with such.   5
He gave it scarcely a touch,
And was off on his duty run.
Yet if he encountered one
Of the hive's enquiry squad
Whose work is to find out God   10
And the nature of time and space,
He would put him onto the case.
Ants are a curious race;
One crossing with hurried tread
The body of one of their dead   15
Isn't given a moment's arrest—
Seems not even impressed.
But he no doubt reports to any
With whom he crosses antennae,
And they no doubt report   20
To the higher-up at court.
Then word goes forth in Formic:
"Death's come to Jerry McCormic,

Our selfless forager Jerry.
Will the special Janizary   25
Whose office it is to bury
The dead of the commissary
Go bring him home to his people.
Lay him in state on a sepal.
Wrap him for shroud in a petal.   30
Embalm him with ichor of nettle.
This the word of your Queen."
And presently on the scene
Appears a solemn mortician;
And taking formal position,   35
With feelers calmly atwiddle,
Seizes the dead by the middle,
And heaving him high in air,
Carries him out of there.
No one stands round to stare.   40
It is nobody else's affair.

It couldn't be called ungentle.
But how thoroughly departmental.

                                                1936

THE GIFT OUTRIGHT

The land was ours before we were the land's.
She was our land more than a hundred years
Before we were her people. She was ours
In Massachusetts, in Virginia,
But we were England's, still colonials,   5
Possessing what we still were unpossessed by,
Possessed by what we now no more possessed.
Something we were withholding made us weak
Until we found it was ourselves
We were withholding from our land of living,   10
And forthwith found salvation in surrender.
Such as we were we gave ourselves outright
(The deed of gift was many deeds of war)
To the land vaguely realizing westward,
But still unstoried, artless, unenhanced,   15
Such as she was, such as she would become.

                                                1942

"Departmental": 25. *Janizary:* a janissary, a soldier in an elite guard of Turkish troops.

Further Reading

Frost, Robert. "The Constant Symbol." *Selected Prose of Robert Frost.* Ed. Hyde Cox and Edward Connery Lathem. New York: Holt, 1966. 23–29. • Pritchard, William H. *Frost: A Literary Life Reconsidered.* New York: Oxford UP, 1984. • Perrine, Laurence. "On Frost's 'The Wood-Pile.'" *Notes on Modern Literature* 6.1 (Spring–Summer 1982): 1. • Monteiro, George. "Swinging." *Robert Frost and the New England Renaissance.* Lexington: UP of Kentucky, 1988. 99–111. • Shurr, William H. "Once More to the 'Woods': A New Point of Entry into Frost's Most Famous Poem." *New England Quarterly* 47.4 (Dec. 1974): 584–94.

Robert Frost, born in a generation full of poetic experimenters, clung to traditional meter and poetic form and wrote many poems about the rural landscape, the most traditional of subjects. Frost had his reasons for doing so, and articulated them often and well, as in the following excerpt from "The Constant Symbol." Some of Frost's readers, however, would agree with Galway Kinnell that beneath the technical accomplishment and commitment to form there was something deeper and darker in Frost that accounts for the power of his best poetry.

Robert Frost: On Metaphor

There are many other things I have found myself saying about poetry, but the chiefest of these is that it is metaphor, saying one thing and meaning another, saying one thing in terms of another, the pleasure of ulteriority. Poetry is simply made of metaphor. So also is philosophy—and science, too, for that matter, if it will take the soft impeachment from a friend. Every poem is a new metaphor inside or it is nothing. And there is a sense in which all poems are the same old metaphor always.

Every single poem written regular is a symbol small or great of the way the will has to pitch into commitments deeper and deeper to a rounded conclusion and then be judged for whether any original intention it had has been strongly spent or weakly lost; be it in art, politics, school, church, business, love, or marriage—in a piece of work or in a career. Strongly spent is synonymous with kept. . . .

The bard has said in effect, Unto these forms did I commend the spirit. It may take him a year after the act to confess he only betrayed the spirit with a rhymster's cleverness and to forgive his enemies the critics for not having listened to his oaths and protestations to the contrary. Had he anything to be true to? Was he true to it? Did he use good words? You couldn't tell unless you made out what idea they were supposed to be good for. Every poem is an epitome of the great predicament; a figure of the will braving alien entanglements.

Take the President in the White House. A study of the success of his intention might have to go clear back to when as a young politician, youth-fully step-careless, he made the choice between the two parties of our system. He may have stood for a moment wishing he knew of a third party nearer the ideal; but only for a moment, since he was practical. And in fact he may have been so little impressed with the importance of his choice that he left his first commitment to be made for him by his friends and relatives. It was only a small commitment anyway, like a kiss. He can scarcely remember how much credit he deserved personally for the decision it took. Calculation is usually no part in the first step in any walk. And behold him now a statesman so multifariously closed in on with obligations and answerabilities that sometimes he loses his august temper. He might as well have got himself into a sestina royal. . . .

There's an indulgent smile I get for the recklessness of the unnecessary commitment I made when I came to the first line in the second stanza of a poem in this book called "Stopping by Woods on a Snowy Evening." I was riding too high to care what trouble I incurred. And it was all right so long as I didn't suffer deflection.

Galway Kinnell

(b. 1927)

FOR ROBERT FROST

1

Why do you talk so much
Robert Frost? One day
I drove up to Ripton to ask,

I stayed the whole day
And never got the chance   5
To put the question.

I drove off at dusk
Worn out and aching
In both ears. Robert Frost,

---

3. *Ripton:* a town in Vermont where Frost lived.

Were you shy as a boy?
Do you go on making up
For some long stint of solitude?   10

Is it simply that talk
Doesn't have to be metered and rhymed?
Or is gab distracting from something worse?   15

2

I saw you once on the TV,
Unsteady at the lectern,
The flimsy white leaf
Of hair standing straight up
In the wind, among top hats,   20
Old farmer and son
Of worse winters than this,
Stopped in the first dazzle

Of the District of Columbia,
Suddenly having to pay   25
For the cheap onionskin,
The worn-out ribbon, the eyes
Wrecked from writing poems
For us—stopped,
Lonely before millions,   30
The paper jumping in your grip,
And as the Presidents
Also on the platform
Began flashing nervously
Their Presidential smiles   35
For the harmless old guy,
And poets watching on the TV
Started thinking, Well that's
The end of *that* tradition,

And the managers of the event   40
Said, Boys this is it,
The sonofabitch poet
Is gonna croak,
Putting the paper aside
You drew forth   45
From your great faithful heart
The poem.

---

16. *TV:* Frost appeared on the televised inauguration of John F. Kennedy, January 20, 1961,
for which he recited his "The Gift Outright."

3

Once, walking in winter in Vermont,
In the snow, I followed a set of footprints
That aimed for the woods. At the verge   50
I could make out, "far in the pillared dark,"
An old creature in a huge, clumsy overcoat,
Lifting his great boots through the drifts,
Going as if to die among "those dark trees"
Of his own country. I watched him go,   55

Past a house, quiet, warm and light,
A farm, a countryside, a woodpile in its slow
Smokeless burning, alder swamps ghastly white,
Tumultuous snows, blanker whitenesses,
Into the pathless woods, one eye weeping,   60
The dark trees, for which no saying is dark enough,
Which mask the gloom and lead on into it,
The bare, the withered, the deserted.

There were no more cottages.
Soft bombs of dust falling from the boughs,   65
The sun shining no warmer than the moon,
He had outwalked the farthest city light,
And there, clinging to the perfect trees,
A last leaf. What was it?
What was that whiteness?—white, uncertain—   70
The night too dark to know.

4

He turned. *Love,*
Love of things, duty, he said.
And made his way back to the shelter
No longer sheltering him, the house   75
Where everything real was turning to words,

Where he would think on the white wave,
Folded back, that rides in place on the obscure
Pouring of this life to the sea—
And invent on the broken lips of darkness   80
The seal of form and the *mot juste.*

5

Poet of the country of white houses,
Of clearings going out to the dark wall of woods

---

81. *mot juste:* right, exact word (French).

Frayed along the skyline, you who nearly foreknew
The next lines of poems you suddenly dropped,   85
Who dwelt in access to that which other men
Have burnt all their lives to get near, who heard
The high wind, in gusts, seething
From far off, headed through the trees exactly
To this place where it must happen, who spent   90
Your life on the point of giving away your heart
To the dark trees, the dissolving woods,
Into which you go at last, heart in hand, deep in:
When we think of a man who was cursed
Neither with the mystical all-lovingness of Walt Whitman   95
Nor with Melville's anguish to know and to suffer,
And yet cursed . . . a man, what shall I say,
Vain, not fully convinced he was dying, whose calling
Was to set up in the wilderness of his country,
At whatever cost, a man, who would be his own man,   100
We think of you. And from the same doorway
At which you lived, between the house and the woods,
We see your old footprints going away across
The great Republic, Frost, up memorized slopes,
Down hills floating by heart on the bulldozed land.   105

1964

RAINER MARIA RILKE

(1875–1926)

ARIEL

(After reading Shakespeare's Tempest*)*

translated from the German by Stephen Mitchell

Once, somewhere, somehow, you had set him free
with that sharp jolt which as a young man tore you
out of your life and vaulted you to greatness.
Then he grew willing; and, since then, he serves,
after each task impatient for his freedom.   5
And half imperious, half almost ashamed,
you make excuses, say that you still need him
for this and that, and, ah, you must describe
how you helped him. Yet you feel, yourself,

that everything held back by his detention   10
is missing from the air. How sweet, how tempting:
to let him go—to give up all your magic,
submit yourself to destiny like the others,
and know that his light friendship, without strain now,
with no more obligations, anywhere,   15
an intensifying of this space you breathe,
is working in the element, thoughtlessly.
Henceforth dependent, never again empowered
to shape the torpid mouth into that call
at which he dived. Defenseless, aging, poor,   20
and yet still breathing *him* in, like a fragrance
spread endlessly, which makes the invisible
complete for the first time. Smiling that you ever
could summon him and feel so much at home
in that vast intimacy. Weeping too, perhaps,   25
when you remember how he loved and yet
wished to leave you: always both, at once.

(Have I let go already? I look on,
terrified by this man who has become
a duke again. How easily he draws   30
the wire through his head and hangs himself
up with the other puppets; then steps forward
to ask the audience for their applause
and their indulgence. . . . What consummate power:
to lay aside, to stand there nakedly   35
with no strength but one's own, "which is most faint.")

1913, trans. 1982

EXPOSED ON THE CLIFFS OF
THE HEART

translated from the German by Stephen Mitchell

Exposed on the cliffs of the heart. Look, how tiny down there,
look: the last village of words and, higher,
(but how tiny) still one last
farmhouse of feeling. Can you see it?
Exposed on the cliffs of the heart. Stoneground   5
under your hands. Even here, though,
something can bloom; on a silent cliff-edge
an unknowing plant blooms, singing, into the air.
But the one who knows? Ah, he began to know
and is quiet now, exposed on the cliffs of the heart.   10

While, with their full awareness,
many sure-footed mountain animals pass
or linger. And the great sheltered bird flies, slowly
circling, around the peak's pure denial.—But
without a shelter, here on the cliffs of the heart. . . .   15

1914, trans. 1982

ARCHAIC TORSO OF APOLLO

translated from the German by Stephen Mitchell

We cannot know his legendary head
with eyes like ripening fruit. And yet his torso
is still suffused with brilliance from inside,
like a lamp, in which his gaze, now turned to low,

gleams in all its power. Otherwise   5
the curved breast could not dazzle you so, nor could
a smile run through the placid hips and thighs
to that dark center where procreation flared.

Otherwise the stone would seem defaced
beneath the translucent cascade of the shoulders   10
and would not glisten like a wild beast's fur:

would not, from all the borders of itself,
burst like a star; for here there is no place
that does not see you. You must change your life.

1927, trans. 1982

EVENING

translated from the German by Stephen Mitchell

The sky puts on the darkening blue coat
held for it by a row of ancient trees;
you watch: and the lands grow distant in your sight,
one journeying to heaven, one that falls;

and leave you, not at home in either one,   5
not quite so still and dark as the darkened houses,
not calling to eternity with the passion
of what becomes a star each night, and rises;

"*Archaic Torso of Apollo*": *Apollo:* one of the greatest classical gods; he was identified with the
sun, but was also the god of healing, music, and poetry, and the leader of the Muses.

and leave you (inexpressibly to unravel)
your life, with its immensity and fear,   10
so that, now bounded, now immeasurable,
it is alternately stone in you and star.

                                                             1927, trans. 1982

AUTUMN DAY

translated from the German by Stephen Mitchell

Lord: it is time. The huge summer has gone by.
Now overlap the sundials with your shadows,
and on the meadows let the wind go free.

Command the fruits to swell on tree and vine;
grant them a few more warm transparent days,   5
urge them on to fulfillment then, and press
the final sweetness into the heavy wine.

Whoever has no house now, will never have one.
Whoever is alone will stay alone,
will sit, read, write long letters through the evening,   10
and wander on the boulevards, up and down,
restlessly, while the dry leaves are blowing.

                                                             1927, trans. 1982

THE PANTHER

In the Jardin des Plantes, Paris

translated from the German by Stephen Mitchell

His vision, from the constantly passing bars,
has grown so weary that it cannot hold
anything else. It seems to him there are
a thousand bars; and behind the bars, no world.

As he paces in cramped circles, over and over,   5
the movement of his powerful soft strides
is like a ritual dance around a center
in which a mighty will stands paralyzed.

Only at times, the curtain of the pupils
lifts, quietly—. An image enters in,   10
rushes down through the tensed, arrested muscles,
plunges into the heart and is gone.

                                                             1927, trans. 1982

THE GAZELLE

Gazella Dorcas

translated from the German by Stephen Mitchell

Enchanted thing: how can two chosen words
ever attain the harmony of pure rhyme
that pulses through you as your body stirs?
Out of your forehead branch and lyre climb,

and all your features pass in simile, through   5
the songs of love whose words, as light as rose-
petals, rest on the face of someone who
has put his book away and shut his eyes:

to see you: tenses, as if each leg were a gun
loaded with leaps, but not fired while your neck   10
holds your head still, listening: as when,

while swimming in some isolated place,
a girl hears leaves rustle, and turns to look:
the forest pool reflected in her face.

1927, trans. 1982

Further Reading

Hass, Robert. "Looking for Rilke." Introduction to *The Selected Poems of Rainer
Maria Rilke.* Ed. Stephen Mitchell. New York: Random, 1982. xi–xliv. • Brodsky,
Patricia Pollock. *Rainer Maria Rilke.* Boston: Twayne, 1988. 85–88. • Mandel,
Siegfried. *Rainer Maria Rilke: The Poetic Instinct.* Carbondale; Southern Illinois UP,
1965. • Bly, Robert. Introduction to "New Poems." *Selected Poems of Rainer Maria
Rilke.* New York: Harper, 1981. 133–37. • Fitzgerald, William. "Articulating the
Unarticulated: Form, Death and Other in Keats and Rilke." *Modern Language Notes*
100.5 (Dec. 1985): 949–67.

*One of Rilke's remarkable qualities is his ability in a single poem both to
bring us face to face with life's interesting surfaces and to suggest that these
surfaces are not enough. Robert Hass has described this quality admirably in
his analysis of a passage from Rilke's* Duino Elegies *(1923).*

Robert Hass: On Rilke's Calling Us from the Things of This World

Rilke's special gift as a poet is that he does not seem to speak from the middle of life, that he is always calling us away from it. His poems have the feeling of being written from a great depth in himself. What makes them so seductive is that they also speak to the reader so intimately. They seem whispered or crooned into our inmost ear, insinuating us toward the same depth in ourselves. The effect can be hypnotic. When Rilke was dying in 1926—of a rare and particularly agonizing blood disease—he received a letter from the young Russian poet Marina Tsvetayeva. "You are not the poet I love most," she wrote to him. " 'Most' already implies comparison. You are poetry itself." And one knows that this is not hyperbole. That voice of Rilke's poems, calling us out of ourselves, or calling us into the deepest places in ourselves, is very near to what people mean by poetry. It is also what makes him difficult to read thoughtfully. He induces a kind of trance, as soon as the whispering begins:

> Yes—the springtimes needed you. Often a star
> was waiting for you to notice it. A wave rolled toward you
> out of the distant past, or as you walked
> under an open window, a violin
> yielded itself to your hearing. All this was mission.
> But could you accomplish it? Weren't you always
> distracted by expectation, as if every event
> announced a beloved? (Where can you find a place
> to keep her, with all the huge strange thoughts inside you
> going and coming and often staying all night.)

Look at how he bores into us. That caressing voice seems to be speaking to the solitary walker in each of us who is moved by springtimes, stars, oceans, the sound of music. And then he reminds us that those things touch off in us a deeper longing. First, there is the surprising statement that the world is a mission, and the more surprising question about our fitness for it. Then, with another question, he brings us to his intimacy with our deeper hunger. And then he goes below that, to the still more solitary self with its huge strange thoughts. It is as if he were peeling off layers of the apparent richness of the self, arguing us back to the poverty of a great, raw, objectless longing.

WALLACE STEVENS

(1879–1955)

SUNDAY MORNING

1

Complacencies of the peignoir, and late
Coffee and oranges in a sunny chair,
And the green freedom of a cockatoo
Upon a rug mingle to dissipate
The holy hush of ancient sacrifice.   5
She dreams a little, and she feels the dark
Encroachment of that old catastrophe,
As a calm darkens among water-lights.
The pungent oranges and bright, green wings
Seem things in some procession of the dead   10
Winding across wide water, without sound.
The day is like wide water, without sound,
Stilled for the passing of her dreaming feet
Over the seas, to silent Palestine,
Dominion of the blood and sepulchre.   15

2

Why should she give her bounty to the dead?
What is divinity if it can come
Only in silent shadows and in dreams?
Shall she not find in comforts of the sun,
In pungent fruit and bright, green wings, or else   20
In any balm or beauty of the earth,
Things to be cherished like the thought of heaven?
Divinity must live within herself:
Passions of rain, or moods in falling snow;
Grievings in loneliness, or unsubdued   25
Elations when the forest blooms; gusty
Emotions on wet roads on autumn nights;
All pleasures and all pains, remembering
The bough of summer and the winter branch.
These are the measures destined for her soul.   30

3

Jove in the clouds had his inhuman birth.
No mother suckled him, no sweet land gave
Large-mannered motions to his mythy mind

He moved among us, as a muttering king,
Magnificent, would move among his hinds,   35
Until our blood, commingling, virginal,
With heaven, brought such requital to desire
The very hinds discerned it, in a star.
Shall our blood fail? Or shall it come to be
The blood of paradise? And shall the earth   40
Seem all of paradise that we shall know?
The sky will be much friendlier then than now,
A part of labor and a part of pain,
And next in glory to enduring love,
Not this dividing and indifferent blue.   45

4

She says, "I am content when wakened birds,
Before they fly, test the reality
Of misty fields, by their sweet questionings;
But when the birds are gone, and their warm fields
Return no more, where, then, is paradise?"   50
There is not any haunt of prophecy,
Nor any old chimera of the grave,
Neither the golden underground, nor isle
Melodious, where spirits gat them home,
Nor visionary south, nor cloudy palm   55
Remote on heaven's hill, that has endured
As April's green endures; or will endure
Like her remembrance of awakened birds,
Or her desire for June and evening, tipped
By the consummation of the swallow's wings.   60

5

She says, "But in contentment I still feel
The need of some imperishable bliss."
Death is the mother of beauty; hence from her,
Alone, shall come fulfilment to our dreams
And our desires. Although she strews the leaves   65
Of sure obliteration on our paths,
The path sick sorrow took, the many paths
Where triumph rang its brassy phrase, or love
Whispered a little out of tenderness,
She makes the willow shiver in the sun   70
For maidens who were wont to sit and gaze
Upon the grass, relinquished to their feet.
She causes boys to pile new plums and pears
On disregarded plate. The maidens taste
And stray impassioned in the littering leaves.   75

6

Is there no change of death in paradise?
Does ripe fruit never fall? Or do the boughs
Hang always heavy in that perfect sky,
Unchanging, yet so like our perishing earth,
With rivers like our own that seek for seas   80
They never find, the same receding shores
That never touch with inarticulate pang?
Why set the pear upon those river-banks
Or spice the shores with odors of the plum?
Alas, that they should wear our colors there,   85
The silken weavings of our afternoons,
And pick the strings of our insipid lutes!
Death is the mother of beauty, mystical,
Within whose burning bosom we devise
Our earthy mothers waiting, sleeplessly.   90

7

Supple and turbulent, a ring of men
Shall chant in orgy on a summer morn
Their boisterous devotion to the sun,
Not as a god, but as a god might be,
Naked among them, like a savage source.   95
Their chant shall be a chant of paradise,
Out of their blood, returning to the sky;
And in their chant shall enter, voice by voice,
The windy lake wherein their lord delights,
The trees, like serafin, and echoing hills,   100
That choir among themselves long afterward.
They shall know well the heavenly fellowship
Of men that perish and of summer morn.
And whence they came and whither they shall go
The dew upon their feet shall manifest.   105

8

She hears, upon that water without sound,
A voice that cries, "The tomb in Palestine
Is not the porch of spirits lingering.
It is the grave of Jesus, where he lay."
We live in an old chaos of the sun,   110
Or old dependency of day and night,
Or island solitude, unsponsored, free,
Of that wide water, inescapable.
Deer walk upon our mountains, and the quail
Whistle about us their spontaneous cries;   115

Sweet berries ripen in the wilderness;
And, in the isolation of the sky,
At evening, casual flocks of pigeons make
Ambiguous undulations as they sink,
Downward to darkness, on extended wings.   120

                                                            1923

THE EMPEROR OF ICE-CREAM

Call the roller of big cigars,
The muscular one, and bid him whip
In kitchen cups concupiscent curds.
Let the wenches dawdle in such dress
As they are used to wear, and let the boys   5
Bring flowers in last month's newspapers.
Let be be finale of seem.
The only emperor is the emperor of ice-cream.

Take from the dresser of deal,
Lacking the three glass knobs, that sheet   10
On which she embroidered fantails once
And spread it so as to cover her face.
If her horny feet protrude, they come
To show how cold she is, and dumb.
Let the lamp affix its beam.   15
The only emperor is the emperor of ice-cream.

                                                        1923

ANECDOTE OF THE JAR

I placed a jar in Tennessee,
And round it was, upon a hill.
It made the slovenly wilderness
Surround that hill.

The wilderness rose up to it,   5
And sprawled around, no longer wild.
The jar was round upon the ground
And tall and of a port in air.

It took dominion everywhere.
The jar was gray and bare.   10
It did not give of bird or bush,
Like nothing else in Tennessee.

                                                        1923

DISILLUSIONMENT OF TEN O'CLOCK

The houses are haunted
By white night-gowns
None are green,
Or purple with green rings,
Or green with yellow rings,   5
Or yellow with blue rings.
None of them are strange,
With socks of lace
And beaded ceintures.
People are not going   10
To dream of baboons and periwinkles.
Only, here and there, an old sailor,
Drunk and asleep in his boots,
Catches tigers
In red weather.   15

1923

A POSTCARD FROM THE VOLCANO

Children picking up our bones
Will never know that these were once
As quick as foxes on the hill;

And that in autumn, when the grapes
Made sharp air sharper by their smell   5
These had a being, breathing frost;

And least will guess that with our bones
We left much more, left what still is
The look of things, left what we felt

At what we saw. The spring clouds blow   10
Above the shuttered mansion-house,
Beyond our gate and the windy sky

Cries out a literate despair.
We knew for long the mansion's look
And what we said of it became   15

A part of what is . . . Children,
Still weaving budded aureoles,
We will speak our speech and never know,

Will say of the mansion that it seems
As if he that lived there left behind   20
A spirit storming in blank walls,

A dirty house in a gutted world,
A tatter of shadows peaked to white,
Smeared with the gold of the opulent sun.

1936

STUDY OF TWO PEARS

1

Opusculum paedagogum
The pears are not viols,
Nudes or bottles.
They resemble nothing else.

2

They are yellow forms   5
Composed of curves
Bulging toward the base.
They are touched red.

3

They are not flat surfaces
Having curved outlines.   10
They are round
Tapering toward the top.

4

In the way they are modelled
There are bits of blue.
A hard dry leaf hangs   15
From the stem.

5

The yellow glistens.
It glistens with various yellows,
Citrons, oranges and greens
Flowering over the skin.   20

6

The shadows of the pears
Are blobs on the green cloth.
The pears are not seen
As the observer wills.

1942

"Study of Two Pears": 1. *Opusculum paedagogum:* a little study, a practice piece.

Wallace Stevens   *673*

Further Reading

Vendler, Helen. *Wallace Stevens.* Knoxville: U of Tennessee P, 1984. • Stern, Herbert J. *Wallace Stevens: Art of Uncertainty.* Ann Arbor: U of Michigan P, 1966. • Carroll, Joseph. *Wallace Stevens' Supreme Fiction: A New Romanticism.* Baton Rouge: Louisiana State UP, 1987. • Blackmur, R. P. "Examples of Wallace Stevens." *The Achievement of Wallace Stevens.* Ed. Ashley Brown and Robert S. Haller. New York: Lippincott, 1962. 52–80. • Rehder, Robert. "The Grand Poem: Preliminary Minutiae." Chapter 2 of *The Poetry of Wallace Stevens.* London: Macmillan, 1988. 56–86, spec. 65–86. • Keyser, Samuel Jay. "Wallace Stevens: Form and Meaning in Four Poems." *College English* 37.6 (Feb. 1976): 578–98, spec. 585–89.

Although many poets have expressed great admiration for Wallace Stevens's work, few have been successful in explaining what qualities make it admirable. Marianne Moore once said that his virtue was in understatement: "one is safe from 'harangue,' 'ado,' and the ambitious page" because Stevens sees "the difference between the grand and the grandiose." Randall Jarrell sees somewhat different virtues.

Randall Jarrell: On Stevens's Sense of Wonder

At the bottom of Stevens's poetry there is wonder and delight, the child's or animal's or savage's—man's—joy in his own existence, and thankfulness for it. He is the poet of well-being: "One might have thought of sight, but who could think/Of what it sees, for all the ill it sees?" This sigh of awe, of wondering pleasure, is underneath all these poems that show us the "celestial possible," everything that has not yet been transformed into the infernal impossibilities of our everyday earth. Stevens is full of the natural or Aristotelian virtues; he is, in the terms of Hopkins's poem, all windhover and no Jesuit. There is about him, under the translucent glazes, a Dutch solidity and weight; he sits surrounded by all the good things of this earth, with rosy cheeks and fresh clear blue eyes, eyes not going out to you but shining in their place, like fixed stars—or else he moves off, like the bishop in his poem, "globed in today and tomorrow." If he were an animal he would be, without a doubt, that rational, magnanimous, voluminous animal, the elephant.

WILLIAM CARLOS WILLIAMS

(1883–1963)

THE RED WHEELBARROW

so much depends
upon

a red wheel
barrow

glazed with rain   5
water

beside the white
chickens.

1923

QUEEN-ANNE'S-LACE

Her body is not so white as
anemone petals nor so smooth—nor
so remote a thing. It is a field
of the wild carrot taking
the field by force; the grass   5
does not raise above it.
Here is no question of whiteness,
white as can be, with a purple mole
at the center of each flower.
Each flower is a hand's span   10
of her whiteness. Wherever
his hand has lain there is
a tiny purple blemish. Each part
is a blossom under his touch
to which the fibers of her being   15
stem one by one, each to its end,
until the whole field is a
white desire, empty, a single stem,
a cluster, flower by flower,
a pious wish to whiteness gone over—   20
or nothing.

1925

THE BOTTICELLIAN TREES

The alphabet of
the trees

is fading in the
song of the leaves

the crossing   5
bars of the thin

letters that spelled
winter

and the cold
have been illumined   10

with
pointed green

by the rain and sun—
The strict simple

principles of   15
straight branches

are being modified
by pinched-out

ifs of color, devout
conditions   20

the smiles of love—
· · · · · ·

until the stript
sentences

move as a woman's   25
limbs under cloth

and praise from secrecy
quick with desire

love's ascendancy
in summer—   30

In summer the song
sings itself

above the muffled words—

1931

THIS IS JUST TO SAY

I have eaten
the plums
that were in
the icebox

and which
you were probably   5
saving
for breakfast

Forgive me
they were delicious   10
so sweet
and so cold

1934

TO A POOR OLD WOMAN

munching a plum on
the street a paper bag
of them in her hand

They taste good to her
They taste good   5
to her. They taste
good to her

You can see it by
the way she gives herself
to the one half   10
sucked out in her hand

Comforted
a solace of ripe plums
seeming to fill the air
They taste good to her   15

1938

YOUNG WOMAN AT A WINDOW

She sits with
tears on

her cheek
her cheek on

              her hand
              the child

              in her lap
              his nose

              pressed
              to the glass   10

                                                    1951

THE YELLOW FLOWER

What shall I say, because talk I must?
        That I have found a cure
                for the sick?

I have found no cure
        for the sick   5
                but this crooked flower
which only to look upon
        all men
                are cured. This
is that flower   10
        for which all men
                sing secretly their hymns
of praise. This
        is that sacred
                flower!   15

Can this be so?
        A flower so crooked
                and obscure? It is
a mustard flower,
        and not a mustard flower,   20
                a single spray
topping the deformed stem
        of fleshy leaves
                in this freezing weather
under glass.   25

An ungainly flower and
        an unnatural one,
                in this climate; what
can be the reason
        that it has picked me out   30
                to hold me, openmouthed,
rooted before this window

in the cold,
                my will
drained from me   35
            so that I have only eyes
                    for these yellow,
twisted petals   .   ?

That the sight,
            though strange to me,   40
                    must be a common one,
is clear: there are such flowers
            with such leaves
                    native to some climate
which they can call   45
            their own.

But why the torture
            and the escape through
                    the flower? It is
as if Michelangelo   50
            had conceived the subject
                    of his *Slaves* from this
—or might have done so.
            And did he not make
                    the marble bloom? I   55
am sad
            as he was sad
                    in his heroic mood.
But also
            I have eyes   60
                    that are made to see and if
they see ruin for myself
            and all that I hold
                    dear, they see
also   65
            through the eyes
                    and through the lips
and tongue the power
            to free myself
                    and speak of it, as   70
Michelangelo through his hands
            had the same, if greater,
                    power.

Which leaves, to account for,
            the tortured bodies   75
                    of

the slaves themselves
                and
                        the tortured body of my flower
which is not a mustard flower at all   80
                but some unrecognized
                        and unearthly flower
for me to naturalize
                and acclimate
                        and choose it for my own.   85

1954

Further Reading

Terrell, Carroll F., ed. *William Carlos Williams: Man and Poet.* Orono: U of Maine P, 1983. • Whitaker, Thomas R. *William Carlos Williams,* rev. ed. Boston: Twayne, 1989. • Townley, Rod. *The Early Poetry of William Carlos Williams.* Ithaca: Cornell UP, 1975. • Altieri, Charles. "A Test Case of Action Description: Interpreting Williams' 'This Is Just to Say.' " *Act and Quality: A Theory of Literary Meaning and Humanistic Understanding.* Amherst: U of Massachusetts P, 1981. 160–75. • Rapp, Carl. "Thinking as Salvation." *William Carlos Williams and Romantic Idealism.* Hanover: UP of New England, 1984. 121–48, spec. 136–40. • Glowka, Arthur W. "Williams' 'Queen Anne's Lace.' " *Explicator* 39.4 (Summer 1981): 25–26. Verdier, Douglas L. "Williams' 'Queen Anne's Lace.' " *Explicator* 40.1 (Fall 1981): 46–47.

William Carlos Williams's influence on contemporary American poetry has been enormous, not only because his poems were so widely admired but because his attitude toward poetry drew to him followers tired of poetry in the European tradition. This attitude shows in the following quotations drawn from various interviews.

William Carlos Williams: On the Poetry Made from American Prose

"Forcing twentieth-century America into a sonnet—gosh, how I hate sonnets—is like putting a crab into a square box. You've got to cut his legs off to make him fit. When you get through, you don't have a crab any more."

*   *   *   *

We were speaking straight ahead about what concerned us, and if I could have overheard what I was saying then, that would have given me a hint of how to phrase myself, to say what I had to say. Not after the establishment, but speaking straight ahead. I would gladly have traded what I have tried to say, for what came off my tongue, naturally. . . . I couldn't speak like the academy. It had to be modified by the conversation about me. As Marianne Moore used to say, a language dogs and cats could understand. So I think she agrees with me fundamentally. Not the speech of English country people, which would have something artificial about it; not that, but language modified by *our* environment; the American environment.

* * * *

The commonest situations in the world have the very essence of poetry if looked at correctly. If I take a dirty old woman in the street, it is not necessary to put her in the situation of a princess. All poets have a tendency to dress up an ordinary person, as Yeats does. It has to be a special treatment to be poetic, and I don't acknowledge this at all. I'd rather look at an old woman paring her nails as the essence of the "anti-poetic."

* * * *

I had a violent feeling that Eliot had betrayed what I believed in. He was looking backward; I was looking forward. He was a conformist, with wit, learning which I did not possess. He knew French, Latin, Arabic, God knows what. I was interested in that. But I felt he had rejected America and I refused to be rejected and so my reaction was violent. I realized the responsibility I must accept. I knew he would influence all subsequent American poets and take them out of my sphere. I had envisaged a new form of poetic composition, a form for the future. It was a shock to me that he was so tremendously successful; my contemporaries flocked to him— away from what I wanted. It forced me to be successful.

Not every poet is convinced, however, that Williams's influence has been benign. Robert Bly speaks for several others when he questions some of Williams's assumptions about what poetry should do.

Robert Bly: On the Dangers of Williams's Ideas

William Carlos Williams's work shows a similar attachment to objects. "No ideas but in things!" he said. His poems show great emotional life mingled with the drive of the intelligence to deal with outward things—but no inward life, if by inward life we mean an interest in spiritual development. Williams was a noble man, of all the poets in his generation the warmest and most human. Still, his ideas contained something destructive: there is in them a drive toward the extinction of personality. Williams's "No ideas but in things!" is a crippling program. Besides the ideas in things there are ideas in images and in feelings. True, bits of broken glass are preferable for poetry to fuzzy generalities such as virtue or patriotism. But images like Lorca's "black horses and dark people are riding over the deep roads of the guitar" also contain ideas and give birth to ideas. Williams asked poetry to confine itself to wheelbarrows, bottlecaps, weeds—with the artist "limited to the range of his contact with the objective world." Keeping close to the surface becomes an obsession. The effect of Williams's thought, therefore, was to narrow the language of poetry—to narrow it to general remarks mixed with bits of glass and paper bags, with what Pound called "natural objects." Williams says, "The good poetry is where the vividness comes up true like in prose but better. That's poetry."

BETWEEN WALLS

The back wings
of the

hospital where
nothing

will grow lie
cinders

in which shine
the broken

pieces of a green
bottle

In that Williams poem the personality and the imagination are merely two among many guests. The imagination has to exist as best it can in a poem crowded with objects. In the bare poems of some of Williams's followers the personality of the poet is diffused among lampposts and matchfolders, and vanishes. The poet appears in the poem only as a disembodied anger or an immovable eye.

MARIANNE MOORE

(1887–1972)

POETRY

I, too, dislike it: there are things that are important beyond all this
        fiddle.
    Reading it, however, with a perfect contempt for it, one discovers
            in it
    after all, a place for the genuine.

Hands that can grasp, eyes
    that can dilate, hair that can rise   5
        if it must, these things are important not because a

high-sounding interpretation can be put upon them but because they
        are
    useful. When they become so derivative as to become
        unintelligible,
    the same thing may be said for all of us, that we
        do not admire what   10
        we cannot understand: the bat
           holding on upside down or in quest of something to

eat, elephants pushing, a wild horse taking a roll, a tireless wolf under
    a tree, the immovable critic twitching his skin like a horse that
        feels a flea, the base-
    ball fan, the statistician—   15
        nor is it valid
        to discriminate against 'business documents and

school-books'; all these phenomena are important. One must make a
        distinction
    however: when dragged into prominence by half poets, the result is
        not poetry,
    nor till the poets among us can be   20
        'literalists of
        the imagination'—above
        insolence and triviality and can present

for inspection, imaginary gardens with real toads in them, shall we
        have
    it. In the meantime, if you demand on the one hand,   25
    the raw material of poetry in
        all its rawness and
        that which is on the other hand
        genuine, then you are interested in poetry.

1921

SILENCE

My father used to say,
"Superior people never make long visits,
have to be shown Longfellow's grave
or the glass flowers at Harvard.
Self-reliant like the cat—   5
that takes its prey to privacy,
the mouse's limp tail hanging like a shoelace from its mouth—

they sometimes enjoy solitude,
and can be robbed of speech
by speech which has delighted them.   10
The deepest feeling always shows itself in silence;
not in silence, but restraint."
Nor was he insincere in saying, "Make my house your inn."
Inns are not residences.

                                                                1921

THE FISH

wade
through black jade.
　　Of the crow-blue mussel shells, one keeps
　　adjusting the ash heaps;
　　　　opening and shutting itself like   5

an
injured fan.
　　The barnacles which encrust the side
　　of the wave, cannot hide
　　　　there for the submerged shafts of the   10

sun,
split like spun
　　glass, move themselves with spotlight swiftness
into the crevices—
　　in and out, illuminating   15

the
turquoise sea
　　of bodies. The water drives a wedge
　　of iron through the iron edge
　　　　of the cliff; whereupon the stars,   20

pink
rice-grains, ink-
　　bespattered jellyfish, crabs like green
　　lilies, and submarine
　　　　toadstools, slide each on the other.   25

All
external
　　marks of abuse are present on this
　　defiant edifice—
　　　　all the physical features of   30

ac-
cident—lack
   of cornice, dynamite grooves, burns, and
   hatchet strokes, these things stand
      out on it; the chasm side is   35

dead.
Repeated
   evidence has proved that it can live
   on what can not revive
      its youth. The sea grows old in it.   40

1921

PETER

   Strong and slippery,
built for the midnight grass-party
confronted by four cats, he sleeps his time away—
the detached first claw on the foreleg corresponding
to the thumb, retracted to its tip; the small tuft of fronds   5
or katydid-legs above each eye numbering all units
in each group; the shadbones regularly set about the mouth
to droop or rise in unison like porcupine-quills.
He lets himself be flattened out by gravity,
as seaweed is tamed and weakened by the sun,   10
compelled when extended, to lie stationary.
Sleep is the result of his delusion that one must
do as well as one can for oneself,
sleep—epitome of what is to him the end of life.
Demonstrate on him how the lady placed a forked stick   15
on the innocuous neck-sides of the dangerous southern snake.
One need not try to stir him up; his prune-shaped head
and alligator-eyes are not party to the joke.
Lifted and handled, he may be dangled like an eel
or set up on the forearm like a mouse;   20
his eyes bisected by pupils of a pin's width,
are flickeringly exhibited, then covered up.
May be? I should have said might have been;
when he has been got the better of in a dream—
as in a fight with nature or with cats, we all know it.   25
Profound sleep is not with him a fixed illusion.
Springing about with froglike accuracy, with jerky cries
when taken in hand, he is himself again;
to sit caged by the rungs of a domestic chair
would be unprofitable—human. What is the good of hypocrisy?   30

it is permissible to choose one's employment,
to abandon the nail, or roly-poly,
when it shows signs of being no longer a pleasure,
to score the nearby magazine with a double line of strokes.
He can talk but insolently says nothing. What of it?   35
 When one is frank, one's very presence is a compliment.
It is clear that he can see the virtue of naturalness,
that he does not regard the published fact as a surrender.
As for the disposition invariably to affront,
an animal with claws should have an opportunity to use them.   40
The eel-like extension of trunk into tail is not an accident.
To leap, to lengthen out, divide the air, to purloin, to pursue.
To tell the hen: fly over the fence, go in the wrong way
in your perturbation—this is life;
to do less would be nothing but dishonesty.   45

1935

FOUR QUARTZ CRYSTAL CLOCKS

There are four vibrators, the world's exactest clocks;
   and these quartz timepieces that tell
time intervals to other clocks,
   these worksless clocks work well;
independently the same, kept in   5
   the 41 Bell
     Laboratory time

vault. Checked by a comparator with Arlington,
   they punctualize the "radio,
cinéma," and "presse"—a group the   10
   Giraudoux truth-bureau
of hoped-for accuracy has termed
   "instruments of truth." We know—
     as Jean Giraudoux says

certain Arabs have not heard—that Napoleon   15
   is dead; that a quartz prism when
the temperature changes, feels
   the change and that the then
electrified alternate edges
   oppositely charged, threaten   20
     careful timing; so that

"*Four Quartz Crystal Clocks*": 11. *Jean Giraudoux* (1882–1944); a French novelist and dramatist.

this water-clear crystal as the Greeks used to say,
    this "clear ice" must be kept at the
same coolness. Repetition, with
    the scientist, should be   25
synonymous with accuracy.
    The lemur-student can see
        that an aye-aye is not

an angwan-tibo, potto, or loris. The sea-
    side burden should not embarrass   30
the bell-boy with the buoy-ball
    endeavoring to pass
hotel patronesses; nor could a
    practiced ear confuse the glass
        eyes for taxidermists   35

with eyeglasses from the optometrist. And as
    MEridian-seven one-two
one-two gives, each fifteenth second
    in the same voice, the new
data—"The time will be" so and so—   40
    you realize that "when you
        hear the signal," you'll be

hearing Jupiter or jour pater, the day god—
    the salvaged son of Father Time—
telling the cannibal Chronos   45
    (eater of his proxime
newborn progeny) that punctuality
    is not a crime.

                                                              1941

ELEPHANTS

Uplifted and waved till immobilized
wistaria-like, the opposing opposed
mouse-gray twined proboscises' trunk formed by two
trunks, fights itself to a spiraled inter-nosed

deadlock of dyke-enforced massiveness. It's a   5
knock-down drag-out fight that asks no quarter? Just

"*Four Quartz Crystal Clocks*": 28. *aye-aye:* a lemur.   29. *angwan-tibo:* a small African
primate.   *potto:* a small African primate.   *loris:* a small Asian primate.   43. *jour pater:* "day
father"; Jupiter is the god of day and son of Time.   45. *Chronos:* devoured all his children
except Jupiter (air), Neptune (water), and Pluto (the grave), which Time cannot consume.

a pastime, as when the trunk rains on itself
the pool siphoned up; or when—since each must

provide his forty-pound bough dinner—he broke
the leafy branches. These templars of the Tooth,   10
these matched intensities, take master care of
master tools. One, sleeping with the calm of youth,

at full length in the half-dry sun-flecked stream-bed,
rests his hunting-horn-curled trunk on shallowed stone.
The sloping hollow of the sleeper's body   15
cradles the gently breathing eminence's prone

mahout, asleep like a lifeless six-foot
frog, so feather light the elephant's stiff
ear's unconscious of the crossed feet's weight. And the
defenseless human thing sleeps as sound as if   20

incised with hard wrinkles, embossed with wide ears,
invincibly tusked, made safe by magic hairs!
As if, as if, it is all ifs; we are at
much unease. But magic's masterpiece is theirs—

Houdini's serenity quelling his fears.   25
Elephant-ear-witnesses-to-be of hymns
and glorias, these ministrants all gray or
gray with white on legs or trunk, are a pilgrims'

pattern of revery not reverence—a
religious procession without any priests,   30
the centuries-old carefullest unrehearsed
play. Blessed by Buddha's Tooth, the obedient beasts

themselves as toothed temples blessing the street, see
the white elephant carry the cushion that
carries the casket that carries the Tooth.   35
Amenable to what, matched with him, are gnat

trustees, he does not step on them as the white-
canopied blue-cushioned Tooth is augustly
and slowly returned to the shrine. Though white is
the color of worship and of mourning, he   40

is not here to worship and he is too wise
to mourn—a life prisoner but reconciled.
With trunk tucked up compactly—the elephant's
sign of defeat—he resisted, but is the child

---

17. *mahout:* the elephant keeper and driver.   27. *glorias:* hymns of praise.   32. *Buddha's Tooth:* Ceylonese elephants guard the tooth-relic of the Buddha, "the Enlightened one," in Kandy, a mountain city.

of reason now. His straight trunk seems to say: when   45
what we hoped for came to nothing, we revived.
As loss could not ever alter Socrates'
tranquillity, equanimity's contrived

by the elephant. With the Socrates of
animals as with Sophocles the Bee, on whose   50
tombstone a hive was incised, sweetness tinctures
his gravity. His held-up foreleg for use

as a stair, to be climbed or descended with
the aid of his ear, expounds the brotherhood
of creatures to man the encroacher, by the   55
small word with the dot, meaning know—the verb bůd.

These knowers "arouse the feeling that they are
allied to man" and can change roles with their trustees.
Hardship makes the soldier; then teachableness
makes him the philosopher—as Socrates,   60

prudently testing the suspicious thing, knew
the wisest is he who's not sure that he knows.
Who rides on a tiger can never dismount;
asleep on an elephant, that is repose.

1944

Further Reading

Hall, Donald. *Marianne Moore: The Cage and the Animal.* New York: Pegasus, 1970.
• Engel, Bernard. *Marianne Moore.* New York: Twayne, 1964. • Nitchie, George W.
Marianne Moore: An Introduction to the Poetry. New York: Columbia UP, 1969.
• Stapleton, Laurence. *Marianne Moore: The Poet's Advance.* Princeton: Princeton
UP, 1978. • Slatin, John M. *The Savage's Romance: The Poetry of Marianne Moore.*
University Park: The Pennsylvania State UP, 1986. • Plumly, Stanley. "Absent
Things." *Field: Contemporary Poetry and Poetics* 37 (Fall 1987): 31–34.

*In Marianne Moore's poems, animals and things are viewed with a clarity
that some readers have found too precise, too cold, too clinical. Robert Bly,
for instance, has complained that the animals in Moore's poems are always
really trophies of animals, suitable for display in a living room. The most*

---

47. *Socrates:* (470–399 B.C.); one of the earliest and greatest of Greek philosophers, known as
a seeker of virtue and tranquillity. 56. *bůd:* the Sanskrit verb for "knowing."

Marianne Moore   689

enthusiastic readers of Marianne Moore's poetry, however, respond to the concentration and affection she lavishes on the things of the world.

William Carlos Williams: On Moore's Simplicity of Design

There are two elements essential to Miss Moore's scheme of composition, the hard and unaffected concept of the apple itself as an idea, then its edge-to-edge contact with the things which surround it—the coil of a snake, leaves at various depths, or as it may be; and without connectives unless it be poetry, the inevitable connective, if you will. . . .

. . .

There must be edges. This casts some light I think on the simplicity of design in much of Miss Moore's work. There must be recognizable edges against the ground which cannot, as she might desire it, be left entirely white. Prose would be all black, a complete black painted or etched over, but solid.

There is almost no overlaying at all. The effect is of every object sufficiently uncovered to be easily recognizable. This simplicity, with the light coming through from between the perfectly plain masses, is however extremely bewildering to one who has been accustomed to look upon the usual "poem," the commonplace opaque board covered with vain curlicues. They forget, those who would read Miss Moore aright, that white circular discs grouped closely edge to edge upon a dark table make black six-pointed stars.

The "useful result" is an accuracy to which this simplicity of design greatly adds. The effect is for the effect to remain "true"; nothing loses its identity because of the composition, but the parts in their assembly remain quite as "natural" as before they were gathered. There is no "sentiment"; the softening effect of word upon word is nil; everything is in the style. To make this ten times evident is Miss Moore's constant care. There seems to be almost too great a wish to be transparent and it is here if anywhere that Miss Moore's later work will show a change, I think.

Elizabeth Bishop: On Moore's Visit to the Circus

I got to Madison Square Garden very early—we had settled on the hour because we wanted to see the animals before the show began—but Marianne was there ahead of me. She was loaded down: two blue cloth bags, one on each arm, and two huge brown paper bags, full of something. I was given one of these. They contained, she told me, stale brown bread for the elephants, because stale brown bread was one of the things they liked best to eat. (I later suspected that they might like stale white bread just as much but that Marianne had been thinking of their health.) As we went in and down to the lower level, where we could hear (and smell) the animals, she told me her preliminary plan for the circus. Her brother, Warner, had given her an elephant-hair bracelet, of which she was very fond, two or three strands of black hairs held together with gold clasps. One of the elephant hairs had fallen out and been lost. As I probably knew, elephant hairs grow only on the tops of the heads of very young elephants. In her bag, Marianne had a pair of strong nail scissors. I was to divert the adult elephants with the bread, and, if we were lucky, the guards wouldn't observe her at the end of the line where the babies were, and she could take out her scissors and snip a few hairs from a baby's head, to repair her bracelet.

She was quite right; the elephants adored stale brown bread and started trumpeting and pushing up against each other to get it. I stayed at one end of the line, putting slices of bread into the trunks of the older elephants, and Miss Moore went rapidly down to the other end, where the babies were. The large elephants were making such a to-do that a keeper did come up my way, and out of the corner of my eye I saw Miss Moore leaning forward over the rope on tiptoe, scissors in hand. Elephant hairs are tough; I thought she would never finish her hair-cutting. But she did, and triumphantly we handed out the rest of the bread and set off to see the other animals. She opened her bag and showed me three or four coarse, grayish hairs in a piece of Kleenex.

T. S. ELIOT

(1888–1965)

THE LOVE SONG OF J. ALFRED PRUFROCK

S'io credesse che mia risposta fosse
A persona che mai tornasse al mondo,
Questa fiamma staria senza piu scosse.
Ma perciocche giammai di questo fondo
Non torno vivo alcun, s'i'odo il vero,
Senza tema d'infamia ti rispondo.

"*The Love Song of J. Alfred Prufrock*": *S'io credesse . . . rispondo:* from Dante's *Inferno*, Canto 27: 61–66; Guido de Montefeltro, enclosed in a flame, tells Dante of the shame of his evil life: "If I thought that my reply would be to one who would ever return to the world [and tell others], this flame would move no more [with his speech]; but since no one has ever returned alive from such depth, if what I hear is true, I will answer without fear of being further disgraced."

Let us go then, you and I,
When the evening is spread out against the sky
Like a patient etherized upon a table;
Let us go, through certain half-deserted streets,
The muttering retreats   5
Of restless nights in one-night cheap hotels
And sawdust restaurants with oyster-shells:
Streets that follow like a tedious argument
Of insidious intent
To lead you to an overwhelming question . . .   10
Oh, do not ask, "What is it?"
Let us go and make our visit.

In the room the women come and go
Talking of Michelangelo.

The yellow fog that rubs its back upon the window-panes   15
The yellow smoke that rubs its muzzle on the window-panes
Licked its tongue into the corners of the evening,
Lingered upon the pools that stand in drains,
Let fall upon its back the soot that falls from chimneys,
Slipped by the terrace, made a sudden leap,   20
And seeing that it was a soft October night,
Curled once about the house, and fell asleep.

And indeed there will be time
For the yellow smoke that slides along the street,
Rubbing its back upon the window-panes;   25
There will be time, there will be time
To prepare a face to meet the faces that you meet;
There will be time to murder and create,
And time for all the works and days of hands
That lift and drop a question on your plate;   30
Time for you and time for me,
And time yet for a hundred indecisions,
And for a hundred visions and revisions,
Before the taking of a toast and tea.

In the room the women come and go   35
Talking of Michelangelo.

And indeed there will be time
To wonder, "Do I dare?" and, "Do I dare?"
Time to turn back and descend the stair,
With a bald spot in the middle of my hair—   40
[They will say: "How his hair is growing thin!"]

---

14. *Michelangelo:* the great sixteenth-century painter and sculptor.

My morning coat, my collar mounting firmly to the chin,
My necktie rich and modest, but asserted by a simple pin—
[They will say: "But how his arms and legs are thin!"]
Do I dare   45
Disturb the universe?
In a minute there is time
For decisions and revisions which a minute will reverse.

For I have known them all already, known them all:
Have known the evenings, mornings, afternoons,   50
I have measured out my life with coffee spoons;
I know the voices dying with a dying fall
Beneath the music from a farther room.
    So how should I presume?

And I have known the eyes already, known them all—   55
The eyes that fix you in a formulated phrase,
And when I am formulated, sprawling on a pin,
When I am pinned and wriggling on the wall,
Then how should I begin
To spit out all the butt-ends of my days and ways?   60
    And how should I presume?

And I have known the arms already, known them all—
Arms that are braceleted and white and bare

[But in the lamplight, downed with light brown hair!]
Is it perfume from a dress   65
That makes me so digress?
Arms that lie along a table, or wrap about a shawl.
    And should I then presume?
    And how should I begin?
            .   .   .   .   .
Shall I say, I have gone at dusk through narrow streets   70
And watched the smoke that rises from the pipes
Of lonely men in shirt-sleeves, leaning out of windows? . . .

I should have been a pair of ragged claws
Scuttling across the floors of silent seas.
            .   .   .   .   .
And the afternoon, the evening, sleeps so peacefully!   75
Smoothed by long fingers,
Asleep . . . tired . . . or it malingers,
Stretched on the floor, here beside you and me.
Should I, after tea and cakes and ices,
Have the strength to force the moment to its crisis?   80
But though I have wept and fasted, wept and prayed,
Though I have seen my head [grown slightly bald] brought in upon a
    platter,

I am no prophet—and here's no great matter;
I have seen the moment of my greatness flicker,   85
And I have seen the eternal Footman hold my coat, and snicker,
And in short, I was afraid.

And would it have been worth it, after all,
After the cups, the marmalade, the tea,
Among the porcelain, among some talk of you and me,   90
Would it have been worth while,
To have bitten off the matter with a smile,
To have squeezed the universe into a ball
To roll it toward some overwhelming question,
To say: "I am Lazarus, come from the dead,   95
Come back to tell you all, I shall tell you all"—
If one, settling a pillow by her head,
     Should say: "That is not what I meant at all.
     That is not it, at all."

And would it have been worth it, after all,   100
Would it have been worth while,
After the sunsets and the dooryards and the sprinkled streets,
After the novels, after the teacups, after the skirts that trail along the
          floor—
And this, and so much more?—
It is impossible to say just what I mean!   105
But as if a magic lantern threw the nerves in patterns on a screen:
Would it have been worth while
If one, settling a pillow or throwing off a shawl,
And turning toward the window, should say:
     "That is not it at all,   110
     That is not what I meant, at all."

                     .   .   .   .   .   .

No! I am not Prince Hamlet, nor was meant to be;
Am an attendant lord, one that will do
To swell a progress, start a scene or two,
Advise the prince; no doubt, an easy tool,   115
Deferential, glad to be of use,
Politic, cautious, and meticulous;
Full of high sentence, but a bit obtuse;
At times, indeed, almost ridiculous—
Almost, at times, the Fool.   120

I grow old . . . I grow old . . .
I shall wear the bottoms of my trousers rolled.

Shall I part my hair behind? Do I dare to eat a peach?
I shall wear white flannel trousers, and walk upon the beach.
I have heard the mermaids singing, each to each.   125

I do not think that they will sing to me.

I have seen them riding seaward on the waves
Combing the white hair of the waves blown back
When the wind blows the water white and black.

We have lingered in the chambers of the sea   130
By sea-girls wreathed with seaweed red and brown
Till human voices wake us, and we drown.

1915

PRELUDES

1

The winter evening settles down
With smell of steaks in passageways.
Six o'clock.
The burnt-out ends of smoky days.
And now a gusty shower wraps   5
The grimy scraps
Of withered leaves about your feet
And newspapers from vacant lots;
The showers beat
On broken blinds and chimney-pots,   10
And at the corner of the street
A lonely cab-horse steams and stamps.
And then the lighting of the lamps.

2

The morning comes to consciousness
Of faint stale smells of beer   15
From the sawdust-trampled street
With all its muddy feet that press
To early coffee-stands.
With the other masquerades
That time resumes,   20
One thinks of all the hands
That are raising dingy shades
In a thousand furnished rooms.

3

You tossed a blanket from the bed,
You lay upon your back, and waited;   25

T. S. Eliot   695

You dozed, and watched the night revealing
The thousand sordid images
Of which your soul was constituted;
And when all the world came back
And the light crept up between the shutters   30
And you heard the sparrows in the gutters,
And had such a vision of the street
As the street hardly understands;
Sitting along the bed's edge, where
You curled the papers from your hair,   35
Or clasped the yellow soles of feet
in the palms of both soiled hands.

4

His soul stretched tight across the skies
That fade behind a city block,
Or trampled by insistent feet   40
At four and five and six o'clock;
And short square fingers stuffing pipes,
And evening newspapers, and eyes
Assured of certain certainties,
The conscience of a blackened street   45
Impatient to assume the world.

    I am moved by fancies that are curled
Around these images, and cling:
The notion of some infinitely gentle
Infinitely suffering thing.   50

    Wipe your hand across your mouth, and laugh;
The worlds revolve like ancient women
Gathering fuel in vacant lots.

1917

JOURNEY OF THE MAGI

'A cold coming we had of it,
Just the worst time of the year

"Journey of the Magi": Magi: the Wise Men who visited Christ in Chapter 2 of Matthew. *[First
5 lines]* Eliot is quoting from Bishop Lancelot Andrewes's Christmas sermon of 1622.

For a journey, and such a long journey:
The ways deep and the weather sharp,
The very dead of winter.'   5
And the camels galled, sore-footed, refractory,
Lying down in the melting snow.
There were times we regretted
The summer palaces on slopes, the terraces,
And the silken girls bringing sherbet.   10
Then the camel men cursing and grumbling
And running away, and wanting their liquor and women,
And the night-fires going out, and the lack of shelters,
And the cities hostile and the towns unfriendly
And the villages dirty and charging high prices: 15
A hard time we had of it.
At the end we preferred to travel all night,
Sleeping in snatches,
With the voices singing in our ears, saying
That this was all folly.   20

Then at dawn we came down to a temperate valley,
Wet, below the snow line, smelling of vegetation;
With a running stream and a water-mill beating the darkness,
And three trees on the low sky,
And an old white horse galloped away in the meadow.   25
Then we came to a tavern with vine-leaves over the lintel,
Six hands at an open door dicing for pieces of silver,
And feet kicking the empty wine-skins.
But there was no information, and so we continued
And arrived at evening, not a moment too soon   30
Finding the place; it was (you may say) satisfactory.

All this was a long time ago, I remember,
And I would do it again, but set down
This set down
This: were we led all that way for   35
Birth or Death? There was a Birth, certainly,
We had evidence and no doubt. I had seen birth and death,
But had thought they were different; this Birth was
Hard and bitter agony for us, like Death, our death.
We returned to our places, these Kingdoms,   40
But no longer at ease here, in the old dispensation,
With an alien people clutching their gods.
I should be glad of another death.

1927

ANIMULA

'Issues from the hand of God, the simple soul'
To a flat world of changing lights and noise,
To light, dark, dry or damp, chilly or warm;
Moving between the legs of tables and of chairs,
Rising or falling, grasping at kisses and toys,   5
Advancing boldly, sudden to take alarm,
Retreating to the corner of arm and knee,
Eager to be reassured, taking pleasure
In the fragrant brilliance of the Christmas tree,
Pleasure in the wind, the sunlight and the sea;   10
Studies the sunlit pattern on the floor
And running stags around a silver tray;
Confounds the actual and the fanciful,
Content with playing-cards and kings and queens,
What the fairies do and what the servants say.   15
The heavy burden of the growing soul
Perplexes and offends more, day by day;
Week by week, offends and perplexes more
With the imperatives of 'is and seems'
And may and may not, desire and control.   20
The pain of living and the drug of dreams
Curl up the small soul in the window seat
Behind the *Encyclopedia Britannica*.
Issues from the hand of time the simple soul
Irresolute and selfish, misshapen, lame,   25
Unable to fare forward or retreat,
Fearing the warm reality, the offered good,
Denying the importunity of the blood,
Shadow of its own shadows, spectre in its own gloom,
Leaving disordered papers in a dusty room;   30
Living first in the silence after the viaticum.

    Pray for Guiterriez, avid of speed and power,
For Boudin, blown to pieces,
For this one who made a great fortune,
And that one who went in his own way.   35
Pray for Floret, by the boarhound slain between the yew trees,
Pray for us now and at the hour of our birth.

1929

Animula: "a little soul" (Latin).   1. *Issues . . . soul:* taken from Dante's *Purgatorio,* Canto 16:
85–93; in response to Dante's question about the origin of evil, Marco Lombardo locates it in
man, particularly in evil leaders.

THE HOLLOW MEN

Mistah Kurtz—he dead.

A penny for the Old Guy

1

We are the hollow men
We are the stuffed men
Leaning together
Headpiece filled with straw. Alas!
Our dried voices, when   5
We whisper together
Are quiet and meaningless
As wind in dry grass
Or rats' feet over broken glass
In our dry cellar   10

    Shape without form, shade without color,
Paralysed force, gesture without motion;

    Those who have crossed
With direct eyes, to death's other Kingdom
Remember us—if at all—not as lost   15
Violent souls, but only
As the hollow men
The stuffed men.

2

Eyes I dare not meet in dreams
In death's dream kingdom   20
These do not appear:
There, the eyes are
Sunlight on a broken column
There, is a tree swinging
And voices are   25
In the wind's singing
More distant and more solemn
Than a fading star.

    Let me be no nearer
In death's dream kingdom   30
Let me also wear

"The Hollow Men": Mistah Kurtz—he dead: from Joseph Conrad's *Heart of Darkness;* Kurtz is a
"lost violent soul." *A penny . . . Guy:* In the annual celebration of Guy Fawkes Day, children
beg money for fireworks to set off in honor of the defeat of Fawkes's "gunpowder plot"
against King James I.

Such deliberate disguises
Rat's coat, crowskin, crossed staves
In a field
Behaving as the wind behaves   35
No nearer—

   Not that final meeting
In the twilight kingdom

                     3

This is the dead land
This is cactus land   40
Here the stone images
Are raised, here they receive
The supplication of a dead man's hand
Under the twinkle of a fading star.

   Is it like this   45
In death's other kingdom
Waking alone
At the hour when we are
Trembling with tenderness
Lips that would kiss   50
Form prayers to broken stone.

                     4

The eyes are not here
There are no eyes here
In this valley of dying stars
In this hollow valley   55
This broken jaw of our lost kingdoms

   In this last of meeting places
We grope together
And avoid speech
Gathered on this beach of the tumid river   60

   Sightless, unless
The eyes reappear
As the perpetual star
Multifoliate rose
Of death's twilight kingdom   65
The hope only
Of empty men.

                     5

Here we go round the prickly pear
Prickly pear prickly pear

Here we go round the prickly pear   70
At five o'clock in the morning.

   Between the idea
And the reality
Between the motion
And the act   75
Falls the shadow
     For Thine is the Kingdom

   Between the conception
And the creation
Between the emotion   80
And the response
Falls the Shadow
     Life is very long

   Between the desire
And the spasm   85
Between the potency
And the existence
Between the essence
And the descent
Falls the Shadow.   90
     For Thine is the Kingdom

   For Thine is
Life is
For Thine is the

   This is the way the world ends   95
This is the way the world ends
This is the way the world ends
Not with a bang but a whimper.

1936

Further Reading

Eliot, T. S. "Tradition and the Individual Talent." *The Sacred Wood: Essays on Poetry and Criticism.* New York: Methuen, 1920. 47–59. • Smith, Grover. *T. S. Eliot's Poetry and Plays.* 2nd ed. Chicago: U of Chicago P, 1974. • Raffel, Burton. *T. S. Eliot.* New York: Ungar, 1982. 8–18. • Pinion, F. B. *A T. S. Eliot Companion.* London: Macmillan, 1986. • Everett, Barbara. "In Search of Prufrock." *Critical*

Inquiry 16.2 (Summer 1974): 101–21. • Franklin, Rosemary. "The Satisfactory Journey of Eliot's Magus." *English Studies* 49.6 (Dec. 1969): 559–61.

T. S. Eliot's emphasis on the separation of the poet's personality from the poem itself has caused considerable controversy. Some poets agree that their job is not to describe an emotion, but to create an "objective correlative" of the emotion. Poet and reader, experiencing the correlative, will have the emotion rise from it. Other poets find Eliot's methods too cold, too distanced.

William Butler Yeats: On Monotony in Eliot

Eliot has produced his great effect upon his generation because he has described men and women that get out of bed or into it from mere habit; in describing this life that has lost heart his own art seems grey, cold, dry. He is an Alexander Pope, working without apparent imagination, producing his effects by a rejection of all rhythms and metaphors used by the more popular romantics rather than by the discovery of his own, this rejection giving his work an unexaggerated plainness that has the effect of novelty. He has the rhythmical flatness of the *Essay on Man*—despite Miss Sitwell's advocacy I see Pope as Blake and Keats saw him—later, in *The Waste Land,* amid much that is moving in symbol and imagery there is much monotony of accent:

> When lovely woman stoops to folly and
> Paces about her room again, alone,
> She smooths her hair with automatic hand,
> And puts a record on the gramophone.

I was affected, as I am by these lines, when I saw for the first time a painting by Manet. I longed for the vivid colour and light of Rousseau and Courbet, I could not endure the grey middle-tint—and even to-day Manet gives me an incomplete pleasure; he had left the procession. Nor can I put the Eliot of these poems among those that descend from Shakespeare and the translators of the Bible. I think of him as satirist rather than poet. Once only does that early work speak in the great manner:

> The host with someone indistinct
> Converses at the door apart,
> The nightingales are singing near
> The Convent of the Sacred Heart,
>
> And sang within the bloody wood
> When Agamemnon cried aloud,
> And let their liquid siftings fall
> To stain the stiff dishonoured shroud.

Not until *The Hollow Men* and *Ash-Wednesday,* where he is helped by the short lines, and in the dramatic poems where his remarkable sense of actor, chanter, scene, sweeps him away, is there rhythmical animation.

T. S. Eliot: On Feeling Rather Than Emotion in Poetry

The progress of an artist is a continual self-sacrifice, a continual extinction of personality.

There remains to define this process of depersonalization and its relation to the sense of tradition. It is in this depersonalization that art may be said to approach the condition of science. I shall, therefore, invite you to consider, as a suggestive analogy, the action which takes place when a bit of finely filiated platinum is introduced into a chamber containing oxygen and sulphur dioxide. . . .

When the two gases . . . are mixed in the presence of a filament of platinum, they form sulphurous acid. This combination takes place only if the platinum is present; nevertheless the newly formed acid contains no trace of platinum, and the platinum itself is apparently unaffected; has remained inert, neutral, and unchanged. The mind of the poet is the shred of platinum. It may partly or exclusively operate upon the experience of the man himself; but, the more perfect the artist, the more completely separate in him will be the man who suffers and the mind which creates; the more perfectly will the mind digest and transmute the passions which are its material.

The experience, you will notice, the elements which enter the presence of the transforming catalyst, are of two kinds: emotions and feelings. The effect of a work of art upon the person who enjoys it is an experience different in kind from any experience not of art. It may be formed out of one emotion, or may be a combination of several; and various feelings, inhering for the writer in particular words or phrases or images, may be added to compose the final result. Or great poetry may be made without the direct use of any emotion whatever: composed out of feelings solely. . . .

The poet's mind is in fact a receptacle for seizing and storing up numberless feelings, phrases, images, which remain there until all the particles which can unite to form a new compound are present together.

If you compare several representative passages of the greatest poetry you see how great is the variety of types of combination, and also how completely any semi-ethical criterion of 'sublimity' misses the mark. For it is not the 'greatness', the intensity, of the emotions, the components, but the intensity of the artistic process, the pressure, so to speak, under which the fusion takes place, that counts.

EDNA ST. VINCENT MILLAY

(1892–1950)

RECUERDO

We were very tired, we were very merry—
We had gone back and forth all night on the ferry.
It was bare and bright, and smelled like a stable—
But we looked into a fire, we leaned across a table,
We lay on a hill-top underneath the moon;   5
And the whistles kept blowing, and the dawn came soon.

We were very tired, we were very merry—
We had gone back and forth all night on the ferry;
And you ate an apple, and I ate a pear,
From a dozen of each we had bought somewhere;   10
And the sky went wan, and the wind came cold,
And the sun rose dripping, a bucketful of gold.

We were very tired, we were very merry,
We had gone back and forth all night on the ferry.
We hailed, "Good morrow, mother!" to a shawl-
   covered head,   15
And bought a morning paper, which neither of us read;
And she wept, "God bless you!" for the apples and pears,
And we gave her all our money but our subway fares.

1920

SPRING

To what purpose, April, do you return again?
Beauty is not enough.
You can no longer quiet me with the redness
Of little leaves opening stickily.
I know what I know.   5
The sun is hot on my neck as I observe
The spikes of the crocus.
The smell of the earth is good.
It is apparent that there is no death.
But what does that signify?   10
Not only under ground are the brains of men

"Recuerdo": Recuerdo: "reminiscence" (Spanish).

Eaten by maggots.
Life in itself
Is nothing,
An empty cup, a flight of uncarpeted stairs.   15
It is not enough that yearly, down this hill,
April
Comes like an idiot, babbling and strewing flowers.

1921

LOVE IS NOT ALL: IT IS NOT MEAT NOR DRINK

Love is not all: it is not meat nor drink
Nor slumber nor a roof against the rain;
Nor yet a floating spar to men that sink
And rise and sink and rise and sink again;
Love can not fill the thickened lung with breath,   5
Nor clean the blood, nor set the fractured bone;
Yet many a man is making friends with death
Even as I speak, for lack of love alone.
It well may be that in a difficult hour,
Pinned down by pain and moaning for release,   10
Or nagged by want past resolution's power,
I might be driven to sell your love for peace,
Or trade the memory of this night for food.
It well may be. I do not think I would.

1931

FROM A TRAIN WINDOW

Precious in the light of the early sun the Housatonic
Between its not unscalable mountains flows.
Precious in the January morning the shabby fur of the cat-tails by the
    stream.
The farmer driving his horse to the feed-store for a sack of cracked
    corn
Is not in haste; there is no whip in the socket.   5

Pleasant enough, gay even, by no means sad
Is the rickety graveyard on the hill. Those are not cypress trees
Perpendicular among the lurching slabs, but cedars from the
    neighbourhood,
Native to this rocky land, self-sown. Precious
In the early light, reassuring   10

Is the grave-scarred hillside.
As if after all, the earth might know what it is about.

1934

THE OAK-LEAVES

Yet in the end, defeated too, worn out and ready to fall,
Hangs from the drowsy tree with cramped and desperate stem above
    the ditch the last leaf of all.

There is something to be learned, I guess, from looking at the dead
    leaves under the living tree;
Something to be set to a lusty tune and learned and sung, it well
    might be;
Something to be learned—though I was ever a ten-o'clock scholar at
    this school—   5
Even perhaps by me.

But my heart goes out to the oak-leaves that are the last to sigh
"Enough," and loose their hold;
They have boasted to the nudging frost and to the two-and-thirty
    winds that they would never die,
Never even grow old.   10
(These are those russet leaves that cling
All winter, even into the spring,
To the dormant bough, in the wood knee-deep in snow the only
    coloured thing.)

1934

CHILDHOOD IS THE KINGDOM WHERE NOBODY DIES

Childhood is not from birth to a certain age and at a certain age
The child is grown, and puts away childish things.
Childhood is the kingdom where nobody dies.

Nobody that matters, that is. Distant relatives of course
Die, whom one never has seen or has seen for an hour,   5
And they gave one candy in a pink-and-green striped bag, or a
    jack-knife,
And went away, and cannot really be said to have lived at all.

And cats die. They lie on the floor and lash their tails,
And their reticent fur is suddenly all in motion
With fleas that one never knew were there,   10
Polished and brown, knowing all there is to know,

Trekking off into the living world.
You fetch a shoe-box, but it's much too small, because she won't curl
    up now:
So you find a bigger box, and bury her in the yard, and weep.   15
But you do not wake up a month from then, two months,
A year from then, two years, in the middle of the night
And weep, with your knuckles in your mouth, and say Oh, God! Oh,
    God!
Childhood is the kingdom where nobody dies that matters,—mothers
    and fathers don't die.

And if you have said, "For heaven's sake, must you always be kissing a
    person?"   20
Or, "I do wish to gracious you'd stop tapping on the window with
    your thimble!"
Tomorrow, or even the day after tomorrow if you're busy having fun,
Is plenty of time to say, "I'm sorry, mother."

To be grown up is to sit at the table with people who have died, who
    neither listen nor speak;
Who do not drink their tea, though they always said   25
Tea was such a comfort.

Run down into the cellar and bring up the last jar of raspberries; they
    are not tempted.
Flatter them, ask them what was it they said exactly
That time, to the bishop, or to the overseer, or to Mrs. Mason;   30
They are not taken in.
Shout at them, get red in the face, rise,
Drag them up out of their chairs by their stiff shoulders and shake
    them and yell at them;
They are not startled, they are not even embarrassed; they slide back
    into their chairs.

Your tea is cold now.   35
You drink it standing up,
And leave the house.

1934

MODERN DECLARATION

I, having loved ever since I was a child a few things, never having
    wavered
In these affections; never through shyness in the houses of the rich
    or in the presence of clergymen having denied these loves;   5
Never when worked upon by cynics like chiropractors having grunted
    or clicked a vertebra to the discredit of these loves;

Never when anxious to land a job having diminished them by a
    conniving smile; or when befuddled by drink
Jeered at them through heartache or lazily fondled the   10
 fingers of their alert enemies; declare

That I shall love you always.
No matter what party is in power;
No matter what temporarily expedient combination of allied interests
    wins the war;   15
Shall love you always.

1939

AN ANCIENT GESTURE

I thought, as I wiped my eyes on the corner of my apron:
Penelope did this too.
And more than once: you can't keep weaving all day
And undoing it all through the night;
Your arms get tired, and the back of your neck gets tight;   5
And along towards morning, when you think it will never be light,
And your husband has been gone, and you don't know where, for
    years,
Suddenly you burst into tears;
There is simply nothing else to do.   10

And I thought, as I wiped my eyes on the corner of my apron:
This is an ancient gesture, authentic, antique,
In the very best tradition, classic, Greek;
Ulysses did this too.
But only as a gesture,—a gesture which implied   15
To the assembled throng that he was much too moved to speak.
He learned it from Penelope . . .
Penelope, who really cried.

1954

Further Reading

Brittin, Norman A. *Edna St. Vincent Millay*. Boston: Twayne, 1982. • Gould, Jean.
The Poet and Her Book. New York: Dodd, 1969. • Tanselle, G. Thomas. "Millay, Dell,
and 'Recuerdo.'" *Colby Library Quarterly* 6 (Mar. 1963): 202–05. • Fried, Debra.
"Andromeda Unbound: Gender and Genre in Millay's Sonnets." *Twentieth Century*

Literature 31.4 (Winter 1985): 1–22. • Libera, Sharon Mayer. "Maine Remembered." *Parnassus* 5.1 (Fall–Winter 1976): 200–12.

Edna St. Vincent Millay's early poetry appealed to a wide audience in the 1920s, when women were emerging from traditional roles and asserting a new independence of thought and action. Serious readers of her later poetry seldom doubted her talent, but some wondered whether her themes matured as she grew older. Louise Bogan, her contemporary, reviewed the poems in Wine from These Grapes *(1934) with great enthusiasm, feeling that Millay had made "a successful passage from the emotions and point of view of a rebellious girl to that of a maturely contemplative woman." Reviewing* Huntsman, What Quarry? *(1939), she was somewhat disappointed.*

Louise Bogan: On Millay's Strengths and Weaknesses

It is difficult to say what a woman poet should concern herself with as she grows older, because woman poets who have produced an impressively bulky body of work are few. But is there any reason to believe that a woman's spiritual fibre is less sturdy than a man's? Is it not possible for a woman to come to terms with herself, if not with the world; to withdraw more and more, as time goes on, her own personality from her productions; to stop childish fears of death and eschew charming rebellions against facts? Certainly some fragments of Sappho are more "mature" than others. And Christina Rossetti, who lived an anonymous life and somewhat resembled, according to the cruel wit of Max Beerbohm, "a pew-opener," explored regions which Miss Millay has not yet entered. And there is the case of Emily Dickinson.

Miss Millay has always fought, and is still fighting, injustice. She is still subject to moods of self-disgust as well as to moods of mutiny against mankind's infringements on its own human decency. Once or twice she contemplates a truce which "slackens the mind's allegiance to despair." And twice—in the poem just quoted and in the recessively titled "The Princess Recalls Her One Adventure"—she writes as beautiful lyrics as she has ever written. But what has happened to the kind of development announced in *Wine from These Grapes,* the most kindly disposed reader cannot say. If Miss Millay should give up for good the idea that "wisdom" and "peace" are stuffy concepts, perhaps that development might be renewed.

WILFRED OWEN

(1893–1918)

ANTHEM FOR DOOMED YOUTH

What passing-bells for these who die as cattle?
   Only the monstrous anger of the guns.
   Only the stuttering rifles' rapid rattle
Can patter out their hasty orisons.
No mockeries now for them; no prayers nor bells,   5
   Nor any voice of mourning save the choirs—
The shrill, demented choirs of wailing shells;
   And bugles calling for them from sad shires.

What candles may be held to speed them all?
   Not in the hands of boys, but in their eyes   10
Shall shine the holy glimmers of good-byes.
   The pallor of girls' brows shall be their pall;
Their flowers the tenderness of patient minds,
And each slow dusk a drawing-down of blinds.

1920

ARMS AND THE BOY

Let the boy try along this bayonet-blade
How cold steel is, and keen with hunger of blood;
Blue with all malice, like a madman's flash;
And thinly drawn with famishing for flesh.

Lend him to stroke these blind, blunt bullet-heads   5
Which long to nuzzle in the hearts of lads,
Or give him cartridges of fine zinc teeth,
Sharp with the sharpness of grief and death.

For his teeth seem for laughing round an apple
There lurk no claws behind his fingers supple;   10
And God will grow no talons at his heels,
Nor antlers through the thickness of his curls.

1920

DULCE ET DECORUM EST

Bent double, like old beggars under sacks,
Knock-kneed, coughing like hags, we crushed through sludge,

Till on the haunting flares we turned our backs
And towards our distant rest began to trudge.
Men marched asleep. Many had lost their boots   5
But limped on, blood-shod. All went lame; all blind;
Drunk with fatigue; deaf even to the hoots
Of tired, outstripped Five-Nines that dropped behind.

Gas! Gas! Quick, boys!—An ecstasy of fumbling,
Fitting the clumsy helmets just in time;   10
But someone still was yelling out and stumbling
And flound'ring like a man in fire or lime . . .
Dim, through the misty panes and thick green light,
As under a green sea, I saw him drowning.

In all my dreams, before my helpless sight,   15
He plunges at me, guttering, choking, drowning.

If in some smothering dreams you too could pace
Behind the wagon that we flung him in,
And watch the white eyes writhing in his face,
His hanging face, like a devil's sick of sin;   20
If you could hear, at every jolt, the blood
Come gargling from the froth-corrupted lungs,
Obscene as cancer, bitter as the cud
Of vile, incurable sores on innocent tongues,—
My friend, you would not tell with such high zest   25
To children ardent for some desperate glory,
The old Lie: Dulce et decorum est
Pro patria mori.

1920

DISABLED

He sat in a wheeled chair, waiting for dark,
And shivered in his ghastly suit of grey,
Legless, sewn short at elbow. Through the park
Voices of boys rang saddening like a hymn,
Voices of play and pleasure after day,   5
Till gathering sleep had mothered them from him.

About this time Town used to swing so gay
When glow-lamps budded in the light blue trees,
And girls glanced lovelier as the air grew dim,—

"*Dulce et Decorum Est*": 8. *Five-Nines:* 5.9 caliber shells.   27–28. *Dulce . . . mori:* "It is sweet
and honorable to die for one's country."—Horace.

In the old times, before he threw away his knees.   10
Now he will never feel again how slim
Girls' waists are, or how warm their subtle hands;
All of them touch him like some queer disease.

There was an artist silly for his face,
For it was younger than his youth, last year.   15
Now, he is old; his back will never brace;
He's lost his color very far from here,
Poured it down shell-holes till the veins ran dry,
And half his lifetime lapsed in the hot race,
And leap of purple spurted from his thigh.   20

One time he liked a blood-smear down his leg,
After the matches, carried shoulder-high
It was after football, when he'd drunk a peg.
He thought he'd better join.—He wonders why.
Someone had said he'd look a god in kilts,   25
That's why; and may be, too, to please his Meg;
Aye, that was it, to please the giddy jilts
He asked to join. He didn't have to beg;
Smiling they wrote his lie; aged nineteen years.
Germans he scarcely thought of; all their guilt,   30
And Austria's, did not move him. And no fears
Of Fear came yet. He thought of jeweled hilts
For daggers in plaid socks; of smart salutes;
And care of arms; and leave; and pay arrears;
Esprit de corps; and hints for young recruits.   35
And soon, he was drafted out with drums and cheers.

Some cheered him home, but not as crowds cheer Goal.
Only a solemn man who brought him fruits
Thanked him; and then inquired about his soul.
Now, he will spend a few sick years in Institutes,   40
And do what things the rules consider wise,
And take whatever pity they may dole.
Tonight he noticed how the women's eyes
Passed from him to the strong men that were whole.
How cold and late it is! Why don't they come   45
And put him into bed? Why don't they come?

                                                        1920

---

23. *peg:* a shot of liquor   27. *jilts:* women who discard their lovers.   37. *cheer Goal:* that is, cheer for a goal in a soccer match.

Further Reading

Stallworthy, Jon. *Wilfred Owen.* London: Oxford UP, 1974. 217–28. • Lane, Arthur E. *An Adequate Response: The War Poetry of Wilfred Owen and Siegfried Sassoon.* Detroit: Wayne State UP, 1972. 134–37, 150–51. • White, Gertrude M. *Wilfred Owen.* New York: Twayne, 1969. • Lomas, Herbert. "The Critic and the Anti-Hero: War Poetry." *Hudson Review* 38.3 (Autumn 1985): 376–89.

The poet who writes about war has two great obstacles to overcome. First, a subject so public may not produce poems that either writer or reader can feel as personal statements. Second, the poet's theme is predictable: rarely (in this century at least) will we find poems in praise of war, and it is difficult to write a fresh poem deploring what has so often been deplored before. If we look at several war poems together, we get a sense of the different ways poets have overcome these obstacles.

Some War Poems Before and After Wilfred Owen

Niccolò Degli Albizzi

(13th century)

PROLONGED SONNET
WHEN THE TROOPS
WERE RETURNING FROM MILAN

translated from the Italian by Dante Gabriel Rossetti

If you could see, fair brother, how dead beat
   The fellows look who come through Rome to-day,—
   Black-yellow smoke-dried visages,—you'd say
   They thought their haste at going all too fleet.
Their empty victual-wagons up the street   5
   Over the bridge dreadfully sound and sway;
   Their eyes, as hanged men's, turning the wrong way;
   And nothing on their backs, or heads, or feet.
One sees the ribs and all the skeletons
   Of their gaunt horses; and a sorry sight   10

Are the torn saddles, crammed with straw and stones.
They are ashamed, and march throughout the night,
    Stumbling, for hunger, on their marrowbones;
    Like barrels rolling, jolting, in this plight.
    Their arms all gone, not even their swords are saved;   15
    And each as silent as a man being shaved.

ca. 1300

Walt Whitman

(1819–1892)

I SAW THE VISION OF ARMIES

I saw the vision of armies;
And I saw, as in noiseless dreams, hundreds of battle-flags;
Borne through the smoke of the battles, and pierc'd with missiles, I
    saw them,
And carried hither and yon through the smoke, and torn and bloody;

And at last but a few shreds of the flags left on the staffs, (and all in
    silence,)   5
And the staffs all splinter'd and broken.

I saw battle-corpses, myriads of them,
And the white skeletons of young men—I saw them;
I saw the debris and debris of all dead soldiers;
But I saw they were not as was thought;   10
They themselves were fully at rest—they suffer'd not;
The living remain'd and suffer'd—the mother suffer'd,
And the wife and the child, and the musing comrade suffer'd,
And the armies that remained suffer'd.

1865

Thomas Hardy

(1840–1928)

CHANNEL FIRING

That night your great guns, unawares,
Shook all our coffins as we lay,

And broke the chancel window-squares,
We thought it was the Judgment-day

And sat upright. While drearisome   5
Arose the howl of wakened hounds:
The mouse let fall the altar-crumb,
The worms drew back into the mounds,

The glebe cow drooled. Till God called, "No;
It's gunnery practice out at sea   10
Just as before you went below;
The world is as it used to be:

"All nations striving strong to make
Red war yet redder. Mad as hatters
They do no more for Christés sake   15
Than you who are helpless in such matters.

"That this is not the judgment-hour
For some of them's a blessed thing,
For if it were they'd have to scour
Hell's floor for so much threatening. . . .   20

"Ha, ha. It will be warmer when
I blow the trumpet (if indeed
I ever do; for you are men,
And rest eternal sorely need)."

So down we lay again. "I wonder,   25
Will the world ever saner be,"
Said one, "than when He sent us under
In our indifferent century!"

And many a skeleton shook his head.—
"Instead of preaching forty year,"   30
My neighbour Parson Thirdly said,
"I wish I had stuck to pipes and beer."

Again the guns disturbed the hour,
Roaring their readiness to avenge,
As far inland as Stourton Tower,   35
And Camelot, and starlit Stonehenge.

                                                              1914

---

9. *glebe:* a small plot of land granted to a clergyman.   35. *Stourton Tower:* in the ninth
century, King Alfred's Tower.   36. *Camelot:* the legendary site of King Arthur's court. *Stonehenge:* Hardy associated this prehistoric circle of stones with legendary prophets and
sorcerers, the Druids.

Arthur Rimbaud

(1854–1891)

THE SLEEPER IN THE VALLEY

translated from the French by Robert Lowell

The swollen river sang through the green hole,
and madly hooked white tatters on the grass.
Light escaladed the hot hills. The whole
valley bubbled with sunbeams like a beer-glass.

The conscript was open-mouthed; his bare head   5
and neck swam in the bluish water cress.
He slept. The mid-day soothed his heaviness,
sunlight was raining into his green bed,

and baked the bruises from his body, rolled
as a sick child might hug itself asleep . . .   10
Oh Nature, rock him warmly, he is cold.

The flowers no longer make his hot eyes weep.
The river sucks his hair. His blue eye rolls.
He sleeps. In his right side are two red holes.

1870, trans. 1961

Joy Davidman

(1915–1960)

SNOW IN MADRID

Softly, so casual,
Lovely, so light, so light,
The cruel sky lets fall
Something one does not fight.

How tenderly to crown   5
The brutal year

"Snow in Madrid": Madrid: the Nationalist forces in the Spanish Civil War bombed Madrid in
1937.

The clouds send something down
That one need not fear.

Men before perishing
See with unwounded eye   10
For once a gentle thing
Fall from the sky.

                                                        1938

Anthony Hecht

(b. 1923)

"MORE LIGHT! MORE LIGHT!"

for Heinrich Blücher and Hannah Arendt

Composed in the Tower before his execution
These moving verses, and being brought at that time
Painfully to the stake, submitted, declaring thus:
"I implore my God to witness that I have made no crime."

Nor was he forsaken of courage, but the death was horrible,   5
The sack of gunpowder failing to ignite.
His legs were blistered sticks on which the black sap
Bubbled and burst as he howled for the Kindly Light.

And that was but one, and by no means one of the worst;
Permitted at least his pitiful dignity;   10
And such as were by, made prayers in the name of Christ,
That shall judge all men, for his soul's tranquillity.

We move now to outside a German wood.
Three men are there commanded to dig a hole
In which the two Jews are ordered to lie down   15
And be buried alive by the third, who is a Pole.

Not light from the shrine at Weimar beyond the hill
Nor light from heaven appeared. But he did refuse.

"*More Light! More Light!*": *More light:* The last words spoken by the German poet Goethe
before he died. *Heinrich Blücher and Hannah Arendt:* German husband and wife who
emigrated to the United States in 1941; she is known as the author of several books on totali-
tarianism. 1. *Tower:* Tower of London. 8. *Kindly Light:* "Lead, Kindly Light" is a hymn
written by John Henry Newman in 1833. 17. *Weimar:* the setting of the poem is Buchen-
wald, a Nazi concentration camp north of Weimar; Goethe spent most of his life in Weimar,
which is now the site of the Goethe National Museum.

A Luger settled back deeply in its glove.
He was ordered to change places with the Jews.   20

Much casual death had drained away their souls.
The thick dirt mounted toward the quivering chin.
When only the head was exposed the order came
To dig him out again and to get back in.

No light, no light in the blue Polish eye.   25
When he finished a riding boot packed down the earth.
The Luger hovered lightly in its glove.
He was shot in the belly and in three hours bled to death.

1961

Denise Levertov

(b. 1923)

LIFE AT WAR

The disasters numb within us
caught in the chest, rolling
in the brain like pebbles. The feeling
resembles lumps of raw dough

weighing down a child's stomach on baking day.   5
Or Rilke said it, 'My heart . . .
Could I say of it, it overflows
with bitterness . . . but no, as though

its contents were simply balled into
formless lumps, thus   10
do I carry it about.'
The same war

continues.
We have breathed the grits of it in, all our lives,
our lungs are pocked with it,   15
the mucous membrane of our dreams
coated with it, the imagination
filmed over with the gray filth of it:

the knowledge that humankind,

"More Light! More Light!": 19. *Luger:* a German automatic pistol.

delicate Man, whose flesh
responds to a caress, whose eyes
are flowers that perceive the stars,   20

whose music excels the music of birds,
whose laughter matches the laughter of dogs,
whose understanding manifests designs   25
fairer than the spider's most intricate web,

still turns without surprise, with mere regret
to the scheduled breaking open of breasts whose milk
runs out over the entrails of still-alive babies,
transformation of witnessing eyes to pulp-fragments,   30
implosion of skinned penises into carcass-gulleys.

We are the humans, men who can make;
whose language imagines *mercy*,
lovingkindness; we have believed one another
mirrored forms of a God we felt as good—   35

who do these acts, who convince ourselves
it is necessary; these acts are done
to our own flesh; burned human flesh
is smelling in Viet Nam as I write.

Yes, this is the knowledge that jostles for space   40
in our bodies along with all we
go on knowing of joy, of love;

our nerve filaments twitch with its presence
day and night,
nothing we say has not the husky phlegm of it in the saying,   45
nothing we do has the quickness, the sureness,
the deep intelligence living at peace would have.

1965

E. E. CUMMINGS

(1894–1962)

All in green went my love riding

All in green went my love riding
on a great horse of gold
into the silver dawn.

four lean hounds crouched low and smiling
the merry deer ran before. 5

Fleeter be they than dappled dreams
the swift sweet deer
the red rare deer.

Four red roebuck at a white water
the cruel bugle sang before. 10

Horn at hip went my love riding
riding the echo down
into the silver dawn.

four lean hounds crouched low and smiling
the level meadows ran before. 15

Softer be they than slippered sleep
the lean lithe deer
the fleet flown deer.

Four fleet does at a gold valley
the famished arrow sang before. 20

Bow at belt went my love riding
riding the mountain down
into the silver dawn.

four lean hounds crouched low and smiling
the sheer peaks ran before. 25

Paler be they than daunting death
the sleek slim deer
the tall tense deer.

Four tall stags at a green mountain
the lucky hunter sang before. 30

All in green went my love riding
on a great horse of gold
into the silver dawn.

four lean hounds crouched low and smiling
my heart fell dead before. 35

1923

the Cambridge ladies who live in furnished souls

the Cambridge ladies who live in furnished souls
are unbeautiful and have comfortable minds

(also, with the church's protestant blessings
daughters, unscented shapeless spirited)
they believe in Christ and Longfellow, both dead,   5
are invariably interested in so many things—
at the present writing one still finds
delighted fingers knitting for the is it Poles?
perhaps. While permanent faces coyly bandy
scandal of Mrs. N and Professor D   10
. . . . the Cambridge ladies do not care, above
Cambridge if sometimes in its box of
sky lavender and cornerless, the
moon rattles like a fragment of angry candy

                                                        1923

in Just-

in Just-
spring   when the world is mud-
luscious the little
lame balloonman

whistles   far   and wee   5

and eddieandbill come
running from marbles and
piracies and it's
spring

when the world is puddle-wonderful   10

the queer
old balloonman whistles
far   and   wee
and bettyandisbel come dancing

from hop-scotch and jump-rope and   15

it's
spring
and
    the

            goat-footed   20

balloonMan   whistles

"*the cambridge ladies*": 5. *Longfellow:* Henry Wadsworth Longfellow (1807–1882), the first
American poet of international reputation. He was known for his moralistic and romantic
narrative poetry.

far
and
wee

1923

Buffalo Bill's

Buffalo Bill's
defunct
            who used to
            ride a watersmooth-silver
                                        stallion   5
and break onetwothreefourfive pigeonsjustlikethat
                                        Jesus

he was a handsome man
                    and what i want to know is
how do you like your blueeyed boy   10
Mister Death

1923

i sing of Olaf glad and big

i sing of Olaf glad and big
whose warmest heart recoiled at war:
a conscientious object-or

his wellbelovéd colonel (trig
westpointer most succinctly bred)   5
took erring Olaf soon in hand;
but—though an host of overjoyed
noncoms (first knocking on the head
him) do through icy waters roll
that helplessness which others stroke   10
with brushes recently employed
anent this muddy toiletbowl,
while kindred intellects evoke
allegiance per blunt instruments—
Olaf (being to all intents   15
a corpse and wanting any rag
upon what God unto him gave)
responds, without getting annoyed
"I will not kiss your f.ing flag"

straightway the silver bird looked grave   20
(departing hurriedly to shave)

but—though all kinds of officers
(a yearning nation's blueeyed pride)
their passive prey did kick and curse
until for wear their clarion   25
voices and boots were much the worse,
and egged the firstclassprivates on
his rectum wickedly to tease
by means of skilfully applied
bayonets roasted hot with heat—   30
Olaf (upon what were once knees)
does almost ceaselessly repeat
"there is some s. I will not eat"

our president,being of which
assertions duly notified   35
threw the yellowsonofabitch
into a dungeon,where he died

Christ (of His mercy infinite)
i pray to see; and Olaf,too

preponderatingly because   40
unless statistics lie he was
more brave than me:more blond than you.

1931

r-p-o-p-h-e-s-s-a-g-r

                    r-p-o-p-h-e-s-s-a-g-r
                              who
a)s w(e loo)k
upnowgath
            PPEGORHRASS   5
                        eringint(o-
aThe):l
        eA
          !p:
S   a   10
                                   (r
rIvInG   .gRrEaPsPhOs)
                      to
rea(be)rran(com)gi(e)ngly
,grasshopper;   15

                                        1935

Further Reading

Kidder, Rushworth M. *E. E. Cummings: An Introduction to the Poetry.* New York: Columbia UP, 1979. • Wegner, Robert E. *The Poetry and Prose of E. E. Cummings.* New York: Harcourt, 1965. • Lane, Gary. *I Am: A Study of E. E. Cummings' Poems.* Lawrence: UP of Kansas, 1976. • Dumas, Bethany K. *E. E. Cummings: A Remembrance of Miracles.* New York: Barnes, 1974. • Triem, Eve. *E. E. Cummings.* Minneapolis: U of Minnesota P, 1969.

A poet as innovative as E. E. Cummings was naturally watched with interest by fellow poets. Among the more thoughtful comments on his work are those by Louise Bogan and Randall Jarrell.

Louise Bogan: On Cummings as a Satirist

Cummings, whose relation to the 1914–1918 war was close and cruel, brought into American postwar poetry a bittersweet mixture of satire and sentiment. His typographical experiments, which gave him an early notoriety, today seem less important than his persistent attempts to break taboos —to bring back into formal verse vital material that Victorian taste had outlawed. Today, as we read Cummings's lyric output from beginning to end, we are struck by the directness with which he has presented himself— his adolescent daydreams as well as his more mature desires; his small jealousies and prejudices, along with his big hatreds; his negative malice and his fears, beside his positive hopes. His awareness of tradition, too, comes out plainly; he has reworked traditional forms as often as he has invented new ones, turning not only the sonnet to his own purposes but also the ballad, the nursery rhyme, the epigrammatic quatrain, and the incantatory rune. His habit of projecting a continuing present, avoiding any expression of remorse or regret, gave a glitter to his middle period; nothing in it casts a shadow. The pathos of his later elegies is all the more remarkable because no one could foresee its occurrence. But it is his satire that remains focal and sharp as his main contribution to the reinvigoration of modern verse. His targets have been, for the most part, well chosen, and he has made his stand clear—for the rights and value of the individual as opposed to the demands of the crowd and the standards of the machine. He scornfully stuck to his guns in times of crisis, when many of his contemporaries were deserting theirs. It is this underlying passion for simple justice that has given Cummings the power to uncover, point to, and stigmatize those dead areas of custom as only a satirist can effectively do it.

Randall Jarrell: On Cummings's Faults

So many critics have been more than just to Cummings's virtues—who could overlook so much life, individuality, charm, freshness, ingenuity?—that I should like to be unjust about his faults. Some of his sentimentality, his easy lyric sweetness I enjoy in the way one enjoys a rather commonplace composer's half-sweet, half-cloying melodies, but much of it is straight ham, straight corn. All too often Cummings splits man into a delicate unique Ariel, drifting through dew like moonlight, and into a Brooklyn Caliban who says, to prostitutes, dese, dem and dose. Some of all that Sex is there to shock, but more of it is there for its own sweet sake. And there is so much love—love infinite and eternal; love in the movie moonlight, after the prop champagne—that one values all the more the real love affair in Cummings's play *Him.*

To Cummings words are things, exciting things excitingly manipulable: he sits at the Muse's door making mobiles. He is a magical but shallow rhetorician who specializes in turning inside out, fooling around with the rhetoric of popular songs, advertisements, bad romantic poetry. He invents a master stroke, figures out the formula for it, and repeats it fifty times. The best rhetoric is less interested in itself, more interested in what it describes, than Cummings's.

Some of Cummings's humor is genuinely funny, some is crude and expected. He is, alas! a monotonous poet. Everything a poem does is, to old readers, expected. "Type Four," they murmur. "Well done!" Then they yawn. "Change in all things is sweet," said Aristotle; "They must often change who would be constant in happiness or wisdom," said Confucius; "Change the name of Arkansas? Never!" said Senator James Kimbrough Jones. Would that Cummings had listened to Aristotle and Confucius.

What I like least about Cummings's poems is their pride in Cummings and their contempt for most other people; the difference between the *I* and *you* of the poems, and other people, is the poems' favorite subject. All his work thanks God that he is not as other men are; none of it says, "Lord, be merciful to me, a sinner."

Although Louise Bogan may be right about the relative unimportance of Cummings's typographical experiments, they have attracted a great deal of attention. It might be useful to examine them in the light of other "concrete" poems written before and after Cummings's own. (Note that "Acrostic" can be read in three ways: left to right, top to bottom, and right to left then left to right in alternating lines.)

Anonymous

(Sixteenth century)

ACROSTIC

Your face	Your tongue	Your wit
so faire	so smooth	so sharp
first drew	then mov'd	then knit
mine eye	mine eare	my heart
Mine eye	Mine eare	My heart
thus drawn	thus mov'd	thus knit
affects	hangs on	yeelds to
Your face	Your tongue	Your wit

5

George Herbert

(1593–1633)

EASTER-WINGS

Lord, who createdst man in wealth and store,
Though foolishly he lost the same,
Decaying more and more
Till he became
Most poor:
With thee
Oh let me rise
As larks, harmoniously,
And sing this day thy victories:
Then shall the fall further the flight in me.

My tender age in sorrow did begin:
And still with sicknesses and shame
Thou didst so punish sin,
That I became
Most thin.
With thee
Let me combine,
And feel this day thy victory:
For, if I imp my wing on thine,
Affliction shall advance the flight in me.

1633

May Swenson

(b. 1919)

HOW EVERYTHING HAPPENS (Based on a Study of the Wave)

<pre>
                                        happen.
                                     to
                                  up
                            stacking
                         is   5
                   something
When nothing is happening

When it happens
                      something
                            pulls   10
                         back
                      not
                   to
                      happen.
When   has happened.   15
      pulling back   stacking up
            happens

         has happened   stacks up.
When it   something   nothing
                   pulls back while   20
Then nothing is happening.

                            happens.
                         and
                      forward
                   pushes
                up
            stacks   25
         something
Then
</pre>

                                                 1967

LOUISE BOGAN

(1897–1970)

MEDUSA

I had come to the house, in a cave of trees,
Facing a sheer sky.
Everything moved,—a bell hung ready to strike,
Sun and reflection wheeled by.

When the bare eyes were before me   5
And the hissing hair,
Held up at a window, seen through a door.
The stiff bald eyes, the serpents on the forehead
Formed in the air.

This is a dead scene forever now.   10
Nothing will ever stir.
The end will never brighten it more than this,
Nor the rain blur.

The water will always fall, and will not fall,
And the tipped bell make no sound.   15
The grass will always be growing for hay
Deep on the ground.

And I shall stand here like a shadow
Under the great balanced day,
My eyes on the yellow dust, that was lifting in the wind,   20
And does not drift away.

1923

THE ENGINE

The secure pulses of the heart
Drive and rock in dark precision,
Though life brings fever to the mouth
And the eyes vision.

Whatever joy the body takes,   5
Whatever sound the voice makes purer,

"Medusa": Medusa: In Greek mythology, whoever looked on the face of this serpent-haired
sorceress was turned to stone.

Will never cause their beat to faint
Or become surer.

These perfect chambers, and their springs,
So fitly sealed against remorse   10
That keep the lifting shaft of breath
To its cool course,

Cannot delay, and cannot dance—
Until, wrung out to the last drop,
The brain, knowing time and love, must die,   15
And they must stop.

1931

TO MY BROTHER

Killed: Chaumont Wood, October 1918

O you so long dead,
You masked and obscure,
I can tell you, all things endure:
The wine and the bread;

The marble quarried for the arch;   5
The iron become steel;
The spoke broken from the wheel;
The sweat of the long march;

The haystacks cut through like loaves,
And the hundred flowers from the seed.   10

All things indeed,
Though struck by the hooves

Of disaster, of time due,
Of fell loss and gain,
All things remain,   15
I can tell you, this is true,

Though burned down to stone,
Though lost from the eye,
I can tell you, and not lie—
Save of peace alone.   20

1935

COME, BREAK WITH TIME

Come, break with time,
You who were lorded

By a clock's chime
So ill afforded.
If time is allayed   5
Be not afraid.

I shall break, if I will.
Break, since you must.
Time has its fill,
Sated with dust.   10
Long the clock's hand
Burned like a brand.

Take the rocks' speed
And earth's heavy measure.
Let buried seed   15
Drain out time's pleasure,
Take time's decrees.
Come, cruel ease.

1941

THE DREAM

O God, in the dream the terrible horse began
To paw at the air, and make for me with his blows.
Fear kept for thirty-five years poured through his mane,
And retribution equally old, or nearly, breathed through his nose.

Coward complete, I lay and wept on the ground   5
When some strong creature appeared, and leapt for the rein.
Another woman, as I lay half in a swound,
Leapt in the air, and clutched at the leather and chain.

Give him, she said, something of yours as a charm.
Throw him, she said, some poor thing you alone claim.   10
No, no, I cried, he hates me; he's out for harm,
And whether I yield or not, it is all the same.

But, like a lion in a legend, when I flung the glove
Pulled from my sweating, my cold right hand,
The terrible beast, that no one may understand,   15
Came to my side, and put down his head in love.

1941

EVENING IN THE SANITARIUM

The free evening fades, outside the windows fastened with decorative
   iron grilles.

The lamps are lighted; the shades drawn; the nurses are watching a
    little.
It is the hour of the complicated knitting on the safe bone needles; of
    the games of anagrams and bridge;
The deadly game of chess; the book held up like a mask.

The period of the wildest weeping, the fiercest delusion, is over.   5
The women rest their tired half-healed hearts; they are almost well.
Some of them will stay almost well always: the blunt-faced woman
    whose thinking dissolved
Under academic discipline; the manic-depressive girl
Now leveling off; one paranoiac afflicted with jealousy.
Another with persecution. Some alleviation has been possible.   10

O fortunate bride, who never again will become elated after
    childbirth!
O lucky older wife, who has been cured of feeling unwanted!
To the suburban railway station you will return, return,
To meet forever Jim home on the 5:35.
You will be again as normal and selfish and heartless as anybody else. 15

There is life left: the piano says it with its octave smile.
The soft carpets pad the thump and splinter of the suicide to be.
Everything will be splendid: the grandmother will not drink
    habitually.
The fruit salad will bloom on the plate like a bouquet
And the garden produce the blue-ribbon aquilegia.   20
The cats will be glad; the fathers feel justified; the mothers relieved.

The sons and husbands will no longer need to pay the bills.
Childhoods will be put away, the obscene nightmare abated.

At the ends of the corridors the baths are running.
Mrs. C. again feels the shadow of the obsessive idea.   25
Miss R. looks at the mantel-piece, which must mean something.

1941

ZONE

We have struck the regions wherein we are keel or reef
The wind breaks over us,
And against high sharp angles almost splits into words
And these are of fear or grief.

Like a ship, we have struck expected latitudes   5
Of the universe, in March.
Through one short segment's arch
Of the zodiac's round

We pass,
Thinking: Now we hear   10
What we heard last year,
And bear the wind's rude touch
And its ugly sound
Equally with so much
We have learned how to bear.   15

1941

THE DRAGONFLY

You are made of almost nothing
But of enough
To be great eyes
And diaphanous double vans;
To be ceaseless movement,   5
Unending hunger
Grappling love.

Link between water and air,
Earth repels you.
Light touches you only to shift into iridescence   10
Upon your body and wings.
Twice-born, predator,
You split into the heat.
Swift beyond calculation or capture
You dart into the shadow   15
Which consumes you.

You rocket into the day.
But at last, when the wind flattens the grasses,
For you, the design and purpose stop.

And you fall   20
With the other husks of summer.

1961

Further Reading

Roethke, Theodore. "The Poetry of Louise Bogan." *On the Poet and His Craft:
Selected Prose of Theodore Roethke.* Ed. Ralph J. Mills, Jr. Seattle: U of Washington P,
1965. 133–48. • Ridgeway, Jacqueline. *Louise Bogan.* Boston: Twayne, 1984. •

Collins, Martha, ed. *Critical Essays on Louise Bogan.* Boston: Hall, 1984. • Frank, Elizabeth. *Louise Bogan: A Portrait.* New York: Knopf, 1985. • Peterson, Douglas L. "The Poetry of Louise Bogan." *Southern Review* 19.1 (Jan. 1983): 73–87.

Louise Bogan once said of lyric poetry, "The chances of getting away with pure fakery within it are very small. One cannot fib—it shows. One cannot manipulate—it spoils." Her most enthusiastic readers respond strongly to the intellectual and emotional honesty of her work.

Theodore Roethke: On Bogan's Emotional Discipline

Two of the charges most frequently levelled against poetry by women are lack of range—in subject matter, in emotional tone—and lack of a sense of humor. And one could, in individual instances among writers of real talent, add other aesthetic and moral shortcomings: the spinning-out; the embroidering of trivial themes; a concern with the mere surfaces of life—that special province of the feminine talent in prose—hiding from the real agonies of the spirit; refusing to face up to what existence is; lyric or religious posturing; running between the boudoir and the altar, stamping a tiny foot against God; or lapsing into a sententiousness that implies the author has re-invented integrity; carrying on excessively about Fate, about time; lamenting the lot of the woman; caterwauling; writing the same poem about fifty times, and so on.

But Louise Bogan is something else. True, a very few of her earliest poems bear the mark of fashion, but for the most part she writes out of the severest lyrical tradition in English. Her real spiritual ancestors are Campion, Jonson, the anonymous Elizabethan song writers. The word order is usually direct, the plunge straight into the subject, the music rich and subtle (she has one of the best ears of our time), and the subject invariably given its due and no more. As a result, her poems, even the less consequential, have a finality, a comprehensiveness, the sense of being all of a piece, that we demand from the short poem at its best. . . .

One definition of a serious lyric—it may come from Stanley Kunitz—would call it a revelation of a tragic personality. Behind the Bogan poems is a woman intense, proud, strong-willed, never hysterical or silly; who scorns the open unabashed caterwaul so usual with the love poet, male or female; who never writes a serious poem until there is a genuine "up-welling" from the unconscious; who shapes emotion into an inevitable-seeming, an endurable, form.

For love, passion, its complexities, its tensions, its betrayals, is one of Louise Bogan's chief themes. And this love, along with marriage itself, is a virtual battle-ground. But the enemy is respected, the other is there, given his due; the experience, whatever its difficulties, shared.

LANGSTON HUGHES

(1902–1967)

THE NEGRO SPEAKS OF RIVERS

I've known rivers:
I've known rivers ancient as the world and older than the flow of
   human blood in human veins.

My soul has grown deep like the rivers.

I bathed in the Euphrates when dawns were young.   5
I built my hut near the Congo and it lulled me to sleep.
I look upon the Nile and raised the pyramids above it.
I heard the singing of the Mississippi when Abe Lincoln went down
   to New Orleans, and I've seen its muddy bosom turn all golden in
   the sunset.   10

I've known rivers:
Ancient, dusky rivers.

My soul has grown deep like the rivers.

1921

EPILOGUE

I, too, sing America.

I am the darker brother.
They send me to eat in the kitchen
When company comes,
But I laugh,   5
And eat well,
And grow strong.

Tomorrow,
I'll sit at the table
When company comes.   10
Nobody'll dare
Say to me,
"Eat in the kitchen,"
Then.

Besides,   15
They'll see how beautiful I am
And be ashamed,—

I, too, am America.

1926

AFRO-AMERICAN FRAGMENT

So long,
So far away
Is Africa,
Not even memories alive
Save those that history books create,   5
Save those that songs
Beat back into the blood—
Beat out of blood with words sad-sung
In strange un-Negro tongue—
So long,   10
So far away
Is Africa.

Subdued and time-lost
Are the drums—and yet
Through some vast mist of race   15
There comes this song
I do not understand,
This song of atavistic land,
Of bitter yearnings lost
Without a place—   20
So long,
So far away
Is Africa's
Dark face.

1930

HARLEM SWEETIES

Have you dug the spill
Of Sugar Hill?

"Harlem Sweeties": 2. *Sugar Hill:* in Hughes's time, a wealthy section of Harlem.

Cast your gims
On this sepia thrill:
Brown sugar lassie,   5
Caramel treat,
Honey-gold baby
Sweet enough to eat.
Peach-skinned girlie,
Coffee and cream,   10
Chocolate darling
Out of a dream.
Walnut tinted
Or cocoa brown,
Pomegranate-lipped   15
Pride of the town.
Rich cream-colored
To plum-tinted black,
Feminine sweetness
In Harlem's no lack.   20
Glow of the quince
To blush of the rose.
Persimmon bronze
To cinnamon toes.
Blackberry cordial,   25
Virginia Dare wine—
All those sweet colors
Flavor Harlem of mine!
Walnut or cocoa,
Let me repeat: 30
Caramel, brown sugar,
A chocolate treat.
Molasses taffy,
Coffee and cream,
Licorice, clove, cinnamon   35
To a honey-brown dream.
Ginger, wine-gold,
Persimmon, blackberry,
All through the spectrum
Harlem girls vary—   40
So if you want to know beauty's
Rainbow-sweet thrill,
Stroll down luscious,
Delicious, *fine* Sugar Hill.

1942

---

3. *gims:* eyes, possibly a variant of the slang word "glims."

THEME FOR ENGLISH B

The instructor said,

> *Go home and write*
> *a page tonight.*
> *And let that page come out of you—*
> *Then, it will be true.*   5

I wonder if it's that simple?
I am twenty-two, colored, born in Winston-Salem.
I went to school there, then Durham, then here
to this college on the hill above Harlem.
I am the only colored student in my class.   10
The steps from the hill lead down into Harlem,
through a park, then I cross St. Nicholas,
Eighth Avenue, Seventh, and I come to the Y,
the Harlem Branch Y, where I take the elevator
up to my room, sit down, and write this page: 15

It's not easy to know what is true for you or me
at twenty-two, my age. But I guess I'm what
I feel and see and hear, Harlem, I hear you:
hear you, hear me—we two—you, me, talk on this page.
(I hear New York, too.) Me—who?   20
Well, I like to eat, sleep, drink, and be in love.
I like to work, read, learn, and understand life.
I like a pipe for a Christmas present,
or records—Bessie, bop, or Bach.
I guess being colored doesn't make me *not* like   25
the same things other folks like who are other races.
So will my page be colored that I write?
Being me, it will not be white.
But it will be
a part of you, instructor.   30
You are white—
yet a part of me, as I am a part of you.
That's American.
Sometimes perhaps you don't want to be a part of me.
Nor do I often want to be a part of you.   35
But we are, that's true!
As I learn from you,
I guess you learn from me—

"Theme for English B": 9. *college:* Columbia University.   24. *Bessie:* Bessie Smith (1894–1937), the great blues singer.

although you're older—and white—
and somewhat more free.   40

This is my page for English B.

1950

HARLEM

What happens to a dream deferred?

    Does it dry up
    like a raisin in the sun?
    Or fester like a sore—
    And then run?   5
    Does it stink like rotten meat?
    Or crust and sugar over—
    like a syrupy sweet?

    Maybe it just sags
    like a heavy load.   10

    Or does it explode?

1951

SAME IN BLUES

I said to my baby,
Baby, take it slow.
I can't, she said, I can't!
I got to go!

    There's a certain   5
    amount of traveling
    in a dream deferred.

Lulu said to Leonard,
I want a diamond ring.
Leonard said to Lulu,   10
You won't get a goddamn thing!

    A certain
    amount of nothing
    in a dream deferred.

Daddy, daddy, daddy,   15
All I want is you.

You can have me, baby—
but my lovin' days is through.

   A certain
   amount of impotence   20
   in a dream deferred.

Three parties
On my party line—
But that third party,
Lord, ain't mine!   25

   There's liable
   to be confusion
   in a dream deferred.

From river to river,
Uptown and down,   30
There's liable to be confusion
when a dream gets kicked around.

                                                    1951

Further Reading

Hughes, Langston. "The Negro Artist and the Racial Mountain." *Five Black Writers: Essays on Wright, Ellison, Baldwin, Hughes, and LeRoi Jones.* New York: New York UP, 1970. 225–29. • Davis, Arthur P. "Langston Hughes: Cool Poet." *Langston Hughes, Black Genius: A Critical Evaluation.* Ed. Therman B. O'Daniel. New York: Morrow, 1971. 18–38. • Emanuel, James A. *Langston Hughes.* New York: Twayne, 1967. • Miller, R. Baxter. "'Some Mark to Make': The Lyrical Image of Langston Hughes." *Critical Essays on Langston Hughes.* Ed. Edward J. Mullen. Boston: Hall, 1986. 154–66. • Davis, Arthur P. "The Harlem of Langston Hughes' Poetry." *Critical Essays on Langston Hughes.* Ed. Edward J. Mullen. Boston: Hall, 1986. 135–43. • Rampersad, Arnold. "The Origins of Poetry in Langston Hughes." *Southern Review* 21.3 (July 1985): 695–705.

While E. E. Cummings was breaking away from the traditions of English verse by taking up forbidden subject matter and developing novel treatments, Langston Hughes was breaking from tradition by making poetry based on the life, language, and culture of Harlem. Among the readers who had a mixed response to Hughes's experiments was Countee Cullen, another great figure of the Harlem Renaissance.

Countee Cullen: On Hughes's Overemphasis on Race

If I have the least powers of prediction, the first section of this book, *The Weary Blues,* will be most admired, even if less from intrinsic poetical worth than because of its dissociation from the traditionally poetic. Never having been one to think all subjects and forms proper for poetic consideration, I regard these jazz poems as interlopers in the company of the truly beautiful poems in other sections of the book. They move along with the frenzy and electric heat of a Methodist or Baptist revival meeting, and affect me in much the same manner. The revival meeting excites me, cooling and flushing me with alternate chills and fevers of emotion; so do these poems. But when the storm is over, I wonder if the quiet way of communing is not more spiritual for the God-seeking heart; and in the light of reflection I wonder if jazz poems really belong to that dignified company, that select and austere circle of high literary expression which we call poetry. Surely, when in *Negro Dancers* Mr. Hughes says

> Me an' ma baby's
> Got two mo' ways,
> Two mo' ways to do de buck!

he voices, in lyrical, thumb-at-nose fashion the happy careless attitude, akin to poetry, that is found in certain types. And certainly he achieves one of his loveliest lyrics in *Young Singer.* Thus I find myself straddling a fence. It needs only *The Cat and The Saxaphone,* however, to knock me over completely on the side of bewilderment, and incredulity. This creation is a *tour de force* of its kind, but is it a poem:

> EVERYBODY
>
> Half-pint,—
> Gin?
> No, make it
>
> LOVES MY BABY
>
> corn. You like
> don't you, honey?
> BUT MY BABY. . . . .

In the face of accomplished fact, I cannot say *This will never do,* but I feel that it ought never to have been done.

Taken as a group the selections in this book seem one-sided to me. They tend to hurl this poet into the gaping pit that lies before all Negro writers, in the confines of which they become racial artists instead of artists pure and simple. There is too much emphasis here on strictly Negro themes; and this is probably an added reason for my coldness toward the jazz poems—they seem to set a too definite limit upon an already limited field.

Dull books cause no schisms, raise no dissensions, create no parties. Much will be said of *The Weary Blues* because it is a definite achievement, and because Mr. Hughes, in his own way, with a first book that cannot be dismissed as merely *promising,* has arrived.

Langston Hughes: On Embracing Black Culture

One of the most promising of the young Negro poets said to me once, "I want to be a poet—not a Negro poet," meaning, I believe, "I want to write like a white poet"; meaning subconsciously, "I would like to be a white poet"; meaning behind that, "I would like to be white." And I was sorry the young man said that, for no great poet has ever been afraid of being himself. And I doubted then that, with his desire to run away spiritually from his race, this boy would ever be a great poet. But this is the mountain standing in the way of any true Negro art in America—this urge within the race toward whiteness, the desire to pour racial individuality into the mold of American standardization, and to be as little Negro and as much American as possible. . . .

Let the blare of Negro jazz bands and the bellowing voice of Bessie Smith singing Blues penetrate the closed ears of the colored near-intellectuals until they listen and perhaps understand. Let Paul Robeson singing Water Boy, and Rudolph Fisher writing about the streets of Harlem, and Jean Toomer holding the heart of Georgia in his hands, and Aaron Douglas drawing strange black fantasies cause the smug Negro middle class to turn from their white, respectable, ordinary books and papers to catch a glimmer of their own beauty. We younger Negro artists who create now intend to express our individual dark-skinned selves without fear or shame. If white people are pleased we are glad. If they are not, it doesn't matter. We know we are beautiful. And ugly too. The tom-tom cries and the tom-tom laughs. If colored people are pleased we are glad. If they are not, their displeasure doesn't matter either. We build our temples for tomorrow, strong as we know how, and we stand on top of the mountain, free within ourselves.

COUNTEE CULLEN

(1903–1946)

INCIDENT

Once riding in old Baltimore,
   Heart-filled, head-filled with glee,
I saw a Baltimorean
   Keep looking straight at me.

Now I was eight and very small,   5
   And he was no whit bigger,
And so I smiled, but he poked out
   His tongue and called me, "Nigger."

I saw the whole of Baltimore
   From May until December: 10
Of all the things that happened there
   That's all that I remember.

1925

YET DO I MARVEL

I doubt not God is good, well-meaning, kind,
And did He stoop to quibble could tell why
The little buried mole continues blind,
Why flesh that mirrors Him must some day die,
Make plain the reason tortured Tantalus   5
Is baited by the fickle fruit, declare
If merely brute caprice dooms Sisyphus
To struggle up a never-ending stair.
Inscrutable His ways are, and immune
To catechism by a mind too strewn   10
With petty cares to slightly understand
What awful brain compels His awful hand.
Yet do I marvel at this curious thing:
To make a poet black, and bid him sing!

1925

"Yet Do I Marvel": 5. *Tantalus:* a mythical king punished by having to stand up to his chin in
water under a loaded fruit tree; both fruit and water retreated whenever he reached to satisfy
his hunger or thirst.   7. *Sisyphus:* a mythical king condemned in Hades to roll a huge stone
up a hill perpetually; whenever he reached the top of the hill, the stone rolled back down.

TO JOHN KEATS, POET, AT SPRINGTIME

I cannot hold my peace, John Keats;
There never was a spring like this;
It is an echo, that repeats
My last year's song and next year's bliss.
I know, in spite of all men say   5
Of Beauty, you have felt her most.
Yea, even in your grave her way
Is laid. Poor, troubled, lyric ghost,
Spring never was so fair and dear
As Beauty makes her seem this year.   10

I cannot hold my peace, John Keats;
I am as helpless in the toil
Of Spring as any lamb that bleats
To feel the solid earth recoil
Beneath his puny legs. Spring beats   15
Her tocsin call to those who love her,
And lo! the dogwood petals cover
Her breast with drifts of snow, and sleek
White gulls fly screaming to her, and hover
About her shoulders, and kiss her cheek,   20
While white and purple lilacs muster
A strength that bears them to a cluster
Of color and odor; for her sake
All things that slept are now awake.

And you and I, shall we lie still,   25
John Keats, while Beauty summons us?
Somehow I feel your sensitive will
Is pulsing up some tremulous
Sap road of a maple tree, whose leaves
Grow music as they grow, since your   30
Wild voice is in them, a harp that grieves
For life that opens death's dark door.
Though dust, your fingers still can push
The Vision Splendid to a birth,
Though now they work as grass in the hush   35
Of the night on the broad sweet page of the earth.

"John Keats is dead," they say, but I
Who hear your full insistent cry
In bud and blossom, leaf and tree,
Know John Keats still writes poetry.   40
And while my head is earthward bowed

To read new life sprung from your shroud,
Folks seeing me must think it strange
That merely spring should so derange
My mind. They do not know that you,   45
John Keats, keep revel with me, too.

1925

FOR A POET

I have wrapped my dreams in a silken cloth,
And laid them away in a box of gold;
Where long will cling the lips of the moth,
I have wrapped my dreams in a silken cloth;
I hide no hate; I am not even wroth   5
Who found earth's breath so keen and cold;
I have wrapped my dreams in a silken cloth,
And laid them away in a box of gold.

1925

FROM THE DARK TOWER

To Charles S. Johnson

We shall not always plant while others reap
The golden increment of bursting fruit,
Not always countenance, abject and mute,
That lesser men should hold their brothers cheap;
Not everlastingly while others sleep   5
Shall we beguile their limbs with mellow flute,
Not always bend to some more subtle brute;
We were not made eternally to weep.

The night whose sable breast relieves the stark,
White stars is no less lovely being dark,   10
And there are buds that cannot bloom at all
In light, but crumple, piteous, and fall;
So in the dark we hide the heart that bleeds,
And wait, and tend our agonizing seeds.

1927

BLACK MAJESTY

These men were kings, albeit they were black,
Christophe and Dessalines and L'Ouverture;
Their majesty has made me turn my back
Upon a plaint I once shaped to endure.
These men were black, I say, but they were crowned   5
And purple-clad, however brief their time.
Stifle your agony; let grief be drowned;
We know joy had a day once and a clime.

Dark gutter-snipe, black sprawler-in-the-mud,
A thing men did a man may do again.   10
What answer filters through your sluggish blood
To these dark ghosts who knew so bright a reign?
"Lo, I am dark, but comely," Sheba sings.
"And we were black," three shades reply, "but kings."

1929

ONLY THE POLISHED SKELETON

The heart has need of some deceit
    To make its pistons rise and fall;
For less than this it would not beat,
    Nor flush the sluggish vein at all.

With subterfuge and fraud the mind   5
    Must fend and parry thrust for thrust,
With logic brutal and unkind
    Beat off the onslaughts of the dust.

Only the polished skeleton,
    Of flesh relieved and pauperized,   10
Can rest at ease and think upon
    The worth of all it so despised.

1935

"Black Majesty": 2. *Christophe:* Henri Christophe (1767–1820), king of Haiti (1811–1820), was the most trusted general of L'Ouverture. *Dessalines:* Jean Dessalines (1758–1806), emperor of Haiti (1805–06), was second in command under L'Ouverture and known for his cruelty. *L'Ouverture:* Dominique Toussaint L'Ouverture (1743–1803), president of Haiti (1801–02), stripped the French commissioners of their power and temporarily revolutionized social conditions for black Haitians.

Further Reading

Shucard, Alan R. *Countee Cullen*. Boston: Twayne, 1984. • Wagner, Jean. "Countee Cullen." *Black Poets of the U.S.* Trans. Kenneth Douglas. Urbana: U of Illinois P, 1973. 283–347. • Baker, Houston A., Jr. *A Many-Colored Coat of Dreams: The Poetry of Countee Cullen*. Detroit: Broadside Press, 1974. • Davis, Arthur P. "Countee Cullen." *From the Dark Tower: Afro-American Writers, 1900–1960*. Washington, D.C.: Howard UP, 1974. 73–83. • Primeau, Ronald. "Countee Cullen and Keats's 'Vale of Soul-Making.'" *Papers on Language and Literature* 12.1 (Winter 1976): 73–86.

Although Countee Cullen rejected the idea that black poets should limit themselves to poems about race, many of his most familiar poems protest the treatment and status of American blacks in the 1920s and '30s. Poetry about injustice, like war poetry (see pages 710–719), always runs the danger of becoming too cliché-riddled and predictable to be effective. The following collection of poems shows a range of approaches to keeping the poetry fresh.

Some Protest Poems Before and After Countee Cullen

Percy Bysshe Shelley

(1792–1822)

OZYMANDIAS

I met a traveler from an antique land
Who said: Two vast and trunkless legs of stone
Stand in the desert. . . . Near them, on the sand,
Half sunk, a shattered visage lies, whose frown,
And wrinkled lip, and sneer of cold command,   5
Tell that its sculptor well those passions read
Which yet survive, stamped on these lifeless things,
The hand that mocked them, and the heart that fed:
And on the pedestal these words appear:
"My name is Ozymandias, King of Kings: 10
Look on my works, ye Mighty, and despair!"

Nothing beside remains. Round the decay
Of that colossal wreck, boundless and bare
The lone and level sands stretch far away.

1817

Dennis Brutus

(b. 1924)

NIGHTSONG: CITY

Sleep well, my love, sleep well:
the harbour lights glaze over restless docks.
police cars cockroach through the tunnel streets

from the shanties creaking iron-sheets
violence like a bug-infested rag is tossed   5
and fear is immanent as sound in the wind-swung bell;

the long day's anger pants from sand and rocks;
but for this breathing night at least,
my land, my love, sleep well.

1963

Carter Revard

(b. 1931)

DISCOVERY OF THE NEW WORLD

The creatures that we met this morning
marveled at our green skins
and scarlet eyes.
They lack antennae
and can't be made to grasp   5
your proclamation that they are
our lawful food and prey and slaves,
nor can they seem to learn
their body-space is needed to materialize
our oxygen-absorbers—   10

which they conceive are breathing
        and thinking creatures whom they implore
at first as angels, then as devils,
            when they are being snuffed out
                by an absorber swelling   15
                into their space.
Their history bled from one this morning,
        while we were tasting his brain,
            in holographic rainbows,
which we assembled into quite an interesting   20
        set of legends—
            that's all it came to, though
the colors were quite lovely before we
        poured them into our time;
            the blue shift bleached away   25
meaningless circumstances, and they would not fit
        any of our truth-matrices—
            there was, however,
            a curious visual echo in their history
                of our own coming to their earth;   30
a certain General Sherman said
        about one group of them precisely what
            we have been telling you about these creatures:
it is our destiny to asterize this planet,
            and they WILL not be asterized,   35
                so they must be wiped out.
        WE NEED their space and nitrogen
            which they do not know how to *use,*
nor will they breathe ammonia, as we do;
        yet they will not give up their "air" unforced,   40
            so it is clear,
                whatever our "agreements" made this
                            morning,
        we'll have to kill them all:
            the more we cook this orbit,
        the fewer next time round.   45
We've finished lazing all their crops and stores,
        we've killed their meat-slaves, now
                they'll have to come into our pens
and we can use them for our final studies
        of how our heart attacks and cancers spread
                            among them,   50
        since they seem not immune to these.
—If we didn't have this mission it might be sad
        to see such helpless creatures die

chanting their sacred psalms and bills of rights; but

never fear

the riches of this globe are ours   55
and worth whatever pains others may have to

feel.

We'll soon have it cleared
completely, as it now is, at the poles, and then
we will be safe, and rich, and happy here, forever.

1975

Wole Soyinka

(b. 1934)

TELEPHONE CONVERSATION

The price seemed reasonable, location
Indifferent. The landlady swore she lived
Off premises. Nothing remained
But self-confession. 'Madam,' I warned,
'I hate a wasted journey—I am African.'   5
Silence. Silenced transmission of
Pressurized good-breeding. Voice, when it came,
Lipstick coated, long gold-rolled
Cigarette-holder pipped. Caught I was, foully.
'HOW DARK?'. . . I had not misheard. . . .'ARE YOU LIGHT   10
OR VERY DARK?' Button B. Button A. Stench
Of rancid breath of public hide-and-speak.
Red booth. Red pillar-box. Red double-tiered
Omnibus squelching tar. It *was* real! Shamed
By ill-mannered silence, surrender   15
Pushed dumbfoundment to beg simplification.
Considerate she was, varying the emphasis—
'ARE YOU DARK? OR VERY LIGHT?' Revelation came.
'You mean—like plain or milk chocolate?'
Her assent was clinical, crushing in its light   20
Impersonality. Rapidly, wave-length adjusted.
I chose. 'West African sepia'—and as afterthought,

"*Telephone Conversation*": 13–14. *Red . . . Omnibus:* phone booths, post office "pillars," and
buses are painted red in London.

'Down in my passport.' Silence for spectroscopic
Flight of fancy, till truthfulness clanged her accent
Hard on the mouthpiece. 'WHAT'S THAT?' conceding   25
'DON'T KNOW WHAT THAT IS.' 'Like brunette.'
'THAT'S DARK, ISN'T IT?' 'Not altogether.
Facially, I am brunette, but madam, you should see
The rest of me. Palm of my hand, soles of my feet
Are a peroxide blonde. Friction, caused—   30
Foolishly madam—by sitting down, has turned
My bottom raven black—One moment madam!'—sensing
Her receiver rearing on the thunderclap
About my ears—'Madam,' I pleaded, 'wouldn't you rather
See for yourself?'   35

1960

Olga Broumas

(b. 1949)

CINDERELLA

. . . the joy that isn't shared
I heard, dies young.
    Anne Sexton, 1928–1974

Apart from my sisters, estranged
from my mother, I am a woman alone
in a house of men
who secretly
call themselves princes, alone   5
with me usually, under cover of dark. I am the one allowed in

to the royal chambers, whose small foot conveniently
fills the slipper of glass. The woman writer, the lady
umpire, the madam chairman, anyone's wife.
I know what I know.   10
And I once was glad

of the chance to use it, even alone
in a strange castle, doing overtime on my own, cracking
the royal code. The princes spoke
in their fathers' language, were eager to praise me   15
my nimble tongue. I am a woman in a state of siege, alone

as one piece of laundry, strung on a windy clothesline a
mile long. A woman co-opted by promises: the lure
of a job, the ruse of a choice, a woman forced
to bear witness, falsely   20
against my kind, as each
other sister was judged inadequate, bitchy, incompetent,
jealous, too thin, too fat. I know what I know.
What sweet bread I make

for myself in this prosperous house   25
is dirty, what good soup I boil turns
in my mouth to mud. Give
me my ashes. A cold stove, a cinder-block pillow, wet
canvas shoes in my sisters', my sisters' hut. Or I swear

I'll die young   30
like those favored before me, hand-picked each one
for her joyful heart.

1977

PABLO NERUDA

(1904–1973)

HERE I LOVE YOU

translated from the Spanish by W. S. Merwin

Here I love you.
In the dark pines the wind disentangles itself.
The moon glows like phosphorous on the vagrant waters.
Days, all one kind, go chasing each other.

The snow unfurls in dancing figures.   5
A silver gull slips down from the west.
Sometimes a sail. High, high stars.

Oh the black cross of a ship.
Alone.
Sometimes I get up early and even my soul is wet.   10
Far away the sea sounds and resounds.
This is a port.
Here I love you.

Here I love you and the horizon hides you in vain.
I love you still among these cold things.   15
Sometimes my kisses go on those heavy vessels
that cross the sea towards no arrival.
I see myself forgotten like those old anchors.
The piers sadden when the afternoon moors there.
My life grows tired, hungry to no purpose.   20
I love what I do not have. You are so far.
My loathing wrestles with the slow twilights.
But night comes and starts to sing to me.

The moon turns its clockwork dream.
The biggest stars look at me with your eyes.   25
And as I love you, the pines in the wind
want to sing your name with their leaves of wire.

1924, trans. 1969

RITUAL OF MY LEGS

translated from the Spanish by Donald Walsh

For a long time I have stayed looking at my long legs,
with infinite and curious tenderness, with my accustomed passion,
as if they had been the legs of a divine woman,
deeply sunk in the abyss of my thorax:
and, to tell the truth, when time, when time passes   5
over the earth, over the roof, over my impure head,
and it passes, time passes, and in my bed I do not feel at night
that a woman is breathing sleeping naked and at my side,
then strange, dark things take the place of the absent one,
vicious, melancholy thoughts   10
sow heavy possibilities in my bedroom,
and thus, then, I look at my legs as if they belonged to another body
and were stuck strongly and gently to my insides.

Like stems or feminine adorable things,
from the knees they rise, cylindrical and thick,   15
with a disturbed and compact material of existence
like brutal, thick goddess arms,
like trees monstrously dressed as human beings,
like fatal, immense lips thirsty and tranquil,
they are, there, the best part of my body: 20
the entirely substantial part, without complicated content
of senses or tracheas or intestines or ganglia
nothing but the pure, the sweet, and the thick part of my own life

nothing but form and volume existing,
guarding life, nevertheless, in a complete way.   25

People cross through the world nowadays
scarcely remembering that they possess a body and life within it,
and there is fear, in the world there is fear of the words that designate
    the body,
and one talks favorably of clothes,
it is possible to speak of trousers, of suits,   30
and of women's underwear (of "ladies'" stockings and garters)
as if the articles and the suits went completely empty through the
    streets
and a dark and obscene clothes closet occupied the world.

Suits have existence, color, form, design,
and a profound place in our myths, too much of a place,   35
there is too much furniture and there are too many rooms in the
    world
and my body lives downcast among and beneath so many things,
with an obsession of slavery and chains.

Well, my knees, like knots,
private, functional, evident,   40
separate neatly the halves of my legs:
and really two different worlds, two different sexes
are not so different as the two halves of my legs.

From the knee to the foot a hard form,
mineral, coldly useful, appears,   45
a creature of bone and persistence,
and the ankles are now nothing but the naked purpose,
exactitude and necessity definitively disposed.

Without sensuality, short and hard, and masculine,
my legs exist, there, and endowed   50
with muscular groups like complementary animals,
and there too a life, a solid, subtle, sharp life
endures without trembling, waiting and performing.

At my feet ticklish
and hard like the sun, and open like flowers,   55
and perpetual, magnificent soldiers
in the gray war of space,
everything ends, life definitively ends at my feet,
what is foreign and hostile begins there:
the names of the world, the frontier and the remote,   60
the substantive and the adjectival too great for my heart
originate there with dense and cold constancy.

Always,
manufactured products, stockings, shoes,
or simply infinite air.   65
There will be between my feet and the earth
stressing the isolated and solitary part of my being,
something tenaciously involved between my life and the earth,
something openly unconquerable and unfriendly.

1933, trans. 1973

HORSES

translated from the Spanish by Alastair Reid

From the window I saw the horses.

I was in Berlin, in winter. The light
was without light, the sky skyless.

The air white like a moistened loaf.

From my window, I could see a deserted arena,   5
a circle bitten out by the teeth of winter.

All at once, led out by a single man,
ten horses were stepping, stepping into the snow.

Scarcely had they rippled into existence
like flame, than they filled the whole world of my eyes,   10
empty till now. Faultless, flaming,
they stepped like ten gods on broad, clean hoofs,
their manes recalling a dream of salt spray.

Their rumps were globes, were oranges.

Their colour was amber and honey, was on fire.   15

Their necks were towers
carved from the stone of pride,
and in their furious eyes, sheer energy
showed itself, a prisoner inside them.

And there, in the silence, at the mid-   20
point of the day, in a dirty, disgruntled winter,
the horses' intense presence was blood,
was rhythm, was the beckoning light of all being.

I saw, I saw, and seeing, I came to life.
There was the unwitting fountain, the dance of gold, the sky,   25
the fire that sprang to life in beautiful things.

I have obliterated that gloomy Berlin winter.

I shall not forget the light from these horses.

1958, trans. 1972

LOVE

translated from the Spanish by Alastair Reid

So many days, oh so many days
seeing you so tangible and so close,
how do I pay, with what do I pay?

The bloodthirsty spring
has awakened in the woods.   5
The foxes start from their earths,
the serpents drink the dew,
and I go with you in the leaves
between the pines and the silence,
asking myself how and when   10
I will have to pay for my luck.

Of everything I have seen,
it's you I want to go on seeing;
of everything I've touched,
it's your flesh I want to go on touching.   15
I love your orange laughter.
I am moved by the sight of you sleeping.

What am I to do, love, loved one?
I don't know how others love
or how people loved in the past.   20
I live, watching you, loving you.
Being in love is my nature.

You please me more each afternoon.

Where is she? I keep on asking
if your eyes disappear.   25
How long she's taking! I think, and I'm hurt.
I feel poor, foolish and sad,
and you arrive and you are lightning
glancing off the peach trees.

That's why I love you and yet not why.   30
There are so many reasons, and yet so few,
for love has to be so,
involving and general,

Pablo Neruda   755

particular and terrifying,
honoured and yet in mourning,   35
flowering like the stars,
and measureless as a kiss.

                                                        1958, trans. 1972

SWEETNESS, ALWAYS

translated from the Spanish by Alastair Reid

Why such harsh machinery?
Why, to write down the stuff
and people of every day,
must poems be dressed up in gold,
in old and fearful stone?   5

I want verses of felt or feather
which scarcely weigh, mild verses
with the intimacy of beds
where people have loved and dreamed.
I want poems stained   10
by hands and everydayness.

Verses of pastry which melt
into milk and sugar in the mouth,
air and water to drink,
the bites and kisses of love.   15
I long for eatable sonnets,
poems of honey and flour.

Vanity keeps prodding us
to lift ourselves skyward
or to make deep and useless   20
tunnels underground.
So we forget the joyous
love-needs of our bodies.
We forget about pastries.
We are not feeding the world.   25

In Madras a long time since,
I saw a sugary pyramid,
a tower of confectionery—
one level after another,
and in the construction, rubies,   30

"*Sweetness, Always*": 26. *Madras:* an industrial city in India.

and other blushing delights,
medieval and yellow.

Someone dirtied his hands
to cook up so much sweetness.

Brother poets from here   35
and there, from earth and sky,
from Medellín, from Veracruz,
Abyssinia, Antofagasta,
do you know the recipe for honeycombs?

Let's forget about all that stone.   40

Let your poetry fill up
the equinoctial pastry shop
our mouths long to devour—
all the children's mouths
and the poor adults' also.   45
Don't go on without seeing,
relishing, understanding
all these hearts of sugar.

Don't be afraid of sweetness.

With us or without us,   50
sweetness will go on living
and is infinitely alive,
forever being revived,
for it's in a man's mouth,
whether he's eating or singing,   55
that sweetness has its place.

1958, trans. 1972

LOVE SONNET VI

translated from the Spanish by Stephen Tapscott

Lost in the forest, I broke off a dark twig
and lifted its whisper to my thirsty lips:
maybe it was the voice of the rain crying,
a cracked bell, or a torn heart.

Something from far off: it seemed   5
deep and secret to me, hidden by the earth,

"Sweetness, Always": 37. *Medellín:* a city in Colombia notable for its coffee industry.
37. *Veracruz:* one of Mexico's chief seaports.   38. *Abyssinia:* Ethiopia.

a shout muffled by huge autumns,
by the moist half-open darkness of the leaves.

And there, awaking from the dreaming forest, the hazel-sprig
sang under my tongue, its drifting fragrance   10
climbed up through my conscious mind

as if suddenly the roots I had left behind
cried out to me, the land I had lost with my childhood—
and I stopped, wounded by the wandering scent.

1960, trans. 1985

THE DANGER

translated from the Spanish by Ben Belitt

Careful, they said: don't slip
on the wax of the ballroom:
look out for the ice and the rain and the mud.
Right, we all answered: this winter
we'll live without slippage!   5
And what happened? Under our feet
we felt something give way
and there we were, flat on our fannies:

in the blood of a century.

It seeped under the typist-stenographers,   10
the sweep of the snowdrifts,
staircases of marble;
it crossed meadows and cities,
editor's desks and theaters,
warehouses of ashes,   15
the colonel's grilled windows—
blood flowed in the ditches,
spurted from one war to another,
millions of corpses whose eyes
saw nothing but blood.   20

All this happened just as I tell it.

Maybe others will live out their lives with
no more than an occasional spill on the ice.

I live with this horror; when I tumble,
I go down into blood.   25

1969, trans. 1974

Further Reading

Bly, Robert. "Refusing to Be Theocritus." Introduction to *Neruda and Vallejo: Selected Poems*. Ed. Robert Bly. Boston: Beacon, 1971. 3–15. • Agosin, Marjorie. *Pablo Neruda*. Trans. Lorraine Roses. Boston: Twayne, 1986. • Durán, Manuel, and Margery Safir. *Earth Tones: The Poetry of Pablo Neruda*. Bloomington: Indiana UP, 1981. • Guibert, Rita. "The Art of Poetry XIV: Pablo Neruda." Trans. Ronald Christ. *Paris Review* 51 (Winter 1971): 149–75.

The poet Howard Moss once said in irritation that everyone being published in America in the 1970s was trying to sound like a translation of Pablo Neruda. Both Robert Bly's prose comment from an introduction to Neruda's poems and his elegy touch on the qualities that have made Neruda so appealing as a model.

Robert Bly: On Neruda's Revolutionary Poetry

We tend to associate the modern imagination with the jerky imagination, which starts forward, stops, turns around, switches from subject to subject. In Neruda's poems, the imagination drives forward, joining the entire poem in a rising flow of imaginative energy. In the underworld of the consciousness, in the thickets where Freud, standing a short distance off, pointed out incest bushes, murder trees, half-buried primitive altars, and unburied bodies, Neruda's imagination moves with utter assurance, sweeping from one spot to another almost magically. The starved emotional lives of notary publics he links to the whiteness of flour, sexual desire to the shape of shoes, death to the barking sound where there is no dog. His imagination sees the hidden connections between conscious and unconscious substances with such assurance that he hardly bothers with metaphors—he links them by tying their hidden tails. He is a new kind of creature moving about under the surface of everything. Moving under the earth, he knows everything from the bottom up (which is the right way to learn the nature of a thing) and therefore is never at a loss for its name. Compared to him, most American poets resemble blind men moving gingerly along the ground from tree to tree, from house to house, feeling each thing for a long time, and then calling out "House!" when we already know it is a house.

Neruda has confidence in what is hidden. The Establishment respects only what the light has fallen on, but Neruda likes the unlit just as well. He writes of small typists without scorn, and of the souls of huge, sleeping snakes.

He violates the rules for behavior set up by the wise. The convention-
ally wise assure us that to a surrealist the outer world has no reality—only
his inner flow of images is real. Neruda's work demolishes this banality.
Neruda's poetry is deeply surrealist, and yet entities of the outer world like
the United Fruit Company have greater force in his poems than in those of
any strictly "outward" poet alive. Once a poet takes a political stand, the
wise assure us that he will cease writing good poetry. Neruda became a
Communist in the middle of his life and has remained one: at least half of his
greatest work, one must admit, was written after that time. He has written
great poetry at all times of his life.

Finally, many critics in the United States insist the poem must be hard-
bitten, impersonal, and rational, lest it lack sophistication. Neruda is wildly
romantic, and more sophisticated than Hulme or Pound could dream of
being. He has few literary theories. Like Vallejo, Neruda wishes to help
humanity, and tells the truth for that reason.

Robert Bly

(b. 1926)

MOURNING PABLO NERUDA

Water is practical,
especially
in August.
Faucet water
falls   5
into the buckets
I carry
to the young
willow trees
whose leaves   10
have been eaten
off
by grasshoppers.
Or this jar of water
that lies   15
next to me
on the car seat
as I drive
to my shack.
When I look down,   20
the seat all

around the jar
is dark,
for water doesn't intend
to give, it gives   25
anyway
and the jar of water
lies
there quivering
as I drive   30
through a countryside
of granite quarries,
stones
soon to be shaped
into blocks for the dead,   35
the only
thing they have
left that is theirs.

For the dead remain inside
us, as water   40
remains inside granite—
hardly at all—
for their job is to
go
away,   45
and not come back,
even when we ask them,
but water
comes to us—
it doesn't care   50
about us; it goes
around us, on the way
to the Minnesota River,
to the Mississippi River,
to the Gulf,   55
always closer
to where
it has to be.

No one lays flowers
on the grave   60
of water,
for it is not
here,
it is
gone.   65

1981

W. H. AUDEN

(1907–1973)

MUSÉE DES BEAUX ARTS

About suffering they were never wrong,
The Old Masters: how well they understood
Its human position; how it takes place
While someone else is eating or opening a window or just walking
    dully along;
How, when the aged are reverently, passionately waiting   5
For the miraculous birth, there always must be
Children who did not specially want it to happen, skating
On a pond at the edge of the wood:
They never forgot
That even the dreadful martyrdom must run its course   10
Anyhow in a corner, some untidy spot
Where the dogs go on with their doggy life and the torturer's horse
Scratches its innocent behind on a tree.

In Breughel's *Icarus,* for instance: how everything turns away
Quite leisurely from the disaster; the ploughman may   15
Have heard the splash, the forsaken cry,
But for him it was not an important failure; the sun shone
As it had to on the white legs disappearing into the green
Water; and the expensive delicate ship that must have seen
Something amazing, a boy falling out of the sky,   20
Had somewhere to get to and sailed calmly on.

1938

THE SPHINX

Did it once issue from the carver's hand
Healthy? Even the earliest conqueror saw
The face of a sick ape, a bandaged paw,
An ailing lion crouched on dirty sand.

"Musée des Beaux Arts": 14. *Icarus:* This painting (c. 1558) depicts a scene from Greek
mythology. The craftsman Daedalus made wax wings on which both he and his son Icarus
were to escape imprisonment. Ignoring his father's warning, Icarus flew too near the sun and
his wings melted, so that he fell to death in the sea. In the painting Icarus is a tiny figure in the
background, only his legs visible above the surface of a bay busy with ships and boats. In the
foreground a ploughman and shepherd are at work.

We gape, then go uneasily away: 5
It does not like the young nor love nor learning.
Time hurt it like a person: it lies turning
A vast behind on shrill America,

And witnesses. The huge hurt face accuses
And pardons nothing, least of all success: 10
What counsel it might offer it refuses
To those who face akimbo its distress.

'Do people like me?' *No.* The slave amuses
The lion. 'Am I to suffer always?' *Yes.*

                                                                    1940

THE UNKNOWN CITIZEN

(To JS/07/M/378 This Marble Monument Is Erected by the State)

He was found by the Bureau of Statistics to be
One against whom there was no official complaint,
And all the reports on his conduct agree
That, in the modern sense of an old-fashioned word, he was a saint,
For in everything he did he served the Greater Community.   5
Except for the War till the day he retired
He worked in a factory and never got fired,
But satisfied his employers, Fudge Motors Inc.
Yet he wasn't a scab or odd in his views,
For his Union reports that he paid his dues,   10
(Our report on his Union shows it was sound)
And our Social Psychology workers found
That he was popular with his mates and liked a drink.
The Press are convinced that he bought a paper every day
And that his reactions to advertisements were normal in every way.   15
Policies taken out in his name prove that he was fully insured.
And his Health-card shows he was once in hospital but left it cured.
Both Producers Research and High-Grade Living declare
He was fully sensible to the advantages of the Installment Plan
And had everything necessary to the Modern Man,   20
A phonograph, a radio, a car and a frigidaire.
Our researchers into Public Opinion are content
That he held the proper opinions for the time of year;
When there was peace, he was for peace; when there was war, he
     went.
He was married and added five children to the population,   25
Which our Eugenist says was the right number for a
     parent of his generation,

And our teachers report that he never interfered with their
    education.
Was he free? Was he happy? The question is absurd:
Had anything been wrong, we should certainly have heard.

1940

IN MEMORY OF W. B. YEATS

1

He disappeared in the dead of winter:
The brooks were frozen, the airports almost deserted,
The snow disfigured the public statues;
The mercury sank in the mouth of the dying day.
O all the instruments agree   5
The day of his death was a dark cold day.

Far from his illness
The wolves ran on through the evergreen forests,
The peasant river was untempted by the fashionable quays;
By mourning tongues   10
The death of the poet was kept from his poems.

But for him it was his last afternoon as himself,
An afternoon of nurses and rumours;
The provinces of his body revolted,
The squares of his mind were empty,   15
Silence invaded the suburbs,
The current of his feeling failed: he became his admirers.

Now he is scattered among a hundred cities
And wholly given over to unfamiliar affections;
To find his happiness in another kind of wood   20
And be punished under a foreign code of conscience.
The words of a dead man
Are modified in the guts of the living.

But in the importance and noise of tomorrow
When the brokers are roaring like beasts on the floor
    of the Bourse,   25
And the poor have the sufferings to which they are fairly
    accustomed,
And each in the cell of himself is almost convinced of his freedom;
A few thousand will think of this day
As one thinks of a day when one did something slightly unusual.
O all the instruments agree   30
The day of his death was a dark cold day.

You were silly like us: your gift survived it all;
The parish of rich women, physical decay,
Yourself; mad Ireland hurt you into poetry.
Now Ireland has her madness and her weather still,   35
For poetry makes nothing happen: it survives
In the valley of its saying where executives
Would never want to tamper; it flows south
From ranches of isolation and the busy griefs,
Raw towns that we believe and die in; it survives,   40
A way of happening, a mouth.

Earth, receive an honoured guest;
William Yeats is laid to rest:
Let the Irish vessel lie
Emptied of its poetry.   45

Time that is intolerant
Of the brave and innocent,
And indifferent in a week
To a beautiful physique,

Worships language and forgives   50
Everyone by whom it lives;
Pardons cowardice, conceit,
Lays its honours at their feet.

Time that with this strange excuse
Pardoned Kipling and his views,   55
And will pardon Paul Claudel,
Pardons him for writing well.

In the nightmare of the dark
All the gods of Europe bark,
And the living nations wait,   60
Each sequestered in its hate;

Intellectual disgrace
Stares from every human face,
And the seas of pity lie
Locked and frozen in each eye.   65

Follow, poet, follow right
To the bottom of the night,
With your unconstraining voice
Still persuade us to rejoice;

With the farming of a verse   70
Make a vineyard of the curse,
Sing of human unsuccess
In a rapture of distress;

In the deserts of the heart
Let the healing fountain start,   75
In the prison of his days
Teach the free man how to praise.

1940

SPAIN, 1937

Yesterday all the past. The language of size
Spreading to China along the trade-routes; the diffusion
      Of the counting-frame and the cromlech;
Yesterday the shadow-reckoning in the sunny climates.

Yesterday the assessment of insurance by cards,   5
The divination of water; yesterday the invention
      Of cart-wheels and clocks, the taming of
Horses; yesterday the bustling world of navigators.

Yesterday the abolition of fairies and giants;
The fortress like a motionless eagle eyeing the valley,   10
      The chapel built in the forest;
Yesterday the carving of angels and of frightening gargoyles.

The trial of heretics among the columns of stone;
Yesterday the theological feuds in the taverns
      And the miraculous cure at the fountain;   15
Yesterday the Sabbath of Witches. But to-day the struggle.

Yesterday the installation of dynamos and turbines;
The construction of railways in the colonial desert;
      Yesterday the classic lecture
On the origin of Mankind. But to-day the struggle.   20
Yesterday the belief in the absolute value of Greek;
The fall of the curtain upon the death of a hero;
      Yesterday the prayer to the sunset,
And the adoration of madmen. But to-day the struggle.

As the poet whispers, startled among the pines   25
Or, where the loose waterfall sings, compact, or upright

"*Spain, 1937*": *1937*: the Spanish Civil War, precursor to World War II in its brutal conflict
between fascism and communism, was at its height in 1937.   16. *Sabbath of Witches:* a painting
by the Spanish painter Francisco José de Goya Lucientes (1746–1828).

On the crag by the leaning tower:
'O my vision. O send me the luck of the sailor.'

And the investigator peers through his instruments
At the inhuman provinces, the virile bacillus   30
     Or enormous Jupiter finished:
'But the lives of my friends. I inquire, I inquire.'

And the poor in their fireless lodgings dropping the sheets
Of the evening paper: 'Our day is our loss. O show us
     History the operator, the   35
Organizer, Time the refreshing river.'

And the nations combine each cry, invoking the life
That shapes the individual belly and orders
     The private nocturnal terror:
'Did you not found once the city state of the sponge,   40

'Raise the vast military empires of the shark
And the tiger, establish the robin's plucky canton?
     Intervene, O descend as a dove or
A furious papa or a mild engineer: but descend.'

And the life, if it answers at all, replies from the heart   45
And the eyes and the lungs, from the shops and squares of
    the city:
     'O no, I am not the Mover,
Not to-day, not to you. To you I'm the
Yes-man, the bar-companion, the easily-duped: 50
I am whatever you do; I am your vow to be
     Good, your humorous story;
I am your business voice; I am your marriage.

'What's your proposal? To build the Just City? I will.
I agree. Or is it the suicide pact, the romantic   55
     Death? Very well, I accept, for
I am your choice, your decision: yes, I am Spain.'

Many have heard it on remote peninsulas,
On sleepy plains, in the aberrant fishermen's islands,
     In the corrupt heart of the city;   60
Have heard and migrated like gulls or the seeds of a flower.

They clung like burrs to the long expresses that lurch
Through the unjust lands, through the night, through the
    alpine tunnel;
     They floated over the oceans;   65
They walked the passes: they came to present their lives.

On that arid square, that fragment nipped off from hot
Africa, soldered so crudely to inventive Europe,

On that tableland scored by rivers,
Our fever's menacing shapes are precise and alive.   70

To-morrow, perhaps, the future: the research on fatigue
And the movements of packers; the gradual exploring
    of all the
        Octaves of radiation;
To-morrow the enlarging of consciousness by diet and
    breathing.   75

To-morrow the rediscovery of romantic love;
The photographing of ravens; all the fun under
    Liberty's masterful shadow;
To-morrow the hour of the pageant-master and the musician.
To-morrow, for the young, the poets exploding like bombs,   80
The walks by the lake, the winter of perfect communion;
    To-morrow the bicycle races
Through the suburbs on summer evenings: but to-day
    the struggle.

To-day the inevitable increase in the chances of death;
The conscious acceptance of guilt in the fact of murder;   85
    To-day the expending of powers
On the flat ephemeral pamphlet and the boring meeting.

To-day the makeshift consolations; the shared cigarette;
The cards in the candle-lit barn and the scraping concert,
    The masculine jokes; to-day the   90
Fumbled and unsatisfactory embrace before hurting.

The stars are dead; the animals will not look:
We are left alone with our day, and the time is short and
    History to the defeated
May say Alas but cannot help or pardon.   95

1940

LUTHER

With conscience cocked to listen for the thunder,
He saw the Devil busy in the wind,
Over the chiming steeples and then under
The doors of nuns and doctors who had sinned.

What apparatus could stave off disaster   5
Or cut the brambles of man's error down?
Flesh was a silent dog that bites its master,
World a still pond in which its children drown.

The fuse of Judgement spluttered in his head:
'Lord, smoke these honeyed insects from their hives.   10
All works, Great Men, Societies are bad.
The Just shall live by Faith . . .' he cried in dread.

And men and women of the world were glad,
Who'd never cared or trembled in their lives.

1945

VOLTAIRE AT FERNEY

Almost happy now, he looked at his estate.
An exile making watches glanced up as he passed
And went on working; where a hospital was rising fast,
A joiner touched his cap; an agent came to tell
Some of the trees he'd planted were progressing well.   5
The white alps glittered. It was summer. He was very great.

Far off in Paris where his enemies
Whispered that he was wicked, in an upright chair
A blind old woman longed for death and letters. He would write,
"Nothing is better than life." But was it? Yes, the fight   10
Against the false and the unfair
Was always worth it. So was gardening. Civilize.

Cajoling, scolding, scheming, cleverest of them all,
He'd led the other children in a holy war
Against the infamous grown-ups; and, like a child, been sly   15
And humble, when there was occasion for
The two-faced answer or the plain protective lie,
But, patient like a peasant, waited for their fall.

And never doubted, like D'Alembert, he would win:
Only Pascal was a great enemy, the rest
Were rats already poisoned; there was much, though, to be done,   20
And only himself to count upon.
Dear Diderot was dull but did his best;
Rousseau, he'd always known, would blubber and give in.

Yet, like a sentinel, he could not sleep. The night was full of wrong,
Earthquakes and executions: Soon he would be dead,   25

"*Voltaire at Ferney*": *Voltaire:* the great French philosopher (1694–1778) whose rationalism led
him to attack bigotry, cruelty, tyranny, and the church. Among his allies were the encyclopedists Diderot and D'Alembert. Jean-Jacques Rousseau (1712–1778), once an ally to the
Encyclopedists, turned against them partly because he was influenced by the writings of Blaise
Pascal (1623–1662), the great mathematician and advocate of religious faith.

And still all over Europe stood the horrible nurses
Itching to boil their children. Only his verses
Perhaps could stop them: He must go on working: Overhead,
The uncomplaining stars composed their lucid song.

1948

THE SHIELD OF ACHILLES

> She looked over his shoulder
>   For vines and olive trees,
> Marble well-governed cities
>   And ships upon untamed seas,
> But there on the shining metal   5
>   his hands had put instead
> An artificial wilderness
>   And a sky like lead.

A plain without a feature, bare and brown,
  No blade of grass, no sign of neighbourhood,   10
Nothing to eat and nowhere to sit down,
  Yet, congregated on its blankness, stood
  An unintelligible multitude,
A million eyes, a million boots in line,
Without expression, waiting for a sign.   15

Out of the air a voice without a face
  Proved by statistics that some cause was just
In tones as dry and level as the place:
  No one was cheered and nothing was discussed;
  Column by column in a cloud of dust   20
They marched away enduring a belief
Whose logic brought them, somewhere else, to grief.

> She looked over his shoulder
>   For ritual pieties,
> White flower-garlanded heifers,   25
>   Libation and sacrifice,
> But there on the shining metal
>   Where the altar should have been,
> She saw by his flickering forge-light
>   Quite another scene.   30

Barbed wire enclosed an arbitrary spot
  Where bored officials lounged (one cracked a joke)

"*The Shield of Achilles*": *Shield of Achilles:* In Homer's *Iliad,* after Patroclus is killed wearing his friend Achilles' armor, Hephaestos, the blacksmith of the gods, makes him new armor, including a beautiful shield on which are portrayed the earth, sea, and heavens.

And sentries sweated for the day was hot:
    A crowd of ordinary decent folk
    Watched from without and neither moved nor spoke   35
As three pale figures were led forth and bound
To three posts driven upright in the ground.

The mass and majesty of this world, all
    That carries weight and always weighs the same
Lay in the hands of others; they were small   40
    And could not hope for help and no help came:
    What their foes liked to do was done, their shame
Was all the worst could wish; they lost their pride
And died as men before their bodies died.

      She looked over his shoulder   45
        For athletes at their games,
      Men and women in a dance
        Moving their sweet limbs
      Quick, quick, to music,
        But there on the shining shield   50
      His hands had set no dancing-floor
        But a weed-choked field.

A ragged urchin, aimless and alone,
    Loitered about that vacancy, a bird
Flew up to safety from his well-aimed stone: 55
    That girls are raped, that two boys knife a third,
    Were axioms to him, who'd never heard
Of any world where promises were kept,
Or one could weep because another wept.

      The thin-lipped armourer,   60
        Hephaestos hobbled away,
      Thetis of the shining breasts
        Cried out in dismay
      At what the god had wrought
        To please her son, the strong   65
      Iron-hearted man-slaying Achilles
        Who would not live long.

1952

Further Reading

Spears, Monroe K., ed. *Auden: A Collection of Critical Essays.* Englewood Cliffs, NJ: Prentice, 1964. • Bluestone, Max. "The Iconographic Sources of Auden's 'Musée des Beaux Arts.' " *Modern Language Notes* 76.4 (Apr. 1961): 331–36. • McDiarmid, Lucy S. "Poetry's Landscape in Auden's Elegy for Yeats." *Modern Language Quarterly* 38.2 (June 1977): 167–77. • Buell, Frederick. "Experiments in Political Voice." Chapter 4 of *W. H. Auden as Social Poet.* Ithaca: Cornell UP, 1973. 118–57, spec. 148–57. • Johnson, Richard. "The Early History of Late Man." *Man's Place: An Essay on Auden.* Ithaca: Cornell UP, 1973. 126–71, spec. 168–71.

The range of W. H. Auden's poetic subjects, styles, and tones is so wide that some readers have found it disturbing. Some have been particularly distressed by the contrast between the poet committed to social justice and the poet of light verse and poetic gamesmanship. When Auden edited The Oxford Book of Light Verse, *he wrote in the introduction a statement that can help us reconcile these two Audens.*

W. H. Auden: On His Recognition of the Romantic Tradition

Wordsworth's case is paralleled by the history of most of the Romantic poets, both of his day and of the century following. Isolated in an amorphous society with no real communal ties, bewildered by its complexity, horrified by its ugliness and power, and uncertain of an audience, they turned away from the life of their time to the contemplation of their own emotions and the creation of imaginary worlds, Wordsworth to Nature, Keats and Mallarmé to a world of pure poetry, Shelley to a future Golden Age, Baudelaire and Hölderlin to a past,

> . . . ces époques nues
> Dont Phoebus se plaisait à dorer les statues.

Instead of the poet regarding himself as an entertainer, he becomes the prophet, 'the unacknowledged legislator of the world', or the Dandy who sits in the café, 'proud that he is less base than the passers-by, saying to himself as he contemplates the smoke of his cigar: "What does it matter to me what becomes of my perceptions?"'

This is not, of course, to condemn the Romantic poets, but to explain why they wrote the kind of poetry they did, why their best work is personal, intense, often difficult, and generally rather gloomy.

The release from social pressure was, at first, extremely stimulating. The private world was a relatively unexplored field, and the technical discoveries made were as great as those being made in industry. But the feel-

---

W. H. Auden: On His Recognition of the Romantic Tradition: ces epoques . . . statues: "those naked ages/When Phoebus loved to gild statues." The quotation is from Baudelaire's *Flowers of Evil* and is part of a poem contrasting the ancient world's pleasure in healthy, naked young bodies with modern prudery and degeneracy. *"What does . . . perceptions?":* the quotation is from Baudelaire's *Intimate Journals.*

ing of excitement was followed by a feeling of loss. For if it is true that the closer bound the artist is to his community the harder it is for him to see with a detached vision, it is also true that when he is too isolated, though he may see clearly enough what he does see, that dwindles in quantity and importance. He 'knows more and more about less and less'. It is significant that so many of these poets either died young like Keats, or went mad like Hölderlin, or ceased producing good work like Wordsworth, or gave up writing altogether like Rimbaud—'I must ask forgiveness for having fed myself on lies, and let us go. . . . One must be absolutely modern.' For the private world is fascinating, but it is exhaustible. Without a secure place in society, without an intimate relation between himself and his audience, without, in fact, those conditions which make for Light Verse, the poet finds it difficult to grow beyond a certain point. . . .

The problem for the modern poet, as for every one else to-day, is how to find or form a genuine community, in which each has his valued place and can feel at home. The old pre-industrial community and culture are gone and cannot be brought back. Nor is it desirable that they should be. They were too unjust, too squalid, and too custom-bound. Virtues which were once nursed unconsciously by the forces of nature must now be recovered and fostered by a deliberate effort of the will and the intelligence. In the future, societies will not grow of themselves. They will either be made consciously or decay. A democracy in which each citizen is as fully conscious and capable of making a rational choice, as in the past has been possible only for the wealthier few, is the only kind of society which in the future is likely to survive for long.

In such a society, and in such alone, will it be possible for the poet, without sacrificing any of his subtleties of sensibility or his integrity, to write poetry which is simple, clear, and gay.

For poetry which is at the same time light and adult can only be written in a society which is both integrated and free.

THEODORE ROETHKE

(1908–1963)

MY PAPA'S WALTZ

The whiskey on your breath
Could make a small boy dizzy;
But I hung on like death:
Such waltzing was not easy.

We romped until the pans
Slid from the kitchen shelf; 5

My mother's countenance
Could not unfrown itself.

The hand that held my wrist
Was battered on one knuckle;   10
At every step you missed
My right ear scraped a buckle.

You beat time on my head
With a palm caked hard by dirt,
Then waltzed me off to bed   15
Still clinging to your shirt.

1942

BIG WIND

Where were the greenhouses going,
Lunging into the lashing
Wind driving water
So far down the river
All the faucets stopped?   5
So we drained the manure-machine
For the steam plant,
Pumping the stale mixture
Into the rusty boilers,
Watching the pressure gauge   10
Waver over to red,
As the seams hissed
And the live steam
Drove to the far
End of the rose-house,   15
Where the worst wind was,
Creaking the cypress window-frames,
Cracking so much thin glass
We stayed all night,
Stuffing the holes with burlap;   20
But she rode it out,
That old rose-house,
She hove into the teeth of it,
The core and pith of that ugly storm,
Ploughing with her stiff prow,   25
Bucking into the wind-waves
That broke over the whole of her,
Flailing her sides with spray,
Flinging long strings of wet across the roof-top,

Finally veering, wearing themselves out, merely   30
Whistling thinly under the wind-vents;
She sailed until the calm morning,
Carrying her full cargo of roses.

1948

ROOT CELLAR

Nothing would sleep in that cellar, dank as a ditch,
Bulbs broke out of boxes hunting for chinks in the dark,
Shoots dangled and drooped,
Lolling obscenely from mildewed crates,
Hung down long yellow evil necks, like tropical snakes.   5
And what a congress of stinks!
Roots ripe as old bait,
Pulpy stems, rank, silo-rich,
Leaf-mold, manure, lime, piled against slippery planks
Nothing would give up life: 10
Even the dirt kept breathing a small breath.

1948

CHILD ON TOP OF A GREENHOUSE

The wind billowing out the seat of my britches,
My feet crackling splinters of glass and dried putty,
The half-grown chrysanthemums staring up like accusers,
Up through the streaked glass, flashing with sunlight,
A few white clouds all rushing eastward,   5
A line of elms plunging and tossing like horses,
And everyone, everyone pointing up and shouting!

1948

FRAU BAUMAN, FRAU SCHMIDT, AND
FRAU SCHWARTZE

Gone the three ancient ladies
Who creaked on the greenhouse ladders,
Reaching up white strings
To wind, to wind
The sweet-pea tendrils, the smilax,   5
Nasturtiums, the climbing

Roses, to straighten
Carnations, red
Chrysanthemums; the stiff
Stems, jointed like corn,
They tied and tucked,—
These nurses of nobody else.
Quicker than birds, they dipped
Up and sifted the dirt;
They sprinkled and shook;
They stood astride pipes,
Their skirts billowing out wide into tents,
Their hands twinkling with wet;
Like witches they flew along rows
Keeping creation at ease;
With a tendril for needle
They sewed up the air with a stem;
They teased out the seed that the cold kept asleep,—
All the coils, loops, and whorls.
They trellised the sun; they plotted for more than themselves.

I remember how they picked me up, a spindly kid,
Pinching and poking my thin ribs
Till I lay in their laps, laughing,
Weak as a whiffet;
Now, when I'm alone and cold in my bed,
They still hover over me,
These ancient leathery crones,
With their bandannas stiffened with sweat,
And their thorn-bitten wrists,
And their snuff-laden breath blowing lightly over me in my first
    sleep.

10

15

20

25

30

35

1953

I KNEW A WOMAN

I knew a woman, lovely in her bones,
When small birds sighed, she would sigh back at them;
Ah, when she moved, she moved more ways than one:
The shapes a bright container can contain!
Of her choice virtues only gods should speak,
Or English poets who grew up on Greek
(I'd have them sing in chorus, cheek to cheek).

5

How well her wishes went! She stroked my chin,
She taught me Turn, and Counter-turn, and Stand;
She taught me Touch, that undulant white skin; 10
I nibbled meekly from her proffered hand;
She was the sickle; I, poor I, the rake,
Coming behind her for her pretty sake
(But what prodigious mowing we did make).

Love likes a gander, and adores a goose: 15
Her full lips pursed, the errant note to seize;
She played it quick, she played it light and loose,
My eyes, they dazzled at her flowing knees;
Her several parts could keep a pure repose,
Or one hip quiver with a mobile nose 20
(She moved in circles, and those circles moved).

Let seed be grass, and grass turn into hay:
I'm martyr to a motion not my own;
What's freedom for? To know eternity.
I swear she cast a shadow white as stone. 25
But who would count eternity in days?
These old bones live to learn her wanton ways:
(I measure time by how a body sways).

1954

Further Reading

Roethke, Theodore. "Some Remarks on Rhythm." *On the Poet and His Craft: Selected Prose of Theodore Roethke.* Ed. Ralph J. Mills, Jr. Seattle: U of Washington P, 1965. 71–84. • Wolff, George. *Theodore Roethke.* Boston: Twayne, 1981. • Heyen, William, ed. *Profile of Theodore Roethke.* Columbus, O.: Merrill, 1971. • Martz, Louis L. "Theodore Roethke: A Greenhouse Eden." *The Poem of the Mind: Essays on Poetry, English and American.* New York: Oxford UP, 1966. • Galvin, Brendan. "Kenneth Burke and Theodore Roethke's 'Lost Son' Poems." *Northwest Review* 11.3 (Summer 1971): 67–96. • Ramsey, Jarold. "Roethke in the Greenhouse." *Western Humanities Review* 26.1 (Winter 1972): 35–47.

---

9. *Turn . . . Stand:* in classical Greek drama, divisions of a Pindaric ode, corresponding to the movement of the chorus as it chanted the lines.

Louise Bogan once remarked that Theodore Roethke and Robert Lowell are alike in their fascination with memories that stretch back to childhood, but unalike in their methods. Roethke, she said, combines "a close recording of the actual with a kind of lyrical incantation" absent from Lowell. Roethke himself has discussed this "lyrical incantation" in "Some Remarks on Rhythm."

Theodore Roethke: On Rhythm and Association

What do *I* like? Listen:

> Hinx, minx, the old witch winks!
> The fat begins to fry!
> There's nobody home but Jumping Joan,
> And father, and mother, and I.

Now what makes that "catchy," to use Mr. Frost's word? For one thing: the rhythm. Five stresses out of a possible six in the first line, though maybe "old" doesn't take quite as strong a stress as the others. And three—keep noticing that magic number—internal rhymes, *hinx, minx, winks.* And notice too the apparent mysteriousness of the action: something happens right away—the old witch winks and she sets events into motion. The fat begins to fry, literally and symbolically. She commands—no old fool witch this one. Notice that the second line, "The fat begins to fry," is absolutely regular metrically. It's all iambs, a thing that often occurs when previous lines are sprung or heavily counterpointed. The author doesn't want to get too far from his base, from his ground beat. The third line varies again with an anapaest and variations in the "o" and "u" sounds. "There's nobody home but Jumping Joan." Then the last line—anapaest lengthening the line out to satisfy the ear, "And father, and mother, and I." Sometimes we are inclined to feel that Mother Goose, or the traditional kind of thing, is almost infallible as memorable speech—the phrase is Auden's. . . .

It's nonsense, of course, to think that memorableness in poetry comes solely from rhetorical devices, or the following of certain sound patterns, or contrapuntal rhythmical effects. We all know that poetry is shot through with appeals to the unconsciousness, to the fears and desires that go far back into our childhood, into the imagination of the race. And we know that some words, like *hill, plow, mother, window, bird, fish,* are so drenched with human association, they sometimes can make even bad poems evocative.

ELIZABETH BISHOP

(1911-1979)

THE PRODIGAL

The brown enormous odor he lived by
was too close, with its breathing and thick hair,
for him to judge. The floor was rotten; the sty
was plastered halfway up with glass-smooth dung.
Light-lashed, self-righteous, above moving snouts,   5
the pigs' eyes followed him, a cheerful stare—
even to the sow that always ate her young—
till, sickening, he leaned to scratch her head.
But sometimes mornings after drinking bouts
(he hid the pints behind a two-by-four),   10
the sunrise glazed the barnyard mud with red;
the burning puddles seemed to reassure.
And then he thought he almost might endure
his exile yet another year or more.

But evenings the first star came to warn.   15
The farmer whom he worked for came at dark
to shut the cows and horses in the barn
beneath their overhanging clouds of hay,
with pitchforks, faint forked lightnings, catching light,
safe and companionable as in the Ark.   20
The pigs stuck out their little feet and snored.
The lantern—like the sun, going away—
laid on the mud a pacing aureole.

Carrying a bucket along a slimy board,
he felt the bats' uncertain staggering flight,   25
his shuddering insights, beyond his control,
touching him. But it took him a long time
finally to make his mind up to go home.

1951

Prodigal: See Luke 15:11–32.

FILLING STATION

Oh, but it is dirty!
—this little filling station,
oil-soaked, oil-permeated
to a disturbing, over-all
black translucency.   5
Be careful with that match!

Father wears a dirty,
oil-soaked monkey suit
that cuts him under the arms,
and several quick and saucy   10
and greasy sons assist him
(it's a family filling station),
all quite thoroughly dirty.

Do they live in the station?
It has a cement porch   15
behind the pumps, and on it
a set of crushed and grease-
impregnated wickerwork;
on the wicker sofa
a dirty dog, quite comfy.   20

Some comic books provide
the only note of color—
of certain color. They lie
upon a big dim doily
draping a taboret   25
(part of the set), beside
a big hirsute begonia.

Why the extraneous plant?
Why the taboret?
Why, oh why, the doily?   30
(Embroidered in daisy stitch
with marguerites, I think,
and heavy with gray crochet.)
Somebody embroidered the doily.
Somebody waters the plant,   35
or oils it, maybe. Somebody
arranges the rows of cans
so that they softly say:
ESSO—SO—SO—SO
to high-strung automobiles.   40
Somebody loves us all.

1955

THE ARMADILLO

(For Robert Lowell)

This is the time of year
when almost every night
the frail, illegal fire balloons appear.
Climbing the mountain height,

rising toward a saint   5
still honored in these parts,
the paper chambers flush and fill with light
that comes and goes, like hearts.

Once up against the sky it's hard
to tell them from the stars—   10
planets, that is—the tinted ones:
Venus going down, or Mars,

or the pale green one. With a wind,
they flare and falter, wobble and toss;
but if it's still they steer between   15
the kite sticks of the Southern Cross,

receding, dwindling, solemnly
and steadily forsaking us,
or, in the downdraft from a peak,
suddenly turning dangerous.   20

Last night another big one fell.
It splattered like an egg of fire
against the cliff behind the house.
The flame ran down. We saw the pair

of owls who nest there flying up   25
and up, their whirling black-and-white
strained bright pink underneath, until
they shrieked up out of sight.

The ancient owls' nest must have burned.
Hastily, all alone,   30
a glistening armadillo left the scene,
rose-flecked, head down, tail down,

and then a baby rabbit jumped out,
short-eared, to our surprise.
So soft!—a handful of intangible ash   35
with fixed, ignited eyes.

Too pretty, dreamlike mimicry!
O falling fire and piercing cry

and panic, and a weak mailed fist
clenched ignorant against the sky!   40

1965

QUESTIONS OF TRAVEL

There are too many waterfalls here; the crowded streams
hurry too rapidly down to the sea,
and the pressure of so many clouds on the mountaintops
makes them spill over the sides in soft slow-motion,
turning to waterfalls under our very eyes.   5
—For if those streaks, those mile-long, shiny, tearstains,
aren't waterfalls yet,
in a quick age or so, as ages go here,
they probably will be.
But if the streams and clouds keep travelling, travelling,   10
the mountains look like the hulls of capsized ships,
slime-hung and barnacled.

Think of the long trip home.
Should we have stayed at home and thought of here?
Where should we be today?   15
Is it right to be watching strangers in a play
in this strangest of theatres?
What childishness is it that while there's a breath of life
in our bodies, we are determined to rush
to see the sun the other way around?   20
The tiniest green hummingbird in the world?
To stare at some inexplicable old stonework,
inexplicable and impenetrable,
at any view,
instantly seen and always, always delightful?   25
Oh, must we dream our dreams
and have them, too?
And have we room
for one more folded sunset, still quite warm?

But surely it would have been a pity   30
not to have seen the trees along this road,
really exaggerated in their beauty,
not to have seen them gesturing
like noble pantomimists, robed in pink.
—Not to have had to stop for gas and heard   35
the sad, two-noted, wooden tune
of disparate wooden clogs
carelessly clacking over

a grease-stained filling-station floor.
(In another country the clogs would all be tested.   40
Each pair there would have identical pitch.)
—A pity not to have heard
the other, less primitive music of the fat brown bird
who sings above the broken gasoline pump
in a bamboo church of Jesuit baroque: 45
three towers, five silver crosses.
—Yes, a pity not to have pondered,
blurr'dly and inconclusively,
on what connection can exist for centuries
between the crudest wooden footwear   50
and, careful and finicky,
the whittled fantasies of wooden cages.
—Never to have studied history in
the weak calligraphy of songbirds' cages.
—And never to have had to listen to rain   55
so much like politicians' speeches:
two hours of unrelenting oratory
and then a sudden golden silence
in which the traveller takes a notebook, writes:

"Is it lack of imagination that makes us come   60
to imagined places, not just stay at home?
Or could Pascal have been not entirely right
about just sitting quietly in one's room?

Continent, city, country, society:
the choice is never wide and never free.   65
And here, or there . . . No. Should we have stayed at home,
wherever that may be?"

                                                            1965

IN THE WAITING ROOM

In Worcester, Massachusetts,
I went with Aunt Consuelo
to keep her dentist's appointment
and sat and waited for her
in the dentist's waiting room.   5
It was winter. It got dark
early. The waiting room
was full of grown-up people,

"Questions of Travel": 62. *Pascal:* The French geometrician and philosopher (1623–1662)
secluded himself in the Jansenist monastery of Port Royal after 1654.

arctics and overcoats,
lamps and magazines.   10
My aunt was inside
what seemed like a long time
and while I waited I read
the *National Geographic*
(I could read) and carefully   15
studied the photographs:
the inside of a volcano,
black, and full of ashes;
then it was spilling over
in rivulets of fire.   20
Osa and Martin Johnson
dressed in riding breeches,
laced boots, and pith helmets.
A dead man slung on a pole
—"Long Pig," the caption said.   25
Babies with pointed heads
wound round and round with string;
black, naked women with necks
wound round and round with wire
like the necks of light bulbs.   30
Their breasts were horrifying.
I read it right straight through.
I was too shy to stop.
And then I looked at the cover:
the yellow margins, the date.   35

Suddenly, from inside,
came an *oh!* of pain
—Aunt Consuelo's voice—
not very loud or long.
I wasn't at all surprised;   40
even then I knew she was
a foolish, timid woman.
I might have been embarrassed,
but wasn't. What took me
completely by surprise   45
was that it was *me:*
my voice, in my mouth.
Without thinking at all
I was my foolish aunt,
I—we—were falling, falling,   50
our eyes glued to the cover
of the *National Geographic,*
February, 1918.

I said to myself: three days
and you'll be seven years old.   55
I was saying it to stop
the sensation of falling off
the round, turning world
into cold, blue-black space.
But I felt: you are an *I*,   60
you are an *Elizabeth*,
you are one of *them*.
Why should you be one, too?
I scarcely dared to look
to see what it was I was.   65
I gave a sidelong glance
—I couldn't look any higher—
at shadowy gray knees,
trousers and skirts and boots
and different pairs of hands   70
lying under the lamps.
I knew that nothing stranger
had ever happened, that nothing
stranger could ever happen.
Why should I be my aunt,   75
or me, or anyone?
What similarities—
boots, hands, the family voice
I felt in my throat, or even
the *National Geographic*   80
and those awful hanging breasts–
held us all together
or made us all just one?
How—I didn't know any
word for it—how "unlikely". . .   85
How had I come to be here,
like them, and overhear
a cry of pain that could have
got loud and worse but hadn't?

The waiting room was bright   90
and too hot. It was sliding
beneath a big black wave,
another, and another.

Then I was back in it.
The War was on. Outside,   95
in Worcester, Massachusetts,
were night and slush and cold,

and it was still the fifth
of February, 1918.

1976

CRUSOE IN ENGLAND

A new volcano has erupted,
the papers say, and last week I was reading
where some ship saw an island being born:

at first a breath of steam, ten miles away;
and then a black fleck—basalt, probably—   5
rose in the mate's binoculars
and caught on the horizon like a fly.
They named it. But my poor old island's still
un-rediscovered, un-renamable.
None of the books has ever got it right.   10

Well, I had fifty-two
miserable, small volcanoes I could climb
with a few slithery strides—
volcanoes dead as ash heaps.
I used to sit on the edge of the highest one   15
and count the others standing up,
naked and leaden, with their heads blown off.
I'd think that if they were the size
I thought volcanoes should be, then I had
become a giant;   20
and if I had become a giant,
I couldn't bear to think what size
the goats and turtles were,
or the gulls, or the over-lapping rollers
—a glittering hexagon of rollers   25
closing and closing in, but never quite,
glittering and glittering, though the sky
was mostly overcast.

My island seemed to be
a sort of cloud-dump. All the hemisphere's   30
left-over clouds arrived and hung
above the craters—their parched throats
were hot to touch.
Was that why it rained so much?

"Crusoe in England": *Crusoe:* shipwrecked hero of Daniel Defoe's *Robinson Crusoe* (1719).

And why sometimes the whole place hissed? 35
The turtles lumbered by, high-domed,
hissing like teakettles.
(And I'd have given years, or taken a few,
for any sort of kettle, of course.)
The folds of lava, running out to sea, 40
would hiss. I'd turn. And then they'd prove
to be more turtles.

The beaches were all lava, variegated,
black, red, and white, and gray;
the marbled colors made a fine display. 45
And I had waterspouts. Oh,
half a dozen at a time, far out,
they'd come and go, advancing and retreating,
their heads in cloud, their feet in moving patches
of scuffed-up white. 50
Glass chimneys, flexible, attenuated,
sacerdotal beings of glass . . . I watched
the water spiral up in them like smoke.
Beautiful, yes, but not much company.

I often gave way to self-pity. 55
"Do I deserve this? I suppose I must.
I wouldn't be here otherwise. Was there
a moment when I actually chose this?
I don't remember, but there could have been."
What's wrong about self-pity, anyway? 60
With my legs dangling down familiarly
over a crater's edge, I told myself
"Pity should begin at home." So the more
pity I felt, the more I felt at home.

The sun set in the sea; the same odd sun 65
rose from the sea,
and there was one of it and one of me.
The island had one kind of everything:
one tree snail, a bright violet-blue
with a thin shell, crept over everything, 70
over the one variety of tree,
a sooty, scrub affair.
Snail shells lay under these in drifts
and, at a distance,
you'd swear that they were beds of irises. 75
There was one kind of berry, a dark red.
I tried it, one by one, and hours apart.
Sub-acid, and not bad, no ill effects;

and so I made home-brew. I'd drink
the awful, fizzy, stinging stuff   80
that went straight to my head
and play my home-made flute
(I think it had the weirdest scale on earth)
and, dizzy, whoop and dance among the goats.
Home-made, home-made! But aren't we all?   85
I felt a deep affection for
the smallest of my island industries.
No, not exactly, since the smallest was
a miserable philosophy.

Because I didn't know enough.   90
Why didn't I know enough of something?
Greek drama or astronomy? The books
I'd read were full of blanks;
the poems—well, I tried
reciting to my iris-beds,   95
"They flash upon that inward eye,
which is the bliss . . ." The bliss of what?
One of the first things that I did
when I got back was look it up.

The island smelled of goat and guano.   100
The goats were white, so were the gulls,
and both too tame, or else they thought
I was a goat, too, or a gull.
Baa, baa, baa and *shriek, shriek, shriek,*
baa . . . shriek . . . baa . . . I still can't shake   105
them from my ears; they're hurting now.
The questioning shrieks, the equivocal replies
over a ground of hissing rain
and hissing, ambulating turtles
got on my nerves.   110

When all the gulls flew up at once, they sounded
like a big tree in a strong wind, its leaves.
I'd shut my eyes and think about a tree,
an oak, say, with real shade, somewhere.
I'd heard of cattle getting island-sick.   115
I thought the goats were.
One billy-goat would stand on the volcano
I'd christened *Mont d'Espoir* or *Mount Despair*
(I'd time enough to play with names),
and bleat and bleat, and sniff the air.   120
I'd grab his beard and look at him.
His pupils, horizontal, narrowed up

and expressed nothing, or a little malice.
I got so tired of the very colors!
One day I dyed a baby goat bright red   125
with my red berries, just to see
something a little different.
And then his mother wouldn't recognize him.

Dreams were the worst. Of course I dreamed of food
and love, but they were pleasant rather   130
than otherwise. But then I'd dream of things
like slitting a baby's throat, mistaking it
for a baby goat. I'd have
nightmares of other islands
stretching away from mine, infinities   135
of islands, islands spawning islands,
like frogs' eggs turning into polliwogs
of islands, knowing that I had to live
on each and every one, eventually,
for ages, registering their flora,   140
their fauna, their geography.

Just when I thought I couldn't stand it
another minute longer, Friday came.
(Accounts of that have everything all wrong.)
Friday was nice.   145
Friday was nice, and we were friends.
If only he had been a woman!
I wanted to propagate my kind,
and so did he, I think, poor boy.
He'd pet the baby goats sometimes,   150
and race with them, or carry one around.
—Pretty to watch; he had a pretty body.
And then one day they came and took us off.

Now I live here, another island,
that doesn't seem like one, but who decides?   155
My blood was full of them; my brain
bred islands. But that archipelago
has petered out. I'm old.
I'm bored, too, drinking my real tea,
surrounded by uninteresting lumber.   160
The knife there on the shelf—
it reeked of meaning, like a crucifix.
It lived. How many years did I
beg it, implore it, not to break?
I knew each nick and scratch by heart,   165
the bluish blade, the broken tip,

the lines of wood-grain on the handle . . .
Now it won't look at me at all.
The living soul has dribbled away.
My eyes rest on it and pass on.   170

The local museum's asked me to
leave everything to them:
the flute, the knife, the shrivelled shoes,
my shedding goatskin trousers
(moths have got in the fur),   175
the parasol that took me such a time
remembering the way the ribs should go.
It still will work but, folded up,
looks like a plucked and skinny fowl.
How can anyone want such things?   180
—And Friday, my dear Friday, died of measles
seventeen years ago come March.

                                                            1976

ONE ART

The art of losing isn't hard to master;
so many things seem filled with the intent
to be lost that their loss is no disaster.

Lose something every day. Accept the fluster
of lost door keys, the hour badly spent.   5
The art of losing isn't hard to master.

Then practice losing farther, losing faster:
places, and names, and where it was you meant
to travel. None of these will bring disaster.

I lost my mother's watch. And look! my last, or   10
next-to-last, of three loved houses went.
The art of losing isn't hard to master.

I lost two cities, lovely ones. And, vaster,
some realms I owned, two rivers, a continent.
I miss them, but it wasn't a disaster.   15

—Even losing you (the joking voice, a gesture
I love) I shan't have lied. It's evident
the art of losing's not too hard to master
though it may look like (*Write* it!) like disaster.

                                                            1976

Further Reading

Pinsky, Robert. "Poetry and the World." *Claims for Poetry.* Ed. Donald Hall. Ann Arbor: U of Michigan P, 1982. 331–44. • Vendler, Helen. "Domestication, Domesticity, and the Otherworldly." *Part of Nature, Part of Us: Modern American Poets.* Cambridge: Harvard UP, 1980. 97–110. • Diehl, Joanne Fiet. "At Home with Loss: Elizabeth Bishop and the American Sublime." *Coming to Light: American Women Poets in the Twentieth Century.* Ed. Diane Wood Middlebrook and Marilyn Yalom. Ann Arbor: U of Michigan P, 1985. • *Field: Contemporary Poetry and Poetics* 31 (Fall 1984): entire issue.

The attentive observation that makes Elizabeth Bishop's poems so unusual also shows in her reading of other poets. Poet and translator Dana Gioia, who took Bishop's class in modern poetry at Harvard in 1975, gives us an account of Bishop's attitude toward William Carlos Williams's work in particular and poetry in general.

Dana Gioia: On Bishop as a Teacher

We began with poems from "Spring and All," by William Carlos Williams. We worked through each poem as slowly as if it had been written in a foreign language, and Miss Bishop provided a detailed commentary: biographical information, publication dates, geographical facts, and personal anecdotes about her meetings with the poet. She particularly admired the passage with which Williams opened the title poem of "Spring and All":

> By the road to the contagious hospital
> under the surge of the blue
> mottled clouds driven from the
> northeast—a cold wind. Beyond, the
> waste of broad, muddy fields
> brown with dried weeds, standing
>   and fallen
>
> patches of standing water
> the scattering of tall trees
>
> All along the road the reddish
> purplish, forked, upstanding, twiggy
> stuff of bushes and small trees
> with dead, brown leaves under them
> leafless vines

It took us about an hour to work through this straightforward passage, not because Miss Bishop had any thesis to prove but because it reminded her of so many things—wildflowers, New Jersey, the medical profession, modern painting. Her remarks often went beyond the point at hand, but frequently she made some phrase or passage we might have overlooked in the poem come alive through a brilliant, unexpected observation. . . .

The poem of Williams' that she enjoyed talking about most was "The Sea-Elephant," which begins:

Trundled from
the strangeness of the sea—
a kind of
heaven—

Ladies and Gentlemen!
the greatest
sea-monster ever exhibited
alive

the gigantic
sea-elephant! O wallow
of flesh where
are

there fish enough for
that
appetite stupidity
cannot lessen?

One thing she found particularly fascinating about the poem was the way Williams made transitions. The poem moves quickly from one voice to the next, from one mood to another. It switches effortlessly from wonder to pathos, then to burlesque, and then back to wonder. I think this was the side of Williams' work closest to Bishop's own poetry. She, too, was a master of swift, unexpected transitions, and her poems move as surprisingly from amusement to wonder, from quiet pathos to joy. But with "The Sea-Elephant" the subject alone was enough to light up her interest. She loved talking about exotic animals or flowers, and, not surprisingly, she proved formidably well informed about sea elephants. And she admitted that for her the high point of the poem was the word that Williams invented to imitate the sea elephant's roar: "Blouaugh." It was music to her ears. . . . She never articulated her philosophy in class, but she practiced it so consistently that it is easy—especially now, a decade later—to see what she was doing. She wanted us to see poems, not ideas. Poetry was the particular way the world could be talked about only in verse, and here, as one of her fellow-Canadians once said, the medium was the message. One did not interpret poetry; one experienced it. Showing us how to experience it clearly, intensely, and, above all, directly was the substance of her teaching.

One did not need a sophisticated theory. One needed only intelligence, intuition, and a good dictionary. There was no subtext, only the text. A painter among Platonists, she preferred observation to analysis, and poems to poetry.

RANDALL JARRELL

(1914–1965)

THE DEATH OF THE BALL TURRET GUNNER

From my mother's sleep I fell into the State,
And I hunched in its belly till my wet fur froze.
Six miles from earth, loosed from its dream of life,
I woke to black flak and the nightmare fighters.
When I died they washed me out of the turret with a hose.   5

1944

THE SNOW-LEOPARD

His pads furring the scarp's rime,
Weightless in greys and ecru, gliding
Invisibly, incuriously
As the crystals of the cirri wandering
A mile below his absent eyes,   5
The leopard gazes at the caravan.

The yaks groaning with tea, the burlaps
Lapping and lapping each stunned universe
That gasps like a kettle for its thinning life
Are pools in the interminable abyss   10
That ranges up through ice, through air, to night.
Raiders of the unminding element,
The last cold capillaries of their kind,
They move so slowly they are motionless
To any eye less stubborn than a man's. . . .   15
From the implacable jumble of the blocks
The grains dance icily, a scouring plume,
Into the breath, sustaining, unsustainable,
They trade to that last stillness for their death.
They sense with misunderstanding horror, with desire,   20

Behind the world their blood sets up in mist
The brute and geometrical necessity:
The leopard waving with a grating purr
His six-foot tail; the leopard, who looks sleepily—
Cold, fugitive, secure—at all that he knows,   25
At all that he is: the heart of heartlessness.

1945

NESTUS GURLEY

Sometimes waking, sometimes sleeping,
Late in the afternoon, or early
In the morning, I hear on the lawn,
On the walk, on the lawn, the soft quick step.
The sound half song, half breath: a note or two   5
That with a note or two would be a tune.
It is Nestus Gurley.

It is an old
Catch or snatch or tune
In the Dorian mode: the mode of the horses   10
That stand all night in the fields asleep
Or awake, the mode of the cold
Hunter, Orion, wheeling upside-down,
All space and stars, in cater-cornered Heaven.
When, somewhere under the east,   15
The great march begins, with birds and silence;
When, in the day's first triumph, dawn
Rides over the houses, Nestus Gurley
Delivers to me my lot.

As the sun sets, I hear my daughter say: 20
"He has four routes and makes a hundred dollars."
Sometimes he comes with dogs, sometimes with children,
Sometimes with dogs and children.
He collects, today.
I hear my daughter say: 25
"Today Nestus has got on his derby."
And he says, after a little: "It's two-eighty."
"How could it be two-eighty?"
"Because this month there're five Sundays: it's two-eighty."

He collects, delivers. Before the first, least star   30
Is lost in the paling east; at evening
While the soft, side-lit, gold-leafed day
Lingers to see the stars, the boy Nestus

Delivers to me the Morning Star, the Evening Star
—Ah no, only the Morning *News,* the Evening *Record*   35
Of what I have done and what I have not done
Set down and held against me in the Book
Of Death, on paper yellowing
Already, with one morning's sun, one evening's sun.

Sometimes I only dream him. He brings then   40
News of a different morning, a judgment not of men.
The bombers have turned back over the Pole,
Having met a star. . . . I look at that new year
And, waking, think of our Moravian Star
Not lit yet, and the pure beeswax candle   45
With its red flame-proofed paper pompom
Not lit yet, and the sweetened
Bun we brought home from the love-feast, still not eaten,
And the song the children sang: *O Morning Star—*

And at this hour, to the dew-hushed drums   50
Of the morning, Nestus Gurley
Marches to me over the lawn; and the cat Elfie,
Furred like a musk-ox, coon-tailed, gold-leaf-eyed,
Looks at the paper boy without alarm
But yawns, and stretches, and walks placidly   55
Across the lawn to his ladder, climbs it, and begins to purr.

I let him in,
Go out and pick up from the grass the paper hat
Nestus has folded: this tricorne fit for a Napoleon
Of our days and institutions, weaving   60
Baskets, being bathed, receiving
Electric shocks, Rauwolfia. . . . I put it on
—Ah no, only unfold it.
There is dawn inside; and I say to no one
About—   65
            it is a note or two
That with a note or two would—
                          say to no one
About nothing: "He delivers dawn."

When I lie coldly   70
—Lie, that is, neither with coldness nor with warmth—
In the darkness that is not lit by anything,
In the grave that is not lit by anything
Except our hope: the hope
That is not proofed against anything, but pure   75
And shining as the first, least star
That is lost in the east on the morning of Judgment—

May I say, recognizing the step
Or tune or breath. . . .
                            recognizing the breath,   80
May I say, "It is Nestus Gurley."

                                                                       1960

FIELD AND FOREST

When you look down from the airplane you see lines,
Roads, ruts, braided into a net or web—
Where people go, what people do: the ways of life.

Heaven says to the farmer: 'What's your field?'
And he answers: 'Farming,' with a field,   5
Or: 'Dairy-farming,' with a herd of cows.
They seem a boys' toy cows, seen from this high.

Seen from this high,
The fields have a terrible monotony.

But between the lighter patches there are dark ones.   10
A farmer is separated from a farmer
By what farmers have in common: forests,
Those dark things—what the fields were to begin with.
At night a fox comes out of the forest, eats his chickens.
At night the deer come out of the forest, eat his crops.   15

If he could he'd make farm out of all the forest,
But it isn't worth it: some of it's marsh, some rocks,
There are things there you couldn't get rid of
With a bulldozer, even—not with dynamite.
Besides, he likes it. He had a cave there, as a boy;   20
He hunts there now. It's a waste of land,
But it would be a waste of time, a waste of money,
To make it into anything but what it is.

At night, from the airplane, all you see is lights,
A few lights, the lights of houses, headlights,   25
And darkness. Somewhere below, beside a light,
The farmer, naked, takes out his false teeth:
He doesn't eat now. Takes off his spectacles:
He doesn't see now. Shuts his eyes:
If he were able to he'd shut his ears,   30
And as it is, he doesn't hear with them.
Plainly, he's taken out his tongue: he doesn't talk.
His arms and legs: at least, he doesn't move them.

They are knotted together, curled up, like a child's.
And after he has taken off the thoughts   35
It has taken him his life to learn,
He takes off, last of all, the world.

When you take off everything what's left? A wish,
A blind wish; and yet the wish isn't blind,
What the wish wants to see, it sees.   40

There in the middle of the forest is the cave
And there, curled up inside it, is the fox.
He stands looking at it.
Around him the fields are sleeping: the fields dream.
At night there are no more farmers, no more farms.   45
At night the fields dream, the fields *are* the forest.
The boy stands looking at the fox
As if, if he looked long enough—
                              he looks at it.
Or is it the fox that's looking at the boy?   50
The trees can't tell the two of them apart.

                                                        1966

IN MONTECITO

In a fashionable suburb of Santa Barbara,
Montecito, there visited me one night at midnight
A scream with breasts. As it hung there in the sweet air
That was always the right temperature, the contractors
Who had undertaken to dismantle it, stripped off   5
The lips, let the air out of the breasts.
                              People disappear
Even in Montecito. Greenie Taliaferro,
In her white maillot, her good figure almost firm,
Her old pepper-and-salt hair stripped by the hairdresser   10
To nothing and dyed platinum—Greenie has left her Bentley.
They have thrown away her electric toothbrush, someone else slips
The key into the lock of her safety-deposit box
At the Crocker-Anglo Bank, her seat at the cricket matches
Is warmed by buttocks less delectable than hers.   15
Greenie's girdle is empty.
                      A scream hangs there in the night:
They strip off the lips, let the air out of the breasts,
And Greenie has gone into the Greater Montecito
That surrounds Montecito like the echo of a scream.   20

                                                        1966

Further Reading

Ferguson, Suzanne. *The Poetry of Randall Jarrell*. Baton Rouge: Louisiana State UP, 1971. • *Field: Contemporary Poetry and Poetics* 35 (Fall 1986): entire issue. • Ferguson, Suzanne, ed. *Critical Essays on Randall Jarrell*. Boston: Hall, 1983. • Lowell, Robert, Peter Taylor, and Robert Penn Warren. *Randall Jarrell: 1914–1965*. New York: Farrar, 1967. • Quinn, Sister Bernetta, OSF. *Randall Jarrell*. Boston: Twayne, 1981.

Randall Jarrell's description of the writing of "The Woman at the Washington Zoo" is one of the most thorough and lucid accounts ever written of the way that poets work. It also gives us insight into themes important to all of Jarrell's poetry and criticism.

Randall Jarrell: On the Composition of "The Woman at the Washington Zoo"

Late in the summer of 1956 my wife and I moved to Washington. We lived with two daughters, a cat, and a dog, in Chevy Chase; every day I would drive to work through Rock Creek Park, past the zoo. I worked across the street from the Capitol, at the Library of Congress. I knew Washington fairly well, but had never lived there; I had been in the army, but except for that had never worked for the government.

Some of the new and some of the old things there—I was often reminded of the army—had a good deal of effect on me: after a few weeks I began to write a poem. I have most of what I wrote, though the first page is gone; the earliest lines are:

> any color
> My print, that has clung to its old colors
> Through many washings; this dull null
> Navy I wear to work, and wear from work, and so
> ~~And so to bed~~   To bed
> With no complaint, no comment—neither from my chief,
> nor
> The Deputy Chief Assistant, ~~from~~ his chief,
> Nor   nor
> ~~From~~ Congressmen, ~~from~~ their constituents—
> ~~thin~~
> Only I complain; this ~~poor~~ worn serviceable . . .

The woman talking is a near relation of women I was seeing there in Washington—some at close range, at the Library—and a distant relation of women I had written about before, in "The End of the Rainbow" and "Cinderella" and "Seele im Raum." She is a kind of aging machine part. I wrote, as they say in suits, "acting as next friend"; I had for her the sympathy of an aging machine part. (If I was also something else, that was just personal; and she also was something else.) I felt that one of these hundreds of thousands of government clerks might feel all her dresses one dress, a faded navy-blue print, and that dress her body. This work or life uniform of hers excites neither complaint, nor comment, nor the mechanically protective *No comment* of the civil servant; excites them neither from her "chief," the Deputy Chief Assistant, nor from his, nor from any being on any level of that many-leveled machine: all the system is silent, except for her own cry, which goes unnoticed just as she herself goes unnoticed. (I had met a Deputy Chief Assistant, who saw nothing remarkable in the title.) The woman's days seem to her the going-up-to-work and coming-down-from-work of a worker; each ends in *And so to bed,* the diarist's conclusive unvarying entry in the daybook of his life.

These abruptly opening lines are full of duplications and echoes, like what they describe. And they are wrong in the way in which beginnings are wrong: either there is too much of something or it is not yet there. The lines break off with *this worn serviceable*—the words can apply either to her dress or to her body, but anything so obviously suitable to the dress must be intended for the body. *Body that no sunlight dyes, no hand suffuses,* the page written the next day goes on; then after a space there is *Dome-shadowed, withering among columns, / Wavy upon the pools of fountains, small beside statues* . . . No sun colors, no hand suffuses with its touch, this used, still-useful body. It is subdued to the element it works in: is shadowed by the domes, grows old and small and dry among the columns, of the buildings of the capital; becomes a reflection, its material identity lost, upon the pools of the fountains of the capital; is dwarfed beside the statues of the capital—as year by year it passes among the public places of this city of space and trees and light, city sinking beneath the weight of its marble, city of graded voteless workers.

The word *small,* as it joins the reflections in the pools, the trips to the public places, brings the poem to its real place and subject—to its title, even: next there is *small and shining,* then (with the star beside it that means *use, don't lose*) *small, far-off, shining in the eyes of animals;* the woman ends at the zoo, looking so intently into its cages that she sees her own reflection in *the eyes of animals, these wild ones trapped / As I am trapped but not, themselves, the trap* . . . The lines have written above them *The Woman at the Washington Zoo.*

The next page has the title and twelve lines:

This print, that has kept the memory of color
Alive through many cleanings; this dull null

Navy I wear to work, and wear from work, and so
To bed (with no complaints, no comment: neither from my chief,
The Deputy Chief Assistant, nor her chief,
Nor his, nor Congressmen, nor their constituents

—Only I complain); this ~~plain~~, worn, serviceable
        sunlight
Body that no ~~sunset~~ dyes, no hand suffuses
But, dome-shadowed, withering among columns,
Wavy beneath fountains—small, far-off, shining
        ~~wild~~
In the eyes of animals, these beings trapped
As I am trapped but not, themselves, the trap . . .

(above "plain" the struck word ~~wan~~ appears)

Written underneath this, in the rapid, ugly, disorganized handwriting of most of the pages, is *bars of my body burst blood breath breathing—lives aging but without knowledge of age / Waiting in their safe prisons for death, knowing not of death;* immediately this is changed into two lines, *Aging, but without knowledge of their age, / Kept safe here, knowing not of death, for death*—and out at the side, scrawled heavily, is: *O bars of my own body, open, open!* She recognizes herself in the animals—and recognizes herself, also, in the cages.

Written across the top of this page is *2nd and 3rd alphabets.* Streets in Washington run through a one-syllable, a two-syllable, and a three-syllable (Albermarle, Brandywine, Chesapeake . . .) alphabet, so that people say about an address: "Let's see, that's in the second alphabet, isn't it?" It made me think of Kronecker's "God made the integers, all else is the work of man"; but it seemed right for Washington to have alphabets of its own—I made up the title of a detective story, *Murder in the Second Alphabet.* The alphabets were a piece of Washington that should have fitted into the poem, but didn't; but the zoo was a whole group of pieces, a little Washington, into which the poem itself fitted.

Rock Creek Park, with its miles of heavily wooded hills and valleys, its rocky stream, is like some National Forest dropped into Washington by mistake. Many of the animals of the zoo are in unroofed cages back in its ravines. My wife and I had often visited the zoo, and now that we were living in Washington we went to it a great deal. We had made friends with a lynx that was very like our cat that had died the spring before, at the age of sixteen. We would feed the lynx pieces of liver or scraps of chicken and turkey; we fed liver, sometimes, to two enormous white timber wolves that lived at the end of one ravine. Eager for the meat, they would stand up against the bars on their hind legs, taller than a man, and stare into our eyes; they reminded me of Akela, white with age, in *The Jungle Books,* and of the wolves who fawn at the man Mowgli's brown feet in "In the Rukh." In one of the buildings of the zoo there was a lioness with two big cubs; when the keeper came she would come over, purring her bass purr, to rub her head against the bars almost as our lynx would rub his head against the turkey skin, in rapture, before he finally gulped it down. In the lions' building there were two black leopards; when you got close to them you saw they had not lost the spots of the ordinary leopards—were the ordinary leopards, but spotted black on black, dingy somehow.

On the way to the wolves one went by a big unroofed cage of foxes curled up asleep; on the concrete floor of the enclosure there would be scattered two or three white rats—stiff, quite untouched—that the foxes had left. (The wolves left their meat, too—big slabs of horse meat, glazing, covered with flies.) Twice when I came to the foxes' cage there was a turkey buzzard that had come down for the rats; startled at me, he flapped up heavily, with a rat dangling underneath. (There are usually vultures circling over the zoo; nearby, at the tennis courts of the Sheraton-Park, I used to see vultures perched on the tower of WTTG, above the court on which Defense Secretary McElroy was playing doubles—so that I would say to myself, like Peer Gynt: "Nature is witty.") As a child, coming around the bend of a country road, I had often seen a turkey buzzard, with its black wings and naked red head, flap heavily up from the mashed body of a skunk or possum or rabbit.

A good deal of this writes itself on the next page, almost too rapidly for line endings or punctuation: *to be and never know I am   when the vulture buz-zard comes for the white rat that the foxes left   May he take off his black wings, the red flesh of his head, and step to me as man—a man at whose brown feet the white wolves fawn—to whose hand of power / The lioness stalks, leaving her cubs play-ing / and rubs her head along the bars as he strokes it.* Along the side of the page, between these lines, two or three words to a line, is written *the animals who are trapped but are not themselves the trap   black leopards   spots, light and darkened, hidden except to the close eyes of love, in their life-long darkness, so I in decent black, navy blue.*

As soon as the zoo came into the poem, everything else settled into it and was at home there; on this page it is plain even to the writer that all the things in the poem come out of, and are divided between, color and color-lessness. Colored women and colored animals and colored cloth—all that the woman sees as her own opposite—come into the poem to begin it. Beside the typed lines are many hurried phrases, most of them crossed out: *red and yellow as October maples   rosy, blood seen through flesh in summer colors wild and easy natural   leaf-yellow cloud-rose leopard-yellow, cloth from another planet   the leopards look back at their wearers, hue for hue   the women look back at the leopard.* And on the back of the vulture's page there is a flight of ideas, almost a daydream, coming out of these last phrases: *we have never mistaken you for the others   among the legations one of a different architecture women, saris of a different color   envoy   impassive clear bulletproof glass lips, through the clear glass of a rose sedan color of blood   you too are represented on this earth . . .*

One often sees on the streets of Washington—fairly often sees at the zoo—what seem beings of a different species: women from the embassies of India and Pakistan, their sallow skin and black hair leopard-like, their yellow or rose or green saris exactly as one imagines the robes of Greek statues before the statues had lost their colors. It was easy for me to see the saris as cloth from another planet or satellite; I have written about a sick child who wants "a ship from some near star / To land in the yard and beings to come out / And think to me: 'So this is where you are!' " and about an old man who says that it is his ambition to be the pet of visitors from another planet; as an old reader of science fiction, I am used to looking at the sun red over the hills, the moon white over the ocean, and saying to my wife in a sober voice: "It's like another planet." After I had worked a little longer, the poem began as it begins now:

> The saris go by me from the embassies.
>
> Cloth from the moon. Cloth from another planet.
> They look back at the leopard like the leopard.
>
> And I . . . This print of mine, that has kept its color
> Alive through so many cleanings; this dull null
> Navy I wear to work, and wear from work, and so
> To my bed, so to my grave, with no
> Complaints, no comment: neither from my chief,
> The Deputy Chief Assistant, nor his chief—
> Only I complain; this serviceable
> Body that no sunlight dyes, no hand suffuses
> But, dome-shadowed, withering among columns,
> Wavy beneath fountains—small, far-off, shining
> In the eyes of animals, these beings trapped
> As I am trapped but not, themselves, the trap,
> Aging, but without knowledge of their age,
> Kept safe here, knowing not of death, for death
> —Oh, bars of my own body, open, open!

It is almost as if, once all the materials of the poem were there, the middle and end of the poem made themselves, as the beginning seemed to make itself. After the imperative *open, open!* there is a space, and the middle of the poem begins evenly—since her despair is beyond expression—in a statement of accomplished fact: *The world goes by my cage and never sees me.* Inside the mechanical official cage of her life, her body, she lives invisibly; no one feeds this animal, reads out its name, pokes a stick through the bars at it— the cage is empty. She feels that she is even worse off than the other animals of the zoo: they are still wild animals—since they do not know how to change into domesticated animals, beings that are their own cages—and they are surrounded by a world that does not know how to surrender them, still thinks them part of itself. This natural world comes through or over the bars of the cages, on its continual visits to those within: to those who are not machine parts, convicts behind the bars of their penitentiary, but wild animals—the free beasts come to their imprisoned brothers and never know

802   *Poetry*

that they are not also free. Written on the back of one page, crossed out, is *Come still, you free;* on the next page this becomes:

> The world goes by my cage and never sees me.
> And there come not to me, as come to these,
> The wild ~~ones~~ beasts, sparrows pecking the llamas' grain,
> Pigeons ~~fluttering to~~ settling on the bears' bread,
>   turkey-buzzards
> ~~Coming with grace first, then with horror Vulture seizing~~
>   Tearing the meat the flies have clouded . . .

In saying mournfully that the wild animals do not come to her as they come to the animals of the zoo, she is wishing for their human equivalent to come to her. But she is right in believing that she has become her own cage —she has changed so much, in her manless, childless, fleshless existence, that her longing wish has inside it an increasing repugnance and horror: the innocent sparrows *pecking* the llamas' grain become larger in the pigeons *settling on* (not *fluttering to*) the bears' bread; and these grow larger and larger, come (with grace first, far off in the sky, but at last with horror) as turkey buzzards seizing, no, *tearing* the meat the flies have clouded. She herself is that stale leftover flesh, nauseating just as what comes to it is horrible and nauseating. The series *pecking, settling on,* and *tearing* has inside it a sexual metaphor: the stale flesh that no one would have is taken at last by the turkey buzzard with his naked red neck and head.

Her own life is so terrible to her that, to change, she is willing to accept even this, changing it as best she can. She says: *Vulture* [it is a euphemism that gives him distance and solemnity], *when you come for the white rat that the foxes left* [to her the rat is so plainly herself that she does not need to say so; the small, white, untouched thing is more accurately what she is than was the clouded meat—but, also, it is euphemistic, more nearly bearable], *take off the red helmet of your head* [the bestiality, the obscene sexuality of the flesh-eating death-bird is really—she hopes or pretends or desperately is sure—merely external, *clothes,* an intentionally frightening war garment like a Greek or Roman helmet], *the black wings that have shadowed me* [she feels that their inhuman colorless darkness has always, like the domes of the inhuman city, shadowed her; the wings are like a black parody of the wings the Swan Brothers wear in the fairy tale, just as the whole costume is like that of the Frog Prince or the other beast-princes of the stories] *and step* [as a human being, not fly as an animal] *to me as* [what you really are under the disguising clothing of red flesh and black feathers] *man*—not the machine part, the domesticated animal that is its own cage, but man as he was first, still must be, is: the animals' natural lord,

> The wild brother at whose feet the white wolves fawn,
> To whose hand of power the great lioness
> Stalks, purring . . .

And she ends the poem when she says to him:

> You know what I was,
> You see what I am: change me, change me!

Here is the whole poem:

THE WOMAN AT THE WASHINGTON ZOO

The saris go by me from the embassies.

Cloth from the moon. Cloth from another planet.
They look back at the leopard like the leopard.

And I . . .
         This print of mine, that has kept its color   5
Alive through so many cleanings; this dull null
Navy I wear to work, and wear from work, and so
To my bed, so to my grave, with no
Complaints, no comment: neither from my chief,
The Deputy Chief Assistant, nor his chief—   10
Only I complain; this serviceable
Body that no sunlight dyes, no hand suffuses
But, dome-shadowed, withering among columns,
Wavy beneath fountains—small, far-off, shining
In the eyes of animals, these beings trapped   15
As I am trapped but not, themselves, the trap,
Aging, but without knowledge of their age,
Kept safe here, knowing not of death, for death
—Oh, bars of my own body, open, open!

The world goes by my cage and never sees me.   20
And there come not to me, as come to these,
The wild beasts, sparrows pecking the llamas' grain,
Pigeons settling on the bears' bread, buzzards
Tearing the meat the flies have clouded . . .
         Vulture,   25
When you come for the white rat that the foxes left,
Take off the red helmet of your head, the black
Wings that have shadowed me, and step to me as man,
The wild brother at whose feet the white wolves fawn,
To whose hand of power the great lioness   30
Stalks, purring . . .
         You know what I was,
You see what I am: change me, change me!

DYLAN THOMAS

(1914–1953)

THE FORCE THAT THROUGH THE GREEN FUSE DRIVES THE FLOWER

The force that through the green fuse drives the flower
Drives my green age; that blasts the roots of trees
Is my destroyer.
And I am dumb to tell the crooked rose
My youth is bent by the same wintry fever. 5

The force that drives the water through the rocks
Drives my red blood; that dries the mouthing streams
Turns mine to wax.
And I am dumb to mouth unto my veins
How at the mountain spring the same mouth sucks. 10

The hand that whirls the water in the pool
Stirs the quicksand; that ropes the blowing wind
Hauls my shroud sail.
And I am dumb to tell the hanging man
How of my clay is made the hangman's lime. 15

The lips of time leech to the fountain head;
Love drips and gathers, but the fallen blood
Shall calm her sores.
And I am dumb to tell a weather's wind
How time has ticked a heaven round the stars. 20

And I am dumb to tell the lover's tomb
How at my sheet goes the same crooked worm.

1934

THE HUNCHBACK IN THE PARK

The hunchback in the park
A solitary mister
Propped between trees and water
From the opening of the garden lock
That lets the trees and water enter 5
Until the Sunday somber bell at dark

Eating bread from a newspaper
Drinking water from the chained cup

That the children filled with gravel
In the fountain basin where I sailed my ship   10
Slept at night in a dog kennel
But nobody chained him up.

Like the park birds he came early
Like the water he sat down
And Mister they called Hey mister   15
The truant boys from the town
Running when he had heard them clearly
On out of sound

Past lake and rockery
Laughing when he shook his paper   20
Hunchbacked in mockery
Through the loud zoo of the willow groves
Dodging the park keeper
With his stick that picked up leaves.

And the old dog sleeper   25
Alone between nurses and swans
While the boys among willows
Made the tigers jump out of their eyes
To roar on the rockery stones
And the groves were blue with sailors   30

Made all day until bell time
A woman figure without fault
Straight as a young elm
Straight and tall from his crooked bones
That she might stand in the night   35
After the locks and chains

All night in the unmade park
After the railings and shrubberies
The birds the grass the trees the lake
And the wild boys innocent as strawberries   40
Had followed the hunchback
To his kennel in the dark.

1942

POEM IN OCTOBER

It was my thirtieth year to heaven
Woke to my hearing from harbor and neighbor wood
And the mussel pooled and the heron
Priested shore

The morning beckon   5
With water praying and call of seagull and rook
And the knock of sailing boats on the net webbed wall
   Myself to set foot
    That second
  In the still sleeping town and set forth.   10

  My birthday began with the water-
Birds and the birds of the winged trees flying my name
  Above the farms and the white horses
    And I rose
   In rainy autumn   15
And walked abroad in a shower of all my days.
High tide and the heron dived when I took the road
   Over the border
    And the gates
  Of the town closed as the town awoke.   20

  A springful of larks in a rolling
Cloud and the roadside bushes brimming with whistling
  Blackbirds and the sun of October
    Summery
   On the hill's shoulder,   25
Here were fond climates and sweet singers suddenly
Come in the morning where I wandered and listened
   To the rain wringing
    Wind blow cold
  In the wood faraway under me.   30

  Pale rain over the dwindling harbor
And over the sea wet church the size of a snail
  With its horns through mist and the castle
    Brown as owls
   But all the gardens   35
Of spring and summer were blooming in the tall tales
Beyond the border and under the lark full cloud.
   There could I marvel
    My birthday
  Away but the weather turned around.   40

  It turned away from the blithe country
And down the other air and the blue altered sky
  Streamed again a wonder of summer
    With apples
   Pears and red currants   45
And I saw in the turning so clearly a child's
Forgotten mornings when he walked with his mother
   Through the parables

               Of sun light
      And the legends of the green chapels   50

     And the twice told fields of infancy
That his tears burned my cheeks and his heart moved in mine.
    These were the woods the river and sea
         Where a boy
           In the listening   55
Summertime of the dead whispered the truth of his joy
To the trees and the stones and the fish in the tide.
       And the mystery
         Sang alive
     Still in the water and singingbirds.   60

     And there could I marvel my birthday
Away but the weather turned around. And the true
    Joy of the long dead child sang burning
        In the sun.
      It was my thirtieth   65
Year to heaven stood there then in the summer noon
Though the town below lay leaved with October blood.
       O may my heart's truth
         Still be sung
     On this high hill in a year's turning.   70

1946

OVER SIR JOHN'S HILL

Over Sir John's hill,
The hawk on fire hangs still;
In a hoisted cloud, at drop of dusk, he pulls to his claws
And gallows, up the rays of his eyes the small birds of the bay
And the shrill child's play   5
Wars
Of the sparrows and such who swansing, dusk, in wrangling hedges.
And blithely they squawk
To fiery tyburn over the wrestle of elms until
The flashed the noosed hawk   10
Crashes, and slowly the fishing holy stalking heron
In the river Towy below bows his tilted headstone.

Flash, and the plumes crack,
And a black cap of jack-
Daws Sir John's just hill dons, and again the gulled birds hare   15
To the hawk on fire, the halter height, over Towy's fins,
In a whack of wind.
There

Where the elegiac fisherbird stabs and paddles
In the pebbly dab-filled
Shallow and sedge, and 'dilly dilly,' calls the loft hawk,   20
'Come and be killed,'
I open the leaves of the water at a passage
Of psalms and shadows among the pincered sandcrabs prancing

And read, in a shell,   25
Death clear as a buoy's bell:
All praise of the hawk on fire in hawk-eyed dusk be sung,
When his viperish fuse hangs looped with flames under the brand
Wing, and blest shall
Young   30
Green chickens of the bay and bushes cluck, 'dilly dilly,
Come let us die.'
We grieve as the blithe birds, never again, leave shingle and elm,
The heron and I,
I young Aesop fabling to the near night by the dingle   35
Of eels, saint heron hymning in the shell-hung distant

Crystal harbour vale
Where the sea cobbles sail,
And wharves of water where the walls dance and the white cranes
   stilt.
It is the heron and I, under judging Sir John's elmed   40
Hill, tell-tale the knelled
Guilt
Of the led-astray birds whom God, for their breast of whistles,
Have mercy on,
God in his whirlwind silence save, who marks the sparrows hail,   45
For their souls' song.
Now the heron grieves in the weeded verge. Through windows
Of dusk and water I see the tilting whispering

Heron, mirrored, go,
As the snapt feathers snow,   50
Fishing in the tear of the Towy. Only a hoot owl
Hollows, a grassblade blown in cupped hands, in the looted elms
And no green cocks or hens
Shout
Now on Sir John's hill. The heron, ankling the scaly   55
Lowlands of the waves
Makes all the music; and I who hear the tune of the slow,
Wear-willow river, grave,
Before the lunge of the night, the notes on this time-shaken
Stone for the sake of the souls of the slain birds sailing.   60

1950

POEM ON HIS BIRTHDAY

In the mustardseed sun,
By full tilt river and switchback sea
   Where the cormorants scud,
In his house on stilts high among beaks
   And palavers of birds   5
This sandgrain day in the bent bay's grave
   He celebrates and spurns
His driftwood thirty-fifth wind turned age;
   Herons spire and spear.

   Under and round him go   10
Flounders, gulls, on their cold, dying trails,
   Doing what they are told,
Curlews aloud in the congered waves
   Work at their ways to death,
And the rhymer in the long tongued room,   15
   Who tolls his birthday bell,
Toils towards the ambush of his wounds;
   Herons, steeple stemmed, bless.

   In the thistledown fall,
He sings towards anguish; finches fly   20
   In the claw tracks of hawks
On a seizing sky; small fishes glide
   Through wynds and shells of drowned
Ship towns to pastures of otters. He
   In his slant, racking house   25
And the hewn coils of his trade perceives
   Herons walk in their shroud,

   The livelong river's robe
Of minnows wreathing around their prayer;
   And far at sea he knows,   30
Who slaves to his crouched, eternal end
   Under a serpent cloud,
Dolphins dive in their turnturtle dust,
   The rippled seals streak down
To kill and their own tide daubing blood   35
   Slides good in the sleek mouth.

   In a cavernous, swung
Wave's silence, wept white angelus knells.
   Thirty-five bells sing struck
On skull and scar where his loves lie wrecked,   40
   Steered by the falling stars.
And to-morrow weeps in a blind cage
   Terror will rage apart

Before chains break to a hammer flame
   And love unbolts the dark   45

   And freely he goes lost
In the unknown, famous light of great
   And fabulous, dear God.
Dark is a way and light is a place,
   Heaven that never was   50
Nor will be ever is always true,
   And, in that brambled void,
Plenty as blackberries in the woods
   The dead grow for His joy.

There he might wander bare   55
With the spirits of the horseshoe bay
   Or the stars' seashore dead,
Marrow of eagles, the roots of whales
   And wishbones of wild geese,
With blessed, unborn God and His Ghost,   60
   And every soul His priest,
Gulled and chanter in young Heaven's fold
   Be at cloud quaking peace,

   But dark is a long way.
He, on the earth of the night, alone   65
   With all the living, prays,
Who knows the rocketing wind will blow
   The bones out of the hills,
And the scythed boulders bleed, and the last
   Rage shattered waters kick   70
Masts and fishes to the still quick stars,
   Faithlessly unto Him

   Who is the light of old
And air shaped Heaven where souls grow wild
   As horses in the foam: 75
Oh, let me midlife mourn by the shrined
   And druid herons' vows
The voyage to ruin I must run
   Dawn ships clouted aground,
Yet, though I cry with tumbledown tongue,   80
   Count my blessings aloud:

   Four elements and five
Senses, and man a spirit in love
   Tangling through this spun slime
To his nimbus bell cool kingdom come   85
   And the lost, moonshine domes,
And the sea that hides his secret selves

Deep in its black, base bones,
Lulling of spheres in the seashell flesh,
   And this last blessing most,   90

   That the closer I move
To death, one man through his sundered hulks,
   The louder the sun blooms
And the tusked, ramshackling sea exults;
   And every wave of the way   95
And gale I tackle, the whole world then,
   With more triumphant faith
That ever was since the world was said,
   Spins its morning of praise,

   I hear the bouncing hills   100
Grow larked and greener at berry brown
   Fall and the dew larks sing
Taller this thunderclap spring, and how
   More spanned with angels ride
The mansouled fiery islands! Oh,   105
   Holier then their eyes,
And my shining men no more alone
   As I sail out to die.

1951

DO NOT GO GENTLE INTO THAT
GOOD NIGHT

Do not go gentle into that good night,
Old age should burn and rave at close of day;
Rage, rage against the dying of the light.

Though wise men at their end know dark is right,
Because their words had forked no lightning they   5
Do not go gentle into that good night.

Good men, the last wave by, crying how bright
Their frail deeds might have danced in a green bay,
Rage, rage against the dying of the light.

Wild men who caught and sang the sun in flight,   10
And learn, too late, they grieved it on its way,
Do not go gentle into that good night.

Grave men, near death, who see with blinding sight
Blind eyes could blaze like meteors and be gay,
Rage, rage against the dying of the light.   15

And you, my father, there on the sad height,
Curse, bless, me now with your fierce tears, I pray.
Do not go gentle into that good night.
Rage, rage against the dying of the light.

1952

Further Reading

Emery, Clark. *The World of Dylan Thomas.* Coral Gables: U of Miami P, 1962. •
Ackerman, John. *Dylan Thomas: His Life and Work.* London: Oxford UP, 1964. •
Brand, Sister Helena, SNJM. "Structure Signals in 'The Hunchback in the Park.' "
English Journal 59.2 (Feb. 1970): 195–200. • Maud, Ralph. "Last Poems." *Dylan
Thomas: A Collection of Critical Essays.* Englewood Cliffs, NJ: Prentice, 1966. 74–83.
• Murphy, Michael W. "Thomas's 'Do Not Go Gentle into That Good Night.' "
Explicator 28.6 (Feb. 1970): 55.

*Dylan Thomas's poetry, sometimes surrealist, sometimes traditional, often
exuberant, is so different from the sort of poetry William Carlos Williams
advocated and wrote that Williams's appreciation of it has special meaning.*

William Carlos Williams: On Thomas's "Drunken Poetry"

Politer verse, more in the english style, appears to have been impossible for
Thomas, it's a constitutional matter, in which a man has no choice. At least
I don't think it was a choice that was open to him. Thomas was a lyric poet
and, I think, a great one. Such memorable poems as "Over Sir John's Hill"
and, even more to be emphasized, "On His Birthday," are far and away
beyond the reach of any contemporary english or american poet. Not only
in the contrapuntal metaphors which he uses, the fuguelike overlay of his
language does he excel but he is outstanding in the way he packs the
thought in among the words. For it is not all sound and image, but the ability to think is there also with a flaming conviction that clinches each point as
the images mount. The clarity of his thought is not obscured by his images
but rather emphasized.

The wind does "whack" as the hawk which is "on fire" hangs still in the
sky. This devotional poem which in its packed metaphors shows a man
happy in his fate though soon to die shows Dylan Thomas in a triumphant
mood, exultant. What else can a man say or be? He carries the image
through to a definite conclusion and as a lyric poet at his best does show the

sparks of light which convinces us that he means what he says. He includes the whole world in his benisons.

The second poem, "Poem on His Birthday," is demonic, you have to chortle with glee at some of the figures. But it is the way the metaphors are identified with the meaning to emphasize it and to universalize and dignify it that is the proof of the poet's ability. You may not like such poems but prefer a more reasoned mode but this is impassioned poetry, you might call it drunken poetry, it smacks of the divine—as Dylan Thomas does also.

The analytic spirit that might have made him backtrack and reconsider, building a rational system of thought and technique, was not his. He had passion and a heart which carried him where he wanted to go but it cannot be said that he did not choose what he wanted.

JOHN BERRYMAN

(1914–1972)

THE BALL POEM

What is the boy now, who has lost his ball,
What, what is he to do? I saw it go
Merrily bouncing, down the street, and then
Merrily over—there it is in the water!
No use to say 'O there are other balls':   5
An ultimate shaking grief fixes the boy
As he stands rigid, trembling, staring down
All his young days into the harbour where
His ball went. I would not intrude on him,
A dime, another ball, is worthless. Now   10
He senses first responsibility
In a world of possessions. People will take balls,
Balls will be lost always, little boy,
And no one buys a ball back. Money is external.
He is learning, well behind his desperate eyes,   15
The epistemology of loss, how to stand up
Knowing what every man must one day know
And most know many days, how to stand up.
And gradually light returns to the street,
A whistle blows, the ball is out of sight,   20
Soon part of me will explore the deep and dark
Floor of the harbor . . I am everywhere,
I suffer and move, my mind and my heart move

With all that move me, under the water
Or whistling, I am not a little boy.   25

1942

SONNET 25

Sometimes the night echoes to prideless wailing
Low as I hunch home late and fever-tired,
Near you not, nearing the sharer I desired,
Toward whom till now I sailed back; but that sailing
Yaws, from the cabin orders like a failing   5
Dribble, the stores disordered and then fired
Skid wild, the men are glaring, the mate has wired
Hopeless: locked in, and humming, the Captain's nailing
A false log to the lurching table. Lies
And passion sing in the cabin on the voyage home,   10
The burgee should fly Jolly Roger: wind
Madness like the tackle of a crane (outcries
Ascend) around to heave him from the foam
Irresponsible, since all the stars rain blind.

1952

DREAM SONG 1

Huffy Henry hid the day,
unappeasable Henry sulked.
I see his point,—a trying to put things over.
It was the thought that they thought
they could *do* it made Henry wicked & away.   5
But he should have come out and talked.

All the world like a woolen lover
once did seem on Henry's side.
Then came a departure.
Thereafter nothing fell out as it might or ought.   10
I don't see how Henry, pried
open for all the world to see, survived.

What he has now to say is a long
wonder the world can bear & be.
Once in a sycamore I was glad   15
all at the top, and I sang.
Hard on the land wears the strong sea
and empty grows every bed.

1959

DREAM SONG 4

Filling her compact & delicious body
with chicken páprika, she glanced at me
twice.
Fainting with interest, I hungered back
and only the fact of her husband & four other people   5
kept me from springing on her

or falling at her little feet and crying
'You are the hottest one for years of night
Henry's dazed eyes
have enjoyed, Brilliance.' I advanced upon   10
(despairing) my spumoni. —Sir Bones: is stuffed,
de world, wif feeding girls.

—Black hair, complexion Latin, jewelled eyes
downcast . . . The slob beside her feasts . . . What wonders is
she sitting on, over there?   15
The restaurant buzzes. She might as well be on Mars.
Where did it all go wrong? There ought to be a law against Henry.
—Mr. Bones: there is.

1959

DREAM SONG 14

Life, friends, is boring. We must not say so.
After all, the sky flashes, the great sea yearns,
we ourselves flash and yearn,
and moreover my mother told me as a boy
(repeatingly) 'Ever to confess you're bored   5
means you have no

Inner Resources.' I conclude now I have no
inner resources, because I am heavy bored.
Peoples bore me,
literature bores me, especially great literature,   10
Henry bores me, with his plights & gripes
as bad as achilles,

who loves people and valiant art, which bores me.
And the tranquil hills, & gin, look like a drag
and somehow a dog   15
has taken itself & its tail considerably away
into mountains or sea or sky, leaving
behind: me, wag.

1959

[UNDER NEW MANAGEMENT, YOUR MAJESTY]

6

Under new management, Your Majesty:
Thine. I have solo'd mine since childhood, since
my father's suicide when I was twelve
blew out my most bright candle faith, and look at me.

I served at Mass six dawns a week from five,   5
adoring Father Boniface & you,
memorizing the Latin he explained.
Mostly we worked alone. One or two women.

Then my poor father frantic. Confusions & afflictions
followed my days. Wives left me.   10
Bankrupt I closed my doors. You pierced the roof
twice & again. Finally you opened my eyes.

My double nature fused in that point of time
three weeks ago day before yesterday.
Now, brooding thro' a history of the early Church,   15
I identify with everybody, even the heresiarchs.

1970

Further Reading

Linebarger, J. M. *John Berryman*. New York: Twayne, 1974. • Haffendon, John.
John Berryman: A Critical Commentary. New York: New York UP, 1980. • Hickey,
Donna. "John Berryman and the Art of *The Dream Songs.*" *Chicago Review* 32.4
(Spring 1981): 34–43. • Hahn, Robert. "Berryman's *Dream Songs: Missing Poet
Beyond the Poet.*" *Massachusetts Review* 23 (Spring 1982): 117–28. • Vonalt, Larry P.
"Berryman's *The Dream Songs.*" *Sewanee Review* 79.3 (July–Sept. 1971): 464–69.

*In 1965, responding to a request from fellow poet Howard Nemerov, John
Berryman answered a series of questions about his poetry. One of his
answers sheds light both on the influences that shaped his work and the complexity of his effort to "sound like myself." Even in his early poem "Winter
Landscape," the "self" in the poem refuses with "stubborn incredulity" to
understand the world quite as completely as the poet behind the self.*

John Berryman: On the Origins of "Winter Landscape"

The question was this: "Do you see your work as having essentially changed in character or style since you began?"

I would reply: *of course.* I began work in verse-making as a burning, trivial disciple of the great Irish poet William Butler Yeats, and I hope I have moved off from there. One is obsessed at different times by different things and by different ways of putting them. Naturally there are catches in the question. What does "essentially" mean? What is "character"? What is "style"? Still the question, if semantically murky, is practically clear, and I respond to it with some personal history.

When I said just now "work in verse-making" I was leaving out some months of protoapprenticeship during which I was so inexperienced that I didn't imitate *anybody.* Then came Yeats, whom I didn't so much wish to resemble as to *be,* and for several fumbling years I wrote in what it is convenient to call "period style," the Anglo-American style of the 1930's, with no voice of my own, learning chiefly from middle and later Yeats and from the brilliant young Englishman W. H. Auden. Yeats somehow saved me from the then crushing influences of Ezra Pound and T. S. Eliot—luckily, as I now feel—but he could not teach me to sound like myself (whatever that was) or tell me what to write about. The first poem, perhaps, where those dramatic-to-me things happened was (is) called "Winter Landscape." It is mounted in five five-line stanzas, unrhymed, all one sentence. (I admit there is a colon near the middle of the third stanza.)

WINTER LANDSCAPE

The three men coming down the winter hill
In brown, with tall poles and a pack of hounds
At heel, through the arrangement of the trees
Past the five figures at the burning straw,
Returning cold and silent to their town,   5

Returning to the drifted snow, the rink
Lively with children, to the older men,
The long companions they can never reach,
The blue light, men with ladders, by the church
The sledge and shadow in the twilit street,   10

Are not aware that in the sandy time
To come, the evil waste of history
Outstretched, they will be seen upon the brow
Of that same hill: when all their company
Will have been irrecoverably lost,   15

These men, this particular three in brown
Witnessed by birds will keep the scene and say
By their configuration with the trees,
The small bridge, the red houses and the fire,
What place, what time, what morning occasion   20

Sent them into the wood, a pack of hounds
At heel and the tall poles upon their shoulders,
Thence to return as now we see them and
Ankle-deep in snow down the winter hill
Descend, while three birds watch and the fourth flies.   25

1948

This does not sound, I would say, like either Yeats or Auden—or Rilke or
Lorca or Corbiére or any of my other passions of those remote days. It
derives its individuality, if I am right, from a peculiar steadiness of somber
tone (of which I'll say more presently) and from its peculiar relation to its
materials—drawn, of course, from Brueghel's famous painting. The poem
is sometimes quoted and readers seem to take it for either a verbal *equivalent* to the picture or (like Auden's fine Brueghel poem, "Musée des Beaux
Arts," written later) an *interpretation* of it. Both views I would call wrong,
though the first is that adopted in a comparative essay on picture and poem
recently published by two aestheticians at the University of Notre Dame.
After a competent study, buttressed by the relevant scholarship, of
Brueghel's painting, they proceed to the poem—where, there being no relevant scholarship, they seem less at ease—and so to the relation between
the two. Some of the points made are real, I believe. To quote the two with
which they begin: they say the poem's "elaborative sequence urged on by
the sweeping carry-over lines"—they mean run-on—"within the stanza or
between stanzas—preserves the same order of presentation and the same
grouping of elements as the Brueghel composition. . . . Purposively restricting himself to a diction as sober, direct, and matter-of-fact as the painter's
treatment of scene and objects, Berryman so composes with it that he
achieves an insistent and animated pattern of strong poetic effect." And so
on, to the end of the article where the "disclosed affinities" of the two works
are found testifying to the "secret friendship" of the arts. Nowhere is anything said as to what the poem is *about,* nor is any interest expressed in that
little topic; the relation between the works is left obscure except for the
investigation of affinities. An investigation of *differences* would have taken
them farther.

Very briefly, the poem's extreme sobriety would seem to represent a
reaction, first, against Yeats's gorgeous and seductive rhetoric and, second,
against the hysterical political atmosphere of the period. It dates from
1938–1939 and was written in New York following two years' residence in

England, during recurrent crises, with extended visits to France and Germany, especially one of the Nazi strongholds, Heidelberg. So far as I can make out, it is a war poem, of an unusual negative kind. The common title of the picture is *Hunters in the Snow* and of course the poet knows this. But he pretends not to, and calls their spears (twice) "poles," the resultant governing emotion being a certain stubborn incredulity—as the hunters are loosed while the peaceful nations plunge again into war. This is not the subject of Brueghel's painting at all, and the interpretation of *the event of the poem* proves that the picture has merely provided necessary material from a tranquil world for what is necessary to be said—but which the poet refuses to say—about a violent world.

You may wonder whether I dislike aestheticians. I do.

GWENDOLYN BROOKS

(b. 1917)

A STREET IN BRONZEVILLE: SOUTHEAST CORNER

The School of Beauty's a tavern now.
The Madam is underground.
Out at Lincoln, among the graves
Her own is early found.
Where the thickest, tallest monument   5
Cuts grandly into the air
The Madam lies, contentedly.
Her fortune, too, lies there,
Converted into cool hard steel
And right red velvet lining;   10
While over her tan impassivity
Shot silk is shining.

1945

WE REAL COOL

The Pool Players.
Seven at the Golden Shovel.

We real cool. We
Left school. We

Lurk late. We
Strike straight. We

Sing sin. We   5
Thin gin. We

Jazz June. We
Die soon.

1957–1958

THE CHICAGO DEFENDER SENDS A
MAN TO LITTLE ROCK

Fall, 1957

In Little Rock the people bear
Babes, and comb and part their hair
And watch the want ads, put repair
To roof and latch. While wheat toast burns
A woman waters multiferns.   5

Time upholds or overturns
The many, tight, and small concerns.

In Little Rock the people sing
Sunday hymns like anything,
Through Sunday pomp and polishing.   10

And after testament and tunes,
Some soften Sunday afternoons
With lemon tea and Lorna Doones.

I forecast
And I believe   15
Come Christmas Little Rock will cleave
To Christmas tree and trifle, weave,
From laugh and tinsel, texture fast.

In Little Rock is baseball; Barcarolle.
That hotness in July . . . the uniformed figures raw and implacable   20
And not intellectual,
Batting the hotness or clawing the suffering dust.

"*The Chicago Defender Sends a Man to Little Rock*": *Little Rock:* The desegregation of Central
High in Little Rock, Arkansas, in 1957 was resisted by both the local population and state
authorities. President Eisenhower eventually had to send in federal troops to maintain order.

The Open Air Concert, on the special twilight
   green. . . .
When Beethoven is brutal or whispers to lady-like air.
Blanket-sitters are solemn, as Johann troubles to lean   25
To tell them what to mean. . . .

There is love, too, in Little Rock. Soft women softly
Opening themselves in kindness,
Or, pitying one's blindness,
Awaiting one's pleasure   30
In azure
Glory with anguished rose at the root. . . .
To wash away old semi-discomfitures.
They re-teach purple and unsullen blue.
The wispy soils go. And uncertain   35
Half-havings have they clarified to sures.

In Little Rock they know
Not answering the telephone is a way of rejecting life,
That it is our business to be bothered, is our business
To cherish bores or boredom, be polite   40
To lies and love and many-faceted fuzziness.

I scratch my head, massage the hate-I-had.
I blink across my prim and pencilled pad.
The saga I was sent for is not down.
Because there is a puzzle in this town.   45
The biggest News I do not dare
Telegraph to the Editor's chair:
"They are like people everywhere."

The angry Editor would reply
In hundred harryings of Why.   50

And true, they are hurling spittle, rock,
Garbage and fruit in Little Rock.
And I saw coiling storm a-writhe
On bright madonnas. And a scythe
Of men harassing brownish girls.   55
(The bows and barrettes in the curls
And braids declined away from joy.)

I saw a bleeding brownish boy. . . .

The lariat lynch-wish I deplored.

The loveliest lynchee was our Lord.   60

1960

THE BLACKSTONE RANGERS

1

AS SEEN BY DISCIPLINES

There they are.
Thirty at the corner.
Black, raw, ready.
Sores in the city
that do not want to heal.   5

2

THE LEADERS

Jeff. Gene. Geronimo. And Bop.
They cancel, cure and curry.
Hardly the dupes of the downtown thing
the cold bonbon,
the rhinestone thing. And hardly   10
in a hurry.
Hardly Belafonte, King,
Black Jesus, Stokely, Malcolm X or Rap.
Bungled trophies.
Their country is a Nation on no map.   15

Jeff, Gene, Geronimo and Bop
in the passionate noon,
in bewitching night
are the detailed men, the copious men.
They curry, cure,   20
they cancel, cancelled images whose Concerts
are not divine, vivacious; the different tins
are intense last entries; pagan argument;
translations of the night.

The Blackstone bitter bureaus   25
(bureaucracy is footloose) edit, fuse
unfashionable damnations and descent;
and exulting, monstrous hand on monstrous hand,
construct, strangely, a monstrous pearl or grace.

Blackstone Rangers: a Chicago street gang.

3

GANG GIRLS

A Rangerette

Gang Girls are sweet exotics.   30
Mary Ann
uses the nutrients of her orient,
but sometimes sighs for Cities of blue and jewel
beyond her Ranger rim of Cottage Grove.
(Bowery Boys, Disciples, Whip-Birds will   35
dissolve no margins, stop no savory sanctities.)

Mary is
a rose in a whiskey glass.

Mary's
Februaries shudder and are gone. Aprils   40
fret frankly, lilac hurries on.
Summer is a hard irregular ridge.
October looks away.
And that's the Year!
            Save for her bugle-love.   45
Save for the bleat of not-obese devotion.
Save for Somebody Terribly Dying, under
the philanthropy of robins. Save for her Ranger
bringing
an amount of rainbow in a string-drawn bag.   50
"Where did you get the diamond?" Do not ask:
but swallow, straight, the spirals of his flask
and assist him at your zipper; pet his lips
and help him clutch you.

Love's another departure.   55
Will there be any arrivals, confirmations?
Will there be gleaning?

Mary, the Shakedancer's child
from the rooming-flat, pants carefully, peers at
her laboring lover. . . .   60
            Mary! Mary Ann!
Settle for sandwiches! settle for stocking caps!
for sudden blood, aborted carnival,
the props and niceties of non-loneliness—
the rhymes of Leaning.   65

1968

RIOT

A riot is the language of the unheard.
          —Martin Luther King

John Cabot, out of Wilma, once a Wycliffe,
all whitebluerose below his golden hair,
wrapped richly in right linen and right wool,
almost forgot his Jaguar and Lake Bluff;
almost forgot Grandtully (which is The   5
Best Thing That Ever Happened To Scotch); almost
forgot the sculpture at the Richard Gray
and Distelheim; the kidney pie at Maxim's,
the Grenadine de Boeuf at Maison Henri.

Because the Negroes were coming down the street.   10

Because the Poor were sweaty and unpretty
(not like Two Dainty Negroes in Winnetka)

and they were coming toward him in rough ranks.
In seas. In windsweep. They were black and loud.
And not detainable. And not discreet.   15

Gross. Gross. *"Que tu es grossier!"* John Cabot
itched instantly beneath the nourished white
that told his story of glory to the World.
"Don't let It touch me! the blackness! Lord!" he whispered
to any handy angel in the sky.   20

But, in a thrilling announcement, on It drove
and breathed on him: and touched him. In that breath
the fume of pig foot, chitterling and cheap chili,
malign, mocked John. And, in terrific touch, old
averted doubt jerked forward decently,   25
cried "Cabot! John! You are a desperate man,
and the desperate die expensively today."

John Cabot went down in the smoke and fire
and broken glass and blood, and he cried "Lord!
Forgive these nigguhs that know not what they do."   30

                                                                   1969

---

4. *Lake Bluff:* township in Chicago.   7–8. *Richard Gray . . . Distelheim:* art galleries.
8–9. *Maxim's . . . Maison Henri:* restaurants.   12. *Winnetka:* township in Chicago.   16. *Que
tue es grossier!:* How gross you (singular) are! (French).

THE CHICAGO PICASSO

August 15, 1967
"Mayor Daley tugged a white ribbon, loosing the blue percale wrap. A hearty cheer
went up as the covering slipped off the big steel sculpture that looks at once like a
bird and a woman."

—Chicago *Sun-Times*

(Seiji Ozawa leads the Symphony.
The Mayor smiles.
And 50,000 See.)

Does man love Art? Man visits Art, but squirms.
Art hurts. Art urges voyages—   5
and it is easier to stay at home,
the nice beer ready.
   In commonrooms
we belch, or sniff, or scratch.
Are raw.   10

But we must cook ourselves and style ourselves for Art, who
is a requiring courtesan.
We squirm.
We do not hug the Mona Lisa.
We   15
may touch or tolerate
an astounding fountain, or a horse-and-rider.
At most, another Lion.

Observe the tall cold of a Flower
which is as innocent and as guilty,   20
as meaningful and as meaningless as any
other flower in the western field.

1973

Further Reading

Melhem, D. H. *Gwendolyn Brooks: Poetry and the Heroic Voice.* Lexington: U of
Kentucky P, 1987. • Shaw, Harry B. *Gwendolyn Brooks.* Boston: Twayne, 1980. •
Mootry, Maria K., and Gary Smith, ed. *A Life Distilled: Gwendolyn Brooks, Her Poetry
and Fiction.* Urbana: U of Illinois P, 1987. • Hudson, Clenora F. "Racial Themes in
the Poetry of Gwendolyn Brooks." *CLA Journal* 17:1 (Sept. 1973): 16–20. •
Hansell, William H. "Aestheticism v. Political Militancy in Gwendolyn Brooks's
'The Chicago Picasso' and 'The Wall'" *CLA Journal* 17.1 (Sept. 1973): 11–15. •

Stavros, George. "An Interview with Gwendolyn Brooks." *Contemporary Literature* 11.1 (Winter 1970): 1–20.

In midcareer, Gwendolyn Brooks's work underwent a change. Her first fame had been established on the basis of A Street in Bronzeville *(1945) and the Pulitzer Prize-winning* Annie Allen *(1949). In these early collections, racial and social themes are usually one face of lyrics multifaceted as cut glass. The later poems deal more directly with race. In her autobiography,* Report from Part One, *Brooks gives an account of a critical moment in the change.*

Gwendolyn Brooks: On a Belated Discovery of Blackness

Until 1967 my own blackness did not confront me with a shrill spelling of itself. I knew that I was what most people were calling "a Negro"; I called myself that, although always the word fell awkwardly on a poet's ear; I had never liked the sound of it (Caucasian has an ugly sound, too, while the name Indian is beautiful to look at and to hear). *And* I knew that people of my coloration and distinctive history had been bolted to trees and sliced or burned or shredded; knocked to the back of the line; provided with separate toilets, schools, neighborhoods; denied, when possible, voting rights; hounded, hooted at, or shunned, or patronizingly patted. . . . Yet, although almost secretly, I had always felt that to be black was good. Sometimes, there would be an approximate whisper around me: *others* felt, it seemed, that to be black was good. The translation would have been something like "Hey—being black is *fun*." Or something like "Hey—our folks have got stuff to be proud of!" Or something like "Hey—since we are so good why aren't we treated like the other 'Americans?'"

Suddenly there was New Black to meet. In the spring of 1967 I met some of it at the Fisk University Writers' Conference in Nashville. Coming from white white white South Dakota State College I arrived in Nashville, Tennessee, to give one more "reading." But blood-boiling surprise was in store for me. First, I was aware of a general energy, an electricity, in look, walk, speech, *gesture* of the young blackness I saw all about me. I had been "loved" at South Dakota State College. Here, I was coldly Respected. . . . I didn't know what to make of what surrounded me, of what with hot sureness began almost immediately to invade me. *I* had never been, before, in the general presence of such insouciance, such live firmness, such confident vigor, such determination to mold or carve something DEFINITE.

Up against the wall, white man! was the substance of the Baraka shout, at the evening reading he shared with fierce Ron Milner among intoxicating drum-beats, heady incense and organic underhumming. Up against the wall! And a pensive (until that moment) white man of thirty or thirty three abruptly shot himself into the heavy air, screaming "Yeah! *Yeah!* Up against the wall, Brother! KILL 'EM ALL! KILL 'EM *ALL!*"

I thought that was interesting. . . .

I—who have "gone the gamut" from an almost angry rejection of my dark skin by some of my brainwashed brothers and sisters to a surprised queenhood in the new black sun—am qualified to enter at least the kindergarten of new consciousness now. New consciousness and trudge-toward-progress.

I have hopes for myself.

ROBERT LOWELL

(1917–1977)

THE DRUNKEN FISHERMAN

Wallowing in this bloody sty,
I cast for fish that pleased my eye
(Truly Jehovah's bow suspends
No pots of gold to weight its ends);
Only the blood-mouthed rainbow trout   5
Rose to my bait. They flopped about
My canvas creel until the moth
Corrupted its unstable cloth.

A calendar to tell the day;
A handkerchief to wave away   10
The gnats; a couch unstuffed with storm
Pouching a bottle in one arm;
A whiskey bottle full of worms;
And bedroom slacks: are these fit terms
To mete the worm whose molten rage   15
Boils in the belly of old age?

Once fishing was a rabbit's foot—
O wind blow cold, O wind blow hot,
Let suns stay in or suns step out:
Life danced a jig on the sperm-whale's spout— 20
The fisher's fluent and obscene
Catches kept his conscience clean.
Children, the raging memory drools
Over the glory of past pools.

1944

WAKING IN THE BLUE

The night attendant, a B. U. sophomore,
rouses from the mare's-nest of his drowsy head
propped on *The Meaning of Meaning*.
He catwalks down our corridor.
Azure day   5
makes my agonized blue window bleaker.
Crows maunder on the petrified fairway.
Absence! My heart grows tense
as though a harpoon were sparring for the kill.
(This is the house for the "mentally ill.")   10

What use is my sense of humor?
I grin at Stanley, now sunk in his sixties,
once a Harvard all-American fullback,
(if such were possible!)
still hoarding the build of a boy in his twenties,   15
as he soaks, a ramrod
with the muscle of a seal
in his long tub,
vaguely urinous from the Victorian plumbing.
A kingly granite profile in a crimson golf-cap,   20
worn all day, all night,
he thinks only of his figure,
of slimming on sherbet and ginger ale—
more cut off from words than a seal.

This is the way day breaks in Bowditch Hall at McLean's;   25
the hooded night lights bring out "Bobbie,"
Porcellian '29,
a replica of Louis XVI
without the wig—
redolent and roly-poly as a sperm whale,   30
as he swashbuckles about in his birthday suit
and horses at chairs.

These victorious figures of bravado ossified young.

In between the limits of day,
hours and hours go by under the crew haircuts   35
and slightly too little nonsensical bachelor twinkle
of the Roman Catholic attendants.
(There are no Mayflower
screwballs in the Catholic Church.)

---

1. *B.U.:* Boston University.   25. *McLean's:* a private mental hospital in Belmont, Massachusetts.   27. *Porcellian:* an exclusive club at Harvard.

After a hearty New England breakfast,   40
I weigh two hundred pounds
this morning. Cock of the walk,
I strut in my turtle-necked French sailor's jersey
before the metal shaving mirrors,

and see the shaky future grow familiar   45
in the pinched, indigenous faces
of these thoroughbred mental cases,
twice my age and half my weight.
We are all old-timers,
each of us holds a locked razor.   50

1959

FOR THE UNION DEAD

*"Relinquunt omnia
servare rem publicam."*

The old South Boston Aquarium stands
in a Sahara of snow now. Its broken windows are boarded.
The bronze weathervane cod has lost half its scales.
The airy tanks are dry.

Once my nose crawled like a snail on the glass;   5
my hand tingled
to burst the bubbles
drifting from the noses of the cowed, compliant fish.

My hand draws back, I often sigh still
for the dark downward and vegetating kingdom   10
of the fish and reptile. One morning last March,
I pressed against the new barbed and galvanized

fence on the Boston Common. Behind their cage,
yellow dinosaur steamshovels were grunting
as they cropped up tons of mush and grass   15
to gouge their underworld garage.

Parking spaces luxuriate like civic
sandpiles in the heart of Boston.

"For the Union Dead": Relinquunt . . . publicam: "They gave up everything to preserve the
Republic." A slightly different form of this quotation appears on the monument on Boston
Common dedicated to Colonel Robert Gould Shaw (1837–1863) and the black troops he led in
an assault on Fort Wagner, South Carolina, on July 18, 1863.

A girdle of orange, Puritan-pumpkin colored girders
braces the tingling Statehouse,   20

shaking over the excavations, as it faces Colonel Shaw
and his bell-cheeked Negro infantry
on St. Gaudens' shaking Civil War relief,
propped by a plank splint against the garage's earthquake.

Two months after marching through Boston,   25
half the regiment was dead;
at the dedication,
William James could almost hear the bronze Negroes breathe.

Their monument sticks like a fishbone
in the city's throat.   30
Its Colonel is as lean
as a compass-needle.

He has an angry wrenlike vigilance,
a greyhound's gentle tautness;
he seems to wince at pleasure,   35
and suffocate for privacy.

He is out of bounds now. He rejoices in man's lovely,
peculiar power to choose life and death—
when he leads his black soldiers to death,
he cannot bend his back.   40

On a thousand small town New England greens,
the old white churches hold their air
of sparse, sincere rebellion; frayed flags
quilt the graveyards of the Grand Army of the Republic.

The stone statues of the abstract Union Soldier   45
grow slimmer and younger each year—
wasp-waisted, they doze over muskets
and muse through their sideburns . . .

Shaw's father wanted no monument
except the ditch,   50
where his son's body was thrown
and lost with his "niggers."

The ditch is nearer.
There are no statues for the last war here;
on Boylston Street, a commercial photograph   55
shows Hiroshima boiling

over a Mosler Safe, the "Rock of Ages"
that survived the blast. Space is nearer.

When I crouch to my television set,
the drained faces of Negro school-children rise like balloons.   60

Colonel Shaw
is riding on his bubble,
he waits
for the blessed break.

The Aquarium is gone. Everywhere,   65
giant finned cars nose forward like fish;
a savage servility
slides by on grease.

1959

NIGHT SWEAT

Work-table, litter, books and standing lamp,
plain things, my stalled equipment, the old broom—
but I am living in a tidied room,
for ten nights now I've felt the creeping damp
float over my pajamas' wilted white . . .   5
Sweet salt embalms me and my head is wet,
everything streams and tells me this is right;
my life's fever is soaking in night sweat—
one life, one writing! But the downward glide
and bias of existing wrings us dry—   10
always inside me is the child who died,
always inside me is his will to die—
one universe, one body . . . in this urn
the animal night sweats of the spirit burn.
Behind me! You! Again I feel the light   15
lighten my leaded eyelids, while the gray
skulled horses whinny for the soot of night.
I dabble in the dapple of the day,
a heap of wet clothes, seamy, shivering,
I see my flesh and bedding washed with light,   20
my child exploding into dynamite,
my wife . . . your lightness alters everything,
and tears the black web from the spider's sack,
as your heart hops and flutters like a hare.
Poor turtle, tortoise, if I cannot clear   25
the surface of these troubled waters here,
absolve me, help me, Dear Heart, as you bear
this world's dead weight and cycle on your back.

1964

THE NEO-CLASSICAL URN

I rub my head and find a turtle shell
stuck on a pole,
each hair electrical
with charges, and the juice alive
with ferment. Bubbles drive   5
the motor, always purposeful . . .
Poor head!
How its skinny shell once hummed,
as I sprinted down the colonnade
of bleaching pines, cylindrical   10
clipped trunks without a twig between them. Rest!
I could not rest. At full run on the curve,
I left the caste stone statue of a nymph,
her soaring armpits and her one bare breast,
gray from the rain and graying in the shade,   15
as on, on, in sun, the pathway now a dyke,
I swerved between two water bogs,
two seines of moss, and stooped to snatch
the painted turtles on dead logs.

In that season of joy;   20
my turtle catch
was thirty-three,
dropped splashing in our garden urn,
like money in the bank,
the plop and splash   25
of turtle on turtle,
fed raw gobs of hash . . .

Oh neo-classical white urn, Oh nymph,
Oh lute! The boy was pitiless who strummed
their elegy,   30
for as the month wore on,
the turtles rose,
and popped up dead on the stale scummed
surface—limp wrinkled heads and legs withdrawn
in pain. What pain? A turtle's nothing. No   35
grace, no cerebration, less free will
than the mosquito I must kill—
nothings! Turtles! I rub my skull,
that turtle shell,
and breathe their dying smell,   40
still watch their crippled last survivors pass,
and hobble humpbacked through the grizzled grass.

1964

EPILOGUE

Those blessed structures, plot and rhyme—
why are they no help to me now
I want to make
something imagined, not recalled?
I hear the noise of my own voice: 5
The painter's vision is not a lens,
it trembles to caress the light.
But sometimes everything I write
with the threadbare art of my eye
seems a snapshot,   10
lurid, rapid, garish, grouped,
heightened from life,
yet paralyzed by fact.
All's misalliance.
Yet why not say what happened?   15
Pray for the grace of accuracy
Vermeer gave to the sun's illumination
stealing like the tide across a map
to his girl solid with yearning.
We are poor passing facts,   20
warned by that to give
each figure in the photograph
his living name.

1975

Further Reading

Fein, Richard J. *Robert Lowell.* 2nd ed. Boston: Twayne, 1979. • Bell, Vereen M.
Robert Lowell: Nihilist as Hero. Cambridge: Harvard UP, 1983. • Perloff, Marjorie
G. "Lowell and Some Contemporaries: A Portrait of the Artist as Mental Patient."
The Poetic Art of Robert Lowell. Ithaca: Cornell UP, 1973. 164–84. • Giles, Ronald
K. "Symbol and Tone in 'For the Union Dead.'" *College Literature* 13.3 (1986):
266–71. • Deese, Helen. "Lowell and the Visual Arts." *Robert Lowell: Essays on the
Poetry.* Ed. Stephen Gould Axelrod and Helen Deese. Cambridge, Eng.: Cambridge
UP, 1986. 180–216, spec. 184–98. • Seidel, Frederick. "Robert Lowell." *Robert
Lowell: A Collection of Critical Essays.* Ed. Thomas Parkinson. Englewood Cliffs, NJ:
Prentice, 1968. 12–35.

---

17. *Vermeer:* Jan Vermeer (1632–1675), the Dutch painter; the reference is probably to his
painting "Woman Reading a Letter."

Robert Lowell, like William Butler Yeats, was never completely satisfied with his poetry and searched restlessly for an appropriate style. Early in his career he became a master of highly formal verse. In Life Studies *(1959) he broke with formalism and treated autobiographical subjects in a free verse that approached prose. Later, he returned to a somewhat more reserved and formal style. In an interview with Frederick Seidel, Lowell discussed the relationship between the formality of verse and the informality of prose.*

Robert Lowell: On the Advantages of Prose

But there's another point about this mysterious business of prose and poetry, form and content, and the reason for breaking forms. I don't think there's any very satisfactory answer. I seesaw back and forth between something highly metrical and something free; there isn't any one way to write. But it seems to me we've gotten into a sort of Alexandrian age. Poets of my generation and particularly younger ones have gotten terribly proficient at these forms. They write a very musical, difficult poem with tremendous skill, perhaps there's never been such skill. Yet the writing seems divorced from the culture. It's become too much something specialized that can't handle much experience. It's become a craft, purely a craft, and there must be some breakthrough back into life. Prose is in many ways better off than poetry. It's quite hard to think of a young poet who has the vitality, say, of Salinger or Saul Bellow. Yet prose tends to be very diffuse. The novel is really a much more difficult form than it seems; few people have the wind to write anything that long. Even a short story demands almost poetic perfection. Yet, on the whole, prose is less cut off from life than poetry is. Now, some of this Alexandrian poetry is very brilliant, you would not have it changed at all. But I thought it was getting increasingly stifling. I couldn't get my experience into tight metrical forms.

RICHARD WILBUR

(b. 1921)

PRAISE IN SUMMER

Obscurely yet most surely called to praise,
As sometimes summer calls us all, I said
The hills are heavens full of branching ways

Where star-nosed moles fly overhead the dead;
I said the trees are mines in air, I said   5
See how the sparrow burrows in the sky!
And then I wondered why this mad *instead*
Perverts our praise to uncreation, why
Such savor's in this wrenching things awry.
Does sense so stale that it must needs derange   10
The world to know it? To a praiseful eye
Should it not be enough of fresh and strange
That trees grow green, and moles can course in clay,
And sparrows sweep the ceiling of our day?

1947

THE DEATH OF A TOAD

    A toad the power mower caught,
Chewed and clipped off a leg, with a hobbling hop has got
  To the garden verge, and sanctuaried him
    Under the cineraria leaves, in the shade
      Of the ashen heartshaped leaves, in a dim,   5
        Low, and a final glade.

    The rare original heartsblood goes,
Spends on the earthen hide, in the folds and wizening, flows
  In the gutters of the banked and staring eyes. He lies
    As still as if he would return to stone,   10
      And soundlessly attending, dies
        Toward some deep monotone,

      Toward misted and ebullient seas
And cooling shores, toward lost Amphibia's emperies.
  Day dwindles, drowning, and at length is gone   15
    In the wide and antique eyes, which still appear
      To watch, across the castrate lawn,
        The haggard daylight steer.

1950

STILL, CITIZEN SPARROW

Still, citizen sparrow, this vulture which you call
Unnatural, let him but lumber again to air
Over the rotten office, let him bear
The carrion ballast up, and at the tall

Tip of the sky lie cruising. Then you'll see   5
That no more beautiful bird is in heaven's height,
No wider more placid wings, no watchfuller flight
He shoulders nature there, the frightfully free,

The naked-headed one. Pardon him, you
Who dart in the orchard aisles, for it is he   10
Devours death, mocks mutability,
Has heart to make an end, keeps nature new.

Thinking of Noah, childheart, try to forget
How for so many bedlam hours his saw
Soured the song of birds with its wheezy gnaw,   15
And the slam of his hammer all the day beset

The people's ears. Forget that he could bear
To see the towns like coral under the keel,
And the fields so dismal deep. Try rather to feel
How high and weary it was, on the waters where   20

He rocked his only world, and everyone's.
Forgive the hero, you who would have died
Gladly with all you knew; he rode that tide
To Ararat; all men are Noah's sons.

                                                     1950

LOVE CALLS US TO THE THINGS OF THIS WORLD

    The eyes open to a cry of pulleys,
And spirited from sleep, the astounded soul
Hangs for a moment bodiless and simple
As false dawn.
               Outside the open window   5
The morning air is all awash with angels.

    Some are in bed-sheets, some are in blouses,
Some are in smocks: but truly there they are.
Now they are rising together in calm swells
Of halcyon feeling, filling whatever they wear   10
With the deep joy of their impersonal breathing;

    Now they are flying in place, conveying
The terrible speed of their omnipresence, moving
And staying like white water; and now of a sudden
They swoon down into so rapt a quiet   15

That nobody seems to be there.
                    The soul shrinks

    From all that it is about to remember,
From the punctual rape of every blessèd day,
And cries,   20
            "Oh, let there be nothing on earth but laundry,
Nothing but rosy hands in the rising steam
And clear dances done in the sight of heaven."

    Yet, as the sun acknowledges
With a warm look the world's hunks and colors,   25
The soul descends once more in bitter love
To accept the waking body, saying now
In a changed voice as the man yawns and rises,

    "Bring them down from their ruddy gallows;
Let there be clean linen for the backs of thieves;   30
Let lovers go fresh and sweet to be undone,
And the heaviest nuns walk in a pure floating
Of dark habits,
            keeping their difficult balance."

                                                        1956

THE UNDEAD

        Even as children they were late sleepers,
Preferring their dreams, even when quick with monsters,
        To the world with all its breakable toys,
                Its compacts with the dying;

        From the stretched arms of withered trees   5
They turned, fearing contagion of the mortal,
        And even under the plums of summer
                Drifted like winter moons.

        Secret, unfriendly, pale, possessed
Of the one wish, the thirst for mere survival,   10
        They came, as all extremists do
                In time, to a sort of grandeur:

        Now, to their Balkan battlements
Above the vulgar town of their first lives,
        They rise at the moon's rising. Strange   15
                That their utter self-concern

        Should, in the end, have left them selfless:
Mirrors fail to perceive them as they float

Through the great hall and up the staircase;
    Nor are the cobwebs broken.   20

Into the pallid night emerging,
Wrapped in their flapping capes, routinely maddened
    By a wolf's cry, they stand for a moment
        Stoking the mind's eye

    With lewd thoughts of the pressed flowers   25
And bric-a-brac of rooms with something to lose,—
    Of love-dismembered dolls, and children
        Buried in quilted sleep.

Then they are off in a negative frenzy,
Their black shapes cropped into sudden bats   30
    That swarm, burst, and are gone. Thinking
        Of a thrush cold in the leaves

Who has sung his few summers truly,
Or an old scholar resting his eyes at last,
    We cannot be much impressed with vampires,   35
        Colorful though they are;

Nevertheless their pain is real,
And requires our pity. Think how sad it must be
    To thirst always for a scorned elixir,
        The salt quotidian blood   40

Which, if mistrusted, has no savor;
To prey on life forever and not possess it,
    As rock-hollows, tide after tide,
        Glassily strand the sea.

1961

HAMLEN BROOK

    At the alder-darkened brink
    Where the stream slows to a lucid jet
I lean to the water, dinting its top with sweat,
    And see, before I can drink,

    A startled inchling trout   5
    Of spotted near-transparency,
Trawling a shadow solider than he.
    He swerves now, darting out

    To where, in a flicked slew
    Of sparks and glittering silt, he weaves   10

Through stream-bed rocks, disturbing foundered leaves,
    And butts then out of view

    Beneath a sliding glass
  Crazed by the skimming of a brace
Of burnished dragon-flies across its face,   15
    In which deep cloudlets pass

    And a white precipice
  Of mirrored birch-trees plunges down
Toward where the azures of the zenith drown.
    How shall I drink all this?   20

    Joy's trick is to supply
  Dry lips with what can cool and slake,
Leaving them dumbstruck also with an ache
    Nothing can satisfy.

                                                    1982

Further Reading

Salinger, Wendy. *Richard Wilbur's Creation.* Ann Arbor: U of Michigan P, 1983. •
Cummins, Paul F. *Richard Wilbur: A Critical Essay.* Grand Rapids, Mich.: Eerdmans,
1971. • Hill, Donald L. *Richard Wilbur.* New York: Twayne, 1967. • Littler, Frank.
"Wilbur's 'Love Calls Us to the Things of This World.'" *Explicator* 40.3 (Spring
1982): 53–55. • Stitt, Peter, Ellesa Clay High, and Helen McCloy Ellison. "The Art
of Poetry: Richard Wilbur." *Paris Review* 72 (Winter 1973): 68–105.

*Asked by fellow poet Howard Nemerov in 1965 to comment on how his
approach to poetry had changed over the years, Richard Wilbur responded
with a brief essay on two poetic styles he associates with phases in his career.
It is typical of Wilbur that he finds in both styles, opposed as they are, "a true
view of poetry."*

Richard Wilbur: On the Meditative Lyric and the Dramatic Poem

Most American poets of my generation were taught to admire the English
Metaphysical poets of the seventeenth century and such contemporary
masters of irony as John Crowe Ransom. We were led by our teachers and
by the critics whom we read to feel that the most adequate and convincing

poetry is that which accommodates mixed feelings, clashing ideas, and incongruous images. Poetry could not be honest, we thought, unless it began by acknowledging the full discordancy of modern life and consciousness.

I still believe that to be a true view of poetry, and therefore I can still stand behind the poem I am about to read you, the title of which is "A Baroque Wall-Fountain in the Villa Schiarra." It is, in the first place, a minutely descriptive poem, in which I portray a wall-fountain in one of the public gardens of Rome, and then proceed across town to describe the celebrated fountains in St. Peter's Square. At the same time the poem presents, by way of its contrasting fountains, a clash between the ideas of pleasure and joy, of acceptance and transcendence.

A BAROQUE WALL-FOUNTAIN IN THE VILLA SCHIARRA

Under the bronze crown
Too big for the head of the stone cherub whose feet
   A serpent has begun to eat,
Sweet water brims a cockle and braids down

   Past spattered mosses, breaks   5
On the tipped edge of a second shell, and fills
   The massive third below. It spills
In threads then from the scalloped rim, and makes

   A scrim or summery tent
For a faun-menage and their familiar goose.   10
   Happy in all that ragged, loose
Collapse of water, its effortless descent

   And flatteries of spray,
The stocky god upholds the shell with ease,
   Watching, about his shaggy knees,   15
The goatish innocence of his babes at play;

   His fauness all the while
Leans forward, slightly, into a clambering mesh
   Of water-lights, her sparkling flesh
In a saecular ecstasy, her blinded smile   20

   Bent on the sand floor
Of the trefoil pool, where ripple-shadows come
   And go in swift reticulum,
More addling to the eye than wine, and more

   Interminable to thought   25
Than pleasure's calculus. Yet since this all
   Is pleasure, flash, and waterfall,
Must it not be too simple? Are we not

More intricately expressed
In the plain fountains that Maderna set
   Before St. Peter's—the main jet   30
Struggling aloft until it seems at rest

   In the act of rising, until
The very wish of water is reversed,
   That heaviness borne up to burst   35
In a clear, high, cavorting head, to fill

   With blaze, and then in gauze
Delays, in a gnatlike shimmering, in a fine
   Illumined version of itself, decline,
And patter on the stones its own applause?   40

   If that is what men are
Or should be, if those water-saints display
   The pattern of our areté,
What of those showered fauns in their bizarre,

   Spangled, and plunging house?   45
They are at rest in fullness of desire
   For what is given, they do not tire
Of the smart of the sun, the pleasant water-douse

   And riddled pool below,
Reproving our disgust and our ennui   50
   With humble insatiety.
Francis, perhaps, who lay in sister snow

   Before the wealthy gate
Freezing and praising, might have seen in this
   No trifle, but a shade of bliss—   55
That land of tolerable flowers, that state

   As near and far as grass
Where eyes become the sunlight, and the hand
   Is worthy of water: the dreamt land
Toward which all hungers leap, all pleasures pass.   60

                                                              1956

It may be that the poem I have just read arrives at some sort of reconciliation between the claims of pleasure and joy, acceptance and transcendence; but what one hears in most of it is a single meditative voice balancing
argument and counterargument, feeling and counterfeeling. I now want to
read you a somewhat later poem on very much the same subject, in which
there are two distinct voices speaking, both of them dramatic. The title of
the poem is "Two Voices in a Meadow," and the speakers are a milkweed
and a stone. The milkweed speaks first:

Anonymous as cherubs
Over the crib of God,
White seeds are floating
Out of my burst pod.
What power had I   5
Before I learned to yield?
Shatter me, great wind:
I shall possess the field.

And now the stone speaks:

As casual as cow-dung
Under the crib of God,   10
I lie where chance would have me,
Up to the ears in sod.
Why should I move? To move
Befits a light desire.
The sill of Heaven would founder,   15
Did such as I aspire.

    The virtue of the ironic meditative poem is that the poet speaks out of his whole nature, acknowledging the contradictions which inhere in life. The limitation of such a poem is that the atmosphere of contradiction can stifle passion and conduce to a bland evasiveness. The virtue of the dramatic poem is that, while it may not represent the whole self of the poet, it can (like the love song, hymn, or curse) give free expression to some one compelling mood or attitude. The fact is that we are not always divided in spirit and that we sometimes yield utterly to a feeling or idea. Each of these kinds of poem, then, has its own truth to life and without abandoning the first, I have lately been writing more and more of the second.

AMY CLAMPITT

(b. 1923)

THE BURNING CHILD

After a few hours' sleep, the father had a dream that his child was standing beside his bed, caught him by the arm and whispered reproachfully: "Father, don't you see I'm burning?"

—Freud, *The Interpretation of Dreams*

Dreamwork, the mnemonic flicker
of the wave of lost particulars—
whose dream, whose child, where, when, all lost
except the singed reprieve, its fossil ardor
burnished to a paradigm of grief,   5
half a century before the cattle cars,
the shunted parceling—*links, rechts*—
in a blaspheming parody of judgment
by the Lord of burning: the bush, the lava flow,
the chariot, the pillar. What is, even so,   10
whatever breathes but a reprieve, a risk,
a catwalk stroll between the tinder
and the nurture whose embrace is drowning?

The dream redacted cannot sleep; it whimpers
so relentlessly of lost particulars, I can't   15
help thinking of the dreamer as your father,
sent for by the doctors the night he said the *Sh'ma*
over the dim phoenix-nest of scars
you were, survivor
pulled from behind a blazing gas tank   20
that summer on the Cape, those many years
before we two, by a shuttlecock-and-battle-
dore, a dreamworklike accretion of nitwit
trouvées, were cozened into finding how
minute particulars might build themselves   25
into a house that almost looks substantial:
just as I think of how, years earlier,
the waves at Surfside on Nantucket, curveting
like herded colts, subsiding, turned
against my staggering thighs, a manacle   30
of iron cold I had to be pulled out of. Drowning,
since, has seemed a native region's ocean,
that anxiety whose further shores are lurid
with recurrences of burning.

The people herded from the cattle cars   35
first into barracks, then to killing chambers,
stripped of clothes, of names, of chattels—all those
of whom there would remain so few particulars:
I think of them, I think of how your mother's
people made the journey, and of how   40
                              unlike

---

7. *links, rechts:* left, right (German).   17. *Sh'ma:* Shema Yihsrael, "Hear, O Israel."

my own forebears who made the journey,
when the rush was on, aboard a crowded
train from Iowa to California, where,
hedged by the Pacific's lunging barricades,   45
they brought into the world the infant
who would one day be my father, and
(or the entire astonishment, for me, of
having lived until this moment would
have drowned unborn, unburied without   50
ever having heard of Surfside) chose
to return, were free to stay or go
back home, go anywhere at all—
                                    not one
outlived the trip whose terminus was burning.   55

The catwalk shadows of the cave, the whimper
of the burning child, the trapped
reprieve of nightmare between the
tinder and the nurture whose
embrace is drowning.   60

                                                    1979

BEACH GLASS

While you walk the water's edge,
turning over concepts
I can't envision, the honking buoy
serves notice that at any time
the wind may change,   5
the reef-bell clatters
its treble monotone, deaf as Cassandra
to any note but warning. The ocean,
cumbered by no business more urgent
than keeping open old accounts   10
that never balanced,
goes on shuffling its millenniums
of quartz, granite, and basalt.
                                    It behaves
toward the permutations of novelty—   15
driftwood and shipwreck, last night's
beer cans, spilt oil, the coughed-up
residue of plastic—with random

"*Beach Glass*": 7. *Cassandra:* in Greek mythology, the Trojan princess and prophetess who
warned Troy about the wooden horse of the Greeks.

impartiality, playing catch or tag
or touch-last like a terrier,   20
turning the same thing over and over,
over and over. For the ocean, nothing
is beneath consideration.
                        The houses
of so many mussels and periwinkles   25
have been abandoned here, it's hopeless
to know which to salvage. Instead
I keep a lookout for beach glass—
amber of Budweiser, chrysoprase
of Almadén and Gallo, lapis   30
by way of (no getting around it,
I'm afraid) Phillips'
Milk of Magnesia, with now and then a rare
translucent turquoise or blurred amethyst
of no known origin.   35
                        The process
goes on forever: they came from sand,
they go back to gravel,
along with the treasuries
of Murano, the buttressed   40
astonishments of Chartres,
which even now are readying
for being turned over and over as gravely
and gradually as an intellect
engaged in the hazardous   45
redefinition of structures
no one has yet looked at.

                                                         1980

LINDENBLOOM

Before midsummer density
opaques with shade the checker-
tables underneath, in daylight
unleafing lindens burn
green-gold a day or two,   5
no more, with intimations
of an essence I saw once,

"*Beach Glass*": 29. *chrysoprase: brilliant to light green.   40. Murano:* island and town northeast
of Venice, famous for its glass manufacturing and cathedrals.   41. *Chartres:* a city in
northern France famous for its cathedral.

in what had been the pleasure-
garden of the popes
at Avignon, dishevel   10
into half (or possibly three-
quarters of) a million
hanging, intricately
tactile, blond bell-pulls
of bloom, the in-mid-air   15
resort of honeybees'
hirsute cotillion
teasing by the milligram
out of those necklaced
nectaries, aromas   20
so intensely subtle,
strollers passing under
looked up confused,
as though they'd just
heard voices, or   25
inhaled the ghost
of derelict splendor
and/or of seraphs shaken
into pollen dust
no transubstantiating   30
pope or antipope could sift
or quite precisely ponder.

1981

THE WOODLOT

Clumped murmuring above a sump of loam—
grass-rich, wood-poor—that first the plow,
then the inventor (his name plowed under
somewhere in the Patent Office) of barbed wire,
taught, if not fine manners, how at least to follow   5
the surveyor's rule, the woodlot nodes of willow,
evergreen or silver maple gave the prairie grid
what little personality it had.
               Who could
have learned fine manners where the air,   10
that rude nomad, still domineered,

"*Lindenbloom*": 10. *Avignon:* a city in southeast France. During the thirteenth and fourteenth
centuries, Roman popes, facing instability in the Vatican, fled to Avignon and made it a papal
territory.

without a shape it chose to keep,
oblivious of section lines, in winter
whisking its wolfish spittle to a froth
that turned whole townships into   15
one white wallow? Barbed wire
kept in the cattle but would not abrade
the hide or draw the blood
of gales hurled gnashing like seawater over fences'
laddered apertures, rigging the landscape   20
with the perspective of a shipwreck. Land-chained,
the blizzard paused to caterwaul
at every windbreak, a rage the worse
because it was in no way personal.
                                        Against   25
the involuted tantrums of spring and summer—
sackfuls of ire, the frightful udder
of the dropped mammocumulus
become all mouth, a lamprey
swigging up whole farmsteads, suction   30
dislodging treetrunks like a rotten tooth—
luck and a cellarhole were all
a prairie dweller had to count on.
                                        Whether
the inventor of barbed wire was lucky   35
finally in what he found himself
remembering, who knows? Did he
ever, even once, envision
the spread of what he'd done
across a continent: whale-song's   40
taut dulcimer still thrumming as it strung together
orchard, barnyard, bullpen, feedlot,
windbreak: wire to be clambered over,
crawled through or slid under, shepherded—
the heifers staring—to an enclosure   45
whose ceiling's silver-maple tops
stir overhead, uneasy, in the interminably
murmuring air? Deep in it, under
appletrees like figures in a ritual, violets
are thick, a blue cellarhole   50
of pure astonishment.
                        It is
the earliest memory. Before it,

---

28. *mammocumulus:* mammatocumulus, a cumulus storm cloud with breast-shaped protuber-
ances below.

I/you, whatever that conundrum may yet
prove to be, amounts to nothing.   55

1981

DANCERS EXERCISING

Frame within frame, the evolving conversation
is dancelike, as though two could play
at improvising snowflakes'
six-feather-vaned evanescence,
no two ever alike. All process   5
and no arrival: the happier we are,
the less there is for memory to take hold of,
or—memory being so largely a predilection
for the exceptional—come to a halt
in front of. But finding, one evening   10
on a street not quite familiar,
inside a gated
November-sodden garden, a building
of uncertain provenance,
peering into whose vestibule we were   15
arrested—a frame within a frame,
a lozenge of impeccable clarity—
by the reflection, no, not
of our two selves, but of
dancers exercising in a mirror,   20
at the center
of that clarity, what we saw
was not stillness
but movement: the perfection
of memory consisting, it would seem,   25
in the never-to-be completed.
We saw them mirroring themselves,
never guessing the vestibule
that defined them, frame within frame,
contained two other mirrors.   30

1981

ANO PRINIOS

Transport was what we'd come in search of.
A hill village where no bus goes—

———
"*Ano Prinios*": *Ano Prinios:* the name of a small Greek village.

we caught a lift there in a pickup truck,
hopped down onto cobblestones. Dank plane trees,
root, branch and foliage, engulfed the square.   5
The mountain slope behind spoke, murmurous,
in tongues of torrents. In what was actually
someone's living room, a small bar at the back,
two men sat by the window, drinking coffee.
We asked for ouzo. Olives on a bed of herbs   10
came with it, and feta, freshly made.
What next? Conversation halted, stumbling,
drew repeated blanks. The woman of the house
sat half-retired, hands busy, needle-glint
releasing a slow rill of thread lace.   15
What it was for—a tablecloth, a baby's
christening robe perhaps—I tried to ask,
she tried to tell me, but the filament fell short.
The plane trees dripped. The old man,
the proprietor, moved in and out. A course   20
we hadn't asked for—two fishes, mountain trout
they must have been, served on a single plate—
was set between us: seasoned with leeks,
I could not guess what else, the ridged
flesh firm and delicate.   25
Later, as I came from the latrine,
the old man, intercepting, showed me
the rooms we might have slept in—hangings
vivid over whitewash, the blankets rough.
A disappointed avarice—how could we, savoring   30
a poverty rarer than any opulence, begin
to grasp how dear our fickle custom was?—
gloomed, hurtful as a bruise, on
our departure: the rooted and the footloose
each looking past the other, for something missed.   35
A scruple over how to deal with matters so
fundamental, and so unhandsome, restrained me,
for two years and more, from writing
of what happened in between: how happiness
asperged, redeemed, made the occasion   40
briefly articulate. One of the coffee-drinkers,
having vanished, came back in. He brought,
dripping as from a fountain, a branch just severed
from some fruit tree, loaded with drupes
that were, though still green, delectable.   45
Turning to the woman, I asked what
they were called in Greek. She answered,

"Damaskēno." Damson, damask, damascene:
the word hung, still hangs there,
glistening among its cognates.   50

1987

MAN FEEDING PIGEONS

It was the form of the thing, the unmanaged
symmetry of it, of whatever it was
he convoked as he knelt on the sidewalk
and laid out from his unfastened briefcase
a benefaction of breadcrumbs—this band   5

arriving of the unhoused and opportune
we have always with us, composing
as they fed, heads together, wing tip
and tail edge serrated like chicory
(that heavenly weed, that cerulean   10

commoner of waste places) but with a
glimmer in it, as though the winged
beings of all the mosaics of Ravenna
had gotten the message somehow and come
flying in to rejoin the living: plump-   15

contoured as the pomegranates and pears
in a Della Robbia holiday wreath that had
put on the bloom, once again, of the soon
to perish, to begin to decay, to reënter
that dance of freewheeling dervishes,   20

the breakdown of order: it was the form
of the thing, if a thing is what it was,
and not the merest wisp of a part of
a process—this unravelling inkling
of the envisioned, of states of being   25

past alteration, of all that we've
never quite imagined except by way of
the body: the winged proclamations,
the wheelings, the stairways, the
vast, concentric, paradisal rose.   30

1987

Further Reading

Vendler, Helen. "On the Thread of Language." *New York Review of Books* 30 (3 Mar. 1983): 19–22. • Howard, Richard. "The Hazardous Definition of Structures." *Parnassus* 11.1 (Spring–Summer 1983): 271–75. • Olson, Paul A. "The Marryings of All Likeness." *Prairie Schooner* 51.1 (Spring 1983): 99–102. • Rudman, Mark. "Voluptuaries and Maximalists." *New York Times Book Review* 20 Dec. 1987: 12.

Amy Clampitt's career has been complicated by her absolute independence from the poetic fashions. Some of the great poets of her generation created an audience with a taste for poetry that was confessional and hard-edged. Her own interest was in poetry richer in sound, less openly confessional, and more openly tied to the literature and culture of the past. So unfashionable were these standards that when Clampitt began to write seriously, she had no anticipation of the popularity she has enjoyed in recent years. Echos of this unusual poetic career appear in a 1986 interview with Laura Fairchild.

Amy Clampitt: On Sound and Allusion

Fairchild: Your work seems to have a special emphasis on sound. Are you particularly interested in the aural tradition of verse?

Clampitt: Aural tradition—I'm not sure that I would say that. Certainly the sound is what I start out with. I write for the ear. I don't really know what I've got until I've read it aloud to someone. I can't read things aloud to myself. . . .

As I was growing up the poetry that appealed to me was certainly aural. For a while I had a crush on Swinburne. I got over it. I decided there was a little bit too much mellifluousness there. It goes so smoothly that you hardly notice that he's saying anything, and he is saying something. I never wanted to sound so pretty that no one would think that there was any meaning to it. Just lately I've been attacked very harshly by a reviewer who said, "All her prosodies tend toward cacophony." (*Laughing*) . . . I guess I know what she means. I don't try to be pretty all the time. I kind of like all of these mouth-filling, bumpy sounds. English is full of them.

Fairchild: What about all this use of allusion? Do you feel that poetry should help to preserve literary and cultural history?

I was writing for quite a while without any sense that I would ever be published at all, out of what I heard in my head. I can't exactly say what I was doing. But certainly all of those voices out of the past were there. I still heard them and I could not shut them out. I'm feeling now somewhat chastened by a couple of reviews objecting to so many literary allusions. The truth is I am not an academic; I am not a scholar at all. I just get excited about books. But it may be that the best poetry does come out of direct experience. That I am drawn by subjects that go back into previous literature may be a sign of something reprehensible, I don't know.

I'm fascinated by Greek literature. And although I'm not good at it at all, I've studied classical Greek. I decided it was worth doing, to take an intensive course; we got through Attic grammar in one semester. I liked Homer. There is something about the worn-smooth sense you get line by line, although the sound of Greek is rather harsh. It has a lot of diphthongs, it has a lot of consonants, and so they kind of jamb against each other. I'm drawn by that kind of harsh sound. It's harsh and at the same time tempered in some kind of way that no other literature I know has. It's just wonderful to be reading and to feel that you are going back through time to the sources of things.

Travelling in Greece was more exciting to me than anything. There is so much to be found in Homer that no one has yet surpassed, the sad knowledge of what human beings are really like, told in this very straightforward and unpretentious way—grown men acting like children. They still do.

ROBERT BLY

(b. 1926)

MY FATHER'S WEDDING 1924

Today, lonely for my father, I saw
a log, or branch,
long, bent, ragged, bark gone.
I felt lonely for my father when I saw it.
It was the log   5
that lay near my uncle's old milk wagon.

Some men live with an invisible limp,
stagger, or drag

a leg. Their sons are often angry.
Only recently I thought: 10
Doing what you want . . .
Is that like limping? Tracks of it show in sand.

Have you seen those giant bird-
men of Bhutan?
Men in bird masks, with pig noses, dancing,   15
teeth like a dog's, sometimes
dancing on one bad leg!
They do what they want, the dog's teeth say that!

But I grew up without dogs' teeth,
showed a whole body,   20
left only clear tracks in sand.
I learned to walk swiftly, easily,
no trace of a limp.
I even leaped a little. Guess where my defect is!

Then what? If a man, cautious   25
hides his limp,
Somebody has to limp it! Things
do it; the surroundings limp.
House walls get scars,
the car breaks down; matter, in drudgery, takes it up.   30

On my father's wedding day,
no one was there
to hold him. Noble loneliness
held him. Since he never asked for pity
his friends thought he   35
was whole. Walking alone, he could carry it.

He came in limping. It was a simple
wedding, three
or four people. The man in black,
lifting the book, called for order.   40
And the invisible bride
stepped forward, before his own bride.

He married the invisible bride, not his own.
In her left
breast she carried the three drops   45
that wound and kill. He already had
his barklike skin then,
made rough especially to repel the sympathy

he longed for, didn't need, and wouldn't accept.
They stopped. So   50

the words are read. The man in black
speaks the sentence. When the service
is over, I hold him
in my arms for the first time and the last.

After that he was alone   55
and I was alone.
No friends came; he invited none.
His two-story house he turned
into a forest,
where both he and I are the hunters.   60

1981

FOR MY SON NOAH, TEN YEARS OLD

Night and day arrive, and day after day goes by,
and what is old remains old, and what is young remains young, and
    grows old.
The lumber pile does not grow younger, nor the two-by-fours lose
    their darkness,
but the old tree goes on, the barn stands without help so many years;
The advocate of darkness and night is not lost.   5

The horse steps up, swings on one leg, turns its body,
the chicken flapping claws onto the roost, its wings whelping and
    walloping,
but what is primitive is not to be shot out into the night and the dark.
And slowly the kind man comes closer, loses his rage, sits down at
    table.

So I am proud only of those days that pass in undivided tenderness,   10
when you sit drawing, or making books, stapled, with messages to the
    world,
or coloring a man with fire coming out of his hair.
Or we sit at a table, with small tea carefully poured.
So we pass our time together, calm and delighted.

1981

WORDS RISING

I open my journal, write a few
sounds with green ink, and suddenly
fierceness enters me, stars
begin to revolve, and pick up
alligator dust from under the ocean.   5

The music comes, I feel the bushy
tail of the Great Bear
reach down and brush the seafloor.

All those lives we lived in the sunlit
shelves of the Dordogne, the thousand   10
tunes we sang to the skeletons
of Papua, the many times
we died—wounded—under the cloak
of an animal's sniffing, all of these
return, and the grassy nights   15
we ran for hours in the moonlight.

Watery syllables come welling up.
Anger that barked and howled in the cave,
the luminous head of barley
the priest holds up, growls   20
from under fur, none of that is lost.
The old earth fragrance remains
in the word "and." We experience
"the" in its lonely suffering.

We are bees then; our honey is language.   25
Now the honey lies stored in caves
beneath us, and the sound of words
carries what we do not.
When a man or woman feeds a few words
with private grief, the shames we knew   30
before we could invent the wheel,
then words grow. We slip out

into farmyards, where rabbits lie
stretched out on the ground for buyers.
Wicker baskets and hanged men   35
come to us as stanzas and vowels.
We see a crowd with dusty
palms turned up inside each
verb. There are eternal vows
held inside the word "Jericho."   40

Blessings then on the man who labors
in his tiny room, writing stanzas on the lamb;
blessings on the woman who picks the brown

---

10. *Dordogne:* region of central France containing significant remains of Stone Age people,
including the cave paintings at Lascaux.   12. *Papua:* formerly the name for British New
Guinea; now the entire country is named Papua New Guinea.   40. *Jericho:* God promised the
city of Jericho to Joshua; see Joshua 6:2.

seeds of solitude in afternoon light
out of the black seeds of loneliness.   45
And blessings on the dictionary maker, huddled among
his bearded words, and on the setter of songs
who sleeps at night inside his violin case.

1981

IN RAINY SEPTEMBER

In rainy September, when leaves grow down to the dark,
I put my forehead down to the damp, seaweed-smelling sand.
The time has come. I have put off choosing for years,
perhaps whole lives. The fern has no choice but to live;
for this crime it receives earth, water, and night.   5

We close the door. "I have no claim on you."
Dusk comes. "The love I have had with you is enough."
We know we could live apart from one another.
The sheldrake floats apart from the flock.
The oaktree puts out leaves alone on the lonely hillside.   10

Men and women before us have accomplished this.
I would see you, and you me, once a year.
We would be two kernels, and not be planted.
We stay in the room, door closed, lights out.
I weep with you without shame and without honor.   15

1984

THE INDIGO BUNTING

I go to the door often.
Night and summer. Crickets
lift their cries.
I know you are out.
You are driving   5
late through the summer night.

I do not know what will happen.
I have no claim on you.
I am one star
you have as guide; others   10
love you, the night
so dark over the Azores.

You have been working outdoors,
gone all week. I feel you

Robert Bly   857

in this lamp lit
so late. As I reach for it
I feel myself
driving through the night.

I love a firmness in you
that disdains the trivial
and regains the difficult.
You become part then
of the firmness of night,
the granite holding up walls.

There were women in Egypt who
supported with their firmness the stars
as they revolved,
hardly aware
of the passage from night
to day and back to night.

I love you where you go
through the night, not swerving,
clear as the indigo
bunting in her flight,
passing over two
thousand miles of ocean.

1985

Further Reading

Nelson, Howard. *Robert Bly: An Introduction to the Poetry.* New York: Columbia UP, 1984. • Sugg, Richard P. *Robert Bly.* Boston: Twayne, 1986. • Shakarchi, Joseph. "An Interview with Robert Bly." *Massachusetts Review* 23 (Summer 1982): 226–43. • Perloff, Marjorie. "Soft Touch." *Parnassus* 10 (Spring–Summer 1982): 221–30. • Molesworth, Charles. Review. *Western American Literature* 17.3 (Nov. 1982): 282–84.

Robert Bly came to poetic maturity in an era when poets like T. S. Eliot, William Carlos Williams, and Marianne Moore were predominant. He, however, did not adopt their "objectivist" views of poetry. Instead, he looked for inspiration to non-English-speaking poets, notably Federico García Lorca, Rainer Maria Rilke, and Pablo Neruda. Following their example, he sought to produce poetry that would "transfer an intuition from poet to reader" rather than direct the reader's attention to objects that would carry the emotions "in dehydrated form."

Robert Bly: On True Metaphor and Forgotten Relations

The image belongs with the simile, the metaphor, and the analogy as an aspect of metaphorical language. Shelley said: "Metaphorical language marks the before unapprehended relations of things." Owen Barfield remarks in his marvelous book called *Poetic Diction* (which is about many other things as well) that he would like to alter only one detail in Shelley's sentence. He would change "before unapprehended relations" to "forgotten relations." Ancient man stood in the center of a wheel of relations coming to the human being from objects. The Middle Ages were aware of a relationship between a woman's body and a tree, and Jung reproduces in one of his books an old plate showing a woman taking a baby from a tree trunk. That would be an example of a forgotten relationship recently retrieved; and Greek myths, when studied, turn up others. Many relationships then have been forgotten—by us. They can be recovered. "For though they were never yet apprehended they were at one time seen," Barfield says. "And imagination can see them again." Whenever a poet through imagination discovers a true analogy, he or she is bringing up into consciousness a relationship that has been forgotten for centuries; the object is then not only more seen, but the poet receives a permanent addition to his knowledge.

The power of the image is the power of seeing resemblances, a discipline important to the growth of intelligence, and essential to a poet's intelligence. Emerson said of true analogies:

> It is easily seen that there is nothing lucky or capricious in these
> analogies, but that they are constant, and pervade nature. These are
> not the dreams of a few poets, here and there, but man is an analogist,
> and studies relations in all objects. He is placed in the center of
> beings, and a ray of relation passes from every other being to him.

Remembering forgotten relationships is then one of the great joys that comes from making up poetry. Of course not every image the mind makes up is a true one, and we have the right to ask of every image in a poem: Does this image help us to remember a forgotten relationship, or is it merely a silly juxtaposition, which is amusing and no more?

W. S. MERWIN

(b. 1927)

GRANDMOTHER WATCHING AT HER WINDOW

There was always the river or the train
Right past the door, and someone might be gone
Come morning. When I was a child I mind
Being held up at a gate to wave
Good-bye, good-bye to I didn't know who,   5
Gone to the War, and how I cried after.
When I married I did what was right
But I knew even that first night
That he would go. And so shut my soul tight
Behind my mouth, so he could not steal it   10
When he went. I brought the children up clean
With my needle, taught them that stealing
Is the worst sin; knew if I loved them
They would be taken away, and did my best
But must have loved them anyway   15
For they slipped through my fingers like stitches.
Because God loves us always, whatever
We do. You can sit all your life in churches
And teach your hands to clutch when you pray
And never weaken, but God loves you so dearly   20
Just as you are, that nothing you are can stay,
But all the time you keep going away, away.

1960

NOAH'S RAVEN

Why should I have returned?
My knowledge would not fit into theirs.
I found untouched the desert of the unknown,
Big enough for my feet. It is my home.
It is always beyond them. The future   5
Splits the present with the echo of my voice.
Hoarse with fulfilment, I never made promises.

1963

"Noah's Raven": See Genesis 8:7–9; God sent out a raven before the dove.

FOR THE ANNIVERSARY OF MY DEATH

Every year without knowing it I have passed the day
When the last fires will wave to me
And the silence will set out
Tireless traveller
Like the beam of a lightless star   5
Then I will no longer
Find myself in life as in a strange garment
Surprised at the earth
And the love of one woman
And then shamelessness of men   10
As today writing after three days of rain
Hearing the wren sing and the falling cease
And bowing not knowing to what

1967

THE LAST ONE

Well they'd made up their minds to be everywhere because why not.
Everywhere was theirs because they thought so.
They with two leaves they whom the birds despise.
In the middle of stones they made up their minds.
They started to cut.   5

Well they cut everything because why not.
Everything was theirs because they thought so.
It fell into its shadows and they took both away.
Some to have some for burning.

Well cutting everything they came to the water.   10
They came to the end of the day there was one left standing.
They would cut it tomorrow they went away.
The night gathered in the last branches.
The shadow of the night gathered in the shadow on the water.
The night and the shadow put on the same head.   15
And it said Now.

Well in the morning they cut the last one.
Like the others the last one fell into its shadow.
It fell into its shadow on the water.
They took it away its shadow stayed on the water.   20

Well they shrugged they started trying to get the shadow away.
They cut right to the ground the shadow stayed whole.
They laid boards on it the shadow came out on top.
They shone lights on it the shadow got blacker and clearer.

They exploded the water the shadow rocked. 25
They built a huge fire on the roots.
They sent up black smoke between the shadow and the sun.
The new shadow flowed without changing the old one.
They shrugged they went away to get stones.

They came back the shadow was growing. 30
They started setting up stones it was growing.
They looked the other way it went on growing.
They decided they would make a stone out of it.
They took stones to the water they poured them into the shadow.
They poured them in they poured them in the stones vanished. 35
The shadow was not filled it went on growing.
That was one day.

The next day was just the same it went on growing.
They did all the same things it was just the same.
They decided to take its water from under it. 40
They took away water they took it away the water went down.
The shadow stayed where it was before.
It went on growing it grew onto the land.
They started to scrape the shadow with machines.
When it touched the machines it stayed on them. 45
They started to beat the shadow with sticks.
Where it touched the sticks it stayed on them.
They started to beat the shadow with hands.
Where it touched the hands it stayed on them.
That was another day. 50

Well the next day started about the same it went on growing.
They pushed lights into the shadow.
Where the shadow got onto them they went out.
They began to stomp on the edge it got their feet.
And when it got their feet they fell down. 55
It got into eyes the eyes went blind.

The ones that fell down it grew over and they vanished.
The ones that went blind and walked into it vanished.
The ones that could see and stood still
It swallowed their shadows. 60
Then it swallowed them too and they vanished.
Well the others ran.

The ones that were left went away to live if it would let them.
They went as far as they could.
The lucky ones with their shadows. 65

1968

THE DIFFERENT STARS

I could never have come to the present without you
remember that
from whatever stage we may again
watch it appear

with its lines clear   5
pain
having gone from there

so that we may well wonder
looking back on us here what tormented us
what great difficulty invisible   10
in a time that by then looks simple
and is irrevocable

pain having come from there
my love
I tend to think of division as the only evil   15
when perhaps it is merely my own

that unties
one day the veins one the arteries
that prizes less
as it receives than as it loses   20
that breaks the compasses
cannot be led or followed
cannot choose what to carry
into grief
even   25
unbinds will unbind
unbinds our hands
pages of the same story
what is it
they say can turn even this into wisdom   30
and what is wisdom if it is not
now
in the loss that has not left this place

oh if we knew
if we knew what we needed if we even knew   35
the stars would look to us to guide them

1970

THE JUDGMENT OF PARIS

For Anthony Hecht

Long afterwards
the intelligent could deduce what had been offered
and not recognized
and they suggest that bitterness should be confined
to the fact that the gods chose for their arbiter   5
a mind and character so ordinary
albeit a prince

and brought up as a shepherd
a calling he must have liked
for he had returned to it   10

when they stood before him
the three
naked feminine deathless
and he realized that he was clothed
in nothing but mortality   15
the strap of his quiver of arrows crossing
between his nipples
making it seem stranger

and he knew he must choose
and on that day   20

the one with the gray eyes spoke first
and whatever she said he kept
thinking he remembered
but remembered it woven with confusion and fear
the two faces that he called father   25
the first sight of the palace
where the brothers were strangers

and the dogs watched him and refused to know him
she made everything clear she was dazzling she
offered it to him   30
to have for his own but what he saw
was the scorn above her eyes
and her words of which he understood few

In Greek mythology, Paris was the son of Priam, King of Troy. Asked to decide who was the fairest among Athena, Juno, and Aphrodite, Paris chose Aphrodite, who promised him the fairest woman for his wife. By abducting Helen, wife of the Spartan King Menelaus (and later called Helen of Troy), whom Aphrodite had destined for him, Paris caused the Trojan War.

all said to him *Take wisdom*
take power   35
you will forget anyway

the one with the dark eyes spoke
and everything she said
he imagined he had once wished for
but in confusion and cowardice   40
the crown
of his father the crowns the crowns bowing to him
his name everywhere like grass
only he and the sea
triumphant   45
she made everything sound possible she was
dazzling she offered it to him
to hold high but what he saw
was the cruelty around her mouth
and her words of which he understood more   50
all said to him *Take pride*
take glory
you will suffer anyway

the third one the color of whose eyes
later he could not remember   55
spoke last and slowly and
of desire and it was his
though up until then he had been
happy with his river nymph
here was his mind   60
filled utterly with one girl gathering
yellow flowers
and no one like her
the words
made everything seem present   65
almost present
present
they said to him *Take*
her
you will lose her anyway   70

it was only when he reached out to the voice
as though he could take the speaker
herself
that his hand filled with
something to give   75
but to give to only one of the three

an apple as it is told
discord itself in a single fruit its skin
already carved
To the fairest   80

then a mason working above the gates of Troy
in the sunlight thought he felt the stone
shiver

in the quiver on Paris's back the head
of the arrow for Achilles' heel   85
smiled in its sleep

and Helen stepped from the palace to gather
as she would do every day in that season
from the grove the yellow ray flowers tall
as herself   90

Whose roots are said to dispel pain

1970

EMIGRÉ

You will find it is
much as you imagined
in some respects
which no one can predict
you will be homesick   5
at times for something you can describe
and at times without being able to say
what you miss
just as you used to feel when you were at home

some will complain from the start   10
that you club together
with your own kind
but only those who have
done what you have done
conceived of it longed for it   15
lain awake waiting for it
and have come out with
no money no papers nothing
at your age
know what you have done   20
what you are talking about
and will find you a roof and employers

others will say from the start
that you avoid
those of your country   25
for a while
as your country becomes
a category in the new place
and nobody remembers the same things
in the same way   30
and you come to the problem
of what to remember after all
and of what is your real
language
where does it come from what does it   35
sound like
who speaks it

if you cling to the old usage
do you not cut yourself off
from the new speech   40
but if you rush to the new lips
do you not fade like a sound cut off
do you not dry up like a puddle
is the new tongue to be trusted

what of the relics of your childhood   45
should you bear in mind pieces
of dyed cotton and gnawed wood
lint of voices untranslatable stories
summer sunlight on dried paint
whose color continues to fade in the   50
growing brightness of the white afternoon
ferns on the shore of the transparent lake
or should you forget them
as you float between ageless languages
and call from one to the other who you are   55

1986

HISTORY

Only I never came back

the gates stand open
where I left the barnyard in the evening
as the owl was bringing the mouse home
in the gold sky   5

at the milking hour
and I turned to the amber hill and followed
along the gray fallen wall
by the small mossed oaks and the bushes of rusting
arches bearing the ripe   10
blackberries into the long shadow
and climbed the ancient road
through the last songs of the blackbirds

passing the last live farms
their stones running with dark liquid   15
and the ruined farms their windows without frames
facing away
looking out across the pastures of dead shepherds
whom nobody ever knew
grown high with the dry flowers of a late summer   20
their empty doorways gazing
toward the arms of the last oaks
and at night their broken chimneys watching
the cold of the meteors
the beams had fallen together   25
to rest in brown herds around the fireplaces
and in the shade of black trees the houses were full
of their own fragrance at last
mushrooms and owls
and the song of the cicadas   30

there was a note on a page
made at the time
and the book was closed
and taken on a journey
into a country where no one   35
knew the language
no one could read
even the address
inside the cover
and there the book was   40
of course lost

it was a book full of words to remember
this is how we manage without them
this is how they manage
without us   45

I was not going to be long

1986

Further Reading

Davis, Cheri. *W. S. Merwin.* Boston: Twayne, 1981. • Folsom, Ed, and Cary Nelson, eds. "'Fact Has Two Faces': Interview." *Regions of Memory: Uncollected Prose, 1949–82.* Urbana: U of Illinois P, 1987. 320–61. • Ramsey, Jarold. "The Continuities of W. S. Merwin: 'What Has Escaped Us We Bring with Us.'" *Massachusetts Review* 14.3 (Summer 1973): 569–90, spec. 588–89. • Howard, Richard. "W. S. Merwin: 'We Survived the Selves That We Remembered.'" *Alone in America: Essays on the Art of Poetry in the United States Since 1950.* New York: Atheneum, 1969. 349–81.

W. S. Merwin, like Robert Bly, has been profoundly affected by poetry that comes from outside the Anglo-American tradition. We see in the excerpt below (from a conversation with Ed Folsom and Cary Nelson) that many of his poems are nonetheless attempts to find the layers that underlie a life lived on the apparently stable surface of twentieth-century America.

W. S. Merwin: On Looking Back Through Layers of Time

I don't think it's possible for me to see or to approach that subject—it never has been—without . . . this feeling of inhabiting a palimpsest. However long the culture may have left, we are not just sitting here on a Sunday afternoon. Insofar as there is any historical or temporal continuity at all, that continuity involves these many layers, many of them invisible, and they are not different at all from the repressed, pressed, and forgotten layers of our own experience. And if we really are so dishonest and so mutilated that we can't make any sense of the world, or come to any terms with them, then our lives are maimed and truncated accordingly—our imaginative lives and probably our physical lives too. You know I've felt various things about that over the years and very often the rage that you, Ed, said that your father felt when he saw what was happening to the soil of this country—I can imagine feeling it about the soil, too. For a while I used to think of it in terms of two myths, two Western myths, one of them the myth of Orpheus obviously— the important thing there is that Orpheus is singing with the animals all around him listening—and one can take that as a myth of arrogation or as a myth of harmony. It's both, you know, it is homocentric but it's also inclusive, and everything is there in the act of singing. And the other is the myth of Phaeton, who says "Daddy, I want to drive those horses," and ends up with a holocaust . . . and the beginning of racism. It's probably not as simple as that, but at one point I kept seeing it in terms of those two myths—harmonious interaction with the living world, or envy and exploitation of it. . . .

You know, one can begin to see differently the great phony myth of the "winning of the West"—it was the *destruction* of the West. It *was* heroic, but it was heroic in an incredibly cramped and vicious way. People did suffer and were magnificent, but they were also broken and cruel, and in the long run incredibly destructive, irreversibly destructive. What we've done to this continent is something *unbelievable*—to think that one species could have done this in a hundred years. Right where we're sitting. And this is our lives. This is not something to have an opinion about, this is what we live with, this is our bodies and our minds, this is what our words come out of, and we should know.

ADRIENNE RICH

(b. 1929)

AUNT JENNIFER'S TIGERS

Aunt Jennifer's tigers prance across a screen,
Bright topaz denizens of a world of green.
They do not fear the men beneath the tree;
They pace in sleek chivalric certainty.

Aunt Jennifer's fingers fluttering through her wool   5
Find even the ivory needle hard to pull.
The massive weight of Uncle's wedding band
Sits heavily upon Aunt Jennifer's hand.

When Aunt is dead, her terrified hands will lie
Still ringed with ordeals she was mastered by.   10
The tigers in the panel that she made
Will go on prancing, proud and unafraid.

1951

LOVE IN THE MUSEUM

Now will you stand for me, in this cool light,
Infanta reared in ancient etiquette,

"Love in the Museum": 2. *Infanta:* probably refers to "The Maids of Honor," a painting by Diego Rodriquez Velázquez (1599–1660), the Spanish painter.

A point-lace queen of manners—at your feet,
The doll-like royal dog demurely set
Upon a chequered floor of black and white.   5

Or be a Louis' mistress, by Boucher,
Lounging on cushions, silken feet asprawl
Upon a couch where casual cupids play,
While on your arms and shoulders seems to fall
The tired extravagance of a sunset day.   10

Or let me think I pause beside a door
And see you in a bodice by Vermeer,
Where light falls quartered on the polished floor
And rims the line of water tilting clear
Out of an earthen pitcher as you pour.   15

But art requires a distance; let me be
Always the connoisseur of your perfection.
Stay where the spaces of the gallery
Flow calm between your pose and my inspection,
Lest one imperfect gesture make demands   20
As troubling as the touch of human hands.

1954

TWO SONGS

1

Sex, as they harshly call it,
I fell into this morning
at ten o'clock, a drizzling hour
of traffic and wet newspapers.
I thought of him who yesterday   5
clearly didn't
turn me to a hot field
ready for plowing,
and longing for that young man
piercéd me to the roots   10
bathing every vein, etc.
All day he appears to me
touchingly desirable,
a prize one could wreck one's peace for.
I'd call it love if love   15

"Love in the Museum": 6. *Boucher:* François Boucher (1703–1770), the French painter; the
painting is probably his "Young Girl Resting."   12. *Vermeer:* Jan Vermeer (1632–1675), the
Dutch painter; the painting is probably his "Girl Pouring Milk."

didn't take so many years
but lust too is a jewel
a sweet flower and what
pure happiness to know
all our high-toned questions   20
breed in a lively animal.

2

That "old last act"!
And yet sometimes
all seems post coitum triste
and I a mere bystander.   25
Somebody else is going off,
getting shot to the moon.
Or, a moon-race!
Split seconds after
my opposite number lands   30
I make it—
we lie fainting together
at a crater-edge
heavy as mercury in our moonsuits
till he speaks—   35
in a different language
yet one I've picked up
through cultural exchanges . . .
we murmur the first moonwords:
Spasibo. Thanks. O.K.   40

1964

ORION

Far back when I went zig-zagging
through tamarack pastures
you were my genius, you
my cast-iron Viking, my helmed
lion-heart king in prison.   5
Years later now you're young

my fierce half-brother, staring
down from that simplified west
your breast open, your belt dragged down
by an oldfashioned thing, a sword   10

"*Orion*": Orion: a giant and hunter favored by the goddess Diana, who placed him among the
stars where he appears with his dog Sirius.

the last bravado you won't give over
though it weighs you down as you stride

and the stars in it are dim
and maybe have stopped burning.
But you burn, and I know it;   15
as I throw back my head to take you in
an old transfusion happens again:
divine astronomy is nothing to it.

Indoors I bruise and blunder,
break faith, leave ill enough   20
alone, a dead child born in the dark.
Night cracks up over the chimney,
pieces of time, frozen geodes
come showering down in the grate.

A man reaches behind my eyes   25
and finds them empty
a woman's head turns away
from my head in the mirror
children are dying my death
and eating crumbs of my life.   30

Pity is not your forte.
Calmly you ache up there
pinned aloft in your crow's nest,
my speechless pirate!
You take it all for granted   35
and when I look you back

it's with a starlike eye
shooting its cold and egotistical spear
where it can do least damage.
Breathe deep! No hurt, no pardon   40
out here in the cold with you
you with your back to the wall.

1965

GABRIEL

There are no angels   yet
here comes an angel   one
with a man's face   young

"*Gabriel*": *Gabriel:* the angel who announced the birth of John the Baptist to Zachary (Luke
1:11–20) and the birth and life of Christ to Mary (Luke 1:26–38).

shut-off   the dark
side of the moon   turning to me   5
and saying: I am the plumed
          serpent   the beast
          with fangs of fire   and a gentle
          heart

But he doesn't say that   His message   10
drenches his body
he'd want to kill me
for using words to name him

I sit in the bare apartment
reading   15
words stream past me   poetry
twentieth-century rivers
disturbed surfaces   reflecting clouds
reflecting wrinkled neon
but clogged   and mostly   20
nothing alive left
in their depths

The angel is barely
speaking   to me
Once in a horn of light   25
he stood   or someone like him
salutations in gold-leaf
ribboning from his lips
Today again   the hair streams
to his shoulders   30
the eyes reflect something
like a lost country   or so I think
but the ribbon has reeled itself
up
    he isn't giving   35
or taking any shit
We glance miserably
across the room   at each other

It's true   there are moments
closer and closer together   40
when words stick   in my throat
               'the art of love'
               'the art of words'
I get your message Gabriel
just   will you stay looking   45

straight at me
awhile longer

1969

DIVING INTO THE WRECK

First having read the book of myths,
and loaded the camera,
and checked the edge of the knife-blade,
I put on
the body-armor of black rubber   5
the absurd flippers
the grave and awkward mask.
I am having to do this
not like Cousteau with his
assiduous team   10
aboard the sun-flooded schooner
but here alone.

There is a ladder.
The ladder is always there
hanging innocently   15
close to the side of the schooner.
We know what it is for,
we who have used it.
Otherwise
it's a piece of maritime floss   20
some sundry equipment.

I go down.
Rung after rung and still
the oxygen immerses me
the blue light   25
the clear atoms
of our human air.
I go down.
My flippers cripple me,
I crawl like an insect down the ladder   30
and there is no one
to tell me when the ocean
will begin.

"Diving into the Wreck": 9. *Cousteau:* Jacques Yves Cousteau (1906–   ), the French underwater explorer, film producer, and author.

First the air is blue and then
it is bluer and then green and then
black I am blacking out and yet
my mask is powerful
it pumps my blood with power
the sea is another story
the sea is not a question of power
I have to learn alone
to turn my body without force
in the deep element.

And now: it is easy to forget
what I came for
among so many who have always
lived here
swaying their crenellated fans
between the reefs
and besides
you breathe differently down here.

I came to explore the wreck.
The words are purposes.
The words are maps.
I came to see the damage that was done
and the treasures that prevail.
I stroke the beam of my lamp
slowly along the flank
of something more permanent
than fish or weed

the thing I came for:
the wreck and not the story of the wreck
the thing itself and not the myth
the drowned face always staring
toward the sun
the evidence of damage
worn by salt and sway into this threadbare beauty
the ribs of the disaster
curving their assertion
among the tentative haunters.

This is the place.
And I am here, the mermaid whose dark hair
streams black, the merman in his armored body
We circle silently
about the wreck
we dive into the hold.
I am she: I am he

whose drowned face sleeps with open eyes
whose breasts still bear the stress
whose silver, copper, vermeil cargo lies   80
obscurely inside barrels
half-wedged and left to rot
we are the half-destroyed instruments
that once held to a course
the water-eaten log   85
the fouled compass

We are, I am, you are
by cowardice or courage
the one who find our way
back to this scene   90
carrying a knife, a camera
a book of myths
in which
our names do not appear.

1973

ORIGINS AND HISTORY OF CONSCIOUSNESS

1

Night-life. Letters, journals, bourbon
sloshed in the glass. Poems crucified on the wall,
dissected, their bird-wings severed
like trophies. No one lives in this room
without living through some kind of crisis.   5

No one lives in this room
without confronting the whiteness of the wall
behind the poems, planks of books,
photographs of dead heroines.
Without contemplating last and late   10
the true nature of poetry. The drive
to connect. The dream of a common language.

Thinking of lovers, their blind faith, their
experienced crucifixions,
my envy is not simple. I have dreamed of going to bed   15
as walking into clear water ringed by a snowy wood
white as cold sheets, thinking, *I'll freeze in there.*
My bare feet are numbed already by the snow
but the water
is mild, I sink and float   20

like a warm amphibious animal
that has broken the net, has run
through fields of snow leaving no print;
this water washes off the scent—
You are clear now   25
of the hunter, the trapper
the wardens of the mind—

yet the warm animal dreams on
of another animal
swimming under the snow-flecked surface of the pool,   30
and wakes, and sleeps again.

No one sleeps in this room without
the dream of a common language.

2

It was simple to meet you, simple to take your eyes
into mine, saying: these are eyes I have known   35
from the first. . . . It was simple to touch you
against the hacked background, the grain of what we
had been, the choices, years. . . . It was even simple
to take each other's lives in our hands, as bodies.

What is not simple: to wake from drowning   40
from where the ocean beat inside us like an afterbirth
into this common, acute particularity
these two selves who walked half a lifetime untouching—
to wake to something deceptively simple: a glass
sweated with dew, a ring of the telephone, a scream   45
of someone beaten up far down in the street
causing each of us to listen to her own inward scream

knowing the mind of the mugger and the mugged
as any woman must who stands to survive this city,
this century, this life . . .   50

each of us having loved the flesh in its clenched or loosened beauty
better than trees or music (yet loving those too
as if they were flesh—and they are—but the flesh
of beings unfathomed as yet in our roughly literal life).

3

It's simple to wake from sleep with a stranger,   55
dress, go out, drink coffee,
enter a life again. It isn't simple
to wake from sleep into the neighborhood
of one neither strange nor familiar
whom we have chosen to trust. Trusting, untrusting,   60

we lowered ourselves into this, let ourselves
downward hand over hand as on a rope that quivered
over the unsearched. . . . We did this. Conceived
of each other, conceived each other in a darkness
which I remember as drenched in light.   65
                                    I want to call this, life.

But I can't call it life until we start to move
beyond this secret circle of fire
where our bodies are giant shadows flung on a wall
where the night becomes our inner darkness, and sleeps   70
like a dumb beast, head on her paws, in the corner.

                                                            1974

Further Reading

Rich, Adrienne. "When We Dead Awaken: Writing as Re-vision." *Claims for Poetry.*
Ed. Donald Hall. Ann Arbor: U of Michigan P, 1982. 345–61. • Keyes, Claire. *The
Aesthetics of Power: The Poetry of Adrienne Rich.* Athens: U of Georgia P, 1986. •
Cooper, Jane Roberta. *Reading Adrienne Rich: Reviews and Re-Visions, 1951–81.*
Ann Arbor: U of Michigan P, 1984. • Morris, John N. "The Songs Protect Us, in a
Way." *Hudson Review* 28.3 (Autumn 1975): 446–50. • Vendler, Helen. "Adrienne
Rich: Diving into the Wreck." *Part of Nature, Part of Us: Modern American Poets.*
Cambridge: Harvard UP, 1980. 237–62.

*Adrienne Rich's essay "When We Dead Awaken" describes a change in her
attitude toward being a female poet comparable in many ways to Gwendolyn
Brooks's changed attitude toward being a black poet (see page 827). It
also shows the relationship between this change and the style of the poems in
various stages of Rich's career.*

Adrienne Rich: On Learning to Write as a Woman

I know that my style was formed first by male poets: by the men I was reading as an undergraduate—Frost, Dylan Thomas, Donne, Auden, MacNeice,
Stevens, Yeats. What I chiefly learned from them was craft.* But poems

---

*A.R., 1978: Yet I spent months, at sixteen, memorizing and writing imitations of Millay's
sonnets: and in notebooks of that period I find what are obviously attempts to imitate
Dickinson's metrics and verbal compression. I knew H.D. only through anthologized lyrics;
her epic poetry was not then available to me.

are like dreams: in them you put what you don't know you know. Looking back at poems I wrote before I was twenty-one, I'm startled because beneath the conscious craft are glimpses of the split I even then experienced between the girl who wrote poems, who defined herself in writing poems, and the girl who was to define herself by her relationships with men. "Aunt Jennifer's Tigers" (1951), written while I was a student, looks with deliberate detachment at this split. . . . In writing this poem, composed and apparently cool as it is, I thought I was creating a portrait of an imaginary woman. But this woman suffers from the opposition of her imagination, worked out in tapestry, and her life-style, "ringed with ordeals she was mastered by." It was important to me that Aunt Jennifer was a person as distinct from myself as possible—distanced by the formalism of the poem, by its objective, observant tone—even by putting the woman in a different generation.

In those years formalism was part of the strategy—like asbestos gloves, it allowed me to handle materials I couldn't pick up bare-handed.

In the late fifties I was able to write, for the first time, directly about experiencing myself as a woman. The poem was jotted in fragments during children's naps, brief hours in a library, or at 3:00 A.M. after rising with a wakeful child. I despaired of doing any continuous work at this time. Yet I began to feel that my fragments and scraps had a common consciousness and a common theme, one which I would have been very unwilling to put on paper at an earlier time because I had been taught that poetry should be "universal," which meant, of course, nonfemale. Until then I had tried very much *not* to identify myself as a female poet. Over two years I wrote a ten-part poem called "Snapshots of a Daughter-in-Law" (1958–60), in a longer looser mode than I'd ever trusted myself with before. It was an extraordinary relief to write that poem. It strikes me now as too literary, too dependent on allusion; I hadn't found the courage yet to do without authorities, or even to use the pronoun "I"—the woman in the poem is always "she." One section of it, No. 2, concerns a woman who thinks she is going mad; she is haunted by voices telling her to resist and rebel, voices which she can hear but not obey.

2

Banging the coffee-pot into the sink
she hears the angels chiding, and looks out
past the raked gardens to the sloppy sky.
Only a week since They said: *Have no patience.*

The next time it was: *Be insatiable.*   5
Then: *Save yourself; others you cannot save.*
Sometimes she's let the tapstream scald her arm,
a match burn to her thumbnail,

or held her hand above the kettle's snout
right in the woolly steam. They are probably angels,   10
since nothing hurts her anymore, except
eacjh morning's grit blowing into her eyes.

SYLVIA PLATH

(1932–1963)

BLACK ROOK IN RAINY WEATHER

On the stiff twig up there
Hunches a wet black rook
Arranging and rearranging its feathers in the rain.
I do not expect miracle
Or an accident   5

To set the sight on fire
In my eye, nor seek
Any more in the desultory weather some design,
But let spotted leaves fall as they fall,
Without ceremony, or portent   10

Although, I admit, I desire,
Occasionally, some backtalk
From the mute sky, I can't honestly complain:
A certain minor light may still
Leap incandescent   15

Out of kitchen table or chair
As if a celestial burning took
Possession of the most obtuse objects now and then—
Thus hallowing an interval
Otherwise inconsequent   20

By bestowing largesse, honor,
One might say love. At any rate, I now walk
Wary (for it could happen
Even in this dull, ruinous landscape); skeptical,
Yet politic; ignorant   25

Of whatever angel may choose to flare
Suddenly at my elbow. I only know that a rook
Ordering its black features can so shine

As to seize my senses, haul
My eyelids up, and grant   30

A brief respite from fear
Of total neutrality. With luck,
Trekking stubborn through this season
Of fatigue, I shall
Patch together a content   35

Of sorts. Miracles occur,
If you care to call those spasmodic
Tricks of radiance miracles. The wait's begun again,
The long wait for the angel,
For that rare, random descent.   40

                                                        1960

MEDALLION

By the gate with star and moon
Worked into the peeled orange wood
The bronze snake lay in the sun

Inert as a shoelace; dead
But pliable still, his jaw   5
Unhinged and his grin crooked,

Tongue a rose-colored arrow.
Over my hand I hung him.
His little vermilion eye

Ignited with a glassed flame   10
As I turned him in the light;
When I split a rock one time

The garnet bits burned like that.
Dust dulled his back to ochre
The way sun ruins a trout.   15

Yet his belly kept its fire
Going under the chainmail,
The old jewels smoldering there

In each opaque belly-scale:
Sunset looked at through milk glass.   20
And I saw white maggots coil

Thin as pins in the dark bruise
Where his innards bulged as if
He were digesting a mouse.

Knifelike, he was chaste enough,   25
Pure death's-metal. The yardman's
Flung brick perfected his laugh.

1960

TULIPS

The tulips are too excitable; it is winter here.
Look how white everything is, how quiet, how snowed-in!
I am learning peacefulness, lying by myself quietly
As the light lies on these white walls, this bed, these hands.
I am nobody; I have nothing to do with explosions.   5
I have given my name and my day-clothes up to the nurses
And my history to the anesthetist and my body to surgeons.

They have propped my head between the pillow and the sheet-cuff
Like an eye between two white lids that will not shut.
Stupid pupil, it has to take everything in.   10
The nurses pass and pass; they are no trouble;
They pass the way gulls pass inland in their white caps,
Doing things with their hands, one just the same as another,
So it is impossible to tell how many there are.

My body is a pebble to them; they tend it as water   15
Tends to the pebbles it must run over, smoothing them gently.
They bring me numbness in their bright needles, they bring me sleep.
Now I have lost myself, I am sick of baggage—
My patent-leather overnight case like a black pillbox,
My husband and child smiling out of the family photo.   20
Their smiles catch onto my skin, little smiling hooks.

I have let things slip, a thirty-year-old cargo boat
Stubbornly hanging onto my name and address.
They have swabbed me clear of my loving associations,
Scared and bare on the green plastic-pillowed trolley,   25
I watched my tea set, my bureaus of linen, my books
Sink out of sight, and the water went over my head.
I am a nun now; I have never been so pure.

I didn't want any flowers, I only wanted
To lie with my hands turned up and be utterly empty.   30
How free it is, you have no idea how free!
The peacefulness is so big it dazes you,
And it asks nothing—a name tag, a few trinkets.
It is what the dead close on, finally; I imagine them
Shutting their mouths on it, like a Communion tablet.   35

The tulips are too red in the first place; they hurt me.
Even through the gift paper I could hear them breathe
Lightly, through their white swaddlings, like an awful baby.
Their redness talks to my wound, it corresponds.
They are subtle: they seem to float, though they weigh me down,   40
Upsetting me with their sudden tongues and their color,
A dozen red lead sinkers round my neck.

Nobody watched me before; now I am watched.
The tulips turn to me and the window behind me,
Where, once a day, the light slowly widens and slowly thins,   45
And I see myself, flat, ridiculous, a cut-paper shadow
Between the eye of the sun and the eyes of the tulips,
And I have no face. I have wanted to efface myself.
The vivid tulips eat my oxygen.

Before they came, the air was calm enough,   50
Coming and going, breath by breath, without any fuss.
Then the tulips filled it up like a loud noise.
Now the air snags and eddies round them the way a river
Snags and eddies round a sunken rust-red engine.
They concentrate my attention that was happy   55
Playing and resting without committing itself.

The walls, also, seem to be warming themselves.
The tulips should be behind bars, like dangerous animals;
They are opening like the mouth of some great African cat,
And I am aware of my heart: it opens and closes   60
Its bowl of red blooms out of sheer love of me.
The water I taste is warm and salt, like the sea,
And comes from a country far away as health.

1961

THE ARRIVAL OF THE BEE BOX

I ordered this, this clean wood box
Square as a chair and almost too heavy to lift.
I would say it was the coffin of a midget
Or a square baby
Were there not such a din in it.   5

The box is locked, it is dangerous.
I have to live with it overnight
And I can't keep away from it.
There are no windows, so I can't see what is in there.
There is only a little grid, no exit.   10

I put my eye to the grid.
It is dark, dark,
With the swarmy feeling of African hands
Minute and shrunk for export,
Black on black, angrily clambering.   15

How can I let them out?
It is the noise that appalls me most of all,
The unintelligible syllables.
It is like a Roman mob,
Small, taken one by one, but my god, together!   20

I lay my ear to furious Latin.
I am not a Caesar.
I have simply ordered a box of maniacs.
They can be sent back.
They can die, I need feed them nothing, I am the owner.   25

I wonder how hungry they are.
I wonder if they would forget me
If I just undid the locks and stood back and turned into a tree.
There is the laburnum, its blond colonnades,
And the petticoats of the cherry.   30

They might ignore me immediately
In my moon suit and funeral veil.
I am no source of honey
So why should they turn on me?
Tomorrow I will be sweet God, I will set them free.   35

The box is only temporary.

1962

CUT

for Susan O'Neill Roe

What a thrill——
My thumb instead of an onion.
The top quite gone
Except for a sort of a hinge

Of skin,   5
A flap like a hat,
Dead white.
Then that red plush.

Little pilgrim,
The Indian's axed your scalp.   10

Your turkey wattle
Carpet rolls

Straight from the heart.
I step on it,
Clutching my bottle
Of pink fizz.   15

A celebration, this is.
Out of a gap
A million soldiers run,
Redcoats, every one.   20

Whose side are they on?
O my
Homunculus, I am ill.
I have taken a pill to kill

The thin   25
Papery feeling.
Saboteur,
Kamikaze man——

The stain on your
Gauze Ku Klux Klan   30
Babushka
Darkens and tarnishes and when

The balled
Pulp of your heart
Confronts its small   35
Mill of silence

How you jump——
Trepanned veteran,
Dirty girl,
Thumb stump.   40

1965

DADDY

You do not do, you do not do
Any more, black shoe
In which I have lived like a foot
For thirty years, poor and white,
Barely daring to breathe or Achoo.   5

Daddy, I have had to kill you.
You died before I had time——

Marble-heavy, a bag full of God,
Ghastly statue with one grey toe
Big as a Frisco seal   10

And a head in the freakish Atlantic
Where it pours bean green over blue
In the waters off beautiful Nauset.
I used to pray to recover you.
Ach, du.   15

In the German tongue, in the Polish town
Scraped flat by the roller
Of wars, wars, wars.
But the name of the town is common.
My Polack friend   20

Says there are a dozen or two.
So I never could tell where you
Put your foot, your root,
I never could talk to you.
The tongue stuck in my jaw.   25

It stuck in a barb wire snare.
Ich, ich, ich, ich,
I could hardly speak.
I thought every German was you.
And the language obscene   30

An engine, an engine
Chuffing me off like a Jew.
A Jew to Dachau, Auschwitz, Belsen.
I began to talk like a Jew.
I think I may well be a Jew.   35

The snows of the Tyrol, the clear beer of Vienna
Are not very pure or true.
With my gypsy ancestress and my weird luck
And my Taroc pack and my Taroc pack
I may be a bit of a Jew.   40

I have always been scared of *you,*
With your Luftwaffe, your gobbledygoo.
And your neat moustache
And your Aryan eye, bright blue.
Panzer-man, panzer-man, O You——   45

---

15. *Ach, du:* ah, you (German).   27. *Ich, ich, ich, ich:* I, I, I, I (German).   33. *Dachau, Auschwitz, Belsen:* German concentration camps.   36. *Tyrol:* Tirol, a west Austrian alpine province.

Not God but a swastika
So black no sky could squeak through.
Every woman adores a Fascist,
The boot in the face, the brute
Brute heart of a brute like you.   50

You stand at the blackboard, daddy,
In the picture I have of you,
A cleft in your chin instead of your foot
But no less a devil for that, no not
Any less the black man who   55

Bit my pretty red heart in two.
I was ten when they buried you.
At twenty I tried to die
And get back, back, back to you.
I thought even the bones would do.   60

But they pulled me out of the sack,
And they stuck me together with glue.
And then I knew what to do.
I made a model of you,
A man in black with a Meinkampf look   65

And a love of the rack and the screw.
And I said I do, I do.
So daddy, I'm finally through.
The black telephone's off at the root,
The voices just can't worm through.   70

If I've killed one man, I've killed two——
The vampire who said he was you
And drank my blood for a year,
Seven years, if you want to know.
Daddy, you can lie back now.   75

There's a stake in your fat black heart
And the villagers never liked you.
They are dancing and stamping on you.
They always *knew* it was you.
Daddy, daddy, you bastard, I'm through.   80

1965

---

65. *Meinkampf: Mein Kampf* (*My Battle*), Hitler's political autobiography.

LADY LAZARUS

I have done it again.
One year in every ten
I manage it——

A sort of walking miracle, my skin
Bright as a Nazi lampshade,   5
My right foot

A paperweight
My face a featureless, fine
Jew linen.

Peel off the napkin   10
O my enemy.
Do I terrify?——

The nose, the eye pits, the full set of teeth?
The sour breath
Will vanish in a day.   15

Soon, soon the flesh
The grave cave ate will be
At home on me

And I a smiling woman.
I am only thirty.   20
And like the cat I have nine times to die.

This is Number Three.
What a trash
To annihilate each decade.

What a million filaments.   25
The peanut-crunching crowd
Shoves in to see

Them unwrap me hand and foot——
The big strip tease.
Gentleman, ladies,   30

These are my hands,
My knees.
I may be skin and bone,

Nevertheless, I am the same, identical woman.
The first time it happened I was ten.   35
It was an accident.

Lazarus: Jesus raised Lazarus from the dead; see John 11:44.

The second time I meant
To last it out and not come back at all.
I rocked shut

As a seashell.   40
They had to call and call
And pick the worms off me like sticky pearls.

Dying
Is an art, like everything else.
I do it exceptionally well.   45

I do it so it feels like hell.
I do it so it feels real.
I guess you could say I've a call.

It's easy enough to do it in a cell.
It's easy enough to do it and stay put.   50
It's the theatrical

Comeback in broad day
To the same place, the same face, the same brute
Amused shout:

"A miracle!"   55
That knocks me out.
There is a charge

For the eyeing of my scars, there is a charge
For the hearing of my heart——
It really goes.   60

And there is a charge, a very large charge,
For a word or a touch
Or a bit of blood

Or a piece of my hair or my clothes.
So, so, Herr Doktor.   65
So, Herr Enemy.

I am your opus,
I am your valuable,
The pure gold baby

That melts to a shriek.   70
I turn and burn.
Do not think I underestimate your great concern.

Ash, ash—
You poke and stir.
Flesh, bone, there is nothing there——   75

A cake of soap,
A wedding ring,
A gold filling.

Herr God, Herr Lucifer,
Beware   80
Beware.

Out of the ash
I rise with my red hair
And I eat men like air.

1965

Further Reading

Alexander, Paul, ed. *Ariel Ascending: Writings About Sylvia Plath.* New York: Harper,
1985. • Broe, Mary Lynn. *Protean Poetic: The Poetry of Sylvia Plath.* Columbia: U of
Missouri P, 1980. • Ballif, Gene. "Facing the Worst: A View from Minerva's
Buckler." *Parnassus* 5.1 (Fall–Winter 1976): 231–59. • Perloff, Marjorie. "Angst
and Animism in the Poetry of Sylvia Plath." *Journal of Modern Literature* 1.1 (1970):
57–74, spec. 69–73. • Kamel, Rose. "'A Self to Recover': Sylvia Plath's Bee Cycle
Poems." *Modern Poetry Studies* 4.3 (Winter 1973): 304–18. • Van Dyne, Susan.
"Fueling the Phoenix Fire: Sylvia Plath's 'Lady Lazarus.'" *Massachusetts Review* 24
(Summer 1983): 395–410.

*Though Sylvia Plath was one of the most skillful nature poets of the twen-
tieth century, her reputation has been largely shaped by her anguished confessional poetry. Even poets whose own work is very different in approach
from Plath's have admired this poetry. "Some of it," Amy Clampitt says,
"is so beautiful that I'm drawn to it in spite of the confessional tone." Richard Wilbur's description of a meeting with Plath tells us a great deal about
both poets.*

Richard Wilbur

(b. 1921)

COTTAGE STREET, 1953

Framed in her phoenix fire-screen, Edna Ward
Bends to the tray of Canton, pouring tea

For frightened Mrs. Plath; then, turning toward
The pale, slumped daughter, and my wife, and me,

Asks if we would prefer it weak or strong.   5
Will we have milk or lemon, she enquires?
The visit seems already strained and long.
Each in his turn, we tell her our desires.

It is my office to exemplify
The published poet in his happiness,   10
Thus cheering Sylvia, who has wished to die;
But half-ashamed, and impotent to bless,

I am a stupid life-guard who has found,
Swept to his shallows by the tide, a girl
Who, far from shore, has been immensely drowned,   15
And stares through water now with eyes of pearl.

How large is her refusal; and how slight
The genteel chat whereby we recommend
Life, of a summer afternoon, despite
The brewing dusk which hints that it may end.   20

And Edna Ward shall die in fifteen years,
After her eight-and-eighty summers of
Such grace and courage as permit no tears,
The thin hand reaching out, the last word *love*,

Outliving Sylvia who, condemned to live,   25
Shall study for a decade, as she must,
To state at last her brilliant negative
In poems free and helpless and unjust.

                                                   1976

LUCILLE CLIFTON

(b. 1936)

THE LOST BABY POEM

the time i dropped your almost body down
down to meet the waters under the city
and run one with the sewage to the sea
what did i know about waters rushing back

what did i know about drowning   5
or being drowned

you would have been born into winter
in the year of the disconnected gas
and no car   we would have made the thin
walk over Genesee hill into the Canada wind   10
to watch you slip like ice into strangers' hands
you would have fallen naked as snow into winter
if you were here i could tell you these
and some other things

if i am ever less than a mountain   15
for your definite brothers and sisters
let the rivers pour over my head
let the sea take me for a spiller
of seas   let black men call me stranger
always   for your never named sake   20

                                             1972

GOD'S MOOD

these daughters are bone,
they break.
He wanted stone girls
and boys with branches for arms
that He could lift His life with   5
and be lifted by.
these sons are bone.

He is tired of years that keep turning into age
and flesh that keeps widening.
He is tired of waiting for His teeth to   10
bite Him and walk away.

He is tired of bone,
it breaks.
He is tired of eve's fancy and
adam's whining ways.   15

                                             1974

SHE UNDERSTANDS ME

it is all blood and breaking,
blood and breaking. the thing

drops out of its box squalling
into the light. they are both squalling,
animal and cage. her bars lie wet, open   5
and empty and she has made herself again
out of flesh out of dictionaries,
she is always emptying and it is all
the same wound the same blood the same breaking.

1974

[THERE IS A GIRL INSIDE]

there is a girl inside.
she is randy as a wolf.
she will not walk away
and leave these bones
to an old woman.   5

she is a green tree
in a forest of kindling.
she is a green girl
in a used poet.

she has waited   10
patient as a nun
for the second coming,
when she can break through gray hairs
into blossom

and her lovers will harvest   15
honey and thyme
and the woods will be wild
with the damn wonder of it.

1977

FOR THE MUTE

they will blow from your mouth one morning
like from a shook bottle
and you will try to keep them for
tomorrow's conversation but
your patience will be broken when the   5
bottle bursts
and you will spill all of your
extraordinary hearings for there are

too many languages for
one mortal tongue.   10

1978

FOR THE LAME

happen you will rise,
lift from grounded in a spin
and begin to forget the geography
of fixed things.
happen you will walk past   5
where you meant to stay,
happen you will wonder at the way
it seemed so marvelous to move.

1980

PERHAPS

i am going blind.
my eyes exploding,
seeing more than is there
until they burst into nothing

or going deaf, these sounds   5
the feathered hum of silence

or going away from my self, the cool
fingers of lace on my skin
the fingers of madness

or perhaps   10
in the palace of time
our lives are a circular stair
and i am turning

1980

MY DREAM ABOUT FALLING

a fruitful woman
such as myself
is
falling
notices   5

Lucille Clifton   **895**

she is
an apple
thought
that the blossom
was always   10
thought
that the tree
was forever
fruitful
a woman   15
such as
myself.

the fact is the falling.
the dream is the tree.

1987

Further Reading

Clifton, Lucille. "A Simple Language." *Black Women Writers (1950–1980): A Critical Evaluation.* Ed. Mari Evans. Garden City, NY: Anchor, 1984. 137–38. • McCluskey, Audrey. "Tell the Good News: A View of the Works of Lucille Clifton." *Black Women Writers (1950–1980): A Critical Evaluation.* Ed. Mari Evans. Garden City, NY: Anchor, 1984. 139–49. • Madhubuti, Haki. "Lucille Clifton: Warm Water, Greased Legs, and Dangerous Poetry." *Black Women Writers (1950–1980): A Critical Evaluation.* Ed. Mari Evans. Garden City, NY: Anchor, 1984. 150–60. • Rosenberg, Liz. "Simply American and Mostly Free." *New York Times Book Review* 19 Feb. 1989: 24.

There is an absolute confidence and independence about the voice that we hear in Lucille Clifton's poetry. It seems not to depend on the voice of any particular literary predecessor (though she does acknowledge the importance of Walt Whitman). Instead it seems to come directly from a life lived among people who talk well and frankly and deeply.

Lucille Clifton: On Strength Gotten from Others

When I was 5 years old I forgot my piece. It was the annual Christmas program of Macedonia Baptist Church—a splendid affair—and all of the young Sunday school members had been given poems and recitations to memorize. I forgot mine. I remember standing there on stage in my new Christmas dress, trying not to cry as the church mothers smiled, nodded and murmured encouragement from the front row.

"Go 'head, baby."

"Say it now, Luc."

"Come on now, baby."

But I couldn't remember, and to hide my deep humiliation, my embarrassment, I became sullen, angry.

"I don' wanna."

And I stood there with my mouth poked out.

It was a scandal! This fresh young nobody baby standing in front of the Lord in His own house talking about what she don't want! I could feel the disapproval pouring over my new dress. Then, like a great tidal wave from the ocean of God, my sanctified mother poured down the Baptist aisle, huge as love, her hand outstretched toward mine.

"Come on, baby," she smiled, then turned to address the church: "She don't have to do nothing she don't want to do."

And I was at the same time empowered and made free. . . .

In November of 1984 my beloved husband of almost 30 years died. I am making it because of my daughters, my sons, my woman friends. When I retreat into my room to just sit and stare or cry I can hear my mama speak through my four daughters. "She don't have to act strong if she don't want to." And they still love me.

We talk a lot, these four women and I, but then we always did. They grew up hearing stories I heard from mama and aunts and the old mothers of the church. It was, it is, the way we have continued in this country, passing on our own and the wider history and culture of America. Not just of Black America, of all of it, so that we know what life was like among Black people as well as white ones during slavery time because we heard and overheard the tales of Ole Miz and what happened when. It has been, it is, our strength, this talking and listening, because we have traditionally shared not only the outward cold and definite facts, but also the inward feeling and meaning of things.

ROBERT HASS

(b. 1941)

PALO ALTO: THE MARSHES

For Mariana Richardson (1830–1891)

1

She dreamed along the beaches of this coast.
Here where the tide rides in to desolate
the sluggish margins of the bay,
sea grass sheens copper into distances.
Walking, I recite the hard   5
explosive names of birds:
egret, killdeer, bittern, tern.
Dull in the wind and early morning light,
the striped shadows of the cattails
twitch like nerves.   10

2

Mud, roots, old cartridges, and blood.
High overhead, the long silence of the geese.

3

"We take no prisoners," John Fremont said
and took California for President Polk.
That was the Bear Flag War.   15
She watched it from the Mission San Rafael,
named for the archangel (the terrible one)
who gently laid a fish across the eyes
of saintly, miserable Tobias
that he might see.   20
The eyes of fish. The land
shimmers fearfully.
No archangels here, no ghosts,
and terns rise like seafoam
from the breaking surf.   25

4

Kit Carson's antique .45, blue,
new as grease. The roar
flings up echoes,
row on row of shrieking avocets.

The blood of Francisco de Haro,
Ramon de Haro, José de los Reyes Berryessa
runs darkly to the old ooze.

                              5

The star thistles: erect, surprised,

                              6

and blooming
violet caterpillar hairs. One   35
of the de Haros was her lover,
the books don't say which.
They were twins.

                              7

In California in the early spring
there are pale yellow mornings
when the mist burns slowly into day.   40
The air stings
like autumn, clarifies
like pain.

                              8

Well I have dreamed this coast myself.   45
Dreamed Mariana, since here father owned the land
where I grew up. I saw her picture once:
a wraith encased in a high-necked black silk
dress so taut about the bones there were hardly ripples
for the light to play in. I knew her eyes   50
had watched the hills seep blue with lupine after rain,
seen the young peppers, heavy and intent,
first rosy drupes and then the acrid fruit,
the ache of spring. Black as her hair
the unreflecting venom of those eyes   55
is an aftermath I know, like these brackish,
russet pools a strange life feeds in
or the old fury of land grants, maps,
and deeds of trust. A furious dun-
colored mallard knows my kind   60
and skims across the edges of the marsh
where the dead bass surface
and their flaccid bellies bob.

                              9

A chill tightens the skin
around my bones. The other California   65

and its bitter absent ghosts
dance to a stillness in the air:
the Klamath tribe was routed and they disappeared.
Even the dust seemed stunned,
tools on the ground, fishnets.   70
Fires crackled, smouldering.
No movement but the slow turning
of the smoke, no sound but jays
shrill in the distance and flying further off.
The flicker of lizards, dragonflies.   75
And beyond the dry flag-woven lodges
a faint persistent slapping.
Carson found ten wagonloads
of fresh-caught salmon, silver
in the sun. The flat eyes stared.   80
Gills sucked the thin annulling air.
They flopped and shivered,
ten wagonloads. Kit Carson
burned the village to the ground.
They rode some twenty miles that day   85
and still they saw the black smoke
smear the sky above the pines.

10

Here everything seems clear,
firmly etched against the pale
smoky sky: sedge, flag, owl's clover,   90
rotting wharves. A tanker lugs silver
bomb-shaped napalm tins toward
port at Redwood City. Again,
my eye performs
the lobotomy of description.   95
Again, almost with yearning,
I see the malice of her ancient eyes.
The mud flats hiss as the tide turns.
They say she died in Redwood City,
cursing "the goddamned Anglo-Yankee yoke."   100

11

The otters are gone from the bay
and I have seen five horses
easy in the grassy marsh
beside three snowy egrets.

Bird cries and the unembittered sun,   105
wings and the white bodies of the birds,

it is morning. Citizens are rising
to murder in their moral dreams.

1973

HEROIC SIMILE

When the swordsman fell in Kurosawa's *Seven Samurai*
in the gray rain,
in Cinemascope and the Tokugawa dynasty,
he fell straight as a pine, he fell
as Ajax fell in Homer   5
in chanted dactyls and the tree was so huge
the woodsman returned for two days
to that lucky place before he was done with the sawing
and on the third day he brought his uncle.

They stacked logs in the resinous air,   10
hacking the small limbs off,
tying those bundles separately.
The slabs near the root
were quartered and still they were awkwardly large;
the logs from midtree they halved: 15
ten bundles and four great piles of fragrant wood,
moons and quarter moons and half moons
ridged by the saw's tooth.

The woodsman and the old man his uncle
are standing in midforest   20
on a floor of pine silt and spring mud.
They have stopped working
because they are tired and because
I have imagined no pack animal
or primitive wagon. They are too canny   25
to call in neighbors and come home
with a few logs after three days' work.
They are waiting for me to do something
or for the overseer of the Great Lord
to come and arrest them.   30

How patient they are!
The old man smokes a pipe and spits.
The young man is thinking he would be rich
if he were already rich and had a mule.
Ten days of hauling   35
and on the seventh day they'll probably

be caught, go home empty-handed
or worse. I don't know
whether they're Japanese or Mycenaean
and there's nothing I can do.   40
The path from here to that village
is not translated. A hero, dying,
gives off stillness to the air.
A man and a woman walk from the movies
to the house in the silence of separate fidelities.   45
There are limits to imagination.

1978

MEDITATION AT LAGUNITAS

All the new thinking is about loss.
In this it resembles all the old thinking.
The idea, for example, that each particular erases
the luminous clarity of a general idea. That the clown-
faced woodpecker probing the dead sculpted trunk   5
of that black birch is, by his presence,
some tragic falling off from a first world
of undivided light. Or the other notion that,
because there is in this world no one thing
to which the bramble of *blackberry* corresponds,   10
a word is elegy to what it signifies.
We talked about it late last night and in the voice
of my friend, there was a thin wire of grief, a tone
almost querulous. After a while I understood that,
talking this way, everything dissolves: *justice,*   15
pine, hair, woman, you and *I.* There was a woman
I made love to and I remembered how, holding
her small shoulders in my hands sometimes,
I felt a violent wonder at her presence
like a thirst for salt, for my childhood river   20
with its island willows, silly music from the pleasure boat,
muddy places where we caught the little orange-silver fish
called *pumpkinseed.* It hardly had to do with her.
Longing, we say, because desire is full
of endless distances. I must have been the same to her.   25
But I remember so much, the way her hands dismantled bread,
the thing her father said that hurt her, what
she dreamed. There are moments when the body is as numinous
as words, days that are the good flesh continuing.

Such tenderness, those afternoons and evenings,   30
saying *blackberry, blackberry, blackberry.*

1978

THIN AIR

What if I did not mention death to get started
or how love fails in our well-meaning hands
or what my parents in the innocence of their malice
toward each other did to me. What if I let the light
pour down on the mountan meadow, mule ears   5
dry already in the August heat, and the sweet
heavy scent of sage rising into it, marrying
what light it can, a wartime marriage,
summer is brief in these mountains, the
ticker-tape parade of snow will bury it   10
in no time, in the excess the world gives
up there, and down here, you want snow? you think
you have seen infinity watching the sky shuffle
the pink cards of thirty thousand flamingoes
on the Serengeti Plain? this is my blush,   15
she said, turning toward you, eyes downcast
demurely, a small smile playing at her mouth
playing what? house, playing I am the sister
and author of your sorrow, playing the Lord
God loves the green earth and I am a nun   20
of his Visitations, you want snow, I'll give you
snow, she said, this is my flamingoes-in-migration
blush. Winter will bury it. You had better
sleep through that cold, or sleep in a solitary bed
in a city where the stone glistens darkly   25
in the morning rain, you are allowed a comforter,
silky in texture though it must be blue,
and you can listen to music in the morning,
the notes nervous as light reflected in a fountain,
and you can drink your one cup of fragrant tea   30
and rinse the cup and sweep your room and
the sadness you are fighting off while the gulls'
calls beat about the church towers out the window
and you smell the salt smell of the sea
is the dream you don't remember of the meadow   35
sleeping under fifteen feet of snow though you half
recall the tracks of some midsized animal,
a small fox or a large hare, and the deadly

Robert Hass   **903**

silence, and the blinded-eye gray of the winter sky:
it is sleeping, the meadow, don't wake it.   40
You have to go to the bottom of the raveling.
The surgical pan, and the pump, and the bits
of life that didn't take floating in the smell
of alcohol, or the old man in the bed spitting up
black blood like milk of the other world, or the way   45
middle-aged women from poorer countries are the ones
who clean up after and throw the underwear away.
Hang on to the luxury of the way she used
to turn to you, don't abandon it, summer
is short, no one ever told you differently,   50
this is a good parade, this is the small hotel,
the boathouse on the dock, and the moon thin,
just silvering above the pines, and you are starting
to sweat now, having turned north out of the meadow
and begun the ascent up granite and through buckthorn   55
to the falls. There is a fine film on your warm skin
that you notice. You are water, light and water and thin air,
and you're breathing deeply now—a little dead marmot
like a rag of auburn hair swarms with ants beside the trail—
and you can hear the rush of water in the distance   60
as it takes its leap into the air and falls. In the winter
city she is walking toward you or away from you,
the fog condensing and dripping from the parapets
of old apartments and from the memory of intimate garments
that dried on the balcony in summer, even in the spring.   65
Do you understand? You can brew your one cup of tea
and you can drink it, the leaves were grown in Ceylon,
the plump young man who packed them was impatient,
he is waiting for news of a scholarship to Utrecht,
he is pretty sure he will rot in this lousy place   70
if he doesn't get it, and you can savor the last sip,
rinse the cup, and put it on the shelf,
and then you go outside or you sit down at the desk.
You go into yourself, the sage scent rising in the heat.

1989

OLD DOMINION

The shadows of late afternoon and the odors
of honeysuckle are a congruent sadness.
Everything is easy but wrong. I am walking
across thick lawns under maples in borrowed tennis whites.

It is like the photographs of Randall Jarrell   5
I stared at on the backs of books in college.
He looked so sad and relaxed in the pictures.
He was translating Chekhov and wore tennis whites.
It puzzled me that in his art, like Chekhov's,
everyone was lost, that the main chance was never seized   10
because it is only there as a thing to be dreamed of
or because someone somewhere had set the old words
to the old tune: we live by habit and it doesn't hurt.
Now the *thwack . . . thwack* of tennis balls being hit
reaches me and it is the first sound of an ax   15
in the cherry orchard or the sound of machine guns
where the young terrorists are exploding
among poor people on the streets of Los Angeles.
I begin making resolutions: to take risks, not to stay
in the south, to somehow do honor to Randall Jarrell,   20
never to kill myself. Through the oaks I see the courts,
the nets, the painted boundaries, and the people in tennis
whites who look so graceful from this distance.

1978

WEED

  Horse is Lorca's word, fierce as wind,
or melancholy, gorgeous, Andalusian:
    white horse grazing near the river dust;
and parsnip is hopeless,
    second cousin to the rhubarb   5
which is already second cousin
    to an apple pie. Marrying the words
to the coarse white umbels sprouting
    on the first of May is history
but conveys nothing; it is not the veined   10
    body of Queen Anne's lace
I found, bored, in a spring classroom
    from which I walked hands tingling
for the breasts that are meadows in New Jersey
    in 1933; it is thick, shaggier, and the name   15
is absurd. It speaks of durable
    unimaginative pleasures: reading Balzac,
fixing the window sash, rising
    to a clean kitchen, the fact
that the car starts & driving to work   20
    through hills where the roadside thickens

with the green ungainly stalks,
   the bracts and bright white flowerets
      of horse-parsnips.

1978

Further Reading

Rudman, Mark. "A Review of *Praise.*" *American Poetry Review* 9 (Sept–Oct. 1980): 12–16. • Shapiro, Alan. "'And There Are Always Melons,' Some Thoughts on Robert Hass." *Chicago Review* 33.3 (Winter 1983): 84–90. • Miklitsch, Robert. *"Praise:* The Poetry of Robert Hass." *Hollins Critic* 17.1 (Feb. 1980): 2–13. • Remmick, David. "A Conversation with Robert Hass." *Chicago Review* 32.4 (Spring 1981): 17–26.

Robert Hass brings together threads that connect several contemporary poets. Like Amy Clampitt and Maxine Kumin, he reminds us of the historical underlayers of the present moment. Like Robert Bly and W. S. Merwin, he is an enthusiastic reader of poets from other cultures. He also writes lucid prose about the values that connect him with poets of all periods.

Robert Hass: On the Discovery of Order

I've been trying to think about form in poetry and my mind keeps returning to a time in the country in New York when I was puzzled that my son Leif was getting up a little earlier every morning. I had to get up with him, so it exasperated me. I wondered about it until I slept in his bed one night. His window faced east. At six-thirty I woke to brilliant sunlight. The sun had risen. . . .

The first fact of the world is that it repeats itself. I had been taught to believe that the freshness of children lay in their capacity for wonder at the vividness and strangeness of the particular, but what is fresh in them is that they still experience the power of repetition, from which our first sense of the power of mastery comes. Though *predictable* is an ugly little word in daily life, in our first experience of it we are clued to the hope of a shapeliness in things. To see that power working on adults, you have to catch them out: the look of foolish happiness on the faces of people who have just sat down to dinner is their knowledge that dinner will be served.

Probably, that is the psychological basis for the power and the necessity of artistic form. I think of our children when they first came home from the hospital, wide, staring eyes, wet mouths, fat, uncontrollable tongues. I thought they responded when I bent over their cribs because they were beginning to recognize me. Now I think it was because they were coming to recognize themselves. They were experiencing in the fluidity of things a certain orderliness: footsteps, a face, the smell of hair and tobacco, cooing syllables. One would gradually have the sense that looking-out-of-the-eyes was a point around which phenomena organized themselves; thinking *this is going to happen* and having it happen might be, then, the authentic source of the experience of being, of identity, that word which implies that a lot of different things are the same thing.

Robert Hass: On Images

Images haunt. There is a whole mythology built on this fact: Cézanne painting till his eyes bled, Wordsworth wandering the Lake Country hills in an impassioned daze. Blake describes it very well, and so did the colleague of Tu Fu who said to him, "It is like being alive twice." Images are not quite ideas, they are stiller than that, with less implication outside themselves. And they are not myth, they do not have that explanatory power; they are nearer to pure story. Nor are they always metaphors; they do not say this is that, they say this is. In the nineteenth century one would have said that what compelled us about them was a sense of the eternal. And it is something like that, some feeling in the arrest of the image that what perishes and what lasts forever have been brought into conjunction, and accompanying that sensation is a feeling of release from the self. Antonio Machado wrote, *"Hoy es siempre todavía."* Yet today is always. And Czeslaw Milosz, *"Tylko trwa wieczna chwila."* Only the moment is eternal.

For me, at least, there is a delicate balance in this matter. Walking through the rooms of my house on a moonlit August night, with a sharp sense of my children each at a particular moment in their lives and changing, with three or four shed, curled leaves from a Benjamin fig on the floor of the dining room and a spider, in that moonlight, already set to work in one of them, and the dark outline of an old Monterey pine against the sky outside the window, the one thing about the house that seems not to have changed in the years of my living in it, it is possible to feel my life, in a quiet ecstatic helplessness, as a long slow hurtle through the forms of things. I think I resist that sensation because there is a kind of passivity in it; I suppose that I fear it would make me careless of those things that need concentration to attend to.

SHARON OLDS

(b. 1942)

THE ELDER SISTER

When I look at my elder sister now
I think how she had to go first, down through the
birth canal, to force her way
head-first through the tiny channel,
the pressure of Mother's muscles on her brain,   5
the tight walls scraping her skin.
Her face is still narrow from it, the long
hollow cheeks of a Crusader on a tomb,
and her inky eyes have the look of someone who has
been in prison a long time and   10
knows they can send her back. I look at her
body and think how her breasts were the first to
rise, slowly, like swans on a pond.
By the time mine came along, they were just
two more birds in the flock, and when the hair   15
rose on the white mound of her flesh, like
threads of water out of the ground, it was the
first time, but when mine came
they knew about it. I used to think
only in terms of her harshness, sitting and   20
pissing on me in bed, but now I
see I had her before me always
like a shield. I look at her wrinkles, her clenched
jaws, her frown-lines—I see they are
the dents on my shield, the blows that did not reach me.   25
She protected me, not as a mother
protects a child, with love, but as a
hostage protects the one who makes her
escape as I made my escape, with my sister's
body held in front of me.   30

1984

THE VICTIMS

When Mother divorced you, we were glad. She took it and
took it, in silence, all those years and then
kicked you out, suddenly, and her

kids loved it. Then you were fired, and we
grinned inside, the way people grinned when   5
Nixon's helicopter lifted off the South
Lawn for the last time. We were tickled
to think of your office taken away,
your secretaries taken away,
your lunches with three double bourbons,   10
your pencils, your reams of paper. Would they take your
suits back, too, those dark
carcasses hung in your closet, and the black
noses of your shoes with their large pores?
She had taught us to take it, to hate you and take it   15
until we pricked with her for your
annihilation, Father. Now I
pass the bums in doorways, the white
slugs of their bodies gleaming through slits in their
suits of compressed silt, the stained   20
flippers of their hands, the underwater
fire of their eyes, ships gone down with the
lanterns lit, and I wonder who took it and
took it from them in silence until they had
given it all away and had nothing   25
left but this.

1984

BATHING THE NEW BORN

I love with a fearful love to remember the
first baths I gave this boy—
my second child, so my hands knew what to do,
I laid the tiny torso along my
left forearm, nape of the noodle   5
neck in the crook of my elbow, hips
tiny as a bird's hips against my wrist, and the
thigh the thickness of a thick pencil held
loosely in the loop of my thumb and forefinger, the
sign that means perfect. I'd soap him slowly, the   10
long thin cold feet, the
scrotum tight and wrinkled as a rosy
shell so new it was flexible yet, the
miniature underweight athlete's chest, the
gummy furze of the scalp. If I got him too   15
soapy he'd get so slippery he'd
slide in my grip like an armful of white
buttered noodles, but I'd hold him not too tight,

I knew I was so good for him, and I'd
talk to him the whole time, I'd   20
tell him about his wonderful body
and the wonderful soap, the whole world made of love,
and he'd look up at me, one week old,
his eyes still wide and apprehensive of his
new life. I love that time   25
when you croon and croon to them, you can see the
calm slowly entering them, you can
feel it in your anchoring hand, the
small necklace of the spine against the
muscle of your forearm, you feel the fear   30
leaving their bodies, he lay in the blue
oval plastic baby tub and
looked at me in wonder and began to
move his silky limbs at will in the water.

1984

SEX WITHOUT LOVE

How do they do it, the ones who make love
without love? Beautiful as dancers,
gliding over each other like ice-skaters
over the ice, fingers hooked
inside each other's bodies, faces   5
red as steak, wine, wet as the
children at birth whose mothers are going to
give them away. How do they come to the
come to the   come to the   God   come to the
still waters, and not love   10
the one who came there with them, light
rising slowly as steam off their joined
skin? These are the true religious,
the purists, the pros, the ones who will not
accept a false Messiah, love the   15
priest instead of the God. They do not
mistake the lover for their own pleasure,
they are like great runners: they know they are alone
with the road surface, the cold, the wind,
the fit of their shoes, their over-all cardio-   20
vascular health—just factors, like the partner
in the bed, and not the truth, which is the
single body alone in the universe
against its own best time.

1985

THE RACE

When I got to the airport I rushed up to the desk
and they told me the flight was cancelled. The doctors had
said my father would not live through the night
and the flight was cancelled. A young man with a
dark blond moustache told me   5
another airline had a non-stop
leaving in seven minutes—see that
elevator over there well go
down to the first floor, make a right you'll
see a yellow bus, get off at the   10
second Pan Am terminal—I
ran, I who have no sense of direction
raced exactly where he'd told me, like a fish
slipping upstream deftly against the
flow of the river. I jumped off that bus with my   15
heavy bags and ran, the bags
wagged me from side to side as if to
prove I was under the claims of the material, I
ran up to a man with a white flower on his breast,
I who always go to the end of the line, I said   20
Help me. He looked at my ticket, he said make a
left and then a right go up the moving stairs and then
run. I raced up the moving stairs
two at a time, at the top I saw the
long hollow corridor and   25
then I took a deep breath, I said
goodbye to my body, goodbye to comfort, I
used my legs and heart as if I would
gladly use them up for this, to
touch him again in this life. I ran and the   30
big heavy dark bags
banged me, wheeled and swam around me like
planets in wild orbits—I have seen
pictures of women running down roads with their
belongings tied in black scarves   35
grasped in their fists, running under serious
gray historical skies—I blessed my
long legs he gave me, my strong
heart I abandoned to its own purpose, I
ran to Gate 17 and they were   40
just lifting the thick white
lozenge of the door to fit it into the
socket of the plane. Like the man who is not
too rich, I turned to the side and
slipped through the needle's eye, and then I   45

walked down the aisle toward my father. The jet was
full and people's hair was shining, they were
smiling, the interior of the plane was filled with a
mist of gold endorphin light,
I wept as people weep when they enter heaven,   50
in massive relief. We lifted up
gently from one tip of the continent and
did not stop until we set down lightly on the
other edge, I walked into his room and
watched his chest rise slowly and   55
sink again, all night
I watched him breathe.

1985

SUMMER SOLSTICE, NEW YORK CITY

By the end of the longest day of the year he could not stand it,
he went up the iron stairs through the roof of the building
and over the soft, tarry surface
to the edge, put one leg over the complex green tin cornice
and said if they came a step closer that was it.   5
Then the huge machinery of the earth began to work for his life,
the cops came in their suits blue-gray as the sky on a cloudy evening,
and one put on a bulletproof vest, a
black shell around his own life,
life of his children's father, in case   10
the man was armed, and one, slung with a
rope like the sign of his bounden duty,
came up out of a hole in the top of the neighboring building,
like the gold hole they say is in the top of the head,
and began to lurk toward the man who wanted to die.   15
The tallest cop approached him directly,
softly, slowly, talking to him, talking, talking,
while the man's leg hung over the lip of the next world,
and the crowd gathered in the street, silent, and the
dark hairy net with its implacable grid was   20
unfolded near the curb and spread out and
stretched as the sheet is prepared to receive at a birth.
Then they all came a little closer
where he squatted next to his death, his shirt
glowing its milky glow like something   25
growing in a dish at night in the dark in a lab, and then
everything stopped
as his body jerked and he
stepped down from the parapet and went toward them

and they closed on him, I thought they were going to   30
beat him up, as a mother whose child has been
lost will scream at the child when it's found, they
took him by the arms and held him up and
leaned him against the wall of the chimney and the
tall cop lit a cigarette   35
in his own mouth, and gave it to him, and
then they all lit cigarettes, and the
red glowing ends burned like the
tiny campfires we lit at night
back at the beginning of the world.   40

1986

THE CHUTE

When I was a kid, my father built a
hole down through the center of the house.
It started in the upstairs closet, a
black, square mouth like a well
with a lid on it, it plummeted down   5
behind the kitchen wall, and the raw
pine cloaca tip of it was
down in the basement where the twisted wicker
basket lay on the cement floor,
so when someone dropped in laundry at the top, it would   10
drop with the speed of sheer falling—in the
kitchen you'd hear that whisk of pure
descent behind the wall. And halfway
down there was an electric fixture for the
doorbell—that bell my father would ring and   15
ring years later when he stood at the door with that
blood on him, like a newborn's caul,
ringing ringing to enter. But back
then he was only halfway down, a
wad of sheets stuck in the chute,   20
he could still fix the doorbell when it busted.
He'd stand his kids in front of him,
three skinny scared braggart kids,
and run his gaze over them, a
surgeon running his eyes over the tray,   25
and he'd select a kid, and take that kid by the
ankles and slowly feed that kid
down the chute. First you'd do a handstand on the
lip of it and then he'd lower you in,
the smell of pine and dirty laundry,   30

his grip on your ankles like the steel he sold,
he'd lower you until your whole body was in it
and you'd find the little wires, red and
blue, like a vein and a nerve, and you'd tape them together.
We thought it was such an honor to be chosen,   35
and like all honors it was mostly terror, not
only the blood in your head like a sac of
worms in wet soil, but how could you believe he would
not let go? He would joke about it,
standing there, holding his kid like a   40
bottle brush inside a bottle, or the
way they drown people, he'd lower us down as if
dipping us into the darkness before birth
and he'd pretend to let go—he loved to hear
passionate screaming in a narrow space—   45
how could you trust him? And then if you were
his, half him, your left hand maybe and your
left foot dipped in the gleaming
murky liquor of his nature, how could you
trust yourself? What would it feel like   50
to be on the side of life? How did the
good know they were good, could they look at their
hand and see, under the skin, the
greenish light? We hung there in the dark
and yet, you know, he never dropped us   55
or meant to, he only liked to say he would,
so although it's a story with some cruelty in it,
finally it's a story of love
and release, the way the father pulls you out of nothing
and stands there foolishly grinning.   60

1987

Further Reading

Harris, Peter. "Poetry Chronicle: Four Salvers Salvaging: New Works by Voigt,
Olds, Dove, and McHugh." *Virginia Quarterly Review* 64.2 (Spring 1988): 262–76,
spec. 265–69. • McEwen, Christian. "Soul Substance." *Nation* 244 (Apr. 11, 1987):
472–75. • Stitt, Peter. "Liars and Truth-Tellers, Fancy and Plain." *Georgia Review*
41 (Fall 1987): 585–601, spec. 598–601. • Wright, Carolyne. "On Sharon Olds."
Iowa Review 15.1 (Winter 1985): 151–61. • Kinzie, Mary. "Idiom and Error."
American Poetry Review 13.5 (Sept.–Oct. 1984): 38–47.

Perhaps because the nineteenth century produced so much sentimental poetry about romantic love and family relationships, twentieth-century poets have approached these subjects very carefully, often very obliquely. In 1947 Louise Bogan noticed that women poets, particularly, were so anxious to avoid "feminine" subjects that they had begun to imitate "the work of male verbalizers and poetic logicians." Bogan urged these women not to abandon "their contact with, and their expression of, deep and powerful emotional streams." Toddlers when Bogan wrote this, Sharon Olds and Tess Gallagher seem belatedly to be answering her call to women to "keep open the emotional channels of literature."

Tess Gallagher

(b. 1943)

EACH BIRD WALKING

Not while, but long after he had told me,
I thought of him, washing his mother, his
bending over the bed and taking back
the covers. There was a basin of water
and he dipped a washrag in and   5
out of the basin, the rag
dripping a little onto the sheet as he
turned from the bedside to the nightstand
and back, there being no place

on her body he shouldn't touch because   10
he had to and she helped him, moving
the little she could, lifting so he could
wipe under her arms, a dipping motion
in the hollow. Then working up from
the feet, around the ankles, over the   15
knees. And this last, opening
her thighs and running the rag firmly
and with the cleaning thought
up through her crotch, between the lips,
over the V of thin hairs—   20

as though he were a mother
who had the excuse of cleaning to touch
with love and indifference,

the secret parts of her child, to graze
the sleepy sexlessness in its waiting   25
to find out what to do for the sake
of the body, for the sake of what only
the body can do for itself.

So his hand, softly at the place
of his birth-light. And she, eyes deepened   30
and closed in the dim room.
And because he told me her death was
important to his being with her,
I could love him another way. Not
of the body alone, or of its making,   35
but carried in the white spires of trembling
until what spirit, what breath we were
was shaken from us. Small then,
the word *holy*.

He turned her on her stomach   40
and washed the blades of her shoulders, the
small of the back. "That's good," she said,
"that's enough."
On our lips that morning, the tart juice
of the mothers, so strong in remembrance, no   45
asking, no giving, and what you said, this
being the end of our loving, so as not to hurt
the closer one to you, made me look
to see what was left of us
with our sex taken away. "Tell me," I said,   50
"something I can't forget." Then the story of
your mother, and when you finished
I said, "That's good, that's enough."

                                                                        1984

LOUISE GLÜCK

(b. 1943)

FOR MY MOTHER

It was better when we were
together in one body.
Thirty years. Screened

through the green glass
of your eye, moonlight   5
filtered into my bones
as we lay
in the big bed, in the dark,
waiting for my father.
Thirty years. He closed   10
your eyelids with
two kisses. And then spring
came and withdrew from me
the absolute
knowledge of the unborn,   15
leaving the brick stoop
where you stand, shading
your eyes, but it is
night, the moon
is stationed in the beech tree,   20
round and white among
the small tin markers of the stars:
Thirty years. A marsh
grows up around the house.
Schools of spores circulate   25
behind the shades, drift through
gauze flutterings of vegetation.

                                                       1975

THE APPLE TREES

Your son presses against me
his small intelligent body.

I stand beside his crib
as in another dream
you stood among trees hung   5
with bitten apples
holding out your arms.
I did not move
but saw the air dividing
into panes of color—at the very last   10
I raised him to the window saying
See what you have made
and counted out the whittled ribs,
the heart on its blue stalk
as from among the trees   15
the darkness issued:

In the dark room your son sleeps.
The walls are green, the walls
are spruce and silence.
I wait to see how he will leave me.   20
Already on his hand the map appears
as though you carved it there,
the dead fields, women rooted to the river.

1975

METAMORPHOSIS

1. Night

The angel of death flies
low over my father's bed.
Only my mother sees. She and my father
are alone in the room.

She bends over him to touch   5
his hand, his forehead. She is
so used to mothering
that now she strokes his body
as she would the other children's,
first gently, then   10
inured to suffering.

Nothing is any different.
Even the spot on the lung
was always there.

2. Metamorphosis

My father has forgotten me   15
in the excitement of dying.
Like a child who will not eat,
he takes no notice of anything.

I sit at the edge of his bed
while the living circle us   20
like so many tree stumps.

Once, for the smallest
fraction of an instant, I thought
he was alive in the present again;
then he looked at me   25
as a blind man stares
straight into the sun, since

whatever it could do to him
is done already.

Then his flushed face   30
turned away from the contract.

3. For My Father

I'm going to live without you
as I learned once
to live without my mother.
You think I don't remember that?   35
I've spent my whole life trying to remember.

Now, after so much solitude,
death doesn't frighten me,
not yours, not mine either.
And those words, *the last time,*   40
have no power over me. I know
intense love always leads to mourning.

For once, your body doesn't frighten me.
From time to time, I run my hand over your face
lightly, like a dustcloth.   45
What can shock me now? I feel
no coldness that can't be explained.
Against your cheek, my hand is warm
and full of tenderness.

1985

THE TRIUMPH OF ACHILLES

In the story of Patroclus
no one survives, not even Achilles
who was nearly a god.
Patroclus resembled him; they wore
the same armor.   5

Always in these friendships
one serves the other, one is less than the other:
the hierarchy
is always apparent, though the legends
cannot be trusted—   10
their source is the survivor,
the one who has been abandoned.

What were the Greek ships on fire
compared to this loss?

In his tent, Achilles   15
grieved with his whole being
and the gods saw

he was a man already dead, a victim
of the part that loved,
the part that was mortal.   20

1985

HORSE

What does the horse give you
that I cannot give you?

I watch you when you are alone,
when you ride into the field behind the dairy,
your hands buried in the mare's   5
dark mane.

Then I know what lies behind your silence:
scorn, hatred of me, of marriage. Still,
you want me to touch you; you cry out
as brides cry, but when I look at you I see   10
there are no children in your body.
Then what is there?

Nothing, I think. Only haste
to die before I die.

In a dream, I watched you ride the horse   15
over the dry fields and then
dismount: you two walked together;
in the dark, you had no shadows.
But I felt them coming toward me
since at night they go anywhere,   20
they are their own masters.

Look at me. You think I don't understand?
What is the animal
if not passage out of this life?

1985

NIGHT SONG

Look up into the light of the lantern.
Don't you see? The calm of darkness
is the horror of heaven.

We've been apart too long, too painfully separated.
How can you bear to dream,   5
to give up watching? I think you must be dreaming,
your face is full of mild expectancy.

I need to wake you, to remind you that there isn't a future.
That's why we're free. And now some weakness in me
has been cured forever, so I'm not compelled   10
to close my eyes, to go back, to rectify—

The beach is still; the sea, cleansed of its superfluous life,
opaque, rocklike. In mounds, in vegetal clusters,
seabirds sleep on the jetty. Terns, assassins—

You're tired; I can see that.   15
We're both tired, we have acted a great drama.
Even our hands are cold, that were like kindling.
Our clothes are scattered on the sand; strangely enough,
they never turned to ashes.

I have to tell you what I've learned, that I know now   20
what happens to the dreamers.
They don't feel it when they change. One day
they wake, they dress, they are old.

Tonight I'm not afraid
to feel the revolutions. How can you want sleep   25
when passion gives you that peace?
You're like me tonight, one of the lucky ones.
You'll get what you want. You'll get your oblivion.

1985

Further Reading

Glück, Louise. "The Dreamer and the Watcher." *Singular Voices: American Poetry Today.* Ed. Stephen Berg. New York: Avon, 1985. 75–82. • Vendler, Helen. "In the Zoo of the New." *New York Review of Books* 33 (23 Oct. 1986): 47. • Hirsch, Edward. "The Watcher." *American Poetry Review* 15.6 (Nov.–Dec. 1986): 33. • Bedient, Calvin. "Birth, Not Death, Is the Hard Loss." *Parnassus* 9.1 (Spring–Summer 1981): 168–86. • Stitt, Peter. "Contemporary American Poems: Exclusive and Inclusive." *Georgia Review* 39.4 (Winter 1985): 849–63.

The critic Helen Vendler points out that Louise Glück's poems are often "cryptic narratives," pared to the bare minimum so that the reader must construct plot, character, theme, and action. Glück's own account of the writing of "Night Song" shows the same sort of cryptic quality from the poet's perspective: the surprisingly indirect relation between the external events that stimulate a poem and the "messages" the poet is "equipped to receive."

Louise Glück: On Change and Loss

In April of 1980, my house was destroyed by fire. . . . Gradually, certain benefits became apparent. I felt grateful; the vivid sense of escape conferred on daily life an aura of blessedness. I felt lucky to wake up, lucky to make the beds, lucky to grind the coffee. There was also, after a period of devastating grief, a strange exhilaration. Having nothing, I was no longer hostage to possessions. . . .

That first summer after the fire was a period of rare happiness. I mean, by that word, not ecstasy but another state, one more balanced, serene, attentive. . . .

It was clear to me long ago that any hope I had of writing real poetry depended on my living through common experiences. The privileged, the too-protected, the mandarin in my nature would have to be checked. At the same time, I was wary of drama, of disaster too deliberately courted: I have always been too at ease with extremes. What had to be cultivated, beyond a necessary neutrality, was the willingness to be identified with others. . . .

Major experiences vary in form—what reader and writer learn to do is recognize analogies. I watched my house burn—in the category of major losses, this made only the most modest start. Nor was it unexpected: I had spent twenty years waiting to undergo the losses I knew to be inevitable. I was obsessed with loss; not surprisingly, I was also acquisitive, possessive. The two tendencies fed each other; every impulse to extend my holdings increased the fundamental anxiety. Actual loss, loss of mere property, was a release, an abrupt transition from anticipation to expertise. In passing, I learned something about fire, about its appetite. I watched the destruction of all that had been, all that would not be again, and all that remained took on a radiance.

These are, in the deepest sense, ordinary experiences. On the subject of change, of loss, we all attain to authority. In my case, the timing was efficient. I was in my late thirties; perhaps I'd learned all I could about preparation, about gathering. The next lesson is abandon, letting go.

Perhaps, too, in all this there were other messages to be heard. And perhaps "Night Song" sounds much more of a piece with my other work than this suggests. It wouldn't surprise me. It seems these are the messages I'm equipped to receive.

DRAMA

Reading Drama: The Space in Which the Words Are Spoken

An attractive hypothesis about the relation of drama to fiction is that a play is a short story told by acting it out. If we put the hypothesis to the test, however, we are forced to discard or change it. We might try, for example, to "dramatize" a passage that comes about five hundred words into Anton Chekhov's story "The Lady with the Pet Dog." We have learned that the principal character, Dmitry Dmitrich Gurov, is a married man under forty, "bored and ill at ease" in the presence of men, who has been repeatedly unfaithful to his wife and who regards women as "the inferior race."

> One evening while he was dining in the public garden the lady in the beret walked up without haste to take the next table. Her expression, her gait, her dress, and the way she did her hair told him that she belonged to the upper class, that she was married, that she was in Yalta for the first time and alone, and that she was bored there. The stories told of the immorality in Yalta are to a great extent untrue; he despised them, and knew that such stories were made up for the most part by persons who would have been glad to sin themselves if they had had the chance; but when the lady sat down at the next table three paces

from him, he recalled these stories of easy conquests, of trips to the mountains, and the tempting thought of a swift, fleeting liaison, a romance with an unknown woman of whose very name he was ignorant suddenly took hold of him.

He beckoned invitingly to the Pomeranian, and when the dog approached him, shook his finger at it. The Pomeranian growled; Gurov threatened it again.

The lady glanced at them and at once dropped her eyes.

"He doesn't bite," she said and blushed.

"May I give him a bone?" he asked; and when she nodded he inquired affably, "Have you been in Yalta long?"

"About five days."

"And I am dragging out the second week here."

There was a short silence.

"Time passes quickly, and yet it is so dull here!" she said, not looking at him.

A great dramatist as well as a great fiction writer, Chekhov has given us promising material here: external action that need only be converted into stage directions, some practical hints for costuming and set. Here is the scene as we might work it up in an adaptation for the stage.

> *[A public garden, with tables, about half of them occupied, at which people sit eating.* Gurov *occupies a table alone.* Anna, *a fair-haired young lady of medium height, fashionably dressed, enters with a Pomeranian on a leash. She sits at the table next to* Gurov, *about fifteen feet away.* Gurov *drops his hand to his side and wiggles his fingers to attract the dog's attention. When the dog approaches, he shakes his finger at it. The dog growls and* Gurov *shakes his finger again.* Anna *glances at* Gurov *and drops her eyes.]*

Anna: *(blushing)* He doesn't bite.

Gurov: May I give him a bone? *(Anna nods.) (affably)* Have you been in Yalta long?

Anna: About five days.

Gurov: I am dragging out the second week here.

Anna: *(after a short pause, not looking at him)* Time passes quickly and yet it is so dull here.

In some ways this is not a bad bit of scriptwriting: the presence of the dog not only creates an interesting bit of stage business but leads naturally to dialogue that reveals something about the characters of Gurov and Anna. The problem, however, is that the Gurov our viewers will see on stage is not the same one that we read about in the story. They can see by the way that he entices the dog and then shakes his finger at it that Gurov is trying to find a way to draw the lady into conversation. But they may—if they have watched enough romantic movies, they probably will—assume that Gurov is a bachelor who has seen an unmarried woman. Even if we show him to be married (perhaps we could bring on a waiter at the beginning of the scene to deliver a letter from his wife?), there will be nothing to show his contempt for women or his habit of using them to fill up the emptiness of his life.

How can we show Gurov's inner life to the audience? Three tactics come to mind. We could supply Gurov with a confidant to whom he could talk about his feelings, but this method can work only if the character has a confiding nature, which Gurov does not. He confides in neither men nor women: his isolation is essential to his character. We could have him address an occasional aside directly to the audience. After Anna says, "Time passes quickly, and yet it is so dull here," for instance, he might say, "And so it is as I thought: here is a woman ripe for a fleeting affair." But a character who confides in the audience hardly seems isolated, and asides like these would make the play seem like a melodrama rather than the subtle story Chekhov has provided us. We might write another scene in which

Gurov, alone on the stage, reveals his thoughts in a soliloquy. But soliloquies require characters (like Hamlet) who are inclined to search their souls: Gurov's soul-searching will come later in the story, when he discovers that he has one to search.

A good playwright could find a way around some of these difficulties of presenting a character's psychological state in dramatic form[1] but some of them are inherent in the form of drama. A play depends upon external actions and on words spoken while standing in a particular place: it is a physical art form. This physical form imposes some limitations on drama, but it also opens up possibilities, for action, spoken words, and a sense of place are powerful tools.

THE SOCIAL NATURE OF DRAMA: GREEK DRAMA

Toward the end of "The Lady with the Pet Dog," Chekhov says this: "The personal life of every individual is based on secrecy, and perhaps it is partly for that reason that civilized man is so nervously anxious that personal privacy should be respected." This statement is profoundly true, but it does not exhaust the truth. Humans are public creatures as well as private ones, and "the personal life of every individual" comes largely from a relation to the society in which he or she lives. Private musing, joys, and heartaches have tremendous weight; so too do external actions and words spoken aloud to the community.

The ancient Greeks very strongly felt the importance of this public side of human nature, nowhere more clearly expressed than in Aristotle's statement that "man is a political animal." Translation here obscures Aristotle's meaning slightly. It might be better to say that a human is a creature of the *polis*, the community: from it the individual derives the values that allow a fully human life; to it the individual is ultimately answerable.

Implied in this emphasis on "political" life is the Greek love of talk, games, debate, public worship, song, dance: all the things that bind people together on public occasions. The Greek view did not assume that life's true center was in private relations that were separated by a wide moat from an alien public life. The Greek public life penetrated what we would view as private sanctuaries. This penetration is crucial to Greek drama, as we can see in a play like Sophocles' *Antigone,* where the grief of a sister for the death of her brother raises an enormous public issue: duty to the *polis* versus duty to the gods.

Euripides' *Medea*, too, treats in a surprisingly "political" way a subject most of us would see as extremely personal. Medea, a foreigner in Corinth, discovers that her husband is abandoning her to marry the king's daughter,

---

1. See, for example, Samuel Beckett's play *Krapp's Last Tape.*

and she is enraged by the betrayal. A chorus of Corinthian women enters to console Medea, but also—very much in the Greek fashion—to investigate the situation and discuss it. To them Medea delivers the opening speech, which sounds rather like a lawyer's opening argument before a jury.

> *Medea:* Women of Corinth, I have come outside to you
> Lest you should be indignant with me; for I know
> That many people are overproud, . . .
> But on me this thing has fallen so unexpectedly,
> It has broken my heart. I am finished. I let go
> All my life's joy. . . .
> Of all things which are living and can form a judgment
> We women are the most unfortunate creatures.
> Firstly, with an excess of wealth it is required
> For us to buy a husband and take for our bodies
> A master; for not to take one is even worse. . . .
> And if we work out all this well and carefully,
> And the husband lives with us and lightly bears his yoke,
> Then life is enviable. If not, I'd rather die.
> A man, when he's tired of the company in his home,
> Goes out of the house and puts an end to his boredom
> And turns to a friend or companion of his own age.
> But we are forced to keep our eyes on one alone.
> What they say of us is that we have a peaceful time
> Living at home, while they do the fighting in war.
> How wrong they are! I would very much rather stand
> Three times in the front of battle than bear one child.
> Yet what applies to me does not apply to you.
> You have a country. Your family home is here.
> You enjoy life and the company of your friends.
> But I am deserted, a refugee, thought nothing of
> By my husband—something he won in a foreign land.
> I have no mother or brother, nor any relation
> With whom I can take refuge in this sea of woe.
> This much then is the service I would beg from you:
> If I can find the means or devise any scheme
> To pay my husband back for what he has done to me—
> Him and his father-in-law and the girl who married him—
> Just to keep silent. For in other ways a woman
> Is full of fear, defenseless, dreads the sight of cold
> Steel; but, when once she is wronged in the matter of love,
> No other soul can hold so many thoughts of blood.

> *Chorus:* This I will promise. You are in the right, Medea
> In paying your husband back. I am not surprised at you
> For being sad.

Medea has given a stirring speech, and one full of passion, but not in Chekhov's sense a *personal* speech. Always her emphasis is on the central questions of the *polis:* justice, equity, propriety, participation in (or exclusion from) the life of the community. Her complaint is not in a sense peculiar to herself: she talks about "we women" or "a woman," as if what she feels might be felt (sometimes must be felt) by all the women in the chorus or by any stranger in the polis. And the chorus is temporarily won over.

Consider for a moment the circumstances in which this scene was originally enacted. The amphitheater in Athens held an audience of almost 14,000 and of course was in the open air. The average theatergoer was two hundred feet away from the actors. So far away were the actors that they wore oversized masks with exaggerated facial expressions, stood in elevator shoes about six inches high, and dressed in bold, stylized costumes (Medea's would have declared her at great distance to be a regal woman from the East). Built into the masks of the actors was a sort of megaphone that allowed their voices to carry to the back rows—provided, of course, that they spoke very loudly. None of this can have encouraged an easy identification with Medea as an individual human. But shoulder to shoulder with the average spectator and quite visible to him in the broad daylight were the members of his community, listening intently to Medea's speech, weighing its justice, considering the treatment of women and strangers in the *polis,* watching as the play unfolds the horrifying effects of pride and unchecked passion. In this context a Greek tragedy gathers a force that a short story, read silently by a single reader, can never have. Works like *Medea* and *Antigone* are "social documents," as Arthur Miller says, "not just piddling private conversations."

Adding to this force of public performance was the atmosphere of the spring festival of Dionysius, during which the drama was performed. Religious in origin, the festival had become in the days of Sophocles and Euripides a celebration of the glory of the Athenian *polis,* a very civic event. All citizens attended the plays: those who could not afford the price of admission were admitted at the expense of the city. The cost of the production was borne as a civic duty and honor by a rich man the *polis* elected. The city was small enough that the theatergoer would have known the producer, the playwright, the actors, and the members of the chorus. The audience must have felt on the day of a performance that "we" were coming together to enjoy, consider, and argue about a thing "we" all valued and were building together: a shared understanding of life.

TRANSPARENT DECEPTION: ELIZABETHAN DRAMA

The whole of the Globe, Shakespeare's theater in London, could have fit in the orchestra of the theater in Athens. The change in scale signals a change in all aspects of drama. English public theaters in the time of Elizabeth I

(1558–1603) and James I (1603–1625) were not places where the whole society gathered for a religious and civic celebration. They were places where a fraction of the city's population paid for entertainment, just as they paid to watch the animals tormented at the Bear Garden or at the Bull Baiting. An Elizabethan tragedian did not have the Athenian's advantages in achieving high seriousness and civic involvement.

On the other hand, the Elizabethan playwright reaped advantages from the smaller theater. A full house at the Globe might have consisted of about two thousand people, some six hundred "groundlings" standing in the "yard" that surrounded the stage on three sides, more wealthy patrons seated in the galleries built one above the other a bit further back, and a few seated on the stage itself. Those seated on the stage could have seen the wrinkles in an actor's face. Even those seated in the back of the third gallery would have been only about sixty feet away: close enough to see ordinary gestures—shrugging the shoulders, clenching the fists, running fingers nervously through the hair. Under these circumstances plays could assume a sort of realism they had never had in the ancient world. A man[2] standing on platform shoes, wearing a carved mask, and chanting in a voice that could be heard a hundred yards away might *represent* Medea to an audience willing to use its imagination. But a man dressed in fairly ordinary costume, his features mobile and expressive and his voice varying naturally in volume and inflection, might *impersonate* Prince Hamlet so well that the audience would for a moment see life itself on the stage. In *Hamlet,* the Prince tells a group of actors that the purpose of drama is "to hold, as 't were, the mirror up to nature." The older style of acting, he says, is out of fashion:

> O! there be players that I have seen play—and heard others praise,
> and that highly—not to speak it profanely, that, neither having th'
> accent of Christians nor the gait of Christian, pagan, nor man, have so
> strutted and bellow'd that I have thought some of Nature's journey-
> men had made men, and not made them well, they imitated humanity
> so abominably.

Holding the mirror up to nature was not, however, the whole mission, and one of the pleasures of Elizabethan drama is the counterpoint between the illusion on stage and the reality of a London afternoon in a bustling theater. Like the Athenian amphitheater, Elizabethan public theaters were open to the sky, and the spectators could see each other quite as well as they could see the players. In fact, the audience was part of the attraction. One observer reported that "in the playhouses at London, it is the fashion of youths to go first into the yard, and there to carry their eye through every gallery" in search of beautiful women. When they find them "thither they

---

2. Men and boys played women's roles in both Greek and Elizabethan theater.

fly, and press as near to the fairest as they can" where "they dally with their garments to pass the time."

The awareness of other spectators was so strong that playwrights occasionally incorporated references to the audience in their plays. In his speech to the players, Hamlet says, "O, it offends me to the soul to hear a robustious periwig-pated fellow tear a passion to tatters, to very rags, to spleet the ears of the groundlings, who for the most part are capable of nothing but inexplicable dumb shows and noise. . . ." The groundlings, standing within a few yards of the player delivering these lines, *must* have reacted, visibly if not audibly, and the people in the galleries must have watched for the groundlings' reactions as if they were part of the play. At the beginning of *The Careless Shepherd*, a play produced in a theater much like the Globe, two supposed spectators rise up from their seats at the edge of the stage and talk about moving into the gallery. A third "spectator" gets up and follows them, commenting that he knew that they would have preferred to sit on stage "To show their cloak and Sute," and that they were undoubtedly moving into the gallery only because they feared they might have creditors in the audience. Then the "real" play begins.

In reading some passages of Shakespearean drama, we can sense the pleasure playwright, players, and audience felt when they could do acrobatics on the tightwire stretched between reality and illusion. In Act I, scene 5, of *Twelfth Night*, for example, Viola disguises herself as a boy and becomes a page to Orsino, Duke of Illyria. The audience, knowing that all women on the Elizabethan stage were played by boys, has an interesting idea to play with: the boy actor had been dressed as a woman to play Viola, now Viola decides to dress as a eunuch named Cesario. Very well: a boy is playing a girl who is playing a boy. Dressed as Cesario, she becomes a page to Orsino, with whom she secretly falls in love. Orsino, not knowing these things, makes Cesario/Viola a messenger to speak words of love to Olivia. Now the audience is quite aware that two boy actors are about to play a love scene in which one is pretending to be a woman and the other is pretending to be a woman pretending to be a boy. Viola/Cesario arrives at Olivia's house where Olivia, her face covered, is standing with her maid, Maria:

Viola: The honorable lady of the house, which is she?

Olivia: Speak to me, I shall answer for her. Your will?

Viola: Most radiant, exquisite, and unmatchable beauty—I pray you tell me if this be the lady of the house, for I never saw her. I would be loath to cast away my speech; for, besides that it is excellently well penn'd, I have taken great pains to con it. Good beauties, let me sustain no scorn; I am very comptible,[3] even to the least sinister usage.

---

3. *Comptible* means sensitive or susceptible. For other notes on this scene, see pages 1022–1023.

Olivia:	Whence came you, sir?
Viola:	I can say little more than I have studied, and that question's out of my part. Good gentle one, give me modest assurance if you be the lady of the house, that I may proceed in my speech.
Olivia:	Are you a comedian?
Viola:	No, my profound heart; and yet (by the very fangs of malice I swear) I am not that I play. Are you the lady of the house?
Olivia:	If I do not usurp myself, I am.

When the boy playing Viola says that she/he has taken "great pains to con" an "excellently well penn'd" speech, the audience can step *into* the illusion of the play and hear Viola talking about her relation to her writer/master Orsino, but can also step *out of* the illusion to hear the boy actor talking about his relation to the playwright. When she/he swears that she is "not that I play," the levels of revealed make-believe are deliciously complicated:

- The boy actor must pretend to be a woman.
- Viola must pretend to be Cesario.
- Cesario must pretend to be Olivia's lover.

All these levels of illusion are plain to the audience and are part of the comedy. And yet for all the humor that comes from admitting that the play is a performance, the characters eventually develop such definite personalities that the audience comes to believe in them.

Viola:	Most certain, if you are she, you do usurp yourself; for what is yours to bestow is not yours to reserve. But this is from my commission; I will on with my speech in your praise, and then show you the heart of my message.
Olivia:	Come to what is important in 't. I forgive you the praise.
Viola:	Alas, I took great pains to study it, and 'tis poetical.
Olivia:	It is the more like to be feign'd, I pray you keep it in. I heard you were saucy at my gates, and allow'd your approach rather to wonder at you than to hear you. If you be not mad, be gone. If you have reason, be brief. 'Tis not that time of moon with me to make one in so skipping a dialogue.

The wit of this dialogue absorbs the audience's attention, and two extraordinarily interesting characters begin to emerge—intelligent, sharp-tongued, resourceful, hard-shelled, and (as we later learn) tender-hearted women. The boys stand in women's costumes in broad daylight on the bare stage, with no curtain to hide their exits and entrances, no scenery in the background, and very few stage props. But they "imitate humanity" so convincingly that the audience can sometimes forget the stage and the other spectators. The playwright reminds us that the characters are only actors delivering lines, and yet slowly they seem to assume a reality more intense than that of the groundlings or the spectators on stools at the edge of the stage. This sort of magic is characteristic of Shakespearean drama and distinguishes it both from the ritual drama of Athens and the realistic drama of the nineteenth and twentieth centuries.

TOTAL ILLUSION: REALISTIC DRAMA IN THIS CENTURY

Realism in drama is difficult to define and depends partly on a system of contrasts. In the context of Greek drama, with its larger-than-human scale, its dance and song, and its masked actors, Medea may have seemed a surprisingly realistic character because her emotions seem to imitate those of actual humans. But if the same actor represented Medea by the same methods at the Globe theater, where gestures and speech were more natural and the range of emotions wider and more fluid, he would be less convincing than the bombastic players Prince Hamlet criticizes. On a typical twentieth-century stage, however, an actor playing Viola or Hamlet in the Elizabethan fashion would not strike us as remarkably realistic.[4] We would probably find that he or she delivered the lines with too much attention to their poetry and too little attention to motivation, and we would be distracted by the soliloquies, asides, and gestures addressed frankly to the audience. The way that Elizabethan actors hovered between artifice and reality is consistent with the way their parts are written. These characters speak far more cleverly than anyone we have met, and their lives, filled with unlikely events, are lived at an emotional pitch no one sustains for long. They are created for a theater where the literal reproduction of reality was neither possible nor desirable.

After the seventeenth century, theater became increasingly an indoor business, and an indoor theater gave directors an opportunity to control the audience's perceptions more completely than before. The standard theater acquired a proscenium, the arch at the stage front through which the audience looks, a curtain to cover the proscenium between acts, and footlights that made the actors highly visible while leaving the audience in darkness. With the addition of carefully contrived scenery, it became possible to reproduce the visible world on stage, sometimes with breathtaking

---

4. I am not saying that the plays do not work on the modern stage, of course: they are still among the most popular plays ever written. The point is that one rarely leaves a contemporary Shakespearean performance thinking how much Hamlet and Ophelia resemble the couple next door, or how we meet Violas every day.

accuracy. When in 1898 the curtain went up on the Moscow Art Theatre's production of Anton Chekhov's *The Seagull*, the audience saw a convincing outdoor scene: a dark summer evening, the distant sounds of a drunkard singing and a dog howling, the croaking of frogs, the crake of a marsh bird, the tolling of a distant church bell, flashes of lightning, faint thunder in the distance. By the light of a lantern on top of a lamppost, the audience could see trees and bushes surrounding a clearing in which a workman was humming a tune as he hammered a nail into a crude stage for an amateur play. A white sheet was draped across the front of the stage the workman was building. A man smoking a cigarette and a woman cracking nuts strolled in from the right and began a conversation, sometimes facing directly away from the audience as they talked. The illusion was so nearly perfect that the auditorium in which the spectators sat now seemed to look into a real world, extending indefinitely into space. Midway through the first act, the white sheet came down and the audience saw a lake gleaming in the moonlit distance.

In a sense, this production of *The Seagull* was the logical culmination of three centuries of movement toward realistic theater. In another sense, it was an absolute revolution, one we associate with the writer Chekhov and the actor/directors Constantine Stanislavsky and Vladimir Nemirovich-Danchenko. These three men, objecting to the artificial conventions of the nineteenth-century Russian theater,[5] began to build a drama on new principles. Ultimately, the purpose of the spectacularly realistic setting of plays like *The Seagull* was to make possible a new sort of drama, one where actors seemed to stand in the real world and act like real people. In the old drama, actors addressed their lines to the audience and used conventional gestures and intonations to convey their emotions; when they were not talking, they simply waited for their next line to come up. In the new drama, the actors addressed their comments to each other, listened to the responses, and adopted whatever gestures, accents, and intonations seemed realistic for a person of the character's region, education, and disposition. In the old drama, there were recognizable stars in the play, stars who would bow to the audience and receive an ovation the minute they came onstage. In the new drama, the actor was completely subordinated to the character, and the star of one play might have the smallest part in another. In the old theater, the script presented characters who were in many ways larger than life, involved in extraordinarily dramatic situations, and expressing extraordinarily strong and unmixed emotions. In the new drama, the scale had shrunk to truly human proportions. The characters were people as ordinary as ourselves.

A Moscow Art Theatre production of a Chekhov play was so bold a departure into realism that it put everyone's nerves on edge. Was there an

---

5. Russian theater had lagged behind, for instance, the Norwegian theater of Ibsen.

audience for drama about genuinely ordinary people? *The Seagull* opened with a cast so edgy that the actors took tranquilizers and made signs of the cross before they made their entrances. Stanislavsky managed to sit through the performance, but his legs twitched so violently that he had to hold them with both hands. Nemirovich-Danchenko stood out in the foyer for the whole first act, dreading a bad reaction. Chekhov was in Yalta, very ill with tuberculosis, and his sister had warned the company that a failure of the play might be his deathblow. Stanislavsky's description of the company's mood at the end of the last act deserves quotation:

> There was a gravelike silence. Knipper fainted on stage. All of us could hardly keep our feet. In the throes of despair we began moving to our dressing rooms. Suddenly there was a roar in the auditorium, and a shriek of joy or fright on the stage. The curtain was lifted, fell, was lifted again, showing the whole auditorium our amazed and astounded immovability. It fell again, it rose; it fell, it rose, and we could not even gather enough sense to bow.

At the end of the performance Nemirovich-Danchenko suggested to the audience that Chekhov be sent a congratulatory telegram. The ovation was enormous and prolonged.

This success made it possible for Chekhov to write still more realistic drama of the sort we find in *The Three Sisters,* where the dialogue is lifelike to the point of imitating the pointlessness of everyday conversation.

Fedotik: I will now show you a new kind of solitaire. . . .

[He lays out the cards.
They bring in the samovar; Anfisa stands by it; a little later Natasha comes in and begins to straighten things on the table; Solyony enters, is greeted, and sits down at the table.]

Vershinin: What a wind!

Masha: Yes. I'm bored with winter. I've forgotten what summer's like.

Irina: I'm going to go out, I can see it. We're going to get to Moscow!

Fedotik: No it's not—see, that eight's on the deuce of spades. *(He laughs)* So, you're not going to get to Moscow.

Chebutykin: *(Reading the newspaper)* Tsitsikar. Smallpox is raging here.

Anfisa: *(Going up to Masha)* Masha, have some tea, darling. *(To Vershinin)* Please, your honor. . . . Excuse me, sir, I've forgotten your name. . . .

Masha: Bring it over here, nurse. I'm not going there.

Irina:	Nurse!
Anfisa:	Coming-g!

Natasha: (*To* Solyony) Babies, little babies still at the breast—they understand perfectly. "Good morning, Bobik!" I say. "Good morning, sweetheart!" Then he looks up at me in a very special way. You think I'm just saying that because I'm a mother, but that isn't so, no indeed it isn't so! He really is the most amazing child.

Solyony: If that child were mine I'd fry him in a frying pan and then eat him.

[*He picks up his glass, goes into the living room, and sits down in a corner*]

Natasha: (*Covering.her face with her hands*) Rude, common man!

Masha: If you're happy you don't notice whether it's summer or winter. It seems to me that if I were in Moscow I wouldn't care what the weather was like.

Despite the success of *The Seagull,* the script of *The Three Sisters* once again challenged the nerves of the Moscow Art Theatre. Some of the dismayed actors and actresses complained that it was not a play, that it could not be acted. It seemed to be an uncomposed photograph of life rather than an orderly imitation of it. Eventually, actors and audiences discovered in Chekhov's dialogue a "music of life"[6] that reveals individual characters and also portrays the connections and disconnections of the small society on stage. Chekhov's music, so different from the literal music of Greek or Elizabethan drama, gave order to the realistic action of the play.

A word of warning about realism is in order at this point. The historical accident that gave us Greek drama before Elizabethan, and Elizabethan drama before Chekovian realism, might deceive us into thinking that the theater has progressed toward a goal. Progress is hardly the issue. Some of today's playwrights have more in common with Euripides than with Chekhov. Some very deliberately turn their back on the capacity of twentieth-century stagecraft (or cinematography) to produce a fictional world as detailed as the everyday world. Even Chekhov complained that technical realism could interfere with drama: when characters are too busy slapping mosquitoes to establish the reality of an outdoor setting, the heart of the play can be overlooked. Although complete illusions of reality are easier to create now than they were at the turn of the century, many playwrights have

---

6. The phrase is Nemirovich-Danchenko's. He is referring particularly to the way that Chekhov writes dialogue full of pauses "in which were expressed unspoken feelings, insinuations as to character, the semitones. The atmosphere gradually deepened, gathered itself into one harmonious whole, became, as it were, the music of life."

stepped back from extreme realism in setting or performance and preferred the more symbolic patterns we associate with Greek drama or the
half-illusion we associate with Elizabethan drama.

READING THE PLAY SILENTLY

Obviously, a play we read silently cannot have exactly the same impact on us
that a performed play does. As silent readers we gain because we can
approach the text at our own pace, rereading passages that are difficult or
interesting and carefully comparing one scene to another. We lose because
we cannot get a complete sense of the action onstage, the sound of the performance, or the interaction between audience and players. The loss, however, need not be complete. There are steps we can take to overcome our
disadvantages.

First, we can pay attention to the setting and to the degree of detailed
realism the author seems to expect in the set. In Greek or Shakespearean
drama, where scenery and stage properties were severely limited, much of
the setting was conveyed in the language of the play. Thus, at the beginning
of *Hamlet,* two sentries help create a setting by their words:

Barnardo: 'Tis now stroock twelf. Get thee to bed, Francisco.

Francisco: For this relief much thanks. 'Tis bitter cold,
And I am sick at heart.

We get the time, temperature, and general mood conveyed in dialogue.
Chekhov and Stanislavsky would probably have done the same work visually, but the Shakespearean stage could not be darkened or converted
visually to the gloomy walls of Elsinore castle.

In a play where setting is written into dialogue, we are not likely to
overlook it, but many novice readers fail to read the description most modern playwrights insert before the action begins. At the beginning of *Death of
a Salesman,* for instance, Arthur Miller spends over six hundred words
describing the set in a way that also defines the play's relation to reality.
The kitchen of Willy Loman's house should seem "actual enough," with a
kitchen table, three chairs, and a refrigerator, but "no other fixtures are
seen." In the other rooms of the house are a few pieces of actual furniture.
But most of the walls are missing, so that actors can occasionally walk right
through them when the action is not in the present time. Around the house
are "towering, angular shapes" that as the lights come up are revealed as "a
solid vault of apartment building around the small, fragile-seeming home."
This both is and is not the real world. Miller says that the set should have
"the air of a dream rising out of reality." He is preparing the audience for a
type of drama intermediate between Chekhov's realism and the Greek theater of ideas and symbolic actions. Spectators can take all this in subconsciously, but as readers we need to give it conscious thought.

Second, we can notice the playwright's use of action, dialogue, and music. In the first hundred lines of *Twelfth Night* Shakespeare manages to give the audience music, poetic language, the background information on two story lines, a bit of imaginary geography, and the description of a ship-wreck: all through the mouths of characters who have motives to say what they say. Twice in *The Three Sisters* Chekhov manages to solve the technical problem mentioned at the beginning of this chapter, that of getting an essentially uncommunicative character into a situation where he will reveal his innermost thoughts. Andrei talks freely to Ferapont in Act 2 because Ferapont is too hard of hearing to understand him, and Chebutykin gets so drunk in Act 3 that he begins to talk to himself in what he thinks is an empty room. This sort of virtuosity deserves to be consciously savored.

Third, we can take time early to get the firmest possible grip on the identity of the characters: to know their ages, relations to each other, and general dispositions. Modern playwrights often help us by a thumbnail description in the list of characters that precedes the text of the play. In *Crimes of the Heart* Beth Henley gives brief physical descriptions when the character enters, and also makes the initial words and actions typical. Chick Boyle, for instance, opens the play shouting:

Chick's Voice: Lenny! Oh, Lenny! Lenny *quickly blows out the candle and stuffs the cookie and candle into her dress pocket. Chick, twenty-nine, enters from the back door. She is a brightly dressed matron with yellow hair and shiny red lips.*

Chick: Hi! I saw your car pull up.

Lenny: Hi.

Chick: Well, did you see today's paper?

Lenny *nods.*

Chick: It's just too awful! It's just way too awful! How I'm gonna con-tinue holding my head up high in this community, I do not know. Did you remember to pick up those pantyhose for me?

Lenny: They're in the sack.

Chick: Well, thank goodness, at least I'm not gonna have to go into town wearing holes in my stockings. *She gets the package, tears it open, and proceeds to take off one pair of stockings and put on another throughout the following scene. There should be something slightly grotesque about this woman changing her stockings in the kitchen.*

We should pause a moment to fix our image of Chick: a twenty-nine-year-old woman, brightly dressed, with red lipstick, struggling into pantyhose and talking about holding her head up in this community. The essential Chick is all there, and every subsequent speech she makes is more interesting if we can keep the image clearly in mind.

The image is crucial to drama. Medea with the bloody corpses of her children escaping in a chariot drawn by dragons, the pompous Malvolio appearing onstage with his trousers rolled up to reveal yellow stockings and crossed garters, Chekhov's three sisters embracing in the garden of the home they must soon leave: these images move us whether we see them on a literal stage or only on the stage of our imagination. As a boy, the eighteenth-century writer Samuel Johnson sat in the basement kitchen of his house, reading plays by firelight. When he read the opening scenes of *Hamlet*, the ghost scenes worked so vividly on his imagination that he ran up the stairs onto the street so "that he might have people about him." If we could all read with this sort of intensity, we would not need textbooks or classrooms to learn what drama is about.

SOPHOCLES

(496–406 B.C.)

ANTIGONE

translated from the Greek by Elizabeth Wyckoff

CHARACTERS

Antigone
Ismene
Chorus of Theban Elders
Creon
A Guard
Haemon
Teiresias
A Messenger
Eurydice

Scene: Thebes, before the royal palace.

(Antigone and Ismene emerge from its great central door.)

Antigone: My sister, my Ismene, do you know
of any suffering from our father sprung
that Zeus does not achieve for us survivors?
There's nothing grievous, nothing free from doom,
not shameful, not dishonored, I've not seen.   5
Your sufferings and mine.
And now, what of this edict which they say
the commander has proclaimed to the whole people?
Have you heard anything? Or don't you know
that the foes' trouble comes upon our friends?   10
Ismene: I've heard no word, Antigone, of our friends.
Not sweet nor bitter, since that single moment
when we two lost two brothers
who died on one day by a double blow.
And since the Argive army[1] went away   15
this very night, I have no further news
of fortune or disaster for myself.

---

1. The army from Argos had been led against Thebes by Antigone's brother Polyneices. Her other brother, Eteocles, had helped lead the defense.

Antigone: I knew it well, and brought you from the house
    for just this reason, that you alone may hear.
   Ismene: What is it? Clearly some news has clouded you.   20
Antigone: It has indeed. Creon will give the one
    of our two brothers honor in the tomb;
    the other none.
    Eteocles, with just entreatment treated,
    as law provides he has hidden under earth   25
    to have full honor with the dead below.
    But Polyneices' corpse who died in pain,
    they say he has proclaimed to the whole town
    that none may bury him and none bewail,
    but leave him unwept, untombed, a rich sweet sight   30
    for the hungry birds' beholding.
    Such orders they say the worthy Creon gives
    to you and me—yes, yes, I say to *me*—
    and that he's coming to proclaim it clear
    to those who know it not.   35
    Further: he has the matter so at heart
    that anyone who dares attempt the act
    will die by public stoning in the town.
    So there you have it and you soon will show
    if you are noble, or fallen from your descent.   40
   Ismene: If things have reached this stage, what can I do,
    poor sister, that will help to make or mend?
Antigone: Think will you share my labor and my act.
   Ismene: What will you risk? And where is your intent?
Antigone: Will you take up that corpse along with me?   45
   Ismene: To bury him you mean, when it's forbidden?
Antigone: My brother, and yours, though you may wish he were not.
    I never shall be found to be his traitor.
   Ismene: O hard of mind! When Creon spoke against it!
Antigone: It's not for him to keep me from my own.   50
   Ismene: Alas. Remember, sister, how our father
    perished abhorred, ill-famed.
    Himself with his own hand, through his own curse
    destroyed both eyes.
    Remember next his mother and his wife   55
    finishing life in the shame of the twisted strings.[2]
    And third two brothers on a single day,
    poor creatures, murdering, a common doom
    each with his arm accomplished on the other.

---

2. Oedipus blinded himself when he learned that he had unknowingly killed his father, Laius, and married his mother, Jocasta. Jocasta hanged herself.

And now look at the two of us alone.   60
We'll perish terribly if we force law
and try to cross the royal vote and power.
We must remember that we two are women
so not to fight with men.
And that since we are subject to strong power   65
we must hear these orders, or any that may be worse.
So I shall ask of them beneath the earth
forgiveness, for in these things I am forced,
and shall obey the men in power. I know
that wild and futile action makes no sense.   70
Antigone: I wouldn't urge it. And if now you wished
to act, you wouldn't please me as a partner.
Be what you want to; but that man shall I
bury. For me, the doer, death is best.
Friend shall I lie with him, yes friend with friend,   75
when I have dared the crime of piety.
Longer the time in which to please the dead
than that for those up here.
There shall I lie forever. You may see fit
to keep from honor what the gods have honored.   80
Ismene: I shall do no dishonor. But to act
against the citizens. I cannot.
Antigone: That's your protection. Now I go, to pile
the burial-mound for him, my dearest brother.
Ismene: Oh my poor sister. How I fear for you!   85
Antigone: For me, don't borrow trouble. Clear your fate.
Ismene: At least give no one warning of this act;
you keep it hidden, and I'll do the same.
Antigone: Dear God! Denounce me. I shall hate you more
if silent, not proclaiming this to all.   90
Ismene: You have a hot mind over chilly things.
Antigone: I know I please those whom I most should please.
Ismene: If but you can. You crave what can't be done.
Antigone: And so, when strength runs out, I shall give over.
Ismene: Wrong from the start, to chase what cannot be.   95
Antigone: If that's your saying, I shall hate you first,
and next the dead will hate you in all justice.
But let me and my own ill-counselling
suffer this terror. I shall suffer nothing
as great as dying with a lack of grace.   100
Ismene: Go, since you want to. But know this: you go
senseless indeed, but loved by those who love you.

*(Ismene returns to the palace; Antigone leaves by one of the side entrances. The
Chorus now enters from the other side.)*

Chorus: Sun's own radiance, fairest light ever shone on the gates of
    Thebes,
  then did you shine, O golden day's
  eye, coming over Dirce's stream,   105
  on the Man who had come from Argos with all his armor
  running now in headlong fear as you shook his bridle free.

    He was stirred by the dubious quarrel of Polyneices.
    So, screaming shrill,
    like an eagle over the land he flew,   110
    covered with white-snow wing,
    with many weapons,
    with horse-hair crested helms.

  He who had stood above our halls, gaping about our seven gates,
  with that circle of thirsting spears.   115
  Gone, without our blood in his jaws,
  before the torch took hold on our tower-crown.
  Rattle of war at his back; hard the fight for the dragon's foe.

    The boasts of a proud tongue are for Zeus to hate.
    So seeing them streaming on   120
    in insolent clangor of gold,
    he struck with hurling fire him who rushed
    for the high wall's top,
    to cry conquest abroad.

  Swinging, striking the earth he fell   125
  fire in hand, who in mad attack,
  had raged against us with blasts of hate.
  He failed. He failed of his aim.
  For the rest great Ares[3] dealt his blows about,
  first in the war-team.   130

    The captains stationed at seven gates
    fought with seven and left behind
    their brazen arms as an offering
    to Zeus who is turner of battle.
    All but those wretches, sons of one man,   · 135
    one mother's sons, who sent their spears
    each against each and found the share
    of a common death together.

  Great-named Victory comes to us
  answering Thebes' warrior-joy.   140
  Let us forget the wars just done

---

3. God of war.

and visit the shrines of the gods.
All, with night-long dance which Bacchus[4] will lead,
who shakes Thebes' acres.

(Creon enters from the palace.)

Now here he comes, the king of the land,   145
Creon, Menoeceus' son,
newly named by the gods' new fate.
What plan that beats about his mind
has made him call this council-session,
sending his summons to all?   150

Creon: My friends, the very gods who shook the state
with mighty surge have set it straight again.
So now I sent for you, chosen from all,
first that I knew you constant in respect
to Laius' royal power; and again   155
when Oedipus had set the state to rights,
and when he perished, you were faithful still
in mind to the descendants of the dead.
When they two perished by a double fate,
on one day struck and striking and defiled   160
each by his own hand, now it comes that I
hold all the power and the royal throne
through close connection with the perished men.
You cannot learn of any man the soul,
the mind, and the intent until he shows   165
his practise of the government and law.
For I believe that who controls the state
and does not hold to the best plans of all,
but locks his tongue up through some kind of fear,
that he is worst of all who are or were.   170
And he who counts another greater friend
than his own fatherland, I put him nowhere.
So I—may Zeus all-seeing always know it—
could not keep silent as disaster crept
upon the town, destroying hope of safety.   175
Nor could I count the enemy of the land
friend to myself, not I who know so well
that she it is who saves us, sailing straight,
and only so can we have friends at all.
With such good rules shall I enlarge our state.   180
And now I have proclaimed their brother-edict.
In the matter of the sons of Oedipus,

---

4. God of wine; the great Greek tragedies were performed at festivals dedicated to him.

citizens, know: Eteocles who died,
defending this our town with champion spear,
is to be covered in the grave and granted   185
all holy rites we give the noble dead.
But his brother Polyneices whom I name
the exile who came back and sought to burn
his fatherland, the gods who were his kin,
who tried to gorge on blood he shared, and lead   190
the rest of us as slaves—
it is announced that no one in this town
may give him burial or mourn for him.
Leave him unburied, leave his corpse disgraced,
a dinner for the birds and for the dogs.   195
Such is my mind. Never shall I, myself,
honor the wicked and reject the just.
The man who is well-minded to the state
from me in death and life shall have his honor.
Chorus: This resolution, Creon, is your own,   200
in the matter of the traitor and the true.
For you can make such rulings as you will
about the living and about the dead.
  Creon: Now you be sentinels of the decree.
Chorus: Order some younger man to take this on.   205
  Creon: Already there are watchers of the corpse.
Chorus: What other order would you give us, then?
  Creon: Not to take sides with any who disobey.
Chorus: No fool is fool as far as loving death.
  Creon: Death is the price. But often we have known   210
men to be ruined by the hope of profit.

(Enter, from the side, a guard.)

  Guard: Lord, I can't claim that I am out of breath
from rushing here with light and hasty step,
for I had many haltings in my thought
making me double back upon my road.   215
My mind kept saying many things to me:
"Why go where you will surely pay the price?"
"Fool, are you halting? And if Creon learns
from someone else, how shall you not be hurt?"
Turning this over, on I dilly-dallied.   220
And so a short trip turns itself to long.
Finally, though, my coming here won out.
If what I say is nothing, still I'll say it.
For I come clutching to one single hope
that I can't suffer what is not my fate.   225
  Creon: What is it that brings on this gloom of yours?

Guard: I want to tell you first about myself.
   I didn't do it, didn't see who did it.
   It isn't right for me to get in trouble.
Creon: Your aim is good. You fence the fact around.   230
   It's clear you have some shocking news to tell.
Guard: Terrible tidings make for long delays.
Creon: Speak out the story, and then get away.
Guard: I'll tell you. Someone left the corpse just now,
   burial all accomplished, thirsty dust   235
   strewn on the flesh, the ritual complete.
Creon: What are you saying? What man has dared to do it?
Guard: I wouldn't know. There were no marks of picks,
   no grubbed-out earth. The ground was dry and hard,
   no trace of wheels. The doer left no sign.   240
   When the first fellow on the day-shift showed us,
   we all were sick with wonder.
   For he was hidden, not inside a tomb,
   light dust upon him, enough to turn the curse,
   no wild beast's track, nor track of any hound   245
   having been near, nor was the body torn.
   We roared bad words about, guard against guard,
   and came to blows. No one was there to stop us.
   Each man had done it, nobody had done it
   so as to prove it on him—we couldn't tell.   250
   We were prepared to hold to red-hot iron,
   to walk through fire, to swear before the gods
   we hadn't done it, hadn't shared the plan,
   when it was plotted or when it was done.
   And last, when all our sleuthing came out nowhere,   255
   one fellow spoke, who made our heads to droop
   low toward the ground. We couldn't disagree.
   We couldn't see a chance of getting off.
   He said we had to tell you all about it.
   We couldn't hide the fact.   260
   So he won out. The lot chose poor old me
   to win the prize. So here I am unwilling,
   quite sure you people hardly want to see me.
   Nobody likes the bringer of bad news.
Chorus: Lord, while he spoke, my mind kept on debating.   265
   Isn't this action possibly a god's?
Creon: Stop now, before you fill me up with rage,
   or you'll prove yourself insane as well as old.
   Unbearable, your saying that the gods
   take any kindly forethought for this corpse.   270
   Would it be they had hidden him away,

honoring his good service, his who came
to burn their pillared temples and their wealth,
even their land, and break apart their laws?
Or have you seen them honor wicked men?   275
It isn't so.
No, from the first there were some men in town
who took the edict hard, and growled against me,
who hid the fact that they were rearing back,
not rightly in the yoke, no way my friends.   280
These are the people—oh it's clear to me—
who have bribed these men and brought about the deed.
No current custom among men as bad
as silver currency. This destroys the state;
this drives men from their homes; this wicked teacher   285
drives solid citizens to acts of shame.
It shows men how to practise infamy
and know the deeds of all unholiness.
Every least hireling who helped in this
brought about then the sentence he shall have.   290
But further, as I still revere great Zeus,
understand this, I tell you under oath,
if you don't find the very man whose hands
buried the corpse, bring him for me to see,
not death alone shall be enough for you   295
till living, hanging, you make clear the crime.
For any future grabbings you'll have learned
where to get pay, and that it doesn't pay
to squeeze a profit out of every source.
For you'll have felt that more men come to doom   300
through dirty profits than are kept by them.
Guard: May I say something? Or just turn and go?
Creon: Aren't you aware your speech is most unwelcome?
Guard: Does it annoy your hearing or your mind?
Creon: Why are you out to allocate my pain?   305
Guard: The doer hurts your mind. I hurt your ears.
Creon: You are a quibbling rascal through and through.
Guard: But anyhow I never did the deed.
Creon: And you the man who sold your mind for money!
Guard: Oh!   310
    How terrible to guess, and guess at lies!
Creon: Go pretty up your guesswork. If you don't
    show me the doers you will have to say
    that wicked payments work their own revenge.
Guard: Indeed, I pray he's found, but yes or no,   315
    taken or not as luck may settle it,

you won't see me returning to this place.
Saved when I neither hoped nor thought to be,
I owe the gods a mighty debt of thanks.

(Creon enters the palace. The Guard leaves by the way he came.)

Chorus: Many the wonders but nothing walks stranger than man.   320
This thing crosses the sea in the winter's storm,
making his path through the roaring waves.
And she, the greatest of gods, the earth—
ageless she is, and unwearied—he wears her away
as the ploughs go up and down from year to year   325
and his mules turn up the soil.

Gay nations of birds he snares and leads,
wild beast tribes and the salty brood of the sea,
with the twisted mesh of his nets, this clever man.
He controls with craft the beasts of the open air,   330
walkers on hills. The horse with his shaggy mane
he holds and harnesses, yoked about the neck,
and the strong bull of the mountain.

Language, and thought like the wind
and the feelings that make the town,   335
he has taught himself, and shelter against the cold,
refuge from rain. He can always help himself.
He faces no future helpless. There's only death
that he cannot find an escape from. He has contrived
refuge from illnesses once beyond all cure.   340

Clever beyond all dreams
the inventive craft that he has
which may drive him one time or another to well or ill.
When he honors the laws of the land and the gods' sworn right
high indeed is his city; but stateless the man   345
who dares to dwell with dishonor. Not by my fire,
never to share my thoughts, who does these things.

(The Guard enters with Antigone.)

My mind is split at this awful sight.
I know her. I cannot deny
Antigone is here.   350
Alas, the unhappy girl,
her unhappy father's child.
Oh what is the meaning of this?
It cannot be you that they bring
for breaking the royal law,   355
caught in open shame.

Guard: This is the woman who has done the deed.
　　　We caught her at the burying. Where's the king?

(Creon enters.)

　　Chorus: Back from the house again just when he's needed.
　　　Creon: What must I measure up to? What has happened?　　360
　　Guard: Lord, one should never swear off anything.
　　　Afterthought makes the first resolve a liar.
　　　I could have vowed I wouldn't come back here
　　　after your threats, after the storm I faced.
　　　But joy that comes beyond the wildest hope　　365
　　　is bigger than all other pleasure known.
　　　I'm here, though I swore not to be, and bring
　　　this girl. We caught her burying the dead.
　　　This time we didn't need to shake the lots;
　　　mine was the luck, all mine.　　370
　　　So now, lord, take her, you, and question her
　　　and prove her as you will. But I am free.
　　　And I deserve full clearance on this charge.
　　Creon: Explain the circumstance of the arrest.
　　Guard: She was burying the man. You have it all.　　375
　　Creon: Is this the truth? And do you grasp its meaning?
　　Guard: I saw her burying the very corpse you had forbidden. Is
　　　this adequate?
　　Creon: How was she caught and taken in the act?
　　Guard: It was like this: when we got back again　　380
　　　struck with those dreadful threatenings of yours,
　　　we swept away the dust that hid the corpse.
　　　We stripped it back to slimy nakedness.
　　　And then we sat to windward on the hill
　　　so as to dodge the smell.　　385
　　　We poked each other up with growling threats
　　　if anyone was careless of his work.
　　　For some time this went on, till it was noon.
　　　The sun was high and hot. Then from the earth
　　　up rose a dusty whirlwind to the sky,　　390
　　　filling the plain, smearing the forest-leaves,
　　　clogging the upper air. We shut our eyes,
　　　sat and endured the plague the gods had sent.
　　　So the storm left us after a long time.
　　　We saw the girl. She cried the sharp and shrill　　395
　　　cry of a bitter bird which sees the nest
　　　bare where the young birds lay.
　　　So this same girl, seeing the body stripped,
　　　cried with great groanings, cried a dreadful curse
　　　upon the people who had done the deed.　　400

Soon in her hands she brought the thirsty dust,
and holding high a pitcher of wrought bronze
she poured the three libations for the dead.
We saw this and surged down. We trapped her fast;
and she was calm. We taxed her with the deeds   405
both past and present. Nothing was denied.
And I was glad, and yet I took it hard.
One's own escape from trouble makes one glad;
but bringing friends to trouble is hard grief.
Still, I care less for all these second thoughts   410
than for the fact that I myself am safe.
  Creon: You there, whose head is drooping to the ground,
do you admit this, or deny you did it?
Antigone: I say I did it and I don't deny it.
  Creon (to the Guard): Take yourself off wherever you wish to go   415
free of a heavy charge.
  Creon (to Antigone): You—tell me not at length but in a word.
You knew the order not to do this thing?
Antigone: I knew, of course I knew. The word was plain.
  Creon: And still you dared to overstep these laws?   420
Antigone: For me it was not Zeus who made that order.
Nor did that Justice who lives with the gods below
mark out such laws to hold among mankind.
Nor did I think your orders were so strong
that you, a mortal man, could over-run   425
the gods' unwritten and unfailing laws.
Not now, nor yesterday's, they always live,
and no one knows their origin in time.
So not through fear of any man's proud spirit
would I be likely to neglect these laws,   430
draw on myself the gods' sure punishment.
I knew that I must die; how could I not?
even without your warning. If I die
before my time, I say it is a gain.
Who lives in sorrows many as are mine   435
how shall he not be glad to gain his death?
And so, for me to meet this fate, no grief.
But if I left that corpse, my mother's son,
dead and unburied I'd have cause to grieve
as now I grieve not.   440
And if you think my acts are foolishness
the foolishness may be in a fool's eye.
  Chorus: The girl is bitter. She's her father's child.
She cannot yield to trouble; nor could he.
  Creon: These rigid spirits are the first to fall.   445
The strongest iron, hardened in the fire,

most often ends in scraps and shatterings.
Small curbs bring raging horses back to terms.
Slave to his neighbor, who can think of pride?
This girl was expert in her insolence   450
when she broke bounds beyond established law.
Once she had done it, insolence the second,
to boast her doing, and to laugh in it.
I am no man and she the man instead
if she can have this conquest without pain.   455
She is my sister's child, but were she child
of closer kin than any at my hearth,
she and her sister should not so escape
their death and doom. I charge Ismene too.
She shared the planning of this burial.   460
Call her outside. I saw her in the house,
maddened, no longer mistress of herself.
The sly intent betrays itself sometimes
before the secret plotters work their wrong.
I hate it too when someone caught in crime   465
then wants to make it seem a lovely thing.

Antigone: Do you want more than my arrest and death?
  Creon: No more than that. For that is all I need.
Antigone: Why are you waiting? Nothing that you say
fits with my thought. I pray it never will.   470
Nor will you ever like to hear my words.
And yet what greater glory could I find
than giving my own brother funeral?
All these would say that they approved my act
did fear not mute them.   475
(A king is fortunate in many ways,
and most, that he can act and speak at will.)
  Creon: None of these others see the case this way.
Antigone: They see, and do not say. You have them cowed.
  Creon: And you are not ashamed to think alone?   480
Antigone: No, I am not ashamed. When was it shame
to serve the children of my mother's womb?
  Creon: It was not your brother who died against him, then?
Antigone: Full brother, on both sides, my parents' child.
  Creon: Your act of grace, in his regard, is crime.   485
Antigone: The corpse below would never say it was.
  Creon: When you honor him and the criminal just alike?
Antigone: It was a brother, not a slave, who died.
  Creon: Died to destroy this land the other guarded.
Antigone: Death yearns for equal law for all the dead.   490
  Creon: Not that the good and bad draw equal shares.
Antigone: Who knows that this is holiness below?

Creon: Never the enemy, even in death, a friend.

Antigone: I cannot share in hatred, but in love.

Creon: Then go down there, if you must love, and love   495
  the dead. No woman rules me while I live.

(Ismene is brought from the palace under guard.)

Chorus: Look there! Ismene is coming out.
  She loves her sister and mourns,
  with clouded brow and bloodied cheeks,
  tears on her lovely face.   500

Creon: You, lurking like a viper in the house,
  who sucked me dry. I looked the other way
  while twin destruction planned against the throne.
  Now tell me, do you say you shared this deed?
  Or will you swear you didn't even know?   505

Ismene: I did the deed, if she agrees I did.
  I am accessory and share the blame.

Antigone: Justice will not allow this. You did not
  wish for a part, nor did I give you one.

Ismene: You are in trouble, and I'm not ashamed   510
  to sail beside you into suffering.

Antigone: Death and the dead, they know whose act it was.
  I cannot love a friend whose love is words.

Ismene: Sister, I pray, don't fence me out from honor,
  from death with you, and honor done the dead.   515

Antigone: Don't die along with me, nor make your own
  that which you did not do. My death's enough.

Ismene: When you are gone what life can be my friend?

Antigone: Love Creon. He's your kinsman and your care.

Ismene: Why hurt me, when it does yourself no good?   520

Antigone: I also suffer, when I laugh at you.

Ismene: What further service can I do you now?

Antigone: To save yourself. I shall not envy you.

Ismene: Alas for me. Am I outside your fate?

Antigone: Yes. For you chose to live when I chose death.   525

Ismene: At least I was not silent. You were warned.

Antigone: Some will have thought you wiser. Some will not.

Ismene: And yet the blame is equal for us both.

Antigone: Take heart. You live. My life died long ago.
  And that has made me fit to help the dead.   530

Creon: One of these girls has shown her lack of sense
  just now. The other had it from her birth.

Ismene: Yes, lord. When people fall in deep distress
  their native sense departs, and will not stay.

Creon: You chose your mind's distraction when you chose   535
  to work out wickedness with this wicked girl.

Ismene: What life is there for me to live without her?
 Creon: Don't speak of her. For she is here no more.
Ismene: But will you kill your own son's promised bride?
 Creon: Oh, there are other furrows for his plough. 540
Ismene: But where the closeness that has bound these two?
 Creon: Not for my sons will I choose wicked wives.
Ismene: Dear Haemon, your father robs you of your rights.
 Creon: You and your marriage trouble me too much.
Ismene: You will take away his bride from your own son? 545
 Creon: Yes. Death will help me break this marriage off.
Chorus: It seems determined that the girl must die.
 Creon: You helped determine it. Now, no delay!
       Slaves, take them in. They must be women now.
       No more free running. 550
       Even the bold will fly when they see Death
       drawing in close enough to end their life.

(Antigone and Ismene are taken inside.)

 Chorus: Fortunate they whose lives have no taste of pain.
       For those whose house is shaken by the gods
       escape no kind of doom. It extends to all the kin 555
       like the wave that comes when the winds of Thrace
       run over the dark of the sea.
       The black sand of the bottom is brought from the depth;
       the beaten capes sound back with a hollow cry.

       Ancient the sorrow of Labdacus'[5] house, I know. 560
       Dead men's grief comes back, and falls on grief.
       No generation can free the next.
       One of the gods will strike. There is no escape.
       So now the light goes out
       for the house of Oedipus, while the bloody knife 565
       cuts the remaining root. Folly and Fury have done this.

       What madness of man, O Zeus, can bind your power?
       Not sleep can destroy it who ages all,
       nor the weariless months the gods have set. Unaged in time
       monarch you rule of Olympus' gleaming light. 570
       Near time, far future, and the past,
       one law controls them all:
       any greatness in human life brings doom.

       Wandering hope brings help to many men.
       But others she tricks from their giddy loves, 575

---

5. Father of Laius, thus grandfather of Oedipus.

and her quarry knows nothing until he has walked into flame.
Word of wisdom it was when someone said,
"The bad becomes the good
to him a god would doom."
Only briefly is that one from under doom.   580

(Haemon enters from the side.)

    Here is your one surviving son.
    Does he come in grief at the fate of his bride,
    in pain that he's tricked of his wedding?
Creon: Soon we shall know more than a seer could tell us.
    Son, have you heard the vote condemned your bride?   585
    And are you here, maddened against your father,
    or are we friends, whatever I may do?
Haemon: My father, I am yours. You keep me straight
    with your good judgment, which I shall ever follow.
    Nor shall a marriage count for more with me   590
    than your kind leading.
Creon: There's my good boy. So should you hold at heart
    and stand behind your father all the way.
    It is for this men pray they may beget
    households of dutiful obedient sons,   595
    who share alike in punishing enemies,
    and give due honor to their father's friends.
    Whoever breeds a child that will not help
    what has he sown but trouble for himself,
    and for his enemies laughter full and free?   600
    Son, do not let your lust mislead your mind,
    all for a woman's sake, for well you know
    how cold the thing he takes into his arms
    who has a wicked woman for his wife.
    What deeper wounding than a friend no friend?   605
    Oh spit her forth forever, as your foe.
    Let the girl marry somebody in Hades.
    Since I have caught her in the open act,
    the only one in town who disobeyed,
    I shall not now proclaim myself a liar,   610
    but kill her. Let her sing her song of Zeus
    who guards the kindred.
    If I allow disorder in my house
    I'd surely have to licence it abroad.
    A man who deals in fairness with his own,   615
    he can make manifest justice in the state.
    But he who crosses law, or forces it,
    or hopes to bring the rulers under him,
    shall never have a word of praise from me.

The man the state has put in place must have   620
obedient hearing to his least command
when it is right, and even when it's not.
He who accepts this teaching I can trust,
ruler, or ruled, to function in his place,
to stand his ground even in the storm of spears,   625
a mate to trust in battle at one's side.
There is no greater wrong than disobedience.
This ruins cities, this tears down our homes,
this breaks the battle-front in panic-rout.
If men live decently it is because   630
discipline saves their very lives for them.
So I must guard the men who yield to order,
not let myself be beaten by a woman.
Better, if it must happen, that a man
should overset me.   635
I won't be called weaker than womankind.
Chorus: We think—unless our age is cheating us—
that what you say is sensible and right.
Haemon: Father, the gods have given men good sense,
the only sure possession that we have.   640
I couldn't find the words in which to claim
that there was error in your late remarks.
Yet someone else might bring some further light.
Because I am your son I must keep watch
on all men's doing where it touches you,   645
their speech, and most of all, their discontents.
Your presence frightens any common man
from saying things you would not care to hear.
But in dark corners I have heard them say
how the whole town is grieving for this girl,   650
unjustly doomed, if ever woman was,
to die in shame for glorious action done.
She would not leave her fallen, slaughtered brother
there, as he lay, unburied, for the birds
and hungry dogs to make an end of him.   655
Isn't her real desert a golden prize?
This is the undercover speech in town.
Father, your welfare is my greatest good.
What loveliness in life for any child
outweighs a father's fortune and good fame?   660
And so a father feels his children's faring.
Then, do not have one mind, and one alone
that only your opinion can be right.
Whoever thinks that he alone is wise,
his eloquence, his mind, above the rest,   665

come the unfolding, shows his emptiness.
A man, though wise, should never be ashamed
of learning more, and must unbend his mind.
Have you not seen the trees beside the torrent,
the ones that bend them saving every leaf,   670
while the resistant perish root and branch?
And so the ship that will not slacken sail,
the sheet drawn tight, unyielding, overturns.
She ends the voyage with her keel on top.
No, yield your wrath, allow a change of stand.   675
Young as I am, if I may give advice,
I'd say it would be best if men were born
perfect in wisdom, but that failing this
(which often fails) it can be no dishonor
to learn from others when they speak good sense.   680

Chorus: Lord, if your son has spoken to the point
you should take his lesson. He should do the same.
Both sides have spoken well.

Creon: At my age I'm to school my mind by his?
This boy instructor is my master, then?   685
Haemon: I urge no wrong. I'm young, but you should watch
my actions, not my years, to judge of me.
Creon: A loyal action, to respect disorder?
Haemon: I wouldn't urge respect for wickedness.
Creon: You don't think she is sick with that disease?   690
Haemon: Your fellow-citizens maintain she's not.
Creon: Is the town to tell me how I ought to rule?
Haemon: Now there you speak just like a boy yourself.
Creon: Am I to rule by other mind than mine?
Haemon: No city is property of a single man.   695
Creon: But custom gives possession to the ruler.
Haemon: You'd rule a desert beautifully alone.
Creon (to the Chorus): It seems he's firmly on the woman's side.
Haemon: If you're a woman. It is you I care for.
Creon: Wicked, to try conclusions with your father.   700
Haemon: When you conclude unjustly, so I must.
Creon: Am I unjust, when I respect my office?
Haemon: You tread down the gods' due. Respect is gone.
Creon: Your mind is poisoned. Weaker than a woman!
Haemon: At least you'll never see me yield to shame.   705
Creon: Your whole long argument is but for her.
Haemon: And you, and me, and for the gods below.
Creon: You shall not marry her while she's alive.
Haemon: Then she shall die. Her death will bring another.
Creon: Your boldness has made progress. Threats, indeed!   710
Haemon: No threat, to speak against your empty plan.

Creon: Past due, sharp lessons for your empty brain.
Haemon: If you weren't father, I should call you mad.
Creon: Don't flatter me with "father," you woman's slave.
Haemon: You wish to speak but never wish to hear.   715
Creon: You think so? By Olympus, you shall not
    revile me with these tauntings and go free.
    Bring out the hateful creature; she shall die
    full in his sight, close at her bridegroom's side.
Haemon: Not at my side her death, and you will not   720
    ever lay eyes upon my face again.
    Find other friends to rave with after this.

(Haemon leaves, by one of the side entrances.)

Chorus: Lord, he has gone with all the speed of rage.
    When such a man is grieved his mind is hard.
Creon: Oh, let him go, plan superhuman action.   725
    In any case the girls shall not escape.
Chorus: You plan for both the punishment of death?
Creon: Not her who did not do it. You are right.
Chorus: And what death have you chosen for the other?
Creon: To take her where the foot of man comes not.   730
    There shall I hide her in a hollowed cave
    living, and leave her just so much to eat
    as clears the city from the guilt of death.
    There, if she prays to Death, the only god
    of her respect, she may manage not to die.   735
    Or she may learn at last and even then
    how much too much her labor for the dead.

(Creon returns to the palace.)

Chorus: Love unconquered in fight, love who falls on our havings.
    You rest in the bloom of a girl's unwithered face.
    You cross the sea, you are known in the wildest lairs.   740
    Not the immortal gods can fly,
    nor men of a day. Who has you within him is mad.

    You twist the minds of the just. Wrong they pursue and are
      ruined.
    You made this quarrel of kindred before us now.
    Desire looks clear from the eyes of a lovely bride: 745
    power as strong as the founded world.
    For there is the goddess at play with whom no man can fight.

(Antigone is brought from the palace under guard.)

    Now I am carried beyond all bounds.
    My tears will not be checked.

I see Antigone depart   750
to the chamber where all men sleep.
Antigone: Men of my fathers' land, you see me go
my last journey. My last sight of the sun,
then never again. Death who brings all to sleep
takes me alive to the shore   755
of the river underground.
Not for me was the marriage-hymn nor will anyone start the song
at a wedding of mine. Acheron[6] is my mate.
Chorus: With praise as your portion you go
in fame to the vault of the dead.   760
Untouched by wasting disease,
not paying the price of the sword,
of your own motion you go.
Alone among mortals will you descend
in life to the house of Death.   765
Antigone: Pitiful was the death that stranger died,
our queen once, Tantalus'[7] daughter. The rock
it covered her over, like stubborn ivy it grew.
Still, as she wastes, the rain
and snow companion her.   770
Pouring down from her mourning eyes comes the water that
soaks the stone.
My own putting to sleep a god has planned like hers.
Chorus: God's child and god she was.
We are born to death.   775
Yet even in death you will have your fame,
to have gone like a god to your fate,
in living and dying alike.
Antigone: Laughter against me now. In the name of our fathers'
gods,
could you not wait till I went? Must affront be thrown in my
face?   780
O city of wealthy men.
I call upon Dirce's[8] spring,
I call upon Thebes' grove in the armored plain,
to be my witnesses, how with no friend's mourning,
by what decree I go to the fresh-made prison-tomb.   785
Alive to the place of corpses, an alien still,
never at home with the living nor with the dead.
Chorus: You went to the furthest verge

---

6. Underworld River of Sorrow.
7. Niobe, whose boasting drove Apollo and Artemis to kill her 14 children; Niobe was
transformed into a stone from which a stream of water flowed.
8. For her cruelty to Antiope, a princess of Thebes, Dirce was brutally killed and her body
thrown into a spring.

of daring, but there you found
the high foundation of justice, and fell. 790
Perhaps you are paying your father's pain.
Antigone: You speak of my darkest thought, my pitiful father's fame,
spread through all the world, and the doom that haunts our
house,
the royal house of Thebes.
My mother's marriage-bed. 795
Destruction where she lay with her husband-son,
my father. These are my parents and I their child.
I go to stay with them. My curse is to die unwed.
My brother, you found your fate when you found your bride,
found it for me as well. Dead, you destroy my life. 800
Chorus: You showed respect for the dead.
So we for you: but power
is not to be thwarted so.
Your self-sufficiency has brought you down.
Antigone: Unwept, no wedding-song, unfriended, now I go 805
the road laid down for me.
No longer shall I see this holy light of the sun.
No friend to bewail my fate.

(Creon enters from the palace.)

Creon: When people sing the dirge for their own deaths
ahead of time, nothing will break them off 810
if they can hope that this will buy delay.
Take her away at once, and open up
the tomb I spoke of. Leave her there alone.
There let her choose: death, or a buried life.
No stain of guilt upon us in this case, 815
but she is exiled from our life on earth.
Antigone: O tomb, O marriage-chamber, hollowed out
house that will watch forever, where I go.
To my own people, who are mostly there;
Persephone has taken them to her. 820
Last of them all, ill-fated past the rest,
shall I descend, before my course is run.
Still when I get there I may hope to find
I come as a dear friend to my dear father,
to you, my mother, and my brother too. 825
All three of you have known my hand in death.
I washed your bodies, dressed them for the grave,
poured out the last libation at the tomb.
Last, Polyneices knows the price I pay
for doing final service to his corpse. 830
And yet the wise will know my choice was right.
Had I had children or their father dead,

I'd let them moulder. I should not have chosen
in such a case to cross the state's decree.
What is the law that lies behind these words?   835
One husband gone, I might have found another,
or a child from a new man in first child's place,
but with my parents hid away in death,
no brother, ever, could spring up for me.
Such was the law by which I honored you.   840
But Creon thought the doing was a crime,
a dreadful daring, brother of my heart.
So now he takes and leads me out by force.
No marriage-bed, no marriage-song for me,
and since no wedding, so no child to rear.   845
I go, without a friend, struck down by fate,
live to the hollow chambers of the dead.
What divine justice have I disobeyed?
Why, in my misery, look to the gods for help?
Can I call any of them my ally?   850
I stand convicted of impiety,
the evidence my pious duty done.
Should the gods think that this is righteousness,
in suffering I'll see my error clear.
But if it is the others who are wrong   855
I wish them no greater punishment than mine.
  Chorus: The same tempest of mind
    as ever, controls the girl.
   Creon: Therefore her guards shall regret
    the slowness with which they move.   860
Antigone: That word comes close to death.
   Creon: You are perfectly right in that.
Antigone: O town of my fathers in Thebes' land,
    O gods of our house.
    I am led away at last.   865
    Look, leaders of Thebes,
    I am last of your royal line,
    Look what I suffer, at whose command,
    because I respected the right.

(Antigone is led away. The slow procession should begin during the preceding passage.)

  Chorus: Danaë[9] suffered too.
    She went from the light to the brass-built room,   870

---

9. Danaë was locked in a room by her father so that she could not conceive the son destined to kill him. Zeus took the form of a shower of gold to impregnate her.

chamber and tomb together. Like you, poor child,
she was of great descent, and more, she held and kept
the seed of the golden rain which was Zeus.
Fate has terrible power. 875
You cannot escape it by wealth or war.
No fort will keep it out, no ships outrun it.

Remember the angry king,
son of Dryas,[10] who raged at the god and paid,
pent in a rock-walled prison. His bursting wrath 880
slowly went down. As the terror of madness went,
he learned of his frenzied attack on the god.
Fool, he had tried to stop
the dancing women possessed of god,
the fire of Dionysus, the songs and flutes. 885

Where the dark rocks divide
sea from sea in Thrace
is Salmydessus whose savage god
beheld the terrible blinding wounds
dealt to Phineus'[11] sons by their father's wife. 890
Dark the eyes that looked to avenge their mother.
Sharp with her shuttle she struck, and blooded her hands.

Wasting they wept their fate,
settled when they were born
to Cleopatra, unhappy queen. 895
She was a princess too, of an ancient house,
reared in the cave of the wild north wind, her father.
Half a goddess but, child, she suffered like you.

(Enter, from the side, Teiresias, the blind prophet, led by a boy attendant.)

Teiresias: Elders of Thebes, we two have come one road,
two of us looking through one pair of eyes. 900
This is the way of walking for the blind.
Creon: Teiresias, what news has brought you here?
Teiresias: I'll tell you. You in turn must trust the prophet.
Creon: I've always been attentive to your counsel.
Teiresias: And therefore you have steered this city straight. 905
Creon: So I can say how helpful you have been.
Teiresias: But now you are balanced on a razor's edge.
Creon: What is it? How I shudder at your words!

---

10. Lycurgus; for insulting Bacchus and opposing worship of him, Lycurgus was driven mad and killed his own son. He was eventually torn to pieces by wild horses.
11. King Phineus divorced and imprisoned his first wife, Cleopatra, in order to marry Idaea. Idaea then persuaded Phineus that his sons by Cleopatra had violated her, and she put their eyes out.

Teiresias: You'll know, when you hear the signs that I have marked
　　　I sat where every bird of heaven comes　　　　　　　　　910
　　　in my old place of augury, and heard
　　　bird-cries I'd never known. They screeched about
　　　goaded by madness, inarticulate.
　　　I marked that they were tearing one another
　　　with claws of murder. I could hear the wing-beats.　　　915
　　　I was afraid, so straight away I tried
　　　burnt sacrifice upon the flaming altar.
　　　No fire caught my offerings. Slimy ooze
　　　dripped on the ashes, smoked and sputtered there.
　　　Gall burst its bladder, vanished into vapor;　　　　　　920
　　　the fat dripped from the bones and would not burn.
　　　These are the omens of the rites that failed,
　　　as my boy here has told me. He's my guide
　　　as I am guide to others.
　　　Why has this sickness struck against the state?　　　　　925
　　　Through your decision.
　　　All of the altars of the town are choked
　　　with leavings of the dogs and birds; their feast
　　　was on that fated, fallen Polyneices.
　　　So the gods will have no offering from us,　　　　　　　930
　　　not prayer, nor flame of sacrifice. The birds
　　　will not cry out a sound I can distinguish,
　　　gorged with the greasy blood of that dead man.
　　　Think of these things, my son. All men may err
　　　but error once committed, he's no fool　　　　　　　　935
　　　nor yet unfortunate, who gives up his stiffness
　　　and cures the trouble he has fallen in.
　　　Stubbornness and stupidity are twins.
　　　Yield to the dead. Why goad him where he lies?
　　　What use to kill the dead a second time?　　　　　　　940
　　　I speak for your own good. And I am right.
　　　Learning from a wise counsellor is not pain
　　　if what he speaks are profitable words.
Creon: Old man, you all, like bowmen at a mark,
　　　have bent your bows at me. I've had my share　　　　　945
　　　of seers. I've been an item in your accounts.
　　　Make profit, trade in Lydian silver-gold,
　　　pure gold of India; that's your chief desire.
　　　But you will never cover up that corpse.
　　　Not if the very eagles tear their food　　　　　　　　950
　　　from him, and leave it at the throne of Zeus.
　　　I wouldn't give him up for burial
　　　in fear of that pollution. For I know
　　　no mortal being can pollute the gods.

O old Teiresias, human beings fall;   955
        the clever ones the furthest, when they plead
        a shameful case so well in hope of profit.
Teiresias: Alas!
        What man can tell me, has he thought at all . . .
    Creon: What hackneyed saw is coming from your lips?   960
Teiresias: How better than all wealth is sound good counsel.
    Creon: And so is folly worse than anything.
Teiresias: And you're infected with that same disease.
    Creon: I'm reluctant to be uncivil to a seer . . .
Teiresias: You're that already. You have said I lie.   965
    Creon: Well, the whole crew of seers are money-mad.
Teiresias: And the whole tribe of tyrants grab at gain.
    Creon: Do you realize you are talking to a king?
Teiresias: I know. Who helped you save this town you hold?
    Creon: You're a wise seer, but you love wickedness.   970
Teiresias: You'll bring me to speak the unspeakable, very soon.
    Creon: Well, speak it out. But do not speak for profit.
Teiresias: No, there's no profit in my words for you.
    Creon: You'd better realise that you can't deliver
        my mind, if you should sell it, to the buyer.   975
Teiresias: Know well, the sun will not have rolled its course
        many more days, before you come to give
        corpse for these corpses, child of your own loins.
        For you've confused the upper and lower worlds.
        You sent a life to settle in a tomb;   980
        you keep up here that which belongs below
        the corpse unburied, robbed of its release.
        Not you, nor any god that rules on high
        can claim him now.
        You rob the nether gods of what is theirs.   985
        So the pursuing horrors lie in wait
        to track you down. The Furies sent by Hades[12]
        and by all gods will even you with your victims.
        Now say that I am bribed! At no far time
        shall men and women wail within your house.   990
        And all the cities that you fought in war
        whose sons had burial from wild beasts, or dogs,
        or birds that brought the stench of your great wrong
        back to each hearth, they move against you now.
        A bowman, as you said, I send my shafts,   995
        now you have moved me, straight. You'll feel the wound.

---

12. *Furies:* avenging spirits who punished crimes beyond the reach of human justice; *Hades:* god of the underworld.

Boy, take me home now. Let him spend his rage
on younger men, and learn to calm his tongue,
and keep a better mind than now he does.

(Exit.)

Chorus: Lord, he has gone. Terrible prophecies!   1000
　　And since the time when I first grew grey hair
　　his sayings to the city have been true.
　Creon: I also know this. And my mind is torn.
　　To yield is dreadful. But to stand against him.
　　Dreadful to strike my spirit to destruction.   1005
Chorus: Now you must come to counsel, and take advice.
　Creon: What must I do? Speak, and I shall obey.
Chorus: Go free the maiden from that rocky house.
　　Bury the dead who lies in readiness.
　Creon: This is your counsel? You would have me yield?   1010
Chorus: Quick as you can. The gods move very fast
　　when they bring ruin on misguided men.
　Creon: How hard, abandonment of my desire.
　　But I can fight necessity no more.
Chorus: Do it yourself. Leave it to no one else.   1015
　Creon: I'll go at once. Come, followers, to your work.
　　You that are here round up the other fellows.
　　Take axes with you, hurry to that place
　　that overlooks us.
　　Now my decision has been overturned   1020
　　shall I, who bound her, set her free myself.
　　I've come to fear it's best to hold the laws
　　of old tradition to the end of life.

(Exit.)

Chorus: God of the many names, Semele's golden child,
　　Child of Olympian thunder, Italy's lord.   1025
　　Lord of Eleusis, where all men come
　　to mother Demeter's plain.
　　Bacchus, who dwells in Thebes,
　　by Ismenus' running water,
　　where wild Bacchic women[13] are at home,   1030
　　on the soil of the dragon seed.

　　Seen in the glaring flame, high on the double mount,
　　with the nymphs of Parnassus at play on the hill,
　　seen by Kastalia's flowing stream.
　　You come from the ivied heights,   1035

---

13. The Maenads, frenzied devotees of Bacchus.

from green Euboea's shore.
In immortal words we cry
your name, lord, who watch the ways,
the many ways of Thebes.

This is your city, honored beyond the rest,   1040
the town of your mother's miracle-death.
Now, as we wrestle our grim disease,
come with healing step from Parnassus' slope
or over the moaning sea.

Leader in dance of the fire-pulsing stars,   1045
overseer of the voices of night,
child of Zeus, be manifest,
with due companionship of Maenad maids
whose cry is but your name.

(Enter one of those who left with Creon, as messenger.)

Messenger: Neighbors of Cadmus, and Amphion's[14] house,   1050
    there is no kind of state in human life
    which I now dare to envy or to blame.
    Luck sets it straight, and luck she overturns
    the happy or unhappy day by day.
    No prophecy can deal with men's affairs.   1055
    Creon was envied once, as I believe,
    for having saved this city from its foes
    and having got full power in this land.
    He steered it well. And he had noble sons.
    Now everything is gone.   1060
    Yes, when a man has lost all happiness,
    he's not alive. Call him a breathing corpse.
    Be very rich at home. Live as a king.
    But once your joy has gone, though these are left
    they are smoke's shadow to lost happiness.   1065
  Chorus: What is the grief of princes that you bring?
Messenger: They're dead. The living are responsible.
  Chorus: Who died? Who did the murder? Tell us now.
Messenger: Haemon is gone. One of his kin drew blood.
  Chorus: But whose arm struck? His father's or his own?   1070
Messenger: He killed himself. His blood is on his father.
  Chorus: Seer, all too true the prophecy you told!
Messenger: This is the state of things. Now make your plans.

---

14. *Cadmus:* founder of Thebes; *Amphion:* son of Antiope who killed Dirce to avenge his
mother. As King of Thebes, Amphion played such beautiful music that he moved stones to
build a wall around the city. Married to Niobe, he took his own life when their children were
killed.

(Enter, from the palace, Eurydice.)

   Chorus: Eurydice is with us now, I see.
          Creon's poor wife. She may have come by chance.   1075
          She may have heard something about her son.
Eurydice: I heard your talk as I was coming out
          to greet the goddess Pallas with my prayer.
          And as I moved the bolts that held the door
          I heard of my own sorrow.   1080
          I fell back fainting in my women's arms.
          But say again just what the news you bring.
          I, whom you speak to, have known grief before.
Messenger: Dear lady, I was there, and I shall tell,
          leaving out nothing of the true account.   1085
          Why should I make it soft for you with tales
          to prove myself a liar? Truth is right.
          I followed your husband to the plain's far edge,
          where Polyneices' corpse was lying still
          unpitied. The dogs had torn him all apart.   1090
          We prayed the goddess of all journeyings,
          and Pluto, that they turn their wrath to kindness,
          we gave the final purifying bath,
          then burned the poor remains on new-cut boughs,
          and heaped a high mound of his native earth.   1095
          Then turned we to the maiden's rocky bed,
          death's hollow marriage-chamber.
          But, still far off, one of us heard a voice
          in keen lament by that unblest abode.
          He ran and told the master. As Creon came   1100
          he heard confusion crying. He groaned and spoke:
          "Am I a prophet now, and do I tread
          the saddest of all roads I ever trod?
          My son's voice crying! Servants, run up close,
          stand by the tomb and look, push through the crevice   1105
          where we built the pile of rock, right to the entry.
          Find out if that is Haemon's voice I hear
          or if the gods are tricking me indeed."
          We obeyed the order of our mournful master
          In the far corner of the tomb we saw   1110
          her, hanging by the neck, caught in a noose
          of her own linen veiling.
          Haemon embraced her as she hung, and mourned
          his bride's destruction, dead and gone below,
          his father's actions, the unfated marriage.   1115
          When Creon saw him, he groaned terribly,
          and went toward him, and called him with lament:

"What have you done, what plan have you caught up,
what sort of suffering is killing you?
Come out, my child, I do beseech you, come!"   1120
The boy looked at him with his angry eyes,
spat in his face and spoke no further word.
He drew his sword, but as his father ran,
he missed his aim. Then the unhappy boy,
in anger at himself, leant on the blade.   1125
It entered, half its length, into his side.
While he was conscious he embraced the maiden,
holding her gently. Last, he gasped out blood,
red blood on her white cheek.
Corpse on a corpse he lies. He found his marriage.   1130
Its celebration in the halls of Hades.
So he has made it very clear to men
that to reject good counsel is a crime.

(Eurydice returns to the house.)

   Chorus: What do you make of this? The queen has gone
      in silence. We know nothing of her mind.   1135
Messenger: I wonder at her, too. But we can hope
      that she has gone to mourn her son within
      with her own women, not before the town.
      She knows discretion. She will do no wrong.
   Chorus: I am not sure. This muteness may portend   1140
      as great disaster as a loud lament.
Messenger: I will go in and see if some deep plan
      hides in her heart's wild pain. You may be right.
      There can be heavy danger in mute grief.

(The messenger goes into the house. Creon enters with his followers. They are carrying Haemon's body on a bier.)

   Chorus: But look, the king draws near.   1145
      His own hand brings
      the witness of his crime,
      the doom he brought on himself.
   Creon: O crimes of my wicked heart,
      harshness bringing death.   1150
      You see the killer, you see the kin he killed.
      My planning was all unblest.
      Son, you have died too soon.
      Oh, you have gone away
      through my fault, not your own.   1155
   Chorus: You have learned justice, though it comes too late.
   Creon: Yes, I have learned in sorrow. It was a god who struck,

who has weighted my head with disaster; he drove me to wild
   strange ways,
his heavy heel on my joy.
Oh sorrows, sorrows of men.   1160

(Re-enter the messenger, from a side door of the palace.)

Messenger: Master, you hold one sorrow in your hands
   but you have more, stored up inside the house.
   Creon: What further suffering can come on me?
Messenger: Your wife has died. The dead man's mother in deed,
   poor soul, her wounds are fresh.   1165
   Creon: Hades, harbor of all,
   you have destroyed me now.
   Terrible news to hear, horror the tale you tell.
   I was dead, and you kill me again.
   Boy, did I hear you right?   1170
   Did you say the queen was dead,
   slaughter on slaughter heaped?

(The central doors of the palace begin to open.)

   Chorus: Now you can see. Concealment is all over.

(The doors are open, and the corpse of Eurydice is revealed.)

   Creon: My second sorrow is here. Surely no fate remains
   which can strike me again. Just now, I held my son in my arms. 1175
   And now I see her dead.
   Woe for the mother and son.
Messenger: There, by the altar, dying on the sword,
   her eyes fell shut. She wept her older son
   who died before, and this one. Last of all   1180
   she cursed you as the killer of her children.
   Creon: I am mad with fear. Will no one strike
   and kill me with cutting sword?
   Sorrowful, soaked in sorrow to the bone!
Messenger: Yes, for she held you guilty in the death   1185
   of him before you, and the elder dead.
   Creon: How did she die?
Messenger: Struck home at her own heart
   when she had heard of Haemon's suffering.
   Creon: This is my guilt, all mine. I killed you, I say it clear. 1190
   Servants, take me away, out of the sight of men.
   I who am nothing more than nothing now.
   Chorus: Your plan is good—if any good is left.
   Best to cut short our sorrow.
   Creon: Let me go, let me go. May death come quick,   1195
   bringing my final day.
   O let me never see tomorrow's dawn.

> Chorus: That is the future's. We must look to now.
> What will be is in other hands than ours.
> Creon: All my desire was in that prayer of mine. 1200
> Chorus: Pray not again. No mortal can escape
> the doom prepared for him.
> Creon: Take me away at once, the frantic man who killed
> my son, against my meaning. I cannot rest.
> My life is warped past cure. My fate has struck me down. 1205

(Creon and his attendants enter the house.)

> Chorus: Our happiness depends
> on wisdom all the way.
> The gods must have their due.
> Great words by men of pride
> bring greater blows upon them. 1210
> So wisdom comes to the old.

Further Reading

Woodard, Thomas. Introduction. *Sophocles: A Collection of Critical Essays*. Englewood Cliffs, NJ: Prentice, 1966. 1–15. • Kitto, H. D. F. "The Antigone." *Greek Tragedy: A Literary Study*. London: Methuen, 1939. 125–31. • Bowra, C. M. "Antigone." *Sophoclean Tragedy*. London: Oxford UP, 1944. 63–115. • Segal, Charles Paul. "Sophocles' Praise of Man and the Conflicts of the *Antigone*." *Sophocles: A Collection of Critical Essays*. Ed. Thomas Woodard. Englewood Cliffs, NJ: Prentice, 1966. 62–85. • Knox, Bernard. "Antigone I." *The Heroic Temper: Studies in Sophoclean Tragedy*. Berkeley: U of California P, 1964. 62–90. • Waldock, A. J. A. "Romantic Tragedy: The *Antigone*." *Sophocles the Dramatist*. Cambridge: Cambridge UP, 1966. 104–42.

In 1944 the French playwright Jean Anouilh rewrote Sophocles's Antigone. *His version was not a simple translation or adaptation, but a reinterpretation of Antigone's story. The passage below is part of a long speech Creon makes to Antigone soon after she is captured. It gives a sufficient glimpse of Anouilh's Creon to allow us to see how the character differs from and conforms to Sophocles's Creon.*

Jean Anouilh: Creon's Defense

You come of people for whom the human vestment is a kind of straitjacket: it cracks at the seams. You spend your lives wriggling to get out of it. Nothing less than a cosy tea party with death and destiny will quench your thirst. The happiest hour of your father's life came when he listened greedily to the story of how, unknown to himself, he had killed his own father and dishonored the bed of his own mother. Drop by drop, word by word, he drank in the dark story that the gods had destined him first to live and then to hear. How avidly men and women drink the brew of such a tale when their names are Oedipus—and Antigone! And it is so simple, afterwards, to do what your father did, to put out one's eyes and take one's daughter begging on the highways.

Let me tell you, Antigone: those days are over for Thebes. Thebes has a right to a king without a past. My name, thank God, is only Creon. I stand here with both feet firm on the ground; with both hands in my pockets; and I have decided that so long as I am king—being less ambitious than your father was—I shall merely devote myself to introducing a little order into this absurd kingdom; if that is possible.

Don't think that being a king seems to me romantic. It is my trade; a trade a man has to work at every day; and like every other trade, it isn't all beer and skittles. But since it is my trade, I take it seriously. And if, tomorrow, some wild and bearded messenger walks in from some wild and distant valley—which is what happened to your dad—and tells me that he's not quite sure who my parents were, but thinks that my wife Eurydice is actually my mother, I shall ask him to do me the kindness to go back where he came from; and I shan't let a little matter like that persuade me to order my wife to take a blood test and the police to let me know whether or not my birth certificate was forged. Kings, my girl, have other things to do than to surrender themselves to their private feelings. *[He looks at her and smiles.]* Hand *you* over to be killed! *[He rises, moves to end of table and sits on the top of table.]* I have other plans for you. You're going to marry Haemon; and I want you to fatten up a bit so that you can give him a sturdy boy. Let me assure you that Thebes needs that boy a good deal more than it needs your death. You will go to your room, now, and do as you have been told; and you won't say a word about this to anybody. Don't fret about the guards: I'll see that their mouths are shut. And don't annihilate me with those eyes. I know that you think I am a brute, and I'm sure you must consider me very prosaic. But the fact is, I have always been fond of you, stubborn though you always were. Don't forget that the first doll you ever had came from me.

EURIPIDES

(480–406 B.C.)

MEDEA

translated from the Greek by Rex Warner

CHARACTERS

> *Medea, princess of Colchis and wife of*
> *Jason, son of Aeson, king of Iolcus*
> *Two children of Medea and Jason*
> *Creon, king of Corinth*
> *Aegeus, king of Athens*
> *Nurse to Medea*
> *Tutor to Medea's children*
> *Messenger*
> *Chorus of Corinthian Women*

> Scene: *In front of Medea's house in Corinth. Enter from the*
> *house Medea's nurse.*

Nurse: How I wish the Argo never had reached the land
Of Colchis,[1] skimming through the blue Symplegades,
Nor ever had fallen in the glades of Pelion
The smitten fir-tree to furnish oars for the hands
Of heroes who in Pelias' name attempted   5
The Golden Fleece! For then my mistress Medea
Would not have sailed for the towers of the land of Iolcus,
Her heart on fire with passionate love for Jason;
Nor would she have persuaded the daughters of Pelias
To kill their father, and now be living here   10
In Corinth with her husband and children. She gave
Pleasure to the people of her land of exile,
And she herself helped Jason in every way.
This is indeed the greatest salvation of all—
For the wife not to stand apart from the husband.   15
But now there's hatred everywhere, Love is diseased.

---

1. In order to obtain his rightful crown from his uncle Pelias, Jason had to sail to Colchis and return with the Golden Fleece. With his band of followers, Jason launched from the city of Iolcus in his ship, the *Argo*. Arriving at Colchis, Jason persuaded Medea, the king's daughter and a sorceress, to help him secure the Fleece. He then married her and the two fled to Corinth.

For, deserting his own children and my mistress,
Jason has taken a royal wife to his bed,
The daughter of the ruler of this land, Creon.
And poor Medea is slighted, and cries aloud on the   20
Vows they made to each other, the right hands clasped
In eternal promise. She calls upon the gods to witness
What sort of return Jason has made to her love.
She lies without food and gives herself up to suffering,
Wasting away every moment of the day in tears.   25
So it has gone since she knew herself slighted by him.
Not stirring an eye, not moving her face from the ground,
No more than either a rock or surging sea water
She listens when she is given friendly advice.
Except that sometimes she twists back her white neck and   30
Moans to herself, calling out on her father's name,
And her land, and her home betrayed when she came away with
A man who now is determined to dishonor her.
Poor creature, she has discovered by her sufferings
What it means to one not to have lost one's country.   35
She has turned from the children and does not like to see them.
I am afraid she may think of some dreadful thing,
For her heart is violent. She will never put up with
The treatment she is getting. I know and fear her
Lest she may sharpen a sword and thrust to the heart,   40
Stealing into the palace where the bed is made,
Or even kill the king and the new-wedded groom,
And thus bring a greater misfortune on herself.
She's a strange woman. I know it won't be easy
To make an enemy of her and come off best.   45
But here the children come. They have finished playing.
They have no thought at all of their mother's trouble.
Indeed it is not usual for the young to grieve.

*Enter from the right the slave who is the tutor to Medea's two small children. The
children follow him.*

    Tutor: You old retainer of my mistress' household,
        Why are you standing here all alone in front of the   50
        Gates and moaning to yourself over your misfortune?
        Medea could not wish you to leave her alone.
    Nurse: Old man, and guardian of the children of Jason,
        If one is a good servant, it's a terrible thing
        When one's master's luck is out; it goes to one's heart.   55
        So I myself have got into such a state of grief
        That a longing stole over me to come outside here
        And tell the earth and air of my mistress' sorrows.
    Tutor: Has the poor lady not given up her crying?

Nurse: Given up? She's at the start, not halfway through her tears. 60
Tutor: Poor fool—if I may call my mistress such a name—
    How ignorant she is of trouble more to come.
Nurse: What do you mean, old man? You needn't fear to speak.
Tutor: Nothing. I take back the words which I used just now.
Nurse: Don't, by your beard, hide this from me, your
    fellow-servant. 65
    If need be, I'll keep quiet about what you tell me.
Tutor: I heard a person saying, while I myself seemed
    Not to be paying attention, when I was at the place
    Where the old draught-players sit, by the holy fountain,
    That Creon, ruler of the land, intends to drive 70
    These children and their mother in exile from Corinth.
    But whether what he said is really true or not
    I do not know. I pray that it may not be true.
Nurse: And will Jason put up with it that his children
    Should suffer so, though he's no friend to their mother? 75
Tutor: Old ties give place to new ones. As for Jason, he
    No longer has a feeling for this house of ours.
Nurse: It's black indeed for us, when we add new to old
    Sorrows before even the present sky has cleared.
Tutor: But you be silent, and keep all this to yourself. 80
    It is not the right time to tell our mistress of it.
Nurse: Do you hear, children, what a father he is to you?
    I wish he were dead—but no, he is still my master.
    Yet certainly he has proved unkind to his dear ones.
Tutor: What's strange in that? Have you only just discovered 85
    That everyone loves himself more than his neighbor?
    Some have good reason, others get something out of it.
    So Jason neglects his children for the new bride.
Nurse: Go indoors, children. That will be the best thing.
    And you, keep them to themselves as much as possible. 90
    Don't bring them near their mother in her angry mood
    For I've seen her already blazing her eyes at them
    As though she meant some mischief and I am sure that
    She'll not stop raging until she has struck at someone.
    May it be an enemy and not a friend she hurts! 95

Medea is heard inside the house.

Medea: Ah, wretch! Ah, lost in my sufferings,
    I wish, I wish I might die.
Nurse: What did I say, dear children? Your mother
    Frets her heart and frets it to anger.
    Run away quickly into the house, 100
    And keep well out of her sight.
    Don't go anywhere near, but be careful

Of the wildness and bitter nature
Of that proud mind.
Go now! Run quickly indoors.   105
It is clear that she soon will put lightning
In that cloud of her cries that is rising
With a passion increasing. O, what will she do,
Proud-hearted and not to be checked on her course,
A soul bitten into with wrong?   110

The Tutor takes the children into the house.

   Medea: Ah, I have suffered
What should be wept for bitterly. I hate you,
Children of a hateful mother. I curse you
And your father. Let the whole house crash.
   Nurse: Ah, I pity you, you poor creature.   115
How can your children share in their father's
Wickedness? Why do you hate them? Oh children,
How much I fear that something may happen!
Great people's tempers are terrible, always
Having their own way, seldom checked,   120
Dangerous they shift from mood to mood.
How much better to have been accustomed
To live on equal terms with one's neighbors.
I would like to be safe and grow old in a
Humble way. What is moderate sounds best,   125
Also in practice *is* best for everyone.
Greatness brings no profit to people.
God indeed, when in anger, brings
Greater ruin to great men's houses.

*Enter, on the right, a Chorus of Corinthian women. They have come to inquire
about Medea and to attempt to console her.*

   Chorus: I heard the voice, I heard the cry   130
Of Colchis' wretched daughter.
Tell me, mother, is she not yet
At rest? Within the double gates
Of the court I heard her cry. I am sorry
For the sorrow of this home. O, say, what has happened?   135
   Nurse: There is no home. It's over and done with.
Her husband holds fast to his royal wedding,
While she, my mistress, cries out her eyes
There in her room, and takes no warmth from
Any word of any friend.   140
   Medea: O, I wish
That lightning from heaven would split my head open.
Oh, what use have I now for life?

I would find my release in death
And leave hateful existence behind me.   145
Chorus: O God and Earth and Heaven!
Did you hear what a cry was that
Which the sad wife sings?
Poor foolish one, why should you long
For that appalling rest?   150
The final end of death comes fast.
No need to pray for that.
Suppose your man gives honor
To another woman's bed.
It often happens. Don't be hurt.   155
God will be your friend in this.
You must not waste away
Grieving too much for him who shared your bed.
Medea: Great Themis, lady Artemis,[2] behold
The things I suffer, though I made him promise,   160
My hateful husband. I pray that I may see him,
Him and his bride and all their palace shattered
For the wrong they dare to do me without cause.
Oh, my father! Oh, my country! In what dishonor
I left you, killing my own brother for it.   165
Nurse: Do you hear what she says, and how she cries
Oh Themis, the goddess of Promises, and on Zeus,
Whom we believe to be the Keeper of Oaths?
Of this I am sure, that no small thing
Will appease my mistress' anger.   170
Chorus: Will she come into our presence?
Will she listen when we are speaking
To the words we say?
I wish she might relax her rage
And temper of her heart.   175
My willingness to help will never
Be wanting to my friends.
But go inside and bring her
Out of the house to us,
And speak kindly to her: hurry,   180
Before she wrongs her own.
This passion of hers moves to something great.
Nurse: I will, but I doubt if I'll manage
To win my mistress over.
But still I'll attempt it to please you.   185
Such a look she will flash on her servants

---

2. *Themis:* goddess of justice; *Artemis:* goddess of the moon and protector of women.

If any comes near with a message,
Like a lioness guarding her cubs.
It is right, I think, to consider
Both stupid and lacking in foresight   190
Those poets of old who wrote songs
For revels and dinners and banquets,
Pleasant sounds for men living at ease;
But none of them all has discovered
How to put to an end with their singing   195
Or musical instruments grief,
Bitter grief, from which death and disaster
Cheat the hopes of a house. Yet how good
If music could cure men of this! But why raise
To no purpose the voice at a banquet? For *there* is   200
Already abundance of pleasure for men
With a joy of its own.

The Nurse goes into the house.

Chorus: I heard a shriek that is laden with sorrow.
Shrilling out her hard grief she cries out
Upon him who betrayed both her bed and her marriage.   205
Wronged, she calls on the gods,
On the justice of Zeus, the oath sworn,
Which brought her away
To the opposite shore of the Greeks
Through the gloomy salt straits to the gateway   210
Of the salty unlimited sea.

Medea, attended by servants, comes out of the house.

Medea: Women of Corinth, I have come outside to you
Lest you should be indignant with me; for I know
That many people are overproud, some when alone,
And others when in company. And those who live   215
Quietly, as I do, get a bad reputation.
For a just judgment is not evident in the eyes
When a man at first sight hates another, before
Learning his character, being in no way injured;
And a foreigner especially must adapt himself.   220
I'd not approve of even a fellow-countryman
Who by pride and want of manners offends his neighbors.
But on me this thing has fallen so unexpectedly,
It has broken my heart. I am finished. I let go
All my life's joy. My friends, I only want to die.   225
It was everything to me to think well of one man,
And he, my own husband, has turned out wholly vile.
Of all things which are living and can form a judgment

We women are the most unfortunate creatures.
Firstly, with an excess of wealth it is required 230
For us to buy a husband and take for our bodies
A master; for not to take one is even worse.
And now the question is serious whether we take
A good or bad one; for there is no easy escape
For a woman, nor can she say no to her marriage. 235
She arrives among new modes of behavior and manners,
And needs prophetic power, unless she has learned at home,
How best to manage him who shares the bed with her.
And if we work out all this well and carefully,
And the husband lives with us and lightly bears his yoke, 240
Then life is enviable. If not, I'd rather die.
A man, when he's tired of the company in his home,
Goes out of the house and puts an end to his boredom
And turns to a friend or companion of his own age.
But we are forced to keep our eyes on one alone. 245
What they say of us is that we have a peaceful time
Living at home, while they do the fighting in war.
How wrong they are! I would very much rather stand
Three times in the front of battle than bear one child.
Yet what applies to me does not apply to you. 250
You have a country. Your family home is here.
You enjoy life and the company of your friends.
But I am deserted, a refugee, thought nothing of
By my husband—something he won in a foreign land.
I have no mother or brother, nor any relation 255
With whom I can take refuge in this sea of woe.
This much then is the service I would beg from you:
If I can find the means or devise any scheme
To pay my husband back for what he has done to me—
Him and his father-in-law and the girl who married him— 260
Just to keep silent. For in other ways a woman
Is full of fear, defenseless, dreads the sight of cold
Steel; but, when once she is wronged in the matter of love,
No other soul can hold so many thoughts of blood.
Chorus: This I will promise. You are in the right, Medea, 265
In paying your husband back. I am not surprised at you
For being sad.
But look! I see our King Creon[3]
Approaching. He will tell us of some new plan.

Enter, from the right, Creon, with attendants.

---

3. In ancient Greece, "Creon" was synonymous with "king"; here, the proper name of the
king of Corinth.

Creon: You, with that angry look, so set against your husband,   270
    Medea, I order you to leave my territories
    An exile, and take along with you your two children,
    And not to waste time doing it. It is my decree,
    And I will see it done. I will not return home
    Until you are cast from the boundaries of my land.   275
Medea: Oh, this is the end for me. I am utterly lost.
    Now I am in the full force of the storm of hate
    And have no harbor from ruin to reach easily.
    Yet still, in spite of it all, I'll ask the question:
    What is your reason, Creon, for banishing me?   280
Creon: I am afraid of you—why should I dissemble it?—
    Afraid that you may injure my daughter mortally.
    Many things accumulate to support my feeling.
    You are a clever woman, versed in evil arts,
    And are angry at having lost your husband's love.   285
    I hear that you are threatening, so they tell me,
    To do something against my daughter and Jason
    And me, too. I shall take my precautions first.
    I tell you, I prefer to earn your hatred now
    Than to be soft-hearted and afterward regret it.   290
Medea: This is not the first time, Creon. Often previously
    Through being considered clever I have suffered much.
    A person of sense ought never to have his children
    Brought up to be more clever than the average.
    For, apart from cleverness bringing them no profit,   295
    It will make them objects of envy and ill-will.
    If you put new ideas before the eyes of fools
    They'll think you foolish and worthless into the bargain;
    And if you are thought superior to those who have
    Some reputation for learning, you will become hated.   300
    I have some knowledge myself of how this happens;
    For being clever, I find that some will envy me,
    Others object to me. Yet all my cleverness
    Is not so much.
                Well, then, are you frightened, Creon,   305
    That I should harm you? There is no need. It is not
    My way to transgress the authority of a king.
    How have you injured me? You gave your daughter away
    To the man you wanted. Oh, certainly I hate
    My husband, but you, I think, have acted wisely;   310
    Nor do I grudge it you that your affairs go well.
    May the marriage be a lucky one! Only let me
    Live in this land. For even though I have been wronged,
    I will not raise my voice, but submit to my betters.
Creon: What you say sounds gentle enough. Still in my heart   315

I greatly dread that you are plotting some evil,
And therefore I trust you even less than before.
A sharp-tempered woman, or, for that matter, a man,
Is easier to deal with than the clever type
Who holds her tongue. No. You must go. No need for more   320
Speeches. The thing is fixed. By no manner of means
Shall you, an enemy of mine, stay in my country.

Medea: I beg you. By your knees, by your new-wedded girl.

Creon: Your words are wasted. You will never persuade me.

Medea: Will you drive me out, and give no heed to my prayers?   325

Creon: I will, for I love my family more than you.

Medea: O my country! How bitterly now I remember you!

Creon: I love my country too—next after my children.

Medea: Oh what an evil to men is passionate love!

Creon: That would depend on the luck that goes along with it.   330

Medea: O God, do not forget who is the cause of this!

Creon: Go. It is no use. Spare me the pain of forcing you.

Medea: I'm spared no pain. I lack no pain to be spared me.

Creon: Then you'll be removed by force by one of my men.

Medea: No, Creon, not that! But do listen, I beg you.   335

Creon: Woman, you seem to want to create a disturbance.

Medea: I *will* go into exile. *This* is not what I beg for.

Creon: Why then this violence and clinging to my hand?

Medea: Allow me to remain here just for this one day,
So I may consider where to live in my exile,   340
And look for support for my children, since their father
Chooses to make no kind of provision for them.
Have pity on them! You have children of your own.
It is natural for you to look kindly on them.
For myself I do not mind if I go into exile.   345
It is the children being in trouble that I mind.

Creon: There is nothing tyrannical about my nature,
And by showing mercy I have often been the loser.
Even now I know that I am making a mistake.
All the same you shall have your will. But this I tell you,   350
That if the light of heaven tomorrow shall see you,
You and your children in the confines of my land,
You die. This word I have spoken is firmly fixed.
But now, if you must stay, stay for this day alone.
For in it you can do none of the things I fear.   355

Exit Creon with his attendants.

Chorus: Oh, unfortunate one! Oh, cruel!
   Where will you turn? Who will help you?
   What house or what land to preserve you
   From ill can you find?

Medea, a god has thrown suffering   360
          Upon you in waves of despair.
Medea: Things have gone badly every way. No doubt of that
          But not these things this far, and don't imagine so.
          There are still trials to come for the new-wedded pair,
          And for their relations pain that will mean something.   365
          Do you think that I would ever have fawned on that man
          Unless I had some end to gain or profit in it?
          I would not even have spoken or touched him with my hands.
          But he has got to such a pitch of foolishness
          That, though he could have made nothing of all my plans   370
          By exiling me, he has given me this one day
          To stay here, and in this I will make dead bodies
          Of three of my enemies—father, the girl, and my husband.
          I have many ways of death which I might suit to them,
          And do not know, friends, which one to take in hand;   375
          Whether to set fire underneath their bridal mansion,
          Or sharpen a sword and thrust it to the heart,
          Stealing into the palace where the bed is made.
          There is just one obstacle to this. If I am caught
          Breaking into the house and scheming against it,   380
          I shall die, and give my enemies cause for laughter.
          It is best to go by the straight road, the one in which
          I am most skilled, and make away with them by poison.
          So be it then.
          And now suppose them dead. What town will receive me?   385
          What friend will offer me a refuge in his land,
          Or the guaranty of his house and save my own life?
          There is none. So I must wait a little time yet,
          And if some sure defense should then appear for me,
          In craft and silence I will set about this murder.   390
          But if my fate should drive me on without help,
          Even though death is certain, I will take the sword
          Myself and kill, and steadfastly advance to crime.
          It shall not be—I swear it by her, my mistress,
          Whom most I honor and have chosen as partner,   395
          Hecate,[4] who dwells in the recesses of my hearth—
          That any man shall be glad to have injured me.
          Bitter I will make their marriage for them and mournful,
          Bitter the alliance and the driving me out of the land.
          Ah, come, Medea, in your plotting and scheming   400
          Leave nothing untried of all those things which you know.
          Go forward to the dreadful act. The test has come

———————
4. Goddess of sorcery and witchcraft.

For resolution. You see how you are treated. Never
Shall you be mocked by Jason's Corinthian wedding,
Whose father was noble, whose grandfather Helius.⁵   405
You have the skill. What is more, you were born a woman,
And women, though most helpless in doing good deeds,
Are of every evil the cleverest of contrivers.
Chorus: Flow backward to your sources, sacred rivers,
And let the world's great order be reversed.   410
It is the thoughts of *men* that are deceitful,
Their pledges that are loose.

Story shall now turn my condition to a fair one,
Women are paid their due.
No more shall evil-sounding fame be theirs.   415

Cease now, you muses of the ancient singers,
To tell the tale of my unfaithfulness;
For not on us did Phoebus,⁶ lord of music,
Bestow the lyre's divine
Power, for otherwise I should have sung an answer   420
To the other sex. Long time
Has much to tell of us, and much of them.

You sailed away from your father's home,
With a heart on fire you passed
The double rocks of the sea.   425
And now in a foreign country
You have lost your rest in a widowed bed,
And are driven forth, a refugee
In dishonor from the land.

Good faith has gone, and no more remains   430
In great Greece a sense of shame.
It has flown away to the sky.
No father's house for a haven
Is at hand for you now, and another queen
Of your bed has dispossessed you and   435
Is mistress of your home.

Enter Jason, with attendants.

Jason: This is not the first occasion that I have noticed
How hopeless it is to deal with a stubborn temper.
For, with reasonable submission to our ruler's will,
You might have lived in this land and kept your home.   440
As it is you are going to be exiled for your loose speaking.
Not that I mind myself. You are free to continue

———————
5. God of the sun.   6. Phoebus, meaning "bright," is the epithet of Apollo, the sun god.

Telling everyone that Jason is a worthless man.
But as to your talk about the king, consider
Yourself most lucky that exile is your punishment.   445
I, for my part, have always tried to calm down
The anger of the king, and wished you to remain.
But you will not give up your folly, continually
Speaking ill of him, and so you are going to be banished.
All the same, and in spite of your conduct, I'll not desert   450
My friends, but have come to make some provision for you,
So that you and the children may not be penniless
Or in need of anything in exile. Certainly
Exile brings many troubles with it. And even
If you hate me, I cannot think badly of you.   455
Medea: O coward in every way—that is what I call you,
With bitterest reproach for your lack of manliness,
You have come, you, my worst enemy, have come to me!
It is not an example of overconfidence
Or of boldness thus to look your friends in the face,   460
Friends you have injured—no, it is the worst of all
Human diseases, shamelessness. But you did well
To come, for I can speak ill of you and lighten
My heart, and you will suffer while you are listening.
And first I will begin from what happened first.   465
I saved your life, and every Greek knows I saved it,
Who was a shipmate of yours aboard the Argo,
When you were sent to control the bulls that breathed fire
And yoke them, and when you would sow that deadly field.
Also that snake, who encircled with his many folds   470
The Golden Fleece and guarded it and never slept,
I killed, and so gave you the safety of the light.
And I myself betrayed my father and my home,
And came with you to Pelias' land of Iolcus.
And then, showing more willingness to help than wisdom,   475
I killed him, Pelias, with a most dreadful death
At his own daughters' hands, and took away your fear.
This is how I behaved to you, you wretched man,
And you forsook me, took another bride to bed,
Though you had children; for, if that had not been,   480
You would have had an excuse for another wedding.
Faith in your word has gone. Indeed, I cannot tell
Whether you think the gods whose names you swore by then
Have ceased to rule and that new standards are set up,
Since you must know you have broken your word to me.   485
O my right hand, and the knees which you often clasped
In supplication, how senselessly I am treated
By this bad man, and how my hopes have missed their mark!

Come, I will share my thoughts as though you were a friend—
You! Can I think that you would ever treat me well?   490
But I will do it, and these questions will make you
Appear the baser. Where am I to go? To my father's?
Him I betrayed and his land when I came with you.
To Pelias' wretched daughters? What a fine welcome
They would prepare for me who murdered their father!   495
For this is my position—hated by my friends
At home, I have, in kindness to you, made enemies
Of others whom there was no need to have injured.
And how happy among Greek women you have made me
On your side for all this! A distinguished husband   500
I have—for breaking promises. When in misery
I am cast out of the land and go into exile,
Quite without friends and all alone with my children,
That will be a fine shame for the new-wedded groom,
For his children to wander as beggars and she who saved him.   505
O God, you have given to mortals a sure method
Of telling the gold that is pure from the counterfeit;
Why is there no mark engraved upon men's bodies,
By which we could know the true ones from the false ones?
Chorus: It is a strange form of anger, difficult to cure,   510
    When two friends turn upon each other in hatred.
  Jason: As for me, it seems I must be no bad speaker.
    But, like a man who has a good grip of the tiller,
    Reef up his sail, and so run away from under
    This mouthing tempest, women, of your bitter tongue.   515
    Since you insist on building up your kindness to me,
    My view is that Cypris[7] was alone responsible
    Of men and gods for the preserving of my life.
    You are clever enough—but really I need not enter
    Into the story of how it was love's inescapable   520
    Power that compelled you to keep my person safe.
    On this I will not go into too much detail.
    In so far as you helped me, you did well enough.
    But on this question of saving me, I can prove
    You have certainly got from me more than you gave.   525
    Firstly, instead of living among barbarians,
    You inhabit a Greek land and understand our ways,
    How to live by law instead of the sweet will of force.
    And all the Greeks considered you a clever woman.
    You were honored for it; while, if you were living at   530
    The ends of the earth, nobody would have heard of you.

---

7. Aphrodite, goddess of love and beauty.

For my part, rather than stores of gold in my house
Or power to sing even sweeter songs than Orpheus,[8]
I'd choose the fate that made me a distinguished man.
There is my reply to your story of my labors.   535
Remember it was you who started the argument.
Next for your attack on my wedding with the princess:
Here I will prove that, first, it was a clever move,
Secondly, a wise one, and, finally, that I made it
In your best interests and the children's. Please keep calm.   540
When I arrived here from the land of Iolcus,
Involved, as I was, in every kind of difficulty,
What luckier chance could I have come across than this,
An exile to marry the daughter of the king?
It was not—the point that seems to upset you—that I   545
Grew tired of your bed and felt the need of a new bride;
Nor with any wish to outdo your number of children.
We have enough already. I am quite content.
But—this was the main reason—that we might live well,
And not be short of anything. I know that all   550
A man's friends leave him stone-cold if he becomes poor.
Also that I might bring my children up worthily
Of my position, and, by producing more of them
To be brothers of yours, we would draw the families
Together and all be happy. You need no children.   555
And it pays me to do good to those I have now
By having others. Do you think this a bad plan?
You wouldn't if the love question hadn't upset you.
But you women have got into such a state of mind
That, if your life at night is good, you think you have   560
Everything; but, if in that quarter things go wrong,
You will consider your best and truest interests
Most hateful. It would have been better far for men
To have got their children in some other way, and women
Not to have existed. Then life would have been good.   565
Chorus: Jason, though you have made this speech of yours look well,
Still I think, even though others do not agree,
You have betrayed your wife and are acting badly.
Medea: Surely in many ways I hold different views
From others, for I think that the plausible speaker   570
Who is a villain deserves the greatest punishment.
Confident in his tongue's power to adorn evil,
He stops at nothing. Yet he is not really wise.
As in your case. There is no need to put on the airs

---

8. Poet and musician whose music moved even inanimate objects.

Of a clever speaker, for one word will lay you flat.   575
    If you were not a coward, you would not have married
    Behind my back, but discussed it with me first.
Jason: And you, no doubt, would have furthered the proposal.
    If I had told you of it, you who even now
    Are incapable of controlling your bitter temper.   580
Medea: It was not that. No, you thought it was not respectable
    As you got on in years to have a foreign wife.
Jason: Make sure of this: it was not because of a woman
    I made the royal alliance in which I now live,
    But, as I said before, I wished to preserve you   585
    And breed a royal progeny to be brothers
    To the children I have now, a sure defense to us.
Medea: Let me have no happy future that brings pain with it,
    Or prosperity which is upsetting to the mind!
Jason: Change your ideas of what you want, and show more sense. 590
    Do not consider painful what is good for you,
    Nor, when you are lucky, think yourself unfortunate.
Medea: You can insult me. You have somewhere to turn to.
    But I shall go from this land into exile, friendless.
Jason: It was what you chose yourself. Don't blame others for it. 595
Medea: And how did I choose it? Did I betray my husband?
Jason: You called down wicked curses on the king's family.
Medea: A curse, that is what I am become to your house too.
Jason: I do not propose to go into all the rest of it;
    But, if you wish for the children or for yourself   600
    In exile to have some of my money to help you,
    Say so, for I am prepared to give with open hand,
    Or to provide you with introductions to my friends
    Who will treat you well. You are a fool if you do not
    Accept this. Cease your anger and you will profit.   605
Medea: I shall never accept the favors of friends of yours,
    Nor take a thing from you, so you need not offer it.
    There is no benefit in the gifts of a bad man.
Jason: Then, in any case, I call the gods to witness that
    I wish to help you and the children in every way,   610
    But you refuse what is good for you. Obstinately
    You push away your friends. You are sure to suffer for it.
Medea: Go! No doubt you hanker for your virginal bride,
    And are guilty of lingering too long out of her house.
    Enjoy your wedding. But perhaps—with the help of God—   615
    You will make the kind of marriage that you will regret.

Jason goes out with his attendants.

Chorus: When love is in excess
    It brings a man no honor

Nor any worthiness.
But if in moderation Cypris comes,   620
There is no other power at all so gracious.
O goddess, never on me let loose the unerring
Shaft of your bow in the poison of desire.

Let my heart be wise.
It is the gods' best gift.   625
On me let mighty Cypris
Inflict no wordy wars or restless anger
To urge my passion to a different love.
But with discernment may she guide women's weddings,
Honoring most what is peaceful in the bed.   630

O country and home,
Never, never may I be without you,
Living the hopeless life,
Hard to pass through and painful,
Most pitiable of all.   635
Let death first lay me low and death
Free me from this daylight.
There is no sorrow above
The loss of a native land.

I have seen it myself,   640
Do not tell of a secondhand story.
Neither city nor friend
Pitied you when you suffered
The worst of sufferings.
O let him die ungraced whose heart   645
Will not reward his friends,
Who cannot open an honest mind
No friend will he be of mine.

Enter Aegeus, king of Athens, an old friend of Medea.

Aegeus: Medea, greeting! This is the best introduction
   Of which men know for conversation between friends.   650
Medea: Greeting to you too, Aegeus, son of King Pandion.[9]
   Where have you come from to visit this country's soil?
Aegeus: I have just left the ancient oracle of Phoebus.
Medea: And why did you go to earth's prophetic center?
Aegeus: I went to inquire how children might be born to me.   655
Medea: Is it so? Your life still up to this point is childless?
Aegeus: Yes. By the fate of some power we have no children.
Medea: Have you a wife, or is there none to share your bed?

---

9. King of Athens.

Aegeus:	There is. Yes, I am joined to my wife in marriage.	
Medea:	And what did Phoebus say to you about children?	660
Aegeus:	Words too wise for a mere man to guess their meaning.	
Medea:	It is proper for me to be told the god's reply?	
Aegeus:	It is. For sure what is needed is cleverness.	
Medea:	Then what was his message? Tell me, if I may hear.	
Aegeus:	I am not to loosen the hanging foot of the wine-skin . . .	665
Medea:	Until you have done something, or reached some country?	
Aegeus:	Until I return again to my hearth and house.	
Medea:	And for what purpose have you journeyed to this land?	
Aegeus:	There is a man called Pittheus, king of Troezen.	
Medea:	A son of Pelops,[10] they say, a most righteous man.	670
Aegeus:	With him I wish to discuss the reply of the god.	
Medea:	Yes. He is wise and experienced in such matters.	
Aegeus:	And to me also the dearest of all my spear-friends.	
Medea:	Well, I hope you have good luck, and achieve your will.	
Aegeus:	But why this downcast eye of yours, and this pale cheek?	675
Medea:	O Aegeus, my husband has been the worst of all to me.	
Aegeus:	What do you mean? Say clearly what has caused this grief.	
Medea:	Jason wrongs me, though I have never injured him.	
Aegeus:	What has he done? Tell me about it in clearer words.	
Medea:	He has taken a wife to his house, supplanting me.	680
Aegeus:	Surely he would not dare to do a thing like that.	
Medea:	Be sure he has. Once dear, I now am slighted by him.	
Aegeus:	Did he fall in love? Or is he tired of your love?	
Medea:	He was greatly in love, this traitor to his friends.	
Aegeus:	Then let him go, if, as you say, he is so bad.	685
Medea:	A passionate love—for an alliance with the king.	
Aegeus:	And who gave him his wife? Tell me the rest of it.	
Medea:	It was Creon, he who rules this land of Corinth.	
Aegeus:	Indeed, Medea, your grief was understandable.	
Medea:	I am ruined. And there is more to come: I am banished.	690
Aegeus:	Banished? By whom? Here you tell me of a new wrong.	
Medea:	Creon drives me an exile from the land of Corinth.	
Aegeus:	Does Jason consent? I cannot approve of this.	
Medea:	He pretends not to, but he will put up with it.	

Ah, Aegeus, I beg and beseech you, by your beard　　　　695
And by your knees I am making myself your suppliant,
Have pity on me, have pity on your poor friend,
And do not let me go into exile desolate,
But receive me in your land and at your very hearth.
So may your love, with God's help, lead to the bearing　　700
Of children, and so may you yourself die happy.

---

10. *Pittheus:* grandfather of Theseus, founder of Athens; *Pelops:* son of Tantalus who killed, boiled, and served his son to the gods at the banquet. Pelops was later restored to life.

You do not know what a chance you have come on here.
I will end your childlessness, and I will make you able
To beget children. The drugs I know can do this.
Aegeus: For many reasons, woman, I am anxious to do 705
This favor for you. First, for the sake of the gods,
And then for the birth of children which you promise,
For in that respect I am entirely at my wits' end.
But this is my position: if you reach my land,
I, being in my rights, will try to befriend you. 710
But this much I must warn you of beforehand:
I shall not agree to take you out of this country;
But if you by yourself can reach my house, then you
Shall stay there safely. To none will I give you up
But from this land you must make your escape yourself, 715
For I do not wish to incur blame from my friends.
Medea: It shall be so. But, if I might have a pledge from you
For this, then I would have from you all I desire.
Aegeus: Do you not trust me? What is it rankles with you?
Medea: I trust you, yes. But the house of Pelias hates me, 720
And so does Creon. If you are bound by this oath,
When they try to drag me from your land, you will not
Abandon me; but if our pact is only words,
With no oath to the gods, you will be lightly armed,
Unable to resist their summons. I am weak, 725
While they have wealth to help them and a royal house.
Aegeus: You show much foresight for such negotiations.
Well, if you will have it so, I will not refuse.
For, both on my side this will be the safest way
To have some excuse to put forward to your enemies, 730
And for you it is more certain. You may name the gods.
Medea: Swear by the plain of Earth, and Helius, father
Of my father, and name together all the gods. . .
Aegeus: That I will act or not act in what way? Speak.
Medea: That you yourself will never cast me from your land, 735
Nor, if any of my enemies should demand me,
Will you, in your life, willingly hand me over.
Aegeus: I swear by the Earth, by the holy light of Helius,
By all the gods, I will abide by this you say.
Medea: Enough. And, if you fail, what shall happen to you? 740
Aegeus: What comes to those who have no regard for heaven.
Medea: Go on your way. Farewell. For I am satisfied.
And I will reach your city as soon as I can,
Having done the deed I have to do and gained my end.

Aegeus goes out.

Chorus: May Hermes, god of travelers, 745
Escort you, Aegeus, to your home!

And may you have the things you wish
So eagerly; for you
Appear to me to be a generous man.
Medea: God, and God's daughter, justice, and light of Helius!   750
Now, friends, has come the time of my triumph over
My enemies, and now my foot is on the road.
Now I am confident they will pay the penalty.
For this man, Aegeus, has been like a harbor to me
In all my plans just where I was most distressed.   755
To him I can fasten the cable of my safety
When I have reached the town and fortress of Pallas.[11]
And now I shall tell to you the whole of my plan.
Listen to these words that are not spoken idly.
I shall send one of my servants to find Jason   760
And request him to come once more into my sight.
And when he comes, the words I'll say will be soft ones.
I'll say that I agree with him, that I approve
The royal wedding he has made, betraying me.
I'll say it was profitable, an excellent idea.   765
But I shall beg that my children may remain here:
Not that I would leave in a country that hates me
Children of mine to feel their enemies' insults,
But that by a trick I may kill the king's daughter.
For I will send the children with gifts in their hands   770
To carry to the bride, so as not to be banished—
A finely woven dress and a golden diadem.
And if she takes them and wears them upon her skin
She and all who touch the girl will die in agony;
Such poison will I lay upon the gifts I send.   775
But there, however, I must leave that account paid.
I weep to think of what a deed I have to do
Next after that; for I shall kill my own children.
My children, there is none who can give them safety.
And when I have ruined the whole of Jason's house,   780
I shall leave the land and flee from the murder of my
Dear children, and I shall have done a dreadful deed.
For it is not bearable to be mocked by enemies.
So it must happen. What profit have I in life?
I have no land, no home, no refuge from my pain.   785
My mistake was made the time I left behind me
My father's house, and trusted the words of a Greek,
Who, with heaven's help, will pay me the price for that.
For those children he had from me he will never
See alive again, nor will he on his new bride   790

---

11. A shrine in Athens.

Beget another child, for she is to be forced
To die a most terrible death by these my poisons.
Let no one think me a weak one, feeble-spirited,
A stay-at-home, but rather just the opposite,
One who can hurt my enemies and help my friends;   795
For the lives of such persons are most remembered.
Chorus: Since you have shared the knowledge of your plan with us,
    I both wish to help you and support the normal
    Ways of mankind, and tell you not to do this thing.
Medea: I can do no other thing. It is understandable   800
    For you to speak thus. You have not suffered as I have.
Chorus: But can you have the heart to kill your flesh and blood?
Medea: Yes, for this is the best way to wound my husband.
Chorus: And you, too. Of women you will be most unhappy.
Medea: So it must be. No compromise is possible.   805

She turns to the Nurse.

    Go, you, at once, and tell Jason to come to me.
    You I employ on all affairs of greatest trust.
    Say nothing of these decisions which I have made,
    If you love your mistress, if you were born a woman.
Chorus: From of old the children of Erechtheus[12] are   810
    Splendid, the sons of blessed gods. They dwell
    In Athens' holy and unconquered land,
    Where famous Wisdom feeds them and they pass gaily
    Always through that most brilliant air where once, they say,
    That golden Harmony gave birth to the nine   815
    Pure Muses of Pieria.

    And beside the sweet flow of Cephisus' stream,
    Where Cypris sailed, they say, to draw the water,
    And mild soft breezes breathed along her path,
    And on her hair were flung the sweet-smelling garlands   820
    Of flowers of roses by the Lovers, the companions
    Of Wisdom, her escort, the helpers of men
    In every kind of excellence.

    How then can these holy rivers
    Or this holy land love you,   825
    Or the city find you a home,
    You, who will kill your children,
    You, not pure with the rest?
    O think of the blow at your children
    And think of the blood that you shed.   830
    O, over and over I beg you,

---

12. Mythical king of Athens who killed some of his own children to save the city.

By your knees I beg you do not
Be the murderess of your babes!

O where will you find the courage
Or the skill of hand and heart,   835
When you set yourself to attempt
A deed so dreadful to do?
How, when you look upon them,
Can you tearlessly hold the decision
For murder? You will not be able,   840
When your children fall down and implore you,
You will not be able to dip
Steadfast your hand in their blood.

Enter Jason with attendants.

   Jason: I have come at your request. Indeed, although you are
      Bitter against me, this you shall have: I will listen   845
      To what new thing you want, woman, to get from me.
  Medea: Jason, I beg you to be forgiving toward me
      For what I said. It is natural for you to bear with
      My temper, since we have had much love together.
      I have talked with myself about this and I have   850
      Reproached myself. "Fool," I said, "why am I so mad?
      Why am I set against those who have planned wisely?
      Why make myself an enemy of the authorities
      And of my husband, who does the best thing for me
      By marrying royalty and having children who   855
      Will be as brothers to my own? What is wrong with me?
      Let me give up anger, for the gods are kind to me.
      Have I not children, and do I not know that we
      In exile from our country must be short of friends?"
      When I considered this I saw that I had shown   860
      Great lack of sense, and that my anger was foolish.
      Now I agree with you. I think that you are wise
      In having this other wife as well as me, and I
      Was mad. I should have helped you in these plans of yours,
      Have joined in the wedding, stood by the marriage bed,   865
      Have taken pleasure in attendance on your bride.
      But we women are what we are—perhaps a little
      Worthless; and you men must not be like us in this,
      Nor be foolish in return when we are foolish.
      Now, I give in, and admit that then I was wrong.   870
      I have come to a better understanding now.

She turns toward the house.

Children, come here, my children, come outdoors to us!
Welcome your father with me, and say goodbye to him,

And with your mother, who just now was his enemy,
Join again in making friends with him who loves us.   875

Enter the children, attended by the Tutor.

We have made peace, and all our anger is over.
Take hold of his right hand—O God, I am thinking
Of something which may happen in the secret future.
O children, will you just so, after a long life,
Hold out your loving arms at the grave? O children,   880
How ready to cry I am, how full of foreboding!
I am ending at last this quarrel with your father,
And, look my soft eyes have suddenly filled with tears.
Chorus: And the pale tears have started also in my eyes.
O may the trouble not grow worse than now it is!   885
Jason: I approve of what you say. And I cannot blame you
Even for what you said before. It is natural
For a woman to be wild with her husband when he
Goes in for secret love. But now your mind has turned
To better reasoning. In the end you have come to   890
The right decision, like the clever woman you are.
And of you, children, your father is taking care.
He has made, with God's help, ample provision for you.
For I think that a time will come when you will be·
The leading people in Corinth with your brothers.   895
You must grow up. As to the future, your father
And those of the gods who love him will deal with that.
I want to see you, when you have become young men,
Healthy and strong, better men than my enemies.
Medea, why are your eyes all wet with pale tears?   900
Why is your cheek so white and turned away from me?
Are not these words of mine pleasing for you to hear?
Medea: It is nothing. I was thinking about these children.
Jason: You must be cheerful. I shall look after them well.
Medea: I will be. It is not that I distrust your words,   905
But a woman is a frail thing, prone to crying.
Jason: But why then should you grieve so much for these children?
Medea: I am their mother. When you prayed that they might live
I felt unhappy to think that these things will be.
But come, I have said something of the things I meant   910
To say to you, and now I will tell you the rest.
Since it is the king's will to banish me from here—
And for me, too, I know that this is the best thing,
Not to be in your way by living here or in
The king's way, since they think me ill-disposed to them—   915
I then am going into exile from this land;
But do you, so that you may have the care of them,
Beg Creon that the children may not be banished.

Jason: I doubt if I'll succeed, but still I'll attempt it.
Medea: Then you must tell your wife to beg from her father   920
    That the children may be reprieved from banishment.
Jason: I will, and with her I shall certainly succeed.
Medea: If she is like the rest of us women, you will.
    And I, too, will take a hand with you in this business,
    For I will send her some gifts which are far fairer,   925
    I am sure of it, than those which now are in fashion,
    A finely woven dress and a golden diadem,
    And the children shall present them. Quick, let one of you
    Servants bring here to me that beautiful dress.

One of her attendants goes into the house.

    She will be happy not in one way, but in a hundred,   930
    Having so fine a man as you to share her bed,
    And with this beautiful dress which Helius of old,
    My father's father, bestowed on his descendants.

Enter attendant carrying the poisoned dress and diadem.

    There, children, take these wedding presents in your hands.
    Take them to the royal princess, the happy bride,   935
    And give them to her. She will not think little of them.
Jason: No, don't be foolish, and empty your hands of these.
    Do you think the palace is short of dresses to wear?
    Do you think there is no gold there? Keep them, don't give them
    Away. If my wife considers me of any value,   940
    She will think more of me than money, I am sure of it.
Medea: No, let me have my way. They say the gods themselves
    Are moved by gifts, and gold does more with men than words.
    Hers is the luck, her fortune that which god blesses;
    She is young and a princess; but for my children's reprieve   945
    I would give my very life, and not gold only.
    Go children, go together to that rich palace,
    Be suppliants to the new wife of your father,
    My lady, beg her not to let you be banished.
    And give her the dress—for this is of great importance,   950
    That she should take the gift into her hand from yours.
    Go, quick as you can. And bring your mother good news
    By your success of those things which she longs to gain.

*Jason goes out with his attendants, followed by the Tutor and the children carrying
the poisoned gifts.*

Chorus: Now there is no hope left for the children's lives.
    Now there is none. They are walking already to murder.   955
    The bride, poor bride, will accept the curse of the gold,
    Will accept the bright diadem.

Around her yellow hair she will set that dress
Of death with her own hands.

The grace and the perfume and glow of the golden robe   960
Will charm her to put them upon her and wear the wreath,
And now her wedding will be with the dead below,
Into such a trap she will fall,
Poor thing, into such a fate of death and never
Escape from under that curse.   965

You, too, O wretched bridegroom, making your match with
        kings,
You do not see that you bring
Destruction on your children and on her,
Your wife, a fearful death.
Poor soul, what a fall is yours!   970
In your grief, too, I weep, mother of little children,
You who will murder your own,
In vengeance for the loss of married love
Which Jason has betrayed
As he lives with another wife.   975

Enter the Tutor with the children.

Tutor: Mistress, I tell you that these children are reprieved,
        And the royal bride has been pleased to take in her hands
        Your gifts. In that quarter the children are secure.
        But come,
        Why do you stand confused when you are fortunate?   980
        Why have you turned round with your cheek away from me?
        Are not these words of mine pleasing for you to hear?
Medea: Oh! I am lost!
Tutor: That word is not in harmony with my tidings.
Medea: I am lost, I am lost!   985
Tutor: Am I in ignorance telling you
        Of some disaster, and not the good news I thought?
Medea: You have told what you have told. I do not blame you.
Tutor: Why then this downcast eye, and this weeping of tears?
Medea: Oh, I am forced to weep, old man. The gods and I,   990
        I in a kind of madness, have contrived all this.
Tutor: Courage! You, too, will be brought home by your children.
Medea: Ah, before that happens I shall bring others home.
Tutor: Others before you have been parted from their children.
        Mortals must bear in resignation their ill luck.   995
Medea: That is what I shall do. But go inside the house,
        And do for the children your usual daily work.

The Tutor goes into the house. Medea turns to her children.

O children, O my children, you have a city,
You have a home, and you can leave me behind you,
And without your mother you may live there forever.   1000
But I am going into exile to another land
Before I have seen you happy and taken pleasure in you,
Before I have dressed your brides and made your marriage beds
And held up the torch at the ceremony of wedding.
Oh, what a wretch I am in this my self-willed thought!   1005
What was the purpose, children, for which I reared you?
For all my travail and wearing myself away?
They were sterile, those pains I had in the bearing of you.
Oh surely once the hopes in you I had, poor me,
Were high ones: you would look after me in old age,   1010
And when I died would deck me well with your own hands;
A thing which all would have done. Oh but now it is gone,
That lovely thought. For, once I am left without you,
Sad will be the life I'll lead and sorrowful for me.
And you will never see your mother again with   1015
Your dear eyes, gone to another mode of living.
Why, children, do you look upon me with your eyes?
Why do you smile so sweetly that last smile of all?
Oh, Oh, what can I do? My spirit has gone from me,
Friends, when I saw that bright look in the children's eyes.   1020
I cannot bear to do it. I renounce my plans
I had before. I'll take my children away from
This land. Why should I hurt their father with the pain
They feel, and suffer twice as much of pain myself?
No, no, I will not do it. I renounce my plans   1025
Ah, what is wrong with me? Do I want to let go
My enemies unhurt and be laughed at for it?
I must face this thing. Oh, but what a weak woman
Even to admit to my mind these soft arguments.
Children, go into the house. And he whom laws forbids   1030
To stand in attendance at my sacrifices,
Let him see to it. I shall not mar my handiwork.
Oh! Oh!
Do not, O my heart, you must not do these things!
Poor heart, let them go, have pity upon the children.   1035
If they live with you in Athens they will cheer you.
No! By Hell's avenging furies it shall not be—
This shall never be, that I should suffer my children
To be the prey of my enemies' insolence.
Every way is it fixed. The bride will not escape.   1040
No, the diadem is now upon her head; and she,
The royal princess, is dying in the dress, I know it.
But—for it is the most dreadful of roads for me

To tread, and them I shall send on a more dreadful still—
I wish to speak to the children.   1045

She calls the children to her.

                                        Come, children, give
Me your hands, give your mother your hands to kiss them.
Oh the dear hands, and O how dear are these lips to me,
And the generous eyes and the bearing of my children!
I wish you happiness, but not here in this world.   1050
What is here your father took. Oh how good to hold you!
How delicate the skin, how sweet the breath of children!
Go, go! I am no longer able, no longer
To look upon you. I am overcome by sorrow.

The children go into the house.

I know indeed what evil I intend to do,   1055
But stronger than all my afterthoughts is my fury,
Fury that brings upon mortals the greatest evils.

She goes out to the right, toward the royal palace.

Chorus: Often before
I have gone through more subtle reasons,
And have come upon questionings greater   1060
Than a woman should strive to search out.
But we too have a goddess to help us
And accompany us into wisdom.
Not all of us. Still you will find
Among many women a few,   1065
And our sex is not without learning.
This I say, that those who have never
Had children, who know nothing of it,
In happiness have the advantage
Over those who are parents.   1070
The childless, who never discover
Whether children turn out as a good thing
Or as something to cause pain, are spared
Many troubles in lacking this knowledge.
And those who have in their homes   1075
The sweet presence of children, I see that their lives
Are all wasted away by their worries.
First they must think how to bring them up well and
How to leave them something to live on.
And then after this whether all their toil   1080
Is for those who will turn out good or bad,
Is still an unanswered question.

And of one more trouble, the last of all,
That is common to mortals I tell.
For suppose you have found them enough for their living,　　　1085
Suppose that the children have grown into youth
And have turned out good, still, if God so wills it,
Death will away with your children's bodies,
And carry them off into Hades.
What is our profit, then, that for the sake of　　　1090
Children the gods should pile upon mortals
After all else
This most terrible grief of all?

Enter Medea, from the spectators' right.

   Medea:　Friends, I can tell you that for long I have waited
For the event. I stare toward the place from where　　　1095
The news will come. And now, see one of Jason's servants
Is on his way here, and that labored breath of his
Shows he has tidings for us, and evil tidings.

Enter, also from the right, the Messenger.

Messenger:　Medea, you have done such a dreadful thing,
So outrageous, run for your life, take what you can,　　　1100
A ship to bear you hence or chariot on land.
   Medea:　And what is the reason deserves such flight as this?
Messenger:　She is dead, only just now, the royal princess,
And Creon dead, too, her father, by your poisons.
   Medea:　The finest words you have spoken. Now and hereafter　　　1105
I shall count you among my benefactors and friends.
Messenger:　What! Are you right in the mind? Are you not mad,
Woman? The house of the king is outraged by you.
Do you enjoy it? Not afraid of such doings?
   Medea:　To what you say I on my side have something too　　　1110
To say in answer. Do not be in a hurry, friend,
But speak. How did they die? You will delight me twice
As much again if you say they died in agony.
Messenger:　When those two children, born of you, had entered in,
Their father with them, and passed into the bride's house,　　　1115
We were pleased, we slaves who were distressed by your wrongs.
All through the house we were talking of but one thing,
How you and your husband had made up your quarrel.
Some kissed the children's hands and some their yellow hair,
And I myself was so full of my joy that I　　　1120
Followed the children into the women's quarters.
Our mistress, whom we honor now instead of you,
Before she noticed that your two children were there,

Was keeping her eye fixed eagerly on Jason.
Afterwards, however, she covered up her eyes,   1125
Her cheek paled, and she turned herself away from him,
So disgusted was she at the children's coming there.
But your husband tried to end the girl's bad temper,
And said "You must not look unkindly on your friends.
Cease to be angry. Turn your head to me again.   1130
Have as your friends the same ones as your husband has.
And take these gifts, and beg your father to reprieve
These children from their exile. Do it for my sake."
She, when she saw the dress, could not restrain herself.
She agreed with all her husband said, and before   1135
He and the children had gone far from the palace,
She took the gorgeous robe and dressed herself in it,
And put the golden crown around her curly locks,
And arranged the set of the hair in a shining mirror,
And smiled at the lifeless image of herself in it.   1140
Then she rose from her chair and walked about the room,
With her gleaming feet stepping most soft and delicate,
All overjoyed with the present. Often and often
She would stretch her foot out straight and look along it.
But after it was a fearful thing to see.   1145
The color of her face changed, and she staggered back,
She ran, and her legs trembled, and she only just
Managed to reach a chair without falling flat down.
An aged woman servant who, I take it, thought
This was some seizure of Pan[13] or another god,   1150
Cried out "God bless us," but that was before she saw
The white foam breaking through her lips and her rolling
The pupils of her eyes and her face all bloodless.
Then she raised a different cry from that "God bless us,"
A huge shriek, and the women ran, one to the king,   1155
One to the newly wedded husband to tell him
What had happened to his bride; and with frequent sound
The whole of the palace rang as they were running.
One walking quickly round the course of a race-track
Would now have turned the bend and be close to the goal,   1160
When she, poor girl, opened her shut and speechless eye,
And with a terrible groan she came to herself.
For a twofold pain was moving up against her.
The wreath of gold that was resting around her head
Let forth a fearful stream of all-devouring fire,   1165

_____

13. God of nature known to incite fear among mortals.

And the finely woven dress your children gave to her,
Was fastening on the unhappy girl's fine flesh.
She leapt up from the chair, and all on fire she ran,
Shaking her hair now this way and now that, trying
To hurl the diadem away; but fixedly   1170
The gold preserved its grip, and, when she shook her hair,
Then more and twice as fiercely the fire blazed out.
Till, beaten by her fate, she fell down to the ground,
Hard to be recognized except by a parent.
Neither the setting of her eyes was plain to see,   1175
Nor the shapeliness of her face. From the top of
Her head there oozed out blood and fire mixed together.
Like the drops on pine-bark, so the flesh from her bones
Dropped away, torn by the hidden fang of the poison.
It was a fearful sight; and terror held us all   1180
From touching the corpse. We had learned from what had
     happened.
But her wretched father, knowing nothing of the event,
Came suddenly to the house, and fell upon the corpse,
And at once cried out and folded his arms about her,
And kissed her and spoke to her, saying, "O my poor child,   1185
What heavenly power has so shamefully destroyed you?
And who has set me here like an ancient sepulcher,
Deprived of you? O let me die with you, my child!"
And when he had made an end of his wailing and crying,
Then the old man wished to raise himself to his feet;   1190
But, as the ivy clings to the twigs of the laurel,
So he stuck to the fine dress, and he struggled fearfully.
For he was trying to lift himself to his knee,
And she was pulling him down, and when he tugged hard
He would be ripping his aged flesh from his bones.   1195
At last his life was quenched, and the unhappy man
Gave up the ghost, no longer could hold up his head.
There they lie close, the daughter and the old father,
Dead bodies, an event he prayed for in his tears.
As for your interests, I will say nothing of them,   1200
For you will find your own escape from punishment.
Our human life I think and have thought a shadow,
And I do not fear to say that those who are held
Wise among men and who search the reasons of things
Are those who bring the most sorrow on themselves.   1205
For of mortals there is no one who is happy.
If wealth flows in upon one, one may be perhaps
Luckier than one's neighbor, but still not happy.

Exit.

Chorus: Heaven, it seems, on this day has fastened many
        Evils on Jason, and Jason has deserved them.   1210
        Poor girl, the daughter of Creon, how I pity you
        And your misfortunes, you who have gone quite away
        To the house of Hades because of marrying Jason.
Medea: Women, my task is fixed: as quickly as I may
        To kill my children, and start away from this land,   1215
        And not, by wasting time, to suffer my children
        To be slain by another hand less kindly to them.
        Force every way will have it they must die, and since
        This must be so, then I, their mother, shall kill them.
        Oh, arm yourself in steel, my heart! Do not hang back   1220
        From doing this fearful and necessary wrong.
        Oh, come, my hand, poor wretched hand, and take the sword,
        Take it, step forward to this bitter starting point,
        And do not be a coward, do not think of them,
        How sweet they are, and how you are their mother. Just for   1225
        This one short day be forgetful of your children,
        Afterward weep; for even though you will kill them,
        They were very dear—Oh, I am an unhappy woman!

With a cry she rushes into the house.

Chorus: O Earth, and the far shining
        Ray of the Sun, look down, look down upon   1230
        This poor lost woman, look, before she raises
        The hand of murder against her flesh and blood.
        Yours was the golden birth from which
        She sprang, and now I fear divine
        Blood may be shed by men.   1235
        O heavenly light, hold back her hand,
        Check her, and drive from out the house
        The bloody Fury raised by fiends of Hell.
        Vain waste, your care of children;
        Was it in vain you bore the babes you loved,   1240
        After you passed the inhospitable strait
        Between the dark blue rocks, Symplegades?
        O wretched one, how has it come,
        This heavy anger on your heart,
        This cruel bloody mind?   1245
        For God from mortals asks a stern
        Price for the stain of kindred blood
        In like disaster falling on their homes.

A cry from one of the children is heard.

Chorus: Do you hear the cry, do you hear the children's cry?
        O you hard heart, O woman fated for evil!   1250

One of the Children (from within):
>What can I do and how escape my mother's hands?

Another child (from within):
>O my dear brother, I cannot tell. We are lost.

>*Chorus:* Shall I enter the house? Oh, surely I should
>Defend the children from murder.

A Child (from within):
>O help us, in God's name, for now we need your help.   1255
>Now, now we are close to it. We are trapped by the sword.

>*Chorus:* O your heart must have been made of rock or steel,
>You who can kill
>With your own hand the fruit of your own womb.
>Of one alone I have heard, one woman alone   1260
>Of those of old who laid her hands on her children,
>Ino, sent mad by heaven when the wife of Zeus
>Drove her out from her home and made her wander;
>And because of the wicked shedding of blood
>Of her own children she threw   1265
>Herself, poor wretch, into the sea and stepped away
>Over the sea-cliff to die with her two children.
>What horror more can be? O women's love,
>So full of trouble,
>How many evils have you caused already!   1270

Enter Jason, with attendants.

>*Jason:* You women, standing close in front of this dwelling,
>Is she, Medea, she who did this dreadful deed,
>Still in the house, or has she run away in flight?
>For she will have to hide herself beneath the earth,
>Or raise herself on wings into the height of air,   1275
>If she wishes to escape the royal vengeance.
>Does she imagine that, having killed our rulers,
>She will herself escape uninjured from this house?
>But I am thinking not so much of her as for
>The children—her the king's friends will make to suffer   1280
>For what she did. So I have come to save the lives
>Of my boys, in case the royal house should harm them
>While taking vengeance for their mother's wicked deed.

>*Chorus:* O Jason, if you but knew how deeply you are
>Involved in sorrow, you would not have spoken so.   1285

>*Jason:* What is it? That she is planning to kill me also?

>*Chorus:* Your children are dead, and by their own mother's hand.

>*Jason:* What! That is it? O woman, you have destroyed me!

>*Chorus:* You must make up your mind your children are no more.

>*Jason:* Where did she kill them? Was it here or in the house?   1290

Chorus: Open the gates and there you will see them murdered.
  Jason: Quick as you can unlock the doors, men, and undo
      The fastenings and let me see this double evil,
      My children dead and her—Oh her I will repay.

His attendants rush to the door. Medea appears above the house in a chariot drawn by dragons. She has the dead bodies of her children with her.

  Medea: Why do you batter these gates and try to unbar them,   1295
      Seeking the corpses and for me who did the deed?
      You may cease your trouble, and, if you have need of me,
      Speak, if you wish. You will never touch me with your hand,
      Such a chariot has Helius, my father's father,
      Given me to defend me from my enemies.   1300
  Jason: You hateful thing, you woman most utterly loathed
      By the gods and me and by all the race of mankind,
      You who have had the heart to raise a sword against
      Your children, you, their mother, and left me childless—
      You have done this, and do you still look at the sun   1305
      And at the earth, after these most fearful doings?
      I wish you dead. Now I see it plain, though at that time
      I did not, when I took you from your foreign home
      And brought you to a Greek house, you, an evil thing,
      A traitress to your father and your native land.   1310
      The gods hurled the avenging curse of yours on me.
      For your own brother you slew at your own hearthside,
      And then came aboard that beautiful ship, the Argo.
      And that was your beginning. When you were married
      To me, your husband, and had borne children to me,
      For the sake of pleasure in the bed you killed them.   1315
      There is no Greek woman who would have dared such deeds,
      Out of all those whom I passed over and chose you
      To marry instead, a bitter destructive match,
      A monster, not a woman, having a nature
      Wilder than that of Scylla[14] in the Tuscan sea.   1320
      Ah! no, not if I had ten thousand words of shame
      Could I sting you. You are naturally so brazen.
      Go, worker in evil, stained with your children's blood.
      For me remains to cry aloud upon my fate,
      Who will get no pleasure from my newly wedded love,   1325
      And the boys whom I begot and brought up, never
      Shall I speak to them alive. Oh, my life is over!
  Medea: Long would be the answer which I might have made to

---

14. A sea nymph changed into a dangerous rock, facing the whirlpool Charybdis.

These words of yours, if Zeus the father did not know
How I have treated you and what you did to me.   1330
No, it was not to be that you should scorn my love,
And pleasantly live your life through, laughing at me;
Nor would the princess, nor he who offered the match,
Creon, drive me away without paying for it.
So now you may call me a monster, if you wish,   1335
A Scylla housed in the caves of the Tuscan sea.
I too, as I had to, have taken hold of your heart.
Jason: You feel the pain yourself. You share in my sorrow.
Medea: Yes, and my grief is gain when you cannot mock it.
Jason: O children, what a wicked mother she was to you!   1340
Medea: They died from a disease they caught from their father.
Jason: I tell you it was not my hand that destroyed them.
Medea: But it was your insolence, and your virgin wedding.
Jason: And just for the sake of that you chose to kill them.
Medea: Is love so small a pain, do you think, for a woman?   1345
Jason: For a wise one, certainly. But you are wholly evil.
Medea: The children are dead. I say this to make you suffer.
Jason: The children, I think, will bring down curses on you.
Medea: The gods know who was the author of this sorrow.
Jason: Yes, the gods know indeed, they know your loathsome
heart.   1350
Medea: Hate me. But I tire of your barking bitterness.
Jason: And I of yours. It is easier to leave you.
Medea: How then? What shall I do? I long to leave you too.
Jason: Give me the bodies to bury and to mourn them.
Medea: No, that I will not. I will bury them myself,   1355
Bearing them to Hera's[15] temple on the promontory;
So that no enemy may evilly treat them
By tearing up their grave. In this land of Corinth
I shall establish a holy feast and sacrifice
Each year for ever to atone for the blood guilt.   1360
And I myself go to the land of Erechtheus
To dwell in Aegeus' house, the son of Pandion.
While you, as is right, will die without distinction,
Struck on the head by a piece of the Argo's timber,
And you will have seen the bitter end of my love.   1365
Jason: May a Fury for the children's sake destroy you,
And justice, Requitor of blood.
Medea: What heavenly power lends an ear
To a breaker of oaths, a deceiver?

---

15. Wife and sister of Zeus, king of gods.

Jason: Oh, I hate you, murderess of children.   1370
Medea: Go to your palace. Bury your bride.
Jason: I go, with two children to mourn for.
Medea: Not yet do you feel it. Wait for the future.
Jason: Oh, children I loved!
Medea: I loved them, you did not.   1375
Jason: You loved them, and killed them.
Medea: To make you feel pain.
Jason: Oh, wretch that I am, how I long
    To kiss the dear lips of my children!
Medea: Now you would speak to them, now you would kiss them.   1380
    Then you rejected them.
Jason: Let me, I beg you,
    Touch my boys' delicate flesh.
Medea: I will not. Your words are all wasted.
Jason: O God, do you hear it, this persecution,   1385
    These my sufferings from this hateful
    Woman, this monster, murderess of children?
    Still what I can do that I will do:
    I will lament and cry upon heaven,
    Calling the gods to bear me witness   1390
    How you have killed my boys and prevent me from
    Touching their bodies or giving them burial.
    I wish I had never begot them to see them
    Afterward slaughtered by you.
Chorus: Zeus in Olympus is the overseer   1395
    Of many doings. Many things the gods
    Achieve beyond our judgment. What we thought
    Is not confirmed and what we thought not god
    Contrives. And so it happens in this story.

Curtain

Further Reading

Knox, Bernard. "Euripides: The Poet as Prophet." *Directions in Euripidean Criticism: A Collection of Essays.* Ed. Peter Burian. Durham: Duke UP, 1985. 1–12. • Con-acher, D. J. "The *Medea.*" *Euripidean Drama: Myth, Theme, and Structure.* Toronto: U of Toronto P, 1967. 183–98. • Schlesinger, Eilhard. "On Euripides' *Medea.*" A translation of "Zu Euripides *Medea.*" *Euripides: A Collection of Critical Essays.* Ed. Erich Segal. Englewood Cliffs, NJ: Prentice, 1968. 70–89. • Sale, William. *Existentialism and Euripides: Sickness, Tragedy and Divinity in the "Medea," the*

"Hippolytus" and the "Bacchae." Berwick, Victoria, Aust.: Aureal, 1977. 13–34. •
Flory, Stewart. "Medea's Right Hand: Promises and Revenge." *Transactions of the
American Philological Association* 108 (1978): 69–74.

*The introduction of the major characters is crucial in establishing the tone
and theme of a play. We can get a clear sense of the effect created by Euripides' introduction of Medea by comparing it to the following fragments of
the opening scenes of Seneca's* Medea *(circa* A.D. *50) and Jean Anouilh's*
Medea *(1946).*

Seneca: Medea's Entrance

Scene:—Before the house of *Jason* in Corinth. The
palace of *Creon* is near.

ACT ONE

Scene I

(Enter Medea.*)*

> *Medea:* Ye gods of wedlock, thou the nuptial couch's guard,
> Lucina, thou from whom that tamer of the deep,
> The Argo's pilot, learned to guide his pristine bark,
> And Neptune, thou stern ruler of the ocean's depths,
> And Titan, by whose rays the shining day is born,
> Thou triformed maiden Hecate, whose conscious beams
> With splendour shine upon the mystic worshippers—
> Upon ye all I call, the powers of heaven, the gods
> By whose divinity false Jason swore; and ye
> Whose aid Medea may more boldly claim, thou world
> Of endless night, th' antipodes of heavenly realms,
> Ye damnéd ghosts, thou lord of hades' dark domain,
> Whose mistress was with trustier pledge won to thy side—
> Before ye all this baleful prayer I bring: Be near!
> Be near! Ye crime-avenging furies, come and loose
> Your horrid locks with serpent coils entwined, and grasp
> With bloody hands the smoking torch; be near as once
> Ye stood in dread array beside my wedding couch.
> Upon this new-made bride destruction send, and death
> Upon the king and all the royal line! But he,
> My husband, may he live to meet some heavier doom;
> This curse I imprecate upon his head; may he,
> Through distant lands, in want, in exile wander, scorned
> And houseless.

Jean Anouilh: Medea's Entrance

When the curtain rises, Medea *and the* Nurse *are seen squatting on the ground before a wagon. Vague music and singing are heard in the distance. They listen.*

Medea: Do you hear it?

Nurse: What?

Medea: Happiness. Prowling around.

Nurse: They are singing in the village. Today may be a feast day for them.

Medea: I hate their feast days. I hate their joy.

Nurse: It does not concern us. [A *silence.*] At home our feast days came earlier. In June. The girls put flowers in their hair and the boys paint their faces red with their blood, and then in the small hours of the morning, after the first sacrifices, they begin to fight. How handsome our Colchis boys look when they fight!

Medea: Be still.

Nurse: Afterward they spend all day taming wild animals. And in the evening they set large fires before your father's palace— large yellow bonfires made with herbs that smelled so strongly. Have you forgotten the fragrance of our native plants, child?

Medea: Be still. Not another word, good woman.

Nurse: Ah, I am old now and the way is so long. . . . Why, why did we leave, Medea?

Medea [*shouts*]: We left because I loved Jason, because I stole from my father for him, because I killed my brother for him! Be still, good woman. Be still. Do you think it is wise to repeat these things over and over again?

Nurse: You had a palace with walls of gold and now we squat here like two beggars before a fire which always dies out.

Medea: Go and fetch some wood.

The Nurse *gets up moaning and walks away.*

WILLIAM SHAKESPEARE

(1564–1616)

TWELFTH NIGHT,
or WHAT YOU WILL

edited by G. Blakemore Evans

CHARACTERS

Orsino, Duke of Illyria
Sebastian, brother to Viola
Antonio, a sea captain, friend to Sebastian
Sea Captain, friend to Viola
Valentine
Curio
} *gentlemen attending on the Duke*
Sir Toby Belch, uncle to Olivia
Sir Andrew Aguecheek
Malvolio, steward to Olivia
Fabian
Feste, a clown
} *servants to Olivia*
Olivia, a rich countess
Viola, sister to Sebastian
Maria, Olivia's gentlewoman

Lords, Priests, Sailors, Officers, Musicians, Gentlewoman,
Servant, and other Attendants

Scene: A city in Illyria, and the sea-coast near it.

ACT I

Scene I

Enter Orsino, *Duke of Illyria,* Curio, *and other* Lords: [Musicians *attending*].

Duke: If music be the food of love, play on,
    Give me excess of it; that surfeiting,

Words and passages enclosed in square brackets in the text above are either emendations of the First Folio (1623) or additions to it. O.s.d. is an abbreviation for opening stage direction.

I.i. Location: The Duke's palace. o.s.d. *Illyria:* a country extending along the east coast of the Adriatic, in large part approximating modern Jugoslavia. 1. *music . . . love:* Cf. *Antony and Cleopatra,* II.v. 1–2, "music, moody food / Of us that trade in love." The whole speech is concerned, using a figure of nausea (surfeiting), with the insatiable, but paradoxically quickly sated, quality of love as Orsino here sees it—a kind of glutton that devours dainties only to vomit them up. In a real sense, the play is about a rectification of this view of love.

The appetite may sicken, and so die.
That strain again, it had a dying fall;
O, it came o'er my ear like the sweet sound   5
That breathes upon a bank of violets,
Stealing and giving odor. Enough, no more,
'Tis not so sweet now as it was before.
O spirit of love, how quick and fresh art thou,
That notwithstanding thy capacity   10
Receiveth as the sea, nought enters there,
Of what validity and pitch soe'er,
But falls into abatement and low price
Even in a minute. So full of shapes is fancy
That it alone is high fantastical.   15
Curio: Will you go hunt, my lord?
Duke: What, Curio?
Curio: The hart.
Duke: Why, so I do, the noblest that I have.
O, when mine eyes did see Olivia first,
Methought she purg'd the air of pestilence!
That instant was I turn'd into a hart,   20
And my desires, like fell and cruel hounds,
E'er since pursue me.

Enter Valentine.

                    How now, what news from her?
Valentine: So please my lord, I might not be admitted,
But from her handmaid do return this answer:
The element itself, till seven years' heat,   25
Shall not behold her face at ample view;
But like a cloistress she will veiled walk,
And water once a day her chamber round
With eye-offending brine; all this to season
A brother's dead love, which she would keep fresh   30
And lasting in her sad remembrance.
Duke: O, she that hath a heart of that fine frame

---

3. *appetite:* i.e. love's appetite for music.   4. *fall:* cadence.   9. *quick:* lively, vigorous. *fresh:* keen.   10. *capacity:* power to take in.   12. *validity:* value. *pitch:* high worth (a term from falconry, designating the highest point of a hawk's flight; or perhaps *validity and pitch* is better taken as a hendiadys, meaning "high valuation."   13. *abatement:* depreciation. *price:* esteem.   14. *shapes:* fanciful forms. *fancy:* love.   15. *it . . . fantastical:* it carries imagination to unique heights.   16. *hart:* Orsino plays on *heart.*   20–22. *turn'd . . . me:* Alluding to the story of Actaeon who, having seen Diana naked, was turned into a stag, whereupon his own hounds hunted him down and killed him.   21. *fell:* fierce.   25. *element:* sky. *heat:* course (?) or progress of the sun through the zodiac (?).   26. *ample:* unrestricted.   27. *cloistress:* cloistered nun.   29. *season:* preserve (with play on preserving food in brine).   30. *A brother's dead love:* a dead brother's love (referring both to her love for him and the memory of his for her).   32. *frame:* framing, construction.

To pay this debt of love but to a brother,
How will she love when the rich golden shaft
Hath kill'd the flock of all affections else   35
That live in her; when liver, brain, and heart,
These sovereign thrones, are all supplied and fill'd
Her sweet perfections with one self king!
Away before me to sweet beds of flow'rs,
Love-thoughts lie rich when canopied with bow'rs.   *Exeunt.* 40

Scene II

Enter Viola, *a* Captain, *and* Sailors.

    Viola: What country, friends, is this?
 Captain: This is Illyria, lady.
    Viola: And what should I do in Illyria?
        My brother he is in Elysium.
        Perchance he is not drown'd—what think you, sailors?   5
 Captain: It is perchance that you yourself were saved.
    Viola: O my poor brother! and so perchance may he be.
 Captain: True, madam, and to comfort you with chance,
        Assure yourself, after our ship did split,
        When you, and those poor number saved with you,   10
        Hung on our driving boat, I saw your brother,
        Most provident in peril, bind himself
        (Courage and hope both teaching him the practice)
        To a strong mast that liv'd upon the sea;
        Where like [Arion] on the dolphin's back,   15
        I saw him hold acquaintance with the waves
        So long as I could see.
    Viola: For saying so, there's gold.
        Mine own escape unfoldeth to my hope,
        Whereto thy speech serves for authority,   20
        The like of him. Know'st thou this country?

---

34. *golden shaft:* Cupid's gold-tipped arrow, which caused love. He had also a lead-tipped
arrow, which produced loathing.   35. *affections else:* other emotions (than love) (?) or other
loves (?).   36. *liver . . . heart:* The supposed seats of the passions (and especially love),
thought or judgment, and the feelings or sentiments respectively.   37. *supplied:* Synonymous
with *fill'd.*   37–38. *and . . . perfections:* and her sweet perfections filled.   38. *one self king:*
one and the same lord, the person whom she loves wholly.

I.ii. Location: The sea-coast.   4. *Elysium:* i.e. heaven. The classical name is used to play on
Illyria.   5–6. *Perchance . . .perchance:* perhaps . . . by mere chance.   8. *chance:* i.e. a
favorable possibility.   11. *driving:* drifting.   12. *Most provident:* showing great foresight.
14. *liv'd:* i.e. remained afloat.   15. *Arion . . . back:* Arion, a Greek poet and musician, on a
voyage from Sicily to Greece charmed dolphins with his singing and playing on the lyre. When
he leaped overboard to escape murder by the sailors, he was saved by a dolphin on whose
back he rode to shore.   19. *unfoldeth:* discloses.   21. *like of him:* i.e. chance that he escaped
likewise.

Captain: Ay, madam, well, for I was bred and born
        Not three hours' travel from this very place.
Viola: Who governs here?
Captain: A noble duke, in nature as in name.   25
Viola: What is his name?
Captain: Orsino.
Viola: Orsino! I have heard my father name him.
        He was a bachelor then.
Captain: And so is now, or was so very late;   30
        For but a month ago I went from hence,
        And then 'twas fresh in murmur (as you know
        What great ones do, the less will prattle of)
        That he did seek the love of fair Olivia.
Viola: What's she?   35
Captain: A virtuous maid, the daughter of a count
        That died some twelvemonth since, then leaving her
        In the protection of his son, her brother,
        Who shortly also died; for whose dear love,
        They say, she hath abjur'd the [company]   40
        And [sight] of men.
Viola: O that I serv'd that lady,
        And might not be delivered to the world
        Till I had made mine own occasion mellow
        What my estate is!
Captain: That were hard to compass,
        Because she will admit no kind of suit,   45
        No, not the Duke's.
Viola: There is a fair behavior in thee, captain,
        And though that nature with a beauteous wall
        Doth oft close in pollution, yet of thee
        I will believe thou hast a mind that suits   50
        With this thy fair and outward character.
        I prithee (and I'll pay thee bounteously)
        Conceal me what I am, and be my aid
        For such disguise as haply shall become
        The form of my intent. I'll serve this duke;   55
        Thou shalt present me as an eunuch to him,
        It may be worth thy pains; for I can sing
        And speak to him in many sorts of music

---

32. *murmur:* rumor.   42–44. *might . . . is:* that my position in life *(estate)* might not be
revealed to the world until the moment is ripe for me.   44. *compass:* achieve.   46. *not:* not
even.   47. *behavior:* appearance and conduct, the "outward character" of line 51.
54. *become:* be suitable to.   55. *form . . . intent:* nature of my purpose (with *form* in the sense
of "shape" looking back to *disguise,* line 54).   56. *as an eunuch:* i.e. as a *castrato* or male
soprano singer; thus her high voice will not be incongruous with her male disguise. Actually,
Viola becomes his page.

That will allow me very worth his service.
What else may hap, to time I will commit,   60
Only shape thou thy silence to my wit.
Captain: Be you his eunuch, and your mute I'll be;
When my tongue blabs, then let mine eyes not see.
Viola: I thank thee. Lead me on.   *Exeunt.*

Scene III

Enter Sir Toby [Belch] *and* Maria.

Sir Toby: What a plague means my niece to take the death of her
brother thus? I am sure care's an enemy to life.
Maria: By my troth, Sir Toby, you must come in earlier a' nights.
Your cousin, my lady, takes great exceptions to your ill hours.
Sir Toby: Why, let her except before excepted.   5
Maria: Ay, but you must confine yourself within the modest limits
of order.
Sir Toby: Confine? I'll confine myself no finer than I am. These
clothes are good enough to drink in, and so be these boots too;
and they be not, let them hang themselves in their own straps.   10
Maria: That quaffing and drinking will undo you. I heard my lady
talk of it yesterday; and of a foolish knight that you brought in
one night here to be her wooer.
Sir Toby: Who, Sir Andrew Aguecheek?
Maria: Ay, he.   15
Sir Toby: He's as tall a man as any's in Illyria.
Maria: What's that to th' purpose?
Sir Toby: Why, he has three thousand ducats a year.
Maria: Ay, but he'll have but a year in all these ducats. He's a very
fool and a prodigal.   20
Sir Toby: Fie, that you'll say so! He plays o' th' viol-de-gamboys, and
speaks three or four languages word for word without book,
and hath all the good gifts of nature.
Maria: He hath indeed, almost natural; for besides that he's a
fool, he's a great quarreller; and but that he hath the gift of a 25

---

59. *allow . . . service:* cause me to be acknowledged as worthy to serve him. 61. *shape:*
fashion. *wit:* plan, device. 62. *mute:* i.e. silent servant (suggested by *eunuch*, both being
servants in the Turkish court).

I.iii. Location: Olivia's house. 3. *a':* of. 4. *cousin:* kinswoman. 5. *except before excepted:* A
quibble on the legal phrase *exceptis excipiendis* = with the exceptions aforesaid. Sir Toby
apparently means that Olivia's objections are an old story and that she is welcome to go on
making them. 6. *modest:* moderate. 7. *order:* orderly conduct. 8. *confine:* Quibbling on
the sense "dress." 10. *and:* if. 11. *undo you:* be the ruin of you. 14. *Aguecheek:*
Suggestive of a thin, pale face, like that of a man with ague. 16. *tall:* valiant, stalwart.
19. *he'll . . . ducats:* i.e. he'll run through his estate in a year (at the rate he's going). *very:* true,
utter. 21. *viol-de-gamboys:* viola da gamba ("leg-viol"), the bass of the viol family. 22. *without book:* by memory. 24. *almost natural:* almost like a "natural" or halfwit.

coward to allay the gust he hath in quarrelling, 'tis thought
among the prudent he would quickly have the gift of a grave.

Sir Toby: By this hand, they are scoundrels and substractors that say
so of him. Who are they?

Maria: They that add moreov'r, he's drunk nightly in your 30
company.

Sir Toby: With drinking healths to my niece. I'll drink to her as long
as there is a passage in my throat, and drink in Illyria. He's a
coward and a coystrill that will not drink to my niece till his
brains turn o' th' toe like a parish-top. What, wench! *Castiliano* 35
vulgo! for here comes Sir Andrew Agueface.

Enter Sir Andrew [Aguecheek].

Sir Andrew: Sir Toby Belch! How now, Sir Toby Belch?

Sir Toby: Sweet Sir Andrew!

Sir Andrew: Bless you, fair shrew.

Maria: And you too, sir.   40

Sir Toby: Accost, Sir Andrew, accost.

Sir Andrew: What's that?

Sir Toby: My niece's chambermaid.

[*Sir Andrew:*] Good Mistress Accost, I desire better acquaintance.

Maria: My name is Mary, sir.   45

Sir Andrew: Good Mistress Mary Accost—

Sir Toby: You mistake, knight. "Accost" is front her, board her, woo
her, assail her.

Sir Andrew: By my troth, I would not undertake her in this company.
Is that the meaning of "accost"?   50

Maria: Fare you well, gentlemen.

Sir Toby: And thou let part so, Sir Andrew, would thou mightst
never draw sword again.

Sir Andrew: And you part so, mistress, I would I might never draw
sword again. Fair lady, do you think you have fools in hand?   55

Maria: Sir, I have not you by th' hand.

---

26. *gust:* relish, gusto.   28. *substractors:* i.e. detractors.   34. *coystrill:* knave.   35. *parish-top:*
Parishes kept large tops for the amusement and exercise of their people in winter; they were
made to spin by means of whips.   35–36. *Castiliano vulgo:* Meaning uncertain; perhaps
Maria is urged to act with the proverbial gravity and decorum of the Castilians to impress Sir
Andrew.   36. *Agueface:* Perhaps a slip on Shakespeare's part which was later received into
the text as an intentional jest.   41. *Accost:* address (her). Sir Toby's gloss (lines 47–48)
includes the several suggestive connotations of the word.   43. *chambermaid:* lady in waiting.
In a household like Olivia's such a term does not imply low social position. Maria is clearly a
gentlewoman.   47. *board:* approach closely (as in boarding a ship in naval warfare).
48. *assail:* i.e. attack with offers of love. Both *board* and *assail* illustrate the common practice
of applying the language of war to amorous activity.   49. *undertake:* have to do (a word
frequently used in a bawdy sense).   52. *And . . . so:* i.e. if you let her go thus.   55. *have . . .*
hand: are dealing with fools.

Sir Andrew: Marry, but you shall have—and here's my hand.

Maria: Now, sir, thought is free. I pray you bring your hand to th' butt'ry-bar, and let it drink.

Sir Andrew: Wherefore, sweetheart? What's your metaphor? 60

Maria: It's dry, sir.

Sir Andrew: Why, I think so. I am not such an ass but I can keep my hand dry. But what's your jest?

Maria: A dry jest, sir.

Sir Andrew: Are you full of them? 65

Maria: Ay, sir, I have them at my fingers' ends. Marry, now I let go your hand, I am barren. *Exit Maria.*

Sir Toby: O knight, thou lack'st a cup of canary. When did I see thee so put down?

Sir Andrew: Never in your life I think, unless you see canary put me 70 down. Methinks sometimes I have no more wit than a Christian or an ordinary man has; but I am a great eater of beef, and I believe that does harm to my wit.

Sir Toby: No question.

Sir Andrew: And I thought that, I'd forswear it. I'll ride home to- 75 morrow, Sir Toby.

Sir Toby: Pourquoi, my dear knight?

Sir Andrew: What is *"pourquoi"*? Do, or not do? I would I had bestow'd that time in the tongues that I have in fencing, dancing, and bear-baiting. O had I but follow'd the arts! 80

Sir Toby: Then hadst thou had an excellent head of hair.

Sir Andrew: Why, would that have mended my hair?

Sir Toby: Past question, for thou seest it will not [curl by] nature.

Sir Andrew: But it becomes [me] well enough, does't not?

Sir Toby: Excellent, it hangs like flax on a distaff; and I hope to see a 85 huswife take thee between her legs, and spin it off.

Sir Andrew: Faith, I'll home to-morrow, Sir Toby. Your niece will not

---

57. *Marry:* indeed (a weakened oath, "by the Virgin Mary"). *you shall have:* An unfortunate choice of words. 58. *thought is free:* i.e. I may think what I like (proverbial); an unreassuring answer to his question in line 55. 59. *butt'ry-bar:* entrance to the buttery, the room where butts of air and wine were stored and from which drinks were dispensed. 61. *dry:* (1) thirsty; (2) lacking in moisture (a dry hand was associated with age and impotence). 62–63. *I . . . dry:* Alluding to a proverb to the effect that even a fool knows enough to come in out of the rain. 64. *dry jest:* (1) ironic joke; (2) barren old laughingstock. 66. *at . . . ends:* (1) in readiness; (2) held by my hand. 67. *barren:* i.e. destitute of dry jests. 68. *canary:* a sweet wine from the Canary Islands. 69. *put down:* confounded, overcome. 70–71. *put me down:* make me drunk. 73. *I . . . wit:* This reflects a current belief. 75. *forswear:* swear off. 77. *Pourquoi:* why. 79. *bestow'd:* employed. *tongues:* languages. 80. *follow'd the arts:* applied myself to learning. 82. *mended:* improved. 83. *it . . . nature:* Sir Toby's jest takes advantage of the phonetic similarity of *tongues* and *tongs* (= curling-tongs) and of a second meaning of *arts,* "artificial methods." 85. *distaff:* three-foot cleft staff used in spinning wool or flax. 86. *huswife . . . off:* With second meaning involving *huswife* (housewife) in the sense "hussy, whore" and a reference to loss of hair from venereal disease.

be seen, or if she be, it's four to one she'll none of me. The Count himself here hard by woos her.

Sir Toby: She'll none o' th' Count. She'll not match above her 90 degree, neither in estate, years, nor wit; I have heard her swear't. Tut, there's life in't, man.

Sir Andrew: I'll stay a month longer. I am a fellow o' th' strangest mind i' th' world; I delight in masques and revels sometimes altogether. 95

Sir Toby: Art thou good at these kickshawses, knight?

Sir Andrew: As any man in Illyria, whatsoever he be, under the degree of my betters, and yet I will not compare with an old man.

Sir Toby: What is thy excellence in a galliard, knight?

Sir Andrew: Faith, I can cut a caper. 100

Sir Toby: And I can cut the mutton to't.

Sir Andrew: And I think I have the back-trick simply as strong as any man in Illyria.

Sir Toby: Wherefore are these things hid? Wherefore have these gifts a curtain before 'em? Are they like to take dust, like Mis- 105 tress Mall's picture? Why dost thou not go to church in a gal- liard, and come home in a coranto? My very walk should be a jig. I would not so much as make water but in a sink-a-pace. What dost thou mean? Is it a world to hide virtues in? I did think by the excellent constitution of thy leg, it was form'd 110 under the star of a galliard.

Sir Andrew: Ay, 'tis strong; and it does indifferent well in a [dun-]- color'd stock. Shall we [set] about some revels?

Sir Toby: What shall we do else? were we not born under Taurus?

Sir Andrew: Taurus? That['s] sides and heart. 115

Sir Toby: No, sir, it is legs and thighs. Let me see thee caper. Ha, higher! Ha, ha, excellent! *Exeunt.*

---

89. *hard by:* near by. 90–91. *above her degree:* with her superior. 91. *estate:* social position. 96. *kickshawses:* elegant trifles (the singular *kickshaws* is an anglicization of French *quelque chose*). 97–98. *under . . . betters:* except for those that excel me. 98. *old man:* experienced man, expert (?). 99. *galliard:* a lively dance in triple time. 100. *cut a caper:* execute a leap. Sir Toby's reply quibbles on *caper* as a condiment often served with mutton. 102. *back-trick:* steps taken backwards in the galliard. 105. *like:* likely. *take:* gather. 105–106. *Mistress Mall's picture:* A topical allusion has been suspected, but the reference is probably general (*Mall* = Moll). Pictures were often protected from fading by curtains; see I.v.198. 107. *coranto:* a quick running dance. *should:* would. 108. *sink-a-pace:* cinquepace (French *cinque-pas*), a dance resembling the galliard. 109. *virtues:* talents, accomplishments. There is probably an allusion here to Jesus' parable of the talents (Matthew 25:14-30). 11. *star . . . galliard:* i.e. star favorable to dancing. Cf. Beatrice's "There was a star danc'd, and under that was I born" (*Much Ado*, II.i.335) 112. *indifferent:* moderately. 113. *stock:* stocking. 114. *Taurus:* the zodiacal sign that according to a few authorities controls "legs and thighs" (line 116), but neck and throat according to the majority. 115. *sides and heart:* Sir Andrew errs as usual; the sign for this region is Leo.

Scene IV

Enter Valentine, *and* Viola *in man's attire.*

Valentine: If the Duke continue these favors towards you, Cesario,
you are like to be much advanc'd; he hath known you but three
days, and already you are no stranger.
Viola: You either fear his humor or my negligence, that you call in
question the continuance of his love. Is he inconstant, sir, in 5
his favors?
Valentine: No, believe me.

Enter Duke, Curio, *and* Attendants.

Viola: I thank you. Here comes the Count.
Duke: Who saw Cesario, ho?
Viola: On your attendance, my lord, here.   10
Duke: Stand you awhile aloof. Cesario,
Thou know'st no less but all. I have unclasp'd
To thee the book even of my secret soul.
Therefore, good youth, address thy gait unto her,
Be not denied access, stand at her doors,   15
And tell them, there thy fixed foot shall grow
Till thou have audience.
Viola: Sure, my noble lord,
If she be so abandon'd to her sorrow
As it is spoke, she never will admit me.
Duke: Be clamorous, and leap all civil bounds,   20
Rather than make unprofited return.
Viola: Say I do speak with her, my lord, what then?
Duke: O then, unfold the passion of my love,
Surprise her with discourse of my dear faith;
It shall become thee well to act my woes: 25
She will attend it better in thy youth
Than in a nuntio's of more grave aspect.
Viola: I think not so, my lord.
Duke: Dear lad, believe it;
For they shall yet belie thy happy years,
That say thou art a man. Diana's lip   30
Is not more smooth and rubious; thy small pipe

I.iv. Location: The Duke's palace.   4. *his humor . . . negligence:* change of mood on his part
or neglect of duty on mine.   10. *On your attendance:* waiting to attend upon you.   11. *you:*
Addressed to all except Viola-Cesario.   14. *address thy gait:* go.   17. *audience:* a hearing (of
the Duke's love-suit).   20. *civil bounds:* i.e. bounds of good manners.   21. *unprofited:*
profitless.   24. *Surprise:* overpower. *dear:* loving, heartfelt.   26. *attend:* heed, give ear to.
27. *nuntio's:* messenger's.   29. *yet:* as yet.   31. *rubious:* ruby-red. *pipe:* throat.

Is as the maiden's organ, shrill and sound,
And all is semblative a woman's part.
I know thy constellation is right apt
For this affair. Some four or five attend him—   35
All, if you will; for I myself am best
When least in company. Prosper well in this,
And thou shalt live as freely as thy lord,
To call his fortunes thine
Viola: I'll do my best
To woo your lady. [*Aside.*] Yet a barful strife!   40
Whoe'er I woo, myself would be his wife.   *Exeunt.*

Scene V

Enter Maria *and* Clown [Feste].

Maria: Nay, either tell me where thou hast been, or I will not open
my lips so wide as a bristle may enter, in way of thy excuse. My
lady will hang thee for thy absence.

Clown: Let her hang me! He that is well hang'd in this world needs
to fear no colors.   5

Maria: Make that good.

Clown: He shall see none to fear.

Maria: A good lenten answer. I can tell thee where that saying
was born, of "I fear no colors."

Clown: Where, good Mistress Mary?   10

Maria: In the wars, and that may you be bold to say in your
foolery.

Clown: Well, God give them wisdom that have it; and those that are
fools, let them use their talents.

Maria: Yet you will be hang'd for being so long absent, or to be   15
turn'd away—is not that as good as a hanging to you?

Clown: Many a good hanging prevents a bad marriage; and for
turning away, let summer bear it out.

Maria: You are resolute then?

Clown: Not so, neither, but I am resolv'd on two points—   20

---

32. *shrill and sound:* high and clear (uncracked).   33. *semblative:* resembling. *part:* role (cf.
act, line 25).   34. *constellation:* i.e. nature (as determined by position of the stars at one's
birth).   38. *freely:* generously.   40. *barful strife:* i.e. an endeavor to which there is (for me) a
serious impediment.

I.v. Location: Olivia's house.   o.s.d. *Feste:* This name is known only from II.iv.11.   5. *fear no
colors:* Proverbial for "fear nothing" (*colors* = worldy deceptions). Feste puns on *collars* =
hangman's nooses.   8. *lenten:* meagre (in wit).   11. *In the wars:* Maria quibbles on *colors* in
the sense "military standards."   14. *talents:* (1) natural abilities; (2) talons (with a pun on *fools /
fowls*).   16. *turn'd away:* With a play on *turned off* = hanged.   17. *for:* as for.   18. *let . . . out:*
let the fact that summer is coming make it endurable.   20. *points:* Maria's rejoinder quibbles
on the sense "laces support the breeches or hose."

Maria: That if one break, the other will hold; or if both break, your gaskins fall.

Clown: Apt, in good faith, very apt. Well, go thy way, if Sir Toby would leave drinking, thou wert as witty a piece of Eve's flesh as any in Illyria. 25

Maria: Peace, you rogue, no more o' that. Here comes my lady. Make your excuse wisely, you were best. *[Exit.]*

Enter Lady Olivia *with* Malvolio [*and* Attendants].

Clown: Wit, and't be thy will, put me into good fooling! Those wits that think they have thee do very oft prove fools; and I that am sure I lack thee, may pass for a wise man. For what says Quina- 30 palus? "Better a witty fool than a foolish wit."—God bless thee, lady!

Olivia: Take the fool away.

Clown: Do you not hear, fellows? Take away the lady.

Olivia: Go to, y' are a dry fool; I'll no more of you. Besides, you 35 grow dishonest.

Clown: Two faults, madonna, that drink and good counsel will amend; for give the dry fool drink, then is the fool not dry; bid the dishonest man mend himself: if he mend, he is no longer dishonest; if he cannot, let the botcher mend him. Any thing 40 that's mended is but patch'd; virtue that transgresses is but patch'd with sin, and sin that amends is but patch'd with vir- tue. If that this simple syllogism will serve, so; if it will not, what remedy? As there is no true cuckold but calamity, so beauty's a flower. The lady bade take away the fool, therefore 45 I say again, take her away.

Olivia: Sir, I bade them take away you.

Clown: Misprision in the highest degree! Lady, *"Cucullus non facit monachum"*: that's as much to say as I wear not motley in my brain. Good madonna, give me leave to prove you a fool. 50

Olivia: Can you do it?

---

22. *gaskins:* breeches. 23. *go thy way:* run along. 24–25. *thou . . . Illyria:* i.e. you'd make him a good match. 28. *and't:* if it. *good fooling:* good form for jesting. 29. *thee:* i.e. wit. 30–31. *Quinapalus:* Feste's invention. 35. *Go to:* a conventional phrase of reproof. *dry:* dull, stale. 36. *dishonest:* wanton, wicked. 37. *madonna:* my lady (Italian *mia donna*). 39. *mend:* reform. 40. *let . . . him:* let him be mended by someone who can do the job (*botcher* = one who mends shoes or clothes, a cobbler or a tailor). 41–43. *virtue . . . virtue:* Feste warns that he, like all men, will be imperfect after he reforms, as he was before. *Patch'd* plays on Feste's motley, the conventional parti-colored dress for jesters. 43. *so:* well and good. 44. *what remedy:* i.e. there's nothing more I can say or do. 44–45. *As . . . flower:* A difficult passage. Dover Wilson explains: "Olivia has wedded calamity by taking her vow, and has proved herself a fool, since women are proverbially unfaithful to their weeds and beauty fades like the flower." 48. *Misprision:* mistaking one thing for another. 48–49. *Cucullus . . . monachum:* the cowl does not make the monk.

Clown: Dexteriously, good madonna.

Olivia: Make your proof.

Clown: I must catechize you for it, madonna. Good my mouse of
   virtue, answer me.   55

Olivia: Well, sir, for want of other idleness, I'll bide your proof.

Clown: Good madonna, why mourn'st thou?

Olivia: Good fool, for my brother's death.

Clown: I think his soul is in hell, madonna.

Olivia: I know his soul is in heaven, fool.   60

Clown: The more fool, madonna, to mourn for your brother's
   soul, being in heaven. Take away the fool, gentlemen.

Olivia: What think you of this fool, Malvolio? doth he not mend?

Malvolio: Yes, and shall do till the pangs of death shake him. Infirmity, that decays the wise, doth ever make the better fool.   65

Clown: God send you, sir, a speedy infirmity, for the better
   increasing your folly! Sir Toby will be sworn that I am no fox,
   but he will not pass his word for twopence that you are no fool.

Olivia: How say you to that, Malvolio?

Malvolio: I marvel your ladyship takes delight in such a barren ras- 70
   cal. I saw him put down the other day with an ordinary fool
   that has no more brain than a stone. Look you now, he's out of
   his guard already. Unless you laugh and minister occasion to
   him, he is gagg'd. I protest I take these wise men that crow so
   at these set kind of fools no better than the fools' zanies.   75

Olivia: O, you are sick of self-love, Malvolio, and taste with a distemper'd appetite. To be generous, guiltless, and of free disposition, is to take those things for bird-bolts that you deem
   cannon-bullets. There is no slander in an allow'd fool, though
   he do nothing but rail; nor no railing in a known discreet man,   80
   though he do nothing but reprove.

Clown: Now Mercury indue thee with leasing, for thou speak'st
   well of fools!

Enter Maria.

---

52. *Dexteriously:* dexterously (a true variant, not Feste's coinage).   54–55. *Good . . . virtue:*
my good virtuous mouse. The transpositions in *Good my* is common in forms of address (e.g.
good my lord).   56. *other idleness:* any other way of wasting time.   62. *being:* when it is.
63. *mend:* equivalent to "become a better fool"; Olivia uses it in the sense "become a more
amusing fool," Malvolio in the sense "become more and more foolish."   67. *fox:* crafty
fellow.   68. *pass:* pledge.   71. *with:* by.   72–73. *out . . . guard:* without a witty riposte (a
figure from fencing).   73. *minister occasion:* give opportunity, provide openings.   74. *protest:*
declare, avow.   75. *set kind:* artificial sort.   *fools' zanies:* fools' fools. A zany (a character in the
commedia dell'arte) was a clown's attendant who aped his master on stage.   76. *of:* with.   *self-
love:* The key to Malvolio's character.   76–77. *distemper'd:* unhealthy.   77. *free:* open.
78. *bird-bolts:* blunt-headed arrows for shooting birds. The passage has reference to the
proverb "A fool's bolt is soon shot."   79. *allow'd:* given license to speak his mind.
80. *known discreet:* of recognized judgment.   82. *Mercury:* god of guile and trickery.   *leasing:*
lying.

Maria: Madam, there is at the gate a young gentleman much desires to speak with you.   85

Olivia: From the Count Orsino, is it?

Maria: I know not, madam. 'Tis a fair young man, and well attended.

Olivia: Who of my people hold him in delay?

Maria: Sir Toby, madam, your kinsman.   90

Olivia: Fetch him off, I pray you, he speaks nothing but madman; fie on him! [*Exit Maria.*] Go you, Malvolio; if it be a suit from the Count, I am sick, or not at home—what you will, to dismiss it. (*Exit Malvolio.*) Now you see, sir, how your fooling grows old, and people dislike it.   95

Clown: Thou hast spoke for us, madonna, as if thy eldest son should be a fool; whose skull Jove cram with brains! for—here he comes—one of thy kin has a most weak *pia mater.*

Enter Sir Toby.

Olivia: By mine honor, half drunk. What is he at the gate, cousin?

Sir Toby: A gentleman.   100

Olivia: A gentleman? What gentleman?

Sir Toby: 'Tis a gentleman here—a plague o' these pickle-herring! How now, sot?

Clown: Good Sir Toby!

Olivia: Cousin, cousin, how have you come so early by this   105
lethargy?

Sir Toby: Lechery! I defy lechery. There's one at the gate.

Olivia: Ay, marry, what is he?

Sir Toby: Let him be the devil and he will, I care not; give me faith say I. Well, it's all one.   *Exit.*   110

Olivia: What's a drunken man like, fool?

Clown: Like a drown'd man, a fool, and a madman. One draught above heat makes him a fool, the second mads him, and a third drowns him.

Olivia: Go thou and seek the crowner, and let him sit o' my coz;   115
for he's in the third degree of drink, he's drown'd. Go look after him.

Clown: He is but mad yet, madonna, and the fool shall look to the madman.   *[Exit.]*

Enter Malvolio.

---

91. *madman:* i.e. mad talk.   95. *old:* i.e. stale (cf. line 35).   98. *pia mater:* brain (properly, the membrane enveloping the brain).   99. *What:* what sort of man.   102. *a plague . . . pickle-herring:* Sir Toby thus excuses a belch.   103. *sot:* fool.   106. *lethargy:* stupor. 109. *give me faith:* As protection in confrontation with the devil.   110. *it's all one:* no matter.   113. *above heat:* i.e. above the point of feeling a pleasant warmth.   115. *crowner:* coroner.   *sit . . . coz:* i.e. hold an inquest on my kinsman.

Malvolio: Madam, yond young fellow swears he will speak with you. 120
  I told him you were sick; he takes on him to understand so
  much, and therefore comes to speak with you. I told him you
  were asleep; he seems to have a foreknowledge of that too, and
  therefore comes to speak with you. What is to be said to him,
  lady? he's fortified against any denial. 125
Olivia: Tell him he shall not speak with me.
Malvolio: H'as been told so; and he says he'll stand at your door like a
  sheriff's post, and be the supporter to a bench, but he'll speak
  with you.
Olivia: What kind o' man is he? 130
Malvolio: Why, of mankind.
Olivia: What manner of man?
Malvolio: Of very ill manner: he'll speak with you, will you or no.
Olivia: Of what personage and years is he?
Malvolio: Not yet old enough for a man, nor young enough for a boy; 135
  as a squash is before 'tis a peascod, or a codling when 'tis
  almost an apple. 'Tis with him in standing water, between boy
  and man. He is very well-favor'd, and he speaks very shrewish-
  ly. One would think his mother's milk were scarce out of him.
Olivia: Let him approach. Call in my gentlewoman. 140
Malvolio: Gentlewoman, my lady calls. *Exit.*

Enter Maria.

Olivia: Give me my veil; come throw it o'er my face.
  We'll once more hear Orsino's embassy.

Enter [Viola].

Viola: The honorable lady of the house, which is she?
Olivia: Speak to me, I shall answer for her. Your will? 145
Viola: Most radiant, exquisite, and unmatchable beauty—I pray
  you tell me if this be the lady of the house, for I never saw her.
  I would be loath to cast away my speech; for besides that it is
  excellently well penn'd, I have taken great pains to con it.
  Good beauties, let me sustain no scorn; I am very comptible, 150
  even to the least sinister usage.
Olivia: Whence came you, sir?
Viola: I can say little more than I have studied, and that ques-

---

122. *therefore:* for that very reason. 127. *H'as:* he has. 128. *sheriff's post:* a decorative post
set up outside the sheriff's office. 131. *of mankind:* of the human race, i.e. just an ordinary
man. 134. *personage:* physical appearance. 136. *squash:* unripe pea pod. *peascod:* pea
pod. *codling:* unripe apple. 137. *in standing water:* i.e. at the turn of the tide. 138. *well-
favor'd:* handsome. 138–39. *shrewishly:* ill-temperedly, sharply. 148. *cast away:* waste (by
delivering it to the wrong person). 149. *con:* memorize. 150. *comptible:* sensitive,
susceptible. 151. *least sinister usage:* slightest uncivil treatment.

tion's out of my part. Good gentle one, give me modest assurance if you be the lady of the house, that I may proceed in my 155
speech.

Olivia: Are you a comedian?

Viola: No, my profound heart; and yet (by the very fangs of malice I swear) I am not that I play. Are you the lady of the house?

Olivia: If I do not usurp myself, I am. 160

Viola: Most certain, if you are she, you do usurp yourself; for what is yours to bestow is not yours to reserve. But this is from my commission; I will on with my speech in your praise, and then show you the heart of my message.

Olivia: Come to what is important in't. I forgive you the praise. 165

Viola: Alas, I took great pains to study it, and 'tis poetical.

Olivia: It is the more like to be feign'd, I pray you keep it in. I heard you were saucy at my gates, and allow'd your approach rather to wonder at you than to hear you. If you be not mad, be gone. If you have reason, be brief. 'Tis not that time of 170 moon with me to make one in so skipping a dialogue.

Maria: Will you hoist sail, sir? Here lies your way.

Viola: No, good swabber, I am to hull here a little longer. Some mollification for your giant, sweet lady. Tell me your mind—I am a messenger. 175

Olivia: Sure you have some hideous matter to deliver, when the courtesy of it is so fearful. Speak your office.

Viola: It alone concerns your ear. I bring no overture of war, no taxation of homage; I hold the olive in my hand; my words are as full of peace as matter. 180

Olivia: Yet you began rudely. What are you? What would you?

Viola: The rudeness that hath appear'd in me have I learn'd from my entertainment. What I am, and what I would, are as secret as maidenhead: to your ears, divinity; to any other's, profanation. 185

---

154. *out . . . part:* not in my lines. *modest:* befitting. 157. *comedian:* actor (continuing the theatrical metaphor of line 154). 158. *my profound heart:* my very wise lady (?). 160. *do . . . myself:* am not an impostor. 161. *usurp yourself:* possess yourself wrongfully (by refusing to give yourself to a husband). 162–63. *from my commission:* i.e. beyond my instructions. 165. *forgive you:* excuse you from. 167. *keep it in:* do not utter it. 169. *not mad:* i.e. not utterly mad (?). Some editors emend to *but mad* (Staunton conjecture). 170. *reason:* your wits. 170–71. *time of moon:* Certain phases of the moon were supposed to have a bad influence, particularly on lunacy. 171. *make one:* take part. *skipping:* flighty. 173. *swabber:* Continuing Maria's nautical metaphor. A swabber was a petty officer charged with keeping the decks clean. *hull:* drift with sails furled. 174. *mollification:* appeasement. *your giant:* Referring ironically to Maria, who is apparently diminutive (see II.v.11, III.ii.56), and alluding to giants as guardians of ladies in romantic tales. *Tell . . . mind:* Assigned by many editors (following Warburton) to Olivia. 176–77. *when . . . fearful:* i.e. when what should be the courteous manner of its introduction is so threatening (?). 177. *office:* business. 179. *taxation of homage:* demand for tribute. 180. *matter:* significant meaning. 183. *entertainment:* manner of reception. 184. *maidenhead:* virginity.

Olivia: Give us the place alone, we will hear this divinity. [*Exeunt Maria and Attendants.*] Now, sir, what is your text?

  Viola: Most sweet lady—

Olivia: A comfortable doctrine, and much may be said of it. Where lies your text?   190

  Viola: In Orsino's bosom.

Olivia: In his bosom? In what chapter of his bosom?

  Viola: To answer by the method, in the first of his heart.

Olivia: O, I have read it; it is heresy. Have you no more to say?

  Viola: Good madam, let me see your face.   195

Olivia: Have you any commission from your lord to negotiate with my face? You are now out of your text; but we will draw the curtain, and show you the picture. Look you, sir, such a one I was this present. [*Unveiling.*] Is't not well done?

  Viola: Excellently done, if God did all.   200

Olivia: 'Tis in grain, sir, 'twill endure wind and weather.

  Viola: 'Tis beauty truly blent, whose red and white Nature's own sweet and cunning hand laid on.
Lady, you are the cruell'st she alive
If you will lead these graces to the grave,   205
And leave the world no copy.

Olivia: O, sir, I will not be so hard-hearted. I will give out divers schedules of my beauty. It shall be inventoried, and every particle and utensil labell'd to my will: as *item,* two lips, indifferent red; *item,* two grey eyes, with lids to them; *item,* one neck, one 210 chin, and so forth. Were you sent hither to praise me?

  Viola: I see you what you are, you are too proud;
But if you were the devil, you are fair.
My lord and master loves you. O, such love
Could be but recompens'd, though you were crown'd   215
The nonpareil of beauty.

Olivia: How does he love me?

---

187. *what . . . text:* Picking up *divinity* (line 184), Olivia suggests that Viola-Cesario is going to proceed like a preacher in setting forth the text of a sermon. She continues this figure, with Viola's cooporation, through line 194.   189. *comfortable:* full of comfort.   193. *by the method:* according to the accepted form in beginning a sermon.   197. *out of:* wandering from.   198–99. *such . . . present:* Olivia begins as if displaying a portrait of herself painted at an earlier time, then ends with "at the present time" (*this present*).   200. *if . . . all:* if it is all natural (unaided by cosmetics).   201. *'Tis in grain:* it is fast-dyed, i.e. it won't wash off. 202. *blent:* blended.   203. *cunning:* skilled.   204–206. *Lady . . . copy:* Reminiscent of the argument in Shakespeare's first seventeen sonnets.   204. *she:* woman.   206. *copy:* i.e. a child inheriting your beauty. Olivia plays on the sense "transcript, record."   208. *schedules:* itemized lists, inventories.   208–209. *particle and utensil:* particular and item.   209. *labell'd:* attached. *item:* a term (= also) usually preceding each item after the first (signalled by *imprimis* = in the first place) in a list, but sometimes, as here, preceding the first as well. *indifferent:* moderately.   211. *praise:* With a quibble on "appraise."   213. *if:* even if. *the devil:* The supreme example of pride.   215. *Could . . . though:* could be no more than evenly repaid even though.   216. *nonpareil:* one that has no equal.

Viola: With adorations, fertile tears,
　　With groans that thunder love, with sighs of fire.
Olivia: Your lord does know my mind, I cannot love him,
　　Yet I suppose him virtuous, know him noble, 220
　　Of great estate, of fresh and stainless youth;
　　In voices well divulg'd, free, learn'd, and valiant,
　　And in dimension, and the shape of nature,
　　A gracious person. But yet I cannot love him.
　　He might have took his answer long ago. 225
Viola: If I did love you in my master's flame,
　　With such a suff'ring, such a deadly life,
　　In your denial I would find no sense,
　　I would not understand it.
Olivia: 　　　　　　　　Why, what would you?
Viola: Make me a willow cabin at your gate, 230
　　And call upon my soul within the house;
　　Write loyal cantons of contemned love,
　　And sing them loud even in the dead of night;
　　Hallow your name to the reverberate hills,
　　And make the babbling gossip of the air 235
　　Cry out "Olivia!" O, you should not rest
　　Between the elements of air and earth
　　But you should pity me!
Olivia: 　　　　　　　　You might do much.
　　What is your parentage?
Viola: Above my fortunes, yet my state is well: 240
　　I am a gentleman.
Olivia: 　　　　　　　Get you to your lord.
　　I cannot love him; let him send no more—
　　Unless (perchance) you come to me again
　　To tell me how he takes it. Fare you well.
　　I thank you for your pains. Spend this for me. 245
Viola: I am no fee'd post, lady; keep your purse;
　　My master, not myself, lacks recompense.
　　Love make his heart of flint that you shall love,
　　And let your fervor like my master's be
　　Plac'd in contempt! Farewell, fair cruelty. *Exit.* 250

---

217. *fertile:* abundant, ever-flowing. 221. *stainless:* unstained. 222. *In . . . divulg'd:* well reputed by general opinion *(voices).* 223. *dimension . . . nature:* form and physique. 224. *gracious person:* pleasing figure of a man. 226. *flame:* passion. 227. *deadly:* death-like. 230. *willow cabin:* hut of willow boughs. Willow was the symbol of unrequited love. 231. *my soul:* i.e. Olivia. 232. *cantons:* cantos, songs. *contemned:* despised, scornfully rejected. 234. *Hallow:* halloo, shout. *reverberate:* resounding. 235. *babbling . . . air:* echo. 237. *Between . . . earth:* i.e. anywhere on the face of the earth. 238. *But:* but that. 240. *state:* condition. 246. *fee'd post:* messenger who should be tipped. 248. *Love . . . love:* may love give a heart of flint to the man you fall in love with. 250. *cruelty:* cruel person.

Olivia: "What is your parentage?"
    "Above my fortunes, yet my state is well:
    I am a gentleman." I'll be sworn thou art;
    Thy tongue, thy face, thy limbs, actions, and spirit
    Do give thee fivefold blazon. Not too fast! soft, soft!   255
    Unless the master were the man. How now?
    Even so quickly may one catch the plague?
    Methinks I feel this youth's perfections
    With an invisible and subtle stealth
    To creep in at mine eyes. Well, let it be.   260
    What ho, Malvolio!

Enter Malvolio.

 Malvolio: Here, madam, at your service.
  Olivia: Run after that same peevish messenger,
    The [County's] man. He left this ring behind him,
    Would I or not. Tell him I'll none of it.
    Desire him not to flatter with his lord,   265
    Nor hold him up with hopes: I am not for him.
    If that the youth will come this way to-morrow,
    I'll give him reasons for't. Hie thee, Malvolio.
 Malvolio: Madam, I will.   *Exit.*
  Olivia: I do I know not what, and fear to find   270
    Mine eye too great a flatterer for my mind.
    Fate, show thy force: ourselves we do not owe;
    What is decreed must be; and be this so.   *[Exit.]*

ACT II

Scene I

Enter Antonio *and* Sebastian.

  Antonio: Will you stay no longer? nor will you not that I go with you?
  Sebastian: By your patience, no. My stars shine darkly over me. The
    malignancy of my fate might perhaps distemper yours; there-
    fore I shall crave of you your leave, that I may bear my evils

---

255. *give . . . blazon:* i.e. proclaim you a gentleman five times over as surely as if they were coats of arms. A blazon is a heraldic description of armorial bearings. *soft:* stay.
260. *creep . . .eyes:* It was a conventional idea that love entered through the eyes.   262. *peevish:* pettish, childish.   263. *County's:* Count's, i.e. Duke's.   265. *flatter with:* encourage.
268. *Hie:* hasten.   270–71. *fear . . .mind:* am afraid I shall find that my eyes (i.e. senses) have seduced my mind.   272. *owe:* own, control.

II.i. Location: The sea-coast.   2. *patience:* sufferance.   3. *malignancy:* virulent condition, (1) in its medical sense = deadly contagion, (2) in its astrological sense = evil stellar influence. *distemper:* infect.

alone. It were a bad recompense for your love, to lay any of 5
them on you.

Antonio: Let me yet know of you whither you are bound.

Sebastian: No, sooth, sir; my determinate voyage is mere extravagancy. But I perceive in you so excellent a touch of modesty,
that you will not extort from me what I am willing to keep in; 10
therefore it charges me in manners the rather to express
myself. You must know of me then, Antonio, my name is Sebastian, which I call'd Rodorigo; my father was that Sebastian of
Messaline, whom I know you have heard of. He left behind him
myself and a sister, both born in an hour. If the heavens had 15
been pleas'd, would we had so ended! But you, sir, alter'd that,
for some hour before you took me from the breach of the sea
was my sister drown'd.

Antonio: Alas the day!

Sebastian: A lady, sir, though it was said she much resembled me, was 20
yet of many accounted beautiful; but though I could not with
such estimable wonder overfar believe that, yet thus far I will
boldly publish her: she bore a mind that envy could not but call
fair. She is drown'd already, sir, with salt water, though I seem
to drown her remembrance again with more. 25

Antonio: Pardon me, sir, your bad entertainment.

Sebastian: O good Antonio, forgive me your trouble.

Antonio: If you will not murther me for my love, let me be your
servant.

Sebastian: If you will not undo what you have done, that is, kill him 30
whom you have recover'd, desire it not. Fare ye well at once;
my bosom is full of kindness, and I am yet so near the manners
of my mother, that upon the least occasion more mine eyes will
tell tales of me. I am bound to the Count Orsino's court.
Farewell. *Exit.* 35

Antonio: The gentleness of all the gods go with thee!
I have many enemies in Orsino's court,
Else would I very shortly see thee there.
But come what may, I do adore thee so
That danger shall seem sport, and I will go. *Exit.* 40

---

8. *sooth:* truly (shortened form of *in sooth*). *determinate:* intended. 8–9. *mere extravagancy:*
utter vagabondage. 9. *touch:* feeling. 10. *willing . . . in:* desirous of keeping secret.
11. *it charges me:* it is incumbent on me. *in manners:* by the requirements of good manners, in
courtesy. 14. *Messaline:* Not identified. 15. *in an hour:* within the same hour.
17. *breach . . . sea:* breaking waves, surf. 22. *such estimable wonder:* estimation reflecting so
much admiration. 23. *publish:* proclaim. *envy:* i.e. even malice. 26. *your bad entertainment:*
the humble hospitality I have offered you. 28. *murther me:* i.e. be the cause of my death.
31. *recover'd:* rescued. 32. *kindness:* natural feeling, i.e. a brother's grief. 32–33. *yet . . .
mother:* i.e. still so newly a man. Such apologies by men for womanish tears are numerous in
Shakespeare.

Scene II

Enter Viola *and* Malvolio *at several doors.*

> *Malvolio:* Were you not ev'n now with the Countess Olivia?
> *Viola:* Even now, sir; on a moderate pace I have since arriv'd but hither.
> *Malvolio:* She returns this ring to you, sir. You might have sav'd me my pains, to have taken it away yourself. She adds moreover, 5 that you should put your lord into a desperate assurance she will none of him. And one thing more, that you be never so hardy to come again in his affairs, unless it be to report your lord's taking of this. Receive it so.
> *Viola:* She took the ring of me, I'll none of it. 10
> *Malvolio:* Come, sir, you peevishly threw it to her, and her will is, it should be so return'd. If it be worth stooping for, there it lies, in your eye; if not, be it his that finds it. *Exit.*
> *Viola:* I left no ring with her. What means this lady?
> Fortune forbid my outside have not charm'd her! 15
> She made good view of me; indeed so much
> That methought her eyes had lost her tongue,
> For she did speak in starts distractedly.
> She loves me sure, the cunning of her passion
> Invites me in this churlish messenger. 20
> None of my lord's ring? Why, he sent her none.
> I am the man! If it be so, as 'tis,
> Poor lady, she were better love a dream.
> Disguise, I see thou art a wickedness
> Wherein the pregnant enemy does much. 25
> How easy is it for the proper-false
> In women's waxen hearts to set their forms!
> Alas, [our] frailty is the cause, not we,
> For such as we are made [of,] such we be.
> How will this fadge? My master loves her dearly, 30
> And I (poor monster) fond as much on him;
> And she (mistaken) seems to dote on me.
> What will become of this? As I am man,

II.ii. Location: A street. o.s.d. *several:* separate. 2. *on:* at. 5. *to have taken:* by taking. 6. *desperate assurance:* certainty without hope of change. 8. *hardy:* bold. 9. *taking of this:* i.e. reception of Olivia's message of rejection. 12. *so return'd:* i.e. thrown back at you. 13. *in your eye:* in plain view. 15. *forbid . . . not:* Modern idiom would omit *not.* 16. *made . . . me:* examined me closely. 17. *lost:* i.e. made her lose. 18. *in starts:* by fits and starts. *distract-edly:* disjointedly. 20. *in:* by means of, through. 25. *the pregnant enemy:* the devil, always ready (to take advantage of our evil for his own evil ends). 26. *proper-false:* i.e. men who are handsome but false. 27. *waxen:* i.e. impressionable. The image is from sealing. *set their forms:* stamp their images. 28. *frailty:* human weakness. 29. *such . . . of:* i.e. frail flesh. 30. *fadge:* work out, come off. 31. *monster:* i.e. being both a man and woman. *fond:* dote.

My state is desperate for my master's love;
As I am woman (now alas the day!),   35
What thriftless sighs shall poor Olivia breathe!
O time, thou must untangle this, not I,
It is too hard a knot for me t' untie.   *[Exit.]*

Scene III
Enter Sir Toby *and* Sir Andrew.

Sir Toby: Approach, Sir Andrew. Not to be a-bed after midnight is
    to be up betimes, and *"deliculo surgere,"* thou know'st—
Sir Andrew: Nay, by my troth, I know not; but I know, to be up late is to
    be up late.
Sir Toby: A false conclusion. I hate it as an unfill'd can. To be up 5
    after midnight and to go to bed then, is early; so that to go to
    bed after midnight is to go to bed betimes. Does not our lives
    consist of the four elements?
Sir Andrew: Faith, so they say, but I think it rather consists of eating
    and drinking.   10
Sir Toby: Th' art a scholar; let us therefore eat and drink. Marian, I
    say, a stoup of wine!

Enter Clown.

Sir Andrew: Here comes the fool, i' faith.
    Clown: How now, my hearts? Did you never see the picture of "we
        three"?   15
Sir Toby: Welcome, ass. Now let's have a catch.
Sir Andrew: By my troth, the fool has an excellent breast. I had rather
    than forty shillings I had such a leg, and so sweet a breath to
    sing, as the fool has. In sooth, thou wast in very gracious fool-
    ing last night, when thou spok'st of Pigrogromitus, of the 20
    Vapians passing the equinoctial of Queubus. 'Twas very good,
    i' faith. I sent thee sixpence for thy leman; hadst it?
    Clown: I did impeticos thy gratillity; for Malvolio's nose is no

---

36. *thriftless:* unprofitable.

II.iii. Location: Olivia's house. 2. *betimes:* in good season. *deliculo surgere:* From a well-
known Latin maxim, *Diluculo surgere saluberrimum est,* "to get up at dawn is very healthful."
3. *by my troth:* on my word. 5. *can:* tankard. 8. *four elements:* earth, water, air, and fire,
supposed the constituents of all created things. 11. *Th' art a scholar:* i.e. I'll accept your
authority on that point. 12. *stoup:* large drinking-cup. 14–15. *picture of "we three":* i.e. a
picture of two fools or ass-heads inscribed "we three," the viewer being the third. 16. *catch:*
round. 17. *breast:* i.e. breath, voice. 18. *leg:* graceful bow or obeisance (?) or fine leg for
dancing (?). Relevance uncertain. 19. *gracious:* delightful. 20–21. *Pigrogromitus . . .
Queubus:* Feste's mock scholarship. 21. *equinoctial:* equator. 22. *leman:* sweetheart.
23. *impeticos:* impetticoat, i.e. pocket (?) or, possibly, spend on a woman (?). *gratillity:* little tip
(invented diminutive of *gratuity*).

whipstock. My lady has a white hand, and the Mermidons are
no bottle-ale houses. 25

Sir Andrew: Excellent! Why, this is the best fooling, when all is done.
Now a song.

  Sir Toby: Come on, there is sixpence for you. Let's have a song.

Sir Andrew: There's a testril of me too. If one knight give a—

  Clown: Would you have a love-song, or a song of good life? 30

  Sir Toby: A love-song, a love-song.

Sir Andrew: Ay, ay. I care not for good life.

Clown sings.

> O mistress mine, where are you roaming?
> O, stay and hear, your true-love's coming,
>   That can sing both high and low. 35
> Trip no further, pretty sweeting;
> Journeys end in lovers meeting,
>   Every wise man's son doth know.

Sir Andrew: Excellent good, i' faith.

  Sir Toby: Good, good. 40

Clown [sings].

> What is love? 'Tis not hereafter;
> Present mirth hath present laughter;
>   What's to come is still unsure.
> In delay there lies no plenty,
> Then come kiss me sweet and twenty; 45
>   Youth's a stuff will not endure.

Sir Andrew: A mellifluous voice, as I am true knight.

  Sir Toby: A contagious breath.

Sir Andrew: Very sweet and contagious, i' faith.

  Sir Toby: To hear by the nose, it is dulcet in contagion. But shall we 50
make the welkin dance indeed? Shall we rouse the night-owl in
a catch that will draw three souls out of one weaver? Shall we
do that?

---

24. *whipstock:* whip handle, i.e. whip. The apparent meaning is that Malvolio's nose is stuck
into everything but is no real deterrent. *has . . . hand:* is gently bred (?) or has ladylike tastes
(?). *Mermidons:* Presumably a tavern, with a sign displaying Myrmidons (Achilles' troop).
25. *bottle-ale houses:* i.e. low-class taverns.   29. *testril:* sixpence (invented diminutive of *tester;*
Sir Andrew seems to be aping Feste, with absurd effect).   30. *of good life:* conducive to virtue,
edifying.   36. *sweeting:* sweet one.   37. *in lovers meeting:* when lovers meet.   43. *still:* ever,
always.   46. *sweet and twenty:* sweet and twenty more times sweet. *Twenty* is used as an
intensive.   48. *contagious breath:* (1) catchy song; (2) bad breath.   50. *To . . . contagion:* if we
could both hear and smell with our noses, we could call it sweetly stinking.   51. *welkin:*
heavens, i.e. heavenly bodies.   52. *draw three souls:* It was a conventional notion that music
could draw the soul from the body. These three singers will have three times that
effect. *weaver:* Weavers were supposedly given to singing psalms.

Sir Andrew: And you love me, let's do't. I am dog at a catch.

    Clown: By'r lady, sir, and some dogs will catch well.   55

Sir Andrew: Most certain. Let our catch be "Thou knave."

    Clown: "Hold thy peace, thou knave," knight? I shall be constrain'd in't to call thee knave, knight.

Sir Andrew: 'Tis not the first time I have constrain'd one to call me knave. Begin, fool. It begins, "Hold thy peace."   60

    Clown: I shall never begin if I hold my peace.

Sir Andrew: Good, i' faith. Come, begin.   *Catch sung.*

Enter Maria.

    Maria: What a caterwauling do you keep here! If my lady have not called up her steward Malvolio and bid him turn you out of doors, never trust me.   65

    Sir Toby: My lady's a Cataian, we are politicians, Malvolio's a Peg-a-Ramsey, and [*sings*] "Three merry men be we." Am I not consanguineous? Am I not of her blood? Tilly-vally! Lady! [*Sings.*] "There dwelt a man in Babylon, lady, lady."

    Clown: Beshrew me, the knight's in admirable fooling.   70

Sir Andrew: Ay, he does well enough if he be dispos'd, and so do I too. He does it with a better grace, but I do it more natural.

    Sir Toby: [*Sings.*] "O' the twelf day of December"—

    Maria: For the love o' God, peace!

Enter Malvolio.

    Malvolio: My masters, are you mad? Or what are you? Have you no 75 wit, manners, nor honesty, but to gabble like tinkers at this time of night? Do ye make an alehouse of my lady's house, that ye squeak out your coziers' catches without any mitigation or remorse of voice? Is there no respect of place, persons, nor time in you?   80

    Sir Toby: We did keep time, in our catches. Sneck up!

    Malvolio: Sir Toby, I must be round with you. My lady bade me tell

---

54. *dog:* i.e. very good, expert. 55. *By'r lady:* by Our Lady. 56. *"Thou knave.":* The words of the catch are: "Hold thy peace, thou knave; and I prithee hold thy peace." Each singer in turn thus calls another a knave. 59–60. *constrain'd . . . knave:* compelled someone to challenge me to a duel (but as usual Sir Andrew's form of words is unfortunate). 63. *keep:* keep up. 66. *Cataian:* Cathayan (i.e., Chinese); slang for one whose word cannot be trusted (?). *politicians:* schemers, intriguers. 66–67. *Peg-a-Ramsey:* A term of contempt, alluding to a character in a coarse ballad. 67. *"Three . . . we.":* A fragment of an old song. 68. *Tilly-vally! Lady!:* fiddle-faddle, lady indeed! Perhaps Sir Toby is annoyed by Maria's "my lady" instead of "your cousin" as elsewhere. 69. *There . . . lady:* The first line of the *Ballad of Constant Susanna,* with the song's "burden" (*lady, lady*) added. 70. *Beshrew me:* a mild oath (originally = curse me). 71. *dispos'd:* inclined to mirth. 72. *natural:* (1) naturally; (2) like a fool. 73. *"O' . . . December":* The opening line of another ballad (*twelf* = twelfth). 76. *honesty:* decorum, decency. 78. *coziers':* cobblers'. 78–79. *mitigation or remorse:* i.e. softening. 79 *respect:* regard. 81. *Sneck up:* go hang. 82. *round:* plain-spoken.

you, that though she harbors you as her kinsman, she's nothing
allied to your disorders. If you can separate yourself and your
misdemeanors, you are welcome to the house; if not, and it   85
would please you to take leave of her, she is very willing to bid
you farewell.

Sir Toby: [*Sings.*] "Farewell, dear heart, since I must needs be
          gone."

Maria: Nay, good Sir Toby.   90

Clown: [*Sings.*] "His eyes do show his days are almost done."

Malvolio: Is't even so?

Sir Toby: [*Sings.*] "But I will never die."

Clown: Sir Toby, there you lie.

Malvolio: This is much credit to you.   95

Sir Toby: [*Sings.*] "Shall I bid him go?"

Clown: [*Sings.*] "What and if you do?"

Sir Toby: [*Sings.*] "Shall I bid him go, and spare not?"

Clown: [*Sings.*] "O no, no, no, no, you dare not."

Sir Toby: [*To Clown.*] Out o' tune, sir! ye lie. *[To Malvolio.]* Art any   100
          more than a steward? Dost thou think because thou art virtu-
          ous there shall be no more cakes and ale?

Clown: Yes, by Saint Anne, and ginger shall be hot i' th' mouth too.

Sir Toby: Th' art i' th' right. Go, sir, rub your chain with crumbs. A
          stope of wine, Maria!   105

Malvolio: Mistress Mary, if you priz'd my lady's favor at any thing
          more than contempt, you would not give means for this uncivil
          rule. She shall know of it, by this hand.   *Exit.*

Maria: Go shake your ears.

Sir Andrew: 'Twere as good a deed as to drink when a man's a-hungry,   110
          to challenge him the field, and then to break promise with him,
          and make a fool of him.

Sir Toby: Do't, knight. I'll write thee a challenge, or I'll deliver thy
          indignation to him by word of mouth.

Maria: Sweet Sir Toby, be patient for to-night. Since the youth of   115
          the Count's was to-day with my lady, she is much out of quiet.
          For Monsieur Malvolio, let me alone with him. If I do not gull

---

83. *harbors you:* allows you residence.   83–84. *nothing allied:* no kin at all.   88–89. *Farewell
. . . gone:* From the ballad *Corydon's Farewell to Phillis.* The subsequent lines sung by Sir Toby
and Feste are slightly adapted to the occasion.   94. *Sir . . . Lie:* It seems likely that Feste sings
this line too.   97. *and if:* if.   100. *Out o' tune:* i.e. false (quibbling on *false* as in "a false
note," but with intended meaning "lying"); like the following *ye lie,* a reference to Feste's
"you dare not [bid him go]."   102. *cakes and ale:* Proverbial for revelry.   103. *ginger:* A
common addition to ale.   104. *rub . . . crumbs:* i.e. polish your steward's chain (a reminder of
his position as a servant).   105. *stope:* stoup.   107. *give means:* i.e. provide drinks.
108. *rule:* course of conduct.   109. *Go . . . ears:* Implying that Malvolio is an ass.
111. *field:* i.e. duelling-ground.   117. *let . . . him:* leave him to me. *gull:* befool.

him into an ayword, and make him a common recreation, do
not think I have wit enough to lie straight in my bed. I know I
can do it.   120

Sir Toby: Possess us, possess us, tell us something of him.

Maria: Marry, sir, sometimes he is a kind of puritan.

Sir Andrew: O, if I thought that, I'd beat him like a dog!

Sir Toby: What, for being a puritan? Thy exquisite reason, dear
knight?   125

Sir Andrew: I have no exquisite reason for't, but I have reason good
enough.

Maria: The dev'l a puritan that he is, or any thing constantly but a
time-pleaser, an affection'd ass, that cons state without book,
and utters it by great swarths; the best persuaded of himself, so 130
cramm'd (as he thinks) with excellencies, that it is his grounds
of faith that all that look on him love him; and on that vice in
him will my revenge find notable cause to work.

Sir Toby: What wilt thou do?

Maria: I will drop in his way some obscure epistles of love, where- 135
in by the color of his beard, the shape of his leg, the manner of
his gait, the expressure of his eye, forehead, and complexion,
he shall find himself most feelingly personated. I can write very
like my lady your niece; on a forgotten matter we can hardly
make distinction of our hands.   140

Sir Toby: Excellent, I smell a device.

Sir Andrew: I have't in my nose too.

Sir Toby: He shall think by the letters that thou wilt drop that they
come from my niece, and that she's in love with him.

Maria: My purpose is indeed a horse of that color.   145

Sir Andrew: And your horse now would make him an ass.

Maria: Ass, I doubt not.

Sir Andrew: O, 'twill be admirable!

Maria: Sport royal, I warrant you. I know my physic will work

---

118. *an ayword:* a byword or proverb (*ay* = ever). The F1 form is here retained, since
Shakespeare seems to have been the first to use the phrase and its etymology is doubtful.
Editors (following Rowe) usually read *a nayword,* a form that occurs twice in *The Merry Wives
of Windsor,* where, however, the sense required seems to be "password." *common recreation:*
general laughingstock.   121. *Possess:* tell, inform.   122. *puritan:* i.e. one who professes to be
extremely precise in morals; frequently (as Malvolio has just shown himself to be), one who is
complacent about his own moral superiority and highly censorious of the lapses or fancied
lapses of others. Apparently Sir Andrew in line 124 takes Maria to be charging him with
being a member of the Puritan party in the Anglican Church, and Maria in line 128 rejects
the idea.   124. *exquisite:* ingenious.   128. *constantly:* consistently, steadily.   129. *time-
pleaser:* self-seeking flatterer. *affection'd:* full of affectation. *cons . . . book:* commits to memory
the speech and behavior of the great.   130. *utters:* (1) repeats; (2) discharges. *swarths:*
swaths, i.e. masses. *the best . . . himself:* having the highest opinion of himself.
131–32. *grounds of faith:* firm belief.   137. *expressure:* expressive quality.   138. *feelingly
personated:* exactly represented.   140. *hands:* handwriting.   146. *Ass:* A quibble on *as* / *ass*
(= Sir Andrew).   149. *physic:* medicine.

with him. I will plant you two, and let the fool make a third, 150
where he shall find the letter; observe his construction of it.
For this night, to bed, and dream on the event. Farewell. *Exit.*

Sir Toby: Good night, Penthesilea.

Sir Andrew: Before me, she's a good wench.

Sir Toby: She's a beagle true-bred, and one that adores me. What o' 155
that?

Sir Andrew: I was ador'd once too.

Sir Toby: Let's to bed, knight. Thou hadst need send for more
money.

Sir Andrew: If I cannot recover your niece, I am a foul way out. 160

Sir Toby: Send for money, knight; if thou hast her not i' th' end, call
me cut.

Sir Andrew: If I do not, never trust me, take it how you will.

Sir Toby: Come, come, I'll go burn some sack, 'tis too late to go to
bed now. Come, knight, come, knight. *Exeunt.* 165

Scene IV

Enter Duke, Viola, Curio, *and others.*

Duke: Give me some music. Now good morrow, friends.
Now, good Cesario, but that piece of song,
That old and antique song we heard last night;
Methought it did relieve my passion much,
More than light airs and recollected terms 5
Of these most brisk and giddy-paced times.
Come, but one verse.

Curio: He is not here, so please your lordship, that should sing it.

Duke: Who was it?

Curio: Feste the jester, my lord, a fool that the Lady Olivia's 10
father took much delight in. He is about the house.

Duke: Seek him out, and play the tune the while.
[Exit Curio.] Music plays.
Come hither, boy. If ever thou shalt love,
In the sweet pangs of it remember me;

---

150. *fool . . . third:* Actually it is not Feste but Fabian who makes the third (see II.v). Maria's
words imply that Feste is no longer present. He last speaks at line 103; perhaps Malvolio
waves him out as he leaves at line 108.   151. *construction:* interpretation.   152. *event:*
outcome.   153. *Penthesilea:* queen of the Amazons (an ironical allusion to Maria's size).
154. *Before me:* i.e. on my soul (formed on the pattern of such oaths as *before God* and *before
heaven*).   155. *beagle:* small hunting-dog.   157. *I . . . too:* A line that suddenly, as elsewhere
in Shakespeare, reveals the human being as a hitherto ridiculous figure of fun.   160. *recover:*
win (with a suggestion of making good on his expenditure, as in *recover a debt*). *foul way out:*
wretchedly out of pocket.   162. *cut:* a horse with a docked tail.   164. *burn some sack:* prepare
some warm sack (Spanish wine) and sugar.

II.iv. Location: The Duke's palace.   2. *but:* just (let us have).   3. *antique:* quaint.   5. *light:*
trivial (?) or quick in tempo (?). *recollected:* Meaning uncertain; variously explained as
"refined," "studied," "farfetched," and so on.

For such as I am, all true lovers are,   15
Unstaid and skittish in all motions else,
Save in the constant image of the creature
That is belov'd. How dost thou like this tune?
Viola: It gives a very echo to the seat
Where Love is thron'd.
Duke: Thou dost speak masterly.   20
My life upon't, young though thou art, thine eye
Hath stay'd upon some favor that it loves.
Hath it not, boy?
Viola: A little, by your favor.
Duke: What kind of woman is't?
Viola: Of your complexion.
Duke: She is not worth thee then. What years, i' faith?   25
Viola: About your years, my lord.
Duke: Too old, by heaven. Let still the woman take
An elder than herself, so wears she to him;
So sways she level in her husband's heart.
For, boy, however we do praise ourselves,   30
Our fancies are more giddy and unfirm,
More longing, wavering, sooner lost and worn,
Than women's are.
Viola: I think it well, my lord.
Duke: Then let thy love be younger than thyself,
Or thy affection cannot hold the bent;   35
For women are as roses, whose fair flow'r
Being once display'd, doth fall that very hour.
Viola: And so they are; alas, that they are so!
To die, even when they to perfection grow!

Enter Curio *and* Clown.

Duke: O fellow, come, the song we had last night.   40
Mark it, Cesario, it is old and plain.
The spinsters and the knitters in the sun,
And the free maids that weave their thread with bones,

---

16. *Unstaid and skittish:* giddy and fickle. *motions else:* other thoughts and feelings.
18–19. *gives . . . thron'd:* i.e. it expresses what the heart feels.   20. *masterly:* like one who has
had experience (of love).   22. *stay'd upon:* attended (?) or lingered upon (?). *favor:* face.
23. *by your favor:* if you please (a polite phrase), but with obvious quibbles on "near your
face" and "thanks to you."   24. *complexion:* appearance, good looks.   27. *still:* ever,
always.   28. *wears:* adapts herself (like a garment adjusting itself to the wearer).   29. *sways:*
(1) holds sway; (2) swings. *level:* in perfect balance.   31. *fancies:* loves. *unfirm:* fickle.
32. *worn:* spent.   33. *think it well:* think so too.   35. *hold the bent:* maintain its fullness and
intensity (as a bow is kept bent to its full extent under high tension).   37. *display'd:* fully
opened.   39. *even when:* just when.   40. *fellow:* here, a familiar term of address to one of
lower station (without derogatory implication).   42. *spinsters:* spinning-women.   43. *free:*
carefree. *weave . . . bones:* make bone or thread lace with bone bobbins.

Do use to chant it. It is silly sooth,
And dallies with the innocence of love,   45
Like the old age.
Clown: Are you ready, sir?
Duke: Ay, prithee sing.   *Music.*

THE SONG

[Clown]: Come away, come away, death,
             And in sad cypress let me be laid.   50
         [Fly] away, [fly] away, breath,
             I am slain by a fair cruel maid.
         My shroud of white, stuck all with yew,
                 O, prepare it!
         My part of death, no one so true   55
             Did share it.

         Not a flower, not a flower sweet
             On my black coffin let there be strown.
         Not a friend, not a friend greet
             My poor corpse, where my bones shall be thrown.   60
         A thousand thousand sighs to save,
                 Lay me, O, where
         Sad true lover never find my grave,
                 To weep there.

Duke: There's for thy pains.   65
Clown: No pains, sir, I take pleasure in singing, sir.
Duke: I'll pay thy pleasure then.
Clown: Truly, sir, and pleasure will be paid, one time or another.
Duke: Give me now leave to leave thee.
Clown: Now the melancholy god protect thee, and the tailor make 70
thy doublet of changeable taffeta, for thy mind is a very
opal. I would have men of such constancy put to sea, that
their business might be every thing and their intent every
where, for that's it that always makes a good voyage of nothing.
Farewell.   *Exit.* 75

---

44. *Do use:* are accustomed. *silly sooth:* simple truth. 45. *dallies:* plays lovingly. 46. *Like
. . . age:* as in the good old days.   49. *Come away:* come hither.   50. *cypress:* i.e. a coffin of
cypress wood, or a bier covered with cypress boughs. Cypress trees, like yews (line 53), were
often planted in graveyards and were emblematic of death. 55–56. *My . . . it:* i.e. I had to
enact alone my role of dying, unsupported by one of equal constancy. 68. *pleasure . . .
another:* i.e. indulgence exacts payment sooner or later.   69. *leave to leave:* permission to take
leave of.   70. *the melancholy god:* i.e. the god to whom you pay your devotion. Feste clearly
implies that Orsino's melancholy is a self-indulgence.   71. *doublet:* close-fitting
jacket. *changeable taffeta:* taffeta (thin silk) woven of threads of different colors, so that its
color shifts with movement.   72–75. *I . . . nothing:* Intended ironically; men of such
changeable mind arrive at no destination and bring nothing home.

Duke: Let all the rest give place.

[Curio and Attendants retire.]

Once more, Cesario,
Get thee to yond same sovereign cruelty.
Tell her, my love, more noble than the world,
Prizes not quantity of dirty lands;
The parts that fortune hath bestow'd upon her,   80
Tell her, I hold as giddily as fortune;
But 'tis that miracle and queen of gems
That nature pranks her in attracts my soul.

Viola: But if she cannot love you, sir?

Duke: [I] cannot be so answer'd.

Viola: Sooth, but you must.   85
Say that some lady, as perhaps there is,
Hath for your love as great a pang of heart
As you have for Olivia. You cannot love her;
You tell her so. Must she not then be answer'd?

Duke: There is no woman's sides   90
Can bide the beating of so strong a passion
As love doth give my heart; no woman's heart
So big, to hold so much; they lack retention.
Alas, their love may be call'd appetite,
No motion of the liver, but the palate,   95
That suffer surfeit, cloyment, and revolt,
But mine is all as hungry as the sea,
And can digest as much. Make no compare
Between that love a woman can bear me
And that I owe Olivia.

Viola: Ay, but I know—   100

Duke: What dost thou know?

Viola: Too well what love women to men may owe:
In faith, they are as true of heart as we.
My father had a daughter lov'd a man
As it might be perhaps, were I a woman,   105
I should your lordship.

Duke: And what's her history?

---

76. *give place:* withdraw.   77. *sovereign cruelty:* supremely cruel person, "cruell'st she alive"
(I.v.204).   80. *parts:* worldly goods.   81. *hold . . . fortune:* esteem as lightly as fortune does
(which could sweep them away in a moment).   82. *miracle . . . gems:* i.e. her beauty.
83. *nature:* As contrasted with fortune. *pranks:* adorns.   87. *for your love:* for love of you.
89. *be answer'd:* accept your answer.   90–91. *There . . . Olivia:* True to his changeable
nature, the Duke now contradicts the opinion he voiced in lines 30–31.   91. *bide:* endure.
93. *retention:* power of retaining.   95. *No . . . liver:* no impulse of the liver, i.e. not the
passion of true love. *the palate:* i.e. a motion of the palate, a sensual appetite.   96. *suffer:*
experience. *cloyment:* satiety. *revolt:* revulsion of appetite. Cf. lines 94–98 with Orsino's
opening speech in I.i; there is considerable irony in what he here attributes to women's love
and what to his own.   99. *owe:* bear.

Viola: A blank, my lord; she never told her love,
　　　But let concealment like a worm i' th' bud
　　　Feed on her damask cheek; she pin'd in thought,
　　　And with a green and yellow melancholy   110
　　　She sate like Patience on a monument,
　　　Smiling at grief. Was not this love indeed?
　　　We men may say more, swear more, but indeed
　　　Our shows are more than will; for still we prove
　　　Much in our vows, but little in our love.   115
Duke: But died thy sister of her love, my boy?
Viola: I am all the daughters of my father's house.
　　　And all the brothers too—and yet I know not.
　　　Sir, shall I to this lady?
Duke:　　　　　　　　　Ay, that's the theme,
　　　To her in haste; give her this jewel; say   120
　　　My love can give no place, bide no denay.   *Exeunt.*

Scene V

Enter Sir Toby, Sir Andrew, *and* Fabian.

Sir Toby: Come thy ways, Signior Fabian.
Fabian: Nay, I'll come. If I lose a scruple of this sport, let me be
　　boil'd to death with melancholy.
Sir Toby: Wouldst thou not be glad to have the niggardly rascally
　　sheep-biter come by some notable shame?   5
Fabian: I would exult, man. You know he brought me out o' favor
　　with my lady about a bear-baiting here.
Sir Toby: To anger him we'll have the bear again, and we will fool
　　him black and blue, shall we not, Sir Andrew?
Sir Andrew: And we do not, it is pity of our lives.   10

Enter Maria.

Sir Toby: Here comes the little villain. How now, my metal of India?
Maria: Get ye all three into the box-tree; Malvolio's coming down
　　this walk. He has been yonder i' the sun practicing behavior to

---

109. *damask:* pink and white, like a damask rose.　110. *green and yellow:* pale and sallow.
111. *sate:* sat. *like . . . monument:* like a sculptured figure of Patience on a tomb.　114. *more
than will:* greater than our desire. *still:* ever, always.　121. *give . . . denay:* yield no ground
and endure no denial.
II.v. Location: Olivia's garden.　1. *Come they ways:* come along.　2. *Nay:* Implying that Sir
Toby need not urge. *scruple:* tiniest bit.　3. *boil'd . . . melancholy:* With a pun on *boil/bile*
(pronounced alike). Black bile was the cause of melancholy.　5. *sheep-biter:* i.e. malicious
sneak.　7. *bear-baiting:* A type of entertainment that Malvolio would naturally disapprove of
(with some reason).　8. *fool:* mock.　9. *black and blue:* i.e. thoroughly (used figuratively with
fool instead of the usual *beat*).　10. *it . . . lives:* "life won't be worth living" (Kittredge).
11. *metal of India:* i.e. gold; here = girl worth her weight in gold.　13. *behavior:* courtly
manners.

his own shadow this half hour. Observe him, for the love of
mockery; for I know this letter will make a contemplative idiot 15
of him. Close, in the name of jesting! [*The men hide themselves.*] Lie thou there [*throws down a letter*]; for here comes the
trout that must be caught with tickling.   *Exit.*

Enter Malvolio.

Malvolio: 'Tis but fortune, all is fortune. Maria once told me she did
    affect me, and I have heard herself come thus near, that should 20
    she fancy, it should be one of my complexion. Besides, she uses
    me with a more exalted respect than any one else that follows
    her. What should I think on't?
  Sir Toby: Here's an overweening rogue!
    Fabian: O, peace! Contemplation makes a rare turkey-cock of 25
    him. How he jets under his advanc'd plumes!
Sir Andrew: 'Slight, I could so beat the rogue!
  Sir Toby: Peace, I say!
  Malvolio: To be Count Malvolio!
  Sir Toby: Ah, rogue!   30
Sir Andrew: Pistol him, pistol him!
  Sir Toby: Peace, peace!
  Malvolio: There is example for't: The lady of the Strachy married the
    yeoman of the wardrobe.
Sir Andrew: Fie on him, Jezebel!   35
    Fabian: O, peace! now he's deeply in. Look how imagination blows
    him.
  Malvolio: Having been three months married to her, sitting in my
    state—
  Sir Toby: O, for a stone-bow, to hit him in the eye!   40
  Malvolio: Calling my officers about me, in my branch'd velvet gown;
    having come from a day-bed, where I have left Olivia
    sleeping—
  Sir Toby: Fire and brimstone!
    Fabian: O, peace, peace!   45

15–16. *make . . . him:* make him sit and daydream like an idiot staring into space.   16. *Close:*
keep hidden.   18. *tickling:* (1) stroking under the gills (trout were actually taken by this
means); (2) flattery.   19. *she:* i.e. Olivia.   19–20. *did affect:* was fond of.   21. *fancy:* fall in
love.   22–23. *follows her:* is in her service.   24. *overweening:* arrogant, presumptuous.
25. *Contemplation:* Looking back to lines 15–16.   26. *jets:* struts. *advanc'd:* raised.
27. *'Slight:* by God's light.   33. *example:* precedent. *Lady . . . Strachy:* Not certainly identified.   34. *yeoman . . . wardrobe:* servant in charge of clothing and linen in a nobleman's
household.   35. *Jezebel:* the cruel and arrogant wife of Ahab, king of Israel (the application
of the word to Malvolio is typical of Sir Andrew).   36–37. *blows him:* puffs him up.
39. *state:* chair of state (as Count).   40. *stone-bow:* crossbow that shot stones instead of
arrows.   41. *officers:* household staff. *branch'd:* figured with a pattern of leaves or flowers.
42. *day-bed:* couch.

Malvolio: And then to have the humor of state; and after a demure
    travel of regard—telling them I know my place as I would they
    should do theirs—to ask for my kinsman Toby—

  Sir Toby: Bolts and shackles!

    Fabian: O, peace, peace, peace! Now, now.   50

Malvolio: Seven of my people, with an obedient start, make out for
    him. I frown the while, and perchance wind up my watch, or
    play with my—some rich jewel. Toby approaches; curtsies
    there to me—

  Sir Toby: Shall this fellow live?   55

    Fabian: Though our silence be drawn from us with cars, yet peace.

Malvolio: I extend my hand to him thus, quenching my familiar smile
    with an austere regard of control—

  Sir Toby: And does not Toby take you a blow o' the lips then?

Malvolio: Saying, "Cousin Toby, my fortunes, having cast me on your 60
    niece, give me this prerogative of speech"—

  Sir Toby: What, what?

Malvolio: "You must amend your drunkenness."

  Sir Toby: Out, scab!

    Fabian: Nay, patience, or we break the sinews of our plot!   65

Malvolio: "Besides, you waste the treasure of your time with a foolish
    knight"—

Sir Andrew: That's me, I warrant you.

  Malvolio: "One Sir Andrew"—

Sir Andrew: I knew 'twas I, for many do call me fool.   70

  Malvolio: What employment have we here?   *[Taking up the letter.]*

    Fabian: Now is the woodcock near the gin.

  Sir Toby: O, peace, and the spirit of humors intimate reading aloud
    to him!

  Malvolio: By my life, this is my lady's hand. These be her very c's, her 75
    u's, and her t's, and thus makes she her great P's. It is, in con-
    tempt of question, her hand.

---

46. *have . . . state:* i.e. adopt the manner of the great.   46–47. *after . . . regard:* having gravely
allowed my eyes to travel from one to another.   47. *telling:* indicating to.   51. *with . . . start:*
in obedient haste. *make out:* sally forth.   53. *my— . . . jewel:* Malvolio is on the verge of
saying "my chain" (his insignia of office as steward) but catches himself in time.   56. *with
cars.* The general meaning is clearly "by main force." *Cars* is sometimes explained as meaning
"carts" (with citation of III.ii.50, "oxen and wain-ropes cannot hale them together"), but
Shakespeare elsewhere uses *car* only in the sense *chariot,* usually with reference to the
sun-god's chariot; Johnson therefore proposed emending to *carts.* Possibly a reference to
some form of torture is intended; the line would then mean "it is torture to remain silent" and
would present a witty reversal of the usual purpose of torture, which is to draw speech from
the silent. The emendation most often adopted, however, is Hanmer's *by th' ears,* which
implies reluctance or resistance on the part of what is drawn.   57. *familiar:* friendly.
58. *austere . . . control:* look of stern authority.   59. *take:* give.   64. *scab:* scurvy
fellow. *employment:* business.   72. *woodcock:* A proverbially stupid bird, easily caught. *gin:*
trap, snare (short form of *engine* = contrivance).   73. *humors:* caprice.   75–76. *c's . . .t's:*
Malvolio has unwittingly spelled out *cut,* slang for the female pudenda. The "joke" is
compounded by *great P's,* line 76.   76. *great:* capital.   76–77. *in . . . question:* beyond
dispute.

Sir Andrew: Her c's, her u's, and her t's: why that?

Malvolio: [*Reads.*] "To the unknown belov'd, this, and my good
    wishes":—her very phrases! By your leave, wax. Soft! And the 80
    impressure her Lucrece, with which she uses to seal. 'Tis my
    lady. To whom should this be?

Fabian: This wins him, liver and all.

Malvolio: [*Reads.*]
    "Jove knows I love.
      But who?   85
    Lips, do not move;
    No man must know."
    "No man must know." What follows? The numbers alter'd!
    "No man must know." If this should be thee, Malvolio?

Sir Toby: Marry, hand thee, brock!   90

Malvolio: [*Reads.*]
    "I may command where I adore,
      But silence, like a Lucrece knife,
    With bloodless stroke my heart doth gore;
      M. O. A. I. doth sway my life."

Fabian: A fustian riddle!   95

Sir Toby: Excellent wench, say I.

Malvolio: "M. O. A. I. doth sway my life." Nay, but first let me see,
    let me see, let me see.

Fabian: What dish a' poison has she dress'd him!

Sir Toby: And with what wing the [staniel] checks at it!   100

Malvolio: "I may command where I adore." Why, she may com-
    mand me: I serve her, she is my lady. Why, this is evident to any
    formal capacity, there is no obstruction in this. And the end—
    what should that alphabetical position portend? If I could
    make that resemble something in me! Softly! M. O. A. I.— 105

Sir Toby: O ay, make up that. He is now at a cold scent.

Fabian: Sowter will cry upon't for all this, though it be as rank as a
    fox.

Malvolio: M—Malvolio; M—why, that begins my name.

---

80. *By your leave:* with your permission (addressed to the seal as he breaks it). *Soft:* not so fast,
wait a moment.   81. *impressure:* device impressed on the wax. *Lucrece:* i.e. a figure of the
virtuous Roman matron Lucretia, who stabbed herself after her rape by Tarquin—an emblem
of chastity. *uses:* is accustomed.   83. *wins:* conquers. *liver:* i.e. his love.   88. *The numbers
alter'd:* the metre changed.   90. *brock:* badger, i.e. stinker.   95. *fustian:* worthless, nonsensical.   99. *What:* what a. *dress'd:* prepared.   100. *wing:* flight, i.e. speed. *staniel:* inferior
hawk. *checks:* is diverted from its proper quarry by an inferior prey, i.e. is led astray.
103. *formal capacity:* normal understanding. *Obstruction:* obstacle, difficulty.   104. *alphabetical position:* arrangement of letters.   106. *O, ay:* Sir Toby seems to echo two of the letters that
Malvolio has just read (*ay* is spelled *I,* as usual in F1). *make up that:* piece that together, work
that out. *cold scent:* faint, hence difficult, trail.   107. *Sowter:* a hound's name; literally,
cobbler, i.e. bungler. *cry upon't:* give tongue as if he had found the scent.
107–08. *though . . . fox:* though the deception is as easy to smell out as a stinking (*rank*) fox.

Fabian: Did not I say he would work it out? The cur is excellent at 110
faults.

Malvolio: M—but then there is no consonancy in the sequel that suffers under probation: A should follow, but O does.

Fabian: And O shall end, I hope.

Sir Toby: Ay, or I'll cudgel him, and make him cry O! 115

Malvolio: And then I comes behind.

Fabian: Ay, and you had any eye behind you, you might see more detraction at your heels than fortunes before you.

Malvolio: M. O. A. I. This simulation is not as the former; and yet, to crush this a little, it would bow to me, for every one of these let- 120 ters are in my name. Soft, here follows prose.

[*Reads.*] "If this fall into thy hand, revolve. In my stars I am above thee, but be not afraid of greatness. Some are [born] great, some [achieve] greatness, and some have greatness thrust upon 'em. Thy Fates open their hands, let thy blood and 125 spirit embrace them, and to inure thyself to what thou art like to be, cast thy humble slough and appear fresh. Be opposite with a kinsman, surly with servants; let thy tongue tang arguments of state; put thyself into the trick of singularity. She thus advises thee that sighs for thee. Remember who commended 130 thy yellow stockings, and wish'd to see thee ever cross-garter'd: I say, remember. Go to, thou art made if thou desir'st to be so; if not, let me see thee a steward still, the fellow of servants, and not worthy to touch Fortune's fingers. Farewell. She that would alter services with thee, 135

                   The Fortunate-Unhappy."

Daylight and champian discovers not more. This is open. I will be proud, I will read politic authors, I will baffle Sir Toby, I will wash off gross acquaintance, I will be point-devise the very

---

110–11. *excellent at faults:* not put off the trail by breaks in the scent (with ironic implication that he is very likely to pick up a false scent). 112. *consonancy:* agreement, correspondence. *sequel:* i.e. following letter(s). 112–13. *suffers:* endures, stands up. *probation:* testing, examination. 113. *O:* i.e. a hangman's noose. 118. *detraction:* defamation. 119. *simulation:* representation, disguised meaning. 120. *crush:* force. *bow to:* (1) yield its meaning to; (2) point to, indicate. 122. *revolve:* consider. *stars:* fortunates, i.e. rank and wealth. 125. *open their hands:* i.e. are ready to give. 125–26. *let . . . them:* i.e. welcome their gifts with the whole force of your being. *Blood and spirit* = either "body and soul" or "passion and mettle." 126. *inure:* accustom. 127. *cast . . . slough:* cast off your lowly demeanor. The figure is of a snake sloughing off its old skin. *opposite:* quarrelsome. 128. *tang:* sound loud with. 128–29. *arguments of state:* political topics, matters of statecraft. *trick:* custom, habit. 129. *put . . . singularity:* cultivate individuality, adopt eccentric habits. 131. *cross-garter'd:* wearing the garters crossed at the back so that in front they pass both above and below the knee. 133. *still:* always (so also in line 151). 135. *alter services:* exchange duties, i.e. make you master and myself your servant. 137. *champian:* champaign, open country. *discovers:* reveals. *open:* evident, obvious. 138. *proud:* lofty. *politic authors:* writers on political science. *baffle:* treat with disdain. 139. *wash of:* rid myself of. *gross:* low. *point-devise:* correctly in every detail, precisely.

man. I do not now fool myself, to let imagination jade me; for 140
every reason excites to this, that my lady loves me. She did
commend my yellow stockings of late, she did praise my leg
being cross-garter'd, and in this she manifests herself to my
love, and with a kind of injunction drives me to these habits of
her liking. I thank my stars, I am happy. I will be strange, 145
stout, in yellow stockings, and cross-garter'd, even with the
swiftness of putting on. Jove and my stars be prais'd! Here is
yet a postscript.

[*Reads.*] "Thou canst not choose but know who I am. If thou
entertain'st my love, let it appear in thy smiling; thy smiles 150
become thee well. Therefore in my presence still smile, dear
my sweet, I prithee."

Jove, I thank thee. I will smile, I will do every thing that thou
wilt have me.   *Exit.*

Fabian: I will not give my part of this sport for a pension of thou- 155
sands to be paid from the Sophy.

Sir Toby: I could marry this wench for this device—

Sir Andrew: So could I too.

Sir Toby: And ask no other dowry with her but such another jest.

Enter Maria.

Sir Andrew: Nor I neither.   160

Fabian: Here comes my noble gull-catcher.

Sir Toby: Wilt thou set thy foot o' my neck?

Sir Andrew: Or o' mine either?

Sir Toby: Shall I play me freedom at tray-trip, and become thy
bond-slave?   165

Sir Andrew: I' faith, or I either?

Sir Toby: Why, thou hast put him in such a dream, that when the
image of it leaves him he must run mad.

Maria: Nay, but say true, does it work upon him?

Sir Toby: Like aqua-vitae with a midwife.   170

Maria: If you will then see the fruits of the sport, mark his first
approach before my lady. He will come to her in yellow stockings, and 'tis a color she abhors, and cross-garter'd, a fashion
she detests; and he will smile upon her, which will now be so

---

140. *I . . . me:* I am not foolishly allowing imagination to trick me.   141. *every . . . this:* every
piece of evidence urges this conclusion.   145. *happy:* blessed by fortune. *strange:* distant,
reserved.   146. *stout:* haughty.   147, 153. *Jove.* Here and elsewhere (III.iv.67, 73, and
particularly IV. ii.10), possibly a replacement for an original *God,* to comply with the
anti-profanity statute of 1606.   150. *entertain'st:* acceptest.   156. *Sophy:* the Shah of
Persia.   161. *gull-catcher:* tricker of credulous fools.   162. *set . . . neck:* i.e. as a symbol of
conquest.   164. *play:* gamble. *tray-trip:* a game of dice in which the best throw was three *(tray
= trey).*   170. *aqua-vitae:* brandy or other spirits.

unsuitable to her disposition, being addicted to a melancholy as   175
she is, that it cannot but turn him into a notable contempt. If
you will see it, follow me.

Sir Toby: To the gates of Tartar, thou most excellent devil of wit!

Sir Andrew: I'll make one too.   *Exeunt.*

ACT III

Scene I

Enter Viola, *and* Clown [*with a tabor*].

> *Viola:*   'Save thee, friend, and thy music! Dost thou live by thy
> tabor?
>
> *Clown:*   No, sir, I live by the church.
>
> *Viola:*   Art thou a churchman?
>
> *Clown:*   No such matter, sir. I do live by the church; for I do live at   5
> my house, and my house doth stand by the church.
>
> *Viola:*   So thou mayst say the [king] lies by a beggar, if a beggar
> dwells near him; or the church stands by thy tabor, if thy tabor
> stand by the church.
>
> *Clown:*   You have said, sir. To see this age! A sentence is but a   10
> chev'ril glove to a good wit. How quickly the wrong side may be
> turn'd outward!
>
> *Viola:*   Nay, that's certain. They that dally nicely with words may
> quickly make them wanton.
>
> *Clown:*   I would therefore my sister had had no name, sir.   15
>
> *Viola:*   Why, man?
>
> *Clown:*   Why, sir, her name's a word, and to dally with that word
> might make my sister wanton. But indeed, words are very ras-
> cals since bonds disgrac'd them.
>
> *Viola:*   Thy reason, man?   20
>
> *Clown:*   Troth, sir, I can yield you none without words, and words
> are grown so false, I am loath to prove reason with them.
>
> *Viola:*   I warrant thou art a merry fellow, and car'st for nothing.

---

178. *Tartar:* Tartarus, hell.   179. *make one:* go along.

III.i. Location: Olivia's garden.   o.s.d. *tabor:* small drum.   1. *'Save:* God save. *music:* Feste
probably has also a pipe (played with the help of one hand while the tabor was beaten with
the other).   3. *live by:* earn a living by. Feste quibbles on "dwell near."   4. *churchman:* man
in holy orders.   7. *So . . . beggar:* in the same fashion you could say what would be taken to
mean "the king lies with a beggar." (Similarly, *stands by*, line 8, could be taken to mean "is
supported by.")   10. *A sentence:* any utterance.   11. *chev'ril:* kidskin (soft and pliable).
13. *dally nicely:* play sophistically.   13–14. *make them wanton:* allow them to get out of hand.
17. *dally:* toy amorously.   18. *wanton:* unchaste. Dover Wilson suggests a pun on *want one*,
i.e. lack a (good) name.   19. *bonds disgrac'd them:* Quibbling on *bonds* as (1) sworn statements
(in place of a man's plain word or promise); (2) fetters (betokening criminality).   22. *reason:*
"the reasonableness of any proposition" (Kittredge).   23. *car'st for nothing:* dost not worry
about anything. Feste then proceeds to play on other meanings of *care*.

Clown: Not so, sir, I do care for something; but in my conscience, sir, I do not care for you. If that be to care for nothing, sir, I would it would make you invisible. 25

Viola: Art not thou the Lady Olivia's fool?

Clown: No, indeed, sir, the Lady Olivia has no folly. She will keep no fool, sir, till she be married, and fools are as like husbands as pilchers are to herrings, the husband's the bigger. I am indeed 30 not her fool, but her corrupter of words.

Viola: I saw thee late at the Count Orsino's.

Clown: Foolery, sir, does walk about the orb like the sun, it shines every where. I would be sorry, sir, but the fool should be as oft with your master as with my mistress. I think I saw your wisdom 35 there.

Viola: Nay, and thou pass upon me, I'll no more with thee. Hold, there's expenses for thee.

Clown: Now Jove, in his next commodity of hair, send thee a beard! 40

Viola: By my troth, I'll tell thee, I am almost sick for one—[*aside*] though I would not have it grow on my chin. Is thy lady within?

Clown: Would not a pair of these have bred, sir?

Viola: Yes, being kept together, and put to use.

Clown: I would play Lord Pandarus of Phrygia, sir, to bring a 45 Cressida to this Troilus.

Viola: I understand you, sir. 'Tis well begg'd.

Clown: The matter, I hope, is not great, sir—begging but a beggar: Cressida was a beggar. My lady is within, sir. I will conster to them whence you come; who you are, and what you would, 50 are out of my welkin—I might say "element," but the word is overworn. *Exit.*

Viola: This fellow is wise enough to play the fool,

---

24. *in my conscience:* to let you into a secret. 25–26. *I . . . invisible.* Viola ought to be invisible, by Feste's process of thought, since if he cares for something and does not care for Viola, then Viola is nothing. 30. *pilchers:* pilchards, small fish resembling herring. 32. *late:* recently. 33. *orb:* earth, as the centre about which the sun courses *(walks)* in the Ptolemaic system. 34. *but:* unless. 35. *your wisdom:* An ironic form of address on the model of *your honor* or *your worship.* 37. *pass upon me:* fence with me (using sharp words as your weapon). *Hold:* take this. 38. *expenses:* something for you to spend. 39–40. *Jove . . . beard.* Feste follows the usual practice of one who received alms by invoking God's blessing on the giver. 39. *commodity:* consignment, lot. 41. *one:* a beard, i.e. a man (Orsino). 42. *my chin:* The stress belongs on *my.* 43. *pair of these:* i.e. two coins. *bred:* multiplied. 44. *put to use:* loaned at interest. 45. *Pandarus:* Cressida's uncle, and the go-between in her love affair with Troilus. 48. *The matter:* i.e. the amount begged. 49. *Cressida . . . beggar.* Alluding to the tradition stemming from Henryson's *Testament of Cresseid* that Cressida became a leper and a beggar. *conster:* construe, explain. 51. *welkin, element. Element* in the sense "sky" is synonymous with *welkin,* but it can have other senses as well, as of course it has in the phrase *out of my element* (= here "outside the range of my information"). Feste gives a final example of how words can be made "wanton." 53. *play the fool.* Feste, like Touchstone in *As You Like It,* is a shrewd, sharp person who makes his living by playing the fool; he is not, like the Fool in *King Lear,* a "natural" or halfwit.

And to do that well craves a kind of wit.
He must observe their mood on whom he jests,   55
The quality of persons, and the time;
And like the haggard, check at every feather
That comes before his eye. This is a practice
As full of labor as a wise man's art;
For folly that he wisely shows is fit,   60
But wise [men], folly-fall'n, quite taint their wit.

Enter Sir Toby *and* Sir Andrew.

   Sir Toby: 'Save you, gentleman.
     Viola: And you, sir.
Sir Andrew: Dieu vous garde, monsieur.
     Viola: Et vous aussi; votre serviteur.   65
Sir Andrew: I hope, sir, you are, and I am yours.
   Sir Toby: Will you encounter the house? My niece is desirous you
     should enter, if you trade be to her.
     Viola: I am bound to your niece, sir; I mean she is the list of my
     voyage.   70
   Sir Toby: Taste your legs, sir, put them to motion.
     Viola: My legs do better understand me, sir, than I understand
     what you mean by bidding me taste my legs.
   Sir Toby: I mean, to go, sir, to enter.
     Viola: I will answer you with gait and entrance—but we are   75
     prevented.

Enter Olivia *and* Gentlewoman.

     Most excellent accomplish'd lady, the heavens rain odors on
     you!
Sir Andrew: That youth's a rare courtier—"rain odors," well.
     Viola: My matter hath no voice, lady, but to your own most preg-   80
     nant and vouchsafed ear.
Sir Andrew: "Odors," "pregnant," and "vouchsafed"; I'll get 'em all
     three all ready.

---

54. *wit:* intelligence.   55. *their mood:* the mood of those.   56. *quality:* character.
57. *haggard:* a hawk taken in maturity and hence difficult to train. *check:* See the note on
II.v.100.   58. *practice:* exercise of skill.   59. *art:* skill.   60. *wisely shows:* assumes judiciously. *fit:* proper.   61. *folly-fall'n:* lapsed into folly. *taint:* discredit.   64. *Dieu . . .
monsieur:* God keep you, sir.   65. *Et . . . serviteur:* And you too; your servant.   67. *encounter:*
Pedantry for "enter."   68. *trade:* business. The word suggests to Viola a trading voyage.
69. *I . . . to:* i.e. my destination is. *list:* limit, utmost point.   71. *Taste:* i.e. make trial of,
test.   73. *understand me:* stand under me, hold me up.   75. *gait and entrance:* going and
entering (answering to go and enter in line 74); with a play on "gate and entrance."
76. *prevented:* anticipated.   80. *hath no voice:* cannot be spoken.   82. *pregnant and vouchsafed:* receptive and graciously bestowed.   83. *all ready:* i.e. all ready for use in future
conversation.

Olivia: Let the garden door be shut, and leave me to my hearing.
[*Exeunt all but Olivia and Viola.*] Give me your hand, sir.   85
   Viola: My duty, madam, and most humble service.
Olivia: What is your name?
   Viola: Cesario is your servant's name, fair princess.
Olivia: My servant, sir. 'Twas never merry world
   Since lowly feigning was call'd compliment.   90
   Y' are servant to the Count Orsino, youth.
   Viola: And he is yours, and his must needs be yours:
   Your servant's servant is your servant, madam.
Olivia: For him, I think not on him. For his thoughts,
   Would they were blanks, rather than fill'd with me.   95
   Viola: Madam, I come to whet your gentle thoughts
   On his behalf.
Olivia: O, by your leave, I pray you:
   I bade you never speak again of him;
   But would you undertake another suit,
   I had rather hear you to solicit that   100
   Than music from the spheres.
   Viola: Dear lady—
Olivia: Give me leave, beseech you. I did send,
   After the last enchantment you did here,
   A ring in chase of you; so did I abuse
   Myself, my servant, and I fear me you.   105
   Under your hard construction must I sit,
   To force that on you in a shameful cunning
   Which you knew none of yours. What might you think?
   Have you not set mine honor at the stake,
   And baited it with all th' unmuzzled thoughts   110
   That tyrannous heart can think? To one of your receiving
   Enough is shown; a cypress, not a bosom,
   Hides my heart. So let me hear you speak.
   Viola: I pity you.
Olivia: That's a degree to love.

---

84. *hearing:* audience, interview.   89. *'Twas . . . world:* life has never been as pleasant
(proverbial).   90. *lowly feigning:* pretending humility, i.e. calling oneself "your servant."   *was
call'd:* was first called, began to be called.   94. *For: as for.*   98. *by your leave:* a polite phrase
of interruption: "please say no more" (so also *Give me leave,* line 103).   101. *music . . .
spheres:* A reference to the notion that the revolution of the spheres in which the heavenly
bodies were fixed produced ravishing music, inaudible to human ears.   103. *enchantment you
did:* charm you worked, spell you cast.   104. *abuse:* dishonor.   106. *construction:* interpretation.   107. *To force:* for forcing.   109. *at the stake.* The figure in 109–10 is from bear-baiting; Olivia's honor is set upon by Cesario's thoughts as the bear is set upon by dogs to tear
and worry it.   111. *tyrannous:* cruel.   *receiving:* power to apprehend.   112. *cypress:* a nearly
transparent black fabric.   114. *degree:* step; *grize* in line 115 is a synonym.

Viola: No, not a grize; for 'tis a vulgar proof   115
    That very oft we pity enemies.
Olivia: Why then methinks 'tis time to smile again.
    O world, how apt the poor are to be proud!
    If one should be a prey, how much the better
    To fall before the lion than the wolf!   *Clock strikes.* 120
    The clock upbraids me with the waste of time.
    Be not afraid, good youth, I will not have you,
    And yet when wit and youth is come to harvest,
    Your wife is like to reap a proper man.
    There lies your way, due west.
Viola: Then westward-ho!   125
    Grace and good disposition attend your ladyship!
    You'll nothing, madam, to my lord by me?
Olivia: Stay!
    I prithee tell me what thou think'st of me.
Viola: That you do think you are not what you are.   130
Olivia: If I think so, I think the same of you.
Viola: Then think you right: I am not what I am.
Olivia: I would you were as I would have you be.
Viola: Would it be better, madam, than I am?
    I wish it might, for now I am your fool.   135
Olivia: [*Aside.*] O, what a deal of scorn looks beautiful
    In the contempt and anger of his lip!
    A murd'rous guilt shows not itself more soon
    Than love that would seem hid: love's night is noon.—
    Cesario, by the roses of the spring,   140
    By maidhood, honor, truth, and every thing,
    I love thee so, that maugre all thy pride,
    Nor wit nor reason can my passion hide.
    Do not extort thy reasons from this clause,
    For that I woo, thou therefore hast no cause;   145

---

115. *'tis . . . proof:* i.e. everybody knows from experience.   117. *then:* i.e. if you are my enemy. *smile:* i.e. abandon love and its pangs.   118. *apt:* ready.   *119. should be:* were to be. 120. *lion . . . wolf:* i.e. Orsino . . . Cesario.   122. *have you:* have you for a husband. 123. *proper:* worthy.   124. *due west:* i.e. where the sun disappears from sight; a clear dismissal.   125. *westward-ho:* the cry of watermen on the Thames when they were about to put off westward.   126. *good disposition:* a tranquil mind.   130. *That . . . what you are:* i.e. that you are mistaken in supposing you are in love with a man, not a woman.   131. *If . . . you:* Presumably she interprets his remark as meaning that she is mad but doesn't know it. 135. *now . . . fool:* i.e. you have put me into a foolish position (in a sense that she cannot guess).   136. *deal:* large amount.   139. *love's . . . noon:* love's attempted secrecy is like broad daylight to everybody else.   142. *maugre:* in spite of.   143. *Nor:* neither.   144–45. *Do . . . cause:* do not wrest reasons for not loving me from this proposition that because I woo, you have no cause to accept my love.

But rather reason thus with reason fetter:
Love sought is good, but given unsought is better.
Viola: By innocence I swear, and by my youth,
I have one heart, one bosom, and one truth,
And that no woman has, nor never none   150
Shall mistress be of it, save I alone.
And so adieu, good madam, never more
Will I my master's tears to you deplore.
Olivia: Yet come again; for thou perhaps mayst move
That heart which now abhors, to like his love.   *Exeunt.* 155

Scene II
Enter Sir Toby, Sir Andrew, *and* Fabian.

Sir Andrew: No, faith, I'll not stay a jot longer.
  Sir Toby: Thy reason, dear venom, give thy reason.
  Fabian: You must needs yield your reason, Sir Andrew.
Sir Andrew: Marry, I saw your niece do more favors to the Count's
    servingman than ever she bestow'd upon me. I saw't i' th' 5
    orchard.
  Sir Toby: Did she see [thee] the while, old boy? tell me that.
Sir Andrew: As plain as I see you now.
  Fabian: This was a great argument of love in her toward you.
Sir Andrew: 'Slight! will you make an ass o' me?   10
  Fabian: I will prove it legitimate, sir, upon the oaths of judgment
    and reason.
  Sir Toby: And they have been grand-jurymen since before Noah was
    a sailor.
  Fabian: She did show favor to the youth in your sight only to exas- 15
    perate you, to awake your dormouse valor, to put fire in your
    heart, and brimstone in your liver. You should then have
    accosted her, and with some excellent jests, fire-new from the
    mint, you should have bang'd the youth into dumbness. This
    was look'd for at your hand, and this was balk'd. The double 20
    gilt of this opportunity you let time wash off, and you are now
    sail'd into the north of my lady's opinion, where you will hang

---

146. *rather . . . fetter:* instead bind together these two reasons (to accept my love).
147. *Love . . . better:* Olivia will receive a love that she sued for, which is good; Cesario will
receive a love for which he did not have to sue, which is better.   153. *deplore:* lament,
describe.

III.ii. Location: Olivia's house.   2. *venom:* venomous one.   6. *orchard:* garden.   9. *argument:* evidence.   11. *oaths:* i.e. sworn testimony.   13. *grand-jurymen:* i.e. experts in
evaluating evidence.   16. *dormouse:* i.e. sleepy.   18. *fire-new:* brand-new.   20. *balk'd:*
neglected, let slip.   20–21. *double gilt:* double plating with gold; perhaps referring to Sir
Andrew's double opportunity to prove his love and valor.   22. *north:* i.e. cold regions (of disfavor).

like an icicle on a Dutchman's beard, unless you do redeem it by
some laudable attempt either of valor or policy.

Sir Andrew: And't be any way, it must be with valor, for policy I hate. I 25
had as lief be a Brownist as a politician.

Sir Toby: Why then build me thy fortunes upon the basis of valor.
Challenge me the Count's youth to fight with him, hurt him in
eleven places—my niece shall take note of it, and assure thyself,
there is no love-broker in the world can more prevail in man's 30
commendation with woman than report of valor.

Fabian: There is no way but this, Sir Andrew.

Sir Andrew: Will either of you bear me a challenge to him?

Sir Toby: Go, write it in a martial hand, be curst and brief. It is no
matter how witty, so it be eloquent and full of invention. Taunt 35
him with the license of ink. If thou thou'st him some thrice, it
shall not be amiss; and as many lies as will lie in thy sheet of
paper, although the sheet were big enough for the bed of Ware
in England, set 'em down. Go about it. Let there be gall
enough in thy ink, though thou write with a goose-pen, no mat- 40
ter. About it.

Sir Andrew: Where shall I find you?

Sir Toby: We'll call thee at the cubiculo. Go.　　　*Exit Sir Andrew.*

Fabian: This is a dear manikin to you, Sir Toby.

Sir Toby: I have been dear to him, lad, some two thousand strong, or 45
so.

Fabian: We shall have a rare letter from him; but you'll not
deliver't?

Sir Toby: Never trust me then; and by all means stir on the youth to
an answer. I think oxen and wain-ropes cannot hale them 50
together. For Andrew, if he were open'd and you find so much
blood in his liver as will clog the foot of a flea, I'll eat the rest of
th' anatomy.

---

23. *icicle . . . beard:* Perhaps an allusion to William Barentz, a Dutchman who travelled to the
Arctic in 1596–97 and wrote an account of his experiences which was entered in the
Stationers' Register in June 1598 (earliest extant edition, 1609).　25. *policy:* cunning,
strategy.　26. *Brownist:* a follower of Robert Browne, founder of the Congregationalist
sect. *politician:* contriver, schemer.　27. *build me:* build (a colloquialism); cf. *Challenge me,*
line 28.　30. *love-broker:* go-between in love matters.　31. *report:* reputation.　34. *curst:*
bad-tempered, insulting.　35. *so:* provided that, so long as. *invention:* imagination. (Sir Toby
is being intentionally contradictory in lines 34–35).　36. *with . . . ink:* i.e. with the freedom
that writing affords (arising in this case from its comparative safety). *If . . . him: Thou* instead
of *you* was the form of address used to friends and to social inferiors, hence an insult to a
comparative stranger.　38. *bed of Ware:* This bed (which may be seen in the Victoria and
Albert Museum, London) is eleven feet square.　39. *gall:* (1) an ingredient of ink; (2)
acrimony.　40. *goose-pen:* quill pen made from a goose feather (with an implication that the
letter will be couched in foolish terms).　43. *call thee:* call for you. *cubiculo:* little chamber.
44. *dear . . . you:* puppet dear to you (referring to Sir Toby's manipulation of him).　45. *dear:*
expensive.　49. *then:* i.e. if I don't.　50. *wain-ropes:* wagon ropes. *hale:* drag.　52. *blood . . .
liver:* Cowards were thought to have white (bloodless) livers.　53. *anatomy:* a medical term
meaning either "body" or "skeleton." In view of Sir Andrew's thinness, Sir Toby may intend
the latter.

Fabian: And his opposite, the youth, bears in his visage no great presage of cruelty.   55

Enter Maria.

Sir Toby: Look where the youngest wren of [nine] comes.
Maria: If you desire the spleen, and will laugh yourselves into stitches, follow me. Yond gull Malvolio is turn'd heathen, a very renegado; for there is no Christian that means to be sav'd by believing rightly can ever believe such impossible passages of   60
grossness. He's in yellow stockings.
Sir Toby: And cross-garter'd?
Maria: Most villainously; like a pedant that keeps a school i' th' church. I have dogg'd him like his murtherer. He does obey every point of the letter that I dropp'd to betray him. He does   65
smile his face into more lines than is in the new map, with the augmentation of the Indies; you have not seen such a thing as 'tis. I can hardly forbear hurling things at him. I know my lady will strike him. If she do, he'll smile, and take't for a great favor.   70
Sir Toby: Come bring us, bring us where he is.   *Exeunt omnes.*

Scene III

Enter Sebastian *and* Antonio.

Sebastian: I would not by my will have troubled you,
But since you make your pleasure of your pains,
I will no further chide you.
Antonio: I could not stay behind you. My desire
(More sharp than filed steel) did spur me forth,   5
And not all love to see you (though so much
As might have drawn one to a longer voyage)
But jealousy what might befall your travel,
Being skilless in these parts; which to a stranger,
Unguided and unfriended, often prove   10
Rough and unhospitable. My willing love,

---

54. *opposite:* adversary.   56. *youngest . . . nine:* i.e. the very smallest of wrens.   57. *the spleen:* extreme mirth. The spleen was regarded as the source of immoderate or uncontrollable laughter.   58. *gull:* dupe.   59. *renegado:* regegade, i.e. renouncer of his religion.
60–61. *such . . . grossness:* such obviously impossible expressions (as the letter contains).
63. *pedant:* schoolmaster (the point of the reference to his holding a school in the church is unexplained).   65. *betray:* expose, ensnare.   66–67. *lines . . . Indies.* Probably referring to a map prepared by Edward Wright, Richard Hakluyt, and John Davis, and printed in 1600. It was the first English map based on Mercator's projection, and therefore showed North America *(the Indies)* as proportionately larger than in earlier maps. It is crisscrossed by numerous rhumb lines.

III.iii. Location: A street.   6. *all:* entirely, only.   8. *jealousy:* suspicion, anxiety.   9. *skilless in:* unfamiliar with.

The rather by these arguments of fear,
Set forth in your pursuit.
Sebastian: My kind Antonio,
I can no other answer make but thanks,
And thanks; and ever oft good turns   15
Are shuffled off with such uncurrent pay;
But were my worth as is my conscience firm,
You should find better dealing. What's to do?
Shall we go see the reliques of this town?
Antonio: To-morrow, sir; best first go see your lodging.   20
Sebastian: I am not weary, and 'tis long to night;
I pray you let us satisfy our eyes
With the memorials and the things of fame
That do renown this city.
Antonio: Would you'ld pardon me.
I do not without danger walk these streets.   25
Once in a sea-fight 'gainst the Count his galleys
I did some service, of such note indeed,
That were I ta'en here, it would scarce be answer'd.
Sebastian: Belike you slew great number of his people?
Antonio: Th' offense is not of such a bloody nature,   30
Albeit the quality of the time and quarrel
Might well have given us bloody argument.
It might have since been answer'd in repaying
What we took from them, which for traffic's sake
Most of our city did. Only myself stood out,   35
For which if I be lapsed in this place
I shall pay dear.
Sebastian: Do not then walk too open.
Antonio: It doth not fit me. Hold, sir, here's my purse.
In the south suburbs at the Elephant
Is best to lodge. I will bespeak our diet,   40
Whiles you beguile the time, and feed your knowledge
With viewing of the town. There shall you have me.

---

15. *And . . . turns:* A much-emended line. Sense can be made of it by taking *ever oft* as "it has always been true that frequently," but the awkwardness of this and the metrical deficiency of the line strongly suggest corruption. Most editors adopt Theobald's *And thanks, and ever thanks: and oft good turns.*   16. *shuffled off:* shrugged off. *uncurrent pay:* payment in worthless money, i.e. mere thanks. An uncurrent coin is one not accepted as legal tender.   17. *worth:* wealth. *conscience:* awareness (of my indebtedness).   19. *reliques:* relics of the past, ancient monuments (see line 23).   24. *renown:* make famous.   26. *Count his:* Count's.   28. *it . . . answer'd:* it would be difficult for me to make a defense.   29. *Belike:* probably.   31. *quality:* i.e. circumstances.   32. *bloody argument:* occasion for bloodshed.   34. *for traffic's sake:* in order to resume trading.   36. *lapsed:* caught napping, taken by surprise (literally, slipped).   38. *fit:* behoove.   39. *Elephant:* the name of an inn.   40. *bespeak our diet:* order our food.   42. *have me:* know where to find me.

Sebastian: Why I your purse?

Antonio: Haply your eye shall light upon some toy
    You have desire to purchase; and your store   45
    I think is not for idle markets, sir.

Sebastian: I'll be your purse-bearer, and leave you
    For an hour.

Antonio: To th' Elephant.

Sebastian: I do remember.   *Exeunt.*

Scene IV

Enter Olivia *and* Maria.

Olivia: [*Aside.*] I have sent after him; he says he'll come.
    How shall I feast him? What bestow of him?
    For youth is bought more oft than begg'd or borrow'd.
    I speak too loud.—
    Where's Malvolio? He is sad and civil,   5
    And suits well for a servant with my fortunes.
    Where is Malvolio?

Maria: He's coming, madam, but in very strange manner. He is
    sure possess'd, madam.

Olivia: Why, what's the matter? does he rave?   10

Maria: No, madam, he does nothing but smile. Your ladyship
    were best to have some guard about you, if he come, for sure
    the man is tainted in 's wits.

Olivia: Go call him hither.

Enter Malvolio.

                        I am as mad as he,
    If sad and merry madness equal be.   15
    How now, Malvolio?

Malvolio: Sweet lady, ho, ho.

Olivia: Smil'st thou? I sent for thee upon a sad occasion.

Malvolio: Sad, lady? I could be sad. This does make some obstruc-
    tion in the blood, this cross-gartering, but what of that? If it 20
    please the eye of one, it is with me as the very true sonnet is,
    "Please one, and please all."

Olivia: Why, how dost thou, man? What is the matter with thee?

---

44. *Haply:* perchance. *toy:* trifle.   45. *store:* supply of money.   46. *idle markets:* luxuries.

III.iv. Location: Olivia's garden.   1. *he . . . come:* In view of lines 52–53, this apparently
means "if he says he'll come."   5. *sad:* sober, serious (so also in line 18). *civil:* seemly,
decorous.   6. *suits:* accords.   9. *possess'd:* i.e. possessed of an evil spirit.   10. *rave:* talk
incoherently.   13. *tainted:* infected, disordered.   21. *sonnet:* poem.   22. *Please . . . all:* i.e.
if I please you, I please everyone I care to please (the first line and refrain of a popular ballad
published in 1592).

Malvolio: Not black in my mind, though yellow in my legs. It did come to his hands, and commands shall be executed. I think we do know the sweet Roman hand. 25

Olivia: Wilt thou go to bed, Malvolio?

Malvolio: To bed? Ay, sweet heart, and I'll come to thee.

Olivia: God comfort thee! Why dost thou smile so, and kiss thy hand so oft? 30

Maria: How do you, Malvolio?

Malvolio: At your request! Yes, nightingales answer daws.

Maria: Why appear you with this ridiculous boldness before my lady?

Malvolio: "Be not afraid of greatness": 'twas well writ. 35

Olivia: What mean'st thou by that, Malvolio?

Malvolio: "Some are born great"—

Olivia: Ha?

Malvolio: "Some achieve greatness"—

Olivia: What say'st thou? 40

Malvolio: "And some have greatness thrust upon them."

Olivia: Heaven restore thee!

Malvolio: "Remember who commended thy yellow stockings"—

Olivia: Thy yellow stockings?

Malvolio: "And wish'd to see thee cross-garter'd." 45

Olivia: Cross-garter'd?

Malvolio: "Go to, thou art made, if thou desir'st to be so"—

Olivia: Am I made?

Malvolio: "If not, let me see thee a servant still."

Olivia: Why, this is very midsummer madness. 50

Enter Servant.

Servant: Madam, the young gentleman of the Count Orsino's is return'd. I could hardly entreat him back. He attends your ladyship's pleasure.

Olivia: I'll come to him. [*Exit Servant.*] Good Maria, let this fellow be look'd to. Where's my cousin Toby? Let some of my people have a special care of him. I would not have him miscarry for the half of my dowry. *Exit [with Maria].* 55

---

24. *Not . . . legs:* Meaning not entirely clear. *To wear yellow hose* meant "to be jealous," and Malvolio may mean "Though I wear yellow on my legs, my thoughts are not black, i.e. I don't wear yellow because I am jealous." His main intent, of course, is to call attention to the stockings. 26. *Roman hand:* The Italian script, resembling our own, which was beginning to replace the English or secretary hand. 32. *At . . . daws:* i.e. am I to notice a question from you? O, certainly, a nightingale should answer a crow. (Malvolio is being "surly with servants," as instructed.) 50. *midsummer madness:* Proverbial; the midsummer moon was traditionally associated with insanity. 52. *attends:* awaits. 54–55. *fellow:* man (used of a servant or social inferior, without contemptuous sense). 56–57. *miscarry:* come to harm.

Malvolio: O ho, do you come near me now? No worse man than Sir
   Toby to look to me! This concurs directly with the letter: she
   sends him on purpose, that I may appear stubborn to him; for 60
   she incites me to that in the letter. "Cast thy humble slough,"
   says she; "be opposite with a kinsman, surly with servants; let
   thy tongue [tang] with arguments of state; put thyself into the
   trick of singularity"; and consequently sets down the manner
   how: as a sad face, a reverend carriage, a slow tongue, in the 65
   habit of some sir of note, and so forth. I have lim'd her, but it is
   Jove's doing, and Jove make me thankful! And when she went
   away now, "Let this fellow be look'd to"; "fellow"! not "Malvolio," nor after my degree, but "fellow." Why, every thing
   adheres together, that no dram of a scruple, no scruple of a 70
   scruple, no obstacle, no incredulous or unsafe circumstance—
   What can be said? Nothing that can be can come between me
   and the full prospect of my hopes. Well, Jove, not I, is the doer
   of this, and he is to be thank'd.

Enter Sir Toby, Fabian, *and* Maria.

   Sir Toby: Which way is he, in the name of sanctity? If all the devils of 75
   hell be drawn in little, and Legion himself possess'd him, yet I'll
   speak to him.
   Fabian: Here he is, here he is. How is't with you, sir?
   [Sir Toby:] How is't with you, man?
   Malvolio: Go off, I discard you. Let me enjoy my private. Go off. 80
   Maria: Lo, how hollow the fiend speaks within him! Did not I tell
   you? Sir Toby, my lady prays you to have a care of him.
   Malvolio: Ah ha, does she so?
   Sir Toby: Go to, go to; peace, peace, we must deal gently with him.
   Let me alone. How do you, Malvolio? How is't with you? 85
   What, man, defy the devil! Consider, he's an enemy to
   mankind.
   Malvolio: Do you know what you say?

---

58. *come near:* begin to understand.   60. *stubborn:* rude, harsh.   61. *incites:* encourages.
64. *consequently:* thereafter.   65. *reverend:* dignified. *slow tongue:* deliberate manner of
speaking.   66. *habit . . . note:* attire of a kind suitable for a distinguished gentleman. *lim'd:*
caught as with birdlime (a sticky substance spread on bushes to ensnare small birds).
68. *fellow:* Malvolio takes the word to mean "companion."   69. *after my degree:* according to
my place, i.e. "steward."   70. *adheres together:* hangs together. *dram:* small quantity
(one-eighth of a fluid ounce). *scruple:* (1) doubt; (2) smallest quantity (one-third of a dram).
71. *incredulous:* incredible. *unsafe:* uncertain.   73. *prospect:* range, scope.   75. *in . . .
sanctity:* in the name of all that is holy.   76. *drawn in little:* contracted into small compass (so
that they could all find room in Malvolio's bosom). *Legion:* Alluding to Mark 5:8–9: "For he
[Jesus] said unto him, Come out of the man, thou unclean spirit. And he asked him, What is
thy name? And he answered, saying, My name is Legion: for we are many" (Geneva).
80. *discard:* cast off, want nothing to do with. *private:* privacy.   81. *hollow:* deep, resounding
(adverbial).   82. *have . . . of:* be attentive to, take care of.   85. *Let me alone:* leave him to
me.   86. *defy:* renounce.

Maria: La you, and you speak ill of the devil, how he takes it at
    heart! Pray God he be not bewitch'd!   90
Fabian: Carry his water to th' wise woman.
Maria: Marry, and it shall be done to-morrow morning if I live.
    My lady would not lose him for more than I'll say.
Malvolio: How now, mistress?
  Maria: O Lord!   95
Sir Toby: Prithee hold thy peace, this is not the way. Do you not see
    you move him? Let me alone with him.
  Fabian: No way but gentleness, gently, gently. The fiend is rough,
    and will not be roughly us'd.
Sir Toby: Why, how now, my bawcock? How dost thou, chuck?   100
Malvolio: Sir!
Sir Toby: Ay, biddy, come with me. What, man, 'tis not for gravity to
    play at cherry-pit with Sathan. Hang him, foul collier!
  Maria: Get him to say his prayers, good Sir Toby, get him to pray.
Malvolio: My prayers, minx!   105
  Maria: No, I warrant you, he will not hear of godliness.
Malvolio: Go hang yourselves all! You are idle shallow things, I am
    not of your element. You shall know more hereafter.   *Exit.*
Sir Toby: Is't possible?
  Fabian: If this were play'd upon a stage now, I could condemn it as 110
    an improbable fiction.
Sir Toby: His very genius hath taken the infection of the device,
    man.
  Maria: Nay, pursue him now, lest the device take air, and taint.
  Fabian: Why, we shall make him mad indeed.   115
  Maria: The house will be the quieter.
Sir Toby: Come, we'll have him in a dark room and bound. My niece
    is already in the belief that he's mad. We may carry it thus, for
    our pleasure and his penance, till our very pastime, tir'd out of
    breath, prompt us to have mercy on him; at which time we will 120
    bring the device to the bar and crown thee for a finder of mad-
    men. But see, but see.

---

89. *La you:* an exclamation. *and:* if, when.   90. *bewitch'd:* Demoniac possession was
sometimes attributed to witchcraft.   91. *water:* urine (for analysis).   97. *move him:* make him
angry.   98. *rough:* violent.   99. *us'd:* treated.   100. *bawcock:* fine fellow (from French *beau
coq*). *chuck:* chick (a term of endearment).   102. *biddy:* child's name for a chicken. *gravity:* a
grave man.   103. *cherry-pit:* a child's game in which cherry stones are thrown into a hole. Sir
Toby provokingly talks to Malvolio as if he were a child and at the same time warns him that
his soul is in danger. *foul collier:* filthy coal-miner. Devils were always represented as
coal-black, and they worked in hell-pit.   105. *minx:* impudent woman.   107. *idle:* foolish.
I . . . element: i.e. I do not belong to your earthy level. *know more:* hear about this.
112. *genius:* governing principle of his being (literally, attendant spirit).   114. *take . . . taint:*
(1) be exposed to (noxious) air and corrupt; (2) become known and be spoiled.
117. *dark . . . bound.* A common treatment at this time for the insane.   118. *carry it:* keep it
going.   121. *bar:* i.e. bar of judgment.

Enter Sir Andrew.

> *Fabian:* More matter for a May morning.
>
> *Sir Andrew:* Here's the challenge, read it. I warrant there's vinegar
> and pepper in't. 125
>
> *Fabian:* Is't so saucy?
>
> *Sir Andrew:* Ay, is't! I warrant him. Do but read.
>
> *Sir Toby:* Give me. [*Reads.*] "Youth, whatsoever thou art, thou art
> but a scurvy fellow."
>
> *Fabian:* Good, and valiant. 130
>
> *Sir Toby:* [*Reads.*] "Wonder not, nor admire not in thy mind, why I
> do call thee so, for I will show thee no reason for't."
>
> *Fabian:* A good note, that keeps you from the blow of the law.
>
> *Sir Toby:* [*Reads.*] "Thou com'st to the Lady Olivia, and in my sight
> she uses thee kindly. But thou liest in thy throat, that is not the 135
> matter I challenge thee for."
>
> *Fabian:* Very brief, and to exceeding good sense—less.
>
> *Sir Toby:* [*Reads.*] "I will waylay thee going home, where if it be thy
> chance to kill me"—
>
> *Fabian:* Good. 140
>
> *Sir Toby:* [*Reads.*] "Thou kill'st me like a rogue and a villain."
>
> *Fabian:* Still you keep o' th' windy side of the law; good.
>
> *Sir Toby:* [*Reads.*] "Fare thee well, and God have mercy upon one of
> our souls! He may have mercy upon mine, but my hope is bet-
> ter, and so look to thyself. Thy friend as thou usest him, and 145
> thy sworn enemy, Andrew Aguecheek." If this letter move him
> not, his legs cannot. I'll give't him.
>
> *Maria:* You may have very fit occasion for't; he is now in some
> commerce with my lady, and will by and by depart.
>
> *Sir Toby:* Go, Sir Andrew, scout me for him at the corner of the 150
> orchard like a bum-baily. So soon as ever thou seest him, draw,
> and as thou draw'st, swear horrible; for it comes to pass oft that
> a terrible oath, with a swaggering accent sharply twang'd off,
> gives manhood more approbation than ever proof itself would
> have earn'd him. Away! 155

---

123. *matter . . . morning:* material for a May-day comedy. 126. *saucy:* (1) highly spiced; (2) insolent. 127. *I warrant him:* I guarantee he (Cesario) will be taken care of. 131. *admire:* marvel. 133. *A . . . law:* i.e. a carefully worded challenge, that safeguards you from a charge of slander. 135. *in thy throat:* in the most heinous degree. 142. *windy side:* windward, i.e. safe (because, as before, the abuse is too feeble to be defamatory, but perhaps also because *like a rogue and a villain* can be taken to modify *me,* not *thou*). 145. *Thy . . . him:* your friend insofar as you behave in a friendly fashion toward him. 146. *move him:* stir him up (with following quibble). 148. *fit:* convenient. 149. *commerce:* dealing, business. *will . . . depart:* is on the verge of departing. 150. *scout me:* keep watch. 151. *bum-baily:* petty sheriff's officer who arrested for debt. 154. *gives . . . approbation:* gives valor a higher reputation. i.e. gives a man a higher reputation for valor. *proof:* actual trial, performance.

Sir Andrew: Nay, let me alone for swearing.   *Exit.*

Sir Toby: Now will not I deliver his letter; for the behavior of the
young gentleman gives him out to be of good capacity and
breeding; his employment between his lord and my niece confirms no less. Therefore this letter, being so excellently igno- 160
rant, will breed no terror in the youth; he will find it comes
from a clodpole. But, sir, I will deliver his challenge by word of
mouth, set upon Aguecheek a notable report of valor, and
drive the gentleman (as I know his youth will aptly receive it)
into a most hideous opinion of his rage, skill, fury, and impe- 165
tuosity. This will so fright them both that they will kill one
another by the look, like cockatrices.

Enter Olivia *and* Viola.

Fabian: Here he comes with your niece. Give them way till he take
leave, and presently after him.
Sir Toby: I will meditate the while upon some horrid message for a 170
challenge.   *[Exeunt Sir Toby, Fabian, and Maria.]*
Olivia: I have said too much unto a heart of stone,
And laid mine honor too unchary on't.
There's something in me that reproves my fault;
But such a headstrong potent fault it is   175
That it but mocks reproof.
Viola: With the same havior that your passion bears
Goes on my master's griefs.
Olivia: Here, wear this jewel for me, 'tis my picture.
Refuse it not, it hath no tongue to vex you;   180
And I beseech you come again to-morrow.
What shall you ask of me that I'll deny,
That honor, sav'd, may upon asking give?
Viola: Nothing but this—your true love for my master.
Olivia: How with mine honor may I give him that   185
Which I have given to you?
Viola: I will acquit you.
Olivia: Well, come again to-morrow. Fare thee well.
A fiend like thee might bear my soul to hell.   *[Exit.]*

Enter Sir Toby *and* Fabian.

---

156. *let . . . swearing:* have no fears about my ability to swear.   158. *gives him out:* declares
him. *capacity:* ability.   161. *find:* detect, see.   162. *clodpole:* knucklehead (variant form of
clodpoll).   164. *youth:* i.e. inexperience. *aptly receive it:* readily credit the report.   166. *cockatrices:* basilisks, fabulous serpents that were supposedly able to kill by their glance alone.
168. *Give them way:* stay out of their way.   169. *presently:* immediately.   173. *laid:*
hazarded. *unchary:* carelessly.   175. *potent:* powerful.   177. *havior:* behavior.   179. *jewel:*
Used of any product of the jeweller's art; here a brooch or locket with Olivia's picture set in
it.   183. *sav'd:* i.e. without injury to itself, safely.   187. *acquit:* waive all claim to.   189. *like
thee:* in your likeness. *might:* i.e. could without resistance from me.

Sir Toby: Gentleman, God save thee!

Viola: And you, sir.   190

Sir Toby: That defense thou hast, betake thee to't. Of what nature the wrongs are thou hast done him, I know not; but thy intercepter, full of despite, bloody as the hunter, attends thee at the orchard-end. Dismount thy tuck, be yare in thy preparation, for thy assailant is quick, skillful, and deadly.   195

Viola: You mistake, sir, I am sure; no man hath any quarrel to me. My remembrance is very free and clear from any image of offense done to any man.

Sir Toby: You'll find it otherwise, I assure you; therefore, if you hold your life at any price, betake you to your guard; for your oppo- 200 site hath in him what youth, strength, skill, and wrath can furnish man withal.

Viola: I pray you, sir, what is he?

Sir Toby: He is knight, dubb'd with unhatch'd rapier, and on carpet consideration, but he is a devil in private brawl. Souls and 205 bodies hath he divorc'd three, and his incensement at this moment is so implacable, that satisfaction can be none but by pangs of death and sepulchre. Hob, nob, is his word; give't or take't.

Viola: I will return again into the house, and desire some conduct 210 of the lady. I am no fighter. I have heard of some kind of men that put quarrels purposely on others, to taste their valor. Belike this is a man of that quirk.

Sir Toby: Sir, no; his indignation derives itself out of a very [compe-tent] injury; therefore get you on, and give him his desire. Back 215 you shall not to the house, unless you undertake that with me which with as much safety you might answer him; therefore on, or strip your sword stark naked; for meddle you must, that's certain, or forswear to wear iron about you.

Viola: This is as uncivil as strange. I beseech you do me this cour- 220 teous office, as to know of the knight what my offense to him is. It is something of my negligence, nothing of my purpose.

---

191. *That defense:* whatever skill in fencing.   193. *intercepter:* ambusher. *despite:* contempt and hatred.   193. *bloody . . . hunter:* i.e. as intent on bloodshed as the hunting dog tracking down its prey.   194. *Dismount thy tuck:* draw your rapier. *yare:* ready, brisk.   196. *quarrel to:* reason to quarrel with.   197. *remembrance:* memory.   200. *price:* value.   200–01. *opposite:* adversary.   202. *withal:* with.   204. *unhatch'd:* unhacked, undented (i.e. never used in battle).   204–05. *on carpet consideration:* A carpet knighthood was one not given on the bat-tlefield for services performed there, hence often one given for political reasons; *consideration* suggests a bought knighthood.   208. *Hob, nob:* have it, have it not; i.e. "give't or take't." *word:* motto.   210. *conduct:* protective escort.   212. *taste:* make trial of. 214–15. *competent:* sufficient.   216. *that:* i.e. a duel.   218. *strip . . . naked:* draw your sword now (and fight with me). *meddle:* have to do, be involved. Cf. line 240, where *not meddle with* = have nothing to do with.   219. *forswear . . . you:* renounce your right to wear a sword. 221. *know of:* ascertain from.   222. *of:* arising from. *purpose:* intention.

Sir Toby: I will do so. Signior Fabian, stay you by this gentleman till my return. *Exit Sir Toby.*

Viola: Pray you, sir, do you know of this matter? 225

Fabian: I know the knight is incens'd against you, even to a mortal arbitrement, but nothing of the circumstance more.

Viola: I beseech you, what manner of man is he?

Fabian: Nothing of that wonderful promise, to read him by his form, as you are like to find him in the proof of his valor. He is 230 indeed, sir, the most skillful, bloody, and fatal opposite that you could possibly have found in any part of Illyria. Will you walk towards him? I will make your peace with him if I can.

Viola: I shall be much bound to you for't. I am one that had rather go with sir priest than sir knight. I care not who knows 235 so much of my mettle. *Exeunt.*

Enter Sir Toby *and* Sir Andrew.

Sir Toby: Why, man, he's a very devil, I have not seen such a firago. I had a pass with him, rapier, scabbard, and all; and he gives me the stuck in with such a mortal motion that it is inevitable; and on the answer, he pays you as surely as your feet hit the ground 240 they step on. They say he has been fencer to the Sophy.

Sir Andrew: Pox on't, I'll not meddle with him.

Sir Toby: Ay, but he will not now be pacified. Fabian can scarce hold him yonder.

Sir Andrew: Plague on't, and I thought he had been valiant, and so 245 cunning in fence, I'd have seen him damn'd ere I'd have challeng'd him. Let him let the matter slip, and I'll give him my horse, grey Capilet.

Sir Toby: I'll make the motion. Stand here, make a good show on't; this shall end without the perdition of souls. [*Aside.*] Marry, 250 I'll ride your horse as well as I ride you.

Enter Fabian *and* Viola.

[*To Fabian:*] I have his horse to take up the quarrel. I have persuaded him the youth's a devil.

226–27. *to . . . arbitrement:* to a point requiring settlement by a duel to the death. 229–30. *read . . . form:* judge him by his appearance. 235. *sir priest.* Priests were often addressed by the courtesy title *sir.* 236. *mettle:* temperament. 237. *firago:* virago. Schmidt suggests that Sir Toby uses this word, applicable only to a woman (its original meaning is "acting like a man"), as a linguistic joke on Sir Andrew, who has not studied languages (I.iii.92–93); if so, there is a joke on Sir Toby also. 238. *pass:* bout. *gives me:* gives. 239. *stuck in:* stoccado (or stoccato), thrust. 240. *answer:* return hit. *pays:* repays. 245. *and . . . been:* if I had supposed he was. 248. *Capilet:* a name meaning "little horse." It is typical of Sir Andrew's imagination that he should name a little horse "little horse." 249. *motion:* offer. *make . . . show:* put a good face. 250. *perdition of souls:* loss of lives. 252. *take up:* settle.

Fabian: He is as horribly conceited of him; and pants and looks
pale, as if a bear were at his heels.   255
Sir Toby: [*To Viola.*] There's no remedy, sir, he will fight with you for
's oath sake. Marry, he hath better bethought him of his quarrel, and he finds that now scarce to be worth talking of; therefore draw, for the supportance of his vow. He protests he will
not hurt you.   260
  Viola: [*Aside.*] Pray God defend me! A little thing would make
me tell them how much I lack of a man.
  Fabian: Give ground if you see him furious.
Sir Toby: Come, Sir Andrew, there's no remedy, the gentleman will
for his honor's sake have one bout with you. He cannot by the   265
duello avoid it; but he has promis'd me, as he is a gentleman
and a soldier, he will not hurt you. Come on, to't.
Sir Andrew: Pray God he keep his oath!

Enter Antonio.

  Viola: I do assure you, 'tis against my will.   *[They draw.]*
Antonio: Put up your sword. If this young gentleman   270
Have done offense, I take the fault on me;
If you offend him, I for him defy you.
Sir Toby: You, sir? Why, what are you?
Antonio: One, sir, that for his love dares yet do more
Than you have heard him brag to you he will.   275
Sir Toby: Nay, if you be an undertaker, I am for you.— *[They draw.]*

Enter Officers.

  Fabian: O good Sir Toby, hold! here come the officers.
Sir Toby: [*To Antonio.*] I'll be with you anon.
                              [Steps aside to avoid the Officers.]
  Viola: Pray, sir, put your sword up, if you please.
Sir Andrew: Marry, will I, sir; and for that I promis'd you, I'll be as 280
good as my word. He will bear you easily, and reins well.
1. Officer: This is the man, do thy office.
2. Officer: Antonio, I arrest thee at the suit of Count Orsino.
  Antonio: You do mistake me, sir.
1. Officer: No, sir, no jot. I know your favor well,   285
Though now you have no sea-cap on your head.
Take him away, he knows I know him well.

---

254. *He . . . him:* i.e. the youth has as dreadful a conception of Sir Andrew.   256–57. *for's:*
for his.   257–58. *bethought . . . quarrel:* considered the grounds for his challenge.
259. *supportance:* upholding. *protests:* solemnly promises.   266. *duello:* the code of duelling.
276. *undertaker:* i.e. one who takes up a challenge for another.   278. *be . . . anon:* be back
right away.   280. *that . . . you:* i.e. the horse Capilet (about which of course Viola knows
nothing).   281. *easily:* smoothly.   282. *office:* duty, function.   285. *favor:* face.

Antonio: I must obey. *[To Viola.]* This comes with seeking you;
    But there's no remedy, I shall answer it.
    What will you do, now my necessity   290
    Makes me to ask you for my purse? It grieves me
    Much more for what I cannot do for you
    Than what befalls myself. You stand amaz'd,
    But be of comfort.
2. Officer: Come, sir, away.   295
  Antonio: I must entreat of you some of that money.
   Viola: What money, sir?
    For the fair kindness you have show'd me here,
    And part being prompted by your present trouble,
    Out of my lean and low ability   300
    I'll lend you something. My having is not much;
    I'll make division of my present with you.
    Hold, there's half my coffer.
  Antonio: Will you deny me now?
    Is't possible that my deserts to you
    Can lack persuasion? Do not tempt my misery,   305
    Lest that it make me so unsound a man
    As to upbraid you with those kindnesses
    That I have done for you.
   Viola: I know of none,
    Nor know I you by voice or any feature.
    I hate ingratitude more in a man   310
    Than lying, vainness, babbling, drunkenness,
    Or any taint of vice whose strong corruption
    Inhabits our frail blood.
  Antonio: O heavens themselves!
2. Officer: Come, sir, I pray you go.
  Antonio: Let me speak a little. This youth that you see here   315
    I snatch'd one half out of the jaws of death,
    Reliev'd him with such sanctity of love,
    And to his image, which methought did promise
    Most venerable worth, did I devotion.
1. Officer: What's that to us? The time goes by; away!   320
  Antonio: But O, how vild an idol proves this god!
    Thou hast, Sebastian, done good feature shame.

---

289. *answer it:* i.e. make what defence I can. 293. *amaz'd:* bewildered. 299. *part:* in part. 300. *ability:* means. 301. *My having:* what I possess. 302. *present:* ready money. 303. *coffer:* store of wealth (literally, strong-box). 305. *lack persuasion:* fail to persuade you. *tempt:* try too far. 306. *unsound:* unhealthy (used figuratively). 311. *vainness:* vanity. *babbling:* foolish, loose talk. 312. *any . . . vice:* the taint of any fault. 316. *one . . . death:* out of the jaws of death which had half-swallowed him. 317. *such:* Used here with intensive force. 318. *his image:* what he appeared to be (with play on *image* in the sense "religious statue"). 319. *venerable worth:* worthiness of veneration. 321. *vild:* vile. 322. *Thou . . . shame:* Alluding to the belief that physical beauty is a reflection of spiritual beauty. *feature:* physical form.

In nature there's no blemish but the mind;
None can be call'd deform'd but the unkind.
Virtue is beauty, but the beauteous evil   325
Are empty trunks o'erflourish'd by the devil.

1. Officer: The man grows mad, away with him! Come, come, sir.

Antonio: Lead me on.   *Exit [with Officers].*

   Viola: Methinks his words do from such passion fly
That he believes himself; so do not I.   330
Prove true, imagination, O, prove true,
That I, dear brother, be now ta'en for you!

Sir Toby: Come hither, knight; come hither, Fabian; we'll whisper
o'er a couplet or two of most sage saws.

   Viola: He nam'd Sebastian. I my brother know   335
Yet living in my glass; even such and so
In favor was my brother, and he went
Still in this fashion, color, ornament,
For him I imitate. O, if it prove,
Tempests are kind and salt waves fresh in love.   340

                                    [Exit.]

Sir Toby: A very dishonest paltry boy, and more a coward than a
hare. His dishonesty appears in leaving his friend here in
necessity, and denying him; and for his cowardship, ask Fabian.

Fabian: A coward, a most devout coward, religious in it.

Sir Andrew: 'Slid, I'll after him again, and beat him.   345

Sir Toby: Do, cuff him soundly, but never draw thy sword.

Sir Andrew: And I do not—   *[Exit.]*

   Fabian: Come, let's see the event.

Sir Toby: I dare lay any money 'twill be nothing yet.   *Exeunt.*

ACT IV

Scene I

Enter Sebastian *and* Clown.

   Clown: Will you make me believe that I am not sent for you?

Sebastian: Go to, go to, thou art a foolish fellow,
Let me be clear of thee.

   Clown: Well held out, i' faith! No, I do not know you, nor I am not

---

324. *unkind:* unnatural. The unnatural quality with which he is charging the supposed
Sebastian is of course ingratitude. 326. *trunks o'erflourish'd:* (1) chests covered over with
elaborate carvings; (2) bodies made externally beautiful. 330. *so . . . I:* I do not believe
myself, i.e. I don't quite dare to believe what all this suggests to me (that my brother is alive).
334. *saws:* sayings, maxims. 335–36. *I . . . glass:* I know that the appearance of my brother
is still alive every time I look in a mirror (i.e. I am the living image of my brother). 337–
38. *went Still in:* always wore. 339. *prove:* prove true. 341. *dishonest:* dishonorable. *more a
coward:* more cowardly. 345. *'Slid:* by God's eyelid. 347. *And:* if. 348. *event:* outcome.
349. *yet:* now as before(?) or nevertheless (?) or after all (?).

IV.i. Location: Before Olivia's house. 3. *clear:* rid. 4. *held out:* persisted in.

sent to you by my lady, to bid you come speak with her, nor your 5
name is not Master Cesario, nor this is not my nose neither:
nothing that is so is so.

Sebastian: I prithee vent thy folly somewhere else,
    Thou know'st not me.

Clown: Vent my folly! He has heard that word of some great man, 10
and now applies it to a fool. Vent my folly! I am afraid this
great lubber the world will prove a cockney. I prithee now
ungird thy strangeness, and tell me what I shall vent to my lady.
Shall I vent to her that thou art coming?

Sebastian: I prithee, foolish Greek, depart from me. 15
    There's money for thee. If you tarry longer,
    I shall give worse payment.

Clown: By my troth, thou hast an open hand. These wise men that
give fools money get themselves a good report—after fourteen
years' purchase. 20

Enter Sir Andrew, Sir Toby, *and* Fabian.

Sir Andrew: Now, sir, have I met you again? There's for you.
                                    [Strikes Sebastian.]

Sebastian: Why, there's for thee, and there, and there. *[Strikes Sir
    Andrew.]* Are all the people mad?
                                    [Draws his dagger.]

Sir Toby: Hold, sir, or I'll throw your dagger o'er the house.
                                    [Seizes Sebastian's arm.]

Clown: This will I tell my lady straight; I would not be in some of 25
your coats for twopence.   *[Exit.]*

Sir Toby: Come on, sir, hold!

Sir Andrew: Nay, let him alone. I'll go another way to work with him;
    I'll have an action of battery against him, if there be any law in
    Illyria. Though I strook him first, yet it's no matter for that. 30

Sebastian: Let go thy hand.

Sir Toby: Come, sir, I will not let you go. Come, my young soldier,
    put up your iron; you are well flesh'd. Come on.

Sebastian: I will be free from thee. *[Breaks away and draws his sword.]*
    What wouldst thou now? If thou dar'st tempt me further, draw 35
    thy sword.

Sir Toby: What, what? Nay then I must have an ounce or two of this
    malapert blood from you.   *[Draws.]*

Enter Olivia.

---

11. *vent thy folly:* utter your foolish talk. *Vent* was in common use, and it is hard to understand
why Feste chooses to think it affected.   12. *lubber:* clumsy stupid fellow, lout. *cockney:*
overnice, effeminate fellow.   13. *ungird thy strangeness:* put off your pretense of being a
stranger.   15. *Greek:* i.e. jester.

Olivia: Hold, Toby, on thy life I charge thee hold!

Sir Toby: Madam— 40

Olivia: Will it be ever thus? Ungracious wretch,
    Fit for the mountains and the barbarous caves,
    Where manners ne'er were preach'd! Out of my sight!
    Be not offended, dear Cesario.
    Rudesby, be gone!   *[Exeunt Sir Toby, Sir Andrew, and Fabian.]*
                    I prithee, gentle friend, 45
    Let thy fair wisdom, not thy passion, sway
    In this uncivil and unjust extent
    Against thy peace. Go with me to my house,
    And hear thou there how many fruitless pranks
    This ruffian hath botch'd up, that thou thereby 50
    Mayst smile at this. Thou shalt not choose but go,
    Do not deny. Beshrew his soul for me,
    He started one poor heart of mine, in thee.

Sebastian: What relish is in this? How runs the stream?
    Or I am mad, or else this is a dream. 55
    Let fancy still my sense in Lethe steep;
    If it be thus to dream, still let me sleep!

Olivia: Nay, come, I prithee. Would thou'dst be rul'd by me!

Sebastian: Madam, I will.

Olivia: O, say so, and so be!   *Exeunt.*

Scene II

Enter Maria *and* Clown.

Maria: Nay, I prithee put on this gown and this beard, make him
    believe thou art Sir Topas the curate, do it quickly. I'll call Sir
    Toby the whilst.   *[Exit.]*

Clown: Well, I'll put it on, and I will dissemble myself in't, and I
    would I were the first that ever dissembled in such a gown. I am 5
    not tall enough to become the function well, nor lean enough
    to be thought a good studient; but to be said an honest man and

---

52. *Beshrew:* Here much closer to its original sense "curse" than in II.iii.70.   53. *He . . . thee:*
"He that offends thee, attacks one of my hearts, or as the ancients expressed it, half my heart"
(Johnson). There may also be a glancing play on *hart,* suggested by *started.*   54. *relish:* taste,
i.e. quality, nature.   55. *Or:* either.   56. *fancy:* imagination. *Lethe:* the river of forgetfulness
in the underworld.

IV.ii. Location: Olivia's house.   2. *Sir Topas:* Shakespeare may have borrowed the name
from Chaucer's "Rime of Sir Thopas" in *The Canterbury Tales.* On *Sir* see the note to
III.iv.235.   3. *the whilst:* in the meantime.   4. *dissemble:* disguise.   5. *dissembled:* created a
false impression, concealed his true nature.   6. *tall:* The sense here is probably "large,
well-fleshed," in contrast to *lean,* line 6. Feste seems to be glancing jestingly at two traditional
notions, that clerics are given to the pleasures of the table and that scholars lead ascetic
lives. *become . . . well:* grace the priestly office.   7. *studient:* scholar (a variant form of *student,*
not Feste's inverent. Most scholars were churchmen). *said:* known as.

a good house-keeper goes as fairly as to say a careful man and a great scholar. The competitors enter.

Enter Sir Toby [*and* Maria].

   Sir Toby: Jove bless thee, Master Parson.   10
     Clown: *Bonos dies*, Sir Toby: for as the old hermit of Prague, that never saw pen and ink, very wittily said to a niece of King Gorboduc, "That that is is"; so I, being Master Parson, am Master Parson; for what is "that" but "that," and "is" but "is"?
   Sir Toby: To him, Sir Topas.   15
     Clown: What ho, I say! Peace in this prison!
   Sir Toby: The knave counterfeits well; a good knave.
  Malvolio: *(Within.)* Who calls there?
     Clown: Sir Topas the curate, who comes to visit Malvolio the lunatic.   20
  Malvolio: Sir Topas, Sir Topas, good Sir Topas, go to my lady.
     Clown: Out, hyperbolical fiend! how vexest thou this man! Talkest thou nothing but of ladies?
   Sir Toby: Well said, Master Parson.
  Malvolio: Sir Topas, never was man thus wrong'd. Good Sir Topas, 25
do not think I am mad; they have laid me here in hideous darkness.
     Clown: Fie, thou dishonest Sathan! I call thee by the most modest terms, for I am one of those gentle ones that will use the devil himself with courtesy. Say'st thou that house is dark?   30
  Malvolio: As hell, Sir Topas.
     Clown: Why, it hath bay windows transparent as barricadoes, and the [clerestories] toward the south north art as lustrous as ebony; and yet complainest thou of obstruction?
  Malvolio: I am not mad, Sir Topas, I say to you this house is dark. 35
     Clown: Madman, thou errest. I say there is not darkness but ignorance, in which thou art more puzzled than the Egyptians in their fog.
  Malvolio: I say this house is as dark as ignorance, though ignorance were as dark as hell; and I say there was never man thus abus'd. 40
I am no more mad than you are; make the trial of it in any constant question.

---

8. *good house-keeper:* good manager of his household. *goes as fairly:* sounds as well. *careful:* highly respected duties.   9. *competitors:* partners, confederates.   11. *Bonos dies:* for *bonus dies,* good day. *hermit of Prague:* Now that Feste is a priest, the authority he invents is a man of religion.   12. *wittily:* cleverly.   12–13. *Gorboduc:* a legendary king of England.   22. *hyperbolical:* vehement (a rhetorical term, meaning "exaggerated in style"). *fiend:* i.e. the devil by whom Malvolio is possessed.   28. *modest:* moderate.   30. *house:* i.e. room.   32. *barricadoes:* barricades.   33. *clerestories:* windows in the upper wall.   34. *obstruction:* shutting out of light. 37. *puzzled:* greatly perplexed.   37–38. *Egyptians . . . fog:* An allusion to Exodus 10:22, "And Moses stretched forth his hand toward heaven; and there was a black darkness in all the land of Egypt three days" (Geneva).   41–42. *constant question:* topic for rational discourse.

Clown: What is the opinion of Pythagoras concerning wild-fowl?
Malvolio: That the soul of our grandam might happily inhabit a bird.
Clown: What think'st thou of his opinion? 45
Malvolio: I think nobly of the soul, and no way approve his opinion.
Clown: Fare thee well. Remain thou still in darkness. Thou shalt
hold th' opinion of Pythagoras ere I will allow of thy wits, and
fear to kill a woodcock lest thou dispossess the soul of thy gran-
dam. Fare thee well. 50
Malvolio: Sir Topas, Sir Topas!
Sir Toby: My most exquisite Sir Topas!
Clown: Nay, I am for all waters.
Maria: Thou mightst have done this without thy beard and gown,
he sees thee not. 55
Sir Toby: To him in thine own voice, and bring me word now thou
find'st him. I would we were well rid of this knavery. If he may
be conveniently deliver'd, I would he were, for I am now so far
in offense with my niece that I cannot pursue with any safety
this sport [t'] the upshot. Come by and by to my chamber. 60

Exit [with Maria].

Clown: [Sings.]
"Hey, Robin, jolly Robin,
Tell me how thy lady does."

Malvolio: Fool! 65
Clown: "My lady is unkind, perdie."
Malvolio: Fool!
Clown: "Alas, why is she so?"
Malvolio: Fool, I say!
Clown: "She loves another"—Who calls, ha?
Malvolio: Good fool, as ever thou wilt deserve well at my hand, help
me to a candle, and pen, ink, and paper. As I am a gentleman, I 70
will live to be thankful to thee for't.
Clown: Master Malvolio?
Malvolio: Ay, good fool.
Clown: Alas, sir, how fell you besides your five wits?
Malvolio: Fool, there was never man so notoriously abus'd; I am as 75
well in my wits, fool, as thou art.

---

43. *Pythagoras . . . wild-fowl:* Referring to the Pythagorean doctrine of transmigration of
souls.   44. *happily:* haply, perchance.   48. *allow . . . wits:* grant that you are sane.
49. *woodcock:* Proverbial for its stupidity.   52. *exquisite:* consummately accomplished.
53. *for all waters:* i.e. ready for anything (a phrase of unknown origin).   58. *deliver'd:* set
free.   58–59. *far in offense:* deeply in disgrace.   60. *upshot:* conclusion (the decisive shot in
an archery contest).   61–62. *Hey . . . does:* These lines, with 66, 68, 70, are from an old song,
a version of which is attributed to Sir Thomas Wyatt.   66. *perdie:* indeed (a weakened oath,
like French *pardieu,* literally "by God").   74. *besides:* out of. *five wits:* Usually listed as
common wit (common sense), fantasy, memory, judgment, and imagination.   75. *notoriously
abus'd:* egregiously misused.

Clown: But as well! Then you are mad indeed, if you be no better
in your wits than a fool.

Malvolio: They have here propertied me, keep me in darkness, send
ministers to me, asses, and do all they can to face me out of my   80
wits.

Clown: Advise you what you say; the minister is here.—Malvolio,
Malvolio, thy wits the heavens restore! Endeavor thyself to
sleep, and leave thy vain bibble babble.

Malvolio: Sir Topas!   85

Clown: Maintain no words within, good fellow.—Who, I, sir? Not
I, sir. God buy you, good Sir Topas.—Marry, amen.—I will,
sir, I will.

Malvolio: Fool, fool, fool, I say!

Clown: Alas, sir, be patient. What say you, sir? I am shent for   90
speaking to you.

Malvolio: Good fool, help me to some light and some paper. I tell
thee I am as well in my wits as any man in Illyria.

Clown: Well-a-day that you were, sir!

Malvolio: By this hand, I am. Good fool, some ink, paper, and light;   95
and convey what I will set down to my lady. It shall advantage
thee more than ever the bearing of letter did.

Clown: I will help you to't. But tell me true, are you not mad
indeed, or do you but counterfeit?

Malvolio: Believe me I am not, I tell thee true.   100

Clown: Nay, I'll ne'er believe a madman till I see his brains. I will
fetch you light and paper and ink.

Malvolio: Fool, I'll require it in the highest degree. I prithee be
gone.

Clown: [Sings.]

> I am gone, sir,   105
> And anon, sir,
>   I'll be with you again;
> In a trice,
> Like to the old Vice,
>   Your need to sustain;   110

---

79. *propertied me:* i.e. stowed me away like a piece of furniture (perhaps with play on stage
properties).   80–81. *face . . . wits:* brazenly deny that I am sane.   82. *Advise you:* consider
well.   83–84. *Malvolio . . . babble:* Feste here impersonates Sir Topas again, and in his next
speech takes both parts in a dialogue between Sir Topas and himself.   83. *Endeavor thyself:*
strive.   87. *God buy you:* God be with you, goodby.   90. *shent:* rebuked.   94. *Well-a-day:*
alas.   96. *advantage:* benefit.   108. *trice:* moment.   109. *Vice:* the comic character in the
morality plays and interludes in which he often beat the Devil with his "dagger of lath" and
threatened to trim his long nails with it. Feste here compares himself to the Vice (whose role
was an ancestor of the Clown's role), and his impudent remarks to the devil by whom Malvolio
is supposedly possessed are by implication addressed to Malvolio himself.

Who with dagger of lath,
In his rage and his wrath,
  Cries, ah, ha! to the devil;
Like a mad lad,
Pare thy nails, dad.   115
  Adieu, goodman devil.   *Exit.*

Scene III

Enter Sebastian.

Sebastian: This is the air, that is the glorious sun,
This pearl she gave me, I do feel't and see't,
And though 'tis wonder that enwraps me thus,
Yet 'tis not madness. Where's Antonio then?
I could not find him at the Elephant,   5
Yet there he was, and there I found this credit,
That he did range the town to seek me out.
His counsel now might do me golden service,
For though my soul disputes well with my sense,
That this may be some error, but no madness,   10
Yet doth this accident and flood of fortune
So far exceed all instance, all discourse,
That I am ready to distrust mine eyes,
And wrangle with my reason that persuades me
To any other trust but that I am mad,   15
Or else the lady's mad; yet if 'twere so,
She could not sway her house, command her followers,
Take and give back affairs, and their dispatch,
With such a smooth, discreet, and stable bearing
As I perceive she does. There's something in't   20
That is deceivable. But here the lady comes.

Enter Olivia *and* Priest.

Olivia: Blame not this haste of mine. If you mean well,
Now go with me, and with this holy man,
Into the chantry by; there, before him,

---

116. *goodman devil:* A final insult to Malvolio, who is addressed by the title proper for those below the rank of gentleman.

IV.iii. Location: Olivia's garden. 6. *was:* had been. *found this credit:* learned that they believed as follows. 7. *range:* go about. 9. *my soul . . . sense:* i.e. my reason and my senses both maintain (*disputes with* = "argues together with"). 11. *accident . . . fortune:* chance occurrence and (i.e. which is a brimming over of good fortune. 12. *instance:* example, precedent. *discourse:* reasoning, logic. 15. *trust:* belief, conviction. 17. *sway:* rule, manage. *followers:* servants. 18. *Take . . . dispatch:* i.e. take business in hand and give instructions for its prompt execution. *Take* governs *affairs; give back* governs *dispatch.*
19. *discreet:* judicious. 21. *deceivable:* deceptive. 24. *chantry:* a small private chapel where mass was sung daily for the souls of the dead. *by:* near by.

And underneath that consecrated roof, 25
Plight me the full assurance of your faith,
That my most jealous and too doubtful soul
May live at peace. He shall conceal it
Whiles you are willing it shall come to note,
What time we will our celebration keep 30
According to my birth. What do you say?
Sebastian: I'll follow this good man, and go with you,
And having sworn truth, ever will be true.
Olivia: Then lead the way, good father, and heavens so shine
That they may fairly note this act of mine! *Exeunt.* 35

ACT V

Scene I

Enter Clown *and* Fabian.

Fabian: Now as thou lov'st me, let me see his letter.
Clown: Good Master Fabian, grant me another request.
Fabian: Any thing.
Clown: Do not desire to see this letter.
Fabian: This is to give a dog and in recompense desire my dog 5
again.

Enter Duke, Viola, Curio, *and* Lords.

Duke: Belong you to the Lady Olivia, friends?
Clown: Ay, sir, we are some of her trappings.
Duke: I know thee well; how dost thou, my good fellow?
Clown: Truly, sir, the better for my foes and the worse for my 10
friends.
Duke: Just the contrary: the better for thy friends.
Clown: No, sir, the worse.
Duke: How can that be?
Clown: Marry, sir, they praise me, and make an ass of me. Now my 15
foes tell me plainly I am an ass; so that by my foes, sir, I profit in

---

26. *Plight:* pledge. The ceremony in question here is the betrothal, regarded as a binding contract; the marriage will be solemnized later (lines 30–31). 27. *jealous:* mistrustful (variant form of *jealous*). *doubtful:* apprehensive. 29. *Whiles:* until. *come to note:* become publicly known. 30. *What:* at which. 31. *birth:* rank, social position.

V.i. Location: Before Olivia's house. 5–6. *This . . . again:* Manningham in his *Diary* (in which the Middle Temple performance of *Twelfth Night* is recorded; see the introduction) relates a similar incident involving Queen Elizabeth and a Dr. Bullein, her kinsman, the owner of the dog. But whether Shakespeare knew of the incident is uncertain.

the knowledge of myself, and by my friends I am abus'd; so that, conclusions to be as kisses, if your four negatives make your two affirmatives, why then the worse for my friends and the better for my foes. 20

Duke: Why, this is excellent.

Clown: By my troth, sir, no; though it please you to be one of my friends.

Duke: Thou shalt not be the worse for me, there's gold.

Clown: But that it would be double-dealing, sir, I would you could 25 make it another.

Duke: O, you give me ill counsel.

Clown: Put your grace in your pocket, sir, for this once, and let your flesh and blood obey it.

Duke: Well, I will be so much a sinner to be a double-dealer. 30 There's another.

Clown: *Primo, secundo, tertio,* is a good play, and the old saying is, the third pays for all. The triplex, sir, is a good tripping measure, or the bells of Saint Bennet, sir, may put you in mind— one, two, three. 35

Duke: You can fool no more money out of me at this throw. If you will let your lady know I am here to speak with her, and bring her along with you, it may awake my bounty further.

Clown: Marry, sir, lullaby to your bounty till I come again. I go, sir, but I would not have you to think that my desire of having is 40 the sin of covetousness; but as you say, sir, let your bounty take a nap, I will awake it anon. *Exit.*

Enter Antonio *and* Officers.

Viola: Here comes the man, sir, that did rescue me.

Duke: That face of his I do remember well,
Yet when I saw it last, it was besmear'd 45
As black as Vulcan in the smoke of war.

---

17. *abus'd:* deceived.   17–20. *so . . .foes:* This jest has never been satisfactorily paraphrased. Dover Wilson's explication may be given as one of many: "a kiss is made by four lips (contraries or negatives) brought together by two ardent mouths (affirmatives); if conclusions are like this, says Feste, then the conclusion that I am not an ass is only half the value of the conclusion that I am one."   25. *But:* except for the fact. *double-dealing:* (1) duplicity; (2) giving two coins.   28. *Put . . . pocket:* (1) pocket up (set aside) your virtue; (2) let your Grace dip into your purse (with further sense in *grace* of "favor" or "generosity").   29. *flesh and blood:* frail human nature. *it:* i.e. the "ill counsel."   32. *Primo, secundo, tertio:* Perhaps with reference to a game of dice, perhaps to a child's game.   33. *the third . . . all:* Proverbial; cf. "The third time's the charm." *triplex:* triple time in music.   34. *Saint Bennet:* Saint Benedict; possibly alluding to the London parish church of St. Bennet Hithe on Paul's Wharf, just across the Thames from the Globe.   36. *fool:* (1) befool, cheat; (2) obtain by your jester's wit. *throw:* (1) time; (2) throw of the dice.   46. *Vulcan:* the smith of the gods, blackened by the smoky fire in his smithy.

A baubling vessel was he captain of,
For shallow draught and bulk unprizable,
With which such scathful grapple did he make
With the most noble bottom of our fleet,   50
That very envy, and the tongue of loss,
Cried fame and honor on him. What's the matter?

1. Officer: Orsino, this is that Antonio
That took the *Phoenix* and her fraught from Candy,
And this is he that did the *Tiger* board,   55
When your young nephew Titus lost his leg.
Here in the streets, desperate of shame and state,
In private brabble did we apprehend him.

Viola: He did me kindness, sir, drew on my side,
But in conclusion put strange speech upon me.   60
I know not what 'twas but distraction.

Duke: Notable pirate, thou salt-water thief!
What foolish boldness brought thee to their mercies
Whom thou in terms so bloody and so dear
Hast made thine enemies?

Antonio: Orsino, noble sir,   65
Be pleas'd that I shake off these names you give me.
Antonio never yet was thief or pirate,
Though I confess, on base and ground enough,
Orsino's enemy. A witchcraft drew me hither:
That most ingrateful boy there by your side   70
From the rude sea's enrag'd and foamy mouth
Did I redeem; a wrack past hope he was.
His life I gave him, and did thereto add
My love, without retention or restraint,
All his in dedication. For his sake   75
Did I expose myself (pure for his love)
Into the danger of this adverse town,
Drew to defend him when he was beset;
Where being apprehended, his false cunning
(Not meaning to partake with me in danger)   80

---

47. *baubling:* trifling, toylike.   48. *For . . . unprizable:* valueless because of its shallow
draught and small size. For another *bauble / shallow / bulk* cluster see *Troilus and Cressida,* I.
iii.34–37.   49. *scathful:* damaging.   50. *bottom:* ship.   51. *envy:* enmity, i.e. (we) his
enemies. *loss:* i.e. the losers.   54. *fraught:* freight, cargo *from Candy:* returning from Candia
(Crete).   57. *desperate . . . state:* i.e. with reckless disregard of disgrace and danger. *Shame*
refers perhaps to his involvement in a street brawl, *state* to his dangerous position as a public
enemy.   58. *brabble:* brawl.   59. *drew . . . side:* drew his sword in my defense.   60. *put . . .
me:* spoke very strangely to me.   61. *but distraction:* unless it was insanity.   62. *Notable:*
notorious.   64. *in terms:* in a manner. *dear:* grievous.   66. *Be pleas'd:* permit.   68. *base and
ground:* The nouns are synonyms.   72. *wrack:* wreck.   74. *retention:* reservation.   76. *pure:*
solely.   77. *Into:* to. *adverse:* hostile.   80. *Not . . . partake:* having no intention of sharing.

Taught him to face me out of his acquaintance,
And grew a twenty years removed thing
While one would wink; denied me mine own purse,
Which I had recommended to his use
Not half an hour before.
Viola: How can this be?   85
Duke: When came he to this town?
Antonio: To-day, my lord; and for three months before,
No int'rim, not a minute's vacancy,
Both day and night did we keep company.

Enter Olivia *and* Attendants.

Duke: Here comes the Countess, now heaven walks on earth.   90
But for thee, fellow—fellow, thy words are madness.
Three months this youth hath tended upon me,
But more of that anon. Take him aside.
Olivia: What would my lord, but that he may not have,
Wherein Olivia may seem serviceable?   95
Cesario, you do not keep promise with me.
Viola: Madam—
Duke: Gracious Olivia—
Olivia: What do you say, Cesario? Good my lord—
Viola: My lord would speak, my duty hushes me.   100
Olivia: If it be aught to the old tune, my lord,
It is as fat and fulsome to mine ear
As howling after music.
Duke: Still so cruel?
Olivia: Still so constant, lord.
Duke: What, to perverseness? You uncivil lady.   105
To whose ingrate and unauspicious altars
My soul the faithfull'st off'rings have breath'd out
That e'er devotion tender'd! What shall I do?
Olivia: Even what it please my lord, that shall become him.
Duke: Why should I not (had I the heart to do it),   110
Like to th' Egyptian thief at point of death,
Kill what I love? (a savage jealousy

---

81. *face . . . acquaintance:* deny brazenly that he knew me.   82–83. *grew . . . wink:* in the
twinkling of an eye became as distant as if we had not seen each other for twenty years.
84. *recommended:* commended, committed.   88. *vacancy:* gap, interval.   94. *but . . . have:*
i.e. except what I cannot give him (i.e. her love).   95. *seem serviceable:* show her duty.
102. *fat and fulsome:* gross and distasteful.   105. *uncivil:* inhumane.   106. *ingrate:*
ungrateful. *unauspicious:* unpropitious.   108. *tender'd:* offered.   111. *Egyptian thief:*
Referring to an episode in Heliodorus' *Ethiopica* in which Thyamis, an Egyptian robber
captain who has taken Chariclea captive and fallen in love with her, finds himself in danger of
death at his enemies' hands and attempts to kill Chariclea first.

That sometime savors nobly), but hear me this:
Since you to non-regardance cast my faith,
And that I partly know the instrument   115
That screws me from my true place in your favor,
Live you the marble-breasted tyrant still.
But this your minion, whom I know you love,
And whom, by heaven I swear, I tender dearly,
Him will I tear out of that cruel eye,   120
Where he sits crowned in his master's spite.
Come, boy, with me, my thoughts are ripe in mischief.
I'll sacrifice the lamb that I do love,
To spite a raven's heart within a dove.

Viola: And I most jocund, apt, and willingly,   125
To do you rest, a thousand deaths would die.

Olivia: Where goes Cesario?

Viola: After him I love
More than I love these eyes, more than my life,
More by all mores than e'er I shall love wife.
If I do feign, you witnesses above   130
Punish my life for tainting of my love!

Olivia: Ay me, detested! how am I beguil'd!

Viola: Who does beguile you? who does do you wrong?

Olivia: Hast thou forgot thyself? Is it so long? Call forth the holy
father.

Duke: Come, away!   135

Olivia: Whither, my lord? Cesario, husband, stay.

Duke: Husband?

Olivia: Ay, husband. Can he that deny?

Duke: Her husband, sirrah?

Viola: No, my lord, not I.

Olivia: Alas, it is the baseness of thy fear
That makes thee strangle thy propriety.   140
Fear not, Cesario, take thy fortunes up,
Be that thou know'st thou art, and then thou art
As great as that thou fear'st.

Enter Priest.

O, welcome, father!

---

113. *savors nobly:* has a noble quality about it.   114. *non-regardance:* disregard, neglect. *faith:*
constancy.   115. *that:* Repeating the sense of *Since,* line 114.   116. *screws:* forces.
117. *marble-breasted:* stony-hearted.   118. *minion:* darling.   119. *tender:* regard.
121. *in . . . spite:* in defiance of his master.   125. *apt:* ready.   126. *do you rest:* give you
peace.   129. *mores:* (such) comparisons.   131. *tainting . . . love:* bringing my love into discredit.   132. *detested:* renounced, rejected.   138. *sirrah:* form of address to an inferior.
140. *strangle thy propriety:* i.e. disown your identity as my husband.   141. *take . . . up:* receive
your fortune.   143. *that thou fear'st:* i.e. Orsino.

Father, I charge thee by thy reverence
Here to unfold, though lately we intended   145
To keep in darkness what occasion now
Reveals before 'tis ripe, what thou dost know
Hath newly pass'd between this youth and me.
    Priest: A contract of eternal bond of love,
Confirm'd by mutual joinder of your hands,   150
Attested by the holy close of lips,
Strength'ned by interchangement of your rings,
And all the ceremony of this compact
Seal'd in my function, by my testimony;
Since when, my watch hath told me, toward my grave   155
I have travell'd but two hours.
    Duke: O thou dissembling cub! what wilt thou be
When time hath sow'd a grizzle on thy case?
Or will not else thy craft so quickly grow,
That thine own trip shall be thine overthrow?   160
Farewell, and take her, but direct thy feet
Where thou and I (henceforth) may never meet.
    Viola: My lord, I do protest—
    Olivia: O, do not swear!
Hold little faith, though thou hast too much fear.

Enter Sir Andrew.

Sir Andrew: For the love of God, a surgeon! Send one presently to Sir   165
    Toby.
    Olivia: What's the matter?
Sir Andrew: H'as broke my head across, and has given Sir Toby a
    bloody coxcomb too. For the love of God, your help! I had
    rather than forty pound I were at home.   170
    Olivia: Who has done this, Sir Andrew?
Sir Andrew: The Count's gentleman, one Cesario. We took him for a
    coward, but he's the very devil incardinate.
    Duke: My gentleman, Cesario?
Sir Andrew: 'Od's lifelings, here he is! You broke my head for nothing,   175
    and that that I did, I was set on to do't by Sir Toby.
    Viola: Why do you speak to me? I never hurt you.

---

147. *occasion:* necessity.   148. *newly:* recently.   150. *joinder:* joining.   151. *close:* union.
154. *Seal'd:* ratified, attested. *in my function:* i.e. by my authority as priest.   158. *a grizzle:*
grey hair. *case:* skin (of a fox); Orsino is thus calling Viola-Cesario a fox-cub.   160. *trip:*
attempt to trip up (or trap) another.   163. *protest:* avow, swear.   164. *Hold little:* keep a little.   165. *presently:* immediately.   168. *H'as . . . across:* he has given me a cut on the head.
169. *coxcomb:* head (with a suggestion of the cap traditionally worn by the professional fool in
its applicability to Sir Toby and Sir Andrew).   173. *incardinate:* Apparently Sir Andrew's slip
for *incarnate.*   175. *'Od's lifelings:* by God's little lives.

> You drew your sword upon me without cause,
> But I bespake you fair, and hurt you not.

Enter Sir Toby *and* Clown.

Sir Andrew: If a bloody coxcomb be a hurt, you have hurt me. I think 180
    you set nothing by a bloody coxcomb. Here comes Sir Toby
    halting—you shall hear more. But if he had not been in drink,
    he would have tickled you othergates than he did.
    Duke: How now, gentleman? how is't with you?
  Sir Toby: That's all one. H'as hurt me, and there's th' end on't. Sot, 185
    didst see Dick surgeon, sot?
    Clown: O, he's drunk, Sir Toby, an hour agone; his eyes were set at
    eight i' th' morning.
  Sir Toby: Then he's a rogue, and a passy-measures [pavin]. I hate a
    drunken rogue. 190
    Olivia: Away with him! Who hath made this havoc with them?
Sir Andrew: I'll help you, Sir Toby, because we'll be dress'd together.
  Sir Toby: Will you help?—an ass-head and a coxcomb and a knave, a
    thin-fac'd knave, a gull!
    Olivia: Get him to bed, and let his hurt be look'd to. 195

[Exeunt Clown, Fabian, Sir Toby, and Sir Andrew.]

Enter Sebastian.

  Sebastian: I am sorry, madam, I have hurt your kinsman,
> But had it been the brother of my blood,
> I must have done no less with wit and safety.
> You throw a strange regard upon me, and by that
> I do perceive it hath offended you. 200
> Pardon me, sweet one, even for the vows
> We made each other but so late ago.
    Duke: One face, one voice, one habit, and two persons,
> A natural perspective, that is and is not!
  Sebastian: Antonio, O my dear Antonio! 205
> How have the hours rack'd and tortur'd me,

---

179. *bespake you fair:* spoke courteously to you.　181. *set nothing by:* regard as nothing.
182. *halting:* limping. *But if:* if only. *in drink:* drunk.　183. *tickled:* chastised. *othergates:*
otherwise.　185. *That's all one:* no matter. *there's . . . on't:* that's that. *Sot:* fool.　187. *set:*
extinguished (as in *the sun sets*). *passy-measures pavin:* Naylor explains
passy-measures (from Italian *passamezzo*) as a dance tune with "strains" consisting of eight bars
each (hence suggested to Sir Toby by Feste's "set at eight"). The pavin or pavan(e) was a slow
and stately dance. Sir Toby obviously expects no speedy aid from Dick surgeon.　192. *be
dress'd:* have our wounds cared for.　193. *coxcomb:* fool.　194. *gull:* dupe.　198. *with . . .
safety:* i.e. with due regard for my own safety.　199. *throw . . .me:* look at me as if I were a
stranger.　203. *habit:* dress.　204. *natural perspective:* i.e. an optical illusion produced by
nature, not by a perspective glass (an optical device that makes the viewer see an object
differently). *that . . . not:* i.e. that must be an illusion and yet is not.

　　　　　Since I have lost thee!
　　Antonio:　Sebastian are you?
Sebastian:　　　　　　　　Fear'st thou that, Antonio?
　　Antonio:　How have you made division of yourself?
　　　　　An apple, cleft in two, is not more twin　　　　　　　210
　　　　　Than these two creatures. Which is Sebastian?
　　Olivia:　Most wonderful!
Sebastian:　Do I stand there? I never had a brother;
　　　　　Nor can there be that deity in my nature
　　　　　Of here and every where. I had a sister,　　　　　　　215
　　　　　Whom the blind waves and surges have devour'd.
　　　　　Of charity, what kin are you to me?
　　　　　What countryman? What name? What parentage?
　　Viola:　Of Messaline; Sebastian was my father,
　　　　　Such a Sebastian was my brother too;　　　　　　　220
　　　　　So went he suited to his watery tomb.
　　　　　If spirits can assume both form and suit,
　　　　　You come to fright us.
Sebastian:　　　　　　　　A spirit I am indeed,
　　　　　But am in that dimension grossly clad
　　　　　Which from the womb I did participate.　　　　　　　225
　　　　　Were you a woman, as the rest goes even,
　　　　　I should my tears let fall upon your cheek,
　　　　　And say, "Thrice welcome, drowned Viola!"
　　Viola:　My father had a mole upon his brow.
Sebastian:　And so had mine.　　　　　　　230
　　Viola:　And died that day when Viola from her birth
　　　　　Had numb'red thirteen years.
Sebastian:　O, that record is lively in my soul!
　　　　　He finished indeed his mortal act
　　　　　That day that made my sister thirteen years.　　　　　　　235
　　Viola:　If nothing lets to make us happy both
　　　　　But this my masculine usurp'd attire,
　　　　　Do not embrace me till each circumstance
　　　　　Of place, time, fortune, do cohere and jump
　　　　　That I am Viola—which to confirm,　　　　　　　240
　　　　　I'll bring you to a captain in this town,
　　　　　Where lie my maiden weeds; by whose gentle help
　　　　　I was preserv'd to serve this noble count.

214. *deity:* divine attribute.　215. *here . . . where:* omnipresence.　216. *blind:* ruthless.
217. *Of charity:* (tell me) out of kindness.　221. *suited:* dressed.　224. *in . . . clad:* clothed in
that corporeal frame.　225. *participate:* share existence with.　226. *as . . . even:* i.e. as (is
likely since) all the rest accords. A common type of ellipsis; for another example see line
252.　233. *lively:* vivid.　236. *lets:* hinders.　239. *cohere:* agree. *jump:* coincide, agree.
242. *Where:* at whose house. *weeds:* clothes.

All the occurrence of my fortune since
Hath been between this lady and this lord. 245
Sebastian: [To Olivia.] So comes it, lady, you have been mistook;
But Nature to her bias drew in that.
You would have been contracted to a maid,
Nor are you therein, by my life, deceiv'd,
You are betroth'd both to a maid and man. 250
Duke: Be not amaz'd, right noble is his blood.
If this be so, as yet the glass seems true,
I shall have share in this most happy wrack.
[To Viola.] Boy, thou hast said to me a thousand times
Thou never shouldst love woman like to me. 255
Viola: And all those sayings will I over swear,
And all those swearings keep as true in soul
As doth that orbed continent the fire
That severs day from night.
Duke: Give me thy hand,
And let me see thee in thy woman's weeds. 260
Viola: The captain that did bring me first on shore
Hath my maid's garments. He upon some action
Is now in durance, at Malvolio's suit,
A gentleman, and follower of my lady's.
Olivia: He shall enlarge him; fetch Malvolio hither. 265
And yet, alas, now I remember me,
They say, poor gentleman, he's much distract.

Enter Clown *with a letter, and* Fabian.

A most extracting frenzy of mine own
From my remembrance clearly banish'd his.
How does he, sirrah? 270
Clown: Truly, madam, he holds Belzebub at the stave's end as well
as a man in his case may do. H'as here writ a letter to you; I
should have given't you to-day morning. But as a madman's
epistles are no gospels, so it skills not much when they are
deliver'd. 275

---

247. *Nature . . . that:* i.e. your nature was true to its own bent when you fell in love with one
who is the perfect likeness of me. 248. *contracted:* betrothed. 250. *maid:* virgin (here
applied to a man). 251. *amaz'd:* astounded, dazed (a much stronger word than in modern
usage). 252. *glass:* i.e. the "natural perspective" of line 204. 256. *over:* again.
258. *As . . . fire:* i.e. as the sun's sphere keeps the fire. *Continent* = container. 262. *action:*
legal charge. 263. *durance:* prison. 265. *enlarge:* release. 266. *remember me:* recall.
267. *distract:* distracted, out of his wits. 268. *extracting frenzy:* i.e. madness that took other
things out of my mind. 269. *his:* i.e. remembrance of his frenzy. 271. *holds . . . end:* keeps
the devil (who possesses him) at a distance. "To hold the devil at stave's end" was proverbial.
273–74. *a madman's . . . gospels:* i.e. a madman's letters are not to be taken as gospel truth
(with play on the reading of appointed passages from the epistles and the gospels in a church
service). 274. *it . . . much:* doesn't matter much.

Olivia: Open't and read it.

Clown: Look then to be well edified when the fool delivers the
madman. *[Reads madly.]* "By the Lord, madam,"—

Olivia: How now, art thou mad?

Clown: No, madam, I do but read madness. And your ladyship 280
will have it as it ought to be, you must allow *vox.*

Olivia: Prithee read i' thy right wits.

Clown: So I do, madonna; but to read his right wits is to read thus;
therefore perpend, my princess, and give ear.

Olivia: *[To Fabian.]* Read it you, sirrah. 285

Fabian: *(Reads.)* "By the Lord, madam, you wrong me, and the
world shall know it. Though you have put me into darkness,
and given your drunken cousin rule over me, yet have I the
benefit of my senses as well as your ladyship. I have your own
letter that induc'd me to the semblance I put on; with the which 290
I doubt not but to do myself much right, or you much shame.
Think of me as you please. I leave my duty a little unthought of,
and speak out of my injury.

The madly-us'd Malvolio."

Olivia: Did he write this? 295

Clown: Ay, madam.

Duke: This savors not much of distraction.

Olivia: See him deliver'd, Fabian, bring him hither. *[Exit Fabian.]*
My lord, so please you, these things further thought on,
To think me as well a sister as a wife, 300
One day shall crown th' alliance on't, so please you,
Here at my house and at my proper cost.

Duke: Madam, I am most apt t' embrace your offer.
[To Viola.] Your master quits you; and for your service done
him, 305
So much against the mettle of your sex,
So far beneath your soft and tender breeding,
And since you call'd me master for so long,
Here is my hand—you shall from this time be
Your master's mistress.

Olivia: A sister! you are she.

Enter [Fabian *with*] Malvolio.

Duke: Is this the madman? 310

---

277. *delivers:* presents, speaks the words of. 280. *And:* if. 281. *vox:* voice, i.e. dramatic
reading. 284. *perpend:* consider. 290. *the which:* i.e. the letter (as proof). 292. *my duty:*
the duty I owe you as your servant. 298. *deliver'd:* released. 300. *think . . . wife:* regard me
as favorably as a sister-in-law as you would have as a wife. 301. *crown . . . on't:* i.e. see the
performance of the two weddings that will create that relationship. 302. *proper cost:* own
expense. 303. *apt:* ready. 304. *quits:* frees, withdraws all claim to. 306. *mettle:*
disposition.

Olivia: Ay, my lord, this same.
          How now, Malvolio?
Malvolio: Madam, you have done me wrong,
          Notorious wrong.
Olivia: Have I, Malvolio? No.
Malvolio: Lady, you have. Pray you peruse that letter.
          You must not now deny it is your hand;   315
          Write from it if you can, in hand or phrase,
          Or say 'tis not your seal, not your invention.
          You can say none of this. Well, grant it then,
          And tell me, in the modesty of honor,
          Why you have given me such clear lights of favor,   320
          Bade me come smiling and cross-garter'd to you,
          To put on yellow stockings, and to frown
          Upon Sir Toby and the lighter people;
          And acting this in an obedient hope,
          Why have you suffer'd me to be imprison'd,   325
          Kept in a dark house, visited by the priest,
          And made the most notorious geck and gull
          That e'er invention play'd on? Tell me why!
Olivia: Alas, Malvolio, this is not my writing,
          Though I confess much like the character;   330
          But out of question 'tis Maria's hand.
          And now I do bethink me, it was she
          First told me thou wast mad. Then cam'st in smiling,
          And in such forms which here were presuppos'd
          Upon thee in the letter. Prithee be content.   335
          This practice hath most shrewdly pass'd upon thee;
          But when we know the grounds and authors of it,
          Thou shalt be both the plaintiff and the judge
          Of thine own cause.
Fabian: Good madam, here me speak,
          And let no quarrel nor no brawl to come   340
          Taint the condition of this present hour,
          Which I have wond'red at. In hope it shall not,
          Most freely I confess, myself and Toby
          Set this device against Malvolio here,
          Upon some stubborn and uncourteous parts   345
          We had conveiv'd against him. Maria writ

---

316. *from it:* differently. *hand or phrase:* handwriting or phraseology. 317. *invention:* composition. 319. *in . . . honor:* with the sense of propriety of an honorable person. 320. *clear lights:* i.e. sure signs. 323. *lighter:* lesser. 327. *geck:* fool. 328. *invention:* devising. 331. *out of:* beyond. 333. *cam'st:* cam'st thou. 334. *which:* as. *presuppos'd:* suggested beforehand. 336. *shrewdly:* grievously. *pass'd upon:* imposed upon. 342. *wond'red:* marvelled. 345. *Upon:* (which) in consequence of. *stubborn:* rude, haughty. *parts:* acts. 346. *conceiv'd:* devised.

The letter at Sir Toby's great importance,
In recompense whereof he hath married her.
How with a sportful malice it was follow'd
May rather pluck on laughter than revenge,   350
If that the injuries be justly weigh'd
That have on both sides pass'd.
    Olivia: Alas, poor fool, how have they baffled thee!
    Clown: Why, "some are born great, some achieve greatness, and
some have greatness thrown upon them." I was one, sir, in this   355
enterlude—one Sir Topas, sir, but that's all one. "By the Lord,
fool, I am not mad." But do you remember? "Madam, why
laugh you at such a barren rascal? And you smile not, he's
gagg'd." And thus the whirligig of time brings in his revenges.
Malvolio: I'll be reveng'd on the whole pack of you.   *[Exit.]* 360
    Olivia: He hath been most notoriously abus'd.
    Duke: Pursue him, and entreat him to a peace;
He hath not told us of the captain yet.
When that is known, and golden time convents,
A solemn combination shall be made   365
Of our dear souls. Mean time, sweet sister,
We will not part from hence. Cesario, come—
For so you shall be while you are a man;
But when in other habits you are seen,
Orsino's mistress, and his fancy's queen. *Exeunt [all but Clown].* 370

Clown sings.

    When that I was and a little tine boy,
       With hey ho, the wind and the rain,
    A foolish thing was but a toy,
       For the rain it raineth every day.

    But when I came to man's estate,   375
       With hey ho, etc.
    'Gainst knaves and thieves men shut their gate,
       For the rain, etc.

    But when I came, alas, to wive,
       With hey ho, etc.   380

---

347. *importance:* importunity.   349. *sportful:* jesting. *follow'd:* carried through.   350. *pluck on:* draw on, induce.   353. *baffled thee:* put you down.   356. *enterlude:* interlude, i.e. comedy.   359. *whirligig of time:* time's circling course. A whirligig is a spinning top or toy.
361. *He . . . abus'd:* Olivia thus repeats Malvolio's own judgment at IV.ii.75.   363. *captain:* See lines 240–43, 261–64.   364. *convents:* suits.   365. *combination:* marriage.
371. *tine:* tiny. Cf. with lines 389 ff. the song in *King Lear,* III.ii.74–77, in which the variant spelling *tine* again appears.   373. *A . . . toy:* i.e. my mischief was not taken seriously.
377. *'Gainst . . . gate:* i.e. my mischief caused men to shut their doors against me as a knave and a thief.

By swaggering could I never thrive,
  For the rain, etc.
But when I came unto my beds,
  With hey ho, etc.
With toss-pots still had drunken heads,   385
  For the rain, etc.
A great while ago the world begun,
  [With] hey ho, etc.
But that's all one, our play is done,
  And we'll strive to please you every day.   *[Exit.]* 390

Further Reading

Woolf, Virginia. "Twelfth Night at the Old Vic." *The Death of the Moth.* New York: Harcourt, 1942. 45–50. • King, Walter N. Introduction. *Twentieth Century Interpretations of "Twelfth Night."* Ed. Walter N. King. Englewood Cliffs, NJ: Prentice, 1968. 1–14. • Summers, Joseph H. "The Masks of Twelfth Night." *Twentieth Century Interpretations of "Twelfth Night."* Ed. Walter N. King. Englewood Cliffs, NJ: Prentice, 1968. 15–23. • Auden, W. H. "Music in Shakespeare." *The Dyer's Hand.* New York: Random, 1962. 500–27, spec. 520–22. • Williams, Porter, Jr. "Mistakes in *Twelfth Night* and Their Resolution: A Study in Some Relationships of Plot and Theme." *Twentieth Century Interpretations of "Twelfth Night."* Ed. Walter N. King. Englewood Cliffs, NJ: Prentice, 1968. 31–44. • Krieger, Elliot. "Twelfth Night." *A Marxist Study of Shakespeare's Comedies.* New York: Barnes, 1979. 97–130.

That drama is meant to be acted by players on a stage—that it is written to be brought literally to life before an audience—is easy enough to forget when we sit solitary, silent, reading the printed page. The "sport and play" of words, especially the words of Shakespeare, can overtake us, and we can feel that the play's essence is imprinted on our consciousness. But many nuances, intonations, and downright interpretations can only be conveyed by voice and gesture, thus the reader's understanding is often different from that of the viewer. As Virginia Woolf reminds us in a review of a performance of Twelfth Night, *to see the play enacted is to be made "to pause and think about it," to recognize that playwrights write "for the body and the mind simultaneously."*

---

381. *swaggering:* bullying, blustering.   383. *unto my beds:* to old age (?)   385. *toss-pots:* drunkards.

Virginia Woolf: On a Performance of *Twelfth Night*

Certainly there is a good deal to be said for reading *Twelfth Night* in the book if the book can be read in a garden, with no sound but the thud of an apple falling to the earth, or of the wind ruffling the branches of the trees. For one thing there is time—time not only to hear "the sweet sound that breathes upon a bank of violets" but to unfold the implications of that very subtle speech as the Duke winds into the nature of love. There is time, too, to make a note in the margin; time to wonder at queer jingles like "that live in her; when liver, brain, and heart" . . . "and of a foolish knight that you brought in one night" and to ask oneself whether it was from them that was born the lovely, "And what should I do in Illyria? My brother he is in Elysium." For Shakespeare is writing, it seems, not with the whole of his mind mobilized and under control but with feelers left flying that sport and play with words so that the trail of a chance word is caught and followed recklessly. From the echo of one word is born another word, for which reason, perhaps, the play seems as we read it to tremble perpetually on the brink of music. They are always calling for songs in *Twelfth Night,* "O fellow come, the song we had last night." Yet Shakespeare was not so deeply in love with words but that he could turn and laugh at them. "They that do dally with words do quickly make them wanton." There is a roar of laughter and out burst Sir Toby, Sir Andrew, Maria. Words on their lips are things that have meaning; that rush and leap out with a whole character packed in a little phrase. When Sir Andrew says "I was adored once," we feel that we hold him in the hollow of our hands; a novelist would have taken three volumes to bring us to that pitch of intimacy. And Viola, Malvolio, Olivia, the Duke —the mind so brims and spills over with all that we know and guess about them as they move in and out among the lights and shadows of the mind's stage that we ask why should we imprison them within the bodies of real men and women? Why exchange this garden for the theatre? The answer is that Shakespeare wrote for the stage and presumably with reason. . . .

The play gains immensely in robustness, in solidity. The printed word is changed out of all recognition when it is heard by other people. We watch it strike upon this man or woman; we see them laugh or shrug their shoulders, or turn aside to hide their faces. The word is given a body as well as a soul. Then again as the actors pause, or topple over a barrel, or stretch their hands out, the flatness of the print is broken up as by crevasses or precipices; all the proportions are changed. Perhaps the most impressive effect in the play is achieved by the long pause which Sebastian and Viola make as they stand looking at each other in a silent ecstasy of recognition. The reader's eye may have slipped over that moment entirely. Here we are made to pause and think about it; and are reminded that Shakespeare wrote for the body and for the mind simultaneously.

But now that the actors have done their proper work of solidifying and intensifying our impressions, we begin to criticize them more minutely and to compare their version with our own. We make Mr. Quartermaine's Malvolio stand beside our Malvolio. And to tell the truth, wherever the fault may lie, they have very little in common. Mr. Quartermaine's Malvolio is a splendid gentleman, courteous, considerate, well bred; a man of parts and humour who has no quarrel with the world. He has never felt a twinge of vanity or a moment's envy in his life. If Sir Toby and Maria fool him he sees through it, we may be sure, and only suffers it as a fine gentleman puts up with the games of foolish children. Our Malvolio, on the other hand, was a fantastic complex creature, twitching with vanity, tortured by ambition. There was cruelty in his teasing, and a hint of tragedy in his defeat; his final threat had a momentary terror in it. But when Mr. Quartermaine says "I'll be revenged on the whole pack of you," we feel merely that the powers of the law will be soon and effectively invoked. What, then, becomes of Olivia's "He hath been most notoriously abused"? Then there is Olivia. Madame Lopokova has by nature that rare quality which is neither to be had for the asking nor to be subdued by the will—the genius of personality. She has only to float on to the stage and everything round her suffers, not a sea change, but a change into light, into gaiety; the birds sing, the sheep are garlanded, the air rings with melody and human beings dance towards each other on the tips of their toes possessed of an exquisite friendliness, sympathy and delight. But our Olivia was a stately lady; of sombre complexion, slow moving, and of few sympathies. She could not love the Duke nor change her feeling. Madame Lopokova loves everybody. She is always changing. Her hands, her face, her feet, the whole of her body, are always quivering in sympathy with the moment. She could make the moment, as she proved when she walked down the stairs with Sebastian, one of intense and moving beauty; but she was not our Olivia. . . .

Nevertheless, the play has served its purpose. It has made us compare our Malvolio with Mr. Quartermaine's; our Olivia with Madame Lopokova's; our reading of the whole play with Mr. Guthrie's; and since they all differ, back we must go to Shakespeare. We must read *Twelfth Night* again.

WILLIAM SHAKESPEARE

(1564–1616)

THE TRAGEDY OF HAMLET, PRINCE OF DENMARK

edited by G. Blakemore Evans

CHARACTERS

Claudius, King of Denmark
Hamlet, son to the late King Hamlet, and nephew to the
   present King
Polonius, Lord Chamberlain
Horatio, friend to Hamlet
Laertes, son to Polonius
Voltemand ⎫
Cornelius ⎪
Rosencrantz ⎬ *courtiers*
Guildenstern ⎪
Osric ⎪
Gentleman ⎭
Marcellus ⎫ *officers*
Barnardo ⎭
Francisco, a soldier
Reynaldo, servant to Polonius
Fortinbras, Prince of Norway
Norwegian Captain
Doctor of Divinity
Players
Two Clowns, gravediggers
English Ambassadors
Gertrude, Queen of Denmark, and mother to Hamlet
Ophelia, daughter to Polonius
Ghost of Hamlet's Father
Lords, Ladies, Officers, Soldiers, Sailors, Messengers, and
   Attendants

Scene: Denmark

Words and passages enclosed in square brackets in the text above are either emendations of the Second Quarto (1604–1605) or additions to it. The following abbreviations appear in the notes: F1 (First Folio), Q2 (Second Quarto), Q3 (Third Quarto), o.s.d. (opening stage direction), and s.d. (stage direction).

ACT I

Scene I

Enter Barnardo *and* Francisco, *two sentinels, [meeting].*

    Barnardo: Who's there?
    Francisco: Nay, answer me. Stand and unfold yourself.
    Barnardo: Long live the King!
    Francisco: Barnardo.
    Barnardo: He.   5
    Francisco: You come most carefully upon your hour.
    Barnardo: 'Tis now strook twelf. Get thee to bed, Francisco.
    Francisco: For this relief much thanks. 'Tis bitter cold,
        And I am sick at heart.
    Barnardo: Have you had quiet guard?
    Francisco: Not a mouse stirring.   10
    Barnardo: Well, good night.
        If you do meet Horatio and Marcellus,
        The rivals of my watch, bid them make haste.

Enter Horatio *and* Marcellus.

    Francisco: I think I hear them. Stand ho! Who is there?
    Horatio: Friends to this ground.
    Marcellus: And liegemen to the Dane.   15
    Francisco: Give you good night.
    Marcellus: O, farewell, honest [soldier].
        Who hath reliev'd you?
    Francisco: Barnardo hath my place.
        Give you good night.   *Exit Francisco.*
    Marcellus: Holla, Barnardo!
    Barnardo: Say—
        What, is Horatio there?
    Horatio: A piece of him.
    Barnardo: Welcome, Horatio, welcome, good Marcellus.   20
    Horatio: What, has this thing appear'd again to-night?
    Barnardo: I have seen nothing.
    Marcellus: Horatio says 'tis but our fantasy,
        And will not let belief take hold of him
        Touching this dreaded sight twice seen of us;   25
        Therefore I have entreated him along,

I.i. Location: Elsinore. A guard-platform of the castle.   2. *answer me:* i.e. *you* answer *me.*
Francisco is on watch; Barnardo has come to relieve him.   *unfold yourself:* make known who
you are.   3. *Long . . . King:* Perhaps a password, perhaps simply an utterance to allow the
voice to be recognized.   7. *strook twelf:* struck twelve.   9. *sick at heart:* in low spirits.
13. *rivals:* partners.   15. *liegemen . . . Dane:* loyal subjects to the King of Denmark.
16. *Give:* God give.   23. *fantasy:* imagination.

> With us to watch the minutes of this night,
> That if again this apparition come,
> He may approve our eyes and speak to it.
Horatio: Tush, tush, 'twill not appear.
Barnardo: Sit down a while,   30
> And let us once again assail your ears,
> That are so fortified against our story,
> What we have two nights seen.
Horatio: Well, sit we down,
> And let us hear Barnardo speak of this.
Barnardo: Last night of all,   35
> When yond same star that's westward from the pole
> Had made his course t' illume that part of heaven
> Where now it burns, Marcellus and myself,
> The bell then beating one—

Enter Ghost.

Marcellus: Peace, break thee off! Look where it comes again!   40
Barnardo: In the same figure like the King that's dead.
Marcellus: Thou art a scholar, speak to it, Horatio.
Barnardo: Looks 'a not like the King? Mark it, Horatio.
Horatio: Most like; it [harrows] me with fear and wonder.
Barnardo: It would be spoke to.
Marcellus: Speak to it, Horatio.   45
Horatio: What art thou that usurp'st this time of night,
> Together with that fair and warlike form
> In which the majesty of buried Denmark
> Did sometimes march? By heaven I charge thee speak!
Marcellus: It is offended.
Barnardo: See, it stalks away!   50
Horatio: Stay! Speak, speak, I charge thee speak!   *Exit Ghost.*
Marcellus: 'Tis gone, and will not answer.
Barnardo: How now, Horatio? you tremble and look pale.
> Is not this something more than fantasy?
> What think you on't?   55
Horatio: Before my God, I might not this believe
> Without the sensible and true avouch
> Of mine own eyes.
Marcellus: Is it not like the King?
Horatio: As thou art to thyself.

---

29. *approve:* corroborate.   36. *pole:* pole star.   37. *his:* its (the commonest form of the neuter possessive singular in Shakespeare's day).   41. *like:* in the likeness of.   42. *a scholar:* i.e. one who knows how best to address it.   43. *'a:* he.   45. *It . . . to:* A ghost had to be spoken to before it could speak.   46. *usurp'st:* The ghost, a supernatural being, has invaded the realm of nature.   48. *majesty . . . Denmark:* late King of Denmark.   49. *sometimes:* formerly.   57. *sensible:* relating to the senses.   *avouch:* guarantee.

Such was the very armor he had on   60
When he the ambitious Norway combated.
So frown'd he once when in an angry parle
He smote the sledded [Polacks] on the ice.
'Tis strange.

Marcellus: Thus twice before, and jump at this dead hour,   65
With martial stalk hath he gone by our watch.

Horatio: In what particular thought to work I know not,
But in the gross and scope of mine opinion,
This bodes some strange eruption to our state.

Marcellus: Good now, sit down, and tell me, he that knows,   70
Why this same strict and most observant watch
So nightly toils the subject of the land,
And [why] such daily [cast] of brazen cannon,
And foreign mart for implements of war,
Why such impress of shipwrights, whose sore task   75
Does not divide the Sunday from the week,
What might be toward, that this sweaty haste
Doth make the night joint-laborer with the day:
Who is't that can inform me?

Horatio: That can I,
At least the whisper goes so: our last king,   80
Whose image even but now appear'd to us,
Was, as you know, by Fortinbras of Norway,
Thereto prick'd on by a most emulate pride,
Dar'd to the combat; in which our valiant Hamlet
(For so this side of our known world esteem'd him)   85
Did slay this Fortinbras, who, by a seal'd compact
Well ratified by law and heraldry,
Did forfeit (with his life) all [those] his lands
Which he stood seiz'd of, to the conqueror;
Against the which a moi'ty competent   90
Was gaged by our king, which had [return'd]
To the inheritance of Fortinbras,
Had he been vanquisher; as by the same comart
And carriage of the article [design'd],
His fell to Hamlet. Now, sir, young Fortinbras,   95

---

61. *Norway:* King of Norway. 62. *parle:* parley. 63. *sledded:* using sleds or sledges.
Polacks: Poles. 65. *jump:* precisely. 67-68. *In . . . opinion:* while I have no precise theory
about it, my general feeling is that. *Gross* = wholeness, totality; *scope* = range. 69. *eruption:*
upheaval. 72. *toils:* causes to work. *subject:* subjects. 74. *foreign mart:* dealing with foreign
markets. 75. *impress:* forced service. 77. *toward:* in preparation. 83. *emulate:* emulous,
proceeding from rivalry. 87. *law and heraldy:* heraldic law (governing combat). *Heraldy* is a
variant of *heraldry.* 89. *seiz'd of:* possessed of. 90. *moi'ty:* portion. *competent:* adequate, i.e.
equivalent. 91. *gaged:* pledged. *had:* would have. 92. *inheritance:* possession. 93. *comart:*
bargain. 94. *carriage:* tenor. *design'd:* drawn up.

Of unimproved mettle hot and full,
Hath in the skirts of Norway here and there
Shark'd up a list of lawless resolutes
For food and diet to some enterprise
That hath a stomach in't, which is no other,   100
As it doth well appear unto our state,
But to recover of us, by strong hand
And terms compulsatory, those foresaid lands
So by his father lost; and this, I take it,
Is the main motive of our preparations,   105
The source of this our watch, and the chief head
Of this post-haste and romage in the land.

Barnardo: I think it be no other but e'en so.
Well may it sort that this portentous figure
Comes armed through our watch so like the King   110
That was and is the question of these wars.

Horatio: A mote it is to trouble the mind's eye.
In the most high and palmy state of Rome,
A little ere the mightiest Julius fell,
The graves stood [tenantless] and the sheeted dead   115
Did squeak and gibber in the Roman streets.
As stars with trains of fire, and dews of blood,
Disasters in the sun; and the moist star
Upon whose influence Neptune's empire stands
Was sick almost to doomsday with eclipse.   120
And even the like precurse of [fear'd] events,
As harbingers preceding still the fates
And prologue to the omen coming on,
Have heaven and earth together demonstrated
Unto our climatures and countrymen.   125

Enter Ghost.

But soft, behold! lo where it comes again!
                                   It spreads his arms.
I'll cross it though it blast me. Stay, illusion!

---

96. *unimproved:* untried (?) or not directed to any useful end (?). 97. *skirts:* outlying
territories. 98. *Shark'd up:* gathered up hastily and indiscriminately. 100. *stomach:* relish
of danger (?) or demand for courage (?). 106. *head:* source. 107. *romage:* rummage,
bustling activity. 109. *sort:* fit. *portentous:* ominous. 116. One or more lines may have been
lost between this line and the next. 118. *Disasters:* ominous signs. *moist star:* moon.
119. *Neptune's empire stands:* the seas are dependent. 120. *sick . . . doomsday:* i.e. almost
totally darkened. When the Day of Judgment is imminent, says Matthew 24:29, "the moon
shall not give her light." *eclipse:* There were a solar and two total lunar eclipses visible in
England in 1598; they caused gloomy speculation. 121. *precurse:* foreshadowing.
122. *harbingers:* advance messengers. *still:* always. 123. *omen:* i.e. the events portended.
125. *climatures:* regions. 126 s.d. *his:* its. 127. *cross it:* cross its path, confront it directly.
blast: wither (by supernatural means).

If thou hast any sound or use of voice,
Speak to me.
If there be any good thing to be done   130
That may to thee do ease, and grace to me,
Speak to me.
If thou art privy to thy country's fate,
Which happily foreknowing may avoid,
O speak!   135
Or if thou hast uphoarded in thy life
Extorted treasure in the womb of earth,
For which, they say, our spirits oft walk in death,
Speak of it, stay and speak! *(The cock crows.)* Stop it,
Marcellus.   140
Marcellus: Shall I strike it with my partisan?
   Horatio: Do, if it will not stand.
Barnardo: 'Tis here!
   Horatio: 'Tis here!
Marcellus: 'Tis gone!   [*Exit Ghost.*]
We do it wrong, being so majestical,
To offer it the show of violence,
For it is as the air, invulnerable,   145
And our vain blows malicious mockery.
Barnardo: It was about to speak when the cock crew.
   Horatio: And then it started like a guilty thing
Upon a fearful summons. I have heard
The cock, that is the trumpet to the morn,   150
Doth with his lofty and shrill-sounding throat
Awake the god of day, and at his warning,
Whether in sea or fire, in earth or air,
Th' extravagant and erring spirit hies
To his confine, and of the truth herein   155
This present object made probation.
Marcellus: It faded on the crowing of the cock.
Some say that ever 'gainst that season comes
Wherein our Saviour's birth is celebrated,
This bird of dawning singeth all night long,   160
And then they say no spirit dare stir abroad,
The nights are wholesome, then no planets strike,
No fairy takes, nor witch hath power to charm,
So hallowed, and so gracious, is that time.

---

134. *happily:* haply, perhaps.   138. *your:* Colloquial and impersonal; cf. I.v.167, IV.iii.20,
22. Most editors adopt *you* from F1.   141. *partisan:* long-handled spear.   146. *malicious
mockery:* mockery of malice, i.e. empty pretenses of harming it.   150. *trumpet:* trumpeter.
154. *extravagant:* wandering outside its proper bounds. *erring:* wandering abroad. *hies:*
hastens.   156. *object:* sight. *probation:* proof.   158. *'gainst:* just before.   162. *strike:* exert
malevolent influence.   163. *takes:* bewitches, charms.   164. *gracious:* blessed.

Horatio: So have I heard and do in part believe it.   165
        But look, the morn in russet mantle clad
        Walks o'er the dew of yon high eastward hill.
        Break we our watch up, and by my advice
        Let us impart what we have seen to-night
        Unto young Hamlet, for, upon my life,   170
        This spirit, dumb to us, will speak to him.
        Do you consent we shall acquaint him with it,
        As needful in our loves, fitting our duty?
Marcellus: Let's do't, I pray, and I this morning know
        Where we shall find him most convenient.   *Exeunt.* 175

Scene II

Flourish.   Enter Claudius, King of Denmark, Gertrude the Queen; Council:
as Polonius; *and his son* Laertes, Hamlet, *cum aliis* [*including* Voltemand *and*
Cornelius].

        King: Though yet of Hamlet our dear brother's death
        The memory be green, and that it us befitted
        To bear our hearts in grief, and our whole kingdom
        To be contracted in one brow of woe,
        Yet so far hath discretion fought with nature   5
        That we with wisest sorrow think on him
        Together with remembrance of ourselves.
        Therefore our sometime sister, now our queen,
        Th' imperial jointress to this warlike state,
        Have we, as 'twere with a defeated joy,   10
        With an auspicious, and a dropping eye,
        With mirth in funeral, and with dirge in marriage,
        In equal scale weighing delight and dole,
        Taken to wife; nor have we herein barr'd
        Your better wisdoms, which have freely gone   15
        With this affair along. For all, our thanks.
        Now follows that you know young Fortinbras,
        Holding a weak supposal of our worth,
        Or thinking by our late dear brother's death
        Our state to be disjoint and out of frame,   20
        Co-leagued with this dream of his advantage,
        He hath not fail'd to pester us with message

---

166. *russet:* coarse greyish-brown cloth.
I.ii. Location: The castle.   o.s.d. *Flourish:* trumpet fanfare. *cum aliis:* with others.
2. *befitted:* would befit.   4. *contracted in:* (1) reduced to; (2) knit or wrinkled in. *brow of woe:*
mournful brow.   9. *jointress:* joint holder.   10. *defeated:* impaired.   11. *auspicious . . .
dropping:* cheerful . . . weeping.   15. *freely:* fully, without reservation.   17. *know:* be
informed, learn.   18. *supposal:* conjecture, estimate.   21. *Co-leagued:* joined.   22. *pester
. . . message:* trouble me with persistent messages (the original sense of *pester* is "overcrowd").

Importing the surrender of those lands
Lost by his father, with all bands of law,
To our most valiant brother. So much for him.   25
Now for ourself, and for this time of meeting,
Thus much the business is: we have here writ
To Norway, uncle of young Fortinbras—
Who, impotent and bedred, scarcely hears
Of this his nephew's purpose—to suppress   30
His further gait herein, in that the levies,
The lists, and full proportions are all made
Out of his subject; and we here dispatch
You, good Cornelius, and you, Voltemand,
For bearers of this greeting to old Norway,   35
Giving to you no further personal power
To business with the King, more than the scope
Of these delated articles allow.   *[Giving a paper.]*
Farewell, and let your haste commend your duty.
Cornelius, Voltemand: In that, and all things, will we show our duty.   40
    King: We doubt it nothing; heartily farewell.
                      [Exeunt Voltemand and Cornelius.]
And now, Laertes, what's the news with you?
You told us of some suit, what is't, Laertes?
You cannot speak of reason to the Dane
And lose your voice. What wouldst thou beg, Laertes,   45
    That shall not be my offer, not thy asking?
The head is not more native to the heart,
The hand more instrumental to the mouth,
Than is the throne of Denmark to thy father.
What wouldst thou have, Laertes?
  Laertes: My dread lord,   50
Your leave and favor to return to France,
From whence though willingly I came to Denmark
To show my duty in your coronation,
Yet now I must confess, that duty done,
My thoughts and wishes bend again toward France,   55
And bow them to your gracious leave and pardon.
    King: Have you your father's leave? What says Polonius?
  Polonius: H'ath, my lord, wrung from me my slow leave
By laborsome petition, and at last
Upon his will I seal'd my hard consent.   60

---

23. *Importing:* having as import.   24. *bands:* bonds, binding terms.   29. *impotent and bedred:*
feeble and bedridden.   31. *gait:* proceeding.   31-33. *in . . . subject:* since the troops are all
drawn from his subjects.   38. *delated:* extended, detailed (a variant of *dilated*).   41. *nothing:*
not at all.   45. *lose:* waste.   47. *native:* closely related.   48. *instrumental:* serviceable.
51. *leave and favor:* gracious permission.   56. *pardon:* permission to depart.   58. *H'ath:* he
hath.   60. *hard:* reluctant.

                I do beseech you give him leave to go.
        King: Take thy fair hour, Laertes, time be thine,
                And thy best graces spend it at thy will!
                But now, my cousin Hamlet, and my son—
Hamlet: *[Aside.]* A little more than kin, and less than kind.   65
        King: How is it that the clouds still hang on you?
Hamlet: Not so, my lord, I am too much in the sun.
        Queen: Good Hamlet, cast thy nighted color off,
                And let thine eye look like a friend on Denmark.
                Do not for ever with thy vailed lids   70
                Seek for thy noble father in the dust.
                Thou know'st 'tis common, all that lives must die,
                Passing through nature to eternity.
Hamlet: Ay, madam, it is common.
        Queen: If it be,
                Why seems it so particular with thee?   75
Hamlet: Seems, madam? nay, it is, I know not "seems."
                'Tis not alone my inky cloak, [good] mother,
                Nor customary suits of solemn black,
                Nor windy suspiration of forc'd breath,
                No, nor the fruitful river in the eye,   80
                Nor the dejected havior of the visage,
                Together with all forms, moods, [shapes] of grief,
                That can [denote] me truly. These indeed seem,
                For they are actions that a man might play,
                But I have that within which passes show,   85
                These but the trappings and the suits of woe.
        King: 'Tis sweet and commendable in your nature, Hamlet,
                To give these mourning duties to your father.
                But you must know your father lost a father,
                That father lost, lost his, and the survivor bound   90
                In filial obligation for some term
                To do obsequious sorrow. But to persever
                In obstinate condolement is a course
                Of impious stubbornness, 'tis unmanly grief,
                It shows a will most incorrect to heaven,   95
                A heart unfortified, or mind impatient,
                An understanding simple and unschool'd:
                For what we know must be, and is as common

---

64. *cousin:* kinsman (used in familiar address to any collateral relative more distant than a brother or sister; here to a nephew). 65. *A little . . . kind:* closer than a nephew, since you are my mother's husband; yet more distant than a son, too (and not well disposed to you). 67. *sun:* With obvious quibble on *son.* 70. *vailed:* downcast. 72. *common:* general, universal. 75. *particular:* individual, personal. 80. *fruitful:* copious. 92. *obsequious:* proper to obsequies. 93. *condolement:* grief. 95. *incorrect:* unsubmissive.

As any the most vulgar thing to sense,
Why should we in our peevish opposition   100
Take it to heart? Fie, 'tis a fault to heaven,
A fault against the dead, a fault to nature,
To reason most absurd, whose common theme
Is death of fathers, and who still hath cried,
From the first corse till he that died to-day,   105
"This must be so." We pray you throw to earth
This unprevailing woe, and think of us
As of a father, for let the world take note
You are the most immediate to our throne,
And with no less nobility of love   110
Than that which dearest father bears his son
Do I impart toward you. For your intent
In going back to school in Wittenberg,
It is most retrograde to our desire,
And we beseech you bend you to remain   115
Here in the cheer and comfort of our eye,
Our chiefest courtier, cousin, and our son.
Queen: Let not thy mother lose her prayers, Hamlet,
    I pray thee stay with us, go not to Wittenberg.
Hamlet: I shall in all my best obey you, madam.   120
  King: Why, 'tis a loving and a fair reply.
    Be as ourself in Denmark. Madam, come.
    This gentle and unforc'd accord of Hamlet
    Sits smiling to my heart, in grace whereof,
    No jocund health that Denmark drinks to-day,   125
    But the great cannon to the clouds shall tell,
    And the King's rouse the heaven shall bruit again,
    Respeaking earthly thunder. Come away.
               Flourish. Exeunt all but Hamlet.
Hamlet: O that this too too sallied flesh would melt,
    Thaw, and resolve itself into a dew!   130
    Or that the Everlasting had not fix'd
    His canon 'gainst [self-]slaughter! O God, God,
    How [weary], stale, flat, and unprofitable
    Seem to me all the uses of this world!
    Fie on't, ah fie! 'tis an unweeded garden   135
    That grows to seed, things rank and gross in nature
    Possess it merely. That it should come [to this]!

---

99. *any . . . sense:* what is perceived to be commonest.   101. *to:* against.   103. *absurd:*
contrary.   107. *unprevailing:* unavailing.   111. *dearest:* most loving.   112. *impart:* i.e.
impart love.   127. *rouse:* bumper, drink. *bruit:* loudly declare.   129. *sallied:* sullied. Many
editors prefer the F1 reading, *solid.*   132. *canon:* law.   134. *uses:* customs.   137. *merely:*
utterly.

But two months dead, nay, not so much, not two.
So excellent a king, that was to this
Hyperion to a satyr, so loving to my mother   140
That he might not beteem the winds of heaven
Visit her face too roughly. Heaven and earth,
Must I remember? Why, she should hang on him
As if increase of appetite had grown
By what it fed on, and yet, within a month—   145
Let me not think on't! Frailty, thy name is woman!—
A little month, or ere those shoes were old
With which she followed my poor father's body,
Like Niobe, all tears—why, she, [even she]—
O God, a beast that wants discourse of reason   150
Would have mourn'd longer—married with my uncle,
My father's brother, but no more like my father
Than I to Hercules. Within a month,
Ere yet the salt of most unrighteous tears
Had left the flushing in her galled eyes,   155
She married—O most wicked speed: to post
With such dexterity to incestious sheets,
It is not, nor it cannot come to good,
But break my heart, for I must hold my tongue.

Enter Horatio, Marcellus, *and* Barnardo.

   Horatio: Hail to your lordship!
   Hamlet: I am glad to see you well.   160
      Horatio—or I do forget myself.
   Horatio: The same, my lord, and your poor servant ever.
   Hamlet: Sir, my good friend—I'll change that name with you.
      And what make you from Wittenberg, Horatio? Marcellus.
  Marcellus: My good lord.   165
   Hamlet: I am very glad to see you. *[To Barnardo.]* Good even,
      sir.—
      But what, in faith, make you from Wittenberg?
   Horatio: A truant disposition, good my lord.
   Hamlet: I would not hear your enemy say so,   170
      Nor shall you do my ear that violence
      To make it truster of your own report
      Against yourself. I know you are no truant.

---

139. *to:* in comparison with.   140. *Hyperion:* the sun-god.   141. *beteem:* allow.   147. *or ere:*
before.   149. *Niobe:* She wept endlessly for her children, whom Apollo and Artemis had
killed.   150. *wants . . . reason:* lacks the power of reason (which distinguishes men from
beasts).   154. *unrighteous:* i.e. hypocritical.   155. *flushing:* redness. *galled:* inflamed.
157. *incestious:* incestuous. The marriage of a man to his brother's widow was so regarded
until long after Shakespeare's day.   163. *change:* exchange.   164. *what . . . from:* what are
you doing away from.   169. *truant disposition:* inclination to play truant.

But what is your affair in Elsinore?
We'll teach you to drink [deep] ere you depart.   175
Horatio: My lord, I came to see your father's funeral.
Hamlet: I prithee do not mock me, fellow studient,
    I think it was to [see] my mother's wedding.
Horatio: Indeed, my lord, it followed hard upon.
Hamlet: Thrift, thrift, Horatio, the funeral bak'd meats   180
    Did coldly furnish forth the marriage tables.
    Would I had met my dearest foe in heaven
    Or ever I had seen that day, Horatio!
    My father—methinks I see my father.
Horatio: Where, my lord?   185
Hamlet: In my mind's eye, Horatio.
Horatio: I saw him once, 'a was a goodly king.
Hamlet: 'A was a man, take him for all in all,
    I shall not look upon his like again.
Horatio: My lord, I think I saw him yesternight.
Hamlet: Saw, who?   190
Horatio: My lord, the King your father.
Hamlet: The King my father?
Horatio: Season your admiration for a while
    With an attent ear, till I may deliver,
    Upon the witness of these gentlemen,   195
    This marvel to you.
Hamlet: For God's love let me hear!
Horatio: Two nights together had these gentlemen,
    Marcellus and Barnardo, on their watch,
    In the dead waste and middle of the night,
    Been thus encount'red: a figure like your father,   200
    Armed at point exactly, cap-a-pe,
    Appears before them, and with solemn march
    Goes slow and stately by them; thrice he walk'd
    By their oppress'd and fear-surprised eyes
    Within his truncheon's length, whilst they, distill'd   205
    Almost to jelly with the act of fear,
    Stand dumb and speak not to him. This to me
    In dreadful secrecy impart they did,
    And I with them the third night kept the watch,

---

177. *studient:* student.   181. *coldly:* when cold.   182. *dearest:* most intensely hated.
183. *Or:* ere, before.   193. *Season:* temper. *admiration:* wonder.   194. *deliver:* report.
199. *waste:* empty expanse.   201. *at point exactly:* in every particular. *cap-a-pe:* from head to
foot.   204. *fear-surprised:* overwhelmed by fear.   205. *truncheon:* short staff carried as a
symbol of military command.   206. *act:* action, operation.   208. *dreadful:* held in awe, i.e.
solemnly sworn.

	Where, as they had delivered, both in time,	210
	Form of the thing, each word made true and good,	
	The apparition comes. I knew your father,	
	These hands are not more like.	
Hamlet:	But where was this?	
Marcellus:	My lord, upon the platform where we watch.	
Hamlet:	Did you not speak to it?	
Horatio:	My lord, I did,	215
	But answer made it none. Yet once methought	
	It lifted up it head and did address	
	Itself to motion like as it would speak;	
	But even then the morning cock crew loud,	
	And at the sound it shrunk in haste away	220
	And vanish'd from our sight.	
Hamlet:	'Tis very strange.	
Horatio:	As I do live, my honor'd lord, 'tis true,	
	And we did think it writ down in our duty	
	To let you know of it.	
Hamlet:	Indeed, [indeed,] sirs. But this troubles me.	225
	Hold you the watch to-night?	
Marcellus, Barnardo:	We do, my lord.	
Hamlet:	Arm'd, say you?	
Marcellus, Barnardo:	Arm'd, my lord.	
Hamlet:	From top to toe?	
Marcellus, Barnardo:	My lord, from head to foot.	
Hamlet:	Then saw you not his face.	230
Horatio:	O yes, my lord, he wore his beaver up.	
Hamlet:	What, look'd he frowningly?	
Horatio:	A countenance more	
	In sorrow than in anger.	
Hamlet:	Pale, or red?	
Horatio:	Nay, very pale.	
Hamlet:	And fix'd his eyes upon you?	
Horatio:	Most constantly.	
Hamlet:	I would I had been there.	235
Horatio:	It would have much amaz'd you.	
Hamlet:	Very like, [very like]. Stay'd it long?	
Horatio:	While one with moderate haste might tell a hundreth.	
Both [Marcellus, Barnardo]:	Longer, longer.	
Horatio:	Not when I saw't.	
Hamlet:	His beard was grisl'd, no?	240

---

213. *are . . . like:* i.e. do not resemble each other more closely than the apparition resembled
him.   217. *it:* its.   217–218. *address . . . motion:* begin to make a gesture.   231. *beaver:*
visor.   238. *tell a hundreth:* count a hundred.   240. *grisl'd:* grizzled, mixed with grey.

Horatio: It was, as I have seen it in his life,
    A sable silver'd.
Hamlet: I will watch to-night,
    Perchance 'twill walk again.
Horatio: I warr'nt it will.
Hamlet: If it assume my noble father's person,
    I'll speak to it though hell itself should gape   245
    And bid me hold my peace. I pray you all,
    If you have hitherto conceal'd this sight,
    Let it be tenable in your silence still,
    And whatsomever else shall hap tonight,
    Give it an understanding but no tongue.   250
    I will requite your loves. So fare you well.
    Upon the platform 'twixt aleven and twelf
    I'll visit you.
All: Our duty to your honor.
Hamlet: Your loves, as mine to you; farewell.

                          Exeunt [all but Hamlet].

    My father's spirit—in arms! All is not well,   255
    I doubt some foul play. Would the night were come!
    Till then sit still, my soul. [Foul] deeds will rise,
    Though all the earth o'erwhelm them, to men's eyes.   *Exit.*

Scene III

Enter Laertes *and* Ophelia, *his sister.*

Laertes: My necessaries are inbark'd. Farewell.
    And, sister, as the winds give benefit
    And convey [is] assistant, do not sleep,
    But let me hear from you.
Ophelia: Do you doubt that?
Laertes: For Hamlet, and the trifling of his favor,   5
    Hold it a fashion and a toy in blood,
    A violet in the youth of primy nature,
    Forward, not permanent, sweet, not lasting,
    The perfume and suppliance of a minute—
    No more.
Ophelia: No more but so?
Laertes: Think it no more: 10
    For nature crescent does not grow alone

---

248. *tenable:* held close.   252. *aleven:* eleven.   256. *doubt:* suspect.

I.iii. Location: Polonius' quarters in the castle.   1. *inbark'd:* embarked, abroad.   3. *convey is assistant:* means of transport is available.   6. *a fashion:* i.e. standard behavior for a young man. *toy in blood:* idle fancy of youthful passion.   7. *primy:* springlike.   8. *Forward:* early of growth.   9. *suppliance:* pastime.   11. *crescent:* growing, increasing.

In thews and [bulk], but as this temple waxes,
The inward service of the mind and soul
Grows wide withal. Perhaps he loves you now,
And now no soil nor cautel doth besmirch   15
The virtue of his will, but you must fear,
His greatness weigh'd, his will is not his own,
[For he himself is subject to his birth:]
He may not, as unvalued persons do,
Carve for himself, for on his choice depends   20
The safety and health of this whole state,
And therefore must his choice be circumscrib'd
Unto the voice and yielding of that body
Whereof he is the head. Then if he says he loves you,
It fits your wisdom so far to believe it   25
As he in his particular act and place
May give his saying deed, which is no further
Than the main voice of Denmark goes withal.
Then weigh what loss your honor may sustain
If with too credent ear you list his songs,   30
Or lose your heart, or your chaste treasure open
                  To his unmast'red importunity.
Fear it, Ophelia, fear it, my dear sister,
And keep you in the rear of your affection,
Out of the shot and danger of desire.   35
The chariest maid is prodigal enough
If she unmask her beauty to the moon.
Virtue itself scapes not calumnious strokes.
The canker galls the infants of the spring
Too oft before their buttons be disclos'd,   40
And in the morn and liquid dew of youth
Contagious blastments are most imminent.
Be wary then, best safety lies in fear:
Youth to itself rebels, though none else near.
Ophelia: I shall the effect of this good lesson keep   45
As watchman to my heart. But, good my brother,
Do not, as some ungracious pastors do,
Show me the steep and thorny way to heaven,
Whiles, [like] a puff'd and reckless libertine,

---

12. *thews:* muscles, sinews.   12-14. *as . . . withal:* as the body develops, the powers of mind
and spirit grow along with it.   15. *soil:* stain. *cautel:* deceit.   16. *will:* desire.   17. *His
greatness weigh'd:* considering his princely status.   19. *unvalued:* of low rank.   20. *Carve for
himself:* indulge his own wishes.   23. *voice:* vote, approval. *yielding:* consent. *that body:* i.e. the
state.   26. *in . . . place:* i.e. acting as he must act in the position he occupies.   28. *main:*
general. *goes withal:* accord with.   30. *credent:* credulous.   35. *shot:* range.   39. *canker:*
canker-worm.   40. *buttons:* buds. *disclos'd:* opened.   42. *blastments:* withering blights.
44. *to:* of.   47. *ungracious:* graceless.   49. *puff'd:* bloated.

Himself the primrose path of dalliance treads,   50
And reaks not his own rede.
Laertes: O, fear me not.

Enter Polonius.

I stay too long—but here my father comes.
A double blessing is a double grace,
Occasion smiles upon a second leave.
Polonius: Yet here, Laertes? Aboard, aboard, for shame!   55
The wind sits in the shoulder of your sail,
And you are stay'd for. There—*[laying his hand on* Laertes'
head] my blessing with thee!
And these few precepts in thy memory
Look thou character. Give thy thoughts no tongue,   60
Nor any unproportion'd thought his act.
Be thou familiar, but by no means vulgar:
Those friends thou hast, and their adoption tried,
Grapple them unto thy soul with hoops of steel,
But do not dull thy palm with entertainment   65
Of each new-hatch'd, unfledg'd courage. Beware
Of entrance to a quarrel, but being in,
Bear't that th' opposed may beware of thee.
Give every man thy ear, but few thy voice,
Take each man's censure, but reserve thy judgment.   70
Costly thy habit as thy purse can buy,
But not express'd in fancy, rich, not gaudy,
For the apparel oft proclaims the man,
And they in France of the best rank and station
[Are] of a most select and generous chief in that.   75
Neither a borrower nor a lender [be],
For [loan] oft loses both itself and friend,
And borrowing dulleth [th'] edge of husbandry.
This above all: to thine own self be true,
And it must follow, as the night the day,   80
Thou canst not then be false to any man.
Farewell, my blessing season this in thee!
Laertes: Most humbly do I take my leave, my lord.
Polonius: The time invests you, go, your servants tend.

---

51. *reaks:* recks, heeds. *rede:* advice. *fear me not:* don't worry about me.   54. *Occasion:*
opportunity (here personified, as often). *smiles upon:* i.e. graciously bestows.   60. *character:*
inscribe.   61. *unproportion'd:* unfitting.   62. *familiar:* affable, sociable. *vulgar:* friendly with
everybody.   63. *their adoption tried:* their association with you tested and proved.   66. *courage:* spirited, young blood.   68. *Bear't that:* manage it in such a way that.   70. *Take:* listen to.
censure: opinion.   75. *generous:* noble. *chief:* eminence (?). But the line is probably corrupt.
Perhaps *of a* is intrusive, in which case *chief* = chiefly.   78. *husbandry:* thrift.   82. *season:*
preserve (?) or ripen, make fruitful (?).   84. *invests:* besieges. *tend:* wait.

Laertes: Farewell, Ophelia, and remember well   85
    What I have said to you.
Ophelia: 'Tis in my memory lock'd,
    And you yourself shall keep the key of it.
Laertes: Farewell.   *Exit Laertes.*
Polonius: What is't, Ophelia, he hath said to you?
Ophelia: So please you, something touching the Lord Hamlet.
Polonius: Marry, well bethought.   90
    'Tis told me, he hath very oft of late
    Given private time to you, and you yourself
    Have of your audience been most free and bounteous.
    If it be so—as so 'tis put on me,
    And that in way of caution—I must tell you,   95
    You do not understand yourself so clearly
    As it behooves my daughter and your honor.
    What is between you? Give me up the truth.
Ophelia: He hath, my lord, of late made many tenders
    Of his affection to me.   100
Polonius: Affection, puh! You speak like a green girl,
    Unsifted in such perilous circumstance.
    Do you believe his tenders, as you call them?
Ophelia: I do not know, my lord, what I should think.
Polonius: Marry, I will teach you: think yourself a baby   105
    That you have ta'en these tenders for true pay,
    Which are not sterling. Tender yourself more dearly,
    Or (not to crack the wind of the poor phrase,
    [Wringing] it thus) you'll tender me a fool.
Ophelia: My lord, he hath importun'd me with love   110
    In honorable fashion.
Polonius: Ay, fashion you may call it. Go to, go to.
Ophelia: And hath given countenance to his speech, my lord,
    With almost all the holy vows of heaven.
Polonius: Ay, springes to catch woodcocks. I do know,   115
    When the blood burns, how prodigal the soul
    Lends the tongue vows. These blazes, daughter,
    Giving more light than heat, extinct in both
    Even in their promise, as it is a-making,
    You must not take for fire. From this time   120
    Be something scanter of your maiden presence,

---

90. *Marry:* indeed (originally the name of the Virgin Mary used as an oath). 94. *put on:* told
to. 99. *tenders:* offers. 102. *Unsifted:* untried. 106. *tenders:* With play on the sense
"money offered in payment" (as in *legal tender*). 107. *Tender:* hold, value. 109. *Wringing:*
straining, forcing to the limit. *tender . . . fool:* (1) show me that you are a fool; (2) make me look
like a fool; (3) present me with a (bastard) grandchild. 112. *fashion:* See note on line 6.
113. *countenance:* authority. 115. *springes:* snares. *woodcocks:* Proverbially gullible birds.

Set your entreatments at a higher rate
Than a command to parle. For Lord Hamlet,
Believe so much in him, that he is young,
And with a larger teder may he walk   125
Than may be given you. In few, Ophelia,
Do not believe his vows, for they are brokers,
Not of that dye which their investments show,
But mere [implorators] of unholy suits,
Breathing like sanctified and pious bonds,   130
The better to [beguile]. This is for all:
I would not, in plain terms, from this time forth
Have you so slander any moment leisure
As to give words or talk with the Lord Hamlet.
Look to't, I charge you. Come your ways.   135
   Ophelia: I shall obey, my lord.   *Exeunt.*

[Scene IV]

Enter Hamlet, Horatio, *and* Marcellus.

     Hamlet: The air bites shrowdly, it is very cold.
     Horatio: It is [a] nipping and an eager air.
     Hamlet: What hour now?
     Horatio: I think it lacks of twelf.
  Marcellus: No, it is strook.
     Horatio: Indeed? I heard it not. It then draws near the season   5
Wherein the spirit held his wont to walk.

A flourish of trumpets, and two pieces goes off [within].

What does this mean, my lord?
     Hamlet: The King doth wake to-night and takes his rouse,
Keeps wassail, and the swagg'ring up-spring reels;
And as he drains his draughts of Rhenish down,   10
The kettle-drum and trumpet thus bray out
The triumph of his pledge.

122-23. *Set . . . parle:* place a higher value on your favors; do not grant interviews simply because he asks for them. Polonius uses a military figure: *entreatments* = negotiations for surrender; *parle* = parley, discuss terms.   124. *so . . . him:* no more than this with respect to him.   125. *larger teder:* longer tether.   127. *brokers:* procurers.   128. *Not . . . show:* not of the color that their garments (*investments*) exhibit, i.e. not what they seem.   129. *mere:* out-and-out.   130. *bonds:* (lover's) vows or assurances. Many editors follow Theobald in reading *bawds.*   133. *slander:* disgrace. *moment:* momentary.   135. *Come your ways:* come along.

I.iv. Location: The guard-platform of the castle. 1. *shrowdly:* shrewdly, wickedly.   2. *eager:* sharp.   6. s.d. *pieces:* cannon.   8. *doth . . . rouse:* i.e. holds revels far into the night. 9. *wassail:* carousal. *up-spring:* wild dance.   10. *Rhenish:* Rhine wine.   12. *triumph . . . pledge:* accomplishment of his toast (by draining his cup at a single draught).

Horatio: Is it a custom?

Hamlet: Ay, marry is't,
     But to my mind, though I am native here
     And to the manner born, it is a custom   15
     More honor'd in the breach than the observance.
     This heavy-headed revel east and west
     Makes us traduc'd and tax'd of other nations.
     They clip us drunkards, and with swinish phrase
     Soil our addition, and indeed it takes   20
     From our achievements, though perform'd at height,
     The pith and marrow of our attribute.
     So, oft it chances in particular men,
     That for some vicious mole of nature in them,
     As in their birth, wherein they are not guilty   25
     (Since nature cannot choose his origin),
     By their o'ergrowth of some complexion
     Oft breaking down the pales and forts of reason,
     Or by some habit, that too much o'er-leavens
     The form of plausive manners—that these men,   30
     Carrying, I say, the stamp of one defect,
     Being nature's livery, or fortune's star,
     His virtues else, be they as pure as grace,
     As infinite as man may undergo,
     Shall in the general censure take corruption   35
     From that particular fault: the dram of [ev'l]
     Doth all the noble substance of a doubt
     To his own scandal.

Enter Ghost.

Horatio: Look, my lord, it comes!

Hamlet: Angels and ministers of grace defend us!
     Be thou a spirit of health, or goblin damn'd,   40
     Bring with thee airs from heaven, or blasts from hell,
     Be thy intents wicked, or charitable,

---

15. *manner:* custom (of carousing). 16. *More . . . observance:* which it is more honorable to break than to observe. 18. *tax'd of:* censured by. 19. *clip:* clepe, call. 20. *addition:* titles of honor. 21. *at height:* most excellently. 22. *attribute:* reputation. 23. *particular:* individual. 24. *vicious . . . nature:* small natural blemish. 26. *his:* its. 27. *By . . . complexion:* by the excess of some one of the humors (which were thought to govern the disposition). 28. *pales:* fences. 29. *o'er-leavens:* makes itself felt throughout (as leaven works in the whole mass of dough). 30. *plausive:* pleasing. 32. *Being . . . star:* i.e. whether they were born with it, or got it by misfortune. *Star* means "blemish." 34. *undergo:* carry the weight of, sustain. 35. *general censure:* popular opinion. 36. *dram:* minute amount. *ev'l:* evil, with a pun on *eale,* "yeast" (cf. *o'er-leavens* in line 29). 37. *of a doubt:* A famous crux, for which many emendations have been suggested, the most widely accepted being Steevens' *often dout* (i.e. extinguish). 38. *To . . . scandal:* i.e. so that it all shares in the disgrace. 40. *of health:* wholesome, good.

Thou com'st in such a questionable shape
That I will speak to thee. I'll call thee Hamlet,
King, father, royal Dane. O, answer me!   45
Let me not burst in ignorance, but tell
Why thy canoniz'd bones, hearsed in death,
Have burst their cerements; why the sepulchre,
Wherein we saw thee quietly [inurn'd,]
Hath op'd his ponderous and marble jaws   50
To cast thee up again. What may this mean,
That thou, dead corse, again in complete steel
Revisits thus the glimpses of the moon,
Making night hideous, and we fools of nature
So horridly to shake our disposition   55
With thoughts beyond the reaches of our souls?
Say why is this? wherefore? what should we do?
                              [Ghost] beckons [Hamlet].

Horatio: It beckons you to go away with it,
    As if it some impartment did desire
    To you alone.
Marcellus: Look with what courteous action   60
    It waves you to a more removed ground,
    But do not go with it.
Horatio: No, by no means.
Hamlet: It will not speak, then I will follow it.
Horatio: Do not, my lord.
Hamlet: Why, what should be the fear?
    I do not set my life at a pin's fee,   65
    And for my soul, what can it do to that,
    Being a thing immortal as itself?
    It waves me forth again, I'll follow it.
Horatio: What if it tempt you toward the flood, my lord,
    Or to the dreadful summit of the cliff   70
    That beetles o'er his base into the sea,
    And there assume some other horrible form
    Which might deprive your sovereignty of reason,
    And draw you into madness? Think of it.
    The very place puts toys of desperation,   75
    Without more motive, into every brain
    That looks so many fadoms to the sea
    And hears it roar beneath.

---

43. *questionable:* inviting talk.   47. *canoniz'd:* buried with the prescribed rites.   48. *cerements:*
grave-clothes.   52. *complete steel:* full armor.   53. *Revisits:* The *-s* ending in the second
person singular is common.   54. *fools of nature:* the children (or the dupes) of a purely natural
order, baffled by the supernatural.   55. *disposition:* nature.   59. *impartment:* communication.   65. *fee:* worth.   73. *deprive . . . reason:* unseat reason from the rule of your mind.
75. *toys of desperation:* fancies of desperate action, i.e. inclinations to jump off.   77. *fadoms:*
fathoms.

Hamlet:	It waves me still.—
	Go on, I'll follow thee.
Marcellus:	You shall not go, my lord.
Hamlet:	Hold off your hands.
Horatio:	Be rul'd, you shall not go.
Hamlet:	My fate cries out,

Hamlet: It waves me still.—
Go on, I'll follow thee.
Marcellus: You shall not go, my lord.
Hamlet: Hold off your hands. 80
Horatio: Be rul'd, you shall not go.
Hamlet: My fate cries out,
And makes each petty artere in this body
As hardy as the Nemean lion's nerve.
Still am I call'd. Unhand me, gentlemen. 85
By heaven, I'll make a ghost of him that lets me!
I say away!—Go on, I'll follow thee.

Exeunt Ghost and Hamlet.

Horatio: He waxes desperate with [imagination].
Marcellus: Let's follow. 'Tis not fit thus to obey him.
Horatio: Have after. To what issue will this come? 90
Marcellus: Something is rotten in the state of Denmark.
Horatio: Heaven will direct it.
Marcellus: Nay, let's follow him. *Exeunt.*

[Scene V]

Enter Ghost *and* Hamlet.

Hamlet: Whither wilt thou lead me? Speak, I'll go no further.
Ghost: Mark me.
Hamlet: I will.
Ghost: My hour is almost come
When I to sulph'rous and tormenting flames
Must render up myself.
Hamlet: Alas, poor ghost!
Ghost: Pity me not, but lend thy serious hearing 5
To what I shall unfold.
Hamlet: Speak, I am bound to hear.
Ghost: So art thou to revenge, when thou shalt hear.
Hamlet: What?
Ghost: I am thy father's spirit,
Doom'd for a certain term to walk the night, 10
And for the day confin'd to fast in fires,
Till the foul crimes done in my days of nature
Are burnt and purg'd away. But that I am forbid
To tell the secrets of my prison-house,
I could a tale unfold whose lightest word 15
Would harrow up thy soul, freeze thy young blood,

---

83. *artere:* variant spelling of *artery;* here, ligament, sinew.   84. *Nemean lion:* Slain by
Hercules as one of his twelve labors. *nerve:* sinew.   86. *lets:* hinders.   92. *it:* i.e. the issue.
I.v. Location: On the battlements of the castle. 11. *fast:* do penance.   12. *crimes:* sins.

Make thy two eyes like stars start from their spheres,
Thy knotted and combined locks to part,
And each particular hair to stand an end,
Like quills upon the fearful porpentine.   20
But this eternal blazon must not be
To ears of flesh and blood. List, list, O, list!
If thou didst ever thy dear father love—

Hamlet: O God!

Ghost: Revenge his foul and most unnatural murther.   25

Hamlet: Murther!

Ghost: Murther most foul, as in the best it is,
But this most foul, strange, and unnatural.

Hamlet: Haste me to know't, that I with wings as swift
As meditation, or the thoughts of love,   30
May sweep to my revenge.

Ghost: I find thee apt,
And duller shouldst thou be than the fat weed
That roots itself in ease on Lethe wharf,
Wouldst thou not stir in this. Now, Hamlet, hear:
'Tis given out that, sleeping in my orchard,   35
A serpent stung me, so the whole ear of Denmark
Is by a forged process of my death
Rankly abus'd; but know, thou noble youth,
The serpent that did sting thy father's life
Now wears his crown.

Hamlet: O my prophetic soul!   40
My uncle?

Ghost: Ay, that incestuous, that adulterate beast,
With witchcraft of his wits, with traitorous gifts—
O wicked wit and gifts that have the power
So to seduce!—won to his shameful lust   45
The will of my most seeming virtuous queen.
O Hamlet, what [a] falling-off was there
From me, whose love was of that dignity
That it went hand in hand even with the vow
I made to her in marriage, and to decline   50
Upon a wretch whose natural gifts were poor
To those of mine!
But virtue, as it never will be moved,

---

17. *spheres:* eye-sockets; with allusion to the revolving spheres in which, according to the Ptolemaic astronomy, the stars were fixed.   19. *an end:* on end.   20. *fearful porpentine:* frightened porcupine.   21. *eternal blazon:* revelation of eternal things.   30. *meditation:* thought.   33. *Lethe:* river of Hades, the water of which made the drinker forget the past. *wharf:* bank.   35. *orchard:* garden.   37. *forged process:* false account.   38. *abus'd:* deceived. 42. *adulterate:* adulterous.

Though lewdness court it in a shape of heaven,
So [lust], though to a radiant angel link'd,   55
Will [sate] itself in a celestial bed
And prey on garbage.
But soft, methinks I scent the morning air,
Brief let me be. Sleeping within my orchard,
My custom always of the afternoon,   60
Upon my secure hour thy uncle stole,
With juice of cursed hebona in a vial,
And in the porches of my ears did pour
The leprous distillment, whose effect
Holds such an enmity with blood of man   65
That swift as quicksilver it courses through
The natural gates and alleys of the body,
And with a sudden vigor it doth [posset]
And curd, like eager droppings into milk,
The thin and wholesome blood. So did it mine,   70
And a most instant tetter bark'd about,
Most lazar-like, with vile and loathsome crust
All my smooth body.
Thus was I, sleeping, by a brother's hand
Of life, of crown, of queen, at once dispatch'd,   75
Cut off even in the blossoms of my sin,
Unhous'led, disappointed, unanel'd,
No reck'ning made, but sent to my account
With all my imperfections on my head.
O, horrible, O, horrible, most horrible!   80
If thou hast nature in thee, bear it not,
Let not the royal bed of Denmark be
A couch for luxury and damned incest.
But howsomever thou pursues this act,
Taint not thy mind, nor let thy soul contrive   85
Against thy mother aught. Leave her to heaven,
And to those thorns that in her bosom lodge
To prick and sting her. Fare thee well at once!
The glow-worm shows the matin to be near,
And gins to pale his uneffectual fire.   90
Adieu, adieu, adieu! remember me.   *[Exit.]*
  Hamlet: O all you host of heaven! O earth! What else?

---

54. *shape of heaven:* angelic form.   61. *secure:* carefree.   62. *hebona:* ebony (which Shakespeare, following a literary tradition, and perhaps also associating the word with *henbane,* thought the name of a poison).   68. *posset:* curdle.   69. *eager:* sour.   71. *tetter:* scabby eruption. *bark'd:* formed a hard covering, like bark on a tree.   72. *lazar-like:* leper-like. 75. *at once:* all at the same time. *dispatch'd:* deprived.   77. *Unhous'led:* without the Eucharist. *disappointed:* without (spiritual) preparation. *unanel'd:* unanointed, without extreme unction. 81. *nature:* natural feeling.   83. *luxury:* lust.   89. *matin:* morning.   90. *gins:* begins.

And shall I couple hell? O fie, hold, hold, my heart,
And you, my sinows, grow not instant old,
But bear me [stiffly] up. Remember thee!   95
Ay, thou poor ghost, whiles memory holds a seat
In this distracted globe. Remember thee!
Yea, from the table of my memory
I'll wipe away all trivial fond records,
All saws of books, all forms, all pressures past   100
That youth and observation copied there,
And thy commandement all alone shall live
Within the book and volume of my brain,
Unmix'd with baser matter. Yes, by heaven!
O most pernicious woman!   105
O villain, villain, smiling, damned villain!
My tables—meet it is I set it down
That one may smile, and smile, and be a villain!
At least I am sure it may be so in Denmark.   *[He writes.]*
So, uncle, there you are. Now to my word.   110
It is "Adieu, adieu! remember me."
I have sworn't.

   Horatio: [Within.]   My lord, my lord!
 Marcellus: [Within.]   Lord Hamlet!

Enter Horatio *and* Marcellus.

   Horatio: Heavens secure him!
   Hamlet: So be it!
 Marcellus: Illo, ho, ho, my lord!   115
   Hamlet: Hillo, ho, ho, boy! Come, [bird,] come.
 Marcellus: How is't, my noble lord?
   Horatio: What news, my lord?
   Hamlet: O, wonderful!
   Horatio: Good my lord, tell it.
   Hamlet: No, you will reveal it.
   Horatio: Not I, my lord, by heaven.
 Marcellus: Nor I, my lord.   120
   Hamlet: How say you then, would heart of man once think it?—
    But you'll be secret?

                         Both [Horatio, Marcellus]:
                  Ay, by heaven, [my lord].
   Hamlet: There's never a villain dwelling in all Denmark
    But he's an arrant knave.

---

94. *sinows:* sinews.   97. *globe:* head.   98. *table:* writing tablet.   99. *fond:* foolish.
100. *saws:* wise sayings. *forms:* shapes, images. *pressures:* impressions.   110. *word:* i.e. word of
command from the Ghost.   116. *Hillo . . . come:* Hamlet answers Marcellus' halloo with a
falconer's cry.

Horatio: There needs no ghost, my lord, come from the grave   125
    To tell us this.
Hamlet: Why, right, you are in the right,
    And so, without more circumstance at all,
    I hold it fit that we shake hands and part,
    You, as your business and desire shall point you,
    For every man hath business and desire,   130
    Such as it is, and for my own poor part,
    I will go pray.
Horatio: These are but wild and whirling words, my lord.
Hamlet: I am sorry they offend you, heartily,
    Yes, faith, heartily.
Horatio: There's no offense, my lord.   135
Hamlet: Yes, by Saint Patrick, but there is, Horatio,
    And much offense too. Touching this vision here,
    It is an honest ghost, that let me tell you.
    For your desire to know what is between us,
    O'ermaster't as you may. And now, good friends,   140
    As you are friends, scholars, and soldiers,
    Give me one poor request.
Horatio: What is't, my lord, we will.
Hamlet: Never make known what you have seen to-night.
                        Both [Horatio, Marcellus]:
    My lord, we will not.
Hamlet: Nay, but swear't.
Horatio: In faith,   145
    My lord, not I.
Marcellus: Nor I, my lord, in faith.
Hamlet: Upon my sword.
Marcellus: We have sworn, my lord, already.
Hamlet: Indeed, upon my sword, indeed.
                        Ghost cries under the stage.
  Ghost: Swear.
Hamlet: Ha, ha, boy, say'st thou so? Art thou there, truepenny?   150
    Come on, you hear this fellow in the cellarage,
    Consent to swear.
Horatio: Propose the oath, my lord.
Hamlet: Never to speak of this that you have seen,
    Swear by my sword.
  Ghost: *[Beneath.]*   Swear.   155
Hamlet: Hic et ubique? Then we'll shift our ground.
    Come hither, gentlemen,

---

127. *circumstance:* ceremony. 138. *honest:* true, genuine. 143. *What is't:* whatever it is.
147. *Upon my sword:* i.e. on the cross formed by the hilt. 150. *truepenny:* trusty fellow.
156. *Hic et ubique:* here and everywhere.

And lay your hands again upon my sword.
　　　　Swear by my sword
　　　　Never to speak of this that you have heard.　　　　　　　160
　　Ghost: *[Beneath.]* 　Swear by his sword.
　Hamlet: 　Well said, old mole, canst work i' th' earth so fast?
　　　　A worthy pioner! Once more remove, good friends.
　Horatio: 　O day and night, but this is wondrous strange!
　Hamlet: 　And therefore as a stranger give it welcome.　　　　165
　　　　There are more things in heaven and earth, Horatio,
　　　　Than are dreamt of in your philosophy.
　　　　But come—
　　　　Here, as before, never, so help you mercy,
　　　　How strange or odd some'er I bear myself—　　　　　　170
　　　　As I perchance hereafter shall think meet
　　　　To put an antic disposition on—
　　　　That you, at such times seeing me, never shall,
　　　　With arms encumb'red thus, or this headshake,
　　　　Or by pronouncing of some doubtful phrase,　　　　　　175
　　　　As "Well, well, we know," or "We could, and if we would,"
　　　　Or "If we list to speak," or "There be, and if they might,"
　　　　Or such ambiguous giving out, to note
　　　　That you know aught of me—this do swear,
　　　　So grace and mercy at your most need help you.　　　　180
　Ghost: 　*[Beneath.]* 　Swear.　　　　　　　　　　*[They swear.]*
　Hamlet: 　Rest, rest, perturbed spirit! So, gentlemen,
　　　　With all my love I do commend me to you,
　　　　And what so poor a man as Hamlet is
　　　　May do t' express his love and friending to you,　　　185
　　　　God willing, shall not lack. Let us go in together,
　　　　And still your fingers on your lips, I pray.
　　　　The time is out of joint—O cursed spite,
　　　　That ever I was born to set it right!
　　　　Nay, come, let's go together.　　　　　　　　*Exeunt.*　190

ACT II

Scene I

Enter old Polonius *with his man* [Reynaldo].

　Polonius: 　Give him this money and these notes, Reynaldo.
　Reynaldo: 　I will, my lord.

----

163. *pioner:* digger, miner (variant of *pioneer*).　165. *as . . . welcome:* give it the welcome due
in courtesy to strangers.　167. *your:* See note on I.i.138. *philosophy:* i.e. natural philosophy,
science.　172. *put . . . on:* behave in some fantastic manner, act like a madman.
174. *encumb'red:* folded.　176. *and if:* if.　177. *list:* cared, had a mind.　178. *note:*
indicate.　187. *still:* always.　190. *Nay . . . together:* They are holding back to let him go first.
II.i. Location: Polonius' quarters in the castle.

Polonius: You shall do marvell's wisely, good Reynaldo,
    Before you visit him, to make inquire
    Of his behavior.
Reynaldo: My lord, I did intend it.   5
Polonius: Marry, well said, very well said. Look you, sir,
    Inquire me first what Danskers are in Paris,
    And how, and who, what means, and where they keep,
    What company, at what expense; and finding
    By this encompassment and drift of question   10
    That they do know my son, come you more nearer
    Than your particular demands will touch it.
    Take you as 'twere some distant knowledge of him,
    As thus, "I know his father and his friends,
    And in part him." Do you mark this, Reynaldo?   15
Reynaldo: Ay, very well, my lord.
Polonius: "And in part him—but," you may say, "not well.
    But if't be he I mean, he's very wild,
    Addicted so and so," and there put on him
    What forgeries you please: marry, none so rank   20
    As may dishonor him, take heed of that,
    But, sir, such wanton, wild, and usual slips
    As are companions noted and most known
    To youth and liberty.
Reynaldo: As gaming, my lord.
Polonius: Ay, or drinking, fencing, swearing, quarreling,   25
    Drabbing—you may go so far.
Reynaldo: My lord, that would dishonor him.
Polonius: Faith, as you may season it in the charge:
    You must not put another scandal on him,
    That he is open to incontinency—   30
    That's not my meaning. But breathe his faults so quaintly
    That they may seem the taints of liberty,
    The flash and outbreak of a fiery mind,
    A savageness in unreclaimed blood,
    Of general assault.
Reynaldo: But, my good lord—   35
Polonius: Wherefore should you do this?
Reynaldo: Ay, my lord,
    I would know that.
Polonius: Marry, sir, here's my drift,

---

3. *marvell's:* marvellous(ly).   7. *Danskers:* Danes.   8. *keep:* lodge.   10. *encompassment:*
circuitousness. *drift of question:* directing of the conversation.   12. *particular demands:* direct
questions.   20. *forgeries:* invented charges.   22. *wanton:* sportive.   26. *Drabbing:* whoring.
28. *Faith:* Most editors read *Faith, no,* following F1; this makes easier sense. *season:* qualify,
temper.   30. *open to incontinency:* habitually profligate.   31. *quaintly:* artfully.   33. *unre-
claimed:* untamed.   34. *Of general assault:* i.e. to which young men are generally subject.

And I believe it is a fetch of wit:
You laying these slight sallies on my son,
As 'twere a thing a little soil'd [wi' th'] working,   40
Mark you,
Your party in converse, him you would sound,
Having ever seen in the prenominate crimes
The youth you breathe of guilty, be assur'd
He closes with you in this consequence: 45
"Good sir," or so, or "friend," or "gentleman,"
According to the phrase or the addition
Of man and country.
Reynaldo: Very good, my lord.
Polonius: And then, sir, does 'a this—'a does—what was I about
to say?   50
By the mass, I was about to say something.
Where did I leave?
Reynaldo: At "closes in the consequence."
Polonius: At "closes in the consequence," ay, marry.
He closes thus: "I know the gentleman.
I saw him yesterday, or th' other day,   55
Or then, or then, with such or such, and as you say,
There was 'a gaming, there o'ertook in 's rouse,
There falling out at tennis"; or, perchance,
"I saw him enter such a house of sale,"
Videlicet, a brothel, or so forth. See you now,   60
Your bait of falsehood take this carp of truth,
And thus do we of wisdom and of reach,
With windlasses and with assays of bias,
By indirections find directions out;
So by my former lecture and advice   65
Shall you my son. You have me, have you not?
Reynaldo: My lord, I have.
Polonius: God buy ye, fare ye well.
Reynaldo: Good my lord.
Polonius: Observe his inclination in yourself.
Reynaldo: I shall, my lord.   70
Polonius: And let him ply his music.

---

38. *fetch of wit:* ingenious device.   39. *sallies:* sullies, blemishes.   40. *soil'd . . . working:* i.e.
shopworn.   43. *Having:* if he has. *prenominate crimes:* aforementioned faults.   45. *closes:*
falls in. *in this consequence:* as follows.   47. *addition:* style of address.   57. *o'ertook in 's rouse:*
overcome by drink.   62. *reach:* capacity, understanding.   63. *windlasses:* roundabout
methods. *assays of bias:* indirect attempts (a figure from the game of bowls, in which the player
must make allowance for the curving course his bowl will take toward its mark).   64. *direc-*
tions: the way things are going.   66. *have me:* understand me.   67. *God buy ye:* good-bye (a
contraction of *God be with you*).   69. *in:* by. Polonius asks him to observe Laertes directly, as
well as making inquiries.   71. *let him ply:* see that he goes on with.

Reynaldo: Well, my lord.
Polonius: Farewell.   *Exit Reynaldo.*

Enter Ophelia.

                    How now, Ophelia, what's the matter?
Ophelia: O my lord, my lord, I have been so affrighted!
Polonius: With what, i' th' name of God?
Ophelia: My lord, as I was sewing in my closet,   75
          Lord Hamlet, with his doublet all unbrac'd,
          No hat upon his head, his stockins fouled,
          Ungart'red, and down-gyved to his ankle,
          Pale as his shirt, his knees knocking each other,
          And with a look so piteous in purport   80
          As if he had been loosed out of hell
          To speak of horrors—he comes before me.
Polonius: Mad for thy love?
Ophelia: My lord, I do not know,
          But truly I do fear it.
Polonius: What said he?
Ophelia: He took me by the wrist, and held me hard,   85
          Then goes he to the length of all his arm,
          And with his other hand thus o'er his brow,
          He falls to such perusal of my face
          As 'a would draw it. Long stay'd he so.
          At last, a little shaking of mine arm,   90
          And thrice his head thus waving up and down,
          He rais'd a sigh so piteous and profound
          As it did seem to shatter all his bulk
          And end his being. That done, he lets me go,
          And with his head over his shoulder turn'd,   95
          He seem'd to find his way without his eyes,
          For out a' doors he went without their helps,
          And to the last bended their light on me.
Polonius: Come, go with me. I will go seek the King.
          This is the very ecstasy of love,   100
          Whose violent property fordoes itself,
          And leads the will to desperate undertakings
          As oft as any passions under heaven
          That does afflict our natures. I am sorry—
          What, have you given him any hard words of late?   105
Ophelia: No, my good lord, but as you did command

---

75. *closet:* private room.   76. *unbrac'd:* unlaced.   77. *stockins fouled:* stockings dirty.
78. *down-gyved:* hanging down like fetters on a prisoner's legs.   93. *bulk:* body.   100. *ecstasy:*
madness.   101. *property:* quality. *fordoes:* destroys.

I did repel his letters, and denied
His access to me.

Polonius: That hath made him mad.
I am sorry that with better heed and judgment
I had not coted him. I fear'd he did but trifle   110
And meant to wrack thee, but beshrow my jealousy!
By heaven, it is as proper to our age
To cast beyond ourselves in our opinions,
As it is common for the younger sort
To lack discretion. Come, go we to the King.   115
This must be known, which, being kept close, might move
More grief to hide, than hate to utter love.
Come.   *Exeunt.*

Scene II

Flourish.   Enter King *and* Queen, Rosencrantz *and* Guildenstern *[cum aliis].*

King: Welcome, dear Rosencrantz and Guildenstern!
Moreover that we much did long to see you,
The need we have to use you did provoke
Our hasty sending. Something have you heard
Of Hamlet's transformation; so call it,   5
Sith nor th' exterior nor the inward man
Resembles that it was. What it should be,
More than his father's death, that thus hath put him
So much from th' understanding of himself,
I cannot dream of. I entreat you both   10
That, being of so young days brought up with him,
And sith so neighbored to his youth and havior,
That you voutsafe your rest here in our court
Some little time, so by your companies
To draw him on to pleasures, and to gather   15
So much as from occasion you may glean,
Whether aught to us unknown afflicts him thus,
That, open'd, lies within our remedy.

Queen: Good gentlemen, he hath much talk'd of you,
And sure I am two men there is not living   20
To whom he more adheres. If it will please you

---

110. *coted:* observed.   111. *beshrow:* beshrew, plague take. *jealousy:* suspicious mind.
112. *proper . . . age:* characteristic of men of my age.   113. *cast beyond ourselves:* overshoot,
go too far (by way of caution).   116. *close:* secret.   116-17. *move . . . love:* cause more
grievous consequences by its concealment than we shall incur displeasure by making it known.

II.ii. Location: The castle. 2. *Moreover . . . you:* besides the fact that we wanted to see you
for your own sakes. 6. *Sith:* since. 11. *of:* from. 13. *voutsafe your rest:* vouchsafe to
remain. 21. *more adheres:* is more attached.

To show us so much gentry and good will
As to expend your time with us a while
For the supply and profit of our hope,
Your visitation shall receive such thanks   25
As fits a king's remembrance.
Rosencrantz: Both your Majesties
Might, by the sovereign power you have of us,
Put your dread pleasures more into command
Than to entreaty.
Guildenstern: But we both obey,
And here give up ourselves, in the full bent,   30
To lay our service freely at your feet,
To be commanded.
    King: Thanks, Rosencrantz and gentle Guildenstern.
    Queen: Thanks, Guildenstern and gentle Rosencrantz.
And I beseech you instantly to visit   35
My too much changed son. Go some of you
And bring these gentlemen where Hamlet is.
Guildenstern: Heavens make our presence and our practices
Pleasant and helpful to him!
    Queen: Ay, amen!

Exeunt Rosencrantz *and* Guildenstern *[with some Attendants].*
Enter Polonius.

Polonius: Th' embassadors from Norway, my good lord,   40
Are joyfully return'd.
    King: Thou still hast been the father of good news.
Polonius: Have I, my lord? I assure my good liege
I hold my duty as I hold my soul,
Both to my God and to my gracious king;   45
And I do think, or else this brain of mine
Hunts not the trail of policy so sure
As it hath us'd to do, that I have found
The very cause of Hamlet's lunacy.
    King: O, speak of that, that do I long to hear.   50
Polonius: Give first admittance to th' embassadors;
My news shall be the fruit to that great feast.
    King: Thyself do grace to them, and bring them in.
                                                     [*Exit Polonius.*]
He tells me, my dear Gertrude, he hath found
The head and source of all your son's distemper.   55

---

22. *gentry:* courtesy.   24. *supply and profit:* support and advancement.   30. *in . . . bent:* to
our utmost.   40. *embassadors:* ambassadors.   42. *still:* always.   43. *liege:* sovereign.
47. *policy:* statecraft.   52. *fruit:* dessert.   55. *head:* Synonymous with *source. distemper:*
(mental) illness.

Queen: I doubt it is no other but the main,
His father's death and our [o'erhasty] marriage.

Enter [Polonius *with* Voltemand *and* Cornelius, *the*] *Embassadors.*

    King: Well, we shall sift him.—Welcome, my good friends!
    Say, Voltemand, what from our brother Norway?
Voltemand: Most fair return of greetings and desires. 60
    Upon our first, he sent out to suppress
    His nephew's levies, which to him appear'd
    To be a preparation 'gainst the Polack;
    But better look'd into, he truly found
    It was against your Highness. Whereat griev'd, 65
    That so his sickness, age, and impotence
    Was falsely borne in hand, sends out arrests
    On Fortinbras, which he, in brief, obeys,
    Receives rebuke from Norway, and in fine,
    Makes vow before his uncle never more 70
    To give th' assay of arms against your Majesty.
    Whereon old Norway, overcome with joy,
    Gives him threescore thousand crowns in annual fee,
    And his commission to employ those soldiers,
    So levied, as before, against the Polack, 75
    With an entreaty, herein further shown,   *[Giving a paper.]*
    That it might please you to give quiet pass
    Through your dominions for this enterprise,
    On such regards of safety and allowance
    As therein are set down.
  King: It likes us well, 80
    And at our more considered time we'll read,
    Answer, and think upon this business.
    Mean time, we thank you for your well-took labor.
    Go to your rest, at night we'll feast together.
    Most welcome home!   *Exeunt Embassadors [and Attendants].*
  Polonius: This business is well ended. 85
    My liege, and madam, to expostulate
    What majesty should be, what duty is,
    Why day is day, night night, and time is time,
    Were nothing but to waste night, day, and time;
    Therefore, [since] brevity is the soul of wit, 90
    And tediousness the limbs and outward flourishes,
    I will be brief. Your noble son is mad:

---

56. *doubt:* suspect. *main:* main cause.   61. *Upon our first:* at our first representation.
65. *griev'd:* aggrieved, offended.   67. *borne in hand:* taken advantage of.   69. *in fine:* in the end.   71. *assay:* trial.   79. *On . . . allowance:* with such safeguards and provisos.   80. *likes:* pleases.   81. *consider'd:* suitable for consideration.   86. *expostulate:* expound.   90. *wit:* understanding, wisdom.

Mad call I it, for to define true madness,
What is't but to be nothing else but mad?
But let that go.

Queen: More matter with less art. 95

Polonius: Madam, I swear I use no art at all.
That he's mad, 'tis true, 'tis true 'tis pity,
And pity 'tis 'tis true—a foolish figure,
But farewell it, for I will use no art.
Mad let us grant him then, and now remains 100
That we find out the cause of this effect,
Or rather say, the cause of this defect,
For this effect defective comes by cause:
Thus it remains, and the remainder thus.
Perpend. 105
I have a daughter—have while she is mine—
Who in her duty and obedience, mark,
Hath given me this. Now gather, and surmise.

[Reads the salutation of the letter.]
"To the celestial and my soul's idol, the most beautified
Ophelia"— 110
That's an ill phrase, a vile phrase, "beautified" is a vile
phrase. But you shall hear. Thus:
"In her excellent white bosom, these, etc."

Queen: Came this from Hamlet to her?

Polonius: Good madam, stay awhile. I will be faithful. 115

[Reads the] letter.
"Doubt thou the stars are fire,
Doubt that the sun doth move,
Doubt truth to be a liar,
But never doubt I love.
O dear Ophelia, I am ill at these numbers. I have not art to 120
reckon my groans, but that I love thee best, O most best,
believe it. Adieu.
Thine evermore, most dear lady,
whilst this machine is to him, Hamlet."
This in obedience hath my daughter shown me, 125
And more [above], hath his solicitings,
As they fell out by time, by means, and place,
All given to mine ear.

King: But how hath she
Receiv'd his love?

---

95. *art:* i.e., rhethorical art.   98. *figure:* figure of speech.   103. *For . . . cause:* for this effect
(which shows as a defect in Hamlet's reason) is not merely accidental, and has a cause we may
trace.   105. *Perpend:* consider.   109. *beautified:* beautiful (not an uncommon usage).
118. *Doubt:* suspect.   120. *ill . . . numbers:* bad at versifying.   121. *reckon:* count (with a
quibble on *numbers*).   124. *machine:* body.   126. *more above:* furthermore.

William Shakespeare **1117**

Polonius: What do you think of me?
    King: As of a man faithful and honorable.   130
Polonius: I would fain prove so. But what might you think,
        When I had seen this hot love on the wing—
        As I perceiv'd it (I must tell you that)
        Before my daughter told me—what might you,
        Or my dear Majesty your queen here, think,   135
        If I had play'd the desk or table-book,
        Or given my heart a [winking,] mute and dumb,
        Or look'd upon this love with idle sight,
        What might you think? No, I went round to work,
        And my young mistress thus I did bespeak: 140
        "Lord Hamlet is a prince out of thy star;
        This must not be"; and then I prescripts gave her,
        That she should lock herself from [his] resort,
        Admit no messengers, receive no tokens.
        Which done, she took the fruits of my advice;   145
        And he repell'd, a short tale to make,
        Fell into a sadness, then into a fast,
        Thence to a watch, thence into a weakness,
        Thence to [a] lightness, and by this declension,
        Into the madness wherein now he raves,   150
        And all we mourn for.
    King: Do you think ['tis] this?
    Queen: It may be, very like.
Polonius: Hath there been such a time—I would fain know that—
        That I have positively said, "'Tis so,"
        When it prov'd otherwise?
    King: Not that I know.   155
Polonius: [Points to his head and shoulder.] Take this from this, if
        this be otherwise.
        If circumstances lead me, I will find
        Where truth is hid, though it were hid indeed
        Within the centre.
    King: How may we try it further?   160
Polonius: You know sometimes he walks four hours together
        Here in the lobby.
    Queen: So he does indeed.
Polonius: At such a time I'll loose my daughter to him.
        Be you and I behind an arras then,

---

131. *fain:* willingly, gladly.   136. *play'd . . . table-book:* i.e. noted the matter secretly.
137. *winking:* closing of the eyes.   138. *idle sight:* noncomprehending eyes.   139. *round:*
straightforwardly.   140. *bespeak:* address.   141. *star:* i.e. sphere, lot in life.   145. *took . . . of:*
profited by, i.e. carried out.   146. *repell'd:* repulsed.   148. *watch:* sleeplessness.
149. *lightness:* lightheadedness.   159. *centre:* i.e. of the earth (which in the Ptolemaic system
is also the centre of the universe).   163. *arras:* hanging tapestry.

Mark the encounter: if he love her not,   165
And be not from his reason fall'n thereon,
Let me be no assistant for a state,
But keep a farm and carters.
    King: We will try it.

Enter Hamlet *[reading on a book.]*

   Queen: But look where sadly the poor wretch comes reading.
  Polonius: Away, I do beseech you, both away.   170
         I'll board him presently.   *Exeunt King and Queen.*
                          O, give me leave,
How does my good Lord Hamlet?
   Hamlet: Well, God-a-mercy.
  Polonius: Do you know me, my lord?
   Hamlet: Excellent well, you are a fishmonger.   175
  Polonius: Not I, my lord.
   Hamlet: Then I would you were so honest a man.
  Polonius: Honest, my lord?
   Hamlet: Ay, sir, to be honest, as this world goes, is to be one man
      pick'd out of ten thousand.   180
  Polonius: That's very true, my lord.
   Hamlet: For if the sun breed maggots in a dead dog, being a good
      kissing carrion—Have you a daughter?
  Polonius: I have, my lord.
   Hamlet: Let her not walk i' th' sun. Conception is a blessing, but 185
      as your daughter may conceive, friend, look to't.
  Polonius: *[Aside.]* How say you by that? still harping on my daugh-
      ter. Yet he knew me not at first, 'a said I was a fishmonger. 'A
      is far gone. And truly in my youth I suff'red much extremity
      for love—very near this. I'll speak to him again.—What do 190
      you read, my lord?
   Hamlet: Words, words, words.
  Polonius: What is the matter, my lord?
   Hamlet: Between who?
  Polonius: I mean, the matter that you read, my lord.   195
   Hamlet: Slanders, sir; for the satirical rogue says here that old
      men have grey beards, that their faces are wrinkled, their eyes
      purging thick amber and plumtree gum, and that they have a
      plentiful lack of wit, together with most weak hams; all which,
      sir, though I most powerfully and potently believe, yet I hold 200

---

166. *thereon:* because of that.   171. *board:* accost. *presently:* at once.   173. *God-a-mercy:*
thank you.   175. *fishmonger:* Usually explained as slang for "bawd," but no evidence has been
produced for such a usage in Shakespeare's day.   182–83. *good kissing carrion:* flesh good
enough for the sun to kiss.   185. *Conception:* understanding (with following play on the sense
"conceiving a child").   193. *matter:* subject; but Hamlet replies as if he had understood
Polonius to mean "cause for a quarrel."

it not honesty to have it thus set down, for yourself, sir, shall
grow old as I am, if like a crab you could go backward.

Polonius: *[Aside.]* Though this be madness, yet there is method
in't.—Will you walk out of the air, my lord?

Hamlet: Into my grave.   205

Polonius: Indeed that's out of the air. *[Aside.]* How pregnant
sometimes his replies are! a happiness that often madness
hits on, which reason and [sanity] could not so prosperously
be deliver'd of. I will leave him, [and suddenly contrive the
means of meeting between him] and my daughter.—My lord, 210
I will take my leave of you.

Hamlet: You cannot take from me any thing that I will not more
willingly part withal—except my life, except my life, except
my life.

Polonius: Fare you well, my lord.   215

Hamlet: These tedious old fools!

Enter Guildenstern *and* Rosencrantz.

Polonius: You go to seek the Lord Hamlet, there he is.

Rosencrantz: *[To Polonius.]* God save you, sir!   *[Exit Polonius.]*

Guildenstern: My honor'd lord!

Rosencrantz: My most dear lord!   220

Hamlet: My [excellent] good friends! How dost thou, Guildenstern? Ah, Rosencrantz! Good lads, how do you both?

Rosencrantz: As the indifferent children of the earth.

Guildenstern: Happy, in that we are not [over-]happy, on Fortune's
[cap] we are not the very button.   225

Hamlet: Nor the soles of her shoe?

Rosencrantz: Neither, my lord.

Hamlet: Then you live about her waist, or in the middle of her
favors?

Guildenstern: Faith, her privates we.   230

Hamlet: In the secret parts of Fortune? O, most true, she is a
· strumpet. What news?

Rosencrantz: None, my lord, but the world's grown honest.

Hamlet: Then is doomsday near. But your news is not true. [Let
me question more in particular. What have you, my good 235
friends, deserv'd at the hands of Fortune, that she sends you
to prison hither?

Guildenstern: Prison, my lord?

Hamlet: Denmark's a prison.

---

201. *honesty:* a fitting thing.   203. *method:* orderly arrangement, sequence of ideas. *out . . .*
air: Outdoor air was thought to be bad for invalids.   206. *pregnant:* apt.   209. *suddenly:* at
once.   223. *indifferent:* average.   230. *privates:* (1) intimate friends; (2) genitalia.
232. *strumpet:* A common epithet for Fortune, because she grants favors to all men.

Rosencrantz: Then is the world one. 240

Hamlet: A goodly one, in which there are many confines, wards, and dungeons, Denmark being one o' th' worst.

Rosencrantz: We think not so, my lord.

Hamlet: Why then 'tis none to you; for there is nothing either good or bad, but thinking makes it so. To me it is a prison. 245

Rosencrantz: Why then your ambition makes it one. 'Tis too narrow for your mind.

Hamlet: O God, I could be bounded in a nutshell, and count myself a king of infinite space—were it not that I have bad dreams. 250

Guildenstern: Which dreams indeed are ambition, for the very substance of the ambitious is merely the shadow of a dream.

Hamlet: A dream itself is but a shadow.

Rosencrantz: Truly, and I hold ambition of so airy and light a quality that it is but a shadow's shadow. 255

Hamlet: Then are our beggars bodies, and our monarchs and outstretch'd heroes the beggars' shadows. Shall we to th' court? for, by my fay, I cannot reason.

Both [Rosencrantz, Guildenstern]:
We'll wait upon you.

Hamlet: No such matter. I will not sort you with the rest of my 260 servants; for to speak to you like an honest man, I am most dreadfully attended.] But in the beaten way of friendship, what make you at Elsinore?

Rosencrantz: To visit you, my lord, no other occasion.

Hamlet: Beggar that I am, I am [even] poor in thanks—but I 265 thank you, and sure, dear friends, my thanks are too dear a halfpenny. Were you not sent for? is it your own inclining? is it a free visitation? Come, come, deal justly with me. Come, come—nay, speak.

Guildenstern: What should we say, my lord? 270

Hamlet: Any thing but to th' purpose. You were sent for, and there is a kind of confession in your looks, which your modesties have not craft enough to color. I know the good King and Queen have sent for you.

Rosencrantz: To what end, my lord? 275

Hamlet: That you must teach me. But let me conjure you, by the

---

241. *wards:* cells.   256. *bodies:* i.e. not shadows (since they lack ambition).   256-57. *outstretch'd:* i.e. with their ambition extended to the utmost (and hence producing stretched-out or elongated shadows).   258. *fay:* faith.   259. *wait upon you:* attend you thither.   260. *sort:* associate.   262. *dreadfully:* execrably.   266-67. *too . . . halfpenny:* too expensively priced at a halfpenny, i.e. not worth much.   268. *justly:* honestly.   271. *but:* Ordinarily punctuated with a comma preceding, to give the sense "provided that it is"; but Q2 has no comma, and Hamlet may intend, or include, the sense "except."   272-73. *modesties:* sense of shame.

rights of our fellowship, by the consonancy of our youth, by
the obligation of our ever-preserv'd love, and by what more
dear a better proposer can charge you withal, be even and
direct with me, whether you were sent for or no!   280

Rosencrantz: [Aside to Guildenstern.] What say you?

Hamlet: [Aside.] Nay then I have an eye of you!—If you love me,
hold not off.

Guildenstern: My lord, we were sent for.

Hamlet: I will tell you why, so shall my anticipation prevent your 285
discovery, and your secrecy to the King and Queen moult no
feather. I have of late—but wherefore I know not—lost all
my mirth, forgone all custom of exercises; and indeed it goes
so heavily with my disposition, that this goodly frame, the
earth, seems to me a sterile promontory; this most excellent 290
canopy, the air, look you, this brave o'erhanging firmament,
this majestical roof fretted with golden fire, why, it appeareth
nothing to me but a foul and pestilent congregation of
vapors. What [a] piece of work is a man, how noble in reason,
how infinite in faculties, in form and moving, how express 295
and admirable in action, how like an angel in apprehension,
how like a god! the beauty of the world; the paragon of animals; and yet to me what is this quintessence of dust? Man
delights not me—nor women neither, though by your smiling
you seem to say so.   300

Rosencrantz: My lord, there was no such stuff in my thoughts.

Hamlet: Why did ye laugh then, when I said, "Man delights not
me"?

Rosencrantz: To think, my lord, if you delight not in man, what lenten
entertainment the players shall receive from you. We coted 305
them on the way, and hither are they coming to offer you
service.

Hamlet: He that plays the king shall be welcome—his Majesty
shall have tribute on me, the adventerous knight shall use his
foil and target, the lover shall not sigh gratis, the humorous 310
man shall end his part in peace, [the clown shall make those

---

277. *consonancy . . . youth:* similarity of our ages.   279. *charge:* urge, adjure. *even:* frank,
honest (cf. modern "level with me").   282. *of:* on.   285-86. *prevent your discovery:* forestall
your disclosure (of what the King and Queen have said to you in confidence).   286-87. *moult
no feather:* not be impaired in the least.   288. *custom of exercises:* my usual athletic activities.
291. *brave:* splendid.   292. *fretted:* ornamented as with fretwork.   294. *piece of work:*
masterpiece.   295. *how infinite . . . god:* F1 shows different punctuation.   295. *express:*
exact.   298. *quintessence:* finest and purest extract.   304-05. *lenten entertainment:* meagre
reception.   305. *coted:* outstripped.   309. *on:* of, from.   *adventerous:* adventurous, i.e.
wandering in search of adventure.   310. *foil and target:* light fencing sword and small shield.
gratis: without reward. *humorous:* dominated by some eccentric trait (like the melancholy
Jaques in *As You Like It*).

laugh whose lungs are [tickle] a' th' sere,] and the lady shall
say her mind freely, or the [blank] verse shall halt for't. What
players are they?

Rosencrantz: Even those you were wont to take such delight in, the tra- 315
gedians of the city.

Hamlet: How chances it they travel? Their residence, both in reputation and profit, was better both ways.

Rosencrantz: I think their inhibition comes by the means of the late
innovation. 320

Hamlet: Do they hold the same estimation they did when I was in
the city? Are they so follow'd?

Rosencrantz: No indeed are they not.

[Hamlet: How comes it? do they grow rusty?

Rosencrantz: Nay, their endeavor keeps in the wonted pace; but there 325
is, sir, an aery of children, little eyases, that cry out on the top
of question, and are most tyrannically clapp'd for't. These
are now the fashion, and so [berattle] the common stages—
so they call them—that many wearing rapiers are afraid of
goose-quills and dare scarce come thither. 330

Hamlet: What, are they children? Who maintains 'em? How are
they escoted? Will they pursue the quality no longer than
they can sing? Will they not say afterwards, if they should
grow themselves to common players (as it is [most like], if
their means are [no] better), their writers do them wrong, to 335
make them exclaim against their own succession?

Rosencrantz: Faith, there has been much to do on both sides, and the
nation holds it no sin to tarre them to controversy. There was

---

312. *tickle . . . sere:* i.e. easily made to laugh (literally, describing a gun that goes off easily; *sere*
= a catch in the gunlock; *tickle* = easily affected, highly sensitive to stimulus). 313. *halt:*
limp, come off lamely (the verse will not scan if she omits indecent words). 319. *inhibition:*
hindrance (to playing in the city). The word could be used of an official prohibition. See next
note. 320. *innovation:* Shakespeare elsewhere uses this word of a political uprising or revolt,
and lines 319-20 are often explained as meaning that the company had been forbidden to play
in the city as the result of some disturbance. It is commonly conjectured that the allusion is to
the Essex rebellion of 1601, but it is known that Shakespeare's company, though to some
extent involved on account of the special performance of *Richard II* they were commissioned
to give on the eve of the rising, were not in fact punished by inhibition. A second interpretation explains *innovation* as referring to the new theatrical vogue described in lines 326 ff., and
conjectures that *inhibition* may allude to a Privy Council order of 1600 restricting the number
of London playhouses to two and the number of performances to two a week. 324-44. *How
. . . too:* This passage refers topically to the "War of the Theatres" between the child actors
and their poet Jonson on the one side, and on the other the adults, with Dekker, Marston, and
possibly Shakespeare as spokesmen, in 1600-1601. 326. *aery:* nest. *eyases:* unfledged
hawks. 326-27. *cry . . . question:* cry shrilly above others in controversy. 327. *tyrannically:*
outrageously. 328. *berattle:* cry down, satirize. *common stages:* public theatres (the children
played at the Blackfriars, a private theatre). 330. *goose-quills:* pens (of satirical playwrights). 332. *escoted:* supported. *quality:* profession (of acting). 332-33. *no . . . sing:*
i.e. only until their voices change. 336. *succession:* future. 337. *to do:* ado. 338. *tarre:*
incite.

for a while no money bid for argument, unless the poet and
the player went to cuffs in the question.   340
    Hamlet: Is't possible?
Guildenstern: O, there has been much throwing about of brains.
    Hamlet: Do the boys carry it away?
Rosencrantz: Ay, that they do, my lord—Hercules and his load too.]
    Hamlet: It is not very strange, for my uncle is King of Denmark, 345
        and those that would make mouths at him while my father
        liv'd, give twenty, forty, fifty, a hundred ducats a-piece for his
        picture in little. 'Sblood, there is something in this more than
        natural, if philosophy could find it out.

                                            A flourish [for the Players].

Guildenstern: There are the players.   350
    Hamlet: Gentlemen, you are welcome to Elsinore. Your hands,
        come then: th' appurtenance of welcome is fashion and cere-
        mony. Let me comply with you in this garb, [lest my] extent
        to the players, which, I tell you, must show fairly outwards,
        should more appear like entertainment than yours. You are 355
        welcome; but my uncle-father and aunt-mother are deceiv'd.
Guildenstern: In what, my dear lord?
    Hamlet: I am but mad north-north-west. When the wind is south-
        erly I know a hawk from a hand-saw.

Enter Polonius.

    Polonius: Well be with you, gentlemen!   360
    Hamlet: [*Aside to them.*] Hark you, Guildenstern, and you too—at
        each ear a hearer—that great baby you see there is not yet
        out of his swaddling-clouts.
Rosencrantz: Happily he is the second time come to them, for they say
        an old man is twice a child.   365
    Hamlet: I will prophesy, he comes to tell me of the players, mark
        it. [*Aloud.*] You say right, sir, a' Monday morning, 'twas then
        indeed.
    Polonius: My lord, I have news to tell you.
    Hamlet: My lord, I have news to tell you. When Roscius was an 370
        actor in Rome—

---

339. *argument:* plot of a play.   340. *in the question:* i.e. as part of the script.   343. *carry it
away:* win.   344. *Hercules . . . too:* Hercules in the course of one of his twelve labors
supported the world for Atlas; the children do better, for they carry away the world and
Hercules as well. There is an allusion to the Globe playhouse, which reportedly had for its
sign the figure of Hercules upholding the world.   346. *mouths:* derisive faces.   348. *'Sblood:*
by God's (Christ's) blood.   353. *comply:* observe the formalities. *garb:* fashion, manner. *my
extent:* i.e. the degree of courtesy I show.   354-55. *more . . . yours:* seem to be a warmer
reception than I have given you.   359. *hawk, hand-saw:* Both cutting-tools; but also both
birds, if *hand-saw* quibbles on *henshaw,* "heron," a bird preyed upon by the hawk.
363. *swaddling-clouts:* swaddling clothes.   364. *Happily:* haply, perhaps.   365. *twice:* i.e. for
the second time.   370. *Roscius:* the most famous of Roman actors (died 62 B.C.). News about
him would be stale news indeed.

Polonius: The actors are come hither, my lord.

Hamlet: Buzz, buzz!

Polonius: Upon my honor—

Hamlet: "Then came each actor on his ass"— 375

Polonius: The best actors in the world, either for tragedy, comedy, history, pastoral, pastoral-comical, historical-pastoral, [tragi-cal-historical, tragical-comical-historical-pastoral,] scene in-dividable, or poem unlimited; Seneca cannot be too heavy, nor Plautus too light, for the law of writ and the liberty: these 380 are the only men.

Hamlet: O Jephthah, judge of Israel, what a treasure hadst thou!

Polonius: What a treasure had he, my lord?

Hamlet: Why—

"One fair daughter, and no more, 385
The which he loved passing well."

Polonius: *[Aside.]* Still on my daughter.

Hamlet: Am I not i' th' right, old Jephthah?

Polonius: If you call me Jephthah, my lord, I have a daughter that I love passing well. 390

Hamlet: Nay, that follows not.

Polonius: What follows then, my lord?

Hamlet: Why—

"As by lot, God wot,"
and then, you know, 395
"It came to pass, as most like it was"—
the first row of the pious chanson will show you more, for look where my abridgment comes.

Enter the Players, *[four or five]*.

You are welcome, masters, welcome all. I am glad to see thee well. Welcome, good friends. O, old friend! why, thy face is 400 valanc'd since I saw thee last; com'st thou to beard me in Denmark? What, my young lady and mistress! by' lady, your ladyship is nearer to heaven than when I saw you last, by the altitude of a chopine. Pray God your voice, like a piece of

---

373. *Buzz:* exclamation of impatience at someone who tells news already known. 378-79. *scene individable:* play observing the unity of place. 379. *poem unlimited:* play ignoring rules such as the three unities. 400. *Seneca:* Roman writer of tragedies. 380. *Plautus:* Roman writer of comedies. *for . . . liberty:* for strict observance of the rules, or for freedom from them (with possible allusion to the location of playhouses, which were not built in properties under city jurisdiction, but in the "liberties"—land once monastic and now outside the jurisdiction of the city authorities). 381. *only:* very best (a frequent use). 382. *Jephthah . . . Israel:* title of a ballad, from which Hamlet goes on to quote. For the story of Jephthah and his daughter, see Judges 11. 397. *row:* stanza. *chanson:* song, ballad. 398. *abridgment:* (1) interruption; (2) pastime. 401. *valanc'd:* fringed, i.e. bearded. 424. *beard:* confront boldly (with obvious pun). 402. *by' lady:* by Our Lady. 404. *chopine:* thick-soled shoe.

uncurrent gold, be not crack'd within the ring. Masters, you 405
are all welcome. We'll e'en to't like [French] falc'ners—fly at
any thing we see; we'll have a speech straight. Come give us a
taste of your quality, come, a passionate speech.

    [1.] Player: What speech, my good lord?

    Hamlet: I heard thee speak me a speech once, but it was never 410
acted, or if it was, not above once; for the play, I remember,
pleas'd not the million, 'twas caviary to the general, but it was
—as I receiv'd it, and others, whose judgments in such
matters cried in the top of mine—an excellent play, well
digested in the scenes, set down with as much modesty as 415
cunning. I remember one said there were no sallets in the
lines to make the matter savory, nor no matter in the phrase
that might indict the author of affection, but call'd it an
honest method, as wholesome as sweet, and by very much
more handsome than fine. One speech in't I chiefly lov'd, 420
'twas Aeneas' [tale] to Dido, and thereabout of it especially
when he speaks of Priam's slaughter. If it live in your mem-
ory, begin at this line—let me see, let me see:
"The rugged Pyrrhus, like th' Hyrcanian beast—"
'Tis not so, it begins with Pyrrhus: 425
"The rugged Pyrrhus, he whose sable arms,
Black as his purpose, did the night resemble
When he lay couched in th' ominous horse,
Hath now this dread and black complexion smear'd
With heraldy more dismal: head to foot 430
Now is he total gules, horridly trick'd
With blood of fathers, mothers, daughters, sons,
Bak'd and impasted with the parching streets,
That lend a tyrannous and a damned light
To their lord's murther. Roasted in wrath and fire, 435
And thus o'er-sized with coagulate gore,
With eyes like carbuncles, the hellish Pyrrhus

---

405. *crack'd . . . ring:* i.e. broken to the point where you can no longer play female roles. A
coin with a crack extending far enough in from the edge to cross the circle surrounding the
stamp of the sovereign's head was unacceptable in exchange (*uncurrent*).   407. *straight:*
straightway.   408. *quality:* professional skill.   412. *caviary . . . general:* caviare to the
common people, i.e. too choice for the multitude.   414. *cried . . . of:* were louder than, i.e.,
carried more authority than.   416. *sallets:* salads, i.e. spicy jokes.   417. *savory:* zesty.
418. *affection:* affectation.   420. *fine:* showily dressed (in language).   422. *Priam's slaughter:*
the slaying of Priam (at the fall of Troy).   424. *Pyrrhus:* another name for Neoptolemus,
Achilles' son. *Hyrcanian beast:* Hyrcania in the Caucasus was notorious for its tigers.
426. *sable arms:* The Greeks within the Trojan horse had blackened their skin so as to be
inconspicuous when they emerged at night.   430. *heraldy:* heraldry. *dismal:* ill-boding.
431. *gules:* red (heraldic term). *trick'd:* adorned.   433. *Bak'd:* caked. *impasted:* crusted. *with*
. . . streets: i.e. by the heat from the burning streets.   436. *o'er-sized:* covered over as with a
coat of sizing.   437. *carbuncles:* jewels believed to shine in the dark.

Old grandsire Priam seeks."
So proceed you.
Polonius: 'Fore God, my lord, well spoken, with good accent and   440
good discretion.
[1.] Player: "Anon he finds him
Striking too short at Greeks. His antique sword,
Rebellious to his arm, lies where it falls,
Repugnant to command. Unequal match'd,   445
Pyrrhus at Priam drives, in rage strikes wide,
But with the whiff and wind of his fell sword
Th' unnerved father falls. [Then senseless Ilium,]
Seeming to feel this blow, with flaming top
Stoops to his base, and with a hideous crash   450
Takes prisoner Pyrrhus' ear; for lo his sword,
Which was declining on the milky head
Of reverent Priam, seem'd i' th' air to stick.
So as a painted tyrant Pyrrhus stood
[And,] like a neutral to his will and matter,   455
Did nothing.
But as we often see, against some storm,
A silence in the heavens, the rack stand still,
The bold winds speechless, and the orb below
As hush as death, anon the dreadful thunder   460
Doth rend the region; so after Pyrrhus' pause,
A roused vengeance sets him new a-work,
And never did the Cyclops' hammers fall
On Mars's armor forg'd for proof eterne
With less remorse than Pyrrhus' bleeding sword   465
Now falls on Priam.
Out, out, thou strumpet Fortune! All you gods,
In general synod take away her power!
Break all the spokes and [fellies] from her wheel,
And bowl the round nave down the hill of heaven   470
As low as to the fiends!"
Polonius: This is too long.
Hamlet: It shall to the barber's with your beard. Prithee say on,
he's for a jig or a tale of bawdry, or he sleeps. Say on, come to
Hecuba.   475

---

445. *Repugnant:* resistant, hostile.   447. *fell:* cruel.   448. *unnerved:* drained of strength.
senseless: insensible. *Ilium:* the citadel of Troy.   453. *reverent:* reverend, aged.   455. *like . . .
matter:* i.e. poised midway between intention and performance.   457. *against:* just before.
458. *rack:* cloud-mass.   461. *region:* i.e. air.   463. *Cyclops:* giants who worked in Vulcan's
smithy, where armor was made for the gods.   464. *proof eterne:* eternal endurance.
465. *remorse:* pity.   469. *fellies:* rims.   470. *nave:* hub.   474. *jig:* song-and-dance entertainment performed after the main play.

[1.] Player: "But who, ah woe, had seen the mobled queen"—
  Hamlet: "The mobled queen"?
  Polonius: That's good, ["[mobled] queen" is good].
[1.] Player: "Run barefoot up and down, threat'ning the flames
    With bisson rheum, a clout upon that head   480
    Where late the diadem stood, and for a robe,
    About her lank and all o'er-teemed loins,
    A blanket, in the alarm of fear caught up—
    Who this had seen, with tongue in venom steep'd,
    'Gainst Fortune's state would treason have pronounc'd.   485
    But if the gods themselves did see her then,
    When she saw Pyrrhus make malicious sport
    In mincing with his sword her [husband's] limbs,
    The instant burst of clamor that she made,
    Unless things mortal move them not at all,   490
    Would have made milch the burning eyes of heaven,
    And passion in the gods."
  Polonius: Look whe'er he has not turn'd his color and has tears in 's
    eyes. Prithee no more.
   Hamlet: 'Tis well, I'll have thee speak out the rest of this soon.   495
    Good my lord, will you see the players well bestow'd? Do you
    hear, let them be well us'd, for they are the abstract and brief
    chronicles of the time. After your death you were better have
    a bad epitaph than their ill report while you live.
  Polonius: My lord, I will use them according to their desert.   500
   Hamlet: God's bodkin, man, much better: use every man after his
    desert, and who shall scape whipping? Use them after your
    own honor and dignity—the less they deserve, the more
    merit is in your bounty. Take them in.
  Polonius: Come, sirs.   *[Exit.]* 505
   Hamlet: Follow him, friends, we'll hear a play to-morrow. *[Exeunt
    all the Players but the First.]* Dost thou hear me, old friend?
    Can you play "The Murther of Gonzago"?
[1.] Player: Ay, my lord.
   Hamlet: We'll ha't to-morrow night. You could for need study a   510
    speech of some dozen lines, or sixteen lines, which I would
    set down and insert in't, could you not?
[1.] Player: Ay, my lord.
   Hamlet: Very well. Follow that lord, and look you mock him not.
    [Exit First Player.] My good friends, I'll leave you [till] night.   515
    You are welcome to Elsinore.

---

476. *mobled:* muffled.   480. *bisson rheum:* blinding tears. *clout:* cloth.   482. *o'er-teemed:*
worn out by childbearing.   485. *state:* rule, government.   491. *milch:* moist (literally, milky).
492. *passion:* grief.   493. *Look . . . not:* i.e. note how he has.   496. *bestow'd:* lodged. *us'd:*
treated.   501. *God's bodkin:* by God's (Christ's) little body.   510. *for need:* if necessary.

Rosencrantz: Good my lord!

   Hamlet: Ay so, God buy to you. it1

                       Exeunt [Rosencrantz and Guildenstern].

Now I am alone.

O, what a rogue and peasant slave am I!   520

Is it not monstrous that this player here,

But in a fiction, in a dream of passion,

Could force his soul so to his own conceit

That from her working all the visage wann'd,

Tears in his eyes, distraction in his aspect,   525

A broken voice, an' his whole function suiting

With forms to his conceit? And all for nothing,

For Hecuba!

What's Hecuba to him, or he to [Hecuba],

That he should weep for her? What would he do   530

    Had he the motive and [the cue] for passion

That I have? He would drown the stage with tears,

And cleave the general ear with horrid speech,

Make mad the guilty, and appall the free,

Confound the ignorant, and amaze indeed   535

The very faculties of eyes and ears. Yet I,

A dull and muddy-mettled rascal, peak

Like John-a-dreams, unpregnant of my cause,

And can say nothing; no, not for a king,

Upon whose property and most dear life   540

A damn'd defeat was made. Am I a coward?

Who calls me villain, breaks my pate across,

Plucks off my beard and blows it in my face,

Tweaks me by the nose, gives me the lie i' th' throat

As deep as to the lungs? Who does me this?   545

Hah, 'swounds, I should take it; for it cannot be

But I am pigeon-liver'd, and lack gall

To make oppression bitter, or ere this

I should 'a' fatted all the region kites

With this slave's offal. Bloody, bawdy villain!   550

Remorseless, treacherous, lecherous, kindless villain!

Why, what an ass am I! This is most brave,

That I, the son of a dear [father] murthered,

---

523. *conceit:* imaginative conception.   526. *his whole function:* the operation of his whole body.   527. *forms:* actions, expressions.   534. *free:* innocent.   535. *amaze:* confound. 537. *muddy-mettled:* dull-spirited. *peak:* mope.   538. *John-a-dreams:* a sleepy fellow. *unpregnant of:* unquickened by.   541. *defeat:* destruction.   544-45. *gives . . . lungs:* calls me a liar in the extremest degree.   546. *'swounds:* by God's (Christ's) wounds. *should:* would certainly. 547. *am . . . gall:* i.e. am constitutionally incapable of resentment. That doves were mild because they had no gall was a popular belief.   549. *region kites:* kites of the air.   550. *offal:* entrails.   551. *kindless:* unnatural.

Prompted to my revenge by heaven and hell,
Must like a whore unpack my heart with words,   555
And fall a-cursing like a very drab,
A stallion. Fie upon't, foh!
About, my brains! Hum—I have heard
That guilty creatures sitting at a play
Have by the very cunning of the scene   560
Been strook so to the soul, that presently
They have proclaim'd their malefactions:
For murther, though it have no tongue, will speak
With most miraculous organ. I'll have these players
Play something like the murther of my father   565
Before mine uncle. I'll observe his looks,
I'll tent him to the quick. If 'a do blench,
I know my course. The spirit that I have seen
May be a [dev'l], and the [dev'l] hath power
T' assume a pleasing shape, yea, and perhaps,   570
Out of my weakness and my melancholy,
As he is very potent with such spirits,
Abuses me to damn me. I'll have grounds
More relative than this—the play's the thing
Wherein I'll catch the conscience of the King.   *Exit.*   575

ACT III

Scene I

Enter King, Queen, Polonius, Ophelia, Rosencrantz, Guildenstern, Lords.

    King: An' can you by no drift of conference
        Get from him why he puts on this confusion,
        Grating so harshly all his days of quiet
        With turbulent and dangerous lunacy?
Rosencrantz: He does confess he feels himself distracted,   5
        But from what cause 'a will by no means speak.
Guildenstern: Nor do we find him forward to be sounded,
        But with a crafty madness keeps aloof
        When we would bring him on to some confession
        Of his true state.
    Queen: Did he receive you well?   10

---

557. *stallion:* male whore. Most editors adopt the F1 reading *scullion,* "kitchen menial."
558. *About:* to work.   561. *presently:* at once, then and there.   567. *tent:* probe. *blench:*
flinch.   572. *spirits:* states of temperament.   573. *Abuses:* deludes.   574. *relative:* closely
related (to fact), i.e. conclusive.

III.i. Location: The castle. 1. *An':* and. *drift of conference:* leading on of conversation.
7. *forward:* readily willing. *sounded:* plumbed, probed.   8. *crafty madness:* i.e. mad craftiness,
the shrewdness that mad people sometimes exhibit.

Rosencrantz: Most like a gentleman.	
Guildenstern: But with much forcing of his disposition.	
Rosencrantz: Niggard of question, but of our demands	
Most free in his reply.	
Queen: Did you assay him	
To any pastime?	15
Rosencrantz: Madam, it so fell out that certain players	
We o'erraught on the way; of these we told him,	
And there did seem in him a kind of joy	
To hear of it. They are here about the court,	
And as I think, they have already order	20
This night to play before him.	
Polonius: 'Tis most true,	
And he beseech'd me to entreat your Majesties	
To hear and see the matter.	
King: With all my heart, and it doth much content me	
To hear him so inclin'd.	25
Good gentlemen, give him a further edge,	
And drive his purpose into these delights.	
Rosencrantz: We shall, my lord. *Exeunt Rosencrantz and Guildenstern.*	
King: Sweet Gertrude, leave us two,	
For we have closely sent for Hamlet hither,	
That he, as 'twere by accident, may here	30
Affront Ophelia. Her father and myself,	
We'll so bestow ourselves that, seeing unseen,	
We may of their encounter frankly judge,	
And gather by him, as he is behav'd,	
If 't be th' affliction of his love or no	35
That thus he suffers for.	
Queen: I shall obey you.	
And for your part, Ophelia, I do wish	
That your good beauties be the happy cause	
Of Hamlet's wildness. So shall I hope your virtues	
Will bring him to his wonted way again,	40
To both your honors.	
Ophelia: Madam, I wish it may. *[Exit Queen.]*	
Polonius: Ophelia, walk you here.—Gracious, so please you,	
We will bestow ourselves. *[To Ophelia.]* Read on this book,	
That show of such an exercise may color	
Your [loneliness]. We are oft to blame in this—	45
'Tis too much prov'd—that with devotion's visage	

---

12. *disposition:* inclination. 13. *question:* conversation. *demands:* questions. 14. *assay:* attempt to win. 17. *o'erraught:* passed (literally, overreached). 26. *edge:* stimulus. 27. *into:* on to. 29. *closely:* privately. 31. *Affront:* meet. 33. *frankly:* freely. 44. *exercise:* i.e. religious exercise (as the next sentence makes clear). 44-45. *color Your loneliness:* make your solitude seem natural. 46. *too much prov'd:* too often proved true.

And pious action we do sugar o'er
The devil himself.

King: [Aside.] O, 'tis too true!
How smart a lash that speech doth give my conscience!
The harlot's cheek, beautied with plast'ring art,   50
Is not more ugly to the thing that helps it
Than is my deed to my most painted word.
O heavy burthen!

Polonius: I hear him coming. Withdraw, my lord.

                                        [Exeunt King and Polonius.]

Enter Hamlet.

Hamlet: To be, or not to be, that is the question: 55
Whether 'tis nobler in the mind to suffer
The slings and arrows of outrageous fortune,
Or to take arms against a sea of troubles,
And by opposing, end them. To die, to sleep—
No more, and by a sleep to say we end   60
The heart-ache and the thousand natural shocks
That flesh is heir to; 'tis a consummation
Devoutly to be wish'd. To die, to sleep—
To sleep, perchance to dream—ay, there's the rub,
For in that sleep of death what dreams may come,   65
When we have shuffled off this mortal coil,
Must give us pause; there's the respect
That makes calamity of so long life:
For who would bear the whips and scorns of time,
Th' oppressor's wrong, the proud man's contumely,   70
The pangs of despis'd love, the law's delay,
The insolence of office, and the spurns
That patient merit of th' unworthy takes,
When he himself might his quietus make
With a bare bodkin; who would fardels bear,   75
To grunt and sweat under a weary life,
But that the dread of something after death,
The undiscover'd country, from whose bourn
No traveller returns, puzzles the will,
And makes us rather bear those ills we have,   80

----

47. *action:* demeanor.   51. *to . . . it:* in comparison with the paint that makes it look
beautiful.   55-89. See the Textual Notes for the version of this soliloquy in Q1.   56. *suffer:*
submit to, endure patiently.   62. *consummation:* completion, end.   64. *rub:* obstacle (a term
from the game of bowls).   66. *shuffled off:* freed ourselves from. *this mortal coil:* the turmoil
of this mortal life.   67. *respect:* consideration.   68. *of . . . life:* so long-lived.   69. *time:* the
world.   74. *his quietus make:* write paid to his account.   75. *bare bodkin:* mere dagger. *fardels:*
burdens.   78. *undiscover'd:* not disclosed to knowledge; about which men have no information. *bourn:* boundary, i.e. region.   79. *puzzles:* paralyzes.

Than fly to others that we know not of?
Thus conscience does make cowards [of us all],
And thus the native hue of resolution
Is sicklied o'er with the pale cast of thought,
And enterprises of great pitch and moment   85
With this regard their currents turn awry,
And lose the name of action.—Soft you now,
The fair Ophelia. Nymph, in thy orisons
Be all my sins rememb'red.

Ophelia: Good my lord,
How does your honor for this many a day?   90

Hamlet: I humbly thank you, well, [well, well].

Ophelia: My lord, I have remembrances of yours
That I have longed long to redeliver.
I pray you now receive them.

Hamlet: No, not I,
I never gave you aught.   95

Ophelia: My honor'd lord, you know right well you did,
And with them words of so sweet breath compos'd
As made these things more rich. Their perfume lost,
Take these again, for to the noble mind
Rich gifts wax poor when givers prove unkind.   100
There, my lord.

Hamlet: Ha, ha! are you honest?

Ophelia: My lord?

Hamlet: Are you fair?

Ophelia: What means your lordship?   105

Hamlet: That if you be honest and fair, [your honesty] should
admit no discourse to your beauty.

Ophelia: Could beauty, my lord, have better commerce than with
honesty?

Hamlet: Ay, truly, for the power of beauty will sooner transform 110
honesty from what it is to a bawd than the force of honesty
can translate beauty into his likeness. This was sometime a
paradox, but now the time gives it proof. I did love you once.

Ophelia: Indeed, my lord, you made me believe so.

Hamlet: You should not have believ'd me, for virtue cannot so 115
[inoculate] our old stock but we shall relish of it. I lov'd you
not.

---

82. *conscience:* reflection (but with some of the modern sense, too).   83. *native hue:* natural
(ruddy) complexion.   84. *pale cast:* pallor. *thought:* i.e. melancholy thought, brooding.
85. *pitch:* loftiness (a term from falconry, signifying the highest point of a hawk's flight).
88. *orisons:* prayers.   102. *honest:* chaste.   112. *sometime:* formerly.   113. *paradox:* tenet
contrary to accepted belief.   115-16. *virtue . . . it:* virtue, engrafted on our old stock (of
viciousness), cannot so change the nature of the plant that no trace of the original will remain.

Ophelia: I was the more deceiv'd.

Hamlet: Get thee [to] a nunn'ry, why wouldst thou be a breeder of sinners? I am myself indifferent honest, but yet I could 120 accuse me of such things that it were better my mother had not borne me: I am very proud, revengeful, ambitious, with more offenses at my beck than I have thoughts to put them in, imagination to give them shape, or time to act them in. 125 What should such fellows as I do crawling between earth and heaven? We are arrant knaves, believe none of us. Go thy ways to a nunn'ry. Where's your father?

Ophelia: At home, my lord.

Hamlet: Let the doors be shut upon him, that he may play the fool 130 no where but in 's own house. Farewell.

Ophelia: O, help him, you sweet heavens!

Hamlet: If thou dost marry, I'll give thee this plague for thy dowry: be thou as chaste as ice, as pure as snow, thou shalt not escape calumny. Get thee to a nunn'ry, farewell. Or if thou wilt needs marry, marry a fool, for wise men know well 135 enough what monsters you make of them. To a nunn'ry, go, and quickly too. Farewell.

Ophelia: Heavenly powers, restore him!

Hamlet: I have heard of your paintings, well enough. God hath given you one face, and you make yourselves another. You jig 140 and amble, and you [lisp,] you nickname God's creatures and make your wantonness [your] ignorance. Go to, I'll no more on't, it hath made me mad. I say we will have no moe marriage. Those that are married already (all but one) shall live, the rest shall keep as they are. To a nunn'ry, go.   *Exit.* 145

Ophelia: O, what a noble mind is here o'erthrown!
The courtier's, soldier's, scholar's, eye, tongue, sword,
Th' expectation and rose of the fair state,
The glass of fashion and the mould of form,
Th' observ'd of all observers, quite, quite down!   150
And I, of ladies most deject and wretched,
That suck'd the honey of his [music] vows,
Now see [that] noble and most sovereign reason
Like sweet bells jangled out of time, and harsh;
That unmatch'd form and stature of blown youth   155

---

120. *indifferent honest:* tolerably virtuous.   136. *monsters:* Alluding to the notion that the husbands of unfaithful wives grew horns.   *you:* you women.   141. *You . . . creatures:* i.e. you walk and talk affectedly.   142. *make . . . ignorance:* excuse your affectation as ignorance. 143. *moe:* more.   148. *expectation:* hope. *rose:* ornament. *fair:* Probably proleptic: "(the kingdom) made fair by his presence."   149. *glass:* mirror. *mould of form:* pattern of (courtly) behavior.   150. *observ'd . . . observers:* Shakespeare uses *observe* to mean not only "behold, mark attentively" but also "pay honor to."   155. *blown:* in full bloom.

Blasted with ecstasy. O, woe is me
T' have seen what I have seen, see what I see!

[Ophelia withdraws.]

Enter King *and* Polonius.

King: Love? his affections do not that way tend,
Nor what he spake, though it lack'd form a little,
Was not like madness. There's something in his soul   160
O'er which his melancholy sits on brood,
And I do doubt the hatch and the disclose
Will be some danger; which for to prevent,
I have in quick determination
Thus set it down: he shall with speed to England   165
For the demand of our neglected tribute.
Haply the seas, and countries different,
With variable objects, shall expel
This something-settled matter in his heart,
Whereon his brains still beating puts him thus   170
From fashion of himself. What think you on't?
Polonius: It shall do well; but yet do I believe
The origin and commencement of his grief
Sprung from neglected love. *[Ophelia comes forward.]* How
now, Ophelia?   175
You need not tell us what Lord Hamlet said,
We heard it all. My lord, do as you please,
But if you hold it fit, after the play
Let his queen-mother all alone entreat him
To show his grief. Let her be round with him,   180
And I'll be plac'd (so please you) in the ear
Of all their conference. If she find him not,
To England send him, or confine him where
Your wisdom best shall think.
King: It shall be so.
Madness in great ones must not [unwatch'd] go.   *Exeunt.* 185

Scene II

Enter Hamlet *and three of the* Players.

Hamlet: Speak the speech, I pray you, as I pronounc'd it to you,
trippingly on the tongue, but if you mouth it, as many of our

---

156. *Blasted:* withered. *ecstasy:* madness.   158. *affections:* inclinations, feelings.   162. *doubt:*
fear. *disclose:* Synonymous with *hatch;* see also V.i.263.   166. *neglected:* unrequited.
173. *his grief:* what is troubling him. *round:* blunt, outspoken.   182. *find him:* learn the truth
about him.

III.ii. Location: The castle. 2. *mouth:* pronounce with exaggerated distinctness or declama-
tory effect.

players do, I had as live the town-crier spoke my lines. Nor do
not saw the air too much with your hand, thus, but use all
gently, for in the very torrent, tempest, and, as I may say, 5
whirlwind of your passion, you must acquire and beget a tem-
perance that may give it smoothness. O, it offends me to the
soul to hear a robustious periwig-pated fellow tear a passion
to totters, to very rags, to spleet the ears of the groundlings,
who for the most part are capable of nothing but inexplicable 10
dumb shows and noise. I would have such a fellow whipt for
o'erdoing Termagant, it out-Herods Herod, pray you avoid
it.

[1.] Player: I warrant your honor.

Hamlet: Be not too tame neither, but let your own discretion be 15
your tutor. Suit the action to the word, the word to the
action, with this special observance, that you o'erstep not the
modesty of nature: for any thing so o'erdone is from the purpose of playing, whose end, both at the first and now, was and
is, to hold as 'twere the mirror up to nature: to show virtue 20
her feature, scorn her own image, and the very age and body
of the time his form and pressure. Now this overdone, or
come tardy off, though it makes the unskillful laugh, cannot
but make the judicious grieve; the censure of which one must
in your allowance o'erweigh a whole theatre of others. O, 25
there be players that I have seen play—and heard others
[praise], and that highly—not to speak it profanely, that, neither having th' accent of Christians nor the gait of Christian,
pagan, nor man, have so strutted and bellow'd that I have
thought some of Nature's journeymen had made men, and 30
not made them well, they imitated humanity so abominably.

[1.] Player: I hope we have reform'd that indifferently with us, [sir].

Hamlet: O, reform it altogether. And let those that play your
clowns speak no more than is set down for them, for there be
of them that will themselves laugh to set on some quantity of 35
barren spectators to laugh too, though in the mean time
some necessary question of the play be then to be consider'd.
That's villainous, and shows a most pitiful ambition in the
fool that uses it. Go make you ready.   *[Exeunt Players.]*

---

3. *live:* lief, willingly.   9. *totters:* tatters. *spleet:* split.   *groundlings:* those who paid the lowest
admission price and stood on the ground in the "yard" or pit of the theatre.   10. *capable of:*
able to take in.   12. *Termagant:* a supposed god of the Saracens, whose role in medieval
drama, like that of Herod (line 12), was noisy and violent.   18. *modesty:* moderation. *from:*
contrary to.   21. *scorn:* i.e. that which is worthy of scorn.   22. *pressure:* impression (as of a
seal), exact image.   23. *tardy:* inadequately.   24. *censure:* judgment. *which one:* (even) one of
whom.   26. *allowance:* estimation.   27. *profanely:* irreverently.   30-31. *some . . . abominably:*
i.e. they were so unlike men that it seemed Nature had not made them herself, but had
delegated the task to mediocre assistants.   32. *indifferently:* pretty well.   35. *of them:* some
of them.   39. *fool:* (1) stupid person; (2) actor playing a fool's role. *uses it:* an interesting
passage follows these words in Q1.

Enter Polonius, Guildenstern, *and* Rosencrantz.

How now, my lord? Will the King hear this piece of work?   40
  Polonius: And the Queen too, and that presently.
    Hamlet: Bid the players make haste.   *[Exit Polonius.]*
          Will you two help to hasten them?
Rosencrantz: Ay, my lord.   *Exeunt they two.*
    Hamlet: What ho, Horatio!   45

Enter Horatio.

    Horatio: Here, sweet lord, at your service.
    Hamlet: Horatio, thou art e'en as just a man
      As e'er my conversation cop'd withal.
    Horatio: O my dear lord—
    Hamlet: Nay, do not think I flatter,
      For what advancement may I hope from thee   50
      That no revenue hast but thy good spirits
      To feed and clothe thee? Why should the poor be flatter'd?
      No, let the candied tongue lick absurd pomp,
      And crook the pregnant hinges of the knee
      Where thrift may follow fawning. Dost thou hear?   55
      Since my dear soul was mistress of her choice
      And could of men distinguish her election,
      Sh' hath seal'd thee for herself, for thou hast been
      As one in suff'ring all that suffers nothing,
      A man that Fortune's buffets and rewards   60
      Hast ta'en with equal thanks; and blest are those
      Whose blood and judgment are so well co-meddled,
      That they are not a pipe for Fortune's finger
      To sound what stop she please. Give me that man
      That is not passion's slave, and I will wear him   65
      In my heart's core, ay, in my heart of heart,
      As I do thee. Something too much of this.
      There is a play to-night before the King,
      One scene of it comes near the circumstance
      Which I have told thee of my father's death.   70
      I prithee, when thou seest that act afoot,
      Even with the very comment of thy soul
      Observe my uncle. If his occulted guilt
      Do not itself unkennel in one speech,
      It is a damned ghost that we have seen,   75

---

40. *piece of work:* masterpiece (said jocularly).   41. *presently:* at once.   47. *thou . . . man:* i.e.
you come as close to being what a man should be (*just* = exact, precise).   48. *my . . . withal:*
my association with people has brought me into contact with.   53. *candied:* sugared, i.e.
flattering. *absurd:* tasteless (Latin sense).   54. *pregnant:* moving readily.   55. *thrift:* thriving,
profit.   62. *blood:* passions. *co-meddled:* mixed, blended.   66. *my heart of heart:* the heart of
my heart.   72. *very . . . soul:* your most intense critical observation.   73. *occulted:* hidden.
74. *unkennel:* bring into the open.   75. *damned ghost:* evil spirit, devil.

And my imaginations are as foul
As Vulcan's stithy. Give him heedful note,
For I mine eyes will rivet to his face,
And after we will both our judgments join
In censure of his seeming.

Horatio: Well, my lord.   80
If 'a steal aught the whilst this play is playing,
And scape [detecting], I will pay the theft.

[Sound a flourish. Danish march.] Enter Trumpets and Kettle-drums, King,
Queen, Polonius, Ophelia, [Rosencrantz, Guildenstern, *and other* Lords
attendant, with his Guard *carrying torches].*

Hamlet: They are coming to the play. I must be idle;
    Get you a place.

King: How fares our cousin Hamlet?   85

Hamlet: Excellent, i' faith, of the chameleon's dish: I eat the air,
    promise-cramm'd—you cannot feed capons so.

King: I have nothing with this answer, Hamlet, these words are
    not mine.

Hamlet: No, nor mine now. *[To Polonius.]* My lord, you play'd 90
    once i' th' university, you say?

Polonius: That did I, my lord, and was accounted a good actor.

Hamlet: What did you enact?

Polonius: I did enact Julius Caesar. I was kill'd i' th' Capitol;
    Brutus kill'd me.   95

Hamlet: It was a brute part of him to kill so capital a calf there. Be
    the players ready?

Rosencrantz: Ay, my lord, they stay upon your patience.

Queen: Come hither, my dear Hamlet, sit by me.

Hamlet: No, good mother, here's metal more attractive.   100

                              [Lying down at Ophelia's feet.]

Polonius: *[To the King.]* O ho, do you mark that?

Hamlet: Lady, shall I lie in your lap?

Ophelia: No, my lord.

[Hamlet: I mean, my head upon your lap?

Ophelia: Ay, my lord.]   105

Hamlet: Do you think I meant country matters?

Ophelia: I think nothing, my lord.

Hamlet: That's a fair thought to lie between maids' legs.

Ophelia: What is, my lord?

---

77. *stithy:* forge.   79. *censure . . . seeming:* reaching a verdict on his behavior.   83. *be idle:*
act foolish, pretend to be crazy.   85. *fares:* Hamlet takes up this word in another sense.
86. *chameleon's dish:* Chameleons were thought to feed on air. Hamlet says that he subsists on
an equally nourishing diet, the promise of succession. There is probably a pun on *air/heir.*
88. *have nothing with:* do not understand.   89. *mine:* i.e. an answer to my question.
96. *part:* action.   106. *country matters:* indecency.

Hamlet: Nothing. 110
Ophelia: You are merry, my lord.
Hamlet: Who, I?
Ophelia: Ay, my lord.
Hamlet: O God, your only jig-maker. What should a man do but
be merry, for look you how cheerfully my mother looks, and 115
my father died within 's two hours.
Ophelia: Nay, 'tis twice two months, my lord.
Hamlet: So long? Nay then let the dev'l wear black, for I'll have a
suit of sables. O heavens, die two months ago, and not forgotten yet? Then there's hope a great man's memory may 120
outlive his life half a year, but, by'r lady, 'a must build
churches then, or else shall 'a suffer not thinking on, with the
hobby-horse, whose epitaph is, "For O, for O, the hobby-
horse is forgot."

The trumpets sounds. Dumb show follows.

*Enter a King and a Queen [very lovingly], the Queen embracing him and he her.
[She kneels and makes show of protestation unto him.] He takes her up and declines
his head upon her neck. He lies him down upon a bank of flowers. She, seeing him
asleep, leaves him. Anon comes in another man, takes off his crown, kisses it, pours
poison in the sleeper's ears, and leaves him. The Queen returns, finds the King
dead, makes passionate action. The pois'ner with some three or four [mutes] come
in again, seem to condole with her. The dead body is carried away. The pois'ner
woos the Queen with gifts; she seems harsh [and unwilling] awhile, but in the end
accepts love. [Exeunt.]*

Ophelia: What means this, my lord? 125
Hamlet: Marry, this' [miching] mallecho, it means mischief.
Ophelia: Belike this show imports the argument of the play.

Enter Prologue.

Hamlet: We shall know by this fellow. The players cannot keep
[counsel], they'll tell all.
Ophelia: Will 'a tell us what this show meant? 130
Hamlet: Ay, or any show that you will show him. Be not you
asham'd to show, he'll not shame to tell you what it means.
Ophelia: You are naught, you are naught. I'll mark the play.

---

114. *only:* very best. *jig-maker:* one who composed or played in the farcical song-and-dance
entertainments that followed plays. 116. *'s:* this. 118-19. *let . . . sables:* i.e. to the devil
with my garments; after so long a time I am ready for the old man's garb of sables (fine fur).
122. *not thinking on:* not being thought of, i.e. being forgotten. 123-24. *For . . . forgot:* line
from a popular ballad lamenting puritanical suppression of such country sports as the
May-games, in which the hobby-horse, a character costumed to resemble a horse, traditionally
appeared. 126. *this' miching mallecho:* this is sneaking mischief. 127. *argument:* subject,
plot. 129. *counsel:* secrets. 131. *Be not you:* if you are not. 133. *naught:* wicked.

> *Prologue:* For us, and for our tragedy,
>   Here stooping to your clemency,   135
>   We beg your hearing patiently.   *[Exit.]*
>   *Hamlet:* Is this a prologue, or the posy of a ring?
>   *Ophelia:* 'Tis brief, my lord.
>   *Hamlet:* As woman's love.

Enter [two Players,] King and Queen.

> *[Player] King:* Full thirty times hath Phoebus' cart gone round   140
>   Neptune's salt wash and Tellus' orbed ground,
>   And thirty dozen moons with borrowed sheen
>   About the world have times twelve thirties been,
>   Since love our hearts and Hymen did our hands
>   Unite comutual in most sacred bands.   145
> *[Player] Queen:* So many journeys may the sun and moon
>   Make us again count o'er ere love be done!
>   But woe is me, you are so sick of late,
>   So far from cheer and from [your] former state,
>   That I distrust you. Yet though I distrust,   150
>   Discomfort you, my lord, it nothing must,
>   [For] women's fear and love hold quantity,
>   In neither aught, or in extremity.
>   Now what my [love] is, proof hath made you know,
>   And as my love is siz'd, my fear is so.   155
>   Where love is great, the littlest doubts are fear;
>   Where little fears grow great, great love grows there.
> *[Player] King:* Faith, I must leave thee, love, and shortly too;
>   My operant powers their functions leave to do,
>   And thou shalt live in this fair world behind,   160
>   Honor'd, belov'd, and haply one as kind
>   For husband shalt thou—
> *[Player] Queen:*   O, confound the rest!
>   Such love must needs be treason in my breast.
>   In second husband let me be accurs'd!
>   None wed the second but who kill'd the first.   165
>   *Hamlet:* *[Aside.]* That's wormwood!
> *[Player Queen:]* The instances that second marriage move
>   Are base respects of thrift, but none of love.

---

137. *posy . . . ring:* verse motto inscribed in a ring (necessarily short). 140-58. The Q1 text reads differently. 140. *Phoebus' cart:* the sun-god's chariot. 141. *Tellus:* goddess of the earth. 144. *Hymen:* god of marriage. 145. *bands:* bonds. 150. *distrust:* fear for. 152. *hold quantity:* are related in direct proportion. 154. *proof:* experience. 159. *operant:* active, vital. *leave to do:* cease to perform. 163. *confound the rest:* may destruction befall what you are about to speak of—a second marriage on my part. 167. *instances:* motives. *move:* give rise to. 168. *respects of thrift:* considerations of advantage.

A second time I kill my husband dead,
When second husband kisses me in bed.   170
[Player] King: I do believe you think what now you speak,
But what we do determine, oft we break.
Purpose is but the slave to memory,
Of violent birth, but poor validity,
Which now, the fruit unripe, sticks on the tree,   175
But fall unshaken when they mellow be.
Most necessary 'tis that we forget
To pay ourselves what to ourselves is debt.
What to ourselves in passion we propose,
The passion ending, doth the purpose lose.   180
The violence of either grief or joy
Their own enactures with themselves destroy.
Where joy most revels, grief doth most lament;
Grief [joys], joy grieves, on slender accident.
This world is not for aye, nor 'tis not strange   185
That even our loves should with our fortunes change:
For 'tis a question left us yet to prove,
Whether love lead fortune, or else fortune love.
The great man down, you mark his favorite flies,
The poor advanc'd makes friends of enemies.   190
And hitherto doth love on fortune tend,
For who not needs shall never lack a friend,
And who in want a hollow friend doth try,
Directly seasons him his enemy.
But orderly to end where I begun,   195
Our wills and fates do so contrary run
That our devices still are overthrown,
Our thoughts are ours, their ends none of our own:
So think thou wilt no second husband wed,
But die thy thoughts when thy first lord is dead.   200
[Player] Queen: Nor earth to me give food, nor heaven light,
Sport and repose lock from me day and night,
To desperation turn my trust and hope,
[An] anchor's cheer in prison be my scope!
Each opposite that blanks the face of joy   205
Meet what I would have well and it destroy!

---

174. *validity:* strength, power to last.   177-78. *Most . . . debt:* i.e. such resolutions are debts
we owe to ourselves, and it would be foolish to pay such debts.   179. *passion:* violent
emotion.   181-82. *The violence . . . destroy:* i.e. both violent grief and violent joy fail of their
intended acts because they destroy themselves by their very violence.   184. *slender accident:*
slight occasion.   194. *seasons:* ripens, converts into.   197. *devices:* devisings, intentions. *still:*
always.   204. *anchor's cheer:* hermit's fare. *my scope:* the extent of my comforts.   205. *blanks:*
blanches, makes pale (a symptom of grief).

Both here and hence pursue me lasting strife,
If once I be a widow, ever I be a wife!

Hamlet: If she should break it now!

[Player] King: 'Tis deeply sworn. Sweet, leave me here a while,   210
My spirits grow dull, and fain I would beguile
The tedious day with sleep.   *[Sleeps.]*

[Player] Queen: Sleep rock thy brain,
and never come mischance between us twain!   *Exit.*

Hamlet: Madam, how like you this play?

Queen: The lady doth protest too much, methinks.   215

Hamlet: O but she'll keep her word.

King: Have you heard the argument? is there no offense in't?

Hamlet: No, no, they do but jest, poison in jest—no offense i' th'
world.

King: What do you call the play?   220

Hamlet: "The Mouse-trap." Marry, how? tropically: this play is
the image of a murther done in Vienna; Gonzago is the
duke's name, his wife, Baptista. You shall see anon. 'Tis a
knavish piece of work, but what of that? Your Majesty, and
we that have free souls, it touches us not. Let the gall'd jade   225
winch, our withers are unwrung.

Enter Lucianus.

This is one Lucianus, nephew to the king.

Ophelia: You are as good as a chorus, my lord.

Hamlet: I could interpret between you and your love, if I could
see the puppets dallying.   230

Ophelia: You are keen, my lord, you are keen.

Hamlet: It would cost you a groaning to take off mine edge.

Ophelia: Still better, and worse.

Hamlet: So you mistake your husbands. Begin, murtherer, leave
thy damnable faces and begin. Come, the croaking raven 235
doth bellow for revenge.

Lucianus: Thoughts black, hands apt, drugs fit, and time agreeing,
[Confederate] season, else no creature seeing,

---

217. *offense:* offensive matter (but Hamlet quibbles on the sense "crime"). 218. *jest:* i.e.
pretend. 221. *tropically:* figuratively (with play on *trapically*—which is the reading of
Q1—and probably with allusion to the children's saying *marry trap,* meaning "now you're
caught"). 222. *image:* representation. 225. *free souls:* clear consciences. 225. *gall'd jade:*
chafed horse. 226. *winch:* wince. *withers:* ridge between a horse's shoulders. *unwrung:* not
rubbed sore. 228. *chorus:* i.e. one who explains the forthcoming action. 229–30. *I . . .
dallying:* I could speak the dialogue between you and your lover like a puppet-master (with an
indecent jest). 231. *keen:* bitter, sharp. 233. *better, and worse:* i.e. more pointed and less
decent. 234. *So:* i.e. "for better, for worse," in the words of the marriage service. *mistake:* i.e.
mis-take, take wrongfully. Their vows, Hamlet suggests, prove false. 235. *faces:* facial
expressions 235-36. *the croaking . . . revenge:* Misquoted from an old play, *The True Tragedy
of Richard III.* 238. *Confederate season:* the time being my ally.

Thou mixture rank, of midnight weeds collected,
With Hecat's ban thrice blasted, thrice [infected],   240
Thy natural magic and dire property
On wholesome life usurps immediately.

[Pours the poison in his ears.]

Hamlet: 'A poisons him i' th' garden for his estate. His name's
Gonzago, the story is extant, and written in very choice Ital-
ian. You shall see anon how the murtherer gets the love of 245
Gonzago's wife.

Ophelia: The King rises.

[Hamlet: What, frighted with false fire?]

Queen: How fares my lord?

Polonius: Give o'er the play.   250

King: Give me some light. Away!

Polonius: Lights, lights, lights!

Exeunt all but Hamlet *and* Horatio.

Hamlet: "Why, let the strooken deer go weep,
            The hart ungalled play,
        For some must watch while some must sleep,   255
            Thus runs the world away."
    Would not this, sir, and a forest of feathers—if the rest of my
    fortunes turn Turk with me—with [two] Provincial roses on
    my raz'd shoes, get me a fellowship in a cry of players?

Horatio: Half a share.   260

Hamlet: A whole one, I.
        "For thou dost know, O Damon dear,
            This realm dismantled was
        Of Jove himself, and now reigns here
            A very, very"—pajock.   265

Horatio: You might have rhym'd.

Hamlet: O good Horatio, I'll take the ghost's word for a thousand
    pound. Didst perceive?

Horatio: Very well, my lord.

Hamlet: Upon the talk of the pois'ning?   270

Horatio: I did very well note him.

Hamlet: Ah, ha! Come, some music! Come, the recorders!

---

240. *Hecat's ban:* the curse of Hecate, goddess of witchcraft.   248. *false fire:* i.e. a blank
cartridge.   253. *strooken:* struck, i.e. wounded.   254. *ungalled:* unwounded.   255. *watch:*
stay awake.   257. *feathers:* the plumes worn by tragic actors.   258. *turn Turk:* i.e. go to the
bad.   *Provincial roses:* rosettes designed to look like a variety of French rose.   259. *raz'd:*
with decorating slashing. *fellowship:* partnership.   *cry:* company.   263. *dismantled:* divested,
deprived.   265. *pajock:* peacock (substituting for the rhyme-word *ass*). The natural history of
the time attributed many vicious qualities to the peacock.

<blockquote>
For if the King like not the comedy,
Why then belike he likes it not, perdy.
Come, some music!
</blockquote>

275

Enter Rosencrantz *and* Guildenstern.

Guildenstern: Good my lord, voutsafe me a word with you.

Hamlet: Sir, a whole history.

Guildenstern: The King, sir—

Hamlet: Ay, sir, what of him?

280

Guildenstern: Is in his retirement marvellous distemp'red.

Hamlet: With drink, sir?

Guildenstern: No, my lord, with choler.

Hamlet: Your wisdom should show itself more richer to signify this to the doctor, for for me to put him to his purgation would perhaps plunge him into more choler.

285

Guildenstern: Good my lord, put your discourse into some frame, and [start] not so wildly from my affair.

Hamlet: I am tame, sir. Pronounce.

Guildenstern: The Queen, your mother, in most great affliction of spirit, hath sent me to you.

290

Hamlet: You are welcome.

Guildenstern: Nay, good my lord, this courtesy is not of the right breed. If it shall please you to make me a wholesome answer, I will do your mother's commandement; if not, your pardon and my return shall be the end of [my] business.

295

Hamlet: Sir, I cannot.

Rosencrantz: What, my lord?

Hamlet: Make you a wholesome answer—my wit's diseas'd. But, sir, such answer as I can make, you shall command, or rather, as you say, my mother. Therefore no more, but to the matter: my mother, you say—

300

Rosencrantz: Then thus she says: your behavior hath strook her into amazement and admiration.

Hamlet: O wonderful son, that can so stonish a mother! But is there no sequel at the heels of this mother's admiration? Impart.

305

Rosencrantz: She desires to speak with you in her closet ere you go to bed.

Hamlet: We shall obey, were she ten times our mother. Have you any further trade with us?

310

---

274. *perdy:* assuredly (French *pardieu,* "by God"). 283. *choler:* anger (but Hamlet willfully takes up the word in the sense "biliousness"). 285. *put . . . purgation:* i.e. prescribe for what's wrong with him. 287. *frame:* logical structure. 294. *wholesome:* sensible, rational. 295. *pardon:* permission for departure. 304. *amazement and admiration:* bewilderment and wonder. 305. *stonish:* astound. 308. *closet:* private room.

Rosencrantz: My lord, you once did love me.

Hamlet: And do still, by these pickers and stealers.

Rosencrantz: Good my lord, what is your cause of distemper? You do surely bar the door upon your own liberty if you deny your griefs to your friend. 315

Hamlet: Sir, I lack advancement.

Rosencrantz: How can that be, when you have the voice of the King himself for your succession in Denmark?

Hamlet: Ay, sir, but "While the grass grows"—the proverb is something musty. 320

Enter the Players *with recorders.*

O, the recorders! Let me see one.—To withdraw with you— why do you go about to recover the wind of me, as if you would drive me into a toil?

Guildenstern: O my lord, if my duty be too bold, my love is too unmannerly. 325

Hamlet: I do not well understand that. Will you play upon this pipe?

Guildenstern: My lord, I cannot.

Hamlet: I pray you. 330

Guildenstern: Believe me, I cannot.

Hamlet: I do beseech you.

Guildenstern: I know no touch of it, my lord.

Hamlet: It is as easy as lying. Govern these ventages with your fingers and [thumbs], give it breath with your mouth, and it will discourse most eloquent music. Look you, these are the stops. 335

Guildenstern: But these cannot I command to any utt'rance of harmony. I have not the skill.

Hamlet: Why, look you now, how unworthy a thing you make of me! You would play upon me, you would seem to know my stops, you would pluck out the heart of my mystery, you would sound me from my lowest note to [the top of] my compass; and there is much music, excellent voice, in this little organ, yet cannot you make it speak. 'Sblood, do you think I am easier to be play'd on than a pipe? Call me what instrument you will, though you fret me, [yet] you cannot play upon me. 340 345

---

313. *pickers and stealers:* hands, which, as the Catechism says, we must keep "from picking and stealing." 320. *proverb:* i.e. "While the grass grows, the steed starves." 321. *something musty:* somewhat stale. 323. *recover the wind:* get to windward. 324. *toil:* snare. 334. *ventages:* stops. 345. *organ:* instrument. 347. *fret:* (1) finger (an instrument); (2) vex.

Enter Polonius.

        God bless you, sir.

Polonius: My lord, the Queen would speak with you, and presently. 350
  Hamlet: Do you see yonder cloud that's almost in shape of a
    camel?
Polonius: By th' mass and 'tis, like a camel indeed.
  Hamlet: Methinks it is like a weasel.
Polonius: It is back'd like a weasel. 355
  Hamlet: Or like a whale.
Polonius: Very like a whale.
  Hamlet: Then I will come to my mother by and by. *[Aside.]* They
    fool me to the top of my bent.—I will come by and by.
[Polonius]: I will say so.   *[Exit.]* 360
  Hamlet: "By and by" is easily said. Leave me, friends.
                                    [Exeunt all but Hamlet.]
'Tis now the very witching time of night,
When churchyards yawn and hell itself [breathes] out
Contagion to this world. Now could I drink hot blood,
And do such [bitter business as the] day 365
Would quake to look on. Soft, now to my mother.
O heart, lose not thy nature! let not ever
The soul of Nero enter this firm bosom,
Let me be cruel, not unnatural;
I will speak [daggers] to her, but use none. 370
My tongue and soul in this be hypocrites—
How in my words somever she be shent,
To give them seals never my soul consent!   *Exit.*

Scene III

Enter King, Rosencrantz, *and* Guildenstern.

  King: I like him not, nor stands it safe with us
    To let his madness range. Therefore prepare you.
    I your commission will forthwith dispatch,
    And he to England shall along with you.
    The terms of our estate may not endure   5
    Hazard so near 's as doth hourly grow
    Out of his brows.
Guildenstern: We will ourselves provide.

---

350. *presently:* at once.   358-59. *They . . . bent:* they make me play the fool to the limit of my
ability.   *by and by:* at once.   362. *witching:* i.e. when the powers of evil are at large.
367. *nature:* natural affection, filial feeling.   368. *Nero:* Murderer of his mother.
372. *shent:* rebuked.   373. *give them seals:* confirm them by deeds.

III.iii. Location: The castle.   1. *him:* i.e. his state of mind, his behavior.   3. *dispatch:* have
drawn up.   5. *terms:* conditions, nature. *our estate:* my position (as king).   7. *his brows:* the
madness visible in his face (?)

Most holy and religious fear it is
To keep those many many bodies safe
That live and feed upon your Majesty.   10
Rosencrantz: The single and peculiar life is bound
With all the strength and armor of the mind
To keep itself from noyance, but much more
That spirit upon whose weal depends and rests
The lives of many. The cess of majesty   15
Dies not alone, but like a gulf doth draw
What's near it with it. Or it is a massy wheel
Fix'd on the summit of the highest mount,
To whose [huge] spokes ten thousand lesser things
Are mortis'd and adjoin'd, which when it falls,   20
Each small annexment, petty consequence,
Attends the boist'rous [ruin]. Never alone
Did the King sigh, but [with] a general groan.
King: Arm you, I pray you, to this speedy viage,
For we will fetters put about this fear,   25
Which now goes too free-footed.
Rosencrantz: We will haste us.

Exeunt Gentlemen   [*Rosencrantz and Guildenstern*].

Enter Polonius.

Polonius: My lord, he's going to his mother's closet.
Behind the arras I'll convey myself
To hear the process. I'll warrant she'll tax him home,
And as you said, and wisely was it said,   30
'Tis meet that some more audience than a mother,
Since nature makes them partial, should o'erhear
The speech, of vantage. Fare you well, my liege,
I'll call upon you ere you go to bed,
And tell you what I know.
King: Thanks, dear my lord.   35

                                              Exit [Polonius].

O, my offense is rank, it smells to heaven,
It hath the primal eldest curse upon't,
A brother's murther. Pray can I not,
Though inclination be as sharp as will.

---

8. *fear:* concern.   11. *single and peculiar:* individual and private.   13. *noyance:* injury.
15. *cess:* cessation, death.   16. *gulf:* whirlpool.   20. *mortis'd:* fixed.   22. *Attends:* accompanies. *ruin:* fall.   24. *Arm:* prepare. *viage:* voyage.   25. *fear:* object of fear.   29. *process:*
course of the talk. *tax him home:* take him severely to task.   33. *of vantage:* from an advantageous position (?) or in addition (?).   36-72. The Q1 text reads differently.   37. *primal eldest
curse:* i.e. God's curse on Cain, who also slew his brother.   39. *Though . . . will:* though my
desire is as strong as my resolve to do so.

My stronger guilt defeats my strong intent,   40
And, like a man to double business bound,
I stand in pause where I shall first begin,
And both neglect. What if this cursed hand
Were thicker than itself with brother's blood,
Is there not rain enough in the sweet heavens   45
To wash it white as snow? Whereto serves mercy
But to confront the visage of offense?
And what's in prayer but this twofold force,
To be forestalled ere we come to fall,
Or [pardon'd] being down? then I'll look up.   50
My fault is past, but, O, what form of prayer
Can serve my turn? "Forgive me my foul murther"?
That cannot be, since I am still possess'd
Of those effects for which I did the murther:
My crown, mine own ambition, and my queen.   55
May one be pardon'd and retain th' offense?
In the corrupted currents of this world
Offense's gilded hand may [shove] by justice,
And oft 'tis seen the wicked prize itself
Buys out the law, but 'tis not so above: 60
There is no shuffling, there the action lies
In his true nature, and we ourselves compell'd,
Even to the teeth and forehead of our faults,
To give in evidence. What then? What rests?
Try what repentance can. What can it not?   65
Yet what can it, when one can not repent?
O wretched state! O bosom black as death!
O limed soul, that struggling to be free
Art more engag'd! Help, angels! Make assay,
Bow, stubborn knees, and heart, with strings of steel,   70
Be soft as sinews of the new-born babe!
All may be well.   *[He kneels.]*

Enter Hamlet.

    Hamlet: Now might I do it [pat], now 'a is a-praying;
      And now I'll do't—and so 'a goes to heaven,
      And so am I [reveng'd]. That would be scann'd: 75

---

41. *bound:* committed.   43. *neglect:* omit.   46-47. *Whereto . . . offense:* i.e. what function has
mercy except when there has been sin.   56. *th' offense:* i.e. the "effects" or fruits of the
offense.   57. *currents:* courses.   58. *gilded:* i.e. bribing.   59. *wicked prize:* rewards of vice.
61. *shuffling:* evasion. *the action lies:* the charge comes for legal consideration.   63. *Even . . .
forehead:* i.e. fully recognizing their features, extenuating nothing.   64. *rests:* remains.
68. *limed:* caught (as in birdlime, a sticky substance used for catching birds).   69. *engag'd:*
entangled.   75. *would be scann'd:* must be carefully considered.

A villain kills my father, and for that
I, his sole son, do this same villain send
To heaven.
Why, this is [hire and salary], not revenge.
'A took my father grossly, full of bread,   80
With all his crimes broad blown, as flush as May,
And how his audit stands who knows save heaven?
But in our circumstance and course of thought
'Tis heavy with him. And am I then revenged,
To take him in the purging of his soul,   85
When he is fit and season'd for his passage?
No!
Up, sword, and know thou a more horrid hent:
When he is drunk asleep, or in his rage,
Or in th' incestious pleasure of his bed,   90
At game a-swearing, or about some act
That has no relish of salvation in't—
Then trip him, that his heels may kick at heaven,
And that his soul may be as damn'd and black
As hell, whereto it goes. My mother stays,   95
This physic but prolongs thy sickly days.   *Exit.*
    King: [Rising.] My words fly up, my thoughts remain below:
    Words without thoughts never to heaven go.   *Exit.*

Scene IV

Enter [Queen] Gertrude *and* Polonius.

    Polonius: 'A will come straight. Look you, lay home to him.
    Tell him his pranks have been too broad to bear with,
    And that your Grace hath screen'd and stood between
    Much heat and him. I'll silence me even here;
    Pray you be round [with him].   5
    Queen: I'll [warr'nt] you, fear me not. Withdraw,
    I hear him coming.   [*Polonius hides behind the arras.*]

Enter Hamlet.

    Hamlet: Now, mother, what's the matter?
    Queen: Hamlet, thou hast thy father much offended.
    Hamlet: Mother, you have my father much offended.   10

---

80. *grossly:* in a gross state; not spiritually prepared.   81. *crimes:* sins. *broad blown:* in full
bloom. *flush:* lusty, vigorous.   82. *audit:* account.   83. *in . . . thought:* i.e. to the best of our
knowledge and belief.   88. *Up:* into the sheath. *know . . . hent:* be grasped at a more dreadful
time.   92. *relish:* trace.   96. *physic:* (attempted) remedy, i.e. prayer.

III.iv. Location: The Queen's closet in the castle.   1. *lay . . . him:* reprove him severely.
2. *broad:* unrestrained.   5. *round:* plain-spoken.   6. *fear me not:* have no fears about my handling of the situation.

Queen: Come, come, you answer with an idle tongue.

Hamlet: Go, go, you question with a wicked tongue.

Queen: Why, how now, Hamlet?

Hamlet: What's the matter now?

Queen: Have you forgot me?

Hamlet: No, by the rood, not so:

You are the Queen, your husband's brother's wife,   15

And would it were not so, you are my mother.

Queen: Nay, then I'll set those to you that can speak.

Hamlet: Come, come, and sit you down, you shall not boudge;

You go not till I set you up a glass

Where you may see the [inmost] part of you.   20

Queen: What wilt thou do? Thou wilt not murther me?

Help ho!

Polonius: *[Behind.]* What ho, help!

Hamlet: *[Drawing.]* How now? A rat? Dead, for a ducat, dead!

                                    [Kills Polonius *through the arras.]*

Polonius: *[Behind.]* O, I am slain.

Queen: O me, what hast thou done?   25

Hamlet: Nay, I know not, is it the King?

Queen: O, what a rash and bloody deed is this!

Hamlet: A bloody deed! almost as bad, good mother,

As kill a king, and marry with his brother.

Queen: As kill a king!

Hamlet: Ay, lady, it was my word.   30

                              [Parts the arras and discovers Polonius.]

Thou wretched, rash, intruding fool, farewell!

I took thee for thy better. Take thy fortune;

Thou find'st to be too busy is some danger.—

Leave wringing of your hands. Peace, sit you down,

And let me wring your heart, for so I shall   35

If it be made of penetrable stuff,

If damned custom have not brass'd it so

That it be proof and bulwark against sense.

Queen: What have I done, that thou dar'st wag thy tongue

In noise so rude against me?

Hamlet: Such an act   40

That blurs the grace and blush of modesty,

Calls virtue hypocrite, takes off the rose

From the fair forehead of an innocent love

And sets a blister there, makes marriage vows

---

11. *idle:* foolish.   14. *rood:* cross.   18. *boudge:* budge.   24. *for a ducat:* I'll wager a ducat.
33. *busy:* officious, meddlesome.   37. *damned custom:* i.e. the habit of ill-doing. *brass'd:*
hardened, literally, plated with brass.   38. *proof:* armor. *sense:* feeling.   44. *blister:* brand of
shame.

As false as dicers' oaths, O, such a deed   45
As from the body of contraction plucks
The very soul, and sweet religion makes
A rhapsody of words. Heaven's face does glow
O'er this solidity and compound mass
With heated visage, as against the doom;   50
Is thought-sick at the act.
Queen: Ay me, what act,
That roars so loud and thunders in the index?
Hamlet: Look here upon this picture, and on this,
The counterfeit presentment of two brothers.
See what a grace was seated on this brow: 55
Hyperion's curls, the front of Jove himself,
An eye like Mars, to threaten and command,
A station like the herald Mercury
New lighted on a [heaven-]kissing hill,
A combination and a form indeed,   60
Where every god did seem to set his seal
To give the world assurance of a man.
This was your husband. Look you now what follows:
Here is your husband, like a mildewed ear,
Blasting his wholesome brother. Have you eyes?   65
Could you on this fair mountain leave to feed,
And batten on this moor? ha, have you eyes?
You cannot call it love, for at your age
The heyday in the blood is tame, it's humble,
And waits upon the judgment, and what judgment   70
Would step from this to this? Sense sure you have,
Else could you not have motion, but sure that sense
Is apoplex'd, for madness would not err,
Nor sense to ecstasy was ne'er so thrall'd
But it reserv'd some quantity of choice   75
To serve in such a difference. What devil was't
That thus hath cozen'd you at hoodman-blind?
Eyes without feeling, feeling without sight,
Ears without hands or eyes, smelling sans all,

---

46. *contraction:* the making of contracts, i.e. the assuming of solemn obligation.   47. *religion:*
i.e. sacred vows.   48. *rhapsody:* miscellaneous collection, jumble. *glow:* i.e. with anger.
49. *this . . . mass:* i.e. the earth. *Compound* = compounded of the four elements.   50. *as . . .
doom:* as if for Judgment Day.   52. *index:* i.e. table of contents. The index was formerly
placed at the beginning of a book.   54. *counterfeit presentment:* painted likenesses.
56. *Hyperion's:* the sun-god's. *front:* forehead.   58. *station:* bearing.   64. *ear:* i.e. of grain.
67. *batten:* gorge.   69. *heyday:* excitement.   71. *Sense:* sense perception, the five senses.
73. *apoplex'd:* paralyzed.   73-76. *madness . . . difference:* i.e. madness itself could not go so far
astray, nor were the senses ever so enslaved by lunacy that they did not retain the power to
make so obvious a distinction.   77. *cozen'd:* cheated. *hoodman-blind:* blindman's bluff.
79. *sans:* without.

Or but a sickly part of one true sense   80
Could not so mope. O shame, where is thy blush?
Rebellious hell,
If thou canst mutine in a matron's bones,
To flaming youth let virtue be as wax
And melt in her own fire. Proclaim no shame   85
When the compulsive ardure gives the charge,
Since frost itself as actively doth burn,
And reason [panders] will.
   Queen: O Hamlet, speak no more!
Thou turn'st my [eyes into my very] soul,
And there I see such black and [grained] spots   90
As will [not] leave their tinct.
Hamlet: Nay, but to live
In the rank sweat of an enseamed bed,
Stew'd in corruption, honeying and making love
Over the nasty sty!
   Queen: O, speak to me no more!
These words like daggers enter in my ears.   95
No more, sweet Hamlet!
Hamlet: A murtherer and a villain!
A slave that is not twentith part the [tithe]
Of your precedent lord, a Vice of kings,
A cutpurse of the empire and the rule,
That from a shelf the precious diadem stole,   100
And put it in his pocket—
   Queen: No more!

Enter Ghost [*in his night-gown*].

Hamlet: A king of shreds and patches—
Save me, and hover o'er me with your wings,
You heavenly guards! What would your gracious figure?
Queen: Alas, he's mad!   105
Hamlet: Do you not come your tardy son to chide,
That, laps'd in time and passion, lets go by
Th' important acting of your dread command?
O, say!

---

81. *mope:* be dazed.   83. *mutine:* rebel.   85-88. *Proclaim . . . will:* do not call it sin when the
hot blood of youth is responsible for lechery, since here we see people of calmer age on fire
for it; and reason acts as procurer for desire, instead of restraining it. *Ardure* = ardor.
90. *grained:* fast-dyed, indelible.   91. *leave their tinct:* lose their color.   92. *enseamed:*
greasy.   97. *twentith:* twentieth.   98. *precedent:* former. *Vice:* buffoon (like the Vice of the
morality plays).   101 s.d. *night-gown:* dressing gown.   102. *of . . . patches:* clownish (alluding
to the motley worn by jesters) (?) or patched-up, beggarly (?).   107. *laps'd . . . passion:*
"having suffered time to slip and passion to cool" (Johnson).   108. *important:* urgent.

Ghost: Do not forget! This visitation   110
      Is but to whet thy almost blunted purpose.
      But look, amazement on thy mother sits,
      O, step between her and her fighting soul.
      Conceit in weakest bodies strongest works,
      Speak to her, Hamlet.
Hamlet: How is it with you, lady?   115
Queen: Alas, how is't with you,
      That you do bend your eye on vacancy,
      And with th' incorporal air do hold discourse?
      Forth at your eyes your spirits wildly peep,
      And as the sleeping soldiers in th' alarm,   120
      Your bedded hair, like life in excrements,
      Start up and stand an end. O gentle son,
      Upon the heat and flame of thy distemper
      Sprinkle cool patience. Whereon do you look?
Hamlet: On him, on him! look you how pale he glares!   125
      His form and cause conjoin'd, preaching to stones,
      Would make them capable.—Do not look upon me,
      Lest with this piteous action you convert
      My stern effects, then what I have to do
      Will want true color—tears perchance for blood.   130
Queen: To whom do you speak this?
Hamlet: Do you see nothing there?
Queen: Nothing at all, yet all that is I see.
Hamlet: Nor did you nothing hear?
Queen: No, nothing but ourselves.
Hamlet: Why, look you there, look how it steals away!
      My father, in his habit as he lived!   135
      Look where he goes, even now, out at the portal! *Exit Ghost.*
Queen: This is the very coinage of your brain,
      This bodiless creation ecstasy
      Is very cunning in.
Hamlet: [Ecstasy?]
      My pulse as yours doth temperately keep time,   140
      And makes as healthful music. It is not madness
      That I have utt'red. Bring me to the test,
      And [I] the matter will reword, which madness
      Would gambol from. Mother, for love of grace,

---

112. *amazement:* utter bewilderment. 114. *Conceit:* imagination. 120. *in th' alarm:* when
the call to arms is sounded. 121. *excrements:* outgrowths; here, hair (also used of nails).
122. *an end:* on end. 124. *patience:* self-control. 126. *His . . . cause:* his appearance and
what he has to say. 127. *capable:* sensitive, receptive. 128. *convert:* alter. 129. *effects:*
(purposed) actions. 130. *want true color:* lack its proper appearance. 135. *habit:* dress.
137-216. The Q1 conclusion of this scene is different. 138. *ecstasy:* madness. 144. *gambol:*
start, jerk away.

Lay not that flattering unction to your soul,   145
That not your trespass but my madness speaks;
It will but skin and film the ulcerous place,
Whiles rank corruption, mining all within,
Infects unseen. Confess yourself to heaven,
Repent what's past, avoid what is to come,   150
And do not spread the compost on the weeds
To make them ranker. Forgive me this my virtue,
For in the fatness of these pursy times
Virtue itself of vice must pardon beg,
Yea, curb and woo for leave to do him good.   155

Queen: O Hamlet, thou hast cleft my heart in twain.

Hamlet: O, throw away the worser part of it,
And [live] the purer with the other half.
Good night, but go not to my uncle's bed—
Assume a virtue, if you have it not.   160
That monster custom, who all sense doth eat,
Of habits devil, is angel yet in this,
That to the use of actions fair and good
He likewise gives a frock or livery
That aptly is put on. Refrain [to-]night,   165
And that shall lend a kind of easiness
To the next abstinence, the next more easy;
For use almost can change the stamp of nature,
And either [....] the devil or throw him out
With wondrous potency. Once more good night,   170
And when you are desirous to be blest,
I'll blessing beg of you. For this same lord,

                                    [*Pointing to Polonius.*]

I do repent; but heaven hath pleas'd it so
To punish me with this, and this with me,
That I must be their scourge and minister.   175
I will bestow him, and will answer well
The death I gave him. So again good night.
I must be cruel only to be kind.
This bad begins and worse remains behind.
One word more, good lady.

---

145. *flattering unction:* soothing ointment.   151. *compost:* manure.   153. *pursy:* puffy, out of condition.   155. *curb and woo:* bow and entreat.   161. *all . . . eat:* wears away all natural feeling.   162. *Of habits devil:* i.e. though it acts like a devil in establishing bad habits. Most editors read (in lines 161-62) *eat / Of habits evil,* following Theobald.   164-165. *frock . . . on:* i.e. a "habit" or customary garment, readily put on without need of any decision.   168. *use:* habit.   169. A word seems to be wanting after *either.*   171. *desirous . . . blest:* i.e. repentant. 175. *scourge and minister:* the agent of heavenly justice against human crime. *Scourge* suggests a permissive cruelty (Tamburlaine was the "scourge of God"), but "woe to him by whom the offense cometh"; the scourge must suffer for the evil it performs.   176. *bestow:* dispose of. *answer:* answer for.   179. *behind:* to come.

Queen: What shall I do?   180
Hamlet: Not this, by no means, that I bid you do:
          Let the bloat king tempt you again to bed,
          Pinch wanton on your cheek, call you his mouse,
          And let him, for a pair of reechy kisses,
          Or paddling in your neck with his damn'd fingers,   185
          Make you to ravel all this matter out,
          That I essentially am not in madness,
          But mad in craft. 'Twere good you let him know,
          For who that's but a queen, fair, sober, wise,
          Would from a paddock, from a bat, a gib,   190
          Such dear concernings hide? Who would do so?
          No, in despite of sense and secrecy,
          Unpeg the basket on the house's top,
          Let the birds fly, and like the famous ape,
          To try conclusions in the basket creep,   195
          And break your own neck down.
Queen: Be thou assur'd, if words be made of breath,
          And breath of life, I have no life to breathe
          What thou hast said to me.
Hamlet: I must to England, you know that?
Queen: Alack,   200
          I had forgot. 'Tis so concluded on.
Hamlet: There's letters seal'd, and my two schoolfellows,
          Whom I will trust as I will adders fang'd,
          They bear the mandate, they must sweep my way
          And marshal me to knavery. Let it work,   205
          For 'tis the sport to have the enginer
          Hoist with his own petar, an't shall go hard
          But I will delve one yard below their mines,
          And blow them at the moon. O, 'tis most sweet
          When in one line two crafts directly meet.   210
          This man shall set me packing;
          I'll lug the guts into the neighbor room.
          Mother, good night indeed. This counsellor
          Is now most still, most secret, and most grave,
          Who was in life a foolish prating knave.   215
          Come, sir, to draw toward an end with you.
          Good night, mother.
                    Exeunt [severally, Hamlet tugging in Polonius].

---

184. *reechy:* filthy.   190. *paddock:* toad. *gib:* tom-cat.   191. *dear concernings:* matters of
intense concern.   193. *Unpeg the basket:* open the door of the cage.   194. *famous ape:* The
actual story has been lost.   195. *conclusions:* experiments (to see whether he too can fly if he
enters the cage and then leaps out).   196. *down:* by the fall.   205. *knavery:* some knavish
scheme against me.   206. *enginer:* deviser of military "engines" or contrivances.   207. *Hoist
with:* blown up by. *petar:* petard, bomb.   210. *crafts:* plots.   211. *packing:* (1) taking on a
load; (2) leaving in a hurry.   216. *draw . . . end:* finish my conversation.

ACT IV

Scene I

Enter King *and* Queen *with* Rosencrantz *and* Guildenstern.

    King: There's matter in these sighs, these profound heaves—
      You must translate, 'tis fit we understand them.
      Where is your son?
    Queen: Bestow this place on us a little while.

                  [Exeunt Rosencrantz and Guildenstern.]
      Ah, mine own lord, what have I seen to-night!   5
    King: What, Gertrude? How does Hamlet?
    Queen: Mad as the sea and wind when both contend
      Which is the mightier. In his lawless fit,
      Behind the arras hearing something stir,
      Whips out his rapier, cries, "A rat, a rat!"   10
      And in this brainish apprehension kills
      The unseen good old man.
    King: O heavy deed!
      It had been so with us had we been there.
      His liberty is full of threats to all,
      To you yourself, to us, to every one.   15
      Alas, how shall this bloody deed be answer'd?
      It will be laid to us, whose providence
      Should have kept short, restrain'd, and out of haunt
      This mad young man; but so much was our love,
      We would not understand what was most fit,   20
      But like the owner of a foul disease,
      To keep it from divulging, let it feed
      Even on the pith of life. Where is he gone?
    Queen: To draw apart the body he hath kill'd,
      O'er whom his very madness, like some ore   25
      Among a mineral of metals base,
      Shows itself pure: 'a weeps for what is done.
    King: O Gertrude, come away!
      The sun no sooner shall the mountains touch,
      But we will ship him hence, and this vile deed   30
      We must with all our majesty and skill
      Both countenance and excuse. Ho, Guildenstern!

Enter Rosencrantz *and* Guildenstern.

IV.i. Location: The castle. 11. *brainish apprehension:* crazy notion. 16. *answer'd:* i.e. satisfactorily accounted for to the public. 17. *providence:* foresight. 18. *short:* on a short leash. *out of haunt:* away from other people. 22. *divulging:* being revealed. 25. *ore:* vein of gold. 26. *mineral:* mine.

Friends both, go join you with some further aid:
Hamlet in madness hath Polonius slain,
And from his mother's closet hath he dragg'd him,   35
Go seek him out, speak fair, and bring the body
Into the chapel. I pray you haste in this.
                         [*Exeunt Rosencrantz and Guildenstern.*]
Come, Gertrude, we'll call up our wisest friends
And let them know both what we mean to do
And what's untimely done, [....]   40
Whose whisper o'er the world's diameter,
As level as the cannon to his blank,
Transports his pois'ned shot, may miss our name,
And hit the woundless air. O, come away!
My soul is full of discord and dismay.   *Exeunt.* 45

Scene II

Enter Hamlet.

   Hamlet: Safely stow'd.
[Gentlemen: (Within.) Hamlet! Lord Hamlet!]
   [Hamlet:] But soft, what noise? Who calls on Hamlet? O, here they
   come.

Enter Rosencrantz *and* [Guildenstern].

Rosencrantz: What have you done, my lord, with the dead body?   5
   Hamlet: [Compounded] it with dust, whereto 'tis kin.
Rosencrantz: Tell us where 'tis, that we may take it thence,
          And bear it to the chapel.
   Hamlet: Do not believe it.
Rosencrantz: Believe what?   10
   Hamlet: That I can keep your counsel and not mine own. Besides,
          to be demanded of a spunge, what replication should be
          made by the son of a king?
Rosencrantz: Take you me for a spunge, my lord?
   Hamlet: Ay, sir, that soaks up the King's countenance, his   15
          rewards, his authorities. But such officers do the King best
          service in the end: he keeps them, like [an ape] an apple, in
          the corner of his jaw, first mouth'd, to be last swallow'd.
          When he needs what you have glean'd, it is but squeezing
          you, and, spunge, you shall be dry again.   20

---

40. Some words are wanting at the end of the line. Capell's conjecture, *so, haply, slander,*
probably indicates the intended sense of the passage.   42. *As level:* with aim as good. *blank:*
target.   44. *woundless:* incapable of being hurt.

IV.ii. Location: The castle.   12. *demanded of:* questioned by. *spunge:* sponge. *replication:*
reply.   15. *countenance:* favor.

Rosencrantz: I understand you not, my lord.

    Hamlet: I am glad of it, a knavish speech sleeps in a foolish ear.

Rosencrantz: My lord, you must tell us where the body is, and go with
    us to the King.

    Hamlet: The body is with the King, but the King is not with the   25
    body. The King is a thing—

Guildenstern: A thing, my lord?

    Hamlet: Of nothing, bring me to him. [Hide fox, and all after.]

                                             Exeunt.

Scene III

Enter King *and two or three.*

    King: I have sent to seek him, and to find the body.
    How dangerous is it that this man goes loose!
    Yet must not we put the strong law on him.
    He's lov'd of the distracted multitude,
    Who like not in their judgment, but their eyes,   5
    And where 'tis so, th' offender's scourge is weigh'd,
    But never the offense. To bear all smooth and even,
    This sudden sending him away must seem
    Deliberate pause. Diseases desperate grown
    By desperate appliance are reliev'd,   10
    Or not at all.

Enter Rosencrantz.

                     How now, what hath befall'n?

Rosencrantz: Where the dead body is bestow'd, my lord,
    We cannot get from him.

    King: But where is he?

Rosencrantz: Without, my lord, guarded, to know your pleasure.

    King: Bring him before us.

Rosencrantz: Ho, bring in the lord.   15

They [Hamlet *and* Guildenstern] *enter.*

    King: Now, Hamlet, where's Polonius?

    Hamlet: At supper.

    King: At supper? where?

---

22. *sleeps:* is meaningless.   25-26. *The body . . . the body:* Possibly alluding to the legal fiction
that the king's dignity is separate from his mortal body.   28. *Of nothing:* of no account. Cf.
"Man is like a thing of nought, his time passeth away like a shadow" (Psalm 144:4 in the
Prayer Book version). "Hamlet at once insults the King and hints that his days are numbered"
(Dover Wilson).   *Hide . . . after:* Probably a cry in some game resembling hide-and-seek.

IV.iii. Location: The castle.   4. *distracted:* unstable.   6. *scourge:* i.e. punishment.   7. *bear:*
manage.   8-9. *must . . . pause:* i.e. must be represented as a maturely considered decision.

Hamlet: Not where he eats, but where 'a is eaten; a certain convo- 20
cation of politic worms are e'en at him. Your worm is your
only emperor for diet: we fat all creatures else to fat us, and
we fat ourselves for maggots; your fat king and your lean beggar is but variable service, two dishes, but to one table—
that's the end.

King: Alas, alas! 25

Hamlet: A man may fish with the worm that hath eat of a king, and
eat of the fish that hath fed of that worm.

King: What dost thou mean by this?

Hamlet: Nothing but to show you how a king may go a progress
through the guts of a beggar. 30

King: Where is Polonius?

Hamlet: In heaven, send thither to see; if your messenger find him
not there, seek him i' th' other place yourself. But if indeed
you find him not within this month, you shall nose him as you
go up the stairs into the lobby. 35

King: *[To Attendants.]* Go seek him there.

Hamlet: 'A will stay till you come.   *[Exeunt Attendants.]*

King: Hamlet, this deed, for thine especial safety—
Which we do tender, as we dearly grieve
For that which thou hast done—must send thee hence 40
[With fiery quickness]; therefore prepare thyself,
The bark is ready, and the wind at help,
Th' associates tend, and every thing is bent
For England.

Hamlet: For England.

King: Ay, Hamlet.

Hamlet: Good.

King: So is it, if thou knew'st our purposes. 45

Hamlet: I see a cherub that sees them. But come, for England!
Farewell, dear mother.

King: Thy loving father, Hamlet.

Hamlet: My mother: father and mother is man and wife, man and
wife is one flesh—so, my mother. Come, for England! *Exit.* 50

King: Follow him at foot, tempt him with speed aboard.
Delay it not, I'll have him hence to-night.
Away, for every thing is seal'd and done
That else leans on th' affair. Pray you make haste.

---

20. *politic:* crafty, prying; "such worms as might breed in a politician's corpse" (Dowden).
e'en: even now.   21. *for diet:* with respect to what it eats.   23. *variable service:* different
courses of a meal.   29. *progress:* royal journey of state.   39. *tender:* regard with tenderness,
hold dear. *dearly:* with intense feeling.   42. *at help:* favorable.   43. *Th':* thy. *tend:* await. *bent:*
made ready.   46. *I . . . them:* i.e. heaven sees them.   51. *at foot:* at his heels, close behind.
54. *leans on:* relates to.

And, England, if my love thou hold'st at aught— 55
As my great power thereof may give thee sense,
Since yet thy cicatrice looks raw and red
After the Danish sword, and thy free awe
Pays homage to us—thou mayst not coldly set
Our sovereign process, which imports at full, 60
By letters congruing to that effect,
The present death of Hamlet. Do it, England,
For like the hectic in my blood he rages,
And thou must cure me. Till I know 'tis done,
How e'er my haps, my joys [were] ne'er [begun]. *Exit.* 65

Scene IV

Enter Fortinbras *with his army over the stage.*

Fortinbras: Go, captain, from me greet the Danish king.
Tell him that by his license Fortinbras
Craves the conveyance of a promis'd march
Over his kingdom. You know the rendezvous.
If that his Majesty would aught with us, 5
We shall express our duty in his eye,
And let him know so.
Captain: I will do't, my lord.
Fortinbras: Go softly on. [*Exeunt all but the Captain.*]

Enter Hamlet, Rosencrantz, [Guildenstern,] *etc.*

Hamlet: Good sir, whose powers are these?
Captain: They are of Norway, sir. 10
Hamlet: How purpos'd, sir, I pray you?
Captain: Against some part of Poland.
Hamlet: Who commands them, sir?
Captain: The nephew to old Norway, Fortinbras.
Hamlet: Goes it against the main of Poland, sir, 15
Or for some frontier?
Captain: Truly to speak, and with no addition,
We go to gain a little patch of ground
That hath in it no profit but the name.
To pay five ducats, five, I would not farm it; 20

---

55. *England:* King of England.   57. *cicatrice:* scar.   58-59. *thy . . . Pays:* your fear makes you pay voluntarily.   59. *coldly set:* undervalue, disregard.   60. *process:* command.   61. *congruing to:* in accord with.   62. *present:* immediate.   63. *hectic:* continuous fever.   65. *haps:* fortunes.

IV.iv. Location: The Danish coast, near the castle.   3. *conveyance of:* escort for.   6. *eye:* presence.   8. *softly:* slowly.   9. *powers:* forces.   15. *main:* main territory.   20. *To pay:* i.e. for an annual rent of. *farm:* lease.

Nor will it yield to Norway or the Pole
A ranker rate, should it be sold in fee.
Hamlet: Why then the Polack never will defend it.
Captain: Yes, it is already garrison'd.
Hamlet: Two thousand souls and twenty thousand ducats   25
Will not debate the question of this straw.
This is th' imposthume of much wealth and peace,
That inward breaks, and shows no cause without
Why the man dies. I humbly thank you, sir.
Captain: God buy you, sir.   *[Exit.]*
Rosencrantz: Will't please you go, my lord? 30
Hamlet: I'll be with you straight—go a little before.
                                [Exeunt all but Hamlet.]
How all occasions do inform against me,
And spur my dull revenge! What is a man,
If his chief good and market of his time
Be but to sleep and feed? a beast, no more.   35
Sure He that made us with such large discourse,
Looking before and after, gave us not
That capability and godlike reason
To fust in us unus'd. Now whether it be
Bestial oblivion, or some craven scruple   40
Of thinking too precisely on th' event—
A thought which quarter'd hath but one part wisdom
And ever three parts coward—I do not know
Why yet I live to say, "This thing's to do,"
Sith I have cause, and will, and strength, and means   45
To do't. Examples gross as earth exhort me:
Witness this army of such mass and charge,
Led by a delicate and tender prince,
Whose spirit with divine ambition puff'd
Makes mouths at the invisible event,   50
Exposing what is mortal and unsure
To all that fortune, death, and danger dare,
Even for an egg-shell. Rightly to be great
Is not to stir without great argument,
But greatly to find quarrel in a straw   55
When honor's at the stake. How stand I then,
That have a father kill'd, a mother stain'd,

---

22. *ranker:* higher. *in fee:* outright.   26. *Will not debate:* i.e. will scarcely be enough to fight
out.   27. *imposthume:* abscess.   32. *inform against:* denounce, accuse.   34. *market:*
purchase, profit.   36. *discourse:* reasoning power.   39. *fust:* grow mouldy.   40. *oblivion:*
forgetfulness.   41. *event:* outcome.   46. *gross:* large, obvious.   47. *mass and charge:* size and
expense.   50. *Makes mouths at:* treats scornfully. *invisible:* i.e. unforeseeable.   54. *Is not to:*
i.e. is *not* not to. *argument:* cause.   55. *greatly:* nobly.

Excitements of my reason and my blood,
And let all sleep, while to my shame I see
The imminent death of twenty thousand men,   60
That for a fantasy and trick of fame
Go to their graves like beds, fight for a plot
Whereon the numbers cannot try the cause,
Which is not tomb enough and continent
To hide the slain? O, from this time forth,   65
My thoughts be bloody, or be nothing worth!   *Exit.*

Scene V

Enter Horatio, [Queen] Gertrude, *and a* Gentleman.

    Queen: I will not speak with her.
Gentleman: She is importunate, indeed distract.
    Her mood will needs be pitied.
    Queen: What would she have?
Gentleman: She speaks much of her father, says she hears
    There's tricks i' th' world, and hems, and beats her heart,   5
    Spurns enviously at straws, speaks things in doubt
    That carry but half sense. Her speech is nothing,
    Yet the unshaped use of it doth move
    The hearers to collection; they yawn at it,
    And botch the words up fit to their own thoughts,   10
    Which as her winks and nods and gestures yield them,
    Indeed would make one think there might be thought,
    Though nothing sure, yet much unhappily.
Horatio: 'Twere good she were spoken with, for she may strew
    Dangerous conjectures in ill-breeding minds.   15
[Queen:] Let her come in.   *[Exit Gentleman.]*
    [Aside.] To my sick soul, as sin's true nature is,
    Each toy seems prologue to some great amiss,
    So full of artless jealousy is guilt,
    It spills itself in fearing to be spilt.   20

Enter Ophelia [*distracted, with her hair down, playing on a lute*].

    Ophelia: Where is the beauteous majesty of Denmark?

---

58. *Excitements of:* urgings by. 61. *fantasy:* caprice. *trick:* trifle. 63. *Whereon . . . cause:*
which isn't large enough to let the opposing armies engage upon it. 64. *continent:* container.

IV.v. Location: The castle. 1–20. The text in Q1 reads differently. 6. *Spurns . . . straws:*
spitefully takes offense at trifles. *in doubt:* obscurely. 7. *Her speech:* what she says.
8. *unshaped use:* distracted manner. 9. *collection:* attempts to gather the meaning. *yawn at:*
gape eagerly (as if to swallow). Most editors adopt the F1 reading *aim at.* 10. *botch:* patch.
11. *Which:* i.e. the words. 12. *thought:* inferred, conjectured. 15. *ill-breeding:* conceiving ill
thoughts, prone to think the worst. 18. *toy:* trifle. *amiss:* calamity. 19. *artless jealousy:*
uncontrolled suspicion. 20. *spills:* destroys.

Queen: How now, Ophelia?

Ophelia: "How should I your true-love know   *She sings.*
      From another one?
    By his cockle hat and staff,   25
      And his sandal shoon."

Queen: Alas, sweet lady, what imports this song?

Ophelia: Say you? Nay, pray you mark.
    "He is dead and gone, lady,   *Song.*
      He is dead and gone,   30
    At his head a grass-green turf,
      At his heels a stone."
  O ho!

Queen: Nay, but, Ophelia—

Ophelia: Pray you mark.   35
    [Sings.] "White his shroud as the mountain snow"—

Enter King.

Queen: Alas, look here, my lord.

Ophelia: "Larded all with sweet flowers,   *Song.*
      Which bewept to the ground did not go
      With true-love showers."   40

King: How do you, pretty lady?

Ophelia: Well, God dild you! They say the owl was a baker's
    daughter. Lord, we know what we are, but know not what
    we may be. God be at your table!

King: Conceit upon her father.   45

Ophelia: Pray let's have no words of this, but when they ask you
    what it means, say you this:
    "To-morrow is Saint Valentine's day,   *Song.*
      All in the morning betime,
    And I a maid at your window,   50
      To be your Valentine.

    "Then up he rose and donn'd his clo'es,
      And dupp'd the chamber-door,
    Let in the maid, that out a maid
      Never departed more."   55

23-24. These lines resemble a passage in an earlier ballad beginning "As you came from the holy land / Of Walsingham." Probably all the song fragments sung by Ophelia were familiar to the Globe audience, but only one other line (185) is from a ballad still extant.   25. *cockle hat:* hat bearing a cockle shell, the badge of a pilgrim to the shrine of St. James of Compostela in Spain. *staff:* Another mark of a pilgrim.   26. *shoon:* shoes (already an archaic form in Shakespeare's day).   38. *Larded:* adorned.   39. *not:* Contrary to the expected sense, and unmetrical; explained as Ophelia's alteration of the line to accord with the facts of Polonius' burial (see line 83).   42. *dild:* yield, reward. *owl:* Alluding to the legend of a baker's daughter whom Jesus turned into an owl because she did not respond generously to his request for bread.   45. *Conceit:* fanciful brooding.   53. *dupp'd:* opened.

King: Pretty Ophelia!

Ophelia: Indeed without an oath I'll make an end on't.

[*Sings.*] "By Gis, and by Saint Charity,
　　　　Alack, and fie for shame!
　　　　Young men will do't if they come to't,　　　　　　60
　　　　By Cock, they are to blame.

　　　　"Quoth she, 'Before you tumbled me,
　　　　You promis'd me to wed.'"

(He answers.)
　　　　"'So would I 'a' done, by yonder sun,　　　　　　65
　　　　And thou hadst not come to my bed.'"

King: How long hath she been thus?

Ophelia: I hope all will be well. We must be patient, but I cannot
choose but weep to think they would lay him i' th' cold
ground. My brother shall know of it, and so I thank you for　70
your good counsel. Come, my coach! Good night, ladies,
good night. Sweet ladies, good night, good night.　　*[Exit.]*

King: Follow her close, give her good watch, pray you.

　　　　　　　　　　　　　　　　　　　　　[Exit Horatio.]

O, this is the poison of deep grief, it springs
All from her father's death—and now behold!　　　　　　75
O Gertrude, Gertrude,
When sorrows come, they come not single spies,
But in battalions: first, her father slain;
Next, your son gone, and he most violent author
Of his own just remove; the people muddied,　　　　　　80
Thick and unwholesome in [their] thoughts and whispers
For good Polonius' death; and we have done but greenly
In hugger-mugger to inter him; poor Ophelia
Divided from herself and her fair judgment,
Without the which we are pictures, or mere beasts;　　　　85
Last, and as much containing as all these,
Her brother is in secret come from France,
Feeds on this wonder, keeps himself in clouds,
And wants not buzzers to infect his ear
With pestilent speeches of his father's death,　　　　　　90
Wherein necessity, of matter beggar'd,
Will nothing stick our person to arraign
In ear and ear. O my dear Gertrude, this,

---

58. *Gis:* contraction of *Jesus.*　61. *Cock:* corruption of *God.*　66. *And:* if.　77. *spies:* i.e.
soldiers sent ahead of the main force to reconnoiter, scouts.　80. *muddied:* confused.
82. *greenly:* unwisely.　83. *In hugger-mugger:* secretly and hastily.　88. *in clouds:* i.e. in
cloudy surmise and suspicion (rather than the light of fact).　89. *wants:* lacks. *buzzers:*
whispering informers.　92. *of matter beggar'd:* destitute of facts.　92–93. *nothing . . . arraign:*
scruple not at all to charge me with the crime.

Like to a murd'ring-piece, in many places
Gives me superfluous death.   *A noise within.*
[Queen: Alack, what noise is this?]   95
    King: Attend!
      Where is my Swissers? Let them guard the door.

Enter a Messenger.

        What is the matter?
    Messenger: Save yourself, my lord!
      The ocean, overpeering of his list,
      Eats not the flats with more impiteous haste   100
      Than young Laertes, in a riotous head,
      O'erbears your officers. The rabble call him lord,
      And as the world were now but to begin,
      Antiquity forgot, custom not known,
      The ratifiers and props of every word,   105
      [They] cry, "Choose we, Laertes shall be king!"
      Caps, hands, and tongues applaud it to the clouds,
      "Laertes shall be king, Laertes king!"   *A noise within.*
    Queen: How cheerfully on the false trail they cry!
      O, this is counter, you false Danish dogs!   110

Enter Laertes *with others.*

    King: The doors are broke.
  Laertes: Where is this king? Sirs, stand you all without.
    All: No, let 's come in.
  Laertes: I pray you give me leave.
    All: We will, we will.
  Laertes: I thank you, keep the door. [*Exeunt* Laertes' *followers.*]   115
      O thou vile king,
      Give me my father!
    Queen: Calmly, good Laertes.
  Laertes: That drop of blood that's calm proclaims me bastard,
      Cries cuckold to my father, brands the harlot
      Even here between the chaste unsmirched brow   120
      Of my true mother.
    King: What is the cause, Laertes,
      That thy rebellion looks so giant-like?
      Let him go, Gertrude, do not fear our person:
      There's such divinity doth hedge a king
      That treason can but peep to what it would,   125

---

94. *murd'ring-piece:* cannon firing a scattering charge. 98. *Swissers:* Swiss guards.
99. *overpeering . . . list:* rising higher than its shores. 101. *in . . . head:* with a rebellious
force. 103. *as:* as if. 105. *word:* pledge, promise. 110. *counter:* on the wrong scent (literally, following the scent backward). 123. *fear:* fear for. 125. *would:* i.e. would like to do.

Acts little of his will. Tell me, Laertes,
Why thou art thus incens'd. Let him go, Gertrude.
Speak, man.

Laertes: Where is my father?

King: Dead.

Queen: But not by him.

King: Let him demand his fill.   130

Laertes: How came he dead? I'll not be juggled with.
To hell, allegiance! vows, to the blackest devil!
Conscience and grace, to the profoundest pit!
I dare damnation. To this point I stand,
That both the worlds I give to negligence,   135
Let come what comes, only I'll be reveng'd
Most throughly for my father.

King: Who shall stay you?

Laertes: My will, not all the world's:
And for my means, I'll husband them so well,
They shall go far with little.

King: Good Laertes,   140
If you desire to know the certainty
Of your dear father, is't writ in your revenge
That, swoopstake, you will draw both friend and foe,
Winner and loser?

Laertes: None but his enemies.

King: Will you know them then?   145

Laertes: To his good friends thus wide I'll ope my arms,
And like the kind life-rend'ring pelican,
Repast them with my blood.

King: Why, now you speak
Like a good child and a true gentleman.
That I am guiltless of your father's death,   150
And am most sensibly in grief for it,
It shall as level to your judgment 'pear
As day does to your eye.

                            A noise within: "Let her come in!"

Laertes: How now, what noise is that?

Enter Ophelia.

O heat, dry up my brains! tears seven times salt   155
Burn out the sense and virtue of mine eye!

---

135. *both . . . negligence:* i.e. I don't care what the consequences are in this world or in the
next.   137. *throughly:* thoroughly.   138. *world's:* i.e. world's will.   143. *swoopstake:*
sweeping up everything without discrimination (modern *sweepstake*).   147. *pelican:* The
female pelican was believed to draw blood from her own breast to nourish her young.
149. *good child:* faithful son.   151. *sensibly:* feelingly.   152. *level:* plain.   156. *virtue:*
faculty.

By heaven, thy madness shall be paid with weight
[Till] our scale turn the beam. O rose of May!
Dear maid, kind sister, sweet Ophelia!
O heavens, is't possible a young maid's wits   160
Should be as mortal as [an old] man's life?
[Nature is fine in love, and where 'tis fine,
It sends some precious instance of itself
After the thing it loves.]

Ophelia: "They bore him barefac'd on the bier,   *Song.* 165
    [Hey non nonny, nonny, hey nonny,]
    And in his grave rain'd many a tear"—
Fare you well, my dove!

Laertes: Hadst thou thy wits and didst persuade revenge,
It could not move thus.   170

Ophelia: You must sing, "A-down, a-down," and you call him a-
down-a. O how the wheel becomes it! It is the false steward,
that stole his master's daughter.

Laertes: This nothing's more than matter.

Ophelia: There's rosemary, that's for remembrance; pray you,   175
love, remember. And there is pansies, that's for thoughts.

Laertes: A document in madness, thoughts and remembrance
fitted.

Ophelia: [*To* Claudius.] There's fennel for you, and columbines.
[*To* Gertrude.] There's rue for you, and here's some for me;   180
we may call it herb of grace a' Sundays. You may wear your
rue with a difference. There's a daisy. I would give you some
violets, but they wither'd all when my father died. They say 'a
made a good end—
[*Sings.*] "For bonny sweet Robin is all my joy."   185

Laertes: Thought and afflictions, passion, hell itself,
She turns to favor and to prettiness.

Ophelia: "And will 'a not come again?   *Song.*
    And will 'a not come again?
      No, no, he is dead,   190
      Go to thy death-bed,
    He never will come again.

---

162. *fine in:* refined or spiritualized by.   163. *instance:* proof, token. So delicate is Ophelia's
love for her father that her sanity has pursued him into the grave.   169. *persuade:* argue
logically for.   171-72. *and . . . a-down-a:* "if he indeed agrees that Polonius is 'a-down,' i.e.
fallen low" (Dover Wilson).   172. *wheel:* refrain (?) or spinning-wheel, at which women sang
ballads (?).   174. *matter:* lucid speech.   177. *A document in madness:* a lesson contained in
mad talk.   179. *fennel, columbines:* Symbols respectively of flattery and ingratitude.
180. *rue:* Symbolic of sorrow and repentance.   182. *with a difference:* i.e. to represent a
different cause of sorrow. *Difference* is a term from heraldry, meaning a variation in a coat of
arms made to distinguish different members of a family.   182-83. *daisy, violets:* Symbolic
respectively of dissembling and faithfulness. It is not clear who are the recipients of these.
186. *Thought:* melancholy.   187. *favor:* grace, charm.

"His beard was as white as snow,
[All] flaxen was his pole,
   He is gone, he is gone,   195
   And we cast away moan,
God 'a' mercy on his soul!"

And of all Christians' souls, [I pray God]. God buy you.

                                                  [Exit.]

Laertes: Do you [see] this, O God?

   King: Laertes, I must commune with your grief,   200
Or you deny me right. Go but apart,
Make choice of whom your wisest friends you will,
And they shall hear and judge 'twixt you and me.
If by direct or by collateral hand
They find us touch'd, we will our kingdom give,   205
Our crown, our life, and all that we call ours,
To you in satisfaction; but if not,
Be you content to lend your patience to us,
And we shall jointly labor with your soul
To give it due content.

Laertes: Let this be so.   210
His means of death, his obscure funeral—
No trophy, sword, nor hatchment o'er his bones,
No noble rite nor formal ostentation—
Cry to be heard, as 'twere from heaven to earth,
That I must call't in question.

King: So you shall,   215
And where th' offense is, let the great axe fall.
I pray you go with me.   *Exeunt.*

Scene VI

Enter Horatio *and others.*

   Horatio: What are they that would speak with me?

 Gentleman: Sea-faring men, sir. They say they have letters for you.

   Horatio: Let them come in.   *[Exit* Gentleman.]
I do not know from what part of the world
I should be greeted, if not from Lord Hamlet.   5

Enter Sailors.

  [1.] Sailor: God bless you, sir.

---

194. *flaxen:* white. *pole:* poll, head.   204. *collateral:* i.e. indirect.   205. *touch'd:* guilty.
212. *trophy:* memorial. *hatchment:* heraldic memorial tablet.   213. *formal ostentation:* fitting
and customary ceremony.   214. *That:* so that.

IV.vi. Location: The castle.   See the Textual Notes for a scene unique to Q1.

Horatio: Let him bless thee too.

[1.] Sailor: 'A shall, sir, and['t] please him. There's a letter for you,
sir—it came from th' embassador that was bound for Eng-
land—if your name be Horatio, as I am let to know it is.   10

Horatio: [*Reads.*] "Horatio, when thou shalt have overlook'd this,
give these fellows some means to the King, they have letters
for him. Ere we were two days old at sea, a pirate of very warlike appointment gave us chase. Finding ourselves too slow
of sail, we put on a compell'd valor, and in the grapple I   15
boarded them. On the instant they got clear of our ship, so I
alone became their prisoner. They have dealt with me like
thieves of mercy, but they knew what they did: I am to do a
[good] turn for them. Let the King have the letters I have
sent, and repair thou to me with as much speed as thou would-   20
est fly death. I have words to speak in thine ear will make
thee dumb, yet are they much too light for the [bore] of the
matter. These good fellows will bring thee where I am.
Rosencrantz and Guildenstern hold their course for England, of them I have much to tell thee. Farewell.   25

                [He] that thou knowest thine,

                               Hamlet."

Come, I will [give] you way for these your letters,
And do't the speedier that you may direct me
To him from whom you brought them.   *Exeunt.*

Scene VII

Enter King *and* Laertes.

    King: Now must your conscience my acquittance seal,
        And you must put me in your heart for friend,
        Sith you have heard, and with a knowing ear,
        That he which hath your noble father slain
        Pursued my life.

    Laertes: It well appears. But tell me   5
        Why you [proceeded] not against these feats
        So criminal and so capital in nature,
        As by your safety, greatness, wisdom, all things else
        You mainly were stirr'd up.

    King: O, for two special reasons,
        Which may to you perhaps seem much unsinow'd,   10

---

18. *thieves of mercy:* merciful thieves.   22. *bore:* calibre, size (gunnery term).

IV.vii. Location: The castle.   1. *my acquittance seal:* ratify my acquittal, i.e. acknowledge my
innocence in Polonius' death.   6. *feats:* acts.   8. *safety:* i.e. regard for your own safety.
9. *mainly:* powerfully.   10. *unsinow'd:* unsinewed, i.e. weak.

But yet to me th' are strong. The Queen his mother
Lives almost by his looks, and for myself—
My virtue or my plague, be it either which—
She is so [conjunctive] to my life and soul,
That, as the star moves not but in his sphere,   15
I could not but by her. The other motive,
Why to a public count I might not go,
Is the great love the general gender bear him,
Who, dipping all his faults in their affection,
Work like the spring that turneth wood to stone,   20
Convert his gyves to graces, so that my arrows,
Too slightly timber'd for so [loud a wind],
Would have reverted to my bow again,
But not where I have aim'd them.
Laertes: And so have I a noble father lost,   25
A sister driven into desp'rate terms,
Whose worth, if praises may go back again,
Stood challenger on mount of all the age
For her perfections—but my revenge will come.
King: Break not your sleeps for that. You must not think   30
That we are made of stuff so flat and dull
That we can let our beard be shook with danger
And think it pastime. You shortly shall hear more.
I lov'd your father, and we love ourself,
And that, I hope, will teach you to imagine—   35

Enter a Messenger *with letters.*

[How now? What news?
Messenger: Letters, my lord, from Hamlet:]
These to your Majesty, this to the Queen.
King: From Hamlet? Who brought them?
Messenger: Sailors, my lord, they say, I saw them not.
They were given me by Claudio. He receiv'd them   40
Of him that brought them.
King: Laertes, you shall hear them.
—Leave us.   [*Exit Messenger.*]
[*Reads.*] "High and mighty, You shall know I am set naked on
your kingdom. To-morrow shall I beg leave to see your kingly

---

13. *either which:* one or the other.   14. *conjunctive:* closely joined.   15. *in his sphere:* by the
movement of the sphere in which it is fixed (as the Ptolemaic astronomy taught).   17. *count:*
reckoning.   18. *the general gender:* everybody.   21. *gyves:* fetters.   26. *terms:* condition.
27. *go back again:* i.e. refer to what she was before she went mad.   28. *on mount:* pre-emi-
nent.   30. *for that:* i.e. for fear of losing your revenge.   31. *flat:* spiritless.   32. *let . . .
shook:* To ruffle or tweak a man's beard was an act of insolent defiance that he could not disregard without loss of honor. Cf. II.ii.543. *with:* by.   43. *naked:* destitute.

eyes, when I shall, first asking you pardon thereunto, recount   45
the occasion of my sudden [and more strange] return.
                    [Hamlet.]"
What should this mean? Are all the rest come back?
Or is it some abuse, and no such thing?

Laertes: Know you the hand?

King: 'Tis Hamlet's character. "Naked"!   50
And in a postscript here he says "alone."
Can you devise me?

Laertes: I am lost in it, my lord. But let him come,
It warms the very sickness in my heart
That I [shall] live and tell him to his teeth,   55
"Thus didst thou."

King: If it be so, Laertes—
As how should it be so? how otherwise?—
Will you be rul'd by me?

Laertes: Ay, my lord,
So you will not o'errule me to a peace.

King: To thine own peace. If he be now returned   60
As [checking] at his voyage, and that he means
No more to undertake it, I will work him
To an exploit, now ripe in my device,
Under the which he shall not choose but fall;
And for his death no wind of blame shall breathe,   65
But even his mother shall uncharge the practice,
And call it accident.

Laertes: My lord, I will be rul'd,
The rather if you could devise it so
That I might be the organ.

King: It falls right.
You have been talk'd of since your travel much,   70
And that in Hamlet's hearing, for a quality
Wherein they say you shine. Your sum of parts
Did not together pluck such envy from him
As did that one, and that, in my regard,
Of the unworthiest siege.

Laertes: What part is that, my lord?   75

King: A very riband in the cap of youth,
Yet needful too, for youth no less becomes

---

45. *pardon thereunto:* permission to do so.   48. *abuse:* deceit.   50. *character:* handwriting.
52. *devise me:* explain it to me.   57. *As . . . otherwise:* How can he have come back? Yet he
obviously has.   59. *So:* provided that.   61. *checking at:* turning from (like a falcon diverted
from its quarry by other prey).   66. *uncharge the practice:* adjudge the plot no plot, i.e. fail to
see the plot.   67. *organ:* instrument, agent.   71. *quality:* skill.   72. *Your . . . parts:* all your
(other) accomplishments put together.   74. *unworthiest:* i.e. least important (with no
implication of unsuitableness). *siege:* status, position.

The light and careless livery that it wears
Than settled age his sables and his weeds,
Importing health and graveness. Two months since   80
Here was a gentleman of Normandy:
I have seen myself, and serv'd against, the French,
And they can well on horseback, but this gallant
Had witchcraft in't, he grew unto his seat,
And to such wondrous doing brought his horse,   85
As had he been incorps'd and demi-natur'd
With the brave beast. So far he topp'd [my] thought,
That I in forgery of shapes and tricks
Come short of what he did.
Laertes: A Norman was't?
King: A Norman.   90
Laertes: Upon my life, Lamord.
King: The very same.
Laertes: I know him well. He is the brooch indeed
And gem of all the nation.
King: He made confession of you,
And gave you such a masterly report   95
For art and exercise in your defense,
And for your rapier most especial,
That he cried out 'twould be a sight indeed
If one could match you. The scrimers of their nation
He swore had neither motion, guard, nor eye,   100
If you oppos'd them. Sir, this report of his
Did Hamlet so envenom with his envy
That he could nothing do but wish and beg
Your sudden coming o'er to play with you.
Now, out of this—
Laertes: What out of this, my lord?   105
King: Laertes, was your father dear to you?
Or are you like the painting of a sorrow,
A face without a heart?
Laertes: Why ask you this?
King: Not that I think you did not love your father,
But that I know love is begun by time,   110
And that I see, in passages of proof,
Time qualifies the spark and fire of it.

---

79. *weeds:* (characteristic) garb.   80. *Importing . . . graveness:* signifying prosperity and
dignity.   83. *can . . . horseback:* are excellent riders.   86. *incorps'd:* made one body.
demi-natur'd: i.e. become half of a composite animal.   88. *forgery:* mere imagining.
93. *brooch:* ornament (worn in the hat).   94. *made . . . you:* acknowledged your excellence.
99. *scrimers:* fencers.   104. *sudden:* speedy.   110. *time:* i.e. a particular set of circumstances.   111. *in . . . proof:* i.e. by the test of experience, by actual examples.   112. *qualifies:*
moderates.

There lives within the very flame of love
A kind of week or snuff that will abate it,
And nothing is at a like goodness still,   115
For goodness, growing to a plurisy,
Dies in his own too much. That we would do,
We should do when we would; for this "would" changes,
And hath abatements and delays as many
As there are tongues, are hands, are accidents,   120
And then this "should" is like a spendthrift's sigh,
That hurts by easing. But to the quick of th' ulcer:
Hamlet comes back. What would you undertake
To show yourself indeed your father's son
More than in words?
Laertes: To cut his throat i' th' church.   125
  King: No place indeed should murther sanctuarize,
Revenge should have no bounds. But, good Laertes,
Will you do this, keep close within your chamber.
Hamlet return'd shall know you are come home.
We'll put on those shall praise your excellence,   130
And set a double varnish on the fame
The Frenchman gave you, bring you in fine together,
And wager o'er your heads. He, being remiss,
Most generous, and free from all contriving,
Will not peruse the foils, so that with ease,   135
Or with a little shuffling, you may choose
A sword unbated, and in a [pass] of practice
Requite him for your father.
Laertes: I will do't,
And for [that] purpose I'll anoint my sword.
I bought an unction of a mountebank,   140
So mortal that, but dip a knife in it,
Where it draws blood, no cataplasm so rare,
Collected from all simples that have virtue
Under the moon, can save the thing from death
That is but scratch'd withal. I'll touch my point   145

---

114. *week:* wick. 115. *nothing . . . still:* nothing remains forever at the same pitch of
perfection. 116. *plurisy:* plethora (a variant spelling of *pleurisy,* which was erroneously
related to *plus,* stem *plur-,* "more, overmuch." 117. *too much:* excess. 121. *spendthrift's
sigh:* A sigh was supposed to draw blood from the heart. 122. *hurts by easing:* injures us at the
same time that it gives us relief. 126. *sanctuarize:* offer asylum to. 128. *Will . . . this:* if you
want to undertake this. 130. *put on those:* incite those who. 131. *double varnish:* second
coat of varnish. 132. *in fine:* finally. 133. *remiss:* careless, overtrustful. 134. *generous:*
noble-minded. *free . . . contriving:* innocent of sharp practices. 135. *peruse:* examine.
136. *shuffling:* cunning exchange. 137. *unbated:* not blunted. *pass of practice:* tricky thrust.
140. *unction:* ointment. *mountebank:* travelling quack-doctor. 141. *mortal:* deadly.
142. *cataplasm:* poultice. 143. *simples:* medicinal herbs. *virtue:* curative power.

With this contagion, that if I gall him slightly,
It may be death.
King: Let's further think of this,
Weigh what convenience both of time and means
May fit us to our shape. If this should fail,
And that our drift look through our bad performance,   150
'Twere better not assay'd; therefore this project
Should have a back or second, that might hold
If this did blast in proof. Soft, let me see.
We'll make a solemn wager on your cunnings—
I ha't!   155
When in your motion you are hot and dry—
As make your bouts more violent to that end—
And that he calls for drink, I'll have preferr'd him
A chalice for the nonce, whereon but sipping,
If he by chance escape your venom'd stuck,   160
Our purpose may hold there. But stay, what noise?

Enter Queen.

Queen: One woe doth tread upon another's heel,
So fast they follow. Your sister's drown'd, Laertes.
Laertes: Drown'd! O, where?
Queen: There is a willow grows askaunt the brook,   165
That shows his hoary leaves in the glassy stream,
Therewith fantastic garlands did she make
Of crow-flowers, nettles, daisies, and long purples
That liberal shepherds give a grosser name,
But our cull-cold maids do dead men's fingers call them.   170
There on the pendant boughs her crownet weeds
Clamb'ring to hang, an envious sliver broke,
When down her weedy trophies and herself
Fell in the weeping brook. Her clothes spread wide,
And mermaid-like awhile they bore her up,   175
Which time she chaunted snatches of old lauds,
As one incapable of her own distress,
Or like a creature native and indued
Unto that element. But long it could not be

---

146. *gall:* graze.   149. *fit . . . shape:* i.e. suit our purposes best.   150. *drift:* purpose. *look
through:* become visible, be detected.   152. *back or second:* i.e. a second plot in reserve for
emergency.   153. *blast in proof:* blow up while being tried (an image from gunnery).
157. *As:* i.e. and you should.   158. *preferr'd:* offered to. Most editors adopt the F1 reading
prepar'd.   159. *nonce:* occasion.   160. *stuck:* thrust (from *stoccado*, a fencing term).
165. *askaunt:* sideways over.   166. *hoary:* grey-white.   167. *Therewith:* i.e. with willow
branches.   168. *long purples:* wild orchids.   169. *liberal:* free-spoken.   170. *cull-cold:*
chaste.   171. *crownet:* made into coronets.   172. *envious sliver:* malicious branch.
176. *lauds:* hymns.   177. *incapable:* insensible.   178. *indued:* habituated.

Till that her garments, heavy with their drink,   180
Pull'd the poor wretch from her melodious lay
To muddy death.
Laertes: Alas, then she is drown'd?
Queen: Drown'd, drown'd.
Laertes: Too much of water hast thou, poor Ophelia,
And therefore I forbid my tears; but yet   185
It is our trick, Nature her custom holds,
Let shame say what it will; when these are gone,
The woman will be out. Adieu, my lord,
I have a speech a' fire that fain would blaze,
But that this folly drowns it.   *Exit.*
King: Let's follow, Gertrude.   190
How much I had to do to calm his rage!
Now fear I this will give it start again,
Therefore let's follow.   *Exeunt.*

ACT V

Scene I

Enter two Clowns [*with spades and mattocks*].

1. Clown: Is she to be buried in Christian burial when she willfully
seeks her own salvation?

2. Clown: I tell thee she is, therefore make her grave straight. The
crowner hath sate on her, and finds it Christian burial.

1. Clown: How can that be, unless she drown'd herself in her own 5
defense?

2. Clown: Why, 'tis found so.

1. Clown: It must be [*se offendendo*], it cannot be else. For here lies
the point: if I drown myself wittingly, it argues an act, and an
act hath three branches—it is to act, to do, to perform;   10
[*argal*], she drown'd herself wittingly.

2. Clown: Nay, but hear you, goodman delver—

1. Clown: Give me leave. Here lies the water; good. Here stands
the man; good. If the man go to this water and drown himself, it is, will he, nill he, he goes, mark you that. But if the 15
water come to him and drown him, he drowns not himself;

---

186. *It:* i.e. weeping. *trick:* natural way.   187. *these:* these tears.   188. *The woman . . . out:*
my womanish traits will be gone for good.

V.i. Location: A churchyard.   o.s.d. *Clowns:* rustics.   3. *straight:* immediately. *crowner:*
coroner.   8. *se offendendo:* blunder for *se defendendo,* "in self-defense."   11. *argal:* blunder
for *ergo,* "therefore."   13-18. *Here . . . life:* Alluding to a very famous suicide case, that of Sir
James Hales, a judge who drowned himself in 1554; it was long cited in the courts. The clown
gives a garbled account of the defense summing-up and the verdict.   15. *nill he:* will he not.

argal, he that is not guilty of his own death shortens not his own life.

2. *Clown:* But is this law?

1. *Clown:* Ay, marry, is't—crowner's quest law.   20

2. *Clown:* Will you ha' the truth an't? If this had not been a gentle-woman, she should have been buried out a' Christian burial.

1. *Clown:* Why, there thou say'st, and the more pity that great folk should have count'nance in this world to drown or hang themselves, more than their even-Christen. Come, my 25
spade. There is no ancient gentlemen but gard'ners, ditchers, and grave-makers; they hold up Adam's profession.

2. *Clown:* Was he a gentleman?

1. *Clown:* 'A was the first that ever bore arms.

[2. *Clown:* Why, he had none.   30

1. *Clown:* What, art a heathen? How dost thou understand the Scripture? The Scripture says Adam digg'd; could he dig without arms?] I'll put another question to thee. If thou answerest me not to the purpose, confess thyself—

2. *Clown:* Go to.   35

1. *Clown:* What is he that builds stronger than either the mason, the shipwright, or the carpenter?

2. *Clown:* The gallows-maker, for that outlives a thousand tenants.

1. *Clown:* I like thy wit well, in good faith. The gallows does well; but how does it well? It does well to those that do ill. Now 40
thou dost ill to say the gallows is built stronger than the church; argal, the gallows may do well to thee. To't again, come.

2. *Clown:* Who builds stronger than a mason, a shipwright, or a carpenter?   45

1. *Clown:* Ay, tell me that, and unyoke.

2. *Clown:* Marry, now I can tell.

1. *Clown:* To't.

2. *Clown:* Mass, I cannot tell.

Enter Hamlet *and* Horatio [*afar off*].

1. *Clown:* Cudgel thy brains no more about it, for your dull ass will 50
not mend his pace with beating, and when you are ask'd this question next, say "a grave-maker": the houses he makes lasts till doomsday. Go get thee in, and fetch me a sup of liquor.

[*Exit Second Clown. First Clown digs.*]

"In youth when I did love, did love,   *Song.*
Methought it was very sweet,   55

---

20. *quest:* inquest. 25. *even-Christen:* fellow-Christians. 30. *none:* i.e. no coat of arms.
46. *unyoke:* i.e. cease to labor, call it a day. 49. *Mass:* by the mass.

To contract—O—the time for—a—my behove,
O, methought there—a—was nothing—a—meet."

Hamlet: Has this fellow no feeling of his business? 'a sings in
grave-making.
Horatio: Custom hath made it in him a property of easiness.   60
Hamlet: 'Tis e'en so, the hand of little employment hath the
daintier sense.
1. Clown: "But age with his stealing steps   *Song.*
        Hath clawed me in his clutch,
        And hath shipped me into the land,   65
        As if I had never been such."

                [*Throws up a shovelful of earth with a skull in it.*]

Hamlet: That skull had a tongue in it, and could sing once. How
the knave jowls it to the ground, as if 'twere Cain's jaw-bone,
that did the first murder! This might be the pate of a politician, which this ass now o'erreaches, one that would circum-   70
vent God, might it not?
Horatio: It might, my lord.
Hamlet: Or of a courtier, which could say, "Good morrow, sweet
lord! How dost thou, sweet lord?" This might be my Lord
Such-a-one, that prais'd my Lord Such-a-one's horse when 'a   75
[meant] to beg it, might it not?
Horatio: Ay, my lord.
Hamlet: Why, e'en so, and now my Lady Worm's, chopless, and
knock'd about the [mazzard] with a sexton's spade. Here's
fine revolution, and we had the trick to see't. Did these   80
bones cost no more the breeding, but to play at loggats with
them? Mine ache to think on't.
1. Clown: "A pickaxe and a spade, a spade,   *Song.*
        For and a shrouding sheet:
        O, a pit of clay for to be made   85
        For such a guest is meet."   [*Throws up another skull.*]

Hamlet: There's another. Why may not that be the skull of a lawyer? Where be his quiddities now, his quillities, his cases, his
tenures, and his tricks? Why does he suffer this mad knave

---

56. *contract . . . behove:* shorten, i.e. spend agreeably . . . advantage. The song, punctuated by
the grunts of the clown as he digs, is a garbled version of a poem by Thomas Lord Vaux,
entitled "The Aged Lover Renounceth Love."   60. *Custom:* habit.   *a property of easiness:* i.e.
a thing he can do with complete ease of mind.   62. *daintier sense:* more delicate sensitivity.
68. *jowls:* dashes.   69-70. *politician:* schemer, intriguer.   70. *o'erreaches:* gets the better of
(with play on the literal sense). 70-71. *circumvent God:* bypass God's law.   78. *chopless:* lacking
the lower jaw.   79. *mazzard:* head.   80. *revolution:* change. *and:* if.   *trick:* knack, ability.
80-81. *Did . . . cost:* were . . . worth.   81. *loggats:* a game in which blocks of wood were
thrown at a stake.   88. *quiddities:* subtleties, quibbles.   *quillities:* fine distinctions.
89. *tenures:* titles to real estate.

now to knock him about the sconce with a dirty shovel, and 90
will not tell him of his action of battery? Hum! This fellow
might be in 's time a great buyer of land, with his statutes, his
recognizances, his fines, his double vouchers, his recoveries.
[Is this the fine of his fines, and the recovery of his recoveries,] to have his fine pate full of fine dirt? Will [his] vouchers 95
vouch him no more of his purchases, and [double ones too],
than the length and breadth of a pair of indentures? The very
conveyances of his lands will scarcely lie in this box, and must
th' inheritor himself have no more, ha?

Horatio: Not a jot more, my lord. 100

Hamlet: Is not parchment made of sheep-skins?

Horatio: Ay, my lord, and of calves'-skins too.

Hamlet: They are sheep and calves which seek out assurance in
that. I will speak to this fellow. Whose grave's this, sirrah?

1. Clown: Mine, sir. 105

[*Sings.*]   "[O], a pit of clay for to be made
[For such a guest is meet]."

Hamlet: I think it be thine indeed, for thou liest in't.

1. Clown: You lie out on't, sir, and therefore 'tis not yours; for my
part, I do not lie in't, yet it is mine. 110

Hamlet: Thou dost lie in't, to be in't and say it is thine. 'Tis for the
dead, not for the quick; therefore thou liest.

1. Clown: 'Tis a quick lie, sir, 'twill away again from me to you.

Hamlet: What man dost thou dig it for?

1. Clown: For no man, sir. 115

Hamlet: What woman then?

1. Clown: For none neither.

Hamlet: Who is to be buried in't?

1. Clown: One that was a woman, sir, but, rest her soul, she's dead.

Hamlet: How absolute the knave is! we must speak by the card, or 120
equivocation will undo us. By the Lord, Horatio, this three
years I have took note of it: the age is grown so pick'd that the
toe of the peasant comes so near the heel of the courtier, he
galls his kibe. How long hast thou been grave-maker?

1. Clown: Of [all] the days i' th' year, I came to't that day that our 125
last king Hamlet overcame Fortinbras.

---

90. *sconce:* head.   92–93. *statutes, recognizances:* bonds securing debts by attaching land and property.   93. *fines . . . recoveries:* procedures for converting an entailed estate to freehold.
93. *double vouchers:* documents guaranteeing title to real estate, signed by two persons.
94. *fine:* end.   97. *pair of indentures:* legal document cut into two parts which fitted together on a serrated edge. Perhaps Hamlet thus refers to the two rows of teeth in the skull, or to the bone sutures.   98. *conveyances:* documents relating to transfer of property. *this box:* i.e. the skull itself.   99. *inheritor:* owner.   104. *sirrah:* term of address to inferiors.   120. *absolute:* positive. *by the card:* by the compass, i.e. punctiliously.   121. *equivocation:* ambiguity.
122. *pick'd:* refined.   124. *galls his kibe:* rubs the courtier's chilblain.

Hamlet: How long is that since?

1. Clown: Cannot you tell that? Every fool can tell that. It was that very day that young Hamlet was born—he that is mad, and sent into England. 130

Hamlet: Ay, marry, why was he sent into England?

1. Clown: Why, because 'a was mad. 'A shall recover his wits there, or if 'a do not, 'tis no great matter there.

Hamlet: Why?

1. Clown: 'Twill not be seen in him there, there the men are as mad 135 as he.

Hamlet: How came he mad?

1. Clown: Very strangely, they say.

Hamlet: How strangely?

1. Clown: Faith, e'en with losing his wits. 140

Hamlet: Upon what ground?

1. Clown: Why, here in Denmark. I have been sexton here, man and boy, thirty years.

Hamlet: How long will a man lie i' th' earth ere he rot?

1. Clown: Faith, if 'a be not rotten before 'a die—as we have many 145 pocky corses, that will scarce hold the laying in—'a will last you some eight year or nine year. A tanner will last you nine year.

Hamlet: Why he more than another?

1. Clown: Why, sir, his hide is so tann'd with his trade that 'a will 150 keep out water a great while, and your water is a sore decayer of your whoreson dead body. Here's a skull now hath lien you i' th' earth three and twenty years.

Hamlet: Whose was it?

1. Clown: A whoreson mad fellow's it was. Whose do you think it 155 was?

Hamlet: Nay, I know not.

1. Clown: A pestilence on him for a mad rogue! 'a pour'd a flagon of Rhenish on my head once. This same skull, sir, was, sir, Yorick's skull, the King's jester. 160

Hamlet: This?   *[Takes the skull.]*

1. Clown: E'en that.

Hamlet: Alas, poor Yorick! I knew him, Horatio, a fellow of infinite jest, of most excellent fancy. He hath bore me on his back a thousand times, and now how abhorr'd in my imagina- 165 tion it is! my gorge rises at it. Here hung those lips that I have kiss'd I know not how oft. Where be your gibes now, your gambols, your songs, your flashes of merriment, that were wont to set the table on a roar? Not one now to mock

---

146. *pocky:* rotten with venereal disease. *hold . . . in:* last out the burial.

your own grinning—quite chop-fall'n. Now get you to my 170
lady's [chamber], and tell her, let her paint an inch thick, to
this favor she must come; make her laugh at that. Prithee,
Horatio, tell me one thing.

Horatio: What's that, my lord?

Hamlet: Dost thou think Alexander look'd a' this fashion i' th' 175
earth?

Horatio: E'en so.

Hamlet: And smelt so? pah!   *[Puts down the skull.]*

Horatio: E'en so, my lord.

Hamlet: To what base uses we may return, Horatio! Why may not 180
imagination trace the noble dust of Alexander, till 'a find it
stopping a bunghole?

Horatio: 'Twere to consider too curiously, to consider so.

Hamlet: No, faith, not a jot, but to follow him thither with mod-
esty enough and likelihood to lead it: Alexander died, Alex- 185
under was buried, Alexander returneth to dust, the dust is
earth, of earth we make loam, and why of that loam whereto
he was converted might they not stop a beer-barrel?
Imperious Caesar, dead and turn'd to clay,
Might stop a hole to keep the wind away.   190
O that that earth which kept the world in awe
Should patch a wall t' expel the [winter's] flaw!
But soft, but soft awhile, here comes the King,

Enter King, Queen, Laertes, *and* [a Doctor of Divinity, *following*] *the corse,*
[*with* Lords *attendant*].

The Queen, the courtiers. Who is this they follow?
And with such maimed rites? This doth betoken   195
The corse they follow did with desp'rate hand
Foredo it own life. 'Twas of some estate.
Couch we a while and mark.   *[Retiring with Horatio.]*

Laertes: What ceremony else?

Hamlet: That is Laertes, a very noble youth. Mark.   200

Laertes: What ceremony else?

Doctor: Her obsequies have been as far enlarg'd
As we have warranty. Her death was doubtful,
And but that great command o'ersways the order,
She should in ground unsanctified been lodg'd   205

---

170. *chop-fall'n:* (1) lacking the lower jaw; (2) downcast.   172. *favor:* appearance.
183. *curiously:* closely, minutely.   184–85. *modesty:* moderation.   187. *loam:* a mixture of
moistened clay with sand, straw, etc.   189. *Imperious:* imperial.   192. *flaw:* gust.
195. *maimed rites:* lack of customary ceremony.   197. *Foredo:* fordo, destroy. *it:* its. *estate:*
rank.   198. *Couch we:* let us conceal ourselves.   203. *doubtful:* i.e. the subject of an "open
verdict."   204. *order:* customary procedure.   205. *should:* would certainly.

Till the last trumpet; for charitable prayers,
[Shards,] flints, and pebbles should be thrown on her.
Yet here she is allow'd her virgin crants,
Her maiden strewments, and the bringing home
Of bell and burial.   210
Laertes: Must there no more be done?
Doctor: No more be done:
We should profane the service of the dead
To sing a requiem and such rest to her
As to peace-parted souls.
Laertes: Lay her i' th' earth,
And from her fair and unpolluted flesh   215
May violets spring! I tell thee, churlish priest,
A minist'ring angel shall my sister be
When thou liest howling.
Hamlet: What, the fair Ophelia!
Queen: [*Scattering flowers.*]   Sweets to the sweet, farewell!
I hop'd thou shouldst have been my Hamlet's wife.   220
I thought thy bride-bed to have deck'd, sweet maid,
And not have strew'd thy grave.
Laertes: O, treble woe
Fall ten times [treble] on that cursed head
Whose wicked deed thy most ingenious sense
Depriv'd thee of! Hold off the earth a while,   225
Till I have caught her once more in mine arms.
                                       [*Leaps in the grave.*]
Now pile your dust upon the quick and dead,
Till of this flat a mountain you have made
T' o'ertop old Pelion, or the skyish head
Of blue Olympus.   230
Hamlet: [*Coming forward.*]   What is he whose grief
Bears such an emphasis, whose phrase of sorrow
Conjures the wand'ring stars and makes them stand
Like wonder-wounded hearers? This is I,
Hamlet the Dane!   [*Hamlet leaps in after Laertes.*] 235
Laertes: The devil take thy soul!   [*Grappling with him.*]
Hamlet: Thou pray'st not well.
I prithee take thy fingers from my throat.
For though I am not splenitive [and] rash,

---

206. *for:* instead of.   208. *crants:* garland.   209. *maiden strewments:* flowers scattered on the
grave of an unmarried girl.   209–10. *bringing . . . burial:* i.e. burial in consecrated ground,
with the bell tolling.   213. *requiem:* dirge.   219. *Sweets:* flowers.   224. *ingenious:* intelligent.   229–230. *Pelion, Olympus:* mountains in northeastern Greece.   232. *emphasis,
phrase:* Rhetorical terms, here used in disparaging reference to Laertes' inflated language.
233. *Conjures:* puts a spell upon. *wand'ring stars:* planets.   235. *the Dane:* This title normally
signifies the King.   238. *splenitive:* impetuous.

Yet have I in me something dangerous,
    Which let thy wisdom fear. Hold off thy hand!   240
King: Pluck them asunder.
Queen: Hamlet, Hamlet!
    All: Gentlemen!
Horatio: Good my lord, be quiet.

[*The Attendants part them, and they come out of the grave.*]

Hamlet: Why, I will fight with him upon this theme
    Until my eyelids will no longer wag.
Queen: O my son, what theme?   245
Hamlet: I lov'd Ophelia. Forty thousand brothers
    Could not with all their quantity of love
    Make up my sum. What wilt thou do for her?
King: O, he is mad, Laertes.
Queen: For love of God, forbear him.   250
Hamlet: 'Swounds, show me what thou't do.
    Woo't weep, woo't fight, woo't fast, woo't tear thyself?
    Woo't drink up eisel, eat a crocadile?
    I'll do't. Dost [thou] come here to whine?
    To outface me with leaping in her grave?   255
    Be buried quick with her, and so will I.
    And if thou prate of mountains, let them throw
    Millions of acres on us, till our ground,
    Singeing his pate against the burning zone,
    Make Ossa like a wart! Nay, and thou'lt mouth,   260
    I'll rant as well as thou.
Queen: This is mere madness,
    And [thus] a while the fit will work on him;
    Anon, as patient as the female dove,
    When that her golden couplets are disclosed,
    His silence will sit drooping.
Hamlet: Hear you, sir,   265
    What is the reason that you use me thus?
    I lov'd you ever. But it is no matter.
    Let Hercules himself do what he may,
    The cat will mew, and dog will have his day.   *Exit Hamlet.*
King: I pray thee, good Horatio, wait upon him.   270

                                                    [*Exit*] *Horatio.*

_____

251. *thou't:* thou wilt.   252. *Woo't:* wilt thou.   253. *eisel:* vinegar. *crocadile:* crocodile.
257. *if . . . mountains:* Referring to lines 227–30.   259. *burning zone:* sphere of the sun.
260. *Ossa:* another mountain in Greece, near Pelion and Olympus. *mouth:* talk bombast
(synonymous with *rant* in the next line).   262. *mere:* utter.   263. *patient:* calm.   264. *golden
couplets:* pair of baby birds, covered with yellow down. *disclosed:* hatched.   268–69. *Let . . .
day:* i.e. nobody can prevent another from making the scenes he feels he has a right to.

[*To* Laertes.]   Strengthen your patience in our last night's
speech,
We'll put the matter to the present push.—
Good Gertrude, set some watch over your son.
This grave shall have a living monument.   275
An hour of quiet [shortly] shall we see,
Till then in patience our proceeding be.   *Exeunt.*

Scene II

Enter Hamlet *and* Horatio.

> *Hamlet:* So much for this, sir, now shall you see the other—
> You do remember all the circumstance?
> *Horatio:* Remember it, my lord!
> *Hamlet:* Sir, in my heart there was a kind of fighting
> That would not let me sleep. [Methought] I lay   5
> Worse than the mutines in the [bilboes]. Rashly—
> And prais'd be rashness for it—let us know
> Our indiscretion sometime serves us well
> When our deep plots do pall, and that should learn us
> There's a divinity that shapes our ends,   10
> Rough-hew them how we will—
> *Horatio:*   That is most certain.
> *Hamlet:* Up from my cabin,
> My sea-gown scarf'd about me, in the dark
> Grop'd I to find out them, had my desire,
> Finger'd their packet, and in fine withdrew   15
> To mine own room again, making so bold,
> My fears forgetting manners, to [unseal]
> Their grand commission; where I found, Horatio—
> Ah, royal knavery!—an exact command,
> Larded with many several sorts of reasons,   20
> Importing Denmark's health and England's too,
> With, ho, such bugs and goblins in my life,

271–76. These lines are replaced in Q1.   271. *in:* i.e. by recalling.   272. *present push:*
immediate test.   275. *living:* enduring (?) or in the form of a lifelike effigy (?).

V.ii. Location: The castle.   1. *see the other:* i.e. hear the other news I have to tell you (hinted at
in the letter to Horatio, IV.vi.24-25).   6. *mutines:* mutineers (but the term *mutiny* was in
Shakespeare's day used of almost any act of rebellion against authority). *bilboes:* fetters
attached to a heavy iron bar. *Rashly:* on impulse.   7. *know:* recognize, acknowledge.   9. *pall:*
lose force, come to nothing. *learn:* teach.   10. *shapes our ends:* gives final shape to our
designs.   11. *Rough-hew them:* block them out in initial form.   15. *Finger'd:* filched,
"pinched."   20. *Larded:* garnished.   21. *Importing:* relating to.   22. *bugs . . . life:* terrifying
things in prospect if I were permitted to remain alive. *Bugs* = bugaboos.

That, on the supervise, no leisure bated,
No, not to stay the grinding of the axe,
My head should be strook off.
Horatio: Is't possible? 25
Hamlet: Here's the commission, read it at more leisure.
But wilt thou hear now how I did proceed?
Horatio: I beseech you.
Hamlet: Being thus benetted round with [villainies],
Or I could make a prologue to my brains, 30
They had begun the play. I sat me down,
Devis'd a new commission, wrote it fair.
I once did hold it, as our statists do,
A baseness to write fair, and labor'd much
How to forget that learning, but, sir, now 35
It did me yeman's service. Wilt thou know
Th' effect of what I wrote?
Horatio: Ay, good my lord.
Hamlet: An earnest conjuration from the King,
As England was his faithful tributary,
As love between them like the palm might flourish, 40
As peace should still her wheaten garland wear
And stand a comma 'tween their amities,
And many such-like [as's] of great charge,
That on the view and knowing of these contents,
Without debatement further, more or less, 45
He should those bearers put to sudden death,
Not shriving time allow'd.
Horatio: How was this seal'd?
Hamlet: Why, even in that was heaven ordinant.
I had my father's signet in my purse,
Which was the model of that Danish seal; 50
Folded the writ up in the form of th' other,
[Subscrib'd] it, gave't th' impression, plac'd it safely,
The changeling never known. Now the next day
Was our sea-fight, and what to this was sequent
Thou knowest already. 55

---

23. *supervise:* perusal. *bated:* deducted (from the stipulated speediness).   24. *stay:* wait for.
30. *Or:* before.   32. *fair:* i.e. in a beautiful hand (such as a professional scribe would use).
33. *statists:* statesmen, public officials.   34. *A baseness:* i.e. a skill befitting men of low rank.
36. *yeman's:* yeoman's, i.e. solid, substantial.   37. *effect:* purport, gist.   42. *comma:*
connective, link.   43. *as's . . . charge:* (1) weighty clauses beginning with *as;* (2) asses with
heavy loads.   47. *shriving time:* time for confession and absolution.   48. *ordinant:* in charge,
guiding.   50. *model:* small copy.   52. *Subscrib'd:* signed.   53. *changeling:* i.e. Hamlet's
letter, substituted secretly for the genuine letter, as fairies substituted their children for
human children. *never known:* never recognized as a substitution (unlike the fairies'
changelings).

Horatio: So Guildenstern and Rosencrantz go to't.

Hamlet: [Why, man, they did make love to this employment,]
    They are not near my conscience. Their defeat
    Does by their own insinuation grow.
    'Tis dangerous when the baser nature comes   60
    Between the pass and fell incensed points
    Of mighty opposites.

Horatio: Why, what a king is this!

Hamlet: Does it not, think thee, stand me now upon—
    He that hath kill'd my king and whor'd my mother,
    Popp'd in between th' election and my hopes,   65
    Thrown out his angle for my proper life,
    And with such coz'nage—is't not perfect conscience
    [To quit him with this arm? And is't not to be damn'd,
    To let this canker of our nature come
    In further evil?   70

Horatio: It must be shortly known to him from England
    What is the issue of the business there.

Hamlet: It will be short; the interim's mine,
    And a man's life's no more than to say "one."
    But I am very sorry, good Horatio,   75
    That to Laertes I forgot myself,
    For by the image of my cause I see
    The portraiture of his. I'll [court] his favors.
    But sure the bravery of his grief did put me
    Into a tow'ring passion.

Horatio: Peace, who comes here?]   80

Enter [young Osric,] a courtier.

    Osric: Your lordship is right welcome back to Denmark.

Hamlet: I [humbly] thank you, sir.—Dost know this water-fly?

Horatio: No, my good lord.

Hamlet: Thy state is the more gracious, for 'tis a vice to know him.
    He hath much land, and fertile; let a beast be lord of beasts, 85
    and his crib shall stand at the King's mess. 'Tis a chough, but,
    as I say, spacious in the possession of dirt.

---

56. *go to't:* i.e. are going to their death.   58. *defeat:* ruin, overthrow.   59. *insinuation:*
winding their way into the affair.   60. *baser:* inferior.   61. *pass:* thrust. *fell:* fierce.
62. *stand . . . upon:* i.e. rest upon me as a duty.   65. *election:* i.e. as King of Denmark.
66. *angle:* hook and line. *proper:* very.   67. *coz'nage:* trickery.   68. *quit him:* pay him back.
69. *canker:* cancerous sore.   69-70. *come In:* grow into.   74. *a man's . . . more:* i.e. to kill a
man takes no more time. *say "one":* Perhaps this is equivalent to "deliver one sword thrust";
see line 257 below, where Hamlet says "One" as he makes the first hit.   77. *image:* likeness.
79. *bravery:* ostentatious expression.   82. *water-fly:* i.e. tiny, vainly agitated creature.
84. *gracious:* virtuous.   85-86. *let . . . mess:* i.e. if a beast owned as many cattle as Osric, he
could feast with the King.   86. *chough:* jackdaw, a bird that could be taught to speak.

Osric: Sweet lord, if your lordship were at leisure, I should impart a thing to you from his Majesty.

Hamlet: I will receive it, sir, with all diligence of spirit. [Put] your 90 bonnet to his right use, 'tis for the head.

Osric: I thank your lordship, it is very hot.

Hamlet: No, believe me, 'tis very cold, the wind is northerly.

Osric: It is indifferent cold, my lord, indeed.

Hamlet: But yet methinks it is very [sultry] and hot [for] my 95 complexion.

Osric: Exceedingly, my lord, it is very sultry—as 'twere—I cannot tell how. My lord, his Majesty bade me signify to you that 'a has laid a great wager on your head. Sir, this is the matter— 100

Hamlet: I beseech you remember.

[*Hamlet moves him to put on his hat.*]

Osric: Nay, good my lord, for my ease, in good faith. Sir, here is newly come to court Laertes, believe me, an absolute [gentleman], full of most excellent differences, of very soft society, and great showing; indeed, to speak sellingly of him, he is the 105 card or calendar of gentry; for you shall find in him the continent of what part a gentleman would see.

Hamlet: Sir, his definement suffers no perdition in you, though I know to divide him inventorially would dozy th' arithmetic of memory, and yet but yaw neither in respect of his quick sail; 110 but in the verity of extolment, I take him to be a soul of great article, and his infusion of such dearth and rareness as, to make true diction of him, his semblable is his mirror, and who else would trace him, his umbrage, nothing more.

Osric: Your lordship speaks most infallibly of him. 115

Hamlet: The concernancy, sir? Why do we wrap the gentleman in our more rawer breath?

Osric: Sir?

---

91. *bonnet:* hat.   94. *indifferent:* somewhat.   95. *complexion:* temperament.   102. *for my ease:* i.e. I am really more comfortable with my hat off (a polite insistence on maintaining ceremony).   103. *absolute:* complete, possessing every quality a gentleman should have. 104. *differences:* distinguishing characteristics, personal qualities. *soft:* agreeable.   105. *great showing:* splendid appearance. *sellingly:* i.e. like a seller to a prospective buyer; in a fashion to do full justice. Most editors follow Q3 in reading *feelingly* = with exactitude, as he deserves. 106. *card or calendar:* chart or register, i.e. compendious guide. *gentry:* gentlemanly behavior.   106–07. *the continent . . . part:* one who contains every quality.   108. *perdition:* loss.   109. *dozy:* make dizzy.   110. *yaw:* keep deviating erratically from its course (said of a ship). *neither:* for all that. *in respect of:* compared with.   111. *in . . . extolment:* to praise him truly.   112. *article:* scope (?) or importance (?). *infusion:* essence, quality. *dearth:* scarceness. 113. *make true diction:* speak truly. *his semblable:* his only likeness or equal.   113–14. *who . . . him:* anyone else who tries to follow him.   114. *umbrage:* shadow.   116. *concernancy:* relevance.   117. *more rawer breath:* i.e. words too crude to describe him properly.

Horatio: Is't not possible to understand in another tongue? You
    will to't, sir, really.   120
Hamlet: What imports the nomination of this gentleman?
   Osric: Of Laertes?
Horatio: His purse is empty already: all 's golden words are spent.
Hamlet: Of him, sir.
   Osric: I know you are not ignorant—   125
Hamlet: I would you did, sir, yet, in faith, if you did, it would not
    much approve me. Well, sir?
   Osric: You are not ignorant of what excellence Laertes is—
Hamlet: I dare not confess that, lest I should compare with him in
    excellence, but to know a man well were to know himself.   130
   Osric: I mean, sir, for [his] weapon, but in the imputation laid
    on him by them, in his meed he's unfellow'd.
Hamlet: What's his weapon?
   Osric: Rapier and dagger.
Hamlet: That's two of his weapons—but well.   135
   Osric: The King, sir, hath wager'd with him six Barbary horses,
    against the which he has impawn'd, as I take it, six French
    rapiers and poniards, with their assigns, as girdle, [hangers],
    and so. Three of the carriages, in faith, are very dear to
    fancy, very responsive to the hilts, most delicate carriages, 140
    and of very liberal conceit.
Hamlet: What call you the carriages?
Horatio: I knew you must be edified by the margent ere you had
    done.
   Osric: The [carriages], sir, are the hangers.   145
Hamlet: The phrase would be more germane to the matter if we
    could carry a cannon by our sides; I would it [might be]
    hangers till then. But on: six Barb'ry horses against six
    French swords, their assigns, and three liberal-conceited car-
    riages; that's the French bet against the Danish. Why is this 150
    all [impawn'd, as] you call it?
   Osric: The King, sir, hath laid, sir, that in a dozen passes
    between yourself and him, he shall not exceed you three hits;

---

119. *in another tongue:* i.e. when someone else is the speaker.   119–20. *You . . . really:* i.e. you
can do it if you try.   121. *nomination:* naming, mention.   127. *approve:* commend.
129–30. *compare . . . excellence:* i.e. seem to claim the same degree of excellence for myself.
130. *but:* The sense seems to require *for. himself:* i.e. oneself.   131-32. *in . . . them:* i.e. in
popular estimation.   132. *meed:* merit.   137. *impawn'd:* staked.   138. *assigns:* appurten-
ances. *hangers:* straps on which the swords hang from the girdle.   139. *carriages:* properly,
gun-carriages; here used affectedly in place of *hangers.*   140. *fancy:* taste. *very responsive to:*
matching well.   141. *liberal conceit:* elegant design.   143. *must . . . margent:* would require
enlightenment from a marginal note.   152. *laid:* wagered.   153. *he . . . hits:* Laertes must
win by at least eight to four (if none of the "passes" or bouts are draws), since at seven to five
he would be only two up.

he hath laid on twelve for nine; and it would come to immediate trial, if your lordship would vouchsafe the answer.   155

Hamlet: How if I answer no?

Osric: I mean, my lord, the opposition of your person in trial.

Hamlet: Sir, I will walk here in the hall. If it please his Majesty, it is the breathing time of day with me. Let the foils be brought, the gentleman willing, and the King hold his purpose, I will   160
win for him and I can; if not, I will gain nothing but my shame and the odd hits.

Osric: Shall I deliver you so?

Hamlet: To this effect, sir—after what flourish your nature will.

Osric: I commend my duty to your lordship.   165

Hamlet: Yours. *[Exit Osric.]* ['A] does well to commend it himself, there are no tongues else for 's turn.

Horatio: This lapwing runs away with the shell on his head.

Hamlet: 'A did [comply], sir, with his dug before 'a suck'd it. Thus has he, and many more of the same breed that I know the   170
drossy age dotes on, only got the tune of the time, and out of an habit of encounter, a kind of [yesty] collection, which carries them through and through the most [profound] and [winnow'd] opinions, and do but blow them to their trial, the bubbles are out.   175

Enter a Lord.

Lord: My lord, his Majesty commended him to you by young Osric, who brings back to him that you attend him in the hall. He sends to know if your pleasure hold to play with Laertes, or that you will take longer time.

Hamlet: I am constant to my purposes, they follow the King's   180
pleasure. If his fitness speaks, mine is ready; now or whensoever, provided I be so able as now.

Lord: The King and Queen and all are coming down.

Hamlet: In happy time.

---

154. *he . . . nine:* Not satisfactorily explained despite much discussion. One suggestion is that Laertes has raised the odds against himself by wagering that out of twelve bouts he will win nine.   155. *answer:* encounter (as Hamlet's following quibble forces Osric to explain in his next speech).   159. *breathing . . . me:* my usual hour for exercise.   164. *after what flourish:* with whatever embellishment of language.   165. *commend my duty:* offer my dutiful respects (but Hamlet picks up the phrase in the sense "praise my manner of bowing").   168. *lapwing:* a foolish bird which upon hatching was supposed to run with part of the eggshell still over its head. (Osric has put his hat on at last.)   169. *comply . . . dug:* bow politely to his mother's nipple.   171. *drossy:* i.e. worthless. *tune . . . time:* i.e. fashionable ways of talk. *habit of encounter:* mode of social intercourse.   172. *yesty:* yeasty, frothy. *collection:* i.e. anthology of fine phrases.   174. *winnow'd:* sifted, choice. *opinions:* judgments. *blow . . . trial:* test them by blowing on them, i.e. make even the least demanding trial of them.   175. *out:* blown away (?) or at an end, done for (?).   181. *If . . . ready:* i.e. if this is a good moment for him, it is for me also.

Lord: The Queen desires you to use some gentle entertainment 185
to Laertes before you fall to play.

Hamlet: She well instructs me.   [*Exit Lord.*]

Horatio: You will lose, my lord.

Hamlet: I do not think so; since he went into France I have been in
continual practice. I shall win at the odds. Thou wouldst not 190
think how ill all's here about my heart—but it is no matter.

Horatio: Nay, good my lord—

Hamlet: It is but foolery, but it is such a kind of [gain-]giving, as
would perhaps trouble a woman.

Horatio: If your mind dislike any thing, obey it. I will forestall 195
their repair hither, and say you are not fit.

Hamlet: Not a whit, we defy augury. There is special providence
in the fall of a sparrow. If it be [now], 'tis not to come; if it be
not to come, it will be now; if it be not now, yet it [will] come
—the readiness is all. Since no man, of aught he leaves, 200
knows what is't to leave betimes, let be.

*A table prepar'd, [and flagons of wine on it. Enter] Trumpets, Drums, and Officers
with cushions, foils, daggers; King, Queen, Laertes, [Osric,] and all the State.*

King: Come, Hamlet, come, and take this hand from me.
              [*The* King *puts* Laertes' *hand into* Hamlet's.]

Hamlet: Give me your pardon, sir. I have done you wrong,
But pardon't as you are a gentleman.
This presence knows,   205
And you must needs have heard, how I am punish'd
With a sore distraction. What I have done
That might your nature, honor, and exception
Roughly awake, I here proclaim was madness.
Was't Hamlet wrong'd Laertes? Never Hamlet!   210
If Hamlet from himself be ta'en away,
And when he's not himself does wrong Laertes,
Then Hamlet does it not, Hamlet denies it.
Who does it then? His madness. If't be so,
Hamlet is of the faction that is wronged,   215
His madness is poor Hamlet's enemy.
[Sir, in this audience,]
Let my disclaiming from a purpos'd evil
Free me so far in your most generous thoughts,

---

185. *gentle entertainment:* courteous greeting.   193. *gain-giving:* misgiving.   197–98. *special
. . . sparrow:* See Matthew 10:29.   200. *of aught:* i.e. whatever.   201. *knows . . . betimes:*
knows what is the best time to leave.   202 s.d. *State:* nobles.   205. *presence:* assembled
court.   206. *punish'd:* afflicted.   208. *exception:* objection.   218. *my . . . evil:* my declaration that I intended no harm.   219. *Free:* absolve.

That I have shot my arrow o'er the house   220
And hurt my brother.
Laertes: I am satisfied in nature,
Whose motive in this case should stir me most
To my revenge, but in my terms of honor
I stand aloof, and will no reconcilement
Till by some elder masters of known honor   225
I have a voice and president of peace
To [keep] my name ungor'd. But [till] that time
I do receive your offer'd love like love,
And will not wrong it.
Hamlet: I embrace it freely,
And will this brothers' wager frankly play.   230
Give us the foils. [Come on.]
Laertes: Come, one for me.
Hamlet: I'll be your foil, Laertes; in mine ignorance
Your skill shall like a star i' th' darkest night
Stick fiery off indeed.
Laertes: You mock me, sir.
Hamlet: No, by this hand.   235
King: Give them the foils, young Osric. Cousin Hamlet,
You know the wager?
Hamlet: Very well, my lord.
Your Grace has laid the odds a' th' weaker side.
King: I do not fear it, I have seen you both;
But since he is [better'd], we have therefore odds.   240
Laertes: This is too heavy; let me see another.
Hamlet: This likes me well. These foils have all a length?
                                        [Prepare to play.]
Osric: Ay, my good lord.
King: Set me the stoups of wine upon that table.
If Hamlet give the first or second hit,   245
Or quit in answer of the third exchange,
Let all the battlements their ord'nance fire.
The King shall drink to Hamlet's better breath,
And in the cup an [union] shall he throw,
Richer than that which four successive kings   250

---

222. *in nature:* so far as my personal feelings are concerned.   223. *in . . . honor:* i.e. as a man
governed by an established code of honor.   226–27. *have . . . ungor'd:* can secure an opinion
backed by precedent that I can make peace with you without injury to my reputation.
230. *brothers':* i.e. amicable, as if between brothers. *frankly:* freely, without constraint.
232. *foil:* thin sheet of metal placed behind a jewel to set it off.   233. *Stick . . . off:* blaze out
in contrast.   238. *laid the odds:* i.e. wagered a higher stake (horses to rapiers).   240. *is
better'd:* has perfected his skill. *odds:* i.e. the arrangement that Laertes must take more bouts
than Hamlet to win.   242. *likes:* pleases. *a length:* the same length.   244. *stoups:* tankards.
246. *quit . . . exchange:* pays back wins by Laertes in the first and second bouts by taking the
third.   249. *union:* an especially fine pearl.

In Denmark's crown have worn. Give me the cups,
And let the kettle to the trumpet speak,
The trumpet to the cannoneer without,
The cannons to the heavens, the heaven to earth,
"Now the King drinks to Hamlet." Come begin;   255

Trumpets the while.

And you, the judges, bear a wary eye.

Hamlet: Come on, sir.

Laertes: Come, my lord.

[*They play and Hamlet scores a hit.*]

Hamlet: One.

Laertes: No.

Hamlet: Judgment.

Osric: A hit, a very palpable hit.

Laertes: Well, again.

King: Stay, give me drink. Hamlet, this pearl is thine,
Here's to thy health! Give him the cup.   260

Drum, trumpets [sound] flourish. A piece goes off [within].

Hamlet: I'll play this bout first, set it by a while.
Come. [*They play again.*] Another hit; what say you?

Laertes: [A touch, a touch,] I do confess't.

King: Our son shall win.

Queen: He's fat, and scant of breath.
Here, Hamlet, take my napkin, rub thy brows.   265
The Queen carouses to thy fortune, Hamlet.

Hamlet: Good madam!

King: Gertrude, do not drink.

Queen: I will, my lord, I pray you pardon me.

King: [*Aside.*] It is the pois'ned cup, it is too late.

Hamlet: I dare not drink yet, madam; by and by.   270

Queen: Come, let me wipe thy face.

Laertes: My lord, I'll hit him now.

King: I do not think't.

Laertes: [*Aside.*] And yet it is almost against my conscience.

Hamlet: Come, for the third, Laertes, you do but dally.
I pray you pass with your best violence;   275
I am sure you make a wanton of me.

Laertes: Say you so? Come on.   [*They play.*]

Osric: Nothing, neither way.

Laertes: Have at you now!

[Laertes *wounds* Hamlet; *then, in scuffling, they change rapiers.*]

---

252. *kettle:* kettle-drum.   264. *fat:* sweaty.   266. *carouses:* drinks a toast.   276. *make . . .
me:* i.e. are holding back in order to let me win, as one does with a spoiled child (*wanton*).

| King: | Part them, they are incens'd. |
| Hamlet: | Nay, come again. |

[Hamlet *wounds* Laertes. *The* Queen *falls.*]

Osric:	Look to the Queen there ho!	280
Horatio:	They bleed on both sides. How is it, my lord?	
Osric:	How is't, Laertes?	
Laertes:	Why, as a woodcock to mine own springe, Osric:	
	I am justly kill'd with mine own treachery.	
Hamlet:	How does the Queen?	
King:	She sounds to see them bleed.	285
Queen:	No, no, the drink, the drink—O my dear Hamlet—	
	The drink, the drink! I am pois'ned. *[Dies.]*	
Hamlet:	O villainy! Ho, let the door be lock'd!	
	Treachery! Seek it out.	
Laertes:	It is here, Hamlet. [Hamlet,] thou art slain.	290
	No med'cine in the world can do thee good;	
	In thee there is not half an hour's life.	
	The treacherous instrument is in [thy] hand,	
	Unbated and envenom'd. The foul practice	
	Hath turn'd itself on me. Lo here I lie,	295
	Never to rise again. Thy mother's pois'ned.	
	I can no more—the King, the King's to blame.	
Hamlet:	The point envenom'd too!	
	Then, venom, to thy work. *[Hurts the King.]*	
All:	Treason! treason!	300
King:	O, yet defend me, friends, I am but hurt.	
Hamlet:	Here, thou incestious, [murd'rous], damned Dane,	
	Drink [off] this potion! Is [thy union] here?	
	Follow my mother! *[King dies.]*	
Laertes:	He is justly served,	
	It is a poison temper'd by himself.	305
	Exchange forgiveness with me, noble Hamlet.	
	Mine and my father's death come not upon thee,	
	Nor thine on me! *[Dies.]*	
Hamlet:	Heaven make thee free of it! I follow thee.	
	I am dead, Horatio. Wretched queen, adieu!	310
	You that look pale, and tremble at this chance,	
	That are but mutes or audience to this act,	
	Had I but time—as this fell sergeant, Death,	
	Is strict in his arrest—O, I could tell you—	
	But let it be. Horatio, I am dead,	315

---

283. *springe:* snare. 285. *sounds:* swoons. 294. *Unbated:* not blunted. *foul practice:* vile plot. 299 s.d. *Hurts:* wounds. 305. *temper'd:* mixed. 309. *make thee free:* absolve you. 312. *mutes or audience:* silent spectators. 313. *fell:* cruel. *sergeant:* sheriff's officer.

Thou livest. Report me and my cause aright
To the unsatisfied.
Horatio: Never believe it;
I am more an antique Roman than a Dane.
Here's yet some liquor left.
Hamlet: As th' art a man,
Give me the cup. Let go! By heaven, I'll ha't!   320
O God, Horatio, what a wounded name,
Things standing thus unknown, shall I leave behind me!
If thou didst ever hold me in thy heart,
Absent thee from felicity a while,
And in this harsh world draw thy breath in pain   325
To tell my story.   *A march afar off [and a shot within].*
What warlike noise is this?
                                    [Osric goes to the door and returns.]
Osric: Young Fortinbras, with conquest come from Poland,
To th' embassadors of England gives
This warlike volley.
Hamlet: O, I die, Horatio,
The potent poison quite o'er-crows my spirit.   330
I cannot live to hear the news from England,
But I do prophesy th' election lights
On Fortinbras, he has my dying voice.
So tell him, with th' occurrents more and less
Which have solicited—the rest is silence.   *[Dies.]* 335
Horatio: Now cracks a noble heart. Good night, sweet prince,
And flights of angels sing thee to thy rest!   *[March within.]*
Why does the drum come hither?

Enter Fortinbras *with the* [English] Embassadors, [*with Drum, Colors,
and Attendants*].

Fortinbras: Where is this sight?
Horatio: What is it you would see?
If aught of woe or wonder, cease your search.   340
Fortinbras: This quarry cries on havoc. O proud death,
What feast is toward in thine eternal cell,
That thou so many princes at a shot
So bloodily hast strook?
[1.] Embassador: The sight is dismal,
And our affairs from England come too late.   345
The ears are senseless that should give us hearing,

317. *antique Roman:* i.e. one who will commit suicide on such an occasion.   330. *o'ercrows:*
triumphs over (a term derived from cockfighting). *spirit:* vital energy.   333. *voice:* vote.
334. *occurrents:* occurrences.   335. *solicited:* instigated.   341. *This . . . havoc:* this heap of
corpses proclaims a massacre.   342. *toward:* in preparation.

To tell him his commandment is fulfill'd,
That Rosencrantz and Guildenstern are dead.
Where should we have our thanks?

Horatio: Not from his mouth,
Had it th' ability of life to thank you.   350
He never gave commandement for their death.
But since so jump upon this bloody question,
You from the Polack wars, and you from England,
Are here arrived, give order that these bodies
High on a stage be placed to the view,   355
And let me speak to [th'] yet unknowing world
How these things came about. So shall you hear
Of carnal, bloody, and unnatural acts,
Of accidental judgments, casual slaughters,
Of deaths put on by cunning and [forc'd] cause,   360
And in this upshot, purposes mistook
Fall'n on th' inventors' heads: all this can I
Truly deliver.

Fortinbras: Let us haste to hear it,
And call the noblest to the audience.
For me, with sorrow I embrace my fortune.   365
I have some rights, of memory in this kingdom,
Which now to claim my vantage doth invite me.

Horatio: Of that I shall have also cause to speak,
And from his mouth whose voice will draw [on] more.
But let this same be presently perform'd   370
Even while men's minds are wild, lest more mischance
On plots and errors happen.

Fortinbras: Let four captains
Bear Hamlet like a soldier to the stage,
For he was likely, had he been put on,
To have prov'd most royal; and for his passage,   375
The soldiers' music and the rite of war
Speak loudly for him.
Take up the bodies. Such a sight as this
Becomes the field, but here shows much amiss.
Go bid the soldiers shoot.   380

Exeunt [marching; after the which a peal of ordinance are shot off].

----

349. *his:* i.e. the King's. 352. *jump:* precisely, pat. *question:* matter. 355. *stage:* platform.
359. *judgments:* retributions. *casual:* happening by chance. 360. *put on:* instigated. 366. *of
memory:* unforgotten. 367. *my vantage:* i.e. my opportune presence at a moment when the
throne is empty. 369. *his . . . more:* the mouth of one (Hamlet) whose vote will induce others
to support your claim. 370. *presently:* at once. 371. *wild:* distraught. 374. *put on:* put to
the test (by becoming king). 375. *passage:* death. 379. *Becomes . . . amiss:* befits the
battlefield, but appears very much out of place here.

Further Reading

Mack, Maynard. "The World of Hamlet." *Shakespeare: Modern Essays in Criticism.*
Rev. ed. Ed. Leonard F. Dean. New York: Oxford UP, 1967. 242–62. • Bradley,
A. C. "Shakespeare's Tragic Period—Hamlet." *Twentieth Century Interpretations of
"Hamlet."* Ed. David Bevington. Englewood Cliffs, NJ: Prentice, 1968. 13–21. •
Knights, L. C. "Prince Hamlet." *Explorations: Essays in Criticism.* New York:
Stewart, 1947. 82–93. • Gardner, Helen. "Hamlet and the Tragedy of Revenge."
Shakespeare: Modern Essays in Criticism. Rev. ed. Ed. Leonard F. Dean. New York:
Oxford UP, 1967. 218–26. • Jones, Ernest. "Hamlet and Oedipus." *Shakespeare:
Hamlet.* Ed. John Jump. Nashville: Aurora, 1970. 51–63. • Everett, Barbara.
"Hamlet: A Time to Die." *Young Hamlet: Essays on Shakespeare's Tragedies.* Oxford:
Clarendon, 1989. 124–36.

Shakespearean tragedy differs so greatly from Greek tragedy and from modern tragedy that it is hard to find a single adequate definition of the genre. Most of us, if forced to attempt a definition, would be tempted to say that a tragedy is a sad play, one that ends in disaster. But as Arthur Miller points out, sadness (pathos) is not quite the issue. His much more penetrating definition of tragedy provides a particularly useful way to think about Hamlet.

Arthur Miller: On Joy in Tragedy

It is my view—or my prejudice—that when a man is seen whole and round and so characterized, when he is allowed his life on the stage over and beyond the mould and purpose of the story, hope will show its face in his, just as it does, even so dimly, in life. As the old saying has it, there is some good in the worst of us. I think that the tragedian, supposedly the saddest of citizens, can never forget this fact, and must strive always to posit a world in which that good might have been allowed to express itself instead of succumbing to the evil. I began by saying that tragedy would probably never be wholly defined. I end by offering you a definition. It is not final for me, but at least it has the virtue of keeping mere pathos out.

You are witnessing a tragedy when the characters before you are wholly and intensely realized, to the degree that your belief in their reality is all but complete. The story in which they are involved is such as to force their complete personalities to be brought to bear upon the problem, to the degree that you are able to understand not only why they are ending in sadness, but how they might have avoided their end. The demeanor, so to speak, of the story is most serious—so serious that you have been brought to the state of outright fear for the people involved, as though for yourself.

And all this, not merely so that your senses shall have been stretched and your glands stimulated, but that you may come away with the knowledge that man, by reason of his intense effort and desire, which you have just seen demonstrated, is capable of flowering on this earth.

Tragedy arises when we are in the presence of a man who has missed accomplishing his joy. But the joy must be there, the promise of the right way of life must be there. Otherwise pathos reigns, and an endless, meaningless, and essentially untrue picture of man is created—man helpless under the falling piano, man wholly lost in a universe which by its very nature is too hostile to be mastered.

HENRIK IBSEN

(1828–1906)

A DOLL'S HOUSE

translated from the Norwegian by James McFarlane

CHARACTERS

Torvald Helmer, a lawyer
Nora, his wife
Dr. Rank
Mrs. Kristine Linde
Nils Krogstad
Anne Marie, the nursemaid
Helene, the maid
The Helmers' three children
A porter

The action takes place in the Helmers' flat.

ACT I

A pleasant room, tastefully but not expensively furnished. On the back wall, one door on the right leads to the entrance hall, a second door on the left leads to Helmer's study. Between these two doors, a piano. In the middle of the left wall, a door; and downstage from it, a window. Near the window a round table with armchairs and a small sofa. In the right wall, upstage, a door; and on the same wall downstage, a porcelain stove with a couple of armchairs and a rocking-chair. Between the stove and the door a small table. Etchings on the walls. A whatnot with china and other small objets d'art; a small bookcase with books in handsome bindings. Carpet on the floor; a fire burns in the stove. A winter's day.

The front door-bell rings in the hall; a moment later, there is the sound of the front door being opened. Nora *comes into the room, happily humming to herself. She is dressed in her outdoor things, and is carrying lots of parcels which she then puts down on the table, right. She leaves the door into the hall standing open; a* Porter *can be seen outside holding a Christmas tree and a basket; he hands them to the* Maid *who has opened the door for them.*

> *Nora:* Hide the Christmas tree away carefully, Helene. The children mustn't see it till this evening when it's decorated. *[To the* Porter, *taking out her purse.]* How much?

Porter: Fifty öre.

Nora: There's a crown. Keep the change.

[*The* Porter *thanks her and goes.* Nora *shuts the door. She continues to laugh quietly and happily to herself as she takes off her things. She takes a bag of macaroons out of her pocket and eats one or two; then she walks stealthily across and listens at her husband's door.*]

Nora: Yes, he's in.

[*She begins humming again as she walks over to the table, right.*]

Helmer: [*in his study*] Is that my little sky-lark chirruping out there?

Nora: [*busy opening some of the parcels*] Yes, it is.

Helmer: Is that my little squirrel frisking about?

Nora: Yes!

Helmer: When did my little squirrel get home?

Nora: Just this minute. [*She stuffs the bag of macaroons in her pocket and wipes her mouth.*] Come on out, Torvald, and see what I've bought.

Helmer: I don't want to be disturbed! [*A moment later, he opens the door and looks out, his pen in his hand.*] 'Bought', did you say? All that? Has my little spendthrift been out squandering money again?

Nora: But, Torvald, surely this year we can spread ourselves just a little. This is the first Christmas we haven't had to go carefully.

Helmer: Ah, but that doesn't mean we can afford to be extravagant, you know.

Nora: Oh yes, Torvald, surely we can afford to be just a little bit extravagant now, can't we? Just a teeny-weeny bit. You are getting quite a good salary now, and you are going to earn lots and lots of money.

Helmer: Yes, after the New Year. But it's going to be three whole months before the first pay cheque comes in.

Nora: Pooh! We can always borrow in the meantime.

Helmer: Nora! [*Crosses to her and takes her playfully by the ear.*] Here we go again, you and your frivolous ideas! Suppose I went and borrowed a thousand crowns today, and you went and spent it all over Christmas, then on New Year's Eve a slate fell and hit me on the head and there I was. . . .

Nora: [*putting her hand over his mouth*] Sh! Don't say such horrid things.

Helmer: Yes, but supposing something like that did happen . . . what then?

Nora: If anything as awful as that did happen, I wouldn't care if I owed anybody anything or not.

Helmer: Yes, but what about the people I'd borrowed from?

Nora: Them? Who cares about them! They are only strangers!

Helmer: Nora, Nora! Just like a woman! Seriously though, Nora, you know what I think about these things. No debts! Never borrow! There's always something inhibited, something unpleasant, about a home built on credit and borrowed money. We two have managed to stick it out so far, and that's the way we'll go on for the little time that remains.

Nora: [walks over to the stove] Very well, just as you say, Torvald.

Helmer: [following her] There, there! My little singing bird mustn't go drooping her wings, eh? Has it got the sulks, that little squirrel of mine? *[Takes out his wallet.]* Nora, what do you think I've got here?

Nora: [quickly turning round] Money!

Helmer: There! *[He hands her some notes.]* Good heavens, I know only too well how Christmas runs away with the housekeeping.

Nora: [counts] Ten, twenty, thirty, forty. Oh, thank you, thank you, Torvald! This will see me quite a long way.

Helmer: Yes, it'll have to.

Nora: Yes, yes, I'll see that it does. But come over here, I want to show you all the things I've bought. And so cheap! Look, some new clothes for Ivar . . . and a little sword. There's a horse and a trumpet for Bob. And a doll and a doll's cot for Emmy. They are not very grand but she'll have them all broken before long anyway. And I've got some dress material and some handkerchiefs for the maids. Though, really, dear old Anne Marie should have had something better.

Helmer: And what's in this parcel here?

Nora: [shrieking] No, Torvald! You mustn't see that till tonight!

Helmer: All right. But tell me now, what did my little spendthrift fancy for herself?

Nora: For me? Puh, I don't really want anything.

Helmer: Of course you do. Anything reasonable that you think you might like, just tell me.

Nora: Well, I don't really know. As a matter of fact, though, Torvald . . .

Helmer: Well?

Nora: [toying with his coat buttons, and without looking at him] If you did want to give me something, you could . . . you could always . . .

Helmer: Well, well, out with it!

Nora: [quickly] You could always give me money, Torvald. Only what you think you could spare. And then I could buy myself something with it later on.

Helmer: But Nora . . .

Nora: Oh, please, Torvald dear! Please! I beg you. Then I'd wrap the money up in some pretty gilt paper and hang it on the Christmas tree. Wouldn't that be fun?

Helmer: What do we call my pretty little pet when it runs away with all the money?

Nora: I know, I know, we call it a spendthrift. But please let's do what I said, Torvald. Then I'll have a bit of time to think about what I need most. Isn't that awfully sensible, now, eh?

Helmer: [smiling] Yes, it is indeed—that is, if only you really could hold on to the money I gave you, and really did buy something for yourself with it. But it just gets mixed up with the housekeeping and frittered away on all sorts of useless things, and then I have to dig into my pocket all over again.

Nora: Oh but, Torvald . . .

Helmer: You can't deny it, Nora dear. *[Puts his arm round her waist.]* My pretty little pet is very sweet, but it runs away with an awful lot of money. It's incredible how expensive it is for a man to keep such a pet.

Nora: For shame! How can you say such a thing? As a matter of fact I save everything I can.

Helmer: [laughs] Yes, you are right there. Everything you *can*. But you simply can't.

Nora: [hums and smiles quietly and happily] Ah, if you only knew how many expenses the likes of us sky-larks and squirrels have, Torvald!

Helmer: What a funny little one you are! Just like your father. Always on the look-out for money, wherever you can lay your hands on it; but as soon as you've got it, it just seems to slip through your fingers. You never seem to know what you've done with it. Well, one must accept you as you are. It's in the blood. Oh yes, it is, Nora. That sort of thing is hereditary.

Nora: Oh, I only wish I'd inherited a few more of Daddy's qualities.

Helmer: And I wouldn't want my pretty little song-bird to be the least bit different from what she is now. But come to think of it, you look rather . . . rather . . . how shall I put it? . . . rather guilty today. . . .

Nora: Do I?

Helmer: Yes, you do indeed. Look me straight in the eye.

Nora: [looks at him] Well?

Helmer: [wagging his finger at her] My little sweet-tooth surely didn't forget herself in town today?

Nora: No, whatever makes you think that?

Helmer: She didn't just pop into the confectioner's for a moment?

Nora: No, I assure you, Torvald . . . !

Helmer: Didn't try sampling the preserves?

Nora: No, really I didn't.

Helmer: Didn't go nibbling a macaroon or two?

Nora: No, Torvald, honestly, you must believe me. . . !

Helmer: All right then! It's really just my little joke. . . .

Nora: [crosses to the table] I would never dream of doing anything you didn't want me to.

Helmer: Of course not, I know that. And then you've given me your word. . . . [Crosses to her.] Well then, Nora dearest, you shall keep your little Christmas secrets. They'll all come out tonight, I dare say, when we light the tree.

Nora: Did you remember to invite Dr. Rank?

Helmer: No. But there's really no need. Of course he'll come and have dinner with us. Anyway, I can ask him when he looks in this morning. I've ordered some good wine. Nora, you can't imagine how I am looking forward to this evening.

Nora: So am I. And won't the children enjoy it, Torvald!

Helmer: Oh, what a glorious feeling it is, knowing you've got a nice, safe job, and a good fat income. Don't you agree? Isn't it wonderful, just thinking about it?

Nora: Oh, it's marvellous!

Helmer: Do you remember last Christmas? Three whole weeks beforehand you shut yourself up every evening till after midnight making flowers for the Christmas tree and all the other splendid things you wanted to surprise us with. Ugh, I never felt so bored in all my life.

Nora: I wasn't the least bit bored.

Helmer: [smiling] But it turned out a bit of an anticlimax, Nora.

Nora: Oh, you are not going to tease me about that again! How was I to know the cat would get in and pull everything to bits?

Helmer: No, of course you weren't. Poor little Nora! All you wanted was for us to have a nice time—and it's the thought behind it that counts, after all. All the same, it's a good thing we've seen the back of those lean times.

Nora: Yes, really it's marvellous.

Helmer: Now there's no need for me to sit here all on my own, bored to tears. And you don't have to strain your dear little eyes, and work those dainty little fingers to the bone. . . .

Nora: [clapping her hands] No, Torvald, I don't, do I? Not any more. Oh, how marvellous it is to hear that! [Takes his arm.] Now I want to tell you how I've been thinking we might arrange things, Torvald. As soon as Christmas is over. . . . [The door-bell rings in the hall.] Oh, there's the bell. [Tidies one or two things in the room.] It's probably a visitor. What a nuisance!

Helmer: Remember I'm not at home to callers.

Maid: *[in the doorway]* There's a lady to see you, ma'am.

Nora: Show her in, please.

Maid: *[to Helmer]* And the doctor's just arrived, too, sir.

Helmer: Did he go straight into my room?

Maid: Yes, he did, sir.

[Helmer goes into his study. The Maid shows in Mrs. Linde, who is in travelling clothes, and closes the door after her.]

Mrs. Linde: *[subdued and rather hesitantly]* How do you do, Nora?

Nora: *[uncertainly]* How do you do?

Mrs. Linde: I'm afraid you don't recognize me.

Nora: No, I don't think I . . . And yet I seem to. . . . *[Bursts out suddenly.]* Why! Kristine! Is it really you?

Mrs. Linde: Yes, it's me.

Nora: Kristine! Fancy not recognizing you again! But how was I to, when . . . *[Gently.]* How you've changed, Kristine!

Mrs. Linde: I dare say I have. In nine . . . ten years. . . .

Nora: Is it so long since we last saw each other? Yes, it must be. Oh, believe me these last eight years have been such a happy time. And now you've come up to town, too? All that long journey in wintertime. That took courage.

Mrs. Linde: I just arrived this morning on the steamer.

Nora: To enjoy yourself over Christmas, of course. How lovely! Oh, we'll have such fun, you'll see. Do take off your things. You are not cold, are you? *[Helps her.]* There now! Now let's sit down here in comfort beside the stove. No, here, you take the armchair, I'll sit here on the rocking-chair. *[Takes her hands.]* Ah, now you look a bit more like your old self again. It was just that when I first saw you. . . . But you are a little paler, Kristine . . . and perhaps even a bit thinner!

Mrs. Linde: And much, much older, Nora.

Nora: Yes, perhaps a little older . . . very, very little, not really very much. *[Stops suddenly and looks serious.]* Oh, what a thoughtless creature I am, sitting here chattering on like this! Dear, sweet Kristine, can you forgive me?

Mrs. Linde: What do you mean, Nora?

Nora: *[gently]* Poor Kristine, of course you're a widow now.

Mrs. Linde: Yes, my husband died three years ago.

Nora: Oh, I remember now. I read about it in the papers. Oh, Kristine, believe me I often thought at the time of writing to you. But I kept putting it off, something always seemed to crop up.

Mrs. Linde: My dear Nora, I understand so well.

Nora: No, it wasn't very nice of me, Kristine. Oh, you poor

thing, what you must have gone through. And didn't he leave you anything?

Mrs. Linde: No.

Nora: And no children?

Mrs. Linde: No.

Nora: Absolutely nothing?

Mrs. Linde: Nothing at all . . . not even a broken heart to grieve over.

Nora: [looks at her incredulously] But, Kristine, is that possible?

Mrs. Linde: [smiles sadly and strokes Nora's *hair]* Oh, it sometimes happens, Nora.

Nora: So utterly alone. How terribly sad that must be for you. I have three lovely children. You can't see them for the moment, because they're out with their nanny. But now you must tell me all about yourself. . . .

Mrs. Linde: No, no, I want to hear about you.

Nora: No, you start. I won't be selfish today. I must think only about your affairs today. But there's just one thing I really must tell you. Have you heard about the great stroke of luck we've had in the last few days?

Mrs. Linde: No. What is it?

Nora: What do you think? My husband has just been made Bank Manager!

Mrs. Linde: Your husband? How splendid!

Nora: Isn't it tremendous! It's not a very steady way of making a living, you know, being a lawyer, especially if he refuses to take on anything that's the least bit shady—which of course is what Torvald does, and I think he's quite right. You can imagine how pleased we are! He starts at the Bank straight after New Year, and he's getting a big salary and lots of commission. From now on we'll be able to live quite differently . . . we'll do just what we want. Oh, Kristine, I'm so happy and relieved. I must say it's lovely to have plenty of money and not have to worry. Isn't it?

Mrs. Linde: Yes. It must be nice to have enough, at any rate.

Nora: No, not just enough, but pots and pots of money.

Mrs. Linde: [smiles] Nora, Nora, haven't you learned any sense yet? At school you used to be an awful spendthrift.

Nora: Yes, Torvald still says I am. *[Wags her finger.]* But little Nora isn't as stupid as everybody thinks. Oh, we haven't really been in a position where I could afford to spend a lot of money. We've both had to work.

Mrs. Linde: You too?

Nora: Yes, odd jobs—sewing, crochet-work, embroidery and things like that. *[Casually.]* And one or two other things, besides. I suppose you know that Torvald left the Ministry when we got married. There weren't any prospects of promotion in his department, and of course he needed to earn more money than he had before. But the first year he wore himself out completely. He had to take on all kinds of extra jobs, you know, and he found himself working all hours of the day and night. But he couldn't go on like that; and he became seriously ill. The doctors said it was essential for him to go South.

Mrs. Linde: Yes, I believe you spent a whole year in Italy, didn't you?

Nora: That's right. It wasn't easy to get away, I can tell you. It was just after I'd had Ivar. But of course we had to go. Oh, it was an absolutely marvellous trip. And it saved Torvald's life. But it cost an awful lot of money, Kristine.

Mrs. Linde: That I can well imagine.

Nora: Twelve hundred dollars. Four thousand eight hundred crowns. That's a lot of money, Kristine.

Mrs. Linde: Yes, but in such circumstances, one is very lucky if one has it.

Nora: Well, we got it from Daddy, you see.

Mrs. Linde: Ah, that was it. It was just about then your father died, I believe, wasn't it?

Nora: Yes, Kristine, just about then. And do you know, I couldn't even go and look after him. Here was I expecting Ivar any day. And I also had poor Torvald, gravely ill, on my hands. Dear, kind Daddy! I never saw him again, Kristine. Oh, that's the saddest thing that has happened to me in all my married life.

Mrs. Linde: I know you were very fond of him. But after that you left for Italy?

Nora: Yes, we had the money then, and the doctors said it was urgent. We left a month later.

Mrs. Linde: And your husband came back completely cured?

Nora: Fit as a fiddle!

Mrs. Linde: But . . . what about the doctor?

Nora: How do you mean?

Mrs. Linde: I thought the maid said something about the gentleman who came at the same time as me being a doctor.

Nora: Yes, that was Dr. Rank. But this isn't a professional visit. He's our best friend and he always looks in at least once a day. No, Torvald has never had a day's illness since. And the children are fit and healthy, and so am I. *[Jumps up and claps her hands.]* Oh God, oh God, isn't it marvellous to be alive, and to be happy, Kristine! . . . Oh, but I ought to be ashamed of myself . . . Here I go on talking about nothing but myself. *[She sits on a low stool near* Mrs. Linde *and lays her arms on her lap.]* Oh, please, you mustn't be angry with me! Tell me, is it really true that you didn't love your husband? What made you marry him, then?

Mrs. Linde: My mother was still alive; she was bedridden and help-less. And then I had my two young brothers to look after as well. I didn't think I would be justified in refusing him.

Nora: No, I dare say you are right. I suppose he was fairly wealthy then?

Mrs. Linde: He was quite well off, I believe. But the business was shaky. When he died, it went all to pieces, and there just wasn't anything left.

Nora: What then?

Mrs. Linde: Well, I had to fend for myself, opening a little shop, run-ning a little school, anything I could turn my hand to. These last three years have been one long relentless drudge. But now it's finished, Nora. My poor dear mother doesn't need me any more, she's passed away. Nor the boys either; they're at work now, they can look after themselves.

Nora: What a relief you must find it. . . .

Mrs. Linde: No, Nora! Just unutterably empty. Nobody to live for any more. *[Stands up restlessly.]* That's why I couldn't stand it any longer being cut off up there. Surely it must be a bit easier here to find something to occupy your mind. If only I could manage to find a steady job of some kind, in an office perhaps. . . .

Nora: But, Kristine, that's terribly exhausting; and you look so worn out even before you start. The best thing for you would be a little holiday at some quiet little resort.

Mrs. Linde: *[crosses to the window]* I haven't any father I can fall back on for the money, Nora.

Nora: *[rises]* Oh, please, you mustn't be angry with me!

Mrs. Linde: *[goes to her]* My dear Nora, you mustn't be angry with me either. That's the worst thing about people in my position, they become so bitter. One has nobody to work for, yet one has to be on the look-out all the time. Life has to go on, and one starts thinking only of oneself. Believe it or not, when you told me the good news about your step up, I was pleased not so much for your sake as for mine.

Nora: How do you mean? Ah, I see. You think Torvald might be able to do something for you.

Mrs. Linde: Yes, that's exactly what I thought.

Nora: And so he shall, Kristine. Just leave things to me. I'll bring it up so cleverly . . . I'll think up something to put him in a good mood. Oh, I do so much want to help you.

Mrs. Linde: It is awfully kind of you, Nora, offering to do all this for me, particularly in your case, where you haven't known much trouble or hardship in your own life.

Nora: When I . . . ? I haven't known much . . . ?

Mrs. Linde: *[smiling]* Well, good heavens, a little bit of sewing to do and a few things like that. What a child you are, Nora!

Nora: [*tosses her head and walks across the room*] I wouldn't be too
  sure of that, if I were you.
Mrs. Linde: Oh?
  Nora: You're just like the rest of them. You all think I'm useless
    when it comes to anything really serious. . . .
Mrs. Linde: Come, come. . . .
  Nora: You think I've never had anything much to contend with
    in this hard world.
Mrs. Linde: Nora dear, you've only just been telling me all the things
    you've had to put up with.
  Nora: Pooh! They were just trivialities! [*Softly.*] I haven't told
    you about the really big thing.
Mrs. Linde: What big thing? What do you mean?
  Nora: I know you rather tend to look down on me, Kristine.
    But you shouldn't, you know. You are proud of having
    worked so hard and so long for your mother.
Mrs. Linde: I'm sure I don't look down on anybody. But it's true
    what you say; I am both proud and happy when I think of
    how I was able to make Mother's life a little easier towards
    the end.
  Nora: And you are proud when you think of what you have
    done for your brothers, too.
Mrs. Linde: I think I have every right to be.
  Nora: I think so too. But now I'm going to tell you something,
    Kristine. I too have something to be proud and happy
    about.
Mrs. Linde: I don't doubt that. But what is it you mean?
  Nora: Not so loud. Imagine if Torvald were to hear! He must
    never on any account . . . nobody must know about it, Kris-
    tine, nobody but you.
Mrs. Linde: But what is it?
  Nora: Come over here. [*She pulls her down on the sofa beside
    her.*] Yes, Kristine, I too have something to be proud and
    happy about. I was the one who saved Torvald's life.
Mrs. Linde: Saved . . . ? How . . . ?
  Nora: I told you about our trip to Italy. Torvald would never
    have recovered but for that. . . .
Mrs. Linde: Well? Your father gave you what money was
    necessary. . . .
  Nora: [*smiles*] That's what Torvald thinks, and everybody else.
    But . . .
Mrs. Linde: But . . . ?
  Nora: Daddy never gave us a penny. I was the one who raised
    the money.
Mrs. Linde: You? All that money?
  Nora: Twelve hundred dollars. Four thousand eight hundred
    crowns. What do you say to that!

Mrs. Linde: But, Nora, how was it possible? Had you won a sweepstake or something?

Nora: [contemptuously] A sweepstake? Pooh! There would
have been nothing to it then.

Mrs. Linde: Where did you get it from, then?

Nora: [hums and smiles secretively] H'm, tra-la-la!

Mrs. Linde: Because what you couldn't do was borrow it.

Nora: Oh? Why not?

Mrs. Linde: Well, a wife can't borrow without her husband's consent.

Nora: [tossing her head] Ah, but when it happens to be a wife
with a bit of a sense for business . . . a wife who knows her
way about things, then. . . .

Mrs. Linde: But, Nora, I just don't understand. . . .

Nora: You don't have to. I haven't said I did borrow the
money. I might have got it some other way. [Throws herself
back on the sofa.] I might even have got it from some admirer.
Anyone as reasonably attractive as I am. . . .

Mrs. Linde: Don't be so silly!

Nora: Now you must be dying of curiosity, Kristine.

Mrs. Linde: Listen to me now, Nora dear—you haven't done anything rash, have you?

Nora: [sitting up again] Is it rash to save your husband's life?

Mrs. Linde: I think it was rash to do anything without telling him. . . .

Nora: But the whole point was that he mustn't know anything.
Good heavens, can't you see! He wasn't even supposed to
know how desperately ill he was. It was me the doctors came
and told his life was in danger, that the only way to save him
was to go South for a while. Do you think I didn't try talking
him into it first? I began dropping hints about how nice it
would be if I could be taken on a little trip abroad, like other
young wives. I wept, I pleaded. I told him he ought to show
some consideration for my condition, and let me have a bit of
my own way. And then I suggested he might take out a loan.
But at that he nearly lost his temper, Kristine. He said I was
being frivolous, that it was his duty as a husband not to give
in to all these whims and fancies of mine—as I do believe he
called them. All right, I thought, somehow you've got to be
saved. And it was then I found a way. . . .

Mrs. Linde: Did your husband never find out from your father that
the money hadn't come from him?

Nora: No, never. It was just about the time Daddy died. I'd
intended letting him into the secret and asking him not to
give me away. But when he was so ill . . . I'm sorry to say it
never became necessary.

Mrs. Linde: And you never confided in your husband?

Nora: Good heavens, how could you ever imagine such a thing!
When he's so strict about such matters! Besides, Torvald is a

man with a good deal of pride—it would be terribly embarrassing and humiliating for him if he thought he owed anything to me. It would spoil everything between us; this happy home of ours would never be the same again.

Mrs. Linde: Are you never going to tell him?

Nora: [reflectively, half-smiling] Oh yes, some day perhaps . . . in many years time, when I'm no longer as pretty as I am now. You mustn't laugh! What I mean of course is when Torvald isn't quite so much in love with me as he is now, when he's lost interest in watching me dance, or get dressed up, or recite. Then it might be a good thing to have something in reserve. . . . *[Breaks off.]* What nonsense! That day will never come. Well, what have you got to say to my big secret, Kristine? Still think I'm not much good for anything? One thing, though, it's meant a lot of worry for me, I can tell you. It hasn't always been easy to meet my obligations when the time came. You know in business there is something called quarterly interest, and other things called instalments, and these are always terribly difficult things to cope with. So what I've had to do is save a little here and there, you see, wherever I could. I couldn't really save anything out of the housekeeping, because Torvald has to live in decent style. I couldn't let the children go about badly dressed either—I felt any money I got for them had to go on them alone. Such sweet little things!

Mrs. Linde: Poor Nora! So it had to come out of your own allowance?

Nora: Of course. After all, I was the one it concerned most. Whenever Torvald gave me money for new clothes and suchlike, I never spent more than half. And always I bought the simplest and cheapest things. It's a blessing most things look well on me, so Torvald never noticed anything. But sometimes I did feel it was a bit hard, Kristine, because it is nice to be well dressed, isn't it?

Mrs. Linde: Yes, I suppose it is.

Nora: I have had some other sources of income, of course. Last winter I was lucky enough to get quite a bit of copying to do. So I shut myself up every night and sat and wrote through to the small hours of the morning. Oh, sometimes I was so tired, so tired. But it was tremendous fun all the same, sitting there working and earning money like that. It was almost like being a man.

Mrs. Linde: And how much have you been able to pay off like this?

Nora: Well, I can't tell exactly. It's not easy to know where you are with transactions of this kind, you understand. All I know is I've paid off just as much as I could scrape together.

Many's the time I was at my wit's end. *[Smiles.]* Then I used to sit here and pretend that some rich old gentleman had fallen in love with me. . . .

Mrs. Linde: What! What gentleman?

Nora: Oh, rubbish! . . . and that now he had died, and when they opened his will, there in big letters were the words: 'My entire fortune is to be paid over, immediately and in cash, to charming Mrs. Nora Helmer.'

Mrs. Linde: But my dear Nora—who *is* this man?

Nora: Good heavens, don't you understand? There never was any old gentleman; it was just something I used to sit here pretending, time and time again, when I didn't know where to turn next for money. But it doesn't make very much difference; as far as I'm concerned, the old boy can do what he likes, I'm tired of him; I can't be bothered any more with him or his will. Because now all my worries are over. *[Jumping up.]* Oh God, what a glorious thought, Kristine! No more worries! Just think of being without a care in the world . . . being able to romp with the children, and making the house nice and attractive, and having things just as Torvald likes to have them! And then spring will soon be here, and blue skies. And maybe we can go away somewhere. I might even see something of the sea again. Oh yes! When you're happy, life is a wonderful thing!

[The door-bell is heard in the hall.]

Mrs. Linde: *[gets up]* There's the bell. Perhaps I'd better go.

Nora: No, do stay, please. I don't suppose it's for me; it's probably somebody for Torvald. . . .

Maid: *[in the doorway]* Excuse me, ma'am, but there's a gentleman here wants to see Mr. Helmer, and I didn't quite know . . . because the Doctor is in there. . . .

Nora: Who is the gentleman?

Krogstad: *[in the doorway]* It's me, Mrs. Helmer.

[Mrs. Linde starts, then turns away to the window.]

Nora: *[tense, takes a step towards him and speaks in a low voice]* You? What is it? What do you want to talk to my husband about?

Krogstad: Bank matters . . . in a manner of speaking. I work at the bank, and I hear your husband is to be the new manager. . . .

Nora: So it's . . .

Krogstad: Just routine business matters, Mrs. Helmer. Absolutely nothing else.

Nora: Well then, please go into his study.

[She nods impassively and shuts the hall door behind him; then she walks across and sees to the stove.]

Mrs. Linde: Nora . . . who was that man?

Nora: His name is Krogstad.

Mrs. Linde: So it really was him.

Nora: Do you know the man?

Mrs. Linde: I used to know him . . . a good many years ago. He was a solicitor's clerk in our district for a while.

Nora: Yes, so he was.

Mrs. Linde: How he's changed!

Nora: His marriage wasn't a very happy one, I believe.

Mrs. Linde: He's a widower now, isn't he?

Nora: With a lot of children. There, it'll burn better now.

[She closes the stove door and moves the rocking chair a little to one side.]

Mrs. Linde: He does a certain amount of business on the side, they say?

Nora: Oh? Yes, it's always possible. I just don't know. . . . But let's not think about business . . . it's all so dull.

[Dr. Rank comes in from Helmer's study.]

Dr. Rank: *[still in the doorway]* No, no, Torvald, I won't intrude. I'll just look in on your wife for a moment. *[Shuts the door and notices Mrs. Linde.]* Oh, I beg your pardon. I'm afraid I'm intruding here as well.

Nora: No, not at all! *[Introduces them.]* Dr. Rank . . . Mrs. Linde.

Rank: Ah! A name I've often heard mentioned in this house. I believe I came past you on the stairs as I came in.

Mrs. Linde: I have to take things slowly going upstairs. I find it rather a trial.

Rank: Ah, some little disability somewhere, eh?

Mrs. Linde: Just a bit run down, I think, actually.

Rank: Is that all? Then I suppose you've come to town for a good rest—doing the rounds of the parties?

Mrs. Linde: I have come to look for work.

Rank: Is that supposed to be some kind of sovereign remedy for being run down?

Mrs. Linde: One must live, Doctor.

Rank: Yes, it's generally thought to be necessary.

Nora: Come, come, Dr. Rank. You are quite as keen to live as anybody.

Rank: Quite keen, yes. Miserable as I am, I'm quite ready to let things drag on as long as possible. All my patients are the same. Even those with a moral affliction are no different.

As a matter of fact, there's a bad case of that kind in talking with Helmer at this very moment. . . .

Mrs. Linde: [softly] Ah!

Nora: Whom do you mean?

Rank: A person called Krogstad—nobody you would know. He's rotten to the core. But even he began talking about having to *live*, as though it were something terribly important.

Nora: Oh? And what did he want to talk to Torvald about?

Rank: I honestly don't know. All I heard was something about the Bank.

Nora: I didn't know that Krog . . . that this Mr. Krogstad had anything to do with the Bank.

Rank: Oh yes, he's got some kind of job down there. *[To* Mrs. Linde.*]* I wonder if you've got people in your part of the country too who go rushing round sniffing out cases of moral corruption, and then installing the individuals concerned in nice, well-paid jobs where they can keep them under observation. Sound, decent people have to be content to stay out in the cold.

Mrs. Linde: Yet surely it's the sick who most need to be brought in.

Rank: [shrugs his shoulders] Well, there we have it. It's that attitude that's turning society into a clinic.

[Nora, lost in her own thoughts, breaks into smothered laughter and claps her hands.]

Rank: Why are you laughing at that? Do you know in fact what society is?

Nora: What do I care about your silly old society? I was laughing about something quite different . . . something frightfully funny. Tell me, Dr. Rank, are all the people who work at the Bank dependent on Torvald now?

Rank: Is *that* what you find so frightfully funny?

Nora: [smiles and hums] Never you mind! Never you mind! *[Walks about the room.]* Yes, it really is terribly amusing to think that we . . . that Torvald now has power over so many people. *[She takes the bag out of her pocket.]* Dr. Rank, what about a little macaroon?

Rank: Look at this, eh? Macaroons. I thought they were forbidden here.

Nora: Yes, but these are some Kristine gave me.

Mrs. Linde: What? I . . . ?

Nora: Now, now, you needn't be alarmed. You weren't to know that Torvald had forbidden them. He's worried in case they ruin my teeth, you know. Still . . . what's it matter once in a while! Don't you think so, Dr. Rank? Here! *[She pops a mac-*

aroon into his mouth.] And you too, Kristine. And I shall have one as well; just a little one . . . or two at the most. *[She walks about the room again.]* Really I am so happy. There's just one little thing I'd love to do now.

Rank: What's that?

Nora: Something I'd love to say in front of Torvald.

Rank: Then why can't you?

Nora: No, I daren't. It's not very nice.

Mrs. Linde: Not very nice?

Rank: Well, in that case it might not be wise. But to us, I don't see why. . . . What is this you would love to say in front of Helmer?

Nora: I would simply love to say: 'Damn'.

Rank: Are you mad!

Mrs. Linde: Good gracious, Nora. . . !

Rank: Say it! Here he is!

Nora: *[hiding the bag of macaroons]* Sh! Sh!

*[*Helmer *comes out of his room, his overcoat over his arm and his hat in his hand.]*

Nora: *[going over to him]* Well, Torvald dear, did you get rid of him?

Helmer: Yes, he's just gone.

Nora: Let me introduce you. This is Kristine, who has just arrived in town. . . .

Helmer: Kristine. . . ? You must forgive me, but I don't think I know . . .

Nora: Mrs. Linde, Torvald dear. Kristine Linde.

Helmer: Ah, indeed. A school-friend of my wife's, presumably.

Mrs. Linde: Yes, we were girls together.

Nora: Fancy, Torvald, she's come all this long way just to have a word with you.

Helmer: How is that?

Mrs. Linde: Well, it wasn't really. . . .

Nora: The thing is, Kristine is terribly clever at office work, and she's frightfully keen on finding a job with some efficient man, so that she can learn even more. . . .

Helmer: Very sensible, Mrs. Linde.

Nora: And then when she heard you'd been made Bank Manager—there was a bit in the paper about it—she set off at once. Torvald please! You *will* try and do something for Kristine, won't you? For my sake?

Helmer: Well, that's not altogether impossible. You are a widow, I presume?

Mrs. Linde: Yes.

Helmer: And you've had some experience in business?

Mrs. Linde: A fair amount.

Helmer: Well, it's quite probable I can find you a job, I think. . . .

Nora: [clapping her hands] There, you see!

Helmer: You have come at a fortunate moment, Mrs. Linde. . . .

Mrs. Linde: Oh, how can I ever thank you. . . ?

Helmer: Not a bit. [He puts on his overcoat.] But for the present I must ask you to excuse me. . . .

Rank: Wait. I'm coming with you.

[He fetches his fur coat from the hall and warms it at the stove.]

Nora: Don't be long, Torvald dear.

Helmer: Not more than an hour, that's all.

Nora: Are you leaving too, Kristine?

Mrs. Linde: [putting on her things] Yes, I must go and see if I can't find myself a room.

Helmer: Perhaps we can all walk down the road together.

Nora: [helping her] What a nuisance we are so limited for space here. I'm afraid it just isn't possible. . . .

Mrs. Linde: Oh, you mustn't dream of it! Goodbye, Nora dear, and thanks for everything.

Nora: Goodbye for the present. But . . . you'll be coming back this evening, of course. And you too, Dr. Rank? What's that? If you are up to it? Of course you'll be up to it. Just wrap yourself up well.

[They go out, talking, into the hall; children's voices can be heard on the stairs.]

Nora: Here they are! Here they are! [She runs to the front door and opens it. Anne Marie, the Nursemaid, enters with the children.] Come in! Come in! [She bends down and kisses them.] Ah! my sweet little darlings. . . . You see them, Kristine? Aren't they lovely!

Rank: Don't stand here chattering in this draught!

Helmer: Come along, Mrs. Linde. The place now becomes unbearable for anybody except mothers.

[Dr. Rank, Helmer and Mrs. Linde go down the stairs: the Nursemaid comes into the room with the children, then Nora, shutting the door behind her.]

Nora: How fresh and bright you look! My, what red cheeks you've got! Like apples and roses. [During the following, the children keep chattering away to her.] Have you had a nice time? That's splendid. And you gave Emmy and Bob a ride on your sledge? Did you now! Both together! Fancy that! There's a clever boy, Ivar. Oh, let me take her a little while, Anne Marie. There's my sweet little baby-doll! [She takes the youngest of the children from the Nursemaid and dances with her.] All right, Mummy will dance with Bobby too. What? You've been throwing snowballs? Oh, I wish I'd been there.

No, don't bother, Anne Marie, I'll help them off with their things. No, please, let me—I like doing it. You go on in, you look frozen. You'll find some hot coffee on the stove. *[The Nursemaid goes into the room, left. Nora takes off the children's coats and hats and throws them down anywhere, while the children all talk at once.]* Really! A great big dog came running after you? But he didn't bite. No, the doggies wouldn't bite my pretty little dollies. You mustn't touch the parcels, Ivar! What are they? Wouldn't you like to know! No, no, that's nasty. Now? Shall we play something? What shall we play? Hide and seek? Yes, let's play hide and seek. Bob can hide first. Me first? All right, let me hide first.

[She and the children play, laughing and shrieking, in this room and in the adjacent room on the right. Finally Nora hides under the table; the children come rushing in to look for her but cannot find her; they hear her stifled laughter, rush to the table, lift up the tablecloth and find her. Tremendous shouts of delight. She creeps out and pretends to frighten them. More shouts. Meanwhile there has been a knock at the front door, which nobody has heard. The door half opens, and Krogstad can be seen. He waits a little; the game continues.]

Krogstad: I beg your pardon, Mrs. Helmer. . . .

Nora: *[turns with a stifled cry and half jumps up]* Ah! What do you want?

Krogstad: Excuse me. The front door was standing open. Somebody must have forgotten to shut it. . . .

Nora: *[standing up]* My husband isn't at home, Mr. Krogstad.

Krogstad: I know.

Nora: Well . . . what are you doing here?

Krogstad: I want a word with you.

Nora: With . . . ? *[Quietly, to the children.]* Go to Anne Marie. What? No, the strange man won't do anything to Mummy. When he's gone we'll have another game. *[She leads the children into the room, left, and shuts the door after them; tense and uneasy.]* You want to speak to me?

Krogstad: Yes, I do.

Nora: Today? But it isn't the first of the month yet. . . .

Krogstad: No, it's Christmas Eve. It depends entirely on you what sort of Christmas you have.

Nora: What do you want? Today I can't possibly . . .

Krogstad: Let's not talk about that for the moment. It's something else. You've got a moment to spare?

Nora: Yes, I suppose so, though . . .

Krogstad: Good. I was sitting in Olsen's café, and I saw your husband go down the road . . .

Nora: Did you?

Krogstad: . . . with a lady.

Nora: Well?

Krogstad: May I be so bold as to ask whether that lady was a Mrs. Linde?

Nora: Yes.

Krogstad: Just arrived in town?

Nora: Yes, today.

Krogstad: And she's a good friend of yours?

Nora: Yes, she is. But I can't see . . .

Krogstad: I also knew her once.

Nora: I know.

Krogstad: Oh? So you know all about it. I thought as much. Well, I want to ask you straight: is Mrs. Linde getting a job in the Bank?

Nora: How dare you cross-examine me like this, Mr. Krogstad? You, one of my husband's subordinates? But since you've asked me, I'll tell you. Yes, Mrs. Linde *has* got a job. And I'm the one who got it for her, Mr. Krogstad. Now you know.

Krogstad: So my guess was right.

Nora: [*walking up and down*] Oh, I think I can say that some of us have a little influence now and again. Just because one happens to be a woman, that doesn't mean. . . . People in subordinate positions ought to take care they don't offend anybody . . . who . . . hm . . .

Krogstad: . . . has influence?

Nora: Exactly.

Krogstad: [*changing his tone*] Mrs. Helmer, will you have the goodness to use your influence on my behalf?

Nora: What? What do you mean?

Krogstad: Will you be so good as to see that I keep my modest little job at the Bank?

Nora: What do you mean? Who wants to take it away from you?

Krogstad: Oh, you needn't try and pretend to me you don't know. I can quite see that this friend of yours isn't particularly anxious to bump up against me. And I can also see now whom I can thank for being given the sack.

Nora: But I assure you. . . .

Krogstad: All right, all right. But to come to the point: there's still time. And I advise you to use your influence to stop it.

Nora: But, Mr. Krogstad, I *have* no influence.

Krogstad: Haven't you? I thought just now you said yourself . . .

Nora: I didn't mean it that way, of course. Me? What makes you think I've got any influence of that kind over my husband?

Krogstad: I know your husband from our student days. I don't suppose he is any more steadfast than other married men.

Nora: You speak disrespectfully of my husband like that and I'll show you the door.

Krogstad: So the lady's got courage.

Nora: I'm not frightened of you any more. After New Year I'll soon be finished with the whole business.

Krogstad: [*controlling himself*] Listen to me, Mrs. Helmer. If necessary I shall fight for my little job in the Bank as if I were fighting for my life.

Nora: So it seems.

Krogstad: It's not just for the money, that's the last thing I care about. There's something else . . . well, I might as well out with it. You see it's like this. You know as well as anybody that some years ago I got myself mixed up in a bit of trouble.

Nora: I believe I've heard something of the sort.

Krogstad: It never got as far as the courts; but immediately it was as if all paths were barred to me. So I started going in for the sort of business you know about. I had to do something, and I think I can say I haven't been one of the worst. But now I have to get out of it. My sons are growing up; for their sake I must try and win back what respectability I can. That job in the Bank was like the first step on the ladder for me. And now your husband wants to kick me off the ladder again, back into the mud.

Nora: But in God's name, Mr. Krogstad, it's quite beyond my power to help you.

Krogstad: That's because you haven't the will to help me. But I have ways of making you.

Nora: You wouldn't go and tell my husband I owe you money?

Krogstad: Suppose I did tell him?

Nora: It would be a rotten shame. [*Half choking with tears.*] That secret is all my pride and joy—why should he have to hear about it in this nasty, horrid way . . . hear about it from *you.* You would make things horribly unpleasant for. . . .

Krogstad: Merely unpleasant?

Nora: [*vehemently*] Go on, do it then! It'll be all the worse for you. Because then my husband will see for himself what a bad man you are, and then you certainly won't be able to keep your job.

Krogstad: I asked whether it was only a bit of domestic unpleasantness you were afraid of?

Nora: If my husband gets to know about it, he'll pay off what's owing at once. And then we'd have nothing more to do with you.

Krogstad: [*taking a pace towards her*] Listen, Mrs. Helmer, either you haven't a very good memory, or else you don't understand much about business. I'd better make the position a little bit clearer for you.

Nora: How do you mean?

Krogstad: When your husband was ill, you came to me for the loan of twelve hundred dollars.

Nora: I didn't know of anybody else.

Krogstad: I promised to find you the money. . . .

Nora: And you did find it.

Krogstad: I promised to find you the money on certain conditions. At the time you were so concerned about your husband's illness, and so anxious to get the money for going away with, that I don't think you paid very much attention to all the incidentals. So there is perhaps some point in reminding you of them. Well, I promised to find you the money against an IOU which I drew up for you.

Nora: Yes, and which I signed.

Krogstad: Very good. But below that I added a few lines, by which your father was to stand security. This your father was to sign.

Nora: Was to . . . ? He did sign it.

Krogstad: I had left the date blank. The idea was that your father was to add the date himself when he signed it. Remember?

Nora: Yes, I think. . . .

Krogstad: I then gave you the IOU to post to your father. Wasn't that so?

Nora: Yes.

Krogstad: Which of course you did at once. Because only about five or six days later you brought it back to me with your father's signature. I then paid out the money.

Nora: Well? Haven't I paid the instalments regularly?

Krogstad: Yes, fairly. But . . . coming back to what we were talking about . . . that was a pretty bad period you were going through then, Mrs. Helmer.

Nora: Yes, it was.

Krogstad: Your father was seriously ill, I believe.

Nora: He was very near the end.

Krogstad: And died shortly afterwards?

Nora: Yes.

Krogstad: Tell me, Mrs. Helmer, do you happen to remember which day your father died? The exact date, I mean.

Nora: Daddy died on 29 September.

Krogstad: Quite correct. I made some inquiries. Which brings up a rather curious point *[takes out a paper]* which I simply cannot explain.

Nora: Curious . . . ? I don't know . . .

Krogstad: The curious thing is, Mrs. Helmer, that your father signed this document three days after his death.

Nora: What? I don't understand. . . .

Krogstad: Your father died on 29 September. But look here. Your father has dated his signature 2 October. Isn't that rather curious, Mrs. Helmer? [Nora *remains silent.*] It's also remarkable that the words '2 October' and the year are not in your father's handwriting, but in a handwriting I rather think I recognize. Well, perhaps that could be explained. Your father might have forgotten to date his signature, and then somebody else might have made a guess at the date later, before the fact of your father's death was known. There is nothing wrong in that. What really matters is the signature. And *that* is of course genuine, Mrs. Helmer? It really was your father who wrote his name here?

Nora: [after a moment's silence, throws her head back and looks at him defiantly] No, it wasn't. It was me who signed father's name.

Krogstad: Listen to me. I suppose you realize that that is a very dangerous confession?

Nora: Why? You'll soon have all your money back.

Krogstad: Let me ask you a question: why didn't you send that document to your father?

Nora: It was impossible. Daddy was ill. If I'd asked him for his signature, I'd have had to tell him what the money was for. Don't you see, when he was as ill as that I couldn't go and tell him that my husband's life was in danger. It was simply impossible.

Krogstad: It would have been better for you if you had abandoned the whole trip.

Nora: No, that was impossible. This was the thing that was to save my husband's life. I couldn't give it up.

Krogstad: But did it never strike you that this was fraudulent . . . ?

Nora: That wouldn't have meant anything to me. Why should I worry about you? I couldn't stand you, not when you insisted on going through with all those cold-blooded formalities, knowing all the time what a critical state my husband was in.

Krogstad: Mrs. Helmer, it's quite clear you still haven't the faintest idea what it is you've committed. But let me tell you, my own offence was no more and no worse than that, and it ruined my entire reputation.

Nora: You? Are you trying to tell me that you once risked everything to save your wife's life?

Krogstad: The law takes no account of motives.

Nora: Then they must be very bad laws.

Krogstad: Bad or not, if I produce this document in court, you'll be condemned according to them.

Nora: I don't believe it. Isn't a daughter entitled to try and save her father from worry and anxiety on his deathbed? Isn't a wife entitled to save her husband's life? I might not know very much about the law, but I feel sure of one thing: it must say somewhere that things like this are allowed. You mean to say you don't know that—you, when it's your job? You must be a rotten lawyer, Mr. Krogstad.

Krogstad: That may be. But when it comes to business transactions —like the sort between us two—perhaps you'll admit I know something about *them*? Good. Now you must please your-self. But I tell you this: if I'm pitched out a second time, you are going to keep me company.

[He bows and goes out through the hall.]

Nora: [stands thoughtfully for a moment, then tosses her head] Rub-bish! He's just trying to scare me. I'm not such a fool as all that. *[Begins gathering up the children's clothes; after a moment she stops.]* Yet . . . ? No, it's impossible! I did it for love, didn't I?

The Children: [in the doorway, left] Mummy, the gentleman's just gone out of the gate.

Nora: Yes, I know. But you mustn't say anything to anybody about that gentleman. You hear? Not even to Daddy!

The Children: All right, Mummy. Are you going to play again?

Nora: No, not just now.

The Children: But Mummy, you promised!

Nora: Yes, but I can't just now. Off you go now, I have a lot to do. Off you go, my darlings. *[She herds them carefully into the other room and shuts the door behind them. She sits down on the sofa, picks up her embroidery and works a few stitches, but soon stops.]* No! *[She flings her work down, stands up, goes to the hall door and calls out.]* Helene! Fetch the tree in for me, please. *[She walks across to the table, left, and opens the drawer; again pauses.]* No, really, it's quite impossible!

Maid: [with the Christmas tree] Where shall I put it, ma'am?

Nora: On the floor there, in the middle.

Maid: Anything else you want me to bring?

Nora: No, thank you. I've got what I want.

[The Maid *has put the tree down and goes out.]*

Nora: [busy decorating the tree] Candles here . . . and flowers here.—Revolting man! It's all nonsense! There's nothing to worry about. We'll have a lovely Christmas tree. And I'll do anything you want me to, Torvald; I'll sing for you, dance for you. . . .

[Helmer, *with a bundle of documents under his arm, comes in by the hall door.*]

Nora: Ah, back again already?

Helmer: Yes. Anybody been?

Nora: Here? No.

Helmer: That's funny. I just saw Krogstad leave the house.

Nora: Oh? O yes, that's right. Krogstad was here a minute.

Helmer: Nora, I can tell by your face he's been asking you to put a good word in for him.

Nora: Yes.

Helmer: And you were to pretend it was your own idea? You were to keep quiet about his having been here. He asked you to do that as well, didn't he?

Nora: Yes, Torvald. But . . .

Helmer: Nora, Nora, what possessed you to do a thing like that? Talking to a person like him, making him promises? And then on top of everything, to tell me a lie!

Nora: A lie . . . ?

Helmer: Didn't you say that nobody had been here? *[Wagging his finger at her.]* Never again must my little song-bird do a thing like that! Little song-birds must keep their pretty little beaks out of mischief; no chirruping out of tune! *[Puts his arm round her waist.]* Isn't that the way we want things to be? Yes, of course it is. *[Lets her go.]* So let's say no more about it. *[Sits down by the stove.]* Ah, nice and cosy here!

[He glances through his papers.]

Nora: *[busy with the Christmas tree, after a short pause]* Torvald!

Helmer: Yes.

Nora: I'm so looking forward to the fancy dress ball at the Stenborgs on Boxing Day.

Helmer: And I'm terribly curious to see what sort of surprise you've got for me.

Nora: Oh, it's too silly.

Helmer: Oh?

Nora: I just can't think of anything suitable. Everything seems so absurd, so pointless.

Helmer: Has my little Nora come to *that* conclusion?

Nora: *[behind his chair, her arms on the chairback]* Are you very busy, Torvald?

Helmer: Oh. . . .

Nora: What are all those papers?

Helmer: Bank matters.

Nora: Already?

Helmer: I have persuaded the retiring manager to give me authority to make any changes in organization or personnel I think necessary. I have to work on it over the Christmas week. I want everything straight by the New Year.

Nora: So that was why that poor Krogstad. . . .

Helmer: Hm!

Nora: [*still leaning against the back of the chair, running her fingers through his hair*] If you hadn't been so busy, Torvald, I'd have asked you to do me an awfully big favour.

Helmer: Let me hear it. What's it to be?

Nora: Nobody's got such good taste as you. And the thing is I do so want to look my best at the fancy dress ball. Torvald, couldn't you give me some advice and tell me what you think I ought to go as, and how I should arrange my costume?

Helmer: Aha! So my impulsive little woman is asking for somebody to come to her rescue, eh?

Nora: Please, Torvald, I never get anywhere without your help.

Helmer: Very well, I'll think about it. We'll find something.

Nora: That's sweet of you. [*She goes across to the tree again; pause.*] How pretty these red flowers look.—Tell me, was it really something terribly wrong this man Krogstad did?

Helmer: Forgery. Have you any idea what that means?

Nora: Perhaps circumstances left him no choice?

Helmer: Maybe. Or perhaps, like so many others, he just didn't think. I am not so heartless that I would necessarily want to condemn a man for a single mistake like that.

Nora: Oh no, Torvald, of course not!

Helmer: Many a man might be able to redeem himself, if he honestly confessed his guilt and took his punishment.

Nora: Punishment?

Helmer: But that wasn't the way Krogstad chose. He dodged what was due to him by a cunning trick. And that's what has been the cause of his corruption.

Nora: Do you think it would . . . ?

Helmer: Just think how a man with a thing like that on his conscience will always be having to lie and cheat and dissemble; he can never drop the mask, not even with his own wife and children. And the children—*that's* the most terrible part of it, Nora.

Nora: Why?

Helmer: A fog of lies like that in a household, and it spreads disease and infection to every part of it. Every breath the children take in that kind of house is reeking with evil germs.

Nora: [*closer behind him*] Are you sure of that?

Helmer: My dear Nora, as a lawyer I know what I'm talking

about. Practically all juvenile delinquents come from homes where the mother is dishonest.

Nora: Why mothers particularly?

Helmer: It's generally traceable to the mothers, but of course fathers can have the same influence. Every lawyer knows that only too well. And yet there's Krogstad been poisoning his own children for years with lies and deceit. That's the reason I call him morally depraved. *[Holds out his hands to her.]* That's why my sweet little Nora must promise me not to try putting in any more good words for him. Shake hands on it. Well? What's this? Give me your hand. There now! That's settled. I assure you I would have found it impossible to work with him. I quite literally feel physically sick in the presence of such people.

Nora: *[draws her hand away and walks over to the other side of the Christmas tree]* How hot it is in here! And I still have such a lot to do.

Helmer: *[stands up and collects his papers together]* Yes, I'd better think of getting some of this read before dinner. I must also think about your costume. And I might even be able to lay my hands on something to wrap in gold paper and hang on the Christmas tree. *[He lays his hand on her head.]* My precious little singing bird.

[He goes into his study and shuts the door behind him.]

Nora: *[quietly, after a pause]* Nonsense! It can't be. It's impossible. It *must* be impossible.

Nursemaid: *[in the doorway, left]* The children keep asking so nicely if they can come in and see Mummy.

Nora: No, no, don't let them in! You stay with them, Anne Marie.

Nursemaid: Very well, ma'am.

[She shuts the door.]

Nora: *[pale with terror]* Corrupt my children . . . ! Poison my home? *[Short pause; she throws back her head.]* It's not true! It could never, never be true!

ACT II

The same room. In the corner beside the piano stands the Christmas tree, stripped, bedraggled and with its candles burnt out. Nora's outdoor things lie on the sofa. Nora, alone there, walks about restlessly; at last she stops by the sofa and picks up her coat.

Nora: *[putting her coat down again]* Somebody's coming! *[Crosses to the door, listens.]* No, it's nobody. Nobody will come today, of course, Christmas Day—nor tomorrow, either. But perhaps. . . . *[She opens the door and looks out.]* No, nothing in the letter box; quite empty. *[Comes forward.]* Oh, nonsense! He didn't mean it seriously. Things like that *can't* happen. It's impossible. Why, I have three small children.

[The Nursemaid *comes from the room, left, carrying a big cardboard box.]*

Nursemaid: I finally found it, the box with the fancy dress costumes.

Nora: Thank you. Put it on the table, please.

Nursemaid: [does this] But I'm afraid they are in an awful mess.

Nora: Oh, if only I could rip them up into a thousand pieces!

Nursemaid: Good heavens, they can be mended all right, with a bit of patience.

Nora: Yes, I'll go over and get Mrs. Linde to help me.

Nursemaid: Out again? In this terrible weather? You'll catch your death of cold, ma'am.

Nora: Oh, worse things might happen.—How are the children?

Nursemaid: Playing with their Christmas presents, poor little things, but . . .

Nora: Do they keep asking for me?

Nursemaid: They are so used to being with their Mummy.

Nora: Yes, Anne Marie, from now on I can't be with them as often as I was before.

Nursemaid: Ah well, children get used to anything in time.

Nora: Do you think so? Do you think they would forget their Mummy if she went away for good?

Nursemaid: Good gracious—for good?

Nora: Tell me, Anne Marie—I've often wondered—how on earth could you bear to hand your child over to strangers?

Nursemaid: Well, there was nothing else for it when I had to come and nurse my little Nora.

Nora: Yes but . . . how could you *bring* yourself to do it?

Nursemaid: When I had the chance of such a good place? When a poor girl's been in trouble she must make the best of things. Because *he* didn't help, the rotter.

Nora: But your daughter will have forgotten you.

Nursemaid: Oh no, she hasn't. She wrote to me when she got confirmed, and again when she got married.

Nora: [putting her arms round her neck] Dear old Anne Marie, you were a good mother to me when I was little.

Nursemaid: My poor little Nora never had any other mother but me.

Nora: And if my little ones only had you, I know you would. . . . Oh, what am I talking about! *[She opens the box.]* Go in to them. I must . . . Tomorrow I'll let you see how pretty I am going to look.

Nursemaid: Ah, there'll be nobody at the ball as pretty as my Nora.

[She goes into the room, left.]

> *Nora: [begins unpacking the box, but soon throws it down]* Oh, if only I dare go out. If only I could be sure nobody would come. And that nothing would happen in the meantime here at home. Rubbish—nobody's going to come. I mustn't think about it. Brush this muff. Pretty gloves, pretty gloves! I'll put it right out of my mind. One, two, three, four, five, six. . . . *[Screams.]* Ah, they are coming. . . . *[She starts towards the door, but stops irresolute. Mrs. Linde comes from the hall, where she has taken off her things.]* Oh, it's you, Kristine. There's nobody else out there, is there? I'm so glad you've come.

Mrs. Linde: I heard you'd been over looking for me.

> *Nora:* Yes, I was just passing. There's something you must help me with. Come and sit beside me on the sofa here. You see, the Stenborgs are having a fancy dress party upstairs tomorrow evening, and now Torvald wants me to go as a Neapolitan fisher lass and dance the tarantella. I learned it in Capri, you know.

Mrs. Linde: Well, well! So you are going to do a party piece?

> *Nora:* Torvald says I should. Look, here's the costume, Torvald had it made for me down there. But it's got all torn and I simply don't know. . . .

Mrs. Linde: We'll soon have that put right. It's only the trimming come away here and there. Got a needle and thread? Ah, here's what we are after.

> *Nora:* It's awfully kind of you.

Mrs. Linde: So you are going to be all dressed up tomorrow, Nora? Tell you what—I'll pop over for a minute to see you in all your finery. But I'm quite forgetting to thank you for the pleasant time we had last night.

> *Nora: [gets up and walks across the room]* Somehow I didn't think yesterday was as nice as things generally are.—You should have come to town a little earlier, Kristine.—Yes, Torvald certainly knows how to make things pleasant about the place.

Mrs. Linde: You too, I should say. You are not your father's daughter for nothing. But tell me, is Dr. Rank always as depressed as he was last night?

> *Nora:* No, last night it was rather obvious. He's got something seriously wrong with him, you know. Tuberculosis of the spine, poor fellow. His father was a horrible man, who used to have mistresses and things like that. That's why the son was always ailing, right from being a child.

Mrs. Linde: [lowering her sewing] But my dear Nora, how do you come to know about things like that?

Nora: [walking about the room] Huh! When you've got three children, you get these visits from . . . women who have had a certain amount of medical training. And you hear all sorts of things from them.

Mrs. Linde: [begins sewing again; short silence] Does Dr. Rank call in every day?

Nora: Every single day. He was Torvald's best friend as a boy, and he's a good friend of *mine,* too. Dr. Rank is almost like one of the family.

Mrs. Linde: But tell me—is he really genuine? What I mean is: doesn't he sometimes rather turn on the charm?

Nora: No, on the contrary. What makes you think that?

Mrs. Linde: When you introduced me yesterday, he claimed he'd often heard my name in this house. But afterwards I noticed your husband hadn't the faintest idea who I was. Then how is it that Dr. Rank should. . . .

Nora: Oh yes, it was quite right what he said, Kristine. You see Torvald is so terribly in love with me that he says he wants me all to himself. When we were first married, it even used to make him sort of jealous if I only as much as mentioned any of my old friends from back home. So of course I stopped doing it. But I often talk to Dr. Rank about such things. He likes hearing about them.

Mrs. Linde: Listen, Nora! In lots of ways you are still a child. Now, I'm a good deal older than you, and a bit more experienced. I'll tell you something: I think you ought to give up all this business with Dr. Rank.

Nora: Give up what business?

Mrs. Linde: The whole thing, I should say. Weren't you saying yesterday something about a rich admirer who was to provide you with money. . . .

Nora: One who's never existed, I regret to say. But what of it?

Mrs. Linde: Has Dr. Rank money?

Nora: Yes, he has.

Mrs. Linde: And no dependents?

Nora: No, nobody. But . . . ?

Mrs. Linde: And he comes to the house every day?

Nora: Yes, I told you.

Mrs. Linde: But how can a man of his position want to pester you like this?

Nora: I simply don't understand.

Mrs. Linde: Don't pretend, Nora. Do you think I don't see now who you borrowed the twelve hundred from?

Nora: Are you out of your mind? Do you really think that? A friend of ours who comes here every day? The whole situation would have been absolutely intolerable.

Mrs. Linde: It *really* isn't him?

Nora: No, I give you my word. It would never have occurred to me for one moment. . . . Anyway, he didn't have the money to lend then. He didn't inherit it till later.

Mrs. Linde: Just as well for you, I'd say, my dear Nora.

Nora: No, it would never have occurred to me to ask Dr. Rank. . . . All the same I'm pretty certain if I were to ask him . . .

Mrs. Linde: But of course you won't.

Nora: No, of course not. I can't ever imagine it being necessary. But I'm quite certain if ever I were to mention it to Dr. Rank. . . .

Mrs. Linde: Behind your husband's back?

Nora: I have to get myself out of that other business. That's also behind his back. I *must* get myself out of that.

Mrs. Linde: Yes, that's what I said yesterday. But . . .

Nora: [walking up and down] A man's better at coping with these things than a woman. . . .

Mrs. Linde: Your own husband, yes.

Nora: Nonsense! [Stops.] When you've paid everything you owe, you do get your IOU back again, don't you?

Mrs. Linde: Of course.

Nora: And you can tear it up into a thousand pieces and burn it —the nasty, filthy thing!

Mrs. Linde: [looking fixedly at her, puts down her sewing and slowly rises] Nora, you are hiding something from me.

Nora: Is it so obvious?

Mrs. Linde: Something has happened to you since yesterday morning. Nora, what is it?

Nora: [going towards her] Kristine! [Listens.] Hush! There's Torvald back. Look, you go and sit in there beside the children for the time being. Torvald can't stand the sight of mending lying about. Get Anne Marie to help you.

Mrs. Linde: [gathering a lot of the things together] All right, but I'm not leaving until we have thrashed this thing out.

[She goes into the room, left; at the same time Helmer comes in from the hall.]

Nora: [goes to meet him] I've been longing for you to be back, Torvald, dear.

Helmer: Was that the dressmaker. . . ?

Nora: No, it was Kristine; she's helping me with my costume. I think it's going to look very nice. . . .

Helmer: Wasn't that a good idea of mine, now?

Nora: Wonderful! But wasn't it also nice of me to let you have your way?

Helmer: [*taking her under the chin*] Nice of you—because you let your husband have his way? All right, you little rogue, I know you didn't mean it that way. But I don't want to disturb you. You'll be wanting to try the costume on, I suppose.

Nora: And I dare say you've got work to do?

Helmer: Yes. [*Shows her a bundle of papers.*] Look at this. I've been down at the Bank. . . .

[*He turns to go into his study.*]

Nora: Torvald!

Helmer: [*stopping*] Yes.

Nora: If a little squirrel were to ask ever so nicely . . . ?

Helmer: Well?

Nora: Would you do something for it?

Helmer: Naturally I would first have to know what it is.

Nora: Please, if only you would let it have its way, and do what it wants, it'd scamper about and do all sorts of marvellous tricks.

Helmer: What is it?

Nora: And the pretty little sky-lark would sing all day long. . . .

Helmer: Huh! It does that anyway.

Nora: I'd pretend I was an elfin child and dance a moonlight dance for you, Torvald.

Helmer: Nora—I hope it's not that business you started on this morning?

Nora: [*coming closer*] Yes, it is, Torvald. I implore you!

Helmer: You have the nerve to bring that up again?

Nora: Yes, yes, you *must* listen to me. You must let Krogstad keep his job at the Bank.

Helmer: My dear Nora, I'm giving his job to Mrs. Linde.

Nora: Yes, it's awfully sweet of you. But couldn't you get rid of somebody else in the office instead of Krogstad?

Helmer: This really is the most incredible obstinacy! Just because you go and make some thoughtless promise to put in a good word for him, you expect me . . .

Nora: It's not that, Torvald. It's for your own sake. That man writes in all the nastiest papers, you told me that yourself. He can do you no end of harm. He terrifies me to death. . . .

Helmer: Aha, now I see. It's your memories of what happened before that are frightening you.

Nora: What do you mean?

Helmer: It's your father you are thinking of.

Nora: Yes . . . yes, that's right. You remember all the nasty insinuations those wicked people put in the papers about

Daddy? I honestly think they would have had him dismissed if the Ministry hadn't sent you down to investigate, and you hadn't been so kind and helpful.

Helmer: My dear little Nora, there is a considerable difference between your father and me. Your father's professional conduct was not entirely above suspicion. Mine is. And I hope it's going to stay that way as long as I hold this position.

Nora: But nobody knows what some of these evil people are capable of. Things could be so nice and pleasant for us here, in the peace and quiet of our home—you and me and the children, Torvald! That's why I implore you. . . .

Helmer: The more you plead for him, the more impossible you make it for me to keep him on. It's already known down at the Bank that I am going to give Krogstad his notice. If it ever got around that the new manager had been talked over by his wife. . . .

Nora: What of it?

Helmer: Oh, nothing! As long as the little woman gets her own stubborn way. . . ! Do you want me to make myself a laughing stock in the office? . . . Give people the idea that I am susceptible to any kind of outside pressure? You can imagine how soon I'd feel the consequences of that! Anyway, there's one other consideration that makes it impossible to have Krogstad in the Bank as long as I am manager.

Nora: What's that?

Helmer: At a pinch I might have overlooked his past lapses. . . .

Nora: Of course you could, Torvald!

Helmer: And I'm told he's not bad at his job, either. But we knew each other rather well when we were younger. It was one of those rather rash friendships that prove embarrassing in later life. There's no reason why you shouldn't know we were once on terms of some familiarity. And he, in his tactless way, makes no attempt to hide the fact, particularly when other people are present. On the contrary, he thinks he has every right to treat me as an equal, with his 'Torvald this' and 'Torvald that' every time he opens his mouth. I find it extremely irritating, I can tell you. He would make my position at the Bank absolutely intolerable.

Nora: Torvald, surely you aren't serious?

Helmer: Oh? Why not?

Nora: Well, it's all so petty.

Helmer: What's that you say? Petty? Do you think I'm petty?

Nora: No, not at all, Torvald dear! And that's why . . .

Helmer: Doesn't make any difference! . . . You call my motives petty; so I must be petty too. Petty! Indeed! Well, we'll put a stop to that, once and for all. *[He opens the hall door and calls.]* Helene!

Nora: What are you going to do?

Helmer: *[searching among his papers]* Settle things. *[The Maid comes in.]* See this letter? I want you to take it down at once. Get hold of a messenger and get him to deliver it. Quickly. The address is on the outside. There's the money.

Maid: Very good, sir.

[She goes with the letter.]

Helmer: *[putting his papers together]* There now, my stubborn little miss.

Nora: *[breathless]* Torvald . . . what was that letter?

Helmer: Krogstad's notice.

Nora: Get it back, Torvald! There's still time! Oh, Torvald, get it back! Please for my sake, for your sake, for the sake of the children! Listen, Torvald, please! You don't realize what it can do to us.

Helmer: Too late.

Nora: Yes, too late.

Helmer: My dear Nora, I forgive you this anxiety of yours, although it is actually a bit of an insult. Oh, but it is, I tell you! It's hardly flattering to suppose that anything this miserable pen-pusher wrote could frighten *me*! But I forgive you all the same, because it is rather a sweet way of showing how much you love me. *[He takes her in his arms.]* This is how things must be, my own darling Nora. When it comes to the point, I've enough strength and enough courage, believe me, for whatever happens. You'll find I'm man enough to take everything on myself.

Nora: *[terrified]* What do you mean?

Helmer: Everything, I said. . . .

Nora: *[in command of herself]* That is something you shall never, never do.

Helmer: All right, then we'll share it, Nora—as man and wife. That's what we'll do. *[Caressing her.]* Does that make you happy now? There, there, don't look at me with those eyes, like a little frightened dove. The whole thing is sheer imagination.—Why don't you run through the tarantella and try out the tambourine? I'll go into my study and shut both the doors, then I won't hear anything. You can make all the noise you want. *[Turns in the doorway.]* And when Rank comes, tell him where he can find me.

[He nods to her, goes with his papers into his room, and shuts the door behind him.]

Nora: [*wild-eyed with terror, stands as though transfixed*] He's quite capable of doing it! He would do it! No matter what, he'd do it.—No, never in this world! Anything but that! Help? Some way out. . . ? [*The door-bell rings in the hall.*] Dr. Rank. . . ! Anything but that, *anything!* [*She brushes her hands over her face, pulls herself together and opens the door into the hall.* Dr. Rank *is standing outside hanging up his fur coat. During what follows it begins to grow dark.*] Hello, Dr. Rank. I recognized your ring. Do you mind not going in to Torvald just yet, I think he's busy.

Rank: And you?

[Dr. Rank *comes into the room and she closes the door behind him.*]

Nora: Oh, you know very well I've always got time for you.

Rank: Thank you. A privilege I shall take advantage of as long as I am able.

Nora: What do you mean—as long as you are able?

Rank: Does that frighten you?

Nora: Well, it's just that it sounds so strange. Is anything likely to happen?

Rank: Only what I have long expected. But I didn't think it would come quite so soon.

Nora: [*catching at his arm*] What have you found out? Dr. Rank, you must tell me!

Rank: I'm slowly sinking. There's nothing to be done about it.

Nora: [*with a sigh of relief*] Oh, it's *you* you're . . . ?

Rank: Who else? No point in deceiving oneself. I am the most wretched of all my patients, Mrs. Helmer. These last few days I've made a careful analysis of my internal economy. Bankrupt! Within a month I shall probably be lying rotting up there in the churchyard.

Nora: Come now, what a ghastly thing to say!

Rank: The whole damned thing is ghastly. But the worst thing is all the ghastliness that has to be gone through first. I only have one more test to make; and when that's done I'll know pretty well when the final disintegration will start. There's something I want to ask you. Helmer is a sensitive soul; he loathes anything that's ugly. I don't want him visiting me. . . .

Nora: But Dr. Rank. . . .

Rank: On no account must he. I won't have it. I'll lock the door on him.—As soon as I'm absolutely certain of the worst, I'll send you my visiting card with a black cross on it. You'll know then the final horrible disintegration has begun.

Nora: Really, you are being quite absurd today. And here was I hoping you would be in a thoroughly good mood.

Rank: With death staring me in the face? Why should I suffer for another man's sins? What justice is there in that? Somewhere, somehow, every single family must be suffering some such cruel retribution. . . .

Nora: [stopping up her ears] Rubbish! Do cheer up!

Rank: Yes, really the whole thing's nothing but a huge joke. My poor innocent spine must do penance for my father's gay subaltern life.

Nora: [by the table, left] Wasn't he rather partial to asparagus and *pâté de foie gras?*

Rank: Yes, he was. And truffles.

Nora: Truffles, yes. And oysters, too, I believe?

Rank: Yes, oysters, oysters, of course.

Nora: And all the port and champagne that goes with them. It does seem a pity all these delicious things should attack the spine.

Rank: Especially when they attack a poor spine that never had any fun out of them.

Nora: Yes, that is an awful pity.

Rank: [looks at her sharply] Hm. . . .

Nora: [after a pause] Why did you smile?

Rank: No, it was you who laughed.

Nora: No, it was you who smiled, Dr. Rank!

Rank: [getting up] You are a bigger rascal than I thought you were.

Nora: I feel full of mischief today.

Rank: So it seems.

Nora: [putting her hands on his shoulders] Dear, dear Dr. Rank, you mustn't go and die on Torvald and me.

Rank: You wouldn't miss me for long. When you are gone, you are soon forgotten.

Nora: [looking at him anxiously] Do you think so?

Rank: People make new contacts, then . . .

Nora: Who make new contacts?

Rank: Both you and Helmer will, when I'm gone. You yourself are already well on the way, it seems to me. What was this Mrs. Linde doing here last night?

Nora: Surely you aren't jealous of poor Kristine?

Rank: Yes, I am. She'll be my successor in this house. When I'm done for, I can see this woman. . . .

Nora: Hush! Don't talk so loud, she's in there.

Rank: Today as well? There you are, you see!

Nora: Just to do some sewing on my dress. Good Lord, how absurd you are! *[She sits down on the sofa.]* Now Dr. Rank, cheer up. You'll see tomorrow how nicely I can dance. And you can pretend I'm doing it just for you—and for Torvald as well, of course. *[She takes various things out of the box.]* Come here, Dr. Rank. I want to show you something.

Rank: [sits] What is it?

Nora: Look!

Rank: Silk stockings.

Nora: Flesh-coloured! Aren't they lovely! Of course, it's dark here now, but tomorrow. . . . No, no, no, you can only look at the feet. Oh well, you might as well see a bit higher up, too.

Rank: Hm. . . .

Nora: Why are you looking so critical? Don't you think they'll fit?

Rank: I couldn't possibly offer any informed opinion about that.

Nora: [looks at him for a moment] Shame on you. *[Hits him lightly across the ear with the stockings.]* Take that! *[Folds them up again.]*

Rank: And what other delights am I to be allowed to see?

Nora: Not another thing. You are too naughty. *[She hums a little and searches among her things.]*

Rank: [after a short pause] Sitting here so intimately like this with you, I can't imagine . . . I simply cannot conceive what would have become of me if I had never come to this house.

Nora: [smiles] Yes, I rather think you do enjoy coming here.

Rank: [in a low voice, looking fixedly ahead] And the thought of having to leave it all . . .

Nora: Nonsense. You aren't leaving.

Rank: [in the same tone] . . . without being able to leave behind even the slightest token of gratitude, hardly a fleeting regret even . . . nothing but an empty place to be filled by the first person that comes along.

Nora: Supposing I were to ask you to . . . ? No . . .

Rank: What?

Nora: . . . to show me the extent of your friendship . . .

Rank: Yes?

Nora: I mean . . . to do me a tremendous favour. . . .

Rank: Would you really, for once, give me that pleasure?

Nora: You have no idea what it is.

Rank: All right, tell me.

Nora: No, really I can't, Dr. Rank. It's altogether too much to ask . . . because I need your advice and help as well. . . .

Rank: The more the better. I cannot imagine what you have in mind. But tell me anyway. You do trust me, don't you?

Nora: Yes, I trust you more than anybody I know. You are my best and my most faithful friend. I know that. So I will tell you. Well then, Dr. Rank, there is something you must help me to prevent. You know how deeply, how passionately Torvald is in love with me. He would never hesitate a moment to sacrifice his life for my sake.

Rank: [*bending towards her*] Nora . . . do you think he's the only one who . . . ?

Nora: [*stiffening slightly*] Who . . . ?

Rank: Who wouldn't gladly give his life for your sake.

Nora: [*sadly*] Oh!

Rank: I swore to myself you would know before I went. I'll never have a better opportunity. Well, Nora! Now you know. And now you know too that you can confide in me as in nobody else.

Nora: [*rises and speaks evenly and calmly*] Let me past.

Rank: [*makes way for her, but remains seated*] Nora. . . .

Nora: [*in the hall doorway*] Helene, bring the lamp in, please. [*Walks over to the stove.*] Oh, my dear Dr. Rank, that really was rather horrid of you.

Rank: [*getting up*] That I have loved you every bit as much as anybody? Is *that* horrid?

Nora: No, but that you had to go and tell me. When it was all so unnecessary. . . .

Rank: What do you mean? Did you know. . . ?

[*The* Maid *comes in with the lamp, puts it on the table, and goes out again.*]

Rank: Nora . . . Mrs. Helmer . . . I'm asking you if you knew?

Nora: How can I tell whether I did or didn't. I simply can't tell you. . . . Oh, how could you be so clumsy, Dr. Rank! When everything was so nice.

Rank: Anyway, you know now that I'm at your service, body and soul. So you can speak out.

Nora: [*looking at him*] After this?

Rank: I beg you to tell me what it is.

Nora: I can tell you nothing now.

Rank: You must. You can't torment me like this. Give me a chance—I'll do anything that's humanly possible.

Nora: You can do nothing for me now. Actually, I don't really need any help. It's all just my imagination, really it is. Of course! [*She sits down in the rocking-chair, looks at him and smiles.*] I must say, you are a nice one, Dr. Rank! Don't you feel ashamed of yourself, now the lamp's been brought in?

Rank: No, not exactly. But perhaps I ought to go—for good?

Nora: No, you mustn't do that. You must keep coming just as you've always done. You know very well Torvald would miss you terribly.

Rank: And *you*?

Nora: I always think it's tremendous fun having you.

Rank: That's exactly what gave me wrong ideas. I just can't
puzzle you out. I often used to feel you'd just as soon be
with me as with Helmer.

Nora: Well, you see, there are those people you love and those
people you'd almost rather *be* with.

Rank: Yes, there's something in that.

Nora: When I was a girl at home, I loved Daddy best, of course.
But I also thought it great fun if I could slip into the maids'
room. For one thing they never preached at me. And they
always talked about such exciting things.

Rank: Aha! So it's their role I've taken over!

Nora: *[jumps up and crosses to him]* Oh, my dear, kind Dr. Rank,
I didn't mean that at all. But you can see how it's a bit with
Torvald as it was with Daddy. . . .

[The Maid *comes in from the hall.]*

Maid: Please, ma'am. . . !

[She whispers and hands her a card.]

Nora: *[glances at the card]* Ah!

[She puts it in her pocket.]

Rank: Anything wrong?

Nora: No, no, not at all. It's just . . . it's my new costume. . . .

Rank: How is that? There's your costume in there.

Nora: That one, yes. But this is another one. I've ordered it.
Torvald mustn't hear about it. . . .

Rank: Ah, so that's the big secret, is it!

Nora: Yes, that's right. Just go in and see him, will you? He's in
the study. Keep him occupied for the time being. . . .

Rank: Don't worry. He shan't escape me.

[He goes into Helmer's *study.]*

Nora: *[to the maid]* Is he waiting in the kitchen?

Maid: Yes, he came up the back stairs. . . .

Nora: But didn't you tell him somebody was here?

Maid: Yes, but it was no good.

Nora: Won't he go?

Maid: No, he won't till he's seen you.

Nora: Let him in, then. But quietly. Helene, you mustn't tell
anybody about this. It's a surprise for my husband.

Maid: I understand, ma'am. . . .

[She goes out.]

Nora: Here it comes! What I've been dreading! No, no, it can't happen, it *can't* happen.

[She walks over and bolts Helmer's *door. The* Maid *opens the hall door for* Krogstad *and shuts it again behind him. He is wearing a fur coat, over-shoes, and a fur cap.]*

Nora: [goes towards him] Keep your voice down, my husband is at home.

Krogstad: What if he is?

Nora: What do you want with me?

Krogstad: To find out something.

Nora: Hurry, then. What is it?

Krogstad: You know I've been given notice.

Nora: I couldn't prevent it, Mr. Krogstad, I did my utmost for you, but it was no use.

Krogstad: Has your husband so little affection for you? He knows what I can do to you, yet he dares. . . .

Nora: You don't imagine he knows about it!

Krogstad: No, I didn't imagine he did. It didn't seem a bit like my good friend Torvald Helmer to show that much courage. . . .

Nora: Mr. Krogstad, I must ask you to show some respect for my husband.

Krogstad: Oh, sure! All due respect! But since you are so anxious to keep this business quiet, Mrs. Helmer, I take it you now have a rather clearer idea of just what it is you've done, than you had yesterday.

Nora: Clearer than *you* could ever have given me.

Krogstad: Yes, being as I am such a rotten lawyer. . . .

Nora: What do you want with me?

Krogstad: I just wanted to see how things stood, Mrs. Helmer. I've been thinking about you all day. Even a mere money-lender, a hack journalist, a—well, even somebody like me has a bit of what you might call feeling.

Nora: Show it then. Think of my little children.

Krogstad: Did you or your husband think of mine? But what does it matter now? There was just one thing I wanted to say: you needn't take this business too seriously. I shan't start any proceedings, for the present.

Nora: Ah, I knew you wouldn't.

Krogstad: The whole thing can be arranged quite amicably. Nobody need know. Just the three of us.

Nora: My husband must never know.

Krogstad: How can you prevent it? Can you pay off the balance?

Nora: No, not immediately.

Krogstad: Perhaps you've some way of getting hold of the money in the next few days.

Nora: None I want to make use of.

Krogstad: Well, it wouldn't have been very much help to you if you had. Even if you stood there with the cash in your hand and to spare, you still wouldn't get your IOU back from me now.

Nora: What are you going to do with it?

Krogstad: Just keep it—have it in my possession. Nobody who isn't implicated need know about it. So if you are thinking of trying any desperate remedies . . .

Nora: Which I am. . . .

Krogstad: . . . if you happen to be thinking of running away . . .

Nora: Which I am!

Krogstad: . . . or anything worse . . .

Nora: How did you know?

Krogstad: . . . forget it!

Nora: How did you know I was thinking of *that*?

Krogstad: Most of us think of *that*, to begin with. I did, too; but I didn't have the courage. . . .

Nora: *[tonelessly]* I haven't either.

Krogstad: *[relieved]* So you haven't the courage either, eh?

Nora: No, I haven't! I haven't!

Krogstad: It would also be very stupid. There'd only be the first domestic storm to get over. . . . I've got a letter to your husband in my pocket here. . . .

Nora: And it's all in there?

Krogstad: In as tactful a way as possible.

Nora: *[quickly]* He must never read the letter. Tear it up. I'll find the money somehow.

Krogstad: Excuse me, Mrs. Helmer, but I've just told you. . . .

Nora: I'm not talking about the money I owe you. I want to know how much you are demanding from my husband, and I'll get the money.

Krogstad: I want no money from your husband.

Nora: What do you want?

Krogstad: I'll tell you. I want to get on my feet again, Mrs. Helmer; I want to get to the top. And your husband is going to help me. For the last eighteen months I've gone straight; all that time it's been hard going; I was content to work my way up, step by step. Now I'm being kicked out, and I won't stand for being taken back again as an act of charity. I'm going to get to the top, I tell you. I'm going back into that Bank— with a better job. Your husband is going to create a new vacancy, just for me. . . .

Nora: He'll never do that!

Krogstad: He will do it. I know him. He'll do it without so much as a whimper. And once I'm in there with him, you'll see what's what. In less than a year I'll be his right-hand man. It'll be

Nils Krogstad, not Torvald Helmer, who'll be running that Bank.

Nora: You'll never live to see that day!

Krogstad: You mean you . . . ?

Nora: Now I have the courage.

Krogstad: You can't frighten me! A precious pampered little thing like you. . . .

Nora: I'll show you! I'll show you!

Krogstad: Under the ice, maybe? Down in the cold, black water? Then being washed up in the spring, bloated, hairless, unrecognizable. . . .

Nora: You can't frighten me.

Krogstad: You can't frighten me, either. People don't do that sort of thing, Mrs. Helmer. There wouldn't be any point to it, anyway, I'd still have him right in my pocket.

Nora: Afterwards? When I'm no longer . . .

Krogstad: Aren't you forgetting that your reputation would then be entirely in my hands? *[Nora stands looking at him, speechless.]* Well, I've warned you. Don't do anything silly. When Helmer gets my letter, I expect to hear from him. And don't forget: it's him who is forcing me off the straight and narrow again, your own husband! That's something I'll never forgive him for. Goodbye, Mrs. Helmer.

[He goes out through the hall. Nora *crosses to the door, opens it slightly, and listens.]*

Nora: He's going. He hasn't left the letter. No, no, that would be impossible! *[Opens the door further and further.]* What's he doing? He's stopped outside. He's not going down the stairs. Has he changed his mind? Is he . . . ? *[A letter falls into the letter-box. Then* Krogstad's *footsteps are heard receding as he walks downstairs.* Nora *gives a stifled cry, runs across the room to the sofa table; pause.]* In the letter-box! [She creeps stealthily across to the hall door.] There it is! Torvald, Torvald! It's hopeless now!

Mrs. Linde: [comes into the room, left, carrying the costume] There, I think that's everything. Shall we try it on?

Nora: [in a low, hoarse voice] Kristine, come here.

Mrs. Linde: [throws the dress down on the sofa] What's wrong with you? You look upset.

Nora: Come here. Do you see that letter? *There,* look! Through the glass in the letter-box.

Mrs. Linde: Yes, yes, I can see it.

Nora: It's a letter from Krogstad.

Mrs. Linde: Nora! It was Krogstad who lent you the money!

Nora: Yes. And now Torvald will get to know everything.

Mrs. Linde: Believe me, Nora, it's best for you both.

Nora: But there's more to it than that. I forged a signature. . . .

Mrs. Linde: Heavens above!

Nora: Listen, I want to tell you something, Kristine, so you can be my witness.

Mrs. Linde: What do you mean 'witness'? What do you want me to . . . ?

Nora: If I should go mad . . . which might easily happen . . .

Mrs. Linde: Nora!

Nora: Or if anything happened to me . . . which meant I couldn't be here. . . .

Mrs. Linde: Nora, Nora! Are you out of your mind?

Nora: And if somebody else wanted to take it all upon himself, the whole blame, you understand. . . .

Mrs. Linde: Yes, yes. But what makes you think . . . ?

Nora: Then you must testify that it isn't true, Kristine. I'm not out of my mind; I'm quite sane now. And I tell you this: nobody else knew anything, I alone was responsible for the whole thing. Remember that!

Mrs. Linde: I will. But I don't understand a word of it.

Nora: Why should you? You see something miraculous is going to happen.

Mrs. Linde: Something miraculous?

Nora: Yes, a miracle. But something so terrible as well, Kristine —oh, it must *never* happen, not for anything.

Mrs. Linde: I'm going straight over to talk to Krogstad.

Nora: Don't go. He'll only do you harm.

Mrs. Linde: There was a time when he would have done anything for me.

Nora: Him!

Mrs. Linde: Where does he live?

Nora: How do I know . . . ? Wait a minute. *[She feels in her pocket.]* Here's his card. But the letter, the letter . . . !

Helmer: *[from his study, knocking on the door]* Nora!

Nora: *[cries out in terror]* What's that? What do you want?

Helmer: Don't be frightened. We're not coming in. You've locked the door. Are you trying on?

Nora: Yes, yes, I'm trying on. It looks so nice on me, Torvald.

Mrs. Linde: *[who has read the card]* He lives just round the corner.

Nora: It's no use. It's hopeless. The letter is there in the box.

Mrs. Linde: Your husband keeps the key?

Nora: Always.

Mrs. Linde: Krogstad must ask for his letter back unread, he must find some sort of excuse. . . .

Nora: But this is just the time that Torvald generally . . .

Mrs. Linde: Put him off! Go in and keep him busy. I'll be back as soon as I can.

[She goes out hastily by the hall door. Nora walks over to Helmer's door, opens it and peeps in.]

Nora: Torvald!

Helmer: [in the study] Well, can a man get into his own living-room again now? Come along, Rank, now we'll see . . . *[In the doorway.]* But what's this?

Nora: What, Torvald dear?

Helmer: Rank led me to expect some kind of marvellous transformation.

Rank: [in the doorway] That's what I thought too, but I must have been mistaken.

Nora: I'm not showing myself off to anybody before tomorrow.

Helmer: Nora dear, you look tired. You haven't been practising too hard?

Nora: No, I haven't practised at all yet.

Helmer: You'll have to, though.

Nora: Yes, I certainly must, Torvald. But I just can't get anywhere without your help: I've completely forgotten it.

Helmer: We'll soon polish it up.

Nora: Yes, do help me, Torvald. Promise? I'm so nervous. All those people. . . . You must devote yourself exclusively to me this evening. Pens away! Forget all about the office! Promise me, Torvald dear!

Helmer: I promise. This evening I am wholly and entirely at your service . . . helpless little thing that you are. Oh, but while I remember, I'll just look first . . .

[He goes towards the hall door.]

Nora: What do you want out there?

Helmer: Just want to see if there are any letters.

Nora: No, don't, Torvald!

Helmer: Why not?

Nora: Torvald, *please*! There aren't any.

Helmer: Just let me see.

[He starts to go. Nora, at the piano, plays the opening bars of the tarantella.]

Helmer: [at the door, stops] Aha!

Nora: I shan't be able to dance tomorrow if I don't rehearse it with you.

Helmer: [walks to her] Are you really so nervous, Nora dear?

Nora: Terribly nervous. Let me run through it now. There's still time before supper. Come and sit here and play for me,

Torvald dear. Tell me what to do, keep me right—as you always do.

Helmer: Certainly, with pleasure, if that's what you want.

[He sits at the piano. Nora snatches the tambourine out of the box, and also a long gaily-coloured shawl which she drapes round herself, then with a bound she leaps forward.]

Nora: [shouts] Now play for me! Now I'll dance.

[Helmer plays and Nora dances; Dr. Rank stands at the piano behind Helmer and looks on.]

Helmer: [playing] Not so fast! Not so fast!
Nora: I can't help it.
Helmer: Not so wild, Nora!
Nora: This is how it has to be.
Helmer: [stops] No, no, that won't do at all.
Nora: [laughs and swings the tambourine] Didn't I tell you?
Rank: Let me play for her.
Helmer: [gets up] Yes, do. Then I'll be better able to tell her what to do.

[Rank sits down at the piano and plays. Nora dances more and more wildly. Helmer stands by the stove giving her repeated directions as she dances; she does not seem to hear them. Her hair comes undone and falls about her shoulders; she pays no attention and goes on dancing. Mrs. Linde enters.]

Mrs. Linde: [standing as though spellbound in the doorway] Ah . . . !
Nora: [dancing] See what fun we are having, Kristine.
Helmer: But my dear darling Nora, you are dancing as though your life depended on it.
Nora: It does.
Helmer: Stop, Rank! This is sheer madness. Stop, I say.

[Rank stops playing and Nora comes to a sudden halt.]

Helmer: [crosses to her] I would never have believed it. You have forgotten everything I ever taught you.
Nora: [throwing away the tambourine] There you are, you see.
Helmer: Well, some more instruction is certainly needed there.
Nora: Yes, you see how necessary it is. You must go on coaching me right up to the last minute. Promise me, Torvald?
Helmer: You can rely on me.
Nora: You mustn't think about anything else but me until after tomorrow . . . mustn't open any letters . . . mustn't touch the letter-box.
Helmer: Ah, you are still frightened of what that man might . . .
Nora: Yes, yes, I am.

Helmer: I can see from your face there's already a letter there from him.

Nora: I don't know. I think so. But you mustn't read anything like that now. We don't want anything horrid coming between us until all this is over.

Rank: [softly to Helmer*]* I shouldn't cross her.

Helmer: [puts his arm round her] The child must have her way. But tomorrow night, when your dance is done. . . .

Nora: Then you are free.

Maid: [in the doorway, right] Dinner is served, madam.

Nora: We'll have champagne, Helene.

Maid: Very good, madam.

[She goes.]

Helmer: Aha! It's to be quite a banquet, eh?

Nora: With champagne flowing until dawn. *[Shouts.]* And some macaroons, Helene . . . lots of them, for once in a while.

Helmer: [seizing her hands] Now, now, not so wild and excitable! Let me see you being my own little singing bird again.

Nora: Oh yes, I will. And if you'll just go in . . . you, too, Dr. Rank. Kristine, you must help me to do my hair.

Rank: [softly, as they leave] There isn't anything . . . anything as it were, impending, is there?

Helmer: No, not at all, my dear fellow. It's nothing but these childish fears I was telling you about.

[They go out to the right.]

Nora: Well?

Mrs. Linde: He's left town.

Nora: I saw it in your face.

Mrs. Linde: He's coming back tomorrow evening. I left a note for him.

Nora: You shouldn't have done that. You must let things take their course. Because really it's a case for rejoicing, waiting like this for the miracle.

Mrs. Linde: What is it you are waiting for?

Nora: Oh, you wouldn't understand. Go and join the other two. I'll be there in a minute.

*[*Mrs. Linde *goes into the dining-room.* Nora *stands for a moment as though to collect herself, then looks at her watch.]*

Nora: Five. Seven hours to midnight. Then twenty-four hours till the next midnight. Then the tarantella will be over. Twenty-four and seven? Thirty-one hours to live.

Helmer: [in the doorway, right] What's happened to our little
    sky-lark?
    Nora: [running towards him with open arms] Here she is!

ACT III

*The same room. The round table has been moved to the centre of the room, and the
chairs placed round it. A lamp is burning on the table. The door to the hall stands
open. Dance music can be heard coming from the floor above.* Mrs. Linde *is sitting by the table, idly turning over the pages of a book; she tries to read, but does not
seem able to concentrate. Once or twice she listens, tensely, for a sound at the front
door.*

Mrs. Linde: [looking at her watch] Still not here. There isn't much
    time left. I only hope he hasn't . . . [She listens again.] Ah,
    there he is. [She goes out into the hall, and cautiously opens the
    front door. Soft footsteps can be heard on the stairs. She whis-
    pers.] Come in. There's nobody here.
Krogstad: [in the doorway] I found a note from you at home. What
    does it all mean?
Mrs. Linde: I *had* to talk to you.
Krogstad: Oh? And did it have to be here, in this house?
Mrs. Linde: It wasn't possible over at my place, it hasn't a separate
    entrance. Come in. We are quite alone. The maid's asleep
    and the Helmers are at a party upstairs.
Krogstad: [comes into the room] Well, well! So the Helmers are out
    dancing tonight! Really?
Mrs. Linde: Yes, why not?
Krogstad: Why not indeed!
Mrs. Linde: Well then, Nils. Let's talk.
Krogstad: Have we two anything more to talk about?
Mrs. Linde: We have a great deal to talk about.
Krogstad: I shouldn't have thought so.
Mrs. Linde: That's because you never really understood me.
Krogstad: What else was there to understand, apart from the old,
    old story? A heartless woman throws a man over the
    moment something more profitable offers itself.
Mrs. Linde: Do you really think I'm so heartless? Do you think I
    found it easy to break it off?
Krogstad: Didn't you?
Mrs. Linde: You didn't really believe that?
Krogstad: If that wasn't the case, why did you write to me as you
    did?
Mrs. Linde: There was nothing else I could do. If I had to make the
    break, I felt in duty bound to destroy any feeling that you
    had for me.

Krogstad: [*clenching his hands*] So that's how it was. And all that . . . was for money!

Mrs. Linde: You mustn't forget I had a helpless mother and two young brothers. We couldn't wait for you, Nils. At that time you hadn't much immediate prospect of anything.

Krogstad: That may be. But you had no right to throw me over for somebody else.

Mrs. Linde: Well, I don't know. Many's the time I've asked myself whether I was justified.

Krogstad: [*more quietly*] When I lost you, it was just as if the ground had slipped away from under my feet. Look at me now: a broken man clinging to the wreck of his life.

Mrs. Linde: Help might be near.

Krogstad: It was near. Then you came along and got in the way.

Mrs. Linde: Quite without knowing, Nils. I only heard today it's you I'm supposed to be replacing at the Bank.

Krogstad: If you say so, I believe you. But now you do know, aren't you going to withdraw?

Mrs. Linde: No, that wouldn't benefit you in the slightest.

Krogstad: Benefit, benefit. . . ! I would do it just the same.

Mrs. Linde: I have learned to go carefully. Life and hard, bitter necessity have taught me that.

Krogstad: And life has taught me not to believe in pretty speeches.

Mrs. Linde: Then life has taught you a very sensible thing. But deeds are something you surely must believe in?

Krogstad: How do you mean?

Mrs. Linde: You said you were like a broken man clinging to the wreck of his life.

Krogstad: And I said it with good reason.

Mrs. Linde: And I am like a broken woman clinging to the wreck of her life. Nobody to care about, and nobody to care for.

Krogstad: It was your own choice.

Mrs. Linde: At the time there was no other choice.

Krogstad: Well, what of it?

Mrs. Linde: Nils, what about us two castaways joining forces.

Krogstad: What's that you say?

Mrs. Linde: Two of us on *one* wreck surely stand a better chance than each on his own.

Krogstad: Kristine!

Mrs. Linde: Why do you suppose I came to town?

Krogstad: You mean, you thought of me?

Mrs. Linde: Without work I couldn't live. All my life I have worked, for as long as I can remember; that has always been my one great joy. But now I'm completely alone in the world, and feeling horribly empty and forlorn. There's no pleasure in

working only for yourself. Nils, give me somebody and
something to work for.

Krogstad: I don't believe all this. It's only a woman's hysteria,
wanting to be all magnanimous and self-sacrificing.

Mrs. Linde: Have you ever known me hysterical before?

Krogstad: Would you really do this? Tell me—do you know all
about my past?

Mrs. Linde: Yes.

Krogstad: And you know what people think about me?

Mrs. Linde: Just now you hinted you thought you might have been a
different person with me.

Krogstad: I'm convinced I would.

Mrs. Linde: Couldn't it still happen?

Krogstad: Kristine! You know what you are saying, don't you? Yes,
you do. I can see you do. Have you really the courage . . . ?

Mrs. Linde: I need someone to mother, and your children need a
mother. We two need each other. Nils, I have faith in what,
deep down, you are. With you I can face anything.

Krogstad: [seizing her hands] Thank you, thank you, Kristine. And
I'll soon have everybody looking up to me, or I'll know the
reason why. Ah, but I was forgetting. . . .

Mrs. Linde: Hush! The tarantella! You must go!

Krogstad: Why? What is it?

Mrs. Linde: You hear that dance upstairs? When it's finished they'll
be coming.

Krogstad: Yes, I'll go. It's too late to do anything. Of course, you
know nothing about what steps I've taken against the
Helmers.

Mrs. Linde: Yes, Nils, I do know.

Krogstad: Yet you still want to go on. . . .

Mrs. Linde: I know how far a man like you can be driven by despair.

Krogstad: Oh, if only I could undo what I've done!

Mrs. Linde: You still can. Your letter is still there in the box.

Krogstad: Are you sure?

Mrs. Linde: Quite sure. But . . .

Krogstad: [regards her searchingly] Is that how things are? You want
to save your friend at any price? Tell me straight. Is that it?

Mrs. Linde: When you've sold yourself *once* for other people's sake,
you don't do it again.

Krogstad: I shall demand my letter back.

Mrs. Linde: No, no.

Krogstad: Of course I will, I'll wait here till Helmer comes. I'll tell
him he has to give me my letter back . . . that it's only about
my notice . . . that he mustn't read it. . . .

Mrs. Linde: No, Nils, don't ask for it back.

Krogstad: But wasn't that the very reason you got me here?

Mrs. Linde: Yes, that was my first terrified reaction. But that was yesterday, and it's quite incredible the things I've witnessed in this house in the last twenty-four hours. Helmer must know everything. This unhappy secret must come out. Those two must have the whole thing out between them. All this secrecy and deception, it just can't go on.

Krogstad: Well, if you want to risk it. . . . But one thing I can do, and I'll do it at once. . . .

Mrs. Linde: [listening] Hurry! Go, go! The dance has stopped. We aren't safe a moment longer.

Krogstad: I'll wait for you downstairs.

Mrs. Linde: Yes, do. You must see me home.

Krogstad: I've never been so incredibly happy before.

[He goes out by the front door. The door out into the hall remains standing open.]

Mrs. Linde: [tidies the room a little and gets her hat and coat ready] How things change! How things change! Somebody to work for . . . to live for. A home to bring happiness into. Just let me get down to it. . . . I wish they'd come. . . . *[Listens.]* Ah, there they are. . . . Get my things.

[She takes her coat and hat. The voices of Helmer *and* Nora *are heard outside. A key is turned and* Helmer *pushes* Nora *almost forcibly into the hall. She is dressed in the Italian costume, with a big black shawl over it. He is in evening dress, and over it a black cloak, open.]*

Nora: [still in the doorway, reluctantly] No, no, not in here! I want to go back up again. I don't want to leave so early.

Helmer: But my dearest Nora . . .

Nora: Oh, please, Torvald, I beg you. . . . *Please,* just for another hour.

Helmer: Not another minute, Nora my sweet. You remember what we agreed. There now, come along in. You'll catch cold standing there.

[He leads her, in spite of her resistance, gently but firmly into the room.]

Mrs. Linde: Good evening.

Nora: Kristine!

Helmer: Why, Mrs. Linde. You here so late?

Mrs. Linde: Yes. You must forgive me but I did so want to see Nora all dressed up.

Nora: Have you been sitting here waiting for me?

Mrs. Linde: Yes, I'm afraid I wasn't in time to catch you before you went upstairs. And I felt I couldn't leave again without seeing you.

Helmer: [removing Nora's *shawl]* Well take a good look at her. I think I can say she's worth looking at. Isn't she lovely, Mrs. Linde?

Mrs. Linde: Yes, I must say. . . .

Helmer: Isn't she quite extraordinarily lovely? That's what everybody at the party thought, too. But she's dreadfully stubborn . . . the sweet little thing! And what shall we do about that? Would you believe it, I nearly had to use force to get her away.

Nora: Oh Torvald, you'll be sorry you didn't let me stay, even for half an hour.

Helmer: You hear that, Mrs. Linde? She dances her tarantella, there's wild applause—which was well deserved, although the performance was perhaps rather realistic . . . I mean, rather more so than was strictly necessary from the artistic point of view. But anyway! The main thing is she was a success, a tremendous success. Was I supposed to let her stay after that? Spoil the effect? No thank you! I took my lovely little Capri girl—my capricious little Capri girl, I might say —by the arm, whisked her once round the room, a curtsey all round, and then—as they say in novels—the beautiful vision vanished. An exit should always be effective, Mrs. Linde. But I just can't get Nora to see that. Phew! It's warm in here. *[He throws his cloak over a chair and opens the door to his study.]* What? It's dark. Oh yes, of course. Excuse me. . . .

[He goes in and lights a few candles.]

Nora: [quickly, in a breathless whisper] Well?

Mrs. Linde: [softly] I've spoken to him.

Nora: And . . . ?

Mrs. Linde: Nora . . . you must tell your husband everything.

Nora: [tonelessly] I knew it.

Mrs. Linde: You've got nothing to fear from Krogstad. But you must speak.

Nora: I won't.

Mrs. Linde: Then the letter will.

Nora: Thank you, Kristine. Now I know what's to be done. Hush . . . !

Helmer: [comes in again] Well, Mrs. Linde, have you finished admiring her?

Mrs. Linde: Yes. And now I must say good night.

Helmer: Oh, already? Is this yours, this knitting?

Mrs. Linde: [takes it] Yes, thank you. I nearly forgot it.

Helmer: So you knit, eh?

Mrs. Linde: Yes.

Helmer: You should embroider instead, you know.

Mrs. Linde: Oh? Why?

 Helmer: So much prettier. Watch! You hold the embroidery like
this in the left hand, and then you take the needle in the right
hand, like this, and you describe a long, graceful curve. Isn't
that right?

Mrs. Linde: Yes, I suppose so. . . .

 Helmer: Whereas knitting on the other hand just can't help being
ugly. Look! Arms pressed into the sides, the knitting needles going up and down—there's something Chinese about
it. . . . Ah, that was marvellous champagne they served
tonight.

Mrs. Linde: Well, good night, Nora! And stop being so stubborn.

 Helmer: Well said, Mrs. Linde!

Mrs. Linde: Good night, Mr. Helmer.

 Helmer: [accompanying her to the door] Good night, good night!
You'll get home all right, I hope? I'd be only too pleased to
. . . But you haven't far to walk. Good night, good night!
[She goes; he shuts the door behind her and comes in again.]
There we are, got rid of her at last. She's a frightful bore,
that woman.

 Nora: Aren't you very tired, Torvald?

 Helmer: Not in the least.

 Nora: Not sleepy?

 Helmer: Not at all. On the contrary, I feel extremely lively. What
about you? Yes, you look quite tired and sleepy.

 Nora: Yes, I'm very tired. I just want to fall straight off to sleep.

 Helmer: There you are, you see! Wasn't I right in thinking we
shouldn't stay any longer.

 Nora: Oh, everything you do is right.

 Helmer: [kissing her forehead] There's my little sky-lark talking
common sense. Did you notice how gay Rank was this
evening?

 Nora: Oh, was he? I didn't get a chance to talk to him.

 Helmer: I hardly did either. But it's a long time since I saw him in
such a good mood. [Looks at Nora *for a moment or two, then
comes nearer her.]* Ah, it's wonderful to be back in our own
home again, and quite alone with you. How irresistibly
lovely you are, Nora!

 Nora: Don't look at me like that, Torvald!

 Helmer: Can't I look at my most treasured possession? At all this
loveliness that's mine and mine alone, completely and utterly
mine.

 Nora: [walks round to the other side of the table] You mustn't talk
to me like that tonight.

 Helmer: [following her] You still have the tarantella in your blood,
I see. And that makes you even more desirable. Listen! The

guests are beginning to leave now. *[Softly.]* Nora . . . soon the whole house will be silent.

Nora: I should hope so.

Helmer: Of course you do, don't you, Nora my darling? You know, whenever I'm out at a party with you . . . do you know why I never talk to you very much, why I always stand away from you and only steal a quick glance at you now and then . . . do you know why I do that? It's because I'm pretending we are secretly in love, secretly engaged and nobody suspects there is anything between us.

Nora: Yes, yes. I know your thoughts are always with me, of course.

Helmer: And when it's time to go, and I lay your shawl round those shapely, young shoulders, round the exquisite curve of your neck . . . I pretend that you are my young bride, that we are just leaving our wedding, that I am taking you to our new home for the first time . . . to be alone with you for the first time . . . quite alone with your young and trembling loveliness! All evening I've been longing for you, and nothing else. And as I watched you darting and swaying in the tarantella, my blood was on fire . . . I couldn't bear it any longer . . . and that's why I brought you down here with me so early. . . .

Nora: Go away, Torvald! Please leave me alone. I won't have it.

Helmer: What's this? It's just your little game isn't it, my little Nora. Won't! Won't! Am I not your husband. . . ?

[There is a knock on the front door.]

Nora: [startled] Listen. . .!

Helmer: [going towards the hall] Who's there?

Rank: [outside] It's me. Can I come in for a minute?

Helmer: [in a low voice, annoyed] Oh, what does he want now? *[Aloud.]* Wait a moment. *[He walks across and opens the door.]* How nice of you to look in on your way out.

Rank: I fancied I heard your voice and I thought I would just look in. *[He takes a quick glance round.]* Ah yes, this dear, familiar old place! How cosy and comfortable you've got things here, you two.

Helmer: You seemed to be having a pretty good time upstairs yourself.

Rank: Capital! Why shouldn't I? Why not make the most of things in this world? At least as much as one can, and for as long as one can. The wine was excellent. . . .

Helmer: Especially the champagne.

Rank: You noticed that too, did you? It's incredible the amount I was able to put away.

Nora: Torvald also drank a lot of champagne this evening.

Rank: Oh?

Nora: Yes, and that always makes him quite merry.

Rank: Well, why shouldn't a man allow himself a jolly evening after a day well spent?

Helmer: Well spent? I'm afraid I can't exactly claim that.

Rank: [clapping him on the shoulder] But I can, you see!

Nora: Dr. Rank, am I right in thinking you carried out a certain laboratory test today?

Rank: Exactly.

Helmer: Look at our little Nora talking about laboratory tests!

Nora: And may I congratulate you on the result?

Rank: You may indeed.

Nora: So it was good?

Rank: The best possible, for both doctor and patient—certainty!

Nora: [quickly and searchingly] Certainty?

Rank: Absolute certainty. So why shouldn't I allow myself a jolly evening after that?

Nora: Quite right, Dr. Rank.

Helmer: I quite agree. As long as you don't suffer for it in the morning.

Rank: Well, you never get anything for nothing in this life.

Nora: Dr. Rank . . . you are very fond of masquerades, aren't you?

Rank: Yes, when there are plenty of amusing disguises. . . .

Nora: Tell me, what shall we two go as next time?

Helmer: There's frivolity for you . . . thinking about the next time already!

Rank: We two? I'll tell you. You must go as Lady Luck. . . .

Helmer: Yes, but how do you find a costume to suggest *that*?

Rank: Your wife could simply go in her everyday clothes. . . .

Helmer: That was nicely said. But don't you know what you would be?

Rank: Yes, my dear friend, I know exactly what I shall be.

Helmer: Well?

Rank: At the next masquerade, I shall be invisible.

Helmer: That's a funny idea!

Rank: There's a big black cloak . . . haven't you heard of the cloak of invisibility? That comes right down over you, and then nobody can see you.

Helmer: [suppressing a smile] Of course, that's right.

Rank: But I'm clean forgetting what I came for. Helmer, give me a cigar, one of the dark Havanas.

Helmer: With the greatest of pleasure.

[He offers his case.]

Rank: [takes one and cuts the end off] Thanks.

Nora: [strikes a match] Let me give you a light.

Rank: Thank you. *[She holds out the match and he lights his cigar.]* And now, goodbye!

Helmer: Goodbye, goodbye, my dear fellow!

  Nora: Sleep well, Dr. Rank.

Rank: Thank you for that wish.

  Nora: Wish me the same.

Rank: You? All right, if you want me to. . . . Sleep well. And thanks for the light.

[He nods to them both, and goes.]

Helmer: [subdued] He's had a lot to drink.

  Nora: [absently] Very likely.

[Helmer takes a bunch of keys out of his pocket and goes out into the hall.]

  Nora: Torvald . . . what do you want there?

Helmer: I must empty the letter-box, it's quite full. There'll be no room for the papers in the morning. . . .

  Nora: Are you going to work tonight?

Helmer: You know very well I'm not. Hello, what's this? Somebody's been at the lock.

  Nora: At the lock?

Helmer: Yes, I'm sure of it. Why should that be? I'd hardly have thought the maids . . . ? Here's a broken hair-pin. Nora, it's one of yours. . . .

  Nora: [quickly] It must have been the children. . . .

Helmer: Then you'd better tell them not to. Ah . . . there . . . I've managed to get it open. *[He takes the things out and shouts into the kitchen.]* Helene! . . . Helene, put the light out in the hall. *[He comes into the room again with the letters in his hand and shuts the hall door.]* Look how it all mounts up. *[Runs through them.]* What's this?

  Nora: The letter! Oh no, Torvald, no!

Helmer: Two visiting cards . . . from Dr. Rank.

  Nora: From Dr. Rank?

Helmer: [looking at them] Dr. Rank, Medical Practitioner. They were on top. He must have put them in as he left.

  Nora: Is there anything on them?

Helmer: There's a black cross above his name. Look. What an uncanny idea. It's just as if he were announcing his own death.

  Nora: He is.

Helmer: What? What do you know about it? Has he said anything to you?

  Nora: Yes. He said when these cards came, he would have

taken his last leave of us. He was going to shut himself up and die.

Helmer: Poor fellow! Of course I knew we couldn't keep him with us very long. But so soon. . . . And hiding himself away like a wounded animal.

Nora: When it has to happen, it's best that it should happen without words. Don't you think so, Torvald?

Helmer: *[walking up and down]* He had grown so close to us. I don't think I can imagine him gone. His suffering and his loneliness seemed almost to provide a background of dark cloud to the sunshine of our lives. Well, perhaps it's all for the best. For him at any rate. *[Pauses.]* And maybe for us as well, Nora. Now there's just the two of us. *[Puts his arms round her.]* Oh, my darling wife, I can't hold you close enough. You know, Nora . . . many's the time I wish you were threatened by some terrible danger so I could risk everything, body and soul, for your sake.

Nora: *[tears herself free and says firmly and decisively]* Now you must read your letters, Torvald.

Helmer: No, no, not tonight. I want to be with you, my darling wife.

Nora: Knowing all the time your friend is dying. . . ?

Helmer: You are right. It's been a shock to both of us. This ugly thing has come between us . . . thoughts of death and decay. We must try to free ourselves from it. Until then . . . we shall go our separate ways.

Nora: *[her arms round his neck]* Torvald . . . good night! Good night!

Helmer: *[kisses her forehead]* Good night, my little singing bird. Sleep well, Nora, I'll just read through my letters.

[He takes the letters into his room and shuts the door behind him.]

Nora: *[gropes around her, wild-eyed, seizes Helmer's cloak, wraps it round herself, and whispers quickly, hoarsely, spasmodically]* Never see him again. Never, never, never. *[Throws her shawl over her head.]* And never see the children again either. Never, never. Oh, that black icy water. Oh, that bottomless . . . ! If only it were all over! He's got it now. Now he's reading it. Oh no, no! Not yet! Torvald, goodbye . . . and my children. . . .

[She rushes out in the direction of the hall; at the same moment Helmer *flings open his door and stands there with an open letter in his hand.]*

Helmer: Nora!

Nora: *[shrieks]* Ah!

Helmer: What is this? Do you know what is in this letter?

Nora: Yes, I know. Let me go! Let me out!

Helmer: [holds her back] Where are you going?

Nora: [trying to tear herself free] You mustn't try to save me, Torvald!

Helmer: [reels back] True! Is it true what he writes? How dreadful! No, no, it can't possibly be true.

Nora: It *is* true. I loved you more than anything else in the world.

Helmer: Don't come to me with a lot of paltry excuses!

Nora: [taking a step towards him] Torvald. . . !

Helmer: Miserable woman . . . what is this you have done?

Nora: Let me go. I won't have you taking the blame for me. You mustn't take it on yourself.

Helmer: Stop play-acting! *[Locks the front door.]* You are staying here to give an account of yourself. Do you understand what you have done? Answer me! Do you understand?

Nora: [looking fixedly at him, her face hardening] Yes, now I'm really beginning to understand.

Helmer: [walking up and down] Oh, what a terrible awakening this is. All these eight years . . . this woman who was my pride and joy . . . a hypocrite, a liar, worse than that, a criminal! Oh, how utterly squalid it all is! Ugh! Ugh! *[Nora remains silent and looks fixedly at him.]* I should have realized something like this would happen. I should have seen it coming. All your father's irresponsible ways. . . . Quiet! All your father's irresponsible ways are coming out in you. No religion, no morals, no sense of duty. . . . Oh, this is my punishment for turning a blind eye to him. It was for your sake I did it, and this is what I get for it.

Nora: Yes, this.

Helmer: Now you have ruined my entire happiness, jeopardized my whole future. It's terrible to think of. Here I am, at the mercy of a thoroughly unscrupulous person; he can do whatever he likes with me, demand anything he wants, order me about just as he chooses . . . and I daren't even whimper. I'm done for, a miserable failure, and it's all the fault of a feather-brained woman!

Nora: When I've left this world behind, you will be free.

Helmer: Oh, stop pretending! Your father was just the same, always ready with fine phrases. What good would it do me if you left this world behind, as you put it? Not the slightest bit of good. He can still let it all come out, if he likes; and if he does, people might even suspect me of being an accomplice in these criminal acts of yours. They might even think I was the one behind it all, that it was I who pushed you into it!

And it's you I have to thank for this . . . and when I've taken such good care of you, all our married life. Now do you understand what you have done to me?

Nora: [*coldly and calmly*] Yes.

Helmer: I just can't understand it, it's so incredible. But we must see about putting things right. Take that shawl off. Take it off, I tell you! I must see if I can't find some way or other of appeasing him. The thing must be hushed up at all costs. And as far as you and I are concerned, things must appear to go on exactly as before. But only in the eyes of the world, of course. In other words you'll go on living here; that's understood. But you will not be allowed to bring up the children, I can't trust you with them. . . . Oh, that I should have to say this to the woman I loved so dearly, the woman I still. . . . Well, that must be all over and done with. From now on, there can be no question of happiness. All we can do is save the bits and pieces from the wreck, preserve appearances. . . . [*The front door-bell rings.* Helmer *gives a start.*] What's that? So late? How terrible, supposing. . . If he should . . . ? Hide, Nora! Say you are not well.

[Nora *stands motionless.* Helmer *walks across and opens the door into the hall.*]

Maid: [*half dressed, in the hall*] It's a note for Mrs. Helmer.

Helmer: Give it to me. [*He snatches the note and shuts the door.*] Yes, it's from him. You can't have it. I want to read it myself.

Nora: You read it then.

Helmer: [*by the lamp*] I hardly dare. Perhaps this is the end, for both of us. Well, I *must* know. [*He opens the note hurriedly, reads a few lines, looks at another enclosed sheet, and gives a cry of joy.*] Nora! [Nora *looks at him inquiringly.*] Nora! I must read it again. Yes, yes, it's true! I am saved! Nora, I am saved!

Nora: And me?

Helmer: You too, of course, we are both saved, you as well as me. Look, he's sent your IOU back. He sends his regrets and apologies for what he has done. . . . His luck has changed. . . . Oh, what does it matter what he says. We are saved, Nora! Nobody can do anything to you now. Oh, Nora, Nora . . . but let's get rid of this disgusting thing first. Let me see. . . . [*He glances at the IOU.*] No, I don't want to see it. I don't want it to be anything but a dream. [*He tears up the IOU and both letters, throws all the pieces into the stove and watches them burn.*] Well, that's the end of that. He said in his note you'd known since Christmas Eve. . . . You must have had three terrible days of it, Nora.

Nora: These three days haven't been easy.

Helmer: The agonies you must have gone through! When the
     only way out seemed to be. . . . No, let's forget the whole
     ghastly thing. We can rejoice and say: It's all over! It's all
     over! Listen to me, Nora! You don't seem to understand: it's
     all over! Why this grim look on your face? Oh, poor little
     Nora, of course I understand. You can't bring yourself to
     believe I've forgiven you. But I have, Nora, I swear it. I for-
     give you everything. I know you did what you did because
     you loved me.

Nora: That's true.

Helmer: You loved me as a wife should love her husband. It was
     simply that you didn't have the experience to judge what was
     the best way of going about things. But do you think I love
     you any the less for that; just because you don't know how to
     act on your own responsibility? No, no, you just lean on me,
     I shall give you all the advice and guidance you need. I
     wouldn't be a proper man if I didn't find a woman doubly
     attractive for being so obviously helpless. You mustn't dwell
     on the harsh things I said in that first moment of horror,
     when I thought everything was going to come crashing down
     about my ears. I have forgiven you, Nora, I swear it! I have
     forgiven you!

Nora: Thank you for your forgiveness.

[She goes out through the door, right.]

Helmer: No, don't go! *[He looks through the doorway.]* What are
     you doing in the spare room?

Nora: Taking off this fancy dress.

Helmer: [standing at the open door] Yes, do. You try and get some
     rest, and set your mind at peace again, my frightened little
     song-bird. Have a good long sleep; you know you are safe
     and sound under my wing. *[Walks up and down near the door.]*
     What a nice, cosy little home we have here, Nora! Here you
     can find refuge. Here I shall hold you like a hunted dove I
     have rescued unscathed from the cruel talons of the hawk,
     and calm your poor beating heart. And that will come, grad-
     ually, Nora, believe me. Tomorrow you'll see everything
     quite differently. Soon everything will be just as it was
     before. You won't need me to keep on telling you I've for-
     given you; you'll feel convinced of it in your own heart. You
     don't really imagine me ever thinking of turning you out, or
     even of reproaching you? Oh, a real man isn't made that
     way, you know, Nora. For a man, there's something inde-
     scribably moving and very satisfying in knowing that he has
     forgiven his wife—forgiven her, completely and genuinely,
     from the depths of his heart. It's as though it made her his
     property in a double sense: he has, as it were, given her a new

life, and she becomes in a way both his wife and at the same time his child. That is how you will seem to me after today, helpless, perplexed little thing that you are. Don't you worry your pretty little head about anything, Nora. Just you be frank with me, and I'll take all the decisions for you. . . . What's this? Not in bed? You've changed your things?

Nora: [*in her everyday dress*] Yes, Torvald, I've changed.

Helmer: What for? It's late.

Nora: I shan't sleep tonight.

Helmer: But my dear Nora. . . .

Nora: [*looks at her watch*] It's not so terribly late. Sit down, Torvald. We two have a lot to talk about.

[*She sits down at one side of the table.*]

Helmer: Nora, what is all this? Why so grim?

Nora: Sit down. It'll take some time. I have a lot to say to you.

Helmer: [*sits down at the table opposite her*] You frighten me, Nora. I don't understand you.

Nora: Exactly. You don't understand me. And I have never understood you, either—until tonight. No, don't interrupt. I just want you to listen to what I have to say. We are going to have things out, Torvald.

Helmer: What do you mean?

Nora: Isn't there anything that strikes you about the way we two are sitting here?

Helmer: What's that?

Nora: We have now been married eight years. Hasn't it struck you this is the first time you and I, man and wife, have had a serious talk together?

Helmer: Depends what you mean by 'serious'.

Nora: Eight whole years—no, more, ever since we first knew each other—and never have we exchanged one serious word about serious things.

Helmer: What did you want me to do? Get you involved in worries that you couldn't possibly help me to bear?

Nora: I'm not talking about worries. I say we've never once sat down together and seriously tried to get to the bottom of anything.

Helmer: But, my dear Nora, would that have been a thing for you?

Nora: That's just it. You have never understood me . . . I've been greatly wronged, Torvald. First by my father, and then by you.

Helmer: What! Us two! The two people who loved you more than anybody?

Nora: [*shakes her head*] You two never loved me. You only thought how nice it was to be in love with me.

Helmer: But, Nora, what's this you are saying?

Nora: It's right, you know, Torvald. At home, Daddy used to tell me what he thought, then I thought the same. And if I thought differently, I kept quiet about it, because he wouldn't have liked it. He used to call me his baby doll, and he played with me as I used to play with my dolls. Then I came to live in your house. . . .

Helmer: What way is that to talk about our marriage?

Nora: [imperturbably] What I mean is: I passed out of Daddy's hands into yours. You arranged everything to your tastes, and I acquired the same tastes. Or I pretended to . . . I don't really know . . . I think it was a bit of both, sometimes one thing and sometimes the other. When I look back, it seems to me I have been living here like a beggar, from hand to mouth. I lived by doing tricks for you, Torvald. But that's the way you wanted it. You and Daddy did me a great wrong. It's your fault that I've never made anything of my life.

Helmer: Nora, how unreasonable . . . how ungrateful you are! Haven't you been happy here?

Nora: No, never. I thought I was, but I wasn't really.

Helmer: Not . . . not happy!

Nora: No, just gay. And you've always been so kind to me. But our house has never been anything but a play-room. I have been your doll wife, just as at home I was Daddy's doll child. And the children in turn have been my dolls. I thought it was fun when you came and played with me, just as they thought it was fun when I went and played with them. That's been our marriage, Torvald.

Helmer: There is some truth in what you say, exaggerated and hysterical though it is. But from now on it will be different. Play-time is over; now comes the time for lessons.

Nora: Whose lessons? Mine or the children's?

Helmer: Both yours and the children's, my dear Nora.

Nora: Ah, Torvald, you are not the man to teach me to be a good wife for you.

Helmer: How can you say that?

Nora: And what sort of qualifications have I to teach the children?

Helmer: Nora!

Nora: Didn't you say yourself, a minute or two ago, that you couldn't trust me with that job.

Helmer: In the heat of the moment! You shouldn't pay any attention to that.

Nora: On the contrary, you were quite right. I'm not up to it. There's another problem needs solving first. I must take steps to educate myself. You are not the man to help me there. That's something I must do on my own. That's why I'm leaving you.

Helmer: [*jumps up*] What did you say?

Nora: If I'm ever to reach any understanding of myself and the things around me, I must learn to stand alone. That's why I can't stay here with you any longer.

Helmer: Nora! Nora!

Nora: I'm leaving here at once. I dare say Kristine will put me up for tonight. . . .

Helmer: You are out of your mind! I won't let you! I forbid you!

Nora: It's no use forbidding me anything now. I'm taking with me my own personal belongings. I don't want anything of yours, either now or later.

Helmer: This is madness!

Nora: Tomorrow I'm going home—to what used to be my home, I mean. It will be easier for me to find something to do there.

Helmer: Oh, you blind, inexperienced . . .

Nora: I must set about *getting* experience, Torvald.

Helmer: And leave your home, your husband and your children? Don't you care what people will say?

Nora: That's no concern of mine. All I know is that this is necessary for *me*.

Helmer: This is outrageous! You are betraying your most sacred duty.

Nora: And what do you consider to be my most sacred duty?

Helmer: Does it take me to tell you that? Isn't it your duty to your husband and your children?

Nora: I have another duty equally sacred.

Helmer: You have not. What duty might *that* be?

Nora: My duty to myself.

Helmer: First and foremost, you are a wife and mother.

Nora: That I don't believe any more. I believe that first and foremost I am an individual, just as much as you are—or at least I'm going to try to be. I know most people agree with you, Torvald, and that's also what it says in books. But I'm not content any more with what most people say, or with what it says in books. I have to think things out for myself, and get things clear.

Helmer: Surely you are clear about your position in your own home? Haven't you an infallible guide in questions like these? Haven't you your religion?

Nora: Oh, Torvald, I don't really know what religion is.

Helmer: What do you say!

Nora: All I know is what Pastor Hansen said when I was confirmed. He said religion was this, that and the other. When

I'm away from all this and on my own, I'll go into that, too. I want to find out whether what Pastor Hansen told me was right—or at least whether it's right for *me*.

Helmer: This is incredible talk from a young woman! But if religion cannot keep you on the right path, let me at least stir your conscience. I suppose you do have some moral sense? Or tell me—perhaps you don't?

Nora: Well, Torvald, that's not easy to say. I simply don't know. I'm really very confused about such things. All I know is my ideas about such things are very different from yours. I've also learnt that the law is different from what I thought; but I simply can't get it into my head that that particular law is right. Apparently a woman has no right to spare her old father on his death-bed, or to save her husband's life, even. I just don't believe it.

Helmer: You are talking like a child. You understand nothing about the society you live in.

Nora: No, I don't. But I shall go into that too. I must try to discover who is right, society or me.

Helmer: You are ill, Nora. You are delirious. I'm half inclined to think you are out of your mind.

Nora: Never have I felt so calm and collected as I do tonight.

Helmer: Calm and collected enough to leave your husband and children?

Nora: Yes.

Helmer: Then only one explanation is possible.

Nora: And that is?

Helmer: You don't love me any more.

Nora: Exactly.

Helmer: Nora! Can you say that!

Nora: I'm desperately sorry, Torvald. Because you have always been so kind to me. But I can't help it. I don't love you any more.

Helmer: [*struggling to keep his composure*] Is that also a 'calm and collected' decision you've made?

Nora: Yes, absolutely calm and collected. That's why I don't want to stay here.

Helmer: And can you also account for how I forfeited your love?

Nora: Yes, very easily. It was tonight, when the miracle didn't happen. It was then I realized you weren't the man I thought you were.

Helmer: Explain yourself more clearly. I don't understand.

Nora: For eight years I have been patiently waiting. Because, heavens, I knew miracles didn't happen every day. Then this devastating business started, and I became absolutely convinced the miracle *would* happen. All the time Krogstad's letter lay there, it never so much as crossed my mind that you would ever submit to that man's conditions. I was absolutely convinced you would say to him: Tell the whole wide world if you like. And when that was done . . .

Helmer: Yes, then what? After I had exposed my own wife to dishonour and shame . . . !

Nora: When that was done, I was absolutely convinced you would come forward and take everything on yourself, and say: I am the guilty one.

Helmer: Nora!

Nora: You mean I'd never let you make such a sacrifice for my sake? Of course not. But what would my story have counted for against yours?—That was the miracle I went in hope and dread of. It was to prevent it that I was ready to end my life.

Helmer: I would gladly toil day and night for you, Nora, enduring all manner of sorrow and distress. But nobody sacrifices his *honour* for the one he loves.

Nora: Hundreds and thousands of women have.

Helmer: Oh, you think and talk like a stupid child.

Nora: All right. But you neither think nor talk like the man I would want to share my life with. When you had got over your fright—and you weren't concerned about me but only about what might happen to you—and when all danger was past, you acted as though nothing had happened. I was your little sky-lark again, your little doll, exactly as before; except you would have to protect it twice as carefully as before, now that it had shown itself to be so weak and fragile. *[Rises.]* Torvald, that was the moment I realised that for eight years I'd been living with a stranger, and had borne him three children. . . . Oh, I can't bear to think about it! I could tear myself to shreds.

Helmer: *[sadly]* I see. I see. There is a tremendous gulf dividing us. But, Nora, is there no way we might bridge it?

Nora: As I am now, I am no wife for you.

Helmer: I still have it in me to change.

Nora: Perhaps . . . if you have your doll taken away.

Helmer: And be separated from you! No, no, Nora, the very thought of it is inconceivable.

Nora: *[goes into the room, right]* All the more reason why it must be done.

[She comes back with her outdoor things and a small travelling bag which she puts on the chair beside the table.]

Helmer: Nora, Nora, not now! Wait till the morning.

Nora: *[putting on her coat]* I can't spend the night in a strange man's room.

Helmer: Couldn't we go on living here like brother and sister. . . ?

Nora: [tying on her hat] You know very well that wouldn't last. *[She draws the shawl round her.]* Goodbye, Torvald. I don't want to see the children. I know they are in better hands than mine. As I am now, I can never be anything to them.

Helmer: But some day, Nora, some day. . . ?

Nora: How should I know? I've no idea what I might turn out to be.

Helmer: But you are my wife, whatever you are.

Nora: Listen, Torvald, from what I've heard, when a wife leaves her husband's house as I am doing now, he is absolved by law of all responsibility for her. I can at any rate free you from all responsibility. You must not feel in any way bound, any more than I shall. There must be full freedom on both sides. Look, here's your ring back. Give me mine.

Helmer: That too?

Nora: That too.

Helmer: There it is.

Nora: Well, that's the end of that. I'll put the keys down here. The maids know where everything is in the house—better than I do, in fact. Kristine will come in the morning after I've left to pack up the few things I brought with me from home. I want them sent on.

Helmer: The end! Nora, will you never think of me?

Nora: I dare say I'll often think about you and the children and this house.

Helmer: May I write to you, Nora?

Nora: No, never. I won't let you.

Helmer: But surely I can send you . . .

Nora: Nothing, nothing.

Helmer: Can't I help you if ever you need it?

Nora: I said 'no'. I don't accept things from strangers.

Helmer: Nora, can I never be anything more to you than a stranger?

Nora: [takes her bag] Ah, Torvald, only by a miracle of miracles. . . .

Helmer: Name it, this miracle of miracles!

Nora: Both you and I would have to change to the point where . . . Oh, Torvald, I don't believe in miracles any more.

Helmer: But I *will* believe. Name it! Change to the point where . . . ?

Nora: Where we could make a real marriage of our lives together. Goodbye!

[She goes out through the hall door.]

Helmer: [sinks down on a chair near the door, and covers his face with his hands] Nora! Nora! *[He rises and looks round.]* Empty! She's gone! *[With sudden hope.]* The miracle of miracles. . . ?

[The heavy sound of a door being slammed is heard from below.]

Further Reading

Meyer, Michael. Introduction. *A Doll's House.* By Henrik Ibsen. London: Eyre, 1974. 9–19. • Archer, William. "A Doll's House." *William Archer on Ibsen.* Ed. Thomas Postlewait. Westport, CT: Greenwood, 1984. 205–215. • Shaw, George B. "A Doll's House." *The Quintessence of Ibsenism.* New York: Brentano's, 1913. 88–92. • Downs, Brian W. "A Doll's House." *A Study of Six Plays by Ibsen.* Cambridge: Cambridge UP, 1950. 104–146. • Weigand, Hermann J. "A Doll's House." *Henrik Ibsen.* Ed. James McFarlane. Middlesex, Eng.: Penguin, 1970. 359–69. • Hardwick, Elizabeth. "A Doll's House." *Seduction and Betrayal: Women and Literature.* New York: Random, 1974. 33–48.

"Before I write down one word," Ibsen once said, "I have to have the character in mind through and through. I always proceed from the individual; the stage setting, the dramatic ensemble, all of that comes naturally and does not cause me any worry, as soon as I am certain of the individual in every aspect of his humanity." Ibsen's preliminary notes for A Doll's House *show his earliest attempt to envision his play by describing the character that would become Nora Helmer.*

Henrik Ibsen: Preliminary Notes for *A Doll's House* (1878)

NOTES FOR THE TRAGEDY OF MODERN TIMES, ROME, 19 OCTOBER 1878

There are two kinds of moral law, two kinds of conscience, one in man and a completely different one in woman. They do not understand each other; but in matters of practical living the woman is judged by man's law, as if she were not a woman but a man.

The wife in the play ends up quite bewildered and not knowing right from wrong; her natural instincts on the one side and her faith in authority on the other leave her completely confused.

A woman cannot be herself in contemporary society, it is an exclusively male society with laws drafted by men, and with counsel and judges who judge feminine conduct from the male point of view.

She has committed a crime, and she is proud of it; because she did it for love of her husband and to save his life. But the husband, with his conventional views of honour, stands on the side of the law and looks at the affair with male eyes.

Mental conflict. Depressed and confused by her faith in authority, she loses faith in her moral right and ability to bring up her children. Bitterness. A mother in contemporary society, just as certain insects go away and die when she has done her duty in the propagation of the race [sic]. Love of life, of home and husband and children and family. Now and then, womanlike, she shrugs off her thoughts. Sudden return of dread and terror. Everything must be borne alone. The catastrophe approaches, ineluctably, inevitably. Despair, resistance, defeat.

ANTON CHEKHOV

(1860–1904)

THE THREE SISTERS

translated from the Russian by Randall Jarrell

CHARACTERS

Prozorov, Andrei Sergeevich
Natalya [Natasha] Ivanovna, his fiancée, then his wife
Olga
Masha } *his sisters*
Irina
Kulygin, Fyodor Ilich, a high school teacher, husband of Masha
Vershinin, Alexander Ignatyevich, Lieutenant Colonel, Battery Commander
Tuzenbach, Nikolai Lvovich, Baron, Lieutenant
Solyony, Vasili Vasilevich, Staff Captain
Chebutykin, Ivan Romanovich, Military Doctor
Fedotik, Alexei Petrovich, Second Lieutenant
Rode, Vladimir Karlovich, Second Lieutenant
Ferapont, janitor from the county board, an old man
Anfisa, nurse, an old woman of eighty

The action takes place in a provincial city.

ACT 1

The living room in the house of the Prozorovs—*a row of columns separates it from a large dining room at the back. Midday; outside it is sunny and bright. In the dining room the table is being set for lunch.* Olga, *in the dark blue uniform of a teacher in a girls' high school, is correcting papers, standing or walking to and fro.* Masha, *in a black dress, her hat on her knees, is sitting reading a book.* Irina, *in a white dress, stands lost in thought.*

Olga: Just a year ago, a year ago on this very day, Father died— on your birthday, Irina, on the fifth of May. It was very cold, the snow was falling. I thought I'd never live through it; you had fainted, and lay there as if you were dead. But now a year's gone by and we can remember it calmly; you're already wearing white, your face is radiant. . . .

[The clock strikes twelve]

And the clock struck just the same way then. *(A pause)* I
remember that as they took Father there the band was playing,
they fired a volley over his grave. He was a general, he was in
command of a whole brigade, and yet there weren't many people. Of course, it was raining. Raining hard—rain and snow.

Irina: Why think about it?

*[Behind the columns, in the dining room, Baron Tuzenbach, Chebutykin, and
Solyony appear]*

Olga: It's warm today, we can have the windows wide open—and
yet there still aren't any leaves on the birches. They gave
Father his brigade, we left Moscow with him, eleven years ago,
and I remember distinctly that in Moscow at this time, at the
start of May, everything is already in bloom; it's warm, everything is bathed in sunshine. That was eleven years ago, and yet
I remember it all as if we'd left it yesterday. Oh, God! When I
woke up this morning I saw that everything was light, that it
was spring, and I thought my heart would burst with joy. I
longed so passionately to go home.

Chebutykin: The devil it is!

Tuzenbach: Of course, it's all nonsense. (Masha, *brooding over her book,
softly whistles a tune*)

Olga: Don't *whistle*, Masha! How can you? *(A pause)* Being at
school every day and then giving lessons all afternoon—it
makes my head ache all the time, the thoughts I have are an old
woman's thoughts already. Really and truly, these four years
I've been at the high school I've felt the strength and the youth
being squeezed out of me day by day, drop by drop. And just
one dream grows stronger and stronger.

Irina: To go back to Moscow! To sell the house, finish up everything here, and—off to Moscow!

Olga: Yes! As soon as we possibly can, to Moscow! (Chebutykin
and Tuzenbach *laugh*)

Irina: Brother will probably be a professor, he won't be living
here anyway. The only thing wrong is poor Masha.

Olga: Masha's going to come and spend the whole summer in
Moscow every summer. (Masha *softly begins to whistle a tune*)

Irina: Please God, it will all come out right! *(She looks out of the
window)* It's such a beautiful day, I don't know why I feel so
happy. This morning I remembered it's my birthday, and all at
once I felt joyful and remembered my childhood, when
Mother was still alive. And what marvelous thrilling thoughts I
had—what thoughts!

Olga: You're radiant today—I've never seen you lovelier. And
Masha looks lovely, too. And Andrei would be good-looking,
only he's got so fat; it isn't a bit becoming. And I've got older

and so much thinner—I suppose it's because I get so cross at the girls at school. Today now, I'm free, I'm at home, my head doesn't ache, I feel so much younger to myself than I did yesterday. I'm only twenty-eight. . . . It's all good, it's all as God means it to be, but it seems to me that if I were married and stayed home all day it would be better. *(A pause)* I'd love my husband.

Tuzenbach: You talk such nonsense I'm sick of listening to you. *(Coming into the living room)* I forgot to tell you. Today you are to be visited by our new battery commander. His name's Vershinin.

   Olga: Really? I'm delighted.

   Irina: Is he old?

Tuzenbach: No, not very. Forty or so—forty-five at the most. He seems quite nice—and he's certainly no fool. Only he talks a lot.

   Irina: Is he interesting?

Tuzenbach: Yes, interesting enough—only there's a wife, a mother-in-law, and two little girls. What's more, she's his second wife. He goes around calling on people and telling them he has a wife and two little girls. He'll tell you that. His wife isn't exactly all there: she has long braids like a girl's, talks only of lofty things, philosophizes, and regularly tries to commit suicide—to annoy her husband, evidently. If I were Vershinin I'd have left such a woman long ago, but he puts up with it and just complains.

   Solyony: *(Entering the living room with* Chebutykin*)* With one hand I can only lift sixty pounds, but with two hands I can lift a hundred and eighty-two—two hundred, even. From that I deduce that two men aren't twice as strong, they're three times as strong as one man . . . or even stronger. . . .

Chebutykin: *(Reading a newspaper as he comes in)* For falling hair: Two ounces of naphtha in half a pint of alcohol . . . dissolve and apply daily. *[He writes it down in his notebook]* Let's make a note of it! *[To* Solyony*]* So remember what I told you, you want to cork the bottle tight and push a glass tube down through the cork. Then you take a pinch of alum, plain ordinary alum—

   Irina: Ivan Romanich, dear Ivan Romanich!

Chebutykin: What is it, my child, my treasure?

   Irina: Tell me, why is it I'm so happy today? As if I were sailing along with the wide blue sky over me and great white birds floating across it. Why is that? Why?

Chebutykin: *(Kissing both her hands tenderly)* My white bird . . .

   Irina: When I woke up this morning and got up and bathed, all at once I felt as if everything in the world were clear to me, and I understood the way one ought to live. Dear Ivan Romanich, I understand everything. A man must work, must make his

bread by the sweat of his brow, it doesn't matter who he is—
and it is in this alone that he can find the purpose and meaning
of his life, his happiness, his ecstasies. Oh, how good it is to be
a workman who gets up at dawn and breaks stones in the street,
or a shepherd, or a schoolteacher who teaches children, or a
locomotive engineer! My God, it's better to be an ox, it's better to be a plain horse, and *work*, than to be a girl who wakes up
at twelve o'clock, has coffee in bed, and then takes two hours to
get dressed. . . . Oh, how awful that is! Sometimes I—I *thirst*
for work the way on a hot day you thirst for water. And if I
don't get up early and work, give me up forever, Ivan
Romanich!

Chebutykin: *(Tenderly)* I will, I will.

Olga: Father trained us to get up at seven. Now Irina wakes up at
seven and lies there till nine at least, and thinks about something. And she does look so serious! *(Laughing)*

Irina: You're so used to considering me a child that you're surprised I should ever be serious. I am twenty!

Tuzenbach: That thirst for work—good God, how well I understand it!
I've never worked a day in my life. I was born in Petersburg,
cold, lazy Petersburg—born into a family that never knew what
work or worry meant. I remember that when I'd get home
from cadet school a footman would pull my boots off for me,
and I'd do something idiotic and my mother would look at me
in awe, and then be surprised when everybody else didn't. I've
been sheltered from work. But they've hardly succeeded in
sheltering me forever—hardly! The time has come: a thunder-
cloud is hanging over us all, a great healthy storm is gathering;
it's coming, it's already almost upon us, and is going to sweep
out of our society the laziness, the indifference, the contempt
for work, the rotten boredom. I'll work—and in another
twenty-five or thirty years everybody will work. Everybody!

Chebutykin: *I'm* not going to work.

Tuzenbach: You don't count.

Solyony: In another twenty-five years, thank God, you won't be here
on this earth. In two or three years either you'll get apoplexy
or I'll lose control of myself and put a bullet through your
head, my angel. *(He takes a little bottle of perfume from his pocket
and sprinkles it over his chest and hands)*

Chebutykin: I really never have done a thing. Since I left the university
I haven't lifted a finger, I haven't opened a book—I just read
the newspapers. *(He takes another newspaper out of his pocket)*
Here we are. I know from the papers that there was, say, some-
body named Dobrolyubov, but what he wrote I don't know.
God only knows. *(A knock is heard from the floor below)* Listen.
They want me downstairs, somebody's come to see me. . . .

I'm coming right away. Wait a minute. . . . *(He goes out hurriedly, combing his beard)*

Irina: He's up to something.

Tuzenbach: Yes. He went out looking solemn—plainly, he's about to bring you a present.

Irina: What a nuisance!

Olga: Yes, it's awful. He's always doing something silly.

Masha: By the curved seastrand a green oak stands, / A chain of gold upon it . . . *(She gets up and hums softly)*

Olga: You're not very cheerful today, Masha. *(Masha, humming, puts on her hat)* Where are you going?

Masha: Home.

Irina: That's strange.

Tuzenbach: To walk out on a birthday party!

Masha: What's the difference? I'll be back this evening. Goodbye, my darling. . . . *(She kisses Irina)* I'll wish all over again: may you always be well and happy! In the old days, when Father was alive, there'd always be thirty or forty officers here on our birthdays, there was lots of noise, and today there's a man and a half and it's as silent as the tomb. . . . I'm going. I'm depressed today, I feel miserable—don't you listen to me. *(She smiles through her tears)* We'll talk afterwards—good-bye till then, dearest, I'm going.

Irina: *(Discontentedly)* Oh, how can you be so . . .

Olga: *(In tears)* I understand you, Masha.

Solyony: If a man philosophizes, you get philosophy or, anyway, something that looks like philosophy; but if a woman philosophizes, or two do, you might just as well suck your thumb.

Masha: And what is that supposed to mean, you terribly dreadful man?

Solyony: Nothing. Before he'd time to get his breath / The bear was hugging him to death. *(A pause)*

Masha: *(To Olga, angrily)* Don't sit there sniveling!

[Enter Anfisa *and* Ferapont *with a cake]*

Anfisa: In here, uncle. Come on in, your feet are clean. *(To Irina)* From the county board, from Mikhail Ivanich Protopopov—a cake.

Irina: Thank you. And thank him for me, please.

Ferapont: How's that?

Irina: *(Louder)* Thank him!

Anfisa: Come on, Ferapont Spiridonich. Come on. . . .

[She goes out with Ferapont*]*

Masha: I don't like that Protopopov, that Mikhail Potapich or Ivanich or whatever it is. He ought not to be invited.

Irina: I didn't invite him.

Masha: That's fine!

[Chebutykin *enters, behind him an orderly with a silver samovar; there is a hum of amazement and displeasure*]

Olga: *(Covering her face with her hands)* A samovar! This is awful!

[*She goes to the table in the dining room*]

Irina: Darling Ivan Romanich, what can have possessed you?

Tuzenbach: *(Laughing)* I told you so.

Masha: Ivan Romanich, you're simply shameless.

Chebutykin: My darlings, my blessed girls, you are all that I have left, to me you are the most precious treasures that there are upon this earth. Soon I'll be sixty years old: I'm an old man, a lonely worthless old man. The only good that there is in me is my love for you—if it weren't for you I should have left this world long ago. *(To* Irina) My darling, my own little girl, I've known you since the day you were born. . . . I carried you in these arms. . . . I loved your sainted mother. . . .

Irina: But why such expensive presents?

Chebutykin: *(Through his tears, angrily)* Expensive presents! Oh, get out! *(To the* Orderly) Carry the samovar over there. *(Mimicking)* Expensive presents!

[*The* Orderly *carries the samovar into the dining room*]

Anfisa: [*Walking through the living room*] My dears, there's a strange colonel. He's already taken off his overcoat, children, he's coming in here. Irina darling, now you be a nice polite little girl. *(As she goes out)* And it was time for lunch hours ago. . . . The Lord have mercy!

Tuzenbach: It must be Vershinin.

[Vershinin *enters*]

Tuzenbach: Lieutenant Colonel Vershinin!

Vershinin: I have the honor of introducing myself: Vershinin. I'm so glad, so very glad to be here in your house at last. But how you've grown! My, my!

Irina: Do sit down. We're delighted.

Vershinin: How glad I am! How glad I am! But surely there are three of you sisters. I remember—three little girls. I can't remember your faces any longer, but your father, Colonel Prozorov, had three little girls—that I remember distinctly; I saw them with my own eyes. How time does fly! My, my, how time does fly!

Tuzenbach: Alexander Ignatyevich is from Moscow.

Irina: From Moscow? You're from Moscow?

Vershinin: Yes, from Moscow. Your father, God bless him, was a battery commander there, and I was an officer in the same brigade. *(To* Masha*)* Now that I—it seems to me I do remember your face a little.

Masha: Yours—I—no!

Irina: Olga! Olga! *(She calls into the dining room)* Olga! Come here!

[Olga *comes in from the dining room*]

Irina: It seems Colonel Vershinin's from Moscow.

Vershinin: You must be Olga Sergeevna, the eldest. . . . And you're Marya. . . . And you're Irina, the youngest.

Olga: You're from Moscow?

Vershinin: Yes, I went to school in Moscow and went into the service in Moscow, I was stationed there for many years, and finally they gave me a battery here and I've moved here, as you see. I don't exactly remember you, I just remember that there were you three sisters. But I remember your father so well: if I shut my eyes I can see him standing there as plain as life. I used to come to see you in Moscow. . . .

Olga: It seemed to me I remembered everybody, and now all at once. . . .

Vershinin: My name is Alexander Ignatyevich.

Irina: Alexander Ignatyevich, so you're from Moscow! What a surprise!

Olga: We're about to move there, you know.

Irina: We'll be there by this fall, we expect. It's our home town, we were born there. . . . On Old Basmanny Street. *(They both laugh with delight)*

Masha: We've met someone from home—and so unexpectedly! *(Animatedly)* Now I remember! Remember, Olga, they used to talk to us about "the love-sick major." You were a lieutenant then, and in love with somebody, and for some reason they'd all call you major to tease you.

Vershinin: *(Laughing)* That's it! That's it! The love-sick major. That was it!

Masha: You just had a moustache then. But how old you've got! *(Tearfully)* How old you've got!

Vershinin: Yes, when they used to call me the love-sick major I was young, I was in love. It's different now.

Olga: But you still haven't a single gray hair. You've got older, but you're still not old.

Vershinin: Just the same, I'm forty-two. Has it been long since you left Moscow?

Irina: Eleven years. Oh, Masha, what are you crying for, you crazy thing? *(Through her tears)* You've made me cry, too.

Masha: I'm all right. What street did you live on?

Vershinin: On Old Basmanny.

Olga: We did, too.

Vershinin: For a while I lived on Nyemetski Street. From there I used to go back and forth to the Red Barracks. On the way there's a gloomy-looking bridge, you can hear the water under it. A lonely man gets melancholy there. *(A pause)* But here you've such a broad, such a splendid river! A wonderful river!

Olga: Yes . . . only it's so cold. It's so cold here, and there're mosquitoes.

Vershinin: How can you say that? You have such a splendid, healthy, Russian climate here. The forest, the river . . . and there're birches here, too. Dear, modest birches—of all the trees I love birches best. It's good to live here. The only queer thing, the railroad station is ten miles away. . . . And nobody knows why.

Solyony: I know why. *(Everyone looks at him)* Because if the station were here it wouldn't be way off there; and if it's way off there, then of course it can't be here. *(An awkward silence)*

Tuzenbach: He's a joker, Vasili Vasilich.

Olga: Now I've remembered you. I remember.

Vershinin: I knew your mother.

Chebutykin: She was a lovely woman, bless her soul.

Irina: Mother is buried in Moscow.

Olga: In the Novo Devichy. . . .

Masha: Imagine, I'm already beginning to forget her face. And the same way, they won't remember us. They'll forget us.

Vershinin: Yes. They'll forget us. That is our fate, there is nothing we can do about it. Everything that seems to us serious, significant, profoundly important—the time will come when it will be forgotten or will seem unimportant. . . . *(A pause)* And what's so interesting is that there's no way for us to know what it is that's going to seem great and important, and what it is that's going to seem pitiful and ridiculous. Take Copernicus or Columbus, for instance—didn't their discoveries seem useless or ridiculous at first, and some fool's empty nonsense seem the truth? And it may be that the life we lead now, the life we reconcile ourselves to so easily, will seem strange some day, uncomfortable, unintelligent, not clean enough—perhaps, even, wrong.

Tuzenbach: Who knows? Or perhaps our life will be called great and be remembered with respect. We don't torture people any more, we've no more executions and invasions—but just the same, how much suffering there is still!

Solyony: *(In a high-pitched voice)* He-ere, chicky, chicky, chicky! Don't feed the baron chicken feed, just let him philosophize.

Tuzenbach: Vasili Vasilich, leave me alone, please. *(He sits down in another place)* After all, this sort of thing gets to be boring.

Solyony: (In a high-pitched voice) He-ere, chicky, chicky, chicky!

Tuzenbach: The suffering we see now—there's still so much of it— itself is a sign that our society has reached a certain level of moral development. . . .

Vershinin: Yes, yes, of course.

Chebutykin: You said just now, Baron, that they'll call our life great: just the same, people are very small. *(He stands up)* Look how small I am. If anybody were to say that my life is something great, something that makes sense, he'd just be saying it to make me feel good.

[Behind the scene someone is playing the violin]

Masha: That's Andrei playing, our brother.

Irina: He's the scholar of the family. We expect he'll be a professor someday. Father was a military man, but his son has chosen an academic career.

Masha: Father wanted him to.

Olga: We've been teasing him all morning. It looks as if he's a little bit in love.

Irina: With one of the local girls. She'll probably be here before long.

Masha: The way she does dress! It's not that her clothes are ugly or old-fashioned, somehow they're just pathetic. Some sort of queer gaudy yellowish skirt with a cheap fringe on it—and a red blouse. And her cheeks scrubbed till they shine! Andrei isn't in love with her—I refuse to admit it, he does have some taste—he's just making fun of us, playing some sort of joke on us. I heard yesterday that she's going to marry Protopopov, the chairman of the county board. That would be perfect. *(Through the side door)* Andrei, come in here! Just for a minute, darling!

[Andrei enters]

Olga: This is my brother, Andrei Sergeevich.

Vershinin: Vershinin.

Andrei: Prozorov. *(He wipes the sweat off his face)* You're our new battery commander?

Olga: Just imagine, Alexander Ignatyevich is from Moscow.

Andrei: You are? Well then, I congratulate you—my sisters won't give you a moment's peace.

Vershinin: I've already succeeded in boring your sisters.

Irina: Look at the frame Andrei gave me today! *(Showing the frame)* He made it himself.

Vershinin: (Looking at the frame and not knowing what to say) Yes. It's . . . it's a thing . . .

[Andrei *waves his hand in disgust and walks away*]

> *Olga:* He's our scholar, and he plays the violin, and he can make *anything* with his fretsaw. In fact, he's a kind of universal expert. Don't go away, Andrei! That's the way he is, always going off by himself. Come back here!

[Masha *and* Irina *take him by the arms and, laughing, lead him back*]

> *Masha:* Come along! Come along!
> *Andrei:* Please let me alone.
> *Masha:* Isn't he absurd! They used to call Alexander Ignatyevich the love-sick major, and he never got angry, not even once.
> *Vershinin:* Not even once!
> *Masha:* I think we ought to call you the love-sick violinist!
> *Irina:* Or the love-sick professor!
> *Olga:* He's in love! Our little Andrei's in love!
> *Irina: (Applauding)* Bravo! Bravo! Encore! Our little Andrei's in love!
> *Chebutykin: (Coming up behind* Andrei *and putting both hands around his waist)* Male and female created He them! *(He laughs. He still has the newspaper.)*
> *Andrei:* Well, that's enough, that's enough. . . . *(He wipes his face)* I couldn't sleep all night and this morning I'm not quite myself, as the phrase goes. I read till four o'clock and then went to bed, but it wasn't any use. I'd think of something, and then think of something else—and it gets light so early here: the sunlight simply pours into my bedroom. This summer while I'm here there's this English book I want to translate . . .
> *Vershinin:* You read English?
> *Andrei:* Yes. Father, God bless him, absolutely loaded us down with education. It's absurd, it's idiotic, but just the same I've got to admit that after his death I began to gain weight—in a year I've got fat like this, just as if my body had taken the chance to break loose from him. Thanks to Father my sisters and I know French, German, and English, and Irina even knows Italian. But what's the use of that?
> *Masha:* In this town knowing three languages is a useless luxury. Not even a luxury but a sort of useless appendage, like a sixth finger. We know a lot that isn't any use.
> *Vershinin:* Really now! *(He laughs)* You know a lot that isn't any use! I don't think that there is a town, that there can be a town, so boring and so dismal that it doesn't need intelligent, cultivated people. Suppose that among the hundred thousand inhabitants of this town—this obviously crude, obviously backward

place—suppose that there're only three people like you. It's plain that you won't be able to get the better of the darkness and ignorance around you; as you go on living, little by little you'll have to give up, you'll be lost in this crowd of a hundred thousand human beings, their life will choke you out. But you'll have been here, you'll not disappear without a trace: later on others like you will come, perhaps only six at first, then twenty, and so on, until at last people like you will be in the majority. In two or three hundred years life on earth will be unimaginably wonderful. Mankind needs such a life—and if it isn't here yet then we must look forward to it, wait, dream of it, prepare for it; and to do that we must see and know more than our fathers and grandfathers saw and knew. *(He laughs)* And you say you know a lot that isn't any use!

   Masha: (Taking off her hat) I'm staying to lunch.

   Irina: (Sighing) Really, all that ought to be written down.

[Andrei *is not there; he has gone out unnoticed*]

   Tuzenbach: After many years, you say, life on earth will be beautiful, wonderful. That is true. But to have a share in it now, even from a distance, we must get ready for it, we must work.

   Vershinin: Yes. *(He gets up)* But what a lot of flowers you have! *(He looks around)* And this beautiful house. I envy you! My whole life has been spent in little apartments with two chairs, a sofa, and a stove that keeps smoking all the time. It's just such flowers as these that have been missing in my life. *(He rubs his hands together)* Well, there's nothing to be done about it now. . . .

   Tuzenbach: Yes, we must work. Probably you're thinking: the German is getting sentimental. But I give you my word of honor, I'm Russian, I can't even speak German. My father's Orthodox. . . . *(A pause)*

   Vershinin: I often think, suppose it were possible for us to begin life over again—and consciously, this time. If only the first life, the one we've lived through already, were a rough draft, so to speak, and the other the final copy! I believe that each of us would try above all not to repeat himself—or at least would create a different set of circumstances for his life, would manage to live in a house like this, with flowers, with plenty of light. . . . I have a wife and two little girls, and not only that, my wife's an invalid, and so forth and so on—well, if I were to begin life over again, I'd never get married. . . . Never, never!

[Kulygin *enters, in a schoolteacher's uniform*]

   Kulygin: (Going up to Irina) Dear sister, allow me to congratulate you on the day of your birth—and to wish for you, sincerely and from the bottom of my heart, health and everything else that's appropriate for a girl of your age. And to offer you as a gift this little book. *(He hands her a book)* An insignificant little book, written only because I had nothing else to do, but just the same, read it. Good morning, gentlemen! *(To* Vershinin*)* Kulygin, teacher in the local high school, court councillor. *(To* Irina*)* In this book you will find a list of everyone who has graduated from our high school in the last fifty years. *Feci, quod potui, faciant meliora potentes.*[1] *(He kisses* Masha*)*

Irina: But you gave me one Easter!

Kulygin: *(He laughs)* Impossible! Well, in that case give it back—or better still, give it to the colonel. Take it, Colonel. Some day when you're bored, read it.

Vershinin: Thank you. *(He is about to leave)* I'm extremely glad to have made your acquaintance—

Olga: You're leaving? No, no!

Irina: Surely you'll stay and have lunch with us. Please.

Olga: I beg you.

Vershinin: I can see I've happened in on a party for your birthday. Forgive me, I didn't know—I haven't congratulated you.

[He goes into the dining room with Olga*]*

Kulygin: Today, gentlemen, is a Sunday, a day of rest, so let us rest, let us rejoice, each in accordance with his age and position. The rugs must be taken up for the summer and put away till winter . . . with moth balls or naphthalene. . . . The Romans were healthy because they knew both how to work and how to rest, they had *mens sana in corpore sano.*[2] Their lives were organized into a definite routine. Our principal is fond of saying that the most important thing in any life is its routine. . . . That which loses its routine loses its very existence—and it is exactly the same in our everyday life. *(He takes* Masha *by the waist, laughing)* Masha loves me. My wife loves me. And the curtains too, along with the carpets. I am gay today, in the very best of spirits. Masha, at four o'clock today we are due at the principal's. An outing has been arranged for the teachers and their families.

Masha: I'm not going.

Kulygin: *(Aggrieved)* But dear Masha, why?

Masha: We'll talk about it later. . . . *(Angrily)* Oh, all right, I'll go, only please leave me alone. . . .

---

1. "Do what you can, let those who are able do better." (Latin)
2. "A sound mind in a sound body." (Latin)

[She walks away]

Kulygin: And afterwards we're to spend the evening at the principal's. In spite of the precarious condition of his health, that man tries above all else to be sociable. A stimulating, an outstanding personality! Yesterday after the faculty meeting he said to me, "I am tired, Fyodor Ilich! I am tired!" *(He looks at the clock on the wall, then at his watch)* Your clock is seven minutes fast. "Yes," he said, "I am tired!"

[Behind the scene a violin is playing]

Olga: Ladies and gentlemen, please come to lunch. There's a meat pie.

Kulygin: Ah, Olga, my dear Olga! Yesterday I worked from early morning till eleven o'clock at night, and I was tired, literally exhausted—and today I am happy. *(He goes into the dining room by the table)* Ah, my dear . . .

Chebutykin: *(Putting the newspaper into his pocket and combing his beard)* A meat pie? Splendid!

Masha: *(To Chebutykin, sternly)* Only—listen to me!—nothing to drink today. Do you hear? It's bad for you.

Chebutykin: Oh, come on, that's ancient history. I haven't been drunk for two years. *(Impatiently)* And, my dear girl, what's the difference anyway?

Masha: Difference or no difference, don't you dare drink! Don't you dare! *(Angrily, but so that her husband doesn't hear)* Oh, damnation, damnation! for another whole evening to sit and be bored to death at that principal's!

Tuzenbach: If I were you I just wouldn't go. It's perfectly simple.

Chebutykin: Don't you go, my darling!

Masha: Yes, don't you go! . . . A damnable life! an insufferable life!

[She goes into the dining room]

Chebutykin: *(Going after her)* Now, now!

Solyony: *(Going into the dining room)* He-ere, chicky, chicky, chicky!

Tuzenbach: That's enough, Vasili Vasilich. Stop it!

Solyony: He-ere, chicky, chicky, chicky!

Kulygin: *(Cheerfully)* Your health, Colonel! I am a pedagogue, you know, and here in this house I'm one of the family, Masha's husband. . . . She is kind—so kind. . . .

Vershinin: I'll have some of this dark vodka here. *(Drinking)* Your health! *(To Olga)* I feel so good here at your house! . . .

[Only Irina and Tuzenbach are left in the living room]

Irina: Masha's not in a very good humor today. She was married when she was eighteen, and he seemed to her the most intelligent of men. It's different now. He's the kindest of men, but not the most intelligent.

Olga: (*Impatiently*) Andrei, *please* come on. After all! . . .

Andrei: (*Offstage*) This minute.

[*He comes in and goes over to the table*]

Tuzenbach: What are you thinking about?

Irina: This: I don't like that Solyony of yours, I'm afraid of him. Everything he says is so stupid. . . .

Tuzenbach: He's a strange man. I'm sorry for him and irritated at him too, but mostly I'm sorry for him. It seems to me he's shy. . . . When he's alone with you he's quite intelligent and pleasant, but when there're other people around he's rude, a sort of bully. Don't go, let's let them sit down without us. Let me be near you a little. What are you thinking about? (*A pause*) You're twenty, I'm not thirty yet. How many years we still have left—so many days, row on row of them, all full of my love for you. . . .

Irina: Nikolai Lvovich, don't talk to me about love.

Tuzenbach: (*Not listening*) I long so passionately to live, to struggle, to work—and because I love you, Irina, the longing's stronger than ever: it's as if you were meant to be so beautiful, and life seems to me just as beautiful. What are you thinking about?

Irina: You say life is beautiful. Yes, but suppose it only seems that way! For us three sisters life hasn't been beautiful, it's—it's choked us out, the way weeds choke out grass. I'm crying. . . . (*She quickly wipes her eyes and smiles*) I mustn't cry. We must work, work. We're so unhappy, we take such a gloomy view of life, because we don't work. We come from people who despised work.

[*Natalya (Natasha) Ivanovna enters; she has on a pink dress and a bright green belt*]

Natasha: They've already sat down to the table. . . . I'm late. . . . (*As she goes by it she looks into the mirror and tidies herself*) My hair seems to be all right. . . . (*Seeing* Irina) Many happy returns of the day, dear Irina Sergeevna! (*She gives her a vigorous and prolonged kiss*) You've got such a lot of visitors, I really do feel embarrassed. . . . How do you do, Baron!

Olga: (*Entering the living room*) Why, here's Natalya Ivanovna! How are you, dear?

[*They kiss*]

Natasha: Many happy returns! You've got so much company I really do feel terribly embarrassed.

Olga: You mustn't, it's only the family. *(In an undertone, alarmed)* You have on a green belt! Dear, that's too bad—

Natasha: What's wrong, is it bad luck?

Olga: No, it's just that it doesn't go with . . . somehow it looks a little strange.

Natasha: (In a tearful voice) It—it does? But it isn't really green, it's more a sort of a neutral shade.

[She follows Olga *into the dining room. In the dining room they sit down to lunch; there is no one left in the living room.]*

Kulygin: I wish you, Irina, a good fiancé! It's time you were getting married.

Chebutykin: Natalya Ivanovna, I wish you a fiancé too.

Kulygin: Natalya Ivanovna already has a fiancé.

Masha: I'll have a little drink! What the—life's a bed of roses! Come on, take a chance!

Kulygin: For that you get a C-minus in deportment.

Vershinin: This liqueur's good—what's it made of?

Solyony: Cockroaches.

Irina: Ugh! How disgusting!

Olga: For dinner we're having roast turkey and apple pie. Thank the Lord, I'll be home all day today and home all evening. Everybody must come this evening.

Vershinin: Let me come this evening, too.

Olga: Please do.

Natasha: They certainly don't wait to be asked twice around here.

Chebutykin: Male and female created He them! *(He laughs)*

Andrei: (Angrily) Oh, stop it, everybody! Don't you ever get tired of it?

[Fedotik and Rode *enter with a big basket of flowers]*

Fedotik: Look, they're already having lunch. . . .

Rode: (Loudly and affectedly) Already having lunch? That's right, they're already having lunch.

Fedotik: Hold still a minute! *(He takes a photograph)* One! Wait, just one more! *(He takes another photograph)* Two! Now it's all right.

[They pick up the basket and go on into the dining room, where they are greeted noisily]

Rode: (Loudly) Many happy returns! I wish you everything, everything! It's wonderful out today, absolutely magnificent. I've been out all morning with the high school boys, on a hike. I teach the gym class at the high school, you know.

Fedotik: You can move, Irina Sergeevna, you can move now. *(He takes a photograph)* You look simply beautiful today. *(He takes a top out of his pocket)* By the way, here's a little top. . . . It makes the most wonderful sound. . . .

Irina: How *nice!*

Masha: By the curved seastrand a green oak stands,
A chain of gold upon it . . .
A chain of gold upon it . . . *(Tearfully)* What am I saying that for? It's been going through my head all day. . . .

Kulygin: Thirteen at table!

Rode: *(Loudly)* But surely, ladies and gentlemen, you do not actually take such superstitions as these seriously? *(Laughter)*

Kulygin: If there're thirteen at table it means that one of them's in love. It's not you by any chance, Ivan Romanovich? *(Laughter)*

Chebutykin: I'm an old reprobate, but why Natalya Ivanovna is so embarrassed I simply can't imagine.

[Loud laughter. Natalya runs out of the dining room into the living room; Andrei follows her.]

Andrei: Please don't pay any attention to them! Wait. . . . Don't go, please don't. . . .

Natasha: I'm ashamed. . . . I don't know what's the matter with me, and they're all making fun of me. I know it's bad manners for me to leave the table like this, but I just can't help it. . . . I just can't. . . .

[She covers her face with her hands]

Andrei: Dear, I beg you, I implore you, don't let them upset you. Honestly, they're only joking, they mean well. They have such kind hearts—my darling, my dearest, they're all such good, kindhearted people, they love both of us. Come over here by the window, they can't see us here. . . . *(He looks around)*

Natasha: I'm just not used to being in society!

Andrei: Ah, youth, marvelous, beautiful youth! My darling, my dearest, please don't be upset! Believe me, believe me. . . . I'm so happy, so in love—I'm so blissfully happy. . . . Oh, they can't see us! They can't see us at all! Why I first fell in love with you, when I first fell in love with you—I don't know . . . My dearest, my darling, my innocent one, be my wife! I love you, love you as nobody ever—

[They kiss.
Two Officers *come in and seeing the two kissing, stop in amazement.]*

CURTAIN

ACT 2

The scene is that of the first act. It is eight o'clock at night. The faint sound of an accordion comes up from the street. The room is dark. Natalya Ivanovna enters in a dressing gown, with a candle; she walks over and stops at the door of Andrei's room.

Natasha: Andrei . . . dear, what are you doing? Reading? Nothing, I just . . . *(She goes to another door, opens it, looks inside, and then shuts it)* No, there isn't one. . . .

Andrei: (Entering with a book in his hand) What, Natasha?

Natasha: I was looking to see whether there's a light. . . . Now it's carnival week the servants are simply impossible, you have to be on the lookout every minute to make sure nothing goes wrong. Last night at midnight I went through the dining room, and there on the table was a lighted candle! Now, who lit it? I still haven't been able to get a straight answer. *(She puts down her candle)* What time is it?

Andrei: (Looking at his watch) Quarter after eight.

Natasha: And Olga and Irina not in yet. They aren't in yet. Still hard at work, poor things! Olga at the teachers' council and Irina at the telegraph office. . . . *(She sighs)* I was saying to your sister just this morning, "Irina darling," I said, "you simply must take better care of yourself." But she just won't listen. . . . Quarter after eight, you said? I'm worried, I'm afraid our Bobik just isn't well. Why is he so cold? Yesterday he had a temperature and today he's cold all over. . . . I am so worried!

Andrei: It's all right, Natasha. The boy's all right.

Natasha: Just the same, I think we'd better put him on a diet. I *am* worried. And tonight at almost ten o'clock those carnival people are going to be here, they said—it would be better if they didn't come, Andrei dear.

Andrei: I don't know. They *have* been asked, you know.

Natasha: This morning the little thing woke up and looked at me, and all of a sudden he gave a big smile: he knew me! "Good morning, Bobik!" I said. "Good morning, sweetheart!" And he laughed. . . . Babies understand, they understand perfectly. So Andrei dear, I'm going to tell them they mustn't let those carnival people in.

Andrei: (Indecisively) But that's up to my sisters, you know. This is their house.

Natasha: Yes, theirs too. I'll speak to them. They're so kind. . . . *(She starts to leave)* I've ordered cottage cheese for your supper. The doctor says you mustn't eat anything but cottage cheese or you won't ever get any thinner. *(She stops)* Bobik is *cold.* I'm afraid he must be cold in that room of his. At least till it's warm weather, we ought to put him in a different room.

For instance, Irina's room is a perfect room for a child, it's dry and the sun simply pours in all day long. I must speak to her about it. She could stay in Olga's room with her, for the time being. . . . It won't make any difference to her, she's never at home in the daytime anyway, she only spends the night there. . . . *(A pause)* Andrei-Wandrei, why don't you say something?

Andrei: I was just thinking. . . . Anyway, there isn't anything to say. . . .

Natasha: Uh-huh. . . . There was something I meant to tell you about. . . . Now I remember: Ferapont's here from the county board, he wants to see you.

Andrei: (Yawning) Send him on in.

[Natasha *goes out.* Andrei, *stooping over the candle she has left, reads his book.* Ferapont *comes in; he is in a worn-out old overcoat, the collar turned up, a scarf over his ears.*]

Andrei: How are you, Ferapont, old man? What have you got to tell me?

Ferapont: The chairman's sent you a little book and some kind of paper. Here . . . *(He gives a book and an envelope to* Andrei)

Andrei: Thanks. That's fine. But what did you come so late for? It's already past eight, you know.

Ferapont: How's that?

Andrei: (Louder) I said you're late, it's past eight.

Ferapont: That's right. I got here when it was still light but they wouldn't let me in. The master's busy, they said. Well, if you're busy you're busy, I'm not in any hurry. *(Thinking that* Andrei *has said something)* How's that?

Andrei: Nothing. *(He examines the book)* Tomorrow's Friday, we don't have any meeting, but I'll come anyway. . . . I'll do something. It's boring at home. *(A pause)* Ferapont, old man, it's funny how life changes, how it fools you. Today out of pure boredom, just because I hadn't anything else to do, I picked up this book here, some old university lectures, and I couldn't help laughing. . . . Good God! I'm the secretary of the county board, the board Protopopov's the head of; I'm the secretary, and the very most I can ever hope for is—to be a member of the board! I a member of a county board—I who dream every night that I'm a professor at the University of Moscow, a famous scholar of whom all Russia is proud!

Ferapont: I couldn't rightly say . . . I'm a little hard of hearing. . . .

Andrei: If you could hear as you ought I might not be talking to you like this. I've got to talk to somebody and my wife doesn't understand me, I'm afraid of my sisters, somehow—I'm afraid they'll make fun of me, make me feel ashamed. . . . You know,

I don't drink, I don't like cafés, but . . . good old Ferapont, what I'd give to be sitting in Moscow right now, at Testov's or the Great Muscovite!

Ferapont: In Moscow, there was a contractor at the board the other day that said so, there were some merchants eating pancakes, and it seems as how one of them ate forty pancakes and he died. It was either forty or fifty. I don't remember.

Andrei: In Moscow you sit in the main room at a restaurant, you don't know anybody and nobody knows you, but just the same you don't feel like a stranger. And here you know everybody and everybody knows you, and you're a stranger, a stranger . . . a stranger and lonely.

Ferapont: How's that? *(A pause)* And the contractor said—maybe he was lying, though—that there's a rope stretched all the way across Moscow.

Andrei: What for?

Ferapont: I couldn't rightly say. The contractor said so.

Andrei: That's nonsense. *(He reads)* Have you ever been to Moscow?

Ferapont: *(After a pause)* I never have. It wasn't God's will I should. *(A pause)* Shall I go now?

Andrei: You can go. Good-bye. *(Ferapont goes out)* Good-bye. *(Reading)* In the morning come back and get these papers. . . . You can go. . . . *(A pause)* He's gone. *(The bell rings)* Yes, it's a nuisance. . . .

[He stretches and walks slowly into his room. Behind the scene the Nurse is singing, rocking the baby. Masha and Vershinin enter. While they talk, a Maid is lighting the lamp and candles.]

Masha: I don't know. *(A pause)* I don't know. Of course, a lot of it is just habit. For instance, after Father's death it took us a long time to get used to not having orderlies in the house. But even if you disregard habit, it's only fair to say that—maybe it's not so in other places—that in our town the nicest people, the decentest people, the best-mannered people, really are the ones in the army.

Vershinin: I'm thirsty. I'd certainly like some tea.

Masha: It'll be here before long. They married me when I was eighteen, and I was afraid of my husband because he was a teacher and I was barely out of school. He seemed terribly learned to me then, intelligent, and important. It's different now, unfortunately.

Vershinin: I see . . . yes.

Masha: I'm not talking about my husband, I'm used to him, but among civilians in general there're so many coarse, unpleasant, ill-bred people. Coarseness upsets me—insults me; when I see that a man isn't polite enough, isn't refined or delicate enough, I suffer. When I'm with the teachers, my husband's colleagues, I'm simply miserable.

Vershinin: Yes. . . . But it seems to me it doesn't make any difference —whether they're army men or civilians, they're equally uninteresting . . . in this town, at any rate. It makes no difference! If you listen to one of the local intellectuals, civilian or military, all you ever hear is that he's sick and tired of his wife, sick and tired of his house, sick and tired of his estate, sick and tired of his horses. . . . When it comes to lofty ideas, thinking on an exalted plane, a Russian is extraordinary, but will you tell me why it is he aims so low in life? Why?

Masha: Why?

Vershinin: Why is a Russian always sick and tired of his children, sick and tired of his wife? And why are his wife and children always sick and tired of him?

Masha: You're a little depressed today.

Vershinin: Perhaps. I didn't have any dinner—I've had nothing to eat since breakfast. One of my daughters isn't exactly well, and when my little girls are ill I get anxious about them, my conscience torments me for having given them such a mother. If you could have seen her today! What a miserable creature! We began quarreling at seven in the morning, and at nine I slammed the door and walked away. . . . *(A pause)* I never mention it to anybody—it's strange, it's only to you that I complain. *(He kisses her hand)* Don't be angry with me. If it weren't for you I'd have no one—no one. *(A pause)*

Masha: Listen to the chimney! Just before Father died there was a howling in the chimney—there, just like that!

Vershinin: You're superstitious?

Masha: Yes.

Vershinin: That's strange. *(He kisses her hand)* You're a splendid woman, a wonderful woman. Splendid, wonderful! It's dark in here, but I can see how your eyes sparkle.

Masha: *(Moving to another chair)* The light's better over here.

Vershinin: I love, love, love . . . love your eyes, the way you move, I see them in my dreams. . . . Splendid, wonderful woman!

Masha: *(Laughing softly)* When you talk to me like that, somehow, I don't know why, I laugh, even when it frightens me. But don't do it again, please don't. . . . *(In a low voice)* No, you can, though—it doesn't make any difference to me. . . . *(She covers her face with her hands)* It doesn't make any difference to me. Someone's coming. Talk about something else.

[Irina and Tuzenbach *come in through the dining room]*

Tuzenbach: I've got three last names, my name is Baron Tuzenbach-

Krone-Altschauer, and yet I'm Russian and Orthodox, just like you. There's hardly anything German left in me—nothing, maybe, except the patience and obstinacy with which I keep boring you. Every single night I see you home.

Irina: I'm so tired!

Tuzenbach: And every single day for ten years, for twenty years, I'll come to the telegraph office and see you home, as long as you don't drive me away. . . . *(Seeing* Masha *and* Vershinin, *delightedly)* Oh, it's you! How are you!

Irina: Here I am, home at last! *(To* Masha*)* Just before I left a lady came in—she was wiring her brother in Saratov that her son had died today, and she couldn't manage to remember the address. So she sent it without any address, just to Saratov. She was crying. And for no reason whatsoever, I was rude to her. I said, "I simply haven't the time." It was so stupid! Are the carnival people coming tonight?

Masha: Yes.

Irina: *(Sitting down in an armchair)* I'll rest. I'm so tired.

Tuzenbach: *(Smiling)* When you come home from work you seem so young and so unhappy. . . . *(A pause)*

Irina: I'm tired. No, I don't like working there, I don't like it.

Masha: You've got thinner . . . *(She begins to whistle)* And younger, and your face looks like a little boy's.

Tuzenbach: That's the way she does her hair.

Irina: I must try to find some other job, this one's not right for me. What I longed for so, what I dreamed about, is exactly what's missing. It's work without poetry, without sense, even . . . *(A knock on the floor)* The Doctor's knocking. . . . *(To* Tuzenbach*)* You knock, dear. . . . I can't . . . I'm so tired. *(*Tuzenbach *knocks on the floor)* He'll be right up. Some way or other we've got to do something about it. Yesterday he and Andrei were at the club, and they lost again. They say Andrei lost two hundred rubles.

Masha: *(Indifferently)* Well, there's nothing we can do about it now.

Irina: Two weeks ago he lost, in December he lost. If only he'd hurry up and lose everything, maybe then we'd get out of this town. My God, every night I dream of Moscow, it's as if I were possessed. *(She laughs)* We're moving there in June, from now to June leaves—February, March, April, May . . . almost half a year!

Masha: The only thing is, Natasha mustn't hear anything about what he's lost.

Irina: I don't think it makes any difference to her.

[Chebutykin, *just out of bed—He has taken a nap after dinner—enters the dining room combing his beard, then sits down at the table and takes a newspaper from his pocket]*

Masha: So, he arrives. . . . Has he paid anything on his apartment?

Irina: (Laughing) No. For eight months, not a kopeck. Evidently he's forgotten.

Masha: (Laughing) How grandly he sits there! *(Everybody laughs. A pause.)*

Irina: Why are you so silent, Alexander Ignatich?

Vershinin: I don't know. I'd like some tea. I'd sell my soul for a glass of tea! I've had nothing to eat since breakfast. . . .

Chebutykin: Irina Sergeevna!

Irina: What is it?

Chebutykin: Please come here. *Venez ici! (*Irina *goes and sits down at the table)* I simply cannot do without you.

Vershinin: Well, if they won't give us any tea, at least let's philosophize.

Tuzenbach: Yes, let's. What about?

Vershinin: What about? Let's dream . . . for instance, about the life that will come after us, in two or three hundred years.

Tuzenbach: Well, after us they'll fly in balloons, their clothes will be different, they'll discover a sixth sense, maybe, and then develop it; but life will stay the same, a difficult life, full of mysteries, and happy. And in a thousand years people will be sighing, the same as now: "Ah, life is hard!"—and along with that, exactly the same as now, they'll be frightened of death and not want to die.

Vershinin: (After a moment's thought) How shall I put it? It seems to me that everything on earth must change, little by little, and that it is already changing before our eyes. In two or three hundred, in a thousand years—the length of time doesn't matter—a new and happy life will come. We can have no share in it, of course, but we are living for it, working for it, yes, suffering for it: we are creating it—and in that and in that alone is the aim of our existence and, if you wish, our happiness. (Masha *laughs softly)*

Tuzenbach: What's the matter with you?

Masha: I don't know. All day today, ever since morning, I've been laughing.

Vershinin: I finished school there where you did, I didn't go on to the Academy; I read a lot, but I don't know how to choose the books, and what I read, maybe, isn't exactly what I need to read. But the longer I live the more I want to know. My hair's getting gray, I'm an old man, almost, and yet I know so little, oh, so little! Still, though, it seems to me that what matters most, what's absolutely essential—that I do know, and know very well. If only I could make you see that there *is* no happiness, that there should not be, and that there will not be, for us. . . . We must only work and work, and happiness—that is the lot of our remote descendants. *(A pause)* Not mine but, at least, that of the descendants of my descendants.

[Fedotik and Rode *appear in the dining room; they sit down and softly begin to sing, one of them playing on the guitar.]*

Tuzenbach: According to you, we ought not even to dream of happiness! But suppose I *am* happy?

Vershinin: No.

Tuzenbach: (Throwing up his hands and laughing) Obviously we don't understand each other. Well, how am I going to convince you? *(*Masha *laughs softly)*

Tuzenbach: (Showing her his finger) Laugh! *(To* Vershinin*)* Not just in two or three hundred but in a million years, even, life will be the same: it doesn't change, it goes on the same as ever, obeying laws of its own—laws that are none of our business or, anyhow, that we'll never be able to discover. Migratory birds, cranes for instance, fly and fly, and no matter what thoughts, great or small, wander into their heads, they'll still keep on flying, they don't know where, they don't know why. They fly and will fly, no matter what philosophers appear among them; and they can philosophize as much as they please, just so long as they still fly.

Masha: But still, it means something?

Tuzenbach: Means something. . . . Look, it's snowing. What does that mean? *(A pause)*

Masha: It seems to me a man must believe or search for some belief, or else his life is empty, empty. . . . To live and not know why the cranes fly, why children are born, why there are stars in the sky. . . . Either you know what you're living for or else it's all nonsense, hocus-pocus.

Vershinin: Still, it's a pity one's youth is over.

Masha: Gogol says: Life on this earth is a dull proposition, gentlemen! I give up.

Chebutykin: (Reading a newspaper) Balzac was married in Berdichev. *(*Irina *softly begins to sing)* I really ought to write that down in my book. *(He writes it down)* Balzac was married in *Berdichev. (He reads his newspaper)*

Irina: (Pensively, as she lays out the cards for solitaire) Balzac was married in Berdichev.

Tuzenbach: The die is cast. You know, I've handed in my resignation, Marya Sergeevna.

Masha: So I hear. But I don't see anything good about that. I don't like civilians.

Tuzenbach: What's the difference? *(He gets up)* I'm not handsome, what sort of soldier am I? Well, anyway, what's the difference?. . . I'm going to work. If only for one day in my life, work so that I come home at night, fall in bed exhausted, and go right to sleep. *(He goes into the dining room)* Surely workmen must sleep soundly!

Fedotik: I got these crayons for you—on Moscow Street, at Pyzikov's. . . . And this little penknife. . . .

Irina: You keep on treating me as if I were a little girl, but I'm grown up now, you know. . . . *(Taking the crayons and the knife, joyfully)* How lovely!

Fedotik: And I bought myself a knife. . . . Look. . . . One blade, two, three, this is to clean your ears with, a pair of scissors, this is to clean your nails with. . . .

Rode: *(Loudly)* Doctor, how old are you?

Chebutykin: I? Thirty-two. *(Laughter)*

Fedotik: I will now show you a new kind of solitaire. . . .

[He lays out the cards.

They bring in the samovar; Anfisa *stands by it; a little later* Natasha *comes in and begins to straighten things on the table;* Solyony *enters, is greeted, and sits down at the table.]*

Vershinin: What a wind!

Masha: Yes. I'm bored with winter. I've forgotten what summer's like.

Irina: I'm going to go out, I can see it. We're going to get to Moscow!

Fedotik: No it's not—see, that eight's on the deuce of spades. *(He laughs)* So you're not going to get to Moscow.

Chebutykin: *(Reading the newspaper)* Tsitsikar. Smallpox is raging here.

Anfisa: *(Going up to* Masha*)* Masha, have some tea, darling. *(To* Vershinin*)* Please, your honor. . . . Excuse me, sir, I've forgotten your name. . . .

Masha: Bring it over here, nurse. I'm not going there.

Irina: Nurse!

Anfisa: Coming-g!

Natasha: *(To* Solyony*)* Babies, little babies still at the breast—they understand perfectly. "Good morning, Bobik!" I say. "Good morning, sweetheart!" Then he looks up at me in a very special way. You think I'm just saying that because I'm a mother, but that isn't so, no indeed it isn't so! He really is the most amazing child.

Solyony: If that child were mine I'd fry him in a frying pan and then eat him.

[He picks up his glass, goes into the living room, and sits down in a corner]

Natasha: *(Covering her face with her hands)* Rude, common man!

Masha: If you're happy you don't notice whether it's summer or winter. It seems to me that if I were in Moscow I wouldn't care what the weather was like.

Vershinin: The other day I was reading the diary of some French cabinet minister—he's been sent to prison because of that Panama affair. With what rapture, with what delight he describes the birds he sees from the window of his cell . . . birds he'd never noticed in the days when he was a minister. Now that they've let him out again, of course, it's the same as it used to be: he doesn't notice the birds. Just as when you live in Moscow again, you won't notice it. We aren't happy, we never will be, we only long to be.

Tuzenbach: (*Picking up a box from the table*) What's become of the candy?

Irina: Solyony ate it.

Tuzenbach: All of it?

Anfisa: (*Serving tea*) A letter for you, sir.

Vershinin: For me? (*He takes the letter*) From my daughter. (*He reads*) Yes, of course. . . . Forgive me, Marya Sergeevna, I'll slip out quietly. No tea for me. (*He gets up, disturbed*) The same old story. . . .

Masha: What is it? It's not a secret?

Vershinin: (*In a low voice*) My wife's poisoned herself again. I must go. I'll slip out so no one will notice. All this is horribly unpleasant. (*He kisses* Masha's *hand*) My good, darling, wonderful woman. . . . I'll just slip out quietly. . . .

Anfisa: Where on earth's he going now? After I've poured out his tea. . . . If he isn't a . . .

Masha: (*Losing her temper*) Stop it! Bothering everybody to death, you never give us a moment's peace. . . . (*She goes over to the table with her cup*) I'm bored with you, old woman!

Anfisa: What are you so mad about? Darling girl!

Andrei's Voice: (*Offstage*) Anfisa!

Anfisa: (*Mimicking him*) Anfisa! There he sits . . .

[*She goes out*]

Masha: (*By the table in the dining room, angrily*) Let me sit down! (*She mixes up the cards on the table*) Sprawling all over the place with your cards. Drink your tea!

Irina: Masha, you're just mean.

Masha: Well if I'm mean don't talk to me. Don't bother me!

Chebutykin: (*Laughing*) Don't bother her, don't bother her. . . .

Masha: You're sixty years old and yet you behave like a spoiled child, always jabbering the devil knows what. . . .

Natasha: (*She sighs*) Dear Masha, why *must* you use such expressions in conversation? With your looks you'd be simply fascinating in society if only it weren't for these—I'm going to be frank with you—for these expressions of yours. Excuse me for mentioning it, Masha, but your manners *are* a little coarse.

Tuzenbach: (*Trying to keep from laughing*) Give me . . . Give me . . . It seems to me there's some cognac somewhere. . . .

Natasha: It looks like my little Bobik isn't asleep any more, he's waked up. He isn't well today. I must go to him, excuse me. . . .

[She goes out]

Irina: And where's Alexander Ignatich gone?

Masha: Home. Something about his wife again—something odd.

Tuzenbach: (*Going over to* Solyony *with a decanter of cognac*) You always sit by yourself thinking about something, and there's no telling what it is. Come on, let's make peace. Let's have some cognac. (*They drink*) I'll have to play the piano all night tonight, I expect—all sorts of trash. . . . Well, come what may!

Solyony: Why make peace? I'm not mad at you.

Tuzenbach: You always give me the feeling that something's gone wrong between us. You're a strange character, you've got to admit it.

Solyony: (*Declaiming*) I am strange, and yet, who is not strange? Ah, be not wroth, Aleko!

Tuzenbach: You see! How'd that Aleko get in? (*A pause*)

Solyony: When I'm alone with anybody I'm all right, I'm just like everybody else, but when there are people around I get depressed and shy and . . . just talk nonsense. But just the same, I'm more honest and sincere than lots of people—lots and lots of people. And I can prove it.

Tuzenbach: I'm always getting angry at you, you keep bothering me so when there're other people around, but I like you just the same . . . why I don't know. . . . Come what may, I'm going to get drunk tonight. Let's have another!

Solyony: Yes, let's! (*He drinks*) I never have had anything against you, Baron. But I have a disposition like Lermontov's. . . . (*In a low voice*) I even look a little like Lermontov . . . so I'm told. . . . (*He takes a bottle of perfume from his pocket and sprinkles some over his hands*)

Tuzenbach: I've sent in my resignation. Finished! For five years I've been thinking about it and at last I've made up my mind. I'm going to work.

Solyony: (*Declaiming*) Ah, be not wroth, Aleko. . . . Forget, forget thy dreams. . . .

[While they are talking Andrei *comes in quietly, a book in his hand, and sits down by a candle]*

Tuzenbach: I'm going to work.

Chebutykin: (*Coming into the living room with* Irina) And besides that, they had real Caucasian food for me—onion soup, and for the meat course *chekhartma.*

Solyony: *Cheremsha* isn't meat at all, it's a vegetable like an onion.

Chebutykin: No indeed, my angel. . . . *Chekhartma* isn't onion, it's roast lamb.

Solyony: And I tell you, *cheremsha*'s onion.

Chebutykin: And I tell you, *chekhartma*'s lamb.

Solyony: And I tell you, *cheremsha*'s onion.

Chebutykin: What's the use of arguing with you! You never were in the Caucasus, you never ate any *chekhartma.*

Solyony: I never ate it because I hate it. *Cheremsha* smells—it smells like garlic.

Andrei: (*Imploringly*) That's enough, gentlemen! I beg you.

Tuzenbach: When are the carnival people coming?

Irina: They promised about nine—and that means any minute.

Tuzenbach: (*Embracing* Andrei *and singing*) "O my porch, O my porch, O my new porch . . ."[3]

Andrei: (*Dancing and singing*) "My new porch, my maple porch . . ."

Chebutykin: (*Dancing*) "Porch with my new trellis!" (*Laughter*)

Tuzenbach: (*Embracing* Andrei) Ah, the devil take it, let's have a drink! Old Andrei, let's drink to our eternal friendship! And Andrei, I'm going right along to Moscow with you, to the University.

Solyony: To which university? There's two universities in Moscow.

Andrei: There's one university in Moscow.

Solyony: And I tell you, there're two.

Andrei: There can be three for all I care. The more the better.

Solyony: There's two universities in Moscow! (*Murmurs of protest; people say,* "Sh!") There're two universities in Moscow, the old one and the new one. And if you don't want to listen to me, if my words annoy you, then I don't have to talk. I can even go in the other room. . . .

[He goes out through one of the doors]

Tuzenbach: Bravo, bravo! (*He laughs*) Get ready, ladies and gentlemen, I'm about to sit down at the piano! That Solyony, he's a funny one!

[He sits down at the piano and plays a waltz]

Masha: (*Waltzing by herself*) The Ba-ron's drunk, the Ba-ron's drunk, the Ba-a-ron is dru-unk! (Natasha *comes in*)

Natasha: (*To* Chebutykin) Ivan Romanich!

---

3. See Randall Jarrell's comment, p. 1320.

[She speaks about something with Chebutykin, *then quietly goes out.* Chebutykin *touches* Tuzenbach *on the shoulder and whispers to him.]*

Irina: What's the matter?

Chebutykin: It's time we were going. Good-bye.

Tuzenbach: Good night. Time we were going.

Irina: But—but what do you mean? What about the carnival people?

Andrei: (Embarrassed) There aren't going to be any carnival people. You see, my dear, Natasha says that Bobik doesn't feel very good, and so . . . To tell the truth, I don't know anything about it, it doesn't make any difference to me.

Irina: (Shrugging her shoulders) Bobik doesn't feel good!

Masha: Oh, what's the difference! If they run us out, then we've got to go. *(To* Irina) There's nothing wrong with Bobik, there's something wrong with her. . . . Here! *(She taps her forehead)* Common little creature!

[Andrei goes into his room; Chebutykin *follows him; in the dining room they are saying good-bye]*

Fedotik: What a shame! I was counting on spending the evening, but if the little baby's sick then of course . . . Tomorrow I'll bring him a little toy. . . .

Rode: (Loudly) I took a long nap this afternoon on purpose, just because I thought I was going to get to dance all night. Why, it's only nine o'clock!

Masha: Let's go on out and talk things over there. We'll decide about everything.

[Sounds of "Good night!" "Good-bye!" Tuzenbach *is heard laughing gaily. Everyone goes out.* Anfisa *and a* Maid *clear the table and put out the lights. The* Nurse *is heard singing.* Andrei, *in a hat and overcoat, and* Chebutykin *come in.]*

Chebutykin: I never did manage to get married, because life's gone by me like lightning, and because I was crazy about your mother and she was married. . . .

Andrei: People shouldn't get married. They shouldn't because it's boring.

Chebutykin: Maybe so, maybe so, but the loneliness! You can philosophize as much as you please, but loneliness is a terrible thing, Andrei boy. . . . Though on the other hand, really . . . of course, it doesn't make any difference one way or the other!

Andrei: Let's hurry.

Chebutykin: What's the hurry? We'll make it.

Andrei: I'm afraid my wife might stop me.

Chebutykin: Oh!

Andrei: Tonight I won't play any myself, I'll just sit and watch. I don't feel very good. . . . Sometimes I feel as if I had asthma—what should I do for it, Ivan Romanich?

Chebutykin: Why ask me? *I* don't remember, Andrei boy. I don't know. . . .

Andrei: Let's go out through the kitchen.

[They go out. A ring, then another ring; voices and laughter. Irina *enters.]*

Irina: What's that?

Anfisa: (Whispering) The carnival people! (Another ring)

Irina: Nurse dear, tell them there isn't anyone at home. They'll have to excuse us.

*[*Anfisa *goes out.* Irina *walks back and forth, lost in thought; she seems disturbed.* Solyony *comes in.]*

Solyony: (Perplexed) Nobody here. . . . Where is everybody?

Irina: Gone home.

Solyony: That's funny. You're alone here?

Irina: Alone. (A pause) Good-bye.

Solyony: A little while ago I lost control of myself, I wasn't tactful. But you are different from the rest of them, you are exalted, pure, you see the truth. . . . You are the only one there is that can understand me. I love you so, I'll love you to the end of—

Irina: Good-bye. Go away.

Solyony: I can't live without you. *(Following her)* Oh, my ideal! *(Through his tears)* Oh, bliss! Those marvelous, glorious, incredible eyes—eyes like no other woman's I've ever seen. . . .

Irina: (Coldly) Stop it, Vasili Vasilich!

Solyony: For the first time I'm speaking to you of love, and it's as if I were no longer on this earth, but on another planet. *(He runs his hand across his forehead)* Well, it doesn't make any difference. I can't make you love me, of course. . . . But rivals, happy rivals—I can't stand those . . . can't stand them. I swear to you by all that is holy, I shall kill any rival. . . . Oh, wonderful one!

*[*Natasha *comes in, a candle in her hand. She looks into one room, then into another, but walks by her husband's door without stopping.]*

Natasha: There Andrei is. Let him read! Excuse me, Vasili Vasilich, I hadn't any idea you were in here. I'm not dressed.

Solyony: It doesn't make any difference to me. Good-bye!

[He goes out]

Natasha: And you're tired, dear—my poor little girl! *(She kisses* Irina) If only you would go to bed a little earlier!

Irina: Is Bobik asleep?

Natasha: Asleep. But not sound asleep. By the way, dear, I keep
  meaning to speak to you about it, but either you're not home
  or else I haven't the time. . . . It seems to me that it's so cold
  and damp for Bobik in the nursery he has now. And your
  room is simply ideal for a child. My darling, my precious, do
  move in with Olga for a while!
Irina: (*Not understanding*) Where?

[*A troika with bells is heard driving up to the house*]

Natasha: You and Olga will be in one room, for the time being, and
  your room will be for Bobik. He's such a little dear, this morning I said to him, "Bobik, you're mine! Mine!" And he looked
  up at me with those darling little eyes of his. (*A ring*) That
  must be Olga. How late she is!

[*A* Maid *comes in and whispers in* Natasha's *ear*]

Natasha: Protopopov! What a funny man! Protopopov's here and
  wants me to go for a ride in his troika with him. (*She laughs*)
  Men are so funny! (*A ring*) Someone else's come. I suppose I
  might go, just for a few minutes. (*To the* Maid) Tell him just a
  minute. . . . (*A ring*) There's that doorbell again, it must be
  Olga.

[*She goes out*]

[*The* Maid *runs out;* Irina *sits thinking;* Kulygin *and* Olga *enter,* Vershinin *just
behind*]

Kulygin: Well, this is a fine state of affairs! And they said they were
  going to have a party!
Vershinin: Strange. I left a little while ago, a half hour ago, and they
  were expecting the carnival people.
Irina: They've all gone.
Kulygin: And Masha's gone too? Where's she gone? And why's
  Protopopov waiting down there in his troika? Who's he wait-
  ing for?
Irina: Don't ask questions. . . . I'm tired.
Kulygin: Little crosspatch!
Olga: The meeting lasted till just this minute. I'm exhausted.
  Our headmistress is ill and I've had to take her place. My head,
  how my head aches, my head . . . (*She sits down*) Andrei lost
  two hundred rubles yesterday, playing cards. Everybody in
  town is talking about it. . . .
Kulygin: Yes, and I got tired at the meeting, too.
Vershinin: My wife decided to give me a scare just now, she almost
  poisoned herself. Everything's turned out all right, and I certainly am glad—I can relax now. . . . Then of course, we ought

to leave? Well then, let me wish you good-bye. Fyodor Ilich, come somewhere with me! I can't go home tonight, I absolutely can't. . . . Come on!

Kulygin: I am tired. I'm not going. *(He gets up)* I am tired. Has my wife gone home?

Irina: I suppose so.

Kulygin: *(Kissing* Irina's *hand)* Good-bye. Tomorrow and the day after tomorrow I'm going to rest all day long. Good-bye! *(He goes)* I surely would like some tea. I'd been counting on spending the evening in congenial company and—*O, fallacem hominum spem!* Accusative of exclamation. . . .

Vershinin: It means I go by myself.

[He goes out with Kulygin, *whistling]*

Olga: My head aches, my head . . . Andrei's lost—everybody in town's talking about it. . . . I'll go lie down. *(She starts to go)* Tomorrow I'm free. . . . O my God, what a relief that is! Tomorrow I'm free, the day after tomorrow I'm free. . . . My head aches, my head . . .

[She goes out]

Irina: *(Alone)* They've all gone. There's no one left.

[An accordion is heard in the street, the Nurse *is singing in the next room]*

Natasha: *(Crossing the dining room in a fur coat and cap, followed by a* Maid*)* I'll be back in half an hour. I'll only go for a short drive.

[She goes out]

Irina: *(Alone, yearningly)* To Moscow! To Moscow! To Moscow!

CURTAIN

ACT 3

Olga's *and* Irina's *room. To the left and right are beds, with screens around them. It is past two o'clock in the morning. Offstage a fire bell is being rung, for a fire that began a long time ago. No one in the house has gone to bed yet.* Masha *is lying on the sofa, dressed as usual in a black dress.* Olga *and* Anfisa *come in.*

Anfisa: They're down there now, just sitting by the stairs. I said, "Come upstairs. Please," I said, "you can't just sit here like this!"—they were crying. "Papa," they said, "we don't know where he is—" they said, "Maybe he's burned to death." What a thing to think of! And there're some people in the yard—they're not dressed either. . . .

Olga: *(Taking dresses from a wardrobe)* Here, this gray one, take it . . . and this one here . . . the blouse, too. . . . And this skirt—

take it, nurse dear. . . . My God, what a thing to happen—all Kirsanov Street's burned down, evidently. . . . Take this. . . . Take this. . . . *(She piles the clothes in* Anfisa's *arms)* The Vershinins, poor things, certainly did get a fright. . . . Their house nearly burned down. They must spend the night here with us. . . . We can't send them home. . . . Poor Fedotik's had everything he owns burnt, there isn't a thing left. . . .

Anfisa: You'll have to call Ferapont, Olga darling, or else I can't carry it. . . .

Olga: (Ringing) Nobody answers. *(She calls through the door)* Come here, whoever's down there. *(A window, red with the glow of the fire, can be seen through the open door; the fire department is heard going past the house)* How terrible it all is! And how sick of it I am!

[Ferapont comes in]

Olga: Here, take these downstairs. . . . The Kelotilin girls are down there by the staircase—give them to them. Give them this, too. . . .

Ferapont: Yes'm. In the year '12 Moscow burned too.[4] Good God Almighty! The Frenchmen were flabbergasted.

Olga: Go on, get along. . . .

Ferapont: Yes'm.

[He goes out]

Olga: Nurse darling, give it all away. We don't need anything, give it all away, nurse. . . . I'm so tired I can hardly stand on my feet. . . . We *can't* allow the Vershinins to go home. The little girls can sleep in the living room, and put Alexander Ignatich downstairs at the Baron's . . . Fedotik at the Baron's, too, or else in our dining room. . . . The Doctor's drunk, terribly drunk, just as if he'd done it on purpose—we can't put anyone in with him. And put Vershinin's wife in the living room too.

Anfisa: (Wearily) Olga darling, don't drive me away! Don't drive me away!

Olga: You're talking nonsense, nurse. Nobody's driving you away.

Anfisa: (Laying her head on Olga's *breast)* My own treasure, I do the best I can, I do work. . . . I'm getting weak, they'll all say, "Get out!" And where is there for me to go? Where? Eighty years old . . . my eighty-second year. . . .

Olga: You sit down, nurse darling. . . . You're tired, poor thing. . . . *(She gets her to sit down)* Rest, my darling. How pale you look!

---

4. In 1812, when the French invaded Russia, the Moscovites burned down their own city.

[Natasha enters]

Natasha: They're saying we ought to organize a committee right
away to aid the victims of the fire. Well, why not? It's a fine
idea. After all, we ought to help the poor, that's the duty of the
rich. Bobik and Baby Sophie are both sound asleep—sleeping
as if nothing had happened! . . . There're people here everywhere, wherever you go the house is full of them. And there's
all this flu in town now, I'm so afraid the children may catch it.

Olga: *(Not listening to her)* From this room you can't see the fire,
it's peaceful here. . . .

Natasha: Uh-huh. . . . I must be a sight. *(In front of the mirror)* They
keep saying I've gained. . . . And it's not so! It's not a bit so!
And Masha's fast asleep—dead tired, poor thing. . . . *(To
Anfisa, coldly)* Don't you dare sit down in my presence! Get
up! Get out of here! *(Anfisa goes out. A pause)* What you keep
that old woman for I simply do not understand!

Olga: *(Taken aback)* I beg your pardon, I don't understand
either. . . .

Natasha: She's around here for no reason whatsoever. She's a peasant, she ought to be in the country where she belongs. . . . It's
simply spoiling them! I like for everything in the house to have
its proper place! There ought not to be these useless people
cluttering up the house. *(She strokes* Olga's *cheek)* Poor girl,
you're tired. Our headmistress is tired. When my little Sophie
gets to be a big girl and goes to the high school, I'm going to be
so afraid of you.

Olga: I'm not going to be headmistress.

Natasha: You're sure to be, Olga. It's already settled.

Olga: I won't accept. I can't . . . I'm not strong enough. . . . *(She
drinks some water)* You were so rude to nurse just now. Forgive
me, I just haven't the strength to bear it. . . . It's getting all
black before my eyes. . . .

Natasha: *(Agitated)* Forgive me, Olga, forgive me. . . . I didn't mean
to upset you.

[Masha gets up, takes her pillow, and goes out angrily]

Olga: Try to understand, dear . . . perhaps we've been brought
up in an unusual way, but I can't bear this. This sort of thing
depresses me so, I get sick. . . . I just despair!

Natasha: Forgive me, forgive me. *(She kisses her)*

Olga: The least rudeness, even, an impolite word—it upsets
me. . . .

Natasha: Sometimes I do say more than I should, that's so, but you
must admit, my dear, she *could* live in the country.

Olga: She's been with us thirty years already.

Natasha: But now she just can't do anything, you know that! Either I don't understand you or you don't want to understand me. She's not fit for any work, she just sleeps or sits.

Olga: Well, let her sit.

Natasha: *(Surprised)* What do you mean, let her sit? Why, she's a servant. *(Tearfully)* I simply cannot understand you, Olga. I've got a nurse, a wet nurse, we've got a maid, we've got a cook. . . . What do we have to have that old woman for too? What *for?*

[Behind the scene a fire alarm rings]

Olga: Tonight I have aged ten years.

Natasha: We've got to settle things, Olga. You're at the high school, I'm at home; you have the teaching, and I have the housekeeping. And if I say something about the servants, I know what I'm talking about: *I—know—what—I'm—talking—about . . .* and tomorrow morning that old thief, that old wretch *(She stamps her foot),* that witch is going to be out of this house! Don't you dare irritate me! Don't you dare! *(Collecting herself)* Honestly, if you don't move downstairs we'll be quarreling like this for the rest of our lives. This is awful!

[Kulygin comes in]

Kulygin: Where's Masha? It's time to go home. They say the fire's dying down. *(He stretches)* In spite of all the wind, only one block's burned—at first it looked as if the whole town would burn. *(He sits down)* I am exhausted, Olga my dear. . . . I often think if it hadn't been Masha I'd have married you, Olga dear. You have such a generous nature. . . . I am exhausted. *(He listens for something)*

Olga: What is it?

Kulygin: As if he'd done it on purpose, the Doctor's got drunk, he's terribly drunk. As if he'd done it on purpose! *(He gets up)* I do believe he's coming up here. . . . Hear him? Yes, up here. . . . *(He laughs)* If he isn't the . . . I'll hide. *(He goes to the wardrobe and stands between it and the wall)* What a rascal!

Olga: For two years he doesn't drink, and now all of a sudden he goes and gets drunk. . . .

[She follows Natasha to the back of the room.

Chebutykin *enters; without staggering, like a sober person, he crosses the room, stops, looks around, then goes to the washbasin and begins to wash his hands]*

Chebutykin: *(Gloomily)* The devil take every one of them . . . every one of them. . . . They think I'm a doctor, know how to treat anything there is, and I don't know a thing, I've forgotten everything I ever did know, I remember nothing, absolutely nothing.

[Olga *and* Natasha *leave the room without his noticing*]

Chebutykin: The devil take them. Last Wednesday I treated a woman at Zasyp—dead, and it's my fault she's dead. Yes. . . . Twenty-five years ago I used to know a little something, but now I don't remember a thing. One single thing. Maybe I'm not a man at all, but just look like one—maybe it just looks like I've got arms and legs and a head. Maybe I don't even exist, and it only looks like I walk and eat and sleep. *(He cries)* Oh, if only I didn't exist! *(He stops crying; gloomily)* The devil only knows. . . . Day before yesterday they were talking at the club; they talked about Shakespeare, Voltaire. . . . I haven't read them, I never have read them at all, but I looked like I'd read them. And the others did too, the same as me. So cheap! So low! And that woman I killed Wednesday—she came back to me, and it all came back to me, and everything inside me felt all twisted, all vile, all nauseating. . . . I went and got drunk. . . .

[Irina, Vershinin, *and* Tuzenbach *come in;* Tuzenbach *is wearing new and stylish civilian clothes*]

    Irina: Let's sit in here. Nobody will be coming in here.

Vershinin: If it hadn't been for the soldiers the whole town would have burnt up. Brave men, those! *(He rubs his hands with pleasure)* The salt of the earth! Ah, those are first-rate men!

    Kulygin: *(Going up to them)* What's the time, gentlemen?

Tuzenbach: Going on four. It's getting light.

    Irina: They're all sitting there in the dining room, nobody thinks of leaving, and that Solyony of yours sits there. . . . *(To* Chebutykin*)* Oughtn't you to go to bed, Doctor?

Chebutykin: Doesn't matter. . . . Thank you. . . . *(He combs his beard)*

    Kulygin: *(Laughing)* You're tight, Ivan Romanich! *(He slaps him on the back)* Bravo! *In vino veritas*,[5] as the ancients used to say.

Tuzenbach: Everybody keeps asking me to get up a concert to help the people whose houses burned.

    Irina: Yes, but who's there to . . . ?

Tuzenbach: We could arrange one if we wanted to. Marya Sergeevna, in my opinion, is a wonderful pianist.

    Kulygin: Yes indeed, wonderful.

    Irina: She's forgotten how, by now. She hasn't played for three years—four.

Tuzenbach: Here in this town there is not a soul who understands music, not a single soul; but I, I do understand it, and I give you my word of honor that Marya Sergeevna plays magnificently, almost with genius.

---

5. "In wine there is truth." (Latin)

Kulygin: You're right, Baron. I love her very much, Masha. She's wonderful.

Tuzenbach: To be able to play so beautifully and all the time to know that no one, no one, understands you!

Kulygin: (Sighing) Yes. . . . But would it be proper for her to appear in a public concert? (A pause) Really, gentlemen, I know nothing about it. Perhaps it would be quite all right. You have to admit that our principal is a fine man, in fact a very fine man, very intelligent, too; but his views *are* a little . . . Of course, it isn't any of his affair, but just the same, if you think I ought to, I'll speak to him about it.

[Chebutykin picks up a porcelain clock and examines it]

Vershinin: I got all covered with dirt at the fire—I look pretty disreputable. (A pause) Yesterday just by accident I heard someone say that they may be sending our brigade a long way off—some of them said to Poland, some of them said to Siberia, to Chita.

Tuzenbach: I heard that too. Well, what is there you can do? The town will be completely empty.

Irina: And we'll leave too!

Chebutykin: (Drops the clock, smashing it) To smithereens!

[A pause; everyone looks embarrassed and upset]

Kulygin: (Picking up the pieces) To break such an expensive thing— oh, Ivan Romanich, Ivan Romanich! You get a zero-minus in deportment!

Irina: That's Mother's clock.

Chebutykin: Maybe. . . . If it's Mother's, then it's Mother's. Maybe I didn't break it but it only looks like I broke it. Maybe it only looks like we exist, and really we don't. I don't know anything, nobody knows anything. (At the door) What are you staring at? Natasha's having an affair with Protopopov, and you don't see that. You sit there and see nothing, and Natasha's having an affair with Protopopov. . . . (Singing) "Tell me how you like this little present!"

[He goes out]

Vershinin: Yes. . . . (He laughs) How strange all this is, in reality! When the fire started I rushed home; I got there, looked around . . . the house was safe and sound, not in any danger at all, but there my two little girls were, standing in the doorway in just their underwear, their mother gone, people rushing around, horses running by, dogs, and my little girls' faces were so anxious and terrified and beseeching and—I don't know what; it wrung my heart to look at those faces. My God, I thought, what these girls still have to go through in the rest of their lives, in all the years to come! I picked them up and ran, and I kept thinking one thing: what they still have to live through in this world! *(Fire alarm; a pause)* I got here and here was their mother—she was shouting, she got angry.

[Masha *comes in with the pillow and sits down on the sofa*]

Vershinin: And while my little girls were standing in the doorway in just their underwear, and the street was red with the fire, the noise was terrible, I started thinking that it's almost what happened long ago, when the enemy attacked unexpectedly, looting and burning. . . . And yet, in reality, what a difference there is between what things are now and what they were then! And when a little more time has passed, two or three hundred years, people will look in horror and mockery at this life we live now, and everything we do now will seem to them clumsy, and difficult, and terribly uncomfortable and strange. Oh, what life will be like then! What life will be like then! *(He laughs)* Sorry, I've started philosophizing again. But do let me go on, ladies and gentlemen. I feel terribly like philosophizing, I'm in just the right frame of mind. *(A pause)* Looks like they're all asleep. So I say: What life will be like then! Can you imagine! Here in this town there are only three of your kind now, but in the generations to come there will be more and more and more; the time will come when everything will get to be the way you want it to be, everybody will live like you, and then after a while you yourselves will be out-of-date, there'll be people born who'll be better than you. . . . *(He laughs)* I'm in a most peculiar frame of mind tonight. I want like the devil to live. *(He sings)* "Unto love all ages bow, its pangs are blest . . ."

Masha: Da-da-dum . . .
Vershinin: Da-dum . . .
Masha: Da-da-da?
Vershinin: Da-da-da! *(He laughs)*

[Fedotik *comes in*]

Fedotik: *(Dancing)* Burnt to ashes! Burnt to ashes! Everything I had in this world! *(Laughter)*
Irina: What kind of joke is that? Is it really all burnt?
Fedotik: *(Laughing)* Every single last thing! There's not one thing left! The guitar's burnt, and the camera burnt, and all my letters are burnt. . . . And I meant to give you a little notebook, and it's burnt too. . . .

[Solyony *enters*]

Irina: No, please go away, Vasili Vasilich. You can't come in here.
Solyony: But why is it the Baron can and I can't?

Vershinin: We ought to be going, really. How's the fire?

Solyony: They say it's dying down. No, it's a very strange thing to me, why is it the Baron can and I can't? *(He takes out a bottle of perfume and sprinkles it on himself)*

Vershinin: Da-da-dum?

Masha: Da-dum!

Vershinin: *(Laughing, to* Solyony*)* Let's go on in the dining room.

Solyony: All right, but there'll be a note made of this. "This moral could be made more clear. But 'twould annoy the geese, I fear."[6] *(He looks at* Tuzenbach*)* He-ere, chicky, chicky, chicky!

[He goes out with Vershinin *and* Fedotik*]*

Irina: That Solyony! There's smoke all over everything.... *(In surprise)* The Baron's asleep! Baron! Baron!

Tuzenbach: *(Waking up)* I'm tired, only I . . . the brickyard . . . I'm not delirious, I really am going to start work there soon.... I've already talked it over with them. *(To* Irina, *tenderly)* You're so pale and beautiful and enchanting.... It seems to me your paleness brightens the dark air like light . . . You're sad, you're dissatisfied with life.... Oh, come away with me, let's go and work together!

Masha: Nikolai Lvovich, go away from here!

Tuzenbach: *(Laughing)* You're here? I didn't see you. *(He kisses* Irina's *hand)* Good-bye, I'm going. I look at you now, and it reminds me of how long ago on your birthday you were so happy and cheerful, and talked about the joy of work.... And what a happy life I saw before me then! Where is it? *(He kisses her hand)* You have tears in your eyes. Go to bed, it's already getting light.... It's beginning to be morning.... If only I might give my life for you!

Masha: Nikolai Lvovich, go away! Why, really, what . . .

Tuzenbach: I'm going.

[He goes out]

Masha: *(Lying down)* Are you asleep, Fyodor?

Kulygin: What?

Masha: You should go home.

Kulygin: My darling Masha, my precious Masha . . .

Irina: She's worn out.... Let her rest, Fyodor dear.

Kulygin: I'll go in just a minute. My good, wonderful wife . . . I love you, my only one. . . .

Masha: *(Angrily)* Amo, amas, amat, amamus, amatis, amant.[7]

---

6. The concluding lines of "The Geese," by Ivan Andreyevich Krylov (1768–1844).
7. "I love, you love," etc. (Latin)

Kulygin: *(Laughing)* No, really, she's amazing. I've been married to you for seven years, and it seems as if we were married only yesterday. Word of honor! No, really, you're an amazing woman. I am satisfied, I am satisfied, I am satisfied!

Masha: Bored, bored, bored! . . . *(She sits up)* I can't get it out of my head. It's simply revolting. It sticks in my head like a nail, I can't keep quiet about it any longer. I mean about Andrei . . . he's mortgaged this house at the bank and his wife's got hold of all the money. But the house doesn't belong just to him, it belongs to the four of us! He ought to know that if he's a decent man.

Kulygin: Must you, Masha? What's it to you? Poor Andrei's in debt to everybody—well, God help him!

Masha: Just the same, it's revolting. *(She lies down)*

Kulygin: You and I aren't poor. I work, I go to the high school, I give lessons afterwards. . . . I'm an honest man . . . a simple man. . . . *Omnia mea mecum porto,*[8] as the saying goes.

Masha: I don't need anything, but the injustice of it nauseates me. *(A pause)* Go on, Fyodor.

Kulygin: *(Kissing her)* You're tired, rest for half an hour, and I'll sit there and wait. . . . Sleep. . . . *(He starts to leave)* I am satisfied, I am satisfied, I am satisfied.

[He goes out]

Irina: No, really, how petty our Andrei's become, how lifeless and old he's got, at the side of that woman! Once he was preparing to be a professor, a scholar, and yesterday he was boasting that he's finally managed to get made a member of the county board. He a member, Protopopov chairman. . . . Everybody in town is talking about it, laughing at it, and he's the only one that knows nothing, that sees nothing. . . . And now everybody's run off to the fire, and he sits there in his room and doesn't pay any attention to anything, he just plays the violin. *(Nervously)* Oh, it's awful, awful, awful! *(She cries)* I can't stand any more, I can't stand it! . . . I can't, I can't. . . .

[Olga comes in and begins to straighten her dressing table]

Irina: *(Sobbing loudly)* Throw me out, throw me out, I can't stand any more!

Olga: *(Alarmed)* What is it, what is it? Darling!

Irina: *(Sobbing)* Where? Where's it all gone? Where is it? Oh, my God, my God! I've forgotten everything, forgotten . . . it's all mixed up in my head, I don't remember what *window* is in

---

8. "All that is mine I carry with me." (Latin)

Italian, or—or *ceiling*. . . . I'm forgetting everything, every day I forget, and life goes by and won't ever come back, won't ever, we'll never go to Moscow, we won't ever . . . now I see that we won't ever . . .

Olga: Darling, darling . . .

Irina: (Trying to control herself) Oh, I'm miserable . . . I can't work, I'm not ever going to work. That's enough, that's enough! First I worked at the telegraph office, now I work at the county board, and I hate and despise every last thing they have me do. . . . I'm already almost twenty-four, I've been working for years and years already, my brain is drying up, I'm getting thin, getting ugly, getting old, and there's nothing, nothing—there isn't the least satisfaction of any kind—and the years are going by, and every day, over and over, everything's getting farther away from any real life, beautiful life, everything's going farther and farther into some abyss. . . . I am in despair, I can't understand how I'm alive, how I haven't killed myself long ago. . . .

Olga: Don't cry, my own little girl, don't cry. . . . I suffer, too.

Irina: I'm not crying, I'm not crying. . . . That's enough. . . . See, now I'm not crying any more. . . . That's enough, that's enough!

Olga: Darling, I tell you as your sister, as your friend: If you want my advice, marry the Baron!

[Irina *weeps silently*]

Olga: You know you respect him, you think so much of him. . . . He's ugly, it's true, but he's such an honest man, such a good man. . . . You know, people don't marry for love, but for duty. At least, I think so, and I would marry without being in love. If someone proposed to me, no matter who it was, I'd marry him, as long as he was a decent man. I'd marry an old man, even. . . .

Irina: I was always waiting till we moved to Moscow, I'd meet the real one there—I used to dream about him, love him. . . . But it's all turned out nonsense, all nonsense!

Olga: (Embracing her sister) My dear, beautiful sister, I understand it all: When Baron Nikolai Lvovich left the army and came to see us in his civilian clothes, he looked so homely to me I absolutely started to cry. . . . He said, "Why are you crying?" How could I tell him! But if it were God's will he should marry you, I'd be happy. That would be different, you know, completely different.

[Natasha, *with a candle, comes out of the door on the right, crosses the stage, and goes out through the door on the left, without speaking*]

Masha: (Sitting up) She walks like the one that started the fire.

Olga: Masha, you're silly. The silliest one in the whole family—that's you. Please forgive me. *(A pause)*

Masha: I want to confess, dear sisters. Inside I—I can't keep on this way any longer. I'll confess to you and then never again to anybody, never again. . . . In a minute I'll say it. *(In a low voice)* It's my secret, but you ought to know it. . . . I can't keep quiet any longer. . . . *(A pause)* I love, love . . . I love that man. . . . The one you just saw. . . . Oh, why not say it? In one word, I love Vershinin.

Olga: (Going behind her screen) Stop it. Anyway, I don't hear you.

Masha: What is there I can do? *(She holds her head in her hands)* At first he seemed strange to me, then I felt sorry for him . . . then I fell in love with him, fell in love with his voice, his words, his misfortunes, his two little girls. . . .

Olga: (Behind the screen) Anyway, I don't hear you. Whatever silly things you're saying, anyway, I don't hear you.

Masha: Oh, you're so silly, Olga. I love him—it means, it's my fate. It means, it's my lot. . . . And he loves me. . . . It's all so strange. Yes? It isn't good? *(She takes* Irina *by the hand and draws her close to her)* Oh my darling, how are we going to live our lives, what is going to become of us? When you read some novel then it all seems so old and so easy to understand, but when you're in love yourself you see that no one knows anything, and everyone has to decide for himself. . . . My darlings, my sisters, I've confessed to you, now I'll be silent. . . . From now on I'll be like Gogol's madman . . . silence . . . silence . . .

[Andrei comes in, followed by Ferapont*]*

Andrei: (Angrily) What is it you want? I don't understand.

Ferapont: (Standing in the doorway, impatiently) Andrei Sergeevich, I've told you ten times already.

Andrei: In the first place, to you I am not Andrei Sergeevich, but your honor!

Ferapont: The firemen, your honor, want to know if you'll please let them go to the river through your garden. Because the way it is they have to go around and around, they're getting all worn out.

Andrei: All right. Tell them all right.

[Ferapont leaves]

Andrei: What a bore! . . . Where's Olga? *(Olga comes out from behind the screen)* I've come to get the key to the cupboard from you, I've lost mine. You've got one of those little keys. . . . *(Olga hands him the key, without speaking.* Irina *goes behind her screen. A pause)* What a tremendous fire! It's started to die down now. . . . The devil, that Ferapont made me lose my temper—that was stupid to say that. . . . Your honor. . . . *(A pause)* Why don't you say something, Olga? *(A pause)* It's about time you stopped this silliness . . . pouting like this without rhyme or reason. . . . Masha, you're here, Irina's here, well, that's just fine—let's get things settled once and for all. What is it you've got against me? What is it?

Olga: Let it go now, Andrei dear. We'll straighten things out tomorrow. *(In an agitated voice)* What a dreadful night!

Andrei: *(In great confusion and embarrassment)* Don't get all upset. I'm asking you perfectly calmly: What is it you've got against me? Come right out with it.

Vershinin's Voice: *(Offstage)* Da-da-dum!

Masha: *(In a loud voice, getting up)* Da-da-dah! *(To Olga)* Goodbye, Olga, God bless you! *(She goes behind the screen and kisses Irina)* Have a good sleep. . . . Good-bye, Andrei. Leave them alone now, they're worn out. . . . Tomorrow we can straighten things out.

[She goes out]

Olga: That's right, Andrei dear, let's put it off until tomorrow. . . . *(She goes behind the screen on her side of the room)* It's time to go to sleep.

Andrei: I'll only say this much and go. Right away. . . . In the first place, you've got something against Natasha, my wife, and I've seen that from the very first day we were married. Natasha is a splendid, honest person, straightforward and sincere—that is my opinion. I love and respect my wife—respect her, you understand, and I demand that others respect her too. I repeat, she's an honest, sincere person, and anything you've got against her, if I may say so, is just your imagination. . . . *(A pause)* In the second place, you seem to be angry with me because I'm not a professor, don't in some way advance knowledge. But I am in the service of the government, I am a member of the county board, and this service of mine is to me just as sacred and lofty as the service of knowledge. I am a member of the county board and I am proud of it, if you want to know. . . . *(A pause)* In the third place. . . . I have something else to say. . . . I've mortgaged the house without your permission. . . . For that I am to blame, I admit it, and I beg you to forgive me. My debts forced me to. . . . Thirty-five thousand. . . . I no longer play cards, gave them up long ago, but the main thing I can say to justify myself is this, that you—that you're girls, you get a pension, I, though, didn't get . . . earnings, so to speak. . . . *(A pause)*

Kulygin: (*At the door*) Isn't Masha here? (*Anxiously*) But where is she? This is strange. . . .

[*He goes out*]

Andrei: They won't listen. Natasha's a splendid, honest person. (*He walks up and down silently, then stops*) When I got married I thought we'd be happy . . . all of us happy . . . but my God! . . . (*He cries*) My dearest sisters, darling sisters, don't believe me, don't believe . . .

[*He goes out*]

Kulygin: (*at the door anxiously*) Where's Masha? Isn't Masha here? What an extraordinary thing!

[*He goes out*]

[*Fire alarm; the stage is empty*]

Irina: (*Behind the screen*) Olga! Who's that knocking on the floor?

Olga: It's the Doctor, it's Ivan Romanich. He's drunk.

Irina: What a miserable night! (*A pause*) Olga! (*She looks out from behind the screen*) Did you hear? They're taking the brigade away from us, sending it way off somewhere.

Olga: It's only a rumor.

Irina: Then we'll be left all alone. . . . Olga!

Olga: Well?

Irina: Dearest sister, darling sister, I respect the Baron, I admire the Baron, he's a marvelous person, I'll marry him, I agree, only let's go to Moscow! Let's go, oh please let's go! There's nothing in this world better than Moscow! Let's go, Olga! Let's go!

CURTAIN

ACT 4

The old garden of the Prozorovs' *house. At the end of a long avenue of fir trees there is the river. On the other bank of the river is a forest. To the right of the house there is a terrace. Here on a table there are bottles and glasses; it is evident that they have just been drinking champagne. Occasionally people from the street cut through the garden to get to the river; five or six soldiers go through, walking fast.* Chebutykin, *in a genial mood which does not leave him during the act, is sitting in an easy chair in the garden; he wears his uniform cap and is holding a walking stick.* Irina, Kulygin *with a decoration around his neck and with no moustache, and* Tuzenbach *are standing on the terrace saying good-bye to* Fedotik *and* Rode, *who are coming down the steps; both officers are in parade uniform.*

Tuzenbach: (*Embracing* Fedotik) You're a fine man, we got along so well together. *(He embraces* Rode*)* One more time. . . . Good-bye, old man. . . .

Irina: *Au revoir!*

Fedotik: It isn't *au revoir*, it's good-bye; we'll never see each other again!

Kulygin: Who knows? *(He wipes his eyes and smiles)* Here I've started crying.

Irina: Some day or other we'll meet again.

Fedotik: In ten years—fifteen? By then we'll hardly recognize each other, we'll say "How do you do" coldly. . . . *(He takes a photograph)* Stand still. . . . One more time, it's the last time.

Rode: *(Embracing* Tuzenbach*)* We'll never see each other again. . . . *(He kisses* Irina's *hand)* Thank you for everything, for everything!

Fedotik: *(Annoyed)* Oh, stand still!

Tuzenbach: Please God, we'll see each other again. Write us now. Be sure to write us.

Rode: *(Looking around the garden)* Good-bye, trees! *(He shouts)* Yoo-hoo! *(A pause)* Good-bye, echo!

Kulygin: With any luck you'll get married there in Poland. . . . Your Polish wife will hug you and call you *kochany!*[9] *(He laughs)*

Fedotik: *(Looking at his watch)* We've less than an hour left. Solyony's the only one from our battery that's going on the barge, the rest of us are going with the enlisted men. Three batteries are leaving today, three more tomorrow—and then peace and quiet will descend on the town.

Tuzenbach: And awful boredom.

Rode: But where's Marya Sergeevna?

Kulygin: Masha's in the garden.

Fedotik: We must say good-bye to her.

Rode: Good-bye. We must go, otherwise I'll start crying. *(He hurriedly embraces* Tuzenbach *and* Kulygin, *and kisses* Irina's *hand)* It was so nice living here.

Fedotik: *(To* Kulygin*)* This is for you to remember us by . . . a notebook with a pencil. . . . We'll go on down to the river this way. . . .

[They go off, both looking back]

Rode: *(Shouting)* Yoo-hoo!

Fedotik: *(Shouting)* Good-bye!

[At the back of the stage Fedotik *and* Rode *meet* Masha *and say good-bye to her; she goes off with them]*

Irina: They're gone. . . .

---

9. Beloved. (Polish)

[She sits down on the bottom step of the terrace]

Chebutykin: And forgot to say good-bye to me.

    Irina: And what about you?

Chebutykin: Well, I forgot, somehow. Anyway, I'll be seeing them again
    soon, I'm leaving tomorrow. Yes. . . . Only one more day. In
    a year more they'll retire me, I'll come back again and live out
    the rest of my days near you. . . . Only one more year and I get
    my pension. . . . *(He puts a newspaper in his pocket, takes a news-*
    paper out of his pocket) I'll come back here to you and lead a
    completely new life. I'll get to be such a sober, Gu-Gu-God-
    fearing, respectable man.

    Irina: Yes, you really ought to, my dove. Somehow or other you
    ought.

Chebutykin: Yes. I feel so. *(He begins to sing softly)* Ta-ra-ra-boom-de-
    aye . . . / Sit on a log I may . . .

    Kulygin: You're incorrigible, Ivan Romanich! You're incorrigible!

Chebutykin: Yes, if only I had *you* for a teacher! Then I'd reform.

    Irina: Fyodor's shaved off his moustache. I can't bear to look at
    him.

    Kulygin: And what of it?

Chebutykin: I could say what that face of yours looks like now—but I
    don't dare.

    Kulygin: Well, what of it? It's the accepted thing, it's the *modus*
    vivendi. . . . Our principal's shaved off his moustache, so when
    they made me the assistant principal I shaved mine off too.
    Nobody likes it, but it doesn't make any difference to me. I am
    satisfied. With a moustache or without a moustache, I am
    satisfied. . . .

[He sits down.

Andrei *walks across the back of the stage, wheeling a baby carriage with the baby
asleep in it.]*

    Irina: Ivan Romanich, my dove, my darling, I'm terribly wor-
    ried. You were on the boulevard yesterday, tell me, what hap-
    pened there?

Chebutykin: What happened? Nothing. Piffle! *(He reads the newspaper)*
    What's the difference!

    Kulygin: What they say is that Solyony and the Baron met each other
    yesterday on the boulevard, up by the theater—

Tuzenbach: Stop it! Why, really, what . . .

[He waves his hand and goes into the house]

    Kulygin: Up by the theater . . . Solyony started bothering the Baron,
    and the Baron wouldn't stand for it, he said something insult-
    ing . . .

Chebutykin: I don't know. It's all nonsense.

Kulygin: There was a teacher in some seminary that wrote *Nonsense!* on a theme, and the pupil thought it was *Nonesuch!*—thought it was Latin. *(He laughs)* Amazingly funny! They say it looks like Solyony's in love with Irina, and he hates the Baron. . . . That's understandable. Irina is a very nice girl. She's quite like Masha, even—always thinking about something. Only you have a milder disposition, Irina. Though as a matter of fact Masha has a fine disposition too. I love her, Masha.

[At the rear of the garden, behind the stage, someone shouts: "Yoo-hoo!"]

Irina: *(Shivering)* Somehow everything frightens me today. *(A pause)* I've got everything packed already, I'm sending my things off right after dinner. The Baron and I are getting married tomorrow, tomorrow we leave for the brickyard, and day after tomorrow I'll already be at school, the new life will have begun. Somehow God will help me! When I passed my teacher's examination I wept for joy . . . so grateful . . . *(A pause)* In a little while the horse and the cart will be here for my things. . . .

Kulygin: That's all right, only somehow it isn't serious. It's all just ideas, and hardly anything really serious. Still, though, I wish you luck from the bottom of my heart.

Chebutykin: *(With emotion)* My dearest, my treasure. . . . My wonderful girl. . . . You have gone on far ahead, I'll never catch up with you. I'm left behind like a bird that's grown old, too old to fly. Fly on, my dears, fly on and God be with you! *(A pause)* It's a shame you shaved off your moustache, Fyodor Ilich.

Kulygin: That's enough from you! *(He sighs)* Well, the soldiers leave today, and then everything will be the way it used to be. No matter what they say, Masha is a good, honest woman, I love her very much, and I'm thankful for my fate. . . . People have such different fates. . . . There's a man named Kozyrev that works in the tax department here. He went to school with me, but they expelled him from high school because he just couldn't manage to understand *ut consecutivum.*[10] Now he's terribly poor, sick, and when we meet each other I say to him, "Hello, *ut consecutivum!*" Yes, he says, that's it, *consecutivum,* and he coughs. . . . And I've been lucky all my life, I've even got the Order of Stanislav Second Class, I myself am teaching others, now, that *ut consecutivum.* Of course, I'm an intelligent man, more intelligent than lots of people, but happiness doesn't consist in that. . . .

[Inside the house someone plays "The Maiden's Prayer" on the piano]

---

10. A grammatical construction in Latin

Irina: Tomorrow evening I won't be hearing that "Maiden's
Prayer" any more, I won't be meeting that Protopopov. . . . *(A
pause)* And Protopopov's sitting there in the living room—
he's come today too. . . .

Kulygin: The headmistress still hasn't arrived?

Irina: No. They've sent for her. If only you knew how hard it is
for me to live here alone, without Olga. . . . She lives at the
high school; she's the headmistress, all day she's busy with her
job, and I'm alone, I'm bored, there's nothing to do, I hate the
very room I live in. . . . So I just made up my mind: If it's fated
for me not to live in Moscow, then that's that. It means, it's
fate. There's nothing to be done about it. . . . It's all in God's
hands, that's the truth. Nikolai Lvovich proposed to me. . . .
Well? I thought it over and made up my mind. He's a good
man, it really is extraordinary how good . . . and all at once it
was as if my soul had wings, I was happy, I felt all relieved, I
wanted to work all over again, to work! . . . Only something
happened yesterday, there's something mysterious hanging
over me. . . .

Chebutykin: Nonesuch. Nonsense.

Natasha: (At the window) The headmistress!

Kulygin: The headmistress has arrived. Let's go on in.

[He and Irina *go into the house]*

Chebutykin: (Reading the newspaper and singing softly to himself) Ta-ra-ra-
boom-de-aye . . . / Sit on a log I may . . .

[Masha comes up; Andrei *passes across the back of the stage wheeling the baby
carriage]*

Masha: He sits there. There he sits.

Chebutykin: So what?

Masha: (Sitting down) Nothing. . . . *(A pause)* Did you love my
mother?

Chebutykin: Very much.

Masha: And she loved you?

Chebutykin: (After a pause) I don't remember any more.

Masha: Is my man here? That's the way our cook Marfa used to
talk about her policeman—my man. Is my man here?

Chebutykin: Not yet.

Masha: When you get happiness in snatches, in shreds, and then
lose it the way I'm losing it, little by little you get coarse, you get
furious. *(She points to her breast)* In here I'm boiling. . . . *(She
looks at* Andrei, *who again crosses the stage with the baby carriage)*
There's that little brother of ours, our Andrei. . . . All our
hopes vanished. Once upon a time there was a great bell,
thousands of people were raising it, ever so much work and

money had gone into it, and all of a sudden it fell and broke. All of a sudden, for no reason at all. And that's Andrei.

Andrei: Aren't they ever going to quiet down in the house? What a hubbub!

Chebutykin: In a little. *(He looks at his watch)* I've got an old-fashioned watch, it strikes. . . . *(He winds the watch, it strikes)* The first and the second and the fifth batteries leave at one o'clock sharp. *(A pause)* And I leave tomorrow.

Masha: For good?

Chebutykin: I don't know. Maybe I'll be back in a year. Except . . . the devil knows. . . . What's the difference! . . .

[Somewhere in the distance a harp and violin are playing]

Andrei: The town will be deserted. It will be as if they'd put all the lights out. *(A pause)* Something happened yesterday up by the theater—everybody's talking about it, but I haven't any idea.

Chebutykin: Nothing. Just nonsense. Solyony started bothering the Baron, and he got mad and insulted him, and finally Solyony had to challenge him to a duel. *(He looks at his watch)* It's already about time. . . . At half past twelve, in the state forest over there, the one you can see across the river. . . . Piff-Paff! *(He laughs)* Solyony's got the idea he's Lermontov, and even writes little poems. A joke is a joke, but this is his third duel already.

Masha: Whose?

Chebutykin: Solyony's.

Masha: And the Baron?

Chebutykin: What about the Baron? *(A pause)*

Masha: It's all mixed up in my head. . . . Just the same, I say it isn't right to allow them to. He might wound the Baron or even kill him.

Chebutykin: The Baron's a good man, but one baron more, one baron less—what's the difference?

[Someone shouts from beyond the garden: "Yoo-hoo!"]

You wait. That's Skvortsov shouting, one of the seconds. He's in the boat. *(A pause)*

Andrei: In my opinion, to take part in a duel, to be present at one even in the capacity of a doctor, is simply immoral.

Chebutykin: It only looks that way. . . . We're not here, there's nothing in this world, we don't exist, it looks like we exist. . . . And what's the difference anyway!

Masha: That's how it is—the whole day long they talk, talk. . . . *(She walks away)* To live in a climate where you have to expect it to snow every minute—and then on top of it, that's the way they talk. *(She stops)* I won't go into that house, I can't bear it. . . . Tell me when Vershinin comes. . . . *(She goes off along the avenue of trees)* And the birds are flying south already. . . . Swans or geese. . . . *(She looks up)* My beautiful ones, my happy ones. . . .

[She goes out]

Andrei: Our house will be deserted. The officers are leaving, you're leaving, my sister's getting married, and I'll be the only one left.

Chebutykin: And your wife?

[Ferapont comes in with some papers]

Andrei: A wife's a wife. She's honest, sincere—well, kind, but at the same time there's something in her that makes her a kind of blind, petty, hairy animal. In any case, she's not a human being. I'm saying this to you as my friend, the only one I can really talk to. I love Natasha, that's so, but sometimes she seems to me astonishingly vulgar, and then I just despair, I can't understand why I love her as much as I do—or anyway, did. . . .

Chebutykin: *(Getting up)* Brother, I'm going away tomorrow, we may never see each other again, so here's my advice to you. Put on your hat, take your walking stick in your hand, and get out . . . get out, keep going, don't ever look back. And the farther you go the better.

[Solyony walks across the back of the stage, along with two Officers; seeing Chebutykin, he turns toward him—the other Officers walk on]

Solyony: Doctor, it's time! It's already half past twelve. *(He shakes hands with Andrei)*

Chebutykin: In a minute. I'm sick of all of you. *(To Andrei)* If anybody wants me, Andrei boy, tell them I'll be back in a minute. . . . *(He sighs)* Oh—oh—oh!

Solyony: Before he'd time to get his breath /
The bear was hugging him to death. *(He goes with him)* What are you groaning about, old man?

Chebutykin: Well . . .

Solyony: How're you feeling?

Chebutykin: *(Angrily)* As snug as a bug in a rug!

Solyony: The old man's unduly excited. I'm only going to indulge myself a little, I'll just shoot him like a snipe. *(He takes out a bottle of perfume and sprinkles it on his hands)* I've used up the whole bottle today, and they still smell. They smell like a corpse. *(A pause)* So. . . . Remember the poem? "But he, the rebel, seeks

the storm /
As if in tempests there were peace . . ."[11]

Chebutykin: Uh-huh. "Before he'd time to get his breath
The bear was hugging him to death."

[*He and* Solyony *go out.*

People shout, "Yoo-hoo! Yoo-hoo!" Andrei *and* Ferapont *come in.*]

Ferapont: Papers to sign. . . .
Andrei: (*Nervously*) Leave me alone! Leave me alone! *I beg you!*

[*He goes off with the carriage*]

Ferapont: But that's what papers are for, you know, to sign.

[*He goes to the back of the stage.*

Irina *and* Tuzenbach *come in; he is wearing a straw hat.* Kulygin *crosses the stage, calling:* "Yoo-hoo, Masha! Yoo-hoo!"]

Tuzenbach: I believe he's the only person in town that's glad the sol-
diers are leaving.
Irina: That's understandable. (*A pause*) The town's getting all
empty.
Tuzenbach: (*After looking at his watch*) Dear, I'll be back in a minute.
Irina: Where are you going?
Tuzenbach: I have to go in to town, to—to say good-bye to my friends.
Irina: That's not so. . . . Nikolai, why are you so upset today? (*A
pause*) What happened yesterday, by the theater?
Tuzenbach: (*With a movement of impatience*) In an hour I'll come back
and be with you again. (*He kisses her hands*) My beloved . . .
(*He looks into her face*) For five years now I've been in love with
you, and still I can't get used to it, and you seem more beautiful
to me all the time. What marvelous, wonderful hair! What
eyes! Tomorrow I'll take you away, we'll work, we'll be rich, my
dreams will come true. You'll be happy. Only there's one
thing wrong, just one thing wrong: you don't love me!
Irina: It isn't in my power! I'll be your wife, I'll be faithful and
obedient, but it's not love, oh, what is there I can do? (*She
cries*) I never have been in love in my life, not even once. Oh,
I've dreamed so about love, dreamed about love so long now,
day and night, but my soul is like some expensive piano that's
locked and the key lost. (*A pause*) You look so worried.
Tuzenbach: I didn't sleep all night. There isn't anything in my life terrible enough to frighten me, only that lost key tortures me, it

---

11. Concluding lines of "The Sail" by Mikhail Yuryevich Lermontov (1814–1841).

won't let me sleep. Say something to me. *(A pause)* Say something to me. . . .

Irina: What? What is there to say? What?

Tuzenbach: Something.

Irina: That's enough, that's enough! . . . *(A pause)*

Tuzenbach: What senseless things, what idiotic little things suddenly, for no reason, start to matter in your life! You laugh at them the way you did before, you know they're senseless, and yet you go on and on and haven't the strength to stop. Oh, let's not talk about it! I'm happy. It's as if I were seeing for the first time in my life these firs and maples and birches, and they are all looking at me curiously and waiting. What beautiful trees, and how beautiful life ought to be under them! *(A shout: "Yoo-hoo!")* I must go, it's already time. . . . See that tree, it's dried up, but the wind moves it with the others just the same. So it seems to me that if I die, still, some way or other I'll have a share in life. Good-bye, my darling. . . . *(He kisses her hands)* The papers you gave me are on my table under the calendar.

Irina: I'm going with you.

Tuzenbach: *(Uneasily)* No, no! *(He goes away quickly, then stops by the avenue of trees)* Irina!

Irina: What?

Tuzenbach: *(Not knowing what to say)* I didn't have any coffee this morning. Tell them to make me some. . . .

[*He goes out quickly.*

Irina *stands lost in thought, then goes to the back of the stage and sits down in the swing.*

Andrei *comes in with the baby carriage;* Ferapont *appears.*]

Ferapont: Andrei Sergeevich, they're not my papers, you know, they're the government's. I didn't think them up.

Andrei: Oh, where's it gone, what's become of it—my past, when I was young and gay and clever, when I had such beautiful dreams, such beautiful thoughts, when my present and future were bright with hope? Why is it that, almost before we've begun to live, we get boring, drab, uninteresting, lazy, indifferent, useless, unhappy? . . . Our town's been in existence for two hundred years, there's a hundred thousand people living in it, and there's not one of them that's not exactly the same as the others; there never has been in it, either in the past or in the present, a single saint, a single scholar, a single artist, a single person famous enough for anybody to envy him or try to be like him. . . . They just eat, drink, sleep, and then die. . . . And some more are born and they too eat, drink, sleep, and so as not to die of boredom they fill their lives with nasty gossip, vodka, cards, affairs, and the wives deceive their husbands and the husbands lie and pretend they don't see anything, and a kind of inexorable vulgarity oppresses the children, and the divine spark within them dies, and they become the same pitiful, absolutely identical corpses that their mothers and fathers were before them. . . . *(To* Ferapont, *angrily)* What do you want?

Ferapont: What? Papers to sign.

Andrei: I'm sick of you.

Ferapont: A while ago the doorman at the courthouse was saying—in Petersburg last winter, he says, it seems as how it was two hundred degrees below zero.

Andrei: The present's disgusting, but on the other hand, when I think of the future—oh, then it's so good! I feel so light, so free: Off there in the distance the light dawns, I see freedom, I see my children and myself freed from laziness, from vodka, from goose with cabbage, from naps after dinner, from all this laziness and cowardice. . . .

Ferapont: It seems as how two thousand people were frozen to death. He says people were terrified. Either it was Petersburg or Moscow, I don't remember.

Andrei: *(Suddenly overcome with tenderness)* My own darling sisters, my wonderful sisters . . . *(Tearfully)* Masha, my own sister . . .

Natasha: Who's that making all that noise out there? Is that you, Andrei? You'll wake Baby Sophie! You know you ought not to make any noise, Sophie's asleep. You're as clumsy as a bear. If you want to talk, then give the baby carriage and the baby to someone else! Ferapont, take the baby carriage from your master.

Ferapont: Yes'm.

Andrei: *(Embarrassed)* I was speaking in a low voice.

Natasha: *(Behind the window, petting Bobik)* Bobik! Naughty Bobik! Bad Bobik!

Andrei: *(Glancing through the papers)* All right, I'll look them over and sign the ones that have to be signed, and you can take them back to the board. . . .

[He goes into the house, reading the papers.

Ferapont *pushes the baby carriage toward the back of the garden.]*

Natasha: Bobik, tell Mother what's her name! You darling, you darling! And who's that over there? That's Aunt Olga. Say to your Aunt Olga: "How do you do, Olga!"

[Two street Musicians, *a* Man *and a* Girl, *come in and begin to play on a violin*

and harp; Vershinin, Olga, *and* Anfisa *come out of the house and listen silently for a moment;* Irina *comes up]*

   Olga: Our garden's like a vacant lot, they walk right through it. Nurse dear, give the musicians something.

   Anfisa: (Giving something to the Musicians*)* Good-bye and God bless you! *(The* Musicians *bow and go out)* Poor things! If you've enough to eat you don't go around playing. *(To* Irina*)* Good morning, little Irina! *(She kisses her)* M-m-m-m, child, the life I lead! the life I lead! At the high school in a lovely government apartment, there with little Olga—that's what the Lord has vouchsafed me in my old age! Sinner that I am, never in my whole life have I lived the way I live now! . . . A big apartment, a government one, and I've a little room all to myself, a little bed—all government property! I go to sleep at night and—O Lord! Mother of God, there's nobody in the whole world happier than I am!

Vershinin: We're leaving right away, Olga Sergeevna. It's time I was going. *(A pause)* I wish you everything, everything. . . . Where is Marya Sergeevna?

   Irina: She's somewhere in the garden. I'll go look for her.

Vershinin: Please do. I haven't much time.

   Anfisa: I'll go look too. *(She calls)* Little Masha, yoo-hoo! *(She goes with* Irina *toward the back of the garden)* Yoo-hoo! Yoo-hoo!

Vershinin: Everything comes to an end. And so we too must part. *(He looks at his watch)* The town gave us a sort of lunch, we drank champagne, the mayor made a speech, I ate and listened, but my soul was here with you. . . . *(He looks around the garden)* I'll miss you.

   Olga: Shall we see each other again, someday?

Vershinin: Most likely not. *(A pause)* My wife and my two little girls will be staying for two months more; please, if anything should happen, if they should need anything . . .

   Olga: Yes, yes, of course. Don't even think about it. *(A pause)* By tomorrow there won't be a single soldier left in town, it will all be only a memory—and of course a new life will begin for us. . . . *(A pause)* Nothing turns out the way we want it to. I didn't want to be a headmistress, and just the same I've become one. It means we won't live in Moscow. . . .

Vershinin: Well. . . . Thank you for everything. Forgive me if anything wasn't what it should have been. . . . I've talked a lot, such a lot—and forgive me for that, don't hold it against me. . . .

   Olga: (Wiping her eyes) Why doesn't Masha come on . . .

Vershinin: What is there left for me to say to you, in farewell? What's left to philosophize about? . . . *(He laughs)* Life is hard. It seems to many of us lonely and hopeless—but just the same you've got to admit it's gradually getting clearer and lighter, and plainly the time isn't too far away when it will be entirely bright. *(He looks at his watch)* It's time for me to leave, it's time! In the old days mankind was busy with wars, its whole existence was filled with campaigns, invasions, conquests, but nowadays we've outlived all that. It's left behind an enormous vacuum which, so far, there is nothing to fill; mankind is passionately searching for it and of course will find it. Ah, if only it would come more quickly! *(A pause)* You know, if only industry could be added to education, and education to industry . . . *(He looks at his watch)* But it's time I was going. . . .

Olga: Here she comes.

Vershinin: I came to say good-bye. . . .

[Olga goes off a little to the side, in order to let them say good-bye]

Masha: *(Looking into his face)* Good-bye. . . . *(A long kiss)*

Olga: There, there . . . (Masha *is sobbing violently*)

Vershinin: Write me. . . . Don't forget me! Let me go . . . it's time. . . . Olga Sergeevna, take her, I'm already . . . it's time . . . I'm late . . .

[Moved, he kisses Olga's *hands, then once again embraces* Masha *and quickly goes out]*

Olga: There, Masha, there. . . . Stop, darling. . . .

[Kulygin enters]

Kulygin: *(Embarrassed)* It's all right, let her cry, let her. . . . My good Masha, my sweet Masha. . . . You're my wife, and I'm happy, no matter what happens. . . . I don't complain, I don't reproach you for a single thing. There's Olga, she'll be our witness. . . . Let's start over and live the way we used to, and I won't by so much as a single word, by the least hint . . .

Masha: *(Stifling her sobs)* By the curved seastrand a green oak stands, /
A chain of gold upon it . . . a chain of gold upon it . . . I'm going out of my mind. . . . By the curved seastrand . . . a green oak . . .

Olga: Hush, Masha. . . . Hush. . . . Give her some water.

Masha: I'm not crying any more. . . .

Kulygin: She's not crying any more. . . . She's a good girl. . . .

[A muffled, far-off shot is heard]

Masha: By the curved seastrand a green oak stands, /
A chain of gold upon it . . . a green cat . . . a green oak . . . I'm

all mixed up. . . . *(She takes a drink of water)* My life's all wrong. I don't want anything any more. . . . I'll be all right in a minute. . . . What difference is anything anyway? . . . What does it mean, *by the curved seastrand?* Why do I keep saying that? My thoughts are all mixed up.

[Irina enters]

Olga: Hush, Masha. Now you're being a sensible girl. . . . Let's go on in. . . .

Masha: (Angrily) I won't go in there. *(She sobs, but immediately stops herself)* I don't go in that house any more, and I won't now. . . .

Irina: Let's just sit together for a while and not say anything. . . . Tomorrow I'm going, you know. . . .

Kulygin: Yesterday I took this moustache and beard away from one of the boys in my class. . . . *(He puts on the moustache and beard)* I look just like the German teacher. . . . *(He laughs)* Don't I? They're funny, those boys. . . .

Masha: You really do look just like that German of yours.

Olga: (Laughing) You do. *(Masha cries)*

Irina: There, Masha, there!

Kulygin: Just like . . .

[Natasha comes in]

Natasha: (To the maid) What? Protopopov's going to sit with Baby Sophie, and Andrei Sergeevich can take Bobik for a ride. Children are so much trouble. . . . *(To* Irina*)* Irina, you're leaving tomorrow—such a pity! Do stay at least one week more! *(She catches sight of* Kulygin *and shrieks; he laughs and takes off his moustache and beard)* What on earth—get out, how you did scare me! *(To* Irina*)* I'll miss you—do you think having you leave is going to be easy for me? I've told them to put Andrei and his violin in your room—let him saw away in there!—and we're going to put Baby Sophie in his room. That wonderful, marvelous child! What a girl! Today she looked up at me with the most extraordinary expression in her eyes and—"Mama!"

Kulygin: A beautiful child, that's so.

Natasha: So tomorrow I'll be all alone here. *(She sighs)* First of all I'm going to have them chop down all those fir trees along the walk, and then that maple. . . . In the evening it's so ugly. . . . *(To* Irina*)* Dear, that belt isn't a bit becoming to you. . . . It's in bad taste—you need something a little brighter. . . . And I'm having them plant darling little flowers everywhere—how they will smell! *(Sternly)* What's this fork doing lying around on this bench? *(She goes into the house; to the* Maid*)* Will you tell me what this fork is doing lying around on this bench? *(She shouts)* Don't you dare talk back to me!

Kulygin: There she goes again!

[Behind the scene a band is playing a march; everybody listens]

    Olga: They are leaving.

[She goes away.

Chebutykin *comes in.]*

    Masha: Our friends are leaving. Well, let's wish them a happy journey! *(To her husband)* We must go home. Where are my hat and cape?

    Kulygin: I took them indoors. . . . I'll get them right away.

[He goes into the house]

    Olga: Yes, now we can all go home. It's time.

Chebutykin: Olga Sergeevna!

    Olga: What is it? *(A pause)* What is it?

Chebutykin: Nothing. . . . I don't know how to tell you. . . . *(He whispers in her ear)*

    Olga: *(Alarmed)* It's not possible!

Chebutykin: Yes. . . . What a mess! . . . I'm worn out, I'm sick and tired of it. I don't want to say another word. . . . *(Irritably)* Anyway, what's the difference!

    Masha: What's happened?

    Olga: *(Putting her arms around* Irina*)* This is a terrible day. I don't know how to tell you, my darling. . . .

    Irina: What? Tell me right away, what? For God's sake! *(She cries)*

Chebutykin: A little while ago the Baron was killed in a duel.

    Irina: *(Crying softly)* I knew, I knew. . . .

Chebutykin: *(Sitting down on a bench at the back of the stage)* I'm worn out. . . . *(He takes a newspaper out of his pocket)* Let 'em cry. . . . *(He sings softly)* Ta-ra-ra-boom-de-aye . . . / Sit on a log I may . . . What's the difference anyway? *(The* Three Sisters *stand nestled against one another)*

    Masha: Oh, how the music is playing! They are leaving us, one is really gone, really, gone forever and ever; we'll stay here alone, to begin our life over again. We must live . . . we must live . . .

    Irina: *(Putting her head on* Olga's *breast)* The time will come when everyone will know why all this is, what these sufferings are for, there will be no more secrets—but in the meantime we must live . . . must work, only work! Tomorrow I'll go away alone, I'll teach in the school and give my life to those who'll need it, perhaps. It's fall now, soon the winter will come and cover everything with snow, and I will work, I will work . . .

Olga: (Putting her arms around both her sisters) The music is playing so gaily, so eagerly, and one wants so to live! Oh, my God! Time will pass, and we shall be gone forever, they will forget us —they'll forget our faces, our voices, and how many of us there were, but our sufferings will change into joy for those who will live after us, happiness and peace will come on earth, and they'll be reminded and speak tenderly of those who are living now, they will bless them. Oh, dear sisters, our life isn't over yet. We shall live! The music is playing so gaily, so joyfully, and it seems as though a little more and we shall know why we live, why we suffer. . . . If only we knew, if only we knew!

[The music grows fainter and fainter; Kulygin, *smiling happily, brings the hat and cape;* Andrei *pushes* Bobik *across the stage in the baby carriage]*

Chebutykin: (Singing softly) Ta-ra-ra-boom-de-aye. . . / Sit on a log I may . . . *(He reads the newspaper)* What's the difference anyway! What's the difference!

Olga: If only we knew, if only we knew!

CURTAIN

Further Reading

Jarrell, Randall. "About *The Three Sisters*: Notes." *The Three Sisters*. By Anton Chekhov. Trans. Randall Jarrell. London: Macmillan, 1969. 103–60. • Golomb, Harai. "Communicating Relationships in Chekhov's *Three Sisters*." *Anton Chekhov Rediscovered: A Collection of New Studies with a Comprehensive Bibliography*. Ed. Savely Senderovich and Munir Sendich. East Lansing, Mich.: Russian Language Journal, 1987. 9–33. • Stroeva, M. N. "*The Three Sisters* in the Production of the Moscow Art Theater." *Chekhov: A Collection of Critical Essays*. Trans. and ed. Robert Louis Jackson. Englewood Cliffs: Prentice, 1967. 121–35. • Magarshack, David. *Chekhov the Dramatist*. London: Eyre Methuen, 1980. 226–63. • Barricelli, Jean-Pierre, ed. *Chekhov's Great Plays: A Critical Anthology*. New York: New York UP, 1981. • Tufts, Carol Strongin. "Prisoners of Their Plots: Literary Allusion and the Satiric Drama of Self-Consciousness in Chekhov's *Three Sisters*." *Modern Drama* 32.5 (Dec. 1989): 485—501.

The realism of Anton Chekhov's plays, their mixture of themes and moods, makes them sometimes almost as hard to interpret as life itself. When The Three Sisters *was first read by the actors of the Moscow Art Theater, for example, they felt primarily its note of melancholy and took it for a tragedy. Chekhov, who was present at the reading, was embarrassed and troubled because he saw the play as a comedy. Randall Jarrell, who translated the play in 1964, saw it neither as a tragedy nor a comedy but emphasized its blend of loneliness and music.*

Randall Jarrell: On Chekhov's Loneliness and His Music

Loneliness (hardly a value or a philosophy) becomes a sort of ghost that haunts Andrei all the time, Irina until she gets older, and Solyony under cover of his Lermontov personality. Loneliness pervaded Chekhov's own life in similar ways. He wrote someone, "I positively cannot live without guests. When I am alone, for some reason I become terrified, just as though I were in a frail little boat on a great ocean." . . .

For years he wore a seal ring with these words: "To the lonely man the world is a desert." He keeps us conscious of the loneliness underneath the general animation. At the birthday party in Act I, there is Vershinin's line about the gloomy-looking bridge in Moscow where the water under it could be heard: "It makes a lonely man feel sad." Later on we hear again when Chebutykin tells Andrei about being unmarried, even if marriage is boring: "But the loneliness! You can philosophize as much as you please, but loneliness is a terrible thing, Andrei. . . ." With the "good-bye trees" and "good-bye echo" and the embraces, tears, *au revoir*'s and farewells, loneliness has built up like entropy as the good social group—that partly kept people from being lonely—has been broken into by the inferior outside world. The organized enclave of Act I, after being invaded by the relatively unorganized environment, loses its own organization like a physical system and runs down to almost nothing . . . Andrei.

The musical side of Russian life, and Chekhov, comes into the play in every act: Masha whistles, the carnival people play offstage, Chebutykin sings nervously after the duel. Specifically, Act I opens with Olga remembering the band's funeral march after the father's death and Act IV ends with the band playing a march as the brigade leaves and Olga has her last, summarizing speech. The "yoo-hoos" beforehand have imparted a faintly musical nostalgia to the scene, too. In Acts I and II there are guitar and piano and singing. "My New Porch" is a song everyone knows like "Old MacDonald Had a Farm," so that when Tuzenbach starts it off, even lonely Andrei and old Chebutykin can carry it along. Masha and Vershinin's duet becomes a witty—but entirely different—parallel of this formula. The camaraderie at the bottom of the first is countered with the romantic insinuation of the second. "Unto love all ages bow, its pangs are blest . . ." leaves nothing in doubt, and when Masha sings a refrain of this and Vershinin adds another, they make a musical declaration of love. This is an excellent preparation for Act III when, after Masha's love confession, it would have been awkward for Vershinin and her to appear together on stage. Their intimacy is even strengthened, in our minds, by his off-stage song to Masha which she hears, comprehends, and answers in song before leaving the stage to join him.

There was always a piano in Chekhov's house, and having someone play helped him to write when he got stuck. Rhythms came naturally to him, and just as he has varied them in the lines of *The Three Sisters*—from the shortest (sounds, single words) to the arias and big set speeches—similarly there is a rhythmic pattern like that on a railway platform where all the people know each other and little groups leave, say good-bye, meet.

SUSAN GLASPELL

(1882–1948)

TRIFLES

CHARACTERS

George Henderson, County Attorney
Henry Peters, Sheriff
Lewis Hale, A Neighboring Farmer
Mrs. Peters
Mrs. Hale

Scene: *The kitchen in the now abandoned farmhouse of* John Wright, *a gloomy kitchen, and left without having been put in order—unwashed pans under the sink, a loaf of bread outside the breadbox, a dish towel on the table—other signs of incompleted work. At the rear the outer door opens and the* Sheriff *comes in followed by the* County Attorney *and* Hale. *The* Sheriff *and* Hale *are men in middle life, the* County Attorney *is a young man; all are much bundled up and go at once to the stove. They are followed by two women—the* Sheriff's *wife first; she is a slight wiry woman, a thin nervous face.* Mrs. Hale *is larger and would ordinarily be called more comfortable looking, but she is disturbed now and looks fearfully about as she enters. The women have come in slowly, and stand close together near the door.*

County Attorney: [Rubbing his hands.] This feels good. Come up to the fire, ladies.
    Mrs. Peters: [After taking a step forward.] I'm not—cold.
    Sheriff: [Unbuttoning his overcoat and stepping away from the stove as if to mark the beginning of official business.] Now, Mr. Hale, before we move things about, you explain to Mr. Henderson just what you saw when you came here yesterday morning.
County Attorney: By the way, has anything been moved? Are things just as you left them yesterday?
    Sheriff: [Looking about.] It's just the same. When it dropped below zero last night I thought I'd better send Frank out this morning to make a fire for us—no use getting pneumonia with a big case on, but I told him not to touch anything except the stove—and you know Frank.
County Attorney: Somebody should have been left here yesterday.
    Sheriff: Oh—yesterday. When I had to send Frank to Morris Center for that man who went crazy—I want you to know

I had my hands full yesterday, I knew you could get back from Omaha by today and as long as I went over everything here myself—

County Attorney: Well, Mr. Hale, tell just what happened when you came here yesterday morning.

Hale: Harry and I had started to town with a load of potatoes. We came along the road from my place and as I got here I said, "I'm going to see if I can't get John Wright to go in with me on a party telephone." I spoke to Wright about it once before and he put me off, saying folks talked too much anyway, and all he asked was peace and quiet—I guess you know about how much he talked himself; but I thought maybe if I went to the house and talked about it before his wife, though I said to Harry that I didn't know as what his wife wanted made much difference to John—

County Attorney: Let's talk about that later, Mr. Hale. I do want to talk about that, but tell now just what happened when you got to the house.

Hale: I didn't hear or see anything; I knocked at the door, and still it was all quiet inside. I knew they must be up, it was past eight o'clock. So I knocked again, and I thought I heard somebody say, "Come in." I wasn't sure, I'm not sure yet, but I opened the door—this door *[Indicating the door by which the two women are still standing]* and there in that rocker—*[Pointing to it.]* sat Mrs. Wright. *[They all look at the rocker.]*

County Attorney: What—was she doing?

Hale: She was rockin' back and forth. She had her apron in her hand and was kind of—pleating it.

County Attorney: And how did she—look?

Hale: Well, she looked queer.

County Attorney: How do you mean—queer?

Hale: Well, as if she didn't know what she was going to do next. And kind of done up.

County Attorney: How did she seem to feel about your coming?

Hale: Why, I don't think she minded—one way or other. She didn't pay much attention. I said, "How do, Mrs. Wright, it's cold, ain't it?" And she said, "Is it?"—and went on kind of pleating at her apron. Well, I was surprised; she didn't ask me to come up to the stove, or to set down, but just sat there, not even looking at me, so I said, "I want to see John." And then she—laughed. I guess you would call it a laugh. I thought of Harry and the team outside, so I said a little sharp: "Can't I see John?" "No," she says, kind o' dull like. "Ain't he home?" says I. "Yes," says she, "he's home." "Then why can't I see him?" I asked her, out of patience. " 'Cause he's dead," says she. "*Dead?*" says I. She just nodded her head, not getting a bit excited, but rockin' back and forth. "Why—where is he?" says I, not knowing what to say. She just pointed upstairs —like that [*Himself pointing to the room above*]. I got up, with the idea of going up there. I walked from there to here—then I says, "Why, what did he die of?" "He died of a rope round his neck," says she, and just went on pleatin' at her apron. Well, I went out and called Harry. I thought I might—need help. We went upstairs and there he was lyin'—

County Attorney: I think I'd rather have you go into that upstairs where you can point it all out. Just go on now with the rest of the story.

Hale: Well, my first thought was to get that rope off. It looked . . . [*Stops, his face twitches.*] . . . but Harry, he went up to him, and he said, "No, he's dead all right, and we'd better not touch anything." So we went back down stairs. She was still sitting that same way. "Has anybody been notified?" I asked. "No," says she, unconcerned. "Who did this, Mrs. Wright?" said Harry. He said it businesslike —and she stopped pleatin' of her apron. "I don't know," she says. "You don't *know?*" says Harry. "No," says she. "Weren't you sleepin' in the bed with him?" says Harry. "Yes," says she, " but I was on the inside." "Somebody slipped a rope round his neck and strangled him and you didn't wake up?" says Harry. "I didn't wake up," she said after him. We must 'a looked as if we didn't see how that could be, for after a minute she said, "I sleep sound." Harry was going to ask her more questions but I said maybe we ought to let her tell her story first to the coroner, or the sheriff, so Harry went fast as he could to Rivers' place, where there's a telephone.

County Attorney: And what did Mrs. Wright do when she knew that you had gone for the coroner?

Hale: She moved from that chair to this one over here [*Pointing to a small chair in the corner.*] and just sat there with her hands held together and looking down. I got a feeling that I ought to make some conversation, so I said I had come in to see if John wanted to put in a telephone, and at that she started to laugh, and then she stopped and looked at me—scared. [*The* County Attorney, *who has had his notebook out, makes a note.*] I dunno, maybe it wasn't scared. I wouldn't like to say it was. Soon Harry got back, and then Dr. Lloyd came, and you, Mr. Peters, and so I guess that's all I know that you don't.

County Attorney: *[Looking around.]* I guess we'll go upstairs first—and
        then out to the barn and around there. *[To the* Sheriff*]*
        You're convinced that there was nothing important here
        —nothing that would point to any motive.
    Sheriff: Nothing here but kitchen things.

[The County Attorney, *after again looking around the kitchen, opens the door of a
cupboard closet. He gets up on a chair and looks on a shelf. Pulls his hand away,
sticky.]*

County Attorney: Here's a nice mess.

[The women draw nearer.]

    Mrs. Peters: *[To the other woman.]* Oh, her fruit; it did freeze. *[To
      the* County Attorney*]* She worried about that when it
      turned so cold. She said the fire'd go out and her jars
      would break.
    Sheriff: Well, can you beat the women! Held for murder and
      worryin' about her preserves.
County Attorney: I guess before we're through she may have something
      more serious than preserves to worry about.
    Hale: Well, women are used to worrying over trifles.

[The two women move a little closer together.]

County Attorney: *[With the gallantry of a young politician.]* And yet, for
      all their worries, what would we do without the ladies?
      *[The women do not unbend. He goes to the sink, takes a dipper-
      ful of water from the pail and, pouring it into a basin, washes
      his hands. Starts to wipe them on the roller towel, turns it for a
      cleaner place.]* Dirty towels! *[Kicks his foot against the pans
      under the sink.]* Not much of a housekeeper, would you
      say, ladies?
    Mrs. Hale: *[Stiffly.]* There's a great deal of work to be done on a
      farm.
County Attorney: To be sure. And yet *[With a little bow to her]* I know
      there are some Dickson county farmhouses which do not
      have such roller towels.

[He gives it a pull to expose its full length again.]

    Mrs. Hale: Those towels get dirty awful quick. Men's hands
      aren't always as clean as they might be.
County Attorney: Ah, loyal to your sex, I see. But you and Mrs. Wright
      were neighbors. I suppose you were friends, too.
    Mrs. Hale: *[Shaking her head.]* I've not seen much of her of late
      years. I've not been in this house—it's more than a year.
County Attorney: And why was that? You didn't like her?

Mrs. Hale: I liked her all well enough. Farmers' wives have their hands full, Mr. Henderson. And then—

County Attorney: Yes—?

Mrs. Hale: [*Looking about.*] It never seemed a very cheerful place.

County Attorney: No—it's not cheerful. I shouldn't say she had the homemaking instinct.

Mrs. Hale: Well, I don't know as Wright had, either.

County Attorney: You mean that they didn't get on very well?

Mrs. Hale: No, I don't mean anything. But I don't think a place'd be any cheerfuller for John Wright's being in it.

County Attorney: I'd like to talk more of that a little later. I want to get the lay of things upstairs now.

[*He goes to the left, where three steps lead to a stair door.*]

Sheriff: I suppose anything Mrs. Peters does'll be all right. She was to take in some clothes for her, you know, and a few little things. We left in such a hurry yesterday.

County Attorney: Yes, but I would like to see what you take, Mrs. Peters, and keep an eye out for anything that might be of use to us.

Mrs. Peters: Yes, Mr. Henderson.

[*The women listen to the men's steps on the stairs, then look about the kitchen.*]

Mrs. Hale: I'd hate to have men coming into my kitchen, snooping around and criticising.

[*She arranges the pans under sink which the* County Attorney *had shoved out of place.*]

Mrs. Peters: Of course it's no more than their duty.

Mrs. Hale: Duty's all right, but I guess that deputy sheriff that came out to make the fire might have got a little of this on. [*Gives the roller towel a pull.*] Wish I'd thought of that sooner. Seems mean to talk about her for not having things slicked up when she had to come away in such a hurry.

Mrs. Peters: [*Who has gone to a small table in the left rear corner of the room, and lifted one end of a towel that covers a pan.*] She had bread set.

[*Stands still.*]

Mrs. Hale: [*Eyes fixed on a loaf of bread beside the breadbox, which is on a low shelf at the other side of the room. Moves slowly toward it.*] She was going to put this in there. [*Picks up loaf, then abruptly drops it. In a manner of returning to familiar things.*] It's a shame about her fruit. I wonder if it's all gone. *[Gets up on the chair and looks.]* I think there's some here that's all right, Mrs. Peters. Yes—here; *[Holding it toward the window.]* this is cherries, too. *[Looking again.]* I declare I believe that's the only one. *[Gets down, bottle in her hand. Goes to the sink and wipes it off on the outside.]* She'll feel awful bad after all her hard work in the hot weather. I remember the afternoon I put up my cherries last summer.

[She puts the bottle on the big kitchen table, center of the room. With a sigh, is about to sit down in the rocking-chair. Before she is seated realizes what chair it is; with a slow look at it, steps back. The chair which she has touched rocks back and forth.]

Mrs. Peters: Well, I must get those things from the front room closet. *[She goes to the door at the right, but after looking into the other room, steps back.]* You coming with me, Mrs. Hale? You could help me carry them.

[They go in the other room; reappear, Mrs. Peters *carrying a dress and skirt,* Mrs. Hale *following with a pair of shoes.]*

Mrs. Peters: My, it's cold in there.

[She puts the clothes on the big table, and hurries to the stove.]

Mrs. Hale: *[Examining her skirt.]* Wright was close. I think maybe that's why she kept so much to herself. She didn't even belong to the Ladies Aid. I suppose she felt she couldn't do her part, and then you don't enjoy things when you feel shabby. She used to wear pretty clothes and be lively, when she was Minnie Foster, one of the town girls singing in the choir. But that—oh, that was thirty years ago. This all you was to take in?

Mrs. Peters: She said she wanted an apron. Funny thing to want, for there isn't much to get you dirty in jail, goodness knows. But I suppose just to make her feel more natural. She said they was in the top drawer in this cupboard. Yes, here. And then her little shawl that always hung behind the door. *[Opens stair door and looks.]* Yes, here it is.

[Quickly shuts door leading upstairs.]

Mrs. Hale: *[Abruptly moving toward her.]* Mrs. Peters?
Mrs. Peters: Yes, Mrs. Hale?
Mrs. Hale: Do you think she did it?
Mrs. Peters: *[In a frightened voice.]* Oh, I don't know.
Mrs. Hale: Well, I don't think she did. Asking for an apron and her little shawl. Worrying about her fruit.
Mrs. Peters: *[Starts to speak, glances up, where footsteps are heard in the*

room above. In a low voice.] Mr. Peters says it looks bad for her. Mr. Henderson is awful sarcastic in a speech and he'll make fun of her sayin' she didn't wake up.

Mrs. Hale: Well, I guess John Wright didn't wake when they was slipping that rope under his neck.

Mrs. Peters: No, it's strange. It must have been done awful crafty and still. They say it was such a—funny way to kill a man, rigging it all up like that.

Mrs. Hale: That's just what Mr. Hale said. There was a gun in the house. He says that's what he can't understand.

Mrs. Peters: Mr. Henderson said coming out that what was needed for the case was a motive; something to show anger, or— sudden feeling.

Mrs. Hale: *[Who is standing by the table.]* Well, I don't see any signs of anger around here. *[She puts her hand on the dish towel which lies on the table, stands looking down at table, one half of which is clean, the other half messy.]* It's wiped to here. *[Makes a move as if to finish work, then turns and looks at loaf of bread outside the breadbox. Drops towel. In that voice of coming back to familiar things.]* Wonder how they are finding things upstairs. I hope she had it a little more red-up up there. You know, it seems kind of *sneaking.* Locking her up in town and then coming out here and trying to get her own house to turn against her!

Mrs. Peters: But Mrs. Hale, the law is the law.

Mrs. Hale: I s'pose 'tis. *[Unbuttoning her coat.]* Better loosen up your things, Mrs. Peters. You won't feel them when you go out.

[Mrs. Peters takes off her fur tippet, goes to hang it on hook at back of room, stands looking at the under part of the small corner table.]

Mrs. Peters: She was piecing a quilt.

[She brings the large sewing basket and they look at the bright pieces.]

Mrs. Hale: It's log cabin pattern. Pretty, isn't it? I wonder if she was goin' to quilt it or just knot it?

[Footsteps have been heard coming down the stairs. The Sheriff enters followed by Hale and the County Attorney.]

Sheriff: They wonder if she was going to quilt it or just knot it!

[The men laugh; the women look abashed.]

County Attorney: *[Rubbing his hands over the stove.]* Frank's fire didn't do much up there, did it? Well, let's go out to the barn and get that cleared up.

[The men go outside.]

> Mrs. Hale: *[Resentfully.]* I don't know as there's anything so strange, our takin' up our time with little things while we're waiting for them to get the evidence. *[She sits down at the big table smoothing out a block with decision.]* I don't see as it's anything to laugh about.
>
> Mrs. Peters: *[Apologetically.]* Of course they've got awful important things on their minds.

[Pulls up a chair and joins Mrs. Hale *at the table.]*

> Mrs. Hale: *[Examining another block.]* Mrs. Peters, look at this one. Here, this is the one she was working on, and look at the sewing! All the rest of it has been so nice and even. And look at this! It's all over the place! Why, it looks as if she didn't know what she was about!

[After she has said this they look at each other, then start to glance back at the door. After an instant Mrs. Hale *has pulled at a knot and ripped the sewing.]*

> Mrs. Peters: Oh, what are you doing, Mrs. Hale?
>
> Mrs. Hale: *[Mildly.]* Just pulling out a stitch or two that's not sewed very good. *[Threading a needle.]* Bad sewing always made me fidgety.
>
> Mrs. Peters: *[Nervously.]* I don't think we ought to touch things.
>
> Mrs. Hale: I'll just finish up this end. *[Suddenly stopping and leaning forward.]* Mrs. Peters?
>
> Mrs. Peters: Yes, Mrs. Hale?
>
> Mrs. Hale: What do you suppose she was so nervous about?
>
> Mrs. Peters: Oh—I don't know. I don't know as she was nervous. I sometimes sew awful queer when I'm just tired. *[*Mrs. Hale *starts to say something, looks at* Mrs. Peters, *then goes on sewing.]* Well, I must get these things wrapped up. They may be through sooner than we think. *[Putting apron and other things together.]* I wonder where I can find a piece of paper, and string.
>
> Mrs. Hale: In that cupboard, maybe.
>
> Mrs. Peters: *[Looking in cupboard.]* Why, here's a birdcage. *[Holds it up.]* Did she have a bird, Mrs. Hale?
>
> Mrs. Hale: Why, I don't know whether she did or not—I've not been here for so long. There was a man around last year selling canaries cheap, but I don't know as she took one; maybe she did. She used to sing real pretty herself.
>
> Mrs. Peters: *[Glancing around.]* Seems funny to think of a bird here. But she must have had one, or why would she have a cage? I wonder what happened to it.

Mrs. Hale: I s'pose maybe the cat got it.

Mrs. Peters: No, she didn't have a cat. She's got that feeling some people have about cats—being afraid of them. My cat got in her room and she was real upset and asked me to take it out.

Mrs. Hale: My sister Bessie was like that. Queer, ain't it?

Mrs. Peters: *[Examining the cage.]* Why, look at this door. It's broke. One hinge is pulled apart.

Mrs. Hale: *[Looking too.]* Looks as if someone must have been rough with it.

Mrs. Peters: Why, yes.

[She brings the cage forward and puts it on the table.]

Mrs. Hale: I wish if they're going to find any evidence they'd be about it. I don't like this place.

Mrs. Peters: But I'm awful glad you came with me, Mrs. Hale. It would be lonesome for me sitting here alone.

Mrs. Hale: It would, wouldn't it? *[Dropping her sewing.]* But I tell you what I do wish, Mrs. Peters. I wish I had come over sometimes when *she* was here. I—*[Looking around the room.]*—wish I had.

Mrs. Peters: But of course you were awful busy. Mrs. Hale—your house and your children.

Mrs. Hale: I could've come. I stayed away because it weren't cheerful—and that's why I ought to have come. I—I've never liked this place. Maybe because it's down in a hollow and you don't see the road. I dunno what it is but it's a lonesome place and always was. I wish I had come over to see Minnie Foster sometimes. I can see now—

[Shakes her head.]

Mrs. Peters: Well, you mustn't reproach yourself, Mrs. Hale. Somehow we just don't see how it is with other folks until —something comes up.

Mrs. Hale: Not having children makes less work—but it makes a quiet house, and Wright out to work all day, and no company when he did come in. Did you know John Wright, Mrs. Peters?

Mrs. Peters: Not to know him; I've seen him in town. They say he was a good man.

Mrs. Hale: Yes—good; he didn't drink, and kept his word as well as most, I guess, and paid his debts. But he was a hard man, Mrs. Peters. Just to pass the time of day with him—*[Shivers.]* Like a raw wind that gets to the bone. *[Pauses, her eye falling on the cage.]* I should think she would 'a wanted a bird. But what do you suppose went with it?

Mrs. Peters: I don't know, unless it got sick and died.

[She reaches over and swings the broken door, swings it again. Both women watch it.]

Mrs. Hale: You weren't raised round here, were you? *[Mrs. Peters shakes her head.]* You didn't know—her?

Mrs. Peters: Not till they brought her yesterday.

Mrs. Hale: She—come to think of it, she was kind of like a bird herself—real sweet and pretty, but kind of timid and—fluttery. How—she—did—change. *[Silence; then as if struck by a happy thought and relieved to get back to everyday things.]* Tell you what, Mrs. Peters, why don't you take the quilt in with you? It might take up her mind.

Mrs. Peters: Why, I think that's a real nice idea, Mrs. Hale. There couldn't possibly be any objection to it, could there? Now, just what would I take? I wonder if her patches are in here—and her things.

[They look in the sewing basket.]

Mrs. Hale: Here's some red. I expect this has got sewing things in it. *[Brings out a fancy box.]* What a pretty box. Looks like something somebody would give you. Maybe her scissors are in here. *[Opens box. Suddenly puts her hand to her nose.]* Why—*[Mrs. Peters bends nearer, then turns her face away.]* There's something wrapped up in this piece of silk.

Mrs. Peters: Why, this isn't her scissors.

Mrs. Hale: [Lifting the silk.] Oh, Mrs. Peters—it's—

[Mrs. Peters bends closer.]

Mrs. Peters: It's the bird.

Mrs. Hale: [Jumping up.] But, Mrs. Peters—look at it! Its neck! Look at its neck! It's all—other side *to.*

Mrs. Peters: Somebody—wrung—its—neck.

[Their eyes meet. A look of growing comprehension, of horror. Steps are heard outside. Mrs. Hale slips box under quilt pieces, and sinks into her chair. Enter Sheriff and County Attorney. Mrs. Peters rises.]

County Attorney: [As one turning from serious things to little pleasantries.] Well, ladies, have you decided whether she was going to quilt it or knot it?

Mrs. Peters: We think she was going to—knot it.

County Attorney: Well, that's interesting, I'm sure. *[Seeing the birdcage.]* Has the bird flown?

Mrs. Hale: [Putting more quilt pieces over the box.] We think the— cat got it.

County Attorney: [Preoccupied.] Is there a cat?

[Mrs. Hale glances in a quick covert way at Mrs. Peters.]

Mrs. Peters: Well, not now. They're superstitious, you know. They leave.

County Attorney: [To Sheriff Peters, continuing an interrupted conversation.] No sign at all of anyone having come from the outside. Their own rope. Now let's go up again and go over it piece by piece. [They start upstairs.] It would have to have been someone who knew just the—

[Mrs. Peters sits down. The two women sit there not looking at one another, but as if peering into something and at the same time holding back. When they talk now it is in the manner of feeling their way over strange ground, as if afraid of what they are saying, but as if they can not help saying it.]

Mrs. Hale: She liked the bird. She was going to bury it in that pretty box.

Mrs. Peters: [In a whisper.] When I was a girl—my kitten—there was a boy took a hatchet, and before my eyes—and before I could get there—[Covers her face an instant.] If they hadn't held me back I would have—[Catches herself, looks upstairs where steps are heard, falters weakly.]—hurt him.

Mrs. Hale: [With a slow look around her.] I wonder how it would seem never to have had any children around. [Pause.] No, Wright wouldn't like the bird—a thing that sang. She used to sing. He killed that, too.

Mrs. Peters: [Moving uneasily.] We don't know who killed the bird.

Mrs. Hale: I knew John Wright.

Mrs. Peters: It was an awful thing was done in this house that night, Mrs. Hale. Killing a man while he slept, slipping a rope around his neck that choked the life out of him.

Mrs. Hale: His neck. Choked the life out of him.

[Her hand goes out and rests on the birdcage.]

Mrs. Peters: [With rising voice.] We don't know who killed him. We don't know.

Mrs. Hale: [Her own feeling not interrupted.] If there'd been years and years of nothing, then a bird to sing to you, it would be awful—still, after the bird was still.

Mrs. Peters: [Something within her speaking.] I know what stillness is. When we homesteaded in Dakota, and my first baby died—after he was two years old, and me with no other then—

Mrs. Hale: [Moving.] How soon do you suppose they'll be through, looking for the evidence?

Mrs. Peters: I know what stillness is. *[Pulling herself back.]* The law has got to punish crime, Mrs. Hale.

Mrs. Hale: [Not as if answering that.] I wish you'd seen Minnie Foster when she wore a white dress with blue ribbons and stood up there in the choir and sang. *[A look around the room.]* Oh, I *wish* I'd come over here once in a while! That was a crime! That was a crime! Who's going to punish that?

Mrs. Peters: [Looking upstairs.] We mustn't—take on.

Mrs. Hale: I might have known she needed help! I know how things can be—for women. I tell you, it's queer, Mrs. Peters. We live close together and we live far apart. We all go through the same things—it's all just a different kind of the same thing. *[Brushes her eyes; noticing the bottle of fruit, reaches out for it.]* If I was you I wouldn't tell her her fruit was gone. Tell her it *ain't.* Tell her it's all right. Take this in to prove it to her. She—she may never know whether it was broke or not.

Mrs. Peters: [Takes the bottle, looks about for something to wrap it in; takes petticoat from the clothes brought from the other room, very nervously begins winding this around the bottle. In a false voice.] My, it's a good thing the men couldn't hear us. Wouldn't they just laugh! Getting all stirred up over a little thing like a—dead canary. As if that could have anything to do with—with—wouldn't they *laugh!*

[The men are heard coming down stairs.]

Mrs. Hale: [Under her breath.] Maybe they would—maybe they wouldn't.

County Attorney: No, Peters, it's all perfectly clear except a reason for doing it. But you know juries when it comes to women. If there was some definite thing. Something to show—something to make a story about—a thing that would connect up with this strange way of doing it—

[The women's eyes meet for an instant. Enter Hale from outer door.]

Hale: Well, I've got the team around. Pretty cold out there.

County Attorney: I'm going to stay here a while by myself. *[To the Sheriff.]* You can send Frank out for me, can't you? I want to go over everything. I'm not satisfied that we can't do better.

Sheriff: Do you want to see what Mrs. Peters is going to take in?

[The County Attorney *goes to the table, picks up the apron, laughs.]*

County Attorney: Oh, I guess they're not very dangerous things the ladies have picked out. *[Moves a few things about, disturbing the quilt pieces which cover the box. Steps back.]* No, Mrs. Peters doesn't need supervising. For that matter, a sheriff's wife is married to the law. Ever think of it that way, Mrs. Peters?

Mrs. Peters: Not—just that way.

Sheriff: *[Chuckling.]* Married to the law. *[Moves toward the other room.]* I just want you to come in here a minute, George. We ought to take a look at these windows.

County Attorney: *[Scoffingly.]* Oh, windows!

Sheriff: We'll be right out, Mr. Hale.

*[*Hale *goes outside. The* Sheriff *follows the* County Attorney *into the other room. Then* Mrs. Hale *rises, hands tight together, looking intensely at* Mrs. Peters, *whose eyes make a slow turn, finally meeting* Mrs. Hale*'s. A moment* Mrs. Hale *holds her, then her own eyes point the way to where the box is concealed. Suddenly* Mrs. Peters *throws back quilt pieces and tries to put the box in the bag she is wearing. It is too big. She opens box, starts to take bird out, cannot touch it, goes to pieces, stands there helpless. Sound of a knob turning in the other room.* Mrs. Hale *snatches the box and puts it in the pocket of her big coat. Enter* County Attorney *and* Sheriff.*]*

County Attorney: *[Facetiously.]* Well, Henry, at least we found out that she was not going to quilt it. She was going to—what is it you call it, ladies?

Mrs. Hale: *[Her hand against her pocket.]* We call it—knot it, Mr. Henderson.

CURTAIN

Further Reading

Bigsby, C. W. E. Introduction. *Plays by Susan Glaspell.* Cambridge: Cambridge UP, 1987. 1–31. • Waterman, Arthur E. *Susan Glaspell.* New York: Twayne, 1966. 68–69. • Lewisohn, Ludwig. *Expressions in America.* New York: Harper, 1932. 393–94. • Sutherland, Cynthia. "American Women Playwrights as Mediators of the 'Woman Problem.'" *Modern Drama* 21.3 (Sept. 1978): 319–36, spec. 322–24. • "Mr. Hornblow Goes to the Play." *Theatre* 25 (Jan. 1917): 21.

Though she had previous experience as a newspaper reporter and as a writer of rather sentimental fiction, Glaspell was a relative newcomer to theater when she wrote Trifles. *She had been plunged into the world of drama by her husband, George Cram Cook, who, along with the great playwright Eugene O'Neill, founded the Provincetown Players in 1915. In the following passage from her biography of Cook, Glaspell explains how he (nicknamed "Jig") pushed her into writing plays and how she responded.*

Susan Glaspell: On the Origin of *Trifles*

"Now, Susan," he said to me, briskly, "I have announced a play of yours for the next bill."

"But I have no play!"

"Then you will have to sit down to-morrow and begin one."

I protested. I did not know how to write a play. I had never "studied it."

"Nonsense," said Jig. "You've got a stage, haven't you?"

So I went out on the wharf, sat alone on one of our wooden benches without a back, and looked a long time at that bare little stage. After a time the stage became a kitchen—a kitchen there all by itself. I saw just where the stove was, the table, and the steps going upstairs. Then the door at the back opened, and people all bundled up came in—two or three men, I wasn't sure which, but sure enough about the two women, who hung back, reluctant to enter that kitchen. When I was a newspaper reporter out in Iowa, I was sent down-state to do a murder trial, and I never forgot going into the kitchen of a woman locked up in town. I had meant to do it as a short story, but the stage took it for its own, so I hurried in from the wharf to write down what I had seen. Whenever I got stuck, I would run across the street to the old wharf, sit in that leaning little theater under which the sea sounded, until the play was ready to continue. Sometimes things written in my room would not form on the stage, and I must go home and cross them out. "What playwrights need is a stage," said Jig, "their own stage."

SAMUEL BECKETT

(1906–1989)

KRAPP'S LAST TAPE

A late evening in the future.

Krapp's den.

Front centre a small table, the two drawers of which
open towards audience.

*Sitting at the table, facing front, i.e. across from the drawers, a bearish old man:
Krapp.*

*Rusty black narrow trousers too short for him. Rusty black sleeveless waistcoat, four
capacious pockets. Heavy silver watch and chain. Grimy white shirt open at neck,
no collar. Surprising pair of dirty white boots, size ten at least, very narrow and
pointed.*

White face. Purple nose. Disordered grey hair. Unshaven.

Very near-sighted (but unspectacled). Hard of hearing.

Cracked voice. Distinctive intonation.

Laborious walk.

*On the table a tape-recorder with microphone and a number of cardboard boxes con-
taining reels of recorded tapes.*

*Table and immediately adjacent area in strong white light. Rest of stage in
darkness.*

*Krapp remains a moment motionless, heaves a great sigh, looks at his watch, fum-
bles in his pockets, takes out an envelope, puts it back, fumbles, takes out a small
bunch of keys, raises it to his eyes, chooses a key, gets up and moves to front of table.
He stoops, unlocks first drawer, peers into it, feels about inside it, takes out a reel of
tape, peers at it, puts it back, locks drawer, unlocks second drawer, peers into it, feels
about inside it, takes out a large banana, peers at it, locks drawer, puts keys back in
his pocket. He turns, advances to edge of stage, halts, strokes banana, peels it, drops
skin at his feet, puts end of banana in his mouth and remains motionless, staring
vacuously before him. Finally he bites off the end, turns aside and begins pacing to
and fro at edge of stage, in the light, i.e. not more than four or five paces either way,
meditatively eating banana. He treads on skin, slips, nearly falls, recovers himself,
stoops and peers at skin and finally pushes it, still stooping, with his foot over the
edge of stage into pit. He resumes his pacing, finishes banana, returns to table, sits
down, remains a moment motionless, heaves a great sigh, takes keys from his
pockets, raises them to his eyes, chooses key, gets up and moves to front of table,*

unlocks second drawer, takes out a second large banana, peers at it, locks drawer, puts back keys in his pocket, turns, advances to edge of stage, halts, strokes banana, peels it, tosses skin into pit, puts end of banana in his mouth and remains motionless, staring vacuously before him. Finally he has an idea, puts banana in his waistcoat pocket, the end emerging, and goes with all the speed he can muster backstage into darkness. Ten seconds. Loud pop of cork. Fifteen seconds. He comes back into light carrying an old ledger and sits down at table. He lays ledger on table, wipes his mouth, wipes his hands on the front of his waistcoat, brings them smartly together and rubs them.

Krapp: *[briskly.]* Ah! *[He bends over ledger, turns the pages, finds the entry he wants, reads.]* Box . . . thrree . . . spool . . . five. *[He raises his head and stares front. With relish.]* Spool! *[Pause.]* Spooool! *[Happy smile. Pause. He bends over table, starts peering and poking at the boxes.]* Box . . . thrree . . . thrree . . . four . . . two . . . *[with surprise]* nine! good God! . . . seven . . . ah! the little rascal! *[He takes up box, peers at it.]* Box thrree. *[He lays it on table, opens it and peers at spools inside.]* Spool . . . *[he peers at ledger]* . . . five . . . *[he peers at spools]* . . . five . . . five . . . ah! the little scoundrel! *[He takes out a spool, peers at it.]* Spool five. *[He lays it on table, closes box three, puts it back with the others, takes up the spool.]* Box thrree, spool five. *[He bends over the machine, looks up. With relish.]* Spooool! *[Happy smile. He bends, loads spool on machine, rubs his hands.]* Ah! *[He peers at ledger, reads entry at foot of page.]* Mother at rest at last . . . Hm . . . The black ball . . . *[He raises his head, stares blankly front. Puzzled.]* Black ball? . . . *[He peers again at ledger, reads.]* The dark nurse . . . *[He raises his head, broods, peers again at ledger, reads.]* Slight improvement in bowel condition . . . Hm . . . Memorable . . . what? *[He peers closer.]* Equinox, memorable equinox. *[He raises his head, stares blankly front. Puzzled.]* Memorable equinox? . . . *[Pause. He shrugs his shoulders, peers again at ledger, reads.]* Farewell to—*[he turns the page]*—love.

He raises his head, broods, bends over machine, switches on and assumes listening posture, i.e. leaning forward, elbows on table, hand cupping ear towards machine, face front.

Tape: *[strong voice, rather pompous, clearly Krapp's at a much earlier time.]* Thirty-nine today, sound as a—*[Settling himself more comfortably he knocks one of the boxes off the table, curses, switches off, sweeps boxes and ledger violently to the ground, winds tape back to beginning, switches on, resumes posture.]* Thirty-nine today, sound as a bell, apart from my old weakness, and intellectually I have now every reason to suspect at the . . . *[hesitates]* . . . crest of the wave—or thereabouts. Celebrated the awful occasion, as in recent years, quietly at the Winehouse. Not a soul. Sat before the fire with closed eyes, separating the grain from the husks. Jotted down a few notes, on the back of an envelope. Good to be back in my den, in my old rags. Have just eaten I regret to say three bananas and only with difficulty refrained from a fourth. Fatal things for a man with my condition. *[Vehemently.]* Cut 'em out! *[Pause.]* The new light above my table is a great improvement. With all this darkness round me I feel less alone. *[Pause.]* In a way. *[Pause.]* I love to get up and move about in it, then back here to . . . *[hesitates]* . . . me. *[Pause.]* Krapp.

Pause.

The grain, now what I wonder do I mean by that, I mean . . . *[hesitates]* . . . I suppose I mean those things worth having when all the dust has—when all *my* dust has settled. I close my eyes and try and imagine them.

Pause.

Krapp closes his eyes briefly.

Extraordinary silence this evening, I strain my ears and do not hear a sound. Old Miss McGlome always sings at this hour. But not tonight. Songs of her girlhood, she says. Hard to think of her as a girl. Wonderful woman though. Connaught, I fancy. *[Pause.]* Shall I sing when I am her age, if I ever am? No. *[Pause.]* Did I sing as a boy? No. *[Pause.]* Did I ever sing? No.

Pause.

Just been listening to an old year, passages at random. I did not check in the book, but it must be at least ten or twelve years ago. At that time I think I was still living on and off with Bianca in Kedar Street. Well out of that, Jesus yes! Hopeless business. *[Pause.]* Not much about her, apart from a tribute to her eyes. Very warm. I suddenly saw them again. *[Pause.]* Incomparable! *[Pause.]* Ah well . . . *[Pause.]* These old P.M.s are gruesome, but I often find them—*[Krapp switches off, broods, switches on]*—a help before embarking on a new . . . *[hesitates]* . . . retrospect. Hard to believe I was ever that young whelp. The voice! Jesus! And the aspirations! *[Brief laugh in which Krapp joins.]* And the resolutions! *[Brief laugh in which Krapp joins.]* To drink less, in particular. *[Brief laugh of Krapp alone.]* Statistics. Seventeen hundred hours, out of the preceding eight thousand odd, consumed on licensed premises alone. More than 20%, say 40% of his waking life. *[Pause.]* Plans for a less . . . *[hesitates]* . . . engrossing sexual life. Last illness of his father. Flagging pursuit of happiness. Unattainable laxation. Sneers at what he calls his youth and thanks to God that it's over. *[Pause.]* False ring there. *[Pause.]* Shadows of the opus . . . magnum. Closing with a—*[brief laugh]*—yelp to Providence. *[Prolonged laugh in which Krapp joins.]* What remains of all that misery? A girl in a shabby green coat, on a railway-station platform? No?

Pause.

When I look—

Krapp switches off, broods, looks at his watch, gets up, goes backstage into darkness. Ten seconds. Pop of cork. Ten seconds. Second cork. Ten seconds. Third cork. Ten seconds. Brief burst of quavering song.

Krapp: *[sings].* Now the day is over,
Night is drawing nigh-igh,
Shadows—

Fit of coughing. He comes back into light, sits down, wipes his mouth, switches on, resumes his listening posture.

Tape: —back on the year that is gone, with what I hope is perhaps a glint of the old eye to come, there is of course the house on the canal where mother lay a-dying, in the late autumn, after her long viduity *[Krapp gives a start],* and the—*[Krapp switches off, winds back tape a little, bends his ear closer to machine, switches on]*—a-dying, after her long viduity, and the—

Krapp switches off, raises his head, stares blankly before him. His lips move in the syllables of "viduity." No sound. He gets up, goes backstage into darkness, comes back with an enormous dictionary, lays it on table, sits down and looks up the word.

Krapp: *[reading from dictionary.]* State—or condition of being—or remaining—a widow—or widower. *[Looks up. Puzzled.]* Being—or remaining? . . . *[Pause. He peers again at dictionary. Reading.]* "Deep weeds of viduity" . . . Also of an animal, especially a bird . . . the vidua or weaver-bird . . . Black plumage of male . . . *[He looks up. With relish.]* The vidua-bird!

Pause. He closes dictionary, switches on, resumes listening posture.

Tape: —bench by the weir from where I could see her window. There I sat, in the biting wind, wishing she were gone. *[Pause.]* Hardly a soul, just a few regulars, nursemaids, infants, old men, dogs. I got to know them quite well—oh by appearance of course I mean! One dark young beauty I recollect particularly, all white and starch, incomparable bosom, with a big black hooded perambulator, most funereal thing. Whenever I looked in her direction she had her eyes on me. And yet when I was bold enough to speak to her—not having been introduced—she threatened to call a policeman. As if I had designs on her virtue! *[Laugh. Pause.]* The face she had! The eyes! Like . . . *[hesitates]* . . . chrysolite! *[Pause.]* Ah well . . . *[Pause.]* I was there when— *[Krapp switches off, broods, switches on again]*—the blind went down, one of those dirty brown roller affairs, throwing a ball for a little white dog, as chance would have it. I happened to look up and there it was. All over and done with, at last. I sat on for a few moments with the ball in my hand and the dog yelping and pawing at me. *[Pause.]* Moments. Her moments, my moments. *[Pause.]* The dog's moments. *[Pause.]* In the end I held it out to him and he took it in his mouth, gently, gently. A small, old, black, hard, solid rubber ball. *[Pause.]* I might have kept it. *[Pause.]* But I gave it to the dog.

Pause.

Ah well . . .

Pause.

Spiritually a year of profound gloom and indigence until that memorable night in March, at the end of the jetty, in the howling wind, never to be forgotten, when suddenly I saw the whole thing. The vision, at last. This I fancy is what I have chiefly to record this evening, against the day when my work will be done and perhaps no place left in my memory, warm or cold, for the miracle that . . . *[hesitates]* . . . for the fire that set it alight. What I suddenly saw then was this, that the belief I had been going on all my life, namely—*[Krapp switches off impatiently, winds tape forward, switches on again]*—great granite rocks the foam flying up in the light of the lighthouse and the wind-gauge spinning like a propellor, clear to me at last that the dark I have always struggled to keep under is in reality my most—*[Krapp curses, switches off, winds tape forward, switches on again]*—unshatterable association until my dissolution of storm and night with the light of the understanding and the fire —*[Krapp curses louder, switches off, winds tape forward, switches on again]*—my face in her breasts and my hand on her. We lay there without moving. But under us all moved, and moved us, gently, up and down, and from side to side.

Pause.

Past midnight. Never knew such silence. The earth might be uninhabited.

Pause.

Here I end—

Krapp switches off, winds tape back, switches on again.

—upper lake, with the punt, bathed off the bank, then pushed out into the stream and drifted. She lay stretched out on the floor-boards with her hands under her head and her eyes closed. Sun blazing down, bit of a breeze, water nice and lively. I noticed a scratch on her thigh and asked her how she came by it. Picking gooseberries, she said. I said again I thought it was hopeless and no good going on, and she agreed, without opening her eyes. *[Pause.]* I asked her to look at me and after a few moments—*[pause]*—after a few moments she did, but the eyes just slits, because of the glare. I bent over her to get them in the shadow and they opened. *[Pause. Low.]* Let me in. *[Pause.]* We drifted in among the flags and stuck. The way they went down, sighing, before the stem! *[Pause.]* I lay down across her with my face in her breasts and my hand on her. We lay there without moving. But under us all moved, and moved us, gently, up and down, and from side to side.

Pause.

Past midnight. Never knew—

Krapp switches off, broods. Finally he fumbles in his pockets, encounters the banana, takes it out, peers at it, puts it back, fumbles, brings out the envelope, fumbles, puts back envelope, looks at his watch, gets up and goes backstage into darkness. Ten seconds. Sound of bottle against glass, then brief siphon. Ten seconds. Bottle against glass alone. Ten seconds. He comes back a little unsteadily into light, goes to front of table, takes out keys, raises them to his eyes, chooses key, unlocks first drawer, peers into it, feels about inside, takes out reel, peers at it, locks drawer, puts keys back in his pocket, goes and sits down, takes reel off machine, lays it on dictionary, loads virgin reel on machine, takes envelope from his pocket, consults back of it, lays it on table, switches on, clears his throat and begins to record.

Krapp: Just been listening to that stupid bastard I took myself for thirty years ago, hard to believe I was ever as bad as that. Thank God that's all done with anyway. *[Pause.]* The eyes she had! *[Broods, realizes he is recording silence, switches off, broods. Finally.]* Everything there, everything, all the—*[Realizes this is not being recorded, switches on.]* Everything there, everything on this old muckball, all the light and dark and famine and feasting of . . . *[hesitates]* . . . the ages! *[In a shout.]* Yes! *[Pause.]* Let that go! Jesus! Take his mind off his homework! Jesus! *[Pause. Weary.]* Ah well, maybe he was right. *[Pause.]* Maybe he was right. *[Broods. Realizes. Switches off. Consults envelope.]* Pah! *[Crumples it and throws it away. Broods. Switches on.]* Nothing to say, not a squeak. What's a year now? The sour cud and the iron stool. *[Pause.]* Revelled in the word spool. *[With relish.]* Spooool! Happiest moment of the past half million. *[Pause.]* Seventeen copies sold, of which eleven at trade price to free circulating libraries beyond the seas. Getting known. *[Pause.]* One pound six and something, eight I have little doubt. *[Pause.]* Crawled out once or twice, before the summer was cold. Sat shivering in the park, drowned in dreams and burning to be gone. Not a soul. *[Pause.]* Last fancies. *[Vehemently.]* Keep 'em under! *[Pause.]* Scalded the eyes out of me reading *Effie* again, a page a day, with tears again. Effie . . . *[Pause.]* Could have been happy with her, up there on the Baltic, and the pines, and the dunes. *[Pause.]* Could I? *[Pause.]* And she? *[Pause.]* Pah! *[Pause.]* Fanny came in a couple of times. Bony old ghost of a whore. Couldn't do much, but I suppose better than a kick in the crutch. The last time wasn't so bad. How do you manage it, she said, at your age? I told her I'd been saving up for her all my life. *[Pause.]* Went to Vespers once, like when I was in short trousers. *[Pause. Sings.]*

> Now the day is over,
> Night is drawing nigh-igh,
> Shadows—*[coughing, then almost inaudible]*—of the evening
> Steal across the sky.

[Gasping.] Went to sleep and fell off the pew. *[Pause.]* Sometimes wondered in the night if a last effort mightn't—*[Pause.]* Ah finish your booze now and get to your bed. Go on with this drivel in the morning. Or leave it at that. *[Pause.]* Leave it at that. *[Pause.]* Lie propped up in the dark—and wander. Be again in the dingle on a Christmas Eve, gathering holly, the red-berried. *[Pause.]* Be again on Croghan on a Sunday morning, in the haze, with the bitch, stop and listen to the bells. *[Pause.]* And so on. *[Pause.]* Be again, be again. *[Pause.]* All that old misery. *[Pause.]* Once wasn't enough for you. *[Pause.]* Lie down across her.

Long pause. He suddenly bends over machine, switches off, wrenches off tape, throws it away, puts on the other, winds it forward to the passage he wants, switches on, listens staring front.

Tape: —gooseberries, she said. I said again I thought it was hopeless and no good going on, and she agreed, without opening her eyes. *[Pause.]* I asked her to look at me and after a few moments— *[pause]*—after a few moments she did, but the eyes just slits, because of the glare. I bent over her to get them in the shadow and they opened. *[Pause. Low.]* Let me in. *[Pause.]* I lay down across her with my face in her breasts and my hand on her. We lay there without moving. But under us all moved, and moved us, gently, up and down, and from side to side.

Pause.

Krapp's lips move. No sound.

Past midnight. Never knew such silence. The earth might be uninhabited.

Pause.

Here I end this reel. Box—*[pause]*—three, spool—*[pause]*—five. *[Pause.]* Perhaps my best years are gone. When there was a chance of happiness. But I wouldn't want them back. Not with the fire in me now. No, I wouldn't want them back.

Krapp motionless staring before him. The tape runs on in silence.

CURTAIN

Further Reading

Cohn, Ruby. *Back to Beckett.* Princeton: Princeton UP, 1973. 165–72. • Homan, Sidney. *Beckett's Theaters: Interpretations for Performance.* London: Associated U Presses, 1984. 96–104. • Ben-Zvi, Linda. *Samuel Beckett.* Boston: Twayne, 1986. 152–55. • Fletcher, Beryl S. and John. *A Student's Guide to the Plays of Samuel Beckett.* 2nd ed. London: Faber, 1985. 119–33. • Brustein, Robert. "Krapp and a Little Claptrap." *New Republic* 142 (22 Feb. 1960): 21–22. • Brien, Alan. "Waiting for Beckett." *Spectator* 201 (7 Nov. 1958): 609.

The "absurdist" plays of Samuel Beckett show characters whose lives seem to be reduced to a least common denominator rather than enlarged to the dimensions we associate with tragedy. The result according to some critics is a fine mixture of tragic and comic elements; other critics find Beckett's view of life too bleak to rise above mere pathos. Arthur Miller's distinction between the tragic and the pathetic can help us clarify the issue, regardless of which side we finally take.

Arthur Miller: On the Difference Between Tragedy and Pathos

Let me put it this way. When Mr. B., while walking down the street, is struck on the head by a falling piano, the newspapers call this a tragedy. In fact, of course, this is only the pathetic end of Mr. B. Not only because of the accidental nature of his death; that is elementary. It is pathetic because it merely arouses our feelings of sympathy, sadness, and possibly of identification. What the death of Mr. B. does not arouse is the tragic feeling.

To my mind the essential difference, and the precise difference, between tragedy and pathos is that tragedy brings us not only sadness, sympathy, identification and even fear; it also, unlike pathos, brings us knowledge or enlightenment.

But what sort of knowledge? In the largest sense, it is knowledge pertaining to the right way of living in the world. The manner of Mr. B.'s death was not such as to illustrate any principle of living. In short, there was no illumination of the ethical in it. And to put it all in the same breath, the reason we confuse the tragic with the pathetic, as well as why we create so few tragedies, is twofold: in the first place many of our writers have given up trying to search out the right way of living, and secondly, there is not among us any commonly accepted faith in a way of life that will give us not only material gain but satisfaction.

Our modern literature has filled itself with an attitude which implies that despite suffering, nothing important can really be learned by man that might raise him to a happier condition. The probing of the soul has taken the path of behaviorism. By this method it is sufficient for an artist simply to spell out the anatomy of disaster. Man is regarded as essentially a dumb animal moving through a preconstructed maze toward his inevitable sleep.

Such a concept of man can never reach beyond pathos, for enlightenment is impossible within it, life being regarded as an immutably disastrous fact. Tragedy, called a more exalted kind of consciousness, is so called because it makes us aware of what the character might have been. But to say or strongly imply what a man might have been requires of the author a soundly based, completely believed vision of man's great possibilities. As Aristotle said, the poet is greater than the historian because he presents not only things as they were, but foreshadows what they might have been. We forsake literature when we are content to chronicle disaster.

ARTHUR MILLER

(b. 1915)

DEATH OF A SALESMAN

CHARACTERS

Willy Loman
Linda
Biff
Happy
Bernard
The Woman
Charley
Uncle Ben
Howard Wagner
Jenny
Stanley
Miss Forsythe
Letta

The action takes place in Willy Loman's house and yard and in various places he visits in the New York and Boston of today.

Throughout the play, in the stage directions, left and right mean stage left and stage right.

ACT ONE

A melody is heard, played upon a flute. It is small and fine, telling of grass and trees and the horizon. The curtain rises.

Before us is the Salesman's house. We are aware of towering, angular shapes behind it, surrounding it on all sides. Only the blue light of the sky falls upon the house and forestage; the surrounding area shows an angry glow of orange. As more light appears, we see a solid vault of apartment houses around the small, fragile-seeming home. An air of the dream clings to the place, a dream rising out of reality. The kitchen at center seems actual enough, for there is a kitchen table with three chairs, and a refrigerator. But no other fixtures are seen. At the back of the kitchen there is a draped entrance, which leads to the living-room. To the right of the kitchen, on a level raised two feet, is a bedroom furnished only with a brass bedstead and a straight chair. On a shelf over the bed a silver athletic trophy stands. A window opens onto the apartment house at the side.

Behind the kitchen, on a level raised six and a half feet, is the boys' bedroom, at present barely visible. Two beds are dimly seen, and at the back of the room a dormer window. (This bedroom is above the unseen living-room.) At the left a stairway curves up to it from the kitchen.

The entire setting is wholly or, in some places, partially transparent. The roof-line of the house is one-dimensional; under and over it we see the apartment buildings. Before the house lies an apron, curving beyond the forestage into the orchestra. This forward area serves as the back yard as well as the locale of all Willy's imaginings and of his city scenes. Whenever the action is in the present the actors observe the imaginary wall-lines, entering the house only through its door at the left. But in the scenes of the past these boundaries are broken, and characters enter or leave a room by stepping "through" a wall onto the forestage.

From the right, Willy Loman, the Salesman, enters, carrying two large sample cases. The flute plays on. He hears but is not aware of it. He is past sixty years of age, dressed quietly. Even as he crosses the stage to the doorway of the house, his exhaustion is apparent. He unlocks the door, comes into the kitchen, and thankfully lets his burden down, feeling the soreness of his palms. A word-sigh escapes his lips—it might be "Oh, boy, oh, boy." He closes the door, then carries his cases out into the living-room, through the draped kitchen doorway.

Linda, his wife, has stirred in her bed at the right. She gets out and puts on a robe, listening. Most often jovial, she has developed an iron repression of her exceptions to Willy's behavior—she more than loves him, she admires him, as though his mercurial nature, his temper, his massive dreams and little cruelties, served her only as sharp reminders of the turbulent longings within him, longings which she shares but lacks the temperament to utter and follow to their end.

> *Linda, (hearing* Willy *outside the bedroom, calls with some trepidation):* Willy!
>
> *Willy:* It's all right. I came back.
>
> *Linda:* Why? What happened? *(Slight pause.)* Did something happen, Willy?
>
> *Willy:* No, nothing happened.
>
> *Linda:* You didn't smash the car, did you?
>
> *Willy, (with casual irritation):* I said nothing happened. Didn't you hear me?
>
> *Linda:* Don't you feel well?
>
> *Willy:* I'm tired to the death. *(The flute has faded away. He sits on the bed beside her, a little numb.)* I couldn't make it. I just couldn't make it, Linda.
>
> *Linda, (very carefully, delicately):* Where were you all day? You look terrible.
>
> *Willy:* I got as far as a little above Yonkers. I stopped for a cup of coffee. Maybe it was the coffee.
>
> *Linda:* What?

Willy, (after a pause): I suddenly couldn't drive any more. The car kept going off onto the shoulder, y'know?

Linda, (helpfully): Oh. Maybe it was the steering again. I don't think Angelo knows the Studebaker.

Willy: No, it's me, it's me. Suddenly I realize I'm goin' sixty miles an hour and I don't remember the last five minutes. I'm—I can't seem to—keep my mind to it.

Linda: Maybe it's your glasses. You never went for your new glasses.

Willy: No, I see everything. I came back ten miles an hour. It took me nearly four hours from Yonkers.

Linda, (resigned): Well, you'll just have to take a rest, Willy, you can't continue this way.

Willy: I just got back from Florida.

Linda: But you didn't rest your mind. Your mind is overactive, and the mind is what counts, dear.

Willy: I'll start out in the morning. Maybe I'll feel better in the morning. *(She is taking off his shoes.)* These goddam arch supports are killing me.

Linda: Take an aspirin. Should I get you an aspirin? It'll soothe you.

Willy, (with wonder): I was driving along, you understand? And I was fine. I was even observing the scenery. You can imagine, me looking at scenery, on the road every week of my life. But it's so beautiful up there, Linda, the trees are so thick, and the sun is warm. I opened the windshield and just let the warm air bathe over me. And then all of a sudden I'm goin' off the road! I'm tellin' ya, I absolutely forgot I was driving. If I'd've gone the other way over the white line I might've killed somebody. So I went on again—and five minutes later I'm dreamin' again, and I nearly— *(He presses two fingers against his eyes.)* I have such thoughts, I have such strange thoughts.

Linda: Willy, dear. Talk to them again. There's no reason why you can't work in New York.

Willy: They don't need me in New York. I'm the New England man. I'm vital in New England.

Linda: But you're sixty years old. They can't expect you to keep traveling every week.

Willy: I'll have to send a wire to Portland. I'm supposed to see Brown and Morrison tomorrow morning at ten o'clock to show the line. Goddammit, I could sell them! *(He starts putting on his jacket.)*

Linda, (taking the jacket from him): Why don't you go down to the place tomorrow and tell Howard you've simply got to work in New York? You're too accommodating, dear.

Willy: If old man Wagner was alive I'd a been in charge of New York now! That man was a prince, he was a masterful man. But that boy of his, that Howard, he don't appreciate. When I went north the first time, the Wagner Company didn't know where New England was!

Linda: Why don't you tell those things to Howard, dear?

Willy, (encouraged): I will, I definitely will. Is there any cheese?

Linda: I'll make you a sandwich.

Willy: No, go to sleep. I'll take some milk. I'll be up right away. The boys in?

Linda: They're sleeping. Happy took Biff on a date tonight.

Willy, (interested): That so?

Linda: It was so nice to see them shaving together, one behind the other, in the bathroom. And going out together. You notice? The whole house smells of shaving lotion.

Willy: Figure it out. Work a lifetime to pay off a house. You finally own it, and there's nobody to live in it.

Linda: Well, dear, life is a casting off. It's always that way.

Willy: No, no, some people—some people accomplish something. Did Biff say anything after I went this morning?

Linda: You shouldn't have criticized him, Willy, especially after he just got off the train. You mustn't lose your temper with him.

Willy: When the hell did I lose my temper? I simply asked him if he was making any money. Is that a criticism?

Linda: But, dear, how could he make any money?

Willy, (worried and angered): There's such an undercurrent in him. He became a moody man. Did he apologize when I left this morning?

Linda: He was crestfallen, Willy. You know how he admires you. I think if he finds himself, then you'll both be happier and not fight any more.

Willy: How can he find himself on a farm? Is that a life? A farmhand? In the beginning, when he was young, I thought, well, a young man, it's good for him to tramp around, take a lot of different jobs. But it's more than ten years now and he has yet to make thirty-five dollars a week!

Linda: He's finding himself, Willy.

Willy: Not finding yourself at the age of thirty-four is a disgrace!

Linda: Shh!

Willy: The trouble is he's lazy, goddammit!

Linda: Willy, please!

Willy: Biff is a lazy bum!

Linda: They're sleeping. Get something to eat. Go on down.

Willy: Why did he come home? I would like to know what brought him home.

Linda: I don't know. I think he's still lost, Willy. I think he's very lost.

Willy: Biff Loman is lost. In the greatest country in the world a young man with such—personal attractiveness, gets lost. And such a hard worker. There's one thing about Biff— he's not lazy.

Linda: Never.

Willy, (with pity and resolve): I'll see him in the morning; I'll have a nice talk with him. I'll get him a job selling. He could be big in no time. My God! Remember how they used to follow him around in high school? When he smiled at one of them their faces lit up. When he walked down the street . . . *(He loses himself in reminiscences.)*

Linda, (trying to bring him out of it): Willy, dear, I got a new kind of American-type cheese today. It's whipped.

Willy: Why do you get American when I like Swiss?

Linda: I just thought you'd like a change—

Willy: I don't want a change! I want Swiss cheese. Why am I always being contradicted?

Linda, (with a covering laugh): I thought it would be a surprise.

Willy: Why don't you open a window in here, for God's sake?

Linda, (with infinite patience): They're all open, dear.

Willy: The way they boxed us in here. Bricks and windows, windows and bricks.

Linda: We should've bought the land next door.

Willy: The street is lined with cars. There's not a breath of fresh air in the neighborhood. The grass don't grow any more, you can't raise a carrot in the back yard. They should've had a law against apartment houses. Remember those two beautiful elm trees out there? When I and Biff hung the swing between them?

Linda: Yeah, like being a million miles from the city.

Willy: They should've arrested the builder for cutting those down. They massacred the neighborhood. *(Lost):* More and more I think of those days, Linda. This time of year it was lilac and wisteria. And then the peonies would come out, and the daffodils. What fragrance in this room!

Linda: Well, after all, people had to move somewhere.

Willy: No, there's more people now.

Linda: I don't think there's more people. I think—

Willy: There's more people! That's what's ruining this country! Population is getting out of control. The competition is maddening! Smell the stink from that apartment house!

And another one on the other side . . . How can they whip cheese?

On Willy's *last line,* Biff *and* Happy *raise themselves up in their beds, listening.*

    Linda: Go down, try it. And be quiet.

    Willy, (turning to Linda, *guiltily):* You're not worried about me, are you, sweetheart?

    Biff: What's the matter?

    Happy: Listen!

    Linda: You've got too much on the ball to worry about.

    Willy: You're my foundation and my support, Linda.

    Linda: Just try to relax, dear. You make mountains out of molehills.

    Willy: I won't fight with him any more. If he wants to go back to Texas, let him go.

    Linda: He'll find his way.

    Willy: Sure. Certain men just don't get started till later in life. Like Thomas Edison, I think. Or B. F. Goodrich. One of them was deaf. *(He starts for the bedroom doorway.)* I'll put my money on Biff.

    Linda: And Willy—if it's warm Sunday we'll drive in the country. And we'll open the windshield, and take lunch.

    Willy: No, the windshields don't open on the new cars.

    Linda: But you opened it today.

    Willy: Me? I didn't. *(He stops.)* Now isn't that peculiar! Isn't that a remarkable— *(He breaks off in amazement and fright as the flute is heard distantly.)*

    Linda: What, darling?

    Willy: That is the most remarkable thing.

    Linda: What, dear?

    Willy: I was thinking of the Chevvy. *(Slight pause.)* Nineteen twenty-eight . . . when I had that red Chevvy— *(Breaks off.)* That funny? I coulda sworn I was driving that Chevvy today.

    Linda: Well, that's nothing. Something must've reminded you.

    Willy: Remarkable. Ts. Remember those days? The way Biff used to simonize that car? The dealer refused to believe there was eighty thousand miles on it. *(He shakes his head.)* Heh! *(To* Linda*):* Close your eyes, I'll be right up. *(He walks out of the bedroom.)*

    Happy, (to Biff*):* Jesus, maybe he smashed up the car again!

    Linda, (calling after Willy*):* Be careful on the stairs, dear! The cheese is on the middle shelf! *(She turns, goes over to the bed, takes his jacket, and goes out of the bedroom.)*

Light has risen on the boys' room. Unseen, Willy *is heard talking to himself,* "Eighty thousand miles," *and a little laugh.* Biff *gets out of bed, comes downstage a bit, and stands attentively.* Biff *is two years older than his brother* Happy, *well built, but in these days bears a worn air and seems less self-assured. He has succeeded less, and his dreams are stronger and less acceptable than* Happy's. *Happy is tall, powerfully made. Sexuality is like a visible color on him, or a scent that many women have discovered. He, like his brother, is lost, but in a different way, for he has never allowed himself to turn his face toward defeat and is thus more confused and hard-skinned, although seemingly more content.*

> *Happy, (getting out of bed):* He's going to get his license taken away if he keeps that up. I'm getting nervous about him, y'know, Biff?
>
> *Biff:* His eyes are going.
>
> *Happy:* No, I've driven with him. He sees all right. He just doesn't keep his mind on it. I drove into the city with him last week. He stops at a green light and then it turns red and he goes. *(He laughs.)*
>
> *Biff:* Maybe he's color-blind.
>
> *Happy:* Pop? Why he's got the finest eye for color in the business. You know that.
>
> *Biff, (sitting down on his bed):* I'm going to sleep.
>
> *Happy:* You're not still sour on Dad, are you, Biff?
>
> *Biff:* He's all right, I guess.
>
> *Willy, (underneath them, in the living-room):* Yes, sir, eighty thousand miles—eighty-two thousand!
>
> *Biff:* You smoking?
>
> *Happy, (holding out a pack of cigarettes):* Want one?
>
> *Biff, (taking a cigarette):* I can never sleep when I smell it.
>
> *Willy:* What a simonizing job, heh!
>
> *Happy, (with deep sentiment):* Funny, Biff, y'know? Us sleeping in here again? The old beds. *(He pats his bed affectionately.)* All the talk that went across those two beds, huh? Our whole lives.
>
> *Biff:* Yeah. Lotta dreams and plans.
>
> *Happy, (with a deep and masculine laugh):* About five hundred women would like to know what was said in this room.

They share a soft laugh.

> *Biff:* Remember that big Betsy something—what the hell was her name—over on Bushwick Avenue?
>
> *Happy, (combing his hair):* With the collie dog!
>
> *Biff:* That's the one. I got you in there, remember?
>
> *Happy:* Yeah, that was my first time—I think. Boy, there was a pig! *(They laugh, almost crudely.)* You taught me everything I know about women. Don't forget that.
>
> *Biff:* I bet you forgot how bashful you used to be. Especially with girls.
>
> *Happy:* Oh, I still am, Biff.

Biff: Oh, go on.

Happy: I just control it, that's all. I think I got less bashful and you got more so. What happened, Biff? Where's the old humor, the old confidence? *(He shakes* Biff's *knee.* Biff *gets up and moves restlessly about the room.)* What's the matter?

Biff: Why does Dad mock me all the time?

Happy: He's not mocking you, he—

Biff: Everything I say there's a twist of mockery on his face. I can't get near him.

Happy: He just wants you to make good, that's all. I wanted to talk to you about Dad for a long time, Biff. Something's— happening to him. He—talks to himself.

Biff: I noticed that this morning. But he always mumbled.

Happy: But not so noticeable. It got so embarrassing I sent him to Florida. And you know something? Most of the time he's talking to you.

Biff: What's he say about me?

Happy: I can't make it out.

Biff: What's he say about me?

Happy: I think the fact that you're not settled, that you're still kind of up in the air . . .

Biff: There's one or two other things depressing him, Happy.

Happy: What do you mean?

Biff: Never mind. Just don't lay it all to me.

Happy: But I think if you just got started—I mean—is there any future for you out there?

Biff: I tell ya, Hap, I don't know what the future is. I don't know—what I'm supposed to want.

Happy: What do you mean?

Biff: Well, I spent six or seven years after high school trying to work myself up. Shipping clerk, salesman, business of one kind or another. And it's a measly manner of existence. To get on that subway on the hot mornings in summer. To devote your whole life to keeping stock, or making phone calls, or selling or buying. To suffer fifty weeks of the year for the sake of a two-week vacation, when all you really desire is to be outdoors, with your shirt off. And always to have to get ahead of the next fella. And still—that's how you build a future.

Happy: Well, you really enjoy it on a farm? Are you content out there?

Biff, (with rising agitation): Hap, I've had twenty or thirty different kinds of jobs since I left home before the war, and it always turns out the same. I just realized it lately. In Nebraska when I herded cattle, and the Dakotas, and Arizona, and now in Texas. It's why I came home now, I guess, because I realized it. This farm I work on, it's spring there now, see? And they've got about fifteen new colts. There's nothing more inspiring or—beautiful than the sight of a mare and a new colt. And it's cool there now, see? Texas is cool now, and it's spring. And whenever spring comes to where I am, I suddenly get the feeling, my God, I'm not gettin' anywhere! What the hell am I doing, playing around with horses, twenty-eight dollars a week! I'm thirty-four years old, I oughta be makin' my future. That's when I come running home. And now, I get here, and I don't know what to do with myself. *(After a pause):* I've always made a point of not wasting my life, and everytime I come back here I know that all I've done is to waste my life.

Happy: You're a poet, you know that, Biff? You're a—you're an idealist!

Biff: No, I'm mixed up very bad. Maybe I oughta get married. Maybe I oughta get stuck into something. Maybe that's my trouble. I'm like a boy. I'm not married, I'm not in business, I just—I'm like a boy. Are you content, Hap? You're a success, aren't you? Are you content?

Happy: Hell, no!

Biff: Why? You're making money, aren't you?

Happy, (moving about with energy, expressiveness): All I can do now is wait for the merchandise manager to die. And suppose I get to be merchandise manager? He's a good friend of mine, and he just built a terrific estate on Long Island. And he lived there about two months and sold it, and now he's building another one. He can't enjoy it once it's finished. And I know that's just what I would do. I don't know what the hell I'm workin' for. Sometimes I sit in my apartment —all alone. And I think of the rent I'm paying. And it's crazy. But then, it's what I always wanted. My own apartment, a car, and plenty of women. And still, goddammit, I'm lonely.

Biff, (with enthusiasm): Listen, why don't you come out West with me?

Happy: You and I, heh?

Biff: Sure, maybe we could buy a ranch. Raise cattle, use our muscles. Men built like we are should be working out in the open.

Happy, (avidly): The Loman Brothers, heh?

Biff, (with vast affection): Sure, we'd be known all over the counties!

Happy, (enthralled): That's what I dream about, Biff. Sometimes I want to just rip my clothes off in the middle of the store and outbox that goddam merchandise manager. I mean I can outbox, outrun, and outlift anybody in that store, and I have to take orders from those common, petty sons-of-bitches till I can't stand it any more.

Biff: I'm tellin' you, kid, if you were with me I'd be happy out there.

Happy, (enthused): See, Biff, everybody around me is so false that I'm constantly lowering my ideals . . .

Biff: Baby, together we'd stand up for one another, we'd have someone to trust.

Happy: If I were around you—

Biff: Hap, the trouble is we weren't brought up to grub for money. I don't know how to do it.

Happy: Neither can I!

Biff: Then let's go!

Happy: The only thing is—what can you make out there?

Biff: But look at your friend. Builds an estate and then hasn't the peace of mind to live in it.

Happy: Yeah, but when he walks into the store the waves part in front of him. That's fifty-two thousand dollars a year coming through the revolving door, and I got more in my pinky finger than he's got in his head.

Biff: Yeah, but you just said—

Happy: I gotta show some of those pompous, self-important executives over there that Hap Loman can make the grade. I want to walk into the store the way he walks in. Then I'll go with you, Biff. We'll be together yet, I swear. But take those two we had tonight. Now weren't they gorgeous creatures?

Biff: Yeah, yeah, most gorgeous I've had in years.

Happy: I get that any time I want, Biff. Whenever I feel disgusted. The only trouble is, it gets like bowling or something. I just keep knockin' them over and it doesn't mean anything. You still run around a lot?

Biff: Naa. I'd like to find a girl—steady, somebody with substance.

Happy: That's what I long for.

Biff: Go on! You'd never come home.

Happy: I would! Somebody with character, with resistance! Like Mom, y'know? You're gonna call me a bastard when I tell you this. That girl Charlotte I was with tonight is engaged to be married in five weeks. *(He tries on his new hat.)*

Biff: No kiddin'!

Happy: Sure, the guy's in line for the vice-presidency of the store. I don't know what gets into me, maybe I just have an overdeveloped sense of competition or something, but I went and ruined her, and furthermore I can't get rid of her. And he's the third executive I've done that to. Isn't that a crummy characteristic? And to top it all, I go to their weddings! *(Indignantly, but laughing):* Like I'm not supposed to take bribes. Manufacturers offer me a hundred-dollar bill now and then to throw an order their way. You know how honest I am, but it's like this girl, see. I hate myself for it. Because I don't want the girl, and, still I take it and—I love it!

Biff: Let's go to sleep.

Happy: I guess we didn't settle anything, heh?

Biff: I just got one idea that I think I'm going to try.

Happy: What's that?

Biff: Remember Bill Oliver?

Happy: Sure, Oliver is very big now. You want to work for him again?

Biff: No, but when I quit he said something to me. He put his arm on my shoulder, and he said, "Biff, if you ever need anything, come to me."

Happy: I remember that. That sounds good.

Biff: I think I'll go to see him. If I could get ten thousand or even seven or eight thousand dollars I could buy a beautiful ranch.

Happy: I bet he'd back you. 'Cause he thought highly of you, Biff. I mean, they all do. You're well liked, Biff. That's why I say to come back here, and we both have the apartment. And I'm tellin' you, Biff, any babe you want . . .

Biff: No, with a ranch I could do the work I like and still be something. I just wonder though. I wonder if Oliver still thinks I stole that carton of basketballs.

Happy: Oh, he probably forgot that long ago. It's almost ten years. You're too sensitive. Anyway, he didn't really fire you.

Biff: Well, I think he was going to. I think that's why I quit. I was never sure whether he knew or not. I know he thought the world of me, though. I was the only one he'd let lock up the place.

Willy, (below): You gonna wash the engine, Biff?

Happy: Shh!

Biff *looks at* Happy, *who is gazing down, listening.* Willy *is mumbling in the parlor.*

Happy: You hear that?

They listen. Willy *laughs warmly.*

Biff, (growing angry): Doesn't he know Mom can hear that?

Willy: Don't get your sweater dirty, Biff!

A look of pain crosses Biff's *face.*

> *Happy:* Isn't that terrible? Don't leave again, will you? You'll
> find a job here. You gotta stick around. I don't know what
> to do about him, it's getting embarrassing.
>
> *Willy:* What a simonizing job!
>
> *Biff:* Mom's hearing that!
>
> *Willy:* No kiddin', Biff, you got a date? Wonderful!
>
> *Happy:* Go on to sleep. But talk to him in the morning, will you?
>
> *Biff, (reluctantly getting into bed):* With her in the house.
> Brother!
>
> *Happy, (getting into bed):* I wish you'd have a good talk with him.

The light on their room begins to fade.

> *Biff, (to himself in bed):* That selfish, stupid . . .
>
> *Happy:* Sh . . . Sleep, Biff.

Their light is out. Well before they have finished speaking, Willy's *form is dimly
seen below in the darkened kitchen. He opens the refrigerator, searches in there,
and takes out a bottle of milk. The apartment houses are fading out, and the entire
house and surroundings become covered with leaves. Music insinuates itself as the
leaves appear.*

> *Willy:* Just wanna be careful with those girls, Biff, that's all.
> Don't make any promises. No promises of any kind.
> Because a girl, y'know, they always believe what you tell
> 'em, and you're very young, Biff, you're too young to be
> talking seriously to girls.

Light rises on the kitchen. Willy, *talking, shuts the refrigerator door and comes
downstage to the kitchen table. He pours milk into a glass. He is totally immersed
in himself, smiling faintly.*

> *Willy:* Too young entirely, Biff. You want to watch your school-
> ing first. Then when you're all set, there'll be plenty of
> girls for a boy like you. *(He smiles broadly at a kitchen chair.)*
> That so? The girls pay for you? *(He laughs.)* Boy, you must
> really be makin' a hit.

Willy *is gradually addressing—physically—a point offstage, speaking through
the wall of the kitchen, and his voice has been rising in volume to that of a normal
conversation.*

> *Willy:* I been wondering why you polish the car so careful. Ha!
> Don't leave the hubcaps, boys. Get the chamois to the
> hubcaps. Happy, use newspaper on the windows, it's the
> easiest thing. Show him how to do it, Biff! You see,
> Happy? Pad it up, use it like a pad. That's it, that's it, good
> work. You're doin' all right, Hap. *(He pauses, then nods in*

approbation for a few seconds, then looks upward.) Biff, first thing we gotta do when we get time is clip that big branch over the house. Afraid it's gonna fall in a storm and hit the roof. Tell you what. We get a rope and sling her around, and then we climb up there with a couple of saws and take her down. Soon as you finish the car, boys, I wanna see ya. I got a surprise for you, boys.

Biff, (offstage): Whatta ya got, Dad?

Willy: No, you finish first. Never leave a job till you're finished —remember that. *(Looking toward the "big trees"):* Biff, up in Albany I saw a beautiful hammock. I think I'll buy it next trip, and we'll hang it right between those two elms. Wouldn't that be something? Just swingin' there under those branches. Boy, that would be . . .

Young Biff *and* Young Happy *appear from the direction* Willy *was addressing.* Happy *carries rags and a pail of water.* Biff, *wearing a sweater with a block "S," carries a football.*

Biff, (pointing in the direction of the car offstage): How's that, Pop, professional?

Willy: Terrific. Terrific job, boys. Good work, Biff.

Happy: Where's the surprise, Pop?

Willy: In the back seat of the car.

Happy: Boy! *(He runs off.)*

Biff: What is it, Dad? Tell me, what'd you buy?

Willy, (laughing, cuffs him): Never mind, something I want you to have.

Biff, (turns and starts off): What is it, Hap?

Happy, (offstage): It's a punching bag!

Biff: Oh, Pop!

Willy: It's got Gene Tunney's signature on it!

Happy *runs onstage with a punching bag.*

Biff: Gee, how'd you know we wanted a punching bag?

Willy: Well, it's the finest thing for the timing.

Happy, (lies down on his back and pedals with his feet): I'm losing weight, you notice, Pop?

Willy, (to Happy*):* Jumping rope is good too.

Biff: Did you see the new football I got?

Willy, (examining the ball): Where'd you get a new ball?

Biff: The coach told me to practice my passing.

Willy: That so? And he gave you the ball, heh?

Biff: Well, I borrowed it from the locker room. *(He laughs confidentially.)*

Willy, (laughing with him at the theft): I want you to return that.

Happy: I told you he wouldn't like it!

Biff, (angrily): Well, I'm bringing it back!

Willy, (stopping the incipient argument, to Happy*):* Sure, he's gotta practice with a regulation ball, doesn't he? *(To* Biff*):* Coach'll probably congratulate you on your initiative!

Biff: Oh, he keeps congratulating my initiative all the time, Pop.

Willy: That's because he likes you. If somebody else took that ball there'd be an uproar. So what's the report, boys, what's the report?

Biff: Where'd you go this time, Dad? Gee we were lonesome for you.

Willy, (pleased, puts an arm around each boy and they come down to the apron): Lonesome, heh?

Biff: Missed you every minute.

Willy: Don't say? Tell you a secret, boys. Don't breathe it to a soul. Someday I'll have my own business, and I'll never have to leave home any more.

Happy: Like Uncle Charley, heh?

Willy: Bigger than Uncle Charley! Because Charley is not— liked. He's liked, but he's not—well liked.

Biff: Where'd you go this time, Dad?

Willy: Well, I got on the road, and I went north to Providence. Met the Mayor.

Biff: The Mayor of Providence!

Willy: He was sitting in the hotel lobby.

Biff: What'd he say?

Willy: He said, "Morning!" And I said, "You got a fine city here, Mayor." And then he had coffee with me. And then I went to Waterbury. Waterbury is a fine city. Big clock city, the famous Waterbury clock. Sold a nice bill there. And then Boston—Boston is the cradle of the Revolution. A fine city. And a couple of other towns in Mass., and on to Portland and Bangor and straight home!

Biff: Gee, I'd love to go with you sometime, Dad.

Willy: Soon as summer comes.

Happy: Promise?

Willy: You and Hap and I, and I'll show you all the towns. America is full of beautiful towns and fine, upstanding people. And they know me, boys, they know me up and down New England. The finest people. And when I bring you fellas up, there'll be open sesame for all of us, 'cause one thing, boys: I have friends. I can park my car in any street in New England, and the cops protect it like their own. This summer, heh?

Biff and Happy, (together): Yeah! You bet!

    Willy: We'll take our bathing suits.

    Happy: We'll carry your bags, Pop!

    Willy: Oh, won't that be something! Me comin' into the Boston stores with you boys carryin' my bags. What a sensation!

Biff *is prancing around, practicing passing the ball.*

    Willy: You nervous, Biff, about the game?

    Biff: Not if you're gonna be there.

    Willy: What do they say about you in school, now that they made you captain?

    Happy: There's a crowd of girls behind him every time the classes change.

    Biff, (taking Willy's *hand):* This Saturday, Pop, this Saturday —just for you, I'm going to break through for a touchdown.

    Happy: You're supposed to pass.

    Biff: I'm takin' one play for Pop. You watch me, Pop, and when I take off my helmet, that means I'm breakin' out. Then you watch me crash through that line!

    Willy, (kisses Biff*):* Oh, wait'll I tell this in Boston!

Bernard *enters in knickers. He is younger than* Biff, *earnest and loyal, a worried boy.*

    Bernard: Biff, where are you? You're supposed to study with me today.

    Willy: Hey, looka Bernard. What're you lookin' so anemic about, Bernard?

    Bernard: He's gotta study, Uncle Willy. He's got Regents next week.

    Happy, (tauntingly, spinning Bernard *around):* Let's box, Bernard!

    Bernard: Biff! *(He gets away from* Happy.*)* Listen, Biff, I heard Mr. Birnbaum say that if you don't start studyin' math he's gonna flunk you, and you won't graduate. I heard him!

    Willy: You better study with him, Biff. Go ahead now.

    Bernard: I heard him!

    Biff: Oh, Pop, you didn't see my sneakers! *(He holds up a foot for* Willy *to look at.)*

    Willy: Hey, that's a beautiful job of printing!

    Bernard, (wiping his glasses): Just because he printed University of Virginia on his sneakers doesn't mean they've got to graduate him, Uncle Willy!

    Willy, (angrily): What're you talking about? With scholarships to three universities they're gonna flunk him?

Bernard: But I heard Mr. Birnbaum say—

Willy: Don't be a pest, Bernard! *(To his boys):* What an anemic!

Bernard: Okay, I'm waiting for you in my house, Biff.

Bernard *goes off. The* Lomans *laugh.*

Willy: Bernard is not well liked, is he?

Biff: He's liked, but he's not well liked.

Happy: That's right, Pop.

Willy: That's just what I mean. Bernard can get the best marks in school, y'understand, but when he gets out in the business world, y'understand, you are going to be five times ahead of him. That's why I thank Almighty God you're both built like Adonises. Because the man who makes an appearance in the business world, the man who creates personal interest, is the man who gets ahead. Be liked and you will never want. You take me, for instance. I never have to wait in line to see a buyer. "Willy Loman is here!" That's all they have to know, and I go right through.

Biff: Did you knock them dead, Pop?

Willy: Knocked 'em cold in Providence, slaughtered 'em in Boston.

Happy, (on his back, pedaling again): I'm losing weight, you notice, Pop?

Linda *enters, as of old, a ribbon in her hair, carrying a basket of washing.*

Linda, (with youthful energy): Hello, dear!

Willy: Sweetheart!

Linda: How'd the Chevvy run?

Willy: Chevrolet, Linda, is the greatest car ever built. *(To the boys):* Since when do you let your mother carry wash up the stairs?

Biff: Grab hold there, boy!

Happy: Where to, Mom?

Linda: Hang them up on the line. And you better go down to your friends, Biff. The cellar is full of boys. They don't know what to do with themselves.

Biff: Ah, when Pop comes home they can wait!

Willy, (laughs appreciatively): You better go down and tell them what to do, Biff.

Biff: I think I'll have them sweep out the furnace room.

Willy: Good work, Biff.

Biff, (goes through wall-line of kitchen to doorway at back and calls down): Fellas! Everybody sweep out the furnace room! I'll be right down!

Voices: All right! Okay, Biff.

Biff: George and Sam and Frank, come out back! We're hangin' up the wash! Come on, Hap, on the double! *(He and Happy carry out the basket.)*

Linda: The way they obey him!

Willy: Well, that's training, the training. I'm tellin' you, I was sellin' thousands and thousands, but I had to come home.

Linda: Oh, the whole block'll be at that game. Did you sell anything?

Willy: I did five hundred gross in Providence and seven hundred gross in Boston.

Linda: No! Wait a minute, I've got a pencil. *(She pulls pencil and paper out of her apron pocket.)* That makes your commission . . . Two hundred—my God! Two hundred and twelve dollars!

Willy: Well, I didn't figure it yet, but . . .

Linda: How much did you do?

Willy: Well, I—I did—about a hundred and eighty gross in Providence. Well, no—it came to—roughly two hundred gross on the whole trip.

Linda, (without hesitation): Two hundred gross. That's . . . *(She figures.)*

Willy: The trouble was that three of the stores were half closed for inventory in Boston. Otherwise I woulda broke records.

Linda: Well, it makes seventy dollars and some pennies. That's very good.

Willy: What do we owe?

Linda: Well, on the first there's sixteen dollars on the refrigerator—

Willy: Why sixteen?

Linda: Well, the fan belt broke, so it was a dollar eighty.

Willy: But it's brand new.

Linda: Well, the man said that's the way it is. Till they work themselves in, y'know.

They move through the wall-line into the kitchen.

Willy: I hope we didn't get stuck on that machine.

Linda: They got the biggest ads of any of them!

Willy: I know, it's a fine machine. What else?

Linda: Well, there's nine-sixty for the washing machine. And for the vacuum cleaner there's three and a half due on the fifteenth. Then the roof, you got twenty-one dollars remaining.

Willy: It don't leak, does it?

Linda: No, they did a wonderful job. Then you owe Frank for the carburetor.

Willy: I'm not going to pay that man! That goddam Chevrolet, they ought to prohibit the manufacture of that car!

Linda: Well, you owe him three and a half. And odds and ends, comes to around a hundred and twenty dollars by the fifteenth.

Willy: A hundred and twenty dollars! My God, if business don't pick up I don't know what I'm gonna do!

Linda: Well, next week you'll do better.

Willy: Oh, I'll knock 'em dead next week. I'll go to Hartford. I'm very well liked in Hartford. You know, the trouble is, Linda, people don't seem to take to me.

They move onto the forestage.

Linda: Oh, don't be foolish.

Willy: I know it when I walk in. They seem to laugh at me.

Linda: Why? Why would they laugh at you? Don't talk that way, Willy.

Willy *moves to the edge of the stage.* Linda *goes into the kitchen and starts to darn stockings.*

Willy: I don't know the reason for it, but they just pass me by. I'm not noticed.

Linda: But you're doing wonderful, dear. You're making seventy to a hundred dollars a week.

Willy: But I gotta be at it ten, twelve hours a day. Other men— I don't know—they do it easier. I don't know why—I can't stop myself—I talk too much. A man oughta come in with a few words. One thing about Charley. He's a man of few words, and they respect him.

Linda: You don't talk too much, you're just lively.

Willy, (smiling): Well, I figure, what the hell, life is short, a couple of jokes. *(To himself):* I joke too much! *(The smile goes.)*

Linda: Why? You're—

Willy: I'm fat. I'm very—foolish to look at, Linda. I didn't tell you, but Christmas time I happened to be calling on F.H. Stewarts, and a salesman I know, as I was going in to see the buyer I heard him say something about—walrus. And I—I cracked him right across the face. I won't take that. I simply will not take that. But they do laugh at me. I know that.

Linda: Darling . . .

Willy: I gotta overcome it. I know I gotta overcome it. I'm not dressing to advantage, maybe.

Linda: Willy, darling, you're the handsomest man in the world—

Willy: Oh, no, Linda.

Linda: To me you are. *(Slight pause.)* The handsomest.

From the darkness is heard the laughter of a woman. Willy *doesn't turn to it, but it continues through* Linda's *lines.*

> *Linda:* And the boys, Willy. Few men are idolized by their children the way you are.

Music is heard as behind a scrim, to the left of the house, The Woman, *dimly seen, is dressing.*

> *Willy, (with great feeling):* You're the best there is, Linda, you're a pal, you know that? On the road—on the road I want to grab you sometimes and just kiss the life outa you.

The laughter is loud now, and he moves into a brightening area at the left, where The Woman *has come from behind the scrim and is standing, putting on her hat, looking into a "mirror" and laughing.*

> *Willy:* 'Cause I get so lonely—especially when business is bad and there's nobody to talk to. I get the feeling that I'll never sell anything again, that I won't make a living for you, or a business, a business for the boys. *(He talks through* The Woman's *subsiding laughter;* The Woman *primps at the "mirror.")* There's so much I want to make for—
>
> *The Woman:* Me? You didn't make me, Willy. I picked you.
>
> *Willy, (pleased):* You picked me?
>
> *The Woman, (who is quite proper-looking,* Willy's *age):* I did. I've been sitting at that desk watching all the salesmen go by, day in, day out. But you've got such a sense of humor, and we do have such a good time together, don't we?
>
> *Willy:* Sure, sure. *(He takes her in his arms.)* Why do you have to go now?
>
> *The Woman:* It's two o'clock . . .
>
> *Willy:* No, come on in! *(He pulls her.)*
>
> *The Woman:* . . . my sisters'll be scandalized. When'll you be back?
>
> *Willy:* Oh, two weeks about. Will you come up again?
>
> *The Woman:* Sure thing. You do make me laugh. It's good for me. *(She squeezes his arm, kisses him.)* And I think you're a wonderful man.
>
> *Willy:* You picked me, heh?
>
> *The Woman:* Sure. Because you're so sweet. And such a kidder.
>
> *Willy:* Well, I'll see you next time I'm in Boston.
>
> *The Woman:* I'll put you right through to the buyers.
>
> *Willy, (slapping her bottom):* Right. Well, bottoms up!
>
> *The Woman, (slaps him gently and laughs):* You just kill me, Willy. *(He suddenly grabs her and kisses her roughly.)* You kill me. And thanks for the stockings. I love a lot of stockings. Well, good night.
>
> *Willy:* Good night. And keep your pores open!
>
> *The Woman:* Oh, Willy!

The Woman bursts out laughing, *and* Linda's *laughter blends in. The Woman* disappears into the dark. *Now the area at the kitchen table brightens.* Linda *is sitting where she was at the kitchen table, but now is mending a pair of her silk stockings.*

> Linda: You are, Willy. The handsomest man. You've got no reason to feel that—
>
> Willy, *(coming out of* The Woman's *dimming area and going over to* Linda): I'll make it all up to you, Linda, I'll—
>
> Linda: There's nothing to make up, dear. You're doing fine, better than—
>
> Willy, *(noticing her mending):* What's that?
>
> Linda: Just mending my stockings. They're so expensive—
>
> Willy, *(angrily, taking them from her):* I won't have you mending stockings in this house! Now throw them out!

Linda *puts the stockings in her pocket.*

> Bernard, *(entering on the run):* Where is he? If he doesn't study!
>
> Willy, *(moving to the forestage, with great agitation):* You'll give him the answers!
>
> Bernard: I do, but I can't on a Regents! That's a state exam! They're liable to arrest me!
>
> Willy: Where is he? I'll whip him, I'll whip him!
>
> Linda: And he'd better give back that football, Willy, it's not nice.
>
> Willy: Biff! Where is he? Why is he taking everything?
>
> Linda: He's too rough with the girls, Willy. All the mothers are afraid of him!
>
> Willy: I'll whip him!
>
> Bernard: He's driving the car without a license!

The Woman's *laugh is heard.*

> Willy: Shut up!
>
> Linda: All the mothers—
>
> Willy: Shut up!
>
> Bernard, *(backing quietly away and out):* Mr. Birnbaum says he's stuck up.
>
> Willy: Get outa here!
>
> Bernard: If he doesn't buckle down he'll flunk math! *(He goes off.)*
>
> Linda: He's right, Willy, you've gotta—
>
> Willy, *(exploding at her):* There's nothing the matter with him! You want him to be a worm like Bernard? He's got spirit, personality . . .

As he speaks, Linda, *almost in tears, exits into the living-room.* Willy *is alone in the kitchen, wilting and staring. The leaves are gone. It is night again, and the apartment houses look down from behind.*

Willy: Loaded with it. Loaded! What is he stealing? He's giving it back, isn't he? Why is he stealing? What did I tell him? I never in my life told him anything but decent things.

Happy *in pajamas has come down the stairs;* Willy *suddenly becomes aware of* Happy's *presence.*

 Happy: Let's go now, come on.
 Willy, (sitting down at the kitchen table): Huh! Why did she have to wax the floors herself? Everytime she waxes the floors she keels over. She knows that!
 Happy: Shh! Take it easy. What brought you back tonight?
 Willy: I got an awful scare. Nearly hit a kid in Yonkers. God! Why didn't I go to Alaska with my brother Ben that time! Ben! That man was a genius, that man was success incarnate! What a mistake! He begged me to go.
 Happy: Well, there's no use in—
 Willy: You guys! There was a man started with the clothes on his back and ended up with diamond mines!
 Happy: Boy, someday I'd like to know how he did it.
 Willy: What's the mystery? The man knew what he wanted and went out and got it! Walked into a jungle, and comes out, the age of twenty-one, and he's rich! The world is an oyster, but you don't crack it open on a mattress!
 Happy: Pop, I told you I'm gonna retire you for life.
 Willy: You'll retire me for life on seventy goddam dollars a week? And your women and your car and your apartment, and you'll retire me for life! Christ's sake, I couldn't get past Yonkers today! Where are you guys, where are you? The woods are burning! I can't drive a car!

Charley *has appeared in the doorway. He is a large man, slow of speech, laconic, immovable. In all he says, despite what he says, there is pity, and, now, trepidation. He has a robe over pajamas, slippers on his feet. He enters the kitchen.*

 Charley: Everything all right?
 Happy: Yeah, Charley, everything's . . .
 Willy: What's the matter?
 Charley: I heard some noise. I thought something happened. Can't we do something about the walls? You sneeze in here, and in my house hats blow off.
 Happy: Let's go to bed, Dad. Come on.

Charley *signals to* Happy *to go.*

 Willy: You go ahead, I'm not tired at the moment.
 Happy, (to Willy): Take it easy, huh? (He exits.)
 Willy: What're you doin' up?

Charley, (sitting down at the kitchen table opposite Willy*):* Couldn't sleep good. I had a heartburn.

Willy: Well, you don't know how to eat.

Charley: I eat with my mouth.

Willy: No, you're ignorant. You gotta know about vitamins and things like that.

Charley: Come on, let's shoot. Tire you out a little.

Willy, (hesitantly): All right. You got cards?

Charley, (taking a deck from his pocket): Yeah, I got them. Someplace. What is it with those vitamins?

Willy, (dealing): They build up your bones. Chemistry.

Charley: Yeah, but there's no bones in a heartburn.

Willy: What are you talkin' about? Do you know the first thing about it?

Charley: Don't get insulted.

Willy: Don't talk about something you don't know anything about.

They are playing. Pause.

Charley: What're you doin' home?

Willy: A little trouble with the car.

Charley: Oh. *(Pause.)* I'd like to take a trip to California.

Willy: Don't say.

Charley: You want a job?

Willy: I got a job, I told you that. *(After a slight pause):* What the hell are you offering me a job for?

Charley: Don't get insulted.

Willy: Don't insult me.

Charley: I don't see no sense in it. You don't have to go on this way.

Willy: I got a good job. *(Slight pause.)* What do you keep comin' in here for?

Charley: You want me to go?

Willy, (after a pause, withering): I can't understand it. He's going back to Texas again. What the hell is that?

Charley: Let him go.

Willy: I got nothin' to give him, Charley, I'm clean, I'm clean.

Charley: He won't starve. None a them starve. Forget about him.

Willy: Then what have I got to remember?

Charley: You take it too hard. To hell with it. When a deposit bottle is broken you don't get your nickel back.

Willy: That's easy enough for you to say.

Charley: That ain't easy for me to say.

Willy: Did you see the ceiling I put up in the living-room?

Charley: Yeah, that's a piece of work. To put up a ceiling is a mystery to me. How do you do it?

Willy: What's the difference?

Charley: Well, talk about it.

Willy: You gonna put up a ceiling?

Charley: How could I put up a ceiling?

Willy: Then what the hell are you bothering me for?

Charley: You're insulted again.

Willy: A man who can't handle tools is not a man. You're disgusting.

Charley: Don't call me disgusting, Willy.

Uncle Ben, *carrying a valise and an umbrella, enters the forestage from around the right corner of the house. He is a stolid man, in his sixties, with a mustache and an authoritative air. He is utterly certain of his destiny, and there is an aura of far places about him. He enters exactly as* Willy *speaks.*

Willy: I'm getting awfully tired, Ben.

Ben's *music is heard.* Ben *looks around at everything.*

Charley: Good, keep playing; you'll sleep better. Did you call me Ben?

Ben *looks at his watch.*

Willy: That's funny. For a second there you reminded me of my brother Ben.

Ben: I only have a few minutes. *(He strolls, inspecting the place.* Willy *and* Charley *continue playing.)*

Charley: You never heard from him again, heh? Since that time?

Willy: Didn't Linda tell you? Couple of weeks ago we got a letter from his wife in Africa. He died.

Charley: That so.

Ben, (chuckling): So this is Brooklyn, eh?

Charley: Maybe you're in for some of his money.

Willy: Naa, he had seven sons. There's just one opportunity I had with that man . . .

Ben: I must make a train, William. There are several properties I'm looking at in Alaska.

Willy: Sure, sure! If I'd gone with him to Alaska that time, everything would've been totally different.

Charley: Go on, you'd froze to death up there.

Willy: What're you talking about?

Ben: Opportunity is tremendous in Alaska, William. Surprised you're not up there.

Willy: Sure, tremendous.

Charley: Heh?

Willy: There was the only man I ever met who knew the answers.

Charley: Who?

Ben: How are you all?

Willy, (taking a pot, smiling): Fine, fine.

Charley: Pretty sharp tonight.

Ben: Is Mother living with you?

Willy: No, she died a long time ago.

Charley: Who?

Ben: That's too bad. Fine specimen of a lady, Mother.

Willy, (to Charley*):* Heh?

Ben: I'd hoped to see the old girl.

Charley: Who died?

Ben: Heard anything from Father, have you?

Willy, (unnerved): What do you mean, who died?

Charley, (taking a pot): What're you talkin' about?

Ben, (looking at his watch): William, it's half-past eight!

Willy, (as though to dispel his confusion he angrily stops Charley's *hand):* That's my build!

Charley: I put the ace—

Willy: If you don't know how to play the game I'm not gonna throw my money away on you!

Charley, (rising): It was my ace, for God's sake!

Willy: I'm through, I'm through!

Ben: When did Mother die?

Willy: Long ago. Since the beginning you never knew how to play cards.

Charley, (picks up the cards and goes to the door): All right! Next time I'll bring a deck with five aces.

Willy: I don't play that kind of game!

Charley, (turning to him): You ought to be ashamed of yourself!

Willy: Yeah?

Charley: Yeah! *(He goes out.)*

Willy, (slamming the door after him): Ignoramus!

Ben, (as Willy *comes toward him through the wall-line of the kitchen):* So you're William.

Willy, (shaking Ben's *hand):* Ben! I've been waiting for you so long! What's the answer? How did you do it?

Ben: Oh, there's a story in that.

Linda *enters the forestage, as of old, carrying the wash basket.*

Linda: Is this Ben?

Ben, (gallantly): How do you do, my dear.

Linda: Where've you been all these years? Willy's always wondered why you—

Willy, (pulling Ben *away from her impatiently):* Where is Dad? Didn't you follow him? How did you get started?

Ben: Well, I don't know how much you remember.

Willy: Well, I was just a baby, of course, only three or four years old—

Ben: Three years and eleven months.

Willy: What a memory, Ben!

Ben: I have many enterprises, William, and I have never kept books.

Willy: I remember I was sitting under the wagon in—was it Nebraska?

Ben: It was South Dakota, and I gave you a bunch of wild flowers.

Willy: I remember you walking away down some open road.

Ben, (laughing): I was going to find Father in Alaska.

Willy: Where is he?

Ben: At that age I had a very faulty view of geography, William. I discovered after a few days that I was heading due south, so instead of Alaska, I ended up in Africa.

Linda: Africa!

Willy: The Gold Coast!

Ben: Principally diamond mines.

Linda: Diamond mines!

Ben: Yes, my dear. But I've only a few minutes—

Willy: No! Boys! Boys! *(Young* Biff *and* Happy *appear.)* Listen to this. This is your Uncle Ben, a great man! Tell my boys, Ben!

Ben: Why, boys, when I was seventeen I walked into the jungle, and when I was twenty-one I walked out. *(He laughs.)* And by God I was rich.

Willy, (to the boys): You see what I been talking about? The greatest things can happen!

Ben, (glancing at his watch): I have an appointment in Ketchikan Tuesday week.

Willy: No, Ben! Please tell about Dad. I want my boys to hear. I want them to know the kind of stock they spring from. All I remember is a man with a big beard, and I was in Mamma's lap, sitting around a fire, and some kind of high music.

Ben: His flute. He played the flute.

Willy: Sure, the flute, that's right!

New music is heard, a high, rollicking tune.

Ben: Father was a very great and a very wild-hearted man. We would start in Boston, and he'd toss the whole family into the wagon, and then he'd drive the team right across the country; through Ohio, and Indiana, Michigan, Illinois, and all the Western states. And we'd stop in the towns and sell the flutes that he'd made on the way. Great inventor,

Father. With one gadget he made more in a week than a man like you could make in a lifetime.

Willy: That's just the way I'm bringing them up, Ben—rugged, well liked, all-around.

Ben: Yeah? *(To* Biff*):* Hit that, boy—hard as you can. *(He pounds his stomach.)*

Biff: Oh, no, sir!

Ben, (taking boxing stance): Come on, get to me! *(He laughs.)*

Willy: Go to it, Biff! Go ahead, show him!

Biff: Okay! *(He cocks his fists and starts in.)*

Linda, (to Willy*):* Why must he fight, dear?

Ben, (sparring with Biff*):* Good boy! Good boy!

Willy: How's that, Ben, heh?

Happy: Give him the left, Biff!

Linda: Why are you fighting?

Ben: Good boy! *(Suddenly comes in, trips* Biff, *and stands over him, the point of his umbrella poised over* Biff's *eye.)*

Linda: Look out, Biff!

Biff: Gee!

Ben, (patting Biff's *knee):* Never fight fair with a stranger, boy. You'll never get out of the jungle that way. *(Taking* Linda's *hand and bowing):* It was an honor and a pleasure to meet you, Linda.

Linda, (withdrawing her hand coldly, frightened): Have a nice—trip.

Ben, (to Willy*):* And good luck with your—what do you do?

Willy: Selling.

Ben: Yes. Well . . . *(He raises his hand in farewell to all.)*

Willy: No, Ben, I don't want you to think . . . *(He takes* Ben's *arm to show him.)* It's Brooklyn, I know, but we hunt too.

Ben: Really, now.

Willy: Oh, sure, there's snakes and rabbits and—that's why I moved out here. Why, Biff can fell any one of these trees in no time! Boys! Go right over to where they're building the apartment house and get some sand. We're gonna rebuild the entire front stoop right now! Watch this, Ben!

Happy, (as he and Biff *run off):* I lost weight, Pop, you notice?

Charley *enters in knickers, even before the boys are gone.*

Charley: Listen, if they steal any more from that building the watchman'll put the cops on them!

Linda, (to Willy*):* Don't let Biff . . .

Ben *laughs lustily.*

Willy: You shoulda seen the lumber they brought home last week. At least a dozen six-by-tens worth all kinds a money.

Charley: Listen, if that watchman—

Willy: I gave them hell, understand. But I got a couple of fearless characters there.

Charley: Willy, the jails are full of fearless characters.

Ben, (clapping Willy *on the back, with a laugh at* Charley*):* And the stock exchange, friend!

Willy, (joining in Ben's *laughter):* Where are the rest of your pants?

Charley: My wife bought them.

Willy: Now all you need is a golf club and you can go upstairs and go to sleep. *(To* Ben*):* Great athlete! Between him and his son Bernard they can't hammer a nail!

Bernard, (rushing in): The watchman's chasing Biff!

Willy, (angrily): Shut up! He's not stealing anything!

Linda, (alarmed, hurrying off left): Where is he? Biff, dear! *(She exits.)*

Willy, (moving toward the left, away from Ben*):* There's nothing wrong. What's the matter with you?

Ben: Nervy boy. Good!

Willy, (laughing): Oh, nerves of iron, that Biff!

Charley: Don't know what it is. My New England man comes back and he's bleedin', they murdered him up there.

Willy: It's contacts, Charley, I got important contacts!

Charley, (sarcastically): Glad to hear it, Willy. Come in later, we'll shoot a little casino. I'll take some of your Portland money. *(He laughs at* Willy *and exits.)*

Willy (turning to Ben*):* Business is bad, it's murderous. But not for me, of course.

Ben: I'll stop by on my way back to Africa.

Willy, (longingly): Can't you stay a few days? You're just what I need, Ben, because I—I have a fine position here, but I— well, Dad left when I was such a baby and I never had a chance to talk to him and I still feel—kind of temporary about myself.

Ben: I'll be late for my train.

They are at opposite ends of the stage.

Willy: Ben, my boys—can't we talk? They'd go into the jaws of hell for me, see, but I—

Ben: William, you're being first-rate with your boys. Outstanding, manly chaps!

Willy, (hanging on to his words): Oh, Ben, that's good to hear! Because sometimes I'm afraid that I'm not teaching them the right kind of— Ben, how should I teach them?

Ben, (giving great weight to each word, and with a certain vicious audacity): William, when I walked into the jungle, I was seventeen. When I walked out I was twenty-one. And, by God, I was rich! *(He goes off into darkness around the right corner of the house.)*

Willy: . . . was rich! That's just the spirit I want to imbue them with! To walk into a jungle! I was right! I was right! I was right!

Ben is gone, but Willy *is still speaking to him as* Linda, *in nightgown and robe, enters the kitchen, glances around for* Willy, *then goes to the door of the house, looks out and sees him. Comes down to his left. He looks at her.*

Linda: Willy, dear? Willy?

Willy: I was right!

Linda: Did you have some cheese? *(He can't answer.)* It's very late, darling. Come to bed, heh?

Willy, *(looking straight up):* Gotta break your neck to see a star in this yard.

Linda: You coming in?

Willy: Whatever happened to that diamond watch fob? Remember? When Ben came from Africa that time? Didn't he give me a watch fob with a diamond in it?

Linda: You pawned it, dear. Twelve, thirteen years ago. For Biff's radio correspondence course.

Willy: Gee, that was a beautiful thing. I'll take a walk.

Linda: But you're in your slippers.

Willy, *(starting to go around the house at the left):* I was right! I was! *(Half to* Linda, *as he goes, shaking his head):* What a man! There was a man worth talking to. I was right!

Linda, *(calling after* Willy): But in your slippers, Willy!

Willy *is almost gone when* Biff, *in his pajamas, comes down the stairs and enters the kitchen.*

Biff: What is he doing out there?

Linda: Sh!

Biff: God Almighty, Mom, how long has he been doing this?

Linda: Don't, he'll hear you.

Biff: What the hell is the matter with him?

Linda: It'll pass by morning.

Biff: Shouldn't we do anything?

Linda: Oh, my dear, you should do a lot of things, but there's nothing to do, so go to sleep.

Happy *comes down the stair and sits on the steps.*

Happy: I never heard him so loud, Mom.

Linda: Well, come around more often; you'll hear him. *(She sits down at the table and mends the lining of* Willy's *jacket.)*

Biff: Why didn't you ever write me about this, Mom?

Linda: How would I write to you? For over three months you had no address.

Biff: I was on the move. But you know I thought of you all the time. You know that, don't you, pal?

Linda: I know, dear, I know. But he likes to have a letter. Just to know that there's still a possibility for better things.

Biff: He's not like this all the time, is he?

Linda: It's when you come home he's always the worst.

Biff: When I come home?

Linda: When you write you're coming, he's all smiles, and talks about the future, and—he's just wonderful. And then the closer you seem to come, the more shaky he gets, and then, by the time you get here, he's arguing, and he seems angry at you. I think it's just that maybe he can't bring himself to —to open up to you. Why are you so hateful to each other? Why is that?

Biff, (evasively): I'm not hateful, Mom.

Linda: But you no sooner come in the door than you're fighting!

Biff: I don't know why. I mean to change. I'm tryin', Mom, you understand?

Linda: Are you home to stay now?

Biff: I don't know. I want to look around, see what's doin'.

Linda: Biff, you can't look around all your life, can you?

Biff: I just can't take hold, Mom. I can't take hold of some kind of a life.

Linda: Biff, a man is not a bird, to come and go with the springtime.

Biff: Your hair . . . *(He touches her hair.)* Your hair got so gray.

Linda: Oh, it's been gray since you were in high school. I just stopped dyeing it, that's all.

Biff: Dye it again, will ya? I don't want my pal looking old. *(He smiles.)*

Linda: You're such a boy! You think you can go away for a year and . . . You've got to get it into your head now that one day you'll knock on this door and there'll be strange people here—

Biff: What are you talking about? You're not even sixty, Mom.

Linda: But what about your father?

Biff, (lamely): Well, I meant him too.

Happy: He admires Pop.

Linda: Biff, dear, if you don't have any feeling for him, then you can't have any feeling for me.

Biff: Sure I can, Mom.

Linda: No. You can't just come to see me, because I love him. *(With a threat, but only a threat, of tears):* He's the dearest man in the world to me, and I won't have anyone making him feel unwanted and low and blue. You've got to make up your mind now, darling, there's no leeway any more. Either he's your father and you pay him that respect, or else you're not to come here. I know he's not easy to get along with—nobody knows that better than me—but . . .

Willy, *(from the left, with a laugh):* Hey, hey, Biffo!

Biff, *(starting to go out after* Willy): What the hell is the matter with him? (Happy *stops him.)*

Linda: Don't—don't go near him!

Biff: Stop making excuses for him! He always, always wiped the floor with you. Never had an ounce of respect for you.

Happy: He's always had respect for—

Biff: What the hell do you know about it?

Happy, *(surlily):* Just don't call him crazy!

Biff: He's got no character— Charley wouldn't do this. Not in his own house—spewing out that vomit from his mind.

Happy: Charley never had to cope with what he's got to.

Biff: People are worse off than Willy Loman. Believe me, I've seen them!

Linda: Then make Charley your father, Biff. You can't do that, can you? I don't say he's a great man. Willy Loman never made a lot of money. His name was never in the paper. He's not the finest character that ever lived. But he's a human being, and a terrible thing is happening to him. So attention must be paid. He's not to be allowed to fall into his grave like an old dog. Attention, attention must be finally paid to such a person. You called him crazy—

Biff: I didn't mean—

Linda: No, a lot of people think he's lost his—balance. But you don't have to be very smart to know what his trouble is. The man is exhausted.

Happy: Sure!

Linda: A small man can be just as exhausted as a great man. He works for a company thirty-six years this March, opens up unheard-of territories to their trademark, and now in his old age they take his salary away.

Happy, *(indignantly):* I didn't know that, Mom.

Linda: You never asked, my dear! Now that you get your spending money someplace else you don't trouble your mind with him.

Happy: But I gave you money last—

Linda: Christmas time, fifty dollars! To fix the hot water it cost ninety-seven fifty! For five weeks he's been on straight commission, like a beginner, an unknown!

Biff: Those ungrateful bastards!

Linda: Are they any worse than his sons? When he brought

them business, when he was young, they were glad to see him. But now his old friends, the old buyers that loved him so and always found some order to hand him in a pinch— they're all dead, retired. He used to be able to make six, seven calls a day in Boston. Now he takes his valises out of the car and puts them back and takes them out again and he's exhausted. Instead of walking he talks now. He drives seven hundred miles, and when he gets there no one knows him any more, no one welcomes him. And what goes through a man's mind, driving seven hundred miles home without having earned a cent? Why shouldn't he talk to himself? Why? When he has to go to Charley and borrow fifty dollars a week and pretend to me that it's his pay? How long can that go on? How long? You see what I'm sitting here and waiting for? And you tell me he has no character? The man who never worked a day but for your benefit? When does he get the medal for that? Is this his reward—to turn around at the age of sixty-three and find his sons, who he loved better than his life, one a philandering bum—

Happy: Mom!

Linda: That's all you are, my baby! *(To* Biff*):* And you! What happened to the love you had for him? You were such pals! How you used to talk to him on the phone every night! How lonely he was till he could come home to you!

Biff: All right, Mom. I'll live here in my room, and I'll get a job. I'll keep away from him, that's all.

Linda: No, Biff. You can't stay here and fight all the time.

Biff: He threw me out of this house, remember that.

Linda: Why did he do that? I never knew why.

Biff: Because I know he's a fake and he doesn't like anybody around who knows!

Linda: Why a fake? In what way? What do you mean?

Biff: Just don't lay it all at my feet. It's between me and him —that's all I have to say. I'll chip in from now on. He'll settle for half my pay check. He'll be all right. I'm going to bed. *(He starts for the stairs.)*

Linda: He won't be all right.

Biff, (turning on the stairs, furiously): I hate this city and I'll stay here. Now what do you want?

Linda: He's dying. Biff.

Happy *turns quickly to her, shocked.*

Biff, (after a pause): Why is he dying?

Linda: He's been trying to kill himself.

Biff, (with great horror): How?

Linda: I live from day to day.

Biff: What're you talking about?

Linda: Remember I wrote you that he smashed up the car again? In February?

Biff: Well?

Linda: The insurance inspector came. He said that they have evidence. That all these accidents in the last year —weren't—weren't—accidents.

Happy: How can they tell that? That's a lie.

Linda: It seems there's a woman . . . *(She takes a breath as)*

Biff, (sharply but contained): What woman?

Linda, (simultaneously): . . . and this woman . . .

Linda: What?

Biff: Nothing. Go ahead.

Linda: What did you say?

Biff: Nothing. I just said what woman?

Happy: What about her?

Linda: Well, it seems she was walking down the road and saw his car. She says that he wasn't driving fast at all, and that he didn't skid. She says he came to that little bridge, and then deliberately smashed into the railing, and it was only the shallowness of the water that saved him.

Biff: Oh, no, he probably just fell asleep again.

Linda: I don't think he fell asleep.

Biff: Why not?

Linda: Last month . . . *(With great difficulty):* Oh, boys, it's so hard to say a thing like this! He's just a big stupid man to you, but I tell you there's more good in him than in many other people. *(She chokes, wipes her eyes.)* I was looking for a fuse. The lights blew out, and I went down the cellar. And behind the fuse box—it happened to fall out—was a length of rubber pipe—just short.

Happy: No kidding?

Linda: There's a little attachment on the end of it. I knew right away. And sure enough, on the bottom of the water heater there's a new little nipple on the gas pipe.

Happy, (angrily): That—jerk.

Biff: Did you have it taken off?

Linda: I'm—I'm ashamed to. How can I mention it to him? Every day I go down and take away that little rubber pipe. But, when he comes home, I put it back where it was. How can I insult him that way? I don't know what to do. I live from day to day, boys. I tell you, I know every thought in his mind. It sounds so old-fashioned and silly, but I tell you he put his whole life into you and you've turned your backs on him. *(She is bent over in the chair, weeping, her face in her hands.)* Biff, I swear to God! Biff, his life is in your hands!

Happy, (to Biff): How do you like that damned fool!

Biff, (kissing her): All right, pal, all right. It's all settled now. I've been remiss. I know that, Mom. But now I'll stay, and I swear to you, I'll apply myself. *(Kneeling in front of her, in a fever of self-reproach):* It's just—you see, Mom, I don't fit in business. Not that I won't try. I'll try, and I'll make good.

Happy: Sure you will. The trouble with you in business was you never tried to please people.

Biff: I know, I—

Happy: Like when you worked for Harrison's. Bob Harrison said you were tops, and then you go and do some damn fool thing like whistling whole songs in the elevator like a comedian.

Biff, (against Happy*):* So what? I like to whistle sometimes.

Happy: You don't raise a guy to a responsible job who whistles in the elevator!

Linda: Well, don't argue about it now.

Happy: Like when you'd go off and swim in the middle of the day instead of taking the line around.

Biff, (his resentment rising): Well, don't you run off? You take off sometimes, don't you? On a nice summer day?

Happy: Yeah, but I cover myself!

Linda: Boys!

Happy: If I'm going to take a fade the boss can call any number where I'm supposed to be and they'll swear to him that I just left. I'll tell you something that I hate to say, Biff, but in the business world some of them think you're crazy.

Biff, (angered): Screw the business world!

Happy: All right, screw it! Great, but cover yourself!

Linda: Hap, Hap!

Biff: I don't care what they think! They've laughed at Dad for years, and you know why? Because we don't belong in this nuthouse of a city! We should be mixing cement on some open plain, or—or carpenters. A carpenter is allowed to whistle!

Willy *walks in from the entrance of the house, at left.*

Willy: Even your grandfather was better than a carpenter. *(Pause. They watch him.)* You never grew up. Bernard does not whistle in the elevator, I assure you.

Biff, (as though to laugh Willy *out of it):* Yeah, but you do, Pop.

Willy: I never in my life whistled in an elevator! And who in the business world thanks I'm crazy?

Biff: I didn't mean it like that, Pop. Now don't make a whole thing out of it, will ya?

Willy: Go back to the West! Be a carpenter, a cowboy, enjoy yourself!

Linda: Willy, he was just saying—

Willy: I heard what he said!

Happy, (trying to quiet Willy): Hey, Pop, come on now . . .

Willy, (continuing over Happy's line): They laugh at me, heh? Go to Filene's, go to the Hub, go to Slattery's, Boston. Call out the name Willy Loman and see what happens! Big shot!

Biff: All right, Pop.

Willy: Big!

Biff: All right!

Willy: Why do you always insult me?

Biff: I didn't say a word. *(To Linda):* Did I say a word?

Linda: He didn't say anything, Willy.

Willy, (going to the doorway of the living-room): All right, good night, good night.

Linda: Willy, dear, he just decided . . .

Willy, (to Biff): If you get tired hanging around tomorrow, paint the ceiling I put up in the living-room.

Biff: I'm leaving early tomorrow.

Happy: He's going to see Bill Oliver, Pop.

Willy, (interestedly): Oliver? For what?

Biff, (with reserve, but trying, trying): He always said he'd stake me. I'd like to go into business, so maybe I can take him up on it.

Linda: Isn't that wonderful?

Willy: Don't interrupt. What's wonderful about it? There's fifty men in the City of New York who'd stake him. *(To Biff):* Sporting goods?

Biff: I guess so. I know something about it and—

Willy: He knows something about it! You know sporting goods better than Spalding, for God's sake! How much is he giving you?

Biff: I don't know, I didn't even see him yet, but—

Willy: Then what're you talkin' about?

Biff, (getting angry): Well, all I said was I'm gonna see him, that's all!

Willy, (turning away): Ah, you're counting your chickens again.

Biff, (starting left for the stairs): Oh, Jesus, I'm going to sleep!

Willy, (calling after him): Don't curse in this house!

Biff, (turning): Since when did you get so clean?

Happy, (trying to stop them): Wait a . . .

Willy: Don't use that language to me! I won't have it!

Happy, (grabbing Biff, shouts): Wait a minute! I got an idea. I got a feasible idea. Come here, Biff, let's talk this over now, let's talk some sense here. When I was down in Florida last time, I thought of a great idea to sell sporting goods. It just came back to me. You and I, Biff—we have a line, the Loman Line. We train a couple of weeks, and put on a couple of exhibitions, see?

Willy: That's an idea!

Happy: Wait! We form two basketball teams, see? Two water-polo teams. We play each other. It's a million dollars' worth of publicity. Two brothers, see? The Loman Brothers. Displays in the Royal Palms—all the hotels. And banners over the ring and the basketball court: "Loman Brothers." Baby, we could sell sporting goods!

Willy: That is a one-million-dollar idea!

Linda: Marvelous!

Biff: I'm in great shape as far as that's concerned.

Happy: And the beauty of it is, Biff, it wouldn't be like a business. We'd be out playin' ball again . . .

Biff, (enthused): Yeah, that's . . .

Willy: Million-dollar . . .

Happy: And you wouldn't get fed up with it, Biff. It'd be the family again. There'd be the old honor, and comradeship, and if you wanted to go off for a swim or somethin'—well, you'd do it! Without some smart cooky gettin' up ahead of you!

Willy: Lick the world! You guys together could absolutely lick the civilized world.

Biff: I'll see Oliver tomorrow. Hap, if we could work that out . . .

Linda: Maybe things are beginning to—

Willy, (wildly enthused, to Linda*):* Stop interrupting! *(To* Biff*):* But don't wear sport jacket and slacks when you see Oliver.

Biff: No, I'll—

Willy: A business suit, and talk as little as possible, and don't crack any jokes.

Biff: He did like me. Always liked me.

Linda: He loved you!

Willy, (to Linda*):* Will you stop! *(To* Biff*):* Walk in very serious. You are not applying for a boy's job. Money is to pass. Be quiet, fine, and serious. Everybody likes a kidder, but nobody lends him money.

Happy: I'll try to get some myself, Biff. I'm sure I can.

Willy: I see great things for you kids, I think your troubles are over. But remember, start big and you'll end big. Ask for fifteen. How much you gonna ask for?

Biff: Gee, I don't know—

Willy: And don't say "Gee." "Gee" is a boy's word. A man walking in for fifteen thousand dollars does not say "Gee!"

Biff: Ten, I think, would be top though.

Willy: Don't be so modest. You always started too low. Walk in with a big laugh. Don't look worried. Start off with a couple of your good stories to lighten things up. It's not what you say, it's how you say it—because personality always wins the day.

Linda: Oliver always thought the highest of him—

Willy: Will you let me talk?

Biff: Don't yell at her, Pop, will ya?

Willy, (angrily): I was talking, wasn't I?

Biff: I don't like you yelling at her all the time, and I'm tellin' you, that's all.

Willy: What're you, takin' over this house?

Linda: Willy—

Willy, (turning on her): Don't take his side all the time, goddammit!

Biff, (furiously): Stop yelling at her!

Willy, (suddenly pulling on his cheek, beaten down, guilt ridden): Give my best to Bill Oliver—he may remember me. *(He exits through the living-room doorway.)*

Linda, (her voice subdued): What'd you have to start that for? *(Biff turns away.)* You see how sweet he was as soon as you talked hopefully? *(She goes over to* Biff.*)* Come up and say good night to him. Don't let him go to bed that way.

Happy: Come on, Biff, let's buck him up.

Linda: Please, dear. Just say good night. It takes so little to make him happy. Come. *(She goes through the living-room doorway, calling upstairs from within the living-room):* Your pajamas are hanging in the bathroom, Willy!

Happy, (looking toward where Linda *went out):* What a woman! They broke the mold when they made her. You know that, Biff?

Biff: He's off salary. My God, working on commission!

Happy: Well, let's face it: he's no hot-shot selling man. Except that sometimes, you have to admit, he's a sweet personality.

Biff, (deciding): Lend me ten bucks, will ya? I want to buy some new ties.

Happy: I'll take you to a place I know. Beautiful stuff. Wear one of my striped shirts tomorrow.

Biff: She got gray. Mom got awful old. Gee, I'm gonna go in to Oliver tomorrow and knock him for a—

Happy: Come on up. Tell that to Dad. Let's give him a whirl. Come on.

Biff, (steamed up): You know, with ten thousand bucks, boy!

Happy, (as they go into the living-room): That's the talk, Biff, that's the first time I've heard the old confidence out of you!

(From within the living-room, fading off): You're gonna live with me, kid, and any babe you want just say the word . . . *(The last lines are hardly heard. They are mounting the stairs to their parents' bedroom.)*

Linda, *(entering her bedroom and addressing* Willy, *who is in the bathroom. She is straightening the bed for him):* Can you do anything about the shower? It drips.

Willy, *(from the bathroom):* All of a sudden everything falls to pieces! Goddam plumbing, oughta be sued, those people. I hardly finished putting it in and the thing . . . *(His words rumble off.)*

Linda: I'm just wondering if Oliver will remember him. You think he might?

Willy, *(coming out of the bathroom in his pajamas):* Remember him? What's the matter with you, you crazy? If he'd've stayed with Oliver he'd be on top by now! Wait'll Oliver gets a look at him. You don't know the average caliber any more. The average young man today—*(he is getting into bed)*—is got a caliber of zero. Greatest thing in the world for him was to bum around.

Biff *and* Happy *enter the bedroom. Slight pause.*

Willy, *(stops short, looking at Biff):* Glad to hear it, boy.

Happy: He wanted to say good night to you, sport.

Willy, *(to Biff):* Yeah. Knock him dead, boy. What'd you want to tell me?

Biff: Just take it easy, Pop. Good night. *(He turns to go.)*

Willy, *(unable to resist):* And if anything falls off the desk while you're talking to him—like a package or something—don't you pick it up. They have office boys for that.

Linda: I'll make a big breakfast—

Willy: Will you let me finish? *(To Biff):* Tell him you were in the business in the West. Not farm work.

Biff: All right, Dad.

Linda: I think everything—

Willy, *(going right through her speech):* And don't undersell yourself. No less than fifteen thousand dollars.

Biff, *(unable to bear him):* Okay. Good night, Mom. *(He starts moving.)*

Willy: Because you got a greatness in you, Biff, remember that. You got all kinds a greatness . . . *(He lies back, exhausted. Biff walks out.)*

Linda, *(calling after Biff):* Sleep well, darling!

Happy: I'm gonna get married, Mom. I wanted to tell you.

Linda: Go to sleep, dear.

Happy, *(going):* I just wanted to tell you.

Willy: Keep up the good work. *(Happy exits.)* God . . . remember that Ebbets Field game? The championship of the city?

Linda: Just rest. Should I sing to you?

Willy: Yeah. Sing to me. *Linda hums a soft lullaby.* When that team came out—he was the tallest, remember?

Linda: Oh, yes. And in gold.

Biff *enters the darkened kitchen, takes a cigarette, and leaves the house. He comes downstage into a golden pool of light. He smokes, staring at the night.*

Willy: Like a young god. Hercules—something like that. And the sun, the sun all around him. Remember how he waved to me? Right up from the field, with the representatives of three colleges standing by? And the buyers I brought, and the cheers when he came out—Loman, Loman, Loman! God Almighty, he'll be great yet. A star like that, magnificent, can never really fade away!

The light on Willy *is fading. The gas heater begins to glow through the kitchen wall, near the stairs, a blue flame beneath red coils.*

Linda, (timidly): Willy dear, what has he got against you?

Willy: I'm so tired. Don't talk any more.

Biff *slowly returns to the kitchen. He stops, stares toward the heater.*

Linda: Will you ask Howard to let you work in New York?

Willy: First thing in the morning. Everything'll be all right.

Biff *reaches behind the heater and draws out a length of rubber tubing. He is horrified and turns his head toward* Willy's *room, still dimly lit, from which the strains of* Linda's *desperate but monotonous humming rise.*

Willy, (staring through the window into the moonlight): Gee, look at the moon moving between the buildings!

Biff *wraps the tubing around his hand and quickly goes up the stairs.*

CURTAIN

ACT TWO

Music is heard, gay and bright. The curtain rises as the music fades away. Willy, *in shirt sleeves, is sitting at the kitchen table, sipping coffee, his hat in his lap.* Linda *is filling his cup when she can.*

Willy: Wonderful coffee. Meal in itself.

Linda: Can I make you some eggs?

Willy: No. Take a breath.

Linda: You look so rested, dear.

Willy: I slept like a dead one. First time in months. Imagine, sleeping till ten on a Tuesday morning. Boys left nice and early, heh?

Linda: They were out of here by eight o'clock.

Willy: Good work!

Linda: It was so thrilling to see them leaving together. I can't get over the shaving lotion in this house!

Willy, (smiling): Mmm—

Linda: Biff was very changed this morning. His whole attitude seemed to be hopeful. He couldn't wait to get downtown to see Oliver.

Willy: He's heading for a change. There's no question, there simply are certain men that take longer to get—solidified. How did he dress?

Linda: His blue suit. He's so handsome in that suit. He could be a—anything in that suit!

Willy *gets up from the table.* Linda *holds his jacket for him.*

Willy: There's no question, no question at all. Gee, on the way home tonight I'd like to buy some seeds.

Linda, (laughing): That'd be wonderful. But not enough sun gets back there. Nothing'll grow any more.

Willy: You wait, kid, before it's all over we're gonna get a little place out in the country, and I'll raise some vegetables, a couple of chickens . . .

Linda: You'll do it yet, dear.

Willy *walks out of his jacket.* Linda *follows him.*

Willy: And they'll get married, and come for a weekend. I'd build a little guest house. 'Cause I got so many fine tools. All I'd need would be a little lumber and some peace of mind.

Linda, (joyfully): I sewed the lining . . .

Willy: I could build two guest houses, so they'd both come. Did he decide how much he's going to ask Oliver for?

Linda, (getting him into the jacket): He didn't mention it, but I imagine ten or fifteen thousand. You going to talk to Howard today?

Willy: Yeah. I'll put it to him straight and simple. He'll just have to take me off the road.

Linda: And Willy, don't forget to ask for a little advance, because we've got the insurance premium. It's the grace period now.

Willy: That's a hundred . . . ?

Linda: A hundred and eight, sixty-eight. Because we're a little short again.

Willy: Why are we short?

Linda: Well, you had the motor job on the car . . .

Willy: That goddam Studebaker!

Linda: And you got one more payment on the refrigerator . . .

Willy: But it just broke again!

Linda: Well, it's old, dear.

Willy: I told you we should've bought a well-advertised machine. Charley bought a General Electric and it's twenty years old and it's still good, that son-of-a-bitch.

Linda: But, Willy—

Willy: Whoever heard of a Hastings refrigerator? Once in my life I would like to own something outright before it's broken! I'm always in a race with the junkyard! I just finished paying for the car and it's on its last legs. The refrigerator consumes belts like a goddam maniac. They time those things. They time them so when you finally paid for them, they're used up.

Linda, (buttoning up his jacket as he unbuttons it): All told, about two hundred dollars would carry us, dear. But that includes the last payment on the mortgage. After this payment, Willy, the house belongs to us.

Willy: It's twenty-five years!

Linda: Biff was nine years old when we bought it.

Willy: Well, that's a great thing. To weather a twenty-five year mortgage is—

Linda: It's an accomplishment.

Willy: All the cement, the lumber, the reconstruction I put in this house! There ain't a crack to be found in it any more.

Linda: Well, it served its purpose.

Willy: What purpose? Some stranger'll come along, move in, and that's that. If only Biff would take this house, and raise a family . . . *(He starts to go.)* Good-by, I'm late.

Linda, (suddenly remembering): Oh, I forgot! You're supposed to meet them for dinner.

Willy: Me?

Linda: At Frank's Chop House on Forty-eighth near Sixth Avenue.

Willy: Is that so! How about you?

Linda: No, just the three of you. They're gonna blow you to a big meal!

Willy: Don't say! Who thought of that?

Linda: Biff came to me this morning, Willy, and he said, "Tell Dad, we want to blow him to a big meal." Be there six o'clock. You and your two boys are going to have dinner.

Willy: Gee whiz! That's really somethin'. I'm gonna knock Howard for a loop, kid. I'll get an advance, and I'll come home with a New York job. Goddammit, now I'm gonna do it!

Linda: Oh, that's the spirit, Willy!

Willy: I will never get behind a wheel the rest of my life!

Linda: It's changing, Willy, I can feel it changing!

Willy: Beyond a question. G'by, I'm late. *(He starts to go again.)*

Linda, *(calling after him as she runs to the kitchen table for a handkerchief):* You got your glasses?

Willy, *(feels for them, then comes back in):* Yeah, yeah, got my glasses.

Linda, *(giving him the handkerchief):* And a handkerchief.

Willy: Yeah, handkerchief.

Linda: And your saccharine?

Willy: Yeah, my saccharine.

Linda: Be careful on the subway stairs.

She kisses him, and a silk stocking is seen hanging from her hand. Willy *notices it.*

Willy: Will you stop mending stockings? At least while I'm in the house. It gets me nervous. I can't tell you. Please.

Linda *hides the stocking in her hand as she follows* Willy *across the forestage in front of the house.*

Linda: Remember, Frank's Chop House.

Willy, *(passing the apron):* Maybe beets would grow out there.

Linda, *(laughing):* But you tried so many times.

Willy: Yeah. Well, don't work hard today. *(He disappears around the right corner of the house.)*

Linda: Be careful!

As Willy *vanishes,* Linda *waves to him. Suddenly the phone rings. She runs across the stage and into the kitchen and lifts it.*

Linda: Hello? Oh, Biff! I'm so glad you called, I just . . . Yes, sure, I just told him. Yes, he'll be there for dinner at six o'clock, I didn't forget. Listen, I was just dying to tell you. You know that little rubber pipe I told you about? That he connected to the gas heater? I finally decided to go down the cellar this morning and take it away and destroy it. But it's gone! Imagine? He took it away himself, it isn't there! *(She listens.)* When? Oh, then you took it. Oh—nothing, it's just that I'd hoped he'd taken it away himself. Oh, I'm not worried, darling, because this morning he left in such high spirits, it was like the old days! I'm not afraid any more. Did Mr. Oliver see you? . . . Well, you wait there then. And make a nice impression on him, darling. Just don't perspire too much before you see him. And have a nice time with Dad. He may have big news too! . . . That's right, a New York job. And be sweet to him tonight, dear. Be loving to him. Because he's only a little boat looking for a harbor. *(She is trembling with sorrow and joy.)* Oh, that's wonderful, Biff, you'll save his life. Thanks, darling. Just put your arm around him when he comes into the restaurant. Give him a smile. That's the boy . . . Good-by, dear. . . . You got your comb? . . . That's fine. Good-by, Biff dear.

In the middle of her speech, Howard Wagner, *thirty-six, wheels on a small type-writer table on which is a wire-recording machine and proceeds to plug it in. This is on the left forestage. Light slowly fades on* Linda *as it rises on* Howard. *Howard is intent on threading the machine and only glances over his shoulder as* Willy *appears.*

Willy: Pst! Pst!
Howard: Hello, Willy, come in.
Willy: Like to have a little talk with you, Howard.
Howard: Sorry to keep you waiting. I'll be with you in a minute.
Willy: What's that, Howard?
Howard: Didn't you ever see one of these? Wire recorder.
Willy: Oh. Can we talk a minute?
Howard: Records things. Just got delivery yesterday. Been driving me crazy, the most terrific machine I ever saw in my life. I was up all night with it.
Willy: What do you do with it?
Howard: I bought it for dictation, but you can do anything with it. Listen to this. I had it home last night. Listen to what I picked up. The first one is my daughter. Get this. *(He flicks the switch and "Roll out the Barrel" is heard being whistled.)* Listen to that kid whistle.
Willy: That is lifelike, isn't it?
Howard: Seven years old. Get that tone.
Willy: Ts, ts. Like to ask a little favor if you . . .

The whistling breaks off, and the voice of Howard's *daughter is heard.*

His Daughter: "Now you, Daddy."
Howard: She's crazy for me! *(Again the same song is whistled.)* That's me! Ha! *(He winks.)*
Willy: You're very good!

The whistling breaks off again. The machine runs silent for a moment.

Howard: Sh! Get this now, this is my son.
His Son: "The capital of Alabama is Montgomery; the capital of Arizona is Phoenix; the capital of Arkansas is Little Rock; the capital of California is Sacramento . . ." *(and on, and on.)*

Howard, (holding up five fingers): Five years old, Willy!

    Willy: He'll make an announcer some day!

His Son, (continuing): "The capital . . ."

Howard: Get that—alphabetical order! *(The machine breaks off suddenly.)* Wait a minute. The maid kicked the plug out.

    Willy: It certainly is a—

Howard: Sh, for God's sake!

His Son: "It's nine o'clock, Bulova watch time. So I have to go to sleep."

    Willy: That really is—

Howard: Wait a minute! The next is my wife.

They wait.

Howard's Voice: "Go on, say something." *(Pause.)* "Well, you gonna talk?"

    His Wife: "I can't think of anything."

Howard's Voice: "Well, talk—it's turning."

    His Wife, (shyly, beaten): "Hello." *(Silence.)* "Oh, Howard, I can't talk into this . . ."

Howard, (snapping the machine off): That was my wife.

    Willy: That is a wonderful machine. Can we—

Howard: I tell you, Willy, I'm gonna take my camera, and my bandsaw, and all my hobbies, and out they go. This is the most fascinating relaxation I ever found.

    Willy: I think I'll get one myself.

Howard: Sure, they're only a hundred and a half. You can't do without it. Supposing you wanna hear Jack Benny, see? But you can't be at home at that hour. So you tell the maid to turn the radio on when Jack Benny comes on, and this automatically goes on with the radio . . .

    Willy: And when you come home you . . .

Howard: You can come home twelve o'clock, one o'clock, any time you like, and you get yourself a Coke and sit yourself down, throw the switch, and there's Jack Benny's program in the middle of the night!

    Willy: I'm definitely going to get one. Because lots of times I'm on the road, and I think to myself, what I must be missing on the radio!

Howard: Don't you have a radio in the car?

    Willy: Well, yeah, but who ever thinks of turning it on?

Howard: Say, aren't you supposed to be in Boston?

    Willy: That's what I want to talk to you about, Howard. You got a minute? *(He draws a chair in from the wing.)*

Howard: What happened? What're you doing here?

    Willy: Well . . .

Howard: You didn't crack up again, did you?

Willy: Oh, no. No . . .

Howard: Geez, you had me worried there for a minute. What's the trouble?

Willy: Well, tell you the truth, Howard. I've come to the decision that I'd rather not travel any more.

Howard: Not travel! Well, what'll you do?

Willy: Remember, Christmas time, when you had the party here? You said you'd try to think of some spot for me here in town.

Howard: With us?

Willy: Well, sure.

Howard: Oh, yeah, yeah. I remember. Well, I couldn't think of anything for you, Willy.

Willy: I tell ya, Howard. The kids are all grown up, y'know. I don't need much any more. If I could take home—well, sixty-five dollars a week, I could swing it.

Howard: Yeah, but Willy, see I—

Willy: I tell ya why, Howard. Speaking frankly and between the two of us, y'know—I'm just a little tired.

Howard: Oh, I could understand that, Willy. But you're a road man, Willy, and we do a road business. We've only got a half-dozen salesmen on the floor here.

Willy: God knows, Howard, I never asked a favor of any man. But I was with the firm when your father used to carry you in here in his arms.

Howard: I know that, Willy, but—

Willy: Your father came to me the day you were born and asked me what I thought of the name of Howard, may he rest in peace.

Howard: I appreciate that, Willy, but there just is no spot here for you. If I had a spot I'd slam you right in, but I just don't have a single solitary spot.

He looks for his lighter. Willy *has picked it up and gives it to him. Pause.*

Willy, (with increasing anger): Howard, all I need to set my table is fifty dollars a week.

Howard: But where am I going to put you, kid?

Willy: Look, it isn't a question of whether I can sell merchandise, is it?

Howard: No, but it's a business, kid, and everybody's gotta pull his own weight.

Willy, (desperately): Just let me tell you a story, Howard—

Howard: 'Cause you gotta admit, business is business.

Willy, (angrily): Business is definitely business, but just listen for a minute. You don't understand this. When I was a boy —eighteen, nineteen—I was already on the road. And there was a question in my mind as to whether selling had a future for me. Because in those days I had a yearning to go to Alaska. See, there were three gold strikes in one month in Alaska, and I felt like going out. Just for the ride, you might say.

Howard, (barely interested): Don't say.

Willy: Oh, yeah, my father lived many years in Alaska. He was an adventurous man. We've got quite a little streak of self-reliance in our family. I thought I'd go out with my older brother and try to locate him, and maybe settle in the North with the old man. And I was almost decided to go, when I met a salesman in the Parker House. His name was Dave Singleman. And he was eighty-four years old, and he'd drummed merchandise in thirty-one states. And old Dave, he'd go up to his room, y'understand, put on his green velvet slippers—I'll never forget—and pick up his phone and call the buyers, and without ever leaving his room, at the age of eighty-four, he made his living. And when I saw that, I realized that selling was the greatest career a man could want. 'Cause what could be more satisfying than to be able to go, at the age of eighty-four, into twenty or thirty different cities, and pick up a phone, and be remembered and loved and helped by so many different people? Do you know? when he died—and by the way he died the death of a salesman, in his green velvet slippers in the smoker of the New York, New Haven and Hartford, going into Boston—when he died, hundreds of salesmen and buyers were at his funeral. Things were sad on a lotta trains for months after that. *(He stands up.* Howard *has not looked at him.)* In those days there was personality in it, Howard. There was respect, and comradeship, and gratitude in it. Today, it's all cut and dried, and there's no chance for bringing friendship to bear—or personality. You see what I mean? They don't know me any more.

Howard, (moving away, to the right): That's just the thing, Willy.

Willy: If I had forty dollars a week—that's all I'd need. Forty dollars, Howard.

Howard: Kid, I can't take blood from a stone, I—

Willy, (desperation is on him now): Howard, the year Al Smith was nominated, your father came to me and—

Howard, (starting to go off): I've got to see some people, kid.

Willy, (stopping him): I'm talking about your father! There were promises made across this desk! You mustn't tell me you've got people to see—I put thirty-four years into this firm, Howard, and now I can't pay my insurance! You can't eat the orange and throw the peel away—a man is not a

piece of fruit! *(After a pause):* Now pay attention. Your
father—in 1928 I had a big year. I averaged a hundred and
seventy dollars a week in commissions.

Howard, (impatiently): Now, Willy, you never averaged—

Willy, (banging his hand on the desk): I averaged a hundred and
seventy dollars a week in the year of 1928! And your father
came to me—or rather, I was in the office here—it was
right over this desk—and he put his hand on my shoulder—

Howard, (getting up): You'll have to excuse me, Willy, I gotta see
some people. Pull yourself together. *(Going out):* I'll be
back in a little while.

On Howard's *exit, the light on his chair grows very bright and strange.*

Willy: Pull myself together! What the hell did I say to him? My
God, I was yelling at him! How could I! (Willy *breaks off,
staring at the light, which occupies the chair, animating it. He
approaches this chair, standing across the desk from it.)* Frank,
Frank, don't you remember what you told me that time?
How you put your hand on my shoulder, and Frank . . . *(He
leans on the desk and as he speaks the dead man's name he accidentally switches on the recorder, and instantly)*

Howard's Son: ". . . of New York is Albany. The capital of Ohio is Cincinnati, the capital of Rhode Island is . . ." *(The recitation
continues.)*

Willy, (leaping away with fright, shouting): Ha! Howard! Howard! Howard!

Howard, (rushing in): What happened?

*Willy, (pointing at the machine, which continues nasally, childishly,
with the capital cities):* Shut it off! Shut it off!

Howard, (pulling the plug out): Look, Willy . . .

Willy, (pressing his hands to his eyes): I gotta get myself some coffee. I'll get some coffee . . .

Willy *starts to walk out.* Howard *stops him.*

Howard, (rolling up the cord): Willy, look . . .

Willy: I'll go to Boston.

Howard: Willy, you can't go to Boston for us.

Willy: Why can't I go?

Howard: I don't want you to represent us. I've been meaning to
tell you for a long time now.

Willy: Howard, are you firing me?

Howard: I think you need a good long rest, Willy.

Willy: Howard—

Howard: And when you feel better, come back, and we'll see if we
can work something out.

Willy: But I gotta earn money, Howard. I'm in no position
to—

Howard: Where are your sons? Why don't your sons give you a
   hand?

Willy: They're working on a very big deal.

Howard: This is no time for false pride, Willy. You go to your sons
   and you tell them that you're tired. You've got two great
   boys, haven't you?

Willy: Oh, no question, no question, but in the meantime . . .

Howard: Then that's that, heh?

Willy: All right, I'll go to Boston tomorrow.

Howard: No, no.

Willy: I can't throw myself on my sons. I'm not a cripple!

Howard: Look, kid, I'm busy this morning.

Willy, (grasping Howard's *arm):* Howard, you've got to let me
   go to Boston!

Howard, (hard, keeping himself under control): I've got a line of people to see this morning. Sit down, take five minutes, and
   pull yourself together, and then go home, will ya? I need
   the office, Willy. *(He starts to go, turns, remembering the
   recorder, starts to push off the table holding the recorder.)* Oh,
   yeah. Whenever you can this week, stop by and drop off the
   samples. You'll feel better, Willy, and then come back and
   we'll talk. Pull yourself together, kid, there's people
   outside.

Howard *exits, pushing the table off left.* Willy *stares into space, exhausted. Now
the music is heard*—Ben's *music—first distantly, then closer, closer. As* Willy
speaks, Ben *enters from the right. He carries valise and umbrella.*

Willy: Oh, Ben, how did you do it? What is the answer? Did
   you wind up the Alaska deal already?

Ben: Doesn't take much time if you know what you're doing.
   Just a short business trip. Boarding ship in an hour.
   Wanted to say good-by.

Willy: Ben, I've got to talk to you.

Ben, (glancing at his watch): Haven't the time, William.

Willy, (crossing the apron to Ben*):* Ben, nothing's working out. I
   don't know what to do.

Ben: Now, look here, William. I've bought timberland in
   Alaska and I need a man to look after things for me.

Willy: God, timberland! Me and my boys in those grand
   outdoors!

Ben: You've a new continent at your doorstep, William. Get
   out of these cities, they're full of talk and time payments and
   courts of law. Screw on your fists and you can fight for a
   fortune up there.

Willy: Yes, yes! Linda, Linda!

Linda *enters as of old, with the wash.*

Linda: Oh, you're back?

Ben: I haven't much time.

Willy: No, wait! Linda, he's got a proposition for me in Alaska.

Linda: But he's got— *(To Ben):* He's got a beautiful job here.

Willy: But in Alaska, kid, I could—

Linda: You're doing well enough, Willy!

Ben, (to Linda): Enough for what, my dear?

Linda, (frightened of Ben and angry at him): Don't say those things to him! Enough to be happy right here, right now. *(To Willy, while Ben laughs):* Why must everybody conquer the world? You're well liked, and the boys love you, and someday—*(to Ben)*—why, old man Wagner told him just the other day that if he keeps it up he'll be a member of the firm, didn't he, Willy?

Willy: Sure, sure. I am building something with this firm, Ben, and if a man is building something he must be on the right track, mustn't he?

Ben: What are you building? Lay your hand on it. Where is it?

Willy, (hesitantly): That's true, Linda, there's nothing.

Linda: Why? *(To Ben):* There's a man eighty-four years old—

Willy: That's right, Ben, that's right. When I look at that man I say, what is there to worry about?

Ben: Bah!

Willy: It's true, Ben. All he has to do is go into any city, pick up the phone, and he's making his living and you know why?

Ben, (picking up his valise): I've got to go.

Willy, (holding Ben back): Look at this boy!

Biff, *in his high school sweater, enters carrying suitcase.* Happy *carries* Biff's *shoulder guards, gold helmet, and football pants.*

Willy: Without a penny to his name, three great universities are begging for him, and from there the sky's the limit, because it's not what you do, Ben. It's who you know and the smile on your face! It's contacts, Ben, contacts! The whole wealth of Alaska passes over the lunch table at the Commodore Hotel, and that's the wonder, the wonder of this country, that a man can end with diamonds here on the basis of being liked! *(He turns to Bill.)* And that's why when you get out on that field today it's important. Because thousands of people will be rooting for you and loving you. *(To Ben, who has again begun to leave):* And Ben! when he walks into a business office his name will sound out like a bell and all the doors will open to him! I've seen it, Ben, I've seen it a thousand times! You can't feel it with your hand like timber, but it's there!

Ben: Good-by, William.

Willy: Ben, am I right? Don't you think I'm right? I value your advice.

Ben: There's a new continent at your doorstep, William. You could walk out rich. Rich! *(He is gone.)*

Willy: We'll do it here, Ben! You hear me? We're gonna do it here!

Young Bernard *rushes in. The gay music of the Boys is heard.*

Bernard: Oh, gee, I was afraid you left already!

Willy: Why? What time is it?

Bernard: It's half-past one!

Willy: Well, come on, everybody! Ebbets Field next stop! Where's the pennants? *(He rushes through the wall-line of the kitchen and out into the living-room.)*

Linda, (to Biff*):* Did you pack fresh underwear?

Biff, (who has been limbering up): I want to go!

Bernard: Biff, I'm carrying your helmet, ain't I?

Happy: No, I'm carrying the helmet.

Bernard: Oh, Biff, you promised me.

Happy: I'm carrying the helmet.

Bernard: How am I going to get in the locker room?

Linda: Let him carry the shoulder guards. *(She puts her coat and hat on in the kitchen.)*

Bernard: Can I, Biff? 'Cause I told everybody I'm going to be in the locker room.

Happy: In Ebbets Field it's the clubhouse.

Bernard: I meant the clubhouse. Biff!

Happy: Biff!

Biff, (grandly, after a slight pause): Let him carry the shoulder guards.

Happy, (as he gives Bernard *the shoulder guards):* Stay close to us now.

Willy *rushes in with the pennants.*

Willy, (handing them out): Everybody wave when Biff comes out on the field. *(Happy and* Bernard *run off.)* You set now, boy?

The music has died away.

Biff: Ready to go, Pop. Every muscle is ready.

Willy, (at the edge of the apron): You realize what this means?

Biff: That's right, Pop.

Willy, (feeling Biff's *muscles):* You're comin' home this afternoon captain of the All-Scholastic Championship Team of the City of New York.

Biff: I got it, Pop. And remember, pal, when I take off my helmet, that touchdown is for you.

Willy: Let's go! *(He is starting out, with his arm around* Biff, *when* Charley *enters, as of old, in knickers.)* I got no room for you, Charley.

Charley: Room? For what?

Willy: In the car.

Charley: You goin' for a ride? I wanted to shoot some casino.

Willy, (furiously): Casino? *(Incredulously):* Don't you realize what today is?

Linda: Oh, he knows, Willy. He's just kidding you.

Willy: That's nothing to kid about!

Charley: No, Linda, what's goin' on?

Linda: He's playing in Ebbets Field.

Charley: Baseball in this weather?

Willy: Don't talk to him. Come on, come on! *(He is pushing them out.)*

Charley: Wait a minute, didn't you hear the news?

Willy: What?

Charley: Don't you listen to the radio? Ebbets Field just blew up.

Willy: You go to hell! *(Charley laughs. Pushing them out):* Come on, come on! We're late.

Charley, (as they go): Knock a homer, Biff, knock a homer!

Willy, (the last to leave, turning to Charley*):* I don't think that was funny, Charley. This is the greatest day of his life.

Charley: Willy, when are you going to grow up?

Willy: Yeah, heh? When this game is over, Charley, you'll be laughing out of the other side of your face. They'll be calling him another Red Grange. Twenty-five thousand a year.

Charley, (kidding): Is that so?

Willy: Yeah, that's so.

Charley: Well, then, I'm sorry, Willy. But tell me something.

Willy: What?

Charley: Who is Red Grange?

Willy: Put up your hands. Goddam you, put up your hands!

Charley, *chuckling, shakes his head and walks away, around the left corner of the stage.* Willy *follows him. The music rises to a mocking frenzy.*

Willy: Who the hell do you think you are, better than everybody else? You don't know everything, you big, ignorant, stupid . . . Put up your hands!

Light rises, on the right side of the forestage, on a small table in the reception room of Charley's *office. Traffic sounds are heard.* Bernard, *now mature, sits whistling to himself. A pair of tennis rackets and an overnight bag are on the floor beside him.*

Willy, (offstage): What are you walking away for? Don't walk away! If you're going to say something say it to my face! I know you laugh at me behind my back. You'll laugh out of the other side of your goddam face after this game. Touchdown! Touchdown! Eighty thousand people! Touchdown! Right between the goal posts.

Bernard *is a quiet, earnest, but self-assured young man.* Willy's *voice is coming from right upstage now.* Bernard *lowers his feet off the table and listens.* Jenny, *his father's secretary, enters.*

    Jenny, (distressed): Say, Bernard, will you go out in the hall?
    Bernard: What is that noise? Who is it?
    Jenny: Mr. Loman. He just got off the elevator.
    Bernard, (getting up): Who's he arguing with?
    Jenny: Nobody. There's nobody with him. I can't deal with him any more, and your father gets all upset everytime he comes. I've got a lot of typing to do, and your father's waiting to sign it. Will you see him?
    Willy, (entering): Touchdown! Touch— *(He sees* Jenny.*)* Jenny, Jenny, good to see you. How're ya? Workin'? Or still honest?
    Jenny: Fine. How've you been feeling?
    Willy: Not much any more, Jenny. Ha, ha! *(He is surprised to see the rackets.)*
    Bernard: Hello, Uncle Willy.
    Willy, (almost shocked): Bernard! Well, look who's here! *(He comes quickly, guiltily, to* Bernard *and warmly shakes his hand.)*
    Bernard: How are you? Good to see you.
    Willy: What are you doing here?
    Bernard: Oh, just stopped by to see Pop. Get off my feet till my train leaves. I'm going to Washington in a few minutes.
    Willy: Is he in?
    Bernard: Yes, he's in his office with the accountant. Sit down.
    Willy, (sitting down): What're you going to do in Washington?
    Bernard: Oh, just a case I've got there, Willy.
    Willy: That so? *(Indicating the rackets):* You going to play tennis there?
    Bernard: I'm staying with a friend who's got a court.
    Willy: Don't say. His own tennis court. Must be fine people, I bet.
    Bernard: They are, very nice. Dad tells me Biff's in town.
    Willy, (with a big smile): Yeah, Biff's in. Working on a very big deal, Bernard.
    Bernard: What's Biff doing?
    Willy: Well, he's been doing very big things in the West. But he

decided to establish himself here. Very big. We're having dinner. Did I hear your wife had a boy?

Bernard: That's right. Our second.

Willy: Two boys! What do you know!

Bernard: What kind of a deal has Biff got?

Willy: Well, Bill Oliver—very big sporting-goods man—he wants Biff very badly. Called him in from the West. Long distance, carte blanche, special deliveries. Your friends have their own private tennis court?

Bernard: You still with the old firm, Willy?

Willy, (after a pause): I'm—I'm overjoyed to see how you made the grade, Bernard, overjoyed. It's an encouraging thing to see a young man really—really— Looks very good for Biff —very— *(He breaks off, then):* Bernard— *(He is so full of emotion, he breaks off again.)*

Bernard: What is it, Willy?

Willy, (small and alone): What—what's the secret?

Bernard: What secret?

Willy: How—how did you? Why didn't he ever catch on?

Bernard: I wouldn't know that, Willy.

Willy, (confidentially, desperately): You were his friend, his boy-hood friend. There's something I don't understand about it. His life ended after that Ebbets Field game. From the age of seventeen nothing good ever happened to him.

Bernard: He never trained himself for anything.

Willy: But he did, he did. After high school he took so many correspondence courses. Radio mechanics; television; God knows what, and never made the slightest mark.

Bernard, (taking off his glasses): Willy, do you want to talk candidly?

Willy, (rising, faces Bernard): I regard you as a very brilliant man, Bernard. I value your advice.

Bernard: Oh, the hell with the advice, Willy. I couldn't advise you. There's just one thing I've always wanted to ask you. When he was supposed to graduate, and the math teacher flunked him—

Willy: Oh, that son-of-a-bitch ruined his life.

Bernard: Yeah, but, Willy, all he had to do was go to summer school and make up that subject.

Willy: That's right, that's right.

Bernard: Did you tell him not to go to summer school?

Willy: Me? I begged him to go. I ordered him to go!

Bernard: Then why wouldn't he go?

Willy: Why? Why! Bernard, that question has been trailing me like a ghost for the last fifteen years. He flunked the sub-ject, and laid down and died like a hammer hit him!

Bernard: Take it easy, kid.

Willy: Let me talk to you—I got nobody to talk to. Bernard, Bernard, was it my fault? Y'see? It keeps going around in my mind, maybe I did something to him. I got nothing to give him.

Bernard: Don't take it so hard.

Willy: Why did he lay down? What is the story there? You were his friend!

Bernard: Willy, I remember, it was June, and our grades came out. And he'd flunked math.

Willy: That son-of-a-bitch!

Bernard: No, it wasn't right then. Biff just got very angry, I remember, and he was ready to enroll in summer school.

Willy, (surprised): He was?

Bernard: He wasn't beaten by it at all. But then, Willy, he disappeared from the block for almost a month. And I got the idea that he'd gone up to New England to see you. Did he have a talk with you then?

Willy *stares in silence.*

Bernard: Willy?

Willy, (with a strong edge of resentment in his voice): Yeah, he came to Boston. What about it?

Bernard: Well, just that when he came back—I'll never forget this, it always mystifies me. Because I'd thought so well of Biff, even though he'd always taken advantage of me. I loved him, Willy, y'know? And he came back after that month and took his sneakers—remember those sneakers with "University of Virginia" printed on them? He was so proud of those, wore them every day. And he took them down in the cellar, and burned them up in the furnace. We had a fist fight. It lasted at least half an hour. Just the two of us, punching each other down in the cellar, and crying right through it. I've often thought of how strange it was that I knew he'd given up his life. What happened in Boston, Willy?

Willy *looks at him as at an intruder.*

Bernard: I just bring it up because you asked me.

Willy, (angrily): Nothing. What do you mean, "What happened?" What's that got to do with anything?

Bernard: Well, don't get sore.

Willy: What are you trying to do, blame it on me? If a boy lays down is that my fault?

Bernard: Now, Willy, don't get—

Willy: Well, don't—don't talk to me that way! What does that mean, "What happened?"

Charley *enters. He is in his vest, and he carries a bottle of bourbon.*

>Charley: Hey, you're going to miss that train. *(He waves the bottle.)*
>Bernard: Yeah, I'm going. *(He takes the bottle.)* Thanks, Pop. *(He picks up his rackets and bag.)* Good-by, Willy, and don't worry about it. You know, "If at first you don't succeed . . ."
>Willy: Yes, I believe in that.
>Bernard: But sometimes, Willy, it's better for a man just to walk away.
>Willy: Walk away?
>Bernard: That's right.
>Willy: But if you can't walk away?
>Bernard, *(after a slight pause):* I guess that's when it's tough. *(Extending his hand):* Good-by, Willy.
>Willy, *(shaking* Bernard's *hand):* Good-by, boy.
>Charley, *(an arm on* Bernard's *shoulder):* How do you like this kid? Gonna argue a case in front of the Supreme Court.
>Bernard, *(protesting):* Pop!
>Willy, *(genuinely shocked, pained, and happy):* No! The Supreme Court!
>Bernard: I gotta run. 'By, Dad!
>Charley: Knock 'em dead, Bernard!

Bernard *goes off.*

>Willy, *(as* Charley *takes out his wallet):* The Supreme Court! And he didn't even mention it!
>Charley, *(counting out money on the desk):* He don't have to—he's gonna do it.
>Willy: And you never told him what to do, did you? You never took any interest in him.
>Charley: My salvation is that I never took any interest in anything. There's some money—fifty dollars. I got an accountant inside.
>Willy: Charley, look . . . *(With difficulty):* I got my insurance to pay. If you can manage it—I need a hundred and ten dollars.

Charley *doesn't reply for a moment; merely stops moving.*

>Willy: I'd draw it from my bank but Linda would know, and I . . .
>Charley: Sit down, Willy.
>Willy, *(moving toward the chair):* I'm keeping an account of everything, remember. I'll pay every penny back. *(He sits.)*
>Charley: Now listen to me, Willy.
>Willy: I want you to know I appreciate . . .

Charley, (sitting down on the table): Willy, what're you doin'? What the hell is goin' on in your head?

Willy: Why? I'm simply . . .

Charley: I offered you a job. You can make fifty dollars a week. And I won't send you on the road.

Willy: I've got a job.

Charley: Without pay? What kind of a job is a job without pay? *(He rises.)* Now, look, kid, enough is enough. I'm no genius but I know when I'm being insulted.

Willy: Insulted!

Charley: Why don't you want to work for me?

Willy: What's the matter with you? I've got a job.

Charley: Then what're you walkin' in here every week for?

Willy, (getting up): Well, if you don't want me to walk in here—

Charley: I am offering you a job.

Willy: I don't want your goddam job!

Charley: When the hell are you going to grow up?

Willy, (furiously): You big ignoramus, if you say that to me again I'll rap you one! I don't care how big you are! *(He's ready to fight.)*

Pause.

Charley, (kindly, going to him): How much do you need, Willy?

Willy: Charley, I'm strapped. I'm strapped. I don't know what to do. I was just fired.

Charley: Howard fired you?

Willy: That snotnose. Imagine that? I named him. I named him Howard.

Charley: Willy, when're you gonna realize that them things don't mean anything? You named him Howard, but you can't sell that. The only thing you got in this world is what you can sell. And the funny thing is that you're a salesman, and you don't know that.

Willy: I've always tried to think otherwise, I guess. I always felt that if a man was impressive, and well liked, that nothing—

Charley: Why must everybody like you? Who liked J. P. Morgan? Was he impressive? In a Turkish bath he'd look like a butcher. But with his pockets on he was very well liked. Now listen, Willy, I know you don't like me, and nobody can say I'm in love with you, but I'll give you a job because—just for the hell of it, put it that way. Now what do you say?

Willy: I—I just can't work for you, Charley.

Charley: What're you, jealous of me?

Willy: I can't work for you, that's all, don't ask me why.

Charley, (angered, takes out more bills): You been jealous of me all your life, you damned fool! Here, pay your insurance. *(He puts the money in* Willy's *hand.)*

Willy: I'm keeping strict accounts.

Charley: I've got some work to do. Take care of yourself. And pay your insurance.

Willy, *(moving to the right):* Funny, y'know? After all the highways, and the trains, and the appointments, and the years, you end up worth more dead than alive.

Charley: Willy, nobody's worth nothin' dead. *(After a slight pause):* Did you hear what I said?

Willy *stands still, dreaming.*

Charley: Willy!

Willy: Apologize to Bernard for me when you see him. I didn't mean to argue with him. He's a fine boy. They're all fine boys, and they'll end up big—all of them. Someday they'll all play tennis together. Wish me luck, Charley. He saw Bill Oliver today.

Charley: Good luck.

Willy, *(on the verge of tears):* Charley, you're the only friend I got. Isn't that a remarkable thing? *(He goes out.)*

Charley: Jesus!

Charley *stares after him a moment and follows. All light blacks out. Suddenly raucous music is heard, and a red glow rises behind the screen at right.* Stanley, *a young waiter, appears, carrying a table, followed by* Happy, *who is carrying two chairs.*

Stanley, *(putting the table down):* That's all right, Mr. Loman, I can handle it myself. *(He turns and takes the chairs from* Happy *and places them at the table.)*

Happy, *(glancing around):* Oh, this is better.

Stanley: Sure, in the front there you're in the middle of all kinds a noise. Whenever you got a party, Mr. Loman, you just tell me and I'll put you back here. Y'know, there's a lotta people they don't like it private, because when they go out they like to see a lotta action around them because they're sick and tired to stay in the house by theirself. But I know you, you ain't from Hackensack. You know what I mean?

Happy, *(sitting down):* So how's it coming, Stanley?

Stanley: Ah, it's a dog's life. I only wish during the war they'd a took me in the Army. I coulda been dead by now.

Happy: My brother's back, Stanley.

Stanley: Oh, he come back, heh? From the Far West.

Happy: Yeah, big cattle man, my brother, so treat him right. And my father's coming too.

Stanley: Oh, your father too!

Happy: You got a couple of nice lobsters?

Stanley: Hundred per cent, big.

Happy: I want them with the claws.

Stanley: Don't worry, I don't give you no mice. *(Happy laughs.)* How about some wine? It'll put a head on the meal.

Happy: No. You remember, Stanley, that recipe I brought you from overseas? With the champagne in it?

Stanley: Oh, yeah, sure. I still got it tacked up yet in the kitchen. But that'll have to cost a buck apiece anyways.

Happy: That's all right.

Stanley: What'd you, hit a number or somethin'?

Happy: No, it's a little celebration. My brother is—I think he pulled off a big deal today. I think we're going into business together.

Stanley: Great! That's the best for you. Because a family business, you know what I mean?—that's the best.

Happy: That's what I think.

Stanley: 'Cause what's the difference? Somebody steals? It's in the family. Know what I mean? *(Sotto voce):* Like this bartender here. The boss is goin' crazy what kinda leak he's got in the cash register. You put it in but it don't come out.

Happy, (raising his head): Sh!

Stanley: What?

Happy: You notice I wasn't lookin' right or left, was I?

Stanley: No.

Happy: And my eyes are closed.

Stanley: So what's the—?

Happy: Strudel's comin'.

Stanley, (catching on, looks around): Ah, no, there's no—

He breaks off as a furred, lavishly dressed girl enters and sits at the next table. Both follow her with their eyes.

Stanley: Geez, how'd ya know?

Happy: I got radar or something. *(Staring directly at her profile):* Oooooooo . . . Stanley.

Stanley: I think that's for you, Mr. Loman.

Happy: Look at that mouth. Oh, God. And the binoculars.

Stanley: Geez, you got a life, Mr. Loman.

Happy: Wait on her.

Stanley, (going to the girl's table): Would you like a menu, ma'am?

Girl: I'm expecting someone, but I'd like a—

Happy: Why don't you bring her—excuse me, miss, do you mind? I sell champagne, and I'd like you to try my brand. Bring her a champagne, Stanley.

Girl: That's awfully nice of you.

Happy: Don't mention it. It's all company money. *(He laughs.)*

Girl: That's a charming product to be selling, isn't it?

Happy: Oh, gets to be like everything else. Selling is selling, y'know.

Girl: I suppose.

Happy: You don't happen to sell, do you?

Girl: No, I don't sell.

Happy: Would you object to a compliment from a stranger? You ought to be on a magazine cover.

Girl, (looking at him a little archly): I have been.

Stanley *comes in with a glass of champagne.*

Happy: What'd I say before, Stanley? You see? She's a cover girl.

Stanley: Oh, I could see, I could see.

Happy, (to the Girl*):* What magazine?

Girl: Oh, a lot of them. *(She takes the drink.)* Thank you.

Happy: You know what they say in France, don't you? "Champagne is the drink of the complexion"—Hya, Biff!

Biff *has entered and sits with* Happy.

Biff: Hello, kid. Sorry I'm late.

Happy: I just got here. Uh, Miss—?

Girl: Forsythe.

Happy: Miss Forsythe, this is my brother.

Biff: Is Dad here?

Happy: His name is Biff. You might've heard of him. Great football player.

Girl: Really? What team?

Happy: Are you familiar with football?

Girl: No, I'm afraid I'm not.

Happy: Biff is quarterback with the New York Giants.

Girl: Well, that is nice, isn't it? *(She drinks.)*

Happy: Good health.

Girl: I'm happy to meet you.

Happy: That's my name. Hap. It's really Harold, but at West Point they called me Happy.

Girl, (now really impressed): Oh, I see. How do you do? *(She turns her profile.)*

Biff: Isn't Dad coming?

Happy: You want her?

Biff: Oh, I could never make that.

Happy: I remember the time that idea would never come into your head. Where's the old confidence, Biff?

Biff: I just saw Oliver—

Happy: Wait a minute. I've got to see that old confidence again. Do you want her? She's on call.

Biff: Oh, no. *(He turns to look at the* Girl.*)*

Happy: I'm telling you. Watch this. *(Turning to the* Girl*):* Honey? *(She turns to him.)* Are you busy?

Girl: Well, I am . . . but I could make a phone call.

Happy: Do that, will you, honey? And see if you can get a friend. We'll be here for a while. Biff is one of the greatest football players in the country.

Girl, (standing up): Well, I'm certainly happy to meet you.

Happy: Come back soon.

Girl: I'll try.

Happy: Don't try, honey, try hard.

The Girl *exits.* Stanley *follows, shaking his head in bewildered admiration.*

Happy: Isn't that a shame now? A beautiful girl like that? That's why I can't get married. There's not a good woman in a thousand. New York is loaded with them, kid!

Biff: Hap, look—

Happy: I told you she was on call!

Biff, (strangely unnerved): Cut it out, will ya? I want to say something to you.

Happy: Did you see Oliver?

Biff: I saw him all right. Now look, I want to tell Dad a couple of things and I want you to help me.

Happy: What? Is he going to back you?

Biff: Are you crazy? You're out of your goddam head, you know that?

Happy: Why? What happened?

Biff, (breathlessly): I did a terrible thing today, Hap. It's been the strangest day I ever went through. I'm all numb, I swear.

Happy: You mean he wouldn't see you?

Biff: Well, I waited six hours for him, see? All day. Kept sending my name in. Even tried to date his secretary so she'd get me to him, but no soap.

Happy: Because you're not showin' the old confidence, Biff. He remembered you, didn't he?

Biff, (stopping Happy *with a gesture):* Finally, about five o'clock, he comes out. Didn't remember who I was or anything. I felt like such an idiot, Hap.

Happy: Did you tell him my Florida idea?

Biff: He walked away. I saw him for one minute. I got so mad I could've torn the walls down! How the hell did I ever get the idea I was a salesman there? I even believed myself that I'd been a salesman for him! And then he gave me one look and—I realized what a ridiculous lie my whole life has been! We've been talking in a dream for fifteen years. I was a shipping clerk.

Happy: What'd you do?

Biff, (with great tension and wonder): Well, he left, see. And the
secretary went out. I was all alone in the waiting-room. I
don't know what came over me, Hap. The next thing I
know I'm in his office—paneled walls, everything. I can't
explain it. I—Hap, I took his fountain pen.
Happy: Geez, did he catch you?
Biff: I ran out. I ran down all eleven flights. I ran and ran
and ran.
Happy: That was an awful dumb—what'd you do that for?
Biff, (agonized): I don't know, I just—wanted to take some-
thing, I don't know. You gotta help me, Hap, I'm gonna tell
Pop.
Happy: You crazy? What for?
Biff: Hap, he's got to understand that I'm not the man some-
body lends that kind of money to. He thinks I've been spit-
ing him all these years and it's eating him up.
Happy: That's just it. You tell him something nice.
Biff: I can't.
Happy: Say you got a lunch date with Oliver tomorrow.
Biff: So what do I do tomorrow?
Happy: You leave the house tomorrow and come back at night
and say Oliver is thinking it over. And he thinks it over for a
couple of weeks, and gradually it fades away and nobody's
the worse.
Biff: But it'll go on forever!
Happy: Dad is never so happy as when he's looking forward to
something!

Willy *enters.*

Happy: Hello, scout!
Willy: Gee, I haven't been here in years!

Stanley *has followed* Willy *in and sets a chair for him.* Stanley *starts off but*
Happy *stops him.*

Happy: Stanley!

Stanley *stands by, waiting for an order.*

Biff, (going to Willy *with guilt, as to an invalid):* Sit down, Pop.
You want a drink?
Willy: Sure, I don't mind.
Biff: Let's get a load on.
Willy: You look worried.
Biff: N-no. *(To Stanley):* Scotch all around. Make it doubles.
Stanley: Doubles, right. *(He goes.)*
Willy: You had a couple already, didn't you?

Biff: Just a couple, yeah.

Willy: Well, what happened, boy? *(Nodding affirmatively, with a smile):* Everything go all right?

Biff, (takes a breath, then reaches out and grasps Willy's *hand):* Pal . . . *(He is smiling bravely, and* Willy *is smiling too.)* I had an experience today.

Happy: Terrific, Pop.

Willy: That so? What happened?

Biff, (high, slightly alcoholic, above the earth): I'm going to tell you everything from first to last. It's been a strange day. *(Silence. He looks around, composes himself as best he can, but his breath keeps breaking the rhythm of his voice.)* I had to wait quite a while for him, and—

Willy: Oliver?

Biff: Yeah, Oliver. All day, as a matter of cold fact. And a lot of—instances—facts, Pop, facts about my life came back to me. Who was it, Pop? Who ever said I was a salesman with Oliver?

Willy: Well, you were.

Biff: No, Dad, I was a shipping clerk.

Willy: But you were practically—

Biff, (with determination): Dad, I don't know who said it first, but I was never a salesman for Bill Oliver.

Willy: What're you talking about?

Biff: Let's hold on to the facts tonight, Pop. We're not going to get anywhere bullin' around. I was a shipping clerk.

Willy, (angrily): All right, now listen to me—

Biff: Why don't you let me finish?

Willy: I'm not interested in stories about the past or any crap of that kind because the woods are burning, boys, you understand? There's a big blaze going on all around. I was fired today.

Biff, (shocked): How could you be?

Willy: I was fired, and I'm looking for a little good news to tell your mother, because the woman has waited and the woman has suffered. The gist of it is that I haven't got a story left in my head, Biff. So don't give me a lecture about facts and aspects. I am not interested. Now what've you got to say to me?

Stanley *enters with three drinks. They wait until he leaves.*

Willy: Did you see Oliver?

Biff: Jesus, Dad!

Willy: You mean you didn't go up there?

Happy: Sure he went up there.

Biff: I did. I—saw him. How could they fire you?

Willy, (on the edge of his chair): What kind of a welcome did he give you?

Biff: He won't even let you work on commission?

Willy: I'm out! *(Driving):* So tell me, he gave you a warm welcome?

Happy: Sure, Pop, sure!

Biff, (driven): Well, it was kind of—

Willy: I was wondering if he'd remember you. *(To* Happy*):* Imagine, man doesn't see him for ten, twelve years and gives him that kind of a welcome!

Happy: Damn right!

Biff, (trying to return to the offensive): Pop, look—

Willy: You know why he remembered you, don't you? Because you impressed him in those days.

Biff: Let's talk quietly and get this down to the facts, huh?

Willy, (as though Biff *had been interrupting):* Well, what happened? It's great news, Biff. Did he take you into his office or'd you talk in the waiting-room?

Biff: Well, he came in, see, and—

Willy, (with a big smile): What'd he say? Betcha he threw his arm around you.

Biff: Well, he kinda—

Willy: He's a fine man. *(To* Happy*):* Very hard man to see, y'know.

Happy, (agreeing): Oh, I know.

Willy, (to Biff*):* Is that where you had the drinks?

Biff: Yeah, he gave me a couple of—no, no!

Happy, (cutting in): He told him my Florida idea.

Willy: Don't interrupt. *(To* Biff*):* How'd he react to the Florida idea?

Biff: Dad, will you give me a minute to explain?

Willy: I've been waiting for you to explain since I sat down here! What happened? He took you into his office and what?

Biff: Well—I talked. And—and he listened, see.

Willy: Famous for the way he listens, y'know. What was his answer?

Biff: His answer was— *(He breaks off, suddenly angry.)* Dad, you're not letting me tell you what I want to tell you!

Willy, (accusing, angered): You didn't see him, did you?

Biff: I did see him!

Willy: What'd you insult him or something? You insulted him, didn't you?

Biff: Listen, will you let me out of it, will you just let me out of it!

Happy: What the hell!

Willy: Tell me what happened!

Biff, (to Happy*):* I can't talk to him!

A single trumpet note jars the ear. The light of green leaves stains the house, which holds the air of night and a dream. Young Bernard *enters and knocks on the door of the house.*

Young Bernard, (frantically): Mrs. Loman, Mrs. Loman!

    Happy: Tell him what happened!

    Biff, (to Happy*):* Shut up and leave me alone!

    Willy: No, no! You had to go and flunk math!

    Biff: What math? What're you talking about?

Young Bernard: Mrs. Loman, Mrs. Loman!

    Linda *appears in the house, as of old.*

    Willy, (wildly): Math, math, math!

    Biff: Take it easy, Pop!

Young Bernard: Mrs. Loman!

    Willy, (furiously): If you hadn't flunked you'd've been set by now!

    Biff: Now, look, I'm gonna tell you what happened, and you're going to listen to me.

Young Bernard: Mrs. Loman!

    Biff: I waited six hours—

    Happy: What the hell are you saying?

    Biff: I kept sending in my name but he wouldn't see me. So finally he . . . *(He continues unheard as light fades low on the restaurant.)*

Young Bernard: Biff flunked math!

    Linda: No!

Young Bernard: Birnbaum flunked him! They won't graduate him!

    Linda: But they have to. He's gotta go to the university. Where is he? Biff! Biff!

Young Bernard: No, he left. He went to Grand Central.

    Linda: Grand— You mean he went to Boston!

Young Bernard: Is Uncle Willy in Boston?

    Linda: Oh, maybe Willy can talk to the teacher. Oh, the poor, poor boy!

    Light on house area snaps out.

    Biff, (at the table, now audible, holding up a gold fountain pen): . . . so I'm washed up with Oliver, you understand? Are you listening to me?

    Willy, (at a loss): Yeah, sure. If you hadn't flunked—

    Biff: Flunked what? What're you talking about?

    Willy: Don't blame everything on me! I didn't flunk math— you did! What pen?

Happy: That was awful dumb, Biff, a pen like that is worth—

Willy, (seeing the pen for the first time): You took Oliver's pen?

Biff, (weakening): Dad, I just explained it to you.

Willy: You stole Bill Oliver's fountain pen!

Biff: I didn't exactly steal it! That's just what I've been explaining to you!

Happy: He had it in his hand and just then Oliver walked in, so he got nervous and stuck it in his pocket!

Willy: My God, Biff!

Biff: I never intended to do it, Dad!

Operator's Voice: Standish Arms, good evening!

Willy, (shouting): I'm not in my room!

Biff, (frightened): Dad, what's the matter? *(He and Happy stand up.)*

Operator: Ringing Mr. Loman for you!

Willy: I'm not there, stop it!

Biff, (horrified, gets down on one knee before Willy): Dad, I'll make good, I'll make good. *(Willy tries to get to his feet. Biff holds him down.)* Sit down now.

Willy: No, you're no good, you're no good for anything.

Biff: I am, Dad, I'll find something else, you understand? Now don't worry about anything. *(He holds up Willy's face):* Talk to me, dad.

Operator: Mr. Loman does not answer. Shall I page him?

Willy, (attempting to stand, as though to rush and silence the Operator): No, no, no!

Happy: He'll strike something, Pop.

Willy: No, no . . .

Biff, (desperately, standing over Willy): Pop, listen! Listen to me! I'm telling you something good. Oliver talked to his partner about the Florida idea. You listening? He—he talked to his partner, and he came to me . . . I'm going to be all right, you hear? Dad, listen to me, he said it was just a question of the amount!

Willy: Then you . . . got it?

Happy: He's gonna be terrific, Pop!

Willy, (trying to stand): Then you got it, haven't you? You got it! You got it!

Biff, (agonized, holds Willy down): No, no. Look, Pop. I'm supposed to have lunch with them tomorrow. I'm just telling you this so you'll know that I can still make an impression, Pop. And I'll make good somewhere, but I can't go tomorrow, see?

Willy: Why not? You simply—

Biff: But the pen, Pop!

Willy: You give it to him and tell him it was an oversight!

Happy: Sure, have lunch tomorrow!

Biff: I can't say that—

Willy: You were doing a crossword puzzle and accidentally used his pen!

Biff: Listen, kid, I took those balls years ago, now I walk in with his fountain pen? That clinches it, don't you see? I can't face him like that! I'll try elsewhere.

Page's Voice: Paging Mr. Loman!

Willy: Don't you want to be anything?

Biff: Pop, how can I go back?

Willy: You don't want to be anything, is that what's behind it?

Biff, (now angry at Willy *for not crediting his sympathy):* Don't take it that way! You think it was easy walking into that office after what I'd done to him? A team of horses couldn't have dragged me back to Bill Oliver!

Willy: Then why'd you go?

Biff: Why did I go? Why did I go! Look at you! Look at what's become of you!

Off left, The Woman *laughs.*

Willy: Biff, you're going to go to that lunch tomorrow, or—

Biff: I can't go. I've got no appointment!

Happy: Biff, for . . . !

Willy: Are you spiting me?

Biff: Don't take it that way! Goddammit!

Willy, (strikes Biff *and falters away from the table):* You rotten little louse! Are you spiting me?

The Woman: Someone's at the door, Willy!

Biff: I'm no good, can't you see what I am?

Happy, (separating them): Hey, you're in a restaurant! Now cut it out, both of you! *(The girls enter.)* Hello, girls, sit down.

The Woman *laughs, off left.*

Miss Forsythe: I guess we might as well. This is Letta.

The Woman: Willy, are you going to wake up?

Biff, (ignoring Willy*):* How're ya, miss, sit down. What do you drink?

Miss Forsythe: Letta might not be able to stay long.

Letta: I gotta get up very early tomorrow. I got jury duty. I'm so excited! Were you fellows ever on a jury?

Biff: No, but I been in front of them! *(The girls laugh.)* This is my father.

Letta: Isn't he cute? Sit down with us, Pop.

Happy: Sit him down, Biff!

Biff, (going to him): Come on, slugger, drink us under the table. To hell with it! Come on, sit down, pal.

On Biff's *last insistence,* Willy *is about to sit.*

The Woman, (now urgently): Willy, are you going to answer the door!

The Woman's call pulls Willy *back. He starts right, befuddled.*

> *Biff:* Hey, where are you going?
> *Willy:* Open the door.
> *Biff:* The door?
> *Willy:* The washroom . . . the door . . . where's the door?
> *Biff,* (leading Willy to the left): Just go straight down.

Willy *moves left.*

> *The Woman:* Willy, Willy, are you going to get up, get up, get up, get up?

Willy *exits left.*

> *Letta:* I think it's sweet you bring your daddy along.
> *Miss Forsythe:* Oh, he isn't really your father!
> *Biff,* (at left, turning to her resentfully): Miss Forsythe, you've just seen a prince walk by. A fine, troubled prince. A hardworking, unappreciated prince. A pal, you understand? A good companion. Always for his boys.
> *Letta:* That's so sweet.
> *Happy:* Well, girls, what's the program? We're wasting time. Come on, Biff. Gather round. Where would you like to go?
> *Biff:* Why don't you do something for him?
> *Happy:* Me!
> *Biff:* Don't you give a damn for him, Hap?
> *Happy:* What're you talking about? I'm the one who—
> *Biff:* I sense it, you don't give a good goddam about him. (He takes the rolled-up hose from his pocket and puts it on the table in front of Happy.) Look what I found in the cellar, for Christ's sake. How can you bear to let it go on?
> *Happy:* Me? Who goes away? Who runs off and—
> *Biff:* Yeah, but he doesn't mean anything to you. You could help him—I can't! Don't you understand what I'm talking about? He's going to kill himself, don't you know that?
> *Happy:* Don't I know it! Me!
> *Biff:* Hap, help him! Jesus . . . help him . . . Help me, help me, I can't bear to look at his face! (Ready to weep, he hurries out, up right.)
> *Happy,* (starting after him): Where are you going?
> *Miss Forsythe:* What's he so mad about?
> *Happy:* Come on, girls, we'll catch up with him.
> *Miss Forsythe,* (as Happy pushes her out): Say, I don't like that temper of his!
> *Happy:* He's just a little overstrung, he'll be all right!

Willy, *(off left, as* The Woman *laughs):* Don't answer! Don't answer!

Letta: Don't you want to tell your father—

Happy: No, that's not my father. He's just a guy. Come on, we'll catch Biff, and, honey, we're going to paint this town! Stanley, where's the check! Hey, Stanley!

They exit. Stanley *looks toward left.*

Stanley, *(calling to* Happy *indignantly):* Mr. Loman! Mr. Loman!

Stanley *picks up a chair and follows them off. Knocking is heard off left.* The Woman *enters, laughing.* Willy *follows her. She is in a black slip; he is buttoning his shirt. Raw, sensuous music accompanies their speech.*

Willy: Will you stop laughing? Will you stop?

The Woman: Aren't you going to answer the door? He'll wake the whole hotel.

Willy: I'm not expecting anybody.

The Woman: Whyn't you have another drink, honey, and stop being so damn self-centered?

Willy: I'm so lonely.

The Woman: You know you ruined me, Willy? From now on, whenever you come to the office, I'll see that you go right through to the buyers. No waiting at my desk any more, Willy. You ruined me.

Willy: That's nice of you to say that.

The Woman: Gee, you are self-centered! Why so sad? You are the saddest, self-centeredest soul I ever did see-saw. *(She laughs. He kisses her.)* Come on inside, drummer boy. It's silly to be dressing in the middle of the night. *(As knocking is heard):* Aren't you going to answer the door?

Willy: They're knocking on the wrong door.

The Woman: But I felt the knocking. And he heard us talking in here. Maybe the hotel's on fire!

Willy, *(his terror rising):* It's a mistake.

The Woman: Then tell him to go away!

Willy: There's nobody there.

The Woman: It's getting on my nerves, Willy. There's somebody standing out there and it's getting on my nerves!

Willy, *(pushing her away from him):* All right, stay in the bathroom here, and don't come out. I think there's a law in Massachusetts about it, so don't come out. It may be that new room clerk. He looked very mean. So don't come out. It's a mistake, there's no fire.

The knocking is heard again. He takes a few steps away from her, and she vanishes into the wing. The light follows him, and now he is facing Young Biff, *who carries a suitcase.* Biff *steps toward him. The music is gone.*

Biff: Why didn't you answer?

Willy: Biff! What are you doing in Boston?

Biff: Why didn't you answer? I've been knocking for five minutes, I called you on the phone—

Willy: I just heard you. I was in the bathroom and had the door shut. Did anything happen home?

Biff: Dad—I let you down.

Willy: What do you mean?

Biff: Dad . . .

Willy: Biffo, what's this about? *(Putting his arm around Biff)*: Come on, let's go downstairs and get you a malted.

Biff: Dad, I flunked math.

Willy: Not for the term?

Biff: The term. I haven't got enough credits to graduate.

Willy: You mean to say Bernard wouldn't give you the answers?

Biff: He did, he tried, but I only got a sixty-one.

Willy: And they wouldn't give you four points?

Biff: Birnbaum refused absolutely. I begged him, Pop, but he won't give me those points. You gotta talk to him before they close the school. Because if he saw the kind of man you are, and you just talked to him in your way, I'm sure he'd come through for me. The class came right before practice, see, and I didn't go enough. Would you talk to him? He'd like you, Pop. You know the way you could talk.

Willy: You're on. We'll drive right back.

Biff: Oh, Dad, good work! I'm sure he'll change it for you!

Willy: Go downstairs and tell the clerk I'm checkin' out. Go right down.

Biff: Yes, sir! See, the reason he hates me, Pop—one day he was late for class so I got up at the blackboard and imitated him. I crossed my eyes and talked with a lithp.

Willy, (laughing): You did? The kids like it?

Biff: They nearly died laughing!

Willy: Yeah? What'd you do?

Biff: The thquare root of thixthy twee is . . . *(Willy bursts out laughing; Biff joins him.)* And in the middle of it he walked in!

Willy *laughs and* The Woman *joins in offstage.*

Willy, (without hesitation): Hurry downstairs and—

Biff: Somebody in there?

Willy: No, that was next door.

The Woman *laughs offstage.*

Biff: Somebody got in your bathroom!

Willy: No, it's the next room, there's a party—

The Woman, (enters, laughing. She lisps this): Can I come in? There's something in the bathtub, Willy, and it's moving!

Willy *looks at* Biff, *who is staring open-mouthed and horrified at* The Woman.

Willy: Ah—you better go back to your room. They must be finished painting by now. They're painting her room so I let her take a shower here. Go back, go back . . . *(He pushes her.)*

The Woman, (resisting): But I've got to get dressed, Willy, I can't—

Willy: Get out of here! Go back, go back . . . *(Suddenly striving for the ordinary):* This is Miss Francis, Biff, she's a buyer. They're painting her room. Go back, Miss Francis, go back . . .

The Woman: But my clothes, I can't go out naked in the hall!

Willy, (pushing her offstage): Get outa here! Go back, go back!

Biff *slowly sits down on his suitcase as the argument continues offstage.*

The Woman: Where's my stockings? You promised me stockings, Willy!

Willy: I have no stockings here!

The Woman: You had two boxes of size nine sheers for me, and I want them!

Willy: Here, for God's sake, will you get outa here!

The Woman, (enters holding a box of stockings): I just hope there's nobody in the hall. That's all I hope. *(To* Biff): Are you football or baseball?

Biff: Football.

The Woman, (angry, humiliated): That's me too. G'night. *(She snatches her clothes from* Willy, *and walks out.)*

Willy, (after a pause): Well, better get going. I want to get to the school first thing in the morning. Get my suits out of the closet. I'll get my valise. *(*Biff *doesn't move.)* What's the matter? *(*Biff *remains motionless, tears falling.)* She's a buyer. Buys for J. H. Simmons. She lives down the hall— they're painting. You don't imagine— *(He breaks off. After a pause):* Now listen, pal, she's just a buyer. She sees merchandise in her room and they have to keep it looking just so . . . *(Pause. Assuming command):* All right, get my suits. *(*Biff *doesn't move.)* Now stop crying and do as I say. I gave you an order. Biff, I gave you an order! Is that what you do when I give you an order? How dare you cry! *(Putting his arm around* Biff): Now look, Biff, when you grow up you'll understand about these things. You mustn't—you mustn't overemphasize a thing like this. I'll see Birnbaum first thing in the morning.

Biff: Never mind.

Willy, (getting down beside Biff): Never mind! He's going to give you those points. I'll see to it.

   Biff: He wouldn't listen to you.

Willy: He certainly will listen to me. You need those points for the U. of Virginia.

   Biff: I'm not going there.

Willy: Heh? If I can't get him to change that mark you'll make it up in summer school. You've got all summer to—

Biff, (his weeping breaking from him): Dad . . .

Willy, (infected by it): Oh, my boy . . .

   Biff: Dad . . .

Willy: She's nothing to me, Biff. I was lonely, I was terribly lonely.

   Biff: You—you gave her Mama's stockings! *(His tears break through and he rises to go.)*

Willy, (grabbing for Biff): I gave you an order!

   Biff: Don't touch me, you—liar!

Willy: Apologize for that!

   Biff: You fake! You phony little fake! You fake! *(Overcome, he turns quickly and weeping fully goes out with his suitcase. Willy is left on the floor on his knees.)*

Willy: I gave you an order! Biff, come back here or I'll beat you! Come back here! I'll whip you!

Stanley *comes quickly in from the right and stands in front of* Willy.

   Willy, (shouts at Stanley): I gave you an order . . .

Stanley: Hey, let's pick it up, pick it up, Mr. Loman. *(He helps* Willy *to his feet.)* Your boys left with the chippies. They said they'll see you home.

A second waiter watches some distance away.

   Willy: But we were supposed to have dinner together.

Music is heard, Willy's *theme.*

   Stanley: Can you make it?

   Willy: I'll—sure, I can make it. *(Suddenly concerned about his clothes):* Do I—I look all right?

Stanley: Sure, you look all right. *(He flicks a speck off* Willy's *lapel.)*

   Willy: Here—here's a dollar.

Stanley: Oh, your son paid me. It's all right.

Willy, (putting it in Stanley's *hand):* No, take it. You're a good boy.

Stanley: Oh, no, you don't have to . . .

   Willy: Here—here's some more, I don't need it any more. *(After a slight pause):* Tell me—is there a seed store in the neighborhood?

Stanley: Seeds? You mean like to plant?

As Willy *turns,* Stanley *slips the money back into his jacket pocket.*

> *Willy:* Yes. Carrots, peas . . .
>
> *Stanley:* Well, there's hardware stores on Sixth Avenue, but it may be too late now.
>
> *Willy, (anxiously):* Oh, I'd better hurry. I've got to get some seeds. *(He starts off to the right.)* I've got to get some seeds, right away. Nothing's planted. I don't have a thing in the ground.

Willy *hurries out as the light goes down.* Stanley *moves over to the right after him, watches him off. The other waiter has been staring at* Willy.

> *Stanley, (to the waiter):* Well, whatta you looking at?

The waiter picks up the chairs and moves off right. Stanley *takes the table and follows him. The light fades on this area. There is a long pause, the sound of the flute coming over. The light gradually rises on the kitchen, which is empty.* Happy *appears at the door of the house, followed by* Biff. Happy *is carrying a large bunch of long-stemmed roses. He enters the kitchen, looks around for* Linda. *Not seeing her, he turns to* Biff, *who is just outside the house door, and makes a gesture with his hands, indicating "Not here, I guess." He looks into the living-room and freezes. Inside,* Linda, *unseen, is seated,* Willy's *coat on her lap. She rises ominously and quietly and moves toward* Happy, *who backs up into the kitchen, afraid.*

> *Happy:* Hey, what're you doing up? (Linda *says nothing but moves toward him implacably.)* Where's Pop? *(He keeps backing to the right, and now* Linda *is in full view in the doorway to the living-room.)* Is he sleeping?
>
> *Linda:* Where were you?
>
> *Happy, (trying to laugh it off):* We met two girls, Mom, very fine types. Here, we brought you some flowers. *(Offering them to her):* Put them in your room, Ma.

She knocks them to the floor at Biff's *feet. He has now come inside and closed the door behind him. She stares at* Biff, *silent.*

> *Happy:* Now what'd you do that for? Mom, I want you to have some flowers—
>
> *Linda, (cutting* Happy *off, violently to* Biff): Don't you care whether he lives or dies?
>
> *Happy, (going to the stairs):* Come upstairs, Biff.
>
> *Biff, (with a flare of disgust, to* Happy): Go away from me! *(To* Linda): What do you mean, lives or dies? Nobody's dying around here, pal.
>
> *Linda:* Get out of my sight! Get out of here!
>
> *Biff:* I wanna see the boss.
>
> *Linda:* You're not going near him!

Biff: Where is he? *(He moves into the living-room and* Linda *follows.)*

Linda, (shouting after Biff*):* You invite him for dinner. He looks forward to it all day—(Biff *appears in his parents' bedroom, looks around, and exits)*—and then you desert him there. There's no stranger you'd do that to!

Happy: Why? He had a swell time with us. Listen, when I—(Linda *comes back into the kitchen)*—desert him I hope I don't outlive the day!

Linda: Get out of here!

Happy: Now look, Mom . . .

Linda: Did you have to go to women tonight? You and your lousy rotten whores!

Biff *re-enters the kitchen.*

Happy: Mom, all we did was follow Biff around trying to cheer him up! *(To* Biff*):* Boy, what a night you gave me!

Linda: Get out of here, both of you, and don't come back! I don't want you tormenting him any more. Go on now, get your things together! *(To* Biff*):* You can sleep in his apartment. *(She starts to pick up the flowers and stops herself.)* Pick up this stuff, I'm not your maid any more. Pick it up, you bum, you!

Happy *turns his back to her in refusal.* Biff *slowly moves over and gets down on his knees, picking up the flowers.*

Linda: You're a pair of animals! Not one, not another living soul would have had the cruelty to walk out on that man in a restaurant!

Biff, (not looking at her): Is that what he said?

Linda: He didn't have to say anything. He was so humiliated he nearly limped when he came in.

Happy: But, Mom, he had a great time with us—

Biff, (cutting him off violently): Shut up!

Without another word, Happy *goes upstairs.*

Linda: You! You didn't even go in to see if he was all right!

Biff, (still on the floor in front of Linda, *the flowers in his hand; with self-loathing):* No. Didn't. Didn't do a damned thing. How do you like that, heh? Left him babbling in a toilet.

Linda: You louse. You . . .

Biff: Now you hit it on the nose! *(He gets up, throws the flowers in the wastebasket.)* The scum of the earth, and you're looking at him!

Linda: Get out of here!

Biff: I gotta talk to the boss, Mom. Where is he?

Linda: You're not going near him. Get out of this house!

Biff, (with absolute assurance, determination): No. We're gonna have an abrupt conversation, him and me.

Linda: You're not talking to him!

Hammering is heard from outside the house, off right. Biff turns toward the noise.

Linda, (suddenly pleading): Will you please leave him alone?

Biff: What's he doing out there?

Linda: He's planting the garden!

Biff, (quietly): Now? Oh, my God!

Biff *moves outside,* Linda *following. The light dies down on them and comes up on the center of the apron as* Willy *walks into it. He is carrying a flashlight, a hoe, and a handful of seed packets. He raps the top of the hoe sharply to fix it firmly, and then moves to the left, measuring off the distance with his foot. He holds the flashlight to look at the seed packets, reading off the instructions. He is in the blue of night.*

Willy: Carrots . . . quarter-inch apart. Rows . . . one-foot rows. *(He measures it off.)* One foot. *(He puts down a package and measures off.)* Beets. *(He puts down another package and measures again.)* Lettuce. *(He reads the package, puts it down.)* One foot—*(He breaks off as* Ben *appears at the right and moves slowly down to him.)* What a proposition, ts, ts. Terrific, terrific. 'Cause she's suffered, Ben, the woman has suffered. You understand me? A man can't go out the way he came in, Ben, a man has to to add up to something. You can't, you can't—*(Ben moves toward him as though to interrupt.)* You gotta consider, now. Don't answer so quick. Remember, it's a guaranteed twenty-thousand-dollar proposition. Now look, Ben, I want you to go through the ins and outs of this thing with me. I've got nobody to talk to, Ben, and the woman has suffered, you hear me?

Ben, (standing still, considering): What's the proposition?

Willy: It's twenty thousand dollars on the barrelhead. Guaranteed, gilt-edged, you understand?

Ben: You don't want to make a fool of yourself. They might not honor the policy.

Willy: How can they dare refuse? Didn't I work like a coolie to meet every premium on the nose? And now they don't pay off? Impossible!

Ben: It's called a cowardly thing, William.

Willy: Why? Does it take more guts to stand here the rest of my life ringing up a zero?

Ben, (yielding): That's a point, William. *(He moves, thinking, turns.)* And twenty thousand—that *is* something one can feel with the hand, it is there.

Willy, (now assured, with rising power): Oh, Ben, that's the whole beauty of it! I see it like a diamond, shining in the dark, hard and rough, that I can pick up and touch in my hand. Not like—like an appointment! This would not be another damned-fool appointment, Ben, and it changes all the aspects. Because he thinks I'm nothing, see, and so he spites me. But the funeral— *(Straightening up):* Ben, that funeral will be massive! They'll come from Maine, Massachusetts, Vermont, New Hampshire! All the old-timers with the strange license plates—that boy will be thunder-struck, Ben, because he never realized—I am known! Rhode Island, New York, New Jersey—I am known, Ben, and he'll see it with his eyes once and for all. He'll see what I am, Ben! He's in for a shock, that boy!

Ben, (coming down to the edge of the garden): He'll call you a coward.

Willy, (suddenly fearful): No, that would be terrible.

Ben: Yes. And a damned fool.

Willy: No, no, he mustn't, I won't have that! *(He is broken and desperate.)*

Ben: He'll hate you, William.

The gay music of the Boys is heard.

Willy: Oh, Ben, how do we get back to all the great times? Used to be so full of light, and comradeship, the sleigh-riding in winter, and the ruddiness on his cheeks. And always some kind of good news coming up, always something nice coming up ahead. And never even let me carry the valises in the house, and simonizing, simonizing that little red car! Why, why can't I give him something and not have him hate me?

Ben: Let me think about it. *(He glances at his watch.)* I still have a little time. Remarkable proposition, but you've got to be sure you're not making a fool of yourself.

Ben *drifts off upstage and goes out of sight.* Biff *comes down from the left.*

Willy, (suddenly conscious of Biff, *turns and looks up at him, then begins picking up the packages of seeds in confusion):* Where the hell is that seed? *(Indignantly):* You can't see nothing out here! They boxed in the whole goddam neighborhood!

Biff: There are people all around here. Don't you realize that?

Willy: I'm busy. Don't bother me.

Biff, (taking the hoe from Willy): I'm saying good-by to you, Pop. *(Willy looks at him, silent, unable to move.)* I'm not coming back any more.

Willy: You're not going to see Oliver tomorrow?

Biff: I've got no appointment, Dad.

Willy: He put his arm around you, and you've got no appointment?

Biff: Pop, get this now, will you? Everytime I've left it's been a fight that sent me out of here. Today I realized something about myself and I tried to explain it to you and I—I think I'm just not smart enough to make any sense out of it for you. To hell with whose fault it is or anything like that. *(He takes* Willy's *arm.)* Let's just wrap it up, heh? Come on in, we'll tell Mom. *(He gently tries to pull* Willy *to left.)*

Willy, (frozen, immobile, with guilt in his voice): No, I don't want to see her.

Biff: Come on! *(He pulls again, and* Willy *tries to pull away.)*

Willy, (highly nervous): No, no, I don't want to see her.

Biff, (tries to look into Willy's *face, as if to find the answer there):* Why don't you want to see her?

Willy, (more harshly now): Don't bother me, will you?

Biff: What do you mean, you don't want to see her? You don't want them calling you yellow, do you? This isn't your fault; it's me, I'm a bum. Now come inside! (Willy *strains to get away.)* Did you hear what I said to you?

Willy *pulls away and quickly goes by himself into the house.* Biff *follows.*

Linda, (to Willy): Did you plant, dear?

Biff, (at the door, to Linda): All right, we had it out. I'm going and I'm not writing any more.

Linda, (going to Willy *in the kitchen):* I think that's the best way, dear. 'Cause there's no use drawing it out, you'll just never get along.

Willy *doesn't respond.*

Biff: People ask where I am and what I'm doing, you don't know, and you don't care. That way it'll be off your mind and you can start brightening up again. All right? That clears it, doesn't it? (Willy *is silent, and* Biff *goes to him.)* You gonna wish me luck, scout? *(He extends his hand.)* What do you say?

Linda: Shake his hand, Willy.

Willy, (turning to her, seething with hurt): There's no necessity to mention the pen at all, y'know.

Biff, (gently): I've got no appointment, Dad.

Willy, (erupting fiercely): He put his arm around . . . ?

Biff: Dad, you're never going to see what I am, so what's the use of arguing? If I strike oil I'll send you a check. Meantime forget I'm alive.

Willy, (to Linda): Spite, see?

Biff: Shake hands, Dad.

Willy: Not my hand.

Biff: I was hoping not to go this way.

Willy: Well, this is the way you're going. Good-by.

Biff *looks at him a moment, then turns sharply and goes to the stairs.*

Willy, (stops him with): May you rot in hell if you leave this house!

Biff, (turning): Exactly what is it that you want from me?

Willy: I want you to know, on the train, in the mountains, in the valleys, wherever you go, that you cut down your life for spite!

Biff: No, no.

Willy: Spite, spite, is the word for your undoing! And when you're down and out, remember what did it. When you're rotting somewhere beside the railroad tracks, remember, and don't you dare blame it on me!

Biff: I'm not blaming it on you!

Willy: I won't take the rap for this, you hear?

Happy *comes down the stairs and stands on the bottom step, watching.*

Biff: That's just what I'm telling you!

Willy, (sinking into a chair at the table, with full accusation): You're trying to put a knife in me—don't think I don't know what you're doing!

Biff: All right, phony! Then let's lay it on the line. *(He whips the rubber tube out of his pocket and puts it on the table.)*

Happy: You crazy—

Linda: Biff! *(She moves to grab the hose, but* Biff *holds it down with his hand.)*

Biff: Leave it there! Don't move it!

Willy, (not looking at it): What is that?

Biff: You know goddam well what that is.

Willy, (caged, wanting to escape): I never saw that.

Biff: You saw it. The mice didn't bring it into the cellar! What is this supposed to do, make a hero out of you? This supposed to make me sorry for you?

Willy: Never heard of it.

Biff: There'll be no pity for you, you hear it? No pity!

Willy, (to Linda): You hear the spite!

Biff: No, you're going to hear the truth—what you are and what I am!

Linda: Stop it!

Willy: Spite!

Happy, (coming down toward Biff): You cut it now!

Biff, (to Happy): The man don't know who we are! The man is gonna know! *(To* Willy): We never told the truth for ten minutes in this house!

Happy: We always told the truth!

Biff, (turning on him): You big blow, are you the assistant buyer? You're one of the two assistants to the assistant, aren't you?

Happy: Well, I'm practically—

Biff: You're practically full of it! We all are! And I'm through with it. *(To* Willy): Now hear this, Willy, this is me.

Willy: I know you!

Biff: You know why I had no address for three months? I stole a suit in Kansas City and I was in jail. *(To* Linda, *who is sobbing):* Stop crying. I'm through with it.

Linda *turns away from them, her hands covering her face.*

Willy: I suppose that's my fault!

Biff: I stole myself out of every good job since high school!

Willy: And whose fault is that?

Biff: And I never got anywhere because you blew me so full of hot air I could never stand taking orders from anybody! That's whose fault it is!

Willy: I hear that!

Linda: Don't, Biff!

Biff: It's goddam time you heard that! I had to be boss big shot in two weeks, and I'm through with it!

Willy: Then hang yourself! For spite, hang yourself!

Biff: No! Nobody's hanging himself, Willy! I ran down eleven flights with a pen in my hand today. And suddenly I stopped, you hear me? And in the middle of that office building, do you hear this? I stopped in the middle of that building and I saw—the sky. I saw the things that I love in this world. The work and the food and time to sit and smoke. And I looked at the pen and said to myself, what the hell am I grabbing this for? Why am I trying to become what I don't want to be? What am I doing in an office, making a contemptuous, begging fool of myself, when all I want is out there, waiting for me the minute I say I know who I am! Why can't I say that, Willy? *(He tries to make* Willy *face him, but* Willy *pulls away and moves to the left.)*

Willy, (with hatred, threateningly): The door of your life is wide open!

Biff: Pop! I'm a dime a dozen, and so are you!

Willy, (turning on him now in an uncontrolled outburst): I am not a dime a dozen! I am Willy Loman, and you are Biff Loman!

Biff *starts for* Willy, *but is blocked by* Happy. *In his fury,* Biff *seems on the verge of attacking his father.*

Biff: I am not a leader of men, Willy, and neither are you. You were never anything but a hard-working drummer who landed in the ash can like all the rest of them! I'm one dollar an hour, Willy! I tried seven states and couldn't raise it. A buck an hour! Do you gather my meaning? I'm not bringing home any prizes any more, and you're going to stop waiting for me to bring them home!

Willy, (directly to Biff*):* You vengeful, spiteful mut!

Biff *breaks from* Happy. Willy, *in fright, starts up the stairs.* Biff *grabs him.*

Biff, (at the peak of his fury): Pop, I'm nothing! I'm nothing, Pop. Can't you understand that? There's no spite in it any more. I'm just what I am, that's all.

Biff's *fury has spent itself, and he breaks down, sobbing, holding on to* Willy, *who dumbly fumbles for* Biff's *face.*

Willy, (astonished): What're you doing? What're you doing? *(To* Linda*):* Why is he crying?

Biff, (crying, broken): Will you let me go, for Christ's sake? Will you take that phony dream and burn it before something happens? *(Struggling to contain himself, he pulls away and moves to the stairs.)* I'll go in the morning. Put him—put him to bed. *(Exhausted,* Biff *moves up the stairs to his room.)*

Willy, (after a long pause, astonished, elevated): Isn't that—isn't that remarkable? Biff—he likes me!

Linda: He loves you, Willy!

Happy, (deeply moved): Always did, Pop.

Willy: Oh, Biff! *(Staring wildly):* He cried! Cried to me. *(He is choking with his love, and now cries out his promise):* That boy—that boy is going to be magnificent!

Ben *appears in the light just outside the kitchen.*

Ben: Yes, outstanding, with twenty thousand behind him.

Linda, (sensing the racing of his mind, fearfully, carefully): Now come to bed, Willy. It's all settled now.

Willy, (finding it difficult not to rush out of the house): Yes, we'll sleep. Come on. Go to sleep, Hap.

Ben: And it does take a great kind of a man to crack the jungle.

In accents of dread, Ben's *idyllic music starts up.*

Happy, (his arm around Linda*):* I'm getting married, Pop, don't forget it. I'm changing everything. I'm gonna run that department before the year is up. You'll see, Mom. *(He kisses her.)*

Ben: The jungle is dark but full of diamonds, Willy.

Willy *turns, moves, listening to* Ben.

Linda: Be good. You're both good boys, just act that way, that's all.

Happy: 'Night, Pop. *(He goes upstairs.)*

Linda, (to Willy*):* Come, dear.

  Ben, (with greater force): One must go in to fetch a diamond out.

Willy, (to Linda, *as he moves slowly along the edge of the kitchen, toward the door):* I just want to get settled down, Linda. Let me sit alone for a little.

Linda, (almost uttering her fear): I want you upstairs.

Willy, (taking her in his arms): In a few minutes, Linda. I couldn't sleep right now. Go on, you look awful tired. *(He kisses her.)*

  Ben: Not like an appointment at all. A diamond is rough and hard to the touch.

Willy: Go on now. I'll be right up.

Linda: I think this is the only way, Willy.

Willy: Sure, it's the best thing.

  Ben: Best thing!

Willy: The only way. Everything is gonna be—go on, kid, get to bed. You look so tired.

Linda: Come right up.

Willy: Two minutes.

Linda *goes into the living-room, then reappears in her bedroom.* Willy *moves just outside the kitchen door.*

Willy: Loves me. *(Wonderingly):* Always loved me. Isn't that a remarkable thing? Ben, he'll worship me for it!

  Ben, (with promise): It's dark there, but full of diamonds.

Willy: Can you imagine that magnificence with twenty thousand dollars in his pocket?

Linda, (calling from her room): Willy! Come up!

Willy, (calling into the kitchen): Yes! Yes. Coming! It's very smart, you realize that, don't you, sweetheart! Even Ben sees it. I gotta go, baby. 'By! 'By! *(Going over to* Ben, *almost dancing):* Imagine? When the mail comes he'll be ahead of Bernard again!

  Ben: A perfect proposition all around.

Willy: Did you see how he cried to me? Oh, if I could kiss him, Ben!

  Ben: Time, William, time!

Willy: Oh, Ben, I always knew one way or another we were gonna make it, Biff and I!

  Ben, (looking at his watch): The boat. We'll be late. *(He moves slowly off into the darkness.)*

Willy, (elegiacally, turning to the house): Now when you kick off, boy, I want a seventy-yard boot, and get right down the field under the ball, and when you hit, hit low and hit hard, because it's important, boy. *(He swings around and faces the audience.)* There's all kinds of important people in the stands, and the first thing you know . . . *(Suddenly realizing he is alone):* Ben! Ben, where do I . . . ? *(He makes a sudden movement of search.)* Ben, how do I . . . ?

Linda, *(calling):* Willy, you coming up?

Willy, *(uttering a gasp of fear, whirling about as if to quiet her):* Sh! *(He turns around as if to find his way; sounds, faces, voices, seem to be swarming in upon him and he flicks at them, crying),* Sh! Sh! *(Suddenly music, faint and high, stops him. It rises in intensity, almost to an unbearable scream. He goes up and down on his toes, and rushes off around the house.)* Shhh!

Linda: Willy?

There is no answer. Linda waits. Biff gets up off his bed. He is still in his clothes. Happy sits up. Biff stands listening.

Linda, *(with real fear):* Willy, answer me! Willy!

There is the sound of a car starting and moving away at full speed.

Linda: No!

Biff, *(rushing down the stairs):* Pop!

As the car speeds off, the music crashes down in a frenzy of sound, which becomes the soft pulsation of a single cello string. Biff slowly returns to his bedroom. He and Happy gravely don their jackets. Linda slowly walks out of her room. The music has developed into a dead march. The leaves of day are appearing over everything. Charley and Bernard, somberly dressed, appear and knock on the kitchen door. Biff and Happy slowly descend the stairs to the kitchen as Charley and Bernard enter. All stop a moment when Linda, in clothes of mourning, bearing a little bunch of roses, comes through the draped doorway into the kitchen. She goes to Charley and takes his arm. Now all move toward the audience, through the wall-line of the kitchen. At the limit of the apron, Linda lays down the flowers, kneels, and sits back on her heels. All stare down at the grave.

REQUIEM

Charley: It's getting dark, Linda.

Linda *doesn't react. She stares at the grave.*

Biff: How about it, Mom? Better get some rest, heh? They'll be closing the gate soon.

Linda *makes no move. Pause.*

Happy, *(deeply angered):* He had no right to do that. There was no necessity for it. We would've helped him.

Charley, (*grunting*): Hmmm.

    Biff: Come along, Mom.

    Linda: Why didn't anybody come?

Charley: It was a very nice funeral.

    Linda: But where are all the people he knew? Maybe they blame him.

Charley: Naa. It's a rough world, Linda. They wouldn't blame him.

    Linda: I can't understand it. At this time especially. First time in thirty-five years we were just about free and clear. He only needed a little salary. He was even finished with the dentist.

Charley: No man only needs a little salary.

    Linda: I can't understand it.

    Biff: There were a lot of nice days. When he'd come home from a trip; or on Sundays, making the stoop; finishing the cellar; putting on the new porch; when he built the extra bathroom; and put up the garage. You know something, Charley, there's more of him in that front stoop than in all the sales he ever made.

Charley: Yeah. He was a happy man with a batch of cement.

    Linda: He was so wonderful with his hands.

    Biff: He had the wrong dreams. All, all wrong.

Happy, (*almost ready to fight* Biff): Don't say that!

    Biff: He never knew who he was.

Charley, (*stopping* Happy's *movement and reply. To* Biff): Nobody dast blame this man. You don't understand: Willy was a salesman. And for a salesman, there is no rock bottom to the life. He don't put a bolt to a nut, he don't tell you the law or give you medicine. He's a man way out there in the blue, riding on a smile and a shoeshine. And when they start not smiling back—that's an earthquake. And then you get yourself a couple of spots on your hat, and you're finished. Nobody dast blame this man. A salesman is got to dream, boy. It comes with the territory.

    Biff: Charley, the man didn't know who he was.

Happy, (*infuriated*): Don't say that!

    Biff: Why don't you come with me, Happy?

Happy: I'm not licked that easily. I'm staying right in this city, and I'm gonna beat this racket! (*He looks at* Biff, *his chin set.*) The Loman Brothers!

    Biff: I know who I am, kid.

Happy: All right, boy. I'm gonna show you and everybody else that Willy Loman did not die in vain. He had a good dream. It's the only dream you can have—to come out number-one man. He fought it out here, and this is where I'm gonna win it for him.

Biff, (with a hopeless glance at Happy, bends toward his mother): Let's go, Mom.

Linda: I'll be with you in a minute. Go on, Charley. (He hesitates.) I want to, just for a minute. I never had a chance to say good-by.

Charley moves away, followed by Happy. Biff remains a slight distance up and left of Linda. She sits there, summoning herself. The flute begins, not far away, playing behind her speech.

Linda: Forgive me, dear. I can't cry. I don't know what it is, but I can't cry. I don't understand it. Why did you ever do that? Help me, Willy, I can't cry. It seems to me that you're just on another trip. I keep expecting you. Willy, dear, I can't cry. Why did you do it? I search and search and I search, and I can't undrstand it, Willy. I made the last payment on the house today. Today, dear. And there'll be nobody home. (A sob rises in her throat.) We're free and clear. (Sobbing more fully, released): We're free. (Biff comes slowly toward her.) We're free . . . We're free . . .

Biff lifts her to her feet and moves out up right with her in his arms. Linda sobs quietly. Bernard and Charley come together and follow them, followed by Happy. Only the music of the flute is left on the darkening stage as over the house the hard towers of the apartment buildings rise into sharp focus, and

THE CURTAIN FALLS

Further Reading

Huftel, Sheila. "Miller on Playwriting." *Arthur Miller: The Burning Glass.* New York: Citadel, 1965. 60–75. • Dennis Welland. "Death of a Salesman." *Miller: The Playwright.* 3rd ed. New York: Methuen, 1985. 36–53. • de Schweinitz, George. "*Death of a Salesman:* A Note on Epic and Tragedy." *Western Humanities Review* 14 (1960): 91–96. • Clark, Eleanor. Review. *Partisan Review* 16 (1949): 631–35. • Eisinger, Chester E. "Focus on Arthur Miller's *Death of Salesman:* The Wrong Dreams." *American Dreams, American Nightmares.* Ed. David Madden. Carbondale: Southern Illinois UP, 1970. 165–74. • Foster, Richard J. "Confusion and Tragedy: The Failure of Miller's *Salesman.*" *Two Modern American Tragedies: Reviews and Criticism of "Death of a Salesman" and "A Streetcar Named Desire."* Ed. John Hurrell. New York: Scribner's, 1961.

Arthur Miller's drama seems to bring two planes of experience together. On one hand, he is committed to a realistic and often unflattering portrayal of society, and his plays often show his impatience with the less humane aspects

of American capitalism. On the other hand, he shares a vision of life that links him with the Greek tragedians, whose characters were certainly not the sort of "common men" who inhabit the social world Miller sets out to explore. In "Tragedy and the Common Man," Miller discusses the elements of tragedy that link a character like Willy Loman to a character like Antigone.

Arthur Miller: On Personal Dignity and Tragedy

As a general rule, to which there may be exceptions unknown to me, I think the tragic feeling is evoked in us when we are in the presence of a character who is ready to lay down his life, if need be, to secure one thing—his sense of personal dignity. From Orestes to Hamlet, Medea to Macbeth, the underlying struggle is that of the individual attempting to gain his "rightful" position in his society.

Sometimes he is one who has been displaced from it, sometimes one who seeks to attain it for the first time, but the fateful wound from which the inevitable events spiral is the wound of indignity, and its dominant force is indignation. Tragedy, then, is the consequence of a man's total compulsion to evaluate himself justly.

In the sense of having been initiated by the hero himself, the tale always reveals what has been called his "tragic flaw," a failing that is not peculiar to grand or elevated characters. Nor is it necessarily a weakness. The flaw, or crack in the character, is really nothing—and need be nothing—but his inherent unwillingness to remain passive in the face of what he conceives to be a challenge to his dignity, his image of his rightful status. Only the passive, only those who accept their lot without active retaliation, are "flawless." Most of us are in that category.

But there are among us today, as there always have been, those who act against the scheme of things that degrades them, and in the process of action everything we have accepted out of fear or insensitivity or ignorance is shaken before us and examined, and from this total onslaught by an individual against the seemingly stable cosmos surrounding us—from this total examination of the "unchangeable" environment—comes the terror and the fear that is classically associated with tragedy.

SAM SHEPARD

(b. 1943)

TRUE WEST

CHARACTERS

Austin: early thirties, light blue sports shirt, light tan cardigan sweater, clean blue jeans, white tennis shoes

Lee: his older brother, early forties, filthy white t-shirt, tattered brown overcoat covered with dust, dark blue baggy suit pants from the Salvation Army, pink suede belt, pointed black forties dress shoes scuffed up, holes in the soles, no socks, no hat, long pronounced sideburns, "Gene Vincent" hairdo, 2 days' growth of beard, bad teeth

Saul Kimmer: late forties, Hollywood producer, pink and white flower print sports shirt, white sports coat with matching polyester slacks, black and white loafers

Mom: early sixties, mother of the brothers, small woman, conservative white skirt and matching jacket, red shoulder bag, two pieces of matching red luggage

SET

All nine scenes take place on the same set; a kitchen and adjoining alcove of an older home in a Southern California suburb, about 40 miles east of L.A. The kitchen takes up the majority of the playing area to stage left *[from the actor's point of view, facing the audience]*. The kitchen consists of a sink, upstage center, surrounded by counter space, a wall telephone, cupboards and a small window just above it bordered by neat yellow curtains. Stage left of sink is a stove. Stage right, a refrigerator. The alcove adjoins the kitchen to stage right. There is no wall division or door to the alcove. It is open and easily accessible from the kitchen and defined only by the objects in it: A small round glass breakfast table mounted on white iron legs, Two matching white iron chairs set across from each other. The two exterior walls of the alcove which prescribe a corner in the upstage right are composed of many small windows beginning from a solid wall about three feet high and extending to the ceiling. The windows look out to bushes and citrus trees. The alcove is filled with all sorts of house plants in various pots, mostly Boston ferns hanging in planters at different levels. The floor of the alcove is composed of green synthetic grass.

All entrances and exits are made stage left from the kitchen. There is no door. The actors simply go off and come onto the playing area.

ACT I

Scene 1

Night, sound of crickets in dark, candlelight appears in alcove illuminating Austin seated at glass table hunched over a writing notebook, pen in hand, cigarette burning in ashtray, cup of coffee, typewriter on table, stacks of paper, candle burning on table, soft moonlight fills kitchen illuminating Lee, beer in hand, six pack on counter behind him, he's leaning against sink, mildly drunk, takes slug of beer.

Lee: So, Mom took off for Alaska huh?

Austin: Yeah.

Lee: Sorta' left you in charge.

Austin: Well, she knew I was coming down here so she offered me the place.

Lee: You keepin' the plants watered?

Austin: Yeah.

Lee: Keepin' the sink clean? She don't like even a single tea leaf in the sink ya' know.

Austin: *[Trying to concentrate on writing]* Yeah, I know.

[Pause.]

Lee: She gonna' be up there a long time?

Austin: I don't know.

Lee: Kinda' nice for you, huh? Whole place to yourself.

Austin: Yeah, it's great.

Lee: Ya' got crickets anyway. Tons a' crickets out there. *[Looks around kitchen]* Ya' got groceries? Coffee?

Austin: *[Looking up from writing]* What?

Lee: You got coffee?

Austin: Yeah.

Lee: At's good. *[Short pause]* Real coffee? From the bean?

Austin: Yeah. You want some?

Lee: Naw. I brought some uh—*[Motions to beer]*

Austin: Help yourself to whatever's—*[Motions to refrigerator]*

Lee: I will. Don't worry about me. I'm not the one to worry about.
I mean I can uh—*[Pause]* You always work by candlelight?

Austin: No—un—Not always.

Lee: Just sometimes?

Austin: *[Puts pen down, rubs his eyes]* Yeah. Sometimes it's soothing.

Lee: Isn't that what the old guys did?

Austin: What old guys?

Lee: The Forefathers. You know.

Austin: Forefathers?

Lee: Isn't that what they did? Candlelight burning into the night? Cabins in the wilderness.

Austin: *[Rubs hand through his hair]* I suppose.

Lee: I'm not botherin' you am I? I mean I don't wanna break into yer uh—concentration or nothin'.

Austin: No, it's all right.

Lee: That's good. I mean I realize that yer line a' work demands a lota' concentration.

Austin: It's okay.

Lee: You probably think that I'm not fully able to comprehend somethin' like that, huh?

Austin: Like what?

Lee: That stuff yer doin'. That art. You know. Whatever you call it.

Austin: It's just a little research.

Lee: You may not know it but I did a little art myself once.

Austin: You did?

Lee: Yeah! I did some a' that. I fooled around with it. No future in it.

Austin: What'd you do?

Lee: Never mind what I did! Just never mind about that. *[Pause]* It was ahead of its time.

[Pause.]

Austin: So, you went out to see the old man, huh?

Lee: Yeah, I seen him.

Austin: How's he doing?

Lee: Same. He's doin' just about the same.

Austin: I was down there too, you know.

Lee: What d'ya' want, an award? You want some kinda' metal? You were down there. He told me all about you.

Austin: What'd he say?

Lee: He told me. Don't worry.

[Pause.]

Austin: Well—

Lee: You don't have to say nothin'.

Austin: I wasn't.

Lee: Yeah, you were gonna' make somethin' up. Somethin' brilliant.

[Pause.]

Austin: You going to be down here very long, Lee?

Lee: Might be. Depends on a few things.

Austin: You got some friends down here?

Lee: [*Laughs*] I know a few people. Yeah.

Austin: Well, you can stay here as long as I'm here.

Lee: I don't need your permission do I?

Austin: No.

Lee: I mean she's my mother too, right?

Austin: Right.

Lee: She might've just as easily asked me to take care of her place as you.

Austin: That's right.

Lee: I mean I know how to water plants.

[Long pause.]

Austin: So you don't know how long you'll be staying then?

Lee: Depends mostly on houses, ya' know.

Austin: Houses?

Lee: Yeah. Houses. Electric devices. Stuff like that. I gotta' make a little tour first.

[Short pause.]

Austin: Lee, why don't you just try another neighborhood, all right?

Lee: [*Laughs*] What'sa' matter with this neighborhood? This is a great neighborhood. Lush. Good class a' people. Not many dogs.

Austin: Well, our uh—Our mother just happens to live here. That's all.

Lee: Nobody's gonna' know. All they know is somethin's missing. That's all. She'll never even hear about it. Nobody's gonna' know.

Austin: You're going to get picked up if you start walking around here at night.

Lee: Me? I'm gonna' git picked up? What about you? You stick out like a sore thumb. Look at you. You think yer regular lookin'?

Austin: I've got too much to deal with here to be worrying about—

Lee: Yer not gonna' have to worry about me! I've been doin' all right without you. I haven't been anywhere near you for five years! Now isn't that true?

Austin: Yeah.

Lee: So you don't have to worry about me. I'm a free agent.

Austin: All right.

Lee: Now all I wanna' do is borrow yer car.

Austin: No!

Lee: Just fer a day. One day.

Austin: No!

    Lee: I won't take it outside a twenty mile radius. I promise ya'. You can check the speedometer.

Austin: You're not borrowing my car! That's all there is to it.

[Pause.]

    Lee: Then I'll just take the damn thing.

Austin: Lee, look—I don't want any trouble, all right?

    Lee: That's a dumb line. That is a dumb fuckin' line. You git paid fer dreamin' up a line like that?

Austin: Look, I can give you some money if you need money.

*[*Lee *suddenly lunges at* Austin, *grabs him violently by the shirt and shakes him with tremendous power.]*

    Lee: Don't you say that to me! Don't you ever say that to me!

[Just as suddenly he turns him loose, pushes him away and backs off.]

You may be able to git away with that with the Old Man. Git him tanked up for a week! Buy him off with yer Hollywood blood money, but not me! I can git my own money my own way. Big money!

Austin: I was just making an offer.

    Lee: Yeah, well keep it to yourself!

[Long pause.]

Those are the most monotonous fuckin' crickets I ever heard in my life.

Austin: I kinda' like the sound.

    Lee: Yeah. Supposed to be able to tell the temperature by the number a' pulses. You believe that?

Austin: The temperature?

    Lee: Yeah. The air. How hot it is.

Austin: How do you do that?

    Lee: I don't know. Some woman told me that. She was a Botanist. So I believed her.

Austin: Where'd you meet her?

    Lee: What?

Austin: The woman Botanist?

    Lee: I met her on the desert. I been spendin' a lota' time on the desert.

Austin: What were you doing out there?

    Lee: [Pause, stares in space] I forgit. Had me a Pit Bull there for a while but I lost him.

Austin: Pit Bull?

    Lee: Fightin' dog. Damn I made some good money off that little dog. Real good money.

[Pause.]

Austin: You could come up north with me, you know.

    Lee: What's up there?

Austin: My family.

    Lee: Oh, that's right, you got the wife and kiddies now don't ya'. The house, the car, the whole slam. That's right.

Austin: You could spend a couple days. See how you like it. I've got an extra room.

    Lee: Too cold up there.

[Pause.]

Austin: You want to sleep for a while?

    Lee: *[Pause, stares at* Austin*]* I don't sleep.

[Lights to black.]

END SCENE 1

Scene 2

Morning, Austin *is watering plants with a vaporizer,* Lee *sits at glass table in alcove drinking beer.*

    Lee: I never realized the old lady was so security-minded.

Austin: How do you mean?

    Lee: Made a little tour this morning. She's got locks on everything. Locks and double-locks and chain-locks and—what's she got that's so valuable?

Austin: Antiques I guess. I don't know.

    Lee: Antiques? Brought everything with her from the old place, huh. Just the same crap we always had around. Plates and spoons.

Austin: I guess they have personal value to her.

    Lee: Personal value. Yeah just a lota' junk. Most of its phony anyway. Idaho decals. Now who in the hell wants to eat offa' plate with the State of Idaho starin' ya' in the face. Every time ya' take a bite ya' get to see a little bit more.

Austin: Well it must mean something to her or she wouldn't save it.

    Lee: Yeah, well personally I don't wanna' be invaded by Idaho when I'm eatin'. When I'm eatin' I'm home. Ya' know what I'm sayin'? I'm not driftin', I'm home. I don't need my thoughts swept off to Idaho. I don't need that!

[Pause.]

Austin: Did you go out last night?

    Lee: Why?

Austin: I thought I heard you go out.

    Lee: Yeah, I went out. What about it?

Austin: Just wondered.

   Lee: Damn coyotes kept me awake.

Austin: Oh yeah, I heard them. That must've killed somebody's dog or
   something.

   Lee: Yappin' their fool heads off. They don't yap like that on the
   desert. They howl. These are city coyotes here.

Austin: Well, you don't sleep anyway do you?

[Pause, Lee *stares at him.]*

   Lee: You're pretty smart aren't ya?

Austin: How do you mean?

   Lee: I mean you never had any more on the ball than I did. But here
   you are gettin' invited into prominent people's houses. Sittin'
   around talkin' like you know somethin'.

Austin: They're not so prominent.

   Lee: They're a helluva' lot more prominent than the houses I get
   invited into.

Austin: Well you invite yourself.

   Lee: That's right. I do. In fact I probably got a wider range a'
   choices than you do, come to think of it.

Austin: I wouldn't doubt it.

   Lee: In fact I been inside some pretty classy places in my time. And
   I never even went to an Ivy League school either.

Austin: You want some breakfast or something?

   Lee: Breakfast?

Austin: Yeah. Don't you eat breakfast?

   Lee: Look, don't worry about me pal. I can take care a' myself. You
   just go ahead as though I wasn't even here, all right?

[Austin goes into kitchen, makes coffee.]

Austin: Where'd you walk to last night?

[Pause.]

   Lee: I went up in the foothills there. Up in the San Gabriels. Heat
   was drivin' me crazy.

Austin: Well, wasn't it hot out on the desert?

   Lee: Different kinda' heat. Out there it's clean. Cools off at night.
   There's a nice little breeze.

Austin: Where were you, the Mojave?

   Lee: Yeah. The Mojave. That's right.

Austin: I haven't been out there in years.

   Lee: Out past Needles there.

Austin: Oh yeah.

   Lee: Up here it's different. This country's real different.

Austin: Well, it's been built up.

Lee: Built up? Wiped out is more like it. I don't even hardly recognize it.

Austin: Yeah. Foothills are the same though, aren't they?

Lee: Pretty much. It's funny goin' up in there. The smells and everything. Used to catch snakes up there, remember?

Austin: You caught snakes.

Lee: Yeah. And you'd pretend you were Geronimo or some damn thing. You used to go right out to lunch.

Austin: I enjoyed my imagination.

Lee: That what you call it? Looks like yer still enjoyin' it.

Austin: So you just wandered around up there, huh?

Lee: Yeah. With a purpose.

Austin: See any houses?

[Pause.]

Lee: Couple. Couple a' real nice ones. One of 'em didn't even have a dog. Walked right up and stuck my head in the window. Not a peep. Just a sweet kinda' suburban silence.

Austin: What kind of a place was it?

Lee: Like a paradise. Kinda' place that sorta' kills ya' inside. Warm yellow lights. Mexican tile all around. Copper pots hangin' over the stove. Ya' know like they got in the magazines. Blonde people movin' in and outa' the rooms, talkin' to each other. *[Pause]* Kinda' place you wish you sorta' grew up in, ya' know.

Austin: That's the kind of place you wish you'd grown up in?

Lee: Yeah, why not?

Austin: I thought you hated that kind of stuff.

Lee: Yeah, well you never knew too much about me did ya'?

[Pause.]

Austin: Why'd you go out to the desert in the first place?

Lee: I was on my way to see the old man.

Austin: You mean you just passed through there?

Lee: Yeah. That's right. Three months of passin' through.

Austin: Three months?

Lee: Somethin' like that. Maybe more. Why?

Austin: You lived on the Mojave for three months?

Lee: Yeah. What'sa' matter with that?

Austin: By yourself?

Lee: Mostly. Had a couple a' visitors. Had that dog for a while.

Austin: Didn't you miss people?

Lee: *[Laughs]* People?

Austin: Yeah. I mean I go crazy if I have to spend three nights in a motel by myself.

Lee: Yer not in a motel now.

Austin: No, I know. But sometimes I have to stay in motels.

Lee: Well, they got people in motels don't they?

Austin: Strangers.

Lee: Yer friendly aren't ya'? Aren't you the friendly type?

[Pause.]

Austin: I'm going to have somebody coming by here later, Lee.

Lee: Ah! Lady friend?

Austin: No, a producer.

Lee: Aha! What's he produce?

Austin: Film. Movies. You know.

Lee: Oh, movies. Motion Pictures! A Big Wig huh?

Austin: Yeah.

Lee: What's he comin' by here for?

Austin: We have to talk about a project.

Lee: Whadya' mean, "a project"? What's "a project"?

Austin: A script.

Lee: Oh. That's what yer doin' with all these papers?

Austin: Yeah.

Lee: Well, what's the project about?

Austin: We're uh—it's a period piece.

Lee: What's "a period piece"?

Austin: Look, it doesn't matter. The main thing is we need to discuss this alone. I mean—

Lee: Oh, I get it. You want me outa' the picture.

Austin: Not exactly. I just need to be alone with him for a couple of hours. So we can talk.

Lee: Yer afraid I'll embarrass ya' huh?

Austin: I'm not afraid you'll embarrass me!

Lee: Well, I tell ya' what—Why don't you just gimme the keys to yer car and I'll be back here around six o'clock or so. That give ya' enough time?

Austin: I'm not loaning you my car, Lee.

Lee: You want me to just git lost huh? Take a hike? Is that it? Pound the pavement for a few hours while you bullshit yer way into a million bucks.

Austin: Look, it's going to be hard enough for me to face this character on my own without—

Lee: You don't know this guy?

Austin: No I don't know—He's a producer. I mean I've been meeting with him for months but you never get to know a producer.

Lee: Yer tryin' to hustle him? Is that it?

Austin: I'm not trying to hustle him! I'm trying to work out a deal! It's not easy.

Lee: What kinda' deal?

Austin: Convince him it's a worthwhile story.

Lee: He's not convinced? How come he's comin' over here if he's
   not convinced? I'll convince him for ya'.
Austin: You don't understand the way things work down here.
   Lee: How do things work down here?

[Pause.]

Austin: Look, if I loan you my car will you have it back here by six?
   Lee: On the button. With a full tank a' gas.
Austin: *[Digging in his pocket for keys]* Forget about the gas.
   Lee: Hey, these days gas is gold, old buddy.

[Austin hands the keys to Lee.]

   You remember that car I used to loan you?
Austin: Yeah.
   Lee: Forty Ford. Flathead.
Austin: Yeah.
   Lee: Sucker hauled ass didn't it?
Austin: Lee, it's not that I don't want to loan you my car—
   Lee: You are loanin' me yer car.

[Lee gives Austin a pat on the shoulder, pause.]

Austin: I know. I just wish—
   Lee: What? You wish what?
Austin: I don't know. I wish I wasn't—I wish I didn't have to be doing
   business down here. I'd like to just spend some time with you.
   Lee: I though it was "Art" you were doin'.

[Lee moves across kitchen toward exit, tosses keys in his hand.]

Austin: Try to get it back here by six, okay?
   Lee: No sweat. Hey, ya' know, if that uh—story of yours doesn't go
   over with the guy—tell him I got a couple a' "projects" he might
   be interested in. Real commercial. Full a' suspense. True-to-life
   stuff.

*[Lee exits, Austin stares after Lee then turns, goes to papers at table, leafs through
pages, lights fade to black.]*

END SCENE 2

Scene 3
Afternoon, alcove, Saul Kimmer *and* Austin *seated across from each other at table.*

   Saul: Well, to tell you the truth Austin, I have never felt so confident
   about a project in quite a long time.
Austin: Well, that's good to hear Saul.
   Saul: I am absolutely convinced we can get this thing off the ground.
   I mean we'll have to make a sale to television and that means get-

ting a major star. Somebody bankable. But I think we can do it. I really do.

Austin: Don't you think we need a first draft before we approach a star?

Saul: No, no, not at all. I don't think it's necessary. Maybe a brief synopsis. I don't want you to touch the typewriter until we have some seed money.

Austin: That's fine with me.

Saul: I mean it's a great story. Just the story alone. You've really managed to capture something this time.

Austin: I'm glad you like it, Saul.

[Lee enters abruptly into kitchen carrying a stolen television set, short pause.]

Lee: Aw shit, I'm sorry about that. I am really sorry Austin.

Austin: [Standing] That's all right.

Lee: [Moving toward them] I mean I thought it was way past six already. You said to have it back here by six.

Austin: We were just finishing up. *[To Saul]* This is my uh—brother, Lee.

Saul: [Standing] Oh, I'm very happy to meet you.

[Lee sets T.V. on sink counter, shakes hands with Saul.]

Lee: I can't tell ya' how happy I am to meet you sir.

Saul: Saul Kimmer.

Lee: Mr. Kipper.

Saul: Kimmer.

Austin: Lee's been living out on the desert and he just uh—

Saul: Oh, that's terrific! *[To Lee]* Palm Springs?

Lee: Yeah. Yeah, right. Right around in that area. Near uh—Bob Hope Drive there.

Saul: Oh I love it out there. I just love it. The air is wonderful.

Lee: Yeah. Sure is. Healthy.

Saul: And the golf. I don't know if you play golf, but the golf is just about the best.

Lee: I play a lota' golf.

Saul: Is that right?

Lee: Yeah. In fact I was hoping I'd run into somebody out here who played a little golf. I've been lookin' for a partner.

Saul: Well, I uh—

Austin: Lee's just down for a visit while our mother's in Alaska.

Saul: Oh, your mother's in Alaska?

Austin: Yes. She went up there on a little vacation. This is her place.

Saul: I see. Well isn't that something. Alaska.

Lee: What kinda' handicap do ya' have, Mr. Kimmer?

Saul: Oh I'm just a Sunday duffer really. You know.

Lee: That's good 'cause I haven't swung a club in months.

Saul: Well we ought to get together sometime and have a little game. Austin, do you play?

[Saul *mimes a Johnny Carson golf swing for* Austin.]

Austin: No. I don't uh—I've watched it on T.V.
  Lee: [*To* Saul] How 'bout tomorrow morning? Bright and early. We could get out there and put in eighteen holes before breakfast.
  Saul: Well, I've got uh—I have several appointments—.
  Lee: No, I mean real early. Crack a'dawn. While the dew's still thick on the fairway.
  Saul: Sounds really great.
  Lee: Austin could be our caddie.
  Saul: Now that's an idea. [*Laughs*]
Austin: I don't know the first thing about golf.
  Lee: There's nothin' to it. Isn't that right, Saul? He'd pick it up in fifteen minutes.
  Saul: Sure. Doesn't take long. 'Course you have to play for years to find your true form. [*Chuckles*]
  Lee: [*To* Austin] We'll give ya' a quick run-down on the club faces. The irons, the woods. Show ya' a couple pointers on the basic swing. Might even let ya' hit the ball a couple times. Whadya' think, Saul?
  Saul: Why not. I think it'd be great. I haven't had any exercise in weeks.
  Lee: At's the spirit! We'll have a little orange juice right afterwards.

[Pause.]

  Saul: Orange juice?
  Lee: Yeah! Vitamin C! Nothin' like a shot a' orange juice after a round a' golf. Hot shower. Snappin' towels at each other's privates. Real sense a' fraternity.
  Saul: [*Smiles at* Austin] Well, you make it sound very inviting, I must say. It really does sound great.
  Lee: Then it's a date.
  Saul: Well, I'll call the country club and see if I can arrange something.
  Lee: Great! Boy, I sure am sorry that I busted in on ya' all in the middle of yer meeting.
  Saul: Oh that's quite all right. We were just about finished anyway.
  Lee: I can wait out in the other room if you want.
  Saul: No really—
  Lee: Just got Austin's color T.V. back from the shop. I can watch a little amateur boxing now.

[Lee *and* Austin *exchange looks.*]

Saul: Oh—Yes.

Lee: You don't fool around in Television, do you Saul?

Saul: Uh—I have in the past. Produced some T.V. Specials. Network stuff. But it's mainly features now.

Lee: That's where the big money is huh?

Saul: Yes. That's right.

Austin: Why don't I call you tomorrow, Saul and we'll get together. We can have lunch or something.

Saul: That'd be terrific.

Lee: Right after the golf.

[*Pause.*]

Saul: What?

Lee: You can have lunch right after the golf.

Saul: Oh, right.

Lee: Austin was tellin' me that yer interested in stories.

Saul: Well, we develop certain projects that we feel have commercial potential.

Lee: What kinda' stuff do ya' go in for?

Saul: Oh, the usual. You know. Good love interest. Lots of action. [*Chuckles at* Austin]

Lee: Westerns?

Saul: Sometimes.

Austin: I'll give you a ring, Saul.

[Austin *tries to move* Saul *across the kitchen but* Lee *blocks their way.*]

Lee: I got a Western that'd knock yer lights out.

Saul: Oh really?

Lee: Yeah. Contemporary Western. Based on a true story. 'Course I'm not a writer like my brother here. I'm not a man of the pen.

Saul: Well—

Lee: I mean I can tell ya' a story off the tongue but I can't put it down on paper. That don't make any difference though does it?

Saul: No, not really.

Lee: I mean plenty a guys have stories don't they? True-life stories. Musta' been a lota' movies made from real life.

Saul: Yes. I suppose so.

Lee: I haven't seen a good Western since 'Lonely Are the Brave'. You remember that movie?

Saul: No, I'm afraid I—

Lee: Kirk Douglas. Helluva' movie. You remember that movie, Austin?

Austin: Yes.

Lee: [*To Saul*] The man dies for the love of a horse.

Saul: Is that right.

Lee: Yeah. Ya' hear the horse screamin' at the end of it. Rain's comin' down. Horse is screamin'. Then there's a shot. BLAM! Just a single shot like that. Then nothin' but the sound of rain. And Kirk Douglas is ridin' in the ambulance. Ridin' away from the scene of the accident. And when he hears that shot he knows that his horse has died. He knows. And you see his eyes. And his eyes die. Right inside his face. And then his eyes close. And you know that he's died too. You know that Kirk Douglas has died from the death of his horse.

Saul: [Eyes Austin nervously] Well, it sounds like a great movie. I'm sorry I missed it.

Lee: Yeah, you shouldn't a' missed that one.

Saul: I'll have to try to catch it some time. Arrange a screening or something. Well, Austin, I'll have to hit the freeway before rush hour.

Austin: [Ushers him toward exit] It's good seeing you, Saul.

[Austin and Saul shake hands.]

Lee: So ya' think there's room for a real Western these days? A true-to-life Western?

Saul: Well, I don't see why not. Why don't you uh—tell the story to Austin and have him write a little outline.

Lee: You'd take a look at it then?

Saul: Yes. Sure. I'll give it a read-through. Always eager for new material. [Smiles at Austin]

Lee: That's great! You'd really read it then huh?

Saul: It would just be my opinion of course.

Lee: That's all I want. Just an opinion. I happen to think it has a lota' possibilities.

Saul: Well, it was great meeting you and I'll—

[Saul and Lee shake.]

Lee: I'll call you tomorrow about the golf.

Saul: Oh. Yes, right.

Lee: Austin's got your number, right?

Saul: Yes.

Lee: So long Saul. [Gives Saul a pat on the back]

[Saul exits, Austin turns to Lee, looks at T.V. then back to Lee.]

Austin: Give me the keys.

[Austin extends his hand toward Lee, Lee doesn't move, just stares at Austin, smiles, lights to black.]

END SCENE 3

Scene 4

Night, coyotes in distance, fade, sound of typewriter in dark, crickets, candlelight in *alcove, dim light in kitchen, lights reveal* Austin *at glass table typing,* Lee *sits across from him, foot on table, drinking beer and whiskey, the T.V. is still on sink counter,* Austin *types for a while then stops.*

   Lee: All right, now read it back to me.
Austin: I'm not reading it back to you, Lee. You can read it when we're finished. I can't spend all night on this.
   Lee: You got better things to do?
Austin: Let's just go ahead. Now what happens when he leaves Texas?
   Lee: Is he ready to leave Texas yet? I didn't know we were that far along. He's not ready to leave Texas.
Austin: He's right at the border.
   Lee: *[Sitting up]* No, see, this is one a' the crucial parts. Right here. *[Taps paper with beer can]* We can't rush through this. He's not right at the border. He's a good fifty miles from the border. A lot can happen in fifty miles.
Austin: It's only an outline. We're not writing an entire script now.
   Lee: Well ya' can't leave things out even if it is an outline. It's one a' the most important parts. Ya' can't go leavin' it out.
Austin: Okay, okay. Let's just—get it done.
   Lee: All right. Now. He's in the truck and he's got his horse trailer and his horse.
Austin: We've already established that.
   Lee: And he sees this other guy comin' up behind him in another truck. And that truck is pullin' a gooseneck.
Austin: What's a gooseneck?
   Lee: Cattle trailer. You know the kind with a gooseneck, goes right down in the bed a' the pick-up.
Austin: Oh. All right. *[Types]*
   Lee: It's important.
Austin: Okay. I got it.
   Lee: All these details are important.

[Austin types as they talk.]

Austin: I've got it.
   Lee: And this other guy's got his horse all saddled up in the back a' the gooseneck.
Austin: Right.
   Lee: So both these guys have got their horses right along with 'em, see.
Austin: I understand.
   Lee: Then this first guy suddenly realizes two things.
Austin: The guy in front?
   Lee: Right. The guy in front realizes two things almost at the same time. Simultaneous.

Austin: What were the two things?

    Lee: Number one, he realizes that the guy behind him is the hus-
band of the woman he's been—

[Lee *makes gesture of screwing by pumping his arm.*]

Austin: [*Sees* Lee's *gesture*] Oh. Yeah.

    Lee: And number two, he realizes he's in the middle of Tornado
Country.

Austin: What's "Tornado Country"?

    Lee: Panhandle.

Austin: Panhandle?

    Lee: Sweetwater. Around in that area. Nothin'. Nowhere. And
number three—

Austin: I thought there was only two.

    Lee: There's three. There's a third unforeseen realization.

Austin: And what's that?

    Lee: That he's runnin' outa' gas.

Austin: [*Stops typing*] Come on, Lee.

[Austin *gets up, moves to kitchen, gets a glass of water.*]

    Lee: Whadya' mean, "come on"? That's what it is. Write it down!
He's runnin' outa' gas.

Austin: It's too—

    Lee: What? It's too what? It's too real! That's what ya' mean isn't
it? It's too much like real life!

Austin: It's not like real life! It's not enough like real life. Things don't
happen like that.

    Lee: What! Men don't fuck other men's women?

Austin: Yes. But they don't end up chasing each other across the Panhandle. Through "Tornado Country".

    Lee: They do in this movie!

Austin: And they don't have horses conveniently along with them when
they run out of gas! And they don't run out of gas either!

    Lee: These guys run outa' gas! This is my story and one a' these guys
runs outa' gas!

Austin: It's just a dumb excuse to get them into a chase scene. It's
contrived.

    Lee: It is a chase scene! It's already a chase scene. They been
chasin' each other fer days.

Austin: So now they're supposed to abandon their trucks, climb on
their horses and chase each other into the mountains?

    Lee: [*Standing suddenly*] There aren't any mountains in the Panhan-
dle! It's flat!

[Lee *turns violently toward windows in alcove and throws beer can at them.*]

Lee: Goddamn these crickets! *[Yells at crickets]* Shut up out there! *[Pause, turns back toward table]* This place is like a fuckin' rest home here. How're you supposed to think!

Austin: You wanna' take a break?

Lee: No, I don't wanna' take a break! I wanna' get this done! This is my last chance to get this done.

Austin: *[Moves back into alcove]* All right. Take it easy.

Lee: I'm gonna' be leavin' this area. I don't have time to mess around here.

Austin: Where are you going?

Lee: Never mind where I'm goin'! That's got nothin' to do with you. I just gotta' get this done. I'm not like you. Hangin' around bein' a parasite offa' other fools. I gotta' do this thing and get out.

[Pause.]

Austin: A parasite? Me?

Lee: Yeah, you!

Austin: After you break into people's houses and take their televisions?

Lee: They don't need their televisions! I'm doin' them a service.

Austin: Give me back my keys, Lee.

Lee: Not until you write this thing! You're gonna write this outline thing for me or that car's gonna' wind up in Arizona with a different paint job.

Austin: You think you can force me to write this? I was doing you a favor.

Lee: Git off yer high horse will ya'! Favor! Big favor. Handin' down favors from the mountain top.

Austin: Let's just write it, okay? Let's sit down and not get upset and see if we can just get through this.

[Austin sits at typewriter.]

[Long pause.]

Lee: Yer not gonna' even show it to him, are ya'?

Austin: What?

Lee: This outline. You got no intention of showin' it to him. Yer just doin' this 'cause yer afraid a' me.

Austin: You can show it to him yourself.

Lee: I will, boy! I'm gonna' read it to him on the golf course.

Austin: And I'm not afraid of you either.

Lee: Then how come yer doin' it?

Austin: *[Pause]* So I can get my keys back.

[Pause as Lee takes keys out of his pocket slowly and throws them on table, long pause, Austin stares at keys.]

Lee: There. Now you got yer keys back.

[Austin looks up at Lee but doesn't take keys.]

    Lee: Go ahead. There's yer keys.

[Austin slowly takes keys off table and puts them back in his own pocket.]

        Now what're you gonna' do? Kick me out?

Austin: I'm not going to kick you out, Lee.

    Lee: You couldn't kick me out, boy.

Austin: I know.

    Lee: So you can't even consider that one. *[Pause]* You could call the Police. That'd be the obvious thing.

Austin: You're my brother.

    Lee: That don't mean a thing. You go down to the L.A. Police Department there and ask them what kinda' people kill each other the most. What do you think they'd say?

Austin: Who said anything about killing?

    Lee: Family people. Brothers. Brothers-in-Law. Cousins. Real American-type people. They kill each other in the heat mostly. In the Smog-Alerts. In the Brush Fire Season. Right about this time a' year.

Austin: This isn't the same.

    Lee: Oh no? What makes it different?

Austin: We're not insane. We're not driven to acts of violence like that. Not over a dumb movie script. Now sit down.

[Long pause, Lee considers which way to go with it.]

    Lee: Maybe not. *[He sits back down at table across from Austin]* Maybe you're right. Maybe we're too intelligent huh? *[Pause]* We got our heads on our shoulders. One of us has even got a Ivy League diploma. Now that means somethin' don't it? Doesn't that mean somethin'?

Austin: Look, I'll write this thing for you, Lee. I don't mind writing it. I just don't want to get all worked up about it. It's not worth it. Now, come on. Let's just get through it, okay?

    Lee: Nah. I think there's easier money. Lotsa' places I could pick up thousands. Maybe millions. I don't need this shit. I could go up to Sacramento Valley and steal me a diesel. Ten thousand a week dismantling one a' those suckers. Ten thousand a week!

[Lee opens another beer, puts his foot back up on table.]

Austin: No, really, look, I'll write it out for you. I think it's a great idea.

    Lee. Nah, you got yer own work to do. I don't wanna' interfere with yer life.

Austin: I mean it'd be really fantastic if you could sell this. Turn it into a movie. I mean it.

[Pause.]

Lee: Ya' think so huh?

Austin: Absolutely. You could really turn your life around, you know. Change things.

Lee: I could get me a house maybe.

Austin: Sure you could get a house. You could get a whole ranch if you wanted to.

Lee: *[Laughs]* A ranch? I could get a ranch?

Austin: 'Course you could. You know what a screenplay sells for these days?

Lee: No. What's it sell for?

Austin: A lot. A whole lot of money.

Lee: Thousands?

Austin: Yeah. Thousands.

Lee: Millions?

Austin: Well—

Lee: We could get the old man outa' hock then.

Austin: Maybe.

Lee: Maybe? Whadya' mean, maybe?

Austin: I mean it might take more than money.

Lee: You were just tellin' me it'd change my whole life around. Why wouldn't it change his?

Austin: He's different.

Lee: Oh, he's of a different ilk huh?

Austin: He's not gonna' change. Let's leave the old man out of it.

Lee: That's right. He's not gonna' change but I will. I'll just turn myself right inside out. I could be just like you then huh? Sittin' around dreamin' stuff up. Gettin' paid to dream. Ridin' back and forth on the freeway just dreamin' my fool head off.

Austin: It's not all that easy.

Lee: It's not huh?

Austin: No. There's a lot of work involved.

Lee: What's the toughest part? Deciding whether to jog or play tennis?

[Long pause.]

Austin: Well, look. You can stay here—do whatever you want to. Borrow the car. Come in and out. Doesn't matter to me. It's not my house. I'll help you write this thing or—not. Just let me know what you want. You tell me.

Lee: Oh. So now suddenly you're at my service. Is that it?

Austin: What do you want to do Lee?

[Long pause, Lee stares at him then turns and dreams at windows.]

Lee: I tell ya' what I'd do if I still had that dog. Ya' wanna' know what I'd do?

Austin: What?

Lee: Head out to Ventura. Cook up a little match. God that little dog could bear down. Lota' money in dog fightin'. Big money.

[Pause.]

Austin: Why don't we try to see this through, Lee. Just for the hell of it. Maybe you've really got something here. What do you think?

[Pause, Lee *considers.]*

Lee: Maybe so. No harm in tryin' I guess. You think it's such a hot idea. Besides, I always wondered what'd be like to be you.
Austin: You did?
Lee: Yeah, sure. I used to picture you walkin' around some campus with yer arms fulla' books. Blondes chasin' after ya'.
Austin: Blondes? That's funny.
Lee: What's funny about it?
Austin: Because I always used to picture you somewhere.
Lee: Where'd you picture me?
Austin: Oh, I don't know. Different places. Adventures. You were always on some adventure.
Lee: Yeah.
Austin: And I used to say to myself, 'Lee's got the right idea. He's out there in the world and here I am. What am I doing?'
Lee: Well you were settin' yourself up for somethin'.
Austin: I guess.
Lee: We better get started on this thing then.
Austin: Okay.

[Austin sits up at typewriter, puts new paper in.]

Lee: Oh. Can I get the keys back before I forget?

[Austin hesitates.]

You said I could borrow the car if I wanted, right? Isn't that what you said?
Austin: Yeah. Right.

[Austin takes keys out of his pocket, sets them on table, Lee *takes keys slowly, plays with them in his hand.]*

Lee: I could get a ranch huh?
Austin: Yeah. We have to write it first though.
Lee: Okay. Let's write it.

[Lights start dimming slowly to end of scene as Austin *types,* Lee *speaks.]*

So they take off after each other straight into an endless black prairie. The sun is just comin' down and they can feel the night on their backs. What they don't know is that each one of 'em is afraid see. Each one separately thinks that he's the only one that's afraid. And they keep ridin' like that straight into the night. Not knowing. And the one who's chasin' doesn't know where the other one is taking him. And the one who's being chased doesn't know where he's going.

[Lights to black, typing stops in the dark, crickets fade.]

END ACT 1

[Music in Act break: Hank Williams' *"Ramblin Man".]*

ACT II

Scene 5

Morning, Lee *at table in alcove with a set of golf clubs in a fancy leather bag,* Austin *at sink washing a few dishes.*

Austin: He really liked it huh?
 Lee: He wouldn't a' gave me these clubs if he didn't like it.
Austin: He gave you the clubs?
 Lee: Yeah. I told ya' he gave me the clubs. The bag too.
Austin: I thought he just loaned them to you.
 Lee: He said it was part a' the advance. A little gift like. Gesture of his good faith.
Austin: He's giving you an advance?
 Lee: Now what's so amazing about that? I told ya' it was a good story. You even said it was a good story.
Austin: Well that is really incredible Lee. You know how many guys spend their whole lives down here trying to break into this business? Just trying to get in the door?
 Lee: *[Pulling clubs out of bag, testing them]* I got no idea. How many?

[Pause.]

Austin: How much of an advance is he giving you?
 Lee: Plenty. We were talkin' big money out there. Ninth hole is where I sealed the deal.
Austin: He made a firm commitment?
 Lee: Absolutely.
Austin. Well, I know Saul and he doesn't fool around when he says he likes something.
 Lee: I though you said you didn't know him.
Austin: Well, I'm familiar with his tastes.
 Lee: I let him get two up on me goin' into the back nine. He was sure he had me cold. You shoulda' seen his face when I pulled out the old pitching wedge and plopped it pin-high, two feet from the cup. He 'bout shit his pants. "Where'd a guy like you ever learn how to play golf like that?", he says.

[Lee laughs, Austin *stares at him.]*

Austin: 'Course there's no contract yet. Nothing's final until it's on paper.

   Lee: It's final, all right. There's no way he's gonna' back out of it now. We gambled for it.

Austin: Saul, gambled?

   Lee: Yeah, sure. I mean he liked the outline already so he wasn't risking that much. I just guaranteed it with my short game.

[Pause.]

Austin: Well, we should celebrate or something. I think Mom left a bottle of Champagne in the refrigerator. We should have a little toast.

[Austin gets glasses from cupboard, goes to refrigerator, pulls out bottle of Champagne.]

   Lee: You shouldn't oughta' take her Champagne, Austin. She's gonna' miss that.

Austin: Oh, she's not going to mind. She'd be glad we put it to good use. I'll get her another bottle. Besides, it's perfect for the occasion.

[Pause.]

   Lee: Yer gonna' get a nice fee fer writin' the script a' course. Straight fee.

[Austin stops, stares at Lee, puts glasses and bottle on table, pause.]

Austin: I'm writing the script?

   Lee: That's what he said. Said we couldn't hire a better screenwriter in the whole town.

Austin: But I'm already working on a script. I've got my own project. I don't have time to write two scripts.

   Lee: No, he said he was gonna' drop that other one.

[Pause.]

Austin: What? You mean mine? He's going to drop mine and do yours instead?

   Lee: [Smiles] Now look, Austin, it's jest beginner's luck ya' know. I mean I sank a fifty foot putt for this deal. No hard feelings.

[Austin goes to phone on wall, grabs it, starts dialing.]

      He's not gonna' be in, Austin. Told me he wouldn't be in 'til late this afternoon.

Austin: [Stays on phone, dialing, listens] I can't believe this. I just can't believe it. Are you sure he said that? Why would he drop mine?

   Lee: That's what he told me.

Austin: He can't do that without telling me first. Without talking to me at least. He wouldn't just make a decision like that without talking to me!

Lee: Well I was kinda' surprised myself. But he was real enthusiastic about my story.

[Austin hangs up phone violently, paces.]

Austin: What'd he say! Tell me everything he said!

Lee: I been tellin' ya'! He said he liked the story a whole lot. It was the first authentic Western to come along in a decade.

Austin: He liked that story? Your story?

Lee: Yeah! What's so surprisin' about that?

Austin: It's stupid! It's the dumbest story I ever heard in my life.

Lee: Hey, hold on! That's my story yer talkin' about!

Austin: It's a bullshit story! It's idiotic. Two lamebrains chasing each other across Texas! Are you kidding? Who do you think's going to go see a film like that?

Lee: It's not a film! It's a movie. There's a big difference. That's somethin' Saul told me.

Austin: Oh he did huh?

Lee: Yeah, he said, "In this business we make Movies, American Movies. Leave the Films to the French."

Austin: So you got real intimate with old Saul huh? He started pouring forth his vast knowledge of Cinema.

Lee: I think he liked me a lot, to tell ya' the truth. I think he felt I was somebody he could confide in.

Austin: What'd you do, beat him up or something?

Lee: *[Stands fast]* Hey, I've about had it with the insults buddy! You think yer the only one in the brain department here? Yer the only one that can sit around and cook things up? There's other people got ideas too, ya' know!

Austin: You must've done something. Threatened him or something. Now what'd you do Lee?

Lee: I convinced him!

[Lee makes sudden menacing lunge toward Austin, wielding golf club above his head, stops himself, frozen moment, long pause, Lee lowers club.]

Austin: Oh, Jesus. You didn't hurt him did you?

[Long silence, Lee sits back down at table.]

Lee! Did you hurt him?

Lee: I didn't do nothin' to him! He liked my story. Pure and simple. He said it was the best story he's come across in a long, long time.

Austin: That's what he told me about my story! That's the same thing he said to me.

Lee: Well, he musta' been lyin'. He musta' been lyin' to one of us anyway.

Austin: You can't come into this town and start pushing people around. They're gonna' put you away!

Lee: I never pushed anybody around! I beat him fair and square. *[Pause]* They can't touch me anyway. They can't put a finger on me. I'm gone. I can come in through the window and go out through the door. They never knew what hit 'em. You, yer stuck. Yer the one that's stuck. Not me. So don't be warnin' me to do in this town.

[Pause, Austin *crosses to table, sits at typewriter, rest.]*

Austin: Lee, come on, level with me will you? It doesn't make any sense that suddenly he'd throw my idea out the window. I've been talking to him for months. I've got too much at stake. Everything's riding on this project.

Lee: What's yer idea?

Austin: It's just a simple love story.

Lee: What kinda' love story?

Austin: *[Stands, crosses into kitchen]* I'm not telling you!

Lee: Ha! 'Fraid I'll steal it huh? Competition's gettin' kinda' close to home isn't it?

Austin: Where did Saul say he was going?

Lee: He was gonna' take my story to a couple studios.

Austin: That's *my* outline you know! I wrote that outline! You've got no right to be peddling it around.

Lee: You weren't ready to take credit for it last night.

Austin: Give me my keys!

Lee: What?

Austin: Give me my keys!

Lee: What?

Austin: The keys! I want my keys back!

Lee: Where you goin'?

Austin: Just give me my keys! I gotta' take a drive. I gotta' get out of here for a while.

Lee: Where you gonna' go, Austin?

Austin: *[Pause.]* I might just drive out to the desert for a while. I gotta' think.

Lee: You can think here just as good. This is the perfect set-up for thinkin'. We got some writin' to do here, boy. Now let's just have us a little toast. Relax. We're partners now.

*[*Lee *pops the cork of the Champagne bottle, pours two drinks as the lights fade to black.]*

END SCENE 5

Scene 6

Afternoon, Lee *and* Saul *in kitchen,* Austin *in alcove.*

Lee: Now you tell him. You tell him, Mr. Kipper.

Saul: Kimmer.

Lee: Kimmer. You tell him what you told me. He don't believe me.

Austin: I don't want to hear it.

Saul: It's really not a big issue, Austin. I was simply amazed by your brother's story and —

Austin: Amazed? You lost a bet! You gambled with my material!

Saul: That's really beside the point, Austin. I'm ready to go all the way with your brother's story. I think it has a great deal of merit.

Austin: I don't want to hear about it, okay? Go tell it to the executives! Tell it to somebody who's going to turn it into a package deal or something. A T.V. series. Don't tell it to me.

Saul: But I want to continue with your project too, Austin. It's not as though we can't do both. We're big enough for that aren't we?

Austin: "We"? *I* can't do both! I don't know about "we".

Lee: *[To* Saul*]* See, what'd I tell ya'. He's totally unsympathetic.

Saul: Austin, there's no point in our going to another screenwriter for this. It just doesn't make sense. You're brothers. You know each other. There's a familiarity with the material that just wouldn't be possible otherwise.

Austin: There's no familiarity with the material! None! I don't know what "Tornado Country" is. I don't know what a "gooseneck" is. and I don't want to know! *[Pointing to* Lee*]* He's a hustler! He's a bigger hustler than you are! If you can't see that then—

Lee: *[To* Austin*]* Hey, now hold on. I didn't have to bring this bone back to you, boy. I persuaded Saul here that you were the right man for the job. You don't have to go throwin' up favors in my face.

Austin: Favors! I'm the one who wrote the fuckin' outline! You can't even spell.

Saul: *[To* Austin.*]* Your brother told me about the situation with your father.

[Pause.]

Austin: What? *[Looks at* Lee*]*

Saul: That's right. Now we have a clear cut deal here, Austin. We have big studio money standing behind this thing. Just on the basis of your outline.

Austin: *[To* Saul*]* What'd he tell you about my father?

Saul: Well—that he's destitute. He needs money.

Lee: That's right. He does.

[Austin shakes his head, stares at them both.*]*

Austin: [*To* Lee] And this little assignment is supposed to go toward the old man? A charity project? Is that what this is? Did you cook this up on the ninth green too?

Saul: It's a big slice, Austin.

Austin: [*To* Lee] I gave him money! I already gave him money. You know that. He drank it all up!

Lee: This is a different deal here.

Saul: We can set up a trust for your father. A large sum of money. It can be doled out to him in parcels so he can't mis-use it.

Austin: Yeah, and who's doing the doling?

Saul: Your brother volunteered.

[*Austin laughs.*]

Lee: That's right. I'll make sure he uses it for groceries.

Austin: [*To* Saul] I'm not doing this script! I'm not writing this crap for you or anybody else. You can't blackmail me into it. You can't threaten me into it. There's no way I'm doing it. So just give it up. Both of you.

[*Long pause.*]

Saul: Well, that's it then. I mean this is an easy three hundred grand. Just for a first draft. It's incredible, Austin. We've got three different studios all trying to cut each other's throats to get this material. In one morning. That's how hot it is.

Austin: Yeah, well you can afford to give me a percentage on the out-line then. And you better get the genius here an agent before he gets burned.

Lee: Saul's gonna' be my agent. Isn't that right, Saul?

Saul: That's right. [*To* Austin] Your brother has really got something, Austin. I've been around too long not to recognize it. Raw talent.

Austin: He's got a lota' balls is what he's got. He's taking you right down the river.

Saul: Three hundred thousand, Austin. Just for a first draft. Now you've never been offered that kind of money before.

Austin: I'm not writing it.

[*Pause.*]

Saul: I see. Well—

Lee: We'll just go to another writer then. Right, Saul? Just hire us somebody with some enthusiasm. Somebody who can recognize the value of a good story.

Saul: I'm sorry about this, Austin.

Austin: Yeah.

Saul: I mean I was hoping we could continue both things but now I don't see how it's possible.

Austin: So you're dropping my idea altogether. Is that it? Just trade horses in mid-stream? After all these months of meetings.

Saul: I wish there was another way.

Austin: I've got everything riding on this, Saul. You know that. It's my only shot. If this falls through—

Saul: I have to go with what my instincts tell me—

Austin: Your instincts!

Saul: My gut reaction.

Austin: You lost! That's your gut reaction. You lost a gamble. Now you're trying to tell me you like his story? How could you possibly fall for that story? It's as phony as Hopalong Cassidy. What do you see in it? I'm curious.

Saul: It has the ring of truth, Austin.

Austin: *[Laughs]* Truth?

 Lee: It is true.

Saul: Something about the real West.

Austin: Why? Because it's got horses? Because it's got grown men acting like little boys?

Saul: Something about the land. Your brother is speaking from experience.

Austin: So am I!

Saul: But nobody's interested in love these days, Austin. Let's face it.

 Lee: That's right.

Austin: *[To Saul]* He's been camped out on the desert for three months. Talking to cactus. What's he know about what people wanna' see on the screen! I drive on the freeway every day. I swallow the smog. I watch the news in color. I shop in the Safeway. I'm the one who's in touch! Not him!

Saul: I have to go now, Austin.

[Saul starts to leave.]

Austin: There's no such thing as the West anymore! It's a dead issue! It's dried up, Saul, and so are you.

[Saul stops and turns to Austin.]

Saul: Maybe you're right. But I have to take the gamble, don't I?

Austin: You're a fool to do this, Saul.

Saul: I've always gone on my hunches. Always. And I've never been wrong. *[To Lee]* I'll talk to you tomorrow, Lee.

 Lee: All right, Mr. Kimmer.

Saul: Maybe we could have some lunch.

 Lee: Fine with me. *[Smiles at Austin]*

Saul: I'll give you a ring.

[Saul exits, lights to black as brothers look at each other from a distance.]

END SCENE 6

Scene 7

Night, coyotes, crickets, sound of typewriter in dark, candlelight up on Lee *at type-writer struggling to type with one finger system,* Austin *sits sprawled out on kitchen floor with whiskey bottle, drunk.*

Austin: *[Singing, from floor]*
  "RED SAILS IN THE SUNSET
  WAY OUT ON THE BLUE
  PLEASE CARRY MY LOVED ONE
  HOME SAFELY TO ME

  RED SAILS IN THE SUNSET—"
  Lee: *[Slams first on table]* Hey! Knock it off will ya'! I'm tryin' to
      concentrate here.
Austin: *[Laughs]* You're tryin' to concentrate?
  Lee: Yeah. That's right.
Austin: Now you're tryin' to concentrate.
  Lee: Between you, the coyotes and the crickets a thought don't have
      much of a chance.
Austin: "Between me, the coyotes and the crickets." What a great title.
  Lee: I don't need a title! I need a thought.
Austin: *[Laughs]* A thought! Here's a thought for ya'—
  Lee: I'm not askin' fer yer thoughts! I got my own. I can do this
      thing on my own.
Austin: You're going to write an entire script on your own?
  Lee: That's right.

[Pause.]

Austin: Here's a thought. Saul Kimmer—
  Lee: Shut up will ya'!
Austin: He thinks we're the same person.
  Lee: Don't get cute.
Austin: He does! He's lost his mind. Poor old Saul. *[Giggles]* Thinks
      we're one in the same.
  Lee: Why don't you ease up on that Champagne.
Austin: *[Holding up bottle]* This isn't Champagne any more. This is seri-
      ous stuff. The days of Champagne are long gone.
  Lee: Well go outside and drink it.
Austin: I'm enjoying your company, Lee. For the first time since your
      arrival I am finally enjoying your company. And now you want
      me to go outside and drink alone?
  Lee: That's right.

[Lee reads through paper in typewriter, makes an erasure.]

Austin: You think you'll make more progress if you're alone? You might drive yourself crazy.

Lee: I could have this thing done in a night if I had a little silence.

Austin: Well you'd still have the crickets to contend with. The coyotes. The sounds of the Police Helicopters prowling above the neighborhood. Slashing their searchlights down through the streets. Hunting for the likes of you.

Lee: I'm a screenwriter now! I'm legitimate.

Austin: *[Laughing]* A screenwriter!

Lee: That's right. I'm on salary. That's more'n I can say for you. I got an advance coming.

Austin: This is true. This is very true. An advance. *[Pause]* Well, maybe I oughta' go out and try my hand at your trade. Since you're doing so good at mine.

Lee: Ha!

[Lee attempts to type some more but gets the ribbon tangled up, starts trying to re-thread it as they continue talking.]

Austin: Well why not? You don't think I've got what it takes to sneak into people's houses and steal their T.V.'s?

Lee: You couldn't steal a toaster without losin' yer lunch.

[Austin stands with a struggle, supports himself by the sink.]

Austin: You don't think I could sneak into somebody's house and steal a toaster?

Lee: Go take a shower or somethin' will ya!

[Lee gets more tangled up with the typewriter ribbon, pulling it out of the machine as though it was fishing line.]

Austin: You really don't think I could steal a crumby toaster? How much you wanna' bet I can't steal a toaster! How much? Go ahead! You're a gambler aren't you? Tell me how much yer willing to put on the line. Some part of your big advance? Oh, you haven't got that yet have you. I forgot.

Lee: All right. I'll bet you your car that you can't steal a toaster without gettin' busted.

Austin: You already got my car!

Lee: Okay, your house then.

Austin: What're you gonna' give me! I'm not talkin' about my house and my car. I'm talkin' about what are you gonna' give me. You don't have nothin' to give me.

Lee: I'll give you—shared screen credit. How 'bout that? I'll have it put in the contract that this was written by the both of us.

Austin: I don't want my name on that piece of shit! I want something of value. You got anything of value? You got any tidbits from the

desert? Any Rattlesnake bones? I'm not a greedy man. Any little
personal treasure will suffice.

Lee: I'm gonna' just kick yer ass out in a minute.

Austin: Oh, so now you're gonna' kick me out! Now I'm the intruder.
I'm the one who's invading your precious privacy.

Lee: I'm trying to do some screenwriting here!!

*[*Lee *stands, picks up typewriter, slams it down hard on table, pause, silence except
for crickets.]*

Austin: Well, you got everything you need. You got plenty a' coffee?
Groceries. You got a car. A contract. *[Pause]* Might need a new
typewriter ribbon but other than that you're pretty well fixed. I'll
just leave ya' alone for a while.

*[*Austin *tries to steady himself to leave,* Lee *makes a move toward him.]*

Lee: Where you goin'?

Austin: Don't worry about me. I'm not the one to worry about.

*[*Austin *weaves toward exit, stops.]*

Lee: What're you gonna' do? Just go wander out into the night?

Austin: I'm gonna' make a little tour.

Lee: Why don't ya' just go to bed for Christ's sake. Yer makin' me
sick.

Austin: I can take care a' myself. Don't worry about me.

*[*Austin *weaves badly in another attempt to exit, he crashes to the floor,* Lee *goes to
him but remains standing.]*

Lee: You want me to call your wife for ya' or something?

Austin: *[From floor]* My wife?

Lee: Yeah. I mean maybe she can help ya' out. Talk to ya' or
somethin'.

Austin: *[Struggles to stand again]* She's five hundred miles away.
North. North of here. Up in the North country where things are
calm. I don't need any help. I'm gonna' go outside and I'm
gonna' steal a toaster. I'm gonna' steal some other stuff too. I
might even commit bigger crimes. Bigger than you ever dreamed
of. Crimes beyond the imagination!

*[*Austin *manages to get himself vertical, tries to head for exit again.]*

Lee: Just hang on a minute, Austin.

Austin: Why? What for? You don't need my help, right? You got a
handle on the project. Besides, I'm lookin' forward to the smell
of the night. The bushes. Orange blossoms. Dust in the drive-
ways. Rain bird sprinklers. Lights in people's houses. You're
right about the lights, Lee. Everybody else is livin' the life.

Indoors. Safe. This is a Paradise down here. You know that?
We're livin' in a Paradise. We've forgotten about that.

Lee: You sound just like the old man now.

Austin: Yeah, well we all sound alike when we're sloshed. We just sorta'
echo each other.

Lee: Maybe if we could work on this together we could bring him
back out here. Get him settled down some place.

*[Austin turns violently toward Lee, takes a swing at him, misses and crashes to the
floor again, Lee stays standing.]*

Austin: I don't want him out here! I've had it with him! I went all the
way out there! I went out of my way. I gave him money and all he
did was play Al Jolson records and spit at me! I gave him money!

[Pause.]

Lee: Just help me a little with the characters, all right? You know
how to do it, Austin.

Austin: *[On floor, laughs]* The characters!

Lee: Yeah. You know. The way they talk and stuff. I can hear it in
my head but I can't get it down on paper.

Austin: What characters?

Lee: The guys. The guys in the story.

Austin: Those aren't characters.

Lee: Whatever you call 'em then. I need to write somethin' out.

Austin: Those are illusions of characters.

Lee: I don't give a damn what ya' call 'em! You know what I'm talkin' about!

Austin: Those are fantasies of a long lost boyhood.

Lee: I gotta' write somethin' out on paper!!

[Pause.]

Austin: What for? Saul's gonna' get you a fancy screenwriter isn't he?

Lee: I wanna' do it myself!

Austin: Then do it! Yer on your own now old buddy. You bulldogged
yer way into contention. Now you gotta' carry it through.

Lee: I will but I need some advice. Just a couple a' things. Come
on, Austin. Just help me get 'em talkin' right. It won't take
much.

Austin: Oh, now you're having a little doubt huh? What happened?
The pressure's on, boy. This is it. You gotta' come up with it
now. You don't come up with a winner on your first time out they
just cut your head off. They don't give you a second chance ya'
know.

Lee: I got a good story! I know it's a good story. I just need a little
help is all.

Austin: Not from me. Not from yer little old brother. I'm retired.

Lee: You could save this thing for me, Austin. I'd give ya' half the money. I would. I only need half anyway. With this kinda' money I could be a long time down the road. I'd never bother ya' again. I promise. You'd never even see me again.

Austin: [*Still on floor*] You'd disappear?

Lee: I would for sure.

Austin: Where would you disappear to?

Lee: That don't matter. I got plenty a' places.

Austin: Nobody can disappear. The Old Man tried that. Look where it got him. He lost his teeth.

Lee: He never had any money.

Austin: I don't mean that. I mean his teeth! His real teeth. First he lost his real teeth, then he lost his false teeth. You never knew that did ya'? He never confided in you.

Lee: Nah, I never knew that.

Austin: You wanna' drink?

[Austin *offers bottle to* Lee, Lee *takes it, sits down on kitchen floor with* Austin, *they share the bottle.*]

Yeah, he lost his real teeth one at a time. Woke up every morning with another tooth lying on the mattress. Finally, he decides he's gotta' get 'em all pulled out but he doesn't have any money. Middle of Arizona with no money. Middle of Arizona with no money and no insurance and every morning another tooth is lying on the mattress. [*Takes a drink*] So what does he do?

Lee: I dunno'. I never knew about that.

Austin: He begs the government. G.I. Bill or some damn thing. Some pension plan he remembers in the back of his head. And they send him out the money.

Lee: They did?

[*They keep trading the bottle between them, taking drinks.*]

Austin: Yeah. They send him the money but it's not enough money. Costs a lot to have all yer teeth yanked. They charge by the individual tooth, ya' know. I mean one tooth isn't equal to another tooth. Some are more expensive. Like the big ones in the back—

Lee: So what happened?

Austin: So he locates a Mexican dentist in Juarez who'll do the whole thing for a song. And he takes off hitchhiking to the border.

Lee: Hitchhiking?

Austin: Yeah. So how long you think it takes him to get to the border? A man his age.

Lee: I dunno.

Austin: Eight days it takes him. Eight days in the rain and the sun and every day he's droppin' teeth on the blacktop and nobody'll pick him up 'cause his mouth's full a' blood.

[Pause, they drink.]

So finally he stumbles into the dentist. Dentist takes all his money and all his teeth. And there he is, in Mexico, with his gums sewed up and his pockets empty.

[Long silence, Austin *drinks.]*

Lee: That's it?

Austin: Then I go out to see him, see. I go out there and I take him out for a nice Chinese dinner. But he doesn't eat. All he wants to do is drink Martinis outa' plastic cups. And he takes his teeth out and lays 'em on the table 'cause he can't stand the feel of 'em. And we ask the waitress for one a' those doggie bags to take the Chop Suey home in. So he drops his teeth in the doggie bag along with the Chop Suey. And then we go out to hit all the bars up and down the highway. Says he wants to introduce me to all his buddies. And in one a' those bars, in one a' those bars up and down the highway, he left that doggie bag with his teeth laying in the Chop Suey.

Lee: You never found it?

Austin: We went back but we never did find it. *[Pause]* Now that's a true story. True to life.

[They drink as lights fade to black.]

END SCENE 7

Scene 8

Very early morning, between night and day, no crickets, coyotes yapping feverishly in distance before light comes up, a small fire blazes up in the dark from alcove area, sound of Lee *smashing typewriter with a golf club, lights coming up,* Lee *seen smashing typewriter methodically then dropping pages of his script into a burning bowl set on the floor of alcove, flames leap up,* Austin *has a whole bunch of stolen toasters lined up on the sink counter along with* Lee's *stolen T.V., the toasters are of a wide variety of models, mostly chrome,* Austin *goes up and down the line of toasters, breathing on them and polishing them with a dish towel, both men are drunk, empty whiskey bottles and beer cans litter floor of kitchen, they share a half empty bottle on one of the chairs in the alcove,* Lee *keeps periodically taking deliberate ax-chops at the typewriter using a nine-iron as* Austin *speaks, all of their mother's house plants are dead and drooping.*

Austin: *[Polishing toasters]* There's gonna' be a general lack of toast in the neighborhood this morning. Many, many unhappy, bewildered breakfast faces. I guess it's best not to even think of the victims. Not to even entertain it. Is that the right psychology?

Lee: *[Pauses]* What?

Austin: Is that the correct criminal psychology? Not to think of the victims?

   Lee: What victims?

[Lee takes another swipe at typewriter with nine-iron, adds pages to the fire.]

Austin: The victims of crime. Of breaking and entering. I mean is it a prerequisite for a criminal not to have a conscience?

   Lee: Ask a criminal.

[Pause, Lee *stares at* Austin.*]*

What're you gonna' do with all those toasters? That's the dumbest thing I ever saw in my life.

Austin: I've got hundreds of dollars worth of household appliances here. You may not realize that.

   Lee: Yeah, and how many hundreds of dollars did you walk right past?

Austin: It was toasters you challenged me to. Only toasters. I ignored every other temptation.

   Lee: I never challenged you! That's no challenge. Anybody can steal a toaster.

[Lee smashes typewriter again.]

Austin: You don't have to take it out on my typewriter ya' know. It's not the machine's fault that you can't write. It's a sin to do that to a good machine.

   Lee: A sin?

Austin: When you consider all the writers who never even had a machine. Who would have given an eyeball for a good typewriter. Any typewriter.

[Lee smashes typewriter again.]

Austin: [Polishing toasters] All the ones who wrote on matchbook covers. Paper bags. Toilet paper. Who had their writing destroyed by their jailers. Who persisted beyond all odds. Those writers would find it hard to understand your actions.

[Lee comes down on typewriter with one final crushing blow of the nine-iron then collapses in one of the chairs, takes a drink from bottle, pause.]

Austin: [After pause] Not to mention demolishing a perfectly good golf club. What about all the struggling golfers? What about Lee Trevino? What do you think he would've said when he was batting balls around with broom sticks at the age of nine. Impoverished.

[Pause.]

   Lee: What time is it anyway?

Austin: No idea. Time stands still when you're havin' fun.

Lee: Is it too late to call a woman? You know any women?

Austin: I'm a married man.

Lee: I mean a local woman.

[Austin *looks out at light through window above sink.*]

Austin: It's either too late or too early. You're the nature enthusiast. Can't you tell the time by the light in the sky? Orient yourself around the North Star or something?

Lee: I can't tell anything.

Austin: Maybe you need a little breakfast. Some toast! How 'bout some toast?

[Austin *goes to cupboard, pulls out loaf of bread and starts dropping slices into every toaster,* Lee *stays sitting, drinks, watches* Austin.]

Lee: I don't need toast. I need a woman.

Austin: A woman isn't the answer. Never was.

Lee: I'm not talkin' about permanent. I'm talkin' about temporary.

Austin: [Putting toast in toasters] We'll just test the merits of these little demons. See which brands have a tendency to burn. See which one can produce a perfectly golden piece of fluffy toast.

Lee: How much gas you got in yer car?

Austin: I haven't driven my car for days now. So I haven't had an opportunity to look at the gas gauge.

Lee: Take a guess. You think there's enough to get me to Bakersfield?

Austin: Bakersfield? What's in Bakersfield?

Lee: Just never mind what's in Bakersfield! You think there's enough goddamn gas in the car!

Austin: Sure.

Lee: Sure. You could care less, right. Let me run outa' gas on the Grapevine. You could give a shit.

Austin: I'd say there was enough gas to get you just about anywhere, Lee. With your determination and guts.

Lee: What the hell time is it anyway?

[Lee *pulls out his wallet, starts going through dozens of small pieces of paper with phone numbers written on them, drops some on the floor, drops others in the fire.*]

Austin: Very early. This is the time of morning when the coyotes kill people's Cocker Spaniels. Did you hear them? That's what they were doing out there. Luring innocent pets away from their homes.

Lee: [Searching through his papers] What's the area code for Bakersfield? You know?

Austin: You could always call the operator.

Lee: I can't stand that voice they give ya'.

Austin: What voice?

Lee: That voice that warns you that if you'd only tried harder to find the number in the phone book you wouldn't have to be calling the operator to begin with.

[Lee *gets up, holding a slip of paper from his wallet, stumbles toward phone on wall, yanks receiver, starts dialing.]*

Austin: Well I don't understand why you'd want to talk to anybody else anyway. I mean you can talk to me. I'm your brother.

Lee: *[Dialing]* I wanna talk to a woman. I haven't heard a woman's voice in a long time.

Austin: Not since the Botanist?

Life: What?

Austin: Nothing. *[Starts singing as he tends toast]*
"RED SAILS IN THE SUNSET
WAY OUT ON THE BLUE
PLEASE CARRY MY LOVED ONE
HOME SAFELY TO ME"

Lee: Hey, knock it off will ya'! This is long distance here.

Austin: Bakersfield?

Lee: Yeah, Bakersfield. It's Kern County.

Austin: Well, what County are *we* in?

Lee: You better get yerself a 7-Up, boy.

Austin: One County's as good as another.

*[*Austin *hums "Red Sails" softly as* Lee *talks on phone.]*

Lee: *[To phone]* Yeah, operator look—first off I wanna' know the area code for Bakersfield. Right. Bakersfield! Okay. Good. Now I wanna' know if you can help me track somebody down. *[Pause]* No, no I mean a phone number. Just a phone number. Okay. *[Holds piece of paper up and reads it]* Okay, the name is Melly Ferguson. Melly. *[Pause]* I dunno'. Melly. Maybe. Yeah. Maybe Melanie. Yeah. Melanie Ferguson. Okay. *[Pause]* What? I can't hear ya' so good. Sounds like yer under the ocean. *[Pause]* You got ten Melanie Fergusons? How could that be? Ten Melanie Fergusons in Bakersfield? Well gimme all of 'em then. *[Pause]* What d'ya' mean? Gimme all ten Melanie Fergusons! That's right. Just a second. *[To* Austin*]* Gimme a pen.

Austin: I don't have a pen.

Lee: Gimme a pencil then!

Austin: I don't have a pencil.

Lee: *[To phone]* Just a second operator. *[To* Austin*]* Yer a writer and ya' don't have a pen or a pencil!

Austin: I'm not a writer. You're a writer.

Lee: I'm on the phone here! Get me a pen or a pencil.

Austin: I gotta' watch the toast.

Lee: *[To phone]* Hang on a second, operator.

[Lee lets the phone drop then starts pulling all the drawers in the kitchen out on the floor and dumping the contents, searching for a pencil, Austin *watches him casually.]*

Lee: *[Crashing through drawers, throwing contents around kitchen]* This is the last time I try to live with people, boy! I can't believe it. Here I am! Here I am again in a desperate situation! This would never happen out on the desert. I would never be in this kinda' situation out on the desert. Isn't there a pen or a pencil in this house! Who lives in this house anyway!

Austin: Our mother.

Lee: How come she don't have a pen or a pencil! She's a social person isn't she? Doesn't she have to make shopping lists? She gotta' have a pencil. *[Finds a pencil]* Aaha! *[He rushes back to phone, picks up receiver]* All right operator. Operator? Hey! Operator! Goddamnit!

[Lee rips the phone off the wall and throws it down, goes back to chair and falls into it, drinks, long pause.]

Austin: She hung up?

Lee: Yeah, she hung up. I knew she was gonna' hang up. I could hear it in her voice.

[Lee starts going through his slips of paper again.]

Austin: Well, you're probably better off staying here with me anyway. I'll take care of you.

Lee: I don't need takin' care of! Not by you anyway.

Austin: Toast is almost ready.

[Austin starts buttering all the toast as it pops up.]

Lee: I don't want any toast!

[Long pause.]

Austin: You gotta' eat something. Can't just drink. How long have we been drinking, anyway?

Lee: *[Looking through slips of paper]* Maybe it was Fresno. What's the area code for Fresno? How could I have lost that number! She was beautiful.

[Pause.]

Austin: Why don't you just forget about that, Lee. Forget about the woman.

Lee: She had green eyes. You know what green eyes do to me?

Austin: I know but you're not gonna' get it on with her now anyway. It's dawn already. She's in Bakersfield for Christ's sake.

[Long pause, Lee *considers the situation.]*

> *Lee:* Yeah. *[Looks at windows]* It's dawn?
Austin: Let's just have some toast and—
> *Lee:* What is this bullshit with the toast anyway! You make it sound like salvation or something. I don't want any goddamn toast! How many times I gotta' tell ya'!

[Lee *gets up, crosses upstage to windows in alcove, looks out,* Austin *butters toast.]*

Austin: Well it is like salvation sort of. I mean the smell. I love the smell of toast. And the sun's coming up. It makes me feel like anything's possible. Ya' know?
> *Lee:* *[Back to* Austin, *facing windows upstage]* So go to church why don't ya'.
Austin: Like a beginning. I love beginnings.
> *Lee:* Oh yeah. I've always been kinda' partial to endings myself.
Austin: What if I come with you, Lee?
> *Lee:* *[Pause as* Lee *turns toward* Austin*]* What?
Austin: What if I come with you out to the desert?
> *Lee:* Are you kiddin'?
Austin: No. I'd just like to see what it's like.
> *Lee:* You wouldn't last a day out there pal.
Austin: That's what you said about the toasters. You said I couldn't steal a toaster either.
> *Lee:* A toaster's got nothing' to do with the desert.
Austin: I could make it, Lee. I'm not that helpless. I can cook.
> *Lee:* Cook?
Austin: I can.
> *Lee:* So what! You can cook. Toast.
Austin: I can make fires. I know how to get fresh water from condensation.

[Austin stacks buttered toast up in a tall stack on plate.]

[Lee *slams table.]*

> *Lee:* It's not somethin' you learn out of a Boy Scout Handbook!
Austin: Well how do you learn it then! How're you supposed to learn it!

[Pause.]

> *Lee:* Ya' just learn it, that's all. Ya' learn it 'cause ya' have to learn it. You don't *have* to learn it.
Austin: You could teach me.
> *Lee:* *[Stands]* What're you, crazy or somethin'? You went to col-

lege. Here, you are down here, rollin' in bucks. Floatin' up and down in elevators. And you wanna' learn how to live on the desert!

Austin: I do, Lee. I really do. There's nothin' down here for me. There never was. When we were kids here it was different. There was a life here then. But now—I keep comin' down here thinkin' it's the fifties or somethin'. I keep finding myself getting off the freeway at familiar landmarks that turn out to be unfamiliar. On the way to appointments. Wandering down streets I thought I recognized that turn out to be replicas of streets I remember. Streets I misremember. Streets I can't tell if I lived on or saw in a postcard. Fields that don't even exist anymore.

Lee: There's no point cryin' about that now.

Austin: There's nothin' real down here, Lee! Least of all me!

Lee: Well I can't save you from that!

Austin: You can let me come with you.

Lee: No dice, pal.

Austin: You could let me come with you, Lee!

Lee: Hey, do you actually think I chose to live out in the middle a' nowhere? Do ya'? Ya' think it's some kinda' philosophical decision I took or somethin'? I'm livin' out there 'cause I can't make it here! And yer bitchin' to me about all yer success!

Austin: I'd cash it all in in a second. That's the truth.

Lee: [Pause, shakes his head] I can't believe this.

Austin: Let me go with you.

Lee: Stop sayin' that will ya'! Yer worse than a dog.

[Austin *offers out the plate of neatly stacked toast to* Lee.]

Austin: You want some toast?

[Lee *suddenly explodes and knocks the plate out of* Austin's *hand, toast goes flying, long frozen moment where it appears* Lee *might go all the way this time when* Austin *breaks it by slowly lowering himself to his knees and begins gathering the scattered toast from the floor and stacking it back on the plate,* Lee *begins to circle* Austin *in a slow, predatory way, crushing pieces of toast in his wake, no words for a while,* Austin *keeps gathering toast, even the crushed pieces.]*

Lee: Tell ya' what I'll do little brother. I might just consider makin' you a deal. Little trade. [Austin *continues gathering toast as* Lee *circles him through this]* You write me up this screenplay thing just like I tell ya'. I mean you can use all yer usual tricks and stuff. Yer fancy language. Yer artistic hocus pocus. But ya' gotta write everything like I say. Every move. Every time they run outa' gas, they run outa' gas. Every time they wanna' jump on a horse, they do just that. If they wanna' stay in Texas, by God they'll stay in Texas! [Keeps circling] And you finish the whole thing up for me. Top to bottom. And you put my name on it. And I own all the rights. And every dime goes in my pocket. You do all that and I'll sure enough take ya' with me to the desert. *[Lee stops, pause, looks down at* Austin*]* How's that sound?

[Pause as Austin *stands slowly holding plate of demolished toast, their faces are very close, pause.]*

Austin: It's a deal.

*[*Lee *stares straight into* Austin's *eyes, then he slowly takes a piece of toast off the plate, raises it to his mouth and takes a huge crushing bite never taking his eyes off* Austin's, *as* Lee *crunches into the toast the lights black out.]*

END SCENE 8

Scene 9

Mid-day, no sound, blazing heat, the stage is ravaged; bottles, toasters, smashed typewriter, ripped out telephone, etc. All the debris from previous scene is now starkly visible in intense yellow light, the effect should be like a desert junkyard at high noon, the coolness of the preceding scenes is totally obliterated. Austin *is seated at table in alcove, shirt open, pouring with sweat, hunched over a writing notebook, scribbling notes desperately with a ball-point pen.* Lee *with no shirt, beer in hand, sweat pouring down his chest is walking a slow circle around the table, picking his way through the objects, sometimes kicking them aside.*

    Lee: [As he walks] All right, read it back to me. Read it back to me!
Austin: [Scribbling at top speed] Just a second.
    Lee: Come on, come on! Just read what ya' got.
Austin: I can't keep up! It's not the same as if I had a typewriter.
    Lee: Just read what we got so far. Forget about the rest.
Austin: All right. Let's see—okay—*[Wipes sweat from his face, reads as* Lee *circles]* Luke says uh—
    Lee: Luke?
Austin: Yeah.
    Lee: His name's Luke? All right, all right—we can change the names later. What's he say? Come on, come on.
Austin: He says uh—*[Reading]* "I told ya' you were a fool to follow me in here. I know this prairie like the back a' my hand."
    Lee: No, no, no! That's not what I said. I never said that.
Austin: That's what I wrote.
    Lee: It's not what I said. I never said "like the back a' my hand". That's stupid. That's one a' those—whadya' call it? Whadya' call that?
Austin: What?
    Lee: Whadya' call it when somethin's been said a thousand times before. Whadya' call that?
Austin: Um—a cliche?
    Lee: Yeah. That's right. Cliche. That's what that is. A cliche. "The back a' my hand." That's stupid.

Austin: That's what you said.

　Lee: I never said that! And even if I did, that's where yer supposed to come in. That's where yer supposed to change it to somethin' better.

Austin: Well how am I supposed to do that and write down what you say at the same time?

　Lee: Ya' just do, that's all! You hear a stupid line you change it. That's yer job.

Austin: All right. *[Makes more notes]*

　Lee: What're you changin' it to?

Austin: I'm not changing it. I'm just trying to catch up.

　Lee: Well change it! We gotta' change that, we can't leave that in there like that. ". . . . the back a' my hand." That's dumb.

Austin: *[Stops writing, sits back]* All right.

　Lee: *[Pacing]* So what'll we change it to?

Austin: Um—How 'bout—"I'm on intimate terms with this prairie."

　Lee: *[To himself considering line as he walks]* "I'm on intimate terms with this prairie." Intimate terms, intimate terms. Intimate— that means like uh—sexual right?

Austin: Well—yeah—or—

　Lee: He's on sexual terms with the prairie? How dya' figure that?

Austin: Well it doesn't necessarily have to mean sexual.

　Lee: What's it mean then?

Austin: It means uh—close—personal—

　Lee: All right. How's it sound? Put it into the uh—the line there. Read it back. Let's see how it sounds. *[To himself]* "Intimate terms."

Austin: *[Scribbles in notebook]* Okay. It'd go something like this: *[Reads]* "I told ya' you were a fool to follow me in here. I'm on intimate terms with this prairie."

　Lee: That's good. I like that. That's real good.

Austin: You do?

　Lee: Yeah. Don't you?

Austin: Sure.

　Lee: Sounds original now. "Intimate terms." That's good. Okay. Now we're cookin'! That has a real ring to it.

[Austin makes more notes, Lee walks around, pours beer on his arms and rubs it over his chest feeling good about the new progress, as he does this Mom enters unobtrusively down left with her luggage, she stops and stares at the scene still holding luggage as the two men continue, unaware of her presence, Austin absorbed in his writing, Lee cooling himself off with beer.]

　Lee: *[Continues]* "He's on intimate terms with this prairie." Sounds real mysterious and kinda' threatening at the same time.

Austin: *[Writing rapidly]* Good.

　Lee: Now—*[Lee turns and suddenly sees* Mom, *he stares at her for a while, she stares back,* Austin *keeps writing feverishly, not noticing,* Lee *walks slowly over to* Mom *and takes a closer look, long pause.]*

Lee: Mom?

[Austin *looks up suddenly from his writing, sees* Mom, *stands quickly, long pause,* Mom *surveys the damage.]*

Austin: Mom. What're you doing back?

Mom: I'm back.

Lee: Here, lemme take those for ya.

[Lee *sets beer on counter then takes both her bags but doesn't know where to set them down in the sea of junk so he just keeps holding them.]*

Austin: I wasn't expecting you back so soon. I thought uh—How was Alaska?

Mom: Fine.

Lee: See any igloos?

Mom: No. Just glaciers.

Austin: Cold huh?

Mom: What?

Austin: It must've been cold up there?

Mom: Not really.

Lee: Musta' been colder than this here. I mean we're havin' a real scorcher here.

Mom: Oh? *[She looks at damage]*

Lee: Yeah. Must be in the hundreds.

Austin: You wanna' take your coat off, Mom?

Mom: No. *[Pause, she surveys space]* What happened in here?

Austin: Oh um—Me and Lee were just sort of celebrating and uh—

Mom: Celebrating?

Austin: Yeah. Uh—Lee sold a screenplay. A story, I mean.

Mom: Lee did?

Austin: Yeah.

Mom: Not you?

Austin: No. Him.

Mom: *[To* Lee*]* You sold a screenplay?

Lee: Yeah. That's right. We're just sorta' finishing it up right now. That's what we're doing here.

Austin: Me and Lee are going out to the desert to live.

Mom: You and Lee?

Austin: Yeah. I'm taking off with Lee.

Mom: *[She looks back and forth at each of them, pause]* You gonna go live with your father?

Austin: No. We're going to a different desert Mom.

Mom: I see. Well, you'll probably wind up on the same desert sooner or later. What're all these toasters doing here?

Austin: Well—we had kind of a contest.

Mom: Contest?

Lee: Yeah.

Austin: Lee won.

Mom: Did you win a lot of money, Lee?

Lee: Well not yet. It's comin' in any day now.

Mom: [To Lee] What happened to your shirt?

Lee: Oh. I was sweatin' like a pig and I took it off.

[Austin grabs Lee's shirt off the table and tosses it to him, Lee sets down suitcases and puts his shirt on.]

Mom: Well it's one hell of a mess in here isn't it?

Austin: Yeah, I'll clean it up for you, Mom. I just didn't know you were coming back so soon.

Mom: I didn't either.

Austin: What happened?

Mom: Nothing. I just started missing all my plants.

[She notices dead plants.]

Austin: Oh.

Mom: Oh, they're all dead aren't they. [She crosses toward them, examines them closely] You didn't get a chance to water I guess.

Austin: I was doing it and then Lee came and—

Lee: Yeah I just distracted him a whole lot here, Mom. It's not his fault.

[Pause, as Mom stares at plants.]

Mom: Oh well, one less thing to take care of I guess. [Turns toward brothers] Oh, that reminds me—You boys will probably never guess who's in town. Try and guess.

[Long pause, brothers stare at her.]

Austin: Whadya' mean, Mom?

Mom: Take a guess. Somebody very important has come to town. I read it, coming down on the Greyhound.

Lee: Somebody very important?

Mom: See if you can guess. You'll never guess.

Austin: Mom—we're trying to uh—[Points to writing pad]

Mom: Picasso. [Pause] Picasso's in town. Isn't that incredible? Right now.

[Pause.]

Austin: Picasso's dead, Mom.

Mom: No, he's not dead. He's visiting the museum. I read it on the bus. We have to go down there and see him.

Austin: Mom—

Mom: This is the chance of a lifetime. Can you imagine? We could all go down and meet him. All three of us.

Lee: Uh—I don't think I'm really up fer meetin' anybody right now. I'm uh—What's his name?

Mom: Picasso! Picasso! You've never heard of Picasso? Austin, you've heard of Picasso.

Austin: Mom, we're not going to have time.

Mom: It won't take long. We'll just hop in the car and go down there. An opportunity like this doesn't come along every day.

Austin: We're gonna' be leavin' here, Mom!

[Pause.]

Mom: Oh.

Lee: Yeah.

[Pause.]

Mom: You're both leaving?

Lee: *[Looks at* Austin] Well we were thinkin' about that before but now I—

Austin: No, we are! We're both leaving. We've got it all planned.

Mom: *[To* Austin] Well you can't leave. You have a family.

Austin: I'm leaving. I'm getting out of here.

Lee: *[To* Mom] I don't really think Austin's cut out for the desert do you?

Mom: No. He's not.

Austin: I'm going with you, Lee!

Mom: He's too thin.

Lee: Yeah, he'd just burn up out there.

Austin: *[To* Lee] We just gotta' finish this screenplay and then we're gonna' take off. That's the plan. That's what you said. Come on, let's get back to work, Lee.

Lee: I can't work under these conditions here. It's too hot.

Austin: Then we'll do it on the desert.

Lee: Don't be tellin' me what we're gonna do!

Mom: Don't shout in the house.

Lee: We're just gonna' have to postpone the whole deal.

Austin: I can't postpone it! It's gone past postponing! I'm doing everything you said. I'm writing down exactly what you tell me.

Lee: Yeah, but you were right all along see. It is a dumb story. "Two lamebrains chasin' each other across Texas." That's what you said, right?

Austin: I never said that.

*[*Lee *sneers in* Austin's *face then turns to* Mom.]*

Lee: I'm gonna' just borrow some a your antiques, Mom. You don't mind do ya'? Just a few plates and things. Silverware.

[Lee *starts going through all the cupboards in kitchen pulling out plates and stacking them on counter as* Mom *and* Austin *watch.*]

    Mom: You don't have any utensils on the desert?

    Lee: Nah, I'm fresh out.

  Austin: [*To* Lee] What're you doing?

    Mom: Well some of those are very old. Bone China.

    Lee: I'm tired of eatin' outa' my bare hands, ya' know. It's not civilized.

  Austin: [*To* Lee] What're you doing? We made a deal!

    Mom: Couldn't you borrow the plastic ones instead? I have plenty of plastic ones.

    Lee: [*As he stacks plates*] It's not the same. Plastic's not the same at all. What I need is somethin' authentic. Somethin' to keep me in touch. It's easy to get outa' touch out there. Don't worry I'll get 'em back to ya'.

[Austin *rushes up to* Lee, *grabs him by shoulders.*]

  Austin: You can't just drop the whole thing, Lee!

[Lee *turns, pushes* Austin *in the chest knocking him backwards into the alcove,* Mom *watches numbly,* Lee *returns to collecting the plates, silverware, etc.*]

    Mom: You boys shouldn't fight in the house. Go outside and fight.

    Lee: I'm not fightin'. I'm leavin'.

    Mom: There's been enough damage done already.

    Lee: [*His back to* Austin *and* Mom, *stacking dishes on counter*] I'm clearin' outa' here once and for all. All this town does is drive a man insane. Look what it's done to Austin there. I'm not lettin' that happen to me. Sell myself down the river. No sir. I'd rather be a hundred miles from nowhere than let that happen to me.

[*During this* Austin *has picked up the ripped out phone from the floor and wrapped the cord tightly around both his hands, he lunges at* Lee *whose back is still to him, wraps the cord around* Lee's *neck, plants a foot in* Lee's *back and pulls back on the cord, tightening it,* Lee *chokes desperately, can't speak and can't reach* Austin *with his arms,* Austin *keeps applying pressure on* Lee's *back with his foot, bending him into the sink,* Mom *watches.*]

  Austin: [*Tightening cord*] You're not goin' anywhere! You're not takin' anything with you. You're not takin' my car! You're not takin' the dishes! You're not takin' anything! You're stayin' right here!

    Mom: You'll have to stop fighting in the house. There's plenty of room outside to fight. You've got the whole outdoors to fight in.

[Lee *tries to tear himself away, he crashes across the stage like an enraged bull dragging* Austin *with him, he snorts and bellows but* Austin *hangs on and manages to keep clear of* Lee's *attempts to grab him, they crash into the table, to the floor,*

Lee *is face down thrashing wildly and choking,* Austin *pulls cord tighter, stands with one foot planted on* Lee's *back and the cord stretched taut.]*

Austin: *[Holding cord]* Gimme back my keys, Lee! Take the keys out! Take 'em out!

*[*Lee *desperately tries to dig in his pockets, searching for the car keys,* Mom *moves closer.]*

  Mom: *[Calmly to* Austin*]* You're not killing him are you?
Austin: I don't know. I don't know if I'm killing him. I'm stopping him. That's all. I'm just stopping him.

*[*Lee *thrashes but* Austin *is relentless.]*

  Mom: You oughta' let him breathe a little bit.
Austin: Throw the keys out, Lee!

*[*Lee *finally gets keys out and throws them on floor but out of* Austin's *reach,* Austin *keeps pressure on cord, pulling* Lee's *neck back,* Lee *gets one hand to the cord but can't relieve the pressure.]*

        Reach me those keys would ya', Mom.
  Mom: *[Not moving]* Why are you doing this to him?
Austin: Reach me the keys!
  Mom: Not until you stop choking him.
Austin: I can't stop choking him! He'll kill me if I stop choking him!
  Mom: He won't kill you. He's your brother.
Austin: Just get me the keys would ya'!

[Pause. Mom *picks keys up off floor, hands them to* Austin.]

Austin: *[To* Mom*]* Thanks.
  Mom: Will you let him go now?
Austin: I don't know. He's not gonna' let me get outa' here.
  Mom: Well you can't kill him.
Austin: I can kill him! I can easily kill him. Right now. Right here. All I gotta' do is just tighten up. See? *[He tightens cord,* Lee *thrashes wildly,* Austin *releases pressure a little, maintaining control]* Ya' see that?
  Mom: That's a savage thing to do.
Austin: Yeah well don't tell me I can't kill him because I can. I can just twist. I can just keep twisting.

*[*Austin *twists the cord tighter,* Lee *weakens, his breathing changes to a short rasp.]*

  Mom: Austin!

*[*Austin *relieves pressure,* Lee *breathes easier but* Austin *keeps him under control.]*

Austin: *[Eyes on* Lee, *holding cord]* I'm goin' to the desert. There's nothing stopping me. I'm going by myself to the desert.

[Mom moving toward her luggage.]

   Mom: Well, I'm going to go check into a motel. I can't stand this
      anymore.
Austin: Don't go yet!

[Mom pauses.]

   Mom: I can't stay here. This is worse than being homeless.
Austin: I'll get everything fixed up for you, Mom. I promise. Just stay
      for a while.
   Mom: *[Picking up luggage]* You're going to the desert.
Austin: Just wait!

[Lee thrashes, Austin subdues him, Mom watches holding luggage, pause.]

   Mom: It was the worst feeling being up there. In Alaska. Staring out
      a window. I never felt so desperate before. That's why when I
      saw that article on Picasso I thought—
Austin: Stay here, Mom. This is where you live.

[She looks around the stage.]

   Mom: I don't recognize it at all.

*[She exits with luggage, Austin makes a move toward her but Lee starts to struggle
and Austin subdues him again with cord, pause.]*

Austin: *[Holding cord]* Lee? I'll make ya' a deal. You let me get outa'
      here. Just let me get to my car. All right, Lee? Gimme a little
      headstart and I'll turn you loose. Just gimme a little headstart.
      All right?

*[Lee makes no response, Austin slowly releases tension on cord, still nothing from
Lee.]*

Austin: Lee?

*[Lee is motionless, Austin very slowly begins to stand, still keeping a tenuous hold
on the cord and his eyes riveted to Lee for any sign of movement, Austin slowly
drops the cord and stands, he stares down at Lee who appears to be dead.]*

Austin: *[Whispers]* Lee?

*[Pause. Austin considers, looks toward exit, back to Lee, then makes a small move-
ment as if to leave. Instantly Lee is on his feet and moves toward exit, blocking
Austin's escape. They square off to each other, keeping a distance between them,
pause, a single coyote heard in distance, lights fade softly into moonlight, the figures of the brothers now appear to be caught in a vast desert-like landscape, they are
very still but watchful for the next move, lights go slowly to black as the after-image
of the brothers pulses in the dark, coyote fades.]*

END ACT 2

Further Reading

Cott, Jonathan. "Sam Shepard: The *Rolling Stone* Interview." *Rolling Stone* (18 Dec. 1986): 166ff. • Gilman, Richard. Introduction. *Seven Plays.* By Sam Shepard. New York: Bantam Books, 1981. ix–xxv. • Patraka, Vivian M., and Mark Siegel. *Sam Shepard.* Boise, Idaho: Boise State University, 1985. 42–44. • Orbison, Tucker. "Mythic Levels in Shepard's *True West.*" In *Essays on Modern American Drama: Williams, Miller, Albee, and Shepard.* Ed. Dorothy Parker. Toronto: U of Toronto P, 1987. 188–202. • Mottram, Ron. "The Family: 'Fist Fights Across the Table.' " *Inner Landscapes: The Theater of Sam Shepard.* Columbia: U of Missouri P, 1984. 132–57, spec. 144–49. • Rich, Frank. "Shepard's *True West:* Myths v. Reality." *New York Times* 24 Dec. 1980: 3.9.

Sam Shepard, perhaps because he writes plays set in the American West and makes free use of the mythology of the cowboy, is sometimes seen as a sort of primitive, writing plays that are unrelated to the great traditions of drama. Interviewed by Jonathan Cott for Rolling Stone, *however, Shepard showed a literary allegiance that few people would have expected.*

Sam Shepard: On the Impact of Greek Drama

Interviewer: You seem to like Marlowe a lot. When did you first read him?

Shepard: I'll tell you—aside from assigned reading in high school, I didn't read any plays except for a couple of Brecht things when I was living in New York City. I avoided reading out of arrogance, really. But when I went to England in the early Seventies, I suddenly found myself having a kind of dry spell. It was difficult for me to write, so I started to read. And I read most of the Greek guys—Aeschylus, Sophocles. . . . I studied up on those guys, and I'm glad I did. I was just amazed by the simplicity of the ancient Greek plays, for instance—they were dead simple. Nothing complex or tricky . . . which surprised the hell out of me, because I'd assumed they were beyond me. But now I began to comprehend what they were talking about, and they turned out to be accessible.

Interviewer: They're a lot about the family romance, aren't they?

Shepard: They're all about destiny! That's the most powerful thing. Everything is foreseen, and we just play it out.

Interviewer:	You don't think a person can shape his own destiny?
Shepard:	Oh, maybe. But first you have to know what your destiny is.
Interviewer:	When did you think you knew your own?
Shepard:	I'm not so sure I do. I'm not saying I know my destiny; I'm saying that it exists. It exists, and it can become a duty to discover it. Or it can be shirked. But if you take it on as your duty, then it becomes a different thing from dismissing it altogether and just imagining that it'll work itself out anyway. I mean, it will. But it's more interesting to try to find it and know it.
Interviewer:	The words also pass by unnoticed because they're so well rooted in intense but simple colloquial speech.
Shepard:	I think you have to start in that colloquial territory, and from there move on and arrive in poetic country . . . but not the other way around. I've noticed that even with the Greek guys, especially with Sophocles, there's a very simple, rawboned language. The choruses are poetic, but the speech of the characters themselves is terse, cut to the bone and pointed to the heart of the problem. It's like Merle Haggard tunes like "My Own Kind of Hat"—I do this, that and some other thing, but I wear my own kind of hat. . . . Real simple.

AUGUST WILSON

(b. 1945)

JOE TURNER'S COME AND GONE

CHARACTERS

Seth Holly, owner of the boardinghouse
Bertha Holly, his wife
Bynum Walker, a rootworker
Rutherford Selig, a peddler
Jeremy Furlow, a resident
Herald Loomis, a resident
Zonia Loomis, his daughter
Mattie Campbell, a resident
Reuben Scott, boy who lives next door
Molly Cunningham, a resident
Martha Loomis, Herald Loomis's wife

SETTING

August, 1911. A boardinghouse in Pittsburgh. At right
is a kitchen. Two doors open off the kitchen. One
leads to the outhouse and Seth's workshop. The other
to Seth's and Bertha's bedroom. At left is a parlor.
The front door opens into the parlor, which gives
access to the stairs leading to the upstairs rooms.
There is a small outside playing area.

THE PLAY

It is August in Pittsburgh, 1911. The sun falls out of
heaven like a stone. The fires of the steel mill rage with
a combined sense of industry and progress. Barges
loaded with coal and iron ore trudge up the river to the
mill towns that dot the Monongahela and return with
fresh, hard, gleaming steel. The city flexes its muscles.
Men throw countless bridges across the rivers, lay
roads, and carve tunnels through the hills sprouting
with houses.
     From the deep and the near South the sons and
daughters of newly freed African slaves wander into the

city. Isolated, cut off from memory, having forgotten the names of the gods and only guessing at their faces, they arrive dazed and stunned, their hearts kicking in their chests, with a song worth singing. They arrive carrying Bibles and guitars, their pockets lined with dust and fresh hope, marked men and women seeking to scrape from the narrow, crooked cobbles and the fiery blasts of the coke furnace a way of bludgeoning and shaping the malleable parts of themselves into a new identity as free men of definite and sincere worth.

Foreigners in a strange land, they carry as part and parcel of their baggage a long line of separation and dispersement which informs their sensibilities and marks their conduct as they search for ways to reconnect, to reassemble, to give clear and luminous meaning to the song which is both a wail and a whelp of joy.

ACT ONE

Scene One

The lights come up on the kitchen. Bertha *busies herself with breakfast preparations.* Seth *stands looking out the window at* Bynum *in the yard.* Seth *is in his early fifties. Born of Northern free parents, a skilled craftsman, and owner of the boardinghouse, he has a stability that none of the other characters have.* Bertha *is five years his junior. Married for over twenty-five years, she has learned how to negotiate around* Seth's *apparent orneriness.*

Seth: *(at the window, laughing.)* If that ain't the damndest thing I seen. Look here, Bertha.

Bertha: I done seen Bynum out there with them pigeons before.

Seth: Naw . . . Naw . . . look at this. That pigeon flopped out of Bynum's hand and he about to have a fit.

(Bertha *crosses over to the window.*)

He down there on his hands and knees behind that bush looking all over for that pigeon and it on the other side of the yard. See it over there?

Bertha: Come on and get your breakfast and leave that man alone.

Seth: Look at him . . . he still looking. He ain't seen it yet. All that old mumbo jumbo nonsense. I don't know why I put up with it.

Bertha: You don't say nothing when he bless the house.

Seth: I just go along with that 'cause of you. You around here sprinkling salt all over the place . . . got pennies lined up across the threshold . . . all that heebie-jeebie stuff. I just put up with that 'cause of you. I don't pay that kind of stuff no mind. And you going down there to the church and wanna come home and sprinkle salt all over the place.

Bertha: It don't hurt none. I can't say if it help . . . but it don't hurt none.

Seth: Look at him. He done found that pigeon and now he's talking to it.

Bertha: These biscuits be ready in a minute.

Seth: He done drew a big circle with that stick and now he's dancing around. I know he'd better not . . .

(Seth *bolts from the window and rushes to the back door.*)

Hey, Bynum! Don't be hopping around stepping in my vegetables.

Hey, Bynum . . . Watch where you stepping!

Bertha: Seth, leave that man alone.

Seth: (*coming back into the house.*) I don't care how much he be dancing around . . . just don't be stepping in my vegetables. Man got my garden all messed up now . . . planting them weeds out there . . . burying them pigeons and whatnot.

Bertha: Bynum don't bother nobody. He ain't even thinking about your vegetables.

Seth: I know he ain't! That's why he out there stepping on them.

Bertha: What Mr. Johnson say down there?

Seth: I told him if I had the tools I could go out here and find me four or five fellows and open up my own shop instead of working for Mr. Olowski. Get me four or five fellows and teach them how to make pots and pans. One man making ten pots is five men making fifty. He told me he'd think about it.

Bertha: Well, maybe he'll come to see it your way.

Seth: He wanted me to sign over the house to him. You know what I thought of that idea.

Bertha: He'll come to see you're right.

Seth: I'm going up and talk to Sam Green. There's more than one way to skin a cat. I'm going up and talk to him. See if he got more sense that Mr. Johnson. I can't get nowhere working for Mr. Olowski and selling Selig five or six pots on the side. I'm going up and see Sam Green. See if he loan me the money.

(Seth *crosses back to the window.*)

Now he got that cup. He done killed that pigeon and now he's putting its blood in that little cup. I believe he drink that blood.

Bertha: Seth Holly, what is wrong with you this morning? Come on and get your breakfast so you can go to bed. You know Bynum don't be drinking no pigeon blood.

Seth: I don't know what he do.

Bertha: Well, watch him, then. He's gonna dig a little hole and bury that pigeon. Then he's gonna pray over that blood . . . pour it on top . . . mark out his circle and come on into the house.

Seth: That's what he doing . . . he pouring that blood on top.

Bertha: When they gonna put you back working daytime? Told me two
 months ago he was gonna put you back working daytime.

Seth: That's what Mr. Olowski told me. I got to wait till he say when.
 He tell me what to do. I don't tell him. Drive me crazy to specu-
 late on the man's wishes when he don't know what he want to do
 himself.

Bertha: Well, I wish he go ahead and put you back working daytime.
 This working all hours of the night don't make no sense.

Seth: It don't make no sense for that boy to run out of here and get
 drunk so they lock him up either.

Bertha: Who? Who they got locked up for being drunk?

Seth: That boy that's staying upstairs . . . Jeremy. I stopped down
 there on Logan Street on my way home from work and one of the
 fellows told me about it. Say he seen it when they arrested him.

Bertha: I was wondering why I ain't seen him this morning.

Seth: You know I don't put up with that. I told him when he
 came . . .

(Bynum *enters from the yard carrying some plants. He is a short, round man in his
early sixties. A conjure man, or rootworker, he gives the impression of always being
in control of everything. Nothing ever bothers him. He seems to be lost in a world of
his own making and to swallow any adversity or interference with his grand
design.*)

What you doing bringing them weeds in my house? Out there
 stepping on my vegetables and now wanna carry them weeds in my
 house.

Bynum: Morning, Seth. Morning, Sister Bertha.

Seth: Messing up my garden growing them things out there. I ought
 to go out there and pull up all them weeds.

Bertha: Some gal was by here to see you this morning, Bynum. You was
 out there in the yard . . . I told her to come back later.

Bynum: (*To* Seth.) You look sick. What's the matter, you ain't eating
 right?

Seth: What if I was sick? You ain't getting near me with none of that
 stuff.

(Bertha *sets a plate of biscuits on the table.*)

Bynum: My . . . my . . . Bertha, your biscuits getting fatter and fatter.

(Bynum *takes a biscuit and begins to eat.*)

Where Jeremy? I don't see him around this morning. He usually
 be around riffing and raffing on Saturday morning.

Seth: I know where he at. I know just where he at. They got him
 down there in the jail. Getting drunk and acting a fool. He down
 there where he belong with all that foolishness.

Bynum: Mr. Piney's boys got him, huh? They ain't gonna do nothing but hold on to him for a little while. He's gonna be back here hungrier than a mule directly.

Seth: I don't go for all that carrying on and such. This is a respectable house. I don't have no drunkards or fools around here.

Bynum: That boy got a lot of country in him. He ain't been up here but two weeks. It's gonna take a wile before he can work that country out of him.

Seth: These niggers coming up here with that old backward country style of living. It's hard enough now without all that ignorant kind of acting. Ever since slavery got over with there ain't been nothing but foolish-acting niggers. Word get out they need men to work in the mill and put in these roads . . . and niggers drop everything and head North looking for freedom. They don't know the white fellows looking too. White fellows coming from all over the world. White fellow come over and in six months got more than what I got. But these niggers keep on coming. Walking . . . riding . . . carrying their Bibles. That boy done carried a guitar all the way from North Carolina. What he gonna find out? What he gonna do with that guitar? This the city.

(There is a knock on the door.)

Niggers coming up here from the backwoods . . . coming up here from the country carrying Bibles and guitars looking for freedom. They got a rude awakening.

(Seth goes to answer the door. Rutherford Selig enters. About Seth's age, he is a thin white man with greasy hair. A peddler, he supplies Seth with the raw materials to make pots and pans which he then peddles door to door in the mill towns along the river. He keeps a list of his customers as they move about and is known in the various communities as the People Finder. He carries squares of sheet metal under his arm.)

Ho! Forgot you was coming today. Come on in.

Bynum: If it ain't Rutherford Selig . . . the People Finder himself.

Selig: What say there, Bynum?

Bynum: I say about my shiny man. You got to tell me something. I done give you my dollar . . . I'm looking to get a report.

Selig: I got eight here, Seth.

Seth: (*Taking the sheet metal.*) What is this? What you giving me here? What I'm gonna do with this?

Selig: I need some dustpans. Everybody asking me about dustpans.

Seth: Gonna cost you fifteen cents apiece. And ten cents to put a handle on them.

Selig: I'll give you twenty cents apiece with the handles.

Seth: Alright. But I ain't gonna give you but fifteen cents for the sheet metal.

Selig: It's twenty-five cents apiece for the metal. That's what we agreed on.

Seth: This low-grade sheet metal. They ain't worth but a dime. I'm doing you a favor giving you fifteen cents. You know this metal ain't worth no twenty-five cents. Don't come talking that twenty-five cent stuff to me over no low-grade sheet metal.

Selig: Alright, fifteen cents apiece. Just make me some dustpans out of them.

(Seth *exits with the sheet metal out the back door.*)

Bertha: Sit on down there, Selig. Get you a cup of coffee and a biscuit.

Bynum: Where you coming from this time?

Selig: I been upriver. All along the Monongahela. Past Rankin and all up around Little Washington.

Bynum: Did you find anybody?

Selig: I found Sadie Jackson up in Braddock. Her mother's staying down there in Scotchbottom say she hadn't heard from her and she didn't know where she was at. I found her up in Braddock on Enoch Street. She bought a frying pan from me.

Bynum: You around here finding everybody how come you ain't found my shiny man?

Selig: The only shiny man I saw was the Nigras working on the road gang with the sweat glistening on them.

Bynum: Naw, you'd be able to tell this fellow. He shine like new money.

Selig: Well, I done told you I can't find nobody without a name.

Bertha: Here go one of these hot biscuits, Selig.

Bynum: This fellow don't have no name. I call him John 'cause it was up around Johnstown where I seen him. I ain't even so sure he's one special fellow. That shine could pass on to anybody. He could be anybody shining.

Selig: Well, what's he look like beside being shiny? There's lots of shiny Nigras.

Bynum: He's just a man I seen out on the road. He ain't had no special look. Just a man walking toward me on the road. He come up and asked me which way the road went. I told him everything I knew about the road, where it went and all, and he asked me did I have anything to eat 'cause he was hungry. Say he ain't had nothing to eat in three days. Well, I never be out there on the road without a piece of fried meat. Or an orange or an apple. So I give this fellow an orange. He take and eat that orange and told me to come and go along the road a little ways with him, that he had something he wanted to show me. He had a look about him made me wanna go with him, see what he gonna show me.

    We walked on a bit and it's getting kind of far from where I met him when it come up on me all of a sudden, we wasn't going the way he had come from, we was going back my way. Since he said he ain't knew nothing about the road, I asked him about this. He say he had a voice inside him telling him which way to go and if I come and go along with him he was gonna show me the Secret of Life. Quite naturally I followed him. A fellow that's gonna show you the Secret of Life ain't to be taken lightly. We get near this bend in the road . . .

(Seth *enters with an assortment of pots.*)

Seth: I got six here, Selig.

Selig: Wait a minute, Seth. Bynum's telling me about the secret of life. Go ahead, Bynum. I wanna here this.

(Seth *sets the pots down and exits out the back.*)

Bynum: We get near this bend in the road and he told me to hold out my hands. Then he rubbed them together with his and I looked down and see they got blood on them. Told me to take and rub it all over me . . . say that was a way of cleaning myself. Then we went around the bend in that road. Got around that bend and it seem like all of a sudden we ain't in the same place. Turn around that bend and everything look like it was twice as big as it was. The trees and everything bigger than life! Sparrows big as eagles! I turned around to look at this fellow and he had this light coming out of him. I had to cover up my eyes to keep from being blinded. He shining like new money with that light. He shined until all the light seemed like it seeped out of him and then he was gone and I was by myself in this strange place where everything was bigger than life.

I wandered around there looking for that road, trying to find my way back from this big place . . . and I looked over and seen my daddy standing there. He was the same size he always was, except for his hands and his mouth. He had a great big old mouth that look like it took up his whole face and his hands were as big as hams. Look like they was too big to carry around. My daddy called me to him. Said he had been thinking about me and it grieved him to see me in the world carrying other people's songs and not having one of my own. Told me he was gonna show me how to find my song. Then he carried me further into this big place until we come to this ocean. Then he showed me something I ain't got words to tell you. But if you stand to witness it, you done seen something there. I stayed in that place awhile and my daddy taught me the meaning of this thing that I had seen and showed me how to find my song. I asked him about the shiny man and he told me he was the One Who Goes Before and Shows the Way. Said there was lots of shiny men and if I ever saw one again before I died then I would know that my song had been accepted and worked its full power in the world and I could lay down and die a happy man. A man who done left his mark on life. On the way people cling to each other out of the truth they find in themselves. Then he showed me how to get back to the road. I came out to where everything was its own size and I had my song. I had the Binding Song. I choose that song because that's what I seen most when I was traveling . . . people walking away and leaving one another. So I takes the power of my song and binds them together.

(Seth enters from the yard carrying cabbages and tomatoes.)

Been binding people ever since. That's why they call me Bynum. Just like glue I sticks people together.

Seth: Maybe they ain't supposed to be stuck sometimes. You ever think of that?

Bynum: Oh, I don't do it lightly. It cost me a piece of myself every time I do. I'm a Binder of What Clings. You got to find out if they cling first. You can't bind what don't cling.

Selig: Well, how is that the Secret of Life? I thought you said he was gonna show you the secret of life. That's what I'm waiting to find out.

Bynum: Oh, he showed me alright. But you still got to figure it out. Can't nobody figure it out for you. You got to come to it on your own. That's why I'm looking for the shiny man.

Selig: Well, I'll keep my eye out for him. What you got there, Seth?

Seth: Here go some cabbage and tomatoes. I got some green beans coming in real nice. I'm gonna take and start me a grapevine out there next year. Butera says he gonna give me a piece of his vine and I'm gonna start that out there.

Selig: How many of them pots you got?

Seth: I got six. That's six dollars minus eight on top of fifteen for the sheet metal come to a dollar twenty out the six dollars leave me four dollars and eighty cents.

Selig: *(Counting out the money.)* There's four dollars . . . and . . . eighty cents.

Seth: How many of them dustpans you want?

Selig: As many as you can make out them sheets.

Seth: You can use that many? I get to cutting on them sheets figuring how to make them dustpans . . . ain't no telling how many I'm liable to come up with.

Selig: I can use them and you can make me some more next time.

Seth: Alright, I'm gonna hold you to that, now.

Selig: Thanks for the biscuit, Bertha.

Bertha: You know you welcome anytime, Selig.

Seth: Which way you heading?

Selig: Going down to Wheeling. All through West Virginia there.

I'll be back Saturday. They putting in new roads down that way. Makes traveling easier.

Seth: That's what I hear. All up around here too. Got a fellow staying here working on that road by the Brady Street Bridge.

Selig: Yeah, it's gonna make traveling real nice. Thanks for the cabbage, Seth. I'll see you on Saturday.

(Selig exits.)

Seth: *(To* Bynum.*)* Why you wanna start all that nonsense talk with that man? All that shiny man nonsense.

Bynum: You know it ain't no nonsense. Bertha know it ain't no nonsense. I don't know if Selig know or not.

Bertha: Seth, when you get to making them dustpans make me a coffeepot.

Seth: What's the matter with your coffee? Ain't nothing wrong with your coffee. Don't she make some good coffee, Bynum?

Bynum: I ain't worried about the coffee. I know she makes some good biscuits.

Seth: I ain't studying no coffeepot, woman. You heard me tell the man I was gonna cut as many dustpans as them sheets will make . . . and all of a sudden you want a coffeepot.

Bertha: Man, hush up and go on and make me that coffeepot.

(Jeremy enters the front door. About twenty-five, he gives the impression that he has the world in his hand, that he can meet life's challenges head on. He smiles a lot. He is a proficient guitar player, though his spirit has yet to be molded into song.)

Bynum: I hear Mr. Piney's boys had you.

Jeremy: Fined me two dollars for nothing! Ain't done nothing.

Seth: I told you when you come on here everybody know my house. Know these is respectable quarters. I don't put up with no foolishness. Everybody know Seth Holly keep a good house. Was my daddy's house. This house been a decent house for a long time.

Jeremy: I ain't done nothing, Mr. Seth. I stopped by the Workmen's Club and got me a bottle. Me and Roper Lee from Alabama. Had us a half pint. We was fixing to cut that half in two when they came up on us. Asked us if we was working. We told them we was putting in the road over yonder and that it was our payday. They snatched hold of us to get that two dollars. Me and Roper Lee ain't even had a chance to take a drink when they grabbed us.

Seth: I don't go for all that kind of carrying on.

Bertha: Leave the boy alone, Seth. You know the police do that. Figure there's too many people out on the street they take some of them off. You know that.

Seth: I ain't gonna have folks talking.

Bertha: Ain't nobody talking nothing. That's all in your head. You
want some grits and biscuits, Jeremy?

Jeremy: Thank you, Miss Bertha. They didn't give us a thing to eat last
night. I'll take one of them big bowls if you don't mind.

*(There is a knock at the door. Seth goes to answer it. Enter Herald Loomis and
his eleven-year-old daughter, Zonia. Herald Loomis is thirty-two years old. He
is at times possessed. A man driven not by the hellhounds that seemingly bay at his
heels, but by his search for a world that speaks to something about himself. He is
unable to harmonize the forces that swirl around him, and seeks to recreate the
world into one that contains his image. He wears a hat and a long wool coat.)*

Loomis: Me and my daughter looking for a place to stay, mister. You
got a sign say you got rooms.

(Seth stares at Loomis, sizing him up.)

Mister, if you ain't got no rooms we can go somewhere else.

Seth: How long you plan on staying?

Loomis: Don't know. Two weeks or more maybe.

Seth: It's two dollars a week for the room. We serve meals twice a
day. It's two dollars for room and board. Pay up in advance.

(Loomis reaches into his pocket.)

It's a dollar extra for the girl.

Loomis: The girl sleep in the same room.

Seth: Well, do she eat off the same plate? We serve meals twice a
day. That's a dollar extra for food.

Loomis: Ain't got no extra dollar. I was planning on asking your missus
if she could help out with the cooking and cleaning and whatnot.

Seth: Her helping out don't put no food on the table. I need that
dollar to buy some food.

Loomis: I'll give you fifty cents extra. She don't eat much.

Seth: Okay . . . but fifty cents don't buy but half a portion.

Bertha: Seth, she can help me out. Let her help me out. I can use
some help.

Seth: Well, that's two dollars for the week. Pay up in advance. Saturday to Saturday. You wanna stay on then it's two more come
Saturday.

(Loomis pays Seth the money.)

Bertha: My name's Bertha. This my husband, Seth. You got Bynum
and Jeremy over there.

Loomis: Ain't nobody else live here?

Bertha: They the only ones live here now. People come and go. They
the only ones here now. You want a cup of coffee and a biscuit?

Loomis: We done ate this morning.

Bynum: Where you coming from, Mister . . . I didn't get your name.

Loomis: Name's Herald Loomis. This my daughter, Zonia.

Bynum: Where you coming from?

Loomis: Come from all over. Whicheverway the road take us that's the way we go.

Jeremy: If you looking for a job, I'm working putting in that road down there by the bridge. They can't get enough mens. Always looking to take somebody on.

Loomis: I'm looking for a woman named Martha Loomis. That's my wife. Got married legal with the papers and all.

Seth: I don't know nobody named Loomis. I know some Marthas but I don't know no Loomis.

Bynum: You got to see Rutherford Selig if you wanna find somebody. Selig's the People Finder. Rutherford Selig's a first-class People Finder.

Jeremy: What she look like? Maybe I seen her.

Loomis: She a brownskin woman. Got long pretty hair. About five feet from the ground.

Jeremy: I don't know. I might have seen her.

Bynum: You got to see Rutherford Selig. You give him one dollar to get her name on his list . . . and after she get her name on his list Rutherford Selig will go right on out there and find her. I got him looking for somebody for me.

Loomis: You say he find people. How you find him?

Bynum: You just missed him. He's gone downriver now. You got to wait till Saturday. He's gone downriver with his pots and pans. He come to see Seth on Saturdays. You got to wait till then.

Seth: Come on, I'll show you to your room.

(Seth, Loomis, *and* Zonia *exit up the stairs.*)

Jeremy: Miss Bertha, I'll take that biscuit you was gonna give that fellow, if you don't mind. Say, Mr. Bynum, they got somebody like that around here sure enough? Somebody that find people?

Bynum: Rutherford Selig. He go around selling pots and pans and every house he come to he write down the name and address of whoever lives there. So if you looking for somebody, quite naturally you go and see him . . . 'cause he's the only one who know where everybody live at.

Jeremy: I ought to have him look for this old gal I used to know. It be nice to see her again.

Bertha: (*Giving* Jeremy *a biscuit.*) Jeremy, today's the day for you to pull them sheets off the bed and set them outside your door. I'll set you out some clean ones.

Bynum: Mr. Piney's boys done ruined your good time last night, Jeremy . . . what you planning for tonight?

Jeremy: They got me scared to go out, Mr. Bynum. They might grab me again.

Bynum: You ought to take your guitar and go down to Seefus. Seefus got a gambling place down there on Wylie Avenue. You ought to take your guitar and go down there. They got guitar contest down there.

Jeremy: I don't play no contest, Mr. Bynum. Had one of them white fellows cure me of that. I ain't been nowhere near a contest since.

Bynum: White fellow beat you playing guitar?

Jeremy: Naw, he ain't beat me. I was sitting at home just fixing to sit down and eat when somebody come up to my house and got me. Told me there's a white fellow say he was gonna give a prize to the best guitar player he could find. I take up my guitar and go down there and somebody had gone up and got Bobo Smith and brought him down there. Him and another fellow called Hooter. Old Hooter couldn't play no guitar, he do more hollering than playing, but Bobo could go at it awhile.

This fellow standing there say he the one that was gonna give the prize and me and Bobo started playing for him. Bobo play something and then I'd try to play something better than what he played. Old Hooter, he just holler and bang at the guitar. Man was the worst guitar player I ever seen. So me and Bobo played and after a while I seen where he was getting the attention of this white fellow. He'd play something and while he was playing it he be slapping on the side of the guitar, and that made it sound like he was playing more than he was. So I started doing it too. White fellow ain't knew no difference. He ain't knew as much about guitar playing as Hooter did. After we play awhile, the white fellow called us to him and said he couldn't make up his mind, say all three of us was the best guitar player and we'd have to split the prize between us. Then he give us twenty-five cents. That's eight cents apiece and a penny on the side. That cured me of playing contest to this day.

Bynum: Seefus ain't like that. Seefus give a whole dollar and a drink of whiskey.

Jeremy: What night they be down there?

Bynum: Be down there every night. Music don't know no certain night.

Bertha: You go down to Seefus with them people and you liable to end up in a raid and go to jail sure enough. I don't know why Bynum tell you that.

Bynum: That's where the music at. That's where the people at. The people down there making music and enjoying themselves. Some things is worth taking the chance going to jail about.

Bertha: Jeremy ain't got no business going down there.

Jeremy: They got some women down there, Mr. Bynum?

Bynum: Oh, they got women down there, sure. They got women everywhere. Women be where the men is so they can find each other.

Jeremy: Some of them old gals come out there where we be putting in that road. Hanging around there trying to snatch somebody.

Bynum: How come some of them ain't snatched hold of you?

Jeremy: I don't want them kind. Them desperate kind. Ain't nothing worse than a desperate woman. Tell them you gonna leave them and they get to crying and carrying on. That just make you want to get away quicker. They get to cutting up your clothes and things trying to keep you staying. Desperate women ain't nothing but trouble for a man.

(Seth *enters from the stairs.*)

    Seth: Something ain't setting right with that fellow.

Bertha: What's wrong with him? What he say?

    Seth: I take him up there and try to talk to him and he ain't for no talking. Say he been traveling . . . coming over from Ohio. Say he a deacon in the church. Say he looking for Martha Pentecost. Talking about that's his wife.

Bertha: How you know it's the same Martha? Could be talking about anybody. Lots of people named Martha.

    Seth: You see that little girl? I didn't hook it up till he said it, but that little girl look just like her. Ask Bynum. (*To* Bynum.) Bynum. Don't that little girl look just like Martha Pentecost?

Bertha: I still say he could be talking about anybody.

    Seth: The way he described her wasn't no doubt about who he was talking about. Described her right down to her toes.

Bertha: What did you tell him?

    Seth: I ain't told him nothing. The way that fellow look I wasn't gonna tell him nothing. I don't know what he looking for her for.

Bertha: What else he have to say?

    Seth: I told you he wasn't for no talking. I told him where the out-house was and to keep that gal off the front porch and out of my garden. He asked if you'd mind setting a hot tub for the gal and that was about the gist of it.

Bertha: Well, I wouldn't let it worry me if I was you. Come on get your sleep.

Bynum: He says he looking for Martha and he a deacon in the church.

    Seth: That's what he say. Do he look like a deacon to you?

Bertha: He might be, you don't know. Bynum ain't got no special say on whether he a deacon or not.

    Seth: Well, if he the deacon I'd sure like to see the preacher.

Bertha: Come on get your sleep. Jeremy, don't forget to set them sheets outside the door like I told you.

(Bertha *exits into the bedroom.*)

    Seth: Something ain't setting right with that fellow, Bynum. He's

one of them mean-looking niggers look like he done killed somebody gambling over a quarter.

Bynum: He ain't no gambler. Gamblers wear nice shoes. This fellow
got on clodhoppers. He been out there walking up and down
them roads.

(Zonia *enters from the stairs and looks around.*)

Bynum: You looking for the back door, sugar? There it is. You can go
out there and play. It's alright.

  Seth: (*Showing her the door.*) You can go out there and play. Just
don't get in my garden. And don't go messing around in my
workshed.

(Seth *exits into the bedroom. There is a knock on the door.*)

Jeremy: Somebody at the door.

(Jeremy *goes to answer the door. Enter* Mattie Campbell. *She is a young woman
of twenty-six whose attractiveness is hidden under the weight and concerns of a dissatisfied life. She is a woman in an honest search for love and companionship. She
has suffered many defeats in her search, and though not always uncompromising,
still believes in the possibility of love.*)

Mattie: I'm looking for a man named Bynum. Lady told me to come
back later.

Jeremy: Sure, he here. Mr. Bynum, somebody here to see you.

Bynum: Come to see me, huh?

Mattie: Are you the man they call Bynum? The man folks say can fix
things?

Bynum: Depend on what need fixing. I can't make no promises. But I
got a powerful song in some matters.

Mattie: Can you fix it so my man come back to me?

Bynum: Come on in . . . have a sit down.

Mattie: You got to help me. I don't know what else to do.

Bynum: Depend on how all the circumstances of the thing come
together. How all the pieces fit.

Mattie: I done everything I knowed how to do. You got to make him
come back to me.

Bynum: It ain't nothing to make somebody come back. I can fix it so he
can't stand to be away from you. I got my roots and powders, I
can fix it so wherever he's at this thing will come up on him and he
won't be able to sleep for seeing your face. Won't be able to eat
for thinking of you.

Mattie: That's what I want. Make him come back.

Bynum: The roots is a powerful thing. I can fix it so one day he'll walk
out his front door . . . won't be thinking of nothing. He won't
know what it is. All he knows is that a powerful dissatisfaction

done set in his bones and can't nothing he do make him feel satisfied. He'll set his foot down on the road and the wind in the trees be talking to him and everywhere he step on the road, that road'll give back your name and something will pull him right up to your doorstep. Now, I can do that. I can take my roots and fix that easy. But maybe he ain't supposed to come back. And if he ain't supposed to come back . . . then he'll be in your bed one morning and it'll come up on him that he's in the wrong place. That he's lost outside of time from his place that he's supposed to be in. Then both of you be lost and trapped outside of life and ain't no way for you to get back into it. 'Cause you lost from yourselves and where the places come together, where you're supposed to be alive, your heart kicking in your chest with a song worth singing.

Mattie: Make him come back to me. Make his feet say my name on the road. I don't care what happens. Make him come back.

Bynum: What's your man's name?

Mattie: He go by Jack Carper. He was born in Alabama then he come to West Texas and find me and we come here. Been here three years before he left. Say I had a curse prayer on me and he started walking down the road and ain't never come back. Somebody told me, say you can fix things like that.

Bynum: He just got up one day, set his feet on the road, and walked away?

Mattie: You got to make him come back, mister.

Bynum: Did he say goodbye?

Mattie: Ain't said nothing. Just started walking. I could see where he disappeared. Didn't look back. Just keep walking. Can't you fix it so he come back? I ain't got no curse prayer on me. I know I ain't.

Bynum: What made him say you had a curse prayer on you?

Mattie: 'Cause the babies died. Me and Jack had two babies. Two little babies that ain't lived two months before they died. He say it's because somebody cursed me not to have babies.

Bynum: He ain't bound to you if the babies died. Look like somebody trying to keep you from being bound up and he's gone on back to whoever it is 'cause he's already bound up to her. Ain't nothing to be done. Somebody else done got a powerful hand in it and ain't nothing to be done to break it. You got to let him go find where he's supposed to be in the world.

Mattie: Jack done gone off and you telling me to forget about him. All my life I been looking for somebody to stop and stay with me. I done already got too many things to forget about. I take Jack Carper's hand and it feel so rough and strong. Seem like he's the strongest man in the world the way he hold me. Like he's bigger than the whole world and can't nothing bad get to me. Even when he act mean sometimes he still make everything seem okay with the world. Like there's part of it that belongs just to you. Now you telling me to forget about him?

Bynum: Jack Carper gone off to where he belong. There's somebody searching for your doorstep right now. Ain't no need you fretting over Jack Carper. Right now he's a strong thought in your mind. But every time you catch yourself frettin over Jack Carper you push that thought away. You push it out your mind and that thought will get weaker and weaker till you wake up one morning and you won't even be able to call him up on your mind.

(Bynum *gives her a small cloth packet.*)

Take this and sleep with it under your pillow and it'll bring good luck to you. Draw it to you like a magnet. It won't be long before you forget all about Jack Carper.

Mattie: How much . . . do I owe you?

Bynum: Whatever you got there . . . that'll be alright.

(Mattie *hands* Bynum *two quarters. She crosses to the door.*)

You sleep with that under your pillow and you'll be alright.

(Mattie *opens the door to exit and* Jeremy *crosses over to her.* Bynum *overhears the first part of their conversation, then exits out the back.*)

Jeremy: I overheard what you told Mr. Bynum. Had me an old gal did that to me. Woke up one morning and she was gone. Just took off to parts unknown. I woke up that morning and the only thing I could do was look around for my shoes. I woke up and got out of there. Found my shoes and took off. That's the only thing I could think of to do.

Mattie: She ain't said nothing?

Jeremy: I just looked around for my shoes and got out of there.

Mattie: Jack ain't said nothing either. He just walked off.

Jeremy: Some mens do that. Womens too. I ain't gone off looking for her. I just let her go. Figure she had a time to come to herself. Wasn't no use of me standing in the way. Where you from?

Mattie: Texas. I was born in Georgia but I went to Texas with my mama. She dead now. Was picking peaches and fell dead away. I come up here with Jack Carper.

Jeremy: I'm from North Carolina. Down around Raleigh where they got all that tobacco. Been up here about two weeks. I likes it fine except I still got to find me a woman. You got a nice look to you. Look like you have mens standing in your door. Is you got mens standing in your door to get a look at you?

Mattie: I ain't got nobody since Jack left.

Jeremy: A woman like you need a man. Maybe you let me be your man. I got a nice way with the women. That's what they tell me.

Mattie: I don't know. Maybe Jack's coming back.

Jeremy: I'll be your man till he come. A woman can't be by her lonesome. Let me be your man till he come.

Mattie: I just can't go through life piecing myself out to different
mens. I need a man who wants to stay with me.

Jeremy: I can't say what's gonna happen. Maybe I'll be the man. I
don't know. You wanna go along the road a little ways with me?

Mattie: I don't know. Seem like life say it's gonna be one thing and
end up being another. I'm tired of going from man to man.

Jeremy: Life is like you got to take a chance. Everybody got to take a
chance. Can't nobody say what's gonna be. Come on . . . take a
chance with me and see what the year bring. Maybe you let me
come and see you. Where you staying?

Mattie: I got me a room up on Bedford. Me and Jack had a room
together.

Jeremy: What's the address? I'll come by and get you tonight and we
can go down to Seefus. I'm going down there and play my guitar.

Mattie: You play guitar?

Jeremy: I play guitar like I'm born to it.

Mattie: I live at 1727 Bedford Avenue. I'm gonna find out if you can
play guitar like you say.

Jeremy: I plays it, sugar, and that ain't all I do. I got a ten-pound hammer and I knows how to drive it down. Good god . . . you ought to
hear my hammer ring!

Mattie: Go on with that kind of talk, now. If you gonna come by and
get me I got to get home and straighten up for you.

Jeremy: I'll be by at eight o'clock. How's eight o'clock? I'm gonna
make you forget all about Jack Carper.

Mattie: Go on, now. I got to get home and fix up for you.

Jeremy: Eight o'clock, sugar.

(The lights go down in the parlor and come up on the yard outside. Zonia *is singing and playing a game.)*

Zonia:
>I went downtown
>To get my grip
>I came back home
>Just a pullin' the skiff
>
>I went upstairs
>To make my bed
>I made a mistake
>And I bumped my head
>Just a pullin' the skiff
>
>I went downstairs
>To milk the cow

I made a mistake
And I milked the sow
Just a pullin' the skiff

Tomorrow, tomorrow
Tomorrow never comes
The marrow the marrow
The marrow in the bone.

(Reuben *enters*.)

Reuben: Hi.

  Zonia: Hi.

Reuben: What's your name?

  Zonia: Zonia.

Reuben: What kind of name is that?

  Zonia: It's what my daddy named me.

Reuben: My name's Reuben. You staying in Mr. Seth's house?

  Zonia: Yeah.

Reuben: That your daddy I seen you with this morning?

  Zonia: I don't know. Who you see me with?

Reuben: I saw you with some man had on a great big old coat. And you
    was walking up to Mr. Seth's house. Had on a hat too.

  Zonia: Yeah, that's my daddy.

Reuben: You like Mr. Seth?

  Zonia: I ain't see him much.

Reuben: My grandpap say he a great big old windbag. How come you
    living in Mr. Seth's house? Don't you have no house?

  Zonia: We going to find my mother.

Reuben: Where she at?

  Zonia: I don't know. We got to find her. We just go all over.

Reuben: Why you got to find her? What happened to her?

  Zonia: She ran away.

Reuben: Why she run away?

  Zonia: I don't know. My daddy say some man named Joe Turner did
    something bad to him once and that made her run away.

Reuben: Maybe she coming back and you don't have to go looking for
    her.

  Zonia: We ain't there no more.

Reuben: She could have come back when you wasn't there.

  Zonia: My daddy said she ran off and left us so we going looking for
    her.

Reuben: What he gonna do when he find her?

  Zonia: He didn't say. He just say he got to find her.

Reuben: Your daddy say how long you staying in Mr. Seth's house?

  Zonia: He don't say much. But we never stay too long nowhere. He
    say we got to keep moving till we find her.

Reuben: Ain't no kids hardly live around here. I had me a friend but he died. He was the best friend I ever had. Me and Eugene used to keep secrets. I still got his pigeons. He told me to let them go when he died. He say, "Reuben, promise me when I die you'll let my pigeons go." But I keep them to remember him by. I ain't never gonna let them go. Even when I get to be grown up. I'm just always gonna have Eugene's pigeons.

(Pause.)

Mr. Bynum a conjure man. My grandpap scared of him. He don't like me to come over here too much. I'm scared of him too. My grandpap told me not to let him get close enough to where he can reach out his hand and touch me.

Zonia: He don't seem scary to me.

Reuben: He buys pigeons from me . . . and if you get up early in the morning you can see him out in the yard doing something with them pigeons. My grandpap say he kill them. I sold him one yesterday. I don't know what he do with it. I just hope he don't spook me up.

Zonia: Why you sell him pigeons if he's gonna spook you up?

Reuben: I just do like Eugene do. He used to sell Mr. Bynum pigeons. That's how he got to collecting them to sell to Mr. Bynum. Sometime he give me a nickel and sometime he give me a whole dime.

(Loomis enters from the house.)

Loomis: Zonia!

Zonia: Sir?

Loomis: What you doing?

Zonia: Nothing.

Loomis: You stay around this house, you hear? I don't want you wandering off nowhere.

Zonia: I ain't wandering off nowhere.

Loomis: Miss Bertha set that hot tub and you getting a good scrubbing. Get scrubbed up good. You ain't been scrubbing.

Zonia: I been scrubbing.

Loomis: Look at you. You growing too fast. Your bones getting bigger everyday. I don't want you getting grown on me. Don't you get grown on me too soon. We gonna find your mamma. She around here somewhere. I can smell her. You stay on around this house now. Don't you go nowhere.

Zonia: Yes, sir.

(Loomis exits into the house.)

Reuben: Wow, your daddy's scary!

Zonia: He is not! I don't know what you talking about.

Reuben: He got them mean-looking eyes!

Zonia: My daddy ain't got no mean-looking eyes!

Reuben: Aw, girl, I was just messing with you. You wanna go see Eugene's pigeons? Got a great big coop out the back of my house. Come on, I'll show you.

(Reuben *and* Zonia *exit as the lights go down.*)

Scene Two

It is Saturday morning, one week later. The lights come up on the kitchen. Bertha *is at the stove preparing breakfast while* Seth *sits at the table.*

Seth: Something ain't right about that fellow. I been watching him all week. Something ain't right, I'm telling you.

Bertha: Seth Holly, why don't you hush up about that man this morning?

Seth: I don't like the way he stare at everybody. Don't look at you natural like. He just be staring at you. Like he trying to figure out something about you. Did you see him when he come back in here?

Bertha: That man ain't thinking about you.

Seth: He don't work nowhere. Just go out and come back. Go out and come back.

Bertha: As long as you get your boarding money it ain't your cause about what he do. He don't bother nobody.

Seth: Just go out and come back. Going around asking everybody about Martha. Like Henry Allen seen him down at the church last night.

Bertha: The man's allowed to go to church if he want. He say he a deacon. Ain't nothing wrong about him going to church.

Seth: I ain't talking about him going to church. I'm talking about him hanging around *outside* the church.

Bertha: Henry Allen say that?

Seth: Say he be standing around outside the church. Like he be watching it.

Bertha: What on earth he wanna be watching the church for, I wonder?

Seth: That's what I'm trying to figure out. Looks like he fixing to rob it.

Bertha: Seth, now do he look like the kind that would rob the church?

Seth: I ain't saying that. I ain't saying how he look. It's how he do. Anybody liable to do anything as far as I'm concerned. I ain't never thought about how no church robbers look . . . but now that you mention it, I don't see where they look no different than how he look.

Bertha: Herald Loomis ain't the kind of man who would rob no church.

Seth: I ain't even so sure that's his name.

Bertha: Why the man got to lie about his name?

Seth: Anybody can tell anybody anything about what their name is. That's what you call him . . . Herald Loomis. His name is liable to be anything.

Bertha: Well, until he tell me different that's what I'm gonna call him. You just getting yourself all worked up about the man for nothing.

Seth: Talking about Loomis: Martha's name wasn't no Loomis nothing. Martha's name is Pentecost.

Bertha: How you so sure that's her right name? Maybe she changed it.

Seth: Martha's a good Christian woman. This fellow here look like he owe the devil a day's work and he's trying to figure out how he gonna pay him. Martha ain't had a speck of distrust about her the whole time she was living here. They moved the church out there to Rankin and I was sorry to see her go.

Bertha: That's why he be hanging around the church. He looking for her.

Seth: If he looking for her, why don't he go inside and ask? What he doing hanging around outside the church acting sneaky like?

(Bynum *enters from the yard.*)

Bynum: Morning, Seth. Morning, Sister Bertha.

(Bynum *continues through the kitchen and exits up the stairs.*)

Bertha: That's who you should be asking the questions. He been out there in that yard all morning. He was out there before the sun come up. He didn't even come in for breakfast. I don't know what he's doing. He had three of them pigeons line up out there. He dance around till he get tired. He sit down awhile then get up and dance some more. He come through here a little while ago looking like he was mad at the world.

Seth: I don't pay Bynum no mind. He don't spook me up with all that stuff.

Bertha: That's how Martha come to be living here. She come to see Bynum. She come to see him when she first left from down South.

Seth: Martha was living here before Bynum. She ain't come on here when she first left from down there. She come on here after she went back to get her little girl. That's when she come on here.

Bertha: Well, where was Bynum? He was here when she came.

Seth: Bynum ain't come till after her. That boy Hiram was staying up there in Bynum's room.

Bertha: Well, how long Bynum been here?

Seth: Bynum ain't been here no longer than three years. That's what I'm trying to tell you. Martha was staying up there and sewing and cleaning for Doc Goldblum when Bynum came. This the longest he ever been in one place.

Bertha: How you know how long the man been in one place?

Seth: I know Bynum. Bynum ain't no mystery to me. I done seen a hundred niggers like him. He's one of them fellows never could stay in one place. He was wandering all around the country till he got old and settled here. The only thing different about Bynum is he bring all this heebie-jeebie stuff with him.

Bertha: I still say he was staying here when she came. That's why she came . . . to see him.

Seth: You can say what you want. I know the facts of it. She come on here four years ago all heartbroken 'cause she couldn't find her little girl. And Bynum wasn't nowhere around. She got mixed up in that old heebie-jeebie nonsense with him after he came.

Bertha: Well, if she came on before Bynum I don't know where she stayed. 'Cause she stayed up there in Hiram's room. Hiram couldn't get along with Bynum and left out of here owing you two dollars. Now, I know you ain't forgot about that!

Seth: Sure did! You know Hiram ain't paid me that two dollars yet. So that's why he be ducking and hiding when he see me down on Logan Street. You right. Martha did come on after Bynum. I forgot that's why Hiram left.

Bertha: Him and Bynum never could see eye to eye. They always rubbed each other the wrong way. Hiram got to thinking that Bynum was trying to put a fix on him and he moved out. Martha came to see Bynum and ended up taking Hiram's room. Now, I know what I'm taking about. She stayed on here three years till they moved the church.

Seth: She out there in Rankin now. I know where she at. I know where they moved the church to. She right out there in Rankin in that place used to be shoe store. Used to be Wolf's shoe store. They moved to a bigger place and they put that church in there. I know where she at. I know just where she at.

Bertha: Why don't you tell the man? You see he looking for her.

Seth: I ain't gonna tell that man where that woman is! What I wanna do that for? I don't know nothing about that man. I don't know why he looking for her. He might wanna do her a harm. I ain't gonna carry that on my hands. He looking for her, he gonna have to find her for himself. I ain't gonna help him. Now, if he had come and presented himself as a gentleman—the way Martha Pentecost's husband would have done—then I would have told him. But I ain't gonna tell this old wild-eyed mean-looking nigger nothing!

Bertha: Well, why don't you get a ride with Selig and go up there and tell her where he is? See if she wanna see him. If that's her little girl . . . you say Martha was looking for her.

Seth: You know me, Bertha. I don't get mixed up in nobody's business.

(Bynum enters from the stairs.)

Bynum: Morning, Seth. Morning, Bertha. Can I still get some breakfast? Mr. Loomis been down here this morning?

Seth: He done gone out and come back. He up there now. Left out of here early this morning wearing that coat. Hot as it is, the man wanna walk around wearing a big old heavy coat. He come back in here paid me for another week, sat down there waiting on Selig. Got tired of waiting and went on back upstairs.

Bynum: Where's the little girl?

Seth: She out there in the front. Had to chase her and that Reuben off the front porch. She out there somewhere.

Bynum: Look like if Martha was around here he would have found her by now. My guess is she ain't in the city.

Seth: She ain't! I know where she at. I know just where she at. But I ain't gonna tell him. Not the way he look.

Bertha: Here go your coffee, Bynum.

Bynum: He says he gonna get Selig to find her for him.

Seth: Selig can't find her. He talk all that . . . but unless he get lucky and knock on her door he can't find her. That's the only way he find anybody. He got to get lucky. But I know just where she at.

Bertha: Here go some biscuits, Bynum.

Bynum: What else you got over there, Sister Bertha? You got some grits and gravy over there? I could go for some of that this morning.

Bertha: *(Sets a bowl on the table.)* Seth, come on and help me turn this mattress over. Come on.

Seth: Something ain't right with that fellow, Bynum. I don't like the way he stare at everybody.

Bynum: Mr. Loomis alright, Seth. He just a man got something on his mind. He just got a straightforward mind, that's all.

Seth: What's that fellow that they had around here? Moses, that's Moses Houser. Man went crazy and jumped off the Brady Street Bridge. I told you when I seen him something wasn't right about him. And I'm telling you about this fellow now.

(There is a knock on the door. Seth goes to answer it. Enter Rutherford Selig.)

Ho! Come on in, Selig.

Bynum: If it ain't the People Finder himself.

Selig: Bynum, before you start . . . I ain't seen no shiny man now.

Bynum: Who said anything about that? I ain't said nothing about that. I just called you a first-class People Finder.

Selig: How many dustpans you get out of that sheet metal, Seth?

Seth: You walked by them on your way in. They sitting out there on the porch. Got twenty-eight. Got four out of each sheet and made Bertha a coffeepot out the other one. They a little small but they got nice handles.

Selig: That was twenty cents apiece, right? That's what we agreed on.

Seth: That's five dollars and sixty cents. Twenty on top of twenty-eight. How many sheets you bring me?

Selig: I got eight out there. That's a dollar twenty makes me owe you. . . .

Seth: Four dollars and forty cents.

Selig: *(Paying him.)* Go on and make me some dustpans. I can use all you can make.

*(*Loomis *enters from the stairs.)*

Loomis: I been watching for you. He say you find people.

Bynum: Mr. Loomis here wants you to find his wife.

Loomis: He say you find people. Find her for me.

Selig: Well, let see here . . . find somebody, is it?

*(*Selig *rummages through his pockets. He has several notebooks and he is searching for the right one.)*

Alright now . . . what's the name?

Loomis: Martha Loomis. She my wife. Got married legal with the paper and all.

Selig: *(Writing.)* Martha . . . Loomis. How tall is she?

Loomis: She five feet from the ground.

Selig: Five feet . . . tall. Young or old?

Loomis: She a young woman. Got long pretty hair.

Selig: Young . . . long . . . pretty . . . hair. Where did you last see her?

Loomis: Tennessee. Nearby Memphis.

Selig: When was that?

Loomis: Nineteen hundred and one.

Selig: Nineteen . . . hundred and one. I'll tell you, mister . . . you better off without them. Now you take me . . . old Rutherford Selig could tell you a thing or two about these women. I ain't met one yet I could understand. Now, you take Sally out there. That's all a man needs is a good horse. I say giddup and she go. Say whoa and she stop. I feed her some oats and she carry me wherever I want to go. Ain't had a speck of trouble out of her since I had her. Now, I been married. A long time ago down in Kentucky. I got up one morning and I saw this look on my wife's face. Like way down deep inside her she was wishing I was dead. I walked around that morning and every time I looked at her she had that look on her face. It seem like she knew I could see it on her. Every time I looked at her I got smaller and smaller. Well, I wasn't gonna stay around there and just shrink away. I walked out on the porch and closed the door behind me. When I closed the door she locked it. I went out and bought me a horse. And I ain't been without one since! Martha Loomis, huh? Well, now I'll do the best I can do. That's one dollar.

Loomis: *(Holding out dollar suspiciously.)* How you find her?

Selig: Well now, it ain't no easy job like you think. You can't just go out there and find them like that. There's a lot of little tricks to it. It's not an easy job keeping up with you Nigras the way you move about so. Now you take this woman you looking for . . . this Martha Loomis. She could be anywhere. Time I find her, if you don't keep your eye on her, she'll be gone off someplace else. You'll be thinking she over here and she'll be over there. But like I say there's a lot of little tricks to it.

Loomis: You say you find her.

Selig: I can't promise anything but we been finders in my family for a long time. Bringers and finders. My great-granddaddy used to bring Nigras across the ocean on ships. That's wasn't no easy job either. Sometimes the winds would blow so hard you'd think the hand of God was set against the sails. But it set him well in pay and he settled in this new land and found him a wife of good Christian charity with a mind for kids and the like and well . . . here I am, Rutherford Selig. You're in good hands, mister. Me and my daddy have found plenty Nigras. My daddy, rest his soul, used to find runaway slaves for the plantation bosses. He was the best there was at it. Jonas B. Selig. Had him a reputation stretched clean across the country. After Abraham Lincoln give you all Nigras your freedom papers and with you all looking all over for each other . . . we started finding Nigras for Nigras. Of course, it don't pay as much. But the People Finding business ain't so bad.

Loomis: *(Hands him the dollar.)* Find her. Martha Loomis. Find her for me.

Selig: Like I say, I can't promise you anything. I'm going back upriver, and if she's around in them parts I'll find her for you. But I can't promise you anything.

Loomis: When you coming back?

Selig: I'll be back on Saturday. I come and see Seth to pick up my order on Saturday.

Bynum: You going upriver, huh? You going up around my way. I used to go all up through there. Blawknox . . . Clairton. Used to go up to Rankin and take that first righthand road. I wore many a pair of shoes out walking around that way. You'd have thought I was a missionary spreading the gospel the way I wandered all around them parts.

Selig: Okay, Bynum. See you on Saturday.

Seth: Here, let me walk out with you. Help you with them dustpans.

(Seth and Selig *exit out the back.* Bertha *enters from the stairs carrying a bundle of sheets.)*

Bynum: Herald Loomis got the People Finder looking for Martha.

Bertha: You can call him a People Finder if you want to. I know Rutherford Selig carries people away too. He done carried a whole
bunch of them away from here. Folks plan on leaving plan by
Selig's timing. They wait till he get ready to go, then they hitch a
ride on his wagon. Then he charge folks a dollar to tell them
where he took them. Now, that's the truth of Rutherford Selig.
This old People Finding business is for the birds. He ain't never
found nobody he ain't took away. Herald Loomis, you just wasted
your dollar.

(Bertha exits into the bedroom.)

Loomis: He say he find her. He say he find her by Saturday. I'm gonna
wait till Saturday.

(The lights fade to black.)

Scene Three

It is Sunday morning, the next day. The lights come up on the kitchen. Seth *sits
talking to* Bynum. *The breakfast dishes have been cleared away.*

Seth: They can't see that. Neither one of them can see that. Now,
how much sense it take to see that? All you got to do is be able to
count. One man making ten pots is five men making fifty pots.
But they can't see that. Asked where I'm gonna get my five men.
Hell, I can teach anybody how to make a pot. I can teach you. I
can take you out there and get you started right now. Inside of
two weeks you'd know how to make a pot. All you got to do is
want to do it. I can get five men. I ain't worried about getting no
five men.

Bertha: *(Calls from the bedroom.)* Seth. Come on and get ready now.
Reverend Gates ain't gonna be holding up his sermon 'cause you
sitting out there talking.

Seth: Now, you take the boy, Jeremy. What he gonna do after he put
in that road? He can't do nothing but go put in another one
somewhere. Now, if he let me show him how to make some pots
and pans . . . then he'd have something can't nobody take away
from him. After a while he could get his own tools and go off
somewhere and make his own pots and pans. Find him somebody
to sell them to. Now, Selig can't make no pots and pans. He can
sell them but he can't make them. I get me five men with some
tools and we'd make him so many pots and pans he'd have to open
up a store somewhere. But they can't see that. Neither Mr.
Cohen nor Sam Green.

Bertha: *(Calls from the bedroom.)* Seth . . . time be wasting. Best be getting on.

Seth: I'm coming, woman! *(To Bynum.)* Want me to sign over the house to borrow five hundred dollars. I ain't that big a fool. That's all I got. Sign it over to them and then I won't have nothing.

(Jeremy *enters waving a dollar and carrying his guitar.*)

Jeremy: Look here, Mr. Bynum . . . won me another dollar last night down at Seefus! Me and that Mattie Campbell went down there again and I played contest. Ain't no guitar players down there. Wasn't even no contest. Say, Mr. Seth, I asked Mattie Campbell if she wanna come by and have Sunday dinner with us. Get some fried chicken.

Seth: It's gonna cost you twenty-five cents.

Jeremy: That's alright. I got a whole dollar here. Say Mr. Seth . . . me and Mattie Campbell talked it over last night and she gonna move in with me. If that's alright with you.

Seth: Your business is your business . . . but it's gonna cost her a dollar a week for her board. I can't be feeding nobody for free.

Jeremy: Oh, she know that, Mr. Seth. That's what I told her, say she'd have to pay for her meals.

Seth: You say you got a whole dollar there . . . turn loose that twenty-five cents.

Jeremy: Suppose she move in today, then that make seventy-five cents more, so I'll give you the whole dollar for her now till she gets here.

(Seth *pockets the money and exits into the bedroom.*)

Bynum: So you and that Mattie Campbell gonna take up together?

Jeremy: I told her she don't need to be by her lonesome, Mr. Bynum. Don't make no sense for both of us to be by our lonesome. So she gonna move in with me.

Bynum: Sometimes you got to be where you supposed to be. Sometimes you can get all mixed up in life and come to the wrong place.

Jeremy: That's just what I told her, Mr. Bynum. It don't make no sense for her to be all mixed up and lonesome. May as well come here and be with me. She a fine woman too. Got them long legs. Knows how to treat a fellow too. Treat you like you wanna be treated.

Bynum: You just can't look at it like that. You got to look at the whole thing. Now, you take a fellow go out there, grab hold to a woman and think he got something 'cause she sweet and soft to the touch. Alright. Touching's part of life. It's in the world like everything else. Touching's nice. It feels good. But you can lay your hand upside a horse or a cat, and that feels good too. What's the difference? When you grab hold to a woman, you got something there. You got a whole world there. You got a way of life kicking up under your hand. That woman can take and make you feel like

something. I ain't just talking about in the way of jumping off
into bed together and rolling around with each other. Anybody
can do that. When you grab hold to that woman and look at the
whole thing and see what you got . . . why, she can take and make
something out of you. Your mother was a woman. That's enough
right there to show you what a woman is. Enough to show you
what she can do. She made something out of you. Taught you
converse, and all about how to take care of yourself, how to see
where you at and where you going tomorrow, how to look out to
see what's coming in the way of eating, and what to do with yourself when you get lonesome. That's a mighty thing she did. But
you can't look at a woman to jump off into bed with her. That's a
foolish thing to ignore a woman like that.

Jeremy: Oh, I ain't ignoring her, Mr. Bynum. It's hard to ignore a
woman got legs like she got.

Bynum: Alright. Let's try it this way. Now, you take a ship. Be out
there on the water traveling about. You out there on that ship
sailing to and from. And then you see some land. Just like you see
a woman walking down the street. You see that land and it don't
look like nothing but a line out there on the horizon. That's all it
is when you first see it. A line that cross your path out there on
the horizon. Now, a smart man know when he see that land, it
ain't just a line setting out there. He know that if you get off the
water to go take a good look . . . why, there's a whole world right
there. A whole world with everything imaginable under the sun.
Anything you can think of you can find on that land. Same with a
woman. A woman is everything a man need. To a smart man she
water and berries. And that's all a man need. That's all he need to
live on. You give me some water and berries and if there ain't
nothing else I can live a hundred years. See, you just like a man
looking at the horizon from a ship. You just seeing a part of it.
But it's a blessing when you learn to look at a woman and see in
maybe just a few strands of her hair, the way her cheek curves . . .
to see in that everything there is out of life to be gotten. It's a
blessing to see that. You know you done right and proud by your
mother to see that. But you got to learn it. My telling you ain't
gonna mean nothing. You got to learn how to come to your own
time and place with a woman.

Jeremy: What about your woman, Mr. Bynum? I know you done had
some woman.

Bynum: Oh, I got them in memory time. That lasts longer than any of
them ever stayed with me.

Jeremy: I had me an old gal one time . . .

(There is a knock on the door. Jeremy *goes to answer it. Enter* Molly Cunningham. *She is about twenty-six, the kind of woman that "could break in on a*

dollar anywhere she goes." She carries a small cardboard suitcase, and wears a colorful dress of the fashion of the day. Jeremy's heart jumps out of his chest when he sees her.)

Molly: You got any rooms here? I'm looking for a room.
Jeremy: Yeah . . . Mr. Seth got rooms. Sure . . . wait till I get Mr. Seth. *(Calls.)* Mr. Seth! Somebody here to see you! *(To* Molly.*)* Yeah, Mr. Seth got some rooms. Got one right next to me. This a nice place to stay, too. My name's Jeremy. What's yours?

(Seth enters dressed in his Sunday clothes.)

Seth: Ho!
Jeremy: This here woman looking for a place to stay. She say you got any rooms.
Molly: Mister, you got any rooms? I seen your sign say you got rooms.
Seth: How long you plan to staying?
Molly: I ain't gonna be here long. I ain't looking for no home or nothing. I'd be in Cincinnati if I hadn't missed my train.
Seth: Rooms cost two dollars a week.
Molly: Two dollars!
Seth: That includes meals. We serve two meals a day. That's breakfast and dinner.
Molly: I hope it ain't on the third floor.
Seth: That's the only one I got. Third floor to the left. That's pay up in advance week to week.
Molly: (Going into her bosom.) I'm gonna pay you for one week. My name's Molly. Molly Cunningham.
Seth: I'm Seth Holly. My wife's name is Bertha. She do the cooking and taking care of around here. She got sheets on the bed. Towels twenty-five cents a week extra if you ain't got none. You get breakfast and dinner. We got fried chicken on Sundays.
Molly: That sounds good. Here's two dollars and twenty-five cents. Look here, Mister. . . ?
Seth: Holly. Seth Holly.
Molly: Look here, Mr. Holly. I forgot to tell you. I likes me some company from time to time. I don't like being by myself.
Seth: Your business is your business. I don't meddle in nobody's business. But this is a respectable house. I don't have no riffraff around here. And I don't have no women hauling no men up to their rooms to be making their living. As long as we understand each other then we'll be alright with each other.
Molly: Where's the outhouse?
Seth: Straight through the door over yonder.
Molly: I get my own key to the front door?
Seth: Everybody get their own key. If you come in late just don't be

making no whole lot of noise and carrying on. Don't allow no fussing and fighting around here.

Molly: You ain't got to worry about that, mister. Which way you say that outhouse was again?

Seth: Straight through that door over yonder.

*(*Molly *exits out the back door.* Jeremy *crosses to watch her.)*

Jeremy: Mr. Bynum, you know what? I think I know what you was talking about now.

(The lights go down on the scene.)

Scene Four

The lights come up on the kitchen. It is later the same evening. Mattie *and all the residents of the house, except* Loomis, *sit around the table. They have finished eating and most of the dishes have been cleared.*

Molly: That sure was some good chicken.

Jeremy: That's what I'm talking about. Miss Bertha, you sure can fry some chicken. I thought my mama could fry some chicken. But she can't do half as good as you.

Seth: I know it. That's why I married her. She don't know that, though. She think I married her for something else.

Bertha: I ain't studying you, Seth. Did you get your things moved in alright, Mattie?

Mattie: I ain't had that much. Jeremy helped me with what I did have.

Bertha: You'll get to know your way around here. If you have any questions about anything just ask me. You and Molly both. I get along with everybody. You'll find I ain't no trouble to get along with.

Mattie: You need some help with the dishes?

Bertha: I got me a helper. Ain't I, Zonia? Got me a good helper.

Zonia: Yes, ma'am.

Seth: Look at Bynum sitting over there with his belly all poked out. Ain't saying nothing. Sitting over there half asleep. Ho, Bynum!

Bertha: If Bynum ain't saying nothing what you wanna start him up for?

Seth: Ho, Bynum!

Bynum: What you hollering at me for? I ain't doing nothing.

Seth: Come on, we gonna Juba.

Bynum: You know me, I'm always ready to Juba.

Seth: Well, come on, then.

*(Seth *pulls a harmonica and blows a few notes.)*

Come on there, Jeremy. Where's your guitar? Go get your guitar. Bynum say he's ready to Juba.

Jeremy: Don't need no guitar to Juba. Ain't you never Juba without a guitar?

(Jeremy *begins to drum on the table.*)

   Seth: It ain't that. I ain't never Juba with one! Figured to try it and see how it worked.

Bynum: (*Drumming on the table.*) You don't need no guitar. Look at Molly sitting over there. She don't know we Juba on Sunday. We gonna show you something tonight. You and Mattie Campbell both. Ain't that right, Seth?

   Seth: You said it! Come on, Bertha, leave them dishes be for a while. We gonna Juba.

Bynum: Alright. Let's Juba down!

(*The Juba is reminiscent of the Ring Shouts of the African slaves. It is a call and response dance. Bynum sits at the table and drums. He calls the dance as others clap hands, shuffle, and stomp around the table. It should be as African as possible, with the performers working themselves up into a near frenzy. The words can be improvised, but should include some mention of the Holy Ghost. In the middle of the dance* Herald Loomis *enters.*)

Loomis: (*In a rage.*) Stop it! Stop!

(*They stop and turn to look at him.*)

   You all sitting up here singing about the Holy Ghost. What's so holy about the Holy Ghost? You singing and singing. You think the Holy Ghost coming? You singing for the Holy Ghost to come? What he gonna do, huh? He gonna come with tongues of fire to burn up your woolly heads? You gonna tie onto the Holy Ghost and get burned up? What you got then? Why God got to be so big? Why he got to be bigger than me? How much big is there? How much big do you want?

(Loomis *starts to unzip his pants.*)

   Seth: Nigger, you crazy!

Loomis: How much big you want?

   Seth: You done plumb lost your mind!

(Loomis *begins to speak in tongues and dance around the kitchen.* Seth *starts after him.*)

 Bertha: Leave him alone, Seth. He ain't in his right mind.

Loomis: (*Stops suddenly.*) You all don't know nothing about me. You don't know what I done seen. Herald Loomis done seen some things he ain't got words to tell you.

(Loomis *starts to walk out the front door and is thrown back and collapses, terror-stricken by his vision.* Bynum *crawls to him.*)

Bynum: What you done seen, Herald Loomis?

Loomis: I done seen bones rise up out the water. Rise up and walk across the water. Bones walking on top of the water.

Bynum: Tell me about them bones, Herald Loomis. Tell me what you seen.

Loomis: I come to this place . . . to this water that was bigger than the whole world. And I looked out . . . and I seen these bones rise up out the water. Rise up and begin to walk on top of it.

Bynum: Wasn't nothing but bones and they walking on top of the water.

Loomis: Walking without sinking down. Walking on top of the water.

Bynum: Just marching in a line.

Loomis: A whole heap of them. They come up out the water and started marching.

Bynum: Wasn't nothing but bones and they walking on top of the water.

Loomis: One after the other. They just come up out the water and start to walking.

Bynum: They walking on the water without sinking down. They just walking and walking. And then . . . what happened, Herald Loomis?

Loomis: They just walking across the water.

Bynum: What happened, Herald Loomis? What happened to the bones?

Loomis: They just walking across the water . . . and then . . . they sunk down.

Bynum: The bones sunk into the water. They all sunk down.

Loomis: All at one time! They just all fell in the water at one time.

Bynum: Sunk down like anybody else.

Loomis: When they sink down they made a big splash and this here wave come up . . .

Bynum: A big wave, Herald Loomis. A big wave washed over the land.

Loomis: It washed them out of the water and up on the land. Only . . . only . . .

Bynum: Only they ain't bones no more.

Loomis: They got flesh on them! Just like you and me!

Bynum: Everywhere you look the waves is washing them up on the land right on top of one another.

Loomis: They black. Just like you and me. Ain't no difference.

Bynum: Then what happened, Herald Loomis?

Loomis: They ain't moved or nothing. They just laying there.

Bynum: You just laying there. What you waiting on, Herald Loomis?

Loomis: I'm laying there . . . waiting.

Bynum: What you waiting on, Herald Loomis?

Loomis: I'm waiting on the breath to get into my body.

Bynum: The breath coming into you, Herald Loomis. What you gonna
do now?

Loomis: The wind's blowing the breath into my body. I can feel it. I'm
starting to breathe again.

Bynum: What you gonna do, Herald Loomis?

Loomis: I'm gonna stand up. I got to stand up. I can't lay here no
more. All the breath coming into my body and I got to stand up.

Bynum: Everybody's standing up at the same time.

Loomis: The ground's starting to shake. There's a great shaking. The
world's busting half in two. The sky's splitting open. I got to
stand up.

(Loomis *attempts to stand up.*)

My legs . . . my legs won't stand up!

Bynum: Everybody's standing and walking toward the road. What you
gonna do, Herald Loomis?

Loomis: My legs won't stand up.

Bynum: They shaking hands and saying goodbye to each other and
walking every whichaway down the road.

Loomis: I got to stand up!

Bynum: They walking around here now. Mens. Just like you and me.
Come right up out the water.

Loomis: Got to stand up.

Bynum: They walking, Herald Loomis. They walking around here
now.

Loomis: I got to stand up. Get up on the road.

Bynum: Come on, Herald Loomis.

(Loomis *tries to stand up.*)

Loomis: My legs won't stand up! My legs won't stand up!

(Loomis *collapses on the floor as the lights go down to black.*)

ACT TWO

Scene One

The lights come up on the kitchen. Bertha busies herself with breakfast preparations. Seth *sits at the table.*

   Seth: I don't care what his problem is! He's leaving here!

Bertha: You can't put the man out and he got that little girl. Where
they gonna go then?

   Seth: I don't care where he go. Let him go back where he was before
he come here. I ain't asked him to come here. I knew when I first
looked at him something wasn't right with him. Dragging that lit-

tle girl around with him. Looking like he be sleeping in the woods somewhere. I knew all along he wasn't right.

Bertha: A fellow get a little drunk he's liable to say or do anything. He ain't done no big harm.

Seth: I just don't have all that carrying on in my house. When he come down here I'm gonna tell him. He got to leave here. My daddy wouldn't stand for it and I ain't gonna stand for it either.

Bertha: Well, if you put him out you have to put Bynum out too. Bynum right there with him.

Seth: If it wasn't for Bynum ain't no telling what would have happened. Bynum talked to that fellow just as nice and calmed him down. If he wasn't here ain't no telling what would have happened. Bynum ain't done nothing but talk to him and kept him calm. Man acting all crazy with that foolishness. Naw, he's leaving here.

Bertha: What you gonna tell him? How you gonna tell him to leave?

Seth: I'm gonna tell him straight out. Keep it nice and simple. Mister, you got to leave here!

(Molly enters from the stairs.)

Molly: Morning.

Bertha: Did you sleep alright in that bed?

Molly: Tired as I was I could have slept anywhere. It's a real nice room, though. This is a nice place.

Seth: I'm sorry you had to put up with all that carrying on last night.

Molly: It don't bother me none. I done seen that kind of stuff before.

Seth: You won't have to see it around here no more.

(Bynum is heard singing offstage.)

I don't put up with all that stuff. When that fellow come down here I'm gonna tell him.

Bynum: (singing)
Soon my work will all be done
Soon my work will all be done
Soon my work will all be done

I'm going to see the king.

Bynum: (Enters.) Morning, Seth. Morning, Sister Bertha. I see we got Molly Cunningham down here at breakfast.

Seth: Bynum, I wanna thank you for talking to that fellow last night and calming him down. If you hadn't been here ain't no telling what might have happened.

Bynum: Mr. Loomis alright, Seth. He just got a little excited.

Seth: Well, he can get excited somewhere else 'cause he leaving here.

(Mattie enters from the stairs.)

Bynum: Well, there's Mattie Campbell.

Mattie: Good morning.

Bertha: Sit on down there, Mattie. I got some biscuits be ready in a minute. The coffee's hot.

Mattie: Jeremy gone already?

Bynum: Yeah, he leave out of here early. He got to be there when the sun come up. Most working men got to be there when the sun come up. Everybody but Seth. Seth work at night. Mr. Olowski so busy in his shop he got fellows working at night.

(Loomis enters from the stairs.)

Seth: Mr. Loomis, now . . . I don't want no trouble. I keeps me a respectable house here. I don't have no carrying on like what went on last night. This has been a respectable house for a long time. I'm gonna have to ask you to leave.

Loomis: You got my two dollars. That two dollars say we stay till Saturday.

(Loomis and Seth glare at each other.)

Seth: Alright. Fair enough. You stay till Saturday. But come Saturday you got to leave here.

Loomis: (Continues to glare at Seth. He goes to the door and calls.) Zonia. You stay around this house, you hear? Don't you go anywhere.

(Loomis exits out the front door.)

Seth: I knew it when I first seen him. I knew something wasn't right with him.

Bertha: Seth, leave the people alone to eat their breakfast. They don't want to hear that. Go on out there and make some pots and pans. That's the only time you satisfied is when you out there. Go on out there and make some pots and pans and leave them people alone.

Seth: I ain't bothering anybody. I'm just stating the facts. I told you, Bynum.

(Bertha shoos Seth out the back door and exits into the bedroom.)

Molly: (To Bynum.) You one of them voo-doo people?

Bynum: I got a power to bind folks if that what you talking about.

Molly: I thought so. The way you talked to that man when he started all that spooky stuff. What you say you had the power to do to people? You ain't the cause of him acting like that, is you?

Bynum: I binds them together. Sometimes I help them find each other.

Molly: How do you do that?

Bynum: With a song. My daddy taught me how to do it.

Molly: That's what they say. Most folks be what they daddy is. I wouldn't want to be like my daddy. Nothing ever set right with him. He tried to make the world over. Carry it around with him everywhere he go. I don't want to be like that. I just take life as it come. I don't be trying to make it over.

(Pause.)

Your daddy used to do that too, huh? Make people stay together?

Bynum: My daddy used to heal people. He had the Healing Song. I got the Binding Song.

Molly: My mama used to believe in all that stuff. If she got sick she would have gone and saw your daddy. As long as he didn't make her drink nothing. She wouldn't drink nothing nobody give her. She was always afraid somebody was gonna poison her. How your daddy heal people?

Bynum: With a song. He healed people by singing over them. I seen him do it. He sung over this little white girl when she was sick. They made a big to-do about it. They carried the girl's bed out in the yard and had all her kinfolk standing around. The little girl laying up there in the bed. Doctors standing around can't do nothing to help her. And they had my daddy come up and sing his song. It didn't sound no different than any other song. It was just somebody singing. But the song was its own thing and it come out and took upon this little girl with its power and it healed her.

Molly: That's sure something else. I don't understand that kind of thing. I guess if the doctor couldn't make me well I'd try it. But otherwise I don't wanna be bothered with that kind of thing. It's too spooky.

Bynum: Well, let me get on out here and get to work.

(Bynum gets up and heads out the back door.)

Molly: I ain't meant to offend you or nothing. What's your name . . . Bynum? I ain't meant to say nothing to make you feel bad now.

(Bynum exits out the back door.)

(to Mattie.) I hope he don't feel bad. He's a nice man. I don't wanna hurt nobody's feelings or nothing.

Mattie: I got to go on up to Doc Goldblum's and finish this ironing.

Molly: Now, that's something I don't never wanna do. Iron no clothes. Especially somebody else's. That's what I believe killed my mama. Always ironing and working, doing somebody else's work. Not Molly Cunningham.

Mattie: It's the only job I got. I got to make it someway to fend for myself.

Molly: I thought Jeremy was your man. Ain't he working?

Mattie: We just be keeping company till maybe Jack come back.

Molly: I don't trust none of these men. Jack or nobody else. These men liable to do anything. They wait just until they get one woman tied and locked up with them . . . then they look around to see if they can get another one. Molly don't pay them no mind. One's just as good as the other if you ask me. I ain't never met one that meant nobody no good. You got any babies?

Mattie: I had two for my man, Jack Carper. But they both died.

Molly: That be the best. These men make all these babies, then run off and leave you to take care of them. Talking about they wanna see what's on the other side of the hill. I make sure I don't get no babies. My mama taught me how to do that.

Mattie: Don't make me no mind. That be nice to be a mother.

Molly: Yeah? Well, you go on, then. Molly Cunningham ain't gonna be tied down with no babies. Had me a man one time who I thought had some love in him. Come home one day and he was packing his trunk. Told me the time come when even the best of friends must part. Say he was gonna send me a Special Delivery some old day. I watched him out the window when he carried that trunk out and down to the train station. Said if he was gonna send me a Special Delivery I wasn't gonna be there to get it. I done found out the harder you try to hold onto them, the easier it is for some gal to pull them away. Molly done learned that. That's why I don't trust nobody but the good Lord above, and I don't love nobody but my mama.

Mattie: I got to get on. Doc Goldblum gonna be waiting.

(Mattie *exits out the front door.* Seth *enters from his workshop with his apron, gloves, goggles, etc. He carries a bucket and crosses to the sink for water.*)

Seth: Everybody gone but you, huh?

Molly: That little shack out there by the outhouse . . . that's where you make them pots and pans and stuff?

Seth: Yeah, that's my workshed. I go out there . . . take these hands and make something out of nothing. Take that metal and bend and twist it whatever way I want. My daddy taught me that. He used to make pots and pans. That's how I learned it.

Molly: I never knew nobody made no pots and pans. My uncle used to shoe horses.

(Jeremy *enters at the front door.*)

Seth: I thought you was working? Ain't you working today?

Jeremy: Naw, they fired me. White fellow come by told me to give him fifty cents if I wanted to keep working. Going around to all the colored making them give him fifty cents to keep hold to their jobs. Them other fellows, they was giving it to him. I kept hold to mine and they fired me.

Seth: Boy, what kind of sense that make? What kind of sense it make to get fired from a job where you making eight dollars a week and all it cost you is fifty cents. That's seven dollars and fifty cents profit! This way you ain't got nothing.

Jeremy: It didn't make no sense to me. I don't make but eight dollars. Why I got to give him fifty cents of it? He go around to all the colored and he got ten dollars extra. That's more than I make for a whole week.

Seth: I see you gonna learn the hard way. You just looking at the facts of it. See, right now, without the job, you ain't got nothing. What you gonna do when you can't keep a roof over your head? Right now, come Saturday, unless you come up with another two dollars, you gonna be out there in the streets. Down up under one of them bridges trying to put some food in your belly and wishing you had given that fellow that fifty cents.

Jeremy: Don't make me no difference. There's a big road out there. I can get my guitar and always find me another place to stay. I ain't planning on staying in one place for too long noway.

Seth: We gonna see if you feel like that come Saturday!

(Seth *exits out the back.* Jeremy *sees* Molly.)

Jeremy: Molly Cunningham. How you doing today, sugar?

Molly: You can go on back down there tomorrow and go back to work if you want. They won't even know who you is. Won't even know it's you. I had me a fellow did that one time. They just went ahead and signed him up like they never seen him before.

Jeremy: I'm tired of working anyway. I'm glad they fired me. You sure look pretty today.

Molly: Don't come telling me all that pretty stuff. Beauty wanna come in and sit down at your table asking to be fed. I ain't hardly got enough for me.

Jeremy: You know you pretty. Ain't no sense in you saying nothing about that. Why don't you come on and go away with me?

Molly: You tied up with that Mattie Campbell. Now you talking about running away with me.

Jeremy: I was just keeping her company 'cause she lonely. You ain't the lonely kind. You the kind that know what she want and how to get it. I need a woman like you to travel around with. Don't you wanna travel around and look at some places with Jeremy? With a woman like you beside him, a man can make it nice in the world.

Molly: Molly can make it nice by herself too. Molly don't need nobody leave her cold in hand. The world rough enough as it is.

Jeremy: We can make it better together. I got my guitar and I can play. Won me another dollar last night playing guitar. We can go around and I can play at the dances and we can just enjoy life. You can make it by yourself alright, I agrees with that. A woman

like you can make it anywhere she go. But you can make it better
if you got a man to protect you.

Molly: What places you wanna go around and look at?

Jeremy: All of them! I don't want to miss nothing. I wanna go everywhere and do everything there is to be got out of life. With a
woman like you it's like having water and berries. A man got everything he need.

Molly: You got to be doing more than playing that guitar. A dollar a
day ain't hardly what Molly got in mind.

Jeremy: I gambles real good. I got a hand for it.

Molly: Molly don't work. And Molly ain't up for sale.

Jeremy: Sure, baby. You ain't got to work with Jeremy.

Molly: There's one more thing.

Jeremy: What's that, sugar?

Molly: Molly ain't going South.

(The lights go down on the scene.)

Scene Two

The lights come up on the parlor. Seth *and* Bynum *sit playing a game of dominoes.* Bynum *sings to himself.*

Bynum: (Singing.)

>They tell me Joe Turner's come and gone
>Ohhh Lordy
>They tell me Joe Turner's come and gone
>Ohhh Lordy
>Got my man and gone
>
>Come with forty links of chain
>Ohhh Lordy
>Come with forty links of chain
>Ohhh Lordy
>Got my man and gone

Seth: Come on and play if you gonna play.

Bynum: I'm gonna play. Soon as I figure out what to do.

Seth: You can't figure out if you wanna play or you wanna sing.

Bynum: Well sir, I'm gonna do a little bit of both.

(Playing.)

>There. What you gonna do now?

(Singing.)

>They tell me Joe Turner's come and gone
>Ohhh Lordy

They tell me Joe Turner's come and gone
Ohhh Lordy
Seth: Why don't you hush up that noise.
Bynum: That's a song the women sing down around Memphis. The women down there made up that song. I picked it up down there about fifteen years ago.

(Loomis *enters from the front door.*)

Bynum: Evening, Mr. Loomis.
Seth: Today's Monday, Mr. Loomis. Come Saturday your time is up. We done ate already. My wife roasted up some yams. She got your plate sitting in there on the table. (*To* Bynum.) Whose play is it?
Bynum: Ain't you keeping up with the game? I thought you was a domino player. I just played so it got to be your turn.

(Loomis *goes into the kitchen, where a plate of yams is covered and set on the table. He sits down and begins to eat with his hands.*)

Seth: (*Plays.*) Twenty! Give me twenty! You didn't know I had that ace five. You was trying to play around that. You didn't know I had that lying there for you.
Bynum: You ain't done nothing. I let you have that to get mine.
Seth: Come on and play. You ain't doing nothing but talking. I got a hundred and forty points to your eighty. You ain't doing nothing but talking. Come on and play.
Bynum: (*Singing.*)
They tell me Joe Turner's come and gone
Ohhh Lordy
They tell me Joe Turner's come and gone
Ohhh Lordy
Got my man and gone

He come with forty links of chain
Ohhh Lordy
Loomis: Why you singing that song? Why you singing about Joe Turner?
Bynum: I'm just singing to entertain myself.
Seth: You trying to distract me. That's what you trying to do.
Bynum: (*Singing.*)
Come with forty links of chain
Ohhh Lordy
Come with forty links of chain
Ohhh Lordy
Loomis: I don't like you singing that song, mister!
Seth: Now, I ain't gonna have no more disturbance around here,

Herald Loomis. You start any more disturbance and you leavin' here, Saturday or no Saturday.

Bynum: The man ain't causing no disturbance, Seth. He just say he don't like the song.

Seth: Well, we all friendly folk. All neighborly like. Don't have no squabbling around here. Don't have no disturbance. You gonna have to take that someplace else.

Bynum: He just say he don't like the song. I done sung a whole lot of songs people don't like. I respect everybody. He here in the house too. If he don't like the song, I'll sing something else. I know lots of songs. You got "I Belong to the Band," "Don't You Leave Me Here." You got "Praying on the Old Campground," "Keep Your Lamp Trimmed and Burning" . . . I know lots of songs.

(Sings.)

> Boys, I'll be so glad when payday come
> Captain, Captain, when payday comes
> Gonna catch that Illinois Central
> Going to Kankakee

Seth: Why don't you hush up that hollering and come on and play dominoes.

Bynum: You ever been to Johnstown, Herald Loomis? You look like a fellow I seen around there.

Loomis: I don't know no place with that name.

Bynum: That's around where I seen my shiny man. See, you looking for this woman. I'm looking for a shiny man. Seem like everybody looking for something.

Seth: I'm looking for you to come and play these dominoes. That's what I'm looking for.

Bynum: You a farming man, Herald Loomis? You look like you done some farming.

Loomis: Same as everybody. I done farmed some, yeah.

Bynum: I used to work at farming . . . picking cotton. I reckon everybody done picked some cotton.

Seth: I ain't! I ain't never picked no cotton. I was born up here in the North. My daddy was a freedman. I ain't never even seen no cotton!

Bynum: Mr. Loomis done picked some cotton. Ain't you, Herald Loomis? You done picked a bunch of cotton.

Loomis: How you know so much about me? How you know what I done? How much cotton I picked?

Bynum: I can tell from looking at you. My daddy taught me how to do that. Say when you look at a fellow, if you taught yourself to look for it, you can see his song written on him. Tell you what kind of man he is in the world. Now, I can look at you, Mr. Loomis, and see you a man who done forgot his song. Forgot how to sing it. A fellow forget that and he forget who he is. Forget how he's supposed to mark down life. Now, I used to travel all up and down this road and that . . . looking here and there. Searching. Just like you, Mr. Loomis. I didn't know what I was searching for. The only thing I knew was something was keeping me dissatisfied. Something wasn't making my heart smooth and easy. Then one day my daddy gave me a song. That song had a weight to it that was hard to handle. That song was hard to carry. I fought against it. Didn't want to accept that song. I tried to find my daddy to give him back the song. But I found out it wasn't his song. It was my song. It had come from way deep inside me. I looked long back in memory and gathered up pieces and snatches of things to make that song. I was making it up out of myself. And that song helped me on the road. Made it smooth to where my footsteps didn't bite back at me. All the time that song getting bigger and bigger. That song growing with each step of the road. It got so I used all of myself up in the making of that song. Then I was the song in search of itself. That song rattling in my throat and I'm looking for it. See, Mr. Loomis, when a man forgets his song he goes off in search of it . . . till he find out he's got it with him all the time. That's why I can tell you one of Joe Turner's niggers. 'Cause you forgot how to sing your song.

Loomis: You lie! How you see that? I got a mark on me? Joe Turner done marked me to where you can see it? You telling me I'm a marked man. What kind of mark you got on you?

(Bynum *begins singing.*)

Bynum:

    They tell me Joe Turner's come and gone
    Ohhh Lordy
    They tell me Joe Turner's come and gone
    Ohhh Lordy
    Got my man and gone

Loomis: Had a whole mess of men he catched. Just go out hunting regular like you go out hunting possum. He catch you and go home to his wife and family. Ain't thought about you going home to yours. Joe Turner catched me when my little girl was just born. Wasn't nothing but a little baby sucking on her mama's titty when he catched me. Joe Turner catched me in nineteen hundred and one. Kept me seven years until nineteen hundred and eight. Kept everybody seven years. He'd go out hunting and bring back forty men at a time. And keep them seven years.

    I was walking down this road in this little town outside of Memphis. Come up on these fellows gambling. I was a deacon in the Abundant Life Church. I stopped to preach to these fellows to see if maybe I could turn some of them from their sinning when Joe Turner, brother of the Governor of the great sovereign state of Tennessee, swooped down on us and grabbed everybody there. Kept us all seven years.

My wife Martha gone from me after Joe Turner catched me. Got out from under Joe Turner on his birthday. Me and forty other men put in our seven years and he let us go on his birthday. I made it back to Henry Thompson's place where me and Martha was sharecropping and Martha's gone. She taken my little girl and left her with her mama and took off North. We been looking for her ever since. That's been going on four years now we been looking. That's the only thing I know to do. I just wanna see her face so I can get me a starting place in the world. The world got to start somewhere. That's what I been looking for. I been wandering a long time in somebody else's world. When I find my wife that be the making of my own.

Bynum: Joe Turner tell why he caught you? You ever asked him that?

Loomis: I ain't never seen Joe Turner. Seen him to where I could touch him. I asked one of them fellows one time why he catch niggers. Asked him what I got he want? Why don't he keep on to himself? Why he got to catch me going down the road by my lonesome? He told me I was worthless. Worthless is something you throw away. Something you don't bother with. I ain't seen him throw me away. Wouldn't even let me stay away when I was by my lonesome. I ain't tried to catch him when he going down the road. So I must got something he want. What I got?

Seth: He just want you to do his work for him. That's all.

Loomis: I can look at him and see where he big and strong enough to do his own work. So it can't be that. He must want something he ain't got.

Bynum: That ain't hard to figure out. What he wanted was your song. He wanted to have that song to be his. He thought by catching you he could learn that song. Every nigger he catch he's looking for the one he can learn that song from. Now he's got you bound up to where you can't sing your own song. Couldn't sing it them seven years 'cause you was afraid he would snatch it from under you. But you still got it. You just forgot how to sing it.

Loomis: (To Bynum.*)* I know who you are. You one of them bones people.

(The lights go down to black.)

Scene Three

The lights come up on the kitchen. It is the following morning. Mattie *and* Bynum *sit at the table.* Bertha *busies herself at the stove.*

Bynum: Good luck don't know no special time to come. You sleep with that up under your pillow and good luck can't help but come to you. Sometimes it come and go and you don't even know it's been there.

Bertha: Bynum, why don't you leave that gal alone? She don't wanna be hearing all that. Why don't you go on and get out the way and leave her alone?

Bynum: (Getting up.) Alright, alright. But you mark what I'm saying. It'll draw it to you just like a magnet.

(Bynum *exits up the stairs and* Loomis *enters.*)

Bertha: I got some grits here, Mr. Loomis.

(Bertha *sets a bowl on the table.*)

If I was you, Mattie, I wouldn't go getting all tied up with Bynum in that stuff. That kind of stuff, even if it do work for a while, it don't last. That just get people more mixed up than they is already. And I wouldn't waste my time fretting over Jeremy either. I seen it coming. I seen it when she first come here. She that kind of woman run off with the first man got a dollar to spend on her. Jeremy just young. He don't know what he getting into. That gal don't mean him no good. She's just using him to keep from being by herself. That's the worst use of a man you can have. You ought to be glad to wash him out of your hair. I done seen all kind of men. I done seen them come and go through here. Jeremy ain't had enough to him for you. You need a man who's got some understanding and who willing to work with that understanding to come to the best he can. You got your time coming. You just tries too hard and can't understand why it don't work for you. Trying to figure it out don't do nothing but give you a troubled mind. Don't no man want a woman with a troubled mind.

You get all that trouble off your mind and just when it look like you ain't never gonna find what you want . . . you look up and it's standing right there. That's how I met my Seth. You gonna look up one day and find everything you want standing right in front of you. Been twenty-seven years now since that happened to me. But life ain't no happy-go-lucky time where everything be just like you want it. You got your time coming. You watch what Bertha's saying.

(Seth *enters.*)

Seth: Ho!

Bertha: What you doing come in here so late?

Seth: I was standing down there on Logan Street talking with the fellows. Henry Allen tried to sell me that old piece of horse he got.

(He sees Loomis.*)*

Today's Tuesday, Mr. Loomis.

Bertha: (Pulling him toward the bedroom.) Come on in here and leave that man alone to eat his breakfast.

Seth: I ain't bothering nobody. I'm just reminding him what day it is.

*(*Seth *and* Bertha *exit into the bedroom.)*

Loomis: That dress got a color to it.

Mattie: Did you really see them things like you said? Them people come up out the ocean?

Loomis: It happened just like that, yeah.

Mattie: I hope you find your wife. It be good for your little girl for you to find her.

Loomis: Got to find her for myself. Find my starting place in the world. Find me a world I can fit in.

Mattie: I ain't never found no place for me to fit. Seem like all I do is start over. It ain't nothing to find no starting place in the world. You just start from where you find yourself.

Loomis: Got to find my wife. That be my starting place.

Mattie: What if you don't find her? What you gonna do then if you don't find her?

Loomis: She out there somewhere. Ain't no such thing as not finding her.

Mattie: How she got lost from you? Jack just walked away from me.

Loomis: Joe Turner split us up. Joe Turner turned the world upside-down. He bound me on to him for seven years.

Mattie: I hope you find her. It be good for you to find her.

Loomis: I been watching you. I been watching you watch me.

Mattie: I was just trying to figure out if you seen things like you said.

Loomis: (Getting up.) Come here and let me touch you. I been watching you. You a full woman. A man needs a full woman. Come on and be with me.

Mattie: I ain't got enough for you. You'd use me up too fast.

Loomis: Herald Loomis got a mind seem like you a part of it since I first seen you. It's been a long time since I seen a full woman. I can smell you from here. I know you got Herald Loomis on your mind, can't keep him apart from it. Come on and be with Herald Loomis.

*(*Loomis *has crossed to* Mattie. *He touches her awkwardly, gently, tenderly. Inside he howls like a lost wolf pup whose hunger is deep. He goes to touch her but finds he cannot.)*

I done forgot how to touch.

(The lights fade to black.)

Scene Four

It is early the next morning. The lights come up on Zonia *and* Reuben *in the yard.*

Reuben: Something spooky going on around here. Last night Mr. Bynum was out in the yard singing and talking to the wind . . . and the wind it just be talking back to him. Did you hear it?

Zonia: I heard it. I was scared to get up and look. I thought it was a storm.

Reuben: That wasn't no storm. That was Mr. Bynum. First he say something . . . and the wind it say back to him.

Zonia: I heard it. Was you scared? I was scared.

Reuben: And then this morning . . . I seen Miss Mabel!

Zonia: Who Miss Mabel?

Reuben: Mr. Seth's mother. He got her picture hanging up in the house. She been dead.

Zonia: How you seen her if she been dead?

Reuben: Zonia . . . if I tell you something you promise you won't tell anybody?

Zonia: I promise.

Reuben: It was early this morning . . . I went out to the coop to feed the pigeons. I was down on the ground like this to open up the door to the coop . . . when all of a sudden I seen some feets in front of me. I looked up . . . and there was Miss Mabel standing there.

Zonia: Reuben, you better stop telling that! You ain't seen nobody!

Reuben: Naw, it's the truth. I swear! I seen her just like I see you. Look . . . you can see where she hit me with her cane.

Zonia: Hit you? What she hit you for?

Reuben: She says, "Didn't you promise Eugene something?" Then she hit me with her cane. She say, "Let them pigeons go." Then she hit me again. That's what made them marks.

Zonia: Jeez man . . . get away from me. You done see a haunt!

Reuben: Shhhh. You promised, Zonia!

Zonia: You sure it wasn't Miss Bertha come over there and hit you with her hoe?

Reuben: It wasn't no Miss Bertha. I told you it was Miss Mabel. She was standing right there by the coop. She had this light coming out of her and then she just melted away.

Zonia: What she had on?

Reuben: A white dress. Ain't even had no shoes or nothing. Just had on that white dress and them big hands . . . and that cane she hit me with.

Zonia: How you reckon she knew about the pigeons? You reckon Eugene told her?

Reuben: I don't know. I sure ain't asked her none. She say Eugene was waiting on them pigeons. Say he couldn't go back home till I let them go. I couldn't get the door to the coop open fast enough.

Zonia: Maybe she an angel? From the way you say she look with that white dress. Maybe she an angel.

Reuben: Mean as she was . . . how she gonna be an angel? She used to chase us out her yard and frown up and look evil all the time.

Zonia: That don't mean she can't be no angel 'cause of how she looked and 'cause she wouldn't let no kids play in her yard. It go by if you got any spots on your heart and if you pray and go to church.

Reuben: What about she hit me with her cane? An angel wouldn't hit me with her cane.

Zonia: I don't know. She might. I still say she was an angel.

Reuben: You reckon Eugene the one who sent old Miss Mabel?

Zonia: Why he send her? Why he don't come himself?

Reuben: Figured if he send her maybe that'll make me listen. 'Cause she old.

Zonia: What you think it feel like?

Reuben: What?

Zonia: Being dead.

Reuben: Like being sleep only you don't know nothing and can't move no more.

Zonia: If Miss Mabel can come back . . . then maybe Eugene can come back too.

Reuben: We can go down to the hideout like we used to! He could come back everyday! It be just like he ain't dead.

Zonia: Maybe that ain't right for him to come back. Feel kinda funny to be playing games with a haunt.

Reuben: Yeah . . . what if everybody came back? What if Miss Mabel came back just like she ain't dead? Where you and your daddy gonna sleep then?

Zonia: Maybe they go back at night and don't need no place to sleep.

Reuben: It still don't seem right. I'm sure gonna miss Eugene. He's the bestest friend anybody ever had.

Zonia: My daddy say if you miss somebody too much it can kill you. Say he missed me till it liked to killed him.

Reuben: What if your mama's already dead and all the time you looking for her?

Zonia: Naw, she ain't dead. My daddy say he can smell her.

Reuben: You can't smell nobody that ain't here. Maybe he smelling old Miss Bertha. Maybe Miss Bertha your mama?

Zonia: Naw, she ain't. My mamma got long pretty hair and she five feet from the ground!

Reuben: Your daddy say when you leaving?

(Zonia *doesn't respond.*)

Maybe you gonna stay in Mr. Seth's house and don't go looking for your mama no more.

Zonia: He say we got to leave on Saturday.

Reuben: Dag! You just only been here for a little while. Don't seem like nothing ever stay the same.

Zonia: He say he got to find her. Find him a place in the world.

Reuben: He could find him a place in Mr. Seth's house.

Zonia: It don't look like we never gonna find her.

Reuben: Maybe he find her by Saturday then you don't have to go.

Zonia: I don't know.

Reuben: You look like a spider!

Zonia: I ain't no spider!

Reuben: Got them long skinny arms and legs. You look like one of them Black Widows.

Zonia: I ain't no Black Widow nothing! My name is Zonia!

Reuben: That's what I'm gonna call you . . . Spider.

Zonia: You can call me that, but I don't have to answer.

Reuben: You know what? I think maybe I be your husband when I grow up.

Zonia: How you know?

Reuben: I ask my grandpap how you know and he say when the moon falls into a girl's eyes that how you know.

Zonia: Did it fall into my eyes?

Reuben: Not that I can tell. Maybe I ain't old enough. Maybe you ain't old enough.

Zonia: So there! I don't know why you telling me that lie!

Reuben: That don't mean nothing 'cause I can't see it. I know it's there. Just the way you look at me sometimes look like the moon might have been in your eyes.

Zonia: That don't mean nothing if you can't see it. You supposed to see it.

Reuben: Shucks, I see it good enough for me. You ever let anybody kiss you?

Zonia: Just my daddy. He kiss me on the cheek.

Reuben: It's better on the lips. Can I kiss you on the lips?

Zonia: I don't know. You ever kiss anybody before?

Reuben: I had a cousin let me kiss her on the lips one time. Can I kiss you?

Zonia: Okay.

(Reuben *kisses her and lays his head against her chest.*)

What you doing?

Reuben: Listening. Your heart singing!

Zonia: It is not.

Reuben: Just beating like a drum. Let's kiss again.

(*They kiss again.*)

Now you mine, Spider. You my girl, okay?

Zonia: Okay.
Reuben: When I get grown, I come looking for you.
Zonia: Okay.

(*The lights fade to black.*)

Scene Five

The lights come up on the kitchen. It is Saturday. Bynum, Loomis, *and* Zonia *sit at the table.* Bertha *prepares breakfast.* Zonia *has on a white dress.*

Bynum: With all this rain we been having he might have ran into some washed-out roads. If that wagon got stuck in the mud he's liable to be still upriver somewhere. If he's upriver then he ain't coming until tomorrow.
Loomis: Today's Saturday. He say he be here on Saturday.
Bertha: Zonia, you gonna eat your breakfast this morning.
Zonia: Yes, ma'am.
Bertha: I don't know how you expect to get any bigger if you don't eat. I ain't never seen a child that didn't eat. You about as skinny as a bean pole.

(Pause.)

Mr. Loomis, there's a place down on Wylie. Zeke Mayweather got a house down there. You ought to see if he got any rooms.

(Loomis doesn't respond.)

Well, you're welcome to some breakfast before you move on.

(Mattie enters from the stairs.)

Mattie: Good morning.
Bertha: Morning, Mattie. Sit on down there and get you some breakfast.
Bynum: Well, Mattie Campbell, you been sleeping with that up under your pillow like I told you?
Bertha: Bynum, I done told you to leave that gal alone with all that stuff. You around here meddling in other people's lives. She don't want to hear all that. You ain't doing nothing but confusing her with that stuff.
Mattie: (*To* Loomis.) You all fixing to move on?
Loomis: Today's Saturday. I'm paid up till Saturday.
Mattie: Where you going to?
Loomis: Gonna find my wife.
Mattie: You going off to another city?
Loomis: We gonna see where the road take us. Ain't no telling where we wind up.
Mattie: Eleven years is a long time. Your wife . . . she might have taken

up with someone else. People do that when they get lost from each other.

Loomis: Zonia. Come on, we gonna find your mama.

(Loomis *and* Zonia *cross to the door.*)

Mattie: (To Zonia.) Zonia, Mattie got a ribbon here match your dress. Want Mattie to fix your hair with her ribbon?

(Zonia *nods.* Mattie *ties the ribbon in her hair.*)

There . . . it got a color just like your dress. *(To* Loomis.) I hope you find her. I hope you be happy.

Loomis: A man looking for a woman be lucky to find you. You a good woman, Mattie. Keep a good heart.

(Loomis *and* Zonia *exit.*)

Bertha: I been watching that man for two weeks . . . and that's the closest I come to seeing him act civilized. I don't know what's between you all, Mattie . . . but the only thing that man needs is somebody to make him laugh. That's all you need in the world is love and laughter. That's all anybody needs. To have love in one hand and laughter in the other.

(Bertha *moves about the kitchen as though blessing it and chasing away the huge sadness that seems to envelop it. It is a dance and demonstration of her own magic, her own remedy that is centuries old and to which she is connected by the muscles of her heart and the blood's memory.*)

You hear me, Mattie? I'm talking about laughing. The kind of laugh that comes from way deep inside. To just stand and laugh and let life flow right through you. Just laugh to let yourself know you're alive.

(She *begins to laugh. It is a near-hysterical laughter that is a celebration of life, both its pain and its blessing.* Mattie *and* Bynum *join in the laughter.* Seth *enters from the front door.*)

Seth: Well, I see you all having fun.

(Seth *begins to laugh with them.*)

That Loomis fellow standing up there on the corner watching the house. He standing right up there on Manila Street.

Bertha: Don't you get started on him. The man done left out of here and that's the last I wanna hear of it. You about to drive me crazy with that man.

Seth: I just say he standing up there on the corner. Acting sneaky like he always do. He can stand up there all he want. As long as he don't come back in here.

(There is a knock on the door. Seth *goes to answer it.* Enter Martha Loomis [Pentecost]. *She is a young woman about twenty-eight. She is dressed as befitting a member of an Evangelist church.* Rutherford Selig *follows.)*

Seth: Look here, Bertha. It's Martha Pentecost. Come on in, Martha. Who that with you? Oh . . . that's Selig. Come on in, Selig.

Bertha: Come on in, Martha. It's sure good to see you.

Bynum: Rutherford Selig, you a sure enough first-class People Finder!

Selig: She was right out there in Rankin. You take that first right-hand road . . . right there at that church on Wooster Street. I started to go right past and something told me to stop at the church and see if they needed any dustpans.

Seth: Don't she look good, Bertha.

Bertha: Look all nice and healthy.

Martha: Mr. Bynum . . . Selig told me my little girl was here.

Seth: There's some fellow around here say he your husband. Say his name is Loomis. Say you his wife.

Martha: Is my little girl with him?

Seth: Yeah, he got a little girl with him. I wasn't gonna tell him where you was. Not the way this fellow look. So he got Selig to find you.

Martha: Where they at? They upstairs?

Seth: He was standing right up there on Manila Street. I had to ask him to leave 'cause of how he was carrying on. He come in here one night—

(The door opens and Loomis *and* Zonia *enter.* Martha *and* Loomis *stare at each other.)*

Loomis: Hello, Martha.

Martha: Herald . . . Zonia?

Loomis: You ain't waited for me, Martha. I got out the place looking to see your face. Seven years I waited to see your face.

Martha: Herald, I been looking for you. I wasn't but two months behind you when you went to my mama's and got Zonia. I been looking for you ever since.

Loomis: Joe Turner let me loose and I felt all turned around inside. I just wanted to see your face to know that the world was still there. Make sure everything still in its place so I could reconnect myself together. I got there and you was gone, Martha.

Martha: Herald . . .

Loomis: Left my little girl motherless in the world.

Martha: I didn't leave her motherless, Herald. Reverend Toliver wanted to move the church up North 'cause of all the trouble the colored folks was having down there. Nobody knew what was gonna happen traveling them roads. We didn't even know if we was gonna make it up here or not. I left her with my mama so she be safe. That was better than dragging her out on the road having to duck and hide from people. Wasn't no telling what was gonna happen to us. I didn't leave her motherless in the world. I been looking for you.

Loomis: I come up on Henry Thompson's place after seven years of living in hell, and all I'm looking to do is see your face.

Martha: Herald, I didn't know if you was ever coming back. They told me Joe Turner had you and my whole world split half in two. My whole life shattered. It was like I had poured it in a cracked jar and it all leaked out the bottom. When it go like that there ain't nothing you can do to put it back together. You talking about Henry Thompson's place like I'm still gonna be working the land by myself. How I'm gonna do that? You wasn't gone but two months and Henry Thompson kicked me off his land and I ain't had no place to go but to my mama's. I stayed and waited there for five years before I woke up one morning and decided that you was dead. Even if you weren't, you was dead to me. I wasn't gonna carry you with me no more. So I killed you in my heart. I buried you. I mourned you. And then I picked up what was left and went on to make life without you. I was a young woman with life at my beckon. I couldn't drag you behind me like a sack of cotton.

Loomis: I just been waiting to look on your face to say my goodbye. That goodbye got so big at times, seem like it was gonna swallow me up. Like Jonah in the whale's belly I sat up in that goodbye for three years. That goodbye kept me out on the road searching. Not looking on women in their houses. It kept me bound up to the road. All the time that goodbye swelling up in my chest till I'm about to bust. Now that I see your face I can say my goodbye and make my own world.

(Loomis *takes* Zonia's *hand and presents her to* Martha.)

Martha . . . here go your daughter. I tried to take care of her. See that she had something to eat. See that she was out of the elements. Whatever I know I tried to teach her. Now she need to learn from her mother whatever you got to teach her. That way she won't be no one-sided person.

(Loomis *stoops to* Zonia.)

Zonia, you go live with your mama. She a good woman. You go on with her and listen to her good. You my daughter and I love you like a daughter. I hope to see you again in the world somewhere. I'll never forget you.

Zonia: (*Throws her arms around* Loomis *in a panic.*) I won't get no bigger! My bones won't get no bigger! They won't! I promise! Take me with you till we keep searching and never finding. I won't get no bigger! I promise!

Loomis: Go on and do what I told you now.

Martha: (Goes to Zonia *and comforts her.)* It's alright, baby. Mama's here. Mama's here. Don't worry. Don't cry.

*(*Martha *turns to* Bynum.*)*

Mr. Bynum, I don't know how to thank you. God bless you.

Loomis: It was you! All the time it was you that bind me up! You bound me to the road!

Bynum: I ain't bind you, Herald Loomis. You can't bind what don't cling.

Loomis: Everywhere I go people wanna bind me up. Joe Turner wanna bind me up! Reverend Toliver wanna bind me up. You wanna bind me up. Everybody wanna bind me up. Well, Joe Turner's come and gone and Herald Loomis ain't for no binding. I ain't gonna let nobody bind me up!

*(*Loomis *pulls out a knife.)*

Bynum: It wasn't you, Herald Loomis. I ain't bound you. I bound the little girl to her mother. That's who I bound. You binding yourself. You bound onto your song. All you got to do is stand up and sing it, Herald Loomis. It's right there kicking at your throat. All you got to do is sing it. Then you be free.

Martha: Herald . . . look at yourself! Standing there with a knife in your hand. You done gone over to the devil. Come on . . . put down the knife. You got to look to Jesus. Even if you done fell away from the church you can be saved again. The Bible say, "The Lord is my shepherd I shall not want. He maketh me to lie down in green pastures. He leads me beside the still water. He restoreth my soul. He leads me in the path of righteousness for His name's sake. Even though I walk through the shadow of death—"

Loomis: That's just where I be walking!

Martha: "I shall fear no evil. For Thou art with me. Thy rod and thy staff, they comfort me."

Loomis: You can't tell me nothing about no valleys. I done been all across the valleys and the hills and the mountains and the oceans.

Martha: "Thou preparest a table for me in the presence of my enemies."

Loomis: And all I seen was a bunch of niggers dazed out of their woolly heads. And Mr. Jesus Christ standing there in the middle of them, grinning.

Martha: "Thou anointest my head with oil, my cup runneth over."

Loomis: He grin that big old grin . . . and niggers wallowing at his feet.

Martha: "Surely goodness and mercy shall follow me all the days of my life, and I shall dwell in the house of the Lord forever."

Loomis: Great big old white man . . . your Mr. Jesus Christ. Standing there with a whip in one hand and tote board in another, and them niggers swimming in a sea of cotton. And he counting. He tallying up the cotton. "Well, Jeremiah . . . what's the matter, you ain't picked but two hundred pounds of cotton today? Got to put you on half rations." And Jeremiah go back and lay up there on his half rations and talk about what a nice man Mr. Jesus Christ is 'cause he give him salvation after he die. Something wrong here. Something don't fit right!

Martha: You got to open your heart and have faith, Herald. This world is just a trial for the next. Jesus offers you salvation.

Loomis: I been wading in the water. I been walking all over the River Jordan. But what it get me, huh? I done been baptized with the blood of the lamb and the fire of the Holy Ghost. But what I got, huh? I got salvation? My enemies all around me picking the flesh from my bones. I'm choking on my own blood and all you got to give me is salvation?

Martha: You got to be clean, Herald. You got to be washed with the blood of the lamb.

Loomis: Blood make you clean? You clean with blood?

Martha: Jesus bled for you. He's the Lamb of God who takest away the sins of the world.

Loomis: I don't need nobody to bleed for me! I can bleed for myself.

Martha: You got to be something, Herald. You just can't be alive. Life don't mean nothing unless it got a meaning.

Loomis: What kind of meaning you got? What kind of clean you got, woman? You want blood? Blood make you clean? You clean with blood?

(Loomis *slashes himself across the chest. He rubs the blood over his face and comes to a realization.*)

I'm standing! I'm standing. My legs stood up! I'm standing now!

(*Having found his song, the song of self-sufficiency, fully resurrected, cleansed, and given breath, free from any encumbrance other than the workings of his own heart and the bonds of the flesh, having accepted the responsibility for his own presence in the world, he is free to soar above the environs that weighed and pushed his spirit into terrifying contractions.*)

Goodbye, Martha.

(Loomis *turns and exits, the knife still in his hands.* Mattie *looks about the room and rushes out after him.*)

Bynum: Herald Loomis, you shining! You shining like new money!

(*The lights go down to BLACK.*)

Further Reading

Freedman, Samuel G. "A Voice from the Streets." *New York Times Magazine* 15 Mar. 1986: 36+ • Seibert, Gary. Rev. of *Joe Turner's Come and Gone*. *America* 158 (16 Apr. 1988): 410–11. • Oliver, Edith. Rev. of *Joe Turner's Come and Gone*. *The New Yorker* 64 (11 Apr. 1988): 107. • Disch, Thomas M. Rev. of *Joe Turner's Come and Gone*. *The Nation* 245 (12 Dec. 1987): 726. • Simon, John. Rev. of *Joe Turner's Come and Gone*. *New York* 21 (11 Apr. 1988): 118.

Joe Turner's Come and Gone, which won the New York Critics' Circle Award for the best play of the 1987–88 season, is part of a projected cycle of ten plays that trace, decade by decade, the struggles of black Americans in the twentieth century. In 1987 Wilson made the following statements about these struggles to a reporter for the New York Times. *Both show us something about Wilson's intentions as a dramatist.*

August Wilson: On the Historical Battle of Black Americans

I think it was Amiri Baraka who said that when you look in the mirror you should see your God. All over the world, nobody has a God who doesn't resemble them. Except black Americans. They can't even see they're worshipping someone else's God, because they want so badly to assimilate, to get the fruits of society. The message of American society is "Leave your Africanness outside the door." My message is "Claim what's yours."

* * *

For a long time, I thought the most valuable blacks were those in the penitentiary. They were the people with the warrior spirit. How they chose to battle may have been wrong, but you need people who will battle. You need someone who says, "I won't shine shoes for $40 a week. I have a woman and two kids, and I will put a gun in my hand and take, and my kids will have Christmas presents." Just like there were people who didn't accept slavery. There were Nat Turners. And that's the spirit Levee had [in *Ma Rainey's Black Bottom*], and Troy has [in *Fences*], and Herald Loomis has [in *Joe Turner's Come and Gone*].

BETH HENLEY

(b. 1952)

CRIMES OF THE HEART

CHARACTERS

Lenny MaGrath, thirty, the oldest sister
Chick Boyle, twenty-nine, the sister's first cousin
Doc Porter, thirty, Meg's old boyfriend
Meg MaGrath, twenty-seven, the middle sister
Babe Botrelle, twenty-four, the youngest sister
Barnette Lloyd, twenty-six, Babe's lawyer

The Setting: The setting of the entire play is the kitchen in the MaGrath sisters' house in Hazlehurst, Mississippi, a small Southern town. The old-fashioned kitchen is unusually spacious, but there is a lived-in, cluttered look about it. There are four different entrances and exits to the kitchen: the back door, the door leading to the dining room and the front of the house, a door leading to the downstairs bedroom, and a staircase leading to the upstairs room. There is a table near the center of the room, and a cot has been set up in one of the corners.

The Time: In the fall, five years after Hurricane Camille.

ACT ONE

The lights go up on the empty kitchen. It is late afternoon. Lenny MaGrath, *a thirty-year-old woman with a round figure and face, enters from the back door carrying a white suitcase, a saxophone case, and a brown paper sack. She sets the suitcase and the sax case down and takes the brown sack to the kitchen table. After glancing quickly at the door, she gets the cookie jar from the kitchen counter, a box of matches from the stove, and then brings both objects back to the kitchen table. Excitedly, she reaches into the brown sack and pulls out a package of birthday candles. She quickly opens the package and removes a candle. She tries to stick the candle onto a cookie—it falls off. She sticks the candle in again, but the cookie is too hard and it crumbles. Frantically, she gets a second cookie from the jar. She strikes a match, lights the candle, and begins dripping wax onto the cookie. Just as she is beginning to smile we hear* Chick's *voice from offstage.*

Chick's Voice: Lenny! Oh, Lenny! Lenny *quickly blows out the candle and stuffs the cookie and candle into her dress pocket.* Chick, *twenty-nine, enters from the back door. She is a brightly dressed matron with yellow hair and shiny red lips.*

    Chick: Hi! I saw your car pull up.
    Lenny: Hi.
    Chick: Well, did you see today's paper?

Lenny *nods.*

    Chick: It's just too awful! It's just way too awful! How I'm gonna
        continue holding my head up high in this community, I do not
        know. Did you remember to pick up those pantyhose for me?
    Lenny: They're in the sack.
    Chick: Well, thank goodness, at least I'm not gonna have to go into
        town wearing holes in my stockings. *She gets the package, tears it
        open, and proceeds to take off one pair of stockings and put on another
        throughout the following scene. There should be something slightly
        grotesque about this woman changing her stockings in the kitchen.*
    Lenny: Did Uncle Watson call?
    Chick: Yes, Daddy has called me twice already. He said Babe's ready
        to come home. We've got to get right over and pick her up
        before they change their simple minds.
    Lenny: hesitantly: Oh, I know, of course, it's just—
    Chick: What?
    Lenny: Well, I was hoping Meg would call.
    Chick: Meg?
    Lenny: Yes, I sent her a telegram: about Babe, and—
    Chick: A telegram?! Couldn't you just phone her up?
    Lenny: Well, no, 'cause her phone's . . . out of order.
    Chick: Out of order?
    Lenny: Disconnected. I don't know what.
    Chick: Well, that sounds like Meg. My, these are snug. Are you sure
        you bought my right size?
    Lenny: looking at the box: Size extra-petite.
    Chick: Well, they're skimping on the nylon material. *Struggling to
        pull up the stockings:* That's all there is to it. Skimping on the
        nylon. *She finishes one leg and starts the other.* Now, just what all
        did you say in this "telegram" to Meg?
    Lenny: I don't recall exactly. I, well, I just told her to come on home.
    Chick: To come on home! Why, Lenora Josephine, have you lost
        your only brain, or what?
    *Lenny: nervously, as she begins to pick up the mess of dirty stockings and
        plastic wrappings:* But Babe wants Meg home. She asked me to
        call her.

Chick: I'm not talking about what Babe wants.

Lenny: Well, what then?

Chick: Listen, Lenora, I think it's pretty accurate to assume that after this morning's paper, Babe's gonna be incurring some mighty negative publicity around this town. And Meg's appearance isn't gonna help out a bit.

Lenny: What's wrong with Meg?

Chick: She had a loose reputation in high school.

Lenny: weakly: She was popular.

Chick: She was known all over Copiah County as cheap Christmas trash, and that was the least of it. There was that whole sordid affair with Doc Porter, leaving him a cripple.

Lenny: A cripple—he's got a limp. Just kind of, barely a limp.

Chick: Well, his mother was going to keep *me* out of the Ladies' Social League because of it.

Lenny: What?

Chick: That's right. I never told you, but I had to go plead with that mean old woman and convinced her that I was just as appalled with what Meg had done as she was, and that I was only a first cousin anyway and I could hardly be blamed for all the skeletons in the MaGraths' closet. It was humiliating. I tell you, she even brought up your mother's death. And that poor cat.

Lenny: Oh! Oh! Oh, please, Chick! I'm sorry. But you're in the Ladies' League now.

Chick: Yes. That's true, I am. But frankly, if Mrs. Porter hadn't developed that tumor in her bladder, I wouldn't be in the club today, much less a committee head. *As she brushes her hair:* Anyway, you be a sweet potato and wait right here for Meg to call, so's you can convince her not to come back home. It would make things a whole lot easier on everybody. Don't you think it really would?

Lenny: Probably.

Chick: Good, then suit yourself. How's my hair?

Lenny: Fine.

Chick: Not pooching out in the back, is it?

Lenny: No.

Chick: cleaning the hair from her brush: All right then, I'm on my way. I've got Annie May over there keeping an eye on Peekay and Buck Jr., but I don't trust her with them for long periods of time. *Dropping the ball of hair onto the floor:* Her mind is like a loose sieve. Honestly it is. *As she puts the brush back into her purse:* Oh! Oh! Oh! I almost forgot. Here's a present for you. Happy birthday to Lenny, from the Buck Boyles! *She takes a wrapped package from her bag and hands it to* Lenny.

Lenny: Why, thank you, Chick. It's so nice to have you remember my birthday every year like you do.

Chick: modestly: Oh, well, now, that's just the way I am, I suppose. That's just the way I was brought up to be. Well, why don't you go on and open up the present?

Lenny: All right. *She starts to unwrap the gift.*

Chick: It's a box of candy—assorted crèmes.

Lenny: Candy—that's always a nice gift.

Chick: And you have a sweet tooth, don't you?

Lenny: I guess.

Chick: Well, I'm glad you like it.

Lenny: I do.

Chick: Oh, speaking of which, remember that little polk-a-dot dress you got Peekay for her fifth birthday last month?

Lenny: The red-and-white one?

Chick: Yes; well, the first time I put it in the washing machine, I mean the very first time, it fell all to pieces. Those little polka dots just dropped right off in the water.

Lenny: crushed: Oh, no. Well, I'll get something else for her, then— a little toy.

Chick: Oh, no, no, no, no, no! We wouldn't hear of it! I just wanted to let you know so you wouldn't go and waste any more of your hard-earned money on that make of dress. Those inexpensive brands just don't hold up. I'm sorry, but not in these modern washing machines.

Doc Porter's Voice: Hello! Hello, Lenny!

Chick: taking over: Oh, look, it's Doc Porter! Come on in, Doc! Please come right on in!

Doc Porter enters through the back door. He is carrying a large sack of pecans. Doc is an attractively worn man with a slight limp that adds rather than detracts from his quiet seductive quality. He is thirty years old, but appears slightly older.

Chick: Well, how are you doing? How in the world are you doing?

Doc: Just fine, Chick.

Chick: And how are you liking it now that you're back in Hazlehurst?

Doc: Oh, I'm finding it somewhat enjoyable.

Chick: Somewhat! Only somewhat! Will you listen to him! What a silly, silly, silly man! Well, I'm on my way. I've got some people waiting on me. *Whispering to Doc:* It's Babe. I'm on my way to pick her up.

Doc: Oh.

Chick: Well, goodbye! Farewell and goodbye!

Lenny: 'Bye.

Chick exits.

Doc: Hello.

Lenny: Hi. I guess you heard about the thing with Babe.

Doc: Yeah.

Lenny: It was in the newspaper.

Doc: Uh huh.

Lenny: What a mess.

Doc: Yeah.

Lenny: Well, come on and sit down. I'll heat us up some coffee.

Doc: That's okay. I can only stay a minute. I have to pick up Scott; he's at the dentist.

Lenny: Oh; well, I'll heat some up for myself. I'm kinda thirsty for a cup of hot coffee. *She puts the coffeepot on the burner.*

Doc: Lenny—

Lenny: What?

Doc: *not able to go on:* Ah . . .

Lenny: Yes?

Doc: Here, some pecans for you. *He hands her the sack.*

Lenny: Why, thank you, Doc. I love pecans.

Doc: My wife and Scott picked them up around the yard.

Lenny: Well, I can use them to make a pie. A pecan pie.

Doc: Yeah. Look, Lenny, I've got some bad news for you.

Lenny: What?

Doc: Well, you know, you've been keeping Billy Boy out on our farm; he's been grazing out there.

Lenny: Yes—

Doc: Well, last night, Billy Boy died.

Lenny: He died?

Doc: Yeah. I'm sorry to tell you when you've got all this on you, but I thought you'd want to know.

Lenny: Well, yeah. I do. He died?

Doc: Uh huh. He was struck by lightning.

Lenny: Struck by lightning? In that storm yesterday?

Doc: That's what we think.

Lenny: Gosh, struck by lightning. I've had Billy Boy so long. You know. Ever since I was ten years old.

Doc: Yeah. He was a mighty old horse.

Lenny: *stung:* Mighty old.

Doc: Almost twenty years old.

Lenny: That's right, twenty years. 'Cause; ah, I'm thirty years old today. Did you know that?

Doc: No, Lenny, I didn't know. Happy birthday.

Lenny: Thanks. *She begins to cry.*

Doc: Oh, come on now, Lenny. Come on. Hey, hey, now. You know I can't stand it when you MaGrath women start to cry. You know it just gets me.

Lenny: Oh ho! Sure! You mean when Meg cries! Meg's the one you could never stand to watch cry! Not me! I could fill up a pig's trough!

Doc: Now, Lenny . . . stop it. Come on. Jesus!

Lenny: Okay! Okay! I don't know what's wrong with me. I don't
   mean to make a scene. I've been on this crying jag. *She blows her
   nose.* All this stuff with Babe, and Old Granddaddy's gotten
   worse in the hospital, and I can't get in touch with Meg.
Doc: You tried calling Meggy?
Lenny: Yes.
Doc: Is she coming home?
Lenny: Who knows. She hasn't called me. That's what I'm waiting
   here for—hoping she'll call.
Doc: She still living in California?
Lenny: Yes; in Hollywood.
Doc: Well, give me a call if she gets in. I'd like to see her.
Lenny: Oh, you would, huh?
Doc: Yeah, Lenny, sad to say, but I would.
Lenny: It is sad. It's very sad indeed.

They stare at each other, then look away. There is a moment of tense silence.

Doc: Hey, Jell-O Face, your coffee's boiling.
Lenny: going to check: Oh, it is? Thanks. *After she checks the pot:*
   Look, you'd better go on and pick Scott up. You don't want him
   to have to wait for you.
Doc: Yeah, you're right. Poor kid. It's his first time at the dentist.
Lenny: Poor thing.
Doc: Well, 'bye. I'm sorry to have to tell you about your horse.
Lenny: Oh, I know. Tell Joan thanks for picking up the pecans.
Doc: I will. *He starts to leave.*
Lenny: Oh, how's the baby?
Doc: She's fine. Real pretty. She, ah, holds your finger in her
   hand; like this.
Lenny: Oh, that's cute.
Doc: Yeah. 'Bye, Lenny.
Lenny: 'Bye.

Doc *exits.* Lenny *stares after him for a moment, then goes and sits back down at
the kitchen table. She reaches into her pocket and pulls out a somewhat crumbled
cookie and a wax candle. She lights the candle again, lets the wax drip onto the
cookie, then sticks the candle on top of the cookie. She begins to sing the "Happy
Birthday" song to herself. At the end of the song she pauses, silently makes a wish,
and blows out the candle. She waits a moment, then relights the candle, and repeats
her actions, only this time making a different wish at the end of the song. She starts
to repeat the procedure for the third time, as the phone rings. She goes to answer it.*

Lenny: Hello . . . Oh, hello, Lucille, how's Zackery? . . . Oh, no! . . .
   Oh, I'm so sorry. Of course, it must be grueling for you . . . Yes,
   I understand. Your only brother . . . No, she's not here yet.
   Chick just went to pick her up . . . Oh, now, Lucille, she's still his
   wife, I'm sure she'll be interested . . . Well, you can just tell me

the information and I'll relate it all to her . . . Uh hum, his liver's saved. Oh, that's good news! . . . Well, of course, when you look at it like that . . . Breathing stabilized . . . Damage to the spinal column, not yet determined . . . Okay . . . Yes, Lucille, I've got it all down . . . Uh huh, I'll give her that message. 'Bye, 'bye.

Lenny *drops the pencil and paper. She sighs deeply, wipes her cheeks with the back of her hand, and goes to the stove to pour herself a cup of coffee. After a few moments, the front door is heard slamming.* Lenny *starts. A whistle is heard, then* Meg's *voice.*

Meg's Voice: I'm home! *She whistles the family whistle.* Anybody home?
    Lenny: Meg? Meg!

Meg, *twenty-seven, enters from the dining room. She has sad, magic eyes and wears a hat. She carries a worn-out suitcase.*

    Meg: dropping her suitcase, running to hug Lenny: Lenny—
    Lenny: Well, Meg! Why, Meg! Oh, Meggy! Why didn't you call? Did you fly in? You didn't take a cab, did you? Why didn't you give us a call?
    Meg: overlapping: Oh, Lenny! Why, Lenny! Dear Lenny! *Then she looks at* Lenny's *face.* My God, we're getting so old! Oh, I called, for heaven's sake. Of course, I called!
    Lenny: Well, I never talked to you—
    Meg: Well, I know! I let the phone ring right off the hook!
    Lenny: Well, as a matter of fact, I was out most of the morning seeing to Babe—
    Meg: Now, just what's all this business about Babe? How could you send me such a telegram about Babe? And Zackery! You say somebody's shot Zackery?
    Lenny: Yes, they have.
    Meg: Well, good Lord! Is he dead?
    Lenny: No. But he's in the hospital. He was shot in his stomach.
    Meg: In his stomach! How awful! Do they know who shot him? Lenny *nods.* Well, who? Who was it? Who? Who?
    Lenny: Babe! They're all saying Babe shot him! They took her to jail! And they're saying she shot him! They're all saying it! It's horrible! It's awful!
    Meg: overlapping: Jail! Good Lord, jail! Well, who? Who's saying it? Who?
    Lenny: Everyone! The policemen, the sheriff, Zackery, even Babe's saying it! Even Babe herself!
    Meg: Well, for God's sake. For God's sake.
    Lenny: overlapping as she falls apart: It's horrible! It's horrible! It's just horrible!
    Meg: Now calm down, Lenny. Just calm down. Would you like a Coke? Here, I'll get you some Coke. *She gets a Coke from the*

refrigerator. She opens it and downs a large swig. Why? Why would she shoot him? Why? *She hands the Coke bottle to* Lenny.

Lenny: I talked to her this morning and I asked her that very question. I said, "Babe, why would you shoot Zackery? He was your own husband. Why would you shoot him?" And do you know what she said? Meg *shakes her head.* She said, " 'Cause I didn't like his looks. I just didn't like his looks."

Meg: after a pause: Well, I don't like his looks.

Lenny: But you didn't shoot him! You wouldn't shoot a person 'cause you didn't like their looks! You wouldn't do that! Oh, I hate to say this—I do hate to say this—but I believe Babe is ill. I mean in-her-head ill.

Meg: Oh, now, Lenny, don't you say that! There're plenty of good sane reasons to shoot another person, and I'm sure that Babe had one. Now, what we've got to do is get her the best lawyer in town. Do you have any ideas on who's the best lawyer in town?

Lenny: Well, Zackery is, of course; but he's been shot!

Meg: Well, count him out! Just count him and his whole firm out!

Lenny: Anyway, you don't have to worry, she's already got her lawyer.

Meg: She does? Who?

Lenny: Barnette Lloyd. Annie Lloyd's boy. He just opened his office here in town. And Uncle Watson said we'd be doing Annie a favor by hiring him up.

Meg: Doing Annie a favor? Doing Annie a favor! Well, what about Babe? Have you thought about Babe? Do we want to do her a favor of thirty or forty years in jail? Have you thought about that?

Lenny: Now, don't snap at me! Just don't snap at me! I try to do what's right! All this responsibility keeps falling on my shoulders, and I try to do what's right!

Meg: Well, boo hoo, hoo, hoo! And how in the hell could you send me such a telegram about Babe!

Lenny: Well, if you had a phone, or if you didn't live way out there in Hollywood and not even come home for Christmas, maybe I wouldn't have to pay all that money to send you a telegram!

Meg: overlapping: BABE'S IN TERRIBLE TROUBLE—STOP! ZACKERY'S BEEN SHOT—STOP! COME HOME IMMEDIATELY—STOP! STOP! STOP!

Lenny: And what was that you said about how old we're getting? When you looked at my face, you said, "My God, we're getting so old!" But you didn't mean we—you meant me! Didn't you? I'm thirty years old today and my face is getting all pinched up and my hair is falling out in the comb.

Meg: Why, Lenny! It's your birthday, October 23. How could I forget. Happy birthday!

Lenny: Well, it's not. I'm thirty years old and Billy Boy died last night. He was struck by lightning. He was struck dead.

Meg: reaching for a cigarette: Struck dead. Oh, what a mess. What a mess. Are you really thirty? Then I must be twenty-seven and Babe is twenty-four. My God, we're getting so old.

They are silent for several moments as Meg *drags off her cigarette and* Lenny *drinks her Coke.*

Meg: What's the cot doing in the kitchen?

Lenny: Well, I rolled it out when Old Granddaddy got sick. So I could be close and hear him at night if he needed something.

Meg: glancing toward the door leading to the downstairs bedroom: Is Old Granddaddy here?

Lenny: Why, no. Old Granddaddy's at the hospital.

Meg: Again?

Lenny: Meg!

Meg: What?

Lenny: I wrote you all about it. He's been in the hospital over three months straight.

Meg: He has?

Lenny: Don't you remember? I wrote you about all those blood vessels popping in his brain?

Meg: Popping—

Lenny: And how he was so anxious to hear from you and to find out about your singing career. I wrote it all to you. How they have to feed him through those tubes now. Didn't you get my letters?

Meg: Oh, I don't know, Lenny. I guess I did. To tell you the truth, sometimes I kinda don't read your letters.

Lenny: What?

Meg: I'm sorry. I used to read them. It's just, since Christmas reading them gives me these slicing pains right here in my chest.

Lenny: I see. I see. Is that why you didn't use that money Old Granddaddy sent you to come home Christmas; because you hate us so much? We never did all that much to make you hate us. We didn't!

Meg: Oh, Lenny! Do you think I'd be getting slicing pains in my chest if I didn't care about you? If I hated you? Honestly, now, do you think I would?

Lenny: No.

Meg: Okay, then. Let's drop it. I'm sorry I didn't read your letters. Okay?

Lenny: Okay.

Meg: Anyway, we've got this whole thing with Babe to deal with. The first thing is to get her a good lawyer and get her out of jail.

Lenny: Well, she's out of jail.

Meg: She is?

Lenny: That young lawyer, he's gotten her out.

Meg: Oh, he has?

Lenny: Yes, on bail. Uncle Watson's put it up. Chick's bringing her back right now—she's driving her home.

Meg: Oh; well, that's a relief.

Lenny: Yes, and they're due home any minute now; so we can just wait right here for 'em.

Meg: Well, good. That's good. *As she leans against the counter:* So, Babe shot Zackery Botrelle, the richest and most powerful man in all of Hazlehurst, slap in the gut. It's hard to believe.

Lenny: It certainly is. Little Babe—shooting off a gun.

Meg: Little Babe.

Lenny: She was always the prettiest and most perfect of the three of us. Old Granddaddy used to call her his Dancing Sugar Plum. Why, remember how proud and happy he was the day she married Zackery.

Meg: Yes, I remember. It was his finest hour.

Lenny: He remarked how Babe was gonna skyrocket right to the heights of Hazlehurst society. And how Zackery was just the right man for her whether she knew it now or not.

Meg: Oh, Lordy, Lordy. And what does Old Granddaddy say now?

Lenny: Well, I haven't had the courage to tell him all about this as yet. I thought maybe tonight we could go to visit at the hospital, and you could talk to him and . . .

Meg: Yeah; well, we'll see. We'll see. Do we have anything to drink around here—to the tune of straight bourbon?

Lenny: No. There's no liquor.

Meg: Hell. *She gets a Coke from the refrigerator and opens it.*

Lenny: Then you *will* go with me to see him tonight?

Meg: Of course. *She goes to her purse and gets out a bottle of Empirin. She takes out a tablet and puts it on her tongue.* Brother, I know he's gonna go on about my singing career. Just like he always does.

Lenny: Well, how is your career going?

Meg: It's not.

Lenny: Why, aren't you still singing at that club down on Malibu beach?

Meg: No. Not since Christmas.

Lenny: Well, then, are you singing someplace new?

Meg: No, I'm not singing. I'm not singing at all.

Lenny: Oh. Well, what do you do then?

Meg: What I do is I pay cold-storage bills for a dog-food company. That's what I do.

Lenny: trying to be helpful: Gosh, don't you think it'd be a good idea to stay in the show business field?

Meg: Oh, maybe.

Lenny: Like Old Granddaddy says, "With your talent, all you need is exposure. Then you can make your own breaks!" Did you hear his suggestion about getting your foot put in one of those blocks of cement they've got out there? He thinks that's real important.

Meg: Yeah. I think I've heard that. And I'll probably hear it again when I go to visit him at the hospital tonight; so let's just drop it. Okay? *She notices the sack of pecans.* What's this? Pecans? Great, I love pecans! *She takes out two pecans and tries to open them by cracking them together.* Come on . . . Crack, you demons! Crack!

Lenny: We have a nutcracker!

Meg: trying with her teeth: Ah, where's the sport in a nutcracker? Where's the challenge?

Lenny: getting the nutcracker: It's over here in the utensil drawer.

As Lenny *gets the nutcracker,* Meg *opens the pecan by stepping on it with her shoe.*

Meg: There! Open! *She picks up the crumbled pecan and eats it.* Mmmm, delicious. Delicious. Where'd you get the fresh pecans?

Lenny: Oh . . . I don't know.

Meg: They sure are tasty.

Lenny: Doc Porter brought them over.

Meg: Doc. What's Doc doing here in town?

Lenny: Well, his father died a couple of months ago. Now he's back home seeing to his property.

Meg: Gosh, the last I heard of Doc, he was up in the East painting the walls of houses to earn a living. *Amused:* Heard he was living with some Yankee woman who made clay pots.

Lenny: Joan.

Meg: What?

Lenny: Her name's Joan. She came down here with him. That's one of her pots. Doc's married to her.

Meg: Married—

Lenny: Uh huh.

Meg: Doc married a Yankee?

Lenny: That's right; and they've got two kids.

Meg: Kids—

Lenny: A boy and a girl.

Meg: God. Then his kids must be half Yankee.

Lenny: I suppose.

Meg: God. That really gets me. I don't know why, but somehow that really gets me.

Lenny: I don't know why it should.

Meg: And what a stupid-looking pot! Who'd buy it, anyway?

Lenny: Wait—I think that's them. Yeah, that's Chick's car! Oh, there's Babe! Hello, Babe! They're home, Meg! They're home.

Meg hides.

Babe's Voice: Lenny! I'm home! I'm free!

Babe, twenty-four, enters exuberantly. She has an angelic face and fierce, volatile eyes. She carries a pink pocketbook.

> *Babe:* I'm home!

Meg jumps out of hiding.

> *Babe:* Oh, Meg— Look it's Meg! *Running to hug her:* Meg! When did you get home?
> *Meg:* Just now!
> *Babe:* Well, it's so good to see you! I'm so glad you're home! I'm so relieved.

Chick enters.

> *Meg:* Why, Chick; hello.
> *Chick:* Hello, Cousin Margaret. What brings you back to Hazlehurst?
> *Meg:* Oh, I came on home . . . *Turning to* Babe: I came on home to see about Babe.
> *Babe: running to hug* Meg: Oh, Meg—
> *Meg:* How are things with you, Babe?
> *Chick:* Well, they are dismal, if you want my opinion. She is refusing to cooperate with her lawyer, that nice-looking young Lloyd boy. She won't tell any of us why she committed this heinous crime, except to say that she didn't like Zackery's looks—
> *Babe:* Oh, look, Lenny brought my suitcase from home! And my saxophone! Thank you! *She runs over to the cot and gets out her saxophone.*
> *Chick:* Now, that young lawyer is coming over here this afternoon, and when he gets here he expects to get some concrete answers! That's what he expects! No more of this nonsense and stubbornness from you, Rebecca MaGrath, or they'll put you in jail and throw away the key!
> *Babe: overlapping to* Meg: Meg, come look at my new saxophone. I went to Jackson and bought it used. Feel it. It's so heavy.
> *Meg: overlapping* Chick: It's beautiful.

The room goes silent.

> *Chick:* Isn't that right, won't they throw away the key?
> *Lenny:* Well, honestly, I don't know about that—
> *Chick:* They will! And leave you there to rot. So, Rebecca, what are you going to tell Mr. Lloyd about shooting Zackery when he gets here? What are your reasons going to be?

Babe: glaring: That I didn't like his looks! I just didn't like his stinking looks! And I don't like yours much, either, Chick the Stick! So just leave me alone! I mean it! Leave me alone! Oooh! *She exits up the stairs.*

There is a long moment of silence.

Chick: Well, I was only trying to warn her that she's going to have to help herself. It's just that she doesn't understand how serious the situation is. Does she? She doesn't have the vaguest idea. Does she, now?

Lenny: Well, it's true, she does seem a little confused.

Chick: And that's putting it mildly, Lenny honey. That's putting it mighty mild. So, Margaret, how's your singing career going? We keep looking for your picture in the movie magazines.

Meg moves to light a cigarette.

Chick: You know, you shouldn't smoke. It causes cancer. Cancer of the lungs. They say each cigarette is just a little stick of cancer. A little death stick.

Meg: That's what I like about it, Chick—taking a drag off of death. *She takes a long, deep drag.* Mmm! Gives me a sense of controlling my own destiny. What power! What exhilaration! Want a drag?

Lenny: trying to break the tension: Ah, Zackery's liver's been saved! His sister called up and said his liver was saved. Isn't that good news?

Meg: Well, yes, that's fine news. Mighty fine news. Why, I've been told that the liver's a powerful important bodily organ. I believe it's used to absorb all of our excess bile.

Lenny: Yes—well—it's been saved.

The phone rings. Lenny *gets it.*

Meg: So! Did you hear all that good news about the liver, Little Chicken?

Chick: I heard it. And don't you call me Chicken! Meg *clucks like a chicken.* I've told you a hundred times if I've told you once not to call me Chicken. You cannot call me Chicken.

Lenny: . . . Oh, no! . . . Of course, we'll be right over! 'Bye! *She hangs up the phone.* That was Annie May—Peekay and Buck Jr. have eaten paint!

Chick: Oh, no! Are they all right? They're not sick? They're not sick, are they?

Lenny: I don't know. I don't know. Come on. We've got to run on next door.

Chick: overlapping: Oh, God! Oh, please! Please let them be all right! Don't let them die! Please, don't let them die!

Chick *runs off howling, with* Lenny *following after.* Megs *sits alone, finishing her cigarette. After a moment,* Babe's *voice is heard.*

Babe's Voice: Pst—Psst!

Meg *looks around.* Babe *comes tiptoeing down the stairs.*

Babe: Has she gone?

Meg: She's gone. Peekay and Buck Jr. just ate their paints.

Babe: What idiots.

Meg: Yeah.

Babe: You know, Chick's hated us ever since we had to move here from Vicksburg to live with Old Grandmama and Old Granddaddy.

Meg: She's an idiot.

Babe: Yeah. Do you know what she told me this morning while I was still behind bars and couldn't get away?

Meg: What?

Babe: She told me how embarrassing it was for her all those years ago, you know, when Mama—

Meg: Yeah, down in the cellar.

Babe: She said our mama had shamed the entire family, and we were known notoriously all through Hazlehurst. *About to cry:* Then she went on to say how I would now be getting just as much bad publicity, and humiliating her and the family all over again.

Meg: Ah, forget it, Babe. Just forget it.

Babe: I told her, "Mama got national coverage! National!" And if Zackery wasn't a senator from Copiah County, I probably wouldn't even be getting statewide.

Meg: Of course you wouldn't.

Babe: *after a pause:* Gosh, sometimes I wonder . . .

Meg: What?

Babe: Why she did it. Why Mama hung herself.

Meg: I don't know. She had a bad day. A real bad day. You know how it feels on a real bad day.

Babe: And that old yellow cat. It was sad about that old cat.

Meg: Yeah.

Babe: I bet if Daddy hadn't of left us, they'd still be alive.

Meg: Oh, I don't know.

Babe: 'Cause it was after he left that she started spending whole days just sitting there and smoking on the back porch steps. She'd sling her ashes down onto the different bugs and ants that'd be passing by.

Meg: Yeah. Well, I'm glad he left.

Babe: That old yellow cat'd stay back there with her. I thought if she felt something for anyone it woulda been that old cat. Guess I musta been mistaken.

Meg: God, he was a bastard. Really, with his white teeth. Daddy was such a bastard.

Babe: Was he? I don't remember.

Meg *blows out a mouthful of smoke.*

Babe: after a moment, uneasily: I think I'm gonna make some lemonade. You want some?

Meg: Sure.

Babe *cuts lemons, dumps sugar, stirs ice cubes, etc., throughout the following exchange.*

Meg: Babe. Why won't you talk? Why won't you tell anyone about shooting Zackery?

Babe: Oooh—

Meg: Why not? You must have had a good reason. Didn't you?

Babe: I guess I did.

Meg: Well, what was it?

Babe: I . . . I can't say.

Meg: Why not? *Pause.* Babe, why not? You can tell me.

Babe: 'Cause . . . I'm sort of . . . protecting someone.

Meg: Protecting someone? Oh, Babe, then you really didn't shoot him! I knew you couldn't have done it! I knew it!

Babe: No, I shot him. I shot him all right. I meant to kill him. I was aiming for his heart, but I guess my hands were shaking and I— just got him in the stomach.

Meg: collapsing: I see.

Babe: stirring the lemonade: So I'm guilty. And I'm just gonna have to take my punishment and go on to jail.

Meg: Oh, Babe—

Babe: Don't worry, Meg, jail's gonna be a relief to me. I can learn to play my new saxophone. I won't have to live with Zackery anymore. And I won't have his snoopy old sister, Lucille, coming over and pushing me around. Jail will be a relief. Here's your lemonade.

Meg: Thanks.

Babe: It taste okay?

Meg: Perfect.

Babe: I like a lot of sugar in mine. I'm gonna add some more sugar.

Babe *goes to add more sugar to her lemonade as* Lenny *bursts through the back door in a state of excitement and confusion.*

Lenny: Well, it looks like the paint is primarily on their arms and faces, but Chick wants me to drive them all over to Dr. Winn's just to make sure. *She grabs her car keys from the counter, and as she does so, she notices the mess of lemons and sugar.* Oh, now, Babe, try not to make a mess here; and be careful with this sharp knife.

Honestly, all that sugar's gonna get you sick. Well, 'bye, 'bye. I'll
be back as soon as I can.

Meg: 'Bye, Lenny.

Babe: 'Bye.

Lenny *exits.*

Babe: Boy, I don't know what's happening to Lenny.

Meg: What do you mean?

Babe: "Don't make a mess; don't make yourself sick; don't cut yourself with that sharp knife." She's turning into Old Grandmama.

Meg: You think so?

Babe: More and more. Do you know she's taken to wearing Old
Grandmama's torn sunhat and her green garden gloves?

Meg: Those old lime-green ones?

Babe: Yeah; she works out in the garden wearing the lime-green
gloves of a dead woman. Imagine wearing those gloves on your
hands.

Meg: Poor Lenny. She needs some love in her life. All she does is
work out at that brick yard and take care of Old Granddaddy.

Babe: Yeah. But she's so shy with men.

Meg: biting into an apple: Probably because of that *shrunken* ovary
she has.

Babe: slinging ice cubes: Yeah, that *deformed* ovary.

Meg: Old Granddaddy's the one who's made her feel self-conscious
about it. It's his fault. The old fool.

Babe: It's so sad.

Meg: God—you know what?

Babe: What?

Meg: I bet Lenny's never even slept with a man. Just think, thirty
years old and never even had it once.

Babe: slyly: Oh, I don't know. Maybe she's . . . had it once.

Meg: She has?

Babe: Maybe. I think so.

Meg: When? When?

Babe: Well . . . maybe I shouldn't say—

Meg: Babe!

Babe: rapidly telling the story: All right, then. It was after Old
Granddaddy went back to the hospital this second time. Lenny
was really in a state of deep depression, I could tell that she was.
Then one day she calls me up and asks me to come over and to
bring along my Polaroid camera. Well, when I arrive she's waiting for me out there in the sun parlor wearing her powder-blue
Sunday dress and this old curled-up wig. She confided that she
was gonna try sending in her picture to one of those lonely-hearts
clubs.

Meg: Oh, my God.

Babe: Lonely Hearts of the South. She'd seen their ad in a magazine.

Meg: Jesus.

Babe: Anyway, I take some snapshots and she sends them on in to the club, and about two weeks later she receives in the mail this whole load of pictures of available men, most of 'em fairly odd-looking. But of course she doesn't call any of 'em up 'cause she's real shy. But one of 'em, this Charlie Hill from Memphis, Tennessee, he calls her.

Meg: He does?

Babe: Yeah. And time goes on and she says he's real funny on the phone, so they decide to get together to meet.

Meg: Yeah?

Babe: Well, he drives down here to Hazlehurst 'bout three or four different times and has supper with her; then one weekend she goes up to Memphis to visit him, and I think that is where it happened.

Meg: What makes you think so?

Babe: Well, when I went to pick her up from the bus depot, she ran off the bus and threw her arms around me and started crying and sobbing as though she'd like to never stop. I asked her, I said, "Lenny, what's the matter?" And she said, "I've done it, Babe! Honey, I have done it!"

Meg: whispering: And you think she meant that she'd done *it?*

Babe: whispering back, slyly: I think so.

Meg: Well, goddamn!

They laugh.

Babe: But she didn't say anything else about it. She just went on to tell me about the boot factory where Charlie worked and what a nice city Memphis was.

Meg: So, what happened to this Charlie?

Babe: Well, he came to Hazlehurst just one more time. Lenny took him over to meet Old Granddaddy at the hospital, and after that they broke it off.

Meg: 'Cause of Old Granddaddy?

Babe: Well, she said it was on account of her missing ovary. That Charlie didn't want to marry her on account of it.

Meg: Ah, how mean. How hateful.

Babe: Oh, it was. He seemed like such a nice man, too—kinda chubby, with red hair and freckles, always telling these funny jokes.

Meg: Hmmm, that just doesn't seem right. Something about that doesn't seem exactly right. *She paces about the kitchen and comes across the box of candy Lenny got for her birthday.* Oh, God. "Happy birthday to Lenny, from the Buck Boyles."

Babe: Oh, no! Today's Lenny's birthday!

Meg: That's right.

Babe: I forgot all about it!

Meg: I know. I did, too.

Babe: Gosh, we'll have to order up a big cake for her. She always loves to make those wishes on her birthday cake.

Meg: Yeah, let's get her a big cake! A huge one! *Suddenly noticing the plastic wrapper on the candy box:* Oh, God, that Chick's so cheap!

Babe: What do you mean?

Meg: This plastic has poinsettias on it!

Babe: running to see: Oh, let me see—*She looks at the package with disgust.* Boy, oh, boy! I'm calling that bakery and ordering the very largest size cake they have! That jumbo deluxe!

Meg: Good!

Babe: Why, I imagine they can make one up to be about—*this* big. *She demonstrates.*

Meg: Oh, at least; at least that big. Why, maybe it'll even be *this* big. *She makes a very, very, very large-size cake.*

Babe: You think it could be *that* big?

Meg: Sure!

Babe: after a moment, getting the idea: Or, or what if it were *this* big? *She maps out a cake that covers the room.* What if we get the cake and it's *this* big? *She gulps down a fistful of cake.* Gulp! Gulp! Gulp! Tasty treat!

Meg: Hmmm—I'll have me some more! Give me some more of that birthday cake!

Suddenly there is a loud knock at the door.

Barnette's Voice: Hello . . . Hello! May I come in?

Babe: to Meg, in a whisper, as she takes cover: Who's that?

Meg: I don't know.

Barnette's Voice: He is still knocking. Hello! Hello, Mrs. Botrelle!

Babe: Oh, shoot! It's that lawyer. I don't want to see him.

Meg: Oh, Babe, come on. You've got to see him sometime.

Babe: No, I don't! *She starts up the stairs.* Just tell him I died. I'm going upstairs.

Meg: Oh, Babe! Will you come back here!

Babe: as she exits: You talk to him, please, Meg. Please! I just don't want to see him—

Meg: Babe—Babe! Oh, shit . . . Ah, come on in! Door's open!

Barnette Lloyd, twenty-six, enters carrying a briefcase. He is a slender, intelligent young man with an almost fanatical intensity that he subdues by sheer will.

Barnette: How do you do. I'm Barnette Lloyd.

Meg: Pleased to meet you. I'm Meg MaGrath, Babe's older sister.

Barnette: Yes, I know. You're the singer.

Meg: Well, yes . . .

Barnette: I came to hear you five different times when you were singing at that club in Biloxi. Greeny's I believe was the name of it.

Meg: Yes, Greeny's.

Barnette: You were very good. There was something sad and moving about how you sang those songs. It was like you had some sort of vision. Some special sort of vision.

Meg: Well, thank you. You're very kind. Now . . . about Babe's case—

Barnette: Yes?

Meg: We've just got to win it.

Barnette: I intend to.

Meg: Of course. But, ah . . . *She looks at him.* Ah, you know, you're very young.

Barnette: Yes. I am. I'm young.

Meg: It's just, I'm concerned, Mr. Lloyd—

Barnette: Barnette. Please.

Meg: Barnette; that, ah, just maybe we need someone with, well, with more experience. Someone totally familiar with all the ins and outs and the this and thats of the legal dealings and such. As that.

Barnette: Ah, you have reservations.

Meg: relieved: Reservations. Yes, I have . . . reservations.

Barnette: Well, possibly it would help you to know that I graduated first in my class from Ole Miss Law School. I also spent three different summers taking advanced courses in criminal law at Harvard Law School. I made A's in all the given courses. I was fascinated!

Meg: I'm sure.

Barnette: And even now, I've just completed one year working with Jackson's top criminal law firm, Manchester and Wayne. I was invaluable to them. Indispensable. They offered to double my percentage if I'd stay on; but I refused. I wanted to return to Hazlehurst and open my own office. The reason being, and this is a key point, that I have a personal vendetta to settle with one Zackery F. Botrelle.

Meg: A personal vendetta?

Barnette: Yes, ma'am. You are correct. Indeed, I do.

Meg: Hmmm. A personal vendetta . . . I think I like that. So you have some sort of a personal vendetta to settle with Zackery?

Barnette: Precisely. Just between the two of us, I not only intend to keep that sorry s.o.b. from ever being reelected to the state senate by exposing his shady, criminal dealings; but I also intend to decimate his personal credibility by exposing him as a bully, a brute, and a red-neck thug!

Meg: Well; I can see that you're—fanatical about this.

Barnette: Yes, I am. I'm sorry if I seem outspoken. But for some reason I feel I can talk to you . . . those songs you sang. Excuse me; I feel like a jackass.

Meg: It's all right. Relax. Relax, Barnette. Let me think this out a minute. *She takes out a cigarette. He lights it for her.* Now just exactly how do you intend to get Babe off? You know, keep her out of jail.

Barnette: It seems to me that we can get her off with a plea of self-defense, or possible we could go with innocent by reason of temporary insanity. But basically I intend to prove that Zackery Botrelle brutalized and tormented this poor woman to such an extent that she had no recourse but to defend herself in the only way she knew how!

Meg: I like that!

Barnette: Then, of course, I'm hoping this will break the ice and we'll be able to go on to prove that the man's a total criminal, as well as an abusive bully and contemptible slob!

Meg: That sounds good! To me that sounds very good!

Barnette: It's just our basic game plan.

Meg: But now, how are you going to prove all this about Babe being brutalized? We don't want anyone perjured. I mean to commit perjury.

Barnette: Perjury? According to my sources, there'll be no need for perjury.

Meg: You mean it's the truth?

Barnette: This is a small town, Miss MaGrath. The word gets out.

Meg: It's really the truth?

Barnette: opening his briefcase: Just look at this. It's a photostatic copy of Mrs. Botrelle's medical chart over the past four years. Take a good look at it, if you want your blood to boil!

Meg: looking over the chart: What! What! This is maddening. This is madness! Did he do this to her? I'll kill him; I will—I'll fry his blood! Did he do this?

Barnette: alarmed: To tell you the truth, I can't say for certain what was accidental and what was not. That's why I need to talk with Mrs. Botrelle. That's why it's very important that I see her!

Meg: her eyes are wild, as she shoves him toward the door: Well, look, I've got to see her first. I've got to talk to her first. What I'll do is I'll give you a call. Maybe you can come back over later on—

Barnette: Well, then, here's my card—

Meg: Okay. Goodbye.

Barnette: 'Bye!

Meg: Oh, wait! Wait! There's one problem with you.

Barnette: What?

Meg: What if you get so fanatically obsessed with this vendetta thing that you forget about Babe? You forget about her and sell her down the river just to get at Zackery. What about that?

Barnette: I—wouldn't do that.

Meg: You wouldn't?

Barnette: No.

Meg: Why not?

Barnette: Because I'm—I'm fond of her.

Meg: What do you mean you're fond of her?

Barnette: Well, she . . . she sold me a pound cake at a bazaar once. And I'm fond of her.

Meg: All right; I believe you. Goodbye.

Barnette: Goodbye. *He exits.*

Meg: Babe! Babe, come down here! Babe!

Babe *comes hurrying down the stairs.*

Babe: What? What is it? I called about the cake—

Meg: What did Zackery do to you?

Babe: They can't have it for today.

Meg: Did he hurt you? Did he? Did he do that?

Babe: Oh, Meg, please—

Meg: Did he? Goddamnit, Babe—

Babe: Yes, he did.

Meg: Why? Why?

Babe: I don't know! He started hating me, 'cause I couldn't laugh at his jokes. I just started finding it impossible to laugh at his jokes the way I used to. And then the sound of his voice got to where it tired me out awful bad to hear it. I'd fall asleep just listening to him at the dinner table. He'd say, "Hand me some of that gravy!" Or, "This roast beef is too damn bloody." And suddenly I'd be out cold like a light.

Meg: Oh, Babe. Babe, this is very important. I want you to sit down here and tell me what all happened right before you shot Zackery. That's right, just sit down and tell me.

Babe: after a pause: I told you, I can't tell you on account of I'm protecting someone.

Meg: But, Babe, you've just got to talk to someone about all this. You just do.

Babe: Why?

Meg: Because it's a human need. To talk about our lives. It's an important human need.

Babe: Oh. Well, I do feel like I want to talk to someone. I do.

Meg: Then talk to me; please.

Babe: making a decision: All right. *After thinking a minute:* I don't know where to start.

Meg: Just start at the beginning. Just there at the beginning.

Babe: after a moment: Well, do you remember Willie Jay? *Meg shakes her head.* Cora's youngest boy?

Meg: Oh, yeah, that little kid we used to pay a nickel to, to run down to the drugstore and bring us back a cherry Coke.

Babe: Right. Well, Cora irons at my place on Wednesday now, and she just happened to mention that Willie Jay'd picked up this old stray dog and that he'd gotten real fond of him. But now they couldn't afford to feed him anymore. So she was gonna have to tell Willie Jay to set him loose in the woods.

Meg: trying to be patient: Uh huh.

Babe: Well, I said I liked dogs, and if he wanted to bring the dog over here, I'd take care of him. You see, I was alone by myself most of the time 'cause the senate was in session and Zackery was up in Jackson.

Meg: Uh huh. *She reaches for* Lenny's *box of birthday candy. She takes little nibbles out of each piece throughout the rest of the scene.*

Babe: So the next day, Willie Jay brings over this skinny old dog with these little crossed eyes. Will, I asked Willie Jay what his name was, and he said they called him Dog. Well, I liked the name, so I thought I'd keep it.

Meg: getting up: Uh huh. I'm listening. I'm just gonna get me a glass of cold water. Do you want one?

Babe: Okay.

Meg: So you kept the name—Dog.

Babe: Yeah. Anyway, when Willie Jay was leaving he gave Dog a hug and said, "Goodbye, Dog. You're a fine ole dog." Well, I felt something for him, so I told Willie Jay he could come back and visit with Dog any time he wanted, and his face just kinda lit right up.

Meg: offering the candy: Candy—

Babe: No, thanks. Anyhow, time goes on and Willie Jay keeps coming over and over. And we talk about Dog and how fat he's getting, and then, well, you know, things start up.

Meg: No, I don't know. What things start up?

Babe: Well, things start up. Like sex. Like that.

Meg: Babe, wait a minute—Willie Jay's a boy. A small boy, about this tall. He's about this tall!

Babe: No! Oh, no! He's taller now! He's fifteen now. When you knew him he was only about seven or eight.

Meg: But even so—fifteen. And he's a black boy; a colored boy; a Negro.

Babe: flustered: Well, I realize that, Meg. Why do you think I'm so worried about his getting public exposure? I don't want to ruin his reputation!

Meg: I'm amazed, Babe. I'm really completely amazed. I didn't even know you were a liberal.

Babe: Well, I'm not! I'm not a liberal! I'm a democratic! I was just lonely! I was so lonely. And he was good. Oh, he was so, so good. I'd never had it that good. We'd always go out into the garage and—

Meg: It's okay. I've got the picture; I've got the picture! Now, let's just get back to the story. To yesterday, when you shot Zackery.

Babe: All right, then. Let's see . . . Willie Jay was over. And it was after we'd—

Meg: Yeah! yeah.

Babe: And we were just standing around on the back porch playing with Dog. Well, suddenly Zackery comes from around the side of the house. And he startled me 'cause he's supposed to be away at the office, and there he is coming from round the side of the house. Anyway, he says to Willie Jay, "Hey, boy, what are you doing back here?" And I say, "He's not doing anything. You just go on home, Willie Jay! You just run right on home." Well, before he can move, Zackery comes up and knocks him once right across the face and then shoves him down the porch steps, causing him to skin up his elbow real bad on that hard concrete. Then he says, "Don't you ever come around here again, or I'll have them cut out your gizzard!" Well, Willie Jay starts crying— these tears come streaming down his face—then he gets up real quick and runs away, with Dog following off after him. After that, I don't remember much too clearly; let's see . . . I went on into the living room, and I went right up to the davenport and opened the drawer where we keep the burglar gun . . . I took it out. Then I—I brought it up to my ear. That's right. I put it right inside my ear. Why, I was gonna shoot off my own head! That's what I was gonna do. Then I heard the back door slamming and suddenly, for some reason, I thought about Mama . . . how she'd hung herself. And here I was about ready to shoot myself. Then I realized—that's right, I realized how I didn't want to kill myself! And she—she probably didn't want to kill herself. She wanted to kill him, and I wanted to kill him, too. I wanted to kill Zackery, not myself. 'Cause I—I wanted to live! So I waited for him to come on into the living room. Then I held out the gun, and I pulled the trigger, aiming for his heart but getting him in the stomach. *After a pause:* It's funny that I really did that.

Meg: It's a good thing that you did. It's a damn good thing that you did.

Babe: It was.

Meg: Please, Babe, talk to Barnette Lloyd. Just talk to him and see if he can help.

Babe: But how about Willie Jay?

Meg: *starting toward the phone:* Oh, he'll be all right. You just talk to that lawyer like you did to me. *Looking at the number on the card, she begins dialing.* See, 'cause he's gonna be on your side.

Babe: No! Stop, Meg, stop! Don't call him up! Please don't call him up! You can't! It's too awful. *She runs over and jerks the bottom half of the phone away from* Meg.

Meg *stands, holding the receiver.*

> *Meg:* Babe!

Babe *slams her half of the phone into the refrigerator.*

> *Babe:* I just can't tell some stranger all about my personal life. I just can't.
> *Meg:* Well, hell, Babe; you're the one who said you wanted to live.
> *Babe:* That's right. I did. *She takes the phone out of the refrigerator and hands it to* Meg. Here's the other part of the phone. *She moves to sit at the kitchen table.*

Meg *takes the phone back to the counter.*

> *Babe:* As she fishes a piece of lemon out of her glass and begins sucking on it: Meg.
> *Meg:* What?
> *Babe:* I called the bakery. They're gonna have Lenny's cake ready first thing tomorrow morning. That's the earliest they can get it.
> *Meg:* All right.
> *Babe:* I told them to write on it, *Happy Birthday, Lenny—A Day Late.* That sound okay?
> *Meg:* at the phone: It sounds nice.
> *Babe:* I ordered up the very largest size cake they have. I told them chocolate cake with white icing and red trim. Think she'll like that?
> *Meg:* dialing the phone: Yeah, I'm sure she will. She'll like it.
> *Babe:* I'm hoping.

CURTAIN

ACT TWO

The lights go up on the kitchen. It is evening of the same day. Meg's *suitcase has been moved upstairs.* Babe's *saxophone has been taken out of the case and put together.* Babe *and* Barnette *are sitting at the kitchen table.* Barnette *is writing and rechecking notes with explosive intensity.* Babe, *who has changed into a casual shift, sits eating a bowl of oatmeal, slowly.*

Barnette: to himself: Hmm huh! Yes! I see, I see! Well, we can work on that! And of course, this is mere conjecture! Difficult, if not impossible, to prove. Ha! Yes. Yes, indeed. Indeed—
Babe: Sure you don't want any oatmeal?

Barnette: What? Oh, no. No, thank you. Let's see; ah, where were we?

Babe: I just shot Zackery.

Barnette: looking at his notes: Right. Correct. You've just pulled the trigger.

Babe: Tell me, do you think Willie Jay can stay out of all this?

Barnette: Believe me, it is in our interest to keep him as far out of this as possible.

Babe: Good.

Barnette: throughout the following, Barnette *stays glued to* Babe's *every word:* All right, you've just shot one Zackery Botrelle, as a result of his continual physical and mental abuse—what happens now?

Babe: Well, after I shot him, I put the gun down on the piano bench, and then I went out into the kitchen and made up a pitcher of lemonade.

Barnette: Lemonade?

Babe: Yes, I was dying of thirst. My mouth was just as dry as a bone.

Barnette: So in order to quench this raging thirst that was choking you dry and preventing any possibility of you uttering intelligible sounds or phrases, you went out to the kitchen and made up a pitcher of lemonade?

Babe: Right. I made it just the way I like it, with lots of sugar and lots of lemon—about ten lemons in all. Then I added two trays of ice and stirred it up with my wooden stirring spoon.

Barnette: Then what?

Babe: Then I drank three glasses, one right after the other. They were large glasses—about this tall. Then suddenly my stomach kind of swole all up. I guess what caused it was all that sour lemon.

Barnette: Could be.

Babe: Then what I did was . . . I wiped my mouth off with the back of my hand, like this . . . *She demonstrates.*

Barnette: Hmmm.

Babe: I did it to clear off all those little beads of water that had settled there.

Barnette: I see.

Babe: Then I called out to Zackery. I said, "Zackery, I've made some lemonade. Can you use a glass?"

Barnette: Did he answer? Did you hear an answer?

Babe: No. He didn't answer.

Barnette: So what'd you do?

Babe: I poured him a glass anyway and took it out to him.

Barnette: You took it out to the living room?

Babe: I did. And there he was, lying on the rug. He was looking up at me trying to speak words. I said, "What? . . . Lemonade? . . . You don't want it? Would you like a Coke instead?" Then I got the idea—he was telling me to call on the phone for medical help. So I got on the phone and called up the hospital. I gave my name and address, and I told them my husband was shot and he was lying on the rug and there was plenty of blood. *She pauses a minute, as* Barnette *works frantically on his notes.* I guess that's gonna look kinda bad.

Barnette: What?

Babe: Me fixing that lemonade before I called the hospital.

Barnette: Well, not . . . necessarily.

Babe: I tell you, I think the reason I made up the lemonade, I mean besides the fact that my mouth was bone dry, was that I was afraid to call the authorities. I was afraid. I—I really think I was afraid they would see that I had tried to shoot Zackery, in fact, that I *had* shot him, and they would accuse me of possible murder and send me away to jail.

Barnette: Well, that's understandable.

Babe: I think so. I mean, in fact, that's what did happen. That's what is happening—'cause here I am just about ready to go right off to the Parchment Prison Farm. Yes, here I am just practically on the brink of utter doom. Why, I feel so all alone.

Barnette: Now, now, look— Why, there's no reason for you to get yourself so all upset and worried. Please don't. Please.

They look at each other for a moment.

Barnette: You just keep filling in as much detailed information as you can about those incidents on the medical reports. That's all you need to think about. Don't you worry, Mrs. Botrelle, we're going to have a solid defense.

Babe: Please don't call me Mrs. Botrelle.

Barnette: All right.

Babe: My name's Becky. People in the family call me Babe, but my real name's Becky.

Barnette *and* Babe *stare at each other for a long moment.*

Babe: Are you sure you didn't go to Hazlehurst High?

Barnette: No, I went away to a boarding school.

Babe: Gosh, you sure do look familiar. You sure do.

Barnette: Well, I—I doubt you'll remember, but I did meet you once.

Babe: You did? When?

Barnette: At the Christmas bazaar, year before last. You were selling cakes and cookies and . . . candy.

Babe: Oh, yes! You bought the orange pound cake!

Barnette: Right.

Babe: Of course, and then we talked for a while. We talked about the Christmas angel.

Barnette: You do remember.

    Babe: I remember it very well. You were even thinner then than you are now.

Barnette: Well, I'm surprised. I'm certainly . . . surprised.

The phone rings.

    Babe: as she goes to answer the phone: This is quite a coincidence! Don't you think it is? Why, it's almost a fluke. *She answers the phone.* Hello . . . Oh, hello, Lucille . . . Oh, he is? . . . Oh, he does? . . . Okay. Oh, Lucille, wait! Has Dog come back to the house? . . . Oh, I see . . . Okay. Okay. *After a brief pause:* Hello, Zackery? How are you doing? . . . Uh huh . . . uh huh . . . Oh, I'm sorry . . . Please don't scream . . . Uh huh . . . uh huh . . . You want what? . . . No, I can't come up there now . . . Well, for one thing, I don't even have the car. Lenny and Meg are up at the hospital right now, visiting with Old Granddaddy . . . What? . . . Oh, really? . . . Oh, really? . . . Well, I've got me a lawyer that's over here right now, and he's building me up a solid defense! . . . Wait just a minute, I'll see. *To* Barnette: He wants to talk to you. He says he's got some blackening evidence that's gonna convict me of attempting to murder him in the first degree!

Barnette: disgustedly: Oh, bluff! He's bluffing! Here, hand me the phone. *He takes the phone and becomes suddenly cool and suave.* Hello, this is Mr. Barnette Lloyd speaking. I'm Mrs. . . . ah, Becky's attorney . . . Why, certainly, Mr. Botrelle, I'd be more than glad to check out any pertinent information that you may have . . . Fine, then I'll be right on over. Goodbye. *He hangs up the phone.*

    Babe: What did he say?

Barnette: He wants me to come see him at the hospital this evening. Says he's got some sort of evidence. Sounds highly suspect to me.

    Babe: Oooh! Didn't you just hate his voice? Doesn't he have the most awful voice? I just hate—I can't bear to hear it!

Barnette: Well, now—now, wait. Wait just a minute.

    Babe: What?

Barnette: I have a solution. From now on, I'll handle all communications between you two. You can simply refuse to speak with him.

    Babe: All right—I will. I'll do that.

Barnette: starting to pack his briefcase: Well, I'd better get over there and see just what he's got up his sleeve.

    Babe: after a pause: Barnette.

Barnette: Yes?

    Babe: What's the personal vendetta about? You know, the one you have to settle with Zackery.

Barnette: Oh, it's—it's complicated. It's a very complicated matter.

Babe: I see.

Barnette: The major thing he did was to ruin my father's life. He took away his job, his home, his health, his respectability. I don't like to talk about it.

Babe: I'm sorry. I just wanted to say—I hope you win it. I hope you win your vendetta.

Barnette: Thank you.

Babe: I think it's an important thing that a person could win a life-long vendetta.

Barnette: Yes. Well, I'd better be going.

Babe: All right. Let me know what happens.

Barnette: I will. I'll get back to you right away.

Babe: Thanks.

Barnette: Goodbye, Becky.

Babe: Goodbye, Barnette.

Barnette *exits.* Babe *looks around the room for a moment, then goes over to her white suitcase and opens it up. She takes out her pink hair curlers and a brush. She begins brushing her hair.*

Babe: Goodbye, Becky. Goodbye, Barnette. Goodbye, Becky. Oooh.

Lenny *enters. She is fuming.* Babe *is rolling her hair throughout most of the following scene.*

Babe: Lenny, hi!

Lenny: Hi.

Babe: Where's Meg?

Lenny: Oh, she had to go by the store and pick some things up. I don't know what.

Babe: Well, how's Old Granddaddy?

Lenny: as she picks up Babe's *bowl of oatmeal:* He's fine. Wonderful! Never been better!

Babe: Lenny, what's wrong? What's the matter?

Lenny: It's Meg! I could just wring her neck! I could just wring it!

Babe: Why? Wha'd she do?

Lenny: She lied! She sat in that hospital room and shamelessly lied to Old Granddaddy. She went on and on telling such untrue stories and lies.

Babe: Well, what? What did she say?

Lenny: Well, for one thing, she said she was gonna have an RCA record coming out with her picture on the cover, eating pineapples under a palm tree.

Babe: Well, gosh, Lenny, maybe she is! Don't you think she really is?

Lenny: Babe, she sat here this very afternoon and told me how all that she's done this whole year is work as a clerk for a dog-food company.

Babe: Oh, shoot. I'm disappointed.

Lenny: And then she goes on to say that she'll be appearing on the Johnny Carson show in two weeks' time. Two weeks' time! Why, Old Granddaddy's got a TV set right in his room. Imagine what a letdown it's gonna be.

Babe: Why, mercy me.

Lenny: slamming the coffeepot on: Oh, and she told him the reason she didn't use the money he sent her to come home Christmas was that she was right in the middle of making a huge multimillion-dollar motion picture and was just under too much pressure.

Babe: My word!

Lenny: The movie's coming out this spring. It's called *Singing in a Shoe Factory.* But she only has a small leading role—not a large leading role.

Babe: laughing: For heaven's sake—

Lenny: I'm sizzling. Oh, I just can't help it! I'm sizzling!

Babe: Sometimes Meg does such strange things.

Lenny: slowly, as she picks up the opened box of birthday candy: Who ate this candy?

Babe: hesitantly: Meg.

Lenny: My one birthday present, and look what she does! Why, she's taken one little bite out of each piece and then just put it back in! Ooh! That's just like her! That is just like her!

Babe: Lenny, please—

Lenny: I can't help it! It gets me mad! It gets me upset! Why, Meg's always run wild—she started smoking and drinking when she was fourteen years old; she never made good grades—never made her own bed! But somehow she always seemed to get what she wanted. She's the one who got singing and dancing lessons, and a store-bought dress to wear to her senior prom. Why, do you remember how Meg always got to wear twelve jingle bells on her petticoats, while we were only allowed to wear three apiece? Why?! Why should Old Grandmama let her sew twelve golden jingle bells on her petticoats and us only three!

Babe: who has heard all this before: I don't know! Maybe she didn't jingle them as much!

Lenny: I can't help it! It gets me mad! I resent it. I do.

Babe: Oh, don't resent Meg. Things have been hard for Meg. After all, she was the one who found Mama.

Lenny: Oh, I know; she's the one who found Mama. But that's always been the excuse.

Babe: But I tell you, Lenny, after it happened, Meg started doing all sorts of these strange things.

Lenny: She did? Like what?

Babe: Like things I never even wanted to tell you about.

Lenny: What sort of things?

Babe: Well, for instance, back when we used to go over to the library, Meg would spend all her time reading and looking through this old black book called *Diseases of the Skin.* It was full of the most sickening pictures you've ever seen. Things like rotting-away noses and eyeballs drooping off down the sides of people's faces, and scabs and sores and eaten-away places all over all parts of people's bodies.

Lenny: trying to pour her coffee: Babe, please! That's enough.

Babe: Anyway, she'd spend hours and hours just forcing herself to look through this book. Why, it was the same way she'd force herself to look at the poster of crippled children stuck up in the window at Dixieland Drugs. You know, that one where they want you to give a dime. Meg would stand there and stare at their eyes and look at the braces on their little crippled-up legs—then she'd purposely go and spend her dime on a double-scoop ice cream cone and eat it all down. She'd say to me, "See, I can stand it. I can stand it. Just look how I'm gonna be able to stand it."

Lenny: That's awful.

Babe: She said she was afraid of being a weak person. I guess 'cause she cried in bed every night for such a long time.

Lenny: Goodness mercy. *After a pause:* Well, I suppose you'd have to be a pretty hard person to be able to do what she did to Doc Porter.

Babe: exasperated: Oh, shoot! It wasn't Meg's fault that hurricane wiped Biloxi away. I never understood why people were blaming all that on Meg—just because that roof fell in and crunched Doc's leg. It wasn't her fault.

Lenny: Well, it was Meg who refused to evacuate. Jim Craig and some of Doc's other friends were all down there, and they kept trying to get everyone to evacuate. But Meg refused. She wanted to stay on because she thought a hurricane would be— oh, I don't know—a lot of fun. Then everyone says she baited Doc into staying there with her. She said she'd marry him if he'd stay.

Babe: taken aback by this new information: Well, he has a mind of his own. He could have gone.

Lenny: But he didn't. 'Cause . . . 'cause he loved her. And then, after the roof caved in and they got Doc to the high school gym, Meg just left. She just left him here to leave for California— 'cause of her career, she says. I think it was a shameful thing to do. It took almost a year for his leg to heal, and after that he gave up his medical career altogether. He said he was tired of hospitals. It's such a sad thing. Everyone always knew he was gonna be a doctor. We've called him Doc for years.

Babe: I don't know. I guess I don't have any room to talk; 'cause I just don't know. *Pause.* Gosh, you look so tired.

Lenny: I feel tired.

Babe: They say women need a lot of iron . . . so they won't feel tired.

Lenny: What's got iron in it? Liver?

Babe: Yeah, liver's got it. And vitamin pills.

After a moment, Meg *enters. She carries a bottle of bourbon that is already minus a few slugs, and a newspaper. She is wearing black boots, a dark dress, and a hat. The room goes silent.*

Meg: Hello.

Babe: fooling with her hair: Hi, Meg.

Lenny *quietly sips her coffee.*

Meg: handing the newspaper to Babe: Here's your paper.

Babe: Thanks. *She opens it.* Oh, here it is, right on the front page.

Meg *lights a cigarette.*

Babe: Where're the scissors, Lenny?

Lenny: Look in there in the ribbon drawer.

Babe: Okay. *She gets the scissors and glue out of the drawer and slowly begins cutting out the newspaper article.*

Meg: after a few moments, filled only with the snipping of scissors: All right—I lied! I lied! I couldn't help it . . . these stories just came pouring out of my mouth! When I saw how tired and sick Old Granddaddy'd gotten—they just flew out! All I wanted was to see him smiling and happy. I just wasn't going to sit there and look at him all miserable and sick and sad! I just wasn't!

Babe: Oh, Meg, he is sick, isn't he—

Meg: Why, he's gotten all white and milky—he's almost evaporated!

Lenny: gasping and turning to Meg: But still you shouldn't have lied! It just was wrong for you to tell such lies—

Meg: Well, I know that! Don't you think I know that? I hate myself when I lie for that old man. I do. I feel so weak. And then I have to go and do at least three or four things that I know he'd despise just to get even with that miserable, old, bossy man!

Lenny: Oh, Meg, please don't talk so about Old Granddaddy! It sounds so ungrateful. Why, he went out of his way to make a home for us, to treat us like we were his very own children. All he ever wanted was the best for us. That's all he ever wanted.

Meg: Well, I guess it was; but sometimes I wonder what we wanted.

Babe: taking the newspaper article and glue over to her suitcase: Well, one thing I wanted was a team of white horses to ride Mama's coffin to her grave. That's one thing I wanted.

Lenny *and* Meg *exchange looks.*

Babe: Lenny, did you remember to pack my photo album?

Lenny: It's down there at the bottom, under all that night stuff.

Babe: Oh, I found it.

Lenny: Really, Babe, I don't understand why you have to put in the articles that are about the unhappy things in your life. Why would you want to remember them?

Babe: pasting the article in: I don't know. I just like to keep an accurate record, I suppose. There. *She begins flipping through the book.* Look, here's a picture of me when I got married.

Meg: Let's see.

They all look at the photo album.

Lenny: My word, you look about twelve years old.

Babe: I was just eighteen.

Meg: You're smiling, Babe. Were you happy then?

Babe: laughing: Well, I was drunk on champagne punch. I remember that!

They turn the page.

Lenny: Oh, there's Meg singing at Greeny's!

Babe: Oooh, I wish you were still singing at Greeny's! I wish you were!

Lenny: You're so beautiful!

Babe: Yes, you are. You're beautiful.

Meg: Oh, stop! I'm not—

Lenny: Look, Meg's starting to cry.

Babe: Oh, Meg—

Meg: I'm not—

Babe: Quick, better turn the page; we don't want Meg crying—*She flips the pages.*

Lenny: Why, it's Daddy.

Meg: Where'd you get that picture, Babe? I thought she burned them all.

Babe: Ah, I just found it around.

Lenny: What does it say here? What's that inscription?

Babe: It says "Jimmy—clowning at the beach—1952."

Lenny: Well, will you look at that smile.

Meg: Jesus, those white teeth—turn the page, will you; we can't do any worse than this!

They turn the page. The room goes silent.

Babe: It's Mama and the cat.

Lenny: Oh, turn the page—

Babe: That old yellow cat. You know, I bet if she hadn't of hung that old cat along with her, she wouldn't have gotten all that national coverage.

Meg: after a moment, hopelessly: Why are we talking about this?

Lenny: Meg's right. It was so sad. It was awfully sad. I remember how we all three just sat up on that bed the day of the service all dressed up in our black velveteen suits crying the whole morning long.

Babe: We used up one whole big box of Kleenexes.

Meg: And then Old Granddaddy came in and said he was gonna take us out to breakfast. Remember, he told us not to cry anymore 'cause he was gonna take us out to get banana splits for breakfast.

Babe: That's right—banana splits for breakfast!

Meg: Why, Lenny was fourteen years old, and he thought that would make it all better—

Babe: Oh, I remember he said for us to eat all we wanted. I think I ate about five! He kept shoving them down us!

Meg: God, we were so sick!

Lenny: Oh, we were!

Meg: laughing: Lenny's face turned green—

Lenny: I was just as sick as a dog!

Babe: Old Grandmama was furious!

Lenny: Oh, she was!

Meg: The thing about Old Granddaddy is, he keeps trying to make us happy, and we end up getting stomachaches and turning green and throwing up in the flower arrangements.

Babe: Oh, that was me! I threw up in the flowers! Oh, no! How embarrassing!

Lenny: laughing: Oh, Babe—

Babe: hugging her sisters: Oh, Lenny! Oh, Meg!

Meg: Oh, Babe! Oh, Lenny! It's so good to be home!

Lenny: Hey, I have an idea—

Babe: What?

Lenny: Let's play cards!!

Babe: Oh, let's do!

Meg: All right!

Lenny: Oh, good! It'll be just like when we used to sit around the table playing hearts all night long.

Babe: I know! *Getting up:* I'll fix us up some popcorn and hot chocolate—

Meg: getting up: Here, let me get out that old black popcorn pot.

Lenny: getting up: Oh, yes! Now, let's see, I think I have a deck of cards around here somewhere.

Babe: Gosh, I hope I remember all the rules— Are hearts good or bad?

Meg: Bad, I think. Aren't they, Lenny?

Lenny: That's right. Hearts are bad, but the Black Sister is the worst of all—

Meg: Oh, that's right! And the Black Sister is the Queen of Spades.

Babe: figuring it out: And spades are the black cards that aren't the puppy dog feet?

Meg: thinking a moment: Right. And she counts a lot of points.

Babe: And points are bad?

Meg: Right. Here, I'll get some paper so we can keep score.

The phone rings.

Lenny: Oh, here they are!

Meg: I'll get it—

Lenny: Why, look at these cards! They're years old!

Babe: Oh, let me see!

Meg: Hello . . . No, this is Meg MaGrath . . . Doc. How are you? . . . Well, good . . . You're where? . . . Well, sure. Come on over . . . Sure I'm sure . . . Yeah, come right on over . . . All right. 'Bye. *She hangs up.* That was Doc Porter. He's down the street at Al's Grill. He's gonna come on over.

Lenny: He is?

Meg: He said he wanted to come see me.

Lenny: Oh. *After a pause.* Well, do you still want to play?

Meg: No, I don't think so.

Lenny: All right. *She starts to shuffle the cards, as* Meg *brushes her hair.* You know, it's really not much fun playing hearts with only two people.

Meg: I'm sorry; maybe after Doc leaves I'll join you.

Lenny: I know; maybe Doc'll want to play. Then we can have a game of bridge.

Meg: I don't think so. Doc never liked cards. Maybe we'll just go out somewhere.

Lenny: putting down the cards. Babe *picks them up:* Meg—

Meg: What?

Lenny: Well, Doc's married now.

Meg: I know. You told me.

Lenny: Oh. Well, as long as you know that. *Pause.* As long as you know that.

Meg: still primping: Yes, I know. She made the pot.

Babe: How many cards do I deal out?

Lenny: leaving the table: Excuse me.

Babe: All of 'em, or what?

Lenny: Ah, Meg, could I—could I ask you something?

Babe *proceeds to deal out all the cards.*

Meg: What?

Lenny: I just wanted to ask you—

Meg: What?

Unable to go on with what she really wants to say, Lenny *runs and picks up the box of candy.*

> Lenny: Well, just why did you take one little bite out of each piece of candy in this box and then just put it back in?
>
> Meg: Oh. Well, I was looking for the ones with nuts.
>
> Lenny: The ones with nuts.
>
> Meg: Yeah.
>
> Lenny: But there are none with nuts. It's a box of assorted crèmes—all it has in it are crèmes!
>
> Meg: Oh.
>
> Lenny: Why couldn't you just read on the box? It says right here, *Assorted Crèmes,* not nuts! Besides, this was a birthday present to me! My one and only birthday present; my only one!
>
> Meg: I'm sorry. I'll get you another box.
>
> Lenny: I don't want another box. That's not the point!
>
> Meg: What is the point?
>
> Lenny: I don't know; it's—it's— You have no respect for other people's property! You just take whatever you want. You just take it! Why, remember how you had layers and layers of jingle bells sewed onto your petticoats while Babe and I only had three apiece?!
>
> Meg: Oh, God! She's starting up about those stupid jingle bells!
>
> Lenny: Well, it's an example! A specific example of how you always got what you wanted!
>
> Meg: Oh, come on, Lenny, you're just upset because Doc called.
>
> Lenny: Who said anything about Doc? Do you think I'm upset about Doc? Why, I've long since given up worrying about you and all your men.
>
> Meg: *turning in anger:* Look, I know I've had too many men. Believe me, I've had way too many men. But it's not my fault you haven't had any—or maybe just that one from Memphis.
>
> Lenny: *stopping:* What one from Memphis?
>
> Meg: *slowly:* The one Babe told me about. From the—club.
>
> Lenny: Babe!
>
> Babe: Meg!
>
> Lenny: How could you! I asked you not to tell anyone! I'm so ashamed! How could you? Who else have you told? Did you tell anyone else?
>
> Babe: *overlapping, to* Meg: Why'd you have to open your big mouth?
>
> Meg: *overlapping:* How am I supposed to know? You never said not to tell!
>
> Babe: Can't you use your head just for once? *To* Lenny: No, I never told anyone else. Somehow it just slipped out to Meg. Really, it just flew out of my mouth—
>
> Lenny: What do you two have—wings on your tongues?

Babe: I'm sorry, Lenny. Really sorry.

Lenny: I'll just never, never, never be able to trust you again—

Meg: furiously coming to Babe's *defense:* Oh, for heaven's sake, Lenny, we were just worried about you! We wanted to find a way to make you happy!

Lenny: Happy! Happy! I'll never be happy!

Meg: Well, not if you keep living your life as Old Granddaddy's nursemaid—

Babe: Meg, shut up!

Meg: I can't help it! I just know that the reason you stopped seeing this man from Memphis was because of Old Granddaddy.

Lenny: What— Babe didn't tell you the rest of the story—

Meg: Oh, she said it was something about your shrunken ovary.

Babe: Meg!

Lenny: Babe!

Babe: I just mentioned it!

Meg: But I don't believe a word of that story!

Lenny: Oh, I don't care what you believe! It's so easy for you—you always have men falling in love with you! But I have this under-developed ovary and I can't have children and my hair is falling out in the comb—so what man can love me? What man's gonna love me?

Meg: A lot of men!

Babe: Yeah, a lot! A whole lot!

Meg: Old Granddaddy's the only one who seems to think otherwise.

Lenny: 'Cause he doesn't want to see me hurt! He doesn't want to see me rejected and humiliated.

Meg: Oh, come on now, Lenny, don't be so pathetic! God, you make me angry when you just stand there looking so pathetic! Just tell me, did you really ask the man from Memphis? Did you actually ask that man from Memphis all about it?

Lenny: breaking apart: No, I didn't. I didn't. Because I just didn't want him not to want me—

Meg: Lenny—

Lenny: furious: Don't talk to me anymore! Don't talk to me! I think I'm gonna vomit— I just hope all this doesn't cause me to vomit! *She exits up the stairs sobbing.*

Meg: See! See! She didn't even ask him about her stupid ovary! She just broke it all off 'cause of Old Granddaddy! What a jack-ass fool!

Babe: Oh, Meg, shut up! Why do you have to make Lenny cry? I just hate it when you make Lenny cry! *She runs up the stairs.* Lenny! Oh, Lenny—

Meg *gives a long sigh and goes to get a cigarette and a drink.*

Meg: I feel like hell. *She sits in despair, smoking and drinking bourbon. There is a knock at the back door. She starts. She brushes her hair out of her face and goes to answer the door. It is* Doc.

Doc: Hello, Meggy.

Meg: Well, Doc. Well, it's Doc.

Doc: after a pause: You're home, Meggy.

Meg: Yeah, I've come home. I've come on home to see about Babe.

Doc: And how's Babe?

Meg: Oh, fine. Well, fair. She's fair.

Doc *nods.*

Meg: Hey, do you want a drink?

Doc: Whatcha got?

Meg: Bourbon.

Doc: Oh, don't tell me Lenny's stocking bourbon.

Meg: Well, no. I've been to the store. *She gets him a glass and pours them each a drink. They click glasses.*

Meg: So, how's your wife?

Doc: She's fine.

Meg: I hear ya got two kids.

Doc: Yeah. Yeah, I got two kids.

Meg: A boy and a girl.

Doc: That's right, Meggy, a boy and a girl.

Meg: That's what you always said you wanted, wasn't it? A boy and a girl.

Doc: Is that what I said?

Meg: I don't know. I thought it's what you said.

They finish their drinks in silence.

Doc: Whose cot?

Meg: Lenny's. She's taken to sleeping in the kitchen.

Doc: Ah. Where is Lenny?

Meg: She's in the upstairs room. I made her cry. Babe's up there seeing to her.

Doc: How'd you make her cry?

Meg: I don't know. Eating her birthday candy; talking on about her boyfriend from Memphis. I don't know. I'm upset about it. She's got a lot on her. Why can't I keep my mouth shut?

Doc: I don't know, Meggy. Maybe it's because you don't want to.

Meg: Maybe.

They smile at each other. Meg *pours each of them another drink.*

Doc: Well, it's been a long time.

Meg: It has been a long time.

Doc: Let's see—when was the last time we saw each other?

Meg: I can't quite recall.

Doc: Wasn't it in Biloxi?

Meg: Ah, Biloxi. I believe so.

Doc: And wasn't there a—a hurricane going on at the time?

Meg: Was there?

Doc: Yes, there was; one hell of a hurricane. Camille, I believe they called it. Hurricane Camille.

Meg: Yes, now I remember. It was a beautiful hurricane.

Doc: We had a time down there. We had quite a time. Drinking vodka, eating oysters on the half shell, dancing all night long. And the wind was blowing.

Meg: Oh, God, was it blowing.

Doc: Goddamn, was it blowing.

Meg: There never has been such a wind blowing.

Doc: Oh, God, Meggy. Oh, God.

Meg: I know, Doc. It was my fault to leave you. I was crazy. I thought I was choking. I felt choked!

Doc: I felt like a fool.

Meg: No.

Doc: I just kept on wondering why.

Meg: I don't know why . . . 'Cause I didn't want to care. I don't know. I did care, though. I did.

Doc: after a pause: Ah, hell— *He pours them both another drink.* Are you still singing those sad songs?

Meg: No.

Doc: Why not?

Meg: I don't know, Doc. Things got worse for me. After a while, I just couldn't sing anymore. I tell you, I had one hell of a time over Christmas.

Doc: What do you mean?

Meg: I went nuts. I went insane. Ended up in L.A. County Hospital. Psychiatric ward.

Doc: Hell. Ah, hell, Meggy. What happened?

Meg: I don't really know. I couldn't sing anymore, so I lost my job. And I had a bad toothache. I had this incredibly painful toothache. For days I had it, but I wouldn't do anything about it. I just stayed inside my apartment. All I could do was sit around in chairs, chewing on my fingers. Then one afternoon I ran screaming out of the apartment with all my money and jewelry and valuables, and tried to stuff it all into one of those March of Dimes collection boxes. That was when they nabbed me. Sad story. Meg goes mad.

Doc *stares at her for a long moment. He pours them both another drink.*

Doc: after quite a pause: There's a moon out.

Meg: Is there?

Doc: Wanna go take a ride in my truck and look out at the moon?

Meg: I don't know, Doc. I don't wanna start up. It'll be too hard if we start up.

Doc: Who says we're gonna start up? We're just gonna look at the moon. For one night just you and me are gonna go for a ride in the country and look out at the moon.

Meg: One night?

Doc: Right.

Meg: Look out at the moon?

Doc: You got it.

Meg: Well . . . all right. *She gets up.*

Doc: Better take your coat. *He helps her into her coat.* And the bottle— *He takes the bottle.* Meg *picks up the glasses.* Forget the glasses—

Meg *shuts off the kitchen lights, leaving the kitchen with only a dim light over the kitchen sink.* Meg *and* Doc *leave. After a moment,* Babe *comes down the stairs in her slip.*

Babe: Meg—Meg? *She stands for a moment in the moonlight wearing only a slip. She sees her saxophone, then moves to pick it up. She plays a few shrieking notes. There is a loud knock on the back door.*

Barnette's Voice: Becky! Becky, is that you?

Babe *puts down the saxophone.*

Babe: Just a minute. I'm coming. *She puts a raincoat on over her slip and goes to answer the door.* Hello, Barnette. Come on in.

Barnette *comes in. He is troubled but is making a great effort to hide the fact.*

Barnette: Thank you.

Babe: What is it?

Barnette: I've, ah, I've just come from seeing Zackery at the hospital.

Babe: Oh?

Barnette: It seems . . . Well, it seems his sister, Lucille, was somewhat suspicious.

Babe: Suspicious?

Barnette: About you?

Babe: Me?

Barnette: She hired a private detective: he took these pictures.

He hands Babe *a small envelope containing several photographs.* Babe *opens the envelope and begins looking at the pictures in stunned silence.*

Barnette: They were taken about two weeks ago. It seems she wasn't going to show them to Botrelle straightaway. She, ah, wanted to wait till the time was right.

The phone rings one and a half times. Barnette *glances uneasily toward the phone.*

Barnette: Becky!

The phone stops ringing.

> *Babe: looking up at* Barnette, *slowly:* These are pictures of Willie Jay
> and me . . . out in the garage.

Barnette: looking away: I know.

> *Babe:* You looked at these pictures?

Barnette: Yes—I—well . . . professionally, I looked at them.

> *Babe:* Oh, mercy. Oh, mercy! We can burn them, can't we? Quick,
> we can burn them—

Barnette: It won't do any good. They have the negatives.

> *Babe: Holding the pictures, as she bangs herself hopelessly into the stove,
> table, cabinets, etc.:* Oh, no; oh, no; oh, no! Oh, no—

Barnette: There—there, now—there—

Lenny's Voice: Babe? Are you all right? Babe—

> *Babe: hiding the pictures:* What? I'm all right. Go on back to bed.

Babe *hides the pictures as* Lenny *comes down the stairs. She is wearing a coat and
wiping white night cream off of her face with a washrag.*

> *Lenny:* What's the matter? What's going on down here?
>
> *Babe:* Nothing! *Then as she begins dancing ballet style around the
> room:* We're —we're just dancing. We were just dancing around
> down here. *Signaling to* Barnette *to dance.*

Lenny: Well, you'd better get your shoes on, 'cause we've got—

> *Babe:* All right, I will! That's a good idea! *She goes to get her shoes.*
> Now, you go on back to bed. It's pretty late and—

Lenny: Babe, will you listen a minute—

> *Babe: holding up her shoes:* I'm putting 'em on—

Lenny: That was the hospital that just called. We've got to get over
there. Old Granddaddy's had himself another stroke.

> *Babe:* Oh. All right. My shoes are on. *She stands.*

They all look at each other as the lights black out.

CURTAIN

ACT THREE

*The lights go up on the empty kitchen. It is the following morning. After a few
moments, Babe enters from the back door. She is carrying her hair curlers in her
hands. She lies down on the cot. A few moments later, Lenny enters. She is tired
and weary. Chick's voice is heard.*

Chick's Voice: Lenny! Oh, Lenny!

Lenny *turns to the door.* Chick *enters energetically.*

> *Chick:* Well . . . how is he?

Lenny: He's stabilized; they say for now his functions are all stabilized.

Chick: Well, is he still in the coma?

Lenny: Uh huh.

Chick: Hmmm. So do they think he's gonna be . . . passing on?

Lenny: He may be. He doesn't look so good. They said they'd phone us if there were any sudden changes.

Chick: Well, it seems to me we'd better get busy phoning on the phone ourselves. *Removing a list from her pocket:* Now, I've made out this list of all the people we need to notify about Old Grand-daddy's predicament. I'll phone half, if you'll phone half.

Lenny: But—what would we say?

Chick: Just tell them the facts: that Old Granddaddy's got himself in a coma, and it could be he doesn't have long for this world.

Lenny: I—I don't know. I don't feel like phoning.

Chick: Why, Lenora, I'm surprised; how can you be this way? I went to all the trouble of making up the list. And I offered to phone half of the people on it, even though I'm only one-fourth of the granddaughters. I mean, I just get tired of doing more than my fair share, when people like Meg can suddenly just disappear to where they can't even be reached in case of emergency!

Lenny: All right; give me the list. I'll phone half.

Chick: Well, don't do it just to suit me.

Lenny: wearily tearing the list in half: I'll phone these here.

Chick: taking her half of the list: Fine then. Suit yourself. Oh, wait— let me call Sally Bell. I need to talk to her, anyway.

Lenny: All right.

Chick: So you add Great-uncle Spark Dude to your list.

Lenny: Okay.

Chick: Fine. Well, I've got to get on back home and see to the kids. It is gonna be an uphill struggle till I can find someone to replace that good-for-nothing Annie May Jenkins. Well, you let me know if you hear any more.

Lenny: All right.

Chick: Goodbye, Rebecca. I said goodbye. Babe *blows her sax.* Chick *starts to exit in a flurry, then pauses to add:* And you really ought to try to get that phoning done before twelve noon. *She exits.*

Lenny: after a long pause: Babe, I feel bad. I feel real bad.

Babe: Why, Lenny?

Lenny: Because yesterday I—I wished it.

Babe: You wished what?

Lenny: I wished that Old Granddaddy would be put out of his pain. I wished it on one of my birthday candles. I did. And now he's in this coma, and they say he's feeling no pain.

Babe: Well, when did you have a cake yesterday? I don't remember you having any cake.

Lenny: Well, I didn't . . . have a cake. But I just blew out the candles, anyway.

Babe: Oh. Well, those birthday wishes don't count, unless you have a cake.

Lenny: They don't?

Babe: No. A lot of times they don't even count when you do have a cake. It just depends.

Lenny: Depends on what?

Babe: On how deep your wish is, I suppose.

Lenny: Still, I just wish I hadn't of wished it. Gosh, I wonder when Meg's coming home.

Babe: Should be soon.

Lenny: I just wish we wouldn't fight all the time. I don't like it when we do.

Babe: Me, neither.

Lenny: I guess it hurts my feelings, a little, the way Old Granddaddy's always put so much stock in Meg and all her singing talent. I think I've been, well, envious of her 'cause I can't seem to do too much.

Babe: Why, sure you can.

Lenny: I can?

Babe: Sure. You just have to put your mind to it, that's all. It's like how I went out and bought that saxophone, just hoping I'd be able to attend music school and start up my own career. I just went out and did it. Just on hope. Of course, now it looks like . . . Well, it just doesn't look like things are gonna work out for me. But I know they would for you.

Lenny: Well, they'll work out for you, too.

Babe: I doubt it.

Lenny: Listen, I heard up at the hospital that Zackery's already in fair condition. They say soon he'll probably be able to walk and everything.

Babe: Yeah. And life sure can be miserable.

Lenny: Well, I know, 'cause—day before yesterday, Billy Boy was struck down by lightning.

Babe: He was?

Lenny: *nearing sobs:* Yeah. He was struck dead.

Babe: *crushed:* Life sure can be miserable.

They sit together for several moments in morbid silence. Meg *is heard singing a loud happy song. She suddenly enters through the dining room door. She is exuberant! Her hair is a mess, and the heel of one shoe has broken off. She is laughing radiantly and limping as she sings into the broken heel.*

Meg: spotting her sisters: Good morning! Good morning! Oh, it's a wonderful morning! I tell you, I am surprised I feel this good. I should feel like hell. By all accounts, I should feel like utter hell! *She is looking for the glue.* Where's that glue? This damn heel has broken off my shoe. La, la, la, la, la! Ah, here it is! Now, let me just get these shoes off. Zip, zip, zip, zip, zip! Well, what's wrong with you two? My God, you look like doom!

Babe *and* Lenny *stare helplessly at* Meg.

Meg: Oh, I know, you're mad at me 'cause I stayed out all night long. Well, I did.

Lenny: No, we're—we're not mad at you. We're just . . . depressed. *She starts to sob.*

Meg: Oh, Lenny, listen to me, now; everything's all right with Doc. I mean, nothing happened. Well, actually a lot did happen, but it didn't come to anything. Not because of me, I'm afraid. *Smearing glue on her heel:* I mean, I was out there thinking, What will I say when he begs me to run away with him? Will I have pity on his wife and those two half-Yankee children? I mean, can I sacrifice their happiness for mine? Yes! Oh, yes! Yes, I can! But . . . he didn't ask me. He didn't even want to ask me. I could tell by this certain look in his eyes that he didn't even want to ask me. Why aren't I miserable! Why aren't I morbid! I should be humiliated! Devastated! Maybe these feelings are coming—I don't know. But for now it was . . . just such fun. I'm happy. I realized I could care about someone. I could want someone. And I sang! I sang all night long! I sang right up into the trees! But not for Old Granddaddy. None of it was to please Old Granddaddy!

Lenny *and* Babe *look at each other.*

Babe: Ah, Meg—

Meg: What—

Babe: Well, it's just— It's . . .

Lenny: It's about Old Granddaddy—

Meg: Oh, I know; I know. I told him all those stupid lies. Well, I'm gonna go right over there this morning and tell him the truth. I mean every horrible thing. I don't care if he wants to hear it or not. He's just gonna have to take me like I am. And if he can't take it, if it sends him into a coma, that's just too damn bad!

Babe *and* Lenny *look at each other.* Babe *cracks a smile.* Lenny *cracks a smile.*

Babe: You're too late— Ha, ha, ha!

They both break up laughing.

Lenny: Oh, stop! Please! Ha, ha, ha!

Meg: What is it? What's so funny?

Babe: still laughing: It's not— It's not funny!

Lenny: still laughing: No, it's not! It's not a bit funny!

Meg: Well, what is it, then? What?

Babe: trying to calm down: Well, it's just—it's just—

Meg: What?

Babe: Well, Old Granddaddy—he—he's in a coma!

Babe *and* Lenny *break up again.*

Meg: He's what?

Babe: shrieking: In a coma!

Meg: My God! That's not funny!

Babe: calming down: I know. I know. For some reason, it just struck us as funny.

Lenny: I'm sorry. It's—it's not funny. It's sad. It's very sad. We've been up all night long.

Babe: We're really tired.

Meg: Well, my God. How is he? Is he gonna live?

Babe *and* Lenny *look at each other.*

Babe: They don't think so!

They both break up again.

Lenny: Oh, I don't know why we're laughing like this. We're just sick! We're just awful!

Babe: We are—we're awful!

Lenny: as she collects herself: Oh, good; now I feel bad. Now I feel like crying. I do; I feel like crying.

Babe: Me, too. Me, too.

Meg: Well, you've gotten me depressed!

Lenny: I'm sorry. I'm sorry. It, ah, happened last night. He had another stroke.

They laugh again.

Meg: I see.

Lenny: But he's stabilized now. *She chokes up once more.*

Meg: That's good. You two okay?

Babe *and* Lenny *nod.*

Meg: You look like you need some rest.

Babe *and* Lenny *nod again.*

Meg: going on, about her heel: I hope that'll stay. *She puts the top back on the glue. A realization:* Oh, of course, now I won't be able to tell him the truth about all those lies I told. I mean, finally I get my wits about me, and he conks out. It's just like him. Babe, can I wear your slippers till this glue dries?

Babe: Sure.

Lenny: after a pause: Things sure are gonna be different around here . . . when Old Granddaddy dies. Well, not for you two really, but for me.

Meg: It'll work out.

Babe: depressed: Yeah. It'll work out.

Lenny: I hope so. I'm just afraid of being here all by myself. All alone.

Meg: Well, you don't have to be alone. Maybe Babe'll move back in here.

Lenny *looks at* Babe *hopefully.*

Babe: No, I don't think I'll be living here.

Meg: realizing her mistake: Well, anyway, you're your own woman. Invite some people over. Have some parties. Go out with strange men.

Lenny: I don't know any strange men.

Meg: Well . . . you know that Charlie.

Lenny: shaking her head: Not anymore.

Meg: Why not?

Lenny: breaking down: I told him we should never see each other again.

Meg: Well, if you told him, you can just untell him.

Lenny: Oh, no, I couldn't. I'd feel like a fool.

Meg: Oh, that's not a good enough reason! All people in love feel like fools. Don't they, Babe?

Babe: Sure.

Meg: Look, why don't you give him a call right now? See how things stand.

Lenny: Oh, no! I'd be too scared—

Meg: But what harm could it possibly do? I mean, it's not gonna make things any worse than this never seeing him again, at all, forever.

Lenny: I suppose that's true—

Meg: Of course it is; so call him up! Take a chance, will you? Just take some sort of chance!

Lenny: You think I should?

Meg: Of course! You've got to try— You do!

Lenny *looks over at* Babe.

Babe: You do, Lenny— I think you do.

Lenny: Really? Really, really?

Meg: Yes! Yes!

Babe: You should!

Lenny: All right. I will! I will!

Meg: Oh, good!

Babe: Good!

Lenny: I'll call him right now, while I've got my confidence up!

Meg: Have you got the number?

Lenny: Uh huh. But, ah, I think I wanna call him upstairs. It'll be more private.

Meg: Ah, good idea.

Lenny: I'm just gonna go on and call him up and see what happens— *She has started up the stairs.* Wish me good luck!

Meg: Good luck!

Babe: Good luck, Lenny!

Lenny: Thanks.

Lenny *gets almost out of sight when the phone rings. She stops;* Meg *picks up the phone.*

Meg: Hello? *Then, in a whisper:* Oh, thank you very much . . . Yes, I will. 'Bye, 'bye.

Lenny: Who was it?

Meg: Wrong number. They wanted Weed's Body Shop.

Lenny: Oh. Well, I'll be right back down in a minute. *She exits.*

Meg: after a moment, whispering to Babe: That was the bakery; Lenny's cake is ready!

Babe: who has become increasingly depressed: Oh.

Meg: I think I'll sneak on down to the corner and pick it up. *She starts to leave.*

Babe: Meg—

Meg: What?

Babe: Nothing.

Meg: You okay?

Babe *shakes her head.*

Meg: What is it?

Babe: It's just—

Meg: What?

Babe *gets the envelope containing the photographs.*

Babe: Here. Take a look.

Meg: taking the envelope: What is it?

Babe: It's some evidence Zackery's collected against me. Looks like my goose is cooked.

Meg *opens the envelope and looks at the photographs.*

Meg: My God, it's—it's you and . . . is *that* Willie Jay?

Babe: Yah.

Meg: Well, he certainly *has* grown. You were right about that. My, oh, my.

Babe: Please don't tell Lenny. She'd hate me.

Meg: I won't. I won't tell Lenny. *Putting the pictures back into the envelope:* What are you gonna do?

Babe: What can I do?

There is a knock on the door. Babe *grabs the envelope and hides it.*

Meg: Who is it?

Barnette's Voice: It's Barnette Lloyd.

Meg: Oh. Come on in, Barnette.

Barnette *enters. His eyes are ablaze with excitement.*

Barnette: as he paces around the room: Well, good morning! *Shaking* Meg's *hand:* Good morning, Miss MaGrath. *Touching* Babe *on the shoulder:* Becky. *Moving away:* What I meant to say is, How are you doing this morning?

Meg: Ah—fine. Fine.

Barnette: Good. Good. I—I just had time to drop by for a minute.

Meg: Oh.

Barnette: So, ah, how's your granddad doing?

Meg: Well, not very, ah—ah, he's in this coma. *She breaks up laughing.*

Barnette: I see . . . I see. *To* Babe: Actually, the primary reason I came by was to pick up that—envelope. I left it here last night in all the confusion. *Pause.* You, ah, still do have it?

Babe *hands him the envelope.*

Barnette: Yes. *Taking the envelope:* That's the one. I'm sure it'll be much better off in my office safe. *He puts the envelope into his coat pocket.*

Meg: I'm sure it will.

Barnette: Beg your pardon?

Babe: It's all right. I showed her the pictures.

Barnette: Ah; I see.

Meg: So what's going to happen now, Barnette? What are those pictures gonna mean?

Barnette: after pacing a moment: Hmmm. May I speak frankly and openly?

Babe: Uh huh.

Meg: Please do—

Barnette: Well, I tell you now, at first glance, I admit those pictures had me considerably perturbed and upset. Perturbed to the point that I spent most of last night going over certain suspect papers and reports that had fallen into my hands—rather recklessly.

Babe: What papers do you mean?

Barnette: Papers that, pending word from three varied and unbiased experts, could prove graft, fraud, forgery, as well as a history of unethical behavior.

Meg: You mean about Zackery?

Barnette: Exactly. You see, I now intend to make this matter just as sticky and gritty for one Z. Botrelle as it is for us. Why, with the amount of scandal I'll dig up, Botrelle will be forced to settle this affair on our own terms!

Meg: Oh, Babe! Did you hear that?

Babe: Yes! Oh, yes! So you've won it! You've won your lifelong vendetta!

Barnette: Well . . . well, now of course it's problematic in that, well, in that we won't be able to expose him openly in the courts. That was the original game plan.

Babe: But why not? Why?

Barnette: Well, it's only that if, well, if a jury were to—to get, say, a glance at these, ah, photographs, well . . . well, possibly . . .

Babe: We could be sunk.

Barnette: In a sense. But! On the other hand, if a newspaper were to get a hold of our little item, Mr. Zackery Botrelle could find himself boiling in some awfully hot water. So what I'm looking for, very simply, is—a deal.

Babe: A deal?

Meg: Thank you, Barnette. It's a sunny day, Babe. *Realizing she is in the way:* Ooh, where's that broken shoe? *She grabs her boots and runs upstairs.*

Babe: So, you're having to give up your vendetta?

Barnette: Well, in a way. For the time. It, ah, seems to me you shouldn't always let your life be ruled by such things as, ah, personal vendettas. *Looking at* Babe *with meaning:* Other things can be important.

Babe: I don't know, I don't exactly know. How 'bout Willie Jay? Will he be all right?

Barnette: Yes, it's all been taken care of. He'll be leaving incognito on the midnight bus—heading north.

Babe: North.

Barnette: I'm sorry, it seemed the only . . . way.

Barnette *moves to her; she moves away.*

Babe: Look, you'd better be getting on back to your work.

Barnette: awkwardly: Right—'cause I—I've got those important calls out. *Full of hope for her:* They'll be pouring in directly. *He starts to leave, then says to her with love:* We'll talk.

Meg: reappearing in her boots: Oh, Barnette—

Barnette: Yes?

Meg: Could you give me a ride just down to the corner? I need to stop at Helen's Bakery.

Barnette: Be glad to.

Meg: Thanks. Listen, Babe, I'll be right back with the cake. We're gonna have the best celebration! Now, ah, if Lenny asks where I've gone, just say I'm . . . Just say, I've gone out back to, ah, pick up some pawpaws! Okay?

Babe: Okay.

Meg: Fine; I'll be back in a bit. Goodbye.

Babe: 'Bye.

Barnette: Goodbye, Becky.

Babe: Goodbye, Barnette. Take care.

Meg *and* Barnette *exit.* Babe *sits staring ahead, in a state of deep despair.*

Babe: Goodbye, Barnette. Goodbye, Becky. *She stops when* Lenny *comes down the stairs in a fluster.*

Lenny: Oh! Oh! Oh! I'm so ashamed! I'm such a coward! I'm such a yellow-bellied chicken! I'm so ashamed! Where's Meg?

Babe: suddenly bright: She's, ah—gone out back—to pick up some pawpaws.

Lenny: Oh. Well, at least I don't have to face her! I just couldn't do it! I couldn't make the call! My heart was pounding like a hammer. Pound! Pound! Pound! Why, I looked down and I could actually see my blouse moving back and forth! Oh, Babe, you look so disappointed. Are you?

Babe: despondently: Uh huh.

Lenny: Oh, no! I've disappointed Babe! I can't stand it! I've gone and disappointed my little sister, Babe! Oh, no! I feel like howling like a dog!

Chick's Voice: Oooh, Lenny! *She enters dramatically, dripping with sympathy.* Well, I just don't know what to say! I'm so sorry! I am so sorry for you! And for little Babe here, too. I mean, to have such a sister as that!

Lenny: What do you mean?

Chick: Oh, you don't need to pretend with me. I saw it all from over there in my own back yard; I saw Meg stumbling out of Doc Porter's pickup truck, not fifteen minutes ago. And her looking such a disgusting mess. You must be so ashamed! You must just want to die! Why, I always said that girl was nothing but cheap Christmas trash!

Lenny: Don't talk that way about Meg.

Chick: Oh, come on now, Lenny honey, I know exactly how you feel about Meg. Why, Meg's a low-class tramp and you need not have one more blessed thing to do with her and her disgusting behavior.

Lenny: I said, don't you ever talk that way about my sister Meg again.

Chick: Well, my goodness gracious, Lenora, don't be such a noodle —it's the truth!

Lenny: I don't care if it's the Ten Commandments. I don't want to hear it in my home. Not ever again.

Chick: In your home?! Why, I never in all my life— This is my grandfather's home! And you're just living here on his charity; so don't you get high-falutin' with me, Miss Lenora Josephine MaGrath!

Lenny: Get out of here—

Chick: Don't you tell me to get out! What makes you think you can order me around? Why, I've had just about my fill of you trashy MaGraths and your trashy ways: hanging yourselves in cellars; carrying on with married men; shooting your own husbands!

Lenny: Get out!

Chick: to Babe: And don't you think she's not gonna end up at the state prison farm or in some—mental institution. Why, it's a clear-cut case of manslaughter with intent to kill!

Lenny: Out! Get out!

Chick: running on: That's what everyone's saying, deliberate intent to kill! And you'll pay for that! Do you hear me? You'll pay!

Lenny: picking up a broom and threatening Chick *with it:* And I'm telling you to get out!

Chick: You—you put that down this minute— Are you a raving lunatic?

Lenny: beating Chick *with the broom:* I said for you to get out! That means out! And never, never, never come back!

Chick: overlapping, as she runs around the room: Oh! Oh! Oh! You're crazy! You're crazy!

Lenny: chasing Chick *out the door:* Do you hear me, Chick the Stick! This is my home! This is my house! Get out! Out!

Chick: overlapping: Oh! Oh! Police! Police! You're crazy! Help! Help!

Lenny *chases* Chick *out of the house. They are both screaming. The phone rings.* Babe *goes and picks it up.*

Babe: Hello? . . . Oh, hello, Zackery! . . . Yes, he showed them to me! . . . You're what! . . . What do you mean? . . . What! . . . You can't put me out to Whitfield . . . 'Cause I'm not crazy . . . I'm not! I'm not! . . . She wasn't crazy, either . . . Don't you call my mother crazy! . . . No, you're not! You're not gonna. You're not! *She slams the phone down and stares wildly ahead.* He's not. He's not. *As she walks over to the ribbon drawer:* I'll do it. I will. And he won't . . . *She opens the drawer, pulls out the rope, becomes terrified, throws the rope back in the drawer, and slams it shut.*

Lenny *enters from the back door swinging the broom and laughing.*

Lenny: Oh, my! Oh, my! You should have seen us! Why, I chased
    Chick the Stick right up the mimosa tree. I did! I left her right
    up there screaming in the tree!
  Babe: laughing; she is insanely delighted. Oh, you did!
Lenny: Yes, I did! And I feel so good! I do! I feel good! I feel good!
  Babe: overlapping: Good! Good, Lenny! Good for you!

They dance around the kitchen.

Lenny: stopping: You know what—
  Babe: What?
Lenny: I'm gonna call Charlie! I'm gonna call him up right now!
  Babe: You are?
Lenny: Yeah, I feel like I can really do it!
  Babe: You do?
Lenny: My courage is up; my heart's in it; the time is right! No more
    beating around the bush! Let's strike while the iron is hot!
  Babe: Right! Right! No more beating around the bush! Strike
    while the iron is hot!

Lenny *goes to the phone.* Babe *rushes over to the ribbon drawer. She begins tearing through it.*

Lenny: with the receiver in her hand: I'm calling him up, Babe—I'm
    really gonna do it!
  Babe: still tearing through the drawer: Good! Do it! Good!
Lenny: as she dials: Look. My hands aren't even shaking.
  Babe: pulling out a red rope: Don't we have any stronger rope than
    this?
Lenny: I guess not. All the rope we've got's in that drawer. *About her
    hands:* Now they're shaking a little.

Babe *takes the rope and goes up the stairs.* Lenny *finishes dialing the number.
She waits for an answer.*

Lenny: Hello? . . . Hello, Charlie. This is Lenny MaGrath . . . Well,
    I'm fine. I'm just fine. *An awkward pause:* I was, ah, just calling
    to see—how you're getting on . . . Well, good. Good . . . Yes, I
    know I said that. Now I wish I didn't say it . . . Well, the reason I
    said that before, about not seeing each other again, was 'cause of
    me, not you . . . Well, it's just I—I can't have any children. I—
    have this ovary problem . . . Why, Charlie, what a thing to say! . . .
    Well, they're not all little snot-nosed pigs! . . . You think they are!
    . . . Oh, Charlie, stop, stop! You're making me laugh . . . Yes, I
    guess I was. I can see now that I was . . . You are? . . . Well, I'm
    dying to see you, too . . . Well, I don't know when, Charlie . . .
    soon. How about, well, how about tonight? . . . You will? . . . Oh,
    you will! . . . All right, I'll be here. I'll be right here . . . Goodbye,
    then, Charlie. Goodbye for now. *She hangs up the phone in a*

daze. Babe. Oh, Babe! He's coming. He's coming! Babe! Oh, Babe, where are you? Meg! Oh . . . out back—picking up paw-paws. *As she exits through the back door:* And those pawpaws are just ripe for picking up!

There is a moment of silence; then a loud, horrible thud is heard coming from upstairs. The telephone begins ringing immediately. It rings five times before Babe *comes hurrying down the stairs with a broken piece of rope hanging around her neck. The phone continues to ring.*

> Babe: *to the phone:* Will you shut up! *She is jerking the rope from around her neck. She grabs a knife to cut it off.* Cheap! Miserable! I hate you! I hate you! *She throws the rope violently across the room. The phone stops ringing.* Thank God. *She looks at the stove, goes over to it, and turns the gas on. The sound of gas escaping is heard. She sniffs at it.* Come on. Come on . . . Hurry up . . . I beg of you— hurry up! *Finally, she feels the oven is ready; she takes a deep breath and opens the oven door to stick her head into it. She spots the rack and furiously jerks it out. Taking another breath, she sticks her head into the oven. She stands for several moments tapping her fingers furiously on top of the stove. She speaks from inside the oven:* Oh, please. Please. *After a few moments, she reaches for the box of matches with her head still in the oven. She tries to strike a match. It doesn't catch.* Oh, Mama, please! *She throws the match away and is getting a second one.* Mama . . . Mama . . . So that's why you done it! *In her excitement she starts to get up, bangs her head, and falls back in the oven.*

Meg *enters from the back door, carrying a birthday cake in a pink box.*

> Meg: Babe! *She throws the box down and runs to pull* Babe's *head out of the oven.* Oh, my God! What are you doing? What the hell are you doing?
> Babe: *dizzily:* Nothing. I don't know. Nothing.

Meg *turns off the gas and moves* Babe *to a chair near the open door.*

> Meg: Sit down. Sit down! Will you sit down!
> Babe: I'm okay. I'm okay.
> Meg: Put your head between your knees and breathe deep!
> Babe: Meg—
> Meg: Just do it! I'll get you some water. *She gets some water for* Babe. Here.
> Babe: Thanks.
> Meg: Are you okay?
> Babe: Uh huh.
> Meg: Are you sure?
> Babe: Yeah, I'm sure. I'm okay.
> Meg: *getting a damp rag and putting it over her own face:* Well, good. That's good.

Babe: Meg—

Meg: Yes?

Babe: I know why she did it.

Meg: What? Why who did what?

Babe: with joy: Mama. I know why she hung that cat along with her.

Meg: You do?

Babe: with enlightenment: It's 'cause she was afraid of dying all alone.

Meg: Was she?

Babe: She felt so unsure, you know, as to what was coming. It seems the best thing coming up would be a lot of angels and all of them singing. But I imagine they have high, scary voices and little gold pointed fingers that are as sharp as blades and you don't want to meet 'em all alone. You'd be afraid to meet 'em all alone. So it wasn't like what people were saying about her hating that cat. Fact is, she loved that cat. She needed him with her 'cause she felt so all alone.

Meg: Oh, Babe . . . Babe. Why, Babe? Why?

Babe: Why what?

Meg: Why did you stick your head into the oven?!

Babe: I don't know, Meg. I'm having a bad day. It's been a real bad day; those pictures, and Barnette giving up his vendetta; then Willie Jay heading north; and—and Zackery called me up. *Trembling with terror:* He says he's gonna have me classified insane and then send me on out to the Whitfield asylum.

Meg: What! Why, he could never do that!

Babe: Why not?

Meg: 'Cause you're not insane.

Babe: I'm not?

Meg: No! He's trying to bluff you. Don't you see it? Barnette's got him running scared.

Babe: Really?

Meg: Sure. He's scared to death—calling you insane. Ha! Why, you're just as perfectly sane as anyone walking the streets of Hazlehurst, Mississippi.

Babe: I am?

Meg: More so! A lot more so!

Babe: Good!

Meg: But, Babe, we've just got to learn how to get through these real bad days here. I mean, it's getting to be a thing in our family. *Slight pause as she looks at* Babe: Come on, now. Look, we've got Lenny's cake right here. I mean, don't you wanna be around to give her her cake, watch her blow out the candles?

Babe: realizing how much she wants to be here: Yeah, I do, I do. 'Cause she always loves to make her birthday wishes on those candles.

Meg: Well, then we'll give her her cake and maybe you won't be so miserable.

Babe: Okay.

Meg: Good. Go on and take it out of the box.

Babe: Okay. *She takes the cake out of the box. It is a magical moment.* Gosh, it's a pretty cake.

Meg: handing her some matches: Here now. You can go on and light up the candles.

Babe: All right. *She starts to light the candles.* I love to light up candles. And there are so many here. Thirty pink ones in all, plus one green one to grow on.

Meg: watching her light the candles: They're pretty.

Babe: They are. *She stops lighting the candles.* And I'm not like Mama. I'm not so all alone.

Meg: You're not.

Babe: as she goes back to lighting candles: Well, you'd better keep an eye out for Lenny. She's supposed to be surprised.

Meg: All right. Do you know where she's gone?

Babe: Well, she's not here inside—so she must have gone on outside.

Meg: Oh, well, then I'd better run and find her.

Babe: Okay; 'cause these candles are gonna melt down.

Meg *starts out the door.*

Meg: Wait—there she is coming. Lenny! Oh, Lenny! Come on! Hurry up!

Babe: overlapping and improvising as she finishes lighting candles: Oh, no! No! Well, yes— Yes! No, wait! Wait! Okay! Hurry up!

Lenny *enters.* Meg *covers* Lenny's *eyes with her hands.*

Lenny: terrified: What? What is it? What?

Meg and Babe: Surprise! Happy birthday! Happy birthday to Lenny!

Lenny: Oh, no! Oh, me! What a surprise! I could just cry! Oh, look: *Happy birthday, Lenny—A Day Late!* How cute! My! Will you look at all those candles—it's absolutely frightening.

Babe: a spontaneous thought: Oh, no, Lenny, it's good! 'Cause— 'cause the more candles you have on your cake, the stronger your wish is.

Lenny: Really?

Babe: Sure!

Lenny: Mercy! Meg *and* Babe *start to sing.*

Lenny: interrupting the song: Oh, but wait! I—can't think of my wish! My body's gone all nervous inside.

Meg: For God's sake, Lenny— Come on!

Babe: The wax is all melting!

Lenny: My mind is just a blank, a total blank!

  Meg: Will you please just—

  Babe: overlapping: Lenny, hurry! Come on!

Lenny: Okay! Okay! Just go!

Meg *and* Babe *burst into the* "Happy Birthday" *song. As it ends,* Lenny *blows out all the candles on the cake.* Meg *and* Babe *applaud loudly.*

  Meg: Oh, you made it!

  Babe: Hurray!

Lenny: Oh, me! Oh, me! I hope that wish comes true! I hope it does!

  Babe: Why? What did you wish for?

Lenny: as she removes the candles from the cake: Why, I can't tell you that.

  Babe: Oh, sure you can—

Lenny: Oh, no! Then it won't come true.

  Babe: Why, that's just superstition! Of course it will, if you made it deep enough.

  Meg: Really? I didn't know that.

Lenny: Well, Babe's the regular expert on birthday wishes.

  Babe: It's just I get these feelings. Now, come on and tell us. What was it you wished for?

  Meg: Yes, tell us. What was it?

Lenny: Well, I guess it wasn't really a specific wish. This—this vision just sort of came into my mind.

  Babe: A vision? What was it of?

Lenny: I don't know exactly. It was something about the three of us smiling and laughing together.

  Babe: Well, when was it? Was it far away or near?

Lenny: I'm not sure; but it wasn't forever; it wasn't for every minute. Just this one moment and we were all laughing.

  Babe: Then, what were we laughing about?

Lenny: I don't know. Just nothing, I guess.

  Meg: Well, that's a nice wish to make.

Lenny *and* Meg *look at each other a moment.*

  Meg: Here, now, I'll get a knife so we can go ahead and cut the cake in celebration of Lenny being born!

  Babe: Oh, yes! And give each one of us a rose. A whole rose apiece!

Lenny: cutting the cake nervously: Well, I'll try—I'll try!

  Meg: licking the icing off a candle: Mmmm—this icing is delicious! Here, try some!

  Babe: Mmmm! It's wonderful! Here, Lenny!

Lenny: laughing joyously as she licks icing from her fingers and cuts huge pieces of cake that her sisters bite into ravenously: Oh, how I do love having birthday cake for breakfast! How I do!

The sisters freeze for a moment laughing and catching cake. The lights change and frame them in a magical, golden, sparkling glimmer; saxophone music is heard. The lights dim to blackout, and the saxophone continues to play.

CURTAIN

Further Reading

Simon, John. "Living Beings, Cardboard Symbols." *New York Magazine* 16 Nov. 1981: 125–26. • Kerr, Walter. "Offbeat—But a Beat Too Far." *New York Times* 15 Nov. 1981: 3, 31. • Gill, Brendan. "Backstage." *New Yorker* 57.39 (16 Nov. 1981): 182–83. • Fox, Terry Curtis. "The Acting's the Thing." *Village Voice* 26.2 (7–13 Jan. 1981): 71. • Rochlin, Margy. "The Eccentric Genius of *Crimes of the Heart*." *Ms.* 15 (Feb. 1987): 12–13.

When contemporary comedy runs aground, it is often because the characters are not well enough developed to take seriously: they seem to exist only for the sake of the humor that can be wrung out of them. Beth Henley's admirers see her as a playwright who has avoided this problem and brought credible comic characters to the stage, but critics hold varying opinions, as we can see from the following reviews of Crimes of the Heart.

John Simon: On Henley's Credibility

This is a loving and teasing look back at deep-southern, small-town life, at the effect of constricted living and confined thinking on three different yet not wholly unalike sisters amid Chekhovian boredom in honeysuckle country, and, above all, at the sorely tried but resilient affection and loyalty of these sisters for one another. However far misunderstandings, quarrels, exasperation may stretch their bond, they bounce back into embraces, Indian dances, leaps of joy, or, more simply, love.

For this is one of those rare plays about a family love that you can believe and participate in, because that love is never sappy or piously cloying, but, rather, irreverently prankish and often even acerb. Warmhearted Lenny is also an irritating fussbudget and martyr; Meg is selfish and irresponsible as well as sensible and ultimately generous; Babe, though blessed with the queer wisdom of the unreconstructed child, is also obtuse and infuriating. It is the ties of sympathy—or, if you will, the bloodline—among these three that form the play's crazy, convoluted, but finally exhilarating tracery: sisterly trajectories that diverge, waver, and explosively reunite. Laughter is squeezed from anguish as the logical consequence of looking absurd reality in the eye and just plain outstaring it. Babe's explanation of her mother's real and her own attempted suicide is the same: "a bad day"—nothing Freudian, only what happens when you do not gaze back at life unblinkingly enough.

The wonderful thing about the young author is that she understands a great deal about people and living.

Walter Kerr: On Henley's Lack of Credibility

I found myself often grinning at what might have been gruesome, sometimes cocking my head sharply to catch a rueful inflection before it turned into a comic one, and always, always admiring the actresses involved. I also found myself, rather too often, and in spite of everything, disbelieving—simply and flatly disbelieving. Since this is scarcely the prevailing opinion, I'd best be specific. . . .

We do understand the ground-rules of matter-of-fact Southern grotesquerie, and we know that they're by no means altogether artificial. People do such things and, having done them, react in surprising ways. When Miss Dillon [as Babe], finally confiding some of the homelier details of the shooting to her siblings, reveals that immediately after pumping a bullet into her husband Zachery's stomach she went into the kitchen and made herself a pitcher of lemonade, we're still all right. As Miss Dillon says, she had a simply terrible thirst. Shock and a terrible thirst go very nicely together. It could have—no doubt *has*—happened. And the actress is personally persuasive.

Where my doubting psyche draws the line is a few seconds further along in Miss Dillon's narrative. Having refreshed herself with the lemonade, she bethought herself of her husband, lying conscious on the floor in the blood flowing from his open wound. "Zach," she called out, "I've made lemonade, do you want a glass?" I submit that we've now pressed the offbeat too far, that we've chased a notion past Carson McCullers country straight through Flannery O'Connor country and on into Joke country.

HANDBOOK OF LITERATURE
WRITING ABOUT LITERATURE
BIOGRAPHICAL SKETCHES
INDEXES

ANTH

Handbook of Literature

NOTE: *Titles of works that are collected in* THE RIVERSIDE ANTHOLOGY *appear in italic type enclosed in quotation marks.*

Allegory: See *Figures of Speech.*

Allusion: an implicit reference to another work of art, a person, or an event. In making an allusion, the writer does not pause to explain the significance of the reference but assumes that the reader shares his or her experience and knowledge well enough to register the impact. Because the Bible is one of the most deeply read books in Western culture, allusions to it are particularly common. In T. S. Eliot's *"The Love Song of J. Alfred Prufrock,"* for instance, Prufrock says that he has seen his head "brought in upon a platter" (p. 693), an allusion to the fate of John the Baptist. Allusions to Greek and Roman myths are almost as common as allusions to the Bible. Writers quite frequently and naturally allude to other writers whose work they admire: in *"Old Dominion"* (pp. 904–905), for example, Robert Hass alludes to the life, work, and suicide of Randall Jarrell. Such an allusion can present a momentary stumbling block to readers who know little about the person or thing alluded to, but the ultimate effect is to import into a work the emotional and intellectual force of other works and lives.

Antagonist: a character in a literary work who opposes or resists the action of the protagonist. The antagonist is not necessarily an evil or immoral character but merely one who directly or indirectly creates conflict for that character whose actions most directly affect the course of the work. Since Creon may be called the **protagonist** of Sophocles' *"Antigone"* (pp. 942–72), Antigone may be the antagonist although she possesses many heroic qualities and possibly the audience's sympathy as well. See also *Protagonist.*

Antithesis: See *Figures of Speech.*

Apostrophe: See *Figures of Speech.*

Blank Verse: unrhymed iambic pentameter. See *Sound of Poetry.*

Caesura: a pause inside a line of verse. In some cases such a pause occurs regularly at the midpoint, breaking the line in halves and becoming an element in the meter.

> And all the way,//to guide their chime,
> With falling oars//they kept the time.
> (Marvell, *"Bermudas,"* p. 496)

More often, caesuras appear irregularly, forced by the prose sense of the passage, and become one way that prose rhythm and verse rhythm are counterpointed. See also *Dieresis, Dipodic Meter, Enjambment.*

CHARACTERIZATION

Characterization is the creation from mere words of persons who appear so human and alive that we respond to them much as we respond to the people in our everyday lives. E. M. Forster, in "Aspects of the Novel," claims that we can know fictional characters more completely than we know real people, for unlike even our closest friends, fictional people have no secret places in their lives or minds. They are no more than a story or poem tells us they are, no matter how mysterious or complex the writer makes them seem.

Within this framework that literature imposes on characterization, Forster has developed a system for understanding the range of possible character types. He first labels characters "flat" or "round," noting at once that both qualities can exist in varying degrees, and then adds "dynamic" and "static" to these two. Flat characters lack complication because they possess only one dominant trait; they provide contrast for round ones and sometimes add humor. The concerned husband in Gilman's *"The Yellow Wallpaper"* (pp. 138–51) is flat because he is never more than a concerned husband throughout the story. Round characters, according to Forster, are "capable of surprising in a convincing way." They are complex with several well-developed traits, and their personalities are surprisingly true to human nature. In *"Hamlet"* (pp. 1085–1194), Hamlet's indecision, despair, and continuing search for nonexistent certainty make him a round character who incorporates the essential nature of human existence.

A dynamic character, like the narrator in Melville's "Bartleby the Scrivener" (pp. 42–71), demonstrates an internal and substantial change in the course of the work. A static one, like Elisa's husband in John Steinbeck's *"The Chrysanthemums"* (pp. 246–55), is not internally affected by circumstances. We often assume that major characters will be both round and dynamic, but such consistency is not found in literature. Satan, in Milton's *"Paradise Lost"* (pp. 479–87) is round, but fails to change in the course of the poem. It can also be argued that the grandmother in Flannery O' Connor's *"A Good Man Is Hard To Find"* (pp. 329–42) is dynamic, but lacks the roundness expected in such a focal character.

Narration and point of view directly influence characterization, for they determine how a character is made known to the reader. In fiction and poetry, the author may tell us everything about a character through physical description and by entering the character's mind and reporting her thoughts. The author then may tell us about the character's past, explain her motivations, or report the opinions others have of her. The author may even give us a personal judgment of the character. But in drama the spoken words and actions of the characters alone reveal their personalities. The author can relate something about a character's inner life by using asides and soliloquies, which allow characters to express those inner emotions and thoughts intended for the audience alone. But in the play, characterization depends as much on the efforts of the director and actors as on the skill of the author.

COMEDY

In Shakespeare's comedy "A Midsummer Night's Dream," the character Puck gives what could be a standard formula for the comic plot:

Jack shall have Jill,
Nought will go ill,
The man shall have his mare again, and all shall be well.

Like tragedy, comedy begins with the introduction of disorder into an orderly society and ends with the restoration of a new order. It is oversimple to say that tragedy always ends in death and comedy in marriage, but the oversimplification points to a useful distinction: that the new order in tragedy involves a sense of loss, while the new order in comedy suggests a world grown brighter.

This is not to say, however, that the comic writer has a higher opinion of human nature than the tragic writer. Comedy sometimes has a cold, unsympathetic quality: it holds its characters up to scrutiny at arm's length, limiting the audience's emotional involvement with them. Often it ridicules inconsistencies and incongruities like Sir Andrew Aguecheek's combination of egotism and stupidity:

> *Sir Andrew:* ... Methinks sometimes I have no more wit than a Christian or an ordinary man has; but I am a great eater of beef, and I believe that does harm to my wit.
>
> *Sir Toby:* No question.
>
> *Sir Andrew:* And I thought that, I'd forswear it. I'll ride home tomorrow, Sir Toby.
>
> *Sir Toby:* *Pourquoi,* my dear knight?
>
> *Sir Andrew:* What is *"pourquoi"*? Do, or not do? I would I had bestow'd that time in the tongues that I have in fencing, dancing, and bear-baiting. O had I but follow'd the arts!
>
> *Sir Toby:* Then hadst thou had an excellent head of hair.
>
> (*Twelfth Night,* Act 1, scene 3, lines 71-81, p. 1015)

Comic characters tend to be simpler than tragic ones: we know all that there is to know about Sir Andrew from the few sentences above, and we can enjoy laughing at him partly because we do not see him as a fully rounded human being.

The satiric, intellectual quality of a "high comedy" can be contrasted with "lower" types. The comic tendency to simplify characters can become caricature, and the use of the incongruous can become horseplay: at this point comedy has become farce. The audience can identify with a sympathetic character and become emotionally involved in his or her successful struggle: at this point we have sentimental comedy. A sentimental comedy can depend on a strong love interest; it then becomes romantic comedy, a type familiar to everyone who watches evening television. Many comedies, including *"Twelfth Night"* (pp. 1009–1082) are a blend of high comedy, farce, and sentimental or romantic comedy.

Conceit: See *Figures of Speech.*

Connotation: the set of implications and associations a word carries regardless of its denotation, or "objective" meaning. In his "To be or not to be" soliloquy of *"Hamlet"* (Act 3, scene 1, pp. 1132–33), the Prince wonders why anyone would "grunt and sweat under a weary life." An eighteenth-century editor changed *grunt* to *groan,* because the original word could "hardly be born by modern ears." The alteration does not significantly affect denotation, but it eliminates the demeaning connotation of a word more often used of pigs or oxen than of well-bred gentlefolk. The connotation is, however, part of Shakespeare's meaning; the Prince feels like a coarse animal and his words express his emotional state. See *Diction*.

Couplet: See *Poetic Forms*.

CRITICISM: THE MAJOR APPROACHES

Literary criticism is the analysis and evaluation of a work of literature through a particular set of principles, as well as the justification of the principles used. The practice of criticism is commonly recognized as beginning with the Greeks in the third century B.C. While criticism continues to expand and take new forms yearly, all types find their roots in four basic approaches to literature. The clearest explanation of these approaches is given by M. H. Abrams in "The Mirror and the Lamp," which locates each critical theory in one of these elements being stressed above the others: (1) the universe; (2) the artist or creator; (3) the work of literature produced; (4) the audience to whom the work is directed.

Oldest of the four is a focus on the universe through what is called the *mimetic theory of art*. Aristotle, the great ancient champion of this view, felt that the aim of art was to "delight and instruct" by showing us what the world is like. Until the eighteenth century, writers and critics who defended and evaluated literature did so in light of its verisimilitude, or affinity with what they saw as truth. Some might have complained that Shakespeare frequently violated Aristotle's dictum concerning the unity of time, space, and action, which argues that the existence of time, space, and action on stage should mimetically reflect their existence off stage. Focus on the work's relation to the universe does not always, however, involve this sort of concern with accurate imitation of the natural world. Twentieth-century ideological criticism, notably Marxist and feminist criticism, has focused on the world view expressed by the work. An ideological critic examining Shakespeare's *"Hamlet"* (pp. 1085–1194) might be primarily concerned about the nature of the political system in the play.

A focus on the author, found in expressive theory, tends to single out the artist as one gifted with a heightened ability to see the world; the emotions and perceptions of the artist, then, must prevail in art. The Romantic movement, best represented by the nineteenth-century poets William Wordsworth and Samuel Taylor Coleridge, ushered in a period of self-expression that continues today. Yet criticism that emerged from an interest in the author has taken many different forms. Historical criticism took hold in the eighteenth century as critics began to wonder about the life of an artist and how it shaped his or her work. While a historical critic would study the cultural, social, and personal life of a writer like Shakespeare, a psychological critic would probe even deeper, attempting to study Shakespeare's unconscious. Freudian criticism, for example, may even look at the relationship between Hamlet and his mother for signs of psychological tension or repression within Shakespeare.

When the work itself is the center of attention, the approach is called *objective criticism*. The nineteenth-century "art for art's sake" movement, supported by writers such as Walter Pater and Charles Baudelaire, appreciated art for its inherent worth, regardless of its moral or social value. Similarly, the New Critics of the twentieth century attempted to interpret and evaluate a piece of literature in complete isolation from external reality—especially biography and history. Objective criticism may include the examination of the work in light of the conventions appropriate to works of its kind (tragedy or comedy, for example), but has in recent years concentrated on the work's internal structure. A contemporary objective critic might focus attention, for instance, on conflicts in the diction of a character in the play.

M. H. Abrams claims, however, that the pragmatic approach with its focus on the audience is most significant to the Western world. Advocates of this approach sometimes attempt to analyze a work by re-creating the audience for which it was intended. For example, a study of this type might consider the attitudes, beliefs, and economic standings of the audience for Shakespeare's *"Twelfth Night"* (pp. 1009–82) in order to understand not only his methods (the types of humor, the allusions, etc.) but also the impact he strove to create. Recent reader-response critics pay less attention to the relations between writer and audience than to the interaction between the reader and the text. Their study concerns the manipulation of a reader's thoughts and emotions by a text that holds back information or floods the reader with particular images.

It is important to note, however, that no single form of criticism is the best method of analyzing every work of art. Most critics are relativists and use whatever type, or blend of types, that best enlightens the work. See also *Literary Movements and Periods*.

Deus ex machina: meaning "god out of the machine," a phrase that comes from a practice in some Greek drama of using stage machinery to lower onto the stage a god who could rescue the hero, untangle the plot, or set the world in order before the play closed. The term now refers to any contrivance by which an unexpected person or happening is introduced to solve the conflict and lead to a neat, positive ending. The deus ex machina is often regarded as a device by which an unskillful writer saves a plot that has somehow gotten out of control.

DICTION

Though, by definition, diction means no more than "the choice of words," this choice is so crucial that it deserves special scrutiny. Dictionaries ordinarily recognize at least four levels of diction: the formal, the informal, the colloquial, and the slang. Some writers operate almost exclusively within one of these levels. Milton's *"Paradise Lost,"*(pp. 479–87), for example, is notably formal in its diction, full of words that belong in serious books and grave public discourse: Eve mentions to Adam at one point that "casual discourse" "intermits" the day's work. If the diction were informal, she might have said that conversation lightens the day's work; if colloquial, that a chance to talk breaks up the day; if slang, that it's always good to take a break and shoot the breeze.

Some poets, particularly those of the seventeenth and eighteenth centuries, choose to limit the range of words in their poems to achieve a "pure" or "poetic" diction limited largely to the formal and informal level. The Romantic poets sometimes adopt this pure diction (as in *"Tintern Abbey,"* pp. 517–21), but sometimes deliberately violate it: Wordsworth clearly enjoys violating the decorum of the drawing room by mentioning "leeches" (p. 527), in *"Resolution and Independence"* and "A stump of rotten wood" in "Simon Lee." Though the range of diction easily accepted in poetry today is much wider than it was a century or two ago, there are still words that raise the reader's eyebrows. When Sharon Olds, for instance, uses words like "pissing" and "cardiovascular," she is extending the diction of the poem further into vulgarity on one hand and medical terminology on the other than some poets would be inclined to do. When Richard Wilbur uses *quotidian* in *"The Undead"* (p. 839), he is admitting a word to the poem that W. S. Merwin would probably resist as unnatural in his own poems.

In fiction and drama, diction is obviously useful for characterization. In Toni Cade Bambara's *"The Lesson"* (pp. 400–407), the conflict between Miss Moore and the children echoes in the clash of their slang and her relatively formal speech. Shakespeare relishes the contrast between the diction of his "high" characters, well-bred and educated, and his "low" characters. See the graveyard scene (Act 5, scene 1, pp. 1175–83) in *"Hamlet,"* where the Prince's eloquence is contrasted with the speech of a gravedigger who tells him, for instance, that "your water is a sore decayer of your whoreson dead body." See also *Connotation.*

Dieresis: though used in various senses, usually refers to the practice of ending words at the end of metrical feet, so that there is no conflict between the rhythm established by the slight pause between words and the rhythm established by the slight pause between metrical feet. Shakespeare's *"Sonnet 73"* (p. 464) observes strict dieresis in its first line.

> That time/ of year/ thou mayst/ in me/ behold

but breaks the pattern with the second word of the second line

> When yel/low leaves,/ or none,/ or few,/ do hang

Dieresis helps establish the poem's underlying meter, but if continued for long becomes monotonous. See *Sound of Poetry.*

Dipodic Meter: a meter in which feet with heavy stresses alternate with feet with light stresses. See, for example, Andrew Marvell's *"Bermudas"* (p. 496):

> And all/the way,/to guide/their chime,
> With fal/ling oars,/ they kept/ the time.

The effect here is nearly the same as if the basic foot were four syllables long ($\smile$ / $\smile$ $\smile$). The dipodic meter swings from strong stress to strong stress with very little interference from intervening syllables, giving the poem the rhythm of a song. Anapestic and dactylic passages also develop a rhythmic swing because there are two unstressed syllables for each beat. Without the dipodic effect (that is, the effect of two feet acting as one), iambic and trochaic meters are much less songlike. See *Sound of Poetry.*

Elegy: a formal poetic meditation on a serious theme. Renaissance love complaints, such as Thomas Wyatt's "They Flee from Me," were called elegiac, but death is the subject of most modern elegies, including Louise Bogan's *"To My Brother"* (p. 729), and Dylan Thomas's *"Do Not Go Gentle into That Good Night"* (pp. 812–13). The **pastoral elegy** is characterized by the classical conventions of an invocation to a Muse, a procession of mourners, the pathetic fallacy, and an exaltation of immortality, while expressing grief over the loss of a friend. Alfred, Lord Tennyson, in *"In Memoriam"* (pp. 569–71), and W. H. Auden, in *"In Memory of W. B. Yeats"* (pp. 764–66), use these conventions to create modern versions of the ancient form.

Enjambment: the running of one poetic line into another without a significant pause created by phrasing or punctuation. The first and second lines of Shakespeare's *"Sonnet 55"* (p. 463) are enjambed. The first line of *"Sonnet 138"* (p. 465), on the other hand, is end-stopped. End-stopped lines help establish a poem's underlying meter, but an unvarying pattern of end-stopped lines, like unvarying dieresis, leads to monotony.

Exposition: the portion of a play, preceding the main action, devoted to establishing the situation, character, and conflict. In fiction, exposition is the injection of such material into the story before or between scenes by resorting to the omniscient point of view.

Expressionism: See *Literary Movements.*

Fairy tale: a traditional story that contains elements of fantasy. The people in a fairy tale are often stock characters, the cruel stepmother or the greedy king, and their lack of individualization is reflected in the substitution of labels for personal names—"a princess" or "a poor man," for example. Generally one character appears human but possesses magical powers; sometimes what appears to be a human is actually a supernatural spirit in disguise. Although these characters can change forms or perform miracles, the fairy tale is often otherwise realistic. Finally innocence triumphs, often through reconciliation or ruthless vengeance, to lead the fairy tale to a happy ending. The Grimm brothers' *"Juniper Tree"* (pp. 16–23) and Marguerite Yourcenar's oriental tale, *"How Wang-Fo Was Saved"* (pp. 284–92), although separated by time and culture, are both characteristic of the fairy tale.

Fantasy: a literary form involving a conscious departure from reality, in which the world imitated is, at least in part, an imaginary one. Often the principles of nature are invented or distorted so that animals can take on human traits, people can become animals or superhumans, and the subconscious mind can create monsters or new worlds. Fantasy can be found as a central element in works ranging from the traditional folk tale, such as "The Juniper Tree" (pp. 16–23), to the contemporary magical realism of García Márquez's *"A Very Old Man with Enormous Wings"* (pp. 348–54). Although some works of fantasy are distinctly philosophical, such as Jorge Luis Borges' *"The Aleph"* (pp. 234–46), fantasy can be written purely for entertainment.

FIGURES OF SPEECH

The special language of science uses words and expressions that, so far as possible, communicate one thing at a time without ambiguity or the danger of confusion. *Polytetrafluoroethylene* probably means the same thing in every sentence in which it appears. It is hard to imagine a circumstance where it could be used ironically and it is unlikely to find its way into a simile or metaphor. The language of literature and common life, however, is filled with words and expressions used figuratively, words that mean in a particular context something more than any dictionary definition would lead us to expect. The figures of speech that create these extra meanings are traditionally divided into TROPES (figures that change the meaning of a word) and RHETORICAL FIGURES (those that change the tone or emphasis of a statement without changing the meaning of individual words).

The Principal Tropes

METAPHOR and SYMBOL are the most important tropes by far. They are discussed in a separate entry that should be read before preceding to the less important tropes listed below. The minor tropes can all be seen as offshoots of metaphor and can all be analyzed in terms of tenor, vehicle, and meaning (for a definition of which, see *Metaphor and Symbol*).

An IMPLIED METAPHOR is one in which either the vehicle or the tenor is not specifically named. When Hamlet asks, "What should such fellows as I do crawling between earth and heaven?" (*"Hamlet,"* Act 3, scene 1, p. 1134) the tenor (Hamlet) is specified, but the vehicle (an insect or other crawling creature) is merely implied.

A SIMILE is a type of metaphor that announces (usually by the use of "like" or "as") the comparison it is making between two essentially different things. In Amy Clampitt's *"Man Feeding Pigeons"* (p. 851), the descending pigeons become "plump-contoured as the pomegranates and pears in a Della Robbia holiday wreath." In Hemingway's *"Hills Like White Elephants"* (pp. 229–34), the title itself is a simile, and understanding the simile is an important aspect of understanding the story. In each example, the two things being compared share at least one common element, shape in the first, and shape and color in the second.

The EPIC SIMILE is one in which the secondary image (vehicle) is substantially expanded until it becomes important in itself and ceases to be a mere illustration of the tenor. Homer uses such similes in the "Iliad" and the "Odyssey," and the epic poets who succeeded him followed his lead. In *"Paradise Lost"* (Book 9, lines 513–516, p. 482), for example, Milton elaborately compares the movement of the serpent to that of a ship near the mouth of a river, guided by a skillful steersman who knows how to shift the sails with the varying winds.

A CONCEIT is a metaphor that draws an elaborate parallel between two things so remarkably different that great ingenuity (or wit) is required to find the connecting meaning. While a conceit can be a simple metaphor, it often encompasses an entire poem. The most common conceits are the Petrarchan, in which frequently a woman or love is compared to a ship or a rose, and the Metaphysical, which are more intellectual and abstract. John Donne's *"A Valediction: Forbidding Mourning"* (pp. 470–71), contains one of the best-known Metaphysical conceits: a man and wife are compared to the arms of a compass.

PERSONIFICATION is a form of metaphor that compares animals, inanimate objects, or abstractions to humans. In *"Spring,"* for example, Edna St. Vincent Millay calls April "an idiot, babbling and strewing flowers" (p.705). Often the personification is an implied metaphor, as when Alexander Pope writes in *"The Rape of the Lock"* that the "sun obliquely shoots his burning ray" (p. 501).

An ALLEGORY is an extended metaphor in which the essential meaning (the tenor) is found outside of the literary work. Allegory, like symbolism, uses characters, setting, and images to suggest meaning beyond themselves, but allegorical signs, unlike symbols, are so obviously used to present religious, moral, or political ideas that they retain little objective meaning. Allegorical characters are flat and unreal personifications of the abstract qualities they represent. Charles D'Orléans' *"The Castle of My Heart"* (p. 461) and John Donne's *"Holy Sonnet 14"* (p. 474) are based on a traditional allegory in which the soul is presented as a maiden in a castle defended by knights with names like Reason and Honor and besieged by others with names like Danger and Sorrow.

METONYMY is the replacement of the name of the thing discussed (the tenor) by the name of a commonly associated object (the vehicle). Orsino, in the opening scene of Shakespeare's *"Twelfth Night,"* looks forward to the time when Olivia will find one man who can simultaneously engage her "liver, brain, and heart" (p. 1011). In the medical lore of Shakespeare's time the liver was associated with passions, as the brain and heart are still associated with intellect and emotion. Thus,

Orsino's statement means that Olivia will find a man who will satisfy her passions, intellect, and emotion.

SYNECDOCHE is a type of metonymy in which a part of a thing signifies the whole, and, occasionally, the whole signifies the parts. The "pair of ragged claws scuttling across the floors of silent seas" (p. 693) in T. S. Eliot's *"The Love Song of J. Alfred Prufrock"* signifies the whole crab.

The Principal Rhetorical Figures

The rhetorical figures affect the spirit in which a statement will be taken, and so are related to tone. **Irony** is generally taken to be the most important of these figures, and is treated in a separate entry.

ANTITHESIS involves a marked contrast in words or clauses, as well as in ideas, in order to emphasize both parts of the contrast. In William Blake's *"Auguries of Innocence,"* the antithesis is extended over four lines (p. 515):

> Every Night & every Morn
> Some to Misery are Born
> Every Morn & every Night
> Some are Born to sweet delight

A successful antithesis provides a balance at both the level of structure and ideas so that the two sides directly play off one another.

An APOSTROPHE addresses an abstract quality or an absent or nonexistent person as if present and listening. Usually the apostrophe involves the expression of deep emotion; it can lend itself to humor and satire. Donne's *"Holy Sonnet 10"* (p. 474) seriously addresses death while his *"The Sun Rising"* (pp. 472–73) is a witty appeal to the rising sun.

HYPERBOLE is conscious overstatement for dramatic or comic effect. Andrew Marvell uses hyperbole in *"To His Coy Mistress"* when the lover tells his mistress that had he time to woo at leisure his "love would grow/Vaster than empires and more slow" (p. 494). When Mary, the storyteller in Ralph Ellison's *"Did You Ever Dream Lucky?"* says that her daughter's eyes "got round as silver dollars" (p. 296), she too is using hyperbole. In both these cases the hyperbole is also a simile.

OXYMORON, Greek for "pointedly foolish," is a linking of terms that seem to contradict each other. The Latin proverb *Festina lente* (hasten slowly) is a famous example of oxymoron. The expression "Dimity Convictions" (p. 606) in Emily Dickinson's *"What Soft—Cherubic Creatures"* is a more subtle example: Dimity is a sheer cotton fabric—pretty, but too insubstantial to be linked with convictions. Claudius uses oxymoron when he says that the period when he buried his brother and married his brother's widow was one of "defeated joy," filled "With mirth in funeral, and with dirge in marriage" (*Hamlet*, Act 1, scene 2, lines 10–12, p. 1091).

UNDERSTATEMENT (or LITOTES) is the opposite of hyperbole, a figure of speech that mutes the expression of an emotion, idea, or situation. The irony created by saying less than one means intensifies the effect. In *"Rape Fantasies,"* for instance, Margaret Atwood underscores the irony of a child's desire for leukemia with an understated rehetorical question: "I didn't understand then that she was going to die and I wanted to have leukemia too so I could get flowers. Kids are funny, aren't they?" (p. 413). Understatement is also common in poetry. Edna St. Vincent Millay's *"Love Is Not All"* (p. 705) questions throughout whether the speaker would betray her lover "in a difficult hour"; the understated conclusion is "I do not think I would." See *Irony* and *Metaphor and Symbol.*

Foil: a person or sometimes an object that illuminates and clarifies the distinctive features of another character by sharply contrasting with him or her. The Prior in Robert Browning's *"Fra Lippo Lippi"* (pp. 575–84) is a foil for Lippi as Bailey is for the grandmother in Flannery O'Connor's "A Good Man Is Hard to Find" (pp. 329–42), and both Horatio and Laertes are foils for Hamlet (pp. 1085–1194). The term originally meant a "leaf" of bright metal that, when placed under a gem or piece of jewelry, enhanced its brilliance.

Foreshadowing: the presentation of information early in a work that hints at events to follow. Foreshadowing can be the establishment of atmosphere, particular facts, or notable character traits. Edgar Allan Poe's ". . . but why *will* you say that I am mad?" in the opening sentence of *"The Tell-Tale Heart"* (p. 37), like the appearance of the ghost in the first act of *"Hamlet"* (p. 1089), prepares the reader both emotionally and intellectually for what is to come.

Frame Story: a story, usually very simple, that creates a context in which a character can tell a second, more extensive story. See, for example, the opening and closing passages of Ralph Ellison's *"Did You Ever Dream Lucky?"* (pp. 293–304).

Genre: a French word referring to a type or category of literature. While literary works are usually categorized by form and technique, sometimes the subject matter also helps define a work. Until the eighteenth century, most literature conformed to the specifications of a certain genre, so much that a writer was acknowledged nearly as much for his or her adherence to convention as for originality. Modern readers are probably more strongly affected than they realize by an awareness of genre conventions. We all acknowledge, for instance, that a detective novel follows different rules from those a science fiction novel follows, and we learn to read each according to its kind. The genres represented in this anthology include the epic, comedy, elegy, gothic, lyric, pastoral, tragedy, and tragicomedy. Classification by genre can be useful because, when we know the elements of a certain form, we have a frame of reference that allows us to appreciate both the author's skillful adherence to some aspects of the form and his or her skillful departure from other aspects.

Gothic: when first applied to literature in the eighteenth century, gothic meant "barbaric": that which defied classical order and dignity. The term was soon associated with dark castles, strange noises, ghosts, storms, horror, and the supernatural found in literature. The wildness and mystery of the gothic appealed to the nineteenth-century romantics and inspired works like Samuel Taylor Coleridge's *"Kubla Khan"* (pp. 532–34) and John Keats's *"La Belle Dame sans Merci"* (p. 555–56). In America, Edgar Allan Poe incorporated gothic elements in his poetry and stories, as in *"The Tell-Tale Heart"* (pp. 37–42). More recently, a number of Southern writers have been recognized for their development of gothic elements. The distorted characters, violence, and obsession found in the works of William Faulkner and Flannery O'Connor have created a "Southern gothic" tradition to which Beth Henley and Leigh Allison Wilson at least partly belong.

Grotesque: first used consistently as a literary term in the eighteenth century, grotesque referred to the bizarre or unnatural, anything that opposed the balance and harmony sought by neoclassical art. Its meaning has been narrowed in this century as more writers have become concerned with the absurdity of humankind and the lack of order in the universe. In fiction and in theater, the grotesque is represented by spiritually or physically deformed characters who carry out abnormal behavior. Writers often use the grotesque for comic effect, as Samuel Beckett does in *"Krapp's Last Tape"* (pp. 1336–43.). Flannery O'Connor, in contrast, uses it allegorically to demonstrate the spiritual condition of the world (see *"A Good Man Is Hard to Find,"* pp. 329–42).

Hyperbole: See *Figures of Speech.*

IMAGERY

An image is a word or group of words that refer to any sensory experience. Notice the range of images in the following lines from Wilfred Owen's *"Dulce et Decorum Est"* (p. 711):

> If you could hear, at every jolt, the blood
> Come gargling from the froth-corrupted lungs,
> Obscene as cancer, bitter as the cud
> Of vile, incurable sores on innocent tongues,—

In these lines, visual, auditory, gustatory (taste), and tactile (feeling) images are most obvious. Also, with each jolt of the moving wagon, a kinaesthetic image, one which pertains to bodily movement, is created. The sound of the blood and the sight of sores on the tongues are both "literal" images, tied to objects that are present in the poem. Sometimes, however, the important images in a work are brought in as figures of speech, as in this simile from Alfred, Lord Tennyson's *"Tears, Idle Tears"* (p. 568):

> Ah, sad and strange as in dark summer dawns
> The earliest pipe of half-awakened birds
> To dying ears, when unto dying eyes
> The casement slowly grows a glimmering square;
> So sad, so strange, the days that are no more.

In some poems the images are so rich and have such psychological weight that they convey the "meaning" of the poem more completely than the prose sense of the sentences in which they occur. Some modern poems, such as Charles Baudelaire's *"Correspondences"* (p. 596) employ **synaesthesia,** the description of one kind of sensation in terms of another: the description of "scents . . . /As mellow as oboes," for instance, crosses an olfactory image with an auditory one.

Although imagery is essential to poetry, it can be very important in fiction and drama as well. The opening images of Ernest Hemingway's *"Hills Like White Elephants"* (p. 229) briefly sets the scene for the reader:

> The hills across the valley of the Ebro were long and white. On this side there was no shade and no trees and the station was between two lines of rails in the sun. Close against the side of the station there was the warm shadow of the building and a curtain, made of strings of bamboo beads, hung across the open door into the bar, to keep out flies. The American and the girl with him sat at a table in the shade, outside the building. It was very hot and the express from Barcelona would come in forty minutes.

The imagery is visual and tactile. The reader's sight moves from the large features of the hills and the river valley, to the details of bamboo beads, to the specific location of the story's characters; and the reader feels the pervasive heat of sun that reaches even into the shadows.

Imagism: See *Literary Movements and Periods.*

Impressionism: See *Literary Movements and Periods.*

Initiation Story: a story about the development of a young person from childhood or adolescence to maturity. The internal conflicts that the innocent individual has to face and resolve "initiate" him or her into the world of experience. James Joyce's *"Araby"* (pp. 163–68) and William Faulkner's *"Barn Burning"* (pp. 214–28) are initiation stories.

IRONY
Ancient histories tell us that when the Emperor Croesus of Lydia planned his campaign against the Emperor Cyrus of Persia, he took the precaution of asking the Oracle (a kind of fortune teller) at Delphi for a prediction of the outcome. The Oracle responded that if Croesus invaded, "a great empire would be destroyed." Croesus, hearing in this prophecy only what he wanted to hear, launched the invasion. The result, of course, was the fall of Lydia. This incident illustrates the characteristic grim humor of irony. It also shows its central principle: truth appears in a mask that disguises it. The mask may be verbal, created by an ambiguity in the meaning of an expression (as in the line "She lies not down to weep" in A. E. Housman's *"Is My Team Ploughing,"* p. 627). It may be dramatic, created by the misunderstanding of a character who knows less than the audience (as in Act 3 of Beth Henley's *"Crimes of the Heart"* (pp. 1532–87), where Meg does not know that Old Granddaddy is in a coma). It may be situational, created by juxtapositions that suggest grim humor (as in Charles Baudelaire's *"The Little Old Women"* (pp. 599–602), where we see that old people dwindle in stature until they can be buried in coffins made for children).

Crisp, clear examples of verbal, dramatic, and situational irony are relatively uncommon. Far more common are passages or whole works where the tone is ironic. An author or character says something as if with a wink or grimace to show the discrepancy between the words and the meaning. Hamlet, for instance, seems to praise Gertrude for remarrying immediately after his father's burial: "Thrift, thrift, Horatio! the funeral bak'd meats/Did coldly furnish forth the marriage tables" (*"Hamlet,"* Act 1, scene 2, p. 1096). Neither the audience nor Horatio needs to be told that Hamlet's supposed praise is a mask which both hides and reveals his actual outrage. See also *Wit.*

LITERARY MOVEMENTS AND PERIODS
While some writers represented in this book consciously set out to create a literary movement, others, by virtue of birth and convention, were necessarily assigned to one. No writer escapes being associated with or influenced by the characteristics of some literary movement; knowing the background against which a particular writer has written may prove helpful in fully appreciating his or her work. The following is a discussion of major literary movements and periods.

The RENAISSANCE acquired its name from the French word meaning "rebirth," a word that captures the creative energy and optimism of a society expanding, geographically and culturally, beyond the limits of the medieval period. Harkening back to the humanism of classical times, Renaissance painting, sculpture, and literature often celebrated the beauty of humanity and the physical world. The English Renaissance flowered under Elizabeth I (1533–1603) and James I (1603–1625) and waned in the second half of the seventeenth century. It infused English literature with a range of allusion enriched by scholarship and travel and a poetic sensibility enlarged by European as well as classical influences. The breadth of Shakespeare's drama and Milton's epic poetry demonstrate the unlimited creativity of Renaissance writers.

The NEOCLASSICAL PERIOD arose as a reaction against the unrestrained energy and humanism of the Renaissance. During the eighteenth century, the neoclassicists stressed the imperfections and limitations of humanity. They imposed a new order and decorum on life and art. Art was valued for its exaltation of reason and its restraint of emotion and the imagination. Alexander Pope exemplified both these values in his *"Rape of the Lock"* (pp. 500–503), a mock-epic poem that ridiculed the pettiness of humanity in witty and flawless couplets. An essentially neoclassic sensibility sometimes appears in the twentieth century, as in W. H. Auden's *"The Unknown Citizen"* (pp. 763–64), with its ironic distance, restraint, and wit.

ROMANTICISM began as a movement when William Wordsworth and Samuel Taylor Coleridge published their "Lyrical Ballads" in 1798. Reacting against neoclassical order and restraint, the English Romantic poets enthusiastically embraced supernatural themes, the wildness of nature, imagination, and self-expression. In diction and poetic form, their verse often resembled impassioned prose or folk balladry. In England, William Blake, William Wordsworth, Samuel Taylor Coleridge, John Keats, and Percy Bysshe Shelley were the leading Romantic poets. In America, fiction was equally influenced by the movement. American romanticism tended toward symbolism and gothic elements while maintaining the imaginative qualities of the early romantics. The movement in America was led by Nathaniel Hawthorne, Herman Melville, Edgar Allan Poe, Walt Whitman, and Emily Dickinson.

The array of movements that followed romanticism are all "modern" in their decisive break from former literary traditions. While all can be roughly located in time, each presents a method of literary expression that continues to appear in literature to the present.

REALISM, first, is the attempt to reproduce the actual world in literature. It arose in the nineteenth century as a reaction against the sentimental, supernatural, and optimistic elements of romanticism. Realists generally choose the common or ordinary for subject matter, and they focus on the presentation of character instead of on plot. In drama, Henrik Ibsen and Anton Chekhov are responsible for the turn to realism on stage; Guy de Maupassant, Henry James, and Edith Wharton are forerunners of realism in fiction.

NATURALISM grew out of realism around the turn of this century. Although related to realism, naturalism moves beyond literary principles to scientific ones that govern both human nature and the order of the universe. Scientific determinism leaves characters defeated by both the natural world and their own animalistic nature, neither of which they can understand or control; social and economic determinism takes from them the power to direct their own destinies. Although Maupassant preferred to avoid being labeled, he is aligned with the naturalistic tradition.

SYMBOLISM began as a movement in France during the second half of the nineteenth century as a reaction against realism. The symbolists believed that the objective world was not the true reality, but rather a mere reflection of an Absolute one, with which the artist was closely attuned. Art revealed reality by re-creating the emotional response of the artist, but because emotional states cannot be shared directly, the symbolists believed a system of symbols was necessary to express what they experienced. They also relied on the musical and connotative qualities of words to evoke a response in the reader. Charles Baudelaire was the primary force behind symbolism, especially in his use of synaesthesia, the description of one kind of sensation in terms of another. The influence of the movement is apparent in the poetry of William Butler Yeats, the foremost English symbolist, and Louise Bogan.

IMAGISM was initiated in 1909 by American and English poets as a response to symbolism. To counteract the loosely defined images of the Symbolists, the Imagists set out to give poetry a new concreteness. Influenced in part by Japanese haiku, the Imagists used precise language to create solid, sharply defined representations of objects. Their ideal was a visual creation that would appeal to the intellect while its sound evoked emotion. Imagism continues to influence poets; its traits are seen, for example, in William Carlos Williams's *"The Red Wheelbarrow"* (p. 675).

MODERNISM, when defined specifically, refers to a direction in style and attitude taken by twentieth-century literature. "Modern" does not refer to a specific time period but rather to a conscious break with traditional forms. Rejecting objective truth as a source of meaning, the moderns believe that the individual creates meaning by perception, action, and imagination. Symbolism and personal mythmaking become the means of self-expression. Yet the glorification of the inner being leads the modern to alienation and a sense of loss and despair. William Butler Yeats, T. S. Eliot, James Joyce, Virginia Woolf, William Faulkner, and Samuel Beckett are among the many modern writers.

IMPRESSIONISM is a movement in literature in which things are portrayed as they would be perceived by a particular consciousness and point of view rather than as they objectively appear. Taking their method from the impressionistic painters of the nineteenth century, such as Renoir and Monet, the literary impressionists attempt to imitate, through words, the delicate brush strokes and varying patterns of light created in such art. The result is the reproduction of a fleeting impression upon the mind of how something momentarily looked or felt. Although impressionism is like expressionism in that it uses objects merely to portray the human consciousness, it differs in that it does not distort or abstract them. Virginia Woolf's *"Solid Objects"* (pp. 168–73), for example, is an impressionistic story.

EXPRESSIONISM, a term coined at the beginning of the twentieth century, describes art and literature that emphasize the internal emotions and experience of the artist. External objects merely transmit the artist's psyche and are not significant in themselves; therefore they are often substantially distorted. Expressionism in drama is characterized by symbolic and anti-realistic staging, and in fiction takes the form of stream of consciousness narration and dreamlike situations, as in Franz Kafka's *"A Hunger Artist"* (pp. 174–81).

Finally, SURREALISM is a movement in art and literature that began during World War I in France. Influenced primarily by the psychology of Freud and poetry of Charles Baudelaire and Arthur Rimbaud, the surrealists believed that the illogical and uncontrolled thoughts and associations of the mind better represented objective truth than ideas controlled by convention and imposed rationality. Presenting a dreamlike world through free-form writing and leaving interpretation to the reader alone, the surrealists asserted their freedom from reason and moral purpose. Although the movement ended at the beginning of World War II, surrealism continued to influence contemporary writers. Robert Bly's *"Words Rising"* (pp. 855–57) and Pablo Neruda's *"Love Sonnet VI"* (pp. 757–58) both demonstrate surrealistic qualities.

Lyric: a relatively brief poem that expresses the personal emotions of a single speaker, usually love or sorrow, longing or tranquility. Many of the early and memorable lyrics in English, such as the anonymous "Western Wind," were written to be sung, as popular song lyrics are today. Some later and more "literary" lyrics, such as Alfred, Lord Tennyson's *"Now Sleeps the Crimson Petal"* (p. 568) are still at least nominally songs for music. Others, such as John Keats's *"When I Have Fears That I May Cease to Be"* (pp. 553–54) and Elizabeth Bishop's *"One Art"* (p. 790) were probably never intended to be sung but retain the tight metrical construction of a song lyric. In a somewhat looser sense, lyric is opposed to dramatic and epic as one of the three major genres of poetry: it is the genre of a single voice presenting a single mood or impression.

Melodrama: a term that literally means "a play with music" and that originally referred to a type of musical play popular in England in the nineteenth century. Today the term no longer implies that songs and music will be part of the performance. What is implied is a heavy-handed appeal to emotions: characters who are unrealistically good are pitted in a dire and apparently futile struggle against other characters who are unrealistically bad. When the audience's feelings of horror and pity have been sufficiently exercised, the plot usually turns (often via a deus ex machina) and the audience feels a rush of joy as the play comes to a happy ending. To call a play or story "melodramatic" is to condemn it because it manipulates the emotions of the audience and fails to satisfy their intelligence. But we should remember that the "correct" balance of emotional and intellectual appeal in a work has varied greatly from period to period and from culture to culture. Were it not preserved from the criticism by its antiquity, *Medea* (pp. 973–1008) might be called melodramatic: the literary establishment in ancient Greece seems to have been less put off by appeals to strong and predictable emotions than the majority of critics and literature professors in twentieth-century Britain and America.

METAPHOR AND SYMBOL
In Herman Melville's *"Bartleby the Scrivener"* (pp. 42–71), the narrator first describes Bartleby as ". . . a scrivener, the strangest I ever saw, or heard of." As the story progresses, however, the narrator and the reader alike begin to see Bartleby, with his continuous assertion of his own preferences and refusal to play by society's rules, as more than merely an odd scrivener. By the end of the story, he has in fact come to represent humanity itself, both for the narrator, with his final "Ah, Bartleby! Ah, humanity!" and for the reader, who sees his destiny as the destiny of the individual in a modern bureaucratic society. This representation of one thing by another is the essential characteristic of all the figures of speech.

Most figures of speech are variations on the metaphor, and if we understand how it works, we will understand the rest. Following the practice of the critic I. A. Richards, we can divide the metaphor into three parts: the "tenor" is the thing being described; the "vehicle" is the image the tenor is compared to; the "meaning" is the point of the comparison, the similarity between tenor and vehicle. In *"Bartleby the Scrivener,"* the vehicle of Bartleby is applied to the tenor of the modern individual in mass society with the meaning that the fate of the individual in such a society is not a pleasant one. In the simplest metaphors, the nature of the comparison being made is perfectly clear. Alexander Pope tells us that at *"Timon's Villa"* "his building is a Town" and his "pond an Ocean" (p. 505). The master of the house, on the other hand, is "A puny insect, shiv'ring at a breeze!" All here is so clear that we can construct a chart:

tenor		meaning		vehicle
building is	so remarkable in its	*size*	that we can compare it to	a *town*
pond is		*size*		an *ocean*
master is		*puniness*		an *insect*

More complex metaphors cannot be charted so easily. Dennis Brutus's *"Night-song: City"* gives us the image of police cars that "cockroach through the tunnel streets"(p. 747) of a South African shantytown. Here we know the tenor and the vehicle, but what shall we say the meaning is? Is a police car like a cockroach because its appearance is black and buglike? Because it is a despised intruder in (or among) people's homes? Because it crawls through the streets that are dim, narrow, filthy and crooked like the tunnels insects find behind walls and under floors?

Such metaphors approach the rather hazy border that divides metaphor from symbol. The "vehicle" (the cockroach) is becoming so significant in its own right, so laden with meaning, that it points to several meanings in the tenor. We would probably not call it a symbol, however, because its presence in the poem depends on the presence of the police car; it has no independent existence, it is merely a rhetorical figure. A "fixed symbol" like the garden in Milton's *"Paradise Lost"* (pp. 479–489) is almost indistinguishable from this sort of metaphor. The garden (vehicle) represets good (tenor) because within it are attributes of God such as order, harmony, and the control of wilderness or chaos, itself an attribute of evil (meaning).

The distinction between metaphor and symbol is easier to see when the symbol is "freer." Look at Louise Bogan's poem *"The Dragonfly"* (p. 732) and you will find an image that is tied neither to a particular tenor nor to a particular meaning. Bogan's dragonfly, is a thing represented in its own right and not reduced to an illustration of some abstract meaning. Tenors and meanings may attach themselves to it, but it does not exist solely to carry them (it is no longer merely a vehicle). Yet Bogan writes about the dragonfly in a way that invites the meanings to attach themselves: the dragonfly, we might say, is like the human soul because it is nearly bodiless, because it is airborne and swift, because earth "repels" it. Or we might say that it is like the personality of certain people—restless, subject to an unending hunger. Or we might say that it is like the spirit of people who are "twice-born," who "split into the heat" of the mid-summer of their lives and attack life with a sudden energy before they fall "With the other husks of summer." Symbols like Bogan's dragonfly, the birthmark in Hawthorne's *"The Birthmark"* (pp. 24–37) and the dog in José Donoso's *"Paseo"* (pp. 315–28) become magnets that attract a range of tenors and meanings so wide and complex that we cannot list them definitively.

The metaphor, we can say, is an image (or action) intended primarily to represent an aspect of some other thing. The symbol is an image intended primarily to stand in its own right and to attract meanings to itself. In *"Bartleby the Scrivener"* (pp. 42–71), Bartleby might be called a metaphor by the reader who sees him as an illustration of a warning about the fate of the individual in modern society. Another reader might view Bartleby as a symbol because he accumulates many other meanings concerning such issues as rebellion, freedom, and dignity. See also *Figures of Speech.*

Meter: the rhythmic pattern of a poem that has a regular rhythm. In some cases, this rhythmic pattern is established by including a fixed number of stresses in a line (see, for example, Gerard Manley Hopkins's *"The Windhover"* (pp. 619–20). In some cases, the pattern depends on a fixed number of syllables per line (see, for example, Marianne Moore's *"The Fish,"* pp. 684–85). More often both stress and syllables are considered. See *Sound of Poetry*.

Metonymy: see *Figures of Speech*.

Modernism: see *Literary Movements and Periods*.

Naturalism: see *Literary Movements and Periods*.

Neoclassical Period: see *Literary Movements and Periods*.

Oxymoron: see *Figures of Speech*.

Pathetic Fallacy: a term coined by John Ruskin in 1856 to refer to the practice of ascribing human emotions to inanimate objects. Though Ruskin used the term pejoratively, it is now used neutrally, to indicate a form of personification created when the speaker's emotion is so powerful that he or she seems to see it echoed by the natural world. William Blake's *"The Sick Rage"* (p. 511) is a good illustration of the pathetic fallacy.

Persona: the voice (literally the mask) which an author of a work speaks through. The persona can be the actual author, a created voice or "implied author," or a character created by the author. The persona in Walt Whitman's *"Song of Myself"* (pp. 589–90), for example, may be Whitman himself in part, but takes on universal dimension in the course of the poem. The persona in Alice Walker's *"Everyday Use"* (pp. 415–23) narrates the story while also revealing herself as a well-rounded character.

Personification: see *Figures of Speech*.

PLOT

E. M. Forster says in "The Art of the Novel" that "the king died and the queen died" is not a plot but merely a report of two incidents. "The king died, and then the queen died of grief," however, Forster will allow to be a plot. The distinction between a mere collection of incidents and a plot, then, is that within a plot one event causes another. A well-formed plot is self-contained "action," a chain of causes and effects: it begins with an event that needs no explanation; this event leads naturally to the next event, which leads to the next, and so the events tumble like carefully arranged dominoes until the last domino falls. The last domino, according to innumerable literary critics dating back to Aristotle, should *seem* like a last domino: that is, it should seem a fitting conclusion to the action the first event triggered and should leave the audience with the feeling that nothing else need follow. It is not surprising that plots very commonly end with the death or marriage of the protagonist: either event seems to satisfy the audience's curiosity about his or her fate.

Because drama depends heavily on plot, most of the terms we use to describe plot come from the writings of dramatic theorists, notably Gustav Freytag, whose "Techniques of the Drama" (1863) introduced the pyramid of rising and falling action that has become a standard tool for explaining the structure of plots.

The introduction (*a*) involves the necessary business of establishing characters, setting, and situation. Once the protagonist becomes determined to pursue a goal, complication sets in, and we have a series of encounters between the protagonist and the forces that oppose the protagonist. The conflict increases in intensity during the phase of rising action (*b*) until it reaches the reversal of fortune at the climax (*c*). Here the conflict comes to a crisis and the protagonist begins a descent to destruction in tragedy or into calm contentment in comedy. This phase of falling action (*d*) is sometimes marked by events that add an element of suspense, but it leads finally to the dénouement (*e*), called the catastrophe in tragedy, which reveals beyond doubt the fate of the protagonist.

The plot pattern of Freytag's pyramid is particularly accurate in describing the development of a classical tragedy like *"Antigone"* (pp. 942–72) Most other works will vary the pattern somewhat. The phase of falling action in most short stories, for instance, is much shorter than the phase of rising action. Some writers present their story in an order that varies from the chronological order of the plot. Alice Munro's *"Circle of Prayer"* (pp. 354–70), for example, begins in the middle of things (*in medias res* is the classical term) with the protagonist throwing a jug across the room, then establishes by a flashback the circumstances that led up to the incident. Some writers present us with double plot: in Shakespeare's *"Twelfth Night"* (pp. 1009–1082) the main plot that culminates with Viola's marriage to Orsino is interwoven with a subplot that culminates in the humiliation of Malvolio. See also *Deus ex machina, Foreshadowing, Initiation Story.*

POETIC FORMS

Repetition and variation, two sources of artistic pleasure, pull us in opposite directions when we consider the issue of poetic form. As Robert Hass points out, a regular meter, a repeated rhyme, or a pattern of stanzas can appeal to "the hope of a shapeliness in things": we crave order, and the world outside the poem sometimes seems to have very little of it. On the other hand, an invariable order can produce monotony: a hundred lines of slavishly correct iambic pentameter couplets would rock a listener to sleep and probably drain the poet of any inspiration he or she had. The attempt to reconcile (or explore) the tension between repetition and variation has led some poets, among them Walt Whitman and W. S. Merwin, to favor free (that is, unmetered) verse and an "open form" that defines itself as the poem unfolds rather than being fixed by tradition.

Those who have continued to work in the "closed forms," many of them legacies from the Middle Ages or the Renaissance, find ways to surprise the reader within the established pattern. See, for example, the discussion on Emily Dickinson's *"A Bird came down the Walk"* on page 458. This sense of surprise, however, depends on a knowledge of what the standard forms are. A basic knowledge of the **Sound of Poetry** including meter and rhyme, is assumed in the following discussion of poetic forms that occur repeatedly in *The Riverside Anthology of Literature.*

The COUPLET is simply a pair of rhymed lines. When the couplet is a self-contained statement, it is easy to remember ("Red sky at morning,/Sailor take warning"). It lends itself to wit, as in the couplet Pope wrote for a royal dog's collar: "I am his majesty's dog at Kew./Pray tell me, Sir, whose dog are you?" Though a couplet can be a self-contained poem, it more often is the basic unit of a longer poem, as in Alexander Pope's "Essay on Criticism," which is written in iambic pentameter ("heroic") couplets.

A TERCET or TRIPLET is a three-line stanza, either rhyming in every line, as in Robert Frost's "Provide, Provide" or rhyming *aba* as part of a terza rima poem like his *"Acquainted with the Night"* (p. 655). In TERZA RIMA, the unrhymed line from one stanza provides the rhyme for the next stanza, so that the rhymes link the stanzas into a chain: *aba bcb cdc*, etc.

The QUATRAIN is simply a four-line unit of poetry, usually with at least one rhyme (on the second and fourth line: *abcb*) to give it definition. See, for example, Tennyson's *"Break, Break, Break"* (p. 567). The quatrain can be more elaborately rhymed (*abab, abba,* etc.), and it is a common stanza form in traditional ballads, popular songs, and hymns. Particularly frequent users of the ballad form are William Blake, William Wordsworth, Samuel Taylor Coleridge, Emily Dickinson, and A. E. Housman.

The RHYME ROYAL is a seven-line stanza in iambic pentameter that rhymes *ababbcc*. An alexandrine (hexameter) often comprises the final line. Wordsworth's *"Resolution and Independence"* (pp. 525–28) uses the rhyme royal.

The SONNET, like the ballad, was originally written to be sung. In its basic form it is fourteen lines long, most commonly written in iambic pentameter, and rhymed on one of two patterns. The English or Shakespearian pattern is *abab cdcd efef gg;* the Italian or Petrarchan pattern is *abba abba cde cde*. The number of variations on the sonnet form is enormous, however: see, for example, Niccolò degli Albizzi's *"Prolonged Sonnet"* (pp. 713–14) and Gerard Manley Hopkins's "curtal" sonnet, *"Pied Beauty"* (p. 620).

In reading sonnets on the English pattern it is worth noting that the three quatrains often allow the poet to develop a series of three related images or ideas. The closing couplet lends itself to (or sometimes seems to demand) a neat resolution to the tensions introduced by the quatrains. The Italian sonnet breaks naturally between the first eight lines (the octave) and the last six (the sestet). Even poets who are not following the Italian form precisely may be attracted to its tradition of introducing a problem or tension in the octave and commenting on it in the sestet. See, for instance, William Wordsworth's *"The World Is Too Much with Us"* (p. 523). Among the most important sonneteers in English are Shakespeare, John Donne, Milton, William Wordsworth, John Keats, Christina Rossetti, Edwin Arlington Robinson, Robert Frost, Edna St. Vincent Millay, and Countee Cullen. Of poets represented in *The Riverside Anthology* in translation, the Chilean Pablo Neruda and the Austrian Rainer Maria Rilke are masters of the sonnet form.

The VILLANELLE is a nineteen-line poem using only two rhymes: *aba aba aba aba abba*. The first line is repeated verbatim as lines 6, 12, and 18. The third line is repeated as line 9, 15, and 19. This abstract description does little to clarify the form and nothing to show the emotional effect it can have when masterfully done. See Elizabeth Bishop's *"One Art"* (p. 790) and Dylan Thomas's *"Do Not Go Gentle into That Good Night"* (pp. 812–13)

POINT OF VIEW

One of the most important tools of the storyteller is the ability to choose the point of view from which events will be described. In their pure form, the principal points of view can be seen as vertices of a triangle. At one corner is the omniscient point of view, in which the author freely uses all that he or she knows about the world of the story, moving into and out of the minds of characters at will and also making observations that no character in the story is capable of making. This method is commonly used in tales like the Grimms' *"The Juniper Tree"* (pp. 16–23). At another corner of the triangle is the dramatic point of view, so named because it is the natural perspective of the dramatic performance. The writer limits his or her observations to what the senses of an objective observer can take in; the actions and spoken words of the characters are recorded, therefore, but not their thoughts. The purely dramatic point of view is very rare in fiction, but Ernest Hemingway's

"Hills Like White Elephants" (pp. 229–34) employs it, limiting the reader to only what is objectively seen and heard by the narrator. At the third corner of the triangle is the limited point of view, which restricts itself to the observations of a single character in the story. First person stories are generally limited in this way (see Elizabeth Tallent's *"No One's a Mystery,"* pp. 10–12).

It is unusual for a modern short story or novel to use any of the three points of view purely. The most common perspective for fiction is, in fact, a hybrid called the limited omniscient point of view. This mixed method allows the writer to descend into the consciousness of characters so that the reader can see the world through their eyes, but it also allows her to escape from their limited horizons to make an observation on her own behalf or to move the story along with simple exposition.

The descent from omniscience into the consciousness of a character is like the movement from the perspective of the general looking at the map of the battle to that of the soldier at the front. The soldier's view is in some ways more realistic, since he sees the face of battle; but it can be less reliable since he sees only a part of the field and may conclude that the battle is being won even at the moment that, just out of sight, the enemy is surrounding him. One of the pleasures of reading fiction is looking at the world through the eyes of a naive or unreliable narrator like Sylvia in Toni Cade Bambara's *"The Lesson"* (pp. 400–407) and watching her understanding of what she sees gradually increase.

Protagonist: in a play or story, the principal actor or character, whose pursuit of a goal provides the work with its plot. The protagonist is not necessarily a hero, because the leading figure in a work often is not endowed with heroic qualities. Creon best represents the protagonist in Sophocles' *"Antigone"* (pp. 942–72), although Antigone may obtain the audience's greater sympathy. See also *Antagonist*.

Quatrain: See *Poetic Forms*.

Renaissance: See *Literary Movements and Periods*.

Rhyme: a term often synonymous with true rhyme (see *Sound of Poetry*). Variations on true rhyme include double-rhyme (plaster/master) and triple rhyme (admonish you/astonish you). Poets since Emily Dickinson have often substituted assonance (wave/sail) or consonance (wave/sieve) for true rhyme, a practice called half-rhyme, near rhyme, or slant-rhyme. Some, like Marianne Moore, have also rhymed on an unstressed syllable, a practice called light rhyme (full/eagle).

Romanticism: See *Literary Movements and Periods*.

Rhyme Royal: See *Poetic Forms*.

SETTING AND SCENE

Setting does for fiction (a story, play, or narrative poem) what the background does for a painting. Both establish a fixed context of detail against which the characters are portrayed and the action takes place. On the physical level, setting includes both general and specific geography, the state of Mississippi as well as the back porch of a house; likewise, both the era and the time of day or night are the temporal elements of setting. But the setting in a literary work, in addition, provides the cultural and psychological locale that illuminate the background and mental life of the characters.

Eudora Welty's *"Livvie"* (pp. 273–84) begins with five long paragraphs that seem to do little more than describe the setting. The opening lines, however, also establish an overwhelming sense of isolation.

> Solomon carried Livvie twenty-one miles away from her home when he married her. He carried her away up on the Old Natchez Trace into the deep country to live in his house. She was sixteen—an only girl, then. Once people said he thought nobody would ever come along there.

Soon we also learn that Solomon is an old, dying man who scarcely allows Livvie to leave his side. Yet as the paragraphs continue to describe the house, the tall scrolled rocker, the jelly glass with pretty hen feathers in it, the snow-white curtains, the pickled peaches, fig preserves, and blackberry jam, we begin to see the place as Livvie sees it despite her constant loneliness. "It was a nice house," repeated through the description, become the words of Livvie's perception. By the time we hear of Livvie's attraction to angels and fear of ghosts, the setting has introduced us to a delightful and imaginative young girl, without giving any direct description of her. The parallel between the physical setting and the character's psychology has created the illusion of a concrete world and of a real person as well.

The setting in a dramatic work is of equal importance. As in fiction, dramatic settings should parallel the psychological conditions of the characters. The setting of Samuel Beckett's *"Krapp's Last Tape"* (pp. 1336–43), for example, is a room devoid of everything but a desk, which is surrounded by darkness. This setting reflects the isolation, meaningless, and despair of Krapp.

Fiction and drama are alike in that each establishes scene as well as setting. In drama, a scene is a division of an act, but its purpose can be defined in various ways. The break between scenes may complete an action, signify an emotional break, emphasize the entrance or speech of an important character, or work as a transition. It may or may not involve a change in location, but it does require a clearing of the stage, producing a break in the action and a lapse in time. A new scene, then, creates a new setting. Defining the dramatic scene as a period of continuous action, we will find its counterpart in fiction. The short story writer creates characters and then places them in a particular situation in which action occurs. Scene change is again noted through a change in setting, a transition normally achieved by exposition. In some stories, such as Herman Melville's *"Bartleby the Scrivener"* (pp. 42–71), the progression of scenes builds intensity (see *Plot*). In others, such as Alice Munro's *"Circle of Prayer"* (pp. 354–70), the repetition of a particular scene adds both depth and unity.

SHORT STORY

We have all grown so familiar with the short story that we tend to think of it as a form that is somehow natural or spontaneous. In fact, though storytelling is part of human nature, the literary short story is an invented or developed form, not much more natural than the sonnet or the villanelle, though considerably harder to define. Among the more important "inventors" of the form were Nathaniel Hawthorne, Edgar Allan Poe, and Guy de Maupassant, and if we look at what these writers set out to do, we will gain a sense of how much the short story differs from the story that happens to be short.

Hawthorne's fiction, long or short, borrows from the fable a tendency to moralize, but adds to this an exploration of psychological truths that defy neat moral application. *"The Birthmark"* (pp. 24–37), for example, seems to have a simple moral concerning the danger of aspiring to perfection in a world defined by imperfection. In Hawthorne's hands, however, the story defies such simplistic explanation; within this didactic frame is a complex exploration of the human relationships with love and knowledge.

When, in 1842, Poe reviewed Hawthorne's "Twice-Told Tales," he established an explicit definition of the short story: it should occupy no more than two hours reading time and it should encompass "a certain unique or single effect." Poe insisted that the short story was not a pared-down novel, any more than a lyric poem was a shortened epic. Because the story was short enough to be taken in at a sitting, the reader could keep it all in mind, could see how each part related to each other part, and could be kept in an unbroken mood of excitement, dread, anticipation, horror, or sorrow. Everything should work toward the effect, description and dialogue no less than action. Charles Baudelaire, who read both Poe's literary works and his critical writing with interest, took Poe's views on the short story to their logical conclusion when he developed such prose poems as *"Knock Down the Poor!"* (pp. 1621–22).

Although it seems implicit in Poe's definition of the short story, a third characteristic of the genre did not manifest itself fully until Maupassant's enormously popular stories began to exert their influence in the 1880s and 1890s. This characteristic is an absolute economy of style that strips away every detail or word not essential to the story's "unique or single effect."

If we combine Hawthorne's interest in exploring psychological and moral truth with Poe's interest in a "poetic" unity and Maupassant's insistence on a lean, economical style, we have a fairly good definition of the central qualities of the short story. Anton Chekhov's *"The Lady with the Pet Dog"* (pp. 124–38) and Nadine Gordimer's *"The Catch"* (pp. 304–14) display these qualities to great advantage and are close to the heart of the genre. This is not to say that being near the heart is essential to success. Toni Cade Bambara's *"The Lesson"* (pp. 400–407) moves in the direction of the novel, where unity of effect is often traded for variety and a reflection of the bustle of life. Virginia Woolf's *"Solid Objects"* (pp. 168–73) and Gabriel García Márquez's *"A Very Old Man with Enormous Wings"* (348–54) have turned away from the moral intentness that Hawthorne brought to the genre. Margaret Atwood's *"Rape Fantasies"* (pp. 407–15) uses a narrative technique that Maupassant would surely find uneconomical.

Nonetheless, the central qualities of the short story are so firmly established that even writers who choose to avoid them seem to be defining their art by that act. See also *Plot, Fairy Tale*.

Simile: See *Figures of Speech*.

Sonnet: See *Poetic Forms*.

THE SOUND OF POETRY

When the poet W. H. Auden was an undergraduate at Oxford University he heard Professor J. R. R. Tolkien read a passage of Old English poetry. The passage was complete nonsense to Auden, who had not studied Old English, but the sound enchanted him. An encounter like Auden's with the music of a poem as a thing separate from the meaning is a good starting point when we study the sound in poetry. Consider the first two stanzas of Lewis Carroll's "Jabberwocky":

> 'Twas brillig, and the slithy* toves
>   Did gyre* and gimble in the wabe
> All mimsy were the borogoves,
>   And the mome raths outgrabe.
>
> "Beware the Jabberwock, my son!
>   The jaws that bite, the claws that catch!
> Beware the Jubjub bird, and shun
>   The frumious Bandersnatch."

There is very little to understand here, but a great deal to listen to, and thousands of people who have no idea what the words "brillig" and "slithy" and "gimble" mean remember them because they fit so well into the structure of vowel and consonant sounds that stitch the poem together. Assonance, the repetition of vowel sounds, runs through this entire quatrain: listen to the short "i" in

> br*i*ll*i*g g*i*mble m*i*msy.

Even more extensive is the use of repeated consonant sounds:

> *b*rilli*g* gim*b*le *m*i*m*sey *b*oro*g*oves *m*ome out*g*ra*b*e.

These connections are more obvious in some cases than others. Alliteration, the repetition of the first consonant sound in a word, can be particularly conspicuous ("claws that catch"). True rhyme, which requires an exact match in the vowel of a stressed syllable and any subsequent consonant (t*oves*/borog*oves*, w*abe*/outgr*abe*), is, of course, the most obvious sound echo of all. We expect it most often at the end of verses, but internal rhyme ("The j*aws* that bite, the cl*aws* that catch!") is not uncommon.

In addition to echoing each other in a way that unites the poem, the sounds of vowels and consonants combine in ways that are sweet (euphonious) or harsh (cacophonous) to our ears. Euphony and cacophony exist in the ear of the listener; they are subjective. It is hard to say how much they depend on meaning rather than pure sound: if *murmur* sounds pleasant and *murder* sounds harsh, the difference must depend more on definition than phonetics. Nonetheless, a Bandersnatch sounds like an ugly creature, even if we have never seen one. It seems that certain consonants and clusters of consonants *(ck, g, gr, k, scr, sk, st, str, tch)* sound harsh, especially when they are crowded together without the leavening of long, open vowels. Open vowels and such liquid consonants as *l, m, n,* and *r* tend to be more pleasing. When John Milton wants the corrupt clergymen of "Lycidas" to sound cacophonous, he says that their songs "Grate on their scrannel pipes of wretched straw." When Robert Herrick wants to make his Julia's voice sound euphonious, he says that it is capable of "Melting melodious notes to lutes of amber."

Euphony and cacophony may be indirectly related to onomatopoeia, the use of words that imitate sounds or that match the sound with the sense. *Snap* and *scratch,* for instance, seem to originate in the imitation of abrupt, harsh sounds. *Snatch,* as in "Bandersnatch," is not itself onomatopoeic, but its final syllable is made up of sounds that recollect some of the grating noises of the world. In the final lines of Alfred, Lord Tennyson's *"Come Down, O Maid"* (p. 569) we get onomatopoeia

---

* *Slithy* is pronounced with a long *i,* as in *slimy; gyre* in *gyroscope.*

linked with euphony: "the moaning of doves," and the "murmuring of innumerable bees."

The aspect of a poem's sound most laboriously studied in literature classes is its rhythm. What makes the study so laborious and frustrating is that the rhythm can be very complex, and the system we use to analyze it is complicated without being complete. Linguists can identify at least half a dozen factors that determine the rhythm of ordinary prose. When we add to these factors the special demands of the poetic line, we have a very complex situation, indeed. To simplify the situation, we limit our attention to the regular beat of syllables per line or to accents (stresses*) per line, or both.

Our two stanzas from "Jabberwocky" contain a fairly fixed number of syllables: 8,8,8,6 in the first stanza, 8,8,8,7 in the second. (The third and fourth stanzas, by the way, are 8,8,9,6 and 8,8,8,6: that the slight irregularities are not *heard* as errors indicates that the fingers and the ear experience rhythm differently.) Which of these syllables are stressed? Since stress is related to (not quite synonymous with) volume, we could approach this question by reading the poem into a tape recorder, then watching the needle on the volume indicator as we play it back. Here is my reading of the first stanza, with volume levels noted above each syllable:

$$25 \quad 30 \; 10 \quad 15 \quad 10 \quad 25 \; 20 \; 25$$
'Twas bril lig, and the slith y toves
$$15 \quad 60 \quad 25 \quad 40 \quad 20 \; 25 \; 25 \quad 50$$
Did gyre and gim ble in the wabe
$$45 \; 50 \; 20 \; 20 \quad 15 \; 60 \; 15 \quad 20$$
All mim sy were the bo ro goves,
$$20 \; 20 \quad 60 \quad 50 \; 35 \quad 40$$
And the mome raths out grabe.

Others would undoubtedly read the poem with a different stress, depending partly on their notions of the "meaning" of some words. I read *brillig* as a relatively insignificant word, equal to *morning*. If I read it as a more important word like *ghastly* or *horrid*, it would get more stress.

The traditional method of scansion is to divide the line into feet, a process that can be made simpler by some toe-tapping: the foot is presumably so named because if we were to dance or march to the rhythm of the verse, our foot would strike the ground one time for each of these units. We would expect our foot to hit on a stressed syllable, of course, and some theorists argue therefore that every foot must contain a stress. Traditionally we mark the more heavily stressed syllables in each foot with an accent mark (/) and less stressed with a droop. (⌣).

'Twas bril/lig, and/the slith/y toves
Did gyre/and gim/ble in/the wabe
All mim/sy were/the bo/rogoves,

Notice that the traditional method corresponds much more closely to our actual reading in line 2 than in any other. Traditional scansion is a very imperfect way of recording the actual rhythm of the line as we read it; it usually records a compromise between actual rhythm and a more regular rhythm toward which the line tends. The fourth line is so irregular that it makes traditional scansion difficult. We might try

$$\breve{} \ \breve{} \ / \quad / \quad \breve{} \ /$$
And the/mome/raths/outgrabe.

which corresponds well to what we hear, or

$$\breve{} \ \breve{} \ / \quad / \quad \breve{} \ /$$
And the/mome raths/outgrabe.

which fits the conventions more neatly. At this point, the rules of scansion become as cumbersome as the instructions on a tax form. We all grow up with an instinct for the rhythms of the language; if the sheet music becomes too confusing to us, we can lay it aside and play by ear.

Each foot available in the traditional method has a name: iamb ($\breve{}/$), trochee ($/\breve{}$), anapest ($\breve{}\,\breve{}/$), dactyl ($/\breve{}\,\breve{}$), spondee ($/\!/$), pyrrhic ($\breve{}\,\breve{}$). The stanza above could therefore be described as

> spondee/iamb/iamb/iamb
> iamb/iamb/iamb/iamb
> spondee/pyrrhic/iamb/iamb
> pyrrhic/spondee/iamb

Or, scanned by other readers, it might be

iamb/iamb/iamb/iamb	OR	iamb/pyrrhic/iamb/iamb
iamb/iamb/iamb/iamb		iamb/iamb/pyrrhic/iamb
iamb/iamb/iamb/iamb		iamb/pyrrhic/iamb/iamb
pyrrhic/trochee/spondee		pyrrhic/spondee/iamb

Notice that the last reading reduces the number of stresses in the lines and makes them swing along like a chant (see *Dipodic Meter*). The whole poem could be described as one in which each stanza consists of three lines of iambic tetrameter (*tetra* is Greek for four) followed by one of iambic trimeter. Some lines, of course, vary from this pattern, but the pattern itself is quite clear. Regularly metered poetic lines can thus be described by a binomial system where the first word designates the predominant foot (iambic, trochaic, anapestic, dactylic) and the second gives the number of feet, using Greek prefixes: monometer, dimeter, trimeter, tetrameter, pentameter, hexameter, heptameter. See related entries on *Meter, Poetic Forms, Rhyme.*

Stream of consciousness: a technique in which the writer assumes the point of view of a character so completely that every passing thought or impression of the character is recorded.

Substitution: the replacement of one metrical foot (an iamb, for example) by another (a trochee, for example). This variation in stress is produced when the natural speech rhythm of a verse passage conflicts with the rhythm created by the underlying meter. The first two lines of William Wordsworth's sonnet *"Composed upon Westminster Bridge"* (p. 524) illustrate such a substitution.

$$\text{Earth has/not anything/to show/more fair:}$$
$$\text{Dull would/he be/of soul/who could/pass by}$$

The prose sense of the passage here demands that stress be placed on *Earth* and *Dull* even though a mechanically iambic reading of the lines would leave them unstressed. One effect of such a substitution is to vary the rhythm and avoid monotony. Another effect is to highlight the rhetorical emphasis that caused the substitution. The attentive reader conscious of the underlying iambic rhythm registers the displaced stress with special force and so thinks harder about Wordsworth's meaning and feeling. The stress on *Earth* then seems so strong as to suggest an antithesis (*Earth* has nothing to show more fair; *heaven* might). The special stress on *Dull* seems to add to its force (*very* dull). See *Sound of Poetry*.

Surrealism: see *Literary Movements and Periods*.

Symbol: see *Figures of Speech* and *Metaphor and Symbol*.

Symbolism: see *Literary Movements and Periods*.

Synecdoche: see *Figures of Speech*.

Tercet: see *Poetic Forms*.

Theater of the Absurd: a term applied to the works of several dramatists of the 1950s who expounded the absurdity of both humanity and the universe. Influenced by the farcical comedy of the Renaissance, by Surrealism, and by the philosophy of French writer Albert Camus, dramatists such as Harold Pinter and Samuel Beckett presented human beings as ridiculous creatures attempting to make sense of an irrational world. To emphasize their existential beliefs, the dramatists created plays that defy many of the conventions that give drama its apparent order, so that both their content and their form reflect a loss of direction and purpose.

Theme: the central idea of a literary work. Generally we think of this theme as a general statement about the human condition expressable in a sentence. One might state the theme of Edwin Arlington Robinson's *"Richard Cory"* (pp. 642–43) as "Even the most apparently fortunate person may be on the brink of despair." Too often, naive readers assume that every literary work exists solely for the purpose of illustrating a theme. In fact, good literary works often succeed with themes so faint or ambiguous that readers cannot agree on what they are, and many writers say that the theme cannot be completely stated except as it is embodied in the work. Nonetheless, most literary works derive partly from the writer's desire to deal with general truths, and the attempt to state the theme (even when it is impossible to do so definitively) can help us see what large issues lie beneath the surface of the poem, play, or story. See *Tone*.

TONE

Literature textbooks usually define tone as the author's implied attitude toward the audience and the subject. This literary definition has its roots in a more general meaning of the word, the meaning that a mother has in mind when she says to her daughter, "Don't take that tone with me, young lady!" The tone of a statement cannot be settled by *what* was said; the question is, *in what spirit* were the words spoken?

The tone of a remark made in conversation is relatively easy to establish because we can hear the speaker's inflections and see her gestures and facial expressions. The tone of a remark made by a character in a play or story will very often be clarified by the context or by the author's comment. Arthur Miller's *"Death of a Salesman"* (pp. 1345–1426), for example, is sprinkled with stage directions to help establish the spirit in which the character speaks:

> Willy, *(now assured, with rising power):* Oh, Ben, that's the whole beauty of it! I see it like a diamond, shining in the dark, hard and rough. . . .

In his very next speech, however, we see

> Willy, *(suddenly fearful)* . . .

and the tone has completely changed (p. 1418).

The author's tone is much more difficult to detect than the character's. Even when we know that Willy's attitude is assured or fearful, how do we know what Miller's attitude toward Willy is?

Clearly, the author can establish a tone by speaking directly to the audience. When the author chooses not to address the audience directly, he or she may delegate to one of the characters the role of making judgments that establish the tone. In *"Medea"* (pp. 973–1008), for instance, Jason makes a long and clever speech justifying his actions in abandoning his wife so that he may marry the king's daughter. So effective is the speech that it might sway the audience, might give the impression that Euripides' sympathies are with Jason and that he approves of his actions. The chorus, however, immediately speaks (p. 986):

> Chorus: Jason, though you have made this speech of yours look well,
> Still, I think, even though others do not agree,
> You have betrayed your wife and are acting badly.

The judgment of the chorus leaves little doubt about Euripides' tone of disapproval. The narrator in a story like José Donoso's *"Paseo"* (pp. 315–28) functions almost as a chorus. We should be careful, though, not to assume that the chorus-figure in a story reflects the attitudes of the writer precisely. Toni Cade Bambara begins *"The Lesson"* with a sentence that separates her somewhat from the narrator of the story: "Back in the days when everyone was old and stupid or young and foolish and me and Sugar were the only ones just right, this lady . . . " (p. 400). We see immediately that hiding behind the point of view of the young narrator will be the mature perspective of a grown woman: the tone will be humorous, the author's attitude toward her protagonist will be a combination of admiration and condescension.

When the writer does not establish the tone by direct comment and does not establish a character clearly intended to register his or her values, we can apprehend the tone only by looking very carefully at the style and substance of what is said. Alfred, Lord Tennyson's *"Ulysses"* (pp. 565–67), for example, establishes its highly serious tone by **diction** that is uniformly elevated and by the use of blank verse, a form long used for contemplative and heroic poems. Robert Frost's *"Departmental"* (pp. 656–57), on the other hand, establishes its humorous tone partly by a combination of high and low diction and partly by a number of outrageous rhymes (any/antennae; Formic McCormic; Jerry/Janizary; atwiddle/middle). See also *Irony.*

TRAGEDY

The first tragedies were religious dramas performed before the citizens of ancient Greek city-states, assembled to consider the largest questions of the human struggle with destiny. The most notable of the Greek tragedies were performed in Athens in the fifth century B.C. and reflected an attitude that helped define Greek culture and gave the Athenian citizen an elevated view of human dignity. Aristotle, defining tragedy about 350 B.C., emphasized its highly serious tone and its plot, which carries a person of extraordinary virtue from a state of happiness to a state of misery. This downfall is caused by what Aristotle calls *hamartia,* an error or frailty—very often the error of pride. Error leads the hero to *anagnorsis* (recognition of the dark truth of his or her life) and *peripeteia* (reversal of good fortune). Though this is hardly the outline of a cheerful plot, Aristotle found the effect of tragedy to be finally uplifting. The audience gains a renewed sense of human dignity by the nobility with which the protagonist faces the truth, and experiences a feeling of *catharsis* (purging of the emotions of fear and pity that the play creates).

Exactly what Aristotle meant by *catharsis* is hard to say, but the purgation may come from the shape of the play. The audience begins by seeing the precarious order of the individual and community life shattered by dangerous emotions and injustice. In the end, the audience sees order restored: the suffering of the protagonist has led to new knowledge that helps create this new order.

Aristotle's description of tragedy applies most clearly to the plays of Sophocles, who was confident about the justice of the gods and the possibility of redemptive knowledge leading to a new order. Euripides and most other tragedians, ancient and modern, have been less confident. A useful supplement to Aristotle's definition—useful in examining both ancient and modern drama—is Friedrich Hegel's notion that tragedy comes from the conflict of two almost equally powerful principles of life. Certainly no single definition will adequately cover all the works that have been called tragic. Shakespeare's tragedies, for instance, mix scenes of high seriousness (like *"Hamlet,"* Act 3, scene 3, pp. 1148–49 where the prince contemplates killing Claudius) with scenes of comic relief (like *"Hamlet,"* Act 5, scene 1, pp.1176–80. where the prince trades wisecracks with the gravediggers). Shakespearian tragedy also places less emphasis than classical tragedy on unity of plot (certainly it ignores the classical "unities" that required the play to represent a single day, a single setting, and a single chain of causes and effects). It places more emphasis, however, on the realistic representation of the central characters.

Modern tragedies sometimes (as in Arthur Miller's *"Death of a Salesman"* (pp. 1345–1426) preserve the unity of plot, the high seriousness, the *anagnorsis* (discovery), *peripeteia* (reversal), and *catharsis* (purging) of Greek tragedy. In a democratic society, however, as Miller points out in "Tragedy and the Common Man," the protagonist will naturally be born without royal status, and his or her fall will produce domestic tragedy without the political upheaval we see in Greek or Shakespearian tragedy. Many other modern plays, like Anton Chekhov's *"The Three Sisters"* (pp. 1263–1319), blend a note of tragedy into compositions that defy the neat traditional distinction between tragedy and comedy. See also *Tragicomedy* and *Melodrama.*

Tragicomedy: a term that is, in its narrow sense, used to characterize a play that seems for most of its length to be a **tragedy,** but that by a sudden reversal of fortune achieves the happy ending appropriate to **comedy.** Shakespeare's "Measure for Measure" would fit this narrow definition very well if the audience were not informed until the final act that the Duke is in Vienna, disguised as a Friar, ready to save the day. Were this information withheld, the audience would have reason to fear that Angelo might actually have his way with Isabella and that Claudio might actually be executed; this fear would be suddenly lifted by the apparently miraculous appearance of the Duke. Clearly this sort of tragicomedy is related to **melodrama.** In a broader sense, tragicomedy is applied to plays which balance tragic and comic elements so closely that neither clearly predominates. In this sense, both "Measure for Measure," and *"The Three Sisters"* (pp. 1263–1319) might be classed tragicomedies.

Understatement: see *Figures of Speech.*

Villanelle: see *Poetic Forms.*

Voice: see *Persona.*

Well-made Play: a type of play, popular in France during the nineteenth century, with a prescribed orderly structure. The plot had to make use of a secret, revealed at the climax to produce a reversal and a favorable ending. The suspense, then, was commonly created by a misplaced document, a mistaken identity, or precise, timely entrances and exits. Finally, a battle of wits had to lead the protagonist to success so that a neat, logical resolution could end the play. Sometimes these characteristics were incorporated into each act as well as into the overall play. Henrik Ibsen directed several well-made plays before he began writing his own drama. His plays contain elements of the formula, but do not adhere to it slavishly. Today the term refers to the neatly constructed plays that loosely carry out the tradition.

Wit: a quality that has been defined very differently in different periods of literary history, largely because most writers want to claim they have it. In the early seventeenth century, poets like John Donne cultivated a species of "Metaphysical" wit that involved unlikely and even far-fetched comparisons. Thus, in *"The Good-Morrow"* (pp. 471–72) a lover's eyes are compared to the earth's hemispheres. The comparison ingeniously brings together two otherwise unrelated ideas: that the curve of the eyes echoes the curve of the earth, and that a person looking into the eyes of his lover is seeing everything that counts in the world. If we were to define wit narrowly, we would probably say that it is the writer's ability to bring together such ideas and to have the comparison both surprise us and please us by its appropriateness.

Later in the seventeenth and throughout the eighteenth century, poets like Alexander Pope rejected the Metaphysical conception of wit because they believed it violently joined together ideas and images that were separate in nature. They attempted to replace the older concept with something more consistent with the neoclassical ideal of precise observation of men and manners:

> True wit is nature to advantage dress'd,
> What oft was thought, but ne'er so well express'd.
> (Pope, "Essay on Criticism")

The modern conception of wit includes elements of both the Metaphysical and the neoclassical, and almost always involves humor as well. W. H. Auden, Edna St. Vincent Millay, Robert Frost, and Richard Wilbur are among the wittier poets of the twentieth century. Samuel Beckett is notable for the wit of his plays, and Jorge Luis Borges, Gabriel García Márquez, and Flannery O'Connor for the wit of their stories.

Writing About Literature

A textbook's general principles on writing about literature are not likely to help you much when you sit down to write a paper of your own. It is as hard to learn to write from general instructions as it is to learn to draw a still life or shoot a hook shot from general instructions. On the other hand, a series of example essays thrown together without guiding principles can be as useless as a drawer full of odd socks. The plan of this chapter is, therefore, to alternate between general observations ("the hook shot has five parts") and demonstration ("now watch me do it").

A word of warning about this method is in order before we proceed. The hook shot has one clear and undisputable goal, and its method of execution varies only slightly from one competent basketball player to another. The essay about literature may have a number of goals: some teachers may value originality more than careful research, others vice-versa; some may insist that the work be discussed without direct reference to your reaction as a reader, others may prefer that your personal reactions be taken into consideration. And the writing methods of one individual will naturally vary from those of another. The advice given in this chapter should, therefore, be read cautiously, as a basis for further discussion between yourself and your teacher.

In the course of this chapter you will be looking at two drafts and two completed essays based on the following prose-poem by Charles Baudelaire.

Knock Down the Poor!

I had provided myself with the popular books of the day
(this was sixteen or seventeen years ago), and for two weeks I
had never left my room. I am speaking now of those books
that treat of the art of making nations happy, wise and rich in
twenty-four hours. I had therefore digested—swallowed, I
should say—all the lucubrations of all the authorities on the
happiness of society—those who advise the poor to become
slaves, and those who persuade them that they are all
dethroned kings. So it is not astonishing if I was in a state of
mind bordering on stupidity or madness. Only it seemed to
me that deep in my mind, I was conscious of an obscure germ
of an idea, superior to all the old wives' formulas whose
dictionary I had just been perusing. But it was only the idea
of an idea, something infinitely vague. And I went out with a
great thirst, for a passionate taste for bad books engenders a
proportionate desire for the open air and for refreshments.

As I was about to enter a tavern, a beggar held out his hat
to me, and gave me one of those unforgettable glances which
might overturn thrones if spirit could move matter, and if the

eyes of a mesmerist could ripen grapes. At the same time I heard a voice whispering in my ear, a voice I recognized: it was that of a good Angel, or of a good Demon, who is always following me about. Since Socrates had his good Demon, why should I not have my good Angel, and why should I not have the honour, like Socrates, of obtaining my certificate of folly, signed by the subtle Lelut and by the sage Baillarger? There is this difference between Socrates' Demon and mine: his did not appear except to defend, warn or hinder him, whereas mine deigns to counsel, suggest, or persuade. Poor Socrates had only a prohibitive Demon; mine is a great master of affirmations, mine is a Demon of action, a Demon of combat. And his voice was now whispering to me: "He alone is the equal of another who proves it, and he alone is worthy of liberty who knows how to obtain it."

Immediately, I sprang at the beggar. With a single blow of my fist, I closed one of his eyes, which became, in a second, as big as a ball. In breaking two of his teeth I split a nail; but being of a delicate constitution from birth, and not used to boxing, I didn't feel strong enough to knock the old man senseless; so I seized the collar of his coat with one hand, grasped his throat with the other, and began vigorously to beat his head against a wall. I must confess that I had first glanced around carefully, and had made certain that in this lonely suburb I should find myself, for a short while, at least, out of immediate danger from the police.

Next, having knocked down this feeble man of sixty with a kick in the back sufficiently vicious to have broken his shoulder blades, I picked up a big branch of a tree which lay on the ground, and beat him with the persistent energy of a cook pounding a tough steak.

All of a sudden—O miracle! O happiness of the philosopher proving the excellence of his theory!—I saw this ancient carcass turn, stand up with an energy I should never have suspected in a machine so badly out of order, and with a glance of hatred which seemed to me of good omen, the decrepit ruffian hurled himself upon me, blackened both my eyes, broke four of my teeth, and with the same tree-branch, beat me to a pulp. Thus by an energetic treatment, I had restored to him his pride and his life.

Then I motioned to him to make him understand that I considered the discussion ended, and getting up, I said to him, with all the satisfaction of a Sophist of the Porch: "Sir, you are my equal! Will you do me the honour of sharing my purse, and will you remember, if you are really philanthropic, that you must apply to all the members of your profession, when they seek alms from you, the theory it has been my misfortune to practice on your back?"

He swore to me that he had understood my theory, and that he would carry out my advice.

STEP 1: FIND A GOOD PROBLEM

Most of us read a literary work, like it or dislike it, and have no particular desire to complicate either our like or dislike by too much analysis. This is a valid response. Many things that are significant about a work of art require no analysis: they are self-evident to every competent reader. If we have read *"Twelfth Night"* (pp. 1009–1082) no one needs to tell us that a great deal of the pleasure of the play comes from the use of disguises. Important as this self-evident truth might be, it is not likely to be a basis for a good essay. A student writing on the thesis " 'Knock Down the Poor!' describes an action most people find offensive" might seem to be on safe ground. In fact, he or she is in great peril of spending several boring hours producing a paper that will bore the teacher. An essay about literature needs to demonstrate something about the work that *needs* demonstration.

A good way to find a topic to write about is to concentrate on what you do not understand about a work rather than what you do understand. Find a difficulty or ambiguity you could not resolve on the basis of your first reading. Sometimes your teacher will assign topics that point toward such a problem ("What is the tone in Baudelaire's 'Knock Down the Poor!'?"), but it is up to you to discover why this problem *is* problematic and interesting, to put your lack of understanding to good use. Discussion inside class or out can be a great help: sometimes an hour spent talking with a friend about a literary work will uncover a number of interesting problems. Usually, though, the serious search for a problem will lead us to another sort of conversation, one we have with ourselves on paper.

It is an unhappy fact that for most writers every finished page is preceded by other pages that go into the wastebasket or the desk drawer. The mind is a leaky bucket, and if we try to sort out a paper without committing anything to writing, our thoughts trickle out about as fast as they trickle in, leaving us very nearly where we started. Some writers solve this problem by doing several drafts, each written *as if* it were the last, each collecting thoughts that can be carefully scrutinized because they have been gotten out of the leaky bucket and onto the page. Others write their early drafts very informally, sometimes as journal entries or "free writings" meant for their eyes only. Such private jottings may be written without much attention to form or coherence. Here are mine on "Knock Down the Poor!"

Example 1: Freewriting to Discover a Problem

What interests me most about this story is the tone. In some ways it seems like Baudelaire intends just to shock us—sort of a man-bites-dog story to get our attention. The idea that he can seriously boast about beating a beggar is hardly credible, unless what he is boasting about is his ability to boast about it— a sort of intellectual or moral one-upsmanship. This would be consistent with the talk in the first paragraph about the "popular books" about poverty. He may be simply showing that he is above fashion.

> The wording here is far less formal, less correct, than it will be in the final paper.

But is this all, and is it serious? Sometimes Baudelaire is clearly just being funny. The bit about the passion for reading bad books making him thirsty,

> A sentence fragment— unacceptable in a final paper, natural here.

for instance. I don't think this a good joke, but I think I can see that Baudelaire does, or (since the whole tone is so murky) that his protagonist is making a joke that he (the protagonist) thinks is funny, though Baudelaire may find it feeble. How closely does Baudelaire identify with the protagonist? How can we tell?

Speculation about the author's intent must be more cautious in a critical paper. In a free writing, it is often useful.

Better humor, I think, when Baudelaire/protagonist admits that he looks around for the police before beating the beggar, or when he admits that he is too feeble to do a good job of beating him. And, of course, the whole thing is a sort of shaggy-dog story. We can't believe that such a thing would happen.

Another fragment.

Nonetheless, I think there is something serious here, and beneath all its outrageousness, the point is worth making. Sticking out at us as moral is the good Angel's statement that "He alone is the equal of another who proves it, and he alone is worthy of liberty who knows how to obtain it." Maybe. Actually, the statement stands just to one side of what the story says to me. Dorothy H. once told me (accusing, in a friendly way) that when I went out of my way to spare people's feelings, I was actually being condescending and avoiding dealing with them as equals and friends. Her view was that real friends could give it to each other with both barrels, criticism, affection, anger, feeling always the implied compliment of not holding back. Baudelaire may be serious about applying his story to the problem of the poor, but I feel it moving out to other things.

An entirely personal and idiosyncratic reaction. Useful here, forbidden in the final paper.

Lots of things I don't know about in this story. Socrates' Demon. Is Baudelaire using Demon and Angel interchangeably. I think the Greek word is probably Daemon, and means something neutral like spirit. Where, if anywhere, was this story published in B's lifetime? Who are Lelut and Baillarger? Psychologists?

The question with the question mark carelessly omitted will turn out to be very important.

As a finished paper, this effort would rate a flat "F." It is ungrammatical, incoherent, and given to private observations that have little to do with the work. But in the half-hour I spent writing it, I found the germs of the essays that will follow.

STEP 2: WRITE A DRAFT THAT HAS THE FORM AND SUBSTANCE OF A FINAL PRODUCT

Just what the proper "form and substance" will be depends on your teacher's expectations, some of which will be made explicit by the assignment. Many of these expectations, however, may be so obvious to your teacher that he or she will not

1624   **Writing About Literature**

mention them explicitly. They are the usually unstated conventions of writing about literature.

Bear in mind when you sit down to write a serious draft that your teacher will eventually read the final product by the standards of a well-established profession. Because your teacher knows you as an individual, he or she might *personally* be very interested in every aspect of your response to Baudelaire's story, including your feelings about Baudelaire's condemnation of the middle class, your thoughts on violence and human equality, and even personal anecdotes the story brings to mind. In fact, your teacher may enjoy your free-form journal entries on a story more than your more formal critical writing. But as a *professional* teaching a literature class, he or she must evaluate you on your ability to respond to the work *as literature* rather than as a springboard for non-literary thoughts.

The teacher, therefore, reads your essay as a representative of a larger professional audience that knows nothing about you personally and that is interested in your essay only insofar as it casts light on the work discussed. The members of this professional audience are assumed to have these characteristics:

- They are careful readers familiar with the work; therefore, they will not be interested in mere summary. ("Charles Baudelaire's 'Knock Down the Poor!' is the story of a man who spends two weeks alone in his room reading books that teach the poor how to be happy with their role in life. After he has read these books, he goes out for fresh air and a drink. On his way into a bar, he sees a beggar. . . . ")

- They are skeptical, and they will not accept your generalizations without adequate evidence.

- They expect a writer to be reasonably well informed. This does not mean that you have to do exhaustive research before you can hazard an opinion. It does mean, however, that you would do well to look at a few sources before you undertake an essay, even though the assignment does not call for research. In preparing to write my own draft, I did what research I could within the confines of *The Riverside Anthology*. The short biography of Baudelaire on pages 1643–44 mentions that his "dandyism" was "partly outrageous display, partly strict aesthetic discipline." The passage from his journal on page 603 shows how much "debasement of the human heart" he found in his bourgeois fellow citizens. His poems collected on pages 595–602 gave me a sense of the tone of his other writings.

- They demand objectivity. Most professionals in literature are suspicious of discussions that place too much emphasis on the emotions a work inspires rather than on the work itself ("The reader's heart is touched when . . ."). They are equally suspicious of analyses that assume too much insight into the intentions of the author ("What Baudelaire is trying to do here is . . ."). The creature on the laboratory bench, so to speak, is the literary work, not the heart of the reader or the mind of the author.

- They expect an essay that follows certain rules of behavior. The action in a literary work should be reported in present tense ("The protagonist *beats* the beggar"). Quotations from the story, poem, or play should be worked into the essay without being intrusive or overlong. Contractions and colloquialisms should be avoided. Standard terms of literary analysis ("theme," "tone") should be used where they are appropriate. The writer should refer to himself or herself ("I think," "my own feeling") sparingly, if at all.

Frankly, this is not an audience most of us feel comfortable writing for, and one of the problems of writing an effective essay about literature is to avoid losing heart when we face it. One way to keep your courage and your direction is to think of yourself as part of the audience and try to keep yourself interested.

Example 2: A First Draft on "Knock Down the Poor!"

The Theme of "Knock Down the Poor!"

The theme of Charles Baudelaire's "Knock Down the Poor!" seems on first reading to be precisely what the protagonist's Demon announces it to be midway through the prose poem: "He alone is the equal of another who proves it, and he alone is worthy of liberty who knows how to obtain it." Careful readers, however, will find reason to doubt that the theme can be so easily located or neatly expressed.

> It is standard practice to mention the name of the author and work early in the essay.

> A thesis of sorts, but see comments below.

"Knock Down the Poor!," like many of Baudelaire's other poems, involves a good deal of theatricality. Offended by what he perceives to be the hypocrisies of bourgeois life, Baudelaire puts himself in a pose that will offend bourgeois sensibilities. The prose poem begins with an irritant, the "popular books" that middle-class Frenchmen used to salve their consciences. Disgust with books "that advise the poor to become willing slaves" or that encourage them to live in a fantasy world is really at the heart of the story. The first-person protagonist—Baudelaire's pose in this work—outraged by this hypocrisy, dramatizes the real attitude of the bourgeois toward the poor when he beats the old beggar mercilessly in order to teach him self-reliance (after carefully checking to make sure that the police were out of sight). The theme of the story, then, is not really that the poor must earn equality and liberty, but rather that the middle-class insistence that they do so is really an excuse for the worst sort of inhumanity. The Demon is a demon and what he says is naturally the opposite of the truth.

> The use of short quotations from the poem keeps the essay "in contact" with it, and so adds credibility to the argument. By integrating these quotations into my own sentences, I avoid an awkward interruption of the essay. If the poem were longer, I would need to give page or line numbers.

> The end (at last) of a bad sentence.

> Yet another sentence that is far too convoluted.

We cannot rest comfortably here, however, because the story's plot turns at the end in a direction inconsistent with the hypothesis that the protagonist is mimicking the behavior of the middle class: the bourgeois people Baudelaire so despises would hardly divide their wealth evenly with the poor, and hardly be happy to have the poor drub them more soundly than they have been drubbed. At this point, the protagonist appears to be behaving like a saint, taking very seriously the equality of rich and poor, young and old. Now it seems that the Demon is a good angel after all, since his advice leads to the happy conclusion.

It is unclear who "they" are.

There are perhaps two ways out of the quandary created by the ambiguity of the story. One is to say that we should apply the Demon's words equally to the protagonist and to the beggar. The protagonist (the typical bourgeois) must prove that he is equal to the beggar by treating him as an equal, show that he is worthy of liberty by breaking away from the conventional but unacceptable attitudes of society. The other way is to say that <u>any</u> action that strips away the layers of hypocrisy, even an act of frank violence and brutality, will get us closer to the understanding that all of us are brothers.

The conclusion proposes a solution to the problem, as it should; but see comments below.

STEP 3: EVALUATE THE FIRST DRAFT HONESTLY

When we try to evaluate our own writing, both pride and humility stand in the way. Sometimes we convince ourselves that a bad passage is good; sometimes we raise niggling objections to something that any objective observer would find perfectly acceptable. Nothing is more helpful at this point than friends willing to give frank opinions, and most successful writers learn to cherish such friends. The essayist E. B. White used to call his wife, the editor Katharine Sergeant White, his "B.F. and M.S.C." Anyone familiar with marriage and writing will catch his meaning: Best Friend and Most Severe Critic.

Not everyone has the advantage of being married to a brilliant editor, of course, and even the comments of the best editor must be held at arm's length. The essay is ours: only we know its intentions, only we will be responsible for its final form. Eventually, with or without the help of friends, we must arrive at our own evaluation of the essay's strengths and weaknesses. Writing this evaluation out as a "revision agenda" sometimes increases objectivity and helps the memory. Like a free writing, a revision agenda need not conform to the standard rules of usage.

Example 3: A Revision Agenda

STRENGTHS OF THE FIRST DRAFT

1. Saying that the theme is stated by the Demon, but that we don't know how to *understand* the Demon, is good. I had missed the ambiguity of the Demon's statement entirely when I first read the poem, and I think many other readers must miss it.

2. I like the turn the paper takes in the third paragraph. The poem forces us to do a double take when the protagonist behaves so well at the end, and it is a pleasure to recreate that double take by "solving" the problem of theme, then saying, "We cannot rest comfortably here. . . ." I like the way the word "saint" works here, too, since the shock of calling this mugger a saint is consistent with the shock of the story.

3. The stuff in the second paragraph about self-dramatization and offending the bourgeoisie is pretty useful because it helps solve the problem of tone. If B. is posing, and even clowning, he is doing so with a serious intent. We don't have to choose between a serious reading and a comic reading. The tone is both serious and comic.

4. I *feel* after completing this draft that I understand the poem better than I did before I began to write. I *think* that some other readers would understand the poem better if they read this paper.

WEAKNESSES

1. The thesis and title are both vague and weak, even deceptive. It doesn't tell the reader much to say that the "careful reader" will be skeptical about an easy interpretation. "Careful readers" are always skeptical about this. What direction should their skepticism take? I need to be more direct.

2. The organization of the paper is not clear. If I am saying that there are two ways to read the story, each shedding light on the theme, then I should have a neat, self-contained discussion of each one. The theatricality discussion, much as I like it, muddies the water.

3. The conclusion is not crisp. I say, in effect, "Look, the theme *is* just what the Demon says, but we've got to *apply* it right." Then I turn right around and say that, if you prefer, the theme is no such thing, that the theme has something (rather vague) to do with violence as an antidote to hypocrisy. Stand firm, Hunt, stop moving your feet.

4. I confuse things unnecessarily by talking about whether the Demon is lying or telling the truth. This is a red herring. Eventually, I will have to say that the Demon is telling the truth. The real question is whether it is a demonic truth or an angelic truth.

5. Several of the sentences are murky and overlong, just the sort of pseudo-academic prose I love to hate.

STEP 4: REWRITE THE PAPER

The standard advice at this point is to *revise* the paper, but too often we think of revision as a conservative process that leaves the essay essentially intact. Relatively few first drafts deserve such gentle treatment. Most need to be dismantled and rebuilt, sometimes more than once. Of the twenty sentences in the rewritten paper below only four are taken essentially unchanged from the rough draft.

Example 4: A Rewritten Paper

Ambiguity in the Theme of Baudelaire's "Knock Down the Poor!"

The "good Angel, or good Demon" in Charles Baudelaire's "Knock Down the Poor!" seems to announce the theme of the prose poem at its midpoint: "He alone is the equal of another who proves it, and he alone is worthy of liberty who knows how to obtain it." The poem's tone is generally hard to establish, however; it hovers between humor and serious social criticism. With the general tone so uncertain, the reader naturally has difficulty deciding how to interpret a statement that may come either from hell or from heaven. One way to work out the riddle and find the theme is to read the poem first on the assumption that the Demon is tempting the protagonist to sin, then on the assumption that he is an angel instructing him in virtue.

A statement that the theme *seems* perfectly clear.

A statement of the problem.

A thesis that the problem can be solved by reading the poem two ways.

The hypothesis that the Demon is a tempter has a good deal of evidence on its side. Offended by what he perceives to be the hypocrisies of bourgeois life, Baudelaire often holds a distorting mirror up to his readers, one that exaggerates our faults to the same degree that most of us are inclined to exaggerate our virtues. "Knock Down the Poor!" begins with satiric comments on the "popular books" that deceive the poor and salve the consciences of the middle class. After the protagonist has "swallowed" down the notions contained in these books, he finds the "obscure germ of an idea" grander than the "old wives' formulas" these books contain. The idea becomes concrete when he beats the old beggar mercilessly in order to teach him self-reliance. He is acting out in an exaggerated way the unspoken attitude of the middle class: "Let's knock down the poor if they can't take care of themselves, and if there are no police watching." The theme of the story, then, is not that the poor must rise to the equality and liberty of the middle class, since the inhumanity of middle-class people puts them far below the level of beggars. The Demon is a demon, speaking the most degraded thoughts of the ungenerous bourgeoisie.

Straightforward step to first way of reading poem. Clear topic sentence for the paragraph.

Generalization about Baudelaire's technique, followed by evidence of that technique at work in poem.

Analysis closely tied to text of poem by quotations and echoes of Baudelaire's wording.

Statement of what the theme is *not*.

Sentence to round off investigation of first hypothesis.

We cannot rest comfortably here, however, because the story's plot turns at the end in a direction inconsistent with the hypothesis that the protagonist and his Demon are mimicking the attitudes of the middle class. The people Baudelaire so despises would never divide their wealth with beggars, and never be happy

Move to second hypothesis.

Generalization and evidence.

to have the poor drub them more soundly than they
have drubbed the poor. At this point, the protagonist
is behaving like a saint, taking very seriously the
equality of rich and poor, young and old. Now it
seems that the Demon is a good angel after all, since
his advice leads to saintly behavior and a happy
conclusion.   *Again, a rounding off.*

    The best way to resolve the ambiguity of the story
is probably to assume that, like many oracular   *Statement of result of*
statements, the Demon's statement is true in an   *investigation.*
unexpected way. His words apply to the protagonist
at least as much as to the beggar. The protagonist
(representing the bourgeoisie) must prove that he is
equal to the beggar by treating him as an equal, show
that he is worthy of liberty by breaking away from
conventional and hypocritical attitudes toward the
poor. The poem's theme is that equality and liberty
must be earned by merit, but the bourgeoisie are the   *Clear statement of what*
ones who most need to earn them.   *the theme really is.*

STEP 5: EVALUATE THE REWRITTEN ESSAY OBJECTIVELY

Essays often seem to be finished on the second draft because we want to be rid of
them and because we have invested so much intellectual energy in them that we have
an irrational faith in their quality. Once again, though, we should evaluate the essay
objectively before we let it go. There is a fair chance that the essay would improve
significantly if taken through another draft or two. Even if we decide not to change
it, the re-evaluation may give us ideas worth pursuing.

Example 5: Evaluation of the Second Draft

STRENGTHS

1. The essay is more clearly organized than before. I think any reader
   could now see my thesis—that the theme can be found by giving the
   poem both a demonic and an angelic reading. I am clear (maybe clearly
   wrong, but clear) about what I believe the theme to be: that the solid citizen must earn equality and freedom.

2. The individual paragraphs are organized as miniature essays, each
   proving a point.

3. The bits of quotation establish enough contact with the poem to keep
   the reader from thinking that I am drifting into freewheeling speculation, but the quotations don't get in the way of the argument.

4. Focusing on the *purpose* of the Demon's statement—to damn or to save
   —seems more useful than focusing on its *truth*. I've got my red herring
   out.

WEAKNESSES

1. I think I've sold the poem short. Reconciling the angelic and demonic aspects of the poem pointing out the irony of the Demon's statement is clever, but it is shallow. The more I think about it, the less sure I am that the ambiguity is really there. I'm sure that Baudelaire does resent the hypocrisy of the middle class, but there must be more to it than this. Baudelaire *has* to use a Demon to speak angelic truth, for reasons I've not yet fathomed.

2. I've not come to grips with the grotesque humor in the poem, the thing that first attracted me to it.

3. I know too little about Baudelaire's politics to be at all sure what his attitude toward the poor actually was. In a poem where the tone is so uncertain, I've no rock to stand on.

The essay is not yet entirely satisfactory, but I feel it has gone about as far as it can within the limits of a 500-word non-research paper. An additional revision of the essay within these limits would improve it slightly, but I now feel the need to do more research.

WRITING A RESEARCH PAPER

There is a tendency to talk about the research papers as if they were all cast from the same mold and served the same purpose. In fact, essays that involve research can be expressions of essentially independent opinion, reinforced slightly by a reference to one or two sources, or they can be works of exhaustive scholarship in which almost every sentence is justified by the citation of an authority. Most will fall somewhere between. If you are assigned a research paper, you should check with your teacher to see where on the spectrum he or she expects the paper to lie. (The sample paper below is somewhere near the midpoint.)

A few general observations about writing a research paper are worth making:

- Go into the research with a notion of what you are looking for, what you *think* your essay will prove and what sort of evidence is necessary for the proof. It may well be that your tentative thesis will be overthrown by the research, but unless you have some idea of what you intend to prove, you may find yourself wallowing in data that has no particular significance. Sometimes it is wise to write a very brief "pilot paper" giving your hypothesis and general line of reasoning before you become too deeply involved in the research.

- Take time to be methodical in your search for sources. Working carefully through the card catalogue, computer catalogue, and periodical indices* before you begin reading at random will save you time in the long run. So, too, will compiling a set of notecards with the bibliographic information needed for the "works cited" page: the few

---

* Those most useful for research in literature are the *PMLA* and the *Humanities* indices.

minutes spent jotting down this information every time you locate a potentially useful source can save you hours of frustration as the paper develops.

■ Make notes in a convenient form. Otherwise, the physical problem of trying to shuffle several books will distract you when you write. So, too, will the confusion created by having more than one note on a page or having notes on the back of a page. The time-honored method of using one side of a 4″ × 6″ note card for each note and carefully recording the source and page number remains the most efficient.

■ Be prepared to discard most of the information you uncover. Attempts to use every scrap of research almost always produce papers that are disorganized. It should be clear to the reader that you are selecting information judiciously. Beware, on the other hand, of *physically* discarding note cards or bibliography cards too soon. The information that seems irrelevant at one point may later become important.

■ Pay attention to the credibility of the source as well as the usefulness of the information. Primary sources (works by the author you are discussing) generally have more weight than secondary sources (works by critics and commentators). Works by commentators with undeniable expertise (the scholars other scholars quote) have more weight than works by commentators who are relatively unknown. When you introduce a quotation or paraphrase from a source, be sure that the reader can tell immediately whether the source is primary or secondary.

■ Remember that the proper citation of sources serves three practical purposes. It (a) gives your reader a guide to other sources he or she may want to read, (b) gives your sources credit for the intellectual debt you owe them, and (c) gives you the chance to reinforce your points by showing that other commentators agree with you. Sources that give historical background, biographical data, and other "general information" need not be cited; the reader can find such information in any number of places, and you are not indebted to or relying on the work of a particular thinker.

Sample Research Paper
"Knock Down the Poor!" as Satanic Comedy

Charles Baudelaire's "Knock Down the Poor!" is built on a paradox: by beating a beggar nearly to death, the protagonist gives him back "his pride and his life" (<u>Prose and Poetry</u> 83). This paradox[1] makes it very hard to determine the theme of the prose poem. Some critics find it a political statement about the resilience of the poor and the possibility of an honest relation between social classes. Others see it as an example of Baudelaire's dwelling on the perversity of human nature. Both views are correct; they can be reconciled by seeing the poem as a satanic comedy in which the urge to evil, followed to its conclusion, leads the protagonist to good.

Politically, the poem is related to the wave of utopian socialism that swept France from 1840 to 1848 and helped cause the overthrow of the monarchy in the Revolution of 1848. Baudelaire makes this connection clear by placing the poem's action "sixteen or seventeen years" before the date of the poem's composition and intended publication in 1865 (Hyslop 98). The socialists and their opponents flooded France with tracts, many of them silly (". . . the art of making nations happy, wise, and rich in twenty-four hours"),

Citations in the essay give the minimum information necessary to identify who is being quoted, from what work, and from which pages. Since full information appears on the "works cited" page, titles are sometimes given in abbreviated form.

I insert the explanatory footnote because the bit of information it gives, while it reinforces my point, is not essential and would interrupt the paragraph needlessly.

The opening paragraph previews the main lines of development.

"Satanic comedy" is not a standard literary term, but one I've had to coin to cover the occasion. Therefore, it needs immediate definition.

I cite Hyslop here not because he gives the year that Baudelaire attempted publication (a fact that would fall under the "general knowledge" rule) but because he told me how to understand this fact (as a reference to the Revolution of 1848).

Short quotations from the work discussed keep the essay in contact with the poem.

some of them dishonest and self-serving (Prose and Poetry 81). Though the protagonist of the poem dismisses his interest in the tracts as "a passionate taste for bad books," Baudelaire himself was strongly influenced by one of the socialist writers: Pierre Joseph Proudhon (Hyslop 99-125). Proudhon was not a middle-class liberal attempting to salve his conscience by expressing liberal views. He was a radical from the working class who believed laborers were superior to the money-hungry bourgeoisie, and that if the economic system did not repress them they would be able to escape from poverty ("Proudhon" 744-45). F. W. J. Hemmings argues that "Knock Down the Poor!" illustrates a theme from Proudhon: that it is better for the poor to secure justice for themselves than to rely on the help of "utopian dreamers whose remedies, if applied, would prove more devitalizing than the social evils they are proposing to abolish" (Hemmings 95).[2] Lois Hyslop agrees that Baudelaire's message in the poem is political, and that the protagonist is "the beggar's benefactor" acting "out of his intention to restore the man's dignity and self-pride" (123).

Such interpretations of the poem make the protagonist seem a thoroughly well-meaning political philosopher. But well-meaning philosophers do not

The quotation about "passionate taste" so clearly comes from the same portion of the poem as the description of the tracts that no citation is necessary.

I cite a whole section of Hyslop's article because the whole section proves the Baudelaire/Proudhon connection.

Unsigned encyclopedia articles are poor sources for many purposes. The information they contain is either opinion, in which case we would like to know whose, or it is "general knowledge" requiring no citation. Here, however, the background information is useful, and I want to show the reader the basis of my very sweeping generalizations about Proudhon's philosophy.

The politically optimistic interpretations of the poem strike me as so intuitively unlikely (though finally reasonably convincing) that I want to show two reputable examples. Otherwise, the reader may think that this line of interpretation is largely a figment of my imagination.

I allow my skepticism about the adequacy of the

ordinarily take up tree limbs and thrash old men nearly to death. To get at the motive for the beating we need to look at a second level of the poem: the demonic. The voice that advises the protagonist is that "of a good Angel, or of a good Demon" (82). Demons have a peculiar role in Baudelaire's view of morality and psychology. In "The Evil Glazier," for example, Baudelaire's protagonist, about to torment a poor man for no good reason, says

> "I have more than once been the victim of these crises and of these impulses that appear to be the action of malicious Demons that possess us and, unknown to ourselves, make us accomplish their most absurd desires" (Prose and Poetry 11).

In "Beatrice" the poet is surrounded by a cloud of demons who accuse him of being a bad actor mouthing the lines they write (Fleurs 132-33). In "Knock Down the Poor!" Baudelaire pauses to make a caustic comment about Lelut and Baillarger, psychologists who had declared Socrates insane because he mentions demons who controlled human actions:[3] Baudelaire believed that even the sanest of men could be controlled by evil impulses (in effect, demons) far stronger than their sanity. Critics like George Ross Ridge see "Knock Down the Poor!" as an example of

political interpretations to show, but decide not to refute them: only to say that though they are right on one level, there *must* be more.

Primary sources (in this case, Baudelaire's own poems) are generally more convincing than secondary sources. The route to these poems was via a concordance that allowed me to locate every reference to demons in *The Flowers of Evil.*

Quotations longer than four lines are usually indented and typed without quotation marks.

Once again, a concordance helped. In this case, it allowed me to find out what Socrates said about demons in Plato's dialogues. The information is not important enough to mention in the text, but I add it as an explanatory footnote.

I draw my conclusion about Baudelaire's fascination from accumulated reading of the poems and several secondary sources. No particular source gives it to me directly, so I cite

Baudelaire's emphasis on this demonic side of human psychology: "As sadist, satanist, artist, aesthete, the hero of the prose poem is always the imp of the perverse. His acts are gratuitous, unmotivated; hence, they are pure evil" (20). The distressing implication of the poem is that all humans, even those who read and write Utopian tracts, share the perversity of the protagonist. Those who do not cudgel the poor honestly in the street repress them with a system of hypocritical, degrading charity.

The political and the demonic readings of the poem seem at first to be irreconcilable. One makes the protagonist seem a saint motivated by a good angel;[4] one makes him seem a villain motivated by a demon. The only possible way to a reconciliation is to accept the idea that the prompting voice may be that of a good demon. This view makes the protagonist into a comic figure, a man who surrenders to an evil impulse and ends up, surprisingly, doing something better than all the people who set out to do good.

The idea that a poem about beating a beggar should be humorous is shocking, but Baudelaire is often shocking, and the evidence of humor is everywhere. Sometimes this humor shows in sarcasm: in the parody of the political tracts and the statement

nothing and stand on my own authority. If I were writing a more scholarly paper, I would look for an authority to confirm my opinion.

I like the obvious conflict between the Ridge quotation and the earlier Hyslop quotation.

Having outlined the two apparently opposite views, I re-announce my plan for reconciliation. Notice that I am reminding the reader of the thesis.

I go to perhaps excessive lengths to show the humorous side of the poem because I have found very little commentary on it, and I am afraid that some readers don't see it—are perhaps reluctant to see it.

that reading them makes a person thirsty, for instance. Sometimes it shows in a grotesque turn of phrase, as when the protagonist beats the old beggar "with the persistent energy of a cook pounding a tough steak" (82). There are a series of passages in which the protagonist humorously undercuts his own dignity: when he mentions that his high-minded philosophical experiment needed to be conducted "out of immediate danger from the police," for example, and when he observes that he was so inept as a mugger that he broke a fingernail in the process of smashing two of the man's teeth (82). The denouement of the poem is almost certain to produce an uneasy smile. When the beggar turns on the protagonist, the violence that has made us cringe is doubled--two black eyes for one, four broken teeth for two--very much in the manner of the violent pantomimes popular in Baudelaire's time. And, like the violence in the pantomimes, it never really hurts: the protagonist, though "beat to a pulp" (83), is delighted to have his hypothesis verified.

The mention of the pantomimes prepares the reader for the next paragraph. It also helps the reader see the comedy in the poem by comparing it to a more generally accepted genre that links violence and laughter. I suppose that the present-day equivalents of these cruel and funny pantomimes are some Saturday morning cartoons and a number of comic strips.

Of course, the poem could have these humorous elements without being comic in the sense of achieving a happy ending, but "Knock Down the Poor!" ends happily on both the political level and the "demonic"

level of Baudelaire's view of human nature. The
political happy ending is obvious: the beggar rises out
of his misery to a new independence. The demonic
happy ending is harder to articulate and can perhaps
be best seen by analogy to an English pantomime
Baudelaire loved and wrote about in his essay "The
Essence of Laughter."

In the pantomime, Pierrot is a notorious pick-
pocket, eager to steal absolutely anything. In one
scene he meets a woman who is trying to wash her
doorstep. Not only does he steal her money, but he
also tries to stuff everything else he finds into his
pockets: "the mop, the broom, and the pail--even the
water" (125). Pierrot persists in a wanton and lawless
life until he is condemned to the guillotine. His head
is chopped off, rolling noisily across the stage and
displaying "the bleeding circle of the neck, the severed
vertebrae," and other gory details added courtesy of a
local butcher shop:

Here is a primary source
of a particularly valuable
kind. A critical essay by an
author whose creative
writing is being evaluated
often casts a fascinating
indirect light. It may
make a useful observation
about literature in
general and at the same
time open a window on
the author's attitude
toward his or her own
work.

I include the gory details
so that the reader will
connect them with the
violence in the poem.

> But, suddenly, the decapitated trunk, revived by
>
> the force of the creature's irresistible thievish
>
> monomania, got to its feet, and triumphantly made
>
> off with its head, which like a ham or a bottle of
>
> wine, and far more sagaciously than St. Denis, it
>
> stuffed into its pocket. (126)

The humor here is certainly laced with cruelty, and Baudelaire believed that laughter was "one of the more obvious marks of the satanic in man" (Essence 115). He also believed, however, that there were higher and lower forms of laughter. We sometimes laugh because we feel superior to some unfortunate person who deserves our sympathy, but we sometimes laugh because a person's behavior makes us feel "the superiority of Man to Nature" (130). Pierrot goes to the guillotine as a miserable clown, but he rises from the guillotine as a man whose vices, even, are stronger than death.

This paraphrase of a very complex argument from Baudelaire's essay does not do it full justice. To develop it in greater detail, however, would have taken us too far from "Knock Down the Poor!" I paraphrase briefly, with as little distortion as possible.

What the pantomime does with physical humor, "Knock Down the Poor!" does with psychological or moral humor. Just as Pierrot persists in his crime so thoroughly that it eventually saves him from death, Baudelaire's protagonist persists in his demonic behavior until it proves a kind of salvation not only for the beggar, but for himself. Baudelaire, never optimistic about the sanctioned roads to political improvement or to individual grace (Murray 95-96), suspected that the unsanctioned roads might lead to the same destination:

From my first exposure to this prose poem, I have wanted to insist that the issue is not the beggar's financial or political welfare, but the protagonist's spiritual welfare. My sources have now shifted my thinking somewhat, so I concede that Baudelaire is talking spiritually and politically at the same time.

"... with tears a man may wash away man's sufferings, and with laughter sometimes soften men's hearts and draw them to him. For the phenomena that engendered the Fall can become the means to salvation" (<u>Essence</u> 113).

Baudelaire believed in excess as fervently as some philosophers believe in moderation. "Knock Down the Poor!" is a comedy of excess in which a degenerate man, "sadist, satanist, artist, aesthete," becomes useful to the poor precisely because he avoids the hypocrisy of seeming to be charitable. Instead he follows the prompting of his authentic demon, however cruel that demon might be, until he achieves at the end an unexpected saintliness.

I state Baudelaire's position as strongly as possible in order to tie down the argument of the essay. As a personal matter, I don't agree with Baudelaire. I could get on my soapbox and declare that charity can be real, that people can care for each other in ways that have nothing to do with dominance and submission, and that the angelic forces of the personality are often strong enough to hold the demons at bay. But my job in this paper is to clarify Baudelaire's work, not to preach.

Notes

[1] The original title of the poem was, in fact, "Le Paradoxe l'aumone" ("The Paradox of Charity") (<u>Oeuvres</u> I: 1349).

Explanatory footnotes include citations on the same principles as the main text of the essay.

[2] Supporting Hemmings's position is the fact that the manuscript version of the poem ended with the sentence "Qu'en dis-tu, Citoyen Proudhon?" ("What do you say about it, Citizen Proudhon?").

[3] In the <u>Phaedrus</u>, Socrates says that every person has a demon. He also says, in a passage that might have interested Baudelaire, that a person trying to control his passion is like a charioteer trying to rein in two horses--one good and one evil.

The information may be of interest to those concerned about Socrates's reputation. It is, however, so peripheral to the essay that I give only a casual citation, not noting edition or page number.

⁴ Monroe says that the "bon Ange" may be a composite of Proudhon and Charles-Augustin Sainte-Beuve, Baudelaire's literary mentor (184).

Works Cited

Baudelaire, Charles. "The Essence of Laughter." Trans. Gerard Hopkins. The Essence of Laughter and other Essays, Journals, and Letters. Ed. Peter Quennell. New York: Meridian, 1956.

———. Les Fleurs du Mal. Trans. Richard Howard. Boston: Godine, 1982.

———. Oeuvres Completes. Ed. Charles Pichois. Paris: Gallimard, 1975.

———. Prose and Poetry. Trans. Arthur Symons. New York: Albert and Charles Boni, 1926.

Drost, Wolfgang. "Baudelaire between Marx, Sade, and Satan." Baudelaire, Mallarme, Valéry: New Essays in Honour of Lloyd Austin. Cambridge UP, 1982.

Hemmings, F. W. J. Baudelaire the Damned. New York: Scribner's, 1982.

Hyslop, Lois Boe. Baudelaire: Man of His Time. New Haven: Yale UP, 1980.

Monroe, Jonathan. "Baudelaire's Poor: The Petite Poems en Prose and the Social Reincarnation of the Lyric." Stanford French Review 9 (1985): 169-88.

The rather unusual form of the first entry reflects the importance of noting the translator of a literary work. Had translation not been an issue, I could have gone from Baudelaire's name directly to the title.

Publishers' names are shortened when familiar enough for the reader to easily identify.

Note that three hyphens are used to avoid repeating the author's name.

Cite the full name of those publishers less familiar to the reader.

"UP" is a standard abbreviation for University Press.

"9" is the volume number for the periodical.

Murry, John Middleton. "Baudelaire." Baudelaire: A

Collection of Critical Essays. Ed. Henri Peyre.

Englewood Cliffs: Prentice, 1962.

"Proudhon, Pierre Joseph." Encyclopedia Britannica.

1986 ed.

Ridge, George Ross. "Images of Original Sin in

Baudelaire's Prose Poems." Kentucky Foreign

Language Quarterly 7.1 (1960): 19-21.

Unsigned articles are
alphabetized by title.

"7.1" means "volume 7,
issue number 1," a
citation form necessary
when each issue is
separately paginated.

Biographical Sketches

Chinua Achebe (b. 1932) was born in Ogidi, Nigeria, and has been a professor of English at the University of Nigeria, Nsukku, since 1975, receiving the title of Professor Emeritus in 1985. Although he is a native of Africa and has lived most of his life there, Achebe has taught at several universities in the United States and actually does most of his writing in English. Achebe's concern for preserving African culture in the midst of European influence is revealed in his writing, which is often permeated with Ibo proverbs. His works include *Things Fall Apart* (1958), *Arrow of God* (1969), *Beware Soul-Brother and Other Poems* (1971), *African Short Stories* (1985), and *Anthills of the Savannah* (1987), plus essays and children's books.

Niccolò degli Albizzi (fourteenth century) was a member of the noble Florentine family of Albizzi, which produced several writers of poetry. "Prolonged Sonnet" is the only known poem by Niccolò.

Jean Anouilh (1910–1987) has been one of the most popular French playwrights since the 1930s. He is the author of over forty plays, many of which focus on historical figures. Anouilh characterizes his plays as either "rosy" or "black," corresponding to comedy or tragedy. He also attempts to create characters with strong inner vision, a vision that can blind them to the outer reality. *Antigone* (1944), *Joan of Arc* (1956), and *Becket; or, The Honour of God* (1959) are among his many works.

Margaret Atwood (b. 1939) has been a cashier and a filmscript writer, an editor with one of Canada's largest presses, and a professor of English literature. Born in Ottawa, Ontario, Atwood began writing as a child. Recently relating her love for domestic life to her literary career, Atwood claimed that "if Shakespeare could have kids and avoid suicide" then so could she. The fiction she produces ranges from serious probing into the psychological effects of modern culture to light and humorous stories. Her nonfiction works include *Survival: A Thematic Guide to Canadian Literature* (1972) and *Second Words: Selected Critical Prose* (1982); *Surfacing* (1972), *Bodily Harm* (1982), *The Handmaid's Tale* (1986), and *Cat's Eye* (1988) are among her novels; *Power Politics* (1971), a collection of poems, produced a wave of critical controversy; *Bluebeard's Egg and Other Stories* (1986) is her most recent collection of stories.

W(ystan) H(ugh) Auden (1907–1973) was born in England and educated at Oxford. He was the principal British poet of his generation, using a vocabulary conspicuous for its technical formality and colloquial tone. Like many of his peers he learned wit and irony from T.S. Eliot and metrical techniques from Gerard Manley Hopkins and Wilfred Owen. Of his later volumes, *Nones* (1951) shows the manner in which he combined wit and deep, if unsentimental, feeling. He was at first influenced by Marxism and wrote poems concerned with England's social ills, but later he cultivated a more religious view of personal responsibility and conventional values. As opposed to T.S. Eliot, who moved from America to England in search of tradition, Auden moved to America in search of variety. There he taught before returning to England to live at Oxford. Among his works are *About the House* (1967), *City Without Walls* (1970), and a collection of prose writings, *The Dyer's Hand and Other Essays* (1968). His poetry is collected in *W.H. Auden: Collected Poems* (1976).

Toni Cade Bambara (b. 1939) was born in New York City and was educated there as well as in Paris. While most interested in linguistics and dance, Bambara worked as a social investigator and a psychiatric department recreation director before becoming a professor of English. She has taught and lectured at several colleges and universities across the country. Bambara's writing reflects her diversified life (she calls herself a Pan-Africanist-socialist-feminist); she writes about the experiences of black women in order to "tap Black potential" and "join the chorus of voices that argue that exploitation and misery are neither inevitable nor necessary." Her works include a novel *The Black Woman* (1970) and collections of stories, *Gorilla, My Love* (1972) and *The Sea Birds Are Still Alive* (1977).

Charles Baudelaire (1821–1867) was born in Paris, were he spent most of his life. When Baudelaire was six his father died, and a year later his mother married General (later Ambassador) Aupick. Baudelaire's relations with his parents prefigured his bitter relationship with the bourgeois Parisian critics and public. At eighteen Baudelaire was expelled from college on disciplinary grounds. He lived a life of dandyism (which was partly outrageous display, partly strict aesthetic discipline) until the Aupicks restricted the income from his inheritance. In 1845 Baudelaire published his first art criticism and poetry, followed two years later by a novel *La Fanfarlo* (1847). Attacks on his writing peaked with the publication of *Les Fleurs du mal* in 1857, when he received a 300-franc fine for immorality. Despite the setback, he continued working on his *Petits Poemes en prose* (1868), *Les Paradis artificiels* (1860), and a revised edition of *Les Fleurs du mal* (1861). Inventor of the term "modernism", Baudelaire struggled to define a place for the artist in a world he saw as corrupt and materialistic. His work is known for its images of evil and ugliness, yet Baudelaire was also a worshipper of beauty and called imagination the "queen of faculties."

Samuel Beckett (1906–1989), a native of Dublin, Ireland, wrote most of his important works in French. He began a career teaching both French and English, but abandoned academics when he decided that it was absurd to teach what he felt he could not know himself, the nature of language. This peculiar attitude toward language permeates his works, which emphasize silence as much as sound, voices speaking in isolation, and expression without definite meaning. After World War II Beckett began writing seriously and became a leading figure of the "Theatre of the Absurd," producing plays such as *Waiting for Godot* (1952), *Endgame* (1957), *Krapp's Last Tape* (1958), and *Happy Days* (1961). While Beckett has been criticized for too often portraying humanity as depraved and grotesque, Harold Pinter claims that Beckett "brings forth a body of beauty" through his writing. Beckett considered himself primarily a novelist; his novels include *Molloy* (1951), *Malone Dies* (1951), *The Unnamable* (1953), and *How It Is* (1961). In 1969 he won the Nobel Prize for Literature.

John Berryman (1914–1972) taught at Brown, Harvard, Princeton, and the University of Minnesota, but was most accomplished as a poet, acquiring both the Pulitzer Prize (1965) and the National Book Award (1969) during his lifetime. Aligned with the confessional poets of the sixties, Berryman wrote extremely personal verse, reacting against the academic poetry common at the time. He is best known for his "Dream Songs," which chronicle the epic-like life of his fictional Henry Pussycat. Berryman's poetry is collected in *The Dispossessed* (1948), *Homage to Mistress Bradstreet* (1956), *The Dream Songs* (1969), and *Henry's Fate and Other Poems, 1967–1972* (1977).

Elizabeth Bishop (1911–1979) was born in Worcester, Massachusetts. Her father died in the year of her birth, and her mother succumbed to mental illness a short time later. Raised by her grandparents in their Nova Scotian village, she attended boarding school in Boston before enrolling at Vassar College. In her senior year she met poet Marianne Moore. Under Moore's influence she abandoned her plans to study medicine and decided to devote her life to writing. The poems of Moore and Bishop have in common a wry intelligence and are formal without being bound by traditional forms. Both write from a detached perspective, closely observing the characteristics of animate and inanimate objects. Many of Bishop's poems evoke her experiences in Key West and in Brazil, where she spent long periods. Bishop's relatively modest poetic production has been disproportionately influential. Seen in the context of postwar women's poetry, that influence is at least partly due to the contrast Bishop's objectivity and concentration on the external world provide to the emotional and subjective poetry of Sylvia Plath and Anne Sexton. Bishop's books of poetry are *North and South* (1946); the Pulitzer Prize-winning *Poems* (1955); *A Question of Travel* (1965); *The Complete Poems* (1965), which received the National Book Award; and *Geography III* (1976). She also translated poems from the Portuguese. Her *Collected Prose* appeared in 1984.

William Blake (1757–1827) was born in London and lived virtually his entire life there. The radical upheavals of the French, American, and Industrial Revolutions are echoed in his poetry. Apprenticed at an early age, he earned his living as a highly skilled engraver and illustrator. With Catherine Boucher, whom he married when he was 24, Blake produced his own books of poems by hand. The first of these, *Songs of Innocence* (1789) and *Songs of Experience* (1794), contain his best-known poems and were admired by Wordsworth and Coleridge. It is in his longer books, including *The Marriage of Heaven and Hell* (1790), *Milton* (1803–1808), and *Jerusalem* (1804–20), that Blake strove for a visionary overview of human existence, past and future. His readings of the Bible, alchemical literature, Plato, and Swedenborg, together with the misery he witnessed on the streets of London, made him sympathetic to revolution. His idiosyncratic genius, though scarcely recognized during his own life, prefigured Romanticism and influenced poets right up to the present.

Robert Bly (b. 1926) was born in Madison, Minnesota, of Norwegian descent. He served in the army during World War II, then entered St. Olaf College. After a year he transferred to Harvard, where he earned his degree in 1950. He lived in New York for several years, but soon returned to rural Minnesota where he and his wife raised their three children. In the tradition of William Blake, Bly's poetry addresses the harsh political realities of his day (he founded Writers Against the Vietnam War) from an intensely spiritual perspective. Like Blake, Bly has sought to remain independent of institutions, making his living by giving readings and leading workshops around the country. Bly's beliefs about poetry—for example, the use of simple syntax so as to approach a visionary world by the most direct means—have influenced many contemporaries, including James Wright, Donald Hall, and Galway Kinnell. He has also been influential as an editor, and as translator of Lorca, Neruda, Rilke, the Sufi poet Kabir, and the Norwegian poet Thomas Transtromer. Bly's first of many books of poems was *Silence in the Snowy Fields* (1962); his most recent was *Loving a Woman in Two Worlds* (1987).

Louise Bogan (1897–1970), born in Livermore Falls, Maine, is considered one of the chief American exponents of the English Metaphysical poets. After traveling to Vienna in the early 1920s on a Guggenheim Fellowship, she published her first collection, *Body of This Death* (1923). From 1931 until a year before her death Bogan was poetry critic for *The New Yorker*. She was honored with a chair of poetry at the Library of Congress in 1945–46 and shared the prestigious Bollingen Prize with Leonie Adams for *Selected Criticism: Poetry and Prose* in 1955. In an effort to bring the contradictions in life to bold relief, Bogan is true to the Metaphysicals, employing psychological analysis of love, religion, and all matters emotional. She did not have a large readership during her lifetime, but her work as poet, critic, translator, and philosopher of art is receiving increasing attention. Among her works are *Dark Summer* (1929), *The Sleeping Fury* (1937), *Poems and New Poems* (1941), *The Blue Estuaries: Poems 1923–1968* (1968), and *A Poet's Alphabet: Reflections on the Literary Art and Vocation* (posthumously in 1970).

Jorge Luis Borges (1899–1986) never received a Nobel Prize but was nominated nineteen times. Born in Buenos Aires, Argentina, Borges became one of the pioneers of *Ultraisme,* a Spanish avant-garde literary movement based on Surrealism and Imagism. Even though the movement drifted too far from conventional literature for even Borges, his mature writing maintained its anti-realistic flavor. Borges is also known for his "literature about literature," found in his essays and sketches that present literary history and human experience simultaneously. His collections of short prose pieces and short stories include *Fictions* (1944), *Labyrinths* (1962), *The Aleph and Other Stories* (1970), and *Doctor Brodie's Report* (1972). His critical views on fiction, poetry, and translation are found in *Borges on Writing* (1973).

Gwendolyn Brooks (b. 1917) began her professional career in 1941 when she attended a workshop for new poets. By 1950 she had won the Pulitzer Prize for *Annie Allen,* written in 1949. A native of Chicago, Brooks was made poet laureate of Illinois in 1969. Her poetry is both social and personal, but her later poems, especially, reflect her belief that she should be writing for and about black people. In order to support other black writers, Brooks conducted a workshop for a group of Chicago teenagers, the Blackstone Rangers, through which she encouraged young people to portray the endurance of blacks despite constant battles against racism. Her use of street language and jazz rhythms also distinguishes her work. *A Street in Bronzeville* (1945), *The Bean-Eaters* (1960), *Beckonings* (1975), *To Disembark* (1981), and *The Jear-Johannesburg Boy and Other Poems* (1986) are among her poetic works. Brooks writes of her own life in *Report from Part One* (1972).

Olga Broumas (b. 1949) was born in Greece and educated at the University of Pennsylvania. Since 1982 she has been on the faculty of Freehand, a learning community for women writers and photographers which she originally founded in Provincetown, Massachusetts. As a feminist lesbian, Broumas writes poetry to explore the relationships possible among women. Her works are collected in *Caritas* (1976), *Soie Sauvage* (1979), *Pastoral Jazz* (1983), *Black Holes, Black Stockings* (1985), and several other volumes, all written in her second language, English. She has translated the poems of Greek Nobel Laureate Odysseas Elytis in *What I Love and Other Poems* (1986). Broumas won the Yale Younger Poets Award in 1977.

Robert Browning (1812–1889) was for many years known primarily as "Elizabeth Barrett's husband." Even today readers retain a fascination in their love affair, which was carried on largely in poems and letters until they eloped in 1846. Browning wrote most of his poetry while living in Italy with Elizabeth, whose fame as a poet was already established. Only after her death and Browning's return

to England was he able to build his reputation, particularly with the publication of *The Ring and the Book* in 1868. Browning was most successful in refining the dramatic monologue; his are famous for their psychological depth and ironic objectivity. Striving to portray the "intensest life," Browning created some of the most vivid characters in English literature. By 1881 he had become so popular that a literary society had been formed in his honor. His other works include *Men and Women* (1855) and *Dramatis Personae* (1864).

Dennis Brutus (b. 1924), born in Zimbabwe of South African parents, has not been allowed into South Africa for over twenty years. Considered too outspoken in his fight against apartheid while teaching in South Africa, Brutus was constantly in political trouble and was finally arrested and sentenced to eighteen months hard labor. After being banned from South Africa, he joined the staff of the English department at Northwestern University. His works include *Sirens, Knuckles, Boots* (1963), *Letters to Martha and Other Poems from a South African Prison* (1968), *Poems from Algiers* (1973), *Thoughts Abroad* (1970), and *A Simple Lust* (1973).

Raymond Carver (1938–1988) was born in Oregon, the son of working-class parents. He earned both A.B. and M.F.A. degrees while supporting his wife and two children by working numerous jobs and occasionally publishing stories. Perhaps because of this background, Carver's stories tend to focus on the everyday lives of the working class, portraying people trapped by unfeeling society, mundane employment, and an inability to communicate with others. Carver has won several awards including *The O. Henry Prize,* a National Endowment of the Arts award, a Guggenheim fellowship, and the Mildred and Harold Strauss Living Award. Among his collections of stories are *Put Yourself in My Shoes* (1974), *Will You Please Be Quiet, Please?* (1976), *What We Talk About When We Talk About Love* (1981), *Cathedral* (1984), and *Where I'm Calling From: New and Selected Stories.* Along with the stories, his poems and essays have been collected in *Fires: Essays, Poems, Stories* (1989).

Anton Chekhov (1860–1904), the Russian physician, short story writer, and playwright, was born in Taganrog, Russia, and educated at the University of Moscow. Preferring his literary life to his medical one, Chekhov had his first story published in 1880 and went on to write over six hundred more stories and sketches by 1887. His acute sensitivity to the psychological and social lives people live is best reflected in stories such as "Ward No. 6" (1892), "Peasants" (1897), "Gooseberries" (1898), and "The Lady with the Pet Dog" (1899). Chekhov's attempt to bring realism to the stage revolutionized the theater; to this day he continues to serve as a major influence on playwrights who strive to present life as it is experienced. Among his plays are *The Seagull* (1896), *The Three Sisters* (1901), and *The Cherry Orchard* (1903).

Kate O'Flaherty Chopin (1851–1904) was born in St. Louis, Missouri, the daughter of a Creole mother and an Irish father. She was educated at a convent and moved to Louisiana, which became the setting for many of her works, following her marriage to Oscar Chopin in 1870. After her husband's death in 1883, Chopin returned to St. Louis with her children and began her writing career in earnest. She produced almost all of her works during the ten years between 1889 and 1899. These include the novels *At Fault* (1890) and *The Awakening* (1899), and the story collections *Bayou Folk* (1894) and *A Night in Acadie* (1897). Although her writings were critical failures during her lifetime (she produced very little following the critical lambasting of *The Awakening*), they are now considered excellent examples of American Realism. Her frequent portrayal of strong women torn between a desire for freedom and the confinement society imposes on them also marks Chopin as a precursor to the contemporary feminist movement.

Amy Clampitt (b. 1923) was born and raised in New Providence, Iowa, of Quaker heritage. After graduating from Grinnell College in Iowa, she moved to New York City where she has lived most of her life. A librarian by career, she never published a poem until 1978, when her work began appearing regularly in *The New Yorker*. Since that time she has published three volumes and has established herself as one of America's major poets. In a style given to literary allusions, Clampitt places nearly as much emphasis upon the aural qualities of the work as on the subject matter itself. Through a montage of vivid sounds, she explores themes of history, political strife, and the social position of women. Her published works include: *The Kingfisher* (1983), *What the Light Was Like* (1985), and *Archaic Figure* (1987).

Lucille Clifton (b. 1936) grew up in New York and was educated at Howard University. When her first book of poems, *Good Times* (1969), was published, she was thirty-three years old and had six children under ten years of age. Since that time she has become a lecturer and professor, has been named poet laureate of Maryland, and has been nominated for the Pulitzer Prize. Clifton's poems, brief like those of Emily Dickinson, typically remake the sounds of black spirituals and blues. Clifton purposely keeps her poems simple, claiming she is not interested if anyone knows whether or not she is "familiar with big words" for she is primarily "interested in trying to render big ideas in a simple way." Her works include *Good News about the Earth* (1972), *An Ordinary Woman* (1974), and *Two-Headed Woman* (1980), as well as a memoir, *Generation* (1976).

Samuel Taylor Coleridge (1772–1834), through his collaboration with Wordsworth in the birth of the Romantic Movement and his own poetic and critical production, established himself as one of the towering figures of English literature. Born in rural Devonshire, Coleridge was sent to school in London and went on to Cambridge University. His brilliant mind was understimulated, and he left without a degree in 1794. A year later and married, he met Wordsworth, and thus began the poetic collaboration that resulted in the *Lyrical Ballads* (1798). During a year in Germany Coleridge studied Kant and other German philoso-

phers. Their ideas helped shape his own philosophic, religious, and aesthetic thought, which is articulated mainly in the *Biographia Literaria* and *The Friend,* a periodical Coleridge founded in 1809. Opposed to the prevailing rationalism, he saw the mind as active and creative, the imagination as a participant in perception. In 1799 Coleridge fell deeply in love with Wordsworth's sister-in-law and at the same time suffered the first of many physical ailments. The next ten years were a nightmare of ill health and drug addiction (opium being the standard cure). In 1810 Coleridge and Wordsworth had a falling out that was not resolved for many years. Coleridge's later years were happier; his early radicalism, like Wordsworth's, turned to a philosophic conservativism, and he returned to the Anglican church. He had the good fortune of being recognized in his own lifetime for his enormous creative accomplishments.

Countee Cullen (1903–1946) was adopted by a Methodist minister and raised in Harlem. By the time he was twenty years old, *Nation, Harper's,* and *Poetry* had published his poems. *Color* (1925), his first collection of poems, was published while he was a student at New York University. Cullen's early poetry brought him immediate fame as the youngest of the black writers who inspired the Harlem Renaissance. However, his next work, *Copper Sun* (1927), disappointed black nationalists with its display of love poems, and with the publication of *The Black Christ* in 1929, Cullen stopped writing poetry. After receiving his master's degree from Harvard, he taught high school in New York City for the rest of his life. His other literary work includes a novel, *One Way to Heaven* (1932), and a version of Euripides' *Medea* (1935).

E(dward) E(stlin) Cummings (1894–1962), from Cambridge, Massachusetts, earned his degree from Harvard where he studied both painting and poetry. During World War I he served as an ambulance driver in France and was mistakenly committed to a French prison camp for three months. His account of this experience, recorded through the prose narrative *The Enormous Room* (1922), attracted international attention. *Tulips and Chimneys* (1923), his first book of poetry, was soon followed by *&* (1925), *XLI Poems* (1925), and *is 5* (1926), all of which demonstrate faith in the loving and carefree individual and denounce the "unman" who possesses intellect without emotion. Cummings is known for his experimental typography, technical skill, and inventive language. His *Complete Poems, 1910–1962* was published in 1980.

Samuel Silas Curry (1847–1921) was born in Chatata, Tennessee, but lived most of his life in New England. Known primarily as an educator, he taught oratory and literature at Harvard and Yale and was founder and president of the Boston School of Oratory. Curry wrote several books on oratory and literature, including *The Vocal and Literary Interpretation of the Bible* (1903), *Foundations of Expression: Studies and Problems for Developing the Voice, Body and Mind in Reading and Speaking* (1907), and *Browning and Dramatic Monologue* (1908).

Joy Davidman (1915–1960) was a high school English teacher in New York City and a communist when her first book, *Letter to a Comrade* (1938), was published. It was this work which won Davidman both the Yale Younger Poets Award (1938) and the Loines Award for Poetry (1939). In 1955 she moved to England and became acquainted with C. S. Lewis, whose books were in part responsible for her conversion to Christianity. The two were married in 1957. Davidman also wrote two novels, *Anya* (1940) and *Weeping Bay* (1950).

Emily Dickinson (1830–1886) lived her entire life in her parents' home in Amherst, Massachusetts. As a young girl she was said to be charming and bright, and a promising student at Mount Holyoke Female Seminary. But with each passing year Dickinson grew more and more withdrawn until finally she would not leave the house at all. Twentieth-century scholarship has attributed her isolation to her passion for a young minister she saw two or three times in 1854. After he moved to California, Dickinson became acutely withdrawn, refused to wear anything but white, and began writing poetry that focused on love and renunciation, referring to herself as a "queen of Calvary." The precise metaphors and images of her poems anticipate the Imagist movement of the twentieth century. Although only seven poems were published during Dickinson's lifetime, nearly 2000 poems were found after her death; many were drastically edited and then published in 1890. In 1955 Thomas Johnson restored Dickinson's poems to their original form and published them in *The Poems of Emily Dickinson*.

John Donne (1572–1631) led a life that brought him the wealth and prestige of the Court, the hunger of absolute poverty, and eventually in 1615, priesthood in the Anglican Church, where he was known for his deeply moving sermons. By the time of his death he had become Dean of St. Paul's Cathedral in London. Donne's status among the English Metaphysical movement of the seventeenth century is unchallenged. Relying less on form than on subtlety of thought, the Metaphysical poets analyzed love and religion from a psychological standpoint, laying bare the contradictions of life. Donne's first collection, *Songs and Sonnets*, was published in 1634, three years after his death; it was not until 1912, with the publication of a scholarly edition of his *Holy Sonnets*, that his work achieved the recognition it deserves.

José Donoso (b. 1924), beginning his career as a shepherd in Patagonia, is now regarded as one of the most significant writers of recent Latin American fiction. Born in Santiago, Chile, Donoso remained unknown as a writer for several years. Even after his first book, *Summertime and Other Stories* (1955), was published, he found himself peddling his first novel, *Coronation* (1957), on the streets of Santiago. Donoso is known for the experimental nature of his works, which range from realistic stories of self-disintegration and madness to those that employ supernatural transformations and mythical monsters. Besides two collections of short stories, *The Charleston* (1960) and *The Major Stories of José Donoso* (1966), he has written novels, *The Obscene Bird of Night* (1973), *A House in the*

Country (1984), and *Curfew* (1988) and literary criticism, *The Boom in Spanish American Literature: A Personal History* (1977).

Charles d'Orléans (1391–1465) lived a life dominated by the political complexities and intrigues of his time. The son of Louis, Duke of Orléans, and Valentina, daughter of the Duke of Milan, he was also the brother of Charles VI. At the age of fifteen he was married to his first wife, the widow of England's Richard II. During Henry V's 1415 invasion of France, Charles was wounded and captured at Agincourt; he was held for ransom in England for the next twenty-five years. During this period, he occupied his time with religous study and writing poetry in both French and English. Following his return to France, he secluded himself in Blois with selected friends, including Villon for a time, where he wrote much of his poetry and where he remained until his death. His poems, most frequently in the form of the *ballade,* are remarkable for their formal sophistication, variety of subject matter, and wit. His works are collected in *Poésies* (1927) and *The English Poems of Charles d'Orléans* (1946).

T(homas) S(tearns) Eliot (1888–1965) dominated the world of English language poetry and criticism between the two world wars. He was born into an influential New England family that had been transplanted to St. Louis. Eliot was never comfortable with either heritage and lived the greater part of his life in England. After graduating from Harvard, he spent a year in France, where he wrote and furthered his exposure to the French Symbolists. He returned to Harvard where he studied philosophy. There he developed an interest in Buddhism and the Buddhist notions of Nirvana. Later he became an Anglican, advocating a return to Christian values and beliefs. His early work, especially "The Love Song of J. Alfred Prufrock" (1916) and "The Waste Land" (1922), profoundly influenced a whole generation of poets. Eliot was also active in bringing French Symbolism into English poetry and reviving interest in the Metaphysical poets. He was enormously influential as a critic and editor for the publishing house of Faber and Faber. His last major work, completed in 1943, was *Four Quartets*, in which he strove to structure a poem on musical principals. He also wrote plays for the stage, *Murder in the Cathedral* (1935) and *The Cocktail Party* (1950) among them. In 1948 he received the Nobel Prize for Literature.

Ralph Ellison (b. 1914) was born in Oklahoma City, Oklahoma, and studied music and composition at Tuskegee Institute. The influence of music, especially jazz, is strongly reflected in both Ellison's method of writing and in the works themselves. Studying T.S. Eliot's poetry provoked Ellison's interest in literature; Richard Wright, who always inspired Ellison with his commitment to racial justice, personally encouraged him to pursue a literary career. Ellison is known for his novel *Invisible Man* (1952), which chronicles the life of a man who is both a black and an artist and who faces in both roles the problem, as Ellison says, "of becoming a man, of becoming visible." He also has produced two collections of essays, *Shadow and Act*

(1964) and *Going to the Territory* (1986), which continue to explore the problem of black identity within the American culture.

Louise Erdrich (b. 1954) was born in Minnesota to Chippewa and German parents. She was raised in North Dakota and educated at Dartmouth College and Johns Hopkins University where she began writing award-winning poetry and fiction. In 1984, Erdrich's first novel, *Love Medicine,* brought her immediate attention as a young writer by winning the National Book Critics Circle Award. This novel's concern for her Native American heritage and its depiction of the North American plains are also reflected in her later novels, *Beet Queen* (1986) and *Tracks* (1988). While producing novels and several short stories of her own, Erdrich also collaborates with her Modoc husband Michael Dorris, most recently on a novel about Christopher Columbus, whose explorations had such a dramatic effect on Native Americans. Erdrich lives in New Hampshire with Dorris and their five children. She has also published one book of poetry, *Jacklight* (1984).

Euripides (480 B.C.–406 B.C.), one of the most reknowned tragedians of ancient Greece, was born on the island of Salamis and became an Athenian citizen. He was said to be very wealthy, yet took no part in public affairs, preferring instead to sit alone in a cave overlooking the sea. His passion for ideas and his pessimistic view of the universe limited Euripides' popularity in his lifetime, during which he won only four prizes at the annual Dionysian drama festival. While Euripides adhered to the formal dramatic structure and drew his plots from ancient legends, he commonly gave his characters contemporary ideas, attitudes, and problems. His heros are not idealized but are instead created as flawed people. Likewise, the supernatural aspects of his plays do not glorify Greek gods but merely imply a divine force uninvolved in human affairs. Among his nineteen surviving plays are *Alcestis, Bacchae, Medea, Ion,* and *Hippolytus.*

William Faulkner (1897–1962), bank clerk, cadet pilot, postmaster, carpenter, coal-shoveler, and finally full-time writer, was born in New Albany, Mississippi. From his experiences in the South, Faulkner created his mythical Yoknapatawpha County, the setting for most of his novels. With the writing of *Sartoris* (1929) Faulkner began the legend of the heroic Col. John Sartoris and his troubled descendents, constantly in conflict with the crafty, savage, landless Snopeses. Faulkner's style is dense and varied, often effectively experimenting with point of view and stream of consciousness. One of the great novelists of this century, he received the Nobel Prize in 1949. His major works include *The Sound and the Fury* (1929), *As I Lay Dying* (1930), *Light in August* (1932), *Absalom, Absalom!* (1936), *The Hamlet* (1940), *Go Down, Moses* (1942), *The Town* (1957), and *The Mansion* (1959).

Gustave Flaubert (1821–1880) was born in Rouen, France, and briefly studied law in Paris before being forced by epilepsy to return home. The remainder of his life was consistently uneventful, lived too near the bourgeois society he despised.

Ironically, it was this mundane setting that was the focus of Flaubert's masterpiece, *Madame Bovary* (1856), a novel condemned in France as pornographic yet praised internationally by other writers. Flaubert is generally considered the initiator of the Realist school of French literature. While his aim in fiction was to create beauty, he insisted on dispassionately recording the lives and minds of his characters. As an escape from the bourgeois reality, he turned to the past, studying the mystical lives of the saints as a means of evoking the romantic interest of his youth. His other works include the novels *Salammbô* (1862), *The Sentimental Education* (1869), *Bouvard and Pecuchet* (1881), and *Three Tales* (1877).

Robert Frost (1874–1963) was born in San Francisco but as a young boy moved to New England, the homeland of the Frost family. While growing up, Frost held many craftsman jobs—in a mill, in a shoe factory, and on a farm—and all influenced his later writing. Although he studied at Harvard with the intention of teaching Latin, Frost bought a poultry farm and settled there to write poetry. His reputation was established a few years later with the publication of *North of Boston* (1914). He went on to win four Pulitzer Prizes. His poetry is characterized by colloquial, restrained verse that implies messages rather than openly expressing them. Also politically active, Frost served as a good-will ambassador for the State Department to South America, Israel, Greece, and Russia. His works include *A Boy's Will* (1913), *New Hampshire* (1923), *A Further Range* (1936), *A Witness Tree* (1942), and *In the Clearing* (1962).

Tess Gallagher (b. 1943) was born into a family of loggers in Washington and now teaches English at Syracuse University in New York. Gallagher writes about family conflicts, departures and returns, and self-exploration. Her poems are collected in *Stepping Outside* (1974), *Instructions to the Double* (1976), *Under Stars* (1978), *Portable Kisses* (1978), *The Lover of Horses* (1986), and *Amplitude* (1987). She has recently written a collection of essays on poetry, *A Concert of Tenses* (1986).

Gabriel García Márquez (b. 1928) was born in Aracataca, Colombia. He studied law until civil war closed the university and then became a journalist, film critic, and fiction writer. His journalism tends toward revolutionary socialism, for which he writes rather controversial arguments. But his foremost contribution to the renaissance of Spanish-language literature is *One Hundred Years of Solitude* (1970), a comic and poignant novel about the magical town of Macondo. Garcia Márquez is known for "magic realism," by which possible events are depicted as wonders, and the impossible as commonplace. In 1982 he won the Nobel Prize for Literature. His other works include *Leaf Storm and Other Stories* (1955), *No One Writes to the Colonel and Other Stories* (1961), *In Evil Hour* (1962), *The Autumn of the Patriarch* (1976), *Chronicle of a Death Foretold* (1982), and *Love in the Time of Cholera* (1988).

Charlotte Perkins Gilman (1860–1935), a lecturer and author from Hartford, Connecticut, is probably best known for her promotion of feminism. Her first major work, *Women and Economics*

(1898), is an appeal for the financial independence of women. Her more startling theories are found in *Concerning Children* (1900), which proposes that children should be cared for collectively by women best suited for child-rearing; and *Man-Made World* (1911), in which she claims women are socially and intellectually superior to men. Gilman also co-founded the Women's Peace Party in 1915. Her success, however, came only after she fought off incipient insanity and left her husband and child. Her last work, *The Living of Charlotte Perkins Gilman* (1935), concludes with a letter to her survivors, written shortly before she took her own life. Gilman also wrote several short stories, collected in *The Charlotte Perkins Gilman Reader* (1980).

Dana Gioia (b. 1959) was born in Los Angeles. He holds B.A. and M.B.A. degrees from Stanford University and an M.A. from Harvard University. Although he worked for General Foods Corporation from 1977 to 1985 and as the manager of New Business Development since 1985, Gioia has also served as the poetry editor for *Inquiry* magazine; has translated, with Jonathan Galassi, *Motetti: Poems of Love* by Eugenio Montale (1990); and is editing, with William J. Smith, *Poems from Italy* (no date set). In 1984 *Esquire* named Gioia as one of the best American writers under forty.

Susan Glaspell (1882–1948) was born in Davenport, Iowa, and educated at Drake University. She worked as a reporter for the Des Moines *News* for two years before beginning a career as a writer of plays and fiction. In 1959, Glaspell, her husband George Cram Cook, and Eugene O'Neill founded the Provincetown Playhouse in Provincetown, Massachusetts, beginning a company that would dramatically influence the course of American theater. Glaspell's first play was the widely acclaimed *Trifles* (1916); it was followed by several others, including *The Inheritors* (1921) and *Alison's House* (1930), a Pulitzer Prize winner based on the life of Emily Dickinson. The fictional version of *Trifles*, "A Jury of Her Peers," was included in *Best American Short Stories* of 1916. Glaspell's plays consistently concern the emergence of the "new woman" and the preservation of the virtues of the pioneer character, as do her novels, includng *The Glory and the Conquered* (1909) and *The Morning Is Near Us* (1940). Glaspell's biography of Cook, *The Road to the Temple*, was published in 1927.

Louise Glück (b. 1943) was born in New York City and raised on Long Island. Her first book was published in 1973. Glück draws on nature and animals to define that which is uniquely human; at the same time she affirms our interdependence with the world around us. In a similar way her poetry probes the issues around gender relations. In what ways are men and women unknowable to each other, and in what ways do we require others to help us know ourselves? These concerns, and her frequent forays into the territory of her familial past, make Glück typical of the poets of her generation (Sharon Olds, for example). Glück now lives in Vermont and teaches at nearby Williams College in western Massachusetts. Her books of poetry include *Firstborn* (1973), *The House on*

Marshland (1975), *Descending Figure* (1980), and *The Triumph of Achilles* (1985).

Nadine Gordimer (b. 1923) has seen three of her works banned in South Africa because of their sensitivity to racial injustice. Although she has lived all her life in South Africa, many of Gordimer's stories were first published in American literary magazines, for her liberal politics and harsh critique of apartheid made them unpublishable in her own country. However, Gordimer's sensitivity to the emotional lives of her characters and her objective portrayal of the customs and beliefs of black and white Africans give her works artistic depth as well as political intent. Among her major works are *The Soft Voice of the Serpent, and Other Stories* (1952), *The Lying Days* (1953), *Six Feet of the Country* (1956), *Friday's Footprint, and Other Stories* (1960), *The Conservationist* (1975), *Burgher's Daughter* (1979), *A Soldier's Embrace* (1980), *Something Out There* (1983), and *A Sport of Nature* (1987).

Jacob (1785–1863) and **Wilhelm** (1786–1859) **Grimm** were both born in Hanau, Germany, studied law and science, and became intensely interested in folklore. From the folk poetry and stories they collected, the brothers recorded over 200 fairy tales of Germany, carefully preserving the imagination, beliefs, and personality of the people. From their work emerged the science of folklore. Their most famous work is *Kinder- und Hausmarchen* (1812–1822), generally known as *Grimms' Fairy Tales* in English (translated by Margaret Hunt, 1944). In addition, Jacob wrote many studies of philology and grammar while Wilhelm continued to research folklore and literary history. Among other works translated into English is *The German Legends of the Brothers Grimm* (1981).

Thomas Hardy (1840–1928) was an architect in London when he first became interested in literature. At thirty he began to write novels and had completed sixteen of them before he turned exclusively to writing poetry, some twenty-five years later. Despite his late start as a poet, Hardy produced eight volumes and is now considered among the greatest twentieth-century poets. Like Wordsworth and Browning, Hardy attempted to meld poetic language with that of common speech but enjoyed experimenting with poetic forms, rhythm, and sound. Among his best-known novels are *Tess of the D'Urbervilles* (1891) and *Jude the Obscure* (1895); his poetry collections include *Wessex Poems* (1898) and *Winter Words* (1928).

Robert Hass (b. 1941) has spent most of his life in the San Francisco Bay area. He was born and raised in San Francisco, and attended St. Mary's College in Oakland (where he now teaches) and Stanford University. His writing is dominated by a strong sense of place; the history, politics, and natural surroundings of northern California are frequent themes. In 1973 his first book, *Field Guide*, won the Yale Series of Younger Poets Award. *Praise*, his second book, appeared in 1979. Hass has also distinguished himself as a gifted prose-stylist and translator. His essays and reviews, collected under the title *Twentieth Century Pleasures: Prose on Poetry* (1984), received the National Book Critics Award for Criticism. He was co-translator of

Czeslaw Milosz's *The Separate Notebooks* (1984) and *Unattainable Earth* (1986).

Nathaniel Hawthorne (1804–1864) was born in Salem, Massachusetts, and continued to live in the state throughout his life. He worked as an editor while beginning his writing career, and in 1837 his *Twice-Told Tales* was published. Although Hawthorne's affinity with New England's Puritan traditions was inconsistent with Transcendentalist optimism, he did join for a time in the utopian experiment at Brook Farm, and his *Blithedale Romance* (1852) grew out of his experience of living there. Hawthorne consistently wrote in the romance tradition, although the realistic period was already well established when he began writing. His best-known novel is *The Scarlet Letter* (1850); he also wrote *The House of the Seven Gables* (1851), *The Marble Faun* (1860), and the stories collected in *Mosses from an Old Manse* (1846).

Anthony Hecht (b. 1923) was born in New York City and served in the U.S. Army in World War II. He has taught at several universities, most recently the University of Rochester. His poetry includes *Hard Hours* (1967), *Millions of Strage Shadows* (1977), *The Venetian Vespers* (1979), and *Obbligati: Essays in Criticism* (1986). Besides writing poetry, Hecht is a translator, collaborating with Helen Bacon on Aeschylus' *Seven Against Thebes.*

Ernest Hemingway (1899–1961), born in Oak Park, Illinois, began his writing career as a journalist. During World War I, he drove an ambulance in Italy and was seriously wounded in combat. After the war he lived in Paris and wrote many of his stories and novels; his *A Moveable Feast* (1964) describes the literary and artistic subculture he found there. During the Spanish Civil War, Hemingway returned to journalism as a war correspondent in Spain. Known for prose stripped of excess adjectives and rhetorical coloring, Hemingway writes with simplicity, allowing the direct experiences of his characters to communicate emotion. His extensive traveling and interest in bullfighting, fishing, and hunting are reflected in many of his works, which include *In Our Time* (1924), *The Sun Also Rises* (1926), *A Farewell to Arms* (1929), *Death in the Afternoon* (1932), and *For Whom the Bell Tolls* (1940). In 1954 Hemingway was awarded the Nobel Prize for Literature.

Beth Henley (b. 1952) was born in Jackson, Mississippi, and began acting and playwriting as a student at Southern Methodist University in Texas. Before she was thirty years old she had seen her award-winning *Crimes of the Heart* (1979) performed on Broadway. Often compared to other Southern writers such as Flannery O'Connor and Tennessee Williams, Henley is known for her blend of off-beat humor and compassion. As she explains, her relationship with the South involves "looking at these people and liking them for who they are" and for their ability to "do outrageous things like throw steaks out your plate glass window." She has also written *Am I Blue* (1973), *The Miss Firecracker Contest* (1980), *The Wake of Jamey Foster* (1982), and *The Moon Watcher* (1983). Henley won the 1981 Pulitzer Prize for Drama.

George Herbert (1593–1633) was born in Wales to a patrician family and received his early education

from his mother, who was a patron and friend of John Donne. He won a scholarship to Trinity College, Cambridge, at seventeen and eventually became the public orator at Cambridge. He was a vigorous supporter of James I and became a royal favorite. The death of James brought Herbert into political disfavor, after which he turned to the church and gained fame both as a preacher of re-knowned oratorical power and as a poet. Only two of his works were published during his lifetime, *Parentalia* (1627), about his parents, and *The Temple: Sacred Poems and Private Ejaculations* (1633). Various other writings were collected in *A Priest to the Temple: Or The Country Parson, His Character and Rule of Life* (1652). Herbert and John Donne stand as the major figures in the English Metaphysical movement of the seventeenth century.

Gerard Manley Hopkins (1844–1889) was a writer, painter, and composer of experimental music as a young man. While at Oxford he left the Anglican church and was accepted into the Roman Catholic by Cardinal Newman. He became a Jesuit priest in 1868 and was ordained in 1877. Also a professor of classics, Hopkins was asked to chair the department of Greek and Latin in Dublin in 1884; he spent his last years there in the failing health and depression reflected in his "terrible sonnets." Although his friends admired his writing, only three poems were actually published during Hopkins's lifetime. In 1918, when a friend published his works, Hopkins gained immediate recognition. Brilliant imagery and "sprung rhythm" (a term he coined for meter based on stresses regardless of syllabic count) most consistently characterize his poetry. Hopkins's poems are collected in *The Poems of Gerard Manley Hopkins,* published in 1967.

Alfred Edward Housman (1859–1936), after failing his finals at Oxford, became a clerk in the Patent Office in London. Extremely capable in interpreting the classics, Housman began publishing his studies of classical authors and was eventually appointed professor of Latin at Cambridge. In 1896 he published *A Shropshire Lad,* a nostalgic collection of ballads about an imaginary Shropshire. Although little noticed at the time, by World War I the collection was immensely popular. Likewise, Housman's *Last Poems* of 1922 was well received. The tragedy of doomed youth is a common theme in Housman's poetry, which is often admired for its lyric beauty and classic perfection. Housman is also remembered for his lecture "The Name and Nature of Poetry," an important and controversial comment on poetic invention.

Langston Hughes (1902–1967) was the leading interpreter of the black experience in the United States. Born in Joplin, Missouri, he attained in his work a cultivated artlessness by combining verse form with spirituals and blues. He attempted dialect poetry under the influence of Paul Laurence Dunbar and experimented with free verse influenced by Carl Sandberg, Vachel Lindsay, and Amy Lowell. He earned his baccalaureate from Lincoln University in 1929, a year that also marked the publication of his first novel, *Not Without Laughter* (1930). Other works include: *Shakespeare in Harlem* (1941), *Fields of Wonder*

(1947), *Montage of a Dream Deferred* (1951), and *Ask Your Mama* (1961).

Zora Neale Hurston (1903–1960) grew up in the all-black community of Eatonville, Florida, the town that became the primary source for her literary and scholarly work. Both a fiction writer and a folklorist, Hurston began her career at Howard University. Her fiction commonly reshapes folk material by synthesizing it with art, thus showing readers lives and places that are both realistic and legendary. She was active in the Harlem Renaissance in the 1920s, during which she wrote a play with Langston Hughes, *Mule Bones: A Comedy of Negro Life in Three Acts* (1931). An important source of black mythology and what Alice Walker calls "racial health," Hurston wrote a novel, *Their Eyes Were Watching God* (1937); short stories, *The Eatonville Anthology* (1927); folklore, *Mules and Men* (1935); and an autobiography, *Dust Tracks on a Road* (1942).

Henrik Ibsen (1828–1906), left his native Norway in 1865 because he found its theatrical tradition old-fashioned and constraining. His plays, however, brought Norwegian theater to the forefront of modern literature. Also a poet and theatrical advisor, Ibsen is best known for breaking away from the romantic tradition in drama in order to portray life realistically. His early social dramas, *A Doll's House* (1879), *Ghosts* (1881), and *Hedda Gabler* (1890), gained worldwide attention by shocking audiences with topics previously unmentionable in public: the problem of venereal disease, controversial roles for women in a male-dominated world, and the hypocrisy of modern society. These studies of how people function within society and his exploration of the unconscious have earned Ibsen the title of "father of modern drama." Also by Ibsen are *Peer Gynt* (1867), *The Pillars of Society* (1877), and *The Master Builder* (1897).

Henry James (1843–1916), was born in New York City and educated in Europe. In 1876 he moved permanently to England; thereafter the clash between European sophistication and American innocence became a dominant theme in his works. Primarily a novelist and short story writer, James focused his energies on creating psychological realism by studying the process of the individual mind. His dense style is complicated by his use of the limited point of view, in which the reader shares the partial perception and gradually increasing awareness of the focal character. Also notable are his critical prefaces, collected in *The Art of Fiction* (1884), in which he explains his theories of literature at length. Among his over seventy short stories and several novels are *The American* (1877), *Daisy Miller* (1879), *The Portrait of a Lady* (1881), *The Bostonians* (1886), *The Wings of the Dove* (1902), *The Ambassadors* (1903), and *The Golden Bowl* (1904). *The Complete Tales of Henry James* was published in 1964.

Randall Jarrell (1914–1965) is recognized as one of the most powerful and eloquent spokespersons on war in the history of American literature. Jarrell's childhood was divided between the South and California. He studied psychology and English at Vanderbilt University, then spent two years as a professor at Kenyon College. During World War II he enlisted in the Army Air Corps, serving as a control tower operator for B-29 crews. Two of his collections—*Little Friend, Little Friend* (1945) and *Losses* (1948)—demonstrate the war's profound effect on him. After the war he returned to the life of professor, poet, and critic; in 1965 he was struck and killed by an automobile. His last book of poetry, *The Lost World*, was published a year later. Other works include *Blood from a Stranger* (1942), and his only published novel, *Pictures from an Institution* (1954).

James Joyce (1882–1941), the most influential Irish novelist of the twentieth century, left the country as a young expatriate in 1904, rejecting his Irish Catholic heritage. In Paris he began writing seriously, working on "Epiphanies," a collection of sketches that depicted sudden flashes of personal insight. The rest of his literary career was marked by preference for Irish subject matter while he developed a highly artistic, stream-of-consciousness style. *Ulysses* (1922), Joyce's first experimental novel, proved decidedly controversial for its convoluted language and open sexuality. The book was banned in the United States until 1933. *Dubliners* (1916), *A Portrait of the Artist as a Young Man* (1916), and *Finnegans Wake* (1939) are his other best-known works.

Franz Kafka (1883–1924) was born into a middle-class Jewish family in Prague, Czechoslovakia. He received a law degree in 1906 and spent most of his life working for an insurance company, publishing very little. Yet because his unpublished manuscripts were not destroyed after his death as he requested, Kafka has now gained worldwide fame as one of the greatest writers of visionary fiction in the twentieth century. His fiction is marked by anxiety, like that he experienced in life from his frustrated love affairs, his struggle against tuberculosis, and his guilt over not living up to his father's expectations. Among his works translated into English are *The Trial* (1925), *The Castle* (1926), and *Amerika* (1927), all novels; *Metamorphosis and Other Stories* (1915) and *The Country Doctor* (1919), both short story collections.

John Keats (1795–1821) was born in London, the eldest son of a stable keeper. Following his early schooling he was apprenticed to a surgeon and licensed by the Society of Apothecaries in 1816; however, his intense literary interests led him to abandon medicine to write poetry. He greatly admired Wordsworth, and together with Byron and Shelley he helped establish the Romantic revolution as a tradition. Their work reveled in emotion, the purest expression of experience, and had a profound effect upon early Victorian poets such as Tennyson, Robert Browning, and Elizabeth Barrett Browning. In an effort to capture the essence of his subject, Keats constantly refined his small but extraordinary body of work. He died at age twenty-six, of tuberculosis.

Walter Kerr (b. 1913) began his career as a movie and drama critic at an early age and has become one of the most important critics of this century. He has written for both *Commonweal* and the *New York Times*, among several other publications, and in 1978 won the Pulitzer Prize for Drama Criticism.

As a conservative critic, Kerr has been denounced for agreeing too closely with the Broadway audiences. He explains that the theater should please people, so the best plays are naturally the popular ones. Kerr has written several books, including *How Not to Write a Play* (1955), *Harold Pinter* (1967), and *Journey to the Center of the Theater* (1979), as well as several plays.

Hugh Kingsmill (1889–1949) was chiefly a biographer, writing the lives of Matthew Arnold (1928), Charles Dickens (1935), and D. H. Lawrence (1938), but during his lifetime he was most popular for his prose and poetic parodies. Captured by Germans during World War I, Kingsmill produced his first novel, *The Will to Live* (1919), while confined in a prison camp. He also wrote literary criticism, found in the essays of *The Progress of a Biographer* (1949) and interjected in his fictional fantasy *The Return of William Shakespeare* (1929); both are included in *The Best of Hugh Kingsmill* (1970).

Galway Kinnell (b. 1927) is the director of creative writing at the University of New York at Binghamton and the 1982 Pulitzer Prize winner for Poetry. Kinnell's poems have always reflected a Christian sensibility, and have become increasingly experimental in both form and tone. For Kinnell, poetry is both myth and prayer; it has been described as producing rhythm like a "shaman's chant." His works include *What a Kingdom It Was* (1960), *The Book of Nightmares* (1971), *Mortal Acts, Mortal Words* (1980), *Selected Poems* (1982), and *The Past* (1985). Kinnell also translates French poetry, including a collection of François Villon's poems published in 1977.

D.H. Lawrence (1885–1930) is one of the most controversial and influential figures of twentieth-century literature. Born in Nottinghamshire, England, the son of a schoolteacher and a coal miner, he won a King's Scholarship to Nottingham University in 1906 and taught at Davidson Road School in London from 1908 to 1911, when recurring pneumonia forced him to resign. He began to write as early as 1905 and published his first novel, *The White Peacock*, in 1911. In 1912 he met and eloped to the continent with Frieda von Richthofen Weekley. Returning to England when the war started in 1914, Lawrence faced official harassment because of Frieda's German lineage and, later, obscenity charges, which would follow him through much of his life. The couple's departure for Italy in 1919 marked the onset of a life of world travel and writing that continued until Lawrence's death in France. Lawrence's writings are distinguished by frank exploration of sexuality, Freudian understanding of physiological realities, and a continuing concern for conflict between the natural and civilized aspects of humanity. His most famous novels include *Sons and Lovers* (1913), *The Rainbow* (1915), *Women in Love* (1920), *The Plumed Serpent* (1926), and *Lady Chatterly's Lover* (1928). Among numerous story collections are *The Prussian Officer and Other Stories* (1914), *The Woman Who Rode Away and Other Stories* (1928), *Love Among the Haystacks and Other Pieces* (1930), and *Modern Lover* (1934).

Denise Levertov (b. 1923), from Essex, England, served as a nurse in World War II. She moved to the United States in 1948 and has taught in several universities. Her poetry reflects the influence of William Carlos Williams while presenting a distinctly female voice. Collections of her poetry include *The Double Image* (1946), *The Jacob's Ladder* (1961), *Oblique Prayers* (1984), and *Stay Alive and Footprints* (1987).

Robert Lowell (1917–1977) was born into a famous New England family whose ancestors included the poets Amy Lowell and James Russell Lowell. He attended Harvard but graduated from Kenyon College, where he studied under John Crowe Ransom. During World War II he first tried, unsuccessfully, to enlist; when he was finally drafted he was so opposed to war that he served six months in prison. His concern with moral and spiritual decline made up much of what was to become his Pulitzer Prize-winning book of poems, *Lord Weary's Castle* (1946). *Life Studies* (1960) and *For the Union Dead* (1969) marked the pinnacle of his career. The first gave full expression to self-revelation, beginning the "confessional" movement of poetry; the second was a departure, starting a wide concern for human suffering that culminated in *History* (1973) and *Day by Day*, published shortly before his death.

Archibald MacLeish (1892–1982) was born in Chicago and graduated both from Yale and from Harvard Law School. He also fought in World War I, was a librarian for the Library of Congress, and served as the Assistant Secretary of State. He wrote over a dozen books of poetry as well as radio and television plays. Both his *Conquistador* (1933) and *Collected Poems: 1917–1952* (1952) were awarded Pulitzer Prizes for Poetry; his *J.B.: A Play in Verse* (1958) won the Pulitzer Prize for Drama. Other volumes of poetry include *Songs for a Summer's Day* (1915), *Songs for Eve* (1954), and *New and Collected Poems: 1917–1984* (1985). MacLeish has also written several other plays, prose works, and librettos.

Andrew Marvell (1621–1678) wrote most of his poetry while tutoring the daughter of Sir Thomas Fairfax, the Lord-General of the Parliamentary forces. In 1657 he was appointed to assist Milton and soon became a member of Parliament: his influence is said to have saved Milton from prison. Although often satirizing contemporary politics, Marvell's poems were seldom taken seriously, and their intellectual depth and insight were frequently overlooked during his lifetime. Many of his poems are casual and witty, and their emphasis on the enjoyment of country life anticipates the work of Wordsworth. Marvell's *Miscellaneous Poems* were published in 1681 and his *Poems on Affairs of State* in 1689. A recent collection of his works, *Poems and Letters*, was published in 1971.

Guy de Maupassant (1850–1893) was born in Normandy, France, and fought in the Franco-Prussian War before beginning his literary career. His distant relative, Gustave Flaubert, then took him in for seven years, during which time Maupassant learned to write and destroyed nearly everything he wrote. His work was first published in 1880, and he produced nearly 300 stories in the next ten years. His work is characterized by realism and a turn away from the sentimental fiction of his time—indeed, he demanded "a more complete, striking, and convincing vision of life than the reality itself." Although sympathetic in his portrayal of characters, Maupassant consistently presents bleak and futile existence. His stories are collected in *Complete Stories* (1903); his novels include *A Life* (1883), *Handsome Friend* (1885), and *Pierre et Jean* (1888).

Herman Melville (1819–1891), born in New York City, was forced by poverty to go to sea as a cabin boy in 1839. His adventures there ranged from whaling to living with cannibals, and many were recounted in the early novels *Typee* (1846), *Omoo* (1847), *Mardi* (1849), *Redburn* (1849), and *White-Jacket* (1850). Melville was attracted to Hawthorne's method of weaving philosophy into fiction, a practice that most influenced the writing of his masterpiece, *Moby-Dick* (1851). Although his reputation declined when *Moby-Dick* proved too difficult for popular interest, Melville was rediscovered in the 1920s and is now acknowledged as one of America's finest writers. Considered "legends of wild and gloomy power," Melville's short stories are collected in *Piazza Tales* (1856). *Billy Budd* (1921), which Melville wrote late in life, was published several years after his death.

W.S. Merwin (b. 1927) was raised in Union City, New Jersey, and Scranton, Pennsylvania. After graduating from Princeton University he made the first of many trips abroad. On the Spanish island of Mallorca he continued his study of Romance languages and completed his first book of poems. *A Mask for Janus*, which received the Yale Series of Younger Poets award in 1954, displays a marked classical influence. From this initial formalism Merwin developed a spare and elusive style, restrained yet urgent, shot through with imagery of darkness and water. His true subject has been described as "the nature of loneliness or separation, the burden of consciousness." Merwin has received most of the significant prizes and fellowships available to contemporary poets, including a Pulitzer Prize for *The Carrier of Ladders* (1970). The most recent of his fifteen volumes of poetry are *Opening the Hand* (1984) and *The Rain in the Trees* (1988). He has also published three books of prose and some twenty books of translation from many languages.

Edna St. Vincent Millay (1892–1950) had already made herself known as an actress, poet, and playwright when she graduated from Vassar in 1917. She then moved to Greenwich Village where she continued to write poetry and involve herself in politics. Part of the crusade to save Sacco and Vanzetti, the alleged anarchists executed in 1927, Millay began using her poetry to speak out politically, and continued doing so through World War II. Her poetry is also notable for its engaging persona, a reckless and romantic New Woman who promoted both sexual and emotional liberation. Millay's works include *Renascence and Other Poems* (1917), *A Few Figs from Thistles* (1920), *The Harp-Weaver* (1923), for which she won the Pulitzer Prize, and *Collected Poems* (1956).

Arthur Miller (b. 1915) was born in New York City and educated at the University of Michigan. He first found employment in a box factory, a job that actually prompted his literary career by giving his mind limitless hours in which to create. By 1944 Miller had a play, *The Man Who Had All the Luck,* performed on Broadway. His *Death of a Salesman* (1949) won the Pulitzer Prize for drama. Miller's works typically involve an individual's struggle for personal dignity within a society that offers nothing but betrayal. Miller's interests, however, were not limited to literature. In 1956 (the same year he married Marilyn Monroe), Miller appeared before the House Un-American Activities Committee to answer questions about his participation in Communist-sponsored activities. Though he answered all questions about his own activities, he was cited for contempt because he refused to implicate others. *All My Sons* (1947), *The Crucible* (1953), *A View from the Bridge* (1965), and *The American Clock* (1980) are among his many plays. Miller is also known for his critical writings, collected in *The Theatre Essays of Arthur Miller* (1978). In 1987 he published his autobiography, *Timebends.*

John Milton (1608–1674) received a classical education at Cambridge, but instead of taking holy orders as expected, he isolated himself in his parents' country home for months of extensive reading. After completing his education by traveling to Italy, Milton returned home and began writing political and social tracts. He became Cromwell's Latin secretary during the civil war between the king and Parliament, answering correspondence and writing Puritan propaganda. When he was forty-three Milton lost his eyesight. He was arrested when the monarchy was restored 1660; his income and his role in public life subsequently declined. In the final fourteen years of his life, however, he produced his epic poems *Paradise Lost* (1667) and *Paradise Regained* (1671) and the tragedy *Samson Agonistes* (1671).

Yukio Mishima (1925–1970) was the pseudonym of Kimitake Hiraoka, the Japanese singer, actor, and swordsman remembered most for his literary works. Born and educated in Tokyo, Mishima was highly concerned with restoring Japan to the samurai tradition free from materialistic Western influence. In 1968 he formed a society of over eighty university men devoted to furthering the samurai cause. Two years later he took his own life in a ritual suicide. Yasunari Kawabata, the Japanese Nobel Prize winner, finds Mishima's writing "far superior" to his own work and believes that such genius "comes along perhaps once every 300 years." Mishima's works translated into English include *Confessions of a Mask* (1949), *The Temple of the Golden Pavilion* (1959), *The Sailor Who Fell from Grace with the Sea* (1965), *Death in Midsummer* (1966), and *The Sea of Fertility* (1975).

Marianne Moore (1887–1972) was born in St. Louis, Missouri, but spent most of her life elsewhere. She attended the Metzger Institute and then Bryn Mawr College. Over the years Moore taught typing and bookkeeping at the Carlisle Indian School, worked at the New York Public Library, and, from 1925 to 1929, edited *The Dial*, a leading review of its time. She never married; in her early adult years, she lived with her mother in a Brooklyn apartment where Elizabeth Bishop and others would visit to drink tea and converse. Moore's generation included the major American modernist poets—Eliot, Ezra Pound, William Carlos Williams, and Wallace Stevens—all of whom she knew. Through her keen perceptions, wit, and idiosyncratic line-breaks, she carved out a significant niche for her work. Often taking as subjects animals and inanimate objects, Moore's poems proceed from the "personalities" that she perceives in them to forge dry and ironic comparisons with humanity. Most of her poems are collected in *The Complete Poems* (1967), which was followed by a final volume in 1969, *The Accented Syllable.*

Alice Munro (b. 1931) is a Canadian writer from Wingham, Ontario. Having grown up on a fox farm in a rural community, Munro focuses her work on small-town living, and particularly on the lives of women. Her women, although quite ordinary and often self-conscious and awkward in society, possess emotional lives of surprising depth. Munro writes short stories almost exclusively, claiming that the genre allows her to present "intense, but not connected, moments of experience." Two of her collections have won the Governor General's Award. Among her books are *Dance of the Happy Shades* (1968), *Lives of Girls and Women* (1971), *Something I've Been Meaning to Tell You* (1974), *The Moons of Jupiter* (1983), *The Beggar Maid* (1984), and *The Progress of Love* (1986).

Pablo Neruda (1904–1973) is regarded as one of this century's greatest poets. He was also a political activist and diplomat, serving his country of Chile as a consular official in many countries from 1924 to 1938. He joined the Communist Party in 1939 and traveled in the USSR, China, and Eastern Europe. He was a fiercely elemental poet, coupling meditations on political oppression with intense personal lyrics on the possibilities of romantic love. His influence on European and American, as well as Latin American, poets has been enormous. His best-known works include *Twenty Love Poems and a Song of Despair* (1924), *Residence on Earth* (three series, 1925–45), *Spain in the Heart* (1937), and *The Captain's Verses* (1953).

Joyce Carol Oates (b. 1938) was born in Lockport, New York, and had written thousands of pages of prose by the time she went to high school. She graduated from Syracuse University as valedictorian, and is now a professor of English at Princeton University. Always a prolific writer, Oates has written over 100 stories and nearly 40 books, as well as critical essays. Fascinated by psychological and social disorder, she often examines in her fiction the moral implications of madness and violence. Her works include *By the North Gate* (1963), *Upon the Sweeping Flood* (1966), *Childwold* (1976), *Marya: A Life* (1985), *Raven's Wing* (1986), and *Because It Is Bitter, and Because It Is My Heart* (1990). *New Heaven, New Earth* (1974) and *Last Days: Stories* (1984) are two of her best-known critical books. Oates also writes poetry, collected in *Invisible Woman: New and Selected Poems* (1982).

Flannery O'Connor (1925–1964) was born in Milledgeville, Georgia, and lived most of her life there on a farm with her mother and pet peacocks. She has been characterized as a Southern writer of gothic humor, but it is her Roman Catholicism that most fervently figures in her works. She once stated that her writing concerns "the conflict between an attraction for the Holy and the disbelief in it" and that since everything is "ultimately saved or lost," she must bring her characters to an awareness of their spiritual depravity. Although sick with lupus most of her life, O'Connor devoted as much time as possible to writing, traveling, and lecturing. She wrote two novels, *Wise Blood* (1952) and *The Violent Bear it Away* (1960), as well as short fiction, collected in *The Complete Short Stories* (1971). O'Connor's essays and speeches, which focus on writing and its relationship to Christianity, are found in *Mystery and Manners: Occasional Prose* (1969).

Sharon Olds (b. 1942) was born in San Francisco and educated at Stanford University. After further study at Columbia University she settled in New York, where she teaches writing at universities and at Goldwater Hospital on Roosevelt Island. Olds's poetry is in many ways "confessional" along the lines of Sylvia Plath or Anne Sexton. In their preoccupation with sexuality, and with family and male-female relationships, these poets examine the political in the personal. Olds has published three books of poems to date: *Satan Says,* for which she was given the inaugural San Francisco Poetry Center Award in 1980; *The Dead and the Living,* which received the National Book Critics Circle Award and was the Lamont Poetry Selection for 1983; and *The Gold Cell* (1987).

Wilfred Owen (1893–1918) was born in Shropshire, England, and educated in Liverpool. He worked temporarily as a teacher of English in Bordeaux, where he met a minor Symbolist poet who inspired him to write. In 1915 he joined the English army and fought in World War I. Trench-fever and a concussion, however, forced Owen to be hospitalized in Edinburgh for several months; during this time he wrote all of his major poetry. He finally returned to the war in 1918 and was killed one week before the Armistice. His poetry is marked by technical accuracy, especially in meter and sound. Writing mainly about his war experiences, Owen expressed his hatred for war and the horrors of combat, as well as his pity for all those involved in it. His poems were collected and published in 1920.

Walter Pater (1839–1894) was a tutor of classics at Oxford who believed that great poetry must combine romanticism and classicism. His writing, similarly, tended to blend poetry and prose, for he considered prose writing an art equal to poetry that must be calculated with equal precision of language and rhythm. Pater's followers exalt him most for turning away from traditional Victorianism, at least in theory, and embracing a form of Epicureanism that stressed the enjoyment of life and art. His works include *Studies in the History of the Renaissance* (1873), *Marius the Epicurean* (1885), and *Appreciations* (1889).

Sylvia Plath (1932–1963), daughter of a Polish immigrant, was raised in rural New England. She won a scholarship to Smith College where, at the end of her junior year, she suffered the emotional breakdown chronicled in her novel *The Bell Jar*. After graduating from Smith Plath went to Cambridge University on a Fulbright. While in England she met and married the English poet Ted Hughes, with whom she had a son and a daughter. Plath taught briefly at Smith, but her writing suffered. She and Hughes returned to England. Her emotional problems grew worse with time, leading to several suicide attempts. Before long the strains on their marriage forced Plath and Hughes to separate. In 1963 she took her own life. Her writing, which typifies what has come to be called "confessional" poetry, embodies the frantic, white-knuckled grip on sanity that her troubled emotional history would suggest. Her best-known works include *Ariel, Uncollected Poems, The Bell Jar* (all published posthumously in 1965), *Crossing the Water* (1971), and *Winter Trees* (1972).

Edgar Allan Poe (1809–1849) was born in Boston and educated in both Europe and the United States. He began writing early, publishing *Tamerlane, and Other Poems* in 1827. Admitted to and then expelled within a year from West Point Military Academy, Poe returned to writing and editing to make a living. Introduced to Europe through the translations of Charles Baudelaire, Poe became a major influence on the Symbolist movement. He was also internationally acclaimed as a romantic writer of poetry, fiction, and essays about art. Walt Whitman described Poe and his writing as an image in the midst of a midnight storm, "enjoying all the terror, the murk, and the dislocation of which he was the centre and the victim." Poe's works are collected in *Poems by Edgar Allan Poe* (1831), *The Raven and Other Poems* (1945), *Tales of the Grotesque* (1940), and *The Prose Romances of Edgar A. Poe* (1843), among others.

Elena Poniatowska (b. 1933), although born in Paris and educated in the United States, is a Latin American writer of Polish descent who writes exclusively in Spanish. Journalism, especially in the form of interviews or aggressive political commentaries, dominates Poniatowska's writing. She considers the writing of short stories, therefore, "a sort of self-indulgence" through which she joins all Latin American writers in creating what she calls a literature "of the barefoot . . . of those who eat dirt . . . of those who take up arms . . . of rage." In the stories of *De Noche Vienes* (1979), Poniatowska presents the oppressive dependency of women who are often cut off from the world beyond their own. Her books translated into English are *Massacre in Mexico* (1971) and *Dear Diego* (1986).

Alexander Pope (1688–1744), a small and sickly man born near London, became one of England's finest poets and satirists. His curvature of the spine and tuberculosis, which stopped his growth when he was only four feet six inches tall, severely limited Pope's activity, and he consequently put his energy into reading and writing. He was largely self-taught, owing not only to his poor health but also to his Catholicism, which precluded a university education. His devotion to the classics eventually produced translations of both the *Iliad* and the *Odyssey*, works so successful they brought him financial independence. Sometimes criticized for writing poetry that is overly artificial, Pope is a master of irony and wit. His works include *Essay on Criticism* (1711), *The Rape of the Lock* (1714), *The Dunciad* (1728), and *An Essay on Man* (1733–34).

Katherine Anne Porter (1890–1980), born in Indian Creek, Texas, was primarily a fiction writer, but she also worked for a Chicago newspaper, played bit-parts in movies, and studied Aztec art in Mexico. Her fiction reflects her concern for situation and character over a sharply defined plot. Although considered a Southern writer, Porter locates her fiction in experiences from her numerous and varied travels; *Ship of Fools* (1962), for example, is drawn from a cruise from Mexico to Europe. Porter's works include *Flowering Judas and Other Stories* (1930), *Noon Wine* (1937), *Pale Horse, Pale Rider: Three Short Novels* (1939), *The Collected Essays and Occasional Writings of Katherine Anne Porter* (1970), and *The Never Ending Wrong* (1977). Her *Collected Stories* (1967) won the Pulitzer Prize and the National Book Award the year it was published.

Ezra Pound (1885–1972), originally from Hailey, Idaho, spent his life in Venice, London, Paris, and finally, Rapallo, Italy. He is known as the founder of the Imagist school of poetry, which stressed the use of free rhythms, concreteness, and precise language and imagery. In addition, Pound frequently advised other writers, most notably James Joyce and T. S. Eliot. While in Italy, Pound became preoccupied with economics and began to support Mussolini's social program. During World War II he was arrested and sent to a U.S. Disciplinary Training Center, then to a mental institution in Washington, before being released and allowed to return to Italy. Pound's best-known poetry is his collection of Cantos, which he began in 1917. In his later years he wrote his much-admired *Pisan Cantos* (1948).

Carter Revard (b. 1931), an Osage Indian, was born in Pawhuska, Oklahoma, and studied as a Rhodes Scholar at Oxford University. After receiving his Ph.D. from Yale University, Revard began teaching and is now a professor of literature and linguistics at Washington University. His research and writing include scholarly works such as *How to Make a New Utopian Dictionary of English* (1973) and *Decipherment of the Four-letter Word in a Medieval Manuscript* (1977), but he also writes poetry, collected in *My Right Hand Don't Leave Me No More* (1970), *Ponca War Dancers* (1978), *The Remembered Earth* (1978), and *Nonymosity* (1980).

Adrienne Rich (b. 1929) was born into a prosperous Jewish family in Baltimore. When she was a senior at Radcliffe College her first book of poems, *A Change of World* (1951), was selected by W.H. Auden for the Yale Series of Younger Poets. She studied at Oxford, then married and had three sons. She called her marriage and motherhood a "radicalizing" experience; so, too, was the Vietnam War, which she actively resisted. Most of her adult life, especially after the death of her estranged husband in 1970, has centered around a commitment to advancing feminism. Her eloquent articulation of woman's place in history and society has made her a leading voice in contemporary poetry. Her numerous volumes of poetry, including *Snapshots of a Daughter-in-Law* (1962), *The Dream of a Common Language* (1978), *Diving into the Wreck* (1973), and *A Wild Patience Has Taken Me This Far* (1981), have won many prizes. She has also published *Of Woman Born* (1976), a study of the institution of motherhood, and *On Lies, Secrets, and Silence* (1979), a collection of essays. Rich now teaches at Stanford University.

Rainer Maria Rilke (1875–1926) was born in Prague of German-speaking parents. Educated in Prague, Munich, and Berlin, he was never fully at home in any one place. He spent most of his life criss-crossing the European continent. His first major trip was to Russia (1899–1900), where he met Tolstoy and other writers and returned a changed man. His first recognition came in 1902 with the publication of *The Book of Images*. During the next twelve years, spent on and off in Paris, Rilke produced some of his greatest work. Serving as secretary to the sculptor Rodin, he learned a sharpness of concentration on the things of the external world that culminated in the *New Poems* (1907–08). He wrote a monograph on Rodin, and an autobiographical novel, *The Notebooks of Malte Laurids Brigge*, in 1910. That same year he began work on the *Duino Elegies*, his overwhelming statement on transformation and transcendence. In 1922, in the small town of Muzot in Switzerland, Rilke in a single month was able both to finish the *Elegies* and write the twenty-nine *Sonnets to Orpheus*. He lived and wrote mainly in Switzerland until his premature death from pneumonia.

Arthur Rimbaud's (1854–1891) writing career spanned only five years, but the two collections of poems he produced during that period defined him as one of the most important and influential figures of the French Symbolist movement. Born in Charleville, France, and briefly educated at the college there, Rimbaud traveled to Paris in 1871 and began a tempestuous relationship, both literary and personal, with Paul Verlaine. Verlaine, infatuated with the young poet, abandoned his family and home to travel with Rimbaud to England and Belgium. Their relationship lasted until 1873 when Verlaine shot and wounded Rimbaud during one of their frequent arguments. Rimbaud returned to France where he finished both *Une Saison en Enfer* (*A Season in Hell*), published in 1873, and *Illuminations (Illuminations)*, published in 1886. Thereafter he gave up writing and traveled throughout Europe, in 1878 making his way to Africa where he worked as a gun runner and, some have argued, a slave trader. He died in Marseille of a leg infection.

Edwin Arlington Robinson (1869–1935) was led to writing poetry by his passionate interest in English blank verse. Born in Maine a descendant of the Puritan Anne Bradstreet, Robinson wrote poems that focus on New England living. His first

collection of poems portrays types of people found in his hometown; the psychological depth of these poems is comparable to that of Robert Browning's dramatic monologues. Throughout his life Robinson was a popular poet, winning three Pulitzer Prizes. Robinson's collections include *The Torrent and the Night Before* (1896), *The Children of the Night* (1897), and *The Man Who Died Twice* (1924).

Theodore Roethke (1908–1963) considered himself a "mad poet" yet enjoyed the poetic vision with which the condition endowed him. Born in Saginaw, Michigan, Roethke grew up near his father's twenty-five-acre greenhouse complex, a place that later acquired symbolic meaning in his poetry. He first worked at Lafayette College as a professor of English and tennis coach, and finally settled at the University of Washington, which appointed him poet-in-residence just one year before he died. Roethke was accomplished as a poet, winning both the Pulitzer Prize (1954) and the National Book Award (1958 and 1965). In his poetry he expressed a concern for details and for the poet's ability to see the world with precision. His reverence for and fear of the physical world was always blended with humor and irony. Roethke's works include *Open House* (1941), *Praise to the End!* (1951), *Sequence, Sometimes Metaphysical* (1963), and *The Collected Poems* (1966).

Christina Rossetti (1830–1894), too sickly to work as a governess, lived as an invalid, spending her time reading and writing. She was briefly engaged to James Collinson, a member of the Pre-Raphaelite Brotherhood founded by her brother, painter-poet Dante Gabriel Rossetti, but her devotion to the Anglican church prohibited their marriage when he converted to Catholicism. Her lyric poetry typically expresses frustration and parting in relationships, rarely happiness and fulfillment. Although Rossetti was intensely religious throughout her life, her poetry contains the erotic as well as the spiritual. The poems range in form from ballads to fantasies to religious sonnets and in tone from melancholy to playful. Her works include *Goblin Market and Other Poems* (1862), *The Prince's Progress and Other Poems* (1866), and *A Pageant and Other Poems* (1881).

Lucius Annaeus Seneca (c.4 B.C.–A.D. 65) was a Roman Stoic philosopher, a tragic poet, and a rhetorician. He became Nero's tutor and later advisor, but when he withdrew from the court in 62 he was accused of conspiracy and forced to commit suicide. Seneca's tragedies are marked by exaggerated rhetoric and gory details reported through narrative speeches rather than acted on stage; they were intended for reading rather than for performance. All nine of his tragedies, including *Phaedra, Medea, Oedipus,* and *Hercules* (dates unknown), were translated into English and frequently imitated by dramatists of the English Renaissance and Restoration. Seneca also wrote several satires and philosophical treatises.

William Shakespeare (1554–1616) is indisputably among the timeless writers in any language. Surprisingly little is known of his life. Church and legal registers show that he married in 1582, had two sons and a daughter, and owned a large house in Stratford. It is known that between 1585 and 1592 he left Stratford for London to begin his career as a playwright and actor. However, no dates of his professional career are recorded, nor is it certain in what order he composed his plays and poems. In fact, were it not for his actors, who recalled the text of his plays largely from memory for the historic *First Folio* (the first collection of Shakespeare's work, published in 1623), many of the plays themselves might never have survived. Shakespeare was tremendously prolific; his approximately 35 plays, as well as the 150 sonnets, were written in a span of 25 years. Working largely within story lines borrowed from Roman, English, French, and Italian sources, he proved himself master of a range of genres, including tragedy, comedy, romance, and historical drama. Moreover, he created some of the most complex and three-dimensional characters in the history of the theater, skillfully interweaving them in single, double, and sometimes triple plots. His sonnets are counted by many as some of the most beautiful and stirring love poems ever written.

Percy Bysshe Shelley (1792–1822) was expelled from Oxford for writing an anti-religious pamphlet, "The Necessity of Atheism." The rest of his short life was equally tumultuous: He left his wife for Mary Godwin, left huge debts in England to settle in Italy, saw two of his young children die, and then drowned in a sailing accident. Shelley began writing gothic romances but soon devoted himself to poetry and criticism, publishing most of his greatest poetic works—*Prometheus Unbound* and *"Ode to the West Wind"*—in 1819, and his *Defense of Poetry* in 1821. His works are collected in a ten-volume series, the *Complete Works* (1930).

Sam Shepard (b. 1943) is one of the outstanding American dramatists of his generation. Born in Fort Sheridan, Illinois, he grew up in the car culture of 1950s Southern California. Before establishing himself as a playwright Shepard worked in horse stables, as a rock musician, and as an actor. In 1967 *La Turista* won an Obie (Off-Broadway) Award. Twelve years later *Buried Child* became the first Off-Broadway play to receive the Pulitzer Prize. Set in the West, and centering around one troubled family's efforts to regenerate lives grown as barren as the land they inhabit, *Buried Child* typifies Shepard's concern with the deterioration of American values and dreams. Prolific and experimental, Shepard's dozens of plays include *Curse of the Starving Class* (1978), *True West* (1980), and *A Lie of the Mind* (1985). An accomplished actor and director, Shepard has appeared in *Days of Heaven* (1978), *Country* (1984), *Crimes of the Heart* (1986), *Steel Magnolias* (1989), and the film version of his own play *Fool for Love* (1985).

John Simon (b. 1925) was born in Yugoslavia and educated at Harvard. He has been a professor of humanities and English, an editor, and a critic; he is currently a theater and film critic for *New York* magazine. Simon is known for his consistently harsh criticism: he has been accused of believing not more than a half-dozen good films have ever been made. He responds that positive reviews are always

passionate and subjective, thus we should not expect less from negative ones. His criticism is gathered in *Acid Test* (1963), *Private Screenings: Views of the Cinema of the Sixties* (1967), *Movies into Film* (1971), and *Singularities: Essays on the Theatre: 1964–1974* (1976), among several others.

Sophocles (496–406 B.C.) wrote over 120 plays, but only 7 have survived. Born in Colonus, near Athens, Sophocles studied under Aeschylus, the master of Greek tragedy whom he later defeated in the annual dramatic festival of Dionysus. He then went on to win over twenty more prizes, a record unmatched by any other tragedian. His protagonists are admirably strong-willed, but their pride and lack of self-knowledge often leads them to tragedy. Unlike Eurpides, Sophocles did not question the justice of the gods: his tragedies imply a divine order to which men must learn to conform. Sophocles also maintained an active public life, holding several official positions and possibly establishing a society for music and literature. His best known plays include *Ajax, Antigone, Trachiniae, Oedipus Tyrannus, Electra,* and *Philoctetes.*

Wole Soyinka (b. 1934) calls himself "a very political animal" both in his lifestyle and art. A controversial social critic, Soyinka has had to flee Nigeria on several occasions for criticizing government policies and has been jailed twice. At the same time, he is Nigeria's leading playwright. He was educated at Leeds University in England and has written fifteen plays along with two novels and three volumes of poetry. His first published play, *Swamp Dwellers,* was staged at a London drama festival in 1958. In 1986 he won the Nobel Prize for Literature. Wanting to write for and about Africa, Soyinka often reveals his compassion and concern for his countrymen by depicting them as victims of natural disasters and social turmoil. His plays include *Lion and the Jewel* (1957), *The Invention* (1959), and *Death and the King's Horseman* (1975); he has also written an autobiography, *The Man Died* (1973).

William Stafford (b. 1914) was born in Kansas and received degrees from the University of Kansas and the State University of Iowa. The father of four children, Stafford is a scholar, serving on the faculty of Lewis and Clark College from 1948 to 1980, and a pacifist committed to work for the Church of the Brethren and other peace churches, as well as a poet. His poetry is known for its simple language and its depictions of the Midwest and Western United States, and it is often compared to the work of Robert Frost. Among his numerous collections of poems are *West of Your City* (1960); *Traveling Through the Dark* (1962), which won the National Book Award in 1962; *Stories That Could Be True: New and Collected Poems* (1977); and *A Glass Face in the Rain: New Poems* (1982). He is also the author of *Writing the Australian Crawl: Views on the Writer's Vocation* (1978).

John Steinbeck (1902–1968), having grown up in California's Salinas Valley where he worked as a fruit-picker and hod-carrier, wrote often about the difficulty of living in rural California. His best-known work, the Pulitzer Prize–winning *The Grapes* of *Wrath* (1939), is about a family from the Dust Bowl that emigrates west and struggles against agricultural exploitation there. Steinbeck consistently sympathized with and wrote about the oppressed in his stories and novels, which are often realistic and sociological. Yet he is also known for a mystical, romantic style blended into his realistic fiction. Other works include *Of Mice and Men* (1937), *The Long Valley* (1938), *Cannery Row* (1945), and *East of Eden* (1952). In 1962 he published *Travels with Charley: In Search of America* and won the Nobel Prize for Literature.

Wallace Stevens (1879–1955) was born in Reading, Pennsylvania, studied under the philosopher George Santayana at Harvard, then went on to earn a law degree at New York University. Except for a few years of private law practice, Stevens worked for the rest of his life at the Hartford Accident and Indemnity Company. The facts of his biography are relatively simple; the complexity of his poetry grows out of a rich inner life. Indeed, it is appropriate that Stevens as a worshipper of the mind and imagination, traveled far less than his poems would suggest. From his first book, *Harmonium* (1923), he established himself as a poet less interested in "the thing itself" (William Carlos Williams) than in "the essential poem at the center of things." His striking imagery generally serves to give weight to such free-floating concepts as time, being, meaning, and poetry itself. As one of the key figures in modernist literature, he profoundly affected the writing of poetry in this country. In 1954 his *Collected Poems*, which included his five previous volumes, was awarded the Pulitzer Prize. Many of the thoughts embodied in his poetry are elucidated in *The Necessary Angel* (1951), a collection of essays. Two volumes were published posthumously: *Opus Posthumous* (1957), plays and poetry not included in earlier books, and *The Palm at the End of the Mind: Selected Poems* (1972).

May Swenson (b. 1919) grew up in Logan, Utah, but eventually settled in New York City where she became an editor at New Directions, an avant-garde publishing house. In 1966 she retired in order to write poetry exclusively, but she continues to give lectures and readings at universities all over the country. Elizabeth Bishop characterized Swenson's poetry as direct and optimistic: The poet "looks, and sees, and rejoices in what she sees." Swenson's works include *Another Animal* (1954), *To Mix with Time: New and Selected Poems* (1963), *Iconographs* (1970), *New and Selected Things Taking Place* (1978), and *In Other Words* (1987).

Elizabeth Tallent (b. 1954) was born in Washington, D.C., but grew up in the Southwest, the location for many of her stories. While in college she first aspired to be an archeologist, but instead established her career as a writer. Publishing stories in *The New Yorker, Esquire,* and *Harper's,* Tallent has won a number of prestigious literary awards. The voice she creates in her stories remains remarkably consistent, as if the same young woman is appearing in each. She writes of modern alienation and the difficulty of people truly knowing one another, often illuminating painful relationships between men and women. In addition to her collection of short stories, *In Constant Flight* (1983),

Tallent has written one novel, *Museum Pieces* (1985), and a critical study, *Married Men and Magic Tricks: John Updike's Erotic Heroes* (1982).

Alfred, Lord Tennyson (1809–1892), who succeeded Wordsworth as the English poet laureate, left his university studies at Cambridge without receiving a degree. Though he devoted himself to poetry from childhood, he received discouraging criticism for his early *Poems, Chiefly Lyrical* (1830). The death of his close Cambridge friend Arthur Hallam inspired Tennyson to write his extended elegy *In Memoriam* (1850), through which he gained the favor of Queen Victoria, was named Lord Tennyson, and became the most popular poet of his time. Although Tennyson's poetry typically focuses on the past and classical mythology, the poet was equally concerned with the present condition of the world, often raising philosophical and technological questions. *Maud, and Other Poems* (1855) and *Idylls of the King* (1859) are among his major works.

Dylan Thomas (1914–1953) was born in Swansea, Wales. Despite his father's exhortations, he shunned all formal education, embarking instead on his life's career as a writer, first of poems, later of plays, short stories, and film scripts. By the age of twenty he had published his first collection, *18 Poems*, to modest acclaim. The core of his vision lies in his fascination with the doubleness of nature. The theme of life springing from death, of "womb in tomb," led Thomas to a philosophy that is decidedly Christian, exulting in life and its endless rejuvenation. Among his works are *Under Milk Wood* (1954), a radio play; *Adventures in the Skin Trade* (1955), an autobiography; and *The Poems of Dylan Thomas* (1974).

James Thurber (1894–1961) was born in Ohio and educated at Ohio State University. Except for a brief stint with the State Department in Paris during World War I, Thurber worked in journalism throughout his life. He began as a reporter for the Columbus *Dispatch* and continued as an editor for the Paris edition of the Chicago *Tribune* before beginning his association with E.B. White and *The New Yorker* in 1927. At *The New Yorker,* Thurber wrote the "Talk of the Town" column and began to publish the works that would put him in the ranks of America's most famous humorists. Among his best-known works are *Is Sex Necessary?* (1929), *My Life and Hard Times* (1933), *The Male Animal* (1940), *Fables for Our Time and Famous Poems Illustrated* (1940), *My World—and Welcome to It* (1942), and *The 13 Clocks* (1950). In the tradition of Mark Twain, Thurber's humorous pieces find their sources in the exaggerations and logical incongruities of the tall tale, but also move beyond the limitations of the genre, as T.S. Eliot said, to possess "a criticism of life" and to endure beyond "the immediate einvironment and time out of which they spring."

Alice Walker (b. 1944) is the daughter of sharecroppers from Eatonton, Georgia. She began writing while at Sarah Lawrence College and published her first book of poetry, *Once,* in 1968. She was active in the Civil Rights movement in Mississippi and worked for the welfare department in New York City; her writing reflects her commitment to social and racial change. Although physical and sexual violence within the black community figures consistently in Walker's fiction, she uses violence to emphasize her hope for spiritual survival, freedom, and the power of community, claiming that "the human spirit can be so much more incredible and beautiful than most people ever dream." Walker's works include two collections of stories, *In Love and Trouble* (1973) and *You Can't Keep a Good Woman Down*, and four novels, *The Third Life of Grange Copeland* (1970), *Meridian* (1976), the Pulitzer Prize–winning *The Color Purple* (1982), and *The Temple of My Familiar* (1989). Her essays are collected in *In Search of Our Mothers' Gardens* (1983).

Eudora Welty (b. 1909) has spent most of her life in Jackson, Mississippi. Temporarily a publicity agent for the WPA during the Depression and staffer on the *New York Times Book Review*, Welty has primarily been a writer of fiction, poetry, and literary criticism. She is known as one of the premier American regionalists, for most of her work captures the atmosphere, language, and lifestyle of the South. Her novels include *Delta Wedding* (1946), *The Ponder Heart* (1954), *Losing Battles* (1970), and *The Optimist's Daughter* (1969), which won the Pulitzer Prize in 1972. More recently Welty wrote an exploration of short fiction, *The Eye of the Story* (1978); had her stories collected in *Collected Stories* (1980); and finished an autobiographical account of her literary career, *One Writer's Beginnings* (1984).

Edith Wharton (1862–1937), although originally from New York City, spent most of her life with the American expatriate community in France. During World War I, she wrote propaganda for the Allied cause and was honored for her work with Belgian orphans. Along with her close friend Henry James, Wharton provided readers with both social history and psychological realism in her works. She was awarded the Pulitzer Prize in 1921. Wharton's first collection of stories, *The Greater Inclination* (1899), was followed by ten others; her novels include *The House of Mirth* (1905), *Ethan Frome* (1911), *The Age of Innocence* (1920), and *The Children* (1928). *The Writing of Fiction*, her analysis of short story and novel writing, was published in 1925.

Walt Whitman (1819–1892), one of nine children of a house-builder, grew up on Long Island and later in Brooklyn. Largely self-educated, Whitman worked as a printer, journalist, and teacher. In 1855, after he received some admiring remarks from Ralph Waldo Emerson, Whitman published *Leaves of Grass*. This first version contained just twelve poems; eventually the book expanded to 122 poems. During the Civil War Whitman served as a battlefield nurse near Washington, D.C. He later worked for the Bureau of Indian Affairs and was discharged when his superior read *Leaves of Grass*. After he suffered a stroke, Whitman went to live with his brother in New Jersey. There he continued to write and receive visitors from abroad, where his reputation was greater than in the United States. He broke many conventional barriers, both in the loose, expansive form of his poetry and in his subjects: the spiritual love of man for man, the union of man and nature, the

goodness of the body, and the visionary role of the poet. He is heir to the Romanticism of Blake and Wordsworth, yet his poetry is distinctly American. William Carlos Williams, Frank O'Hara, Allen Ginsberg and the Beat poets, as well as numerous foreign poets such as Pablo Neruda, have kept the "Whitman tradition" alive.

Richard Wilbur (b. 1921), a native of New York City, earned a B.A from Amherst College and an M.A. from Harvard. He has held teaching positions at Harvard, Wellesley College in Massachusetts, and Wesleyan University in Connecticut. Of the postwar poets, Wilbur is considered to be among the most ordered and refined. Calling upon traditional forms to thrust his sometimes extraordinary perceptions into bold relief, he writes poetry that at times recalls Robert Frost and Robert Lowell. His books of poetry include *The Beautiful Changes* (1947), *Ceremony* (1950), *Things of This World* (Pulitzer Prize and National Book Award, 1956), *The Bestiary* (1955), *Advice to a Prophet* (1961), *The Poems of Richard Wilbur* (1963), *Walking to Sleep* (1969), and *The Mind-Reader* (1976). He is also known for his excellent translations of Molière's plays.

William Carlos Williams (1883–1963) spent almost his entire life as a physician in Rutherford, New Jersey. Yet from the voices of his patients he heard "inarticulate poems" that compelled him to write—snatching minutes between patients to scribble down lines, phrases, and whole poems. As part of the Imagist movement, Williams became a revolutionary poet, breaking all poetic conventions to produce uncluttered lines of colloquial language. Randall Jarrell characterizes Williams's work as "stubborn or invincible joyousness" free from "optimistic blindness." Williams also wrote short stories, most of which come directly from his medical experiences, as well as several novels. His numerous works include *The Complete Collected Poems of William Carlos Williams, 1906–1938* (1938), *Paterson* (complete, 1963), *Pictures from Brueghel and Other Poems* (1962), all poetry; *The Farmers' Daughters: Collected Stories* (1961); and *The Autobiography of William Carlos Williams* (1967).

August Wilson (b. 1945), a self-educated playwright and poet, was born and raised in Pittsburgh, Pennsylvania, where he dropped out of school after the ninth grade. He worked various jobs while writing poetry and became involved in the Black Art movement during the 1960s. Although he had no formal experience with drama, Wilson founded the Black Horizon Theatre of St. Paul, Minnesota, in 1968, and soon began writing plays. His best plays are part of a cycle of ten that chronicle the experience of Afro-Americans thoughout the twentieth century. Included in the cycle are *Ma Rainey's Black Bottom* (1985); *Fences*, (1986), which won the Pulitzer Prize and several Tony Awards; *Joe Turner's Come and Gone* (1988), which won the New York Drama Critics' Circle Award for the Best Play of 1987–88; *The Piano Lesson*, which won Wilson a second Pulitzer Prize in 1990, making him one of four American playwrights to be awarded more than one; and *Two Trains Running*, his latest work, which continues the cycle by focusing on the 1960s. Wilson is known for his poetic language and ability to encapsulate the central issues of Afro-Americans, and he is often compared to Eugene O'Neill.

Leigh Allison Wilson (b. 1957), now a professor of fiction writing at the State University of New York College in Oswego, is from Rogersville, Tennessee, and writes colorful tales of the South. When accused of excessive eccentricity in her characters and plots, Wilson answered that she is drawn to absurdity because it is what surrounds her. She also describes her vision of fiction as a comic one that allows her to "approach things without despairing of them." Wilson's short stories are collected in *From the Bottom Up* (1983) and *Wind Stories* (1989).

Virginia Woolf (1882–1941) broke all the rules of convention when she and her sister Vanessa, as young, unmarried women, moved into their own London flat. The two were later part of the Bloomsbury Group, a literary circle that included E. M. Forster, John Maynard Keynes, and Leonard Woolf. After they were married, Virginia and Leonard founded the Hogarth Press and began publishing Virginia's own work, giving her the freedom to experiment with prose writing. Woolf is known for the stream-of-consciousness style found in most of her novels, which include *The Voyage Out* (1915), *Mrs. Dalloway* (1925), *To the Lighthouse* (1927), and *The Waves* (1931). She also wrote short stories, collected in *A Haunted House and Other Stories* (1953) and *The Collected Short Fiction of Virginia Woolf* (1986), and both feminist essays and literary criticism, collected in *A Room of One's Own* (1929), *The Common Reader* (1925), *The Death of the Moth and Other Essays* (1942), and many other books.

William Wordsworth (1770–1850) was born in England's Lake District and spent much of his life in "drinking in" nature and the rural life. Later, after studying at Cambridge and experiencing firsthand the French Revolution, Wordsworth returned to live in the Lake District with his sister Dorothy. There he collaborated closely with Coleridge on the *Lyrical Ballads* (1798), prefaced (in the 1800 edition) with a call for a poetry "in the real language of men." Wordsworth's poetic production was prodigious and lasted until the end of his life. However, with the exception of *The Excursion* (1814), *Poems in Two Volumes* (1807) marked the apex of his creative powers. *The Prelude*, though revised until his death and published posthumously, was largely complete in 1805. Written to chart "the growth of the poet's mind," *The Prelude* is full of biographical insights. Later in life Wordsworth did marry, but it was his partnerships with his sister Dorothy and friend Coleridge that allowed him to reach the imaginative heights he did. In his later life Wordsworth reaped many of the rewards of recognition, including being appointed poet laureate in 1843.

Richard Wright (1908–1960) was born on a plantation near Natchez, Mississippi, but moved north as a young man. In New York City he became involved with the Communist Party and began concentrating on writing poetry and short stories from a Marxist perspective. His first collection, *Uncle Tom's Children*, portrayed the racial conflict through the harsh voice of an insider and earned him immediate literary prominence. Although he spent the last several years of his life in Paris, Wright continued to write about the racial problem in the United States in such novels as *The Outsider* (1953), *Savage Holiday* (1954), and *The Long Dream* (1958). He is acclaimed equally for the sociological and literary value of his works, through which he speaks for all black people. His autobiography, *Black Boy* (1945), is possibly his most important work, followed by his first novel, *Native Son* (1940).

William Butler Yeats (1865–1939) was born in Dublin into a family of English ancestry, and at a time when Ireland was essentially a colony of England he grew up in both countries. Yeats briefly appeared to be following in the footsteps of his father, a painter. In 1889, after deciding to pursue a literary career, Yeats met Maud Gonne, whose beauty and nationalist passions were a lifelong influence. Ten years later, already a respected poet, Yeats founded the Irish National Theater and subsequently wrote and produced many plays. In Yeats's own view he was different from his contemporaries by virtue of his deep, though unorthodox, religious beliefs. Like Blake, whose work he edited, Yeats fused esoteric spiritual ideas with a highly individualized vision to create complexly symbolic poetry. Yeats was politically active as well, first as a leader of the Irish cultural renaissance, later as a senator when the Irish Free State was formed. His numerous books of poetry, his mastery of Irish folk, Pre-Raphaelite, and modernist styles, include *The Wanderings of Oisin and Other Poems* (1889), *In the Seven Woods* (1903), *The Green Helmet and Other Poems* (1910), *Responsibilities* (1914), *The Wild Swans at Coole* (1919), *The Tower* (1928), and *The Winding Stair* (1933).

Marguerite Yourcenar (1913–1988) is a French author and a classicist who was born in Brussels and lived in Maine. Best known for her historical novels, *Memoirs of Hadrian* (1951) and *The Abyss* (1968), Yourcenar also specialized in retelling tales, first through prose poems in *Fires* (1936), which modernized the legends of ancient Greece, and then through her short-story rendition of *Oriental Tales* (1938). Her works always reflect her fascination with ancient myths and themes; her adaptations of Greek drama show sensitivity to the demands of the modern stage. Yourcenar was admitted to the French Academy as the first female member since its founding in 1635. A translator, literary critic, and biographer, she also published *Mishima, or the Vision of the Void* (1981) and a collection of essays, *The Dark Brain of Piranesi* (1984).

ACKNOWLEDGMENTS (continued from p. iv)

L.S. Dembo. Extract from *Contemporary Literature,* Summer 1970, XI, 3. Reprinted by permission of the University of Wisconsin Press.

José Donoso. "Paseo" from *Cuentos* by José Donoso. © José Donoso, 1971. Reprinted by permission of Carmen Balcells Agencia Literaria, Barcelona.

Ralph Ellison. "Did You Ever Dream Lucky?": Reprinted by permission of William Morris Agency, Inc. on behalf of the author. Copyright © 1954 by Ralph Ellison.

Louise Erdrich. "Snares": Copyright © 1987 by Harper's Magazine. All rights reserved. Reprinted from the May issue by special permission. Extract from "PW Interview: Louise Erdrich," by Miriam Berkeley. From *Publisher's Weekly,* August 15, 1986. Reprinted by permission of Miriam Berkeley.

William Faulkner. "Barn Burning": Copyright 1939 and renewed 1967 by Estelle Faulkner and Jill Faulkner Summers. Reprinted from *Collected Stories of William Faulkner* by permission of Random House, Inc. Extract from "Faith or Fear," an address reprinted in *The Atlantic,* August 1953. Reprinted by permission of The Atlantic.

Gustave Flaubert. "A Simple Heart" from *Three Tales* by Gustave Flaubert, translated by Robert Baldick (Penguin Classics, 1961), copyright © Robert Baldick, 1961.

Gabriel García Márquez. "A Very Old Man with Enormous Wings" from *Collected Stories* by Gabriel García Márquez. Copyright © 1984 by Gabriel García Márquez. Reprinted by permission of Harper & Row, Publishers, Inc. From *Writers at Work: The Paris Review Interviews,* Sixth Series, edited by George Plimpton. Copyright © The Paris Review, Inc., 1974, 1975. Reprinted by permission of the publisher, Viking Penguin, a division of Penguin Books USA Inc.

The Brothers Grimm. "The Juniper Tree" from *The Complete Grimm's Fairy Tales* by Jakob Ludwig Karl Grimm and Wilhelm Karl Grimm, translated by Margaret Hunt and James Stern. Copyright 1944 by Pantheon Books, Inc. and renewed 1972 by Random House, Inc. Reprinted by permission of Pantheon Books, a division of Random House, Inc.

Nadine Gordimer. "The Catch": From *Selected Stories* by Nadine Gordimer. Copyright 1952, © 1956, 1957, 1960, 1961, 1964, 1965, 1968, 1969, 1971, 1975, by Nadine Gordimer. Extract from *Writers at Work: The Paris Review Interviews,* Sixth Series, edited by George Plimpton. Copyright © The Paris Review, Inc., 1984. Both reprinted by permission of the publisher, Viking Penguin, a division of Penguin Books USA Inc.

Ernest Hemingway. "Hills Like White Elephants": Reprinted with permission of Charles Scribner's Sons, an imprint of Macmillan Publishing Company from *Men Without Women* by Ernest Hemingway. Copyright 1927 by Charles Scribner's Sons; renewal copyright © 1955 by Ernest Hemingway.

Zora Neale Hurston. "Spunk": Reprinted by permission of Turtle Island Foundation.

Randall Jarrell. Extract from "Stories" from *A Sad Heart at the Supermarket:* Copyright © 1962 by Randall Jarrell. Reprinted by permission of Mrs. Randall Jarrell.

James Joyce. "Araby": From DUBLINERS by James Joyce. Copyright 1916 by B. W. Huebsch. Definitive text edition Copyright © 1967 by The Estate of James Joyce. Reprinted by permission of the publisher, Viking Penguin, a division of Penguin Books USA Inc.

Franz Kafka. "On Parables" from *Parables and Paradoxes, Bilingual Edition,* by Franz Kafka. Copyright 1946, 1947, 1948, 1953, 1954, © 1958 by Schocken Books Inc. Copyright renewed 1975 by Schocken Books Inc. Reprinted by permission of Schocken Books, published by Pantheon Books, a division of Random House, Inc. "A Hunger Artist" from *The Metamorphosis, The Penal Colony, and Other Stories* by Franz Kafka, translated by Willa and Edwin Muir. Copyright 1948 by Schocken Books Inc. Reprinted by permission of Schocken Books, a division of Random House, Inc.

D. H. Lawrence. Extract from "Why the Novel Matters": From *Phoenix: The Posthumous Papers of D. H. Lawrence,* edited by Edward D. McDonald. Copyright, 1936 by Frieda Lawrence. Renewed © 1964 by the Estate of the late Frieda Lawrence Ravagli. Reprinted by permission of the publisher, Viking Penguin, a division of Penguin Books USA Inc.

Guy de Maupassant. "The String" and extract from "Essay on the Novel": Copyright 1923 and renewed 1951 by Alfred A. Knopf, Inc. Reprinted from *The Collected Novels and Short Stories of Guy de Maupassant,* translated by Ernest Boyd, by permission of the publisher.

Yukio Mishima. "Swaddling Clothes": Yukio Mishima: *Death in Midsummer.* Copyright © 1966 by New Directions Publishing Corporation.

Alice Munro. "Circle of Prayer": From *The Progress of Love* by Alice Munro. Copyright © 1986 by Alice Munro. Reprinted by permission of Alfred A. Knopf Inc. Used by permission of the Canadian Publishers, McClelland and Stewart, Toronto.

Joyce Carol Oates. "Where Are You Going, Where Have You Been?": Copyright © 1965 by Joyce Carol Oates. Reprinted by permission of John Hawkins & Associates, Inc. Extract from "The Short Story": From *Southern Humanities Review,* vol. 5, no. 3 (Summer 1971). Reprinted by permission of Southern Humanities Review.

Flannery O'Connor. Excerpts from *Mystery and Manners* by Flannery O'Connor. Copyright © 1957, 1961, 1963, 1964, 1966, 1967, 1969 by the estate of Mary Flannery O'Connor. "A Good Man Is Hard to Find" from *A Good Man Is Hard to Find and Other Stories,* copyright 1953 by Flannery O'Connor and renewed 1981 by Regina O'Connor, reprinted by permission of Harcourt Brace Jovanovich, Inc.

Elena Poniatowska. "A Little Fairy Tale": Tr. by Magda Bogin. Reprinted from *The Massachusetts Review,* © 1987 The Massachusetts Review, Inc.

Katherine Anne Porter. "The Jilting of Granny Weatherall" from *The Flowering Judas and Other Stories,* copyright 1930 and renewed 1958 by Katherine Anne Porter, reprinted by permission of Harcourt Brace Jovanovich, Inc.

Philip Shabecoff. Excerpt from "You've Heard of Yukio Mishima . . . " Copyright © 1970 by The New York Times Company. Reprinted by permission.

John Steinbeck. "The Chrysanthemums": From THE LONG VALLEY by John Steinbeck. Copyright, John Steinbeck, 1938, renewed, John Steinbeck, 1966. Reprinted by permission of the publisher, Viking Penguin, a division of Penguin Books USA Inc. Extract from *Writers at Work: The Paris Review Interviews,* Fourth Series, edited by George Plimpton. Copyright © The Paris Review, Inc., 1974, 1975. Reprinted by permission of the publisher, Viking Penguin, a division of Penguin Books USA Inc.

Elizabeth Tallent. "No One's a Mystery": From *Harper's,* August 1985. Reprinted by permission of the author.

James Thurber. "The Catbird Seat" and two drawings: Copr. © 1945 James Thurber. Copr. © 1973 Helen Thurber and Rosemary A. Thurber. From *The Thurber Carnival,* published by Harper & Row. Reprinted by permission of Rosemary A. Thurber.

Alice Walker. "Everyday Use" from *In Love & Trouble: Stories of Black Women,* copyright © 1973 by Alice Walker, reprinted by permission of Harcourt Brace Jovanovich, Inc. Extract from *Alice Walker Interviews with Kay Bonetti* (sound recording): (p) 1981 American Audio Prose Library, P.O. Box 842, Columbia, MO 65205.

Eudora Welty. Excerpts: Copyright © 1965 by Eudora Welty. Reprinted from *The Eye of the Story* by Eudora Welty, by permission of Random House, Inc. "Livvie" from *The Wide Net and Other Stories,* copyright 1942 and renewed 1970 by Eudora Welty, reprinted by permission of Harcourt Brace Jovanovich, Inc.

Leigh Allison Wilson. "The Raising": © 1983 by Leigh Allison Wilson. Reprinted by permission of Harold Matson Company, Inc.

Virginia Woolf. Excerpt from *Collected Essays, Volume Two* by Virginia Woolf, copyright 1950 and renewed 1978 by Harcourt Brace Jovanovich, Inc., reprinted by permission of the publisher. Extract from *The Collected Essays of Virginia Woolf,* vol. 4. Reprinted by permission of The Hogarth Press. Excerpts from "Modern Fiction" from *The Common Reader* by Virginia Woolf, copyright 1925 by Harcourt Brace Jovanovich, Inc. and renewed 1953 by Leonard Woolf, reprinted by permission of the publisher. Reprinted by permission of The Hogarth Press. "Solid Objects" from *The Complete Shorter Fiction of Virginia Woolf,* edited by Susan Dick, copyright © 1985 by Quentin Bell and Angelica Garnett, introduction and editorial notes copyright © 1985 by Susan Dick, reprinted by permission of Harcourt Brace Jovanovich. Reprinted by permission of The Hogarth Press.

Richard Wright. Excerpt from "Two Negro Novels": Copyright © 1937 by Richard Wright. Reprinted by permission of

Robert Frost. Extracts from *Robert Frost: Poetry and Prose* edited by Edward Connery Lathem and Lawrence Thompson. Copyright © 1972 by Holt, Rinehart and Winston, Inc. Reprinted by permission of Henry Holt and Company, Inc. Poems from *The Poetry of Robert Frost* edited by Edward Connery Lathem. Copyright 1916, 1923, 1928, 1930, 1939, © 1958 by Robert Frost. Copyright © 1964, 1967, 1970 by Lesley Frost Ballantine. Reprinted by permission of Henry Holt and Company, Inc.

Tess Gallagher. "Each Bird Walking": From *Willingly* by Tess Gallagher. Reprinted by permission of Graywolf Press.

Dana Gioia. Excerpt from "Studying with Miss Bishop": From *The New Yorker*, September 15, 1986. Reprinted by permission of The New Yorker.

Louise Glück. "For My Mother," "Still Life," "The Apple Trees" copyright © 1971, 1972, 1973, 1974, 1975 by Louise Glück. From *The House on the Marshland*, first published by The Ecco Press in 1975. Reprinted by permission. "Metamorphoses," "The Triumph of Achilles," "Horse," excerpt from "Marathon" copyright © 1985 by Louise Glück. From *The Triumph of Achilles*, first published by The Ecco Press. Reprinted by permission. Excerpt from "The Dreamer and the Watcher," *Singular Voices*, reprinted by permission of Stephen Berg and Louise Glück.

Robert Hass. Extract from Introduction to *The Selected Poetry of Ranier Maria Rilke:* Reprinted by permission of Robert Hass. "Thin Air" copyright © 1989 by Robert Hass. From *Human Wishes*, first published by The Ecco Press in 1989. Reprinted by permission. "Palo Alto: The Marshes": From *Field Guide* by Robert Hass. Copyright © 1973. Reprinted by permission of the publisher, Yale University Press. "Heroic Simile," "Meditation at Lagunitas," "Old Dominion," "Weed" copyright © 1974, 1975, 1976, 1977, 1978, 1979 by Robert Hass. From *Praise*, first published by The Ecco Press in 1979. Reprinted by permission. Excerpts from "Robert Hass on Poetry and Repetition," and "Robert Hass on Poetry and Image," copyright © 1984 by Robert Hass. From *Twentieth Century Pleasures*, first published by The Ecco Press in 1984. Reprinted by permission.

Anthony Hecht. "More Light! More Light!" from *Collected Earlier Poems* by Anthony Hecht. Copyright © 1990 by Anthony Hecht. Reprinted by permission of Alfred A. Knopf Inc.

A. E. Housman. Extracts from "The Name and Nature of Poetry": In *Selected Prose*, ed. by John Carter. Copyright © 1961 Cambridge University Press. Reprinted by permission of the publisher. Poems: From *The Collected Poems of A. E. Housman*. Copyright 1924, © 1965 by Holt, Rinehart and Winston, Inc. Reprinted by permission of Henry Holt and Company, Inc.

Langston Hughes. "Harlem" ("Dream Deferred"): Copyright 1951 by Langston Hughes. Reprinted from *The Panther and the Lash* by Langston Hughes, by permission of Alfred A. Knopf Inc. "The Negro Speaks of Rivers," "Epilogue" ("I, Too"): Copyright 1926 by Alfred A. Knopf, Inc. and renewed 1954 by Langston Hughes. Reprinted from *Selected Poems of Langston Hughes*, by permission of Alfred A. Knopf Inc. "Afro-American Fragment": From *Selected Poems of Langston Hughes*. Copyright © 1959 by Langston Hughes, by permission of Alfred A. Knopf, Inc. "Harlem Sweeties": Copyright 1942 by Alfred A. Knopf, Inc. and renewed 1970 by Arna Bontemps & George Houston Bass. Reprinted from *Shakespeare in Harlem* by Langston Hughes, by permission of the publisher. "Same in Blues," "Theme for English B": From *Montage of a Dream Deferred*. Reprinted by permission of Harold Ober Associates Incorporated. Copyright 1951 by Langston Hughes. Copyright renewed 1979 by George Houston Bass. Extract from "The Negro Artist and the Racial Mountain": *The Nation*, June 23, 1926. Copyright © 1926. Reprinted by permission of The Nation Magazine/The Nation Company Inc.

Randall Jarrell. Extract from "Some Lines from Whitman": From *Poetry and the Age*. Copyright © 1953 by Randall Jarrel. Reprinted by permission of Mrs. Randall Jarrell. Extracts from "A Poet's Own Way" and "The Woman at the Washington Zoo" (discussion) from *Kipling, Auden & Co.* by Randall Jarrell. Copyright © 1960, 1980 by Mrs. Randall Jarrell. Reprinted by permission of Farrar, Straus and Giroux, Inc. "In Montecito" and "Field and Forest": Reprinted with permission of Macmillan Publishing Company from *The Lost World* by Randall Jarrell. Copyright © Randall Jarrell 1963, 1965. "In Montecito" originally appeared in *The New Yorker*. "Nestus Gurley" and "Woman at the Washington Zoo" from *Woman at the Washington Zoo*. Copyright © 1960 by Randall Jarrell. Reprinted by permission of Mrs. Randall Jarrell. "The Death of the Ball Turret Gunner" and "The Snow-Leopard" from *The Complete Poems* by Randall Jarrell. Copyright © 1945, 1972 by Mrs. Randall Jarrell. Reprinted by permission of Farrar, Straus and Giroux, Inc.

Hugh Kingsmill. "What, Still Alive": From *The Best of Hugh Kingsmill*.Copyright Hugh Kingsmill. Reproduced by permission of Curtis Brown Ltd., London, on Behalf of the Estate of Hugh Kingsmill.

Galway Kinnell. "For Robert Frost" from *Flower Herding on Mount Monadnock* by Galway Kinnell. Copyright © 1964 by Galway Kinnell. Reprinted by permission of Houghton Mifflin Company.

Denise Levertov. "Life at War": *Poems: 1960–1967*. Copyright 1966 by Denise Levertov Goodeman. First published in *Poetry*. Reprinted by permission of New Directions Publishing Corporation.

Robert Lowell. "For the Union Dead," "The Neo-Classical Urn" and "Night Sweat" from *For the Union Dead* by Robert Lowell. Copyright © 1956, 1960, 1961, 1962, 1963, 1964 by Robert Lowell. Renewal copyright © 1988 by the Estate of Robert Lowell. "Epilogue" from *Day by Day* by Robert Lowell. Copyright © 1975, 1976, 1977 by Robert Lowell. "Walking in the Blue" from *Life Studies* by Robert Lowell. Copyright © 1956, 1959 by Robert Lowell. Renewal copyright 1987 by the Estate of Robert Lowell. All reprinted by permission of Farrar, Straus and Giroux, Inc. "The Drunken Fisherman" from *Lord Weary's Castle*, copyright 1946 and renewed 1974 by Robert Lowell. Reprinted by permission of Harcourt Brace Jovanovich, Inc.

Archibald MacLeish. "You, Andrew Marvell" from *New and Collected Poems 1917–1982* by Archibald MacLeish. Copyright © 1985 by the Estate of Archibald MacLeish. Reprinted by permission of Houghton Mifflin Co.

W. S. Merwin. Extracts from *Regions of Memory* reprinted by permission of the University of Illinois Press. © 1986. "History": From *The New Yorker*, September 22, 1986. Reprinted by permission of The New Yorker. "Emigre" from *Grand Street* (Autumn 1982) © 1982 by W. S. Merwin; "For the Anniversary of My Death" from *The Lice* (Atheneum) © 1967 by W. S. Merwin; "The Last One" from *The Lice* (Atheneum) © 1964 by W. S. Merwin; "Grandmother Watching at Her Window" from *The Drunk in the Furnace* (Atheneum) © 1956, 1957, 1958, 1959, 1960 by W. S. Merwin. All reprinted by permission of Georges Borchardt Inc. and the author. "The Judgment of Paris" and "The Different Stars": Reprinted with permission of Atheneum Publishers, an imprint of Macmillan Publishing Company, from *The Carrier of Ladders* by W. S. Merwin. "The Judgment of Paris" copyright © 1970 by W. S. Merwin. "The Different Stars" copyright © 1969, 1970 by W. S. Merwin. Both originally appeared in *The New Yorker*. "Noah's Raven": Reprinted with permission of Atheneum Publishers, an imprint of Macmillan Publishing Company, from *The Moving Target* by W. S. Merwin. Copyright © 1962, 1963 by W. S. Merwin. Originally appeared in *Poetry*.

Edna St. Vincent Millay. "Spring," "Recuerdo," "An Ancient Gesture," "Modern Declaration," "From a Train Window," "The Oak-Leaves," "Childhood Is the Kingdom Where Nobody Dies," and "Love is not all: it is not meat nor drink" by Edna St. Vincent Millay. From *Collected Poems*, Harper & Row. Copyright © 1921, 1922, 1931, 1939, 1948, 1950, 1954, 1958, 1967, 1982 by Edna St. Vincent Millay and Norma Millay Ellis. Reprinted by permission of Elizabeth Barnett.

Marianne Moore. Poems reprinted with permission of Macmillan Publishing Company from *Collected Poems* by Marianne Moore. "Peter," "The Fish," "Poetry," "Silence": Copyright 1935 by Marianne Moore, renewed 1963 by Marianne Moore and T. S. Eliot. "Four Quartz Crystal Clocks": Copyright 1941, and renewed 1969, by Marianne Moore. "Elephants": Copyright 1944, and renewed 1972, by Marianne Moore.

Pablo Neruda. "Here I Love You": Tr. by W. S. Merwin. Reprinted by permission of Georges Borchardt Inc., and W. S. Merwin. Copyright © 1969 by W. S. Merwin. Reprinted by permission of Jonathan Cape Ltd. "Love" and "Sweetness, Always" from *Extravagaria* by Pablo Neruda, translated by Alastair Reid. English translation copyright © 1969, 1970, 1972, 1974 by Alastair Reid. "Love Sonnet VI": From *100 Love Sonnets* by Pablo Neruda, translated by Stephen Tapscott. © 1986 by the University of Texas Press. Reprinted by permission of the University of Texas Press. "Horses," "Ritual of My Legs," "The Danger": From *Five Decades: Poems 1925–1970*, tr. by Ben Belitt. Reprinted by permission of Grove Weidenfeld. Copyright © 1974 by Grove Press, Inc.

Sharon Olds. "The Chute," "Summer Solstice": From *The Gold Cell* by Sharon Olds. Copyright © 1987 by Sharon Olds. Reprinted by permission of Alfred A. Knopf. Inc. "Sex Without Love," "The Elder Sister," "The Victims": From *The Dead and the Living* by Sharon Olds. Copyright © 1983 by Sharon Olds. Reprinted by permission of Alfred A. Knopf Inc. "Bathing the Newborn": From *The New Yorker*, October 15, 1984. "The Race": From *The New Yorker*, November 25, 1985. Both reprinted by permission of The New Yorker.

Charles D'Orleans. Tr. by Louise Bogan. "Castle of My Heart": From *Journey Around My Room*, by Louise Bogan.

Reprinted by permission of Ruth Limmer, Literary Executor, Estate of Louise Bogan.

Wilfred Owen. Poems: Wilfred Owen, *The Collected Poems of Wilfred Owen*. Copyright © 1963 by Chatto & Windus, Ltd. Reprinted by permission of New Directions Publishing Corporation, Chatto & Windus, and the author's estate.

Sylvia Plath. "Medallion": Copyright © 1962 by Sylvia Plath. Reprinted from *The Colossus and Other Poems* by Sylvia Plath, by permission of Alfred A. Knopf Inc. "Tulips" and "The Arrival of the Bee Box" from *Ariel* by Sylvia Plath. Copyright © 1962, 1963 by Ted Hughes. Reprinted by permission of Harper & Row, Publishers, Inc. "Daddy," "Lady Lazarus," "Cut," and "Black Rook in Rainy Weather" from *The Collected Poems of Sylvia Plath*, edited by Ted Hughes. Copyright © 1960, 1963, 1981 by the Estate of Sylvia Plath. Reprinted by permission of Harper & Row, Publishers, Inc. All poems: *Sylvia Plath Collected Poems*, published by Faber and Faber, Limited, London, copyright Ted Hughes 1965, 1971, 1981. Reprinted by permission of Olwyn Hughes.

Ezra Pound. "Alba," "Mr. Housman's Message": *Personae*. Copyright 1926 by Ezra Pound. Reprinted by permission of New Directions Publishing Corporation.

The Princeton Encyclopedia of Poetry and Poetics. Definition of "alba": Preminger, Alex, et al., eds. Copyright © 1965, enlarged edn. copyright © 1974, by Princeton University Press.

Carter Revard. "Discovery of the New World": Reprinted by permission of the author.

Adrienne Rich. "Origins and History of Consciousness" is reprinted from THE DREAM OF A COMMON LANGUAGE, Poems 1974–1977, by Adrienne Rich, by permission of W. W. Norton & Company, Inc. Copyright © 1978 by W. W. Norton & Company, Inc. "Gabriel" is reprinted from POEMS SELECTED AND NEW, 1950–1974, by Adrienne Rich, by permission of W. W. Norton & Company, Inc. Copyright © 1975, 1973, 1971, 1969, 1966 by W. W. Norton & Company, Inc. Copyright © 1967, 1963, 1962, 1961, 1960, 1959, 1958, 1957, 1956, 1955, 1954, 1953, 1952, 1951 by Adrienne Rich. "Love in the Museum": From *The New Yorker*, April 3, 1954. Reprinted by permission of The New Yorker. Other poems: Reprinted from THE FACT OF A DOORFRAME, Poems Selected and New, 1950–1984, by Adrienne Rich, by permission of W. W. Norton & Company, Inc. Copyright © 1984 by Adrienne Rich. Copyright © 1975, 1978 by W. W. Norton & Company, Inc. Copyright © 1981 by Adrienne Rich. Prose excerpt: Reprinted from "When We Dead Awaken: Writing as Re-Vision" from ON LIES, SECRETS, AND SILENCE, Selected Prose, 1966–1978, by Adrienne Rich. By permission of W. W. Norton & Company, Inc., and the author. Copyright © 1979 by W. W. Norton & Company, Inc.

Ranier Maria Rilke. Poems: From *The Selected Poetry of Ranier Maria Rilke* translated by Stephen Mitchell. Copyright © 1982 by Stephen Mitchell. Reprinted by permission of Random House, Inc.

Arthur Rimbaud. "The Sleeper in the Valley" from *Imitations* by Robert Lowell. Copyright © 1958, 1959, 1960, 1961 by Robert Lowell. Renewal copyright © 1989 by the Estate of Robert Lowell. Reprinted by permission of Farrar, Straus and Giroux, Inc.

Edwin Arlington Robinson. Reprinted with permission of Macmillan Publishing Company from *Collected Poems* by Edwin Arlington Robinson. "The Sheaves": Copyright 1925 by Edwin Arlington Robinson, renewed 1953 by Ruth Nivison and Barbara R. Holt. "Mr. Flood's Party": Copyright 1921 by Edwin Arlington Robinson, renewed 1949 by Ruth Nivison. "The Mill": Copyright 1920 by Edwin Arlington Robinson, renewed 1948 by Ruth Nivison. "Eros Turannos": Copyright 1916 by Edwin Arlington Robinson, renewed 1944 by Ruth Nivison.

Theodore Roethke. Extracts from *On the Poet and His Craft—Selected Prose of Theodore Roethke*, ed. by Ralph J. Mills: Reprinted by permission of University of Washington Press. "Big Wind" copyright 1947 by United Chapters of Phi Beta Kappa, "My Papa's Waltz" copyright 1942 by Hearst Magazines, Inc., "I Knew a Woman" copyright 1954 by Theodore Roethke, "Frau Bauman, Frau Schmidt and Frau Schwartz" copyright 1952 by Theodore Roethke, "Root Cellar" copyright 1943 by Modern Poetry Association, Inc. and "Child on Top of a Greenhouse" copyright 1946 by Editorial Publications, Inc. All poems from *The Collected Poems of Theodore Roethke*. Reprinted by permission of Doubleday Publishing Group.

William Shakespeare. Poems: From *The Riverside Shakespeare*, ed. by G. Blakemore Evans. Copyright © 1974 by Houghton Mifflin Company. Reprinted by permission of the publisher.

Wole Soyinka. "Telephone Conversation": Permission granted by Carl E. Younger.

William Stafford. "Traveling Through the Dark" from *Stories That Could Be True* by William Stafford. Copyright © 1960 by William Stafford. Reprinted by permission of Harper & Row, Publishers, Inc.

Wallace Stevens. "Study of Two Pears": Copyright 1942 by Wallace Stevens and renewed 1970 by Holly Stevens. "A Postcard from the Volcano": Copyright 1936 and renewed 1964 by Holly Stevens. Other poems: Copyright 1923 and renewed 1951 by Wallace Stevens. All reprinted from *The Collected Poems of Wallace Stevens*, by permission of Alfred A. Knopf Inc.

May Swenson. "How Everything Happens—Based on a Study of the Wave" by May Swenson is reprinted by permission of the literary estate of May Swenson. Copyright © 1969 by May Swenson.

Dylan Thomas. *Poems by Dylan Thomas*. Copyright 1939, 1943 by New Directions Publishing Corporation, 1945 by the Trustees for the Copyrights of Dylan Thomas, 1952 by Dylan Thomas. "Poem in October" was first published in *Poetry*. All reprinted by permission of New Directions Publishing Corporation. From *The Poems* by Dylan Thomas, published by Dent. All reprinted by permission of David Higham Associates Limited.

Richard Wilbur. "A Late Aubade" from *Walking to Sleep*, copyright © 1968 by Richard Wilbur, reprinted by permission of Harcourt Brace Jovanovich, Inc. Extract from "All That Is": From *The New Yorker*, May 13, 1985. Reprinted by permission of The New Yorker. "Love Calls Us to the Things of This World" from *Things of This World*, copyright © 1956 and renewed 1984 by Richard Wilbur, reprinted by permission of Harcourt Brace Jovanovich, Inc. "A Baroque Wall-Fountain in the Villa Schiarra" from *Things of This World*, copyright © 1955 and renewed 1983 by Richard Wilbur, reprinted by permission of Harcourt Brace Jovanovich, Inc. "Two Voices in a Meadow" from *Advice to a Prophet and Other Poems*, copyright © 1957 and renewed 1985 by Richard Wilbur, reprinted by permission of Harcourt Brace Jovanovich, Inc. "The Undead" from *Advice to a Prophet and Other Poems*, copyright © 1961 by Richard Wilbur, reprinted by permission of Harcourt Brace Jovanovich, Inc. First published in *The New Yorker*. Excerpt from "Praise in Summer" in *The Beautiful Changes and Other Poems*, copyright 1947 and renewed 1975 by Richard Wilbur, reprinted by permission of Harcourt Brace Jovanovich, Inc. Excerpt from "The Death of a Toad" and "Still, Citizen Sparrow" in *Ceremony and Other Poems*, copyright 1950 and 1978 by Richard Wilbur, reprinted by permission of Harcourt Brace Jovanovich, Inc. "Hamlen Brook" from *New and Collected Poems*, copyright © 1987 by Richard Wilbur, reprinted by permission of Harcourt Brace Jovanovich, Inc. Excerpt from *Responses: Prose Pieces 1953–1976*, copyright © 1976 by Richard Wilbur, reprinted by permission of Harcourt Brace Jovanovich, Inc. "Cottage Street, 1953" from *The Mind Reader: New Poems*, copyright © 1972 by Richard Wilbur, reprinted by permission of Harcourt Brace Jovanovich, Inc.

William Carlos Williams. *Collected Poems, 1909–1939, vol. I*. Copyright 1938 by New Directions Publishing Corporation. Extracts from "Marianne Moore," "Dylan Thomas": William Carlos Williams: *Selected Essays of William Carlos Williams*. Copyright 1954 by William Carlos Williams. All reprinted by permission of New Directions Publishing Corporation.

W. B. Yeats. Reprinted with permission of Macmillan Publishing Company from *Collected Poems* by W. B. Yeats. "The Scholars," "The Cat and the Moon," "The Wild Swans at Coole": Copyright 1919 by Macmillan Publishing Company, renewed 1947 by Bertha Georgie Yeats. "Leda and the Swan," "Sailing to Byzantium," "Among School Children": Copyright 1928 by Macmillan Publishing Company, renewed 1956 by Georgie Yeats. "The Second Coming": Copyright 1924 by Macmillan Publishing Company, renewed 1952 by Bertha Georgie Yeats. "Crazy Jane Talks to the Bishop": Copyright 1933 by Macmillan Publishing Company, renewed 1961 by Bertha Georgie Yeats. Extracts from the Introduction to *The Oxford Book of Modern Verse*: Oxford University Press, 1936. Reprinted by permission of the publisher.

DRAMA

Jean Anouilh. Excerpt from *Antigone* by Jean Anouilh, translated by Lewis Galantiere. Copyright 1946 by Random House, Inc. and renewed 1974 by Lewis Galantiere. Reprinted by permission of Random House, Inc. Excerpt from "Medea" from *Seven Plays, Volume III* by Jean Anouilh. Copyright © 1957 by Arthur Klein. Renewal copyright © 1985 by Luce Klein and Arthur Klein. Reprinted by permission of Hill and Wang, a division of Farrar, Straus and Giroux, Inc.

W. H. Auden. Extract from "An Improbable Life": Reprinted by permission of Curtis Brown, Ltd. Copyright © 1963 The New Yorker Magazine Inc.

Samuel Beckett. "Krapp's Last Tape": Reprinted by permission of Grove Weidenfeld. Copyright © 1957 by Samuel Beckett. Reprinted by permission of Faber and Faber Ltd. from *Krapp's Last Tape* by Samuel Beckett.

Anton Chekhov. "The Three Sisters" translated by Randall Jarrell reprinted by permission of Mary Jarrell. All rights reserved. Performance permission for film, theater, radio and television are solely controlled by Mary Jarrell. Extract from the Introduction to the play used by permission of Mary Jarrell.

Euripides. Extract from *Medea:* Tr. by Frank Miller. From *The Complete Roman Drama* edited by George E. Duckworth. Copyright 1942 and renewed 1970 by Random House, Inc. Reprinted by permission of the publisher. *Medea:* Tr. by Rex Warner. Reprinted by permission of The Bodley Head.

Samuel G. Freedman. Excerpt from "A Voice from the Streets": Copyright © 1987 by The New York Times Company. Reprinted by permission.

Susan Glaspell. "Trifles": Reprinted by permission of Daphne C. Cook (Estate of Susan Glaspell).

Beth Henley. *Crimes of the Heart* by Beth Henley. Copyright © 1981, 1982 by Beth Henley. Reprinted by permission of the publisher, Viking Penguin, a division of Penguin Books USA Inc.

Walter Kerr. Extract from "Stage View: Offbeat—But a Beat Too Far": *The New York Times,* November 15, 1981. Copyright © 1981 by The New York Times Company. Reprinted by permission.

Arthur Miller. From "The Nature of Tragedy" and "Tragedy and the Common Man": *The Theater Essays of Arthur Miller*, by Arthur Miller. Copyright © 1978 by Arthur Miller. Reprinted by permission of the publisher, Viking Penguin, a division of Penguin Books USA Inc. *Death of a Salesman* by Arthur Miller. Copyright © 1949, renewed 1977 by Arthur Miller. Reprinted by permission of the publisher, Viking Penguin, a division of Penguin Books USA Inc.

William Shakespeare. Plays from *The Riverside Shakespeare,* ed. by G. Blakemore Evans. Copyright © 1974 by Houghton Mifflin Company. Used by permission.

Sam Shepard. "True West" From *Seven Plays* by Sam Shepard, copyright © 1981 by Sam Shepard. Used by permission of Bantam Books, a division of Bantam, Doubleday, Dell Publishing Group, Inc.

John Simon. Extract from "Living Beings, Cardboard Symbols": *New York* Magazine, November 16, 1981. Copyright © 1987 by News America Publishing, Inc. Reprinted with the permission of *New York* Magazine.

Sophocles. *Antigone* from David Grene and Richard Lattimore, *Greek Tragedies,* Vol. 1, Elizabeth Wycoff, Trans. reprinted by permission of The University of Chicago Press.

August Wilson. "Joe Turner's Come and Gone": JOE TURNER'S COME AND GONE, a play by August Wilson. Copyright © 1988 by August Wilson. Reprinted by permission of the publisher, Plume, an imprint of New American Library, a division of Penguin Books USA Inc.

Virginia Woolf. Extract: "Twelfth Night at the Old Vic" from *Death of the Moth and Other Essays* by Virginia Woolf, copyright 1942 by Harcourt Brace Jovanovich, Inc. and renewed 1970 by Marjorie T. Parsons Executrix, reprinted by permission of the publisher. Reprinted by permission of The Hogarth Press.

Index of Authors and Titles

Index to First Lines of Poetry

O, never say that I was false of heart, 464
Obscurely yet most surely called to praise, 835
Of Bronze—and Blaze—, 605
Often, for pastime, mariners will ensnare, 602
Oft he to her his charge of quick return, 479
O God, in the dream the terrible horse began, 730
Oh, but it is dirty! 780
Old Eben Flood, climbing alone one night, 646
Old warder of these buried bones, 571
Old Yew, which graspest at the stones, 569
O mistress mine, where are you roaming? 465
Once, somewhere, somehow, you had set him free, 662
Once riding in old Baltimore, 742
On ear and ear two noises too old to end, 621
One face looks out from all his canvases, 612
One that is ever kind said yesterday, 632
Only I never came back, 867
On moonlit heath and lonesome bank, 628
On the stiff twig up there, 881
Opusculum paedagogum, 673
O Rose, thou art sick, 511
Out walking in the frozen swamp one gray day, 652
Over Sir John's hill, 808
O woe, woe, 630
O you so long dead, 729

Precious in the light of the early sun the Housatonic, 705

Round the cape of a sudden came the sea, 575
r-p-o-p-h-e-s-s-a-g-r, 723

Season of mists and mellow fruitfulness, 560
Sex, as they harshly call it, 871
She dreamed along the beaches of this coast, 898
She dwelt among the untrodden ways, 521
She fears him, and will always ask, 644

She had thought the studio would keep itself, 454
She is older than the rocks among which she sits, 641
She looked over his shoulder, 770
She sits with, 677
Since brass, nor stone, nor earth, nor boundless sea, 463
Since I am coming to that holy room, 474
Sleep well, my love, sleep well, 747
Softly, so casual, 716
So long, 735
So many days, oh so many days, 755
Sometimes the night echoes to prideless wailing, 815
Sometimes waking, sometimes sleeping, 794
so much depends, 675
Soul. O, who shall from this dungeon raise, 493
Stars, I have seen them fall, 629
Still, citizen sparrow, this vulture which you call, 836
Strange fits of passion have I known, 521
Strong and slippery, 685

Tears, idle tears, I know not what they mean, 567
'Terence, this is stupid stuff,' 625
That is no country for old men. The young, 636
That night your great guns, unawares, 714
That's my last duchess painted on the wall, 573
That time of year thou mayst in me behold, 464
The alphabet of, 676
The angel of death flies, 918
The art of losing isn't hard to master, 790
The back wings, 682
The brown enormous odor he lived by, 779
the Cambridge ladies who live in furnished souls, 720
The cat went here and there, 634
The creatures that we met this morning, 747
The disasters numb within us, 718
The eyes open to a cry of pulleys, 837
The force that through the green fuse drives the flower, 805